This

Belongs to

Katie Hall

3365 35th Ave

Oakland

Ke2-6133

Jerry + Katie

1st ENGA.

THE FLAGS OF NATIONS

If you have read *Treasure Island,* you will recall that after Squire Trelawney's party had occupied the blockhouse on the island, Captain Smollett could not rest content until the union jack was flying from an improvised flagstaff.

So it has been in all ages. Wherever men have banded themselves together for joint action of any kind, some symbol of their union has seemed a first necessity. If they have marched to battle or sailed the high seas, the symbol has usually been a flag.

Every nation has a national flag. Kings succeed kings, and presidents follow presidents; but the flag of a nation continues to fly, year after year, and century after century, unless there comes a revolution and a change of government, as from a monarchy to a republic. Then, usually, a new national flag replaces the old.

Some of the national flags represented in our color plate are of very ancient origin; others, like the flags of Portugal and Spain, are as young as the twentieth century. Probably the oldest of them all is the flag of Denmark, which was carried into battle and sailed the sea as far back as the fourteenth century. Almost as ancient is the flag of Switzerland, from which (with a reversal of colors) the Red Cross emblem was derived. Another very old flag is the flag of the Netherlands. Originally, its red stripe was not red, but orange. Why the color was changed, about 1650, we do not know; but we do know that when Henry Hudson sailed for the New World in 1608, he flew the orange, white, and blue tricolor at his masthead.

The famous "union jack" of the British Empire was first unfurled in 1606. The ancient flag of England was the "cross of Saint George," a red cross on a white field. The ancient flag of Scotland was the "cross of Saint Andrew," a white X-shaped cross on a blue field. After the two kingdoms had been firmly united under a single monarch, the two crosses were united to form the first "union jack." Remove the red diagonal stripes from the present flag and you will see how the British union flag looked throughout the seventeenth and eighteenth centuries. The red diagonals added in 1800, represent the "cross of Saint Patrick" of Ireland, a red X-shaped cross on a white field.

The red, white, and blue tricolor of France originated in the stormy days of the French Revolution. As originally flown, in 1791, the red stripe was nearest to the flagstaff, and the blue stripe farthest from it, but four years later the positions of the two colors were reversed.

When two national flags look very much alike, there is usually a reason for the resemblance. The flag of Italy resembles the flag of France because it was designed when the French under Napoleon Bonaparte were the actual rulers of Italy. The flag of Mexico is like the flag of Italy because, after Napoleon's fall from power, the green, white, and red tricolor fell into disuse in Italy, and was adopted by Mexico. When, some years later, the kingdom of Italy was established, Mexico refused to relinquish its tricolor. Italy then adopted the selfsame flag, but with the coat-of-arms of its king at the center of the white stripe. Italy now uses the plain flag, while Mexico has its coat-of-arms in the white stripe.

The flags of Colombia and Venezuela are so much alike because both flags were taken from the flag of General Bolivar, who led the people of northern South America in successful revolt against the rule of Spain. Bolivar's flag was like the flag of Colombia.

That some of the flags of the Spanish American republics, such as those of Chile, Cuba, and Panama, should suggest our own stars and stripes, is not at all surprising. The United States was, of course, the first republic in the New World, and its flag is the oldest national flag in America.

Indeed, few national flags are as old as the star-spangled banner. Adopted by Congress on June 14, 1777, it has flown for more than a century and a half, though not always in exactly the form in which we see it today. Originally it had but 13 stars and 13 stripes. Then, from 1794, throughout the war of 1812, and down to 1818, it had 15 stars and 15 stripes, for the original intention was to add a stripe, as well as a star, for each new state admitted to the Union. But after 20 States had been admitted to the Union, it was thought best to fix once and for all the number of stripes, and so, on April 4, 1818, Congress passed a law fixing the number of stripes at 13, one for each of the original 13 states. Since then, the only changes in the flag have been in the number of stars in the blue canton, which finally reached the present number, 49, after the admission of the state of Alaska in 1959.

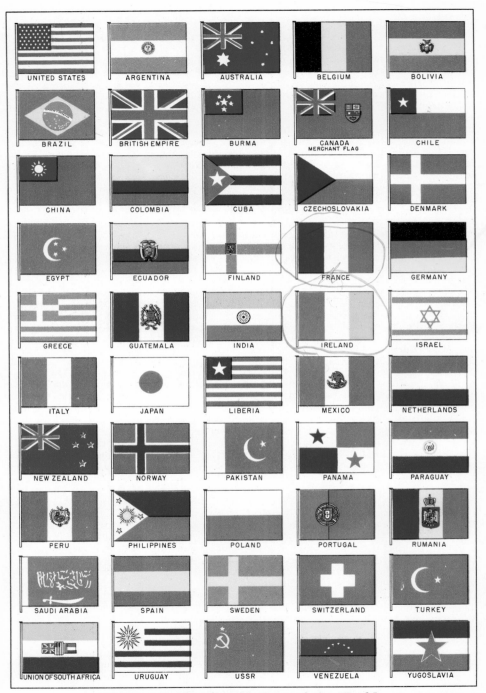

Flags of the Leading Nations of the World. *(See other side.)*

THE WINSTON
DICTIONARY
FOR SCHOOLS

1700 Pictorial Illustrations
10 Color Plates · 16 Maps in Color

THE JOHN C. WINSTON COMPANY
PHILADELPHIA

PREFACE

THIS dictionary is an entirely new work, designed specifically for the use of young people. Choice of vocabulary, definitions, and verbal and pictorial illustrations are all the product of careful study by a staff of scholarly editors which combines thorough knowledge of dictionary technique with first-hand experience with young people.

Look it up in the dictionary. "Look it up in the dictionary" has become a popular slogan in both home and school. Growing knowledge of science encourages the quest for accurate information. World activities presented by the press and on the screen stimulate an expanding interest in human affairs. The speed with which modern life is changing is reflected in our marvelously flexible language. New words are constantly being added. Unfamiliar areas of the globe are mapped and pictured daily in newspapers and magazines, and new words and geographic names are introduced from strange languages. Almost hourly use of a good, up-to-date dictionary is essential to clear understanding.

Ample vocabulary. The New Winston Dictionary for Young People includes over 46,000 terms, by a count made in accordance with the specifications of the United States Government for determining the vocabulary content of dictionaries. It is particularly rich in the new words coming into daily use through motion pictures and the radio, from discoveries in medicine, chemistry, physics, and other physical sciences, from inventions in industry, and from developments in the social sciences. New meanings and new uses of familiar words are clearly explained. The large type of the entry word makes for ease and speed in finding the word wanted.

All entries arranged in one alphabetical list. The confusion involved in looking in different parts of a book for various subjects is obviated by arranging all entries—the standard vocabulary, prefixes, suffixes, and abbreviations, and geographical, Biblical, mythological, and literary names—in a single alphabetical list. The numerous biographical entries furnish hundreds of ready answers to the question: "Who was or *is* he?"

Definitions. The definitions in this dictionary are masterpieces of simplicity. They have been created specifically for this book and are in no case condensed or written down from a larger work. Every word used to define any other word is introduced as an entry in its alphabetical sequence. Like all books of the Winston series, this book follows the basic principle of definition, that every word shall be so defined that its meaning and use can be easily understood. Unintelligible definitions, even though they be scientifically accurate, have no place in this book.

Verbal illustrations. The actual use of a word in a sentence or phrase often clarifies understanding. While a definition—not merely an illustrative phrase—is given at every entry, this dictionary contains thousands of verbal illustrations that show the use of words in context. Such additions to the definitions are particularly valuable in showing idiomatic uses and variations from the usual meaning.

Pictorial illustrations. Completeness of understanding is further served by 1700 black-and-white pictures and ten colored plates. These illustrations are

iii

new, and were nearly all drawn expressly for this book. Particular attention is invited to the ten colored plates. On the back of each of these plates is a discussion of the subject of the picture in simple language. One feature of the illustrations in this book is the size scale, which is included wherever possible and adds to the understanding of the subject. Note also the indication of comparative size on the colored plates of animals.

Pronunciation. The scheme for showing pronunciation by phonetic respelling and diacritical marks is the familiar one that is universally accepted and has stood the test of long use. Markings learned in early school days are easily recognized; this book does not complicate the problem of pronunciation by the use of unfamiliar symbols. The key to pronunciation on each page is adequate, and obviates the necessity of reference to another part of the book. The more extended discussion on pages ix and x is available for careful study. Pronunciations follow the best current usage. Where more than one pronunciation is acceptable, both are given.

Spelling and syllabification. Adequate answers to the numerous problems of spelling and syllabification of plurals, principal parts, and compound words are insured by full treatment, in spite of the added space required. Forms involving difficulties in these particulars are spelled out in full because the familiar device of giving endings alone is often unintelligible to the immature mind.

Parts of speech. Satisfactory treatment of the important problem of classification of a word under different parts of speech with different syllabification and pronunciation has required separate entries for many words, as for the noun *pro'gress* and the verb *pro-gress'*, or the adjective *pres'ent* and the verb *pre-sent'*. Wherever change in the part of speech involves a change in pronunciation without change in syllabification, as in the noun *ab'stract* and the verb *ab-stract'*, the markings indicate the correct usage.

Synonyms. The user of this dictionary will learn from frequent observation the significance of synonyms in our language. Flexibility and charm in speech and writing depend in no small degree on a discriminating resourcefulness in the use of synonyms. For this reason they have been made a prominent feature of this book.

Maps. The dictionary is a reference book. Consequently, the greater its scope, the more frequent will be its use and the more valuable its promotion of the dictionary habit. The present book contains sixteen colored maps, showing the cities, towns, and physical features listed in the vocabulary. Here for the first time in such a book is a ready and adequate reference atlas of the world. Most important of all, except for a very few names of places too small to be shown, each geographic entry in the alphabetical vocabulary refers the user to a specific map for its location.

Type and format. The large, clear type for entry words, facilitating easy reference, has been a consistent feature of the Winston Dictionaries. A new font of type was designed for the pronunciations, with special symbols for such features as primary and secondary accents, long and short hyphens, and diacritical marks. Users of this book will be impressed by the larger format, affording added space for pictures and maps, and by the large type used in the definitions, the quality of paper, the strong binding, and the general beauty of the book.

CONTENTS

COLORED ILLUSTRATIONS

FULL-PAGE AND COMPOSITE ILLUSTRATIONS

DIRECTIONS FOR THE USE OF THIS BOOK
I. GENERAL DIRECTIONS

The Main Listing shows the spelling and syllabification, but not accent nor pronunciation, which, in the interests of simplicity, are given separately.

Hyphens. In the main listing, in which accent is not indicated, a short hyphen is used to mark division into syllables, and a long hyphen to separate the parts of a compound word; as, **self-ev-i-dent.** In the pronunciation, the short hyphen is omitted under an accent, and a double hyphen, retained even under an accent, is used in compound words; as, sĕlf′=ĕv′ĭ-dĕnt. In variants and derivatives printed in boldface at the end of an article, usually without pronunciation, the long hyphen is used in dividing the parts of compound words, even under an accent; the short hyphen is used between syllables, except under an accent.

Variant Spellings. If two or more variations of the spelling of a word exist, as *gauge* and *gage, calcimine* and *kalsomine,* each is listed in its proper alphabetical place, unless the variant is too nearly like the preferred form to require separate entry, as in the case of *catalog, catalogue.*

Proper Names. Included in the main vocabulary is a large selection of names of important persons and places, covering Biblical and mythological characters; persons prominent in literature, legend, or familiar allusion; historical persons; and countries, cities, mountains, rivers, etc. With the names of places is given a map number referring to one of the sixteen colored maps at the back of the book, so that the student can immediately fix the exact location in his mind.

Foreign Words. The vocabulary includes also a large number of words which, though foreign, are so frequently used as to be a part of the educated person's vocabulary. The pronunciation of such of these words as have not yet become entirely Anglicized is admittedly a matter of difficulty; the student is referred to the discussion of the pronunciation of foreign words on page x.

Homographs. Words spelled alike, but of different origin, are given separate listings, each preceded by a small numeral, as ¹**bark**, the outer covering of a tree, ²**bark**, a kind of boat, and ³**bark**, the cry of a dog.

Derivatives. Important derivative words in common use are as a rule listed in the main vocabulary with full definitions. The meanings of some derivatives, however, can be easily and directly inferred from the definition of the basic word, as of *rapidly* from *rapid, whiteness* from *white.* Many such words are given without definition, after the definition of the basic word. They are printed in boldface, with syllabification, accent, and, in case of need, pronunciation. Derivatives which have developed special meanings of their own, as *contractor, adorable, suspenders,* are listed and defined separately.

Prefixes and Suffixes are explained and illustrated. Thus under **-ness** is the entry: "a suffix added to adjectives to form nouns naming a quality or state of being; as, good*ness*, sick*ness.*" It should be noted, however, that a knowledge of the history of the changing forms of English, and of foreign languages, especially Latin, is sometimes necessary for a full understanding of the force of a prefix or suffix. Thus the prefix *ad-* has the general meaning to or toward, and this meaning can be recognized in *adjoin* and *admixture;* but the meaning is not so clear in *admit,* to let (a person) in, or *adore,* originally to pray to, because in English the elements *-mit* and *-ore* do not exist as separate verbs. Special care has been taken in such cases to use illustrative words that really make the force of the prefix or suffix clear.

Abbreviations are entered in their alphabetical order in the main vocabulary.

CONTENTS

judging. There are, however, a few special cases, as *singeing, dyeing,* in which the *e* is retained in order to avoid confusion. In words where final silent *-e* is preceded by a consonant and *l* or *r*, those letters unite with *-ing* to form a single syllable; as, *cou-pling* from *couple.*

(*c*) Final *-y* preceded by a consonant is changed to *i* before *-ed,* but is retained before *-ing;* as, *cried, crying; replied, replying.*

(*d*) Final silent *-e* preceded by *i* is dropped and the *i* is changed to *y* before *-ing;* as, *dying, lying.*

6. Verbs of one syllable, and verbs of more than one syllable if accented on the last syllable, ending in a single consonant preceded by a single vowel, double the final consonant before *-ed* and *-ing;* as, *plan, planned, planning; prefer, preferred, preferring.*

7. A considerable number of verbs have entirely irregular parts; as, *buy, bought, buying; bear,* past tense *bore,* past participle *borne* or *born,* present participle *bearing.* A few are defective, as *can* (no infinitive form), past tense *could.* Many verbs, once regular, have been contracted and now appear to be irregular; as, *put, set,* past tense and past participle *put, set; read* (pronounced rĕd), *kept, slept,* past tense and past participle of *read, keep, sleep.*

8. In British usage, verbs ending in unaccented *-el* double the *l* before *-ed* and *-ing;* as, *travelled, travelling.* In American usage this *l* is not doubled; the principal parts of such verbs are given in the form *traveled, traveling.*

Comparison of Adjectives and Adverbs.

1. Adjectives of one syllable are regularly compared by adding *-er* and *-est* to the positive degree to form respectively the comparative and superlative; as, *old, older, oldest.*

2. Adjectives of more than two syllables are usually compared by using the words *more* and *most* with the positive; as, *beautiful, more beautiful, most beautiful.*

3. Adjectives of two syllables are compared by adding *-er, -est* (but see rule 5), if the resulting form is easily pronounced; as, *yellow, yellower, yellowest;* otherwise they are compared by the use of *more* and *most;* as, *spacious, more spacious, most spacious.* Usage varies according to individual taste; many adjectives can be compared in either way; as, *corrupt, corrupter* or *more corrupt,* etc.

4. Adverbs are usually compared by the use of *more* and *most,* though a few use *-er* and *-est;* as, *near, nearer, nearest; often, oftener, oftenest.* Some adverbs are not compared; as, *here, there, now, then.*

Comparatives and superlatives formed in accordance with the rules stated above are considered regular, and are not given in the Dictionary unless required for some special reason.

The following cases of comparison are considered irregular, and are noted in this book.

5. A final silent *-e* is dropped before the endings *-er* and *-est;* as, *fine, finer, finest; noble, nobler, noblest.*

6. Adjectives of one syllable, and adjectives of more than one syllable if accented on the last syllable, ending in a single consonant preceded by a single vowel, double the final consonant before *-er* and *-est;* as, *big, bigger, biggest.*

7. Adjectives ending in *-y* change the *y* to *i* before *-er* and *-est;* as, *happy, happier, happiest.*

8. A number of the commoner adjectives, and a few adverbs, are entirely irregular; as, *good, better, best; bad, worse, worst; ill* (the adverb), *worse, worst; far, farther, farthest.*

9. Many adverbs which may function also as prepositions have an adjective function when compared, forming the comparative in *-er* and the superlative by adding *-most* to the positive or comparative; as, *in, inner, inmost* or *innermost.* Some adjectives have only the superlative; as, *topmost, uttermost.*

II. SPELLING AND PRONUNCIATION OF INFLECTIONAL FORMS

Plural of Nouns.

1. Add *-s* (pronounced s) if the singular ends in the sound of *f, k, p, t,* or *th* as in *breath*—that is, any sound with which the sound of *s* readily combines; as, *puffs, rakes, tops, hopes, hats, births.* The sound of *th* in a few such words changes in the plural to that of *th* as in *breathe,* and the *s* is pronounced z (see 2 *b* below); as, *baths, mouths.*

2. Add *-s* (pronounced z) if the singular ends:

(*a*) In a vowel sound; as, *trees, laws.*

(*b*) In the sound of *b, d, g, ng, l, m, n, r, v,* or *th* as in *breathe*—that is, any voiced consonant sound with which the sound of *z* readily combines; as, *cabs, odes, bags, tongs, bells, plumes, tins, fires, Slavs, tithes.*

3. Add *-es* (pronounced ĕz) if the singular ends in a sibilant, or hissing sound, whether voiced or unvoiced—that is, in the sound of *s, sh, ch, z, zh,* or *j*—and has no final silent *-e* as, *dresses, marshes, matches, topazes.*

4. Add *-s* if the singular ends in a sibilant sound and has a final silent *-e,* the final *e* combining with the *s* to form an additional syllable (pronounced ĕz); as, *laces, mustaches, avalanches, breezes, garages, edges.*

Plurals formed according to the rules stated above are considered regular, and are not given in the Dictionary, unless required for some special reason.

The following classes of plurals are considered irregular, and are noted in this book.

5. Nouns ending in *-y* preceded by a consonant form the plural by changing the *y* to *i* and adding *-es* (the *-ies* being pronounced ĭz); as, *lady, ladies.* Nouns ending in *-y* preceded by a vowel add *-s* according to rule, but their plurals are usually given; as, *turkey, turkeys.*

6. Nouns ending in *-o* preceded by a vowel form the plural in *-os* (pronounced ōz); as, *cameos, folios;* nouns ending in *-o* preceded by a consonant usually form the plural in *-oes;* as, *echoes, heroes, mos-* quitoes, mottoes, *Negroes, potatoes, tomatoes,* etc.; but musical terms ending in *-o* add *-s* only, whether a vowel or a consonant precedes the *o;* as, *sopranos, altos.*

7. A few nouns ending in the sound of *f* change the *f* to *v* and add *-es* (pronounced z); as, *loaf, loaves.*

8. A few plurals are formed in other ways than by the addition of *-s* or *-es.* Among these are *geese, mice, children, oxen, deer, sheep, dice;* foreign plurals, as *theses, alumni, phenomena, cherubim;* and other scattered cases.

Third Person Singular of Verbs.

The third person singular indicative active of all regular and most irregular verbs is formed according to rules 1–4 for the plural of nouns; as, *gets, hears, wishes, rises.*

Principal Parts of Verbs.

1. Regular verbs add *-ed* to the infinitive to form the past tense and past participle, and *-ing* to form the present participle. The *-ing* is always pronounced as an additional syllable.

2. If the infinitive ends in *-d* or *-t* not silent, the *-ed* is pronounced ĕd; as, *ended, heated.*

3. If the infinitive ends in the sound of *b, g, ng, j, l, m, n, r, v, z, zh,* or *th* as in *breathe*—that is, any voiced consonant except *d*—, or in a vowel sound, the *-ed* is pronounced d; as, *hurled, hurrahed;* but note rules 5 and 6 below.

4. If the infinitive ends in the sound of *f, k, p, s, sh, ch, th* as in *breath*—that is, any unvoiced consonant except *t*—, the *-ed* is pronounced t; as, *amassed, attacked, marched;* but note 5 and 6.

Principal parts derived according to the rules stated above are considered regular, and are not given in the Dictionary unless required for some special reason.

Principal parts formed according to the following rules are considered irregular, and are given in this book.

5. (*a*) Final *-e,* whether silent or not, is dropped before *-ed;* as, *agreed, judged.*

(*b*) Final silent *-e* preceded by a consonant is dropped before *-ing;* as, *racing,*

III. GUIDE TO PRONUNCIATION

The pronunciation of every main listing, and of all forms or derivatives concerning which any doubt could arise, is given by respelling within parentheses according to a simple phonetic key, accessible throughout the Vocabulary at the foot of each page. The following notes are intended as an amplification of this key. It should be borne in mind that these notes are an explanation of the *symbols used in the key*, rather than of English spelling. Each of the symbols stands for one, and only one, specific sound value; but in many cases the sound value is represented in ordinary English spelling by any of several letters or combinations of letters, as shown by the illustrative words.

The principal stress in a word of two or more syllables is indicated by a primary accent [ʹ] placed after the syllable to be stressed. A secondary accent is indicated by this mark in lightface [ʹ]. A word may have a primary accent and no more, as *seaʹman;* a primary and one or more secondary accents, as *earʹmarkʹ, huckʹle-berʹry, auʹto-in-toxʹi-caʹtion;* or, occasionally, two primary accents, as *backʹboneʹ*.

Symbols for English Sounds

ā as in *ate, pale, favor, prevail, weigh, play, steak, veil, they, suède* (long *a*).

ȧ as in *aorta, chaotic:* usually the equivalent of a long *a* sound in an unaccented syllable.

â as in *rare, parent, prepare, there, air, heir:* usually in an accented syllable before *r*.

ă as in *cat, garret, canteen* (short *a*).

ȧ as in *ask, chance* (intermediate *a*).

ä as in *calm, father* (broad or Italian *a*).

å as in *local, affect:* usually equivalent to short *a* in an unaccented syllable ending in a consonant.

a̍ as in *banana, parade, sofa, comma, explanatory* (indeterminate *a*): usually equivalent to intermediate *a* in an unaccented syllable not ending in a consonant.

ē as in *even, stream, meet, seize, people, key, machine, yield, Caesar* (long *e*).

ė as in *event, create:* usually the equivalent of long *e* in an unaccented syllable.

ĕ as in *defect, edge, aesthetic* (short *e*).

ḙ as in *novel, recent:* usually equivalent to short *e* in an unaccented syllable.

ẽ as in *writer, the, conference, elixir, altar, actor:* frequently occurring before *r;* sometimes final; always in an unaccented syllable.

ī as in *fine, delight, idea, fly, aisle, aye, height, eye, tie* (long *i*).

ĭ as in *smith, dissect, myth:* used also for the sound of final unaccented *y*, as in *lovely, seemly;* of *ie* in such forms as *ladies, hurries;* of *a* in *senate, intimate, foliage, savage;* of *u* in *lettuce.*

ō as in *hope, echo, foam, doe, blow, sew, beau, though, yeoman* (long *o*).

ȯ as in *potato, obey:* equivalent to long *o* in an unaccented syllable.

ô as in *cord, adorn, call, law, caught, fought* (intermediate *o*).

o̬ as in *dog, soft, gone* (open *o*): in accented and unaccented syllables.

ŏ as in *bottom, hot, obvious* (short *o*).

o̍ as in *compare, connect:* equivalent to short *o* in an unaccented syllable.

ū as in *cure, unit, yew, few, curfew, feud* (long *u*).

ū as in *unite, circulate, humane:* usually equivalent to long *u* in an unaccented syllable.

û as in *burn, occur, fur, myrtle, word, refer, learn, mirth, amateur:* usually in an accented syllable, before an *r* in the same syllable.

ŭ as in *up, cut, honey, enough* (short *u*).

u̍ as in *focus, support, succeed:* usually equivalent to short *u* in an unaccented syllable.

o͞o as in *boot, fool, do, true, rule, threw, rheumatism, soup.*

o͝o as in *foot, put, could, tearful.*

g as in *g*et, *g*old, *g*host (hard *g*).

j as in *j*oy, a*g*e, *g*em, e*d*ge, cor*di*al (soft *g*).

s as in *s*ing, cea*s*e.

y as in *y*et, *y*ear, *y*ou, oni*o*n.

ng as in so*ng*, tong*u*e, u*n*cle, fi*n*ger.

ch as in *ch*in, ca*tch*, ques*ti*on, righ*te*ous.

sh as in *sh*ow, *s*ure, ac*ti*on, ten*si*on, tena*ci*ous, o*ce*an, ma*ch*ine.

th as in *th*in, ba*th*, e*th*er (voiceless).

th as in *th*en, ba*th*e, ei*th*er (voiced).

hw as in *wh*en, *wh*y, *wh*ere.

zh as in a*z*ure, mea*s*ure, rou*g*e.

b, d, f, h, k, l, m, n, p, r, t, v, w, z, have their ordinary English values.

c, q, x, are not used in indicating pronunciation. The letter *c* in the conventional spelling is generally equivalent to **k** or **s**; *q*(*u*) = **k**(**w**); and *x* = **ks** or **gz**, or, initially, **z**.

Sounds in Foreign Languages

kh for the sound represented by *ch* in German a*ch* (äkh) or i*ch* (ĭkh) and Scottish lo*ch* (lôkh).

ṅ for the French nasal, as in e*n*fant (äṅ′fäṅ′), bie*n* (byăṅ), no*m* (nôṅ).

ö for the sound of umlauted *o* in German (written *ö* or, sometimes, *oe*), as in sch*ö*n (shön), G*oe*the (gö′tĕ); also for *eu* final and before *s, x, z, t* in French words, as in f*eu* (fö), j*eu* (zhö), dans*eu*se (däṅ′söz′). French *eu* in other cases is pronounced like **û** in the key, as in p*eu*r (pûr), dans*eu*r (däṅ′sûr′).

ü for the sound of umlauted *u* in German, as in f*ü*r (für), L*ü*beck (lü′bĕk), and of *u* in French, as in l*u*ne (lün), d*u* (dü).

The symbol **ĕ**, used in English for the unaccented vowel in writer (rīt′ĕr) or in the definite article when unstressed (*th*ĕ), should be reduced in French to almost nothing. Thus *tout de suite* (tōō′ dĕ süēt′) is pronounced almost as tōōt′ süēt′.

The short, open *o*, represented in the key by **ô**, is more quickly pronounced in French and German than in such English words as *dog, soft*.

The symbol **y′** following a vowel in the phonetic respelling of French words, as in *Versailles* (vâr′sày′′), needs special care. The **y′** is pronounced almost like yĕ, but should not be allowed to make an extra syllable. Similarly **r′**, **m′**, **l′** following a consonant should not be sounded as an extra syllable, as in *simple* (săṅpl′′).

In French, all full syllables are pronounced with nearly equal stress; but there is usually a rising inflection or slight stress on the last syllable, which has somewhat the effect of the English accent. In this book, French words are shown with a primary accent on the last syllable, representing this rising inflection or slight stress, and with secondary accents on all other full syllables.

ABBREVIATIONS USED IN THIS BOOK

A.D. . . . . . anno Domini (Latin = in the year of our Lord): used in giving dates

adj . . . . adjective

adv . . . . adverb

B.C. . . . . . before Christ: used in giving dates

cap . . . . capital

comp . . . . comparative

conj . . . . conjunction

def . . . . definition

etc . . . . . et cetera (Latin = and others)

fem . . . . feminine

interj . . . . interjection

masc . . . . masculine

n . . . . noun

neut . . . . neuter

pl . . . . plural

p.p . . . . participle, past

p.pr . . . . participle, present

prep . . . . preposition

pron . . . . pronoun

p.t . . . . past tense

sing . . . . singular

superl . . . . superlative

Syn . . . . synonym(s)

U.S. . . . . United States

U.S.S.R. . . . . . Union of Soviet Socialist Republics

v.i . . . . verb, intransitive

v.t . . . . verb, transitive

THE
WINSTON DICTIONARY

A

¹A, a (ā), *n.* [*pl.* A's, a's], **1** the first letter of the alphabet; **2**, in music, the sixth note in the major scale of C:—**A**, *adj.* **1**, first in order or class; as, an *A* rating; **2**, having the form of an A; as, an *A* tent:—**A 1** (ā′ wŭn′), excellent; first-class.

²a (a; when stressed, ā), *adj.* or *indefinite article*, one; any; as, *a* man was here; *a* man will protect his home: used instead of *an* before words beginning with a consonant or a consonant sound, or with a sounded *h*; as, *a* man, *a* unit, *a* youth, *a* holiday, *a* hotel.

³a (a), *prep.* **1**, for or in each; per; as, twice *a* year: now felt to be the indefinite article; **2**, to, into, in, on, or at; as, *a*float, *a*sleep, *a*-milking: used as a prefix.

A.A.A. abbreviation for *Amateur Athletic Association*, *Automobile Association of America*.

Aa-chen (ä′kĕn), a city in Germany, the ancient capital of Charlemagne's empire. Its French name is *Aix-la-Chapelle*.

Aar (är), a river in Switzerland.

Aar-on (âr′ŭn), in the Bible, the brother of Moses and the first high priest of the Hebrews (Exodus 4:13–17).

A.B. or **B.A.** abbreviation for *bachelor of arts*.

ab- (ăb-), a prefix meaning from; away; as, *ab*duct, *ab*normal.

a-ba-cá (ä′bä-kä′), *n.* Manila hemp; also, the plant which produces it.

a-back (a-băk′), *adv.* backward:—**taken aback**, surprised; disconcerted.

ab-a-cus (ăb′a-kŭs), *n.* [*pl.* abaci (ăb′a-sī) or abacuses (ăb′a-kŭs-ĕz)], **1**, a device used for counting, consisting of beads or balls strung on wires; **2**, in architecture, a flat layer, as of stone, forming the top section of the capital of a column or pillar (see illustration next column).

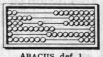
ABACUS, def. 1

a-baft (a-bȧft′), *adv.* at or toward the stern, or back part of a ship; as, go *abaft*:—*prep.* behind; as, *abaft* the bridge.

a-ban-don (a-băn′dŭn), *v.t.* **1**, to give up entirely; as, to *abandon* a house, a ship, or work; **2**, to yield (oneself) without restraint; as, he *abandoned* himself to grief:—*n.* reckless enthusiasm; as, he danced with *abandon*.—*n.* **a-ban′don-ment**.

ABACUS (A), def. 2

Syn., *v.* forsake, desert, leave, quit.

a-ban-doned (a-băn′dŭnd), *adj.* **1**, deserted; as, an *abandoned* house; **2**, wicked; lost to shame; as, an *abandoned* wretch.

a-base (a-bās′), *v.t.* [abased, abas-ing], to humble; as, he *abased* himself.

a-base-ment (a-bās′mĕnt), *n.* humiliation; loss of self-respect.

a-bash (a-băsh′), *v.t.* to embarrass; shame; disconcert; as, the rebuke *abashed* him.

a-bashed (a-băsht′), *adj.* overcome with surprise or shame; confused; disconcerted.

a-bate (a-bāt′), *v.i.* [abat-ed, abat-ing], to decrease; subside; as, the flood has *abated*:—*v.t.* **1**, to put an end to; as, to *abate* a nuisance; **2**, to reduce, as a debt.

a-bate-ment (a-bāt′mĕnt), *n.* **1**, a diminishing, as of pain or a storm; **2**, reduction, as of a debt.

ab-at-toir (ăb′a-twär′), *n.* a building in which animals are killed for market; a slaughterhouse.

ab-bé (a′bā′), *n.* in France, a title given to various persons, not necessarily priests, who wear religious garb.

ab-bess (ăb′ĕs), *n.* the head of a convent; the mother superior of an abbey.

ab-bey (ăb′ĭ), *n.* [*pl.* abbeys], **1**, one or more buildings in which a number of men or women live a religious life apart from the world, governed by an abbot or abbess; **2**, a church that was once part of a monastery; as, Westminster *Abbey*.

āte, āorta, râre, căt, ȧsk, fär, ăllow, sofȧ; ēve, ēvent, ĕll, writẽr, novĕl; bīte, pĭn; nō, ōbey, ôr, dŏg, tŏp, cŏllide; ūnit, ūnite, bûrn, cŭt, focŭs; nōon, fŏŏt; mound; coïn;

go; join; yet; sing; chin; show; thin, *th*en; hw, *wh*y; zh, azure; ü, Ger. für or Fr. lune; ö, Ger. schön or Fr. feu; ṅ, Fr. enfant, nom; kh, Ger. ach or ich.   See pages ix–x.

1

ab·bot (ăb′ŭt), *n.* the head of a monastery; a father superior.

ab·bre·vi·ate (ă-brē′vĭ-āt), *v.t.* [abbreviat-ed, abbreviat-ing], to shorten; especially, to shorten (a word) by writing only a part, as *Apr.* for *April.*

ab·bre·vi·a·tion (ă-brē′vĭ-ā′shŭn), *n.* 1, the act of shortening; especially, the shortening of a word; 2, the shortened form of a word, as *min.* for *minute.*

ab·di·cate (ăb′dĭ-kāt), *v.t.* [abdicat-ed, ab-dicat-ing], to give up, as kingly power; re-sign (a throne):—*v.i.* to give up sovereign power; as, the king *abdicated.*—*n.* **ab′di-ca′tion.**
   Syn. renounce, surrender.

ab·do·men (ăb-dō′měn; ăb′dŏ-měn), *n.* 1, the large cavity of the body below the dia-phragm, containing the digestive organs (see *diaphragm*, illustration); 2, in insects, the rear section of the body.

ab·dom·i·nal (ăb-dŏm′ĭ-năl), *adj.* having to do with the cavity of the body below the diaphragm; as, *abdominal* pains.

ab·duct (ăb-dŭkt′), *v.t.* to kidnap.—*n.* **ab-duc′tor.**—*n.* **ab-duc′tion.**

a·beam (á-bēm′), *adv.* to the side of, or straight across, a ship.

a·bed (á-běd′), *adv.* in bed; as, to lie *abed.*

A·bel (ā′běl), in the Bible, the second son of Adam and Eve, slain by his brother Cain (Genesis 4).

Ab·er·deen (ăb′ēr-dēn′), a city in Scotland on the east coast (map 13).

ab·er·ra·tion (ăb′ēr-ā′shŭn), *n.* 1, a wandering astray; variation from a standard or normal path; as, *aberration* of light; 2, mental disorder.

a·bet (á-bět′), *v.t.* [abet-ted, abet-ting], to encourage or aid, especially in a crime; as, he *abetted* the thief.—*n.* **a-bet′tor.**
   Syn. assist, sanction, support.

a·bey·ance (á-bā′ăns), *n.* state of tempo-rary inactivity; as, Tom's keenness for stamp collecting is in *abeyance.*

ab·hor (ăb-hôr′), *v.t.* [abhorred, abhor-ring], to shrink from with disgust; detest; as, the humane man *abhors* cruelty.

ab·hor·rent (ăb-hôr′ěnt), *adj.* hateful; disgusting; as, treachery is *abhorrent* to me. —*n.* **ab-hor′rence.**

a·bide (á-bīd′), *v.i.* [*p.t.* and *p.p.* abode (á-bōd′) or abid-ed, *p.pr.* abid-ing], 1, to live; dwell; 2, to endure; as, great love *abides*:—**abide by**, to remain faithful to; as, to *abide by* a promise:—*v.t.* 1, to put up with; as, I cannot *abide* him; 2, to watch or wait for; as, I shall *abide* your return.

a·bil·i·ty (á-bĭl′ĭ-tĭ). *n.* [*pl.* abilities], power to do something; as, *ability* to do heavy

work; also, skill; talent; as, a man of *ability.*

ab·ject (ăb′jěkt; ăb-jěkt′), *adj.* 1, de-graded; craven; as, an *abject* coward; 2, contemptible; as, *abject* submission; hope-less; as, *abject* poverty.—*adv.* **ab-ject′ly.**—*n.* **ab-ject′ness.**

ab·jure (ăb-jŏŏr′), *v.t.* [abjured, abjur-ing], to promise solemnly to give up; renounce, as one's religion.—*n.* **ab′ju-ra′tion.**
   Syn. retract, abandon, forswear.

ab·la·tive (ăb′lá-tĭv), *adj.* naming a case, as in Latin grammar, used sometimes with, sometimes without a preposition, to ex-press such ideas as *from, in, by*:—*n.* the ablative case; also, a word in that case.

a·blaze (á-blāz′), *adj.* 1, on fire; as, the hut was *ablaze*; 2, aglow; full of color, as au-tumn woods; 3, ardent; eager.

a·ble (ā′bl), *adj.* [a-bler, a-blest], 1, having power, skill, or means; as, *able* to work hard; is he *able* to drive a car? they are not *able* to buy coal; 2, skilful; unusually clever; as, an *able* lawyer.—*adv.* **a′bly.**

-a·ble (-á-bl), [sometimes, *-ible*], a suffix meaning: 1, able to; as, dur-*able*, delect*able*; 2, capable of being; as, read-*able*; 3, fit to be; as, laud*able*, detest*able*; 4, inclined to; characterized by; as, peace*able*.

ab·lu·tion (ăb-lū′shŭn), *n.* a washing or cleansing of the body or part of the body.

ab·ne·ga·tion (ăb′nē-gā′shŭn), *n.* 1, the act of denying oneself something; self-denial; 2, self-sacrifice.

ab·nor·mal (ăb-nôr′măl), *adj.* differing from what is usual or expected; out of the ordinary; above or below the average; as, an *abnormal* child.—*adv.* **ab-nor′mal-ly.**—*n.* **ab′nor-mal′i-ty.**

a·board (á-bôrd′), *adv.* on or into a ship or railroad train:—*prep.* on board of; in or into; as, to be, or go, *aboard* a ship.

¹a·bode (á-bōd′), one form of the past tense and past participle of *abide.*

²a·bode (á-bōd′), *n.* a place of residence; home; as, this small cottage is my *abode.*

a·bol·ish (á-bŏl′ĭsh), *v.t.* to do away with; put an end to; as, to *abolish* dog racing.

ab·o·li·tion (ăb′ŏ-lĭsh′ŭn), *n.* the destroy-ing of, or doing away with, something; as, the *abolition* of slavery.

ab·o·li·tion·ist (ăb′ŏ-lĭsh′ŭn-ĭst), *n.* a person who wishes to abolish something; especially, one who believed that Negro slavery should be ended in the U.S.

a·bom·i·na·ble (á-bŏm′ĭ-ná-bl), *adj.* hate-ful; odious; as, he is a rude fellow with *abominable* manners.—*adv.* **a-bom′i-na-bly.**

a·bom·i·nate (á-bŏm′ĭ-nāt), *v.t.* [abomi-nat-ed, abominat-ing], to detest; loathe.

āte, āorta, râre, căt. ásk, fär, ăllow, sofá; ēve, ěvent, ĕll, writēr, novĕl; bīte, pĭn; nō, ōbey, ôr, dŏg, tŏp, cŏllide; ūnit, ūnite, bûrn, cŭt, focŭs; nōōn, fŏŏt; mound; coin;

a·bom·i·na·tion (a̯-bŏm/ĭ-nā/shŭn), *n.* **1**, anything vile, hateful, or wicked; a shameful vice; **2**, a feeling of disgust or loathing; as, he held strong drink in *abomination*.

ab·o·rig·i·nes (ăb/ō-rĭj/ĭ-nēz), *n.pl.* the earliest known inhabitants of a country, as the Indians in North America.

a·bor·tion (a̯-bôr/shŭn), *n.* a birth which occurs before the normal time.

a·bound (a̯-bound/), *v.i.* **1**, to exist in great numbers or amount; as, deer *abound* in these hills; **2**, to be richly supplied; as, his speech *abounded* in wit.

a·bout (a̯-bout/), *adv.* **1**, around; on every side; near by; as, they stood *about;* **2**, in a reversed position; as, to face *about;* **3**, in rotation; as, turn *about* is fair play; **4**, in a state of action; as, he is up and *about;* **5**, on the point of; as, I am *about* to shoot; **6**, approximately; as, come at *about* midnight; nearly; as, *about* dead:—*prep.* **1**, concerning; relating to; as, a story *about* a bear; something wrong *about* the plan; **2**, on all sides of; near to; as, trees *about* the lake; **3**, on the person of; as, I haven't a dollar *about* me.

a·bove (a̯-bŭv/), *adv.* **1**, in a higher place; overhead; as, directly *above;* **2**, in heaven; as, up *above;* **3**, before this; as, see page 6 *above:*—*prep.* **1**, over; higher than; **2**, superior to; as, to be *above* deceit; **3**, beyond; as, *above* reproach; **4**, in excess of; as, *above* a dollar:—*adj.* stated previously; as, the *above* objection.

a·bove-board (a̯-bŭv/bôrd/), *adv.* openly; without trickery; as, he acted *aboveboard:*—*adj.* honest; as, he was always *aboveboard.*

Abp. abbreviation for *Archbishop.*

ab·rade (ăb-rād/), *v.t.* [abrad-ed, abrad-ing], to rub off; also, to rub or wear away; as, a glacier *abrades* the rocks at its sides.

A·bra·ham (ā/bra̯-hăm), in the Bible, the first great patriarch of the Hebrews, founder of the race (Genesis 11–25).

ab·ra·sion (ăb-rā/zhŭn), *n.* **1**, an injury to the skin from rubbing or scraping; **2**, a wearing or rubbing away.

ab·ra·sive (ăb-rā/sĭv), *n.* a substance used for grinding and polishing; as, pumice is an *abrasive:*—*adj.* used to grind or polish; as, an *abrasive* substance.

a·breast (a̯-brĕst/), *adv.* side by side; equally advanced; as, the three boys walked *abreast;* to keep *abreast* of the times.

a·bridge (a̯-brĭj/), *v.t.* [abridged, abridg-ing], **1**, to shorten; condense, as a book; **2**, to curtail or cut down, as liberties.

a·bridg·ment or **a·bridge·ment** (a̯-brĭj/mĕnt), *n.* **1**, the act of shortening or reducing; **2**, a shortened form, as of a book.

a·broad (a̯-brôd/), *adv.* **1**, far and wide; as, the news spread *abroad;* **2**, out of doors; as, to walk *abroad;* **3**, in or to a foreign country.

ab·ro·gate (ăb/rō-gāt), *v.t.* [abrogat-ed, abrogat-ing], to repeal or cancel, as a law or privilege.—*n.* **ab/ro·ga/tion.**

ab·rupt (ăb-rŭpt/), *adj.* **1**, steep, as a hill; **2**, sudden; as, an *abrupt* turn; **3**, short or curt; as, an *abrupt* manner.

Ab·sa·lom (ăb/sa̯-lŏm), in the Bible, the favorite son of King David, slain in rebellion against his father (2 Samuel 18).

ab·scess (ăb/sĕs), *n.* pus forming at a certain point, or focus, of infection.

ab·scond (ăb-skŏnd/), *v.i.* to flee secretly, especially after some wrongdoing; as, he *absconded* with the stolen money.

ab·sence (ăb/sĕns), *n.* **1**, a being away, or the period of being away; as, an *absence* of one week; **2**, lack; as, *absence* of heat.

ab·sent (ăb/sĕnt), *adj.* **1**, not present; missing; lacking; **2**, lost in thought; inattentive; as, an *absent* manner:—*v.t.* (ăb-sĕnt/), to withdraw (oneself).—*adv.* **ab/sent·ly.**

ab·sen·tee (ăb/sĕn-tē/), *n.* one who is not present; as, there are three *absentees* today.

ab·sent—mind·ed (ăb/sĕnt-mīn/dĕd), *adj.* lost in thought; hence, inattentive; forgetful.—*adv.* **ab/sent—mind/ed·ly.**—*n.* **ab/-sent—mind/ed·ness.**

ab·so·lute (ăb/sō-lūt), *adj.* **1**, whole; complete; perfect; as, the *absolute* truth; **2**, having power or authority that is not restricted by laws or by a constitution; as, an *absolute* monarch; **3**, positive; certain; as, an *absolute* fact.

Syn. supreme, arbitrary, unconditional.

ab·so·lute·ly (ăb/sō-lūt-lĭ; ăb/sō-lūt/lĭ), *adv.* wholly; positively; as, *absolutely* bad.

ab·so·lu·tion (ăb/sō-lū/shŭn), *n.* **1**, a formal forgiveness of sins; as, the priest pronounced *absolution;* **2**, a release from any obligation, charge, or penalty.

ab·so·lut·ism (ăb/sō-lūt-ĭzm), *n.* the principles and practices of government by a monarch or ruler with unlimited power or authority; autocracy; despotism.—*n.* and *adj.* **ab/so·lut·ist.**

ab·solve (ăb-sŏlv/), *v.t.* [absolved, absolv-ing], **1**, to release or set free, as from a duty; **2**, to acquit; pronounce not guilty; as, the jury *absolved* him of fraud.

ab·sorb (ăb-sôrb/), *v.t.* **1**, to drink in; suck or swallow up; as, a sponge *absorbs* water; **2**, to interest deeply; take all of one's attention; as, baseball *absorbs* John now.

ab·sorb·ent (ăb-sôr/bĕnt), *adj.* having the tendency or ability to absorb; as, *absorbent* cotton:—*n.* an absorbent substance.

---

go; join; yet; sing; chin; show; thin, *th*en; **hw,** *wh*y; **zh,** azure; **ŭ,** Ger. für or Fr. lune; **ö,** Ger. schön or Fr. *feu;* **ṅ,** Fr. *enfant,* nom; **kh,** Ger. a*ch* or i*ch.* See pages ix–x.

ab·sorb·ing (ăb-sôr′bĭng), *adj.* intensely interesting, as a story or drama.

ab·sorp·tion (ăb-sôrp′shŭn), *n.* 1, the process or act of taking or sucking in, or swallowing up; 2, the mental state of being entirely occupied; as, his *absorption* in golf hurts his business.

ab·stain (ăb-stān′), *v.i.* to refrain; keep away; as, to *abstain* from the use of tobacco.—*n.* **ab·stain′er.**

ab·ste·mi·ous (ăb-stē′mĭ-ŭs), *adj.* moderate and sparing in the use of food and drink.—*n.* **ab·ste′mi·ous·ness.**

ab·sti·nence (ăb′stĭ-nĕns), *n.* a refraining from something; especially, the practice of denying oneself certain foods, drinks, pleasures, etc.

Syn. moderation, sobriety, temperance.

ab·stract (ăb′străkt), *n.* a summing up of the main points, as of a book or an argument:—*adj.* (ăb′străkt; ăb·străkt′), 1, considered apart from actual facts or a real situation; as, *abstract* justice; 2, hard to understand; as, philosophy is an *abstract* subject; 3, in grammar, describing a noun which expresses a quality or characteristic but does not name the person or thing that possesses it; thus "strength" is an *abstract* noun, but a word like "wrestler," which names a person, is a *concrete* noun:—*v.t.* (ăb·străkt′), 1, to take away or draw out, especially secretly or dishonestly; 2, to make a summary of (a book).

Syn., v. detach, remove, withdraw, divert.

ab·stract·ed (ăb-străk′tĕd), *adj.* absent-minded; lost in thought.—*adv.* **ab·stract′-ed·ly.**

ab·strac·tion (ăb-străk′shŭn), *n.* 1, the act of drawing out or taking away, as by stealing; 2, an abstract idea; theory; as, nothing can be proved by his *abstractions;* 3, absent-mindedness; inattention.

ab·struse (ăb-stro͞os′), *adj.* hard to understand; obscure, as a difficult problem.

ab·surd (ăb-sûrd′), *adj.* contrary to reason or sense; ridiculous; silly.—*adv.* **ab·surd′ly.**

ab·surd·i·ty (ăb-sûr′dĭ-tĭ), *n.* [*pl.* absurdities], foolishness, as of dress, speech, or conduct; also, a silly act or statement.

a·bun·dance (à-bŭn′dăns), *n.* overflowing quantity or amount; great plenty; as, an *abundance* of food.

a·bun·dant (à-bŭn′dănt), *adj.* ample; more than enough.—*adv.* **a·bun′dant·ly.**

a·buse (à-būz′), *v.t.* [abused, abus-ing], 1, to use improperly; misuse; as, to *abuse* a privilege; 2, to maltreat; as, to *abuse* animals; 3, to use violent language to; as, he *abused* his men; 4, to strain; overtax; as, to *abuse*

one's health:—*n.* (à-būs′), 1, misuse, as of a privilege; 2, cruel treatment, as of animals; 3, violent language; 4, a straining or over-taxing, as of one's health; 5, a corrupt or wrong practice; as, political *abuses.*

Syn., v. reproach, defame, slander.

a·bu·sive (à-bū′sĭv), *adj.* given to cruel treatment or harsh language; also, of language, harsh; insulting.—*adv.* **a·bu′sive·ly.**

a·but (à-bŭt′), *v.i.* [abut-ted, abut-ting], to border (upon); be in contact: followed by *on, upon, against;* as, the house *abuts* on the hill.

a·but·ment (à-bŭt′-mĕnt), *n.* the supporting structure at either end of an arch or bridge, or a wedge-shaped piece on the upstream side of a bridge pier to resist pressure from water or ice.

ABUTMENTS OF AN ARCHED BRIDGE
A, A, arch abutments; B, B, current abutments.

a·bys·mal (à-bĭz′măl), *adj.* deep; vast; profound; as, *abysmal* gloom.

a·byss (à-bĭs′), *n.* 1, a deep hole in the earth; a chasm; 2, anything bottomless or unbounded.

Ab·ys·sin·i·a (ăb′ĭ-sĭn′ĭ-à), an ancient country in eastern Africa. See **Ethiopia.**—*adj.* and *n.* **Ab′ys·sin′i·an.**

A.C. abbreviation for *alternating current.*

ac- (ăk-), *prefix,* a form of *ad-* used before *c.*

a·ca·cia (à-kā′shà), *n.* 1, any of several thorny trees or shrubs growing in warm regions and having, generally, fernlike leaves and clusters of yellow or white flowers; 2, the false acacia, or common locust.

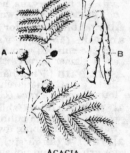

ac·a·dem·ic (ăk′-à-dĕm′ĭk), *adj.* 1, pertaining to a school or college, or to learning; as, *academic* subjects; the *academic* year; 2, theoretical rather than practical; abstract; as, an *academic* discussion. Also, **ac′a·dem′i·cal.**

ACACIA
Showing stem, thorns, leaves, flower (A), and fruit pod (B).

a·cad·e·my (à-kăd′ē-mĭ), *n.* [*pl.* academies], 1, a private high school; 2, a school for special study; as, a military *academy.*

A·ca·di·a (à-kā′dĭ-à), an old poetic name for *Nova Scotia* (map 4). It is sometimes called by its French name, **A′ca′die′** (à′-kä′dē′).—*adj.* and *n.* **A·ca′di·an.**

A·ca·di·a Na·tion·al Park, a national park on Mount Desert Island, Maine.

a·can·thus (*a̍*-kăn′thŭs), *n.* [*pl.* acanthuses (*a̍*-kăn′thŭs-ĕz) or acanthi (*a̍*-kăn′thī)], a plant of southern Europe, characterized by deeply cleft leaves. In Greek art the acanthus is frequently represented on the capitals of Corinthian pillars.

ACANTHUS LEAF

ac·cede (ăk-sēd′), *v.i.* [acced-ed, acced-ing], 1, to agree or yield, as to a request; 2, to succeed, as to a throne.
Syn. assent, consent, acquiesce, comply, coincide, concur, approve.

ac·cel·er·ate (ăk-sĕl′ĕr-āt), *v.t.* [accelerat-ed, accelerat-ing], 1, to cause to move faster; hasten the speed of; as, to *accelerate* an engine; 2, to cause to come sooner; as, death was *accelerated* by grief.
Syn. hurry, promote, quicken, further.

ac·cel·er·a·tion (ăk-sĕl′ĕr-ā′shŭn), *n.* increase in speed; a quickening.

ac·cel·er·a·tor (ăk-sĕl′ĕr-ā′tĕr), *n.* one who or that which increases speed; in an automobile, the pedal which regulates the flow of gasoline, and thus the speed.

ac·cent (ăk′sĕnt), *n.* 1, emphasis; stress; especially, the stress laid upon a syllable of a word or upon a note of music; 2, any of several characters, as [′, ∕], used in writing and printing to show which syllable of a word is to be stressed; 3, a special or peculiar method of pronouncing; as, an Italian is apt to speak English with a foreign *accent*; 4, tone of voice; as, she spoke in *accents* soft and low:—*v.t.* (ăk-sĕnt′; ăk′sĕnt), 1, to utter with special stress, as a word; 2, to mark with an accent; 3, to emphasize; as, his remarks were *accented* by gestures.

ac·cen·tu·ate (ăk-sĕn′tū-āt), *v.t.* [accentuat-ed, accentuat-ing], 1, to emphasize or stress in speech, writing, or music; 2, to heighten; make prominent; as, her youth *accentuated* her beauty.

ac·cept (ăk-sĕpt′), *v.t.* 1, to take gladly, as a gift; consent to take, as an office; take with resignation, as one's fate; 2, to agree to; as, I *accept* your terms; 3, to recognize as true, as a creed; 4, to admit (a person) to favor; as, the club *accepted* the stranger.

ac·cept·a·ble (ăk-sĕp′ta̍-bl), *adj.* pleasing; welcome; also, agreeable; satisfactory; as, an *acceptable* plan.—*adv.* **ac·cept′a·bly.**

ac·cept·ance (ăk-sĕp′tăns), *n.* the taking of, or the willingness to take, something that is offered; as, the *acceptance* of a responsibility or a donation.

ac·cep·ta·tion (ăk′sĕp-tā′shŭn), *n.* the usual meaning; as, he misunderstands the *acceptation* of the word "democracy."

ac·cess (ăk′sĕs), *n.* 1, admittance or approach to a person or place; also, a way of approach; as, a drawbridge gave *access* to the castle; 2, an attack; fit; as, an *access* of coughing; an *access* of rage.

ac·ces·sa·ry (ăk-sĕs′a̍-rĭ), *adj.* and *n.* contributing; that which helps or contributes; accessory. See **accessory**.

ac·ces·si·ble (ăk-sĕs′ĭ-bl), *adj.* 1, easy to reach; as, the book was *accessible* because the shelf was low; 2, approachable, as a person in power who will listen to reason.
—*n.* **ac·ces′si·bil′i·ty.**

ac·ces·sion (ăk-sĕsh′ŭn), *n.* 1, the act of coming to an office, dignity, or throne; as, the *accession* of a king; 2, increase, as of wealth; addition; as, the zoo was improved by the *accession* of a black leopard.

ac·ces·so·ry (ăk-sĕs′ŏ-rĭ), *adj.* 1, contributing to an effect; 2, helping another in crime:—*n.* [*pl.* accessories], an article that adds to the convenience or to the appearance of something else; as, gloves, handbags, neckwear, are *accessories* of dress; 2, a person who assists a criminal before or after a crime. Also spelled **ac·ces′sa·ry.**
Syn., n. ally, confederate, helper.

ac·ci·dent (ăk′sĭ-dĕnt), *n.* 1, an unexpected or unforeseen event, generally unfortunate; 2, something done unintentionally; a mishap; 3, chance; as, to lose or find something by *accident.*
Syn. incident, adventure.

ac·ci·den·tal (ăk′sĭ-dĕn′tăl), *adj.* happening by accident or by chance.—*adv.* **ac′ci·den′tal·ly.**

ac·claim (a̍-klām′), *v.t.* 1, to applaud; 2, to hail or proclaim by shouting; as, to *acclaim* a champion:—*n.* a shout of joy or praise.

ac·cla·ma·tion (ăk′la̍-mā′shŭn), *n.* 1, a general shout of applause or approval; 2, an oral vote on a resolution.

ac·cli·mate (a̍-klī′mĭt; ăk′lĭ-māt), *v.t.* [acclimat-ed, acclimat-ing], to accustom (plants, oneself) to a new climate or to new conditions; as, Eskimos could not be *acclimated* in the Torrid Zone. Also, **ac·cli′ma·tize.**—*n.* **ac·cli·ma′tion; ac·cli′ma·ti·za′tion.**

ac·com·mo·date (a̍-kŏm′ŏ-dāt), *v.t.* [accommodat-ed, accommodat-ing], 1, to be suitable for; as, the room will *accommodate* two persons; to cause to fit or suit; cause (a person or thing) to fall in line; as, I shall gladly *accommodate* my plans to yours; to adapt (oneself), as to circumstances; 2, to

---

go; join; yet; sing; chin; show; thin, *th***en; hw,** *wh***y; zh,** azure; **ü,** Ger. für or Fr. l*u*ne; **ö,** Ger. schön or Fr. f*eu*; **n̄,** Fr. e*n*fant, no*m*; **kh,** Ger. a*ch* or i*ch*. See pages **ix–x.**

render a favor or help to; as, he *accommodated* me with an umbrella; **3**, to supply or furnish (a person) with food or lodging.
Syn. serve, oblige, fit, suit.

ac·com·mo·dat·ing (ă-kŏm′ō-dāt′ĭng), *adj.* obliging; kind.

ac·com·mo·da·tion (ă-kŏm′ō-dā′shŭn), *n.* **1**, the act or process of adjusting or fitting something to something else; as, the *accommodation* of one's plans to those of others; the *accommodation* of the eye to distant objects; **2**, willingness to oblige; **3**, the thing furnished in order to oblige, as a loan of money; **4**, a train stopping at way stations; **5**, **accommodations**, lodgings; as, hotel *accommodations* were scarce.

ac·com·pa·ni·ment (ă-kŭm′pȧ-nĭ-mĕnt), *n.* that which goes with something else; as, a piano *accompaniment* to a song.

ac·com·pa·nist (ă-kŭm′pȧ-nĭst), *n.* a musician who supplies an accompaniment.

ac·com·pa·ny (ă-kŭm′pȧ-nĭ), *v.t.* [accompanied, accompany-ing], **1**, to go with; escort; as, a guide *accompanied* the party; **2**, to supplement or join (with); as, she *accompanied* her words with a glance; **3**, in music, to follow (a singer or player) on an instrument.
Syn. attend, conduct.

ac·com·plice (ă-kŏm′plĭs), *n.* an associate or companion in crime; as, two robbers were caught, but an *accomplice* escaped.
Syn. confederate, accessory, abettor, assistant, partner, colleague, ally.

ac·com·plish (ă-kŏm′plĭsh), *v.t.* **1**, to complete; finish, as a task; **2**, to carry out; fulfil; as, she *accomplished* her purpose.

ac·com·plished (ă-kŏm′plĭsht), *adj.* **1**, brought to fulfilment, as a plan; finished, as a piece of work; **2**, skilful; talented and well-trained; as, an *accomplished* violinist.

ac·com·plish·ment (ă-kŏm′plĭsh-mĕnt), *n.* **1**, fulfilment, as of a purpose; completion, as of a task; **2**, skill; an ability acquired through special training; as, acting was one of his many *accomplishments*.

ac·cord (ă-kôrd′), *v.t.* to give; grant; as, to *accord* due praise:—*v.i.* to be in harmony; agree; as, your point of view *accords* with mine:—*n.* agreement; harmony; as, you and I are in *accord* in respect to the proper way to act:—**of his own accord**, of his own free will; as, he goes to church *of his own accord*.

ac·cord·ance (ă-kôr′dăns), *n.* agreement; as, to act in *accordance* with one's wishes.

ac·cord·ing (ă-kôr′dĭng), *adj.* agreeing; harmonizing.
according as, just as; **according to**, in accordance with; in agreement with; as, *according to* the Bible.

ac·cord·ing·ly (ă-kôr′dĭng-lĭ), *adv.* **1**, in agreement with what might be expected; suitably; as, you are now grown and must act *accordingly;* **2**, consequently; so; therefore; as, *accordingly*, I went.

ac·cor·di·on (ă-kôr′dĭ-ŭn), *n.* a portable musical instrument, consisting of bellows, metal reeds, and a keyboard, played by alternately extending the ends of the instrument and pushing them together, thus forcing air through the reeds:—*adj.* folded and creased like the bellows of an accordion; as, *accordion* pleats.

ACCORDION

ac·cost (ă-kôst′), *v.t.* to speak to first; address; as, a beggar *accosted* me.

ac·count (ă-kount′), *v.i.* **1**, to give a reckoning or make a report of money received and money spent; as, he *accounted* for all the money; **2**, to give an explanation or reason; as, I cannot *account* for his conduct:—*v.t.* to think; consider; as, although he failed, he was *accounted* a hero:—*n.* **1**, a record of business dealings involving money; a bill; as, an *account* with a store; **2**, any reckoning; as, we all have to give an *account* to God; **3**, a record or report, as of events; **4**, cause or explanation; as, give an *account* of your actions; **5**, importance; worth; as, of no *account*; **6**, **accounts**, financial records; bookkeeping records; as, his *accounts* are in order:—**turn to account**, to make use of.
Syn., *n.* description, narration, recital.

ac·count·a·bil·i·ty (ă-koun′tȧ-bĭl′ĭ-tĭ), *n.* responsibility, as for one's conduct.

ac·count·a·ble (ă-koun′tȧ-bl), *adj.* **1**, bound to give an explanation of one's conduct; responsible; answerable; **2**, capable of being explained; as, his failure is *accountable* if you recall his lack of training.

ac·count·an·cy (ă-koun′tăn-sĭ), *n.* the work or position of an accountant.

ac·count·ant (ă-koun′tănt), *n.* one whose business it is to keep financial records, and to go over and examine accounts.

ac·cou·ter (ă-kōō′tẽr), *v.t.* to equip; array; dress; as, *accoutered* for golf; the army was well *accoutered*. Also spelled **ac·cou′tre**.

ac·cou·ter·ments or **ac·cou·tre·ments** (ă-kōō′tẽr-mĕnts), *n.pl.* dress; equipment; as, the *accouterments* of a hunter.

Ac·cra (ăk′rȧ), a seaport town (capital of the Gold Coast) on the Gulf of Guinea, in western Africa (map **14**).

ac·cred·it (ă-krĕd′ĭt), *v.t.* **1**, to send with letters of authority; as, to *accredit* an ambassador to Spain; **2,** to accept or approve as true, up to standard, or the like.

ac·crue (ă-krōō′), *v.i.* [accrued, accru-ing], **1,** to come as a natural result; as, benefits *accruing* from a good education; **2,** to accumulate; be added; as, interest will *accrue* on my savings account.

ac·cu·mu·late (ă-kū′mū-lāt), *v.t.* and *v.i.* [accumulat-ed, accumulat-ing], to collect; gather; pile up; as, to *accumulate* a library; books *accumulate* on a table.—*n.* **ac·cu′mu·la·tor.**—*adj.* **ac·cu′mu·la·tive.**
  Syn. gather, assemble, aggregate, hoard.

ac·cu·mu·la·tion (ă-kū′mū-lā′shŭn), *n.* **1,** the act of collecting; **2,** a pile; heap; collection; as, an *accumulation* of dirt.

ac·cu·ra·cy (ăk′ū-ra̍-sĭ), *n.* correctness; exactness; precision.

ac·cu·rate (ăk′ū-rĭt), *adj.* free from error; as, an *accurate* record; precise; as, an *accurate* person.—*adv.* **ac′cu·rate·ly.**

ac·curs·ed (ă-kûr′sĕd; ă-kûrst′) or **ac·curst** (ă-kûrst′), *adj.* **1,** doomed by a curse; ill-fated; **2,** miserable; hateful; as, poverty made her life *accursed.*

ac·cu·sa·tion (ăk′ū-zā′shŭn), *n.* **1,** a charge of wrongdoing; **2,** the act of charging with wrongdoing.

ac·cu·sa·tive (ă-kū′za̍-tĭv), *adj.* in grammar, naming the case of the direct object of a verb or of a preposition; as, in the sentence "John put the book on the table," "book" and "table" are in the *accusative* case: in English grammar, commonly called *objective:—n.* the accusative case; also, a word in that case.

ac·cuse (ă-kūz′), *v.t.* [accused, accus-ing], to charge with guilt; blame; as, to *accuse* a person of theft.—*n.* **ac·cus′er.**

ac·cus·tom (ă-kŭs′tŭm), *v.t.* to make used to something; to familiarize; as, to *accustom* oneself to new conditions.

ac·cus·tomed (ă-kŭs′tŭmd), *adj.* usual; customary; as, an *accustomed* task:—**accustomed to,** used to.

ace (ās), *n.* **1,** a card or die with a single spot; **2,** an army aviator who has brought down at least five enemy airplanes; **3,** one who excels others in doing some particular thing; as, a football *ace.*

ac·e·tate (ăs′ē-tāt), *n.* in chemistry, a salt of acetic acid.

a·ce·tic (ă-sē′tĭk), *adj.* sour; biting:—**acetic acid,** a sour, colorless liquid, which gives the sour taste to vinegar.

a·cet·y·lene (ă-sĕt′ĭ-lēn), *n.* a gas which burns with a brilliant white light. It is used in welding metals and for lighting.

A·chae·an (a̍-kē′ăn) or **A·cha·ian** (a̍-kā′yăn), *n.* an inhabitant of Achaia in ancient

Greece; hence, a Greek:—*adj.* relating to Achaia; hence, relating to Greece in general.

ache (āk), *n.* continuous pain, bodily or mental; as, tooth*ache;* heart*ache:—v.i.* [ached, ach-ing], **1,** to suffer or be in pain; throb with pain; as, my head *aches;* **2,** to have a strong desire; to long.

Ach·er·on (ăk′ĕr-ŏn), *n.* in Greek and Roman mythology, one of the rivers of Hades; hence, Hades itself.

a·chieve (a̍-chēv′), *v.t.* [achieved, achiev-ing], **1,** to gain or get by effort; as, to *achieve* success; **2,** to accomplish; as, he *achieved* a difficult feat.
  Syn. do, fulfil, execute, win.

a·chieve·ment (a̍-chēv′mĕnt), *n.* **1,** accomplishment; completion; as, the *achievement* of one's purpose; **2,** something accomplished through bravery or skill; a great or heroic deed; as, the discovery of radium was a scientific *achievement.*

A·chil·les (a̍-kĭl′ēz), *n.* the greatest Greek warrior in the Trojan War.

ach·ing (āk′ĭng), *adj.* painful; throbbing with pain; as, an *aching* jaw.

ach·ro·mat·ic (ăk′rō-măt′ĭk), *adj.* without color:—**achromatic lens,** a lens through which light passes without being split up into the colors of the spectrum.

ac·id (ăs′ĭd), *adj.* sharp or biting to the taste, as vinegar; sour:—*n.* **1,** a sour substance, often liquid; **2,** in chemistry, that which combines with a base to form a salt.

a·cid·i·ty (a̍-sĭd′ĭ-tĭ), *n.* sourness.

ack–ack (ăk′-ăk′). *n.* antiaircraft fire, especially that from rapid-firing guns.

ac·knowl·edge (ăk-nŏl′ĕj), *v.t.* [acknowl-edged, acknowledg-ing], **1,** to admit as real or genuine; as, to *acknowledge* a fault or a signature; **2,** to respect; recognize; as, to *acknowledge* Dickens as a great novelist; **3,** to admit the receipt of; express thanks for; as, to *acknowledge* a letter or a gift.
  Syn. avow, grant, allow, concede.

ac·knowl·edg·ment or **ac·knowl·edge·ment** (ăk-nŏl′ĕj-mĕnt), *n.* **1,** a declaration or admission that something is true or genuine; **2,** an expression of appreciation; as, an *acknowledgment* of a gift or favor.

ac·me (ăk′mē), *n.* the highest point; perfection; as, her dancing was the *acme* of grace.

ac·o·lyte (ăk′ō-līt), *n.* an attendant, as the boy who serves a priest in church.

A·con·ca·gua (ä′kôn-kä′gwä), a mountain 22,835 feet high, in Argentina, the highest in the Western Hemisphere (map **11**).

ac·o·nite (ăk′ō-nīt), *n.* **1,** a poisonous plant with blue or purple flowers; the monkshood; **2,** a drug made from aconite.

---

go; join; yet; sing; chin; show; thin, *th*en; hw, *wh*y; zh, azure; ü, Ger. für or Fr. lune; ö, Ger. schön or Fr. feu; ṅ, Fr. enfant, nom; kh, Ger. ach or ich. See pages ix–x.

a·corn (ā′kôrn; ā′kẽrn), *n.* the fruit of the oak, a nut with its base set in a woody cup.

a·cous·tic (*a*-kōōs′tĭk; *a*-kous′tĭk), *adj.* associated with the sense of hearing or with sound; as, the *acoustic* properties of a room:—**acoustics**, *n. pl.* **1,** used as *sing.*, the science of sound; **2,** used as *pl.*, the qualities of a hall that determine how clearly sounds can be heard in it.—*adv* **a·cous′ti·cal·ly.**

ACORN OF WHITE OAK
A, acorn; B, nut; C, cup.

ac·quaint (*a*-kwānt′), *v.t.* to make aware of something; familiarize; as, I *acquainted* him with the contents of this letter.

ac·quaint·ance (*a*-kwān′tăns), *n.* **1,** knowledge of a person or a thing gained by contact or experience; as, an *acquaintance* with a book and with its author; **2,** a person whom one knows slightly.—*n.* **ac·quaint′ance-ship.**

ac·quaint·ed (*a*-kwān′tĕd), *adj.* **1,** having personal knowledge; as, I am *acquainted* with the facts; **2,** known to one another; as, we are *acquainted.*

ac·qui·esce (ăk′wĭ-ĕs′), *v.i.* [acquiesced, acquiesc-ing], to agree in silence; submit or assent without objection; as, she *acquiesced* in her son's decision.—*adj.* **ac′qui·es′cent.**
  Syn. accede, comply, consent.

ac·qui·es·cence (ăk′wĭ-ĕs′ĕns), *n.* the act of submitting; silent assent.

ac·quire (*a*-kwīr′), *v.t.* [acquired, acquir-ing], to gain or obtain, usually by one's own effort; as, she *acquired* speed in swimming; he *acquired* a name for honesty.
  Syn. procure, secure, get.

ac·quire·ment (*a*-kwīr′mĕnt), *n.* **1,** the act of gaining for oneself, as skill, knowledge, etc.; **2,** that which is gained, especially by effort.

ac·qui·si·tion (ăk′wĭ-zĭsh′ŭn), *n.* **1,** the act of obtaining or gaining something; **2,** that which is gained, especially a material possession.

ac·quis·i·tive (*a*-kwĭz′ĭ-tĭv), *adj.* having a strong desire to get or gain for oneself, especially property or money.—*n.* **ac·quis′i·tive-ness.**

ac·quit (*a*-kwĭt′), *v.t.* [acquit-ted, acquit-ting], **1,** to free (a person) from an accusation or an obligation; to set free; as, the jury *acquitted* the prisoner; **2,** to behave or conduct (oneself); as, the soldier *acquitted* himself nobly.

ac·quit·tal (*a*-kwĭt′ăl), *n.* the release of a person by a jury from a charge of wrong-doing, through a verdict of "not guilty."

a·cre (ā′kẽr), *n.* **1,** a measure of land area (43,560 square feet) about equivalent to the area of a field 208 feet square; **2,** a piece of land; a field; **3, acres,** lands or a landed estate; as, ancestral *acres.*

a·cre·age (ā′kẽr-ĭj), *n.* the entire area of a tract of land, measured in acres.

ac·rid (ăk′rĭd), *adj.* **1,** bitter; sharp-tasting; pungent, as smoke; **2,** ill-tempered; bitter; harsh and sharp.—*adv.* **ac′rid-ly.**—*n.* **a·crid′i·ty** (*a*-krĭd′ĭ-tĭ).—*n.* **ac′rid-ness.**

ac·ri·mo·ni·ous (ăk′rĭ-mō′nĭ-ŭs), *adj.* bitter; stinging; cutting; as, *acrimonious* words.—*adv.* **ac′ri·mo′ni·ous-ly.**

ac·ri·mo·ny (ăk′rĭ-mō′nĭ), *n.* bitterness or sharpness, as of temper or speech.

ac·ro·bat (ăk′rō-băt), *n.* one who performs skilled or daring gymnastic feats, such as tumbling, vaulting, etc.

ac·ro·bat·ic (ăk′rō-băt′ĭk), *adj.* pertaining to an acrobat:—**acrobatics,** *n. pl.* **1,** used as *sing.*, the art or profession of an acrobat; **2,** used as *pl.*, the performances of an acrobat; also, similar performances; as, the *acrobatics* of a mountain goat.

ACROBAT

a·crop·o·lis (*a*-krŏp′ō-lĭs), *n.* the highest fortified part, or citadel, of a city of ancient Greece:—**Acropolis,** the citadel of Athens.

a·cross (*a*-krôs′), *prep.* **1,** from one side to the other of; as, she swam *across* the stream; **2,** on the other side of; as, she lives *across* the road:—*adv.* from one side to the other; as, to cut cloth straight *across;* to fly *across.*

act (ăkt), *n.* **1,** a deed; thing done; **2,** the process of doing; as, Mary is in the *act* of cleaning out her desk; **3,** a decree or law; as, an *act* of Congress; **4,** one of the principal divisions of a play or an opera; a separately billed part of a vaudeville performance:—*v.t.* to perform or take the part of, as in a stage or screen play:—*v.i.* **1,** to do something; as, you must *act* quickly; **2,** to behave; as, she *acts* queerly; **3,** to take a part in a play; **4,** to produce an effect; as, the drug *acted* quickly.

act·ing (ăk′tĭng), *adj.* performing the duties of another; as, the *acting* chairman:—*n.* **1,** the art of performing on the stage or screen; **2,** false or insincere behavior; as, his efforts to please are mere *acting.*

ac·tion (ăk′shŭn), *n.* **1,** the doing of something; a deed; as, a kind *action;* **2,** the tendency to act; as, men of *action;* **3,** the effect of one body or substance upon another, as of sunlight on plants; **4,** a suit at law; **5,** the effective or acting part of a mechanism; as, the *action* of our piano needs repair; **6,** the progress of events, as in a play; **7,** a battle; **8, actions,** conscious acts; conduct; behavior; as, we judge a man by his *actions*.

Ac-ti-um (ăk′shǐ-ŭm; ăk′tǐ-ŭm), an ancient town and cape in northwestern Greece (map 1).

ac-tive (ăk′tǐv), *adj*. **1,** given or inclined to action; brisk; lively; as, an *active* body does not always house an *active* mind; **2,** in action or operation; as, an *active* volcano; **3,** in grammar, naming the voice of the verb which represents the subject as the doer of the action of the verb: opposite of *passive.—adv*. **ac′tive-ly.**
  Syn. alert, agile, industrious, quick.

ac-tiv-i-ty (ăk-tǐv′ǐ-tǐ), *n*. [*pl*. activities], **1,** the state of being in motion or operation; briskness; liveliness; **2, activities,** what one does; one's pursuits or occupations; as, political *activities;* athletic *activities*.

ac-tor (ăk′tẽr), *n*. one who takes the part of a character in a play; a theatrical or motion-picture player.—*n.fem*. **ac′tress.**

Acts (ăkts), *n*. a book of the New Testament: called, in full, *The Acts of the Apostles*.

ac-tu-al (ăk′tũ-ăl), *adj*. existing in fact; real; not imaginary.

ac-tu-al-ly (ăk′tũ-ăl-ĭ), *adv*. really; in truth; as a matter of fact.

ac-tu-ar-y (ăk′tũ-ĕr′ĭ), *n*. [*pl*. actuaries], one whose profession it is to calculate insurance risks and premiums.

ac-tu-ate (ăk′tũ-āt), *v.t*. [actuat-ed, actu-at-ing], to impel; move to action; as, he was *actuated* by love of country.

a-cu-men (ă-kū′mĕn). *n*. keenness of insight or understanding; as, business *acumen*.

a-cute (ă-kūt′), *adj*. **1,** sharp-pointed: not blunt; **2,** mentally quick; as, an *acute* person; sensitive; keen; as, an *acute* sense of smell; *acute* insight; **3,** severe; **4,** critical; as, the *acute* stage in a fever.
  acute accent, a sign [′] over a vowel to indicate its sound, as in the French word *café;* **acute angle,** an angle less than a right angle.— *adv*. **a-cute′ly.**—*n*. **a-cute′ness.**

A.D. abbreviation for Latin *anno Domini*, meaning *in the year of the Lord*.

ad- (ăd-), a prefix meaning to, toward, in addition to, etc.: changed to *ab-, ac-, af-, ag-, an-, ap-, ar-, as-, at-* according to the following sound or letter, as in *abbreviate, affect, apply*, etc.

ACUTE ANGLES

ad-age (ăd′ĭj), *n*. a pointed and well-known saying; a proverb. "Waste not, want not," is an *adage*.

a-da-gio (ȧ-dä′jō), *adj*. and *adv*. in music, slow; slowly.

Ad-am (ăd′ăm), in the Bible story of the creation, the first man.

ad-a-mant (ăd′ȧ-mănt; ăd′ȧ-mănt), *n*. a real or imaginary stone of great hardness; any substance of extreme hardness, such as the diamond:—*adj*. extremely hard; inflexible; as, my resolution is *adamant*.

ad-a-man-tine (ăd′ȧ-măn′tĭn; ăd′ȧ-măn′-tĭn; ăd′ȧ-măn′tēn), *adj*. **1,** extremely hard; **2,** unyielding.

Ad-ams (ăd′ămz), **1,** John (1735-1826), the second president of the U.S.; **2,** John Quincy (1767-1848), his son, the sixth president of the U.S.

Ad-am's ap-ple, a cartilage forming the fore part of the human voice box, or larynx, noticeable, especially in men, as an enlargement in the front of the throat.

a-dapt (ȧ-dăpt′), *v.t*. to make suitable; change so as to fit new conditions; as, I must *adapt* myself to the new house.

a-dapt-a-ble (ȧ-dăp′tȧ-bl), *adj*. able to fit oneself easily to new conditions.—*n*. **a-dapt′a-bil′i-ty.**

ad-ap-ta-tion (ăd′ăp-tā′shŭn), *n*. **1,** the act or process of suiting one thing to another; as, the *adaptation* of his eyes to the sudden darkness took several minutes; **2,** a changed or adapted form; as, the screen picture was an *adaptation* of a novel.

add (ăd), *v.t*. **1,** to join or unite into a whole; especially, to sum up (a set of numbers); **2,** to bring (additional items); to put with others; as, to *add* books to a library; **3,** to go on to say.—*n*. **add′er.**

Ad-dams (ăd′ămz), Jane (1860-1935), an American social worker.

ad-dax (ăd′ăks), *n*. a large antelope of North Africa, Syria, and Arabia. (See *antelope*, illustration.)

ad-dend (ăd′ĕnd; ă-dĕnd′), *n*. a number that is to be added to another number in obtaining a sum.

ad-der (ăd′ẽr), *n*. **1,** any of several harmless American snakes; **2,** the poisonous viper of Europe.

ad-dict (ă-dĭkt′), *v.t*. to devote or give (oneself) up to a habit, usually a bad one: —*n*. (ăd′ĭkt), one who is given over to a habit; as, a drug *addict*.—*n*. **ad-dic′tion.**

ad-dict-ed (ă-dĭk′tĕd), *adj*. given or inclined by habit to a practice, pursuit, etc.; as, she is *addicted* to late hours.

Ad-dis A-ba-ba (äd′ĭs ä′bȧ-bä), a city, capital of Ethiopia in Africa (map 14).

---

go; join; yet; sing; chin; show; thin, *th*en; hw, *wh*y; zh, a*z*ure; ü, Ger. f*ür* or Fr. l*u*ne; ö, Ger. sch*ö*n or Fr. f*eu*; ṅ, Fr. e*n*fant, no*m*; kh, Ger. a*ch* or i*ch*. See pages ix-x.

Ad-di-son (ăd/ĭ-sŭn), Joseph (1672–1719), an English writer.

ad-di-tion (ă-dĭsh/ŭn), *n.* **1,** the act, process, or result of summing up numbers, or of adding or joining something to something else; **2,** a thing which is added or joined.

ad-di-tion-al (ă-dĭsh/ŭn-ăl), *adj.* added; extra; more; as, I need *additional* help.— *adv.* **ad-di/tion-al-ly.**

ad-dle (ăd/l), *v.t.* and *v.i.* [ad-dled, ad-dling], **1,** to make or become spoiled or rotten; as, *addled* eggs; **2,** to make or become muddled; as, an *addled* mind:—*adj.* rotten, as an egg:—**addleheaded, addlepated,** or **addlebrained,** weak-brained; muddled.

ad-dress (ă-drĕs/), *v.t.* **1,** to speak or write to; **2,** to direct, as a letter; **3,** to apply or devote (oneself) to a duty, task, or the like: —*n.* **1,** a speech delivered or written; **2,** manners and bearing; **3,** tact; cleverness; **4,** (also ăd/rĕs), the place to which one's mail is directed; also, the direction written on the letter or package.

Syn., v. salute, greet, accost, court.

ad-dress-ee (ăd/rĕs-ē/), *n.* one to whom a letter or a package is directed.

ad-duce (ă-dūs/), *v.t.* [adduced, adduc-ing], to bring forward as a reason; present or offer as proof or evidence; as, to prove his point, he *adduced* a previous decision.

Ad-e-laide (ăd/ĕ-lād), a city, capital of South Australia (map 16).

A-den (ä/dĕn; ā/dĕn), a territory and seaport in southwestern Arabia:—**Gulf of Aden,** a gulf south of Arabia, joining the Red Sea with the Indian Ocean. (Map 15.)

ad-e-noids (ăd/ĕ-noidz), *n.pl.* a growth of spongy or netlike tissue in the passage leading from the nose to the throat, often causing difficulty in breathing.

a-dept (ă-dĕpt/), *adj.* highly skilled:—*n.* (ăd/ĕpt; ă-dĕpt/), one who is fully proficient or skilled in an art; an expert; as, he is an *adept* at diving.

ad-e-qua-cy (ăd/ĕ-kwà-sĭ), *n.* the condition of being suitable or sufficient to what is required; as, we doubted the *adequacy* of the tent to keep us dry.

ad-e-quate (ăd/ĕ-kwĭt), *adj.* equal to requirement; enough to meet a certain need; as, his skill was *adequate* for the job.—*adv.* **ad/e-quate-ly.**—*n.* **ad/e-quate-ness.**

ad-here (ăd-hēr/), *v.i.* [adhered, adher-ing], **1,** to stick fast as if glued; as, candy *adheres* to paper; **2,** to be attached or devoted, as to a person, principle, or party; as, he *adhered* to his resolutions.

ad-her-ence (ăd-hēr/ĕns), *n.* **1,** the act or state of holding fast; **2,** steadfast attachment or devotion.

ad-her-ent (ăd-hēr/ĕnt), *n.* a follower or supporter, as of a party, leader, cult, etc. *Syn.* ally, upholder, defender, backer.

ad-he-sion (ăd-hē/zhŭn), *n.* **1,** the state of sticking fast to something; **2,** continued allegiance, as to a cause or party; **3,** the sticking together, as in a wound, of tissues which normally are separated.

ad-he-sive (ăd-hē/sĭv), *adj.* **1,** holding fast; **2,** sticky; made so as to stick; as, *adhesive* tape:—*n.* a substance used to stick things together, as paste, sealing wax, etc.—*n.* **ad-he/sive-ness.**

a-dieu (à-dū/; à/dyö/), *n.* [*pl.* adieus (à-dūz/) or adieux (à/dyö/)], a farewell:— *interj.* good-by! farewell!

ad-i-pose (ăd/ĭ-pōs), *adj.* pertaining to fat; fatty; as, *adipose* tissue.

Ad-i-ron-dacks (ăd/ĭ-rŏn/dăks), mountains in northern New York (map 6).

adj. abbreviation for *adjective:*—**Adj.** abbreviation for *Adjutant.*

ad-ja-cent (ă-jā/sĕnt), *adj.* **1,** near; adjoining; **2,** in geometry, designating either or both of two angles with a common vertex and a common side between (see illustration at ¹*angle*).—*n.* **ad-ja/cen-cy.** *Syn.* bordering, neighboring.

ad-jec-tive (ăj/ĕk-tĭv), *n.* a part of speech expressing quality or condition; a word used to limit or define a noun or pronoun. —*adj.* **ad/jec-ti/val** (ăj/ĕk-tī/văl).—*adv.* **ad/jec-ti/val-ly.**

ad-join (ă-join/), *v.i.* to lie or be situated so as to touch, as two lots of land:—*v.t.* to lie next to; as, the golf course *adjoins* the highway.

ad-journ (ă-jûrn/), *v.t.* to bring (a meeting) to a close; also, to put off to another time; as, to *adjourn* a debate:—*v.i.* to come to a close, or to cease business for a time; as, the court *adjourned.* *Syn.* postpone, close, end, suspend.

ad-journ-ment (ă-jûrn/mĕnt), *n.* **1,** the act of putting off or postponing; the postponement of a meeting to a specified time, or indefinitely; **2,** the time during which the postponement is effective.

Adjt. or **Adj.** abbreviation for *Adjutant.*

ad-judge (ă-jŭj/), *v.t.* [adjudged, adjudging], **1,** to decide (a dispute) according to law; hence, to declare or sentence by law; as, the defendant was *adjudged* insane; **2,** to award or grant by law; as, the estate was *adjudged* to him.

ad-junct (ăj/ŭngkt), *n.* something added to another thing, but not a necessary part of it; as, a lean-to is an *adjunct* of a house. *Syn.* addition, appendage.

ad-jure (ă-jŏŏr/), *v.t.* [adjured, adjur-ing],

āte, âorta, râre, căt, ȧsk, fär, ăllow, sofȧ; ēve, ĕvent, ĕll, writẽr, novĕl; bīte, pĭn; nō, ōbey, ôr, dŏg, tŏp, cŏllide; ūnit, ûnite, bûrn, cŭt, focŭs; nōon, fŏŏt; mound; coin;

to charge solemnly, as if under oath; entreat earnestly; as, I *adjure* you to tell the truth. —*n.* **ad·ju·ra/tion.**

ad·just (ă-jŭst/), *v.t.* **1,** to harmonize; settle, as accounts, differences, disputes, or the like; **2,** to put in proper order or position; regulate; as, to *adjust* a bicycle brake, eyeglasses, etc.—*n.* **ad·just/er.**

ad·just·a·ble (ă-jŭs/tá-bl), *adj.* capable of being regulated or set as required; as, an *adjustable* wrench.

ad·just·ment (ă-jŭst/mĕnt), *n.* **1,** the act of arranging or putting into order; as, the *adjustment* took only a few minutes; **2,** arrangement; settlement; as, the *adjustment* on my bill was correct.

ad·ju·tant (ăj/ŏo-tănt), *n.* **1,** an assistant; especially, in the army, a regimental staff officer who assists the commanding officer; **2,** a large Old World stork.

Adm. abbreviation for *Admiral.*

ad·min·is·ter (ăd-mĭn/ĭs-tẽr), *v.t.* **1,** to manage or conduct; as, to *administer* the affairs of state; **2,** to supply or give, as justice or relief; **3,** to cause to take; as, he *administered* the oath; **4,** in law, to settle; as, to *administer* an estate:—*v.i.* **1,** to manage affairs; **2,** in law, to settle an estate.

ad·min·is·tra·tion (ăd-mĭn/ĭs-trā/shŭn), *n.* **1,** the act of managing; management; as, his *administration* of the estate was honest; **2,** that part of a government which manages the affairs of a nation, state, city, etc.; also, the body of men who compose the government, or the term of office held by them.

ad·min·is·tra·tive (ăd-mĭn/ĭs-trā/tĭv), *adj.* pertaining to the management of affairs, as of the government; executive.

ad·min·is·tra·tor (ăd-mĭn/ĭs-trā/tẽr), *n.* **1,** one who manages, directs or governs affairs; **2,** one appointed legally to administer an estate; an executor.

ad·mi·ra·ble (ăd/mĭ-rá-bl), *adj.* worthy of wonder and approval; excellent; as, *admirable* behavior.—*adv.* **ad/mi·ra·bly.**

ad·mi·ral (ăd/mĭ-răl), *n.* **1,** a naval officer of the highest rank; a commander of a fleet or navy; **2,** the ship which carries the admiral; the flagship.

ad·mi·ral·ty (ăd/mĭ-răl-tĭ), *n.* [*pl.* admiralties], **1,** the office or rank of admiral; **2,** a department having charge of naval affairs; **3,** the court or law dealing with cases connected with the sea.

ad·mi·ra·tion (ăd/mĭ-rā/shŭn), *n.* **1,** wonder mingled with approval and delight; as, the listeners were filled with *admiration;* **2,** the object of these feelings; as, she was the *admiration* of her classmates.

ad·mire (ăd-mīr/), *v.t.* [admired, admir-ing],

1, to regard with wonder, approval, and delight; **2,** to esteem highly; as, Jane *admires* her teacher.—*adv.* **ad-mir/ing-ly.**

  Syn. esteem, honor, respect.

ad·mir·er (ăd-mīr/ẽr), *n.* one who regards something or someone with pleasure and affection; as, she has many *admirers.*

ad·mis·si·ble (ăd-mĭs/ĭ-bl), *adj.* **1,** worthy of being permitted to enter; **2,** allowable; permissible; as, this form of argument is not *admissible.*—*adv.* **ad-mis/si-bly.**

ad·mis·sion (ăd-mĭsh/ŭn), *n.* **1,** the power or permission to enter; admittance; as, *admission* is limited to certain days; **2,** the price paid for permission to enter; **3,** acknowledgment that something is true; as, he made full *admission* of his guilt.

ad·mit (ăd-mĭt/), *v.t.* [admit-ted, admit-ting] **1,** to permit to enter; **2,** to allow as valid in argument; accept as true; as, I *admit* the justice of your viewpoint; **3,** to permit to have certain privileges: as, to *admit* to bail; **4,** to be capable of; allow; as, the words *admit* no other meaning.

  Syn. own, acknowledge, suffer, tolerate.

ad·mit·tance (ăd-mĭt/ăns), *n.* **1,** the act of letting in; **2,** permission to enter.

ad·mix·ture (ăd-mĭks/tũr), *n.* the act of mixing, or that which is added by mixing.

ad·mon·ish (ăd-mŏn/ĭsh), *v.t.* **1,** to reprove gently; as, she *admonished* the noisy child; **2,** to urge; exhort; as, the pastor *admonished* his flock to be patient

ad·mo·ni·tion (ăd/mŏ-nĭsh/ŭn), *n.* gentle reproof or warning.

a·do (à-dōo/), *n.* fuss; haste; trouble; as, much *ado* about nothing.

a·do·be (à-dō/bĭ), *n.* **1,** unburnt brick dried in the sun, used in southwestern U.S. and Mexico; **2,** a structure made of such brick.

ad·o·les·cence (ăd/ŏ-lĕs/ĕns), *n.* the process of growing up, of changing from a child to a grownup; also, the time of life when this growth occurs, generally the period from about 13 to 23 years of age; hence, youth.

HOUSE OF ADOBE

ad·o·les·cent (ăd/ŏ-lĕs/ĕnt), *adj.* growing up; passing from childhood to manhood or womanhood, youthful:—*n.* a person past childhood, but not yet fully grown.

A·do·nis (à-dō/nĭs; à-dŏn/ĭs), *n.* in mythology, a beautiful youth beloved by Venus.

a·dopt (à-dŏpt/), *v.t.* **1,** to choose or take to be one's own; as, to *adopt* a child, or a plan; **2,** to approve and accept; as, the boys *adopted* his idea.—*adj.* **a-dopt/ed.**—*n.* **a-dopt/er.**—*n.* **a-dop/tion.**

---

go; join; yet; sing; chin; show; thin, *t*hen; hw, *w*hy; zh, azure; **ū,** Ger. f*ü*r or Fr. l*u*ne; **ö,** Ger. sch*ö*n or Fr. f*eu;* **ṅ,** Fr. e*n*fant, no*m;* **kh,** Ger. a*ch* or i*ch.* See pages ix–x.

a·dor·a·ble (a-dôr′a-bl), *adj.* worthy of the utmost love, or of worship.—*adv.* **a·dor′a·bly.**—*n.* **a·dor′a·ble·ness.**

ad·o·ra·tion (ăd′ō-rā′shŭn), *n.* 1, deep reverence and love; 2, worship paid to God.

a·dore (a-dôr′), *v.t.* [adored, ador·ing], 1, to regard with extreme admiration and affection; as, the mother *adores* her baby; 2, to worship; as, to *adore* God.—*n.* **a·dor′er.**

a·dorn (a-dôrn′), *v.t.* to decorate; ornament; as, to *adorn* the room with flowers.

a·dorn·ment (a-dôrn′mĕnt), *n.* ornament; decoration.

a·down (a-doun′), *prep.* and *adv.* Archaic or *Poetic,* down; downward.

ad·re·nal (ăd-rē′năl), *adj.* in anatomy, naming two small ductless glands, called *adrenal glands,* or *suprarenal glands,* near the kidneys in mammals:—*n.* an adrenal gland.

ad·ren·al·in (ăd-rĕn′ăl-ĭn), *n.* a trademark name for a drug made from the secretion of the adrenal glands, used as a heart stimulant. Also, **ad·ren′al·ine.**

A·dri·an·o·ple (ā′drĭ-ăn-ō′pl; ăd′rĭ-ăn-ō′-pl), a city in European Turkey (map 12). Its Turkish name is *Edirne.*

A·dri·at·ic Sea (ā′drĭ-ăt′ĭk; ăd′rĭ-ăt′ĭk), an arm of the Mediterranean, east of Italy (map 12).

a·drift (a-drĭft′), *adj.* and *adv.* floating at random; at the mercy of wind and tide; as, to cast a boat *adrift.*

a·droit (a-droit′), *adj.* clever; expert; skilful.—*adv.* **a·droit′ly.**—*n.* **a·droit′ness.** *Syn.* deft, dexterous, clever.

ad·u·la·tion (ăd′ū-lā′shŭn), *n.* excessive praise or flattery.—*adj.* **ad′u·la·tor·y.**

a·dult (a-dŭlt′; ăd′ŭlt), *adj.* grown to full size:—*n.* a full-grown plant, animal, or person.

a·dul·ter·ate (a-dŭl′tĕr-āt), *v.t.* [adulter·at·ed, adulterat·ing], to make poorer or thinner by mixing in some other substance; as, to *adulterate* milk with water.

a·dul·ter·a·tion (a-dŭl′tĕr-ā′shŭn), *n.* 1, the adding of something inferior to a substance or mixture; 2, the product so adulterated, as milk thinned with water.

a·dul·ter·er (a-dŭl′tĕr-ẽr), *n.* a man who has broken his marriage vow of faithfulness.—*n.fem.* **a·dul′ter·ess.**

a·dul·ter·y (a-dŭl′tẽr-ĭ), *n.* [*pl.* adulteries], the act of breaking the marriage vow of faithfulness.—*adj.* **a·dul′ter·ous.**

adv. abbreviation for *adverb.*

ad va·lor·em (ăd va-lôr′ĕm), according to value:—**ad valorem duty,** an import duty on goods based on their price.

ad·vance (ăd-văns′), *v.i.* [advanced, advanc·ing], 1, to go forward; 2, to rise in rank, price, or the like; as, he *advanced* to the captaincy; the cost of food *advanced:*—*v.t.* 1, to help forward; as, his money *advanced* the work; 2, to promote; as, they *advanced* him to the principalship; 3, to increase, as prices; 4, to offer, as an opinion; 5, to furnish (money) beforehand; as, he *advanced* me a dollar:—*n.* 1, a moving forward; 2, improvement; 3, rise in rank or value; 4, an approach, as to make someone's acquaintance, adjust a quarrel, or the like; as, John was the first to make *advances;* 5, a loan.
  Syn., v. promote, improve, elevate.

ad·vanced (ăd-vănst′), *adj.* far along in life or time, or far ahead of others in any course of action, outlook, or the like; as, a man of *advanced* ideas.

ad·vance·ment (ăd-văns′mĕnt), *n.* moving or helping forward; progress; promotion.

ad·van·tage (ăd-văn′tĭj), *n.* 1, superiority in position, skill, etc.; 2, benefit from favorable circumstances; a useful or helpful result; as, the *advantages* of foreign travel:—*v.t.* [advantaged, advantag·ing], to profit; help; as, lies *advantaged* him little.

ad·van·ta·geous (ăd′văn-tā′jŭs), *adj.* useful; favorable; profitable.

ad·vent (ăd′vĕnt), *n.* a coming or arrival; as, the *advent* of summer:—**Advent,** the period including the four Sundays before Christmas, which prepares for the coming of Jesus Christ.

ad·ven·ture (ăd-vĕn′tũr), *n.* 1, a bold undertaking, involving risk and danger; as, the *adventures* of arctic explorers; 2, the encountering of new and exciting events; as, boys crave *adventure;* 3, an unusual or exciting experience; as, one's first airplane ride is an *adventure:*—*v.t.* and *v.i.* [adventured, adventur·ing], to take a chance; venture.—*adj.* **ad·ven′ture·some.**

ad·ven·tur·er (ăd-vĕn′tũr-ẽr), *n.* 1, one who engages in new and dangerous enterprises; 2, one who lives by his wits, not always respectably or honorably.

ad·ven·tur·ess (ăd-vĕn′tũr-ĕs), *n.* a woman who lives by her wits.

ad·ven·tur·ous (ăd-vĕn′tũr-ŭs), *adj.* 1, inclined to incur danger; rash; as, an *adventurous* explorer; 2, requiring courage; as, an *adventurous* journey.

ad·verb (ăd′vûrb), *n.* a word used: 1, to modify a verb, telling the time, place, or manner of the action; as, you came *early;* he came *here* yesterday; I read *slowly;* 2, to modify an adjective or another adverb, indicating degree; as, *very* pretty; *too* quickly.—*adj.* **ad·ver′bi·al.**

ad-ver-sar-y (ăd′vẽr-sẽr′ĭ), *n.* [*pl.* adversaries], an enemy; opponent; antagonist.

ad-verse (ăd-vûrs′; ăd′vûrs), *adj.* 1, opposed; as, *adverse* winds; 2, unfavorable; as, *adverse* reports.—*adv.* **ad-verse′ly.**

ad-ver-si-ty (ăd-vûr′sĭ-tĭ), *n.* [*pl.* adversities], misfortune; lack of prosperity.
Syn. hardship, trouble, affliction, woe.

ad-vert (ăd-vûrt′), *v.i.* to refer; allude; as, he *adverted* to my former remarks.

ad-ver-tise (ăd′vẽr-tīz; ăd′vẽr-tīz′), *v.t.* [advertised, advertis-ing], to turn the attention of others to; announce, especially by printed matter, radio, or the like; as, to *advertise* a sale; publish:—*v i.* to give public notice, as by circular, newspaper, radio, etc.:—**advertise for,** to ask for by public notice.—*n.* **ad′ver-tis′er.**

ad-ver-tise-ment (ăd-vûr′tĭz-mĕnt; ăd-vûr′tĭs-mĕnt; ăd′vẽr-tīz′mĕnt), *n.* a printed notice or public announcement, especially about something wanted or offered.

ad-vice (ăd-vīs′), *n.* an opinion offered as a guide to someone's action; recommendation; counsel:—**advices,** information from a distance; as, *advices* from Europe.
Syn. counsel, suggestion, caution

ad-vis-a-ble (ăd-vīz′à-bl), *adj.* prudent; sensible; suitable; as, it is *advisable* to drive slowly.—*n.* **ad-vis′a-bil′i-ty.**

ad-vise (ăd-vīz′), *v.t.* [advised, advis-ing], 1, to give advice to; as, he *advised* me to go; 2, to notify; as, he *advised* me of my promotion:—*v.i.* to seek counsel; consult; as, he *advised* with me about his plans.—*n.* **ad-vis′er; ad-vi′sor.**
Syn. instruct, admonish, counsel.

ad-vis-ed-ly (ăd-vīz′ĕd-lĭ), *adv.* not hastily; after careful thought; as, he declined *advisedly* to run for office.

ad-vise-ment (ăd-vīz′mĕnt), *n.* consideration; deliberation; as, keep the matter under *advisement.*

ad-vi-so-ry (ăd-vī′zō-rĭ), *adj.* having power to suggest or to give advice; as, an *advisory* board.

ad-vo-ca-cy (ăd′vō-kà-sĭ), *n.* an urging or supporting; as, *advocacy* of peace.

ad-vo-cate (ăd′vō-kāt), *n.* 1, one who pleads the cause of another, especially in a court of law; 2, one who is in favor of something; as, an *advocate* of peace:—*v.t.* (ăd′vō-kāt), [advocat-ed, advocat-ing], to urge; as, he *advocated* mercy.

adz or **adze** (ădz), *n.* a cutting tool, some-

ADZES
1, shipbuilder's adz; 2, carpenter's adz; 3, cooper's adz.

what like a short, heavy hoe, having a blade at right angles to the handle, and used in shaping and finishing timber. (See illustration in the preceding column.)

Ae-ge-an Sea (ē-jē′ăn), an arm of the Mediterranean, east of Greece (map 12).

Ae-ne-as (ē-nē′ăs), *n.* a Trojan prince and hero in Homer's "Iliad." Vergil's "Aeneid" tells of his wanderings after the fall of Troy, and his plans for founding Rome.

Ae-ne-id (ē-nē′ĭd), *n.* the Latin epic poem by Vergil, telling of the wanderings of Aeneas and his companions from Troy to Italy after the fall of Troy.

ae-o-li-an (ē-ō′lĭ-ăn), *adj.* pertaining to the wind:—**aeolian harp,** a boxlike instrument the strings of which make musical sounds when the wind blows through them.

Ae-o-lus (ē′ō-lŭs), *n.* in Greek and Roman mythology, the god of the winds.

ae-on or **e-on** (ē′ŏn), *n.* a period of time too long to measure; an age.

a-er-ate (ā′ẽr-āt; âr′āt), *v.t.* [aerat-ed, aerating], 1, to charge with gas; force gas into; as, *aerated* water; 2, to expose to air or oxygen; as, the water was *aerated* in a fine spray.—*n.* **a′er-a′tion.**

a-er-i-al (â-ē′rĭ-ăl; âr′ĭ-ăl), *adj.* 1, living in the air, as certain plants; also, produced in the air; as, *aerial* currents; 2, high; lofty; as, *aerial* towers; 3, not real or substantial; imaginary, as, *aerial* flights of fancy:—*n.* in radio systems, one or more wires suspended in the air to receive or radiate energy; an antenna. (See illustration at *radio.*)—*adv.* **a-e′ri-al-ly.**

a-er-ie (ā′ẽr-ĭ; ēr′ĭ), *n.* the nest of an eagle or other bird of prey, often on a lofty crag. Also spelled **ey′rie; ey′ry.**

a-er-o-drome (ā′ẽr-ō-drōm′; âr′ō-drōm′), *n.* an airport so called in Great Britain.

a-er-o-naut (ā′ẽr-ō-nôt; âr′ō-nôt), *n.* one who operates or rides in an aircraft.

a-er-o-nau-tics (ā′ẽr-ō-nô′tĭks; âr′ō-nô′tĭks), *n.pl.* used as *sing.* the science of aviation, or of operating aircraft.—*adj.* **a′er-o-nau′tic; a′er-o-nau′ti-cal.**

a-er-o-plane (ā′ẽr-ō-plān′; âr′ō-plān′), *n.* an airplane. (See illustration at *airplane.*)

aer-o-sol (âr′ō-sŏl′; âr′ō-sōl′), *n.* a suspension of fine particles of a solid or liquid in a gas; as, mist, smoke, or fog.

a-er-o-view (ā′ẽr-ō-vū′; âr′ō-vū′), *n.* a view from an airplane above the earth.

Aes-chy-lus (ĕs′kĭ-lŭs), (525–456 B.C.), a Greek tragic dramatist and poet.

Ae-sop (ē′sŏp), (sixth century B.C.), a Greek writer of fables.

aes-thet-ic or **es-thet-ic** (ĕs-thĕt′ĭk), *adj.* 1, having to do with the sense of beauty; **2,** sensitive to the beautiful in art or nature; having a cultivated, artistic taste; as, the ancient Greeks were an *aesthetic* people.—*adj.* **aes-thet′i-cal.**—*adv.* **aes-thet′i-cal-ly.**

aes-thet-ics or **es-thet-ics** (ĕs-thĕt′ĭks), *n.pl.* used as *sing.* the laws and principles that help to determine what beauty is.

aet. or **aetat.** abbreviation for Latin *aetatis,* meaning *of the age of,* or *aged.*

ae-ther (ē′thẽr), *n.* the upper air. See **ether.**

Aet-na (ĕt′ná), a volcano in Sicily. See **Etna.**

af- (ăf-), *prefix,* a form of *ad-* used before *f,* as in *af*firm.

a-far (á-fär′), *adv.* at, to, or from, a distance; as, he went *afar* in search of work.

af-fa-bil-i-ty (ăf′á-bĭl′ĭ-tĭ), *n.* the quality of being friendly or courteous.

af-fa-ble (ăf′á-bl), *adj.* courteous in speech and manner; friendly.—*adv.* **af′fa-bly.**

af-fair (ă-fâr′), *n.* **1,** concern; proceeding; matter; as, luncheon is a simple *affair;* **2,** that which is done, or is to be done; as, a hard *affair* to manage; **3, affairs,** business of any kind; as, *affairs* of state.

¹af-fect (ă-fĕkt′), *v.t.* to produce an effect upon; as, his tale *affected* me deeply.

²af-fect (ă-fĕkt′), *v.t.* **1,** to pretend to do or to have; as, he *affected* a sympathy he did not feel; **2,** to show a liking for; as, he *affected* loud neckties.

af-fec-ta-tion (ăf′ĕk-tā′shŭn), *n.* the assuming of a manner merely to create an impression; also, an instance of this; as, his *affectations* of speech made us laugh.

af-fect-ed (ă-fĕk′tĕd), *adj.* not natural; assumed; as, *affected* manners.

af-fect-ing (ă-fĕk′tĭng), *adj.* having power to excite the emotions; pathetic; as, the mother's grief was most *affecting.*

af-fec-tion (ă-fĕk′shŭn), *n.* **1,** love; fondness; as, *affection* for animals; **2,** disease; as, an *affection* of the throat.

af-fec-tion-ate (ă-fĕk′shŭn-ĭt), *adj.* having or expressing love; kind; tender; as, she has an *affectionate* nature.—*adv.* **af-fec′tion-ate-ly.**

af-fi-ance (ă-fī′ăns), *v.t.* [affianced, affianc-ing], to betroth, or bind by promise of marriage; as, he is *affianced* to my sister.

af-fi-da-vit (ăf′ĭ-dā′vĭt), *n.* a sworn statement in writing, especially one made before a court or notary public.

af-fil-i-ate (ă-fĭl′ĭ-āt), *v.t.* [affiliat-ed, affili-at-ing], to join; as, to *affiliate* oneself with a certain set of people:—*v.i.* to become connected or associated; as, one company *affiliated* with the other.—*n.* **af-fil′i-a′tion.**

af-fin-i-ty (ă-fĭn′ĭ-tĭ), *n.* [*pl.* affinities], **1,** a close relationship; as, an *affinity* between two races of men, or between two languages; **2,** special attraction; as, the *affinity* of salt for water; **3,** a liking for a person; also, the person liked.

af-firm (ă-fûrm′), *v.t.* and *v.i.* to declare solemnly, as to a court, but without taking oath; to declare vigorously and strongly; as, he *affirmed* his belief in my honesty.—*n.* **af′fir-ma′tion.**
   Syn. maintain, allege, assert, aver.

af-firm-a-tive (ă-fûr′má-tĭv), *n.* the side in a debate which defends a proposition; as, the *affirmative* won:—*adj.* **1,** answering, or consisting of, "yes"; as, an *affirmative* answer; **2,** supporting a proposition; as, we had the *affirmative* side.—*adv.* **af-firm′a-tive-ly.**

af-fix (ă-fĭks′), *v.t.* to attach or add; as, I *affixed* my signature to the letter:—*n.* (ăf′-ĭks), a part added to a word, as a prefix like *ad-* or *un-,* or a suffix like *-able* or *-ness.*

af-flict (ă-flĭkt′), *v.t.* to distress with pain or great trouble; make miserable.

af-flic-tion (ă-flĭk′shŭn), *n.* **1,** a state of pain or distress; as, she was very brave in her *affliction;* **2,** anything that causes suffering or grief; as, cancer is a terrible *affliction.*
   Syn. pain, calamity, misfortune, adversity.

af-flu-ence (ăf′lū-ĕns), *n.* an abundant supply, as of riches, words, or ideas; especially, great wealth.

af-flu-ent (ăf′lū-ĕnt), *adj.* having abundance; wealthy; as, an *affluent* man; *affluent* times.—*adv.* **af′flu-ent-ly.**

af-ford (ă-fôrd′), *v.t.* **1,** to supply; produce; yield; as, singing *affords* him pleasure; **2,** to bear the expense of; as, he cannot *afford* a car; **3,** to manage to give; spare; as, I cannot *afford* the time.

af-fray (ă-frā′), *n.* a noisy quarrel; brawl.

af-fright (ă-frīt′), *v.t.* to frighten; terrify; as, the noise *affrighted* the child.

af-front (ă-frŭnt′), *v.t.* to insult intentionally; as, the boy *affronted* the teacher:—*n.* an insult; as, an *affront* to one's honor.
   Syn., v. annoy, insult, irritate, offend.

Af-ghan (ăf′găn), *adj.* relating to Afghanistan:—*n.* a native of Afghanistan:—**af-ghan,** a crocheted or knitted wool blanket.

Af-ghan-i-stan (ăf-găn′ĭ-stăn; ăf-gän′ĭs-tän′), a country (cap. Kabul) in southern Asia between India and Iran (map 15).

a-field (á-fēld′), *adv.* **1,** to, in, or into the field; as, he turned the cattle *afield;* **2,** to or at a distance; out of the way; as, to go far *afield* for information.

---

a-fire (á-fīr'), *adj.* and *adv.* on fire; as, a house *afire;* to set rubbish *afire.*

A. F. of L. abbreviation for *American Federation of Labor.*

a-flame (á-flām'), *adj.* on fire; blazing; also, ardent; as, *aflame* with patriotism.

a-float (á-flōt'), *adj.* and *adv.* **1,** floating on water, as a vessel; on board ship, as the crew; **2,** awash; covered with water, as a deck; **3,** in circulation; commonly talked about; as, a rumor is *afloat.*

a-foot (á-fŏŏt'), *adj.* and *adv.* **1,** on foot; **2,** astir; as, a conspiracy was *afoot.*

a-fore-said (á-fôr'sĕd), *adj.* mentioned before; as, the *aforesaid* person.

a-fore-thought (á-fôr'thôt), *adj.* planned beforehand; as, malice *aforethought.*

a-foul (á-foul'), *adj.* and *adv.* in a state of entanglement or collision; as, our lines are *afoul;* he ran *afoul* of the law.

Afr. abbreviation for *Africa, African.*

a-fraid (á-frād'), *adj.* filled with fear; frightened; as, he was *afraid* of the dog.

a-fresh (á-frĕsh'), *adv.* again; anew; newly; over again; as, to start *afresh.*

Af-ri-ca (ăf'rĭ-ká), the large continent south of Europe and western Asia (map 14).

Af-ri-can (ăf'rĭ-kăn), *n.* a native of Africa: —*adj.* relating to Africa.

aft (áft), *adj.* and *adv.* toward the back part of a ship; as, the *aft* cabin; to go *aft.*

aft-er (áf'tẽr), *prep.* **1,** in succession to; as, B comes *after* A; **2,** later than; as, John arrived *after* Jim; **3,** in imitation of; in the manner of; as, a painting *after* Raphael; **4,** next below in rank or excellence; as, a captain comes *after* a general; **5,** in pursuit of; as, John ran *after* the dog; **6,** by the name of; as, he is named *after* his father; **7,** in spite of; as, *after* all your help, he failed:—*conj.* following the time when; as, *after* he eats his dinner, he may go:—*adv.* afterward; as, he arrived shortly *after:*—*adj.* **1,** later; as, in *after* days; **2,** in the rear; as, the *after* cabin.

aft-er-math (áf'tẽr-măth), *n.* **1,** a second mowing in a season; **2,** that which follows; result; as, misery is an *aftermath* of war.

aft-er-most (áf'tẽr-mōst), *adj.* [*superl.* of *after*], last; hindmost.

aft-er-noon (áf'tẽr-nōōn'), *n.* the time between noon and evening:—*adj.* (áf'tẽr-nōōn'), occurring in the afternoon.

aft-er-thought (áf'tẽr-thôt'), *n.* a second or later thought about something; especially, one that comes too late; as, the idea came to me as an *afterthought.*

aft-er-ward (áf'tẽr-wẽrd) or **aft-er-wards** (áf'tẽr-wẽrdz), *adv.* at a later time.

ag- (ăg-), *prefix,* a form of *ad-* used before *g,* as in *aggrieved.*

a-gain (á-gĕn'; á-gān'), *adv.* **1,** a second time; once more; as, do it *again;* **2,** in return; as, give the book back *again;* **3,** further; on the other hand; as, then *again,* I need the money.

a-gainst (á-gĕnst'; á-gānst'), *prep.* **1,** in contact with; near to; as, to lean *against* a tree; **2,** opposite to; facing; in the direction of; as, over *against* Jericho; **3,** in opposition to; as, a law *against* speeding.

Ag-a-mem-non (ăg'á-mĕm'nŏn), *n.* a hero in ancient Greek literature, who was king of Mycenae and commander in chief of the Greeks at the siege of Troy.

a-gape (á-gāp'; á-găp'), *adj.* and *adv.* having the mouth wide open, as in wonder.

Ag-as-siz (ăg'á-sē), Louis (1807–1873), an American naturalist of Swiss descent.

ag-ate (ăg'ĭt; ăg'āt), *n.* **1,** a semiprecious stone, with colors in stripes and cloudy patches; **2,** a boy's marble made of agate, or striped like agate; **3,** a small size of type (see illustration under *type*).

a-ga-ve (á-gā'vē), *n.* a plant of the amaryllis family; especially, the century plant and certain others that yield soap and fiber.

AGAVE
Showing bloom cut from plant.

age (āj), *n.* **1,** a particular time or period in life; as, the *age* of six; the *age* of childhood; **2,** a period in history; as, the Elizabethan *age;* **3,** the latter part of life; as, the wisdom of *age;* **4,** *Colloquial,* a long or weary time; as, it's an *age* since I saw you:—**of age,** 21 years old; as, he just came *of age:*—*v.i.* and *v.t.* [aged, ag-ing], to grow old, or cause to grow old.

-age (-āj), a suffix added to a verb or a noun, and meaning: **1,** an act or process; as, pass*age;* **2,** a condition; as, dot*age,* bond*age;* **3,** a collection or sum; as, foli*age,* mile*age;* **4,** a fee charged; as, cart*age;* **5,** a home; as, vicar*age,* parson*age.*

ag-ed (ā'jĕd), *adj.* **1,** old; far on in years; as, an *aged* man; **2,** (ājd), of the age of; as, a child *aged* three.

a-gen-cy (ā'jĕn-sĭ), *n.* [*pl.* agencies], **1,** the business or place of business of one who acts for another; as, a ticket *agency;* **2,** help; active influence; as, crops grow through the *agency* of rain.

a-gent (ā'jĕnt), *n.* **1,** one who acts, especially for another; as, an *agent* for an insurance company; **2,** an active power or cause; as, religion is an *agent* for good.

Syn. doer, factor, operator, performer.

ag·gran·dize (ăg′răn-dīz; ȧ-grăn′dīz), *v.t.* [aggrandized, aggrandiz-ing], to enlarge or increase (a thing); also, to increase the power, rank, or wealth of (a person or state); as, he *aggrandized* himself at the expense of others. —*n.* **ag·gran′dize-ment** (ȧ-grăn′dĭz-mĕnt).

ag·gra·vate (ăg′rȧ-vāt), *v.t.* [aggravat-ed, aggravat-ing], **1,** to increase, as a burden; make worse; as, worry will only *aggravate* your illness; **2,** *Colloquial,* to annoy; irritate; as, his boasting *aggravates* me.— *adj.* **ag′gra-vat′ing.**

ag·gra·va·tion (ăg′rȧ-vā′shŭn), *n.* **1,** the making of a bad thing worse; as, the *aggravation* of a cold by neglect; **2,** anything that increases an evil or distress; as, self-pity is an *aggravation* to grief; **3,** *Colloquial,* exasperation; irritation.

ag·gre·gate (ăg′rē-gāt), *v.t.* [aggregat-ed, aggregat-ing], **1,** to collect or bring together; gather into one whole or mass; **2,** *Colloquial,* to amount to; as, the sales *aggregated* $100:—*n.* (ăg′rē-gȧt), **1,** the entire number; total; as, the *aggregate* of those present exceeded our hope; **2,** a mass formed by the sticking together of similar particles:—*adj.* taken as a whole; total; as, the *aggregate* amount was very small.

ag·gre·ga·tion (ăg′rē-gā′shŭn), *n.* a collection; assemblage; group; as, an *aggregation* of students called on the dean.

ag·gres·sion (ȧ-grĕsh′ŭn), *n.* an unprovoked attack or assault.

ag·gres·sive (ȧ-grĕs′ĭv), *adj.* **1,** energetic; pushing; as, an *aggressive* salesman; **2,** first to attack or quarrel, especially without a cause; as, an *aggressive* nation.— *adv.* **ag·gres′sive-ly.**—*n.* **ag·gres′sive-ness.**

ag·gres·sor (ȧ-grĕs′ẽr), *n.* one who attacks another without just cause; one who begins a quarrel.

ag·grieved (ȧ-grēvd′), *adj.* having a grievance; having cause of grief or offence; as, he felt *aggrieved* at being left out.

a·ghast (ȧ-gȧst′), *adj.* struck with sudden surprise, horror, or terror; as, he stood *aghast* at the damage he had caused.

ag·ile (ăj′ĭl; ăj′īl), *adj.* quick-moving; active; nimble; also, mentally quick; as, an *agile* mind.—*n.* **a·gil′i-ty** (ȧ-jĭl′ĭ-tĭ).

A·gin·court (ȧ′zhăn′kōōr′; ăj′ĭn-kôrt), a village in northern France, where the English defeated the French in 1415.

ag·i·tate (ăj′ĭ-tāt), *v.t.* [agitat-ed, agitat-ing], **1,** to stir violently; as, the storm *agi-*

tates the sea; **2,** to excite; disturb; as, he was *agitated* about losing his job; **3,** to discuss publicly; argue for; as, to *agitate* the repeal of a law:—*v.i.* to stir up public interest, as for a reform; as, to *agitate* for shorter working hours.

ag·i·ta·tion (ăj′ĭ-tā′shŭn), *n.* **1,** disturbance of the feelings; worry; as, *agitation* over a friend's safety; **2,** active discussion or public promotion of a cause; as, *agitation* for war; **3,** the moving of anything to and fro; as, *agitation* of the air.

ag·i·ta·tor (ăj′ĭ-tā′tẽr), *n.* **1,** one who makes a political or industrial disturbance; **2,** an implement for stirring.

a·gley (ȧ-glē′; ȧ-glī′), *adv.* *Scottish,* astray; wrong; as, my plans went *agley.*

a·glow (ȧ-glō′), *adj.* bright; flushed; as, cheeks *aglow* with health or with pleasure.

ag·nos·tic (ăg-nŏs′tĭk), *n.* one who, without denying the existence of God, believes that there is no evidence in man's experience to prove that God exists:—*adj.* relating to the agnostics or their teachings.

ag·nos·ti·cism (ăg-nŏs′tĭ-sĭzm), *n.* the belief or doctrine that it is impossible to know certainly about the existence of God and the origin and real nature of things.

a·go (ȧ-gō′), *adj.* and *adv.* past; in past time; as, an hour *ago;* long *ago.*

a·gog (ȧ-gŏg′), *adj.* aroused; alive with interest; excited; eager; as, we are *agog* with curiosity.

ag·o·nize (ăg′ō-nīz), *v.i.* [agonized, agonizing], to suffer extreme pain or grief:—*v.t.* to torment or torture.

ag·o·ny (ăg′ō-nĭ), *n.* [*pl.* agonies], **1,** intense suffering of body or mind; as, an earache is *agony;* she suffered *agonies* of remorse for her carelessness; **2,** the last struggle of a dying person or animal.

a·gou·ti (ȧ-gōō′tĭ), *n.* a greedy ratlike animal about the size of a rabbit, of Central and South America.

A·gra (ä′grä), an ancient city in northern India, site of the Taj Mahal (map 15).

A·gram (ä′gräm; ŏg′rŏm), the German name for the city of Zagreb. See **Zagreb.**

a·grar·i·an (ȧ-grâr′ĭ-ăn), *adj.* relating to land, or to the right or manner of holding land; as, *agrarian* laws:—*n.* one who is in favor of a redistribution of land.

a·gree (ȧ-grē′), *v.i.* [agreed, agree-ing], **1,** to consent; as, he *agreed* to the plan to go; **2,** to be in harmony; as, I *agree* with you: —**agree with, 1,** in grammar, to correspond with; as, the verb *agrees with* its subject in person and number; **2,** to suit physically; as, fruit *agrees with* me.

Syn. concur, acquiesce, accord.

āte, âorta, râre, căt, ȧsk, fär, ȧllow, sofȧ; ēve, ĕvent, ĕll, writẽr, novĕl; bīte, pĭn; nō, ōbey, ôr, dŏg, tŏp, cŏllide; ūnit, ūnite, bûrn, cŭt, focŭs; nōōn, fŏŏt; mound; coin;

a-gree-a-ble (*à*-grē′*à*-bl), *adj.* **1,** ready or willing to agree; **2,** pleasant; as, an *agreeable* day; having pleasing manners; as, an *agreeable* companion.—*adv.* **a-gree′a-bly.**
   Syn. pleasant, amiable, charming.

a-gree-ment (*à*-grē′mĕnt), *n.* **1,** harmony of opinions or feelings; **2,** in grammar, the correspondence of one word with another in gender, number, case, or person; **3,** a compact; contract; as, the *agreement* for the sale was drawn up and signed.

agric. abbreviation for *agriculture.*

ag-ri-cul-ture (ăg′rĭ-kŭl′tŭr), *n.* the cultivation of the soil; farming.—*adj.* **ag′ri-cul′tur-al.**—*n.* **ag′ri-cul′tur-ist.**

a-ground (*à*-ground′), *adj* and *adv.* stranded or lodged on the bottom in shallow water.

agt. abbreviation for *agent.*

a-gue (ā′gū), *n.* a disease marked by regularly recurring chills and fever.

A-gul-has, Cape (*à*-gŭl′*à*s; ä-gōol′yäs), the southernmost point in Africa (map 14).

ah (ä) and **a-ha** (ä-hä′), *interj.* expressing varied emotions, as pity, scorn, surprise, etc.

A-hab (ā′hăb), (ninth century B.C.), a king of Northern Israel (1 Kings 16–22).

a-head (*à*-hĕd), *adv.* and *adj.* in advance; forward; as, I went *ahead.*

a-hem (*à*-hĕm′), *interj.* a slight cough, or a clearing of the throat, to attract attention.

Ah-mad-a-bad (ä′mŭd-ä-bäd′), a city in India (map 15).

a-hoy (*à*-hoi′), *interj.* a term used in hailing a vessel; as, ship *ahoy!*

aid (ād), *v.t.* to assist; help:—*n.* **1,** help; assistance; **2,** a person or thing that helps.
   Syn., v. sustain, relieve, succor, help.

aide (ād), *n.* one who assists a higher officer in the armed forces; an aide-de-camp

aide–de–camp (ād′-dě⸗kămp′), *n.* [*pl.* aides-de-camp (ādz′—)], an officer who assists a general: often shortened to *aide.*

ai-grette (ā-grĕt′; ā′grĕt), *n.* **1,** the egret, a kind of heron; **2,** a plume of feathers from this heron, worn as a head ornament; also, any similar ornament, as a spray of gems, worn as a headdress.

ail (āl), *v.t.* to trouble with pain or discomfort; as, what *ails* the child?—*v.i.* to feel pain; be ill; as, they are all *ailing.*

ai-ler-on (ā′lĕr-ŏn), *n.* a hinged section on the rear edge of each wing of an airplane, used in tipping or steadying the plane. (See illustration at *airplane.*)

ail-ment (āl′mĕnt), *n.* sickness; illness.

aim (ām), *v.t.* to point (a gun) before firing; hence, to direct; as, the remark was *aimed* at you:—*v.i.* **1,** to point a weapon at something; **2,** to direct one's efforts; as, he *aimed* to succeed:—*n.* **1,** the pointing of a weapon; as, his *aim* is good; **2,** purpose.
   Syn., n. goal, end, mark, object, design.

aim-less (ām′lĕs), *adj.* without a definite intention or purpose; as, an *aimless* stroll.—*adv.* **aim′less-ly.**—*n.* **aim′less-ness.**

ain't (ānt), an incorrect shortened form of *am not, is not, are not, has not, have not.*

air (âr), *n.* **1,** a mixture of gases, consisting chiefly of oxygen and nitrogen, which surrounds the earth; the atmosphere; **2,** a light breeze; **3,** an appearance or manner; as, an *air* of dignity; **4,** a tune or melody; as, she hummed an *air;* **5, airs,** affected manners:—*v.t.* **1,** to expose to the air; ventilate; **2,** to make a public display of; as, he is always *airing* his views

air base, a station for the housing, repairing, and operation of aircraft.

air cas-tle, an idle fancy; a daydream.

air–con-di-tion (âr′-kŏn-dĭsh′ŭn), *v.t.* to provide desirable temperature, humidity, and purity by circulating treated air within a structure.—*n.* **air con-di′tion-ing.**

air-craft (âr′krȧft′), *n.* [*pl.* aircraft], any type of machine for flying, as a balloon, glider, or airplane.

Aire-dale (âr′dāl′), *n.* a large black-and-tan terrier with a rough coat.

air-field (âr′fēld′), *n.* an airport.

air hole, 1, an unfrozen hole in a sheet of ice on a body of water; **2,** an air pocket.

air-i-ness (âr′ĭ-nĕs), *n.* **1,** openness to the air; **2,** delicacy; lightness; **3,** sprightliness.

air-ing (âr′ĭng), *n.* **1,** exposure to air; **2,** exercise in the open air; **3,** public discussion; as, an *airing* of his grievances.

air lift, a military airplane service ferrying supplies and personnel over enemy-held territory. Also **air′lift′.**

air line, *n.* **1,** a straight route between two places on the earth's surface; **2,** a system of transportation by aircraft.

air mail, mail carried by aircraft; also the system of so carrying it.

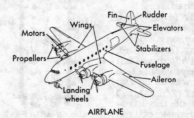

AIRPLANE

air-plane (âr′plān′), *n.* a motor-driven or jet–propelled aircraft, kept aloft by the force of the air upon its winglike planes.

---

air pock·et, a spot or condition in the air, caused by wind and the unevenness of the earth, which causes an airplane to tend to drop suddenly, as if into a hole.

air·port (âr′pôrt′), *n.* a place with facilities for the departure, landing, loading, fueling, or repairing of aircraft.

air raid, a military attack during which bombs are dropped on a target from aircraft.

air·scape (âr′skāp′), *n.* a view or picture of a landscape from a height.

air·ship (âr′shǐp′), *n.* a motor-driven aircraft that is lighter than air; a dirigible. (See illustration at *dirigible balloon*.)

air sleeve, a cone, usually cloth, supported at the larger end and above the ground to show wind direction.

air·strip (âr′strǐp′), *n.* a runway for the take-off and landing of airplanes.

air·tight (âr′tīt′), *adj.* 1, closed or sealed so that no air can get in or out; 2, without flaw; as, he has an *airtight* alibi.

air·way (âr′wā′), *n.* an air route for aircraft from airport to airport.

air·y (âr′ĭ), *adj.* [air-i-er, air-i-est], 1, open to the air; breezy; 2, of the air; as, *airy* spirits; 3, delicate; light; as, *airy* chiffons; 4, gay; lighthearted. —*adv.* **air′i·ly.**

aisle (īl), *n.* 1, a passageway leading to the seats in a church, theater, or the like; 2, in a store, a passageway for customers.

Aisne (ān), a river in France along which many battles in World War I took place.

Aix–la–Cha·pelle (âks′-lȧ-shȧ′pĕl′; âs′-lȧ-shȧ′pĕl′), the French name for Aachen, a city in Germany. See **Aachen.**

¹a·jar (ȧ-jär′), *adv.* and *adj.* slightly open, as a door.

²a·jar (ȧ-jär′), *adv.* and *adj.* out of harmony; as, his temper was much *ajar.*

A·jax (ā′jăks), *n.* 1, one of the heroes at the siege of Troy, next to Achilles the bravest of the Greeks; 2, another Greek hero, often called *the Less*, noted for his fleetness.

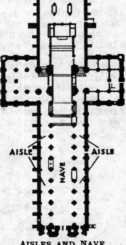

AISLES AND NAVE
In Winchester Cathedral, England.

a·kim·bo (ȧ-kǐm′bō), *adj.* and *adv.* with the hands supported on the hips and the elbows turned outward; as, he stood with arms *akimbo.*

a·kin (ȧ-kǐn′), *adj.* 1, related by blood; 2, of the same kind; near in nature or character; as, the two schemes are closely *akin.*

Ak·ron (ăk′rŭn), a manufacturing city of northeastern Ohio (map **7**).

al- (ăl-), *prefix,* a form of *ad-* used before *l*, as in *al*lure.

-al (-ăl), a suffix meaning: 1, relating to; as, ancestr*al*; 2, an act; as, deni*al*.

Ala. abbreviation for *Alabama.*

Al·a·bam·a (ăl′ȧ-băm′ȧ; ăl′ȧ-bä′mȧ), a southern State (cap. Montgomery) of the U.S. (map **8**).

al·a·bas·ter (ăl′ȧ-băs′tẽr), *n.* a kind of stone, usually white, of fine texture, often carved into vases or ornaments:—*adj.* made of alabaster; white like alabaster.

à la carte (ä lä kärt′; ä lȧ kärt′), according to the bill of fare: used of a meal in which each dish ordered is paid for at a specified price: in contrast with *table d'hôte.*

a·lack (ȧ-lăk′), *interj.* an exclamation expressing sorrow, surprise, or regret; as, *alack* that she should die so young!

a·lac·ri·ty (ȧ-lăk′rĭ-tĭ), *n.* eager readiness to do something; as, he accepted the invitation with *alacrity.*

A·lad·din (ȧ-lăd′ĭn), *n.* the hero of one of the stories in the "Arabian Nights." He possesses a magic lamp and a magic ring, through which his every wish is fulfilled.

A·la·mo, the (ä′lȧ-mō; ăl′ȧ-mō), a church in San Antonio, Texas, where many Texans were killed by Mexicans in 1836.

Al·a·ric (ăl′ȧ-rĭk), (376?-410), a king of the Visigoths who captured Rome.

a·larm (ȧ-lärm′), *n.* 1, a call to arms; hence, a warning of danger; as, he gave the *alarm;* 2, the fear of danger; as, *alarm* seized the camp; 3, a device to warn or awaken persons; as, a fire *alarm:*—*v.t.* to arouse to a sense of danger; startle; as, we were *alarmed* by the smell of smoke.
    Syn., v. frighten, appall, terrify; *n.* fright, terror, dread, panic.

alarm clock, a clock which can be set to ring an alarm at any desired time.

a·larm·ing (ȧ-lär′mǐng), *adj.* causing a fear of danger; terrifying.

a·larm·ist (ȧ-lär′mǐst), *n.* one who exaggerates bad news or foretells calamities.

a·lar·um (ȧ-lăr′ŭm; ȧ-lär′ŭm), *n.* an old spelling of *alarm.* See **alarm.**

a·las (ȧ-làs′), *interj.* an exclamation expressing sorrow, pity, or regret.

āte, âorta, râre, căt, ȧsk, fär, ăllow, sofȧ; ēve, ēvent, ĕll, writẽr, novĕl; bīte, pǐn; nō, ōbey, ôr, dŏg, tŏp, cŏllide; ūnit, ūnite, bûrn, cŭt, focŭs; nōōn, fŏŏt; mound; coin;

A·las·ka (*ȧ*-lăs′kȧ), a State (cap. Juneau) of the U.S., northwest of Canada (map **3**). —*adj.* and *n.* **A·las′kan.**

Al·ba·ni·a (ăl-bā′nĭ-ȧ), a European republic (cap. Tirana) on the Adriatic Sea, northwest of Greece (map **12**).—*adj.* and *n.* **Al·ba′ni·an.**

Al·ba·ny (ôl′bȧ-nĭ), a city, capital of the State of New York (map **6**).

al·ba·tross (ăl′bȧ-trôs), *n.* a very large web-footed sea bird, of southern waters, capable of remarkably long flights from land.

al·be·it (ôl-bē′ĭt), *conj.* ﹐although; even though.

Al·bert I (ăl′bẽrt), (1875–1934), king of Belgium, 1909 to 1934.

ALBATROSS (1⁄30)

Al·bert, Lake (ăl′bẽrt) or **Al·bert Ny·an·za** (nĭ-ăn′zȧ; nyän′zä), a large lake in east central Africa (map **14**).

Al·ber·ta (ăl-bûr′tȧ), a province (cap. Edmonton) of western Canada (map **4**).

al·bi·no (ăl-bī′nō; ăl-bē′nō), *n.* [*pl.* albinos], **1**, a person with white, or unusually light, skin and hair, and pinkish eyes; **2**, an animal or plant of unusually light color.

Al·bi·on (ăl′bĭ-ŭn), an old and poetic name for England.

al·bum (ăl′bŭm), *n.* a book with blank pages, in which to keep a collection of photographs, stamps, autographs, etc.

al·bu·men (ăl-bū′mĕn), *n.* **1**, the white of an egg; **2**, albumin.—*adj.* **al·bu′mi·nous.**

al·bu·min (ăl-bū′mĭn), *n.* a protein found in its purest state in the white of an egg. It occurs in many animal and vegetable tissues and fluids, and is used in sugar refining, calico printing, etc.—*adj.* **al·bu′mi·nous.**

al·che·mist (ăl′kĕ-mĭst), *n.* one who studied or practiced alchemy.

al·che·my (ăl′kĕ-mĭ), *n.* the chemistry of the Middle Ages, the chief purposes of which were to turn common metals into gold and to find a method of prolonging life.

al·co·hol (ăl′kô-hŏl), *n.* a colorless liquid, made by the fermentation of grapes, grain, etc., and forming the intoxicating substance in all fermented and distilled liquors:—**wood alcohol,** a poisonous liquid, much used as a fuel and as a solvent.

al·co·hol·ic (ăl′kô-hŏl′ĭk), *adj.* containing alcohol; as, whisky is an *alcoholic* drink:—*n.* a habitual, heavy drinker.

al·co·hol·ism (ăl′kô-hŏl′ĭzm), *n.* a diseased condition resulting from the excessive use of alcoholic liquors.

Al·cott (ôl′kŭt), Louisa May (1833–1888), an American novelist: "Little Women."

al·cove (ăl′kōv), *n.* a recess in a room, as for a window seat or bookcases; also, a very small room opening into a larger room.

Al·den (ôl′dĕn), John (1599–1687), one of the Pilgrim Fathers of Plymouth.

al·der (ôl′dẽr), *n.* any of several trees and shrubs related to the birches, often growing thickly in moist or swampy places. The bark is used in tanning and dyeing.

al·der·man (ôl′dẽr-măn), *n.* [*pl.* aldermen (-mĕn)], in some cities of the U.S., a member of the city's governing body representing a ward or district.

Al·der·ney (ôl′dẽr-nĭ), an island in the English Channel, famous for a breed of dairy cattle (map **13**).

Al·drich (ôl′drĭch), Thomas Bailey (1836–1907), an American author.

ale (āl), *n.* a strong, fermented liquor like beer, made from malt and hops.

A·lep·po (ȧ-lĕp′ō) or **A·lep** (ȧ′lĕp′), a city in northwest Syria (map **15**).

a·lert (ȧ-lûrt′), *adj.* **1**, watchful; as, an *alert* watchdog; **2**, active; as, an *alert* child:—*n.* warning of an attack:—*v.t.* to warn of an attack:—**on the alert**, ready to act; on the lookout.—*adv.* **a·lert′ly.**—*n.* **a·lert′ness.**

A·leu·tian Is·lands (ȧ-lū′shăn; ȧ-lōō′-shăn), a chain of volcanic islands west of Alaska (map **2**).

Al·ex·an·der (ăl′ĕg-zăn′dẽr), (356–323 B.C.), called *the Great*, king of Macedon.

Al·ex·an·dri·a (ăl′ĕg-zăn′drĭ-ȧ), a seaport in Egypt (maps **1, 14**).

Al·ex·an·drine (ăl′ĕg-zăn′drĭn), *n.* a line of poetry consisting of six iambic feet with a slight pause after the third. An example is: "Our sweet/est songs/ are those //which tell/ of sad/dest thought."

al·fal·fa (ăl-făl′fȧ), *n.* a kind of clover, having purple flowers and very deep roots. In the western U.S. it is grown for hay, of which it yields several cuttings a year.

Al·fon·so XIII (ăl-fŏn′sō), (1886–1941), king of Spain from 1902 until the establishment of the second Spanish Republic in 1931.

Al·fred (ăl′frĕd), (849–901), called *the Great*, a famous king of the West Saxons in England from 871 to 901.

ALFALFA
Showing leaf and bloom.

al·gae (ăl′jē), *n.pl.* [*sing.* alga (ăl′gȧ)], a group of flowerless water plants, including the seaweeds.

---

al·ge·bra (ăl′jĕ-brȧ), *n.* a branch of mathematics which represents quantities by the use of letters and other symbols, instead of by numbers, as in arithmetic.—*adj.* **al′ge-bra′ic; al′ge-bra′i-cal.**—*adv.* **al′ge-bra′i-cal-ly.**

Al·ge·ri·a (ăl-jĭr′ĭ-ȧ), a country (cap. Alger) in northern Africa, under French control (map 14). —*adj.* and *n.* **Al-ge′ri-an.**

Al·giers (ăl-jîrz′), [French **Al-ger** (ȧl′zhā′)], the capital of Algeria, Africa (map 14).

Al·gon·qui·an (ăl-gŏng′kĭ-ăn; -kwĭ-ăn), *adj.* relating to a very large group of Indian tribes of northeastern North America:—*n.* 1, an Indian of an Algonquian tribe; 2, the language of any one of these tribes.

Al·ham·bra (ăl-hăm′brȧ), a former palace of the Moorish kings, at Granada, Spain.

a·li·as (ā′lĭ-ăs), *n.* an assumed name; as, the forger had two *aliases*:—*adv.* otherwise called; as, Max, *alias* Slinky Sam.

al·i·bi (ăl′ĭ-bī), *n.* [*pl.* alibis], 1, the plea, offered by a person accused of a crime, of having been elsewhere when the crime was committed; 2, *Colloquial,* an excuse.

al·ien (āl′yĕn; ā′lĭ-ĕn), *n.* a foreigner; a person who is not a citizen of the country in which he is living:—*adj.* 1, foreign; as, *alien* peoples; 2, strange; unnatural; as, language *alien* to persons of refinement.

al·ien·ate (āl′yĕn-āt; ā′lĭ-ĕn-āt), *v.t.* [alienat-ed, alienat-ing], to estrange (a person); cause (affection) to turn away; as, she was *alienated* from her brother; they *alienated* her affections from me.

al·ien·a·tion (āl′yĕn-ā′shŭn; ā′lĭ-ĕn-ā′-shŭn), *n.* 1, an estrangement or taking away of a feeling, an interest, or the like; as, *alienation* of affections; 2, insanity.

al·ien·ist (āl′yĕn-ĭst; ā′lĭ-ĕn-ĭst), *n.* a physician who specializes in mental diseases.

¹a·light (ȧ-līt′), *adj.* 1, kindled and burning, as a fire; 2, bright in expression; as, the child's face was *alight* with joy.

²a·light (ȧ-līt′), *v.i.* 1, to come down, as from a horse or train; 2, to descend and settle; land, as an airplane.

a·lign (ȧ-līn′), *v.t.* and *v.i.* to put or get into line; as, to *align* troops; the men *aligned* quickly. Also, **a-line**′.

a·lign·ment or **a·line·ment** (ȧ-līn′-mĕnt), *n.* the act of arranging, or an arrangement, in a straight line; as, the *alignment* was good; the sergeant directed the *alignment*.

ALIGNMENT
Blocks 1, 2, 3, 5, 6, are in alignment; block 4 is out of alignment.

a·like (ȧ-līk′), *adj.* resembling one another; similar:—*adv.* in a similar manner.

al·i·ment (ăl′ĭ-mĕnt), *n.* food; nutriment.

al·i·men·ta·ry (ăl′ĭ-mĕn′tȧ-rĭ), *adj.* pertaining to food and nutrition:—**alimentary canal,** the digestive tract of the body, consisting of esophagus, stomach, and intestines, through which food passes.

al·i·mo·ny (ăl′ĭ-mō′nĭ), *n.* an allowance made by a court to a wife from her husband's income or estate, after or pending her separation or divorce from him.

a·line (ȧ-līn′), *v.t.* and *v.i.* [alined, alin-ing], to align. See **align.**

al·i·quot (ăl′ĭ-kwŏt), *adj.* contained by a number an exact number of times, without remainder; as, 3 is an *aliquot* part of 9.

a·live (ȧ-līv′), *adj.* 1, having life; 2, lively; animated; as, John is one of the most *alive* boys we know; 3, attentive; sensitive; as, he is *alive* to his opportunities; 4, full of living things; swarming; as, the stream is *alive* with fish.

al·ka·li (ăl′kȧ-lī; ăl′kȧ-lĭ), *n.* [*pl.* alkalies or alkalis], a substance, as soda or potash, which neutralizes acids and combines with them to form salts; a base.

al·ka·line (ăl′kȧ-lĭn; ăl′kȧ-lĭn), *adj.* containing, or having the properties of, an alkali, as soda or potash.

all (ôl), *adj.* 1, the whole of; every bit of; as, *all* the world; 2, every one of; as, *all* men; 3, as much as possible; as, with *all* speed; 4, nothing but; as, *all* work and no play:—*n.* and *pron.* 1, the whole number or quantity; as, *all* of us, or *all* agreed; 2, one's entire possessions; as, he gave his *all*:—*adv.* wholly; as, *all* wrong:—**all right,** satisfactory or satisfactorily: often used to express mere assent.

Al·lah (ăl′ȧ; ȧl-lä′), the name of God among the Mohammedans.

Al·la·ha·bad (ăl′ȧ-hä-bäd′), a city in northern India; capital of the United Provinces, India (map 15).

al·lay (ă-lā′), *v.t.* to quiet or calm; lessen; as, *allay* your fears.
Syn. lighten, moderate, reduce, relieve.

al·le·ga·tion (ăl′ĕ-gā′shŭn), *n.* 1, the act of asserting; 2, an assertion, whether supported by proof or not.

al·lege (ă-lĕj′), *v.t.* [alleged, alleg-ing], 1, to offer as an argument, plea, or excuse; as, he *alleged* illness for his failure to come; 2, to assert; as, he *alleges* his innocence.

Al·le·ghe·ny (ăl′ĕ-gā′nĭ), a range of mountains in Pennsylvania, Maryland, Virginia, and West Virginia; also, a river in western Pennsylvania (maps 6, 8).

al·le·giance (ă-lē′jăns), *n.* 1, the loyalty or obligation of a person to his sovereign or country; 2, fidelity to a thing, cause, or person; as, we pledge *allegiance* to the flag.

āte, âorta, râre, căt, ȧsk, fär, ăllow, sofȧ; ēve, ĕvent, ĕll, writēr, novĕl; bīte, pĭn; nō, ŏbey, ôr, dŏg, tŏp, cŏllide; ūnit, ūnite, bûrn, cŭt, focŭs; noon, foot; mound; coin;

al·le·gor·y (ăl′ē-gôr′ĭ), *n*. [*pl*. allegories], a story, usually aiming to teach something, as the parables of the Bible or Bunyan's "Pilgrim's Progress," in which the characters stand for ideas or qualities, such as truth, loyalty, or the like.—*adj*. **al′le·gor′i·cal** (ăl′ē-gŏr′ĭ-kăl).—*adv*. **al′le·gor′i·cal·ly**.

al·le·gret·to (ăl′ē-grĕt′ō), *adj*. and *adv*. in music, somewhat fast or lively, between *andante* (slow) and *allegro* (fast).

al·le·gro (ä-lā′grō), *adj*. and *adv*. in music, fast; lively.

al·le·lu·ia, al·le·lu·iah, or **al·le·lu·ja** (ăl′ē-lū′yä), *n*. a song of praise:—*interj*. praise ye Jehovah! See **hallelujah**.

al·ler·gy (ăl′ēr-jĭ), *n*. an unusual sensitivity to specific substances, especially foreign proteins.—*adj*. **al·ler′gic**.

al·le·vi·ate (ă-lē′vĭ-āt), *v.t*. [alleviat-ed, alleviat-ing], to lighten; lessen; make easier; as, a medicine to *alleviate* pain.

¹**al·ley** (ăl′ĭ), *n*. [*pl*. alleys], **1,** a narrow way or back street in a city; **2,** a long, narrow enclosure for games; as, a bowling *alley*.

²**al·ley** (ăl′ĭ), *n*. [*pl*. alleys], in marbles, a shooter, formerly made of alabaster.

All Fools′ Day, a humorous name for the first of April; April Fools′ Day.

All·hal·lows (ôl′hăl′ōz), *n.pl*. used as *sing*. All Saints′ Day, celebrated on November first in honor of all the saints.

al·li·ance (ă-lī′ăns), *n*. **1,** a union between or among nations, groups, or persons; as, an *alliance* by marriage; **2,** a group of persons, societies, or nations united by treaty or agreement; as, the Triple *Alliance*.

al·lied (ă-līd′), past tense and past participle of *ally*.

al·lies (ă-līz′; ăl′īz), plural of *ally*.

al·li·ga·tor (ăl′ĭ-gā′tĕr), *n*. a large, lizard-like, carnivorous animal related to the

ALLIGATOR (₃₀)

crocodiles, with a short, broad head and blunt snout. One kind, growing to about twelve feet, lives in the fresh waters of the southern U. S.

alligator pear, the avocado, a pear-shaped tropical fruit used in salads.

al·lit·er·a·tion (ă-lĭt′ēr-ā′shŭn), *n*. the use of the same initial sound in closely succeeding words, as in "*r*ack and *r*uin," "to *do* or *die*."—*adj*. **al·lit′er·a′tive**.

al·lo·path (ăl′ō-păth), *n*. an allopathic physician: opposite of *homeopath*.

al·lo·path·ic (ăl′ō-păth′ĭk), *adj*. naming, or practicing, the usual method of treating disease. The *homeopathic* method, originally, gave medicines intended to produce the same effects or symptoms as those of the disease; the *allopathic* method gave medicines intended to produce the opposite symptoms, or to do away with the symptoms.

al·lop·a·thy (ă-lŏp′à-thĭ), *n*. the method of treating disease used by an allopathic physician: opposite of *homeopathy*.

al·lot (ă-lŏt′), *v.t*. [allot-ted, allot-ting], to distribute (amounts or shares); assign; as, to *allot* an hour to the work.

al·lot·ment (ă-lŏt′mĕnt), *n*. **1,** a distribution in parts or shares; as, an *allotment* of preferred stock is to be made; **2,** a share or part distributed.

al·low (ă-lou′), *v.t*. **1,** to permit; as, smoking is not *allowed*; **2,** to concede; acknowledge, as a claim; **3,** to set apart; as, to *allow* ten per cent for breakage; **4,** to give; let someone have; as, he *allows* you too much money:—*v.i*. to make concession or provision; as, to *allow* for shrinking.

al·low·a·ble (ă-lou′à-bl), *adj*. permissible; proper; acceptable.

al·low·ance (ă-lou′ăns), *n*. **1,** a quantity or sum allotted; as, she always exceeds her *allowance*; **2,** an amount deducted or added; as, an *allowance* for cash; an *allowance* for stretching:—**make allowance for,** take into consideration.

al·loy (ă-loi′; ăl′oi), *n*. **1,** any mixture of metals; as, steel is an *alloy* of iron and carbon; **2,** a baser metal used in mixture with a finer one; as, copper is often used as an *alloy* with gold; **3,** something that lowers or takes from the value or perfection of something; as, pleasure without *alloy*:—*v.t*. (ă-loi′), **1,** to melt together (two or more metals); **2,** especially, to debase by mixture, as gold with copper; **3,** to lessen by mixing; as, hope *alloyed* with fear.

all right *Colloq*., Correct(ly); satisfactory. *Slang*, certainly.—**alright,** a popular form, but not recognized as good usage.

all—round (ôl′-round′), *adj*. **1,** able to do many things; as, an *all-round* student; **2,** generally useful; as, an *all-round* tool.

All Saints′ Day, a church feast, observed on November first; also, the season of this feast: also called *Allhallows*.

all·spice (ôl′spīs′), *n*. **1,** the berry of the West Indian pimento tree; **2,** a spice made from it, combining the flavors of cinnamon, nutmeg, and cloves.

al·lude (ă-lūd′), *v.i.* [allud-ed, allud-ing], to refer to indirectly or in passing.

al·lure (ă-lūr′), *v.t.* [allured, allur-ing], to tempt by the offer of something desirable; entice; attract.

al·lure·ment (ă-lūr′měnt), *n.* 1, temptation; attraction; as, the salary was an *allurement;* 2, fascination; attractiveness.

al·lur·ing (ă-lūr′ĭng), *adj.* enticing; fascinating; as, an *alluring* perfume.

al·lu·sion (ă-lū′zhŭn), *n.* 1, a passing reference; as, do not make any *allusion* to his loss; 2, a hint or reference, usually to something generally familiar, used by way of illustration; as, a literary *allusion.*

al·lu·vi·al (ă-lū′vĭ-ăl), *adj.* composed of clay, mud, or other material deposited by running water; as, *alluvial* soil.

al·ly (ă-lī′), *v.t.* [allied, ally-ing], to unite or bind, as by marriage, treaty, league, confederacy, or friendship:—*n.* (ă-lī′; ăl′ī), [*pl.* allies (ă-līz′; ăl′īz)], a nation, family, or the like, so united to another; especially, a nation that helps another in war.

Al·ma Ma·ter (ăl′mà mā′tēr; ăl′mà mä′tēr), one's school, college, or university. Also **al′ma ma′ter.**

al·ma·nac (ôl′mà-năk), *n.* a yearbook, or calendar of days, weeks, and months, often giving information about the weather, the sun, moon, stars, tides, festivals, etc.

Al·ma–Tad·e·ma (ăl′mà-tăd′ē-mà), Sir Lawrence (1836–1912), an English painter of Dutch parentage.

al·might·y (ôl-mīt′ĭ), *adj.* having unlimited power; all-powerful:—**the Almighty,** God.

al·mond (ä′mŭnd; ăm′ŭnd), *n.* 1, the nutlike fruit of a small tree somewhat like the peach; 2, the tree itself.

ALMOND
Showing leaf, blossom, nut in hull, and nut with part of hull and part of shell removed.

al·mon·er (ăl′mŭn-ẽr; ä′mŭn-ẽr), *n.* one who is appointed to give out alms.

al·most (ôl′mōst; ôl-mōst′), *adv.* nearly.

alms (ämz), *n.sing.* and *pl.* money given to the poor; charity.

alms·house (ämz′hous′), *n.* a free home for the poor, supported by public funds.

al·oe (ăl′ō), *n.* a plant with thick, spiny leaves found chiefly in South Africa:— **American aloe,** the century plant.

ALOE IN BLOOM

al·oes (ăl′ōz), *n.pl.* commonly used as *sing.* a bitter medicine, made from the juice of aloe leaves.

a·loft (à-lôft′), *adv.* 1, on high; far above the earth; 2, especially, at the masthead, high above the deck of a ship.

a·lone (à-lōn′), *adj.* and *adv.* 1, by oneself; apart; as, he usually walks *alone;* the house stands *alone;* 2, only; as, he *alone* knows it; 3, without the aid of another; as, you can do that job *alone.*

a·long (à-lông′), *prep.* by the length of; lengthwise of; as, *along* the shore:—*adv.* 1, parallel; as, he ran *along* beside me; 2, onward; as, step *along.*

   along with, together with; **all along,** all the time.

a·long·side (à-lông′sīd′), *adv.* by the side; side by side:—*prep.* by the side of; beside: —**alongside of,** beside.

a·loof (à-lōōf′), *adj.* and *adv.* apart; as, he stood *aloof* from the crowd.—*n.* **a-loof′ness.**

a·loud (à-loud′), *adv.* loudly; as, to call *aloud* for help; also, with a normal voice; as, he read *aloud.*

alp (ălp), *n.* a high mountain, or its peak.

al·pac·a (ăl-păk′à), *n.* 1, a domesticated, sheeplike animal of the Andes, with fine long woolly hair; 2, a thin cloth made from this hair, often mixed with silk or cotton.

al·pha (ăl′fà), *n.* the first letter of the Greek alphabet, equivalent to English *a;* hence, the beginning of anything:—**alpha and omega,** the beginning and the end.

al·pha·bet (ăl′fà-bět), *n.* a set of letters used in writing a language; also, these letters arranged in a certain traditional order.

ALPACA (1/30)

al·pha·bet·i·cal (ăl′fà-bět′ĭ-kăl), *adj.* 1, pertaining to the alphabet; 2, in the order in which the alphabet is arranged; as, an *alphabetical* list of names.—*adv.* **al′pha-bet′i-cal-ly.**

al·pha·bet·ize (ăl′fà-bět-īz), *v.t.* [alphabetized, alphabetiz-ing], to arrange, as a list of words, in the order of the alphabet.

Al·pine (ăl′pīn; ăl′pĭn), *adj.* belonging to the Alps:—**alpine,** belonging to high mountains; as, *alpine* snow; *alpine* flowers.

Alps (ălps), a range of lofty mountains in south central Europe (map 12).

al·read·y (ôl-rěd′ĭ), *adv.* previously; before a particular time; beforehand; as, he has *already* left.

Al·sace (ăl′săs; ȧl′zȧs′), a region in France between the Vosges and the Rhine.

Al·sace—Lor·raine (⸗lŏ-rān′; ⸗lô′rân′), a much-disputed border region between France and Germany; now part of France.

al·so (ôl′sō), *adv.* in addition; besides; too.

Al·tai (ăl-tī′; äl-tī′), a range of very high mountains in central Asia (map **15**).

al·tar (ôl′tēr), *n.* **1**, any raised place or structure on which, as in the old days, incense was burned or sacrifices were offered by worshipers; **2**, in some Christian churches, the communion table.

ANCIENT HE-
BREW ALTAR

al·ter (ôl′tēr), *v.t.* and *v.i.* to change; make or become different; as, she *altered* the dress; his manners *altered* for the better.—*adj.* **al′ter·a·ble.**

al·ter·a·tion (ôl′tēr-ā′shŭn), *n.* a change; the act of changing or modifying anything.

al·ter·ca·tion (ôl′tēr-kā′shŭn; ăl′tēr-kā′-shŭn), *n.* a quarrel or dispute; wrangle; as, the baseball pitcher had an *altercation* with the umpire.

al·ter·nate (ôl′tēr-nĭt; ăl′tēr-nĭt; ôl-tûr′-nĭt; ăl-tûr′nĭt), *adj.* **1**, taking place by turns, first one and then the other; as, *alternate* chills and fever; **2**, every other (one) of a series; as, *alternate* months:—*n.* a substitute; as, an *alternate* took the sick man's place:—*v.t.* (ôl′tēr-nāt; ăl′tēr-nāt), [alternat-ed, alternat-ing], to cause to occur by turns; interchange; as, he *alternated* his questions between the boys and the girls:—*v.i.* to act or take place by turns; as. day *alternates* with night.—*adv.* **al′ter·nate·ly.**

al·ter·na·tion (ôl′tēr-nā′shŭn; ăl′tēr-nā′-shŭn), *n.* a following in succession, one after the other; as, the *alternation* of day and night.

☐ ▉ ☐ ▉ ☐
ALTERNATION
White and black squares are arranged in alternation.

al·ter·na·tive (ôl-tûr′nȧ-tĭv; ăl-tûr′nȧ-tĭv), *n.* **1**, a choice between two things or courses of action; as, she had the *alternative* of going to a concert or going to a theater; **2**, either of the two choices; as, she chose the second *alternative*, namely, the theater:—*adj.* giving the choice of two things, only one of which may be taken, done, etc.—*adv.* **al·ter′na·tive·ly.**

Syn., n. option, election, preference.

al·though or **al·tho** (ôl-thō′), *conj.* though; even if.

al·tim·e·ter (ăl-tĭm′ē-tēr), *n.* an instrument for measuring altitude, used in navigation, and especially in aviation.

al·ti·tude (ăl′tĭ-tūd), *n.* **1**, height; height

above sea level; as, the *altitude* of a mountain; **2**, a high place or region.

al·to (ăl′tō), *n.* [*pl.* altos], **1**, the part sung by the lowest female voice; **2**, a person with such a voice, or the voice itself.—*adj.* **al′to.**

al·to·geth·er (ôl′tŏŏ-gĕth′ēr), *adv.* **1**, completely; wholly; entirely; **2**, on the whole; in the main; as, *altogether*, the party was a success.

Al·too·na (ăl-tōō′nȧ), a manufacturing city in central Pennsylvania (map **6**).

al·tru·ism (ăl′trōō-ĭzm), *n.* unselfish regard for the interests of others.—*n.* **al′tru·ist.**

al·tru·is·tic (ăl′trōō-ĭs′tĭk), *adj.* unselfishly concerned with the welfare of others.—*adv.* **al′tru·is′ti·cal·ly.**

al·um (ăl′ŭm), *n.* a transparent, whitish mineral salt, used as a medicine, either externally to stop bleeding, or internally to cause vomiting. It is also used in dyeing and in the purification of water.

a·lu·mi·num (ȧ-lū′mĭ-nŭm), *n.* a bluish-white, very light metal that does not rust, used especially where the combination of lightness and strength is desired.

a·lum·na (ȧ-lŭm′nȧ), *n.fem.* [*pl.* alumnae (ȧ-lŭm′nē)], a girl or woman graduate of a school, college, or university.

a·lum·nus (ȧ-lŭm′nŭs), *n.* [*pl.* alumni (ȧ-lŭm′nī)], a boy or man graduate of a school, college, or university.

al·ways (ôl′wāz), *adv.* at all times.

am (ăm), the first person singular present indicative of *be*.

Am. abbreviation for *America, American.*

A.M. **1**, abbreviation for Latin *ante meridiem* meaning *before noon* (also, **a.m.**); **2**, abbreviation for *Master of Arts* (also **M.A.**); **3**, abbreviation for *amplitude modulation* (also, **AM**).

a·main (ȧ-mān′), *adv.* **1**, forcibly; violently; as, the storm struck the ship *amain*; **2**, at full speed; as, the robbers fled *amain*.

a·mal·gam (ȧ-măl′găm), *n.* **1**, an alloy of one or more metals with mercury; as, silver *amalgam*; **2**, a mixture or compound.

a·mal·ga·mate (ȧ-măl′gȧ-māt), *v.t.* [amalgamat-ed, amalgamat-ing], **1**, to alloy or mix (a metal) with mercury or with another metal; **2**, to mix to form a compound:—*v.i.* to mix or combine so as to become indistinguishable; unite; as, one race of men may *amalgamate* with another.—*n.* **a·mal′ga·ma′tion.**

Syn. join, blend, compound.

a·man·u·en·sis (ȧ-măn′ū-ĕn′sĭs), *n.* [*pl.* amanuenses (ȧ-măn′ū-ĕn′sēz)], one who writes for another, either from dictation or from copy; a secretary.

---

gȯ; join; yet; sing; chin; show; thin, *th*en; hw, *why*; zh, azure; ū, Ger. für or Fr. lune;
ö, Ger. schön or Fr. feu; n̈, Fr. enfant, nom; kh, Ger. ach or ich.   See pages ix–x.

am·a·ranth (ăm′a·rănth), *n*. **1**, an imaginary flower said by poets to be unfading; **2**, any of several plants cultivated for their brilliant green, purple, or crimson flowers.

am·a·ryl·lis (ăm′a·rĭl′ĭs), *n*. any of a family of lilylike, bulbous plants, especially one grown for its large, bright-colored blossoms; also, the blossom.

AMARANTH

a·mass (a·măs′), *v.t.* to collect into a heap; gather; accumulate; as, he *amassed* great wealth.

am·a·teur (ăm′a·tûr′; ăm′a·tūr), *n*. **1**, one who engages in any art, study, or sport for pleasure, and not for money; as, a golf *amateur;* **2**, one whose work lacks professional finish:—*adj.* nonprofessional; as, *amateur* standing in athletics; *amateur* dramatics.

am·a·teur·ish (ăm′a·tûr′ĭsh; ăm′a·tūr·ĭsh), *adj.* lacking in professional finish; inexpert.—*n.* **am′a·teur′ish·ness.**

A·ma·ti (ä·mä′tē), Nicola (1596-1684), a famous Italian violinmaker of Cremona.

am·a·tor·y (ăm′a·tôr′ĭ), *adj.* relating to, or expressive of, love; as, Robert Burns wrote much *amatory* poetry.

a·maze (a·māz′), *v.t.* [amazed, amaz-ing], to overwhelm with astonishment; as, your news *amazes* me.—*adv.* **a·maz′ed·ly.**

a·maze·ment (a·māz′měnt), *n*. astonishment; perplexity or bewilderment arising from sudden surprise.

Syn. awe, wonder, surprise, confusion.

a·maz·ing (a·māz′ĭng), *adj.* astonishing; bewildering.—*adv.* **a·maz′ing·ly.**

¹Am·a·zon (ăm′a·zŏn; ăm′a·zŭn), *n*. one of a fabulous race of female warriors:—**amazon,** a tall, strong, masculine woman.—*adj.* **Am′a·zo′ni·an** (ăm′a·zō′nĭ·ăn).

²Am·a·zon (ăm′a·zŏn; ăm′a·zŭn), a river in South America, the largest in the world (map 11).

am·bas·sa·dor (ăm·băs′a·dẽr), *n*. **1**, a government agent of highest rank representing his country's interests at a foreign capital; **2**, any representative or agent charged with a special mission.

am·ber (ăm′bẽr), *n*. **1**, a yellowish hard resin, or gum, capable of high polish, which is made into beads, cigar holders, etc.; **2**, the reddish-yellow color of amber:—*adj.* made of amber; also, amber-colored.

am·ber·gris (ăm′bẽr-grēs; ăm′bẽr-grĭs), *n*. a waxy substance coming from the sperm whale, used in the manufacture of perfumes.

am·bi·dex·trous (ăm′bĭ·děk′strŭs), *adj.* able to use both hands with equal skill.

am·bi·gu·i·ty (ăm′bĭ·gū′ĭ·tĭ), *n*. [*pl.* ambiguities], **1**, vagueness of meaning; lack of clearness; as, his statement was full of *ambiguity;* **2**, an expression whose meaning can be taken in two or more ways.

am·big·u·ous (ăm·bĭg′ū·ŭs), *adj.* doubtful; having two or more possible meanings; as, *ambiguous* words; *ambiguous* actions.—*adv.* **am·big′u·ous·ly.**—*n.* **am·big′u·ous·ness.**

Syn. uncertain, obscure, vague.

am·bi·tion (ăm·bĭsh′ŭn), *n*. **1**, an eager desire to gain or do something; as, he has an *ambition* to be an explorer; **2**, the thing desired; as, he has attained his *ambition* to be a doctor.

am·bi·tious (ăm·bĭsh′ŭs), *adj.* **1**, full of ambition; determined to succeed; **2**, eager; aspiring; as, *ambitious* for knowledge; **3**, requiring great skill or effort for success; as, they planned an *ambitious* program.—*adv.* **am·bi′tious·ly.**

am·ble (ăm′bl), *v.i.* [am-bled, am-bling], **1**, to walk at an easy pace; meander; **2**, of horses, to pace, or go at a gait in which the animal lifts the two feet on the same side together:—*n.* **1**, the ambling gait of a horse; **2**, any easy gait.—*n.* **am′bler.**

am·bro·si·a (ăm·brō′zhĭ·a; ăm·brō′zĭ·a), *n*. **1**, in mythology, the food of the gods; **2**, anything exquisitely pleasing to taste or smell.—*adj.* **am·bro′si·al.**

am·bu·lance (ăm′bū·lăns), *n*. an enclosed vehicle for carrying the sick and wounded.

am·bus·cade (ăm′bŭs-kād′), *n*. an ambush; a place where troops hide for sudden attack; also, troops so hidden:—*v.i.* [am-buscad-ed, ambuscad-ing], to lie in ambush:—*v.t.* to place (troops) in ambush.

am·bush (ăm′boosh), *n*. **1**, a concealed station from which to attack the enemy unexpectedly; **2**, troops so attacking:—*v.t.* to waylay; attack from ambush.

a·me·ba (a·mē′ba), *n*. [*pl.* amebae (a·mē′bē) or amebas], a one-celled animal; the amoeba. See **amoeba.**

a·meer (a·mēr′), *n*. a Mohammedan noble; an amir. See **amir.**

a·mel·io·rate (a·mēl′yō·rāt), *v.t.* [ameliorat-ed, ameliorat-ing], to make better; as, he wishes to *ameliorate* living conditions:—*v.i.* to grow better; improve.—*adj.* **a·mel′io·ra′tive.**

a·mel·io·ra·tion (a·mēl′yō·rā′shŭn), *n*. improvement; betterment.

a·men (ā′měn′; ä′měn′), *interj.* verily; so be it: a word used at the end of a prayer, blessing, etc., to express solemn assent or approval.—*n.* **a′men′.**

a·me·na·ble (å-mē′nå-bl; å-měn′å-bl), *adj.* 1, easy to lead; ready to accept advice; 2, liable; answerable; as, *amenable* to the law.—*adv.* **a·me′na·bly.**

a·mend (å-měnd′), *v.t.* 1, to change for the better; correct; as, he will *amend* his faults; 2, to change formally; as, to *amend* a law.

a·mend·ment (å-měnd′měnt), *n.* 1, a change for the better; as, an *amendment* in conduct; 2, an alteration or change in a formal document, as in the constitution of a country.

a·mends (å-měndz′), *n.pl.* payment or reparation for loss or injury inflicted on someone else; as, he is willing to make *amends* for the results of his careless driving.

a·men·i·ty (å-měn′ĭ-tĭ; å-mē′nĭ-tĭ), *n.* [*pl.* amenities], pleasantness; agreeableness:—**amenities,** agreeable or polite actions or manners; as, crude people do not observe the *amenities* of life.

Amer. abbreviation for *America, American.*

A·mer·i·ca (å-měr′ĭ-kå), 1, the United States; 2, the lands of the Western Hemisphere, including North America and South America (maps 3, 11).

A·mer·i·can (å-měr′ĭ-kăn), *adj.* 1, pertaining to, or situated in, America; 2, belonging to the U.S.; as, an *American* citizen:—*n.* an inhabitant of America; especially, a citizen of the U.S.

A·mer·i·can·ism (å-měr′ĭ-kăn-ĭzm), *n.* 1, a phrase, word, trait, or custom characteristic of the U.S.; 2, the spirit of loyalty to American ideals and institutions.

A·mer·i·can·ize (å-měr′ĭ-kăn-īz), *v.t.* [Americanized, Americaniz·ing], to bring into agreement or accord with the manners and customs of the U.S.—*n.* **A·mer′i·can·i·za′tion.**

A·mer·i·can plan, in hotels, the inclusion of meals in the fixed rate for a stated period, as contrasted with *European plan.*

A·mer·i·can Rev·o·lu·tion, the war (1775–1783) by which the American colonies became independent of Great Britain.

A·me·ri·go Ves·puc·ci (ä′mä-rē′gŏ věs-pōōt′chē), (1451–1512), an Italian navigator for whom America is named.

am·e·thyst (ăm′ē-thĭst), *n.* a kind of purple or violet quartz, used as a gem.

a·mi·a·ble (ā′mĭ-å-bl), *adj.* friendly; kindly; as, an *amiable* disposition.—*adv.* **a′mi·a·bly.**—*n.* **a′mi·a·bil′i·ty.**

am·i·ca·ble (ăm′ĭ-kå-bl), *adj.* friendly; peaceable; as, an *amicable* discussion.—*adv.* **am′i·ca·bly.**—*n.* **am′i·ca·bil′i·ty.**

a·mid (å-mĭd′), *prep.* in the middle of.

a·mid·ships (å-mĭd′shĭps), *adv.* in the middle of a ship.

a·midst (å-mĭdst′), *prep.* among; amid.

A·miens (å′myăn′; ăm′ĭ-ěnz), a city in northern France, scene of many battles in 1914 and 1918 (map 12).

a·mir or **a·meer** (å-mēr′), *n.* a Mohammedan noble; formerly, the title of the ruler of Afghanistan.

a·miss (å-mĭs′), *adj.* wrong; faulty; as, nothing's *amiss:*—*adv.* wrongly; as, you take my words *amiss.*

am·i·ty (ăm′ĭ-tĭ), *n.* [*pl.* amities], friendship; peaceful relations.

am·me·ter (ăm′mē′tēr; ăm′ē-tēr), *n.* an instrument that measures amperage, or the force of an electric current.

Am·mon (ăm′ŏn), *n.* one of the Egyptian gods, represented with a ram's horns.

am·mo·ni·a (å-mō′nĭ-å; å-mōn′yå), *n.* 1, a clear, sharp-smelling gas readily soluble in water, much used in fertilizers, in cleaning fluids, and in making ice; 2, a solution of this gas in water, for household use.

am·mu·ni·tion (ăm′û-nĭsh′ŭn), *n.* material, as powder and shot, used in charging cannon, firearms, etc.

am·ne·si·a (ăm-nē′zhĭ-å; ăm-nē′zĭ-å), *n.* loss of memory.

am·nes·ty (ăm′něs-tĭ), *n.* [*pl.* amnesties], a general pardon for offenses against the government.

a·moe·ba (å-mē′bå), *n.* [*pl.* amoebae (å-mē′bē) or amoebas], a tiny water animal without definite shape, one of the simplest forms of life. Also spelled **a·me′ba.**

AMOEBA
(highly magnified)

a·mok (å-mŏk′), *adv.* with intent to kill; amuck. See **amuck.**

a·mong (å-mŭng′), *prep.* 1, in the group with; surrounded by; as, *among* friends; *among* all these riches; 2, by the united action of; as, *among* them all, they succeeded; 3, in the time of; as, *among* the ancient Greeks; 4, by distribution to; as, to divide the estate *among* the heirs.

a·mongst (å-mŭngst′), *prep.* among.

am·o·rous (ăm′ŏ-rŭs), *adj.* inclined to love; having to do with love; as, an *amorous* nature; *amorous* letters.

a·mor·phous (å-môr′fŭs), *adj.* 1, formless; shapeless; as, a vase fashioned from *amorphous* clay; 2, not crystallized.

A·mos (ā′mŏs), in the Bible, a Hebrew prophet; also, the book of his prophecies.

a·mount (å-mount′), *v.i.* 1, to be equal or equivalent; as, his answer *amounted* to a threat; 2, to add up; as, it *amounts* to 100: —*n.* 1, the total sum; as, the *amount* is 25 cents; **2**, a measure; quantity; as, an unusual *amount* of courage.

a·mour (ȧ-mŏŏr′), *n.* a secret love affair.

A·moy (ȧ-moi′), a city in China opposite the island of Formosa (map **15**).

am·per·age (ăm-pĭr′ĭj; ăm′pĭr-ĭj), *n.* the strength of an electric current, measured in amperes.

am·pere (ăm′pĭr; ăm-pĭr′), *n.* the unit for measuring the strength of electrical current.

am·phib·i·an (ăm-fĭb′ĭ-ăn), *n.* **1**, a plant or animal that can live both on land and in water; as, frogs are *amphibians*; **2**, an air-

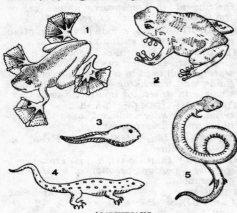

AMPHIBIANS

1, flying frog(⅛); 2, tree toad(⅓); 3, tadpole(⅓); 4, sala-
mander(⅓); 5, congo snake(⅛).

plane that can take off from, and alight upon, either land or water:—*adj.* able to live on land and in water; amphibious.

am·phib·i·ous (ăm-fĭb′ĭ-ŭs), *adj.* able to live or operate both on land and in water.

am·phi·the·a·ter or **am·phi·the·a·tre** (ăm′fĭ-thē′ȧ-tẽr), *n*, **1**, an oval or circular building with rows of seats rising in a slope around a central space, or arena; **2**, anything resembling an amphitheater in shape or purpose. (See illustration next column.)

am·ple (ăm′pl), *adj.* **1**, full; of large size, extent, or volume; **2**, abundant.—*adv.* **am′ply.**

am·pli·fi·ca·tion (ăm′plĭ-fĭ-kā′shŭn), *n.* extension; enlargement, as of a story, by adding details.

am·pli·fi·er (ăm′plĭ-fī′ẽr), *n.* a device to magnify electric impulses, usually including one or more electron tubes. The amplifier in a radio magnifies the sound.

am·pli·fy (ăm′plĭ-fī), *v.t.* [amplified, am-plify-ing], to make larger or fuller; as, she *amplified* her statement.

am·pli·tude (ăm′plĭ-tūd), *n.* **1**, width; breadth; extent or size; as, a park of great *amplitude;* **2**, abundance.

am·pu·tate (ăm′pū-tāt), *v.t.* [amputat-ed, amputat-ing], to cut off, as an arm or leg.

am·pu·ta·tion (ăm′pū-tā′shŭn), *n.* the cutting off of an arm, foot, or the like.

am·pu·tee (ăm′pū-tē′), *n.* a person who, because of injury or disease, has had an arm or leg, or part of an arm or leg, cut off.

Am·ster·dam (ăm′stẽr-dăm), one of the capitals of the Netherlands (map **12**). The other capital is The Hague.

amt. abbreviation for *amount.*

a·muck (ȧ-mŭk′) or **a·mok** (ȧ-mŏk′), *adv.* with intent to kill:—**run amuck,** to run wild.

A·mu Dar·ya (ä-mōō′ där′yä), a river in Asia, flowing into the Aral Sea.

am·u·let (ăm′ū-lĕt), *n.* something worn as a charm against evil or harm; a talisman.

A·mund·sen (ä′mŭn-sĕn), Roald (1872–1928), a Norwegian explorer who dis-covered the South Pole in 1911.

A·mur (ä-mōōr′), a river in Asia about 2,800 miles long, flowing east between Manchuria and the U.S.S.R. (map **15**).

a·muse (ȧ-mūz′), *v t.* [amused, amus-ing], **1**, to entertain; as, to *amuse* children with toys; **2**, to cause to smile or laugh; as, the antics of the clown *amused* her.—*adj.* **a·mus′ing.**—*adv.* **a·mus′ing·ly.**—*n.* **a·muse′-ment.**

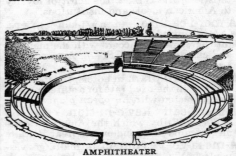

AMPHITHEATER

From a photograph of the amphitheater at Pompeii.

an (ăn), *indefinite sing. article,* a; any; each: used instead of *a* before a vowel sound or silent *h;* as, *an* ell, *an* hour; but *a* hotel, *a* yoke, *a* union.

an- (ăn-), *prefix,* a form of *ad-* used before *n.*

-an (-ăn), a suffix which forms adjectives meaning like or pertaining to; as, republic*an;* the adjective often becoming a noun, meaning: **1**, a person of a given nation-ality or occupation; as, American, librar-i*an;* **2**, a language; as, Italian.

a-nach-ro-nism (a-năk′rô-nĭzm), *n.* the placing of an object in a period to which it does not belong, either because it was not yet known, or because it was no longer used; a chronological error; also, the object so misplaced; as, a hansom cab is an *anachronism* in the era of taxicabs.—*adj.* **a-nach′ro-nis′tic.**

An-a-con-da (ăn′a-kŏn′da), a city in the western part of Montana, noted for its copper mines (map 9).

an-a-con-da (ăn′a-kŏn′da), *n.* a very large tropical South American snake, sometimes 40 feet long, which crushes its prey, usually birds and small animals.

a-nae-mi-a (a-nē′mĭ-a), *n.* a diseased condition of the blood; anemia. See **anemia.** —*adj.* **a-nae′mic.**

an-aes-the-si-a (ăn′ĕs-thē′zhĭ-a; ăn′ĕs-thē′zha; ăn′ĕs-thē′zĭ-a), *n.* insensibility to pain; anesthesia. See **anesthesia.**— *adj.* and *n.* **an′aes-thet′ic.**

an-a-gram (ăn′a-grăm), *n.* a word or phrase obtained by changing the order of the letters of another word or phrase, as "live" from "evil":—**anagrams,** a game in which the players strive to form the largest number of words from any given letters.

a-nal (ā′năl) *adj.* relating to the anus, or lower opening of the large intestine.

a-nal-o-gous (a-năl′ô-gŭs), *adj.* having resemblance; corresponding in certain ways; as, a bird's wing and a human arm are *analogous.*—*adv.* **a-nal′o-gous-ly.**

a-nal-o-gy (a-năl′ô-jĭ), *n.* [*pl.* analogies], a partial agreement or likeness between two things somewhat different; as, the *analogy* between an eye and a camera.

a-nal-y-sis (a-năl′ĭ-sĭs), *n.* [*pl.* analyses (a-năl′ĭ-sēz)], **1,** the separation of a thing into its parts to find out what it is made of; as, a chemical *analysis;* **2,** a critical examination of an idea, book, event, or the like.

an-a-lyst (ăn′a-lĭst), *n.* one who makes a critical examination.

an-a-lyt-ic (ăn′a-lĭt′ĭk) or **an-a-lyt-i-cal** (ăn′a-lĭt′ĭ-kăl). *adj.* separating things into their parts or elements, as for the purpose of study; as, an *analytic* mind.

an-a-lyze (ăn′a-līz). *v.t.* [analyzed, analyz-ing], **1,** to separate into parts or elements; as, to *analyze* a chemical compound; **2,** to examine critically; as, to *analyze* evidence, motives, character, or the like. Also spelled **an′a-lyse.**

an-arch-ism (ăn′ar-kĭzm), *n.* the political belief that all government is unnecessary, and therefore an evil.

an-arch-ist (ăn′ar-kĭst), *n.* **1,** one who regards all government as evil, and believes, as a political ideal, in living without any government; **2,** any person who stirs up violent revolt against established rule.

an-arch-y (ăn′ar-kĭ), *n.* [*pl.* anarchies], the absence or lack of government; hence, a condition of general confusion and terror resulting from the overthrow or disregard of laws.

a-nath-e-ma (a-năth′ê-ma), *n.* **1,** a solemn curse of the church, accompanied by expulsion from the church; **2,** any curse; **3,** a thing or person greatly disliked.

a-nath-e-ma-tize (a-năth′ê-ma-tīz), *v.t.* [anathematized, anathematiz-ing], to pronounce a curse against.

An-a-to-li-a (ăn′a-tō′lĭ-a), the former name of Asia Minor, a peninsula in western Asia. See **Asia Minor.**

an-a-tom-ic (ăn′a-tŏm′ĭk) or **an-a-tom-i-cal** (ăn′a-tŏm′ĭ-kăl), *adj.* relating to the structure of the body.—*adv.* **an′a-tom′i-cal-ly.**

a-nat-o-mist (a-năt′ô-mĭst), *n.* one skilled in anatomy.

a-nat-o-mize (a-năt′ô-mīz), *v.t.* [anatomized, anatomiz-ing], to cut (an animal or plant) apart in order to study the structure.

a-nat-o-my (a-năt′ô-mĭ), *n.* **1,** the science that treats of the structure of the parts of plants and animals, and the relation of these parts to one another; **2,** the cutting up of a plant or an animal to study its structure; **3,** the structure of a plant or animal.

anc. abbreviation for *ancient.*

-ance (-ăns) or **-an-cy** (-ăn-sĭ), a suffix meaning action, process, quality, or state; as, assist*ance,* hindr*ance.*

an-ces-tor (ăn′sĕs′tĕr), *n.* a person from whom one is descended.—*n.fem.* **an′ces′-tress.**

an-ces-tral (ăn-sĕs′trăl), *adj.* belonging to, or inherited from, an ancestor; as, the *ancestral* home.

an-ces-try (ăn′sĕs′trĭ), *n.* [*pl.* ancestries], the line of one's descent traced back through parents, grandparents, etc.; also, one's ancestors.

an-chor (ăng′kẽr), *n.* **1,** a heavy iron or steel implement that, being cast overboard, hooks into the ground and moors a ship in a particular place; **2,** any similar thing to hold fast a movable object:— *v.t.* to make or hold fast, as a ship:—*v.i.* to lie secure in a harbor; as, the ship *anchored* in the bay.

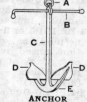

ANCHOR
A, ring; B, stock;
C, shank; D, D,
flukes; E, crown.

an·chor·age (ăng′kẽr-ĭj), *n.* **1,** a place where ships are anchored; **2,** a firm grip, as the hold of an anchor on sea bottom.

an·cho·rite (ăng′kŏ-rīt), *n.* one who forsakes the world and lives alone, as for study or religious meditation; a recluse; hermit.

an·cho·vy (ăn′chŏ-vĭ; ăn-chō′vĭ), *n.* [*pl.* anchovies], a very small Mediterranean herring, used in sauces and as an appetizer.

ANCHOVY (⅓)

an·cient (ān′shĕnt), *adj.* **1,** of very great age; as, *ancient* rocks; **2,** pertaining to times long past; as, *ancient* history:—*n.* **1,** an aged person; **2,** one who lived in olden times:—**the ancients,** civilized peoples of times long past, as the Romans, Greeks, Egyptians, etc.—*adv.* **an′cient·ly.**

-an·cy (-ăn′sĭ), *suffix,* a form of **-ance.**

and (ănd), *conj.* a word connecting two words, phrases, or clauses of equal rank and construction in a sentence; as, John *and* Mary are here; to have *and* to hold.

An·da·lu·sia (ăn′dȧ-lōō′zhȧ; ăn′dȧ-lōō′-shĭ-ȧ), a former division of Spain, on the southern coast.

an·dan·te (än-dän′tā; ăn-dăn′tĕ), *adj.* and *adv.* in music, moderately slow.

An·der·sen (än′dẽr-sĕn), Hans Christian (1805–1875), a Danish writer of fairy stories.

An·des (ăn′dēz), a lofty range of mountains in western South America (map 11).

and·i·ron (ănd′ī′ẽrn), *n.* one of two metal supports or rests for holding logs in a fireplace.

An·dré (än′drā; ăn′drĭ), John, Major (1751–1780), an English officer who conspired with Benedict Arnold in the American Revolution and was executed as a spy.

ANDIRONS
Supporting logs.

An·drew (ăn′drōō), in the Bible, one of the twelve apostles of Jesus.

an·ec·dote (ăn′ĕk-dōt), *n.* a brief story intended to amuse or instruct, often told about a famous person.

a·ne·mi·a or **a·nae·mi·a** (ȧ-nē′mĭ-ȧ), *n.* a diseased condition caused by loss of blood or by lack of red corpuscles in the blood.—*adj.* **a·ne′mic** (ȧ-nē′mĭk).

a·nem·o·ne (ȧ-něm′ŏ-nē), *n.* a plant of the buttercup family; especially, the windflower, or wood anemone, the delicate white flower of which blooms in the woods in early spring.

WOOD
ANEMONE
or windflower.

an·er·oid (ăn′ẽr-oid), *adj.* not containing liquid:—**aneroid barometer,** an instrument in the form of a box from which the air has been partially exhausted, and which indicates variation in air pressure by a pointer controlled by the elastic top of the box.

an·es·the·si·a or **an·aes·the·si·a** (ăn′ĕs-thē′zhĭ-ȧ; ăn′ĕs-thē′zhȧ; ăn′ĕs-thē′zĭ-ȧ), *n.* a partial or complete loss of sensation, due to disease, inhaling of gas, hypnotism, or the like.

an·es·thet·ic or **an·aes·thet·ic** (ăn′ĕs-thĕt′ĭk), *adj.* causing loss of sensation:—*n.* a gas or drug which causes temporary loss of sensation, as ether or chloroform.

a·new (ȧ-nū′), *adv.* a second time; over again.

an·gel (ān′jĕl), *n.* **1,** a messenger of God; one of an order of spiritual beings pictured in human form, but with wings; **2,** an attendant spirit; **3,** a good, innocent, or lovely person; **4,** a gold coin used in England from the 15th to the 17th century.

an·gel·ic (ăn-jĕl′ĭk), *adj.* relating to, or like, the angels; hence, pure; saintly; as, an *angelic* face or disposition.

An·ge·lus (ăn′jĕ-lŭs), *n.* in the Roman Catholic Church, a prayer in memory of the Incarnation, said at morning, noon, and sunset at the ringing of a bell called the *Angelus bell.*

an·ger (ăng′gẽr), *n.* rage; a strong emotion aroused by a sense of injury or wrong:—*v.t.* to provoke to resentment; enrage.

Syn., n. fury, ire. indignation.

¹**an·gle** (ăng′gl), *n.* **1,** the figure formed at the point of intersection of two lines; **2,** the space between such lines; **3,** a corner; a sharp edge; **4,** a point of view; as, he sees it from all *angles.*

A   B   C
ANGLES
A, acute angle; B, right angle; C, obtuse angle.

²**an·gle** (ăng′gl), *v.i.* [an-gled, an-gling], **1,** to fish with hook and line; **2,** to use tricks in obtaining something; as, to *angle* for a compliment.

an·gler (ăng′glẽr), *n.* **1,** a fisherman, especially one who fishes for pleasure; **2,** a salt-water fish with a large, broad head, on which are projections that lure smaller fish within reach of its huge mouth.

ANGLER (¹⁄₂₅), def. 2

An·gles (ăng′glz), *n.pl.* a Germanic tribe which, with the Jutes and Saxons, invaded

Britain in the fifth century A.D. From them England, or "Angleland," got its name.

an·gle–worm (ăng′gl-wûrm′), *n.* an earthworm, often used by anglers as bait.

An·gli·can (ăng′glĭ-kăn), *adj.* **1**, English; **2**, pertaining to the Established Church of England or other churches which have a similar form of worship, as the Protestant Episcopal Church:—*n.* a member of an Anglican Church.—*n.* **An′gli·can·ism.**

an·gli·cize (ăng′glĭ-sīz), *v.t.* [anglicized, angliciz-ing], to bring into accord with English custom, as in dress, pronunciation, etc.; as, we have *anglicized* the French word "valet." Also written **An′gli·cize.**

an·gling (ăng′glĭng), *n.* fishing with hook and line, especially for recreation.

An·glo–E·gyp·tian Su·dan (ăng′glō-ē-jĭp′shăn soō-dän′; soō-dän′), a territory in Africa. See **Sudan.**

An·glo–Sax·on (ăng′glō-săk′sn), *n.* **1**, a member of the people which founded the English nation, descendants of the Jutes, Saxons, and Angles, Germanic tribes from northwestern Europe which invaded Britain in the fifth century A.D.; **2**, the language developed and used by this people, often called *Old English;* **3**, an Englishman, or person of English descent:—*adj.* pertaining to the Anglo-Saxons, or to their language; as, *Anglo-Saxon* customs.

An·go·la (ăng-gō′lá), a Portuguese colony on the west coast of Africa (map **14**). It is also called *Portuguese West Africa.*

¹An·gor·a (ăng-gôr′á), the capital city of Turkey. See **Ankara.**

²An·gor·a (ăng-gôr′á), *n.* the yarn or cloth made from the hair of the Angora goat.

Angora cat, a domestic cat with long, soft hair; **Angora goat,** a domestic goat with long, silky hair; **Angora wool,** the fluffy soft wool of the Angora goat.

ANGORA CAT

an·gri·ly (ăng′grĭ-lĭ), *adv.* in an enraged or resentful manner; wrathfully.

an·gry (ăng′grĭ), *adj.* [an-gri-er, an-gri-est], **1**, feeling or showing wrath, rage, or resentment; as, an *angry* beast; an *angry* look; **2**, inflamed; red; as, an *angry* wound.

an·guish (ăng′gwĭsh), *n.* extreme suffering, especially of mind; as, a mother's *anguish* over the death of her child.

an·gu·lar (ăng′gŭ-lẽr), *adj.* **1**, having angles or points; sharp-cornered; as, *angular* figures; **2**, rawboned; ungainly; awkward; as, an *angular* youth.

an·gu·lar·i·ty (ăng′gŭ-lăr′ĭ-tĭ), *n.* [*pl.* angularities], the state of being sharp-cornered or pointed; also, an angular part or formation; as, *angularities* of figure.

an·i·line (ăn′ĭ-lĭn; ăn′ĭ-lēn) or **an·i·lin** (ăn′ĭ-lĭn), *n.* a colorless, oily liquid, usually obtained from coal tar, and used in making dyes, perfumes, medicines, or the like:—*adj.* made with, or relating to, aniline; as, *aniline* dyes.

an·i·mad·ver·sion (ăn′ĭ-măd-vûr′shŭn; ăn′ĭ-măd-vûr′zhŭn), *n.* a critical remark.

an·i·mal (ăn′ĭ-măl), *n.* **1**, a living being that can feel, and move about of its own will, as a man, dog, sparrow, fish, snake, fly, or the like; **2**, any mammal other than man, as a dog, monkey, or the like:—*adj.* relating to animals; as, the *animal* kingdom; like or characteristic of an animal; as, *animal* spirits.

an·i·mate (ăn′ĭ-māt), *v.t.* [animat-ed, animat-ing], to give life to; inspire with energy or activity; enliven; as, joy *animates* his face:—**animated,** full of spirit and vigor; as, *animated* dialog:—**animated cartoon,** a succession of drawings, each representing a small enough change of position to give the impression of continuous motion when photographed and run through a motion picture projector:—*adj.* (ăn′ĭ-māt), endowed with life; as, biology deals with *animate* beings.

an·i·ma·tion (ăn′ĭ-mā′shŭn), *n.* the state of being full of spirits or vigor; liveliness of appearance or manner.

an·i·mos·i·ty (ăn′ĭ-mŏs′ĭ-tĭ), *n.* [*pl.* animosities], hostility; hatred; enmity.

an·i·mus (ăn′ĭ-mŭs), *n.* [no *pl.*], moving spirit or purpose; strong feeling, especially hostility or malice; as, it is bad manners to exhibit *animus* toward a rival.

an·ise (ăn′ĭs), *n.* **1**, a plant cultivated for its spicy seeds, which are used both in medicine and in flavoring; **2**, the seed of this plant, often called *aniseed.*

An·jou (äṅ′zhoō′; ăn′joō), a former province of France, in the valley of the Loire River.

An·ka·ra (ăng′ká-rá), a city, capital of the Turkish Republic (map **15**). It is sometimes called *Angora.*

an·kle (ăng′kl), *n.* the joint connecting the foot with the leg.

an·klet (ăng′klĕt), *n.* **1**, an ornamental ring or chain for the ankle; **2**, a sock that just covers the ankle.

ANKLETS
def. 1

an·nal·ist (ăn′ăl-ĭst), *n.* a person who records events as they occur year by year.

an·nals (ăn′álz), *n.pl.* **1**, an account or history of events as they happen, written or issued year by year; as, the *Annals* of the Academy are published regularly; **2**, records; history; as, in the *annals* of ancient Rome, we find the reasons for her decline and fall.

An-nam (ă-năm′), a part (cap. Hué) of Indochinese state of Vietnam (map **15**).— *adj.* and *n.* **An-nam-ese** (ăn′ȧ-mēz′; ăn′ȧ-mēs′).

An-nap-o-lis (ă-năp′ṓ-lĭs), a city, capital of Maryland, site of the U.S. Naval Academy (map **6**).

an-neal (ă-nēl′), *v.t.* to heat and then cool slowly, so as to make less brittle; to temper; toughen; as, to *anneal* steel.

an-nex (ă-něks′), *v.t.* to unite, as a smaller thing to a greater; as, to *annex* a province to a kingdom:—*n.* (ăn′ĕks; ă-něks′), a building added to or adjoining another building.

an-nex-a-tion (ăn′ĕk-sā′shŭn), *n.* the act of adding or attaching; addition; as, the *annexation* of Gaul to the Roman Empire.

an-ni-hi-late (ă-nī′ĭ-lāt; ă-nī′hĭ-lāt), *v.t.* [annihilat-ed, annihilat-ing], to blot or wipe out of existence; destroy; as, Pompeii was *annihilated* by the eruption of Vesuvius.

an-ni-hi-la-tion (ă-nī′ĭ-lā′shŭn; ă-nī′hĭ-lā′shŭn), *n.* total destruction; as, the *annihilation* of a regiment in a war.

an-ni-ver-sa-ry (ăn′ĭ-vûr′sȧ-rĭ), *n.* [*pl.* anniversaries], the yearly return of the date of an event; as, we celebrate the *anniversary* of Washington's birth on February 22; a wedding *anniversary*.

an-no Dom-i-ni (ăn′ō dŏm′ĭ-nī), a Latin phrase meaning "in the year of the Lord"; in a given year after the birth of Christ: used, abbreviated (A.D.), with dates; as, *A.D.* 1776.

an-no-tate (ăn′ō-tāt), *v.t.* [annotat-ed, annotat-ing], to make notes upon, by way of comment or criticism; as, to *annotate* a book.

an-no-ta-tion (ăn′ō-tā′shŭn), *n.* the writing of notes in explanation or criticism of a text; also, a note so written.

an-nounce (ă-nouns′), *v.t.* [announced, announc-ing], **1**, to proclaim; make known formally or publicly; publish; as, she *announced* her daughter's engagement; **2**, to state formally the presence or approach of; as, the butler *announced* the guests.
Syn. reveal, herald, proclaim, declare.

an-nounce-ment (ă-nouns′mĕnt), *n.* **1**, the act of announcing or declaring; **2**, the thing declared or made known; **3**, a public notice or advertisement.

an-noy (ă-noi′), *v.t.* to vex or trouble; irritate; as, a dog growls when he is *annoyed*. —*adj.* **an-noy′ing**.

an-noy-ance (ă-noi′ăns), *n.* **1**, the act of causing vexation; as, he finds pleasure in the *annoyance* of his chums; **2**, a sense of being annoyed; vexation; as, my *annoyance* over the delay was great; **3**, the thing or act which bothers or vexes; as, his tardiness was an *annoyance*.
Syn. irritation, nuisance, trouble.

an-nu-al (ăn′ū-ăl), *adj.* **1**, occurring once a year; yearly; as, an *annual* banquet; **2**, taking a year to complete; as, the *annual* rotation of the seasons; **3**, done, reckoned, or published yearly; as, *annual* dues; an *annual* bulletin; **4**, lasting but one year or season, as a plant:—*n.* **1**, a publication appearing once a year; **2**, a plant living only one year or season.—*adv.* **an′nu-al-ly**.

an-nu-i-ty (ă-nū′ĭ-tĭ), *n.* [*pl.* annuities], **1**, a sum of money paid, as by an insurance company, for a specified period in regular instalments; **2**, the right to receive such instalments; as, he invested his money in an *annuity*.

an-nul (ă-nŭl′), *v.t.* [annulled, annul-ling], to abolish or do away with, as a law, decree, or compact; as, the marriage has been *annulled*.—*n.* **an-nul′ment**.

an-nu-lar (ăn′ū-lẽr), *adj.* ring-shaped; as, an *annular* eclipse of the sun.

an-num (ăn′ŭm), *n.* year. See **per an-num**.

An-nun-ci-a-tion, the (ă-nŭn′sĭ-ā′shŭn; ă-nŭn′shĭ-ā′shŭn), *n.* **1**, the announcement to Mary by the angel Gabriel that she was to be the mother of Jesus (Luke 1:28-38); **2**, the feast day, March 25, celebrating this event; **3**, a picture of this scene.

an-nun-ci-a-tor (ă-nŭn′shĭ-ā′tẽr), *n.* an electrically controlled indicator used in hotels, elevators, etc., to show where attendance is required.

an-ode (ăn′ōd), *n.* in electricity, the terminal by which the current enters the substance through which it passes; the positive pole: opposite of *cathode*.

a-noint (ȧ-noint′), *v.t.* **1**, to pour oil or other liquid upon; as, to *anoint* the body with olive oil; **2**, to consecrate, as in a religious ceremony; as, a priest *anoints* a child in baptism.—*n.* **a-noint′ment**.

a-nom-a-ly (ȧ-nŏm′ȧ-lĭ), *n.* [*pl.* anomalies], irregularity; anything that varies from the common rule, or is abnormal or peculiar; as, a winter thunderstorm is an *anomaly*.—*adj.* **a-nom′a-lous**.

a-non (ȧ-nŏn′), *adv.* **1**, soon; in a little while; **2**, at another time; again.

anon. abbreviation for *anonymous*.

a-non-y-mous (ȧ-nŏn′ĭ-mŭs), *adj.* **1**, not known by name; as, an *anonymous* author; **2**, without the author's name; as, an *anon-*

āte, āorta, râre, căt, ȧsk, fär, ăllow, sofȧ; ēve, ĕvent, ĕll, writẽr, novĕl; bīte, pĭn; nō, ōbey, ôr, dôg, tŏp, cŏllide; ūnit, ūnite, bûrn, cŭt, focŭs; nōōn, fŏŏt; mound; coin;

ymous poem.—*adv.* **a-non′y-mous-ly.**—*n.*
an′o-nym′i-ty (ăn/ŏ-nĭm/ĭ-tĭ).

an-oth-er (ă-nŭth/ĕr), *pron.* one more of
the same class or kind; as, I have one hat,
but need *another;* also, a different person
or thing; as, in the dark I took him for
another:—*adj.* **1,** additional; as, please give
me *another* orange; **2,** different; as, he has
become *another* man.

ans. abbreviation for *answer.*

an-swer (ăn/sĕr), *n.* **1,** a response or reply,
as to a letter; **2,** a reply to a charge; as, to say
nothing in *answer* to an accusation; **3,** a
solution, as of a mathematical problem:—
v.t. **1,** to speak, write, or act in reply to;
as, to *answer* the bell; to *answer* a letter;
2, to reply to in defense; as, to *answer* a
charge; **3,** to correspond to; as, he *answers*
the description; **4,** to be sufficient for; as,
this *answers* the purpose:—*v.i.* **1,** to speak,
write, or act in reply; **2,** to be sufficient;
as, this coat will *answer;* **3,** to be accountable; as, I cannot *answer* for this mixture.

an-swer-a-ble (ăn/sĕr-à-bl), *adj.* **1,** accountable; responsible; as, *answerable* to a person
for one's conduct; **2,** capable of being answered or disproved, as an argument.

ant (ănt), *n.* a small insect, famed for its
industry. Ants live in
communities or colo-
nies, in holes which they
burrow in wood or in
the ground.

-ant (-ănt), a suffix
meaning: **1,** doing a certain thing; as, defi*ant,*
dorm*ant;* **2,** one who or
that which does a cer-
tain thing; as, defend*ant,* assist*ant,* serv*ant.*

ANTS
1, female; 2, worker.
Lines indicate actual
length.

ant-ac-id (ănt-ăs/ĭd), *n.* a remedy for an
acid condition, or acidity, especially of
the stomach.

an-tag-o-nism (ăn-tăg/ŏ-nĭzm), *n.* dislike
or opposition between two persons, forces,
parties, etc.; hostility; hatred; as, their *an-
tagonism* was of long standing.

an-tag-o-nist (ăn-tăg/ŏ-nĭst), *n.* one who
fights or competes with another, as in
sports or battle; an opponent; adversary.

an-tag-o-nis-tic (ăn-tăg/ŏ-nĭs/tĭk), *adj.*
contending; opposed; hostile; as, their
antagonistic views; his *antagonistic* spirit.
—*adv.* **an-tag/o-nis/ti-cal-ly.**

an-tag-o-nize (ăn-tăg/ŏ-nīz), *v.t.* [an-
tagonized, antagoniz-ing], to make hostile;
turn into an enemy; as, her rudeness *an-
tagonizes* everyone she meets.

ant-arc-tic (ănt-ärk/tĭk), *adj.* **1,** opposite
to the north-polar, or arctic, regions; **2,**
located in, or relating to, the south-
polar regions:—**Antarctic Circle,** an imag-

inary circle parallel to the equator and
distant 23°27′ from the South Pole.

Ant-arc-tic Con-ti-nent, a body of land,
larger than the U.S., surrounding the
South Pole, and lying within the Antarctic Circle.

Ant-arc-tic O-cean, the body of water
surrounding the Antarctic Continent.

an-te- (ăn/tĕ-), a prefix meaning *before* or
in front of; as, *ante*diluvian, before the
Flood; *ante*room, a room in front of another room.

ant-eat-er (ănt/ēt/ẽr), *n.* an animal which
feeds upon ants. It
has a long, sticky
tongue, with which it
licks up the ants.

ANTEATER (1/70)

an-te-ced-ent (ăn/-
tĕ-sēd/ĕnt), *n.* **1,** some-
one or something that goes before or precedes; **2,** in grammar, a noun, pronoun,
etc., later referred to by a pronoun; as, in
the sentence, "James played football until
he hurt his leg," "James" is the *antecedent* of "he"; **3, antecedents,** the previous
events or influences in a person's life; also,
ancestry; as, his unfortunate *antecedents*
account for his criminal traits:—*adj.* going
before; preceding; as, the events *antecedent*
to the meeting.

an-te-cham-ber (ăn/tĕ-chām/bĕr), *n.* a
room leading into a principal room or
apartment; a waiting room.

an-te-date (ăn/tĕ-dāt/; ăn/tĕ-dāt/), *v.t.*
[antedat-ed, antedat-ing], **1,** to occur at an
earlier time than; as, sailing ships *ante-
dated* steamships; **2,** to mark with an earlier
date than the correct one; as, to *antedate*
a check.

an-te-di-lu-vi-an (ăn/tĕ-dĭ-lū/vĭ-ăn), *adj.*
belonging to or having to do
with the time before the
Flood; hence, ancient; antiquated; as, *antediluvian*
ideas:—*n.* **1,** one who or
that which lived before the
Flood; **2,** an old or old-
fashioned person.

an-te-lope (ăn/tĕ-lōp), *n.*
any of a large group of graceful Old World animals, including the gazelle, eland,
and kudu (see illustration
next page). In western North
America, the name is applied
to the pronghorn, though it is not properly
an antelope.

ANTENNAE (A)
of a beetle. An
insect's antennae
are often longer
than its body.

an-ten-na (ăn-tĕn/à), *n.* [*pl.* antennae
(ăn-tĕn/ē)], **1,** one of the feelers which
grow on the heads of insects, centipedes,
lobsters, etc.; **2,** [*pl.* antennas], in radio,

a wire or set of wires for receiving electric waves or sending them into space.

an·te·pe·nult (ăn′tĕ-pē′nŭlt; ăn′tĕ-pĕ-nŭlt′), *n.* the syllable before the penult; the third syllable from the end of a word; as, "ter" is the *antepenult* in "alteration."

an·te·ri·or (ăn-tîr′ĭ-ẽr), *adj.* 1, fore; toward the front; as, *anterior* lobe; 2, prior; occurring earlier; as, the American Revolution was *anterior* to the French Revolution.

ANTELOPES

1, sable antelope of Africa (₁⁄₇₀); 2, addax (₁⁄₈₀); 3, oryx (₁⁄₇₅); 4, kudu (₁⁄₈₀); 5, gazelle (₁⁄₇₅); 6, eland (₁⁄₉₀).

an·te·room (ăn′tĕ-rōōm′), *n.* a room leading into another; an antechamber.

an·them (ăn′thĕm), *n.* 1, a song of praise or triumph; as, a national *anthem;* 2, a piece of sacred music, usually a passage from the Bible set to music.

an·ther (ăn′thẽr), *n.* in a flower, the part of the stamen which produces the pollen. (See illustration at *flower*.)

an·thol·o·gy (ăn-thŏl′ŏ-jĭ), *n.* [*pl.* anthologies], a collection of choice poems or prose passages from a variety of authors.

An·tho·ny (ăn′thŏ-nĭ), Susan Brownell (1820–1906), a reformer and leader in the struggle for the right of women to vote.

an·thra·cite (ăn′thrȧ-sīt), *n.* a hard coal which burns with little smoke or flame.

an·thrax (ăn′thrăks), *n.* an infectious and usually fatal disease of cattle and sheep. Human beings can catch it from them.

an·thro·poid (ăn′thrŏ-poid), *adj.* manlike; resembling man; as, the chimpanzee is an *anthropoid* ape:—*n.* one of the higher apes resembling man, such as the gorilla.

an·thro·pol·o·gy (ăn′thrŏ-pŏl′ŏ-jĭ), *n.* the study of the development and customs of mankind.—*adj.* **an′thro·po·log′i·cal.**

an·ti (ăn′tī; ăn′tĭ), *Colloquial: n.* [*pl.* antis], a person who is opposed to a policy, movement, law, or the like.

an·ti- (ăn′tĭ-), a prefix meaning against; opposed to; different from; as, *anti*-Christian, *anti*slavery, *anti*climax.

an·ti·bi·ot·ic (ăn′tĭ-bī-ŏt′ĭk), *n.* a chemical substance extracted from living organisms, like molds and fungi, which is able to destroy other organisms, and is therefore useful in treatment of bacterial infection.

an·tic (ăn′tĭk), *n.* a comical trick or action; as, the *antics* of a puppy.

An·ti·christ (ăn′tĭ-krīst′), *n.* the great personal opponent of Christ, expected by many early Christians to appear before the end of the world, bringing evil (1 John 2:18, 22).

an·tic·i·pate (ăn-tĭs′ĭ-pāt), *v.t.* [anticipat-ed, anticipat-ing], 1, to look forward to; expect; especially, to await with pleasure; as, to *anticipate* a party; 2, to foresee (a command, need, wish, etc.) and do ahead of time that which needs doing; as, they *anticipated* our hunger; 3, to be before (another) in doing something; as, A *anticipated* B in the discovery of the new star.

an·tic·i·pa·tion (ăn-tĭs′ĭ-pā′shŭn), *n.* expectation, especially if pleasurable; as, happy in *anticipation* of the picnic.

an·ti·cli·max (ăn′tĭ-klī′măks), *n.* opposite of climax; descent from the sublime to the ridiculous, or from the important to the trivial and uninteresting; as, washing dishes after a party is an *anticlimax.*

an·ti·dote (ăn′tĭ-dōt), *n.* 1, a medicine which counteracts a poison; 2, hence, a remedy, as, hard work served as an *antidote* to his troubles.

An·tie·tam Creek (ăn-tē′tăm), a tributary of the Potomac in Pennsylvania and Maryland. A fiercely fought battle of the War between the States occurred near here.

An·ti·gua (ăn-tē′gwä), one of the Leeward Islands, British West Indies (map 10).

an·ti–im·pe·ri·al·ism (ăn′tĭ-ĭm-pĭr′ĭ-ăl-ĭzm), *n.* opposition to the policy of extending the power of a nation through the acquisition of new territory.

An·til·les (ăn-tĭl′ēz), the West Indies:— **Greater Antilles,** Jamaica, Hispaniola, Cuba, and Puerto Rico; **Lesser Antilles,** a chain of islands southeast of these. (Map 10.)

āte, ȧorta, râre, căt, ȧsk, fär, ăllow, sofȧ; ēve, ĕvent, ĕll, writẽr, novĕl; bīte, pĭn; nō, ōbey, ôr, dôg, tŏp, cŏllide; ūnit, ūnite, bûrn, cŭt, focŭs; nōōn, foŏt; mound; coin;

an·ti·ma·cas·sar (ăn′tĭ-mȧ-kăs′ẽr), *n.* a cover, as of lace, for the back or arms of a chair, sofa, etc.; a tidy.

an·ti·mo·ny (ăn′tĭ-mō′nĭ), *n.* a brittle, white metal which is used in medicine and in important alloys, such as pewter, the metal of printers' type, etc.

An·ti·och (ăn′tĭ-ŏk), a city, the ancient capital of Syria (map 1).

an·tip·a·thy (ăn-tĭp′ȧ-thĭ), *n.* [*pl.* antipathies], a strong, instinctive hatred or a dislike; as, an *antipathy* against snakes.— *adj.* **an′ti-pa-thet′ic.**
   Syn. distaste, hostility, repulsion.

an·tip·o·des (ăn-tĭp′ō-dēz), *n.pl.* places on exactly opposite sides of the earth; as, the North and the South Poles are *antipodes*.

an·ti·quar·i·an (ăn′tĭ-kwâr′ĭ-ăn), *adj.* relating to ancient times or to the relics and ruins of past peoples; as, *antiquarian* studies:—*n.* an antiquary.

an·ti·quar·y (ăn′tĭ-kwẽr′ĭ), *n.* [*pl.* antiquaries], one who collects ancient relics, or who studies the customs, events, and records of ancient or past peoples.

an·ti·quat·ed (ăn′tĭ-kwāt′ĕd), *adj.* old-fashioned; out-of-date; as, *antiquated* clothes; *antiquated* ideas.

an·tique (ăn-tēk′), *adj.* belonging to an age long past; ancient; as, an *antique* vase: —*n.* something of great age; a relic of a much earlier time than the present; as, this chair is an *antique*.

an·tiq·ui·ty (ăn-tĭk′wĭ-tĭ), *n.* [*pl.* antiquities], 1, the early ages, especially before the Middle Ages; as, the pyramids are a relic of *antiquity*; 2, great age; as, the *antiquity* of ruins; 3, **antiquities**, relics that throw light upon ancient times; as, Chinese *antiquities* in a museum.

an·ti·sep·tic (ăn′tĭ-sĕp′tĭk), *adj.* preventing the growth of germs, especially those of disease or decay; as, salt in water makes an *antiseptic* gargle:—*n.* an antiseptic substance, as hydrogen peroxide or iodine.

an·ti·slav·er·y (ăn′tĭ-slāv′ẽr-ĭ), *adj.* opposed to slavery.

an·ti·so·cial (ăn′tĭ-sō′shăl), *adj.* opposed to the interests of society, or of people and citizens as a whole; as, robbery and murder are *antisocial* acts.

an·tith·e·sis (ăn-tĭth′ē-sĭs), *n.* [*pl.* antitheses (ăn-tĭth′ē-sēz)], 1, the exact opposite; as, black is the *antithesis* of white; 2, opposition; contrast; as, an *antithesis* of ideas; 3, an expression that emphasizes contrast. "Give me liberty, or give me death," is an *antithesis*.

an·ti·tox·in (ăn′tĭ-tŏk′sĭn), *n.* a substance formed in the body of a person or animal

suffering from a germ disease, such as diphtheria or scarlet fever, that helps the body to resist the effects of the germs. Antitoxins are used to prevent or cure disease. Some animal is given the disease in a mild form, and an antitoxin is thus produced in its blood. This antitoxin is then drawn off and introduced into the blood of a man or other animal to neutralize the poison of the disease germs.

an·ti·trades (ăn′tĭ-trādz′), *n.pl.* tropical winds blowing steadily above the trade winds, and in an opposite direction; also, prevailing westerly winds of the temperate zones.

ant·ler (ănt′lẽr), *n.* the horn, or a branch of the horn, of a deer.—*adj.* **ant′lered** (ănt′lẽrd).

An·to·ny (ăn′tō-nĭ), Mark, also known as *Marcus Antonius*, (83–30 B.C.), a famous Roman general.

an·to·nym (ăn′tō-nĭm), *n.* a word whose meaning is opposite to that of another word; as, "warm" is the *antonym* of "cool": opposite of *synonym*.

ANTLERS (A)

Ant·werp (ănt′wûrp), a seaport city of Belgium, on the river Scheldt (map 12).

a·nus (ā′nŭs), *n.* the opening at the lower end of the large intestine, through which waste passes from the body.

an·vil (ăn′vĭl), *n.* a block of iron on which metals are hammered and shaped.

anx·i·e·ty (ăng-zī′ĕ-tĭ), *n.* [*pl.* anxieties], 1, mental uneasiness arising from fear of misfortune; as, their *anxiety* increased with the storm; 2, eager desire tinged with fear; as, *anxiety* to make good.
   Syn. concern, dread, trouble, care.

ANVIL

anx·ious (ăngk′shŭs), *adj.* 1, deeply concerned; greatly troubled or worried, as, *anxious* about one's health; 2, desirous; as, *anxious* to please.—*adv.* **anx′ious-ly.**

an·y (ĕn′ĭ), *adj.* 1, one of several, but no matter which; as, you may have *any* book here; 2, some: used with a negative, or in a question; as, I haven't *any* time; 3, every; as, I did what *any* man would do: —*pron.* some; as, give me some nails if you have *any*:—*adv.* to any extent; at all; in any degree; as, don't go *any* farther.

an·y·bod·y (ĕn′ĭ-bŏd′ĭ), *pron.* 1, an ordinary person; any person of a group; as, *anybody* can do it if he tries; 2, someone of importance; as, is he *anybody?*

an·y·how (ĕn′ĭ-hou), *adv.* 1, in any way;

hence, carelessly; in haphazard way; as, she just does her work *anyhow;* **2,** at any rate; as, *anyhow,* you are here now.

an·y·one (ĕn'ĭ-wŭn), *pron.* any person; anybody; as, *anyone* may come who will.

an·y·thing (ĕn'ĭ-thĭng), *pron.* a thing of any sort whatever; as, *anything* can happen.

an·y·way (ĕn'ĭ-wā), *adv.* **1,** in any manner; as, do it *anyway* you like; **2,** nevertheless; as, I am tired, but I'm going *anyway.*

an·y·where (ĕn'ĭ-hwâr), *adv.* in or at any place; as, put it *anywhere.*

an·y·wise (ĕn'ĭ-wīz), *adv.* in any way or degree.

A·o·ran·gi (ä'ō-räng'gē), a mountain, 12,349 feet high, in South Island, New Zealand. It is also called *Mount Cook.*

a·or·ta (ā-ôr'tä), *n.* [*pl.* aortas], the large artery which carries blood away from the heart, subdividing into smaller arteries that supply the entire body.

a·pace (ȧ-pās'), *adv.* quickly; speedily; rapidly; as, the work grew *apace.*

A·pach·e (ȧ-păch'ē), *n.* a member of a warlike tribe of American Indians who formerly roamed the southwestern U. S.

AORTA (A, A)
Showing heart and large blood vessels.

a·pache (ȧ-päsh', à/päsh'), *n.* [*pl.* apaches (ȧ-päsh'ĕz; à/päsh')], a member of a brutal criminal class of Paris; hence, any vicious criminal; a gangster.

a·part (ȧ-pärt'), *adv.* **1,** separately in time or place; as, to live *apart;* **2,** in, or into, pieces; as, it fell *apart;* he took the watch *apart:*—**apart from, 1,** separated from; as, she lives *apart from* her parents; **2,** not considering; leaving out of account; as, *apart from* the plot, the book interested me.

a·part·ment (ȧ-pärt'mĕnt), *n.* a separate room, or suite of rooms, used to live in. —**apartments,** any suite of rooms; **apartment house,** a building containing suites of rooms.

ap·a·thet·ic (ăp'ȧ-thĕt'ĭk), *adj.* without interest; indifferent; as, *apathetic* toward a suggestion.—*adv.* **ap'a·thet'i·cal·ly.**

ap·a·thy (ăp'ȧ-thĭ), *n.* [*pl.* apathies], lack of feeling or interest; indifference; as, to arouse a person from *apathy.*

ape (āp), *n.* **1,** a tail-less monkey, like man in structure and organs, as the gorilla, chimpanzee, orangutan; **2,** a silly mimic:— *v.t.* [aped, ap-ing], to imitate; as, he smoked only to *ape* his elders.

Ap·en·nines (ăp'ĕ-nīnz), a chain of mountains in central Italy (map **12**).

a·pe·ri·ent (ȧ-pē'rĭ-ĕnt), *n.* a mildly laxative medicine or food, such as figs or prunes:—*adj.* mildly laxative.

ap·er·ture (ăp'ĕr-tūr), *n.* an opening; gap; hole; as, an *aperture* in a wall.

a·pex (ā'pĕks), *n.* [*pl.* apexes (ā'pĕk-sēz) or apices (ăp'ĭ-sēz; ā'pĭ-sēz)], the peak or summit of something, as of a mountain.

a·pha·si·a (ȧ-fā'zhĭ-ȧ; ȧ-fā'zhȧ), *n.* a mental disturbance, marked by inability to understand or use words.

a·phid (ā'fĭd; ăf'ĭd), *n.* a small insect that sucks the sap of plants: also called *aphis.*

a·phis (ā'fĭs; ăf'-ĭs), *n.* [*pl.* aphides (ăf'ĭ-dēz)], an aphid.

APHIDS (enlarged)
A, male; B, female.

aph·o·rism (ăf'ō-rĭzm), *n.* a general truth stated forcefully and in very few words; a proverb. "A stitch in time saves nine" is a common aphorism.

Aph·ro·di·te (ăf'rō-dī'tē), *n.* in Greek mythology, the goddess of love and beauty, identified by the Romans with *Venus.*

a·pi·ar·y (ā'pĭ-ĕr'ĭ), *n.* [*pl.* apiaries], a place where bees are kept; also, a collection of beehives.

ap·i·ces (ăp'ĭ-sēz; ā'pĭ-sēz), one form of the plural of *apex.*

a·piece (ȧ-pēs'), *adv.* for each one; as, the pencils cost five cents *apiece.*

a·poc·a·lypse (ȧ-pŏk'ȧ-lĭps), *n.* any writing that professes to reveal the future: —**Apocalypse,** the last book of the New Testament; Revelation.—*adj.* **a·poc'a·lyp'tic.**

a·poc·ry·pha (ȧ-pŏk'rĭ-fȧ), *n.pl.* used as *sing.* writings or statements of doubtful authorship or authority:—**Apocrypha,** certain writings which are included in the Old Testament as used by Roman Catholics, but are not in that used by Protestants.

a·poc·ry·phal (ȧ-pŏk'rĭ-făl), *adj.* **1,** having to do with the Apocrypha; as, *apocryphal* books of the Bible; **2,** of doubtful genuineness; as, an *apocryphal* story.

A·pol·lo (ȧ-pŏl'ō), *n.* the Greek and Roman god of manly youth and beauty. Apollo was also the god of the sun, music, poetry, prophecy, and medicine.

APOLLO
A Greek statue called *Apollo Belvedere,* from its location in a belvedere, or open gallery, in the Vatican.

āte, āorta, râre, căt, ȧsk, fär, ăllow, sofȧ; ēve, ēvent, ĕll, writẽr, novĕl; bīte, pĭn; nō, ōbey, ôr, dŏg, tŏp, cŏllide; ūnit, ūnite, bûrn, cŭt, focŭs; nōōn, fŏŏt; mound; coin;

a-pol-o-get-ic (å-pŏl/ō-jĕt/ĭk) or **a-pol-o-get-i-cal** (-jĕt/ĭ-kăl), *adj.* admitting or excusing a fault or failure; as, his *apologetic* attitude won him a new chance.— *adv.* **a-pol/o-get/i-cal-ly.**

a-pol-o-gist (å-pŏl/ō-jĭst), *n.* **1**, one who makes an apology; **2**, one who speaks or writes in defense of a person or cause; as, an *apologist* for our prison system.

a-pol-o-gize (å-pŏl/ō-jīz), *v.i.* [apologized, apologiz-ing], **1**, to make an excuse; **2**, to express regret for something.

a-pol-o-gy (å-pŏl/ō-jĭ), *n.* [*pl.* apologies], **1**, an excuse or expression of regret for something one has said or done; as, he made an *apology* for being noisy; **2**, something spoken, written, or offered in defense; as, an *apology* for communism; **3**, a poor substitute; a makeshift; as, this drawing is only an *apology* for a map.

a-po-plec-tic (ăp/ō-plĕk/tĭk), *adj.* **1**, afflicted or threatened with apoplexy; **2**, red of face; **3**, hot-tempered; easily angered.

ap-o-plex-y (ăp/ō-plĕk/sĭ), *n.* the sudden loss of consciousness, or of the power to feel or move; a stroke. It is usually caused by the breaking of a blood vessel in the brain.

a-port (å-pôrt/), *adv.* on or toward the left; as, rocks *aport*; to steer hard *aport*.

a-pos-ta-sy (å-pŏs/tå-sĭ), *n.* [*pl.* apostasies], the giving up of what one has professed, believed, or followed; as, religious or political *apostasy*.

a-pos-tate (å-pŏs/tāt), *n.* one who has forsaken his faith or party; as, a Republican *apostate*:—*adj.* false; traitorous; faithless; as, an *apostate* Christian.

a-pos-tle (å-pŏs/l), *n.* **1**, one of the twelve men chosen by Jesus to teach his gospel to the world (Luke 6:13); also, a disciple, like Paul, given the same work to do; **2**, a pioneer missionary; as, Livingstone was the *apostle* to Africa; **3**, a leader of any reform; as, an *apostle* of temperance.

ap-os-tol-ic (ăp/ŏs-tŏl/ĭk) or **ap-os-tol-i-cal** (-tŏl/ĭ-kăl), *adj.* **1**, relating to the twelve apostles of Christ, or their times, doctrine, or practice; **2**, coming from the Pope; papal; as, an *apostolic* blessing.

a-pos-tro-phe (å-pŏs/trō-fē), *n.* **1**, a breaking off in a speech to address a person, usually absent or dead, or an abstract idea or imaginary object; **2**, the sign ['] used to show various things: **a,** a contraction, as *I'll* for *I will*; **b,** the omission of one or more letters from a word, as *can't* for *cannot*; '*49* for *1849*; **c,** the possessive case of nouns, as in *cat's* fur, *Ulysses'* shield; **d,** the plural of letters and figures, as *x's* and *y's*, *6's* and *7's*.

a-poth-e-car-y (å-pŏth/ē-kĕr/ĭ), *n.* [*pl.* apothecaries], one who prepares and sells medicines and drugs; a pharmacist; druggist:—**apothecaries' weight,** a system of weights used in dispensing drugs.

a-poth-e-o-sis (å-pŏth/ē-ō/sĭs; ăp/ō-thē/ō-sĭs), *n.* [*pl.* apotheoses (å-pŏth/ē-ō/sēz; ăp/ō-thē/ō-sēz)], **1**, the raising of a man to the rank of a god; deification; as, the *apotheosis* of a Roman emperor; **2**, glorification; exalted personification of an ideal; as, the *apotheosis* of goodness.

Ap-pa-lach-i-an Moun-tains (ăp/å-lăch/ĭ-ăn; ăp/å-lā/chĭ-ăn), a range of mountains running parallel with the coast in eastern North America (map 5).

ap-pall or **ap-pal** (å-pôl/), *v.t.* [appalled, appall-ing], to frighten; shock; dismay; as, the danger of war *appalled* us.

ap-pa-nage (ăp/å-nĭj), *n.* **1**, money or lands for the support of the younger members of the family of a prince; **2**, anything assumed as a right by virtue of birth, office, etc.; **3**, a dependent territory; **4**, a natural accompaniment; as, truthfulness is an *appanage* of virtue.

ap-pa-ra-tus (ăp/å-rā/tŭs; ăp/å-răt/ŭs), *n.* [*pl.* apparatus or apparatuses], **1**, an outfit of tools, utensils, or instruments for any kind of work; as, laboratory *apparatus*; **2**, the set of organs which performs some natural process; as, the digestive *apparatus*.

ap-par-el (å-păr/ĕl), *n.* clothing; dress; as, boys' *apparel*:—*v.t.* to clothe; fit out.

ap-par-ent (å-păr/ĕnt; å-pâr/ĕnt), *adj.* **1**, open to view; easily seen; **2**, easily understood; evident; **3**, appearing or seeming, rather than true or real; as, his *apparent* remorse fooled us.—*adv.* **ap-par/ent-ly.**

ap-pa-ri-tion (ăp/å-rĭsh/ŭn), *n.* something startling and unreal that suddenly appears; a ghost or specter.

ap-peal (å-pēl/), *v.t.* to transfer or refer to a superior court or judge; as, to *appeal* a case:—*v.i.* **1**, to make an earnest request; as, he *appealed* for aid; **2**, to be of interest; make a favorable impression; as, good music *appeals* to me:—*n.* **1**, a call for aid or sympathy; **2**, interest; attraction; as, your proposal has no *appeal* for me; **3**, the transfer of a case from a lower to a higher court.—*adj.* **ap-peal/ing.**

ap-pear (å-pēr/), *v.i.* **1**, to come into sight; as, the moon *appeared*; **2**, to seem; as, he *appears* to be ill; **3**, to come before the public; as, the book *appeared* in June; this actor *appeared* in "Hamlet."

ap-pear-ance (å-pēr/ăns), *n.* **1**, the act of becoming visible; as, the *appearance* of the sun from behind a cloud; **2**, look; bearing; as, Daniel Webster had a dignified *ap-*

---

go; join; yet; sing; chin; show; thin, *th*en; hw, *wh*y; zh, a*z*ure; ü, Ger. f*ü*r or Fr. l*u*ne; ö, Ger. sch*ö*n or Fr. f*eu*; ṅ, Fr. e*n*fant, no*m*; kh, Ger. a*ch* or i*ch*. See pages ix–x.

pearance; **3,** outward show; as, an *appearance* of humility; **4,** the act of coming before the public; as, an *appearance* in court.

ap-pease (ă-pēz'), *v.t.* [appeased, appeasing], **1,** to quiet; pacify; as, to *appease* an angry person; **2,** to satisfy; as, to *appease* one's hunger or curiosity; **3,** to act contrary to one's principles in an attempt to effect a compromise.—*n.* **ap-pease'ment.**

ap-pel-lant (ă-pĕl'ănt), *n.* one who appeals from a lower to a higher court.

ap-pel-late (ă-pĕl'āt), *adj.* dealing with appeals; as, an *appellate* court.

ap-pel-la-tion (ăp'ĕ-lā'shŭn), *n.* a name or title by which a person or thing is described or known; as, one *appellation* of Pennsylvania is "The Keystone State."

ap-pend (ă-pĕnd'), *v.t.* **1,** to attach or affix, as a seal; **2,** to attach or add, as supplementary matter to a book.

ap-pend-age (ă-pĕn'dĭj), *n.* something attached to a greater thing, and forming a part of it, as a leg to an animal's body, or a porch to a house.
  Syn. attachment, adjunct, addition.

ap-pen-di-ces (ă-pĕn'dĭ-sēz), one form of the plural of *appendix.*

ap-pen-di-ci-tis (ă-pĕn'dĭ-sī'tĭs), *n.* an inflammation of the vermiform appendix.

ap-pen-dix (ă-pĕn'dĭks), *n.* [*pl.* appendixes (ă-pĕn'dĭk-sĕz) or appendices (ă-pĕn'-dĭ-sēz)], **1,** that which is added to give further information; as, the *appendix* to a book; **2,** a wormlike sac, three or four inches long, situated near the entrance to the large intestine, in the lower right-hand side of the abdomen: called in full *vermiform appendix.* (See illustration at *intestines.*)

ap-per-tain (ăp'ĕr-tān'), *v.i.* **1,** to belong by right, nature, or custom; as, these lands *appertain* to the abbey; the right to vote *appertains* to all citizens; **2,** to be related.

ap-pe-tite (ăp'ĕ-tīt), *n.* **1,** a physical craving for food; **2,** a strong and active desire; as, an *appetite* for adventure.

ap-pe-tiz-er (ăp'ĕ-tī'zĕr), *n.* **1,** a food or drink served before a meal to stimulate the desire for food; **2,** anything that arouses interest in things to follow.

ap-pe-tiz-ing (ăp'ĕ-tī'zĭng), *adj.* exciting or pleasing the appetite; as, *appetizing* food.

Ap-pi-an Way (ăp'ĭ-ăn), the most famous of ancient Roman roads, running 366 miles southeast from Rome to the heel of Italy.

ap-plaud (ă-plôd'), *v.t.* **1,** to express approval of, especially by a clapping of the hands; **2,** to commend; as, I *applaud* your stand in the matter:—*v.i.* to clap the hands, or otherwise show approval.

ap-plause (ă-plôz'), *n.* a public expression of approval, as by clapping of the hands.

ap-ple (ăp'l), *n.* **1,** the round, fleshy fruit of a well-known tree, grown in nearly all temperate regions; **2,** the tree itself. (See illustration on page 864.)

ap-pli-ance (ă-plī'ăns), *n.* an article or device for some special use or purpose, as an electric iron or a lawn mower.

ap-pli-ca-ble (ăp'lĭ-kă-bl), *adj.* suitable; appropriate; capable of being used or applied; as, this excuse is not *applicable* to your case.—*n.* **ap'pli-ca-bil'i-ty.**

ap-pli-cant (ăp'lĭ-kănt), *n.* one who asks or applies for something; a candidate; as, an *applicant* for a position.

ap-pli-ca-tion (ăp'lĭ-kā'shŭn), *n.* **1,** the act of putting on; as, the *application* of ice to a sprained ankle; **2,** the thing put on; as, cold *applications;* **3,** practical demonstration or use, as of a theory or law; **4,** close attention, as to work; **5,** a personal or written request, as for a job.

ap-plied (ă-plīd'), *adj.* put to practical use; as, *applied* science.

ap-pli-qué (ăp'lĭ-kā'), *n.* an ornamentation, as for clothes or fancywork, made by cutting figures out of one material and applying them upon another.

ap-ply (ă-plī'), *v.t.* [applied, apply-ing], **1,** to bring into contact with something; lay on; as, to *apply* a bandage; to *apply* a whip; **2,** to put into practice; as, to *apply* a rule; **3,** to devote to a particular purpose; as, *apply* yourself to study:—*v.i.* **1,** to ask; petition; as, *apply* early if you want a ticket; **2,** to have some connection; as, this does not *apply* to you.

ap-point (ă-point'), *v.t.* **1,** to name for an office; as, to *appoint* a chairman; **2,** to set; fix; as, to *appoint* a day for a game.

ap-point-ee (ă-poin'tē'), *n.* a person named to an office; as, political *appointees.*

ap-poin-tive (ă-poin'tĭv), *adj.* filled by appointment, not by election, as an office.

ap-point-ment (ă-point'mĕnt), *n.* **1,** the act of naming or appointing to an office; **2,** the position or office so assigned; **3,** an engagement; mutual agreement to meet: —**appointments,** furniture or equipment.

Ap-po-mat-tox (ăp'ŏ-măt'ŭks), a village in south central Virginia, where Lee surrendered to Grant on April 9, 1865, thus ending the War between the States.

ap-por-tion (ă-pôr'shŭn), *v.t.* to divide and distribute; allot; as, ample rations were *apportioned* to the sailors.
  Syn. assign, appoint, divide, allocate.

ap-por-tion-ment (ă-pôr'shŭn-mĕnt), *n.* distribution; allotment.

āte, âorta, râre, căt, ȧsk, fär, ȁllow, sofȧ; ēve, ĕvent, ĕll, writĕr, novĕl; bīte, pĭn; nō, ōbey, ôr, dŏg, tŏp, cŏllide; ūnit, ūnite, bûrn, cŭt, focŭs; nōōn, fŏŏt; mound; coin;

ap·po·site (ăp′ō-zĭt), *adj.* suitable; to the point; as, an *apposite* remark.

ap·po·si·tion (ăp′ō-zĭsh′ŭn), *n.* **1,** the act of placing together; also, the condition of being in close contact; **2,** in grammar, the relation of a noun to another noun near which it is placed, as its equivalent, or as explanatory of it. In the expression, "Crusoe spoke to Friday, his servant," "servant" is in apposition to "Friday."

ap·pos·i·tive (ă-pŏz′ĭ-tĭv), *adj.* in apposition; explanatory:—*n.* a word or phrase in apposition.—*adv.* **ap·pos′i·tive·ly.**

ap·prais·al (ă-prāz′ăl), *n.* **1,** the setting of a value or price; **2,** the value assigned; valuation; as, the *appraisal* was too high.

ap·praise (ă-prāz′), *v.t.* [appraised, apprais·ing], to estimate or fix the price or value of; as, to *appraise* a man's worth; to *appraise* land for taxation.—*n.* **ap·prais′er.**

ap·pre·ci·a·ble (ă-prē′shĭ-á-bl), *adj.* capable of being estimated; perceptible; as, an *appreciable* gain.—*adv.* **ap·pre′ci·a·bly.**

ap·pre·ci·ate (ă-prē′shĭ·āt), *v.t.* [appreci·at·ed, appreciat·ing], **1,** to value justly; esteem; **2,** to have a cultivated understanding of; be sensitive to; as, to *appreciate* art:—*v.i.* to increase in price or value; as, real estate *appreciates* in good times.

ap·pre·ci·a·tion (ă-prē′shĭ-ā′shŭn; ă-prē′-sĭ-ā′shŭn), *n.* **1,** the just valuation or recognition of worth; **2,** sympathetic and cultivated understanding; as, *appreciation* of music; **3,** a rise in value.

ap·pre·ci·a·tive (ă-prē′shĭ-ā′tĭv; ă-prē′-shĭ-á-tĭv), *adj.* showing appreciation or gratitude.

ap·pre·hend (ăp′rē-hĕnd′), *v.t.* **1,** to lay hold of; seize; arrest; as, to *apprehend* a fugitive; **2,** to take mental hold of; as, I *apprehend* his meaning; **3,** to anticipate with fear; as, to *apprehend* danger:—*v.i.* to catch the meaning.

ap·pre·hen·sion (ăp′rē-hĕn′shŭn), *n.* **1,** arrest; capture, as of a thief; **2,** mental grasp; understanding; as, a good *apprehension* of facts; **3,** dread as to what may happen; as, *apprehension* for a soldier son.

ap·pre·hen·sive (ăp′rē-hĕn′sĭv), *adj.* afraid; fearful, as of trouble; worried, as for someone's safety.—*adv.* **ap′pre·hen′-sive·ly.**—*n.* **ap′pre·hen′sive·ness.**

ap·pren·tice (ă-prĕn′tĭs), *n.* **1,** a person who is learning a trade or craft by practical experience under a skilled worker; formerly, one bound by an agreement to work for a definite length of time in return for his training; **2,** a novice, or one slightly versed in anything:—*v.t.* [apprenticed, apprentic-ing], to put under a master for training in a trade.

ap·pren·tice·ship (ă-prĕn′tĭs-shĭp), *n.* **1,** state of being an apprentice; **2,** time during which one serves as apprentice.

ap·prise (ă-prīz′), *v.t.* [apprised, appris·ing], to give notice to; warn; inform; as, I *apprised* him of danger. Also, **ap·prize′.**

ap·proach (ă-prōch′), *v.i.* to draw near; as, a stranger is *approaching:*—*v.t.* to come near to (a thing, place, or condition); as, to *approach* a church; to *approach* perfection:—*n.* **1,** the act of drawing near; as, we noticed the *approach* of a car; **2,** the way by which one draws near; as, the *approaches* to the city were lined with trees; **3,** in golf, a shot which aims to place the ball on the green.—*adj.* **ap·proach′a·ble.**

ap·pro·ba·tion (ăp′rō-bā′shŭn), *n.* the act of declaring good; commendation; approval; as, the audience clapped in *approbation.*

ap·pro·pri·ate (ă-prō′prĭ-āt), *v.t.* [appropri·at·ed, appropriat·ing], **1,** to take and use for one's own; as, I *appropriated* your pencil; **2,** to set apart for a particular purpose, often by legislative act; as, to *appropriate* money for roads:—*adj.* (ă-prō′prĭ-ĭt), fit; suitable; proper.—*adv.* **ap·pro′pri·ate·ly.**—*n.* **ap·pro′pri·ate·ness.**

ap·pro·pri·a·tion (ă-prō′prĭ-ā′shŭn), *n.* **1,** a setting apart for a particular use or person; **2,** the act of taking to oneself; **3,** a grant of money for a special purpose.

ap·prov·al (ă-prōōv′ăl), *n.* favorable opinion; the thinking well of a person or his act; as, your idea has my *approval.*

ap·prove (ă-prōōv′), *v.t.* [approved, approv·ing], to think or speak well of; commend; accept; as, to *approve* plans:—*v.i.* to express a favorable opinion; as, we *approve* of his friends.—*adv.* **ap·prov′ing·ly.**

ap·prox·i·mate (ă-prŏk′sĭ-mĭt), *adj.* almost equal; nearly correct; not exact but nearly so; as, an *approximate* price:—*v.t.* (ă-prŏk′sĭ-māt), [approximat·ed, approximat·ing], to come close to; as, John's conduct *approximates* folly.—*adv.* **ap·prox′i·mate·ly.**

ap·prox·i·ma·tion (ă-prŏk′sĭ-mā′shŭn), *n.* a near approach; also, a nearly correct estimate, as of the truth.

ap·pur·te·nance (ă-pûr′tē-năns), *n.* that which belongs or goes with something else; as, stables are *appurtenances* of an estate.

Apr. abbreviation for *April.*

a·pri·cot (ā′prĭ-kŏt; ăp′rĭ-kŏt), *n.* **1,** an orange-colored fruit of the plum family, similar to the peach in texture of skin and flesh; **2,** the tree on which it grows.

A·pril (ā′prĭl), *n.* the fourth month of the year, containing 30 days.

April Fools' Day, the first of April.

---

go; join; yet; sing; chin; show; thin, *th*en; hw, *wh*y; zh, azure; ü, Ger. f*ü*r or Fr. l*u*ne; ö, Ger. sch*ö*n or Fr. f*eu*; ṅ, Fr. e*n*fant, no*m*; kh, Ger. a*ch* or i*ch*. See pages ix–x.

a·pron (ā′prŭn), *n.* **1**, a garment, usually made of cloth, rubber, or leather, worn in front to protect one's clothes; **2**, such a garment worn as part of a costume; as, a bishop's *apron.*

ap·ro·pos (ăp′rŏ-pō′), *adv.* with reference (to); as, *apropos* of that remark:—*adj.* appropriate; fitting; as, an *apropos* remark.

apse (ăps), *n.* a semicircular recess covered with a half dome, especially at the pulpit end of a church, beyond the choir as viewed from the nave.

APSE (A)

apt (ăpt), *adj.* **1**, suitable; appropriate; as, an *apt* reply; **2**, inclined; likely; as, he is *apt* to be careless; **3**, quick to learn; as, an *apt* student.—*adv.* **apt′ly.**

ap·ter·yx (ăp′tēr-ĭks), *n.* a tailless New Zealand bird, about the size of a hen, with undeveloped wings hidden under its hairlike feathers. It is nearly extinct.

ap·ti·tude (ăp′tĭ-tūd), *n.* **1**, talent; as, *aptitude* for painting; **2**, fitness; as, the *aptitude* of his remark; **3**, ability or quickness to learn.

apt·ness (ăpt′nĕs), *n.* **1**, fitness; as, the *aptness* of the story; **2**, quickness of understanding; **3**, tendency; inclination.

APTERYX (1/12)

aq·ua·ma·rine (ăk′wȧ-mȧ-rēn′; ā′kwȧ-mȧ-rēn′), *n.* **1**, a transparent semiprecious stone, blue, green, or bluish green in color; **2**, a pale blue-green color:—*adj.* of this color.

aq·ua·plane (ăk′wȧ-plān′; ā′kwȧ-plān′), *n.* a board attached by ropes to the stern of a motorboat, and ridden by a person standing on it:—*v.i.* [aquaplaned, aquaplan-ing], to ride an aquaplane.

AQUAPLANE

a·quar·i·um (ȧ-kwâr′ĭ-ŭm), *n.* [*pl.* aquariums or aquaria (ȧ-kwâr′ĭ-ȧ)], **1**, a tank, bowl, or artificial pond in which living water plants and water animals are kept; **2**, a place devoted to the care and exhibition of large collections of water plants and animals.

a·quat·ic (ȧ-kwăt′ĭk; ȧ-kwŏt′ĭk; ȧ-kwŏt′ĭk), *adj.* **1**, in or on water; as, *aquatic* sports; **2**, growing in water:—*n.* an animal or plant that lives in water.

aq·ue·duct (ăk′wē-dŭkt), *n.* **1**, a pipe or artificial channel for conducting water from a distance; **2**, a bridgelike structure that supports such a pipe or channel.

a·que·ous (ā′kwē-ŭs; ăk′wē-ŭs), *adj.* **1**, of the nature of water; watery; **2**, made from or by water; as, *aqueous* rocks.

aq·ui·line (ăk′wĭ-līn; ăk′wĭ-lĭn), *adj.* curved like an eagle's beak.

A·qui·nas (ȧ-kwī′nȧs), Saint Thomas (1225-1274), an Italian theologian.

Aq·ui·taine (ăk′wĭ-tān′), an ancient division of southwestern France.

ar- (är-), *prefix,* a form of *ad-* used before *r;* as *ar*range, *ar*rive.

-ar (-är), a suffix meaning: **1**, like or pertaining to; as, famili*ar,* simil*ar,* popul*ar;* **2**, a thing like or pertaining to; as, alt*ar,* pill*ar;* **3**, a doer or agent; as, begg*ar.*

Ar·ab (ăr′ăb), *n.* **1**, a native of Arabia; **2**, a member of one of the Arabic tribes of the African and Syrian deserts; **3**, an Arabian horse; **4**, a homeless street boy:—*adj.* relating to Arabia or its people.

ar·a·besque (ăr′ȧ-bĕsk′), *n.* a decoration in low relief or color, representing fruits, flowers, etc., fancifully combined.

ARABESQUE

A·ra·bi·a (ȧ-rā′bĭ-ȧ), a large peninsula in southwestern Asia (map **15**). —*adj.* **A·ra′bi·an:**—**Arabian Nights,** an ancient collection of tales of Persia and Arabia.—*n.* **A·ra′bi·an.**

Arabian Sea, part of the Indian Ocean between India and Arabia (map **15**).

Ar·a·bic (ăr′ȧ-bĭk), *adj.* relating to Arabia or the Arabs:—**Arabic numerals,** the figures 1, 2, 3, 4, etc.: distinguished from Roman numerals, as I, II, III, IV, etc.:—*n.* the language used by the Arabs.

ar·a·ble (ăr′ȧ-bl), *adj.* suitable for cultivation; tillable; as, *arable* land.

Ar·a·by (ăr′ȧ-bĭ), a poetic name for Arabia.

a·rach·nid (ȧ-răk′nĭd), *n.* a member of a class of backboneless animals, including scorpions, mites, and spiders.—*adj.* and *n.* **a·rach′ni·dan.**

A·ra·gon (ăr′ȧ-gŏn), an ancient kingdom in northeastern Spain.

Ar·al Sea (ăr′ăl; ȧ-räl′), an inland sea in U.S.S.R., east of the Caspian Sea (map **15**).

Ar·a·lac (âr′ȧ-lăk), *n.* the trade-mark of a synthetic fiber derived from a natural protein, such as casein; used in producing cloth:—**aralac,** a product by this name; as, a dress of *aralac.*

Ar·a·rat (ăr′ȧ-răt), two mountains (Great and Little Ararat) in eastern Turkey.

ar·bi·ter (är′bĭ-tẽr), *n.* **1,** a person chosen or appointed to settle a dispute; an umpire; **2,** one who has full power to make decisions; as, each man is the *arbiter* of his own life.—*n.fem.* **ar′bi·tress.**

ar·bit·ra·ment (är-bĭt′rá-mĕnt), *n.* **1,** the right or power of settling a dispute; **2,** the settling of a dispute by an arbiter; also, his decision or award.

ar·bi·trar·y (är′bĭ-trẽr′ĭ), *adj.* **1,** ruled only by one's own wishes or ideas in making decisions; despotic; as, he is an intelligent, but *arbitrary* ruler; **2,** based on one's own opinions and wishes, and not on any rule or law; as, an *arbitrary* decision.—*adv.* **ar′bi·trar′i·ly** (är′bĭ-trẽr′ĭ-lĭ; är′bĭ-trâr′ĭ-lĭ).

ar·bi·trate (är′bĭ-trāt), *v.t.* [arbitrat-ed, arbitrat-ing], **1,** to hear as a judge, and decide; as, the father *arbitrated* the family differences; **2,** to refer (a dispute) to others for settlement; as, we decided to *arbitrate* the issue:—*v.i.* to act as arbiter or judge.

ar·bi·tra·tion (är′bĭ-trā′shŭn), *n.* the settlement of a dispute by a group of persons chosen by the parties to the dispute.

ar·bi·tra·tor (är′bĭ-trā′tẽr), *n.* **1,** a person chosen to settle or to assist in settling a dispute between parties; **2,** one who has authority to make decisions.

ar·bor (är′bẽr), *n.* **1,** a bower formed by vines trained over a latticework; as, a grape *arbor;* **2,** a shaded nook or walk.

Arbor Day, a day, generally observed in the U.S., for planting trees and shrubs.

ar·bor·e·al (är-bôr′ē-ăl), *adj.* **1,** like trees; relating to trees; **2,** living in trees, as monkeys and squirrels.

ar·bo·re·tum (är′bō-rē′tŭm), *n.* [*pl.* arboretums or arboreta (är′bō-rē′tá)], a garden in which shrubs and trees, especially rare trees, are cultivated and exhibited.

ar·bor·vi·tae (är′bŏr-vī′tē), *n.* an evergreen tree or shrub with fanlike branches, cultivated for gardens and hedges. (See illustration on page 865.)

ar·bu·tus (är-bū′tŭs), *n.* a trailing plant of eastern North America that bears very fragrant pink and white flowers very early in the spring: also called *trailing arbutus* and *Mayflower.*

arc (ärk), *n.* **1,** part of a curved line; especially, a part of the circumference of a circle; **2,** in electricity, a short band of light, sometimes curved, formed when a powerful electric current passes across a space between two points, generally of carbon, in a broken circuit.

ARCS (A, A, A)

Arc, Jeanne d' (zhän′ därk′), a French national heroine. See **Joan of Arc.**

ar·cade (är-kād′), *n.* **1,** a row of arches supported by pillars; **2,** an arched gallery or passageway, frequently between buildings, especially one lined with shops.

Ar·ca·di·a (är-kā′-dĭ-á) or **Ar·ca·dy** (är′ká-dĭ), a region in ancient Greece, where simple, contented people lived; hence, any place of quiet contentment and peace.—*adj.* and *n.* **Ar·ca′di·an.**

ARCADE, def. 1

¹**arch** (ärch), *n.* **1,** a structure of brick or masonry, the wedge-shaped parts of which follow a curved line, usually forming the top of a door, window, or gateway; **2,** an opening or passage covered by such a structure; an archway; **3,** anything arch-shaped; as, the *arch* of the foot:—*v.t.* **1,** to cover with a curved or arched structure; **2,** to bend or curve; as, the cat *arched* his back:—*v.i.* to form an arch-shaped bend or curve; as, *arching* trees.

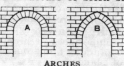

ARCHES
A, round; B, pointed.

²**arch** (ärch), *adj.* **1,** mischievous; roguish; as, an *arch* look; **2,** chief; of the first rank; as, an *arch* villain: often used as a prefix, as in *arch*bishop, *arch*duke.

ar·chae·ol·o·gy or **ar·che·ol·o·gy** (är′kē-ŏl′ō-jĭ), *n.* the science of antiquities; a study of the life of earlier peoples, based on the remains of their towns or villages, and on relics, such as weapons, utensils, or ornaments, found in these remains.

ar·chae·o·log·i·cal or **ar·che·o·log·i·cal** (är′kē-ō-lŏj′ĭ-kăl), *adj.* connected with archaeology; as, *archaeological* research, expeditions, excavations, or the like.

ar·cha·ic (är-kā′ĭk), *adj.* old-fashioned; primitive; of words, no longer in common use; as, the word "methinks" is *archaic.*

ar·cha·ism (är′ká-ĭzm), *n.* a word or expression no longer in common use.

Arch·an·gel (ärk′ăn′jĕl), a seaport town in northern Soviet Russia (map 12).

arch·an·gel (ärk′ăn′jĕl), *n.* a chief angel.

arch·bish·op (ärch′bĭsh′ŭp), *n.* a bishop of highest rank, with authority over a group of dioceses.

arch·bish·op·ric (ärch′bĭsh′ŭp-rĭk), *n.* the office or province of an archbishop.

arch·dea·con (ärch′dē′kŭn), *n.* a chief deacon, immediately below a bishop in rank.

arch·duch·ess (ärch′dŭch′ĕs), *n.* **1,** the

wife of an archduke; **2,** a princess of the former imperial family of Austria.

arch·duke (ärch′dūk′), *n.* a prince of the imperial house of Austria.—*adj.* **arch′du′cal.**—*n.* **arch′duch′y.**

ar·che·ol·o·gy (är′kē-ŏl′ō-jĭ), *n.* study of the life of earlier peoples. See **archaeology.**

arch·er (är′chĕr), *n.* a person skilled in using the bow and arrow.

arch·er·y (är′chĕr-ĭ), *n.* **1,** the use, or skill in the use, of bow and arrow; **2,** a company of archers.

ar·chi·e·pis·co·pal (är′kĭ-ē-pĭs′kō-păl), *adj.* relating to an archbishop.

Ar·chi·me·des (är′kĭ-mē′dēz), (287?-212 B.C.), a Greek mathematician.

ar·chi·pel·a·go (är′kĭ-pĕl′à-gō), *n.* [*pl.* archipelagoes or archipelagos], a sea containing numerous islands; also, a group of islands.

ar·chi·tect (är′kĭ-tĕkt), *n.* one who plans or designs houses, churches, bridges, etc., and superintends their construction.

ar·chi·tec·tur·al (är′kĭ-tĕk′tūr-ăl), *adj.* relating to architecture, or the art of building; as, an *architectural* drawing.

ar·chi·tec·ture (är′kĭ-tĕk′tūr), *n.* **1,** the science and art of building for both use and beauty; **2,** the manner or style of building; as, the White House is an example of colonial *architecture;* **3,** construction; shape; workmanship; as, the *architecture* of this library has many defects.

ar·chi·trave (är′kĭ-trāv), *n.* in architecture, a horizontal part which rests on the columns of a building. (See *frieze,* illustration.)

ar·chive (är′kīv), *n.* a record preserved as evidence:—**archives,** the place in which public records or documents of historical value are kept; also, these documents or records.

arch·ly (ärch′lĭ), *adv.* in a coy manner; roguishly; playfully.

arch·ness (ärch′nĕs), *n.* coyness; roguishness; playfulness.

arch·way (ärch′wā′), *n.* an opening or entrance through an arch; also, a passage under an arch or curved roof.

ARCHWAY through an Etruscan gate in Perugia.

arc·tic (ärk′tĭk), *adj.* located in, or relating to, the region of the North Pole; northern; frigid:—**Arctic Circle,** an imaginary circle parallel to the equator and distant 23° 30′ from the North Pole:—*n.*

in the U.S., a high, warmly lined, waterproof overshoe.

Arc·tic O·cean, the ocean around the North Pole (map 2).

Arc·tu·rus (ärk-tū′rŭs), *n.* a large, bright star in the northern sky.

Ar·den, For·est of (är′dn), a forest in England, near Shakespeare's home.

ar·dent (är′dĕnt), *adj.* blazing; hence, passionate; eager; as, an *ardent* desire.

ar·dor (är′dẽr), *n.* burning heat; hence, warmth of affection; eagerness.

ar·du·ous (är′dū-ŭs), *adj.* **1,** steep; hard to climb; **2,** attended with great labor or exertion; difficult; as, an *arduous* task; **3,** strenuous; as, *arduous* efforts.

¹are (är), present indicative plural of *be;* as, we *are;* you *are;* men *are.*

²are (âr; är), *n.* in the metric system, a measure of surface, especially of land; 100 square meters, equal to 119.6 square yards.

a·re·a (ā′rē-à; âr′ē-à), *n.* [*pl.* areas], **1,** any level, bounded surface; as, the *area* occupied by a house; the shaded *area* of a drawing; **2,** extent of surface, especially of the earth's surface; as, the *area* of the U.S.; **3,** a region; as, a hilly *area;* **4,** scope; range; as, his activities covered a wide *area;* **5,** in geometry, the total surface of a plane or solid figure; as, the *area* of a square or of a cube.

a·re·na (à-rē′nà), *n.* **1,** the enclosed space of a Roman amphitheater, in which fights between gladiators took place; **2,** hence, any scene or field of exertion or rivalry; as, the *arena* of politics.

ar·gent (är′jĕnt), *adj.* made of, or resembling, silver; silvery white: used especially in heraldry; as, a field *argent* in a coat of arms.

Ar·gen·ti·na (är′jĕn-tē′nà), a republic (cap. Buenos Aires) in South America (map 11).—*adj.* and *n.* **Ar′gen-tine** (är′jĕn-tēn; är′jĕn-tīn).

ar·gon (är′gŏn), *n.* a colorless, odorless gaseous element found in the air, and used for filling electric light bulbs.

Ar·gonne (àr′gŏn′), a wooded section in northeastern France, the scene of many battles in 1918.

ar·go·sy (är′gō-sĭ), *n.* [*pl.* argosies], a large merchant vessel.

ar·gue (är′gū), *v.i.* [argued, argu-ing], **1,** to give reasons for or against an opinion, measure, or the like; try to prove or disprove something; as, to *argue* for a lower tariff; **2,** to debate; dispute:—*v.t.* to persuade by force of words; as, you have *argued* me into going along.

ar·gu·ment (är′gū-mĕnt), *n.* **1,** a reason for or against a thing; as, I know of no *argument* against it; **2,** a discussion con-

---

āte, āorta, râre, căt, àsk, fär, ăllow, sof*à;* ēve, êvent, ĕll, writẽr, novĕl; bīte, pĭn; nō, ōbey, ôr, dŏg, tŏp, cŏllide; ūnit, ūnite, bûrn, cŭt, focŭs; nōōn, fŏŏt; mound; coin;

taining reasons for or against something, or trying to prove or disprove something; **3**, the subject, as of a speech or essay; also, an outline or summary, as of a book.

ar·gu·men·ta·tive (är'gū-měn'tȧ-tĭv), *adj.* fond of arguing or discussing; hence, quarrelsome; contentious.

Ar·gus (är'gŭs), *n.* in Greek mythology, a monster which had a hundred eyes.

a·ri·a (ä'rĭ-ȧ; är'ĭ-ȧ), *n.* **1**, an air or tune; **2**, an elaborate solo part in an opera, oratorio, or the like.

Ar·i·ad·ne (ăr'ĭ-ăd'nē), *n.* in mythology, the daughter of Minos, king of Crete, who guided Theseus out of the Labyrinth.

ar·id (ăr'ĭd), *adj.* dry; parched; as, an *arid* desert.

a·rid·i·ty (ȧ-rĭd'ĭ-tĭ), *n.* dryness; barrenness, as of soil.

Ar·i·el (âr'ĭ-ĕl), *n.* **1**, in Shakespeare's play "The Tempest," an airy spirit who serves Prospero; **2**, in Milton's poem "Paradise Lost," one of the rebel angels.

a·right (ȧ-rīt'), *adv.* correctly; in a proper way or form.

a·rise (ȧ-rīz'), *v.i.* [*p.t.* arose (ȧ-rōz'), *p.p.* aris-en (ȧ-rĭz'n), *p.pr.* aris-ing], **1**, to stand up; change to a standing position from one of sitting, kneeling, or lying; get up after sleep; **2**, to ascend; come into view; as, the sun *arose*; **3**, to spring up; begin; as, then a dispute *arose*.

   Syn. spring, proceed, rise, issue.

a·ris·en (ȧ-rĭz'n), past participle of *arise.*

Ar·is·ti·des (ăr'ĭs-tī'dēz), (?–468? B.C.), an Athenian statesman and general.

ar·is·toc·ra·cy (ăr'ĭs-tŏk'rȧ-sĭ), *n.* [*pl.* aristocracies], **1**, government by persons of the highest rank in a state; **2**, a state with such a government; **3**, the nobility; the few who, in rank, wealth, or intellect, are regarded as superior to the many.

a·ris·to·crat (ȧ-rĭs'tō-krăt; ăr'ĭs-tō-krăt), *n.* **1**, a personage of high rank or noble birth, or one who has traits characteristic of such rank; **2**, one who upholds aristocracy or favors government by the few.

a·ris·to·crat·ic (ȧ-rĭs'tō-krăt'ĭk; ăr'ĭs-tō-krăt'ĭk), *adj.* **1**, pertaining to an aristocracy of rank, wealth, or intellect; **2**, like an aristocrat.

Ar·is·toph·a·nes (ăr'ĭs-tŏf'ȧ-nēz), (448?–380? B.C.), a Greek writer of comic plays.

Ar·is·tot·le (ăr'ĭs-tŏt'l), (384–322 B.C.), a Greek philosopher.—*adj.* and *n.* **Ar'is·to·te'li·an** (ăr'ĭs-tō-tē'lĭ-ăn).

a·rith·me·tic (ȧ-rĭth'mĕ-tĭk), *n.* the science of numbers; the art of reckoning by the use of figures.

ar·ith·met·i·cal (ăr'ĭth-mĕt'ĭ-kȧl), *adj.* relating to arithmetic or the science of numbers.—*adv.* **ar'ith·met/i·cal·ly.**—*n.* **a·rith'me·ti'cian** (ȧ-rĭth'mĕ-tĭsh'ăn; ăr'-ĭth-mĕ-tĭsh'ăn).

Ariz. abbreviation for *Arizona.*

Ar·i·zo·na (ăr'ĭ-zō'nȧ), a southwestern State (cap. Phoenix) of the U.S. (map **9**).

ark (ärk), *n.* **1**, a chest; **2**, the oblong box containing the Covenant, or tables of the Law, in the Jewish Tabernacle (Exodus 25); **3**, the ship in which Noah and his family remained during the Flood (Genesis 6).

Ark. abbreviation for *Arkansas.*

Ar·kan·sas (är'kăn-sô), **1**, a south central State (cap. Little Rock) of the U.S. (map **8**); **2**, (är-kăn'zȧs; är'kăn-sô), a river flowing into the Mississippi (map **8**).

Ark·wright (ärk'rīt), Sir Richard (1732–1792), an English manufacturer, inventor of a frame for spinning yarn.

¹**arm** (ärm), *n.* **1**, in man and monkey, one of the two upper limbs; especially, that part of the upper limb between shoulder and hand; **2**, the front or fore limb of any animal having a backbone; **3**, a part resembling, or corresponding to, an arm, as the side piece of a chair, an inlet of the sea, a branch of a tree, or the like.

²**arm** (ärm), *n.* **1**, a weapon; as, the right to bear *arms;* **2**, a branch of the military service, as the infantry or the artillery:—*v.t.* to furnish with arms:—*v.i.* to fit oneself with arms; take up arms.

ar·ma·da (är-mä'dȧ; är-mä'dȧ), *n.* **1**, a fleet of armed vessels; **2**, a fleet of aircraft:—**Armada**, a fleet of ships ·sent against England by Spain in 1588.

ar·ma·dil·lo (är'mȧ-dĭl'ō), *n.* [*pl.* armadillos], any of several South and Central American burrowing animals having the head and body protected by an armor of bony plates. Some kinds when attacked curl up into a ball.

ARMADILLO (⅛)

ar·ma·ment (är'mȧ-mĕnt), *n.* a nation's entire war equipment or military strength; also, equipment in guns and ammunition.

ar·ma·ture (är'mȧ-tūr), *n.* **1**, armor; **2**, an armorlike, protective covering, as the shell of a turtle, or, especially, the wire covering of a cable; **3**, in a dynamo, the rotary iron core in which current is produced; in a motor, the conductors which move when a current is passed through them.

arm·chair (ärm'châr'; ärm'châr'), *n.* a chair with supports for the arms.

---

go; join; yet; sing; chin; show; thin, *th*en; hw, *wh*y; zh, azure; ü, Ger. für or Fr. *l*une; ö, Ger. schön or Fr. *f*eu; n̈, Fr. *en*fant, nom; kh, Ger. a*ch* or i*ch*. See pages ix–x.

Ar·me·ni·a (är-mē′nĭ-a̱), formerly, a kingdom in Asia Minor, now divided among the U.S.S.R., Turkey, and Iran (map 12).— *adj.* and *n.* **Ar·me′ni·an.**

arm·ful (ärm′fool), *n.* [*pl.* armfuls], as much as one arm, or both, can hold.

arm·hole (ärm′hōl′), *n.* in a garment, a hole or opening through which the arm passes or at which the sleeve is attached.

ar·mi·stice (är′mĭ-stĭs), *n.* a pause in war by agreement of both sides; a truce.

Armistice Day, November 11, 1918, the day on which the World War I armistice was declared. The anniversary of it is now called *Veterans Day.*

arm·let (ärm′lĕt), *n.* a decorative band worn around the upper arm.

ar·mor (är′mẽr), *n.* 1, a covering, of metal, leather, or the like, worn of old, to protect the body in battle or in any contest at arms; 2, the steel plating of a warship; 3, any protective covering, as the scales of a fish:—*v.t.* to furnish with a protective covering.—*adj.* **ar′mored.**

ARMLETS

ar·mor—bear·er (är′- mẽr=bâr′ẽr), *n.* in olden times, one who carried the arms and armor of a warrior or knight.

ar·mor—clad (är′mẽr- klăd′), *adj.* protected by armor:—*n.* a war vessel protected by steel plating.

ARMOR

1, chain armor of the 12th century; 2, plate armor of the early 16th century.

ar·mor·er (är′mẽr-ẽr), *n.* 1, formerly, a maker of armor; now, a manufacturer of arms; 2, on a battleship, the man in charge of cleaning and repairing arms.

ar·mor·i·al (är-môr′ĭ-ăl), *adj.* relating to armor or to coats of arms:—**armorial bearings,** a coat of arms.

ar·mor·y (är′mẽr-ĭ), *n.* [*pl.* armories], 1, a place where arms are stored; a large building in which soldiers assemble, and which contains also drill halls, offices, etc.; 2, a place where arms are manufactured.

ar·mour (är′mẽr), a British spelling of *armor.* Similarly, **armour—bearer, armour— clad, armoured, armourer, armoury.**

arm·pit (ärm′pĭt′), *n.* the pit or hollow beneath the arm where it joins the shoulder.

arms (ärmz), *n.pl.* 1, weapons of offense or defense; 2, the military service; as, a call to *arms;* war as a profession; 3, heraldic emblems or devices; as, the coat of *arms* of the United States.

ar·my (är′mĭ), *n.* [*pl.* armies], 1, a large body of men trained and equipped for war; 2, a great number or multitude; a host; as, an *army* of beetles; 3, an organized body of persons engaged in furthering a common cause; as, an *army* of workmen:—**army worm,** the larva of a kind of moth, so called because it spreads over a region like an army, stripping the land of young grain and grasses.

ar·ni·ca (är′nĭ-ka̱), *n.* 1, an herb of the aster family, from which a healing lotion for bruises is made; 2, this lotion.

Ar·no (är′nō), a river of north central Italy, flowing west into the Mediterranean.

Ar·nold (är′nŭld), 1, Benedict (1741– 1801), a general in the American Revolution, who turned traitor; 2, Matthew (1822–1888), an English poet.

a·ro·ma (a̱-rō′ma̱), *n.* a pleasant, spicy odor.

ar·o·mat·ic (ăr′ō-măt′ĭk), *adj.* spicy; fragrant:—*n.* a plant or herb with a fragrant smell, as ginger or cinnamon.

a·rose (a̱-rōz′), past tense of *arise.*

a·round (a̱-round′), *adv.* 1, in a circle; as, to go *around* on a merry-go-round; 2, on every side; round about; as, to rush *around;* 3, near at hand; as, no one is *around:*— *prep.* 1, circling or encircling; as, to walk *around* a tree; a belt *around* a waist; 2, on all sides of; as, the air *around* us; 3, about; as, *around* two o'clock; 4, here and there in; as, to go *around* the city.

a·rouse (a̱-rouz′), *v.t.* [aroused, arous-ing], 1, to awaken; as, she sleeps soundly, but is easily *aroused;* 2, to stir to life; excite to activity; as, his anger is not easily *aroused.*

ar·peg·gio (är-pĕj′ō), *n.* [*pl.* arpeggios], in music, the tones of a chord produced in rapid succession.

ar·que·bus (är′kwĕ-bŭs), *n.* a kind of portable firearm. See **harquebus.**

ar·raign (ă-rān′), *v.t.* 1, to summon (a prisoner) into court to answer a charge; accuse; 2, to find fault with; call in question; as, I do not *arraign* his honesty. *Syn.* charge, cite, impeach, indict.

ar·raign·ment (ă-rān′mĕnt), *n.* 1, a summons to answer a charge in court; also, the state of being so summoned; 2, a finding fault or calling in question; as, the *arraignment* of a man's integrity.

ar·range (ă-rānj′), *v.t.* [arranged, arrang-ing], 1, to put into suitable order; as, to *arrange* flowers or books; 2, to adjust or settle, as a dispute; bring about, as an interview or compromise:—*v.i.* to make preparations in advance; as, I have *arranged* for the use of the hall.

ar·range·ment (ă-rānj′měnt), *n.* **1,** the act of putting into proper form or order; **2,** the method or style of arranging things; as, an orderly *arrangement* of one's tools; **3,** preparation; an agreement upon details, as in getting ready for a meeting; as, *arrangements* for a party.

ar·rant (ăr′ănt), *adj.* notorious; out-and-out; utter; as, an *arrant* coward.

Ar·ras (ăr′ăs; à/räs′), a town near Lille in northern France, the scene of important battles during World War I.

ar·ras (ăr′ăs), *n.* tapestry; also, hangings of tapestry covering the walls of a room.

ar·ray (ă-rā′), *n.* **1,** orderly or formal arrangement; as, troops in battle *array;* **2,** a fine or imposing collection or display; as, an *array* of silver; an *array* of talent; **3,** clothing, especially fine clothing; as, the crowds were in holiday *array:*—*v.t.* **1,** to place or dispose in order; to marshal; as, to *array* troops in battle formation; **2,** to deck or dress; as, the guests were beautifully *arrayed.*

ar·rears (ă-rērz′), *n.pl.* that which should be done or paid, but is still undone or unpaid; as, *arrears* of work or rent:—**in arrears,** behindhand with what should already be done or paid.—*n.* **ar·rear′age.**

ar·rest (ă-rĕst′), *v.t.* **1,** to stop or check; as, to *arrest* a runaway horse; also, to attract and hold; as, bright colors *arrest* the eye; **2,** to seize and hold (a person) by legal authority; take prisoner:—*n.* **1,** the act of checking or stopping; as, the *arrest* of decay; **2,** the act of taking a person prisoner.   *Syn., v.* capture, hold, detain, secure.

ar·riv·al (ă-rīv′ăl), *n.* **1,** the act of coming to a place, or reaching a destination; as, her *arrival* was unexpected; **2,** a person arriving; as, a late *arrival.*

ar·rive (ă-rīv′), *v.i.* [arrived, arriv-ing], **1,** to come to, or reach, a given place; **2,** to reach a result by a process of thought; as, to *arrive* at a conclusion.

ar·ro·gance (ăr′ō-găns), *n.* a display of too great confidence in oneself, or one's abilities; extreme haughtiness; lordly contempt of others.

ar·ro·gant (ăr′ō-gănt), *adj.* overestimating one's importance or ability; haughty and overbearing.   *Syn.* proud, disdainful, insolent, assuming.

ar·ro·gate (ăr′ō-gāt), *v.t.* [arrogat-ed, arrogat-ing], to take unjustly; claim presumptuously as one's own; as, the governor *arrogated* to himself the authority of the

legislators; hence, to usurp.—*n.* **ar′ro·ga′tion.**

ar·row (ăr′ō), *n.* **1,** a slender, pointed shaft, often of wood, usually feathered and barbed, and made to be shot from a bow; **2,** a figure on maps, signboards, or the like, to indicate direction.

ARROWS
1, conventional arrow; 2, English arrow; 3, Japanese arrow; 4, American Indian arrow.

ar·row·head (ăr′ō-hĕd′), *n.* the piercing end or tip of an arrow.

ar·roy·o (ă-roi′ō), *n.* [*pl.* arroyos], a small stream, or the dry bed of a creek or brook.

ar·se·nal (ăr′sĕ-năl), *n.* a public building for storing, making, or repairing military equipment of all kinds.

ar·se·nate (ăr′sĕ-nāt), *n.* in chemistry, a salt of arsenic acid.

ar·se·nic (ăr′sĕ-nĭk; ärs′nĭk), *n.* a poisonous grayish-white chemical element:—*adj.* (är-sĕn′ĭk), containing arsenic.

ar·son (är′sn), *n.* the malicious or intentional act of setting fire to a building or other property.

¹art (ärt), a form of *be* used in old or poetic writings. "Thou art" was used for "you are" in addressing one person.

²art (ärt), *n.* **1,** skill acquired by study or practice; natural aptitude; knack; as, the *art* of sewing; **2,** the body of knowledge and experience related to a particular occupation or profession; as, the *art* of engineering; **3,** the study or creation of beautiful things, as in painting, drawing, sculpture, architecture, music, literature, and dancing: usually called *fine arts;* **4,** the work produced by painters, sculptors, musicians, and the like; **5, arts,** certain branches of learning such as literature, science, history, languages, etc.; **6,** craft; cunning; as, her *art* and wiles failed.

Ar·te·mis (är′tĕ-mĭs), *n.* in Greek mythology, the goddess of the chase and of the moon. The Romans called her *Diana.*

ar·te·ri·al (är-tē′rĭ-ăl), *adj.* **1,** pertaining to the arteries; as, *arterial* blood; **2,** like a main channel or artery; as, an *arterial* highway between two large cities.

ar·ter·y (är′tĕr-ĭ), *n.* [*pl.* arteries], **1,** one of the tubes which carry blood from the heart to all parts of the body; **2,** any great channel or main thoroughfare.

ar·te·sian well (är-tē′zhăn; är-tē′zĭ-ăn), a well made by boring into the ground deep enough to reach water which, from internal pressure, will gush to the surface.

---

go; join; yet; sing; chin; show; thin, *th***en; hw,** *wh***y; zh,** a**z**ure; **ü,** Ger. f*ü*r or Fr. l*u*ne; **ö,** Ger. sch**ö**n or Fr. f*eu*; **ǹ,** Fr. e*n*fant, no*m*; **kh,** Ger. a*ch* or i*ch.* See pages ix-x.

art·ful (ärt′fŏŏl), *adj.* **1,** skilful; clever; as, *artful* decoration; **2,** cunning; crafty; as, her *artful* ways displeased us.

    Syn. sly, tricky, wily, insincere.

Ar·thur (är′thẽr), **1,** a British king of the sixth century, who, with his knights, is the subject of many mythical romances; **2,** Chester Alan (1830–1886), the 21st president of the U.S.

Ar·thu·ri·an (är-thū′rĭ-ăn), *adj.* pertaining to King Arthur or his knights; as, the story of Excalibur is an *Arthurian* legend.

ar·ti·choke (är′tĭ-chōk), *n.* a tall plant the edible flower head of which is used as a vegetable; also, the vegetable.

ar·ti·cle (är′tĭ-kl), *n.* **1,** a thing belonging to a particular class of things; as, an *article* of clothing; **2,** a single section of a written document, as a clause of a contract, treaty, creed, or the like; **3,** a prose composition, complete in

ARTICHOKE

itself, in a newspaper, magazine, etc.; **4,** in grammar, any of the words *a*, *an* or ¹*the:* —*v.t.* [arti-cled, arti-cling], to bind by written agreement; as, he *articled* his son to a carpenter as an apprentice.

ar·tic·u·lar (är-tĭk′ū-lẽr), *adj.* pertaining to the joints; as, *articular* rheumatism.

ar·tic·u·late (är-tĭk′ū-lāt), *v.t.* [articu-lat-ed, articulat-ing], **1,** to unite by means of joints; **2,** to utter in distinct syllables; as, do not mumble, *articulate* your words: —*v.i.* **1,** to utter distinct sounds; **2,** to be jointed:—*adj.* (är-tĭk′ū-lăt), **1,** jointed; **2,** spoken with distinctness; **3,** able to express oneself clearly.—*adv.* **ar·tic′u·late·ly.**

ar·tic·u·la·tion (är-tĭk′ū-lā′shŭn), *n.* **1,** utterance of distinct or articulate sounds; **2,** the state of being jointed; also, a joint.

ar·ti·fact (är′tĭ-făkt), *n.* a product of human skill or workmanship; especially, a simple product of primitive art.

ar·ti·fice (är′tĭ-fĭs), *n.* **1,** skill in invention or design; **2,** a ruse or trick.

    Syn. deceit, cunning, craft.

ar·tif·i·cer (är-tĭf′ĭ-sẽr), *n.* a skilled or artistic worker; craftsman.

ar·ti·fi·cial (är′tĭ-fĭsh′ăl), *adj.* **1,** not natural; made by man in imitation of nature; as, *artificial* teeth or ice; **2,** affected; insincere; as, an *artificial* smile.—*adv.* **ar′ti·fi′cial·ly.**—*n.* **ar′ti·fi′ci·al′i·ty.**

ar·til·ler·y (är-tĭl′ẽr-ĭ), *n.* **1,** cannon, mounted guns, etc., together with their

ammunition; **2,** that branch of an army which uses these arms.—*n.* **ar·til′ler·y·man.**

ar·ti·san (är′tĭ-zăn; är′tĭ-zăn′), *n.* a man specially trained to work with his hands, as a bricklayer or carpenter.

art·ist (är′tĭst), *n.* **1,** a person who practices an art, as painting, sculpture, music, literature, or the like; especially, a painter or sculptor; **2,** in any field, a person who shows creative power in his work; as, your cook is an *artist*.

ar·tis·tic (är-tĭs′tĭk), *adj.* **1,** pertaining to art or artists; **2,** designed and made with skill; **3,** readily responsive to beauty; as, an *artistic* nature.—*adv.* **ar·tis′ti·cal·ly.**

art·ist·ry (är′tĭs-trĭ), *n.* beauty of workmanship or effect; also, artistic skill.

art·less (ärt′lĕs), *adj.* **1,** lacking skill or art; clumsy; **2,** free from guile or deceit; natural.—*adv.* **art′less·ly.**—*n.* **art′less·ness.**

-ar·y (-âr′ĭ), a suffix meaning: **1,** one belonging to or engaged in; as, actu*ary*, mission*ary;* **2,** something connected with or containing; as, libr*ary*, avi*ary;* **3,** of the nature of, or connected with; as, contr*ary*, volunt*ary*.

Ar·y·an (âr′ĭ-ăn; är′yăn), *n.* a member of the family of races which contains most of the chief peoples of western Asia and Europe; also, the family of their languages, including Sanskrit, Persian, Armenian, Greek, Latin, Teutonic, Slavic, and others: —*adj.* relating to the Aryans or the Aryan languages.

as (ăz), *adv.* **1,** equally; similarly; to the same extent; as, paper plates will do *as* well; he swam just *as* far yesterday; **2,** thus; for example: used in introducing an example or illustrative quotation:—*conj.* **1,** because; as, he sat down, *as* he was tired; **2,** while; when; as, they fled *as* we approached; **3,** in the way that; as, we did *as* we were told:—*prep.* in the role of; as, he entered the contest *as* an amateur: —*relative pron.* that; which: used after *such, same,* etc.; as, send me such books *as* you have ready.

as·a·fet·i·da or **as·a·foet·i·da** (ăs′ȧ-fĕt′-ĭ-dȧ), *n.* the gum of any of various Oriental plants of the parsley family. It has the odor and taste of garlic, and is used in nerve-soothing medicines.

as·bes·tos (ăs-bĕs′tŏs; ăz-bĕs′tŏs) or **as·bes·tus** (ăs-bĕs′tŭs; ăz-bĕs′tŭs), *n.* a fibrous, unburnable mineral substance, used in making fireproof materials.

as·cend (ȧ-sĕnd′), *v.t.* and *v.i.* to climb or go up; also, to mount; as, to *ascend* the stairs; we watched the kite *ascend*.

āte, âorta, râre, căt, ȧsk, fär, ȧllow, sofȧ; ēve, ĕvent, ĕll, wrīter, novĕl; bīte, pĭn; nō, ōbey, ôr, dŏg, tŏp, cŏllide; ūnit, ūnite, bûrn, cŭt, focŭs; nōon, fŏŏt; mound; coin;

as·cend·an·cy (ă-sĕn′dăn-sĭ) or **as·cend-en·cy** (ă-sĕn′dĕn-sĭ), *n.* domination; control; as, to gain *ascendancy* over fear.

as·cend·ant (ă-sĕn′dănt) or **as·cend·ent** (ă-sĕn′dĕnt), *adj.* 1, rising; predominant; 2, above the horizon:—**in the ascendant**, in a position of power.

as·cen·sion (ă-sĕn′shŭn), *n.* a moving upward; a rising:—**the Ascension**, Christ's ascent to heaven after his resurrection.

as·cent (ă-sĕnt′), *n.* 1, a rising; as, the *ascent* of an airplane; 2 the act of climbing; as, the *ascent* of a mountain; 3, an upward slope.

as·cer·tain (ăs′ẽr-tān′), *v.t.* to find out definitely; discover; as, it is not always easy to *ascertain* the truth.—*adj.* **as′cer-tain′a·ble.**—*n.* **as′cer-tain′ment.**

as·cet·ic (ă-sĕt′ĭk), *n.* a person who renounces the comforts and pleasures of life and devotes himself to religious duties; also, any person who practices self-denial: —*adj.* self-denying; as, the monks lived *ascetic* lives.—*n.* **as·cet′i·cism.**

as·cribe (ăs-krīb′), *v.t.* [ascribed, ascribing], 1, to regard or speak of (something) as caused by something else; as, she *ascribed* her success to hard work; 2, to regard or speak of (something) as belonging to someone; as, the poem was *ascribed* to Burns; valor is *ascribed* to a hero.—*adj.* **as·crib′a·ble.**

a·sep·tic (ȧ-sĕp′tĭk; ā-sĕp′tĭk), *adj.* free from disease germs; surgically clean; as, *aseptic* bandages.

¹ash (ăsh), *n.* a common timber and shade tree, or its tough, elastic wood.

²ash (ăsh), *n.* 1, what remains of a substance that has been burned; as, wood *ash;* coal *ash;* 2, the color of wood ashes; a whitish or brownish gray.

a·shamed (ȧ-shāmd′), *adj.* 1, feeling shame or regret; as, he was *ashamed* of his rude act; 2, fearful of reproach or scorn; as, *ashamed* to wear patched clothes.

¹ash·en (ăsh′ĕn), *adj.* made of the wood of the ash tree.

²ash·en (ăsh′ĕn), *adj.* of the color of ashes; pale.

ash·es (ăsh′ĕz), *n.pl.* 1, what remains of a thing after it is burned; as, wood *ashes* are good for a garden; 2, the remains of a human body when it is reduced to dust by natural decay or by being burned or cremated.

Ashe·ville (ăsh′vĭl), a city in North Carolina, famous as a health resort (map 8).

a·shore (ȧ-shôr′), *adv.* on shore; to the shore; as, a ship driven *ashore*.

Ash Wednes·day, the first day of Lent.

ash·y (ăsh′ĭ), *adj.* 1, composed of ashes; as, an *ashy* soil; 2, covered with ashes; as, an *ashy* floor; 3, like ashes in color.

A·sia (ā′zhȧ; ā′shȧ), the largest continent, lying east of Europe (map 15).—*adj.* and *n.* **A′sian.**

A·sia Mi·nor (mī′nẽr), a peninsula in western Asia, between the Black Sea and the Mediterranean (map 1). It was formerly called *Anatolia*.

A·si·at·ic (ā′zhĭ-ăt′ĭk; ā′shĭ-ăt′ĭk), *adj.* having to do with Asia or its inhabitants: —*n.* a native of Asia.

a·side (ȧ-sīd′), *adv.* on or to one side; as, to pull a curtain *aside:*—*n.* a remark in a low tone, intended not to be overheard.

as·i·nine (ăs′ĭ-nīn), *adj.* like the ass; hence, stupid; silly; as, an *asinine* remark.

ask (ȧsk), *v.t.* 1, to seek an answer to; as, to *ask* a question; also, to put a question to; as, *ask* her how old she is; 2, to beg or request; as, to *ask* a favor; 3, to inquire about; as, to *ask* the way; 4, to invite; as, I was *asked* to the party; 5, to claim; demand; as, what price do you *ask?*—*v.i.* 1, to make a request; as, to *ask* for money; 2, to inquire; as, to *ask* for the chief.

a·skance (ȧ-skȧns′), *adv.* with a sidelong glance; hence, with suspicion or distrust; as, to look *askance* at a newcomer.

a·skew (ȧ-skū′), *adv.* and *adj.* awry; out of order; off the true or straight; as, the picture is hanging *askew*.

a·slant (ȧ-slȧnt′), *adv.* and *adj.* in a sloping or slanting direction:—*prep.* in a slanting direction over; as, the rays of the sun fell *aslant* the barn.

a·sleep (ȧ-slēp′), *adj.* and *adv.* 1, sleeping; 2, numb; as, my foot is *asleep*.

As·ma·ra (äs-mä′rä), the capital of Eritrea, in eastern Africa.

asp (ăsp), *n.* a small poisonous snake of Egypt.

as·par·a·gus (ăs-păr′ȧ-gŭs), *n.* the tender young stalks of a garden plant of the lily family, used as a vegetable; also, the plant.

ASPARAGUS

As·pa·si·a (ăs-pā′shĭ-ȧ; ăs-pā′zhĭ-ȧ), (470?–410 B.C.), a Greek woman, a friend of Pericles, whose home was a famous literary and social center.

as·pect (ăs′pĕkt), *n.* 1, appearance; look; as, the pirate's fierce *aspect;* 2, a side or part facing a given direction; as, he viewed the southern *aspect* of the fort.

---

go; join; yet; sing; chin; show; thin, *th*en; **hw,** *wh*y; **zh,** azure; **ü,** Ger. für or Fr. *l*une; **ö,** Ger. schön or Fr. *f*eu; **ṅ,** Fr. e*n*fant, no*m*; **kh,** Ger. a*ch* or i*ch*. See pages ix–x.

as·pen (ăs′pĕn; às′pĕn), *n.* a kind of poplar tree whose leaves tremble in the faintest breeze:—*adj.* relating to this tree.

as·per·i·ty (ăs-pĕr′ĭ-tĭ), *n.* [*pl.* asperities], **1**, roughness of surface; unevenness; hence, harshness or sharpness of temper; as, he spoke with *asperity* of the trouble we had caused him.

as·perse (ăs-pûrs′), *v.t.* [aspersed, aspersing], to spread damaging or false reports about (a person or his character); to slander.
  Syn. defame, malign, revile, libel.

as·per·sion (ăs-pûr′shŭn; ăs-pûr′zhŭn), *n.* a damaging or untrue remark about a person.

as·phalt (ăs′fôlt; ăs′fălt), *n.* **1**, a dark-colored, tarlike mineral substance; **2**, a preparation of this substance, used for paving, roofing, and cementing.

as·pho·del (ăs′fō-dĕl), *n.* **1**, a kind of plant with yellow flowers; **2**, in poetical language, the daffodil; **3**, in mythology, the immortal flower of the Elysian fields.

as·phyx·i·ate (ăs-fĭk′sĭ-āt), *v.t.* [asphyxiat-ed, asphyxiat-ing], to cause unconsciousness or death to by cutting off the supply of air; to suffocate.

as·pic (ăs′pĭk), *n.* a clear meat jelly, served cold, and used as a garnish, or to make a mold of meat, fish, or vegetables.

as·pir·ant (ăs-pīr′ănt; ăs′pĭ-rănt), *n.* one who seeks to attain some high object or honor; an ambitious person.

as·pi·rate (ăs′pĭ-rĭt), *n.* the sound of the letter *h* as in "horse":—*v.t.* (ăs′pĭ-rāt), [aspirat-ed, aspirat-ing], to pronounce with the sound of the letter *h*; as, we *aspirate* the *h* in "horse" but not in "honor."

as·pi·ra·tion (ăs′pĭ-rā′shŭn), *n.* **1**, the act of breathing; a breath; **2**, the strong desire to attain a high or noble goal; ambition; as, an *aspiration* to become an artist; **3**, the pronunciation of the letter *h* as in "horse."

as·pire (ăs-pīr′), *v.i.* [aspired, aspir-ing], to have an earnest desire to attain something great or noble; as, he *aspired* to fame as an artist.

as·pi·rin (ăs′pĭ-rĭn), *n.* a drug, usually in the form of white tablets, used as a remedy for rheumatism, headache, colds, etc.

ass (ás), *n.* **1**, an animal of the horse family with longer ears and a shorter mane than the horse; **2**, a dull, stupid person; a dolt.

ASS (ǔ̆s)

as·sa·fet·i·da or **as·sa·foet·i·da** (ăs′à-fĕt′ĭ-dà), *n.* a plant gum that smells and tastes like garlic. See **asafetida**.

as·sa·gai (ăs′à-gī), *n.* a slender, hardwood spear, usually tipped with iron, used in South Africa. It can be hurled, as a javelin, or used as a lance.

as·sail (ă-sāl′), *v.t.* to fall upon or attack violently; also, to attack with words; as, his enemies *assailed* him with threats and jeers.—*adj.* **as·sail′a·ble**.

as·sail·ant (ă-sāl′ănt), *n.* a person who makes an attack or assault.

as·sas·sin (ă-săs′ĭn), *n.* a person who kills secretly or treacherously.

as·sas·si·nate (ă-săs′ĭ-nāt), *v.t.* [assassi-nat-ed, assassinat-ing], to kill by secret or treacherous means.

as·sault (ă-sôlt′), *n.* a violent attack, by physical force, or by force of words; as, an *assault* on the enemy's camp; an *assault* on the character of an opponent:—*v.t.* to attack violently; assail.

as·say (ă-sā′), *n.* **1**, the act or process of analyzing a metallic compound, ore, or alloy; especially, the testing of gold or silver coin or bullion to see if it is of standard purity; **2**, the substance tested:—*v.t.* **1**, to make a chemical analysis of; **2**, to attempt; as, to *assay* a hard task.—*adj.* **as·say′a·ble**.—*n.* **as·say′er**.

as·sem·blage (ă-sĕm′blĭj), *n.* **1**, the act of gathering together; also, the state of being collected in one place; **2**, a group or collection of persons, as a congregation or audience; **3**, the fitting together of parts and pieces, as of a machine.

as·sem·ble (ă-sĕm′bl), *v.t.* [assem-bled, assem-bling], **1**, to gather together into one place or mass; collect; as, he *assem-bled* the committee; **2**, to fit together, as parts of machinery:—*v.i.* to meet or come together; convene; as, the Senate *assembles* today.—*n.* **as·sem′bler**.

as·sem·bly (ă-sĕm′blĭ), *n.* [*pl.* assem-blies], **1**, a collection or company of persons brought together in one place and for a common object; a meeting; congregation; **2**, a legislative body; **3**, the fitting together of parts to make a complete machine; as, the *assembly* of a motorcar.

as·sem·bly·man (ă-sĕm′blĭ-măn), *n.* [*pl.* assemblymen (-mĕn)], a member of an assembly:—**Assemblyman**, in certain States, a member of the lower body of the legislature.

as·sent (ă-sĕnt′), *v.i.* to agree; consent; express agreement; as, to *assent* to a request:—*n.* the act of agreeing; consent; as, I need your *assent* to my plan.

as·sert (ă-sûrt′), *v.t.* **1**, to state positively;

declare with assurance; affirm; as, let me *assert* my belief; **2,** to insist upon; as, to *assert* one's rights; make (oneself) felt; as, he invariably *asserts* himself.

as·ser·tion (ă-sûr′shŭn), *n.* **1,** the act of declaring positively; **2,** a positive declaration or statement.

as·ser·tive (ă-sûr′tĭv), *adj.* inclined to make very positive statements; overconfident; as, an *assertive* person is often disliked.—*n.* **as·ser′tive-ness.**

as·sess (ă-sĕs′), *v.t.* **1,** to fix or determine the amount of; as, *assess* the damages; **2,** to fix or set (a tax), as on property; **3,** to value officially for the purpose of taxation; as, the property was *assessed* at $500.—*adj.* **as·sess′a·ble.**

as·sess·ment (ă-sĕs′mĕnt), *n.* **1,** the act of determining an amount to be paid; **2,** an official valuation for the purpose of taxation; **3,** the tax paid on property; **4,** any fixed tax; a share of joint expenses; as, the *assessment* on each member was a dollar.

as·ses·sor (ă-sĕs′ẽr), *n.* one appointed to estimate the value of property.

as·set (ăs′ĕt), *n.* **1,** anything of value that belongs to a business, a person, etc.; as, integrity is a business *asset;* bank deposits are an *asset;* **2, assets,** all the property of a person, firm, or estate which may be used to pay debts and obligations.

as·sev·er·ate (ă-sĕv′ẽr-āt), *v.t.* [asseverat-ed, asseverat-ing], to declare positively or solemnly; as, the man under arrest *asseverated* his innocence.

Syn. maintain, assert, declare.

as·sev·er·a·tion (ă-sĕv′ẽr-ā′shŭn), *n.* a positive statement; an earnest declaration.

as·si·du·i·ty (ăs′ĭ-dū′ĭ-tĭ), *n.* close and constant attention; persistent endeavor.

as·sid·u·ous (ă-sĭd′ū-ŭs), *adj.* persistent; persevering; hard-working; as, John was an *assiduous* worker for peace.

as·sign (ă-sīn′), *v.t.* **1,** to allot, as seats; **2,** to appoint, as to a duty; **3,** to give out, as lessons; **4,** to settle definitely; as, to *assign* a time for meeting; **5,** to transfer (property) to another.—*n.* **as·sign′er; as′sign-or′.**

as·sign·ee (ăs′ĭ-nē′), *n.* one to whom anything is assigned.

as·sign·ment (ă-sīn′mĕnt), *n.* **1,** a setting apart for some particular person or use; allotment; **2,** a thing given out or allotted, as a lesson; **3,** a legal transfer, as of property.

as·sim·i·late (ă-sĭm′ĭ-lāt), *v.t.* [assimilat-ed, assimilat-ing], to absorb; make a part of oneself:—*v.i.* to be absorbed.

as·sim·i·la·tion (ă-sĭm′ĭ-lā′shŭn), *n.* **1,** a bringing into agreement; **2,** in physiol-

ogy, the absorbing of digested food, and its change into bodily tissue.

as·sist (ă-sĭst′), *v.t.* and *v.i.* to help; aid.

Syn. succor, sustain, support, help.

as·sist·ance (ă-sĭs′tăns), *n.* help; aid.

as·sist·ant (ă-sĭs′tănt), *adj.* **1,** helping; lending aid; **2,** acting under another person of higher authority; as, an *assistant* editor:—*n.* a helper.

as·size (ă-sīz′), *n.* a court of justice, or a session, for the trial by jury of civil or criminal cases.

assn. abbreviation for *association.*

as·so·ci·ate (ă-sō′shĭ-āt), *n.* **1,** a companion; **2,** someone joined with another in an undertaking; partner, as in business; **3,** a member of a society or institution:—*adj.* **1,** joined with someone in interest or purpose; **2,** sharing office or authority; as, an *associate* judge; **3,** admitted to some but not all rights or privileges; as, an *associate* member of a club:—*v.t.* (ă-sō′shĭ-āt), [associat-ed, associat-ing], to unite; combine; connect in thought; as, I *associate* green with grass:—*v.i.* to keep company; as, don't *associate* with evil persons.

Syn., n. partner, colleague, ally.

as·so·ci·a·tion (ă-sō′sĭ-ā′shŭn; ă-sō′shĭ-ā′shŭn), *n.* **1,** a joining together; **2,** fellowship; **3,** a body of persons organized for a common object; a corporation; **4,** a connection between related ideas.

Syn. combination, company, partnership.

as·sort (ă-sôrt′), *v.t.* **1,** to separate into classes; sort; **2,** to agree; as, his actions *assort* well with his character.

as·sort·ed (ă-sôr′tĕd), *adj.* of different kinds; various; as, *assorted* cakes.

as·sort·ment (ă-sôrt′mĕnt), *n.* **1,** a separating and arranging; **2,** a collection of articles of various kinds.

asst. abbreviation for *assistant.*

as·suage (ă-swāj′), *v.t.* [assuaged, assuaging], to lessen; as, time *assuaged* her grief.

as·sume (ă-sūm′), *v.t.* [assumed, assuming], **1,** to take upon oneself, especially without authority; as, to *assume* the leadership; **2,** to take for granted; as, to *assume* that something is true; **3,** to pretend; put on; as, he *assumed* an air of surprise; **4,** to undertake (an office or duty).

as·sump·tion (ă-sŭmp′shŭn), *n.* **1,** the act of taking upon oneself; as, the *assumption* of a task; **2,** the act of taking for granted; supposition; as, he acted on the *assumption* that I was going; **3,** arrogance; a disposition to claim more than one's due:—**the Assumption,** the ascension into heaven of the Virgin Mary; also, a picture of this scene.

---

go; join; yet; sing; chin; show; thin, *th***en; hw,** *wh***y; zh,** a**z**ure; **ü,** Ger. f*ü*r or Fr. l*u*ne; **ö,** Ger. sch*ö*n or Fr. f*eu*; **ṅ,** Fr. e*n*fant, no*m*; **kh,** Ger. a*ch* or i*ch.* See pages **ix–x.**

as-sur-ance (ă-shŏŏr′ăns), *n.* **1**, a statement intended to give certainty or confidence; as, *assurances* of his safety came in every mail; **2**, certain proof; freedom from doubt; utmost certainty; as, we have *assurance* of the success of our plan; **3**, self-reliance; self-confidence; as, frequent speaking in public gave him *assurance;* **4**, impudence; too much self-confidence; as, his *assurance* cost him his job; **5**, insurance.

as-sure (ă-shŏŏr′), *v.t.* [assured, assur-ing], **1**, to make certain; as, practice *assures* skill; **2**, to declare confidently to (a person); promise; as, he *assured* us she would come; **3**, to insure against loss.

as-sured (ă-shŏŏrd′), *adj.* made certain; **2**, confident; **3**, over-confident:—*n.* a person whose life or property is insured.

as-sur-ed-ly (ă-shŏŏr′ĕd-lĭ), *adv.* certainly; without doubt.

As-syr-i-a (ă-sĭr′ĭ-à), an ancient empire (cap. Nineveh) in southwestern Asia.— *n.* and *adj.* **As-syr′i-an.**

as-ter (ăs′tĕr), *n.* a leafy-stemmed plant related to the daisy, with white, pink, blue, or purple flower heads; also, its flower. Asters vary in size from small, star-shaped heads to large, many-flowered heads which often resemble chrysanthemums.

ASTER

as-ter-isk (ăs′tĕr-ĭsk), *n.* the figure of a star [*], used in printing or writing as a reference mark, or to show an omission:—*v.t.* to mark with such a star.

a-stern (à-stûrn′), *adv.* **1**, at or toward the rear end of a ship; **2**, behind a ship.

as-ter-oid (ăs′tĕr-oid), *n.* one of the small planets between Jupiter and Mars.

asth-ma (ăz′mà; ăs′mà), *n.* a disease attended by difficulty in breathing.—*adj.* **asth-mat′ic** (ăz-măt′ĭk; ăs-măt′ĭk).

a-stig-ma-tism (à-stĭg′mà-tĭzm), *n.* a defect in the shape of the eye, causing blurred vision.

a-stir (à-stûr′), *adj.* and *adv.* on the move; in activity; as, to be *astir* early.

as-ton-ish (ăs-tŏn′ĭsh), *v.t.* to strike with sudden wonder; surprise; amaze.

as-ton-ish-ing (ăs-tŏn′ĭsh-ĭng), *adj.* wonderful; surprising.

as-ton-ish-ment (ăs-tŏn′ĭsh-mĕnt), *n.* extreme surprise.

as-tound (ăs-tound′), *v.t.* to strike with amazement; shock.—*adj.* **as-tound′ing.**

a-strad-dle (à-străd′l), *adv.* with one leg on each side of something.

As-tra-khan (ăs′trà-kăn′), a city in southeastern U.S.S.R., on an island at the mouth of the Volga (map **12**).

as-tra-khan or **as-tra-chan** (ăs′trà-kăn). *n.* **1**, the skin of young lambs, with a curly wool like fur; **2**, a cloth imitation of this.

a-stray (à-strā′), *adv.* out of the proper way or place; as, to go *astray:*—*adj.* wandering; confused; as, her thoughts are *astray.*

a-stride (à-strīd′), *adv.* with one leg on each side:—*prep.* straddling.

as-trin-gent (ăs-trĭn′jĕnt), *adj.* tending to pucker or wrinkle the skin, as alum:— *n.* a substance that contracts tissues.

as-tro-labe (ăs′trŏ-lāb), *n.* an instrument formerly used, especially by navigators, for making astronomical observations.

as-trol-o-gy (ăs-trŏl′ŏ-jĭ), *n.* the practice which claims to predict events by the position and mysterious influence on human affairs of the sun, moon, and planets.— *adj.* **as′tro-log′i-cal** (ăs′trŏ-lŏj′ĭ-kăl).—*n.* **as-trol′o-ger.**

as-tron-o-mer (ăs-trŏn′ŏ-mĕr), *n.* a person who studies stars, planets, and other heavenly bodies.

as-tro-nom-i-cal (ăs′trŏ-nŏm′ĭ-kăl), *adj.* having to do with the study of heavenly bodies.—*adv.* **as′tro-nom′i-cal-ly.**

as-tron-o-my (ăs-trŏn′ŏ-mĭ), *n.* the science of the nature and movements of stars, planets, and other heavenly bodies.

as-tute (ăs-tūt′), *adj.* shrewd; cunning; crafty; subtle.—*n.* **as-tute′ness.**
  Syn. acute, sharp, sagacious.

A-sun-ción (ä-sōōn′syōn′), the capital of Paraguay, in South America (map **11**).

a-sun-der (à-sŭn′dĕr), *adv.* apart; into parts; as, he tore the book *asunder.*

As-wân (äs-wän′), a town in Egypt on the Nile, the site of a large dam (map **14**).

a-sy-lum (à-sī′lŭm), *n.* **1**, a place of refuge or security; **2**, an institution for the care of the helpless or insane.

at (ăt; ăt), *prep.* **1**, indicating nearness in place or time; as, to be *at* home *at* noon; **2**, indicating such conditions as occupation, cause, price, etc.; as, *at* play; *at* ten cents; angry *at* a noise; *at* will.

ate (āt), past tense of *eat.*

a tem-po (ä těm′pō), [Italian], in music, in time; return to former tempo, or time.

Ath-a-bas-ka (ăth′à-băs′kà), **1**, a big lake in northern Alberta and Saskatchewan, Canada; **2**, a river in Canada. (Map **4**.)

a-the-ist (ā′thē-ĭst), *n.* one who disbelieves in, or denies, the existence of a God.—*n.* **a′the-ism.**—*adj.* **a′the-is′tic.**

āte, âorta, râre, căt, àsk, fär, ăllow, sofà; ēve, ĕvent, ĕll, writĕr, novĕl; bīte, pĭn; nō, ōbey, ôr, dŏg, tŏp, cŏllide; ūnit, ūnite, bûrn, cŭt, focŭs; nōōn, fŏŏt; mound; coin;

A-the-na (á-thē′ná) or **A-the-ne** (á-thē′-nē), *n.* in mythology, the Greek goddess of wisdom, industrial arts, and free government. The Romans called her *Minerva*.

A-the-ni-an (á-thē′ni-ăn), *adj.* pertaining to Athens, Greece, or to its culture:—*n.* a citizen of Athens.

Ath-ens (ăth′ĕnz), a city, capital of Greece (maps **1, 12**).

a-thirst (á-thûrst′), *adj.* **1**, thirsty; **2**, having a keen desire; eager, as for fame.

ath-lete (ăth′lēt), *n.* a person trained to contend in games of physical strength or endurance:—**athlete's foot**, an infection causing inflammation and itching.

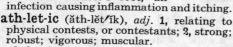

ATHENA

ath-let-ic (ăth-lĕt′ĭk), *adj.* **1**, relating to physical contests, or contestants; **2**, strong; robust; vigorous; muscular.

ath-let-ics (ăth-lĕt′ĭks), *n.pl.* sometimes used as *sing.* athletic sports.

a-thwart (á-thwôrt′), *adv.* from side to side; crosswise:—*prep.* **1**, across the course or direction of; **2**, from side to side of; as, beams set *athwart* the ship.

-a-tion (-ā′shŭn), a suffix meaning: **1**, the act or process of; as, cre*ation*; **2**, the condition or state of; as, starv*ation*, emaci*ation*; **3**, the result of; as, plant*ation*. In many words *-ation* can have more than one of these meanings, as in reserv*ation*.

-a-tive (-ā′tĭv), a suffix meaning: **1**, having to do with; as, narr*ative*; **2**, tending or likely to; as, cur*ative*, restor*ative*.

At-lan-ta (ăt-lăn′tá), a city, the capital of Georgia (map **8**).

At-lan-tic Cit-y (ăt-lăn′tĭk), a city and popular seaside resort in New Jersey (map **6**).

At-lan-tic O-cean, the ocean separating America from Europe and Africa (map **2**).

At-las (ăt′lăs), *n.* in mythology, a giant who had to support the heavens on his shoulders.

at-las (ăt′lăs), *n.* **1**, a bound volume of maps or charts; **2**, the vertebra of the neck which supports the skull.

At-las Moun-tains, a range of mountains in northern Africa (map **14**).

at-mos-phere (ăt′mŏs-fĭr), *n.* **1**, the air which surrounds the earth; **2**, the air in any particular place; as, the damp *atmosphere* of a cellar; **3**, a surrounding or pervading influence; as, an *atmosphere* of peace.

ATLAS

at-mos-pher-ic (ăt′mŏs-fĕr′ĭk), *adj.* relating to the air:—**atmospheric pressure**, pressure exerted by the weight of the air.

at-oll (ăt′ŏl; á-tŏl′), *n.* a circular coral reef surrounding a lake or lagoon.

ATOLL

at-om (ăt′ŭm), *n.* **1**, the smallest distinct chemical unit of a substance, itself composed of electrical particles; **2**, a tiny bit.

a-tom-ic (á-tŏm′ĭk), *adj.* **1**, relating to atoms; **2**, very minute:—**atomic bomb**, a highly destructive bomb, in which the energy released by the splitting of atoms is used to produce explosion:—**atomic theory**, the theory that elements consist of atoms which, when combined with one another, form chemical compounds, and which are composed of smaller electrical particles.

at-om-iz-er (ăt′ŭm-i′zĕr), *n.* a device for changing a liquid to a fine spray.

a-tone-ment (á-tōn′mĕnt), *n.* amends or satisfaction for a wrong that has been done:—**the Atonement**, the sufferings and death of Christ for the sin of mankind. —*v.i.* **a-tone′**.

a-top (á-tŏp′), *adv.* at or to the top:—*prep.* on top of.

a-tri-um (ā′trĭ-ŭm), *n.* the principal room in an ancient Roman house.

a-tro-cious (á-trō′shŭs), *adj.* extremely wicked; outrageous.—*adv.* **a-tro′cious-ly**.

a-troc-i-ty (á-trŏs′ĭ-tĭ), *n.* [*pl.* atrocities], **1**, an outrageous or cruel deed; **2**, *Colloquial*, something ugly or very faulty; as, that hat is an *atrocity*.

at-ro-phy (ăt′rŏ-fĭ), *v.i.* [atrophied (ăt′-rŏ-fĭd), atrophy-ing], to waste or wither away, from lack of food or from disuse:—*n.* a wasting of the body or any part of it.

at-tach (á-tăch′), *v.t.* **1**, to fasten to or upon something; connect; as, to *attach* a check to a letter; **2**, to assign, as to a military company; appoint; **3**, to affix, as a signature; **4**, to attribute; as, to *attach* importance to something; **5**, to bind by ties of affection or self-interest; **6**, to take by law:—*v.i.* to be fixed; adhere.

at-ta-ché (ăt′á-shā′; á-tăsh′á), *n.* [*pl.* attachés], a member of a suite or staff; especially, a subordinate attached to the staff of a foreign minister or ambassador.

at-tach-ment (á-tăch′mĕnt), *n.* **1**, the act of fastening, or the thing fastened; **2**, affection; **3**, something extra that may be connected to something else; as, *attachments* for a vacuum cleaner; **4**, legal seizure of goods or persons.

---

go; join; yet; sing; chin; show; thin, *th*en; **hw**, *wh*y; **zh**, azure; **ü**, Ger. für or Fr. lune; **ö**, Ger. schön or Fr. *feu*; **ṅ**, Fr. enfant, nom; **kh**, Ger. a*ch* or i*ch*. See pages ix–x.

at-tack (ă-tăk′), *v.t.* **1,** to set upon with physical force, or with words; assail; as, to *attack* with sword or pen; **2,** to start to have a harmful effect upon; as, worms are *attacking* our trees; **3,** to begin work on; as, to *attack* a problem:—*v.i.* to make an assault:—*n.* **1,** an assault; onset; **2,** a bitter criticism; **3,** the first step of an undertaking; **4,** a seizure, as of illness.

at-tain (ă-tān′), *v.t.* **1,** to reach; arrive at; as, to *attain* the top of a hill; **2,** to achieve; gain; accomplish; as, to *attain* one's goal:—*v.i.* to arrive.

at-tain-der (ă-tān′dẽr), *n.* the taking away from a person of all civil or legal rights upon sentence for a serious crime.

at-tain-ment (ă-tān′měnt), *n.* **1,** the act of arriving at something, as the result of effort; **2,** that which is reached; an achievement; accomplishment.
Syn. acquisition, achievement.

at-taint (ă-tānt′), *v.t.* to deprive (a condemned person) of all rights.

at-tar (ăt′ẽr), *n.* a fragrant oil extracted from the petals of flowers, chiefly roses.

at-tempt (ă-těmpt′), *v.t.* **1,** to make an effort to do; try; as, to *attempt* a flight, or to fly; **2,** to try to take by force; as, to *attempt* a man's life:—*n.* trial; effort.

at-tend (ă-těnd′), *v.t.* **1,** to wait upon; care for; **2,** to escort; accompany; **3,** to be present at; as, to *attend* a church service:—*v.i.* **1,** to give heed to; as, *attend* to my warning; **2,** to be in waiting, as a bridesmaid at a wedding; **3,** to look after something; as, to *attend* to business.

at-tend-ance (ă-těn′dăns), *n.* **1,** the fact of being present, as at school; **2,** the state of looking after or waiting upon some person or thing; as, the nurse is in *attendance*; **3,** the number of persons present; also, the record of this number; as, to take the *attendance* at school.

at-tend-ant (ă-těn′dănt), *adj.* accompanying or immediately following; as, illness *attendant* on overeating:—*n.* **1,** one who serves or waits upon another; a servant or companion; as, he dismissed his *attendants*; **2,** one who is frequently present, as at church.

at-ten-tion (ă-těn′shŭn), *n.* **1,** the fixing of one's thoughts closely on something; concentration; **2,** an act of courtesy, especially on the part of a man in wooing a woman:—**come to attention, stand at attention,** in army drill, to stand still ready to act on the next command.

BOY SCOUT AT ATTENTION

at-ten-tive (ă-těn′tĭv), *adj.* **1,** heedful;

intent; as, an *attentive* student; **2,** polite; eager to offer courtesies.
Syn. thoughtful, considerate.

at-ten-u-ate (ă-těn′ū-āt), *v.t.* [attenuat-ed, attenuat-ing], to make thin or slender; as, his body was *attenuated* by disease; a rubber band is *attenuated* by stretching; hence, to weaken; dilute.

at-ten-u-a-tion (ă-těn′ū-ā′shŭn), *n.* **1,** the act or process of making thin or slender; **2,** extreme thinness.

at-test (ă-těst′), *v.t.* **1,** to bear witness to; affirm the truth of, especially by signing one's name or by oath; **2,** to give proof of; as, your work *attests* your ability.

At-tic (ăt′ĭk), *adj.* **1,** relating to Attica, in Greece; **2,** pure; refined; classic.

at-tic (ăt′ĭk), *n.* the space immediately beneath the roof of a house; a garret.

At-ti-ca (ăt′ĭ-ká), an ancient Greek state whose capital was Athens:—**Attica and Boeotia,** a department (cap. Athens) of modern Greece.

At-ti-la (ăt′ĭ-lá), (A.D. 406?-453), king of the warlike Huns of central Europe.

at-tire (ă-tīr′), *n.* clothes; finery:—*v.t.* [attired, attir-ing], to clothe; array.

at-ti-tude (ăt′ĭ-tūd), *n.* **1,** bodily position or pose; especially, position assumed to show feeling, purpose, mood, etc.; as, to take a threatening *attitude*; **2,** way of thinking or feeling; as, his *attitude* toward his work was one of indifference.

at-tor-ney (ă-tûr′nĭ), *n.* [*pl.* attorneys], a lawyer; one legally appointed by another to act for him in any legal matter: also called *attorney at law*.

at-tor-ney gen-er-al [*pl.* attorneys general or attorney generals], the chief law officer of a state or nation.

at-tract (ă-trăkt′), *v.t.* **1,** to draw to oneself by personal charm, or the like; as, he *attracts* friends easily; **2,** to cause to approach; as, a magnet *attracts* steel; **3,** to draw forth; win; as, beauty *attracts* attention.

at-trac-tion (ă-trăk′shŭn), *n.* **1,** the power or act of drawing to or toward; **2,** the thing that attracts; as, the dwarf was the great *attraction* in the show.

at-trac-tive (ă-trăk′tĭv), *adj.* having the power to attract; charming; alluring.

at-trib-ut-a-ble (ă-trĭb′ŭt-á-bl), *adj.* owing (to); due (to); as, her success is *attributable* to her hard work.

¹**at-trib-ute** (ă-trĭb′ūt), *v.t.* [attribut-ed, attribut-ing], **1,** to consider (a quality) as belonging to a person or thing; as, we *attribute* grace to a dancer; **2,** to consider (a thing) as being caused by something else; as, I *attribute* Anne's popularity to her beauty.—*n.* **at′tri-bu′tion.**

²**at·tri·bute** (ăt′rĭ-būt), *n.* **1,** a trait or characteristic, thought of as belonging to a person or thing; as, courtesy is an *attribute* of a gentleman; **2,** a symbol; as, the crown is an *attribute* of royalty.

at·trib·u·tive (ă-trĭb′ū-tĭv), *adj.* in grammar, an adjective which immediately precedes the noun which it modifies; as, "red," in the expression "red bricks," is an *attributive* adjective.

at·tune (ă-tūn′), *v.t.* [attuned, attun-ing], **1,** to put in tune; **2,** to bring into harmony; as, his spirit was *attuned* to nature.

atty. abbreviation for *attorney.*

au·burn (ô′bẽrn), *adj.* reddish brown.

Auck·land (ôk′lănd), a seaport of North Island, New Zealand (map 16).

auc·tion (ôk′shŭn), *n.* a public sale of property, which goes to the highest bidder: —**auction bridge,** a card game:—*v.t.* to sell to the highest bidder.

auc·tion·eer (ôk′shŭn-ēr′), *n.* a person who conducts an auction.

au·da·cious (ô-dā′shŭs), *adj.* **1,** bold; daring; **2,** too bold; insolent; impudent.

au·dac·i·ty (ô-dăs′ĭ-tĭ), *n.* [*pl.* audacities], **1,** rash boldness; **2,** impudence.

au·di·ble (ô′dĭ-bl), *adj.* loud enough to be heard.—*adv.* **au′di·bly.**

au·di·ence (ô′dĭ-ĕns), *n.* **1,** a group of persons assembled to hear or to see, as at a lecture or a motion picture; **2,** a formal interview with a person of authority.

au·di·o·vis·u·al aids (ô′dĭ-ō-vĭz′ū-ăl), films, pictures, recordings, and similar materials used in addition to or in conjunction with textbooks.

au·dit (ô′dĭt), *n.* an official examination of claims or accounts:—*v.t.* to examine and adjust, as accounts or claims.

au·di·tor (ô′dĭ-tẽr), *n.* **1,** a listener; **2,** one who examines accounts and claims.

au·di·tor·i·um (ô′dĭ-tôr′ĭ-ŭm), *n.* a building or room designed for public gatherings; also, the part of a theater, or the like, assigned to the audience.

au·di·tor·y (ô′dĭ-tôr′ĭ), *adj.* having to do with hearing or the organs of hearing; as, the *auditory* nerve.

Au·du·bon (ô′dŏŏ-bŏn), John James (1785–1851), an American naturalist, chiefly famous for studies and drawings of birds.

Aug. abbreviation for *August.*

au·ger (ô′gẽr), *n.* a tool for boring holes.

AUGER

aught (ôt), *n.* **1,** any part; anything; as, for *aught* I know; **2,** in arithmetic, a cipher; a naught; nothing.

aug·ment (ôg-mĕnt′), *v.t.* to increase in size or extent; to make bigger; as, the general *augmented* his forces.—*n.* **aug′-men·ta′tion** (ôg′mĕn-tā′shŭn).

Augs·burg (ouks′bŏŏrkh; ôgz′bûrg), a city of Bavaria, Germany (map 12).

au·gur (ô′gẽr), *n.* in Roman times, a religious official who foretold events by signs or omens, such as the flight of birds, thunder, etc.; a soothsayer; prophet:—*v.i.* to foretell events from signs:—*v.t.* to predict; give promise of; as, careful planning *augurs* success for his scheme:—**augurs well** or **ill,** to give reason to expect a good or bad outcome; as, his general weakness *augurs ill* for his recovery.

au·gu·ry (ô′gŭ-rĭ), *n.* [*pl.* auguries], **1,** the art or practice of foretelling events by signs or omens; **2,** an omen; a prediction.

au·gust (ô-gŭst′), *adj.* **1,** majestic; having grandeur and dignity; **2,** of high rank; noble.

Au·gust (ô′gŭst), *n.* the eighth month of the year, having 31 days: named for the first Roman emperor, Augustus Caesar.

Au·gus·ta (ô-gŭs′tà), **1,** a city in eastern Georgia, on the Savannah River (map 8); **2,** a city, capital of Maine (map 6).

Au·gus·tan (ô-gŭs′tăn), *adj.* having to do with Augustus Caesar or with his age, or with any age like his in brilliance and refinement:—*n.* a writer of the classical period of any language.

Au·gus·tine (ô′gŭs-tēn; ô-gŭs′tĭn), **1,** Saint (354–430), a Roman bishop, famous for his writings and sermons; **2,** Saint (?–604), a Roman missionary to England, who became the first Archbishop of Canterbury.—*adj.* and *n.* **Au′gus·tin′i·an.**

Au·gus·tus (ô-gŭs′tŭs), a name, meaning "Majestic," conferred by the Roman Senate upon Octavius, the first emperor, and used as an official title by later emperors.

Au·gus·tus Cae·sar (63 B.C.–A.D. 14), (*Octavius*), the first Roman emperor.

auk (ôk), *n.* a kind of diving bird with small wings used as paddles, and a heavy body. It lives in the colder regions of the Northern Hemisphere.

auld (ôld; äld), *adj. Scottish,* old:—**auld lang syne,** the days of long ago, especially those that seem happy and full of sweet memories.

aunt (ånt), *n.* the sister of one's father or mother; also, an uncle's wife.

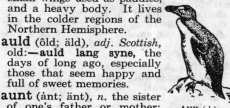

AUK (1⁄20)

au·ra (ô′rà), *n.* an invisible something supposed to issue from a human body, and to surround it like an atmosphere; as, an *aura* of gentleness surrounded the old lady.

Au·re·li·us (ô-rē′lĭ-ŭs; ô-rēl′yŭs), Marcus (A.D. 121–180), a Roman emperor and philosopher.

au·re·ole (ô′rê-ōl), *n.* **1**, a halo or ring of light, as around the sun in a total eclipse; **2**, in Christian art, a halo around the head of a martyr, saint, or other sacred person.

au re·voir (ō′ rĕ-vwår′), good-by till I see you again: a French leave-taking.

au·ri·cle (ô′rĭ-kl), *n.* **1**, the part of the ear outside the head; the outer ear; **2**, either of the two upper chambers of the heart, which receive the blood from the veins and transmit it to the ventricles.

au·ric·u·lar (ô-rĭk′û-lẽr), *adj.* **1**, relating to the ear or to the sense of hearing; **2**, told in private, as to a priest in the confessional; **3**, known by hearing; as, *auricular* evidence; **4**, ear-shaped; **5**, pertaining to the auricles of the heart.

Au·ro·ra (ô-rôr′a), *n.* in Roman mythology, the goddess of dawn:—**aurora, 1**, the dawn; the reddish color of the sky at sunrise; **2**, the aurora borealis.—*adj.* **au·ror′al.**

au·ro·ra bor·e·a·lis (bôr′ê-ā′lĭs; bôr′ê-ăl′ĭs), northern lights; a glow or, more often, streamers of light, supposed to be of electrical origin, appearing in the northern sky at night, best seen in northern latitudes.

aus·pic·es (ôs′pĭ-sĕz), *n.pl.* **1**, omens or signs, as those drawn from birds by the ancient Romans; **2**, protection; patronage; as, a play given under the *auspices* of the club.

aus·pi·cious (ôs-pĭsh′ŭs), *adj.* **1**, promising success or happiness; as, *auspicious* circumstances; **2**, successful; prosperous; as, an *auspicious* year.

aus·tere (ôs-tēr′), *adj.* **1**, rigidly strict in manner of living or thinking; **2**, severely simple; unadorned; as, an *austere* building. —*adv.* **aus·tere′ly.**—*n.* **aus·ter′i·ty.**
Syn. rigid, rigorous, harsh.

Aus·tin (ôs′tĭn), a city, capital of Texas (map 8).

Aus·tral·a·sia (ôs′trăl-ā′zha; ôs′trăl-ā′sha), the lands of the southern Pacific, including Australia, Papua, Tasmania, New Zealand, and smaller islands, lying southeast of Asia (map 16).—*adj.* and *n.* **Aus′tral·a′sian.**

Aus·tral·ia (ôs-trāl′ya; ôs-trā′lĭ-a), an island continent southeast of Asia:—**Commonwealth of Australia,** a self-governing Dominion (cap. Canberra) of the British Empire, comprising Australia, Tasmania, and Territory of Papua (map 16).—*adj.* and *n.* **Aus·tral′ian.**

Aus·tri·a (ôs′trĭ-a), a republic of central Europe (cap. Vienna: map **12**), annexed to Germany from 1938-1945. German name, *Osterreich.*—*n.* and *adj.* **Aus′tri·an.**

Aus·tri·a–Hun·ga·ry (ôs′trĭ-a-hŭng′ga-rĭ), a dual monarchy of central Europe, established in 1867 and dissolved in 1918, allied with Germany during World War I.

au·then·tic (ô-thĕn′tĭk), *adj.* **1**, genuine; original; as, an *authentic* painting by Raphael; **2**, duly authorized; true; trustworthy; as, does the spy bring *authentic* information?—*adv.* **au·then′ti·cal·ly.**—*n.* **au′then·tic′i·ty** (ô′thĕn-tĭs′ĭ-tĭ).

au·then·ti·cate (ô-thĕn′tĭ-kāt), *v.t.* [authenticat-ed, authenticat-ing], to establish as real or genuine, as the authorship of a book, a signature, or the like.—*n.* **au·then′ti·ca′tion.**

au·thor (ô′thẽr), *n.* **1**, one who composes or writes a book, articles, etc.; **2**, a person who begins or originates anything.

au·thor·i·ta·tive (ô-thŏr′ĭ-tā′tĭv), *adj.* **1**, having acknowledged authority; entitled to obedience or acceptance; **2**, commanding in manner; imperative.

au·thor·i·ty (ô-thŏr′ĭ-tĭ), *n.* [*pl.* authorities], **1**, the right to act or command; as, a general's *authority;* **2**, one whose knowledge or judgment on a subject is entitled to acceptance; an expert; as, Audubon is an *authority* on birds; also, a book, quotation, or the like, cited in justification of a statement or action; **3**, **authorities**, government officials.

au·thor·i·za·tion (ô′thẽr-ĭ-zā′shŭn; -ī-zā′shŭn), *n.* **1**, the giving of legal power; **2**, legal right; as, he had no *authorization* to write checks.

au·thor·ize (ô′thẽr-īz), *v.t.* [authorized, authoriz-ing], **1**, to give (a person) the right to act; as, he is *authorized* to act for us; **2**, to approve; allow; as, to *authorize* the purchase of supplies:—**Authorized Version,** the translation of the Bible, made in 1611, commonly used by English-speaking Protestants.

au·thor·ship (ô′thẽr-shĭp), *n.* **1**, the occupation of writing; **2**, origin; source.

au·to (ô′tō), *n.* [*pl.* autos], *Colloquial,* an automobile.

au·to- (ô′tō-), a prefix meaning self, oneself, itself; as, *autobiography,* *automobile.

au·to·bi·og·ra·phy (ô′tō-bī-ŏg′ra-fĭ; ô′tō-bĭ-ŏg′ra-fĭ), *n.* [*pl.* autobiographies], a life history of a person, written by himself.—*n.* **au′to·bi·og′ra·pher.**—*adj.* **au′to·bi′o·graph′ic** (ô′tō-bī′ō-grăf′ĭk); **au′to·bi′o·graph′i·cal.**

au·toc·ra·cy (ô-tŏk′ra-sĭ), *n.* [*pl.* autocracies], government by a person whose will is law; absolute monarchy.

āte, āorta, râre, căt, ȧsk, fär, ăllow, sofȧ; ēve, êvent, ĕll, writẽr, novĕl; bīte, pĭn; nō, ōbey, ôr, dŏg, tŏp, cŏllide; ūnit, ŭnite, bûrn, cŭt, focŭs; nōon, fŏot; mound; coin;

au·to·crat (ô′tŏ-krăt), *n.* **1,** a ruler with unlimited power; **2,** a person who demands obedience to his will; as, Jack's father was an *autocrat* in his home.—*adj.* **au′to-crat′ic.**

Au·to·gi·ro (ô′tŏ-jĭ′rō), *n.* a trade-mark name for an airplane with windmill-like mechanism above, which allows the craft to take off or to land in a small space:— **autogiro,** an airplane bearing this trade-mark. (See illustration at *aviation.*)

ger is held and the ammunition lasts.—*adv.* **au′to-mat′i-cal-ly.**

au·to·ma·tion (ô′tŏ-mā′shŭn), *n.* the operation of machines by other machines rather than by human hands.

au·tom·a·ton (ô-tŏm′à-tŏn), *n.* [*pl.* automata (ô-tŏm′à-tá) or automatons], **1,** a self-acting mechanism, as a robot; **2,** a human being whose actions are mechanical.

au·to·mo·bile (ô′tŏ-mō-bēl′; ô′tŏ-mō′bĭl;

HISTORY OF THE AUTOMOBILE
1, the steam wagon of 1786; 2, a one-cylinder motorcar of 1900, with solid tires; 3, four-cylinder car of 1902, with steering wheel, mudguards, pneumatic tires; 4, a touring car of 1905, with side doors; 5, a limousine of 1908; 6, sedan of 1925; 7, streamlined two-door sedan of 1950.

au·to·graph (ô′tŏ-gráf), *n.* a person's own handwriting or signature:—*v.t.* to write one's signature in or on; as, to *autograph* a book. —*adj.* **au′to-graph′ic; au′to-graph′i-cal.**

au·to·in·tox·i·ca·tion (ô′tŏ-ĭn-tŏk′sĭ-kā′shŭn), *n.* poisoning, or a state of being poisoned, from substances produced in one's own body.

au·to·mat (ô′tŏ-măt), *n.* a restaurant where the proper coin put in a slot mechanically releases a portion of food.

au·to·mat·ic (ô′tŏ-măt′ĭk), *adj.* **1,** designed to work without attention; as, an *automatic* oil burner; **2,** done unconsciously; as, breathing is *automatic:*—*n.* a firearm which continues to fire so long as the trig-

ô′tŏ-mō-bēl′), *n.* a vehicle carrying an engine by which it is propelled; a motorcar: —*adj.* having to do with motorcars.

au·to·mo·bil·ist (ô′tŏ-mō-bē′lĭst; ô′tŏ-mō′bĭl-ĭst), *n.* one who rides in or drives an automobile.

au·to·mo·tive (ô′tŏ-mō′tĭv), *adj.* **1,** moving under its own power; **2,** relating to self-propelling vehicles or mechanisms.

au·ton·o·mous (ô-tŏn′ŏ-mŭs), *adj.* self-governing; independent; as, the Philippines are now *autonomous.*

au·ton·o·my (ô-tŏn′ŏ-mĭ), *n.* [*pl.* autonomies], the right of self-government.

au·top·sy (ô′tŏp-sĭ; ô′tŭp-sĭ), *n.* [*pl.* autopsies], the examination and dissection

---

go; join; yet; sing; chin; show; thin, *th*en; hw, *wh*y; zh, az**ure; ü, Ger. f**ü**r or Fr. l**u**ne; ö, Ger. sch**ö**n or Fr. f**eu**; ṅ, Fr. e**n**fant, no**m**; kh, Ger. a**ch** or i**ch**. See pages ix–x.**

of a dead body to find the cause of death or the effects of a disease or injury.

au·to–truck (ô′tō-trŭk′), *n.* a motor-driven freight vehicle; a motor truck.

au·tumn (ô′tŭm), *n.* the season following summer, beginning, in the Northern Hemisphere, about September 22, and ending about December 21: also called *fall:—adj.* belonging to this season; as, *autumn* fruits.

au·tum·nal (ô-tŭm′năl), *adj.* belonging to or peculiar to autumn; as, *autumnal* foliage.

aux·il·ia·ry (ôg-zĭl′yȧ-rĭ), *adj.* helping; assisting; as, *auxiliary* forces:—*n.* [*pl.* auxiliaries], 1, a helper; an ally; aid of any kind; 2, in grammar, a verb, such as *be, have, may*, which helps to form the moods and tenses of other verbs; as, in "they have come," "have" is the *auxiliary;* 3, auxiliaries, foreign troops in the service of a nation at war.

av. abbreviation for *avoirdupois, avenue.*

A.V. abbreviation for *Authorized Version* (of the Bible).

a·vail (ȧ-vāl′), *v.i.* to be of use or value:—*v.t.* to benefit; help; as, shouting did not *avail* us:—**avail oneself of,** to take advantage of; utilize:—*n.* use; means toward an end; as, crying was of no *avail.*
Syn. n. utility, benefit, advantage.

a·vail·a·ble (ȧ-vāl′ȧ-bl), *adj.* 1, at hand; ready to be used; 2, suitable for one's purpose.—*n.* **a·vail′a·bil′i·ty.**

av·a·lanche (ăv′ȧ-lȧnch), *n.* 1, a large mass of snow or earth sliding down a mountain; 2, anything that overwhelms by speed and volume; as, an *avalanche* of words.

av·a·rice (ăv′ȧ-rĭs), *n.* the passion for hoarding or acquiring wealth; greed.—*adj.* **av′a·ri′cious** (ăv′ȧ-rĭsh′ŭs).
Syn. covetousness, stinginess.

a·vast (ȧ-vàst′), *interj.* a sailors' term meaning stop! cease!

a·vaunt (ȧ-vônt′; ȧ-vänt′), *interj.* away! depart! begone!

ave. or **av.** abbreviation for *avenue.*

A·ve Ma·ri·a (ä′vā mä-rē′ä; ā′vē mȧ-rī′ȧ), Hail Mary! a prayer to the Virgin Mary.

a·venge (ȧ-vĕnj′), *v.t.* [avenged, aveng-ing], 1, to inflict just punishment in return for (a wrong or injury); as, to *avenge* an insult; 2, to exact punishment on behalf of; as, to *avenge* a slain kinsman.—*n.* **a·veng′er.**

av·e·nue (ăv′ē-nū), *n.* 1, a wide roadway or drive; 2, a way of approach to a place or goal; as, an *avenue* to success.

a·ver (ȧ-vûr′), *v.t.* [averred, aver-ring], to state positively; assert; as, the man *averred* that he had not slept.

av·er·age (ăv′ẽr-ĭj), *n.* 1, something of a usual character, midway between extremes, as between too much and too little, very good and very bad, or the like; as, ability above the *average;* 2, the result obtained by dividing the sum of several quantities by the number of quantities; as, the *average* of 5, 8, and 14 is 9:—*adj.* 1, arrived at by dividing the sum of several quantities by their number; as, the *average* height of the boys; 2, ordinary; usual:—*v.t.* [averaged, averag-ing], to find the average of (a series of numbers or the like):—*v.i.* to do, perform, or get as an average rate, sum, amount, or the like; as, the car *averaged* 20 miles an hour.

a·verse (ȧ-vûrs′), *adj.* 1, unwilling; reluctant; 2, having a dislike; as, *averse* to hard work.

a·ver·sion (ȧ-vûr′zhŭn; ȧ-vûr′shŭn), *n.* 1, fixed dislike; 2, the object of dislike.
Syn. hatred, disgust, antipathy.

a·vert (ȧ-vûrt′), *v.t.* 1, to turn aside, as one's eyes; 2, to turn or ward off; 3, to prevent; as, to *avert* a strike.

a·vi·ar·y (ā′vĭ-ĕr′ĭ), *n.* [*pl.* aviaries], a place for the keeping of birds.

a·vi·a·tion (ā′vĭ-ā′shŭn), *n.* the art or science of flying airplanes. (See illustration on opposite page.)

a·vi·a·tor (ā′vĭ-ā′tẽr), *n.* the pilot of an airplane: used of both men and women.—*n.fem.* **a′vi·a′tress; a′vi·a′trix.**

av·id (ăv′ĭd), *adj.* extremely eager; as, *avid* of pleasure; greedy; as, *avid* for food.—*adv.* **av′id·ly.**—*n.* **a·vid′i·ty** (ȧ-vĭd′ĭ-tĭ).

A·vi·gnon (à′vē-nyôn′), an ancient walled city of southeastern France (map **12**).

av·o·ca·do (ăv′ō-kä′dō), *n.* [*pl.* avocados], 1, the pear-shaped, pulpy, green or purple fruit of a tropical American tree; an alligator pear; 2, the tree that bears this fruit.

AVOCADO

av·o·ca·tion (ăv′ō-kā′shŭn), *n.* an activity other than one's occupation; hobby; as, the lawyer's *avocation* is playing the violin.

av·o·cet or **av·o·set** (ăv′ō-sĕt), *n.* a shore bird with webbed feet and a slender, upcurved bill.

a·void (ȧ-void′), *v.t.* to keep away from; shun.—*n.* **a·void′ance.**

av·oir·du·pois (ăv′ẽr-dŭ-poiz′; ăv′ẽr-dŭ-poiz′), *n.* 1, the common system of measuring weight, in

AVOCET (¹⁄₁₆)

āte, āorta, râre, căt, ȧsk, fär, ȧllow, sofȧ; ēve, ĕvent, ĕll, wrītẽr, novĕl; bīte, pĭn; nō, ōbey, ôr, dôg, tŏp, cŏllide; ūnit, ūnite, bûrn, cŭt, focŭs; nōon, fŏot; mound; coin;

pounds of sixteen ounces each: used for weighing all articles except precious metals, gems, and drugs; 2, *Colloquial*, weight; heaviness.

A-von (ā′vŭn; ăv′ŭn), a Celtic word meaning *river* and used in several English place names, as Stratford-on-Avon.

a-vouch (à-vouch′), *v.t.* to declare positively; maintain; affirm; as, the spectators *avouched* that the man was badly hurt; their evidence *avouched* the date of the accident.

as does a judge or an umpire, after careful consideration; 2, to bestow, as a prize:—*n.* 1, a careful and deliberate decision; 2, that which is awarded.

a-ware (à-wâr′), *adj.* conscious; informed; as, he is well *aware* of his shortcomings.— *n.* **a-ware′ness.**

a-wash (à-wŏsh′; à-wôsh′), *adj.* and *adv.* 1, afloat; tossed about by water; 2, covered with water, as a street.

a-way (à-wā′), *adv.* 1, at or to a distance; off; aside; as, to be *away*; to look *away*;

AVIATION

1, seaplane equipped with pontoons for landing on water; 2, amphibian, an airplane with a boatlike body for support in water, and landing wheels for landings on dry ground; 3, flying boat (in this case, a "Clipper" ship, a large seaplane with a number of engines, designed for long journeys over the ocean, carrying passengers, baggage, etc.); 4, autogiro, an aircraft without wings, supported in the air, and, in types like the above, steered, by means of revolving vanes, or blades, hinged to a vertical shaft; 5, glider, an airplane without an engine; 6, ordinary biplane with landing wheels; 7, high-winged monoplane, with streamlined windshields over landing wheels; 8, low-winged monoplane (in this case, a large twin-motored transport plane equipped with landing gear for landings on dry ground only).

a-vow (à-vou′), *v.t.* to declare openly; admit; as, to *avow* one's faults.—*v.t.* **a-vow′al.** —*adj.* **a-vowed′.**—*adv.* **a-vow′ed-ly.**

a-wait (à-wāt′), *v.t.* 1, to wait for; expect; as, to *await* news; 2, to be ready for; as, I *await* your commands; 3, to be in store for; as, happiness *awaits* you.

a-wake (à-wāk′), *v.t.* [*p.t.* and *p.p.* awoke (à-wōk′) or awaked (à-wākt′), *p.pr.* awak-ing], 1, to rouse from sleep; 2, to rouse from inactivity; stimulate; as, to *awake* interest:—*v.i.* 1, to cease to sleep; 2, to rouse oneself; become alert:—*adj.* 1, not asleep; 2, fully aware; on the alert; as, he was *awake* to his danger.

a-wak-en (à-wāk′ĕn), *v.t.* and *v.i.* to rouse from sleep or as if from sleep; awake.—*n.* and *adj.* **a-wak′en-ing.**

a-ward (à-wôrd′), *v.t.* 1, to give or assign,

2, out of one's possession; as, to give *away*; 3, continuously; as, to work *away*; 4, out of existence; as, to die *away*.

awe (ô), *n.* wonder tinged with fear; reverence; as, to live in *awe* of nature:—*v.t.* [awed, aw-ing], to produce feelings of solemn respect or fear in; as, to be *awed* by mountains.

Syn., n. dread, wonder, veneration.

a-wea-ry (à-wē′rĭ), *adj. Poetic,* weary.

awe-some (ô′sŭm), *adj.* majestic and terrifying, as a volcano.—*n.* **awe′some-ness.**

awe-struck (ô′-strŭk′), *adj.* filled with, or overwhelmed by, awe or reverential fear.

aw-ful (ô′fŏol), *adj.* 1, inspiring reverence or fear; 2, appalling, as a calamity; 3, *Colloquial,* extreme in any sense; very bad, great, ugly, etc.; as, *awful* language; an *awful* dress; an *awful* thirst.—*n.* **aw′ful-ness.**

go; join; yet; sing; chin; show; thin, *then;* hw, *why;* zh, azure; ü, Ger. für or Fr. lune; ö, Ger. schön or Fr. feu; n̄, Fr. enfant, nom; kh, Ger. ach or ich. See pages ix–x.

aw-ful-ly (ô′fŏol-ĭ), *adv.* **1,** in an awesome or terrifying manner; **2,** *Colloquial,* very; as, an *awfully* dull book.

a-while (a-hwīl′), *adv.* for a short time.

awk-ward (ôk′wẽrd), *adj.* **1,** unskilful; bungling; clumsy; as, an *awkward* workman; **2,** ungraceful; ungainly in action or form; as, an *awkward* skater; **3,** ill at ease; embarrassed; as, he feels *awkward* in company; **4,** difficult to deal with; embarrassing; as, an *awkward* situation.—*adv.* **awk′-ward-ly.**—*n.* **awk′ward-ness.**

awl (ôl), *n.* a pointed tool for making small holes, as in leather or wood.

AWL

awn-ing (ôn′ĭng), *n.* a rooflike covering, as of canvas, stretched on a frame and used above or before any place as a shelter from rain or sun.

a-woke (a-wōk′), past tense and past participle of *awake.*

AWNING

a-wry (a-rī′), *adv.* and *adj.* **1,** turned or twisted to one side; out of the right line; crooked; **2,** wrong; amiss; as, the plan went *awry.*

ax or **axe** (ăks), *n.* a hewing or chopping tool, consisting of an iron head with a bit, or cutting edge, of steel, fastened on a handle.

ax-i-om (ăk′sĭ-ŭm), *n.* a self-evident truth; a statement accepted without proof. An axiom of geometry is, "The shortest distance between two points is the straight line between them."

AXES

1, hand ax; 2, lumberman's ax; 3, doublebitted ax; 4, fireman's ax.

ax-i-o-mat-ic (ăk′sĭ-ō-măt′ĭk), *adj.* **1,** self-evident; accepted without proof; unquestionably true; **2,** full of maxims.

ax-is (ăk′sĭs), *n.* [*pl.* axes (ăk′sēz)], a straight line, real or imaginary, about which a body turns, or may be supposed to turn; as, the earth's *axis:* **the Axis,** Germany, Italy, Japan, and their allies.

ax-le (ăk′sl), *n.* the bar on which a wheel turns; also, the center rod of a wheel which revolves along with it.

ax-le-tree (ăk′sl-trē′), *n.* a bar between opposite wheels on a vehicle, on the ends of which the wheels turn.

Ax-min-ster (ăks′mĭn-stẽr), *n.* a kind of carpet first made in Axminster, England.

AXIS (AA)
of a globe representing the earth.

¹**aye** or ¹**ay** (ā), *adv.* always; forever;

²**aye** or ²**ay** (ī), *adv.* yes; even so:—*n.* [*pl.* ayes (īz)], a vote, or one who votes, in the affirmative.

Ayr-shire (âr′shĭr; âr′shẽr), *n.* one of a breed of dairy cattle, raised in Scotland.

a-za-le-a (a-zā′lē-a; a-zāl′ya), *n.* a shrub of the heath family, with luxuriant, brilliant flowers.

A-zer-bai-jan (ä′zẽr-bī-jän′; ăz′ẽr-bī-jän′), a small republic (cap. Baku) in southwestern Asia, part of the U.S.S.R., lying on the west coast of the Caspian Sea (map 12).

A-zores (a-zôrz′), a group of Portuguese islands in the northern Atlantic Ocean (map 2).

AZALEA (⅛)

Az-tec (ăz′tĕk), *n.* **1,** a member of the race which founded the Mexican Empire, conquered by Cortes in 1519; **2,** the language of this race:—*adj.* relating to the Aztecs.

az-ure (ăzh′ẽr; ā′zhẽr), *adj.* sky blue:—*n.* **1,** clear blue sky; **2,** a sky-blue color.

B

B, b (bē), *n.* [*pl.* B's, b's], **1,** the second letter of the alphabet, following A; **2,** the seventh tone in the major scale of C.

B.A. or **A.B.** abbreviation *bachelor of arts.*

baa (bä), *v.i.* [baaed (bäd), baa-ing], to bleat or cry as a sheep or lamb:—*n.* the bleating of a sheep or lamb.

Ba-al (bā′ăl), *n.* **1,** in the Bible, a sun god of the ancient Phoenicians, worshiped by the Jews; **2,** a false god or idol.

bab-ble (băb′l), *v.i.* [bab-bled, bab-bling], **1,** to talk indistinctly or imperfectly; **2,** to talk childishly or foolishly; **3,** to chatter;

also, to make a murmuring sound:—*v.t.* **1,** to utter indistinctly or imperfectly; as, he *babbled* his words; **2,** to blab (secrets):—*n.* **1,** foolish talk; **2,** a confused prattle or continuous murmuring.—*n.* **bab′bler.**

babe (bāb), *n.* a young child; baby.

Ba-bel (bā′bĕl), *n.* in the Bible, the city and tower where the confusion of languages took place (Genesis 11):—**babel,** tumult; confusion, as of many persons talking at once.

Bab el Man-deb (băb′ ĕl män′dĕb; băb′ ĕl măn′dĕb), a strait between Africa and the southern tip of Arabia (map 14).

ba·boon (bă-bōon′), *n.* a kind of large, Old World monkey, usually with a short tail and a doglike face.

ba·by (bā′bĭ), *n.* [*pl.* babies], a child in arms; a young or small child.—*adj.* **ba′-by-ish.**

ba·by·hood (bā′bĭ-hŏŏd), *n.* the condition of being a baby; also, the time during which one is a baby.

BABOON (₃₀)
Sacred baboon of the Egyptians.

Bab·y·lon (băb′ĭ-lŏn), an ancient powerful city on the Euphrates River in western Asia, capital of Babylonia (map 15): now applied to any great, rich, or wicked city.

Bab·y·lo·ni·a (băb′ĭ-lō′nĭ-à), an ancient empire of western Asia, in the valley of the Euphrates. Its modern name is *Iraq* (map 15).—*adj.* and *n.* **Bab′y-lo′ni-an.**

ba·by sit·ter, one who cares for a child, usually for a short period of time.

bac·cha·nal (băk′à-năl), *adj.* having to do with Bacchus, the ancient god of wine; wild; riotous; as, a *bacchanal* feast:—*n.* **1,** a follower of Bacchus; **2,** a drunken reveler; **3,** a dance or song in honor of Bacchus; **4,** a drinking party; orgy.—*adj.* and *n.* **bac′cha·na′li·an.**

Bac·chus (băk′ŭs), *n.* in mythology, the god of wine: the same as *Dionysus.*

Bach (bäkh), Johann Sebastian (1685–1750), a German organist and·composer.

bach·e·lor (băch′ĕ-lẽr; băch′lẽr), *n.* **1,** a man who has never married; **2,** one who has taken the first degree at a college or university; as, a *bachelor* of arts or of science.

bach·e·lor's–but·ton (băch′lẽrz=bŭt′n), *n.* a garden plant of the chrysanthemum family; the cornflower.

ba·cil·lus (bà-sĭl′ŭs), *n.* [*pl.* bacilli (bà-sĭl′ī)], any of a large number of tiny one-celled bodies, usually rodlike in shape, visible only under the microscope. The bacilli form a class of bacteria; some cause disease, many are harmless.

back (băk), *n.* **1,** in man and other animals having a backbone, the hinder or upper surface of the body from the neck to the end of the backbone; also, the corresponding part in other animals; **2,** the opposite of the front; the hinder part; as, the kitchen is at the *back* of the house; **3,** the side of anything away from, or out of sight of, the beholder; as, put the inkstand at the *back* of the desk; **4,** the part of a book where the leaves are sewed in; **5,** the part of a knife, sword, etc., opposite to the cutting edge; **6,** the vertical part of a chair, bench, or the like, against which one can lean

when sitting; as, the *back* of a sofa:—*v.t.* **1,** to move backward or to the rear; as, to *back* a car; **2,** to second or support; as, we *back* Jones for president; he *backed* up his proposal with a donation:—*v.i.* to go or move backward or to the rear:—*adj.* **1,** lying or being behind as to time, situation, or direction; as, *back* numbers of a magazine; a *back* porch; **2,** overdue; in arrears; as, *back* pay:—*adv.* **1,** to or toward the rear; **2,** to or toward a former place or state; as, to bring *back* a borrowed book; *back* to normal conditions; **3,** to or toward former time past; **4,** in return; as, to pay *back.*

back·bite (băk′bīt′), *v.t.* [*p.t.* backbit (-bĭt′), *p.p.* backbit·ten (-bĭt′n) or backbit, *p.pr.* backbit·ing], to speak evil of (one who is absent).—*n.* **back′bit′er.**

back·bone (băk′bōn′), *n.* **1,** the spine; **2,** firmness; moral courage.

back·er (băk′ẽr), *n.* one who supports another with money or influence; also, one who ventures money on a contest or a contestant.

back·field (băk′fēld′), *n.* in football, the players behind the line in the offensive line-up.

back·fire (băk′fīr′), *n.* **1,** in a gasoline engine, an explosion of gas that occurs at the wrong time, or in the wrong part of the engine; **2,** a fire started to check a prairie fire by burning a space in its path.

back·gam·mon (băk′găm′ŭn; băk′găm′ŭn), *n.* a game played with dice by two persons with fifteen pieces each, on a specially marked board.

back·ground (băk′ground′), *n.* **1,** the distant parts of any scene or landscape, or the corresponding part of a picture; **2,** a surface upon which patterns or designs are drawn, etc.; **3,** a place out of sight; as, she modestly kept herself in the *background.*

back·hand (băk′hănd′), *n.* **1,** backward-slanting handwriting; **2,** a backhanded stroke:—*adj.* [also **back-hand-ed** (băk′hăn′dĕd)], **1,** made with the back of the hand, or with the hand turned backward; as, a *backhand* stroke; **2,** not straightforward; insincere; as, a *backhanded* warning.

back·ing (băk′ĭng), *n.* **1,** anything used to support, form, or line, a back; **2,** aid or support given to a person or cause.

back·log (băk′lŏg′), *n.* a log at the back of a hearth fire; **2,** *Colloquial,* a reserve supply; as, a *backlog* of orders.

back·slide (băk′slīd′; băk′slīd′), *v.i.* [*p.t.* backslid (-slĭd′), *p.p.* backslid or back-slid-den (-slĭd′n), *p.pr.* backslid-ing], to

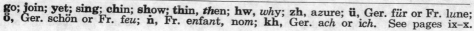

BACKHAND
Tennis player delivering back-handed stroke.

slip back, especially to slip away from a religion, habit, or the like.—*n.* **back′slid′er.**

back-stay (băk′stā′), *n.* a rope extending backward from a mast to the side of a ship, to support the mast.

back-stroke (băk′strōk′), *n.* a style of swimming in which the swimmer moves through the water on his back.

back-ward (băk′wẽrd), *adj.* **1,** directed to the rear; as, a *backward* look; **2,** retiring; bashful; **3,** behind in learning or progress; dull; as, a *backward* pupil; **4,** behindhand; late; as, a *backward* season.—*n.* **back′ward-ness.**

back-ward (băk′wẽrd) or **back-wards** (băk′wẽrdz), *adv* **1,** toward the rear; **2,** with the back coming first or foremost; as, to go into a room *backward;* **3,** in a reverse direction; as, turn the clock *backward.*

back-wa-ter (băk′wô′tẽr), *n.* **1** water held by a dam, or a current turned back by a rising tide; **2,** an unprogressive community.

back-woods (băk′wŏŏdz′), *n.pl.* forests or partly cleared land on the outskirts of a new settlement.—*n.* **back′woods′man.**

Ba-con (bā′kŭn), **1,** Francis (1561-1626), an English writer and philosopher; **2,** Roger (1214-94), called *Friar Bacon,* an English monk and scientist, inventor of spectacles.

ba-con (bā′kŭn), *n.* the salted and dried or smoked flesh of the hog, especially that from the back and sides.

bac-te-ri-a (băk-tĭr′ĭ-á), *n.pl.* [*sing.* bacterium (băk-tĭr′ĭ-ŭm)!, a widely distributed group of tiny plants, invisible without a microscope, living on plant and animal tissues, dead or alive, and causing a great variety of processes and conditions affecting vegetable and animal life,

BACTERIA
(greatly magnified)

as decay, fermentation, soil enrichment, and disease.—*adj.* **bac-te′ri-al.**

bac-te-ri-ol-o-gy (băk-tĭr′ĭ-ŏl′ō-jĭ), *n.* the study of bacteria.—*adj.* **bac-te/ri-o-log′-i-cal.**—*n.* **bac-te/ri-ol′o-gist.**

bac-te-ri-um (băk-tĭr′ĭ-ŭm), *n.* singular of *bacteria.* See **bacteria.**

bad (băd), *adj.* [*comp.* worse, *superl.* worst], **1,** evil; morally wicked; vicious; as, *bad* company; **2,** of poor quality; defective; as, *bad* eggs; *bad* housing conditions; **3,** legally worthless, as a coin; **4,** severe; as, a *bad* cold; **5,** ill; sick:—*n.* that which is wrong, defective, corrupting, or the like.—*adv.* **bad′ly.**—*n.* **bad′ness.**

Syn., adj. wicked, naughty, wrong.

bade (băd), past tense of *bid* except when it means to offer (a price).

Ba-den (bä′děn), a state (cap. Freiburg) in West Germany.

Ba-den–Po-well (bā′děn-pō′ĕl), Sir Robert S. S. (1857-1941), an English general who founded the Boy Scouts.

badge (băj), *n.* a distinctive mark, sign, or token worn to denote occupation or achievements; as, a policeman's *badge;* the Roman toga was the *badge* of manhood.

badg-er (băj′ẽr), *n.* a hairy, flesh-eating, burrowing animal, about two feet long:—*v.t.* to tease; worry; pester: from the former practice of baiting badgers for sport.

BADGER (⅒)

Bad Lands, a large barren region in South Dakota, extending into Nebraska.

bad–tem-pered (băd′-těm′pẽrd), *adj.* peevish; easily angered.

Baf-fin Bay (băf′ĭn), a body of water between Greenland and Baffin Island, northeast of Canada (map 4).

baf-fle (băf′l), *v.t.* [baf-fled, baf-fling], to check or interfere with (a person) by placing difficulties in his way; hence, to foil, check, or hamper (efforts or plans).

bag (băg), *n.* **1,** a sack; pouch; wallet; **2,** the amount contained in a sack; as, a *bag* of grain; **3,** all the game secured by a sportsman in a day:—*v.t.* [bagged bag-ging], **1,** to enclose in a bag; **2,** to secure or capture; as, to *bag* game:—*v.i.* to bulge; hang down like a full bag.

ba-gasse (bá-găs′), *n.* the crushed pulp of sugar cane or sugar beets remaining after the juice is extracted for making sugar.

bag-a-telle (băg′á-těl′), *n.* **1,** a trifle; a matter of no importance; **2,** a kind of game.

Bag-dad (băg′dăd) or **Bagh-dad** (băg-däd′), capital of Iraq, western Asia, on the Tigris River (map 15).

bag-gage (băg′ĭj), *n.* **1,** the tents, clothing, utensils, etc., of an army; **2,** the trunks, packages, etc., which a traveler takes with him; luggage.

bag-gy (băg′ĭ), *adj.* [bag-gi-er, bag-gi-est], having a loose or flabby appearance.

bag-pipe (băg′pīp′), *n.* a shrill Scottish musical instrument consisting of a leather bag

BAGPIPE

from which air is forced by the player's arm into pipes.—*n.* **bag′pip′er.**

Ba·ha·mas (bȧ-hā′mȧz; bȧ-hä′mȧz), a group of islands (cap. Nassau) just off the lower end of Florida (map 10).

Ba·hi·a (bȧ-ē′ȧ), a state (cap. Salvador) of eastern Brazil; also, former name of capital (map 11).

baht (bät), *n.* a silver coin, the monetary unit of Thailand. (See Table, page 943.)

Bai·kal, Lake (bī-käl′), a large freshwater lake in southeastern Siberia (map 15).

¹**bail** (bāl), *v.t.* in law: **1,** to turn over (a defendant or prisoner) to persons who promise to be responsible for his appearance in court when summoned; as, the magistrate *bailed* the accused thief to Mr. Smith; **2,** to obtain the release of (a person) by promising to pay a certain sum if he does not appear in court or when wanted; as, Mr. Smith *bailed* his friend out of jail: —*n.* in law: **1,** temporary freedom given a defendant or prisoner, said to be released *on bail,* when security is entered for his appearance when wanted; **2,** security so given.

²**bail** (bāl), *v.t.* **1,** to dip or throw (water) out of a boat with a cup, bucket, or the like; **2,** to empty (a boat) by this process:—**bail out,** leap, with a parachute, from a flying aircraft:—*n.* the dipper used in bailing.

³**bail** (bāl), *n.* **1,** a semicircular support, as for the cover of a wagon; **2,** the handle of a pail, kettle, or the like.

bail·iff (bā′lĭf), *n.* **1,** a sheriff's officer or constable; **2,** in England, an overseer on an estate.

bait (bāt), *n.* any substance, especially real or sham food, used to entice or allure fish or other animals with a view to catching them:—*v.t.* **1,** to prepare (a fishhook, trap, or snare) by placing bait so as to attract an animal; **2,** to torment or worry with dogs; as, bears were formerly *baited* for sport; to tease or annoy (a person) so as to make him angry.

baize (bāz), *n.* a coarse woolen stuff with a long nap, used for table covers.

bake (bāk), *v.t.* and *v.i.* [baked, bak-ing], **1,** to cook or be cooked in an oven; as, she is *baking* cakes; the cake is *baking;* **2,** to dry or harden by dry heat. —*n.* **bak′er.**

bak·er·y (bā′kẽr-ĭ), *n.* [*pl.* bakeries], a place where bread, cakes, etc., are made or sold.

bak·ing (bā′kĭng), *n.* the quantity of bread, pies, etc., made at one time.

bak·ing pow·der, a white powder used to bring about the quick rising of biscuits, cakes, etc.

bak·ing so·da, bicarbonate of soda.

Ba·ku (bȧ-kōō′), the capital of Azerbaijan, on the Caspian Sea (map 12).

bal. abbreviation for *balance.*

Ba·laam (bā′lăm), in the Bible, a prophet who was rebuked by his ass (Numbers 22:28).

Bal·a·kla·va (băl′ȧ-klä′vȧ; bȧ-lȧ-klä′vȧ), a small seaport in the Crimea, Russia: site of the battle described by Tennyson in "The Charge of the Light Brigade."

bal·ance (băl′ăns), *n.* **1,** an apparatus for weighing, consisting in its simplest form of a beam pivoted at its middle, with hooks, platforms, or pans suspended from the ends; **2,** the condition of a scale when the beam is about horizontal; hence, equality of any opposing forces; equilibrium or steadiness; **3,** general good sense; sanity; **4,** an equality between the two sides of an account; also, the excess shown on either side; **5,** in a watch, the wheel which regulates the rate of running:—*v.t.* [balanced, balanc-ing], **1,** to weigh on a balance; **2,** to weigh in the mind; hence, to compare or estimate; as, we *balanced* the good against the bad; **3,** to find out the difference between the debits and credits of (an account); **4,** to steady: —*v.i.* **1,** to be of the same weight, force, or amount as something else; as, the advantages of the two plans *balance;* **2,** to keep one's balance.

BALANCE, def. 1

Bal·bo·a (băl-bō′ȧ; bäl-bō′ä), (1475–1517), a Spanish soldier who discovered the Pacific by crossing the Isthmus of Panama.

bal·bo·a (băl-bō′ä), *n.* the monetary unit of Panama. (See Table, page 943.)

bal·brig·gan (băl-brĭg′ăn), *n.* a knitted cotton fabric for underwear.

bal·co·ny (băl′kō-nĭ), *n.* [*pl.* balconies], a platform or gallery built to jut out from a wall, and enclosed by a balustrade or railing. It may be either on the outside or the inside of a building.

bald (bôld), *adj.* **1,** bare of hair; **2,** without the natural or usual covering of hair, feathers, fur, or foliage, upon the head, top, or summit; **3,** of birds, having a white head; as, a *bald* eagle; **4,** unadorned; bare; without disguise; as, a *bald* statement of the facts. —*adv.* **bald′ly.** —*n.* **bald′ness.**

BALCONY

bal·dric (bôl′drĭk), *n.* a broad belt, often richly decorated, worn around the waist or over a shoulder, often to support a bugle or sword.

Bâle (bäl), a city in Switzerland. See **Basel**.

bale (bāl), *n.* a large and closely pressed package of merchandise, prepared for storage or transportation: — *v.t.* [baled, bal-ing], to make into bales; as, to *bale* cotton or hay.

Bal·e·ar·ic Is·lands (băl′ē-ăr′ĭk), a group of Spanish islands in the Mediterranean (map 12).

bale·ful (bāl′fŏŏl), *adj.* full of deadly intent; destructive.—*adv.* **bale′ful·ly**.

Ba·li (bä′lē), an island lying east of the island of Java (map 15).

balk (bôk), *v.i.* to stop short and refuse to go, as a stubborn horse:—*v.t.* to hinder or check; prevent (a person) from doing something:—*n.* a barrier or hindrance.

Bal·kan Pen·in·su·la (bôl′kăn; băl-kän′), a peninsula in southeastern Europe, between the Adriatic and Black seas, containing the *Balkan States*, which are Rumania, Yugoslavia, Bulgaria, Albania, Greece, and European Turkey (map 12).

balk·y (bô′kĭ), *adj.* [balk-i-er, balk-i-est], likely to balk; stubborn; obstinate; as, a *balky* mule.

¹**ball** (bôl), *n.* **1**, a round or roundish body or mass; a sphere; especially, such a body, solid or inflated, used in playing a game; **2**, a bullet or other missile shot from firearms; **3**, a game played with a ball; **4**, in baseball, a pitched ball, not struck at, which does not pass over the plate between the levels of the batsman's shoulders and knees:—*v.t.* and *v.i.* to form into a ball.

²**ball** (bôl), *n.* a large, formal, social gathering for dancing.

bal·lad (băl′ăd), *n.* **1**, a short narrative poem, suitable for reciting or singing; **2**, a simple song, often sentimental.

bal·last (băl′ȧst), *n.* **1**, heavy material carried to give steadiness or balance, as in a boat or a balloon; **2**, stones in the spaces between the ties of a railway track; **3**, that which gives strength to the character:—*v.t.* to steady with a weight; as, to *ballast* the bow of a canoe with a rock.

ball bear·ing, a bearing in which a shaft turns smoothly upon balls of metal which turn with it; also, any one of the balls.—*adj.* **ball′-bear′ing**.

bal·let (băl′ā; bă-lā′), *n.* **1**, an elaborate and artistic dance; **2**, the company of persons who perform the dance.

bal·loon (bă-lōōn′), *n.* a large airtight bag of prepared silk or other material, which when filled with a gas that is lighter than air, such as hydrogen or helium, rises and floats in the air:—**balloon tire**, a large automobile tire that is not filled very full of air, so that it rides easily:—*v.i.* **1**, to go up in a balloon; **2**, to expand or swell out.—*n.* **bal·loon′ist**.

BALDRIC (A)

BALLOON

bal·lot (băl′ŭt), *n.* **1**, a ball, ticket, or paper used in voting; **2**, the system of secret voting by use of a printed form; **3**, the act of voting; also, the total number of votes cast:—*v.i.* to vote by ballot.

balm (bäm), *n.* **1**, an oily, gummy substance coming from certain trees or shrubs, used for healing or soothing; balsam; **2**, anything that heals or soothes; as, praise was *balm* to his wounded vanity.—*adj.* **balm′y**.—*n.* **balm′i·ness**.

bal·sa (bôl′sȧ; bäl′sȧ), *n.* **1**, a tree of tropical America, having wood lighter than cork; **2**, a raft or float of the tropics; **3**, a life raft, made over two hollow cylinders of wood or metal.

bal·sam (bôl′săm), *n.* **1**, an oily, fragrant substance obtained from certain trees or shrubs, and used for medicine or in perfumery; balm; **2**, a kind of evergreen tree or shrub, yielding an oily, resinous substance; **3**, a flowering plant, with flowers like those of the lady's-slipper.

Bal·tic Sea (bôl′tĭk), a sea in northern Europe, east of Denmark (map 12).

Bal·tic States (bôl′tĭk), the states on the eastern coast of the Baltic Sea: Estonia, Latvia, and Lithuania (map 12).

Bal·ti·more (bôl′tĭ-môr), a city of Maryland (map 6).

Ba·lu·chi·stan (bȧ-lōō′chĭ-stän′), a state (cap. Kalat) in western Pakistan.

bal·us·ter (băl′ŭs-tẽr), *n.* one of a set of small pillars that support the handrail of a parapet or balustrade.

bal·us·trade (băl′ŭs-trād′), *n.* a row of small pillars, or balusters, topped by a protective rail, as along the edge of a bridge, balcony, or staircase.

BALUSTRADE

Bal·zac (băl′zăk; bȧl′zȧk′), Honoré de (1799–1850), a French novelist.

bam·boo (băm-bōō′), *n.* a tropical, tree-like plant of the grass family, with thick jointed stems, used for poles and canes.

ban (băn), *n.* **1**, the formal forbidding of an act, as by law; as, a *ban* on lotteries; **2**, condemnation, as by public opinion; **3**, a decree of excommunication by the

āte, āorta, râre, căt, ȧsk, fär, ăllow, sofȧ; ēve, ĕvent, ĕll, writẽr, novĕl; bīte, pĭn; nō, ōbey, ôr, dŏg, tŏp, cŏllide; ūnit, ūnite, bûrn, cŭt, focŭs; nōon, fŏŏt; mound; coin;

church:—*v.t.* [banned, ban-ning], **1,** to curse; call evil down upon; **2,** to prohibit; forbid; as, noise is *banned* in the library.

ba-nal (bā′năl; bȧ-năl′; băn′ăl), *adj.* commonplace; trivial; hackneyed; trite; as, "It isn't the heat, it's the humidity," is a *banal* remark.

ba-nal-i-ty (bȧ-năl′ĭ-tĭ), *n.* [*pl.* banalities], a commonplace remark or idea.

ba-nan-a (bȧ-năn′ȧ; bȧ-nä′nȧ), *n.* a tropical tree-like plant which grows 20 feet high and bears a long, hanging cluster of sweet fruit, much used for food; also, the fruit.

BAMBOO

¹band (bănd), *n.* **1,** a thin, flat, flexible strip used for binding or supporting; a strip of trimming or lining, as on a hat or a sleeve; **2,** a stripe; as, a *band* of white around a pole:—*v.t.* to tie or mark with a band.

²band (bănd), *n.* **1,** a company united by a common purpose; as, a *band* of robbers or soldiers; **2,** flock; herd; as, a *band* of sheep; **3,** a company of musicians, especially one playing music suitable for outdoors:—*v.t.* and *v.i.* to unite; bring together into a company.

band-age (băn′dĭj), *n.* a strip of cloth used in dressing and binding wounds, sprains, etc.:—*v.t.* [bandaged, bandag-ing], to dress, cover, or bind, as wounds, with a strip of any soft material.

BANANA AND FRUIT

ban-dan-na or **ban-dan-a** (băn-dăn′ȧ), *n.* a large, colorful silk or cotton handkerchief.

BANDAGES
Method of bandaging a finger, a hand, and an ankle.

band-box (bănd′bŏks′), *n.* a light pasteboard box for holding hats.

ban-dit (băn′dĭt), *n.* [*pl.* bandits or banditti (băn-dĭt′ĭ)], an outlaw; robber.

ban-dy (băn′dĭ), *v.t.* [bandied, bandy-ing], **1,** to knock to and fro, as a ball; **2,** to give and take; exchange; as, to *bandy* words.

ban-dy–leg-ged (băn′dĭ-lĕg′ĕd; ‑lĕgd′), *adj.* bowlegged; having legs bent outward at the knees.

bane (bān), *n.* **1,** originally, poison: still used in names of plants; as, wolfs*bane;* **2,** a cause of ruin or destruction; curse; as, drink is the *bane* of his life.

bane-ful (bān′fŏol), *adj.* harmful; destructive; deadly.—*adv.* **bane′ful-ly.**

¹bang (băng), *v.t.* **1,** to beat noisily; thump; as, to *bang* an anvil or a piano; **2,** to shut or put down noisily; as, to *bang* a door; to *bang* down a book:—*v.i.* **1,** to strike a noisy blow; as, to *bang* upon a piano or a door; **2,** to make a loud or sudden noise; as, the gun *banged:*—*n.* **1,** a heavy, noisy blow; whack; as, I gave the pan a *bang;* **2,** a loud, sudden noise; an explosive sound:—*adv.* suddenly; with a noisy sound; as, *bang* went another tire.

²bang (băng), *v.t.* to cut (the hair over the forehead) straight across:—**bangs,** *n.pl.* or, sometimes, **bang,** *sing.* hair cut to a short fringe over the forehead.

Ban-ga-lore (băng′gȧ-lôr′), a city in southern India (map 15).

Bang-kok (băng′kŏk′; băng′-kŏk), capital city of Thailand, in southeastern Asia (map 15).

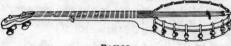

BANGS
Child's hair cut in bangs.

ban-gle (băng′gl), *n.* **1,** an ornamental ring worn upon the wrists and ankles in India and Africa; **2,** one of several slender bracelets worn together.

ban-ian (băn′yăn), *n.* an East Indian tree; the banyan. See **banyan.**

ban-ish (băn′ĭsh), *v.t.* **1,** to drive out; condemn to exile; expel; as, to *banish* an alien from a country; **2,** to drive out of the mind; as, to *banish* care or fear.

ban-ish-ment (băn′ĭsh-mĕnt), *n.* expulsion from a country; exile.

ban-is-ter (băn′ĭs-tẽr), *n.* a baluster:—**banisters,** a balustrade along a stairway.

ban-jo (băn′jō), *n.* [*pl.* banjos], a stringed musical instrument somewhat like a

BANJO

guitar, having a long neck, and a body like a tambourine.—*n.* **ban′jo-ist.**

¹bank (băngk), *n.* **1,** a ridge of earth; **2,** a heap, mound, or large mass; as, a *bank* of clouds or snow; **3,** the land at the edge or margin of a stream; **4,** a shallow place in the sea or at the mouth of a river; a shoal;

5, a slope:—*v.t.* **1**, to cover (a fire) with ashes or packed coal, to prevent rapid burning; **2**, to pile up; as, he *banked* leaves against the wall:—*v.i.* in aeronautics, to tip an airplane when going round a curve.

²**bank** (băngk), *n.* **1**, a rowers' bench in a galley; also, a tier or row of oars; **2**, a row or rank of keys, as on an organ.

³**bank** (băngk), *n.* an institution which receives money from its depositors for safekeeping, lends money at interest, and in many ways assists in transactions requiring the transfer of money:—*v.t.* to place (money) in a bank:—*v.i.* **1**, to have an account with a bank; **2**, *Colloquial*, to rely; count; as, I *bank* on him to do his part.

bank-er (băngk′ẽr), *n.* a person engaged in the business of banking.

bank-ing (băngk′ĭng), *n.* the business of lending, issuing, or caring for money.

bank note, a piece of paper resembling government paper money, and used as money, but actually issued by a bank.

bank-rupt (băngk′rŭpt), *n.* a person who is legally declared to be unable to pay his debts, and whose property is divided among his creditors in proportion to their claims:—*adj.* unable to meet one's debts; insolvent:—*v.t.* to make poor or insolvent; as, the hard times *bankrupted* him.

bank-rupt-cy (băngk′rŭpt-sĭ), *n.* [*pl.* bankruptcies], the state of being legally insolvent, or unable to pay one's debts.

ban-ner (băn′ẽr), *n.* a piece of cloth attached to a pole, and usually worked with some device or motto; an ensign, standard, or flag, as of a state or nation:—*adj.* unusually good; as, a *banner* year.

ban-nock (băn′ŭk), *n.* a thick homemade cake or loaf, usually made without yeast, baked on a hot stone or griddle. The bannock is popular in Scotland.

banns (bănz), *n.pl.* notice, given in church, of a proposed marriage.

ban-quet (băng′kwĕt), *n.* an elaborate or costly feast or large formal dinner:—*v.t.* and *v.i.* to feed or dine (a person) elaborately; to feast.

Ban-quo (băng′kwō), *n.* in Shakespeare's "Macbeth," a brave Scottish noble, who haunts his slayer, Macbeth.

ban-shee (băn′shē), *n.* in the folklore of Ireland and Scotland, a spirit whose wailing was believed to foretell death.

Ban-tam (băn′tăm), *n.* a kind of domestic fowl or chicken, of very small size (see illustration next column):—**bantam**, a very small, often absurdly spirited, person.

ban-ter (băn′tẽr), *n.* good-natured teasing:—*v.t.* to make fun of; tease with good humor.—*adv.* **ban′ter-ing-ly**.

Syn., *n.* chaff, mockery, ridicule, jeering, raillery.

ban-yan or **ban-ian** (băn′yăn), *n.* an East Indian tree, the branches of which send roots down to the ground, so as to form new trunks.

ba-o-bab (bā′ō-băb), *n.* an African tree with an enormously thick trunk and an edible fruit resembling a gourd, called *monkey bread*.

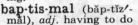

BANTAM
A breed of fighting Bantam.

bap-tism (băp′tĭzm), *n.* **1**, the sacrament of immersion or sprinkling with water, symbolizing the washing away of sin, and admitting to membership in a Christian church; **2**, an experience or trial that purifies; as, a *baptism* of suffering.

bap-tis-mal (băp-tĭz′măl), *adj.* having to do with baptism; as, *baptismal* water.

BANYAN TREE

Bap-tist (băp′tĭst), *n.* a member of that church which believes that Christians should be baptized only after they have become adults, and then by complete immersion rather than by sprinkling.

bap-tis-ter-y (băp′tĭs-tẽr-ĭ), *n.* [*pl.* baptisteries], that part of a church building in which baptism is performed. Also spelled **bap′tist-ry**.

bap-tize (băp-tīz′), *v.t.* [baptized, baptizing], **1**, to sprinkle with water, or immerse in water, as a religious ceremony, especially in admitting to a Christian church; **2**, to purify; **3**, to christen; name; as, the boy was *baptized* John.

bar (bär), *n.* **1**, a rigid piece of wood, metal, or other solid matter, long in proportion to its thickness; **2**, a barrier; **3**, a bank of sand, gravel, or the like, under water, obstructing the passage of ships; **4**, the place in court where prisoners are stationed for trial or sentence; also, the court itself; **5**, those who are permitted to try cases in court; lawyers as a class; **6**, a counter over which liquor is sold as a beverage, or a room containing such a counter; **7**, a band or stripe; as, a *bar* of red in a border; **8**, one of the series of upright lines drawn through a staff of written music, dividing it into equal measures of time; also, the space between two such bars or lines:—*prep.* but; except; as, *bar* none:—*v.t.*

[barred, bar-ring], **1,** to fasten with a bar; **2,** to hinder; obstruct; as, the police *barred* the way.

barb (bärb), *n.* the sharp point extending backward in an arrow, fishhook, etc.:—*v.t.* to furnish with barbs.

Bar-ba-dos (bär-bā′dōz), a British island in the eastern part of the West Indies (map 10).

bar-bar-i-an (bär-bâr′ĭ-ăn), *n.* **1,** in ancient history, a foreigner; one not a Greek or a Roman, and therefore regarded as uncivilized; **2,** a person of uncultivated taste:—*adj.* rude; uncivilized; savage.

BARB (B) on fishhook.

bar-bar-ic (bär-băr′ĭk), *adj.* belonging to, or characteristic of, uncivilized people; as, *barbaric* cruelty; *barbaric* splendor.

bar-ba-rism (bär′bȧ-rĭzm), *n.* **1,** the state of being uncivilized; **2,** rudeness; ignorance of art and literature; **3,** a word or expression not in good use.

bar-bar-i-ty (bär-băr′ĭ-tĭ), *n.* [*pl.* barbarities], brutal or inhuman conduct.

Bar-ba-ros-sa (bär′bȧ-rŏs′ȧ), a surname of *Frederick I* (1121–1190), emperor of Germany and the Holy Roman Empire.

bar-ba-rous (bär′bȧ-rŭs), *adj.* **1,** uncivilized; outlandish; rude; **2,** of language, crude; unpolished; **3,** cruel; inhuman.—*adv.* **bar′ba-rous-ly.**

Syn. brutal, savage, merciless.

Bar-ba-ry (bär′bȧ-rĭ), the Mohammedan countries of northern Africa, except Egypt.

bar-be-cue (bär′bē-kū), *n.* **1,** the carcass of an ox, pig, etc., roasted whole; **2,** an out-of-door feast at which animals are roasted whole:—*v.t.* [barbecued, barbecu-ing], to dress and roast whole, as an ox.

barbed(bärbd),*adj.*having barbs:—**barbed wire,** twisted wire with sharp points.

bar-ber (bär′bĕr), *n.* one whose business is shaving, haircutting, and hairdressing.

bar-ber-ry (bär′bĕr′ĭ), *n.* [*pl.* barberries], a prickly shrub bearing berries which turn red in the fall; also, the berry.

Bar-ce-lo-na (bär′sĕ-lō′nȧ), a province of eastern Spain, on the Mediterranean Sea; also, a city; its capital (map 12).

bard (bärd), *n.* in ancient times, a poet and singer who made and sang verses about heroes and heroic deeds; hence, any poet.

bare (bâr), *adj.* **1,** not covered; as, a *bare* hillside; especially, not covered with clothing; as, *bare* arms; **2,** unadorned; simple; plainly or scantily furnished; as, *bare* lodgings; **3,** scanty; mere; as, he earned a *bare* living:—*v.t.* [bared, bar-ing], to uncover; expose.—*n.* **bare′ness.**

bare-back (bâr′băk′), *adj.* and *adv.* on a horse without a saddle.

bare-faced (bâr′fāst′), *adj.* unconcealed; bold; impudent; as, *barefaced* frauds.

bare-foot (bâr′fŏŏt′), *adj.* and *adv.* with the feet bare.

bare-head-ed (bâr′hĕd′ĕd), *adj.* having no hat or other covering on the head.

bare-ly (bâr′lĭ), *adv.* **1,** only just; hence, hardly; scarcely; as, he had *barely* enough time; **2,** scantily; poorly; as, the room was furnished *barely*.

bar-gain (bär′gĭn), *n.* **1,** an agreement on the terms of a deal; as, they closed the *bargain* at $5 a load; **2,** something offered, bought, or sold, at a low price:—*v.i.* to make a bargain or trade; also, to discuss the terms of an agreement; haggle:—**bargain for,** to be prepared for; expect.

Syn., n. agreement, contract.

barge (bärj), *n.* **1,** a large, roomy, flat-bottomed vessel, used for carrying freight or passengers; **2,** a large boat of a warship, used by a flag officer.—*n.* **barge′man.**

bar-i-tone or **bar-y-tone** (băr′ĭ-tōn), *n.* a male voice between tenor and bass; also, a person who has such a voice:—*adj.* having, or suited to, a baritone voice.

bar-i-um (bâr′ĭ-ŭm; bā′rĭ-ŭm), *n.* a soft, silver-gray metallic element.

¹bark (bärk), *n.* the outer covering of trees and other woody plants:—*v.t.* to strip bark or skin from; as, to *bark* a tree; *bark* one's shin.

BARK, def. 1

²bark or **barque** (bärk), *n.* **1,** a kind of three-masted vessel; **2,** *Poetic,* any small ship.

³bark (bärk), *n.* the sound made by a dog:—*v.i.* to utter a bark, as a dog.

bark-en-tine (bär′kĕn-tēn), *n.* a kind of three-masted vessel. (See illustration under *ship.*)

bar-ley (bär′lĭ), *n.* **1,** a grain used as a food and in the manufacture of malt liquors; **2,** the plant yielding the grain.

Bar-ley-corn, John (bär′lĭ-kôrn′), a humorous name for intoxicating drink.

BARLEY

barn (bärn), *n.* a farm building for housing livestock, keeping tools, and storing hay, grain, and other produce.

bar-na-cle (bär/na-kl), *n.* **1**, a small sea animal living in a white shell and fastening itself to rocks or the bottoms of ships; **2**, a hanger-on.

barn-yard (bärn/-yärd/), *n.* the yard around a barn.

Ba-ro-da (ba-rō/da), a former state of west central India; also, a city (map 15).

BARNACLES
Common barnacles attached to a stick of wood.

ba-rom-e-ter (ba-rŏm/e-tēr), *n.* an instrument for measuring the pressure of the air, used in showing height above sea level and in forecasting weather.—*adj.* **bar/o-met/ric** (băr/ō-mět/-rĭk); **bar/o-met/ri-cal.**

bar-on (băr/ŭn), *n.* **1**, in English history, one who held an estate directly from the king; **2**, in Great Britain and other countries, a noble of the lowest rank within the nobility; also, the rank itself.—*n.fem.* **bar/on-ess.**

bar-on-et (băr/ŭn-ĕt), *n.* a rank of honor between baron and knight; also, a person holding this rank.

BAROMETER

ba-ro-ni-al (ba-rō/nĭ-ăl), *adj.* pertaining to a baron.

bar-o-ny (băr/ō-nĭ), *n.* [*pl.* baronies], the rank or landed property of a baron.

ba-roque (ba-rōk/), *adj.* **1**, odd or irregular in shape; as, a *baroque* pearl; **2**, grotesque; fantastic; **3**, ornate; oddly ornamented; as, *baroque* architecture.

BAROUCHE

ba-rouche (ba-rōōsh/), *n.* a carriage with a driver's seat, two other seats facing each other, and a folding top.

barque (bärk), *n.* a three-masted vessel. See ²**bark.**

bar-racks (băr/ăks), *n.pl.* a large structure or a row of buildings for lodging soldiers or workmen.

bar-rage (ba-räzh/; băr/äzh), *n.* a volley of missiles of any sort, such as a curtain of bursting shells, fired so as to fall just in front of advancing troops, in order to screen and protect them.

bar-rel (băr/ĕl), *n.* **1**, a round, bulging cask or vessel, greater in length than in width, usually of wood, with flat ends or heads; **2**, the quantity which a full barrel contains;

3, a tubelike part; as, the *barrel* of a gun or of a fountain pen:—*v.t.* [barreled, barreling], to put or pack in a barrel.

bar-ren (băr/ĕn), *adj.* **1**, unable to bear, or not bearing, children or young; also, not producing fruit; as, a *barren* plant; **2**, not fertile; as, *barren* land; **3**, without profit; empty; as, *barren* labor:—*n.* (usually *barrens*), a sandy, wooded tract.

bar-rette (bä-rĕt/; ba-rĕt/), *n.* a clasp or bar for holding the loose ends of a woman's hair in place.

bar-ri-cade (băr/ĭ-kād/), *n.* a fortification made of such materials as are nearest to hand, and serving to obstruct an enemy or shield a besieged party:—*v.t.* [barricad-ed, barricad-ing], to obstruct or fortify with a barricade.

Bar-rie (băr/ĭ), Sir James M. (1860–1937), a Scottish dramatist and novelist.

bar-ri-er (băr/ĭ-ēr), *n.* **1**, anything that prevents progress or approach; **2**, a fence or wall to keep people out.

bar-ring (bär/ĭng), *prep.* except for; as, *barring* delay I shall arrive Tuesday.

bar-ris-ter (băr/ĭs-tēr), *n.* in England, a lawyer who argues cases in court.

bar-room (băr/rōōm/), *n.* a room in which liquor is sold over a counter.

Bar-row (băr/ō), the northernmost point of Alaska (map 3).

¹**bar-row** (băr/ō), *n.* a flat, oblong frame with projecting handles at each corner (a *hand-barrow*), or with a wheel at one end and shafts at the other (a *wheelbarrow*), for carrying or wheeling loads.

²**bar-row** (băr/ō), *n.* in early times, a mound of earth or stones raised over a grave.

BARROW

Bart. abbreviation for *Baronet.*

Men carrying a stone on a handbarrow.

bar-ter (băr/tēr), *v.t.* to give in exchange for something; as, to *barter* oats for groceries:—*n.* the trade or exchange of one thing for another without the use of money.

Bar-thol-di (bär/tŏl/dē/), Frédéric Auguste (1834–1904), a French sculptor. The famous Statue of Liberty is his work.

Bar-thol-o-mew (bär-thŏl/ō-mū), one of the twelve apostles of Jesus.

Bar-ton (bär/tn), Clara (1821–1912), an American nurse who founded the American Red Cross Society.

bar-y-tone (băr/ĭ-tōn), *n.* and *adj.* baritone: used of a man's voice of middle range. See **baritone.**

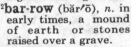

bas·al (bās'ăl), *adj.* having to do with a foundation; used as a base; as, the *basal* parts of a column; also, fundamental; basic.

ba·salt (bȧ-sôlt'; băs'ôlt), *n.* a kind of hard greenish-black rock of volcanic origin.—*adj.* **ba·sal'tic.**

BASE
as used in baseball.

¹**base** (bās), *n.* **1,** the part of a thing on which it rests; as, the *base* of a statue; **2,** one of the principal or fundamental parts of which anything is made; as, the *base* of some soups is meat stock; **3,** the line or point from which an operation starts, as in surveying or in a race; **4,** in baseball and some other games, a station or goal; **5,** a secure or fortified location used as a starting point for operations, for storage of supplies, etc.; as, a military or naval *base*; **6,** in chemistry, a substance that combines with an acid to form a salt; an alkali: —**base hit**, in baseball, a hit on which a batter gets to first base:—*v.t.* [based, bas·ing], **1,** to found; establish; as, he *bases* his hopes on news reports; his business is *based* on honesty; **2,** to set on a base; as, to *base* a statue on concrete.

BASEBALL
In lower illustration shown in section: A, cork; B, rubber; C, yarn; D, horsehide cover.

²**base** (bās), *adj.* [bas·er, bas·est], **1,** inferior in quality; as, *base* materials; **2,** mixed with inferior metal; as, a *base* coin; **3,** morally bad; mean; vile; as, kidnaping is a *base* crime; **4,** low or deep in sound; bass.— *adv.* **base'ly.** —*n.* **base'-ness.**

base·ball (bās'bôl'), *n.* **1,** a game, very popular in the U.S., played with a bat and ball by nine players on a side, on a field

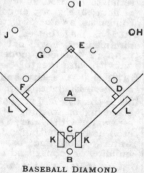

BASEBALL DIAMOND
A, pitcher; B, catcher; C, home plate; D, E, F, first, second, and third bases; G, shortstop; H, I, J, right, center, and left field; K, K, batsman's boxes; L, L, coachers' boxes.

with four stations, or bases, in the shape of a diamond; **2,** the ball used in this game.

base·board (bās'bôrd'), *n.* a wide molding running around the lower part of the wall of a room, against the floor.

base·born (bās'bôrn'), *adj.* **1,** of humble parentage; **2,** born of an unmarried mother.

Ba·sel (bä'zl), a city in northern Switzerland (map 12). Also spelled *Basle.*

base·ment (bās'mĕnt), *n.* the lowest story of a building, usually below the level of the ground.

bash·ful (băsh'fŏol), *adj.* shy; easily embarrassed; as, a *bashful* suitor.—*adv.* **bash'ful·ly.**—*n.* **bash'ful·ness.**

bas·ic (bās'ĭk), *adj.* fundamental; having to do with the base or with the essential quality of a thing; as, *basic* reasons:— **Basic English,** 850 common English words, which, with inflections and derivatives, may serve as the foundation for an international language.—*adv.* **ba'sic·al·ly.**

ba·sil·i·ca (bȧ-sĭl'ĭ-kȧ), *n.* [*pl.* basilicas], **1,** in ancient Rome, an oblong hall with columns along the two sides and a semicircular recess, or apse, at one end; **2,** a church built on such a plan.

bas·i·lisk (băs'ĭ-lĭsk; băz'ĭ-lĭsk), *n.* a fabled lizard of the African desert, whose breath and look were supposed to be fatal.

ba·sin (bā'sn), *n.* **1,** a round, wide vessel for holding water or other liquid; **2,** the quantity such a vessel will hold; **3,** a hollow or enclosed place containing water, as a dock for ships; **4,** all the land drained by a river and its branches.

ba·sis (bā'sĭs), *n.* [*pl.* bases (bā'sēz)], **1,** a reason; cause; foundation; as, a *basis* for doubt; **2,** a fundamental part or ingredient.

bask (bȧsk), *v.i.* to lie in comfortable warmth, as in the sun or before a fire.

bas·ket (bȧs'kĕt), *n.* **1,** a container made

BASKETS
1, peach basket; 2, grape basket; 3, wastebasket; 4, clothesbasket; 5, market basket.

of woven rushes, reeds, or other flexible material; **2,** the amount which such a container will hold.—*n.* **bas′ket-work′.**

bas-ket-ball (bås′kĕt-bôl′), *n.* **1,** a game played by two teams of five (or, for women, six) players each, in which a ball about ten inches in diameter must be thrown into basketlike goals placed ten feet above the floor; **2,** the ball used in the game. Also written **bas′ket ball.**

Basle (bäl), a city in Switzerland. See **Basel.**

Basque (băsk), *n.* **1,** one of a people, of uncertain origin, living in the region of the western Pyrenees in Spain and France; **2,** the language of the Basques: peculiar in that it is not allied to any European language:—*adj.* pertaining to the Basques, their country, or their language.

Bas-ra (bŭs′rȧ), a city and river port in southern Iraq (map 15).

bas-re-lief (bä′-rė-lēf′; bä′-rė-lēf′), *n.* a form of sculpture in which the figures stand out very slightly from the background.

¹bass (băs), *n.* [*pl.* bass or basses], an edible fish found in both fresh and salt water.

²bass (bās), *adj.* low-toned; deep; low in pitch; as, a *bass* note; a *bass* voice:—*n.* **1,** the lowest part in a musical composition; **2,** the lowest tones of a male voice or of an instrument; **3,** a bass viol; **4,** a singer or an instrument with a bass part.

bas-si-net (băs′ĭ-nĕt′; băs′ĭ-nĕt′), *n.* a wicker basket used as a baby's crib.

bas-soon (bă-sōōn′), *n.* a musical wind instrument of deep tone, having a long, curved mouthpiece, and a wooden tube. (See illustration at *musical instrument.*)

bass vi-ol (bās vī′ŭl), a musical instrument similar in shape to the violin, the largest in size and lowest in tone of all the stringed instruments: also called *bass.* (See illustration at *musical instrument.*)

bass-wood (băs′wŏŏd′), *n.* the American linden tree; also, the wood of this tree.

bast (băst), *n.* the tough, inner fibrous bark of various trees, as of the linden, used in making rope or matting.

bas-tard (băs′tẽrd), *n.* a child born of unmarried parents.

¹baste (bāst), *v.t.* [bast-ed, bast-ing], to sew temporarily with long, loose stitches; as, Mary *basted* her dress before she stitched it on the machine.

²baste (bāst), *v.t.* [bast-ed, bast-ing], to moisten (roasting meat), especially with its own juice, to make it tender and juicy.

bas-tille or **bas-tile** (băs-tēl′), *n.* a prison:—**the Bastille,** an old prison in Paris, destroyed by the people in 1789.

bast-ings (bās′tĭngz), *n.pl.* the long, loose stitches used in dressmaking to hold parts of a garment together before the final stitching, and later taken out.

bas-tion (băs′chŭn; băs′tĭ-ŭn), *n.* a part projecting out from the main body of a fortification.

Ba-su-to-land (bȧ-sōō′tō-lănd′), a territory near the southern tip of Africa, southeast of the Orange Free State (map 14).

BASTION
B, bastion; P, parapet; D, ditch, or moat.

¹bat (băt), *n.* **1,** a heavy stick, especially one used to strike the ball in cricket, baseball, etc.; **2,** a turn to hit; as, it is my *bat*; **3,** *Colloquial,* a hard blow; **4,** *Slang,* a carefree good time; a spree:—*v.t.* [bat-ted, bat-ting], to hit with a bat:—*v.i.* to use a bat in games; as, he *batted* once.

²bat (băt), *n.* a small animal which flies by night and feeds on fruit and insects. It has a mouselike body and wings formed of skin stretched between the fore limbs, feet, and tail.

Ba-ta-vi-a (bȧ-tā′vĭ-ȧ), former Dutch name of Indonesian capital, now named Djakarta.

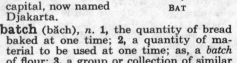
BAT

batch (băch), *n.* **1,** the quantity of bread baked at one time; **2,** a quantity of material to be used at one time; as, a *batch* of flour; **3,** a group or collection of similar things; as, a *batch* of letters.

bate (bāt), *v.t.* [bat-ed, bat-ing], **1,** to lessen; diminish; as, I will not *bate* the bill by a penny; **2,** to check; moderate; as, he looked on with *bated* breath.

Bath (båth), a city and health resort in southern England (map 13).

bath (båth), *n.* [*pl.* baths (båthz)], **1,** a cleansing or washing of the entire body, especially with water; **2,** the water, liquid, etc., used for bathing; **3,** a vessel holding water for bathing; as, a bird*bath*; **4,** a building or room fitted up for bathing.

bathe (bāth), *v.t.* [bathed, bath-ing], **1,** to wash by putting into water or other liquid; **2,** to wet; wash; as, the ocean *bathes* the shore; **3,** to surround; envelop; as, a landscape *bathed* in moonlight:—*v.i.* to take a bath.—*n.* **bath′er.**

bath-robe (băth′rōb′), *n.* a long, loose garment, opening in front like a coat, worn as a lounging or dressing gown.

bath-room (băth′rōōm′), *n.* a room containing a tub or shower for bathing and, usually, other toilet facilities.

Bath-urst (băth′ẽrst), a British island settlement in northwestern Africa, near the mouth of the Gambia River (map 14).

ba-tiste (bȧ-tēst′), *n.* a fine kind of very light, soft, cotton cloth.

ba-ton (bȧ-tôn′; băt′ŭn), *n.* **1,** a staff used as a badge of office or symbol of authority; **2,** the stick used by the leader of a band or orchestra for beating time.

Bat-on Rouge (băt′ŭn rōōzh′), a city, capital of Louisiana (map 8).

bats-man (băts′măn), *n.* [*pl.* batsmen (-mĕn)], in baseball, cricket, etc., the one who wields the bat; the batter.

bat-tal-ion (bȧ-tăl′yŭn), *n.* an army unit made up of two or more companies.

bat-ten (băt′n), *n.* a strip of wood nailed across two boards, to fasten a piece of canvas to the deck of a ship, or the like; a cleat:—*v.t.* to fasten with such strips.

¹bat-ter (băt′ẽr), *v.t.* to strike with heavy, repeated blows; as, the sea *battered* the wall; the champion *battered* his opponent: —*v.i.* to strike repeatedly; as, he *battered* at the door:—*n.* a stiff liquid mixture, as of flour, eggs, etc., beaten together before being cooked.

Syn., v. beat, pound, bruise, demolish.

²bat-ter (băt′ẽr), *n.* one who hits with a bat or club, as in baseball.

bat-ter-ing—ram (băt′ẽr-ĭng-răm′), *n.* a large iron-headed beam, used in ancient days to beat down the walls of besieged places.

BATTERING-RAM
Type used in the Middle Ages.

bat-ter-y (băt′ẽr-ĭ), *n.* [*pl.* batteries], **1,** an unlawful attack on another; as, he was arrested for assault and *battery;* **2,** two or more cannons placed together for combined action, usually under a single command; as, a field *battery;* also, the place where they are stationed; as, the forward *battery* on a battleship; **3,** an apparatus for producing or storing electric current; as, a storage *battery;* **4,** in baseball, the combination of pitcher and catcher; **5,** a number of like things used as a unit; as, a *battery* of lights.

bat-ting (băt′ĭng), *n.* **1,** wool or cotton prepared in sheets, used in making quilts, for quilting garments, etc.; **2,** the act of hitting or striking, as in a ball game.

bat-tle (băt′l), *n.* a fight between opposing forces, especially one between armies or fleets; also, any hard struggle; as, the game was a *battle:*—*v.i.* [bat-tled, bat-tling], to fight; struggle.

Syn., n. conflict, engagement, skirmish.

bat-tle—ax or **bat-tle—axe** (băt′l-ăks′), *n.* a broad-faced ax formerly used as a weapon in battle.

BATTLE-AX
As used in the Middle Ages.

bat-tle-dore (băt′l-dôr), *n.* a kind of light, paddle-shaped racket used in playing a game called *battledore and shuttlecock.*

bat-tle-field (băt′l-fēld′) or **bat-tle-ground** (băt′l-ground′), *n.* a place where a battle is, or has been, fought.

bat-tle-ment (băt′l-mĕnt), *n.* a wall for defense, usually at the top of a building or tower, with openings through which in ancient times defenders shot at the enemy.

BATTLEMENTS
B, B, battlements; E, embrasure; M, merlon.

bat-tle-ship (băt′l-shĭp′), *n.* a large, strongly armored ship carrying heavy guns.

bau-ble (bô′bl), *n.* a trifling piece of finery; anything showy but without real value; as, the prizes at the fair were mere *baubles.*

Bau-douin (bō′dwăn′), (1930–), king of the Belgians from 1951.

baux-ite (bôks′īt; bouks′īt; bō′zīt), *n.* a claylike substance from which aluminum is obtained.

Ba-var-i-a (bȧ-vâr′ĭ-ȧ), a state (cap. Munich) in southern Germany, bordering on Austria.—*n.* and *adj.* **Ba-var′i-an.**

bawd-y (bôd′ĭ), *adj.* immodest; obscene; immoral; indecent; as, *bawdy* talk.

bawl (bôl), *v.i.* to cry out loudly; howl; as, the child *bawled* more from temper than from pain:—*v.t.* to call loudly; shout; as, the captain *bawled* his commands.

¹bay (bā), *n.* an arm of the sea in a sheltered recess or curve in the shore.

²bay (bā), *n.* **1,** a division of a building marked off by pillars, columns, etc.; **2,** a bay window; also, the space added to a room at a bay window; **3,** a place or recess in a barn for storing hay or grain; **4,** any compartment in the fuselage of an airplane, as the bomb bay; **5,** the forward part of a ship between decks, sometimes used as a hospital.

³bay (bā), *n.* **1,** the laurel tree; also, a shrub or tree resembling the laurel; **2,** a garland or crown composed of laurel leaves, formerly given as a mark of honor to conquerors and successful poets.

⁴**bay** (bā), *n.* **1,** the deep-toned prolonged cry of a dog; **2,** the position of a person or animal compelled to turn and face an enemy or a danger when no escape is possible; as, a stag at *bay;* also, the position of the pursuers thus held off; as, the guard held the five robbers at *bay:—v.i.* to bark with a deep sound; as, the hounds *bayed.*

⁵**bay** (bā), *adj.* reddish brown in color:—*n.* a horse of a bay color.

bay-ber-ry (bā′bĕr′ĭ), *n.* [*pl.* bayberries], a low-growing shrub, common along the sea-coast, bearing round gray berries in clusters; also, the waxy berry. Candles are made from the berries, and the fragrant leaves are used to perfume bay rum.

BAYBERRY

Twig of bayberry shrub, showing leaves and berries.

Ba-yeux (bȧ-yōō′; bȧ′-yö′), an ancient town in northern France.

bay-o-net (bā′ŏ-nĕt), *n.* a daggerlike weapon attached to the muzzle end of a rifle:—*v.t.* [bayonet-ed, bayonet-ing], to stab with a bayonet.

BAYONET

(B) fixed to end of rifle barrel (R).

bay-ou (bī′ōō), *n.* [*pl.* bayous], a sluggish, marshy offshoot of a river or lake, especially as found in the southern U.S.

Bay-reuth (bī′roit′), a town of northern Bavaria, famous for its festivals of Wagnerian music.

bay rum, a fragrant toilet liquid, perfumed with the leaves of a species of bayberry.

bay win-dow, the window or windows in a part of a room which extends outward from the line of the wall.

BAY WINDOW

ba-zaar (bȧ-zär′), *n.* **1,** in Oriental countries, a market place or street lined with shops; **2,** a hall or series of rooms with stalls for the sale of goods; **3,** a sale of fancy articles, as in aid of a charity. Also spelled **bazar.**

ba-zoo-ka (bȧ-zōō′kȧ), *n.* a portable anti-tank rocket gun operated by two men.

bbl. [*pl.* bbl., bbls.], abbreviation for *barrel.*

B.C. abbreviation for *before Christ* (used in giving dates); *British Columbia.*

bdl. [*pl.* bdl., bdls.], abbreviation for *bundle.*

be (bē), *v.i.* [*present sing.* I am, you are, he is, *pl.* are; *p.t.* I was, you were, he was, *pl.* were; *p.p.* been; *p.pr.* be-ing], **1,** to exist; as, there *is* a strong feeling against war; **2,** to stay; occupy a certain place; as, the lesson *is* on this page; **3,** to mean; signify; as, it *is* nothing to me; **4,** to coincide with; equal; as, it *is* I; the girl *is* my sister; **5,** to belong to the class or group of; as, the animal *is* a lion; **6,** as a helping verb used to form: **a,** the progressive form of other verbs; as, he *is* going; **b,** the passive voice; as, I *was* hit.

be- (bē-), a prefix meaning: **1,** to cause to be; make; as, *befoul, bedim;* **2,** all over; thoroughly; completely; as, *besmear.*

beach (bēch), *n.* the shore of a body of water which is washed by the waves, especially the sandy or pebbly part:—*v.t.* and *v.i.* to haul up or land on a beach.

beach-head (bēch′hĕd′), *n.* the portion of an enemy shore captured and held for landing of men and supplies, and as a base for further operations.

bea-con (bē′kŭn), *n.* **1,** a fire or light used as a signal of warning or guidance, as for ships or airplanes; also, the structure bearing this signal; **2,** anything which serves as a guide; as, faith was his *beacon.*

Bea-cons-field (bē′kŭnz-fēld), Earl of. See **Disraeli.**

bead (bēd), *n.* **1,** a little ball of any material, such as wood, glass, or pearl, pierced through and intended to be strung with others to form an ornament; **2,** any small round body; a drop or bubble; as, a *bead* of dew; *beads* of perspiration; **3,** a small knob of metal at the end of a gun barrel, used in taking aim.—*adj.* **bead′y.**

bead-ing (bē′dĭng), *n.* **1,** ornamental work made of beads, as on a dress; **2,** a band or molding with beadlike elevations; **3,** a kind of openwork trimming through which ribbon may be run.

bea-dle (bē′dl), *n.* a parish officer with minor duties.

bea-gle (bē′gl), *n.* a small, short-legged hound, used especially in hunting rabbits.

beak (bēk), *n.* **1,** the bill of a bird; also, the long, sharp mouth of some insects and other animals; **2,** anything pointed or shaped like the bill of a bird, as the prow of ancient war vessels.—*adj.* **beaked** (bēkt; bē′kĕd).

BEAGLE (¹⁄₁₅)

beak-er (bē′kẽr), *n.* **1,** a large drinking cup or vessel with a wide mouth; **2,** an open-mouthed vessel with a projecting lip, used as a container in laboratories.

beam (bēm), *n.* 1, a long heavy piece of wood or metal used in the framework of buildings; 2, one of the principal horizontal supports of a ship; 3, the widest part of a ship; 4, the bar of a balance on which the scale pans are hung; 5, the chief timber of a plow; 6, a ray of light given out by the sun or any other luminous body; as, the *beam* from a lamp; 7, a smile:—*v.i.* to gleam; shine; as, his face *beamed* with joy.

BEAM
B, beam of a plow.

beam-ing (bēm′ĭng), *adj.* shining; glowing; bright; as, a face *beaming* with joy.—*adv.* **beam′ing-ly.**

bean (bēn), *n.* 1, the seed or the long pod of a pod-bearing plant used as food; also, the plant itself, as a Lima bean or a string bean; 2, any seed resembling a true bean; as, a coffee *bean.*

BEAN
Part of plant of string bean, showing leaves and pods.

¹**bear** (bâr), *n.* 1, a large four-footed animal with long shaggy fur and a very short tail, as the cinnamon bear, grizzly bear, polar bear; 2, a person with rough, uncouth, or surly manners; 3, on the stock exchange, one who tries to lower prices for his own advantage: opposite of *bull*:—**Bear,** in astronomy, either of two groups of stars in the Northern Hemisphere, called *Great Bear,* containing the *Big Dipper,* and the *Little Bear,* containing the *Little Dipper.*

BEAR (⅛)

²**bear** (bâr), *v.t.* [*p.t.* bore (bôr), *p.p.* borne (bôrn) or born (bôrn), (*born* is properly used only in the passive voice of sense 6 when *by* does not follow; as, a son was *born* to him; he was *born* in 1800; a son *borne by* his first wife), *p.pr.* bear-ing], 1, to support; hold up; as, the pillars *bore* all the weight; 2, to carry; convey; as, this letter *bears* good news; 3, to suffer or endure; stand; as, to *bear* pain or sorrow; 4, to possess, wear, or use, as a weapon; 5, to show; as, his past record *bears* proof of his guilt; 6, to bring forth; as, she *bore* many children; 7, to behave; as, he *bore* himself well:—*v.i.* 1, to be capable of enduring trouble or pain; as, she *bears* up well under her grief; 2, to be fruitful; as, this tree always *bears;* 3, to press or weigh; as, he *bore* too hard on the tool and it broke; 4, to refer; as, this *bears* on our talk.—*adj.* **bear′a-ble.**

Beard (bērd), Daniel Carter (1850-1941), the founder of the Boy Scouts of America.

beard (bērd), *n.* 1, the hair on the chin and cheeks of a man; 2, the long hair on the chin of some animals, as the goat; 3, anything resembling such hair, especially the hairlike growths on the heads of certain grains, as barley:—*v.t.* 1, to take by the beard; pull the beard of; hence, to oppose face to face; defy; 2, to furnish with a beard.—*adj.* **beard′ed.**—*adj.* **beard′less.**

bear-er (bâr′ẽr), *n.* 1, one who or that which carries; 2, one who presents a check or other order for the payment of money.

bear-ing (bâr′ĭng), *n.* 1, the act of one who endures or bears; 2, behavior; as, the *bearing* of a gentleman; 3, meaning; relation; as, this has no *bearing* on the subject; 4, the act or power of producing; 5, a part of a machine in which another part turns; as, ball *bearings;* 6, (usually *bearings*), direction; position; way; as, he lost his *bearings* in the storm.

bear-ish (bâr′ĭsh), *adj.* rude; surly; as, *bearish* behavior.—*n.* **bear′ish-ness.**—*adv.* **bear′ish-ly.**

beast (bēst), *n.* 1, a four-footed animal, as distinguished from a bird, insect, fish, or man; 2, a brutal person.—*adj.* **beast′ly.**—*n.* **beast′li-ness.**

beat (bēt), *v.t.* [*p.t.* beat, *p.p.* beat-en (bēt′n), *p.pr.* beat-ing], 1, to strike with many blows; 2, in hunting, to range over in order to drive out game; as, to *beat* a thicket; 3, to flap; as, the bird *beat* its wings; 4, in cooking, to mix by stirring with a spoon or fork; 5, in music, to measure (time) by strokes; 6, to defeat; conquer; as, the first team *beat* the second:—*v.i.* 1, to strike repeatedly; as, waves *beat* upon rocks; 2, to throb; as, the heart *beats;* 3, to sail against the wind by tacking; as, the boat *beat* along the shore; 4, *Colloquial,* to win in a contest; as, have you been to the game? who *beat?*—*n.* 1, a stroke which is made again and again; as, the *beat* of marching feet; 2, a round or course which is frequently gone over; as, the policeman's *beat;* 3, in music, the rise and fall of the stroke marking the divisions of time.—*n.* **beat′er.**

Syn. smite, bang, pound, batter, bruise, maul, overcome, conquer.

beat-en (bēt′n), *adj.* 1, shaped by beating; as, *beaten* brass; 2, worn by use; as, a *beaten* path; 3, conquered; overcome.

---

go; join; yet; sing; chin; show; thin, *th*en; hw, *wh*y; zh, azure; ü, Ger. f*ü*r or Fr. l*u*ne; ö, Ger. sch*ö*n or Fr. f*eu*; ṅ, Fr. e*n*fant, no*m*; kh, Ger. a*ch* or i*ch*. See pages ix-x.

be·a·tif·ic (bē′à-tĭf′ĭk), *adj.* blissfully happy; as, a *beatific* frame of mind.

be·at·i·fy (bē-ăt′ĭ-fī), *v.t.* [beatified, beatify-ing], **1**, to make happy; **2**, in the Roman Catholic Church, to declare (a dead person) to have attained the rank of "the blessed," and the right to public religious honor.—*n.* **be·at·i·fi·ca′tion.**

beat·ing (bēt′ĭng), *n.* **1**, a striking, as of drums; **2**, a whipping; **3**, a defeat.

be·at·i·tude (bē-ăt′ĭ-tūd), *n.* supreme happiness:—**the Beatitudes,** nine statements made in the Sermon on the Mount (Matthew 5:3–12) blessing and declaring blessed, or supremely happy, those who possess certain virtues.

Beat·ty (bē′tĭ), Sir David (1871–1936), a British admiral, commander of the British fleet 1916–1919.

beau (bō), *n.* [*pl.* beaux (bōz; bō) or beaus (bōz)], **1**, a man who follows the latest fashion in dress; a dandy; **2**, an escort; a lover.

Beau·re·gard (bō′rĕ-gärd), Pierre G. T. (1818–1893), an American Confederate general.

beau·te·ous (bū′tē-ŭs), *adj.* beautiful.—*adv.* **beau′te·ous·ly.**—*n.* **beau′te·ous·ness.** *Syn.* handsome, pretty, comely.

beau·ti·ful (bū′tĭ-fŏŏl), *adj.* possessing qualities which delight the mind and senses; lovely.—*adv.* **beau′ti·ful·ly.**

beau·ti·fy (bū′tĭ-fī), *v.t.* [beautified, beautify-ing], to make beautiful; adorn.—*n.* **beau′ti·fi′er.**

beau·ty (bū′tĭ), *n.* [*pl.* beauties], **1**, that combination of qualities which is pleasing to the eye or ear, or is satisfying in a moral sense; **2**, a particular grace or charm; as, the *beauty* of the country; **3**, a beautiful thing or person; especially, a lovely or beautiful woman.

beaux (bōz; bō), one of the plural forms of *beau.*

BEAVER (⅒)

¹**bea·ver** (bē′vẽr), *n.* **1**, a small fur-bearing animal that lives both in water and on land, having a broad, flat, powerful tail, strong teeth formed for gnawing, and webbed hind feet: remarkable for the way in which it fells trees and dams streams; **2**, the fur of this animal; **3**, a gentleman's high hat, formerly made of beaver fur.

²**bea·ver** (bē′vẽr), *n.* on an ancient helmet, the movable part that served as protection for the lower part of the face.

be·calm (bē-käm′), *v.t.* to make calm or quiet:—**becalmed,** motionless because of a lack of wind, as a sailing vessel.

be·came (bē-kām′), past tense of *become.*

be·cause (bē-kôz′; bē-kŏz′), *conj.* for the reason that; since; as, we came in *because* it rained:—**because of,** on account of; as, I stayed late *because of* my work.

Bech·u·a·na·land (bĕch′ōō-ä′nȧ-lănd′), a British protectorate (cap. Mafeking) in central South Africa (map **14**).

beck (bĕk), *n.* a nod or other silent signal given as a sign of command.

Beck·et (bĕk′ĕt), Thomas à (1118? 1170), a British prelate, Archbishop of Canterbury, who was made a saint in 1772.

beck·on (bĕk′ŭn), *v.i.* and *v.t.* 1772. to signal by a motion of the head or hand; also, to attract; call; as, pleasure *beckons.*

be·cloud (bē-kloud′), *v.t.* to darken; obscure; as, much talk *beclouds* the truth.

be·come (bē-kŭm′), *v.i.* [*p.t.* became (bē-kām′), *p.p.* become, *p.pr.* becom-ing], to pass from one state to another; as, a boy *becomes* a man:—*v.t.* to suit; be suitable for; as, that hat *becomes* you.

be·com·ing (bē-kŭm′ĭng), *adj.* proper; suitable; appropriate; as, a *becoming* hat; a *becoming* pride.—*adv.* **be·com′ing·ly.** *Syn.* decent, seemly, suitable.

bed (bĕd), *n.* **1**, an article of furniture upon which one rests or sleeps; **2**, anything which serves as a bed or resting place; **3**, a portion of a garden; as, a *bed* of pansies; **4**, the base or bottom of anything; as, a *bed* of concrete; the *bed* of a river:—*v.t.* [bed-ded, bed-ding], **1**, to fix for the night; as, I *bedded* the horses; **2**, to plant; **3**, to set; fix; as, to *bed* a pole in concrete.

be·dab·ble (bē-dăb′l), *v.t.* [bedab-bled, be-dab-bling], to spatter all over; splash.

be·daub (bē-dôb′), *v.t.* to smear with something oily or dirty.

bed·bug (bĕd′bŭg′), *n.* a biting, bloodsucking, flat-bodied insect, of vile odor, infesting furniture, especially beds.

bed·cham·ber (bĕd′chām′bẽr), *n.* a bedroom.

bed·clothes (bĕd′klōthz′), *n.pl.* sheets, blankets, etc., used on a bed.

bed·ding (bĕd′ĭng), *n.* **1**, bedclothes; **2**, the materials for a bed; as, straw is used as *bedding* for animals.

Bede (bēd), (673–735), called *the Venerable,* an English monk and historian.

be·deck (bē-dĕk′), *v.t.* to adorn; decorate; as, she *bedecked* herself with jewels.

be·dew (bē-dū′), *v.t.* to moisten with, or as with, dew; as, *bedewed* with tears.

āte, āorta, râre, căt, ȧsk, fär, ăllow, sofȧ; ēve, ĕvent, ĕll, writẽr, novĕl; bīte, pĭn; nō, ōbey, ôr, dŏg, tŏp, cŏllide; ūnit, ūnite, bûrn, cŭt, focŭs; nōōn, fŏŏt; mound; coin;

bed·fel·low (bĕd′fĕl′ō), *n.* one who shares a bed with another.

Bed·ford·shire (bĕd′fĕrd-shĭr) or **Bedford**, a county located in south central England.

be·dight (bē-dīt′), *adj. Archaic*, arrayed; decked out; adorned.

be·dim (bē-dĭm′), *v.t.* [bedimmed, bedim-ming], to darken; cloud; dim; as, a haze *bedimmed* the horizon.

be·diz·en (bē-dĭz′n; bē-dī′zn), *v.t.* to dress or adorn, especially with gaudy finery; as, she *bedizened* the child with cheap jewelry.

bed·lam (bĕd′lăm), *n.* 1, an insane asylum; 2, any scene of uproar and confusion; as, the jail was a *bedlam* during the riot.

Bed·loe's Is·land (bĕd′lō), a small island in New York Bay where the Statue of Liberty stands. It is also called *Liberty Island.*

Bed·ou·in (bĕd′ōō-ĭn; bĕd′ōō-ēn), *n.* 1, a wandering Arab of the deserts of Arabia or northern Africa; 2, hence, any wanderer: —*adj.* pertaining to the Bedouins.

be·drag·gle (bē-drăg′l), *v.t.* [bedrag-gled, bedrag-gling], to make wet or limp and dirty by dragging in mud, dirt, etc.:—**bedraggled**, limp and soiled or mussed; as, a *bedraggled* skirt.

bed·rid (bĕd′rĭd′) or **bed·rid·den** (bĕd′-rĭd′n), *adj.* confined to bed by illness.

bed·rock (bĕd′rŏk′), *n.* 1, the solid rock underlying the looser upper crust of the earth; 2, hence, the lowest state or bottom of a thing; as, my savings account has reached *bedrock.*

bed·room (bĕd′rōōm′), *n.* a room with a bed in it; a sleeping room.

bed·side (bĕd′sīd′), *n.* the side of a bed; as, to sit by the *bedside.*

bed·spread (bĕd′sprĕd′), *n.* a covering for a bed; a counterpane.

bed·stead (bĕd′stĕd; bĕd′stĭd), *n.* the wood or metal framework of a bed.

bed·time (bĕd′tīm′), *n.* the time at which one should go to bed or at which one usually goes to bed.

bee (bē), *n.* 1, a winged insect with sucking and stinging organs; especially, the honey-bee, which lives with many others in a hive where it stores pollen and honey; 2, a social meeting for work or amusement; as, a quilting *bee;* a spelling *bee.*

BEE

bee·bread (bē′brĕd′), *n.* pollen as stored up in the honeycomb. It is mixed with honey by the bees and used as food.

beech (bēch), *n.* a wide-spreading tree with smooth, ash-gray bark and deep-green leaves, yielding hard timber and edible nuts. (See illustration, page 864.)

beech·en (bē′chĕn), *adj.* pertaining to the beech; made of wood of the beech.

Beech·er (bē′chēr), Henry Ward (1813-1887), an American clergyman and lecturer.

beef (bēf), *n.* 1, the flesh of an ox, or cow, used for food; 2, [*pl.* beeves (bēvz) or beefs (bēfs)], a full-grown ox, bull, or cow, especially when fattened for market.

beef·steak (bēf′stāk′), *n.* a thin broad piece, or slice, of beef that can be broiled or fried.

beef·y (bēf′ĭ), *adj.* [beef-i-er, beef-i-est], fat; brawny; fleshy.

bee·hive (bē′hīv′), *n.* a box made to house a swarm of bees and store its honey. (See illustration below.)

bee·line (bē′līn′), *n.* 1, the straight course of a bee returning to the hive with honey or pollen; 2, the most direct way from one point to another; as, I made a *beeline* for home.

Be·el·ze·bub (bē-ĕl′zē-bŭb), *n.* in the Bible, the Devil; also, a devil.

been (bĭn; bēn), past participle of the verb *be.*

beer (bēr), *n.* 1, an alcoholic liquor generally brewed from malted barley and flavored with hops; 2, a nonalcoholic drink made from roots or plants, as root beer, ginger beer, etc.

Be·er·she·ba (bē′ĕr-shē′bà; bēr-shē′bà), a town in Israel, formerly Palestine.

bees·wax (bēz′wăks′), *n.* a tough, yellowish-brown wax that bees make and use for honeycomb:—*v.t.* to rub or polish with beeswax.

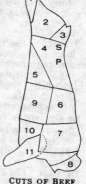

CUTS OF BEEF

1, hind shank; 2, round; 3, rump; 4, loin (S, sirloin steaks; P, porter-house steaks); 5, flank; 6, rib; 7, chuck; 8, neck; 9, plate; 10, brisket; 11, fore shank.

BEEHIVE

A, alighting board; B, bee entrance; C, hive body, or brood chamber; D, comb honey super; E, hive cover; F, inner cover; G, comb honey sections, held in section holder; H, comb foundation in frames; J, frame ends, showing bee spaces; K, bottom board; L, hive stand.

---

go; join; yet; sing; chin; show; thin, *then;* hw, *why;* zh, azure; ü, Ger. für or Fr. lune; ö, Ger. schön or Fr. feu; n̈, Fr. enfant, nom; kh, Ger. ach or ich. See pages ix–x.

beet (bēt), *n.* a plant cultivated for its root, which serves as a vegetable and as a source of sugar; also, the red or white root.

Bee-tho-ven (bā′tō-věn), Ludwig van (1770-1827), a German composer, famous for his symphonies.

¹**bee-tle** (bē′tl), *n.* a kind of insect having four wings, the outer pair being hard and shiny and serving as a protection to the inner pair. (See illustration below.)

²**bee-tle** (bē′tl), *n.* a heavy wooden mallet for hammering, leveling, or crushing.

bee-tle (bē′tl), *v.i.* [bee-tled, bee-tling], to project; overhang.

bee-tling (bē′tlĭng), *adj.* jutting out; prominent; overhanging; as, bare and *beetling* cliffs; a *beetling* brow.

beeves (bēvz), a plural form of *beef.*

be-fall (bē-fôl′), *v.t.* [*p.t.* befell (bē-fěl′), *p.p.* befall-en (bē-fôl′ĕn), *p.pr.* befall-ing], to happen or occur to:—*v.i.* to come to pass; as, whatever *befalls.*

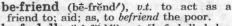

BEET
Beet plant showing leaves and root.

BEETLE

be-fall-en (bē-fôl′ĕn), past participle of *befall.*

be-fell (bē-fěl′), past tense of the verb *befall.*

be-fit (bē-fĭt′), *v.t.* [befit-ted, befit-ting], to be worthy of; be suitable or appropriate for.—*adj.* **be-fit′ting.**

be-fog (bē-fŏg′), *v.t.* [befogged, befog-ging], to envelop in a fog or mist; hence, to confuse; perplex.

be-fore (bē-fôr′), *prep.* 1, in front of; 2, preceding in space, time, or rank; as, the lawn *before* the house; *before* ten o'clock; a general comes *before* a colonel; 3, in the presence or sight of; as, the prisoner was brought *before* the judge:—*adv.* in front; previously; formerly; as, you never looked like that *before:*—*conj.* 1, previous to the time at which; as, I shall finish *before* I leave; 2, rather than; as, he would die *before* he'd betray his country.

be-fore-hand (bē-fôr′hǎnd′), *adv.* in advance; as, copy your notes *beforehand.*

be-foul (bē-foul′), *v.t.* to make dirty; pollute; as, to *befoul* a spring with mud or filth.

be-friend (bē-frěnd′), *v.t.* to act as a friend to; aid; as, to *befriend* the poor.

be-fud-dle (bē-fŭd′l), *v.t.* [befud-dled, befud-dling], to confuse; as, the liquor he drank *befuddled* him.

beg (běg), *v.t.* [begged, beg-ging], 1, to entreat or ask for (food, money, etc.) as an alms or a charity; 2, to beseech; implore; as, I *beg* you to help me; 3, to ask as a favor; as, I *beg* you to hand me that book:—*v.i.* to ask, or to live by asking, alms; as, he *begs* from door to door.

Syn. implore, solicit, supplicate.

be-gan (bē-gǎn′), past tense of *begin.*

be-gat (bē-gǎt′), old past tense of *beget.*

be-get (bē-gět′), *v.t.* [*p.t.* begot (bē-gŏt′) or, *Archaic,* begat (bē-gǎt′), *p.p.* begot or begot-ten (bē-gŏt′n), *p.pr.* beget-ting], 1, to become the father of; 2, to produce; cause; as, idleness *begets* discontent.

beg-gar (běg′ẽr), *n.* 1, one who asks for alms; 2, a very poor person; 3, a fellow: often used humorously; as, he's a cute little *beggar:*—*v.t.* to reduce to poverty.

beg-gar-ly (běg′ẽr-lĭ), *adj.* poor; contemptible; mean; as, *beggarly* rags.

Syn. abject, sordid, wretched, mean.

beg-gar's-lice (běg′ẽrz-līs′), *n.* a weed whose seeds catch on clothing; also, the seed. Also, **beg′gar—lice′.**

beg-gar—ticks (běg′ẽr-tĭks′), *n.pl.* used as *sing.* a kind of weed with seeds that stick to clothing, the fur of animals, etc.; also, the seeds of such a plant. Also, **beg′gar's—ticks′.**

beg-gar-y (běg′ẽr-ĭ), *n.* extreme poverty.

be-gin (bē-gĭn′), *v.i.* [*p.t.* began (bē-gǎn′), *p.p.* begun (bē-gŭn′), *p.pr.* begin-ning], 1, to come into existence; arise; commence; as, life *began* many million years ago; the stream *begins* up in the hills; the story *begins* on page 30; 2, to take the first step or do the first act; start; as, work *begins* tomorrow:—*v.t.* to commence.

be-gin-ner (bē-gĭn′ẽr), *n.* one who is just starting in; one who has had no training or experience; a novice.

be-gin-ning (bē-gĭn′ĭng), *n.* 1, origin; as, the *beginning* of the world; 2, source; as, the *beginning* of all evil; 3, the first part; as, the *beginning* of a book.

be-girt (bē-gûrt′), *adj.* surrounded; as, a castle *begirt* with a wall.

be-gone (bē-gôn′), *interj.* go away!

be-go-ni-a (bē-gō′nĭ-à; bē-gōn′yà), *n.* a plant with

BEGONIA
Spray of plant showing leaves and flowers.

āte, âorta, râre, cǎt, ǎsk, fär, ǎllow, sofà; ēve, ěvent, ěll, writẽr, nověl; bīte, pǐn; nō, ōbey, ôr, dǒg, tǒp, cǒllide; ūnit, ūnite, bûrn, cǔt, focǔs; noŏn, foŏt; mound; coin;

ornamental leaves and red, pink, or white flowers, often grown in the house.

be-got (bĕ-gŏt′), past tense and one of the past participles of *beget:*—**begotten,** one of the past participles of *beget.*

be-grime (bĕ-grīm′), *v.t.* [begrimed, begrim-ing], to soil; make dirty.

be-grudge (bĕ-grŭj′), *v.t.* [begrudged, begrudg-ing], **1,** to envy (a person) the possession of (something); as, I *begrudge* him the honor; **2,** to give reluctantly; as, I *begrudge* the money.—*adv.* **be-grudg′ing-ly.**

be-guile (bĕ-gīl′), *v.t.* [beguiled, beguil-ing], **1,** to deceive; **2,** to cause to pass pleasantly; as, to *beguile* many hours in reading; **3,** to amuse; as, to *beguile* children with stories.

be-gun (bĕ-gŭn′), past participle of *begin.*

be-half (bĕ-hàf′), *n.* used only in phrases: —**in behalf of,** in the defense or interest of; as, he spoke *in behalf of* the plan; **on behalf of,** in the place of; for; as, the agent acts *on behalf of* his employer.

be-have (bĕ-hāv′), *v.t.* and *v.i.* [behaved, behav-ing], to conduct or carry (oneself); act; as, he *behaves* himself well; also, to conduct (oneself) properly; as, make him *behave.*

be-hav-ior (bĕ-hāv′yẽr), *n.* conduct; manners. In British usage, **be-hav′iour.**

be-head (bĕ-hĕd′), *v.t.* to cut off the head of.

be-held (bĕ-hĕld′), past tense and past participle of *behold.*

be-he-moth (bĕ-hē′mŏth; bē′hĕ-mŏth), *n.* in the Bible, an enormous animal (Job 40: 15-24); hence, any very large animal.

be-hest (bĕ-hĕst′), *n.* a command; order.

be-hind (bĕ-hīnd′), *prep.* **1,** at the back of; as, to hide *behind* the door; **2,** inferior to; as, he is *behind* the class in spelling; **3,** in support of; as, there is money *behind* the plan; **4,** remaining after; as, he left nothing but debts *behind* him:—*adv.* **1,** in the rear; as, to remain *behind;* **2,** backward; to the rear; as, look *behind;* **3,** in arrears; as, he is *behind* in his dues.

be-hind-hand (bĕ-hīnd′hănd′), *adj.* and *adv.* late; slow; behind, as in one's work.

be-hold (bĕ-hōld′), *v.t.* [*p.t.* beheld (bĕ-hĕld′), *p.p.* beheld or, *Archaic,* behold-en (bĕ-hōl′dĕn). *p.pr.* behold-ing], to look at; gaze upon; see.—*n.* **be-hold′er.**

be-hold-en (bĕ-hōl′dĕn), *adj.* indebted; as, I am *beholden* to you for your help.

be-hoof (bĕ-hōōf′), *n.* use; benefit; interest: used chiefly in phrases with *for, to, in* or *on;* as, he works for his own *behoof.*

be-hoove (bĕ-hōōv′), *v.t.* [behooved, behoov-ing], to be necessary or proper or fitting for; as, it *behooves* you to apologize. Also spelled **be-hove′** (bĕ-hōv′).

beige (bāzh), *n.* the light-tan color of unbleached wool:—*adj.* of a light-tan color.

be-ing (bē′ĭng), *n.* **1,** existence; life; as; to come into *being;* **2,** that which exists; especially, a person.

Bei-rut (bā′rōōt; bā-rōōt′), a seaport, capital of Lebanon (map 15).

be-jew-el (bĕ-jōō′ĕl), *v.t.* to adorn or deck with jewels.

be-la-bor (bĕ-lā′bẽr), *v.t.* to beat with hard blows. In British usage, **be-la′bour.**

be-lat-ed (bĕ-lā′tĕd), *adj.* delayed; as, a *belated* report; a *belated* arrival.

be-lay (bĕ-lā′), *v.t.* [belayed, belay-ing], in sailors' language, to make fast, as a running rope, by winding around a pin, cleat, or the like:—**belaying pin,** an adjustable pin to which ropes are made fast:—*interj.* stop!

belch (bĕlch), *v.t.* and *v.i.* **1,** to discharge (gas) from the stomach through the mouth; **2,** to throw out with force:—*n.* the act of belching.

BELAYING PIN

Shown in gunwale of a ship, holding a rope.

bel-dam or **bel-dame** (bĕl′-dăm), *n.* an ugly old woman; a hag; witch.

be-lea-guer (bĕ-lē′gẽr), *v.t.* to besiege; surround; as, the enemy *beleaguered* the city.

Be-lém (bā-lĕn′), a seaport in northern Brazil (map 11). It is also called *Pará.*

Bel-fast (bĕl′fàst), a seaport city, capital of Northern Ireland (map 13).

bel-fry (bĕl′frĭ), *n.* [*pl.* belfries], a bell tower, or that part of a tower in which a bell is hung.

Belg. abbreviation for *Belgium, Belgian.*

bel-ga (bĕl′gà), *n.* the monetary unit of Belgium, equivalent to five Belgian francs.

Bel-gi-an (bĕl′jĭ-ăn; bĕl′jăn), *n.* a native or inhabitant of Belgium: —*adj.* relating to Belgium or its people.

BELFRY

Belfry of the Mission of San Juan Capistrano, California.

Bel-gi-an Con-go (kŏng′gō), a large Belgian colony (cap. Léopoldville) of south central Africa (map 14). It was formerly called *Congo Free State.*

Bel-gi-um (bĕl′jĭ-ŭm; bĕl′jŭm), a kingdom (cap. Brussels) in western Europe, between France and the Netherlands (map 12).

Bel-grade (bĕl′grād′; bĕl′grād) or **Be-o-grad** (bĕ-ō′grád), a city, capital of Yugoslavia (map 12).

be-lie (bĕ-lī′), *v.t.* [belied, bely-ing], **1,** to give a false notion of; as, his appearance *belies* his feelings; **2,** to fail to come up to or to accord with; as, his acts *belie* his words.

be-lief (bĕ-lēf′), *n.* **1,** the acceptance of something as true or desirable; confidence; as, a *belief* in physical education; my *belief* in his innocence; **2,** creed; as, a religious *belief*; **3,** opinion; as, it is my *belief* that he is coming.

    Syn. faith, trust, persuasion.

be-lieve (bĕ-lēv′), *v.t.* [believed, believing], **1,** to accept as true; as, I *believe* part of the evidence; **2,** to trust the word of; place confidence in; as, I *believe* him; **3,** to think; as, I *believe* that honesty pays:—*v.i.* to have faith, trust, or confidence; as, to *believe* in God; *believe* in our ability to win. —*adj.* **be-liev′ing.**—*adj.* **be-liev′a-ble.**

be-liev-er (bĕ-lēv′ẽr), *n.* **1,** one who believes; as, a *believer* in the divine right of kings; **2,** one who has faith in a religious doctrine; a Christian.

be-like (bĕ-līk′), *adv. Archaic,* probably.

be-lit-tle (bĕ-lĭt′l), *v.t.* [belit-tled, belittling], **1,** to cause to appear small; as, he *belittled* the danger; **2,** to speak slightingly of; as, he *belittled* my work.

Bell (bĕl), Alexander Graham (1847–1922), a Scottish American, credited with inventing the telephone.

bell (bĕl), *n.* **1,** a hollow metal vessel, usually cup-shaped, which gives a ringing sound when struck with a clapper or hammer; **2,** anything shaped like a bell, as the flare at the mouth of a horn; **3,** on shipboard, the time as indicated by strokes on a bell, each stroke meaning a half hour

BELLS
1, farm bell; 2, hand bell; 3, electric bell.

after 12, 4, or 8 o'clock, so that 1 bell is 12:30, 4:30, or 8:30, 4 bells is 2, 6, or 10, etc.:—*v.t.* to put a bell on; as, to *bell* a cat.

bel-la-don-na (bĕl′a-dŏn′a), *n.* **1,** a poisonous plant of the nightshade family; **2,** a poisonous drug made from the roots and leaves of this plant.

belle (bĕl), *n.* a beautiful woman; a very popular young lady.

bel-li-cose (bĕl′ĭ-kōs; bĕl′ĭ-kōs′), *adj.* inclined to fight; quarrelsome.

bel-lig-er-ent (bĕ-lĭj′ẽr-ĕnt), *adj.* **1,** waging war; as, *belligerent* nations; **2,** quarrelsome; warlike; as, *belligerent* words; a *belligerent* person:—*n.* a nation or person

at war; as, the *belligerents* laid down their arms.—*adv.* **bel-lig′er-ent-ly.**—*n.* **bel-lig′-er-ence; bel-lig′er-en-cy.**

bel-low (bĕl′ō), *v.i.* **1,** to roar like a bull; **2,** to make a similar noise; as, he *bellowed* with rage:—*v.t.* to utter with a loud, full voice; roar:—*n.* **1,** the roar of a bull or similar animal; **2,** a loud, deep cry or voice.

bel-lows (bĕl′ōz), *n.* [*pl.* bellows], **1,** an instrument for producing a current of air, used for various purposes, such as blowing fires or filling the pipes of an organ; **2,** the creased casing that connects the front and back of a camera. (See illustration at *camera.*)

HAND BELLOWS

bell-weth-er (bĕl′wĕth′ẽr), *n.* a male sheep, or wether, wearing a bell, which leads the flock.

bel-ly (bĕl′ĭ), *n.* [*pl.* bellies], **1,** the part of the body of man or animal between the chest and the thighs, containing the stomach, bowels, etc.; the abdomen; **2,** the front or lower surface of the body of man or an animal; **3,** the bulging part of any object; as, the *belly* of a flask:—*v.i.* [bellied, belly-ing], to swell and extend; bulge out, as sails in the wind:—*v.t.* to cause to swell out.

be-long (bĕ-lông′), *v.i.* **1,** to be the duty, concern, or business; as, this work *belongs* to you; **2,** to be the property; as, the coat *belongs* to me; **3,** to be a part or member; as, the button *belongs* to my coat; he *belongs* to the Masons; **4,** to have a characteristic place or niche; as, the book *belongs* on this shelf.

be-long-ings (bĕ-lông′ĭngz), *n.pl.* the things that are one's own; possessions.

be-lov-ed (bĕ-lŭv′ĕd; bĕ-lŭvd′), *adj.* dearly loved:—*n.* one who is greatly loved.

be-low (bĕ-lō′), *prep.* **1,** farther down, or lower than, in place, rank, excellence, value, amount, price, or the like; beneath; **2,** undeserving or unworthy of; beneath; as, *below* your dignity:—*adv.* **1,** into or to a lower place; as, go *below;* **2,** on the earth; as, here *below.*

belt (bĕlt), *n.* **1,** a strip of leather, cloth, or the like, worn around the body as a support for a garment, or as an ornament or mark of rank; **2,** any broad band, strip, or series of things; as, a *belt* of forts; **3,** a region, with a given character, or within which a certain kind of vegetation grows; as, the timber *belt;* **4,** an endless band connecting two wheels or pulleys, and passing motion from one to the other; as, a sewing-machine *belt:*—*v.t.* **1,** to encircle, as with a belt; **2,** to fasten on (a sword) with a belt; **3,** to flog soundly, as with a belt.

āte, āorta, râre, căt, ȧsk, fär, ȧllow, sofȧ; ēve, ĕvent, ĕll, writẽr, novĕl; bīte, pĭn; nō, ōbey, ôr, dŏg, tŏp, cŏllide; ūnit, ūnite, bûrn, cŭt, focŭs; nōōn, fŏŏt; mound; coin;

be-moan (bē-mōn′), *v.t.* to grieve for; bewail; as, to *bemoan* one's lot.

Be-na-res (bĕ-nä′rĭz), the holy city of the Hindus, in India, on the Ganges River (map 15).

bench (bĕnch). *n.* **1,** a long seat; **2,** a strong table on which mechanics do their work; as, a carpenter's *bench;* **3,** the seat where judges sit in court; hence, judges as a class; also, the court.

bend (bĕnd), *v.t.* [bent (bĕnt), bending], **1,** to strain or make taut, as the string of a bow; **2,** to curve or make crooked; as, he *bent* the iron rod; **3,** to turn; deflect; as, the glass *bent* the rays of the sun; **4,** to direct to a certain point; as, we *bent* our energies to the task; **5,** to force to submit or yield; **6,** in nautical language, to fasten, as a sail to a spar:—*v.i.* **1,** to become curved or crooked; as, the board *bent* under his weight; **2,** to turn toward or away from something; as, the road *bends* to the left; **3,** to bow or stoop; hence, to submit; as, I *bend* to fate:—*n.* **1,** a turn or curve; **2,** a knot by which one rope is fastened to another or to some object. (See illustration at *knot.*)

BENCHES
1, carpenter's workbench; 2, lawn bench.

be-neath (bē-nēth′; bē-nēth′), *prep.* **1,** under; as, *beneath* the sky; **2,** under the pressure of; as, to sink *beneath* troubles; **3,** lower than; as, *beneath* the rank of captain; **4,** undeserving of; as, the letter was *beneath* his notice; unworthy of; as, the work was *beneath* him:—*adv.* in a lower place; below.

ben-e-dic-i-te (bĕn′ē-dĭs′ĭ-tē; bĕn′ē-dī′-sĭ-tē), *n.* the asking of a blessing; also, the blessing:—**Benedicite,** a Latin hymn of praise in the Book of Common Prayer, beginning with this word.

Ben-e-dict (bĕn′ē-dĭkt), Saint (480–543), founder of the Benedictines, an order of Catholic monks.

ben-e-dict (bĕn′ē-dĭkt), *n.* a newly married man.

Ben-e-dic-tine (bĕn′ē-dĭk′tĭn; bĕn′ē-dĭk′-tĭn), *n.* a monk or a nun of the order founded by Saint Benedict:—*adj.* pertaining to Saint Benedict or to his order.

ben-e-dic-tion (bĕn′ē-dĭk′shŭn), *n.* a blessing, especially the short blessing pronounced at the end of a church service.

ben-e-fac-tion (bĕn′ē-făk′shŭn), *n.* a charitable gift.

Syn. alms, charity, donation, bequest.

ben-e-fac-tor (bĕn′ē-făk′tēr), *n.* one who has given help, whether in the form of money or service.—*n.fem.* **ben-e-fac′tress.**

ben-e-fice (bĕn′ē-fĭs), *n.* an endowed office or position in the English Church.

be-nef-i-cence (bē-nĕf′ĭ-sĕns), *n.* active kindness; a charitable gift; as, his *beneficence* relieved the poor.—*adj.* **be-nef′i-cent.**

ben-e-fi-cial (bĕn′ē-fĭsh′ăl), *adj.* useful; helpful; profitable; as, *beneficial* climate, advice, or experiences.

ben-e-fi-ci-ar-y (bĕn′ē-fĭsh′ĭ-ĕr′ĭ; bĕn′ē-fĭsh′ēr-ĭ), *n.* [*pl.* beneficiaries], one who receives anything as a gift or benefit; especially, the person named in a will or an insurance policy to receive part or all of the estate or of the insurance.

ben-e-fit (bĕn′ē-fĭt), *n.* **1,** a help; advantage; as, the *benefits* of an education, or of sunshine and fresh air; **2,** a play, concert, or the like, the proceeds of which go to a particular person or cause:—*v.t.* [benefit-ed, benefit-ing], to do good to; help; as, the vacation *benefited* him:—*v.i.* to be helped; improve; as, he *benefited* from his rest.

Syn., n. profit, advantage, service, use.

be-nev-o-lent (bē-nĕv′ō-lĕnt), *adj.* kindly; charitable; generous; as, a *benevolent* disposition.—*n.* **be-nev′o-lence.**

Ben-gal (bĕn-gôl′; bĕng-gôl′), a former province of northeastern India, now divided between India and Pakistan:—*adj.* (bĕn′-gôl; bĕng′gôl), coming from or connected with Bengal:—**Bay of Bengal,** a part of the Indian Ocean between India and the Malay Peninsula (map 15).

be-night-ed (bē-nī′tĕd), *adj.* **1,** overtaken by the darkness of night; **2,** hence, being in moral darkness or ignorance; as, *benighted* savages.

be-nign (bē-nīn′), *adj.* **1,** of a kind or gentle disposition; **2,** favorable; healthful; as, a *benign* sea breeze; **3,** in medical usage, harmless.—*adv.* **be-nign′ly.**

be-nig-ni-ty (bē-nĭg′nĭ-tĭ), *n.* [*pl.* benignities], kindliness of nature; graciousness.—*adj.* **be-nig′nant.**

ben-i-son (bĕn′ĭ-zn; bĕn′ĭ-sn), *n.* a blessing; benediction.

Ben-ja-min (bĕn′ja-mĭn), in the Bible, the youngest son of Jacob; also, the tribe descended from him (Genesis 35:18).

---

go; join; yet; sing; chin; show; thin, *th*en; hw, *wh*y; zh, azure; ŭ, Ger. für or Fr. lune; ö, Ger. schön or Fr. feu; n̄, Fr. enfant, nom; kh, Ger. ach or ich. See pages ix–x.

Ben Lo·mond (bĕn lō′mŭnd), a mountain of west central Scotland, on the eastern shore of Loch Lomond.

Ben Ne·vis (bĕn nē′vĭs; nĕv′ĭs), the loftiest mountain, 4,406 feet high, of the British Isles, in northwestern Scotland.

bent (bĕnt), past tense and past participle of *bend:—adj.* **1,** curved; crooked; **2,** strongly inclined; set; as, he is *bent* on going:—*n.* a natural interest or ability; as, Tom has a *bent* for painting.

be·numb (bĕ-nŭm′), *v.t.* to stupefy; deprive of feeling; as, a foot *benumbed* by cold; a heart *benumbed* by grief.

ben·zene (bĕn′zēn; bĕn-zēn′), *n.* a highly inflammable, colorless liquid obtained from coal tar, used as a motor fuel, in the manufacture of illuminating gas and of dyes, and in other processes.

ben·zine (bĕn′zēn; bĕn-zēn′), *n.* an inflammable liquid obtained from petroleum, used in cleaning, dyeing, painting, and other processes, and as a motor fuel.

Be·o·grad (bĕ-ō′grȧd), a city, capital of Yugoslavia (map 12). Also called **Belgrade.**

be·queath (bĕ-kwēth′), *v.t.* **1,** to give or leave by will; **2,** to hand down; as, the Greeks *bequeathed* to us a love of beauty.

be·quest (bĕ-kwĕst′), *n.* something given or left by will; a legacy; as, small *bequests* of money went to the servants.

be·rate (bĕ-rāt′), *v.t.* [berat-ed, berat-ing], to scold; rebuke severely.

Ber·ber (bûr′bĕr), *n.* a member of a native race of northern Africa:—*adj.* relating to the Berbers.

be·reave (bĕ-rēv′), *v.t.* [bereaved (bĕ-rēvd′) or bereft (bĕ-rĕft′), bereav-ing], to deprive; leave desolate; as, Jacob was *bereaved* of his children; *bereft* of reason.

be·reave·ment (bĕ-rēv′mĕnt), *n.* **1,** the state of being left desolate; **2,** the loss of a relative or friend by death.

be·reft (bĕ-rĕft′), past tense and past participle of *bereave:* used of abstract qualities; as, *bereft* of hope and peace.

be·ret (bĕ-rā′; bĕ′rā), *n.* a round cap of wool or other soft material, without a brim.

berg (bûrg), *n.* a large floating mass of ice; an iceberg.

Ber·gen (bûr′gĕn), a seaport on the west coast of Norway (map 12).

Be·ring Sea (bē′rĭng; bâr′ĭng), a sea between Alaska and Siberia, north of the Aleutian Islands (map 2).—**Bering Strait,** a channel separating Alaska from Siberia.

Berke·ley (bûrk′lĭ), a city of California, on San Francisco Bay (map 9).

Berk·shire (bärk′shĭr; bûrk′shĭr), a county of south central England:—**Berkshire**

Hills (bûrk′shĭr), a group of hills in western Massachusetts (map 6).

Ber·lin (bûr-lĭn′), a city, formerly the capital of Germany, now under Allied military control (map 12).

Ber·mu·da (bĕr-mū′dȧ), a group of British islands in the Atlantic Ocean, about 900 miles east of South Carolina (map 3).

Bern (bûrn; bĕrn), a canton in west central Switzerland; also, a city, capital of Switzerland (map 12). Also, **Berne.**

Ber·nard (bûr′närd; bĕr-närd′), Saint (1091–1153), a famous French abbot and crusader.

Bern·hardt (bĕrn′härt), Sarah (1844–1923), a celebrated French actress.

ber·ry (bĕr′ĭ), *n.* [*pl.* berries], **1,** any small pulpy fruit with many seeds, as the huckleberry; **2,** the dry seed or kernel of certain plants; as, the coffee *berry:—v.i.* [berried, berry-ing], to gather berries.

berth (bûrth), *n.* **1,** a bunk or bed for a passenger, as on a ship, in a railroad car, or the like; **2,** a position or job; as, he has a good *berth* with the government; **3,** in nautical language, a place where a ship ties up or lies at anchor.

Ber·til·lon (bâr′tē′yôn′), Alphonse (1853–1914), a French scientist who devised a system of identifying criminals by records of their measurements, coloring, scars, etc.

ber·yl (bĕr′ĭl), *n.* a semiprecious or precious stone of varying colors, commonly green or greenish blue. The aquamarine and the emerald are beryls.

be·seech (bĕ-sēch′), *v.t.* [besought (bĕ-sôt′), beseech-ing], **1,** to entreat; implore; as, I *beseech* you to hear me; **2,** to beg for; as, I *beseech* your favor.

be·seem (bĕ-sēm′), *v.t.* to be suitable or becoming to; befit; as, it hardly *beseems* you to bully your sister.

be·set (bĕ-sĕt′), *v.t.* [beset, beset-ting], **1,** to assail; harass; as, troubles *beset* him; **2,** to hem in; surround; as, a spy is constantly *beset* with dangers.
Syn. encompass, besiege, attack.

be·side (bĕ-sīd′), *prep.* **1,** at or by the side of; near by; as, sit *beside* me; **2,** in comparison with; as, my work is poor *beside* yours; **3,** away from; as, *beside* the point: —**beside oneself,** out of one's senses.

be·sides (bĕ-sīdz′), *adv.* in addition; also; as well:—*prep.* over and above; in addition to.

be·siege (bĕ-sēj′), *v.t.* [besieged, besieging], **1,** to surround with armed forces; lay siege to; as, to *besiege* a city; **2,** to pester or harass (a person) in any way, as with questions or requests.

āte, âorta, râre, căt, ȧsk, fär, ăllow, sofȧ; ēve, êvent, ĕll, writĕr, novĕl; bīte, pĭn; nō, ōbey, ôr, dŏg, tŏp, cŏllide; ūnit, ûnite, bûrn, cŭt, focŭs; nōon, fŏot; mound; coin;

be·smear (bē-smĭr′), *v.t.* to smear or daub with something greasy or sticky.

be·smirch (bē-smûrch′), *v.t.* **1,** to soil; discolor, as with mud; **2,** to dishonor; sully; as, to *besmirch* a man's reputation.

be·sot·ted (bē-sŏt′ĕd), *adj.* stupefied; made senseless; as, *besotted* with drink.

be·sought (bē-sôt′), past tense and past participle of *beseech*.

be·span·gle (bē-spăng′gl), *v.t.* [bespangled, bespan-gling], to besprinkle or adorn, as with spangles.

be·spat·ter (bē-spăt′ẽr), *v.t.* to soil by splashing with wet mud or the like.

be·speak (bē-spēk′), *v.t.* [*p.t.* bespoke (bē-spōk′), *p.p.* bespo-ken (bē-spō′kĕn), *p.pr.* bespeak-ing], **1,** to ask for beforehand; order in advance; as, I *bespoke* two tickets; **2,** to show or give evidence of; as, his fine playing *bespoke* long practice.

Bes·sa·ra·bi·a (bĕs′ȧ-rā′bĭ-ȧ), a region in southwestern U.S.S.R., formerly a Rumanian province.

Bes·se·mer proc·ess (bĕs′ĕ-mẽr), a process for making steel, in which air is blown through molten cast iron to remove carbon and impurities.

best (bĕst), *adj.* [*superl.* of *good*], **1,** having the highest degree of goodness or excellence; as, he did the *best* work in class; **2,** largest; as, the *best* part of a month:—*n.* **1,** that which is finest; as, the *best* is none too good; **2,** the highest degree of excellence; as, she was at her *best* in the school play:—*adv.* [*superl.* of ²*well*], **1,** in the most successful way; **2,** in the highest degree:—*v.t.* to get the better of; surpass.

bes·tial (bĕst′yăl; bĕs′chăl), *adj.* like the beasts; brutish; savage.—*n.* **bes′ti·al′i·ty** (bĕs′tĭ-ăl′ĭ-tĭ; bĕs′chĭ-ăl′ĭ-tĭ).

be·stir (bē-stûr′), *v.t.* [bestirred, bestirring], to rouse; exert.

be·stow (bē-stō′), *v.t.* to give or confer; as, to *bestow* a medal on a hero.

be·stow·al (bē-stō′ăl), *n.* the act of giving or bestowing; as, the *bestowal* of gifts.

be·strew (bē-strōō′), *v.t.* [*p.t.* bestrewed, *p.p.* bestrewed (bē-strōōd′) or bestrewn (bē-strōōn′), *p.pr.* bestrew-ing], **1,** to cover (a surface) with things scattered; as, to *bestrew* a table with papers; **2,** to scatter (things) about; **3,** to lie scattered over; as, stars *bestrewed* the sky.

be·stride (bē-strīd′), *v.t.* [*p.t.* bestrode (bē-strōd′), *p.p.* bestrid-den (bē-strĭd′n), *p.pr.* bestrid-ing], to mount, sit on, or stand over, with one leg on each side; straddle; as, to *bestride* a horse, a fence, a log, or the like.

bet (bĕt), *v.t.* [bet or bet-ted, bet-ting], to stake, risk, or wager (money or the like) that something will or will not happen, or that a contest or situation will end in a certain way; as, I *bet* a dollar that it will rain today; I *bet* ten dollars on the home team:—*v.i.* to lay a wager; as, to *bet* on a horse:—*n.* **1,** a wager; as, to make a *bet*; **2,** the amount staked or wagered; **3,** that on which a wager is laid; as, this horse is a safe *bet*.

bet. abbreviation for *between*.

be·ta (bē′tȧ; bā′tȧ), *n.* the second letter in the Greek alphabet, corresponding in general to English *b*:—**beta particle** or **beta ray**, an electron moving at very high speed. Beta particles are one of the three products of the disintegration of radioactive substances such as radium. They can also be produced artificially by accelerating electrons to high speeds.

be·take (bē-tāk′), *v.t.* [*p.t.* betook (bē-took′), *p.p.* betak-en (bē-tā′kĕn), *p.pr.* betak-ing], to take (oneself); as, they *betook* themselves to a place of safety.

bête noire (bât′ nwär′), literally, in French, black beast; hence, a bugbear; something that is especially disliked.

Beth·a·ny (bĕth′ȧ-nĭ), a village outside of Jerusalem, in Palestine.

beth·el (bĕth′ĕl), *n.* **1,** a holy place; **2,** chapel; especially, a seamen's chapel.

be·think (bē-thĭngk′), *v.t.* [bethought (bē-thôt′), bethink-ing], to remember: used with *myself*, *himself*, or the like; as, I *bethought* myself of an errand.

Beth·le·hem (bĕth′lĕ-ĕm; bĕth′lĕ-hĕm), a village in Palestine, a few miles south of Jerusalem (map 1).

be·thought (bē-thôt′), past tense and past participle of *bethink*.

be·tide (bē-tīd′), *v.t.* [betid-ed, betid-ing], to happen to; befall; as, what will *betide* us, none can tell:—*v.i.* to come to pass.

be·times (bē-tīmz′), *adv.* early; promptly.

be·to·ken (bē-tō′kĕn), *v.t.* to be a token or sign of; foreshadow; as, a red sunset is said to *betoken* hot weather.
Syn. indicate, portend, signify.

be·took (bē-took′), past tense of *betake*.

be·tray (bē-trā′), *v.t.* **1,** to give into the hands of an enemy by treachery; as, Judas *betrayed* his Master; **2,** to be faithless to; as, to *betray* a trust; **3,** to disclose; reveal, as a secret; **4,** to disclose unintentionally; his manner *betrays* uneasiness.—*n.* **be·tray′er.**—*n.* **be·tray′al.**

be·troth (bē-trôth′; bē-trōth′), *v.t.* to promise to give (a daughter) in marriage: —**betrothed,** *n.* the person to whom one is engaged to be married.

be-troth-al (bē-trô′thăl; bē-trō′thăl), *n.* 1, an engagement or promise to marry; 2, the state of being engaged.

¹**bet-ter** (bĕt′ẽr), *adj.* [*comp.* of *good*], 1, having good qualities in a higher degree; as, your work is *better* than it was; these apples are *better* than those; 2, preferable; as, it is *better* to walk than to wait for a car; 3, improved in health; 4, larger; greater; as, I waited the *better* part of an hour:—*adv.* [*comp.* of ²*well*], 1, in a more excellent manner; as, you swim *better* than you did; 2, more; as, you like swimming *better* now:—*v.t.* 1, to improve; as, he has *bettered* his condition; 2, to surpass, as a record:—*n.* 1, a thing more desirable than another; as, of the two pencils, this is the *better;* 2, advantage; as, to get the *better* of an opponent; 3, **betters,** superiors, as in social standing, education, or the like; as, respect for one's *betters.*

    Syn., v. correct, reform, amend.

²**bet-ter** or **bet-tor** (bĕt′ẽr), *n.* one who wagers, or lays bets.

bet-ter-ment (bĕt′ẽr-mĕnt), *n.* a bettering; an improvement, as of land, a railway, a road, or the like.

be-tween (bē-twēn′), *prep.* 1, in the space or time which separates one thing from another; as, *between* dark and daylight; 2, from one to another of; as, a look passed *between* them; 3, by the joint action of; as, *between* us we shall succeed; 4, by comparison of; as, a choice *between* evils:—*adv.* in a place between other things.

be-twixt (bē-twĭkst′), *prep.* between; as, *betwixt* two perils:—**betwixt and between,** neither one thing nor the other.

bev-el (bĕv′ĕl), *v.t.* [beveled, bevel-ing], to give a sloping edge to; as, to *bevel* the edge of a table:—*v.i.* to slant or incline:—*n.* 1, the slant or angle that one line or surface makes with another; 2, an instrument used for drawing or measuring angles:—*adj.* having a slant; as, a *bevel* edge.

bev-er-age (bĕv′ẽr-ĭj), *n.* any kind of drink, as coffee, lemonade, wine, etc.

bev-y (bĕv′ĭ), *n.* [*pl.* bevies], 1, a company or group, especially of girls or women; 2, a flock of birds, especially of quail or larks.

be-wail (bē-wāl′), *v.t.* to mourn or weep for; lament; as, Shylock *bewailed* his loss.

be-ware (bē-wâr′), *v.i.* and *v.t.* to be on one's guard (against); be wary (of).

be-wil-der (bē-wĭl′dẽr), *v.t.* to perplex; confuse; puzzle; as, the turns and twists in the path *bewildered* us.

    Syn. confound, mystify.

be-wil-der-ment (bē-wĭl′dẽr-mĕnt), *n.* perplexity; confusion; a puzzled state.

be-witch (bē-wĭch′), *v.t.* 1, to cast a spell over as by magic; as, the fairy *bewitched* the cow; 2, hence, to fascinate; charm.

be-witch-ing (bē-wĭch′ĭng), *adj.* fascinating; charming.—*adv.* **be-witch′ing-ly.**

be-wray (bē-rā′), *v.t. Archaic,* to betray.

bey (bā), *n.* 1, a governor of a province or district in Turkey; 2, the title of the rulers of Tunis.

be-yond (bē-yŏnd′), *prep.* 1, on the farther side of; as, *beyond* the hills; 2, farther than; past; as, *beyond* the finish line; *beyond* five o'clock; 3, out of the reach of; as, *beyond* medical aid; 4, outside the experience of; too much for; as, algebra was *beyond* him:—*adv.* at a distance; yonder:—*n.* that which lies on the farther side:—**the Beyond,** life after death.

Bey-routh (bā′rōōt; bā-rōōt′), former French name for capital city of Lebanon. See **Beirut.**

bi- (bī-), a prefix meaning two, twice, or doubly; as, *biped. Bi*monthly means occurring every two months; as, a *bimonthly* report.

bi-an-nu-al (bī-ăn′ū-ăl), *adj.* occurring twice a year.—*adv.* **bi-an′nu-al-ly.**

bi-as (bī′ăs), *adj.* slanting; diagonal; as, a *bias* seam:—*n.* 1, the diagonal direction of a cut, seam, or stitching made to slant across the threads of material; as, to cut a skirt on the *bias;* 2, a leaning of the mind toward a particular thing, desire, or opinion; prejudice:—*v.t.* [biased or biassed, bias-ing or bias-sing], to give a particular direction to; influence; as, the newspapers *bias* our opinions.

bi-ased or **bi-assed** (bī′ăst), *adj.* prejudiced; influenced by prejudice.

bib (bĭb), *n.* a cloth like a small apron placed under a child's chin to protect the clothes; also, the upper part of an apron.

Bib. abbreviation for *Bible, Biblical.*

Bi-ble (bī′bl), *n.* 1, the sacred writings of the Old and New Testaments, whether in the original tongue or translated; 2, a book of the sacred writings of any religion; as, the Koran is the Mohammedan *Bible.*

Bib-li-cal (bĭb′lĭ-kăl), *adj.* pertaining to the Bible; as, *Biblical* criticism.

bib-li-og-ra-phy (bĭb′lĭ-ŏg′rá-fĭ), *n.* [*pl.* bibliographies], 1, the study of books, their authors, material, style of printing, dates, editions, and the like; 2, a list of books relating to a given subject or author. —*n.* **bib′li-og′ra-pher.**—*adj.* **bib′li-o-graph′i-cal** (bĭb′lĭ-ō-grăf′ĭ-kăl).

bib-li-o-phile (bĭb′lĭ-ō-fīl; bĭb′lĭ-ō-fĭl) or **bib-li-o-phil** (bĭb′lĭ-ō-fĭl), *n.* a booklover.

bi-cam-er-al (bī-kăm′ẽr-ăl), *adj.* consisting of two legislative chambers or branches. The U.S. Congress is bicameral.

bi-car-bon-ate (bī-kär′bŏn-āt), *n.* a salt of carbonic acid:—**bicarbonate of soda,** a white substance, in the form of powder or crystals, used as a leaven in cooking, and as a medicine.

bi-cen-ten-ni-al (bī′sĕn-tĕn′ĭ-ăl), *adj.* occurring every 200 years:—*n.* a 200th anniversary or its celebration.

bi-ceps (bī′sĕps), *n.* the large muscle on the front of the upper arm.

bi-chlor-ide(bī-klôr′īd; bī-klôr′-ĭd) or **bi-chlor-id** (bī-klôr′ĭd), *n.* a compound of chlorine; especially, bichloride of mercury, a deadly poison, which is used as an antiseptic.

B, human biceps.

BICEPS

bick-er (bĭk′ẽr), *v.i.* **1,** to squabble; wrangle; as, these two boys always *bicker* over their marbles; **2,** to flow noisily, as a brook:—*n.* an angry or petty dispute.

bi-cus-pid (bī-kŭs′pĭd), *adj.* with two points or cusps:—*n.* in man, one of eight teeth, placed in pairs, two on each side of each jaw, between the canines and the molars. (See illustration at *dentition*.)

bi-cy-cle (bī′sĭk-l), *n.* a light vehicle having a metal frame, two wheels, one behind the other, and a saddlelike seat for the rider, who propels the bicycle by means of pedals, and steers it by means of a handlebar:—*v.i.* [bicy-cled, bicy-cling], to ride on a bicycle.—*n.* **bi′cy-cler.**—*n.* **bi′cy-clist.**

BICYCLE

bid (bĭd), *v.t.* [*p.t.* bade (băd) or, in definition 3, bid, *p.p.* bid-den (bĭd′n) or, in definition 3, bid, *p.pr.* bid-ding], **1,** to command; order; as, he *bade* me tell everything; **2,** to offer by way of greeting; say; as, to *bid* someone welcome or good-by; also, to invite; as, he *bade* me come again; **3,** to propose as a price for something, especially at an auction; as, he *bid* ten dollars for the watch:—*v.i.* to make an offer; offer a price:—*n.* **1,** an offer of a price, as at an auction; also, the amount offered; as, a *bid* of five dollars; **2,** the statement of a price, or the price itself, at which a person will do a piece of work; as, his *bid* on the new house was $15,000.

bid-den (bĭd′n), one of the forms of the past participle of *bid*.

bid-der (bĭd′ẽr), *n.* one who bids, as at an auction, or in competition for a piece of work.

bid-ding (bĭd′ĭng), *n.* **1,** a command; summons; as, I have come at your *bidding*; **2,** the offering of a price in competition with others, as at an auction.

bide (bīd), *v.t.* [*p.t.* bode (bōd) or bid-ed, *p.p.* bid-ed, *p.pr.* bid-ing], to wait for; as, you must *bide* your time.

bi-en-ni-al (bī-ĕn′ĭ-ăl), *adj.* **1,** occurring once in two years; as, a *biennial* convention; **2,** continuing or living for two years; as, *biennial* plants:—*n.* **1,** a plant which produces roots and leaves in the first year, and flowers, fruit, and seed in the second, and then dies; **2,** an event that occurs once in two years.

bier (bēr), *n.* the frame on which a corpse or coffin is placed or carried.

bi-fo-cal (bī-fō′kăl), *adj.* having two focal points, as a lens:—*n.* a lens ground to form a combination of two lenses, one for near and the other for distant objects:—**bifocals,** eyeglasses with this type of lens.

big (bĭg), *adj.* [big-ger, big-gest], **1,** large, bulky; as, a *big* horse; a *big* load; **2,** boastful; pompous; as, *big* talk; **3,** important; serious; as, a *big* issue; a *big* mistake.

big-a-mist (bĭg′á-mĭst), *n.* a man who has two wives, or a woman who has two husbands, at the same time.

big-a-my (bĭg′á-mĭ), *n.* the act of marrying a person while married to another.

big-horn (bĭg′hôrn′), *n.* the wild sheep of the Rocky Mountains.

bight (bīt), *n.* **1,** a bend, as in a coast line or river, forming a bay; **2,** a bay between two headlands; **3,** a loop or bend in a rope.

big-ot (bĭg′ŭt), *n.* a person who is unreasonably and obstinately attached to his beliefs and opinions on such subjects as religion, morals, etc.

BIGHORN (₂⁄₀)

big-ot-ed (bĭg′ŭt-ĕd), *adj.* obstinately attached to one's own beliefs and opinions. *Syn.* intolerant, prejudiced, biased.

big-ot-ry (bĭg′ŭt-rĭ), *n.* [*pl.* bigotries], obstinate and unreasonable attachment to one's beliefs and opinions on religion, morals, politics, or the like; intolerance.

big tree, the giant sequoia of California; also, popularly, the redwood. (See illustration on page 865.)

bi-jou (bē′zhōō; bē′zhōō′), *n.* [*pl.* bijoux (bē′zhōōz; bē′zhōō′)], a trinket; jewel.

bi-lat-er-al (bī-lăt′ẽr-ăl), *adj.* having to do with two sides or two parties; as, a *bilateral* contract.

---

bil·ber·ry (bĭl'bĕr'ĭ), *n.* [*pl.* bilberries], a shrub, somewhat like the blueberry; also, its berry.

bile (bīl), *n.* **1,** the bitter, yellow or greenish fluid secreted by the liver to aid in the digestive processes; **2,** ill-humor; irritation; anger.

bilge (bĭlj), *n.* **1,** the bulging part of a cask; **2,** the bottom of a ship up to the point where the sides become vertical:—**bilge water,** water which gathers in the bottom of a ship, always very disagreeable in odor:—*v.i.* [bilged, bilg-ing], **1,** to spring a leak by a break in the bilge; **2,** to bulge:— *v.t.* to stave in the bottom of (a ship).

bi·lin·gual (bī-lĭng'gwăl), *adj.* **1,** expressed in two languages; as, a *bilingual* inscription; **2,** speaking two languages.

bil·ious (bĭl'yŭs), *adj.* **1,** caused by a disorder of the liver; due to too much bile; as, a *bilious* headache; **2,** bad-tempered; peevish.—*n.* **bil'ious-ness.**

-bil·i·ty (-bĭl'ĭ-tĭ), a suffix meaning state of being, which forms nouns corresponding to adjectives ending in *-ble*; as, possi*bility*, credi*bility*.

¹bill (bĭl), *n.* **1,** a draft of a proposed law presented to a legislature; **2,** an account of money owed for goods sold, services given, or work done; as, a plumbing *bill*; **3,** a piece of paper money; as, a ten-dollar *bill*; **4,** a promissory note; **5,** a printed advertisement; poster; **6,** a paper giving a list of items; as, the *bill* of the races; a *bill* of fare; **7,** in law, a written complaint or accusation:—*v.t.* **1,** to advertise by posters; enter on a program; announce; as, the actor was *billed* to appear in person; **2,** to make a bill of; enter on a bill; make a list of; as, these purchases will be *billed* next month; **3,** to charge (a person); send a statement of indebtedness to; as, please· *bill* me without delay; **4,** to ship by freight; as, *billed* to Chicago.

bill of lading, a receipt for goods shipped issued to the shipper by a railroad or other carrier; **bill of sale,** a formal paper transferring to a buyer the title to personal property.

²bill (bĭl), *n.* **1,** the beak of a bird; **2,** a similar beak in other animals, as the jaw of a turtle:—*v.i.* to join bills; show affection; as, doves *bill* and coo.

bill-board (bĭl'bôrd), *n.* a board set up outdoors for the display of posters.

¹bil·let (bĭl'ĕt), *n.* a thick piece of wood, cut for fuel.

²bil·let (bĭl'ĕt), *n.* **1,** a written order from a military officer directing the person to whom it is addressed to furnish a soldier with board and lodging; **2,** a place where a soldier is lodged; in World War I, a rest camp; **3,** a situation; appointment; as, he had a comfortable *billet* in Washington: —*v.t.* [billet-ed, billet-ing], to quarter or lodge; as, the government *billeted* the soldiers on the peasants.

bill-head (bĭl'hĕd'), *n.* a printed form, with a name and business address at the top, used for making out bills.

bil·liards (bĭl'yĕrdz), *n.* a game played with solid balls and a cue on an oblong, cloth-covered table which is bounded by a raised, cushioned ledge.

bil·lion (bĭl'yŭn), *n.* in the U.S. and France, one thousand millions, written 1,000,000,000; in England and Germany, a million millions, written 1,000,000,000,-000.

bil·low (bĭl'ō), *n.* a great wave of the sea: —*v.i.* **1,** to rise and roll in large waves; **2,** to swell out; bulge; as, the ship's sails *billowed* in the breeze.

bil·low·y (bĭl'ō-ĭ), *adj.* surging; as, the *billowy* ocean.

bil·ly (bĭl'ĭ), *n.* [*pl.* billies], a club, especially a policeman's club.

bi·met·al·lism (bī-mĕt'ăl-ĭzm), *n.* the use of two metals jointly, usually gold and silver, as a standard of value in a monetary system.

bi·month·ly (bī-mŭnth'lĭ), *adj.* occurring once every two months.

bin (bĭn), *n.* a box, crib, or enclosed place, used as a storage place; as, a coal *bin.*

bind (bīnd), *v.t.* [bound (bound), bind-ing], **1,** to tie up, as with a cord or band; **2,** to hold together; confine; restrain; as, cement *binds* bricks; ice *binds* the river in winter; this shoe *binds* my foot; **3,** to hold in bonds of affection, loyalty, duty, or law; as, *bound* by friendship or by a promise; *bound* as an apprentice; **4,** to finish or protect with a band or border; as, to *bind* an edge of a garment; **5,** to bandage; **6,** to fasten together and into a cover; as, to *bind* a book:—*v.i.* **1,** to tie up something; **2,** to have the force of a duty or necessity; as, ties that *bind*; **3,** to stick together in a mass; to become hard or stiff; as, clay *binds* when heated.

bind-er (bīn'dĕr), *n.* **1,** a person who binds; **2,** anything that binds, as tar on roads, or a stiff cover for holding loose sheets of paper; **3,** a machine that cuts and binds grain.

bind-er-y (bīn'dĕr-ĭ), *n.* [*pl.* binderies], a place where books are bound.

bind-ing (bīn'dĭng), *n.* **1,** the act of making fast; **2,** something that binds or ties up, as a bandage; **3,** the cover of a book and the part which holds the pages together; **4,** a narrow strip of material, such as braid, which is sewed over the edge of cloth to keep it from fraying or to serve as trimming:—*adj.* holding a person to his word; as, a *binding* agreement.

Bi·net (bē/nâ/), Alfred (1857–1911), a French psychologist, best known for his work on intelligence tests.

bin·na·cle (bĭn/a-kl), *n.* a case or stand near the steering wheel of a ship containing the ship's compass.

bin·oc·u·lar (bĭn-ŏk/ū-lẽr; bī-nŏk/ū-lẽr), *adj.* adapted to the use of both eyes at the same time; as, *binocular* glasses:—**binoculars,** *n.pl.* field or opera glasses. (See illustration at *field glass.*)

bi·no·mi·al (bī-nō/mĭ-ăl), *n.* in algebra, an expression having two terms connected by the sign plus [+] or minus [−], as $a+b$ or $3-y$:—*adj.* consisting of two terms; as, $a-b$ is a *binomial* expression.

bi·og·ra·pher (bī-ŏg/ra-fẽr; bĭ-ŏg/ra-fẽr), *n.* one who writes the history of a person's life; as, Boswell was Johnson's *biographer.*

bi·o·graph·ic (bī/ō-grăf/ĭk) or **bi·o·graph·i·cal** (-grăf/ĭ-kăl), *adj.* having to do with biography; as, *biographic* material.

bi·og·ra·phy (bī-ŏg/ra-fĭ; bĭ-ŏg/ra-fĭ), *n.* [*pl.* biographies], **1,** a history of a person's life; **2,** the branch of literature dealing with the written history of persons' lives.

bi·o·log·i·cal war·fare, the use of germs which are harmful to animal or plant life as a means of military attack.

bi·ol·o·gist (bī-ŏl/ō-jĭst), *n.* a person who is trained or skilled in biology.

bi·ol·o·gy (bī-ŏl/ō-jĭ), *n.* the science which includes both the study of plants (*botany*) and the study of animals (*zoology*).—*adj.* **bi/o·log/ic** (bī/ō-lŏj/ĭk); **bi/o·log/i·cal.**

bi·ped (bī/pĕd), *n.* an animal with two feet. Men and birds are bipeds.

bi·plane (bī/plān/), *n.* an airplane with two main supporting surfaces, usually one above the other.

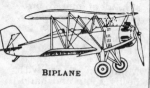

BIPLANE

birch (bûrch), *n.* **1,** a kind of tree, valued for its close-grained wood, with smooth outer bark, which in some varieties may be removed in thin, papery sheets (see illustration page 864); **2,** the wood of this tree; **3,** a whip formed of birch twigs, used for flogging:—*adj.* made of birch; as, *birch* furniture:—*v.t.* to punish with a birch; flog; whip.—*adj.* **birch/en.**

birch bark, the smooth outer bark of the birch, especially the white paper birch:—**birch–bark,** *adj.* made of birch bark.

bird (bûrd), *n.* **1,** any member of a class of warm-blooded, feathered, egg-laying animals, having wings that generally enable it to fly; **2,** any small game bird, as distinguished from a waterfowl; **3,** *Slang,* a fellow; chap; as, he is a queer *bird.*

BIRD

Parts of a bird: 1, bill; 2, forehead; 3, crown; 4, wing; 5, primary feathers; 6, secondary feathers; 7, tail; 8, abdomen; 9, breast; 10, throat; 11, tarsus; 12, first toe; 13, second, third, and fourth toes.

bird of par·a·dise, a bird of New Guinea the male of which has brilliant plumage; **bird of passage, 1,** a bird which moves or migrates from one place to another as the season changes; **2,** *Colloquial,* a person who wanders from place to place; **bird of prey,** any flesh-eating bird, as a hawk.

bird-lime (bûrd/līm/), *n.* a sticky substance smeared on twigs to catch birds.

bird's–eye (bûrdz/–ī/), *adj.* **1,** seen from above, as if by a flying bird; as, a *bird's-eye* view of the city; hence, general; sweeping; not detailed; as, a *bird's-eye* view of the labor problem; **2,** marked with spots resembling a bird's eye; as, *bird's-eye* maple.

Bir·ming·ham (bûr/mĭng-ăm; bûr/mĭng-hăm), **1,** a large manufacturing city in central England (map **13**); **2,** a manufacturing city in central Alabama (map **8**).

birth (bûrth), *n.* **1,** the act of coming into life; **2,** origin; beginning; as, the *birth* of a republic; **3,** descent; lineage; as, Lincoln was a man of humble *birth.*

birth-day (bûrth/dā/), *n.* **1,** the day on which a person is born or on which a beginning is made; **2,** the anniversary of such a day.

birth-mark (bûrth/märk/), *n.* a mark or blemish existing on the skin from birth.

birth-place (bûrth/plās/), *n.* the place of a person's birth; hence, place of origin.

birth rate, the number of births within a given area and time, usually stated as so many births per hundred or thousand inhabitants.

birth-right (bûrth/rīt/), *n.* **1,** any right, privilege, or possession to which a person

---

go; join; yet; sing; chin; show; thin, *th*en; hw, *wh*y; zh, azure; ü, Ger. für or Fr. lune; ö, Ger. schön or Fr. feu; ṅ, Fr. enfant, nom; kh, Ger. ach or ich. See pages ix–x.

is entitled by birth; **2,** the rights or inheritance of the oldest son.

Bi·sa·yas (bē-sä′yäz), a group of islands in the Philippines. See **Visayan Islands.**

Bis·cay, Bay of (bĭs′kā; bĭs′kĭ), a bay north of Spain (map 12).

bis·cuit (bĭs′kĭt), *n.* **1,** a flat cake of unraised bread, baked hard and dry; a cracker; **2,** in the U.S., a small piece of dough, usually unsweetened, raised with baking powder or baking soda, and baked.

bi·sect (bī′sĕkt′), *v.t.* to cut or divide into two, usually equal, parts.— *n.* **bi·sec′tion.**— *n.* **bi·sec′tor.**

bish·op (bĭsh′ŭp), *n.* **1,** a clergyman of high rank, the head of a diocese or church district; **2,** a piece used in playing chess.

BISECT
Line BD bisects the angle ABC.

bish·op·ric (bĭsh′ŭp-rĭk), *n.* **1,** the office of bishop; **2,** a diocese or church district.

[1]**Bis·marck** (bĭz′märk; bĭs′märk), Otto von (1815-1898), a German statesman who unified the German states into the German Empire.

[2]**Bis·marck** (bĭz′märk), a city, the capital of North Dakota (map 7).

bis·muth (bĭz′mŭth; bĭs′mŭth), *n.* a brittle, reddish-white, metallic element, used in alloys. Salts of bismuth are commonly used in medicines and cosmetics.

bi·son (bī′sn; bī′zn), *n.* **1,** a wild, shaggy-maned, oxlike animal of North America, popularly called *buffalo,* extinct except in protected herds; **2,** the European wild ox, now extinct except in protected herds in Lithuania.

BISON (.)
American buffalo.

bisque (bĭsk), *n.* **1,** a thick, rich, cream soup made from meat, fish, or tomatoes; **2,** a kind of ice cream containing finely chopped nuts or macaroons.

bis·ter (bĭs′tẽr), *n.* **1,** a dark-brown pigment made from wood soot and used in water colors; **2,** its color.

[1]**bit** (bĭt), past tense and a form of the past participle of *bite:*— *n.* **1,** a tool for boring holes (see illustration in next column); **2,** the cutting part of a tool, as a blade in a carpenter's plane; **3,** the metal mouthpiece

BIT
Bit on horse's bridle, showing relation to harness and to horse's mouth.

of a bridle; **4,** the part of a key that enters and works a lock (see illustration at *key*).

[2]**bit** (bĭt), *n.* **1,** a small piece of anything; a little; as, a *bit* of bread; **2,** a little while; as, wait a *bit;* **3,** in the southwestern U.S., a money value of 12 1⁄2 cents:—**not a bit,** not at all; none at all.

bitch (bĭch), *n.* the female of the dog, wolf, fox, etc.

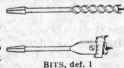
BITS, def. 1

bite (bīt), *v.t.* [*p.t.* bit (bĭt), *p.p.* bitten (bĭt′n) or bit, *p.pr.* bit·ing], **1,** to seize, grip, or cut with the teeth; **2,** to sting; as, a spider *bit* him; **3,** to cut into; as, the saw *bites* the wood; **4,** to cause smarting pain to; as, vinegar *bites* my tongue; **5,** to eat into; as, acid *bites* metal:—**bite the dust,** to fall dead or dying, as in combat; be defeated:—*v.i.* **1,** to seize an object with the teeth; as, the dog *bites;* **2,** to sting or pierce; as, insects *bite;* **3,** to cut or take hold; as, the saw *bites* well; **4,** to smart; as, mustard *bites;* **5,** to take a bait; as, the fish are *biting;* **6,** to eat away; as, acid *bites:*— *n.* **1,** the act of seizing with teeth; **2,** a wound made by the teeth or by a sting; **3,** a mouthful; a slight meal; **4,** a smarting sensation.— *n.* **bit′er.**

bit·ing (bīt′ĭng), *adj.* **1,** sharp, as a taste; **2,** cutting; sarcastic, as speech.

bit·ten (bĭt′n), a form of the past participle of *bite.*

bit·ter (bĭt′ẽr), *adj.* **1,** sharp and unpleasant to the taste, as quinine; **2,** sharp; painful; as, *bitter* cold; grievous; as, *bitter* woe; **3,** severe; sarcastic; as, *bitter* words; **4,** relentless; as, a *bitter* enemy:— *n.* **1,** that which is hard or unpleasant; as, take the *bitter* with the sweet; **2, bitters,** liquor in which herbs or roots have been soaked. —*adv.* **bit′ter·ly.**—*n.* **bit′ter·ness.**—*adj.* **bit′ter·ish.**

bit·tern (bĭt′ẽrn), *n.* a kind of marsh bird, related to the heron. It is noted for its peculiar booming cry.

bit·ter·root (bĭt′ẽr-rōōt′), *n.* a Rocky Mountain plant, with fleshy roots and handsome pink flowers.

bit·ter·sweet (bĭt′ẽr-swēt′), *n.* **1,** a vine of the nightshade family; **2,** an American twining shrub showing in the fall scarlet seeds in open, orange pods:—*adj.* mingling bitter and sweet, or pain and pleasure.

BITTERN (.)

ORIOLE

BOBOLINK

BLUE JAY

RED-WINGED BLACKBIRD

BLUEBIRD

REDSTART

HOUSE WREN

ROBIN

MEADOWLARK

RED-HEADED WOODPECKER

FLICKER

GOLDFINCH

R. BRUCE HORSFALL

All the birds on this page are 1/3 natural size

Familiar Birds of the United States. *(See other side.)*

FAMILIAR BIRDS OF THE UNITED STATES

The pictures on the preceding page represent only a few of our more familiar small birds. There are birds of every size and color, and their habits vary as greatly as their sizes. But whatever a bird's habits, its bill and feet are its working tools. Eagles, hawks, and owls have strong talons for catching and holding their prey and sharp curved beaks for tearing flesh. That old fisherman, the pelican, has a sort of fish-basket bill, and webbed feet for swimming. Woodpeckers have chisel-like bills for drilling in wood. The hummingbird is equipped with a long slender bill for sipping nectar from flowers. Birds, such as the robin, that live on both animal and vegetable matter, have a combination bill, sharp, strong, and comparatively short. A robin will pull an earthworm out of the ground and gobble it down, but more than half of a robin's diet is fruit. It winters as far south as Guatemala, but early in the spring returns north, where it nests in trees about homes and orchards.

The house wren is another friendly visitor to our lawns and orchards, tucking its nest under the eaves of a house or in the cavity of a post. The wren's small body and slender feet are just right for creeping in and about bushes in search of insects. The house wren is noted for its lively curiosity, its merry song, and its large families.

The bluebird is another friendly bird. It builds its nest in crannies of old buildings or in holes in trees, singing merrily as it flashes in and out among the blossoms. It eats a variety of harmful insects.

Joyous, too, is the little goldfinch, perching like a thing of gold on your choicest zinnias or lettuce to eat the ripened seeds. It gathers, too, in family groups on tall thistles. It is also known as the *thistle bird* and *wild canary*.

The Baltimore oriole was named after Lord Baltimore because its colors, black and yellow, are those of the Baltimore family. It builds a stockinglike nest of grass and fiber, attached to the swinging limb of a tree. Such a nest is a great protection against snakes and other egg thieves. The Baltimore oriole is a beautiful singer. Caterpillars, bugs, beetles, and spiders constitute its food.

Gay as the oriole, but naughty, is our blue jay. He leads a double life. Near his nest he is quiet and cautious, away from home he is noisy and bold, ready to bully other birds or attack young squirrels. His stout bill is suited to his diet of acorns, chestnuts, wood-boring insects, and other birds' eggs.

The flicker is a woodpecker, and makes its nest in the hollow of a tree or post, but some of its habits are not unlike those of a thrush. The feet, with two toes turned backward and two turned forward, are meant for tree climbing, and the stiff points on the tail feathers for bracing against a tree while the flicker drills for grubs, but most of its food, especially its favorite insect, the ant, comes from the ground.

The flashy red-headed woodpecker is similar in equipment to the flicker, but it does not feed on the ground. It gets its food from insects that infest trees.

Heading the warblers in beauty is the redstart, so brilliant and so active that it has been called "the little torchbearer." Like most warblers, it builds a rickety nest—a crude affair of bark and fiber, placed in a low bush. But it wages continuous warfare against tree and leaf hoppers, and other insects that do great damage to vegetation. It winters in the West Indies but raises its young as far north as Canada.

The meadow lark delights its listeners with its spirited song. It is of value to man, too, waging war on the boll weevil, alfalfa weevil, cutworms, and ground beetles. Farmers regret that in a few sections of the country it is classed as a game bird.

The bobolink is beloved in the North for its beauty and its song. In the South, it is disliked because on its way to South America for the winter, it stops in the Carolinas just in time to uproot and devour the sprouting rice.

The red-winged blackbird is a delight to the eye, but along the valleys of the Mississippi, where it breeds in great numbers, it destroys much grain. It also eats wasps, spiders, bugs, flies, and the destructive army worm. It winters as far south as Costa Rica.

bi·tu·men (bĭ-tū′mĕn; bĭt′ū-mĕn), *n.* any one of a number of inflammable minerals such as asphalt, petroleum, tar, etc.

bi·tu·mi·nous (bĭ-tū′mĭ-nŭs), *adj.* like or containing bitumen:—**bituminous coal,** coal containing a large amount of bitumen: commonly called *soft coal.*

bi·valve (bī′vălv′), *n.* a shellfish, such as the oyster or clam, with a shell consisting of two valves hinged at one side:—*adj.* having two valves.

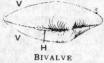

BIVALVE
A clam: V, V, valves; H, hinge.

biv·ou·ac (bĭv′ŏŏ-ăk; bĭv′wăk), *n.* a temporary camp in the open air:—*v.i.* [bivouacked (bĭv′ŏŏ-ăkt; bĭv′wăkt), bivouack-ing], to encamp, as for a night, in the open air.

bi·week·ly (bī-wēk′lĭ), *adj.* occurring or appearing every two weeks:—*n.* [*pl.* bi-weeklies], a periodical issued once in two weeks:—*adv.* once every two weeks.

bi·zarre (bĭ-zär′), *adj.* odd in manner or appearance; fantastic; grotesque.

blab (blăb), *v.t.* [blabbed, blab-bing], to tell thoughtlessly:—*v.i.* to tell tales; talk too much and unwisely:—*n.* one who lets out secrets, or tells tales.

black (blăk), *adj.* 1, of the color of coal: opposite of *white;* 2, almost without light; very dark; as, a *black* cellar; 3, dismal; as, a *black* sky; threatening; sullen; as, *black* looks; 4, without moral goodness; evil; as, *black* deeds; 5, indicating disgrace; as, he got a *black* mark for conduct; 6, dark-skinned, as a Negro; 7, grimy:—*n.* 1, the color of coal; 2, a black color or dye; 3, a Negro; a member of any dark-skinned race; 4, black clothes; mourning: —*v.t.* to blacken, as boots.—*n.* **black′-ness.**—*adv.* **black′ly.**

black·a·moor (blăk′á-mŏŏr), *n.* a Negro; especially, an African Negro.

black art, black magic; the art that witches and conjurers claim to practice.

black·ball (blăk′bôl′), *v.t.* to exclude (a person) from a club or other society by adverse votes recorded by the placing of black balls in the ballot box; hence, to banish from society

black bass, either of two fresh-water game fishes of eastern North America, the *large-mouthed black bass* or the *small-mouthed black bass.*

LARGE-MOUTHED BLACK BASS (⅒)

black·ber·ry (blăk′bĕr′ĭ), *n.* [*pl.* blackberries], 1, a bramble bearing a small, dark, juicy fruit; 2, the fruit itself.

black·bird (blăk′bûrd′), *n.* 1, an English thrush; 2, one of several North American birds related to the bobolink, including the red-winged blackbird and the purple grackle (see illustration below).

BLACKBERRY
Twig of blackberry bush, showing leaves and fruit.

black·board (blăk′bôrd′), *n.* a dark, smooth surface, often of slate, to be written or drawn upon with chalk, or colored crayons.

black buck, 1, the common medium-sized antelope of India; 2, the sable antelope of Africa (see illustration under *antelope*).

black·en (blăk′ĕn), *v.i.* to grow black or dark:—*v.t.* 1, to make black; 2, to speak evil of; as, to *blacken* a person's character.

black—eyed Su·san (blăk′=īd′ sū′zăn; sŏŏ′zăn),a large, orange daisy with a dark-brown center.

RED-WINGED BLACK-BIRD (⅟)

Black For·est, a mountainous region in southwestern Germany.

black·guard (blăg′ärd), *n.* a vicious and abusive scoundrel:—*adj.* low; abusive:—*v.t.* to revile.—*adv.* and *adj.* **black′guard·ly.**

black·ing (blăk′ĭng), *n.* a black paste, cream, or liquid for polishing shoes, etc.

black·jack (blăk′jăk′), *n.* a small club with a weighted head and flexible handle: —*v.t.* to hit with a blackjack.

black list, a list of persons, companies, etc., judged worthy of punishment, exclusion, or the like:—**black—list** (blăk′=līst′), *v.t.* to place the name of (a person or firm) on a black list.

black·mail (blăk′māl′), *n.* 1, money got from a person by a threat to tell something bad about him; 2, an attempt to get money thus:—*v.t.* to get money from (a person) by threats.—*n.* **black′mail·er.**

black·out (blăk′out′), *n.* the covering at night of all lights that would be visible to an airplane pilot flying overhead.

Black Sea, a sea between Europe and Asia Minor (map 12). Its former name was *Euxine Sea.*

black·smith (blăk′smĭth′), *n.* a person who works in iron, by heating it in fire, and then hammering it into shape.

---

go; join; yet; sing; chin; show; thin, *th*en; hw, *wh*y; zh, azure; ü, Ger. f*ür* or Fr. l*u*ne; ö, Ger. sch*ö*n or Fr. f*eu*; ṅ, Fr. *enfant*, *nom*; kh, Ger. a*ch* or i*ch*. See pages ix–x.

black snake or **black-snake** (blăk´-snāk´), *n.* **1**, any of several dark, harmless snakes; **2**, a heavy whip of cowhide.

Black-stone (blăk´stōn), Sir William (1723 1780), an English jurist and writer on law.

blad-der (blăd´ẽr), *n.* **1**, in man and other animals, a sac of elastic muscle in which fluid collects, especially the fluid secreted by the kidneys; **2**, any sac or bag containing fluid or gas.

blade (blād), *n.* **1**, the cutting part of a knife or other instrument; **2**, a long slender leaf, as of grass; **3**, the broad part of any leaf; **4**, a broad, flat object or part; as, the shoulder *blade;* **5**, a sword or swordsman; **6**, a dashing fellow.

BLADE

Knife, showing: B, blade; H, handle.

Blake (blāk), William (1757–1827), an English mystic, poet, and artist.

blam-a-ble (blā´mȧ-bl), *adj.* deserving of blame or censure; faulty.

blame (blām), *n.* **1**, an expression of disapproval; censure; **2**, responsibility for something that goes wrong or is done wrong; as, he bears the *blame:—v.t.* [blamed, blam-ing], **1**, to find fault with; reproach; **2**, to place responsibility for; as, she *blames* her errors on her sister: **—to blame,** at fault; as, she is *to blame.* *Syn.,* v. condemn, upbraid, censure.

blame-less (blām´lĕs), *adj.* free from fault. —*adv.* **blame´less-ly.**—*n.* **blame´less-ness.**

blame-wor-thy (blām´wûr´thǐ), *adj.* deserving reproof.

blanch (blȧnch), *v.t.* **1**, to whiten; **2**, to scald quickly, so as to remove the skin; as, to *blanch* almonds:—*v.i.* to turn pale.

blanc-mange (blȧ-mänzh´), *n.* a jellylike dessert composed of some starchy substance, such as cornstarch, combined with milk, sweetened and flavored.

Blanc, Mont (môn´/blän´), the highest mountain of the Alps, located in France near the Italian border (map 12).

bland (blănd), *adj.* **1**, soft-spoken; gentle; as, a *bland* manner; **2**, mild; soothing; as, a *bland* diet.—*adv.* **bland´ly.**—*n.* **bland´ness.**

blan-dish (blăn´dǐsh), *v.t.* to flatter; coax; wheedle.—*n.* **blan´dish-ment.**

blank (blăngk), *n.* **1**, any empty space; **2**, a printed form with empty spaces to be filled in; as, an order *blank;* **3**, a void; as, his mind was a *blank:—adj.* **1**, free from writing or print; **2**, without variety or interest; as, a *blank* day; **3**, without expression; as, a *blank* look; **4**, unbroken;

unmarked; as, *b..ank* silence; a *blank* wall. —*adv.* **blank´ly.**—*n.* **blank´ness.**

blan-ket (blăng´kĕt), *n.* **1**, a soft piece of cloth, often of wool, used to cover a bed, a horse, a dog, etc.; **2**, a covering of any kind; as, a waterproof *blanket;* a *blanket* of clouds:—*v.t.* to cover with, or as with, a blanket.

blank verse, unrimed verse; especially, in English literature, verse written in unrimed iambic pentameter.

blare (blâr), *n.* a loud sound like that of a trumpet:—*v.i.* [blared, blar-ing], to give forth a loud, brazen sound like that of a trumpet:—*v.t.* to sound loudly.

blar-ney (blär´nǐ), *n.* wheedling flattery:— *v.t.* to win over by smooth talk:—**Blarney Stone,** a stone in the wall of Blarney Castle, in Ireland, said to confer the gift of blarney upon those who kiss it.

blas-pheme (blăs-fēm´), *v.t.* [blasphemed, blasphem-ing], to speak profanely or impiously of (God or sacred things):—*v.i.* to talk irreverently.—*n.* **blas-phem´er.**

blas-phe-my (blăs´fē-mǐ), *n.* [*pl.* blasphemies], irreverent or mocking language about God or sacred things.—*adj.* **blas´-phe-mous.**—*adv.* **blas´phe-mous-ly.**

blast (blăst), *n.* **1**, a strong gust of wind; **2**, a forcible stream of air or gas from an opening; as, a *blast* of heat from a furnace; **3**, a sudden sound, as from a wind instrument; **4**, a sudden harmful influence upon plants or animals; a blight; **5**, an explosion, as of dynamite, used in blowing up rocks; also, the charge so used:—*v.i.* to take-off or operate under rocket power: —*v.t.* **1**, to cause to fade or wither; as, a late frost *blasted* the crops; **2**, to destroy; **3**, to break or shatter by an explosive.

blast fur-nace, a furnace for smelting ores, in which the fire is kept very hot by currents of air admitted under pressure.

bla-tant (blā´tănt), *adj.* **1**, noisy; vociferous; **2**, vulgarly conspicuous; as, a *blatant* display of wealth.—*adv.* **bla´tant-ly.**

¹**blaze** (blāz), *n.* **1**, a fire; bright flame; **2**, intense direct light, as of the sun; **3**, brilliant display; splendor; **4**, a sudden outbreak; as, a *blaze* of fury:—*v.i.* [blazed, blaz-ing], **1**, to burst into flame; burn; **2**, to glow or shine like a flame; as, his eyes *blazed;* **3**, to be lighted up, as a house.

²**blaze** (blāz), *n.* **1**, a white spot on the face of an animal; **2**, a mark made on a tree by removing a piece of the bark:—*v.t.* [blazed, blaz-ing], **1**, to mark (a tree), by chipping off bark; **2**, to indicate (a trail) by marking trees in this way.

³**blaze** (blāz), *v.t.* [blazed, blaz-ing], to spread abroad (news); make public.

āte, âorta, râre, căt, ȧsk, fär, ăllow, sofȧ; ēve, ēvent, ĕll, writẽr, novĕl; bīte, pǐn; nō, ōbey, ôr, dŏg, tŏp, cŏllide; ūnit, ūnite, bûrn, cŭt, focŭs; nōon, fŏot; mound; coin;

blaz-er (blāz′ẽr), *n.* a brightly colored jacket used for sport wear.

bla-zon (blā′zn), *n.* a coat of arms:—*v.t.* **1,** to decorate in color, as a shield; inscribe; **2,** to proclaim; as, his face *blazons* his evil deeds.

bldg. abbreviation for *building*.

bleach (blēch), *v.t.* to whiten by a chemical process or by exposing to the sun's rays:—*v.i.* to become white:—*n.* the process of whitening or bleaching; also, a chemical used in the process.

bleach-ers (blēch′ẽrz), *n.pl.* a roofless or temporary stand providing cheap seats at a game, such as baseball.

bleak (blēk), *adj.* **1,** exposed to wind and cold; unsheltered; as, a *bleak* house; **2,** piercingly cold, as a wind; **3,** cheerless; as, a *bleak* day.—*n.* **bleak′ness.**

blear (blēr), *adj.* sore or dim from a watery discharge; as, *blear* eyes:—*v.t.* **1,** to make (the eyes) sore or watery; **2,** to dim or obscure (the sight).—*adj.* **blear′-eyed′.**—*adj.* **blear′y.**

bleat (blēt), *n.* the cry of a sheep, goat, or calf; also, any similar cry:—*v.i.* to utter any such cry.

bled (blĕd), past tense and past participle of *bleed*.

bleed (blēd), *v.i.* [bled (blĕd), bleed-ing], **1,** to give forth or lose blood; **2,** to lose sap or juice; as, the tree *bled* from trimming; **3,** to be filled with sympathy or pity; as, my heart *bleeds* for you:—*v.t.* **1,** to take blood or sap from; **2,** *Colloquial,* to extort money from.

blem-ish (blĕm′ish), *n.* any defect or flaw:—*v.t.* to injure; mar; disfigure.

¹blench (blĕnch), *v.i.* to start or shrink back; quail; flinch.

²blench (blĕnch), *v.t.* to make white or pale:—*v.i.* to grow pale, as with fear.

blend (blĕnd), *v.t.* [blend-ed or blent (blĕnt), blend-ing], to mix together, as colors, liquids, teas, or the like, so as to secure a certain quality or flavor:—*v.i.* to mingle; as, oil and water do not *blend;* also, to merge; harmonize:—*n.* **1,** a thorough mixture; **2,** a shading or merging, as of one color or flavor into another. *Syn.,* v. fuse, combine, mix.

blent (blĕnt), one of the forms of the past tense and past participle of *blend*.

bless (blĕs), *v.t.* [blessed or blest (blĕst), bless-ing], **1,** to make or declare holy; as, God *blessed* the seventh day; **2,** to call down the favor of God upon; as, the priest *blessed* the altar; **3,** to give happiness or protection to; as, *bless* thy people; **4,** to praise; extol; as, *bless* the Lord.

bless-ed (blĕs′ĕd; *Poetic,* blĕst), *adj.* **1,** holy; hallowed; as, the *blessed* saints; **2,** supremely happy; as, *blessed* day; **3,** bringing comfort or joy; as, *blessed* news. —*adv.* **bless′ed-ly.**—*n.* **bless′ed-ness.**

bless-ing (blĕs′ing), *n.* **1,** the favor of God; **2,** a prayer of thanks for such favor, as at a meal; a benediction; **3,** something which makes for happiness or well-being; as, good health is a *blessing*.

blest (blĕst), one of the forms of the past tense and past participle of *bless*.

blew (blōō), past tense of *blow*.

blight (blīt), *n.* **1,** any disease that causes plants to wither or decay; **2,** insects, fungi, or the like, which cause such a disease; **3,** anything which brings about ruin or decay; as, the *blight* of poverty:—*v.t.* to cause to wither; destroy; as, illness *blighted* his life.

blimp (blĭmp), *n. Colloquial,* a small, motor-driven balloon.

blind (blīnd), *adj.* **1,** sightless; **2,** unable or unwilling to understand, judge, or realize; as, *blind* to one's own faults; **3,** heedless; unthinking; as, *blind* haste; **4,** without reason; as, *blind* instinct; **5,** hidden; as, a *blind* ditch; difficult to follow; as, a *blind* path; **6,** without an opening or outlet; as, a *blind* wall; a *blind* alley:—*n.* **1,** anything designed to obstruct vision, or light, as a window shade, a blinker on a bridle, or the like; **2,** something to mislead the eye or the understanding; a trick; **3,** a place or means of concealment, as in hunting:—*v.t.* **1,** to deprive of sight; also, to dazzle; as, the sunlight *blinded* him; **2,** to deprive of judgment; as, hate *blinded* him.—*adv.* **blind′ly.**—*n.* **blind′ness.**

blind-er (blīn′dẽr), *n.* a blinker on a horse's bridle which prevents him from seeing objects beside or behind him.

blind-fold (blīnd′fōld′), *adj.* **1,** with the eyes covered and unable to see; **2,** without thinking clearly; hence, heedless; reckless; as, *blindfold* extravagance:—*v.t.* to cover the eyes of, as with a bandage.

B, BLINKER

blink (blĭngk), *v.i.* **1,** to wink quickly; **2,** to see through half-shut eyes; as, to *blink* at the sun; **3,** to twinkle; glimmer:—*v.t.* **1,** to wink (the eyes) rapidly; also, to turn (lights) off and on rapidly; **2,** to close the mind to:—*n.* **1,** a rapid winking; **2,** a glimmer, as of light.

blink-er (blĭngk′ẽr), *n.* **1,** a leather flap placed one on each side of a horse's bridle to prevent him from seeing objects beside or behind him; **2,** a blinking light used as a warning signal, as at a crossing.

bliss (blĭs), *n.* great happiness; perfect joy.—*adj.* **bliss'ful.**—*adv.* **bliss'ful·ly.**

blis·ter (blĭs'tẽr), *n.* **1,** a small, bladder-like swelling of the skin, containing watery liquid, resulting from a burn, friction, or the like; **2,** any similar swelling, as of the surface of a leaf, or of paint, an air bubble in glass, or the like:—*v.t.* to raise blisters on:—*v.i.* to become covered with blisters.

blithe (blīth), *adj.* gay; joyous; cheery; happy; as, a *blithe* spirit.—*adj.* **blithe'ly.** —*adj.* **blithe'some.**—*adv.* **blithe'some·ly.**

blitz·krieg (blĭts'krēg), *n.* [Ger.], literally, lightning war; war waged with great speed and intensity of attack.

bliz·zard (blĭz'ẽrd), *n.* a furious wind-storm, with snow and extreme cold.

bloat (blōt), *v.t.* **1,** to cause to swell, as with water or air; **2,** hence, to inflate; make vain; as, *bloated* with pride.

bloat·er (blō'tẽr), *n.* a large herring, salted, smoked, and half dried.

bloc (blŏk), *n.* a number of persons tempo-rarily united and working for a common cause; as, the silver *bloc* in Congress.

block (blŏk), *n.* **1,** a solid piece of wood, stone, metal, or the like; **2,** a form for molding or shaping articles, as hats; **3,** the solid piece of wood on which an execu-tioner chops off heads; **4,** a stand on which articles

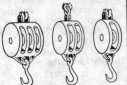

PULLEY BLOCKS

are put up for sale by an auctioneer; **5,** a grooved pulley in a frame: often called *pulley block;* **6,** a connected row of houses or shops; a large building divided into separate houses or shops; **7,** a part of a city bounded by four streets: also called *square;* also, the length of one side of such a square; **8,** a number or section of things taken as a unit; as, a *block* of theater seats; **9,** an obstacle; hindrance; hence, stand-still; as, a traffic *block:*—*v.t.* **1,** to secure or hold up, as by square wooden supports; **2,** to obstruct; hinder; as, do not *block* my way; **3,** to mold on a form; as, to *block* hats; **4,** to outline roughly; plan without details; **5,** in football or basketball, to check the progress of, or interfere with (an opponent or his play).

block·ade (blŏk-ād'), *n.* the shutting up of a place, as a port, by ships or troops in order to prevent anything from coming in or going out, in the hope of forcing sur-render:—**blockade runner,** a ship that evades the enemy's blockade:—*v.t.* [block-ad·ed, blockad·ing], to surround (a place) with a blockade.

block·head (blŏk'hĕd'), *n.* a dunce; dolt.

block·house (blŏk'hous'), *n.* a fort, built of heavy timber, often made with a pro-jecting upper story, and with loopholes in the walls through which to shoot at the enemy.

BLOCKHOUSE

Bloem·fon·tein (blōōm'fŏn-tān), a city, capital of Orange Free State, in Africa.

blond or **blonde** (blŏnd), *adj.* having light hair and a fair skin; fair in coloring. —*n.masc.* **blond.**—*n.fem.* **blonde.**

blood (blŭd), *n.* **1,** in man and other ani-mals, the red fluid which circulates through the body, supplying it with nourishment and oxygen, and carrying away waste matter; **2,** kinship; as, near in *blood;* **3,** de-scent; especially, noble or royal lineage; as, a prince of the *blood;* **4,** bloodshed; as, deeds of *blood;* **5,** a man of spirit; as, a young *blood;* **6,** temper; passion; as, his *blood* was up:—**in cold blood,** deliberately.

blood bank, a reserve supply of blood or plasma for use in transfusion.

blood·ed (blŭd'ĕd), *adj.* of good stock or breed; thoroughbred; as, *blooded* cattle.

blood·hound (blŭd'hound'), *n.* **1,** a powerful hound with long drooping ears, fa-mous for its acute sense of smell, and used chiefly in tracking criminals; **2,** a person keen in pursuit; a de-tective.

BLOODHOUND (¹⁄₁₀)

blood·less (blŭd'lĕs), *adj.* **1,** pale; **2,** lacking emotion or spirit; coldhearted; unfeeling; **3,** without blood-shed; as, a *bloodless* victory.—*adv.* **blood'-less·ly.**—*n.* **blood'less·ness.**

blood mon·ey, money got at the cost of a life, as money received by a murderer for killing someone, or money received for betraying the whereabouts of a fugitive from justice or assisting in his conviction.

blood plas·ma, 1, the fluid portion of un-clotted blood; **2,** treated, and usually dried, blood from which the red cells have been removed.

blood poi·son·ing, a diseased condition of the blood due to poisons or germs.

blood·root (blŭd'rōōt'), *n.* a plant with a red root and red sap, bearing a white flower which blooms in early spring.

blood·shed (blŭd'shĕd'), *n.* the shedding of blood, especially of human beings.

āte, āorta, râre, căt, ȧsk, fär, ăllow, sofȧ; ēve, ĕvent, ĕll, writẽr, novĕl; bīte, pĭn; nō, ōbey, ôr, dŏg, tŏp, cŏllide; ūnit, ūnite, bûrn, cŭt, focŭs; nōōn, fŏŏt; mound; coin;

blood-shot (blŭd′shŏt′), *adj.* red and inflamed; as, *bloodshot* eyes.

blood-stone (blŭd′stōn′), *n.* an opaque green stone, flecked with red.

blood-suck-er (blŭd′sŭk′ẽr), *n.* **1,** an animal that sucks blood; especially, a leech; **2,** one who extorts money from others.

blood-thirst-y (blŭd′-thûrs′tĭ), *adj.* murderous; eager to shed blood.—*adv.* **blood′-thirst′i-ly.**—*n.* **blood′-thirst′i-ness.**

blood type, any one of four classes into which human blood is divided.

blood ves-sel, a tube in which blood circulates in the body, as an artery or vein.

BLOODROOT
Showing root, leaf, and blossom.

blood-y (blŭd′ĭ), *adj.* [blood-i-er, blood-i-est], **1,** stained with blood; as, a *bloody* field; **2,** bleeding; as, a *bloody* nose; **3,** with much bloodshed; as, a *bloody* fight:—*v.t.* [bloodied, bloodying], to stain with blood.—*n.* **blood′i-ness.**

bloom (bloom), *n.* **1,** the flower of a plant; **2,** the state of being in flower or having flowers; as, the tulips are in *bloom*; **3,** a state or period of health and beauty; prime; as, the *bloom* of youth; **4,** a delicate, waxy, or powdery coating on certain fruits or leaves; **5,** a rosy flush on the cheeks:—*v.i.* **1,** to produce blossoms; flower; **2,** to glow with youth and freshness; flourish.

bloom-ers (bloom′ẽrz), *n.pl.* loose, wide trousers gathered and ending at the knees, worn by women in athletic sports; also, an undergarment of similar design.

blos-som (blŏs′ŭm), *n.* **1,** the flower of a plant; **2,** the state of being in bloom; as, trees in *blossom*:—*v.i.* **1,** to put forth flowers; **2,** to flourish.

blot (blŏt), *n.* **1,** a spot or stain; **2,** a spot on the reputation; disgrace:—*v.t.* [blot-ted, blot-ting], **1,** to spot or stain, as with ink; **2,** to dishonor; stain with disgrace; **3,** to dry (ink) with absorbent paper; **4,** to cancel; as, to *blot* out an obligation; **5,** to destroy utterly; as, Sodom was *blotted* out; **6,** to darken or hide; as, a cloud *blots* out the moon:—*v.i.* to become blotted.

blotch (blŏch), *n.* **1,** a large, irregular spot, as of ink; **2,** a disfiguring spot or blemish on the skin:—*v.t.* to mark or disfigure with spots.—*adj.* **blotch′y.**

blot-ter (blŏt′ẽr), *n.* something intended to dry or absorb wet ink; a piece of blotting paper.

blot-ting pa-per, porous, absorbent paper, specially made to dry and absorb wet ink.

blouse (blouz; blous), *n.* **1,** a loose outer garment, like a smock, originally worn by workmen; **2,** any similar garment, especially a waist worn by women and children.

BLOUSES
1, porter's blouse; 2, middy blouse.

¹**blow** (blō), *v.i.* [*p.t.* blew (bloo), *p.p.* blown (blōn), *p.pr.* blow-ing], to burst into bloom or flower.

²**blow** (blō), *v.t.* [*p.t.* blew (bloo), *p.p.* blown (blōn), *p.pr.* blow-ing], **1,** to cause to move or send forward by a current of air; as, the wind *blows* the papers about; **2,** to force air upon, with the mouth or otherwise; as, *blow* out the light; **3,** to make or shape by causing to swell with air; as, to *blow* bubbles; **4,** to cause to sound by forcing air or steam through, as a wind instrument or a whistle; **5,** to clear by forcing air through, as a tube or a nostril; **6,** to shatter by explosives; also, to melt by an electric overcharge, as a fuse; **7,** *Slang,* to spend freely, as money:—*v.i.* **1,** to move flowingly, as the wind; **2,** to send forth air; send up a spout of water, as whales do in breathing out; **3,** to give forth sound when air or steam is forced through; as, the whistle *blew*; **4,** to pant; breathe with quick gasps; **5,** to be moved or carried by the wind; as, the curtains are *blowing*; **6,** *Colloquial,* to brag:—*n.* a gale.

³**blow** (blō), *n.* **1,** a hard stroke with the hand or with a weapon; **2,** a calamity.
Syn. stroke, shock, knock, cuff, lash.

blow-er (blō′ẽr), *n.* **1,** one who blows; as, a glass *blower*; **2,** a device for producing a current of air.

blown (blōn), past participle of ¹*blow* and ²*blow*:—*adj.* **1,** swollen; puffed up with gas: used of cattle; **2,** winded; breathless.

blow-out (blō′out′), *n.* the bursting of something, as a tire, caused by too much pressure from within.

blow-pipe (blō′pīp′), *n.* **1,** a small tube for blowing air into a flame to direct it properly, and to increase its heat; **2,** a primitive gun of cane, from which a dart is blown by the breath: also called *blowgun.*

blowz-y (blou′zĭ), *adj.* [blowz-i-er, blowz-i-est], **1,** red-faced; coarse-complexioned; **2,** frowzy; unkempt.

blub-ber (blŭb′ẽr), *v.i.* to weep noisily:—*v.t.* to utter sobbingly:—*n.* **1,** a noisy weeping; **2,** the fat of whales and some other animals: a source of oil.

---

bludg·eon (blŭj'ŭn), *n.* a short, heavy-headed stick used as a weapon:—*v.t.* to strike with, or as with, a club.—*n.* **bludg'eon·ing.**

blue (bloo), *adj.* [blu-er, blu-est], **1,** of the color of the clear sky; azure; **2,** gloomy; sad; dismal; as, the sad news made her *blue*; **3,** discolored; as, my nose was *blue* with cold:—*n.* **1,** the color of the clear sky; azure; the primary color between green and violet; **2,** a dye or powder that colors blue; **3, the blue,** the sky; the sea; **4, blues: a,** *Colloquial,* usually with *the,* melancholy; low spirits; **b,** a melancholy kind of folk song, of Negro origin, widely adopted in popular music:—*v.t.* [blued, blu-ing or blue-ing], **1,** to make or dye the color of the clear sky, or any hue like it; **2,** to treat with bluing.—*n.* **blue'ness.**

blue blood, 1, in stockbreeding, blood of a pure breed; **2,** blood of a noble or aristocratic family; **blue laws, 1,** certain very strict laws said to have been made by the Puritans of Connecticut; **2,** hence any severe laws, especially in regard to Sunday amusements.

blue·bell (bloo'bĕl'), *n.* any of several plants, bearing blue, bell-shaped flowers, as the harebell.

blue·ber·ry (bloo'bĕr'ĭ), *n.* [*pl.* blueberries], **1,** a shrub of the heath family, bearing round, blue, edible berries; **2,** the berry.

BLUEBERRY
Twig showing leaf and fruit.

blue·bird (bloo'bûrd'), *n.* a songbird of the thrush family. The male has a blue back. (See illustration in next column.)

blue·bot·tle (bloo'bŏt'l), *n.* **1,** a large, flesh-eating steel-blue fly, that buzzes loudly; **2,** a cornflower.

blue·fish (bloo'fĭsh'), *n.* [*pl.* bluefish or bluefishes], a valuable food fish of the Atlantic Coast of the U.S.

blue·grass (bloo'grás'), *n.* a valuable pasture and lawn grass with bluish-gray stems.

blue·ing (bloo'ĭng), *n.* a liquid used in laundering. See **bluing.**

blue·jack·et (bloo'jăk'ĕt), *n.* a sailor; an enlisted man in the navy.

blue jay, a bird of eastern North America, with bright blue plumage and handsome crest.

BLUE JAY (⅓)

blue·print (bloo'prĭnt'), *n.* a photographic print, white on blue paper, used as a plan in building operations, etc.—*adj.* and *v.t.* **blue'print'.**

Blue Ridge, the most easterly ridge of the Appalachian Mountains, extending through North Carolina, Virginia, and Pennsylvania (map **5**).

blu·et (bloo'ĕt), *n.* a low-growing plant of the U.S., with small, bluish flowers, and tufted stems.

COMMON BLUEBIRD OF THE EASTERN UNITED STATES (⅓)

¹bluff (blŭf), *n.* a high, steep bank, cliff, or headland:—*adj.* **1,** rising steeply or boldly, as a cliff; **2,** abrupt but hearty in manner.—*n.* **bluff'ness.**

²bluff (blŭf), *v.t.* and *v.i.* **1,** to mislead or overawe (someone) by assuming a bold or pretentious manner or speech; **2,** to accomplish or attempt by pretense or bravado; as, to *bluff* a test:—*n.* **1,** a show of pretended confidence, knowledge, or the like; **2,** one who bluffs:—**to call one's bluff,** to demand a showdown.—*n.* **bluff'er.**

blu·ing or **blue·ing** (bloo'ĭng), *n.* a bluish preparation used in laundering to make clothes white.

blu·ish (bloo'ĭsh), *adj.* somewhat blue.

blun·der (blŭn'dĕr), *n.* a stupid or careless mistake:—*v.i.* **1,** to make a mistake from stupidity, ignorance, or the like; **2,** to move clumsily, as in a dark room.—*n.* **blun'der·er.**

blun·der·buss (blŭn'dĕr-bŭs), *n.* a short gun of former times, with a flaring muzzle, for shooting at close range.

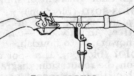
BLUNDERBUSS
S, stand or support.

blunt (blŭnt), *adj.* **1,** having a thick or rounded edge or point; not sharp; as, *blunt* scissors; **2,** dull; not quick-witted; not sensitive; **3,** abrupt in speech or manner; plain-spoken:—*v.t.* **1,** to dull the edge or point of; as, to *blunt* a knife; **2,** to make less keen; as, fatigue *blunted* his wits.—*adv.* **blunt'ly.**—*n.* **blunt'ness.**

blur (blûr), *v.t.* [blurred, blur-ring], **1,** to make indistinct; as, fog *blurred* the road ahead; **2,** to dim (the senses or judgment); **3,** to stain; blemish; as, to *blur* a paper with blots:—*n.* **1,** a smudge; smear, as of ink; **2,** an indistinct or confused effect; as, the page was a *blur* to his tired eyes.

blurt (blûrt), *v.t.* to utter suddenly and without thought; as, to *blurt* out a secret.

blush (blŭsh), *v.i.* **1,** to become red in the face, as from shame or confusion; **2,** to feel shame; as, she *blushed* for his ignorance:—*n.* **1,** a reddening of the face from any emotion; **2,** a rosy tint, as of dawn.

blus-ter (blŭs′tẽr), *v.i.* **1,** to blow gustily, as wind; to be rough and windy, as the weather; **2,** to talk in a noisy, threatening style:—*n.* **1,** the noise and violence of a storm, or of a high wind; **2,** noisy talk; empty threats.—*n.* **blus′ter-er.**—*adj.* **blus′ter-y.**

blvd. abbreviation for *boulevard.*

bo-a (bō′à), *n.* **1,** a large, nonpoisonous snake that crushes its prey by coiling around it; **2,** a long fur or feather neckpiece for women.

bo-a con-stric-tor (kŏn-strĭk′tẽr), a large boa, often eleven to twelve feet in length, found in tropical America, which crushes its prey to death in its coils.

Bo-a-di-ce-a (bō′à-dĭ-sē′à), (?–A.D. 62), the British queen who, in A.D. 61, led an unsuccessful revolt against the Romans.

boar (bôr), *n.* **1,** a male swine; **2,** the wild hog.

board (bôrd), *n.* **1,** a thin, flat piece of sawed timber, longer than it is broad; **2,** a table for food, or spread with food; **3,** food; meals served,

WILD BOAR (⅟₃₀)

especially at a fixed price; **4,** a group of persons with power to act or advise; as, a *Board* of Health; **5,** pasteboard, as for a book cover; **6,** a flat piece of wood or other material prepared for a definite use; as, a diving *board;* a checker*board:*—**on board,** on a ship or other conveyance:—*v.t.* **1,** to cover with boards; **2,** to furnish with food, or food and lodging, in return for money; as, to *board* students; **3,** to cause to be lodged and fed, as a horse at a stable; **4,** to get on (a ship or train):—*v.i.* to get meals, or meals and lodging, regularly, at a fixed charge; as, I *board* at my aunt's.

board-er (bôr′dẽr), *n.* one who regularly takes meals, or gets meals and lodging, at a fixed charge.

board-ing (bôrd′ĭng), *n.* light timber; also, a covering of light timber.

boast (bōst), *v.i.* to brag; praise oneself or one's belongings or deeds in loud terms; to exult:—*v.t.* to possess as a thing to be proud of; as, he *boasted* a fine ranch:—*n.* **1,** a proud, vainglorious speech; bragging; **2,** a cause of pride or vanity; as, his garden was his *boast.*—*n.* **boast′er.**

boast-ful (bōst′fŏŏl), *adj.* **1,** given to bragging; as, a *boastful* winner; **2,** marked by vanity; as, a *boastful* remark.—*adv.* **boast′ful-ly.**—*n.* **boast′ful-ness.**

boat (bōt), *n.* **1,** any kind of small open watercraft, named according to the power by which it moves; as, row*boat;* sail*boat;* motor*boat;* also, a ship; **2,** a long, narrow dish; as, a gravy *boat:*—*v.i.* to ride in a small open vessel; row; sail. —*n.* **boat′ing.**

GRAVY BOAT

boat-house (bōt′hous′), *n.* a house or shed at the water's edge for storing boats.

boat-man (bōt′mǎn), *n.* [*pl.* boatmen (-mĕn)], a mạn who manages or works around boats.

boat-swain (bō′sn; bōt′swān′), *n.* an under officer of a ship in charge of the crew, and of the rigging and anchors.

¹**bob** (bŏb), *n.* **1,** a jerking movement, as of the head; also, a curtsy; **2,** a weight, as on a pendulum or a plumb line; also, a cork or float on a fishing line; **3,** a style of haircut, shoulder length or shorter, for women or children; **4,** a bobsled:—*v.t.* [bobbed, bob-bing], **1,** to move (the head) with short, jerky motions; **2,** to cut (a woman's or child's hair) to shoulder length or shorter:—*v.i.* **1,** to move jerkily; also, to curtsy; **2,** to fish with a float on the line.

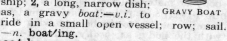

BOB, defs. 3 and 2
1, child wearing bob; **2,** bob of a plumb line.

bob up, to appear suddenly; **bob for,** to try to seize (a floating or hanging apple, cherry, or the like), with the teeth.

²**bob** (bŏb), *n.* [*pl.* bob], in British slang, a shilling.

bob-bin (bŏb′ĭn), *n.* a spool or reel around which thread or yarn is wound.

bob-by (bŏb′ĭ), *n.* [*pl.* bobbies], in British slang, a policeman.

bob-o-link (bŏb′ô-lĭngk), *n.* an American songbird: also called *ricebird* or *reedbird.*

bob-sled (bŏb′slĕd′), *n.* a long sled made of two short sleds joined by a plank; also, either of the two short sleds.

bob-stay (bŏb′stā′), *n.* in a sailing vessel, a rope or chain from the end of the bowsprit to the prow, to hold the bowsprit down.

bob-tail (bŏb′tāl′), *n.* **1,** a short tail or a tail cut short; **2,** hence, an animal with such a tail.—*adj.* **bob′tailed′.**

---

go; join; yet; sing; chin; show; thin, *th*en; hw, *why;* zh, azure; ü, Ger. für or Fr. lune; ö, Ger. schön or Fr. *feu;* ṅ, Fr. *enfant,* nom; kh, Ger. ach or ich. See pages ix–x.

bob-white (bŏb′hwīt′), *n.* **1,** a common American game bird, also known as quail or partridge; **2,** the cry of this bird.

¹bode (bōd), *v.t.* [bod-ed, bod-ing], to be a sign or omen of; betoken; as, his lack of perseverance *bodes* ill for his future.

²bode (bōd), a form of the past tense of *bide.*

bod-ice (bŏd′ĭs), *n.* **1,** the close-fitting waist of a woman's dress; **2,** a wide belt or girdle, laced and tight-fitting.

bod-i-less (bŏd′ĭ-lĕs), *adj.* having no body or material form; as, *bodiless* souls.

bod-i-ly (bŏd′ĭ-lĭ), *adj.* having material form; belonging to the body; having to do with the body; as, *bodily* warmth:—*adv.* completely; in one body; as a whole; as, the class was sent out *bodily.*

bod-kin (bŏd′kĭn), *n.* **1,** a pointed instrument used to pierce holes for embroidery; **2,** a blunt needle with a large eye for drawing tape or ribbon through loops or hems; **3,** a small dagger.

Bod-le-ian (bŏd-lē′ăn; bŏd′lē-ăn), *adj.* pertaining to Sir Thomas Bodley (1545-1613), or to the famous library at Oxford University, England, founded and endowed by him.

bod-y (bŏd′ĭ), *n.* [*pl.* bodies], **1,** the physical form and substance of a person or an animal, living or dead; **2,** the trunk or main portion of a person, animal, or plant; also, the greater part of anything; as, the *body* of a letter; **3,** a person; as, she is a good *body;* **4,** a group of persons or things; as, a legislative *body;* a *body* of facts; **5,** a mass of matter; as, a heavenly *body;* **6,** consistency; substance; as, this silk has very little *body:* —**body politic,** the people of a nation, state, or community, especially when acting as a political unit.

bod-y-guard (bŏd′ĭ-gärd′), *n.* a guard, of one or more, to protect a person.

Boe-o-ti-a (bē-ō′shĭ-à), a division (cap. Thebes) of ancient Greece, northwest of Athens:—**Attica and Boeotia,** a department of modern Greece.

Boer (bōōr; bōr), *n.* a South African of Dutch descent. Most Boers are farmers.

bog (bŏg), *n.* wet, spongy ground composed of partially decayed vegetable matter; a quagmire; marsh:—*v.i.* and *v.t.* [bogged, bog-ging], to sink, or cause to sink, in wet ground; to mire.

bo-gey (bō′gĭ), *n.* [*pl.* bogeys], a bugbear; hobgoblin. Also spelled **bo′gie** or **bo′gy.**

bog-gy (bŏg′ĭ), *adj.* [bog-gi-er, bog-gi-est], full of wet, muddy places; marshy.

Bo-go-tá (bō′gŏ-tä′), a city, capital of Colombia, in South America (map **11**).

bo-gus (bō′gŭs), *adj.* counterfeit; not genuine; sham; as, *bogus* money.

Bo-he-mi-a (bō-hē′mĭ-à), a district (cap. Prague) of western Czechoslovakia; formerly a province of Austria-Hungary.

Bo-he-mi-an (bō-hē′mĭ-ăn), *n.* **1,** a native or inhabitant of Bohemia; **2,** the language of Bohemia; **3,** a gypsy; **4,** a person who is indifferent to established customs, manners, modes of living, and the like; also, an unconventional person:—*adj.* pertaining to the land or language of Bohemia, or to Bohemians.

¹boil (boil), *v.i.* **1,** to bubble from the action of heat; throw off bubbles of vapor; **2,** to be cooked in boiling water; **3,** to be violently agitated; seethe, as if boiling; **4,** to be excited, as by anger:—*v.t.* **1,** to heat (a liquid) to the boiling point, or temperature at which vapor rises in bubbles; **2,** to cook in a boiling liquid:—*n.* a bubbling from the effect of heat.

²boil (boil), *n.* an inflamed, festering sore in the skin, caused by infection.

boil-er (boil′ẽr), *n.* **1,** a strong metal vessel in which steam is produced, as for driving engines; **2,** a tank for storing hot water; **3,** a vessel in which things are boiled.

Boi-se (boi′sĭ), a city, capital of Idaho, on the Boise River (map **9**).

bois-ter-ous (bois′tẽr-ŭs), *adj.* **1,** stormy; rough; as, a *boisterous* sea; **2,** noisily cheerful; as, *boisterous* laughter.

bold (bōld), *adj.* **1,** courageous; fearless; as, a *bold* knight; **2,** steep; abrupt; as, a *bold* headland; **3,** clear; well-marked; as, *bold* strokes of a pen; **4,** showing courage or daring in thought or expression; as, *bold* ideas; **5,** audacious; as, a *bold* front.—*adv.* **bold′ly.**—*n.* **bold′ness.**

bold-face (bōld′fās′), *n.* a particular heavy and conspicuous type:—*adj.* **1,** printing with broad, black lines; as, *boldface* type; **2,** printed in boldface type; as, **this is a boldface line.**—*adj.* **bold′-faced′.**

bole (bōl), *n.* the trunk of a tree.

Bol-i-var (bŏl′ĭ-vẽr; bō-lē′vär), Simon (1783-1830), a Venezuelan patriot.

bol-i-var (bŏl′ĭ-vẽr), *n.* the monetary unit of Venezuela, a silver coin.

Bo-liv-i-a (bō-lĭv′ĭ-à), a republic (caps. La Paz and Sucre) in western South America (map **11**).—*n.* and *adj.* **Bo-liv′i-an.**

bo-li-via-no (bō-lē′vyä′nō), *n.* the monetary unit of Bolivia, a silver coin.

boll (bōl), *n.* the seed pod of a plant, as of cotton:—**boll weevil,** a grayish beetle, about one quarter of an inch long, which lays its eggs in cotton bolls. The larvae cause serious damage to the cotton crop.

bo·lo (bō′lō), *n.* [*pl.* bolos], a large, heavy, swordlike knife used in the Philippines.

Bo·lo·gna (bō-lō′nyä), a province in northeastern Italy; also, a city, its capital (map 12).

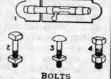

BOLO

Bol·she·vik or **bol·she·vik** (bŏl′shĕ-vĭk; bŏl′shĕ-vĭk), *n.* [*pl.* Bolsheviki (bŏl′shĕ-vē′kē; bŏl′shĕ-vē′kē) or Bolsheviks], 1, a member or supporter of the extreme wing of the Russian Socialist party which has controlled Russia since 1917, now called the *Communist* party; 2, any person with extremely radical views; one who is opposed to the existing order of things.—*adj.* **Bol′she·vik**; **bol′she·vik**.

Bol·she·vism or **bol·she·vism** (bŏl′shĕ-vĭzm; bŏl′shĕ-vĭzm), *n.* the theory of government of the Bolsheviki; revolutionary socialism.—*adj.* and *n.* **Bol′she·vist**; **bol′she·vist**.—*adj.* **Bol′she·vis′tic**; **bol′she·vis′tic**.

bol·ster (bōl′stẽr), *n.* a long pillow; also, a cushioned pad or support:—*v.t.* to support.

¹bolt (bōlt), *n.* 1, a short, heavy-headed arrow for a crossbow; a dart; 2, hence, anything coming dartingly or suddenly; as, a *bolt* of lightning; 3, a metal pin or rod for fastening together parts of machinery, furniture, or the like, threaded to hold a nut; 4, a sliding catch for a door or gate; that part of a lock which is shot or drawn back by the key; 5, a roll of cloth, usually containing about 40 yards; 6, a sudden dashing or darting away, as of a horse; 7, in politics, a refusal to support the policy or nominee of one's own party:—*v.t.* 1, to fasten with a sliding catch, as a door; 2, to fasten together with bolts, as metal plates; 3, to swallow (food) very rapidly, or without chewing; 4, in politics, to break away from (one's party):—*v.i.* to dash away suddenly:—*adv.* stiffly; like a bolt; as, to sit *bolt* upright.

BOLTS
1, door bolt; 2, 4, machine bolts; 3, stove bolt.

²bolt (bōlt), *v.t.* to sift, as flour.

bolt·er (bōl′tẽr), *n.* a machine for separating flour from bran.

bomb (bŏm; bŭm), *n.* a hollow iron ball or shell filled with an explosive, which may be exploded by a time fuse, or by the force with which it strikes:—*v.t.* to attack with bombs; drop bombs on; bombard.

bom·bard (bŏm-bärd′; bŭm-bärd′), *v.t.* 1, to attack with cannon; 2, to assail persistently; as, they *bombarded* me for pennies.—*n.* **bom·bard′ment**.

bom·bast (bŏm′băst), *n.* high-sounding or pompous language.—*adj.* **bom·bas′tic**.

Bom·bay (bŏm-bā′), a province in India; also, a city, its capital, the chief seaport of western India (map 15).

bom·ba·zine (bŏm′bȧ-zēn′; bŏm′bȧ-zēn), *n.* a twilled dress material of silk and wool, or cotton and wool. Also spelled **bom′ba·sine′**.

bomb·er (bŏm′ẽr; bŭm′ẽr), *n.* a heavy airplane, used in offensive warfare for dropping highly destructive missiles.

bomb·shell (bŏm′shĕl′), *n.* 1, a bomb; 2, something sudden and overwhelming.

bo·na fi·de (bō′nȧ fī′dē), in good faith; genuine; as, a *bona fide* offer.

bo·nan·za (bō-năn′zȧ), *n.* a rich vein of ore in a gold or silver mine; hence, anything which brings unexpected wealth.

Bo·na·parte (bō′nȧ-pärt), first emperor of the French. See **Napoleon**.

bon·bon (bŏn′bŏn′), *n.* a sweetmeat; a piece of candy.

¹bond (bŏnd), *n.* 1, that which fastens or confines; 2, **bonds**, fetters; chains; imprisonment; 3, a force or an influence which unites; as, the *bond* of kinship; 4, an agreement binding a person to pay a certain sum of money, if certain conditions are not fulfilled; 5, a certificate issued and sold by a corporation or government, and promising to pay the purchaser a specified sum by a certain date, with interest, usually in instalments; 6, a guarantee that owners of goods, liable to a tax and held in a warehouse pending disposal, will pay the tax when the goods are removed:—*v.t.* 1, to place under the conditions of a bond; as, the firm *bonded* its employees; 2, to put (goods) into a bonded warehouse; 3, to mortgage (property).

²bond (bŏnd), *adj.* in slavery; as, persons both *bond* and free.

bond·age (bŏn′dĭj), *n.* slavery; servitude.

bond·ed (bŏn′dĕd), *adj.* 1, held in bond for payment of taxes or import duties; as, *bonded* goods; 2, working under bond; as, a *bonded* employee:—**bonded warehouse**, a warehouse under bond to the government for the payment of taxes on goods stored in it.

¹bonds·man (bŏndz′măn), *n.* [*pl.* bondsmen (-mĕn)], a person who pledges his credit and assets as guarantee that another will fulfil certain conditions by a given time.

²bonds·man (bŏndz′măn), *n.* [*pl.* bondsmen (-mĕn)], a male slave or serf. Also, **bond′man**.—*n. fem.* **bonds′wom′an**; **bond′wom′an**.

bone (bōn), *n.* **1,** the hard, whitish material composing a skeleton; **2,** one of the separate pieces of this skeleton; **3,** a substance similar to bone, as ivory; **4,** a piece of bone with meat on it; as, a soup *bone:*—*v.t.* [boned, bon-ing], **1,** to remove bones; as, to *bone* a chicken; **2,** to make stiff with whalebone or the like, as a corset.

¹**bon-er** (bōn′ẽr), *n.* a worker who cuts bones from meat.

²**bon-er** (bōn′ẽr), *n. Slang,* a silly, stupid error, either of speech or action.

bon-fire (bŏn′fīr′), *n.* an outdoor fire of refuse or rubbish.

bon-net (bŏn′ĕt), *n.* **1,** a head covering worn by women and children, usually brimless, with ribbons or strings tied under the chin; **2,** in Scotland, a soft woolen cap worn by men.

BONNETS
1, as worn in 1835; 2, as worn in 1850.

bon-ny or **bon-nie** (bŏn′ĭ), *adj.* [bon-ni-er, bon-ni-est], pretty; healthy-looking; as, a *bonny* lass.

bo-nus (bō′nŭs), *n.* a sum paid above what is strictly due.

bon-y (bōn′ĭ), *adj.* [bon-i-er, bon-i-est], **1,** made of bone; like bone; as, *bony* tissue; **2,** full of bones, as a shad; **3,** having prominent bones; as, a *bony* arm.

boo (boō), *interj.* **1,** an exclamation of dislike, disapproval, or contempt; **2,** a sound uttered to frighten someone:—*v.i.* to say boo:—*v.t.* to jeer at in disapproval; as, *boo* a speaker:—*n.* a hoot.

boo-by (boō′bĭ), *n.* [*pl.* boobies], **1,** a dunce; a dull-witted fellow; **2,** in a game, the player ending with the poorest score; **3,** a large tropical sea bird.

book (boōk), *n.* **1,** a collection of sheets of paper or other writing material, bound together in a cover; **2,** a volume containing a long composition or a number of shorter ones; as, a text*book;* a *book* of verse; **3,** a main division or part of a literary composition; as, a *book* of the Bible; **4,** in bridge, a minimum of six tricks, after which the counting of tricks won begins; **5,** in horse racing, a list of horses entered and the bets laid on them:—**the Book,** the Bible:—*v.t.* **1,** to record or register; as, to *book* an order; **2,** to engage beforehand; as, to *book* an orchestra.

book-case (boōk′kās′), *n.* a set of shelves, with or without doors, for holding books.

book-ish (boōk′ĭsh), *adj.* **1,** fond of study; **2,** thoroughly acquainted with books; learned; **3,** making a display of learning; as, *bookish* talk.—*n.* **book′ish-ness.**

book-keep-er (boōk′kēp′ẽr), *n.* a person who keeps accounts, as for a store.

book-keep-ing (boōk′kēp′ĭng), *n.* the work of recording business transactions in an orderly manner; the keeping of accounts.

book-let (boōk′lĕt), *n.* a small book.

book-mark (boōk′märk′), *n.* a loose, flat object put in a book to mark a page.

book-worm (boōk′wûrm′), *n.* **1,** an insect larva that feeds on the paste or leaves of books; **2,** a person very fond of books and reading.

¹**boom** (boōm), *n.* **1,** a long pole or spar attached to a ship's mast to extend the bottom of a sail (see illustration on page 695); **2,** a similar pole attached to a derrick's mast to support or guide the load; **3,** a chain or line of connected floating timbers used on a river to keep logs from drifting away.

BOOM, def. 2
B, boom; M, mast.

²**boom** (boōm), *n.* a deep, rumbling sound, as the roar of breakers:—*v.i.* and *v.t.* to make, or utter with, such a sound.

³**boom** (boōm), *n.* **1,** a sudden increase in business activity or in prices; also, rapid growth, as in population; **2,** a vigorous endorsement of a person for a political office:—*v.i.* to grow or rise rapidly; become suddenly prosperous; as, the town *boomed* when gold was found:—*v.t.* to advertise (a town or a product) widely and actively; to advocate (a candidate) with vigor.

boom-er-ang (boōm′ẽr-ăng), *n.* **1,** a bent, flat piece of wood, used as a weapon by Australian natives, which, when thrown in a certain manner, returns to the thrower; **2,** hence, anything that recoils to the disadvantage of its author.

BOOMERANGS
Showing different types.

¹**boon** (boōn), *n.* a favor; gift; blessing.

²**boon** (boōn), *adj.* jovial; merry; convivial; as, a *boon* companion.

boon-dog-gler (boōn′dŏg′lẽr), *n. Colloquial,* one hired at public expense to do needless work.—*n.* **boon′dog′gling.**

Boone (boōn), Daniel (1735–1820), an American explorer and frontiersman.

boor (boōr), *n.* **1,** a peasant; **2,** a clumsy, ill-mannered person; a lout.—*adj.* **boor′ish.**

boost (boōst), *Colloquial: v.t.* **1,** to lift by pushing from behind; hoist; as, *boost* me over the fence; **2,** to raise; push up; as, to *boost* wages; **3,** to support; promote; as, *boost*

Smith for mayor:—*n.* a push or shove that helps someone to rise or advance.—*n.* **boost'er.**

¹**boot** (boot), *n.* **1,** an outer covering for the foot, usually of leather, coming above the ankle; a high shoe; **2,** especially, in the U.S., such a covering, either of leather or of rubber, and reaching either the knee or the hip; **3,** a place for baggage in a coach, carriage, or automobile:—*v.t.* **1,** to put boots on (someone); **2,** to kick.

BOOTS

1, boy's rubber boot; 2, hunting boot of the 17th century; 3, modern hunting boot.

²**boot** (boot), *n. Archaic,* use; profit:—**to boot,** in addition; into the bargain; as, she gave her time, and her money *to boot:*—*v.t.* and *v.i., Poetic,* to benefit; be of use; as, it *boots* me nothing to go.

boot-black (boot'blăk'), *n.* one who polishes shoes and boots for a living.

booth (booth; boo*th*), *n.* **1,** a temporary stall for the sale of goods, for a puppet show, or the like; **2,** an enclosure to ensure privacy; as, a telephone *booth.*

Booth (booth), **1,** John Wilkes (1838–1865), an American actor, who assassinated Abraham Lincoln; **2,** William (1829–1912), often called *General Booth,* an English clergyman and the founder of the Salvation Army.

boot-jack (boot'jăk'), *n.* a device to hold the heel of a boot while one pulls one's foot out of it.

boot-leg-ger (boot'lĕg'ẽr), *Slang, n.* one who makes or sells something, especially alcoholic liquors, in violation of law.—*v.t., v.i.,* and *adj.* **boot'leg/.**—*n.* **boot'leg'ging.**

BOOTJACK

boot-less (boot'lĕs), *adj.* useless; as, *bootless* efforts.

boots (boots), *n.pl.* used as *sing.* a hotel employee who shines the shoes of the guests.

boo-ty (boo'tĭ), *n.* [*pl.* booties], **1,** food, guns, and the like, taken from the enemy in war; **2,** the plunder of thieves and robbers; **3,** any rich prize or gain.

booze (booz), *Colloquial, v.i.* [boozed, booz-ing], to drink to excess; tipple:—*n.* **1,** liquor; drink; **2,** a spree.

bor. abbreviation for *borough.*

bo-rac-ic (bŏ-răs'ĭk), *adj.* pertaining to, or produced from, boron; boric:—**boracic acid,** a white powder used in solution for antiseptic purposes; boric acid.

bor-ax (bôr'ăks), *n.* a white, crystalline compound of sodium, boron, and oxygen: used as a cleaning agent, antiseptic, water softener, or the like.

¹**Bor-deaux** (bôr'dō'), a French city and port, on the Garonne River (map **12**).

²**Bor-deaux** (bôr'dō'), *n.* a red or white wine made in the region around Bordeaux.

bor-der (bôr'dẽr), *n.* **1,** the edge of anything, as of a lake; **2,** a boundary or frontier, as of a country; **3,** a narrow strip along or around something; as, a handkerchief with a lace *border:*—*v.t.* **1,** to surround or line with a border; as, to *border* a path with flowers; **2,** to come in contact with; lie next to; as, their land *borders* ours:—*v.i.* **1,** to touch; as, the park *borders* on the lake front; **2,** to come near to being; as, his ability *borders* on genius.

Syn., n. rim, brim, brink.

bor-der-land (bôr'dẽr-lănd'), *n.* **1,** land on or near a frontier; **2,** an intermediate state or stage between two distinct states or stages, not belonging entirely to either; as, twilight is the *borderland* between day and night.

¹**bore** (bôr), *v.t.* [bored, bor-ing], **1,** to pierce or drill a hole in; as, to *bore* the ground; **2,** to form (a hole) by piercing or drilling; as, to *bore* a tunnel; **3,** to force (a passage) with effort; as, he *bored* his way through the crowd:—*v.i.* **1,** to make a hole; pierce; as, they *bored* all day; **2,** to be drilled by an instrument; as, this wood *bores* easily:—*n.* **1,** a hole made by piercing or drilling; **2,** hence, the hollow of a gun or tube; **3,** the inside diameter of a drilled hole; caliber.

²**bore** (bôr), *v.t.* [bored, bor-ing], to weary by tiresome repetition or by dulness; as, her complaining *bores* me:—*n.* a tiresome person or thing.—*n.* **bore'dom.**

³**bore** (bôr), *n.* a sudden, violent rush of a flood tide into the mouth of a river.

⁴**bore** (bôr), *n.* past tense of ²*bear.*

Bor-e-as (bôr'ē-ăs), *n.* the north wind.

bor-er (bôr'ẽr), *n.* **1,** one who bores; **2,** an insect or worm that drills holes in wood or plants.

Bor-gia (bôr'jä), the name of a powerful family in Italy in the 15th and 16th centuries.

bor-ic (bôr'ĭk), *adj.* containing boron; boracic:—**boric acid,** a white powder used in solution as an eyewash and an antiseptic; boracic acid.

born (bôrn), one of the past participles of ²*bear* in the meaning brought into life; as, John was *born* in May:—*adj.* natural; so disposed from birth; as, a *born* musician.

borne (bôrn), the usual form of the past participle of ²*bear* when not referring to birth; as, the tree has *borne* fruit: used also in reference to birth when followed by *by*; as, twins were *borne* by the young mother.

Bor-ne-o (bôr′nē-ō), a large island in the East Indies, between Asia and Australia (map **15**).

bor-on (bôr′ŏn), *n.* a nonmetallic element always occurring in combination, as in borax, boric acid, or the like.

bor-ough (bûr′ō), *n.* **1**, an incorporated town; also, in England, a town represented in Parliament; **2**, one of the five political divisions of New York City.

bor-row (bŏr′ō), *v.t.* **1**, to obtain (something) with the understanding that it is to be returned; **2**, to copy; adopt; as, English has *borrowed* many words from Latin:—*v.i.* **1**, to obtain something on the promise to return it; as, he *borrowed* from his son; **2**, to copy or adopt another's thought or words; as, Shakespeare *borrowed* from history and legend.—*n.* **bor′row-er.**

bosh (bŏsh), *Colloquial: n.* absurd or empty talk; utter nonsense:—*interj.* nonsense!

Bos-ni-a (bŏz′nĭ-à), a former Turkish province (cap. Sarajevo) in southeastern Europe, now a part of Yugoslavia.

bos-om (bŏŏz′ŭm; bŏŏ′zŭm), *n.* **1**, the breast of a human being; **2**, the part of a garment which covers the breast; **3**, the breast as the seat of affections, passions, emotions, or desires; the heart; as, my *bosom* swells with pride; **4**, intimacy; privacy; as, in the *bosom* of the family; **5**, anything resembling the breast; as, the *bosom* of the sea:—*adj.* intimate; as, a *bosom* friend.

Bos-po-rus (bŏs′pō-rŭs), a strait joining the Black Sea and the Sea of Marmara and forming part of the boundary between Europe and Asia (map **12**).

¹**boss** (bôs), *n.* a knob which stands out from a flat surface, as on a shield:—*v.t.* to ornament with knobs; to emboss.

²**boss** (bôs), *Colloquial: n.* **1**, a superintendent of workmen; a foreman; also, an employer; **2**, a politician who controls a large number of votes:—*v.t.* to manage:—*v.i.* to be master.—*adj.* **boss′y.**

Bos-ton (bôs′tŭn), a city, capital of Massachusetts, and one of the chief ports and centers of culture of the U.S. (map **6**).—*n.* and *adj.* **Bos-to′ni-an.**

bo-tan-i-cal (bō-tăn′ĭ-kăl) or **bo-tan-ic** (bō-tăn′ĭk), *adj.* relating to botany, the scientific study of plant life.

bot-a-nist (bŏt′à-nĭst), *n.* one who makes a study of plant life.

bot-a-nize (bŏt′à-nīz), *v.i.* [botanized, botaniz-ing], to go into the fields to study plants as they grow.

bot-a-ny (bŏt′à-nĭ), *n.* [*pl.* botanies], the science which treats of plants, their form, growth, classification, distribution, and importance to other forms of life.

botch (bŏch), *n.* bungled work:—*v.t.* to spoil; bungle; do clumsily.—*adj.* **botch′y.**

both (bōth), *adj.* the one and the other; not one only, but two; as, *both* boys were lost:—*pron.* the two; as, take *both*:—*conj.* alike; including; as, *both* men and women.

both-er (bŏth′ēr), *v.t.* to annoy; worry; give trouble to; as, I am busy, don't *bother* me:—*v.i.* to take trouble; as, don't *bother* about dinner:—*n.* **1**, a source of worry; **2**, one who gives trouble.

both-er-a-tion (bŏth′ēr-ā′shŭn), *Colloquial: n.* **1**, the act of annoying; **2**, the state of being vexed:—*interj.* confound it!

both-er-some (bŏth′ēr-sŭm), *adj.* troublesome; annoying; as, a *bothersome* child.

Both-ni-a, Gulf of (bŏth′nĭ-à), the northern arm of the Baltic Sea, between Sweden and Finland (map **12**).

bot-tle (bŏt′l), *n.* **1**, a hollow, narrow-necked vessel without handles, usually of glass; **2**, the contents of a bottle; as, buy a *bottle* of milk:—*v.t.* [bot-tled, bot-tling], **1**, to put into a bottle; **2**, to shut in or hold back; as, to *bottle* up one's feelings.

bot-tle-neck (bŏt′l-nĕk), *n.* figuratively, a stage or condition in a process at which the entire process may be slowed or stopped.

bot-tom (bŏt′ŭm), *n.* **1**, the lowest part of anything, as of a hill; **2**, the part underneath; the base, as of a barrel; **3**, the basis; essential point; as, he got to the *bottom* of the mystery; **4**, the ground under any body of water; **5**, low land bordering a river; **6**, the part of a vessel below the water line; hence, a ship:—*adj.* lowest.

bou-doir (bŏŏ′dwär), *n.* a lady's private sitting room or bedroom.

bough (bou), *n.* a limb or branch of a tree.

bought (bôt), past tense and past participle of *buy*.

bouil-lon (bŏŏ′yôn′; bŏŏl′yŭn), *n.* a clear soup or broth made from beef or other meat.

boul-der (bōl′dēr), *n.* a large, detached stone, rounded by water, weather, or moving ice. Also spelled **bowl′der.**

Boulder Dam, a dam on the Colorado River, at Black Canyon, between Arizona and Nevada, creating a lake 100 miles long. Its official name is now **Hoover Dam.**

bou-le-vard (bŏŏ′lĕ-värd; bŏŏl′ĕ-värd), *n.* **1**, a broad, parklike avenue; **2**, a street reserved for pleasure cars.

Bou-logne (bŏŏ-lōn′; bŏŏ′lôny′), a fortified French port, on the Strait of Dover.

āte, âorta, râre, căt, ȧsk, fär, ăllow, sofȧ; ēve, ĕvent, ĕll, writēr, novĕl; bīte, pĭn; nō, ōbey, ôr, dŏg, tŏp, cŏllide; ūnit, ûnite, bûrn, cŭt, focŭs; nŏŏn, fŏŏt; mound; coin;

bounce (bouns), v.t. [bounced, bounc-ing], to throw or toss (something) so that it will rebound; as, to *bounce* a ball:—v.i. 1, to rebound; as, this ball won't *bounce*; 2, to move suddenly and noisily; as, she *bounced* out of the room:—n. the rebound of an elastic body; a sudden bound or spring; as, she rose with a *bounce*.—n. **bounc′er.**

bounc-ing (boun′sĭng), adj. large; active.

bouncing Bet or **Bess,** a hardy plant of the pink family, growing along roadsides, with narrow leaves and clusters of pinkish-white or red flowers.

¹**bound** (bound), v.i. 1, to leap or spring lightly; as, to *bound* from rock to rock; 2, to rebound; bounce; as does a ball:—n. 1, a light, springing step or leap; a rebound; 2, the space covered by such a leap.

²**bound** (bound), v.t. 1, to form the boundary of; as, the Pacific Ocean *bounds* Oregon on the west; 2, to name the countries or waters surrounding; as, to *bound* Canada:—n. 1, a boundary; limit; 2, **bounds,** extent of territory, as of a state; hence, range of action, thought, or the like; as, within the *bounds* of reason.
  Syn., v. limit, enclose, circumscribe.

³**bound** (bound), past tense and past participle of *bind:*—adj. 1, tied; fastened; as, a prisoner *bound* and gagged; 2, obliged; compelled; as, *bound* to obey; 3, fated; certain; as, *bound* to die; 4, connected; dependent; as, lives *bound* up in one another; 5, under obligations to serve; as, a *bound* apprentice; 6, made fast between covers, as a book; 7, *Colloquial,* determined; resolved; as, *bound* to have his way.

⁴**bound** (bound), adj. ready to start; having started for; destined; as, a train *bound* for New York.

bound-a-ry (boun′dȧ-rĭ), n. [pl. boundaries], that which marks the extent or limit of anything, as a line which bounds a territory on a map, a fence around a property, or the like; also, the limit itself; as, this river forms a *boundary* between the two states.

bound-en (boun′dĕn), archaic past participle of *bind:*—adj. imposed as an obligation; hence, binding; as, his *bounden* duty.

bound-less (bound′lĕs), adj. unlimited; vast; as, the *boundless* prairies.

boun-te-ous (boun′tē-ŭs), adj. 1, giving freely; generous; as, *bounteous* nature; 2, plentiful; as, a *bounteous* harvest.—adv. **boun′te-ous-ly.**

boun-ti-ful (boun′tĭ-fool), adj. 1, liberal; generous; as, a *bountiful* giver; 2, plentiful; yielding abundantly; as, *bountiful* acres. —adv. **boun′ti-ful-ly.**
  Syn. bounteous, abundant, ample.

boun-ty (boun′tĭ), n. [pl. bounties], 1, generosity in giving; also, generous gifts; as, this hospital is supported by the *bounty* of one man; 2, a premium or reward, especially one offered or given by a government; as, to give farmers a *bounty* for destroying excess crops.

bou-quet (bōō-kā′; bō-kā′), n. 1, a bunch of flowers; 2, aroma, as of wine; fragrance.

Bour-bon (bŏŏr′bŭn), n. 1, an ancient royal family of France, Spain, and Naples; 2, a conservative or reactionary person.

¹**bour-geois** (bŏŏr-zhwä′; bŏŏr′zhwä), n. a member of the middle class of society:— adj. belonging to the middle class; having the characteristics of the middle class.

²**bour-geois** (bûr-jois′), n. in printing, a size of type, equivalent to 9 point. (See second illustration under *type.*)

bour-geoi-sie (bŏŏr′zhwä-zē′), [French], n. the middle class.

¹**bourn** or **bourne** (bôrn), n. a brook.

²**bourn** (bôrn; bŏŏrn), n. 1, a boundary; limit; 2, a destination; goal. Also spelled **bourne.**

bout (bout), n. 1, a test of skill, strength, or endurance; a contest; as, a boxing *bout*; 2, a spell or turn at something; as, a *bout* of house cleaning.

bo-vine (bō′vīn; bō′vĭn), adj. 1, relating to, or like, the ox or cow; 2, sluggish; patient; stolid.

¹**bow** (bou), v.t. 1, to bend (the head, body, or knee) to express greeting, thanks, or respect; as, to *bow* the head in prayer; 2, to express (greeting, thanks, or respect) by bending the head, body, or knee; as, he *bowed* his thanks; 3, to oppress; crush; as, sorrow has *bowed* him:—v.i. 1, to bend, as in greeting, thanks, or respect; 2, to yield; as, I *bow* to your wishes:—n. a bending of the head, body, or knee, in greeting, thanks, or respect.

²**bow** (bō), n. 1, anything curved, as a rainbow; 2, a weapon of elastic wood for shooting arrows; 3, a rod strung with tightly stretched horsehair, for playing instruments like the violin; 4, a knot with a loop or loops, as of ribbon: —**bow window,** a bay window:—v.t. to bend or curve like a bow:—v.i. to become bent or curved. —n. **bow′man.**

³**bow** (bou), n. the forward part of a ship, airship, or the like:—adj. situated at or near the bow; as, the *bow* oar.

BOWS, def. 2
1, ancient Greek; 2, medieval; 3, American Indian.

bowels (bou′ĕlz), *n.pl.* **1**, the intestines, especially of man; **2**, the innermost parts, as of the earth; **3**, pity; compassion.

bow-er (bou′ẽr), *n.* **1**, a shelter made of boughs or twining plants; an arbor; **2**, a lady's private apartment.

bow-er-y (bou′ẽr-ĭ), *adj.* shaded; arborlike.

Bow-er-y (bou′ẽr-ĭ), a street in lower New York City, once famous for its cheap, flashy amusements.

bow-ie knife (bō′ĭ; bōō′ĭ), a strong, single-edged hunting knife, about a foot long, with a curved point.

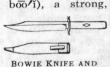

BOWIE KNIFE AND SHEATH

bowl (bōl), *n.* **1**, a kitchen dish or vessel in shape more or less spherical; **2**, the contents of a bowl; as, she drank a *bowl* of milk; **3**, the hollow part of anything, as of a spoon; **4**, anything bowl-shaped, especially an amphitheater for athletics; as, the Yale *bowl*.

bowl (bōl), *n.* **1**, a heavy ball of wood used in ninepins, or similar games; **2**, **bowls**, in England, a game played with such balls; ninepins; tenpins; **3**, the act of rolling a bowl:— *v.i.* **1**, to play at bowling; **2**, to roll a bowl or ball; **3**, to move rapidly and smoothly along; as, we *bowled* along the road in the carriage:—*v.t.* **1**, to knock over; as, he *bowled* him off his feet; **2**, in the game of cricket, to throw (the ball) with a stiff arm.—*n.* **bowl′er**.

bowl-der (bōl′dẽr), *n.* a rounded or worn stone or piece of rock. See **boulder**.

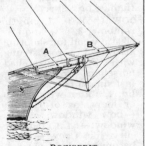

BOWLING IN CRICKET

bow-leg-ged (bō′lĕg′ĕd; bō′-lĕgd′), *adj.* having legs that curve outward.—*n.* **bow′leg′**.

bow-line (bō′lĭn; bō′līn), *n.* a kind of loop knot that will not slip. (See illustration at *knot*.)

bowl-ing (bōl′ĭng), *n.* the game of bowls, ninepins, or tenpins.

BOWSPRIT
A, bowsprit; B, jib boom.

bow-shot (bō′shŏt′), *n.* the distance covered by an arrow shot from a bow.

bow-sprit (bou′sprĭt; bō′sprĭt), *n.* a large spar or boom projecting from the prow, or forward end, of a sailing vessel.

box (bŏks), *n.* a slap on the face or a cuff on the ear:—*v.t.* to strike with the fist or hand:—*v.i.* to fight with fists, usually gloved, as a sport, or for money.

box (bŏks), *n.* an evergreen tree or shrub, much used for borders and hedges.

box (bŏks), *n.* **1**, a case or container, of wood, cardboard, steel, or the like, usually with a lid; **2**, the contents or the quantity that such a container can hold; as, to use up a *box* of soap; **3**, a compartment in a theater, courtroom, or the like; as, the jury *box*; **4**, a shed or stall used as shelter for a sentry; **5**, in baseball, the place where the pitcher or the batsman stands; **6**, the driver's seat on a coach or carriage; **7**, a trunk, especially in British usage:—*v.t.* to enclose in a box; as, to *box* toys; you must *box* up the dog.

box-er (bŏk′sẽr), *n.* a pugilist; one who fights with his fists, usually with padded gloves, for sport or for money:—**Boxer**, a member of the Chinese secret society which in 1900 attempted to rid China of all foreigners by massacre.

box-ing (bŏk′sĭng), *n.* the art of fighting with bare fists or, more generally, with fists covered with padded gloves:—**boxing gloves**, gloves padded for boxing.

box-wood (bŏks′wŏŏd′), *n.* the hard, close-grained wood of the box. See **box**.

boy (boi), *n.* **1**, a male child, up to the age of about fourteen; a lad; **2**, a male servant; as, an errand *boy*.

boy-cott (boi′kŏt), *v.t.* **1**, to refuse, in agreement with others, to buy from, sell to, or have dealings with (a person, firm, nation, etc.); **2**, to refuse as a group to use or purchase (a thing):—*n.* an organized refusal to have any dealings with a person, firm, or nation, or to buy a product, in an effort to force the adoption of a certain course of action.

boy-hood (boi′hŏŏd), *n.* **1**, the state or time of being a boy; **2**, boys as a class; as, the *boyhood* of America.

boy-ish (boi′ĭsh), *adj.* boylike; youthful; as, *boyish* fun.

boy scout, a member of an organization, "Boy Scouts of America," for training boys in character

CARPENTER'S BRACE

and good citizenship by promoting healthy physical and mental activities.

Bp. abbreviation for *Bishop*.

Br. abbreviation for *Britain*, *British*.

brace (brās), *n.* **1**, that which steadies a thing or supports it firmly, as a supporting steel or timber in the framework of a building; also, a bandage or a steel support for a part of the body; **2**, a pair; as a *brace* of pistols; **3**, a curved line as ⎰ or ⎱ connecting two or more lines of print, staffs of music, or the like; **4**, a curved implement used to hold and turn boring tools (see illustration on preceding page); **5**, **braces**, suspenders:—*v.t.* [braced, bracing], to steady; as, to *brace* a ladder; to *brace* one's courage:—*v.i.* to rouse oneself to effort; as, we told him to *brace* up.

brace-let (brās′lĕt), *n.* an ornamental band or chain for the wrist or the arm.

brac-er (brās′ẽr), *n.* **1**, a brace; **2**, *Slang*, a drink of liquor.

brac-ing (brās′ĭng), *adj.* giving strength or vigor; as, *bracing* air.

brack-en (brăk′ĕn), *n.* a large, coarse fern; brake.

brack-et (brăk′ĕt), *n.* **1**, an L-shaped piece or framework of wood or metal projecting from a wall, as to support a shelf; **2**, one of two marks [ ], used to enclose a word, or to separate a certain part of the text from the rest:—*v.t.* **1**, to enclose in brackets; as, to *bracket* a phrase; **2**, to mention or classify (two things) together; as, both speakers *bracketed* the two names.

BRACKETS (B) for shelf.

brack-ish (brăk′ĭsh), *adj.* saltish; salty; as, *brackish* water.

bract (brăkt), *n.* a small leaf at the base of a flower or flower stem, usually small and green, but sometimes brilliantly colored like a petal, as in the dogwood or the poinsettia.

brad (brăd), *n.* a small, thin nail.

Brad-dock (brăd′ŭk), Edward (1695–1755), a British general in the French and Indian War in America.

Brad-ford (brăd′fẽrd), William (1590–1657), the second governor of Plymouth Colony (1621) and one of the leaders of the Pilgrim Fathers.

brae (brā; brē), *n. Scottish*, a hillside.

brag (brăg), *v.i.* [bragged, brag-ging], to boast:—*n.* boasting.—*n.* **brag′ger**.

brag-ga-do-ci-o (brăg′à-dō′shĭ-ō), *n.* empty boasting; brag.

brag-gart (brăg′ẽrt), *n.* a person given to bragging; a boaster:—*adj.* boastful.

Brah-ma (brä′mà), *n.* in Hindu religion, the creator of the world.

Brah-man (brä′măn), *n.* [*pl.* Brahmans], a Hindu of the sacred or priestly caste. Also spelled **Brah′min**.—*n.* **Brah′man-ism**.

Brah-ma-pu-tra (brä′mà-pōō′trà), a river of India, rising in Tibet, where it is called *Tsangpo*, and flowing southeast into the Bay of Bengal (map **15**).

Brahms (brämz), Johannes (1833 1897), a great German composer, famous for his songs and symphonies.

braid (brād), *n.* **1**, something plaited; as, a *braid* of hair; **2**, a flat band made of machine-plaited silk, cotton, or wool, used for binding or trimming:—*v.t.* **1**, to intertwine (three or more strands of hair, silk, or the like); plait; **2**, to trim with braid.

¹**Braille** (brāl; brāy′), Louis (1809 1852), a French educator who invented the Braille system of printing for the blind.

²**Braille** (brāl), *n.* **1**, a system of printing for the blind, in which points raised above the surface are used to represent letters and numbers; **2**, the symbols themselves.

brain (brān), *n.* **1**, the mass of nervous tissue filling the skull; the center of thought and feeling; **2**, **brains**, *pl.* intelligence:—**brain trust**, a small group of advisers who supposedly have intelligence:—*v.t.* to dash out the brains of (a person or animal).

brain-less (brān′lĕs), *adj.* without brains; stupid.—*n.* **brain′less-ness**.

braise (brāz), *v.t.* [braised, brais-ing], to cook (meat) by browning first in fat, and then simmering in very little liquid in a covered vessel.

¹**brake** (brāk), *n.* a device for checking the motion of a locomotive, vehicle, or the like:—*v.t.* [braked, brak-ing], to slow down or stop by applying a brake.

²**brake** (brāk), *n.* a large fern common on waste lands in temperate latitudes.

³**brake** (brāk), *n.* a place overgrown with shrubs, bushes, and the like; a thicket.

brake-man (brāk′măn), *n.* [*pl.* brakemen (-mĕn)], **1**, one who operates the brakes, as on a freight train; **2**, an assistant to the conductor on a passenger train.

bram-ble (brăm′bl), *n.* **1**, any prickly bush or shrub; **2**, the English blackberry.

bran (brăn), *n.* the outer coat or husks of wheat, rye, etc., separated from flour by sifting.

branch (bránch), *n.* **1**, a shoot or limb from the main trunk of a tree or the main bough of a shrub or plant; **2**, any member or part of a body or system; a department or subdivision; as, a *branch* of a family:—*adj.* **1**, turning off from the trunk or main body; as, the *branch* roads of a railway system; **2**, subordinate; as, a *branch* office:—*v.i.* to send out a branch, or branches; to divide into branches.

brand (brănd), *n.* **1,** a charred or burning piece of wood; **2,** a mark burned with a hot iron upon animals, to indicate the owner, or upon things, often to indicate the producer; **3,** a trade-mark; hence, any particular kind or make of goods; as, they do not carry that *brand* of coffee; **4,** a mark burned with a hot iron upon a criminal; hence, a mark of disgrace:—*v.t.* to mark with, or as with, a brand; as, the cattle were *branded;* these words were *branded* upon my mind.

bran-dish (brăn'dĭsh), *v.t.* to move about or wave (a weapon) as a threat, or in preparation for action; as, at sight of the enemy, they *brandished* their rifles.

brand—new (brănd'-nū'), *adj.* quite new.

bran-dy (brăn'dĭ), *n.* [*pl.* brandies], an alcoholic liquor distilled from wine or other fermented fruit juice.

brant (brănt), *n.* a small, dark, wild goose.

brass (bràs), *n.* **1,** an alloy made of copper and zinc; **2,** the deep-yellow color of brass; **3,** *Slang,* impudence; as, he had the *brass* to say that; **4, brasses,** ornaments of brass; also, musical wind instruments made of brass (see illustration at *musical instruments*).

BRANT (2'g)
Canada goose.

brass-ie (bràs'ĭ), *n.* a golf club, with a wooden head, which is weighted with brass or other metal, used for long shots off the fairway. Also spelled **brass'y** or **brass'ey.**

bras-si-ère (bràs'ĭ-âr'; brȧ-zēr'), *n.* an underwaist for supporting the breasts.

brass-y (bràs'ĭ), *adj.* [brass-i-er, brass-i-est], made of brass; like brass.

brat (brăt), *n.* a child, especially an undisciplined or spoiled child.

Bra-ti-sla-va (brä'tĭ-slä'vȧ), a city on the Danube in southwestern Czechoslovakia (map 12). Its German name is *Pressburg.*

Braun-schweig (broun'shvīkh), a city in Germany. See **Brunswick.**

bra-va-do (brȧ-vä'dō), *n.* [*pl.* bravadoes or bravados], pretense of courage or indifference; boastful defiance; as, timid people often assume an air of *bravado.*

brave (brāv), *adj.* [brav-er, brav-est], **1,** fearless; courageous; as, a *brave* deed; **2,** showy; as, a *brave* display of flags:—*n.* a North American Indian warrior:—**the brave,** all those who are brave:—*v.t.* [braved, brav-ing], to face or meet with courage; defy; as, he *braved* the storm.—*adv.* **brave'ly.**

brav-er-y (brāv'ẽr-ĭ), *n.* [*pl.* braveries], **1,**
fearlessness; courage; **2,** splendid appearance; finery.

¹bra-vo (brä'vō), *interj.* well done!—*n.* [*pl.* bravos], a shout of applause.

²bra-vo (brä'vō; brä'vō), *n.* [*pl.* bravoes or bravos], a ruthless villain; a hired assassin.

brawl (brôl), *n.* a noisy quarrel:—*v.i.* **1,** to quarrel or wrangle noisily; **2,** to make a loud noise, as rushing water.—*n.* **brawl'er.**

brawn (brôn), *n.* firm, strong muscles; muscular strength; as, a fighter's *brawn.*

brawn-y (brôn'ĭ), *adj.* [brawn-i-er, brawn-i-est], muscular; strong; as, the blacksmith has a *brawny* arm.

bray (brā), *n.* the loud, harsh cry of the ass; also, any similar sound, as the blast of a trumpet:—*v.i.* to utter a loud, harsh sound or cry.

bra-zen (brā'zn), *adj.* **1,** made of brass; like brass; **2,** loud and harsh; as, a *brazen* voice; **3,** impudent; shameless; as, a *brazen* manner:—*v.t.* to face with impudence; as, to *brazen* out a situation.—*adv.* **bra'zen-ly.**

¹bra-zier (brā'zhẽr), *n.* an open pan for holding burning charcoal or live coals.

²bra-zier (brā'zhẽr), *n.* a worker in brass.

Bra-zil, U-nit-ed States of (brȧ-zĭl'), a republic (cap. Rio de Janeiro), the largest state in South America (map 11).—*n.* and *adj.* **Bra-zil'ian.**

Brazil nut, an oily nut, used as food, consisting of a whitish kernel in a hard, three-sided shell, the seed of a Brazilian tree.

breach (brēch), *n.* **1,** a gap or opening made by breaking through; as, a *breach* in a wall; **2,** the breaking of a law, contract, or other obligation; as, a *breach* of promise; **3,** a break in friendly relations; as, a *breach* between nations.

bread (brĕd), *n.* **1,** an article of food made from flour or meal, moistened, raised, kneaded, and baked; **2,** livelihood; as, he works for his *bread:*—*v.t.* to cover with bread crumbs before cooking; as, to *bread* chops.—*adj.* **bread'ed.**

bread-fruit (brĕd'frōot'), *n.* **1,** the large round fruit of a tree native to the South Pacific islands, which, when roasted, somewhat resembles bread; **2,** the tree which bears this fruit.

bread-stuff (brĕd'stŭf'), *n.* any material such as meal or flour, from which bread is made; also, bread in any form.

breadth (brĕdth), *n.* **1,** the measure of a thing from side to side; width; hence, spaciousness: extent; **2,** a piece of fabric of a certain width; as, a *breadth* of carpet; **3,** freedom from narrowness; liberality; as, *breadth* of mind.

break (brāk), *v.t.* [*p.t.* broke (brōk), *p.p.* bro-ken (brō'kĕn), *p.pr.* break-ing], **1,** to split or smash into pieces by a blow or strain; as, to *break* glasses; fracture, as a bone; **2,** to force (a path, hole, or the like) into or through something; **3,** to destroy the arrangement or completeness of; as, to *break* ranks; to *break* a dollar bill; **4,** to weaken the force of; as, the haystack *broke* my fall; **5,** to set aside, violate, or fail to obey; as, to *break* a promise or a law; also, to escape from; as, he *broke* jail; **6,** to tell cautiously; disclose; as, to *break* news; **7,** to tame, as a horse; **8,** to plow or dig up, as ground; **9,** to make bankrupt; as, he *broke* the bank at Monte Carlo; **10,** to discontinue; as, to *break* off relations; **11,** to exceed; as, to *break* a swimming record; **12,** to interrupt, as silence or an electric circuit:—*v.i.* **1,** to separate into pieces suddenly; burst; as, the plate *broke;* **2,** to change abruptly in gait, tone, etc.; as, the horse *broke* into a gallop; three times his voice *broke* during the questioning; **3,** to fail in health; weaken; **4,** to burst forth violently, as a storm or cry; **5,** to force a way; as, he *broke* into the safe; **6,** to begin to be; as, day *breaks;* **7,** to discontinue relations; as, the firms *broke* with each other; **8,** *Slang,* to occur or turn out in a given way; as, luck *broke* against him:—*n.* **1,** the act of breaking; as, the *break* of day; **2,** something produced by breaking; as, a *break* in a wire; an interruption; as, a *break* in a conversation; **3,** a sudden fall in prices; as, a *break* in the stock market; **4,** *U.S. Colloquial,* a blunder in speech or action; **5,** *Slang,* a turn of fortune; as, it was a lucky *break* for me.—*adj.* **break′a-ble.**

Syn., v. crush, rend, tear, destroy, smash, crack, split, shiver, shatter.

break-age (brāk′ij), *n.* **1,** the act of breaking; **2,** things broken; **3,** loss or damage caused by breaking; or an equivalent in money for such loss or damage.

break-down (brāk′doun′), *n.* **1,** a mental or physical collapse; **2,** a failure; downfall; as, the *breakdown* of the empire; **3,** a noisy, shuffling Negro dance.

break-er (brāk′ẽr), *n.* **1,** one who or that which smashes or breaks; **2,** a machine for crushing coal, rocks, etc.; **3,** a wave which dashes itself upon the shore in foam.

break-fast (brĕk′fȧst), *n.* the first meal of the day:—*v.i.* to eat breakfast.

break-neck (brāk′nĕk′), *adj.* dangerous; risking life; as, a *breakneck* pace.

break-wa-ter (brāk′wô′tẽr), *n.* a wall or dike built to break the force of the waves, as around a harbor.

bream (brēm), *n.* **1,** a deep-bodied, freshwater European fish of the carp family; **2,** in the U.S., a freshwater sunfish.

breast (brĕst), *n.* **1,** the front part of the body between the neck and the abdomen; **2,** either one of the glands found on the chest of man and some other mammals, serving, in the female, for the secretion of milk; **3,** anything resembling the breast; as, the *breast* of a hill; **4,** the seat of the affections:—*v.t.* to face bravely.

breast-bone (brĕst′bōn′), *n.* the thin, flat, vertical bone in the front of the chest to which the seven upper pairs of ribs are attached.

breast-plate (brĕst′plāt′), *n.* in a suit of armor, the metal plate protecting the chest.

breast-work (brĕst′wûrk′), *n.* a hastily constructed wall built breast-high for defense.

breath (brĕth), *n.* **1,** the air drawn into and forced out of the lungs; **2,** a single act of drawing air into or forcing air out from the lungs; hence, an instant; pause; **3,** the power to breathe freely; as, to lose one's *breath;* hence, life; strength; **4,** a light breeze; as, a *breath* of air; **5,** a whisper; as, a *breath* of scandal; **6,** a film produced by the breath, as on a mirror.

BREASTPLATE As worn in the 16th century.

breathe (brē*th*), *v.i.* [breathed, breath-ing], **1,** to use the lungs; be alive; as, the dying man still *breathes;* **2,** to rest from stress or action; pause; as, I can *breathe* again, now that the work is done; **3,** to blow softly, as wind:—*v.t.* **1,** to draw into and force out of the lungs; as, we *breathed* the fresh air; **2,** to exhale; give forth; as, he *breathed* a sigh of relief; the flower *breathes* perfume; **3,** to whisper softly; as, don't *breathe* a word of this.

breath-less (brĕth′lĕs), *adj.* **1,** out of breath, as from exertion or emotion; as, *breathless* from running; *breathless* with fear; **2,** dead.—*adv.* **breath′less-ly.**

bred (brĕd), past tense and past participle of *breed.*

breech (brēch), *n.* the hinder part of anything, especially of firearms.

breech-es (brĭch′ĕz), *n.pl.* **1,** short trousers, fastened below the knee; **2,** *Colloquial,* trousers.

breech-ing (brĭch′ĭng; brēch′ĭng), *n.* in a horse's harness, the heavy strap which passes round the horse's hindquarters. (See illustration under *harness.*)

breed (brēd), *v.t.* [bred (brĕd), breed-ing], **1,** to give birth to; **2,** to mate or raise, as animals or plants, for the purpose of maintaining or improving the stock; **3,** to train; rear; as, I was *bred* to be my father's successor; **4,** to nourish; as, swamps *breed* mosquitoes; poverty *breeds* misery:—*v.i.* **1,** to bear young; **2,** to be born; come into being; as, crime *breeds* in slums:—*n.* race; stock; strain; as, a good *breed* of cattle.

breed·er (brē′dẽr), *n.* a person who raises and breeds animals or plants.

breed·ing (brē′dǐng), *n.* **1,** the producing of young; **2,** the training or bringing up of young; especially, the results of training; good manners; as, a man of *breeding.*
   Syn. nurture, upbringing, culture.

breeze (brēz), *n.* a gentle wind.

breez·y (brē′zǐ), *adj.* [breez-i-er, breez-i-est], **1,** fanned by breezes; windy; as, a *breezy* day; **2,** brisk; vivacious; animated; as, a *breezy* fellow.

Bre·men (brā′mĕn; brĕm′ĕn), a German state, on the North Sea, east of the Netherlands; also, a city, its capital (map **12**).

Bres·lau (brĕs′lou), a city in Poland on the Oder River; now called *Wroclaw* (map **12**).

Brest Li·tovsk (brĕst′ lǐ-tôfsk′), a city in the western part of U.S.S.R. (map **12**).

Bre·tagne (brĕ-tàny′′), a section of France. See **Brittany.**

breth·ren (brĕth′rĕn), *n.pl.* brothers; fellow members of a church or fraternity.

Bret·on (brĕt′ŭn), *adj.* pertaining to Brittany, its language, or its people.—*n.* **Bret′on.**

breve (brēv), *n.* a mark [˘] used to indicate a short vowel or syllable, as in "căt."

bre·vi·ar·y (brē′vǐ-ĕr′ǐ; brĕv′ǐ-ĕr′ǐ), *n.* [*pl.* breviaries], a book containing the daily service and prayers of the Roman Catholic Church.

bre·vier (brĕ-vǐr′), *n.* in printing, a size of type, about equivalent to 8 point. (See second illustration under *type*.)

brev·i·ty (brĕv′ǐ-tǐ), *n.* [*pl.* brevities], briefness; shortness.

brew (brōō), *v.t.* **1,** to make, as beer, from malt and hops, by steeping, boiling, and fermenting; **2,** to make by steeping, as tea, or by mixing, as punch; **3,** to bring about; plot; as, to *brew* mischief:—*v.i.* **1,** to make a liquor by fermentation or steeping; **2,** to gather; grow in force; as, a storm *brews*:—*n.* a drink made by brewing.

brew·er (brōō′ẽr), *n.* a person whose business is making beer, ale, or the like.

brew·er·y (brōō′ẽr-ǐ), *n.* [*pl.* breweries], a place where beer and other malt liquors are made.

brew·ing (brōō′ǐng), *n.* **1,** the making of beer and other malt liquors; **2,** the quantity of such made at one time.

¹**bri·ar** (brī′ẽr), *n.* a thorny bush. See ¹**brier.**

²**bri·ar** (brī′ẽr), *n.* the European white or tree heath. See ²**brier.**

bribe (brīb), *n.* a gift made or promised to a person to influence him to decide or act dishonestly:—*v.t.* [bribed, brib-ing], to influence by a bribe.

brib·er·y (brī′bẽr-ǐ), *n.* [*pl.* briberies], the giving or taking of gifts in return for a dishonest act.

bric–a–brac (brĭk′-á-brăk′), *n.* small articles of artistic or sentimental value, displayed as ornaments; knicknacks.

brick (brĭk), *n.* **1,** a material used in building or paving made from clay molded into blocks, usually oblong, and baked in the sun or in kilns; also, one of these blocks; **2,** anything shaped like such a block; as, a *brick* of ice cream; **3,** *Colloquial*, a good fellow; as, he's a *brick* to do it:—*v.t.* to lay bricks; wall in with bricks; as, to *brick* up a fireplace.

brick·bat (brĭk′băt′), *n.* a piece of brick, or anything similar, thrown in a fight.

brick·lay·er (brĭk′lā′ẽr), *n.* one whose occupation is to lay bricks.

brid·al (brī′dăl), *n.* a wedding:—*adj.* pertaining to a bride or a wedding.

bride (brīd), *n.* a woman newly married, or about to be married.

bride·groom (brīd′grōōm′), *n.* a man newly married, or about to be married.

brides·maid (brīdz′mād′), *n.* a woman who attends a bride at her wedding.

bridge (brĭj), *n.* **1,** a structure built to carry a road or path across a river, valley, or the like (see illustration on next page); **2,** anything shaped like a bridge, as the upper part of the nose, the arch for the strings on a violin, or a mounting for artificial teeth; **3,** an observation platform above the deck of a ship for the officer in charge or the pilot; **4,** a movable passageway from a ship to the shore; **5,** a modern card game developed from the game of whist:—*v.t.* [bridged, bridg-ing], **1,** to build a bridge over; span; **2,** to pass; get over; as, he helped me *bridge* the difficulty.

bridge·head (brĭj′hĕd′), *n.* **1,** a position occupied on the enemy side of a river in advance of a crossing in force; **2,** a fortified position or defensive work to protect the end of a bridge nearest the enemy.

Bridge·port (brĭj′pôrt), a city in Connecticut, on Long Island Sound (map **6**).

bridg·ing (brĭj′ǐng), *n.* wooden braces placed between beams to keep them apart. (See illustration of *frame house*.)

BRIDLE

bri·dle (brī′dl), *n.* **1,** in a horse's harness, the headgear, with the bit and reins, by which the horse is governed; **2,** a check; restraint; as, to put a *bridle* on the tongue: —*v.t.* [bri-dled, bri-dling], **1,** to put a bit and reins on; **2,** to control, as, the temper:—*v.i.* to throw back the head, as in anger or pride; as, she *bridled* at his words.

¹**bri·er** or **bri·ar** (brī′ẽr), *n.* **1,** any thorny plant or shrub; **2,** a thorn, as of a rose; **3,** a patch of thorny bushes.

²**bri·er** or **bri·ar** (brī′ẽr), *n.* **1,** the European white heath; **2,** a tobacco pipe made from its root.

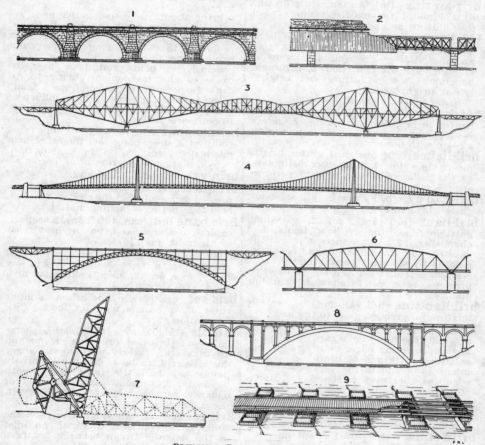

PRINCIPAL TYPES OF BRIDGE

1, stone arch (Roman); 2, wood covered (Colonial); 3, steel cantilever; 4, steel suspension; 5, steel arch; 6, steel truss; 7, steel bascule, a form of drawbridge; 8, concrete arch; 9, wood pontoon (military).

brief (brēf), *adj.* **1,** short; not lengthy; as, a *brief* delay; **2,** said in few words; condensed; as, a *brief* description:—*n.* a summary; especially, a lawyer's outline of the argument of a case.—*adv.* **brief′ly.** *Syn.,* adj. short, concise, abridged.

brief case, a flat leather case, in which papers can be carried flat and unfolded.

brig (brĭg), *n.* a two-masted square-rigged vessel. (See illustration under *ship.*)

Brig. abbreviation for *Brigade, Brigadier.*

bri·gade (brĭ-gād′), *n.* **1,** in the United States Army, a unit consisting of two regiments, under a brigadier general; **2,** an organized body of men acting under authority; as, a fire *brigade.*

go; join; yet; sing; chin; show; thin, *th*en; hw, *why*; zh, azure; ü, Ger. für or Fr. lune; ö, Ger. schön or Fr. *feu*; n̈, Fr. *enfant, nom*; kh, Ger. ach or ich. See pages ix–x.

brig·a·dier (brĭg′ȧ-dēr′), *n.* an officer in command of a brigade, ranking next below a major general: more often called *brigadier general.*

brig·and (brĭg′ănd), *n.* a member of a gang of robbers; bandit.—*n.* **brig′and·age.**

brig·an·tine (brĭg′ăn-tēn; brĭg′ăn-tīn), *n.* a kind of two-masted sailing vessel. (See illustration under *ship.*)

bright (brīt), *adj.* **1**, giving much light; shining, as the sun; **2**, vivid; as, *bright* green; **3**, lively; cheerful; **4**, clever; as, a *bright* idea; a *bright* child; **5**, favorable; hopeful; as, a *bright* future.—*adv.* **bright′- ly.**—*n.* **bright′ness.**
Syn. brilliant, radiant, luminous.

bright·en (brīt′n), *v.i.* to grow clearer, lighter, or brighter; as, the day *brightens:* —*v.t.* to make light or bright; as, to *brighten* a room with flowers.

bril·liance (brĭl′yăns), *n.* **1**, glitter; brightness, as of a star; **2**, excellence; distinction; as, the *brilliance* of the violinist's performance; **3**, outstanding mental ability.

bril·lian·cy (brĭl′yăn-sĭ), *n.* splendor; glitter; brilliance.

bril·liant (brĭl′yănt), *adj.* **1**, sparkling; glittering; as, the *brilliant* light of a chandelier; **2**, very successful; distinguished; as, a *brilliant* reign; **3**, distinguished by splendid mental ability; as, a *brilliant* scientist:—*n.* a diamond or other precious stone, cut to show its sparkling quality.

bril·lian·tine (brĭl′yăn-tēn′), *n.* an oily mixture for giving a gloss to the hair.

brim (brĭm), *n.* **1**, the edge or brink, as of a lake; the rim, as of a cup; **2**, the projecting edge, as of a hat:—*v.i.* [brimmed, brimming], to be full to the very edge; as, her eyes *brimmed* with tears.—*adj.* **brim′less.**

BRIM
B, brim of a hat; C, crown.

brim·ful (brĭm′fŏŏl′; brĭm′- fŏŏl), *adj.* full to the edge; completely filled; as, a *brimful* cup.

brim·stone (brĭm′stōn′), *n.* sulphur.

Brin·di·si (brēn′dē-zē), an Italian seaport on the southeast coast (map **12**). Its ancient name was *Brundisium* or *Brundusium.*

brin·dled (brĭn′dld), *adj.* of a brown or tawny color, with dark spots or streaks.

brine (brīn), *n.* **1**, water that is extremely salty; **2**, the ocean.

bring (brĭng), *v.t.* [brought (brôt), bringing], **1**, to cause (a person or thing) to come along; as, *bring* your cousin home; also, to fetch; as, *bring* me a cake; **2**, to carry; as, the boat *brought* me to land; **3**,

to draw; attract; as, this speaker always *brings* a crowd; **4**, to cause, or to result in; as, winter *brings* snow; sleep *brings* relief; **5**, to sell for (a price); as, diamonds *bring* a large sum; **6**, to recall; as, that *brings* up a story; **7**, to persuade; as, I cannot *bring* myself to go; **8**, in law, to begin; as, to *bring* suit.

bring about, to cause to happen; accomplish; **bring forth,** to give birth to; produce; **bring forward,** to introduce, as a proposal; to carry forward, as a sum; **bring home,** to make vividly clear; prove conclusively; **bring round** or **over,** to cause to change opinions; **bring to,** to cause (a person) to recover from a faint; **bring to bear,** to cause to have influence; **bring to light,** discover; reveal; **bring up,** to rear; educate.

brink (brĭngk), *n.* the edge or top, especially of a steep place; as, the *brink* of a pit; hence, verge; as, on the *brink* of ruin.
Syn. margin, edge, rim, brim, border.

brin·y (brīn′ĭ), *adj.* very salty.

bri·quette or **bri·quet** (brĭ-kĕt′), *n.* a pressed brick of coal dust or other fuel, held together by a binding material.

Bris·bane (brĭz′bān; brĭz′băn), a seaport, capital of Queensland, on the east coast of Australia (map **16**).

brisk (brĭsk), *adj.* **1**, active; lively; swift; nimble; as, a *brisk* walker; **2**, burning freely, as a fire; **3**, keen; enlivening, as a wind.—*adv.* **brisk′ly.**

bris·ket (brĭs′kĕt), *n.* the breast or lower chest of an animal used for food. (See illustration at *beef.*)

bris·tle (brĭs′l), *n.* a short, stiff, coarse hair:—*v.i.* [bris·tled, bris·tling], **1**, to stand up in a stiff, prickly way, as an angry dog's hair; **2**, to be covered with bristly points; as, the battle front *bristles* with bayonets; **3**, to show signs of anger or defiance; as, the class *bristled* with revolt. —*adj.* **bris′tly.**

Bris·tol (brĭs′tl), an English city on the Avon River:—**Bristol Channel,** an inlet of the Atlantic Ocean between southern Wales and England (map **13**).

Bristol board, a hard cardboard with a smooth finish.

Brit. abbreviation for *Britain, British.*

Brit·ain (brĭt′ĕn). See **Great Britain.**

Bri·tan·ni·a (brĭ-tăn′ĭ-ȧ; brĭ-tăn′yȧ), Great Britain; also, the British Empire.

Brit·ish (brĭt′ĭsh), *adj.* **1**, relating to Great Britain or its inhabitants; **2**, relating to the ancient Britons:—*n.* **1**, the people of Great Britain; **2**, the language spoken by the ancient Britons.

āte, âorta, râre, căt, àsk, fär, ȧllow, sofȧ; ēve, ĕvent, ĕll, writẽr, novĕl; bīte, pĭn; nō, ōbey, ôr, dŏg, tŏp, cōllide; ūnit, ŭnite, bûrn, cŭt, focŭs; nōͻn, fŏŏt; mound; coin;

Brit·ish Co·lum·bi·a (kŏ-lŭm′bĭ-a̍), a western province (cap. Victoria) of Canada (map 4).

Brit·ish Em·pire, a community of nations (cap. London, England), including Great Britain, Canada, Australia, New Zealand, the Union of South Africa, and colonies, protectorates, and dependencies. British Commonwealth of Nations.

Brit·ish·er (brĭt′ĭsh-ẽr), *n.* a native or subject of Great Britain; especially, an Englishman.

Brit·ish Hon·du·ras (hŏn-dōō′răs; hŏn-dū′răs), a British colony (cap. Belize) in Central America, north of Honduras (map 10).

Brit·ish In·di·a (ĭn′dĭ-a̍), the part of India formerly wholly or partly subject to British rule. See **India.**

Brit·ish Isles, a group of islands lying off the coast of Europe, including Great Britain, Ireland, and smaller surrounding islands (map 13).

Brit·ish West In·dies, the islands of the West Indies which are colonies of Great Britain, including Jamaica, the Bahamas, the Leeward Islands, and other small islands (map 10).

Brit·on (brĭt′ŭn), *n.* 1, a member of one of the Celtic tribes which occupied ancient Britain or southern England before the Anglo-Saxon and Roman invasions; 2, a native or inhabitant of Great Britain.

Brit·ta·ny (brĭt′a̍-nĭ), an ancient Celtic kingdom occupying the peninsula of northwestern France. French name, *Bretagne.*

brit·tle (brĭt′l), *adj.* easily broken; apt to break, as ice, glass, or thin china. *Syn.* fragile, delicate, frail.

Bro. [*pl.* Bros.], abbreviation for *Brother.*

broach (brōch), *n.* 1, any pointed, spike-shaped tool, as a skewer for roasting meat; 2, any boring tool, especially one used for rounding out irregularly shaped holes in metal:—*v.t.* 1, to tap or pierce, as a keg of wine; 2, to begin to talk about; as, to *broach* an unpleasant subject.

broad (brôd), *adj.* 1, wide from side to side; 2, spacious; vast; as, *broad* estates; 3, liberal; as, *broad* views; 4, open; clear; as, *broad* daylight; 5, evident; plain; as, a *broad* hint; 6, indelicate; as, a *broad* joke.—*adv.* **broad′ly.**

broad·ax or **broad·axe** (brôd′ăks′), *n.* 1, a broad-bladed ax for cutting timber; 2, an ancient weapon with a wide blade.

broad·cast (brôd′kȧst′), *v.t.* [broadcast or broadcast-ed, broadcast-ing], 1, to scatter or throw by hand, as seed; 2, to spread abroad, as news; 3, to send out (messages or sound) by radio from a transmitting station:—*adv.* so as to scatter widely; as, to sow *broadcast:*—*n.* 1, a scattering of seed far and wide; 2, anything broadcast by radio, as a program, speech, or game.

broad·cloth (brôd′klôth′), *n.* 1, a fine woolen cloth with a smooth surface, often used for suits; 2, a fine grade of cotton or silk cloth, much used for shirts, dresses, etc.

broad·en (brô′dn), *v.i.* to grow wide or wider; as, the river *broadens* at this point:—*v.t.* to make wider or more liberal; as, education should *broaden* the mind.

broad jump (brôd), in athletics, a jump made for distance, either from a standing position or from a running start.

broad—mind·ed (brôd′=mīn′dĕd), *adj.* liberal in opinions; tolerant.

broad·side (brôd′sīd′), *n.* 1, the entire side of a ship above the water line; also, the broad unbroken expanse of anything; 2, all the cannon on one side of a warship; also, a discharge from all these at once; 3, a sheet of paper printed on one side only, as a tract or advertisement; 4, *Colloquial,* a printed or verbal attack on some person.

broad·sword (brôd′sôrd′), *n.* a sword with a broad blade.

Broad·way (brôd′wā′), a famous street   BROADSWORD
in New York City, which cuts Manhattan Island diagonally north and south. The brilliantly lighted part called the "Great White Way," centering at Times Square, is the theatrical center of the nation.

bro·cade (brō-kād′), *n.* a silken fabric woven with gold and silver threads, or ornamented with raised designs of flowers, etc.:—*v.t.* [brocad-ed, brocad-ing], to decorate or weave with a raised pattern.—*adj.* **bro·cad′ed.**

broc·co·li (brŏk′ō-lĭ), *n.* a plant of the mustard family, used as a vegetable. It is related to the cabbage and cauliflower.

bro·chure (brō-shūr′), *n.* a printed booklet or any article published in this form.

Brock (brŏk), Sir Isaac (1769–1812), a British general, called the "Hero of Upper Canada."

bro·gan (brō′găn; brō-găn′), *n.* a coarse, heavy shoe. See ¹**brogue.**

¹**brogue** (brōg), *n.* 1, in Ireland and Scotland, a shoe of untanned leather, strapped over the instep; 2, any coarse, low shoe.

²**brogue** (brōg), *n.* a pronunciation characteristic of a dialect; especially, the Irish pronunciation of English.

broi·der (broi′dẽr), *v.t. Archaic,* to embroider.—*adj.* **broi′dered.**

---

go; join; yet; sing; chin; show; thin, *then;* **hw,** *why;* **zh,** azure; **ü,** Ger. **für** or Fr. **l**u**ne;**
ö, Ger. **schön** or Fr. *feu;* **ṅ,** Fr. **e**nfant, nom; **kh,** Ger. **ach** or **i**ch. See pages **ix–x.**

¹**broil** (broil), *v.t.* to cook directly over or under a hot fire:—*v.i.* to be exposed to great heat; as, we fairly *broiled* in the hot sun on the beach:—*n.* a broiled dish.

²**broil** (broil), *n.* a noisy quarrel; brawl.

broil-er (broil′ẽr), *n.* **1**, a utensil or device for cooking food directly over or under a fire; **2**, a young fowl suitable for broiling.

broke (brōk), past tense of *break*.

bro-ken (brō′kĕn), *adj.* **1**, not entire; in pieces; shattered; as, a *broken* dish; **2**, fractured; as, a *broken* bone; **3**, cut into; as, ground *broken* by plowing; **4**, uneven; as, *broken* country; **5**, incomplete; disorganized; as, a *broken* set; *broken* ranks; **6**, interrupted; as, *broken* sleep; **7**, violated; as, a *broken* vow; **8**, trained to obedience; as, a *broken* horse; **9**, enfeebled; weak; as, *broken* health; **10**, subdued; crushed; as, a *broken* spirit; **11**, imperfectly spoken; as, *broken* English.—*adv.* **bro′ken-ly**.

bro-ken-heart-ed (brō′kĕn-här′tĕd), *adj.* crushed in spirit by grief or despair.

bro-ker (brō′kẽr), *n.* an agent for others in buying or selling anything, as real estate, stocks, bonds, or the like.

bro-ker-age (brō′kẽr-ĭj), *n.* the business of a broker; also, his fee or commission.

bro-mide (brō′mīd; brō′mĭd) or **bro-mid** (brō′mĭd), *n.* **1**, a drug often used as a medicine to quiet the nerves; **2**, *Slang*, a commonplace person or remark.

bro-mine (brō′mēn; brō′mĭn) or **bro-min** (brō′mĭn), *n.* a reddish-brown liquid element with a disagreeable odor.

bron-chi (brŏng′kī), *n.pl.* [*sing.* bronchus (brŏng′kŭs)], the two main branches of the windpipe, or trachea.

bron-chi-a (brŏng′-kĭ-à), *n.pl.* the group of tubes into which each of the bronchi divides, forming the larger air passages of the lungs.

bron-chi-al (brŏng′kĭ-ăl), *adj.* having to do with the bronchi or bronchia; as, *bronchial* tubes; a *bronchial* cold.

BRONCHI

Large air passages of the lungs, showing: B, B, bronchi; T, trachea, or windpipe.

bron-chi-tis (brŏn-kī′tĭs; brŏng-kī′tĭs), *n.* an inflammation of the bronchi or their branches.

bron-co or **bron-cho** (brŏng′kō), *n.* [*pl.* broncos, bronchos], in western North America, a small, half-tamed horse.

Bron-të (brŏn′tĭ), **1**, Charlotte (1816–1855), [pen name *Currer Bell*], an English novelist; **2**, Emily (1818–1848), [pen name *Ellis Bell*], her sister, also a novelist.

Bronx (brŏngks), a residential borough, the northeastern part of New York City.

bronze (brŏnz), *n.* **1**, an alloy or metallic mixture of eight or nine parts copper to one of tin; **2**, a work of art cast or wrought in this alloy; **3**, a yellowish or reddish brown, the color of bronze:—*adj.* made of bronze; like bronze:—*v.t.* [bronzed, bronzing], to make of the color of bronze; tan; as, the sun *bronzed* his face.

brooch (brōch; brōōch), *n.* an ornamental pin or clasp, used for fastening the dress, especially at the neck.

brood (brōōd), *n.* **1**, all the young of birds hatched at one time; **2**, all the young of one mother; **3**, the eggs and larvae of bees when in the comb:—*v.i.* **1**, to sit on eggs, as a hen; **2**, to think about something long and moodily; as, to *brood* over losses:—*v.t.* to sit on (eggs) for the purpose of hatching them.

BROOCH

brood-er (brōōd′ẽr), *n.* **1**, a bird that hatches eggs; **2**, a person lost in moody thought; **3**, an artificially heated device for raising young chicks.

¹**brook** (brōōk), *n.* a small, natural stream of water:—**brook trout**, a fresh-water game fish of eastern North America, related to the salmon, and valued highly as food.

²**brook** (brōōk), *v.t.* to bear; put up with; as, I will *brook* no delay.

brook-let (brōōk′lĕt), *n.* a little brook.

Brook-lyn (brōōk′lĭn), a borough of New York City, on Long Island.

broom (brōōm), *n.* **1**, a long-handled brush used for sweeping; **2**, a shrub of the pea family, with stiff, slender branches:—**broom corn**, a cornlike grass, eight to ten feet high, used in making brooms.

broom-stick (brōōm′stĭk′), *n.* the handle of a broom.

broth (brôth), *n.* thin soup made by boiling meat slowly in water.

broth-er (brŭth′ẽr), *n.* **1**, a man or boy who has the same father and mother as another person; **2**, a member of a father-land or race; a fellow man; **3**, one closely united to another or others by a common interest, such as a lodge, church, or the like.

broth-er-hood (brŭth′ẽr-hŏŏd), *n.* **1**, a group of men with similar interests and aims; a fraternity; as, the legal *brotherhood*; **2**, fellowship; kinship; as, the *brotherhood* of man.

broth-er—in—law (brŭth′ẽr-ĭn-lô′), *n.* [*pl.* brothers-in-law], a brother of one's husband or wife, or husband of one's sister.

broth-er-ly (brŭth′ĕr-lĭ), *adj.* like a brother; kind; friendly.—*n.* **broth′er-li-ness.**

brougham (brōōm; brōō′ŭm; brō′ŭm), *n.* a closed automobile or light carriage with the driver's seat outside.

BROUGHAM

brought (brôt), past tense and past participle of *bring.*

brow (brou), *n.* **1,** the forehead; **2,** the arch of hair over the eye; the eyebrow; **3,** the edge of a cliff; the top of a hill.

brow-beat (brou′bēt′), *v.t.* [*p.t.* browbeat (-bēt′), *p.p.* browbeat-en (-bēt′n), *p.pr.* browbeat-ing], to frighten by stern looks or words; bully.

Brown (broun), John (1800–1859), an American abolitionist, convicted of treason for his raid on the arsenal at Harpers Ferry.

brown (broun), *adj.* of a dusky color between black and orange:—*n.* a dark color between black and orange:—*v.i.* and *v.t.* to become or to make brown.

brown-ie (broun′ĭ), *n.* **1,** a good-natured elf supposed to do certain useful household tasks by night, as sweeping, churning, etc.; **2,** a thin flat chocolate cake with nuts in it.

Brown-ing (broun′ĭng), **1,** Elizabeth Barrett (1806–1861), an English poet, the wife of Robert Browning; **2,** Robert (1812–1889), a famous English poet.

brown-stone (broun′stōn′), *n.* a reddish-brown sandstone, used for building purposes, as for the fronts of houses.

browse (brouz), *n.* the tender shoots of shrubs and trees fit for the food of cattle and other animals:—*v.i.* [browsed, browsing], **1,** to nibble off twigs or grass; **2,** to read here and there in books; wander idly, as through an art gallery or the like.

Bruce (brōōs), Robert de (1274–1329), a king of Scotland, 1306–1329, who liberated Scotland from England.

Bru-ges (brōō′jĭz; brōōzh; brüzh), an important city in western Belgium (map **12**).

bru-in (brōō′ĭn), *n.* the brown bear: so called in popular tales.

bruise (brōōz), *n.* an injury to the flesh of an animal or plant which discolors the skin:—*v.t.* [bruised, bruis-ing], to injure or hurt; as, to *bruise* one's leg; to *bruise* a friend's feelings:—*v.i.* to show the effects of bruises; as, I *bruise* easily.

bruit (brōōt), *v.t.* to report; spread abroad; as, the story was *bruited* about.

Brum-mell (brŭm′ĕl), George Bryan

(1778–1840), called *Beau Brummell,* an English fop and society leader.

Brun-di-si-um (brŭn-dĭz′ĭ-ŭm) or **Brun-du-si-um** (brŭn-dū′zhĭ-ŭm), the ancient name of *Brindisi* (map **1**).

bru-net or **bru-nette** (brōō-nĕt′), *adj.* having dark skin, hair, and eyes.—*n. masc.* **bru-net′.**—*n. fem.* **bru-nette′.**

Bruns-wick (brŭnz′wĭk), a city in north Germany (map **12**). The German name is *Braunschweig.*

brunt (brŭnt), *n.* the heaviest part of a shock or strain; as, to bear the *brunt.*

brush (brŭsh), *n.* **1,** an implement made of bristles, feathers, or the like, fixed in a back or handle, used for cleaning, smoothing, applying paint, etc.; **2,** the tail of a fox; **3,** a slight battle; skirmish; **4,** the act of cleaning or smoothing with a brush; **5,** a thicket of small trees; **6,** branches cut from trees; brushwood; **7,** thin metallic plates or wires bound together, to conduct a current to or from an electric motor or dynamo:—*v.t.* **1,** to sweep, cleanse, or rub with a brush; **2,** to remove as with a brush; as, to *brush* crumbs away; **3,** to touch lightly in passing; graze:—*v.i.* to pass quickly with a casual touch; as, he *brushed* by me.—*adj.* **brush′y.**

brush-wood (brŭsh′wŏŏd′), *n.* **1,** a dense growth of bushes; thicket; **2,** cut branches, or the like, suitable for a fire.

brusque (brŭsk; brōōsk), *adj.* abrupt; curt in manner or speech.—*adv.* **brusque′-ly.**—*n.* **brusque′ness.**

Brus-sels (brŭs′ĕlz) or **Bru-xelles** (brü′sĕl′), a city, the capital of Belgium (map **12**).

Brussels sprouts, a food plant of the mustard family, with small, green, cabbagelike heads growing on a stalk.

bru-tal (brōō′tăl), *adj.* savage; cruel; as, *brutal* treatment.—*adv.* **bru′tal-ly.**

bru-tal-i-ty (brōō-tăl′ĭ-tĭ), *n.* [*pl.* brutalities], pitiless cruelty; a savage act.

bru-tal-ize (brōō′tăl-īz), *v.t.* [brutalized, brutaliz-ing], to make cruel or inhuman; as, war tends to *brutalize* men.

brute (brōōt), *adj.* **1,** without intelligence; not human; **2,** like a wild beast; cruel:—*n.* **1,** a beast; especially, a wild beast; **2,** a man without human kindliness.

brut-ish (brōōt′ĭsh), *adj.* uncultured; stupid.—*n.* **brut′ish-ness.**

Bru-tus (brōō′tŭs), Marcus Junius (85–42 B.C.), a Roman politician, one of Julius Caesar's assassins.

Bry-an (brī′ăn). William Jennings (1860–1925), an American politician, reformer, and lecturer.

Bry·ant (brī'ănt), William Cullen (1794–1878), an American poet and journalist.

bu. abbreviation for *bushel, bushels.*

bub·ble (bŭb'l), *n.* **1,** a small, globelike film filled with air or gas; **2,** a small body of air or gas rising in a liquid, as in soda water, or held within a solid, as in ice or glass; **3,** anything unreal or fanciful; a delusion:—*v.i.* [bub-bled, bub-bling], **1,** to rise in bubbles; also, to form bubbles, as soda water; **2,** to make a gurgling sound, as a stream.

bu·bon·ic plague (bū-bŏn'ĭk plāg), a deadly contagious disease, marked by chills, fever, and swellings in the glands of neck, armpit, and groin. It is spread chiefly by the bites of fleas which have fed on infected rats.

buc·ca·neer (bŭk'a-nēr'), *n.* a pirate; a sea robber.

Bu·chan·an (bŭ-kăn'ăn; bū-kăn'ăn), James (1791-1868), the 15th president of the U.S.

Bu·cha·rest (bū'ka-rĕst'; bōō'ka-rĕst'), a city, capital of Rumania (map 12).

buck (bŭk), *n.* **1,** the male of any animal, as the deer or rabbit, of which the female is called *doe;* **2,** a sudden, vertical leap, as of an unruly horse; **3,** in football, a hard plunge into the opponents' line; **4,** *Slang,* a dollar:—*v.i.* to leap suddenly into the air with arched back, as a horse does to throw off a rider:—*v.t.* **1,** to throw off by a sudden leap; **2,** in football, to charge into (the opposing line).

pass the buck, *Slang,* to shift a task or responsibility to another; **buck up,** *Colloquial,* to take heart; revive in spirit.

buck·a·roo (bŭk'a-rōō'; bŭk'a-rōō'), *n.* a cowboy.

buck·board (bŭk'-bôrd'), *n.* a light wagon, with the seat set on a long, flexible board fastened without springs to the axles.

buck·et (bŭk'ĕt), *n.* **1,** a wooden pail for drawing water; **2,** any pail or holder in which something is collected or carried, as the scoop of a dredging machine; **3,** the amount a bucket holds; a bucketful.

BUCKETS

1, wooden water bucket; 2, fire bucket; 3, bucket of a dredging machine.

buck·eye (bŭk'ī'), *n.* another name for the horse-chestnut tree of the U.S.

¹buck·le (bŭk'l), *n.* **1,** a clasp for holding together the ends of a strap or the like; **2,** an ornament of similar shape for a dress, hat, etc.:—*v.t.* [buck-led, buck-ling], **1,** to fasten with a buckle; **2,** to apply (oneself) with energy:—*v.i.* **1,** to be held together by means of a buckle; **2,** to set to work with energy; as, to *buckle* down to studying.

²buck·le (bŭk'l), *v.i.* [buck-led, buck-ling], to bend or warp, as metal, from pressure or heat; crumple up:—*v.t.* to cause to buckle; crumple:—*n.* a bend or kink in a piece of metal.

BUCKLES

1, harness buckle; 2, man's belt buckle; 3, woman's belt buckle.

buck·ler (bŭk'lẽr), *n.* a small, round shield, or similar protection.

buck·ram (bŭk'răm), *n.* a coarse cloth of linen, cotton, or hemp stiffened with glue, used in making hat frames, binding books, etc.:—*adj.* made of, or like, buckram.

buck·saw (bŭk'sô'), *n.* a saw set in a deep, H-shaped frame and used with both hands for sawing firewood, as on a sawhorse.

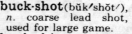

BUCKSAW

buck·shot (bŭk'shŏt'), *n.* coarse lead shot, used for large game.

buck·skin (bŭk'skĭn'), *n.* a soft, pliable leather made from the skin of a deer or sheep:—*adj.* made of buckskin.

buck·wheat (bŭk'hwēt'), *n.* a plant cultivated for its triangular seeds, which are ground into flour; also, the flour.

bu·col·ic (bū-kŏl'ĭk), *adj.* relating to a shepherd's life; pastoral; rustic.

bud (bŭd), *n.* **1,** a growth, as a lump or point, on a plant, that may develop into a branch, stem, leaf, or flower; **2,** a young girl in her first season in society:—*v.t.* [bud-ded, bud-ding], to insert (a bud) into an opening cut in the bark of another plant; graft; as, to *bud* an apple on a quince stock:—*v.i.* to put forth new shoots; sprout.

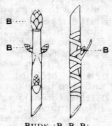

BUDS (B, B, B)

Showing one method of inserting a bud.

Bu·da·pest (bōō'da-pĕst'), a city, capital of Hungary, on the Danube (map 12).

Bud·dha (bood'a), (563 483 B.C.), an East Indian mystic, founder of Buddhism.

āte, āorta, râre, căt, ȧsk, fär, ăllow, sofȧ; ēve, ēvent, ĕll, writẽr, novĕl; bīte, pĭn; nō, ōbey, ôr, dŏg, tŏp, cŏllide; ūnit, ūnite, bûrn, cŭt, focŭs; nōōn, fŏŏt; mound; coin;

Bud·dhism (bood'ĭzm), *n.* a religion of Asia, named for Buddha, its founder, which teaches self-denial, virtue, and wisdom. —*n.* and *adj.* **Bud'dhist.**

budge (bŭj), *v.i.* [budged, budg·ing], to move from one's place; stir:—*v.t.* to cause to move; as, I can't *budge* the box.

budg·et (bŭj'ĕt), *n.* **1,** a quantity or store; as, a *budget* of news; **2,** a statement by a person, corporation, or government, of estimated income and expenses for a definite period; also, a plan for the best division of such income among the expenses:—*v. t.* to plan the spending of (one's income) by making a budget.

Bue·na Vis·ta (bwā'nä vēs'tä), a battlefield of the Mexican War, near Saltillo, in northeastern Mexico.

Bue·nos Ai·res (bwā'nŏs ī'rās; bō'nŏs âr'ēz), a large seaport city, capital of Argentina (map **11**); also, the province in which it is situated.

buff (bŭf), *n.* **1,** a thick, soft, dull-yellow leather made from the skin of a buffalo, ox, or similar animal; **2,** a soldier's coat made from this skin; **3,** a pale or faded yellowish-orange color; **4,** a wheel covered with buff, used for polishing:—*adj.* **1,** made of dull-yellow leather; **2,** of a faded yellowish-orange color:—*v.t.* to polish with a buff.

buf·fa·lo (bŭf'à-lō), *n.* [*pl.* buffaloes, buffalos, or buffalo], **1,** a kind of wild ox, as the Asiatic water buffalo, or the African Cape buffalo; **2,** in U.S. usage, the bison:—**buffalo bug,** a small

AFRICAN BUFFALO

beetle which in its larva stage is destructive to wool, fur, and feathers.

Buf·fa·lo (bŭf'à-lō), a city of New York State, on Lake Erie (map **6**).

Buffalo Bill, an American showman. See Cody, W. F.

¹**buff·er** (bŭf'ẽr), *n.* anything which softens or deadens the shock caused by the striking together of two bodies; especially, an apparatus placed at each end of a railway car:—**buffer state,** a small state between two larger, rival states, serving to lessen the chance of war.

²**buff·er** (bŭf'ẽr), *n.* **1,** a worker who polishes; **2,** a polishing machine or device; as, we have a *buffer* for our silver.

¹**buf·fet** (bŭf'ĕt), *n.* **1,** a blow with the hand; **2,** any blow:—*v.t.* **1,** to strike with the hand or fist; knock about; **2,** to struggle against; as, to *buffet* the waves:—*v.i.* to fight with blows; struggle.

²**buf·fet** (boo-fā'; bŭf'ĕt), *n.* **1,** a cupboard or sideboard for a dining room; **2,** a refreshment counter; also, a restaurant equipped with such counters:—**buffet luncheon,** a light meal served to guests seated or standing about a room.

buf·foon (bŭ-foon'), *n.* one who amuses others by jokes, antics, etc.; a clown.

buf·foon·er·y (bŭ-foon'ẽr-ĭ), *n.* [*pl.* buffooneries], the pranks or jokes of a clown or low comedian; vulgar jesting.

bug (bŭg), *n.* **1,** one of a group of flattened insects, with or without wings, having a piercing or sucking mouth, as the squash bug; **2,** in U.S. usage, any crawling insect; **3,** *Colloquial,* a disease germ.

bug·a·boo (bŭg'à-boo'), *n.* [*pl.* bugaboos], an imaginary creature used to frighten children into obedience; hence, any fancied cause of fear.

STINKBUG

bug·bear (bŭg'bâr'), *n.* **1,** a bugaboo or goblin; **2,** any object of dislike or dread.

bug·gy (bŭg'ĭ), *n.* [*pl.* buggies], a light, one-seated carriage.

bu·gle (bū'gl), *n.* **1,** a hunting horn; **2,** a trumpetlike brass wind instrument used for military calls (see illustration below):—*v.i.* and *v.t.* [bu-gled, bu-gling], to sound on a bugle.

AMERICAN BUGGY

bu·gler (bū'glẽr), *n.* a person who plays or sounds signals on the bugle.

Bug Riv·er (boog), a tributary of the Vistula, flowing through Poland.

build (bĭld), *v.t.* [built (bĭlt), build-ing], **1,** to construct by putting materials or parts together according to some plan or practice; **2,** to base or found; as, he *built* his hopes on his invention; **3,** to establish gradually, as a business:—*v.i.* to construct a building:—*n.* style of construction; as, the *build* of an automobile; also, figure; form; as, a boy of sturdy *build*.

MILITARY BUGLE

build·er (bĭl'dẽr), *n.* **1,** a person whose business is the construction of buildings; **2,** one who creates, organizes, or develops something; as, an empire *builder*.

build·ing (bĭl'dĭng), *n.* **1,** the art or business of erecting houses, churches, etc.; **2,** the act of constructing, raising, or establishing; **3,** a structure covering a piece of land, and designed for some particular use, as a school, house, barn, or the like.

built (bĭlt), the past tense and past participle of *build*.

bulb (bŭlb), *n.* **1,** the rounded part, usually under ground, of some plant, as the onion, the lily, and the narcissus, where the plant food is stored; **2,** a rounded end of a glass tube, as of a thermometer; **3,** a small glass globe containing an electric-light filament. — *adj.* **bulb′ous.**

Bul·gar·i·a (bŭl-gâr′-ĭ-à; bo͝ol-gär′ĭ-à), a country (cap. Sofia) in southeastern Europe, on the Black Sea (map 12). — *n.* and *adj.* **Bul·gar′i-an.**

BULBS

1, bulb of a thermometer; 2, electric-lamp bulb; 3, lily bulb (view and cross section).

bulge (bŭlj), *n.* **1,** a swelling outward, as from pressure; **2,** part of a wall, ship, etc., designed to curve outward: — *v.i.* and *v.t.* [bulged, bulging], to swell or bend outward. — *adj.* **bulg′y.**

bulk (bŭlk), *n.* **1,** mass; volume; great size; **2,** the main mass; the greater part.

bulk·head (bŭlk′hĕd), *n.* **1,** an upright partition in a ship, separating watertight compartments; **2,** a structure built to resist the pressure of water, air, or earth; especially, a sea wall.

bulk·y (bŭl′kĭ), *adj.* [bulk-i-er, bulk-i-est], massive; big; unwieldy. — *n.* **bulk′i-ness.**

¹**bull** (bo͝ol), *n.* **1,** the male of any animal of the ox family or of other large animals, as the whale or elephant; **2,** a person who buys stocks, bonds, etc., because he thinks he can sell at a profit: opposite of *bear.* — *adj.* **bull′ish.**

²**bull** (bo͝ol), *n.* an official document, edict, or decree, especially of the Pope.

³**bull** (bo͝ol), *n.* an absurd blunder.

bull·dog (bo͝ol′dôg′), *n.* a breed of short-haired, medium-sized dog with a heavy head and projecting lower jaw, remarkable for its courage and for its strong grip: — *adj.* having the qualities of a bulldog; courageous; tenacious.

bull·doze (bo͝ol′dōz′), *v.t.* [bulldozed, bulldoz-ing], to bully; compel by threats.

bull·doz·er (bo͝ol′dōz′ẽr), *n.* **1,** a machine for grading and roadbuilding: a powerful tractor, pushing a broad horizontal scraper; **2,** a person who forces another by bluster or violence; also, anything used to threaten, as especially, a weapon; **3,** a heavy, powerful machine for bending and shaping metal into shorter and thicker form.

bul·let (bo͝ol′ĕt), *n.* a small metal ball, made to be fired from a firearm.

bul·le·tin (bo͝ol′ĕ-tĭn), *n.* **1,** a brief official report on some matter of public interest; as, a doctor's *bulletin* on a famous patient's condition; **2,** a magazine published regularly, containing reports of a club or society: — *v.t.* to publish or announce in a brief statement.

bull·fight (bo͝ol′fīt′), *n.* a combat between men and a bull, or bulls, for public amusement. — *n.* **bull′fight′er.** — *n.* **bull′fight′ing.**

BULLDOG (¹⁄₁₈)

bull·finch (bo͝ol′fĭnch′), *n.* a sparrowlike European songbird with a short, strong bill and brilliant plumage.

bull·frog (bo͝ol′frŏg′), *n.* a kind of large, heavy frog with a loud, bellowing croak.

bull·head (bo͝ol′hĕd′), *n.* any of various big-headed fishes, especially the catfish.

bul·lion (bo͝ol′yŭn), *n.* uncoined gold or silver in lumps, bars, or the like.

bul·lock (bo͝ol′ŭk), *n.* an ox; steer.

Bull Run, a stream in northeastern Virginia where two great battles in the War between the States were fought.

bull's-eye (bo͝olz′-ī′), *n.* **1,** a bulging lens used to bring together the rays of light from a lantern upon a small spot; also, a lantern having such a lens; **2,** a round piece of thick glass in a floor or deck to admit light; **3,** the center point of a target, or a shot that hits it; hence, anything especially successful; **4,** a hard, round candy which looks like a marble.

bul·ly (bo͝ol′ĭ), *n.* [*pl.* bullies], a coward who tries to rule his weaker fellows by cruelty or threats: — *v.t.* [bullied, bully-ing], to rule with bluster and threats: — *v.i.* to be noisy and overbearing: — *adj. Colloquial*, excellent.

BULL'S-EYE

In an archer's target.

bul·rush (bo͝ol′rŭsh′), *n.* a large plant with slender stalks, growing in wet places.

bul·wark (bo͝ol′wẽrk′), *n.* **1,** a barrier or wall built for defense; an earthwork; rampart; breakwater; **2,** the boarding round the sides of a ship, above the level of the deck; **3,** any means of protection.

bum (bŭm), *v.i.* [bummed, bum-ming], to idle or loaf: — *v.t.* to get (something) by imposing on somebody; as, he always *bums* rides: — *n.* a loafer: — *adj.* [bum-mer, bummest], worthless. *Slang* in all uses.

bum-ble-bee (bŭm′bl-bē′), *n.* a large bee which makes a loud humming sound.

bump (bŭmp), *n.* 1, a blow; collision; 2, a swelling due to a knock or blow:—*v.t.* 1, to bring violently together; as, to *bump* heads; 2, to strike against; knock into:—*v.i.* to come together heavily.

¹**bump-er** (bŭmp′ẽr), *n.* a device for absorbing shock from a collision, as on an automobile, engine, or the like.

²**bump-er** (bŭmp′ẽr), *n.* 1, an overflowing cup; especially, one used in drinking a toast; 2, *Colloquial*, anything unusually large:—*adj.* very large; as, a *bumper* crop.

bump-kin (bŭmp′kĭn), *n.* a clumsy fellow.

bump-tious (bŭmp′shŭs), *adj.* conceited; self-assertive.—*n.* **bump′tious-ness.**

bun (bŭn), *n.* a sweetened, raised roll.

bunch (bŭnch), *n.* 1, a cluster, as of grapes; a bouquet, as of flowers; 2, a collection of things of the same kind grouped or fastened together; as, a *bunch* of keys:—*v.i.* and *v.t.* 1, to form into a cluster or bouquet; 2, to gather into folds; 3, to group together.

    Syn., *n.* bundle, group, cluster.

bun-co (bŭng′kō), *n.* a swindle. See **bunko.**

bun-combe or **bun-kum** (bŭng′kŭm), *n. Colloquial*, anything said or done for mere show or effect.

bun-dle (bŭn′dl), *n.* 1, a number of things bound together; a parcel; as, a *bundle* of rags; a *bundle* of books; 2, a quantity of something in one mass; as, a *bundle* of carpet:—*v.t.* [bun-dled, bun-dling], 1, to tie in a mass or roll; 2, to send off in a hurry; as, they *bundled* him out of town:—*v.i.* to pack up and start in haste; as, they *bundled* off before daylight.

bung (bŭng), *n.* 1, a stopper of wood or cork for the hole in the side of a cask or barrel; 2, the bunghole:—*v.t.* to close (a bunghole) with a stopper.

bun-ga-low (bŭng′gȧ-lō), *n.* a one-story house.

bung-hole (bŭng′hōl′), *n.* the small, round hole in the side of a cask.

BUNGALOW of India

bun-gle (bŭng′gl), *v.i.* and *v.t.* [bun-gled, bun-gling], to perform in a clumsy and unskilful manner:—*n.* a clumsy performance.—*n.* **bun′gler.**

bun-ion (bŭn′yŭn), *n.* an inflamed swelling on the foot, usually on the first joint of the great toe.

¹**bunk** (bŭngk), *n.* a shelf or recess used for a bed, as in a ship, camp, or the like:—*v.i.* to sleep in a bunk or bed.

²**bunk** (bŭngk), *n. Slang*, sentiments that sound well, but mean nothing; buncombe.

bunk-er (bŭngk′ẽr), *n.* 1, a large bin, especially for coal on a ship; 2, a rough place on a golf course; hence, an obstacle.

Bunk-er Hill, a hill in Charlestown, Boston, Massachusetts, a spur of which, Breed's Hill, was the scene of a famous battle (1775) in the American Revolution.

bun-ko (bŭng′kō), *n.* [*pl.* bunkos], a swindling game or scheme:—*v.t.* to swindle or cheat. Also spelled **bun′co.**

bun-kum (bŭng′kŭm), *n.* anything said or done for effect. See **buncombe.**

bun-ny (bŭn′ĭ), *n.* [*pl.* bunnies], a child's pet name for a rabbit.

bunt (bŭnt), *v.t.* and *v.i.* 1, to butt or push, as with head or horns; 2, in baseball, to tap (the ball) a short distance within the infield by meeting it with a loosely held bat:—*n.* 1, a push, as with horns; 2, in baseball, a bunted ball.

¹**bun-ting** (bŭn′tĭng), *n.* a kind of small, thick-billed bird akin to the finch.

²**bun-ting** (bŭn′tĭng) or **bun-tine** (bŭn′tĭn), *n.* a light fabric used for flags.

Bun-yan (bŭn′yăn), John (1628–1688), an English preacher and writer.

buoy (boo′ĭ; boi), *n.* 1, a floating object to show the position of rocks or shoals, or of a channel; 2, a device to keep a person afloat: usually called *life buoy:*—*v.t.* to support; as, to *buoy* up one's hopes.

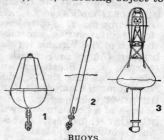
BUOYS
1, conical; 2, spar; 3, gas-lighted.

buoy-an-cy (boo′yăn-sĭ; boi′ăn-sĭ), *n.* 1, the capacity, as of cork, to float in a fluid; 2, the power of a fluid to float an object; as, the *buoyancy* of water; 3, the tendency to be cheerful; lightheartedness.

buoy-ant (boo′yănt; boi′ănt), *adj.* 1, able to float in a fluid, as cork; 2, vivacious; lighthearted; gay.—*adv.* **buoy′ant-ly.**

bur or **burr** (bûr), *n.* 1, a prickly seedcase, or a plant bearing such; 2, a small, rough, or clinging object.

CHESTNUT BUR

Bur-bank (bûr′băngk), Luther (1849–1926), an American natural-

---

go; join; yet; sing; chin; show; thin, *th*en; hw, *wh*y; zh, a*z*ure; ü, Ger. f*ür* or Fr. l*u*ne; ö, Ger. sch*ö*n or Fr. f*eu*; ṅ, Fr. *en*fant, *nom*; kh, Ger. a*ch* or i*ch*. See pages ix–x.

ist, who developed many new varieties of flowers and fruits.

¹bur-den (bûr'dn), *n.* 1, something carried; a load; 2, something endured, as a trouble or sorrow; 3, the bearing of loads or packs; as, a beast of *burden;* 4, the cargo-carrying capacity of a vessel; tonnage:—*v.t.* 1, to load; 2, to put too much upon; oppress. —*adj.* **bur'den-some.**

²bur-den (bûr'dn), *n.* 1, the refrain or chorus of a song; 2, the main theme of a poem, story, or the like.

bur-dock (bûr'dŏk'), *n.* a coarse weed with broad leaves and a prickly, clinging fruit.

bu-reau (bū'rō), *n.* [*pl.* bureaus or bureaux (bū'rōz)], 1, a low chest of drawers for clothing, usually with a mirror; 2, an office or department; as, an employment *bureau;* information *bureau;* 3, a government office or department; as, the *Bureau* of Standards.

BUREAU, def. 1

bu-reauc-ra-cy (bū-rŏk'rȧ-sĭ; bū-rō'krȧ-sĭ), *n.* [*pl.* bureaucracies], 1, government by an organized system of bureaus or departments; 2, officials of such a government, spoken of as a group. —*n.* **bu'reau-crat** (bū'rō-krăt).

bur-gess (bûr'jĕs), *n.* 1, a citizen or freeman of a borough; 2, a town executive; 3, before the Revolution, a member of the lower branch of the Virginia legislature.

burgh (bûrg; in Scottish usage, bŭr'ō; bŭr'ŭ), *n.* a Scottish town with certain local lawmaking rights, which has a voice in sending a member to Parliament.

burgh-er (bûr'gēr), *n.* in former times, a citizen of a borough or town.

bur-glar (bûr'glēr), *n.* one who breaks into a building to steal.

bur-gla-ry (bûr'glȧ-rĭ), *n.* [*pl.* burglaries], the crime of breaking into a building, especially at night, to steal.—*adj.* **bur-glar'i-ous** (bûr-glâr'ĭ-ŭs).

bur-go-mas-ter (bûr'gō-màs'tēr), *n.* in Holland, Flanders, or Germany, the chief magistrate or the mayor of a town.

Bur-goyne (bûr-goin'), John (1722–1792), an English general in the American Revolution.

¹Bur-gun-dy (bûr'gŭn-dĭ), a former duchy of eastern France, which for a time controlled also Holland and Belgium.

²Bur-gun-dy (bûr'gŭn-dĭ), *n.* the name given to certain red and white wines made in the former duchy of Burgundy.

bur-i-al (bĕr'ĭ-ăl), *n.* the act or ceremony of placing a body in the grave.

Burke (bûrk), Edmund (1729–1797), a British statesman, orator, and writer.

bur-lap (bûr'lăp), *n.* a coarse fabric of jute or hemp, used for bags, curtains, etc.

bur-lesque (bûr-lĕsk'), *n.* 1, a ridiculous imitation; a parody; 2, a composition or play in which a trifling subject is treated with mock dignity, or a dignified subject with irreverence:—*v.t.* and *v.i.* [burlesqued, burles-quing], to ridicule by exaggeration: —*adj.* amusingly imitative.

bur-ly (bûr'lĭ), *adj.* [bur-li-er, bur-li-est], strong and muscular.—*n.* **bur'li-ness.**

Bur-ma (bûr'mȧ), formerly the largest province in British India, since 1948 an independent republic on the Bay of Bengal. —*n.* and *adj.* **Bur'man; Bur'mese'.**

¹burn (bûrn), *n.* in Scotland, a brook.

²burn (bûrn), *v.t.* [burned (bûrnd) or burnt (bûrnt), burn-ing], 1, to destroy or damage by fire or heat; 2, to use or consume as fuel for heat or light; as, we *burn* coal; this lamp *burns* kerosene; 3, to affect or injure by heat, acid, or the like; as, the sun *burned* her skin; 4, to expose intentionally to the action of fire, as wood to make charcoal; 5, in surgery, to apply heat or acid to; cauterize:—*v.i.* 1, to be on fire; 2, to suffer from, or be injured by, too much heat; 3, to be inflamed with passion or desire; as, he *burns* to win fame; 4, to feel a sensation of heat; as, his ears *burned;* 5, to blaze; glow; be bright; as, the sky *burned* with color:—*n.* damage or an injury caused by fire or by too much heat.

Syn., v. blaze, sear, scorch, singe.

burn-er (bûr'nēr), *n.* 1, one who burns something; as, a brick *burner;* 2, a device in which something is burned, as an incinerator; 3, the part of a gas lamp or fixture from which the flame comes; also, the fixture itself.

bur-nish (bûr'nĭsh), *v.t.* to polish by rubbing, as metal:—*n.* polish; brightness. —*n.* **bur'nish-er.**

bur-noose (bûr-nōōs'; bûr'-nōōs), *n.* a cloak and hood in one piece, worn by Moors and Arabs. Also spelled **bur-nous'.**

Burns (bûrnz), Robert (1759–1796), a Scottish poet.

burnt (bûrnt), a form of the past tense and past participle of *²burn:*—*adj* charred, damaged, or destroyed by fire.

Burr (bûr), Aaron (1756–1836), an American politician, who was tried for treason, and acquitted, for his plan to found an empire in the southwestern part of the U.S.

ARABIAN BURNOOSE

burr (bûr), *n.* **1,** a thin ridge or roughness left by a tool in cutting or shaping metal; **2,** a small rotating drill used by dentists; **3,** a prickly, clinging seedcase; a bur; **4,** a rough, guttural pronunciation of *r:—v.i.* and *v.t.* to pronounce with a rough or guttural sound; as, to *burr* one's r's.

bur-ro (bûr′ō; bōōr′ō), *n.* [*pl.* burros], in the southwestern U.S., a small donkey used as a pack animal.

bur-row (bûr′ō), *n.* **1,** a hole in the ground, such as is dug by an animal as a refuge or nest; **2,** hence, a secluded dwelling place or place of retreat:—*v.i.* **1,** to dig a hole in the earth, as for shelter; **2,** to lodge in a burrow; **3,** to dig or search; as, he was *burrowing* in an old trunk:—*v.t.* to build by burrowing; as, to *burrow* a cave.

bur-sar (bûr′sẽr), *n.* a treasurer; purser; as, the *bursar* of a college.

burst (bûrst), *v.i.* [burst, burst-ing], **1,** to explode; break open; fly to pieces; as, our steam boiler *burst;* **2,** to break out into sudden action or expression of feeling; as, to *burst* into tears; **3,** to appear or disappear suddenly; as, a scene *burst* upon our view; **4,** to be full to overflowing; as, the bags are *bursting* with mail:—*n.* **1,** a violent or sudden breaking forth; as, a *burst* of applause; **2,** a sudden breaking, as of a gas pipe; **3,** a rush; spurt; as, a *burst* of energy.

bur-y (bĕr′ĭ), *v.t.* [buried, bury-ing], **1,** to place in a grave, tomb, or the like; **2,** to cover from sight; conceal, as treasure; **3,** to keep secret; as, to *bury* one's past; **4,** to engross; as, he *buried* himself in a book.

bus (bŭs), *n.* [*pl.* busses or buses], an omnibus; a large public vehicle.

bush (bŏŏsh), *n.* **1,** a shrub or low-growing plant which develops some wood in its stem; **2,** an uncleared forest region: used especially of land in Australia.

bush-el (bŏŏsh′ĕl), *n.* **1,** a unit of dry measure, containing four pecks, or 32 quarts; **2,** a container holding a bushel.

bush-ing (bŏŏsh′ing), *n.* a detachable lining, usually of metal, within which a shaft or axle turns. The *bushing* protects against friction.

bush-y (bŏŏsh′ĭ), *adj.* [bush-i-er, bush-i-est], **1,** growing thickly; as, *bushy* hair; **2,** overgrown with shrubs.

bus-i-ly (bĭz′ĭ-lĭ), *adv.* in a busy, active manner.

busi-ness (bĭz′nĕs), *n.* **1,** employment; regular occupation; **2,** duty; mission; as, I made it my *business* to see that the job was done; **3,** concern; as, it is no *business* of mine; **4,** affair; matter; as, the trial was an unpleasant *business;* **5,** a commercial enterprise; as, he started a hardware *business;* **6,** activity in trade; as, *business* was good last month:—*adj.* relating to commercial activities; as, a *business* deal.

Syn., n. commerce, trade, profession.

busi-ness-like (bĭz′nĕs-līk′), *adj.* practical; efficient; well-ordered.

bus-kin (bŭs′kĭn), *n.* **1,** a high, laced boot; **2,** a thick-soled boot worn in ancient times by tragic actors and used as a symbol of tragedy; **3,** hence, tragedy.

bust (bŭst), *n.* **1,** the upper front of the body; the breast or bosom, especially of a woman; **2,** a piece of sculpture representing the head and shoulders of a person.

bus-tard (bŭs′tẽrd), *n.* a large, swift-running game bird of the Old World, akin to the cranes and plovers.

¹**bus-tle** (bŭs′l), *n.* noisy activity:—*v.i.* [bus-tled, bustling], to be noisily and fussily busy.

²**bus-tle** (bŭs′l), *n.* a pad, or a framework of wire, formerly worn by women under the skirt at the back, below the waist, to give the proper shape to the dress.

BUST
of Julius Caesar.

bus-y (bĭz′ĭ), *adj.* [bus-i-er, bus-i-est], **1,** at work; active; not idle; **2,** produced by industry or activity; as, the *busy* hum of the factory; **3,** full of activity; as, a *busy* crossing; **4,** in use, as a telephone line:—*v.t.* [busied, busy-ing] to keep constantly occupied; as, *busied* with housework.

Syn., adj. industrious, diligent, engaged.

bus-y-bod-y (bĭz′ĭ-bŏd′ĭ), *n.* [*pl.* busybodies], one who meddles in others' affairs.

but (bŭt), *adv.* only; as, speak *but* a word: —*prep.* except; as, I can bear all *but* that: —*conj.* **1,** still; yet; as, poor *but* honest; **2,** on the contrary; as, you go, *but* I stay; **3,** that; as, I do not doubt *but* it is true; **4,** that not; as, who knows *but* he will succeed: —**but for,** without; except for; as, *but for* that, I could go.

butch-er (bŏŏch′ẽr), *n.* **1,** a person who kills and dresses animals for food; **2,** a meat dealer; **3,** a cruel, bloody murderer:— *v.t.* **1,** to kill and dress (animals) for food; **2,** to murder by violence; **3,** to botch or mangle; ruin.

butch-er-y (bŏŏch′ẽr-ĭ), *n.* [*pl.* butcheries], **1,** the business of killing and dressing animals for food; **2,** cruel and unnecessary slaughter.

But-ler (bŭt′lẽr), Nicholas Murray (1862–1947), an American educator.

but-ler (bŭt′lẽr), *n.* a manservant, usually the chief servant in a household.

---

go; join; yet; sing; chin; show; thin, *th*en; hw, *why;* zh, *a*zure; ü, Ger. f*ü*r or Fr. l*u*ne; ö, Ger. sch*ö*n or Fr. f*eu;* n, Fr. e*n*fant, nom; kh, Ger. a*ch* or i*ch*. See pages ix–x.

¹butt (bŭt), *n.* **1,** the thicker, heavier, or lower part of anything, as of a whip or a gun; **2,** what is left of anything after a part has been cut away or used up.

²butt (bŭt), *v.t.* to strike with, or as with, lowered head:—*v. i.* to bump; collide; as, he *butted* into the table:—*n.* a push or sudden thrust with the head.

³butt (bŭt), *n.* that at which anything is aimed; a target, especially for ridicule; as, to be the *butt* of jokes.

⁴butt (bŭt), *n.* a large cask or barrel, as for wine, ale, or beer.

Butte (būt), a city in Montana (map 9).

butte (būt), *n.* an isolated tablelike hill.

but-ter (bŭt/-ĕr), *n.* **1,** the fatty substance obtained from milk or cream by churning; **2,** any butter-like substance;

BUTTE

as, peanut *butter*; peach *butter*:—*v.t.* to spread or season with butter.—*adj.* **but/ter-y.**

but-ter-cup (bŭt/ĕr-kŭp/), *n.* a common meadow plant with yellow, cup-shaped flowers; also, the flower of this plant.

but-ter-fat (bŭt/ĕr-făt/), *n.* the natural fat in milk.

but-ter-fly (bŭt/-ĕr-flī/), *n.* [*pl.* butterflies], **1,** a day-flying insect with a long sucking beak, two long knobbed feelers, and four wings, frequently brightly colored; **2,** a gay idler:—**butterfly weed,** a milkweed with orange-colored flowers.

MONARCH BUTTERFLY

but-ter-milk (bŭt/ĕr-mĭlk/), *n.* the liquid remaining when cream or milk has been churned and the butter removed.

but-ter-nut (bŭt/ĕr-nŭt/) *n.* the American white walnut tree, or its edible nut.

but-tocks (bŭt/ŭks), *n.pl.* the part of the body on which one sits.

but-ton (bŭt/n), *n.* **1,** a small disk or knob of bone, wood, glass, or the like, used for fastening or ornamenting a garment; **2,** anything like this, as the knob operating an electric switch:—*v.t.* and *v.i.* to fasten with buttons.

but-ton-hole (bŭt/n-hōl/), *n.* a stitched slit for a button to pass through:—*v.t.* [buttonholed, buttonhol-ing], **1,** to furnish with buttonholes; **2,** to edge (cloth) with the stitching used in making buttonholes; **3,** to engage (a person) in conversation, often against his will.

but-ton-wood (bŭt/n-wŏŏd/), *n.* a large North American tree with a round, buttonlike fruit; the plane tree or sycamore.

but-tress (bŭt/rĕs), *n.* **1,** brickwork or masonry constructed against a wall or building to give it strength and support; **2,** any prop or support:—*v.t.* to support with, or as with, a buttress; strengthen; brace.

BUTTRESSES
A, buttress; B, flying buttress.

bux-om (bŭk/sŭm), *adj.* plump, healthy, and full of life.

buy (bī), *v.t.* [bought (bôt), buy-ing], **1,** to get by paying a price agreed on; **2,** to gain at a sacrifice; as, to *buy* peace by yielding; **3,** to be the means of getting; as, money cannot *buy* happiness; **4,** to bribe:—*v.i.* to make a purchase; as, I cannot *buy* without money.

buy-er (bī/ĕr), *n.* one whose business is buying for a firm; a purchasing agent.

buzz (bŭz), *n.* **1,** a continuous humming sound, as of bees; **2,** a confused or blended murmur, as of voices:—*v.i.* to make, or speak with, a low humming sound.

buz-zard (bŭz/ĕrd), *n.* **1,** any of several hawklike birds of prey of America and Europe; **2,** especially, in America, the turkey buzzard, a blackish vulture that feeds only on dead flesh.

Buz-zard's Bay (bŭz/ĕrdz), an inlet of the Atlantic, on the south coast of Massachusetts (map 6).

buzz-er (bŭz/ĕr), *n.* an electric device for quiet signaling.

by- (bī-), a prefix meaning: **1,** not the main; out of the way; as, *by*-path, *by*way; **2,** near; as, *by*stander; also, past; as, *by*gone.

by (bī), *prep.* **1,** beside or near to; as, a chair *by* the window; **2,** along; as, a road *by* the river; over; as, I came *by* the bridge; **3,** in, on, or at; as, *by* night; *by* land; **4,** past and beyond; as, to go *by* the spot; **5,** according to; from; as, known *by* his gait; to judge *by* appearances; **6,** not any later than; as, to finish *by* two o'clock; **7,** through the agency of; as, to send word

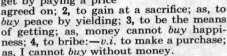

BUZZARD, def. 1
American rough-legged hawk (!)

by a boy; **8,** through the action of; as, a poem *by* Shelley; **9,** because of; as, to succeed *by* industry; **10,** to or in the amount of; as, taller *by* several inches; the game was won *by* one goal; **11,** with regard to; as, he dealt well *by* me; **12,** with the witness of; in the name of; as, to swear *by* the Book; **13,** in the measure of; as, sell tea *by* the pound; **14,** in the manner of; as, *by* accident; **15,** one point in the direction of; as, north *by* east:—*adv.* **1,** near; at hand; as, to stand *by;* **2,** aside; in reserve; as, put *by* some money; lay your armor *by;* **3,** past; as, he drove *by.*

by and by, after a while; before long.

by-and-by (bī′-ănd-bī′), *n.* the future.

bye (bī), *n.* in certain games, the position of a player in a tournament who is not matched with another player, and advances to the next round without playing: —**by the bye** or **by the by,** by the way.

by-gone (bī′gôn′), *adj.* past; gone by:— *n.* a thing of the past.

by-law (bī′lô′), *n.* a rule or law made by an organization for regulating its affairs.

by-pass (bī′-pàs′), *n.* an alternate method or route, as a road, channel, or pipe:—*v.t.* to go around by means of an alternate route or method.

by-path (bī′pàth′), *n.* a side path.

by-play (bī′plā′), *n.* action, often in pantomime, not directly connected with the main situation, especially on the stage.

by-prod-uct (bī′-prŏd′ŭkt), *n.* something that is produced in a manufacturing process, other than the principal product, and has a value of its own, as sawdust in a sawmill; a secondary product.

Byrd (bûrd), Richard Evelyn (1888–1957), an American rear admiral and explorer.

by-road (bī′rōd′), *n.* a side road.

By-ron (bī′rŭn), George Gordon, Lord (1788–1824), an English poet.

by-stand-er (bī′stăn′dẽr), *n.* a person who looks on, but does not take part.

by-way (bī′wā′), *n.* a side path; a road little known or used.

by-word (bī′wûrd′), *n.* **1,** a proverb or saying; **2,** an object of scorn or ridicule; as, her vanity made her a *byword.*

By-zan-tine (bĭ-zăn′tĭn; -tīn; bī-zăn′tĭn; -tīn; bĭz′ăn-tĭn; -tīn), *n.* a native of Byzantium:—*adj.* relating to Byzantium, the Eastern Roman Empire, or a style of art developed there in the fifth and sixth centuries. (See illustration at ²*capital.*)

By-zan-ti-um (bĭ-zăn′shĭ-ŭm; -tĭ-ŭm; bī-zăn′shĭ-ŭm; -tĭ-ŭm), an ancient city, founded 658 B.C.; later called Constantinople (map 1): now called *Istanbul.*

C

C, c (sē), *n.* [*pl.* C's, c's], **1,** the third letter of the alphabet, following B; **2,** the Roman numeral for 100; **3,** in music, the first tone in the major scale of C.

C. abbreviation for *Cape, Catholic, Centigrade, Congress:*—**c.** abbreviation for *cent* or *cents,* and for Latin *circa,* meaning *about.*

cab (kăb), *n.* **1,** an automobile for hire to passengers; a taxicab; **2,** a public carriage drawn by one horse; **3,** on an engine, the shelter for the fireman and engineer.

ca-bal (ka-băl′), *n.* **1,** a secret scheme; **2,** a few people closely united in some secret scheme or plot; as, a *cabal* of five members formed to overthrow the government.

cab-a-ret (kăb′a-rā′; kăb′a-rā), *n.* a restaurant in which guests are entertained with dancing and vaudeville acts; also, the entertainment itself.

cab-bage (kăb′ĭj), *n.* a vegetable with thick curved leaves forming a round, hard head.

cab-in (kăb′ĭn), *n.* **1,** a small hut or cottage; **2,** on a ship, a room for

CABBAGE

officers or passengers; **3,** on an airplane, the enclosed place for passengers.

cab-i-net (kăb′ĭ-nĕt), *n.* **1,** a piece of furniture or a closet having shelves or drawers, in which a number of articles are kept or displayed; as, a curio *cabinet;* a medicine *cabinet;* a filing *cabinet;* **2,** a group of persons chosen by the head of a government to act as his advisers in managing the country's affairs.

CABINET, def. 1

cab-i-net-mak-er (kăb′ĭ-nĕt-māk′ẽr), *n.* a maker of fine woodwork, especially of fine household furniture.

ca-ble (kā′bl), *n.* **1,** a chain or strong rope of hemp or wire strands, variously used, as for supporting suspension bridges, towing automobiles, mooring ships, etc.; **2,** an insulated bundle of electric wires; **3,** a

CABLE, def. 1

message sent by submarine telegraph; as, a *cable* from London; **4**, a cable's length, about 100 fathoms or 600 feet:—*v.t.* and *v.i.* [ca-bled, ca-bling], to send by submarine telegraph; as, *cable* me your answer; he *cabled* today.

ca·ble·gram (kā′bl-grăm), *n.* a message sent by submarine cables.

ca·boose (ka-boos′), *n.* **1**, a kitchen on the deck of a ship; **2**, a small car in which trainmen rest, sleep, or eat, generally attached to the end of a freight train.

Cab·ot (kăb′ŭt), **1**, John (1451?–1498?), an Italian navigator in the English service, who discovered the continent of North America in 1497; **2**, Sebastian (1472?–1557), his son, an English navigator.

cab·ri·o·let (kăb′rĭ-ō-lā′), *n.* **1**, a covered, two-seated carriage drawn by one horse; **2**, an enclosed automobile with a folding top.

ca·ca·o (ka-kā′ō; ka-kā′ō), *n.* **1**, a small evergreen tree of tropical America; **2**, the seeds of this tree, from which cocoa and chocolate are made.

CACAO
1, pod and leaves; 2, pod opened to show seeds.

cache (kăsh), *n.* **1**, a hiding place, as for treasure or supplies; **2**, the material so hidden:—*v.t.* [cached, cach-ing], to hide; conceal; store away; as, the robber *cached* the loot.

cack·le (kăk′l), *n.* **1**, the cry, or clucking, of a hen or goose just after it has laid an egg; **2**, chatter; noisy, idle talk; as, the *cackle* of the diners drowned the music:—*v.i.* [cack-led, cack-ling], **1**, to cry like a goose or a hen; **2**, to giggle; prattle; as, they *cackled* too much to get anything done.

cac·tus (kăk′tŭs), *n.* [*pl.* cacti (kăk′tī) or cactuses], a leafless desert plant with sharp spines or prickles along a fleshy stem and branches. There are many kinds, some bearing very showy flowers.

cad (kăd), *n.* an ill-bred, ungentlemanly man.

ca·dav·er (ka-dăv′ẽr; ka-dā′vẽr), *n.* a dead body, especially of a human being.

ca·dav·er·ous (ka-dăv′ẽr-ŭs), *adj.* corpselike; pale; gaunt.

GIANT CACTUS

cad·die or **¹cad·dy** (kăd′ĭ), *n.* [*pl.* caddies], a person who carries clubs for a golf player:—*v.i.* [caddied, caddy-ing], to carry clubs for a golfer; as, I *caddied* for him all day.

²cad·dy (kăd′ĭ), *n.* [*pl.* caddies], a small box or can; as, a tea *caddy*.

ca·dence (kā′děns), *n.* **1**, the rise and fall of the voice in reading or speaking; **2**, rhythm, as in music; **3**, in music, chords at the end of part of a composition.

ca·det (ka-dĕt′), *n.* **1**, a student in a naval or military academy; **2**, a younger brother or son.—*n.* **ca·det′ship**.

Cá·diz (kā′dĭz; kä′thĕth), a seaport on the southwestern coast of Spain (map **12**).

Cad·mus (kăd′mŭs), *n.* in mythology, a Phoenician prince who introduced the alphabet into Greece. He founded Thebes with the help of five men, who grew from the planted teeth of a dragon he slew.

ca·du·ce·us (ka-dū′sē-ŭs), *n.* [*pl.* caducei (ka-dū′sē-ī)], **1**, the winged, serpent-twined staff of Mercury; **2**, a likeness of this staff used as a symbol of the medical profession.

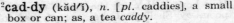

CADUCEUS

¹Cae·sar (sē′zẽr), Gaius Julius (100–44 B.C.), a Roman general and statesman.

²Cae·sar (sē′zẽr), *n.* **1**, the title assumed by Roman emperors; **2**, any dictator.

Caes·a·re·a (sĕs′a-rē′a; sēz′a-rē′a), the Roman capital of Palestine (map **1**).

cae·su·ra (sē-zū′ra; sē-sū′ra), *n.* a slight pause near the middle of a line of verse. It is indicated by a double mark [||]; as, "Jack and Jill || went up the hill."

ca·fé (ka-fā′), *n.* a restaurant, especially for light refreshments.

caf·e·te·ri·a (kăf′ē-tē′rĭ-a), *n.* a restaurant where patrons serve themselves.

caf·fe·ine (kăf′ē-ĭn; kăf′ēn; kăf′ē-ēn) or **caf·fe·in** (kăf′ē-ĭn; kăf′ēn), *n.* the drug or stimulant in coffee and tea.

caf·tan (kăf′tăn; kaf-tän′), *n.* a girdled, long-sleeved garment worn in countries of the Near East.

CAFTAN

cage (kāj), *n.* **1**, a box or enclosure, usually of bars or wire, used to confine birds or animals; **2**, anything like a cage in form or effect; as, a *cage* for baseball practice; an elevator *cage*:—*v.t.* [caged, cag-ing], to confine; shut up in, or as if in, a cage.

CAGE

Cain (kān), in the Bible, the son of Adam and Eve, outlawed because he killed his brother Abel (Genesis 4:1–10).

āte, âorta, râre, căt, ȧsk, fär, ăllow, sofȧ; ēve, ĕvent, ĕll, writẽr, novĕl; bīte, pĭn; nō, ōbey, ôr, dŏg, tŏp, cŏllide; ūnit, ūnite, bûrn, cŭt, focŭs; noon, foot; mound; coin;

cairn (kârn), *n.* a heap of stones serving as a monument or landmark.

Cai-ro (kī′rō), a city, capital of Egypt, on the Nile River (map 14).

cais-son (kā′sŭn), *n.* 1, an ammunition wagon; 2, a water-tight box under water, in which workmen work when building bridges, dams, or piers; 3, a float used to raise sunken vessels.

cai-tiff (kā′tĭf), *n.* a mean, cowardly person; wretch:—*adj.* vile; cowardly.

ca-jole (ka-jōl′), *v.t.* [cajoled, cajol-ing], to coax or deceive by flattery; wheedle; cheat; as, he *cajoled* me into signing the note; he *cajoled* me out of my allowance.

ca-jol-er-y (ka-jō′lĕr-ĭ), *n.* [*pl.* cajoleries], the act of getting one's way through flattery, insincere promises, or the like.

cake (kāk), *n.* 1, a small mass of dough, sweetened and baked; as, layer *cake;* 2, a small portion of thin batter or of ground-up meat, fish, potatoes, etc., cooked on a griddle; 3, any small compressed or flattened mass; as, a *cake* of soap or ice:—*v.i.* and *v.t.* [caked, cak-ing], to form or harden into a hard mass; as, the mud *caked*.

cal-a-bash (kăl′a-băsh), *n.* 1, a tropical American tree, or its hard-shelled, gourdlike fruit; 2, a pipe, bowl, dipper, bottle, or the like, made from the dried shell.

CALABASHES
1, calabash growing; 2, 3, articles made from calabashes.

Ca-la-bri-a (ka-lā′brĭ-a; kä-lä′brē-ä), a peninsula and department of southern Italy.

Cal-ais (kăl′ā; kăl′ĭs; ka-lā′), a seaport city in northwestern France, on the Strait of Dover (map 12).

ca-lam-i-tous (ka-lăm′ĭ-tŭs), *adj.* causing affliction or misery; disastrous.

ca-lam-i-ty (ka-lăm′ĭ-tĭ), *n.* [*pl.* calamities], 1, an event that causes widespread destruction, as a hurricane or an earthquake; 2, a great personal misfortune, as the death of a loved one, loss of sight, etc. *Syn.* accident, mishap, catastrophe.

cal-car-e-ous (kăl-kâr′ē-ŭs), *adj.* containing lime, as do animal bones, shells, etc.

cal-ci-fy (kăl′sĭ-fī), *v.t.* and *v.i.* [calcified, calcify-ing], to make or become hard by the addition of lime.

cal-ci-mine (kăl′sĭ-mīn; kăl′sĭ-mĭn), *n.* a white or tinted wash for decorating walls or ceilings:—*v.t.* [calcimined, calcimin-ing], to cover with such a wash. Also spelled **kal′so-mine.**

cal-cine (kăl-sīn′; kăl′sīn), *v.t.* and *v.i.* [calcined, calcin-ing], to burn to ashes; change into powder by the action of dry heat.

cal-ci-um (kăl′sĭ-ŭm), *n.* a soft, white metal, found only in combination with some other substance, as in lime, marble, chalk, or bone.

calcium carbide, a compound of calcium and carbon, used to make acetylene gas; **calcium chloride,** a compound of calcium and chlorine, used for disinfecting and freezing; **calcium light,** an intense white light: also called *limelight.*

cal-cu-la-ble (kăl′kŭ-la-bl), *adj.* capable of being measured or computed; as, the cost is *calculable.*

cal-cu-late (kăl′kŭ-lāt), *v.t.* [calculat-ed, calculat-ing], 1, to figure out by arithmetic; as, to *calculate* the cost of a house; 2, to estimate in any way; as, to *calculate* the benefits of science; also, chiefly in *p.p.*, to intend; as, a program *calculated* to help business:—*v.i.* 1, to make a computation or estimate; as, he *calculated* wrongly; 2, *Colloquial,* to plan; as, he *calculated* on arriving before dark. *Syn.* compute, number, rate.

cal-cu-la-tion (kăl′kŭ-lā′shŭn), *n.* 1, the use of numbers in solving a problem; also, the result obtained; 2, an estimate; forecast; as, *calculation* of benefits; 3, caution; care; as, to act with *calculation.*

cal-cu-la-tor (kăl′kŭ-lā′tĕr), *n.* 1, a person who reckons; 2, a machine that computes, as an adding machine.

cal-cu-lus (kăl′kŭ-lŭs), *n.* [*pl.* calculi (kăl′kŭ-lī)], 1, a branch of mathematics which deals with problems involving motion, curves, etc.; 2, a hard stonelike mass formed in an organ of the body, as a kidney stone or gallstone.

Cal-cut-ta (kăl-kŭt′a), a city in India, north of the Bay of Bengal (map 15), capital of the former Bengal province.

cal-dron or **caul-dron** (kôl′drŭn), *n.* a large kettle or boiler.

Cal-e-do-ni-a (kăl′ē-dō′nĭ-a; kăl′ē-dŏn′ya), the ancient Latin name of Scotland.

cal-en-dar (kăl′ĕn-dĕr), *n.* 1, a method of reckoning time, especially as to the length and divisions of a year; 2, a printed card, or sheets of paper, setting forth the days, weeks, and months of a year; 3, a list of things to be done in order of time; as, a court *calendar;* the *calendar* for the day:—*v.t.* to register or place on a list.

cal-en-der (kăl′ĕn-dĕr), *n.* a machine with heated rollers for smoothing and glazing paper or cloth:—*v.t.* to press in a smoothing machine, as paper.

¹**calf** (kåf), *n.* [*pl.* calves (kåvz)], 1, the

young of the cow; **2,** the young of certain other large mammals, as of the whale, elephant, or moose; **3,** leather made of the skin of the calf.

²**calf** (kȧf), *n.* [*pl.* calves (kȧvz)], the fleshy hinder part of the human leg, between the knee and the ankle.

calf-skin (kȧf′skĭn′), *n.* **1,** the skin of a calf; **2,** leather made of this skin.

Cal·i·ban (kăl′ĭ-băn), *n.* a deformed, savage slave in Shakespeare's play, "The Tempest"; hence, a man of degraded nature.

cal·i·ber or **cal·i·bre** (kăl′ĭ-bẽr), *n.* **1,** the inside diameter of the barrel of a pistol, gun, etc.; as, a pistol of .22 *caliber* has a bore 22 hundredths of an inch wide; **2,** mental capacity; degree of merit or importance; as, we play teams of our own *caliber.*

cal·i·co (kăl′ĭ-kō), *n.* [*pl.* calicoes or calicos], a cheap cotton cloth, usually printed with figured or flowered patterns:—*adj.* made of calico.

Cal·i·for·ni·a (kăl′ĭ-fôr′nĭ-ȧ; kăl′ĭ-fôrn′yȧ), a Pacific State (cap. Sacramento) in the U.S. (Map 9.)—**Gulf of California,** a gulf lying between Mexico and Lower California.—*n.* and *adj.* **Cal′i-for′ni-an.**

cal·i·pers or **cal·li·pers** (kăl′ĭ-pẽrz), *n. pl.* [*sing.* caliper or calliper], an instrument with two adjustable curved legs, used to measure diameters.

CALIPERS

ca·liph or **ca·lif** (kā′lĭf; kăl′ĭf), *n.* formerly, in Mohammedan countries, especially Turkey, a title for one having supreme power in religion and government. Also spelled **ka′lif** or **kha′lif.**

cal·iph·ate (kăl′ĭ-fāt), *n.* the office, reign, or country of a caliph.

cal·is·then·ics or **cal·lis·then·ics** (kăl′ĭs-thĕn′ĭks), *n.pl.* **1,** setting-up or simple gymnastic exercises; **2,** used as *sing.*, the science or practice of such exercises.—*adj.* **cal′is-then′ic; cal′lis-then′ic.**

¹**calk** or **caulk** (kôk), *v.t.* to drive hemp rope fiber into the seams of (a ship), to stop leaks; also, to seal (a house) by putting a similar substance in cracks, as around doors.—*n.* **calk′er.**—*n.* **calk′ing.**

²**calk** (kôk), *n.* a piece of metal projecting downward from a horseshoe or a man's shoe or boot, to prevent slipping:—*v.t.* to furnish with calks; as, to *calk* shoes.

call (kôl), *v.t.* **1,** to utter in a loud voice; as, to *call* the roll; to announce, especially with authority; as, the announcer *calls* the train; **2,** to summon or request to come; as, to be *called* home; **3,** to appeal to; as,

he *called* God to witness; **4,** to bring up for action; as, to *call* a case in court; **5,** to arouse from sleep; **6,** to invite or summon to meet; as, to *call* Congress together; **7,** to issue a command for; as, to *call* a strike; **8,** to invite to a position; as, to *call* a minister; **9,** to direct; as, to *call* one's attention to something; **10,** to telephone to; as, he *called* me from New York; **11,** to demand payment of (a loan); **12,** to give a name to; **13,** to regard as being; as, I *call* him my friend; **14,** to estimate; as, I should *call* it six miles; **15,** in cards, to require (a player) to show his hand; **16,** in baseball, to designate (a pitched ball) as a strike or a ball; **17,** in sports, to order (a game) to begin or end; as, the game was *called* at two o'clock:—*v.i.* **1,** to cry out loudly; **2,** to make a brief visit; **3,** to communicate with a person by telephone; as, he *called* from New York:—*n.* **1,** a loud shout, as for help; **2,** a summons; **3,** an urge or invitation; as, a *call* to preach; **4,** need; occasion; as, he has no *call* to be offended; **5,** a short visit; **6,** the cry or note of an animal or bird:—*adj.* in business, payable on demand; as, a *call* loan.

   call down, to rebuke sharply; **call for, 1,** to request; as, we *called for* his opinion; **2,** to demand; require; need; as, this *calls for* quick action; **3,** to go to get; as, to *call for* a package; **call off,** to cancel or postpone; as, to *call off* a game because of rain; **call on, 1,** to visit; **2,** to request; as, he *called on* me to make a speech.

cal·la (kăl′ȧ), *n.* a house plant in which the flowers, clustered on a spike, are surrounded by a large, trumpet-shaped, white or yellow sheath, or spathe: often called *calla lily.*

Cal·la·o (käl-yä′ō), a city, the chief seaport of Peru (map **11**).

CALLA
Flower and leaf.

call·ing (kôl′ĭng), *n.* **1,** a summons; **2,** a vocation or profession.

cal·li·o·pe (kȧ-lī′ō-pē; popularly, kăl′ĭ-ōp), *n.* a mechanical organ in which the tones are produced by a series of whistles.

cal·li·pers (kăl′ĭ-pẽrz), *n.pl.* an instrument for measuring. See **calipers.**

cal·lis·then·ics (kăl′ĭs-thĕn′ĭks) *n.pl.* the science of body exercise. See **calisthenics.**

cal·los·i·ty (kă-lŏs′ĭ-tĭ), *n.* [*pl.* callosities], **1,** lack of feeling or sensitiveness; **2,** a hardened place on the skin or on bark.

cal·lous (kăl′ŭs), *adj.* **1,** hardened, as the skin forming a callus; **2,** unfeeling; insensitive; as, he was *callous* to criticism.—*adv.* **cal′lous-ly.**—*n.* **cal′lous-ness.**

āte, ãorta, râre, căt, ȧsk, fär, ăllow, sofȧ; ēve, ĕvent, ĕll, writẽr, novĕl; bīte, pĭn; nō, ōbey, ôr, dŏg, tŏp, cŏllide; ūnit, ūnite, bûrn, cŭt, focŭs; nōōn, fŏŏt; mound; coin;

cal·low (kăl′ō), *adj*. **1**, unfledged; not yet feathered; **2**, young and inexperienced; as, a *callow* youth.—*n*. **cal′low-ness.**

cal·lus (kăl′ŭs), *n*. [*pl*. calluses or calli (kăl′ī)], **1**, a thick, hard place on the skin, as on the palm of the hand; **2**, the bony matter which forms around the ends of fractured bones and helps to knit them.

calm (käm), *adj*. peaceful; undisturbed; as, a *calm* scene:—*n*. stillness; peace and quiet; as, a *calm* after the storm:—*v.t.* to quiet; as, to *calm* an excited child:—*v.i.* to become calm; as, to *calm* down after a fright.—*adv*. **calm′ly.**—*n*. **calm′ness.**
    Syn., *adj.* tranquil, peaceful, serene.

cal·o·mel (kăl′ŏ-mĕl), *n*. a whitish compound of mercury, used as a laxative.

cal·o·rie or **cal·o·ry** (kăl′ŏ-rĭ), *n*. a unit of heat or energy: used also to measure the heat or energy which the body can get from foods. One egg contains about 75 calories.

cal·u·met (kăl′ū-mĕt), *n*. the to-bacco pipe of the North American Indians, smoked  CALUMET
as a part of the ceremonial on important public occasions; the pipe of peace.

ca·lum·ni·ate (ka-lŭm′nĭ-āt), *v.t.* [calumniat-ed, calumniat-ing], to tell harmful untruths about (a person); to slander.—*n*. **ca-lum′ni-a′tion.**—*n*. **ca-lum′ni-a′tor.**

ca·lum·ni·ous (ka-lŭm′nĭ-ŭs), *adj*. slanderous; injurious; as, *calumnious* gossip.

cal·um·ny (kăl′ŭm-nĭ), *n*. [*pl*. calumnies], a slanderous report; slander.

Cal·va·ry (kăl′va-rĭ), *n*. the place where Jesus was crucified (Matthew 27:33).

calve (käv), *v.i.* [calved, calv-ing], to bring forth young. Cows, whales, elephants, and does are said to calve.

calves (kävz), plural of ¹*calf* and ²*calf*.

Cal·vin (kăl′vĭn), John (1509–1564), a celebrated French Protestant reformer.

Cal·y·don (kăl′ĭ-dŏn), an ancient city in Greece.—*n*. and *adj*. **Cal′y-do′ni-an.**

Cal·y·do·ni·an boar (kăl′ĭ-dō′nĭ-ăn bôr), in Greek mythology, a wild boar sent by Artemis to ravage Calydon for neglecting sacrifices, and finally killed by Meleager in a famous hunt.

CALYX, (C)

ca·lyx (kā′lĭks; kăl′ĭks), *n*. [*pl*. calyxes (kā′lĭk-sĕz; kăl′ĭk-sĕz) or calyces (kăl′ĭ-sēz; kā′lĭ-sēz)], the outer sheath of a bud, composed of sepals, usually green.

cam (kăm), *n*. a device used to transform the circular motion of a wheel into a straight-line, back-and-forth motion in another part of the machine.

ca·ma·ra·de·rie (kä/mȧ-rä′dĕ-rē), *n*. comradeship; loyalty; good-fellowship.

cam·bi·um (kăm′bĭ-ŭm), *n*. the layer of soft tissue between the sapwood and the bark of trees, which develops into the new wood and the new bark.

Cam·bo·di·a (kăm-bō′dĭ-ȧ), a kingdom (cap. Phnom Penh), in the Indochina peninsula (map 15).

Cam·bri·an (kăm′brĭ-ăn), *n*. a native of Wales:—*adj*. of Wales or its people.

cam·bric (kām′brĭk), *n*. **1**, a fine, thin, white linen fabric; **2**, a cotton imitation of this in white or plain colors.

Cam·bridge (kām′brĭj), **1**, a city in eastern England, famous for its university (map 13); **2**, a city in eastern Massachusetts, the site of Harvard University (map 6).

Cam·den (kăm′dĕn), a manufacturing city in New Jersey, on the Delaware River (map 6).

came (kām), past tense of *come*.

cam·el (kăm′ĕl), *n*. a large four-footed, cud-chewing animal, of which there are two kinds, the Arabian camel or dromedary, with a single hump, and the Bactrian camel, with two humps. Camels are used as beasts of burden in the desert.

BACTRIAN CAMEL (⅟₈₀)

ca·mel·li·a (ka-mĕl′ĭ-ȧ; ka-mēl′yȧ), *n*. a small, hothouse evergreen from China, India, and Japan, with glossy green leaves and double red or white flowers; also, the flower.

CAMELLIA

Cam·e·lot (kăm′ĕ-lŏt), *n*. in Arthurian legend, the place in England where King Arthur had his court.

cam·e·o (kăm′ē-ō), *n*. [*pl*. cameos], a gem, stone, or shell with a raised design carved upon it: opposite of *intaglio*.

cam·er·a (kăm′ĕr-ȧ), *n*. an apparatus for taking photographs. (See illustration on next page.)

Cam·er·oons (kăm′ĕr-ōonz′), a territory in western equatorial Africa, under British and French trusteeship (map 14).

go; join; yet; sing; chin; show; thin, *th*en; hw, *wh*y; zh, azure; ü, Ger. für or Fr. lune; ö, Ger. schön or Fr. feu; n̈, Fr. enfant, nom; kh, Ger. ach or ich. See pages ix–x.

cam·o·mile (kăm′ō-mīl), *n.* a plant with pungent smell and daisylike flowers, some varieties of which are used in medicine.

cam·ou·flage (kăm′ŏŏ-fläzh), *n.* 1, disguise; concealment; pretense; as, her calm manner is mere *camouflage;* 2, the art or practice of disguising guns, ships, etc., to hide them from the enemy:—*v.t.* [camouflaged, camouflag-ing], to conceal by disguising.

CAMERA (KODAK)
1, case; 2, bellows; 3, finder; 4, lens; 5, release.

camp (kămp), *n.* 1, a collection of tents or other temporary dwellings; also, the ground on which these are set up; 2, the people staying there; as, he belonged to a gypsy *camp;* 3, one side in war, religion, politics, or the like; as, the republican *camp:*—*v.i.* to pitch a camp; live in a camp; as, we *camped* in the open all summer.

cam·paign (kăm-pān′), *n.* 1, a series of military operations, conducted in a definite place, or with a single purpose; 2, action organized to produce a certain result; as, a political *campaign:*—*v.i.* to take an active part in or go on a campaign.—*n.* **cam·paign′er.**

cam·pa·ni·le (kăm′pȧ-nē′lê), *n.* [*pl.* campaniles (kăm′pȧ-nē′lêz) or campanili (kăm′pȧ-nē′lê)], a bell tower, especially one standing apart from another building.

CAMPANILE

camp·fire girl (kămp′fīr′), a member of The Camp Fire Girls of America, an organization aiming to promote useful, healthy womanhood through supervised outdoor activities, especially camping, hiking, etc.

cam·phor (kăm′fẽr), *n.* a whitish crystalline gum with pungent odor, obtained chiefly from the camphor tree of eastern Asia, and used in medicines, moth balls, etc.

cam·pus (kăm′pŭs), *n.* in America, the grounds of a school or a college.

¹**can** (kăn), *verb auxiliary* [*p.t.* could (kŏŏd)], 1, to be able to; have the power to; as, I *can* dance; 2, *Colloquial,* to be permitted to; as, he *can* go now.

MILK CAN

²**can** (kăn), *n.* 1, a metal container for holding or preserving liquids, solids, or powders; as, a coffee *can;* 2, the contents of a can; as, one *can* of peaches

will be enough for lunch:—*v.t.* [canned, can-ning], 1, to preserve in sealed cans, as fruits or vegetables; 2, *Slang,* to stop; as, *can* that noise; also, to discharge.

Can. abbreviation for *Canada* or *Canadian.*

Ca·naan (kā′năn), *n.* 1, the "Promised Land"; Palestine; 2, paradise.

Ca·naan·ite (kā′năn-īt), *n.* a member of an ancient race living in Palestine before the Israelites settled there.

Can·a·da (kăn′ȧ-dȧ), a self-governing federation of British possessions in northern North America (map 4).

Ca·na·di·an (kȧ-nā′dĭ-ăn), *n.* a native or resident of Canada:—*adj.* pertaining to Canada or to its people.

ca·nal (kȧ-năl′), *n.* 1, a man-made water channel, used for either navigation or irrigation; 2, any tubelike part of the body; as, the alimentary *canal.*

Canal Zone, a strip of land about ten miles wide, leased by Panama to the U.S. for the Panama Canal (map 10).

ca·nard (kȧ-närd′), *n.* a false and absurd rumor to deceive the public; a hoax.

ca·nar·y (kȧ-nâr′ĭ), *n.* [*pl.* canaries], 1, a small, yellow songbird, originally from the Canary Islands; 2, a light-yellow color; 3, a light wine from the Canary Islands:—*adj.* of a light-yellow color.

Ca·nar·y Is·lands (kȧ-nâr′ĭ), a group of islands, belonging to Spain, northwest of Africa (map 14).

Can·ber·ra (kăn′bĕr-ȧ), a city, capital of Australia (map 16).

can·cel (kăn′sĕl), *v.t.* [canceled, cancel-ing], 1, to cross out with a line or lines; mark so as to deprive of value; as, to *cancel* a stamp; 2, to take back; withdraw; as, to *cancel* an order; 3, to balance; offset; as, this item *cancels* that; 4, in arithmetic, to strike out (a common factor) from the numerator and the denominator of a fraction. *Syn.* abolish, efface, erase, repeal.

can·cel·la·tion (kăn′sĕ-lā′shŭn), *n.* 1, the act of annulling or revoking; as, the *cancellation* of a privilege, debt, engagement, etc.; 2, the mark used to cancel, as on a postage stamp.

can·cer (kăn′sẽr), *n.* 1, a harmful, often deadly, tumor, or growth, that spreads and eats into the body; 2, the diseased condition resulting from such a growth.

Can·cer, Trop·ic of (kăn′sẽr), the parallel of latitude 23°30″ north of the equator, which marks the northern boundary of the Torrid Zone.

can·de·la·brum (kăn′dĕ-lā′brŭm), *n.* [*pl.* candelabra (kăn′dĕ-lā′brȧ) or candelabrums: **candelabra** is also a *sing.* with

a separate *pl.* candelabras], a large ornamented candlestick with several branches
for holding candles or lights.

can-did (kăn′dĭd), *adj.*
1, outspoken; frank; as,
a *candid* person; a *candid* opinion; **2,** unprej-
udiced; fair.
   Syn. artless, blunt,
frank, truthful.

can-di-da-cy (kăn′dĭ-
dȧ-sĭ), *n.* [*pl.* candi-
dacies], the position of
one who presents him-
self, or is presented by
others, as a contestant

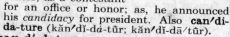

CANDELABRUM

for an office or honor; as, he announced
his *candidacy* for president. Also **can′di-
da-ture** (kăn′dĭ-dȧ-tŭr; kăn′dĭ-dȧ′tŭr).

can-di-date (kăn′dĭ-dāt), *n.* one who offers
himself, or is proposed by others, as a
contestant for an office or honor.

can-died (kăn′dĭd), *adj.* coated, cooked,
or preserved with sugar; as, *candied* apples.

can-dle (kăn′dl), *n.* **1,** a slender stick of
tallow or wax enclosing a wick, burned to
furnish light; **2,** anything resembling a
candle in form or purpose:—*v.t.* [can-dled,
can-dling], to test or examine (eggs) by
holding between the eye and a small light.

can-dle-light (kăn′dl-līt′), *n.* **1,** the light
of a candle; **2,** twilight.

can-dle pow-er, a unit of measure of light;
as, a bulb of 25 *candle power.*

can-dle-stick (kăn′dl-stĭk′), *n.*
a device for holding a candle.

can-dor (kăn′der), *n.* **1,** openness;
frankness, as of speech; **2,** fairness; as, to judge with *candor.*

can-dy (kăn′dĭ), *n.* [*pl.* candies],
something to eat made largely
of sugar, usually cut or formed
into small pieces:—*v.t.* [candied,
candy-ing], to coat, cook, or preserve with sugar:—*v.i.* to turn
into sugar; as, the sirup *candied.*

CANDLE-
STICK

can-dy-tuft (kăn′dĭ-tŭft′), *n.* a low-growing spring plant bearing flat tufts of flowers.

cane (kān), *n.* **1,** the woody, jointed stem
of certain palms or grasses, as the bamboo
or rattan; **2,** sugar cane; **3,** a walking
stick:—*v.t.* [caned, can-ing], **1,** to beat, as
with a walking stick; **2,** to furnish with
parts made of cane; as, to *cane* chairs:—
adj. made of cane, as a chair seat.

Ca-ne-a (kä-nē′ä), a city, capital of the
island of Crete. See **Khania.**

ca-nine (kā′nīn; kȧ-nīn′), *adj.* **1,** pertaining to dogs; doglike; **2,** designating one
of the four sharp-pointed teeth, found in

most mammals, between the incisors and
the bicuspids:—*n.* **1,** one of the canine
teeth (see illustration at *dentition*); **2,**
a dog.

can-is-ter (kăn′ĭs-tẽr), *n.* a box or small
container, usually of metal,
for holding tea, coffee, etc.

can-ker (kăng′kẽr), *n.* **1,**
anything which destroys by
gradual eating or wearing
away, as an ulcer in animals,
or rust in plants; **2,** a white
sore in the mouth, caused by
an upset stomach; **3,** a can-
kerworm.—*adj.* **can′ker-ous.**

CANISTER

can-ker-worm (kăng′kẽr-wûrm′), *n.* a
caterpillar especially destructive to fruit
and shade trees.

can-na (kăn′ȧ), *n.* a tall-
stemmed, cultivated gar-
den plant with large red
or green leaves and single
clusters of red or yellow
flowers.

canned (kănd), *adj.* preserved in sealed tins or
glass jars, as fruit.

can-nel coal (kăn′ĕl),
a soft coal that is used
for making coal oils and
gas: also called *cannel.*

CANNA
Flowering stem and
leaf.

can-ner-y (kăn′ẽr-ĭ), *n.*
[*pl.* canneries], a factory where vegetables,
fish, or other foodstuffs are canned.

Cannes (kăn), a famous resort in France
on the Mediterranean coast.

can-ni-bal (kăn′ĭ-băl), *n.* **1,** a human being
who eats human flesh; **2,** any animal that
eats its own kind:—*adj.* like a cannibal.—
n. **can′ni-bal-ism.**—*adj.* **can′ni-bal-is′tic.**

can-non (kăn′ŭn), *n.* [*pl.* cannons or, collectively, cannon], a large mounted gun.

can-non-ade (kăn′ŭn-ād′), *n.* a continuous discharge of artillery or cannon:—*v.t.*
[cannonad-ed,cannon-
ad-ing], to attack with
artillery; to bombard,
as a fortress.

can-not (kăn′nŏt),
am, is, or are not able
to; as, I *cannot* do this
problem.

can-ny (kăn′ĭ), *adj.*
[can-ni-er, can-ni-est],
1, shrewd; cautious;
as, a *canny* person;
2, thrifty; frugal; **3,**
quiet.—*adv.***can′ni-ly.**

CANOE

ca-noe (kȧ-nōō′), *n.* a light boat made of
bark, canvas, or thin wood and moved by

paddles:—*v.i.* [canoed (ka-nōōd′), canoeing], to paddle, or go in, a canoe.—*n.* ca-noe′ing.—*n.* ca-noe′ist.

¹can·on (kăn′ŭn), *n.* 1, an established standard or principle; as, according to the *canons* of good manners; 2, a law of a church; 3, the books of the Bible accepted as authoritative by the Christian church; 4, a list of saints in the Roman Catholic Church.

²can·on (kăn′ŭn), *n.* a clergyman attached to a cathedral.

ca·ñon (kăn′yŭn), *n.* a narrow deep gorge; canyon. See canyon.

ca·non·i·cal (ka-nŏn′ĭ-kăl), *adj.* 1, pertaining to, or conforming to, a law or rule, especially of the church; as, *canonical* hours of prayer; 2, accepted as a law or standard; as, *canonical* books.

can·on·ize (kăn′ŭn-īz), *v.t.* [canonized, canoniz-ing], to declare (a deceased person) a saint; admit to the list of saints.— *n.* can·on·i·za′tion.

can·o·py (kăn′ō-pĭ), *n.* [*pl.* canopies], 1, a covering fixed above a bed, hung over a throne, or held on poles over an important personage; 2, an overhanging covering, as over an entrance:— *v.t.* [canopied, canopying], to cover with, or as with, a canopy.

CANOPY

canst (kănst), a form of *can* used only in the phrase *thou canst,* equivalent to *you can.*

¹cant (kănt), *n.* 1, the words and phrases peculiar to a certain trade, profession, or group, as the slang used by thieves; 2, the insincere use of religious or moral speech; hypocrisy; 3, a whining manner of speech, especially that used by beggars.

²cant (kănt), *n.* 1, a sloping position; a slant or tilt; as, the *cant* of a roof; 2, a sudden, forceful thrust resulting in a change of course or position:—*v.t.* 1, to give a tilt or slant to; 2, to push or pitch sideways; as, the wind *canted* the sailing vessel:—*v.i.* to lean; lean to one side.

can't (kănt), the contracted form of *cannot* in colloquial use.

can·ta·loupe (kăn′ta-lōp), *n.* a hollow, edible melon with a hard, ridged rind. Also spelled can′ta-loup.

CANTALOUPE
1, entire fruit; 2, fruit opened to show arrangement of seeds.

can·tan·ker·ous (kăn-tăng′kĕr-ŭs), *adj. Colloquial,* ill-tempered; quarrelsome; as,

a *cantankerous* mood; a *cantankerous* person.—*n.* can-tan′ker-ous-ness.

can·ta·ta (kăn-tä′ta), *n.* a story or drama set to music, to be sung by a chorus.

can·teen (kăn-tēn′), *n.* 1, a shop in a military camp, for the sale of food, drink, tobacco, etc.; 2, a metal bottle used for carrying water or other drink when on the march; 3, a box containing mess utensils, for soldiers on active service.

can·ter (kăn′tĕr), *n.* an easy gallop:—*v.i.* and *v.t.* to gallop, or cause (a horse) to gallop, without haste.

Can·ter·bur·y (kăn′tĕr-bĕr′ĭ; kăn′tĕr-bĕr-ĭ), a city in southeastern England, famous for its cathedral (map 13).

can·ti·cle (kăn′tĭ-kl), *n.* 1, a little song; hymn; 2, a passage of the Bible arranged for chanting in church:—Canticles, in the Bible, the Song of Solomon.

can·ti·le·ver (kăn′tĭ-lē′vĕr; kăn′tĭ-lĕv′ĕr), *n.* 1, a bracket or block projecting from the wall of a house, to support a balcony, cornice, etc.; 2, a projecting beam supported only at one end:—cantilever bridge, a bridge each span of which is formed by two trusses, or cantilevers, each attached to a pier, and projecting toward each other and joining (see illustration at *bridge*).

can·to (kăn′tō), *n.* [*pl.* cantos], a part or section of a long poem.

Can·ton (kăn′tŏn), 1, a manufacturing city in northeastern Ohio (map 7); 2, (kăn-tŏn′), a city and treaty port in southeastern China (map 15).

can·ton (kăn′tŏn; kăn-tŏn′), *n.* 1, a division of a country; especially, one of the states in Switzerland; 2, a rectangular division in the corner of a heraldic shield or a flag.

Can·ton flan·nel, a strong cotton cloth with a long, fleecy nap.

can·ton·ment (kăn-tŏn′mĕnt; kăn′tŏn-mĕnt), *n.* the place or quarters assigned to a body of troops.

can·vas (kăn′vas), *n.* 1, a coarse, heavy cloth of hemp, cotton, or flax, used for tents, sails, etc., and as material on which to paint in oil; 2, an oil painting.

can·vas·back (kăn′vas-băk′), *n.* a North American wild duck.

can·vass (kăn′vas), *v.t.* 1, to examine thoroughly; discuss in detail; as, we *canvassed* the subject from A to Z; 2, to visit (a district, house, or person) in order to get votes or contributions, or make sales:—*v.i.* to seek orders, contributions, votes, etc.; as, to *canvass* for a charity:—

CANVASBACK (¹⁄₁₅)

āte, āorta, râre, căt, ȧsk, fär, ȧllow, sofȧ; ēve, ēvent, ĕll, writĕr, novĕl; bīte, pĭn; nō, ōbey, ôr, dŏg, tŏp, cŏllide; ūnit, ūnite, bûrn, cŭt, focŭs; nōōn, fŏŏt; mound; coin;

n. 1, a thorough examination or discussion; 2, a solicitation of votes, orders, etc.—*n.* **can′vass-er.**

can-yon or **ca-ñon** (kăn′yŭn), *n.* a deep gorge or valley made by a river or stream.

caou-tchouc (kōō′chŏŏk; kou-chōōk′; kou′chŏŏk), *n.* rubber; India rubber.

cap (kăp), *n.* 1, a tight-fitting covering, especially one with a peak and without a brim, for a person's head; 2, anything resembling a cap in form or use; as, a *cap* on a bottle; a mushroom *cap;* a nurse's *cap;* a *cap* and gown; 3, a small quantity of explosive, enclosed in paper, for toy pistols, or in metal, for setting off cartridges, artillery, shells, etc.; 4, writing paper of various large sizes; as, foolscap; legal *cap:*—*v.t.* [capped, cap-ping], 1, to cover, as with a cap; as, to *cap* a bottle; snow *caps* the mountain; 2, to match or surpass; as, his story *capped* mine.

ca-pa-bil-i-ty (kā′pȧ-bĭl′ĭ-tĭ), *n.* [*pl.* capabilities], ability to think, or to accomplish things.

ca-pa-ble (kā′pȧ-bl), *adj.* 1, having skill or ability; as, a *capable* servant, student, etc.; 2, having the nature or spirit to do a given thing; as, he is quite *capable* of such a trick.—*adv.* **ca′pa-bly.**
    Syn. able, competent, efficient.

ca-pa-cious (kȧ-pā′shŭs), *adj.* roomy; able to hold much; as, a *capacious* trunk. —*n.* **ca-pa′cious-ness.**

ca-pac-i-ty (kȧ-păs′ĭ-tĭ), *n.* [*pl.* capacities], 1, the power of receiving or holding; also, the amount that can be held; as, the *capacity* of a room, cup, etc.; 2, mental ability; as, a man of great *capacity;* 3, position; relationship; as, he served in the *capacity* of teacher.
    Syn. ability, talent.

ca-par-i-son (kȧ-păr′ĭ-sŭn), *n.* 1, an ornamental covering or harness for a horse; 2, gay or rich clothing.—*v.t.* **ca-par′i-son.**

¹cape (kāp), *n.* 1, a sleeveless outer garment worn loosely over the shoulders; also, a part of a garment similar to this, attached to a cloak or dress; 2, the short feathers on the back of a fowl lying below the hackle (see illustration under *fowl*).

²cape (kāp), *n.* a point of land; a promontory:—**Cape:** for *Cape Cod, Cape of Good Hope, Cape Hatteras,* etc., in which *Cape* refers to a promontory rather than to a district, see *Cod, Good Hope, Hatteras,* etc.

Cape Bret-on (brĭt′ŭn; brĕt′ŭn), an island northeast of Nova Scotia, Canada (map 4).

Cape Col-o-ny (kŏl′ō-nĭ), former name of a province, now called *Cape of Good Hope.*

Cape of Good Hope (gŏŏd hōp), a British self-governing province in the southern part of the Union of South Africa (map 14). It is often called *Cape Province.*

Cape Verde Is-lands (vûrd), islands belonging to Portugal, west of Cape Verde, Africa (map 14).

ca-per (kā′pēr), *n.* 1, a playful leap or spring; 2, a prank:—*v.i.* to skip or jump playfully; frolic.

Cape Town or **Capetown** (kāp′toun′), a city, capital of Cape of Good Hope province and the Union of South Africa (map 14).

cap-il-lar-y (kăp′ĭ-lĕr′ĭ), *n.* [*pl.* capillaries], a slender, hairlike tube; especially, a very minute blood vessel:—*adj.* 1, hairlike; slender; 2, relating to the minute blood vessels of the body:—**capillary tube,** a tube of very small bore.

¹cap-i-tal (kăp′ĭ-tăl), *adj.* 1, punishable by death; involving the death penalty; as, *capital* crime; *capital* punishment; 2, in writing and printing, designating one of the large letters, as A, B, C, etc., used at the beginning of a sentence, line of verse, proper noun, etc.; 3, first in importance; chief; as, the *capital* points in a discussion; 4, first-rate; as, a *capital* plan:—*n.* 1, the city or town which is the seat of government in a country or state; 2, a capital letter; 3, an amount of accumulated wealth available for use in business; as, he has plenty of *capital* to finance the invention; 4, any resources.—*adj.* **cap′i-tal-ly.**
    Syn., adj. leading, important, vital.

²cap-i-tal (kăp′ĭ-tăl), *n.* in architecture, the ornamental head or top of a column.

CAPITALS
1, Doric; 2, Ionic; 3, Corinthian; 4, Byzantine.

cap-i-tal-ism (kăp′ĭ-tăl-ĭzm), *n.* an economic system resting upon private ownership of wealth used in producing goods.

cap-i-tal-ist (kăp′ĭ-tăl-ĭst), *n.* a person whose accumulated wealth is used in business enterprises or in the production of goods.—*adj.* **cap′i-tal-is′tic.**

cap-i-tal-i-za-tion (kăp′ĭ-tăl-ĭ-zā′shŭn; -ĭ-zā′shŭn), *n.* 1, the investment of resources so that they will yield an income; 2, the face value of the stocks and bonds of a business; 3, the act of forming capital letters.

cap-i-tal-ize (kăp′ĭ-tăl-īz), *v.t.* [capitalized, capitaliz-ing], 1, to furnish (a business) with capital; as, the firm was *capitalized* at $10,000; 2, to make profitable use

go; join; yet; sing; chin; show; thin, *th*en; hw, *wh*y; zh, azure; ü, Ger. für or Fr. lune; ö, Ger. schön or Fr. *feu*; n̄, Fr. enfant, nom; kh, Ger. ach or ich. See pages ix-x.

of; as, a guide *capitalizes* his knowledge of the woods; **3,** to print or write with capital letters; start (a word) with, or change (a small letter) to, a capital letter.

Cap·i·tol (kăp′ĭ-tŏl), *n.* **1,** the building at Washington in which Congress meets; **2,** (often *capitol*), the building in which a State legislature meets; a Statehouse.

Cap·i·to·line (kăp′ĭ-tō-līn; kȧ-pĭt′ō-līn), *adj.* pertaining to the Capitol or ancient temple of Jupiter at Rome, or to the hill on which it stood.

ca·pit·u·late (kȧ-pĭt′ū-lāt), *v.i.* [capitulat-ed, capitulat-ing], to surrender on an enemy on conditions agreed upon.

ca·pit·u·la·tion (kȧ-pĭt′ū-lā′shŭn), *n.* **1,** the act of surrender; **2,** a summary of the main points of a topic.

ca·pon (kā′pŏn), *n.* a castrated rooster, specially raised and fattened for the table.

Ca·pri (kä′prē), an Italian island in the Bay of Naples.

ca·price (kȧ-prēs′), *n.* **1,** a sudden, unreasoning change of mind or conduct; whim; as, her refusal to go is mere *caprice;* **2,** the tendency to yield to whims.

ca·pri·cious (kȧ-prĭsh′ŭs), *adj.* controlled by whims; unpredictable; as, a *capricious* appetite.—*adv.* **ca·pri′cious·ly.**
    Syn. changeable, moody, shifting.

Cap·ri·corn, Trop·ic of (kăp′rĭ-kôrn), the parallel of latitude 23°30′ south of the equator, which marks the southern boundary of the Torrid Zone.

cap·size (kăp-sīz′), *v.i.* and *v.t.* [capsized, cap-siz-ing], to upset; turn over (a boat).

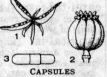

CAPSTAN

cap·stan (kăp′stăn), *n.* an upright drum or cylinder revolving upon a pivot. It may be turned by bars or levers in the top of the drum, or by steam. Around the center of the drum a rope or cable is wound, by means of which heavy weights are raised. It is used especially on ships.

CAPSULES
1, of violet; 2, of poppy; 3, as used in medicine.

cap·sule (kăp′sōōl), *n.* **1,** a small envelope of gelatin enclosing disagreeable medicine; **2,** a seedcase which bursts when ripe; **3,** a skinlike sac enclosing some part or organ of the body.—*adj.* **cap′su·lar.**

Capt. abbreviation for *Captain.*

cap·tain (kăp′tĭn), *n.* **1,** one in authority over others acting in a group; a leader; as,

the *captain* of a football team; **2,** in the army, an officer ranking below a major and above a lieutenant, and usually in command of a company; **3,** in the navy, an officer commanding a man-of-war; **4,** the master of a merchant ship:—*v.t.* to act as leader or captain of; lead.—*n.* **cap′tain-cy.**—*n.* **cap′tain-ship.**

cap·tion (kăp′shŭn), *n.* a brief title to an article, chapter, or the like, set above it in large type; a heading or headline; also, a title or explanation of a picture or design, or an explanation of a motion-picture scene thrown on the screen beforehand.

cap·tious (kăp′shŭs), *adj.* ready to find fault; as, a *captious* critic.—*adv.* **cap′-tious·ly.**—*n.* **cap′tious·ness.**
    Syn. carping, peevish, petulant.

cap·ti·vate (kăp′tĭ-vāt), *v.t.* [captivat-ed, captivat-ing], to attract; charm; fascinate.—*n.* **cap′ti·va′tion.**

cap·tive (kăp′tĭv), *n.* a prisoner, especially one taken in war:—*adj.* taken or held prisoner; as, a *captive* army.

cap·tiv·i·ty (kăp-tĭv′ĭ-tĭ), *n.* the state of being held prisoner, especially in war.

cap·tor (kăp′tẽr; kăp′tôr), *n.* a person who captures a prisoner, or holds him captive.

cap·ture (kăp′tŭr), *v.t.* [captured, captur-ing], to take or seize by force, skill, surprise, trickery, or other means; as, to *capture* a thief; to *capture* the attention:—*n.* **1,** the act of capturing; an arrest; **2,** the person or thing captured.

Cap·u·chin (kăp′ū-chĭn; kăp′ū-shēn′), *n.* a monk of one of the Franciscan orders, distinguished in dress by a long pointed hood:—**capuchin, 1,** a South American monkey with a hoodlike growth of hair on its head; **2,** a woman's hooded cloak, of a shape similar to that of the Capuchin monk.

car (kär), *n.* **1,** a wheeled vehicle, as a railway car, trolley, automobile, etc.; **2,** the part of an airship or balloon in which freight, baggage, or passengers are carried; **3,** the cage of an elevator.

ca·ra·ba·o (kä′rä-bä′ō), *n.* [*pl.* carabaos], in the Philippine Islands, a water buffalo.

CARABAO (¹/₅₀)

Ca·ra·cas (kä-rä′käs), a city, capital of Venezuela, South America (map **11**).

car·a·cul (kăr′ȧ-kŭl), *n.* **1,** a kind of Asiatic sheep; **2,** a kind of fur. See **karakul.**

car·a·mel (kăr′ȧ-mĕl), *n.* **1,** a kind of candy, of various flavors, generally in the shape of a cube; 2, burnt sugar used for coloring and flavoring foods.

car·at or **kar·at** (kăr′ăt), *n.* 1, a unit of weight, one fifth of a gram, for precious stones; 2, a 24th part: a measure of the purity of gold, pure gold being 24 carats; as, gold 22 *carats* fine contains 22 parts gold and 2 parts alloy.

car·a·van (kăr′à-văn; kăr′à-văn′), *n.* 1, a company of persons traveling together for safety, as across a desert or through dangerous country; 2, a large covered wagon.

car·a·van·sa·ry (kăr′à-văn′sà-rĭ), *n.* [*pl.* caravansaries], 1, in the Orient, a kind of inn for caravans, built around a spacious court; 2, a large hotel.

car·a·vel (kăr′à-vĕl) or **car·vel** (kăr′-vĕl), *n.* a small Spanish or Portuguese sailing vessel, such as was used by Columbus, of the 15th and 16th centuries. It had a high stern, three masts, and usually three or more three - cornered sails.

CARAVEL

car·a·way (kăr′à-wā), *n.* a plant of the parsley family, whose seed is used to flavor small cakes, rye bread, etc.

car·bide (kăr′bīd; kăr′bĭd), *n.* a compound of carbon with a metal. Calcium carbide is used to make acetylene gas.

car·bine (kăr′bīn), *n.* a short, light rifle used chiefly by cavalry.

CARBINE

car·bo·hy·drate (kăr′-bō-hī′drāt), *n.* a compound of carbon, hydrogen, and oxygen, as sugar or starch.

car·bo·lat·ed (kăr′bō-lāt′ĕd), *adj.* treated with, or containing, carbolic acid.

car·bol·ic ac·id (kăr-bŏl′ĭk), a poisonous acid, made from coal tar, and used in solution as a disinfectant and antiseptic.

car·bon (kăr′bŏn; kăr′bŏn), *n.* 1, a chemical element occurring pure in nature as the diamond and as graphite, and found in combination in all animal and vegetable substances, especially fuels; 2, either of two rods of hard carbon used in an arc lamp; 3, a piece of carbon paper; also, a copy made by its use.

carbon dioxide, a heavy, colorless gas produced by burning, breathing, fermentation, etc., poisonous to breathe, as in the gas of mines, but refreshing to the taste in soda water, and used in the form of dry ice for freezing foodstuffs; **carbon monoxide**, a colorless, odorless, poisonous gas, found in the exhaust gases from automobiles, produced by an incomplete burning of carbon; **carbon paper**, thin paper which is coated with coloring matter and which, when laid between sheets of paper, transfers marks or letters made on the upper sheet to the lower, as on a typewriter.—*adj.* **car′bo·na′ceous.**

car·bon·ate (kăr′bŏn-āt), *n.* a salt of carbonic acid:—*v.t.* (kăr′bŏn-āt), [carbonat-ed, carbonat-ing], to charge with carbonic-acid gas; as, soda water is *carbonated*.

car·bon·ic ac·id (kăr-bŏn′ĭk), an acid existing only in solution:—**carbonic-acid gas**, carbon dioxide.

car·bon·ize (kăr′bŏn-īz), *v.t.* [carbonized, carboniz-ing], 1, to char, as by fire or acid; 2, to coat with carbon.

Car·bo·run·dum (kăr′bō-rŭn′dŭm), *n.* a trade-mark name for certain very hard substances used in grinding, especially for a compound of carbon and silicon.

car·bun·cle (kăr′bŭng-kl), *n.* 1, a painful inflamed swelling, more severe than a boil; 2, a deep-red garnet.

car·bu·ret·or or **car·bu·ret·tor** (kăr′bū-rā′tẽr), *n.* an apparatus used to mix air with gasoline in the form of a vapor or spray, as in the motor of an automobile.

car·cass or **car·case** (kăr′kàs), *n.* 1, the dead body of an animal; 2, contemptuously, the living or dead body of a human being. *Syn.* body, corpse, remains.

¹**card** (kärd), *n.* 1, a piece of pasteboard, usually small and rectangular in shape; as, a post *card;* a calling *card;* a playing *card;* 2, **cards**, any game or games played with playing cards; card playing.

²**card** (kärd), *n.* a toothed instrument for combing wool, flax, cotton, or the like, to prepare it for spinning:—*v.t.* to comb with a card, as wool.

card-board (kärd′bôrd′), *n.* stiff pasteboard used in making posters, boxes, etc.

car·di·ac (kär′dĭ-ăk), *adj.* relating to, or situated near, the heart.

Car·diff (kär′dĭf), a seaport city in Wales, on the Bristol Channel (map **13**).

car·di·gan (kär′dĭ-găn), *n.* a knitted woolen jacket: also called *cardigan jacket.*

car·di·nal (kär′dĭ-năl), *adj.* 1, chief; of first importance; as, justice is one of the *cardinal* virtues; 2, of a rich red color:— *n.* 1, a high official in the Roman Catholic Church, appointed by the Pope, and of his council; 2, the red color worn by cardinals; 3, the cardinal bird.

cardinal bird, an American songbird, the

male of which has bright-red plumage and a pointed crest: also called *redbird;* **cardinal flower,** a large, bright-red lobelia which blooms in late summer and early fall; **cardinal numbers,** the numbers *one, two, three,* etc., in distinction from the ordinal numbers, *first, second, third,* etc.; **cardinal points,** the main directions of the compass, north, east, south, and west.

CARDINAL (⅟₇)

card-ing (kär′dĭng), *n.* the combing of wool, flax, cotton, or the like, to prepare it for spinning.

care (kâr), *n.* **1,** a burdened state of mind caused by doubt, fear, or anxiety; **2,** the cause of such doubt, fear, or anxiety; as, the *cares* of state weighed heavily upon the king; **3,** heed; caution; pains; as, take *care* in crossing the street; work done with *care;* **4,** charge or oversight; as, under a nurse's *care:—v.i.* [cared, car-ing], **1,** to be anxious, concerned, or interested; as, she *cared* only for dancing; also, to feel affection; as, she *cared* a great deal for her sister; **2,** to provide oversight or protection; as, the nurse *cared* for the children while the mother was away; **3,** to desire; wish; as, I do not *care* to go.

ca-reen (kȧ-rēn′), *v.t.* to turn (a ship) over on one side, in order to clean or repair it:—*v.i.* to incline to one side; to lurch, as a ship in the wind.

ca-reer (kȧ-rēr′), *n.* **1,** a swift or sweeping course; full speed; as, a horse in full *career;* **2,** a course of action in the life of an individual, a nation, etc.; **3,** an occupation or calling; as, a scientific *career:—v.i.* to move rapidly, as a ship.

care-ful (kâr′fool), *adj.* **1,** done or made with care; as, a *careful* piece of work; **2,** attentive; concerned; as, the nurse is *careful* with his diet; **3,** watchful; cautious; as, *careful* with money.—*adv.* **care′-ful-ly.**—*n.* **care′ful-ness.**

  Syn. heedful, prudent, discreet, wary.

care-less (kâr′lĕs), *adj.* **1,** not taking due care; inaccurate; as, a *careless* writer; *careless* work; **2,** unconcerned; heedless; as, *careless* of the consequences.—*adv.* **care′less-ly.**—*n.* **care′less-ness.**

  Syn. indifferent, thoughtless, reckless.

ca-ress (kȧ-rĕs′), *n.* any act expressing affection, as a kiss or embrace:—*v.t.* to touch or stroke lovingly; fondle.

car-et (kăr′ĕt; kâr′ĕt), *n.* a mark [∧] used in writing, or in correcting proof, to indicate where something is to be added.

care-tak-er (kâr′tāk′ẽr), *n.* one who takes care of places, persons, or things for someone else.

care-worn (kâr′wôrn′), *adj.* showing marks of anxiety; wearied by care.

car-go (kär′gō), *n.* [*pl.* cargoes or cargos], the goods or merchandise carried by a ship.

Car-ib-be-an Sea (kăr′ĭ-bē′ăn; kȧ-rĭb′ē-ăn), an arm of the Atlantic Ocean between the West Indies and South America (map **10**).

car-i-bou (kăr′ĭ-boo), *n.* [*pl.* caribou], a North American reindeer.

car-i-ca-ture (kăr′ĭ-kȧ-tūr; kăr′ĭ-kȧ-tūr′), *n.* a picture or description of a person or thing, in which the defects or peculiarities are so exaggerated as to appear ridiculous:—*v.t.* [carica-tured, caricatur-ing], to make or give a caricature of; as, the cartoonist *caricatured* the actor.—*n.* **car′i-ca-tur-ist.**

CARIBOU (₁/₂₅)

  Syn. cartoon, satire, burlesque.

car-il-lon (kăr′ĭ-lŏn; kȧ-rĭl′yŭn), *n.* **1** a set of bells on which tunes may be played; **2,** an air played on such bells.

Carle-ton (kärl′tŭn), Sir Guy (1724-1808), a British general in the American Revolution.

car-load (kär′lōd′), *n.* a load that fills a car; all that a car can carry.

Carls-bad (kärls′bät; kärlz′băd), a town in Czechoslovakia. See **Karlsbad.**

Car-lyle (kär-līl′), Thomas (1795-1881), a British essayist and historian.

Car-mel, Mount (kär′měl), a famous mountain in northwestern Palestine.

car-mine (kär′mĭn; kär′mīn), *n.* **1,** the rich bright-red coloring matter obtained from the cochineal insect; **2,** the color itself.

car-nage (kär′nĭj), *n.* great slaughter, especially in battle.

car-nal (kär′năl), *adj.* fleshly; sensual; as, *carnal* desires.

car-na-tion (kär-nā′shŭn), *n.* a cultivated pink with large red, pink, or white flowers.

CARNATIONS

Car-ne-gie (kär-nā′gĭ; kär-něg′ĭ), Andrew (1837-1919), a Scottish-American philanthropist.

car-nel-ian (kär-nēl′yăn), *n.* a flesh-colored, deep-red, or reddish-white, semi-precious stone, used for jewelry and seals.

car-ni-val (kär′nĭ-văl), *n.* **1,** in Roman Catholic countries, the season just before Lent, devoted to merrymaking; **2,** any revelry or feasting; **3,** an amusement enterprise, with side shows, games, etc.

car-niv-o-rous (kär-nĭv′ō-rŭs), *adj.* flesh-eating; as, the dog is a *carnivorous* animal.

car-ol (kăr′ŭl), *n.* a song of joy or praise: —*v.t.* and *v.i.* [caroled, carol-ing], to sing joyfully.—*n.* **car′ol-er.**

Car-o-li-na (kăr′ō-lī′nȧ), an American colony settled in 1653, later divided into North Carolina and South Carolina (map 8).—*adj.* and *n.* **Car′o-lin′i-an.**

car-om (kăr′ŭm), *n.* the act of striking and rebounding:—*v.i.* to rebound.

ca-rous-al (kȧ-rouz′ăl), *n.* a carouse.

ca-rouse (kȧ-rouz′), *n.* a drinking party: —*v.i.* [caroused, carous-ing], to take part in a drinking party.—*n.* **ca-rous′er.**

car-ou-sel (kăr′ŏŏ-zĕl′), *n.* a merry-go-round; a carrousel.

¹carp (kärp), *v.i.* to find fault; as, to *carp* at someone.—*adj.* **carp′ing.**

²carp (kärp), *n.* a fresh-water fish that lives in ponds.

Car-pa-thi-an Moun-tains (kär-pā′thĭ-ăn), a European mountain range, extending from northeastern Czechoslovakia to northern Rumania (map 12).

CARP (₂⁄₀)

car-pel (kär′pĕl), *n.* the part of a plant which bears seeds; one of the parts of a compound ovary.

car-pen-ter (kär′pĕn-tẽr), *n.* one who works in timber and builds or repairs the woodwork of houses, ships, etc.

car-pen-try (kär′pĕn-trĭ), *n.* the work of a carpenter.

CARPELS (C)

car-pet (kär′pĕt), *n.* **1,** a thick woven or felted fabric used as a floor or stair covering; **2,** a soft covering upon which one may walk; as, a *carpet* of grass:—*v.t.* to cover with, or as with, a carpet.

car-pet-bag (kär′pĕt-băg′), *n.* a traveling bag, originally made of carpet.

car-pet-bag-ger (kär′pĕt-băg′ẽr), *n.* one traveling with only a carpetbag; especially, a Northern political adventurer in the Southern States after the War between the States.

car-pet-ing (kär′pĕt-ĭng), *n.* cloth or material to be used for carpets.

car-port (kär′pôrt′), *n.* a shed, attached to a building, and used as a shelter for an automobile.

Car-ra-ra (kär-rä′rä), a city on the northwest coast of Italy, famous for its marble.

car-riage (kăr′ĭj), *n.* **1,** the act or business of carrying or transporting goods; also, the expense of carrying; **2,** a wheeled vehicle for carrying persons, especially one drawn by horses; **3,** a wheeled support, as for a cannon; **4,** the moving part of a machine which carries another part, as in a typewriter; **5,** the manner of holding one's body; as, an erect *carriage.*

car-rick bend (kăr′ĭk), a kind of knot. (See illustration at *knot.*)

car-ri-er (kăr′ĭ-ẽr), *n.* **1,** a bearer, as of letters; **2,** a person or firm whose business is to transport goods or persons; **3,** a device in a machine for guiding something; as, a slide *carrier* in a magic lantern; **4,** a person or thing that carries disease germs and may communicate them.

car-ri-on (kăr′ĭ-ŭn), *n.* decaying flesh.

Car-roll (kăr′ŭl), Lewis (1832–1898), the pen name of *Charles L. Dodgson,* author of "Alice in Wonderland."

car-rot (kăr′ŭt), *n.* a cultivated plant of the parsley family, with an edible, orange-yellow tapering root.—*adj.* **car′rot-y.**

car-rou-sel or **car-ou-sel** (kăr′ŏŏ-zĕl′), *n.* a merry-go-round.

car-ry (kăr′ĭ), *v.t.* [carried, carry-ing], **1,** to convey; transmit, as a cargo or a message; **2,** to support or sustain; as, the columns *carry* the weight of the building; **3,** to have upon one's person; as, to *carry* a scar; **4,** to hold (oneself); as, she *carries* herself well; also, to conduct (oneself); **5,** to win, as an election; **6,** to secure the passage of, as a bill in Congress; **7,** to keep on hand for sale:—*v.i.* **1,** to bear or convey something; **2,** to have power to reach a distance, as a gun or a voice:—*n.* [*pl.* carries], **1,** the distance over which a gun will hurl a shot; **2,** in the northern U.S. and Canada, the act of carrying between two bodies of water; also, the distance crossed; a portage; **3,** in golf, the distance from the spot where a ball is struck to the point where it first lands.

carry away to move or charm; as, I was

CARROT
1, entire plant; 2, detail of top.

carried away by his eloquence; **carry on,** 1, to continue; as, we *carried on* till dark; 2, *Colloquial*, to behave in a wild manner; **carry out,** to complete; bring to success.

Syn., v. transport, bring, fetch, bear.

car-ry-all (kăr′ĭ-ôl′), *n.* a light, covered carriage for four or more people.

Car-son (kär′sn), Christopher (1809–1868), usually called *Kit Carson,* an American frontiersman and U.S. Indian agent.

Car-son Cit-y (kär′sn), a city, capital of the State of Nevada (map 9).

cart (kärt), *n.* 1, a two-wheeled vehicle for carrying heavy goods; 2, a light delivery wagon used by tradesmen; 3, a light, two-wheeled carriage:—*v.t.* to carry in a cart.

CART

cart-age (kär′tĭj), *n.* transportation in a cart; also, the fee charged for it.

Car-ta-ge-na (kär′tá-jē′ná; kär′tä-hā′nä), 1, a seaport in southeastern Spain (map 12); 2, a seaport on the coast of Colombia, South America (map 11).

carte blanche (kärt′ blänsh′; kärt′), a signed paper given to another to be filled up as he pleases; hence, absolute freedom of action or judgment.

car-tel (kär′tĕl; kär-tĕl′), *n.* 1, a written agreement between hostile states regarding the exchange of prisoners, etc.; 2, a written challenge to single combat; 3, a combination of industrial groups to fix prices, control output, etc.; also, a union of political groups for common action.

Car-thage (kär′thĭj), an ancient city in northern Africa, founded by the Phoenicians and later destroyed by the Romans (map 1).—*n.* and *adj.* **Car′tha-gin′i-an.**

Car-tier (kár′tyā′), Jacques (1494–1557?), a famous French explorer, discoverer of the St. Lawrence River.

car-ti-lage (kär′tĭ-lĭj), *n.* an elastic tissue which composes most of the skeleton of young animals and children, and usually develops into bone; gristle.

car-ti-lag-i-nous (kär′tĭ-lăj′ĭ-nŭs), *adj.* 1, like gristle; 2, having a skeleton composed largely of cartilage, as a shark.

car-ton (kär′tŏn), *n.* a pasteboard or cardboard box.

car-toon (kär-tōōn′), *n.* a picture, especially one in a newspaper or magazine, dealing with a public person or event in an exaggerated or satirical manner; as, the newspaper *cartoons* of the sea disaster aroused much feeling:—*v.t.* to draw a cartoon of:—*v.i.* to draw cartoons.—*n.* **car-toon′ist.**

car-tridge (kär′trĭj), *n.* 1, a case of metal, cardboard, or other material containing powder and a bullet, as for a firearm, or one charge of powder, as of dynamite; 2, a case shaped like a cartridge, used as a container; as, a *cartridge* of films for a camera.

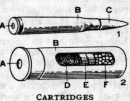
CARTRIDGES
1, for rifle; 2, for shotgun. A, cap; B, shell; C, bullet; D, powder; E, wads; F, shot.

Cart-wright (kärt′rīt), Edmund (1743–1823), an Englishman who invented the power loom.

carve (kärv), *v.t.* [carved, carv-ing], 1, to produce by cutting; as, to *carve* a statue out of marble; 2, to adorn by cutting; as, he *carved* a panel with floral designs; 3, to cut, as meat; 4, to make or get as if by cutting; as, he *carved* out a career for himself:—*v.i.* 1, to work as a sculptor; 2, to cut up meat.—*n.* **carv′er.**—*adj.* **carv′en.**

carv-ing (kär′vĭng), *n.* 1, the act or art of one who carves; 2, a design or figure produced by carving.

Ca-sa-blan-ca (kä′sä-bläng′kä), a seaport in western Morocco, Africa (map 14).

cas-cade (kăs-kād′), *n.* 1, a small, waterfall or a series of small falls; 2, anything like this; as, a *cascade* of ruffles.

Cas-cade Range (kăs-kād′), a mountain range in western North America (map 5).

cas-car-a (kăs-kâr′á), *n.* a medicine made from the bark of a California tree.

¹**case** (kās), *n.* 1, any set of facts, conditions, or circumstances relating to a particular person or thing; as, the *case* of Mr. Jones; a *case* of robbery; 2, an actual state of affairs; as, that was not the *case;* 3, a certain form or instance of disease; also, the person having a given disease; a patient; as, there is a *case* of mumps in the house; 4, a lawsuit; 5, a person, family, or problem under the observation of a social-service organization; 6, in grammar, the relation of a noun or pronoun to other words; as, the subject of a sentence is in the nominative *case;* 7, *Colloquial*, a person who is peculiar in any respect; as, he's a queer *case:*—**in case of,** in the event of; as, *in case of* fire, ring the alarm.

Syn. events, situation, plight.

²**case** (kās), *n.* 1, a covering or container; as, the *case* of a watch; a pillow*case;* 2, a container and its contents; as, a *case* of books; also, the amount of this content; as, to buy canned peas by the *case;* 3, a glass box used for exhibiting goods; a

---

āte, âorta, râre, căt, àsk, fär, ăllow, sofà; ēve, êvent, ĕll, writêr, novĕl; bīte, pĭn; nō, ōbey, ôr, dŏg, tŏp, cŏllide; ūnit, ūnite, bûrn, cŭt, focŭs; nōōn, fŏŏt; mound; coin;

showcase; **4,** a frame or casing, as of a window; **5,** in printing, a tray for type, divided into *upper case,* which contains the capital letters, etc., and *lower case,* which contains small letters, etc.:—*v.t.* [cased, cas-ing], to protect with a case; incase.

case-hard-en (kās′här′dn), *v.t.* **1,** to harden the surface of (metal); **2,** to make insensible to influences; as, he was *case-hardened* by his experiences.

ca-se-in (kā′sē-ĭn), *n.* a substance in milk which forms the main part of cheese.

case-ment (kās′měnt), *n.* a window made to open on hinges like a door.

CASEMENT

cash (kăsh), *n.* **1,** money; especially, ready money; as, I have no *cash* in my pocket; **2,** money paid for an article at the time of purchase; as, sold for *cash;* **3,** in banking, strictly, coin, but also paper money, bank notes, and commercial paper easily exchanged for coin:—*v.t.* to exchange for money in coin or bills; as, to *cash* a check.

cash-book (kăsh′boŏk′), *n.* a book in which an account is kept of money received and paid out.

ca-shew (ká-shoō′; kăsh′oō), *n.* a tropical American tree, or its kidney-shaped nut, which is used for food.

¹cash-ier (kăsh-ēr′), *n.* **1,** in a bank, an executive officer who has charge of the practical affairs of the bank; **2,** a person in a store who pays out and receives cash.

²cash-ier (kăsh-ēr′), *v.t.* to dismiss in disgrace from a position of trust or from military service.

cash-mere (kăsh′mēr; kăsh′mēr′), *n.* **1,** a soft woolen fabric made from the wool of the goats of Kashmir, Tibet, etc.; **2,** a shawl made of this; **3,** a soft woolen imitation of real cashmere.

cas-ing (kās′ĭng), *n.* **1,** a covering, as for a pillow; **2,** a framework, as of a window.

ca-si-no (ká-sē′nō), *n.* [*pl.* casinos or casini (ká-sē′nē)], **1,** in Italy, a summer house; **2,** a public room or building for dancing, gambling, etc.

cask (kăsk), *n.* **1,** a barrel-shaped, wooden vessel for holding liquids; a keg; **2,** the amount contained in a cask; as, a *cask* of molasses was consumed in a month; **3,** the cask and its contents; as, a *cask* of wine was shipped.

cas-ket (kás′kĕt), *n.* **1,** a small chest or box, as for jewels; **2,** a coffin.

Cas-pi-an Sea (kăs′pĭ-ăn), an inland salt sea between Europe and Asia (map 12).

casque (kăsk), *n. Poetic,* a helmet.

Cas-san-dra (ká-săn′drá), *n.* in Greek legend, a Trojan princess, daughter of Priam and Hecuba, endowed with the gift of prophecy, but doomed never to be believed.

cas-sa-va (ká-sä′vá), *n.* a tropical plant with a fleshy root that yields a starch from which tapioca is made: often called the *bitter cassava.*

cas-se-role (kăs′ĕ-rōl), *n.* **1,** a covered glass or earthen dish in which food is baked and served; **2,** food cooked and served in a casserole.

CASSEROLE

cas-si-a (kăsh′ĭ-á; kăs′ĭ-á), *n.* **1,** a herb, shrub, or tree, mostly tropical, from which the drug senna is obtained; **2,** (kăsh′á), the bark of a tree of Brazil, used as cinnamon.

cas-si-mere (kăs′ĭ-mēr), *n.* a thin woolen cloth used for garments.

cas-si-no (ká-sē′nō), *n.* a card game.

cas-sock (kăs′ŭk), *n.* a long, close-fitting gown worn by some clergymen.

cas-so-war-y (kăs′ō-wěr′ĭ), *n.* [*pl.* cassowaries], a large, swift-running bird of Australia and Papua, resembling the ostrich, but smaller.

CASSOWARY (₁′₁₅)

cast (kăst), *v.t.* [*p.t.* and *p.p.* cast, *p.pr.* casting], **1,** to throw; hurl; as, to *cast* a fishing line; to *cast* stones; **2,** to send or turn in a certain direction; as, to *cast* a glance; to *cast* a shadow; **3,** to put off; shed; as, a snake *casts* its skin; **4,** to deposit, as a vote; **5,** to assign, as the parts or actors in a play; **6,** to pour into a certain shape; as, to *cast* a bronze statue; **7,** to add; as, to *cast* up a column of figures:—*v.i.* **1,** to throw a fishing line; as, it was his turn to *cast;* **2,** to receive shape in a mold; **3,** in hunting, to search for game, or for a lost scent; hence, to search; as, he *casts* about for an idea:—*n.* **1,** the act or manner of throwing; the distance to which a thing can be thrown; **2,** a permanent turn, twist, or warp; as, a *cast* in the eye; **3,** calculation; the addition of columns of an account; **4,** the members of a company of actors to whom certain parts are assigned; **5,** something formed by molding; as, a plaster *cast;* **6,** form; style; bent; as, a gloomy *cast* of countenance; **7,** a tinge or hue; as, a grayish *cast;* **8,** in hunting, the scattering of hounds in search of a lost scent:—*adj.* shaped in a mold while fluid.

---

go; join; yet; sing; chin; show; thin, *th*en; hw, *why;* zh, azure; ü, Ger. *für* or Fr. *lune;* ö, Ger. *schön* or Fr. *feu;* ṅ, Fr. *enfant, nom;* kh, Ger. *ach* or *ich.* See pages ix–x.

cas-ta-nets (kăs′tȧ-nĕts′; kăs′tȧ-nĕts), *n.pl.* a pair of spoon-shaped shells of hard wood or ivory, clicked with the fingers to beat time, especially in Spanish dances and music.

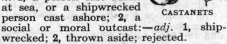

CASTANETS

cast-a-way (kăst′ȧ-wā′), *n.* **1,** a person cast adrift at sea, or a shipwrecked person cast ashore; **2,** a social or moral outcast:—*adj.* **1,** shipwrecked; **2,** thrown aside; rejected.

caste (kăst), *n.* a distinct class of society, especially as in India:—**lose caste**, to lose social rank.

cas-tel-lat-ed (kăs′tĕ-lāt′ĕd), *adj.* built with battlements, like a castle.

¹cast-er (kàs′tẽr), *n.* a person or thing that casts.

²cast-er or **¹cas-tor** (kàs′tẽr), *n.* **1,** a small vessel for salt, vinegar, or the like; a cruet; also, a stand for a number of such vessels; **2,** a small roller on a swivel, or a set of rollers in a frame, used under furniture or other heavy articles to permit easy moving.

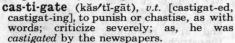

CASTER def. 2

cas-ti-gate (kăs′tĭ-gāt), *v.t.* [castigat-ed, castigat-ing], to punish or chastise, as with words; criticize severely; as, he was *castigated* by the newspapers.

cas-ti-ga-tion (kăs′tĭ-gā′shŭn), *n.* a severe criticism or reproof.

Cas-tile (kăs-tēl′), a former kingdom in the central part of Spain.

Cas-tile soap (kăs′tēl; kăs-tēl′), a soap of fine quality made from pure olive oil, originally manufactured in Castile, Spain.

Cas-til-ian (kăs-tĭl′yăn; kăs-tĭl′ĭ-ăn), *n.* **1,** a native of Castile, Spain; **2,** the standard literary form of the Spanish language: —*adj.* relating to Castile, or to its people or language.

cast-ing (kàs′tĭng), *n.* an object formed by pouring molten metal into a mold and allowing it to harden; also, the process of making it.

cast i-ron, iron which has been melted and shaped by being run into molds:—**cast-iron,** *adj.* **1,** made of cast iron; **2,** like iron; rigid; unyielding; as, a *cast-iron* will.

cas-tle (kàs′l), *n.* **1,** a building or group of buildings fortified for defense; a fortress; **2,** any of these used now as a residence by a nobleman or wealthy person; **3,** anything resembling a castle (see illustration next column); **4,** one of the pieces used in chess: also called *rook*.

cast-off (kàst′ôf′), *adj.* discarded as worthless; thrown away; as, *castoff* shoes.

Cas-tor (kàs′tẽr), *n.* in Greek mythology, a mortal son of Zeus and Leda, who was placed with his immortal twin brother Pollux in the sky as a constellation.

¹cas-tor (kàs′tẽr), *n.* **1,** a cruet or cruet stand; **2,** a small roller on a swivel, used under furniture. See **²caster.**

²cas-tor (kàs′tẽr), *n.* **1,** a hat, especially of beaver fur; **2,** a substance obtained from beaver, used in perfumery and medicine.

ENGLISH NORMAN CASTLE

A, palisade; B, B, moat; C, C, drawbridges; D, D, D, D, towers protecting entrances; E, outer court; F, stables; G, barracks; H, inner court; I, well; J, chapel; K, keep; L, L, corner towers protecting outer walls.

castor bean, the seed of the castor-oil plant, from which castor oil is made.

castor oil, a thick, yellowish oil from the castor bean, used as a physic.—*adj.* **cas′tor—oil′.**

cas-trate (kăs′trāt), *v.t.* [castrat-ed, castrat-ing], to remove the male sex glands of (an animal); as, a steer is a *castrated* bull.

cas-u-al (kăzh′ū-ăl; kăz′ū-ăl), *adj.* **1,** happening by chance; accidental; as, a *casual* meeting; **2,** uncertain; occasional; as, *casual* profits; **3,** having an air of indifference; as, a *casual* manner.

cas-u-al-ty (kăzh′ū-ăl-tĭ; kăz′ū-ăl-tĭ), *n.* [*pl.* casualties], **1,** a disaster; an accident; **2, casualties,** in the army and navy, losses in general, caused by death, wounds, illness, desertion, or discharge; **3,** a soldier unfit for duty, from any cause.

cas-u-ist (kăzh′ū-ĭst; kăz′ū-ĭst), *n.* one who studies questions of right and wrong; especially, one who reasons shrewdly but falsely about them.—*n.* **cas′u-ist-ry.**

cat (kăt), *n.* a small flesh-eating animal, often kept as a household pet; also, any closely related animal, as the lion or tiger.

cat-a-clysm (kăt′ȧ-klĭzm), *n.* **1,** a deluge; flood; **2,** a violent or sudden change of the earth's surface, as from an earthquake; **3,** hence, any social or political upheaval, as the French Revolution.

cat-a-combs (kăt′ȧ-kōmz), *n.pl.* an underground cemetery with long passageways lined with burial niches; as, the early Christian *catacombs* near Rome.

Cat-a-lan (kăt′ȧ-lăn; kăt′ȧ-lăn), *n.* a native of Catalonia, Spain; also, the language of Catalonia:—*adj.* pertaining to Catalonia, or to its language or people.

cat-a-lo (kăt′å-lō), *n.* the hybrid offspring of a bison and a domestic cow.

cat-a-log (kăt′å-lŏg), *n.* a systematic list of names, places, books, etc., usually arranged alphabetically:—*v.t.* [cataloged, catalog-ing], to enter in a list; make a list of; as, to *catalog* a library.   Also spelled **cat′a-logue** [catalogued, catalogu-ing].

Cat-a-lo-ni-a (kăt′å-lō′nĭ-å), an ancient division of northeastern Spain.

ca-tal-pa (kå-tăl′på), *n.* a tree with large leaves, showy white flower clusters, and winged seeds in long pods.

cat-a-ma-ran (kăt′å-må-răn′), *n.* 1, a raft made of logs tied together, and moved by paddles or sails; 2, a vessel with two hulls side by side.

CATAMARAN, def. 2

cat-a-mount (kăt′å-mount), *n.* a wild cat; in North America, especially a lynx, or the cougar.

Ca-ta-nia (kä-tä′nyä), a city on the eastern coast of Sicily (map 12).

cat-a-pult (kăt′å-pŭlt). *n.* 1, in ancient times, a military engine for hurling stones, arrows, or the like; 2, in modern times, a similar device for launching an airplane from the deck of a ship; 3, a slingshot:—*v.t.* to hurl (something) from a catapult:—*v.i.* to rush headlong; hurtle; as, the acrobat was *catapulted* from a cannon into a net.

CATAPULT

cat-a-ract (kăt′å-răkt), *n.* 1, a large waterfall; 2, a furious rush of water; 3, a disease of the eye which causes partial or total blindness.

ca-tarrh (kå-tär′), *n.* an inflammation of any mucous membrane, especially of the air passages in the head and throat.

CATBIRD (⅓)

ca-tas-tro-phe (kå-tăs′trō-fē), *n.* a sudden calamity or widespread disaster.

cat-bird (kăt′bûrd′), *n.* an American song-

bird, slate-gray in color, related to the mockingbird. It utters a catlike mew when disturbed.

cat-boat (kăt′bōt′), *n.* a small sailboat with one mast in the bow, and one large sail. (See *ship*, illustration.)

cat-call (kăt′kôl′), *n.* a loud cry of disapproval, as from the audience in a theater.

catch (kăch), *v.t.* [caught (kôt), catch-ing], 1, to lay hold of; seize; as, the brambles *caught* her dress; to *catch* a bird; to *catch* a ball; 2, to reach or be in time for; as, to *catch* a train; 3, to overtake; as, I will *catch* you; 4, to attract; as, to *catch* the eye or the attention; 5, to learn by hearing, as a tune; 6, to understand; as, to *catch* a meaning; 7, to become infected with, as a disease; 8, to come upon suddenly; surprise; as, to *catch* a thief in the act; the storm *caught* him; 9, to take (fire); 10, please; charm; as, the music *caught* the public's fancy:—*v.i.* 1, to grasp; snatch; as, to *catch* at an opportunity; to *catch* at straws; 2, to be seized and held; as, my dress *caught* in the door; 3, to take hold, as fire; 4, to take and keep hold, as a bolt; 5, to be stuck, as a window:—*n.* 1, a fastening, as a hook, door latch, or the like; 2, a choking sensation in the throat; 3, that which is caught; as, a *catch* of fish; 4, a trick or pitfall; as, a *catch* in a question; 5, in ball games, the seizing of the ball before it touches the ground.

CATCH FOR A DOOR

catch-er (kăch′ẽr), *n.* 1, a person or thing that catches; 2, in baseball, the player who stands behind the plate, to catch the ball thrown by the pitcher.

catch-ing (kăch′ĭng), *adj.* contagious; infectious; spreading from person to person.

catch-pen-ny (kăch′pĕn′ĭ), *n.* [*pl.* catch-pennies], an article of little value made attractive to sell quickly:—*adj.* cheap; made to sell to the unwary or ignorant.

catch-up (kăch′ŭp; kĕch′ŭp) or **cat-sup** (kăt′sŭp), *n.* a sauce made by boiling and spicing fruit, mushrooms, tomatoes, etc.: used cold with meat. Also spelled **ketch′up**.

catch-y (kăch′ĭ), *adj.* quick to win popular fancy; as, a *catchy* tune.

cat-e-chism (kăt′ē-kĭzm), *n.* 1, a small book of questions and answers for instruction in the Christian religion; 2, a method of teaching by questions and answers; 3, a set of questions to be answered.

cat-e-chize (kăt′ē-kīz), *v.t.* [catechized, catechiz-ing], 1, to instruct by questions and answers, especially in the Christian

go; join; yet; sing; chin; show; thin, *th*en; hw, *why*; zh, azure; ŭ, Ger. für or Fr. lune; ö, Ger. schön or Fr. *feu*; ṅ, Fr. enfant, nom; kh, Ger. ach or ich. See pages ix–x.

religion; **2,** to question closely. Also spelled **cat′e-chise.**—*n.* **cat′e-chist.**

cat-e-gor-i-cal (kăt′ē-gŏr′ĭ-kăl), *adj.* absolute; unconditional; as, a *categorical* negative; positive; explicit; as, a *categorical* answer.

cat-e-gory (kăt′ē-gôr′ĭ), *n.* [*pl.* categories], a broad division or classification; as, there are three *categories* of matter, animal, vegetable, and mineral.

ca-ter (kā′tēr), *v.i.* **1,** to provide or supply food; as, to *cater* for a banquet; **2,** to supply what is desired; as, some writers *cater* to popular taste.—*n.* **ca′ter-er.**

cat-er-pil-lar (kăt′ēr-pĭl′ēr), *n.* a wormlike larva, usually of a butterfly or moth: —**Caterpillar tractor,** a trade-mark name for a powerful traction engine, operating on a pair of endless metal belts, used for heavy hauling over uneven ground.

cat-er-waul (kăt′ēr-wôl), *v.i.* to cry, as cats at night; yowl.

cat-fish (kăt′fĭsh′), *n.* [*pl.* catfish or catfishes], a kind of fish, usually without scales, but with long, whiskerlike feelers around the mouth, as the bullhead.

CATFISH (⅛)

cat-gut (kăt′gŭt′), *n.* a dried and twisted cord made from the intestines of animals, usually of sheep. Its chief use is for the strings of musical instruments, tennis rackets, etc.

Cath. abbreviation for *Catholic.*

ca-thar-tic (kȧ-thär′tĭk), *adj.* cleansing the bowels; purgative; as, *cathartic* herbs: —*n.* a purgative medicine; a physic.

Ca-thay (kȧ-thā′), an old name for China, used especially in the Middle Ages.

ca-the-dral (kȧ-thē′drȧl), *n.* **1,** the principal church of a church district under the special charge of the bishop; **2,** in careless use, any church of great size or importance.

Cath-er-ine II (kăth′ēr-ĭn), (1729–1796), called *the Great,* a famous Russian empress.

cath-ode (kăth′ōd), *n.* in an electrolytic cell, vacuum tube, or the like, the negative electron, or the conductor by which the electricity leaves: opposite of *anode.*

cath-o-lic (kăth′ō-lĭk), *adj.* **1,** universal; general; including all; as, he has a *catholic* taste in literature; **2,** liberal, as in thought or sympathies:—**Catholic, 1,** naming or having to do with the universal Christian church; **2,** naming or having to do with the Church of Rome:—*n.* a member of such a church, especially of the Roman Catholic Church.

cath-o-lic-i-ty (kăth′ō-lĭs′ĭ-tĭ), *n.* liberality; tolerance; as, *catholicity* of ideas, mind, or point of view.

Cat-i-line (kăt′ĭ-līn), Lucius Sergius (108?–62 B.C.), a Roman conspirator, denounced by Cicero.

cat-kin (kăt′kĭn), *n.* a hanging, fingerlike flower cluster, as of the willow or birch.

cat-nip (kăt′nĭp), *n.* a common plant of the mint family, so called because cats like its pungent leaves.

Ca-to (kā′tō), (234–149 B.C.), called *the Elder,* a Roman statesman and patriot.

cat-o′-nine-tails (kăt′ᵊ-ō-nīn′ᵊ-tālz′), *n.* **1,** a whip with nine lashes of knotted cord, formerly used for flogging offenders; **2,** popularly, the cattail, a marsh plant with long, furry spikes.

CATKIN OF A WILLOW

Cats-kill Moun-tains (kăts′kĭl), a mountain group, west of the Hudson River, in New York State (map 6).

cat's-paw (kăts′pô′), *n.* **1,** a dupe; a person who is deceived and made use of by another; **2,** a light air that roughens calm water; **3,** a kind of hitch or knot (see *knot* illustration).

cat-sup (kăt′sŭp), *n.* a spicy sauce for meat. See **catchup.**

cat-tail (kăt′tāl′), *n.* a tall marsh plant with long, narrow leaves and brownish, candleshaped spikes of flowers.

cat-tle (kăt′l), *n.pl.* livestock; especially, cows, etc., raised for profit.

Cau-ca-sian (kô-kā′shȧn; kô-kā′zhȧn; kô-kăsh′ȧn; kô-kăzh′ȧn), *adj.* **1,** relating to the Caucasus, a range of mountains between the Black and Caspian seas, or to the inhabitants of this region; **2,** belonging to a division of mankind including the chief races of Europe, northern Africa, and southwestern Asia:—*n.* **1,** a member of the Caucasian race; **2,** a native of the Caucasus.

CATTAIL

Cau-ca-sus (kô′kȧ-sŭs), a mountain group between the Black Sea and Caspian Sea (map 12).

cau-cus (kô′kŭs), *n.* a meeting of political party leaders, to discuss party policies or to choose party candidates.

āte, āorta, râre, căt, ȧsk, fär, ăllow, sofȧ; ēve, ĕvent, ĕll, writēr, novĕl; bīte, pĭn; nō, ōbey, ôr, dŏg, tŏp, cŏllide; ūnit, ūnite, bûrn, cŭt, focŭs; nōon, fŏŏt; mound; coin;

cau-dal (kô′dăl), *adj.* relating to the tail; as, the *caudal* fin of a fish.

caught (kôt), past tense and past participle of *catch*.

caul-dron (kôl′drŭn), *n.* a large kettle or boiler. See **caldron**.

cau-li-flow-er (kô′lĭ-flou′ĕr), *n.* a variety of cabbage with a white, compact flowering head; also, the head, used as a vegetable.

CAULIFLOWER

caulk (kôk), *v.t.* to make watertight. See **calk**.

cause (kôz), *n.* 1, a person who, or a thing which, makes something happen or contributes to a result; as, the boy was the *cause* of the quarrel; hunger is a *cause* of crime; 2, a motive or reason; as, he had no *cause* for being angry; 3, a subject, especially one side of a question of wide interest, which is taken up by a person or group of persons and made into an issue, as in a political campaign; as, the *cause* of child labor; 4, in law, a ground for action; also, a lawsuit:—*v.t.* [caused, caus-ing], to bring about; to effect.—*n.* **cau-sa′tion** (kô-zā′shŭn).

cause-less (kôz′lĕs), *adj.* without cause; without good or sufficient reason.—*adv.* **cause′less-ly**.

cause-way (kôz′wā′), *n.* 1, a raised path or road over wet ground, shallow water, or the like; 2, a raised sidewalk.

caus-tic (kôs′tĭk), *adj.* 1, having the power of gradually eating away or destroying by chemical action; as, *caustic* soda; 2, sarcastic; biting; as, a *caustic* remark:—*n.* a substance which by chemical action burns or eats away animal tissues. —*adv.* **caus′ti-cal-ly**.

cau-ter-ize (kô′tĕr-īz), *v.t.* [cauterized, cauteriz-ing], to burn or sear with a hot iron, or with some caustic agent; as, to *cauterize* a wound.—*n.* **cau′ter-i-za′tion**.

cau-tion (kô′shŭn), *n.* 1, an act, word, or the like, that warns, as against danger; a warning; as, he heeded my *caution* against gambling; 2, heedfulness; care in avoiding danger; as, handle chemicals with *caution*:—*v.t.* to warn of danger.

cau-tion-ar-y (kô′shŭn-ĕr′ĭ), *adj.* giving a warning; as, *cautionary* words.

cau-tious (kô′shŭs), *adj.* taking care to avoid danger or trouble; heedful.—*adv.* **cau′tious-ly**.

Syn. careful, prudent, discreet, wary.

cav-al-cade (kăv′ăl-kād′), *n.* a procession of persons, usually on horseback.

cav-a-lier (kăv′à-lēr′), *n.* 1, a horseman; often, an armed horseman; a knight; 2, a gay adventurer; 3, a lady's escort; a gallant:—*adj.* 1, gay; frank and carefree; 2, haughty; as, a *cavalier* refusal.

cav-al-ry (kăv′ăl-rĭ), *n.* [*pl.* cavalries], soldiers who fight on horseback; mounted troops.—*n.* **cav′al-ry-man**.

cave (kāv), *n.* a large hole in the earth, especially a natural one:—**cave man**, a man of the Stone Age; hence, humorously, any man who is rough or overbearing, especially toward women:—*v.i.* [caved, cav-ing], to fall in or down; as, the road *caved* in.

cav-ern (kăv′ĕrn), *n.* a large, underground hollow or cave.

cav-ern-ous (kăv′ĕr-nŭs), *adj.* 1, hollow like a cavern; 2, containing caverns; as, a *cavernous* mountain.

cav-i-ar (kăv′ĭ-är′; kà′vyàr′), *n.* the roe, or eggs, of certain large fishes, especially the sturgeon, prepared for use as an appetizer or relish. Also spelled **cav′i-are′**.

cav-il (kăv′ĭl; kăv′l), *v.i.* [caviled, caviling], 1, to find fault without good reason; 2, to raise foolish or frivolous objections; as, to *cavil* at a proposed plan:—*n.* a petty or frivolous objection.

cav-i-ty (kăv′ĭ-tĭ), *n.* [*pl.* cavities], a hollow place; a hole or hollow.

ca-vort (kà-vôrt′), *v.i. Colloquial*, to prance or caper about, as does a horse.

caw (kô), *n.* a cry like that of the crow:— *v.i.* to utter such a cry.

Cawn-pore (kôn′pôr′), a city in India, on the Ganges River (map **15**).

Cax-ton (kăk′stŭn), William (1422?–1491), the first English printer.

Cay-enne (kī-ĕn′; kā-ĕn′), a city on the northeastern coast of South America, the capital of French Guiana (map **11**).

cay-enne (kī-ĕn′; kā-ĕn′), *n.* a hot, biting pepper made from the seeds or fruit of certain plants: also called *red pepper*, *cayenne pepper*.

Ca-yu-ga (kà-yōō′gà), *n.* a member of the Cayugas, a tribe of North American Indians formerly living in the central part of New York.

cay-use (kī-ūs′), *n.* in the western U.S., an Indian pony; a mustang.

c.c. abbreviation for *cubic centimeter*.

cease (sēs), *v.i.* [ceased, ceas-ing], to come to an end; stop; as, at nightfall the singing of the birds *ceased*:—*v.t.* to discontinue; as, *cease* your quarreling.

Syn. pause, desist, terminate, refrain.

cease-less (sēs′lĕs), *adj.* without end or pause; as, *ceaseless* chatter.

Ce-bu (sā-bōō′), 1, an island in the Philippines; also, a city, its capital (map **15**).

ce·dar (sē′dẽr), *n.* **1,** an Old World evergreen tree of the pine family, with a very durable and fragrant wood; **2,** any one of several related North American trees, as the white cedar, red cedar, etc. (see illustrations on page 865); **3,** the wood of any of these trees:—*adj.* relating to cedar; made of cedar.

ce·dar-bird (sē′dẽr-bûrd′), *n.* a crested American bird with red patches on its wings; the cedar waxwing. See **waxwing.**

cede (sēd), *v.t.* [ced-ed, ced-ing], **1,** to give up or surrender, as a tract of land; **2,** to grant (a point), as in an argument.

ce·dil·la (sē-dĭl′à), *n.* a mark put under the letter *c* [ç] to show that it has the sound of *s*, as in the word *façade.*

ceil·ing (sēl′ĭng), *n.* **1,** the inner overhead covering of a room; **2,** the greatest height that an airplane can reach, or at which the earth is visible from an airplane; **3,** an upper limit, as of hours of labor per week, or of price for a given commodity.

cel·an·dine (sĕl′ăn-dīn), *n.* a plant of the poppy family, or its yellow flower.

Cel·e·bes (sĕl′ē-bēz; sē-lē′bēz), an island (cap. Makassar), east of Borneo, in Indonesia (map 15).

cel·e·brant (sĕl′ē-brănt), *n.* one who performs a public religious ceremony, especially the priest who officiates at Mass.

cel·e·brate (sĕl′ē-brāt), *v.t.* [celebrat-ed, celebrat-ing], **1,** to perform publicly with suitable ceremonies, as a Mass; **2,** to make known with praise; honor; as, we *celebrate* the names of great men; **3,** to observe suitably, as with a holiday and ceremonies; as, to *celebrate* Christmas.
Syn. commemorate, observe, keep.

cel·e·brat·ed (sĕl′ē-brāt′ĕd), *adj.* famous; illustrious.

cel·e·bra·tion (sĕl′ē-brā′shŭn), *n.* **1,** the performing of a public religious ceremony; **2,** ceremonies or festivities on a special occasion, as Christmas, a birthday, or the like.

ce·leb·ri·ty (sē-lĕb′rĭ-tĭ), *n.* [*pl.* celebrities], **1,** fame; renown; **2,** a renowned or celebrated person; a public character.

ce·ler·i·ty (sē-lĕr′ĭ-tĭ), *n.* rapidity; speed.

cel·er·y (sĕl′ẽr-ĭ), *n.* a garden plant, the stalks of which are bleached, during growth, and eaten as a vegetable; also, a stalk of this plant.

CELERY

ce·les·tial (sē-lĕs′chăl), *adj.* **1,** pertaining to the heavens; as, the stars are *celestial* bodies; **2,** heavenly; divine; as, *celestial* joy.

cel·i·ba·cy (sĕl′ĭ-bà-sĭ; sē-lĭb′à-sĭ), *n.* the state of being unmarried; single life, especially that of one bound by religious vows.

cel·i·bate (sĕl′ĭ-bāt), *n.* an unmarried person:—*adj.* single; unmarried.

cell (sĕl), *n.* **1,** a small, close room, as in a monastery or prison; **2,** a tiny mass of living matter, the unit of structure in both plants and animals; **3,** a small, enclosed space, as in a honeycomb; **4,** in electricity, a vessel containing a fluid and two plates of different materials, or a similar apparatus, used to generate an electric current.

cel·lar (sĕl′ẽr), *n.* a room or group of rooms, generally underground or under a building, most often used for storage.

Cel·li·ni (chĕl-lē′nē), Benvenuto (1500–1571), an Italian artist and goldsmith.

cel·lo (chĕl′ō), *n.* [*pl.* cellos or celli (chĕl′ē)], the violoncello; a musical stringed instrument larger than the violin and deeper in tone (see illustration under *musical instrument*). Also written ′cel′lo.—*n.* cel′list; ′cel′list.

Cel·lo·phane (sĕl′ō-fān), *n.* a trade-mark name for a thin, transparent, waterproof material made from wood pulp, and used as a wrapper for many articles:—**cellophane,** a product bearing this name.

cel·lu·lar (sĕl′ū-lẽr), *adj.* pertaining to a cell; consisting of cells, as tissue.

Cel·lu·loid (sĕl′ū-loid), *n.* a trade-mark name for a compound of camphor and guncotton:—**celluloid,** a material bearing this name, often colored to imitate amber, tortoise shell, or the like, used in making combs, brushes, films, etc.

cel·lu·lose (sĕl′ū-lōs), *n.* a substance related to starch, and forming the main part of plant tissue, linen, paper, etc.

Celt (sĕlt; kĕlt), *n.* a member of any Celtic-speaking people, including the ancient Gauls and Britons, and the modern Irish, Welsh, Highland Scots, and Bretons.

Celt·ic (sĕl′tĭk; kĕl′tĭk), *adj.* pertaining to the Celts or to their language:—*n.* a group of languages now spoken chiefly in the Scottish Highlands, Ireland, Wales, and Brittany.

ce·ment (sē-mĕnt′), *n.* **1,** a substance usually made from clay and limestone and mixed with water to form a kind of mortar which soon hardens to the consistency of stone, used in building walls, laying floors, etc.; **2,** any similar substance which causes things to stick together, as glue or paste; **3,** the bony material which covers the root of a tooth; **4,** in dentistry, a material used for filling cavities:—*v.t.* **1,** to cause to stick together, as bricks; **2,** to cover or pave with cement.

āte, âorta, râre, căt, åsk, fär, ăllow, sofà; ēve, ĕvent, ĕll, wrĩtẽr, novĕl; bīte, pĭn; nō, ōbey, ôr, dŏg, tŏp, cŏllide; ūnit, ūnite, bûrn, cŭt, focŭs; nōōn, fŏŏt; mound; coin;

cem·e·ter·y (sĕm′ē-tĕr′ĭ), *n.* [*pl.* cemeteries], a burial ground; graveyard.

Cen. Am. abbreviation for *Central America.*

cen·ser (sĕn′sẽr), *n.* a vessel with a perforated lid, in which incense is burned.

cen·sor (sĕn′sẽr), *n.* **1,** in ancient Rome, one of the two magistrates who took the census and regulated morals; **2,** an official who examines books, plays, or the like, to prevent anything immoral or offensive in them; **3,** an official who, in time of war, examines all printed matter, to suppress anything that might help the enemy; **4,** one who criticizes manners or morals:—*v.t.* to deal with as a censor.—*n.* **cen′sor·ship.**

cen·sor·i·ous (sĕn-sôr′ĭ-ŭs), *adj.* faultfinding; severely critical.

cen·sure (sĕn′shẽr), *n.* blame; faultfinding; reproof:—*v.t.* [censured, censuring], to find fault with.

Syn., *v.* criticize, blame, upbraid.

cen·sus (sĕn′sŭs), *n.* an official count of population. In ancient Rome, the census was a registration of citizens and property for taxation purposes. In the U.S., the census is taken every ten years, and the information collected includes statistics as to sex, race, age, employment, etc.

cent (sĕnt), *n.* **1,** in the U.S., the 100th part of a dollar; **2,** a coin of this value.

cent. abbreviation for *century, centigrade, central.*

cen·taur (sĕn′tôr), *n.* **1,** in mythology, a creature half man and half horse; **2,** a perfect horseman.

cen·ta·vo (sĕn-tä′vō; thän-tä′vō), *n.* a small copper or nickel coin of some Spanish-speaking countries; worth from a half cent to a cent.

cen·te·nar·i·an (sĕn′tē-nâr′ĭ-ăn), *n.* a person 100 years old or over.

CENTAUR

cen·te·nar·y (sĕn′tē-nẽr′ĭ; sĕn-tĕn′à-rĭ), *n.* [*pl.* centenaries], a period of 100 years; also, a celebration of a 100th anniversary.

cen·ten·ni·al (sĕn-tĕn′ĭ-ăl), *adj.* relating to a period of 100 years:—*n.* the 100th anniversary celebration of any event.

cen·ter or **cen·tre** (sĕn′tẽr), *n.* **1,** that point of a circle or sphere which is equally distant from every point of the circumference; **2,** a point about which something turns, or about which things are collected or people gather; as, the *center* of a wheel; a shopping *center*; **3,** the principal point or object; as, she is the *center* of attention:—*v.t.* **1,** to place (something) at the middle point; **2,** to gather to a point; concentrate,

as the attention:—*v.i.* to gather at one point; converge toward a single point; as, his ambition *centered* on his son.

cen·ter·board (sĕn′tẽr-bôrd′), *n.* a vertical piece of wood or metal, used in place of a keel in certain small boats. It can be raised or lowered through a slot in the bottom of the boat.

cen·ti·grade (sĕn′tĭ-grād), *adj.* having 100 equal divisions called degrees:—**centigrade thermometer**, a thermometer on which the distance between the freezing point of water, marked at 0°, and the boiling point, marked at 100°, is divided into 100 equal degrees.

cen·ti·gram or **cen·ti·gramme** (sĕn′tĭ-grăm), *n.* in the metric system, a weight equal to the 100th part of a gram, or 0.15432 grain, troy.

cen·time (säṅ′tēm; säṅ′tĕm′), *n.* a small French coin equal in value to the 100th part of a franc.

cen·ti·me·ter or **cen·ti·me·tre** (sĕn′-tĭ-mē′tẽr), *n.* in the metric system, a measure of length equal to the 100th part of a meter, or about 0.3937 inch.

cen·ti·pede (sĕn′tĭ-pēd), *n.* a small, wormlike animal with many pairs of legs.

cen·tral (sĕn′trăl), *adj.* **1,** relating to the middle; situated in the middle; **2,** chief; leading; as, the *central* theme of a discussion:—*n.* a telephone exchange; also, a telephone operator working at an exchange.

Cen·tral A·mer·i·ca, the south portion of North America, between Mexico and South America, including Guatemala, British Honduras, Honduras, El Salvador, Nicaragua, Costa Rica, and Panama (map **10**).

CENTI-PEDE (⅓)

cen·tral·i·za·tion (sĕn′trăl-ĭ-zā′shŭn; sĕn′trăl-ī-zā′shŭn), *n.* **1,** the process of bringing to a central point; as, the *centralization* of business in large cities; **2,** the concentration of the powers of government in a central organization; as, successful local self-government will always oppose *centralization.*

cen·tral·ize (sĕn′trăl-īz), *v.t.* [centralized, centraliz-ing], to draw to one central point; to bring under one control; as, to *centralize* a government.

cen·tre (sĕn′tẽr), *n.* the middle point:—*v.t.* and *v.i.* [cen-tred, cen-tring], to gather at a point. See **center.**

cen·trif·u·gal (sĕn-trĭf′ū-găl), *adj.* moving or tending to move away from a center: opposite of *centripetal*:—**centrifugal force,** a force which tends to make a body

---

moving in a curved line fly off along a straight line, as mud is thrown from a moving wheel.

cen·trip·e·tal (sĕn-trĭp′ē-tăl), *adj.* moving or tending to move toward a center: opposite of *centrifugal:*—**centripetal force,** a force which tends to prevent a body moving in a curved line from flying off at a tangent.

cen·tu·ri·on (sĕn-tū′rĭ-ŭn), *n.* in Roman history, an officer commanding a company of about 100 soldiers.

cen·tu·ry (sĕn′tū-rĭ), *n.* [*pl.* centuries], **1,** a group of 100, especially 100 years; **2,** each group of 100 years after some fixed date, as the birth of Christ; as, the years 1801 to 1900 inclusive belong to the 19th *century* A. D.; **3,** a score of 100 points; as, in cricket, to make a *century;* **4,** in Roman history, a group of citizens casting a single vote; also, a company of about 100 soldiers:—**century plant,** the American aloe, a plant with long, fleshy spiny leaves and a treelike flower stalk, formerly supposed to bloom once every 100 years.

ce·ram·ic (sē-răm′ĭk), *adj.* pertaining to pottery; as, the *ceramic* arts:—**ceramics,** *n.pl.* used as *sing.,* **1,** the art of making vases, tiles, or the like, of baked clay; **2,** pieces of pottery.

Cer·ber·us (sûr′bĕr-ŭs), *n.* in mythology, a savage three-headed dog guarding the entrance to Hades.

CERBERUS

ce·re·al (sē′rē-ăl), *n.* **1,** any grass that yields a grain or seed used for food, as rice, wheat, oats, or the like; **2,** any of these grains, in a natural state or as put on the market; **3,** a prepared food, especially a breakfast food, made from any of these grains:—*adj.* pertaining to edible grains or the grasses which produce them.

cer·e·bel·lum (sĕr′ē-bĕl′ŭm), *n.* [*pl.* cerebellums], the smaller of the two chief parts of the brain, lying behind the cerebrum.

cer·e·bral (sĕr′ē-brăl), *adj.* pertaining to the brain, especially to the cerebrum, or larger part of the brain.

cer·e·brum (sĕr′ē-brŭm), *n.* [*pl.* cerebrums], the larger of the two chief parts of the brain, filling practically the entire upper part of the skull cavity.

cere·ment (sēr′mĕnt), *n.* a shroud for a dead body.

cer·e·mo·ni·al (sĕr′ē-mō′nĭ-ăl), *adj.* relating to rites or formalities; as, *ceremonial* garb:—*n.* **1,** a system of rites or ceremonies; as, the *ceremonial* of coronation; **2,** behavior required by custom on a given

social occasion; as, court *ceremonial.*—*adv.* **cer′e-mo′ni-al-ly.**

cer·e·mo·ni·ous (sĕr′ē-mō′nĭ-ŭs), *adj.* **1,** consisting of rites or formalities; formal; as, a *ceremonious* religion; **2,** courteous in a prescribed and formal manner; as, a *ceremonious* bow; a courtier must be *ceremonious.*—*adv.* **cer′e-mo′ni-ous-ly.**—*n.* **cer′e-mo′ni-ous-ness.**

cer·e·mo·ny (sĕr′ē-mō′nĭ), *n.* [*pl.* ceremonies], **1,** a formal rite or observance; as, the marriage *ceremony;* the inaugural *ceremony;* **2,** behavior regulated by the laws of strict etiquette; formality:—**to stand on ceremony,** to insist on the formalities.

Ce·res (sē′rēz), *n.* in mythology, the goddess of growing vegetation. The Greeks called her *Demeter.*

ce·rise (sĕ-rēz′; sĕ-rēs′), *adj.* cherry red; —*n.* a bright, light-red color.

cer·tain (sûr′tĭn), *adj.* **1,** beyond question; sure; as, it is *certain* that day follows night; **2,** destined; inevitable; as, death is the *certain* end for all; **3,** fixed; settled; as, it is *certain* that we leave tomorrow; **4,** confident; as, I am *certain* of your loyalty; **5,** particular; one or some; as, to travel by a *certain* road; *certain* senators disagreed.

cer·tain·ly (sûr′tĭn-lĭ), *adv.* with certainty; without fail; without doubt.

cer·tain·ty (sûr′tĭn-tĭ), *n.* [*pl.* certainties], **1,** the state of being sure; as, there is no *certainty* that we can leave today; **2,** something that is sure to happen; as, death is a *certainty.*

cer·tes (sûr′tēz; sûr′tĭz), *adv. Archaic,* certainly; in truth.

cer·tif·i·cate (sĕr-tĭf′ĭ-kĭt), *n.* a formal, printed or written statement of a fact or privilege, signed by a public official or qualified person; as, a *certificate* of marriage; a medical *certificate;* a teacher's *certificate.*

cer·ti·fi·ca·tion (sûr′tĭ-fĭ-kā′shŭn), *n.* **1,** written confirmation of the truth of something; **2,** a certificate; **3,** a formal notice.

cer·ti·fied mail a class of U.S. mail, not insured, but requiring a signed receipt upon delivery.

cer·ti·fy (sûr′tĭ-fī), *v.t.* [certified, certifying], **1,** to confirm or verify by a signed statement; as, the doctor *certified* that John had been vaccinated; **2,** to guarantee; as, to *certify* a check.

ce·ru·le·an (sĕ-roo′lē-ăn), *adj.* sky-blue.

Cer·van·tes Sa·a·ve·dra (sĕr-vän′tĕs sä′ä-vĕ′drä; sĕr-văn′tēz), Miguel de (1547–1616), a Spanish writer: "Don Quixote."

cer·vi·cal (sûr′vĭ-kăl), *adj.* pertaining to the neck; as, the *cervical* vertebrae.

āte, āorta, râre, căt, ȧsk, fär, ăllow, sofȧ; ēve, ĕvent, ĕll, wrīter, novĕl; bīte, pĭn; nō, ōbey, ôr, dŏg, tŏp, cŏllide; ūnit, ŭnite, bûrn, cŭt, focŭs; nōon, fŏŏt; mound; coin;

ces-sa-tion (sĕ-sā′shŭn), *n.* a ceasing; a pause; stop; as, *cessation* of pain; *cessation* of hostilities.

Syn. intermission, stop, end, close.

ces-sion (sĕsh′ŭn), *n.* a formal giving up to another; as, a *cession* of territory.

cess-pool (sĕs′pōōl′), *n.* a deep pit or well to receive sewage.

ce-ta-cean (sĕ-tā′shăn), *n.* a whale, dolphin, porpoise, or related sea animal.

Cey-lon (sĕ-lŏn′), an island (cap. Colombo) southeast of India, a dominion in the British Commonwealth of Nations. (map 15).

cf. abbreviation for Latin *confer*, meaning *compare.*

cg. abbreviation for *centigram, centigrams.*

ch. abbreviation for *chapter, church.*

Chad (chăd), a lake northeast of Nigeria, in Africa (map 14).

chafe (chāf), *v.t.* [chafed, chaf-ing], 1, to rub with the hand, so as to restore warmth or sensation; as, to *chafe* numb hands; 2, to wear away or make sore by rubbing; as, a frayed collar *chafes* the skin; 3, to fret; irritate:—*v.i.* 1, to rub; 2, to be worn or made sore by rubbing; 3, to be vexed; to fume; as, to *chafe* at the least delay.

¹chaff (chăf), *n.* 1, the husks of grain, separated by threshing and winnowing; 2, straw or hay cut fine for cattle; 3, anything worthless.

²chaff (chăf), *n.* good-natured teasing; banter:—*v.i.* and *v.t.* to tease.

chaf-finch (chăf′ĭnch), *n.* a common European song and cage bird that picks its food from chaff.

chaf-ing dish (chā′-fĭng), a cooking vessel with a handle and a cover, heated by alcohol or electricity, used for cooking at the table.

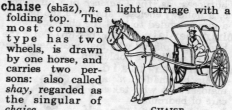

CHAFFINCH (⅓)

Cha-gres (chä′grĕs), a river in Panama, Central America, dammed to form Gatun Lake (map 10).

cha-grin (shȧ-grĭn′), *n.* vexation due to disappointment, failure, or humiliation:—*v.t.* to vex; mortify; as, he was deeply *chagrined* by the loss of his job.

Syn., n. confusion, dismay, shame.

chain (chān), *n.* 1, a series of links or rings joined together; 2, anything which binds or restrains; 3, **chains**, imprisonment or bondage; 4, a connected series or succession; as, a *chain* of events; 5, a measure, used in surveying land, equal to 100 links or 66 feet:—*v.t.* 1, to fasten with a chain; 2, to fetter; restrain.

chair (châr), *n.* 1, a movable single seat with a back; 2, a position of honor or authority; 3, the seat from which a professor delivers his lectures; hence, the office or position of a professor; as, the *chair* of English at a university; 4, the presiding officer of an assembly; chairman; as, to address the *chair.*

chair-man (châr′măn), *n.* [*pl.* chairmen (-mĕn)], the presiding officer of an assembly or committee.—*n. fem.* **chair′wom′an.**

chair-man-ship (châr′măn-shĭp), *n.* the office or work of a chairman.

chaise (shāz), *n.* a light carriage with a folding top. The most common type has two wheels, is drawn by one horse, and carries two persons: also called *shay,* regarded as the singular of *chaise.*

CHAISE

Chal-de-a (kăl-dē′ȧ), an ancient country in southwestern Asia, on the Euphrates River and the Persian Gulf.—*adj.* and *n.* **Chal-de′an.**

cha-let (shȧ-lā′; shăl′ā), *n.* 1, a herdsman's hut or a peasant's cottage in the mountains of Switzerland; 2, a house built in the style of a Swiss chalet.

CHALET

chal-ice (chăl′ĭs), *n.* 1, a goblet; 2, the cup used in celebrating the Eucharist, or Lord's Supper; 3, the cup-shaped head of a flower, as of the tulip.

chalk (chôk), *n.* 1, a soft, whitish limestone, composed chiefly of tiny sea shells; 2, a chalklike material used to make crayons; also, the crayon:—*v.t.* 1, to rub or whiten with chalk; 2, to mark or write with chalk.

CHALICE

chal-lenge (chăl′ĕnj), *n.* 1, a summons or invitation to a duel or contest; a dare; 2, a demand by a sentry that a passerby show who he is; 3, an objection made to a person's serving on a jury:—*v.t.* [challenged, challeng-ing], 1, to summon to a duel or contest; 2, to invite; as, to *challenge* investigation; 3, to take exception to; dispute, as a statement; 4, to claim as due; as, he *challenges* respect by his honesty; 5, to demand identification from; as, the sentry *challenged* him; 6, in law, to object to (a juror).—*n.* **chal′leng-er.**

chal-lis (shăl′ĭ; chăl′ĭs) or **chal-lie**

(shăl′ĭ), *n.* a light, all-wool or wool-and-cotton dress material, usually printed in a small-figured design.

cham·ber (chām′bĕr), *n.* **1,** a room, especially a bedroom; as, in my lady's *chamber;* **2, chambers,** a set of rooms used as a dwelling or business office; **3,** a hall where a legislative or other government body meets; **4,** the government body itself; as, in the U.S., the Senate is the upper *chamber* of Congress; **5,** a group of persons organized for certain business purposes; as, the *Chamber* of Commerce; **6,** a hollow, enclosed space, as the part of a gun intended to hold the charge.

cham·ber·lain (chām′bĕr-lĭn), *n.* the high court official who manages the household of a ruler or nobleman.

cham·ber·maid (chām′bĕr-mād′), *n.* a maidservant who takes care of bedrooms.

cham·bray(shăm′brā), *n.* cotton fabric with a smooth finish, woven of threads of white and one other color.

cha·me·le·on (kȧ-mē′lē-ŭn; kȧ-mēl′yŭn), *n.* **1,** a lizard which has the power to change its color to match its surroundings; **2,** a person of changeable disposition.

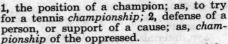

CHAMELEON (⅓)

cham·ois (shăm′ĭ), *n.* [*pl.* chamois], **1,** a small antelope found on high peaks in Europe and Asia; **2,** a soft, thin leather, originally made from the hide of the chamois, but now prepared from other skins, and used for gloves, polishing cloths, etc.

champ (chămp), *v.t.* and *v.i.* to bite or bite upon, noisily or impatiently; as, a horse *champs* the bit.

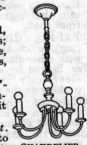

CHAMOIS (1/18)

cham·pagne (shăm-pān′), *n.* **1,** a light, sparkling, almost colorless wine made originally in the northeastern part of France; **2,** in careless use, any sparkling wine.

cham·paign (shăm-pān′), *n.* a flat, open country.

cham·pi·on (chăm′pĭ-ŭn), *n.* **1,** a successful competitor against all rivals; as, lightweight *champion* of the U.S.; **2,** a person who defends another or fights for a cause; as, a *champion* of free speech:—*adj.* above all rivals:—*v.t.* to defend or support.

cham·pi·on·ship (chăm′pĭ-ŭn-shĭp′), *n.*

1, the position of a champion; as, to try for a tennis *championship;* **2,** defense of a person, or support of a cause; as, *championship* of the oppressed.

¹Cham·plain (shăm-plān′), a large lake between Vermont and New York (map 6).

²Cham·plain (shăm-plān′), Samuel de (1567–1635), a French explorer, founder of the first settlements in Canada.

chance (chȧns), *n.* **1,** the way things happen; fate; fortune; as, *chance* willed it; **2,** a possibility; probability; also, opportunity; as, a *chance* of a position; **3,** risk; as, to take a *chance:—adj.* accidental; unforeseen; as, a *chance* meeting:—*v.i.* [chanced, chanc·ing], to happen; as, it *chanced* to rain:—*v.t. Colloquial*, to risk; as, I don't dare *chance* it.

chan·cel (chȧn′sĕl), *n.* in certain churches, the space surrounding the altar, reserved for the clergy and, sometimes, for the choir.

chan·cel·lor (chȧn′sĕ-lĕr), *n.* **1,** in some European countries, the chief minister of state; **2,** in many universities, the president:—**Chancellor,** in Great Britain: **1,** the highest judge of the realm, called *Lord Chancellor;* **2,** the minister of finance, called *Chancellor of the Exchequer.—n.* **chan′cel·lor·ship′.**

chan·cer·y (chȧn′sĕr-ĭ), *n.* **1,** in England, the court of the Lord Chancellor; **2,** in the U.S., a court of equity.

chan·de·lier (shăn′dē-lĭr′), *n.* a hanging light fixture, with branches for two or more gas or electric lights or for candles.

chan·dler (chăn′dlĕr), *n.* **1,** a maker or seller of candles; **2,** a dealer in paint, rope, lanterns, groceries, etc.; as, a ship *chandler.*

Chang·chun (chäng′-chŏŏn′), a city in Manchuria. Under Japanese rule it was called *Hsinking.*

CHANDELIER

change (chānj), *v.t.* [changed, chang·ing], **1,** to make different by substituting one thing for another; as, he *changed* his coat; he *changed* his job; **2,** to alter so as to make different in shape, size, color, or the like; **3,** to exchange; as, to *change* rings with someone; **4,** to give an equivalent for; as, to *change* a dollar bill:—*v.i.* **1,** to vary; as, the weather *changes;* **2,** to be altered, as her appearance has *changed* greatly; **3,** of the moon, to pass from one phase, or state, to another; as, the moon *changes* next week: —*n.* **1,** an alteration; a variation; as, a *change* of scenery; **2,** variety; as, she plays tennis almost every day, but likes golf as a *change;* **3,** small coins taken together; **4,** the difference, returned to a purchaser, between the price of a purchase and the amount paid.

change-a-ble (chān'jȧ-bl), *adj.* likely to change, or to keep changing from moment to moment; variable; as, a *changeable* mood.—*n.* **change'a-ble-ness.**

change-ful (chānj'fŏŏl), *adj.* changeable.

change-less (chānj'lĕs), *adj.* unchanging; constant; continuing without change.

change-ling (chānj'lĭng), *n.* **1,** in folklore, an elf child left by fairies in exchange for a human infant; **2,** any child substituted for another.

Chang-sha (chäng'shä'), a city in south-eastern China (map **15**).

chan-nel (chăn'ĕl), *n.* **1,** the bed of a stream; also, the deepest part of a bay, harbor, etc.; **2,** a strait separating two large bodies of land; as, the English *Channel;* **3,** a long groove or furrow; **4,** a course by which information, thought, or the like, travels; as, news comes through the *channel* of the press:—*v.t.* [channeled, channel-ing], to cut or wear (a groove or way); as, the brook *channeled* its way through the rock.

Chan-nel Is-lands, a group of British islands in the English Channel near France, including Jersey, Guernsey, Alderney, and Sark (map **13**).

chan-son (shăn'sŏn; shäṅ'sôṅ'), *n.* a poem set to music; a song.

chant (chȧnt), *v.t.* **1,** to sing; **2,** to praise in song; **3,** to intone, or sing on one prolonged note; recite musically:—*v.i.* **1,** to make melody with the voice; **2,** to intone; sing slowly and solemnly:—*n.* **1,** a song; especially, a solemn, measured song; **2,** a special musical composition, chanted or intoned, used in church services.—*n.* **chant'er.**

chant-ey (shăn'tĭ; chăn'tĭ), *n.* [*pl.* chanteys], a song sailors sing in rhythm with their work. Also, **chant'y** [*pl.* chanties].

chan-ti-cleer (chăn'tĭ-klēr), *n.* a rooster.

cha-os (kā'ŏs), *n.* **1,** the utter confusion formerly supposed to have existed before the universe; **2,** hence, utter disorder.

cha-ot-ic (kā-ŏt'ĭk), *adj.* confused or disordered, as a mind or a room.

¹**chap** (chăp), *v.t.* [chapped, chap-ping], to cause to crack or become rough; as, cold *chaps* the skin:—*v.i.* to crack or become rough; as, my hands *chap* quickly:—*n.* a crack, as in the skin.

²**chap** (chăp), *n. Colloquial,* a fellow; youth; a man or boy.

chap. [*pl.* chaps.], abbreviation for *chapter.*

chap-el (chăp'ĕl), *n.* **1,** a place of public worship, not so large or important as a church; **2,** a place of worship in a palace, or in a school or other institution; **3,** in Great Britain, a church belonging to neither the Church of England nor the Roman Catholic Church.

chap-er-on (shăp'ĕr-ōn), *n.* an older woman who accompanies a young unmarried woman, or a group of young people, to the theater, a dance, or other social function:—*v.t.* to act as chaperon to. Also, **chap'er-one.**

chap-lain (chăp'lĭn), *n.* a clergyman who performs religious services in the army or navy, or in an institution, etc.

chap-let (chăp'lĕt), *n.* **1,** a wreath or garland for the head; **2,** a string of beads, one third as long as a rosary, for counting prayers; also, the prayers; **3,** any string of beads.

chap-man (chăp'măn), *n.* [*pl.* chapmen (-mĕn)], a peddler.

chaps (chăps; shăps), *n.pl.* leather or fur overbreeches worn by cowboys.

chap-ter (chăp'tĕr), *n.* **1,** a main division of a book; **2,** a local group which is part of a larger religious or fraternal order.

char (chär), *v.t.* [charred, char-ring], **1,** to burn partially; **2,** to change wood into charcoal.

char-ac-ter (kăr'ăk-tĕr), *n.* **1,** a distinctive sign or mark; hence, the written or printed marks for letters and numbers; **2,** individuality; nature; the qualities that make a thing what it is, and different from other things; as, the *character* of the vegetation in a valley is different from that on a mountain; **3,** a person possessing distinctive qualities; as, a great historical *character;* **4,** mental or moral nature; as, a person of high *character;* **5,** reputation; **6,** a testimonial; **7,** a person in literature; as, a Dickens *character.*

char-ac-ter-is-tic (kăr'ăk-tĕr-ĭs'tĭk), *adj.* showing the distinctive qualities or traits of a person or thing; typical; as, her *characteristic* kindness:—*n.* a distinguishing mark or quality; as, the *characteristics* of a scholar.

  Syn., n. feature, trait.

char-ac-ter-ize (kăr'ăk-tĕr-īz), *v.t.* [characterized, characteriz-ing], **1,** to describe as having specific qualities; as, the author *characterizes* his heroines as ugly, but interesting; **2,** to mark or distinguish; be characteristic of; as, obstinacy *characterizes* the donkey.—*n.* **char'ac-ter-i-za'tion.**

---

go; join; yet; sing; chin; show; thin, *th*en; hw, *wh*y; zh, azure; ü, Ger. für or Fr. lune; ö, Ger. schön or Fr. feu; ṅ, Fr. enfant, nom; kh, Ger. ach or ich. See pages ix–x.

cha-rade (shà-rād′; shà-räd′), *n.* a game in which a word is to be guessed from the acting out of each syllable, as *persuaded* from the acting of *purr, sway, dead.*

char-coal (chär′kōl′), *n.* a very dark or black porous substance produced by charring wood in the absence of air. Charcoal is used chiefly as a fuel; charcoal pencils are used in drawing.

charge (chärj), *v.t.* [charged, charg-ing], 1, to load, as a gun with ammunition, or a battery with electricity; 2, to command; instruct; as, the judge then *charged* the jury; 3, to accuse; blame; as, he was *charged* with murder; 4, to demand, as a price; 5, to place (something) on record as not paid for; as, please *charge* this purchase to me; 6, to rush upon or attack:— *v.i.* 1, to demand or set a price or sum due; as, he *charges* reasonably for what he sells; 2, to make an attack:—*n.* 1, a quantity of material with which a firearm or other apparatus is loaded; as, a *charge* of gunpowder; a *charge* of electricity; 2, an office or trust; responsibility; 3, a parish or congregation entrusted to the care of a minister; 4, the price of an object; as, the *charge* is one dollar; 5, an entry or account of what is owed; 6, an accusation; as, a *charge* of theft; 7, a violent onset or attack.—*adj.* **charge′a-ble.**

charg-er (chär′jẽr), *n.* 1, a spirited war horse; 2, a large platter.

char-i-ly (chār′ĭ-lĭ), *adv.* cautiously; sparingly; as, make promises *charily.*

char-i-ness (chār′ĭ-nĕs), *n.* caution; frugality; sparingness.

char-i-ot (chār′ĭ-ŭt), *n.* an ancient two-wheeled car used in war, state processions, and racing, drawn by two horses, or, sometimes, by four.

char-i-ot-eer (chär′ĭ-ŭt-ẽr′), *n.* the driver of a chariot.

EGYPTIAN WAR CHARIOT

char-i-ta-ble (chār′ĭ-tà-bl), *adj.* 1, generous in gifts to the needy; 2, providing for the poor; as, a *charitable* institution; 3, merciful; kindly; forgiving; lenient; as, a *charitable* judge.—*adv.* **char′i-ta-bly.**

char-i-ty (chār′ĭ-tĭ), *n.* [*pl.* charities], 1, generosity to the poor; 2, a gift to the poor; 3, brotherly love and good will; 4, leniency in judging others; 5, an institution, founded by a gift, to help the needy.

char-la-tan (shär′là-tăn), *n.* one who pre-

tends to have knowledge or powers that he does not possess; an imposter; quack.

Char-le-magne (shär′lĕ-mān), (742–814), called *Charles the Great*, king of the Franks and Holy Roman emperor.

Charles (chärlz), the name of two English kings: I (1600–1649); II (1630–1685), his son.

Charles-ton (chärlz′tŭn), 1, a seaport city in South Carolina (map 8); 2, a city, the capital of West Virginia (map 8).

Char-lotte (shär′lŏt), a manufacturing city in North Carolina (map 8).

char-lotte russe (shär′lŏt rōōs′), a dessert of custard or whipped cream surrounded by fingers of sponge cake.

charm (chärm), *n.* 1, originally, a chanted verse supposed to have magic power; 2, hence, anything which has magic power; 3, something worn to bring good luck and avert ill luck; an amulet; 4, a trinket worn on a watch fob; 5, a quality of appearance or personality which attracts others; attractiveness:—*v.t.* 1, to bewitch; put a spell on; 2, hence, to affect as if by magic; as, to *charm* away pain; 3, to fascinate.

charm-ing (chär′mĭng), *adj.* delightful; fascinating; pleasing.—*adv.* **charm′ing-ly.**

char-nel house (chär′nĕl), a vault to hold the bodies or bones of the dead.

Cha-ron (kā′rŏn; kâr′ŏn), *n.* in mythology, the boatman who ferried the souls of the dead across the river Styx to Hades.

chart (chärt), *n.* 1, a map, especially a map of any part of a body of water, marking dangerous ledges, ocean currents, islands, etc., for the use of mariners; 2, the map of a ship's course; 3, a sheet of paper giving information in the form of tables, diagrams, or the like; as, a nurse's *chart:* —*v.t.* 1, to map out; 2, to put (information) in the form of a chart.

char-ter (chär′tẽr), *n.* 1, an official paper bestowing certain rights and privileges; 2, a written permit from the authorities of a society to establish a chapter, lodge, or branch:—*v.t.* 1, to grant a charter or permit to; 2, to hire; as, to *charter* a bus.

char-wom-an (chär′wŏŏm-ăn), *n.* [*pl.* charwomen (-wĭm′ĕn)], a woman hired to do cleaning and scrubbing in office buildings.

char-y (châr′ĭ), *adj.* [char-i-er, char-i-est], 1, careful; cautious; as, she is *chary* of talking to strangers; 2, reserved; shy; 3, frugal or sparing.

Cha-ryb-dis (kà-rĭb′dĭs), *n.* a dangerous whirlpool between Sicily and Italy, lying opposite Scylla (map 1). See **Scylla.**

¹**chase** (chās), *v.t.* [chased, chas-ing], 1, to

pursue with intent to capture or kill, as a fox; to hunt; **2,** to drive away; dispel; as, to *chase* crows; *chase* fears:—*n.* **1,** eager pursuit, especially with the idea of capturing (a criminal) or killing (an animal); **2,** those taking part in the hunt.

²chase (chās), *v.t.* [chased, chas-ing], to decorate (a surface) by embossing or engraving; as, to *chase* silver.

chasm (kăzm), *n.* a deep opening in the earth; a cleft; gap; a vast empty space.

chas-sis (shăs´ĭ; shăs´ĭs), *n.* [*pl.* chassis (shăs´ĭz)], **1,** the frame, machinery, and wheels of an automobile; **2,** the main frame of an airplane.

chaste (chāst), *adj.* **1,** virtuous; pure; **2,** simple and restrained in style or taste; unadorned.

chas-ten (chās´n), *v.t.* **1,** to punish for the purpose of making better; as, God *chastens* his people; **2,** to subdue; bring low; as, ridicule *chastens* a braggart.—*n.* **chas´ten-er.**—*n.* **chas´ten-ing.**

Syn. chastise, punish.

chas-tise (chăs-tīz´), *v.t.* [chastised, chastis-ing], to correct by punishment; as, to *chastise* a child.

chas-tise-ment (chăs´tĭz-mĕnt), *n.* punishment; discipline.

chas-ti-ty (chăs´tĭ-tĭ), *n.* **1,** moral purity; innocence; **2,** simplicity in design or style.

chat (chăt), *v.i.* [chat-ted, chat-ting], to converse in an easy, familiar manner:—*n.* **1,** familiar, easy speech; an informal talk; **2,** a kind of songbird, noted for its song.

châ-teau (shă-tō´; shä-tō´), *n.* [*pl.* châteaux (shă-tōz´; shä-tō´)], **1,** a French feudal castle; **2,** a large country house.

Châ-teau—Thier-ry (shä´tō´-tyâ´rē´), a town on the Marne River, northeast of Paris: the scene of one of the most important battles of World War I.

CHÂTEAU

chat-e-laine (shăt´ĕ-lān; shä´tĕ-lân´), *n.* **1,** the lady of a château; **2,** a chain worn at the waist, as for keys or trinkets.

Chat-ta-noo-ga (chăt´a-nōō´ga), a city in southeastern Tennessee (map 8).

chat-tel (chăt´l), *n.* personal property not including houses or land; a movable possession, such as furniture.

chat-ter (chăt´ẽr), *v.i.* **1,** to utter sounds rapidly and indistinctly, as monkeys; **2,** to talk much and say little; **3,** to rattle, as parts of a machine in motion, or as

teeth when one is shivering:—*n.* **1,** sounds like those of the magpie, monkey, etc.; **2,** idle, rapid talk; **3,** a rattling of the teeth, as from cold or fear.—*n.* **chat´ter-er.**

chat-ty (chăt´ĭ), *adj.* [chat-ti-er, chat-ti-est], talkative in a friendly trifling way.—*n.* **chat´ti-ness.**

Chau-cer (chô´sẽr), Geoffrey (1340?-1400), a great English poet, who wrote the "Canterbury Tales."

chauf-feur (shō-fûr´; shō´fẽr), *n.* one whose business is to drive an automobile.

Chau-tau-qua or **chau-tau-qua** (shă-tô´kwä), *n.* **1,** a system of education by summer schools, programs of lectures, etc., at Chautauqua, New York; later, a similar program conducted by traveling lecturers, musicians, etc.; **2,** a system of home instruction by correspondence.

cheap (chēp), *adj.* **1,** low in price; inexpensive; **2,** low in quality; as, *cheap* goods are expensive in the long run; **3,** well worth the price; as, the car was *cheap* at $200; **4,** easily secured; hence, of little value; as, *cheap* popularity; **5,** connected with things of low price or value; as, a *cheap* street or store.—*adv.* **cheap´ly.**—*n.* **cheap´ness.**

cheap-en (chēp´ĕn), *v.t.* to lower in price or value:—*v.i.* to become cheap.

cheat (chēt), *n.* one who deceives or swindles another:—*v.i.* to act dishonestly; as, to *cheat* at cards:—*v.t.* **1,** to deceive; deprive of by trickery; **2,** to escape; as, to *cheat* the gallows.—*n.* **cheat´er.**

¹check (chĕk), *n.* **1,** a restraint; control; as, to keep one's thoughts in *check;* also, a person or thing imposing restraint; **2,** a stop or interruption; as, a journey without *check;* **3,** a ticket or metal disk which shows that a person has the right to claim something; as, a hat *check;* **4,** (also *cheque*), an order or draft on a bank for money; **5,** an examination into the accuracy of something; as, a *check* of a bank statement; **6,** a mark showing that something has been examined or verified:—*v.t.* **1,** to stop; as, to *check* the advance of the enemy; **2,** to examine for accuracy, or mark, as having been examined or verified; **3,** to deposit for safekeeping; as, to *check* a coat.

²check (chĕk), *n.* **1,** a pattern of squares of alternating colors, as on a checkerboard; **2,** any one of these squares; **3,** cloth woven or printed in this pattern:—*v.t.* to mark in checks.

CHECK

¹check-er (chĕk´ẽr), *n.* one who checks, especially an employee whose duty it is

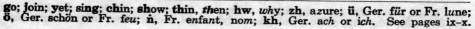

to check all items for price, safekeeping, delivery, etc.; as, a package *checker*.

²**check-er** (chĕk′ẽr), *n.* **1,** one of the squares of a pattern marked in squares of alternate colors; also, the pattern itself; **2,** one of the pieces used in playing checkers; **3, checkers,** a game played on a checkerboard by two persons each with twelve pieces:—*v.t.* to mark with small squares of alternate colors; also, to mark in any similar fashion; as, sunlight through the leaves *checkered* the ground.

check-er-board (chĕk′ẽr-bôrd′), *n.* a board of 64 squares of alternate colors on which the games of chess and checkers are played.

check-mate (chĕk′māt′), *n.* **1,** in chess, the putting of an opponent's king in such a position that he cannot escape; **2,** hence, a complete obstruction or defeat:—*v.t.* [checkmat-ed, checkmat-ing], to obstruct or defeat utterly; as, to *checkmate* a plan.

check-rein (chĕk′rān′), *n.* a short rein running from the bit to the saddle to keep the horse's head up. (See *harness*, illustration.)

cheek (chēk), *n.* **1,** the side of the face below the eye; **2,** *Slang*, saucy speech; bold behavior; impudence.—*adj.* **cheek′y.**

cheep (chēp), *n.* a shrill, feeble noise, as that of a chick or young bird; a peep:—*v.i.* to peep.—*n.* **cheep′er.**

cheer (chēr), *n.* **1,** state of mind; especially, a state of gladness or joy; **2,** that which is furnished in the way of food or entertainment; **3,** a shout of joy, applause or encouragement:—*v.t.* **1,** to gladden; comfort; **2,** to greet, especially with shouts of welcome; **3,** hence, to applaud; encourage:—*v.i.* **1,** to become hopeful or glad; as, he soon *cheered* up; **2,** to applaud.

cheer-ful (chēr′fŏŏl), *adj.* **1,** in good spirits; gay; as, a *cheerful* person; **2,** bringing cheer; as, a *cheerful* fire; **3,** willing; eager; as, a *cheerful* worker.—*adv.* **cheer′-ful-ly.**—*n.* **cheer′ful-ness.**
  Syn. cheery, gay, mirthful.

cheer-less (chēr′lĕs), *adj.* gloomy; forlorn; dismal; as, a damp, *cheerless* day.— *n.* **cheer′less-ness.**

cheer-y (chēr′ĭ), *adj.* [cheer-i-er, cheer-i-est], **1,** cheerful; gay; as, a *cheery* voice; **2,** attractive; bright; as, a *cheery* room.—*n.* **cheer′i-ness.**—*adv.* **cheer′i-ly.**

cheese (chēz), *n.* a food made of the pressed curd of milk.—*adj.* **chees′y.**

cheese-cloth (chēz′klŏth′), *n.* a thin, loosely woven cotton cloth.

chee-tah (chē′tȧ), *n.* an animal of the cat family, found especially in Africa and India, often trained to hunt antelope.

chef (shĕf), *n.* a head cook, as of a hotel or restaurant; hence, any male cook.

Chel-sea (chĕl′sē), a division of the city of London, England.

chem. abbreviation for *chemical, chemist, chemistry*.

chem-i-cal (kĕm′ĭ-kăl), *adj.* **1,** pertaining to chemistry; as, a *chemical* experiment; **2,** produced by, or used in operations of, chemistry; as, a *chemical* compound:—*n.* a substance, such as alcohol, hydrogen, soda, or the like, produced by, or used in, a chemical process.—*adv.* **chem′i-cal-ly.**

che-mise (shē-mēz′), *n.* a woman's sleeveless undergarment, usually knee-length.

chem-ist (kĕm′ĭst), *n.* **1,** one skilled in chemistry; one whose profession is chemistry; **2,** in England, a druggist.

chem-is-try (kĕm′ĭs-trĭ), *n.* the science which treats of the nature of different kinds of substances, and of the laws which govern their combination and behavior under various conditions.

Chem-nitz (kĕm′nĭts), a manufacturing city in Saxony, Germany (map 12).

Che-ops (kē′ŏps), (3700? B.C.), an Egyptian king, sometimes called *Khufu*, builder of the great pyramid at El Giza, Egypt.

cheque (chĕk), *n.* an order or draft on a bank; usually spelled *check*.

Cher-bourg (shâr′bŏŏr′), a fortified seaport and naval arsenal in northern France, on the English Channel (map 12).

cher-ish (chĕr′ĭsh), *v.t.* **1,** to protect; care for tenderly; **2,** to hold dear, as a memory; **3,** to cling to, as a hope.

Cher-o-kee (chĕr′ō-kē′; chĕr′ō-kē′), *n.* a member of a southern tribe of Iroquois Indians.

che-root (shē-rŏŏt′), *n.* a cigar with both ends square.

cher-ry (chĕr′ĭ), *n.* [*pl.* cherries], **1,** a tree related to the plum, bearing a small smooth, fleshy fruit with a stone in the center (see illustration on page 864); also, the fruit or the wood of this tree; **2,** a bright red like that of certain cherries:— *adj.* **1,** of the color of ripe red cherries; **2,** made of cherry wood.

CHERRIES
Leaves and fruit.

cher-ub (chĕr′ŭb), *n.* [*pl.* cherubs], **1,** a representation of a child, or the head of a child, with wings; **2,** a beautiful, innocent child; **3,** [*pl.* cherubim (chĕr′ū-bĭm; chĕr′-ŏŏ-bĭm)], in the Bible, one of an order of angels.—*adj.* **che-ru′bic** (chē-rŏŏ′bĭk).

āte, āorta, râre, căt, ȧsk, fär, ăllow, sofȧ; ēve, ĕvent, ĕll, writẽr, novĕl; bīte, pĭn; nō, ōbey, ôr, dŏg, tŏp, cŏllide; ūnit, ūnite, bûrn, cŭt, focŭs; nōōn, fŏŏt; mound; coin;

cher-u-bim (chĕr′ū-bĭm; chĕr′ŏŏ-bĭm), one of the plural forms of *cherub*.

cher-vo-nets or **cher-vo-netz** (chĕr′vŏ-nĕts), *n.* [*pl.* chervontsi (chĕr-vônt′sē)], a gold coin of the U.S.S.R., equal to ten rubles.

Ches-a-peake Bay (chĕs′ȧ-pēk), an inlet of the Atlantic between the eastern shore of Maryland and Virginia (map **8**).

Chesh-ire cat (chĕsh′ẽr), the cat in "Alice in Wonderland," which converses with Alice from the branch of a tree, and then disappears, bit by bit, until only its grin is left, and finally vanishes.

chess (chĕs), *n.* a game played by two persons, each with sixteen variously shaped pieces, or men, on a checkered board of 64 squares.—*n.* **chess′board′**.—*n.* **chess′man**.

chest (chĕst), *n.* 1, a strong case; a box with a lid; as, a seaman's *chest;* a tool *chest;* 2, the quantity such a box contains; also, the box and the contents; as, a *chest* of tea; 3, a place for keeping a fund of money; hence, the fund itself; as, a community *chest;* 4, the breast or upper front part of the body enclosed by the ribs.

chest-nut (chĕs′nŭt; chĕs′nŭt), *n.* 1, a tree of the beech family, bearing nuts in a prickly bur (see illustration page 864); 2, the nut or the timber of this tree; 3, a reddish-brown color; 4, a horse of such color; 5, *Slang,* an old or stale joke:—*adj.* 1, made of the wood of the chestnut; 2, reddish brown.

CHESTNUT BUR

chev-a-lier (shĕv′ȧ-lĭr′), *n.* 1, a knight; 2, in France, a member of an order of merit, as The Legion of Honor.

chev-i-ot (shĕv′ĭ-ŭt; chĕv′ĭ-ŭt), *n.* 1, a kind of rough woolen fabric; 2, a similar fabric made of cotton.

chev-ron (shĕv′rŭn), *n.* the badge, consisting of two or more stripes meeting at an angle, on the coat sleeve of a noncommissioned officer, a policeman, etc., to show his rank.

CHEVRONS

1, of corporal; 2, of sergeant; 3, of regimental sergeant major.

chew (chōō), *v.t.* to crush and grind with the teeth:—*v.i.* to bite repeatedly with the teeth:—*n.* 1, the act of chewing; 2, that which can be chewed, as a quid of tobacco.

chew-ing gum, a preparation of sweetened and flavored chicle for chewing.

[1]**Chey-enne** (shī-ĕn′), a city, capital of Wyoming (map **9**).

[2]**Chey-enne** (shī-ĕn′), *n.* a member of a western tribe of Algonquian Indians.

chic (shēk; shĭk), *n. Colloquial,* Parisian cleverness in dress; hence, smartness; style:—*adj.* stylish.

Chi-ca-go (shĭ-kô′gō; shĭ-kä′gō), a large city of Illinois on Lake Michigan (map **7**).

chi-can-er-y (shĭ-kā′nẽr-ĭ), *n.* [*pl.* chicaneries], trickery; shrewd or sharp dealing.

chick (chĭk), *n.* 1, the young of a bird, especially of the hen; 2, a child.

chick-a-dee (chĭk′ȧ-dē′), *n.* a small, gray bird with a black cap.

chick-en (chĭk′ĕn), *n.* 1, the young of a fowl, especially of the domestic fowl; 2, a hen or rooster; 3, the flesh of such fowl, prepared for the table; as, roast *chicken*.

CHICKADEE

chicken pox (pŏks), a mild contagious disease of children.

chick-weed (chĭk′wēd′), *n.* a common, white-flowering weed, the seeds and young leaves of which are eaten by birds.

chi-cle (chē′kl), *n.* a gum extracted from certain Central American trees: the chief ingredient of chewing gum.

chic-o-ry (chĭk′ō-rĭ), *n.* 1, a plant with blue flowers, the leaves of which are used as salad; 2, the root of this plant which, when roasted, is used to adulterate coffee.

chid (chĭd), a form of the past tense and past participle of *chide*.

chide (chīd), *v.i.* and *v.t.* [*p.t.* chid (chĭd) or chid-ed (chī′dĕd), *p.p.* chid, chid-den (chĭd′n), or chid-ed, *p.pr.* chid-ing], to find fault (with); scold.

Syn. blame, rebuke, censure, reprimand.

chief (chēf), *n.* a commander, leader, or principal person in an organization or group:—*adj.* principal; leading; most important; as, the *chief* news of the day.

chief-ly (chēf′lĭ), *adv.* principally; for the most part.

chief-tain (chēf′tĭn), *n.* a leader or commander; especially, the military or civil head of a clan or tribe.

chif-fon (shĭf′ŏn; shĭ-fŏn′), *n.* a soft, thin, transparent fabric:—*adj.* very light and sheer in weight; as, *chiffon* hosiery.

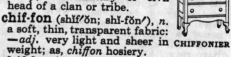

CHIFFONIER

chif-fo-nier (shĭf′ō-nĭr′), *n.* a high chest of drawers, sometimes with a mirror.

chig-ger (chĭg′ẽr), *n.* a mite that burrows under the skin, causing intense itching. Also called **chig′oe** (chĭg′ō).

chil·blain (chĭl′blān′), *n.* an itching sore, usually on the foot or hand, resulting from exposure to cold.

child (chīld), *n.* [*pl.* children (chĭl′drĕn)], 1, a boy or a girl; 2, a son or a daughter; offspring; 3, a baby; 4, a descendant; as, a *child* of Abraham; 5, a product, as of habit, environment, or temperament; as, a *child* of poverty.

child·birth (chīld′bûrth′), *n.* the act of bringing forth a child.

child·hood (chīld′hŏŏd), *n.* 1, the years during which one is a child; 2, the state of being a child.

child·ish (chīld′ĭsh), *adj.* 1, like a child; 2, weak; foolish; as, a *childish* impulse in an adult.—*n.* **child′ish·ness**.

child·less (chīld′lĕs), *adj.* having no child; without offspring.

child·like (chīld′līk′), *adj.* like a child; especially, having the good qualities of a child; hence, dutiful; trustful.

chil·dren (chĭl′drĕn), plural of *child.*

child's play, something easily done; as, winning that set was *child's play.*

Chil·e (chĭl′ē) or **Chil·i** (chĭl′ĭ), a republic (cap. Santiago) in western South America (map 11).—*n.* and *adj.* **Chil′e·an; Chil′i·an**.

chil·i or **chil·li** (chĭl′ĭ), *n.* a tropical plant, the pods of which, red when ripe, are dried and powdered to make cayenne pepper; also, the pods.

chill (chĭl), *n.* 1, coldness; 2, a sudden coldness of body with shivering; as, *chills* and fever; 3, a check upon enthusiasm; as, she put a *chill* on the party:—*adj.* 1, cool; as, a *chill* breeze; 2, unfriendly; not cordial; as, a *chill* welcome:—*v.t.* to make cold:—*v.i.* to become or feel cold.

chill·y (chĭl′ĭ), *adj.* [chill-i-er, chill-i-est], 1, unpleasantly cool; 2, cool in manner.

chime (chīm), *n.* 1, a set of bells musically attuned, as the bells in a clock tower; 2, (often *chimes*), the music of such bells:—*v.i.* [chimed, chim-ing], 1, to sound in harmony; as, hear the bells *chiming;* 2, to agree; as, your opinion *chimes* with mine:—*v.t.* to announce (the hour) by chimes.

chi·me·ra (kĭ-mē′rá; kī-mē′rá), *n.* 1, in mythology, a she-monster, with a lion's head, goat's body, and serpent's tail; 2, hence, a frightful or mad fancy. Also spelled **chi·mae′ra**.

chim·ney (chĭm′nĭ), *n.* [*pl.* chimneys], 1, the upright tube or flue, made of brick, stone, or the like, through which smoke and heated air may escape from a building (see illustration under *frame house);* 2, the part of a flue above a roof; 3, a glass

tube around the flame of a lamp:—**chimney sweep,** a man or boy who cleans chimneys.

chim·pan·zee (chĭm-păn-zē′; chĭm-păn′zē), *n.* a blackish-brown, anthropoid, or man-like ape of Africa, smaller than the go-rilla.

CHIMPANZEE (¹⁄₃₀)

chin (chĭn), *n.* the part of the face below the under lip; also, the rounded tip of the lower jaw:—*v.t.* [chinned, chin-ning], to pull (oneself) up, while hanging by the hands from a hori-zontal bar, until one's chin is on a level with the bar.

Chi·na (chī′ná), a republic (cap. Peiping) in eastern Asia (map 15). It was an em-pire until 1912.

chi·na (chī′ná), *n.* 1, porcelain or porce-lain ware, brought originally from the Far East; 2, porcelain or earthenware dishes of any kind:—*adj.* made of porcelain.

chinch bug (chĭnch), an insect which in the U.S. destroys grass and grains.

chin·chil·la (chĭn-chĭl′á), *n.* 1, a small, South American, gnawing animal with a soft, fine, gray fur; 2, the fur of this ani-mal; 3, a heavy woolen cloth.

CHINCHILLA (¼)

chi·ne·la (chē-nā′lä), *n.* a flat slipper with no heel, worn by Philippine women.

Chi·nese (chī′nēz′; chī′nēs′), *adj.* per-taining to the country, the people, or the language, of China:—*n.* 1, [*pl.* Chinese], a native of China or the descendant of one; 2, the language of the Chinese.

¹**chink** (chĭngk), *n.* a narrow crack or opening; as, you can see through the *chink* in the wall:—*v.t.* 1, to make fissures or cracks in; 2, to fill the cracks of.

²**chink** (chĭngk), *n.* a sharp, ringing sound as of glass or metal struck lightly:—*v.t.* to cause to jingle:—*v.i.* to jingle.

chi·nook (chĭ-nŏŏk′; chī-nŏŏk′), *n.* 1, a warm, damp, southwest wind on the coast of Washington and Oregon, named from the Chinook Indians who once lived there; 2, a warm, dry wind that comes down from the Rocky Mountains.

chintz (chĭnts), *n.* a cotton cloth, printed in colored patterns, often with a smooth, glossy finish.

chip (chĭp), *v.t.* [chipped, chip-ping], **1,** to cut or break small bits or pieces from; **2,** to shape by cutting away small bits; as, to *chip* an arrow from flint:—*v.i.* to break off in small bits; as, these cups *chip* easily:—*n.* **1,** a small piece, as of stone or wood, cut or broken off; also, the gap left; as, a *chip* in the saucer; **2,** a very small piece, as of a diamond; **3,** a counter or disk used in games; as, a poker *chip.*

chip-munk (chĭp′mŭngk), *n.* a small, striped, squirrel-like animal.

chip-ping spar-row, a small sparrow very common in eastern North America.

chi-rop-o-dist (kī-rŏp′ô-dĭst; kĭ-rŏp′ô-dĭst), *n.* one who treats ailments, especially minor ailments, of the feet.

CHIPMUNK (!)

chi-ro-prac-tic (kī′rō-prăk′tĭk), *n.* a system of treatment of bodily disorders by manipulating the joints, especially of the spine, without the use of drugs or surgery:—*adj.* having to do with this method.

chi-ro-prac-tor (kī′rō-prăk′tẽr), *n.* one who treats bodily diseases by manipulating the joints, especially of the spine.

chirp (chûrp), *n.* a short, cheerful note, as that of a bird:—*v.i.* **1,** to utter such a note; **2,** to talk merrily:—*v.t.* to utter (a sound) resembling a chirp.

chir-rup (chĭr′ŭp), *v.i.* and *v.t.* [chirruped, chirrup-ing], to chirp repeatedly, as does a cricket:—*n.* a chirp or chirping.

chis-el (chĭz′l), *n.* a steel-edged tool for cutting wood, stone, or metal:—*v.t.* and *v.i.* [chiseled, chiseling], **1,** to cut or engrave with such a tool; **2,** *Slang:* **a,** to cheat; **b,** to secure (something) by shrewd, often unfair, means.
CHISEL

chiv-al-ric (shĭv′ăl-rĭk; shĭ-văl′rĭk), *adj.* knightly; of courteous spirit.

chiv-al-rous (shĭv′ăl-rŭs), *adj.* **1,** relating to chivalry; **2,** gallant; considerate: used especially of a gentleman in reference to his manner toward a lady.

chiv-al-ry (shĭv′ăl-rĭ), *n.* **1,** the system of knighthood in the Middle Ages; **2,** the characteristics of an ideal knight, as courage, nobility, courtesy, respect for women, and the like; **3,** a body of knights; hence, a company of gallant gentlemen.

chive (chīv), *n.* a plant similar to the onion, used for seasoning.

chlor-al (klôr′ăl; klō-răl′), *n.* a sleep-producing drug.

chlor-ide of lime (klôr′īd; klôr′ĭd), a grayish-white powder, used as a bleach and as a disinfectant.

chlor-ine (klôr′ēn; klôr′ĭn), *n.* a greenish-yellow gaseous element, used for bleaching and for purifying water.

chlor-o-form (klôr′ô-fôrm), *n.* a colorless liquid with sweetish odor, used in surgery to produce unconsciousness:—*v.t.* to make unconscious or to kill with chloroform.

chlor-o-phyll or **chlor-o-phyl** (klôr′ô-fĭl), *n.* the green coloring matter of plants.

chock (chŏk), *n.* **1,** a block or wedge to fill in a space so as to prevent motion; as, to put a *chock* under the wheel of a cart; **2,** on a ship, a metal casting or wooden part for ropes or cables to run through:—*v.t.* to furnish, wedge, or make fast with a chock:—*adv.* as tight or close as possible; as, a car *chock* against the curb.
CHOCK, def. 2

choc-o-late (chŏk′ô-lĭt), *n.* **1,** a food substance obtained by roasting and grinding cacao seeds; **2,** a small piece of candy made of, or coated with, this substance; **3,** a drink made from this food with milk and sugar:—*adj.* **1,** made of, or flavored with, chocolate; **2,** of the dark-brown color of chocolate.

choice (chois), *n.* **1,** selection; as, make your *choice*; also, power of selection; as, you have your *choice*; **2,** the thing or person chosen; as, the president is the *choice* of the nation; **3,** the best or most desirable part or thing; as, this puppy is the *choice* of the litter; **4,** a number large enough to choose from; as, a *choice* of hats:—*adj.* [choic-er, choic-est], **1,** select; particularly fine; as, *choice* meats; **2,** selected with care; appropriate.

choir (kwīr), *n.* **1,** a group of trained singers, especially in a church; **2,** the part of the church in which they sing.

choke (chōk), *v.t.* [choked, chok-ing], **1,** to stop the breath of; stifle; as, this collar *chokes* me; **2,** to check the growth of by stifling, or as if by stifling; as, weeds *choked* the garden; to *choke* the fire; **3,** to cut down the air intake of the carburetor of (a motor) to enrich the mixture; as, to *choke* an engine; **4,** to block up; clog; as, rubbish *choked* the alley; **5,** to suppress (an emotion); as, to *choke* down anger:—*v.i.* to become suffocated:—*n.* **1,** the act or sound of strangling; **2,** in an automobile, the carburetor valve which regulates the air intake.

chol-er (kŏl′ẽr), *n.* anger; irritability.—*adj.* **chol′er-ic.**

chol-er-a (kŏl′ẽr-à), *n.* **1, cholera morbus** (môr′bŭs) or **summer cholera,** an acute, noninfectious inflammation of the digestive tract, occurring in hot summer months; **2, Asiatic cholera,** an infectious and often rapidly fatal disease.

choose (chooz), *v.t.* [*p.t.* chose (chōz), *p.p.* cho-sen (chō′zn), *p.pr.* choos-ing], **1,** to pick; select from a number; as, he *chose* the reddest apple; **2,** to prefer; see fit; as, he *chose* to run:—*v.i.* to make a choice.

¹**chop** (chŏp), *v.t.* [chopped, chop-ping], **1,** to cut with repeated blows; as, to *chop* wood; **2,** to cut into very small pieces; as, to *chop* vegetables; **3,** to cut short, as words:—*v.i.* to make a quick stroke, as with an ax:—*n.* **1,** a small piece of meat containing a rib or section of bone; as, a lamb *chop;* **2,** a short, rough movement of the waves.—*n.* **chop′per.**

²**chop** (chŏp), *v.i.* [chopped, chop-ping], to veer; shift suddenly, as the wind.

³**chop** (chŏp), *n.* **1,** a jaw; **2, chops,** the mouth or the fleshy parts about it.

Cho-pin (shô′păn′), Frédéric François (1809–1849), a French-Polish composer.

¹**chop-py** (chŏp′ĭ), *adj.* [chop-pi-er, chop-pi-est], full of short, rough waves; as, a *choppy* sea.

²**chop-py** (chŏp′ĭ), *adj.* [chop-pi-er, chop-pi-est], changeable; as, a *choppy* wind.

chop-sticks (chŏp′stĭks′), *n.pl.* two small sticks of wood, ivory, or the like, used instead of a fork, especially by the Chinese.

chor-al (kôr′ăl), *adj.* **1,** pertaining to a choir or chorus; as, *choral* singing; **2,** sung by a choir; as, a *choral* service.

¹**chord** (kôrd), *n.* **1,** a string of a musical instrument; **2,** in geometry, a straight line joining two points on the circumference of a circle; **3,** in the body, a chordlike structure; tendon.

²**chord** (kôrd), *n.* in music, a combination of three or more tones sounded together and in harmony.

CHORDS (AB, AC)

chore (chôr), *n.* **1,** a small job; **2, chores,** small or odd jobs; the daily humdrum work of a farm or household.

cho-re-a (kō-rē′à), *n.* a nervous disease characterized by twitching and jerking; St. Vitus's dance.

chor-is-ter (kŏr′is-tẽr), *n.* **1,** a member of a choir; especially, a boy singer; **2,** in the U.S., the leader of a church choir.

chor-tle (chôr′tl), *v.i.* and *v.t.* [chor-tled, chor-tling], to laugh with chuckling sounds or in snorting fashion.

chor-us (kôr′ŭs), *n.* **1,** a group of persons singing together or their song; also, any utterance by a number of persons at one time; as, a *chorus* of shouts; **2,** a piece of music arranged to be sung by a number of voices all together; **3,** a refrain at the end of each verse of a song:—*v.t.* and *v.i.* to sing or utter all together.

chose (chōz), past tense of *choose.*

cho-sen (chō′zn), past participle of *choose.*

Cho-sen (chō′sĕn′), a peninsula east of China, from 1910–1945 part of the Japanese Empire (map 15). Name restored to *Korea* after World War II.

chow (chou) or **chow-chow** (chou′chou′), *n.* a dog of a breed originating in China, having a muscular body, a heavy coat, and a short tail which curls over the back.

chow-der (chou′dẽr), *n.* a soup made by stewing fish, clams, or a vegetable, usually in milk, with bits of pork, onions, etc.

Christ (krīst), *n.* used as a title of Jesus, meaning the Messiah, whose coming was foretold by the Jewish prophets.

chris-ten (krĭs′n), *v.t.* **1,** to baptize; **2,** to name; as, to *christen* a ship; **3,** *Colloquial,* to use for the first time; as, to *christen* the new car.—*n.* **chris′ten-ing.**

Chris-ten-dom (krĭs′n-dŭm), *n.* all Christian lands and peoples.

Chris-tian (krĭs′chăn; krĭst′yăn), *n.* a believer in the religion of Christ; a member of the Christian church:—*adj.* **1,** believing in, or practicing, the religion of Christ; **2,** pertaining to Christ, his followers, or his teachings; **3,** showing Christlike qualities, as gentleness, forbearance, etc.:— **Christian name,** a person's first name.

Chris-ti-an-i-ty (krĭs′chĭ-ăn′ĭ-tĭ; krĭs′-tĭ-ăn′ĭ-tĭ), *n.* **1,** the religion or doctrines taught by Christ; **2,** all who are Christians; **3,** Christian character or qualities.

Chris-tian-ize (krĭs′chăn-īz; krĭst′yăn-īz), *v.t.* [Christianized, Christianiz-ing], to convert to Christianity; make Christian. —*n.* **Chris′tian-i-za′tion.**

Chris-tian Sci-ence, a religion founded by Mary Baker Eddy (1821–1910).

Christ-mas (krĭs′màs), *n.* the yearly festival (December 25) in honor of the birth of Christ.—*n.* **Christ′mas-tide′.**

chro-mat-ic (krō-măt′ĭk), *adj.* pertaining to color:—**chromatic scale,** in music, a scale in which the intervals are half steps, played by striking all the keys, white and black, in order, from any key on a piano to the key an octave above.

chrome (krōm), *n.* chromium.

āte, âorta, râre, căt, ȧsk, fär, ăllow, sofȧ; ēve, ĕvent, ĕll, writẽr, novĕl; bīte, pĭn; nō, ōbey, ôr, dŏg, tŏp, cŏllide; ūnit, ūnite, bûrn, cŭt, focŭs; noon, foot; mound; coin;

chro·mi·um (krō′mĭ-ŭm), *n.* a grayish-white, rust-resisting metallic element, much used for plating and alloys.

chron. abbreviation for *chronological, chronology.*

chron·ic (krŏn′ĭk), *adj.* **1,** continuing for a long time; as, he has a *chronic* cold; **2,** habitual; as, a *chronic* complainer.

chron·i·cle (krŏn′ĭ-kl), *n.* a record of events in the order of their happening:—*v.t.* [chroni-cled, chroni-cling], to enter, as in a record.—*n.* **chron′i·cler.**

Syn., n. annals, archives, record.

Chron·i·cles (krŏn′ĭ-klz), *n.* either of two historical books of the Old Testament.

chron·o·log·i·cal (krŏn′ō-lŏj′-ĭ-kăl), *adj.* arranged in the order of time; as, a *chronological* list of the year's events.

chro·nol·o·gy (krō-nŏl′ō-jĭ), *n.* [*pl.* chronologies], **1,** the science that deals with events and arranges their dates in proper order; **2,** a table of events given in the order of their occurrence; as, a *chronology* of the war.

CHRYSALIS OF A BUTTERFLY

chrys·a·lis (krĭs′ȧ-lĭs), *n.* [*pl.* chrysalises], **1,** the inactive form through which an insect, especially a moth or a butterfly, passes when it leaves the caterpillar stage and before it reaches its winged or perfect form; **2,** the case enclosing the insect during that stage; a cocoon.

chrys·an·the·mum (krĭs-ăn′thē-mŭm; krĭz-ăn′thē-mŭm), *n.* **1,** a plant with showy flowers that blooms late in the fall; **2,** a flower of this plant.

CHRYSANTHEMUMS

chrys·o·lite (krĭs′ō-līt), *n.* an olive-green material, which, when transparent, is used as a gem.

chub (chŭb), *n.* a kind of fresh-water fish.

chub·by (chŭb′ĭ), *adj.* [chub-bi-er, chub-bi-est], plump and round; as, a baby's *chubby* fists.—*n.* **chub′bi·ness.**

¹chuck (chŭk), *v.t.* **1,** to tap or pat under the chin affectionately or playfully; **2,** to fling away; throw; toss; as, *chuck* me the suitcase:—*n.* a light tap; a pat under the chin.

²chuck (chŭk), *n.* **1,** a clamp for holding a tool or piece of work in a lathe or drill press; **2,** the part of a side of beef or of a carcass of lamb or mutton, including most of the neck, the shoulder, and about three ribs (see illustration under *beef*).

chuck·le (chŭk′l), *n.* a quiet, suppressed laugh:—*v.i.* [chuck-led, chuck-ling], to laugh quietly to oneself.

chug (chŭg), *n.* a sharp, explosive sound, as that made by the exhaust from an engine:—*v.i.* [chugged, chug-ging], to make, or move with, such sounds; as, the car *chugged* along.

chum (chŭm), *n.* **1,** a roommate, as at school; **2,** an intimate friend:—*v.i.* [chummed, chum-ming], **1,** to occupy the same room; **2,** to be very friendly.—*adj.* **chum′my.**

Chung·king (chŏong′kĭng′), a city in western China (map 15).

chunk (chŭngk), *n.* a short, thick piece; as, a *chunk* of meat.

church (chûrch), *n.* **1,** a building for public Christian worship; **2,** the entire body of Christians; **3,** (usually *Church*), a particular body or division of Christians; a denomination; as, the Methodist *Church*; **4,** a regular service for Christian worship:—*adj.* having to do with a church; as, *church* music; *church* architecture.

church·man (chûrch′măn), *n.* [*pl.* church-men (-mĕn)], **1,** a clergyman; **2,** a member of a church.

Church of Eng·land, the established episcopal church in England and Wales of which the King of England is the head.

church·ward·en (chûrch′wôr′dn), *n.* in the Episcopal church, a parish officer who looks after church property, finances, etc.

church·yard (chûrch′yärd′), *n.* the ground around a church, part of which is often used for burial.

churl (chûrl), *n.* **1,** formerly, a person of low birth; **2,** a surly, ill-bred person.—*adj.* **churl′ish.**—*adv.* **churl′ish·ly.**

churn (chûrn), *n.* a vessel in which milk or cream is made into butter:—*v.t.* **1,** to make (butter) by violently stirring cream; **2,** to stir by violent motion; as, the propeller *churned* the water:—*v.i.* **1,** to work a churn; **2,** foam; seethe; wash to and fro; as, the water *churns* around the rocks.

chute (shoot), *n.* **1,** a slanting trough for sliding things down; as, a coal *chute*; **2,** a rapid in a stream; a shoot; **3,** a toboggan slide:—*v.t.* [chut-ed, chut-ing], to send down a chute.

D

SIMPLE FORM OF CHURN

D, dasher.

ci·ca·da (sĭ-kā′dȧ; sĭ-kä′dȧ), *n.* [*pl.* ci-cadas], a large insect with four transparent wings, noted for the long, shrill, chirping sound made by the male.

Cic·e·ro (sĭs'ĕ·rō), Marcus Tullius (106–43 B.C.), a Roman writer, orator, and statesman. —*adj.* **Cic'e·ro'ni·an.**

ci·der (sī'dẽr), *n.* apple juice; also, cherry juice: used as a drink or for making vinegar. **hard,** or **sweet, cider,** fermented, or unfermented, apple juice.

CICADA (?)

Cien·fue·gos (syĕn·fwä'gōs), a seaport of Cuba (map **10**).

ci·gar (sĭ·gär'), *n.* a roll of tobacco leaf, used for smoking.

cig·a·rette (sĭg'á·rĕt'), *n.* a small roll made of finely cut tobacco wrapped in thin paper for smoking.

cil·i·a (sĭl'ĭ·á), *n.pl.* **1,** eyelashes; **2,** similar hairlike processes, as on plant leaves, insect wings, etc.—*adj.* **cil'i·ar·y.**

Cim·me·ri·an (sĭ·mē'rĭ·ăn), *adj.* **1,** belonging to the Cimmerii, a people mentioned by Homer as living in constant darkness; **2,** hence, very dark; gloomy.

cinch (sĭnch), *n.* **1,** a saddle girth firmly fastened in place by loops and knots; **2,** *Colloquial,* a sure grip or hold; **3,** *Slang,* a sure or easy thing:—*v.t.* **1,** to put a cinch upon; **2,** *Slang,* to get a sure hold on.

cin·cho·na (sĭn·kō'ná), *n.* an evergreen tree of South America, the dried bark of which is a source of quinine.

Cin·cin·nat·i (sĭn/sĭ·năt'ĭ; sĭn/sĭ·năt/á), a city in Ohio (map **7**).

Cin·cin·na·tus (sĭn/sĭ·nā'tŭs), (519?–439?), a Roman dictator.

cinc·ture (sĭngk'tûr), *n.* a belt or girdle worn round the waist:—*v.t.* [cinctured, cinctur·ing], to surround with a girdle.

cin·der (sĭn'dẽr), *n.* **1,** a piece of partly burned coal or wood which has ceased to flame; **2, cinders,** ashes.

Cin·der·el·la (sĭn/dẽr·ĕl'á), *n.* **1,** in an old fairy tale, a maiden compelled to serve her stepsisters as a drudge until, aided by her fairy godmother, she marries a prince; **2,** hence, a drudge; also, one to whom unexpected good fortune comes.

cin·e·ma (sĭn'ĕ·má), *n.* chiefly British, a motion-picture theater; also, a photoplay.

cin·na·mon (sĭn'á·mŭn), *n.* **1,** an East Indian tree; also, its bark or the spice made from it; **2,** a red-brown color.

C I O or **C. I. O.** abbreviation for *Congress of Industrial Organizations.*

ci·pher or **cy·pher** (sī'fẽr), *n.* **1,** in mathematics, zero; naught [symbol 0]; **2,** hence, a person or thing without value or power; **3,** a secret manner of writing,

or the key to it; a code:—*v.t.* and *v.i.* **1,** to work (arithmetical examples) with figures; calculate; **2,** to write in code.

Cir·cas·si·a (sẽr·kăsh'ĭ·á; sẽr·kăsh'á), the former name of a region on the northeastern shore of the Black Sea.

Cir·ce (sûr'sē), *n.* **1,** in Homer's "Odyssey," an enchantress who changed the companions of Odysseus into swine; **2,** hence, any enchantress.

cir·cle (sûr'kl), *n.* **1,** a plane surface bounded by a single curved line called its circumference, every part of which is equally distant from a point within it, called the center; also, the curve bounding such a surface; **2,** any flat, round body; **3,** anything resembling a circle or part of a circle; as, the family *circle* in a theater; **4,** a completed series; a system; cycle; round; as, the *circle* of the months; **5,** a number of persons grouped around a central interest or person; as, a *circle* of friends:—*v.i.* [cir-cled, cir-cling], to move in a circle; as, the airplane *circled* above:—*v.t.* **1,** to surround; as, a ring *circled* his finger; **2,** to revolve around; as, the earth *circles* the sun.—*n.* **cir'cler.**

CIRCLE

cir·clet (sûr'klĕt), *n.* **1,** a small circle; **2,** a circular ornament for the head, arm, neck, or finger.

cir·cuit (sûr'kĭt), *n.* **1,** the boundary line around an area; also, the space enclosed; **2,** the distance around any space, whether circular or of other form; **3,** the act of going around anything; revolution; as, the *circuit* of the earth around the sun; **4,** the regular traveling from place to place of a judge or other person for the purpose of holding court or performing other specific duties; also, the territory or district over which he travels; **5,** the path of an electric current; **6,** a group of theaters under the same management.

cir·cu·i·tous (sẽr·kū'ĭ·tŭs), *adj.* roundabout; indirect; as, to go by a *circuitous* route.—*adv.* **cir·cu'i·tous·ly.**

cir·cu·lar (sûr'kú·lẽr), *adj.* **1,** of, pertaining to, or like, a circle; as, a *circular* saw; **2,** moving in a circle; as, *circular* motion; **3,** published for distribution to a group of persons; as, a *circular* letter:—*n.* a printed letter or notice for general distribution.—*adv.* **cir'cu·lar·ly.**

cir·cu·lar·ize (sûr'kú·lẽr·īz), *v.t.* [circularized, circulariz·ing], to send printed circulars to, for advertising.

cir·cu·late (sûr'kú·lāt), *v.i.* [circulat·ed, circulat·ing], **1,** to pass from place to place; as, he *circulated* among the guests; **2,** to move around in a course; as, in that heat-

āte, āorta, râre, căt, ȧsk, fär, ȧllow, sofá; ēve, ĕvent, ĕll, writẽr, novĕl; bīte, pĭn; nō, ōbey, ôr, dŏg, tŏp, cŏllide; ūnit, ūnite, bûrn, cŭt, focŭs; noon, fŏŏt; mound; coin;

ing system hot water *circulates* through the pipes; **3,** to be distributed, as a newspaper:—*v.t.* to send round; as, he *circulated* the report.

cir·cu·la·tion (sûr'kū-lā'shŭn), *n.* **1,** the act of moving around, or of passing or sending from place to place; as, the new coins have been put into *circulation;* **2,** the extent to which a thing is distributed or sent; as, the *circulation* of a magazine; **3,** movement in a course which leads back to the starting point; especially, the movement of the blood through the vessels of the body.

cir·cu·la·tor·y (sûr'kū-là-tôr'ĭ), *adj.* pertaining to the movement of the blood through the vessels of the body, or of any similar current of fluid.

cir·cum- (sûr'kŭm-), a prefix meaning around; roundabout; as, *circum*navigate.

cir·cum·cise (sûr'kŭm-sīz), *v.t.* [circumcised, circumcis-ing], to cut off part or all of the foreskin.

cir·cum·ci·sion (sûr'kŭm-sĭzh'ŭn), *n.* **1,** the act of cutting off part or all of the foreskin, a rite practiced by Jews, Mohammedans, and others; **2,** in the Bible, spiritual purification:—**The Circumcision, 1,** in the Bible, the Jews; **2,** a festival commemorating the circumcision of Jesus, observed January 1.

cir·cum·fer·ence (sĕr-kŭm'fĕr-ĕns), *n.* **1,** the line that bounds a circle or any curved plane figure; **2,** the distance around a circular body or area; circuit.

cir·cum·flex (sûr'kŭm-flĕks), *n.* **1,** a mark [^ ˘ ~] over a letter to denote length, contraction, etc.; **2,** the pronunciation or accent given such a letter:—*adj.* pronounced or marked with such an accent.

cir·cum·lo·cu·tion (sûr'kŭm-lō-kū'-shŭn), *n.* the use of many words where but few are necessary; indirect expression.

cir·cum·nav·i·gate (sûr'kŭm-năv'ĭ-gāt), *v.t.* [circumnavigat-ed, circumnavigat-ing], to sail completely around (the earth, an island, etc.).—*n.* **cir'cum·nav'i·ga'tion.**

cir·cum·scribe (sûr'kŭm-skrīb'), *v.t.* [circumscribed, circumscrib-ing], **1,** to draw a line around; **2,** hence, to restrict; as, to *circumscribe* the powers of a king.

cir·cum·spect (sûr'kŭm-spĕkt), *adj.* cautious; considering all sides of a problem before acting.—*n.* **cir'cum·spec'tion.**

cir·cum·stance (sûr'kŭm-stăns), *n.* **1,** an incident, occurrence, or fact relating to another fact, and throwing light on its meaning, importance, etc.; **2,** a detail; as, one *circumstance* was overlooked; **3,** pomp; ceremony; **4, circumstances, a,** the conditions under which an act occurs, such as time, place, or cause, etc.; as, the meeting occurred under peculiar *circumstances;* **b,** a condition or state of affairs; material welfare; as, he is living in poor *circumstances.*

cir·cum·stan·tial (sûr'kŭm-stăn'shăl), *adj.* **1,** consisting of, or based on, particular incidents or apparent facts; not direct; as, *circumstantial* evidence; **2,** detailed; as, a *circumstantial* report.—*adv.* **cir'cum·stan'tial·ly.**

cir·cum·vent (sûr'kŭm-vĕnt'), *v.t.* to get the better of by crafty means; get around; outwit.—*n.* **cir'cum·ven'tion.**

cir·cus (sûr'kŭs), *n.* **1,** a large level space surrounded by seats, usually within a tent, for displaying acrobatic feats, animals, etc.; **2,** the performance in such a space; also, the company of performers; **3,** in ancient Rome, an oblong space surrounded on three sides by tiers of seats, used for chariot races, games, etc.

cir·rus (sĭr'ŭs), *n.* [*pl.* cirri (sĭr'ī)], a cloud formation in which the clouds spread in filmy wisps at a great height.

cis·tern (sĭs'tẽrn), *n.* a tank or artificial reservoir, often underground, for storing water or other liquids.

cit·a·del (sĭt'à-dĕl), *n.* **1,** a fortress, especially one defending a city; **2,** any strongly fortified place; any refuge.

ci·ta·tion (sī-tā'shŭn), *n.* **1,** a summons to appear at a court of law; **2,** the act of quoting, or a passage quoted, as from a book; **3,** mention; especially, in war dispatches, honorable mention for bravery.

cite (sīt), *v.t.* [cit-ed, cit-ing], **1,** to summon to appear in court; **2,** to quote; as, a minister *cites* as his text a passage from the Bible; **3,** to bring forward as proof; as, the lawyer *cited* the evidence; **4,** to give honorable mention to.

cit·i·zen (sĭt'ĭ-zĕn), *n.* **1,** an inhabitant; a resident of a town or city; as, the *citizens* of New York; **2,** a member of a state or nation who enjoys political rights and privileges, and gives in return his allegiance to the government; **3,** a civilian as distinguished from a soldier, policeman, etc.

cit·i·zen·ry (sĭt'ĭ-zĕn-rĭ), *n.* the body of citizens, especially as distinguished from officials or soldiery.

cit·i·zen·ship (sĭt'ĭ-zĕn-shĭp'), *n.* the status of a person who owes allegiance to the government in return for his political rights and privileges.

cit·ric (sĭt'rĭk), *adj.* pertaining to, or derived from lemons, oranges, and other citrus fruits; as, *citric* acid.

cit·ron (sĭt'rŭn), *n.* **1,** a small tree or shrub of oriental origin; **2,** its fruit, like the lemon, but larger and not so acid; **3,** the thick rind of this fruit, used in cooking.

cit-rus or **cit-rous** (sĭt′rŭs), *adj.* of or relating to a group of trees which includes the orange, lemon, lime, citron, etc.

cit-y (sĭt′ĭ), *n.* [*pl.* cities], 1, a large and important town; also, its inhabitants; 2, in the U.S. and Canada, a municipality having local self-government.

Ciu-dad Tru-jil-lo (syōō-thäth′trōō-hēl′-yō), a city, the capital of the Dominican Republic (map 10). Also called *Trujillo.*

civ-et (sĭv′ĕt), *n.*, a thick substance of a yellowish color and a musklike odor, secreted by the the civet cat: used in making perfumes:—**civet cat,** a gray, catlike animal with black stripes and spots.

CIVET CAT (⅒)

civ-ic (sĭv′ĭk), *adj.* of or relating to a city, a citizen, or citizenship; as, *civic* beauty; *civic* rights:—**civics,** *n.pl.* used as *sing.* the study of city government or of good citizenship.

civ-il (sĭv′ĭl), *adj.* 1, of, relating to, or characteristic of, a city, its government, or its citizens; as, *civil* duties; 2, pertaining to civilians; not military or ecclesiastical; 3, formally polite; often, barely polite.—*adv.* **civ′il-ly.**
    Syn. obliging, well-bred, respectful.

ci-vil-ian (sĭ-vĭl′yăn), *n.* one who is neither a soldier nor a sailor.

ci-vil-i-ty (sĭ-vĭl′ĭ-tĭ), *n.* [*pl.* civilities], politeness; an act of courtesy.

civ-i-li-za-tion (sĭv′ĭ-lĭ-zā′shŭn; -lĭ-zā′-shŭn), *n.* 1, the act of making or becoming less savage or barbarous; as, the *civilization* of man has been a slow process; 2, the state of being refined in manners; culture; refinement; also, a particular stage or type of this; as, Greek *civilization* is older than Roman; 3, collectively, those countries which are in a high stage of development.

civ-i-lize (sĭv′ĭ-līz), *v.t.* [civilized, civilizing], to bring out of a savage or barbarous way of living.

civ-il serv-ice, the departments of the government administration which are not naval, military, judiciary, or legislative.

civil war, a war between different sections or parties of the same nation:—**Civil War,** in the U.S., the war (1861–65) between the North and the South.

clack (klăk), *v.i.* 1, to make a sudden, sharp sound; 2, to chatter; 3, to cackle, as a hen:—*n.* 1, a sudden, sharp sound or succession of sounds; as, the *clack* of a typewriter; 2, continual prattle.

clad (klăd), past tense and past participle of *clothe.*

claim (klām), *v.t.* 1, to demand or assert as one's own or one's due; as, to *claim* an inheritance; 2, to call for; deserve; as, this matter *claims* our attention; 3, *Colloquial,* to maintain; as, I *claim* this to be true:—*n.* 1, a demand for something as due; as, he put in a *claim* for damages; 2, an assertion of a right to something; as, I have a *claim* to the property; 3, the thing demanded; especially, a piece of land which a miner marks out.—*n.* **claim′ant.**

clair-voy-ance (klâr-voi′ăns), *n.* 1, the power claimed by some persons of seeing that which others cannot see, or of reading minds; 2, unusual insight.

clair-voy-ant (klâr-voi′ănt), *n.* one who professes to have the power of seeing that which others cannot see, or of reading minds; a medium:—*adj.* relating to the powers of a clairvoyant.

clam (klăm), *n.* an edible shellfish with a hinged double shell, living partly or wholly buried in sand or mud:—*v.i.* [clammed, clam-ming], to dig for clams.

clam-bake (klăm′bāk′), *n.* in the U.S., a picnic where clams are cooked, as on hot stones with a covering of seaweed.

CLAM (¼)

clam-ber (klăm′bĕr), *v.t.* and *v.i.* to ascend or climb with difficulty; as, to *clamber* up a rocky slope.

clam-my (klăm′ĭ), *adj.* [clam-mi-er, clam-mi-est], damp, soft, and cold.

clam-or (klăm′ẽr), *n.* a loud and continued outcry; a loud and persistent demand:—*v.i.* to make noisy demands; as, to *clamor* for food.
    Syn., *n.* uproar, racket, noise, tumult.

clam-or-ous (klăm′ẽr-ŭs), *adj.* noisy; as, a *clamorous* mob.—*adv.* **clam′or-ous-ly.**

clamp (klămp), *n.* a device, as a brace, clasp, or band, usually of wood or metal, used to hold or press things together:—*v.t.* to fasten or bind with a clamp.

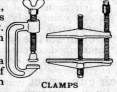

CLAMPS

clan (klăn), *n.* 1, a tribe or association of families, especially in the Scottish Highlands, united under one chieftain, claiming common ancestry, and having the same surname; 2, a group of people closely united by some common interest or pursuit; a set; clique.
    Syn. party, caste, class, club.

clan-des-tine (klăn-dĕs′tĭn), *adj.* secret; private; underhand; as, a *clandestine* meeting.—*adv.* **clan-des′tine-ly.**

clang (klăng), *n.* a loud, ringing, metallic sound; as, the *clang* of an anvil:—*v.i.* to give out such a sound; as, the bells *clanged;*—*v.t* to cause to give out such a sound; as, he *clanged* the cymbals.

clan-gor (klăng′gẽr; klăng′ẽr), *n.* a loud, metallic sound; a clang:—*v.i.* to ring repeatedly and noisily; as, the bells *clangored.* —*adj.* **clan′gor-ous.**

clank (klăngk), *n.* a sharp, harsh, brief, metallic sound:—*v.t.* and *v.i.* to rattle.

clan-nish (klăn′ĭsh), *adj.* closely united, as in a clan; exclusive; prejudiced; as, the mountaineers are a *clannish* people.—*n.* **clan′nish-ness.**

clans-man (klănz′măn), *n.* [*pl.* clansmen (-mĕn)], a member of a clan.

clap (klăp), *v.t.* [clapped, clap-ping], **1,** to strike together with a quick, sharp noise; **2,** to applaud by striking the hands together noisily; **3,** to put, place, etc., quickly and suddenly; as, they *clapped* him in jail; **4,** to strike or slap suddenly; as, he *clapped* me on the back:—*v.i.* **1,** to show approval by striking the hands together; **2,** to come together with a quick, sharp noise; as, the door *clapped* shut:—*n.* **1,** a loud noise made by, or as by, a sudden collision; as, a *clap* of thunder; **2,** applause; **3,** a slap; as, a *clap* on the back.

clap-board (klăp′bôrd; klăb′ẽrd), *n.* a long, narrow board, often wider at one edge than at the other, used to cover the outside of wooden houses:—*v.t.* to cover with such boards; as, to *clapboard* a house.

clap-per (klăp′ẽr), *n.* **1,** one who applauds by clapping; **2,** that which makes a clapping sound, especially the tongue of a bell.

clar-et (klăr′ĕt), *n.* **1,** a red wine; **2,** a deep, purplish-red color:—*adj.* purplish red.

clar-i-fi-ca-tion (klăr′ĭ-fĭ-kā′shŭn), *n.* the act of making clear, or the process of becoming clear; as, a *clarification* of ideas.

clar-i-fy (klăr′ĭ-fī), *v.t.* [clarified, clarify-ing], **1,** to make clear or pure; **2,** to make intelligible or plain; as, to *clarify* a statement:—*v.i.* to become clear, pure, or transparent; as, the sirup *clarified* as it heated.

clar-i-net (klăr′ĭ-nĕt′; klăr′ĭ-nĕt), *n.* a tube-shaped, musical wind instrument. Also, **clar′i-o-net′.**

clar-i-on (klăr′ĭ-ŭn), *n.* a small, high-pitched trumpet; also, its sound:—*adj.* clear and loud; as, a *clarion* call.

CLARINETS
1, clarinet;
2, bass clarinet.

clar-i-ty (klăr′ĭ-tĭ), *n.* clearness; as, the *clarity* of his speech; *clarity* of the air.

Clark or **Clarke** (klärk), William (1770–1838), an American general and explorer, famous as a leader of the Lewis and Clark Expedition.

clash (klăsh), *v.i.* **1,** to make a loud, harsh noise by striking together; as, the cymbals *clashed;* **2,** to be in opposition; disagree; as, their interests *clashed:*—*v.t.* to strike violently together; as, they *clashed* the cymbals:—*n.* **1,** the noise so produced; **2,** opposition; conflict; as, a *clash* of ideas.

clasp (klăsp), *n.* **1,** a hook to hold anything close; a fastening device; **2,** a grasp, as in shaking hands; a close embrace:—*v.t.* **1,** to fasten together with, or as with, a clasp; **2,** to enclose and hold with the arms; **3,** to grasp, as hands in a handshake.

class (klås), *n.* **1,** a number or body of persons with common characteristics, as social status, property, occupation, etc.; as, the middle *class;* **2,** a body of students taught by the same teacher, or engaged in similar studies; as, a *class* in Latin; also, a group of students who are to graduate in the same year; **3,** a division or grading on the basis of quality; as, first *class* on a steamer; mail sent second *class;* **4,** in zoology, a group of animals; in botany, a group of plants:—*v.t.* to arrange according to a system; classify.

clas-sic (klăs′ĭk), *n.* **1,** any book or work of art that is, or may properly be regarded as, a standard; **2,** especially, any Greek or Roman piece of literature or work of art; **3,** any author whose productions are of such excellence that they are regarded as standards:—**the Classics,** the literature of ancient Greece and Rome:—*adj.* **1,** pertaining to the highest class or rank in literature or art; **2,** pertaining to, or like, the Greek or Roman authors.—*n.* **clas′si-cism.**—*n.* **clas′si-cist.**

clas-si-cal (klăs′ĭ-kăl), *adj.* **1,** standard; relating or belonging to the highest rank in literature and art; **2,** having to do with, or following the simple style of, the ancient Greek and Roman authors and artists, or their works; **3,** based on the works of the ancient Greek or Latin authors; as, the *classical* course in college.—*adv.* **clas′si-cal-ly.**

clas-si-fi-ca-tion (klăs′ĭ-fĭ-kā′shŭn), *n.* **1,** the act of grouping according to a system; **2,** any arrangement in orderly groups; as, a *classification* of animals.

clas-si-fy (klăs′ĭ-fī), *v.t.* [classified, classify-ing], to arrange in groups according to a system; as, to *classify* books by subject. —*n.* **clas′si-fi′er.**

class-mate (klås′māt′), *n.* a person who

belongs or belonged to the same class in school as another; as, a college *classmate*.

class-room (klås/room/), *n.* a room in a school where classes are held.

clat-ter (klăt/ẽr), *v.i.* 1, to make a rattling sound; 2, to talk idly and noisily:— *v.t.* to cause to make a rattling sound; as, to *clatter* dishes:—*n.* 1, a rattling noise; 2, commotion; noisy talk.

clause (klôz), *n.* 1, a separate part of a written agreement or document; a distinct condition; as, a *clause* in a treaty; 2, a division of a sentence containing a subject and predicate of its own. In the sentence, "I can go today, but I can't go tomorrow," there are two clauses connected by the conjunction "but."

clav-i-cle (klăv/ĭ-kl), *n.* either of two bones which connect the breastbone and the shoulder blades; a collarbone.

claw (klô), *n.* 1, a sharp, hooked, horny nail on the foot of an animal or bird; 2, the whole foot equipped with these nails; as, the owl held a mouse in his *claw*; 3, the pincers of a shellfish, as a crab or lobster; 4, anything sharp and hooked like a claw, as the curved end of some hammer heads:—*v.t.* and *v.i.* to tear or scratch with, or as with, claws.

Clay (klā), Henry (1777–1852), an American statesman and orator.

clay (klā), *n.* 1, an earthy material, easily molded when moist, but hard when baked, used in making pottery, bricks, etc.; 2, the human body.—*adj.* **clay/ey.**

clean (klēn), *adj.* 1, free from dirt or filth; as, *clean* hands; 2, unmixed with foreign matter; as, *clean* seed; 3, pure; without moral or spiritual stain; as, he lives a *clean* life; 4, even; unobstructed; complete; as, a *clean* field; a *clean* sweep; 5, skilful; well done; as, a *clean* hit; 6, cleanly by habit; as, a *clean* housekeeper; 7, shapely; as, a car with *clean* lines:— *adv.* 1, so as to be clean; as, swept *clean;* 2, wholly; entirely; as, the apple was sound *clean* through:—*v.t.* 1, to remove dirt from; as, to *clean* house; 2, to remove undesirable parts of; as, to *clean* a fish by removing its head, scales, etc.—*n.* **clean/ness.**

clean-er (klēn/ẽr), *n.* a person or thing that removes dirt, stains, etc.

¹**clean-ly** (klĕn/lĭ), *adj.* [clean-li-er, clean-li-est], careful to keep clean; neat.—*n.* **clean/li-ness.**

²**clean-ly** (klēn/lĭ), *adv.* in a clean manner.

cleanse (klĕnz), *v.t.* [cleansed, cleans-ing], to free from filth, guilt, sin, etc.—*n.* **cleans/er.**

clear (klēr), *adj.* 1, bright; unclouded; as, a *clear* day; 2, clean; pure; as, *clear* water;

3, fresh; blooming; as, a *clear* skin; 4, untroubled; as, a *clear* conscience; 5, easily understood; plain; as, a *clear* explanation; 6, audible; distinct; as, a *clear* voice; 7, without further cost to be deducted; net; as, *clear* profit; 8, unobstructed; as, a *clear* view; freed from obstruction; as, land *clear* of stumps:—*adv.* wholly, entirely; clean; as, I broke a piece *clear* off:—*v.t.* 1, to make free from muddiness, cloudiness, smoke, stuffiness, etc.; 2, to make plain; as, to *clear* up a puzzling situation; 3, to free from obstruction; as, to *clear* the way; 4, to remove; as, to *clear* away rubbish; 5, to prove or declare to be innocent; as, to *clear* an accused person; 6, to jump over or pass by without touching; as, the horse *cleared* the fence; 7, to make beyond expenses; as, to *clear* ten dollars:—*v.i.* to become clear; as, the weather *cleared.*—*adv.* **clear/ly.**—*n.* **clear/ness.**

   Syn., *adj.*, bright, transparent, distinct.

clear-ance (klēr/ăns), *n.* 1, removal of obstructions; 2, a legal certificate issued by a customhouse permitting a vessel to leave port; 3, the clear space between two passing objects, or between a vehicle and the top of an arch, bridge, etc.

clear-cut (klēr/-kŭt/), *adj.* 1, having a well-defined outline; as, a *clear-cut* profile; 2, saying much in a few words.

clear-ing (klēr/ĭng), *n.* 1, the act of removing obstructions; as, the *clearing* of land; 2, a tract of land cleared of trees and underbrush.

clear-ing-house (klēr/ĭng-hous/), *n.* an institution through which banks regularly exchange drafts and checks, settling in cash only the balances due.

cleat (klēt), *n.* 1, a piece of wood or metal with branching arms, around which ropes are turned to prevent slipping; 2, a strip of wood or metal fastened across a board, under a shelf, etc., to give support or strength, hold something in position, prevent slipping, or the like; as, the *cleats* on a gangplank, on football shoes, etc.

CLEAT with rope attached.

cleav-age (klēv/ĭj), *n.* 1, the way in which a thing is apt to split; especially, the tendency of anything to split in a particular direction, as rocks; 2, the division resulting from the split.

¹**cleave** (klēv), *v.i.* [*p.t.* cleaved (klēvd) or, *Archaic,* clave (klāv), *p.p.* cleaved, *p.pr.* cleav-ing], to adhere or be faithful to something or someone.

²**cleave** (klēv), *v.t.* [*p.t.* cleft (klĕft),

cleaved (klēvd), clove (klōv), *p.p.* cleft, cleaved, clo-ven (klō′vĕn), *p.pr.* cleav-ing], to cut open; cut a way through; split; as, the ax *cleft* the log; the boat *cleaved* the water:—*v.i.* to split; divide; as, wood *cleaves* along the grain.

Syn. tear, rend, rip.

cleav-er (klēv′ẽr), *n.* a butcher's heavy hatchet or chopper for cutting meat or bone.   CLEAVER

clef (klĕf), *n.* in music, a sign placed at the beginning of the staff to show the pitch of the notes on each line. The line on which the center of the circle of the G clef falls is G; the line on which the dot of the F clef falls is F.

CLEFS
Above, G clef; below two forms of F clef.

¹**cleft** (klĕft), a past tense and past participle of ²*cleave.*

²**cleft** (klĕft), *n.* a crack; crevice; as, the water trickled from a *cleft* in the rock:—*adj.* partly divided.

clem-a-tis (klĕm′a-tĭs), *n.* a vine or bush of the buttercup family, with yellow, blue, purple, or white flowers.

Cle-men-ceau (klĕ-mäṅ′sō′), Georges (1841–1929), called *the Tiger*, a French editor and statesman.

clem-en-cy (klĕm′ĕn-sĭ), *n.* [*pl.* clemencies], 1, compassion; mercy; leniency; as, the jury showed *clemency* to the prisoner; 2, applied to the weather, mildness.

Clem-ens (klĕm′ĕnz), Samuel (1835–1910), an American author, better known by his pen name. See **Twain.**

clem-ent (klĕm′ĕnt), *adj.* 1, forgiving; gentle; kind; as, a *clement* judge; 2, mild; as, *clement* weather.—*adv.* **clem′ent-ly.**

clench (klĕnch), *v.t.* 1, to set closely together, as the teeth; close tightly, as the hands; 2, to clinch or settle, as an argument; 3, to grasp firmly; as, he *clenched* his sword:—*n.* a thing that grips or catches. —*n.* **clench′er.**

Cle-o-pa-tra (klē′ō-pā′tra; klē′ō-pä′tra; klē′ō-pāt′ra), (69–30 B.C.), a famous queen of Egypt.

cler-gy (klûr′jĭ), *n.* [*pl.* clergies], the body of persons ordained for religious service, as ministers, priests, monks, etc.

cler-gy-man (klûr′jĭ-măn), *n.* [*pl.* clergymen (-mĕn)], a properly ordained minister, priest, or preacher.

cler-ic (klĕr′ĭk), *n.* a clergyman.

cler-i-cal (klĕr′ĭ-kăl), *adj.* 1, having to do with the clergy; as, *clerical* garb; 2, pertaining to a clerk, writer, or copyist; as, *clerical* work.—*adv.* **cler′i-cal-ly.**

clerk (klûrk), *n.* 1, a person, not of the clergy, with certain minor church duties; 2, one who keeps records and does routine business; as, the town *clerk;* 3, a general office assistant; typist; secretary; 4, a salesman or saleswoman in a store:—*v.i.* to act as a clerk; as, he *clerks* in a law office.—*n.* **clerk′ship.**

¹**Cleve-land** (klēv′lănd), Stephen Grover (1837–1908), the 22d and 24th president of the U.S.

²**Cleve-land** (klēv′lănd), a city on Lake Erie, in northeastern Ohio (map **7**).

clev-er (klĕv′ẽr), *adj.* 1, skilful; 2, mentally quick; talented.—*adv.* **clev′er-ly.**—*n.* **clev′er-ness.**

Syn. adroit, skilful, deft, expert.

clew or **clue** (klōō), *n.* 1, a ball of thread, yarn, etc.; especially, in mythology, a ball of thread by which one found one's way through a labyrinth; 2, hence, (usually *clue*), a guide or key to a problem, plot, or mystery; 3, a metal loop attached to the lower corner of a sail to hold the ropes that raise or lower the sail:—*v.t.* to draw up (sails) by the lower corners, as for furling.

click (klĭk), *n.* a slight, sharp sound like the turning of a key in a lock:—*v.i.* to make such a sound; as, hail *clicked* against the window.

cli-ent (klī′ĕnt), *n.* one who consults or employs a lawyer, doctor, etc.; hence, a customer or patron.

cliff (klĭf), *n.* a high, steep face of rock; a precipice.

cli-mac-tic (klī-măk′tĭk), *adj.* in the order of importance; forming a climax.

cli-mate (klī′mĭt), *n.* 1, the weather conditions of a place, especially as regards temperature, moisture, etc.; 2, a region with certain conditions of weather, as of heat and cold, sunlight, etc.; as, a sunny *climate.*—*adj.* **cli-mat′ic** (klī-măt′ĭk).

cli-max (klī′măks), *n.* 1, a series of ideas or expressions increasing in force; also, the last of such a series; 2, hence, the highest point of interest, excitement, or development; as, the *climax* of a play.

climb (klīm), *v.t.* 1, to go up or down, especially using both hands and feet; as, to *climb* a ladder; mount; ascend; as, the sun *climbs* the heavens; 2, to ascend by twining; as, a vine *climbs* a trellis:—*v.i.* 1, to go up or down something, using both hands and feet; as, to *climb* into (or out of) a tree; 2, to rise by effort or achievement; as, to *climb* to the head of the class; *climb* to fame:—*n.* the act of climbing; as, a long, hard *climb;* also, a place to be ascended; as, there was a steep *climb* near the top.

climb-er (klĭm′ẽr), *n.* **1**, one who, or that which, climbs; **2**, a climbing plant.

clime (klīm), *n. Poetic,* a place; region.

clinch (klĭnch), *v.t.* **1**, to rivet; to fasten tightly; especially, to turn down the protruding point of (a nail); **2**, to conform or settle, as a bargain or argument; **3**, to grasp tightly:—*v.i.* to grapple; seize one another, as in boxing:—*n.* **1**, the act of making a fastening on both sides of something; **2**, the fastening by which a tight hold is obtained; **3**, in the U.S., a struggle or scuffle at close grips, as in boxing; **4**, a kind of rope fastening (see *knot*, illustration).

cling (klĭng), *v.i.* [clung (klŭng), cling-ing], **1**, to stick together or to something; as, snow *clings* to bushes; **2**, to adhere closely; stick; hold fast by embracing or entwining; hang on; as, a child *clings* to its mother's hand; ivy *clings* to a wall; **3**, hence, to be loyal; remain faithful; as, one *clings* to a friend.

clin-ic (klĭn′ĭk), *n.* **1**, in medicine and surgery, the treatment of patients before a class of students for the instruction of the class; **2**, an institution, or department of a hospital, devoted to the study, and often the free treatment, of disease or of problems of a particular type; as, an eye or a child-guidance *clinic.*—*adj.* **clin′i-cal.**—*adv.* **clin′i-cal-ly.**

clink (klĭngk), *v.t.* to strike so as to make a slight, tinkling sound; as, they *clinked* glasses:—*v.i.* to make a tinkling noise; as, ice *clinks* in a glass:—*n.* a slight, tinkling noise; as, the *clink* of coins.

clink-er (klĭngk′ẽr), *n.* a partly melted, stony mass left from burning coal or other matter, as in a furnace.

¹**clip** (klĭp), *v.t.* [clipped or clipt (klĭpt), clip-ping], to clasp or hold tightly; fasten; as, he *clipped* the papers together:—*n.* a clasp, as for holding papers; any device for gripping.—*n.* **clip′per.**

²**clip** (klĭp), *v.t.* [clipped or clipt (klĭpt), clip-ping], **1**, to cut or trim with shears or scissors, as hair, or the wool from sheep; **2**, to cut short, as final letters, syllables, etc., from words:—*n.* the act of cutting off with, or as with, shears; **2**, the amount of wool obtained from a single shearing season.

³**clip** (klĭp), *v.i. Colloquial,* [clipped, clip-ping], to move swiftly:—*n. Colloquial,* a fast gait; as, to walk at a good *clip.*

CLIPPER, def. 1

clip-per (klĭp′ẽr), *n.* **1**, one who or that which moves swiftly, as a horse or a ship; especially, a kind of fast-sailing vessel, developed in New England; **2**, a large passenger airplane, for long flights; **3**, a tool for cutting hair, wool, etc.

clip-ping (klĭp′ĭng), *n.* **1**, the act of cutting; **2**, a piece cut out of a newspaper.

clique (klēk), *n.* a small, exclusive, social group.—*adj.* **cli′quish** (klē′kĭsh).
    Syn. caste, class, clan, club.

cloak (klōk), *n.* **1**, a loose outer garment, usually sleeveless; **2**, hence, that which covers or conceals; as, night is a *cloak* for crime:—*v.t.* to conceal; cover; disguise; as, to *cloak* grief with laughter.

¹**clock** (klŏk), *n.* a mechanical device for keeping time, larger than a watch, with a moving pair of pointers, or hands, on a dial marked with the hours and minutes.

²**clock** (klŏk), *n.* a woven or embroidered ornament on the ankle of a sock or stocking.—*adj.* **clocked.**

clock-wise (klŏk′wīz′), *adj.* and *adv.* in the same direction in which the hands of a clock turn; circling from left to right.

clock-work (klŏk′wûrk′), *n.* **1**, the machinery of a clock; **2**, any mechanism resembling it in exactness and regularity.

clod (klŏd), *n.* **1**, a lump of earth, turf, or clay; **2**, a stupid fellow.—*adj.* **clod′dy.**

clod-hop-per (klŏd′hŏp′ẽr), *n.* **1**, a country lout; a clown; **2**, **clodhoppers,** heavy shoes, such as are worn by a plowman.

clog (klŏg), *v.t.* [clogged, clog-ging], **1**, to hinder motion with a weight or burden; impede; **2**, hence, to hinder in any way; as, ignorance *clogs* progress; **3**, to obstruct; stop up; as, mud *clogs* a drain:—*v.i.* **1**, to be hindered; **2**, to stick together:—*n.* **1**, a load or weight; hence, any hindrance or restraint; **2**, a shoe with a wooden sole; **3**, a dance by one wearing such shoes.

clois-ter (klois′tẽr), *n.* **1**, a place of religious retirement; a monastery or convent; **2**, an arched way or covered walk along the outside walls of a monastery, college, etc., often surrounding an open court, or connecting buildings of a group:—*v.t.* to confine in, or as if in, a convent or monastery; seclude from the world.—*adj.* **clois′tered.**

CLOISTER

¹**close** (klōz), *v.t.* [closed, clos-ing], **1**, to shut, as a box, the mouth, a door, etc.; **2**, to fill; stop up; obstruct; as, to *close* an opening; **3**, to make an ending to; as, to *close* an argument:—*v.i.* **1**, to come to-

gether; as, the waters *closed* over the diver; **2,** to grapple or fight at close quarters; **3,** to come to an ending:—*n.* conclusion. *Syn., v.* end, conclude, finish.

²**close** (klōs), *adj.* **1,** shut; closed; **2,** contracted; narrow; shut in; as, *close* quarters; **3,** stifling; without ventilation; as, this room is *close;* **4,** stingy; **5,** near in space, time, etc.; **6,** accurate; careful; as, *close* thinking; **7,** firmly knit; compact; tight; as, *close* weaving; **8,** dear; familiar; as, a *close* friend; **9,** almost equal; as, a *close* race or contest; **10,** fitting tightly or snugly, as a turban to the head; **11,** accurate; precise; as, a *close* translation; **12,** confined; kept within bounds; as, a *close* prisoner:—*adv.* **1,** near in space or time; as, follow *close* after me; **2,** tightly; closely together; as, *close* knit; **3,** secretly; in hiding; as, keep *close.*—*adv.* **close′ly.**—*n.* **close′ness.**

closed shop, a shop which will not employ laborers of a certain kind, usually non-union laborers: opposite of *open shop.*

close-fist-ed (klōs′fĭs′tĕd), *adj.* stingy.

clos-et (klŏz′ĕt), *n.* **1,** a small room for privacy or retirement; **2,** a small room for storing things, as clothes, dishes, etc.; a cupboard:—*adj.* private; secret:—*v.t.* to shut up, as in a private room, especially for secret conversation.

clo-sure (klō′zhẽr), *n.* **1,** shutting up; ending; as, the *closure* of a meeting; **2,** in parliamentary law, a way of ending a debate and taking an immediate vote.

clot (klŏt), *v.i.* [clot-ted, clot-ting], to thicken into a soft, sticky, semisolid mass; as, blood *clots:*—*v.t.* to form into lumps of thickened fluid; as, souring *clots* milk:—*n.* a lumpish mass of some thickened fluid, especially blood.—*adj.* **clot′ted.**

cloth (klôth), *n.* [*pl.* cloths (klôthz; klôths)], **1,** a woven fabric of wool, cotton, silk, linen, or the like; **2,** a piece of such fabric made for a certain use; as, a dish*cloth;* a table*cloth;* **3,** one's profession as shown by one's dress, especially the profession of a clergyman:—**the cloth,** the clergy.

clothe (klōth), *v.t.* [clothed or clad (klăd), cloth-ing], **1,** to dress; **2,** to cover with, or as with, a garment; as, flowers *clothed* the field; old age *clothes* a man with dignity.

clothes (klōthz; *Colloquial,* klōz), *n.pl.* **1,** garments; dress; **2,** bedclothes.

clothes-horse (klōthz′hôrs′; klōz′hôrs′), *n.* a folding wooden frame with horizontal bars on which to dry or air clothes.

clothes-pin (klōthz′pĭn′; klōz′pĭn′), *n.* a forked wooden peg, or little clamp, used to fasten clothes on a line. (See illustration under *pin.*)

cloth-ier (klôth′yẽr), *n.* one who makes, or deals in, cloth or clothing.

cloth-ing (klōth′ĭng), *n.* clothes; dress; garments in general.

cloud (kloud), *n.* **1,** a visible mass of condensed water floating above the earth; **2,** a similar mass of smoke or dust; **3,** anything that threatens or darkens, as grief, disgrace, suspicion, etc.; **4,** anything that moves in or like a mass, as a large number of arrows, insects, or horsemen:—*v.t.* **1,** to cover with a mist or cloud; **2,** hence, to make gloomy; as, grief *clouds* a face; **3,** to blacken; trouble; sully; as, a bad record *clouds* his reputation:—*v.i.* to grow cloudy; as, toward afternoon the sky *clouded* over.

cloud-burst (kloud′bûrst′), *n.* a violent, unusually heavy downpour of rain.

cloud-less (kloud′lĕs), *adj.* clear; bright; unshadowed; not overcast.

cloud-y (kloud′ĭ), *adj.* [cloud-i-er, cloud-i-est], **1,** pertaining to a cloud or clouds; **2,** overcast; threatening rain; **3,** vague; obscure; **4,** not transparent; as, a *cloudy* liquid; **5,** gloomy.—*adv.* **cloud′i-ly.**—*n.* **cloud′i-ness.**

clout (klout), *n.* **1,** *Archaic,* a patch; a rag; especially, a dishcloth; **2,** in archery, the white canvas center of a target; also, an arrow that hits the center; **3,** *Colloquial,* a blow on the head with the hand:—*v.t.* **1,** to patch or mend coarsely; **2,** *Colloquial,* to strike; knock.

¹**clove** (klōv), past tense of ²*cleave.*

²**clove** (klōv), *n.* **1,** the dried flower bud of a tropical evergreen tree of the myrtle family, used as spice; **2,** the tree.

clo-ven (klō′vĕn), a form of the past participle of ²*cleave:*—*adj.* divided into two parts; split; as, a *cloven* hoof.

clo-ver (klō′vẽr), *n.* a low-growing plant with three-parted leaves and sweet, round flower heads of red, white, or purple, used for fodder.

clown (kloun), *n.* **1,** a man of coarse manners; a boor; **2,** a jester, especially in a play or circus:—*v.i.* to act the clown.

RED CLOVER

clown-ish (kloun′ĭsh), *adj.* **1,** coarse; awkward; **2,** like a clown; comical; as, a *clownish* fellow.—*adv.* **clown′ish-ly.**—*n.* **clown′ish-ness.**

cloy (kloi), *v.t.* to surfeit or sate with food, especially with rich or sweet food; also, to weary with pleasure.

club (klŭb), *n.* **1,** a heavy stick; **2,** one of

a suit, called *clubs*, of playing cards, marked with a black figure like a clover leaf; **3**, a number of persons united for a common purpose or mutual benefit; **4**, a building or room occupied by such persons; **5**, a stick used to hit the ball in certain games, especially golf:—*v.t.* [clubbed, clubbing], **1**, to beat with a cudgel; **2**, to give to a common cause; as, the town *clubbed* its resources to help the flood victims:— *v.i.* to combine for a common purpose; as, to *club* together to buy a football.

Syn., *n.* organization, society.

cluck (klŭk), *n.* the call of a hen to her chickens; also, a sound resembling this:— *v.i.* to make this sound.

clue or **clew** (klōō), *n.* anything that helps to solve a mystery or difficulty; as, a footprint was the only *clue* to the thief.

clump (klŭmp), *n.* **1**, a cluster or group, as of trees; **2**, a mass; lump, as of earth; **3**, a sound like that of heavy treading:—*v.i.* to tread heavily; as, the laborers *clumped* along the road.

clum-sy (klŭm′zĭ), *adj.* [clum-si-er, clumsi-est], **1**, awkward; heavy; lacking in ease or grace; as, a *clumsy* person or action; **2**, ill-made; unwieldy; as, a *clumsy* tool.— *adv.* **clum′si-ly**.—*n.* **clum′si-ness**.

clung (klŭng), past tense and past participle of *cling*.

clus-ter (klŭs′tẽr), *n.* **1**, a number of things, such as fruits, of the same kind growing or collected together; a bunch; **2**, a group; as, a *cluster* of islands:—*v.i.* and *v.t.* to grow, or gather, in bunches.

clutch (klŭch), *v.t.* to grasp, seize, or grip strongly; as, to *clutch* a dagger:—*v.i.* to snatch or reach out eagerly; as, he *clutched* at the rope:—*n.* **1**, a tight grasp; **2**, **clutches**, grasping claws or hands; as, a bird in the *clutches* of a hawk; **3**, a device for gripping or holding, as in a crane; also, a mechanical device which connects and disconnects the motor of a machine from certain other parts which do the work of the machine, as in an automobile.

clut-ter (klŭt′ẽr), *n.* disorder; litter:—*v.t.* to make untidy; disarrange.

Clyde (klīd), a river in Scotland, famous for its shipbuilding (map **13**).

cm. abbreviation for *centimeter, centimeters*.

Co. abbreviation for *company, county*.

C.O. abbreviation for *commanding officer:* —**c.o.** or **c/o** abbreviation for *care of*.

co- (kō-), *prefix*, a form of *com-* used before vowels and certain consonants.

coach (kōch), *n.* **1**, a large, closed, four-wheeled carriage; **2**, a tutor, especially

one who prepares others for an examination; also, a director of athletics, dramatics, etc.; **3**, a closed, two-door automobile; **4**, a

WESTERN STAGECOACH

railroad passenger car:—*v.t.* to teach; direct; as, to *coach* a team or a play.— *n.* **coach′er.**

coach-man (kōch′măn), *n.* [*pl.* coach-men (-mĕn)], one who drives a coach or any carriage for a living.

co-ad-ju-tor (kŏ-ăj′ŏō-tẽr; kō′ă-jōō′tẽr), *n.* an official helper or assistant.

co-ag-u-late (kŏ-ăg′ū-lāt), *v.t.* [coagulated, coagulat-ing], to clot or curdle; thicken; solidify; as, cooking *coagulates* the white of egg.—*n.* **co-ag′u-la′tion.**

coal (kōl), *n.* **1**, a black, hard, burnable mineral, formed under the earth by the decay of the vegetation of prehistoric times, and used as fuel; **2**, charcoal; **3**, a glowing or charred bit of wood, coal, etc.; an ember:—*v.t.* to furnish with coal, as a vessel: —*v.i.* to take in coal, as a ship.—*n.* **coal′er.**

co-a-lesce (kō′ă-lĕs′), *v.i.* [coalesced, coalesc-ing], **1**, to grow together, as the sides of a wound; **2**, combine; blend; fuse; unite into one body.—*n.* **co′a-les′cence.**

co-a-li-tion (kō′ă-lĭsh′ŭn), *n.* **1**, union into one body or mass; **2**, a temporary combination of different persons or parties for a special purpose.

coal oil, kerosene.

coal tar, a thick, black, sticky substance obtained when gas is distilled from soft coal, yielding paraffin, benzine, dyes, etc.

coarse (kôrs), *adj.* [coars-er, coars-est], **1**, of poor or inferior quality or appearance; as, *coarse* cloth; **2**, large in texture or size; as, *coarse* sand; **3**, not refined; gross; as, *coarse* manners.—*adv.* **coarse′ly.** —*n.* **coarse′ness.**

Syn. rude, rough, unpolished.

coars-en (kôr′sn), *v.t.* and *v.i.* to turn, or become, large, rough, common, etc.

coast (kōst), *n.* **1**, the land forming the margin or boundary of the sea; the seashore; also, the region adjoining the sea; **2**, a slide downhill over snow or ice on a sled, skis, or the like:—*v.i.* **1**, to sail along a shore, or from port to port; **2**, to ride along by the force of gravity, without power, as on a sled.—*adj.* **coast′al.**

Syn., *n.* edge, bank, shore, margin.

coast-er (kōs′tĕr), *n.* **1,** a vessel engaged in trade along a coast; **2,** a person or thing that coasts; **3,** a round, shallow tray for a glass or dish, used to protect a table from heat or dampness.

coast guard, 1, any force organized to guard a coast; **2,** in the U.S., a military service which enforces federal laws to maintain safety and order and to protect life and property in maritime activities.

coast-wise (kōst′wīz′), *adj.* and *adv.* by way of, or along, the coast.

coat (kōt), *n.* **1,** a sleeved, outer garment covering the upper part of the body; **2,** any outside covering, as fur, skin, rind, etc.; also, any outer layer; as, a *coat* of paint:—*v.t.* to cover or spread over.

coat of arms, 1, a group of emblems signifying rank or achievement, originally granted to a knight or person of distinction and adopted by his descendants; **2,** a shield or coat marked with such emblems.

coat of mail, a garment made of metal links, and worn as protective armor.

coat-ing (kō′tĭng), *n.* **1,** a thin layer or covering; **2,** material for coats.

coax (kōks), *v.t.* **1,** to wheedle; urge or influence with soft words or flattery; **2,** to handle with patience and skill; as, to *coax* a fire.—*adv.* **coax′ing-ly.**

cob (kŏb), *n.* **1,** a corncob; **2,** a strong, short-legged horse.

co-balt (kō′bôlt; kō′bŏlt), *n.* **1,** a silver-white metallic element; **2,** a deep-blue coloring matter made from it.

¹cob-ble (kŏb′l), *n.* a round stone, worn smooth by water, especially one of a size used for street paving; a cobblestone:—*v.t.* [cob-bled, cob-bling], to pave with cobblestones.

²cob-ble (kŏb′l), *v.t.* [cob-bled, cob-bling], to mend or patch up coarsely; repair, especially shoes.

cob-bler (kŏb′lĕr), *n.* **1,** one who mends boots and shoes; **2,** a clumsy workman; **3,** a cooling summer drink of iced wine and fruit juices; as, sherry *cobbler;* **4,** a deep-dish fruit pie with one crust.

cob-ble-stone (kŏb′l-stōn′), *n.* a rounded stone used for paving.

Cóbh (kōv), an important seaport in the southern part of Eire, now the Republic of Ireland (map **13**): formerly called *Queenstown*.

co-bra (kō′brà), *n.* a large, poisonous

COBRA (¹⁄₁₆)

snake of Asia and Africa which, when irritated, swells its neck out like a hood.

cob-web (kŏb′wĕb′), *n.* **1,** a spider's web or the material of which it is made; **2,** anything resembling the flimsy or entangling qualities of a cobweb.

co-caine or **co-cain** (kō-kān′; kō′kān), *n.* a powerful drug extracted from the leaves of a South American shrub called coca, used to dull pain and cause sleep.

coc-cyx (kŏk′sĭks), *n.* [*pl.* coccyges (kŏk-sī′jēz)], the last bone of the spinal column. —*adj.* **coc-cyg′e-al** (kŏk-sĭj′ē-ăl).

Co-chin (kō′chĭn; kŏch′ĭn), *n.* a large, domestic fowl of Asiatic breed with thickly feathered legs.

Co-chin Chi-na (kō′chĭn chī′nà; kŏch′ĭn), a part (cap. Saïgon) of the Indo-Chinese state of Vietnam (map **15**).

coch-i-neal (kŏch′ĭ-nēl′), *n.* **1,** a scarlet dye obtained from the dried bodies of an insect found in Mexico, Central America, etc.; **2,** the insect itself.

¹cock (kŏk), *n.* **1,** the male of the common domestic fowl; a rooster; **2,** any male bird; **3,** a weather vane in the shape of a rooster; **4,** a leader; as, *cock* of the school; **5,** a turn valve, tap, faucet, etc.; **6,** the hammer of a firearm, or its position when raised; as, a gun at full *cock.*

¹COCK
def. 5

²cock (kŏk), *n.* a tilting or turning upward, as of a hat or an eye:—*v.t.* **1,** to turn up or set jauntily on one side; tilt defiantly, as a hat; **2,** to raise the hammer of (a gun), in readiness for firing.

³cock (kŏk), *n.* a small, cone-shaped pile, especially of hay:—*v.t.* to stack in piles.

COCKADE (C)
def. 1

cock-ade (kŏk-ād′), *n.* **1,** a rosette or knot of ribbon or leather worn on a hat to signify office or party; **2,** an ornament on a bridle (see *harness,* illustration).

cock-a-too (kŏk′à-tōo′), *n.* a white or brilliantly colored parrot, often with a crest, found chiefly in Australia.

cock-a-trice (kŏk′à-trĭs; kŏk′à-trīs), *n.* a fabulous monster, part cock and part serpent, whose glance was supposed to kill; a basilisk.

COCKATOO (¹⁄₁₆)

cock-er-el (kŏk′ĕr-ĕl), *n.* a young domestic cock.

cock-er span-iel (kŏk′ĕr spăn′yĕl), a

spaniel, usually with long black, red, or cream-colored hair, trained to hunt birds.

cock-fight (kŏk'fīt'), *n.* a fight between cocks, especially those armed with spurs.

¹**cock-le** (kŏk'l), *n.* **1,** an edible shellfish with two heart-shaped fluted shells; **2,** one of its shells: often called *cockleshell;* **3,** a frail or shallow boat:—**cockles of the heart,** the depths of the heart; the feelings.

COCKER SPANIEL (¹⁄₂₀)

²**cock-le** (kŏk'l), *n.* a plant that grows as a weed among grain.

cock-ney (kŏk'nĭ), *n.* [*pl.* cockneys], a Londoner; especially, one born in the East End of London, and speaking a characteristic dialect:—*adj.* of or relating to cockneys.

¹COCKLE, def. 2

cock-pit (kŏk'pĭt'), *n.* **1,** an enclosed space for cockfights; **2,** in small vessels, space aft lower than the deck; **3,** in a war vessel, the quarters of junior officers, used as a hospital during a battle; **4,** in some airplanes, the place where the pilots and passengers sit.

cock-roach (kŏk'rōch'), *n.* a black or brown, beetlelike insect found in kitchens and pantries.

cocks-comb (kŏks'kōm'), *n.* **1,** the comb or crest of a cock; **2,** a garden plant of the amaranth family with a crest-shaped red or yellow flower; **3,** (usually *coxcomb*), the red edge on a jester's cap; also, the cap; **4,** (usually *coxcomb*), a conceited fellow; a fop.

COCKROACH (⅔)

cock-sure (kŏk'shŏor'), *adj.* **1,** absolutely certain or sure; **2,** too sure.

cock-swain (kŏk'sn; kŏk'swān), *n.* the steersman of a boat; a coxswain. See **coxswain.**

cock-tail (kŏk'tāl'), *n.* **1,** an iced, mixed drink made of alcoholic liquors, bitters, fruit juices, etc.; **2,** an appetizer of shellfish, mixed fruits, or the like, served as a first course.

co-co (kō'kō), *n.* [*pl.* cocos], **1,** a palm which produces the coconut: also called *coconut palm;* **2,** the fruit of this tree; a coconut.

co-coa (kō'kō), *n.* **1,** a powder made from the ground seeds of the cacao tree; **2,** a drink made from it.

co-co-nut (kō'kō-nŭt'), *n.* **1,** the fruit of the coco palm; **2,** loosely, the white meaty

substance from it, prepared for use as food. Also spelled **co'coa-nut'.**

co-coon (kō-kōōn'), *n.* the silky case spun by the larvae of many insects, such as caterpillars and silkworms, as a protection while they are developing into butterflies, moths, or the like. (See illustration below.)

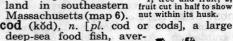
COCONUT
1, tree and fruit; 2, fruit cut in half to show nut within its husk.

C.O.D. abbreviation for *cash on delivery.*

Cod, Cape (kŏd), a hook-shaped point of land in southeastern Massachusetts (map 6).

cod (kŏd), *n.* [*pl.* cod or cods], a large deep-sea food fish, averaging 10 to 30 pounds, found in the northern Atlantic.

cod-dle (kŏd'l), *v.t.* [coddled, cod-dling], **1,** to pet or pamper; treat tenderly; **2,** to stew gently; cook by allowing to stand in hot water.

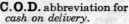
COCOON OF CECROPIA MOTH

code (kōd), *n.* **1,** a body of laws arranged in clear and regular order; as, tʰe civil or penal *code;* **2,** a system of military or naval signals; **3,** any system of symbols used for messages, to secure their brevity or secrecy; **4,** a body of principles or standards governing the conduct of a society, class, or profession, under certain conditions; as, the social *code.*

co-dex (kō'dĕks), *n.* [*pl.* codices (kō'dĭ-sēz; kŏd'ĭ-sēz)], an ancient manuscript of a book, as of the Scriptures or the classics.

cod-fish (kŏd'fĭsh'), *n.* the cod or its flesh, especially when cured and salted, served as food.

cod-i-fy (kŏd'ĭ-fī; kō'dĭ-fī), *v.t.* [codified, codify-ing], to reduce to a system or code, as laws or regulations.

¹**cod-ling** (kŏd'lĭng), *n.* a young cod.

²**cod-ling** (kŏd'lĭng), *n.* an unripe apple: —**codling moth,** a small moth whose larvae damage apples, pears, etc.

cod—liv-er oil (kŏd'₌lĭv'ĕr), a nutritious oil obtained from the liver of the cod.

Co-dy (kō'dĭ), William F. (1846–1917), known as *Buffalo Bill,* an American scout and showman.

co-ed-u-ca-tion (kō'ĕd'ū-kā'shŭn), *n.* the education of both boys and girls in the same school.—*adj.* **co'ed'u-ca'tion-al.**

āte, āorta, râre, căt, àsk, fär, ăllow, sofà; ēve, ĕvent, ĕll, writĕr, novĕl; bīte, pĭn; nō, ōbey, ôr, dŏg, tŏp, cŏllide; ūnit, ūnite, bûrn, cŭt, focŭs; nōōn, fŏŏt; mound; coin;

co·ef·fi·cient (kō′ĕ-fĭsh′ĕnt), *n.* **1,** that which unites with something else in producing a certain effect or result; **2,** in algebra, any sign or group of signs placed before another as a multiplier; as, in the expression "3*y*," the *coefficient* of *y* is 3.

co·erce (kō-ûrs′), *v.t.* [coerced, coerc-ing], to compel by force; as, he *coerced* the prisoner into submission.—*adj.* **co·er′cive.**

co·er·cion (kō-ûr′shŭn), *n.* the act of forcing someone, physically, legally, or morally, to do something against his will.
Syn. force, constraint, violence.

co·e·val (kō-ē′văl), *adj.* **1,** of the same age; **2,** living at the same time; contemporary; **3,** lasting to the same age.

co·ex·ist (kō′ĕg-zĭst′), *v.i.* to exist together.—*n.* **co′ex·ist′ence.**

cof·fee (kôf′ĭ), *n.* **1,** a drink made from the seeds, roasted and ground, of a tropical shrub; **2,** the seeds: often called *coffee beans;* **3,** the shrub or tree.

cof·fer (kôf′ẽr), *n.* **1,** a casket, chest, or trunk in which to keep money or treasure; **2, coffers,** a treasury; funds.

COFFEE
1, branch bearing leaves and fruit; 2, fruit with part of husk removed to show seeds.

cof·fer·dam (kôf′ẽr-dăm′), *n.* a temporary dam or watertight enclosure, open at the top, which may be pumped dry to permit workmen to work on the sea or river bottom.

cof·fin (kôf′ĭn), *n.* the case or chest in which a dead person is buried.

cog (kŏg), *n.* one of a series of teeth on the rim of a wheel, designed to give or transmit motion by interlocking with teeth on another wheel. (See *cogwheel,* illustration.)

co·gent (kō′jĕnt), *adj.* forceful; convincing; as, a *cogent* reason.—*adv.* **co′gent·ly.**—*n.* **co′gen·cy.**

cog·i·tate (kŏj′ĭ-tāt), *v.i.* [cogitat-ed, cogitat-ing], to reflect; ponder; think:—*v.t.* to think over; plan.

cog·i·ta·tion (kŏj′ĭ-tā′shŭn), *n.* deep thought; pondering.

co·gnac (kōn′yăk; kŏn′yăk), *n.* a very fine French brandy.

cog·nate (kŏg′nāt), *adj.* **1,** related by blood; alike in origin, nature, or quality; **2,** related in origin; coming from the same original source; as, *cognate* words or languages:—*n.* a person or thing that is akin to another by blood, derivation, etc.

cog·ni·zance (kŏg′nĭ-zăns; kŏn′ĭ-zăns), *n.* **1,** understanding; notice; as, to take cognizance of a fact; **2,** range of knowledge; as, within a child's *cognizance.*

cog·ni·zant (kŏg′nĭ-zănt; kŏn′ĭ-zănt), *adj.* having knowledge; aware.

cog·no·men (kŏg-nō′mĕn), *n.* **1,** a surname or family name; **2,** a distinguishing name; a nickname; as, King Richard went under the *cognomen* of the Lionhearted.

cog·wheel (kŏg′hwēl′), *n.* a wheel with teeth in its rim; a gear wheel: when small, called *pinion.*

COGWHEELS
a, gear; *b,* pinion.

co·here (kō-hēr′), *v.i.* [cohered, coher-ing], to stick together in a mass, as mud; hold together, as cement and stone.

co·her·ence (kō-hēr′ĕns), *n.* **1,** the state or quality of sticking together; **2,** clearness; consistency, as between the parts of a story, speech, etc. Also, **co·her′en·cy.**

co·her·ent (kō-hēr′ĕnt), *adj.* **1,** sticking together; **2,** logically connected and developed; consistent.—*adv.* **co·her′ent·ly.**

co·he·sion (kō-hē′zhŭn), *n.* a sticking together; specifically, the force by which particles of the same material are held together; as, there is *cohesion* in clay, but not in gravel.—*adj.* **co·he′sive.**—*adv.* **co·he′sive·ly.**—*n.* **co·he′sive·ness.**

co·hort (kō′hôrt), *n.* **1,** in ancient Rome, a body of soldiers of 300 to 600 men, or the tenth part of a legion; **2,** any body of soldiers or band of persons.

coif·fure (kwä-fūr′), *n.* **1,** a headdress; **2,** the manner of arranging the hair.

COIL OF ROPE

coil (koil), *n.* **1,** anything wound in a circle or series of circles; a spiral; as, a *coil* of rope; **2,** a continuous spiral of pipe or wire for conducting hot water, electricity, or the like:—*v.t.* to wind into circles; as, to *coil* a rope:—*v.i.* to form coils.

coin (koin), *n.* **1,** a piece of metal legally stamped to be used as money; **2,** metal money:—*v.t.* **1,** to make (coins) by stamping pieces of metal; also, to change (metal) into coins; **2,** to invent (a word); as, he *coined* the word "cinemactor."

coin·age (koin′ĭj), *n.* **1,** the process of making pieces of money; **2,** the money made; **3,** the system of metal money used in a country; **4,** invention of new words and phrases.

---

go; join; yet; sing; chin; show; thin, *th*en; **hw,** *wh*y; **zh,** *a*zure; **ü,** Ger. f*ü*r or Fr. l*u*ne; **ö,** Ger. sch*ö*n or Fr. f*eu;* **ǹ,** Fr. *en*fant, *nom;* **kh,** Ger. a*ch* or i*ch.* See pages ix-x.

co·in·cide (kō′ĭn-sīd′), *v.i.* [coincid-ed, coincid-ing], **1,** to occur at the same time; as, their rest periods *coincide;* **2,** to occupy the same space exactly; **3,** to agree; be alike; as, my idea *coincides* with yours.—*adj.* **co·in′ci·dent.**—*adj.* **co·in′ci·den′tal.**

co·in·ci·dence (kō-ĭn′sĭ-děns), *n.* **1,** the condition of happening at the same time or of occupying the same space; **2,** agreement; **3,** a remarkable happening together of events, apparently accidental.

coke (kōk), *n.* coal from which some of the gases have been driven by intense heat: used for fuel.

col- (kŏl-), *prefix,* a form of *com-* used before *l.*

Col. abbreviation for *Colorado, Columbia, Colonel.*

COLANDER

col·an·der (kŭl′ăn-dẽr; kŏl′ăn-dẽr), *n.* a strainer; a kitchen utensil pierced with holes, used for draining off liquids from vegetables, etc.

cold (kōld), *adj.* **1,** producing or feeling chilliness; of low temperature: opposite of *hot;* especially, less hot than the human body; as, a *cold* wind; *cold* food; **2,** indifferent; as, the news left him *cold;* **3,** unfriendly; as, a *cold* greeting; **4,** chilling, depressing; as, *cold* comfort; **5,** spiritless; dull; **6,** not fresh, as a scent in hunting:—*n.* **1,** lack of heat; as, to feel the *cold;* **2,** the sensation produced by lack of heat; **3,** in physics, a temperature below the freezing point of water; as, five degrees of *cold;* **4,** cold weather; **5,** the shivering sensation caused by fear or despair; **6,** an inflammation of a mucous membrane, generally of the nose or throat.—*adv.* **cold′ly.**—*n.* **cold′ness.**

cold–blood·ed (kōld′=blŭd′ĕd), *adj.* **1,** having blood that takes its temperature from the surrounding water or air, as fish, snakes, etc.; **2,** sensitive to cold; **3,** unfeeling; deliberately cruel.

cold war, an international situation in which, without armed conflict, and without breaking diplomatic relations, openly hostile nations struggle for political advantage.

cold wave, 1, a period of extremely cold weather; **2,** a chemical process of curling the hair; **3,** the wave so produced.

cole (kōl), *n.* any of certain plants of the mustard family, as cabbage kale, etc.

Cole·ridge (kōl′rĭj), Samuel Taylor (1772–1834), an English writer and poet.

cole·slaw (kōl′slô′), *n.* a salad made of finely cut raw cabbage, with a dressing.

col·ic (kŏl′ĭk), *n.* sharp pain in the abdomen or bowels.—*adj.* **col′ick·y.**

col·i·se·um (kŏl′ĭ-sē′ŭm), *n.* a theater, music hall, or large building for athletic sports:—**Coliseum,** an amphitheater in ancient Rome; the Colosseum: see **Colosseum.**

col·lab·o·rate (kŏ-lăb′ō-rāt), *v.i.* [collaborat-ed, collaborat-ing], **1,** to work with others; **2,** to co-operate with the enemy in time of war, especially during enemy occupation.—*n.* **col·lab′o·ra′tion.**—*n.* **col·lab′o·ra′tor.**—*n.* **col·lab′o·ra′tion·ist.**

col·lapse (kŏ-lăps′), *n.* **1,** a falling in or together, as of a roof; **2,** a sudden and complete failure; **3,** general breakdown; as, a nervous *collapse:*—*v.i.* [collapsed, collapsing], **1,** to shrink together; **2,** to fail completely and suddenly; **3,** to break down physically.—*adj.* **col·laps′i·ble.**

col·lar (kŏl′ẽr), *n.* **1,** the part of any garment which fits around the neck; also, an ornamental piece of lace, linen, silk, etc., worn around the neck; **2,** a leather or metal band for the neck of a dog or other animal; **3,** the part of a horse's harness which fits over the neck and shoulders and bears the strain of the load (see *harness,* illustration); **4,** in mechanics, a connecting ring or band:—*v.t.* **1,** to seize by the collar; **2,** to put a collar on.

col·lar·bone (kŏl′ẽr-bōn′), *n.* either of two bones that connect the breastbone and the shoulder blades.

col·lat·er·al (kŏ-lăt′ẽr-ăl), *adj.* **1,** side by side; parallel; **2,** connected with something but of minor importance; **3,** pertaining to something, as stocks or bonds, offered as security, in addition to one's note, or other promise to pay; **4,** descended from the same stock, but not in a direct line: opposed to *lineal;* as, my sister is my *collateral* relative; my father is my *lineal* relative:—*n.* something given, as stocks or bonds, as a pledge for the repayment of a loan.—*adv.* **col·lat′er·al·ly.**

col·la·tion (kŏ-lā′shŭn), *n.* a light meal, usually cold.

col·league (kŏl′ēg), *n.* an associate in office, or in a profession.

¹col·lect (kŏ-lĕkt′), *v.t.* **1,** to gather; **2,** to secure payment; **3,** to make a hobby of collecting; as, to *collect* stamps:—*v.i.* **1,** to accumulate; as, scum *collects* on stagnant water; **2,** to meet or assemble.

²col·lect (kŏl′ĕkt), *n.* a short prayer.

col·lect·ed (kŏ-lĕk′tĕd), *adj.* calm; cool; undisturbed.—*adv.* **col·lect′ed·ly.**

col·lec·tion (kŏ-lĕk′shŭn), *n.* **1,** the process of gathering or assembling; as, the *collection* of outgoing mail; the *collection* of a crowd at a fire; **2,** any assemblage of persons or things; especially, a group of books, stamps, paintings, or the like, gathered for display or study; **3,** the taking in of money due; also, the amount received; **4,** a contribution asked for; as, they took up two *collections* at church.

col·lec·tive (kŏ-lĕk′tĭv), *adj.* relating to, produced by, or affecting a number of individuals jointly, that is, a number of persons as if they were one body; as, the *collective* wisdom of the ages; *collective* action: —**collective noun,** a singular noun used to name a group or collection of individuals; as, "army" and "audience" are *collective* nouns.—*adv.* **col·lec′tive·ly.**

col·lec·tor (kŏ-lĕk′tẽr), *n.* a person who collects; as, an art *collector;* a tax *collector.*

col·leen (kŏl′ēn; kŏ-lēn′), *n.* a girl: an Irish term.

col·lege (kŏl′ĕj), *n.* **1,** an educational institution above the high school, which gives degrees to its students upon completion of certain courses of study; **2,** the buildings and grounds of such an institution; **3,** a school for special instruction; **4,** an association of men having a common profession; as, the *College* of Physicians.

col·le·gi·an (kŏ-lē′jĭ-ăn; kŏ-lē′jăn), *n.* a college student.

col·le·gi·ate (kŏ-lē′jĭ-ĭt), *adj.* **1,** relating to a college; as, *collegiate* sports; **2,** of a kind used by college students; as, *collegiate* clothes.

col·lide (kŏ-līd′), *v.i.* [collid-ed, collid-ing], to meet and strike together with force; crash; as, the two ships *collided;* also, to clash; conflict.

col·lie (kŏl′ĭ), *n.* a large sheep dog with a shaggy coat.

col·lier (kŏl′yẽr), *n.* **1,** a coal miner; **2,** a ship for carrying coal.

col·lier·y (kŏl′yẽr-ĭ), *n.* [*pl.* collieries], a coal mine and the buildings connected with it.

COLLIE (¹⁄₂₀)

col·li·sion (kŏ-lĭzh′ŭn), *n.* the violent striking together of two bodies; a crash; also, a clash or conflict.

col·lo·ca·tion (kŏl′ō-kā′shŭn), *n.* the arrangement of a number of objects or of words with reference to one another; as, the *collocation* of words in a sentence determines their meaning.

col·lo·di·on (kŏ-lō′dĭ-ŭn), *n.* a solution of guncotton in ether, which hardens in the open air, used especially as a protective covering for wounds.

col·lop (kŏl′ŭp), *n.* a slice of meat, especially of bacon, cooked or to be cooked.

col·lo·qui·al (kŏ-lō′kwĭ-ăl), *adj.* used in ordinary conversation, but not in formal or literary language; as, "movies" is a *colloquial* word.—*adv.* **col·lo′qui·al·ly.**—*n.* **col·lo′qui·al·ism.**

col·lo·quy (kŏl′ō-kwĭ), *n.* [*pl.* colloquies], a conversation; discussion.

col·lu·sion (kŏ-lū′zhŭn), *n.* a secret agreement for an unlawful or evil purpose; as, *collusion* between witnesses in a lawsuit.

Colo. abbreviation for *Colorado.*

co·logne (kŏ-lōn′), *n.* perfumed toilet water.

Co·logne (kŏ-lōn′), a city on the Rhine in Germany, famous for its cathedral (map **12**). Its German name is *Köln.*

Co·lom·bi·a (kŏ-lŏm′bē-ä), a republic (cap. Bogotá), in South America (map **11**). —*adj.* and *n.* **Co·lom′bi·an.**

Co·lom·bo (kŏ-lŏm′bō), a seaport and capital of the island of Ceylon (map **15**).

¹**co·lon** (kō′lŏn), *n.* a punctuation mark [:] used after the formal greeting with which a letter begins, before a quotation of some length, and before a list, as of contents, illustrations, causes, or the like.

²**co·lon** (kō′lŏn), *n.* the large intestine, which in a man is about six feet long. (See illustration at *intestine.*)

³**co·lon** (kŏ-lōn′), *n.* [*pl.* colons (kŏ-lōnz′) or colones (kŏ-lō′nās)], **1,** a coin, the monetary unit of Costa Rica; **2,** a coin, the monetary unit of El Salvador. (See Table, page 943.)

colo·nel (kûr′nĕl), *n.* the commander of a regiment.—*n.* **colo′nel·cy.**

co·lo·ni·al (kŏ-lō′nĭ-ăl), *adj.* relating to a colony or colonies; especially, relating to the thirteen British colonies which united to form the United States of America.

col·o·nist (kŏl′ō-nĭst), *n.* **1,** a person who helps to found a colony; **2,** an inhabitant of a colony.

col·o·nize (kŏl′ō-nīz), *v.t.* [colonized, coloniz-ing], **1,** to migrate to and establish a colony in (a place); as, the Quakers *colonized* Pennsylvania; **2,** to send colonists to; as, England *colonized* New Zealand.— *n.* **col′o·ni·za′tion.**—*n.* **col′o·niz′er.**

col·on·nade (kŏl′ō-nād′), *n.* a row of columns, regularly spaced along the side or sides of a building.

COLONNADE

col·o·ny (kŏl′ō-nĭ), *n.* [*pl.* colonies], **1,** a body of people who leave their native country and settle in another land, but remain subject to the mother country; **2,** the country thus settled; **3,** a group of people allied by race, interests, or the like, living together; as, an artist *colony;* **4,** a group of plants or animals living together; as, a *colony* of honeybees.

col·or (kŭl′ẽr), *n.* **1,** that quality of an object by which one can see whether it is red, blue, green, or the like; **2,** any hue, tint, or shade, sometimes including black and white; **3,** a paint or pigment; **4,** complexion, especially a complexion indicative of good, or bad, health:—**the colors,** the flag; as, a call to *the colors:—v.t.* **1,** to give a color to; dye; **2,** to misrepresent; as, the witness *colored* his story:—*v.i.* to blush.

Col·o·ra·do (kŏl′ō-rä′dō; kŏl′ō-răd′ō), a western State (cap. Denver) in the U.S. (map 9).

Col·o·ra·do Riv·er, a river of Colorado, Utah, and Arizona (map 9).

col·or·a·tion (kŭl′ẽr-ā′shŭn), *n.* arrangement of colors; coloring; as, to admire the *coloration* of a painting, a flower, etc.

col·or–blind (kŭl′ẽr-blīnd′), *adj.* unable to distinguish between certain colors, or, sometimes, to distinguish any color.

col·or·cast (kŭl′ẽr-kăst′), *n.* a telecast intended for color reception.

col·ored (kŭl′ẽrd), *adj.* **1,** having color; not black or white; **2,** belonging to a dark-skinned race: especially the Negro race.

col·or·ful (kŭl′ẽr-fŏŏl), *adj.* **1,** full of striking color or colors; as, a *colorful* parade; **2,** exciting the fancy or imagination; as, *colorful* music.

col·or·ing (kŭl′ẽr-ĭng), *n.* **1,** the act, art, or style of producing color; **2,** a material that gives color; as, to put green *coloring* in jelly; **3,** coloration.

col·or·less (kŭl′ẽr-lĕs), *adj.* **1,** pale; **2,** dull; not vivid; as, a *colorless* story; **3,** clear; as, a *colorless* liquid.

co·los·sal (kō-lŏs′ăl), *adj.* huge; vast.
 Syn. immense, enormous.

Col·os·se·um (kŏl′ō-sē′ŭm), *n.* an amphitheater in ancient Rome in which gladiators fought. Much of it is still standing. Also spelled **Col′i·se′um.**

Co·los·sians (kō-lŏsh′ănz), *n.* a book of the New Testament that contains the Epistle, or letter, of the apostle Paul to the inhabitants of Colossae (kō-lŏs′ē), an ancient city in Asia Minor.

co·los·sus (kō-lŏs′ŭs), *n.* [*pl.* colossi (kō-lŏs′ī) or colossuses (kō-lŏs′ŭs-ĕz)], **1,** an immense statue; **2,** any huge person or object:—**Colossus of Rhodes,** a huge bronze statue of Apollo in ancient Rhodes, one of the Seven Wonders of the World.

col·our (kŭl′ẽr), a British spelling of *color.* Similarly, **colouration, colour-blind, coloured, colourful, colouring, colourless.**

colt (kōlt), *n.* a young horse, ass, zebra, etc.

Co·lum·bi·a (kō-lŭm′bĭ-à), **1,** the poetical name for the U.S.; **2,** a city, capital of South Carolina (map 8).

Co·lum·bi·a Riv·er, a river of British Columbia, Canada, and the northwestern part of the U.S. (maps 4, 9).

col·um·bine (kŏl′ŭm-bīn), *n.* a plant of the buttercup family, having flowers with deeply spurred petals; also, the flowers.

¹Co·lum·bus (kō-lŭm′bŭs), Christopher (1446?–1506), an Italian who discovered America in 1492.

²Co·lum·bus (kō-lŭm′bŭs), a city, capital of Ohio (map 7).

col·umn (kŏl′ŭm), *n.* **1,** an upright pillar supporting or adorning any part of a building or standing alone as a monument; **2,** anything that by its form, position, or use suggests a pillar; as, the spinal *column;* a *column* of mercury; **3,** a vertical division on a printed page; as, the *columns* of a newspaper; **4,** a department in a newspaper, usually written by one person on one general subject; as, the society *column;* **5,** a body or file of soldiers or ships following one after the other.

col·um·nist (kŏl′ŭm-nĭst), *n.* a person who writes a special column of sports, humor, or the like, in a newspaper.

COLUMN

C, capital; S, shaft; B, base.

com- (kŏm-), a prefix meaning together; with; as, *combine, compete:* changed to *col-, cor-, co-, con-,* according to the initial sound of the word to which it is prefixed; as, *collect, correct, co-operate, contract.*

co·ma (kō′mà), *n.* a state of prolonged unconsciousness and insensibility, produced by disease, injury, or poison.

com·a·tose (kŏm′à-tōs; kŏm′à-tōz), *adj.* resembling coma, or a state of insensibility; as, a *comatose* sleep.—*adv.* **com′a·tose·ly.**

comb (kōm), *n.* **1,** a toothed instrument of hard rubber, celluloid, metal, or the like, used to smooth, adjust, or hold in the hair; **2,** a toothed ornament for the hair; **3,** a toothed metal instrument used in grooming horses, separating and cleaning the fibers of flax or wool, etc.; **4,** the crest of a cock (see illustration next page); **5,** a honeycomb (see illustration under *beehive*); **6,** the crest of a hill or wave:—*v.t.* **1,** to dress (the hair)

COMBS, defs. 1 and 2

1, round comb; 2 and 3, ornamental combs; 4, ordinary straight comb.

with a comb; **2,** to cleanse (flax or wool) with a comb; **3,** to search through; as, they *combed* the city for the fugitive.

com·bat (kŏm'băt; kŭm'băt), *n.* a strug-gle; fight:—*v.i.* (kŏm'-băt; kŭm'băt; kŏm-băt'), [combat-ed, combat-ing; if accent-ed on the last syllable, combat-ted, combat-ting], to struggle; as, good *combating* with evil:—*v.t.* to oppose; resist.

COMBS (C, C), def. 4

Syn., n. strife, contest, conflict, battle.

com·bat·ant (kŏm'bȧ-tȧnt; kŭm'bȧ-tȧnt), *n.* a person who takes part in a fight or conflict:—*adj.* fighting.

com·ba·tive (kŏm'bȧ-tĭv; kŭm'bȧ-tĭv; kŏm-băt'ĭv), *adj.* quarrelsome; ready for a battle.—*n.* **com·bat'ive·ness.**

comb·er (kōm'ẽr), *n.* a long, curling wave.

com·bi·na·tion (kŏm'bĭ-nā'shŭn), *n.* **1,** a uniting or being united; **2,** a union or mixing of two or more things to make a new and different thing; **3,** an association of persons for a common object; as, a *combination* of workmen to raise wages; **4,** a one-piece suit of underwear.

com·bine (kŏm-bīn'), *v.t.* [combined, combin-ing], to unite or join; as, to *com-bine* forces; to mix, as ingredients:—*v.i.* to unite; agree; as, two parties will *combine* to defeat a third:—*n.* (kŏm'bīn; kŏm-bīn'), **1,** *Colloquial,* a union; a joining of persons or parties in business or politics to effect a common purpose, sometimes for question-able purposes; **2,** a machine which har-vests and threshes grain at the same time.

com·bus·ti·ble (kŏm-bŭs'tĭ-bl), *adj.* **1,** capable of taking fire and burning; as, wood and coal are *combustible;* **2,** excitable; fierce; as, a *combustible* temper:—*n.* an in-flammable substance, as gasoline.—*n.* **com·bus'ti·bil'i·ty.**

com·bus·tion (kŏm-bŭs'chŭn), *n.* the act or process of burning.

Comdr. abbreviation for *Commander.*

Comdt. abbreviation for *Commandant.*

come (kŭm), *v.i.* [*p.t.* came (kām), *p.p.* come, *p.pr.* com-ing], **1,** to draw near; approach; as, *come* here; spring is *coming;* also, to arrive; **2,** to extend to a given point; as, the farm *comes* as far as the river; **3,** to amount (to); as, the bill *comes* to $50; it all *comes* to the same thing; **4,** to become visible, audible, or the like; as, sounds *come* to the ear; **5,** to be descended; as, he *comes* from a humble family; **6,** to occur as a result; as, accidents *come* from carelessness; **7,** to happen; as, I don't know how we *came* to speak of it.

co·me·di·an (kō-mē'dĭ-ăn), *n.* an actor who plays comic parts.—*n.fem.* **co·me·di·enne'** (kō-mē'dĭ-ĕn').

com·e·dy (kŏm'ĕ-dĭ), *n.* [*pl.* comedies], an amusing play with a happy ending.

come·ly (kŭm'lĭ), *adj.* [come-li-er, come-li-est], fair to look upon; of pleasing appear-ance; as, a *comely* maiden.—*n.* **come'li·ness.**

com·er (kŭm'ẽr), *n.* one who comes; as, a late *comer.*

com·et (kŏm'ĕt), *n.* a heavenly body which moves about the sun. It often has a long, blazing train, or tail.

com·fit (kŭm'fĭt; kŏm'fĭt), *n.* a piece of candied fruit or similar sweetmeat.

com·fort (kŭm'fẽrt), *v.t.* to console or cheer (a person) in pain, grief, or trouble: —*n.* **1,** a person or thing that relieves dis-tress or makes trouble easier to bear; as, a good friend is a *comfort;* **2,** enjoyment of freedom from mental or physical discom-fort; **3,** contentment resulting from the satisfying of wants; also, the things that produce such a state; as, the *comforts* of home.

com·fort·a·ble (kŭm'fẽrt-ȧ-bl), *adj.* **1,** enjoying ease, contentment, or freedom from care; **2,** giving comfort; as, a *com-fortable* chair:—*n.* a wadded bed covering; a comforter.—*adv.* **com'fort·a·bly.**

Syn., adj. snug, contented, satisfied.

com·fort·er (kŭm'fẽrt-ẽr), *n.* **1,** one who consoles or cheers; **2,** a long woolen scarf; **3,** a quilted bed covering of cotton, wool, or feathers; a comfortable.

com·ic (kŏm'ĭk), *adj.* aiming to excite laughter; funny; as, a *comic* song.

com·i·cal (kŏm'ĭ-kăl), *adj.* exciting mirth; laughable; as, the *comical* antics of a monkey.

com·ing (kŭm'ĭng), *n.* **1,** arrival; approach: —*adj.* approaching; impending; as, *coming* events; **2,** *Colloquial,* fairly on the way to fame or success; as, a *coming* man.

com·i·ty (kŏm'ĭ-tĭ), *n.* [*pl.* comities], civility; politeness; especially, the cour-tesy between nations, which consists of recognizing and respecting one another's laws and customs.

com·ma (kŏm'ȧ), *n.* a punctuation mark [,] used to indicate a slight separation of ideas or construction, as to set off a short quotation from the text, to separate words in a series, and the like.

com·mand (kŏ-mănd'), *v.t.* **1,** to give orders to, with authority; **2,** to have au-thority over; control; as, the captain *commands* his ship and crew; **3,** to over-look or dominate, as from a height; **4,** to

---

go; join; yet; sing; chin; show; thin, *th*en; hw, *wh*y; zh, azure; ü, Ger. *für* or Fr. *lune;* ö, Ger. *schön* or Fr. *feu;* ṅ, Fr. *enfant,* nom; kh, Ger. *ach* or *ich.* See pages ix–x.

be able to obtain; as, to *command* good prices; to *command* respect:—*v.i.* to act as leader; rule:—*n.* **1,** authority; the right to command or control; as, a captain is in *command* of a company; **2,** an order; as, he gave the *command* to fire; **3,** a district or a body of troops under a naval or military officer; **4,** mastery; as, the *command* of language; in *command* of one's temper.

com·man·dant (kŏm′ăn-dănt′; kŏm′-ăn-dànt′), *n.* the officer in command of a troop, a fort, a navy yard, or the like.

com·man·deer (kŏm′ăn-dēr′), *v.t.* **1,** to compel (men) to military service; **2,** to take forcibly (food, clothing, horses, etc.) for military purposes; **3,** *Colloquial,* to seize for personal use.

com·mand·er (kŏ-măn′dēr), *n.* **1,** a person in authority; **2,** a military leader or chief; **3,** a naval officer ranking next below a captain: **—commander in chief** [*pl.* commanders in chief], the person in supreme command of the army or the navy, or of both.

com·mand·ing (kŏ-măn′dĭng), *adj.* **1,** in charge; as, a *commanding* officer; **2,** impressive; as, a *commanding* personality.

com·mand·ment (kŏ-mănd′mĕnt), *n.* an order; law; especially, any one of the Ten Commandments given by God to Moses on Mount Sinai (Exodus 20 : 3–17).

com·man·do (kŏ-măn′dō), *n.* [*pl.* commandos or commandoes], a picked force of troops trained for a specific undertaking.

com·mem·o·rate (kŏ-mĕm′ō-rāt), *v.t.* [commemorat-ed, commemorat-ing], to keep alive the memory of (a person, event, etc.), as by a celebration or a monument; as, the Washington Monument *commemorates* George Washington.

Syn. observe, celebrate, keep.

com·mence (kŏ-mĕns′), *v.t.* and *v.i.* [commenced, commenc-ing], to begin.

Syn. start, originate.

com·mence·ment (kŏ-mĕns′mĕnt), *n.* **1,** the beginning; origin; **2,** the occasion when degrees or diplomas are conferred at a school or a college.

com·mend (kŏ-mĕnd′), *v.t.* **1,** to recommend as worthy of notice; as, I *commend* that play to your attention; **2,** to praise; as, to *commend* a child for promptness.

com·mend·a·ble (kŏ-mĕn′dà-bl), *adj.* praiseworthy.—*adv.* **com·mend′a·bly.**

com·men·da·tion (kŏm′ĕn-dā′shŭn), *n.* **1,** praise; approval; as, to win *commendation;* **2,** a quality that wins approval; as, honesty is one's best *commendation.*

com·men·su·rate (kŏ-mĕn′shŏō-rĭt), *adj.* **1,** equal in measure or extent; as, six yards is *commensurate* with eighteen feet; **2,** capable of being measured by the same unit

of measure; as, a room and a box are *commensurate,* but temperature and distance are not; **3,** suitable; proportionate; as, a reward *commensurate* with his effort.

com·ment (kŏm′ĕnt), *n.* **1,** a spoken or written remark; especially, a written note that explains, illustrates, or criticizes; **2,** talk; gossip; as, his unexpected departure caused *comment:*—*v.i.* to make observations or notes; as, to *comment* upon the news.

com·men·ta·ry (kŏm′ĕn-tĕr′ĭ), *n.* [*pl.* commentaries], **1,** an explanation; **2,** a series of explanatory notes, as on passages in the Bible; also, a book of critical or explanatory notes.

com·men·ta·tor (kŏm′ĕn-tā′tēr), *n.* one who writes or makes comments on a book or topic; as, a radio news *commentator.*

com·merce (kŏm′ērs), *n.* the buying and selling of goods on a large scale; trade.

com·mer·cial (kŏ-mûr′shăl), *adj.* **1,** engaged in, resulting from, or having to do with trade or business; as, a *commercial* firm; *commercial* profits; **2,** made to be sold in quantity; as, *commercial* fertilizer: —*n.* the advertising portion of a radio program.—*adv.* **com·mer′cial·ly.**

com·mer·cial·ize (kŏ-mûr′shăl-īz), *v.t.* [commercialized, commercializ-ing], to reduce to a money-making or business basis; as, to *commercialize* football.

com·min·gle (kŏ-mĭng′gl), *v.t.* and *v.i.* [commin-gled, commin-gling], to mix.

com·mis·er·ate (kŏ-mĭz′ēr-āt), *v.t.* [commiserat-ed, commiserat-ing], to feel or express pity for; sympathize with.

com·mis·er·a·tion (kŏ-mĭz′ēr-ā′shŭn), *n.* a feeling of sympathy; also, an expression of this feeling.

com·mis·sar·i·at (kŏm′ĭ-sâr′ĭ-ăt), *n.* **1,** the department of an army that furnishes provisions and other supplies; **2,** the officers in this department; **3,** the supplies furnished.

com·mis·sar·y (kŏm′ĭ-sĕr′ĭ), *n.* [*pl.* commissaries], **1,** one to whom some charge is committed by a superior; a deputy; **2,** in the army, an official in the department which has charge of provisions and supplies; **3,** a company store supplying food and equipment, as in a lumber camp.

com·mis·sion (kŏ-mĭsh′ŭn), *n.* **1,** the doing or performing of some act: often implying wrongdoing; as, the *commission* of a crime; **2,** a matter entrusted to anyone to perform; as, he had a *commission* to buy land; **3,** the fee paid to an agent for doing business for another; as, the *commission* on the sale was $25; **4,** a group of persons appointed to perform certain duties; as, a *commission* to investigate housing; **5,** a

āte, āorta, râre, căt, ȧsk, fär, ȧllow, sofȧ; ēve, ĕvent, ĕll, wrītēr, novĕl; bīte, pĭn; nō, ōbey, ôr, dŏg, tŏp, cŏllide; ūnit, ūnite, bûrn, cŭt, focŭs; nōōn, fŏŏt; mound; coin;

document conferring military or naval rank or authority:—*v.t.* **1,** to empower; delegate; as, I *commission* you to paint the picture; **2,** in the army and navy, to confer rank or authority upon; **3,** to put into service, as a warship.

in commission, 1, into service; as, to put a ship *in commission;* **2,** in working order; as, our radio has been repaired and is now *in commission;* **out of commission,** not in working order.

com·mis·sion·aire (kŏ-mĭsh′ŭn-âr′), *n.* in Europe, the hotel attendant who meets trains and boats, acts as porter, and endeavors to secure patrons.

com·mis·sion·er (kŏ-mĭsh′ŭn-ẽr), *n.* **1,** a person holding authority under a commission, or warrant, especially an officer in charge of some department of the public service; as, the *Commissioner* of Public Works; **2,** in some cities, a member of the governing body.

com·mit (kŏ-mĭt′), *v.t.* [commit-ted, commit-ting], **1,** to give (someone) into another's care for safekeeping, care, custody, or the like; as, to *commit* an invalid to a hospital; to *commit* a man for trial; **2,** to entrust (something) for safekeeping, as by writing down or memorizing; as, to *commit* thoughts to paper or verses to memory; **3,** to do (something foolish or wrong); as, to *commit* a folly or a crime; **4,** to involve (oneself) in difficulties; as, he refused to *commit* himself by talking; also, to pledge; as, I am *committed* to the cause.

com·mit·ment (kŏ-mĭt′mĕnt), *n.* **1,** the act of committing; especially, the act of entrusting or giving in charge; **2,** the sending of a person to prison; also, imprisonment; confinement; **3,** a pledge, or agreement, to do something.

com·mit·tee (kŏ-mĭt′ĭ), *n.* a group of persons elected or appointed to deal with a certain phase of a business, or to act on, consider, or report on, one special matter; as, a *committee* for decorating the hall.

com·mode (kŏ-mōd′), *n.* **1,** a bureau or chest of drawers; **2,** an old-fashioned movable washstand.

com·mo·di·ous (kŏ-mō′dĭ-ŭs), *adj.* roomy; spacious.—*adv.* **com·mo′di·ous·ly.**

com·mod·i·ty (kŏ-mŏd′ĭ-tĭ), *n.* [*pl.* commodities], **1,** something useful; an article of commerce, such as wheat, copper, silk, hogs, or the like; **2, commodities,** goods; merchandise.

com·mo·dore (kŏm′ō-dôr′), *n.* **1,** a naval commanding officer ranking above a captain and below a rear admiral; **2,** a title of courtesy given to the president of a yacht club, the senior captain of a line of merchant ships, etc.

com·mon (kŏm′ŭn), *adj.* **1,** belonging to, or shared by, more than one; general; as, death is the *common* lot; **2,** belonging, or relating, to a group or community; public; as, parks are *common* property; **3,** usual; frequent; as, a *common* saying; a *common* sight; **4,** of the ordinary kind; merely average in rank, ability, etc.; as, the *common* people; a *common* daisy; **5,** low; vulgar:—*n.* **1,** a tract of open public land; as, the village *common;* **2,** the average; as, a man above the *common.*

common noun, a noun which refers to objects as individuals of a class; as, "book," "cars," and "store" are *common nouns:* distinguished from *proper noun,* which names a specific person, place, or the like, as "John," "Chicago"; **common sense,** good judgment in ordinary affairs; **in common,** jointly; as, property held *in common.*—*n.* **com′mon-ness.**

Syn., adj. ordinary, universal, mutual.

com·mon·er (kŏm′ŭn-ẽr), *n.* one of the common people; not a nobleman.

com·mon·ly (kŏm′ŭn-lĭ), *adv.* usually.

com·mon·place (kŏm′ŭn-plās′), *n.* **1,** an ordinary topic of conversation; also, a remark often heard; **2,** an everyday object, action, or event; one that is not uncommon; as, flying has become a *commonplace:*—*adj.* uninteresting; neither new nor striking.

com·mons (kŏm′ŭnz), *n.pl.* **1,** the mass of the people; **2,** in a college or university, meals at a common table; **3,** rations; fare: —**Commons,** the House of Commons, or lower house of Parliament, in Great Britain and Canada.

com·mon·weal (kŏm′ŭn-wēl′), *n.* **1,** the public welfare; **2,** *Archaic,* a commonwealth.

com·mon·wealth (kŏm′ŭn-wĕlth′), *n.* the public; the whole body of people in a state; also, a state in which the people rule.

com·mo·tion (kŏ-mō′shŭn), *n.* **1,** violent physical disturbance; as, the *commotion* of the raging sea; **2,** stir and confusion; tumult; as, a *commotion* in the crowd.

com·mu·nal (kŏm′ū-nǎl; kŏ-mū′nǎl), *adj.* relating to the community; belonging to the people; as, *communal* land.

¹com·mune (kŏm′ūn), *n.* in some countries of Europe, especially France, the smallest political division; hence, a local, self-governing community.

²com·mune (kŏ-mūn′), *v.i.* [commu-ned, commun-ing], **1,** to feel an intimate understanding or hold intimate intercourse; as, to *commune* with nature; **2,** especially in the U.S., to partake of Holy Communion.

com·mu·ni·ca·ble (kŏ-mū′nĭ-kȧ-bl), *adj.* capable of being transmitted from person to person; as, a *communicable* disease.

com·mu·ni·cant (kŏ-mū′nĭ-kănt), *n.* a partaker of the Eucharist, or Lord's Supper; hence, a member of a church.

com·mu·ni·cate (kŏ-mū′nĭ-kāt), *v.t.* [communicat-ed, communicat-ing], 1, to impart; convey; as, to *communicate* happiness; to *communicate* a disease; 2, to make known; tell, as news:—*v.i.* 1, to partake of the Lord's Supper; 2, to be connected; as, the two rooms *communicate*; 3, to get into connection or touch, by letter, telephone, or the like; as, she *communicates* with us regularly.—*adj.* com-mu′ni-ca′tive.

com·mu·ni·ca·tion (kŏ-mū′nĭ-kā′shŭn), *n.* 1, an imparting, as of news; a spreading, as of disease; 2, the exchange of thoughts, opinions, or the like, as between persons, business firms, or countries; as, all *communication* was broken off by the storm; also, the letter, message, etc., so exchanged; as, I just received your *communication* of yesterday; 3, any means of conveying thoughts or information, as the telephone, telegraph, or wireless; 4, the means of passing from place to place; as, there is no *communication* between rooms.

com·mun·ion (kŏ-mūn′yŭn), *n.* 1, fellowship; especially, religious fellowship; an intimate exchange of spiritual thoughts and feelings; 2, a group of persons having the same religious beliefs:—**Communion**, the sacrament of the Lord's Supper.

com·mu·nist (kŏm′ū-nĭst), *n.* one who believes in communism, or the theory that the people should own in common the means of production, such as mines, factories, etc., and should share in both the work and the returns:—**Communist**, a member of a political party holding these views, especially in the U.S.S.R.—*n.* com′mu-nism.—*adj.* com′mu-nis′tic.

com·mu·ni·ty (kŏ-mū′nĭ-tĭ), *n.* [*pl.* communities], 1, all the persons who live in one place, as the people of a town, city, or the like; hence, the public; 2, a group of persons, bound by ties of religion or of common interest; as, a *community* of artists; 3, likeness; similarity; as, *community* of interests.

com·mu·ta·tion (kŏm′ū-tā′shŭn), *n.* 1, the substitution of one kind of payment or service for another; 2, the changing of a penalty to one less severe, as of death to life imprisonment:—**commutation ticket**, a transportation ticket, sold at a reduced rate, for a certain number of trips or for daily trips between neighboring places.

com·mu·ta·tor (kŏm′ū-tā′tẽr), *n.* a device, usually on a motor or generator, for reversing the direction of an electric current, or for changing an alternating into a direct current.

com·mute (kŏ-mūt′), *v.t.* [commut-ed, commut-ing], to exchange for something different; especially, to reduce the severity of; as, to *commute* a sentence of imprisonment from ten to five years:—*v.i.* to travel back and forth daily from a suburb to work in a city.—*n.* com-mut′er.

Co·mo (kō′mô), a lake in Lombardy, Italy, at the foot of the Alps (map **12**).

comp. or **compar.** abbreviation for *comparative.*

¹**com·pact** (kŏm′păkt), *n.* an agreement.

²**com·pact** (kŏm-păkt′; kŏm′păkt), *adj.* 1, closely or firmly united or packed together; solid; 2, condensed; terse; as, a *compact* style:—*v.t.* to press or pack closely; make solid:—*n.* (kŏm′păkt), a small metal case, to be carried in the purse, which contains face powder and rouge.—*adv.* com-pact′ly.—*n.* com-pact′ness.

com·pan·ion (kŏm-păn′yŭn), *n.* 1, a comrade or associate; sometimes, a person paid to live or travel with another; 2, one of a pair or set of objects designed to go together:—*v.t.* to accompany.—*n.* com-pan′ion-ship.

Syn., n. friend, ally, chum.

com·pan·ion·a·ble (kŏm-păn′yŭn-á-bl), *adj.* sociable; agreeable.—*adv.* com-pan′-ion-a-bly.

com·pan·ion·way (kŏm-păn′yŭn-wā′), *n.* on a ship, a stairway leading below from the deck.

com·pa·ny (kŭm′pá-nĭ), *n.* [*pl.* companies], 1, companionship; society; as, I want *company* tonight; 2, companions; associates; as, a man is known by the *company* he keeps; 3, a guest or guests; 4, a group of persons assembled; 5, a business or commercial firm; 6, a troupe of actors; 7, a body of soldiers, especially a section of infantry, normally commanded by a captain.

Syn. assemblage, crowd, host, throng.

compar. abbreviation for *comparative.*

com·pa·ra·ble (kŏm′pá-rá-bl), *adj.* 1, capable of being compared; as, the sound of cannon and of thunder are *comparable*; 2, worthy or fit to be compared; as, the Lincoln Memorial is *comparable* to the Parthenon.—*adv.* com′pa-ra-bly.

com·par·a·tive (kŏm-păr′á-tĭv), *adj.* 1, involving the use of comparison; as, the *comparative* study of animals; 2, measured by comparison with something else; as, we live in *comparative* comfort; 3, in grammar, naming that form of an adjective or adverb, as "longer" or "sooner," that expresses a higher degree of the quality indicated by the simple form:—*n.* the comparative degree; also, a comparative form; as, "better" is the *comparative* of "good."—*adv.* com-par′a-tive-ly.

com-pare (kŏm-pâr′), *v.t.* [compared, compar-ing], **1,** to liken; describe as similar; as, the poets *compare* death to sleep; **2,** to examine in order to discover likeness and unlikeness; as, to *compare* two specimens; **3,** in grammar, to give the positive, comparative, and superlative degrees of an adjective or adverb:—*v.i.* to be worthy of comparison with something else; as, rayon *compares* favorably with silk:—*n.* comparison; as, beauty beyond *compare*.

com-par-i-son (kŏm-păr′ĭ-sŭn), *n.* **1,** an examination of two or more things with a view to discovering likenesses or differences; as, a *comparison* between town and country life; **2,** a description of a thing as like another; a simile; as, "hair white as snow" is a common *comparison*; **3,** in grammar, the change in form of adjectives and adverbs which shows a difference in degree.

com-part-ment (kŏm-pärt′mĕnt), *n.* a separate part or division, as of an enclosed space; a separate section; as, a watertight *compartment* in the hull of a ship; a *compartment* in a European passenger coach.

¹**com-pass** (kŭm′pȧs), *v.t.* **1,** to encircle; surround, as a city with a wall; also, to besiege (a city); **2,** to grasp (ideas) with the mind; **3,** to attain (a goal), or achieve (a task).

²**com-pass** (kŭm′pȧs), *n.* **1,** the boundary of an area; as, within the *compass* of a city; **2,** an instrument for determining direction by means of a needle pointing to the magnetic north; **3,** the range of tones possible to a given voice or instrument; **4,** (usually *compasses*), an instrument for drawing and dividing circles, transferring measurements, etc., consisting of two small, upright rods joined together at the top by a hinge: also called *dividers*.

COMPASS, def. 2

COMPASSES

com-pas-sion (kŏm-păsh′ŭn), *n.* sorrow and pity for the sufferings of others.
Syn. sympathy, mercy, tenderness.

com-pas-sion-ate (kŏm-păsh′ŭn-ĭt), *adj.* merciful.—*adv.* **com-pas′sion-ate-ly**.

com-pat-i-ble (kŏm-păt′ĭ-bl), *adj.* **1,** consistent; able to exist at the same time; as, accuracy may not be *compatible* with speed; **2,** harmonious; mutually agreeable; as, *compatible* people.—*adv.* **com-pat′i-bly**. —*n.* **com-pat′i-bil/i-ty**.

com-pa-tri-ot (kŏm-pā′trĭ-ŭt; kŏm-păt′-rĭ-ŭt), *n.* a fellow countryman.

com-peer (kŏm-pēr′), *n.* **1,** an equal in rank; **2,** an associate or companion.

com-pel (kŏm-pĕl′), *v.t.* [compelled, compel-ling], to oblige; force; as, a guilty conscience *compelled* him to confess.
Syn. coerce, make, drive, necessitate.

com-pen-sate (kŏm′pĕn-sāt), *v.t.* [compensat-ed, compensat-ing], to make a suitable return to; pay; as, to *compensate* you for your time:—*v.i.* to make up for something; supply an equivalent; as, nothing can *compensate* for loss of health.

com-pen-sa-tion (kŏm′pĕn-sā′shŭn), *n.* **1,** whatever makes good any lack or loss; payment; amends; as, the man received *compensation* for his injuries; **2,** something given in return for a service or for something of value; as, he receives inadequate *compensation* for the work he does.

com-pete (kŏm-pēt′), *v.i.* [compet-ed, compet-ing], to enter into a contest or rivalry; contend; as, to *compete* for a prize.

com-pe-tence (kŏm′pē-tĕns), *n.* **1,** fitness; capability; ability; as, no one questions her *competence* to teach; **2,** a modest fortune; enough for comfort. Also, **com′pe-ten-cy**.

com-pe-tent (kŏm′pē-tĕnt), *adj.* able; capable.—*adv.* **com′pe-tent-ly**.

com-pe-ti-tion (kŏm′pē-tĭsh′ŭn), *n.* **1,** the act of competing; rivalry; **2,** a contest; a trial of ability, as in sport; as, the *competition* in skiing drew a crowd; **3,** the effort of rival concerns to secure as much business as possible by making concessions as regards price, terms of payment, etc.—*adj.* **com-pet′i-tive** (kŏm-pĕt′ĭ-tĭv).—*n.* **com-pet′i-tor** (kŏm-pĕt′ĭ-tĕr).
Syn. opposition, strife, emulation.

com-pile (kŏm-pīl′), *v.t.* [compiled, compil-ing], to collect (data, facts, figures, literary extracts, or the like) from various sources and put into new form; as, to *compile* a table of contents or a book of verse.—*n.* **com-pil′er**.—*n.* **com/pi-la′tion**.

com-pla-cence (kŏm-plā′sĕns), *n.* self-satisfaction. Also, **com-pla′cen-cy**.

com-pla-cent (kŏm-plā′sĕnt), *adj.* pleased with oneself; self-satisfied.—*adv.* **com-pla′cent-ly**.

com-plain (kŏm-plān′), *v.i.* **1,** to give voice to grief, pain, resentment, or discontent; as, she *complained* of headache; **2,** to lament mournfully; as, Job *complained* to the Lord; **3,** to find fault with; as, the teacher *complained* of John's tardiness; **4,** to make an accusation; as, the prisoner *complained* of injustice.—*n.* **com-plain′er**. —*adv.* **com-plain′ing-ly**.
Syn. deplore, murmur, repine, bewail.

com-plaint (kŏm-plānt′), *n.* **1,** a verbal expression of discontent, grief, or pain;

2, an ailment or disease; **3,** in law, a formal charge against a person.

com·plai·sant (kŏm-plā′sănt; kŏm-plā′zănt), *adj.* courteous; obliging.—*n.* **com·plai′sance.**

com·ple·ment (kŏm′plē-mĕnt), *n.* **1,** the full number or quantity; a complete set; as, the orchestra has its *complement* of instruments; **2,** that which makes an incomplete thing complete; **3,** one of two parts which together form a whole:—*v.t.* (kŏm′plē-mĕnt), to finish out; make whole.

com·ple·men·ta·ry (kŏm′plē-mĕn′tȧ-rĭ), *adj.* forming, or of the nature of, a complement, or completing part:—**complementary angles,** two angles which make a right angle, or an angle of 90 degrees.

com·plete (kŏm-plēt′), *adj.* **1,** lacking nothing; entire; perfect; full; as, a *complete* deck of cards; **2,** absolute; as, a *complete* surprise; **3,** finished; as, her work is now *complete*:—*v.t.* [complet-ed, complet-ing], to make whole or perfect; finish.—*n.* **com·plete′ness.**
Syn., v. close, end, conclude, terminate.

com·plete·ly (kŏm-plēt′lĭ), *adv.* entirely.

com·ple·tion (kŏm-plē′shŭn), *n.* the act of making, or state of being, whole or perfect; fulfilment.

com·plex (kŏm-plĕks′; kŏm′plĕks), *adj.* **1,** made of various parts; not simple; as, a *complex* business organization; **2,** involved; intricate; as, a *complex* situation; —*n.* (kŏm′plĕks), a habitual emotional attitude toward a particular thing.
Syn. complicated, entangled.

com·plex·ion (kŏm-plĕk′shŭn), *n.* **1,** the color, texture, and appearance of the skin, especially of the face; **2,** general aspect or character; as, his story gave a different *complexion* to the case.—*adj.* **com·plex′ioned.**

com·plex·i·ty (kŏm-plĕk′sĭ-tĭ), *n.* [*pl.* complexities], **1,** the state of being involved or complicated; **2,** a complication.

com·pli·ance (kŏm-plī′ăns), *n.* the act or state of yielding or consenting; submission: —**in compliance with,** in agreement with; in obedience to; yielding to.

com·pli·ant (kŏm-plī′ănt), *adj.* inclined to consent; yielding; obliging.—*adv.* **com·pli′ant·ly.**

com·pli·cate (kŏm′plĭ-kāt), *v.t.* [complicat-ed, complicat-ing], to make confused or hard to understand; to make difficult.—*adj.* **com′pli·cat′ed.**

com·pli·ca·tion (kŏm′plĭ-kā′shŭn), *n.* ·**1,** a combination of things, parts, etc., so mixed together as to cause confusion or difficulty; as, a *complication* of knots; **2,** a confused or troublesome situation; as,

his mistake caused the *complication;* **3,** that which causes difficulty or entanglement; as, traffic *complications.*

com·plic·i·ty (kŏm-plĭs′ĭ-tĭ), *n.* [*pl.* complicities], partnership in wrongdoing or crime.

com·pli·ment (kŏm′plĭ-mĕnt), *n.* **1,** something pleasant said about a person or his work; **2, compliments,** formal greetings; as, the new ambassador paid his *compliments* to the President:—*v.t.* (kŏm′plĭ-mĕnt), to express approval of; praise.

com·pli·men·ta·ry (kŏm′plĭ-mĕn′tȧ-rĭ), *adj.* **1,** conveying approval or admiration; **2,** given free; as, *complimentary* tickets.

com·ply (kŏm-plī′), *v.i.* [complied, comply-ing], to assent; yield; agree; as, we *complied* with his wish to be alone.
Syn. accede, conform, submit.

com·po·nent (kŏm-pō′nĕnt), *adj.* composing; forming part of a whole:—*n.* a necessary part; an ingredient.

com·port (kŏm-pôrt′), *v.t.* to conduct or behave (oneself); as, he did not know how to *comport* himself at the party:—*v.i.* to agree; accord; harmonize; as, his lack of dignity does not *comport* with his position as a judge.—*n.* **com·port′ment.**

com·pose (kŏm-pōz′), *v.t.* [composed, compos-ing], **1,** to form by putting things together; as, bronze is *composed* of copper and tin; **2,** to construct or put together; as, to *compose* a sentence, sermon, piece of music, or picture; **3,** in a printing office, to set (type); **4,** to settle or arrange (any matter) successfully; as, to *compose* a dispute; **5,** to calm; make tranquil; as, to *compose* one's mind.

com·posed (kŏm-pōzd′), *adj.* tranquil; calm; serene; quiet.—*adv.* **com·pos′ed·ly.**

com·pos·er (kŏm-pōz′ẽr), *n.* one who composes; especially, one who composes music.

com·pos·ite (kŏm-pŏz′ĭt), *adj.* **1,** made up of various distinct parts; as, the illustration of *aviation* on page 55 is a *composite* illustration; **2,** in botany, belonging to a group of plants whose flowers are made up of many small flowers, as the dandelion or aster:—*n.* a compound.— *adv.* **com·pos′ite·ly.**

com·po·si·tion (kŏm′pŏ-zĭsh′ŭn), *n.* **1,** the act of creating an artistic work; **2,** the work created, as a picture, a piece of music, a novel, or the like; **3,** a schoolroom exercise written for practice in the use of language; **4,** the setting up of type; **5,** a substance formed by mingling various materials; **6,** the make-up of anything; as, what is the *composition* of this substance?

com·pos·i·tor (kŏm-pŏz′ĭ-tẽr), *n.* one who sets type in a printing office.

com·post (kŏm′pōst), *n.* a mixture of various substances, such as leaf mold, manure, etc., for fertilizing land.

com·po·sure (kŏm-pō′zhẽr), *n.* calmness.

¹com·pound (kŏm-pound′), *v.t.* **1,** to mix or combine together, as two chemicals to make a medicine; **2,** to form by mixing, as a medicine:—*adj.* (kŏm′pound; kŏm-pound′), composed of two or more elements:—*n.* (kŏm′pound), **1,** a combination of two or more elements or parts; **2,** in chemistry, a substance formed of two or more elements united in definite proportions; **3,** in grammar, a word composed of two or more elements, themselves usually words, as "housewife."
Syn., *adj.* complex, combined; *v.* mix, mingle, unite, blend, merge.

²com·pound (kŏm′pound), *n.* in China, the East Indies, etc., an enclosure containing a house, trading station, etc., especially one used by foreigners.

com·pre·hend (kŏm′prē-hĕnd′), *v.t.* **1,** to understand; grasp the meaning of; **2,** to include; take in; as, Europe *comprehends* many nations.
Syn. embrace, contain, embody.

com·pre·hen·si·ble (kŏm′prē-hĕn′sĭ-bl), *adj.* understandable.—*n.* **com′pre·hen′si·bil′i·ty.**—*adv.* **com′pre·hen′si·bly.**

com·pre·hen·sion (kŏm′prē-hĕn′shŭn), *n.* the act of understanding; ability to understand; as, geometry is beyond my *comprehension*.

com·pre·hen·sive (kŏm′prē-hĕn′sĭv), *adj.* **1,** including much; full; complete; as, a *comprehensive* account of the war; **2,** able to understand; comprehending; as, a *comprehensive* mind.—*adv.* **com′pre·hen′sive·ly.**—*n.* **com′pre·hen′sive·ness.**

com·press (kŏm-prĕs′), *v.t.* to press together; condense:—*n.* (kŏm′prĕs), a pad applied hot or cold to some part of the body to reduce inflammation.—*adj.* **com·press′i·ble.**—*n.* **com·press′i·bil′i·ty.**

com·pres·sion (kŏm-prĕsh′ŭn), *n.* **1,** the act of pressing together; **2,** condensation.

com·prise (kŏm-prīz′), *v.t.* [comprised, compris·ing], to consist of; include; as, the house *comprises* ten rooms. Also spelled **com·prize′.**

com·pro·mise (kŏm′prō-mīz), *n.* **1,** a method of settling a dispute whereby each side yields something; as, after hours of dispute they resorted to *compromise*; **2,** an agreement reached by mutual yielding; **3,** a line of action that follows a middle course; as, the plan adopted was a *compromise*:—*v.t.* [compromised, compromising], **1,** to settle by mutual yielding; **2,** to expose to suspicion; endanger; as, such actions will *compromise* your reputation:—*v.i.* to make a compromise.

comp·trol·ler (kŏn-trōl′ẽr), *n.* a public officer who examines and certifies accounts. See **con-trol′ler.**

com·pul·sion (kŏm-pŭl′shŭn), *n.* the act of compelling; force; also, the state of being compelled; constraint.

com·pul·so·ry (kŏm-pŭl′sō-rĭ), *adj.* **1,** exercising force; as, *compulsory* laws; **2,** obligatory; enforced; required; as, vaccination is *compulsory*.—*adv.* **com·pul′so·ri·ly.**

com·punc·tion (kŏm-pŭngk′shŭn), *n.* uneasiness of conscience; mild regret, as for a slight wrong; as, I felt some *compunction* at having kept her waiting.

com·pute (kŏm-pūt′), *v.t.* [comput-ed, comput-ing], to figure; number; reckon; calculate; as, he *computed* his expenses.—*adj.* **com·put′a·ble.**—*n.* **com·put′er.**—*n.* **com′pu·ta′tion.**

com·rade (kŏm′răd; kŏm′rĭd), *n.* a friend; a companion:—**comrades at arms,** fellow soldiers.—*n.* **com′rade-ship.**

¹con (kŏn), *v.t.* [conned, con-ning], to study carefully; hence, to commit to memory.

²con (kŏn), *adv.* on the negative side; as, they argued the matter pro and *con*.

con- (kŏn-), *prefix,* a form of *com-* used before certain consonants.

con·cat·e·na·tion (kŏn-kăt′ē-nā′shŭn), *n.* a series of things or events united like links in a chain.

con·cave (kŏn′kāv; kŏn-kāv′), *adj.* curved inward, as the inside of a circle or ball: opposite of *convex*.

CONCAVE
The inside of the bowl is concave.

con·cav·i·ty (kŏn-kăv′ĭ-tĭ), *n.* [*pl.* concavities], **1,** the state of being concave; **2,** the inner surface of a rounded, hollow body.

con·ceal (kŏn-sēl′), *v.t.* to hide; keep secret.—*adj.* **con·ceal′a·ble.**
Syn. hide, secrete, disguise.

con·ceal·ment (kŏn-sēl′mĕnt), *n.* **1,** the act of hiding or state of being hidden; **2,** a place of hiding; shelter.

con·cede (kŏn-sēd′), *v.t.* [conced-ed, conced-ing], **1,** to admit to be true; yield; as, he *conceded* the point in the debate; **2,** to grant (a right, privilege, etc.); as, they *conceded* an advance in wages.

con·ceit (kŏn-sēt′), *n.* **1,** a too flattering belief in one's own powers; vanity; **2,** a fanciful notion; a quaint thought.

con·ceit·ed (kŏn-sēt′ĕd), *adj.* having too good an opinion of oneself; excessively vain.—*adv.* **con·ceit′ed·ly.**

go; join; yet; sing; chin; show; thin, *then;* **hw,** *why;* **zh,** azure; **ü,** Ger. für or Fr. lune; **ö,** Ger. schön or Fr. feu; **n̈,** Fr. enfant, nom; **kh,** Ger. ach or ich. See pages ix–x.

con·ceive (kŏn-sēv'), *v.t.* [conceived, conceiv-ing], **1**, to think of; imagine; **2**, to form (a purpose, design, etc.) in the mind; devise; as, to *conceive* a plot; **3**, to become pregnant with (young):—*v.i.* **1**, to think; imagine; as, I cannot *conceive* of her doing that; **2**, to become pregnant.—*adj.* **con·ceiv'a·ble**.—*adv.* **con·ceiv'a·bly**.

con·cen·trate (kŏn'sĕn-trāt), *v.t.* [concentrat-ed, concentrat-ing], **1**, to bring to a common center; as, the general *concentrated* his troops in the city; **2**, to fix (the attention or energies) on one course or object; **3**, to increase in strength by reducing bulk; as, to *concentrate* soup by boiling away excess liquid:—*v.i.* **1**, to come together in one place; as, population *concentrates* in the cities; **2**, to fix the attention; as, to *concentrate* on a problem.—*n.* **con·cen·tra'tion**.

con·cen·tra·tion camp, **1**, a place where troops from various areas are assembled; **2**, a place where prisoners of war or enemy aliens are confined.

con·cen·tric (kŏn-sĕn'trĭk), *adj.* having a common center; as, *concentric* circles or spheres.

con·cept (kŏn'sĕpt), *n.* a mental impression of an object; a general notion.

con·cep·tion (kŏn-sĕp'shŭn), *n.* **1**, the act of forming a mental image or impression; **2**, an idea or notion; **3**, the fertilization of the egg and the beginning of a new life in the body of the mother.

CONCENTRIC CIRCLES

con·cern (kŏn-sûrn'), *v.t.* **1**, to affect the welfare of; relate or belong to; interest or engage; as, that affair does not *concern* me; **2**, to make uneasy; as, don't let that *concern* you:—*n.* **1**, that which relates to one; affair; as, that is my *concern;* **2**, interest; anxiety; **3**, a business firm.—*adj.* **con·cerned'**.

Syn., n. solicitude, care, worry.

con·cern·ing (kŏn-sûr'nĭng), *prep.* relating to; regarding.

con·cert (kŏn-sûrt'), *v.t.* to plan together; settle by agreement:—*n.* (kŏn'sûrt), **1**, a musical entertainment; **2**, musical harmony; as, the boys like to sing in *concert;* **3**, agreement; co-operation; **4**, unison of voices; as, to recite in *concert.*

con·cert·ed (kŏn-sûr'tĕd), *adj.* mutually planned or agreed upon; simultaneous; as, *concerted* action is most effective.

con·cer·ti·na (kŏn'sĕr-tē'nà), *n.* a small musical instrument somewhat like an accordion.

CONCERTINA

con·cer·to (kŏn-châr'tō; kŏn-sûr'tō), *n.*[*pl.* concertos], a musical composition, usually in three movements, for one or more instruments accompanied by an orchestra.

con·ces·sion (kŏn-sĕsh'ŭn), *n.* **1**, the act of granting or yielding; **2**, an acknowledgment or admission; **3**, a grant of a privilege, or of land, for some special purpose.

conch (kŏngk), *n.* a large spiral sea shell.

con·cil·i·ate (kŏn-sĭl'ĭ-āt), *v.t.*[conciliat-ed, conciliat-ing], to gain the good will of; win over from hostility; as, her many kind deeds finally *conciliated* her enemy.—*n.* **con·cil'i·a'tion**.

CONCH

con·cil·i·a·tor·y (kŏn-sĭl'ĭ-à-tôr'ĭ), *adj.* tending to pacify or soothe; showing a spirit willing to come half way; as, she adopted a *conciliatory* attitude.

con·cise (kŏn-sīs'), *adj.* terse; brief; expressing much in few words.—*adv.* **con·cise'ly**.—*n.* **con·cise'ness**.

Syn. pithy, succinct, short, curt.

con·clave (kŏn'klāv; kŏng'klāv), *n.* **1**, a private meeting of cardinals for the election of a pope; **2**, the rooms in which such meetings are held; **3**, any secret meeting.

con·clude (kŏn-klōōd'), *v.t.* [conclud-ed, conclud-ing], **1**, to bring to an end; as, to *conclude* a speech; **2**, to arrive at an opinion by reasoning; infer; as, it grew so late, I *concluded* you were not coming; **3**, to settle; bring about as a result; as, after hours of bickering, he *concluded* the agreement:—*v.i.* to come to an end.

Syn. terminate, deduce, arrange.

con·clu·sion (kŏn-klōō'zhŭn), *n.* **1**, the end; termination; as, the *conclusion* of a journey, a book, or the like; **2**, an opinion arrived at by reasoning; an inference; as, after much study he came to this *conclusion;* **3**, a final summing up, as of a speech; **4**, the final result; outcome:—**try conclusions with**, to engage in a trial of skill, strength, or the like.

con·clu·sive (kŏn-klōō'sĭv), *adj.* final; ending argument; as, *conclusive* facts.—*adv.* **con·clu'sive·ly**.—*n.* **con·clu'sive-ness**.

con·coct (kŏn-kŏkt'; kŏn-kŏkt'), *v.t.* **1**, to prepare, as food, by mixing various elements; **2**, to form; make up, as a plot.

con·coc·tion (kŏn-kŏk'shŭn; kŏn-kŏk'shŭn), *n.* **1**, the act of mixing ingredients; **2**, anything, as food or a drink, made by mixing a variety of ingredients; **3**, a scheme.

con·com·i·tant (kŏn-kŏm'ĭ-tănt), *n.* that which accompanies something else; as, happiness is not always a *concomitant* of wealth:—*adj.* accompanying; attending.

āte, āorta, râre, căt, àsk, fär, ăllow, sofà; ēve, ēvent, ĕll, writĕr, novĕl; bīte, pĭn; nō, ōbey, ôr, dŏg, tŏp, cŏllide; ūnit, ūnite, bûrn, cŭt, focŭs; nōon, fŏŏt; mound; coin;

Con·cord (kŏng′kĕrd), **1,** a town in Massachusetts, the scene of an early battle in the Revolutionary War, and later an important literary center; **2,** a city, capital of New Hampshire (map 6).

con·cord (kŏn′kôrd; kŏng′kôrd), *n.* agreement; peace; harmony.

con·cord·ance (kŏn-kôr′dăns; kŏn-kôr′dăns), *n.* **1,** agreement; **2,** a list of words in a book, as the Bible, with references to the places where they occur.

con·course (kŏn′kôrs; kŏng′kôrs), *n.* **1,** a flowing together; as, a *concourse* of waters; **2,** an assembly or crowd; **3,** an open place where crowds gather or roads meet.

con·crete (kŏn′krēt; kŏn-krēt′), *adj.* **1,** actual; specific; capable of being seen, heard, tasted, etc.; not abstract; as, a table is a *concrete* object, but goodness is an abstract quality; **2,** consisting of the substance called *concrete:*—*n.* a hardened mixture of cement, sand, gravel, and water.—*adv.* **con′crete·ly.**

con·cu·bine (kŏng′kū-bĭn), *n.* **1,** a woman who lives with a man without being legally married to him; **2,** in countries where a man may have several wives, a wife of inferior position.

con·cur (kŏn-kûr′), *v.i.* [concurred, concur-ring], to agree or unite in action or opinion; as, the class *concurred* in the decision.—*n.* **con·cur′rence.**

con·cur·rent (kŏn-kûr′ĕnt), *adj.* **1,** acting together; agreeing; **2,** occurring at the same time.—*adv.* **con·cur′rent·ly.**

con·cus·sion (kŏn-kŭsh′ŭn), *n.* **1,** a shaking; shock; **2,** an injury to the brain, spine, or other part, from a blow or collision.

con·demn (kŏn-dĕm′), *v.t.* **1,** to blame; censure; declare to be wrong; **2,** to declare guilty; **3,** to declare to be forfeited or taken for public use; as, to *condemn* land; **4,** to pronounce unfit for use; as, to *condemn* a row of tenements.—*adj.* **con·dem′na·tor·y.**—*n.* **con′dem·na′tion.**

Syn. disapprove, denounce, upbraid.

con·den·sa·tion (kŏn′dĕn-sā′shŭn), *n.* **1,** a reduction in size; compression; as, the *condensation* of a chapter into a paragraph; **2,** something that has been so condensed; **3,** the change from a gaseous to a liquid form, as from water vapor to rain.

con·dense (kŏn-dĕns′), *v.t.* [condensed, condens-ing], **1,** to compress; make more close, compact, or dense; **2,** to reduce to fewer words; **3,** to change from a gas or vapor to a liquid, as steam to water; **4,** to increase in intensity, as an electric charge:—*v.i.* **1,** to become dense; **2,** to pass from gaseous or vaporous to liquid form.—*adj.* **con·den′sa·ble.**

con·dens·er (kŏn-dĕn′sẽr), *n.* **1,** a person or thing that condenses; **2,** a machine for changing gases to liquid or solid form; **3,** a lens for concentrating or bringing together rays of light; **4,** a device for holding or storing an electric charge.

con·de·scend (kŏn′dē-sĕnd′), *v.i.* to stoop or come down voluntarily to the level of one's inferiors; show courtesies, often with a superior air; as, the great man *condescended* to join us.

con·de·scen·sion (kŏn′dē-sĕn′shŭn), *n.* a stooping to the level of inferiors, often with a superior air.

con·di·ment (kŏn′dĭ-mĕnt), *n.* a spicy seasoning for food, as pepper or mustard.

con·di·tion (kŏn-dĭsh′ŭn), *n.* **1,** something that must exist if something else is to be or to take place; as, hard work is one of the *conditions* of success; **2,** state of being or of circumstances; as, the road is in bad *condition*; **3,** state of health; fitness for work, etc.; as, he is in good *condition*; **4,** rank; social position; as, a lady of high *condition*; **5,** in schools of the U.S., a failure that can be made up:—*v.t.* **1,** to render fit; as, to *condition* a boxer; **2,** to be a condition for; as, health *conditions* success.—*adj.* **con·di′tioned.**

con·di·tion·al (kŏn-dĭsh′ŭn-ăl), *adj.* **1,** depending upon certain provisions or conditions; **2,** in grammar, containing a provisional clause.—*adv.* **con·di′tion·al·ly.**

con·dole (kŏn-dōl′), *v.i.* [condoled, condol-ing], to express sympathy; as, we *condoled* with him over his loss.

con·do·lence (kŏn-dō′lĕns), *n.* sympathy expressed for another's grief.

con·done (kŏn-dōn′), *v.t.* [condoned, condon-ing], to forgive or overlook, as a fault or offense.—*n.* **con′do·na′tion.**

con·dor (kŏn′dẽr; kŏn′dôr), *n.* a very large, South American vulture found in the Andes Mountains.

con·duce (kŏn-dūs′), *v.i.* [conduced, conduc-ing], to lead or tend toward a result; contribute.

con·du·cive (kŏn-dū′sĭv), *adj.* leading or tending to a result; as, fresh air is *conducive* to health.

CONDOR (¹⁄₃₀)

con·duct (kŏn-dŭkt′), *v.t.* **1,** to guide; **2,** to manage; direct, as an orchestra; **3,** to behave (oneself); **4,** to carry; as, the canal *conducts* water:—*v.i.* **1,** to direct; lead; **2,** to transmit electricity, heat, etc.:—*n.* (kŏn′dŭkt), **1,** personal behavior or practice; **2,** management; guidance.

go; join; yet; sing; chin; show; thin, *th*en; hw, *wh*y; zh, a*z*ure; ü, Ger. für or Fr. lune; ö, Ger. schön or Fr. feu; ṅ, Fr. enfant, nom; kh, Ger. ach or ich. See pages ix-x.

con-duc-tion (kŏn-dŭk′shŭn), *n.* **1,** the act or process of conveying, as water through a pipe; **2,** transmission, as of heat or electricity, by a conductor.

con-duc-tiv-i-ty (kŏn′dŭk-tĭv′ĭ-tĭ), *n.* the power of an object or body to transmit heat, electricity, etc.

con-duc-tor (kŏn-dŭk′tẽr), *n.* **1,** a leader or guide; **2,** a manager; a director of a chorus or orchestra; **3,** an official who has charge of the passengers, collects fare, etc., on a bus, trolley car, or railway train; **4,** a substance which transmits energy; as, metals are good *conductors* of heat and electricity.

con-duit (kŏn′dĭt; kŏn′dōō-ĭt; kŭn′dĭt), *n.* **1,** a canal or pipe for carrying water, etc.; **2,** an enclosed tube or passage for electric wires.

cone (kōn), *n.* **1,** a solid body which tapers uniformly to a point from a circular base; **2,** anything of similar shape; as, an ice-cream *cone;* **3,** the scaly, cone-shaped fruit of certain trees, as the pine, fir, etc.

CONE
def. 1

co-ney (kō′nĭ; kŭn′ĭ), *n.* [*pl.* co-neys], a small rabbitlike animal; the cony. See **cony.**

con-fec-tion (kŏn-fĕk′shŭn), *n.* anything preserved in sugar; a sweetmeat; candy.

con-fec-tion-er (kŏn-fĕk′shŭn-ẽr), *n.* one who makes or sells candies, cake, etc.

con-fec-tion-er-y (kŏn-fĕk′shŭn-ẽr′ĭ), *n.* [*pl.* confectioneries], **1,** candies, ice cream, cakes, etc.; **2,** the business of a confectioner.

CONES, def. 3
1, white pine; 2, red spruce; 3, balsam fir.

con-fed-er-a-cy (kŏn-fĕd′ẽr-à-sĭ), *n.* [*pl.* con-federacies], a group or league made up of persons, states, or nations united for mutual support of any kind; an alliance; as, a loose *confederacy* of Indian tribes:— **the Confederacy,** the Confederate States of America, a league of eleven southern States that seceded from the United States in 1860 and 1861.

con-fed-er-ate (kŏn-fĕd′ẽr-āt), *v.t.* and *v.i.* [confederat-ed, confederat-ing], to unite in a league:—*adj.* (kŏn-fĕd′ẽr-ĭt), united by a league or agreement:—**Con-federate,** pertaining to the Confederacy:— *n.* (kŏn-fĕd′ẽr-ĭt), **1,** a member of a league or union; **2,** an ally; accomplice:—**Confed-erate,** a person who sided with the Con-federacy; a soldier of the Confederacy.

con-fed-er-a-tion (kŏn-fĕd′ẽr-ā′shŭn), *n.* the act of forming a league; an alliance.

con-fer (kŏn-fûr′), *v.t.* [conferred, con-fer-ring], to give or bestow; as, to *confer* a medal:—*v.i.* to consult with others; dis-cuss; as, to *confer* with one's partner.

Syn. grant, give, bestow, offer.

con-fer-ence (kŏn′fẽr-ĕns), *n.* a meeting for discussing some topic or business; also, the discussion itself.

con-fess (kŏn-fĕs′), *v.t.* **1,** to admit as true; especially, to acknowledge (a fault, crime, debt, etc.); **2,** to profess, as a religious belief; **3,** to hear a confession from: said of a priest:—*v.i.* **1,** to disclose the state of one's conscience to a priest; **2,** to make an acknowledgment or admission. —*adv.* **con-fess′ed-ly.**

con-fes-sion (kŏn-fĕsh′ŭn), *n.* **1,** the act of acknowledging or admitting; **2,** the act of making known one's sins to a priest; **3,** anything confessed.

con-fes-sion-al (kŏn-fĕsh′ŭn-ăl), *n.* a booth where a priest hears confessions.

con-fes-sor (kŏn-fĕs′ẽr), *n.* **1,** one who admits or acknowledges a wrong; **2,** a priest who hears confessions.

con-fet-ti (kŏn-fĕt′ĭ), *n.pl.* used as *sing.* small pieces of colored paper scattered at carnivals, weddings, etc.

con-fi-dant (kŏn′fĭ-dănt′; kŏn′fĭ-dănt′), *n.* an intimate friend to whom private af-fairs are told.—*n.fem.* **con′fi-dante′.**

con-fide (kŏn-fīd′), *v.t.* [confid-ed, con-fid-ing], **1,** to put into another's trust or keeping; entrust; as, I will *confide* my daughter to your care; **2,** to tell in confi-dence; as, *confide* your secret to me:—*v.i.* **1,** to have confidence or trust; as, to *con-fide* in military force; **2,** *Colloquial,* to entrust secrets; as, you can *confide* in me. —*n.* **con-fid′er.**

con-fi-dence (kŏn′fĭ-dĕns), *n.* **1,** belief; trust; as, I have *confidence* in his ability; **2,** boldness; self-assurance; as, he spoke with *confidence;* **3,** trusting intimacy; as, to speak in *confidence;* also, a secret.

con-fi-dent (kŏn′fĭ-dĕnt), *adj.* **1,** assured; self-reliant; bold; as, a *confident* per-former; **2,** convinced; sure; as, he was *confident* of victory.—*adv.* **con′fi-dent-ly.**

con-fi-den-tial (kŏn′fĭ-dĕn′shăl), *adj.* **1,** private; secret; as, *confidential* informa-tion; also, intimate; as, he spoke in a *con-fidential* tone of voice; **2,** entrusted with secret matters; as, a *confidential* secretary. —*adv.* **con′fi-den′tial-ly.**

con-fid-ing (kŏn-fīd′ĭng), *adj.* trustful; trusting.—*adv.* **con-fid′ing-ly.**

con-fig-u-ra-tion (kŏn-fĭg′ū-rā′shŭn), *n.* shape; outline; contour; as, the *configura-tion* of the American continent.

āte, āorta, râre, căt, ȧsk, fär, ȧllow, sofȧ; ēve, êvent, ĕll, writẽr, novĕl; bīte, pĭn; nō, ōbey, ôr, dŏg, tŏp, cŏllide; ūnit, ūnite, bûrn, cŭt, focŭs; nōōn, fŏŏt; mound; coin;

con-fine (kŏn′fīn), *n.* a border, limit, or boundary; as, within the *confines* of a country:—*v.t.* (kŏn-fīn′), [confined, confin-ing], **1,** to restrict within limits; as, high dikes *confined* the sea; **2,** to keep within doors; imprison; as, illness *confined* him to his room.

con-fine-ment (kŏn-fīn′měnt), *n.* **1,** restraint; imprisonment; **2,** a staying indoors or in bed because of illness, especially at childbirth.

con-firm (kŏn-fûrm′), *v.t.* **1,** to establish more firmly; as, the book *confirms* my belief; **2,** to assure the truth of; verify; as, to *confirm* a report; **3,** to receive into church membership.—*adj.* **con-firm′a-ble.** *Syn.* establish, sustain.

con-fir-ma-tion (kŏn′fēr-mā′shŭn), *n.* **1,** the act of verifying, ratifying, making sure, etc.; **2,** admission to full membership, after baptism, in certain Christian churches.

con-firmed (kŏn-fûrmd′), *adj.* settled, as in a habit; as, a *confirmed* drunkard; chronic; as, a *confirmed* invalid.

con-fis-cate (kŏn′fĭs-kāt; kŏn-fĭs′kāt), *v.t.* [confiscat-ed, confiscat-ing], to take over (private property) by public authority, or by any authority; as, the police *confiscated* the smuggled goods; the teacher *confiscated* the boy's marbles.—*adj.* **con-fis′ca-tor-y.** —*n.* **con′fis-ca-tor.**—*n.* **con′fis-ca′tion.**

con-fla-gra-tion (kŏn′flà-grā′shŭn), *n.* a large and destructive fire.

con-flict (kŏn-flĭkt′), *v.i.* to clash; be in opposition; as, his story *conflicts* with mine:—*n.* (kŏn′flĭkt), **1,** a fight; struggle; battle; **2,** a clash between ideas, feelings, or the like; as, the *conflict* between duty and pleasure.

con-flu-ence (kŏn′floo-ĕns), *n.* **1,** a flowing together, as of streams; **2,** a flocking together of persons; hence, an assembly; a crowd.—*adj.* **con′flu-ent.**

con-flux (kŏn′flŭks), *n.* confluence.

con-form (kŏn-fôrm′), *v.t.* to make like or similar; as, I will *conform* my tastes to yours:—*v.i.* to act in agreement with a standard, pattern, etc.; as, to *conform* to rules or to the ways of the world.—*n.* **con-form′er.**—*n.* **con-form′ance.**

con-form-a-ble (kŏn-fôr′mà-bl), *adj.* **1,** like; corresponding; **2,** obedient; submissive.—*adv.* **con-form′a-bly.**

con-for-ma-tion (kŏn′fôr-mā′shŭn), *n.* form; structure; especially, the orderly arrangement of the parts of a thing.

con-form-ist (kŏn-fôr′mĭst), *n.* one who is in agreement; especially, a member of the Established Church of England.

con-form-i-ty (kŏn-fôr′mĭ-tĭ), *n.* [*pl.* con-formities], **1,** a correspondence in form, manner, or character; agreement; as, *conformity* of tastes; **2,** action in agreement with a standard, pattern, etc.; as, *conformity* to fashion.

con-found (kŏn-found′; kŏn-found′), *v.t.* **1,** to perplex; bewilder; confuse; **2,** to mistake for another; mix up; as, he *confounds* Jim with his twin; **3,** to damn: used as a mild curse.

con-front (kŏn-frŭnt′), *v.t.* **1,** to bring face to face; as, to *confront* a prisoner with evidence; **2,** to face defiantly or with hostility; as, to *confront* an enemy.

Con-fu-cius (kŏn-fū′shŭs), (551–478 B.C.), a Chinese philosopher, teacher, and writer. —*adj.* and *n.* **Con-fu′cian.**

con-fuse (kŏn-fūz′), *v.t.* [confused, con-fus-ing], **1,** to bewilder; perplex; embarrass; **2,** to mistake for another. *Syn.* distract, disturb, puzzle, mystify.

con-fus-ed-ly (kŏn-fūz′ĕd-lĭ), *adv.* in a bewildered manner.

con-fu-sion (kŏn-fū′zhŭn), *n.* **1,** perplexity; loss of self-possession; **2,** disorder; tumult.

con-fute (kŏn-fūt′), *v.t.* [confut-ed, con-fut-ing], **1,** to prove to be false or untrue; as, to *confute* a claim; **2,** to prove (a person) to be wrong.

Cong. abbreviation for *Congregational, Congress.*

con-geal (kŏn-jēl′), *v.t.* and *v.i.* to thicken by, or as if by, cold; as, fear *congealed* his blood.

con-gen-ial (kŏn-jēn′yǎl; kŏn-jē′nĭ-ǎl), *adj.* **1,** sympathetic; having the same tastes; as, *congenial* friends; **2,** agreeable; naturally suited to one's nature; as, a *congenial* climate.—*adv.* **con-gen′ial-ly.**

con-gen-i-tal (kŏn-jĕn′ĭ-tǎl), *adj.* existing at birth, and not caused by later influences.—*adv.* **con-gen′i-tal-ly.**

con-ger eel (kŏng′gẽr), a large eel found in the ocean and used for food.

con-gest (kŏn-jĕst′), *v.t.* **1,** to cause (an organ or part of the body) to become too full of blood; **2,** to make too crowded; as, parades *congest* traffic.

con-ges-tion (kŏn-jĕs′chŭn), *n.* **1,** an over-crowded condition, as of traffic; **2,** excessive fulness of a part of the body with blood; as, *congestion* of the lungs.

CONGLOMERATE def. 2

con-glom-er-ate (kŏn-glŏm′ẽr-āt), *v.t.* [conglomerat-ed, con-glomerat-ing], to gather into a mass:—

adj. (kŏn-glŏm/ẽr-ĭt), collected, clustered, or massed together:—*n.* (kŏn-glŏm/ẽr-ĭt), **1,** a mass of varied materials or elements; **2,** a rock composed of pebbles, gravel, etc., held together by hardened clay or the like (see illustration on preceding page).

con·glom·er·a·tion (kŏn-glŏm/ẽr-ā/-shŭn), *n.* **1,** the act of gathering into a mass; **2,** a mixed collection; hodgepodge.

Con·go (kŏng/gō), a large river, 3000 miles long, in west central Africa:—**Congo Free State,** the former name of *Belgian Congo;* **French Congo,** the former name of *French Equatorial Africa.* (Map **14.**)

congo snake, an eel-like creature which lives both on land and in water, found in the southeastern part of the U.S. (See illustration under *amphibian.*)

con·grat·u·late (kŏn-grăt/ū-lāt), *v.t.* [congratulat-ed, congratulat-ing], to express sympathetic pleasure to (a person) on account of some happy event or honor.—*adj.* **con·grat/u·la·tor/y.**

con·grat·u·la·tion (kŏn-grăt/ū-lā/shŭn), *n.* an expression of pleasure to someone because of his success or good fortune: usually in the plural; as, *congratulations* on your election.

con·gre·gate (kŏng/grē-gāt), *v.i.* and *v.t.* [congregat-ed, congregat-ing], to assemble; gather together; as, people *congregated* in the town hall.

con·gre·ga·tion (kŏng/grē-gā/shŭn), *n.* **1,** a gathering or collection of persons or things; **2,** a group of people meeting for religious worship or instruction.

con·gre·ga·tion·al (kŏng/grē-gā/shŭn-ăl), *adj.* relating to a congregation:—**Congregational,** relating to Congregationalism or to Congregationalists.

con·gre·ga·tion·al·ism (kŏng/grē-gā/-shŭn-ăl-ĭzm), *n.* a form of church government in which each congregation governs itself:—**Congregationalism,** the faith and constitution of a religious denomination in which each separate church is self-governing, but is united to the others in fellowship.—*n.* **Con/gre·ga/tion·al·ist.**

con·gress (kŏng/grĕs), *n.* **1,** a meeting, as of delegates for discussion; **2,** the chief lawmaking body of a republic:—**Congress,** the national lawmaking body of the U.S., composed of the Senate and the House of Representatives.—*adj.* **con·gres/sion·al.**

con·gress·man (kŏng/grĕs-măn), *n.* [*pl.* congressmen (-mĕn)], a member of a congress, especially, of the House of Representatives.—*n.fem.* **con/gress·wom/an.**

con·gru·ent (kŏng/grōō-ĕnt), *adj.* agreeing; harmonizing; suitable.—*adv.* **con/-gru·ent·ly.**—*n.* **con/gru·ence.**

con·gru·i·ty (kŏn-grōō/ĭ-tĭ), *n.* [*pl.* congruities], agreement; suitableness.

con·gru·ous (kŏng/grōō-ŭs), *adj.* in accord with what is fitting; suitable.—*adv.* **con/gru·ous·ly.**—*n.* **con/gru·ous·ness.**

con·i·cal (kŏn/ĭ-kăl) or **con·ic** (kŏn/ĭk), *adj.* shaped like a cone.

co·ni·fer (kō/nĭ-fẽr; kŏn/ĭ-fẽr), *n.* a cone-bearing tree, as the spruce or pine.

co·nif·er·ous (kō-nĭf/ẽr-ŭs), *adj.* bearing cones, as the spruce, pine, or hemlock.

conj. abbreviation for *conjunction.*

con·jec·tur·al (kŏn-jĕk/tūr-ăl), *adj.* doubtful; depending on or springing from a guess.—*adv.* **con·jec/tur·al·ly.**

con·jec·ture (kŏn-jĕk/tūr), *n.* the act of forming an opinion without definite proof; a guess:—*v.t.* and *v.i.* [conjectured, conjectur-ing], to guess.

con·join (kŏn-join/), *v.t.* and *v.i.* to join together; connect; unite.

con·joint (kŏn-joint/; kŏn/joint), *adj.* united; associated.—*adv.* **con·joint/ly.**

con·ju·gal (kŏn/jōō-găl), *adj.* of or relating to marriage; as, *conjugal* happiness.—*adv.* **con/ju·gal·ly.**—*n.* **con/ju·gal/i·ty.**

con·ju·gate (kŏn/jōō-gāt), *v.t.* [conjugat ed, conjugat-ing], in grammar, to give the various forms of (a verb) in order, as, "I am, you are, he is; we, you, they are."

con·ju·ga·tion (kŏn/jōō-gā/shŭn), *n.* **1,** the act of joining together; union; **2,** in grammar, the process of giving the various forms of a verb in their proper order; **3,** a group or class of verbs which are conjugated in the same manner.

con·junc·tion (kŏn-jŭngk/shŭn), *n.* **1,** a joining together; union; **2,** in grammar, a word, such as *and, if, but, as, or, though,* which is used to connect two words, phrases, clauses, or sentences.

con·junc·tive (kŏn-jŭngk/tĭv), *adj.* **1,** connective; uniting; **2,** in grammar, possessing the qualities of a conjunction; as, a *conjunctive* adverb.

con·ju·ra·tion (kŏn/jōō-rā/shŭn), *n.* **1,** the practice of magic; **2,** a magic spell.

con·jure (kŭn/jẽr; kŏn/jẽr), *v.t.* [conjured, conjur-ing], **1,** to cause to appear or disappear as if by magic; **2,** (kŏn-jōōr/), to appeal to solemnly; implore; as, he *conjured* us to help:—*v.i.* to practice magical arts; also, to juggle.

con·jur·er or **con·jur·or** (kŭn/jẽr-ẽr), *n.* **1,** a magician; **2,** a juggler.

Conn. abbreviation for *Connecticut.*

con·nect (kŏ-nĕkt/), *v.t.* **1,** to join; **2,** to join by personal relationship; as, to *connect* by marriage; **3,** to associate; as, I did not *connect* his name with his face:—*v.i.* to join; have a close relation.

Syn. combine, join, unite.

Con-nect-i-cut (kŏ-nĕt´ĭ-kŭt), a New England State (cap. Hartford) in the U.S. (map **6**).

con-nec-tion (kŏ-nĕk´shŭn), *n.* **1,** the state of being joined; union; **2,** relationship by blood or marriage; hence, a relative, especially a distant one; **3,** relationship by reason of a common interest or occupation; as, to make a good business *connection;* **4,** the linking of words or ideas in speech or thought.

con-nec-tive (kŏ-nĕk´tĭv), *adj.* serving to join:—*n.* that which joins; especially, in grammar, a conjunction.

con-ning tow-er (kŏn´nĭng tou´ẽr), an armored pilot house on a battleship or submarine, used as a post of observation.

con-niv-ance (kŏ-nīv´ăns), *n.* secret encouragement or consent, as in wrongdoing.

con-nive (kŏ-nīv´), *v.i.* [connived, conniving], to permit or help in secret what one should oppose or prevent; as, the jailer *connived* at his escape.

con-nois-seur (kŏn´ĭ-sûr´; kŏn´ĭ-sūr´), *n.* one who knows enough about an art, or anything regarded as an art, to be a good judge of it; as, a *connoisseur* of painting.

con-note (kŏ-nōt´), *v.t.* [connot-ed, connoting], to imply or suggest in addition to the simple or direct meaning; as, the word "equator" often *connotes* heat.—*n.* **con´no-ta´tion.**

con-nu-bi-al (kŏ-nū´bĭ-ăl), *adj.* relating to marriage; as, *connubial* happiness.

con-quer (kŏng´kẽr), *v.t.* **1,** to subdue by war; as, to *conquer* a country; **2,** to overcome by force of will, as a bad habit:—*v.i.* to be victorious.—*n.* **con´quer-or.**

Syn. vanquish, defeat, subjugate.

con-quest (kŏng´kwĕst), *n.* a winning, subduing, or conquering, especially by war; as, the Norman *conquest* of England; also, that which is conquered, subdued, or won.

Syn. triumph, mastery, victory.

con-quis-ta-dor (kŏn-kwĭs´tá-dôr), *n.* a conqueror; especially, a leader in the Spanish conquest of Mexico.

con-san-guin-i-ty (kŏn´săng-gwĭn´ĭ-tĭ), *n.* blood relationship.

con-science (kŏn´shĕns), *n.* a sense of the rightness or wrongness of one's own acts; as, he has a guilty *conscience.*—*adj.* **con´science-less.**

con-sci-en-tious (kŏn´shĭ-ĕn´shŭs), *adj.* **1,** careful to follow one's sense of right; as, a *conscientious* girl; **2,** arising from

one's feeling of right and wrong; as, *conscientious* objections.—*adv.* **con´sci-en´-tious-ly.**—*n.* **con´sci-en´tious-ness.**

con-scious (kŏn´shŭs), *adj.* **1,** aware; as, *conscious* of a pain; **2,** mentally awake; having possession of one's senses; as, the patient is *conscious;* **3,** known to oneself; as, a *conscious* sin.—*adv.* **con´scious-ly.**

con-scious-ness (kŏn´shŭs-nĕs), *n.* **1,** awareness of one's own existence, or of what is happening; as, when asleep we lose *consciousness;* **2,** all that occurs in one's experience; one's sensations, thoughts, feelings, and actions; the entire mental life of a person.

con-script (kŏn-skrĭpt´), *v.t.* to force (a person) to serve in the army or navy:—*adj.* (kŏn´skrĭpt), forced into military or naval service; as, a *conscript* army:—*n.* (kŏn´skrĭpt), a person so forced.

con-scrip-tion (kŏn-skrĭp´shŭn), *n.* forced enrolment in military or naval service; draft; as, to raise troops by *conscription.*

con-se-crate (kŏn´sĕ-krāt), *v.t.* [consecrat-ed, consecrat-ing], to set apart for a holy purpose; regard as sacred; as, to *consecrate* one's life to God.

con-se-cra-tion (kŏn´sĕ-krā´shŭn), *n.* a setting apart for a holy use or service.

con-sec-u-tive (kŏn-sĕk´ū-tĭv), *adj.* following without a break; as, Monday and Tuesday are *consecutive* days.—*adv.* **con-sec´u-tive-ly.**

con-sen-sus (kŏn-sĕn´sŭs), *n.* general agreement in opinion, testimony, or feeling; as, the *consensus* of the committee.

con-sent (kŏn-sĕnt´), *n.* agreement; approval; compliance; as, by common *consent:*—*v.i.* to comply; yield; agree.

Syn., v. accede, acquiesce, assent.

con-se-quence (kŏn´sĕ-kwĕns), *n.* **1,** outcome; result; as, to suffer the *consequences* of an action; **2,** importance; as, a person of no *consequence.*

con-se-quent (kŏn´sĕ-kwĕnt), *adj.* following as a result; as, the disorder *consequent* to the fire.

con-se-quen-tial (kŏn´sĕ-kwĕn´shăl), *adj.* **1,** following as a result; **2,** self-important; as, a *consequential* official.

con-se-quent-ly (kŏn´sĕ-kwĕnt-lĭ), *adv.* as a result; therefore; as, I overslept, *consequently* I missed the boat.

con-ser-va-tion (kŏn´sẽr-vā´shŭn), *n.* the prevention of waste or loss, especially of natural resources, as forests or water power, or of game birds, wild flowers, etc.

con-serv-a-tism (kŏn-sûr´vá-tĭzm), *n.* the tendency to keep existing laws and customs, and to resist change.

con·serv·a·tive (kŏn-sûr′vȧ-tĭv), *adj*. inclined to prefer existing institutions to new ones:—*n*. a conservative person.—*adv*. **con-serv′a-tive-ly.**

con·serv·a·tor·y (kŏn-sûr′vȧ-tôr′ĭ), *n*. [*pl*. conservatories], **1,** a greenhouse, especially a private one; **2,** a college for special study, as of music.

con·serve (kŏn-sûrv′), *v.t*. [conserved, conserv-ing], **1,** to keep from waste or destruction; as, to *conserve* game; **2,** to preserve with sugar:—*n*. (kŏn-sûrv′; kŏn′-sûrv), preserved or candied fruit:—**con-serves**, preserves.—*n*. **con′ser-va′tor.**

con·sid·er (kŏn-sĭd′ẽr), *v.t*. **1,** to think over with care; as, to *consider* an offer; **2,** to esteem; **3,** to regard as; believe; as, I *consider* him rude:—*v.i*. to reflect; as, to take time to *consider*.
Syn. ponder, weigh, meditate.

con·sid·er·a·ble (kŏn-sĭd′ẽr-ȧ-bl), *adj*. worthy of notice; important; not small; as, a *considerable* sum of money.

con·sid·er·a·bly (kŏn-sĭd′ẽr-ȧ-blĭ), *adv*. much; greatly.

con·sid·er·ate (kŏn-sĭd′ẽr-ĭt), *adj*. thoughtful of others; kindly.

con·sid·er·a·tion (kŏn-sĭd′ẽr-ā′shŭn), *n*. **1,** careful thought; as, to take a thing into *consideration;* **2,** something taken, or worth taking, into account; a reason or motive; **3,** thoughtful regard for others; **4,** payment or compensation for something.

con·sid·er·ing (kŏn-sĭd′ẽr-ĭng), *prep*. taking into account; allowing for; as, crops are good, *considering* the drought.

con·sign (kŏn-sīn′), *v.t*. **1,** to deliver formally; hand over; as, to *consign* a man to jail; **2,** to ship, as merchandise.

con·sign·ee (kŏn′sī-nē′; kŏn′sĭ-nē′), *n*. the person to whom goods are shipped.

con·sign·er (kŏn-sīn′ẽr), *n*. the person who sends goods to another. Also spelled **con-sign′or** (kŏn-sīn′ẽr; kŏn′sĭ-nôr′; kŏn′-sĭ-nôr′).

con·sign·ment (kŏn-sīn′mĕnt), *n*. **1,** a delivering; sending; entrusting; as, the *consignment* of a child to a guardian; **2,** merchandise sent to someone.

con·sist (kŏn-sĭst′), *v.i*. to be composed or made up; as, a day *consists* of 24 hours.

con·sist·ence (kŏn-sĭs′tĕns), *n*. consistency.

con·sist·en·cy (kŏn-sĭs′tĕn-sĭ), *n*. [*pl*. consistencies], **1,** degree of firmness or thickness; as, this liquid has the *consistency* of sirup; **2,** harmony; agreement, as of one's deeds with one's statements.

con·sist·ent (kŏn-sĭs′tĕnt), *adj*. **1,** fitting in; in agreement; as, his story is *consistent*

with facts; **2,** continuing without change, or with adherence to the same principles; as, a *consistent* friend to labor.—*adv*. **con-sist′ent-ly.**

con·sis·to·ry (kŏn-sĭs′tō-rĭ; kŏn′sĭs-tẽr-ĭ), *n*. [*pl*. consistories], a governing assembly or court of a church; especially, a session of the college of cardinals, presided over by the Pope.

con·so·la·tion (kŏn′sō-lā′shŭn), *n*. comfort given or received in distress; as, money is no *consolation* in grief.

con·sol·a·tor·y (kŏn-sŏl′ȧ-tôr′ĭ), *adj*. giving comfort; as, a *consolatory* letter.

¹con·sole (kŏn-sōl′), *v.t*. [consoled, consoling], to comfort in sorrow.

²con·sole (kŏn′sōl), *n*. **1,** the part of a pipe organ at which the organist sits, containing the keyboard, stops, and pedals; **2,** a radio cabinet or a table designed to stand against a wall.

con·sol·i·date (kŏn-sŏl′ĭ-dāt), *v.t*. and *v.i*. [consolidat-ed, consolidat-ing], to unite; combine; as, to *consolidate* two offices.—*n*. **con-sol′i-da′tion.**

con·som·mé (kŏn′sŏ-mā′), *n*. a clear soup made by boiling meat thoroughly.

con·so·nance (kŏn′sō-nȧns), *n*. agreement, as of sounds; harmony.

con·so·nant (kŏn′sō-nȧnt), *n*. **1,** a sound made by closing or narrowing the mouth or throat; **2,** a symbol of such a sound, as *b, c, d*:—*adj*. **1,** like a consonant; as, a *consonant* sound; **2,** harmonious; consistent; agreeing; as, an act *consonant* with one's beliefs.—*adj*. **con′so-nan′tal.**

con·sort (kŏn′sôrt), *n*. **1,** a husband or wife; **2,** a ship accompanying another:—*v.i*. (kŏn-sôrt′), to associate; as, to *consort* with criminals.

con·spic·u·ous (kŏn-spĭk′ū-ŭs), *adj*. **1,** plainly visible; as, a *conspicuous* tower; hence, striking; attracting attention; as, a *conspicuous* costume; **2,** distinguished; notable; as, the play was a *conspicuous* success.—*adv*. **con-spic′u-ous-ly.**—*n*. **con-spic′u-ous-ness.**

con·spir·a·cy (kŏn-spĭr′ȧ-sĭ), *n*. [*pl*. conspiracies], a secret agreement to do something unlawful or evil; a plot.

con·spir·a·tor (kŏn-spĭr′ȧ-tẽr), *n*. a person who takes part in a plot.

con·spire (kŏn-spīr′), *v.i*. [conspired, conspir-ing], **1,** to plan secretly together to do something unlawful; plot; **2,** to work with other circumstances toward a given result; as, events *conspired* to injure him.

con·sta·ble (kŭn′stȧ-bl; kŏn′stȧ-bl), *n*. a police officer.

con·stab·u·lar·y (kŏn′stăb′ū-lẽr′ĭ), *n*. [*pl*.

constabularies], an armed force organized for police duty.

con·stan·cy (kŏn′stăn-sĭ), *n.* steadfastness in one's beliefs or friendships.
Syn. faithfulness, devotion, loyalty.

con·stant (kŏn′stănt), *adj.* **1,** standing firm in one's beliefs or affections; steadfast; faithful; as, a *constant* friend; **2,** regular in a habit; unchanging; as, *constant* in attendance.—*adv.* **con′stant·ly.**

Con·stan·ti·no·ple (kŏn′stăn-tĭ-nō′pl), the former name of a city in Turkey. See **Istanbul.**

con·stel·la·tion (kŏn′stĕ-lā′shŭn), *n.* any group of fixed stars with a special name, as the Big Dipper.

con·ster·na·tion (kŏn′stĕr-nā′shŭn), *n.* terrified astonishment; dismay.

con·sti·pa·tion (kŏn′stĭ-pā′shŭn), *n.* a condition in which the bowels do not move freely enough.—*adj.* **con′sti·pat′ed.**

con·stit·u·en·cy (kŏn′stĭt′ū-ĕn-sĭ), *n.* [*pl.* constituencies], a body of voters which elects a representative, as to Congress.

con·stit·u·ent (kŏn′stĭt′ū-ĕnt), *adj.* necessary in the make-up of something; as, a *constituent* part:—*n.* **1,** a necessary part; as, flour is a *constituent* of cake; **2,** a voter in a given district; as, the senator addressed his *constituents.*

con·sti·tute (kŏn′stĭ-tūt), *v.t.* [constituted, constitut-ing], **1,** to make up or form; compose; as, twelve things *constitute* a dozen; **2,** to appoint; elect; as, he *constituted* himself judge of the contest.

con·sti·tu·tion (kŏn′stĭ-tū′shŭn), *n.* **1,** the way in which a thing is made up; as, the *constitution* of the earth; **2,** bodily strength; vitality; **3,** the fundamental law on which a state or society is organized; as, the national *constitution.*

con·sti·tu·tion·al (kŏn′stĭ-tū′shŭn-ăl), *adj.* **1,** inherent in one's make-up; as, a *constitutional* liability to colds; **2,** relating to the fundamental law of a state or society; as, a *constitutional* amendment; also, in harmony with such law:—*n. Colloquial,* a walk taken for health's sake.

con·sti·tu·tion·al·i·ty (kŏn′stĭ-tū′shŭn-ăl′ĭ-tĭ), *n.* agreement with the constitution, or fundamental law; as, the *constitutionality* of an act of Congress.

con·strain (kŏn′strān′), *v.t.* **1,** to hold in check; restrain; as, the presence of the captain *constrained* the crew; **2,** to urge strongly; compel; as, to *constrain* a child to eat.

con·straint (kŏn′strānt′), *n.* **1,** compulsion; force; necessity; as, to act under *constraint;* **2,** repression of natural behavior; as, to have an air of *constraint.*

con·strict (kŏn-strĭkt′), *v.t.* to bind; squeeze; cramp; as, to *constrict* a vein.

con·stric·tion (kŏn-strĭk′shŭn), *n.* a tightening, as of a bandage; compression; also, anything that binds or cramps.

con·struct (kŏn-strŭkt′), *v.t.* **1,** to fit together; arrange; build, as a house; **2,** to plan; compose; as, to *construct* a play.

con·struc·tion (kŏn-strŭk′shŭn), *n.* **1,** a putting together; the act or method of building; as, fireproof *construction;* also, the thing built; **2,** understanding; as, to put a wrong *construction* on a letter; **3,** in grammar, the way in which words are related to one another in a sentence.

con·struc·tive (kŏn-strŭk′tĭv), *adj.* tending to build up rather than to destroy; creative; as, *constructive* ideas.

con·strue (kŏn-strōō′; kŏn′strōō), *v.t.* [construed, constru-ing], **1,** to interpret; explain; as, his act was *construed* as a favor; **2,** in grammar, to apply the rules of syntax to (a sentence).

con·sul (kŏn′sŭl), *n.* **1,** an official commissioned by a government to promote his country's trade in a foreign city, and to protect its citizens; **2,** one of the two joint chief officials of the Roman Republic.

con·su·lar (kŏn′sū-lĕr), *adj.* relating to the work or office of a consul.

con·su·late (kŏn′sū-lăt), *n.* the office or residence of a consul.

con·sul·ship (kŏn′sŭl-shĭp), *n.* the position or term of a consul.

con·sult (kŏn-sŭlt′), *v.t.* **1,** to ask advice of; **2,** to have regard to; as, he *consulted* my welfare:—*v.i.* to take counsel together; confer.—*n.* **con′sul·ta′tion.**

con·sume (kŏn-sūm′), *v.t.* [consumed, consum-ing], **1,** to destroy, as by fire; **2,** to eat or drink up; use up; waste, as time.

con·sum·er (kŏn-sūm′ĕr), *n.* a person or thing that consumes anything; especially, a person who buys goods to be used by himself.

con·sum·mate (kŏn′sŭ-māt), *v.t.* [consummat-ed, consummat-ing], to complete; finish:—*adj.* (kŏn′sŭm′ĭt), perfect; carried to the highest degree; as, a man of *consummate* skill.

con·sum·ma·tion (kŏn′sŭ-mā′shŭn), *n.* **1,** the successful completion of an undertaking; **2,** a desired end; goal.

con·sump·tion (kŏn′sŭmp′shŭn), *n.* **1,** a using up, as of food or other materials; also, the amount used up; **2,** tuberculosis of the lungs.

con·sump·tive (kŏn′sŭmp′tĭv), *adj.* **1,** wasteful; **2,** ill with tuberculosis of the lungs:—*n.* a person who has consumption.

cont. abbreviation for *continued.*

go; join; yet; sing; chin; show; thin, *then;* hw, *why;* zh, azure; ü, Ger. *für* or Fr. *lune;* ö, Ger. schön or Fr. *feu;* ň, Fr. enfant, nom; kh, Ger. ach or ich. See pages ix-x.

con·tact (kŏn′tăkt), *n.* **1,** a touch; touching; as, the *contact* of cold metal; **2,** a meeting for conversation or consultation; also, acquaintance which makes such a meeting possible; as, he makes advantageous *contacts.*

con·ta·gion (kŏn·tā′jŭn), *n.* **1,** the spreading of a disease from person to person; as, schools are closed to prevent *contagion;* **2,** a disease which can be so spread; **3,** the spreading of thoughts or emotions to others; as, a *contagion* of fear.

con·ta·gious (kŏn·tā′jŭs), *adj.* **1,** spreading easily from person to person; as, a *contagious* disease; **2,** exciting a similar action or feeling in others; as, *contagious* laughter.
    Syn. infectious.

con·tain (kŏn·tān′), *v.t.* **1,** to hold; as, the box *contained* candy; the bucket *contained* water; **2,** to include; as, the book *contains* a good story; **3,** to be equal to; as, a quart *contains* two pints; **4,** to hold in check; as, to *contain* one's anger; **5,** to be a multiple of; as, ten *contains* five.

con·tain·er (kŏn·tān′ẽr), *n.* a receptacle in which goods are kept or shipped.

con·tam·i·nate (kŏn·tăm′ĭ·nāt), *v.t.* [contaminat·ed, contaminat·ing], to pollute; make impure.—*n.* **con·tam′i·na′tion.**
    Syn. corrupt, defile, taint, sully.

con·temn (kŏn·tĕm′), *v.t.* [contemned (kŏn·tĕmd′), contemn·ing (kŏn·tĕm′ĭng; kŏn·tĕm′nĭng)],to despise; treat with scorn.

con·tem·plate (kŏn′tĕm·plāt; kŏn·tĕm′·plāt), *v.t.* [contemplat·ed, contemplat·ing], **1,** to look at or to think about with attention; meditate on; **2,** to intend; purpose; expect:—*v.i.* to meditate; reflect.

con·tem·pla·tion (kŏn′tĕm·plā′shŭn), *n.* **1,** a steady looking at something; **2,** a prolonged thinking on one subject; reflection; meditation; **3,** expectation; intention.

con·tem·pla·tive (kŏn·tĕm′plȧ·tĭv; kŏn′·tĕm·plā′tĭv), *adj.* thoughtful; as, a *con- templative* mood.—*n.* **con·tem′pla·tive- ness.**

con·tem·po·ra·ne·ous (kŏn·tĕm′pō·rā′- nē·ŭs), *adj.* living or occurring at the same time; as, *contemporaneous* events.

con·tem·po·rar·y (kŏn·tĕm′pō·rĕr′ĭ), *adj.* existing or occurring at the same time:— *n.* [*pl.* contemporaries], one who lives at the same time as another; as, Lincoln and Lee were *contemporaries.*

con·tempt (kŏn·tĕmpt′), *n.* **1,** scorn, as of vile or mean acts; disdain; **2,** the state of being despised; disgrace; **3,** disregard of lawful orders; as, *contempt* of court.

con·tempt·i·ble (kŏn·tĕmp′tĭ·bl), *adj.* deserving scorn.—*adv.* **con·tempt′i·bly.**

con·temp·tu·ous (kŏn·tĕmp′tū·ŭs), *adj.* disdainful; scornful; as, a *contemptuous* smile.—*adv.* **con·temp′tu·ous·ly.**

con·tend (kŏn·tĕnd′), *v.i.* **1,** to strive against opponents, as for a prize; **2,** to dispute; debate.—*n.* **con·tend′er.**
    Syn. contest, struggle, combat.

[1]**con·tent**(kŏn′tĕnt; sometimes, kŏn·tĕnt′), *n.* **1,** the subject matter or thought, as of a magazine article; **2,** (usually *contents*), all that is contained, as in a vessel or book; also, the capacity, as of a measure.

[2]**con·tent** (kŏn·tĕnt′), *adj.* **1,** satisfied with one's lot; **2,** willing; as, I am *content* to go:—*v.t.* to satisfy; as, he is easily *con- tented:—n.* ease of mind.

con·tent·ed (kŏn·tĕn′tĕd), *adj.* satisfied; as, *contented* with his toys.—*adv.* **con- tent′ed·ly.**

con·ten·tion (kŏn·tĕn′shŭn), *n.* **1,** a striving or struggling; dispute; quarrel; **2,** a point for which one argues; as, my *contention* is that the price is too high.

con·ten·tious (kŏn·tĕn′shŭs), *adj.* inclined to argue about trifles; quarrelsome.—*n.* **con·ten′tious·ness.**

con·tent·ment (kŏn·tĕnt′mĕnt), *n.* **1,** the state of being satisfied; **2,** freedom from worry or restlessness.

con·test (kŏn·tĕst′), *v.t.* **1,** to strive to win or hold, as a battlefield; **2,** to dispute; call in question; as, to *contest* an election: —*n.* (kŏn′tĕst), a struggle for victory, as a game, fight, lawsuit, etc.
    Syn., n. conflict, combat, quarrel.

con·test·ant (kŏn·tĕs′tănt), *n.* a person who takes part in a struggle, game, debate, lawsuit, or the like.

con·text (kŏn′tĕkst), *n.* those parts of a written or spoken passage which are near a given expression, and which help to fix its meaning.

con·ti·gu·i·ty (kŏn′tĭ·gū′ĭ·tĭ), *n.* the state of being in contact; also, nearness.

con·tig·u·ous(kŏn·tĭg′ū·ŭs), *adj.* touching; adjoining; also, near; as, a field *contiguous* to the village.—*adv.* **con·tig′- u·ous·ly.**

con·ti·nence (kŏn′tĭ·nĕns), *n.* self-control; self-restraint, especially as to passions and desires. Also, **con′ti·nen·cy** (kŏn′tĭ·nĕn·sĭ).

[1]**con·ti·nent** (kŏn′tĭ·nĕnt), *adj.* temperate; exercising self-control.—*adv.* **con′ti·nent·ly.**

[2]**con·ti·nent** (kŏn′tĭ·nĕnt), *n.* one of the large divisions of land on the earth; as, the

CONTINENTAL SOLDIER

continent of North America:—**the Continent,** the mainland of Europe as distinguished from the British Isles.

con-ti-nen-tal (kŏn′tĭ-nĕn′tăl), *adj.* relating to a continent:—**Continental, 1,** relating to the mainland of Europe; **2,** in American history, having to do with the colonies at the time of the Revolution; as, the *Continental* Congress:—*n.* **1,** an American soldier during the Revolution (see illustration on preceding page); **2,** an inhabitant of the mainland of Europe.

con-tin-gen-cy (kŏn-tĭn′jĕn-sĭ), *n.* [*pl.* contingencies], possibility; also, an event which may or may not happen; as, ready for any *contingency.*

con-tin-gent (kŏn-tĭn′jĕnt), *adj.* **1,** possible, but uncertain; also, accidental; **2,** depending on something else, or on chance; as, her coming is *contingent* on the weather: —*n.* any unit or group in a gathering of representative units; as, the Idaho *contingent* at the convention.

con-tin-u-al (kŏn-tĭn′ū-ăl), *adj.* **1,** occurring again and again; **2,** going on without a break; ceaseless.—*adv.* **con-tin′u-al-ly.**

con-tin-u-ance (kŏn-tĭn′ū-ăns), *n.* a keeping on, lasting, or continuing.

con-tin-u-a-tion (kŏn-tĭn′ū-ā′shŭn), *n.* **1,** continuance; the carrying on of an activity without a break; **2,** a taking up after an interruption, as of schooling after illness; also, something continued after a break, as part of a serial story.

con-tin-ue (kŏn-tĭn′ū), *v.t.* [continued, continu-ing], **1,** to keep on doing, without a break; as, he *continued* to sing; also, to persevere in; **2,** to take up again after a break, as a story; **3,** to keep in office; **4,** to postpone, as a law case:—*v.i.* **1,** to remain in a place or condition; stay; as, to *continue* sad; **2,** to last; persist.

con-ti-nu-i-ty (kŏn′tĭ-nū′ĭ-tĭ), *n.* [*pl.* continuities], **1,** unbroken succession; connectedness; **2,** a motion-picture scenario; **3,** remarks by a radio announcer, connecting the items on a program.

con-tin-u-ous (kŏn-tĭn′ū-ŭs), *adj.* connected; unbroken.—*adv.* **con-tin′u-ous-ly.**

con-tort (kŏn-tôrt′), *v.t.* to bend or twist violently out of shape; distort.

con-tor-tion (kŏn-tôr′shŭn), *n.* an unnatural twisting, as of the face or body.

con-tour (kŏn′tŏŏr; kŏn-tŏŏr′), *n.* an outline, as of a body, or of a coast, mountain, or the like; also, an outline drawing.

con-tra- (kŏn′trȧ-), a prefix meaning against; opposite; as, *contradict.*

con-tra-band (kŏn′trȧ-bănd), *n.* **1,** anything forbidden to be brought into or out of a country, as in time of war; also, traffic in such goods; smuggling; **2,** smuggled goods:—*adj.* prohibited; forbidden.

con-tra-bass (kŏn′trȧ-bās′), *n.* a large, deep-toned, violin-shaped instrument.

con-tract (kŏn-trăkt′), *v.t.* **1,** to draw closer together; condense; shorten and thicken, as a muscle; to wrinkle; as, to *contract* the brows; **2,** to enter into (a friendship); incur (a debt, disease, habit, etc.); **3,** (often kŏn′trăkt), to enter upon by agreement, as an alliance or a marriage; **4,** in grammar, to shorten; as, to *contract* "over" to "o'er":—*v.i.* **1,** to shrink; **2,** (often kŏn′trăkt), to make an agreement; as, to *contract* for the removal of snow:—*n.* (kŏn′trăkt), **1,** a legal agreement; also, a written record of such an agreement; **2,** in cards, an undertaking to win a given number of tricks:—**contract** bridge, a card game in which the number of tricks bid is all that may count, if won, toward the game score.

Syn., n. bargain, compact, agreement.

con-trac-tion (kŏn-trăk′shŭn), *n.* **1,** a drawing together; shrinking; shortening; as, *contraction* of a muscle; **2,** a getting into a given condition; as, *contraction* of a debt; **3,** the shortening of a word, as in "can't" for "cannot"; also, a word so shortened.

con-trac-tor (kŏn-trăk′tẽr; kŏn′trăk-tẽr), *n.* **1,** one of the parties to a written agreement; **2,** one who undertakes to supply or construct something for a certain sum.

con-tra-dict (kŏn′trȧ-dĭkt′), *v.t.* **1,** to assert the opposite of (a statement); **2,** to deny the words of (a person).

con-tra-dic-tion (kŏn′trȧ-dĭk′shŭn), *n.* **1,** the act of saying the opposite; denial; also, a statement of this kind; **2,** a thing absolutely opposed to something else.

con-tra-dic-to-ry (kŏn′trȧ-dĭk′tō-rĭ), *adj.* **1,** opposing; inconsistent; as, *contradictory* statements; **2,** given to denying what others say; as, a *contradictory* person.

Syn. inconsistent, opposite, contrary.

con-tral-to (kŏn-trăl′tō), *n.* [*pl.* contraltos], **1,** the lowest female voice or part; **2,** a person with such a voice.

con-trap-tion (kŏn-trăp′shŭn), *n.* Colloquial, a gadget; a makeshift contrivance; (often said in contempt).

con-tra-ry (kŏn′trẽr-ĭ), *adj.* **1,** opposed; contradictory; conflicting; as, *contrary* opinions; **2,** opposite in direction; adverse; as, a *contrary* wind; **3,** (often kŏn-trâr′ĭ), perverse; wayward:—*n.* [*pl.* contraries], the opposite; as, if he says one thing, I believe the *contrary.*

con-trast (kŏn-trăst′), *v.t.* to place or state in such a way as to show differences; compare so as to show unlikeness:—*v.i.* to be very different, as shown by comparison; as, the white rose *contrasts* with her black dress: —*n.* (kŏn′trăst), **1,** striking difference; opposition; **2,** the thing or quality showing such difference.

con·trib·ute (kŏn-trĭb′ūt), *v.t.* [contribut-ed, contribut-ing], to give, as to some fund or purpose, along with others; furnish as a share: —*v.i.* **1,** to help; assist; aid in the accomplishment of a purpose; as, every player *contributed* to the victory; **2,** to be of use: as, play *contributes* to health.

con·tri·bu·tion (kŏn′trĭ-bū′shŭn), *n.* **1,** the giving of a share for a common purpose; **2,** the thing given, as money, food, or clothing; **3,** a writing in a periodical.

con·trib·u·tor (kŏn-trĭb′ū-tẽr), *n.* **1,** one who gives a share toward a common project; **2,** one who furnishes an article for publication.

con·trib·u·tor·y (kŏn-trĭb′ū-tôr′ĭ), *adj.* giving or lending aid; assisting.

con·trite (kŏn′trīt; kŏn-trīt′), *adj.* humble; penitent; repentant.

con·tri·tion (kŏn-trĭsh′ŭn), *n.* sincere sorrow for sin or error; repentance.

con·triv·ance (kŏn-trīv′ăns), *n.* **1,** the working out of some plan or scheme; also, the plan itself; **2,** a device; invention.

con·trive (kŏn-trīv′), *v.t.* [contrived, contriv-ing], **1,** to devise cleverly; invent; plan; **2,** to achieve by clever management; as, to *contrive* an escape.

con·trol (kŏn-trōl′), *n.* **1,** a check; restraint; **2,** effective authority; as, a teacher's *control* over a class; **3,** the apparatus regulating the operation of a machine: —**control stick,** in an airplane, the lever which moves the planes controlling the altitude, direction of flight, etc.: —*v.t.* [controlled, control-ling], **1,** to restrain; hold in check; as, to *control* one's anger; **2,** to govern.

con·trol·ler (kŏn-trōl′ẽr), *n.* **1,** on a machine, a device to regulate speed, pressure, etc.; **2,** (also *comptroller*), a public officer who has charge of financial accounts.

con·tro·ver·sial (kŏn′trŏ-vûr′shăl), *adj* **1,** inclined to dispute or argue; contentious; **2,** likely to provoke argument; as, a *controversial* question.

con·tro·ver·sy (kŏn′trŏ-vûr′sĭ), *n.* [*pl.* controversies], a dispute; an argument. *Syn.* contention, strife, quarrel.

con·tro·vert (kŏn′trŏ-vûrt; kŏn′trŏ-vûrt′), *v.t.* to dispute; oppose; as, to *controvert* an argument.

con·tu·ma·cious (kŏn′tū-mā′shŭs), *adj.* stubborn; scornful; rebellious. —*n.* **con′tu-ma-cy** (kŏn′tū-mȧ-sĭ).

con·tu·me·ly (kŏn′tū-mē′lĭ), *n.* [*pl.* contumelies], **1,** haughty, scornful rudeness; insolent, insulting language or abuse; **2,** an insult. —*adj.* **con′tu-me′li-ous.**

con·tu·sion (kŏn-tū′zhŭn), *n.* a bruise.

co·nun·drum (kō-nŭn′drŭm), *n.* a riddle; also, a puzzling question.

con·va·lesce (kŏn′vȧ-lĕs′), *v.i.* [convalesced, convalesc-ing], to recover strength and health after illness; get better.

con·va·les·cent (kŏn′vȧ-lĕs′ĕnt), *adj.* **1,** getting well; as, a *convalescent* patient; **2,** having to do with recovery from an illness; as, a *convalescent* home: —*n.* one who is getting well. —*n.* **con′va-les′cence.**

con·vene (kŏn-vēn′), *v.i.* and *v.t.* [convened, conven-ing], to come or call together; assemble.

con·ven·ience (kŏn-vēn′yĕns), *n.* **1,** suitability; fitness of place or time; **2,** ease in use or action; a saving of trouble; advantage; as, the *convenience* of a car; **3,** a handy device; **4, conveniences,** things that add to personal comfort, make work easier, or the like.

con·ven·ient (kŏn-vēn′yĕnt), *adj.* **1,** suitable; as, a *convenient* time; **2,** saving work or trouble; handy. —*adv.* **con-ven′ient-ly.**

con·vent (kŏn′vĕnt), *n.* a society, usually of women, living together and devoted to a religious life; also, the building occupied by such a society; a nunnery.

con·ven·tion (kŏn-vĕn′shŭn), *n.* **1,** a formal meeting; an assembly of delegates; as, a political *convention;* **2,** a diplomatic agreement; **3,** a fixed custom or usage.

con·ven·tion·al (kŏn-vĕn′shŭn-ăl), *adj.* in harmony with established customs; customary; regular; lacking in original thought; as, *conventional* evening clothes.

con·ven·tion·al·i·ty (kŏn-vĕn′shŭn-ăl′ĭ-tĭ), *n.* [*pl.* conventionalities], **1,** the following of accepted customs; as, a slave to *conventionality;* **2,** a practice approved by polite society; a formality.

con·verge (kŏn-vûrj′), *v.i.* [converged, converg-ing], to tend to come together, as crowds at a place of interest; to approach each other, as spokes of a wheel, or lines drawn toward a common point.

CONVERGENT LINES
The two lines converge toward the point A.

con·ver·gent (kŏn-vûr′jĕnt), *adj.* gradually approaching one another, as the roads to a city. —*n.* **con-ver′gence.**

con·ver·sant (kŏn′vẽr-sănt), *adj.* familiar; as, to be *conversant* with music.

con-ver-sa-tion (kŏn′vẽr-sā′shŭn), *n.* informal or familiar talk of persons with one another.
Syn. chat, parley, discourse, colloquy.

con-ver-sa-tion-al (kŏn′vẽr-sā′shŭn-ăl), *adj.* **1**, given to chatty talk; **2**, suited to familiar talk; as, a *conversational* tone of voice.—*adv.* **con′ver-sa′tion-al-ly.**

¹con-verse (kŏn-vûrs′), *v.i.* [conversed, convers-ing], to chat with a person:—*n.* (kŏn′vûrs), familiar talk; conversation.

²con-verse (kŏn′vûrs), *adj.* opposite:—*n.* the opposite of something else; as, "hot" is the *converse* of "cold."—*adv.* **con′verse-ly** (kŏn′vûrs-lĭ; kŏn-vûrs′lĭ).

con-ver-sion (kŏn-vûr′shŭn; kŏn-vûr′-zhŭn), *n.* **1**, a change in the form or substance of something; a transformation; as, the *conversion* of cream into butter; **2**, a change from one thing to something else, as by giving one thing for another; as, the *conversion* of a farm into money; **3**, a change in religious belief or attitude, as from disbelief to faith, or from one religion to another.

con-vert (kŏn-vûrt′), *v.t.* **1**, to transform or change, as in form, substance, etc.; **2**, to bring (a person) to belief in a religion, course, opinion, etc.; **3**, to exchange for something else, as land for money:—*n.* (kŏn′vûrt), one who becomes a believer in something, as a religion or a political party; as, a *convert* to Christianity.

con-vert-i-ble (kŏn-vûr′tĭ-bl), *adj.* capable of being changed; as, water is *convertible* into ice.—*n.* **con-vert′i-bil′i-ty.**

con-vex (kŏn′vĕks; kŏn-vĕks′), *adj.* curved out like the outside of a circle or ball; bulging; as, a *convex* mirror: opposite of *concave.*—*n.* **con-vex′i-ty.**

CONVEX
The outside of the bowl is convex.

con-vey (kŏn-vā′), *v.t.* **1**, to carry; transport; as, the train *conveyed* the children to the mountains; **2**, to transmit; be a means of carrying; as, pipes *convey* gas; **3**, to transfer (property) from one person to another.—*n.* **con-vey′er; con-vey′or.**

con-vey-ance (kŏn-vā′ăns), *n.* **1**, the act of carrying from one place or person to another; **2**, anything used for carrying; especially, a vehicle; **3**, a written title or deed to property.

con-vict (kŏn-vĭkt′), *v.t.* to prove or find guilty of a crime or offense:—*n.* (kŏn′vĭkt), **1**, a person found guilty of a crime; **2**, a person serving a term in prison.

con-vic-tion (kŏn-vĭk′shŭn), *n.* **1**, the finding that someone is guilty of a crime or offense; also, the state of being found guilty; **2**, a firm or settled belief.

con-vince (kŏn-vĭns′), *v.t.* [convinced, convinc-ing], to cause (a person) to see or feel the truth of something.—*adj.* **con-vinc′-ing.**—*adv.* **con-vinc′ing-ly.**

con-viv-i-al (kŏn-vĭv′ĭ-ăl), *adj.* **1**, like a feast; festive; **2**, fond of companionship and feasting; jovial; gay.

con-vo-ca-tion (kŏn′vō-kā′shŭn), *n.* **1**, the calling together of a number of people for a meeting; **2**, the meeting itself.

con-voke (kŏn-vōk′), *v.t.* [convoked, convok-ing], to call together for a meeting; as, Parliament was *convoked* in June.

con-vo-lu-tion (kŏn′vō-lū′shŭn), *n.* **1**, a coiling or winding together; **2**, a coil; a fold, as on the surface of the brain.

con-vol-vu-lus (kŏn-vŏl′vū-lŭs), *n.* any of a group of twining or trailing plants with funnel-shaped flowers, including the morning-glory.

con-voy (kŏn-voi′; kŏn-voi′), *v.t.* to accompany on the way, so as to guide or protect; to escort; as, the cruiser *convoyed* our ship into port:—*n.* (kŏn′voi), **1**, a protecting force accompanying ships, goods, persons, etc.; an escort; **2**, the goods, ships, persons, etc., so escorted.

con-vulse (kŏn-vŭls′), *v.t.* [convulsed, convuls-ing], **1**, to agitate or disturb violently; shake; **2**, to affect with spasms, as of laughter or anger.

con-vul-sion (kŏn-vŭl′shŭn), *n.* **1**, (usually *convulsions*), a violent twitching or jerking, caused by an uncontrollable contraction of the muscles; a spasm; a fit; **2**, a violent disturbance; upheaval; tumult.

con-vul-sive (kŏn-vŭl′sĭv), *adj.* marked by violent spasms or disturbances.—*adv.* **con-vul′sive-ly.**—*n.* **con-vul′sive-ness.**

co-ny (kō′nĭ), *n.* [*pl.* conies], **1**, a rabbit; **2**, an Old World animal like a rabbit, but unrelated to it; **3**, the fur of either of these animals. Also spelled **co′ney.**

coo (kōō), *n.* a murmuring sound like that of pigeons:—*v.i.* to utter such a sound.

Cook, Mount (kŏŏk), a mountain in New Zealand. See **Aorangi.**

cook (kŏŏk), *v.t.* **1**, to prepare (food) by applying heat, as in boiling, baking, frying, etc.; **2**, to invent falsely; as, to *cook* up an excuse:—*v.i.* to undergo cooking:—*n.* one who prepares food for the table.

cook-er (kŏŏk′ẽr), *n.* a special apparatus or vessel for cooking food; as, a steam *cooker;* a pressure *cooker.*

cook-er-y (kŏŏk′ẽr-ĭ), *n.* [*pl.* cookeries], the art or practice of preparing food for the table; as, an inn noted for fine *cookery.*

cook-y or **cook-ie** (kŏŏk′ĭ), *n.* [*pl.* cookies], a small, flat, sweet cake.

---

cool (kōol), *adj.* **1,** slightly or moderately cold; **2,** not admitting or retaining heat; as, *cool* clothes; **3,** calm; self-possessed; as, he was the only *cool* one in the mob; **4,** lacking in cordiality; as, a *cool* response:— *v.t.* **1,** to make slightly cold; chill; **2,** to calm; quiet; as, his tears *cooled* my anger: —*v.i.* to become slightly cold:—*n.* a state or time of moderate cold; as, the *cool* of the evening.—*adj.* **cool′ish.**—*adv.* **cool′ly.**—*n.* **cool′ness.**

cool-er (kōol′ẽr), *n.* a device for keeping food or liquids cool; as, a water *cooler*.

Cool-idge (kōol′ĭj), Calvin (1872–1933), the 30th president of the U.S.

coo-lie or **coo-ly** (kōo′lĭ), *n.* [*pl.* coolies], an unskilled laborer, usually a native of China, Japan, or India.

coon (kōon), *n.* a raccoon.

coop (kōop), *n.* a cage or enclosure for fowls, rabbits, etc.; a pen: —*v.t.* to confine in a cage or pen.

Coo-per (kōo′pẽr; kōop′ẽr), James Fenimore (1789–1851), an American novelist.

coop-er (kōop′ẽr), *n.* a maker or mender of barrels, casks, etc.—*n.* **coop′er-age.**

co—op-er-ate (kō-ŏp′ẽr-āt), *v.i.* [co-operat-ed, co-operat-ing], to act or work for a common end; work together; as, everyone *co-operated* in making the play a success. Also, **co-op′er-ate, co-ŏp′er-ate.**

co—op-er-a-tion (kō-ŏp′ẽr-ā′shŭn), *n.* a working together for the same end; hence, mutual help; assistance. Also, **co-op′er-a′tion, co-ŏp′er-a′tion.**

co—op-er-a-tive (kō-ŏp′ẽr-ā′tĭv), *adj.* **1,** working together for common ends; **2,** having to do with an organized group of people who work together for common ends and share their profits and losses; as, a *co-operative* shop for students. Also, **co-op′er-a′tive, co-ŏp′er-a′tive.**

co—or-di-nate (kō-ôr′dĭ-nāt), *v.t.* [co-ordinat-ed, co-ordinat-ing], **1,** to place in the same order or class; to make equal in rank or importance; **2,** to put in harmony; adjust; as, to *co-ordinate* movements in swimming:—*v.i.* to harmonize:—*adj.* (kō-ôr′dĭ-năt), **1,** of the same rank or order, as the clauses of a compound sentence; **2,** pertaining to things of the same rank:—*n.* (kō-ôr′dĭ-năt), a person or thing of the same rank,

COOT (¹⁄₁₁), def. 1

order, or importance as another. Also, **co-or′di-nate, co-ör′di-nate.**—*adv.* **co-or′di-nate-ly.**—*n.* **co-or′di-na′tion.**

coot (kōot), *n.* **1,** a swimming and diving bird somewhat like a duck (see illustration in preceding column); **2,** a scoter.

co-pal (kō′păl; kō′păl), *n.* a resin from a tropical tree, used in making varnishes.

¹cope (kōp), *v.i.* [coped, cop-ing], to struggle successfully; as, to *cope* with difficulties.

²cope (kōp), *n.* **1,** a long cloak or mantle worn by priests on certain occasions; **2,** something like this cloak in shape, as an arched roof.

Co-pen-ha-gen (kō′pĕn-hā′gĕn), a seaport city, capital of Denmark. The Danish name is *København*.

Co-per-ni-cus (kô-pûr′nĭ-kŭs), (1473–1543), a Polish astronomer who discovered that the earth and other planets move around the sun.

cop-i-er (kŏp′ĭ-ẽr), *n.* one who reproduces or imitates something by copying.

cop-ing (kōp′ĭng), *n.* the top layer of a wall, often of brick or stone, usually sloping so as to shed water. (See illustration below.)

coping saw, a narrow saw used for cutting curved patterns. (See ¹*saw*, illustration.)

co-pi-ous (kō′pĭ-ŭs), *adj.* plenteous; ample; abundant; as, a *copious* supply of pencils. —*adv.* **co′pi-ous-ly.**

cop-per (kŏp′ẽr), *n.* **1,** a common, reddish metal, easily worked, and an excellent conductor of heat and electricity; **2,** something made of this metal; **3,** a coin, usually made of copper but sometimes of bronze; in the U.S., a cent:—*adj.* of or like copper.—*adj.* **cop′per-y.**

cop-per-as (kŏp′ẽr-ăs), *n.* a green chemical used in dyeing, in making inks, etc.

cop-per-head (kŏp′ẽr-hĕd′), *n.* a poisonous snake, related to the rattlesnake, with brownish or reddish coloring, found in the eastern part of the U.S.:—**Copperhead,** a Northerner who sympathized with the South during the War between the States.

cop-per-plate (kŏp′ẽr-plāt′), *n.* **1,** a polished copper plate on which something, as a drawing or printing, is cut with acid or a pointed tool; **2,** an impression made from such a plate; as, a *copperplate* engraving.

cop-ra (kŏp′rȧ), *n.* the dried meat of the coconut, which furnishes coconut oil.

WATER COOLER

COPE
Bishop wearing cope (C) and miter (M) and holding crosier (CR).

COPING (C)

copse (kŏps), *n.* a grove or thicket of small trees or bushes; a coppice.

Copt (kŏpt), *n.* a native Egyptian belonging to the race that is descended from the ancient Egyptians.

Cop-tic (kŏp′tĭk), *adj.* having to do with Copts, or native Egyptians, their language, or their church:—*n.* the language of the Copts, not used as common speech since the 16th century, but still in use in the services of the Coptic Church.

cop-y (kŏp′ĭ), *n.* [*pl.* copies], 1, an imitation; a reproduction; as, a *copy* of a portrait or of a will; 2, an exercise written in imitation of a model; also, the model; 3, something, as typewritten matter, to be set up in type; 4, a single one of a number of reproductions, as of a book or magazine, etc.:—*v.t.* [copied, copy-ing], 1, to make a likeness of; reproduce; as, to *copy* a report; 2, to imitate.

   Syn., *n.* facsimile, likeness, counterpart.

cop-y-ist (kŏp′ĭ-ĭst), *n.* one who makes reproductions from originals.

cop-y-right (kŏp′ĭ-rīt′), *n.* the exclusive legal right of an artist or author, or his agent, to reproduce, publish, etc., a literary or artistic work for a certain time:—*v.t.* to secure a copyright for; as, to *copyright* a book.

co-quet (kŏ-kĕt′), *v.i.* [coquet-ted, coquet-ting], to flirt; trifle or dally with love, with danger, or the like.

co-quet-ry (kō′-kĕ-trĭ; kŏ-kĕt′rĭ), *n.* [*pl.* coquetries], the act of exciting the affections of

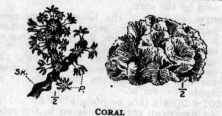

CORACLE

one of the opposite sex in an insincere and trifling manner; flirtation.

co-quette (kŏ-kĕt′), *n.* a woman who trifles with love; a flirt.—*adj.* **co-quet′tish.**—*adv.* **co-quet′tish-ly.**

cor- (kôr-), *prefix*, a form of *com-* used before *r*; as, correspond.

cor-a-cle (kŏr′ȧ-kl), *n.* a small boat made of hides, tarpaulin, or other waterproof material, stretched over a light frame. (See illustration above.)

cor-al (kŏr′ăl), *n.* 1, a hard substance like limestone, varied and often brilliant in color, built up of countless skeletons of certain animals which grow in shallow tropical seas, and often appearing at or above the surface as reefs or islands (see illustration in next column); 2, one of the tiny animals that produce coral; 3, the color of orange red:—*adj.* 1, made of coral; 2, red in color, as coral.

Cor-cy-ra (kôr-sī′rȧ), the ancient name of an island west of Greece. See **Corfu.**

cord (kôrd), *n.* 1, a string or small rope; 2, **cords,** any binding force; as, the *cords* of friendship; 3, a measure of firewood,

CORAL

Branch of red coral showing skeleton (Sk) and polyps (P), and skeleton of a rose coral.

usually the amount in a pile eight feet by four feet by four feet, or 128 cubic feet; 4, any ropelike structure, as a tendon or nerve:—*v.t.* 1, to bind with string or rope; 2, to stack (wood) in cords.

cord-age (kôr′dĭj), *n.* 1, cords and ropes in general, especially as forming the rigging of a ship; 2, a quantity of wood measured in cords.

cor-dial (kôr′jăl; kôrd′yăl), *adj.* 1, tending to revive, as a medicine; 2, hearty-sincere; as, a *cordial* manner:—*n.* 1, a medicine, food, or drink that revives or stimulates; 2, a liqueur.—*adv.* **cor′dial-ly.**

cor-dial-i-ty (kôr-jăl′ĭ-tĭ; kôr′dĭ-ăl′ĭ-tĭ), *n.* sincere good will; heartiness; as, he greeted us with *cordiality.*

cor-dil-ler-a (kôr′dĭl-yâr′ȧ; kôr-dĭl′ĕr-ȧ), *n.* a mountain range.

Cór-do-ba (kôr′dŏ-vä), 1, a province in south central Spain; also, a city, its capital (map 12); 2, (kôr′dŏ-bä), a province in central Argentina, South America; also, a city, its capital (map 11).

cór-do-ba (kôr′dŏ-bä), *n.* a silver coin, the monetary unit of Nicaragua.

cor-don (kôr′dŏn), *n.* 1, a cord or ribbon worn as the badge of an order; 2, a line of men, ships, forts, or the like, forming an extended chain of military posts; 3, a line or circle of persons about a person or place; as, a *cordon* of detectives protected the bank.

Cor-do-van (kôr′dŏ-văn), *adj.* having to do with Córdoba in Spain:—*n.* a native or inhabitant of Córdoba:—**cordovan,** or **cordovan leather,** a fine leather, at one time manufactured chiefly at Córdoba, made of goatskin, pigskin, or horsehide, split so as to retain the grain.

cor-du-roy (kôr′dŭ-roi; kôr′dŭ-roi′), *n.* 1, a stout ribbed or corded cotton cloth with a velvety surface; 2, **corduroys,** trousers, or a suit, made of corduroy:—

---

go; join; yet; sing; chin; show; thin, *th*en; hw, *why*; zh, azure; ü, Ger. *für* or Fr. *lune*; ö, Ger. schön or Fr. *feu*; ṅ, Fr. e*n*fant; nom; kh, Ger. a*ch* or i*ch*. See pages ix–x.

adj. **1**, of or like corduroy; **2**, in the U.S., made of logs laid crosswise, as a road.

cord-wood (kôrd′wŏŏd′), *n.* cut firewood sold by the cord.

core (kôr), *n.* **1**, the heart or innermost part of anything, especially of certain fruits, such as apples; **2**, the substance or essential point, as of an argument or a speech; **3**, a bar of soft iron forming the center of an electromagnet:—*v.t.* [cored, cor-ing], to remove the core from, as an apple.—*n.* **cor′er.**

cor-e-op-sis (kôr′ē-ŏp′sĭs; kôr′ē-ŏp′sĭs), *n.* an American plant belonging to the aster family; also, its daisylike flower.

co-re-spond-ent (kō′rē-spŏn′dĕnt), *n.* a person named along with the husband or wife, as the sharer of guilt in a divorce suit.

Cor-fu (kôr-fōō′; kôr′fū), an island west of Greece, in the Ionian Sea; also, a seaport, its capital. Formerly called *Corcyra.*

Cor-inth (kŏr′ĭnth), a city of Greece, once famed for its luxuries (map 1).

Co-rin-thi-an (kō-rĭn′thĭ-ăn), *n.* a native of Corinth:—*adj.* **1**, pertaining to Corinth, or to its people; **2**, in architecture, designating the most highly ornamented of the three Greek orders, the column having a bell-shaped capital surrounded by acanthus leaves.

CORINTHIAN CAPITAL

Co-rin-thi-ans (kō-rĭn′thĭ-ănz), *n.* in the New Testament, either of two books containing Paul's epistles, or letters, to the Corinthians.

Cor-i-o-la-nus (kôr′ĭ-ō-lā′nŭs), (after 489 B.C.), a Roman hero.

Cork (kôrk), a county in southern Ireland; also, a city, its capital (map 13).

cork (kôrk), *n.* **1**, the light, elastic, outer layer of bark of a certain oak, used for floats, life preservers, stoppers for bottles, etc.; **2**, a stopper for a bottle or cask; especially, one made of cork:—*v.t.* **1**, to stop with a cork, as a bottle; **2**, to restrain; as, to *cork* up one's anger:—*adj.* made of cork. —*adj.* **corked.**

cork-screw (kôrk′skrōō′), *n.* a spiral wire or a screw, fastened to a handle, used for drawing corks from bottles:—*adj.* shaped like a corkscrew; as, a *corkscrew* path: —*v.i.* and *v.t. Colloquial,* to follow, or cause to follow, a winding course.

corm (kôrm), *n.* a bulblike underground plant stem, enlarged for food storage, as in the crocus.

CORK-SCREW

cor-mo-rant (kôr′mō-rănt), *n.* **1**, a large, greedy sea bird that feeds on fish; **2**, a person who is greedy or covetous.

¹corn (kôrn), *n.* **1**, a kernel or seed, especially of a cereal plant; also, the plant producing it; **2**, any kind of cereal grain, as wheat, barley, etc.: in England, usually meaning *wheat;* in Scotland and Ireland, *oats;* in North America and Australia, *Indian corn,* or *maize:*—*v.t.* to preserve in brine; as, to *corn* beef:—**Indian corn, 1**, an American cereal plant producing tall stalks which bear large ears of grain, usually white or yellow when ripe and covered with a husk: called *maize,* in England, but known in the U.S. merely as *corn;* **2**, the grain of this plant, used as food for persons and livestock.

CORMORANT (¹⁄₁₀)

²corn (kôrn), *n.* a horny thickening of the skin, especially on the toe or foot.

corn bread, a kind of hot bread or muffin made of corn meal, without yeast, and baked, usually, in a shallow pan.

EAR OF CORN

corn-cob (kôrn′kŏb′), *n.* **1**, the woody center of an ear of Indian corn, on which the grains are set; **2**, a tobacco pipe made of a corncob.

corn cock-le, a tall weed bearing bright-red flowers, that often grows in cornfields: also called *cornflower.*

corn-crib (kôrn′krĭb′), *n.* a small building used for storing corn.

cor-ne-a (kôr′nē-á), *n.* the front, transparent part of the outer coat of the eyeball, which covers the iris and pupil and admits light to the interior.

Cor-neille (kôr′nāy′), Pierre (1606–84), a French dramatist.

cor-ner (kôr′nẽr), *n.* **1**, an angle; the point where two lines, sides, or edges meet; as, the *corners* of a desk; also, the area near this angle; as, a *corner* of the attic; **2**, the intersection of two or more streets; **3**, a nook; a secluded place; **4**, a remote point; as, the *corners* of the earth; **5**, an awkward situation; as, your question put me in a *corner;* **6**, a monopolizing of the supply of something in order to raise the price:— *v.t.* **1**, to drive into a corner; **2**, to force into a situation having no escape; as, to *corner* a burglar:—*adj.* **1**, located at a corner; as, a *corner* store; **2**, usable in a corner; as, a *corner* cupboard.

cor·ner·stone (kôr/nẽr-stōn/), n. 1. a stone set in place with ceremony at some corner of the foundation of a building; 2, hence, something of basic importance on which other things depend; as, tolerance is the *cornerstone* of friendship.

cor·net (kôr/nĕt; kôr-nĕt/), n. a brass wind instrument similar to a trumpet. —n. cor·net/tist; cor/net·ist.

CORNET

corn·field (kôrn/fēld/), n. a field in which corn is grown.

corn·flow·er (kôrn/flou/ẽr), n. 1, the corn cockle; 2, the bachelor's-button, a plant having showy blue, pink, or white flowers.

cor·nice (kôr/nĭs), n. 1, an ornamental molding on a wall near the ceiling; 2, a horizontal projecting piece forming the top of a wall or column (see *frame house*, illustration).

CORNICE (C)

Cor·nish (kôr/nĭsh), adj. pertaining to Cornwall, or to its language or people: —n. the ancient language of Cornwall.

corn pone, bread made of corn meal: also called *pone*.

corn·starch (kôrn/stärch/), n. a white, floury starch made from Indian corn, used in puddings and as a thickening for foods.

cor·nu·co·pi·a (kôr/nū-kō/pĭ-ȧ), n. [pl. cornucopias], 1, a horn full of fruit and flowers, symbolizing prosperity; 2, hence, plenty; abundance; 3, a cone-shaped paper holder for nuts and candy.

Corn·wall (kôrn/wôl), a county in southwestern England.

Corn·wal·lis (kôrn-wŏl/ĭs;-wôl/ĭs),Charles, Marquis of (1738–1805), an English general who surrendered to Washington, 1781.

co·rol·la (kō-rŏl/ȧ), n. the inner envelope of a flower, usually brightly colored, and made up of the petals.

cor·ol·lar·y (kŏr/ō-lĕr/ĭ), n. [pl. corollaries], 1, a truth which follows naturally from a truth which has been already proved, without requiring further proof; 2, hence, something that follows naturally; a result.

COROLLA (C)

co·ro·na (kō-rō/nȧ), n. [pl. coronas (kō-rō/nȧz) or coronae (kō-rō/nē)], a luminous ring seen around the sun during a total eclipse.

cor·o·na·tion (kŏr/ō-nā/shŭn), n. the act or ceremony of crowning a king or queen.

cor·o·ner (kŏr/ō-nẽr), n. an officer whose chief duty is to find out the cause of any violent or mysterious death.

cor·o·net (kŏr/ō-nĕt), n. 1, a small crown worn to show a high rank below that of a king, as of a duke or earl; 2, an ornamental band or wreath worn around the head.

CORONET

Co·rot (kō/rō/), Jean Baptiste Camille (1796–1875), a French painter.

Corp. abbreviation for *Corporal, Corporation.*

[1]**cor·po·ral** (kôr/pō-rȧl), n. the lowest noncommissioned officer in the army, next below a sergeant, and usually in command of a squad of eight men.

[2]**cor·po·ral** (kôr/pō-rȧl), adj. having to do with the body; as, *corporal* punishment.

cor·po·rate (kôr/pō-rĭt), adj. having to do with a group of persons united into one body and permitted by law to act as one person; as, a *corporate* action.

cor·po·ra·tion (kôr/pō-rā/shŭn), n. a group of persons permitted by law to act as one person in carrying on a given kind of business, work, or the like.

cor·por·e·al (kôr-pôr/ē-ȧl), adj. having to do with the body; material; physical.

corps (kôr), n. [pl. corps (kôrz)], 1, a large unit of an army, containing two or more military divisions; 2, a body of troops for special service; as, the signal *corps;* 3, a body of persons associated in a common work; as, a *corps* of writers.

corpse (kôrps), n. a dead body, usually a human body. *Syn.* remains, carcass, body.

cor·pu·lence (kôr/pū-lĕns), n. stoutness.

cor·pu·lent (kôr/pū-lĕnt), adj. fat; having a large, fleshy body.

cor·pus·cle (kôr/pŭs-l), n. 1, a minute particle of matter; 2, an electron; 3, one of the small cells of the blood.

cor·ral (kŏ-răl/; kô-răl/), n. 1, a pen or enclosure for horses, cattle, or the like; 2, an enclosure or circle of wagons formed to protect an encampment:—v.t. (kŏ-răl/), [corralled, corral-ling], to drive into, or secure in, a pen or enclosure.

cor·rect (kŏ-rĕkt/), v.t. 1, to set straight; make right; remove errors from; mark errors in (something written or printed) for removal; as, to *correct* compositions; 2, to cure; as, to *correct* a bad habit; 3, to reprove; as, the teacher *corrected* the student:—adj. 1, exact; accurate; free from error; 2, measuring up to a standard of morals, taste, manners, etc.; as, *correct* behavior.—n. cor·rect/ness.

cor·rec·tion (kŏ-rĕk′shŭn), *n.* **1,** the act of pointing out mistakes or of changing something to make it right; **2,** a change so made; **3,** reproof; punishment.

cor·rec·tive (kŏ-rĕk′tĭv), *adj.* tending, or having the power, to make right, normal, or healthy; as, *corrective* criticism:—*n.* that which makes right; as, exercise is a *corrective* for physical defects.

cor·re·late (kŏr′ĕ-lāt; kŏr′ĕ-lāt′), *v.i.* [correlat-ed, correlat-ing], to be related by connection, likeness, etc.:—*v.t.* to bring into relation, connection, etc.; as, to *correlate* literature and history.

cor·re·la·tion (kŏr′ĕ-lā′shŭn), *n.* a mutual relationship between things; as, the *correlation* between play and health.

cor·rel·a·tive (kŏ-rĕl′a-tĭv), *adj.* dependent upon, or naturally related to, something else; as, the size and the weight of a stone are *correlative* qualities:—*n.* either of two things related to each other, as, in grammar, two words like "either" and "or" commonly used together.

cor·re·spond (kŏr′ĕ-spŏnd′), *v.i.* **1,** to be similar or equal in use, position, character, or amount; as, our Congress *corresponds* to the British Parliament; **2,** to agree; suit; match; harmonize; as, her actions do not *correspond* to our standards; **3,** to communicate by letter.

cor·re·spond·ence (kŏr′ĕ-spŏn′dĕns), *n.* **1,** communication by letters; **2,** written communications; letters; **3,** agreement; similarity; as, a *correspondence* in size.

cor·re·spond·ent (kŏr′ĕ-spŏn′dĕnt), *adj.* agreeing with; similar:—*n.* **1,** one with whom letters are exchanged; **2,** one who writes news from a particular place for a newspaper or magazine; as, the Geneva *correspondent* for this paper.

cor·re·spond·ing (kŏr′ĕ-spŏn′dĭng), *adj.* **1,** agreeing; matching; **2,** communicating by letter.—*adv.* **cor′re·spond′ing·ly.**

cor·ri·dor (kŏr′ĭ-dôr; kŏr′ĭ-dĕr), *n.* a long passage into which rooms open.

cor·rob·o·rate (kŏ-rŏb′ō-rāt), *v.t.* [corroborat-ed, corroborat-ing], to confirm; make more certain; as, this evidence *corroborates* my opinion.—*n.* **cor·rob′o·ra′-tion.**—*adj.* **cor·rob′o·ra′tive.**—*adj.* **cor·rob′o·ra·tor′y.**

cor·rode (kŏ-rōd′), *v.t.* and *v.i.* [corrod-ed, corrod-ing], to eat away or decay gradually, as by chemical action; disintegrate; rust.

cor·ro·sion (kŏ-rō′zhŭn), *n.* **1,** the act of eating or wearing away, especially by chemical action; **2,** a condition produced by this process, as of metal by rust.

cor·ro·sive (kŏ-rō′sĭv), *adj.* having the power of gradually eating away:—*n.* that which corrodes, as an acid.

cor·ru·gate (kŏr′ŭ-gāt), *v.t.* [corrugat-ed, corrugat-ing], to shape in wrinkles or alternate ridges and grooves:—*v.i.* to contract into wrinkles or folds.—*adj.* **cor′ru·gat′ed.** —*n.* **cor′ru·ga′tion.**

cor·rupt (kŏ-rŭpt′), *v.t.* **1,** to injure; spoil; **2,** to make impure; debase; as, bad associations *corrupted* his morals; **3,** to bribe; as, to *corrupt* a witness:—*adj.* spoiled; depraved; dishonest; as, *corrupt* practices; full of errors; as, he spoke *corrupt* English. —*adv.* **cor·rupt′ly.**—*n.* **cor·rupt′ness.**— *adj.* **cor·rup′tive.**
    Syn., *adj.* polluted, debased.

cor·rupt·i·ble (kŏ-rŭp′tĭ-bl), *adj.* **1,** capable of being changed for the worse; subject to decay; **2,** capable of being bribed. —*n.* **cor·rupt′i·bil′i·ty.**

cor·rup·tion (kŏ-rŭp′shŭn), *n.* **1,** loss of honor, purity, moral principle, etc.; dishonesty; **2,** physical decay; **3,** the bribing of someone to do something wrong.

cor·sage (kôr-säzh′; kôr′sĭj), *n.* **1,** the bodice or waist of a woman's dress; **2,** a bouquet to be worn by a woman.

cor·sair (kôr′sâr), *n.* **1,** formerly, a Turkish or Saracen privateer who attacked the ships and coasts of Christian nations; **2,** a corsair's ship; **3,** a pirate.

corse (kôrs), *n.* a dead body; a corpse.

corse·let or **cors·let** (kôrs′lĕt), *n.* in former times, armor for the body of a soldier or knight; also, the breastplate.

cor·set (kôr′sĕt), *n.* a woman's tight-fitting undergarment, worn to support the figure, or to modify its shape; stays.

Cor·si·ca (kôr′sĭ-ka) or **Corse** (kôrs), a French island (cap. Ajaccio) west of Italy, in the Mediterranean, the birthplace of Napoleon (map 12).—*adj.* and *n.* **Cor′si·can.**

¹**Cor·tes** or **Cor·tez** (kôr′tĕz), (1485–1547), a Spaniard who conquered Mexico.

²**Cor·tes** (kôr′tĕz), *n.* the legislative assembly of Spain or Portugal.

cor·tex (kôr′tĕks), *n.* [*pl.* cortices (kôr′tĭ-sēz)], **1,** a plant tissue lying below the epidermis, often storing starch; **2,** the outer layers of an organ, as of the brain.

cor·ti·cal (kôr′tĭ-kăl), *adj.* having to do with the cortex.

co·run·dum (kŏ-rŭn′dŭm), *n.* next to the diamond the hardest known mineral, used for polishing and grinding. The sapphire, topaz, ruby, etc., are forms of corundum.

cor·vette (kôr-vĕt′) or **cor·vet** (kôr′vĕt), *n.* formerly, a ship of war with one tier of guns, ranking next below a frigate.

āte, āorta, râre, căt, ȧsk, fär, ȧllow, sofȧ; ēve, ēvent, ĕll, writēr, novĕl; bīte, pĭn; nō, ōbey, ôr, dôg, tŏp, cŏllide; ūnit, ŭnite, bûrn, cŭt, focŭs; nōon, fŏŏt; mound; coin;

cos-met-ic (kŏz-mĕt′ĭk), *n.* a preparation, as facial cream, powder, or the like, used to beautify the skin or hair:—*adj.* designed to beautify the complexion.

cos-mic (kŏz′mĭk), *adj.* having to do with the universe and the laws which govern it; hence, vast; mighty:—**cosmic rays**, radiations similar to X rays, but of greater penetrating power, probably coming from outer space.

cos-mog-o-ny (kŏz-mŏg′ô-nĭ), *n.* [*pl.* cosmogonies], a theory or account of the creation of the universe.

cos-mo-pol-i-tan (kŏz′mô-pŏl′ĭ-tăn), *n.* a person of wide information and sympathies:—*adj.* 1, at home anywhere; having broad interests and sympathies; 2, belonging to the world; not restricted to one nation or race; as, *cosmopolitan* ideals.

cos-mos (kŏz′mŏs; kŏz′mŭs), *n.* 1, the world or universe as a well-ordered system; 2, order; harmony; 3, a plant related to the daisy, growing from four to ten feet tall and blooming in the fall with white, red, pink, or rose-colored flowers.

Cos-sack (kŏs′ăk; kŏs′ăk), *n.* a member of a warlike tribe in southern Russia, skilled as horsemen.

cost (kôst), *v.t.* [*p.t.* and *p.p.* cost, *p.pr.* cost-ing], 1, to be obtainable for (a certain price); as, the card *costs* five cents; 2, to cause to spend or lose; as, carelessness *cost* him his job:—*v.i.* to involve or cause expenditure, loss, etc.; as, the accident *cost* dear:—*n.* 1, a charge; expense; the amount asked or paid for anything; as, the *cost* of food; 2, the price in terms of suffering, toil, etc.; as, he made a fortune at the *cost* of health; 3, **costs**, the expenses of a lawsuit.

Cos-ta Ri-ca (kŏs′tà rē′kà), a republic (cap. San José), northwest of Panama, in Central America (map 10).

cos-ter-mon-ger (kŏs′tĕr-mŭng′gĕr), *n.* a peddler of fruit, vegetables, fish, etc.

cos-tive (kŏs′tĭv), *adj.* constipated.

cost-ly (kôst′lĭ), *adj.* [cost-li-er, cost-li-est], involving great cost or expense, as of money or effort.—*n.* **cost′li-ness.**
Syn. dear, expensive, exorbitant.

cos-tume (kŏs′tūm; kŏs-tūm′), *n.* 1, dress in general; style of dress; especially, the dress of a given time, period, class, etc.; 2, historical dress; fancy dress:—*v.t.* (kŏs-tūm′), [costumed, costum-ing], to provide with appropriate dress; as, to *costume* actors for their parts.

cos-tum-er (kŏs-tūm′ĕr; kŏs′tūm-ĕr), *n.* one who makes or sells costumes, as for fancy-dress balls, plays, etc.

co-sy (kō′zĭ), *adj.* [co-si-er, co-si-est], snug: —*n.* [*pl.* cosies], 1, a padded covering for a teapot; 2, a snug seat. See **cozy.**

¹**cot** (kŏt), *n.* 1, a cottage; hut; 2, a cote.

²**cot** (kŏt), *n.* a small, light bed, often portable.

cote (kōt), *n.* a shelter, as for sheep; a coop, as for pigeons.

COT

co-te-rie (kō′tĕ-rĭ; kō′tĕ-rē), *n.* a set of intimate friends; a clique.

co-til-lion (kô-tĭl′yŭn), *n.* 1, a lively dance; a quadrille or german; 2, music for such a dance.

Co-to-pax-i (kō′tô-păk′sē; kō′tô-pä′hē), a volcano in the Andes Mountains in Ecuador, South America (map 11).

cot-tage (kŏt′ĭj), *n.* a small dwelling; also, a house at a summer resort.

cot-tag-er (kŏt′ĭj-ĕr), *n.* one who lives in a cottage.

¹**cot-ter** or **cot-tar** (kŏt′ĕr), *n.* a Scotch farmer who owns a small piece of land.

²**cot-ter** (kŏt′ĕr), *n.* a pin or bolt to fasten together or hold in place parts of machinery; in some forms called *cotter pin.*

COTTON
A, flower; B, boll.

cot-ton (kŏt′n), *n.* 1, a white, fibrous down enclosing the seeds of the cotton plant; 2, the plant producing this; 3, thread or cloth made of cotton:—*adj.* pertaining to cotton.—*adj.* **cot′ton-y.**

cot-ton-seed (kŏt′n-sēd′), *n.* the seed of the cotton plant:—*adj.* made from cotton seeds; as, *cottonseed* oil.

cot-ton-tail (kŏt′n-tāl′), *n.* a wild American rabbit.

cot-ton-wood (kŏt′n-wŏŏd′), *n.* 1, an American poplar, having a fluffy, cottony tuft about the seed; 2, poplar wood.

cot-y-le-don (kŏt′ĭ-lē′dŭn), *n.* a part of a seed containing food for the young root, stem, and first true leaves: often appearing above ground at germination as the seed leaf, and later shriveling up.—*adj.* **cot′y-le′don-ous.**

COTYLEDONS
(C, C)

couch (kouch), *v.t.* 1, to lay upon a bed or other resting place; 2, to put into words; express; as, to *couch* a letter in strong terms; **3,** to lower, as a lance or spear for attack:—*v.i.* **1,** to lie down, as on a bed; **2,** to cower; hide:—*n.* a bed; sofa; lounge.

couch-ant (kouch′ănt), *adj.* in heraldry, crouching, but with the head up.

cou-gar (kōō′gẽr), *n.* a large, tawny American animal of the cat family: also called *puma, catamount, panther,* or *mountain lion.* (See illustration under *puma.*)

cough (kôf), *v.i.* to force air from the lungs suddenly, with a sharp noise:—*v.t.* to expel from the lungs or air passages; as, he *coughed* up the bone:—*n.* **1,** the act or sound of coughing; **2,** an illness marked by a cough; as, to have a dry *cough.*

could (kŏŏd), past tense of *can.*

cou-lee (kōō′lǐ), *n.* **1,** in western U.S., a deep gulch with sides sloping less steeply than those of a canyon; **2,** a sheet of cooled or solid lava.

coun-cil (koun′sĭl), *n.* **1,** a group of persons called together to discuss and settle problems, give advice, etc.; as, a *council* of teachers; **2,** a lawmaking or governing body, as of a city or town; **3,** the deliberation of such a body.

coun-cil-man (koun′sĭl-măn), *n.* [*pl.* councilmen (-měn)], a member of an assembly, especially of the lawmaking body of a city or town.

coun-ci-lor or **coun-cil-lor** (koun′sĭ-lẽr), *n.* a member of an advisory, deliberative, or governing body.

coun-sel (koun′sĕl), *n.* **1,** exchange of opinion; consultation; as, the general took *counsel* with his officers; **2,** instruction; advice; as, he was guided by his mother's *counsel;* **3,** prudence; foresight; **4,** an advocate or lawyer:—*v.t.* [counseled, counseling], **1,** to give advice to; **2,** to recommend; as, I *counsel* patience.

Syn., v. advise, instruct, admonish.

coun-se-lor or **coun-sel-lor** (koun′sĕ-lẽr), *n.* **1,** one who gives advice or counsel; **2,** an advising lawyer or group of lawyers on a case:—**counselor at law,** a lawyer.

¹count (kount), *v.t.* **1,** to tell off (units) in order to find their number; sum up; as, *count* your pennies; **2,** to give the numerals in regular order to a certain point; as, *count* ten before you answer; **3,** to consider; as, she *counts* herself generous; **4,** to include in an enumeration; as, he *counted* only the best:—*v.i.* **1,** to tell off articles or numbers in order; **2,** to rely; as, we *count* on her consent; **3,** to be of worth or value; as, this doesn't *count* much; **4,** to have effect; as, his support *counted* heavily in the victory:—*n.* **1,** the act of numbering; as, a *count* of the boys; **2,** the total ascertained.

²count (kount), *n.* a title of nobility in France, Spain, Italy, etc.: about the same as British *earl.*

coun-te-nance (koun′tĕ-năns), *n.* **1,** the face; **2,** the expression of the face showing feeling or character; as, an angry *countenance;* a noble *countenance;* **3,** approval; support; as, to lend *countenance* to a plan; **4,** composure; as, he kept *countenance* despite the insult:—*v.t.* [countenanced, countenanc-ing], to support; favor; as, he *countenanced* the affair.

¹coun-ter (koun′tẽr), *n.* **1,** a person who keeps count; **2,** a small object used to keep score, as in a game; **3,** a sort of table, as in a store, at which goods are sold or money handled; **4,** a coinlike token.

²coun-ter (koun′tẽr), *adj.* contrary; opposing; as, a *counter* opinion:—*n.* **1,** the opposite or contrary; **2,** in boxing, a blow to ward off a blow:—*v.i.* to make an opposite or contrary attack:—*v.t.* **1,** to return (a blow) by another blow; **2,** to combat; oppose:—*adv.* in a contrary way; against; as, he acted *counter* to our wish.

coun-ter- (koun′tẽr-), a prefix meaning: **1,** in the opposite direction; as, *counter*clockwise, *counter*march; **2,** in opposition to; as, *counter*mand, *counter*claim; **3,** so as to cancel; as, *counter*act; **4,** matching or corresponding; as, *counter*part, *counter*sign; **5,** duplicate; as, *counter*feit.

coun-ter-act (koun′tẽr-ăkt′), *v.t.* to act in opposition to; neutralize; as, one medicine may *counteract* another.

coun-ter-bal-ance (koun′tẽr-băl′ăns), *n.* a weight which balances another; hence, a power or influence that offsets another:—*v.t.* (koun′tẽr-băl′ăns), [counterbalanced, counterbalanc-ing], to balance, as with an equal weight; make up for; as, his unusual mental powers *counterbalance* his lameness.

coun-ter-claim (koun′tẽr-klām′), *n.* an opposing claim; a claim set up by the defendant in a lawsuit:—*v.t.* (koun′tẽr-klām′), to make (an opposing claim).

coun-ter-feit (koun′tẽr-fĭt), *v.t.* to copy or imitate exactly, as money, with intent to deceive or defraud:—*v.i.* to make imitations, especially of money:—*adj.* made to resemble something genuine very closely, with intent to deceive; as, *counterfeit* money:—*n.* a copy made with intent to deceive; a forgery; as, this bill is a *counterfeit.*—*n.* **coun′ter-feit′er.**—*n.* **coun′ter-feit′ing.**

coun-ter-mand (koun′tẽr-mănd′; koun′-tẽr-mănd), *v.t.* **1,** to cancel (a purchase); **2,** to issue instructions reversing (an order, plan, or the like); as, the general *counter-manded* the march:—*n.* (koun′tẽr-mănd), a contrary order.

āte, āorta, râre, căt, àsk, fär, ållow, sofà; ēve, ĕvent, ĕll, writẽr, novĕl; bīte, pĭn; nō, ōbey, ôr, dŏg, tŏp, cŏllide; ūnit, ūnite, bûrn, cŭt, focŭs; nōōn, fŏŏt; mound; coin;

coun-ter-march (koun'tẽr-märch'), *n.* **1,** a reversal; a marching back; returning; **2,** in drilling, a sharp turn, as if around a post, and a march back parallel and close to the line of advance:—*v.i.* (koun'tẽr-märch'; koun'tẽr-märch'), to march back; make a countermarch.

coun-ter-pane (koun'tẽr-pān'), *n.* an outer covering for a bed; a bedspread.

coun-ter-part (koun'tẽr-pärt'), *n.* a person or thing that corresponds closely to another; as, the right foot is a *counterpart* of the left; a duplicate; copy.

coun-ter-point (koun'tẽr-point'), *n.* the art of combining two or more melodies with a main theme, according to the laws of harmony; the art of writing part music.

coun-ter-poise (koun'tẽr-poiz'), *n.* **1,** a force that balances or offsets another; **2,** a condition of balance; as, two weights in *counterpoise:*—*v.t.* [counterpoised, counterpois-ing], to oppose by an equal force; bring into balance; weigh (one thing) against another.

coun-ter-rev-o-lu-tion (koun'tẽr-rĕv'ō-lū'shŭn), *n.* a revolution opposed to a previous revolution or against a government established by a former revolution. —*adj.* and *n.* **coun'ter-rev'o-lu'tion-ar'y.**

coun-ter-sign (koun'tẽr-sīn'; koun'tẽr-sīn'), *v.t.* to sign (a document) already signed by another:—*n.* (koun'tẽr-sīn'), **1,** an additional signature to a document to make it of value; **2,** a word known to a special group, as a secret password.

coun-ter-sink (koun'tẽr-sĭngk'; koun'tẽr-sĭngk'), *v.t.* [countersunk (-sŭngk'; -sŭngk'), countersink-ing], in mechanics: **1,** to widen (a hole) so that it will take the head of a screw or bolt; **2,** to drive (the head of a screw or bolt) into the hole.

count-ess (koun'tĕs), *n.* the wife or widow of a count or an earl; also, a lady who in her own right ranks with an earl or a count.

count-ing-house (koun'tĭng-hous'), *n.* a building or room where business is done and accounts are kept.

count-less (kount'lĕs), *adj.* more than can be counted; innumerable.

coun-try (kŭn'trĭ), *n.* [*pl.* countries], **1,** a tract of land; region; as, level *country;* **2,** rural regions; as, we left the *country* for the city; **3,** one's native or adopted land; **4,** a territory that has a distinct existence as to name, language, government, and the like; as, Spain and other Mediterranean *countries;* **5,** the people of a nation as a whole; the public; as, the *country* voted for lower taxes:—*adj.* **1,** pertaining to the rural regions; as, *country* roads; **2,** unpolished; rustic; as, *country* ways.

coun-try-man (kŭn'trĭ-măn), *n.* [*pl.* countrymen (-mĕn)], **1,** a person who lives in the rural regions; **2,** a person who lives or was born in the same country as another. —*n.fem.* **coun'try-wom'an.**

coun-try-seat (kŭn'trĭ-sēt'), *n.* a mansion or estate situated in a rural district.

coun-try-side (kŭn'trĭ-sīd'), *n.* a rural district; also, the people living there.

coun-ty (koun'tĭ), *n.* [*pl.* counties], **1,** a definite political district of a country; **2,** in all States of the U.S. except Louisiana, the largest political subdivision; also, its people; as, the *county* voted the tax:— *adj.* pertaining to a county; as, *county* officials.

coup (kōō), *n.* a sudden, unexpected, and sometimes brilliantly successful move or stroke:—**coup d'état** (dā'tä'), a sudden political stroke, backed by force, to bring about a change of government.

cou-pe (kōō'pā'), *n.* **1,** a horse-drawn, four-wheeled, closed carriage for two, with an outside driver's seat, **2,** a closed automobile with one seat.

COUPE

cou-ple (kŭp'l), *n.* **1,** two persons or things of the same kind connected or thought of together; as, a *couple* of books; **2,** two persons of opposite sex, closely associated; as, a dancing *couple:*—*v.t.* [cou-pled, cou-pling], **1,** to join together, as railway cars; **2,** *Colloquial,* to unite in pairs; unite in wedlock:—*v.i.* to pair off; mate.—*n.* **cou'-pler.**

cou-plet (kŭp'lĕt), *n.* two successive lines of verse which rime together; as, "Be not the first by whom the new is tried, Nor yet the last to lay the old aside."

cou-pling (kŭp'lĭng), *n.* **1,** the act of joining or mating; **2,** a device for joining two parts of machinery or the like; as, a railroad *coupling.*

cou-pon (kōō'pŏn), *n.* **1,** a detachable slip or part of a ticket, certifying the holder's right to something, as to a theater seat; **2,** a dated, detachable certificate which may be clipped from a bond and presented for collection of interest.

cour-age (kûr'ĭj), *n.* boldness; fearlessness. *Syn.* bravery, valor, pluck.

cou-ra-geous (kŭ-rā'jŭs), *adj.* brave; bold; fearless.—*adv.* **cou-ra'geous-ly.**

cour-i-er (kŏŏr'ĭ-ẽr), *n.* **1,** a messenger, usually entrusted with important letters or documents to be delivered with great speed; **2,** a traveling attendant who arranges all the details of a journey, as tickets, hotel reservations, etc.

---

go; join; yet; sing; chin; show; thin, *th*en; hw, *wh*y; zh, azure; ü, Ger. für or Fr. lune; ö, Ger. schön or Fr. feu; ṅ, Fr. enfant, nom; kh, Ger. ach or ich. See pages ix–x.

course (kôrs), *n.* **1,** the act of moving onward; progress in space; as, the *course* of the earth around the sun; progress in time; as, in the *course* of a week; **2,** ground to be passed over in a regular way; as, a golf *course;* **3,** a path; direction taken; as, a ship's *course;* **4,** a channel through which water flows; as, the *course* of a river; **5,** a succession; series; as, a *course* of lectures; **6,** method of procedure; as, a *course* of action; **7,** the part of a meal served at one time; **8,** in building, a layer of stone or bricks:—**of course,** naturally; as was to be expected:—*v.t.* [coursed, cours-ing], to pursue (game) with hounds:—*v.i.* to run; flow; as, tears *coursed* down her cheeks.

cours-er (kôr′sẽr), *n. Poetic,* a swift horse.

court (kôrt), *n.* **1,** an unroofed space wholly or partly surrounded by buildings or walls; **2,** a level space marked for playing games; **3,** a royal palace; also, the people in attendance at a palace; **4,** a prince or sovereign and his ministers considered as the ruling power; also, an official meeting of a sovereign and his councilors; **5,** a hall of justice; **6,** the judge or judges engaged in administering justice; also, the session at which they preside; **7,** flattering attentions paid to one in power; also, attention paid by a man to a woman in wooing her:—*v.t.* **1,** to pay attention to as a lover; woo; **2,** to seek favor of, by flattery and attention; **3,** to attempt to gain; seek.

cour-te-ous (kûr′tē-ŭs), *adj.* polite.—*adv.* **cour′te-ous-ly.**—*n.* **cour′te-ous-ness.**

cour-te-san or **cour-te-zan** (kôr′tē-zăn), *n.* a loose woman; harlot.

cour-te-sy (kûr′tē-sĭ), *n.* [*pl.* courtesies], **1,** politeness; **2,** an act of kindliness, civility, or respect; **3,** kindness or generosity; as, a program presented through the *courtesy* of a large coal company; **4,** a bow, as made by women or girls; a curtsy.

court-house (kôrt′hous′), *n.* a public building in which courts of law are held.

cour-ti-er (kôr′tĭ-ẽr; kôrt′yẽr), *n.* **1,** a person in attendance at a royal court; **2,** one who pays court to a superior in wealth or station.

court-ly (kôrt′lĭ), *adj.* [court-li-er, court-li-est], polished; elegant; as, *courtly* manners.—*n.* **court′li-ness.**

court—mar-tial (kôrt′ₓmär′shăl), *n.* [*pl.* courts-martial], a court made up of military or naval officers to try offenses against military or naval law; also, a trial by such a court:—*v.t.* to try (a person) by such a court.

court plas-ter, a fine fabric with an adhesive coating on one side, used as covering for wounds or cuts.

court-ship (kôrt′shĭp), *n.* attentions paid by a member of one sex to a member of the other sex, preparatory to marriage or mating.

court-yard (kôrt′yärd′), *n.* an enclosed space adjoining a house or castle.

cous-in (kŭz′n), *n.* a son or daughter of one's uncle or aunt.

cove (kōv), *n.* a sheltered place or pass; especially, an inlet or creek on the coast.

cov-e-nant (kŭv′ĕ-nănt), *n.* a compact or agreement:—*v.t.* and *v.i.* to promise by solemn agreement.

Cov-en-try (kŏv′ĕn-trĭ; kŭv′ĕn-trĭ), a city in Warwickshire, central England (map 13):—**to send to Coventry,** to shut out from society, on account of offensive behavior.

cov-er (kŭv′ẽr), *v.t.* **1,** to lay something over (a person or thing); as, to *cover* a box; **2,** to lie over, so as to close or enclose; as, a lid *covers* the box; a shoe *covers* the foot; **3,** to hide; screen; as, clouds *cover* the mountain; to *cover* a mistake; **4,** to extend or pass over; as, the estate *covers* a wide area; we *covered* ninety miles today; **5,** to include; comprise; as, the book *covers* the subject; **6,** to hold within aim; as, to *cover* a man with a gun:—*n.* **1,** that which is laid on something else; as, a *cover* for a bed; **2,** the binding of a book, or the outside page of a magazine; **3,** protection; as, to escape under *cover* of night; **4,** a thicket that may conceal game; **5,** the table equipment for the use of one person at a meal.

Cov-er-dale (kŭv′ẽr-dāl), Miles (1488–1568), an English bishop, translator of the Bible.

cov-er-ing (kŭv′ẽr-ĭng), *n.* anything that covers; a wrapper; an envelope.

cov-er-let (kŭv′ẽr-lĕt), *n.* the outer cover of a bed; a bedspread.

cov-ert (kŭv′ẽrt), *adj.* secret; disguised; as, a *covert* glance of hate:—*n.* a place that protects or conceals; especially, a shelter for game.—*adv.* **cov′ert-ly.**

cov-et (kŭv′ĕt), *v.t.* to long for (something that belongs to another).

cov-et-ous (kŭv′ĕ-tŭs), *adj.* desirous of what belongs to others.—*adv.* **cov′et-ous-ly.**—*n.* **cov′et-ous-ness.**

cov-ey (kŭv′ĭ), *n.* [*pl.* coveys], a brood or flock of game birds, as quail.

¹**cow** (kou), *n.* [*pl.* cows (kouz), *Poetic* or *Archaic,* kine (kīn)], **1,** a full-grown female of the ox family, especially of domestic cattle; **2,** a female of certain other large mammals, such as the moose, whale, etc.

²**cow** (kou), *v.t.* to make afraid.

cow-ard (kou′ẽrd), *n.* a person lacking in

courage; a shamefully timid person.— *adj.* and *adv.* **cow′ard·ly.**

cow·ard·ice (kou′ẽr-dĭs), *n.* want of courage; shameful fear.

cow-bird (kou′bûrd′), *n.* a small, blackbird of North America, that follows cattle. It builds no nest, but lays its eggs in the nests of other birds.

cow-boy (kou′boi′), *n.* in the western part of Canada and of the U.S., a man who tends cattle, doing his work mostly on horseback.

cow-catch-er (kou′-kăch′ẽr), *n.* a wedge-shaped frame on the front of a locomotive for removing obstructions from the track.

COWBIRD (⅛)

cow-er (kou′ẽr), *v.i.* to crouch down, as from fear or shame.

cow-herd (kou′hûrd′), *n.* one whose occupation is the tending of cattle at pasture.

cow-hide (kou′hīd′), *n.* 1, the skin of a cow, especially when tanned and dressed; 2, a whip made of cowhide:—*adj.* made of cowhide:—*v.t.* [cowhid-ed, cowhid-ing], to flog with a cowhide.

cowl (koul), *n.* 1, a monk's hood, or hood and gown together; 2, the part of an automobile body just forward of the doors and windshield.

cow-lick (kou′lĭk′), *n.* a tuft of hair growing upright, often above the forehead.

COWL def. 1

cow-pea (kou′pē′), *n.* a plant of the bean family, grown for forage and green manure; also, its seed, often used for food.

cow-punch-er (kou′-pŭn′chẽr), *n.* a man who rounds up and tends cattle on a ranch; a cowboy.

cow-slip (kou′slĭp), *n.* 1, in the U.S., the marsh marigold, a yellow-flowered swamp plant; 2, in England, a wild primrose with fragrant flowers.

cox-comb (kŏks′kōm′), *n.* 1, the red edge on a jester's cap; also, the cap; 2, a vain fellow; fop; 3, (usually *cockscomb*), a garden plant with showy flowers.

AMERICAN COWSLIP

cox-swain (kŏk′sn; kŏk′swān), *n.* one who steers or has charge of a boat, especially of a racing shell. Also spelled **cock′swain.**

coy (koi), *adj.* 1, bashful; shy; 2, pretending to be shy; coquettish.

coy-ote (kī′ōt; kī-ō′tě), *n.* the prairie wolf of western North America.

coz (kŭz), *n. Colloquial,* cousin: used formerly in addressing any near relative.

coz-en (kŭz′n), *v.t.* and *v.i.* to cheat in a petty way.

co-zy (kō′zĭ), *adj.* [co-zi-er, co-zi-est], warm and comfortable; snug: —*n.* [*pl.* cozies], 1, a cover, padded, to keep a teapot warm; 2, a corner seat. Also spelled **co′sy.**—*adv.* **co′zi-ly.**—*n.* **co′zi-ness.**

COYOTE (⅟₆₀)

cp. abbreviation for *compare.*

c.p. abbreviation for *candle power.*

C.P.A. abbreviation for *Certified Public Accountant.*

¹**crab** (krăb), *n.* any of various animals, most of which live in the sea, which have a broad, flattened body, ten walking legs, and the abdomen, or so-called tail, curled under the body:—*v.i.* [crabbed, crab-bing], to fish for crabs.

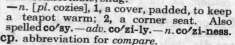

CRAB (⅓)

²**crab** (krăb), *v.i.* [crabbed, crab-bing], *Colloquial,* to find fault; be irritable.

³**crab** (krăb), *n.* 1, a tree bearing small, sour apples, often used in making jelly: usually called *crab apple;* also, the fruit; 2, a surly, ill-tempered person.

crab ap-ple, the crab tree or its fruit.

crab-bed (krăb′ĕd), *adj.* 1, cross; morose; 2, difficult to read.—*n.* **crab′bed-ness.**

crack (krăk), *v.i.* 1, to make a sharp, snapping noise, as a whip; 2, to be broken without dividing completely; as, the cup *cracked* in hot water; 3, to break or become rasping, as a voice:—*v.t.* 1, to cause to pop or snap; as, to *crack* a whip; 2, to break without separating completely; break open; as, to *crack* nuts; 3, to tell (a joke):—*n.* 1, a sudden, sharp noise; as, a *crack* of thunder; 2, an incomplete break; as, a *crack* in the ice; 3, a broken note, as in a boy's voice when changing; 4, *Colloquial,* a sharp blow; as, he gave the boy a *crack* on the head:—*adj. Colloquial,* first-rate; as, a *crack* hunter.

crack-brained (krăk′brānd′), *adj.* crazy; senseless; as, a *crackbrained* person or scheme.

crack-er (krăk′ẽr), *n.* 1, a dry biscuit,

often hard and crisp; **2**, in the southeastern U.S., a poor white from the backwoods; **3**, a firecracker; **4**, a party favor which pops when pulled apart.

crack-le (krăk′l), *v.i.* [crack-led, crack-ling], to make slight rustling or snapping noises, frequently repeated:—*n.* **1**, a slight, sharp, or snapping noise, especially one that is often repeated; as, the *crackle* of a fire; **2**, the finely cracked glaze or surface of a kind of pottery, glass, or porcelain; also, ware having such a surface.

crack-ling (krăk′lĭng), *n.* **1**, small, abrupt, snapping sounds, coming in quick succession; as, the *crackling* of a fire; **2**, the crisp, browned skin of roast pork.

Cra-cow (krā′kō), a city in Poland. See **Kraków**.

cra-dle (krā′dl), *n.* **1**, a baby's crib or bed, often on rockers; **2**, birthplace; origin; as, the *cradle* of liberty; **3**, anything resembling a baby's cradle, as a supporting frame placed under a ship during construction, a trough on rockers used by miners in washing gold-bearing earth, or the like; **4**, a frame of wood, fastened to a scythe, used in harvesting; also, the scythe: —*v.t.* [cra-dled, cra-dling], **1**, to place or rock in a cradle; **2**, to shelter in infancy; as, the two brothers were *cradled* in luxury; **3**, to wash gold-bearing earth in a cradle; **4**, to reap with a cradle scythe.

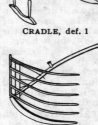

CRADLE, def. 1

GRAIN CRADLE

craft (krȧft), *n.* **1**, skill, especially of the hand; **2**, deceit; cunning; **3**, a trade requiring artistic manual skill; also, those engaged in such a trade; **4**, [*pl.* craft], a ship or boat; also, an airplane or dirigible.
Syn. art, dexterity, ingenuity, trade.

crafts-man (krȧfts′măn), *n.* [*pl.* craftsmen (-měn)], a skilled workman.—*n.* **crafts′man-ship**.

craft-y (krȧf′tĭ), *adj.* [craft-i-er, craft-i-est], deceitful; wily; as, *crafty* schemes.—*adv.* **craft′i-ly**.—*n.* **craft′i-ness**.
Syn. cunning, artful, sly, subtle.

crag (krăg), *n.* a steep, rugged rock; also, a projecting point of rock.

cram (krăm), *v.t.* [crammed, cram-ming], **1**, to stuff; fill to overflowing, as with food; **2**, to pack or crowd in; **3**, *Colloquial*, to study hastily, as for an examination:—*v.i.* **1**, to eat greedily; **2**, *Colloquial*, to study hard for an examination.

¹cramp (krămp), *n.* **1**, an iron bar bent at the ends, used to hold together blocks of stone, timber, or the like; **2**, a piece of iron or steel, resembling a C, with a tightening screw, used for holding two things together: also called *clamp*:—*v.t.* **1**, to fasten or hold by a cramp; **2**, to hinder in action or growth; hamper; as, lack of knowledge *cramped* his progress.

²cramp (krămp), *n.* a sudden, sharp, painful contracting of the muscles, due to sudden chill, strain, or the like:—*v.t.* and *v.i.* to suffer, or cause to suffer, from cramp.

cran-ber-ry (krăn′ber′ĭ), *n.* [*pl.* cranberries], the small, tart, scarlet berry of a kind of bog plant; also, the plant.

CRANBERRY
Stems bearing leaves and berries.

crane (krān), *n.* **1**, a wading bird with very long legs, a long straight bill, and a long neck which it stretches to full length in flight; **2**, a machine for raising and moving heavy weights; **3**, a mechanical arm or support, as an iron arm for utensils in a fireplace:—*v.t.* and *v.i.* [craned, craning], to stretch (the neck), in order to see better.

cra-ni-al (krā′nĭ-ăl), *adj.* relating to the skull or cranium; as, *cranial* nerves.

cra-ni-um (krā′nĭ-ŭm), *n.* the skull, especially the part enclosing the brain.

¹crank (krăngk), *n.* an arm fastened at right angles to a shaft, and used for changing to-and-fro motion to circular motion, as in a grindstone, or the reverse, as in a windmill pump:—*v.t.* **1**, to work with a crank, as a motion-picture camera; **2**, to start (a motor) with a crank.

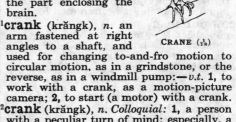

CRANE (⅟₁₈)

²crank (krăngk), *n. Colloquial:* **1**, a person with a peculiar turn of mind; especially, a person who pursues one idea exclusively; **2**, an irritable person.

crank-shaft (krăngk′shȧft′), *n.* a shaft that bears, drives, or is driven by, a crank.

crank-y (krăngk′ĭ), *adj.* [crank-i-er, crank-i-est], **1**, ill-tempered; irritable; **2**, liable to upset, as a boat.—*adv.* **crank′i-ly**.—*n.* **crank′i-ness**.

cran-ny (krăn′ĭ), *n.* [*pl.* crannies], a crack or chink, as in a wall.

---

crape (krāp), *n.* a crinkly black silk fabric, used especially as a sign of mourning.

¹crash (krăsh), *v.i.* **1,** to break to pieces with a loud noise, especially on falling; as, the vase *crashed* to the floor; **2,** to break one's way noisily through something; as, to *crash* through a jungle; **3,** to make a noise as of breakage on a vast scale; as, the thunder *crashed;* **4,** to collide, as two automobiles; also, to come into violent contact with the ground, as an airplane; **5,** to fail, as a business enterprise:—*v.t.* **1,** to break (something) to bits with noise and violence; smash; **2,** to land (an airplane) so as to damage it:—*n.* **1,** a smashing or shattering; **2,** a sudden loud sound, as of violent breakage; as, the *crash* of the orchestra; **3,** an airplane landing in which the craft is damaged; **4,** an automobile collision; **5,** the failure of a business; also, a general business and financial collapse; as, the *crash* of 1929.

²crash (krăsh), *n.* a coarse linen or cotton used for toweling, summer suits, etc.

crass (krăs), *adj.* stupid; dense; as, *crass* ignorance.—*n.* **crass'ness.**

crate (krāt), *n.* a wickerwork basket, or a case made of wooden slats, used for shipping goods:—*v.t.* [crat-ed, crat-ing], to pack in a crate, as apples.

cra-ter (krā'tẽr), *n.* **1,** the cup-shaped cavity forming the mouth of a volcano; **2,** a hole in the earth, caused by an explosion, as of an artillery shell.

Crater Lake National Park, a park in southwestern Oregon (map 9).

cra-vat (krȧ-văt'), *n.* a necktie or neckcloth, usually worn by men.

crave (krāv), *v.t.* [craved, crav-ing], **1,** to beg earnestly for; as, I *crave* your help; **2,** to long for (food).

cra-ven (krā'vĕn), *adj.* cowardly; base; as, a *craven* deserter:—*n.* an abject coward.

crav-ing (krāv'ĭng), *n.* a strong desire or appetite; yearning; as, a *craving* for fame.

craw (krô), *n.* the crop of a bird or insect.

crawl (krôl), *v.i.* **1,** to move slowly by dragging the body along the ground; **2,** to go on hands and knees; **3,** to move very slowly; **4,** to be infested with creeping things; as, the ground *crawls* with ants; **5,** to feel as if live things were creeping over one's body; as, to *crawl* with loathing:—*n.* **1,** the act of creeping, or of making one's way with difficulty; slow motion; **2,** a fast stroke in swimming.—*n.* **crawl'er.** —*adj.* **crawl'y.**

cray-fish (krā'físh'), *n.* [*pl.* crayfish or crayfishes], a shellfish related to, but much smaller than, the lobster, found in fresh water. Also called **craw'fish'.**

cray-on (krā'ŏn), *n.* **1,** a stick or pencil, as of charcoal, chalk, or the like, for drawing or writing; **2,** a drawing made with such material:—*v.t.* to draw with crayon.

craze (krāz), *n.* an intense but passing interest; infatuation; fad:—*v.t.* [crazed, craz-ing], to drive insane.—*adj.* **crazed.**

CRAYFISH (½)

cra-zy (krā'zĭ), *adj.* [cra-zi-er, cra-zi-est], **1,** insane; mad; **2,** shaky; unsound; as, a *crazy* building; **3,** *Colloquial,* foolishly fond or eager; wildly enthusiastic; as, he is *crazy* about music.—*adv.* **cra'zi-ly.** —*n.* **cra'zi-ness.**

creak (krēk), *v.i.* to make a sharp, harsh, squeaking or grating sound:—*n.* a harsh, squeaking sound.

creak-y (krēk'ĭ), *adj.* [creak-i-er, creak-i-est], apt to make harsh, squeaky noises; as, *creaky* floors.

cream (krēm). *n.* **1,** the rich, fat part of milk, which rises to the top; hence, the choicest part of anything; as, the *cream* of a story; **2,** a dessert or sweet made of cream, or like cream; as, ice *cream;* butter *creams;* **3,** a light-yellow color; **4,** a soft cosmetic; as, cold *cream:*—*v.t.* **1,** to skim the cream from (milk); **2,** to put cream into (tea or coffee); **3,** to bring to the consistency of thick cream; as, to *cream* butter, or butter and sugar; **4,** to cook with a dressing of cream or with a sauce of cream-like consistency.

cream-er-y (krēm'ẽr-ĭ), *n.* [*pl.* creameries], a place where cream is bought, and where such products of cream as butter and cheese are manufactured and sold.

cream-y (krēm'ĭ), *adj.* [cream-i-er, cream-i-est], containing cream, or smooth and rich like cream.

crease (krēs), *n.* a mark or wrinkle left by a fold, as in paper:—*v.t.* [creased, creas-ing], to make a fold or wrinkle in; as, to *crease* a pair of trousers:—*v.i.* to fall into folds or wrinkles.

cre-ate (krê-āt'), *v.t.* [creat-ed, creat-ing], to cause to come into existence; make; originate; produce; also, to cause; occasion; as, to *create* a disturbance.

cre-a-tion (krê-ā'shŭn), *n.* **1,** the act of forming or originating; as, the *creation* of a new design; **2,** the thing made or originated; especially, the universe; also, the act by which it was created.

cre-a-tive (krĕ-ā′tĭv), *adj*. having the power to originate; as, *creative* genius.

cre-a-tor (krĕ-ā′tĕr), *n*. one who makes or has the power to bring into existence:— **Creator**, the Supreme Being; God.

crea-ture (krē′tŭr), *n*. **1**, any living being; an animal or a human being; **2**, a person who is the mere tool of another.

cre-dence (krē′dĕns), *n*. belief; as, this rumor is not worthy of *credence*.

cre-den-tials (krĕ-dĕn′shălz), *n. pl.* documents given to a person to be presented by him in proof of his identity, authority, record, or the like; letters of introduction; references.

cred-i-ble (krĕd′ĭ-bl), *adj*. **1**, trustworthy; as, a *credible* witness; **2**, believable; as, a *credible* story.—*adv*. **cred′i-bly**.—*n*. **cred′-i-bil′i-ty**.

cred-it (krĕd′ĭt), *n*. **1**, belief; trust; confidence in the truth of a statement or the truthfulness of a person; as, do not place much *credit* in gossip; **2**, good name; reputation; as, a citizen of *credit* and renown; **3**, acknowledgment of worth; honor; as, he is given *credit* for trying; also, a source of honor; as, he is a *credit* to his family; **4**, the sum remaining at a customer's disposal or in his favor, as on the books of a bank; **5**, a record of satisfactory standing or achievement; as, college entrance *credits;* **6**, an extension of time allowed a customer to pay; as, goods bought on *credit;* **7**, financial standing or reputation; as, his *credit* is good for a charge account; **8**, in bookkeeping, the right-hand side of an account: opposite of *debit:*—*v.t.* **1**, to believe; trust; have confidence in; as, I *credit* her story; **2**, to give (a person) credit or honor; as, I *credit* you with good intentions; **3**, to enter a sum in favor of (a customer or his account); as, *credit* me with ten dollars.

cred-it-a-ble (krĕd′ĭt-à-bl), *adj*. worthy of belief or praise.—*adv*. **cred′it-a-bly**.

cred-i-tor (krĕd′ĭ-tĕr), *n*. one to whom money is owed: opposite of *debtor*.

cre-du-li-ty (krĕ-dū′lĭ-tĭ), *n*. [*pl*. credulities], a readiness to believe what one is told without asking for proof.

cred-u-lous (krĕd′ū-lŭs), *adj*. ready to believe almost anything; easily deceived or imposed upon.—*adv*. **cred′u-lous-ly**.

creed (krēd), *n*. **1**, a brief, authoritative statement of religious belief; as, the Apostles′ *creed;* **2**, a set of opinions or principles on any subject, such as politics, science, etc.; as, a business *creed*.

creek (krēk), *n*. **1**, a small stream; **2**, a long, narrow bay or inlet; also, a stream emptying into a bay or inlet.

creel (krēl), *n*. **1**, a wicker basket for carrying fish; **2**, a wicker trap for fish, lobsters, or the like.

creep (krēp), *v.i.* [crept (krĕpt), creep-ing], **1**, to move with the body near or touching the ground as does a cat stalking a bird, or a human being on hands and knees; **2**, to feel as if touching crawly things; as, my skin *creeps* when I see a snake; **3**, to grow along the ground, or over a surface, as a vine; **4**, to move cautiously or stealthily:—*n*. **creeps**, *Colloquial*, a prickly sensation in the skin or scalp; as, ghost stories give me the *creeps*.

CREEL

creep-er (krēp′ĕr), *n*. **1**, a person or thing that moves slowly, close to or touching the ground; **2**, a plant which clings by rootlets or tendrils to some support; **3**, a bird which creeps up and down tree trunks in search of insects; **4**, a grapnel, or hooked iron instrument for dragging the bottom of a body of water.

creep-y (krēp′ĭ), *adj*. [creep-i-er, creep-i-est], possessed by, or producing, a shivering sense of dread; as, to feel *creepy;* a *creepy* house.

cre-mate (krē′māt; krē-māt′), *v.t.* [cre-mat-ed, cremat-ing], to burn to ashes, as a corpse.—*n*. **cre′ma-tor**.—*n*. **cre-ma′tion**.

cre-ma-tor-y (krē′mȧ-tôr′ĭ; krĕm′ȧ-tôr′ĭ), *n*. [*pl*. crematories], a furnace for burning or cremating dead bodies; an establishment housing such a furnace.

Cre-mo-na (krĕ-mō′nȧ), a city in Lombardy, northern Italy, the home of Amati and Stradivarius, famous violinmakers.

Cre-ole (krē′ōl), *n*. **1**, a person of French or Spanish descent, but born and reared in a colony, especially in the remote tropics; **2**, in the Gulf States, especially in Louisiana, a white person descended from the French or Spanish settlers, and retaining their manners and language; **3**, the French dialect spoken in Louisiana: —*adj*. pertaining to or characteristic of Creoles; as, *Creole* stories; *Creole* customs.

cre-o-sote (krē′ō-sōt), *n*. a heavy, oily liquid with a smoky smell, obtained from coal tar or wood tar: used as an antiseptic in medicine, and as a wood preservative.

crepe or **crêpe** (krāp), *n*. **1**, a soft fabric of silk, wool, cotton, or rayon, with a crinkled or wavy surface; **2**, (usually **crape**), a similar black silk fabric, used as a sign of mourning.

    crepe de Chine (dĕ shēn′), a fine, thin crepe made of raw silk, with an almost smooth surface; **crepe paper**, a crinkly paper, used for paper napkins, etc.

crept (krĕpt), past tense and past participle of *creep.*

cre-scen-do (krĕ-shĕn′dō; krĕ-sĕn′dō), *adv.* and *adj.* in music, gradually increasing in force or loudness.

cres-cent (krĕs′ĕnt), *adj.* 1, increasing; growing, as the moon in its first quarter; 2, shaped like the new moon:—*n.* 1, the figure of the moon in its first or last quarter; 2, anything shaped like the new moon; as, a jeweled *crescent.*

CRESCENT

cress (krĕs), *n.* a green water plant of the mustard family with crisp, peppery leaves, used in salads and for garnishing: also called *water cress.*

cres-set (krĕs′ĕt), *n.* a torch or lantern, consisting of a metal pot or basket in which pitch, oil, or charcoal is burned.

Cres-si-da (krĕs′ĭ-dȧ), *n.* in medieval romances based on Homer's "Iliad," the beautiful daughter of a Trojan priest, who was unfaithful to her lover, Troilus.

crest (krĕst), *n.* 1, a comb or tuft on the head of a bird; 2, a tuft of feathers on a helmet, or the helmet itself; 3, the top, as the ridge of a wave or the summit of a hill or ridge; 4, the device or figure at top of a coat of arms; also, this device used by itself as a decoration or seal:—*v.t.* 1, to serve as the crest of; as, woods *crest* the hills; 2, to rise above; top.—*adj.* **crest′ed.**

CREST (C) OF A COCKATOO

crest-fall-en (krĕst′fôl′ĕn), *adj.* dejected; as, he was *crestfallen* over his failure.

Crete (krēt), a Greek island in the eastern Mediterranean (maps 1, 12).—*n.* and *adj.* **Cre′tan.**

CREST, def. 4

cre-tonne (krĕ-tŏn′; krē′tŏn), *n.* a strong, unglazed cotton fabric, printed on one or both sides, and used for covering chairs, making draperies, etc.

cre-vasse (krĕ-văs′), *n.* 1, a deep crack, as in a glacier; 2, a break in a levee.

crev-ice (krĕv′ĭs), *n.* a narrow split or crack; as, a *crevice* in a wall or rock.

¹crew (krōō), a form of the past tense of *crow.*

²crew (krōō), *n.* 1, the group of men manning a ship or rowing a boat; 2, a gang of men working together; as, a train *crew;* 3, a company or throng; as, a *crew* of gypsies.

crib (krĭb), *n.* 1, a manger for feeding stock; 2, a bin with slatted walls, for storing unshelled corn; 3, a child's bed with high, railed sides; 4, a heavy framework, for strengthening a building that is being moved; 5, *School Slang,* an unfair aid, as a key or translation, used by students:—*v.t.* [cribbed, crib-bing], 1, to put (grain) into a crib; 2, *Colloquial,* to steal and use as one's own; as, to *crib* a thought from Shakespeare:—*v.i. Colloquial,* to use a crib, as in a recitation or test.

CRIB, def. 3

crib-bage (krĭb′ĭj), *n.* a card game for two, three, or four players. The score is kept by means of pegs and a board.

crick (krĭk), *n.* a painful stiffness of the muscles of the neck or back.

¹crick-et (krĭk′ĕt), *n.* a popular English game somewhat like baseball, but with eleven players on each side and two wickets instead of bases.

²crick-et (krĭk′ĕt), *n.* a black, hopping insect. The male makes a chirping sound by rubbing his forewings together. (See illustration below.)

CRICKET
A, wicket keeper; B, wicket; C, batsman.

³crick-et (krĭk′ĕt), *n.* a footstool.

cried (krīd), past tense and past participle of *cry.*

cri-er (krī′ēr), *n.* an officer who publicly utters or cries announcements; as, a court *crier;* a town *crier.*

cries (krīz), plural of *cry.*

crime (krīm), *n.* 1, an act which breaks the law and makes the offender liable to punishment; also, a sinful or wicked deed; 2, wrongdoing; lawbreaking. *Syn.* wickedness, vice, misdemeanor.

CRICKET (½)

Cri-me-a (krī-mē′ȧ; krī-mē′ȧ), a peninsula in southern U.S.S.R., extending into the Black Sea (map 12).—*adj.* **Cri-me′an.**

crim-i-nal (krĭm′ĭ-nȧl), *n.* one who is guilty of a grave offense against the law:—*adj.* having to do with crime; as, *criminal* acts; *criminal* law.—*n.* **crim′i-nal′i-ty.**—*adv.* **crim′i-nal-ly.** *Syn., n.* convict, culprit, felon.

crimp (krĭmp), *v.t.* to fold or press into pleats; impart a wavy appearance to:—*n.* 1, the act of waving, curling, or frilling; 2, **crimps,** curled hair.

crimp-y (krĭmp′ĭ), *adj.* [crimp-i-er, crimp-i-est], crinkled; frizzly, as hair.

go; join; yet; sing; chin; show; thin, *th*en; hw, *why;* zh, azure; ŭ, Ger. *für* or Fr. *lune;* ö, Ger. *schön* or Fr. *feu;* ṅ, Fr. *enfant,* nom; kh, Ger. *ach* or *ich.* See pages ix–x.

crim·son (krĭm′zn), *n.* a deep-red color:—*adj.* deep red:—*v.t.* to color deep red; as, the sunset *crimsons* the lake:—*v.i.* to blush; become red.

cringe (krĭnj), *v.i.* [cringed, cring-ing], 1, to wince with pain; shrink or cower in fear; 2, to fawn; be basely humble in manner, as a beggar:—*n.* a servile bow.—*n.* **cring′er.**

Syn., *v.* stoop, cower, shrink, wince.

crin·kle (krĭng′kl), *v.i.* [crin-kled, crin-kling], 1, to wrinkle; twist; become rippled; as, paper *crinkles*; 2, to rustle, as stiff silk:—*v.t.* to cause to wrinkle or ripple:—*n.* a wrinkle; a fold.—*adj.* **crin′kly.**

crin·o·line (krĭn′ō-lĭn; krĭn′ō-lēn), *n.* 1, a stiff fabric used to expand or stiffen the garments worn over it; 2, a skirt so stiffened; also, a hoop skirt.

crip·ple (krĭp′l), *n.* one who is lame or physically disabled:—*v.t.* [crip-pled, crip-pling], 1, to disable; 2, to weaken; as, the depression *crippled* business.

cri·sis (krī′sĭs), *n.* [*pl.* crises (krī′sēz)], 1, a turning point for better or worse in an illness; 2, a turning point in the progress of anything, as in history.

crisp (krĭsp), *adj.* 1, hard but brittle; as, *crisp* toast; also, flaky; as, *crisp* pastry; 2, brisk; decided; as, *crisp* speech; 3, fresh and firm; as, *crisp* lettuce; 4, fresh and bracing; as, *crisp* air; 5, tightly curling; as, *crisp* hair:—*v.t.* and *v.i.* to make or become crisp.—*n.* **crisp′ness.**

criss-cross (krĭs′krôs′), *adj.* crossing in different directions, as the lines in the letter X:—*adv.* crosswise.

cri·te·ri·on (krī-tē′rĭ-ŭn), *n.* [*pl.* criteria (krī-tē′rĭ-a)], a standard or rule by which to form a judgment; test; as, his words are no *criterion* of his thoughts.

crit·ic (krĭt′ĭk), *n.* 1, a person skilled in judging art, literature, or the like; 2, one who judges harshly.

crit·i·cal (krĭt′ĭ-kăl), *adj.* 1, faultfinding; 2, impartial and careful in forming judgments; 3, decisive; important; as, a *critical* moment; 4, involving risk; as, a *critical* operation.—*adv.* **crit′i-cal-ly.**

crit·i·cism (krĭt′ĭ-sĭzm), *n.* 1, the act or art of judging and defining the merits of a scientific or artistic work; 2, a harsh judgment; faultfinding; 3, the principles or method of judging works of art.

Syn. comment, disapproval, reflection.

crit·i·cize (krĭt′ĭ-sīz), *v.t.* and *v.i.* [criti-cized, criticiz-ing], 1, to judge as a critic; 2, to judge harshly.

cri·tique (krĭ-tēk′), *n.* 1, a careful, written analysis of a literary or artistic work; review; 2, the art of criticism.

croak (krōk), *v.i.* 1, to utter a low, harsh sound like that of a raven or frog; 2, to grumble; forbode evil; 3, *Slang,* to die:—*v.t.* to utter hoarsely or dismally:—*n.* a low, hoarse sound.—*n.* **croak′er.**

Cro·a·ti·a (krō-ā′shǐ-a), formerly, a kingdom northeast of the Adriatic Sea. It is now a part of Yugoslavia.—*n.* and *adj.* **Cro·a′tian.**—*n.* **Cro′at** (krō′ăt).

cro·chet (krō-shā′), *v.t.* [crocheted (krō-shād′), crochet-ing (krō-shā′ĭng)], to make (a fabric or article) by looping a thread into other loops with a single hooked needle; as, to *crochet* a doily:—*v.i.* to make things in this manner; as, to *crochet* all day:—*n.* the kind of fabric thus made; as, a piece of *crochet.*

crock (krŏk), *n.* an earthenware pot or jar, especially for kitchen use.

crock·er·y (krŏk′ẽr-ĭ), *n.* earthenware, especially kitchen dishes, bowls, etc.

Crock·ett (krŏk′ĕt), David (1786–1836), an American frontiersman.

croc·o·dile (krŏk′ō-dĭl), *n.* a tough-skinned, long-tailed, flesh-eating reptile, fourteen to twenty feet long,

CROCODILE (₁⁄₂₀)

with a long, narrow head and pointed snout, found in the fresh waters of Africa, Asia, Australia, and America:—**crocodile tears,** insincere, pretended grief: so called from old tales that crocodiles wept while devouring their prey.

cro·cus (krō′kŭs), *n.* one of the earliest spring-flowering bulbs, bearing purple, yellow, or white flowers.

Croe·sus (krē′sŭs), a king in Asia Minor about the sixth century B.C., famous for his wealth.

croft (krôft), *n.* 1, a small, enclosed field near a house, used for pasture and tillage; 2, in Scotland, a very small farm.—*n.* **croft′er.**

CROCUS

Cro—Ma·gnon (krō-⸗má′nyôṅ′), *adj.* pertaining to a race of European Stone Age men, with large, long heads, low foreheads, and great height, to whom modern man is directly related; so named from the cave in France where in 1868 four skeletons and many relics, such as carved bone figures and stone implements, were found.

Crom·well (krŏm′wĕl; krŭm′wĕl), Oliver (1599–1658), an English general and statesman, who ruled England, as Lord Protector, from 1653 to 1658.

crone (krōn), *n.* a withered old woman.

cro·ny (krō′nĭ), *n.* [*pl.* cronies], a familiar friend; chum.

crook (krŏŏk), *n.* **1,** the bent or curved part of anything; **2,** a bent or hooked article or tool, as a shepherd's staff, **3,** *Colloquial,* a swindler:—*v.t.* to bend; as, to crook one's finger:—*v.i.* to curve; grow crooked.

crook·ed (krŏŏk′ĕd), *adj.* **1,** bent; curved; not straight; as, a *crooked* path; **2,** not upright in conduct; dishonest.—*adv.* **crook′-ed·ly.**—*n.* **crook′ed·ness.**

Syn. twisted, awry, askew.

croon (krōōn), *v.i.* and *v.t.* to sing in a soft, plaintive, or sentimental manner:—*n.* the sound of such singing.—*n.* **croon′er.**

crop (krŏp), *n.* **1,** the amount, as of a grain or fruit, grown and gathered in one season; as, the corn *crop;* **2, crops,** plants grown for food, especially grains and fruits; **3,** anything likened to a season's harvest; as, a *crop* of books; **4,** a pouch in a bird's gullet where food is prepared for digestion; **5,** a stout hunting whip; **6,** hair cut close or short:—*v.t.* [cropped or, *Rare,* cropt (krŏpt), crop·ping], **1,** to mow; **2,** to bite off; as, the horse *cropped* the grass; **3,** to cut short, as hair, tail, ears, etc.:—*v.i.* **1,** to bite the tops off grass, or the like; **2,** to appear unexpectedly; as, an old friend *cropped* up yesterday.

RIDING CROP

crop·per (krŏp′ẽr), *n.* **1,** a tenant who raises crops on shares; **2,** a pigeon with a large crop:—**come a cropper,** *Colloquial,* to fall headlong, as from a horse; hence, to fail unexpectedly.

cro·quet (krō-kā′), *n.* a lawn game in which wooden balls are driven by mallets from a starting stake, through a series of wire wickets to a turning stake, and back.

cro·quette (krō-kĕt′), *n.* a ball of minced meat or fish, seasoned and fried.

cro·sier or **cro·zier** (krō′zhẽr), *n.* a staff resembling a shepherd's crook, the symbol of office of a bishop or abbot.

cross (krôs), *n.* **1,** an upright stake bearing a horizontal bar, or two stakes nailed together to form an X, an ancient Roman instrument of torture and death for slaves or foreign criminals; **2,** a sacred emblem, especially of Christianity, as a symbol of the stake on which Jesus was crucified; **3,** any reproduction of this symbol, used as a shrine or monument; a crucifix; **4,** two intersecting straight lines, as the plus sign

CROSSES
1, Latin; 2, Greek; 3, St. Andrew's; 4, Maltese; 5, papal.

[+] or as the sign of multiplication [×]; **5,** such a mark used as a signature by one who cannot write; **6,** a badge of distinction; as, the Distinguished Service *Cross;* **7,** suffering or affliction to be borne; **8,** an intermixture of breeds or varieties of plants or animals; as, a mule is a *cross* between a horse and an ass:—**sign of the cross, 1,** a figure of Christ's cross, especially that borne on the banners and shields of the Crusaders; **2,** any badge representing the cross of Christ; **3,** a motion of the right hand outlining a cross:—*v.t.* **1,** to put or lay across; as, to *cross* timbers in building; **2,** to draw a mark across; as, to *cross* a *t;* **3,** to go to the opposite side of; as, to *cross* a bridge; **4,** to meet and pass; as, my letter *crossed* his on the way; **5,** to intersect; **6,** to make the sign of the cross upon (oneself); **7,** to cancel; as, I *crossed* out a word; **8,** to thwart; hinder; as, he is not in a mood to be *crossed;* **9,** to cause to interbreed, as plants or animals of different kinds:—*v.i.* **1,** to go, move, or lie from one side to the other; **2,** to meet and pass, going in opposite directions; **3,** to interbreed:—*adj.* **1,** intersecting; **2,** opposed; contrary; as, to work at *cross* purposes; **3,** ill-tempered; peevish.

cross·bar (krôs′bär′), *n.* a bar or line going crosswise, as across a door.

cross·bones (krôs′bōnz′), *n.pl.* a picture of two long bones crossed, often under a picture of a skull, as a symbol of death.

cross·bow (krôs′bō′), *n.* a weapon of the Middle Ages, having a bow across a wooden stock which contained a groove for a stone or an arrow.

CROSSBOW

cross bun, a bun marked with a cross, eaten during Lent, especially on Good Friday.

cross·cut (krôs′kŭt′), *n.* a more direct way than the usual road; a short cut:—**crosscut saw,** a handsaw with teeth set for cutting across the grain; also, a lumberman's two-handed saw (see illustration under ¹*saw*):—*v.t.* [*p.t.* and *p.p.* crosscut, *p.pr.* crosscut·ting], to cut across.

crosse (krôs), *n.* the special racket used in the game of lacrosse.

cross—ex·am·ine (krôs′-ĕg-zăm′ĭn), *v.t.* [cross-examined, cross-examin·ing], to question (a witness) in order to test the truth of previous evidence.—*n.* **cross′-ex·am′i·na′tion.**—*n.* **cross′-ex·am′in·er.**

cross—eyed (krôs′-īd′), *adj.* having one or both eyes turned toward the nose.

cross—grained (krôs′-grānd′), *adj.* **1,** with irregular grain or fiber; **2,** peevish; perverse.

cross·ing (krôs′ĭng), *n.* **1,** a trip across a

body of water, especially an ocean; **2,** an intersection, as of two streets or railroads; also, a place where a street or railroad should be crossed.

cross-jack (krôs′jăk; krôj′ĕk), *n.* a square sail set on the lower yard of the mizzenmast. (See illustration on page 695.)

cross-piece (krôs′pēs′), *n.* a crossbar.

cross—pur-pos-es (krôs′₌pûr′pŭs-ĕz), *n. pl.* **1,** conflicting purposes or intentions; **2,** a game of unrelated, ridiculous questions and answers:—**be at cross purposes,** to argue or work against one another through misunderstanding.

cross—ques-tion (krôs′₌kwĕs′chŭn), *v.t.* to cross-examine; question again and again.

cross ref-er-ence, a reference from one part of a book to another.

cross-road (krôs′rōd′), *n.* **1,** a road that crosses a main road, or runs from one main road to another; **2, crossroads,** the place where two or more roads cross each other.

cross sec-tion, 1, a section cut at right angles to the length of anything; **2,** any group of people or things selected as typical of a greater group.

cross-trees (krôs′trēz′), *n.pl.* short pieces of timber at the upper ends of masts, to support the rigging.

cross-way (krôs′wā′), *n.* a place where two or more roads cross each other; crossroad.

cross-wise (krôs′wīz′), *adv.* **1,** across; athwart; **2,** in the shape of a cross; as, the church was built *crosswise;* **3,** contrarily.

cross-word puz-zle (krôs′wôrd′), a problem of placing letters in a diagram of small squares so as to form intersecting words, some reading across and some down, that fit prescribed definitions.

CROSS-TREES (A, A)

crotch (krŏch), *n.* **1,** a hook or fork; especially, a forked prop or support; **2,** the point of separation into parts or branches; as, a *crotch* of a tree.—*adj.* **crotched** (krŏcht).

crotch-et (krŏch′ĕt), *n.* **1,** a kind of small hook or hooklike instrument; as, a reaping *crotchet;* **2,** a whim or fancy.

crotch-et-y (krŏch′ĕ-tĭ), *adj.* full of odd whims or fancies; eccentric.

crouch (krouch), *v.i.* **1,** to stoop low, as if ready to spring; **2,** to cringe, as if in fear.

¹croup (krōōp), *n.* a child's disease, not infectious, marked by a harsh, gasping cough.—*adj.* **croup′y.**

²croup (krōōp), *n.* the rump, or hind quarters, of a horse. (See *horse,* illustration.)

¹crow (krō), *v.i.* [*p.t.* sometimes in sense 1, crew (krōō); otherwise regular], **1,** to make a shrill sound, like that of a barnyard cock; **2,** to boast in triumph; as, to *crow* over a victory; **3,** to utter a joyous cry:—*n.* the cry of a cock.

²crow (krō), *n.* **1,** a large, black bird, harsh-voiced, highly intelligent, and often destructive; **2,** any closely related bird, as a rook or raven; **3,** a crowbar.

CROW

crow-bar (krō′bär′), *n.* a long, straight iron bar, pointed or wedge-shaped at the working end, used as a lever.

crowd (kroud), *n.* **1,** a number of persons or things collected closely together; **2,** the masses, or common people; **3,** *Colloquial,* a certain set of people; clique: —*v.t.* **1,** to press (people or things) closely together; **2,** to fill too full; pack; stuff; **3,** to force (oneself or one's way) through; shove; push:—*v.i.* **1,** to assemble in large numbers; as, to *crowd* into a hall; **2,** to push; force oneself.

Syn., n. multitude, rabble, throng.

crown (kroun), *n.* **1,** a wreath, as of flowers, for the head; **2,** a headdress of gold and jewels, worn by kings or queens on ceremonial occasions; a diadem; **3,** the monarch himself, or his power; **4,** anything shaped like, or likened to, a crown; as, the *crown* of a hill, hat, or tooth; **5,** the top of the head; also, the head; **6,** completion; perfection; as, wisdom is the *crown* of age; **7,** in England, a coin worth five shillings; **8,** the heavy end of the shank of an anchor (see illustration under *anchor*):—**crown prince,** the immediate heir to a throne; **crown princess,** a woman or girl who is next in succession to a throne; also, the wife of a crown prince:— *v.t.* **1,** to put a crown upon the head of; hence, to invest with regal power; reward; honor; **2,** to occupy the topmost part of; complete; as, a dome *crowns* a building; success *crowns* a career; **3,** in dentistry, to place an artificial top upon (a tooth); **4,** *Colloquial,* to hit on the head.—*n.* **crown′er.**

CROWN, def. 2

crown-piece (kroun′pēs′), *n.* a bridle strap, passing over the head behind the ears. (See *harness,* illustration.)

crow's—nest (krōz′₌nĕst′), *n.* a partly enclosed box or platform on the masthead of a ship, as shelter for the lookout man; any lookout.

CROW'S-NEST

āte, āorta, râre, căt, ȧsk, fär, ăllow, sofȧ; ēve, ĕvent, ĕll, writẽr, novĕl; bīte, pĭn; nō, ōbey, ôr, dŏg, tŏp, cŏllide; ūnit, ūnite, bûrn, cŭt, focŭs; nōōn, fŏŏt; mound; coin;

cro·zier (krō′zhĕr), *n.* the staff of a bishop or abbot. See **crosier**.

cru·cial (krōō′shăl), *adj.* important; decisive; as, a *crucial* test.—*adv.* **cru′cial·ly**.

cru·ci·ble (krōō′sĭ-bl), *n.* an earthenware pot in which ores, metals, and the like, are melted.

cru·ci·fix (krōō′sĭ-fĭks), *n.* any image of Christ on the cross.

cru·ci·fix·ion (krōō′sĭ-fĭk′-shŭn), *n.* death upon a cross:—**Crucifixion,** the death of Christ on the cross; also, a statue or picture representing this scene.

CRUCIBLE

cru·ci·fy (krōō′sĭ-fī), *v.t.* [crucified, crucify-ing], 1, to put (a person) to death by nailing the hands and feet to a cross; 2, to torture in this manner.

crude (krōōd), *adj.* [crud-er, crud-est], 1, in a raw state; unrefined; as, *crude* oil; 2, uncultured; rude; as, *crude* manners; 3, wanting in grace or taste; harsh in color; as, a *crude* painting.—*adv.* **crude′ly.**—*n.* **crude′ness.**—*n.* **cru′di·ty.**

cru·el (krōō′ĕl), *adj.* 1, delighting in giving pain to others; merciless; hardhearted; 2, painful; causing suffering, as a disease.—*adv.* **cru′el·ly.**

Syn. barbarous, brutal, inhuman.

cru·el·ty (krōō′ĕl-tĭ), *n.* [*pl.* cruelties], 1, an inclination to inflict pain and misery; 2, a savage or inhuman deed.

cru·et (krōō′ĕt), *n.* a small glass bottle, especially for vinegar, oil, etc., for the dining table.

Cruik·shank (krōōk′shăngk′), George (1792–1878), an English caricaturist and political satirist, illustrator of Charles Dickens's "Oliver Twist."

cruise (krōōz), *v.t.* [cruised, cruis-ing], to sail about with no special destination; as, pirates *cruised* the China Sea:—*v.i.* 1, to sail about in search of enemy ships or to protect merchant ships in time of war; 2, to travel by boat from port to port; 3, to make a like trip over land:—*n.* a voyage from place to place.

CRUET

cruis·er (krōōz′ĕr), *n.* a swift man-of-war with less armor than a battleship.

crul·ler (krŭl′ĕr), *n.* a ring-shaped or twisted cake, fried brown in deep fat: often called *doughnut.*

crumb (krŭm), *n.* 1, the soft, inner part of bread; 2, a fragment of bread, cake, etc.; 3, a little bit; as, a *crumb* of cheer:—*v.t.* to break (bread) into little pieces.

crum·ble (krŭm′bl), *v.t.* [crum-bled, crum-bling], to break into small pieces:—*v.i.* 1, to fall to pieces; 2, to fall into decay or ruin.—*adj.* **crum′bly.**

crum·pet (krŭm′pĕt), *n.* a soft tea cake or muffin baked on a griddle.

crum·ple (krŭm′pl), *v.t.* [crum-pled, crum-pling], to press into wrinkles; rumple:—*v.i.* to become wrinkled.

crunch (krŭnch), *v.t.* and *v.i.* 1, to crush or grind noisily; as, feet *crunch* the ice; 2, to chew noisily, as does a horse:—*n.* the act or sound of grinding or chewing noisily.

crup·per (krŭp′ĕr; krōōp′ĕr), *n.* in a harness, the leather loop passing under a horse's tail. (See *harness,* illustration.)

cru·sade (krōō-sād′), *n.* 1, any one of seven military expeditions of European Christians, in the 11th, 12th, and 13th centuries, to recover the Holy Land from the Mohammedans; 2, a vigorous movement for some cause, as against crime:—*v.i.* [crusad-ed, crusad-ing], to engage in such a movement.—*n.* **cru·sad′er.**

cruse (krōōs; krōōz), *n. Archaic,* a small vessel for holding oil, water, or the like.

crush (krŭsh), *v.t.* 1, to press between two bodies; break to pieces by pressure; 2, to squeeze; press into a mass; as, to *crush* berries; 3, to bruise so as to change the normal condition; as, to *crush* a leg; 4, to break down; ruin; conquer:—*n.* 1, violent pressure; 2, a crowd; 3, *Colloquial,* a crowded social gathering.—*n.* **crush′er.**

Cru·soe (krōō′sō), **Rob·in·son,** the hero, and the title, of a novel by Daniel Defoe, recounting the adventures day by day of a sailor shipwrecked on a desert island.

crust (krŭst), *n.* 1, the hard outside covering on bread; also, a piece of this or of stale bread; 2, any similar hard outside coating; as, a *crust* of ice over soft snow; 3, the pastry casing of a pie; 4, *Slang,* impudence:—*v.t.* and *v.i.* to cover, or become covered, with a hard outside coating.

crus·ta·cean (krŭs-tā′shăn), *n.* any of a class of animals, most of which live in the water, having a hard outside shell, as crabs, lobsters, shrimps, etc. (See illustration next page.)

crust·y (krŭs′tĭ), *adj.* [crust-i-er, crust-i-est] 1, having, or like, a crust; 2, cross; snappish.—*adv.* **crust′i·ly.**

crutch (krŭch), *n.* 1, a staff with a crosspiece to fit under the arm, used by lame or infirm persons; 2, any forked prop or support.

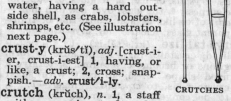

CRUTCHES

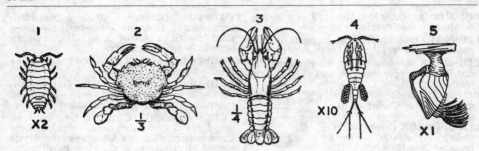

CRUSTACEANS
1, wood louse; 2, crab; 3, crayfish; 4, water flea; 5, barnacle.

crux (krŭks), *n.* [*pl.* cruxes (krŭk′sĕz)], 1, a hard point to settle; 2, the important point on which something depends.

cru·zei·ro (krōō-zâr′ō), *n.* Brazilian monetary unit, a gold coin equivalent to ten milreis.

cry (krī), *v.i.* [cried, cry-ing], 1, to call aloud; complain loudly; wail; exclaim; 2, to shed tears; weep; 3, of an animal or bird, to call loudly:—*v.t.* 1, to announce publicly; as, to *cry* the hour of the night; 2, to advertise or offer for sale; as, the peddler *cries* his wares:—*n.* 1, loud or passionate utterance; as, a *cry* of joy, fear, anger, pain, or the like; 2, outcry; clamor; demand; 3, the calling of goods for sale; as, the peddler's *cry;* 4, common report; rumor; 5, the characteristic call of an animal; as, the *cry* of the wolf; 6, a fit of weeping; 7, a rallying call; as, a battle *cry:*—**a far cry**, a long way.—*adj.* **cry′ing.**

crypt (krĭpt), *n.* an underground vault, especially one under a church.

cryp·tic (krĭp′tĭk), *adj.* hidden; secret; mystical; puzzling; as, he did not understand the *cryptic* message.

cryp·to·gram (krĭp′tṓ-grăm), *n.* a writing in a secret code.

crys·tal (krĭs′tăl), *n.* 1, transparent quartz; 2, a body with regular flat surfaces formed by some substances when they solidify; as, *crystals* of ice; 3, a glass of superior clearness; 4, the glass over a watch dial:—*adj.* of or like crystal; consisting of transparent glass; clear.—*adj.* **crys′tal-line.**

crys·tal·lize (krĭs′tăl-īz), *v.t.* [crystallized, crystalliz-ing], 1, to cause to form grains or become crystalline; 2, to give a fixed shape to; 3, to coat with sugar crystals; as, to *crystallize* ginger:—*v.i.* 1, to be converted into grains or become crystalline; 2, to assume a definite shape; as, his hazy plans *crystallized* into deeds.—*n.* **crys′tal-li-za′tion.**

C.S.A. abbreviation for *Confederate States of America.*

ct. abbreviation for *cent, court.*

cu. abbreviation for *cubic.*

cub (kŭb), *n.* 1, the young of the fox, bear, lion, or the like; 2, a callow youth.

Cu·ba (kū′bȧ), an island republic (cap. Havana) south of Florida, in the Caribbean Sea.—*n.* and *adj.* **Cu′ban** (map 10).

cube (kūb), *n.* 1, in geometry, a regular solid body with six equal square sides or faces; 2, any body resembling this; as, candy *cubes;* 3, the product obtained when a number is multiplied two times by itself; as, $5 \times 5 \times 5 = 125$, the *cube* of 5:—**cube root**, that factor of a number which multiplied twice by itself produces the given number; as, 3 is the *cube root* of 27:—*v.t.* [cubed, cub-ing], 1, to multiply (a number) twice by itself; raise to the third power; 2, to form into cubelike shapes; as, to *cube* potatoes.

CUBE

cu·bic (kū′bĭk) or **cu·bi·cal** (kū′bĭ-kăl), *adj.* 1, having the form of a cube; 2, having three dimensions; as, a *cubic* yard is the volume or capacity of a cube whose edges all measure one yard.

cu·bit (kū′bĭt), *n.* 1, a measure of length among the ancient Hebrews, Egyptians, etc., varying from 12 to 22 inches; 2, in English measure, eighteen inches: originally the length from the elbow to the tip of the middle finger.

cuck·oo (kŏŏk′ōō), *n.* 1, an ash-gray European bird noted for laying its eggs in the nests of other birds, and abandoning them to the care of the nest-owners; 2, an American bird which rears its own

AN AMERICAN CUCKOO (₁/₁₀)

young: both so named from their characteristic two-noted love call; **3,** the call of the cuckoo:—*adj.* **1,** relating to the cuckoo; **2,** *Slang,* silly; unbalanced.

cu·cum·ber (kū′kŭm-bẽr), *n.* **1,** a creeping plant cultivated for its fruit which is used as a salad or pickle; **2,** the fruit itself.

CUCUMBER

cud (kŭd), *n.* food which certain animals, called *ruminants,* bring back into the mouth from the first stomach to be chewed. Cows, sheep, goats, and the like, chew the cud.

cud·dle (kŭd′l), *v.t.* [cud-dled, cud-dling], to embrace closely and lovingly; as, a mother *cuddles* a baby:—*v.i.* to lie close or snug; nestle.

cudg·el (kŭj′ĕl), *n.* a thick stick used as a weapon:—*v.t.* [cudgeled, cudgel-ing], to beat with a stick:—**cudgel one's brains,** to think hard; try to recall something.

¹cue (kū), *n.* **1,** the tapering rod used to strike the ball in playing billiards, pool, and similar games; **2,** a pigtail; queue; **3,** a long line of people waiting. See **queue.**

²cue (kū), *n.* **1,** a hint; a suggestion as to what to do; **2,** the last words of a speech or scene in a play which indicate the time for another actor to enter or speak.

¹cuff (kŭf), *n.* a blow, as with the open hand:—*v.t.* to strike with the open hand.

²cuff (kŭf), *n.* a band worn about the wrist, as on a sleeve; also, a fold about the bottom of a trouser leg.

cui·rass (kwē-răs′), *n.* a piece of armor covering the body from neck to waist; also, the breastplate alone.

cui·ras·sier (kwē′ră-sēr′), *n.* a mounted soldier wearing a breastplate or cuirass.

cui·sine (kwē-zēn′), *n.* the kitchen, as of a hotel; also, the style of preparing and cooking food.

cul—de—sac (kŏŏl′=dē=săk′), *n.* [*pl.* cul-de-sacs], **1,** a blind alley; a passage with an opening only at one end; **2,** hence, a trap.

Cu·le·bra Cut (kōō-lā′brä), a part of the Panama Canal. See **Gaillard Cut.**

cu·li·nar·y (kū′lĭ-nẽr′ĭ), *adj.* pertaining to the kitchen or to cooking.

cull (kŭl), *v.t.* to pick out; select; gather:—*n.* something sorted out from the rest of a group, as inferior or worthless; as, the *culls* of an orchard.

culm (kŭlm), *n.* the jointed, usually hollow, stem of a grass or sedge.

cul·mi·nate (kŭl′mĭ-nāt), *v.i.* [culmi-

nat-ed, culminat-ing], to reach the highest point; come to a climax.—*n.* **cul′mi·na′-tion.**

cul·pa·ble (kŭl′pá-bl), *adj.* guilty; criminal; blameworthy.—*adv.* **cul′pa·bly,**—*n.* **cul′pa·bil′i·ty.**

Syn. guilty, wicked, wrong.

cul·prit (kŭl′prĭt), *n.* **1,** one formally accused of a crime; **2,** one guilty of a crime.

cult (kŭlt), *n.* **1,** a particular system of worship; **2,** devotion to a person, idea, theory, or the like; as, the nudist *cult;* **3,** the group of people so devoted; a body of followers; a sect.

cul·ti·vate (kŭl′tĭ-vāt), *v.t.* [cultivat-ed, cultivat-ing], **1,** to till, as the soil; raise by tillage, as crops; **2,** to improve by care, labor, or study; **3,** to devote oneself to; as, to *cultivate* literature; **4,** to seek the society of (a person or persons); **5,** in the U.S., to loosen the ground about (growing crops).

cul·ti·va·tion (kŭl′tĭ-vā′shŭn), *n.* **1,** tillage; **2,** culture; refinement; **3,** the act of cultivating; development; as, the *cultivation* of musical taste.

cul·ti·va·tor (kŭl′tĭ-vā′tẽr), *n.* **1,** one who tills; **2,** a farm implement for loosening earth about crops.

CULTIVATOR

cul·tur·al (kŭl′tūr-ăl), *adj.* relating to the cultivation of something; especially, having to do with the development and improvement of the mind; broadening; liberal; as, a *cultural* education.

cul·ture (kŭl′tūr), *n.* **1,** care given to the growth and development of animals and plants; **2,** the breeding of germs for scientific study; also, the product of such breeding; **3,** improvement of mind or body by practice or training; as, voice *culture;* physical *culture;* **4,** the training of the mental or moral powers; refinement; **5,** the civilization of a race of people, including religion, arts, and social customs; as, Greek, Zulu, or Navajo *culture.*

Syn. education, training, breeding.

cul·tured (kŭl′tūrd), *adj.* cultivated; refined; educated.

cul·vert (kŭl′vẽrt), *n.* a drain or passage under a road, canal, railroad, etc.

CULVERT

cum·ber (kŭm′bẽr), *v.t.* to burden; hinder.

Cum·ber·land (kŭm′bẽr-lănd), **1,** a group of mountains in Tennessee and Virginia (map 8); **2,** a county in northwestern England, famed for its scenery.

go; join; yet; sing; chin; show; thin, *th*en; hw, *why;* zh, azure; ü, Ger. *für* or Fr. *lune;* ö, Ger. *schön* or Fr. *feu;* ṅ, Fr. *enfant, nom;* kh, Ger. *ach* or *ich.* See pages ix–x.

cum·ber·some (kŭm′bĕr-sŭm), *adj.* burdensome; clumsy.—*adv.* **cum′ber·some·ly.**

cum·brous (kŭm′brŭs), *adj.* troublesome; heavy; weighty.—*adv.* **cum′brous·ly.**

cu·mu·la·tive (kū′mū-lā′tĭv; kū′mū-lá-tĭv), *adj.* growing in number, volume, or strength by repeated additions; formed by one addition after another.

cu·mu·lus (kū′mū-lŭs), *n.* [*pl.* cumuli (kū′mū-lī)], **1,** a heap; **2,** a cloud in the form of a rounded mass heaped up on a flat base.—*adj.* **cu′mu·lous.**

cu·ne·i·form (kū-nē′ĭ-fôrm; kū′nē-ĭ-fôrm′), *adj.* wedge-shaped: said of the wedge-shaped characters of the ancient inscriptions of Assyria and Persia.

CUNEIFORM WRITING

cun·ner (kŭn′ẽr), *n.* a small, food fish found in rocky water along the New England coast: also called *sea perch.*

cun·ning (kŭn′ĭng), *adj.* **1,** skilful; clever; done with skill or ingenuity; as, a *cunning* craftsman; a *cunning* escape; **2,** crafty; sly; esigning; **3,** *Colloquial,* pretty; cute; as, a *cunning* child:—*n.* skill; ability; also, deceit; craftiness.—*adv.* **cun′ning·ly.**

cup (kŭp), *n.* **1,** a small open vessel, usually with a handle, used for drinking or measuring; **2,** something shaped like a cup; as, the *cup* of an acorn; **3,** the amount a cup holds; a cupful; as, two *cups* of milk; **4,** a cup-shaped prize of gold or silver; as, to win the yacht *cup;* **5,** one's portion of happiness or misery; as, to drain the *cup* of sorrow; **6,** cups, intoxication: usually in the expression *in his cups:*—*v.t.* [cupped, cupping], to form a cup with; as, to *cup* one's hands.

CUPS
1, teacup, with saucer; 2, egg cup; 3, tin cup; 4, paper cup.

cup·bear·er (kŭp′bâr′ẽr), *n.* one whose duty it is to fill and serve cups of wine, as at the table of a king.

cup·board (kŭb′ẽrd), *n.* **1,** a closet fitted with shelves for cups, plates, etc.; **2,** any small closet.

cup·ful (kŭp′fŏŏl), *n.* [*pl.* cupfuls], as much as a cup will contain.

CUPBOARD

Cu·pid (kū′pĭd), *n.* in Roman mythology, the god of love, son of Venus.

cu·pid·i·ty (kū-pĭd′ĭ-tĭ), *n.* an eager desire for possession; greed.

cu·po·la (kū′pŏ-lá), *n.* **1,** a domelike roof; a dome; **2,** any small domelike structure above the roof of a building.

CUPOLA

cur (kûr), *n.* **1,** a mongrel; a dog of mixed breed; **2,** a surly, ill-bred person.

cur·a·ble (kūr′á-bl), *adj.* capable of being healed or cured; as, a *curable* disease.

cu·ra·cy (kū′rá-sĭ), *n.* [*pl.* curacies], the office or district of a curate.

cu·rate (kū′rât; kū′rĭt), *n.* an assistant to a priest, rector, or vicar.

cur·a·tive (kūr′á-tĭv), *adj.* having to do with the curing of illness; healing:—*n.* anything which cures; a medicine.

cu·ra·tor (kū-rā′tẽr), *n.* one in charge of a museum, art gallery, or the like.

curb (kûrb), *v.t.* **1,** to restrain; keep within bounds; **2,** to furnish with a protecting rim, as of stone; as, to *curb* a street:—*n.* **1,** that which checks, restrains, or subdues; as, he put a *curb* on his anger; **2,** a chain or strap attached to a horse's bit and used as a check (see *harness,* illustration); **3,** a protecting rim of stone, or the like, bordering a sidewalk; raised path; etc.; a curbstone.
   Syn., v. check, control, subject, repress.

curb·stone (kûrb′stōn′), *n.* the stone or cement edging of a street or sidewalk, between the gutter and the sidewalk.

curd (kûrd), *n.* the thickened part of milk; as, cheese is formed of *curd:*—*v.t.* and *v.i.* to curdle.—*adj.* **curd′y.**

cur·dle (kûr′dl), *v.t.* [cur-dled, cur-dling], to thicken into curd:—*v.i.* to thicken; as, this milk has *curdled.*

cure (kūr), *n.* **1,** the act of healing; as, the *cure* of a cold; **2,** a method of treatment that cures; as, the milk *cure;* the water *cure;* **3,** a remedy; as, quinine is a *cure* for colds:—*v.t.* [cured, cur-ing], **1,** to heal; restore to health; **2,** to remedy or remove (an evil of any kind); as, he *cured* his dread of the dark; **3,** to preserve by salting, drying, etc.; as, to *cure* hams.

cu·ré (kü′rā′), *n.* in France, a Roman Catholic parish priest.

cur·few (kûr′fū), *n.* **1,** in medieval Europe, the ringing of a bell at a fixed hour in the evening as a warning that fires and lights were to be put out; the law which required this; also, the bell itself; **2,** hence, the ringing of a bell at a certain hour in the evening, usually as a signal for children to leave the streets.

Cu·rie (kü′rē′), Pierre (1859–1906), and Marie (1867–1934), his wife, physicists and chemists, discoverers of radium.

cu·ri·o (kū′rĭ-ō), *n.* [*pl.* curios], a rare object of art; a curiosity.

cu·ri·os·i·ty (kū′rĭ-ŏs′ĭ-tĭ), *n.* [*pl.* curiosities], **1,** eager desire to get knowledge; inquisitiveness; **2,** something strange or rare.

cu·ri·ous (kū′rĭ-ŭs), *adj.* **1,** anxious to know; prying; as, *curious* eyes; a *curious* mind; **2,** strange; full of mystery; as, a *curious* silence.—*adv.* **cu′ri·ous·ly.**
    Syn. novel, interesting, prying.

curl (kûrl), *n.* **1,** a small ring of hair; a ringlet; **2,** anything of similar shape; as, a *curl* of smoke; **3,** the act of forming, or state of being formed into a curved or coiled shape; as, the *curl* of a wave; hair kept in *curl*:—*v.t.* to twist into ringlets or coils:—*v.i.* to grow or move in spirals; as, smoke *curled* lazily from the chimney.

cur·lew (kûr′lū), *n.* a long-legged shore bird with a long, downward-curving bill.

curl·ing (kûr′lĭng), *n.* **1,** the act of making ringlets; **2,** a Scottish game played on ice with large, rounded stones.

curl·y (kûr′lĭ), *adj.* [curl-i-er, curl-i-est], having ringlets; as, *curly* hair.

cur·mudg·eon (kẽr-mŭj′ŭn), *n.* a grasping, churlish fellow; miser.

CURLEW (1′₂)

cur·rant (kûr′ănt), *n.* **1,** a small seedless raisin; **2,** a common garden shrub; also, its acid, red, black, or white berry, used for jellies and jams.

cur·ren·cy (kûr′ĕn-sĭ), *n.* [*pl.* currencies], **1,** a passing from person to person; circulation, as of bank notes; **2,** general acceptance; as, the *currency* of a scientific theory; **3,** that which is generally used for money, as notes and coin; as, the *currency* of a nation.

CURRANTS, def. 2

cur·rent (kûr′ĕnt), *adj.* **1,** widely circulated; passing from person to person; **2,** now passing, as time; as, the *current* year; belonging to the present time; as,

the *current* issue of a magazine; **3,** generally accepted; common; as, *current* opinion:—*n.* **1,** a flow or passing; a body of air or water flowing in a certain direction; especially, the swift part of a stream; **2,** the flow, or rate of flow, of electricity; **3,** general course or tendency; as, the *current* of the present time.—*adv.* **cur′rent·ly.**

cur·ric·u·lum (kŭ-rĭk′ū-lŭm), *n.* [*pl.* curriculums (kŭ-rĭk′ū-lŭmz) or curricula (kŭ-rĭk′ū-la)], a regular course of study in a university, school, or the like.

¹**cur·ry** (kûr′ĭ), *v.t.* [curried, curry-ing], **1,** to rub down and clean (an animal) with a currycomb; **2,** to dress, as leather, by scraping, soaking, coloring, etc.:—**curry favor,** to try to win favor by flattery.

²**cur·ry** (kûr′ĭ), *n.* [*pl.* curries], **1,** a highly spiced East Indian sauce; **2,** a dish of meat, rice, or the like, cooked or seasoned with this sauce.

cur·ry·comb (kûr′ĭ-kōm′), *n.* a metal comb used for cleaning horses.

CURRYCOMB

curse (kûrs), *n.* **1,** an oath; **2,** a prayer for injury to someone; **3,** that which brings or causes evil or trouble; also, the evil itself; as, crime is a *curse*:—*v.t.* [cursed or curst (kûrst), curs-ing], **1,** to wish, or bring, evil upon; blaspheme; swear at; **2,** to torment; to afflict; as, to be *cursed* with a bad temper:—*v.i.* to swear.

curs·ed (kûr′sĕd; kûrst), *adj.* **1,** under a curse; **2,** deserving a curse; hateful; detestable; wicked.—*adv.* **curs′ed·ly.**

cur·so·ry (kûr′sō-rĭ), *adj.* hasty; careless; as, he gave the book a *cursory* reading.
    Syn. desultory, fitful, rapid, discursive.

curt (kûrt), *adj.* **1,** short; **2,** abrupt; rude. —*adv.* **curt′ly.**—*n.* **curt′ness.**
    Syn. concise, brusque, uncivil, short.

cur·tail (kûr-tāl′), *v.t.* to cut short; as, rain *curtailed* the exercises; reduce, as expenses.—*n.* **cur·tail′ment.**
    Syn. abbreviate, shorten, lessen.

cur·tain (kûr′tĭn; kûr′tn), *n.* **1,** a hanging covering or screen, usually of cloth, which can be drawn up or aside; as, a window *curtain*; **2,** anything that serves to conceal; as, the fog was like a *curtain* over the city:—*v.t.* to furnish with draperies; enclose with a screen or the like.

curt·sy (kûrt′sĭ), *n.* [*pl.* curtsies], a bow, made by bending the knees and lowering the body:—*v.i.* [curtsied, curtsy-ing], to make a curtsy. Also, **curt′sey.**

cur·va·ture (kûr′va-tūr), *n.* a bending; curving; also, the amount of bending, as of a curved line or surface.

curve (kûrv), *n.* **1,** a bending without

angles; also, that which is bent; **2,** in baseball, a ball so pitched as to turn from its expected course:—*v.t.* [curved, curv-ing], to cause to bend or turn from a straight line:—*v.i.* to bend; to turn.

cur-vet (kûr′vĕt), *n.* a leap of a horse, made by raising the front legs and then, before the front legs have touched the ground, raising the hind legs; a frisk or bound:—*v.i.* and *v.t.* (kûr-vĕt′; kûr′vĕt), [curvet-ted, curvet-ting; when accented on the first syllable, curvet-ed, curvet-ing], to leap, or cause to leap, in this way.

Cush (kŭsh), in the Bible, a country in Africa, identified with Ethiopia.

cush-ion (kŏosh′ŭn), *n.* **1,** a pillow or soft pad to sit, lie, or rest upon; **2,** anything resembling a cushion; as, a *cushion* of leaves:—*v.t.* **1,** to seat on, or as on, a soft pad; **2,** to furnish with a soft pad.

cusp (kŭsp), *n.* a pointed end; a point, as on the crown of a tooth or on the new moon.

cus-pid (kŭs′pĭd), *n.* a tooth with only one point for tearing food; a canine tooth. (See illustration under *tooth*).

cus-pi-dor (kŭs′pĭ-dôr), *n.* a spittoon.

cus-tard (kŭs′tẽrd), *n.* a mixture of eggs, milk, and sugar, baked or boiled.

cus-to-di-an (kŭs-tō′dĭ-ăn), *n.* a keeper or caretaker, as of a public building.

cus-to-dy (kŭs′tō-dĭ), *n.* **1,** guardianship; care; as, the *custody* of the jewels; **2,** restraint of liberty; imprisonment; as, the prisoner was taken into *custody*.

cus-tom (kŭs′tŭm), *n.* **1,** an established practice, habit, or usage; as, it is his *custom* to read in bed; the strange *customs* of the Indians; **2,** the regular buying of goods in one place; as, I give my *custom* to this store; **3, customs,** government taxes on imported or, less frequently, exported goods:—*adj.* **1,** made to order; as, *custom* hats; **2,** doing only work that is ordered; as, *custom* tailors.

cus-tom-ar-y (kŭs′tŭm-ẽr′ĭ), *adj.* habitual; usual.—*adv.* **cus′tom-ar′i-ly.**

cus-tom-er (kŭs′tŭm-ẽr), *n.* one who buys; especially, one who buys regularly at a certain store; a patron.

cus-tom-house (kŭs′tŭm-hous′), *n.* a government building where export or import duties or taxes are paid.

cut (kŭt), *v.t.* [*p.t.* and *p.p.* cut, *p.pr.* cutting], **1,** to slash with a sharp-edged tool; as, to *cut* one's finger; to hew; as, to *cut* down a tree; to pierce; as, the sleet *cut* his skin; **2,** to shape, as a garment, with a sharp instrument; as, she *cut* the sleeves for the dress; **3,** to shorten or reduce in length or extent; trim; as, to *cut*

the hair; *cut* expenses; **4,** figuratively, to grieve or hurt; as, the remark *cut* him to the quick; to penetrate, as if with a sharp-edged tool; as, the wind *cut* him to the bone; **5,** to pretend not to recognize; **6,** to cross; to intersect; as, the two railroad lines *cut* one another; **7,** to dissolve or make less stiff; as, a strong soap will *cut* the grease in washing dishes; **8,** *Colloquial,* to absent oneself from (a lecture, class, or the like):—**to cut teeth,** to have new teeth appear through the gums:—*v.i.* **1,** to make a gash; as, the knife *cuts* well; also, to admit of being cut or divided; as, this meat *cuts* easily; **2,** to pass through or across by a direct route; as, to *cut* across is shorter:—*n.* **1,** the act of slashing or separating by a sharp instrument; also, a slash or wound made by a sharp instrument; **2,** a sharp stroke, as with a whip; **3,** a passage or channel made by digging; as, a *cut* for a railroad track; **4,** that which is severed or detached by a sharp instrument; a slice; as, a *cut* of cake; **5,** a straight, short passage; as, the path is a short *cut* to the house; **6,** the fashion of a garment; style; as, the *cut* of a coat; **7,** a reduction, as in price, expenses, or the like; **8,** absence, as from a lecture, class, or the like; **9,** the deliberate ignoring of an acquaintance; **10,** an engraved block of wood or metal from which a picture or the like is printed; also, the picture made from it:—*adj.* **1,** divided or separated; **2,** gashed, wounded; **3,** having the surface ornamented or fashioned, as a gem; **4,** reduced; as, dresses sold at *cut* prices.

cu-ta-ne-ous (kū-tā′nē-ŭs), *adj.* having to do with the skin.

cute (kūt), *adj.* [cut-er, cut-est], *Colloquial,* **1,** clever; shrewd; **2,** attractive because of daintiness, etc.; as, a *cute* child.

cu-ti-cle (kū′tĭ-kl), *n.* **1,** the outer layer of skin; the epidermis; **2,** dead skin, as that around the base of a fingernail.

cut-lass (kŭt′lȧs), *n.* a short, heavy sword, with a wide, curved blade, used especially by sailors.

CUTLASS

cut-ler (kŭt′lẽr), *n.* one who makes, sells, or repairs knives or other cutting tools.

cut-ler-y (kŭt′lẽr-ĭ), *n.* **1,** edged or cutting tools collectively, as knives, scissors, etc.; especially, implements used in cutting or serving food; **2,** the business of a cutler.

cut-let (kŭt′lĕt), *n.* a slice of meat, generally of veal or mutton, cut from the ribs or leg of an animal, for frying or broiling; also, any preparation of fish, ground meat, or the like, shaped like a cutlet.

āte, āorta, râre, căt, ȧsk, fär, ăllow, sofȧ; ēve, êvent, ĕll, writẽr, novĕl; bīte, pĭn; nō, ōbey, ôr, dŏg, tŏp, cŏllide; ūnit, ŭnite, bûrn, cŭt, focŭs; nōon, fŏot; mound; coin;

cut-off (kŭt′ôf′), *n*. **1,** anything, as a road, which shortens the traveling distance between two points; **2,** a device for stopping a flow, as of steam or water.

cut-out (kŭt′out′), *n*. a design or figure to be cut out, and, sometimes, colored; as, paper doll *cutouts*.

cut-ter (kŭt′ẽr), *n*. **1,** one who cuts out and shapes anything, as garments; **2,** that which cuts; **3,** a light sleigh for two persons; **4,** a small, single-masted sailing vessel, or a boat used by ships of war; **5,** an armed boat used by the coast guard; as, a revenue *cutter*.

CUTTER, def. 4

cut-throat (kŭt′thrōt′), *n*. a murderous villain; an assassin:—*adj*. murderous.

cut-ting (kŭt′ĭng), *adj*. **1,** able to cut; as, the *cutting* edge of a knife; **2,** wounding; sarcastic; as, a *cutting* reply; **3,** piercing; sharp; as, a *cutting* wind:—*n*. **1,** the act of one who cuts; **2,** a piece cut off something; as, a *cutting* from a plant; **3,** an excavation, as for a railway track.

cut-tle-fish (kŭt′l-fĭsh′), *n*. a salt-water shellfish, which has ten arms or tentacles and which gives forth a cloud of black fluid when attacked.

CUTTLE-FISH (¹⁄₁₀)

cut-worm (kŭt′wûrm′), *n*. a destructive caterpillar which destroys the young shoots of cabbage, corn, or the like, by cutting part way through the stalk at or near the ground.

cwt. abbreviation for *hundredweight*.

-cy (-sē), a suffix meaning the state of being; as, bankrupt*cy*.

cyc-la-men (sĭk′lȧ-mĕn), *n*. a plant of the primrose family, with showy, white, pink, or red flowers.

cy-cle (sī′kl), *n*. **1,** a period of time, or a round of events, that takes place regularly; **2,** a complete series; especially, a group of stories surrounding a famous event or hero; as, the Arthurian *cycle*; **3,** an age or long period of time; **4,** a bicycle, tricycle, or motorcycle:—*v.i.*

CYCLAMEN

[*cy-cled, cy-cling*], to ride a cycle; as, he *cycled* to town.

cy-clic (sī′klĭk; sĭk′lĭk), *adj*. pertaining to, belonging to, or moving in, a cycle.

cy-clist (sī′klĭst), *n*. one who rides a bicycle, motorcycle, or tricycle.

cy-clom-e-ter (sī-klŏm′ē-tẽr), *n*. an instrument for recording the revolutions of a wheel or distance covered by a wheel as of a bicycle.

cy-clone (sī′klōn), *n*. **1,** a violent storm in which the wind whirls inward toward a calm center; **2,** loosely, any destructive storm.—*adj*. **cy-clon′ic** (sī-klŏn′ĭk).

cy-clo-pe-di-a or **cy-clo-pae-di-a** (sī′-klō-pē′dĭ-ȧ), *n*. a book containing brief information on all subjects, or on all branches of one subject, usually alphabetically arranged; an encyclopedia.

Cy-clops (sī′klŏps), *n*. [*pl.* Cyclopes (sī-klō′pēz)], in Greek mythology, one of a race of one-eyed giants, appearing in Homer's "Odyssey" as gigantic man-eating shepherds.—*adj*. **Cy′clo-pe′an.**

cyg-net (sĭg′nĕt), *n*. a young swan.

cyl-in-der (sĭl′ĭn-dẽr), *n*. **1,** a solid or hollow body, long and round, with its two ends equal and parallel; **2,** any body having the form of a cylinder, as the piston chamber of a gasoline or steam engine, the barrel of a pump, a roller used in a printing press, etc.

CYLINDER

cy-lin-dri-cal (sī-lĭn′drĭ-kȧl) or **cy-lin-dric** (sī-lĭn′drĭk), *adj*. having the form of a cylinder, as a rolling pin or a gas pipe. —*adv*. **cy-lin′dri-cal-ly.**

cym-bal (sĭm′bȧl), *n*. in music, either of two circular, metal plates which when clashed together produce a ringing sound.

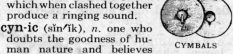

CYMBALS

cyn-ic (sĭn′ĭk), *n*. one who doubts the goodness of human nature and believes that each person has only a desire to further his own interests; hence, a sarcastic, sneering person; a faultfinder:—*adj*. sarcastic; doubting.

cyn-i-cal (sĭn′ĭ-kȧl), *adj*. **1,** sneering; sarcastic; as, a *cynical* remark; **2,** given to doubt in the sincerity of men's motives.

cyn-i-cism (sĭn′ĭ-sĭzm), *n*. the doctrine or belief of a cynic; doubt in the sincerity of men's motives.

cy-no-sure (sī′nō-shŏor; sĭn′ō-shŏor), *n*. a center or object of general attraction; as, she was the *cynosure* of all eyes.

cy-pher (sī′fẽr), *n*. **1,** zero; **2,** secret writing. See **cipher.**

cy-press (sī′prĕs), *n*. **1,** a cone-bearing

evergreen tree of the pine family (see illustration, page 865); **2,** the wood of a cypress tree:—*adj.* pertaining to, or made of, cypress.

Cy-prus (sī′prŭs), an island (cap. Nicosia) south of Turkey, in the Mediterranean. It is a British dependency (map **15**).

Cy-re-ne (sī-rē′nē), an ancient city in Africa, founded by the Greeks (map 1).

Cy-rus (sī′rŭs), (600?–529 B.C.), called *the Great*, founder of the Persian Empire.

cyst (sĭst), *n.* a sac, or pouch, in the body, containing diseased matter.

C.Z. abbreviation for *Canal Zone.*

czar (zär) or **tsar** (tsär), *n.* **1,** the title of the former emperors of Russia; **2,** a dictator; as, the *czar* of an industry.

cza-ri-na (zä-rē′nà) or **tsa-ri-na** (tsä-rē′nà), *n.* the title of the former empresses of Russia; also, the wife of a czar.

Czech (chĕk), *n.* **1,** a member of the most westerly branch of the Slav family, including Bohemians, Moravians, and Slovaks; **2,** their language.—*adj.* and *n.* **Czech/ish.**

Czech-o-slo-vak (chĕk′ō-slō′văk; chĕk′ō-slō-văk′), *adj.* relating to the Czechs and Slovaks or to their language; relating to the people of Bohemia, Moravia, Silesia, and Slovakia, or to their language:—*n.* a member of the Czechish branch of the Slav family; also, the Czechish language.

Czech-o-slo-va-ki-a (chĕk′ō-slō-vä′kĭ-à), a republic (cap. Prague) of central Europe. —*adj.* **Czech/o-slo-vak/i-an.**

D

D, d (dē), *n.* **1,** the fourth letter of the alphabet, following C, or its sound; **2,** in music, the second tone in the major scale of C; **3,** the Roman numeral for 500.

d. abbreviation for Latin *denarius, denarii,* meaning *penny, pence.*

dab (dăb), *v.t.* [dabbed, dab-bing], to strike or touch lightly; smear in spots:—*n.* **1,** a soft blow; **2,** a quick, sharp stroke; **3,** a small, soft lump; **4,** a small portion.

dab-ble (dăb′l), *v.t.* [dab-bled, dab-bling], to wet by dipping; spatter:—*v.i.* **1,** to paddle in water, as with the hands; **2,** to work at or do anything indifferently; as, to *dabble* in art.—*n.* **dab/bler.**

dace (dās), *n.* [*pl.* dace or daces], **1,** a small, European fresh-water fish, like the chub; **2,** a related North American fish.

dachs-hund (däks′hŏont′; däks′hŏond′; däsh′hŭnd′; däsh′-ŭnd′), *n.* a hound, usually black or brown, with a long body and very short, crooked legs.

DACHSHUND (⅒)

dac-tyl (dăk′tĭl), *n.* a metrical foot of one accented syllable followed by two unaccented syllables; as, "Take her up tenderly."—*adj.* **dac-tyl/ic.**

dad (dăd), *n.* a father: used in intimate or informal speech or address.

dad-dy (dăd′ĭ), *n.* [*pl.* daddies], a father.

dad-dy long-legs (dăd′ĭ lông′lĕgz′), a small-bodied spiderlike animal with long, slender legs.

DADDY LONG-LEGS (¼)

daf-fo-dil (dăf′ō-dĭl), *n.* a plant, grown from a bulb, with long, narrow leaves and large yellow flowers.

daft (dàft), *adj.* weak-minded; simple; foolish; crazy.

Da-ge-stan or **Da-ghe-stan** (dä′gĕ-stän′), a self-governing republic, in the U.S.S.R., west of the Caspian Sea.

dag-ger (dăg′ẽr), *n.* **1,** a short, sharp, pointed knife, used for stabbing; **2,** in printing, a mark [†] telling the reader to look elsewhere for more information.

DAFFODIL

Da-gon (dā′gŏn), *n.* in the Old Testament, the chief god, half man, half fish, of the Philistines (1 Samuel 5).

da-guerre-o-type (dà-gĕr′ō-tīp; dà-gĕr′ē-ō-tīp), *n.* an early method of taking photographs on silver-coated plates; also, a photograph made by this method.

DAGGERS

dahl-ia (dăl′yà; dăl′yà; dāl′yà), *n.* **1,** a garden plant that grows from a bulb to a height varying from three to nine feet, and bears in the early autumn large showy flowers of red, yellow, white, etc.; **2,** the bulb or flower of this plant.

Da-ho-mey (dä-hō′mā), a colony in French West Africa, west of Nigeria (map 14).

dai-ly (dā′lĭ), *n.* [*pl.* dailies], a newspaper published every day:—*adj.* occurring, appearing, or done every day:—*adv.* on every day; day by day.
  Syn., adj. diurnal.

dain-ty (dān′tĭ), *n.* [*pl.* dainties], something choice or delicious; a choice bit of food:—*adj.* [dain-ti-er, dain-ti-est], **1,** de-

---

licious; **2,** pretty in a delicate way; **3,** sensitive; having delicate tastes and feelings.
—*adv.* **dain′ti-ly.**

dair-y (dâr′ĭ), *n.* [*pl.* dairies], **1,** a place where milk is kept and made into butter and cheese; **2,** a farm, or part of a farm, which produces and sells milk products; **3,** the cows on such a farm; **4,** a shop where milk products are sold:—**dairy cattle,** cattle raised to produce milk.—*n.* **dair′y-ing.**

dair-y-maid (dâr′ĭ-mād′), *n.* a woman employed in a dairy.

dair-y-man (dâr′ĭ-măn), *n.* [*pl.* dairymen (-měn)], **1,** a man who owns or works in a dairy; **2,** a man who sells dairy products.

da-is (dā′ĭs; dās), *n.* [*pl.* daises (dā′ĭs-ĕz; dās′ĕz)], a raised platform, as for a throne or seats of honor, in a large room or hall.

dai-sy (dā′zĭ), *n.* [*pl.* daisies], a flower of the aster family, with a brown or yellow center surrounded by white, yellow, or pink petals; also, the plant itself. The *English daisy* is low-growing and has white or pink petals, while the common *oxeye daisy*, in the U.S., grows tall and has white petals.—*adj.* **dai′sied.**

Da-kar (dȧ-kär′), a seaport near Cape Verde, capital of French West Africa (map **14**).

Da-ko-ta (dȧ-kō′tȧ), a former territory of the U.S., which in 1889 was made into the States of North Dakota and South Dakota (map **7**).

DAISY

dale (dāl), *n.* a valley; glen; as, they went up hill and down *dale.*

Dal-las (dăl′ȧs), a city in northeastern Texas (map **8**).

dalles (dălz), *n.pl.* in northwestern U.S. and Canada, rapids, especially in a gorge.

dal-li-ance (dăl′ĭ-ăns), *n.* the act of trifling, loitering, or playing.

dal-ly (dăl′ĭ), *v.i.* [dallied, dally-ing], **1,** to make sport; play; trifle, as with affections or an idea; **2,** to waste time; loiter; as, he *dallied* over his work.

Dal-ma-tia (dăl-mā′shȧ), a province of Yugoslavia, on the Adriatic Sea.—*n.* and *adj.* **Dal-ma′tian.**

¹**dam** (dăm), *n.* **1,** a bank or wall built so as to hold back a flow of water; **2,** water so held back:—*v.t.* [dammed, dam-ming], **1,** to provide (a stream) with a dam; as, to *dam* a river or a brook; **2,** to obstruct; restrain; confine.

²**dam** (dăm), *n.* a mother: generally used of certain animals, as sheep.

dam-age (dăm′ĭj), *n.* **1,** injury or harm; as, the flood did *damage* to the town; **2,** dam-

ages, money paid to one for injury or loss through the fault of another; as, the streetcar company paid him *damages:*—*v.t.* [damaged, damag-ing], to injure.

Da-mas-cus (dȧ-măs′kŭs), an ancient city, capital of Syria (maps **1, 15**).

dam-ask (dăm′ȧsk), *n.* **1,** a figured fabric of silk, linen, wool, or other material, used especially for tablecloths: so named from the city of Damascus, where it was originally made; **2,** hard, elastic steel decorated with wavy lines, and formerly used for sword blades; **3,** a deep-pink color:—*adj.* **1,** pertaining to or coming from Damascus; **2,** made of damask; as, a *damask* tablecloth; **3,** of a deep-pink color.

dame (dām), *n.* **1,** formerly, a lady of high rank; **2,** a title used instead of Mistress or Madam; **3,** a matron; an elderly woman.

damn (dăm), *v.t.* [damned (dămd), damning (dăm′nĭng; often dăm′nĭng, except in sense 3)], **1,** to condemn; **2,** to doom to eternal punishment; **3,** to curse; call down a curse upon; **4,** to judge as bad, faulty, or as a failure; as, the critics *damned* the book.—*adj.* **dam′na-tor′y.**

dam-na-ble (dăm′nȧ-bl), *adj.* deserving to be condemned; detestable; as, a *damnable* lie.—*adv.* **dam′na-bly.**

dam-na-tion (dăm-nā′shŭn), *n.* condemnation, especially to eternal punishment; also, eternal punishment.

damned (dămd; *Poetic*, dăm′nĕd), *adj.* **1,** condemned to eternal punishment; **2,** condemned as bad or as a failure; **3,** cursed: used as an oath.

Dam-o-cles (dăm′ō-klēz), a flatterer of a ruler of ancient Syracuse, whose lord caused him to sit at a feast under a sword hung by a single hair.

Da-mon (dā′mŏn), the friend of Pythias. When the latter, condemned to death, asked permission to go home and arrange his affairs, Damon offered his own life as pledge for the return of his friend.

dam-o-zel (dăm′ō-zĕl), *n. Poetic*, a young unmarried woman; damsel. See **damsel.**

damp (dămp), *n.* **1,** moisture; fog; **2,** a poisonous gas sometimes found in coal mines; **3,** depression of spirits:—*adj.* moist; a little wet; as, a *damp* cloth:—*v.t.* **1,** to moisten; **2,** to discourage; depress; **3,** to check; stifle.—*adv.* **damp′ly.**—*n.* **damp′ness.**
Syn., *adj.* moist, dank, wet.

damp-en (dămp′ĕn), *v.t.* **1,** to make moist or wet; **2,** to depress or discourage.

damp-er (dămp′ẽr), *n.* **1,** something which depresses or discourages; as, to put a *damper* on fun; **2,** a movable plate to regulate a draft, as in a stove.

go; join; yet; sing; chin; show; thin, *th*en; hw, *wh*y; zh, azure; ü, Ger. für or Fr. lune; ö, Ger. schön or Fr. feu; ṅ, Fr. enfant, nom; kh, Ger. ach or ich. See pages ix–x.

dam·sel (dăm′zĕl), *n.* a maiden; a girl; a young unmarried woman. Also, *Poetic*, **dam′o·zel** (dăm′ō-zĕl).

dam·son (dăm′zŭn), *n.* a small purple plum, originally from Damascus, or the tree that bears it: also called *damson plum.*

dance (dáns), *v.i.* [danced, danc·ing], **1**, to move the body and feet rhythmically in time to music; **2**, to skip about lightly; as, the child *danced* in glee; sunbeams *dance* in the room:—*v.t.* **1**, to give a dancing motion to; as, to *dance* the baby up and down; **2**, to perform; as, to *dance* a jig:—*n.* **1**, a rhythmical movement of the body and feet, usually to the accompaniment of music; **2**, a dancing party, less formal than a ball; **3**, one round of dancing at such a party; as, may I have this *dance?* **4**, a piece of music for dancing; as, the orchestra played a new *dance.*—*n.* **danc′er**. —*n.* **danc′ing**.

dan·de·li·on (dăn′dē-lī′ŭn), *n.* a common plant having yellow flowers and coarsely toothed leaves; also, its flower.

dan·der (dăn′dĕr), *n. Colloquial*, anger; indignation; as, his *dander* is up.

dan·dle (dăn′dl), *v.t.* [dan·dled, dan·dling], **1**, to dance (an infant) up and down, as on the knee; **2**, to fondle.

DANDELION

dan·druff (dăn′drŭf), *n.* minute scales of dead skin that form on the scalp.—*adj.* **dan′druff·y**.

dan·dy (dăn′dĭ), *n.* [*pl.* dandies], **1**, a man who gives much attention to dress; **2**, *Colloquial*, something unusually fine:—*adj.* [dan-di-er, dan-di-est], *Colloquial*, excellent.

Dane (dān), *n.* a native or inhabitant of Denmark; also, a person of Danish descent.

dan·ger (dān′jĕr), *n.* **1**, peril; exposure to loss, injury, or death; risk; as, the *danger* of an explosion was very grave; **2**, something which may cause loss, injury, etc.

dan·ger·ous (dān′jĕr-ŭs), *adj.* **1**, unsafe; perilous; as, a *dangerous* road; **2**, likely to do harm; as, a *dangerous* criminal.—*adv.* **dan′ger·ous·ly**.

dan·gle (dăng′gl), *v.i.* [dan·gled, dan·gling], **1**, to hang or swing loosely; **2**, to hang about anyone; as, flatterers *dangle* about a king:—*v.t.* to cause to swing loosely; as, he *dangled* the bag.

Dan·iel (dăn′yĕl), **1**, in the Bible, a Hebrew prophet who was a captive at Babylon; **2**, the book of the Old Testament which contains his history and prophecies.

Dan·ish (dān′ĭsh), *n.* the language of the Danes:—*adj.* having to do with Denmark, the Danes, or their language.

Dan·ish West In·dies (ĭn′dĭz), the former name of the *Virgin Islands of the U.S.* See **Virgin Islands**.

dank (dăngk), *adj.* unpleasantly damp; moist; wet; as, *dank* seaweed.

Dan·te A·li·ghie·ri (dăn′tĕ; dän′tā ä/lĕ-gyâ′rē), (1265–1321), an Italian poet, author of "The Divine Comedy."

Dan·ube (dăn′ūb), a river in Europe flowing eastward to the Black Sea (map 12).

Dan·zig (dän′tsĭkh), an ancient Baltic seaport, ruled at different times by several countries; a free city, 1920–1939; part of Poland since 1945: Polish name, *Gdańsk* (map 12).

Daph·ne (dăf′nē), *n.* in Greek mythology, a nymph who in escaping from Apollo was changed into a laurel tree.

dap·per (dăp′ĕr), *adj.* **1**, small and active; **2**, trim and neat in appearance.

dap·ple (dăp′l), *adj.* spotted; as, a *dapple*-gray horse:—*n.* a spotted animal, especially a horse:—*v.t.* [dap-pled, dap-pling], to decorate with spots.—*adj.* **dap′pled**.

D.A.R. abbreviation for *Daughters of the American Revolution.*

Dar·da·nelles (där′dȧ-nĕlz′), a channel between the Marmara and Aegean seas (map 12): formerly called the *Hellespont.*

dare (dâr), *v.i.* [*p.t.* dared (dârd) or durst (dûrst), *p.p.* dared, *p.pr.* dar-ing], to have courage; be bold enough; venture; as, I do not *dare* to enter:—*v.t.* **1**, to have courage for; brave; as, to *dare* the perils of arctic travel; **2**, to challenge; as, he *dared* me to jump:—*n.* a challenge.

dare·dev·il (dâr′dĕv′l), *adj.* bold; reckless:—*n.* a reckless, bold person.

Dar·i·en (dâr′ĭ-ĕn′; dâr′ĭ-ĕn), the former name of a region in Central America now included in Panama.

dar·ing (dâr′ĭng), *n.* bravery; boldness:— *adj.* fearless; bold; venturous.

Da·ri·us I (dȧ-rī′ŭs), (558?–486? B.C.), a king of Persia.

dark (därk), *adj.* **1**, having little or no light; **2**, of colors, nearer black than white; **3**, of a brunet complexion; **4**, gloomy; as, a *dark* mood; **5**, secret; mysterious; as, a *dark* saying; **6**, evil; as, a *dark* deed:— *n.* **1**, darkness; nightfall; **2**, secrecy; as, to work in the *dark;* **3**, ignorance; as, I am in the *dark* on the subject.—*adv.* **dark′ly**.—*n.* **dark′ness**.

dark·en (där′kĕn), *v.t.* to make dark or

 āte, âorta, râre, căt, ȧsk, fär, ăllow, sofȧ; ēve, êvent, ĕll, writĕr, novĕl; bīte, pĭn; nō, ōbey, ôr, dŏg, tŏp, cŏllide; ūnit, ūnite, bûrn, cŭt, focŭs; nōon, fŏŏt; mound; coin;

gloomy; obscure; as, they *darkened* the room:—*v.i.* to become dark or gloomy.

dark-ling (därk′lĭng), *adj.* dimly seen.

dark-room (därk′rōōm′), *n.* a room which has been darkened, or protected from rays, for developing photographic plates.

dark-some (därk′sŭm), *adj. Poetic*, dark; gloomy; hence, wicked; mysterious.

dar-ling (där′lĭng), *n.* one dearly loved: —*adj.* tenderly loved; very dear.

Dar-ling Riv-er (där′lĭng), a river, 1,900 miles long, in New South Wales, Australia (map 16).

darn (därn), *v.t.* to mend, as a hole in a fabric, by interweaving thread or yarn:— *n.* the place so mended.—*n.* **darn′ing.**

dar-nel (där′nĕl), *n.* a common weed of the grass family, found especially in grain fields, growing from one to three feet high, and having prickly green flowers.

darn-ing nee-dle, 1, a long, strong needle used in darning; 2, a dragonfly.

dart (därt), *n.* 1, a thin, pointed weapon, thrown by hand; 2, a swift, sudden movement:—*v.t.* to throw out suddenly; as, to *dart* angry glances:—*v.i.* to move swiftly; as, the child *darted* here and there.

Dar-win (där′wĭn), Charles Robert (1809–1882), an English naturalist.

dash (dăsh), *v.t.* 1, to throw violently or hastily; as, he *dashed* the vase to pieces; 2, to push aside; 3, to spatter; to splash; as, they *dashed* him with water; 4, to ruin; destroy; as, you *dash* my hopes; 5, to do hastily; as, to *dash* off a letter:— *v.i.* 1, to rush with violence; as, he *dashed* madly away; 2, to strike on a surface violently; as, rain *dashed* against the window:—*n.* 1, a violent blow; 2, a little bit; as, a *dash* of pepper; 3, spirit; energy; as, with vim and *dash*; 4, *Colloquial*, a vulgar display; as, to cut a *dash* with fine clothes; 5, a sign [—] used in writing or printing to mark a pause or break; 6, the striking of a liquid against a surface; 7, a sudden rush; as, a *dash* for freedom; 8, a short race; as, a hundred-yard *dash*.

dash-er (dăsh′ẽr), *n.* 1, one who or that which dashes; 2, the part of an ice-cream freezer, etc., which stirs or churns a liquid (see illustration under *churn*).

dash-ing (dăsh′ĭng), *adj.* 1, spirited; bold; as, a *dashing* soldier; 2, showy; gay.

das-tard (dăs′tẽrd), *n.* a base coward:— *adj.* mean; cowardly.

das-tard-ly (dăs′tẽrd-lĭ), *adj.* cowardly.

da-ta (dā′tà; dä′tà), *n.pl.* [*sing.* datum (dā′tŭm; dä′tŭm)], a collection of facts to be used as a basis for study; as, the *data* are not sufficient.

¹**date** (dāt), *n.* 1, the point of time at which something takes place or is done; as, the *date* of his death; 2, the period or era to which anything belongs; as, art of an early *date*; 3, *Colloquial*, an engagement for a fixed time:—*v.t.* [dat-ed, dat-ing], 1, to mark with a definite time; 2, to find the definite time of:—*v.i.* to belong to a certain time; as, this house *dates* from Revolutionary days.

²**date** (dāt), *n.* the edible fruit of the date palm tree, oblong in shape and enclosing a single seed.

date-less (dāt′lĕs), *adj.* 1, not dated; 2, endless; 3, of interest for all times; as, a *dateless* poem.

da-tive (dā′tĭv), *adj.* naming, as in Latin grammar, the case of the indirect object, similar to the case of the indirect object in English:—*n.* the dative case; also, a word in the dative case, as "him" in the sentence "show him your work."

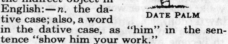

DATE PALM

da-tum (dā′tŭm; dä′tŭm), *n.* [*pl.* data (dā′tà; dä′tà)], something assumed, known, or granted as a basis for study or discussion.

dau. abbreviation for *daughter*.

daub (dôb), *v.t.* 1, to cover or smear with mud, plaster, or the like; 2, to paint coarsely or unskilfully:—*v.i.* 1, to put on plaster, mud, or the like; 2, to paint poor pictures:—*n.* 1, a smear; smudge; 2, a picture poorly painted.—*n.* **daub′er.**

Dau-det (dō′dâ′), Alphonse (1840–1897), a French novelist and writer.

daugh-ter (dô′tẽr), *n.* 1, a female child; 2, a female member of a race, church, or the like; as, a *daughter* of France.

daugh-ter—in—law (dô′tẽr-ĭn-lô′), *n.* [*pl.* daughters—in-law], a son's wife.

daunt (dônt; dänt), *v.t.* to frighten; dishearten; dismay.

daunt-less (dônt′lĕs; dänt′lĕs), *adj.* fearless; intrepid.

dau-phin (dô′fĭn), *n.* formerly, the title of the oldest son of the king of France.

DAVENPORT

dav-en-port (dăv′ĕn-pôrt), *n.* a long upholstered sofa with back and arms; especially, one that can be converted, or changed, into a bed.

go; join; yet; sing; chin; show; thin, *th*en; hw, *why*; zh, azure; ü, Ger. *für* or Fr. *lune*, ö, Ger. *schön* or Fr. *feu*; ṅ, Fr. *enfant*, nom; kh, Ger. *ach* or *ich*. See pages ix–x.

Da·vid (dā'vĭd), a king of Israel, who wrote many of the Psalms in the Bible.

Da·vis (dā'vĭs), Jefferson (1808–1889), an American soldier and statesman, president of the Confederate States of America.

dav·it (dăv'ĭt; dā'vĭt), *n.* one of a pair of iron posts with arms for suspending or lowering boats; also, a small crane for hoisting an anchor.

DAVITS
Davits, with life-boat suspended, ready to launch.

Da·vy (dā'vĭ), Sir Humphry (1778-1829), an English chemist who invented the safety lamp for miners.

Davy Jones, the old man of the sea: a superstition of sailors:—**Davy Jones's locker**, the bottom of the sea; that is, the grave of persons drowned at sea.

daw (dô), *n.* a bird of the crow family; a jackdaw.

daw·dle (dô'dl), *v.i.* [daw-dled, daw-dling], to waste time; loiter; as, to *dawdle* on a walk; *dawdle* over work.—*n.* **daw'dler.**

dawn (dôn), *v.i.* **1**, to begin to grow light; as, when day *dawned*, the attack began; **2**, to become evident or plain; as, the solution of the problem finally *dawned* upon me; **3**, to begin to develop; as, with Pasteur, a new era *dawned* in medicine:—*n.* **1**, the first appearance of daylight; **2**, a beginning or unfolding; as, the *dawn* of history.

day (dā), *n.* **1**, the period of light between sunrise and sunset; daylight; **2**, a period of 24 consecutive hours; **3**, an age or period; as, the *day* of chivalry; *days* of old; **4**, the number of hours per day allowed or permitted for work; as, an eight-hour *day*; **5**, a particular 24-hour period connected with some observance; as, a birth*day*; Armistice *Day*.

day·break (dā'brāk'), *n.* the dawn; the time of morning when light appears.

day·dream (dā'drēm'), *n.* an idle fancy; a castle in the air:—*v.i.* to indulge in fanciful waking dreams.

day·light (dā'līt'), *n.* **1**, the light of day; **2**, the time between dawn and dusk; **3**, daybreak; as, he arose at *daylight*:—**daylight-saving time**, time that is reckoned one hour earlier than standard time and which thus gives an extra hour of daylight in the evening; as, when it is eight o'clock in the evening standard time, it is nine o'clock *daylight-saving time*.

day·spring (dā'sprĭng'), *n.* the dawn; daybreak; hence, a beginning.

day·time (dā'tīm'), *n.* the hours during which the sun gives light.

Day·ton (dā'tŭn), a city in Ohio (map 7).

daze (dāz), *v.t.* [dazed, daz-ing], **1**, to confuse; stupefy; as, he was *dazed* by the blow; **2**, to dazzle; as, the display of jewelry *dazed* the spectators:—*n.* a state of confusion or bewilderment.—*adj.* **dazed.**

daz·zle (dăz'l), *v.t.* [daz-zled, daz-zling], **1**, to confuse with a glare of light; **2**, to bewilder or surprise with splendor; as, the richness of her house *dazzled* the guests:—*n.* glitter.—*adv.* **daz'zling-ly.**

D.C. abbreviation for *direct current*, *District of Columbia*.

D.D. abbreviation for *Doctor of Divinity*.

D.D.S. abbreviation for *Doctor of Dental Surgery*.

DDT, abbreviation for *dichloro-diphenyl-trichloro-ethane*, a powerful insecticide.

de- (dē-), a prefix meaning: **1**, down; as, *depend*, *depress*; **2**, off or away; as, *detract*, *deport*; **3**, entirely: used to intensify the meaning of the word; as, *derelict*, *determine*; **4**, depriving; reversing; as, *decapitate*, *demoralize*.

dea·con (dē'kŭn), *n.* a subordinate church official who assists in certain ceremonies, in caring for the poor, etc. In the Roman Catholic and Protestant Episcopal churches, he is ordained, and ranks just below a priest; in other churches, he is a layman elected to assist the minister.

dead (dĕd), *adj.* **1**, having ceased to live; as, a *dead* man; *dead* wood; **2**, without life; inanimate; as, *dead* matter; **3**, inactive; showing no force, motion, liveliness, or the like; as, a *dead* electric wire; a *dead* tennis ball; **4**, disused; as, a *dead* language; **5**, complete; utter; as, a *dead* loss:—*n.* **1**, one who has died; those who have died; as, the quick and the *dead*; **2**, the time of greatest inactivity or quietness; as, the *dead* of night:—*adv.* **1**, entirely; as, he is *dead* right; **2**, exactly; due; as, *dead* east.

dead letter, **1**, an unclaimed letter that for some reason cannot be delivered; **2**, a belief, custom, or the like, which has died out; especially, a law that is not enforced; **dead reckoning**, the method of reckoning the position of a ship at sea by computing from log and compass the distance and direction traveled.

dead·en (dĕd'n), *v.t.* to deprive of force; lessen; as, medicine to *deaden* pain.

dead·eye (dĕd'ī'), *n.* on ships, a rounded, flat wooden block pierced with holes to receive ropes. (See *shroud*, illustration.)

dead·lock (dĕd'lŏk'), *n.* a standstill; the state of a contest when two opposing sides are so evenly balanced in strength or power that neither will give in and no progress can be made.—*adj.* **dead'locked'.**

āte, âorta, râre, căt, ȧsk, fär, ȧllow, sofȧ; ēve, ĕvent, ĕll, writẽr, novĕl; bīte, pĭn; nō, ōbey, ôr, dŏg, tŏp, cŏllide; ūnit, ûnite, bûrn, cŭt, focŭs; no͞on, fŏŏt; mound; coin;

dead-ly (dĕd'lĭ), *adj.* [dead-li-er, dead-li-est], 1, causing death; fatal; as, Asiatic cholera is a *deadly* disease; 2, relentless; as, a *deadly* enemy; 3, resembling death; as, a *deadly* pallor: —*adv.* 1, like death; as, *deadly* still; 2, *Colloquial*, extremely; as, *deadly* dull reading.

Dead Sea, a salt lake in Palestine, 49 miles long, the lowest body of water on earth, 1,292 feet below the level of the Mediterranean Sea.

deaf (dĕf), *adj.* 1, unable to hear; unable to hear clearly; 2, unwilling to listen; as, *deaf* to persuasion.—*n.* **deaf'ness.**

deaf-en (dĕf'ĕn), *v.t.* to make deaf; stun with noise.—*adj.* **deaf'en-ing.**

deaf-mute (dĕf'₌mūt'), *n.* a person who is deaf and dumb.

¹deal (dēl), *n.* 1, a part; portion; an amount; as, a great *deal* of money; 2, in card games, a distribution of cards to the players; also, a player's turn to distribute the cards; as, it's my *deal;* 3, any distribution or redistribution; as, a new *deal;* 4, a bargain or agreement; also, the result of such an agreement; as, to make a *deal;* to get a square *deal:*—*v.t.* [dealt (dĕlt), deal-ing], 1, to distribute (cards); 2, to deliver; inflict; as, to *deal* a blow:—*v.i.* 1, to buy and sell; trade; as, to *deal* in furs; 2, to behave; as, he *dealt* honorably by his ward; 3, to be concerned; as, the lesson *dealt* with fractions.

²deal (dēl), *n.* fir or pine wood cut into boards of a certain size; also, one of these boards:—*adj.* made of such wood.

deal-er (dē'lẽr), *n.* 1, a person who buys and sells goods; 2, in a card game, the person who has the deal.

deal-ing (dē'lĭng), *n.* 1, conduct towards others; 2, **dealings**, business methods; as, honest *dealings;* also, connections; relations; as, *dealings* with a neighboring country.

dealt (dĕlt), past tense and past participle of *deal.*

dean (dēn), *n.* 1, the head of a group of clergy connected with a cathedral; 2, the member of a college faculty who has charge of the students; 3, the administrative officer of a college or university next below the president; 4, the oldest member, in years of service, among men of similar calling; as, *dean* of the diplomatic corps.

dean-er-y (dē'nẽr-ĭ), *n.* [*pl.* deaneries], 1, the position of a dean or the extent of his authority; 2, the residence of a dean.

dear (dĭr), *adj.* 1, highly esteemed; beloved; often, as in letters, merely a polite form of address; 2, costly; also, charging high prices; as, that is a very *dear* shop; 3, heartfelt; earnest; as, his *dearest* ambition:—*n.* a darling; loved one:—*adv.* at a high price:—*interj.* expressing surprise, pity, or the like.—*adv.* **dear'ly.**

dear-ness (dĭr'nĕs), *n.* 1, lovableness; 2, costliness; as, the *dearness* of food.

dearth (dûrth), *n.* want; lack; scarcity; as, a *dearth* of coal during a strike.

death (dĕth), *n.* 1, the end of life; also, the act of dying; 2, total loss; end; as, the *death* of his hopes; 3, that which causes death; as, his disgrace was the *death* of his father:—**Death**, the destroyer of life; usually represented as a skeleton with a scythe.

death cup, a common, poisonous mushroom; **death rate**, the number of deaths in a given area or group within a given period of time, usually stated as the deaths per thousand of the population.

Syn. departure, decease, extinction.

death-bed (dĕth'bĕd'), *n.* 1, the bed in which a person dies; 2, the last hours of a person's life.

death-less (dĕth'lĕs), *adj.* never ending; never dying; as, *deathless* fame.

death-like (dĕth'līk'), *adj.* like death; deathly; as, a *deathlike* pallor.

death-ly (dĕth'lĭ), *adj.* [death-li-er, death-li-est], 1, fatal; deadly; 2, like death; as, a *deathly* stillness:—*adv.* to a degree like death; as, *deathly* pale.

death's-head (dĕths'₌hĕd'), *n.* a human skull as a symbol of death.

Death Val-ley, a valley in the desert in southeastern California, more than 200 feet below sea level (map 9).

de-bar (dē-bär'), *v.t.* [debarred, debar-ring], to shut out; exclude; as, he was *debarred* from taking the test.

de-bark (dē-bärk'), *v.i.* to go ashore from a vessel:—*v.t.* to remove from a vessel; as, to *debark* troops.—*n.* **de'bar-ka'tion.**

de-base (dē-bās'), *v.t.* [debased, debas-ing], to lower in value, quality, purity, etc.; as, to *debase* the coinage.—*n.* **de-base'ment.**

de-bat-a-ble (dē-bā'tà-bl), *adj.* open to question or debate; not finally settled.

de-bate (dē-bāt'), *v.t.* [debat-ed, debat-ing], to discuss by presenting arguments for and against; as, he *debated* whether or not to go:—*v.i.* to argue or discuss a point:—*n.* 1, an argument; discussion; 2, a formal presentation of arguments on both sides of a question by speakers before an audience.

de-bat-er (dē-bā'tẽr), *n.* a person who takes part in a discussion or debate.

de-bauch (dē-bôch'), *v.t.* to corrupt or seduce (a person):—*n.* an orgy; excessive indulgence in sensual pleasures.

de-bauch-er-y (dē-bô'chẽr-ĭ), *n.* [*pl.* debaucheries], excessive indulgence in sensual pleasures; gluttony; drunkenness.

de-bil-i-tate (dē-bĭl′ĭ-tāt), *v.t.* [debilitated, debilitat-ing], to weaken; as, a bad cold *debilitates* one's health.

de-bil-i-ty (dē-bĭl′ĭ-tĭ), *n.* [*pl.* debilities], a weakness; lack of energy or strength.

deb-it (dĕb′ĭt), *n.* 1, an entry in an account of something due; 2, the left-hand, or debtor, side of an account: opposite of *credit:—v.t.* to charge (a sum due); enter a charge against (a person or an account).

deb-o-nair or **deb-o-naire** (dĕb′ō-nâr′), *adj.* affable; genial; gay and carefree.

de-bris (dĕ-brē′; dĕb′rē) or **dé-bris** (dā-brē′; dā′brē; dĕb′rē), *n.* 1, scattered fragments; rubbish; as, the yard was littered with paper and *debris;* 2, piles of loose rock, as at the base of a mountain.

debt (dĕt), *n.* 1, that which one person owes to another; an amount owed; as, my *debts* total $100; for your kindness to my mother, I owe you a *debt* of gratitude; 2, the state of owing money, especially more than one can pay; as, to be in *debt;* 3, *Archaic,* sin; as, "Forgive us our *debts.*"

debt-or (dĕt′ẽr), *n.* a person who owes money; also, one who is under obligation to another: opposite of *creditor.*

de-but (dā-bū′; dĕ-bū′; dā′bū; dĕb′ū), *n.* 1, the first formal appearance of a girl in society; 2, a first attempt or appearance on the stage, in business, or the like.

deb-u-tante (dĕb′ū-tänt′), *n.* a young woman who is making, or has recently made, her debut, or first appearance, in society.

Dec. abbreviation for *December.*

dec. abbreviation for *deceased.*

dec-a- (dĕk′à-) or **dec-** (dĕk-), a prefix meaning ten; as, *deca*log, *deca*thlon.

dec-ade (dĕk′ād; dē-kād′), *n.* 1, a group of ten; 2, a period of ten consecutive years; as, the census is taken every *decade.*

de-ca-dence (dē-kā′dĕns; dĕk′à-dĕns), *n.* decay, as in morals, character, or quality.

de-ca-dent (dē-kā′dĕnt; dĕk′à-dĕnt), *adj.* decaying or degenerating from a moral, intellectual, or artistic point of view; as, a *decadent* civilization.

dec-a-gon (dĕk′à-gŏn), *n.* a plane figure having ten sides and ten angles.

dec-a-he-dron (dĕk′-à-hē′drŏn), *n.* [*pl.* decahedrons or decahedra (dĕk′à-hē′drà)], a geometrical solid having ten faces.

DECAGON

Dec-a-log or **Dec-a-logue** (dĕk′à-lŏg), *n.* the Ten Commandments given by God to Moses (Exodus 20 : 3–17).

de-camp (dē-kămp′), *v.i.* 1, to break up camp, as an army; 2, to steal away; depart suddenly; as, the treasurer *decamped* with the funds.—*n.* **de-camp′ment.**

de-cant (dē-kănt′), *v.t.* 1, to pour (a solution) off slowly without disturbing the sediment at the bottom; 2, to pour (wine) carefully from a bottle into a decanter.

de-cant-er (dē-kăn′tẽr), *n.* an ornamental glass bottle, with a stopper, used for wine or liquor.

de-cap-i-tate (dē-kăp′ĭ-tāt), *v.t.* [decapitat-ed, decapitat-ing], to cut off the head of; behead.

de-cath-lon (dē-kăth′lŏn), *n.* an athletic contest consisting of ten separate events, in all of which all of the contestants take part.

DECANTER

De-ca-tur (dē-kā′tẽr), Stephen (1779–1820), a commander in the American navy.

de-cay (dē-kā′), *v.i.* 1, to decline from a condition of soundness or health; fail; as, business, beauty, or civilization may *decay;* 2, to rot:—*n.* 1, decline; gradual failure; 2, rot; decomposition; as, I cut out the *decay* and ate the rest of the apple.

de-cease (dē-sēs′), *v.i.* [deceased, deceasing], to die:—*n.* death.

de-ceased (dē-sēst′), *adj.* dead; especially, recently dead:—**the deceased,** the dead person.

de-ce-dent (dē-sē′dĕnt), *n.* in law, one who has died; as, the *decedent* left no will.

de-ceit (dē-sēt′), *n.* 1, the habit or practice of misleading or cheating; as, he justified *deceit* as a means to an end; 2, an instance of misleading; a trick.

Syn. delusion, guile, treachery, sham.

de-ceit-ful (dē-sēt′fŏol), *adj.* given to fraud and trickery; insincere; false.—*adv.* **de-ceit′ful-ly.**—*n.* **de-ceit′ful-ness.**

Syn. misleading, fallacious, fraudulent.

de-ceive (dē-sēv′), *v.t.* [deceived, deceiving], 1, to cause (one) to believe what is untrue; as, do not *deceive* me, tell me the truth; 2, to mislead; as, I was *deceived* by his look of strength.—*n.* **de-ceiv′er.**

Syn. overreach, gull, dupe, cheat.

De-cem-ber (dē-sĕm′bẽr), *n.* the twelfth and last month of the year, containing 31 days.

de-cen-cy (dē′sĕn-sĭ), *n.* [*pl.* decencies], 1, propriety in speech, actions, or dress; decorum; 2, **decencies,** the requirements of a respectable or decent life, such as common courtesy, cleanliness, etc.

āte, āorta, râre, căt, ásk, fär, ăllow, sofà; ēve, ĕvent, ĕll, writẽr, novĕl; bīte, pĭn; nō, ōbey, ôr, dŏg, tŏp, cŏllide; ūnit, ūnite, bûrn, cŭt, focŭs; nōon, fŏot; mound; coin;

de-cen-ni-al (dē-sĕn′ĭ-ăl), *adj.* **1,** consisting of ten years; **2,** occurring every ten years:—*n.* a tenth anniversary.

de-cent (dē′sĕnt), *adj.* **1,** becoming; suitable; proper; as, *decent* behavior; *decent* clothes; **2,** respectable; as, he comes from a *decent* home; **3,** passable; good enough; as, a *decent* living.—*adv.* **de′cent-ly.**

de-cen-tral-ize (dē-sĕn′trăl-īz), *v.t.* [decentralized, decentraliz-ing], to transfer from a central point to outlying points; especially, to give (governmental authority) to communities or states.

de-cep-tion (dē-sĕp′shŭn), *n.* **1,** the act of tricking or cheating; as, *deception* aided his escape; **2,** a piece of trickery; fraud.

de-cep-tive (dē-sĕp′tĭv), *adj.* tending to deceive or mislead; as, appearances are often *deceptive*.—*adv.* **de-cep′tive-ly.**

dec-i- (dĕs′ĭ-), a prefix meaning ten or tenth; as, *deci*mate, *deci*mal.

de-cide (dē-sīd′), *v.t.* [decid-ed, decid-ing], **1,** to settle; bring to a conclusion; as, he *decided* the matter without delay; **2,** to cause to make a decision; as, that trait *decides* me in his favor:—*v.i.* **1,** to make up one's mind; as, I have *decided* to leave early; **2,** to give a judgment or decision.

de-cid-ed (dē-sīd′ĕd), *adj.* **1,** definite; clear; as, *decided* opinions; **2,** determined; resolute; as, a very *decided* person.

de-cid-ed-ly (dē-sīd′ĕd-lĭ), *adv.* definitely; certainly; as, she is *decidedly* pretty.

de-cid-u-ous (dē-sĭd′ū-ŭs), *adj.* **1,** losing foliage every year; not evergreen; as, the oak is a *deciduous* tree; **2,** shed, or falling, at certain seasons; as, *deciduous* leaves.

dec-i-mal (dĕs′ĭ-măl), *adj.* based upon the number ten; as, the *decimal* system:—**decimal fraction,** a fraction having as its denominator ten or some power of ten, usually written as a number preceded by a dot, called the *decimal point*, as .7 = 7/10, .07 = 7/100:—*n.* a decimal fraction.

dec-i-mate (dĕs′ĭ-māt), *v.t.* [decimat-ed, decimat-ing], to destroy one tenth of; more commonly, to destroy a large part of; as, the earthquake *decimated* the population.

de-ci-pher (dē-sī′fẽr), *v.t.* to make out the meaning of; to translate (especially something written in secret characters); as, to *decipher* a code message.

de-ci-sion (dē-sĭzh′ŭn), *n.* **1,** the act of reaching a fixed opinion; also, the opinion or judgment reached; as, he is quick in making *decisions*; **2,** firmness; determination; as, he is a man of *decision*.

de-ci-sive (dē-sī′sĭv), *adj.* **1,** final; conclusive; as, a *decisive* victory; **2,** prompt; positive; determined; as, *decisive* action.

¹deck (dĕk), *n.* **1,** a platform serving as a floor in a ship; also, the space between floors; **2,** a pack of playing cards:—*v.t.* to furnish (a ship) with a deck.

²deck (dĕk), *v.t.* to put finery or ornaments on; adorn; array; as, she *decked* herself out in her Sunday clothes.
Syn. decorate, embellish, ornament.

de-claim (dē-klām′), *v.i.* and *v.t.* **1,** to utter (words) in oratorical style; as, he does not speak naturally, he *declaims*; **2,** to recite in public.—*n.* **de-claim′er.**

dec-la-ma-tion (dĕk′lȧ-mā′shŭn), *n.* **1,** a speech delivered in public; **2,** the act or art of reciting; also, a selection to be recited from memory.

de-clam-a-tor-y (dē-klăm′ȧ-tôr′ĭ), *adj.* **1,** pertaining to, or characterized by, formal discourse; **2,** noisy in style; bombastic.

dec-la-ra-tion (dĕk′lȧ-rā′shŭn), *n.* **1,** the act of announcing or proclaiming; as, the *declaration* of a holiday; **2,** that which is affirmed or proclaimed; also, the document embodying the proclamation; as, the *Declaration* of Independence.

de-clar-a-tive (dē-klăr′ȧ-tĭv), *adj.* making a statement or declaration; as, "The sun shone all day" is a *declarative* sentence.

de-clare (dē-klâr′), *v.t.* [declared, declaring], **1,** to make known; tell openly or publicly; proclaim formally; as, the President *declared* a holiday; she *declared* that nothing would persuade her to go; **2,** to affirm solemnly before witnesses; as, the accused man *declared* his innocence; **3,** to make a complete statement of (dutiable goods or the like); as, a traveler, returning to the U.S., must *declare* his purchases:—*v.i.* to make a statement; take sides for or against something; as, the students *declared* for self-government.—*n.* **de-clar′er.**
Syn. announce, publish.

de-clen-sion (dē-klĕn′shŭn), *n.* in grammar, the changes n form of nouns or pronouns, and, in some languages, adjectives, to correspond to their use in the sentence.

dec-li-na-tion (dĕk′lĭ-nā′shŭn), *n.* **1,** a downward slope; **2,** the deviation of the needle of a compass from true north and south; **3,** a refusal.

de-cline (dē-klīn′), *v.i.* [declined, declining], **1,** to slope, bend, or lean downward; **2,** to sink toward the horizon, as the sun or a star; hence, to draw toward a close; as, day *declined*; **3,** to decay; fail; as, his vigor began to *decline*; **4,** to seek a lower level; as, prices have *declined*; **5,** to refuse; as, I *decline* to go:—*v.t.* **1,** to refuse; as, to *decline* an invitation; **2,** to give the declension of; as, to *decline* a noun:—*n.* **1,** a setting; lessening; decay; as, the *decline* of day, of prices, of fame; **2,** a wasting away with disease; as, she went into a *decline*.

de·cliv·i·ty (dē-klĭv′ĭ-tĭ), *n.* [*pl.* declivities], a downward slope.

dé·col·le·té (dā′kô′lĕ-tā′; dā-kŏl′tā), *adj.* **1,** cut low at the neck; as, a *décolleté* dress; **2,** wearing a low-necked dress.

de·com·pose (dē′kŏm-pōz′), *v.t.* [decomposed, decompos-ing], **1,** to separate (something) into parts; as, a prism *decomposes* sunlight; **2,** to rot:—*v.i.* to decay,—*n.* **de′com-po-si′tion** (dē′kŏm-pô-zĭsh′ŭn).

dec·o·rate (dĕk′ô-rāt), *v.t.* [decorat-ed, decorat-ing], **1,** to adorn; as, to *decorate* a stage; **2,** to confer a badge of honor upon; as, the general was *decorated* for bravery.

dec·o·ra·tion (dĕk′ô-rā′shŭn), *n.* **1,** the act of adorning or ornamenting; **2,** an ornament; **3,** a ribbon or medal to be worn as a badge of honor.

Decoration Day, the holiday (in most States, May 30) officially set apart for decorating the graves of those who have fallen in war: correctly called *Memorial Day*.

dec·o·ra·tive (dĕk′ô-rā′tĭv; dĕk′ô-rȧ-tĭv), *adj.* **1,** used as an ornament; as, a *decorative* vase; **2,** helping to adorn; as, *decorative* curtains.—*adv.* **dec′o-ra′tive-ly.**

dec·o·ra·tor (dĕk′ô-rā′tẽr), *n.* one who beautifies; especially, a person whose business it is to plan interior decorations.

dec·o·rous (dĕk′ô-rŭs; dē-kôr′ŭs), *adj.* seemly; fit; proper; as, *decorous* behavior.—*adv.* **dec′o-rous-ly.**
Syn. staid, sedate, demure, suitable.

de·cor·um (dē-kôr′ŭm), *n.* propriety of dress, language, and conduct; seemliness; dignity; as, to act with *decorum*.

de·coy (dē-koi′), *n.* **1,** a deceptive trick or snare; a lure; **2,** a real or imitation bird used to attract live birds within gunshot; **3,** a person used to lead another into a position of danger:—*v.t.* to draw into danger by a trick; entice.

DECOY

de·crease (dē-krēs′; dē′krēs), *v.i.* [decreased, decreas-ing], to grow less; diminish in number, strength, or the like:—*v.t.* to cause to grow less:—*n.* (dē′krēs; dē-krēs′), a gradual lessening or falling off; also, the amount or degree of lessening.

de·cree (dē-krē′), *n.* **1,** an ordinance; law; edict; **2,** in certain courts, the judgment or award of the court; as, a *decree* of di-

vorce:—*v.t.* [decreed, decree-ing], to establish by law; as, to *decree* an amnesty:—*v.i.* to make a decision or law.
Syn., v. dictate, command, order.

de·crep·it (dē-krĕp′ĭt), *adj.* broken down by age or long use; as, a *decrepit* horse.

de·crep·i·tude (dē-krĕp′ĭ-tūd), *n.* the weakness and feebleness of old age.

de·cre·scen·do (dā′krĕ-shĕn′dô; dē′krĕ-sĕn′dô), *adj.* and *adv.* in music, gradually decreasing in volume of sound:—*n.* in music, a passing from loud to soft.

de·cry (dē-krī′), *v.t.* [decried, decry-ing], **1,** to condemn; censure; as, to *decry* modern dances; **2,** to make little of; as, the ignorant may *decry* the value of education.
Syn. belittle, degrade, discredit.

ded·i·cate (dĕd′ĭ-kāt), *v.t.* [dedicat-ed, dedicat-ing], **1,** to set apart by a solemn act or ceremony; as, to *dedicate* a church; **2,** to devote to some work or duty; as, to *dedicate* ourselves to peace; **3,** to address (a book) formally to a patron or friend.
Syn. consecrate, offer, apportion.

ded·i·ca·tion (dĕd′ĭ-kā′shŭn), *n.* **1,** a devoting to a sacred purpose; as, the *dedication* of a church; **2,** an inscription or address to a patron or friend, expressing gratitude or respect, often prefixed to a book.—*adj.* **ded′i-ca-tor′y** (dĕd′ĭ-kȧ-tôr′ĭ).

de·duce (dē-dūs′), *v.t.* [deduced, deducing], to arrive at (a conclusion) by reasoning; infer; as, from your accurate work I *deduce* that you are an industrious student.

de·duct (dē-dŭkt′), *v.t.* to take away; subtract; as, *deduct* a dollar from the bill.

de·duc·tion (dē-dŭk′shŭn), *n.* **1,** subtraction; also, that which is taken away; as, she expected a *deduction* from her pay; **2,** the drawing of conclusions by reasoning from principles generally accepted as true; also, a conclusion thus reached.

deed (dēd), *n.* **1,** that which is done; an act; **2,** a brave action; exploit; as, *deeds* of prowess; **3,** a legal document for the transfer of ownership of real estate:—*v.t.* to convey by deed; as, he *deeded* the land.
Syn., n. action, feat, performance.

deem (dēm), *v.t.* to think; believe; judge; as, I *deem* it wise to call him back.
Syn. estimate, consider, suppose.

deep (dēp), *adj.* **1,** extending far down from the surface; not shallow; as, a *deep* hole; also, extending well back; as, a *deep* lot; **2,** penetrating; thorough; as, *deep* insight; **3,** difficult to understand; as, a *deep* subject; **4,** absorbed; involved; as, *deep* in study; **5,** low in pitch; as, a *deep* voice; **6,** profound; heavy; as, a *deep* sleep; **7,** dark; rich; as, a *deep* red; **8,** heartfelt; as, *deep* sorrow:—**the deep,** the sea:—*adv.* far

---

āte, āorta, râre, căt, ȧsk, fär, ăllow, sofȧ; ēve, ĕvent, ĕll, wrītẽr, novĕl; bīte, pĭn; nō, ōbey, ôr, dôg, tŏp, cŏllide; ūnit, ūnite, bûrn, cŭt, focŭs; nōōn, fŏŏt; mound; coin;

down; far on; in the heart of; as, dig *deep; deep* in the jungle.—*adv.* **deep/ly.**

deep-en (dēp/ĕn), *v.t.* to extend farther down or back; as, to *deepen* a well; to *deepen* a flower border:—*v.i.* 1, to become deeper; as, the water *deepens* offshore; 2, to become darker, as shadows.

deep—root-ed (dēp/-rōōt/ĕd), *adj.* deeply rooted; profound; as, *deep-rooted* hatred.

deep—seat-ed (dēp/-sēt/ĕd), *adj.* well below the surface; as, a *deep-seated* abscess.

deer (dēr), *n.* [*pl.* deer], a swift, graceful, cud-chewing wild animal. The male deer has branching horns, or antlers, which are shed and renewed every year.

deer-skin (dēr/-skĭn/), *n.* 1, the skin of a deer; also, the leather made from it; 2, a garment made of this leather.

def. abbreviation for *defendant, definition.*

DEER (ŏŏ)

de-face (dē-fās/), *v.t.* [defaced, defac-ing], to mar the appearance of; as, to *deface* a book with pencil marks.—*n.* **de-face/ment.**

de-fal-ca-tion (dē/făl-kā/shŭn; dĕf/ăl-kā/shŭn), *n.* 1, the stealing or dishonest use of money by one to whom it was entrusted; 2, the amount of money taken.

def-a-ma-tion (dĕf/à-mā/shŭn), *n.* malicious injuring of the good name of another: called *slander* if spoken, *libel* if written.

de-fam-a-tor-y (dē-făm/à-tôr/ĭ), *adj.* slanderous; libelous.

de-fame (dē-fām/), *v.t.* [defamed, defaming], to injure or destroy the good name of; speak evil of; slander.—*n.* **de-fam/er.** *Syn.* abuse, malign, slander, asperse.

de-fault (dē-fôlt/), *n.* 1, failure to do something required by law; 2, failure to pay one's debts; 3, failure to start or to finish a game or contest:—*v.t.* and *v.i.* 1, to fail to fulfil (a contract, especially a financial contract); 2, to fail to start or to finish; hence, to lose (a contest) through such a failure.—*n.* **de-fault/er.** *Syn., n.* lapse, forfeit, omission, absence, want, neglect, failure.

de-feat (dē-fēt/), *v.t.* 1, to overthrow or vanquish; as, to *defeat* an enemy; 2, to bring to naught; frustrate; as, to *defeat* a purpose:—*n.* 1, failure; as, the *defeat* of a plan or purpose; also, loss of a game or contest; 2, overthrow, as of an army.

def-e-cate (dĕf/ē-kāt), *v.i.* [defecat-ed,

defecat-ing], to throw off impurities; expel waste matter from the intestines.

de-fect (dē-fĕkt/; dē/fĕkt), *n.* 1, a mental or physical imperfection; 2, error; flaw; as, *defects* in writing; *defects* in masonry.

de-fec-tion (dē-fĕk/shŭn), *n.* the act of abandoning a friend, duty, allegiance, or the like; desertion.

de-fec-tive (dē-fĕk/tĭv), *adj.* 1, imperfect; incomplete; faulty; as, *defective* hearing; a *defective* radio tube; 2, mentally deficient:—*n.* a person who is mentally lacking.—*adv.* **de-fec/tive-ly.**

de-fence (dē-fĕns/), *n.* resistance; protection; defense. See **defense.**

de-fend (dē-fĕnd/), *v.t.* 1, to protect from harm or violence; as, to *defend* a child from danger; 2, to maintain or uphold, as one's legal rights, by argument or evidence; to contest, as a suit.—*n.* **de-fend/er.**

de-fend-ant (dē-fĕn/dănt), *n.* a person ordered to answer a charge in a law court.

de-fense or **de-fence** (dē-fĕns/), *n.* 1, resistance to attack; as, to fight in *defense* of one's country; 2, one who or that which protects; a protector; protection; as, a coat is a *defense* against a cold wind; 3, in law, the reply of the defendant to the charge against him.—*adj.* **de-fense/less.** *Syn.* excuse, plea, bulwark, rampart.

de-fen-si-ble (dē-fĕn/sĭ-bl), *adj.* 1, capable of being protected, as a military position; 2, justifiable, as a point of view.

de-fen-sive (dē-fĕn/sĭv), *adj.* 1, designed to guard or protect; as, *defensive* weapons; 2, carried on in self-defense; as, *defensive* warfare:—*n.* the position of one warding off attack; as, she is always on the *defensive.*—*adv.* **de-fen/sive-ly.**

¹**de-fer** (dē-fûr/), *v.t.* [deferred, defer-ring], to put off until later; delay; postpone; as, he *deferred* final action for a week.

²**de-fer** (dē-fûr/), *v.i.* [deferred, defer-ring], to yield; give in; bow (to); as, I *defer* to your judgment.

def-er-ence (dĕf/ĕr-ĕns), *n.* 1, a yielding to the opinions or wishes of another; 2, respect; as, *deference* to the aged.

def-er-en-tial (dĕf/ĕr-ĕn/shăl), *adj.* showing respect; as, a *deferential* bow.

de-fi-ance (dē-fī/ăns), *n.* 1, the act of challenging; a challenge; 2, resistance; scornful opposition to authority.

de-fi-ant (dē-fī/ănt), *adj.* 1, full of resistance; insolently disobedient; as, a *defiant* child; 2, expressing bold opposition; as, a *defiant* speech.—*adv.* **de-fi/ant-ly.**

de-fi-cien-cy (dē-fĭsh/ĕn-sĭ), *n.* [*pl.* deficiencies], the lack or want of something; a defect; a shortage, as of money.

de-fi-cient (dē-fĭsh'ĕnt), *adj.* lacking; incomplete; defective.
   Syn. short, inadequate, scanty.

def-i-cit (dĕf'ĭ-sĭt), *n.* a shortage, especially of money: opposite of *surplus*.

de-fi-er (dē-fī'ẽr), *n.* one who refuses to obey; as, a *defier* of the law.

¹de-file (dē-fīl'), *v.t.* [defiled, defil-ing], 1, to make foul or impure; as, to *defile* a stream with refuse; 2, to bring dishonor upon; as, to *defile* a person's reputation.— *n.* **de-file'ment.**—*n.* **de-fil'er.**
   Syn. soil, pollute, contaminate, violate.

²de-file (dē-fīl'), *v.i.* [defiled, defil-ing], to march off in a line or in files:—*n.* (dē-fīl'; dē'fīl), a long, narrow pass, as between mountains.

de-fine (dē-fīn'), *v.t.* [defined, defin-ing], 1, to state the exact meaning of; as, to *define* words; 2, to fix the limits of; as, to *define* the extent of a tract of land; 3, to prescribe authoritatively; as, the duties of the treasurer were *defined* in the bylaws. —*adj.* **de-fin'a-ble.**—*n.* **de-fin'er.**
   Syn. fix, settle, limit, explain, describe.

def-i-nite (dĕf'ĭ-nĭt), *adj.* 1, precise; exact; as, *definite* instructions; 2, having fixed or distinct limits; as, a *definite* period of time:—**definite article,** the word *the:* so called because it limits the word it modifies. —*adv.* **def'i-nite-ly.**—*n.* **def'i-nite-ness.**

def-i-ni-tion (dĕf'ĭ-nĭsh'ŭn), *n.* 1, the act of explaining; 2, an exact statement of the meaning of a word, term, or phrase.

de-fin-i-tive (dē-fĭn'ĭ-tĭv), *adj.* final; conclusive; as, a *definitive* answer.

de-flate (dē-flāt'), *v.t.* [deflat-ed, deflat-ing], 1, to release air or gas from; as, to *deflate* a tire; 2, to reduce (prices); also, to reduce the amount of (money in circulation).—*n.* **de-fla'tion.**

de-flect (dē-flĕkt'), *v.t.* to cause to turn from a straight line; as, the wall *deflected* the bullet.—*n.* **de-flec'tion.**

De-foe (dē-fō'), Daniel (1661?–1731), an English author and journalist, famous for "Robinson Crusoe."

de-for-est (dē-fŏr'ĕst), *v.t.* to clear of trees.—*n.* **de-for'est-a'tion.**

de-form (dē-fôrm'), *v.t.* 1, to make ugly or unshapely; disfigure; 2, to mar; deface. —*adj.* **de-formed'.**—*n.* **de-for-ma'tion** (dē'-fôr-mā'shŭn; dĕf'ŏr-mā'shŭn).

de-form-i-ty (dē-fôr'mĭ-tĭ), *n.* [*pl.* deformities], 1, something, as a part of the body, which is not of the proper shape; 2, the state of being disfigured or misshapen; as, the boy was made shy by his *deformity*.

de-fraud (dē-frôd'), *v.t.* to cheat or deceive; deprive (one) of a possession, right,

or the like, by trickery or deceit.
   Syn. trick, swindle, dupe.

de-fray (dē-frā'), *v.t.* to pay; settle; as, to *defray* the cost of a trip.—*n.* **de-fray'al.**

de-frost (dē-frôst'), *v.t.* to remove frost from or cause to thaw.—*n.* **de-frost'er.**

deft (dĕft), *adj.* neat and skilful in action; nimble; as, piano playing requires *deft* fingers.—*adv.* **deft'ly.**—*n.* **deft'ness.**
   Syn. clever, adroit, expert.

de-funct (dē-fŭngkt'), *adj.* dead; extinct: —*n.* a dead person; usually, one who died recently; the dead collectively.

de-fy (dē-fī'), *v.t.* [defied, defy-ing], 1, to challenge or dare; as, to *defy* an enemy; 2, to act in contempt of; as, a criminal *defies* the law; 3, to resist successfully; as, the problem *defied* solution.

deg. abbreviation for *degree, degrees.*

de-gen-er-a-cy (dē-jĕn'ẽr-à-sĭ), *n.* 1, the state of being degraded or worse than formerly; 2, lowness of morals; vice.

de-gen-er-ate (dē-jĕn'ẽr-āt), *v.i.* [degen-erat-ed, degenerat-ing], to sink into a worse state; become inferior in goodness or quality:—*adj.* (dē-jĕn'ẽr-ĭt), below the former or typical standard; degraded; as, *degenerate* times; inferior to the true or former type; as, *degenerate* offspring:—*n.* (dē-jĕn'ẽr-ĭt), a degenerate person.

de-gen-er-a-tion (dē-jĕn'ẽr-ā'shŭn), *n.* the state or process of growing worse; degeneracy; decline.

deg-ra-da-tion (dĕg'rà-dā'shŭn), *n.* the act of lowering, or state of being lowered, in rank, morals, or the like; disgrace.
   Syn. humiliation, dishonor, shame.

de-grade (dē-grād'), *v.t.* [degrad-ed, de-grad-ing], 1, to reduce in grade or rank; deprive of honors, office, or dignity; as, to *degrade* a soldier; 2, to lower morally; as, to tell lies *degrades* one.—*adj.* **de-grad'ed.**

de-gree (dē-grē'), *n.* 1, a step or grade in a series; 2, rank in life; as, a person of low *degree;* 3, a stage in progress; 4, a title conferred by a college or university in recognition of work done or of special distinction; 5, a relative amount, extent, quality; as, a good *degree* of skill; 6, a unit for measuring temperature, as on a Fahrenheit or centigrade scale; 7, a unit division on a mathematical or scientific instrument, as a compass; 8, the 360th part of the circumference of a circle; 9, in grammar, one of the three grades in the comparison of an adjective or adverb:

DEGREES, def. 8

āte, āorta, râre, căt, ȧsk, fär, ăllow, sofȧ; ēve, ēvent, ĕll, writẽr, novĕl; bīte, pĭn; nō, ōbey, ôr, dŏg, tŏp, cŏllide; ūnit, ūnite, bûrn, cŭt, focŭs; nōōn, fŏŏt; mound; coin;

as, "good," "better," "best" are the positive, comparative, and superlative *degrees* of "good"; **10**, in music, a line or a space on the staff for notes; also, a tone of a scale:—**by degrees**, gradually.

Syn. rank, order.

de·horn (dē-hôrn′), *v.t.* to remove the horns from; as, to *dehorn* cattle.

de·hy·drate (dē-hī′drāt), *v.t.* to free of water; as, to *dehydrate* foods:—*v.i.* to undergo loss of water.

de·i·fi·ca·tion (dē′ĭ-fĭ-kā′shŭn), *n.* the act of worshiping as a god; as, the *deification* of a king; extravagant worship; as, the *deification* of the dollar.

de·i·fy (dē′ĭ-fī), *v.t.* [deified, deify-ing], to worship as a god; to make into a god; as, the druids *deified* the oak tree.

deign (dān), *v.i.* to condescend; think fit; as, he did not *deign* to heed our request:—*v.t.* to grant; condescend to give.

de·i·ty (dē′ĭ-tĭ), *n.* [*pl.* deities], **1**, a god or goddess; a being worshiped as divine; **2**, the character, nature, or attributes of God:—**the Deity**, God; Jehovah.

de·jec·tion (dē-jĕk′shŭn), *n.* lowness of spirits; melancholy.—*adj.* **de·ject′ed**. *adv.* **de·ject′ed·ly**.

Del. abbreviation for *Delaware*.

Del·a·ware (dĕl′à-wâr), **1**, a Middle Atlantic State (cap. Dover) in the U.S.; **2**, a river flowing between Pennsylvania and New Jersey to Delaware Bay. (Map 6.)

de·lay (dē-lā′), *v.t.* to put off; postpone; hinder for a time; as, illness *delayed* my journey:—*v.i.* to act or proceed slowly:—*n.* a putting off; postponement; wait; as, a *delay* of two hours.

Syn., v. detain, check, retard, defer.

de·lec·ta·tion (dē′lĕk-tā′shŭn), *n.* delight; pleasure.—*adj.* **de·lec′ta·ble**.—*adv.* **de·lec′ta·bly**.

del·e·gate (dĕl′ē-gāt), *n.* one sent to represent, and act for, others; as, the *delegates* to a convention:—*v.t.* (dĕl′ē-gāt), [delegated, delegat-ing], **1**, to send as an agent, with authority to act; as, I *delegate* you to deliver the message; **2**, to entrust, transfer, or commit; as, we *delegate* to Congress the making of our laws.

Syn., n. agent, deputy, substitute.

del·e·ga·tion (dĕl′ē-gā′shŭn), *n.* **1**, the act of authorizing a person or persons to act for others; **2**, a body of persons chosen so to act; a body of representatives.

de·lete (dē-lēt′), *v.t.* [delet-ed, delet-ing], to take out; strike out; erase; as, certain passages were *deleted* by the editor.

del·e·te·ri·ous (dĕl′ē-tē′rĭ-ŭs), *adj.* harmful; injurious.

de·le·tion (dē-lē′shŭn), *n.* erasure; a taking out; as, the *deletion* of a word.

Delft (dĕlft), a manufacturing city in the Netherlands, famous for its pottery.

delft·ware (dĕlft′wâr′), *n.* a kind of glazed earthenware, made first at Delft, in Holland: also called *delft*.

Del·hi (dĕl′ĭ), a city, former capital of British India (map 15).

de·lib·er·ate (dē-lĭb′ēr-āt), *v.t.* [deliberat-ed, deliberat-ing], to reflect on; think upon; consider carefully; as, to *deliberate* a question:—*v.i.* to take counsel with oneself or others; as, to *deliberate* on a plan:—*adj.* (dē-lĭb′ēr-ĭt), **1**, careful; slow; cautious; **2**, slow in determining or acting; **3**, intended; as, a *deliberate* insult.—*adv.* **de·lib′er·ate·ly** (dē-lĭb′ēr-ĭt-lĭ).

Syn., v. meditate, ponder, debate.

de·lib·er·a·tion (dē-lĭb′ēr-ā′shŭn), *n.* **1**, calm and careful thinking; **2**, slowness in thought or action; as, to speak with *deliberation;* **3**, discussion; as, the *deliberation* of a problem.

del·i·ca·cy (dĕl′ĭ-kà-sĭ), *n.* [*pl.* delicacies], **1**, a dainty; a rare or delightful food; **2**, fineness of form or texture; as, the *delicacy* of a spider web; **3**, fineness of skill or touch; as in writing or painting; **4**, sensitiveness; as, *delicacy* of taste.

Syn. nicety, daintiness, tact, modesty.

del·i·cate (dĕl′ĭ-kĭt), *adj.* **1**, pleasing to the taste; as, a *delicate* flavor; **2**, fine; dainty; exquisite in texture; as, *delicate* lace; **3**, of instruments, minutely accurate; as, a *delicate* scale; **4**, sensitive to injury or disease; as, a *delicate* child or plant; **5**, requiring skill or nicety; as, a *delicate* operation; **6**, soft or subdued, as a color; **7**, capable of making fine distinctions; as, a musician has a *delicate* ear; **8**, finely sensitive; as, a *delicate* touch.

Syn. frail, fragile, brittle.

del·i·ca·tes·sen (dĕl′ĭ-kà-tĕs′ĕn), *n.pl.* **1**, prepared foods, as cooked meats, salads, and preserves; table delicacies; **2**, used as *singular*, a place where these are sold.

de·li·cious (dē-lĭsh′ŭs), *adj.* highly pleasing, especially to the taste.—*adv.* **de·li′cious·ly**.—*n.* **de·li′cious·ness**.

Syn. sweet, palatable, luscious.

de·light (dē-līt′), *v.t.* to gratify or please greatly; charm; as, beauty *delights* the eye:—*v.i.* to take great pleasure or enjoyment; as, to *delight* in dancing:—*n.* **1**, an extreme degree of pleasure; high satisfaction; joy; **2**, that which causes pleasure.—*adj.* **de·light′ed**.

Syn., n. enjoyment, happiness, ecstasy, gladness, rapture, bliss.

de·light·ful (dē-līt′fŏŏl), *adj.* giving enjoyment; pleasing; charming.—*adv.* **de-light'ful-ly.**—*n.* **de-light'ful-ness.**

de-lin-e-ate (dē-lĭn'ē-āt), *v.t.* [delineat-ed, delineat-ing], **1,** to mark out with lines; sketch; draw; **2,** to describe minutely and accurately in words; as, an author *delineates* his characters.—*n.* **de-lin'e-a'tor.**
Syn. trace, depict, outline, portray.

de-lin-e-a-tion (dē-lĭn'ē-ā'shŭn), *n.* **1,** the act or art of picturing or describing; **2,** a sketch, description, or the like.

de-lin-quen-cy (dē-lĭng'kwĕn-sĭ), *n.* [*pl.* delinquencies], neglect of, or failure in, duty; a misdeed; fault.

de-lin-quent (dē-lĭng'kwĕnt), *adj.* **1,** failing in duty; **2,** overdue; not paid, as taxes: —*n.* **1,** one who neglects a duty; **2,** a law-breaker; especially, a youthful offender.
Syn., *adj.* guilty, failing, faulty, remiss.

de-lir-i-ous (dē-lĭr'ĭ-ŭs), *adj.* **1,** raving, as from fever; wandering in mind; **2,** wildly excited.—*adv.* **de-lir'i-ous-ly.**
Syn. mad, crazed.

de-lir-i-um (dē-lĭr'ĭ-ŭm), *n.* **1,** a temporary mental disorder, often caused by fever, and marked by wandering speech; **2,** excitement; wild enthusiasm.

de-liv-er (dē-lĭv'ẽr), *v.t.* **1,** to set free; save; **2,** to yield possession or control of, as a property; **3,** to give; transfer; as, to *deliver* a package; **4,** to send forth vigorously; as, to *deliver* a blow; **5,** to utter; as, to *deliver* a speech.—*n.* **de-liv'er-er.**
Syn. liberate, free, rescue.

de-liv-er-ance (dē-lĭv'ẽr-ăns), *n.* **1,** rescue; release; **2,** a publicly stated opinion.

de-liv-er-y (dē-lĭv'ẽr-ĭ), *n.* [*pl.* deliveries], **1,** the act of releasing; a setting free; **2,** a surrender; transfer; **3,** manner of speaking; as, a lecturer's *delivery;* **4,** a giving from one person to another; as, a mail *delivery;* **5,** the act or manner of pitching a ball; **6,** childbirth.

dell (dĕl), *n.* a secluded valley; glen.

Del-phi (dĕl'fī), a town of central Greece, in ancient times famous for its temple and oracle of Apollo (map 1).—*adj.* **Del'phic.**

del-ta (dĕl'tȧ), *n.* [*pl.* deltas], **1,** the fourth letter of the Greek alphabet, about like English *d;* **2,** a fan-shaped deposit of sand or soil at the mouth of a river.

de-lude (dē-lūd'), *v.t.* [delud-ed, delud-ing], to mislead; deceive; as, to *delude* oneself with false hopes.
Syn. dupe, trick, betray.

del-uge (dĕl'ūj), *n.* **1,** a heavy downpour; **2,** anything that overwhelms or floods; as, a *deluge* of protests greeted the new rules: —**the Deluge,** the great flood of the time of Noah (Genesis 7):—*v.t.* [deluged, del-

ug-ing], **1,** to overflow; **2,** to overwhelm; as, they *deluged* him with questions.

de-lu-sion (dē-lū'zhŭn), *n.* **1,** a misleading of the mind; **2,** a false belief.
Syn. illusion, fallacy, misconception.

de-lu-sive (dē-lū'sĭv), *adj.* likely to mislead; deceptive.—*adv.* **de-lu'sive-ly.**

de luxe (dē lŏoks'; dē lŭks'), of unusually fine quality; luxurious.

delve (dĕlv), *v.i.* [delved, delv-ing], **1,** to work with a spade; **2,** to make earnest search for knowledge; as, to *delve* into a subject.

Dem. abbreviation for *Democrat, Democratic.*

dem-a-gog or **dem-a-gogue** (dĕm'ȧ-gŏg), *n.* a political agitator who gains and uses power by appealing to the ignorance or prejudice of the people.

de-mand (dē-mănd'), *v.t.* **1,** to claim as due; exact; as, to *demand* an apology; **2,** to question with authority; as, to *demand* one's name; **3,** to require; have urgent need for; as, the letter *demands* an answer; **4,** in law, to summon:—*n.* **1,** the act of claiming as due; as, a *demand* for payment; **2,** a desire to obtain; call; as, a great *demand* for books; **3,** the state of being sought after.

de-mar-ca-tion (dē'mär-kā'shŭn), *n.* the act of marking out bounds or limits; a line of separation.

[1]**de-mean** (dē-mēn'), *v.t.* to behave; conduct: used with the reflexive pronoun; as, to *demean* oneself properly.

[2]**de-mean** (dē-mēn'), *v.t.* to debase or degrade; as, to be rude is to *demean* oneself.

de-mean-or (dē-mēn'ẽr), *n.* behavior; bearing. In British usage, **de-mean'our.**

de-ment-ed (dē-mĕn'tĕd), *adj.* insane; mad; out of one's mind.

de-mer-it (dē-mĕr'ĭt), *n.* **1,** something that deserves blame; a fault; **2,** a mark for failure or misconduct.

de-mesne (dē-mān'; dē-mēn'), *n.* **1,** the holding of land as one's own; **2,** a landed estate attached to a manor house; **3,** a region or domain.

De-me-ter (dē-mē'tẽr), *n.* in Greek mythology, the goddess of agriculture, fruitfulness, and marriage: the Roman *Ceres.*

dem-i- (dĕm'ĭ-), a prefix meaning: **1,** half; as, *demi*tasse; **2,** less in size or power; as, *demi*-god.

DEMIJOHN

dem-i-god (dĕm'ĭ-gŏd'), *n.* a minor or lesser god; one who is partly divine; a hero.—*n.fem.* **dem'i-god'dess.**

dem-i-john (dĕm'ĭ-jŏn), *n.* a glass or

stoneware bottle with a small neck and large body, usually incased in wickerwork.

de·mise (ᵈě-mīz′), *n.* death.

dem·i·tasse (dĕm′ĭ-tăs′; dĕm′ĭ-täs′), *n.* a small cup of, or for, black coffee.

de·mo·bi·lize (dē-mō′bĭ-līz), *v.t.* [demobilized, demobiliz·ing], to disband or dismiss, as troops; to change (an army or country) from a war footing to a peace footing.—*n.* **de·mo·bi·li·za′tion.**

de·moc·ra·cy (dē-mŏk′rᴀ-sĭ), *n.* [*pl.* democracies], 1, government by the people; government in which the people hold supreme power and delegate it to elected representatives; also, a nation or state so governed; as, the United States is a *democracy;* 2, political or social equality as opposed to inherited rights and privileges.

dem·o·crat (dĕm′ō-krăt), *n.* one who believes in and upholds the principles of popular government or social equality:— **Democrat,** in the U.S., a member of the Democratic party.

dem·o·crat·ic (dĕm′ō-krăt′ĭk), *adj.* 1, pertaining to democracy, or government by the people; 2, ignoring differences of class; friendly; as, a *democratic* spirit makes one loved:—**Democratic party,** one of the great political groups in the U.S.: so named in 1828.—*adv.* **dem′o·crat′i·cal·ly.**

de·mol·ish (dē-mŏl′ĭsh), *v.t.* to pull down; destroy; as, they *demolished* the old house. *Syn.* raze, ruin, overthrow, destroy.

dem·o·li·tion (dĕm′ō-lĭsh′ŭn; dē′mō-lĭsh′ŭn), *n.* the act of tearing down; destruction.

de·mon (dē′mŭn), *n.* 1, an evil spirit; a devil; 2, a very cruel or fierce person.—*adj.* **de·mon′ic.**

de·mo·ni·ac (dē-mō′nĭ-ăk), *n.* one thought to be possessed of an evil spirit:—*adj.* possessed by an evil spirit; devilish. Also, **de′mo·ni′a·cal** (dē′mō-nī′ᴀ-kᴀl).

de·mon·stra·ble (dē-mŏn′strᴀ-bl), *adj.* capable of being shown or proved.

dem·on·strate (dĕm′ŭn-strāt), *v.t.* [demonstrat·ed, demonstrat·ing], 1, to prove beyond a doubt; 2, to teach by examples; illustrate; 3, to show and explain publicly the good points of (an article or product).

dem·on·stra·tion (dĕm′ŭn-strā′shŭn), *n.* 1, the act of showing or proving; 2, a proof beyond any doubt; 3, an outward expression of feeling; as, a kiss is a *demonstration* of affection; 4, a public exhibition; as, a cooking *demonstration;* 5, a show of military force; 6, a show of public interest and sympathy, as by a street meeting or a parade.

de·mon·stra·tive (dē-mŏn′strᴀ-tĭv), *adj.*

1, having the power of showing or proving; 2, in grammar, serving to point out; as, a *demonstrative* pronoun; 3, showing the feelings, especially affection, openly and strongly:—*n.* a pronoun that serves to point out the object to which it refers, as *this, that, these, those.*

dem·on·stra·tor (dĕm′ŭn-strā′tēr), *n.* 1, one who proves, points out, or shows; 2, one who exhibits and explains a mechanical device, as an automobile, an electric stove, etc.

de·mor·al·ize (dē-mŏr′ăl-īz), *v.t.* [demoralized, demoraliz·ing], 1, to corrupt; lower the morals of; as, bad company will *demoralize* anybody; 2, to weaken the courage, spirit, or energy of; throw into confusion; as, loss of their leader *demoralized* the army.—*n.* **de·mor′al·i·za′tion.**

De·mos·the·nes (dē-mŏs′thē-nēz), [384?- 322 B.C.), an Athenian orator.

de·mote (dē-mōt′), *v.t.* [demot·ed, demot·ing], to put in a lower grade; lower in rank, as an officer in the army.

de·mount·a·ble (dē-moun′tᴀ-bl), *adj.* capable of being taken down or removed.

de·mur (dē-mûr′), *v.i.* [demurred, demur·ring], 1, to hesitate; 2, to raise objections; as, he *demurred* at going so far:—*n.* 1, an objection or exception; 2, hesitation.

de·mure (dē-mūr′), *adj.* [demur·er, demur·est], 1, grave; sober; as, a *demure* child; 2, affectedly modest, as in manner. —*adv.* **de·mure′ly.** *Syn.* prim, sedate, coy, decorous.

den (dĕn), *n.* 1, the lair of a wild beast; 2, a cavern; cave; 3, a cozy, private room; 4, a haunt of criminals.

Den. abbreviation for *Denmark.*

de·na·ture (dē-nā′tūr), *v.t.* [denatured, denatur·ing], to change the nature or character of; as, to *denature* alcohol to render it unfit to drink.—*adj.* **de·na′tured.**

de·ni·al (dē-nī′ăl), *n.* 1, refusal to grant; as, *denial* of a request; 2, contradiction; refusal to admit; as, the prisoner's *denial* of his guilt; 3, refusal to acknowledge.

den·im (dĕn′ĭm), *n.* a coarse cotton material used for overalls, hangings, etc.

den·i·zen (dĕn′ĭ-zĕn), *n.* an inhabitant; dweller; occupant: said of people, animals, and plants; as, the polar bear is a *denizen* of the Arctic.

Den·mark (dĕn′märk), a kingdom (cap. Copenhagen), north of Germany, between the North and Baltic seas (map **12**).

de·nom·i·nate (dē-nŏm′ĭ-nāt), *v.t.* [denominat·ed, denominat·ing], to name; call by name:—*adj.* (dē-nŏm′ĭ-nᴀt), having a specified name.

---

go; join; yet; sing; chin; show; thin, *then;* hw, *why;* zh, azure; ü, Ger. für or Fr. lune; ö, Ger. schön or Fr. feu; n̈, Fr. enfant, nom; kh, Ger. ach or ich. See pages **ix–x.**

de-nom-i-na-tion (dē-nŏm/ĭ-nā/shŭn), *n.* **1**, a name; a descriptive title; **2**, a grouping of people or things under one name; as, botany and chemistry come under the *denomination* of science; **3**, a class or division; especially, a religious sect; as, the Methodist *denomination;* **4**, a name for a certain class or unit in a series; as, in the U.S. we have coins of many *denominations*.

de-nom-i-na-tion-al (dē-nŏm/ĭ-nā/shŭn-ăl), *adj.* having to do with a denomination or class, especially a religious sect.

de-nom-i-na-tor (dē-nŏm/ĭ-nā/tẽr), *n.* in arithmetic, the part of a fraction below the line, showing into how many parts the number or unit is to be divided; the divisor.

de-no-ta-tion (dē/nō-tā/shŭn), *n.* **1**, an indication; sign; also, a name; a designation; **2**, meaning; especially, the exact meaning of a word or expression.

de-note (dē-nōt/), *v.t.* [denot-ed, denoting], **1**, to show; indicate; mark out plainly; as, the hands of a clock *denote* the hour; **2**, to be a sign of; mean or signify; as, the song of a robin *denotes* spring.

de-noue-ment (dā-nōō/mäṅ), *n.* the final solution of the plot of a novel or play.

de-nounce (dē-nouns/), *v.t.* [denounced, denounc-ing], to accuse publicly; condemn; as, to *denounce* a cheat.—*n.* **de-nounce/-ment.**

dense (dĕns), *adj.* **1**, thick; heavy; as, a *dense* fog; closely packed together; as, a *dense* crowd; **2**, stupid; dull; as, a *dense* person.—*adv.* **dense/ly.**—*n.* **dense/ness.**

den-si-ty (dĕn/sĭ-tĭ), *n.* [*pl.* densities], **1**, closeness or compactness; as, the *density* of a forest; **2**, the compactness or crowded state of anything measured by the amount of it in a given space; **3**, stupidity.

dent (dĕnt), *n.* a small hollow or depression:—*v.t.* to make a small hollow in:—*v.i.* to receive dents; as, tin *dents* easily.

den-tal (dĕn/tăl), *adj.* **1**, pertaining to the teeth or to dentistry; as, a *dental* clinic; **2**, pronounced by the aid of the teeth; as, *t* and *d* are *dental* letters:—*n.* a dental sound, as *t*, *d*.

den-ti-frice (dĕn/tĭ-frĭs), *n.* a powder, liquid, or paste used for cleaning teeth.

den-tine (dĕn/tēn; dĕn/tĭn) or **den-tin** (dĕn/tĭn), *n.* the hard, dense tissue which forms the main part of a tooth. (See illustration under *tooth.*)—*adj.* **den/ti-nal.**

den-tist (dĕn/tĭst), *n.* one who treats teeth, as by filling or extracting them.

den-tist-ry (dĕn/tĭs-trĭ), *n.* the science or practice of treating or extracting the teeth; dental surgery.

den-ti-tion (dĕn-tĭsh/ŭn), *n.* **1**, the process or period of cutting teeth; **2**, the arrangement of the teeth.

de-nude (dē-nūd/), *v.t.* [denud-ed, denud-ing], to make bare or naked; as, to *denude* a hillside of trees.

de-nun-ci-a-tion (dē-nŭn/sĭ-ā/shŭn; dē-nŭn/shĭ-ā/shŭn), *n.* a public accusation; also, condemnation of anything.

Den-ver (dĕn/vẽr), a city, capital of Colorado (map 9).

de-ny (dē-nī/), *v.t.* [de-nied, deny-ing], **1**, to refuse to believe or admit; contradict; as, I *deny* his statement; **2**, to withhold; refuse to grant; as, to *deny* help; **3**, to disown; as, to *deny* his son.

Syn. gainsay, dispute, oppose, contest.

de-o-dor-ize (dē-ō/dẽr-īz), *v.t.* [deodorized, deodoriz-ing], to deprive of odor, or smell, as by disinfectants.

de-part (dē-pärt/), *v.i.* **1**, to go away; leave; **2**, to vary; change; as, to *depart* from a habit; **3**, to start on a journey.

Syn. quit, retire, withdraw, leave.

de-part-ment (dē-pärt/mĕnt), *n.* **1**, a distinct division or branch of a whole; **2**, a branch of business, study, or science; **3**, a division of government; as, the *Department* of State; **4**, in France, a division of local government:—**department store,** a store selling many kinds of goods, divided into departments, as for clothing, hardware, groceries, etc.—*adj.* **de/part-men/tal.**

de-par-ture (dē-pär/tūr), *n.* **1**, the act of leaving; going away; **2**, a changing from an old plan, method, or standard; as, a new *departure* in medicine.

de-pend (dē-pĕnd/), *v.i.* **1**, to rely for support; as, the old man *depends* on his son; **2**, to be determined by; rest; as, his answer *depends* on his mood; **3**, to trust or rely; as, I *depend* on your word.

de-pend-a-ble (dē-pĕn/dȧ-bl), *adj.* reliable; trustworthy; as, *dependable* news; a *dependable* servant.—*adv.* **de-pend/a-bly.**

Syn. responsible, faithful.

de-pend-ence (dē-pĕn/dĕns), *n.* **1**, the state of being influenced or determined by something; as, *dependence* of daylight on the sun; **2**, reliance; trust; **3**, that on which one relies; **4**, the state of needing aid; as, the *dependence* of a child on its parents.

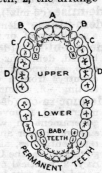

DENTITION

Arrangement of the teeth of a human being. A, incisors; B,B, canines; C,C, bicuspids; D,D, molars.

de·pend·en·cy (dē-pĕn′dĕn-sĭ), *n.* [*pl.* dependencies], **1,** the condition of relying on another; **2,** a country under the control of another country.

de·pend·ent (dē-pĕn′dĕnt), *adj.* **1,** hanging down; **2,** relying on someone or something else for support; **3,** conditioned by something; as, strength is *dependent* on health; **4,** in grammar, subordinate; as, a *dependent* clause:—*n.* one who relies on another for support.

de·pict (dē-pĭkt′), *v.t.* to portray; describe vividly in words.—*n.* **de·pic′tion.**

de·plete (dē-plēt′), *v.t.* [deplet-ed, depleting], to empty; reduce; exhaust; use up; as, illness *depleted* his strength.

de·plor·a·ble (dē-plôr′à-bl), *adj.* **1,** sad; lamentable; grievous; as, a *deplorable* accident; **2,** shameful; regrettable; as, *deplorable* behavior.—*adv.* **de·plor′a·bly.**

de·plore (dē-plôr′), *v.t.* [deplored, deploring], *v.t.* to lament; grieve for.
Syn. mourn, bewail, regret, bemoan.

de·ploy (dē-ploi′), *v.t.* to spread out, as a column of troops, in a line of battle, or to change the position and duties of troops:—*v.i.* to spread out the front line:—*n.* **1,** movement by which a body of troops is spread out in battle line; **2,** a change in the position and duties of troops.—*n.* **de·ploy′ment.**

de·pop·u·late (dē-pŏp′ū-lāt), *v.t.* [depopulat-ed, depopulat-ing], to deprive of inhabitants; reduce the number of people in; as, a severe epidemic *depopulated* the country.—*n.* **de·pop·u·la′tion.**

de·port (dē-pôrt′), *v.t.* **1,** to banish; exile; remove; as, we *deport* criminal aliens; **2,** to behave (oneself); as, he *deported* himself with dignity.—*n.* **de·por·ta′tion.**

de·port·ment (dē-pôrt′mĕnt), *n.* conduct; behavior; manners.
Syn. bearing, carriage, demeanor.

de·pose (dē-pōz′), *v.t.* [deposed, depos-ing], **1,** to remove from a throne or other high station; deprive of office; **2,** to bear witness; testify under oath.—*n.* **de·pos′al.**

de·pos·it (dē-pŏz′ĭt), *v.t.* **1,** to put or set down; place; **2,** to put into a bank, as money; entrust to another for safekeeping:—*n.* **1,** something committed to the care of another; **2,** a pledge; money given as a promise to pay more; as, a small *deposit* on a purchase; **3,** something laid down; especially, solid matter which settles at the bottom of a liquid; sediment.

dep·o·si·tion (dĕp′ō-zĭsh′ŭn; dē′pō-zĭsh′ŭn), *n.* **1,** a putting out of office; dethronement; as, the *deposition* of a king; **2,** a laying down, as of sand or mud by a river; **3,** testimony under oath.

de·pos·i·tor (dē-pŏz′ĭ-tẽr), *n.* one who puts down, or places in trust; especially, one who puts money in a bank.

de·pos·i·to·ry (dē-pŏz′ĭ-tôr′ĭ), *n.* [*pl.* depositories], the place where anything is deposited, as a bank or a warehouse.

de·pot (dē′pō; dĕp′ō), *n.* **1,** in the U.S., a railroad station: (pronounced dē′pō); **2,** a warehouse; **3,** a building for military supplies, food, or the like: (pronounced dĕp′ō).

de·prave (dē-prāv′), *v.t.* [depraved, deprav-ing], to make bad; to corrupt.
Syn. pervert, contaminate, pollute.

de·praved (dē-prāvd′), *adj.* morally bad; evil; corrupt; as, a *depraved* criminal.
Syn. degenerate.

de·prav·i·ty (dē-prăv′ĭ-tĭ), *n.* [*pl.* depravities], **1,** the state of being immoral or corrupt; wickedness; **2,** a wicked act; immoral behavior.

dep·re·cate (dĕp′rē-kāt), *v.t.* [deprecat-ed, deprecat-ing], to express great disapproval of, or regret for; as, to *deprecate* gambling.—*n.* **dep′re·ca′tion.**

de·pre·ci·ate (dē-prē′shĭ-āt), *v.t.* [depreciat-ed, depreciat-ing], **1,** to lower the value of; as, to *depreciate* the currency; **2,** to speak slightingly of; belittle; as, to *depreciate* another's work:—*v.i.* to fall in value; become of less worth; as, buildings *depreciate* if not kept in repair.

de·pre·ci·a·tion (dē-prē′shĭ-ā′shŭn), *n.* **1,** a lessening of value; **2,** a lessening in estimation; disparagement.

dep·re·da·tion (dĕp′rē-dā′shŭn), *n.* a laying waste; a plundering; robbery; as, the *depredations* of the invaders.

de·press (dē-prĕs′), *v.t.* **1,** to thrust down; **2,** to sadden; as, bad news *depresses* us; **3,** to make less active, as trade.
Syn. discourage, dishearten.

de·pres·sion (dē-prĕsh′ŭn), *n.* **1,** a sinking or falling in of a surface; as, a *depression* in the ground; **2,** low spirits; **3,** dulness of trade; also, the period of time in which business is dull.
Syn. gloom, melancholy.

de·prive (dē-prīv′), *v.t.* [deprived, depriving], **1,** to take away from; as, to *deprive* him of his house; **2,** to keep from having, using, or enjoying.—*n.* **dep′ri·va′tion** (dĕp′-rĭ-vā′shŭn).
Syn. strip, bereave, despoil, rob.

dept. abbreviation for *department*.

depth (dĕpth), *n.* **1,** deepness; distance below the surface, or from the observer in any direction; as, the *depth* of a tank; the *depth* of the sky; **2,** profoundness; wisdom; as, the *depths* of learning; a man of *depth*; **3,** richness of tone or color; **4,** the innermost part; as, the *depths* of a forest; the mid part; as, the *depth* of winter; **5,** that which is deep; as, the ocean *depths*.

dep·u·ta·tion (dĕp′ū-tā′shŭn), *n.* **1,** the act of appointing, or giving power to, an agent; **2,** a group of people appointed to act or speak for others; as, a *deputation* of citizens called on the mayor.

dep·u·tize (dĕp′ū-tīz), *v.t.* °⁷ [deputized, deputiz-ing], to appoint as a deputy or agent.—*v.t.* **de·pute′** (dē-pūt′).

dep·u·ty (dĕp′ū-tĭ), *n.* [*pl.* deputies], one appointed to act for another; an agent; as, a policeman is a *deputy* of the law.
   Syn. envoy, agent, delegate.

de·rail (dē-rāl′), *v.t.* to cause (a train or trolley) to leave, or run off, the rails.—*n.* **de·rail′ment.**

de·range (dē-rānj′), *v.t.* [deranged, de-rang-ing], **1,** to disorder; confuse; disturb; **2,** to make insane.—*adj.* **de·ranged′.**

de·range·ment (dē-rānj′mĕnt), *n.* **1,** the act of putting out of order; also, a state of disorder; **2,** insanity.

der·by (dûr′bĭ), *n.* [*pl.* derbies], a stiff felt hat, with a dome-shaped crown and a narrow brim.

Der·by·shire (dûr′bĭ-shĭr; där′bĭ-shĭr) or **Der·by** (dûr′-bĭ; där′bĭ), a county, a city, in England (map 13).

der·e·lict (dĕr′ĕ-lĭkt), *adj.* **1,** abandoned; deserted; **2,** unfaithful; neglectful; as, to be *derelict* in one's duty:— *n.* **1,** anything left, forsaken, or cast away; especially, a waterlogged ship; **2,** a person sunk to the lowest depths of degradation.

DERBY

der·e·lic·tion (dĕr′ĕ-lĭk′shŭn), *n.* **1,** aban-donment; **2,** a falling short or failure in loyalty or duty.

de·ride (dē-rīd′), *v.t.* [derid-ed, derid-ing], to mock; laugh at; jeer.

de·ri·sion (dē-rĭzh′ŭn), *n.* ridicule; scorn; contempt.
   Syn. disrespect, mockery.

de·ri·sive (dē-rī′sĭv), *adj.* expressing ridi-cule or scorn; as, *derisive* laughter.—*adv.* **de·ri′sive·ly.**

der·i·va·tion (dĕr′ĭ-vā′shŭn), *n.* **1,** origin; source; as, the *derivation* of a word; **2,** the obtaining of one thing from another.
   Syn. beginning, cause, root.

de·riv·a·tive (dē-rĭv′a-tĭv), *adj.* obtained from a source; as, *derivative* words:—*n.* something formed from something else; especially, a word formed from another.

de·rive (dē-rīv′), *v.t.* [derived, deriv-ing], **1,** to get from a source; as, to *derive* pleasure from a game; **2,** to trace the origin

of (a word); as, the word "garage" is *derived* from the French.
   Syn. trace, get.

der·o·ga·tion (dĕr′ō-gā′shŭn), *n.* a less-ening in value or estimation; depreciation; disparagement.

de·rog·a·tor·y (dē-rŏg′a-tôr′ĭ), *adj.* tend-ing to discredit; disparaging.

der·rick (dĕr′ĭk), *n.* **1,** a machine equipped

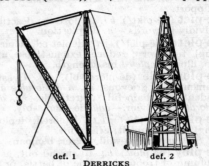

def. 1   def. 2
DERRICKS

with ropes, gears, and pulleys, for lifting heavy weights; **2,** a scaffolding built above an oil well, to which the drilling machinery is attached.

der·rin·ger (dĕr′ĭn-jẽr), *n.* a pistol with a short barrel of large caliber, effective at short range. Also, **der′in·ger.**

der·vish (dûr′vĭsh), *n.* a monk belonging to a Mohammedan religious order, whose members take vows to live a life of poverty and self-denial.

des·cant (dĕs-kănt′), *v.i.* to comment freely:—*n.* (dĕs′kănt), **1,** a strain of melody; song; **2,** a dis-course on one theme.

Des·cartes (dā′kärt′; dā-kärt′), René (1596–1650), a French philosopher and mathematician.

DERRINGERS
Above, old-fash-ioned type; below, modern type.

de·scend (dē-sĕnd′), *v.i.* **1,** to go or come down from a higher to a lower level; as, the rain *descended*; **2,** to fall or come upon in force; as, the soldiers de-*scended* upon the city; **3,** to pass by in-heritance; as, the house *descended* from father to son; also, to come down from earlier times; as, the custom *descended* from the ancient Greeks; **4,** to come down or be derived, as from a source; as, this child *descended* from royalty:—*v.t.* to go down.

de·scend·ant (dē-sĕn′dănt), *n.* one who is descended from a given ancestor; offspring.

de-scent (dė-sĕnt´), *n.* **1,** change from a higher to a lower place; downward motion; **2,** a sudden hostile invasion or attack; **3,** ancestry; as, he is of English *descent;* **4,** a downward slope.
Syn. declivity.

de-scribe (dė-skrīb´), *v.t.* [described, describ-ing], **1,** to give an account of in words; as, he *described* the house; **2,** to draw the outline of; as, to *describe* a circle.—*adj.* **de-scrib´a-ble.**
Syn. portray, illustrate, define, explain.

de-scrip-tion (dė-skrĭp´shŭn), *n.* **1,** the act of giving an oral or written account of something; also, a picture in words; **2,** a class; sort; kind; as, his library contains books of every *description.*
Syn. sketch, portrayal, depiction.

de-scrip-tive (dė-skrĭp´tĭv), *adj.* tending or serving to picture in words.—*adv.* **de-scrip´tive-ly.**

de-scry (dė-skrī´), *v.t.* [descried, descry-ing], to discover with the eye, especially in the distance or through obscurity; catch sight of; as, the shipwrecked sailors *descried* a sail on the horizon.

des-e-crate (dĕs´ė-krāt), *v.t.* [desecrat-ed, desecrat-ing], to treat (something sacred) with contempt: opposite of *consecrate;* as, to *desecrate* the church by throwing stones through the windows.—*n.* **des´e-cra´tion.**

¹de-sert (dė-zûrt´), *v.t.* **1,** to forsake; abandon; **2,** in military usage, to abandon without leave; as, to *desert* the army;—*v.i.* to run from duty; forsake a post.—*n.* **de-sert´er.**
Syn. leave, fail, abandon, forsake.

²de-sert (dė-zûrt´), *n.* often *deserts,* a deserved reward or punishment; as, he received his just *deserts.*
Syn. due, worth, worthiness.

³des-ert (dĕz´ẽrt), *n.* a wilderness; a remote, lonely place; especially, a vast expanse of dry, sandy waste:—*adj.* pertaining to a wilderness; waste; desolate.

de-ser-tion (dė-zûr´shŭn), *n.* **1,** the act of forsaking; a leaving of one's post; **2,** the state of being abandoned.

de-serve (dė-zûrv´), *v.t.* [deserved, deserving], to earn by service; be worthy of; merit; as, he *deserved* his promotion:—*v.i.* to be worthy.—*adj.* **de-serv´ing.**

de-serv-ed-ly (dė-zûr´vĕd-lĭ), *adv.* justly; according to merit.

des-ic-cate (dĕs´ĭ-kāt), *v.t.* [desiccat-ed, desiccat-ing], to dry; preserve by taking the moisture from; as, to *desiccate* fruit:—*desiccated,* dried; as, *desiccated* apples.

de-sign (dė-zīn´), *v.t.* **1,** to draw or plan out; also, to plan and draw in detail; as, to *design* a house or bridge; **2,** to mean;

intend; as, a nod *designed* to warn:—*n.* **1,** an outline or sketch to serve as a pattern, as for a dress; **2,** purpose or intention; also, a plot; as, *designs* against the state; **3,** arrangement of details according to a plan; as, a vase of fancy *design.*
Syn., n. sketch, purpose, intent.

des-ig-nate (dĕz´ĭg-nāt; dĕs´ĭg-nāt), *v.t.* [designat-ed, designat-ing], **1,** to point out; indicate; show; as, to *designate* the boundaries of a county; **2,** to name; nominate; as, the teacher *designated* John and Mary to count the votes.—*n.* **des´ig-na´tor.**

des-ig-na-tion (dĕz´ĭg-nā´shŭn; dĕs´ĭg-nā´shŭn), *n.* **1,** the act of pointing out or indicating; **2,** the act of naming or nominating; **3,** a distinctive mark or title.

de-sign-ed-ly (dė-zīn´ĕd-lĭ), *adv.* intentionally; purposely.

de-sign-er (dė-zīn´ẽr), *n.* one who makes plans, patterns, or original sketches.

de-sign-ing (dė-zīn´ĭng), *adj.* scheming; artful; cunning; as, a *designing* person:—*n.* the art of making plans or sketches.

de-sir-a-ble (dė-zīr´à-bl), *adj.* agreeable; pleasing; worth having; as, *desirable* companions.—*n.* **de-sir´a-bil´i-ty.**
Syn. advisable, acceptable, proper, beneficial, advantageous, profitable.

de-sire (dė-zīr´), *v.t.* [desired, desir-ing], **1,** to wish earnestly for; crave; **2,** to express a wish for; ask; as, I *desire* your help:—*n.* **1,** a longing for the possession of some object; an earnest wish; **2,** a request; **3,** the object longed for.
Syn., n. wish, longing.

de-sir-ous (dė-zīr´ŭs), *adj.* full of desire; eager; as, he was *desirous* of success.

de-sist (dė-zĭst´), *v.i.* to cease; stop; as, *desist* from evil.
Syn. discontinue, quit, abstain.

desk (dĕsk), *n.* a piece of furniture with a tablelike surface to support the paper or book of a writer or reader.

Des Moines (dė moin´), a city, capital of Iowa (map **7**).

des-o-late (dĕs´ô-lāt), *v.t.* [desolat-ed, desolat-ing], **1,** to lay waste; make unfit for inhabitants; as, an earthquake *desolated* the city; **2,** to overwhelm with sorrow:—*adj.* (dĕs´ô-lĭt), **1,** deprived of inhabitants; abandoned; **2,** in a condition of neglect or ruin; **3,** forlorn; miserable.—*adv.* **des´o-late-ly.**—*n.* **des´o-late-ness.**
Syn., adj. lonely, forsaken, deserted.

des-o-la-tion (dĕs´ô-lā´shŭn), *n.* **1,** the act of laying waste; **2,** the state of being laid waste or abandoned; **3,** solitude; ruin; **4,** affliction; melancholy.
Syn. unhappiness, sadness.

De So·to (dē sō′tō; dā sō′tō), Hernando or Ferdinand(1499?–1542), a Spanish explorer.

de·spair (dĕ-spâr′), *v.i.* to lose all hope or expectation:—*n.* **1,** loss of hope or confidence; hopelessness; **2,** that which causes loss of hope; as, she is the *despair* of her mother.—*adj.* **de-spair′ing.**

des·patch (dĕs-păch′), *v.t.* to send off quickly:—*n.* **1,** a news item; **2,** a government document. See **dispatch.**

des·per·a·do (dĕs′pĕr-ä′dō; dĕs′pĕr-ä′dō), *n.* [*pl.* desperadoes or desperados], a bold and reckless criminal.

des·per·ate (dĕs′pĕr-ĭt), *adj.* **1,** without regard to danger; reckless; as, a *desperate* man; **2,** proceeding from despair; frantic; as, the swimmer made a *desperate* effort to reach shore; **3,** beyond hope or cure; as, a *desperate* illness.—*adv.* **des′per-ate-ly.**

des·per·a·tion (dĕs′pĕr-ā′shŭn), *n.* the state of being without hope; the recklessness of despair.

des·pi·ca·ble (dĕs′pĭ-ka-bl), *adj.* contemptible; mean; vile.—*adv.* **des′pi-ca-bly.**

de·spise (dĕ-spīz′), *v.t.* [despised, despis-ing], to look down upon; scorn; disdain.
Syn. abhor, disregard, spurn, slight.

de·spite (dĕ-spīt′), *prep.* notwithstanding; in spite of; as, the player continued in the game *despite* his injuries.

de·spoil (dĕ-spoil′), *v.t.* to rob; deprive of belongings; as, to *despoil* a house of all its treasures.—*n.* **de-spoil′er.**

de·spond (dĕ-spŏnd′), *v.i.* to be cast down in spirits; be greatly depressed; lose heart; as, continued poverty caused him to *despond.*—*adj.* **de-spond′ing.**

de·spond·en·cy (dĕ-spŏn′dĕn-sĭ), *n.* absence of hope; mental depression.—*n.* **de-spond′ence.**

de·spond·ent (dĕ-spŏn′dĕnt), *adj.* blue; depressed.—*adv.* **de-spond′ent-ly.**
Syn. hopeless, discouraged, blue.

des·pot (dĕs′pŏt), *n.* an absolute ruler; tyrant; as, Nero was a *despot.*

des·pot·ic (dĕs-pŏt′ĭk) or **des·pot·i·cal** (dĕs-pŏt′ĭ-kăl), *adj.* absolute in power; tyrannical.—*adv.* **des-pot′i-cal-ly.**

des·pot·ism (dĕs′pŏt-ĭzm), *n.* **1,** absolute government; **2,** any absolute control; tyranny; as, the *despotism* of dictators.

des·sert (dĭ-zûrt′), *n.* a course of fruits, nuts, or sweets, such as pastry or pudding, served last at a meal.

des·ti·na·tion (dĕs′tĭ-nā′shŭn), *n.* **1,** an end or object; goal; **2,** the stated end of a journey; as, Chicago is my *destination.*

des·tine (dĕs′tĭn), *v.t.* [destined, destin-ing], **1,** to appoint to any purpose or end; as, he was *destined* for the ministry; **2,** to

settle in advance; foreordain; as, his hopes were *destined* to be realized.

des·ti·ny (dĕs′tĭ-nĭ), *n.* [*pl.* destinies], **1,** lot or fortune; fate; as, it was his *destiny* to die alone; **2,** the succession of events in life considered as something beyond the power or control of man; as, it is folly to whine against *destiny.*
Syn. decree, doom, end.

des·ti·tute (dĕs′tĭ-tūt), *adj.* **1,** without means; penniless; **2,** being wholly without something necessary or desirable; as, a man *destitute* of honor.

des·ti·tu·tion (dĕs′tĭ-tū′shŭn), *n.* extreme poverty; want; lack.
Syn. indigence, penury, poverty, need.

de·stroy (dĕ-stroi′), *v.t.* **1,** to pull down; overturn; lay waste; undo; **2,** to kill; put an end to; **3,** to render void; as, his acts *destroyed* his influence.
Syn. ruin, demolish.

de·stroy·er (dĕ-stroi′ẽr), *n.* **1,** a person or thing that destroys; **2,** a light, fast war vessel armed with guns, torpedoes, etc.

de·struct·i·ble (dĕ-strŭk′tĭ-bl), *adj.* capable of being destroyed or ruined.—*n.* **de-struct′i-bil′i-ty.**

de·struc·tion (dĕ-strŭk′shŭn), *n.* **1,** the act of destroying; ruin; as, fire completed the *destruction* of the city; **2,** a cause of ruin; as, gambling was his *destruction.*
Syn. desolation, downfall, havoc.

de·struc·tive (dĕ-strŭk′tĭv), *adj.* **1,** causing desolation; ruinous; hurtful; as, the boll weevil is a *destructive* insect; **2,** tearing down without building up; as, a *destructive* critic.—*adv.* **de-struc′tive-ly.**
Syn. detrimental, noxious, injurious.

des·ue·tude (dĕs′wē-tūd), *n.* a state of disuse, as of a custom or fashion.

des·ul·tor·y (dĕs′ŭl-tôr′ĭ), *adj.* passing from one thing to another without order or method; aimless; as, *desultory* reading.—*adv.* **des′ul-tor′i-ly.**—*n.* **des′ul-tor′i-ness.**
Syn rambling, disconnected, fitful.

de·tach (dĕ-tăch′), *v.t.* **1,** to separate; disconnect; **2,** to detail for a special duty; as, to *detach* men to guard a pass.—*adj.* **de-tached′.**
Syn. sever, disjoin, disengage, disunite.

de·tach·a·ble (dĕ-tăch′a-bl), *adj.* something that can be detached; as, some umbrellas have *detachable* handles.

de·tach·ment (dĕ-tăch′mĕnt), *n.* **1,** the act of separating; as, the *detachment* of a key from a key ring; **2,** a body of troops or ships separated from the main body and sent on special service; **3,** a standing apart or aloof; aloofness; isolation.

de·tail (dĕ-tāl′), *v.t.* **1,** to relate minutely;

āte, āorta, râre, căt, ȧsk, fär, ăllow, sofȧ; ēve, êvent, ĕll, writẽr, novĕl; bīte, pĭn; nō, ōbey, ôr, dŏg, tŏp, cŏllide; ūnit, ūnite, bûrn, cŭt, focŭs; nōōn, fŏŏt; mound; coin;

enumerate; as, she *detailed* to us all her troubles; 2, to tell off for a special duty; as, he *detailed* two men for guard duty:—*n.* (dĕ-tāl'; dē'tāl), 1, a small part of a whole; a single item; as, the *details* of a scheme; such items considered together or taken up one by one; as, a subject treated in great *detail*; to go into *detail*; 2, a particular or minute account; 3, a small body of troops assigned to special duty.

de-tain (dē-tān'), *v.t.* 1, to hold back or delay; 2, to keep in custody.

de-tect (dē-tĕkt'), *v.t.* to discover; find out; as, to *detect* a criminal; to *detect* an odor.—*adj.* **de-tect'a-ble; de-tect'i-ble.**

de-tec-tion (dē-tĕk'shŭn), *n.* the act of finding out or discovering.

de-tec-tive (dē-tĕk'tĭv), *n.* a person who investigates crimes and mysteries:—*adj.* fitted for, employed in, or concerned with, finding out; as, a *detective* agency.

de-tec-tor (dē-tĕk'tẽr), *n.* 1, one who or that which finds out or discovers; 2, a device used in radio for making the presence of electric waves known.

de-ten-tion (dē-tĕn'shŭn), *n.* 1, the act of keeping back or withholding; 2, confinement; restraint.

de-ter (dē-tûr'), *v.t.* [deterred, deter-ring], to discourage or hinder, as by fear; restrain; dishearten; as, previous failures did not *deter* us from trying again.

de-ter-gent (dē-tûr'jĕnt), *n.* a substance which cleanses:—*adj.* having cleansing qualities.

de-te-ri-o-rate (dē-tē'rĭ-ō-rāt), *v.t.* [deteriorat-ed, deteriorat-ing], to reduce the quality or value of; as, the rainy spell *deteriorated* the peach crop:—*v.i.* to grow worse; as, a boxer's skill *deteriorates* through idleness.—*n.* **de-te'ri-o-ra'tion.**

de-ter-mi-na-ble (dē-tûr'mĭ-nȧ-bl), *adj.* capable of being decided upon or found out; as, a *determinable* sum.

de-ter-mi-na-tion (dē-tûr'mĭ-nā'shŭn), *n.* 1, the act of deciding; 2, firmness; resolution; as, he spoke with *determination*; 3, measurement or calculation; as, the *determination* of iron in ore.
Syn. firmness, decision, resolve.

de-ter-mine (dē-tûr'mĭn), *v.i.* [determined, determin-ing], to reach a decision; as, he *determined* on quick action:—*v.t.* 1, to put an end to; 2, to settle; as, to *determine* a case in court; 3, to fix or decide upon beforehand; as, to *determine* the date for the game; 4, to find out for oneself; as, to *determine* the facts; 5, to cause to come to a decision; as, this *determined* him to go at once; 6, to establish as a re-

sult, or give a definite direction to; as, an accident *determined* his career.

de-ter-mined (dē-tûr'mĭnd), *adj.* resolute; decided; as, he was a *determined* sort of person.—*adv.* **de-ter'mined-ly** (dē-tûr'-mĭnd-lĭ; dē-tûr'mĭn-ĕd-lĭ).

de-test (dē-tĕst'), *v.t.* to hate intensely; loathe; as, we *detest* people who cheat.

de-test-a-ble (dē-tĕs'tȧ-bl), *adj.* deserving to be loathed; hateful; as, cheating is a *detestable* thing.—*adv.* **de-test'a-bly.**
Syn. odious, loathsome, abominable.

de-tes-ta-tion (dē'tĕs-tā'shŭn), *n.* 1, extreme dislike or loathing; 2, that which is loathed or to which one has an aversion.

de-throne (dē-thrōn'), *v.t.* [dethroned, de-thron-ing], to remove from a throne; deprive of authority.—*n.* **de-throne'ment.**

det-o-nate (dĕt'ō-nāt; dē'tō-nāt), *v.t.* and *v.i.* [detonat-ed, detonat-ing], to explode with a loud report.—*n.* **det'o-na'tion.**

de-tour (dē-tŏŏr'; dē'tŏŏr) or **dé-tour** (dā-tŏŏr'), *n.* a roundabout way; a path or road that is used temporarily because of an obstruction in a main road.

de-tract (dē-trăkt'), *v.t.* and *v.i.* 1, to take away; as, the dark color *detracts* a great deal from the beauty of the hall; 2, to malign; slander.—*n.* **de-trac'tor.**

de-trac-tion (dē-trăk'shŭn), *n.* a taking away from the good name or reputation of another; slander.

det-ri-ment (dĕt'rĭ-mĕnt), *n.* that which injures or reduces in value; injury; damage; loss; harm; as, you cannot do evil without *detriment* to your reputation.

det-ri-men-tal (dĕt'rĭ-mĕn'tăl), *adj.* injurious; hurtful.—*adv.* **det'ri-men'tal-ly.**

de-tri-tus (dē-trī'tŭs), *n.* any loose material, such as sand, gravel, or the like, caused by the wearing away of rocks.

De-troit (dē-troit'), a city in southeastern Michigan, outstanding in the automobile industry (map 7).

¹**deuce** (dūs), *n.* 1, a card or the side of a die marked with two spots; 2, in lawn tennis, an even point score of forty points each, ⟨ ⟩n even game score of five or more games each.

²**deuce** (dūs), *n.* 1, the devil: used as an exclamation of annoyance, preceded by *the*; 2, mischief; havoc; as, to play the *deuce* with one's plans.

deu-ced (dū'sĕd; dūst), *adj.* confounded.

deu-ced-ly (dū'sĕd-lĭ), *adv.* 1, confoundedly; 2, extremely; as, *deucedly* tired.

Deu-ter-on-o-my (dū'tẽr-ŏn'ō-mĭ), *n.* the fifth book of the Old Testament, in which the law of Moses is stated a second time.

dev-as-tate (dĕv'ăs-tāt), *v.t.* [devastat-ed,

devastat-ing], to lay waste; destroy; as, fire *devastated* the town.

dev-as-ta-tion (dĕv′ăs-tā′shŭn), *n.* a laying waste; destruction.

de-vel-op (dē-vĕl′ŭp), *v.t.* **1,** to unfold gradually; make known in detail; as, he *developed* his plans for capturing the city; **2,** to make available for use; as, to *develop* a country's mineral wealth; **3,** to cause to grow; as, fresh air and exercise help to *develop* healthy bodies; **4,** to treat (a photographic plate, print, or film) with chemicals so as to bring out the picture:—*v.i.* to advance from one stage to another; as, boys *develop* into men.

Syn. evolve, amplify, expand, enlarge.

de-vel-op-er (dē-vĕl′ŭp-ẽr), *n.* a chemical mixture for bringing out the picture on photographic plates, films, or prints.

de-vel-op-ment (dē-vĕl′ŭp-mĕnt), *n.* **1,** the act of unfolding; growth; **2,** events; as, recent *developments* in China; **3,** the chemical treatment of photographic plates, films, or prints; **4,** a real-estate tract laid out in lots.—*adj.* **de-vel′op-men′tal.**

de-vi-ate (dē′vĭ-āt), *v.i.* [deviat-ed, deviat-ing], to turn aside or stray, as from a course, custom, plan, or the like.

Syn. swerve, deflect, digress, stray.

de-vi-a-tion (dē′vĭ-ā′shŭn), *n.* a turning away from a rule, custom, or the like.

de-vice (dē-vīs′), *n.* **1,** a scheme; trick; **2,** an invention; apparatus; **3,** a fanciful design or pattern; a heraldic emblem; **3,** fancy or will; as, left to his own *devices.*

dev-il (dĕv′l), *n.* **1,** (usually *Devil*), the supreme spirit of evil; Satan; **2,** a false god or demon; also, a wicked person; **3,** an unfortunate person; as, the poor *devil* deserves pity; **4,** a daring or reckless person; as, he is a *devil* at speeding; **5,** a printer's helper:—*v.t.* to tease; torment.

dev-iled (dĕv′ld), *adj.* chopped and mixed with seasoning or relish; as, *deviled* crabs.

dev-il-fish (dĕv′l-fĭsh′), *n* **1,** any of various odd-shaped sea fishes, as the angler or ray; **2,** a giant octopus.

dev-il-ish (dĕv′l-ĭsh), *adj.* extremely wicked; infernal; as, a *devilish* plot: —*adv. Colloquial,* very; extremely.— *adv.* **dev′il-ish-ly.**— *n.* **dev′il-ish-ness.**

DEVILFISH (½₈)
def. 1

dev-il-ment (dĕv′l-mĕnt), *n.* roguishness; mischief, often without evil intent.

dev-il-try (dĕv′l-trĭ), *n.* [*pl.* deviltries], wanton mischief; wickedness.

de-vi-ous (dē′vĭ-ŭs), *adj.* **1,** indirect; rambling; roundabout; as, *devious* paths; **2,** straying from the way of right and duty; as, he got his wealth by *devious* means.— *adv.* **de′vi-ous-ly.**

de-vise (dē-vīz′), *v.t.* [devised, devis-ing], **1,** to think up or contrive; as, the prisoners *devised* a way to escape; **2,** to bequeath or give by will.

Syn. discover, invent.

de-vi-tal-ize (dē-vī′tăl-īz), *v.t.* [devitalized, devitaliz-ing], to deprive of life or power; make lifeless.

de-void (dē-void′), *adj.* entirely without; lacking; as, *devoid* of sense.

Syn. void, wanting, unendowed, empty.

de-volve (dē-vŏlv′), *v.i.* [devolved, devolv-ing], to be passed down or handed over; as, the duty *devolved* upon him.

Dev-on-shire (dĕv′ŭn-shĭr) or **Dev-on,** a county of southwestern England.

de-vote (dē-vōt′), *v.t.* [devot-ed, devot-ing], **1,** to dedicate or set apart as sacred; as, to *devote* the morning to meditation; **2,** to give up wholly to; as, to *devote* oneself to study or music.

de-vot-ed (dē-vōt′ĕd), *adj.* **1,** wholly given up to some object; loyal; as, a *devoted* mother; **2,** dedicated to some religious purpose; as, priests *devoted* to the service of God; also, doomed; as, troubles gathered round his *devoted* head.—*adv.* **de-vot′ed-ly.**

dev-o-tee (dĕv′ō-tē′), *n.* one entirely given up to a special interest; as, a *devotee* of the theater; one zealous in religion; an enthusiast.

de-vo-tion (dē-vō′shŭn), *n.* **1,** the act of devoting or the state of being devoted; **2,** strong affection; **3, devotions,** religious worship; prayer.—*adj.* **de-vo′tion-al.**— *adv.* **de-vo′tion-al-ly.**

de-vour (dē-vour′), *v.t.* **1,** to swallow greedily or ravenously; as, the hungry man *devoured* the food; **2,** to destroy or lay waste; as, the fire *devoured* much timber; **3,** to take in eagerly with ears or eyes; as, to *devour* a new novel.—*n.* **de-vour′er.**

de-vour-ing (dē-vour′ĭng), *adj.* ravenous; greedy; as, a *devouring* fire.

de-vout (dē-vout′), *adj.* **1,** devoted to religious thoughts and exercises; **2,** expressing piety; as, a *devout* prayer; **3,** sincere; as, accept our *devout* wishes for success.—*adv.* **de-vout′ly.**—*n.* **de-vout′ness.**

dew (dū), *n.* **1,** moisture from the atmosphere condensed in small drops; **2,** anything refreshing like dew.

dew-ber-ry (dū′bĕr′ĭ), *n.* a kind of blackberry.

dew-claw (dū′klô′), *n.* the little inner toe of the foot of certain dogs.

dew-drop (dū′drŏp′), *n.* a small drop of moisture from the air.

Dew-ey (dū′ĭ), George (1837–1917), an American admiral in the Spanish-American War.

dew-lap (dū′lăp′), *n.* the fold of loose skin that hangs from the neck of cattle, dogs, and other animals.

DEWCLAW

dew-y (dū′ĭ), *adj.* [dew-i-er, dew-i-est], moist with dew; as, *dewy* grass; resembling dew.—*n.* **dew′i-ness.**

dex-ter (dĕk′stẽr), *adj.* right: applied in heraldry to the side of a shield on the right side of the person bearing it.

dex-ter-i-ty (dĕks-tẽr′ĭ-tĭ), *n.* 1, skill with the hands; physical skill; as, *dexterity* is necessary to a juggler; 2, cleverness; as, he evaded our questions with *dexterity*.

DEWLAP (D)

Syn. aptitude, expertness, readiness, skill.

dex-ter-ous (dĕk′stẽr-ŭs) or **dex-trous** (dĕks′trŭs), *adj.* 1, skilful with the hands; as, a *dexterous* workman; 2, quick mentally; adroit; clever; 3, done with skill; as, *dexterous* tricks.

DEXTER   SINISTER

Syn. deft, expert, handy, clever, adroit.

DEXTER
Dexter side and sinister side of a shield.

di- (dī-), a prefix meaning: 1, two; twofold; double; as, *di*graph, *di*oxide; 2, away; from: a form of *dis-* before certain consonants; as, *di*late, *di*vert.

di-a- (dī′ȧ-), a prefix meaning through; across; between; thoroughly; as, *dia*meter, *dia*phragm, *dia*log, *dia*gnosis.

di-a-be-tes (dī′ȧ-bē′tēz), *n.* a disease marked by an excessive discharge of, or by an excess of sugar in, the urine.—*adj.* and *n.* **di′a-bet′ic** (dī′ȧ-bĕt′ĭk; dī′ȧ-bē′tĭk).

di-a-bol-ic (dī′ȧ-bŏl′ĭk) or **di-a-bol-i-cal** (dī′ȧ-bŏl′ĭ-kăl), *adj.* devilish; outrageously wicked; cruel; as, he has a *diabolic* temper.—*adv.* **di′a-bol′i-cal-ly.**

di-a-crit-ic (dī′ȧ-krĭt′ĭk), *adj.* diacritical:—*n.* a diacritical mark.

di-a-crit-i-cal (dī′ȧ-krĭt′ĭ-kăl), *adj.* serving to separate or distinguish, as a mark or sign:—**diacritical mark,** a mark used to distinguish particular sounds of letters and to indicate their pronunciation, as in ä, ō.—*adv.* **di′a-crit′i-cal-ly.**

di-a-dem (dī′ȧ-dĕm), *n.* a crown; tiara.

di-ag-nose (dī′ăg-nōs′; [diagnosed, diagnos-ing], nature of something, as the symptoms; as, the her illness as measles.

di-ag-no-sis (dī′ăg-nō′sĭs noses (dī′ăg-nō′sēz)], 1, the recognition of a disease by its symptoms; 2, any explanation based on an examination of facts.—*adj.* and *n.* **di′ag-nos′tic** (dī′ăg-nŏs′tĭk).

di-ag-o-nal (dī-ăg′ō-năl), *adj.* 1, slanting; 2, extending from one corner of a figure, as a square, to its opposite corner:—*n.* 1, a straight line drawn or cut on a slant; 2, a straight line drawn from one angle of a figure, as a square, to any other angle not adjacent; 3, material with an oblique pattern.—*adv.* **di-ag′o-nal-ly**

DIAGONAL

di-a-gram (dī′ȧ-grăm), *n.* 1, a line drawing of something, made for purposes of explanation, and giving in outline the most important parts; a plan or chart, as of a building, machine, or the like; 2, in grammar, an outline of a sentence showing its construction:—*v.t.* [diagramed, diagraming], 1, to illustrate by an outline or drawing; 2, in grammar, to show the construction of (a sentence) by means of a diagram.

di-a-gram-mat-ic (dī′ȧ-grȧ-măt′ĭk) or **di-a-gram-mat-i-cal** (-măt′ĭ-kăl), *adj.* pertaining to, or shown by, line drawing.

di-al (dī′ăl), *n.* 1, a flat surface on which a pointer casts a shadow in such a way as to show the time of day; 2, the face of a watch, clock, or the like; 3, any plate on which a pointer marks revolutions, direction, pressure, or the like; as, the *dial* on a gas meter; 4, in some telephones, a movable device by means of which connections may be made without giving the number to a central operator:—*v.t.* [dialed, dial-ing], 1, to measure or indicate by a dial; as, they *dialed* the speed of the car; 2, in telephoning, to call by operating a movable dial.

DIAL (D), def. 4

di-a-lect (dī′ȧ-lĕkt), *n.* 1, the special form of a language in a given region of the country; as, the Cape Cod *dialect;* also, the customary speech of a class; as, the Negro *dialect;* 2, the special language of a trade or profession.—*adj.* **di′a-lec′tal.**

Syn. tongue, speech, language.

di-a-log or **di-a-logue** (dī′ȧ-lŏg), *n.* a

conversation between two or more persons; also, the conversation in a novel or play.

diam. abbreviation for *diameter*.

di·am·e·ter (dī-ăm′ē-tẽr), *n*. **1**, a straight line through the center of a circle, dividing it in half; **2**, the length of a straight line through the center of an object; hence, thickness; as, the *diameter* of a tree.

DIAMETER

di·a·met·ric (dī′à-mĕt′rĭk) or **di·a·met·ri·cal** (-mĕt′rĭ-kăl), *adj*. pertaining to a diameter.

di·a·met·ri·cal·ly (dī′à-mĕt′rĭ-kăl-ĭ), *adv*. **1**, along the diameter; **2**, entirely; completely; as, *diametrically* opposed.

di·a·mond (dī′à-mŭnd), *n*. **1**, a brilliant, usually colorless, precious stone; crystallized carbon: the hardest known substance; **2**, a plane figure with four equal straight sides and two acute and two obtuse angles; **3**, one of a suit, called *diamonds*, of playing cards, marked with a red figure like a diamond; **4**, in baseball, the space inside the lines connecting the bases; also, the entire playing field:—*adj*. resembling, or made of, a diamond.

DIAMOND

Di·an·a (dī-ăn′à), *n*. in Roman mythology, goddess of the moon and of the hunt: identified with the Greek *Artemis*.

di·a·pa·son (dī′à-pā′zŭn), *n*. **1**, the entire range or compass of a voice or instrument; **2**, harmony of notes or parts; **3**, a recognized musical standard of pitch; **4**, one of the principal stops of an organ.

di·a·per (dī′à-pẽr), *n*. **1**, cotton or linen cloth woven in geometric patterns; **2**, a breech cloth for an infant; **3**, a fabric decoration of one or more simple figures repeated.

di·a·phragm (dī′à-frăm), *n*. **1**, the muscular partition which divides the chest from the abdomen; **2**, a vibrating disk, as in a telephone; **3**, in a camera, optical instrument, or the like, a perforated device for regulating the admission of light. (For illustration of def. 1, see next column.)

DIAPER, def. 3

di·ar·rhe·a or **di·ar·rhoe·a** (dī′à-rē′à), *n*. extreme looseness of the bowels.

di·a·ry (dī′à-rĭ), *n*. [*pl*. diaries], **1**, a personal record of daily events; **2**, a book for daily memoranda.

Di·as or **Di·az** (dē′ăs; dē′äsh), Bartholomeu (1450?–1500), a Portuguese navigator, discoverer of the Cape of Good Hope.

di·a·ton·ic scale (dī′à-tŏn′ĭk), in music, a major or minor scale of eight tones which divides the octave into seven intervals.

di·a·tribe (dī′à-trīb), *n*. an abusive speech; violent and bitter criticism.

dib·ble (dĭb′l), *n*. a pointed gardening tool for making holes in the earth:—*v.t.* [dibbled, dib-bling], to plant with a dibble.

DIAPHRAGM
A, abdominal cavity; C, thoracic cavity; D, diaphragm.

dice (dīs), *n.pl.* [*sing*. die (dī)], small cubes, marked on the sides with one to six spots, used in games of chance:—*v.i.* [diced, dic-ing], to play with dice:—*v.t.* **1**, to decorate with patterns resembling cubes or squares; to checker; **2**, to cut into cubes or squares.—*n*. dic′er.

DIBBLE

Dick·ens (dĭk′ĕnz), Charles (1812–1870), an English novelist, author of "David Copperfield."

dick·er (dĭk′ẽr), *v.i.* in the U.S., to bargain or trade on a small scale; as, to *dicker* with a shopkeeper:—*n*. a small bargain or deal.

DICE

dic·ta (dĭk′tà), *n.pl.* [*sing*. dictum], authoritative assertions.

Dic·ta·phone (dĭk′tà-fōn), *n*. a trademark name for an instrument used to record what is later to be reproduced and written by a stenographer:—**dictaphone**, a machine bearing this trade name.

dic·tate (dĭk′tāt), *v.t.* [dictat-ed, dictat-ing], **1**, to declare with authority; prescribe; **2**, to express orally for another to take down in writing; as, her employer *dictated* ten letters:—*v.i.* to speak with final authority:—*n*. **1**, a command; as, the king's *dictates*; **2**, a controlling principle; as, the *dictates* of conscience.
Syn., *v*. suggest, enjoin, order, command.

dic·ta·tion (dĭk-tā′shŭn), *n*. **1**, the act of speaking words to be written down; also, the words so spoken; **2**, arbitrary command or utterance.

dic·ta·tor (dĭk-tā′tẽr; dĭk′tāt-ẽr), *n*. **1**, one who says something for another to write; **2**, one who rules with absolute powers of government; **3**, one exercising similar authority in any sphere; as, a *dictator* of styles.—*n*. dic·ta/tor-ship.

dic·ta·tor·i·al (dĭk′tà-tôr′ĭ-ăl), *adj*. per-

āte, âorta, râre, căt, ȧsk, fär, ȧllow, sofȧ; ēve, ĕvent, ĕll, writẽr, novĕl; bīte, pĭn; nō, ōbey, ôr, dŏg, tŏp, cŏllide; ūnit, ūnite, bûrn, cŭt, focŭs; nōon, fŏŏt; mound; coin;

taining to one who gives positive commands; overbearing; imperious.
Syn. domineering, arbitrary, tyrannical, autocratic.

dic·tion (dĭk′shŭn), *n.* the manner of expressing ideas in words; choice of words.
Syn. vocabulary, phraseology, style.

dic·tion·ar·y (dĭk′shŭn-ĕr′ĭ), *n.* [*pl.* dictionaries], a book explaining the words of a language arranged alphabetically; a lexicon; vocabulary.

dic·tum (dĭk′tŭm), *n.* [*pl.* dicta], a positive opinion; a dogmatic or authoritative assertion; a current saying.

did (dĭd), past tense of *do*.

di·dac·tic (dī-dăk′tĭk; dĭ-dăk′tĭk), *adj.* pertaining to, or of the nature of, teaching; conveying instruction; as, a *didactic* poem.—*adv.* **di·dac′ti·cal·ly**.

didst (dĭdst), *Archaic*, second person singular, past tense, of *do*.

¹**die** (dī), *v.i.* [died, dy·ing], **1,** to cease to live; expire; **2,** to decay; wither: said of plants or flowers; **3,** to long intensely; as, she is *dying* to hear your secret; **4,** figuratively, to vanish; fade away; as, his fame soon *died*.
Syn. depart, decline, decrease, decay.

²**die** (dī), *n.* [*pl.* dies (dīz)], **1,** a metal form used in stamping coins, medals, or the like; **2,** a tool used in cutting the threads of screws or bolts, or the like; **3,** a metal plate with holes for receiving a punch; also, a form of cutter, used in a press, for shaping leather, paper, sheet metal, or the like; **4,** [*pl.* dice (dīs)], a small cube used in gaming; hence, luck; chance:—**the die is cast,** the decision is irrevocably made.

DIE, def. 2, for threading a pipe or bar, held in a frame or stock.

Die·sel en·gine or **mo·tor** (dē′zĕl), an internal-combustion engine that burns a mixture of compressed air and crude oil.

¹**di·et** (dī′ĕt), *n.* a formal assembly or congress; especially, the parliamentary assembly of some countries.

²**di·et** (dī′ĕt), *n.* **1,** one's customary food; **2,** manner of living, with special reference to food; **3,** a prescribed course of food, intended as a health measure:—*v.t.* to regulate the eating and drinking of (a person); as, he *dieted* himself back to health:—*v.i.* to eat or drink according to prescribed rules.—*n.* **di′et·er.**—*n.* **di′et·ist.**
Syn., *n.* fare, victuals, food.

di·e·tar·y (dī′ĕ-tĕr′ĭ), *adj.* pertaining to diet or to eating; as, *dietary* fads:—*n.* [*pl.* dietaries], **1,** a certain fixed allowance of food; as, the prison *dietary;* **2,** rules for, or a system of, regulating food.

di·e·tet·ic (dī′ĕ-tĕt′ĭk), *adj.* pertaining to diet:—**dietetics,** *n.pl.* used as *sing.* that branch of hygiene relating to diet and its effects.—*adj.* **di′e·tet′i·cal.**

di·e·ti·tian or **di·e·ti·cian** (dī′ĕ-tĭsh′ăn), *n.* one trained to plan meals with a proper proportion of various food elements.

dif·fer (dĭf′ĕr), *v.i.* **1,** to be unlike; **2,** to disagree; dispute; quarrel.

dif·fer·ence (dĭf′ĕr-ĕns), *n.* **1,** the state of being unlike; unlikeness; **2,** controversy; quarrel; **3,** the amount by which numbers differ; remainder after subtraction; as, the *difference* between five and eight is three.
Syn. distinction.

dif·fer·ent (dĭf′ĕr-ĕnt), *adj.* unlike; distinct; not the same.—*adv.* **dif′fer·ent·ly.**
Syn. various, diverse.

dif·fer·en·tial (dĭf′ĕr-ĕn′shăl), *adj.* **1,** creating, pertaining to, or involving, a difference; as, *differential* rates; **2,** pertaining to a differential:—**differential gear,** a device in an automobile which allows one driving wheel to turn faster than the other, as on a curve:—*n.* a differential gear.—*adv.* **dif′fer·en′tial·ly.**

dif·fer·en·ti·ate (dif′ĕr-ĕn′shĭ-āt), *v.t.* [differentiat-ed, differentiat-ing], **1,** to observe or state an unlikeness between; as, to *differentiate* the various breeds of cattle; **2,** to mark (a person or thing) as unlike another; as, size *differentiates* the raven from the crow:—*v.i.* to acquire a distinctive character.
Syn. discriminate, distinguish, contrast.

dif·fer·en·ti·a·tion (dĭf′ĕr-ĕn′shĭ-ā′shŭn), *n.* **1,** the act of separating or classifying; specialization; as, the *differentiation* of labor; **2,** the act of causing, observing, or marking out unlikenesses between things.

dif·fi·cult (dĭf′ĭ-kŭlt), *adj.* **1,** not easy; hard to do, as a problem; **2,** not easily pleased or managed; as, a *difficult* child.
Syn. intricate, involved, obscure, rigorous, exacting, trying, exhausting.

DIFFERENTIAL GEAR

A,B, gears rigidly attached to bevel gear, G, which is turned by pinion on driving shaft, but is not attached to left wheel axle. C,D, gears rigidly attached to left and right wheel axles. A and B, by rotating on their axles, permit wheel axles to turn at different rates when necessary.

dif·fi·cul·ty (dĭf'ĭ-kŭl-tĭ), *n.* [*pl.* difficulties], **1,** the state of being hard to do; as, the *difficulty* of the task; also, great effort; as, he reached home with *difficulty;* **2,** something hard to do; an obstacle; trouble; hard work; as, he had *difficulty* in starting the car; **3,** a scruple; objection; as, he made no *difficulty* about my going; **4, difficulties,** a trying situation; embarrassment; especially, want of money; as, he is in *difficulties.*

dif·fi·dence (dĭf'ĭ-dĕns), *n.* lack of self-reliance; shyness; bashfulness.

dif·fi·dent (dĭf'ĭ-dĕnt), *adj.* lacking self-reliance; shy; modest.—*adv.* **dif'fi·dent·ly.**
  Syn. bashful, coy, demure, shy, modest.

dif·fuse (dĭ-fūz'), *v.t.* [diffused, diffus-ing], **1,** to send out; spread; as, the lamps *diffused* a pale light; **2,** in physics, to spread, as a gas or liquid, by mixing with another gas or liquid; as, to *diffuse* sirup in water:—*v.i.* to spread out in every direction:—*adj.* (dĭ-fūs'), **1,** widely spread; scattered; **2,** wordy; as, a *diffuse* lecture.—*n.* **dif·fuse'ness** (dĭ-fūs'nĕs).

dif·fu·sion (dĭ-fū'zhŭn), *n.* **1,** a spreading or extension; as, the radio will aid the *diffusion* of knowledge; **2,** in physics, the spreading or scattering of heat, light, or the like; also, the intermingling of two or more gases or liquids.

dig (dĭg), *v.i.* [*p.t.* and *p.p.* dug (dŭg) or digged (dĭgd), *p.pr.* dig-ging], **1,** to work with a spade, hands, claws, etc., in casting up earth; **2,** to make a way (under, through, or in); as, they *dug* through the hill; **3,** *Colloquial,* to study hard:—*v.t.* **1,** to loosen or break up (ground) with a spade, hands, claws, or the like; **2,** to make, as a hole, by casting out earth; **3,** to bring up from underground; as, to *dig* potatoes; also, to bring to light; as, to *dig* up information; **4,** to thrust; poke; as, to *dig* spurs into a horse:—*n.* **1,** a poke or thrust; **2,** *Colloquial:* **a,** a cutting or spiteful remark; **b,** a plodding student.

di·gest (dĭ-jĕst'; dī-jĕst'), *v.t.* **1,** to change (food) in the stomach and intestines into a form which the body can use; **2,** to think over carefully until one understands or until the material becomes a part of one's knowledge; as, to *digest* a book; **3,** to arrange in condensed form and systematic order; classify; as, the laws of the state were *digested:*—*v.i.* to undergo change, as food in the stomach and intestines, for use in the body; as, fruits *digest* easily:—*n.* (dī'jĕst), **1,** an orderly and classified arrangement of materials, usually in condensed form; as, a *digest* of the laws of the state; **2,** a brief summary; as, he wrote a *digest* of the book.

di·gest·i·ble (dĭ-jĕs'tĭ-bl; dī-jĕs'tĭ-bl), *adj.* capable of being changed in the stomach and intestines for use in the body.—*adv.* **di·gest'i·bly.**—*n.* **di·gest'i·bil'i·ty.**

di·ges·tion (dĭ-jĕs'chŭn), *n.* the act or process of changing food by action of juices in the stomach and intestines for use in the body; also, the power of digesting; as, a weak *digestion.*

di·ges·tive (dĭ-jĕs'tĭv), *adj.* pertaining to, or promoting, absorption of food by the body.

dig·ger (dĭg'ẽr), *n.* **1,** one who works with a spade or similar tool; **2,** a tool for turning up the soil; **3,** *Slang,* a plodder.

dig·gings (dĭg'ĭngz), *n. pl.* **1,** a place where metals are dug; **2,** *Colloquial,* lodgings.

dig·it (dĭj'ĭt), *n.* **1,** a finger or toe; **2,** any one of the numerals from 1 to 9.

dig·i·ta·lis (dĭj'ĭ-tā'lĭs), *n.* **1,** any of a group of plants of the figwort family bearing spikes of thimble-shaped flowers; especially, the foxglove; **2,** a drug made from the leaves of the purple foxglove, used as a heart stimulant.

dig·ni·fied (dĭg'nĭ-fīd), *adj.* lofty in manner; noble; stately.

dig·ni·fy (dĭg'nĭ-fī), *v.t.* [dignified, dignify-ing], to exalt; confer honor upon; add distinction to; as, his presence *dignified* the meeting.
  Syn. invest, advance, promote, honor.

dig·ni·tar·y (dĭg'nĭ-tẽr'ĭ), *n.* [*pl.* dignitaries], one who holds a position of rank or honor; especially, a high church official; as, a bishop is a *dignitary.*

dig·ni·ty (dĭg'nĭ-tĭ), *n.* [*pl.* dignities], **1,** nobleness; true worth; as, the *dignity* of labor; **2,** stateliness of manner or style; as, to walk with *dignity;* **3,** high rank or office; as, the *dignity* of a king; **4,** a person of high rank; as, the king will meet the other *dignities* of the state.

di·graph (dī'grȧf), *n.* a group of two letters representing one sound, as *ea* in *read* or *th* in *that.*

di·gress (dĭ-grĕs'; dī-grĕs'), *v.i.* to turn aside; get away from the main subject or line of argument.—*n.* **di·gres'sion.**
  Syn. diverge, swerve, wander, deviate.

dike (dīk), *n.* **1,** a ditch; **2,** a mound or bank of earth along a ditch; a causeway; **3,** a dam or bank thrown up as a protection against the sea or floods; as, the *dikes* of Holland:—*v.t.* [diked, dik-ing], **1,** to enclose or

DIKE, def. 3
1, dike; 2, water.

protect with a dike; **2,** to drain by means of ditching or dikes. Also spelled **dyke.**

di-lap-i-dat-ed (dĭ-lăp′ĭ-dā′tĕd), *adj.* in partial ruin; run-down; neglected; as, a *dilapidated* old house.

di-lap-i-da-tion (dĭ-lăp′ĭ-dā′shŭn), *n.* partial ruin through neglect or misuse.

di-late (dī-lāt′; dĭ-lāt′), *v.t.* [dilat-ed, dilat-ing], **1,** to enlarge or widen; as, to *dilate* the eyes; **2,** to distend; as, to *dilate* the lungs with air:—*v.i.* **1,** to be extended or enlarged; **2,** to speak fully and copiously. —*n.* **di-lat′er.**—*n.* **di-la′tion.**

Syn. stretch, expand, swell, inflate.

dil-a-tor-y (dĭl′à-tôr′ĭ), *adj.* tending to cause delay; as, *dilatory* tactics; tardy; as, a *dilatory* reply.—*adv.* **dil′a-tor/i-ly.**

Syn. tardy, procrastinating, behindhand, lagging, dawdling.

di-lem-ma (dĭ-lĕm′à; dī-lĕm′à), *n.* a situation involving a choice between two or more evils; a difficult choice.

dil-et-tan-te (dĭl′ĕ-tăn′tĭ), *n.* [*pl.* dilettanti (dĭl′ĕ-tăn′tē) or dilettantes (dĭl′-ĕ-tăn′tĭz)], **1,** one who pursues the fine arts, literature, or science, only for amusement; **2,** a dabbler.

¹dil-i-gence (dĭl′ĭ-jĕns), *n.* industry; care; zeal; as, to study with *diligence.*

Syn. heed, perseverance, application.

²dil-i-gence (dĭl′ĭ-jĕns), *n.* a stagecoach.

DILIGENCE

dil-i-gent (dĭl′ĭ-jĕnt), *adj.* industrious; careful.—*adv.* **dil′i-gent-ly.**

Syn. persistent, persevering, busy.

dill (dĭl), *n.* a plant whose spicy seeds are used in flavoring:—**dill pickle,** a large pickle seasoned with the seed of the dill.

dil-ly-dal-ly (dĭl′ĭ-dăl′ĭ), *v.i.* [dillydallied, dillydally-ing], *Colloquial,* to loiter; trifle; waver.

di-lute (dĭ-lūt′; dī-lūt′), *v.t.* [dilut-ed, dilut-ing], to weaken or thin by mixture with something, especially by adding water:—*adj.* weakened; thinned; as, a *dilute* mixture.—*adj.* **di-lut′ed.**

di-lu-tion (dĭ-lū′shŭn; dī-lū′shŭn), *n.* **1,** the act of weakening or thinning, as with water; **2,** a weak solution.

dim (dĭm), *adj.* **1,** faint; obscure; not bright; as, the *dim* light of evening; **2,** shedding little light; as, *dim* headlights;

3, hazy; ill-defined; as, a *dim* figure in the shadows; **4,** not understanding or seeing clearly; as, eyes *dim* with tears:—*v.t.* [dimmed, dim-ming], to make less bright or distinct; dull:—*v.i.* to become indistinct; fade.—*adv.* **dim′ly.**—*n.* **dim′ness.**

dim. abbreviation for *diminuendo.*

dime (dīm), *n.* a silver coin of the U. S. worth one tenth of a dollar, or ten cents.

di-men-sion (dĭ-mĕn′shŭn), *n.* **1,** measurement in any one direction, as length, breadth, height, or the like; **2, dimensions, a,** size in terms of these measurements; **b,** size;importance; scope; as, an undertaking of large *dimensions.*—*adj.* **di-men′sion-al.**

di-min-ish (dĭ-mĭn′ĭsh), *v.t.* **1,** to make less in amount, size, number, or the like; as, the long winter *diminished* their supplies; **2,** to weaken; impair; as, the power of wealth was *diminished*:—*v.i.* to grow less in amount or importance; as, his strength *diminished* towards morning.

Syn. contract, decrease, lessen, dwindle.

di-min-u-en-do (dĭ-mĭn′ŭ-ĕn′dō), *adj.* and *adv.* in music, gradually growing softer in sound:—*n.* a gradual decrease in loudness.

dim-i-nu-tion (dĭm′ĭ-nū′shŭn), *n.* a decreasing; a making or growing less.

di-min-u-tive (dĭ-mĭn′ŭ-tĭv), *adj.* **1,** small or little; as, a *diminutive* child; **2,** expressing smallness; as, "-kin" is a *diminutive* ending:—*n.* a word formed from another to express a smaller thing of the same kind; as, *lambkin,* a little *lamb.*—*adv.* **di-min′u-tive-ly.**—*n.* **di-min′u-tive-ness.**

Syn., adj. small, slight, insignificant.

dim-i-ty (dĭm′ĭ-tĭ), *n.* [*pl.* dimities], a cotton cloth with raised ornamental figures.

dim-mer (dĭm′ẽr), *n.* a device used on automobiles to dim the headlights.

dim-ple (dĭm′pl), *n.* a small dent or hollow in the surface of anything, as in the cheek or chin:—*v.i.* [dim-pled, dim-pling], to form dimples:—*v.t.* to mark with dimples.

din (dĭn), *n.* a continued and insistent noise:—*v.t.* [dinned, din-ning], to repeat over and over persistently; as, she *dinned* into him the lesson of honesty:—*v.i.* to make a noise; as, cries *dinning* in his ears.

di-nar (dē-när′), *n.* **1,** a small coin, the monetary unit of Yugoslavia; **2,** the monetary unit of Iraq. (See Table, page 943.)

dine (dīn), *v.i.* [dined, din-ing], to take dinner:—*v.t.* to give a dinner for; feed.

din-er (dī′nẽr), *n.* **1,** one who dines; **2,** a railroad car in which meals are served; **3,** a restaurant resembling a dining car, often made from a converted street car, or built to look like one.

ding (dĭng), *v.i.* to sound like a bell.

---

go; join; yet; sing; chin; show; thin, *th***en; hw,** *wh***y; zh, azure; ü, Ger. für or Fr. lune; ö, Ger. schön or Fr. feu; n̈. Fr. enfant, nom; kh, Ger. ach or ich. See pages ix-x.**

ding-dong (dĭng′dông′), *n.* the sound of the repeated strokes of a bell.

din-ghy, din-gy, or **din-gey** (dĭng′gĭ), *n.* [*pl.* dinghies, dingies, dingeys], any of various kinds of small rowboats or sailboats; especially, the smallest boat of a man-of-war. (See also *ship*, illustration.)

DINGHY

din-gle (dĭng′gl), *n.* a secluded, shady dell.

din-go (dĭng′gō), *n.* [*pl.* dingoes], a wild dog of Australia.

din-gy (dĭn′jĭ), *adj.* [din-gi-er, din-gi-est], grimy; faded; as, a *dingy* room.—*adv.* **din′gi-ly.**—*n.* **din′gi-ness.**

dink-ey (dĭngk′ĭ), *n.* [*pl.* dinkeys], *Colloquial,* a small locomotive used in hauling freight, logging, or the like.

din-ner (dĭn′ẽr), *n.* **1,** the chief meal of the day; **2,** a formal party at which dinner is served.

di-no-saur (dī′nō-sôr), *n.* any of a great variety of large reptiles which lived thousands of years ago.—*adj.* **di′no-sau′ri-an.**

DINOSAUR (⅛₀)

dint (dĭnt), *n.* **1,** a blow; **2,** a mark left by a blow or pressure; a dent; **3,** force or power; as, the trunk was closed by *dint* of much effort:—*v.t.* to mark or dent.

di-oc-e-san (dī-ŏs′ē-săn; dī-ŏs′ē-zăn), *adj.* of or pertaining to a diocese:—*n.* a bishop in charge of a diocese.

di-o-cese (dī′ō-sēs; dī′ō-sĭs), *n.* the district in which a bishop has authority.

Di-og-e-nes (dī-ŏj′ē-nēz), (412?–323 B.C.), a Greek philosopher, a believer in simplicity, said to have lived in a tub and to have gone about with a lantern in search of an honest man.

Di-o-ny-si-us (dī′ō-nĭsh′ĭ-ŭs; dī′ō-nī′sĭ-ŭs), (430?–367 B.C.), called *theElder,* a tyrant, or absolute ruler, of Syracuse.

Di-o-ny-sus (dī′ō-nī′sŭs) or **Di-o-ny-sos** (dī′ō-nī′sŏs), *n.* a Greek god, son of Zeus, first worshiped as the god of vegetation, later as the god and giver of the grape and of wine: indentified with *Bacchus.*

di-ox-ide (dī-ŏk′sīd; dī-ŏk′sĭd), *n.* a compound of two atoms of oxygen and one of a metal or other element.

dip (dĭp), *v.t.* [dipped, dip-ping], **1,** to put quickly into liquid and take out again; immerse; as, to *dip* one's finger in water;

2, to scoop up with a ladle, spoon, bucket, or the like; as, to *dip* water from a brook; **3,** to baptize by putting under water; **4,** to lower and raise quickly, as a flag:—*v.i.* **1,** to immerse oneself; **2,** to enter slightly into anything; as, to *dip* into a book; **3,** to slope downward; as, the road *dips;* **4,** to sink; as, the sun *dipped* below the hills; **5,** to reach into to take something out; as, to *dip* into a barrel for flour:—*n.* **1,** the act of putting into water temporarily; a short plunge; as, a *dip* in the ocean; **2,** a downward slope; as, a *dip* in the road; **3,** a liquid preparation used in cleaning or coloring; **4,** a candle made by frequent dipping of a wick in fat or wax; **5,** in aviation, a quick descent followed by an ascent.

diph-the-ri-a (dĭf-thē′rĭ-à), *n.* an acute contagious disease of the throat.

diph-thong (dĭf′thŏng), *n.* the union of two vowel sounds to form a continuous sound, as in *oil, out, aisle.*

di-plo-ma (dĭ-plō′mà), *n.* an official document conferring some honor or degree; especially, a paper showing the completion of a course of study in school or college.

di-plo-ma-cy (dĭ-plō′mà-sĭ), *n.* [*pl.* diplomacies], **1,** the art or practice of managing relations between states or nations; **2,** skill in conducting affairs; tact.

dip-lo-mat (dĭp′lō-măt), *n.* **1,** a person engaged in managing relations between nations; **2,** a tactful person.

dip-lo-mat-ic (dĭp′lō-măt′ĭk), *adj.* **1,** pertaining to the management of affairs between nations; **2,** skilful in the conduct of affairs; tactful; adroit.—*adv.* **dip′lo-mat′i-cal-ly.**—*n.* **di-plo′ma-tist** (dĭ-plō′mà-tĭst).

dip-per (dĭp′ẽr), *n.* **1,** a vessel with a long handle for scooping up a liquid; **2,** a wrenlike bird skilled in diving; also called *water ouzel:*—**Dipper,** either of two groups of seven stars in the northern heavens, arranged in the outline of a ladle. One is called the *Big Dipper;* the other is called the *Little Dipper.*

DIPPER

dire (dīr), *adj.* [dir-er, dir-est], **1,** dreadful; as, the *dire* news of an explosion; **2,** extreme; as, in *dire* need.—*adv.* **dire′ly.**

di-rect (dĭ-rĕkt′; dī-rĕkt′), *adj.* **1,** straight; as, a *direct* route; **2,** straightforward; sincere; as, a *direct* answer; **3,** immediate; not coming through someone else; as, he had *direct* knowledge; hence, personal; as, under his *direct* supervision; **4,** in an unbroken line of descent; as, a *direct* heir:—*v.t.* **1,** to address (a letter); also, to address with a

definite aim; as, he *directed* his remarks to the students; 2, to aim or point; as, to *direct* one's attention to peace; 3, to show or guide; as, to *direct* him to the station; 4, to conduct or manage; as, to *direct* a chorus; 5, to order or instruct; command: —*v.i.* to act as a guide.—*n.* **di-rect/ness.**
Syn., *v.* order, manage, lead, command, dispose, conduct, govern, control, rule.

di-rec-tion (dĭ-rĕk/shŭn; dī-rĕk/shŭn), *n.* 1, the act of controlling, managing, or guiding; management; 2, instruction or command; as, he left *directions* for the servants; 3, the address on a letter, or the like; 4, a course or line of motion; as, he went in the opposite *direction.*
Syn. course, way, management.

di-rec-tive (dĭ-rĕk/tĭv), *n.* an order, regulation, instruction, or the like.

di-rect-ly (dĭ-rĕkt/lĭ; dī-rĕkt/lĭ), *adv.* 1, in a direct line or manner; 2, at once.
Syn. presently, straightway.

di-rec-tor (dĭ-rĕk/tẽr; dī-rĕk/tẽr), *n.* a person who manages; a manager; especially, a member of the governing board of a company or society.—*n.fem.* **di-rec/tress.**

di-rec-to-rate (dĭ-rĕk/tō-rĭt; dī-rĕk/tō-rĭt), *n.* 1, the office of director; 2, the directors of an organization, as a body.

di-rec-to-ry (dĭ-rĕk/tō-rĭ; dī-rĕk/tō-rĭ), *n.* [*pl.* directories], an alphabetical list of names and addresses; as, a business *directory.*

dire-ful (dīr/fŏŏl), *adj.* dreadful; dire.

dirge (dûrj), *n.* a funeral hymn; a song of mourning.

dir-i-gi-ble (dĭr/ĭ-jĭ-bl), *adj.* capable of being guided; as, a *dirigible* balloon:—*n.* a cigar-shaped balloon driven by motors.

DIRIGIBLE
A, control car; B, B, B, power cars; C, C, vertical fins; D, horizontal fin; E, E, rudder.

dirk (dûrk), *n.* a kind of dagger.

dirt (dûrt), *n.* 1, mud; filth; as, streets full of *dirt;* 2, foulness in action, speech, or thought; also, scandalous gossip; 3, loose earth or soil.

dirt-y (dûr/tĭ), *adj.* [dirt-i-er, dirt-i-est], 1, soiled; as, a *dirty* dress; 2, obscene; as, *dirty* language; 3, mean; as, a *dirty* scoundrel; 4, not clear, as water or color; 5, disagreeable, as weather:—*v.t.* [dirtied, dirty-ing], to soil.—*n.* **dirt/i-ness.**

dis- (dĭs-), a prefix meaning: 1, away; apart; as, *dis*tract, *dis*bar; 2, not; un-; as,

*dis*obliging; 3, a reversal or undoing; as, *dis*entangle. Changed to *di-* or *dif-* in certain cases; as, *di*rect, *dif*ferent.

dis-a-bil-i-ty (dĭs/a-bĭl/ĭ-tĭ), *n.* [*pl.* disabilities], 1, the lack of power or ability to do something; 2, that which deprives of power or ability, as old age or mental or physical illness.

dis-a-ble (dĭs-ā/bl), *v.t.* [disa-bled, disa-bling], to deprive of power or ability; cripple; incapacitate.—*adj.* **dis-a/bled.**

dis-a-buse (dĭs/a-būz/), *v.t.* [disabused, disabus-ing], to undeceive; set free from mistake.

dis-ad-van-tage (dĭs/ăd-vàn/tĭj), *n.* 1, unfavorable condition; obstacle; as, to work under *disadvantages;* 2, loss or harm; as, a rumor to his *disadvantage.*

dis-ad-van-ta-geous (dĭs-ăd/văn-tā/jŭs), *adj.* unfavorable; as, in a *disadvantageous* position.—*adv.* **dis-ad/van-ta/geous-ly.**

dis-af-fect-ed (dĭs/a-fĕk/tĕd), *adj.* discontented; out of sympathy; disloyal.

dis-af-fec-tion (dĭs/a-fĕk/shŭn), *n.* 1, discontent; 2, ill will; disloyalty.
Syn. discontent, dislike, unfriendliness.

dis-a-gree (dĭs/a-grē/), *v.i.* [disagreed, disagree-ing] 1, to differ in opinion; also, to quarrel; as, to *disagree* over money; 2, to be unlike; as, this book *disagrees* with mine; 3, to be unsuitable; as, the climate *disagrees* with him.

dis-a-gree-a-ble (dĭs/a-grē/a-bl), *adj.* unpleasant; distasteful; ill-tempered.—*adv.* **dis/a-gree/a-bly.**

dis-a-gree-ment (dĭs/a-grē/mĕnt), *n.* 1, a difference of opinion; quarrel; 2, lack of similarity; unlikeness.
Syn. discord, dispute, dissension.

dis-al-low (dĭs/ă-lou/), *v.t.* to refuse to admit or allow (a claim or the like).

dis-ap-pear (dĭs/ă-pēr/), *v.i.* to pass from sight or existence.—*n.* **dis/ap-pear/ance.**

dis-ap-point (dĭs/ă-point/), *v.t.* 1, to fail to fulfil the hope of; 2, to balk.—*adj.* **dis/ap-point/ed.**—*n.* **dis/ap-point/ment.**

dis-ap-pro-ba-tion (dĭs/ăp-rō-bā/shŭn), *n.* disapproval; unfavorable opinion.

dis-ap-prov-al (dĭs/ă-prŏŏv/ăl), *n.* unfavorable opinion; disapprobation.

dis-ap-prove (dĭs/ă-prŏŏv/), *v.t.* [disapproved, disapprov-ing], 1, to regard with disfavor; condemn; blame; 2, to refuse assent to:—*v.i.* to express an unfavorable judgment.—*adv.* **dis/ap-prov/ing-ly.**

dis-arm (dĭs-ärm/), *v.t.* 1, to deprive of weapons; 2, to make harmless; as, his frank admission *disarmed* his foes:—*v.i.* to lay aside arms; reduce the size of armed forces; as, the country decided to *disarm.*

dis-ar-ma-ment (dĭs-är′má-mĕnt), *n.* **1,** the laying aside or depriving of weapons; **2,** the reduction of military and naval forces.

dis-ar-range (dĭs′ă-rānj′), *v.t.* [disarranged, disarrang-ing], to put out of order; disturb the order of.—*n.* **dis′ar-range′ment.**

dis-ar-ray (dĭs′á-rā′), *v.t.* **1,** to unrobe; undress; **2,** to throw into disorder:—*n.* **1,** disordered dress; **2,** confusion; disorder.

dis-as-ter (dĭ-zås′tẽr), *n.* a calamity; sudden misfortune; a serious accident. *Syn.* mishap, trouble, adversity.

dis-as-trous (dĭ-zås′trŭs), *adj.* unlucky; unfortunate; calamitous; attended with evil results.—*adv.* **dis-as′trous-ly.**

dis-a-vow (dĭs′á-vou′), *v.t.* to refuse to acknowledge; disclaim.

dis-band (dĭs-bănd′), *v.t.* to break up and dismiss (an organized body of people); as, to *disband* the army after the armistice:—*v.i.* to disperse; as, the club *disbanded* after its meeting.—*n.* **dis-band′ment.**

dis-bar (dĭs-bär′), *v.t.* [disbarred, disbarring], to deprive (a lawyer) of the right to practice as an attorney; expel from the legal profession.—*n.* **dis-bar′ment.**

dis-be-lieve (dĭs′bē-lēv′), *v.t.* and *v.i.* [disbelieved, disbeliev-ing], to refuse to accept as true.—*n.* **dis′be-liev′er.**

dis-bur-den (dĭs-bûr′dn), *v.t.* to relieve of a burden; unload:—*v.i.* to relieve oneself of a burden.

dis-burse (dĭs-bûrs′), *v.t.* [disbursed, disburs-ing], to expend; pay out; as, a treasurer *disburses* money.—*n.* **dis-burs′er; dis-burse′ment.**

disc (dĭsk), *n.* a flat, circular plate or anything resembling it, as a phonograph record; hence, **disc jockey,** a radio announcer on a program of recordings. See **disk.**

disc. abbreviation for *discount, discovered,* or *discoverer.*

dis-card (dĭs-kärd′), *v.t.* **1,** to throw away as useless; **2,** in card playing, to get rid of (a card or cards) as useless or extra:—*v.i.* to throw away a card or cards:—*n.* (dĭs′-kärd), **1,** the act of throwing away weak cards; also, the cards so thrown away; **2,** that which is cast aside as worthless.

dis-cern (dĭ-zûrn′; dĭ-sûrn′), *v.t.* **1,** to make out or perceive with the senses or mind; as, to *discern* a figure in the shadows; he *discerned* danger in the plan; **2,** to distinguish clearly; discriminate; as, to *discern* good from evil:—*v.i.* to see, make, or understand distinctions; as, to *discern* between right and wrong.—*n.* **dis-cern′er.** *Syn.* perceive, distinguish, discriminate.

dis-cern-i-ble (dĭ-zûr′nĭ-bl; dĭ-sûr′nĭ-bl), *adj.* visible; as, the hills are barely *discernible* in the mist.

dis-cern-ing (dĭ-zûr′nĭng; dĭ-sûr′nĭng), *adj.* of keen insight or discriminating judgment; acute.—*adv.* **dis-cern′ing-ly.**

dis-cern-ment (dĭ-zûrn′mĕnt; dĭ-sûrn′-mĕnt), *n.* the act or power of distinguishing or discriminating; keenness of insight. *Syn.* sharpness, acuteness, shrewdness.

dis-charge (dĭs-chärj′), *v.t.* [discharged, discharg-ing], **1,** to relieve of a load or burden; unload, as a ship; **2,** to remove, as a cargo from a ship or passengers from a train; **3,** to let fly, as an arrow; to shoot, as a gun; **4,** to set free; as, to *discharge* a prisoner; **5,** to dismiss, as servants; to end the services of; as, to *discharge* a jury, committee, or the like; **6,** to give off; as, his wound *discharged* pus; **7,** to pay off, as a debt; **8,** to perform, as a duty:—*v.i.* to get rid of a load or burden; to empty; as, the lake *discharged* into a river:—*n.* **1,** an unloading; as, the *discharge* of a ship or a cargo; **2,** that which is unloaded; **3,** a firing or shooting off, as of guns, arrows, dynamite; **4,** release from a burden, debt, accusation, confinement, responsibility; legal release, as of a prisoner; also, a certificate of release; as, a *discharge* from the army; **5,** dismissal; **6,** performance, as of a duty. *Syn., v.* liberate, release, dismiss, accomplish, achieve.

dis-ci-ple (dĭ-sī′pl), *n.* a pupil or follower who accepts the teachings of ə leader or master and who helps to spread them; especially, one of the followers of Jesus.—*n.* **dis-ci′ple-ship.**

dis-ci-pli-nar-i-an (dĭs′ĭ-plĭ-nâr′ĭ-ăn), *n.* one who enforces strict rules and order.

dis-ci-pli-nar-y (dĭs′ĭ-plĭ-nĕr′ĭ), *adj.* pertaining to strict training; corrective.

dis-ci-pline (dĭs′ĭ-plĭn), *n.* **1,** strict training of mind or character; **2,** obedience to rules and commands, as in a school, army, prison, or the like; as, a good teacher enforces *discipline;* **3,** punishment given by way of training or correction:—*v.t.* [disciplined, disciplin-ing], **1,** to train; drill; **2,** to punish. *Syn., n.* order, strictness, training, drill.

dis-claim (dĭs-klām′), *v.t.* to disown; deny any connection with. *Syn.* renounce, disavow, reject.

dis-close (dĭs-klōz′), *v.t.* [disclosed, disclos-ing], **1,** to uncover; bring to light; as, the digging *disclosed* an old treasure; **2,** to make known; as, to *disclose* secrets.

dis-clo-sure (dĭs-klō′zhẽr), *n.* **1,** the act of revealing; **2,** the thing revealed.

---

dis·col·or (dĭs-kŭl′ẽr), *v.t.* to spoil or change the color of; stain:—*v.i.* to change color or fade. In British usage, **dis·col·our**.—*n.* **dis-col′or-a′tion**.

dis·com·fit (dĭs-kŭm′fĭt), *v.t.* to defeat; to upset or throw into confusion; hence, to disconcert; embarrass.
Syn. embarrass, confuse, abash.

dis·com·fi·ture (dĭs-kŭm′fĭ-tūr), *n.* defeat; confusion; embarrassment.

dis·com·fort (dĭs-kŭm′fẽrt), *n.* uneasiness; distress:—*v.t.* to make uneasy.

dis·com·mode (dĭs′kŏ-mōd′), *v.t.* [discommod-ed, discommod-ing], to inconvenience; disturb; annoy.

dis·com·pose (dĭs′kŏm-pōz′), *v.t.* [discomposed, discompos-ing], to disturb the peace or calm of; disarrange.—*n.* **dis′-com-po′sure**.

dis·con·cert (dĭs′kŏn-sûrt′), *v.t.* to disturb the calm or self-possession of; to disorder; as, sickness *disconcerted* his plans.

dis·con·nect (dĭs′kŏ-nĕkt′), *v.t.* to disunite; unfasten.—*n.* **dis′con-nec′tion**.

dis·con·nect·ed (dĭs′kŏ-nĕk′tĕd), *adj.* not connected.—*adv.* **dis′con-nect′ed-ly**.

dis·con·so·late (dĭs-kŏn′sō-lĭt), *adj.* without hope; forlorn; sad or unhappy.—*adv.* **dis-con′so-late-ly**.
Syn. dejected, forlorn, sorrowful.

dis·con·tent (dĭs′kŏn-tĕnt′), *n.* dissatisfaction; restlessness:—*adj.* not satisfied:—*v.t.* to dissatisfy.—*n.* **dis′con-tent′ment**.

dis·con·tent·ed (dĭs′kŏn-tĕn′tĕd), *adj.* dissatisfied; restless.—*adv.* **dis′con-tent′ed-ly**.—*n.* **dis′con-tent′ed-ness**.

dis·con·tin·u·ance (dĭs′kŏn-tĭn′ū-ăns), *n.* a stopping; a breaking off.
Syn. interruption, break, end.

dis·con·tin·ue (dĭs′kŏn-tĭn′ū), *v.t.* [discontinued, discontinu-ing], to stop; cease doing; put an end to:—*v.i.* to cease; come to an end.—*n.* **dis′con-tin′u-a′tion**.

dis·con·tin·u·ous (dĭs′kŏn-tĭn′ū-ŭs), *adj.* broken or interrupted.

dis·cord (dĭs′kôrd), *n.* **1,** difference or lack of agreement; **2,** strife or conflict; **3,** a harsh noise; **4,** in music, lack of harmony.—*n.* **dis-cord′ance; dis-cord′an-cy**.
Syn. difference, contention, clashing.

dis·cord·ant (dĭs-kôr′dănt), *adj.* **1,** not in agreement; clashing; harsh; **2,** in music, not harmonious.—*adv.* **dis-cord′ant-ly**.

dis·count (dĭs′kount), *v.t.* **1,** to deduct from an account, debt, or the like, for early payment; **2,** to get or advance money on, as a note not yet due, deducting interest for the period it still has to run; **3,** to make allowance for exaggeration in; as, they *discounted* his story of the accident; **4,** to reduce the importance of by considering beforehand; as, to *discount* the difficulties of the trip by careful planning:—*n.* (dĭs′kount), **1,** a sum deducted from an account, bill, or the like, for early payment; as, ten per cent *discount* for cash; **2,** a deduction made for interest from the face value of a bill, note, or the like, when it is converted into cash or sold before it is due; **3,** the rate of interest so deducted.—*adj.* **dis′count-a-ble**.

dis·coun·te·nance (dĭs-koun′tē-năns), *v.t.* [discountenanced, discountenanc-ing], **1,** to disapprove of; **2,** to disconcert.

dis·cour·age (dĭs-kûr′ĭj), *v.t.* [discouraged, discourag-ing], **1,** to lessen the courage of; dishearten; **2,** to try to prevent or deter; as, laws *discourage* crime.

dis·cour·age·ment (dĭs-kûr′ĭj-mĕnt), *n.* **1,** the act of disheartening; state of being disheartened; **2,** that which disheartens.
Syn. dejection, despair, hopelessness.

dis·course (dĭs-kôrs′; dĭs′kôrs), *n.* **1,** talk; conversation; **2,** a lecture, treatise, or sermon:—*v.i.* (dĭs-kôrs′) [discoursed, discours-ing], to talk; converse:—*v.t.* to send forth; utter; as, to *discourse* wisdom.

dis·cour·te·ous (dĭs-kûr′tē-ŭs), *adj.* impolite; rude.—*adv.* **dis-cour′te-ous-ly**.
Syn. unmannerly, inconsiderate, blunt.

dis·cour·te·sy (dĭs-kûr′tē-sĭ), *n.* [*pl.* discourtesies], rudeness; an unmannerly act.

dis·cov·er (dĭs-kŭv′ẽr), *v.t.* **1,** to find, find out, or learn for the first time; also, to catch sight of; **2,** *Archaic*, to reveal or make known.—*n.* **dis-cov′er-er**.
Syn. invent, contrive.

dis·cov·er·y (dĭs-kŭv′ẽr-ĭ), *n.* [*pl.* discoveries], **1,** a finding for the first time; **2,** the thing found out or discovered.

dis·cred·it (dĭs-krĕd′ĭt), *v.t.* **1,** to refuse to believe; **2,** to destroy belief in or the reputation of; as, science *discredits* his theories:—*n.* **1,** loss of reputation; disgrace; **2,** doubt or disbelief; as, to bring old beliefs into *discredit*.
Syn., v. depreciate, decry, disgrace.

dis·cred·it·a·ble (dĭs-krĕd′ĭt-à-bl), *adj.* disgraceful; unworthy.—*adv.* **dis-cred′it-a-bly**.

dis·creet (dĭs-krēt′), *adj.* careful in speech and action; as, *discreet* behavior.—*adv.* **dis-creet′ly**.—*n.* **dis-creet′ness**.
Syn. cautious, judicious, prudent.

dis·crep·an·cy (dĭs-krĕp′ăn-sĭ), *n.* [*pl.* discrepancies], a difference; lack of agreement; as, the *discrepancy* between the two accounts.—*adj.* **dis-crep′ant**.
Syn. difference, variance, disparity.

dis·crete (dĭs-krēt′; dĭs′krēt), *adj.* separate; not continuous.

---

go; join; yet; sing; chin; show; thin, *th*en; hw, *why*; zh, azure; ŭ, Ger. f*ür* or Fr. l*u*ne; ö, Ger. sch*ö*n or Fr. f*eu*; ṅ, Fr. *enfant*, no*m*; kh, Ger. a*ch* or i*ch*. See pages ix–x.

dis-cre-tion (dĭs-krĕsh′ŭn), *n.* **1,** prudence; good judgment; **2,** freedom of choice or action; as, use your own *discretion.*

dis-crim-i-nate (dĭs-krĭm′ĭ-nāt), *v.t.* [discriminat-ed, discriminat-ing], to see or mark the difference between; distinguish; as, to *discriminate* good books from bad:— *v.i.* to make a distinction; as, to *discriminate* between good and evil.—*adv.* **dis-crim′i-nate-ly.**—*adj.* **dis-crim′i-na′tive.**
Syn. differentiate, discern, distinguish.

dis-crim-i-na-tion (dĭs-krĭm′ĭ-nā′shŭn), *n.* **1,** the act of distinguishing; **2,** the ability to make fine distinctions; discernment; **3,** a difference, often unfair, in the treatment of persons or things.
Syn. acuteness, judgment, insight.

dis-cur-sive (dĭs-kûr′sĭv), *adj.* wandering from one subject to another; rambling.— *adv.* **dis-cur′sive-ly.**—*n.* **dis-cur′sive-ness.**

dis-cus (dĭs′kŭs), *n.* [*pl.* discuses (dĭs′kŭs-ĕz) or disci (dĭs′ī)], a heavy disk of metal or stone to be thrown in athletic contests.

dis-cuss (dĭs-kŭs′), *v.t.* to debate fully; talk over; consider.

dis-cus-sion (dĭs-kŭsh′ŭn), *n.* full and open consideration or argument; as, the assembly agreed after a two-hour *discussion;* also, talk; as, his absence caused much *discussion.*

DISCUS
Athlete throwing the discus.

dis-dain (dĭs-dān′), *v.t.* to scorn; look upon with contempt; as, he *disdained* our attempts to help:—*n.* contempt; scorn.

dis-dain-ful (dĭs-dān′fŏŏl), *adj.* scornful. —*adv.* **dis-dain′ful-ly.**
Syn. proud, lofty, arrogant.

dis-ease (dĭ-zēz′), *n.* disorder of mind or body marked by definite symptoms; illness; sickness; any particular instance or kind of such disorder; as, heart *disease.*

dis-eased (dĭ-zēzd′), *adj.* **1,** in disordered physical condition; unhealthy; as, the bone is *diseased;* **2,** in mental disorder; depraved; as, a *diseased* imagination.

dis-em-bark (dĭs′ĕm-bärk′), *v.t.* and *v.i.* to remove from, or go ashore from, a vessel; land; as, to *disembark* troops; to *disembark* at Boston.—*n.* **dis-em′bar-ka′tion.**

dis-em-bod-y (dĭs′ĕm-bŏd′ĭ), *v.t.* [disem-bodied, disembody-ing], to set free from the body.—*n.* **dis′em-bod′i-ment.**

dis-en-chant (dĭs′ĕn-chant′), *v.t.* to set free from a charm, spell, or illusion.—*n.* **dis′en-chant′ment.**

dis-en-cum-ber (dĭs′ĕn-kŭm′bẽr), *v.t.* to free from burden.—*n.* **dis′en-cum′brance.**

dis-en-gage (dĭs′ĕn-gāj′), *v.t.* [disengaged, disengag-ing], **1,** to set free; release; as, to *disengage* one from a promise; **2,** to extricate; free (oneself); as, he *disengaged* himself from his bonds:—**dis-en-gaged′,** *adj.* at liberty; not in use.—*n.* **dis′en-gage′ment.**

dis-en-tan-gle (dĭs′ĕn-tăng′gl), *v.t.* [disen-tan-gled, disentan-gling], **1,** to free from confusion; as, to *disentangle* truth from error; **2,** to unravel; as, to *disentangle* a skein of yarn.—*n.* **dis′en-tan′gle-ment.**

dis-es-tab-lish (dĭs′ĕs-tăb′lĭsh), *v.t.* **1,** to end the fixed existence of; **2,** to deprive of state support; as, to *disestablish* a church. —*n.* **dis′es-tab′lish-ment.**

dis-es-teem (dĭs′ĕs-tēm′), *v.t.* to think lightly of; hold in disfavor:—*n.* disfavor.

dis-fa-vor (dĭs-fā′vẽr), *n.* **1,** disapproval; as, to look with *disfavor* on a scheme; **2,** the condition of being regarded with disapproval or dislike; as, he was in *disfavor.*

dis-fig-ure (dĭs-fĭg′ūr), *v.t.* [disfigured, disfigur-ing], to mar or injure in shape, form, or beauty.—*n.* **dis-fig′ure-ment.**

dis-fran-chise (dĭs-frăn′chīz), *v.t.* [dis-franchised, disfranchis-ing], to deprive of the rights of a citizen; especially, to deprive of the right to vote.—*n.* **dis-fran′chise-ment** (dĭs-frăn′chĭz-mĕnt).

dis-gorge (dĭs-gôrj′), *v.t.* [disgorged, disgorg-ing], to discharge from, or as from, the throat with violence; to vomit; hence, also, to give up unwillingly; as, to *disgorge* plunder:—*v.i.* **1,** to discharge contents; **2,** to surrender unlawful gains.

dis-grace (dĭs-grās′), *n.* **1,** shame; dishonor; **2,** the cause of shame; as, the roads are a *disgrace* to the town:—*v.t.* [disgraced, disgrac-ing], to bring shame, reproach, or dishonor upon.
Syn., n. disrepute, odium, reproach.

dis-grace-ful (dĭs-grās′fŏŏl), *adj.* dishonorable; shameful; as, his conduct is *disgraceful.*—*adv.* **dis-grace′ful-ly.**

dis-grun-tle (dĭs-grŭn′tl), *v.t.* [disgrun-tled, disgrun-tling], to put in a bad humor; to make dissatisfied or peevish.— *adj.* **dis-grun′tled.**

dis-guise (dĭs-gīz′), *v.t.* [disguised, disguis-ing], **1,** to change in appearance so as to conceal the identity of (a person); as, they *disguised* him as a woman; **2,** to hide, conceal, or mask; as, to *disguise* one's intentions:—*n.* **1,** anything worn to conceal one's identity; **2,** anything, as a manner of speaking, assumed to deceive.
Syn., n. pretext, simulation; *v.* conceal.

dis-gust (dĭs-gŭst′), *n.* strong distaste;

āte, âorta, râre, căt, ásk, fär, ăllow, sofà; ēve, ĕvent, ĕll, writẽr, novĕl; bīte, pĭn; nō, ōbey, ôr, dŏg, tŏp, cŏllide; ūnit, ūnite, bûrn, cŭt, focŭs; nōōn, fŏŏt; mound; coin;

loathing:—*v.t.* to offend by loathsome appearance, repulsive behavior, or the like.

dish (dĭsh), *n.* **1,** a vessel used for serving food; also, anything so shaped; **2,** any special food; as, ice cream is a popular *dish:—v.t.* to put into a dish for serving.

dis-heart-en (dĭs-härʹtn), *v.t.* to discourage; as, *disheartened* by failure.
Syn. deject, abash, dispirit, depress.

di-shev-el (dĭ-shĕvʹĕl), *v.t.* [disheveled, dishevel-ing], to throw into disorder; to tousle; as, the children *disheveled* his hair.
—*adj.* **di-shevʹeled.**

dis-hon-est (dĭs-ŏnʹĕst), *adj.* **1,** lacking in uprightness or fairness; as, lying is *dishonest;* **2,** inclined to cheat or deceive; as, a *dishonest* person; **3,** designed for unfair use; false; as, *dishonest* scales.

dis-hon-es-ty (dĭs-ŏnʹĕs-tĭ), *n.* deceit; lack of fairness or truth.

dis-hon-or (dĭs-ŏnʹẽr), *v.t.* **1,** to disgrace; bring shame upon; **2,** to refuse to pay (a bill or note):—*n.* disgrace; shame. In British usage, **dis-honʹour.**
Syn., v. degrade, humiliate, insult.

dis-hon-or-a-ble (dĭs-ŏnʹẽr-ȧ-bl), *adj.* **1,** shameful; **2,** lacking in uprightness. In British usage, **dis-honʹour-a-ble.**

dis-il-lu-sion (dĭsʹĭ-lūʹzhŭn), *v.t.* to set free from a mistaken belief in the goodness or value of some person or thing.

dis-in-clined (dĭsʹĭn-klīndʹ), *adj.* unwilling.—*n.* **dis-inʹcli-naʹtion.**

dis-in-fect (dĭsʹĭn-fĕktʹ), *v.t.* to cleanse from infection; purify of disease germs; as, to *disinfect* a room.—*n.* **disʹin-fecʹtion.**

dis-in-fect-ant (dĭsʹĭn-fĕkʹtănt), *n.* a substance capable of destroying disease germs.

dis-in-gen-u-ous (dĭsʹĭn-jĕnʹū-ŭs), *adj.* not frank or candid; insincere; as, a *disingenuous* person; a *disingenuous* remark.

dis-in-her-it (dĭsʹĭn-hĕrʹĭt), *v.t.* to cut off (a natural heir) from property.

dis-in-te-grate (dĭs-ĭnʹtē-grāt), *v.t.* [disintegrat-ed, disintegrat-ing], **1,** to break into pieces; as, frost *disintegrates* rock; **2,** to destroy the unity of; as, to *disintegrate* society:—*v.i.* to crumble to pieces; as, limestone *disintegrates* rapidly.

dis-in-te-gra-tion (dĭs-ĭnʹtē-grāʹshŭn), *n.* a breaking up into parts; a crumbling or wearing down, as of rocks by the weather.

dis-in-ter (dĭsʹĭn-tûrʹ), *v.t.* [disinterred, disinter-ring], to remove from a grave.—*n.* **disʹin-terʹment.**

dis-in-ter-est-ed (dĭs-ĭnʹtẽr-ĕs-tĕd; dĭs-ĭnʹtrĭs-tĕd), *adj.* **1,** not influenced by a selfish motive; **2,** showing a lack of concern or interest.—*adv.* **dis-inʹter-est-ed-ly.**

dis-join (dĭs-joinʹ), *v.t.* to part; separate; detach.

dis-joint (dĭs-jointʹ), *v.t.* **1,** to part at the joints; as, to *disjoint* a turkey; **2,** to put out of joint; as, to *disjoint* one's shoulder: —**disjointed,** *adj.* unconnected; incoherent; as, a *disjointed* speech.

dis-junc-tive (dĭs-jŭngkʹtĭv), *adj.* serving to separate:—*n.* in grammar, a conjunction connecting two or more expressions which are contrasted in meaning, or which permit choice, such as "but," or "either . . . . or."

disk or **disc** (dĭsk), *n.* a flat, circular plate, or anything like it. The spelling **disk** is preferred in some uses; as, *disk* harrow.

dis-like (dĭs-līkʹ), *n.* a feeling of distaste: —*v.t.* [disliked, dislik-ing], to regard with distaste; as, to *dislike* olives.
Syn., n. abhorrence, distaste.

dis-lo-cate (dĭsʹlō-kāt), *v.t.* [dislocat-ed, dislocat-ing], to displace; put out of place; especially, to put out of joint.

dis-lo-ca-tion (dĭsʹlō-kāʹshŭn), *n.* a displacement; a putting out of joint.

dis-lodge (dĭs-lŏjʹ), *v.t.* [dislodged, dislodg-ing], to remove from a resting place; drive from a hiding place.

dis-loy-al (dĭs-loiʹăl), *adj.* false to duty, government, or friends; faithless.—*n.* **dis-loyʹal-ty.**—*adv.* **dis-loyʹal-ly.**
Syn. inconstant, traitorous, untrue.

dis-mal (dĭzʹmăl), *adj.* **1,** gloomy; depressing; as, *dismal* weather; **2,** depressed; melancholy, as a mood.—*adv.* **disʹmal-ly.**

dis-man-tle (dĭs-mănʹtl), *v.t.* [disman-tled, disman-tling], **1,** to strip or deprive of furniture, equipment, or the like; **2,** to take apart; as, to *dismantle* an engine.

dis-may (dĭs-māʹ), *v.t.* **1,** to terrify; **2,** to dispirit; discourage:—*n.* **1,** terrified amazement, as at a great danger or disaster; **2,** discouragement, as at a hopeless task.
Syn., v. frighten, scare, dishearten.

dis-mem-ber (dĭs-mĕmʹbẽr), *v.t.* **1,** to cut or tear limb from limb; **2,** to sever into parts and distribute; divide; as, to *dismember* a kingdom.—*n.* **dis-memʹber-ment.**

dis-miss (dĭs-mĭsʹ), *v.t.* **1,** to send away or permit to depart, as a class; **2,** to discharge from office or employment, as a clerk; **3,** to refuse to consider further; as, to *dismiss* a matter from one's mind.
Syn. discard, banish.

dis-miss-al (dĭs-mĭsʹăl), *n.* **1,** the act of sending away; **2,** removal from office; also, a notice of such removal.

dis-mount (dĭs-mountʹ), *v.i.* to get down, as from a horse:—*v.t.* **1,** to remove (a rider) by force from a horse; **2,** to remove from a carriage, as a cannon; **3,** to remove from a setting, as a jewel.

dis·o·be·di·ence (dĭs/ō·bē/dĭ·ĕns), *n.* neglect or refusal to obey a rule or command.

dis·o·be·di·ent (dĭs/ō·bē/dĭ·ĕnt), *adj.* refusing or neglecting to obey; as, a *disobedient* boy.—*adv.* **dis/o·be/di·ent·ly.**

dis·o·bey (dĭs/ō·bā/), *v.t.* and *v.i.* to refuse or fail to obey; as, to *disobey* parents.

dis·o·blige (dĭs/ō·blīj/), *v.t.* [disobliged, disoblig-ing], to refuse or neglect to accommodate; refuse a favor to.

dis·or·der (dĭs·ôr/dĕr), *n.* **1,** lack of system; confusion; **2,** a commotion; especially, a riot; **3,** mental or physical disease:— *v.t.* **1,** to throw into confusion; disarrange; **2,** to derange in health of mind or body.— *adj.* **dis·or/dered.**

Syn., n. disturbance, tumult, clutter.

dis·or·der·ly (dĭs·ôr/dĕr·lĭ), *adj.* **1,** untidy; as, a *disorderly* room; **2,** unruly; turbulent; lawless; as, he was arrested for *disorderly* conduct.

dis·or·gan·ize (dĭs·ôr/găn·īz), *v.t.* [disorganized, disorganiz-ing], to throw into confusion; as, their arrival *disorganized* the meeting.

dis·own (dĭs·ōn/), *v.t.* **1,** to reject; refuse to claim as one's own; as, to *disown* one's son; **2,** to renounce allegiance to; as, to *disown* one's flag.

dis·par·age (dĭs·păr/ĭj), *v.t.* [disparaged, disparag-ing], to speak slightingly of; belittle; as, to *disparage* a rival.—*adv.* **dis·par/ag·ing·ly.**

Syn. depreciate, discredit, decry.

dis·par·age·ment (dĭs·păr/ĭj·mĕnt), *n.* depreciation; the act of undervaluing; a lowering in esteem or standing; as, the story was a *disparagement* of his friend.

dis·par·i·ty (dĭs·păr/ĭ·tĭ), *n.* [*pl.* disparities], inequality; difference; disproportion; as, a *disparity* in ages.

dis·pas·sion·ate (dĭs·păsh/ŭn·ĭt), *adj.* free from passion; impartial; as, a *dispassionate* speech.—*adv.* **dis·pas/sion·ate·ly.**

dis·patch (dĭs·păch/), *v.t.* **1,** to send off promptly; as, to *dispatch* a messenger; **2,** to finish quickly; as, to *dispatch* a lunch; **3,** to put to death; kill:—*n.* **1,** promptness; as, he did the lesson with *dispatch;* **2,** a message; especially, an official communication; **3,** an item of news; as, a *dispatch* from Paris; **4,** a putting to death; as, the *dispatch* of the spies.

dis·patch·er (dĭs·păch/ĕr), *n.* an official who directs the movements of trains, busses, or airplanes.

dis·pel (dĭs·pĕl/), *v.t.* [dispelled, dispelling], to drive apart; scatter; disperse; as, the wind *dispelled* the fog.

dis·pen·sa·ble (dĭs·pĕn/sȧ·bl), *adj.* that can be done without; unnecessary.

dis·pen·sa·ry (dĭs·pĕn/sȧ·rĭ), *n.* [*pl.* dispensaries], a place where medical advice and medicines are given free or very cheap.

dis·pen·sa·tion (dĭs/pĕn·sā/shŭn), *n.* **1,** distribution; **2,** divine management of the world; also, an instance of this; as, the flood was a *dispensation* of Providence; **3,** permission, especially by a church official, to do something usually forbidden, or to omit something usually required.

dis·pense (dĭs·pĕns/), *v.t.* [dispensed, dispens-ing], **1,** to deal out in portions; **2,** to carry out; apply; as, to *dispense* justice:— **dispense with,** to do without.

dis·pers·al (dĭs·pûr/săl), *n.* distribution; a scattering, as of seed by the wind.

dis·perse (dĭs·pûrs/), *v.t.* [dispersed, dispers-ing], **1,** to scatter; as, to *disperse* a crowd; **2,** to spread; as, to *disperse* funds; also, to cause to vanish; as, the sun *dispersed* the mist:—*v.i.* to break up and depart; as, the meeting *dispersed.*

dis·per·sion (dĭs·pûr/shŭn; dĭs·pûr/zhŭn), *n.* the act of scattering; state of being scattered.

dis·pir·it (dĭs·pĭr/ĭt), *v.t.* to lower the spirits of; dishearten; as, his failure *dispirited* him.—*adj.* **dis·pir/it·ed.**

dis·place (dĭs·plās/), *v.t.* [displaced, displac-ing], **1,** to put out of place; **2,** to remove and replace with something else; as, to *displace* a cart with a truck; **3,** to take the place of; as, the automobile *displaced* the buggy; **4,** to remove from office.

Syn. discharge, remove, disturb.

dis·placed per·son, one taken or driven from his homeland during war. Usually abbreviated *DP.*

dis·place·ment (dĭs·plās/mĕnt), *n.* **1,** the act of putting out of place; **2,** the act of replacing one thing with another; substitution; **3,** the weight or volume of a liquid displaced by a floating body.

dis·play (dĭs·plā/), *v.t.* **1,** to spread out; unfold; as, the peacock *displayed* its feathers; **2,** to exhibit; show off:—*n.* **1,** an exhibit; **2,** a parade or show.

dis·please (dĭs·plēz/), *v.t.* [displeased, displeas-ing], to offend; annoy; make angry.—*adj.* **dis·pleas/ing.**

dis·pleas·ure (dĭs·plĕzh/ẽr), *n.* disapproval; annoyance; indignation.

dis·port (dĭs·pôrt/), *v.t.* to amuse or entertain, especially by frolicsome play; as, we *disported* ourselves on the beach.

dis-pos-al (dĭs-pōz′ăl), *n.* 1, arrangement; as, the *disposal* of goods in a store; 2, a getting rid; as, the *disposal* of rubbish; 3, control; command; as, to place money or other resources at one's *disposal*.

dis-pose (dĭs-pōz′), *v.t.* [disposed, dispos-ing], 1, to arrange; distribute; 2, to make willing; incline; as, weariness *disposed* him to yield.

   dispose of, to get rid of; as, to *dispose of* waste paper; **disposed**, inclined; as, to be kindly *disposed*.

dis-po-si-tion (dĭs′pŏ-zĭsh′ŭn), *n.* 1, the act of placing or arranging; 2, order; arrangement; as, the *disposition* of furniture in a room; 3, the power of managing or distributing; as, to have the *disposition* of property; 4, inclination; temper or habit of mind; as, a *disposition* to jealousy.

   Syn. bent, humor, temperament.

dis-pos-sess (dĭs′pŏ-zĕs′), *v.t.* to oust; put out of possession; as, to *dispossess* a man of his home.—*n.* **dis′pos-ses′sion.**

dis-praise (dĭs-prāz′), *v.t.* [dispraised, disprais-ing], to disparage; censure:—*n.* disapproval; censure.

dis-proof (dĭs-prōōf′), *n.* evidence proving the opposite of what has been asserted; refutation; as, *disproof* of a statement.

dis-pro-por-tion (dĭs′prŏ-pôr′shŭn), *n.* want of balance or symmetry; lack of proper relation in form, size, or the like.

dis-pro-por-tion-ate (dĭs′prŏ-pôr′shŭn-ĭt), *adj.* lacking in proportion or balance; out of proportion.

dis-prove (dĭs-prōōv′), *v.t.* [disproved, disprov-ing], to show to be untrue or unreasonable; as, to *disprove* a statement.

dis-pu-ta-ble (dĭs′pŭ-ta̍-bl; dĭs-pūt′a̍-bl), *adj.* open to question; debatable.

dis-pu-tant (dĭs′pŭ-tănt), *n.* a person who takes part in an argument or debate.

dis-pu-ta-tion (dĭs′pŭ-tā′shŭn), *n.* a debate or argument.

dis-pu-ta-tious (dĭs′pŭ-tā′shŭs), *adj.* inclined to argue or dispute; contentious.

dis-pute (dĭs-pūt′), *v.i.* [disput-ed, disput-ing], to debate; argue; quarrel:—*v.t.* 1, to contend for, by words or actions; as, the soldiers *disputed* every inch of the ground; 2, to question the justice or fairness of; as, to *dispute* an election:—*n.* an argument; also, a quarrel.

   Syn., *v.* wrangle, question; *n.* quarrel, controversy, strife.

dis-qual-i-fy (dĭs-kwŏl′ĭ-fī; dĭs-kwôl′ĭ-fī), *v.t.* [disqualified, disqualify-ing], 1, to make unfit; disable; 2, to deprive of a privilege; as, to *disqualify* a player.—*n.* **dis-qual′i-fi-ca′tion.**

dis-qui-et (dĭs-kwī′ĕt), *v.t.* to make uneasy; worry; as, his absence *disquieted* her:—*n.* uneasiness; anxiety.

dis-qui-e-tude (dĭs-kwī′ĕ-tūd), *n.* a state of mental uneasiness.

dis-qui-si-tion (dĭs′kwĭ-zĭsh′ŭn), *n.* a formal discussion; dissertation.

Dis-rae-li (dĭz-rā′lĭ), Benjamin (1804-1881), Earl of Beaconsfield, a prime minister of England under Queen Victoria.

dis-re-gard (dĭs′rē-gärd′), *v.t.* to fail to notice or give heed to; neglect; as, he *disregarded* instructions:—*n.* lack of attention.

dis-re-pair (dĭs′rē-pâr′), *n.* the state of needing repair; dilapidation.

dis-rep-u-ta-ble (dĭs-rĕp′ū-ta̍-bl), *adj.* of bad reputation; not respectable.

dis-re-pute (dĭs′rē-pūt′), *n.* lack or loss of reputation; dishonor; ill repute.

dis-re-spect (dĭs′rē-spĕkt′), *n.* lack of courtesy or respect, especially toward elders or superiors.

dis-re-spect-ful (dĭs′rē-spĕkt′fŏŏl), *adj.* lacking in respect to elders or superiors.—*adv.* **dis′re-spect′ful-ly.**

dis-robe (dĭs-rōb′), *v.i.* and *v.t.* [disrobed, disrob-ing], to undress.

dis-rupt (dĭs-rŭpt′), *v.t.* to break apart; break up; as, to *disrupt* a government.

dis-rup-tion (dĭs-rŭp′shŭn), *n.* the act of rending or tearing apart; a violent breaking up; as, the *disruption* of a society.

dis-sat-is-fac-tion (dĭs′săt-ĭs-făk′shŭn), *n.* discontent; lack of satisfaction.

dis-sat-is-fy (dĭs-săt′ĭs-fī), *v.t.* [dissatisfied, dissatisfy-ing], to cause discontent to, as by lack of something; to fail to satisfy; as, the house *dissatisfied* her.

dis-sect (dĭ-sĕkt′), *v.t.* 1, to cut in pieces, in order to examine; as, to *dissect* a plant; 2, to examine; analyze; as, to *dissect* a person's motives.—*n.* **dis-sec′tion.**

dis-sem-ble (dĭ-sĕm′bl), *v.t.* [dissem-bled, dissem-bling], to hide under a false appearance; as, to *dissemble* one's feelings:—*v.i.* to conceal the truth by some pretense; as, to *dissemble* in making excuses.—*n.* **dis-sem′bler.**

   Syn. feign, cover, mask, conceal.

dis-sem-i-nate (dĭ-sĕm′ĭ-nāt), *v.t.* [disseminat-ed, disseminat-ing], to scatter, as seed; diffuse; spread abroad; as news.—*n.* **dis-sem′i-na′tion.**

   Syn. spread, circulate, disperse.

dis-sen-sion (dĭ-sĕn′shŭn), *n.* angry disagreement; strife.

   Syn. contention, quarrel, wrangling.

dis-sent (dĭ-sĕnt′), *v.i.* to disagree in

opinion; as, to *dissent* from a judgment:—
n. a disagreement in opinion.

Syn., v. quarrel, differ, vary.

dis-sent-er (dĭ-sĕn'tẽr), *n.* a person who differs from the prevailing opinion:— **Dissenter**, in Great Britain, a member of a Protestant sect which has broken away from the state church.

dis-ser-ta-tion (dĭs/ẽr-tā/shŭn), *n.* a lengthy and formal discourse.

dis-sev-er (dĭ-sĕv/ẽr), *v.t.* to cut off; separate; disjoin.

dis-sim-i-lar (dĭ-sĭm/ĭ-lẽr; dĭs-sĭm/ĭ-lẽr), *adj.* unlike; as, *dissimilar* tastes.—*n.* **dis-sim/i-lar/i-ty.**

dis-sim-u-late (dĭ-sĭm/ū-lāt), *v.i.* and *v.t.* [dissimulat-ed, dissimulat-ing], to dissemble; feign; pretend.

dis-sim-u-la-tion (dĭ-sĭm/ū-lā/shŭn), *n.* pretense; deceit; deception.

dis-si-pate (dĭs/ĭ-pāt), *v.t.* [dissipat-ed, dissipat-ing], **1,** to scatter in different directions; as, the wind *dissipated* the smoke; **2,** to waste foolishly; as, he *dissipated* his fortune:—*v.i.* **1,** to disperse; vanish; **2,** to engage in riotous amusement; especially, to drink to excess.

dis-si-pat-ed (dĭs/ĭ-pāt/ĕd), *adj.* **1,** scattered; dispersed; wasted; **2,** intemperate.

dis-si-pa-tion (dĭs/ĭ-pā/shŭn), *n.* **1,** a scattering, as of fog by sunlight; **2,** a wasting; as, the *dissipation* of one's energies; **3,** intemperate living.

dis-so-ci-ate (dĭ-sō/shĭ-āt), *v.t.* [dissoci-ated, dissociat-ing], to cut off; separate; also, to separate in one's mind; as, to *dissociate* feebleness from old age.

dis-so-lute (dĭs/ō-lūt), *adj.* morally loose; given to vice or dissipation.

Syn. wild, wanton, profligate.

dis-so-lu-tion (dĭs/ō-lū/shŭn), *n.* **1,** the act of separating or breaking up; as, the *dissolution* of a partnership; **2,** decay; ruin; death.

dis-solve (dĭ-zŏlv/), *v.t.* [dissolved, dissolv-ing], **1,** to cause to be absorbed by a liquid; as, to *dissolve* salt in water; **2,** to break up; as, to *dissolve* an assembly; **3,** to put an end to; as, to *dissolve* a partnership:—*v.i.* to be absorbed in a liquid.

dis-so-nance (dĭs/ō-năns), *n.* a disagreeable mingling of sounds; discord.

dis-so-nant (dĭs/ō-nănt), *adj.* harsh in sound; discordant; inharmonious.

dis-suade (dĭ-swād/), *v.t.* [dissuad-ed, dissuad-ing], to advise or counsel against; divert by persuasion from a purpose or action; as, they *dissuaded* him from going.

dis-sua-sion (dĭ-swā/zhŭn), *n.* advice against a purpose or action.

dis-taff (dĭs/tȧf), *n.* a stick on which the wool or flax used for spinning is wound.

dis-tance (dĭs/tăns), *n.* **1,** the extent of space between two objects or points; **2,** a far-off place; as, hills are blue in the *distance;* **3,** lack of familiarity; reserve; coldness; as, to keep one's *distance:*—*v.t.* [distanced, distanc-ing], to leave behind in a race; outstrip; as, to *distance* one's rivals.

DISTAFF
A, distaff; B, spindle.

dis-tant (dĭs/tănt), *adj.* **1,** far off in time, space, or relationship; as, a *distant* event; a *distant* cousin; **2,** reserved; not familiar; cold; as, he is *distant* with his employees.—*adv.* **dis/tant-ly.**

Syn. cold, aloof, unapproachable.

dis-taste (dĭs-tāst/), *n.* dislike; aversion; as, a *distaste* for buttermilk.

dis-taste-ful (dĭs-tāst/fŏŏl), *adj.* **1,** unpleasant to the taste; **2,** disagreeable or displeasing to the feelings.

dis-tem-per (dĭs-tĕm/pẽr), *n.* illness; especially, a disease of animals.

dis-tend (dĭs-tĕnd/), *v.t.* to stretch out or expand; as, to *distend* the stomach:—*v.i.* to swell; enlarge, as a balloon.

dis-ten-tion or **dis-ten-sion** (dĭs-tĕn/-shŭn), *n.* a swelling out or expansion.

dis-til or **dis-till** (dĭs-tĭl/), *v.i.* [distilled, distil-ling], to fall in drops; trickle forth: —*v.t.* **1,** to let fall in drops; **2,** to separate (a liquid) from a mixture by heating so as to form a vapor, which is carried off and condensed by cooling; **3,** to subject (a mixture) to this process.—*n.* **dis/til-la/-tion.**—*n.* **dis-til/ler.**

dis-til-ler-y (dĭs-tĭl/ẽr-ĭ), *n.* [*pl.* distilleries], a place where liquids, especially alcoholic liquors, are distilled.

dis-tinct (dĭs-tĭngkt/), *adj.* **1,** separate; different; **2,** clear to the senses; as, a *distinct* sound or view; **3,** carefully thought out; lucid; as, a *distinct* statement.—*n.* **dis-tinct/ness.**—*adv.* **dis-tinct/ly.**

Syn. obvious, evident, unconfused.

dis-tinc-tion (dĭs-tĭngk/shŭn), *n.* **1,** the act of noting clearly or marking off from others; **2,** a characteristic difference; as, the *distinction* between good and evil; **3,** special honor; eminence; superiority; as, to serve with *distinction.*

Syn. difference.

dis-tinc-tive (dĭs-tĭngk/tĭv), *adj.* marking a difference; characteristic; as, a *distinctive* feature.—*adv.* **dis-tinc/tive-ly.**

dis-tin-guish (dĭs-tĭng/gwĭsh), *v.t.* **1,** to

GREAT DANE

ST. BERNARD

IRISH SETTER

IRISH TERRIER

POMERANIAN

BULLDOG

BOSTON TERRIER

COLLIE

WIRE-HAIRED FOX TERRIER

GREYHOUND

PEKINGESE

POINTER

All the dogs on this page are 1/20 natural size

Twelve Typical Dogs. (*See other side.*)

DOGS

The dog is man's oldest animal friend. No one knows exactly when the friendship started. In the cave homes of ancient peoples, skeletons of dogs have been found beside skeletons of men. One can imagine wild dogs skulking about the caves of primitive man and after each visit becoming a little friendlier. And it is easy to believe that the children of the cave dwellers found and made pets of wild puppies.

The various kinds of dogs have been developed by breeding. The bulldog, that bowlegged fellow with the homely face, did not always look as the artist has pictured him on the preceding page, and he was not always called a bulldog. His story stretches back 800 years, to the time when the sport of bullbaiting started in England. The dogs with the strongest jaws and shortest noses were most successful in this barbarous sport, so the breeders of bullfighting dogs always selected the ones with the heaviest jaws, shortest noses, and greatest tenacity. The result is the bulldog.

At a dog show you might see perhaps 100 different breeds, and behind each one would be a story of careful selection and development, like that of the bulldog. The aristocratic Scotch collie, with his beautiful white collar, silky coat, and pointed head, looks little like his shaggy brother who tends the sheep in the Scottish Highlands.

One of the most extreme types of dog is the greyhound, bred for great speed in hunting such fleet animals as the antelope and the hare. The greyhound has an almost perfect build for speed, muscular back, sloping shoulders, slim legs that can stretch to tremendous reaches. Built on the lines of the greyhound but much larger and more powerful, is the Great Dane, another dog that was bred for hunting. He is also a great protection as a watchdog.

For keenness of scent and cheerful obedience, setters and pointers can hardly be surpassed. In a field where rabbits and mice and various birds have walked and slept, one of these intelligent dogs, while running at high speed, will detect the scent of a quail, and stop several feet away, pointing for the hunter. There are several kinds of setters and all are highly intelligent, obedient, and very beautiful. They have long, silky coats, the Irish setter's being mahogany red. The pointers are shorthaired, of various colors, and lean and muscular.

Terriers were developed by nature as diggers. They got their living by digging out rats, rabbits, and foxes. Their name comes from the French word *terre*, meaning the "earth." Much of the ancient fight and strength has been bred out of dogs, but that can hardly be said of the terriers. At least one of them, the staunch little wire-haired fox terrier, would rather fight than eat. For sheer grit he cannot be beaten. The Irish terrier is also a daredevil and for courage has few equals. He has fine manners and makes a desirable companion. The Boston terrier is of strictly American breeding. His ancestors came to Boston as bulldogs. Now he is less bowlegged than his forefathers, his lungs are better, his body is more compact, and his face has become more intelligent and refined.

The Pomeranians are deep-furred, kitten-footed little toy dogs, with erect ears and pointed noses. They are of various sizes and colors, and have little value except as pets. Equally insignificant is the Pekinese, that pop-eyed, silky-haired favorite, whose useless existence has so dulled his senses that his nose can hardly detect the difference between a cat and a calf.

From a hospice in the Alps comes the St. Bernard, a huge dog whose capacity for service to man is even greater than his size. In his native land, the St. Bernard is trained to obey and serve from the time he is a heavy-footed, clumsy puppy. In due time he is sent out on the snow-covered mountains to rescue travelers lost in the snow. In a small barrel fastened about his neck, he carries wine for the cold wanderer. He will lick the face of a sleeping victim until he wakens and revives enough to hold on to the dog and stagger to the hospice, which is kept open and warm, day and night, the year round. One famous St. Bernard, named "Barry," saved 40 persons, thereby setting a high standard of service for all St. Bernards.

mark off; as, speech *distinguishes* man from apes; **2,** to recognize by special features; as, to *distinguish* cars of different makes; **3,** to see clearly; **4,** to honor by a mark of preference:—*v.i.* to make a distinction; as, to *distinguish* between brown and tan.—*adj.* **dis-tin′guish-a-ble.**

Syn. discern, perceive, discriminate.

dis-tin-guished (dĭs-tĭng′gwĭsht), *adj.* superior in ability, achievement, etc.

Syn. famous, noted, illustrious.

dis-tort (dĭs-tôrt′), *v.t.* **1,** to change from the natural shape; as, to *distort* the features; **2,** to change the meaning of; as, he *distorted* what I said.—*n.* **dis-tor′tion.**

dis-tract (dĭs-trăkt′), *v.t.* **1,** to divert; bewilder; perplex; as, the many changes *distracted* him; **2,** to drive mad; derange.—*adj.* **dis-tract′ed.**—*adv.* **dis-tract′ed-ly.**

dis-trac-tion (dĭs-trăk′shŭn), *n.* **1,** a drawing away of the attention from an object; **2,** anything which diverts attention; **3,** bewilderment; mental confusion or distress; **4,** madness or frenzy.

Syn. disorder, disturbance, diversion.

dis-traught (dĭs-trôt′), *adj.* bewildered; crazy; as, to run about as if *distraught.*

dis-tress (dĭs-trĕs′), *v.t.* to inflict pain or grief upon; grieve:—*n.* **1,** physical or mental anguish; **2,** misfortune; danger; as, a ship in *distress.*

Syn., n. grief, pain, trouble, affliction.

dis-trib-ute (dĭs-trĭb′ŭt), *v.t.* [distribut-ed, distribut-ing], **1,** to deal or give out; allot; as, to *distribute* books; **2,** to spread; scatter; as, to *distribute* fertilizer; **3,** to sort; classify.

Syn. share, dispense, assign, spread, apportion.

dis-tri-bu-tion (dĭs′trĭ-bū′shŭn), *n.* **1,** the act of dealing out or dividing; apportionment; **2,** portions dealt out; as, the *distributions* of food were small; **3,** arrangement; classification.

dis-trib-u-tor (dĭs-trĭb′ū-tẽr), *n.* a person who distributes, as a merchant; also, any device for spreading material or distributing an electric current.

dis-trict (dĭs′trĭkt), *n.* **1,** a section marked off by definite limits for administration; as, a school *district;* **2,** an indefinite region.

Dis-trict of Co-lum-bi-a, a federal territory of the U.S., where Washington, the national capital, is located (map **6**).

dis-trust (dĭs-trŭst′), *n.* want of confidence or reliance; suspicion:—*v.t.* to have no faith in; to doubt; suspect.

Syn., n. misgiving, doubt, suspicion, mistrust, uncertainty, hesitation, question.

dis-trust-ful (dĭs-trŭst′fŏŏl), *adj.* suspicious; lacking confidence.—*adv.* **dis-trust′ful-ly.**—*n.* **dis-trust′ful-ness.**

dis-turb (dĭs-tûrb′), *v.t.* **1,** to trouble; vex; **2,** to throw into confusion; agitate; **3,** to interfere with.—*n.* **dis-turb′er.**

Syn. rouse, interrupt, confuse, annoy.

dis-turb-ance (dĭs-tûr′băns), *n.* **1,** an interruption; **2,** confusion; agitation.

Syn. commotion, tumult, turmoil.

dis-un-ion (dĭs-ūn′yŭn), *n.* **1,** a breaking apart; separation; **2,** lack of agreement.

dis-u-nite (dĭs′ū-nīt′), *v.i.* and *v.t.* [disunit-ed, disunit-ing], to divide; separate.

dis-use (dĭs-ūs′), *n.* the condition of not being in use; neglect.

dis-used (dĭs-ūzd′), *adj.* no longer used.

ditch (dĭch), *n.* a trench cut in the earth:—*v.t.* **1,** to surround with a ditch; **2,** to send into a ditch; as, to *ditch* a car.

dit-to (dĭt′ō), *n.* [*pl.* dittos], the same thing as has been said before:—*adv.* as before; likewise:—**ditto marks,** marks [″] used to avoid repetition.

dit-ty (dĭt′ĭ), *n.* [*pl.* ditties], a little song; especially, one sung by country people.

di-ur-nal (dī-ûr′năl), *adj.* **1,** relating to the day or lasting a day; as, the *diurnal* revolution of the earth; **2,** occurring every day; daily; **3,** active during the daytime; as, *diurnal* insects.—*adv.* **di-ur′nal-ly.**

di-van (dī′văn; dĭ-văn′),*n.* a low cushioned couch without back or ends; a sofa.

DIVAN

dive (dīv), *v.i.* [*p.t.* dived (dīvd) or, *Colloquial,* dove (dōv), *p.p.* dived, *p.pr.* div-ing], **1,** to plunge headforemost, as into water; **2,** to go quickly and completely into a place or an activity; as, to *dive* into a tunnel; he *dived* into his work:—*n.* **1,** a plunge headforemost, as into water; **2,** a low resort:—**dive bomber,** a bombing plane which releases its bomb during a steep dive at the target.

div-er (dīv′ẽr), *n.* **1,** a person who plunges into water; **2,** a person who makes a business of going under water, as for pearls; **3,** any bird of diving habit, as a loon.

DIVER, def. 2
In deep-sea diving suit.

di-verge (dī-vûrj′; dĭ-vûrj′), *v.i.* [diverged, diverg-ing], **1,** to spread out from a point; **2,** to differ, as from a standard.

di-ver-gence (dī-vûr′jĕns; dĭ-vûr′jĕns), *n.* a moving apart; deviation, as from a standard.

di-ver-gent (dī-vûr′jĕnt; dĭ-vûr′jĕnt), *adj.* **1,** tending to move apart; **2,** deviating.

di-vers (dī′vẽrz), *adj.* various; several; as, *divers* points of view.

di-verse (dĭ-vûrs′; dĭ′vûrs; dĭ-vûrs′), *adj.* different; unlike; dissimilar; varied.

di-ver-si-fy (dĭ-vûr′sĭ-fī; dĭ-vûr′sĭ-fī), *v.t.* [diversified, diversify-ing], to make various; give variety to; as, hills *diversify* the view.—*n.* **di-ver′si-fi-ca′tion.**

di-ver-sion (dĭ-vûr′shŭn; dĭ-vûr′zhŭn; dĭ-vûr′shŭn; dĭ-vûr′zhŭn), *n.* **1,** a turning aside from a set course; as, the *diversion* of a river; **2,** a recreation; pastime. *Syn.* sport, game, amusement, fun.

di-ver-si-ty (dĭ-vûr′sĭ-tĭ; dĭ-vûr′sĭ-tĭ), *n.* [*pl.* diversities], difference; variety; as, *diversity* of color.

di-vert (dĭ-vûrt′; dĭ-vûrt′), *v.t.* **1,** to turn from or to any direction or course; draw away; **2,** to entertain; amuse.

di-vest (dĭ-vĕst′; dĭ-vĕst′), *v.t.* **1,** to strip; unclothe; **2,** to deprive, as of rights or office; despoil.

di-vide (dĭ-vīd′), *v.t.* [divid-ed, divid-ing], **1,** to cut into two or more parts; **2,** to separate (a thing) from another or others; **3,** to cause to disagree; as, to *divide* friends; **4,** to share, as money; **5,** in arithmetic, to perform the operation of division on or with; as, to *divide* 30 by 6; to *divide* 6 into 30:—*v.i.* **1,** to be separated into parts; **2,** to perform the operation of division with two numbers:—*n.* a watershed.

div-i-dend (dĭv′ĭ-dĕnd), *n.* **1,** a share of the profits of a company or business; **2,** in arithmetic, a number or quantity to be divided by another number or quantity.

di-vid-ers (dĭ-vīd′ẽrz), *n.pl.* an instrument used in mechanical drawing, for dividing lines, checking distances, or the like.

div-i-na-tion (dĭv′ĭ-nā′shŭn), *n.* **1,** the act of foreseeing or foretelling; **2,** a forecast; guess.

¹**di-vine** (dĭ-vīn′), *adj.* [div-in-er, divin-est], **1,** relating to God; from God; **2,** godlike; holy; **3,** superhumanly excellent:—*n.* a person who knows theology; a priest; clergyman.—*adv.* **di-vine′ly.** *Syn., adj.* heavenly, holy, celestial, sacred, superhuman.

DIVIDERS

²**di-vine** (dĭ-vīn′), *v.t.* [divined, divin-ing], **1,** to foresee or foretell; **2,** to guess; perceive by reason or insight; as, he *divined* my purpose.—*n.* **di-vin′er.**

di-vin-i-ty (dĭ-vĭn′ĭ-tĭ), *n.* [*pl.* divinities], **1,** the state or quality of being godlike; Godhead; **2, the Divinity,** God; **3,** a god or deity; **4,** the study of theology.

di-vis-i-ble (dĭ-vĭz′ĭ-bl), *adj.* **1,** capable of being separated into parts; **2,** in mathematics, capable of division by a specified number without a remainder; as, 6 is *divisible* by 2.—*n.* **di-vis′i-bil′i-ty.**

di-vi-sion (dĭ-vĭzh′ŭn), *n.* **1,** a separation into parts; also, a portion or part; **2,** that which separates, as a partition; a dividing line; **3,** discord; difference in opinion; **4,** a department; as, the selling *division* of a firm; **5,** in the army, a unit complete in itself, comprising several thousand men under a major general; **6,** in the navy, a section or unit of a fleet; **7,** the process of finding how many times one quantity contains, or is contained in, another. *Syn.* share, piece, fraction.

di-vi-sor (dĭ-vī′zẽr), *n.* in arithmetic, the number or quantity by which the dividend is to be divided.

di-vorce (dĭ-vôrs′), *n.* **1,** a legal dissolving of a marriage; **2,** disunion of things formerly united:—*v.t.* [divorced, divorc-ing], **1,** to release from the marriage contract; **2,** to separate; as, to *divorce* church and state.

di-vor-cé (dĭ-vôr′sā′), *n.* a divorced man. —*n.fem.* **di-vor′cée′** (dĭ-vôr′sā′).

di-vulge (dĭ-vŭlj′), *v.t.* [divulged, divulg-ing], to make known, as a secret; tell. *Syn.* impart, reveal.

Dix-ie (dĭk′sĭ), *n.* **1,** the Southern States of the United States; **2,** a popular Confederate war song. Also, **Dix′ie Land.**

diz-zy (dĭz′ĭ), *adj.* [diz-zi-er, diz-zi-est], giddy; also, causing giddiness; as, a *dizzy* height.—*n.* **diz′zi-ness.**

Dja-kar-ta (jä-kär′tȧ), a city (formerly *Batavia*), capital of Indonesia.

Dnep-ro-pe-trovsk (dnĕp′rô-pĕ-trôfsk′), a province and a city, its capital, in southwestern U.S.S.R. (Map 12.)

Dnie-per (nē′pẽr), a river in U.S.S.R., flowing into the Black Sea (map 19). The Russian name is **Dne-pr** (dnĕ′pẽr).

Dnies-ter (nēs′tẽr), a river in southwestern U.S.S.R. (Map 12.)

¹**do** (dōō), *v.t.* [*p.t.* did (dĭd), *p.p.* done (dŭn), *p.pr.* do-ing], **1,** to perform; execute; as, to *do* one's work; **2,** to render; pay; give; as, to *do* a favor; **3,** to produce, especially by art; as, to *do* a painting; **4,** to arrange; as, to *do* one's hair; put in order; as, to *do* a room; also, to prepare, as lessons; **5,** to achieve (a given speed); as, the car *did* fifty miles an hour; **6,** *Colloquial,* to cheat; as, he *did* me out of a job; **7,** *Colloquial,* to visit as a tourist; as, to *do* England:—*v.i.* **1,** to try one's best to succeed; as, to *do* or die; **2,** to fare (well or ill); as, to *do* well in business; **3,** *Colloquial,* to serve the purpose; as, this hat will *do*:

āte, âorta, râre, căt, ȧsk, fär, ăllow, sofȧ; ēve, ĕvent, ĕll, wrīter, novĕl; bīte, pĭn; nō, ōbey, ôr, dŏg, tŏp, cŏllide; ūnit, ūnite, bûrn, cŭt, focŭs; nōōn, fŏŏt; mound; coin;

—auxiliary v. used: **1,** in sentences so phrased as to be emphatic; as, *do* tell me; never *did* I see so large an apple; **2,** in interrogative and negative sentences; as, when *do* you get back? the parade *did* not come this way:—**substitute** v. used to replace a verb or verb construction in order to avoid repetition; as, he walks as his father *does*. *Syn.* effect, accomplish, fulfil, transact.

²do (dō), *n.* in music, the first of the syllables commonly used in singing the scale.

do. abbreviation for *ditto.*

dob·bin (dŏb'ĭn), *n.* a farm horse; also, an old or worn-out horse.

doc·ile (dŏs'ĭl), *adj.* easy to teach; easily managed; amenable; tractable. *Syn.* teachable, compliant, tame.

do·cil·i·ty (dō-sĭl'ĭ-tĭ), *n.* the quality of being gentle or easily managed.

¹dock (dŏk), *n.* a long-rooted, coarse weed with red-veined leaves, and seeds in reddish husks.

²dock (dŏk), *n.* in a courtroom, the place reserved for the prisoner.

³dock (dŏk), *n.* **1,** an artificial basin or waterway for ships; **2,** a waterway between two piers; also, *Colloquial,* a wharf:—*v.t.* to bring to a pier and moor, as a ship:—*v.i.* to arrive at a pier.

⁴dock (dŏk), *n.* the stump of an animal's tail:—*v.t.* **1,** to cut off; **2,** to make a deduction from (wages).

DOCK

dock·et (dŏk'ĕt), *v.t.* to mark (papers) by writing on the back, or by a ticket, to indicate the contents:—*n.* **1,** a label or ticket attached to a package to show the contents; **2,** a list of matters to be acted upon in an assembly; especially, a list of cases for trial in court.

dock·yard (dŏk'yärd'), *n.* a place where ships are built and repaired, and where ships' supplies are kept.

doc·tor (dŏk'tẽr), *n.* **1,** a licensed physician or surgeon; **2,** a person who holds the highest degree conferred by a university: —*v.t. Colloquial:* **1,** to treat medically; as, to *doctor* a cold; **2,** to tamper with.

doc·trine (dŏk'trĭn), *n.* that which is taught; the principles or beliefs of a church, sect, or party.—*adj.* **doc'tri·nal.**

doc·u·ment (dŏk'ū-mĕnt), *n.* a record; an official paper that gives information or evidence, as a birth certificate.

doc·u·men·ta·ry (dŏk'ū-mĕn'tȧ-rĭ), *adj.* relating to written records; derived from official papers; as, *documentary* evidence.

¹dod·der (dŏd'ẽr), *n.* a flowering plant, leafless and with a threadlike twining stem, which attaches itself to other plants by small roots that absorb their sap.

²dod·der (dŏd'ẽr), *v.i.* to shake; tremble; totter, as from weakness or age.

dodge (dŏj), *v.i.* [dodged, dodg-ing], **1,** to move aside quickly so as to escape something; **2,** to practice tricky devices:—*v.t.* to escape from, by dodging; as, to *dodge* a car:—*n.* **1,** an act of evasion; **2,** a clever trick.

Dodg·son (dŏj'sŭn), Charles Lutwidge (1832–1898), an English writer. See **Carroll, Lewis.**

do·do (dō'dō), *n.* [*pl.* do-does or dodos], a large bird, with short legs and wings too small for flight, related to the pigeons. It is now extinct.

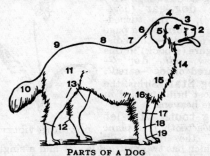

DODO (₁/₁₆)

doe (dō), *n.* the female of the deer; also, the female of the antelope, rabbit, or hare.

do·er (dōō'ẽr), *n.* one who does or achieves things; as, he is a *doer,* not a dreamer.

does (dŭz), third person singular, present indicative active, of **¹do.**

doe·skin (dō'skĭn'), *n.* **1,** leather made from the skin of a female deer; **2,** a fine woolen cloth made with a soft, smooth finish.

DOG (D), def. 2

doff (dŏf), *v.t.* to take off, as one's clothes; raise (one's hat).

dog (dôg), *n.* **1,** a domesticated animal, of which there are many breeds, some an-

PARTS OF A DOG

1, muzzle; 2, nose; 3, stop; 4, dome; 5, ear; 6, neck; 7, shoulder; 8, back; 9, rump; 10, tail; 11, hip; 12, hock, or heel; 13, stifle, or knee; 14, apron; 15, chest; 16, elbow; 17, forearm; 18, wrist; 19, pastern.

cient, found the world over; **2,** a device for bracing, holding, etc.; as, a fire*dog;* also, a catch or ratchet; **3,** *Colloquial,* any sort of fellow; as, a gay *dog;* a sly *dog;* a smart *dog:*—*v.t.* [dogged, dog-ging], to follow; track; trail.

dog-cart (dôg′kärt′), *n.* **1,** a light cart drawn by dogs; **2,** a horse-drawn, two-wheeled carriage with seats back to back.

dog days, a period of hot, sultry weather during July and August, once thought to be due to the rising of the Dog Star.

doge (dōj), *n.* the chief magistrate in the old republics of Venice and Genoa.

dog—ear (dôg′=ēr′), *n.* and *v.* See **dog's-ear.**

dog-fish (dôg′fĭsh′), *n.* any of various small, voracious sharks.

dog-ged (dôg′ĕd), *adj.* stubborn; persistent.

DOGFISH (2⁄5)

dog-ger-el (dôg′ĕr-ĕl), *adj.* of verse, crude; irregular; trivial:—*n.* doggerel verse.

do-gie (dō′gĭ), *n.* in the western U.S., a motherless calf.

dog-ma (dôg′må), *n.* a principle, belief, or doctrine, accepted as authoritative, especially one so accepted by the church.

dog-mat-ic (dôg-măt′ĭk) or **dog-mat-i-cal** (dôg-măt′ĭ-kăl), *adj.* **1,** pertaining to established doctrine or belief; **2,** making assertions in a positive manner, without proof; arrogant; as, a *dogmatic* old man; **3,** asserted positively without proof; as, *dogmatic* opinions.—*adv.* **dog-mat′i-cal-ly.**
Syn. emphatic, imperious.

dog-ma-tism (dôg′må-tĭzm), *n.* **1,** positive assertion of opinion or belief without proof; **2,** the quality of being too positive in opinions or beliefs.

dog's—ear (dôgz′=ēr′) or **dog—ear** (dôg′=ēr′), *n.* the turned-down corner of a page in a book:—*v.t.* to disfigure (a book) in this way.—*adj.* **dog's′-eared** or **dog′—eared′.**

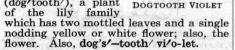

Dog Star, Sirius, the most brilliant star in the heavens.

dog-tooth vi-o-let (dôg′tŏŏth′), a plant of the lily family

DOGTOOTH VIOLET

which has two mottled leaves and a single nodding yellow or white flower; also, the flower. Also, **dog's′—tooth′ vi′o-let.**

dog-trot (dôg′trŏt′), *n.* a slow, easy run.

dog-wood (dôg′wŏŏd′), *n.* any of a group of trees or shrubs with hard, close-grained wood, bearing in spring clusters of flowers, often surrounded by four pink or white petal-like parts.

doi-ly (doi′lĭ), *n.* [*pl.* doilies], a small mat of lace, linen, or the like.

do-ings (dōō′ĭngz), *n.pl.* things done; acts.

doit (doit), *n.* **1,** formerly, a small coin of the Netherlands; **2,** a small thing; trifle.

dol-drums (dŏl′drŭmz), *n.pl.* **1,** the state of being becalmed or at a standstill; as, a ship in the *doldrums;* **2,** a windless region near the equator where ships are often becalmed; **3,** hence, depression of mind.

¹dole (dōl), *n.* the dealing out of money, clothing, food, or the like, for charity; also, the gifts themselves:—*v.t.* [doled, dol-ing], **1,** to give as alms; **2,** hence, to deal out sparingly or in small amounts.

²dole (dōl), *n. Archaic,* woe; grief.

dole-ful (dōl′fŏŏl), *adj.* sad; dismal; gloomy.—*adv.* **dole′ful-ly.**—*n.* **dole′ful-ness.**

doll (dŏl), *n.* **1,** a puppet or toy baby; **2,** a

DOLLS
1, Egyptian; 2, European; 3, American Indian.

girl or woman with a pretty, childish face.

dol-lar (dŏl′ēr), *n.* **1,** a silver coin used in the U.S. and Canada, equal to 100 cents; **2,** a bank note, treasury note, or the like, of the legal value of 100 cents; **3,** any of various large silver coins of other countries; as, a Mexican *dollar.*

do-lor (dō′lēr), *n.* sorrow; pain; grief; lamentation; anguish.—*adj.* **do′lor-ous.**

dol-phin (dŏl′fĭn), *n.* **1,** a whalelike sea mammal, about six feet long, with a long snout; **2,** an edible sea fish remarkable for its

DOLPHIN (⅕0), def. 1

rapid changes of color when dying:—**dol-phin striker,** a spar extending downward from the end of the bowsprit (see illustration on page 695).

dolt (dōlt), *n.* a heavy, stupid fellow; a dunce; blockhead.—*adj.* **dolt′ish.**

-dom (-dŭm), a suffix meaning: **1,** the office or territory of; as, king*dom,* christen-*dom;* **2,** the state or condition of being; as,

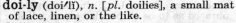

āte, āorta, râre, căt, ȧsk, fär, ȧllow, sofȧ; ēve, ėvent, ĕll, writēr, novĕl; bīte, pĭn; nō, ōbey, ôr, dŏg, tŏp, cŏllide; ūnit, ūnite, bûrn, cŭt, focŭs; nōōn, fŏŏt; mound; coin;

free*dom*, wis*dom;* **3,** the sum total of all of a given class or rank; as, official*dom.*

do-main (dō-mān´), *n.* **1,** an estate owned in one's own right; **2,** a region under the rule of a king or government; dominion; realm; **3,** a field of thought or action; as, the *domain* of science.

dome (dōm), *n.* **1,** a large rounded roof on a circular base; as, the *dome* of the Capitol at Washington; **2,** any domelike object:—*v.t* to top with, or shape like, a dome.

DOME

do-mes-tic (dō-měs´tĭk), *adj.* **1,** relating to one's home or household affairs; as, *domestic* cares; **2,** staying at home; fond of home; **3,** relating to, or made in, one's own country; not foreign; as, *domestic* trade; *domestic* products; **4,** of animals, tame; living with man, as dogs; turned to the use of man, as cattle:—*n.* a household servant.

do-mes-ti-cate (dō-měs´tĭ-kāt), *v.t.* [domesticat-ed, domesticat-ing], **1,** to accustom (a person) to a home or home life; **2,** to turn (an animal or plant) to the use of man; tame or cultivate; **3,** to civilize; as, in some cases savages die out before they can be *domesticated.*—*n.* **do-mes´ti-ca´tion.**

do-mes-tic-i-ty (dō´měs-tĭs´ĭ-tĭ), *n.* the state of being domestic; also, home life.

dom-i-cile (dŏm´ĭ-sĭl), *n.* a place of abode; home:—*v.t.* [domiciled, domiciling], to establish in a fixed residence.

dom-i-nant (dŏm´ĭ-nănt), *adj.* controlling; ruling; also, most important; as, the *dominant* partner in a business.

Syn. governing, principal.

dom-i-nate (dŏm´ĭ-nāt), *v.t.* [dominat-ed, dominat-ing], **1,** to govern or control; rule; as, the Romans once *dominated* Europe; **2,** to occupy a commanding position; as, the mountain *dominates* the valley:—*v.i.* to exercise influence or control; as, the strong *dominate* over the weak. —*n.* **dom´i-na´tion.**

dom-i-neer (dŏm´ĭ-nēr´), *v.i.* to exercise authority arrogantly or tyrannically; be overbearing.—*adj.* **dom´i-neer´ing.**

Dom-i-nic (dŏm´ĭ-nĭk), Saint (1170–1221), a Spaniard, founder of the Dominicans, an order of preaching friars.

Do-min-i-can (dō-mĭn´ĭ-kăn), *adj.* **1,** relating to the religious order founded in A.D. 1215 by Saint Dominic; **2,** relating to the Dominican Republic:—*n.* **1,** a Dominican friar or nun; **2,** a native of the Dominican Republic.

Do-min-i-can Re-pub-lic (dō-mĭn´ĭ-kăn), a republic (cap. Ciudad Trujillo) of eastern Hispaniola, in the West Indies (map 10).

dom-i-nie (dŏm´ĭ-nĭ), *n.* **1,** a schoolmaster; **2,** (usually dō´mĭ-nĭ), a clergyman.

do-min-ion (dō-mĭn´yŭn), *n.* **1,** supreme authority or control; rule; **2,** territory subject to a ruler or government; as, a king's *dominions;* **3,** (usually *Dominion*), a territory with a high degree of self-government, but subject to the control of another government; as, the *Dominion* of Canada.

dom-i-no (dŏm´ĭ-nō), *n.* [*pl.* dominoes or dominos], **1,** a loose cloak with a hood and mask, used as a masquerade costume; **2,** a flat, oblong, dotted piece of bone or wood used in playing a game:—**dominoes,** *n.pl.* used as *sing,* the game so played.

[1]**don** (dŏn), *v.t.* [donned, don-ning], to put on; as, to *don* one's coat.

[2]**don** (dŏn), *n.* **1,** a Spanish lord or gentleman; **2,** at English universities, a fellow, tutor, or head of a college:—**Don** (dŏn), Sir; Mr.: a title used in Spanish-speaking countries.—*n.fem.* **Do´ña** (dō´nyä).

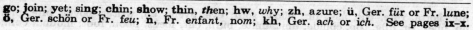

DOMINO, def. 1

do-nate (dō´nāt; dō-nāt´), *v.t.* [donat-ed, donat-ing], to give to charity; contribute.—*n.* **do´na-tor.**

DOMINOES, def. 2

do-na-tion (dō-nā´shŭn), *n.* a charitable gift; present.

Syn. offering, gift.

done (dŭn), past participle of [1]*do:*—*adj.* **1,** cooked sufficiently; **2,** *Colloquial,* cheated.

don-jon (dŭn´jŭn; dŏn´jŭn), *n.* the tower of a medieval castle.

don-key (dŏng´kĭ), *n.* [*pl.* donkeys], **1,** an ass; **2,** a stupid or obstinate fellow:—**donkey engine,** a small, movable steam engine, used when not much power is required.

DONKEY

do-nor (dō´nẽr), *n.* a giver; one who makes a donation or contribution.

Don Quix-ote (dŏn kwĭk´sŏt; dŏn kě-hō´tä), **1,** the title and hero of a Spanish story by Cervantes, ridiculing knights and chivalry; **2,** hence, any person who attempts impossible, romantic deeds.

don't (dōnt), *Colloquial*, contraction of *do not*: incorrectly used for *does not*.

doom (dōōm), *n*. **1,** destiny which cannot be escaped; **2,** destructive fate; **3,** the Last Judgment; as, the crack of *doom*; **4,** judgment; sentence:—*v.t.* **1,** to condemn; sentence; as, to *doom* a man to death; **2,** to destine; as, *doomed* to disappointment.

Syn., n. verdict, condemnation, lot.

dooms-day (dōōmz′dā′), *n*. **1,** the day of the Last Judgment; **2,** any day of judgment.

door (dôr), *n*. **1,** a movable barrier, sliding or swinging on hinges, which opens and closes the entrance to a house, room, or the like; **2,** a means of entrance.

door-keep-er (dôr′kē′pẽr), *n*. one who guards an entrance.

door-step (dôr′stĕp′), *n*. any of the steps leading up to an outside door.

door-way (dôr′wā′), *n*. the opening in which a door is hung; also, the entrance to a room or house.

dope (dōp), *n*. **1,** a varnish-like preparation painted or sprayed on the fabric surfaces of an airplane to strengthen and waterproof them; **2,** a similar substance used in model airplane construction; **3,** *Slang*, narcotic drugs; **4,** information; inside information, as on a horse race:—*v.t.* [doped, doping], *Slang*, to treat or affect with drugs.

DORIC CAPITAL

Dor-ic (dôr′ĭk), *adj*. designating the oldest and simplest form of ancient Greek architecture.

dor-mant (dôr′mănt), *adj*. sleeping; temporarily inactive; as, plants lie *dormant* in the winter; a *dormant* talent.—*n.* **dor-man-cy** (dôr′măn-sĭ).

Syn. latent, unused, inactive.

DORMER WINDOW

dor-mer win-dow (dôr′mẽr), a window built upright in a sloping roof; also, the structure built to contain it.

dor-mi-tor-y (dôr′mĭ-tôr′ĭ), *n*. [*pl*. dormitories], a sleeping room containing several beds; also, a building containing a number of sleeping rooms.

dor-mouse (dôr′mous′), *n*. [*pl*. dormice (dôr′mīs′)], a small, hibernating, squirrel-like animal of Europe and Asia.

DORMOUSE (⅓)

dor-sal (dôr′săl), *adj*. pertaining to, or on or near, the back; as, a *dorsal* muscle.

Dor-set-shire (dôr′sĕt-shĭr) or **Dor-set** (dôr′sĕt), a county in southern England.

dor-y (dôr′ĭ), *n*. [*pl*. dories], a deep flat-bottomed rowboat with a sharp prow and flat, V-shaped stern, used by salt-water fishermen.

DORY

dose (dōs), *n*. a definite quantity of medicine to be taken at one time:—*v.t.* [dosed, dos-ing], to give medicine to.

dost (dŭst), a form of ¹*do* used in old or poetic writings. *Thou dost* means *you do.*

Dos-to-ev-ski (dŏs′tô-yĕf′skē), Feodor Mikhailovich (1821–1881), a Russian novelist.

¹**dot** (dŏt), *n*. a very small spot or point, as over an *i* or *j*; a speck:—*v.t.* [dot-ted, dot-ting], to mark with dots.

²**dot** (dŏt), *n*. property which a bride brings to her husband; dowry.

dot-age (dō′tĭj), *n*. **1,** the childishness of old age; **2,** foolish affection.

do-tard (dō′tẽrd), *n*. one whose mind is weakened by age; a silly, foolish person.

dote (dōt), *v.i.* [dot-ed, dot-ing], **1,** to be feeble and foolish with age; **2,** to show excessive love; as, to *dote* on a grandchild.

doth (dŭth), a form of ¹*do* used in old or poetic writings. *He doth* means *he does.*

Dou-ay Bi-ble (dōō′ā′), an English translation of the Latin version of the Scriptures, made at Douay, France, by English Catholic refugees, about 1609, and commonly accepted by English-speaking Roman Catholics: also called *Douay Version.*

dou-ble (dŭb′l), *adj*. **1,** being in pairs; as, *double* doors; **2,** multiplied by two; twice as much or many; twice the size, strength, value, etc.; as, a *double* amount; **3,** combining two unlike qualities; as, his remark had a *double* meaning; **4,** folded over, as cloth or paper; **5,** in botany, having more than a single row of petals; as, a *double* nasturtium:—*n.* **1,** twice as much; twice the number or quantity; **2,** a substitute or understudy; as, an actor's *double*; **3,** a duplicate; that which looks very much like something else; **4,** in baseball, a two-base hit; **5,** a sharp turn made while running, as by a hunted animal, to get pursuers off the track; hence, an evasive trick:—*v.t.* [dou-bled, dou-bling], **1,** to make twice as much; multiply by two; as, *double* five to get ten; **2,** to fold over; as, to *double* a piece of paper; **3,** to pass around; as a ship *doubles* a cape:—*v.i.* **1,** to increase to twice as much; as, his stock *doubled* in value; **2,** to turn and retrace the same course; as, the fox *doubled* back; **3,** to be a substitute or understudy; as, he *doubles* for Mr. Smith:—*adv.* by twos; in a pair; as, to ride *double*:—**double—dealing,** dishonest action; deceit.

dou·ble—quick (dŭb′l-kwĭk′), *adj.* done with the quickest step in walking or marching:—*n.* such a step or march.

dou·blet (dŭb′lĕt), *n.* **1,** one of a pair; **2,** a couple; **3,** a close-fitting garment for the upper part of the body, worn by men in western Europe from the 15th to the 17th century.

dou·bloon (dŭb-lōon′), *n.* an old Spanish gold coin, worth about $8.00.

DOUBLET

dou·bly (dŭb′lĭ), *adv.* in twice the quantity or degree; twofold.

doubt (dout), *v.i.* to waver in opinion or belief; be uncertain or undecided:—*v.t.* to distrust; question; as, to *doubt* one's eyes:—*n.* **1,** uncertainty of mind; unbelief; as, I have my *doubts;* **2,** an unsettled question; an objection; as, to answer a *doubt;* **3,** a state or condition of uncertainty; as, his life is in *doubt.*—*n.* **doubt′er.**
  Syn., n. question, suspicion, uncertainty.

doubt·ful (dout′fŏŏl), *adj.* **1,** questionable as to result; as, a *doubtful* venture; **2,** questionable as to character; as, *doubtful* people; **3,** undecided; doubting; as, he was *doubtful* of her ability.—*adv.* **doubt′ful·ly.**
  Syn. wavering, distrustful, suspicious.

doubt·less (dout′lĕs), *adv.* assuredly; certainly; without doubt.—*adv.* **doubt′less·ly.**

douche (dōōsh), *n.* **1,** a spray of water for cleansing some part of the body; **2,** the instrument for spraying.

dough (dō), *n.* a spongy paste of flour and other ingredients, especially for bread.

dough·boy (dō′boi′), *n. Colloquial,* in the U.S. army, an infantry soldier.

dough·nut (dō′nŭt′), *n.* a small cake of sweetened dough, fried in deep fat.

dough·ty (dou′tĭ), *adj.* [dough-ti-er, dough-ti-est], brave; strong and bold.

dough·y (dō′ĭ), *adj.* [dough-i-er, dough-i-est], **1,** soft like dough; **2,** flabby; pale; as, a *doughy* skin.

Doug·las (dŭg′lăs), Stephen Arnold (1813–1861), an American political leader, an opponent of Lincoln.

Doug·lass (dŭg′lăs), Frederick (1817–1895), an American Negro antislavery orator and journalist.

Dou·ma (dōō′mä), *n.* the former Russian parliament. See **Duma.**

dour (dōōr), *adj.* stern; hard; obstinate.

douse (dous), *v.t.* [doused, dous-ing], **1,** to plunge into a liquid; **2,** to drench by throwing water.

[1]**dove** (dŭv), *n.* a bird of the pigeon family, known by the cooing sounds it makes.

[2]**dove** (dōv), *Colloquial,* past tense of *dive.*

dove·cot (dŭv′kŏt′) or **dove·cote** (dŭv′kŏt′; -kŏt′), *n.* a small house or box in which doves nest.

Do·ver (dō′vẽr), **1,** a city, capital of Delaware (map 6); **2,** a seaport in southeastern England (map 13): — **Strait of Dover,** a narrow passage of water between England and France (map 13).

DOVE

dove·tail (dŭv′tāl′), *n.* a tongue or a notch shaped like a dove's tail:—*v.t.* to fasten together by interlocking tongues and notches of this shape:—*v.i.* to fit closely and exactly.

dow·a·ger (dou′à-jẽr), *n.* **1,** a widow who holds property or title from her husband; **2,** *Colloquial,* a dignified elderly woman.

DOVETAILS

dow·dy (dou′dĭ), *n.* [*pl.* dowdies], a shabby, poorly dressed woman:—*adj.* [dow-di-er, dow-di-est], lacking style.

dow·el (dou′ĕl), *n.* a pin to fasten two pieces of wood or metal together: also called *dowel pin:*—*v.t.* [dow-eled, dowel-ing], to fasten by such pins.

DOWELS (D)

dow·er (dou′ẽr), *n.* **1,** that part of a deceased husband's estate, usually a third, which the law gives to his widow to use during her life; **2,** dowry; **3,** one's natural talents or abilities:—*v.t.* to furnish with a dower or a dowry; endow.

[1]**down** (doun), *n.* **1,** the first feathers of young birds; **2,** the soft under feathers of birds; **3,** any velvety fuzz, as on a peach.

[2]**down** (doun), *n.* in England, a stretch of high, grassy land used for sheep grazing.

[3]**down** (doun), *adv.* **1,** from a higher to a lower position or degree: opposite of *up;* **2,** from an earlier to a later time; as, heirlooms are handed *down;* **3,** at once, as if on the counter; as, to pay a dollar *down;* **4,** to, or in, a lower state or condition, as of illness, defeat, or the like; as, to come *down* with a cold; to bring *down* one's price; **5,** from a greater to a lesser quantity; as, to boil *down;* **6,** seriously; as, to get *down* to work; **7,** upon paper; as, take *down* what he says:—*adj.* **1,** de-

scending; as, a *down* elevator; 2, in a lowered position; as, the curtain is *down;* 3, in golf, behind one's opponent in holes or points; as, three *down;* 4, ill; inactive; as, he is *down* with a cold:—*prep.* from a higher to a lower point on; as, to row *down* the stream:—*v.t.* to bring or put down; as, *down* the enemy:—*n.* a descent; figuratively, a reverse of fortune; as, to have ups and *downs.*

down-cast (doun'kåst'), *adj.* 1, directed downward; 2, sad; discouraged.
  Syn. downhearted, dejected.

down-fall (doun'fôl'), *n.* 1, a falling downward; 2, a sudden fall from rank, fortune, or reputation; disgrace; 3, capture, as of a city.—*adj.* **down'fall'en.**

down-heart-ed (doun'här'tĕd), *adj.* downcast; sad.—*adv.* **down'heart'ed-ly.**

down-hill (doun'hĭl'), *adv.* down a slope; downward:—*adj.* (doun'hĭl'), descending.

down-pour (doun'pôr'), *n.* a heavy rain.

down-right (doun'rīt'), *adj.* 1, complete; as, *downright* folly; 2, going straight to the point; blunt; as, an honest and *downright* person:—*adv.* (doun'rīt'; doun'rīt'), 1, in plain terms; 2, utterly; extremely.

down-stairs (doun'stârz'), *adv.* on or to a lower floor:—*adj.* (doun'stârz'), on a lower floor.

down-stream (doun'strēm'), *adv.* with the current of a stream; down the stream.

down-town (doun'toun'), *adv.* to or toward the center of a city.

down-trod-den (doun'trŏd'n), *adj.* oppressed; trampled upon.

down-ward (doun'wĕrd), *adj.* moving from a higher to a lower level.

down-ward (doun'wĕrd) or **down-wards** (doun'wĕrdz),*adv.* 1, from a higher to a lower level or condition; 2, from an earlier time.

down-y (dou'nĭ), *adj.* [down-i-er, down-i-est], 1, made of, or covered with, soft feathers, hair, or wool; 2, like down; soft.

dow-ry (dou'rĭ), *n.* [*pl.* dowries], 1, the property a woman brings to her husband at marriage; 2, an endowment or talent.

dox-ol-o-gy (dŏks-ŏl'ŏ-jĭ), *n.* [*pl.* doxologies], a short hymn of praise to God, used in religious services.

doz. abbreviation for *dozen.*

doze (dōz), *v.i.* [dozed, doz-ing], to sleep lightly:—*n.* a light sleep.

doz-en (dŭz'n), *n.* [*pl.* dozen or dozens], twelve things of a kind, taken together.

DP, abbreviation for *displaced person.*

dr. abbreviation for *dram, drams:*—**Dr.** abbreviation for *Doctor, debtor.*

drab (drăb), *adj.* [drab-ber, drab-best], 1, of a dull grayish brown; 2, uninteresting.

drach-ma (drăk'må), *n.* [*pl.* drachmas

or drachmae (drăk'mē)], 1, a small weight or a coin of ancient Greece; 2, a modern Greek coin, the monetary unit of Greece.

draft or **draught** (dråft), *n.* 1, a line drawing or plan, as for an engine or building; 2, a sketch or outline of something to be done; as, the first *draft* of a speech; 3, a written order for the payment of money; also, a drawing of money from a bank or fund; 4, a method of selecting men for compulsory military service; also, the men so selected; 5, the pulling of a load by beasts; as, horses are often used for *draft;* 6, a stream of air; as, a *draft* from an open door; 7, a device for controlling the air stream in a stove, furnace, or the like; 8, a taking away; drain; as, a *draft* on supplies; 9, (usually *draught*), the depth of water to which a ship sinks, especially when loaded; 10, (usually *draught*), the hauling in of a net of fish; also, the quantity of fish caught at one haul; 11, (usually *draught*), a single drink; as, a *draught* of water; also, the act of drawing (liquid) from a cask, barrel, or the like; as, beer on *draught:*—*adj.* 1, used for pulling loads; as, *draft* animals; 2, (usually *draught*), served or drawn from a keg; as, *draught* beer:—*v.t.* 1, to sketch, write, or draw in outline; 2, to select for a special purpose; especially, to select (men) for compulsory military service.

drafts-man (dråfts'măn), *n.* [*pl.* draftsmen (-mĕn)], one who makes plans, mechanical drawings, etc.: sometimes spelled **draughts'man.**

draft-y (dråf'tĭ), *adj.* [draft-i-er, draft-i-est], exposed to currents of air.

drag (drăg), *v.t.* [dragged, drag-ging], 1, to draw along by force; haul; 2, to search the bottom of (a river or lake) with a drag or grapnel:—*v.i.* 1, to trail along the ground; as, her skirt *dragged;* 2, to move or go slowly; hence, to be slow and uninteresting; as, the speech *dragged:*—*n.* 1, a device for searching the bottom of a river or lake; 2, a sledge for hauling loads; 3, a harrow for breaking up soil; 4, anything which holds back progress; 5, a kind of coach; 6, *Slang,* influence; pull.

DRAG, def. 5

drag-gle (drăg'l), *v.t.* [drag-gled, draggling], to wet or soil by drawing in the mud or along the ground:—*v.i.* to drag along the ground and become dirty.

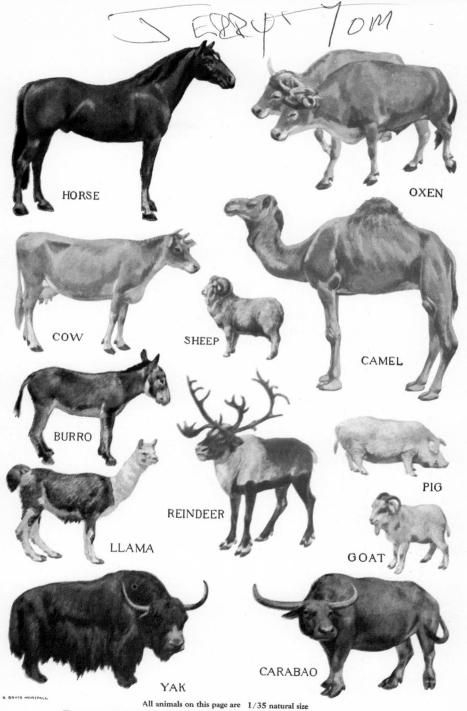

HORSE

OXEN

COW

SHEEP

CAMEL

BURRO

REINDEER

PIG

LLAMA

GOAT

YAK

CARABAO

All animals on this page are 1/35 natural size

Representative Domestic Animals. (*See other side.*)

DOMESTIC ANIMALS

Since prehistoric times, domesticated animals have played a vital part in the history of mankind. They have carried him and his burdens from place to place; they have drawn his wagons and his plows; they have furnished him with food and clothing; they have supplied him with faithful friends and companions.

None of these animals have been of greater value to man than the members of the ox family. The ox was in common use as a draft animal long before the horse was used for the same purpose. Singly, or yoked in pairs, the ox has been used for plowing and for drawing heavy loads since very ancient times. Even today, in many lands, the ox can still be seen performing these humble tasks.

In other lands, the animals of the ox kind are valued chiefly for their meat and their milk, and butter and cheese that are made from the milk. The cow pictured in the previous page is a Jersey, noted for the richness of her milk.

The yak means even more to the people of Tibet than the cow means to us, because, in regions where no other large animal can live, the yak not only furnishes food and milk, but carries men and burdens on its back and draws heavy loads. From its long hair, stout rope and coarse cloth are made. The fur on its shoulders goes into fine cloth. The hide is tanned for leather, and the dried dung is used for fuel.

The carabao came originally from India, but is now to be found in lowlands throughout the Orient, pulling crude, heavily-laden carts, plowing the wet rice fields, or resting in the shallow water of ponds and rivers.

In the northern regions of Europe, the beast of general utility is the reindeer, which can be distinguished from other members of the deer family by the fact that both males and females have antlers. The reindeer provides food, clothing, and a means of travel and transportation to Laplanders and other peoples of the far north. In 1892, reindeer were introduced into Alaska, and now the herd numbers 400,000.

Two closely related beasts of burden are the camel and the llama. The llama is really a small camel without a hump, but the homes of the two animals are far apart. The llama is native to the Andes Mountains, the camel to the deserts of Asia and Africa. The camel is remarkably fitted for long journeys over the desert. It can live on thorny plants, go for days without water, close its nose and curtain its eyes against sand storms. Camels also furnish milk, and their coarse wool has many uses.

The llama is only about three feet high at the shoulder, but it can pick its way up and down narrow mountain trails carrying a load of 120 pounds. The wool of the llama is made into twine and coarse cloth.

The goat has been called the poor man's cow, because it requires much less space than a cow does, and yields a richer milk. In many countries, great herds of goats are raised, for their milk, and their flesh, while certain goats, like the Cashmere goats of India, are valued for their wool.

The world's greatest producer of wool, however, is the sheep. Throughout the ages sheep have been invaluable providers of both food and clothing. The wool goes into yarn and cloth; the tanned hide makes beautiful leather; while the flesh (lamb and mutton) is highly valued as food.

The hog is another animal that was domesticated by man in very remote ages. The hog is the only one of the animals pictured on the previous page that is raised chiefly for food, although its hide is used for leather, and its bristles for brushes.

One of the most beautiful and best loved of animals is the horse. In early times it was prized especially as a steed to carry the warrior or to draw his chariot, but as time went on, horses were bred to other requirements, some for hauling heavy loads, others for all-round purposes, still others for swiftness in running.

In warm dry countries and in mountainous regions, the ass, or donkey, has been more esteemed as a beast of burden than the horse. The donkey is patient and sure-footed, and, like the llama, it will carry heavy burdens on steep mountain paths. The fuzzy little burro is a small breed of donkey that, for a long time, has been very popular in the mountain regions of the western United States.

drag-net (drăg'nĕt'), *n.* a net for drawing along the bottom of a river to catch fish, or along the ground to catch small game.

drag-on (drăg'ŭn), *n.* in mythology or folklore, a huge beast represented as a winged serpent, often many-headed, and breathing fire.

drag-on-fly (drăg'ŭn-flī'), *n.* [*pl.* dragonflies], an insect with a long, slender body, large eyes, and four narrow, finely veined wings: often called *darning needle*.

dra-goon (dra-gōōn'), *n.* a cavalryman or mounted soldier, heavily equipped:—*v.t.* to oppress; force (someone) to do something.

DRAGNET

drain (drān), *v.t.* 1, to draw off (a liquid) gradually; as, to *drain* water from a reservoir; 2, to make empty; as, he *drained* the cup:—*v.i.* to discharge surface water; as, swamps *drain* into ditches: —*n.* 1, a channel or pipe for useless water; 2, a continuous demand; as, a *drain* on one's time.

DRAGON

drain-age (drān'ij), *n.* 1, a flowing off of water; 2, a system of pipes or streams for drawing off water; 3, that which flows away.

DRAGONFLY (½)

Drake (drāk), Sir Francis (1540?–1596), an English admiral who took part in the destruction of the Spanish Armada.

drake (drāk), *n.* a male duck.

dram (drăm), *n.* 1, one eighth of an ounce in apothecaries' weight, or one sixteenth of an ounce in avoirdupois weight; 2, a small drink, especially of alcoholic liquor.

dra-ma (drä'ma; drăm'a), *n.* 1, a play; a work, in prose or verse, intended for acting on a stage; 2, that branch of literature concerned with plays; as, a student of *drama;* 3, any series of human events leading to a climax.

dra-mat-ic (dra-măt'ĭk), *adj.* 1, pertaining to, or like, the drama; as, *dramatic* art; 2, full of intense human interest:—**dramatics,** *n.pl.* dramatic works or performances, especially by amateurs.—*adv.* **dramat-i-cal-ly.**

dram-a-tis per-so-nae (drăm'a-tĭs pĕr-sō'nē), [Latin, *the persons of the drama*], the characters in a play.

dram-a-tist (drăm'a-tĭst), *n.* a writer of plays; a playwright.

dram-a-tize (drăm'a-tīz), *v.t.* [dramatized, dramatiz-ing], 1, to adapt or rewrite for the stage; as, to *dramatize* a novel; 2, to portray anything vividly or in a dramatic manner.—*n.* **dram'a-ti-za'tion.**

drank (drăngk), past tense of *drink.*

drape (drāp), *v.t.* [draped, drap-ing], 1, to cover with cloth; 2, to arrange (cloth or hangings) in folds.

drap-er (drāp'ẽr), *n.* a dealer in cloth: used mainly in Great Britain.

drap-er-y (drā'pẽr-ĭ), *n.* [*pl.* draperies], fabrics used for garments or hangings, especially when hung loosely or in folds; also, the hangings or draped robes.

dras-tic (drăs'tĭk), *adj.* acting rapidly and violently; as, a *drastic* remedy.

draught (draft), *n.* a drink, as of water; the depth of water required to float a boat; a catch of fish:—*adj.* drawn from a keg, as beer. Another spelling of *draft* in some of its uses. See **draft.**

draughts (drafts), *n.pl.* used as *sing.* the game of checkers.

draughts-man (drafts'măn), *n.* [*pl.* draughtsmen (-mĕn)], one who makes drawings; a draftsman. See **draftsman.**

draw (drô), *v.t.* [*p.t.* drew (drōō), *p.p.* drawn (drôn), *p.pr.* draw-ing], 1, to haul or drag; 2, to pull out; haul up, as a fish net; 3, to come to (a conclusion) by reasoning; 4, to extend in length; as, to *draw* out a performance; 5, to extract or bring out; as, to *draw* a cork; to *draw* a sword; 6, to represent on paper with pen or pencil; 7, to write in legal form; as, to *draw* up a will; 8, to require in order to float; as, the boat *draws* ten feet of water; 9, to inhale; as, to *draw* a long breath; 10, to receive; as, to *draw* one's pay; 11, to obtain (money) from a bank; 12, to attract; as, honey *draws* flies; 13, to produce or gain; as, money *draws* interest; 14, to select or obtain (a chance); as, to *draw* lots; 15, to influence (someone) to reveal facts, talents, or the like; as, to *draw* someone out; 16, to get (something) from a source; as, to *draw* inspiration from a book:—*v.i.* 1, to move; as, to *draw* away; *draw* near; 2, to attract; as, a good show always *draws;* 3, to pull or haul something; to move something by pulling; 4, to make a demand; as, to *draw* on a bank; 5, to practice the art of making designs or pictures; 6, to allow a current of air to pass; as, the chimney *draws* well:—*n.* 1, the act or result of drawing; 2, a contest left undecided; a tie; **3,** the movable section of a drawbridge.

draw-back (drô′băk′), *n.* a disadvantage; hindrance.

draw-bridge (drô′brĭj′), *n.* a bridge of which the whole or a part may be lifted up, let down, or drawn aside. (See *bridge,* illustration.)

DRAWBRIDGE
Over moat of a medieval castle.

draw-er (drô′ẽr; drôr), *n.* **1,** one who draws; a draftsman; **2,** (drôr), a sliding compartment in a bureau, table, or the like; **3, drawers** (drôrz), an undergarment for the lower part of the body.

draw-ing (drô′ĭng), *n.* **1,** the act of dragging, pulling, etc.; as, the *drawing* of a load; the *drawing* of a sword; **2,** a picture made with a pen, pencil, chalk, or the like; a sketch; **3,** the art of making such a picture.

drawing room, a room for the reception of company.

drawl (drôl), *v.t.* and *v.i.* to speak in an affected, lazy manner:—*n.* a slow, lazy manner of speaking.

drawn (drôn), past participle of *draw:*—*adj.* **1,** left undecided; as, a *drawn* game; **2,** out of shape; twisted; as, a face *drawn* with grief; **3,** melted; as, *drawn* butter.

dray (drā), *n.* a low, stoutly built cart, without sides, for heavy loads.—*n.* **dray′-man** (drā′măn).

dread (drĕd), *v.t.* to look forward to with shrinking or fear:—*n.* **1,** fear, especially of something to come; **2,** fear mingled with awe:—*adj.* **1,** causing terror; **2,** inspiring fear mingled with awe; as, a *dread* king.
 Syn., n. alarm, fright, terror, panic.

dread-ful (drĕd′fŏŏl), *adj.* arousing fear or awe; as, a *dreadful* disaster.—*adv.* **dread′ful-ly.**—*n.* **dread′ful-ness.**
 Syn. frightful, shocking, awful.

dread-nought or **dread-naught** (drĕd′-nôt′), *n.* a large, heavily armed battleship.

dream (drēm), *n.* **1,** thoughts, feelings, or pictures experienced or seen during sleep; **2,** something imagined; as, a *dream* of greatness:—*v.t.* [*p.t.* and *p.p.* dreamed (drēmd) or dreamt (drĕmt), *p.pr.* dreaming], **1,** to see, think, or feel during sleep; **2,** to imagine or hope for:—*v.i.* **1,** to have thoughts, see pictures, etc., during sleep;

2, to be lost in thought or fancy.—*n.* **dream′er.**—*adj.* **dream′less.**

dream-land (drēm′lănd′), *n.* a land seen in dreams; hence, a land of fancy.

dreamt (drĕmt), one form of the past tense and past participle of *dream.*

dream-y (drēm′ĭ), *adj.* [dream-i-er, dream-i-est], **1,** like a dream; unreal; **2,** not awake to realities; **3,** soothing; as, *dreamy* music.—*adv.* **dream′i-ly.**—*n.* **dream′i-ness.**

drear (drēr), *adj. Poetic,* dreary; dismal or gloomy; as, a *drear* old age.

drear-y (drēr′ĭ), *adj.* [drear-i-er, drear-i-est], cheerless; gloomy; as, a *dreary* day.—*adv.* **drear′i-ly.**—*n.* **drear′i-ness.**

¹**dredge** (drĕj), *n.* **1,** a device for scooping up mud, as from the bottom of a river; **2,** a device for gathering oysters:—*v.t.* [dredged, dredg-ing], **1,** to deepen, as a river channel;

DREDGE

2, to scoop with a dredge.—*n.* **dredg′er.**

²**dredge** (drĕj), *n.* a box with perforated top, used to sprinkle flour, etc.:—*v.t.* [dredged, dredg-ing], to sprinkle with flour.

dregs (drĕgz), *n.pl.* **1,** the sediment of liquids; lees; **2,** hence, the worthless part of anything.

drench (drĕnch), *v.t.* to wet thoroughly.

¹**Dres-den** (drĕz′dĕn), a city in eastern Germany, the capital of Saxony (map 12).

²**Dres-den** (drĕz′dĕn), *n.* a fine porcelain made near Dresden, Saxony.

dress (drĕs), *n.* **1,** clothes; wearing apparel; attire; **2,** a woman's or a child's gown; **3,** any outer garb or appearance; as, trees in autumn *dress:*—*v.t.* **1,** to clothe; as, to *dress* a baby; **2,** to deck out; as, to *dress* a window; **3,** to make ready for use; as, to *dress* meat; **4,** to treat or bind up, as a wound; **5,** to straighten (a line of soldiers) in military drill; **6,** to arrange (hair):—*v.i.* **1,** to put on clothes; **2,** in drilling, to form into a straight line; as, "Right, *dress!*"
 Syn., n. apparel, costume, garb.

dress-er (drĕs′ẽr), *n.* **1,** a chest of drawers with a mirror; **2,** a cupboard for dishes, glass, etc.; **3,** a bench used in dressing or preparing something for use.

DRESSER, def. 2

dress-ing (drĕs′ĭng), *n.* **1,** the act of putting on clothes, treating a wound, etc.; **2,**

material for stiffening fabrics; **3**, sauce or stuffing; **4**, a bandage, compress, or the like, applied to a wound or sore.

dress-mak-ing (drĕs′māk′ĭng), *n.* the process or occupation of making women's and children's clothes.—*n.* **dress′mak′er.**

dress-y (drĕs′ĭ), *adj.* [dress-i-er, dress-i-est], **1**, given to showy dressing; **2**, *Colloquial*, stylish; smart.

drew (drōō), past tense of *draw.*

drib-ble (drĭb′l), *v.i.* [drib-bled, dribbling], to fall in drops:—*v.t.* **1**, to let fall in drops; give out in small portions; **2**, in soccer and hockey, to give slight kicks or shoves to (the ball); **3**, in basketball, to bounce (the ball) rapidly along the floor; **4**, to drool:—*n.* a trickle of water.

drib-let (drĭb′lĕt), *n.* a small quantity; as, to give money in *driblets.*

dried (drīd), past tense and past participle of *dry:*—*adj.* without moisture.

¹dri-er or **dry-er** (drī′ẽr), *n.* **1**, a person or thing that removes moisture; **2**, an oxidized substance added to paint or varnish.

²dri-er (drī′ẽr), comparative of *dry.*

dri-est (drī′ĕst), superlative of *dry.*

drift (drĭft), *n.* **1**, the direction in which anything is driven; tendency; meaning; as, the *drift* of a speech; **2**, that which is driven; as, a snow*drift*; **3**, in geology, loose rocks, earth, etc., carried by a glacier; **4**, the distance a ship is carried from its course by ocean or air currents or an airplane by air currents:—*v.t.* to drive along or heap up; as, the wind *drifts* dry leaves into piles:—*v.i.* **1**, to be carried along by a current or by circumstances; **2**, to gather or collect in heaps.—*n.* **drift′er.**

drift-wood (drĭft′-wŏŏd′), *n.* floating wood cast ashore by water.

drill (drĭl), *n.* **1**, a tool for boring holes; **2**, a machine for sowing seeds in rows; also, a row so planted; **3**, military exercises; **4**, thorough training by frequent repetition:—*v.t.* **1**, to pierce with a drill; bore (holes); **2**, to train (soldiers) in military exercises; **3**, to instruct thoroughly; as, to *drill* pupils; **4**, to sow in rows.

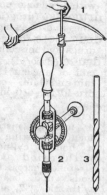

DRILLS, def. 1

1, a primitive form of drill; 2, modern hand drill with (3) enlargement of its bit, or point.

drink (drĭngk), *v.i.* [*p.t.* drank (drăngk), *p.p.* drunk (drŭngk) or drunk-en (drŭngk′ĕn), *p.pr.* drink-ing], **1**, to swallow a liquid; **2**, to take alcoholic liquors habitually:—*v.t.* **1**, to swallow (a liquid); **2**, to absorb; suck in; as, plants *drink* water; **3**, to receive through the senses; as, to *drink* in a scene:—*n.* **1**, any liquid to be swallowed; as, a cool *drink;* **2**, the quantity of liquid to be swallowed; as, a *drink* of water; **3**, strong or intoxicating liquor; as, he took to *drink.*—*adj.* **drink′a-ble.**—*n.* **drink′er.**

drip (drĭp), *v.i.* [dripped, drip-ping], **1**, to fall in drops; as, the oil *drips* on the floor; **2**, to let fall drops; as, your umbrella *drips:*—*v.t.* to let fall in drops; as, the trees *drip* rain:—*n.* **1**, that which falls in drops; **2**, a projecting part so shaped as to throw off rain.

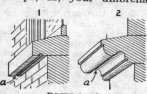

DRIPS (*a, a*)
1, in a window sill; 2, in a cornice.

drip-pings (drĭp′ĭngz), *n.pl.* the fatty juice from roasting meat.

drive (drīv), *v.t.* [*p.t.* drove (drōv), *p.p.* driv-en (drĭv′ĕn), *p.pr.* driv-ing], **1**, to urge forward by force or threats; push forward forcibly; **2**, to control the motion of; steer, as an automobile; also, to carry in a driven vehicle; **3**, to carry on vigorously; to conclude; as, to *drive* a bargain; **4**, to put into a certain state; as, you *drive* me crazy; **5**, to overwork; as, he *drove* his employees to the limit:—*v.i.* **1**, to press, aim, or be moved, forward steadily or with violence; **2**, to travel in a carriage or motor car; **3**, in golf, to strike the ball from a tee:—*n.* **1**, the act of sending forward; **2**, a road, usually one for pleasure vehicles; a driveway; **3**, a trip in a motorcar or carriage; **4**, a gathering together, or rounding up, as of cattle for branding, logs for floating, or the like; **5**, a campaign.

Syn., *v.* compel, impel, press, thrust.

driv-el (drĭv′l), *v.i.* [driveled, drivel-ing], **1**, to let saliva drip from the mouth; slobber; **2**, to talk like a fool:—*n.* **1**, saliva flowing from the mouth; **2**, idiotic talk.—*n.* **driv′el-er.**

driv-en (drĭv′ĕn), past participle of *drive.*

driv-er (drĭv′ẽr), *n.* **1**, one who or that which forces something into motion or directs persons or things in motion; **2**, in golf, a wooden club for driving the ball from a tee. (See *golf club,* illustration.)

driz-zle (drĭz′l), *v.i.* [driz-zled, driz-zling], to rain slightly or mistily:—*n.* fine, misty rain.—*adj.* **driz′zly.**

---

go; join; yet; sing; chin; show; thin, *then;* **hw,** *why;* **zh,** azure; **ŭ,** Ger. für ŏr Fr. l*u*ne; **ŏ,** Ger. schön or Fr. f*eu;* **ṅ,** Fr. *enfant, nom;* **kh,** Ger. a*ch* or i*ch.* See pages ix–x.

droll (drōl), *adj.* queer; odd; amusing; as, a *droll* remark.

Syn. funny, laughable, comic.

droll-er-y (drōl′ĕr-ĭ), *n.* [*pl.* drolleries], dry or quaint humor; jesting.

drom-e-dar-y (drŏm′ē-dĕr′ĭ; drŭm′ē-dĕr′ĭ), *n.* [*pl.* dromedaries], the Arabian, or one-humped, camel, noted for its speed.

DROMEDARY (1/80)

drone (drōn), *v.i.* [droned, dron-ing], to utter a monotonous sound; as, to *drone* through a lesson:—*v.t.* to read or speak in a monotonous tone:—*n.* **1,** a dull, monotonous tone; as, the *drone* of bees; **2,** one of the pipes of a bagpipe; **3,** the male of the honeybee, which produces no honey; **4,** a lazy fellow who will not do his share; **5,** a radio-controlled airplane or boat, carrying no passengers or pilot, used as a target or guided missile.

drool (drōōl), *v.i.* **1,** to run at the mouth; drivel; **2,** to speak foolishly.

droop (drōōp), *v.i.* **1,** to sink or hang down, as from weariness; close, as eyelids; **2,** to fail or flag; as, his spirits *drooped:*—*v.t.* to let hang down; as, to *droop* the head:—*n.* the act of drooping.

drop (drŏp), *v.i.* [dropped, drop-ping], **1,** to fall in small rounded masses of liquid; **2,** to fall; sink to a lower position; as, the hat *dropped;* **3,** to fall behind or below, as in rank; **4,** to grow lower in sound or pitch; as, her voice *dropped* to a whisper; **5,** to cease or end; as, the matter *dropped;* **6,** to come or go naturally or casually; as, to *drop* in for tea:—*v.t.* **1,** to let fall in tiny masses; as, to *drop* medicine from a spoon; **2,** to let fall suddenly; as, I *dropped* the book; **3,** to lower, as one's eyes or voice; **4,** to fell with a blow or weapon; **5,** to have done with; as, to *drop* an argument:—*n.* **1,** a small rounded mass of liquid; as, a *drop* of water; **2,** anything like a small rounded mass of liquid; as, a chocolate *drop;* **3,** any very small quantity; **4,** a sudden descent or fall; as, a *drop* in prices; **5,** the depth or distance of a descent or fall; as, a sheer *drop* of 50 feet; **6,** something arranged to be lowered or hung from above; as, a curtain *drop.*—*n.* **drop′per.**

drop-sy (drŏp′sĭ), *n.* an unnatural collection of watery fluid in cavities or tissues of the body.—*adj.* **drop′si-cal.**

drosh-ky (drŏsh′kĭ), *n.* [*pl.* droshkies], a light four-wheeled open carriage used in Russia.

dross (drôs), *n.* **1,** the scum or refuse of melted metal; **2,** refuse; waste.

drought (drout) or **drouth** (drouth), *n.* continued absence of rain or moisture.

¹drove (drōv), past tense of *drive.*

²drove (drōv), *n.* **1,** a herd of animals driven in a body; **2,** a crowd of people.

Syn. flock, multitude, herd, pack.

dro-ver (drō′vĕr). *n.* **1,** one who drives cattle to market; **2,** a dealer in cattle.

drown (droun), *v.i.* to die from suffocation in water or other liquid:—*v.t.* **1,** to kill by plunging under water; **2,** to overpower; as, the noise *drowned* the music.

drowse (drouz), *v.i.* [drowsed, drows-ing], to be heavy with sleep; doze:—*v.t.* to spend (time) dozing:—*n.* a light sleep, or doze.

drow-sy (drou′zĭ), *adj.* [drow-si-er, drow-si-est], **1,** sleepy; as, a *drowsy* feeling; **2,** making one sleepy; as, a *drowsy* sound.—*adv.* **drow′si-ly.**—*n.* **drow′si-ness.**

drub (drŭb), *v.t.* [drubbed, drub-bing], to beat with a stick.—*n.* **drub′bing.**

drudge (drŭj), *v.i.* [drudged, drudg-ing], to work hard at disagreeable tasks; slave:—*n.* one employed in slavish work.

drudg-er-y (drŭj′ĕr-ĭ), *n.* [*pl.* drudgeries], hard, disagreeable, or servile work.

Syn. toil, labor, work.

drug (drŭg), *n.* **1,** a medicine, or a substance used in making medicine; **2,** a habit-forming substance, or narcotic, such as opium; **3,** an article which sells slowly; as, a *drug* on the market:—*v.t.* [drugged, drug-ging], **1,** to mix drugs with; as, to *drug* wine; **2,** to render stupid or put to sleep with a drug; as, she *drugged* herself with headache powders.

drug-gist (drŭg′ĭst), *n.* a dealer in medicines and their ingredients.

drug-store (drŭg′stôr′), *n.* a shop where drugs and miscellaneous goods are sold.

dru-id (drōō′ĭd), *n.* a priest of a religious cult of ancient Britain and Gaul.—*adj.* **dru-id′ic; dru-id′i-cal.**

drum (drŭm), *n.* **1,** a musical instrument consisting of a hollow cylinder with dried skin stretched across the ends, and beaten with sticks; **2,** anything like a drum, as a cylinder for winding rope or wire, or a cylindrical container, as for oil; **3,** a cavity within the ear; also, less correctly, the membrane or skin

DRUMS
1, kettledrum; 2, tambourine; 3, snare drum; 4, bass drum.

between the outer and middle ear:—*v.i.* [drummed, drum-ming], **1**, to beat or play a drum; **2**, to beat rapidly upon something with the fingers:—*v.t.* **1**, to cause to beat against something; as, to *drum* one's feet on the floor; **2**, to beat (up) or summon; as, to *drum* up trade; **3**, to repeat constantly; as, this idea has been *drummed* into me.

drum-mer (drŭm'ẽr), *n.* **1**, one who plays a drum; **2**, a traveling salesman.

drum-stick (drŭm'stĭk/), *n.* **1**, a stick for beating a drum; **2**, the lower joint of the leg of a dressed chicken, turkey, etc.

drunk (drŭngk), one form of the past participle of *drink*:—*adj.* intoxicated:—*n. Slang:* **1**, a sot; **2**, a spree.

drunk-ard (drŭngk/ẽrd), *n.* one who is habitually intoxicated; a sot.

drunk-en (drŭngk/ĕn), one form of the past participle of *drink*:—*adj.* intoxicated; also, due to drink; as, a *drunken* stupor. —*adv.* **drunk/en-ly.**—*n.* **drunk/en-ness.**

dry (drī), *adj.* [dri-er, dri-est], **1**, without moisture or water; as, *dry* land; **2**, empty of water; as, a *dry* well; also, *Colloquial,* thirsty; **3**, lacking in interest; as, a *dry* speech; **4**, harsh; as, a *dry,* hacking cough; **5**, shrewd and sharp; as, *dry* wit; **6**, naming a measure for grains, vegetables, etc.; **7**, *Colloquial,* forbidding the sale of intoxicants; as, *dry* cities; *dry* laws:—**dry ice,** carbon dioxide gas frozen solid, resembling blocks of snow:—*v.t.* and *v.i.* [dried, drying], to make or become dry:—*n.* [*pl.* drys], *Colloquial,* a prohibitionist.—*n.* **dry/ness.** *Syn., adj.* arid, parched, dull, insipid.

dry-ad (drī'ăd; drī'ăd), *n.* in mythology, a nymph supposed to live in a tree.

Dry-den (drī'dĕn), John (1631–1700), an English poet and dramatist.

dry dock, an artificial basin where ships

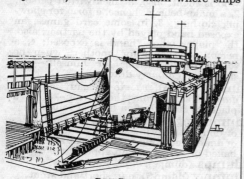

DRY DOCK

are repaired or built. It is so constructed that the water can be pumped out.

dry-er (drī'ẽr), *n.* one who or that which removes moisture. See **drier.**

dry goods, woven or knitted fabrics, such as cloth, lace, ribbon, or the like.

dry-ly (drī'lĭ), *adv.* in an uninteresting manner; without emotion; as, a story *dryly* told.

du-al (dū'ăl), *adj.* pertaining to two; composed of two; twofold; double; as, *dual* ownership.

dub (dŭb), *v.t.* [dubbed, dub-bing], **1**, to bestow knighthood upon, by tapping the shoulder with a sword; **2**, to confer any title, name, or nickname upon; as, they *dubbed* her "Tommy"; **3**, to do awkwardly; as, to *dub* a golf stroke:—*n. Slang,* an awkward player.

du-bi-ous (dū'bĭ-ŭs), *adj.* **1**, doubtful; as, a *dubious* venture; **2**, questionable; as, a man of *dubious* reputation.

Dub-lin (dŭb'lĭn), a city in eastern Ireland, capital of the Republic of Ireland (map 13).

Du-buque (dŭ-būk/), a city in eastern Iowa.

du-cal (dū'kăl), *adj.* pertaining to a duke.

duc-at (dŭk/ăt) *n.* **1**, a gold or silver coin formerly in use in many European countries; **2**, ducats, money; cash.

duch-ess (dŭch/ĕs), *n.* **1**, the wife or widow of a duke; **2**, a woman with the rank or authority of a duke.

duch-y (dŭch/ĭ), *n.* [*pl.* duchies], the territory or dominions of a duke.

¹**duck** (dŭk), *n.* **1**, a flat-billed waterfowl with short legs and neck; **2**, the female duck as distinguished from the male, or *drake;* **3**, *Colloquial,* a pet or favorite.

²**duck** (dŭk), *v.t.* **1**, to plunge (the head) for an instant under water; also, to throw (a person) into the water; **2**, to bend down; as, to *duck* the head; **3**, *Colloquial,* to avoid, as by quickly bowing the head; as, to *duck* a blow:—*v.i.* **1**, to take a quick dip into water; **2**, to move the head or body aside quickly; dodge:—*n.* **1**, a dip or quick plunge under water; **2**, a sudden lowering of the head.

MALLARD DUCK (⅛)

³**duck** (dŭk), *n.* **1**, a linen or cotton fabric for sails and outer clothing; **2**, ducks, *Colloquial,* sailors' trousers made of duck.

⁴**duck** (dŭk), *n.* an amphibious military vehicle used in World War II.

duck-bill (dŭk/bĭl/), *n.* a small water animal of Australia, with webbed feet and a bill like a duck's.

duck-ling (dŭk′lĭng), *n.* a young duck.

duct (dŭkt), *n.* **1,** a canal, tube, or passage by which fluid is carried; **2,** a tube or vessel of the body, especially one for carrying a secretion; **3,** a tube or pipe for cables, wires, or the like.—*adj.* **duct′less.**

duc-tile (dŭk′tĭl), *adj.* **1,** capable of being drawn out into strands; as, copper is highly *ductile;* **2,** easily influenced or led.

dud (dŭd), *n. Slang:* **1,** a shell or bomb that has failed to explode; **2,** a person who fails to make good.

dude (dūd), *n.* a man who is overrefined in manner or dress; a dandy; fop:—**dude ranch,** *Slang,* a ranch at which paying guests are lodged.—*adj.* **dud′ish.**

dudg-eon (dŭj′ŭn), *n.* sullen anger; as, he went away in high *dudgeon.*

due (dū), *adj.* **1,** owed or owing; payable; as, the rent is *due* today; **2,** suitable; proper; as, *due* courtesy; **3,** scheduled or expected; as, *due* at noon; **4,** caused by; as, an accident *due* to carelessness:—*adv.* exactly; directly; as, *due* west:—*n.* **1,** that which rightfully belongs to someone; as, give him his *due;* **2, dues,** the money paid for membership in a club or society.

Syn., adj. just, fair, right, sufficient.

du-el (dū′ĕl), *n.* a combat between two persons, usually planned beforehand and fought with deadly weapons before witnesses:—*v.i.* [dueled, duel-ing], to fight a duel.—*n.* **du′el-ing.**—*n.* **du′el-ist.**

du-en-na (dū-ĕn′à), *n.* an elderly lady who acts as a guardian to a younger one in a Spanish or Portuguese family; a chaperon.

du-et (dū-ĕt′), *n.* a musical composition for two performers.

duff (dŭf), *n.* a stiff flour pudding, boiled in a bag.

dug (dŭg), past tense and past participle of *dig.*

dug-out (dŭg′out′), *n.* **1,** a canoe hollowed out from a log; **2,** a rough shelter dug in the side of a hill or bank.

duke (dūk), *n.* **1,** in England and some other European countries, a member of the nobility next below a prince; **2,** the ruler of a duchy.—*n.* **duke′dom.**

DULCIMER

dul-cet (dŭl′sĕt), *adj.* sweet or pleasant, especially to the ear; as, *dulcet* tones.

dul-ci-mer (dŭl′sĭ-mẽr), *n.* a musical instrument with wire strings, played with two light hammers.

dull (dŭl), *adj.* **1,** not sharp-edged; blunt; as, a *dull* knife; **2,** lacking keenness or liveliness; as, a *dull* fellow; **3,** slow of understanding or action; as, a *dull* pupil; **4,** not clear or vivid; as, *dull* color; a *dull* sound; **5,** pointless; uninteresting; as, a *dull* story:—*v.t.* and *v.i.* to make or become dull.—*adv.* **dull′ly.**—*n.* **dull′ness.**

Syn., adj. gloomy, sad, dismal, stupid.

dull-ard (dŭl′ẽrd), *n.* a stupid person.

dulse (dŭls), *n.* a coarse red seaweed, used in some places as food.

Du-luth (dŏŏ-lōōth′), a city in Minnesota, at the west end of Lake Superior (map 7).

du-ly (dū′lĭ), *adv.* in a fit and becoming manner; regularly; as, *duly* elected officers.

Du-ma or **Dou-ma** (dōō′mä), *n.* the national legislature of Russia from 1905 to 1917.

Du-mas (dü′mä′), **1,** Alexandre (1802–1870), a French author; **2,** Alexandre (1824–1895), his son, also an author.

dumb (dŭm), *adj.* **1,** unable to speak; as, a deaf and *dumb* child; a *dumb* animal; **2,** *Colloquial,* stupid; foolish.—*n.* **dumb′ness.**

Syn. mute, silent, speechless.

dumb-bell (dŭm′bĕl′), *n.* **1,** one of a pair of weights, each consisting of two balls of wood or metal joined by a short bar which serves as a grip, used for gymnastic exercise; **2,** *Slang,* an ignorant or stupid person.

DUMBBELL

dumb–wait-er (dŭm′-wāt′ẽr), *n.* a small elevator for moving dishes or supplies from one floor to another.

dum-found or **dumb-found** (dŭm′-found′), *v.t.* to amaze; make dumb with surprise or fear.

dum-my (dŭm′ĭ), *n.* [*pl.* dummies], **1,** one who is silent; also, a thick-witted person; **2,** a make-believe; hence, a form for showing clothing; **3,** in some card games, an exposed hand played by the partner; also, the player whose hand is exposed; **4,** a person who acts for another, when he seems to be acting for himself:—*adj.* sham; as, a *dummy* drawer.

dump (dŭmp), *v.t.* to unload; as, they *dumped* sand from the barrel:—*n.* **1,** a place for rubbish; **2,** a heap of refuse.

dump-ling (dŭmp′lĭng), *n.* **1,** a small mass of dough boiled in soup or stew; **2,** a shell of dough enclosing fruit or meat and either baked or boiled; as, an apple *dumpling.*

dumps (dŭmps), *n.pl.* low spirits.

dump-y (dŭmp′ĭ), *adj.* short and stout.

¹**dun** (dŭn), *adj.* of a dull or dingy grayish-brown color.

āte, āorta, râre, căt, àsk, fär, ăllow, sofà; ēve, ĕvent, ĕll, wrītẽr, novĕl; bīte, pĭn; nō, ōbey, ôr, dŏg, tŏp, cŏllide; ūnit, ūnite, bûrn, cŭt, focŭs; nōōn, fŏŏt; mound; coin;

²dun (dŭn), *n.* **1**, an urgent request or demand for the payment of a debt; **2**, one who demands payment of a debt repeatedly:—*v.t.* [dunned, dun-ning], to plague by frequent demands for payment.

Dun-bar (dŭn′bär), Paul Laurence (1872–1906), American Negro poet and novelist.

dunce (dŭns), *n.* a dull, ignorant person; especially, a backward student.

Dun-dee (dŭn-dē′), a seaport on the eastern coast of Scotland (map 13).

dune (dūn; dōōn), *n.* a low hill of drifted sand piled up by the wind, especial-ly along a shore.

dung (dŭng), *n.* waste material from animals; manure.

dun-geon (dŭn′-jŭn), *n.* a dark underground cell for prisoners.

DUNES

dung-hill (dŭng′hĭl′), *n.* a heap of dung.

du-o (dōō′ō), *n.* [*pl.* duos or dui (dōō′ē)], in music, a duet.

du-o-de-num (dū′ō-dē′nŭm), *n.* [*pl.* duo-dena (dū′ō-dē′nȧ)], the first part of the small intestine, just below the stomach.

dupe (dūp), *n.* one who is easily tricked, or believes everything he is told:—*v.t.* [duped, dup-ing], to deceive by trickery.

du-plex (dū′plĕks), *adj.* double; twofold.

du-pli-cate (dū′plĭ-kāt), *v.t.* [duplicat-ed, duplicat-ing], to reproduce exactly; make a copy or copies of:—*adj.* (dū′plĭ-kȧt), **1**, corresponding exactly with another; as, a *duplicate* key; **2**, double; twofold:—*n.* (dū′-plĭ-kȧt), **1**, something exactly like an-other; a copy, as of a letter; **2**, exact likeness between two things; as, docu-ments in *duplicate*.—*n.* du′pli-ca′tion.

du-plic-i-ty (dū-plĭs′ĭ-tĭ), *n.* [*pl.* duplic-ities], double-dealing; deceitfulness in speech or action.

Syn. fraud, deception, guile.

du-ra-ble (dūr′ȧ-bl), *adj.* permanent and lasting; resisting wear; as, *durable* cloth.—*adv.* du′ra-bly.—*n.* du′ra-bil′i-ty.

Syn. abiding, persistent, enduring.

dur-ance (dūr′ăns), *n.* imprisonment.

du-ra-tion (dū-rā′shŭn), *n.* the time any-thing lasts; as, the *duration* of a war.

Dur-ban (dûr′băn; dûr-băn′), a seaport on the southeastern coast of Africa, in the Union of South Africa (map 14).

Dü-rer (dü′rẽr), Albrecht (1471–1528), a German painter and engraver.

du-ress (dūr′ĕs; dū-rĕs′), *n.* **1**, imprison-ment; **2**, force; compulsion; as, to make a confession under *duress*.

Dur-ham (dûr′ăm), a city in the northern part of North Carolina (map 8).

dur-ing (dūr′ĭng), *prep.* throughout the period of; in the time of; as, *during* winter.

dur-ra (dŏŏr′ȧ), *n.* a canelike grass grown for its grain: also called *Indian millet.*

durst (dûrst), an old form of the past tense of *dare.*

Du-se (dōō′zä), Eleonora (1859–1924), an Italian actress, famous in tragic roles.

dusk (dŭsk), *adj.* dim; shadowy:—*n.* **1**, the dim light at the beginning and end of day-light; **2**, shadow; gloom.

dusk-y (dŭs′kĭ), *adj.* [dusk-i-er, dusk-i-est], **1**, somewhat dark; as, a *dusky* skin; **2**, gloomy, sad.

Düs-sel-dorf (düs′ĕl-dôrf), a city on the Rhine in Germany.

dust (dŭst), *n.* **1**, fine, dry particles of earth or other matter; a cloud or film of such fine particles; **2**, the earth or its surface; **3**, the remains of a human body after decay; **4**, something worthless:—*v.t.* **1**, to brush away dust from; as, to *dust* the table; **2**, to cover or sprinkle, as with powder; as, to *dust* a cake with sugar.

dust-er (dŭs′tẽr), *n.* **1**, one who dusts; **2**, a cloth, bunch of feathers, or the like, for dusting; **3**, a light outer garment to pro-tect clothing from dust; **4**, a box or can with small holes in the lid for sifting.

dust-y (dŭs′tĭ), *adj.* [dust-i-er, dust-i-est], **1**, filled or covered with dust; as, a *dusty* road; **2**, like dust in color or appearance.

Dutch (dŭch), *adj.* pertaining to, or like, the Netherlands, its people or their lan-guage:—**Dutch treat**, an entertainment in which each person pays for his own share:—*n.* **1**, the inhabitants of the Netherlands, particularly Holland; **2**, the language of the Dutch.

Dutch East In-dies, former colony of the Netherlands. See Indonesia (map 15).

du-te-ous (dū′tē-ŭs), *adj.* obedient; rend-ering service that is due; as, a *duteous* serv-ant.—*adv.* du′te-ous-ly.

du-ti-a-ble (dū′tĭ-ȧ-bl), *adj.* subject to the payment of duty; as, *dutiable* goods.

du-ti-ful (dū′tĭ-fŏŏl), *adj.* obedient and respectful to parents or superiors; as, a *dutiful* child.—*adv.* du′ti-ful-ly.

Syn. compliant, duteous, docile.

du-ty (dū′tĭ), *n.* [*pl.* duties], **1**, the re-spectful behavior due to parents or su-periors; **2**, action required in a certain office or position; as, the *duties* of a chairman; **3**, that which one is morally

go; join; yet; sing; chin; show; thin, *th*en; hw, *wh*y; zh, azure; ŭ, Ger. *für* or Fr. *lune*; ö, Ger. schön or Fr. *feu*; ṅ, Fr. *enfant*, nom; kh, Ger. a*ch* or i*ch*. See pages ix–x.

bound to do; **4,** a tax levied by the government; as, a *duty* on imports.

Syn. obligation, submission.

dwarf (dwôrf), *n.* [*pl.* dwarfs (dwôrfs)], a person, animal, or plant much below average size:—*adj.* of smaller size or height than the average; as, a *dwarf* rose: —*v.t.* **1,** to hinder from growing to natural size; as, the drought *dwarfed* the corn; **2,** to cause to look small by comparison; as, the skyscraper *dwarfs* the church.—*adj.* **dwarf′ish.**

dwell (dwĕl), *v.i.* [dwelt (dwĕlt) or dwelled (dwĕld), dwell-ing], **1,** to reside; live in a place; as, to *dwell* in England; **2,** to linger; as, to *dwell* on a subject.—*n.* **dwell′er.**

Syn. stay, abide, sojourn, tarry.

dwell-ing (dwĕl′ĭng), *n.* a residence.

dwelt (dwĕlt), one form of the past tense and past participle of *dwell.*

dwin-dle (dwĭn′dl), *v.i.* [dwin-dled, dwin-dling], to become gradually less; shrink.

Syn. decrease, diminish, lessen.

dye (dī), *v.i.* [dyed, dye-ing], to stain or color (fabric, fur, or the like):—**dyed-in-the-wool,** dyed while the material was raw and therefore dyed more lastingly; figuratively, thoroughgoing; as, a *dyed-in-the-wool* Republican:—*v.i.* to take color in dyeing; as, this silk *dyes* well:—*n.* **1,** coloring matter used in dyeing; a dyestuff; **2,** a color produced by dyeing.—*n.* **dye′ing.**— *n.* **dy′er.**

dye-stuff (dī′stŭf′), *n.* any substance that yields a dye or stain; also, a dye.

dy-ing (dī′ĭng), present participle of ¹*die*: —*adj.* **1,** passing from life; as, a *dying* man; **2,** drawing to a close; as, the *dying* year; **3,** said or done at the time of death; as,

his *dying* words:—*n.* the act of passing from life.

dyke (dīk), *n.* a bank of earth built as a water barrier. See **dike.**

dy-nam-ic (dī-năm′ĭk; dĭ-năm′ĭk), *adj.* **1,** relating to power or physical energy; **2,** forceful.—*adv.* **dy-nam′i-cal-ly.**

dy-na-mite (dī′nȧ-mīt), *n.* a highly explosive mixture, used for blasting:—*v.t.* [dynamit-ed, dynamit-ing], to destroy or blast by the explosion of dynamite.

dy-na-mo (dī′nȧ-mō), *n.* [*pl.* dynamos], a machine which converts mechanical energy, as that of a steam engine or waterfall, into electric current.

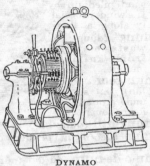

DYNAMO

dy-nas-tic (dī-năs′tĭk; dĭ-năs′tĭk), *adj.* pertaining to a line of sovereigns of the same family.

dy-nas-ty (dī′năs-tĭ), *n.* [*pl.* dynasties], a line or succession of sovereigns of the same family; as, the Tudor *dynasty.*

dys-en-ter-y (dĭs′ĕn-tĕr′ĭ), *n.* a disease of the bowels, marked by severe inflammation and mucous, bloody discharges.

dys-pep-sia (dĭs-pĕp′shȧ; dĭs-pĕp′sĭ-ȧ), *n.* poor digestion; indigestion.

dys-pep-tic (dĭs-pĕp′tĭk), *adj.* relating to indigestion:—*n.* a person with chronic indigestion.

E

E, e (ē), *n.* [*pl.* E's, e's], **1,** the fifth letter of the alphabet, following D; **2,** in music, the third tone of the major scale of C.

E. abbreviation for *east, eastern.*

e- (ē-), a form of the prefix *ex-*, meaning out of; from; as, *evict, emit.* See **ex-.**

ea. abbreviation for *each.*

each (ēch), *pron.* every one of a number considered separately; as, *each* of the girls brings her lunch:—*adj.* every (one) of two or more taken separately; as, they study *each* lesson carefully.

ea-ger (ē′gẽr), *adj.* full of keen desire; impatiently anxious to do or have something; as, he was *eager* to learn.—*adv.* **ea′ger-ly.**

Syn. ardent, fervent, impatient.

ea-gle (ē′gl), *n.* **1,** a bird of prey, akin to the hawks and kites, noted for its strength, size, and keen vision; **2,** the ten-dollar gold piece of the U.S.

ea-glet (ē′glĕt), *n.* a young eagle.

¹**ear** (ēr), *n.* **1,** the entire organ of hearing; also, the outer, visible part of that organ; **2,** the sense of hearing; unusual ability to hear delicate sounds; as, she has an *ear* for music; **3,** attention; heed; as, give *ear* to what I say; **4,** anything like an external ear in shape.

EAGLE (₁⁄₁₆), def. 1

²**ear** (ēr), *n.* the spike of a cereal plant, containing the grains; as, an *ear* of corn or wheat.

ear-ache (ēr′āk), *n.* pain in the ear.

ear-drum (ēr′drŭm), *n.* the middle ear; especially, the thin membrane between the outer and the middle ear.

earl (ûrl), *n.* a British nobleman next below a marquis.— *n.* **earl′dom.**

ear-ly (ûr′lĭ), *adj.* [ear-li-er, ear-li-est], 1, near the beginning; as, *early* spring; 2, before the usual time; in good time; as, an *early* riser:—*adv.* 1, at or near the beginning; as, he arrived *early* in the week; 2, before the usual time; in good time; as, he goes to bed *early.*—*n.* **ear′li-ness.**

EAR OF CORN

ear-mark (ēr′märk), *n.* a mark, such as a slit in the ear of a sheep, cow, etc., used to identify it; hence, any distinguishing mark or characteristic; as, your remark has all the *earmarks* of an insult.

earn (ûrn), *v.t.* 1, to gain or get as just pay for one's labor, service, etc.; as, he *earns* $50 a week; 2, to merit or deserve for one's labor, service, etc.; as, he *earned* his vacation.

Syn. acquire, win, achieve, attain, procure.

¹**ear-nest** (ûr′nĕst), *adj.* 1, zealous; fervent; as, an *earnest* reformer; *earnest* requests; 2, important; grave; as, life is *earnest:*— **in earnest,** serious; as, he is *in earnest* about his work.

Syn. eager, solemn, intent, sincere.

²**ear-nest** (ûr′nĕst), *n.* 1, money or a valuable article given by a buyer to a seller to bind a bargain; 2, a pledge, promise, or indication of what is to follow.

earn-ings (ûr′nĭngz), *n.pl.* money received for services; wages.

ear-phone (ēr′fōn), *n.* a telephone, radio, or telegraph receiver held over the ear by a band worn over the head.

ear-ring (ēr′rĭng), *n.* an ear ornament.

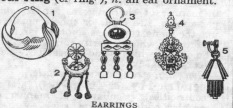

EARRINGS
1, African; 2, ancient Greek; 3, ancient Roman; 4, medieval French; 5, modern.

ear-shot (ēr′shŏt), *n.* the distance within which the voice can be heard; the range of hearing; as, to walk beyond *earshot.*

earth (ûrth), *n.* 1, the planet on which we live, which revolves about the sun; 2, the solid materials which compose it; dry land; 3, ground; soil; as, rich *earth.*

earth-en (ûr′thĕn), *adj.* made of earth; as, *earthen* floors; also, made of baked clay; as, *earthen* jars.

earth-en-ware (ûr′thĕn-wâr), *n.* vessels or other objects made of baked clay.

earth-ly (ûrth′lĭ), *adj.* 1, pertaining to this world or to the present life; material; as, *earthly* possessions; 2, possible; as, he has no *earthly* reason to go.

earth-quake (ûrth′kwāk), *n.* a sudden shaking, often violent, of the earth's surface, usually caused by a splitting and sliding of the rock foundation.

earth-work (ûrth′wûrk), *n.* an embankment made wholly or largely of earth.

earth-worm (ûrth′wûrm), *n.* a burrowing worm that lives in the ground; an angleworm.

EARTHWORM (⅓)

earth-y (ûr′thĭ), *adj.* 1, made of, or like, soil; as, *earthy* colors; 2, material; worldly; as, *earthy* desires.

ear-wig (ēr′wĭg), *n.* 1, an insect, formerly supposed to creep into the ear; 2, a kind of centipede.

ease (ēz), *n.* 1, freedom from pain, labor, worry, trouble, etc.; as, *ease* of body and mind; 2, naturalness; as, *ease* of manner:—*v.t.* [eased, eas-ing], 1, to free from pain, anxiety, stress, etc.; give relief to; as, medicine to *ease* pain; good news *eases* the mind; 2, to loosen anything tight; as, to *ease* a band; also, to move gently; as, to *ease* a stretcher into an ambulance.

EARWIG
(enlarged)
def. 1

Syn., v. calm, pacify, still, allay.

ea-sel (ē′zl), *n.* a frame for supporting an artist's canvas, a blackboard, or the like.

eas-i-er, eas-i-est, comparative and superlative of *easy.*

eas-i-ly (ēz′ĭ-lĭ), *adv.* without difficulty; readily.

east (ēst), *n.* 1, that part of the heavens where the sun is seen to rise; 2, one of the four points of the compass: opposite of *west;* 3, the part of the earth lying toward the sunrise:— **East,** 1 the Orient; the countries of Asia;

EASEL

2, in the U.S., the territory lying between the Mississippi River and the Atlantic Ocean, especially the New England States and New York, Pennsylvania, and New Jersey:—*adj.* from the direction of the east; as, an *east* wind; in the direction of the east; as, the *east* side of the street:—*adv.* in the direction of the east; as, facing *east*.

East Af·ri·ca: British, a region of Africa including Kenya and Uganda, and the islands Zanzibar and Pemba (map 14); **Italian East Africa**, a former Italian colony in eastern Africa; **Portuguese East Africa**, Mozambique (see **Mozambique**).

East Chi·na Sea, a sea lying between China, Japan, and Formosa (map 15).

East·er (ēs′tēr), *n.* a festival of the Christian church to commemorate the resurrection of Jesus Christ, observed on a Sunday between March 21 and April 26.

east·er·ly (ēs′tēr-lǐ), *adj.* **1,** eastward; as, an *easterly* direction; **2,** from the direction of the east; as, an *easterly* wind:—*adv.* in the direction of the east.

east·ern (ēs′tērn), *adj.* **1,** grown or produced in the east; as, *eastern* potatoes; **2,** situated in the east; as, an *eastern* city: —**Eastern**, pertaining to the Orient; Oriental; as, *Eastern* religions.—*n.* **east′ern·er.** —*adj.* **east′ern·most.**

East·ern Church, the Orthodox, or Greek Church, which separated from the Western, or Roman, Church in 1054; the form of the Catholic Church prevailing in Greece, the Balkan States, and the former Russian Empire.

East·ern Hem·i·sphere, that half of the earth which includes Europe, Asia, Africa, Australia, and adjacent islands.

East·ern Shore, Delaware, and the parts of Maryland and Virginia east of Chesapeake Bay (map 6).

East In·di·an, pertaining to the East Indies; also, a native of the East Indies.

East In·dies (ĭn′dǐz), a name used vaguely for India, Indochina, the Malay Archipelago, and the islands between Asia and Australia (map 15).

East Riv·er, a strait, east of the island of Manhattan, connecting Long Island Sound and New York Bay.

¹east·ward (ēst′wērd), *adj.* to or toward the east; as, steer an *eastward* course.

²east·ward (ēst′wērd) or **east·wards** (ēst′wērdz), *adv.* to or toward the east; as, we journeyed *eastward*.

eas·y (ē′zǐ), *adj.* [eas-i-er, eas-i-est], **1,** free from troubles or worry; as, an *easy* life; **2,** comfortable; restful; **3,** not difficult; **4,** moderate; gentle; as, an *easy* pace; **5,** not exacting; as, an *easy* teacher.

eat (ēt), *v.t.* [*p.t.* ate (āt), *p.p.* eat·en (ē′tn), *p.pr.* eat·ing], **1,** to chew and swallow, as food; **2,** to destroy by eating; as, moths *eat* woolen blankets; **3,** to corrode; waste or wear away; as, the river *ate* away the banks:—*v.i.* **1,** to take food; as, we always *eat* here; **2,** to make a way (into), as by eating; as, acids *eat* into metal; expenses *eat* into one's money.—*n.* **eat′er.**

eat·a·ble (ē′tà-bl), *adj.* fit for food; edible: —**eatables,** *n.pl.* food.

eaves (ēvz), *n.pl.* the lower edges of a roof which project a little from the building.

eaves-drop (ēvz′-drŏp′), *v.i.* [eaves-dropped, eavesdrop-ping], to listen secretly to the private conversation of others. --*n.* **eaves′drop′ping. —** *n.* **eaves′drop′per.**

EAVES (E)

ebb (ĕb), *n.* **1,** the going out of the tide; **2,** a decline; low state; as, his courage was at its lowest *ebb*:—**ebb tide,** the receding tide; also, the point or time of lowest tide: opposite of *flood tide*: —*v.i.* **1,** to flow back or return; as, the tide *ebbs* to the sea; **2,** to decline; decay; as, his fortune *ebbs*.

eb·on (ĕb′ŭn), *adj.* made of, or like, ebony; very black; as, *ebon* hair:—*n. Poetic*, ebony.

eb·on·y (ĕb′ŭn-ĭ), *n.* [*pl.* ebonies], a hard, heavy, durable, black-colored wood; also, the tree furnishing it:—*adj.* made of, or like, ebony; as, the *ebony* keys on a piano.

eb·ul·li·tion (ĕb′ŭ-lĭsh′ŭn), *n.* **1,** the act of boiling; **2,** a sudden outburst of feeling.

e.c. abbreviation for Latin *exempli causa*, meaning *for the sake of an example*.

ec- (ĕk-), *prefix*, a form of *ex-* sometimes used before a consonant; as, eccentric.

ec·cen·tric (ĕk-sĕn′trĭk), *adj.* **1,** out of center; not revolving about its center; **2,** not having the same center; as, circles which partly overlap are *eccentric;* **3,** not in the line of a perfect circle, as the earth's course around the sun; **4,** peculiar in manner or character; as, an *eccentric* person:—*n.* **1,** a circle or sphere not having the same center as another circle or sphere with which it partly coinsides; **2,** one who or that which is odd or peculiar.—*adv.* **ec·cen′tri·cal·ly.**

Syn., adj. strange, queer, erratic.

ec·cen·tric·i·ty (ĕk′sĕn·trĭs′ĭ-tĭ), *n.* [*pl.* eccentricities], peculiarity of manner or character; oddity; queerness.

Ec·cle·si·as·tes (ĕ-klē′zĭ-ăs′tēz), *n.* in the Bible, a book of the Old Testament.

ec-cle-si-as-tic (ĕ-klē′zĭ-ăs′tĭk), *adj.* pertaining to the church and its organization or government:—*n.* a person in holy orders; a clergyman; priest.—*adj.* **ec-cle′-si-as′ti-cal.**

ech-o (ĕk′ō), *n.* [*pl.* echoes], **1,** the repetition of a sound caused by the throwing back of sound waves; **2,** any repetition or imitation:—**Echo,** in Greek mythology, a nymph who fell hopelessly in love with Narcissus and pined away until only her voice was left:—*v.i.* [echoed, echo-ing], to give back or repeat a sound; as, the corridors *echoed* with footsteps:—*v.t.* to repeat the sound of; imitate.

é-clair (ā-klâr′), *n* a small, iced, oblong pastry containing whipped cream or custard.

é-clat (ā-klä′), *n.* **1,** brilliant success; as, to perform with *éclat;* **2,** applause; as, the speech was received with *éclat.*

e-clipse (ē-klĭps′), *n.* **1,** the total or partial darkening of the light of the sun, moon, or other heavenly body, caused by its entering the shadow of another body, or by having another body come between it and the observer; **2,** an overshadowing; loss of brilliance or glory:—*v.t.* [eclipsed, eclips-ing], **1,** to darken or conceal, as one body overshadows another; **2,** to outshine; surpass; as, his success *eclipsed* his father's.

ec-logue (ĕk′lŏg), *n.* a poem containing dialogue between shepherds; a pastoral poem.

e-co-nom-ic (ē′kō-nŏm′ĭk; ĕk′ō-nŏm′ĭk), *adj.* relating to the production and use of wealth; as, the *economic* policy of a country:—**economics,** *n.pl.* used as *sing.* the science dealing with the production and use of wealth.

e-co-nom-i-cal (ē′kō-nŏm′ĭ-kăl; ĕk′ō-nŏm′ĭ-kăl), *adj.* prudent in the outlay of money, use of goods, etc.; thrifty.—*adv.* **e′co-nom′i-cal-ly.**
Syn. frugal, saving, sparing, provident.

e-con-o-mist (ē-kŏn′ō-mĭst), *n.* **1,** a person who has made a study of economics; **2,** one who knows how to use time, money, or labor, to the best advantage.

e-con-o-mize (ē-kŏn′ō-mīz), *v.t.* [economized, economiz-ing], **1,** to use sparingly; **2,** to use to the best advantage:—*v.i.* to be careful in spending money; avoid extravagance; as, after two months of unemployment, she began to *economize.*

e-con-o-my (ē-kŏn′ō-mĭ), *n.* [*pl.* economies], **1,** freedom from waste in the use of anything; thrift; **2,** the regulation and management of the resources of a group.

ec-ru (ĕk′rōō; ā′krōō; ā-krōō′), *adj.* pale brown; like unbleached linen in color:—*n.* the color of unbleached linen.

ec-sta-sy (ĕk′stȧ-sĭ), *n.* [*pl.* ecstasies], deep emotion; especially, rapturous joy.
Syn. bliss, exaltation.

ec-stat-ic (ĕk-stăt′ĭk), *adj.* **1,** full of rapture; as, an *ecstatic* moment; **2,** producing rapture; as, *ecstatic* harmonies.

Ec-ua-dor (ĕk′wȧ-dôr), a republic (cap. Quito) on the western coast of South America at the equator (map **11**).

ec-u-men-i-cal (ĕk′ū-mĕn′ĭ-kăl), *adj.* general; universal; especially, pertaining to the Christian church throughout the world; as, an *ecumenical* council.

ec-ze-ma (ĕk′zē-mȧ; ĕk′sē-mȧ), *n.* a skin disease usually attended by the formation of reddish scales and intense itching.

-ed (-ĕd), a suffix, used to form: **1,** the past tense and past participle of many regular verbs; as, sound*ed*, act*ed;* **2,** adjectives meaning having; supplied with; characterized by; as, belt*ed*, long-legg*ed.*

ed. or **edit.** abbreviation for *edited, edition.*

Ed-dy (ĕd′ĭ), Mary Baker Glover (1821–1910), an American religious leader, founder of Christian Science.

ed-dy (ĕd′ĭ), *n.* [*pl.* eddies], a current of air, water, or the like, running opposite to the main current, thus taking on a circular motion; a small whirlpool:—*v.t.* and *v.i.* [eddied, eddy-ing], to move with a circular motion; whirl; as, smoke *eddies* from a chimney.

E-den (ē′dn), *n.* **1,** in the Bible, the garden in which Adam and Eve first lived; **2,** any delightful place; a paradise.

edge (ĕj), *n.* **1,** the thin, sharp, or cutting part of a knife or tool; **2,** extreme border; brink; margin; as, the *edge* of a chair; the *edge* of a brook; **3,** keenness; sharpness; as, her remarks had an *edge:*—*v.t.* [edged, edg-ing], **1,** to make or put an edge upon; sharpen; **2,** to furnish with a border; as, to *edge* a handkerchief with lace; **3,** to move carefully, little by little; as, to *edge* a car into traffic:—*v.i.* to move along little by little; as, to *edge* along a cliff.
Syn., *n.* rim, brim, verge.

edge-ways (ĕj′wāz′) or **edge-wise** (ĕj′-wīz′), *adv.* with the edge foremost; edge first; also, sideways.

edg-ing (ĕj′ĭng), *n.* a narrow border, as of lace, used as trimming.

ed-i-ble (ĕd′ĭ-bl), *adj.* fit to be used for food; as, the salmon is an *edible* fish.

e-dict (ē′dĭkt), *n.* a public order issued by an official authority and having the force of a law; a decree.

ed-i-fi-ca-tion (ĕd′ĭ-fĭ-kā′shŭn), *n.* mental or moral improvement; as, to seek *edification* from serious books.

ed·i·fice (ĕd′ĭ-fĭs), *n.* a building, especially one that is large and imposing.

ed·i·fy (ĕd′ĭ-fī), *v.t.* [edified, edify-ing], to benefit, especially in religion or morals; as, good deeds *edify* us more than words.

Ed·in·burgh (ĕd′ĭn-bŭ-rŭ), a city, capital of Scotland (map **13**).

E·dir·ne (ĕ-dĭr′nĕ), the Turkish name of a city in Turkey. See **Adrianople**.

Ed·i·son (ĕd′ĭ-sŭn), Thomas Alva (1847–1931), American inventor of the phonograph and incandescent lamp.

ed·it (ĕd′ĭt), *v.t.* **1,** to revise and prepare (manuscript) for publication; **2,** to select, arrange, and compile for publication; as, to *edit* a collection of verse; **3,** to direct or be responsible for the work of preparing (a dictionary, encyclopedia, or the like); **4,** to direct the policies of (a newspaper, magazine, or the like).

e·di·tion (ĕ-dĭsh′ŭn), *n.* **1,** the published form of a literary work; **2,** the number of copies, all exactly alike, of a book, magazine, or newspaper, published at or near the same time.

ed·i·tor (ĕd′ĭ-tĕr), *n.* **1,** one who revises or prepares a literary work for publication; **2,** one who directs the policies of a newspaper, magazine, or the like.

ed·i·tor·i·al (ĕd′ĭ-tôr′ĭ-ăl), *adj.* connected with editors, or with their work:—*n.* an article in a newspaper, magazine, or the like, expressing the official opinions of the editors or publishers on some topic.

Ed·mon·ton (ĕd′mŭn-tŭn), a city, capital of Alberta province, Canada (map **4**).

ed·u·cate (ĕd′ū-kāt), *v.t.* [educat-ed, educat-ing], to develop and improve, especially mentally, by teaching or training; instruct; as, to *educate* children.

ed·u·ca·tion (ĕd′ū-kā′shŭn), *n.* **1,** the training of the mental and moral powers, as by a system of study and discipline; also, the system itself; **2,** the knowledge and abilities gained by such training.—*adj.* **ed′u·ca′tion·al.**
Syn. instruction, breeding, culture.

Ed·ward (ĕd′wĕrd), the name of eight kings of England, notably: **1, Edward I** (1239–1307), the conqueror of Wales; **2, Edward VIII** (1894–   ), who became king in January and abdicated in December, 1936.

Ed·wards (ĕd′wĕrdz), **1,** Jonathan (1703–1758), an American clergyman, the third president of Princeton University; **2,** his son, Jonathan, (1745–1801), a clergyman.

-ee (-ē), a suffix, which forms nouns meaning one who is affected by a given action; as, pay*ee*, mortgag*ee*.

eel (ēl), *n.* a long, snakelike fish, smooth and slimy, used for food.

eel-grass (ēl′gras′), *n.* an underwater plant with long, narrow leaves, common along north Atlantic shores.

EELGRASS

e'en (ēn), *adv.* a short form of ²*even*, meaning *exactly:*—*n.* a short form of ¹*even* or *evening*.

e'er (âr; ãr), *adv.* a short form of *ever;* as, the sweetest song that *e'er* I heard.

ee·rie or **ee·ry** (ē′rĭ), *adj.* fearful; weird; as, an *eerie* shriek.—*adv.* **ee′ri·ly.**

ef·face (ĕ-fās′), *v.t.* [effaced, effac-ing], **1,** to erase or blot out (writing); **2,** to wipe out or destroy, as if by erasing; as, time *effaces* sorrow.—*n.* **ef·face′ment.**
Syn. obliterate, expunge, cancel.

ef·fect (ĕ-fĕkt′), *v.t.* to accomplish; bring about; as, to *effect* a change in a plan:—*n.* **1,** result; consequence; **2,** impression; as, to do something for *effect;* **3, effects,** movable goods; personal property; as, household *effects*.
take effect, to become operative; have results; as, the medicine *took effect;* **in effect, 1,** in reality; actually; **2,** in operation, as a rule or law.
Syn., v. perform, achieve, execute.

ef·fec·tive (ĕ-fĕk′tĭv), *adj.* **1,** having the power to produce a desired result; as, an *effective* censorship; **2,** impressive; striking; as, an *effective* picture; **3,** operative; enforced; as, after a law is passed, time may elapse before it becomes *effective*.—*adv.* **ef·fec′tive·ly.**
Syn. effectual, efficient.

ef·fec·tu·al (ĕ-fĕk′tū-ăl), *adj.* producing, or having the ability to produce, a desired result.—*adv.* **ef·fec′tu·al·ly.**
Syn. efficient, effective.

ef·fem·i·nate (ĕ-fĕm′ĭ-nĭt), *adj.* womanish; feeble; lacking in such manly qualities as vigor, endurance, strength, and courage.—*n.* **ef·fem′i·na·cy.**

ef·fer·vesce (ĕf′ĕr-vĕs′), *v.i.* [effervesced, effervesc-ing], **1,** to bubble up; hiss; work, as does new wine; **2,** to be lively and gay.

ef·fer·ves·cence (ĕf′ĕr-vĕs′ĕns), *n.* **1,** a bubbling up or over; **2,** excitement; gaiety; high spirits.—*n.* **ef′fer·ves′cen·cy.**—*adj.* **ef′fer·ves′cent.**

ef·fete (ĕ-fēt′), *adj.* worn out; exhausted.

ef·fi·ca·cious (ĕf′ĭ-kā′shŭs), *adj.* producing, or sure to produce, a desired result; as, an *efficacious* treatment for colds.
Syn. powerful, sure, potent.

āte, āorta, râre, căt, ȧsk, fär, ăllow, sofȧ; ēve, ĕvent, ĕll, writĕr, novĕl; bīte, pĭn; nō, ōbey, ôr, dŏg, tŏp, cŏllide; ūnit, ūnite, bûrn, cŭt, focŭs; nōōn, fŏŏt; mound; coin;

ef-fi-ca-cy (ĕf′ĭ-kȧ-sĭ), *n.* the power to produce desired results; as, the *efficacy* of a remedy.

Syn. energy, potency, strength.

ef-fi-cien-cy (ĕ-fĭsh′ĕn-sĭ), *n.* the quality of producing desired results with the least effort or expense.

Syn. competency, ability.

ef-fi-cient (ĕ-fĭsh′ĕnt), *adj.* capable; competent; able to get results; as, an *efficient* secretary.—*adv.* **ef-fi′cient-ly.**

Syn. effective, effectual.

ef-fi-gy (ĕf′ĭ-jĭ), *n.* [*pl.* effigies], a portrait, image, or other likeness of a person:— **burn in effigy,** burn the image of.

ef-fort (ĕf′ĕrt; ĕf′ôrt), *n.* the putting forth of exertion, physical or mental; as, it takes *effort* to lift a rock or work a problem; also, an attempt or endeavor; as, I shall make an *effort* to come.

Syn. endeavor, struggle.

ef-fron-ter-y (ĕ-frŭn′tĕr-ĭ), *n.* [*pl.* effronteries], shameless impudence or audacity.

Syn. assurance, boldness.

ef-ful-gence (ĕ-fŭl′jĕns), *n.* great luster, brightness, or splendor, as of stars, jewels, or the like.—*adj.* **ef-ful′gent.**

ef-fu-sion (ĕ-fū′zhŭn), *n.* **1,** an act of pouring or gushing forth; as, an *effusion* of blood; **2,** an unrestrained outpouring of thought or feeling.

ef-fu-sive (ĕ-fū′sĭv), *adj.* gushing; extremely demonstrative; as, *effusive* thanks.

eft (ĕft), *n.* a newt or small salamander.

e.g. abbreviation for Latin *exempli gratia,* meaning *for the sake of example, for example.*

EFT (⅓)

Eg-bert (ĕg′bĕrt), (775?–839), the first overlord or "king" of England.

¹**egg** (ĕg), *n.* an animal cell containing the germ of life, which may develop into a new individual; especially, the oval, rounded body produced by birds, insects, fish, and most reptiles, from which the young hatch out.

²**egg** (ĕg), *v.t.* to urge or incite; as, they *egged* him on to try his luck.

egg-nog (ĕg′nŏg′), *n.* a drink made of eggs beaten up with milk, sugar, spices, and wine or other liquor.

egg-plant (ĕg′plănt′), *n.* a cultivated plant or its large, purplish, egg-shaped fruit, used for food.

EGGPLANT
Fruit and leaves.

egg-shell (ĕg′shĕl′), *n.* the shell of an egg:—*adj.* having the color of an eggshell.

eg-lan-tine (ĕg′lăn-tīn), *n.* a wild rose; the sweetbrier.

e-go-ism (ē′gō-ĭzm; ĕg′ō-ĭzm), *n.* the belief that the aim of life is to perfect the self; hence, excessive interest in one's own concerns.

EGLANTINE

e-go-ist (ē′gō-ĭst; ĕg′-ō-ĭst), *n.* a believer in egoism; a selfish person.—*adj.* **e′go-is′tic; e′go-is′ti-cal.**

e-go-tism (ē′gō-tĭzm; ĕg′ō-tĭzm), *n.* the habit of talking or writing too much about oneself; conceit.

Syn. vanity, self-esteem.

e-go-tist (ē′gō-tĭst; ĕg′ō-tĭst), *n.* one who thinks and talks too much of self; a conceited person.

e-go-tis-tic (ē′gō-tĭs′tĭk; ĕg′ō-tĭs′tĭk), *adj.* thinking and talking too much of oneself; conceited. Also, **e′go-tis′ti-cal.**

e-gre-gious (ē-grē′jŭs; ē-grē′jĭ-ŭs), *adj.* extraordinary; shocking; as, an *egregious* blunder.

e-gress (ē′grĕs), *n.* **1,** a departure or going out; **2,** a means of leaving; an exit.

e-gret (ē′grĕt; ĕg′rĕt), *n.* **1,** a large wading bird of the heron family bearing, in the breeding season, long plumes drooping over the tail; **2,** (usually *aigrette*), an egret's plume, often used as a head ornament.

EGRET (½), def. 1

E-gypt (ē′jĭpt), a republic (cap. Cairo) in northeastern Africa, through which the Nile flows (map **14**).

E-gyp-tian (ē-jĭp′shăn), *adj.* pertaining to Egypt or its people:—*n.* **1,** a native of Egypt; **2,** the language of the ancient Egyptians.

eh (ā; ĕ) *interj.* what! an exclamation of doubt, surprise, or inquiry.

ei-der (ī′dĕr), *n.* a large salt-water duck of the northern regions, valued for its downy feathers: also called *eider duck.*

EIDER (⅒)

eider down, 1, the soft breast feathers of the eider duck, used in pillows, coverlets, or the like; **2,** a down quilt.

Eif-fel Tow-er (ī/fĕl), an iron tower in Paris, 984.25 feet high, built in 1889 by A. G. Eiffel.

eight (āt), *adj.* composed of one more than seven:—*n.* **1,** the number consisting of seven plus one; **2,** a sign representing eight units, as 8 or viii; **3,** anything made up of eight members or units, as the crew of a racing shell or a playing card with eight spots.

eight-een (ā/tēn/), *adj.* composed of ten more than eight:—*n.* **1,** the sum of seventeen and one; **2,** a sign representing eighteen units, as 18 or xviii.

eight-eenth (ā/tēnth/), *adj.* next after the 17th: the ordinal of *eighteen:*—*n.* one of the eighteen equal parts of anything.

eighth (ātth), *adj.* next after the seventh: the ordinal of *eight:*—*n.* one of the eight equal parts of anything.

eight-i-eth (ā/tĭ-ĕth), *adj.* next after the 79th: the ordinal of *eighty:*—*n.* one of the 80 equal parts of anything.

eight-y (ā/tĭ), *adj.* composed of one more than 79:—*n.* [*pl.* eighties], **1,** the sum of 79 and one; **2,** a sign representing 80 units, as 80 or lxxx.

Ein-stein (īn/stīn), Albert (1879–1955), an American physicist born in Germany, noted for his theory of relativity.

Eir-e (âr/ĕ), former name for a republic (cap. Dublin), in southern Ireland; called *Irish Free State* from 1922 to 1937; now called *Republic of Ireland* (map **13**).

Ei-sen-how-er (ī/zĕn-hou/ĕr), Dwight David (1890–), an American general in World War II, and 34th president of the U.S.

ei-ther (ē/thĕr; ī/thĕr), *adj.* **1,** one or the other of two; as, come *either* today or tomorrow; **2,** each; as, along *either* bank: —*pron.* one of two; as, *either* of the two boys may go:—*conj.* in one of two cases: the correlative of *or:* `as, *either* confess or die:—*adv.* also: used after a negative; as, he won't go, and she won't *either*.

e-jac-u-late (ē-jăk/ū-lāt), *v.t.* [ejaculat-ed, ejaculat-ing], to utter suddenly or vehemently:—*v.i.* to exclaim suddenly.

e-jac-u-la-tion (ē-jăk/ū-lā/shŭn), *n.* a sudden utterance; an exclamation.

e-ject (ē-jĕkt/), *v.t.* to expel; dismiss (from office); evict or turn out; as, to *eject* a tenant.—*n.* **e-jec/tor.**—*n.* **e-jec/tion.**

¹eke (ēk), *adv.* and *conj.* Archaic, also.

²eke (ēk), *v.t.* [eked, ek-ing], to piece out or add to, little by little; especially, to manage to make (a living) by some means or another; as, to *eke* out a living by writing.

e-lab-o-rate (ē-lăb/ō-rāt), *v.t.* [elaborat-ed, elaborat-ing], to work out with great care and detail:—*adj.* (ē-lăb/ō-rĭt), worked out in detail; highly finished; as, an *elaborate* stage setting; complicated; as, an *elaborate* plan.—*adv.* **e-lab/o-rate-ly.**

e-lab-o-ra-tion (ē-lăb/ō-rā/shŭn), *n.* **1,** the act of producing or working out in detail and with care; **2,** that which has been so produced; **3,** decorative detail.

e-land (ē/lănd), *n.* a large South African antelope, with twisted horns in both sexes. (See *antelope,* illustration.)

e-lapse (ē-lăps/), *v.i.* [elapsed, elaps-ing], to go by; pass, as hours, days, or years.

e-las-tic (ē-lăs/tĭk), *adj.* **1,** having the power of springing back to its original form after being stretched or pressed together, as rubber; **2,** able to rebound from a state of depression; as, an *elastic* disposition; **3,** flexible; easily changed; adaptable:—*n.* **1,** a narrow woven strip or band made in part of India rubber; **2,** a rubber band.—*adv.* **e-las/ti-cal-ly.**

e-las-tic-i-ty (ē-lăs/tĭs/ĭ-tĭ; ē/lăs-tĭs/ĭ-tĭ), *n.* **1,** the power of springing back to its original form after being stretched or pressed together; **2,** the ability to recover from depression; buoyancy.

e-late (ē-lāt/), *v.t.* [elat-ed, elat-ing], to make happy or proud; as, he was *elated* by the applause.—*adj.* **e-lat/ed.**

e-la-tion (ē-lā/shŭn), *n.* a feeling of exultant joy and pride; exaltation.

El-ba (ĕl/bȧ), an Italian island off the northwestern coast of Italy; place of Napoleon's first exile, 1814–1815.

El-be (ĕl/bĕ), a river of Germany flowing northwest into the North Sea (map **12**).

el-bow (ĕl/bō), *n.* **1,** the joint between the forearm and the upper arm; also, the outer part or curve of this joint; **2,** a bend or angle like that of an elbow when the arm is bent; as, the *elbow* of a pipe:—*v.t.* to jostle or push (a person), as with the elbows:—*v.i.* to push rudely along.

El-brus (ĕl/brōōs; āl/brōōz), a mountain, 18,468 feet high, in the Caucasus Mountains, between the Black and Caspian seas (map **12**). It is the highest in Europe.

ELBOWS
1, human elbow; 2, 3, pipe elbows.

eld (ĕld), *n.* Archaic, old age or times.

¹eld-er (ĕl/dĕr), *adj.* [a *comp.* of *old*], older; superior in rank or station; senior; as, an *elder* brother; the *elder* statesmen:— *n.* **1,** one who is older; **2,** a leader or ruler

āte, āorta, râre, căt, ȧsk, fär, ăllow, sofȧ; ēve, ĕvent, ĕll, wrītĕr, novĕl; bīte, pĭn; nō, ōbey, ôr, dŏg, tŏp, cŏllide; ūnit, ūnite, bûrn, cŭt, focŭs; nōon, fŏot; mound; coin;

of a tribe or family; **3,** in certain Protestant churches, especially the Presbyterian, a governing officer.

²**el·der** (ĕl′dẽr), *n.* a shrub with flattened clusters of white or pink flowers, and black, reddish, or purple berries.

el·der·ber·ry (ĕl′dẽr-bĕr′ĭ), *n.* [*pl.* elder-berries], the black, reddish, or purple fruit of the elder; also, the bush.

eld·er·ly (ĕl′dẽr-lĭ), *adj.* somewhat old; beyond middle age.

eld·est (ĕl′dĕst), *adj.* [a *superl.* of *old*], old-est; first-born; as, the *eldest* son inherits the throne.

ELDERBERRY

1, leaves and fruit; 2, flower.

El Do·ra·do (ĕl dō̇-rä′dō), [*pl.* El Dora-dos], an imaginary country rich in gold and precious stones, sought in South America by Spanish adventurers of the 16th century; hence, any region of fab-ulous wealth.

e·lect (ė̇-lĕkt′), *v.t.* **1,** to choose; select; **2,** to choose or select by vote; as, to *elect* a president:—*adj.* chosen for office but not yet in charge; as, the president *elect*:—**the elect, 1,** those divinely chosen for eternal salvation; **2,** hence, those belonging to an exclusive set.

e·lec·tion (ė̇-lĕk′shŭn), *n.* the act of choosing or selecting; especially, the proc-ess of choosing a person or persons for office by vote.

e·lec·tion·eer (ė̇-lĕk′shŭn-ēr′), *v.i.* to work to secure votes for a party or candidate in an election.

e·lec·tive (ė̇-lĕk′tĭv), *adj.* **1,** chosen by election, as an officer; filled by election, as an office; **2,** open to choice; not com-pulsory; as, an *elective* course of study:—*n.* a course of study which a student may choose, as distinguished from one that is compulsory.

e·lec·tor (ė̇-lĕk′tẽr), *n.* **1,** one lawfully qualified to vote; **2,** in the U.S., a member of an electoral college.

e·lec·tor·al (ė̇-lĕk′tẽr-ăl), *adj.* pertaining to electors:—**electoral college,** in the U.S., the body of men chosen every four years by the people of the individual States, to elect a president and vice-president.

e·lec·tor·ate (ė̇-lĕk′tẽr-ĭt), *n.* the whole body of persons entitled to vote.

e·lec·tric (ė̇-lĕk′trĭk) or **e·lec·tri·cal** (ė̇-lĕk′trĭ-kăl), *adj.* **1,** pertaining to or connected with electricity, its production, transmission, or use; as, an *electric* bat-tery; *electric* wires; an *electric* iron; *electric* light; *electric* trains; **2,** figura-tively, as if charged with electricity; thrilling; exciting:—**electric eel,** a South American fish with an eel-like body, growing to a length of six feet, which is able to give a severe electric shock when touched.

ELECTRIC EEL

e·lec·tri·cian (ė̇-lĕk′trĭsh′ăn; ĕl′ĕk-trĭsh′-ăn), *n.* one who makes, repairs, or installs electrical appliances and equipment.

e·lec·tric·i·ty (ė̇-lĕk′trĭs′ĭ-tĭ; ĕl′ĕk-trĭs′ĭ-tĭ), *n.* an invisible force in nature which causes the lightning's flash, the electric spark, and many other phenomena. When artificially produced by man, it is used as an important source of power to produce heat, light, and motion.

e·lec·tri·fy (ė̇-lĕk′trĭ-fī), *v.t.* [electrified, electrify-ing], **1,** to charge with electricity; **2,** to equip for the use of electric power, as a railway; **3,** to thrill; startle; as, the acrobat's feat *electrified* the spectators.

e·lec·tro- (ė̇-lĕk′trō-), a prefix meaning electric or electricity; as, *electro*magnet, *electro*plate.

e·lec·tro·cute (ė̇-lĕk′trō-kūt), *v.t.* [electro-cut-ed, electrocut-ing], **1,** to put (a con-demned criminal) to death by electricity; **2,** to kill accidentally by an electric shock.

e·lec·trode (ė̇-lĕk′trōd), *n.* either pole of an electric battery or of any other source of electricity: when posi-tive, called *anode;* when negative, called *cathode.*

e·lec·trol·y·sis (ė̇-lĕk′trŏl′ĭ-sĭs), *n.* the separa-tion of a chemical com-pound into its several parts by passing an electric current through it.

e·lec·tro·lyte (ė̇-lĕk′trō-līt), *n.* any chemical com-pound which can be sep-arated into its several parts by passing an elec-tric current through it.—*adj.* e·lec′tro·lyt′ic.

e · lec · tro · mag · net (ė̇-lĕk′trō-măg′nĕt), *n.* a piece of soft iron made into a magnet by passing an elec-tric current through a coil of wire wrapped around it.—*adj.* e·lec′tro·mag·net′ic.

e·lec·tro·mag·net·ism (ė̇-lĕk′trō-măg′-nė̇-tĭzm), *n.* **1,** magnetism produced by an

ELECTROMAGNET

An electric current (C,C) passing through the coils of the elec-tromagnet (E) mag-netizes its core so that it is able to lift the weight (W) by magnetic attraction.

electric current; **2,** the science which deals with the relations between electricity and magnetism.

e·lec·tro·mo·tive (ē-lĕk′trŏ-mō′tĭv), *adj.* producing an electric current.

e·lec·tron (ē-lĕk′trŏn), *n.* the smallest known unit of matter; the smallest known quantity of negative electricity in any atom: opposite of *proton.*

e·lec·tron·ics (ē′lĕk-trŏn′ĭks) *n. pl.,* used as *sing.* [see **electric**], the science of the most elementary charge of negative electricity (the *electron*), electrically opposite to the *proton;* the science of using these charges by detaching them from the atoms of which they are normally constituent, and utilizing them in television, radar, the electric eye, etc., or in processes like purifying air and producing high-test gasoline.

e·lec·tro·plate (ē-lĕk′trŏ-plāt′), *v.t.* [electroplat-ed, electroplat-ing], to cover with a coating, as of silver, nickel, or rubber, by means of an electric process.

e·lec·tro·type (ē-lĕk′trŏ-tīp), *n.* a plate for use in printing, made by covering a wax or lead mold of the original type with a thin metal shell by an electric process, and then backing it with molten metal; also, a print made from a plate of this kind.

el·e·gance (ĕl′ē-găns), *n.* refinement; good taste; polish, especially of literary style; careful correctness of dress or manners.

el·e·gant (ĕl′ē-gănt), *adj.* **1,** having refinement and good taste, as dress or manners; **2,** *Colloquial,* excellent.—**el′e·gant·ly.**

el·e·gy (ĕl′ē-jĭ), *n.* [*pl.* elegies], a poem lamenting the dead; a funeral poem.

el·e·ment (ĕl′ē-mĕnt), *n.* **1,** in chemistry, a substance which cannot be broken down into simpler substances, such as gold, hyrdogen, or oxygen; **2,** a simple part; an ingredient; **3,** a main principle of a subject which must be learned first.—**the elements,** in ancient times, air, earth, fire, and water, of which the universe was believed to consist; now, the forces of nature.

el·e·men·tal (ĕl′ē-mĕn′tăl), *adj.* **1,** pertaining to air, earth, fire, and water; also, connected with the forces of nature; as, an earthquake is an *elemental* upheaval; **2,** fundamental; primary.

el·e·men·ta·ry (ĕl′ē-mĕn′tà-rĭ), *adj.* pertaining to first principles; introductory; as, an *elementary* education.

AFRICAN ELEPHANT (₁⁄₁₅)

el·e·phant (ĕl′ē-fănt), *n.* the largest of living land animals, native to India and Africa, with thick, wrinkled hide, a long, flexible snout, or trunk, and two long, curved ivory tusks:—**white elephant,** a possession that costs more in upkeep, or gives more trouble, than it is worth.

el·e·phan·tine (ĕl′ē-făn′tĭn; ĕl′ē-făn′tīn), *adj.* **1,** like an elephant, huge and unwieldy; as, an *elephantine* form; **2,** pertaining to the elephant.

el·e·vate (ĕl′ē-vāt), *v.t.* [elevat-ed, elevat-ing], **1,** to raise to a higher level; lift; as, to *elevate* a goblet before drinking; **2,** to raise in rank, as a lieutenant to a captaincy; **3,** to raise or improve mentally or morally; as, study *elevates* the mind; **4,** to make (the voice) louder or higher in pitch.—*adj.* **el′e·vat′ed.**

 Syn. promote, exalt, dignify.

el·e·va·tion (ĕl′ē-vā′shŭn), *n.* **1,** the act or state of raising; **2,** a raised place; **3,** height; often, height above sea level.

el·e·va·tor (ĕl′ē-vā′tēr), *n.* **1,** a hoisting machine or lift; a cage that can be raised or lowered in a shaft, to carry people or goods from one level to another; **2,** a continuous belt or chain conveyer with buckets for raising sand, earth, etc.; **3,** a warehouse for the storage of grain.

GRAIN ELEVATOR

el·ev·en (ē-lĕv′ĕn), *n.* **1,** the number consisting of ten plus one; **2,** a sign representing eleven units, as 11 or xi; **3,** a football or cricket team.—also *adj.*

el·ev·enth (ē-lĕv′ĕnth), *adj.* next after the tenth: the ordinal of *eleven:*—*n.* one of the eleven equal parts of anything.

elf (ĕlf), *n.* [*pl.* elves (ĕlvz)], **1,** in fairy tales, a tiny goblin, dwarf, or fairy, sometimes mischievous, sometimes helpful, to man; **2,** a small creature.

elf·in (ĕl′fĭn), *adj.* **1,** relating to elves; as, an *elfin* knight; **2,** having the strange charm of an elf; as, *elfin* laughter.

elf·ish (ĕl′fĭsh), *adj.* impish; mischievous.

E·li·a (ē′lĭ-à), the pen name of *Charles Lamb,* author of "Essays of Elia."

e·lic·it (ē-lĭs′ĭt), *v.t.* to draw out; extract; as, to *elicit* a reply.

e·lide (ē-līd′), *v.t.* [elid-ed, elid-ing], to cut off, or slur over, in pronunciation, as a final vowel or syllable.—*n.* **e·li′sion.**

el·i·gi·ble (ĕl′ĭ-jĭ-bl), *adj.* fit to be chosen or elected; meeting given requirements;

as, a disabled soldier is *eligible* for a pension.—*adv.* **el′i·gi·bly.**—*n.* **el′i·gi·bil′i·ty.**

E·li·jah (ē-lī′jå), in the Bible, one of the greatest of the Hebrew prophets.

e·lim·i·nate (ē-lĭm′ĭ-nāt), *v.t.* [eliminated, eliminat-ing], **1,** to get rid of; expel; **2,** to set aside; leave out of consideration.
Syn. eject, oust, dislodge, exclude.

El·i·ot (ĕl′ĭ-ŭt), George (1819–1880), the pen name of *Mary Ann Evans Cross,* an English novelist, author of "Silas Marner."

E·lis (ē′lĭs), a division of the Peloponnesus in ancient Greece; also, a city, its capital (map 1).

E·li·sha (ē-lī′shå), in the Bible, a prophet who carried on the work of Elijah.

e·lite (ā-lēt′), *n.* the best or choicest members, as of a society or a profession.

e·lix·ir (ē-lĭk′sēr), *n.* **1,** a substance formerly believed capable of changing baser metals into gold; also, a liquid formerly believed capable of prolonging life; **2,** hence, a remedy for all diseases or evils.

E·liz·a·beth (ē-lĭz′å-bĕth), the name of two queens of England: Elizabeth I (1533-1603); Elizabeth II (1926–   ), succeeded George VI in 1952.

²E·liz·a·beth (ē-lĭz′å-bĕth), a city and industrial center in northern New Jersey (map 6).

E·liz·a·be·than (ē-lĭz′å-bē′thăn; ē-lĭz′å-bĕth′ăn), *adj.* pertaining to the customs, literature, and spirit of the time of Queen Elizabeth I of England, or the latter half of the 16th century:—*n.* one who lived in that time.

EUROPEAN ELK (⅟₆₀)

elk (ĕlk), *n.* [*pl.* elk], **1,** the largest native deer of Europe and Asia, with spreading antlers; **2,** in North America, the wapiti (see **wapiti**).

¹ell (ĕl), *n.* an old measure of length, chiefly for cloth, varying from 27 to 48 inches.

²ell (ĕl), *n.* an addition to a house at right angles to the main structure.

ELL (E), of a house

el·lipse (ĕ-lĭps′), *n.* a closed curve that differs from an oval in that it has symmetrical ends. (See illustration next column.)

el·lip·sis (ĕ-lĭp′sĭs), *n.* [*pl.* ellipses (ĕ-lĭp′-sēz)], the omission from a sentence of a word or words whose meaning is so clearly implied that they are not needed.

el·lip·tic (ĕ-lĭp′tĭk) or **el·lip·ti·cal** (ĕ-lĭp′-tĭ-kål), *adj.* **1,** relating to, or formed like, an ellipse; **2,** in grammar, having certain words omitted; as, an *elliptic* phrase.

El·lis Is·land (ĕl′ĭs), an immigration station of the U.S., in New York Harbor.

elm (ĕlm), *n.* **1,** a tall, graceful shade tree; **2,** the hard, tough wood of this tree.

el·o·cu·tion (ĕl′-ō-kū′shŭn), *n.* the art which teaches the proper use of voice and gesture in public speaking or reading.

ELM

E. long. abbreviation for *east longitude.*

e·lon·gate (ē-lŏng′gāt; ē′lŏng-gāt), *v.t.* and *v.i.* [elongat-ed, elongat-ing], to lengthen.

e·lope (ē-lōp′), *v.i.* [eloped, elop-ing], to run away with a lover.—*n.* **e·lope′ment.**

el·o·quence (ĕl′ō-kwĕns), *n.* the art of speaking so as to move one's hearers; forceful and vivid use of language.

el·o·quent (ĕl′ō-kwĕnt), *adj.* **1,** speaking in so forceful and vivid a manner as to move one's hearers; **2,** forcefully and vividly expressed.

El Pas·o (ĕl păs′ō), a city in southwest Texas, on the Rio Grande (map 8).

El Sal·va·dor (ĕl săl′vå-dôr; ĕl säl′vä-thôr′), a republic in Central America. See **Salvador, El.**

else (ĕls), *adv.* otherwise; besides; as, eat, *else* you will starve; where *else* shall I hunt? —*adj.* implying someone or something different or additional; as, somebody *else* has the book.

else·where (ĕls′hwâr′), *adv.* in, at, or to, another place; somewhere else.

e·lu·ci·date (ē-lū′sĭ-dāt), *v.t.* [elucidat-ed, elucidat-ing], to make clear; explain.—*n.* **e·lu·ci·da′tion.**

e·lude (ē-lūd′), *v.t.* [elud-ed, elud-ing], to escape or evade through cleverness; as, to *elude* an enemy.

1

2

ELLIPSE
1, ellipse; 2, oval.

e·lu·sive (ē-lū′sĭv), *adj.* tending to slip away or escape; as, an *elusive* criminal; also, hard to get hold of or to understand; as, an *elusive* fact.—*adv.* **e·lu′sive·ly.**

elves (ĕlvz), plural of *elf.*

E·ly·sian (ē-lĭzh′ăn; ē-lĭz′ĭ-ăn), *adj.* heavenly; blissful:—**Elysian fields,** in Greek mythology, the abode of the blessed after death.

E·ly·si·um (ē-lĭzh′ĭ-ŭm; ē-lĭz′ĭ-ŭm), *n.* **1,** in Greek mythology, the abode of the blessed after death; **2,** any place of bliss.

em- (ĕm-), *prefix,* a form of *en-.* See **en-.**

e·ma·ci·ate (ē-mā′shĭ-āt), *v.t.* [emaciat-ed, emaciat-ing], to cause to waste away; to make thin; as, he was *emaciated* by hunger and fatigue.—*adj.* **e·ma′ci·at′ed.**

em·a·nate (ĕm′à-nāt), *v.i.* [emanat-ed, emanat-ing], to flow out, issue, or proceed from a source, as light from the sun.

em·a·na·tion (ĕm′à-nā′shŭn), *n.* **1,** a flowing forth or issuing; **2,** something that flows forth from a source; as, fragrance is an *emanation* from the rose.

e·man·ci·pate (ē-măn′sĭ-pāt), *v.t.* [emancipat-ed, emancipat-ing], to set free from bondage or control; liberate.—*n.* **e·man′-ci·pa′tion.**—*n.* **e·man′ci·pa′tor.**
Syn. deliver, release.

e·mas·cu·late (ē-măs′kū-lāt), *v.t.* [emascul-ed, emasculat-ing], to deprive of vigor.

em·balm (ĕm-bäm′), *v.t.* **1,** to treat (a dead body) to preserve it from decay; **2,** to hold in memory.—*n.* **em·balm′er.**

em·bank·ment (ĕm-băngk′mĕnt), *n.* a structure of earth, stones, etc., built to prevent water from overflowing, to carry a roadway, or for some similar purpose.

em·bar·go (ĕm-bär′gō), *n.* [*pl.* embargoes], **1,** a government act forbidding commercial vessels, especially foreign vessels, to leave or enter its ports; **2,** any restraint imposed on commerce by law:—*v.t.* to lay an embargo on.

em·bark (ĕm-bärk′), *v.i.* **1,** to go on board a vessel; **2,** to engage in any affair; as, to *embark* in business.—*n.* **em′bar·ka′tion.**

em·bar·rass (ĕm-băr′ăs), *v.t.* **1,** to disconcert; fluster; as, her bad manners *embarrassed* her mother; **2,** to worry; hinder; as, he was *embarrassed* by debts.
Syn. entangle, abash, dismay.

em·bar·rass·ment (ĕm-băr′ăs-mĕnt), *n.* **1,** confusion of mind; perplexity; **2,** mortification; **3,** financial difficulties.

em·bas·sy (ĕm′bà-sĭ), *n.* [*pl.* embassies], **1,** the position of an ambassador; also, his official residence; **2,** an ambassador and his assistants.

em·bat·tled (ĕm-băt′ld), *adj.* **1,** in battle order; ready for battle; **2,** fortified; as, an *embattled* frontier.

em·bed (ĕm-bĕd′), *v.t.* [embed-ded, embed-ding], to lay in, or as in, a bed; set firmly in surrounding matter; as, to *embed* a thing in clay. Also, **im-bed′.**

em·bel·lish (ĕm-bĕl′ĭsh), *v.t.* **1,** to beautify or ornament; as, to *embellish* a cloak with fur; **2,** to add fanciful details to (a story).—*n.* **em·bel′lish·ment.**
Syn. adorn, decorate, bedeck.

em·ber (ĕm′bēr), *n.* a live coal or small piece of wood, smouldering in ashes.

em·bez·zle (ĕm-bĕz′l), *v.t.* [embez-zled, embez-zling], to steal (funds entrusted to one's care); as, to *embezzle* a trust fund.—*n.* **em·bez′zler.**—*n.* **em·bez′zle·ment.**

em·bit·ter (ĕm-bĭt′ēr), *v.t.* to make bitter or resentful; as, his scolding *embittered* her because it was unjust.

em·bla·zon (ĕm-blā′zn), *v.t.* **1,** to adorn with heraldic symbols; also, to inscribe, as on a shield; **2,** to display brilliantly; light up; as, stars *emblazoned* the sky; **3,** to praise highly.—*n.* **em·bla′zon·ry.**

em·blem (ĕm′blĕm), *n.* a symbol or representation of an idea; as, the olive branch is an *emblem* of peace.
Syn. token, sign.

em·blem·at·ic (ĕm′blĕ-măt′ĭk) or **em·blem·at·i·cal** (ĕm′blĕ-măt′ĭ-kăl), *adj.* symbolic; serving as an emblem; as, the laurel wreath is *emblematic* of victory.

em·bod·i·ment (ĕm-bŏd′ĭ-mĕnt), *n.* **1,** the act of uniting or concentrating into a whole; **2,** a concrete expression; incarnation; as, she is the *embodiment* of virtue.

em·bod·y (ĕm-bŏd′ĭ), *v.t.* [embodied, embody-ing], **1,** to represent in bodily form; **2,** to express in a definite form; as, to *embody* thought in words; **3,** to collect into a united whole.

em·bold·en (ĕm-bōl′dn), *v.t.* to make bold.

em·bos·om (ĕm-bŏŏz′ŭm; ĕm-bōō′zŭm), *v.t.* **1,** to take to one's heart; **2,** to shelter.

em·boss (ĕm-bôs′), *v.t.* to ornament with raised work; also, to raise above a surface; as, the name was *embossed* on the card.

em·bow·er (ĕm-bou′ēr), *v.t.* to enclose or shelter with flowers, vines, etc.

em·brace (ĕm-brās′), *v.t.* [embraced, embrac-ing], **1,** to hold in the arms with affection; **2,** to adopt; turn to; as, the heathen *embraced* Christianity; **3,** to take up; enter on; as, to *embrace* a profession; **4,** to include; as, biology *embraces* botany and zoology:—*n.* the act of clasping in the arms; a hug.

em·bra·sure (ĕm-brā′zhēr), *n.* **1,** an open-

āte, āorta, râre, căt, àsk, fär, ăllow, sofà; ēve, ēvent, ĕll, writēr, novĕl; bīte, pĭn; nō, ōbey, ôr, dŏg, tŏp, cŏllide; ūnit, ūnite, bûrn, cŭt, focŭs; nōōn, fŏŏt; mound; coin;

ing in a wall or fort from which to fire guns; 2, the space made by the slanting off of the wall at the sides of a door or window.

em·broi·der (ĕm-broi′dẽr), v.t. **1**, to decorate or make beautiful with needlework; **2**, to exaggerate, as a story:—v.i. to do decorative needlework; as, she *embroiders* beautifully.

EMBRASURE, def. 1
A,A, cheeks; B, sole; C, throat, or inner side; D,D, merlons.

em·broi·der·y (ĕm-broi′dẽr-ĭ), n. [pl. embroideries], **1**, ornamental needlework; **2**, exaggeration, as of a story.

em·broil (ĕm-broil′), v.t. to involve in a quarrel; as, he was *embroiled* in a quarrel not of his own making.

EMBROIDERY

em·bry·o (ĕm′brĭ-ō), n. [pl. embryos], **1**, the young of an animal in the earliest stages of its growth before birth or hatching; **2**, an undeveloped plant, contained in a seed; **3**, the first or undeveloped state of anything.

em·bry·on·ic (ĕm′brĭ-ŏn′ĭk), adj. pertaining to an embryo; not yet developed.

e·mend (ē-mĕnd′), v.t. to alter or correct; as, to *emend* a text.—n. e′men·da′tion.

em·er·ald (ĕm′ẽr-ăld), n. **1**, a precious stone of a clear, deep-green color; **2**, the color of this stone.

e·merge (ē-mûrj′), v.i. [emerged, emerging], to rise up; come forth; appear.

e·mer·gence (ē-mûr′jĕns), n. the act of coming forth; as, the *emergence* of a star.

e·mer·gen·cy (ē-mûr′jĕn-sĭ), n. [pl. emergencies], a sudden or unexpected happening or situation, demanding prompt action.

e·mer·i·tus (ē-mĕr′ĭ-tŭs), adj. retired from service with honorary rank and title; as, a professor *emeritus*.

Em·er·son (ĕm′ẽr-sŭn), Ralph Waldo (1803–1882), an American philosopher, essayist, and poet.

em·er·y (ĕm′ẽr-ĭ), n. a very hard, dark mineral substance used, when powdered, for grinding or polishing.

e·met·ic (ē-mĕt′ĭk), adj. causing vomiting:—n. a medicine that causes vomiting.

em·i·grant (ĕm′ĭ-grănt; ĕm′ĭ-grănt), n. one who leaves his own country to settle in another:—adj. moving from one country to settle in another; as, *emigrant* laborers.

em·i·grate (ĕm′ĭ-grāt), v.i. [emigrat-ed, emigrat-ing], to leave one's own country to settle in another; as, many of America's early settlers *emigrated* from England.

em·i·nence (ĕm′ĭ-nĕns), n. **1**, that which is high; an elevation; **2**, a high station or standing in life; as, to attain *eminence* as a lawyer; *eminence* in society.

em·i·nent (ĕm′ĭ-nĕnt), adj. high in office, rank, or reputation; distinguished; as, an *eminent* scholar.—adv. em′i·nent·ly. *Syn.* celebrated, noted, renowned.

e·mir (ē-mēr′), n. **1**, an Arabian prince or chieftain; **2**, a title of certain Turkish officials; **3**, a title given to persons descended from Mohammed.

em·is·sar·y (ĕm′ĭ-sĕr′ĭ), n. [pl. emissaries], a person or agent sent on a mission, especially of a secret nature.

e·mis·sion (ē-mĭsh′ŭn), n. the act of sending out; as, an *emission* of heat; also, something sent out.—adj. e·mis′sive.

e·mit (ē-mĭt′), v.t. [emit-ted, emit-ting], to send forth; as, a stove *emits* heat.

em·met (ĕm′ĕt), n. an ant.

e·mol·li·ent (ē-mŏl′ĭ-ĕnt), adj. softening; soothing to the skin; as, an *emollient* oil:—n. a medicine that has a softening or soothing effect on the skin.

e·mol·u·ment (ē-mŏl′ū-mĕnt), n. profit from an office or job; wages; salary.

e·mo·tion (ē-mō′shŭn), n. **1**, mental excitement; strong feeling; as, he pleaded with *emotion*; **2**, an intense feeling of love, hate, joy, awe, grief, or the like. *Syn.* feeling, passion, sentiment.

e·mo·tion·al (ē-mō′shŭn-ăl), adj. **1**, excitable; easily agitated; as, she has an *emotional* nature; **2**, tending to stir the feelings.—adv. e·mo′tion·al·ly.

em·per·or (ĕm′pẽr-ẽr), n. the supreme ruler of an empire.

em·pha·sis (ĕm′fà-sĭs), n. [pl. emphases (ĕm′fà sēz)], **1**, a particular stress of the voice on a word or words in reading or speaking; **2**, importance; stress; as, to put too much *emphasis* on football.

em·pha·size (ĕm′fà-sīz), v.t. [emphasized, emphasiz-ing], **1**, to pronounce clearly and positively; stress; as, he *emphasized* each word; **2**, to call attention to; as, he *emphasized* the fine points of the picture.

em·phat·ic (ĕm-făt′ĭk), adj. **1**, expressive; forceful; as, an *emphatic* gesture; **2**, positive; striking.—adv. em·phat′i·cal·ly.

em·pire (ĕm′pīr), n. **1**, a group of nations united under one ruler; as, the British *Empire*; **2**, the country or territory ruled over by an emperor; as, the Japanese *Empire*; **3**, supreme power; imperial rule.

go; join; yet; sing; chin; show; thin, *th*en; hw, *why*; zh, azure; ü, Ger. *für* or Fr. *lune*; ö, Ger. schön or Fr. *feu*; ṅ, Fr. *enfant*, nom; kh, Ger. *ach* or *ich*. See pages ix–x.

em·pir·i·cal (ĕm-pĭr'ĭ-kăl), *adj.* based on experience or observation rather than on reasoning or theory.

em·place·ment (ĕm-plās'mĕnt), *n.* the place in a fortification for a gun or guns.

em·ploy (ĕm-ploi'), *v.t.* **1,** to make use of the services of; give occupation to; hire; as, he *employed* ten men; **2,** to make use of; as, he *employed* his knowledge of Spanish in business:—*n.* the state of serving an employer for wages.
Syn., v. use, hire.

em·ploy·ee (ĕm'ploi-ē'; ĕm-ploi'ē), *n.* one who works for another for wages.

em·ploy·er (ĕm-ploi'ĕr), *n.* a person who engages others in paid service.

em·ploy·ment (ĕm-ploi'mĕnt), *n.* **1,** the state of being employed; **2,** business; work.
Syn. profession, trade.

em·por·i·um (ĕm-pôr'ĭ-ŭm), *n.* [*pl.* emporiums or emporia (ĕm-pôr'ĭ-à)], a market place; popularly, a large general store.

em·pow·er (ĕm-pou'ĕr), *v.t.* to give authority to; make able.

em·press (ĕm'prĕs), *n.* a woman ruler of an empire; the wife or widow of an emperor.

em·prise (ĕm-prīz'), *n. Archaic,* an adventure or knightly undertaking.

emp·ty (ĕmp'tĭ), *adj.* [emp-ti-er, emp-ti-est], **1,** containing nothing; as, an *empty* box; **2,** vague; with no possibility of fulfilment; as, *empty* dreams; **3,** having no force or sense; as, *empty* words; **4,** vacant, as an unoccupied house:—*v.t.* [emptied, empty-ing], **1,** to remove the contents from; make vacant; **2,** to pour out; as, to *empty* the milk from the bottle:—*v.i.* **1,** to become empty; **2,** to discharge itself; as, the river *empties* into the ocean.—*adv.* **emp'ti-ly.**—*n.* **emp'ti-ness.**
Syn., adj. hollow, blank.

em·py·re·an (ĕm'pĭ-rē'ăn; ĕm'pī-rē'ăn), *n.* the heavens:
—*adj.* pertaining to the highest heaven; heavenly.—*adj.* **em·pyr'e-al.**

e·mu (ē'mū), *n.* a large, three-toed Australian bird resembling the ostrich.

EMU (₁'₀)

em·u·late (ĕm'ū-lāt), *v.t.* [emulat-ed, emulat-ing], to strive to equal or excel; imitate with the hope of equaling or excelling; as, to *emulate* great men.

em·u·la·tion (ĕm'ū-lā'shŭn), *n.* rivalry; an effort to excel another.

em·u·lous (ĕm'ū-lŭs), *adj.* eager to equal or excel.—*adv.* **em'u-lous-ly.**

e·mul·sion (ē-mŭl'shŭn), *n.* a liquid mixture in which a fatty substance is present in small globules which will not dissolve.—*v.t.* **e-mul'si-fy.**

en- (ĕn-), a prefix meaning in; as, *en*close, *en*velop, *en*liven: becoming **em-** before *p* and *b;* as, *em*ploy, *em*body.

en·a·ble (ĕn-ā'bl), *v.t.* [ena-bled, ena-bling], to make able; as, the airplane *enables* us to travel faster than by train.

en·act (ĕn-ăkt'), *v.t.* **1,** to make into law; as, to *enact* a bill; **2,** to act the part of; as, he *enacted* the hero.

en·act·ment (ĕn-ăkt'mĕnt), *n.* **1,** the act of passing a bill; **2,** a law or decree.

en·am·el (ĕn-ăm'ĕl), *n.* **1,** a hard, glassy substance used in coating the surface of metals, glass, or porcelain for ornamentation or protection; **2,** any hard, glossy covering like enamel; **3,** the hard, white outer coating of the teeth:—*v.t.* [enameled, enamel-ing], **1,** to cover or decorate with enamel; **2,** to apply a glossy surface to.

en·am·or (ĕn-ăm'ĕr), *v.t.* to inspire with love; charm. In British usage, **en-am'our.**

en bloc (ĕn blŏk'), in a block; all together.

en·camp (ĕn-kămp'), *v.t.* to settle in camp:—*v.i.* to make camp; as, let's *encamp* here.

en·case (ĕn-kās'), *v.t.* [encased, encas-ing], to enclose in a box or other container; incase. See **incase.**

-ence (-ĕns), a suffix forming nouns meaning: **1,** an action or a way of acting; as, insist*ence*, diverg*ence;* **2,** a state or quality; as, exist*ence*, depend*ence*.

en·chant (ĕn-chȧnt'), *v.t.* **1,** to charm by magic spells; **2,** to fill with delight.
Syn. captivate, enrapture, fascinate.

en·chant·er (ĕn-chȧn'tĕr), *n.* **1,** one who uses magic or witchcraft; **2,** one who charms or delights.—*n.fem.* **en-chant'ress.**

en·chant·ment (ĕn-chȧnt'mĕnt), *n.* **1,** magic or sorcery; as, a wizard's *enchantment;* **2,** that which delights; charm; as, the *enchantment* of her smile.

en·cir·cle (ĕn-sûr'kl), *v.t.* [encir-cled, encir-cling], **1,** to surround; as, enemies *encircle* us; **2,** to make a circle around; go around; as, to *encircle* the globe.

en·close (ĕn-klōz'), *v.t.* [enclosed, enclosing], **1,** to insert; as, he *enclosed* the check in a letter; **2,** to surround with a barrier. Also, **in-close'.**—*n.* **en-clo'sure.**

en·com·pass (ĕn-kŭm'pȧs), *v.t.* to surround; encircle; as, enemies *encompassed* the city.

āte, âorta, râre, căt, ȧsk, fär, ăllow, sofà; ēve, ēvent, ĕll, writẽr, novĕl; bīte, pĭn; nō, ōbey, ôr, dŏg, tŏp, cŏllide; ūnit, ūnite, bûrn, cŭt, focŭs; nōon, fŏot; mound; coin;

en·core (äng-kôr′), *interj.* once more! again!—*n.* (äng′kôr), a repetition, as of a song, in response to a call by an audience:—*v.t.* (äng-kôr′; äng′kôr), [encored, encor-ing], to call for a repetition of (any part of a performance), by applause; also, to call upon (a person) for an encore.

en·coun·ter (ĕn-koun′tẽr), *v.t.* and *v.i.* 1, to meet in conflict; 2, to meet unexpectedly; as, we *encountered* an old friend this morning:—*n.* 1, a sudden or accidental meeting; 2, a conflict.
Syn., *n.* meeting, engagement, battle.

en·cour·age (ĕn-kûr′ĭj), *v.t.* [encouraged, encourag-ing], 1, to help; foster; 2, to inspire with courage or hope; hearten.
Syn. cheer, support, inspirit.

en·cour·age·ment (ĕn-kûr′ĭj-mĕnt), *n.* 1, the act of inspiring with confidence; 2, that which encourages; an incentive.

en·cour·ag·ing (ĕn-kûr′ĭj-ĭng), *adj.* 1, giving hope; inspiring; 2, aiding; helping. —*adv.* **en·cour′ag·ing·ly.**

en·croach (ĕn-krōch′), *v.i.* 1, to intrude upon another's rights or property; trespass; 2, to go beyond normal limits.—*n.* **en·croach′ment.**

en·crust (ĕn-krŭst′), *v.t.* to cover with a hard coat; incrust. See **incrust.**

en·cum·ber (ĕn-kŭm′bẽr), *v.i.* 1, to impede or hinder; as, her long skirts *encumbered* her; 2, to burden, as with debt. Also, **in·cum′ber.**—*n.* **en·cum′brance.**
Syn. obstruct, hamper.

-en·cy (-ĕn-sĭ), a suffix meaning state or quality; as, flu*ency*, urg*ency.*

ency., encyc., or **encycl.** abbreviation for *encyclopedia.*

en·cy·cli·cal (ĕn-sĭ′klĭ-kăl; ĕn-sĭk′lĭ-kăl), *adj.* circulated generally or widely:—**encyclical letter,** a circular letter from the Pope:—*n.* an encyclical letter.

en·cy·clo·pe·di·a or **en·cy·clo·pae·di·a** (ĕn-sī′klŏ-pē′dĭ-à), *n.* a work in one or more volumes, containing information on all branches of knowledge, with the articles arranged in alphabetical order.—*adj.* **en·cy′clo·pe′dic; en·cy′clo·pae′dic.**

end (ĕnd), *n.* 1, the extreme limit or terminal point of anything; as, the *end* of a railroad; 2, death; 3, that which is left over; as, odds and *ends;* 4, purpose; goal; as, work to some good *end;* 5, conclusion; as, bring the discussion to an *end;* 6, in football, a player stationed at the end of the line:—*v.t.* 1, to finish; 2, to destroy; put to death:—*v.i.* 1, to come to an end; as, the road *ends* here; 2, to result; as, the argument *ended* in a fight; 3, to die.
Syn., *n.* aim, object; *v.* finish, conclude.

en·dan·ger (ĕn-dān′jẽr), *v.t.* to expose to danger; imperil; as, you *endanger* your health when you drink impure water.

en·dear (ĕn-dēr′), *v.t.* to make beloved; make (a person) dear or precious to another; as, his thoughtfulness *endeared* him to us.—*adv.* **en·dear′ing·ly.**

en·dear·ment (ĕn-dēr′mĕnt), *n.* an act or utterance of affection; a caress.

en·deav·or (ĕn-dĕv′ẽr), *v.i.* to strive; attempt; as, the team *endeavored* to win the game:—*n.* an effort or attempt.
Syn., *v.* try, aim, essay.

end·ing (ĕn′dĭng), *n.* end; conclusion.

en·dive (ĕn′dĭv; ĕn′dĭv; än′dēv), *n.* a plant with curling leaves which are used as a salad.

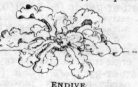
ENDIVE

end·less (ĕnd′lĕs), *adj.* 1, lasting forever; without an end; 2, having no ends; continuous; as, an *endless* chain.—*adv.* **end′less·ly.**
Syn. continual, eternal, everlasting.

en·dorse (ĕn-dôrs′), *v.t.* [endorsed, endors-ing], 1, to approve; as, Congress *endorsed* the President's plan; 2, to write one's name on the back of (a check or other paper); indorse. Also, **in·dorse′.**

en·dorse·ment (ĕn-dôrs′mĕnt), *n.* 1, that which is written on the back of a check or other paper; 2, approval or sanction. Also, **in·dorse′ment.**

en·dow (ĕn-dou′), *v.t.* 1, to bestow a permanent fund or source of income upon; as, to *endow* a college; 2, to equip or furnish; as, Nature *endowed* man with reason.

en·dow·ment (ĕn-dou′mĕnt), *n.* 1, property or a sum of money given to an institution, or devoted permanently to any cause; 2, the act of making such a settlement; 3, any talent that a person possesses by nature.
Syn. aptitude, faculty, capacity, bent.

en·due (ĕn-dū′), *v.t.* [endued, endu-ing], to endow; provide.

en·dur·a·ble (ĕn-dūr′à-bl), *adj.* bearable.

en·dur·ance (ĕn-dūr′ăns), *n.* 1, the ability to hold up without giving way; as, steel girders have great *endurance;* 2, a holding out; bearing; as, *endurance* of torture.
Syn. resignation, sufferance.

en·dure (ĕn-dūr′), *v.t.* [endured, enduring], to bear up under; bear with patience: —*v.i.* 1, to remain firm, as under suffering; 2, to remain in existence; last.
Syn. tolerate, abide, stand, suffer.

---

go; join; yet; sing; chin; show; thin, *th*en; hw, *why;* zh, a*z*ure; **ü,** Ger. f*ü*r or Fr. l*u*ne; **ö,** Ger. sch*ö*n or Fr. f*eu;* **ṅ,** Fr. e*n*fant, no*m;* kh, Ger. a*ch* or i*ch.* See pages **ix-x.**

end·ways (ĕnd′wāz′), *adv.* **1**, on end; **2**, with the end forward; **3**, lengthwise.

end·wise (ĕnd′wīz′), *adv.* endways.

En·dym·i·on (ĕn-dĭm′ĭ-ŏn), *n.* **1**, in Greek mythology, a beautiful shepherd boy, possessing eternal youth, loved by the moon-goddess; **2**, a poem by John Keats.

en·e·ma (ĕn′ē-mȧ; ē-nē′mȧ), *n.* a liquid injected into the rectum; also, the process of injecting it.

en·e·my (ĕn′ē-mĭ), *n.* [*pl.* enemies], **1**, one hostile to another; **2**, anything that harms another person or thing; as, laziness is an *enemy* of success.

   Syn. foe, opponent, adversary.

en·er·get·ic (ĕn′ēr-jĕt′ĭk), *adj.* full of life; active; vigorous; as, she is an *energetic* worker.—*adv.* **en′er·get′i·cal·ly.**

   Syn. industrious, powerful, strenuous.

en·er·gize (ĕn′ēr-jīz), *v.t.* [energized, energiz-ing], to give energy or animation to.

en·er·gy (ĕn′ēr-jĭ), *n.* [*pl.* energies], capacity for work; power; force; vigor; as, he devoted all his *energy* to the task.

   Syn. strength, vigor, might.

en·er·vate (ĕn′ēr-vāt), *v.t.* [enervat-ed, enervat-ing], to deprive of nerve, force, or vigor; weaken.—*n.* **en′er·va′tion.**

en·fee·ble (ĕn-fē′bl), *v.t.* [enfee-bled, enfee-bling], to weaken; make feeble.

en·fold (ĕn-fōld′), *v.t.* to wrap up; infold. See **infold.**

en·force (ĕn-fôrs′), *v.t.* [enforced, enforc-ing], **1**, to carry out; as, to *enforce* a law; **2**, to compel; impose; as, to *enforce* silence. —*adj.* **en·force′a·ble.**

en·force·ment (ĕn-fôrs′mĕnt), *n.* a putting into effect, as of a law.

en·fran·chise (ĕn-frăn′chīz), *v.t.* [enfranchised, enfranchis-ing], **1**, to admit to the right to vote; **2**, to free.—*n.* **en·fran′-chise·ment** (ĕn-frăn′chĭz-mĕnt).

Eng. abbreviation for *England, English.*

eng. abbreviation for *engineer.*

en·gage (ĕn-gāj′), *v.t.* [engaged, engag-ing], **1**, to pledge or bind by oath or contract; **2**, to betroth; **3**, to win and hold; as, to *engage* the attention; **4**, in machinery, to come into gear with; **5**, to secure for aid or employment; as, to *engage* a workman; **6**, to encounter, as in battle; **7**, to occupy the time or attention of; as, to *engage* someone in conversation:—*v.i.* **1**, to promise, or assume an obligation; as, he *engaged* to pay his father's debts; **2**, to occupy oneself; as, to *engage* in business; **3**, to enter a conflict; **4**, in machinery, to interlock.

en·gaged (ĕn-gājd′), *adj.* **1**, busy or occupied; **2**, betrothed.

en·gage·ment (ĕn-gāj′mĕnt), *n.* **1**, betrothal; **2**, occupation; **3**, an appointment; obligation; **4**, in machinery, the state of being in gear; **5**, a battle.

   Syn. conflict, skirmish, action, fight.

en·gag·ing (ĕn-gāj′ĭng), *adj.* winning; pleasing; as, an *engaging* manner.

en·gen·der (ĕn-jĕn′dēr), *v.t.* to beget; cause; as, poverty often *engenders* crime.

en·gine (ĕn′jĭn), *n.* **1**, a machine by which power is used to do work; **2**, an apparatus for converting some form of energy, as heat, into mechanical power; especially, a locomotive; **3**, a tool; an instrument.

en·gi·neer (ĕn′jĭ-nēr′), *n.* **1**, one who designs and constructs machines, bridges, etc.; as, an electrical *engineer;* **2**, one who has charge of and drives an engine or locomotive; **3**, one of an army corps which constructs bridges, roads, etc.:—*v.t.* **1**, to plan or direct; as, he *engineered* the campaign; **2**, to plan and execute the construction of (a road, canal, etc.).

en·gi·neer·ing (ĕn′jĭ-nēr′ĭng), *n.* the science and practice of designing and building machinery, roads, bridges, etc., and of developing natural resources, as water power, minerals, etc.

Eng·land (ĭng′glănd), the largest division of the island of Great Britain, south of Scotland, and east of Wales (map **13**).

Eng·lish (ĭng′glĭsh), *adj.* pertaining to England, its language, or its people:—*n.* the language of England, the United States, and some British colonies.

Eng·lish Chan·nel, a channel separating England and France (map **13**).

Eng·lish horn, a wood-wind instrument larger and deeper in tone than the oboe. (See *musical instrument,* illustration.)

Eng·lish·man (ĭng′glĭsh-măn), *n.* [*pl.* Englishmen (-mĕn)], a citizen of England. —*n.fem.* **Eng′lish·wom′an.**

en·graft (ĕn-grȧft′), *v.t.* to graft; insert (a shoot) in a tree. Also, **in-graft′.**

en·grave (ĕn-grāv′), *v.t.* [*p.t.* engraved, *p.p.* engraved or engrav-en, *p.pr.* engrav-ing], **1**, to cut or carve; as, to *engrave* words on a monument; **2**, to cut (letters, figures, designs, etc.) on stone, wood, or a metal plate, as for printing; **3**, to impress deeply; as, the words were *engraved* upon his mind. —*n.* **en·grav′er.**

en·grav·ing (ĕn-grāv′ĭng), *n.* **1**, the process or art of cutting designs into metal, stone, or hard wood with a tool or with acid; **2**, a design so cut; **3**, a print made from an engraved plate.

en·gross (ĕn-grōs′), *v.t.* to absorb; occupy wholly; as, the book *engrossed* her.

āte, āorta, râre, căt, ȧsk, fär, ăllow, sofȧ; ēve, ĕvent, ĕll, writēr, novĕl; bīte, pĭn; nō, ōbey, ôr, dŏg, tŏp, cŏllide; ūnit, ūnite, bûrn, cŭt, focŭs; nōon, fŏot; mound; coin;

en-gulf (ĕn-gŭlf′), *v.t.* to swallow up, as in a gulf; as, sorrow *engulfed* him.
Syn. absorb, submerge, bury.

en-hance (ĕn-hȧns′), *v.t.* [enhanced, enhanc-ing], to increase in attractiveness or value; add to; as, a good education will *enhance* your earning power.

e-nig-ma (ė-nĭg′mȧ), *n.* a riddle; a remark, act, or person not easily understood.
Syn. conundrum, problem.

e-nig-mat-ic (ē′nĭg-măt′ĭk; ĕn′ĭg-măt′ĭk) or **e-nig-mat-i-cal** (-măt′ĭ-kăl), *adj.* hard to understand; puzzling.

en-join (ĕn-join′) *v.t.* **1,** to direct with authority; command; as, the teacher *enjoined* the students to silence; **2,** to prohibit or restrain by judicial order.
Syn. order, charge, admonish.

en-joy (ĕn-joi′), *v.t.* **1,** to take delight in; as, we *enjoyed* the book; **2,** to have the use or possession of; as, I *enjoy* keen eyesight.

en-joy-a-ble (ĕn-joi′ȧ-bl), *adj.* pleasing; delightful.—*adv.* **en-joy′a-bly.**

en-joy-ment (ĕn-joi′mĕnt), *n.* **1,** pleasure; **2,** a source of joy or satisfaction.
Syn. satisfaction, comfort.

en-kin-dle (ĕn-kĭn′dl), *v.t.* [enkin-dled, enkin-dling], to set on fire; excite; rouse.

en-large (ĕn-lärj′), *v.t.* [enlarged, enlarging], to make larger; increase:—*v.i.* **1,** to become larger; **2,** to speak or write fully; as, he *enlarged* upon his theme.
Syn. augment, broaden, expand, extend.

en-large-ment (ĕn-lärj′mĕnt), *n.* **1,** increase in size; **2,** a photograph reproduced in larger size.

en-light-en (ĕn-līt′n), *v.t.* to furnish with increased knowledge; instruct.—*n.* **en-light′en-ment.**—*n.* **en-light′en-er.**
Syn. illumine, educate, inform.

en-list (ĕn-lĭst′), *v.t.* **1,** to enroll (a person) for military service; **2,** to win over for a cause; as, to *enlist* support for the Red Cross:—*v.i.* to enroll for military service, or in any cause.—*n.* **en-list′ment.**

en-liv-en (ĕn-līv′ĕn), *v.t.* to make lively, active, or gay; to put life into.
Syn. cheer, animate, inspire.

en-mi-ty (ĕn′mĭ-tĭ), *n.* [*pl.* enmities], ill will; hatred; hostility.
Syn. maliciousness, contention.

en-no-ble (ĕ-nō′bl; ĕn-nō′bl), *v.t.* [enno-bled, enno-bling], **1,** to dignify; exalt; **2,** to raise to the nobility.

en-nui (än-nwē′), *n.* boredom from lack of something to do; tedium.

e-nor-mi-ty (ė-nôr′mĭ-tĭ), *n.* [*pl.* enormities], **1,** the state of being outrageous or monstrous; as, the *enormity* of his offense; **2,** a grave offense; **3,** huge size; vastness.

e-nor-mous (ė-nôr′mŭs), *adj.* immense; of very great size or number.—*adv.* **e-nor′mous-ly.**—*n.* **e-nor′mous-ness.**
Syn. huge, vast, colossal.

e-nough (ė-nŭf′), *adj.* sufficient:—*n.* a sufficient amount:—*adv.* in a sufficient degree; sufficiently:—*interj.* stop!

en-rage (ĕn-rāj′), *v.t.* [enraged, enrag-ing], to make intensely angry; provoke to fury.

en-rap-ture (ĕn-răp′tûr), *v.t.* [enraptured, enraptur-ing], to delight; charm; enchant.
Syn. fascinate, bewitch.

en-rich (ĕn-rĭch′), *v.t.* **1,** to increase the wealth of; **2,** to make fertile, as soil; **3,** to improve, as the mind; **4,** to adorn.

en-roll or **en-rol** (ĕn-rōl′), *v.t.* [enrolled, enroll-ing], to insert or write down in a register; enlist; as, to *enroll* men for the army.—*n.* **en-roll′ment; en-rol′ment.**

en route (än root′), on the way; as, *en route* to Paris.

en-san-guine (ĕn-săng′gwĭn), *v.t.* [ensanguined, ensanguin-ing], to stain or cover with blood.

en-sconce (ĕn-skŏns′), *v.t.* [ensconced, ensconc-ing], **1,** to settle comfortably; **2,** to establish in a secret place.

en-sem-ble (än-sŏm′bl; än′sŏm-bl; än′-sänbl′), *n.* **1,** all the parts of anything considered as a whole; **2,** a costume of two or more pieces, worn together.

en-shrine (ĕn-shrīn′), *v.t.* [enshrined, enshrin-ing], to place on an altar or in a holy place; keep sacred.

en-shroud (ĕn-shroud′), *v.t.* to cover completely; hide; as, fog *enshrouds* the city.

en-sign (ĕn′sīn; ĕn′sĭn), *n.* **1,** a flag, especially a national standard; **2,** a badge of office, rank, etc.; **3,** (ĕn′sĭn), in the U.S. navy, a commissioned officer of the lowest rank.

ENSIGN
British naval ensign.

en-si-lage (ĕn′sĭ-lĭj), *n.* fodder stored in a silo.

en-slave (ĕn-slāv′), *v.t.* [enslaved, enslaving], to bring into bondage; deprive of freedom.—*n.* **en-slave′ment.**

en-snare (ĕn-snâr′), *v.t.* [ensnared, ensnaring], to trap; snare. Also, **in-snare′.**

en-sue (ĕn-sū′), *v.i.* [ensued, ensu-ing], to follow; result; come afterward; as, the ship ran aground, and panic *ensued.*

en-sure (ĕn-shoor′), *v.t.* [ensured, ensuring], to make sure; guarantee; as, it is difficult to *ensure* a happy outcome.

---

go; join; yet; sing; chin; show; thin, *th*en; hw, *wh*y; zh, a*z*ure; ü, Ger. f*ü*r or Fr. l*u*ne; ö, Ger. sch*ö*n or Fr. f*eu*; ṅ, Fr. e*n*fant, no*m*; kh, Ger. a*ch* or i*ch.* See pages ix-x.

-ent (-ĕnt), a suffix used to form: 1, adjectives that mean doing the thing referred to in the stem; as, exist*ent*, indulg*ent*; 2, nouns meaning a person or thing that does a specified act; as, correspond*ent*, resid*ent*.

en-tab-la-ture (ĕn-tăb′lȧ-tŭr), *n.* that part of a structure supported by a colonnade which lies between the columns and the upper edge of the cornice, comprising the architrave, frieze, and cornice.

ENTABLATURE
A, entablature; B, cornice; C, frieze; D, architrave.

en-tail (ĕn-tāl′), *v.t.* 1, to leave (property), as money or land, to an heir or line of heirs, so that none of them can give or will it away; 2, to necessitate; require; demand; as, success *entails* hard work.—*n.* **en-tail′ment.**

en-tan-gle (ĕn-tăng′gl), *v.t.* [entan-gled, entan-gling], 1, to twist into a snarl; 2, to ensnare; as, he was *entangled* in a plot; 3, to perplex; bewilder.
Syn. embroil, confuse.

en-tan-gle-ment (ĕn-tăng′gl-mĕnt), *n.* that which entangles; a snare.

en-tente (än′tänt′), *n.* an agreement or understanding; also, the parties involved: —**Triple Entente,** the friendly understanding established between Great Britain, France, and Russia before World War I.

en-ter (ĕn′tẽr), *v.t.* 1, to go or come into; as, he *entered* the house; 2, to set down in writing; as, the clerk *entered* the account in the journal; 3, to join; as, to *enter* a club; 4, to go into or begin, as a business; 5, to enroll as a competitor; as, he *entered* his horse in the race; 6, to gain admission for; as, to *enter* a pupil in a school:—*v.i.* 1, to go or come in; 2, to take part; as, to *enter* into a discussion; 3, to make a beginning, as into business; 4, to come upon the stage, as an actor.

en-ter-prise (ĕn′tẽr-prīz), *n.* 1, an undertaking of importance or danger; as, a daring *enterprise*; 2, readiness to undertake such projects.
Syn. project, endeavor, venture, effort.

en-ter-pris-ing (ĕn′tẽr-prīz′ĭng), *adj.* energetic; active; progressive.

en-ter-tain (ĕn′tẽr-tān′), *v.t.* 1, to receive and treat hospitably; 2, to amuse; as, she *entertained* the children with stories; 3, to harbor, as a grudge; 4, to take into consideration; as, to *entertain* a proposal:— *v.i.* to receive guests.

en-ter-tain-ing (ĕn′tẽr-tān′ĭng), *adj.* amusing; diverting; pleasing.

en-ter-tain-ment (ĕn′tẽr-tān′mĕnt) *n.* 1, that which interests or amuses; 2, provision for the wants of guests.

en-thrall or **en-thral** (ĕn-thrôl′), *v.t.* [enthralled, enthrall-ing], 1, to enslave; 2, to charm.—*n.* **en-thrall′ment; en-thral′-ment.**

en-throne (ĕn-thrōn′), *v.t.* [enthroned, enthron-ing], to place on a seat of power; endow with royal power and authority.

en-thu-si-asm (ĕn-thū′zĭ-ăzm), *n.* keen interest or feeling for something; as, the boys took up football with *enthusiasm*.
Syn. devotion, earnestness, zeal, fervor.

en-thu-si-ast (ĕn-thū′zĭ-ăst), *n.* one who is filled with enthusiasm.

en-thu-si-as-tic (ĕn-thū′zĭ-ăs′tĭk), *adj.* full of zeal.—*adv.* **en-thu′si-as′ti-cal-ly.**

en-tice (ĕn-tīs′), *v.t.* [enticed, entic-ing], to allure; tempt; lead on by arousing hope or desire.—*adv.* **en-tic′ing-ly.**
Syn. decoy, coax, seduce.

en-tire (ĕn-tīr′), *adj.* 1, with no part omitted; whole; unbroken; 2, unqualified; as, my *entire* support.—*n.* **en-tire′ty.**

en-tire-ly (ĕn-tīr′lĭ), *adv.* 1, wholly; 2, solely; as, it is *entirely* his fault.

en-ti-tle (ĕn-tī′tl), *v.t.* [enti-tled, enti-tling], 1, to give a name to; 2 to give a right to; as, this card *entitles* you to a seat.

en-ti-ty (ĕn′tĭ-tĭ), *n.* [*pl.* entities], anything which has real being or existence.

en-tomb (ĕn-tōōm′), *v.t.* to place in a grave or tomb; bury.—*n.* **en-tomb′ment.**

en-to-mol-o-gy (ĕn′tŏ-mŏl′ŏ-jĭ), *n.* [*pl.* entomologies], that branch of zoology which treats of insects.—*adj.* **en′to-mo-log′i-cal.**—*n.* **en′to-mol′o-gist.**

en-trails (ĕn′trālz), *n.pl.* the internal parts of animals; intestines.

en-train (ĕn-trān′), *v.t.* to put aboard a train:—*v.i.* to go aboard a train.

¹**en-trance** (ĕn′trăns), *n.* 1, the act of entering; 2, a door, passage, etc., through which one goes into a place; 3, permission to enter; as, he gained *entrance* at once.
Syn. access, opening, admittance.

²**en-trance** (ĕn-träns′), *v.t.* [entranced, entranc-ing], to throw into a trance; delight; enrapture.—*adv.* **en-tranc′ing-**ly.

en-trant (ĕn′trănt), *n.* one who enters.

en-trap (ĕn-trăp′), *v.t.* [entrapped, entrapping], to catch in a trap; entangle.

en-treat (ĕn-trēt′), *v.t.* to ask earnestly; beg or beseech.
Syn. petition, importune, pray.

en-treat-y (ĕn-trēt′ĭ), *n.* [*pl.* entreaties], an earnest petition or request; prayer.
Syn. supplication, solicitation, appeal.

āte, āorta, râre, căt, ȧsk, fär, ȧllow, sofȧ; ēve, ĕvent, ĕll, writẽr, novĕl; bīte, pĭn; nō, ōbey, ôr, dŏg, tŏp, cŏllide; ūnit, ūnite, bûrn, cŭt, focŭs; nōōn, fŏŏt; mound; coin;

en·tree (än′trā; än′trā′), *n.* **1,** entrance; privilege of entering; **2,** a dish served between the chief courses of a meal.

en·trench (ĕn-trĕnch′) or **in·trench** (ĭn-trĕnch′), *v.t.* to surround or protect with trenches:—*v.i.* to trespass.

en·trench·ment (ĕn-trĕnch′mĕnt) or **in·trench·ment** (ĭn-trĕnch′mĕnt), *n.* **1,** the act of entrenching, or state of being entrenched; **2,** a defensive work, consisting of ditches with a protecting wall of earth, thrown up as a shield against gunfire.

en·trust (ĕn-trŭst′) or **in·trust** (ĭn-trŭst′), *v.t.* **1,** to give (something) in trust to someone; as, to *entrust* funds to a bank; **2,** to confer a trust upon; as, to *entrust* a bank with funds.

en·try (ĕn′trĭ), *n.* [*pl.* entries], **1,** the act of entering; entrance; **2,** a place through which one enters; **3,** the act of writing an item in a list or record; also, the item.

en·twine (ĕn-twīn′), *v.t.* [entwined, entwin-ing], to wind around; twist together.

e·nu·mer·ate (ē-nū′mĕr-āt), *v.t.* [enumer-at-ed, enumerat-ing], to name one by one; count.—*n.* **e·nu′mer·a′tion.**

e·nun·ci·ate (ē-nŭn′shĭ-āt; ē-nŭn′sĭ-āt), *v.t.* [enunciat-ed, enunciat-ing], **1,** to declare; state; **2,** to utter:—*v.i.* to pronounce; as, a public speaker should *enunciate* clearly.—*n.* **e·nun′ci·a′tion.**

en·vel·op (ĕn-vĕl′ŭp), *v.t.* to cover; wrap up or in.—*n.* **en·vel′op·ment.**

en·ve·lope (ĕn′vĕ-lōp; ŏn′vĕ-lōp), *n.* **1,** a paper wrapper for enclosing letters sent by post, messenger, etc.; **2,** any covering.

en·ven·om (ĕn-vĕn′ŭm), *v.t.* **1,** to poison; **2,** to embitter; fill with hate.

en·vi·a·ble (ĕn′vĭ-à-bl), *adj.* arousing a wish for possession; desirable; as, an *enviable* record.—*adv.* **en′vi·a·bly.**

en·vi·ous (ĕn′vĭ-ŭs), *adj.* feeling, or characterized by, a desire to possess something belonging to another; as, an *envious* disposition.—*adv.* **en′vi·ous·ly.**

en·vi·ron (ĕn-vī′rŭn), *v.t.* to surround or enclose; hem in:—**environs,** *n.pl.* places near a town or city; suburbs; any surrounding region.

en·vi·ron·ment (ĕn-vī′rŭn-mĕnt), *n.* the surroundings of one's life; outside conditions which influence growth or character; as, one's home *environment.*

en·voy (ĕn′voi), *n.* a government agent, next in rank to an ambassador; also, a person sent on a special mission.

en·vy (ĕn′vĭ), *v.t.* [envied, envy-ing], **1,** to wish for (what is another's); as, I *envy* his health; **2,** to begrudge the excellence or prosperity of (another):—*n.* [*pl.* en-

vies], **1,** ill will or jealousy felt because of the excellence or good fortune of another; **2,** a person or object exciting such feeling; as, she is the *envy* of her friends.
Syn., *n.* covetousness, jealousy.

en·wrap (ĕn-răp′), *v.t.* [enwrapped, enwrap-ping], to enclose in a wrapping; enfold. Also, **in·wrap′.**

en·zyme (ĕn′zīm; ĕn′zĭm) or **en·zym** (ĕn′zĭm), *n.* any of various substances, made by both plant and animal cells, and able to cause chemical action in other substances, without undergoing any change themselves.

e·on (ē′ŏn), *n.* a period of time too long to measure; an age. See **aeon.**

E·pam·i·non·das (ē-păm′ĭ-nŏn′dăs), (418?–362 B.C.), a Greek general.

ep·au·let or **ep·au·lette** (ĕp′ô-lĕt), *n.* a shoulder ornament on a military or naval uniform, usually signifying rank.

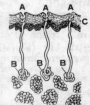

EPAULET

e·phem·er·al (ē-fĕm′ĕr-ăl), *adj.* **1,** living only for a day, as certain insects; **2,** short-lived.
Syn. fleeting, transient, transitory.

E·phe·sians (ē-fē′zhănz; ē-fē′zĭ-ănz), *n.* in the New Testament, an epistle written by Saint Paul to the church in Ephesus, Asia Minor.

eph·od (ĕf′ŏd; ē′fŏd), *n.* a garment worn by a Jewish high priest.

ep·ic (ĕp′ĭk), *adj.* **1,** grand; noble; heroic; **2,** narrative: said of a poem:—*n.* a long narrative poem of heroes and heroic deeds written in a lofty style.

ep·i·cure (ĕp′ĭ-kūr), *n.* a person devoted to pleasure; also, one fond of the delicacies of the table.

ep·i·cu·re·an (ĕp′ĭ-kŭ-rē′ăn), *adj.* **1,** pursuing pleasure as the chief good in life; **2,** devoted to the pleasures of eating:—*n.* an epicure.

Ep·i·cu·rus (ĕp′ĭ-kū′rŭs), (342?–270 B.C.), a Greek philosopher.

ep·i·dem·ic (ĕp′ĭ-dĕm′ĭk), *adj.* attacking many at the same time; as, measles is an *epidemic* disease:—*n.* **1,** a general attack of a disease throughout a locality; **2,** a widespread occurrence of anything; as, an *epidemic* of cheap books.

EPIDERMIS
(greatly enlarged)
A,A,A, pores; B,B,B, sweat glands; C, epidermis.

ep·i·der·mis (ĕp′ĭ-dûr′mĭs), *n.* **1,** the outer layer of an animal's skin; **2,** the outer coating of the leaf or bark of a plant.

ep·i·glot·tis (ĕp/ĭ-glŏt/ĭs), *n.* the leaf-shaped lid of cartilage which covers the upper part of the windpipe, during the act of swallowing.

ep·i·gram (ĕp/ĭ-grăm), *n.* a verse or short poem with a witty point; a witty thought expressed briefly, as "To err is human, to forgive, divine."

ep·i·gram·mat·ic (ĕp/ĭ-gră-măt/ĭk) or **ep·i·gram·mat·i·cal** (ĕp/ĭ-gră-măt/ĭ-kăl), *adj.* witty; pointed and brief. *adv.* **ep/i-gram-mat/i-cal-ly.**

EPIGLOTTIS
A, hard palate; B, soft palate; C, epiglottis; D, windpipe; E, gullet.

ep·i·lep·sy (ĕp/ĭ-lĕp/sĭ), *n.* a chronic nervous disease, often attended by convulsions and loss of consciousness.

ep·i·lep·tic (ĕp/ĭ-lĕp/tĭk), *adj.* pertaining to or having attacks of epilepsy:—*n.* one affected with epilepsy.

ep·i·log or **ep·i·logue** (ĕp/ĭ-lŏg), *n.* **1,** a poem or speech recited at the end of a play; **2,** the conclusion of a literary work.

E·piph·a·ny (ē-pĭf/á-nĭ), *n.* a church festival on January sixth, in honor of the visit of the wise men to the infant Jesus.

E·pi·rus (ē-pī/rŭs), an ancient country in northwestern Greece, opposite the heel of Italy (map 1).

Epis. or **Episc.** abbreviation for *Episcopal.*

e·pis·co·pa·cy (ē-pĭs/kŏ-pá-sĭ), *n.* **1,** church government by bishops; **2,** bishops as a group; as, powers of the *episcopacy.*

e·pis·co·pal (ē-pĭs/kŏ-păl), *adj.* **1,** pertaining to bishops; as, *episcopal* robes; **2,** governed by a bishop:—**Episcopal,** pertaining to the Protestant Episcopal Church.

E·pis·co·pa·li·an (ē-pĭs/kŏ-pā/lĭ-ăn), *adj.* pertaining to the Protestant Episcopal Church:—*n.* a member of that church.

ep·i·sode (ĕp/ĭ-sōd), *n.* an incident within a series of events, connected with but not essential to the series; as, a comic *episode* in a tragic plot; an *episode* of the war.

e·pis·tle (ē-pĭs/l), *n.* a formal letter; a written communication:—**Epistle,** any one of the letters written by the apostles, and recorded in the New Testament.

e·pis·to·lar·y (ē-pĭs/tŏ-lĕr/ĭ); *adj.* pertaining to letters or letter writing; as, a graceful *epistolary* style.

ep·i·taph (ĕp/ĭ-táf), *n.* an inscription or writing on a tomb.

ep·i·thet (ĕp/ĭ-thĕt), *n.* an adjective expressing some characteristic quality, as "empty" in "empty fame"; also, a descriptive title, as "Fat" in "Charles the Fat."

e·pit·o·me (ē-pĭt/ŏ-mē), *n.* [*pl.* epitomes], a brief statement of the contents of a literary work; a summary; synopsis. *Syn.* syllabus, abstract.

ep·och (ĕp/ŏk; ē/pŏk), *n.* **1,** an event or a point of time which marks the beginning of a new period in history; **2,** a period of unusual events; an era.—*adj.* **ep/och-al.**

eq. abbreviation for *equal.*

eq·ua·ble (ĕk/wá-bl; ē/kwá-bl), *adj.* **1,** steady; free from change; as, an *equable* climate; **2,** even and serene in temperament; tranquil.—*adv.* **eq/ua-bly.**

e·qual (ē/kwăl), *adj.* **1,** the same in number, size, or value; the same as; **2,** of the same rank or degree; evenly balanced; **3,** just; fair; as, an *equal* contest; **4,** strong or brave enough; as, *equal* to a task:—*n.* a person or thing of the same rank or value as another:—*v.t.* [equaled, equal-ing], **1,** to have the same size, rank, value, etc., with; match in some way; as, to *equal* another in height; **2,** to make equal; equalize. —*adv.* **e/qual-ly.**

e·qual·i·ty (ē-kwŏl/ĭ-tĭ; ē-kwôl/ĭ-tĭ), *n.* [*pl.* equalities], sameness in size, rank, value, etc.

e·qual·ize (ē/kwăl-īz), *v.t.* [equalized, equaliz-ing], to make the same in size, rank, value, etc.; make equal.

e·qua·nim·i·ty (ē/kwá-nĭm/ĭ-tĭ; ĕk/wá-nĭm/ĭ-tĭ), *n.* evenness of temper or mind; calmness; serenity.

e·quate (ē-kwāt/), *v.t.* [equat-ed, equating], to make equal, or treat as equal; as, to *equate* two quantities.

e·qua·tion (ē-kwā/zhŭn; ē-kwā/shŭn), *n.* in mathematics, a statement that two things are equal; as, "2 + 2 = 4" is an *equation.*

e·qua·tor (ē-kwā/tẽr), *n.* **1,** an imaginary line around the earth, equally distant from the North and South Poles; **2,** a similar line dividing the sphere of the sky in two, called the *celestial equator.*

e·qua·tor·i·al (ē/kwá-tôr/ĭ-ăl), *adj.* pertaining to, or situated near, the equator; characteristic of the Torrid Zone; as, *equatorial* islands; rice is an *equatorial* grain.

EQUATOR (E)

eq·uer·ry (ĕk/wẽr-ĭ), *n.* [*pl.* equerries], an officer in charge of the horses of a prince or nobleman.

e·ques·tri·an (ē-kwĕs/trĭ-ăn), *adj.* **1,** pertaining to horses or horsemanship; performing with horses, as in a circus; **2,**

āte, āorta, râre, căt, ȧsk, fär, ăllow, sofȧ; ēve, ĕvent, ĕll, writẽr, novĕl; bīte, pĭn; nō, ōbey, ôr, dŏg, tŏp, cŏllide; ūnit, ûnite, bûrn, cŭt, focŭs; nōōn, fŏŏt; mound; coin;

mounted; also, showing a figure on horseback; as, an *equestrian* statue:—*n.* a skilled horseman; a performer on horseback.— *n.fem.* **e-ques′tri-enne′** (ĕ-kwĕs′trĭ-ĕn′).

e-qui-dis-tant (ē′kwĭ-dĭs′tănt), *adj.* separated by equal distances; as, the equator is *equidistant* from the North and the South Pole.

e-qui-lat-er-al (ē′kwĭ-lăt′ẽr-ăl), *adj.* having all sides equal.—*adv.* **e′qui-lat′er-al-ly.**

e-qui-lib-ri-um (ē′kwĭ-lĭb′rĭ-ŭm), *n.* **1,** the state of balance between opposing forces, actions, or weights; **2,** even mental balance between opposing influences; hence, neutrality.

EQUILATERAL
TRIANGLE

e-quine (ē′kwīn), *adj.* of, pertaining to, or like, a horse.

e-qui-noc-tial (ē′kwĭ-nŏk′shăl; ĕk′wĭ-nŏk′shăl), *adj.* pertaining to the equinoxes, or having equal day and night; occurring at the time of an equinox; as, an *equinoctial* storm.

e-qui-nox (ē′kwĭ-nŏks; ĕk′wĭ-nŏks), *n.* either of two times when the sun crosses the equator of the sky, making the days and nights of equal length, the *vernal equinox* occurring about March 21, and the *autumnal equinox* about September 22.

e-quip (ĕ-kwĭp′), *v.t.* [equipped, equipping], to fit out for any undertaking; as, to *equip* scouts with tents for camp.

eq-ui-page (ĕk′wĭ-pĭj), *n.* **1,** the arms and outfit of an army, vessel, traveler, etc.; **2,** the carriage, horses, and liveried servants of a person of rank.

e-quip-ment (ĕ-kwĭp′mĕnt), *n.* **1,** all the necessary supplies for any particular service, as for fitting out offices, stores, armies, a fleet, a railway, a person, etc.; **2,** the act of fitting out with supplies; as, the *equipment* of an army takes time.

e-qui-poise (ē′kwĭ-poiz; ĕk′wĭ-poiz), *n.* **1,** balance; equality of weight; **2,** a counterbalancing weight or force.

eq-ui-ta-ble (ĕk′wĭ-tȧ-bl), *adj.* impartial; just; fair; honest; as, an *equitable* decision. —*adv.* **eq′ui-ta-bly.**

eq-ui-ty (ĕk′wĭ-tĭ), *n.* [*pl.* equities], justice; fair dealing.

e-quiv-a-lent (ĕ-kwĭv′ȧ-lĕnt), *adj.* equal in value; the same in meaning or effect; as, cheating is *equivalent* to lying:—*n.* a thing of the same value, weight, power, effect, etc.—*n.* **e-quiv′a-lence.**

e-quiv-o-cal (ĕ-kwĭv′ō-kăl), *adj.* of a doubtful or double meaning; uncertain; as, an *equivocal* reply.

Syn. dubious, doubtful, indefinite.

e-quiv-o-cate (ĕ-kwĭv′ō-kāt), *v.i.* [equivocat-ed, equivocat-ing], to speak with double meaning; evade the truth by making a statement which can be understood in more than one way; lie.—*n.* **e-quiv′o-ca′tion.**

Syn. quibble, shift, evade.

-er (-ẽr), a suffix meaning more; as, high*er*, deep*er*, strong*er*.

-er (-ẽr), a suffix denoting: **1,** one who occupies himself with, or one interested in; as, astronom*er*, lawy*er*, photograph*er*; **2,** a person who does something; as, bak*er*, driv*er*; **3,** an instrument; as, pok*er*; **4,** one living in; as, New York*er*.

e-ra (ē′rȧ), *n.* **1,** a period of time starting from a given point; as, the Christian *era*; **2,** a period of time with notable characteristics; as, the machine *era*; **3,** one of the five great divisions of geologic time.

e-rad-i-cate (ĕ-răd′ĭ-kāt), *v.t.* [eradicat-ed, eradicat-ing], to destroy completely; get rid of; wipe out; as, to *eradicate* crime.— *adj.* **e-rad′i-ca-ble.**

e-rase (ĕ-rās′), *v.t.* [erased, eras-ing], to rub or scrape out, especially something written.—*n.* **e-ra′sure** (ĕ-rā′zhẽr).

Syn. cancel, efface, obliterate.

e-ras-er (ĕ-rās′ẽr), *n.* a device for rubbing out written marks, usually made of rubber or cloth.

E-ras-mus (ĕ-răz′mŭs), (1466?–1536), a Dutch scholar: "Praise of Folly."

ere (âr), *Poetic*, *conj.* **1,** before; as, "the joys that came *ere* I was old"; **2,** rather than; as, I will fight *ere* I will submit:— *prep.* before; as, *ere* daylight.

Er-e-bus (ĕr′ē-bŭs), *n.* in Greek mythology, a place of darkness, through which the dead passed on the way to Hades.

e-rect (ĕ-rĕkt′), *v.t.* **1,** to construct; build, as a house; **2,** to raise upright, as a flagpole; **3,** to set up or establish; as, to *erect* a new government:—*adj.* **1,** upright; as, an *erect* posture; **2,** raised; lifted up; as, to hold a banner *erect*.

e-rec-tion (ĕ-rĕk′shŭn), *n.* **1,** the act of raising a structure, such as a wall or building; also, the state of being constructed; **2,** the structure raised.

ere-long (âr′lông′), *adv.* before long.

er-e-mite (ĕr′ē-mīt), *n.* a religious hermit.

er-go (ûr′gō), [Latin], *conj.* and *adv.* therefore; consequently; hence.

Er-ic-son (ĕr′ĭk-sŭn), Leif, a Norseman, credited with the discovery of Greenland and North America about A.D. 1000.

E-rie (ē′rĭ), **1,** one of the Great Lakes, between the U.S. and Canada; **2,** a city and port on Lake Erie, in northwestern

Pennsylvania:—**Erie Canal**, a waterway connecting Lake Erie and the Hudson River. It is now called *New York State Barge Canal.*(Map 6.)

Er·in (âr′ĭn; ē′rĭn), the ancient Irish name for Ireland: now poetic.

Er·i·tre·a (ĕr′ĭ-trē′á), a former province (cap. Asmara) of Italian East Africa, on the Red Sea (map 14), now federated with Ethiopia.

Er·i·van (ĕr′ē-vän′), a city, capital of Armenian Soviet Socialist Republic.

er·mine (ûr′mĭn), *n.* **1**, a weasel-like animal found in all northern countries, and valued for its fur, especially the white winter coat with black tail tip; **2**, the fur itself; **3**,

ERMINE (⅒)

the dignity or office of a judge, the state robe of European judges being lined with ermine.

e·rode (ē-rōd′), *v.t.* [erod-ed, erod-ing], to wear away; as, running water *erodes* rocks; —*v.i.* to wear away gradually, as rocks.

e·ro·sion (ē-rō′zhŭn), *n.* the act of wearing away; gradual destruction or eating away: used especially of the action of water on rock or soil; as, forests hinder soil *erosion.*

EROSION

Erosion of a cliff by the action of waves of the sea.

err (ûr), *v.i.* **1**, to go astray morally; to sin; **2**, to be mistaken.

er·rand (ĕr′ănd), *n.* **1**, a trip made to attend to some special business; **2**, the object for which the trip is made.

er·rant (ĕr′ănt), *adj.* **1**, roving; wandering in search of adventure; as, a knight-*errant;* **2**, mistaken; not standard; as, *errant* beliefs.—*n.* **er′ran·cy.**

er·ra·ta (ĕ-rā′tá), plural of *erratum.*

er·rat·ic (ĕ-răt′ĭk), *adj.* **1**, having no fixed course; wandering; **2**, irregular; eccentric; queer.—*adv.* **er·rat′i·cal·ly.**
Syn. strange, odd.

er·ra·tum (ĕ-rā′tŭm), *n.* [*pl.* errata (ĕ-rā′tá)], a mistake in printing or writing.

er·ro·ne·ous (ē-rō′nē-ŭs), *adj.* incorrect; mistaken; wrong; as, an *erroneous* belief. —*adv.* **er·ro′ne·ous·ly.**

er·ror (ĕr′ẽr), *n.* **1**, false belief; as, superstition leads to *error;* **2**, a mistake; an inaccuracy; as, an *error* in a sum; **3**, a sin; as, to repent of an *error.*
Syn. blunder, oversight.

erst·while (ûrst′hwīl′; ûrst′hwīl′), *adv. Archaic* or *Poetic,* formerly; long ago.

er·u·dite (ĕr′ŏŏ-dīt; ĕr′ū-dīt), *adj.* learned; scholarly.—*adv.* **er′u·dite·ly.**

er·u·di·tion (ĕr′ŏŏ-dĭsh′ŭn; ĕr′ū-dĭsh′ŭn), *n.* knowledge obtained by study; book learning; scholarship.

e·rupt (ē-rŭpt′), *v.i.* to burst forth, as a volcano:—*v.t.* to hurl out; as, a volcano *erupts* lava.

e·rup·tion (ē-rŭp′shŭn), *n.* **1**, a bursting out or forth, as of a volcano, war, or disease; **2**, that which bursts forth, as water from a geyser; **3**, a rash on the skin.

e·rup·tive (ē-rŭp′tĭv), *adj.* **1**, marked by a breaking out; as, an *eruptive* disease; **2**, bursting forth; as, a volcano is *eruptive* when in action; **3**, caused by volcanic action; as, *eruptive* rocks.

-er·y (-ĕr′ĭ), a suffix meaning: **1**, a place of business, storage, special care, etc.; as, tann*ery*, nurs*ery;* **2**, qualities, conduct, practices, etc.; as, snobb*ery*, trick*ery;* **3**, a class or collection; as, millin*ery*, fin*ery;* **4**, an art or employment; as, arch*ery*, cook*ery;* **5**, a state or condition; as, drudg*ery*, savag*ery.*

er·y·sip·e·las (ĕr′ĭ-sĭp′ĕ-lăs; ĭr′ĭ-sĭp′ĕ-lăs), *n.* an infectious disease of the skin, accompanied by fever and inflammation.

E·sau (ē′sô), in the Old Testament, the son of Isaac and Rebekah, disinherited through the deceit of his younger brother Jacob (Genesis 25:25–34; 27:1–40).

es·ca·la·tor (ĕs′ká-lā′tẽr), *n.* a moving stairway.

es·ca·pade (ĕs′ká-pād′; ĕs′ká-pād), *n.* a breaking loose from restraint; a foolish or reckless adventure.

es·cape (ĕs-kāp′), *v.t.* [escaped, escap-ing], **1**, to flee from; avoid; as, *escape* a task; **2**, be unaffected by; as, he *escaped* the disease; **3**, issue from unawares; as, a sigh *escaped* him; **4**, elude the notice, memory, or understanding of; as, his name *escapes* me; **5**, get away from; be saved from; as, to *escape* danger:—*v.i.* **1**, get out of danger; avoid harm or capture; **2**, break loose from confinement; as, *escape* from prison; **3**, flow out; as, gas *escapes* from a pipe; **4**, slip away; as, *escape* from mind:—*n.* **1**, a successful flight, as from prison; **2**, deliverance from harm or danger; as, a narrow *escape;* **3**, an outlet for water, steam, etc.; **4**, leakage; outflow:— **escape speed,** the velocity at which a body must move to overcome the pull of the earth's gravity and go off into space.

āte, āorta, râre, căt, ȧsk, fär, ȧllow, sofȧ; ēve, ĕvent, ĕll, wrītẽr, novĕl; bīte, pĭn; nō, ōbey, ôr, dŏg, tŏp, cŏllide; ūnit, ūnite, bûrn, cŭt, focŭs; nōon, fŏŏt; mound; coin;

es·cape·ment (ĕs-kāp′mĕnt), *n.* a mechanical device for securing regularity of movement: used in clocks, watches, and motors.

es·carp·ment (ĕs-kärp′mĕnt), *n.* a steep slope to a height, as of a plateau or fortified hill; a cliff.

ESCAPEMENT

es·chew (ĕs-chōō′; ĕs-chū′), *v.t.* to shun; abstain from; avoid; as, to *eschew* bad company; *eschew* strong drink.

es·cort (ĕs′kôrt), *n.* **1,** a body of men, ships, airplanes, automobiles, etc., accompanying a person, another ship, airplane, etc., or goods, for protection or honor; **2,** a person accompanying another as a guard or guide, or to show honor; especially, a gentleman accompanying a lady in public: —*v.t.* (ĕs-kôrt′), to accompany as escort.

es·cu·do (ĕs-kōō′dō; ĕs-kōō′thōō), *n.* [*pl.* escudos], a silver coin, the monetary unit of Portugal. (See Table, page 943.)

es·cutch·eon (ĕs-kŭch′ŭn), *n.* the surface, usually shield-shaped, on which a coat of arms is displayed. Also spelled **scutch′eon.**

ESCUTCHEON
With dexter and sinister sides indicated.

-ese (-ēz; -ēs), a suffix meaning: **1,** pertaining to (a country or the like); also, a native or inhabitant of; as, Chinese; **2,** a language; as, Portuguese.

Es·ki·mo (ĕs′kĭ-mō), *n.* [*pl.* Eskimos or Eskimo], one of a race of people inhabiting arctic North American coasts.

Eskimo dog, a strong, stocky dog with long, gray hair, native to Greenland and Labrador, used by the Eskimos as sled dogs.

ESKIMO DOG (¹⁄₄₀)

e·soph·a·gus or **oe·soph·a·gus** (ē-sŏf′ȧ-gŭs), *n.* the gullet, or tube through which food and drink pass from the throat to the stomach.

es·o·ter·ic (ĕs′ō-tĕr′ĭk), *adj.* **1,** pertaining to and understood only by a select circle; **2,** secret; confidential.

esp. abbreviation for *especially.*

es·pe·cial (ĕs-pĕsh′ăl), *adj.* **1,** particular; chief; special; **2,** exceptional; pre-eminent; as, an *especial* friend.—*adv.* **es·pe′cial·ly.**

Es·pe·ran·to (ĕs′pĕ-rän′tō; ĕs′pĕ-răn′tō), *n.* a language invented by L. L. Zamenhof, a Polish physician, and designed for use as an international or universal language.

es·pi·o·nage (ĕs′pĭ-ō-nĭj; ĕs′pĭ-ō-näzh′; ĕs-pī′ō-nĭj), *n.* **1,** the secret watching of another; spying; **2,** employment of secret agents or spies; especially, systematic spying on an enemy in time of war.

es·pla·nade (ĕs′plȧ-nād′; ĕs′plȧ-näd′), *n.* an open space or road, especially by the water, for public use in walking or driving.

es·pouse (ĕs-pouz′), *v.t.* [espoused, espous-ing], **1,** to give in marriage; **2,** to wed; **3,** to become a follower of; as, to *espouse* a cause.—*n.* **es·pous′al.**

es·prit (ĕs′prē′), [French], *n.* wit; spirit; sprightly intelligence:—**esprit de corps** (dē kôr′), a spirit of unity binding together the members of a group.

es·py (ĕs-pī′), *v.t.* [espied, espy-ing], **1,** to see at a distance; catch sight of; as, to *espy* a ship on the horizon; **2,** to discover or detect (something hard to find).

Esq. or **Esqr.** abbreviation for *Esquire.*

es·quire (ĕs-kwīr′), *n.* **1,** originally, the armor-bearer or attendant of a knight; **2,** a member of the English gentry ranking below a knight:—**Esquire,** a title of courtesy, often written after a man's name.

-ess (-ĕs), a suffix forming a feminine noun; as, countess, tigress.

es·say (ĕs′ā), *n.* **1,** a literary composition on some special subject, usually of moderate length, and expressing the personal views of the author; **2,** (often ĕ-sā′), an attempt; experiment:—*v.t.* (ĕ-sā′), to try.

es·say·ist (ĕs′ā-ĭst), *n.* one who writes in prose, on various subjects.

Es·sen (ĕs′ĕn), a city in the Ruhr Valley, Germany, famous for the Krupp steel and iron works (map 12).

es·sence (ĕs′ĕns), *n.* **1,** the extract of a substance dissolved in alcohol; as, *essence* of peppermint; **2,** a perfume; **3,** that which is the real character of a thing; as, the *essence* of politeness is kindness.

es·sen·tial (ĕ-sĕn′shăl), *adj.* **1,** pertaining to the real character of a thing; as, the *essential* element of a situation; **2,** necessary; indispensable; as, water is *essential* to life:—*n.* that which is a necessary element; as, the three R's are the *essentials* of education.—*adv.* **es·sen′tial·ly.**

Es·sex (ĕs′ĕks), Robert Devereux, Earl of (1567–1601), a favorite of Queen Elizabeth of England.

est. abbreviation for *established.*

-est (-ĕst), a suffix meaning most; as, warm*est,* soon*est,* hard*est.*

---

go; join; yet; sing; chin; show; thin, *then;* hw, *why;* zh, azure; ū, Ger. für or Fr. lune; ŏ, Ger. schön or Fr. feu; n̈, Fr. enfant, nom; kh, Ger. ach or ich. See pages ix–x.

es-tab-lish (ĕs-tăb′lĭsh), *v.t.* **1,** to fix firmly; settle; as, he has *established* a reputation for efficiency; **2,** to prove legally; to prove beyond doubt; as, to *establish* a claim; **3,** to found, as an institution.
Syn. verify, substantiate.

es-tab-lish-ment (ĕs-tăb′lĭsh-mĕnt), *n.* **1,** the act of placing on a sure basis; settlement; as, the *establishment* of a colony; **2,** something firmly placed, founded, or organized; as, his factory is a big *establishment*.

es-tate (ĕs-tāt′), *n.* **1,** condition of life; rank, position, or quality; as, a man of low *estate;* **2,** an order or class of people, politically or socially distinct, as nobles or clergy; **3,** property in land or buildings: used of large possessions; **4,** in law, property in general.

es-teem (ĕs-tēm′), *v.t.* **1,** to value highly; prize; **2,** to think; consider; as, to *esteem* it a privilege:—*n.* a favorable opinion; respect; regard.
Syn., v. appreciate; regard.

Es-ther (ĕs′tẽr), the title and heroine of a book in the Old Testament. Esther, a beautiful Jewess, queen of Ahasuerus, influenced the king to deliver her people from the scheming Persian, Haman.

es-thet-ic (ĕs-thĕt′ĭk), *adj.* pertaining to beauty or love of beauty; having good taste:—**esthetics**, *n.* the science of the beautiful in nature or art; aesthetics. See **aesthetic, aesthetics.**—*n.* **es′thete** (ĕs′thēt).—*adv.* **es-thet′i-cal-ly.**

es-ti-ma-ble (ĕs′tĭ-mȧ-bl), *adj.* **1,** worthy of respect or honor; deserving esteem; **2,** that may be estimated; calculable; as, *estimable* damages.—*adv.* **es′ti-ma-bly.**

es-ti-mate (ĕs′tĭ-māt), *v.t.* [estimat-ed, estimat-ing], **1,** to form an opinion of; as, to *estimate* a man's character; **2,** to reckon approximately; calculate (the amount, cost, or value); as, to *estimate* the cost of a job:—*n.* (ĕs′tĭ-mȧt), **1,** a valuation of qualities; opinion; **2,** a judgment, as of the amount, cost, or value of anything.
Syn., v. appreciate, value, rate.

es-ti-ma-tion (ĕs′tĭ-mā′shŭn), *n.* **1,** a reckoning or judging; as, an *estimation* of the cost; **2,** respect; favorable opinion.

Es-to-ni-a (ĕs-tō′nĭ-ȧ), a former republic (cap. Tallinn) on the Baltic Sea, admitted into the Soviet Union in 1940 (map **12**). —*n.* and *adj.* **Es-to-ni-an.**

Es-to-ni-an So-vi-et So-cial-ist Re-pub-lic, Estonia.

es-trange (ĕs-trānj′), *v.t.* [estranged, estrang-ing], to turn from affection to indifference or dislike; as, to *estrange* one's friends by neglect.—*n.* **es-trange′ment.**

es-tu-ar-y (ĕs′tū-ĕr′ĭ), *n.* [*pl.* estuaries], the wide mouth of a tidal river.

-et (-ĕt), a suffix forming nouns which name something small; as, eagl*et*, isl*et*.

etc. abbreviation for *et cetera.*

et cet-er-a (ĕt sĕt′-ĕr-ȧ), [Latin], and others of the same kind; and so forth.

etch (ĕch), *v.t.* to engrave (a design) upon a copper plate or the like, with an etching needle through a wax coating, which protects the rest of the plate from the acids which eat out the lines:—*v.i.* to practice the art of etching.—*n.* **etch′er.**

ESTUARIES
of some rivers along the Atlantic: 1, Delaware; 2, Susquehanna; 3, Potomac; 4, James; 5, Roanoke.

etch-ing (ĕch′ĭng), *n.* **1,** a picture or design printed from an etched plate; also, the plate itself; **2,** the art or process of making etched plates.

e-ter-nal (ē-tûr′nȧl), *adj.* **1,** without beginning or end; everlasting; **2,** never ceasing; as, *eternal* chatter:—**the Eternal,** God.—*adv.* **e-ter′nal-ly.**
Syn. endless, immortal.

e-ter-ni-ty (ē-tûr′nĭ-tĭ), *n.* [*pl.* eternities], **1,** time without beginning or end; time everlasting; **2,** indefinite time; time that seems endless; as, to wait an *eternity;* **3,** life after death.

-eth (-ĕth) or **-th** (-th), a suffix used: **1,** to make ordinal numbers; as, seven*th*, thirti*eth;* **2,** to make the third singular present indicative of verbs, in archaic language; as, "He stopp*eth* one of three."

e-ther (ē′thẽr), *n.* **1,** the upper, purer air; clear sky; **2,** a liquid anesthetic, the vapor of which, when inhaled, produces unconsciousness and deadens pain; **3,** in physics, a substance believed by many to fill all space, and to carry rays of light. Also, **ae′ther.**

e-the-re-al (ē-thē′rē-ȧl), *adj.* **1,** light; exquisite; airy and delicate; as, *ethereal* music; **2,** heavenly; not earthly.—*adv.* **e-the′re-al-ly.**

eth-i-cal (ĕth′ĭ-kȧl), *adj.* **1,** pertaining to questions of right and wrong; **2,** morally right or good; as, *ethical* behavior.—*adv.* **eth′i-cal-ly.**

eth-ics (ĕth′ĭks), *n. pl.* **1,** used as *sing.,* the science of morals; **2,** used as *pl.,* moral principles or practice; as, every profession has its own *ethics.*

āte, āorta, râre, căt, ȧsk, fär, ȧllow, sofȧ; ēve, ĕvent, ĕll, writẽr, novĕl; bīte, pĭn; nō, ōbey, ôr, dŏg, tŏp, cōllide; ūnit, ūnite, bûrn, cŭt, focŭs; no͞on, fŏŏt; mound; coin;

E·thi·o·pi·a (ē'thĭ-ō'pĭ-á), a kingdom (cap. Addis Ababa) in eastern Africa; conquered by Italy in 1936, but liberated by Great Britain in 1941 (map 14).—*adj.* and *n.* **E'thi·o'pi·an.**

eth·nol·o·gy (ĕth-nŏl'ō-jĭ), *n.* the science that treats of races of men, their characteristics, their relation to one another etc. —*adj.* **eth'no·log'i·cal.**—*n.* **eth·nol'o·gist.**

Eth·yl (ĕth'ĭl), *n.* a trade-mark name for a compound of lead, used in motor fuels to prevent knocking.

et·i·quette (ĕt'ĭ-kĕt), *n.* rules of conduct observed in polite society or in official intercourse; the forms of polite behavior demanded by good breeding.

Et·na (ĕt'ná), an active volcano on the island of Sicily, south of Italy (map 1). It is also spelled **Aet'na.**

E·ton (ē'tn), a town in southeastern England, famous for its boys' school. *n.* and *adj.* **E·to'ni·an** (ē-tō'nĭ-ăn).

E·tru·ri·a (ē-trŏŏr'ĭ-á), an ancient country of northwestern Italy (map 1).—*n.* and *adj.* **E-tru'ri·an.**

E·trus·can (ē-trŭs'kăn), *adj.* pertaining to ancient Etruria, in northwestern Italy: —*n.* a person of this race.

-ette (-ĕt), a suffix forming nouns meaning: **1,** something little; as, kitchen*ette;* **2,** an imitation; as, leather*ette;* **3,** a woman with a given occupation or belief; as, suffrag*ette.*

é·tude (ā'tüd'), [French], *n.* in music, an exercise affording practice and study of some particular point of technique.

et·y·mol·o·gy (ĕt'ĭ-mŏl'ō-jĭ), *n.* [*pl.* etymologies], a statement of the origin of a word and of its history, especially, the history of its changing forms and meanings; also, the science which treats of the origin and history of words.—*n.* **et'y·mol'o·gist.**

EUCALYPTUS

eu· (ū-), a prefix meaning well or good; as, *eu*logy, *eu*phony.

Eu·boe·a (ū-bē'á), the largest island in the Aegean Sea, near Attica and Boeotia.

eu·ca·lyp·tus (ū'ká-lĭp'tŭs), *n.* [*pl.* eucalypti (ū'ká-lĭp'tī) or eucalyptuses], any of various trees of the myrtle family, including the gum tree of Australia, many species of which furnish timber, aromatic gum, and an oil valuable as a medicine.

Eu·cha·rist (ū'ká-rĭst), *n.* **1,** in many Christian churches, the Holy Communion, or the sacrament of the Lord's Supper; **2,** the consecrated bread and wine used in that sacrament.

Eu·clid (ū'klĭd), a Greek mathematician, famous for his works on geometry, written about 300 B.C.

eu·gen·ics (ū-jĕn'ĭks), *n.* the science of improving the human race by mating persons of superior body and mind.

eu·lo·gize (ū'lō-jīz), *v.t.* [eulogized, eulogiz-ing], to praise highly; especially, to praise one who is dead.

eu·lo·gy (ū'lō-jĭ), *n.* [*pl.* eulogies], high praise, either written or spoken, of the life or character of a person, especially of a dead person.

eu·nuch (ū'nŭk), *n.* a castrated man; especially, an attendant in a harem.

eu·phe·mism (ū'fē-mĭzm), *n.* **1,** the use of a mild or pleasing expression in place of one that is plainer or more accurate but which might be offensive or embarrassing, as "you exaggerate" for "you lie"; **2,** the expression so used.—*adj.* **eu'phe·mis'tic.**

eu·pho·ny (ū'fō-nĭ), *n.* [*pl.* euphonies], pleasantness of sound, especially in pronunciation; as, harsh consonants spoil *euphony.*—*adj.* **eu·pho'ni·ous** (ū-fō'nĭ-ŭs).

Eu·phra·tes (ū-frā'tēz), a river flowing from Turkey to the Persian Gulf (map 15).

Eur·a·sia (ūr-ā'zhá; ūr-ā'shá), *n.* Europe and Asia taken as a unit.—*adj.* **Eur-a'sian.**

eu·re·ka (ū-rē'ká), [Greek, "I have found it"], *interj.* an exclamation of triumph over a discovery.

Eu·rip·i·des (ū-rĭp'ĭ-dēz), (480–406 B.C.), a Greek tragic dramatist.

Eu·rope (ū'rŭp), a continent west of Asia and north of Africa (map 12).

Eu·ro·pe·an (ū'rō-pē'ăn), *adj.* belonging or pertaining to Europe:—*n.* a native of Europe.

Eu·ro·pe·an plan, a hotel arrangement by which the fixed rate covers all services but meals. Contrasted with *American plan.*

Eux·ine Sea (ūk'sĭn; ūk'sīn), the ancient name of the *Black Sea* (map 1).

e·vac·u·ate (ē-văk'ū-āt), *v.t.* [evacuat-ed, evacuat-ing], **1,** to empty; **2,** to abandon possession of; as, to *evacuate* a town; also, to withdraw (persons) from a place.

e·vac·u·a·tion (ē-văk'ū-ā'shŭn), *n.* **1,** a withdrawal from a place; also, an emptying or voiding; **2,** discharged matter.

e·vade (ē-vād'), *v.t.* [evad-ed, evad-ing],

1, to escape from by some trick; as, to *evade* pursuers or the law; 2, hence, to baffle or foil; elude.

Syn. avoid, elude, lie.

e-val-u-ate (ē-văl′ū-āt), *v.t.* [evaluat-ed, evaluat-ing], to place a value on; find the worth of; as, to *evaluate* evidence.

ev-a-nes-cent (ĕv′à-nĕs′ĕnt), *adj.* disappearing; vanishing; fleeting; as, the joys of life are *evanescent*.

e-van-gel-i-cal (ē′văn-jĕl′ĭ-kăl; ĕv′ăn-jĕl′-ĭ-kăl), *adj.* 1, pertaining to, or agreeing with the teachings of, the four Gospels; 2, holding certain doctrines, as that of redemption through faith, believed by many Protestants to represent the true teaching of the Gospels. Also, **e′van-gel′ic.**

E-van-gel-i-cal As-so-ci-a-tion, a Christian denomination founded about 1800 in eastern Pennsylvania by Jacob Albright.

E-van-ge-line (ē-văn′jĕ-lēn; ē-văn′jĕ-lĭn), *n.* the title and heroine of a poem by Longfellow.

e-van-ge-lism (ē-văn′jĕ-lĭzm), *n.* the preaching of the gospel of Christ.

e-van-ge-list (ē-văn′jĕ-lĭst), *n.* 1, one of the four writers of the Gospels; 2, one who spreads the gospel; especially, a traveling preacher.—*adj.* **e-van′ge-lis′tic.**

e-van-ge-lize (ē-văn′jĕ-līz), *v.t.* [evangelized, evangeliz-ing], to convert to Christianity; carry the gospel to; as, to *evangelize* the heathen.

Ev-ans-ton (ĕv′ănz-tŭn), a city in northeastern Illinois, on Lake Michigan.

Ev-ans-ville (ĕv′ănz-vĭl), a city in southwestern Indiana on the Ohio (map 7).

e-vap-o-rate (ē-văp′ō-rāt), *v.i* [evaporated, evaporat-ing], 1, to change from solid or liquid into vapor, as water into steam; 2, to pass away without effect; as, his zeal soon *evaporated*.—*v.t.* 1, to change into vapor; as, heat *evaporates* water; 2, to dry or concentrate, by removing moisture; as, to *evaporate* fruit or milk.—*n.* **e-vap′-o-ra′tor.**—*n.* **e-vap′o-ra′tion.**

e-va-sion (ē-vā′zhŭn), *n.* 1, an artful avoidance; as, the *evasion* of a question; 2, an artful escape; 3, an excuse.

e-va-sive (ē-vā′sĭv), *adj.* tending or seeking to avoid; elusive; as, an *evasive* answer.—*adv.* **e-va′sive-ly.**

Eve (ēv), in the Old Testament, the first created woman, wife of Adam.

eve (ēv), *n.* 1, the evening before a church festival or saint's day; as, Christmas *eve*; 2, the period immediately before some important event; as, on the *eve* of departure; 3, *Poetic*, evening.

¹e-ven (ē′vĕn), *n. Poetic*, evening.

²e-ven (ē′vĕn), *adj.* 1, level; smooth; as, an *even* surface; 2, equal in quantity, size, number; 3, on the same line; parallel; as, water *even* with the top of a bucket; 4, divisible by two without a remainder; as, six is an *even* number; 5, impartial; fair; as, *even* justice; 6, satisfied as to an account or grudge; as, to get *even* with a person; 7, calm; unruffled; as, an *even* temper; 8, whole; exact; as, an *even* mile:—*v.t.* 1, to level; make smooth; as, to *even* a lawn; 2, to make equal; as, to *even* up a score:—*adv.* 1, exactly; just; as, *even* so; 2, precisely; just; as, *even* as I spoke; 3, quite; so much as; as, I never *even* spoke; 4, used to emphasize or imply comparison; as, clear *even* to a child.—*adv.* **e′ven-ly.**

eve-ning (ēv′nĭng), *n.* the close of day and beginning of night:—*adj.* pertaining to the latter part of the day; as, the *evening* meal:—**evening star**, a bright planet seen in the west after sunset, especially Venus.

e-vent (ē-vĕnt′), *n.* 1, an occurrence; incident; happening; 2, the fact of something happening; as, in *event* of war; 3, the result or outcome of an action; as, in any *event*; 4, a single item in a program of sports.

Syn. issue, circumstance.

e-vent-ful (ē-vĕnt′fŏŏl), *adj.* full of incidents or happenings; momentous; important.—*adv.* **e-vent′ful-ly.**

e-ven-tide (ē′vĕn-tīd′), *n. Poetic*, evening.

e-ven-tu-al (ē-vĕn′tū-ăl), *adj.* 1, depending on a future or possible event; as, *eventual* succession to a throne; 2, final; as, an *eventual* reward.—*adv.* **e-ven′tu-al-ly.**

e-ven-tu-al-i-ty (ē-vĕn′tū-ăl′ĭ-tĭ), *n.* [*pl.* eventualities], a possible occurrence.

ev-er (ĕv′ẽr), *adv.* 1, at any time; as, if I *ever* go; 2, forever; always; as, the poor are *ever* with us; 3, in any degree: used to strengthen an expression; as, study as hard as *ever* you can:—**ever so**, very; as, *ever so* much better.

Ev-er-est (ĕv′ẽr-ĕst), the highest known mountain in the world, 29,028 feet high, in the Himalayas, Asia (map 15).

Ev-er-ett (ĕv′ẽr-ĕt), Edward (1794–1865), an American statesman and author.

ev-er-glade (ĕv′ẽr-glād), *n.* a low, swampy tract of land.

ev-er-green (ĕv′ẽr-grēn′), *n.* a tree or plant which remains green throughout the year, as the pine, cedar, holly, etc.:—*adj.* always green or fresh.

ev-er-last-ing (ĕv′ẽr-làs′tĭng) *adj.* 1, endless; eternal; as, the *everlasting* hills; 2, never ceasing; lasting too long; as, an *everlasting* noise:—*n.* 1, any of various plants whose flowers keep their form and

āte, āorta, râre, căt, àsk, fär, ăllow, sofà; ēve, ĕvent, ĕll, writẽr, nŏvĕl; bīte, pĭn; nō, ōbey, ôr, dŏg, tŏp, cŏllide; ūnit, ūnite, bûrn, cŭt, focŭs; nōon, fŏŏt; mound; coin;

color when dried; 2, eternity:—**the Everlasting,** God.—*adv.* **ev′er·last′ing·ly.**
Syn., adj. permanent, immortal.

ev·er·more (ĕv′ĕr·môr′; ĕv′ĕr·môr′), *adv.* always; forever.

ev·er·y (ĕv′ĕr·ĭ; ĕv′rĭ), *adj.* 1, all, taken one at a time; each; as, *every* man will do his duty; 2, all possible; as, *every* kindness.

ev·er·y·bod·y (ĕv′ĕr·ĭ·bŏd′ĭ; ĕv′rĭ·bŏd′ĭ), *pron.* every person; everyone.

ev·er·y·day (ĕv′ĕr·ĭ·dā′; ĕv′rĭ·dā′), *adj.* happening on each day; usual; commonplace; as, *everyday* matters.

ev·er·y·one (ĕv′ĕr·ĭ·wŭn′; ĕv′rĭ·wŭn), *pron.* every person; everybody.

ev·er·y·thing (ĕv′ĕr·ĭ·thĭng′; ĕv′rĭ·thĭng′), *pron.* all things; all that relates to a given matter; as, to tell *everything* about it.

ev·er·y·where (ĕv′ĕr·ĭ·hwâr′; ĕv′rĭ·hwâr′), *adv.* in all places or parts; as, they looked *everywhere.*

e·vict (ē·vĭkt′), *v.t.* to put out by force; expel, especially by legal force; as, to *evict* a tenant.—*n.* **e·vic′tion.**

ev·i·dence (ĕv′ĭ·dĕns), *n.* facts from which to judge; proof; testimony; as, *evidence* of guilt:—*v.t.* [evidenced, evidenc-ing], to prove; make evident or plain; indicate:—**in evidence,** conspicuous; perfectly plain.
Syn., n. indication, certainty.

ev·i·dent (ĕv′ĭ·dĕnt), *adj.* clear to the eyes and mind; obvious; as, his dislike was *evident.*—*adv.* **ev′i·dent·ly.**
Syn. apparent, visible.

e·vil (ē′vl; ē′vĭl), *adj.* 1, bad; wicked; sinful; as, *evil* acts; 2, hurtful; disastrous; 3, of ill repute; as, an *evil* name:—**evil eye,** the power to cause harm by a glance: a popular superstition:—*n.* 1, disaster; injury; anything that destroys happiness or well-being; 2, sin; wrongdoing: opposite of *good.*—*adv.* **e′vil·ly.**
Syn., n. harm; *adj.* wrong, corrupt.

e·vil-do·er (ē′vl-dōō′ĕr; ē′vĭl-dōō′ĕr), *n.* one who does evil.

e·vil-mind·ed (ē′vl-mīn′dĕd; ē′vĭl-mīn′dĕd), *adj.* having evil thoughts; bad; wicked.

e·vince (ē·vĭns′), *v.t.* [evinced, evinc-ing], to show; make evident; as, the soldiers *evinced* bravery.—*adj.* **e·vin′ci·ble.**

e·voke (ē·vōk′), *v.t.* [evoked, evok-ing], to call forth; as, to *evoke* an answer.

ev·o·lu·tion (ĕv′ō·lū′shŭn), *n.* 1, development; growth; as, the *evolution* of a moth from a caterpillar; 2, the theory that all present forms of plant and animal life have developed gradually through the ages from lower and simpler forms; also, the long process of this development; 3,

an ordered move or maneuver of troops or ships changing position; 4, a movement that is one of a series of movements; as, an *evolution* in a dance.—*n.* **ev′o·lu′tion·ist.**

ev·o·lu·tion·ar·y (ĕv′ō·lū′shŭn-ĕr′ĭ), *adj.* having to do with evolution; developing; unfolding.—*adj.* **ev′o·lu′tion·al.**

e·volve (ē·vŏlv′), *v.t.* [evolved, evolv-ing], to develop; unfold; expand; as, he *evolved* a new method of doing the work:—*v.i.* to become developed; as, from the invention of the radio a new industry *evolved.*

ewe (ū), *n.* a female sheep.

ew·er (ū′ĕr), *n.* a large water pitcher or jug, usually with a wide mouth.

ex. abbreviation for *example.*

ex- (ĕks-), a prefix, [e- before *b, d, g, h, l, m, n, r,* and *v; ef-* before *f; es-* in combining with French words], 1, out (*extract*); 2, from (*exclude*); 3, beyond (*excessive*); 4, thoroughly (*exasperate*); 5, formerly, but not now (*ex-president*). **EWER**

ex·act (ĕg·zăkt′), *adj.* 1, correct; precise; 2, methodical; thorough; particular:—*v.t.* 1, to require or insist upon; as, to *exact* attention; 2, to compel payment of; demand; as, he *exacted* money from his debtors.—*n.* **ex·act′ness.**
Syn., adj. accurate, strict.

ex·act·ing (ĕg·zăk′tĭng), *adj.* making unreasonable demands; severe; difficult; as, an *exacting* task.

ex·ac·tion (ĕg·zăk′shŭn), *n.* 1, the act of firmly demanding; 2, something demanded, especially more than what is due; an illegal or excessive demand.

ex·act·i·tude (ĕg·zăk′tĭ·tūd), *n.* the quality of being accurate; exactness.

ex·act·ly (ĕg·zăkt′lĭ), *adv.* 1, correctly; in an accurate manner; 2, quite so; just as you say.

ex·ag·ger·ate (ĕg·zăj′ĕr·āt), *v.t.* [exaggerat-ed, exaggerat-ing], to enlarge beyond truth or reason; overstate.

ex·ag·ger·a·tion (ĕg·zăj′ĕr·ā′shŭn), *n.* enlargement beyond reason; overstatement.

ex·alt (ĕg·zôlt′), *v.t.* 1, to raise in rank, position, or dignity; 2, to delight; elate; 3, to glorify; extol; as, *exalt* His holy name.
Syn. ennoble, dignify, promote.

ex·al·ta·tion (ĕg′zôl·tā′shŭn), *n.* 1, a raising or lifting up in position, rank, or dignity; 2, the feeling of being mentally or spiritually uplifted; elation.

ex·am·i·na·tion (ĕg·zăm′ĭ·nā′shŭn), *n.* 1, an investigation; a careful inquiry or inspection; as, an *examination* of the accounts; 2, a test of knowledge, fitness,

go; join; yet; sing; chin; show; thin, *th*en; hw, *why*; zh, azure; ü, Ger. *für* or Fr. *lune*; ö, Ger. schön or Fr. *feu*; ṅ, Fr. *enfant*, nom; kh, Ger. ach or ich. See pages ix–x.

or ability; especially, a written test; **3**, in law, a questioning, as of a witness.

Syn. analysis, search, scrutiny, trial.

ex-am-ine (ĕg-zăm′ĭn), *v.t.* [examined, examin-ing], **1**, to inspect closely; investigate carefully; **2**, in law, to question, as a witness; **3**, to find out the knowledge, qualifications, etc., of (a person) by a spoken or written test; as, he *examined* the class in history.—*n.* **ex-am′in-er.**

ex-am-ple (ĕg-zăm′pl), *n.* **1**, a person, thing, or act fit to be copied; **2**, something that illustrates a rule; as, an *example* in subtraction; **3**, a sample; specimen, as of workmanship; **4**, a warning; as, let his punishment be an *example* to you.

Syn. standard, type, instance.

ex-as-per-ate (ĕg-zăs′pĕr-āt), *v.t.* [exasperat-ed, exasperat-ing], to irritate greatly; enrage; as, delay *exasperates* him.

Syn. annoy, provoke, inflame.

ex-as-per-a-tion (ĕg-zăs′pĕr-ā′shŭn), *n.* extreme irritation; annoyance.

Ex-cal-i-bur (ĕks-kăl′ĭ-bĕr), *n.* King Arthur's sword. By one tradition he pulled it out of a rock.

ex-ca-vate (ĕks′kȧ-vāt), *v.t.* [excavat-ed, excavat-ing], **1**, to dig or hollow out; scoop or cut into; as, to *excavate* a hill; **2**, to bring to light by digging; as, to *excavate* ruins.

ex-ca-va-tion (ĕks′kȧ-vā′shŭn), *n.* the act of digging or hollowing out; anything formed by excavating, as a cellar or tunnel.

ex-ceed (ĕk-sēd′), *v.t.* **1**, to go beyond the limit of; overdo; as, he *exceeded* his authority; **2**, to excel; surpass.

ex-ceed-ing-ly (ĕk-sēd′ĭng-lĭ), *adv.* very; to a remarkable degree; as, she is *exceedingly* studious.

ex-cel (ĕk-sĕl′), *v.i.* [excelled, excel-ling], to possess good qualities in a great degree; as, this tea *excels* in flavor:—*v.t.* to be superior to; outdo in comparison; as, John *excels* Mary in arithmetic.

ex-cel-lence (ĕk′sĕ-lĕns), *n.* superior merit; worth; special virtue.

Syn. superiority, greatness, distinction.

ex-cel-len-cy (ĕk′sĕ-lĕn-sĭ), *n.* [*pl.* excellencies], superior merit:—**Excellency,** a title of honor of various high officials.

ex-cel-lent (ĕk′sĕ-lĕnt), *adj.* of unusually high quality; very good of its kind.

Syn. choice, select, superior, fine.

Ex-cel-si-or (ĕk-sĕl′sĭ-ôr), *adj.* higher; ever upward: the motto of New York State.

ex-cel-si-or (ĕk-sĕl′sĭ-ĕr), *n.* a packing material made of long, fine, wood shavings.

ex-cept (ĕk-sĕpt′), *v.t.* to leave out of account; omit:—*prep.* not including; outside of; as, he knows little *except* music.

ex-cept-ing (ĕk-sĕp′tĭng), *prep.* not including; except.

ex-cep-tion (ĕk-sĕp′shŭn), *n.* **1**, an omission; exclusion; **2**, that which is not included; as, he is an *exception* to the rule; **3**, objection; offense taken; as, to take *exception* to what was said.

ex-cep-tion-al (ĕk-sĕp′shŭn-ăl), *adj.* unusual; uncommon; extraordinary; as, music of *exceptional* beauty.

Syn. remarkable, signal, rare.

ex-cerpt (ĕk-sûrpt′), *v.t.* to take out; select:—*n.* (ĕk′sûrpt; ĕk-sûrpt′), a selection or extract from a book or writing.

ex-cess (ĕk-sĕs′), *n.* **1**, abundance; more than enough; **2**, the amount by which one thing is more than another; **3**, intemperance; **4**, an added charge, as for fare on fast trains:—*adj.* over and above what is ordinary; extra; as, *excess* profits.

Syn. waste, dissipation, lavishness.

ex-ces-sive (ĕk-sĕs′ĭv), *adj.* extreme; unreasonable; immoderate.—*adv.* **ex-ces′sive-ly.**—*n.* **ex-ces′sive-ness.**

ex-change (ĕks-chānj′), *v.t.* [exchanged, exchang-ing], to give in return for something; barter; trade:—*n.* **1**, the giving of one thing for another; barter; **2**, giving and receiving; as, an *exchange* of ideas; **3**, the giving up of one thing for another; as, the *exchange* of country life for city life; **4**, a place for settling special business accounts or where persons, as brokers, meet to carry on particular business transactions; as, a stock *exchange;* **5**, a central office; as, a telephone *exchange.*—*adj.* **ex-change′a-ble.**

ex-cheq-uer (ĕks-chĕk′ĕr; ĕks′chĕk-ĕr), *n.* **1**, a treasury, especially of a government; **2**, cash or funds:—**Exchequer,** in Great Britain, the department of state which controls the national funds.

¹**ex-cise** (ĕk-sīz′; ĕk′sīz), *n.* a tax levied on articles or commodities within the country where they are manufactured, sold, or used:—*adj.* **ex-cis′a-ble.**

²**ex-cise** (ĕk-sīz′), *v.t.* [excised, excis-ing], to cut out; remove by cutting out.

ex-cise-man (ĕk-sīz′măn), *n.* [*pl.* excise-men (-mĕn)], in Great Britain, one who collects certain taxes; a revenue officer.

ex-cit-a-ble (ĕk-sīt′ȧ-bl), *adj.* easily roused or stirred up.—*n.* **ex-cit′a-bil′i-ty.**

Syn. impetuous, fiery, passionate.

ex-cite (ĕk-sīt′), *v.t.* [excit-ed, excit-ing], **1**, to set in motion; stir up; as, to *excite* anger; **2**, to encourage; impel; incite; as, to *excite* men to revolt; **3**, to arouse mentally or emotionally; move; perturb; as, news of the accident *excited* him.—*n.* **ex-cit′er.**

Syn. awaken, provoke, stir.

āte, âorta, râre, căt, ȧsk, fär, ăllow, sofȧ; ēve, ĕvent, ĕll, writẽr, novĕl; bīte, pĭn; nō, ōbey, ôr, dŏg, tŏp, cŏllide; ūnit, ŭnite, bûrn, cŭt, focŭs; no͞on, fo͝ot; mound; coin;

ex·cite·ment (ĕk-sīt′mĕnt), *n.* **1,** the condition of being stirred up; commotion; **2,** the act of stirring up; stimulation.

ex·claim (ĕks-klām′), *v.i.* to speak or cry out suddenly or passionately, as with surprise, anger, pleasure, etc.

ex·cla·ma·tion (ĕks′klȧ-mā′shŭn), *n.* **1,** a sudden crying out; **2,** an expression of surprise, pain, etc.:—**exclamation point,** a mark [!] in writing or printing to denote emotion, surprise, etc.—*adj.* **ex·clam′a·to·ry.**

ex·clude (ĕks-klōōd′), *v.t.* [exclud-ed, exclud-ing], to shut out; keep from entrance or admission; debar; as, they *excluded* him from membership in the club.

Syn. expel, eject, eliminate.

ex·clu·sion (ĕks-klōō′zhŭn), *n.* **1,** the act of shutting out; **2,** the condition of being shut out; rejection.

ex·clu·sive (ĕks-klōō′sĭv), *adj.* **1,** shutting out; **2,** including everything but what is mentioned; as, twenty members *exclusive* of officers; **3,** open to a chosen or privileged number; as, an *exclusive* club; **4,** sole; as, an *exclusive* agency for a certain machine; **5,** entire; complete; as, *exclusive* devotion to work.—*adv.* **ex·clu′sive·ly.**

ex·com·mu·ni·cate (ĕks′kŏ-mū′nĭ-kāt), *v.t.* [excommunicat-ed, excommunicat-ing], **1,** to punish by cutting off from the membership and communion of the church; **2,** to expel from membership in any association or club.—*n.* **ex′com·mu′ni·ca′tion.**

ex·cre·ment (ĕks′krē-mĕnt), *n.* waste matter discharged from the body.

ex·cres·cence (ĕks-krĕs′ĕns), *n.* an unnatural, useless, or disfiguring outgrowth, as a wart.—*adj.* **ex·cres′cent.**

ex·crete (ĕks-krēt′), *v.t.* [excret-ed, excret-ing], to throw off (waste matter) from the body.—*adj.* **ex′cre·tor′y** (ĕks′krē-tôr′ĭ).

ex·cre·tion (ĕks-krē′shŭn), *n.* the act of throwing off waste matter from the body; also, the waste matter thrown off.

ex·cru·ci·at·ing (ĕks-krōō′shĭ-āt′ĭng), *adj.* torturing; extremely painful.

ex·cul·pate (ĕks′kŭl-pāt; ĕks-kŭl′pāt), *v.t.* [exculpat-ed, exculpat-ing], to free from blame; to free from charge of a fault.—*n.* **ex′cul·pa′tion.**

Syn. acquit, absolve, release, exonerate.

ex·cur·sion (ĕks-kûr′zhŭn; ĕks-kûr′shŭn), *n.* **1,** a pleasure trip, often one made by a number of people; also, the persons on such a pleasure trip; **2,** a short or rapid tour.—*n.* **ex·cur′sion·ist.**

Syn. jaunt, ramble, expedition.

ex·cus·a·ble (ĕks-kūz′ȧ-bl), *adj.* deserving to be pardoned; pardonable; as, *excusable* delay.—*adv.* **ex·cus′a·bly.**

ex·cuse (ĕks-kūz′), *v.t.* [excused, excus-ing], **1,** to pardon; as, to *excuse* one for being late; **2,** to free from blame, obligation, or duty; as, the teacher *excused* her from the test; **3,** to make an apology or explanation for; as, illness *excuses* his absence; **4,** to justify; as, only ignorance *excuses* bad grammar:—*n.* (ĕks-kūs′), **1,** a plea offered to justify some fault or neglect of duty; an apology; **2,** a reason; as, an *excuse* for absence.

Syn., n. apology, extenuation.

ex·e·cra·ble (ĕk′sē-krȧ-bl), *adj.* **1,** accursed; outrageous; **2,** very bad; as, *execrable* taste.—*adv.* **ex′e·cra·bly.**

ex·e·crate (ĕk′sē-krāt), *v.t.* [execrat-ed, execrat-ing], **1,** to curse; **2,** to detest; abhor; abominate:—*v.i.* to curse.

ex·e·cra·tion (ĕk′sē-krā′shŭn), *n.* **1,** cursing; **2,** an expression of utter detestation; a curse; **3,** the thing cursed.

ex·e·cute (ĕk′sē-kūt), *v.t.* [execut-ed, execut-ing], **1,** to carry into effect; complete; as, to *execute* a plan; **2,** to make legal by signing or sealing; as, to *execute* a lease; **3,** to put to death under sentence of the law; **4,** to perform, as a musical selection; to make according to a design; as, to *execute* a memorial in marble.

Syn. enforce, manage, perform, accomplish, achieve, effect, kill, assassinate.

ex·e·cu·tion (ĕk′sē-kū′shŭn), *n.* **1,** performance; the carrying of anything into effect; **2,** workmanship; as, a portrait of perfect *execution;* **3,** the making of a legal paper binding; **4,** punishment by death.

ex·e·cu·tion·er (ĕk′sē-kū′shŭn-ẽr), *n.* one who puts to death condemned criminals.

ex·ec·u·tive (ĕg-zĕk′ū-tĭv; ĕk-sĕk′ū-tĭv), *adj.* **1,** pertaining to, or skilful in, the carrying out of plans; as, he has *executive* ability; **2,** referring to that branch of government that administers the laws; as, the *executive* power is distinct from the legislative power:—*n.* **1,** any person charged with putting laws or plans into effect; **2,** the administrative branch of a government.

ex·ec·u·tor (ĕk′sē-kū′tẽr), *n.* **1,** one who carries something into effect; **2,** (ĕg-zĕk′ū-tẽr; ĕk-sĕk′ū-tẽr), a person appointed in a will to see that its terms are carried out.—*n.fem.* **ex·ec′u·trix.**

ex·em·pla·ry (ĕg-zĕm′plȧ-rĭ; ĕg′zĕm-plẽr′ĭ), *adj.* serving as a copy or model; praiseworthy; as, the boy's conduct was *exemplary.*

ex·em·pli·fi·ca·tion (ĕg-zĕm′plĭ-fĭ-kā′shŭn), *n.* the showing or making plain by example; also, an example; illustration.

ex·em·pli·fy (ĕg-zĕm′plĭ-fī), *v.t.* [exemplified, exemplify-ing], to show by example; illustrate; as, a story to *exemplify* honesty.

ex·empt (ĕg-zĕmpt′), *v.t.* to free from an obligation or duty; excuse; release; as, to *exempt* a man from military service:—*adj.* free from a duty, restriction, or other limitation, to which others are subject; as, goods *exempt* from import duties.

ex·emp·tion (ĕg-zĕmp′shŭn), *n.* freedom from a duty or obligation.

ex·er·cise (ĕk′sẽr-sīz), *v.t.* [exercised, exercis-ing], **1,** to train by use; practice; **2,** to employ actively, as the muscles or the mind; **3,** to make anxious; as, the girl's absence *exercised* her mother:—*v.i.* to undergo training:—*n.* **1,** physical or mental activity for the sake of development; **2,** a lesson or example for practice; **3, exercises,** a ceremony; formal program; as, graduation *exercises;* **4,** performance; as, in the *exercise* of duty.

ex·ert (ĕg-zûrt′), *v.t.* to put forth; bring to bear; as, to *exert* one's influence, strength, or ability.

ex·er·tion (ĕg-zûr′shŭn), *n.* the active use of any power; effort.
 Syn. exercise, work, endeavor.

ex·ha·la·tion (ĕks′ha-lā′shŭn; ĕk′sa-lā′-shŭn; ĕg′za-lā′shŭn), *n.* a breathing out; as, the *exhalation* of perfume from a flower; also, that which is breathed or given out.

ex·hale (ĕks-hāl′; ĕg-zāl′), *v.t.* [exhaled, exhal-ing], to breathe out; give off; as, we *exhale* air in breathing; swamps *exhale* mist:—*v.i.* to rise in vapor.

ex·haust (ĕg-zôst′), *v.t.* **1,** to empty by letting out all the contents; drain; **2,** to weaken; wear out; use up, as strength or a supply of money; **3,** to discuss or treat thoroughly; as, to *exhaust* a topic:—*n.* **1,** the drawing off or escape of used fuel, as steam, gas, etc., from an engine; **2,** the steam, gas, etc., that escapes; **3,** an instrument or device for drawing off or letting escape, as bad air from a room, or used fuel from an engine.—*adj.* **ex·haust′ed.**

ex·haus·tion (ĕg-zôs′chŭn), *n.* **1,** the act of draining or the state of being drained; **2,** utter fatigue.

ex·haus·tive (ĕg-zôs′tĭv), *adj.* complete; thorough; as, an *exhaustive* investigation or study.—*adv.* **ex·haus′tive·ly.**

ex·hib·it (ĕg-zĭb′ĭt), *v.t.* **1,** to show; as, the leaves *exhibited* signs of turning color; **2,** to show publicly; present formally or officially; as, to *exhibit* an artist's work:—*n.* **1,** an object or collection of objects offered for public view; as, an *exhibit* of paintings; **2,** in law, an article, paper, etc., marked to be used as evidence.—*n.* **ex·hib′it·er; ex·hib′i·tor.**

ex·hi·bi·tion (ĕk′sĭ-bĭsh′ŭn), *n.* a display; a public showing, as of paintings.

ex·hil·a·rate (ĕg-zĭl′a-rāt), *v.t.* [exhilarat-ed, exhilarat-ing], to make joyous; gladden; enliven.—*adj.* **ex·hil′a·rat′ing.**

ex·hil·a·ra·tion (ĕg-zĭl′a-rā′shŭn), *n.* a feeling of gladness or stimulation.

ex·hort (ĕg-zôrt′), *v.t.* and *v.i.* to urge by appeal or argument, especially to good deeds; to advise; warn.

ex·hor·ta·tion (ĕg′zôr-tā′shŭn; ĕk′sôr-tā′shŭn). *n.* strong urging; earnest warning.

ex·hume (ĕks-hūm′; ĕg-zūm′), *v.t.* [ex-humed, exhum-ing], to dig up (something), especially a buried body.—*n.* **ex′hu·ma·tion** (ĕks′hū-mā′shŭn; ĕks′ū-mā′shŭn).

ex·i·gen·cy (ĕk′sĭ-jĕn′sĭ), *n.* [*pl.* exigencies], **1,** a situation that needs immediate attention; **2,** pressing necessity; urgency. Also, **ex′i·gence.**
 Syn. need, pressure, necessity.

ex·ile (ĕk′sīl; ĕg′zīl), *v.t.* [exiled, exil-ing], to banish from home or country:—*n.* **1,** banishment, either forced or voluntary; as, to live in *exile;* **2,** a person banished from or living out of his own country.
 Syn., v. expel, expatriate.

ex·ist (ĕg-zĭst′), *v.i.* **1,** to have actual being; live; be; **2,** to be found; occur; as, such conditions *exist* only in crowded cities.

ex·ist·ence (ĕg-zĭs′tĕns), *n.* **1,** the state of being; as, the microscope reveals the *existence* of many tiny things; **2,** life; as, food is necessary for *existence;* **3,** manner of life; as, a happy *existence;* **4,** reality; as, savages believe in the *existence* of devils.

ex·ist·ent (ĕg-zĭs′tĕnt), *adj.* existing; as, the amount of money *existent;* current; as, *existent* traffic conditions.

ex·it (ĕk′sĭt; ĕg′zĭt), *n.* **1,** the act of going out; **2,** a way out, as a door; **3,** the departure of an actor from the stage:—*v.i.* to go off or out.

ex·o·dus (ĕk′sō-dŭs), *n.* a going out; departure:—**Exodus, 1,** the departure of the Jews from Egypt, under Moses; **2,** the second book of the Bible, which tells this story.

ex of·fi·ci·o (ĕks ŏ-fĭsh′ĭ-ō), because of right of office and without other authority; as, the president of the U.S. is *ex officio* commander in chief of the army.

ex·on·er·ate (ĕg-zŏn′ẽr-āt), *v.t.* [exonerat-ed, exonerat-ing], to free from blame; as, the jury *exonerated* the accused man.

ex·or·bi·tant (ĕg-zôr′bĭ-tănt), *adj.* going beyond due limits; excessive; as, an *exorbitant* price.—*n.* **ex·or′bi·tance.**
 Syn. immoderate, extravagant, expensive.

ex·or·cise (ĕk′sôr-sīz), *v.t.* [exorcised, exorcis-ing], to expel (an evil spirit), as by religious or magic ceremonies; hence, to deliver or free from evil spirits. Also spelled **ex′or-cize.**—*n.* **ex′or-cis′er.**

ex-or-cism (ĕk′sôr-sĭzm), *n.* the act or process of expelling evil spirits, or of freeing a person from them.—*n.* **ex′or-cist.**

ex-ot-ic (ĕks-ŏt′ĭk; ĕg-zŏt′ĭk), *adj.* foreign; strange; belonging to another part of the world; as, an *exotic* flower.

ex-pand (ĕks-pănd′), *v.t.* **1,** to spread or stretch out; **2,** to dilate; swell; as, to *expand* the chest; **3,** to give more details of; enlarge upon; as, *expand* your topic into an essay:—*v.i.* to increase in size.

ex-panse (ĕks-păns′), *n.* wide extent; uninterrupted stretch or area; as, an *expanse* of ocean or of sky.

ex-pan-sion (ĕks-păn′shŭn), *n.* **1,** a spreading out; **2,** that which is spread out.

ex-pan-sive (ĕks-păn′sĭv), *adj.* **1,** capable of being spread or stretched out; **2,** widely extended; large; **3,** free and unrestrained in the expression of feeling; effusive; as, an *expansive* manner.—*adv.* **ex-pan′sive-ly.**

ex-pa-ti-ate (ĕks-pā′shĭ-āt), *v.i.* [expatiated, expatiat-ing], to talk or write freely and at length; as, to *expatiate* upon the beauty of a view.

ex-pa-tri-ate (ĕks-pā′trĭ-āt), *v.t.* [expatriat-ed, expatriat-ing], to banish (a person) from his native land; exile:—*n.* (ĕks-pā′trĭ-āt), an exile.—*n.* **ex-pa′tri-a′tion.**

ex-pect (ĕks-pĕkt′), *v.t.* **1,** to look forward to as likely to happen; as, I *expect* him to arrive tonight; **2,** *Colloquial,* to suppose; as, I *expect* it is all for the best.

ex-pect-an-cy (ĕks-pĕk′tăn-sĭ), *n.* looking forward to something.

ex-pect-ant (ĕks-pĕk′tănt), *adj.* looking forward with confidence; expecting.—*adv.* **ex-pect′ant-ly.**

ex-pec-ta-tion (ĕks′pĕk-tā′shŭn), *n.* **1,** a looking forward to something; anticipation; as, in *expectation* of a good dinner; **2,** (usually *expectations*), the prospect of future benefit, especially of advancement or wealth; as, his *expectations* are good. *Syn.* hope, trust.

ex-pec-to-rant (ĕks-pĕk′tŏ-rănt), *adj.* helping the discharge of mucus or other fluids from the lungs and throat:—*n.* a medicine that does this.

ex-pec-to-rate (ĕks-pĕk′tŏ-rāt), *v.i.* and *v.t.* [expectorat-ed, expectorat-ing], to discharge (matter) from the mouth, throat, or lungs by coughing or spitting; to spit.

ex-pe-di-en-cy (ĕks-pē′dĭ-ĕn-sĭ), *n.* [*pl.* expediencies], **1,** suitableness; fitness for a purpose; **2,** the doing of something, regardless of fairness or justice, in order to gain a certain end; as, *expediency* made him refuse. Also, **ex-pe′di-ence.**

ex-pe-di-ent (ĕks-pē′dĭ-ĕnt), *adj.* **1,** fit for a special purpose; **2,** helping toward self-interest; as, an *expedient* friendship: —*n.* **1,** that which acts as a means to an end; **2,** a device.—*adv.* **ex-pe′di-ent-ly.** *Syn., adj.* practical, favorable.

ex-pe-dite (ĕks′pē-dīt), *v.t.* [expedit-ed, expedit-ing], **1,** to hasten; help forward; quicken; **2,** to carry out quickly; as, to *expedite* work.

ex-pe-di-tion (ĕks′pē-dĭsh′ŭn), *n.* **1,** haste; dispatch; promptness; as, he did his work with *expedition;* **2,** a journey or voyage for some particular purpose; as, an exploring *expedition;* **3,** the body of persons engaged in such an enterprise.

ex-pe-di-tion-ar-y (ĕks′pē-dĭsh′ŭn-ĕr′ĭ), *adj.* pertaining to or forming an expedition; as, the American *Expeditionary* Forces.

ex-pe-di-tious (ĕks′pē-dĭsh′ŭs), *adj.* effective; speedy.—*adv.* **ex′pe-di′tious-ly.** *Syn.* efficient, energetic, quick, ready.

ex-pel (ĕks-pĕl′), *v.t.* [expelled, expel-ling], **1,** to drive away; force out; as, to *expel* an enemy from a region; **2,** to turn out; send away; as, to *expel* someone from a club, school, or the like. *Syn.* exile, eject, dismiss, banish.

ex-pend (ĕks-pĕnd′), *v.t.* to pay out; spend; as, to *expend* strength, time, or money.

ex-pend-i-ture (ĕks-pĕn′dĭ-tŭr), *n.* **1,** a spending, as of money, time, labor, etc.; **2,** that which is spent.

ex-pense (ĕks-pĕns′), *n.* **1,** money, labor, time, etc., laid out or spent; cost; as, the *expenses* of a college education; he worked long hours at the *expense* of his health; **2,** a source or cause of spending; as, war is a great *expense.*

ex-pen-sive (ĕks-pĕn′sĭv), *adj.* costly; high-priced.—*adv.* **ex-pen′sive-ly.** *Syn.* exorbitant, dear.

ex-pe-ri-ence (ĕks-pē′rĭ-ĕns), *n.* **1,** knowledge or skill gained by direct action, observation, enjoyment, or suffering; **2,** the actual observation of or living through anything, as a series of events, or of feeling anything through sensation; **3,** anything lived through, enjoyed, or felt; as, war *experiences:*—*v.t.* [experienced, experienc-ing], to feel; live through; as, to *experience* hardship.

ex-pe-ri-enced (ĕks-pē′rĭ-ĕnst), *adj.* having experience; made expert by experience.

ex-per-i-ment (ĕks-pĕr′ĭ-mĕnt), *n.* a trial or test to discover something previously unknown, or to confirm or disprove something; as, the *experiment* showed he was right:—*v.i.* (ĕks-pĕr′ĭ-mĕnt), to make tests to find out something; as, Edison *experimented* for years trying to perfect electric lighting.—*n.* **ex-per′i-ment-er.**—*adj.* **ex-per′i-men′tal.**

Syn., *n.* proof, examination.

ex-pert (ĕks-pûrt′; ĕks′pûrt), *adj.* skilful; clever; dexterous:—*n.* (ĕks′pûrt), one who is skilled or thoroughly informed in any particular subject; a specialist; as, a financial *expert.*—*adv.* **ex-pert′ly.**

Syn., *adj.* practiced, facile, deft.

ex-pi-ate (ĕks′pĭ-āt), *v.t.* [expiat-ed, expiat-ing], to atone or make amends for; as, he *expiated* his theft by restoring the plunder.

ex-pi-a-tion (ĕks′pĭ-ā′shŭn), *n.* the act of making amends for an offense; atonement.

ex-pire (ĕk-spīr′), *v.t.* [expired, expir-ing], to breathe out from the lungs:—*v.i.* 1, to die; 2, to come to an end; as, the term *expires* today.—*n.* **ex′pi-ra′tion.**

ex-plain (ĕks-plān′), *v.t.* 1, to make plain or clear; tell the meaning of; as, to *explain* a problem; 2, to account for; as, to *explain* one's conduct.—*adj.* **ex-plain′a-ble.**

Syn. define, describe.

ex-pla-na-tion (ĕks′plă-nā′shŭn), *n.* 1, the act of making clear; interpretation; as, to understand the *explanation* of the lesson; 2, the statement or fact which makes plain or accounts for something; as, to give an *explanation* for lateness.

ex-plan-a-to-ry (ĕks-plăn′ă-tôr′ĭ), *adj.* serving to make clear.

ex-ple-tive (ĕks′plĕ-tĭv), *n.* 1, a word or phrase added merely to fill in or for emphasis; as, the adverb "there" is an *expletive* in the sentence, "there was a fire last night"; 2, an oath; exclamation:—*adj.* filling up; added or inserted for emphasis.

ex-pli-ca-ble (ĕks′plĭ-kà-bl), *adj.* capable of being explained.

ex-plic-it (ĕks-plĭs′ĭt), *adj.* plain; definite; expressed clearly and in detail; as, *explicit* instructions.—*adv.* **ex-plic′it-ly.**—*n.* **ex-plic′it-ness.**

ex-plode (ĕks-plōd′), *v.i.* [explod-ed, explod-ing], 1, to burst with sudden noise and violence; as, the bomb *exploded*; 2, to break forth suddenly into laughter, anger, etc.:—*v.t.* 1, to cause to burst suddenly with a loud noise; as, to *explode* dynamite; 2, to refute or disprove; as, Copernicus *exploded* the theory that the earth was the center of the solar system.

ex-ploit (ĕks-ploit′), *v.t.* 1, to make use of for one's own profit; put to use selfishly; as, to *exploit* one's friends; 2, to make use of; work; develop; as, to *exploit*

natural resources:—*n.* (ĕks′ploit; ĕks-ploit′), a remarkable deed or heroic act.—*n.* **ex-ploit′er.**

ex-ploi-ta-tion (ĕks′ploi-tā′shŭn), *n.* 1, the working and using of something, as lands, mines, water power, etc.; 2, the use of a person or thing for self-profit.

ex-plore (ĕks-plôr′), *v.t.* [explored, explor-ing], 1, to search or examine thoroughly; as, to *explore* a wound; 2, to travel in or over (a region) to discover its geographical characteristics; as, to *explore* unknown islands.—*n.* **ex′plo-ra′tion.**

ex-plor-er (ĕks-plôr′ẽr), *n.* one who travels in far places to find out about them.

ex-plo-sion (ĕks-plō′zhŭn), *n.* 1, a sudden and violent bursting with a loud noise; as, the *explosion* of a bomb; 2, a sudden and violent outburst, as of anger.

ex-plo-sive (ĕks-plō′sĭv), *adj.* pertaining to explosion; likely to explode; as, dynamite is an *explosive* substance:—*n.* any substance, liquid, solid, or gaseous, which will explode or cause an explosion, as gunpowder, TNT, etc.—*adv.* **ex-plo′sive-ly.**

ex-po-nent (ĕks-pō′nĕnt), *n.* 1, one who explains or interprets; as, an *exponent* of democracy; 2, a person or thing that represents a principle or theory; as, Daniel Webster was the *exponent* of the Union.

ex-port (ĕks-pôrt′; ĕks′pôrt), *v.t.* to send or carry out (goods) to another country for sale; as, to *export* cattle:—*n.* (ĕks′pôrt), 1, (usually *exports*), goods sold and sent to a foreign country; also, their amount or value; 2, the act or business of sending goods to a foreign country to be sold; as, the *export* of wheat is an important industry in the U.S.—*n.* **ex′por-ta′tion.**—*adj.* **ex-port′a-ble.**—*n.* **ex-port′er.**

ex-pose (ĕks-pōz′), *v.t.* [exposed, exposing], 1, to lay open to view; uncover; make known; as, to *expose* a secret, an opinion, or a villain; 2, to leave without shelter or defense; as, to *expose* a child to the cold; 3, to lay open or put in the way of; as, to *expose* a plant to the sun; *expose* a friend to blame; 4, in photography, to subject (a film) to the action of light.

Syn. display, publish, exhibit.

ex-po-sé (ĕks′pō-zā′), *n.* 1, a formal recital of the facts of a case; 2, a showing up of something unworthy or shameful.

ex-po-si-tion (ĕks′pō-zĭsh′ŭn), *n.* 1, an explanation or interpretation; a piece of writing that explains or interprets; 2, an exhibition on a large scale.

ex-pos-i-to-ry (ĕks-pŏz′ĭ-tôr′ĭ), *adj.* explanatory; as, *expository* writing.

ex-pos-tu-late (ĕks-pŏs′tū-lāt), *v.i.* [expostulat-ed, expostulat-ing], to plead earnestly, as with a friend about his faults; remonstrate.—*n.* **ex-pos′tu-la′-tion.**

Syn. rebuke, reprimand, reprove.

ex-po-sure (ĕks-pō′zhĕr), *n.* **1,** a revealing or making known; as, the *exposure* of a crime; **2,** the state of being open or subject to attack, contamination, or the like; as, *exposure* to disease; **3,** position; outlook; as, a house with a southern *exposure;* **4,** in photography, an exposing to light.

ex-pound (ĕks-pound′), *v.t.* to set forth, explain, or interpret.—*n.* **ex-pound′er.**

ex-press (ĕks-prĕs′), *adj.* **1,** plainly stated; special; definite; as, an *express* answer or wish; **2,** having to do with quick or direct transportation; as, an *express* train; **3,** pertaining to the business of transporting goods rapidly; as, an *express* company:—*adv.* by express; quickly; as, send the package *express:*—*n.* **1,** a fast railway train stopping only at principal stations; **2,** a system of transportation for mails, goods of small bulk, or the like; also, goods so forwarded:—*v.t.* **1,** to make known, especially by language; utter; as, he *expressed* the idea clearly; **2,** to show; reveal; as, to *express* relief, joy, etc.; **3,** to represent; as, the symbol of the arrow *expresses* direction; **4,** to send by express.—*n.* **ex-press′age.**—*n.* **ex-press′man.**

ex-pres-sion (ĕks-prĕsh′ŭn), *n.* **1,** the act of expressing or revealing, especially in words; manner of speech, change in tone of voice, etc., revealing thought and feeling; as, to speak with *expression;* **2,** a look on the face that betrays feeling; as, a joyous *expression;* **3,** a saying; as, "Never say die" is an old *expression.*

ex-pres-sive (ĕks-prĕs′ĭv), *adj.* full of meaning; serving to point out or express; as, a look *expressive* of sorrow.—*adv.* **ex-pres′sive-ly.**—*n.* **ex-pres′sive-ness.**

ex-press-ly (ĕks-prĕs′lĭ), *adv.* **1,** particularly; specially; **2,** in direct terms; plainly; as, told *expressly* to go home.

ex-pul-sion (ĕks-pŭl′shŭn), *n.* **1,** a forcing out or away; **2,** banishment; as, the *expulsion* of an enemy.—*adj.* **ex-pul′sive.**

ex-punge (ĕks-pŭnj′), *v.t.* [expunged, expung-ing], to blot or rub out; erase; efface.

ex-pur-gate (ĕks′pĕr-gāt; ĕks-pûr′gāt), *v.t.* [expurgat-ed, expurgat-ing], to clean, as a book, by taking out whatever is offensive to good taste or morality.

ex-qui-site (ĕks′kwĭ-zĭt), *adj.* **1,** delicately beautiful; as, *exquisite* lace; *exquisite* workmanship; **2,** intensely or sensitively felt; as, *exquisite* joy.—*adv.* **ex′qui-site-ly.**

Syn. dainty, elegant, fine, rare.

ex-tant (ĕks′tănt; ĕk-stănt′), *adj.* in existence; not destroyed or lost; as, old prints or writings that are still *extant.*

ex-tem-po-ra-ne-ous (ĕks-tĕm′pō-rā′-nē-ŭs), *adj.* made without preparation or study; extemporary.—*adv.* **ex-tem′po-ra′-ne-ous-ly.**

ex-tem-po-rar-y (ĕks-tĕm′pŏ-rĕr′ĭ), *adj.* **1,** without notes or previous study; as, an *extemporary* speech; **2,** made on the spur of the moment.—*adv.* **ex-tem′po-rar′i-ly.**

ex-tem-po-re (ĕks-tĕm′pŏ-rē), *adj.* and *adv.* without preparation; as, to recite *extempore.*

ex-tend (ĕks-tĕnd′), *v.t.* **1,** to lengthen, as a railroad; prolong, as a visit; **2,** to enlarge; increase, as power, influence, etc.; **3,** to straighten out, as the arm; **4,** to offer, as friendship:—*v.i.* to reach, in time or distance; as, the U.S. *extends* from Canada to the Gulf of Mexico.

Syn. prolong, widen, increase.

ex-ten-sion (ĕks-tĕn′shŭn), *n.* **1,** the act of reaching or stretching out; **2,** the state of being lengthened; enlargement; **3,** an addition; as, an *extension* on a house.

ex-ten-sive (ĕks-tĕn′sĭv), *adj.* wide; comprehensive; far-reaching; as, *extensive* business interests; an *extensive* view.—*adv.* **ex-ten′sive-ly.**

ex-tent (ĕks-tĕnt′), *n.* the space or degree to which a thing is extended; size; length; limit; as, the *extent* of his lands.

ex-ten-u-ate (ĕks-tĕn′ū-āt), *v.t.* [extenuat-ed, extenuat-ing], to offer excuses for; lessen the blame for; as, he sought to *extenuate* his fault.

ex-ten-u-a-tion (ĕks-tĕn′ū-ā′shŭn), *n.* the act of making less blamable; that which lessens blame or guilt; as, there can be no *extenuation* of war.

ex-te-ri-or (ĕks-tē′rĭ-ĕr), *adj.* **1,** outward; external; as, the *exterior* covering of a box; **2,** coming, or acting, from without; as, *exterior* aid:—*n.* the outer surface or the outside of anything.

ex-ter-mi-nate (ĕks-tûr′mĭ-nāt), *v.t.* [exterminat-ed, exterminat-ing], to destroy utterly; root out; as, to *exterminate* moths.—*n.* **ex-ter′mi-na′tor.**

Syn. extirpate, eradicate.

ex-ter-mi-na-tion (ĕks-tûr′mĭ-nā′shŭn), *n.* complete destruction.

ex-ter-nal (ĕks-tûr′năl), *adj.* **1,** outside; exterior; as, an *external* force; **2,** foreign; as, the *external* debt of a country; **3,** visible; as, *external* proof; **4,** superficial; as, *external* culture:—*n.* **1,** an outward part; **2,** (often *externals*), outward form or ceremony; as, the *externals* of religion.—*adv.* **ex-ter′nal-ly.**

ex-tinct (ĕks-tĭngkt′), *adj.* **1,** no longer burning; gone out, as a fire; inactive, as a volcano; **2,** destroyed, as life or hope; **3,** no longer living or surviving; as, buffaloes are almost *extinct.*

ex·tinc·tion (ĕks-tĭngk'shŭn), *n.* annihilation; death.

ex·tin·guish (ĕks-tĭng'gwĭsh), *v.t.* **1,** to put out, as a light; **2,** to destroy; as, to *extinguish* hope.—*adj.* **ex·tin'guish·a·ble.**

ex·tin·guish·er (ĕks-tĭng'gwĭsh-ẽr), *n.* one who or that which extinguishes.

ex·tir·pate (ĕk'stẽr-pāt; ĕks-tûr'pāt), *v.t.* [extirpat-ed, extirpat-ing], to root out; completely destroy.

ex·tir·pa·tion (ĕk'stẽr-pā'shŭn), *n.* a rooting out; destruction, as of evil.

ex·tol (ĕks-tŏl'; ĕks-tōl'), *v.t.* [extolled, extol-ling], to praise highly; as, to *extol* the name of God.

ex·tort (ĕks-tôrt'), *v.t.* to obtain by force or threats; as, to *extort* money.

ex·tor·tion (ĕks-tôr'shŭn), *n.* **1,** the act of obtaining by force or threat; **2,** unjust exaction, as of excessive interest on loans; **3,** that which has been exacted unlawfully. —*adj.* **ex·tor'tion·ate.**—*adv.* **ex·tor'tion·ate·ly.**—*n.* **ex·tor'tion·er.**

ex·tra (ĕks'trȧ), *adj.* **1,** more than usual; **2,** unusually good; as, *extra* meats:—*n.* **1,** something additional; **2,** a newspaper edition issued between regular editions:—*adv.* exceptionally; as, *extra* fine silk.

ex·tra- (ĕks'trȧ-), a prefix forming adjectives meaning beyond, outside of besides; as, *extra*ordinary.

ex·tract (ĕks-trăkt'), *v.t.* **1,** to obtain from a substance by some process; as, to *extract* perfume from flowers; **2,** to pull out, as a tooth; **3,** to get by effort; as, to *extract* money from a miser; **4,** to select, as a passage from a book; **5,** in mathematics, to calculate (a specified root, as of a number):—*n.* (ĕks'trăkt), **1,** that which has been extracted, or taken out, as, *extract* of beef; **2,** a passage from a book, speech, etc.—*adj.* **ex·tract'a·ble.**—*n.* **ex·trac'tor.**

ex·trac·tion (ĕks-trăk'shŭn), *n.* **1,** the act of extracting; **2,** origin; descent; as, a person of English *extraction.*

ex·tra·dite (ĕks'trȧ-dīt), *v.t.* [extradit-ed, extradit-ing], **1,** to surrender (a criminal fleeing justice) to the state or nation authorized to try him; **2,** to secure the surrender of (a person) under such conditions.

ex·tra·di·tion (ĕks'trȧ-dĭsh'ŭn), *n.* the surrender by a state or nation of a criminal fleeing justice, to the state or nation in which the crime was committed.

ex·tra·ne·ous (ĕks-trā'nē-ŭs), *adj.* not belonging or proper (to the matter in hand); not essential.

ex·traor·di·nar·y (ĕks-trôr'dĭ-nĕr'ĭ; ĕks'-trȧ-ôr'dĭ-nĕr'ĭ), *adj.* **1,** unusual; **2,** remarkable; rare; **3,** special; as, an envoy *extraordinary.*—*adv.* **ex·traor'ɑi·nar'i·ly.**

ex·trav·a·gant (ĕks-trăv'ȧ-gȧnt), *adj.* **1,** exceeding reasonable limits; **2,** wasteful; needlessly lavish in spending; **3,** very high, as prices.—*adv.* **ex·trav'a·gant·ly.**
Syn. immoderate, profuse, excessive.

ex·treme (ĕks-trēm'), *adj.* **1,** of the highest degree; as, *extreme* old age; *extreme* danger; **2,** outermost; farthest away; as, the *extreme* ends of the world; **3,** most severe or strict; as, *extreme* measures; **4,** excessive; immoderate; as, *extreme* fashions; **5,** advanced; radical; as, *extreme* ideas:—*n.* **1,** the extremity; the very end; **2,** the utmost degree of anything; **3,** excess; as, to go to *extremes.*—*adv.* **ex·treme'ly.**

ex·trem·ist (ĕks-trēm'ĭst), *n.* one who has advanced or radical ideas; one who goes to extremes, as in fashion.

ex·trem·i·ty (ĕks-trĕm'ĭ-tĭ), *n.* [*pl.* extremities], **1,** the farthest point, or end; as, the western *extremity* of the bridge; **2,** an arm, hand, leg, or foot; **3,** the utmost degree; as, an *extremity* of pain; **4,** extreme need or distress; as, people were reduced to *extremity* by the drought.

ex·tri·cate (ĕks'trĭ-kāt), *v.t.* [extricat-ed, extricat-ing], to free or set loose; as, to *extricate* an animal from a trap; also, to free from difficulties; as, to *extricate* oneself from debt.
Syn. release, disengage, relieve.

ex·trin·sic (ĕks-trĭn'sĭk), *adj.* external; not belonging or necessary to a thing; foreign.—*adv.* **ex·trin'si·cal·ly.**
Syn. extraneous, unessential, outward.

ex·u·ber·ance (ĕg-zū'bẽr-ăns), *n.* an overflowing; abundance, as of high spirits.—*adj.* **ex·u'ber·ant.**

ex·ude (ĕks-ūd'; ĕg-zūd'), *v.t.* [exud-ed, exud-ing], to discharge gradually through the pores, as by sweating; give out (moisture):—*v.i.* to ooze out.—*n.* **ex'u·da'tion.**

ex·ult (ĕg-zŭlt'), *v.i.* to rejoice exceedingly; as, to *exult* in victory.—*adv.* **ex·ult'ing·ly.**

ex·ult·ant (ĕg-zŭl'tănt), *adj.* rejoicing exceedingly; as, *exultant* over victory.

ex·ul·ta·tion (ĕk'sŭl-tā'shŭn; ĕg'zŭl-tā'-shŭn), *n.* triumphant joy.

-ey (-ē), a suffix forming words meaning like; full of; as, clay*ey.*

eye (ī), *n.* **1,** the organ of sight; **2,** sight; power to see or appreciate; as, an *eye* for beauty; **3,** a look; gaze; **4,** close observation; as, to keep an *eye* on someone; **5,** estimation; judgment; as, in the *eyes* of the world; **6,** that which resembles an eye;

as, the *eye* of a needle:—*v.t.* [eyed, ey-ing or eye-ing], to look at; watch closely.

eye-ball (ī′bôl′), *n.* all of the eye within the lids and socket.

eye-brow (ī′brou′), *n.* the ridge above either eye; also, the hair on this ridge.

eye-glass (ī′glás′), *n.* 1, a lens for the eye, to improve faulty sight; 2, the lens of a telescope or microscope; 3, **eyeglasses,** a pair of lenses for the eyes.

eye-lash (ī′lăsh′), *n.* the fringe of hair that grows on the edge of the eyelid; also, one of the hairs of this fringe.

eye-less (ī′lĕs), *adj.* without eyes; blind.

eye-let (ī′lĕt), *n.* 1, a small hole to receive a lace or cord; 2, a ring of metal to strengthen such a hole.

eye-lid (ī′lĭd′), *n.* the movable upper or lower cover of skin which closes the eye.

eye-piece (ī′pēs′), *n.* in a telescope or other optical instrument, the lens or system of lenses nearest the eye of the user.

eye-shot (ī′shŏt′), *n.* view; range of vision; also, a glance.

eye-sight (ī′sīt′), *n.* 1, the ability to see; 2, range of vision; as, within *eyesight.*

eye-sore (ī′sôr′), *n.* anything that offends the sight; anything ugly.

eye splice (splīs), a loop on the end of a rope made by turning back the end and interweaving the loose end strands into the strands of the rope. (See illustration under *knot.*)

eye-strain (ī′strān′), *n.* a strained condition of the eye, resulting from poor eyesight, or from overuse of the eyes.

eye-tooth (ī′tōōth′), *n.* [*pl.* eyeteeth (-tēth′)], one of the two canine teeth in the upper jaw, the third tooth from the front on either side.

eye-wink-er (ī′wĭngk′ẽr), *n.* one of the eyelashes.

eye-wit-ness (ī′wĭt′nĕs), *n.* one who has seen something happen; one who can testify to what he has actually seen; as, an *eyewitness* of the crime.

ey-rie (âr′ĭ; ēr′ĭ; ī′rĭ), *n.* the nest or brood of a bird of prey, as an eagle or a hawk; an aerie. Also spelled **ey′ry.**

E-zek-iel (ē-zēk′yĕl; ē-zē′kĭ-ĕl), 1, a great Hebrew prophet; 2, in the Old Testament, the book which contains his prophecies.

Ez-ra (ĕz′rà), 1, a famous Hebrew scribe and priest; 2, a historical book of the Old Testament written by him about his life and teachings.

F

F, f (ĕf), *n.* [*pl.* F's, f's], 1, the sixth letter of the alphabet, following E; 2, the fourth note in the major scale of C.

f. abbreviation for Italian *forte,* meaning *loud:*—**F.** abbreviation for *French, Fahrenheit.*

fa (fä), *n.* in music, the name of the fourth note in the scale.

Fa-bi-us (fā′bĭ-ŭs), Maximus (275?–203 B.C.), called *the Delayer,* a Roman general, opponent of Hannibal.—*adj.* **Fa′bi-an.**

fa-ble (fā′bl), *n.* 1, a story, especially one with a moral, in which, usually, animals talk and act like human beings; 2, an untrue statement; a lie.—*n.* **fab′u-list.**

Fabre (fàbr′), Jean Henri (1823–1915), a French scientist who studied and wrote about insects.

fab-ric (făb′rĭk), *n.* 1, woven or knitted cloth; 2, texture or workmanship; as, cloth of fine *fabric;* 3, structure; as, the social *fabric.*

fab-ri-cate (făb′rĭ-kāt), *v.t.* [fabricat-ed, fabricat-ing], 1, to invent; as, to *fabricate* a tale; 2, to make; manufacture; as, they *fabricate* boxes.—*n.* **fab′ri-ca′tion.**
Syn. frame, concoct, devise.

fab-u-lous (făb′ū-lŭs), *adj.* 1, occurring in fable; legendary; as, Ulysses is a *fabulous* hero; 2, hard to believe; incredible; hence, enormous; amazing; as, *fabulous* wealth.—*adv.* **fab′u-lous-ly.**
Syn. legendary, astonishing, fictitious.

fa-çade (fà-säd′), *n.* the chief front of a building, or any of its principal faces.

face (fās), *n.* 1, the front part of the head; 2, expression or look; as, a happy *face;* also, a grimace; as, don't make a *face* at Ann; 3, impudence; as, she had the *face* to go, uninvited; 4, the principal side, as of a building, clock, card, etc.; 5, reputation; as, to save his *face;* 6, personal presence; sight; as, to say it to his *face:*—*v.t.* [faced, fac-ing], 1, to turn toward; as, she *faced* them; be situated opposite; as, my room *faced* the south; 2, to confront; as, he *faced* danger; 3, to cover, or partly cover, with something in front; as, to *face* a

FAÇADE
of a Greek temple.

fireplace with brick; also, to cover (some part of a garment) with another layer of material; as, to *face* a hem:—*v.i.* to turn the face; stand or front in any given direction.

fac-et (făs′ĕt), *n.* one of the small, polished surfaces of a gem that has been cut.

fa-ce-tious (fá-sē′shŭs), *adj.* humorous; harmlessly teasing; as, a *facetious* remark.—*adv.* **fa-ce′tious-ly.**—*n.* **fa-ce′tious-ness.**

Syn. jocose, laughable, funny, witty.

FACETS
Gem cut with facets: top view and side view.

fa-cial (fā′shăl), *adj.* pertaining to the face; as, *facial* expression:—*n. Colloquial,* a facial massage.

fac-ile (făs′ĭl), *adj.* 1, easily done; 2, quick in doing; fluent; expert; as, a *facile* writer; 3, gentle; mild.

fa-cil-i-tate (fá-sĭl′ĭ-tāt), *v.t.* [facilitat-ed, facilitat-ing], to make easier; as, an electric washer *facilitates* laundering.

fa-cil-i-ty (fá-sĭl′ĭ-tĭ), *n.* [*pl.* facilities], 1, ease; freedom from difficulty; also, skill; as, he writes with *facility;* 2, **facilities,** the devices or means by which anything may be more easily done; as, kitchen *facilities.*

fac-ing (fās′ĭng), *n.* 1, a covering in front, as for ornament; as, the stone *facing* of a house; 2, material applied near the edge of a garment for ornament or protection; as, a gray dress with red sleeve *facings.*

fac-sim-i-le (făk-sĭm′ĭ-lē), *n.* an exact reproduction or copy.

Syn. duplicate, imitation, counterpart.

fact (făkt), *n.* 1, a statement of something that has been done or is strictly true; as, give me the *facts;* 2, the quality of being real or actual; as, a question of *fact* rather than of fancy; 3, that which actually happens or is known to be true; as, the *fact* that fire burns.

Syn. detail, item, circumstance, certainty, truth, reality.

fac-tion (făk′shŭn), *n.* a group of persons who attempt, often by destructive means, to bring about changes, as in government or in the existing state of affairs, usually in order to advance their own interests.—*adj.* **fac′tion-al.**

Syn. cabal, gang, combination, clique.

fac-tious (făk′shŭs), *adj.* tending to form factions; hence, quarrelsome.

fac-ti-tious (făk-tĭsh′ŭs), *adj.* artificial; sham; not natural.—*adv.* **fac-ti′tious-ly.**

fac-tor (făk′tĕr), *n.* 1, any one of the causes of a given result; as, opportunity is one of the great *factors* in success; 2, in arithmetic, any of the numbers which, when multi-

plied together, form a given product; as, two and three are the *factors* of six; 3, in commerce, an agent:—*v.t.* to find the factors of (a number).

fac-to-ry (făk′tō-rĭ), *n.* [*pl.* factories], 1, a place where goods are manufactured; 2, an establishment where factors, or agents, carry on business in a foreign country.

fac-to-tum (făk-tō′tŭm), *n.* a person employed to do many small tasks; a handy man.

fac-tu-al (făk′tū-ăl), *adj.* consisting of or concerned with facts; not theoretical.

fac-ul-ty (făk′ŭl-tĭ), *n.* [*pl.* faculties], 1, the ability to act or do; usually, a special ability; a talent; as, he had a *faculty* for painting; 2, a physical or mental power; as, the *faculty* of hearing; 3, a department of learning in a university; the teaching staff in any school.

Syn. aptitude, gift.

fad (făd), *n.* a passing fancy or fashion; as, large hats were the *fad* that year.

fade (fād), *v.i.* [fad-ed, fad-ing], 1, to grow pale or faint; as, colors *fade* in the sun; the music *faded* in the distance; 2, to wither:—*v.t.* to cause to lose color; as, the sun *faded* the curtains.

fa-er-ie or **fa-er-y** (fā′ĕr-ĭ; fâr′ĭ), an old spelling of *fairy.* See **fairy.**

fag (făg), *v.i.* and *v.t.* [fagged, fag-ging], to work or cause to work until exhausted:—*n.* in England, a schoolboy who runs errands, etc., for an older boy.

fag end, the end of a piece of cloth or the untwisted end of a rope; a remnant; the last and poorest part of anything.

fag-ot or **fag-got** (făg′ŭt), *n.* a bundle of sticks bound together.

Fahr. abbreviation for *Fahrenheit.*

Fahr-en-heit (făr′ĕn-hīt; fär′ĕn-hīt), *adj* naming, or pertaining

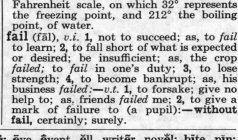

FAGOT

to, the scale on the thermometer introduced by G. D. Fahrenheit:—*n.* the Fahrenheit scale, on which 32° represents the freezing point, and 212° the boiling point, of water.

fail (fāl), *v.i.* 1, not to succeed; as, to *fail* to learn; 2, to fall short of what is expected or desired; be insufficient; as, the crop *failed;* to *fail* in one's duty; 3, to lose strength; 4, to become bankrupt; as, his business *failed:*—*v.t.* 1, to forsake; give no help to; as, friends *failed* me; 2, to give a mark of failure to (a pupil):—**without fail,** certainly; surely.

fail·ing (fāl′ĭng), *n.* a defect; fault.

fail·ure (fāl′ŭr), *n.* **1,** lack of success; as, *failure* in a test; **2,** a falling short of something expected or desired; as, *failure* of crops; *failure* to be on time; **3,** bankruptcy; **4,** an unsuccessful person or thing.

fain (fān), *adv.* willingly; as, *fain* would I do it:—*adj.* glad; willing; as, she was *fain* to keep silence.

faint (fānt), *v.i.* to lose consciousness:—*n.* the act or state of fainting:—*adj.* **1,** weak; about to faint; as, to feel *faint;* **2,** timid; as, a *faint* heart; **3,** dim; indistinct; as, a *faint* sound; **4,** feeble; languid; as, a *faint* attempt.—*n.* **faint′ness.**—*adv.* **faint′ly.**
Syn., *adj.* indistinct, pale, vague.

faint-heart·ed (fānt′här′tĕd), *adj.* timid; lacking courage.

¹fair (fâr), *adj.* **1,** pleasing to the sight; as, a *fair* city; **2,** light in complexion; blond; as, *fair* skin; **3,** without blemish; clean; as, a *fair* name; **4,** not cloudy; clear; as, today will be *fair;* **5,** honest; just; as, *fair* play; **6,** moderately good; as, a *fair* score; **7,** open to lawful pursuit; as, *fair* game:—*adv.* in a fair manner; as, to play *fair.*—*adv.* **fair′ly.**—*n.* **fair′ness.**

²fair (fâr), *n.* **1,** a gathering at a fixed time and place, for the sale or exhibition of farm products, etc.; **2,** a sale of useful and fancy goods, as for charity.

fair-way (fâr′wā′), *n.* in golf, the grassy lane between the tee and the putting green.

fair·y (fâr′ĭ), *n.* [*pl.* fairies], an imaginary being, good or evil, of graceful and tiny human form and supernatural powers:—*adj.* having to do with, or like, fairies. Also spelled **fa′er·ie; fa′er·y.**

fair·y·land (fâr′ĭ-lănd′), *n.* the home of the fairies; hence, an enchanting place.

fairy tale, **1,** a story about fairies, dwarfs, giants, etc.; **2,** hence, any story obviously made up; **3,** a fib.

faith (fāth), *n.* **1,** belief in God; **2,** belief in something without proof; as, he had *faith* that his son was safe; **3,** confidence or trust in another person; as, we had *faith* in the captain; **4,** a promise; as, he broke *faith* with us; **5,** a system of religious belief; as, the Christian *faith.*

faith·ful (fāth′fŏŏl), *adj.* **1,** loyal; as, a *faithful* friend; **2,** trustworthy; as, a *faithful* servant; **3,** accurate; as, a *faithful* copy.—*adv.* **faith′ful·ly.**—*n.* **faith′ful·ness.**
Syn. constant, dependable, devoted.

faith·less (fāth′lĕs), *adj.* **1,** without faith; **2,** untrustworthy; disloyal.—*adv.* **faith′less·ly.**—*n.* **faith′less·ness.**
Syn. unreliable, inconstant, unfaithful.

fake (fāk), *v.t.* [faked, fak-ing], *Colloquial,* **1,** to fix up or change (something) in order

to deceive; **2,** to pretend to have or to do (something) in order to deceive:—*n. Colloquial,* any person, thing, or scheme made to appear different from what it is; a deception.—*n.* **fak′er.**

fa·kir (fȧ-kēr′; fā′kĕr), *n.* in India, a religious beggar.

Fa·lange (fȧ-lănj′), *n.* a political party in Spain, led by Francisco Franco.

fal·chion (fôl′chŭn; fôl′shŭn), *n.* a short, curved sword with a wide blade.

fal·con (fôl′kŭn; fô′kŭn), *n.* any one of several small, swift hawks, especially one trained for hunting.

FALCON (⅟₁₆)

fal·con·er (fôl′kŭn-ẽr; fô′kŭn-ẽr), *n.* one who trains falcons, or hunts game with them.

fal·con·ry (fôl′kŭn-rĭ; fô′kŭn-rĭ), *n.* **1,** the art of training falcons; **2,** the sport of hunting with falcons.

Falk·land Is·lands (fôk′lănd), British islands in the Atlantic Ocean, near the southern end of South America (map 11).

fall (fôl), *v.i.* [*p.t.* fell (fĕl), *p.p.* fall-en (fôl′ĕn), *p.pr.* fall-ing], **1,** to drop from a higher to a lower place; as, the rain *fell;* **2,** to hang down; as, a cloak *falls* in folds; **3,** to be overthrown; as, a city *falls;* **4,** to die; as, to *fall* in battle; **5,** to lose moral dignity or character; as, to *fall* from grace; **6,** to decrease; diminish in value or degree; as, prices *fall;* the thermometer *falls;* **7,** to slope, as land; **8,** to come by chance or by inheritance; as, this part *falls* to me; **9,** to pass gradually into some state of mind or body; as, to *fall* asleep; **10,** to reach or strike; as, moonlight *fell* on the water; **11,** to occur; as, Christmas *fell* on Sunday that year:—*n.* **1,** the act of falling; **2,** something which has fallen; as, a heavy *fall* of rain; **3,** autumn; **4,** ruin or downfall; as, the *fall* of a city; **5,** decrease in price, value, etc.; **6, falls,** *pl.* a cascade.

fall flat, to fail completely; **fall out,** to quarrel; **fall through,** to come to naught.
Syn., v. subside, decline.

fal·la·cious (fȧ-lā′shŭs), *adj.* misleading, due to false reasoning; as, a *fallacious* argument.—*adv.* **fal·la′cious·ly.**

fal·la·cy (făl′ȧ-sĭ), *n.* [*pl.* fallacies], **1,** a mistaken idea; as, it is a *fallacy* that the good die young; **2,** unsound reasoning.

fall·en (fôl′ĕn), *adj.* **1,** ruined; as, a *fallen* empire; **2,** dropped, as leaves, acorns, etc.; **3,** degraded; as, a *fallen* woman; **4,** killed in battle; as, *fallen* soldiers.

fal-li-ble (făl′ĭ-bl), *adj.* liable to be wrong; as, all men are *fallible.*—*n.* **fal′li-bil′i-ty.**

fall-ing star, a shooting star; meteor.

fall—out (fôl′-out′), *n.* the radioactive particles and dust which fall to earth after an atomic explosion.

fal-low (făl′ō), *n.* **1,** land which is plowed, but left unseeded for a season; **2,** the plowing of land without sowing it for a season, in order to increase its fertility:—*adj.* plowed, but not seeded; as, a *fallow* field:—*v.t.* to make or keep fallow.

fallow deer, a small European deer, yellowish in color, with white spots in summer.

Fall Riv-er, a manufacturing city of Massachusetts (map 6).

false (fôls), *adj.* [fals-er, fals-est], **1,** untrue; wrong; as, a *false* idea; **2,** disloyal; **3,** dishonest; lying; as, a *false* witness; **4,** artificial; as, *false* hair; *false* teeth.—*adv.* **false′ly.**—*n.* **false′ness.**
Syn. faithless, counterfeit.

false-hood (fôls′hŏŏd), *n.* a lie.

fal-set-to (fôl-sĕt′ō), *n.* [*pl.* falsettos], a voice, especially a man's voice, pitched unnaturally high; also, one who sings with such a voice:—*adj.* pertaining to a falsetto.

fal-si-fy (fôl′sĭ-fī), *v.t.* [falsified, falsify-ing], **1,** to make false; alter, so as to deceive; as, to *falsify* records; **2,** to prove to be false; disprove.—*n.* **fal′si-fi′er.**—*n.* **fal′si-fi-ca′tion.**

fal-si-ty (fôl′sĭ-tĭ), *n.* [*pl.* falsities], **1,** the quality of being untrue; **2,** that which is untrue; an error; falsehood.

Fal-staff, Sir John (fôl′stȧf), in some of Shakespeare's plays, a fat, jolly knight, noted for his cowardice and his wit.

fal-ter (fôl′tĕr), *v.i.* **1,** to hesitate; waver; as, he started, then *faltered;* **2,** to move unsteadily; **3,** to speak hesitatingly; stammer: —*v.t.* to utter with hesitation.

fame (fām), *n.* reputation; renown.—*adj.* **famed.**
Syn. honor, glory.

fa-mil-iar (fȧ-mĭl′yẽr), *adj.* **1,** well acquainted; intimate; as, *familiar* friends; **2,** well known; as, *familiar* scenes; **3,** taking liberties; bold; **4,** informal; as, a *familiar* greeting.—*adv.* **fa-mil′iar-ly.**

fa-mil-i-ar-i-ty (fȧ-mĭl′ĭ-ăr′ĭ-tĭ), *n.* [*pl.* familiarities], **1,** close acquaintance; **2,** freedom from formality; **3,** an act or speech offensively intimate.

fa-mil-iar-ize (fȧ-mĭl′yẽr-īz), *v.t.* [familiarized, familiariz-ing], **1,** to make (a person) feel well acquainted or at ease with something; as, to *familiarize* oneself with a new job; **2,** to make well known.

fam-i-ly (făm′ĭ-lĭ), *n.* [*pl.* families], **1,** a group of closely related people, as parents and their children; **2,** the children alone of such a group; **3,** a household; a group of persons under one roof; **4,** a body of persons descended from a common ancestor; tribe; clan; **5,** distinguished lineage; as, they are people of good *family;* **6,** a group of things with some common characteristics; as, a mineral *family;* **7,** in biology, a classification of plants or animals, larger than a genus, but smaller than an order; as, the cat *family.*

fam-ine (făm′ĭn), *n.* **1,** extreme scarcity of food; starvation; **2,** shortage of some special thing; as, a cotton *famine.*

fam-ish (făm′ĭsh), *v.t.* to destroy with hunger:—*v.i.* to suffer from extreme hunger.

fa-mous (fā′mŭs), *adj.* renowned; celebrated; as, a *famous* scientist.
Syn. illustrious, eminent, noted.

fa-mous-ly (fā′mŭs-lĭ), *adv.* remarkably well; as, we get on *famously.*

fan (făn), *n.* **1,** any device used to start currents of air; **2,** a small hand device, often one which unfolds into a semicircular shape, used to stir up the air; **3,** anything like a fan in shape; **4,** an enthusiast; as, a football *fan:*—*v.t.* [fanned, fan-ning], **1,** to winnow, or separate, as chaff from grain; **2,** to drive a current of air upon; cool the face of; kindle (a fire); **3,** hence, to rouse, as rage; **4,** *Slang,* in baseball, to strike out (a batter).

fa-nat-ic (fȧ-năt′ĭk), *n.* one who holds extravagant and unreasonable views, especially of religion; one who is carried away by his beliefs:—*adj.* wildly extravagant; extreme.—*adj.* **fa-nat′i-cal.**—*adv.* **fa-nat′i-cal-ly.**—*n.* **fa-nat′i-cism.**

fan-ci-er (făn′sĭ-ẽr), *n.* one who has a special interest in something; as, a cat *fancier;* a bird *fancier.*

fan-ci-ful (făn′sĭ-fŏŏl), *adj.* **1,** led by imagination; **2,** unreal; as, a *fanciful* story; **3,** curiously designed.—*adv.* **fan′ci-ful-ly.** —*n.* **fan′ci-ful-ness.**
Syn. fantastic, imaginative, visionary.

fan-cy (făn′sĭ), *v.t.* [fancied, fancy-ing], **1,** to suppose; as, I *fancy* he will come; **2,** to imagine; as, he *fancies* himself to be king; **3,** to take a liking to:—*adj.* [fan-ci-er, fan-ci-est], **1,** ornamental; not plain; as, *fancy* dress; **2,** extravagant; as, *fancy* prices; **3,** superior to the average; as, *fancy* groceries: —*n.* [*pl.* fancies], **1,** imagination; **2,** an idea; a notion or whim; **3,** a liking.

fane (fān), *n.* *Poetic,* a temple or church.

fan-fare (făn′fâr), *n.* **1,** a flourish of trumpets; **2,** showy display; noisy parade.

ā̆te, ā̆orta, râre, că̆t, ȧsk, fär, ăllow, sofȧ; ēve, ĕvent, ĕll, writẽr, novĕl; bīte, pĭn; nō, ō̆bey, ôr, dŏg, tŏp, cŏllide; ūnit, ūnite, bûrn, cŭt, focŭs; nŏŏn, fŏŏt; mound; coin;

fang (făng), *n.* a long, sharp tooth, as of a dog, wolf, or poisonous snake.

fan-tas-tic (făn-tăs'-tĭk) or **fan-tas-ti-cal** (-tăs'tĭ-kăl), *adj.* 1, imaginary; unreal; as, *fantastic* fears; 2, odd; grotesque; as, shadows assume *fantastic* shapes.—*adv.* **fan-tas'-ti-cal-ly.**
Syn. strange, absurd.

FANGS OF A RATTLE-SNAKE

A, fangs; B, sac containing poison fluid; C, muscle that forces poison through the hollow fang; D, duct leading to sac (B) from gland which secretes the poison.

fan-ta-sy (făn'tȧ-sĭ; făn'tȧ-zĭ), *n.* [*pl.* fan-tasies], 1, imagination; 2, a product of the imagination. Also, **phan'-ta-sy.**

far (fär), *adj.* [far-ther, far-thest], 1, distant in time or space; as, the *far* past; a *far* land; 2, more distant of two; as, the *far* side; 3, reaching to great distances; as, a *far* journey:—*adv.* 1, to or at a great, or definite, distance in time or space; as, to go *far*; to go only so *far*; 2, by a great deal; very much; as, he is *far* wiser than I am.

far-a-way (fär'ȧ-wā'), *adj.* 1, distant; remote; 2, dreamy; as, a *faraway* look.

farce (färs), *n.* 1, a play full of exaggerated situations intended to be very funny; 2, a ridiculous sham; as, the election was a mere *farce.*—*adj.* **far'ci-cal.**—*adv.* **far'-ci-cal-ly.**

fare (fâr), *v.i.* [fared, far-ing], 1, to experience either good or bad fortune; as, to *fare* well or ill; 2, to journey; travel; 3, to be fed; as, I *fared* well at lunch:—*n.* 1, the sum paid for a journey; 2, a person paying this sum; 3, food.

Far East, the East Indies and that part of eastern Asia which includes India, China, Japan, and minor neighboring regions.

fare-well (fâr'wĕl'), *interj.* good-by!—*adj.* final; parting; as, a *farewell* tour:—*n.* (fâr'-wĕl'), 1, a wish of welfare at parting; a good-by; 2, a departure; as, a sad *farewell.*

far-fetched (fär'fĕcht'), *adj.* forced; strained; as, the joke was very *farfetched.*

far–flung (fär'-flŭng'), *adj.* extending to a great distance; extensive.

farm (färm), *n.* 1, a single holding of tillable land with the buildings belonging to it; 2, any other area for breeding or growing anything; as, a peach *farm*, an oyster *farm*: —**farm club,** in sports, a team subsidized by a major league club to develop players: —*v.t.* and *v.i.* to cultivate (land); operate a farm.—*n.* **farm'ing.**—*n.* **farm'er.**

farm-house (färm'hous'), *n.* the dwelling house on a farm.

farm-stead (färm'stĕd), *n.* a farm.

farm-yard (färm'yärd'), *n.* a barnyard; also, the area about farm buildings.

far-o (fâr'ō), *n.* a gambling card game.

far–off (fär'-ôf'), *adj.* distant; remote.

Far-ra-gut (făr'ȧ-gŭt), David Glasgow (1801–1870), an American admiral.

far–reach-ing (fär'rē'chĭng), *adj.* having a wide influence or effect.

far-ri-er (făr'ĭ-ẽr), *n.* one who shoes horses.—*n.* **far'ri-er-y.**

far-row (făr'ō), *n.* a litter of pigs:—*v.i.* and *v.t.* to give birth to (a litter of pigs).

far-see-ing (fär'sē'ĭng), *adj.* having foresight; farsighted.

far-sight-ed (fär'sī'tĕd), *adj.* 1, able to see distant objects more clearly than near ones; 2, having good judgment; prudent.—*n.* **far'sight'ed-ness.**

far-ther (fär'thẽr), *adj.* [*comp.* of *far*], 1, more distant; as, the *farther* side; 2, additional; further; as, to take no *farther* notice:—*adv.* 1, to or at a greater distance; as, to go *farther*; 2, moreover.

far-thest (fär'thĕst), *adj.* [*superl.* of *far*], most distant:—*adv.* to or at the greatest distance.

far-thing (fär'thĭng), *n.* a British coin worth one fourth of a British penny.

far-thin-gale (fär'thĭng-gāl), *n.* a hoop skirt distended by circles of whalebone, worn by women in the 16th and 17th centuries.

FARTHINGALE

fas-ci-nate (făs'ĭ-nāt), *v.t.* [fascinat-ed, fascinat-ing], 1, to bewitch or hold motionless by some strange power; as, snakes are said to *fascinate* small birds; 2, hence, to enchant; charm irresistibly.—*adv.* **fas'ci-nat'ing-ly.**—*n.* **fas'ci-na'tion.**
Syn. enrapture, bewitch, enchant, delight.

Fas-cist (făsh'ĭst; făs'ĭst), *n.* [*pl.* Fascisti (fȧ-shĭs'tē; fä-shē'stē)], a member of an Italian organization (the Fascisti) formed in 1919 to oppose communism, socialism, and the like. Under Mussolini, the organization assumed control of the government in October, 1922.—*n.* **Fas'cism.**

fash-ion (făsh'ŭn), *n.* 1, the shape or form of anything; 2, manner or way of doing something; as, he eats in a queer *fashion*; 3, the prevailing style or custom at any time, especially in dress; as, high shoes are no longer the *fashion*:—*v.t.* to mold, shape, or form.—*n.* **fash'ion-er.**
Syn., n. style, vogue, mode.

fash-ion-a-ble (făsh'ŭn-ȧ-bl), *adj.* 1, according to the prevailing style or fashion at the moment; 2, pertaining to polite society.—adv. **fash′ion-a-bly.**

¹**fast** (fȧst), adj. 1, securely fixed; attached; as, rocks *fast* in the ground; 2, faithful; steadfast; as, *fast* friends; 3, deep; sound; as, a *fast* sleeper; 4, not fading; as, *fast* colors; 5, rapid; swift; as, a *fast* runner; also, allowing quick motion; as, a *fast* track; 6, ahead of the standard time; as, my watch is *fast;* 7, wild; too gay; as, *fast* society:—adv. 1, fixedly; firmly; 2, rapidly; 3, wildly; too gaily; 4, deeply; as, *fast* asleep.

Syn., adj. secure, fleet, swift.

²**fast** (fȧst), v.i. to take little or no food:—n. the act or period of fasting.

fas-ten (fȧs′n), v.t. 1, to fix securely, as a door; cause to hold together, as a dress; to attach to something else; as, to *fasten* a shelf to a wall; 2, to keep fixed steadily, as the attention; 3, to attach, as blame:—v.i. to take hold; become attached.—n. **fas′ten-er.**

fas-ten-ing (fȧs′n-ĭng), n. something that fastens; a lock, chain, clasp, etc.

fas-tid-i-ous (fȧs-tĭd′ĭ-ŭs), adj. hard to please; daintily particular.—adv. **fas-tid′i-ous-ly.**—n. **fas-tid′i-ous-ness.**

fast-ness (fȧst′nĕs), n. 1, swiftness; 2, a stronghold; as, a mountain *fastness.*

fat (făt), adj. [fat-ter, fat-test], 1, plump; fleshy; 2, greasy; rich; as, *fat* gravy; 3, well filled or stocked; as, a *fat* wallet; 4, profitable; as, a *fat* job; 5, fertile; as, a *fat* soil:—n. 1, an oily, yellow or white substance found in animal and vegetable tissues; 2, the best or richest part of anything:—v.t. [fat-ted, fat-ting], to make fat. —n. **fat′ness.**

fa-tal (fā′tăl), adj. 1, causing death; as, a *fatal* accident; 2, causing great harm; as, a *fatal* error.—adv. **fa′tal-ly.**

fa-tal-i-ty (fȧ-tăl′ĭ-tĭ), n. [pl. fatalities], 1, a condition of being doomed by fate; as, a *fatality* attends everything he tries to do; 2, a fatal influence; deadly quality; as, the *fatality* of cancer; 3, a calamity; also, death in a disaster; as, there were only two *fatalities* in the fire.

fate (fāt), n. 1, a power beyond man's control that is believed to determine events; 2, that which is decided by fate; one's lot or destiny:—**the Fates,** in mythology, the three goddesses who preside over the destinies of mankind.—adj. **fat′ed.**

fate-ful (fāt′fŏŏl), adj. 1, important; significant; as, tomorrow is the *fateful* day; 2, prophetic; as, a *fateful* tolling of the bell; 3, deadly; as, a *fateful* blow; 4, controlled by fate.—adv. **fate′ful-ly.**

fa-ther (fä′thĕr), n. 1, a male parent; 2, an ancestor; 3, one who stands in the relation of a father; 4, an originator or founder; 5, a clergyman, especially a Roman Catholic priest:—**Father,** God:—v.t. 1, to beget or adopt (a child); 2, to assume authorship of or accept responsibility for; as, to *father* a plan.—n. **fa′ther-hood.**—adj. **fa′ther-less.**—adj. **fa′ther-ly.**

fa-ther—in—law (fä′thĕr-ĭn-lô′), n. [pl. fathers-in-law], the father of one's husband or of one's wife.

fa-ther-land (fä′thĕr-lănd′), n. one's native country.

fath-om (făth′ŭm), n. a measure of length equal to six feet:—v.t. 1, to find the depth of (water); 2, to reach an understanding of; as, I was able to *fathom* his meaning.

fath-om-less (făth′ŭm-lĕs), adj. 1, so deep that the bottom cannot be reached; 2, not possible to understand; as, a *fathomless* mystery.

fa-tigue (fȧ-tēg′), n. weariness resulting from labor; bodily or mental exhaustion:—v.t. and v.i. [fatigued, fati-guing], to weary; tire or become wearied.

Syn., n. lassitude, tiredness.

fat-ten (făt′n), v.t. and v.i. to make or become fat.

fat-ty (făt′ĭ), adj. [fat-ti-er, fat-ti-est], 1, containing fat; 2, greasy; oily.

fat-u-ous (făt′ū-ŭs), adj. silly; conceitedly vain.—adv. **fat′u-ous-ly.**

fau-cet (fô′sĕt), n. a device for controlling

FAUCETS

1, ordinary faucet, partly cut away; 2, basin faucet; 3, faucet for side of a building, threaded for hose connection; 4, faucet for a barrel, with device for locking.

the flow of liquid from a pipe or other container.

faugh (fô), interj. disgusting!

fault (fôlt), n. 1, a weakness in character; 2, a slight offence; 3, blame or responsibility for something; as, it was not his *fault;* 4, a break in layers of rock that were previously continuous:—**find fault,** to complain.—n. and adj. **fault′find-ing.**

FAULT, def. 4

A,A, line of fault; B,B, strata that at one time connected at the same level.

Syn. error, weakness, flaw, failing.

fault-find-er (fôlt′fīn′dẽr), *n.* one who complains; one who constantly criticizes.

fault-less (fôlt′lĕs), *adj.* without defect; perfect.—*adv.* **fault′less-ly.**

fault-y (fôl′tĭ), *adj.* [fault-i-er, fault-i-est], imperfect; defective.—*adv.* **fault′i-ly.**—*n.* **fault′i-ness.**

faun (fôn), *n.* in mythology, a woodland deity, half-human, with pointed ears, small horns and, sometimes, a goat's tail and hind legs.

fau-na (fô′nȧ), *n.* the animals belonging to a special region or period; as, the *fauna* of the African jungle.

Faust (foust), Johann (1480?–1540?), a German magician and physician, the subject of a drama by Goethe and of an opera by Gounod.

FAUN

fa-vor (fā′vẽr), *n.* **1,** an act of kindness; as, do me a *favor;* **2,** approval; as, he looked on with *favor;* **3,** partiality; special consideration; as, he asked no *favor;* **4,** a small gift or token:—*v.t.* **1,** to regard with good will; approve; **2,** to show partiality to; **3,** to make possible or easy; as, fair weather *favors* our plan; **4,** to oblige; as, *favor* me with your attention; **5,** to look like (a person); as, she *favors* her mother.

fa-vor-a-ble (fā′vẽr-ȧ-bl), *adj.* **1,** expressing approval; as, a *favorable* account; **2,** advantageous; as, *favorable* weather; **3,** giving assent; helpful.—*adv.* **fa′vor-a-bly.** —*n.* **fa′vor-a-ble-ness.**

fa-vored (fā′vẽrd), *adj.* **1,** treated with partiality; as, a *favored* friend; **2,** having a specified aspect; as, ill-*favored.*

fa-vor-ite (fā′vẽr-ĭt), *n.* **1,** one who or that which is particularly liked; **2,** a contestant thought to have the best chance of winning:—*adj.* preferred; best-liked; as, a *favorite* book.

fa-vor-it-ism (fā′vẽr-ĭt-ĭzm), *n.* a showing of undue favor to some while neglecting others.

fa-vour (fā′vẽr), *n.* a British spelling of *favor.* Similarly, **favourable, favourably, favourableness, favoured, favourite, favouritism.**

Fawkes (fôks), Guy (1570–1606), a conspirator in the "Gunpowder Plot" of 1605.

¹**fawn** (fôn), *n.* a deer less than one year old:—*adj.* of a light yellowish brown; as, she bought a *fawn* coat.

²**fawn** (fôn), *v.i.* **1,** to show pleasure or affection by wagging the tail, whining, etc.,

as a dog does; **2,** to seek favor by flattery and cringing behavior.

Syn. stoop, creep, grovel.

fay (fā), *n.* an elf; a fairy.

fe-al-ty (fē′ăl-tĭ), *n.* in the feudal period, the pledge of a vassal to be faithful to his lord; pledge, loyalty; a pledge of allegiance.

fear (fēr), *n.* **1,** a feeling of alarm or dread of possible evil or danger; **2,** reverence; as, the *fear* of God:—*v.t.* **1,** to regard with dread; be afraid of; **2,** to revere:—*v.i.* to be afraid.

Syn., n., horror, fright, terror, panic.

fear-ful (fēr′fool), *adj.* **1,** causing fear or awe; terrible; as, a *fearful* sight; **2,** full of alarm; timid; lacking courage.—*adv.* **fear′-ful-ly.**—*n.* **fear′ful-ness.**

Syn. terrible, frightful, timorous.

fear-less (fēr′lĕs), *adj.* without fear; not afraid; courageous.—*adv.* **fear′less-ly.** —*n.* **fear′less-ness.**

Syn. brave, daring, valorous.

fea-si-ble (fē′zĭ-bl), *adj.* capable of being done; possible; as, a *feasible* scheme.

feast (fēst), *n.* **1,** a lavish meal; **2,** a festival in memory of an event; especially, a religious festival; **3,** anything pleasing to the taste or mind:—*v.t.* **1,** to make a rich meal for; **2,** to delight; as, to *feast* the eyes on beauty:—*v.i.* to partake of a feast.

Syn., n. banquet, celebration, repast.

feat (fēt), *n.* an act or deed displaying great courage, strength, skill, etc.; as, flying the Atlantic is a remarkable *feat.*

Syn. act, exploit, accomplishment.

feath-er (fĕth′ẽr), *n.* one of the light outgrowths from the skin of a bird:—*v.t.* **1,** to cover or line with feathers; **2,** to turn the blade of (an oar) horizontally as it leaves the water:—*v.i.* **1,** to become covered with feathers; **2,** to feather one's oars while rowing.

feath-er-y (fĕth′ẽr-ĭ), *adj.* like a feather in shape, lightness, or softness; as, a *feathery* fern.—*n.* **feath′er-i-ness.**

FEATHER
A, vane; B, quill.

fea-ture (fē′tūr), *n.* **1,** something noticeable about a thing; as, the architectural *features* of a church; **2,** the chief attraction on a program; as, her dance was the *feature;* **3,** any part of the face, as the eyes, chin, etc.; **4,** **features,** the whole face:—*v.t.* [featured, featur-ing], **1,** to portray the features of; outline; **2,** to make prominent; as, to *feature* an actor. —*adj.* **fea′ture-less.**

Syn., n. trait, mark, characteristic.

---

go; join; yet; sing; chin; show; thin, *th*en; hw, *wh*y; zh, azure; ū, Ger. für or Fr. lune; ö, Ger. schön or Fr. *feu*; n̈, Fr. e*n*fant, no*m*; kh, Ger. ach or ich. See pages ix–x.

Feb. abbreviation for *February.*

Feb-ru-ar-y (fĕb′rŏŏ-ĕr′ĭ), *n.* the second month of the year, having 28 days, or 29 days in leap years, which occur every fourth year.

fe-cund (fē′kŭnd; fĕk′ŭnd), *adj.* fruitful; fertile; productive; as, a *fecund* mind.—*n.* **fe-cun′di-ty** (fê-kŭn′dĭ-tĭ).

fed (fĕd), past tense and past participle of *feed.*

fed-er-al (fĕd′ĕr-ăl), *adj.* relating to a nation formed by the union of several smaller states; as, a *federal* republic.

Fed-er-al (fĕd′ĕr-ăl), *adj.* **1,** relating to the government of the United States; as, *Federal* taxes; **2,** favoring the North in the War between the States; as, a *Federal* soldier:—*n.* a person on the side of the Union in the War between the States.

Fed-er-al Cap-i-tal Ter-ri-tor-y, now called Australian Capital Territory, site of Canberra, federal capital of Australia.

Fed-er-al-ist (fĕd′ĕr-ăl-ĭst), *n.* in early U.S. history, one who urged the formation of a strong central government:—**federal-ist,** a person who favors the union of states into one nation.

fed-er-ate (fĕd′ĕr-āt), *v.t.* and *v.i.* [federat-ed, federat-ing], to combine (states or societies) into a union.

fed-er-a-tion (fĕd′ĕr-ā′shŭn), *n.* a union of a number of states or societies, in which each keeps control over its own local affairs; as, a *federation* of clubs.

fee (fē), *n.* **1,** payment for a service or a privilege; as, a lawyer's *fee;* a license *fee;* **2,** under the feudal system, land held from an overlord; also, the terms under which such land was held; a fief; as, to hold land in *fee:*—**fee simple,** an estate held by a person in his own right, without restrictions:—*v.t.* [feed, fee-ing], to give a tip or fee to.

Syn., tip, salary, wage, pay.

fee-ble (fē′bl), *adj.* [fee-bler, fee-blest], **1,** without strength; **2,** lacking in vigor; faint; as, a *feeble* effort.—*n.* **fee′ble-ness.**—*adv.* **fee′bly.**

Syn. slight, frail, decrepit.

fee-ble–mind-ed (fē′bl=mīn′dĕd), *adj.* having very little power to think or to learn.—*n.* **fee′ble–mind′ed-ness.**

feed (fēd), *v.t.* [fed (fĕd), feed-ing], **1,** to supply with food; as, to *feed* a beggar; **2,** to put food into the mouth of; as, to *feed* a baby; **3,** to give as food; as, to *feed* meat to a dog; **4,** to nourish; as, soil *feeds* plants; **5,** to supply (a fire) with fuel:—*v.i.* to take food; as, the pup *fed* eagerly:—*n.* food for animals; fodder.

feed-er (fēd′ẽr), *n.* **1,** an eater; as, a big feeder; **2,** a branch stream, railway, or the like, supplying a main channel or line; **3,** a device supplying material to a machine.

feel (fēl), *v.t.* [felt (fĕlt), feel-ing], **1,** to examine by touch; as, to *feel* a person's pulse; **2,** to be aware of (something) by touch; as, I *felt* rain; **3,** to have a sense of; as, to *feel* pity; **4,** to be moved or disturbed by; as, to *feel* a slight; **5,** to be sure of, without proof; as, I *feel* it to be so:—*v.i.* **1,** to search by touch; grope; as, to *feel* for a match; **2,** to be aware of being in some definite condition of mind or body; as, to *feel* faint; **3,** to have sympathy; as, to *feel* deeply for someone; **4,** to seem to the touch; as, the air *feels* damp:—*n.* a quality perceived by touch; as, the silky *feel* of velvet.

feel-er (fēl′ẽr), *n.* **1,** an organ of touch, as one of a cat's whiskers; **2,** a remark made to draw out the opinions of others; as, to throw out a *feeler.*

FEELERS (F,F) of a cricket.

feel-ing (fēl′ĭng), *n.* **1,** the sense, usually called *touch,* by which a person tells hot from cold, rough from smooth, etc.; **2,** any sensation of the skin, or of the body in general; as, a *feeling* of pain, cold, hunger, etc.; **3,** an emotion of hope, hate, love, or the like; **4,** emotional excitement; as, *feeling* over the game ran high; **5,** opinion; as, it is my *feeling* that you ought to go; **6,** **feelings,** sensitive nature; as, to hurt her *feelings.*

feet (fēt), plural of *foot.*

feign (fān), *v.t.* and *v.i.* to pretend; as, to *feign* illness.—*n.* **feign′er.**

feint (fānt), *n.* a pretense; especially, a pretense of attack at one point while really attacking at another:—*v.i.* to make a sham thrust; as, to *feint* with the left hand and strike with the right.

feld-spar (fĕld′spär′; fĕl′spär′), *n.* a crystalline mineral, usually white or pink, found in many common rocks.

fe-lic-i-tate (fê-lĭs′ĭ-tāt), *v.t.* [felicitat-ed, felicitat-ing], to congratulate; as, to *felici-tate* a boy on winning a prize.—*n.* **fe-lic′-i-ta′tion.**

fe-lic-i-tous (fê-lĭs′ĭ-tŭs), *adj.* well-chosen; as, a *felicitous* compliment.

fe-lic-i-ty (fê-lĭs′ĭ-tĭ), *n.* [*pl.* felicities], **1,** great happiness; also, a source of happiness; **2,** a pleasing way of speaking or writing; also, a well-chosen expression.

Syn. bliss, enjoyment, contentment.

fe-line (fē′līn), *adj.* catlike; as, a *feline* walk; also, sly; treacherous.

¹fell (fĕl), past tense of *fall*.

²fell (fĕl), *n.* an animal's skin or fleece.

³fell (fĕl), *v.t.* **1**, to cause to fall; cut down, as a tree; knock down, as by a blow; **2**, to fold over and sew down flat, as a seam:—*n.* a seam made by felling.

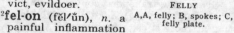

FELLED SEAM

1, stitch the pieces of material, A,B, as at *a*; 2, fold B over A; 3, fold B down upon A and stitch through B and A at *c*.

⁴fell (fĕl), *adj.* cruel; savage; terrible; deadly.

fel-loe (fĕl´ō), *n.* the outer rim of a wheel; a felly. See **felly.**

fel-low (fĕl´ō), *n.* **1**, a companion; as, a *fellow* in misery; **2**, one of a pair; a mate; match; as, the *fellow* of this shoe; **3**, *Colloquial*, a man or boy; anybody; as, a *fellow* has to eat; also, a girl's beau; **4**, an honored member, as of certain learned societies; also, a student supported by an endowment:—*adj.* associated with others; as, *fellow* members.

fel-low-ship (fĕl´ō-shĭp), *n.* **1**, membership in a group, as a church; also, the group itself; as, to admit to *fellowship*; **2**, friendly association; companionship; as, I enjoy his *fellowship*; **3**, a position endowed to enable the holder to continue study, free of expense for board, tuition, etc., as in a university.

Syn. companionship, comradeship.

fel-ly (fĕl´ĭ), *n.* [*pl.* fellies], the outer rim of a wheel. Also, **fel´loe.**

¹fel-on (fĕl´ŭn), *n.* a person who is guilty of a serious crime.

Syn. criminal, convict, evildoer.

FELLY

A,A, felly; B, spokes; C, felly plate.

²fel-on (fĕl´ŭn), *n.* a painful inflammation on a finger or toe, usually near the nail.

fe-lo-ni-ous (fĕ-lō´nĭ-ŭs), *adj.* wicked; criminal.—*adv.* **fe-lo´ni-ous-ly.**

fel-o-ny (fĕl´ō-nĭ), *n.* [*pl.* felonies], a serious crime, as murder or robbery.

¹felt (fĕlt), past tense and past participle of *feel*.

²felt (fĕlt), *n.* a fabric made of wool, hair, and fur, matted or forced together by pressure:—*adj.* made of felt; as, a *felt* hat:—*v.t.* to mat into a mass; as, to *felt* wool together; also, to cover with felt.

fem. abbreviation for *feminine*.

fe-male (fē´māl), *adj.* having to do with or belonging to the sex that bears young:—*n.* a person or an animal of this sex.

fem-i-nine (fĕm´ĭ-nĭn), *adj.* **1**, relating to women; like women; as, *feminine* fashions or ways; **2**, in grammar, of the gender to which names of females belong; as, "doe" is a *feminine* noun.

Syn. womanly, womanish, female.

fe-mur (fē´mẽr), *n.* [*pl.* femurs or femora (fĕm´ō-ra̤)], the thigh bone.

fen (fĕn), *n.* low, marshy land.

fence (fĕns), *n.* **1**, a barrier or boundary of stone, wood, or other material; **2**, a receiver of stolen goods:—*v.t.* [fenced, fencing], to enclose with a fence; as, to *fence* a field:—*v.i.* to practice the use of swords or foils.—*n.* **fenc´er.**

fenc-ing (fĕn´sĭng), *n.* **1**, the art of using a foil or sword; **2**, materials used for making a fence; **3**, the chain of fences on a plot of land.

FENCING, def. 1

fend (fĕnd), *v.t.* to ward off, as a blow:—*v.i.* to provide; as, he must *fend* for himself.

fend-er (fĕn´dẽr), *n.* **1**, a device on the front of a locomotive or a streetcar to prevent or lessen injuries from collisions; **2**, a metal guard in front of a fireplace; **3**, a guard over an automobile or bicycle wheel.

fen-nel (fĕn´ĕl), *n.* a fragrant plant of the carrot family. Its seeds are used in cooking and in medicine.

Fer-di-nand (fûr´dĭ-nănd), (1452–1516), a king of Spain. His wife was Queen Isabella, who befriended Columbus.

FENDERS

1, automobile fender; 2, 3, fenders in front of an open fire.

fer-ment (fûr´mĕnt), *n.* **1**, a substance, as yeast, that causes chemical change with effervescence; **2**, a state of excitement; unrest; as, the town is in a *ferment*:—*v.i.* (fẽr-mĕnt´), **1**, to be in a state of fermentation, as milk when it turns sour, or cider when it begins to bubble; **2**, to become stirred up or excited:—*v.t.* **1**, to cause fermentation in; **2**, to excite or stir up.

fer-men-ta-tion (fûr´mĕn-tā´shŭn), *n.* **1**, a change, such as is caused by yeast, producing gas bubbles, alcohol, or acid, as in the souring of milk, the working of cider, etc.; **2**, excitement; unrest.

fern (fûrn), *n.* any one of many flowerless plants with broad, feathery, leaflike fronds. —*n.* **fern′er-y.**

Fer-nán-dez (fĕr-nän′dĕz; fär-nän′dĕth), Juan (1536–1602?), a Spanish explorer.

fe-ro-cious (fĕ-rō′shŭs), *adj.* savage; fierce; as, a *ferocious* tiger.
   Syn. wild, barbarous, brutal, inhuman.

MAIDENHAIR FERN

fe-roc-i-ty (fĕ-rŏs′ĭ-tĭ), *n.* [*pl.* ferocities], savageness; fierceness; inhuman cruelty.

Fer-ra-ra (fĕr-rä′rä), a province in northern Italy; also, a city, its capital.

fer-ret (fĕr′ĕt), *n.* a weasel-like animal used to hunt rats and rabbits:—*v.t.* **1,** to hunt (rats, etc.) with ferrets; **2,** to search perseveringly for; as, to *ferret* out a secret.—*n.* **fer′ret-er.**

FERRET (⅛)

fer-rule (fĕr′ĭl; fĕr′ōōl), *n.* a metal ring or cap placed around the end of a stick, tool handle, or the like, to strengthen it.

fer-ry (fĕr′ĭ), *n.* [*pl.* ferries], **1,** a ferryboat; **2,** a place where such a boat lands:—*v.t.* [ferried, ferry-ing], **1,** to take across a body of water on a ferry, or across water or other barrier by plane; also, to cross by ferry; as, to *ferry* the lake; **2,** to deliver (planes) by flying them to their destination:—*v.i.* to go by ferry.

fer-ry-boat (fĕr′ĭ-bōt′), *n.* a boat used for carrying people or things across a river, lake, or like body of water.

fer-tile (fûr′tĭl), *adj.* **1,** producing abundantly; fruitful; as, *fertile* land; **2,** capable of producing seed; as, a *fertile* flower; **3,** capable of developing; as, a *fertile* seed or egg.—*n.* **fer-til′i-ty.**
   Syn. plenteous, productive.

fer-ti-lize (fûr′tĭ-līz), *v.t.* [fertilized, fertiliz-ing], to make productive; especially, to supply with plant food; as, to *fertilize* soil.—*n.* **fer′ti-li-za′tion.**

fer-ti-liz-er (fûr′tĭ-lī′zẽr), *n.* any plant food, as manure or bone meal, put on land to make it richer or more fertile.

fer-ule (fĕr′ōōl; fĕr′ĭl), *n.* a stick or ruler used to punish children:—*v.t.* [feruled, ferul-ing], to punish with a ferule.

fer-vent (fûr′vĕnt), *adj.* warmly felt; intense; earnest; as, a *fervent* prayer.—*adv.* **fer′vent-ly.**—*n.* **fer′ven-cy.**

fer-vid (fûr′vĭd), *adj.* fiery in feeling; earnest; as, a *fervid* speech.—*adv.* **fer′vid-ly.**—*n.* **fer′vid-ness.**
   Syn. impetuous, earnest, zealous.

fer-vor (fûr′vẽr), *n.* glowing warmth of feeling; zeal; as, patriotic *fervor*.

fes-cue (fĕs′kū), *n.* any one of several kinds of grasses, some of which are valuable for pasturage or for lawns.

fes-tal (fĕs′tăl), *adj.* relating to a feast or holiday; joyful; as, her birthday was a *festal* occasion.

fes-ter (fĕs′tẽr), *v.i.* **1,** to become filled with pus; as, his wound *festered;* **2,** to linger painfully; cause a sore feeling; rankle; as, the insult *festered* in his mind: —*n.* a pus-forming sore.

fes-ti-val (fĕs′tĭ-văl), *n.* a time of rejoicing and feasting, usually in honor of some great event; a special public celebration; as, a Thanksgiving *festival*.

fes-tive (fĕs′tĭv), *adj.* **1,** suitable to a feast or holiday; **2,** gay; as, a *festive* room.
   Syn. joyful, festal, sportive.

fes-tiv-i-ty (fĕs-tĭv′ĭ-tĭ), *n.* [*pl.* festivities], joyful celebration, as on a holiday; merrymaking; social gaiety.

fes-toon (fĕs-tōōn′), *n.* a decorative chain of flowers, or the like, hung in curves; also, a carved likeness of such a chain:—*v.t.* to decorate with festoons; as, the church was *festooned* with ivy.

FESTOON

fetch (fĕch), *v.t.* **1,** to go after and bring; as, *fetch* me a pen; **2,** to sell for; as, the land *fetched* a high price.
   Syn. carry, transport, convey, bear.

fetch-ing (fĕch′ĭng), *adj. Colloquial,* pleasing; attractive; as, a *fetching* hat.

fête (fāt), *n.* a festival; an entertainment; expecially, an elaborate outdoor entertainment:—*v.t.* [fêt-ed, fêt-ing], to entertain as the guest of honor. Also, **fete.**

fet-id (fĕt′ĭd; fē′tĭd), *adj.* giving forth an offensive smell; stinking.
   Syn. rotten, putrid, noxious.

fe-tish or **fe-tich** (fē′tĭsh; fĕt′ĭsh), *n.* **1,** any object, as a wooden image, supposed to have magic power; **2,** any object of unreasoning devotion; as, money is a miser's *fetish*.—*n.* **fe′tish-ism.**

FETISHES, def. 1

fet·lock (fĕt′lŏk), *n.* a projection on a horse's leg just above and behind the hoof; also, a tuft of hair growing on this projection. (See *horse*, illustration.)

fet·ter (fĕt′ẽr), *n.* **1**, a chain to bind the feet; **2**, a restraint; hindrance; as, the *fetters* of ignorance:—*v.t.* to put in chains; also, to hinder; restrain.

fet·tle (fĕt′l), *n.* the state of being prepared or in condition; as, the runner is in fine *fettle*.

fe·tus or **foe·tus** (fē′tŭs), *n.* the young of an animal in the later stages of development before it is born or hatched.

feud (fūd), *n.* a quarrel, generally of long standing, between clans or families.

feu·dal (fū′dăl), *adj.* relating to the method of holding land in the Middle Ages:—**feudal system**, the form of political organization common in Europe in the Middle Ages, based on the relationship between lord and vassal, the vassal holding land from his lord in return for military and other service.

feu·dal·ism (fū′dăl·ĭzm), *n.* the feudal system; also, its laws and customs.

feu·da·tor·y (fū′dá·tôr′ĭ), *n.* a person who held land in return for service to a feudal superior; a vassal; as, the duke was a *feudatory* of the king:—*adj.* owing feudal service to an overlord.

fe·ver (fē′vẽr), *n.* **1**, a diseased condition marked by weakness, quick pulse, and high body temperature; also, a disease causing such symptoms; **2**, great nervous excitement; as, a *fever* of anxiety.

fe·ver·ish (fē′vẽr·ĭsh), *adj.* **1**, having a fever, especially a slight degree of fever; **2**, restless and fitful; as, *feverish* activity.—*adv.* **fe′ver·ish·ly.**

few (fū), *adj.* small in number; not many; as, his words were *few*.—*n.* **few′ness.**

Fez (fĕz), a commercial city in French Morocco, in northern Africa (map 14).

fez (fĕz), *n.* [*pl.* fezzes], a red felt, tasseled cap, formerly worn by Turkish men.

FEZ

ff. abbreviation for *folios*, *following* (pages or passages), and Italian *fortissimo*, meaning *very loudly*.

fi·an·cé (fē′än·sā′; fē·än′sā; *French*, fyäṅ′sā′), *n.* a man engaged to be married.—*n. fem.* **fi·an·cée** (fē′än·sā′; fē·än′sā; *French*, fyäṅ′sā′).

fi·as·co (fē·ăs′kō), *n.* [*pl.* fiascoes; fiascos], a complete or laughable failure.

fi·at (fī′ăt; fī′ăt), *n.* an official command or decree; as, a royal *fiat*.

fib (fĭb), *n.* a petty lie:—*v.i.* [fibbed, fibbing], to tell fibs.—*n.* **fib′ber.**

fi·ber or **fi·bre** (fī′bẽr), *n.* **1**, one of many slender, threadlike parts forming certain plant and animal substances; as, flax *fibers*; nerve *fibers*; also, a substance made up of such parts; **2**, raw material which can be separated into threads and spun or woven; as, cotton *fiber*; **3**, quality or character; as, a man of tough *fiber*.

fi·brin (fī′brĭn), *n.* a white threadlike substance formed when blood clots.

fi·brous (fī′brŭs), *adj.* **1**, made of threadlike stuff; as, *fibrous* bark; **2**, threadlike in shape; as, *fibrous* roots.

-fi·ca·tion (-fĭ·kā′shŭn), a suffix forming nouns corresponding to verbs ending in *-fy*, and meaning the act or process of; as, electri*fication*.

fick·le (fĭk′l), *adj.* uncertain; changeable; as, *fickle* weather.—*n.* **fick′le·ness.** *Syn.* capricious, freakish, shifting.

fic·tion (fĭk′shŭn), *n.* **1**, novels, short stories, etc., telling of imaginary events and characters; **2**, anything imagined or invented as contrasted with things which are real or true; as, that story of his wealth is a *fiction*.—*adj.* **fic′tion·al.** *Syn.* falsehood, fabrication, fable.

fic·ti·tious (fĭk·tĭsh′ŭs), *adj.* imagined; not real; as, a *fictitious* character. *Syn.* assumed, artificial.

fid·dle (fĭd′l), *n. Colloquial,* a violin:—*v.i.* [fid-dled, fid-dling], **1**, to play the violin; **2**, to trifle; as, to *fiddle* at writing:—*v.t. Colloquial,* to play (a tune) on a violin; as, he can *fiddle* the latest songs.

fid·dler (fĭd′lẽr), *n.* **1**, a violinist; **2**, a kind of burrowing crab having one claw much larger than the other: also called *fiddler crab*.

FIDDLER (⅓), def. 2

fid·dle·stick (fĭd′l·stĭk′), *n.* a violin bow:—**fiddlesticks**, *interj.* nonsense!

fi·del·i·ty (fĭ·dĕl′ĭ·tĭ; fī·dĕl′ĭ·tĭ), *n.* [*pl.* fidelities], faithfulness to a person, cause, or trust; trustworthiness. *Syn.* allegiance, devotion, constancy.

fidg·et (fĭj′ĕt), *v.i.* to be restless and uneasy; as, the boys *fidgeted* during the long play:—*v.t.* to make uneasy; worry; as, the heat *fidgets* me:—*n.* **1**, a restless person; as, the child is a *fidget* in church; **2**, **fidgets**, a state of restlessness; as, to have the *fidgets*.

fidg-et-y (fĭj′ĕ-tĭ), *adj.* nervously restless; as, the noise made me *fidgety.*

fi-du-ci-ar-y (fĭ-dū′shĭ-ĕr′ĭ; fĭ-dū′shȧ-rĭ), *n.* [*pl.* fiduciaries], a trustee.

fie (fī), *interj.* for shame! shame!

fief (fēf), *n.* under the feudal system, land held by a vassal in return for service to an overlord: also called *fee.*

Field (fēld), Eugene (1850–1895), an American journalist and author, especially of poems for children.

field (fēld), *n.* 1, a piece of farm land cleared for cultivation, pasture, etc., often enclosed by a fence or hedge; 2, a plot of ground set aside for a special use; as, a football *field;* 3, a region yielding some natural product; as, oil *fields;* 4, the scene of military operations; a battlefield; also, a battle; 5, in sports, all those who engage or compete in a contest or sport; as, in the fox hunt he led the *field;* 6, in baseball, cricket, or the like, the side not at bat; 7, the background against which a thing is seen; as, stars in a blue *field;* 8, an open space; as, a *field* of snow; 9, a range or sphere of activity; as, the *field* of art:—*v.t.* and *v.i.* in baseball, to catch or stop and return (a ball) from the field.

field-er (fēl′dĕr), *n.* in baseball, a player stationed in the field.

field glass, a small portable telescope, usually double, for use with both eyes.

Field-ing (fēl′dĭng), Henry (1707–1754), an English novelist.

field mar-shal, in Europe, a military officer next below the commander in chief.

field mouse, a kind of mouse that lives in the fields.

field-piece (fēld′pēs′), *n.* a cannon mounted on wheels.

FIELD GLASS
Prism binocular, with the one side cut away to show how a ray of light, after entering the glass, is reflected from one prism to another before reaching the eye.

FIELDPIECE

fiend (fēnd), *n.* 1, an evil spirit; a devil; also, an unnaturally wicked or cruel person; 2, *Colloquial,* a person much given to a habit; as, a drug *fiend;* a speed *fiend.*

fiend-ish (fēn′dĭsh), *adj.* savagely cruel; as, a *fiendish* crime.—*adv.* **fiend′ish-ly.**

fierce (fērs), *adj.* [fierc-er, fierc-est], 1, furiously violent and intense; as, a *fierce* fighter; 2, cruel; savage.—*adv.* **fierce′ly.**—*n.* **fierce′ness.**

fi-er-y (fī′rĭ; fī′ĕr-ĭ), *adj.* [fier-i-er, fier-i-est], 1, hot and lively in feeling; as, a *fiery* speech; 2, having a reddish glow.
Syn. spirited, impetuous, fervid.

fies-ta (fyĕs′tä), *n.* a religious festival; hence, a holiday.

fife (fīf), *n.* a shrill-toned musical instrument of the flute class:—*v.t.* and *v.i.* [fifed, fif-ing], to play (a tune) on a fife.—*n.* **fif′er.**

FIFE

fif-teen (fĭf′tēn′), *adj.* composed of ten more than five:—*n.* 1, the sum of ten and five; 2, a sign representing fifteen units.

fifth (fĭfth), *adj.* next after the fourth: the ordinal of *five:*—*n.* 1, one of the five equal parts of anything; 2, in music, an interval of three steps and a half step:—**fifth column,** a small group working secretly to betray a country to its enemies.

fif-ti-eth (fĭf′tĭ-ĕth), *adj.* next after the 49th: the ordinal of *fifty:*—*n.* one of the 50 equal parts of anything.

fif-ty (fĭf′tĭ), *adj.* composed of ten more than 40:—*n.* [*pl.* fifties], 1, the sum of 49 and one; 2, a sign representing 50 units, as 50 or l.

fig (fĭg), *n.* 1, a small, sweet, pear-shaped fruit, grown in warm countries; also, the tree which bears it; 2, *Colloquial,* the least amount; as, I don't care a *fig.*

fig. abbreviation for *figure.*

fight (fīt), *v.i.* [fought (fôt), fight-ing], 1, to strive in battle or in single combat; as, to die *fighting;* 2, to strive against difficulties or opponents; as, to *fight* for a goal:—*v.t.* 1, to strive against; make war upon; as, to *fight* an enemy, crime, disease, or the like; 2, to engage in (a conflict); as, to *fight* a duel:—*n.* 1, a battle; conflict with firearms, ships, armies, etc.; also, a physical conflict between persons; a brawl; 2, any strife or struggle; as, the *fight* for lower taxes; 3, willingness or eagerness to struggle; as, John is full of *fight.*—*n.* **fight′er.**
Syn., v. contest, struggle; *n.* battle, skirmish, action.

fig-ment (fĭg′mĕnt), *n.* something imagined; as, the weird shapes a child thinks he sees in the dark are *figments* of fancy.

fig-ur-a-tive (fĭg′ūr-ȧ-tĭv), *adj.* expressing an idea or meaning in an unusual way, especially by the use of language which tends to call up a picture; as, "armed to the teeth" is a *figurative* way of saying "completely armed."—*adv.* **fig′ur-a-tive-ly.**

fig-ure (fĭg′ûr), *n.* **1,** a shape; outline; appearance; as, a *figure* in the fog; a girlish *figure;* **2,** a person as he appears to others; as, the old beggar was a pitiful *figure;* **3,** a likeness of something; as, a *figure* on a coin; **4,** an illustrative drawing; **5,** a design or pattern, as in fabrics; also, a movement of a dance; **6,** a symbol of a number, as 1, 2, etc.; **7,** price; as, sold at a high *figure;* **8, figures,** numbers; arithmetic:—**figure of speech,** the saying of something in a fanciful manner in order to make it more striking or forceful:—*v.t.* [figured, figur-ing], **1,** to calculate; estimate; as, to *figure* up the cost; also, to think; as, to *figure* out a way; **2,** to imagine; as, he *figures* himself a hero:—*v.i.* **1,** to be prominent; as, to *figure* in the news; **2,** *Colloquial,* to use arithmetic; as, he likes to *figure.*

Syn., n. allegory, emblem, symbol, sign.

fig-ured (fĭg′ûrd), *adj.* having a design or pattern; as, *figured* cloth.

fig-ure-head (fĭg′ûr-hĕd′), *n.* **1,** a carved image at the prow of a ship; **2,** a person who is important in name only; as, the king was a mere *figurehead.*

fig-wort (fĭg′wûrt′), *n.* any of a group of plants including the mulleins and the snapdragons.

FIGUREHEAD OF A SHIP, def. 1

Fi-ji Is-lands (fē′jē), a group of islands in the Pacific, east of Australia, belonging to Great Britain (map 16).

fil-a-ment (fĭl′à-mĕnt), *n.* **1,** a fine wire or thread; **2,** in a flower, the stalk of a stamen (see *flower,* illustration).

fil-bert (fĭl′bẽrt), *n.* the nut of the hazel.

filch (fĭlch), *v.t.* to take by stealth; to steal.

¹file (fīl), *n.* **1,** a folder or a case, for keeping papers in order; also, papers arranged in order, as letters; **2,** a row of persons or things, one behind another:—*v.t.* [filed, fil-ing], to put (papers) away in order:—*v.i.* to march in line, one behind another.

FILE

²file (fīl), *n.* a steel tool with a rough face for smoothing or wearing away surfaces, as of wood or metal:—*v.t.* [filed, fil-ing], to smooth or cut with a file.

fi-let (fē-lā′; fē′lā), *adj.* made in fine square meshes:—*n.* **1,** lace or crochet work with

a fine square mesh; **2,** a boneless piece of meat or fish; a fillet.

fil-i-al (fĭl′ĭ-ăl; fĭl′yăl), *adj.* due to a parent from a child; as, *filial* respect.

fil-i-bus-ter (fĭl′ĭ-bŭs′tẽr), *n.* **1,** an adventurer who lawlessly invades a foreign country and attempts to stir up revolution; **2,** a legislator who intentionally delays the passing of laws, especially by talking merely to consume time; also, an instance of the use of such a method:—*v.i.* **1,** to invade a country as a military adventurer; **2,** to delay lawmaking by a filibuster.—*n.* **fil′i-bus′ter-er.**

fil-i-gree (fĭl′ĭ-grē), *n.* ornamental lacelike work in gold or silver wire; also, any delicate tracery, as of frost:—*adj.* made of or like such work.

FILIGREE

fil-ing (fīl′ĭng), *n.* a small piece scraped off by a file; as, copper *filings.*

Fil-i-pi-no (fĭl′ĭ-pē′nō), *n.* [*pl.* Filipinos], a native of the Philippine Islands.

fill (fĭl), *v.t.* **1,** to make full; as, to *fill* a glass; **2,** to stop up the pores or cavities of; as, to *fill* teeth; **3,** to satisfy, as with food; **4,** to take up all the space in; as, the crowd *filled* the room; **5,** to supply what is required by; as, to *fill* an order; **6,** to perform the duties of; as, he *fills* the office well:—*v.i.* **1,** to become full; as, her eyes *filled* with tears; **2,** to become full of wind, as sails:—*n.* **1,** enough to satisfy; as, I ate my *fill;* **2,** anything put in to fill up a space; as, a *fill* of sand.

fill-er (fĭl′ẽr), *n.* **1,** a tube or implement for filling something; **2,** anything used to fill a space, cavity, or the like, as sheets of paper for a loose-leaf notebook, a preparation to put on wood before painting, etc.

fil-let (fĭl′ĕt), *n.* **1,** a narrow band, especially one worn around the forehead; **2,** a flat molding separating other moldings; **3,** (often fĭl′ā; fĭl′ĭ), in cooking, a boneless piece of meat or fish: also spelled *filet:* —*v.t.* to bind or ornament with a narrow band.

FILLET, def. 1

fill-ing (fĭl′ĭng), *n.* **1,** material used to fill up a vacant space; **2,** something of inferior quality used to add bulk; as, tin is often used as a *filling* in silk.

fil-lip (fĭl′ĭp), *n.* **1,** a smart tap or snap with a fingertip; **2,** hence, some slight, sharp stimulus serving to excite, or arouse: —*v.t.* **1,** to snap with the fingers; **2,** to incite or arouse.

Fill·more (fĭl′môr), Millard (1800–1874), the 13th president of the U.S.

fil·ly (fĭl′ĭ), *n.* [*pl.* fillies], a young female horse.

film (fĭlm), *n.* **1,** a thin layer, or coating, as of oil on water; **2,** a roll of celluloid for taking photographs; **3,** a motion picture: —*v.t.* **1,** to cover with a thin coating; **2,** to make a motion picture of.—*adj.* **film′y.**— *adj.* **film′like.**

fil·ter (fĭl′tẽr), *n.* any material, as sand or cloth, used to strain out solid matter from liquids; also, an apparatus so used:— *v.t.* and *v.i.* to pass (a liquid) through a filter.—*n.* **fil·tra′tion** (fĭl-trā′shŭn).

filth (fĭlth), *n.* **1,** loathsome dirt; **2,** dirty language or thought.

filth·i·ness (fĭl′thĭ-nĕs), *n.* loathsome dirtiness; foulness.

filth·y (fĭl′thĭ), *adj.* [filth-i-er, filth-i-est], disgustingly dirty; morally or physically unclean.

   Syn. vile, nasty, impure.

fin (fĭn), *n.* one of the fanlike parts of a fish, which helps to move and steer it through the water; also, anything like a fin; as, an airplane *fin.*

fi·nal (fī′nǎl), *adj.* **1,** coming at the end; last; as, the *final* page; **2,** putting an end to doubt; as, a *final* decision:—**finals,** *n.pl.* **1,** the last event or game in a series; **2,** the last examinations of the term.

fi·na·le (fē·nä′lā; fê-nä′lē), *n.* **1,** the final movement of a symphony or other musical composition; **2,** the closing scene of an opera or play.

fi·nal·i·ty (fī-nǎl′ĭ-tĭ), *n.* [*pl.* finalities], **1,** the state of being fully settled; **2,** a conclusive action or utterance.

fi·nal·ly (fī′nǎl-ĭ), *adv.* **1,** lastly; **2,** at last; as, they *finally* came; **3,** once for all; as, to settle a matter *finally.*

fi·nance (fĭ-nǎns′; fī-nǎns′; fī′nǎns), *n.* **1,** the science of the management of money; **2, finances,** income; funds; as, the family *finances* are low:—*v.t.* [financed, financing], to provide the money for; as, the bank *financed* the factory.

fi·nan·cial (fī-nǎn′shǎl; fī-nǎn′shǎl), *adj.* relating to the management of money; as, *financial* advice.

   Syn. fiscal, monetary, pecuniary.

fin·an·cier (fĭn·ăn-sēr′; fī·nǎn-sēr′), *n.* a person skilled in money matters.

FINCH (⅓)

finch (fĭnch), *n.* any of various small song birds, as the bunting, canary, sparrow, etc. (See illustration in preceding column.)

find (fīnd), *v.t.* [found (found), find-ing], **1,** to discover by chance or accident; as, to *find* a dime; **2,** to learn by observation or experiment; as, to *find* the way a thing works; **3,** to reach; get to; as, the arrow *found* its mark; **4,** to determine and declare; as, the jury *found* him guilty; **5,** to succeed in getting; as, to *find* favor:— **find oneself,** to discover one's own powers: —*n.* a valuable discovery; as, the postage stamps on the old letters were a *find.*

find·er (fīn′dẽr), *n.* an extra lens on a camera, used to locate the object in the field of vision and to show on a very small scale the picture to be taken. (See *camera,* illustration.)

¹fine (fīn), *n.* money paid as a penalty for breaking a law:—*v.t.* [fined, fin-ing], to punish by imposing a payment of money.

²fine (fīn), *adj.* [fin-er, fin-est], **1,** of superior quality; as, *fine* silk; *fine* music; **2,** slender; not coarse; as, a *fine* needle; *fine* sand; **3,** delicate; refined; as, a man of *fine* feelings; **4,** excellent in character; as, a *fine* boy; **5,** pleasant; bright; as, a *fine* day:—**fine arts,** arts whose chief concern is with the creation of beauty, as music and painting. —*adv.* **fine′ly.**—*n.* **fine′ness.**

   Syn. dainty, smooth, sensitive.

fin·er·y (fīn′ẽr-ĭ), *n.* [*pl.* fineries], showy clothing or ornaments.

fi·nesse (fĭ-nĕs′), *n.* **1,** cleverness shown against an opponent; cunning; as, the general displayed *finesse* in avoiding the enemy; **2,** grace; delicacy; as, his violin playing showed great *finesse.*

fin·ger (fĭng′gẽr), *n.* **1,** one of the five separate divisions of the hand; especially, any one of four not including the thumb; **2,** any one of many mechanical devices used like a finger; **3,** a division of a glove into which a finger is put:—*v.t.* **1,** to touch; as, to *finger* objects on a counter; **2,** to play (an instrument) with the fingers.

fin·ger·print (fĭng′gẽr-prĭnt′), *n.* an impression of the lines on the inner surface of the thumb or a finger tip, used as means of identification:—*v.t.* to make a fingerprint of.—*n.* **fin′ger·print′ing.**

fin·i·cal (fĭn′ĭ-kǎl), *adj.* too particular; too precise; fussy; as, a *finical* old maid.

fi·nis (fī′nĭs), *n.* the end.

fin·ish (fĭn′ĭsh), *v.t.* **1,** to bring to an end; complete; conclude; as, to *finish* a piece of work; **2,** to fix the surface of in some way; as, to *finish* wood, cloth, etc.; **3,** *Colloquial,* to dispose of; render powerless; kill:—**finished,** done very carefully; excellent; as, a *finished* performance:—*v.i.* to come to an end; stop; as, the book *finished* abruptly:—*n.* 1, the completion; end; as, the *finish* of a race; 2, surface or texture; as, tweed cloth has a rough *finish;* wood with a smooth *finish.*—*n.* **fin′ish-er.** *Syn.*, *v.* perfect, terminate, close.

Fin-is-terre (fĭn′ĭs-târ′), a cape on the northwestern coast of Spain (map 12).

fi-nite (fī′nīt), *adj.* having limits.

Fin-land (fĭn′lănd), a republic (cap. Helsinki) in northern Europe, east of Sweden:—**Gulf of Finland**, a gulf lying between Finland and Estonia. (Map 12.)

¹**Finn** (fĭn), *n.* a native of Finland.—*adj.* **Finn′ic.**—*adj.* and *n.* **Finn′ish.**

²**Finn** (fĭn), (?–283?), the warrior hero of many ancient Celtic legends, noted for his wisdom. He was the father of the poet, Oisin.

fin-nan had-die (fĭn′ăn hăd′ĭ), or **finnan had-dock** (hăd′ŭk), a smoked haddock, a kind of food fish.

fin-ny (fĭn′ĭ), *adj.* 1, having or resembling fins; 2, abounding in fish.

fiord or **fjord** (fyôrd), *n.* a long, narrow inlet, or arm of the sea, between high banks, as on the coast of Norway.

fir (fûr), *n.* a cone-bearing, evergreen tree valued for its resin and timber (see illustration on page 865); also, the timber.

fire (fīr), *n.* 1, the visible heat or light produced by burning; a spark or flame; 2, wood, coal, or other fuel burning; as, a hot *fire* in the stove; 3, a destructive burning; as, a forest *fire;* 4, a discharge of firearms; as, the soldiers heard the *fire* of cannon; 5, strong feeling; spirit; as, the speech lacked *fire;* 6, brilliancy or light; as, the *fire* of a diamond:—*v.t.* [fired, fir-ing], 1, to set on fire; as, to *fire* a haystack; 2, to animate; excite; as, ambition *fires* his genius; 3, to cause to explode; as, to *fire* a gun; 4, to apply intense heat to; as, to *fire* pottery; 5, *Colloquial*, to dismiss; discharge; as, the boss *fired* his secretary:—*v.i.* 1, to become ignited; take fire; 2, to discharge artillery; as, they *fired* at the enemy.

fire-arm (fīr′ärm′), *n.* a small weapon, as a rifle, revolver, etc., from which a shot is discharged by an explosive.

fire-brand (fīr′brănd′), *n.* 1, a piece of burning wood; 2, one who kindles strife; especially, one who inflames the emotions of a crowd.

fire-crack-er (fīr′krăk′ẽr), *n.* a small roll of paper filled with gunpowder and set off by a fuse.

fire-damp (fīr′dămp′), *n.* a dangerous, explosive gas formed in coal mines.

fire-dog (fīr′dôg′), *n.* an andiron or support for wood in a fireplace.

fire en-gine, an apparatus for forcing liquid on a fire to put it out.

FIRE ENGINE

fire es-cape, a ladder or stairway that provides a way of escape from a burning building.

fire ex-tin-guish-er, an apparatus, usually a portable metal tank containing chemicals, for immediate use in putting out a fire.

fire-fly (fīr′flī′), *n.* [*pl.* fireflies], a small beetle which gives forth light.

fire-less (fīr′lĕs), *adj.* having no fire.

fire-light (fīr′līt′), *n.* light from a fire; as, shadows dance in the *firelight.*

fire-man (fīr′măn), *n.* [*pl.* firemen (-mĕn)], 1, one trained to put out fires; 2, one who tends fires; a stoker.

Fi-ren-ze (fē-rĕnt′sä), the Italian name for a city of central Italy. See **Florence.**

fire-place (fīr′plās′), *n.* an opening in a chimney where a fire may be built; a hearth.

fire-proof (fīr′prōōf′), *adj.* made of material that resists fire; as, *fireproof* buildings: —*v.t.* to make proof against burning.

fire-side (fīr′sīd′), *n.* 1, the place near the fire; 2, the hearth; home:—*adj.* pertaining to the home; as, *fireside* comfort.

fire-wa-ter (fīr′wô′tẽr), *n.* spirits; intoxicating liquor: the American Indian's name for strong drink.

fire-wood (fīr′wŏŏd′), *n.* wood for fuel.

fire-works (fīr′wûrks′), *n.pl.* devices, as firecrackers, rockets, etc., used in celebrations to make a noise or a brilliant display of light.

fir-kin (fûr′kĭn), *n.* 1, a small, wooden vessel for butter, lard, etc.; 2, an English liquid measure equal to nine gallons.

¹**firm** (fûrm), *adj.* 1, compact; solid; as, *firm* muscles; 2, not easily moved; stable; as, a *firm* foundation; 3, steady and vigorous; as, a *firm* step; 4, steadfast; loyal; as, a *firm* belief; 5, resolute; positive; as, he is *firm* of purpose:—*v.t.* to compact; fix firmly.—*adv.* **firm′ly.**—*n.* **firm′ness.**

²**firm** (fûrm), *n.* 1, a partnership of two or more persons for doing business; 2, the name under which a partnership does business.

fir-ma-ment (fûr′mȧ-mĕnt), *n.* the sky.

fir-man (fûr′măn; fẽr-män′), *n.* a special order or decree, as of an oriental ruler.

first (fûrst), *adj.* 1, earliest in time or order; as, the *first* page; 2, foremost in importance, time, excellence, etc.; as, he was *first* in his class: also used as the ordinal of *one*:—*adv*. **1,** before everyone else, as in order, place, rank, etc.; **2,** sooner; rather; as, I would die *first*:—*n*. **1,** the beginning; **2,** any person or thing that is first; as, we were the *first* to go.

first aid, temporary treatment given the sick or injured while awaiting regular medical treatment.—*adj*. **first/-aid/**.

first–born (fûrst/=bôrn/), *adj*. earliest produced or born; eldest:—*n*. the eldest.

first–class (fûrst/=klås/), *adj*. of the highest rank or quality:—*adv*. with the best accommodations; as, to travel *first-class*.

first fruits, 1, the earliest harvest of a crop; **2,** the earliest results of any undertaking or attempt.

first–hand (fûrst/hǎnd/), *adj*. obtained directly from the source; as, *firsthand* facts:—*adv*. directly.

first–lings (fûrst/lǐngz), *n.pl*. the earliest of a kind.

first–rate (fûrst/=rāt/), *adj*. **1,** of the highest excellence; very good; as, a *first-rate* writer; **2,** *Colloquial*, very well; as, I feel *first-rate*:—*adv*. *Colloquial*, excellently.

firth (fûrth), *n*. an arm of the sea.

fis-cal (fǐs/kǎl), *adj*. relating to financial matters; financial.

fish (fǐsh), *n*. [*pl*. fish or fishes], **1,** an animal, usually with a scaly body and limbs modified into fins, living in water, and breathing through gills instead of lungs; **2,** the flesh of fish used for food:—*v.i*. **1,** to catch, or try to catch, fish; **2,** to search for anything hidden, buried, etc.; as, he *fished* in his pocket for a match; **3,** to seek to gain something by indirect means; as, he *fished* for information by sly questions:—*v.t*. **1,** to catch or try to catch (fish); **2,** to try to catch fish in; as, to *fish* a stream.

fish-er (fǐsh/ẽr), *n*. **1,** one who fishes for sport or business; as, a pearl *fisher*; **2,** an animal of the weasel family.

FISHER (⅒), def. 2

fish-er-man (fǐsh/ẽr-mǎn), *n*. [*pl*. fishermen (-mĕn)], **1,** one who catches fish as a sport or business; **2,** a fishing boat.

fish-er-y (fǐsh/ẽr-ĭ), *n*. [*pl*. fisheries], **1,** the business of catching fish; **2,** a fishing ground.

fish hawk, a large bird which feeds on fish.

fish-hook (fǐsh/hŏŏk/), *n*. a hook which, when fastened to a line and baited, is used for catching fish.

fish-ing (fǐsh/ǐng), *n*. **1,** the act, art, sport, or business of catching fish; **2,** a fishing ground.

FISHHOOKS
The first three with barbs, the last without a barb.

fish-mon-ger (fǐsh/mŭng/gẽr), *n*. one who buys and sells fish.

fish-wife (fǐsh/wīf/), *n*. [*pl*. fishwives (-wīvz/)], a woman who sells fish.

fish-y (fǐsh/ĭ), *adj*. [fish-i-er, fish-i-est], **1,** like fish or abounding in fish; **2,** *Colloquial*, unlikely; as, the story sounds *fishy*.

fis-sure (fǐsh/ẽr), *n*. a narrow opening; a crack; a cleft; as, a *fissure* in the earth:—*v.t*. or *v.i*. [fissured, fissur-ing], to break or split.

fist (fǐst), *n*. the hand when closed or clenched; as, he struck with his *fist*.

fist-ic (fǐs/tǐk), *adj*. *Colloquial*, pertaining to pugilism or boxing.

fist-i-cuffs (fǐs/tǐ-kŭfs/), *n.pl*. a fight with the fists.

fis-tu-la (fǐs/tū-lá), *n*. [*pl*. fistulas], an abnormal opening or passage, often caused by disease, leading into some internal organ of the body.—*adj*. **fis/tu-lar**.

¹fit (fǐt), *n*. **1,** a sudden, violent attack of disease, as of epilepsy or indigestion; **2,** a sudden outburst, as of laughter or energy.

²fit (fǐt), *adj*. [fit-ter, fit-test], **1,** suitable; proper; as, a dress *fit* for a queen; **2,** ready; prepared; as, the team is *fit* for work; **3,** in good condition; as, I feel *fit* again:—*v.t*. [fit-ted, fit-ting], **1,** to make suitable; adapt; as, I will *fit* my time to yours; **2,** to furnish with what is right in size, shape, etc.; as, can you *fit* me in shoes? **3,** to equip; prepare; as, to *fit* a boy for college; **4,** to be properly adjusted to; be suitable for; as, this dress *fits* me:—*v.i*. to be adapted to one; as, his gloves *fit* well:—*n*. the adaptation of one thing to another; as, this coat is an excellent *fit*.—*adv*. **fit/ly**.—*n*. **fit/ness**.

Syn., adj. seemly, appropriate.

fitch-ew (fǐch/ōō) or **fitch** (fǐch), *n*. the European polecat; also, its yellowish fur.

fit-ful (fǐt/fŏŏl), *adj*. changeable; capricious; also, irregular; restless; as, *fitful* sleep.—*adv*. **fit/ful-ly**.

Syn. jerky, variable, capricious.

fit-ter (fǐt/ẽr), *n*. **1,** one who adjusts or puts the parts of a machine together; as, an engine *fitter*; **2,** one who adjusts and alters clothing to make it fit.

āte, āorta, râre, cǎt, ȧsk, fär, ǎllow, sofȧ; ēve, ĕvent, ĕll, writẽr, novĕl; bīte, pǐn; nō, ōbey, ôr, dŏg, tŏp, cŏllide; ūnit, ūnite, bûrn, cŭt, focŭs; nōōn, fŏŏt; mound; coin;

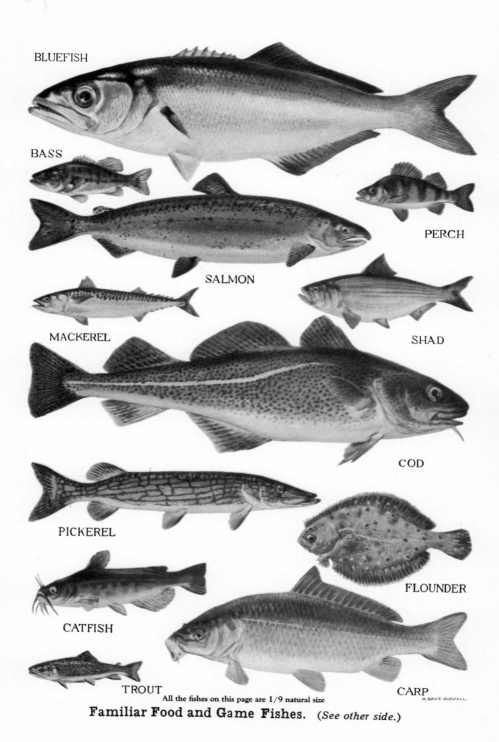

BLUEFISH

BASS

PERCH

SALMON

MACKEREL

SHAD

COD

PICKEREL

FLOUNDER

CATFISH

TROUT

CARP

All the fishes on this page are 1/9 natural size

Familiar Food and Game Fishes. (*See other side.*)

R·BRUCE HORSFALL

FISHES

Although fishes differ among themselves in many ways, they have certain common characteristics which distinguish them from all other animals. They are cold-blooded but have backbones. They have gills by which they get oxygen from the water. For legs and arms, they have fins. Many of them are covered with scales. Fishes have no necks and the front part of the body is heaviest. We say that fishes are boat-shaped, but really we should say that boats are fish-shaped because man evidently got his idea of boat forms from the fishes. A glance at the picture on the preceding page shows that many of them are beautifully streamlined and equipped with a powerful rudder—the tail.

Fishes have developed the particular sense which serves them best in their fight to live. That sense is touch. The least scrape of a fin, or any unusual motion of the water, is enough to send a fish darting away, and often its very life depends upon its speed. But although so sensitive to touch, it feels no pain when wounded. Fishes are shortsighted, and have dull hearing and a poor sense of smell. A few fishes are able to make a noise, but for the most part the "finny folk" live and die in silence.

The fishes pictured on the preceding page are all edible. In the markets of the world the cod ranks above all other food fishes, but in the United States it is of less importance than the salmon. The salmon is also notable because of its life history. It is hatched in the clear, cold, fresh water of northern rivers where it remains for about two years. Then, feeling the call of the sea, off it swims downstream to the ocean. There, for two years it feeds and grows fat, until, following its natural instinct, it returns to its birthplace to spawn—and die. The salmon for canning is caught as soon as possible after it leaves the sea, when it is fat, as the farther upstream it fights its way the thinner it becomes.

Closely related to the salmon is the trout, prized beauty of clear, cold streams. It is noted for its gameness and delicate flavor.

Carp, another fresh-water fish, came to America from Asia by way of Europe. It likes ponds and stagnant streams, lives to a great age, and often reaches a weight of 40 pounds.

The catfish, so called perhaps because of its flowing whiskers, is apt to prove a dangerous fellow because its skin and fins are covered with slime which causes great pain if it gets into a wound. Catfish are found in both fresh and salt water.

In fresh-water streams and lakes, two favorite food and game fishes are the black bass and the perch. Pickerel, also, frequent fresh water where they are a terror to smaller fishes. They are huge feeders and fierce fighters.

Famous for being the first fish to be protected by the United States Fish Commission, is that coast ranger, the shad. It is also noted for its delicious flavor and—for many troublesome bones.

The bluefish is one of the most destructive fishes, repeatedly killing more than it can eat. Its usual weight is under five pounds. It is a favorite food fish and is caught in nets, or with hook and line, in the Atlantic and other seas.

The flat-sided fish with the fancy fins is a flounder, a member of the flatfish family. The flounder makes delicious food and is often sold in restaurants as *filet of sole*.

The fish of perfect proportions is the mackerel. It likes to swim in great schools near the surface of the sea. The kind shown is about 10 inches long, but a giant relative, the tuna, may attain a length of 10 feet and a weight of several hundred pounds.

The average weight of the codfish is 10 pounds but big ones weigh over 70 pounds. Codfish feed on clams and other shellfish, swallowing them shell and all and disgorging the shells after the meat has digested. Where food is plentiful, there codfish are found in great shoals, or schools. That is why immense numbers of codfish are caught, every year off the coast of Newfoundland.

fit·ting (fĭt'ĭng), *adj.* suitable; proper; as, you come at a *fitting* moment:—**fittings**, *n.pl.* the equipment or necessary fixtures of a house, car, shop, etc.

Fitz·ger·ald (fĭts-jĕr'ăld), Edward (1809-1883), an English poet, known for "The Rubáiyát of Omar Khayyám."

Fiu·me (fyōō'mā), former Italian seaport on the Adriatic Sea now called Rijeka (map 12).

five (fīv), *adj.* composed of one more than four:—*n.* **1**, the number consisting of four plus one; **2**, a sign representing five units, as 5 or v.

Five Na·tions, a confederacy, formed about 1570, of Iroquoian Indians of the Mohawk Valley, New York, including the Mohawks, Onondagas, Cayugas, Oneidas, and Senecas.

fix (fĭks), *v.t.* **1**, to make fast or firm; as, they *fixed* a stake in the ground; **2**, to determine; as, they *fixed* the time for the concert; **3**, to place definitely on a person, as blame, responsibility, etc.; **4**, to make fast or permanent, as a color, a photographic negative, or the like; **5**, to direct or hold steadily, as the eyes; **6**, *Colloquial,* to repair; as, the plumber *fixed* the leak; also, to arrange; as, to *fix* one's hair:—*v.i.* to become fixed:—*n. Colloquial,* an awkward situation; as, I'm in a *fix*.
    Syn., v. decide, establish, settle.

fix·a·tion (fĭks-ā'shŭn), *n.* the act or process of making permanent; as, the *fixation* of a photographic film; also, the state of being permanent; as, the *fixation* of a habit.

fixed (fĭkst), *adj.* firmly established; set; as, a *fixed* purpose:—**fixed star**, a star whose position with relation to other stars always seems the same: distinguished from a *planet.—adv.* **fix'ed·ly**.

fix·ture (fĭks'tŭr), *n.* **1**, something permanently attached to an office, house, or the like; as, an electric-light *fixture;* plumbing *fixtures;* **2**, a person permanently placed; as, he's a *fixture* in our town.

fizz or **fiz** (fĭz), *n.* **1**, a hissing sound; **2**, an effervescent or bubbling liquid, as soda water:—*v.i.* [fizzed, fizz-ing], to make a hissing noise.

fiz·zle (fĭz'l), *v.i.* [fiz-zled, fiz-zling], **1**, to make a hissing noise; **2**, *Colloquial,* to fail miserably:—*n.* **1**, a hissing or spluttering; **2**, *Colloquial,* a failure; as, he made a *fizzle* of his part in the play.

fjord (fyôrd), *n.* a narrow arm of the sea, with high rocky banks; a fiord. See fiord.

Fla. abbreviation for *Florida.*

flab·ber·gast·ed (flăb'ẽr-găs'tĕd), *adj. Colloquial,* astonished.

flab·bi·ness (flăb'ĭ-nĕs), *n.* want of firmness; softness; as, *flabbiness* of muscle.

flab·by (flăb'ĭ), *adj.* [flab-bi-er, flab-bi-est], **1**, yielding to the touch; limp; not firm; as, *flabby* cheeks; **2**, feeble; weak; as, a *flabby* will.—*adv.* **flab'bi·ly**.
    Syn. flaccid, soft, yielding.

flac·cid (flăk'sĭd), *adj.* flabby; limp; lacking firmness; as, *flaccid* cheeks.—*adv.* **flac'cid·ly.**—*n.* **flac'cid·ness.**

¹flag (flăg), *n.* a piece of cloth bearing some design or symbol and often attached by one edge to a staff or stick, and intended to be spread or held aloft as a national banner, signal, decoration, etc.:—*v.t.* [flagged, flag-ging], **1**, to signal with, or as with, a flag; as, to *flag* a train; **2**, to place a flag upon; also, to deck with flags.—*n.* **flag'pole'**.

²flag (flăg), *v.i.* [flagged, flagging], to droop; lag; lose strength; as, his courage *flagged.*

³flag (flăg), *n.* a plant with long, narrow leaves and showy flowers; the iris.

³FLAG

⁴flag (flăg), *n.* a large, flat slab of stone for pavements; a flagstone:—*v.t.* [flagged, flag-ging], to pave with flags.

Flag Day, in the U.S., June 14, the anniversary of the day (June 14th, 1777) when Congress adopted the national flag.

flag·el·late (flăj'ĕ-lāt), *v.t.* [flagellat-ed, flagellat-ing], to whip; as, to *flagellate* a criminal.—*n.* **flag'el·la'tion.**

flag·eo·let (flăj'ō-lĕt'), *n.* a small musical wood wind instrument similar to a flute.
FLAGEOLET

flag·ging (flăg'ĭng), *n.* a pavement or walk of flagstones.

fla·gi·tious (flă-jĭsh'ŭs), *adj.* very bad; wicked; highly criminal; as, a *flagitious* deed.—*adv.* **fla·gi'tious·ly.**

flag·on (flăg'ŭn), *n.* a vessel for holding liquors, with a spout, a handle, and often a lid; as, a wine *flagon.*

fla·grant (flā'grănt), *adj.* openly wicked; outrageous; notorious; as, a *flagrant* crime.—*n.* **fla'gran·cy.**

flag·ship (flăg'shĭp'), *n.* a ship that flies the flag of the commander of a fleet.
FLAGON

flag·staff (flăg'stȧf'), *n.* [*pl.* flagstaffs], a pole on which a flag is flown.

flag-stone (flăg′stōn′), *n.* a large, flat stone used especially for paving walks.

flail (flāl), *n.* an instrument consisting of a handle with a short stick hung loosely at one end, used for threshing grain by hand.

flair (flâr), *n.* ability to choose that which is correct; as, she has a *flair* for clothes; also, taste; liking; as, a *flair* for dramatics.

flake (flāk), *n.* a small, thin chip or fragment of anything; as, a *flake* of soap:—*v.i.* [flaked, flak-ing], to break off into flakes; peel or scale off.

flak-y (flā′kĭ), *adj.* [flak-i-er, flak-i-est], consisting of, or like, flakes; as, a *flaky* piecrust.

FLAIL

flam-boy-ant (flăm-boi′ănt), *adj.* 1, flaming; showy; as, *flamboyant* red hair; 2, having a wavy outline like that of a flame; as, *flamboyant* tracery in architecture.—*adv.* **flam-boy′ant-ly.**

flame (flām), *n.* 1, a burning gas or vapor, often tonguelike in shape; 2, a burning emotion or feeling; as, a *flame* of rage; 3, *Colloquial*, a sweetheart; as, she's an old *flame* of mine:—*v.i.* [flamed, flam-ing], to burn with a flame; burst into flame; as, the beacon *flamed* in the night:—*v.t.* 1, to subject to the action of flame; 2, to send (a signal) by fire.
Syn., flare, flash.

fla-min-go (flȧ-mĭng′gō), *n.* [*pl.* flamingos or flamingoes], a long-legged, tropical wading bird, with rosy-white to bright-red plumage.

FLAMINGO (1/20)

Flan-ders (flăn′dĕrz), the coastal region of northern France, Belgium, and the Netherlands, from Calais to the Scheldt (map 12).

flange (flănj), *n.* a raised or projecting rim on a wheel to keep it in place upon a track; or, on a pipe, to give a place for attaching it to a surface.

FLANGE (F)

flank (flăngk), *n.* 1, the fleshy part of an animal, between the ribs and hip (see illustration at *beef*); 2, the side of anything, as of an army, building, etc.; as, the enemy attacked our right *flank*:—*v.t.* 1, to stand at the side of; border; as, large trees *flanked* the road; 2, to attack, go around, or guard the side of.

flan-nel (flăn′ĕl), *n.* 1, a soft, loosely woven cloth, usually made of wool; 2, **flannels,** garments made of this material.

flan-nel-ette (flăn′ĕl-ĕt′), *n.* a soft, cotton material like flannel. Also, **flan′nel-et′.**

flap (flăp), *n.* 1, anything broad and flat, hanging loose, and attached on one side only; as, the *flap* of an envelope; 2, the motion of anything broad and flat swinging loosely and striking against something else; also, the sound thus made; 3, a blow or slap; as, a *flap* of a beaver's tail:—*v.t.* [flapped, flap-ping], 1, to strike with, or as with, a flap; 2, to move to and fro; as, the bird *flaps* its wings:—*v.i.* to sway about loosely, often with a beating noise; as, the shades *flapped* against the windows.

flap-jack (flăp′jăk′), *n.* a cake of thin batter baked on a griddle; a pancake.

flap-per (flăp′ẽr), *n.* 1, something that flaps, as the flipper of a seal or whale; 2, *Colloquial*, a young girl in her teens.

flare (flâr), *n.* 1, a large, unsteady, glaring light; 2, a fire or blaze serving as a signal; 3, a sudden bursting forth; as, a *flare* of trumpets; 4, a spreading outward; as, the vase has a *flare* at the top:—*v.i.* [flared, flar-ing], 1, to burn with a broad, unsteady flame; 2, to spread outward.
Syn., *n.* and *v.* glare, flame, flash.

flash (flăsh), *n.* 1, a sudden burst of light; as, a *flash* of lightning; 2, a sudden outburst, as of merriment, wit, or genius; 3, a momentary light displayed as a signal; 4, cheap display or show; 5, an instant; as, he saw it in a *flash*:—*v.t.* 1, to send forth swiftly or suddenly; as, to *flash* a light; to *flash* a look; 2, to send out in flashes; as, to *flash* a signal:—*v.i.* 1, to shine for a moment with a sudden light; as, beacons *flash* at night; 2, to appear suddenly; pass at great speed; as, the train *flashed* by.
Syn., *n.* flame, spark, gleam, blaze.

flash-back (flăsh′băk′), *n.* in a story, a short interruption during which earlier events are described.

flash-light (flăsh′līt′), *n.* 1, a small, portable electric light; 2, a sudden brilliant light for taking photographs; also, the photograph so taken; 3, a light that comes and goes in flashes, as a signal.

flash-y (flăsh′ĭ), *adj.* [flash-i-er, flash-i-est], 1, brilliant for a moment; 2, gaudy; showy, but cheap-looking; as, *flashy* clothes.—*adv.* **flash′i-ly.**—*n.* **flash′i-ness.**

FLASKS
A, pocket flask; B,C, flasks used in chemical laboratories.

flask (flăsk), *n.* 1, a narrow-necked bottle

made of glass, metal, or leather, for holding liquids, powder, etc.; **2**, a metallic bottle with flat sides; as, a pocket *flask*.

¹flat (flăt), *adj.* [flat-ter, flat-test], **1**, having a level, horizontal surface; as, *flat* country; **2**, stretched or spread out at full length; as, to lie *flat* on the ground; **3**, having a smooth and even surface, or nearly so, whether horizontal or not; as, the *flat* face of a cliff; **4**, broad and smooth, but not very thick; **5**, dull or uninteresting; as, a *flat* sermon; tasteless or stale; as, *flat* food or wine; not clear or sharp; as, a *flat* sound; **6**, unqualified; downright; as, a *flat* refusal; **7**, based on a fixed unit; uniform; as, a *flat* rate for gas; **8**, deflated; as, a *flat* tire; **9**, hence, *Colloquial*, low-spirited; without energy; also, without funds; **10**, dull; not glossy; as, a *flat* paint or finish; **11**, in music: **a**, below the true pitch; as, a *flat* note; **b**, lowered by a half step; as, B *flat*:—*adv.* **1**, in a flat manner; as, he sprawled *flat* on the ground; **2**, positively; directly; as, he came out *flat* against the candidate; **3**, exactly: said of numbers; as, he ran 100 yards in ten seconds *flat*; **4**, in music, below the true pitch; as, she sang slightly *flat*:—*n.* **1**, a level surface or plain; especially, low-lying country; as, the river *flats*; **2**, the smooth, wide part of a thing; as, the *flat* of a sword; **3**, a deflated tire; **4**, in music, a sign [♭] indicating a lowering of pitch by a half step; also, the note so lowered:—*v.t.* and *v.i.* [flat-ted, flat-ting], **1**, to make or become flat; **2**, to lower or become lower in pitch.—*adv.* **flat′ly.**—*n.* **flat′ness.**

Syn., *adj.* level, monotonous.

²flat (flăt), *n.* a set of rooms on one floor, usually planned for a single family and forming complete living quarters.

flat-boat (flăt′bōt′), *n.* a large, roughly-made boat, with a flat bottom and square ends, used for floating bulky freight, especially down rivers or in shallow waters.

flat-car (flăt′kär′), *n.* a railroad car without sides or top.

flat-fish (flăt′fĭsh′) *n.* a fish with a broad, flat body and both eyes on one side, as the flounder.

flat-i-ron (flăt′ī′ĕrn), *n.* a heavy iron with a flat, smooth bottom and a handle on top, used when heated for pressing or smoothing cloth.

flat-ten (flăt′n), *v.t.* **1**, to make level or smooth; **2**, to beat down; as, the rain *flattened* the corn; hence, to sadden or depress; **3**, to make dull or tasteless:—*v.i.* **1**, to become even or level; **2**, to become stale in taste.—*n.* **flat′ten-er.**

flat-ter (flăt′ĕr), *v.t.* **1**, to please, or seek to please, with praise which is usually insin-

cere; as, he got the job by *flattering* the boss; **2**, to portray too favorably; as, the snapshot *flatters* him:—*v.i.* to give false praise.—*n.* **flat′ter-er.**—*adj.* **flat′ter-ing.**

flat-ter-y (flăt′ĕr-ĭ), *n.* [*pl.* flatteries], insincere, false, or undue praise.

flat-tish (flăt′ĭsh), *adj.* rather flat; somewhat flat; as, a *flattish* field.

flat—top (flăt′=tŏp′), *n. Colloquial*, in the Navy, an airplane carrier.

flat-u-lent (flăt′ū-lĕnt), *adj.* **1**, marked by wind, or gas, in the stomach or intestines; **2**, producing, or tending to produce, gases in the stomach; as, *flatulent* foods.

flaunt (flônt; flänt), *v.t.* to show off; display impudently; as, the girl *flaunted* her new clothes:—*v.i.* **1**, to wave showily; as, flags *flaunting* in the wind; **2**, to make a showy appearance.—*adv.* **flaunt′ing-ly.**

Syn. boast, brandish, parade.

fla-vor (flā′vĕr), *n.* **1**, that quality which affects the sense of taste; as, a spicy *flavor* in a cake; **2**, that quality which affects the sense of smell; as, the *flavor* of a perfume; **3**, a substance that gives a particular taste to food or drink; **4**, a particular or characterizing quality; as, his stories have a *flavor* of the sea:—*v.t.* to give flavor to.

Syn., *n.* relish, savor, taste.

fla-vor-ing (flā′vĕr-ĭng), *n.* an extract or substance used to give a particular taste.

flaw (flô), *n.* a blemish; a weak spot; defect; crack; as, a *flaw* in the glass.—*adj.* **flaw′less.**—*adv.* **flaw′less-ly.**

Syn. imperfection, fault.

flax (flăks), *n.* a slender blue-flowered plant whose stem yields the fibers from which linen is spun, and from whose seeds linseed oil is made.

flax-en (flăk′sn), *adj.* **1**, made of, or resembling, flax; **2**, of a pale-yellow color; as, *flaxen* curls.

flax-seed (flăks′sēd′; flăk′-sēd′), *n.* the seed of the flax, much used in medicine and in the making of linseed oil.

flay (flā), *v.t.* **1**, to strip the skin from; skin; **2**, to scold; criticize severely.

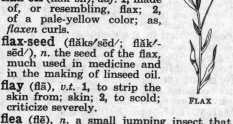

FLAX

flea (flē), *n.* a small jumping insect that sucks the blood of man and some beasts.

fleck (flĕk), *n.* a streak or spot; as, the bird had *flecks* of white on its breast:—*v.t.* to streak or spot; as, clouds *flecked* the sky.

fled (flĕd), past tense and past participle of *flee*.

fledge (flĕj), *v.i.* [fledged, fledg-ing], to acquire the feathers necessary for flight; as,

---

some birds are quicker than others to *fledge* and fly:—*v.t.* to furnish with feathers for flying; as, the young birds are not yet *fledged;* to *fledge* an arrow.

fledg-ling or **fledge-ling** (flĕj′lĭng), *n.* a young bird just able to fly.

flee (flē), *v.t.* [fled (flĕd), flee-ing], to run away from; avoid; shun; as, to *flee* evil:—*v.i.* **1**, to run away, as from danger or evil; as, they *fled* from their burning homes; **2**, to vanish; disappear swiftly.

    Syn. abscond, depart, shun.

fleece (flēs), *n.* **1**, the woolly coat of a sheep; also, all the wool shorn from a sheep at one time; **2**, anything like the coat of a sheep:—*v.t.* [fleeced, fleec-ing], **1**, to shear (a sheep) of its wool; **2**, to rob; strip; as, the thieves *fleeced* him of all his money.—*n.* **fleec′er.**

¹**fleet** (flēt), *adj.* swift; nimble; as, *fleet* as a greyhound:—*v.i.,* *Poetic,* to pass or fly quickly; as, the hours *fleeted* by.—*adv.* **fleet′ly.**—*n.* **fleet′ness.**

    Syn., *adj.* fast, speedy, quick.

²**fleet** (flēt), *n.* a number of warships under one command; hence, a number of vessels or vehicles moving together or under a single ownership; as, a *fleet* of taxicabs.

fleet-ing (flēt′ĭng), *adj.* passing quickly; as, a *fleeting* glance.—*adv.* **fleet′ing-ly.**

Flem-ing (flĕm′ĭng), *n.* a Belgian who speaks the Flemish tongue.

Flem-ish (flĕm′ĭsh), *adj.* pertaining to the Flemings or to Flanders:—*n.* the language of the people of northern Belgium.

flesh (flĕsh), *n.* **1**, the soft muscular tissues beneath the skin of a human or animal body; **2**, the body of animals used as food: more often called *meat;* **3**, soft pulp, as of fruit; **4**, the human body; **5**, kindred, stock, or race; as, his own *flesh* and blood.

    in the flesh, alive; as, I knew him *in the flesh;* **a thorn in the flesh,** an annoyance; as, his disobedience is *a thorn in the flesh.*

flesh-ly (flĕsh′lĭ), *adj.* pertaining to the body; worldly.—*n.* **flesh′li-ness.**

flesh-pot (flĕsh′pŏt′), *n.* **1**, a vessel used for cooking meat; **2**, **fleshpots,** luxury; physical ease and comfort; high living.

flesh-y (flĕsh′ĭ), *adj.* [flesh-i-er, flesh-i-est], **1**, full of flesh, as fruit; plump; **2**, portly; fat.—*n.* **flesh′i-ness.**

fleur—de—lis (flûr′=dē-lē′; flûr′= dē-lēs′), *n.* [*pl.* fleurs-de-lis (flûr′= dē-lēz′)], **1**, the iris; **2**, the emblem of the former royal family of France.

FLEUR-
DE-LIS,
def. 2

flew (flōō), past tense of *fly.*

flex (flĕks), *v.t.* to bend or curve; as, to *flex* the elbow; *flex* the knees.

flex-i-ble (flĕk′sĭ-bl), *adj.* **1**, easily bent without breaking; **2**, yielding to persuasion; hence, easily managed or led; tractable; **3**, adaptable; as, a *flexible* form of government.—*adv.* **flex′i-bly.**—*n.* **flex′i-bil′i-ty.**

    Syn. pliable, limber, supple.

flick (flĭk), *n.* **1**, a light, quick stroke, as of a whip; **2**, a streak or speck; as, a *flick* of dust:—*v.t.* to whip or strike gently with a quick jerk; also, to flip; snap; as, to *flick* the dust off one's coat.

¹**flick-er** (flĭk′ẽr), *v.i.* **1**, to waver, shine, or burn unsteadily, as a flame; **2**, to flutter; vibrate; quiver:—*n.* an unsteady light or movement.—*adj.* and *n.* **flick′er-ing.**—*adv.* **flick′er-ing-ly.**

²**flick-er** (flĭk′ẽr), *n.* the golden-winged woodpecker of North America.

fli-er or **fly-er** (flī′ẽr), *n.* **1**, one who or that which flies, as a bird or an aviator; **2**, anything that moves very rapidly, as an express train; **3**, *Colloquial,* a daring venture; as, he took a *flier* in stocks.

flies (flīz), *plural* of the noun *fly.*

flight (flīt), *n.* **1**, the act, process, manner, or power of flying; **2**, a passage, or the distance traveled, through the air; as, the *flight* of an airplane; hence, a swift passage; as, the *flight* of time; **3**, a hasty departure; as, the enemy took *flight;* **4**, a number of things or creatures, as birds, insects, arrows, or the like, passing through the air together; **5**, a soaring out beyond ordinary bounds; as, a *flight* of the imagination; **6**, a series of steps.

flight-y (flīt′ĭ), *adj.* [flight-i-er, flight-i-est], **1**, given to wild flights, as of fancy, humor, etc.; fickle; unsteady; **2**, mildly crazy.—*n.* **flight′i-ness.**

flim-sy (flĭm′zĭ), *adj.* [flim-si-er, flim-si-est], **1**, thin; weak; without strength; as, a *flimsy* box; **2**, without reason; as, a *flimsy* argument.—*adv.* **flim′si-ly.**—*n.* **flim′si-ness.**

    Syn. feeble, frail, unsubstantial.

flinch (flĭnch), *v.i.* to draw back from pain, danger, an unpleasant duty, or the like.

    Syn. wince, start.

fling (flĭng), *v.t.* [flung (flŭng), fling-ing], **1**, to throw or cast from, or as if from, the hand; as, to *fling* stones into a lake; **2**, to put away violently; as, he was *flung* into prison; **3**, to jerk suddenly; as, he *flung* back his head; **4**, to send out; as, the lantern *flung* out a dim light; **5**, to throw aside or cast off; as, to *fling* caution to the winds:—*v.i.* to rush out or about impatiently; as, to *fling* out of the room:—*n.* **1**, a cast or throw; **2,** a sneer or gibe; as, a *fling* at politicians; **3,** a period, usually brief, of unrestrained pleasure; as, he has had his *fling;* **4,** a lively dance; as, the Highland *fling.*

Flint (flĭnt), a manufacturing city in eastern Michigan (map **7**).

flint (flĭnt), *n.* a hard kind of quartz or rock which strikes sparks from steel.

flint-lock (flĭnt/lŏk/), *n.* an old form of

FLINTLOCK
1, hammer with flint; 2, steel and powder pan.

gun, or the lock of such a gun, in which the charge was set off by a spark from a flint struck on steel.

flint-y (flĭn/tĭ), *adj.* [flint-i-er, flint-i-est], composed of, or like, flint; hard; unyielding; as, a *flinty* heart.—*n.* **flint/i-ness.**

flip (flĭp), *v.t.* [flipped, flip-ping], **1,** to flick with the fingers; tap gently; as, to *flip* the ash from a cigar; to *flip* a horse; **2,** to toss so as to turn over; as, to *flip* a coin:—*v.i.* to move jerkily; flap; as, the fish *flipped* in the boat:—*n.* a short, quick tap or flick:—*adj. Colloquial,* pert; flippant.

flip-pant (flĭp/ănt), *adj.* disrespectfully pert; saucy; as, a *flippant* child or a *flippant* answer.—*adv.* **flip/pant-ly.**—*n.* **flip/pant-ness.**—*n.* **flip/pan-cy.**

flip-per (flĭp/ẽr), *n.* a broad, flat limb or fin adapted for swimming, as those of seals or sea turtles.

flirt (flûrt), *v.t.* **1,** to toss to and fro jerkily; as, the bird *flirts* its tail; **2,** to throw with a jerk; as, they *flirted* water at each other:—*v.i.* **1,** to move jerkily; dart; also, to shift constantly from one thing to another; trifle; **2,** to make love frivolously; play at love; **3,** to play, toy, or dally; as, to *flirt* with an idea:—*n.* **1,** one who plays at making love; **2,** a sudden jerk or toss; as, the *flirt* of a fan.

flir-ta-tion (flûr-tā/shŭn), *n.* a light love affair.—*adj.* **flir-ta/tious.**

flit (flĭt), *v.i.* [flit-ted, flit-ting], **1,** to move lightly from place to place; **2,** to pass or dart along; as, the birds *flit* by.

flitch (flĭch), *n.* the side of a hog salted and cured; as, a *flitch* of bacon.

fliv-ver (flĭv/ẽr), *n. Slang:* **1,** a small, cheap automobile; **2,** a failure; fizzle.

float (flōt), *v.i.* to be buoyed or held up on the surface of a liquid or within a volume of gas; as, a boat *floats;* a balloon *floats:*—*v.t.* **1,** to cause to rest or move gently on the surface of a liquid; as, the tide will *float* the boat again; to *float* a cargo down the river; also, to cause to be suspended or move in a volume of gas; as, to *float* balloons; **2,** to start or set going, as a company, scheme, or rumor:—*n.* **1,** anything that floats, as a raft, an anchored landing place, a life preserver, a cork on a fishing line, a hollow metal ball in a tank or cistern, or the like; **2,** a low platform on wheels to carry an exhibit in a parade, or the exhibit so carried; also, a low underslung platform on wheels for carrying heavy loads.

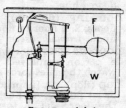

FLOAT, *n.* def. 1
When the water (W) in the tank reaches a certain level, the float (F), rising with the water, closes a valve, thus stopping the inflow of water.

float-er (flōt/ẽr), *n.* **1,** one who or that which floats; **2,** one who moves from place to place to repeat his vote.

¹flock (flŏk), *n.* **1,** a number of animals or birds of one kind keeping together; as, a *flock* of wild ducks; **2,** a large number of persons together; as, they came in great *flocks;* **3,** a group of people in charge of some person; as, the minister preached to his *flock:*—*v.i.* to come together or move in crowds; as, people *flocked* to hear her.

Syn., n. pack, bevy, shoal, drove, swarm, company, family, congregation.

²flock (flŏk), *n.* a tuft of wool or hair.

floe (flō), *n.* a large sheet or mass of drifting ice.

flog (flŏg), *v.t.* [flogged, flog-ging], to whip; beat or strike with a rod.

flood (flŭd), *n.* **1,** a great flow of water; especially, a body of water overflowing its banks; **2,** an abundant supply or outpouring of anything; as, a *flood* of light; a *flood* of music:—*v.t.* to cover or fill with water; as, to *flood* a valley; to supply; fill to excess; as, to *flood* a stage with light.

flood tide, the incoming tide; the point or time of highest tide: opposite of *ebb tide;* **the Flood,** the great deluge in the time of Noah.

flood-gate (flŭd/gāt/), *n.* a gate in a waterway to keep out or let in water.

floor (flôr), *n.* **1,** the bottom surface of a room or hall; as, there is a pine *floor* in the kitchen; **2,** any bottom surface like a floor; as, the *floor* of the ocean; **3,** all the rooms on one level in a building; a story; **4,** the main part of an assembly hall where members sit and speak; hence, the right to speak in an assembly; as, he has the *floor:*—*v.t.* **1,** to cover with a floor; **2,** to strike

go; join; yet; sing; chin; show; thin, *th*en; hw, *wh*y; zh, a*z*ure; ü, Ger. f*ü*r or Fr. l*u*ne; ö, Ger. sch*ö*n or Fr. f*eu*; ṅ, Fr. e*n*fant, no*m*; kh, Ger. a*ch* or i*ch*. See pages ix–x.

down; as, the boxer *floored* his opponent; **3**, to put to silence; as, that argument *floored* him.

floor-ing (flôr'ing), *n.* **1**, materials for floors; **2**, a floor or floors. (See illustration under *frame house*.)

floor-walk-er (flôr'wôk'ẽr), *n.* in the U.S., a person employed in a large store to watch the sales force and direct customers.

flop (flŏp), *v.t.* [flopped, flop-ping], to drop, or let fall heavily; as, to *flop* a suitcase on the floor:—*v.i.* **1**, to strike about; as, the fish *flops* in the boat; flap, as the brim of a hat; **2**, to throw oneself heavily; as, to *flop* down on a chair; **3**, *Colloquial*, to change over suddenly, as from one political party to another; **4**, *Slang*, to fail:—*n.* **1**, *Colloquial*, the act or sound of flopping; **2**, *Slang*, a failure.—*adj. Colloquial*, **flop'py**.

flor-a (flôr'à), *n.* the plants of a particular region or period of time.

flor-al (flôr'ăl), *adj.* of or resembling flowers; as, a *floral* decoration.

Flor-ence (flŏr'ĕns), a city of central Italy, on the Arno River (map **12**). Its Italian name is *Firenze*.

Flor-en-tine (flŏr'ĕn-tēn; flŏr'ĕn-tīn; flŏr'-ĕn-tĭn), *adj.* pertaining to Florence, Italy: —*n.* an inhabitant of Florence.

flor-id (flŏr'ĭd), *adj.* **1**, bright in color; flushed; as, a *florid* complexion; **2**, flowery; richly decorated; showy; as, a *florid* style.

Flor-i-da (flŏr'ĭ-dà), a southern State (cap. Tallahassee) of the U.S. (map **8**).

flor-in (flŏr'ĭn), *n.* **1**, a gold coin, first struck at Florence in 1252, later widely imitated in Europe; **2**, any of various European silver coins, as the British *florin* (two shillings), and the Dutch guilder.

flor-ist (flôr'ĭst; flŏr'ĭst), *n.* one whose business is raising or selling flowers.

floss (flôs), *n.* **1**, strands of silk used in embroidering, crocheting, or the like; **2**, the downy, silky substance in certain pods, as of milkweed.

flo-til-la (flō-tĭl'à), *n.* **1**, a fleet of small vessels; **2**, a small fleet.

flot-sam (flŏt'săm), *n.* pieces of shipwreck or lost cargo found floating.

¹flounce (flouns), *n.* a gathered piece of cloth sewed by its upper border to the skirt of a dress; a deep ruffle:—*v.t.* [flounced, flounc-ing], to trim with deep ruffles.

DRESS WITH FLOUNCES

²flounce (flouns), *n.* a jerk or sudden movement, often showing impatience; as, a

flounce of the head:—*v.i.* [flounced, flounc-ing], to move suddenly and jerkily; as, to *flounce* out of a room.

¹floun-der (floun'dẽr), *v.i.* **1**, to plunge around; struggle awkwardly; as, to *flounder* through a swamp; **2**, to make mistakes; blunder; as, to *flounder* through a speech.

²floun-der (floun'dẽr), *n.* a food fish with

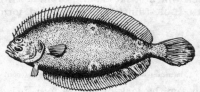

FLOUNDER (¼)

a flat body and both eyes on the same side.

flour (flour), *n.* **1**, the fine meal of ground wheat or other grain; **2**, any fine, soft powder:—*v.t.* **1**, to grind into flour; **2**, to sprinkle flour upon.—*adj.* **flour'y**.

flour-ish (flûr'ĭsh), *v.i.* **1**, to grow; prosper; thrive; be vigorous; as, palm trees *flourish* in the tropics; **2**, to make showy movements, as with a sword; **3**, to make ornamental strokes with a pen:—*v.t.* **1**, to swing about or brandish; as, to *flourish* a sword; **2**, to ornament (letters) in writing:—*n.* **1**, a showy waving; as, a *flourish* of a flag or a weapon; **2**, a decoration in handwriting; **3**, a showy musical passage played by trumpets, bugles, etc.

Syn. v. increase, flaunt, parade.

flout (flout), *v.t.* to insult; mock; disdain; as, to *flout* a kindness:—*n.* a scoffing remark or action.—*adv.* **flout'ing-ly**.

flow (flō), *v.i.* **1**, to move or run along as a fluid; as, water *flows;* blood *flows* in the body; **2**, to abound; be plentiful; as, wine *flows* at a feast; **3**, to pour out easily and plentifully; as, words *flow;* **4**, to come from; proceed; as, energy *flows* from health; **5**, to hang loose; as, her long hair *flows;* **6**, to rise, as the tide:—*n.* **1**, a flowing; as, the *flow* of a river; **2**, the amount of fluid passing through an opening or by a certain point in a given time; **3**, any easy, continuous movement or procedure; as, a *flow* of speech, music, or thought; **4**, the coming in of the tide.

flow-er (flou'ẽr), *n.* **1**, that part of a seed-bearing plant or tree from which the seed develops; a blossom (see illustration next page); **2**, a plant grown for its blossoms; **3**, the best part; as, the *flower* of a nation's youth:—*v.i.* to blossom; as, fruit trees *flower* in the spring.

āte, âorta, râre, căt, ȧsk, fär, ăllow, sofà; ēve, ĕvent, ĕll, writēr, novĕl; bīte, pĭn; nō, ōbey, ôr, dŏg, tŏp, cŏllide; ūnit, ūnite, bûrn, cŭt, focŭs; nōōn, fŏŏt; mound; çoin;

flow-er-et (flou′ĕr-ĕt), *n.* a little flower: also spelled **flow′ret.**

flow-er-pot (flou′ĕr-pŏt′), *n.* a vessel for holding earth in which to grow plants.

f l o w - e r - y (flou′ĕr-ĭ), *adj.* **1,** abounding in, or like, flowers; **2,** full of showy words and phrases; as, *flowery* language.

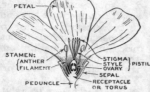
FLOWER, partly cut away to show its parts.

flown (flōn), past participle of *fly.*

flu (flōō), *n. Colloquial,* influenza, a contagious disease, marked by inflamed air passages, muscular pains, headache, digestive disturbances, and exhaustion.

fluc-tu-ate (flŭk′tū-āt), *v.i.* [fluctuat-ed, fluctuat-ing], **1,** to rise and fall like waves; **2,** to keep changing or wavering, as prices or temperature.—*n.* **fluc′tu-a′tion.**
     Syn. waver, oscillate, vacillate, vibrate.

flue (flōō), *n.* **1,** a pipe or passage for smoke, air, etc., as in a chimney; **2,** the opening in an organ pipe.

flu-en-cy (flōō′ĕn-sĭ), *n.* readiness or smoothness, especially in speaking.

flu-ent (flōō′ĕnt), *adj.* **1,** proceeding smoothly; flowing; **2,** ready or easy in the use of words, especially in speaking.
     Syn. glib, lively, talkative.

fluff (flŭf), *n.* light down or fur nap:— *v.t.* to puff up into a light mass; as, to *fluff* the hair.—*adj.* **fluff′y.**—*n.* **fluff′i-ness.**

flu-id (flōō′ĭd), *adj.* capable of flowing; liquid or gaseous:—**fluid dram** or **drachm,** a measure equal to one eighth of a fluid ounce; about a teaspoonful:—**fluid ounce,** a liquid measure of $\frac{1}{16}$ of a pint:—*n.* a substance which is capable of flowing, as a liquid or a gas.

flu-id-i-ty (flōō-ĭd′ĭ-tĭ), *n.* **1,** readiness to flow; **2,** changeableness.

FLUKES (F, F) OF AN ANCHOR

¹fluke (flōōk), *n.* **1,** the flattened, pointed end of an arm of an anchor; **2,** one of the lobes on the tail of a whale; **3,** the head of a harpoon, arrow, or lance.

²fluke (flōōk), *n.* a stroke of good or bad luck, especially in a game.

flume (flōōm), *n.* **1,** an artificial channel for carrying water; **2,** a gap or gorge through which a stream or river flows.

flung (flŭng), past tense and past participle of *fling.*

flunk (flŭngk), *n. Slang,* a complete failure:—*v.i. Colloquial,* to fail completely: —*v.t. Colloquial,* **1,** to fail in; as, to *flunk* history; **2,** to give (a student) a failing grade.

flunk-y or **flunk-ey** (flŭngk′ĭ), *n.* [*pl.* flunkies, flunkeys], **1,** a liveried servant; a footman; **2,** a cringing flatterer.

flu-o-res-cent (flōō′ō-rĕs′ĕnt), *adj.* having the property of converting invisible rays to visible light:—**fluorescent tube,** an electrical lighting tube whose source of light is a fluorescent coating inside the tube

flu-o-ri-date (flōō′ō-rĭ-dāt′), *v.t.* to treat with a compound of fluorine; as, to *fluoridate* water.—*n.* **flu′o-ri-da′tion.**

flu-o-rine (flōō′ō-rēn; flōō′ō-rĭn) or **flu-o-rin** (flōō′ō-rĭn), *n.* a pale, greenish-yellow gas, similar to chlorine.

flur-ry (flûr′ĭ), *v.t.* [flurried, flurry-ing], to excite; confuse; bewilder; as, to be *flurried* by a question:—*n.* [*pl.* flurries], **1,** a sudden commotion or excitement; **2,** a sudden gust of wind, rain, or snow.

¹flush (flŭsh), *v.t.* **1,** to redden; cause to blush; **2,** to excite; fill with elation; as, to be *flushed* with victory; **3,** to wash or cleanse by a strong flow of water:—*v.i.* to blush; glow:—*n.* **1,** a blush; glow; **2,** a sudden rush, as of water; **3,** a thrill, as of excitement, elation, or pleasure:—*adj.* **1,** abundantly supplied, as with money; **2,** even; level; as, nail the board *flush* with the other; **3,** vigorous; spirited; full of life.

²flush (flŭsh), *v.t.* to startle into flight, as birds.

flus-ter (flŭs′tĕr), *v.t.* to confuse; excite; agitate:—*n.* agitation or confusion.

flute (flōōt), *n.* **1,** a musical wind instrument, a wooden pipe with finger stops and a hole

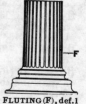
FLUTE, def. 1

on the side across which the player blows; **2,** a long, rounded, decorative groove, as in a column:—*v.i.* [flut-ed, flut-ing], to play on a flute:—*v.t.* to form grooves or folds in; as, to *flute* a ruffle.—*n.* **flut′ist.**

flut-ed (flōō′tĕd), *adj.* **1,** grooved; as, *fluted* columns; **2,** flute-like; clear; as, *fluted* notes.

flut-ing (flōō′tĭng), *n.* **1,** a set of grooves cut lengthwise in a column; **2,** a series of folds in a collar, ruffle, or the like.

FLUTING (F), def.1

flut-ter (flŭt′ĕr), *v.t.* to flap quickly without flying; as, the bird *flutters* his wings.—*v.i.* **1,** to move quickly and irregularly; as, curtains *flutter* in the wind; **2,** to be confused; flit about aimlessly; as, to *flutter* about at odd jobs:—*n.* **1,** a quick, irregular motion; vibration; as, the *flutter* of wings; **2,** a stir; excitement.

flux (flŭks), *n.* **1,** any flow or discharge of matter; **2,** continuous flowing; constant change; as, in a state of *flux;* **3,** a substance used to promote melting in metals: —*v.t.* to fuse or melt; make fluid.

fly (flī), *v.i.* [*p.t.* flew (floo), *p.p.* flown (flōn), *p.pr.* flying], **1,** to move through the air with wings, or as with wings; as, birds *fly;* we *flew* in an airplane; **2,** to float in the air; as, the flag

FLY, *n.* def. 2

flies; **3,** to move or go swiftly; as, he *flies* to her aid; **4,** to run away; flee:— *v.t.* to cause to fly or float; as, to *fly* an airplane:—*n.* [*pl.* flies (flīz)], **1,** any of a large number of insects with a single pair of wings; especially, the common housefly; **2,** a fishhook fitted with feathers to resemble an insect; **3,** in baseball, a ball batted so as to rise high in the air; **4,** a strip of material on a garment to cover or contain fastenings; **5,** a piece of canvas stretched over something to form an extra roof.

fly-a-way (flī'à-wā'), *adj.* **1,** streaming; loose, as a garment; **2,** flighty; as, a *flyaway* person.

fly-catch-er (flī'kăch'ẽr), *n.* **1,** a small bird which feeds on insects, capturing them while flying; **2,** a plant which traps insects, as the pitcher plant.

fly-er (flī'ẽr), *n.* a flier. See **flier.**

fly-ing (flī'ĭng), *adj.* **1,** moving through the air, as on wings; **2,** capable of gliding through the air; as, a *flying* squirrel; **3,** floating or moving freely, as a flag; **4,** moving rapidly; as, a *flying* horse; **5,** fleeting; brief; as, a *flying* visit.

flying boat, a kind of seaplane (see illustration at *aviation*); **flying fish,** any fish with winglike fins by which it can glide a short distance through the air; **flying frog,** a tree frog of the East Indies capable of long, gliding leaps (see illustration at *amphibian*); **fly-ing wing,** an airplane of unusual triangular design.

fly-leaf (flī'lēf'), *n.* [*pl.* flyleaves (-lēvz')], a blank sheet at the beginning or end of a book.

fly-speck (flī'spĕk'), *n.* any small spot, especially the excrement of a housefly.

fly-wheel (flī'hwēl'), *n.* a heavy wheel in a machine to regulate and make more uniform its speed and motion.

F.M. abbreviation for *frequency modulation.*

foal (fōl), *n.* the young of the horse or similar animal; a colt:—*v.i.* to give birth to a foal.

foam (fōm), *n.* the white substance formed on a liquid by shaking or fermentation; froth:—*v.i.* to form or produce foam; as, the dog *foamed* at the mouth.—*adj.* **foam'y.**

fob (fŏb), *n.* **1,** a small pocket for a watch; **2,** a short watch chain or ribbon; also, a small ornament at the end of it.

f.o.b. abbreviation for *free on board,* a commercial term indicating that the price pays for loading on railroad cars at the point mentioned, but not further transportation; as, the price of this car is $700, *f.o.b.* Detroit.

fo-cal (fō'kăl), *adj.* relating to a focus; placed at a central point.

Foch (fôsh), Ferdinand (1851–1929), Marshal of France, commander of the Allied Armies during part of World War I.

fo-cus (fō'kŭs), *n.* [*pl.* focuses (fō'kŭs-ĕz) or foci (fō'sī)], **1,** the point at which rays of heat, light, sound, etc., meet after being bent or

FOCUS, def. 1
Parallel rays of light brought to a focus (F) by a convex lens.

turned from the straight lines in which they radiate; **2,** an adjustment of eyes, glasses, camera lenses, etc., to produce clear sight or images; **3,** a central point; center of interest:—*v.t.* [focused, focusing], **1,** to adjust the focus of (eyes, a telescope, camera, etc.); **2,** to bring into focus; **3,** to center; concentrate; as, he *focused* his attention on history.

fod-der (fŏd'ẽr), *n.* coarse food, such as dried cornstalks, for cattle.

foe (fō), *n.* **1,** an enemy; **2,** anything injurious; as, ill health is a *foe* to happiness. *Syn.* adversary, antagonist, opponent.

foe-tus (fē'tŭs), *n.* the unborn young of animals; a fetus. See **fetus.**

fog (fŏg), *n.* **1,** a cloud of water vapor near the surface of the sea or land; **2,** any haziness, as on a photographic plate; **3,** bewilderment; as, my thoughts are in a *fog:*—**fog bank,** a dense mass of fog on the surface of the sea:—*v.i.* [fogged, fogging], to become clouded, as with a fog:— *v.t.* to cover as with a fog; cloud.

fog-gy (fŏg'ĭ), *adj.* [fog-gi-er, fog-gi-est], **1,** filled or thick with fog; as, a *foggy* day; **2,** hazy; obscure, as a photographic plate; **3,** not clear; confused; as, *foggy* ideas.— *adv.* **fog'gi-ly.**—*n.* **fog'gi-ness.**

fog-horn (fŏg'hôrn'), *n.* a siren or horn for warning ships in a fog.

fo-gy (fō'gĭ), *n.* [*pl.* fogies], a person of old-fashioned or dull habits and ideas.

foi-ble (foi'bl), *n.* a weak point; a failing

āte, ā̇orta, râre, căt, ȧsk, fär, ȧllow, sofà; ēve, ĕvent, ĕll, writẽr, novĕl; bīte, pĭn; nō, ōbey, ôr, dŏg, tŏp, cŏllide; ūnit, ūnite, bûrn, cŭt, focŭs; noon, foot; mound; coin;

Common Wild Flowers of the United States. (*See other side.*)

1, aster; 2, laurel; 3, wood lily; 4, coneflower; 5, lady's-slipper; 6, mountain columbine; 7, eastern columbine; 8, cardinal flower; 9, shooting star; 10, azalea; 11, pasqueflower; 12, fringed gentian; 13, Mariposa lily; 14, pitcher plant; 15, violet; 16, bitterroot; 17, a cactus.

COMMON WILD FLOWERS OF THE UNITED STATES

It has been estimated that in the entire United States there are nearly ten thousand varieties of wild flowers. Some of these varieties are very rare and confined to very limited regions; others are to be found almost everywhere. Those that are pictured on the previous page have been selected as representative of all parts of the United States.

The New England aster (1) and the cone-flower (4) are members of the great "composite" group of plants whose flowers consist of a head, or cluster, made up of small disk flowers, at the center, surrounded by larger petal-like flowers. Both the New England aster and the coneflower are widespread east of the Rocky Mountains, and blossom in the early autumn.

The mountain laurel (2) is a member of the heath family. It blooms on waste, rocky hillsides in early summer, and is widespread in eastern North America. It is closely related to the rhododendron and to the azalea (10).

Though not the largest or showiest of the wild lilies, the wood lily (3) is one of the most widely distributed. In the prairies of the Middle West it is redder than in the East. It blooms in early summer, and, like most members of the lily family, it has three sepals and three petals, all of the same color.

Probably the best known of our wild orchids are the lady's-slippers (5), widely, though not abundantly, spread east of the Rocky Mountains. The name lady's-slipper comes from the large saclike lip which suggests a slipper, or a wooden shoe.

Favorites with lovers of flowers, and also with nectar-sipping insects, are the graceful columbines (6, 7). Each spur of the flower conceals at its base a sac full of nectar, which yields a food for long-tongued insects and certain bees, which obtain the nectar by drilling through the thin wall of the flower.

Most of the lobelias are blue or white, but the cardinal flower (8) is a brilliant exception. It is found, often growing alone, along the water's edge of lakes and streams in the eastern United States and Canada, blooming in late August and early September. Once seen, it is seldom forgotten.

The shooting star (9) belongs to the primrose family. It is a spring flower, blooming abundantly on prairies and moist cliffs, from Manitoba to Texas, and as far east as Pennsylvania and Maryland. Its color varies from a deep magenta to white.

The purple azalea (10) is found growing wild in the eastern United States. Blooming in May, before the leaves are out on the trees, it forms beautiful, shimmering patches of pale or deep rose against a background of brown woods.

The pasqueflower (11) is the most showy of the anemones. The variety pictured may be found blooming in the early spring northwestward of the Mississippi River. It often shoots up through rocks where no other plants appear.

The fringed gentian (12), though not abundant, is the best known flower of the gentian family. It blossoms in the fall, in low grounds, from western Quebec south to Georgia, and westward to Iowa and the Dakotas.

The Mariposa lily (13) is found westward of the Rocky Mountains, bearing bell-shaped flowers, which may be yellow, white, or lilac.

The northern pitcher plant (14) is found in cranberry and peat bogs. Its cuplike leaves usually contain some water, and in the water are usually to be found a number of dead insects. These have found it much easier to crawl in than to crawl out. Their dead bodies are supposed to supply the plant with some of its food. The leaves, as well as the flowers, are beautifully colored in red, brown, and green.

The bird's-foot violet (15), named from the shape of its leaf, is one of the daintiest of the violets. Though not so common as its darker cousins, it is found widely distributed in the eastern and central parts of the country.

The bitterroot (16) and the cactus (17) represent plants that flourish in dry regions of the West. The root of the bitterroot is the main part of the plant, living throughout the year. When the moist season begins, the plant sends up a few slender leaves and bursts into bloom. Then the leaves die down, and the whole plant lies dormant until the next rainy season.

The cactus stores up enough moisture in its thick, fleshy stem to carry it through long dry periods. Its leaves are reduced to mere spines which protect it from animals that would otherwise devour it.

or weakness of character; as, humorists write about the *foibles* of mankind.

¹**foil** (foil), *n.* 1, a thin, flexible sheet of metal; as, tin *foil;* gold *foil;* 2, a thin coat of metal placed on the back of a mirror to reflect light; also, such a coat placed under stones in jewelry to set off their brightness; 3, anything that sets off another thing to advantage by contrast; as, her poor clothes are a *foil* to her beauty.

²**foil** (foil), *n.* a long, thin sword with a blunt point, used in fencing.

FOIL

³**foil** (foil), *v.t.* to baffle; defeat; as, every attempt was *foiled* by the enemy.
   Syn. thwart, overthrow, outwit, balk, frustrate.

foist (foist), *v.t.* to palm off; pass (something false or counterfeit) as genuine; as, to *foist* a false gem on a buyer.

¹**fold** (fōld), *v.t.* 1, to double; bend over; as, to *fold* a letter; 2, to clasp, as the hands; to bend close to the body; as, to *fold* one's arms; a bird *folds* its wings; 3, to envelop; as, peaks *folded* in clouds:—*v.i.* to become closed by bending or doubling; as, the airplane's wings *folded* up:—*n.* a part doubled over another; also, a hollow or crease made by folding.

²**fold** (fōld), *n.* 1, a pen for sheep; 2, a flock of sheep; 3, a body of religious believers:—*v.t.* to shut up (sheep) in a pen.

fold·er (fōl′dẽr), *n.* 1, a small folded circular, map, or the like; 2, a cover for holding loose papers.

fo·li·age (fō′li̇-ij), *n.* leaves; all the leaves of a plant.

fo·li·o (fō′li̇-ō; fōl′yō), *n.* [*pl.* folios], 1, a sheet of paper folded once; 2, a book of the largest size, made of sheets of paper folded only once, with two leaves or four pages to each sheet; 3, the size of a book so made; 4, a folder for carrying music, loose papers, or the like; 5, in printing, the number of a page:—*adj.* consisting of sheets of paper folded once; having the form or size of a folio; as, a *folio* edition:—*v.t.* to number the pages of (a book or manuscript).

folk (fōk), *n.* 1, a race or nation; 2, **folks** or **folk**, *pl.*, people collectively, especially common people; as, town *folk;* some *folks* like to travel; 3, **folks**, *Colloquial,* one's own kindred; as, my *folks* are away:—*adj.* originating with the people; as, a *folk* tale.

folk dance, 1, a dance originating with the common people of any race, and kept up by tradition; 2, the music of such a dance.

folk-lore (fōk′lôr′), *n.* traditions, beliefs, customs, etc., originating long ago among the common people of any nation, and kept alive among them.

folk song, a song originating among the common people, and handed down orally.

fol·li·cle (fŏl′i̇-kl), *n.* 1, a dry seed vessel, as of milkweed; 2, a tiny cavity or sac, as that from which a hair grows.

fol·low (fŏl′ō), *v.t.* 1, to go or come after; as, we *followed* the guide; 2, to come after in time or rank; as, he *followed* his father in office; 3, to go along; as, to *follow* a road; 4, to strive after; aim at; as, to *follow* fame; 5, to copy; imitate; as, your idea *follows* his; 6, to accept as guide; obey; as, to *follow* advice; 7, to practice as a profession; as, he *followed* medicine; 8, to pay attention to; to understand; as, to *follow* a lecture; 9, to result from; as, illness *follows* neglect of health:—*v.i.* 1, to go or come after another; as, go ahead, and we will *follow;* 2, to be inferred; as, it *follows* from your remark that you intend to leave.
   Syn. succeed, pursue, chase.

fol·low·er (fŏl′ō-ẽr), *n.* one who follows another person, or a doctrine, as a disciple, dependent, attendant, or admirer.

fol·low·ing (fŏl′ō-ĭng), *adj.* coming after; next; as, the *following* year; read the *following* page:—*n.* 1, a body of followers or supporters; as, a political leader with a very large *following;* 2, those about to be mentioned; as, the *following* were there.

fol·ly (fŏl′i̇), *n.* [*pl.* follies], 1, lack of sense; want of understanding; foolishness; 2, a foolish act or idea.
   Syn. silliness, senselessness, levity.

fo·ment (fṓ-mĕnt′), *v.t.* 1, to bathe with warm liquids; 2, to foster; excite; stir up; as, to *foment* a riot.—*n.* fo′men·ta′tion.

fond (fŏnd), *adj.* 1, affectionate; loving; 2, interested in; as, *fond* of music; 3, cherished; as, my *fond* hope.—*adv.* **fond′ly.**

fon·dle (fŏn′dl), *v.t.* [fon-dled, fon-dling], to caress; pet; as, to stroke and *fondle* a cat.

¹**font** (fŏnt), *n.* 1, a vessel to hold holy water or water for baptizing; 2, a fountain or spring.

²**font** (fŏnt), *n.* a full assortment of one size and style of type. In British usage, **fount.**

Fon-taine-bleau (fŏn′tân-blō′), a town and forest, southeast of Paris, France, where there is a palace of the former French kings.

BAPTISMAL FONT

Foo·chow (foo'chou'), a city, capital of Fukien province, in southeastern China (map 15).

food (food), *n.* 1, nourishment taken into the body to keep it alive and make it grow; also, any nourishing substance; 2, solid nourishment in contrast to liquid.
Syn. diet, fare.

food-stuff (food'stŭf'), *n.* anything used as food, as meats, cereals, and fruits.

fool (fool), *n.* 1, a person of little sense or intelligence; 2, in former times, a jester or clown; 3, a dupe; a victim of a joke; as, to make a *fool* of him:—*v.t.* to deceive or trick:—*v.i.* to trifle; play the fool.—*adj.* and *n.* **fool'ing.**—*n.* **fool'er·y.**

fool·har·dy (fool'här'dĭ), *adj.* having courage without judgment; heedless of consequences; rash.—*n.* **fool'har'di·ness.**
Syn. venturesome, reckless, bold.

fool·ish (fool'ish), *adj.* 1, without reason or judgment; 2, silly; ridiculous.—*adv.* **fool'ish·ly.**—*n.* **fool'ish·ness.**
Syn. simple, brainless, absurd.

fool-proof (fool'proof'), *adj.* simple or easy enough to be understood by anyone.

fools·cap (foolz'kăp'), *n.* 1, a hat adorned with bells, formerly worn by court jesters; 2, a size of paper about seventeen inches by fourteen inches, originally watermarked with the jester's cap and bells.

foot (foot), *n.* [*pl.* feet (fēt)], 1, that part of the leg on which man and other animals walk or stand; 2, the lowest part; base; as, the *foot* of a tree or a hill; 3, the lowest part in rank; as, the *foot* of the class; 4, the part of a boot or stocking which receives the foot; 5, that part of anything where the feet lie; as, the *foot* of a bed; 6, a measure of length, equal to twelve inches; 7, unmounted soldiers; infantry; 8, in poetry, a group of syllables containing one accented syllable and one or more unaccented syllables; as, the line "Peter,/Peter,/pumpkin/eater" has four metrical *feet:*—*v.t.* 1, to add a foot to, as to a stocking; 2, to add up (a column of figures) and place the total at the bottom; 3, *Colloquial,* to pay; as, to *foot* the bill.
to be carried off one's feet, to be overcome with enthusiasm; **with one foot in the grave,** near death; **to put one's foot down,** to be determined; **to put one's foot in it,** to blunder; **on foot,** 1, walking; 2, astir; under way; as, plans *on foot;* **to foot it,** to go on foot.

foot·ball (foot'bôl'), *n.* 1, a game in which an inflated leather ball must be carried or kicked across the opposing team's goal line; 2, the ball used in this game.

foot·bridge (foot'brĭj'), *n.* a bridge for travelers on foot.

foot·fall (foot'fôl'), *n.* a footstep: the sound of the tread of the foot.

foot·hill (foot'hĭl'), *n.* a low, outlying hill near the base of a mountain range.

foot·hold (foot'hōld'), *n.* a secure place to set foot; firm footing.

foot·ing (foot'ĭng), *n.* 1, firm placing of the feet; foothold; as, to lose one's *footing;* 2, a place to stand or walk; as, there was no *footing* along the cliff; 3, relationship; basis; as, a friendly *footing;* 4, the adding up, or the sum total, of a column of figures.

foot·lights (foot'līts'), *n.pl.* a row of lights along the front of the floor of the stage of a theater.

foot·man (foot'măn), *n.* [*pl.* footmen (-měn)], a male servant, usually in uniform, who attends a carriage, waits on table, etc.

foot·note (foot'nōt'), *n.* a note of explanation at the bottom of a page in a book.

foot·pad (foot'păd'), *n.* a highwayman who goes on foot.

foot·path (foot'påth'), *n.* a path for the use of persons who are walking.

foot—pound (foot'-pound'), *n.* a measure of energy; the amount of energy needed to raise one pound one foot.

foot·print (foot'prĭnt'), *n.* the mark made by a foot, as in mud, snow, or the like.

foot rule, a rule or measure twelve inches long.

foot sol·dier, a soldier who serves on foot; an infantryman.

foot·sore (foot'sôr'), *adj.* having sore feet, as from walking.

foot·step (foot'stĕp'), *n.* 1, an act of stepping; a step; 2, the sound of a step; 3, the mark of a foot, as in the earth; footprint; track.

foot·stool (foot'stool'), *n.* a low block or stool on which to rest the feet.

foot·work (foot'wûrk'), *n.* manner of using the feet, as in tennis, wrestling, etc.

fop (fŏp), *n.* a man who is fond of fine dress; a dandy.—*n.* **fop'per·y.**
Syn. dude, beau, coxcomb.

fop·pish (fŏp'ish), *adj.* vain; like a dandy in dress and manners.—*adv.* **fop'pish·ly.**

for (fôr), *prep.* 1, in place of; as, Jones ran bases *for* Brown; 2, as being; as, I took him *for* an honest man; 3, as equal to, in a trade; as, two pencils *for* five cents; 4, because of; as, he could not walk *for* weakness; 5, because of a hindrance or lack of; as, I'd go but *for* my lessons; pressed *for* time; 6, on account of; in the interest of; as, do it *for* your mother; fear *for* his safety; 7, in favor, support, or defense of;

as, to vote *for* White; **8,** in spite of; as, *for* all his money, he has no influence; **9,** to the amount of; as, a bill *for* five dollars; **10,** as regards; as, so much *for* that point; a love *for* poetry; **11,** in comparison or contrast with; as, wise *for* his years; one success *for* every ten failures; **12,** with the hope, intention, or expectation, of reaching, getting, doing, etc.; as, he left *for* Europe; to try *for* a prize; **13,** with a view to; for the purpose of; as, to go *for* a walk; **14,** suited to; as, a salve *for* burns; the man *for* the job; **15,** about; as, I don't care *for* cards; **16,** for the use of; as, books *for* the class:—*conj.* because; since; seeing that; as, get up, *for* day is here.

for- (fôr-), a prefix meaning: **1,** the opposite or negative of; as, *for*get, *for*bid; **2,** completely; as, *for*lorn, *for*spent.

for. abbreviation for *foreign.*

for-age (fŏr′ĭj), *n.* **1,** food for horses and cattle; **2,** a search for food or provisions for an army:—*v.i.* [foraged, forag-ing], to go in search of provisions:—*v.t.* to strip of provisions; ravage, as a land in wartime.—*n.* **for′ag-er.**

for-ay (fŏr′ā), *n.* in warfare, a raid:—*v.t.* and *v.i.* to plunder or ravage.

for-bade (fôr-băd′), past tense of *forbid.* Also spelled **for-bad′.**

¹**for-bear** (fôr′bâr), *n.* an ancestor; a forebear.

²**for-bear** (fôr-bâr′), *v.t.* [*p.t.* forbore (fôr-bôr′), *p.p.* forborne (fôr-bôrn′), *p.pr.* forbear-ing], to refrain; keep from; as, he *forbore* to ask questions:—*v.i.* to restrain oneself; be patient.

for-bear-ance (fôr-bâr′ăns), *n.* **1,** patient endurance; **2,** lenience towards offenders.

for-bid (fôr-bĭd′), *v.t.* [*p.t.* forbade or forbad (fôr-băd′), *p.p.* forbid-den (fôr-bĭd′n), or, *Archaic,* forbid, *p.pr.* forbidding], **1,** to prohibit; not to allow; **2,** to command (a person) not to do.

for-bid-ding (fôr-bĭd′ĭng), *adj.* stern; discouraging; as, a *forbidding* manner.—*adv.* **for-bid′ding-ly.**

for-bore (fôr-bôr′), past tense of ²*forbear:* —**forborne,** past participle of ²*forbear.*

force (fôrs), *n.* **1,** energy; power; vigor; strength; violence; as, the *force* of a blow; **2,** power to convince or persuade; as, the *force* of an argument; **3,** real meaning, as of a word; **4,** (often *forces*), military or naval strength; armed men; warships or aircraft; **5,** hence, any trained or organized body of persons; as, the police *force;* the night *force* of a hospital; **6,** any powerful person or thing; as, a *force* for social reform; **7,** mental or moral strength; as, *force* of character; **8,** great numbers; as,

the people ran out in *force;* **9,** violence to persons or property; **10,** in physics, anything which causes or changes motion in a body; as, the *force* of gravity, electricity, heat, etc.:—**force pump,** a pump that forces water through valves under pressure:—*v.t.* [forced, forc-ing], **1,** to compel; as, to *force* her to talk; **2,** to push; get by strength; as, to *force* one's way; **3,** to produce by unnatural or special effort; as, to *force* a smile; **4,** to break open; as, to *force* a lock; **5,** to press or impose; as, to *force* a gift on someone; **6,** to hasten the growth of (a plant) artificially.

Syn., n. compulsion, might.

forced (fôrst), *adj.* done under compulsion or by extraordinary effort; strained; as, a *forced* march.

force-ful (fôrs′fŏŏl), *adj.* having vigor; strong; powerful; as, a *forceful* speech.— *adv.* **force′ful-ly.**—*n.* **force′ful-ness.**

for-ceps (fôr′sĕps), *n.* [*pl.* forceps], a pair of pincers used by surgeons for operations, or by dentists for extracting teeth.

for-ci-ble (fôr′sĭ-bl), *adj.* **1,** vivid; convincing; powerful; as, *forcible* speech; **2,** accomplished by violence; as, a *forcible* entry.—*adv.* **for′ci-bly.**

Syn. energetic, mighty, convincing.

ford (fôrd), *n.* a shallow part of a stream, which can be crossed on foot:—*v.t.* and *v.i.* to pass through (water, a stream, etc.,) on foot.

FORCEPS

fore (fôr), *n.* the front part:—*adj.* and *adv.* at or near the front:—*interj.* used as a warning on a golf course.

fore—and—aft (fôr′-ănd-ăft′), *adj.* lengthwise of a ship; as, *fore-and-aft* sails.

¹**fore-arm** (fôr′ärm′), *n.* the arm between the wrist and the elbow.

²**fore-arm** (fôr-ärm′), *v.t.* to arm, or prepare for conflict, beforehand.

fore-bear (fôr′bâr), *n.* an ancestor. Also spelled **for′bear.**

fore-bode (fôr-bōd′), *v.t.* [forebod-ed, forebod-ing], **1,** to have a feeling or suspicion of (coming misfortune); foresee (evil); **2,** to be a sign or warning of; as, conditions *forebode* war.

Syn. portend, prophesy, betoken.

fore-bod-ing (fôr-bōd′ĭng), *n.* a feeling that misfortune is coming.

fore-cast (fôr′kăst′), *n.* a foretelling, as of the weather:—*v.t.* (fôr-kăst′; fôr′kăst′), [forecast or forecast-ed, forecast-ing], to plan or calculate beforehand; to predict.

Syn., n. prophecy, estimate.

fore-cas-tle (fōk′sl; fôr′kȧs-l), *n.* the part of a vessel forward of the foremast.

fore-close (fôr-klōz′), *v.t.* [foreclosed, fore-clos-ing], to terminate (a mortgage) by obtaining the legal right to the property mortgaged.—*n.* **fore-clo′sure.**

fore-doom (fôr-dōom′), *v.t.* to doom beforehand; mark for ruin.

fore-fa-ther (fôr′fä′thẽr), *n.* an ancestor.

fore-fin-ger (fôr′fĭng′gẽr), *n.* the first or index finger, next to the thumb.

fore-foot (fôr′fŏot′), *n.* [*pl.* forefeet (-fēt′)], a front foot of a four-legged animal.

fore-front (fôr′frŭnt′), *n.* the place or part farthest front; foremost place.

fore-gath-er (fôr-găth′ẽr), *v.i.* to come together; forgather. See **forgather.**

fore-go (fôr-gō′), *v.t.* [*p.t.* forewent (fôr-wĕnt′), *p.p.* foregone (fôr-gôn′), *p.pr.* fore-go-ing], to give up. See **forgo.**

fore-go-ing (fôr-gō′ĭng), *adj.* coming ahead of something else; preceding.

fore-gone (fôr-gôn′; fôr′gôn), *adj.* settled in advance; as, a *foregone* conclusion.

fore-ground (fôr′ground′), *n.* that part of a picture, landscape, or scene nearest the observer.

fore-hand (fôr′hănd′), *adj.* in tennis, made, as a stroke, with the arm at the side, not extended across the body.

fore-hand-ed (fôr′hăn′dĕd), *adj.* **1,** ahead of time; **2,** looking to the future; prudent; as, be *forehanded* and save your pennies.

fore-head (fŏr′ĕd), *n.* the part of the face above the eyes; brow.

for-eign (fŏr′ĭn), *adj.* **1,** belonging to another nation or country; as, a *foreign* language; **2,** not native; as, of *foreign* birth; **3,** not belonging or suitable; as, remarks *foreign* to the topic.
    Syn. distant, extraneous, remote, outlandish, alien.

for-eign-er (fŏr′ĭn-ẽr), *n.* a person from some other country.

fore-know (fôr-nō′), *v.t.* [*p.t.* foreknew (fôr-nū′), *p.p.* foreknown (fôr-nōn′), *p.pr.* foreknow-ing], to know beforehand.—*n.* **fore-knowl′edge** (fôr-nŏl′ĕj).

fore-land (fôr′lănd), *n.* a point of land projecting into the sea; a headland.

fore-leg (fôr′lĕg′), *n.* a front leg of a four-footed animal.

fore-lock (fôr′lŏk′), *n.* a lock of hair growing on the front part of the head.

fore-man (fôr′măn), *n.* [*pl.* foremen (-mĕn)], **1,** the man in charge of a group of workmen; **2,** the chairman and spokesman of a jury.—*n. fem.* **fore′wom′an.**

fore-mast (fôr′mȧst′; fôr′mȧst), *n.* the mast nearest the bow of a ship. (See illustration on page 695.)

fore-most (fôr′mōst), *adj.* first; most important; chief.

fore-noon (fôr′nōon′), *n.* the time between sunrise and midday.

fo-ren-sic (fŏ-rĕn′sĭk), *adj.* belonging to the courts of law, or to public debate; as, a *forensic* style of speaking.

fore-or-dain (fôr′ôr-dān′), *v.t.* to appoint beforehand; decree or destine.

fore part, the first or front part of anything. Also written **fore′part′.**

fore-paw (fôr′pô′), *n.* a front foot of any animal that has claws.

fore-run-ner (fôr-rŭn′ẽr), *n.* **1,** a messenger sent in advance; **2,** anything which precedes or foreshadows another.

fore-sail (fôr′sāl′; fôr′sl; fō′sl), *n.* **1,** the largest and lowest sail on the foremast of a square-rigged vessel (see illustration on page 695); **2,** the big fore-and-aft sail on the foremast of a schooner.

fore-see (fôr-sē′), *v.t.* [*p.t.* foresaw (fôr-sô′), *p.p.* foreseen (fôr-sēn′), *p.pr.* foresee-ing], to know or see beforehand.

fore-shad-ow (fôr-shăd′ō), *v.t.* to point to as coming; predict.

fore-short-en (fôr-shôr′tn), *v.t.* in drawing or painting, to shorten (lines or objects) so that they will appear to be at the true distance from the observer, as compared with other lines or objects.

fore-sight (fôr′sīt′), *n.* **1,** knowing or seeing beforehand; **2,** thought for the future; prudence.
    Syn. care, forethought, prevision.

fore-skin (fôr′skĭn′), *n.* the sheath of skin covering the end of the male sex organ.

for-est (fŏr′ĕst), *n.* a growth of trees covering a large tract of land; wild woodland:—*adj.* of or relating to woodland; as, *forest* animals:—*v.t.* to cover with trees or woods.

fore-stall (fôr-stôl′), *v.t.* to hinder or prevent, by action taken in advance.

for-est-a-tion (fŏr′ĕs-tā′shŭn), *n.* extensive planting and care of trees.

fore-stay (fôr′stā′), *n.* a rope from the foremast head forwards to the side of a ship, to support the foremast. (See illustration on page 695.)

for-est-er (fŏr′ĕs-tẽr), *n.* **1,** one skilled in the care of trees; especially, one in charge of a tract of woodland, to guard its game and timber; **2,** a forest dweller.

for-est-ry (fŏr′ĕst-rĭ), *n.* the science of caring for forests.

āte, āorta, râre, căt, ȧsk, fär, ăllow, sofȧ; ēve, ĕvent, ĕll, writẽr, novĕl; bīte, pĭn; nō, ōbey, ôr, dŏg, tŏp, cŏllide; ūnit, ūnite, bûrn, cŭt, focŭs; nōon, fŏot; mound; coin;

fore-taste (fôr-tāst′), *v.t.* [foretast-ed, fore-tast-ing], to taste beforehand:—*n.* (fôr′tāst′), a taste beforehand; anticipation.

fore-tell (fôr-tĕl′), *v.t.* and *v.i.* [foretold (fôr-tōld′), foretell-ing], to tell beforehand; predict; prophesy.
Syn. forecast, portend.

fore-thought (fôr′thôt′), *n.* 1, the planning of something beforehand; 2, heedfulness for the future.

fore-told (fôr-tōld′), past tense and past participle of *foretell.*

fore-top (fôr′tŏp′), *n.* the platform at the head of the foremast of a ship.

for-ev-er (fôr-ĕv′ẽr), *adv.* 1, at all times; as, she was *forever* nagging Rip; 2, through eternity; perpetually.
Syn. endlessly, eternally, always.

fore-warn (fôr-wôrn′), *v.t.* to caution in advance.—*n.* **fore-warn′ing.**

fore-word (fôr′wûrd′), *n.* a preface; remarks introducing a longer discussion.

for-feit (fôr′fĭt), *n.* 1, something lost because of a crime or fault; hence, a fine or penalty; 2, **forfeits**, a game in which one must perform a silly task to regain some article given:—*v.t.* to lose by neglect or fault; as, to *forfeit* a game by coming late: —*adj.* lost by neglect or crime.

for-fei-ture (fôr′fĭ-tŭr), *n.* the losing of some right or possession by one's own fault; also, the thing so lost.

for-fend (fôr-fĕnd′), *v.t. Archaic,* to ward off; prevent, as a disaster.

for-gath-er or **fore-gath-er** (fôr-găth′ẽr), *v.i.* 1, to assemble; come together; 2, to associate.

for-gave (fôr-gāv′), past tense of *forgive.*

¹**forge** (fôrj), *v.i.* [forged, forg-ing], to go on steadily; as, to *forge* ahead.

²**forge** (fôrj), *v.t.* [forged, forg-ing], 1, to shape (metal) by hammering while it is soft with heat; 2, to shape; form; invent; 3, to make a false imitation of; especially, to counterfeit (a signature): —*n.* 1, an open fire for heating metal in preparation for hammering or shaping; 2, a shop for heating and working metal.—*n.* **forg′er.**
Syn., v. counterfeit.

FORGE

for-ger-y (fôr′jẽr-ĭ), *n.* [*pl.* forgeries], 1, the act of copying or imitating something, especially a signature, with intent to deceive; 2, a false signature; 3, anything counterfeit.

for-get (fôr-gĕt′), *v.t.* [*p.t.* forgot (fôr-gŏt′),

p.p. forgot-ten (fôr-gŏt′n) or forgot, *p.pr.* forget-ting], 1, fail to remember or recall; 2, cease to think of; as, he has *forgotten* me; 3, omit to take or do; as, I have *forgotten* my tonic; 4, neglect; disregard; as, to *forget* a debt:—*v.i.* to fail to remember.

for-get-ful (fôr-gĕt′fŏŏl), *adj.* 1, apt not to remember; as, old people are often *forgetful;* 2, neglectful; careless; as, *forgetful* of duty.—*adv.* **for-get′ful-ly.**

for-get—me—not (fôr-gĕt′=mē̆-nŏt′), *n.* a plant with tiny, yellow-eyed blue or white flowers and hairy, rough leaves.

forg-ing (fôr′jĭng), *n.* 1, any piece of forged metal; 2, forgery.

for-give (fôr-gĭv′), *v.t.* [*p.t.* forgave (fôr-gāv′), *p.p.* for-giv-en (fôr-gĭv′ĕn), *p.pr.* forgiv-ing], 1, to cease to resent; to pardon; as, to *forgive* an unkindness; *forgive* him for doing it; 2, to refrain from exacting, as a debt.—*adj.* **for-giv′ing.**—*adv.* **for-giv′ing-ly.**
Syn. condone, excuse, absolve, acquit.

FORGET-ME-NOT

for-giv-en (fôr-gĭv′ĕn), the past participle of *forgive.*

for-give-ness (fôr-gĭv′nĕs), *n.* 1, pardon; remission; as, *forgiveness* of sin; 2, readiness to pardon; as, full of *forgiveness.*
Syn. leniency, forbearance, mercy.

for-go (fôr-gō′), *v.t.* [*p.t.* forwent (fôr-wĕnt′), *p.p.* forgone (fôr-gôn′), *p.pr.* forgoing], to give up; deny oneself. Also, **fore-go′.**

for-got (fôr-gŏt′), past tense and a past participle of *forget:*—**forgotten,** a past participle of *forget.*

fo-rint (fō′rĭnt), *n.* the monetary unit of Hungary. (See table, page 943.)

fork (fôrk), *n.* 1, a farm tool with two or more prongs and a handle, used for digging, picking up, carrying, etc.; as, a pitch*fork;* 2, a small, pronged implement for dining-room or kitchen use; 3, anything branching like a fork; as, a *fork* in a road or a tree:—*v.t.* 1, make in the shape of a fork; 2, raise, throw, or dig with a fork; as, to *fork* hay: —*v.i.* to branch; as, the road *forks* here.

forked (fôrkt; *Poetic,* fôr′kĕd), *adj.* 1, having prongs; 2, opening into two or more parts; as, a *forked* road; a *forked* stick; 3, zigzag; fork-shaped; as, *forked* lightning.

for-lorn (fôr-lôrn′), *adj.* forsaken; miserable; pitiful; as, a *forlorn* beggar.
Syn. abandoned, deserted, desolate, lone, helpless, friendless.

---

go; join; yet; sing; chin; show; thin; *th*en; hw, *why;* zh, azure; ü, Ger. für or Fr. lune; ö, Ger. schön or Fr. feu; ṅ, Fr. enfant, nom; kh, Ger. ach or ich. See pages ix–x.

form (fôrm), *n.* **1,** the outward appearance or shape of anything; **2,** a body, especially the human body; **3,** special arrangement or method of composition; as, poetic *form;* sonata *form;* **4,** established practice or ritual; as, *forms* of worship; **5,** a definite manner of doing something; etiquette; as, the *form* for an introduction; **6,** a standard of conduct; as, tattling is bad *form;* **7,** athletic fitness; as, he's in good *form* to-day; **8,** a mold or pattern; as, a *form* for jelly; **9,** a typewritten or printed blank with spaces left to be filled in; also, a typewritten or printed letter to be sent out in great numbers; **10,** in printing, type locked in a frame ready for printing; **11,** a kind; variety; as, a tree is a *form* of plant life; **12,** a long bench without a back; **13,** a class or grade in a preparatory school; **14,** in grammar, the composition of a word in reference to spelling, pronunciation, inflection, etc.; as, "narcissus" has two plural *forms*, "narcissuses" and "narcissi":—*v.t.* **1,** to give shape to; make; as, to *form* a figure out of clay; **2,** to mold by influence; train; as, education helps to *form* the mind; **3,** to go to make up; as, music *formed* the greater part of the program; **4,** to develop; as, to *form* a habit; **5,** to construct (a word) by grammatical rules; as, to *form* the plural of a noun by adding *s:*—*v.i.* to take shape; as, lumps *formed* in the pudding.
Syn., n. figure, mold, fashion, semblance, rite, formality.

for-mal (fôr′măl), *adj.* **1,** according to established rules or conventions; as, a *formal* ceremony; **2,** having outward show but lacking reality; as, a *formal* friendship.—*adv.* **for′mal-ly.**
Syn. stiff, methodical, affected, precise, stilted.

form-al-de-hyde (fôr-măl′dē-hīd), *n.* a gas, mixed with water and used as a preservative and disinfectant.

For-ma-lin (fôr′mȧ-lĭn), *n.* a trade name for a solution of formaldehyde.

for-mal-ism (fôr′măl-ĭzm), *n.* exact or strict observance of outward forms, especially in religion and art.

for-mal-i-ty (fôr-măl′ĭ-tĭ), *n.* [*pl.* formalities], **1,** rigid observance of forms or established rules; **2,** a regular order of procedure; as, legal *formalities.*
Syn. form, conventionality, ceremony.

for-mat (fôr′măt), *n.* the whole style and size of a book, including the paper, type, and binding.

for-ma-tion (fôr-mā′shŭn), *n.* **1,** molding or shaping; as, *formation* of character; **2,** that which is shaped; structure; as, rock *formations;* also, shape; form; as, the for-

mation of the brain; **3,** arrangement of a body of troops; as, marching *formation.*

for-mer (fôr′mẽr), *adj.* preceding in time or order; as, *former* days; of the two speakers I prefer the *former.*
Syn. previous, prior, foregoing.

for-mer-ly (fôr′mẽr-lĭ), *adv.* in past time; as, he *formerly* lived in France.

for-mi-da-ble (fôr′mĭ-dȧ-bl), *adj.* fear-inspiring; hard to deal with or overcome; as, a *formidable* army.—*adv.* **for′mi-da-bly.**
Syn. terrible, tremendous, alarming.

For-mo-sa (fôr-mō′sȧ), a Chinese island (cap. Taipei) in the China Sea (map 15). Japanese name: Taiwan.

for-mu-la (fôr′mū-lȧ), *n.* [*pl.* formulas or formulae (fôr′mū-lē)], **1,** a set rule for doing something; **2,** the specified way of performing a ceremony or of expressing a faith or doctrine; **3,** a prescription, as for drugs; a recipe.

for-mu-late (fôr′mū-lāt), *v.t.* [formulated, formulat-ing], to put into a definite form; state in definite terms; as, to *formulate* a law.—*n.* **for-mu-la′tion.**

for-ni-ca-tion (fôr′nĭ-kā′shŭn), *n.* unlawful sexual intercourse between unmarried persons.—*n.* **for′ni-ca′tor.**

for-sake (fôr-sāk′), *v.t.* [*p.t.* forsook (fôr-sŏŏk′), *p.p.* forsak-en (fôr-sāk′ĕn), *p.pr.* forsak-ing], to give up; abandon; as, his friends will not *forsake* him.

for-sook (fôr-sŏŏk′), past tense of *forsake.*

for-sooth (fôr-sōōth′), *adv.* indeed; in truth; truly.

for-swear (fôr-swâr′), *v.i.* [forswore (fôr-swôr′), *p.p.* forsworn (fôr-swôrn′), *p.pr.* forswear-ing], to take an oath falsely:—*v.t.* **1,** to deny on oath; **2,** to renounce earnestly; **3,** to perjure (oneself).
Syn. reject, forgo, abjure, perjure.

for-syth-i-a (fôr-sĭth′ĭ-ȧ; fôr-sī′thĭ-ȧ), *n.* an ornamental shrub of the olive family bearing bright yellow flowers in early spring before the leaves appear.

fort (fôrt), *n.* a strongly fortified place; especially, a structure built for defense.

Fort Du-quesne (dŏŏ-kān′; dū-kān′), a former French fort on the site of Pittsburgh, Pennsylvania, captured by the English in 1758 (map 6).

¹forte (fôrt), *n.* one's strong point or special talent; as, his *forte* was music.

²for-te (fôr′tā), *adj.* and *adv.* loud; loudly: a term used in music.

forth (fôrth), *adv.* **1,** onward in time, place, or order; forward; as, from this day *forth;* **2,** out; outward; as, the sun sends *forth* light.

āte, âorta, râre, căt, ȧsk, fär, ăllow, sofȧ; ēve, ĕvent, ĕll, wrītẽr, novĕl; bīte, pĭn; nō, ōbey, ôr, dŏg, tŏp, cŏllide; ūnit, ūnite, bûrn, cŭt, focŭs; nōon, fŏŏt; mound; coin;

Forth, Firth of (fûrth′ ŏv fôrth′), the mouth of the Forth River, in central Scotland, flowing into the North Sea (map **13**).

forth-com-ing (fôrth′kŭm′ĭng), *adj.* ready or about to appear; approaching; as, our *forthcoming* trip; a *forthcoming* answer.

forth-right (fôrth′rīt′; fôrth′rīt′), *adj.* straightforward; decisive; as, a *forthright* reply:—*adv.* at once.

forth-with (fôrth′wĭth′; fôrth′wĭth′), *adv.* immediately; directly.

for-ti-eth (fôr′tĭ-ĕth), *adj.* next after the 39th: the ordinal of *forty:*—*n.* one of the 40 equal parts of anything.

for-ti-fi-ca-tion (fôr′tĭ-fĭ-kā′shŭn), *n.* **1,** the act of building or strengthening military defenses; **2,** a military work erected for defense; a fort.

for-ti-fy (fôr′tĭ-fī), *v.t.* [fortified, fortifying], **1,** to strengthen by forts, walls, etc.; as, to *fortify* a town; **2,** to make strong; as, to *fortify* one's courage.

for-tis-si-mo (fôr-tĭs′ĭ-mō), *adj.* and *adv.* very loud; very loudly: used in music.

for-ti-tude (fôr′tĭ-tūd), *n.* strength of endurance or courage in pain or trouble. *Syn.* endurance, resolution, fearlessness.

Fort Mon-roe (mŭn-rō′), a fortress at the entrance to Chesapeake Bay, in Virginia.

fort-night (fôrt′nīt; fôrt′nĭt), *n.* a period of two weeks.—*adv.* **fort′night-ly.**

for-tress (fôr′trĕs), *n.* a fortified place; a stronghold.

Fort Sum-ter (sŭm′tēr), a fort in Charleston harbor, South Carolina, the attack on which, on April 12, 1861, marked the beginning of the War between the States.

for-tu-i-tous (fôr-tū′ĭ-tŭs), *adj.* happening by chance; accidental; as, a *fortuitous* meeting.—*adv.* **for-tu′i-tous-ly.** *Syn.* incidental, random, casual.

for-tu-nate (fôr′tŭ-nĭt), *adj.* **1,** bringing good fortune; as, a *fortunate* play; **2,** lucky; successful; as, a *fortunate* person.—*adv.* **for′tu-nate-ly.** *Syn.* happy, prosperous, successful.

for-tune (fôr′tŭn), *n.* **1,** the good or ill that happens to a person; chance; luck; as, the good *fortune* to find friends; **2,** wealth; riches; **3,** future fate; as, tell my *fortune.*

for-tune-tell-er (fôr′tŭn-tĕl′ẽr), *n.* one who claims the ability to foretell events in the lives of others.

Fort Wayne (wān), a city in northeastern Indiana (map **7**).

Fort Worth (wûrth), a manufacturing and commercial city in Texas (map **8**).

for-ty (fôr′tĭ), *adj.* composed of one more than 39:—*n.* [*pl.* forties], **1,** the number consisting of 39 plus one; **2,** a sign representing forty units, as 40 or xl.

for-um (fôr′ŭm), *n.* [*pl.* forums or fora (fôr′à)], **1,** the public meeting place in ancient Rome where the law courts, public offices, etc., were situated; **2,** a place or gathering for public discussion.

¹**for-ward** (fôr′wẽrd) or **for-wards** (fôr′-wẽrdz), *adv.* toward the front; on or onward; as, to march *forward:*—*interj.* on!

²**for-ward** (fôr′wẽrd), *adj.* **1,** situated near the front; as, the *forward* ranks; **2,** early; ahead of time; as, *forward* crops; **3,** onward; as, a *forward* movement; **4,** ready; prompt; also, too confident; bold; as, a *forward* manner:—*v.t.* **1,** to help on; advance; as, to *forward* a cause; **2,** to send on or ahead; as, to *forward* mail. *Syn., v.* promote, further, facilitate.

fos-sil (fŏs′ĭl), *n.* **1,** a petrified animal or plant; a trace or remnant of a prehistoric animal or plant, imbedded or preserved in the earth, in rocks, or in caves; **2,** an old-fashioned person:—*adj.* **1,** petrified; like a fossil; **2,** out of date.

fos-ter (fôs′tẽr), *v.t.* **1,** to nourish; rear up; as, to *foster* a child; **2,** to support; cherish; as, to *foster* ideas:—*adj.* giving, receiving, or sharing nurture or care, though not related by blood; as, a *foster* mother; *foster* brother. *Syn., v.* promote, encourage, forward.

fought (fôt), past tense and past participle of *fight.*

foul (foul), *adj.* **1,** offensive; disgusting; as, a *foul* taste; **2,** dirty; soiled; as, *foul* linen; **3,** vulgar; obscene; as, *foul* language; **4,** morally offensive; odious; as, a *foul* deed; **5,** unfair; as, *foul* play; **6,** stormy; as, *foul* weather; **7,** clogged; as, a *foul* chimney; **8,** entangled; as, a *foul* rope; **9,** in collision; as, the ship ran *foul* of the rock:—*n.* **1,** in many games, as football, a play or act that is against the rules; **2,** in baseball, a batted ball which first strikes the ground outside of the lines marking out the playing field:—*v.t.* **1,** to make impure; as, to *foul* the air; **2,** to dishonor; as, to *foul* one's name; **3,** to collide with or entangle; as, to *foul* a cable:—*v.i.* **1,** to become dirty; **2,** to come into collision, as two boats; to become entangled; **3,** in baseball, to hit a foul ball.—*adv.* **foul′ly.**—*n.* **foul′ness.**

fou-lard (foo-lärd′), *n.* a light silk, or silk and cotton, washable dress fabric, satin finished, usually printed.

¹**found** (found), past tense and past participle of the verb *find.*

²**found** (found), *v.t.* to lay the basis of; to originate; establish; as, to *found* a city or an institution.—*n.* **found′er.**

³found (found), *v.t.* to form, as a metal, by melting and pouring into a mold; to cast.

foun-da-tion (foun-dā'shŭn), *n.* **1,** the act of establishing; as, the *foundation* of a school; **2,** the groundwork of a structure; as, a stone *foundation;* basis; as, the rumor has no *foundation;* **3,** an endowment or gift of money to support an institution; **4,** an endowed institution or charity.

foun-der (foun'dĕr), *v.i.* **1,** to fill and sink, as a ship; **2,** to go lame, as a horse; **3,** to fall down; collapse, as a building:—*v.t.* **1,** to cause (a ship) to fill with water and sink; **2,** to make (a horse) break down.

found-ling (found'lĭng), *n.* a child found after having been deserted by its unknown parents.

found-ry (foun'drĭ), *n.* [*pl.* foundries], **1,** the place where metal casting is carried on; as, an iron *foundry;* **2,** the act or process of casting metals.

fount (fount), *n.* a spring of water; a source.

foun-tain (foun'tĭn; foun'tĕn), *n.* **1,** a natural spring of water; **2,** a spring or source; as, a *fountain* of truth; **3,** an artificial jet or spout of water; also, the apparatus for producing it; **4,** a reservoir, as for ink in a pen, or oil in a lamp.

foun-tain-head (foun'tĭn-hĕd'; foun'tĕn-hĕd'), *n.* **1,** the spring from which a stream flows; **2,** a first source; as, the *fountain-head* of truth.

foun-tain pen, a pen having a reservoir for ink in the holder.

four (fōr), *adj.* consisting of one more than three:—*n.* **1,** the sum consisting of three plus one; **2,** a sign representing four units, as 4 or iv.

four-fold (fōr'fōld'), *adj.* having four parts; as, a *fourfold* task:—*adv.* (fōr'fōld'), four times as great or as many.

four-foot-ed (fōr'-foot'ĕd), *adj.* having four feet; as, a dog is a *four-footed* animal.

four-in-hand (fōr'-ĭn-hănd'), *n.* **1,** a team of four horses under one driver, or a coach drawn by it; **2,** a long necktie tied in a slipknot:—*adj.* pertaining to such a coach or necktie.

four-score (fōr'skôr'), *adj.* four times twenty; 80; as, *fourscore* years.

four-some (fōr'sŭm), *n.* in certain games, such as golf, a match in which four players, two on a side, take part.

four-square (fōr'skwâr'), *adj.* **1,** having four equal sides; **2,** honest.

four-teen (fōr'tēn'), *adj.* consisting of one more than thirteen:—*n.* **1,** the number consisting of thirteen plus one; **2,** a sign representing fourteen units, as 14 or xiv.

four-teenth (fōr'tēnth'), *adj.* next after the 13th: the ordinal of *fourteen:*—*n.* one of the fourteen equal parts of anything.

fourth (fōrth), *adj.* next after the third: the ordinal of *four:*—*n.* one of four equal parts of anything; a quarter.

fowl (foul), *n.* [*pl.* fowl or fowls], **1,** a bird; especially, the common rooster or hen; **2,**

FOWL
Parts of a fowl.

the flesh of the domestic fowl used as food:—*v.i.* to hunt wild birds.

fowl-er (foul'ĕr), *n.* one who catches or kills wild birds for sport or food.

fowl-ing piece, a light gun used especially for bird shooting.

Fox (fŏks), George (1624–1691), an English religious leader, founder of the Society of Friends, commonly called *Quakers.*

fox (fŏks), *n.* **1,** a wild animal of the dog family, with pointed ears and a bushy tail, noted for its cunning; **2,** the fur of this animal; **3,** a sly person.

fox-glove (fŏks'glŭv'), *n.* a plant having showy, upright spikes of bell-shaped flowers. Its leaves are used in medicine.

fox-hound (fŏks'hound'), *n.* a hound trained to hunt foxes.

fox ter-ri-er, a small, active, alert dog of the terrier family. There are two kinds, the smooth-haired fox terrier and the wire-haired fox terrier.

fox trot, a modern dance usually having two measures of slow movement followed by two measures of rapid movement; also, the music accompanying this dance:—*v.i.* to dance a fox trot.

FOXGLOVE

fox-y (fŏk'sĭ), *adj.* [fox-i-er, fox-i-est], pertaining to a fox; cunning; crafty.

āte, âorta, râre, căt, ȧsk, fär, ȧllow, sofȧ; ēve, ĕvent, ĕll, wrītĕr, nŏvĕl; bīte, pĭn; nō, ōbey, ôr, dŏg, tŏp, cŏllide; ūnit, ūnite, bûrn, cŭt, focŭs; nōōn, fŏŏt; mound; coin;

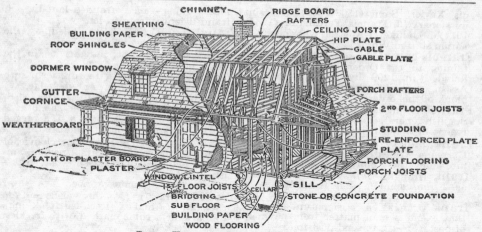

CHIMNEY — RIDGE BOARD — RAFTERS — CEILING JOISTS — HIP PLATE — GABLE — GABLE PLATE — SHEATHING — BUILDING PAPER — ROOF SHINGLES — DORMER WINDOW — GUTTER — CORNICE — WEATHERBOARD — PORCH RAFTERS — 2ND FLOOR JOISTS — STUDDING — RE-ENFORCED PLATE — PLATE — PORCH FLOORING — PORCH JOISTS — LATH OR PLASTER BOARD — PLASTER — WINDOW LINTEL — 1ST FLOOR JOISTS — CELLAR — SILL — BRIDGING — SUB FLOOR — BUILDING PAPER — WOOD FLOORING — STONE OR CONCRETE FOUNDATION

FRAME HOUSE showing details of construction.

foy-er (fwä′yā′; foi′ā; foi′ẽr), *n.* a lobby or entrance hall in a theater, hotel, etc.

fr. abbreviation for *franc:*—**Fr.** abbreviation for *France.*

fra-cas (frā′kás), *n.* [*pl.* fracases], a noisy quarrel; an uproar.

frac-tion (frăk′shŭn), *n.* 1, a fragment; a part; 2, in mathematics, a part, or an indicated number of equal parts of a whole; as, in the *fraction* ⅛ the whole has been divided into eight equal parts of which seven are indicated.—*adj.* **frac′-tion-al.**—*adv.* **frac′tion-al-ly.**

frac-tious (frăk′shŭs), *adj.* unruly; cross; as, a *fractious* child.—*adv.* **frac′tious-ly.**
 Syn. touchy, testy, fretful, rebellious.

frac-ture (frăk′tŭr), *n.* 1, the act of breaking; 2, a break, especially of a bone: —*v.t.* and *v.i.* [fractured, fractur-ing], to break or crack.

frag-ile (frăj′ĭl), *adj.* easily broken; delicate; as, a *fragile* dish.
 Syn. frail, brittle.

frag-ment (frăg′mĕnt), *n.* a part broken off from a whole; a portion, piece, or incomplete part; as, a *fragment* of the story.

frag-men-tar-y (frăg′mĕn-tĕr′ĭ), *adj.* composed of broken parts; disconnected; incomplete; as, a *fragmentary* report.

fra-grance (frā′grăns), *n.* sweetness of smell; an agreeable odor.

fra-grant (frā′grănt), *adj.* sweet-smelling; having a pleasing odor; as, a *fragrant* spice.—*adv.* **fra′grant-ly.**

frail (frāl), *adj.* 1, fragile or easily broken; as, a *frail* stem; 2, physically weak; as, a *frail* child; 3, morally weak.—*adv.* **frail′ly.**

frail-ty (frāl′tĭ), *n.* [*pl.* frailties], 1, weakness; as, *frailty* of character; 2, a failing or sin due to moral weakness.

frame (frām), *v.t.* [framed, fram-ing], 1, to put together; build; as, to *frame* a house; 2, to invent; plan; express; as, to *frame* a conspiracy; 3, to surround or enclose; as, to *frame* a picture:—*n.* 1, anything built or made of parts fitted together; as, the *frame* of a ship; 2, bodily structure; as, the slender *frame* of a girl; 3, a structure for holding, enclosing, or supporting something; as, a door *frame*; an embroidery *frame*; 4, established order; system; as, the *frame* of society; 5, any one of the single pictures on a motion picture film.
 frame of mind, state of mind; humor; **frame house**, a house built largely of wood, or around a wooden frame (see illustration above).—*n.* **fram′er.**
 Syn., v. construct, mold, fashion.

frame-work (frām′wûrk′), *n.* that which supports; a skeleton; as, the *framework* of a house or of the body.

franc (frăngk), *n.* 1, a copper-nickel coin, the monetary unit of France; 2, a silver coin, the monetary unit of Switzerland. (See Table, page 943.)

France (frăns), a republic (cap. Paris) in western Europe (map 12).

fran-chise (frăn′chĭz), *n.* 1, citizenship; the right to vote; 2, a special privilege granted by a government to a person or company; as, a *franchise* to run a bus line.

Fran-cis (frăn′sĭs), 1, Saint, of Assisi (1182–1226), an Italian friar who founded the Franciscan order of monks; 2, **Fran-**

cis **Xavier**, Saint (1506–1552), a Jesuit missionary; **3**, **Francis Ferdinand** (1863–1914), archduke of Austria, whose assassination started World War I.

Fran·cis·can (frăn-sĭs′kăn), *adj.* pertaining to the Order of Saint Francis, founded in 1209 by Saint Francis of Assisi, or to its members:—*n.* a nun or monk of this order.

Fran·co (fräng′kō), Francisco (1892–), Spanish general; chief of state (1939–1947); regent of Spanish monarchy (1947–).

Frank (frăngk), *n.* a member of one of the Germanic tribes that established an empire along the Rhine about A.D. 500.

¹**frank** (frăngk), *adj.* candid; outspoken; as, a *frank* opinion.—*adv.* **frank′ly.**
   Syn. honest, plain, direct, artless.

²**frank** (frăngk), *n.* a signature or mark that exempts mail matter from payment of postage:—*v.t.* to send post-free.

Frank·fort (frăngk′fẽrt), a city, capital of Kentucky (map 7).

Frankfurt (frăngk′fẽrt) **on the Main,** a commercial city of Germany (map 12).

frank·furt·er (frăngk′fẽr-tẽr), *n.* a highly seasoned beef-and-pork sausage.

frank·in·cense (frăngk′ĭn-sĕns), *n.* a fragrant resin from balsam trees, burned as incense.

Frank·lin (frăngk′lĭn), Benjamin (1706–1790), an American statesman, editor, and inventor.

fran·tic (frăn′tĭk), *adj.* wild; frenzied; as, *frantic* cries.—*adv.* **fran′ti·cal·ly.**
   Syn. furious, raving.

fra·ter·nal (frȧ-tûr′năl), *adj.* **1**, pertaining to, or like, a brother or brothers; as, *fraternal* love; **2**, naming or pertaining to a group or society of men who bind themselves together like brothers; as, a *fraternal* order.—*adv.* **fra·ter′nal·ly.**

fra·ter·ni·ty (frȧ-tûr′nĭ-tĭ), *n.* [*pl.* fraternities], **1**, brotherly relationship; **2**, a body of men joined by a common interest, especially such an organization in high schools and colleges.

frat·er·nize (frăt′ẽr-nīz), *v.i.* and *v.t.* [fraternized, fraterniz-ing], to associate as brothers.

frat·ri·cide (frăt′rĭ-sīd; frā′trĭ-sīd), *n.* **1**, the killing of one's own brother or sister; **2**, one who kills his brother or sister.

fraud (frôd), *n.* **1**, deceitfulness; trickery; **2**, a trick; **3**, *Colloquial,* one who cheats.
   Syn. deception, duplicity, guile.

fraud·u·lent (frôd′ū-lĕnt), *adj.* **1**, guilty of trickery; deceitful; dishonest; **2**, characterized by, or obtained by, unfair methods; as, *fraudulent* measures; *fraud-*

ulent gains.—*adv.* **fraud′u·lent·ly.**—*n.* **fraud′u·lence; fraud′u·len·cy.**

fraught (frôt), *adj.* laden; filled; as, the voyage was *fraught* with danger.

¹**fray** (frā), *n.* a riot; a fight; as, in the midst of the *fray.*

²**fray** (frā), *v.t.* and *v.i.* to rub; wear into shreds; as, a sleeve *frayed* at the edge.

fraz·zle (frăz′l), *v.t.* and *v.i.* [fraz-zled, fraz-zling], **1**, to fray or ravel, as cloth; **2**, hence, to tire or wear out:—*n.* **1**, a ragged end; **2**, the state of being exhausted.

freak (frēk), *n.* **1**, a capricious change of mind; whim; **2**, an abnormal person, animal, or plant.—*adj.* **freak′ish.**—*adv.* **freak′-ish·ly.**
   Syn. fancy, humor, caprice.

freck·le (frĕk′l), *n.* a brownish spot on the skin:—*v.t.* and *v.i.* [freck-led, freck-ling], to mark, or become marked, with freckles.—*adj.* **freck′ly.**

Fred·er·ick I (frĕd′ẽr-ĭk), (1121?–1190), called *Barbarossa* or *Redbeard,* emperor of the Holy Roman Empire and leader of the third crusade.

free (frē), *adj.* [fre-er, fre-est], **1**, having full personal and political liberty; as, a *free* people; **2**, loose; not attached; as, the *free* end of a rope; **3**, independent; as, a *free* church; **4**, at liberty; released; not caught or shut up; as, a *free* person or animal; **5**, not following rigid rules of form; as, *free* verse; **6**, not following the original exactly; as, a *free* translation; **7**, frank; also, informal; as, a *free* and easy manner; **8**, lavish; generous; as, *free* with praise; abundant; as, a *free* flow of blood; **9**, clear of obstructions; open; as, a *free* field; a *free* course; **10**, rid of or exempt from; as, *free* from disease or punishment; **11**, unhampered; not influenced by others; as, a *free* choice; **12**, given without cost; as, a *free* ticket; open to all; as, a *free* fight; **13**, impudent; as, a *free* tongue:—*v.t.* [freed, free-ing], **1**, to let go; set at liberty; as, to *free* an animal from a trap; **2**, to rid of; clear; as, to *free* someone of a charge of murder:—*adv.* without charge; as, to get in *free.*

free·boot·er (frē′bo͞o′tẽr), *n.* a buccaneer; pirate.

freed·man (frēd′măn), *n.* [*pl.* freedmen (frēd′mĕn)], a slave who has been set free.—*n.fem.* **freed′wom′an.**

free·dom (frē′dŭm), *n.* **1**, personal and political liberty; independence; as, a slave is given his *freedom;* the colonies won their *freedom;* **2**, free use; as, to be given the *freedom* of a clubhouse; **3**, exemption from; lack of; as, *freedom* from disease; *freedom* from taxes; **4**, state of being clear or unmixed; as, *freedom* from impurities; **5**, ease; as, to move with *freedom;* **6**, frankness; as, *freedom* in expressing his feelings; **7**, undue familiarity; as, he assumes too much *freedom* with his superiors.

Syn. unrestraint, license, immunity.

free-hand (frē/hănd/), *adj.* done or drawn by hand without the aid of ruler, compasses, etc.; as, a *freehand* sketch.

free-hand-ed (frē/hăn/děd), *adj.* generous.

free lance, a writer, actor, or other artist, who is not under contract to any one company.—*adj.* and *v.i.* **free/—lance/**.

free-ly (frē/lǐ), *adv.* in a free manner; without restraint; as, to speak *freely.*

free-man (frē/mǎn), *n.* [*pl.* freemen (-měn)], one who is not a slave.

Free-ma-son (frē/mā/sn; frē/mā/sn), *n.* a member of an ancient and almost worldwide secret society professing principles of brotherly love and mutual aid.

free-stone (frē/stōn/), *n.* **1**, stone suitable for working or cutting without splitting; **2**, a peach whose flesh, when ripe, does not stick to the stone.

free-think-er (frē/thǐngk/ẽr), *n.* one who forms his opinions independently, especially in religious matters.—*adj.* and *n.* **free/think/ing.**

Free-town (frē/toun), a town, capital and chief seaport of the British West African colony of Sierra Leone (map **14**).

free trade, trade not restricted by tariffs or customs duties.—**free trad/er.**

free-will (frē/wǐl/), *adj.* of one's own accord; voluntary; as, a *freewill* gift.

freeze (frēz), *v.t.* [*p.t.* froze (frōz), *p.p.* fro-zen (frō/zn), *p.pr.* freez-ing], **1**, to harden with cold; as, to *freeze* ice cream; **2**, to chill, damage, or kill with cold; as, to *freeze* plants:—*v.i.* **1**, to be changed into or covered with ice; as, the lake *freezes;* **2**, to be killed by cold or frost; as, the plants *froze* last night; **3**, to be very cold; as, I'm *freezing;* **4**, to be chilled with fear or horror; **5**, to stick or adhere because of cold; as, their hands *froze* to the oars.—*n.* **freez/er.**

freight (frāt), *n.* **1**, the goods with which a vessel or car is loaded; cargo; **2**, a method of transporting bulky goods, especially by train; also, a train that carries bulky goods; **3**, the sum paid for hauling goods:—*v.t.* **1**, to load with goods for hauling; **2**, to send (goods) by freight.

freight-age (frā/tǐj), *n.* **1**, transportation of goods, or the charge for it; **2**, a cargo.

freight-er (frā/tẽr), *n.* **1**, one who loads a ship or car; also, one who sends goods by freight; **2**, a vessel for carrying cargoes.

Fré-mont (frē-mŏnt/), John Charles (1813–1890), an American soldier, explorer, and adventurer.

French (frĕnch), *adj.* pertaining to France, its people, or its language:—*n.* the language of France:—**the French**, the people of France.—*n.* **French/man;French/wom/an.**

French E-qua-tor-i-al Af-ri-ca, a French colony (cap. Brazzaville) in central Africa, the territory of which reaches from the Congo valley to the Sahara Desert (map **14**). Formerly called *French Congo.*

French Gui-a-na, a colony in northeastern South America. See **Guiana**.

French Guin-ea, a colony in French West Africa. See **Guinea**.

French horn, a musical wind instrument of the brass group, consisting of a long coiled tube ending in a flaring bell. (See illustration at *musical instrument.*)

French In-di-a (ĭn/dǐ-à), a group of five former French colonies (cap. Pondichéry) in southeastern India (map **15**).

French In-do-Chi-na (ĭn/dō-chī/nà), formerly a French colony (cap. Hanoï), in southeastern Asia, now forming the states of Vietnam, Laos, and Cambodia (map **15**).

French O-ce-an-i-a (ō/shē-ăn/ĭ-à), a group of French islands (cap. Papeete in Tahiti) in the South Pacific.

French Rev-o-lu-tion, the revolution that took place in France, from the storming of the Bastille in 1789 to the proclamation of the Republic in 1792 and the beheading of Louis XVI in 1793.

French So-ma-li-land, a French protectorate in Africa. See **Somaliland**.

French Su-dan, a French colony in Africa. See **Sudan**.

French Un-ion, the Republic of France and its overseas territories.

French West Af-ri-ca, a French colony (cap. Dakar) in western Africa (map **14**).

French West In-dies, a group of French islands, southeast of Florida.

fren-zied (frĕn/zĭd), *adj.* maddened; frantic; as, *frenzied* efforts to swim.

fren-zy (frĕn/zĭ), *n.* [*pl.* frenzies], **1**, violent mental derangement; delirium; **2**, wild excitement or enthusiasm.

Syn. fury, raving, wildness.

fre-quen-cy (frē/kwĕn-sĭ), *n.* [*pl.* frequencies], **1**, the repeated happening of anything at short intervals; as, the *frequency* of storms; **2**, the number of happenings in a given time; rate of occurrence; **3**, the number of complete vibrations, or cycles, per second; as, the radio was tuned to a *frequency* of 990 kilocycles.

go; join; yet; sing; chin; show; thin, *th***en; hw,** *wh***y; zh, a**zure; **ū,** Ger. f**ü**r or Fr. l**u**ne; **ö,** Ger. sch**ö**n or Fr. f**eu**; **ň,** Fr. e**n**fant, no**m**; **kh,** Ger. a**ch** or i**ch**. See pages ix–x.

fre-quent (frē'kwĕnt), *adj.* **1,** occurring often; as, *frequent* delays; **2,** habitual; as, a *frequent* visitor:—*v.t.* (frē-kwĕnt'), to go to often or habitually; as, to *frequent* the theater.—*adv.* **fre'quent-ly.**

Syn., adj. numerous, usual, general.

fres-co (frĕs'kō), *n.* [*pl.* frescoes or frescos], **1,** the method or art of painting on plaster before it has dried; **2,** a painting made in this manner:—*v.t.* [frescoed, fresco-ing], to decorate or paint in fresco.

fresh (frĕsh), *adj.* **1,** new; not known or used before; as, a *fresh* sheet of paper; **2,** additional; different; as, to make a *fresh* start; **3,** recent; just made or arrived; as, a *fresh* report; **4,** newly gathered or produced; as, *fresh* grapes; not faded; as, *fresh* flowers; **5,** pure and cool; refreshing; as, *fresh* air; **6,** not preserved by salting or pickling; as, *fresh* ham; **7,** not salt; as, *fresh* water; **8,** not stale or spoiled; as, *fresh* fish; **9,** lively; not tired; vigorous; as, to feel *fresh* after a nap; **10,** raw; not experienced; as, a *fresh* recruit; **11,** *Slang*, bold; impudent; as, don't get *fresh.*—*adv.* **fresh'ly.**

Syn. sound, unused, good.

fresh-en (frĕsh'ĕn), *v.t.* **1,** to refresh; revive; as, I *freshened* myself after a hard day's work; **2,** to render less salt:—*v.i.* to become brisk; as, the wind *freshens.*

fresh-et (frĕsh'ĕt), *n.* a flood caused by melting snow or heavy rain.

fresh-man (frĕsh'măn), *n.* [*pl.* freshmen (-mĕn)], a college or high-school student in his first year.

¹fret (frĕt), *v.t.* [fret-ted, fret-ting], **1,** to chafe; wear or rub away; as, water *frets* a channel in a rock; **2,** to worry; irritate:—*v.i.* to be irritated; as, she *frets* over little things:—*n.* **1,** a worn spot; **2,** vexation; irritation.

²fret (frĕt), *n.* an ornamental design or pattern, consisting of unbroken combinations of short straight lines.

³fret (frĕt), *n.* a small ridge or bar of wood, metal, ivory, etc., on the neck of certain stringed instruments, as the mandolin, to regulate fingering.

fret-ful (frĕt'fŏŏl), *adj.* peevish; irritable; as, a *fretful* child.—*adv.* **fret'-ful-ly.**—*n.* **fret'ful-ness.**

Syn. testy, captious, querulous.

FRETWORK

fret-work (frĕt'wûrk'), *n.* a kind of carved, raised, or open ornamental work.

Fri. abbreviation for *Friday.*

fri-a-ble (frī'à-bl), *adj.* readily crumbled or reduced to powder.—*n.* **fri'a-bil'i-ty.**

fri-ar (frī'ẽr), *n.* a brother, or member of any of certain religious orders; a monk.

fric-as-see (frĭk'à-sē'), *n.* a dish of chicken, rabbit, or other meat cut into small pieces and stewed in gravy or sauce.

fric-tion (frĭk'shŭn), *n.* **1,** the rubbing of one thing against another; **2,** in machinery, the resistance one thing encounters when moving against another; **3,** conflict; difference of opinion.—*adj.* **fric'tion-al.**

Fri-day (frī'dĭ), *n.* the sixth day of the week.

fried (frīd), past tense and past participle of ²*fry.*

friend (frĕnd), *n.* **1,** a person bound to another by affection, esteem, and intimacy; **2,** a sympathizer; helper; a supporter of a cause; **3,** an ally:—**Friend,** a member of the Religious Society of Friends; a Quaker.

Syn. adherent, companion, comrade.

friend-li-ness (frĕnd'lĭ-nĕs), *n.* cordiality; sociability; good will.

friend-ly (frĕnd'lĭ), *adj.* [friend-li-er, friend-li-est], **1,** like a friend; kind; **2,** not hostile; as, a *friendly* tribe; **3,** played for mere sport; as, a *friendly* contest; **4,** favorable; as, a *friendly* breeze.

Syn. sociable, cordial, amicable, amiable.

Friend-ly Is-lands, a group of islands in the Pacific Ocean. See **Tonga Islands.**

friend-ship (frĕnd'shĭp), *n.* the relationship or attachment between people arising from mutual affection and admiration.

¹frieze (frēz), *n.* **1,** the part of an entablature below the cornice and above the architrave, usually ornamented; **2,** any ornamental or sculptured band around a wall.

²frieze (frēz), *n.* a coarse woolen cloth with a shaggy nap on one side.

FRIEZE

A, cornice; B, frieze; C, architrave.

frig-ate (frĭg'ĭt), *n.* **1,** originally, a light, swift vessel propelled both by oars and sails; **2,** a fast three-masted, square-rigged war vessel of the 18th and early 19th centuries:—**frigate bird,** a large, strong-winged, fish-eating sea bird, found over warm seas: also called *man-of-war bird.*

fright (frīt), *n.* **1,** violent fear; terror; alarm; **2,** *Colloquial*, anything ugly or ridiculous in appearance.

Syn. dread, dismay, horror.

FRIGATE BIRD (1/18)

fright-en (frīt'n), *v.t.* to terrify; alarm; startle.—*adj.* **fright'ened.**

fright-ful (frīt'fŏŏl), *adj.* **1,** terrible; dreadful; frightening; as, a *frightful* accident; **2,** *Colloquial,* grotesque; ugly; as, a *frightful* dress.—*adv.* **fright'ful-ly.**
Syn. fearful, dire, direful, terrific.

frig-id (frĭj'ĭd), *adj.* **1,** very cold; freezing; as, *frigid* weather; **2,** unfriendly; stiff; formal; as, a *frigid* welcome.—*adv.* **frig'-id-ly.**—*n.* **fri-gid'i-ty** (frĭ-jĭd'ĭ-tĭ).

frill (frĭl), *n.* **1,** an ornamental edging made of a strip of material gathered on one edge; a ruffle; **2,** *Colloquial,* an affectation of manner, speech, or dress.

fringe (frĭnj), *n.* **1,** a raveled, frayed edge on a fabric; also, a separate ornamental border of hanging cords, tassels, etc.; **2,** any border or edging like a fringe.

frip-per-y (frĭp'ĕr-ĭ), *n.* [*pl.* fripperies], tawdry finery; cheap gewgaws.

frisk (frĭsk), *v.i.* to skip or dance playfully.

frisk-y (frĭs'kĭ), *adj.* [frisk-i-er, frisk-i-est], lively; playful.—*adv.* **frisk'i-ly.**

frit-il-lar-y (frĭt'ĭ-lĕr'ĭ), *n.* [*pl.* fritillaries], **1,** a plant of the lily family with large, drooping, checkered, bell-shaped flowers; **2,** a kind of butterfly with spotted wings.

¹frit-ter (frĭt'ĕr), *n.* a fried cake made of batter, often containing meat or fruit.

²frit-ter (frĭt'ĕr), *n.* a fragment:—*v.t.* to cut or break into small pieces; hence, to waste; as, to *fritter* away one's time.

fri-vol-i-ty (frĭ-vŏl'ĭ-tĭ), *n.* [*pl.* frivolities], **1,** a trifling thought or act; **2,** light or silly thought, speech, or behavior.

friv-o-lous (frĭv'ŏ-lŭs), *adj.* **1,** of little importance; trivial; as, *frivolous* pastimes; **2,** not serious; giddy; as, *frivolous* people.—*adv.* **friv'o-lous-ly.**

friz or **frizz** (frĭz), *v.t.* and *v.i.* [frizzed, friz-zing], to curl in small, tight curls:—*n.* a small, crisp curl.—*adj.* **friz'zy.**

¹friz-zle (frĭz'l), *v.t.* and *v.i.* [friz-zled, friz-zling], to curl or friz:—*n.* a crisp, curled lock of hair.—*adj.* **friz'zly.**

²friz-zle (frĭz'l), *v.t.* and *v.i.* [friz-zled, friz-zling], to cook with a sputtering noise.

fro (frō), *adv.* away from; backward or back: used only in the phrase *to and fro.*

Fro-bish-er (frō'bĭsh-ĕr; frŏb'ĭsh-ĕr), Sir Martin (1535?-1594), a British navigator who sought a northwest passage to China.

frock (frŏk), *n.* **1,** a loose dress for children or women; **2,** a monk's habit; **3,** a coarse shirtlike garment for men.

frock coat, a double-breasted coat worn by men. It reaches almost to the knees and is the same length in front as behind.

Froe-bel (frö'bĕl), Friedrich (1782-1852), a German educator who started the kindergarten system.

¹frog (frŏg), *n.* **1,** a small, tailless amphibian with smooth skin, webbed feet, and remarkable swimming and leaping ability; **2,** soreness in the throat.

²frog (frŏg), *n.* **1,** a wedge-shaped, horny growth in the middle of the sole of a horse's foot; **2,** a plate used to guide the wheels of a railroad car where one track crosses another, or at a switch.

³FROGS (F), def. 1

³frog (frŏg), *n.* **1,** a covered button that fits into a loop, used as a fastening for cloaks, mantles, etc.; **2,** an attachment at the belt for supporting a sword or bayonet.

frol-ic (frŏl'ĭk), *n.* **1,** a scene of merrymaking or gaiety; **2,** a wild prank:—*v.i.* [frolicked, frolick-ing], to make merry.

frol-ic-some (frŏl'ĭk-sŭm), *adj.* full of sport or gaiety; playful; as, a *frolicsome* mood; a *frolicsome* child.

from (frŏm), *prep.* **1,** indicating a starting point in space, time, or a series; as, a letter *from* home; ten feet *from* a post; *from* morning to night; *from* childhood on; *from* 10 to 20; **2,** indicating a place, person, or thing left behind; as, turn your steps *from* folly; **3,** indicating removal; as, take candy *from* a box; pick berries *from* a bush; steal candy *from* a baby; **4,** indicating separation or freedom; as, excused *from* school; free *from* disease; **5,** indicating some condition changed for another; as, to go *from* bad to worse; **6,** indicating origin or source; as, translated *from* the French; weak *from* hunger; great oaks *from* little acorns grow; **7,** indicating a model or copy; as, drawn *from* life.

frond (frŏnd), *n.* the leaf of a fern, palm, or seaweed.—*adj.* **frond'ed.**

front (frŭnt), *n.* **1,** the foremost part of anything; **2,** the forehead; **3,** land that faces the sea, a river, stream, etc.; as, the beach *front*; the river *front*; **4,** in warfare, the scene of the actual fighting; **5,** a generally respected person who acts as agent for an underworld gang; **6,** a political party uniting several groups in opposition to the conservatives:—*adj.* situated at the foremost part; as, a *front* wall:—*v.t.* **1,** to stand, or be situated, opposite to; as, your house *fronts* mine; **2,** to confront; meet; as, to *front* danger; to *front* an enemy:—*v.i.* to have the front turned in a certain direction; as, his house *fronts* north.

front-age (frŭn'tĭj), *n.* **1,** the extent of a

building or of a piece of land along a street or road; **2,** the land lying between a building and a public roadway.

fron-tal (frŭn′tăl; frŏn′tăl), *adj.* having to do with the front or forehead; as, a *frontal* artery:—*n.* the bone of the forehead.

Fron-te-nac (frŏn′tĕ-năk), (1620?–1698), a French governor of Canada.

fron-tier (frŭn-tēr′; frŏn′tēr), *n.* **1,** the boundary of a country; **2,** the most remote settled part of a country, adjoining wild territory:—*adj.* pertaining to, or situated near, the boundary of a country; as, a *frontier* custom; a *frontier* town.

fron-tiers-man (frŭn-tērz′măn), *n.* [*pl.* frontiersmen (-měn)], **1,** an inhabitant of the border section of a country or of a newly settled region; **2,** a pioneer.

fron-tis-piece (frŭn′tĭs-pēs; frŏn′tĭs-pēs), *n.* an illustration facing the front page or title page of a book.

front-let (frŭnt′lĕt), *n.* **1,** a band worn on the forehead; **2,** the forehead of an animal.

frosh (frŏsh), *n.* in some American colleges, a student in his first term; a freshman.

frost (frôst), *n.* **1,** minute frozen particles of dew or vapor; hoarfrost; **2,** a temperature low enough to cause freezing of water; freezing weather; **3,** *Slang,* a failure: —*v.t.* **1,** to cover with frost, or with something like frost; **2,** to injure by frost; **3,** to cover (a cake) with icing.

frost-bite (frôst′bīt′), *n.* a partially frozen condition of a part of the body.— *adj.* **frost′bit′ten.**

frost-ed (frôs′tĕd), *adj.* **1,** covered with frost; **2,** injured by cold; frostbitten; frozen; **3,** covered with icing, as a cake; **4,** having a dull finish; as, *frosted* glass.

frost-ing (frôs′tĭng), *n.* **1,** a preparation of sugar mixed with a liquid, used in covering or icing cakes or pastry; **2,** a dull finish, as for metal or glass.

frost-y (frôs′tĭ), *adj.* [frost-i-er, frost-i-est], **1,** producing or accompanied by frost; **2,** frozen; covered with frost; as, *frosty* grass; **3,** cold or unfriendly in manner; as, a *frosty* glance.—*adv.* **frost′i-ly.**

froth (frôth), *n.* **1,** a mass of small bubbles formed on the surface of a liquid, as by shaking or fermentation; foam; **2,** shallow knowledge:—*v.i.* to become covered with foam; as, the horse *frothed* at the mouth.

froth-y (frôth′ĭ), *adj.* [froth-i-er, froth-i-est], **1,** full of, or composed of, foam or bubbles; **2,** empty; frivolous or shallow, as talk; without body; fanciful, as ideas.— *adv.* **froth′i-ly.**—*n.* **froth′i-ness.**

fro-ward (frō′wẽrd; frō′ẽrd), *adj.* wilful; disobedient; wayward; contrary.—*adv.* **fro′ward-ly.**—*n.* **fro′ward-ness.**

frown (froun), *n.* a wrinkling of the brow showing displeasure; a scowl; a stern look: —*v.i.* **1,** to contract the brows in anger, deep thought, uncertainty, etc.; **2,** to show disapproval; as, to *frown* upon gambling:—*v.t.* to rebuke or suppress by frowning; as, to *frown* a person down.— *adv.* **frown′ing-ly.**

frowz-y (frouz′ĭ), *adj.* [frowz-i-er, frowz-i-est], untidy; slovenly.

froze (frōz), past tense of *freeze:*—**frozen,** past participle of *freeze.*

fru-gal (frōō′găl), *adj.* **1,** thrifty; economical; not wasteful; **2,** sparingly used or supplied; simple; as, a *frugal* meal.—*adv.* **fru′gal-ly.**—*n.* **fru′gal-ness.**
Syn. provident, saving, sparing, chary.

fru-gal-i-ty (frōō-găl′ĭ-tĭ), *n.* [*pl.* frugalities], thrift; economy.

fruit (frōōt), *n.* **1,** in general, a seed and all its enveloping parts; **2,** usually, a particular fruit, as the apple, peach, pear, etc., generally eaten raw, or cooked with sugar and water and used as a dessert; **3,** any product, result, or profit; as, the *fruit* of labor:—*v.i.* to produce fruit:—**fruited,** *adj.* laden with fruit.

fruit-age (frōōt′ĭj), *n.* a crop of fruit.

fruit-er-er (frōōt′ẽr-ẽr), *n.* one who deals in fruits of all kinds.

fruit-ful (frōōt′fŏŏl), *adj.* yielding fruit; fertile; as, a *fruitful* tree; *fruitful* soil; profitable; productive; as, a *fruitful* venture; a *fruitful* year.—*adv.* **fruit′ful-ly.**—*n.* **fruit′ful-ness.**

fru-i-tion (frōō-ĭsh′ŭn), *n.* **1,** the bearing of fruit; **2,** realization or attainment; as, the *fruition* of his cherished hopes.

fruit-less (frōōt′lĕs), *adj.* **1,** not bearing fruit; **2,** without result; useless; as, a *fruitless* effort.

fruit-y (frōōt′ĭ), *adj.* [fruit-i-er, fruit-i-est], resembling fruit in flavor or odor; as, a *fruity* drink.

frus-trate (frŭs′trāt), *v.t.* [frus-trat-ed, frustrat-ing], to defeat or disappoint; thwart or oppose; bring to nothing; as, to *frustrate* a plan.—*n.* **frus-tra′tion.**
Syn. prevent, hinder, balk.

frus-tum (frŭs′tŭm), *n.* [*pl.* frus-tums or frusta (frŭs′tȧ)], the remainder of a pyramid or cone when the top is cut off.

FRUSTUM
A, frus-tum of cone; B, part cut off.

¹**fry** (frī), *n.* [*pl.* fry], **1,** a young fish; **2,** a large number, especially of young fish; **3,** a number of very unimportant or insignificant persons or objects; as, the police

caught the leaders of the gambling ring, as well as a great number of smaller *fry*.

²**fry** (frī), *v.t.* [fried, fry-ing], to cook with fat or oil in a pan or on a griddle.

ft. abbreviation for *foot, feet*.

fuch-sia (fū′shá; fū′shĭ-á),*n*. **1**, a plant with drooping, tubelike flowers, usually red or pink; **2**, a deep purplish-red color.

fud-dle (fŭd′l), *Colloquial*: *v.t.* [fud-dled, fud-dling], to stupefy or confuse with drink; intoxicate:—*n.* a state of confusion, as from liquor.

FUCHSIA

fudge (fŭj), *n.* **1**, a made-up story; humbug; **2**, a kind of candy, consisting of a sugary mixture flavored with chocolate, maple, or the like:—*interj.* nonsense!

fu-el (fū′ĕl), *n.* **1**, material that can be burned to supply heat, as coal, wood, oil, etc.; **2**, anything that keeps an emotion active; as, the news adds *fuel* to his anger: —*v.t.* [fueled, fuel-ing], to furnish with fuel; as, the vessel was *fueled* enough to last for a long trip.

fu-gi-tive (fū′jĭ-tĭv), *adj.* **1**, fleeting; not lasting very long; as, a *fugitive* idea; **2**, fleeing from danger, pursuit, or duty; as, a *fugitive* slave:—*n.* one who flees; a run-away or deserter; as, a *fugitive* from justice. —*adv.* **fu′gi-tive-ly**.

fugue (fūg), *n.* a musical composition in which a subject or theme is repeated in the various parts.—*n.* **fu′guist** (fū′gĭst).

Fu-ji-ya-ma (fōō′jē-yä′má) or **Fu-ji** (fōō′jē), a mountain, regarded as sacred, in Honshu, the largest island of Japan (map 15).

Fu-kien (fōō′kyĕn′),a Chinese coastal prov-ince (cap. Foochow) opposite Formosa.

-ful (-fōol), a suffix meaning: **1**, full of; containing; characterized by; as, grace*ful;* having the qualities of; as, master*ful;* **2**, able to; likely to; as, forget*ful;* **3**, an amount that would fill; as, hand*ful*, cup*ful*. The plu-ral of nouns ending in *-ful* is formed by adding *-s* to the end of the word; as, hand*fuls*, cup*fuls*, tea-spoon*fuls*.

FULCRUM
A, lever; B, ful-crum; C, weight.

ful-crum (fŭl′krŭm), *n.* [*pl.* fulcrums or fulcra (fŭl′krá)], the support, often wedge-shaped, on which a lever turns when it lifts something.

ful-fil or **ful-fill** (fōol-fĭl′), *v.t.* [fulfilled, fulfil-ling], **1**, to complete or accomplish;

2, to do; carry out (that which is promised, foretold, ordered, or expected); **3**, to satisfy, as a wish.—*n.* **ful-fil′ment; ful-fill′ment**.

Syn. effect, realize, achieve.

¹**full** (fōol), *v.t.* to clean and thicken, as cloth, with moisture and heat.

²**full** (fōol), *adj.* **1**, filled; having no empty space; as, a *full* pail; **2**, well supplied; as, a *full* cellar; **3**, rounded out; plump; as, a *full* figure; **4**, complete; filling the normal allowance, quota, or the like; as, a *full* hour; a *full* orchestra; *full* speed; **5**, having excess material arranged in folds; as, a *full* skirt; **6**, clear; distinct; as, a *full* tone; **7**, *Colloquial*, intoxicated:—*n.* the highest state, extent, or measure; as, enjoy it to the *full*:—*v.t.* to give fulness to; as, to *full* a skirt:—*adv.* completely; quite: often with a hyphen; as, a *full*-blown rose.

full-er (fōol′ĕr), *n.* one who thickens, or fulls, cloth by moistening, heating, and pressing:—**fuller's earth**, a soft, claylike mineral used in cleaning cloth.

full-fledged (fōol′-flĕjd′), *adj.* **1**, mature; of a bird, with all its feathers; **2**, hence, fully developed; as, a *full-fledged* author.

full-y (fōol′ĭ), *adv.* completely; abundantly; as, *fully* equipped for a journey.

ful-mi-nate (fŭl′mĭ-nāt), *v.t.* [fulminat-ed, fulminat-ing], **1**, to cause to explode; **2**, to send out or utter, as a threat:—*v.i.* to ,make a loud noise; explode:—*n.* a material easily exploded.—*n.* **ful′mi-na′tion**.

ful-ness or **full-ness** (fōol′nĕs), *n.* **1**, completeness; abundance; **2**, the amount of gathered material in a garment.

ful-some (fōol′sŭm; fŭl′sŭm), *adj.* offen-sive to good taste; excessive; immoderate; as, *fulsome* flattery.—*adv.* **ful′some-ly**.

Syn. coarse, sickening, rank.

Ful-ton (fōol′tŭn), Robert (1765–1815), an American engineer, credited with the invention of the steamboat.

fum-ble (fŭm′bl), *v.i.* [fum-bled, fum-bling], to grope or feel about in search; as, he *fumbled* in his pocket for a match: —*v.t.* to handle or manage awkwardly, or drop; as, to *fumble* the ball in a game.— *n.* **fum′bler**.

fume (fūm), *n.* smoke, vapor, or gas, espe-cially if offensive; as, the air was thick with tobacco *fumes:—v.i.* [fumed, fum-ing], **1**, to send forth smoke; **2**, to complain angrily; as, he *fumed* over his losses.

fu-mi-gate (fū′mĭ-gāt), *v.t.* [fumigat-ed, fumigat-ing], **1**, to disinfect or purify with fumes; especially, to free of disease germs, insects, etc., with fumes; as, to *fumigate* a sickroom; **2**, to perfume.—*n.* **fu′mi-ga′tion**.—*n.* **fu′mi-ga′tor**.

go; join; yet; sing; chin; show; thin, *then;* hw, *why;* zh, azure; ŭ, Ger. für or Fr. lune; ö, Ger. schön or Fr. feu; ñ, Fr. enfant, nom; kh, Ger. ach or ich. See pages ix–x.

fun (fŭn), *n.* pleasure; mirth; sport; amusement; play.

func·tion (fŭngk′shŭn), *n.* **1,** the special work or use of anything; as, the *function* of the heart is to pump blood; the *function* of a judge is to interpret the law; **2,** a formal social or official ceremony; as, the inauguration was the most important *function* of the year:—*v.i.* to perform the duty for which a person or thing is intended.

func·tion·al (fŭngk′shŭn-ăl), *adj.* pertaining to a function; especially, pertaining to the special work for which anything, as an organ of the body, is intended.

func·tion·ar·y (fŭngk′shŭn-ĕr′ĭ), *n.* [*pl.* functionaries], one who holds an office; an official.

fund (fŭnd), *n.* **1,** a permanent supply of something; a stock; as, a *fund* of information; **2,** money set apart for carrying out some object; as, she has a *fund* saved for vacation; **3,** a stock in reserve; **4,** funds, securities; money.

fun·da·men·tal (fŭn′da-měn′tăl; -měn′tl), *adj.* serving as a foundation or basis; essential; as, a *fundamental* reason:—*n.* a rule or principle that serves as a groundwork of a system; as, a *fundamental* of arithmetic.—*adv.* fun′da·men′tal·ly.

Fun·dy, Bay of (fŭn′dĭ), an inlet of the Atlantic Ocean, between Nova Scotia and New Brunswick, Canada (map 4).

fu·ner·al (fū′nĕr-ăl), *n.* the ceremony of burying a dead human body, or the services that take place at such a time:—*adj.* pertaining to, or fit for, a funeral.

fu·ne·re·al (fū-nē′rē-ăl), *adj.* **1,** suitable for a burial; **2,** mournful; gloomy.—*adv.* fu·ne′re·al·ly.

fun·gi (fŭn′jī), plural of *fungus.*

fun·gi·cide (fŭn′jī-sīd), *n.* anything that kills fungus growths.

fun·gus (fŭng′gŭs), *n.* [*pl.* fungi (fŭn′jī) or funguses (fŭng′gŭs-ĕz)], one of the plants without green color, including bacteria, molds, mushrooms, mildews, toadstools, etc., which feed upon other plants or decaying animal matter:—*adj.* pertaining to, or growing like, a fungus; as, a *fungus* growth.

funk (fŭngk), *Colloquial:* *n.* panic; fright:—*v.i.* to be in a state of cowardly fear:—*v.t.* **1,** to frighten; **2,** to evade; shrink from; as, to *funk* a test.

FUNNELS
1, ordinary funnel; 2, steamship funnel.

fun·nel (fŭn′ĕl), *n.* **1,** a wide-mouthed vessel shaped like a cone with a tube or hole at the bottom, used when pouring liquids into a small opening; **2,** the smokestack of a steamship or steam engine. (See illustration in preceding column.)

fun·ny (fŭn′ĭ), *adj.* [fun-ni-er, fun-ni-est], **1,** comical; droll; causing laughter; **2,** *Colloquial,* strange; odd; queer.

fur (fûr), *n.* **1,** the thick, soft hair of certain animals; **2,** the dressed skin of furbearing animals; also, (often *furs*), clothing made from these dressed skins; **3,** any light, fuzzy covering, as a coating on the tongue:—*adj.* lined or trimmed with fur, or made of fur:—*v.t.* [furred, fur-ring], to cover, line, or trim with fur.—*adj.* **furred.**

fur·be·low (fûr′bē-lō), *n.* **1,** a ruffle, flounce, or the like, used on women's clothing; **2,** furbelows, showy ornamentation; as, the dancer's costume glittered with spangles and other *furbelows* of her profession.

fur·bish (fûr′bĭsh), *v.t.* to make bright by rubbing or polishing; renew.

fu·ri·ous (fū′rĭ-ŭs), *adj.* **1,** very angry; mad; **2,** violent, as a storm.—*adv.* fu′ri·ous·ly.
　Syn. boisterous, vehement, fierce.

furl (fûrl), *v.t.* to roll up and fasten to a mast, pole, or the like, as a sail or flag.

fur·long (fûr′lông), *n.* one eighth of a mile; 40 rods; 220 yards.

fur·lough (fûr′lō), *n.* leave of absence; as, the soldier came home on *furlough*:—*v.t.* to give leave of absence to.

fur·nace (fûr′nĭs), *n.* an apparatus in which fuel is burned to make heat for various purposes, as to melt ores, heat a house, bake pottery, etc.

fur·nish (fûr′nĭsh), *v.t.* **1,** to fit out or fit up with what is needed; as, to *furnish* a house; **2,** to provide; give; as, he *furnished* the money for the trip.

fur·nish·ings (fûr′nĭsh-ĭngz), *n.pl.* **1,** the necessary fittings of a house; **2,** apparatus or fixtures of any kind.

fur·ni·ture (fûr′nĭ-tūr), *n.* the necessary fittings of a house, a ship, or a trade; outfit; especially, the movable articles of a house, as beds, chairs, utensils, etc.

fu·ror (fū′rôr), *n.* **1,** rage; **2,** a great outburst of excitement or enthusiasm.

fur·ri·er (fûr′ĭ-ĕr), *n.* one who prepares or sells furs.

fur·row (fûr′ō), *n.* **1,** a trench made in the ground by a plow; **2,** a groove; a wrinkle:—*v.t.* **1,** to plow; **2,** to make grooves or wrinkles in; as, old age *furrowed* his brow.

fur-ry (fûr′ĭ), *adj.* **1,** covered with fur; as, a *furry* animal; **2,** like fur or made of fur.

fur-ther (fûr′thẽr), *adj.* **1,** more distant; as, the *further* field; **2,** additional; as, he needs *further* help:—*adv.* **1,** to a greater distance or degree; as, to go *further;* **2,** moreover; also; as, she remarked *further* that you were late:—*v.t.* to promote; help forward; as, he *furthered* my plans.

    Syn., v. advance, aid; *adj.* farther.

fur-ther-ance (fûr′thẽr-ăns), *n.* advancement; aid.

fur-ther-more (fûr′thẽr-môr′), *adv.* besides; in addition; also.

fur-ther-most (fûr′thẽr-mōst), *adj.* most distant or remote; as, the *furthermost* point inland.

fur-thest (fûr′thĕst), *adj.* and *adv.* most distant in time or space; as, the *furthest* island of the group.

fur-tive (fûr′tĭv), *adj.* sly; secret; stealthy; as, *furtive* glances or actions.—*adv.* **fur′-tive-ly.**—*n.* **fur′tive-ness.**

fu-ry (fū′rĭ), *n.* [*pl.* furies], **1,** violent anger; rage; **2,** great violence; fierceness; as, the *fury* of the storm; **3,** a violently angry person:—**the Furies,** in Greek mythology, the three goddesses of vengeance.

    Syn. frenzy, madness.

furze (fûrz), *n.* a spiny, evergreen shrub, with yellow flowers, abundant in Europe; gorse.

¹fuse (fūz), *v.t.* [fused, fusing], **1,** to melt, especially by heat, as metals; make liquid; **2,** to join or blend by melting:—*v.i.* **1,** to become melted, as by heat; **2,** to blend, as if melted.—*adj.* **fu′si-ble.**

²fuse (fūz), *n.* **1,** a small tube or casing filled with a material easily set on fire, or a cord saturated with such material, along which fire will run: used for exploding gunpowder, dynamite, etc.; **2,** a piece of metal put in an electric circuit, which melts and breaks the circuit when the current gets too strong for safety:—*v.t.* [fused, fus-ing], to attach a fuse to. Also spelled **fuze.**

FURZE

fu-se-lage (fū′zĕ-lĭj; fū′zĕ-läzh′), *n.* the body of an airplane, to which the wings and the tail are fastened, and which contains the controls, space for the pilot, passengers, cargo, etc. (See illustration at *airplane.*)

fu-sil (fū′zĭl), *n.* a flintlock musket: not now in use.

fu-sil-ier or **fu-sil-eer** (fū′zĭ-lēr′), *n.* **1,** formerly, a soldier armed with a fusil, or flintlock musket; **2,** fusiliers or fusileers, any of several British regiments.

fu-sil-lade (fū′zĭ-lād′), *n.* **1,** the discharge of many firearms at once or in quick succession; **2,** hence, a number of questions or comments made in rapid order:—*v.t.* [fusillad-ed, fusillad-ing], to shoot at in a volley or in quick succession.

fu-sion (fū′zhŭn), *n.* **1,** the act of melting, or state of being melted, together; as, the *fusion* of metals; **2,** a union or blending together; as, a *fusion* of ideas.

fuss (fŭs), *n.* **1,** unnecessary or disturbing activity, especially in small matters; confusion; stir; **2,** a complaint:—*v.i.* **1,** to worry; **2,** to be busy over trifles:—*v.t. Colloquial,* to annoy or embarrass.

fuss-y (fŭs′ĭ), *adj.* [fuss-i-er, fuss-i-est], **1,** worrying; complaining; as, a *fussy* child; **2,** taking great trouble with small matters; as, she was a *fussy* cook; **3,** having much careful detail; requiring minute attention; as, a *fussy* job.

fus-tian (fŭs′chăn), *n.* **1,** a kind of coarse twilled cotton cloth, as corduroy, velveteen, etc.; **2,** high-sounding speech; empty wordiness:—*adj.* **1,** made of fustian; **2,** pretentious.

fust-y (fŭs′tĭ), *adj.* [fust-i-er, fust-i-est], **1,** moldy; musty; stuffy; **2,** antiquated; old-fashioned.

fu-tile (fū′tĭl), *adj.* **1,** without result; useless; as, *futile* shouting; **2,** of no importance; worthless.—*adv.* **fu′tile-ly.**

fu-til-i-ty (fū-tĭl′ĭ-tĭ), *n.* [*pl.* futilities], uselessness; ineffectiveness.

fu-ture (fū′tūr), *adj.* yet to happen or come; as, a *future* event:—*n.* **1,** time yet to come; **2,** the future tense:—**future tense,** in grammar, a tense of the verb indicating action in time to come; as, I *shall go* tomorrow; **future perfect,** in grammar, a tense of the verb indicating action taking place before a future time as, when you arrive, I *shall have finished* the task.

fu-tu-ri-ty (fū-tū′rĭ-tĭ), *n.* [*pl.* futurities], **1,** time to come; **2,** a future event.

fuze (fūz), *n.* a device used to explode a charge of gunpowder, etc. See **²fuse.**

fuzz (fŭz), *n.* tiny particles of down, wool, etc.:—*v.i.* to come off in small fluffy bits.

fuzz-y (fŭz′ĭ), *adj.* [fuzz-i-er, fuzz-i-est], covered with, or like, fuzz or down.—*n.* **fuzz′i-ness.**

-fy (-fī), a suffix meaning to cause to be or to form into; as, simpli*fy*, petri*fy*, lique*fy.*

fyl-fot (fĭl′fŏt), *n.* a crosslike figure, with the ends of the arms bent at right angles and extended to the length of the upright arms; a swastika.

G

G, g (jē), *n.* [*pl.* G's, g's], **1,** the seventh letter of the alphabet, following F; **2,** in music, the fifth tone in the major scale of C.

g. abbreviation for *gram, grams:*— **g** abbreviation for *gravity,* or for the acceleration of gravity: used to represent the unit of acceleration on a scale in which 1g= the acceleration of gravity, or 32 ft. per second per second.

Ga. abbreviation for *Georgia.*

gab (găb), *Colloquial:* n. idle chatter; talkativeness:—*v.i.* [gabbed, gab-bing], to talk idly and much.

gab·ar·dine (găb/ĕr-dēn′; găb/ĕr-dēn), *n.* **1,** a kind of woolen or cotton cloth like serge; **2,** a gaberdine.

gab·ble (găb/l), *v.i.* [gab-bled, gab-bling], **1,** to talk disconnectedly, or without real meaning; to jabber; **2,** to make a clatter of meaningless sounds:— *n.* rapid meaningless sounds; as, the *gabble* of geese.

gab·er·dine or **gab·ar·dine** (găb/ĕr-dēn′; găb/ĕr-dēn), *n.* a long, loose gown or coat; especially, a loose gown worn by the Jews in the Middle Ages.

ga·ble (gā/bl), *n.* **1,** the triangular part of a wall of a building between opposite slopes of a sloping roof; **2,** any similar construction, as over a window.

GABLES (G, G)

Ga·bri·el (gā/brĭ-ĕl), *n.* **1,** in Jewish and Christian legend, one of the seven archangels; **2,** in the Bible, an angel sent as a herald of good tidings and comfort to man.

¹gad (găd), *n.* **1,** a sharp rod; a goad for cattle; **2,** a pointed tool for loosening ore.

²gad (găd), *v.i.* [gad-ded, gad-ding], to go about without purpose; to ramble; as; to *gad* about all day.—*n.* **gad/der.**

Gad (găd), *interj. Archaic,* an exclamation of surprise; a mild oath.

gad·a·bout (găd/ȧ-bout/), *n. Colloquial,* one who wanders about idly.

gad·fly (găd/flī/), *n.* [*pl.* gadflies], any of various flies which sting cattle, horses, etc.

gadg·et (găj/ĕt), *n.* a device; contrivance.

Gael (gāl), *n.* **1,** formerly, a Scottish Highlander; **2,** now, any Celt of Ireland, the Scottish Highlands, or the Isle of Man.

Gael·ic (gā/lĭk), *adj.* pertaining to the Celtic people of the Scottish Highlands, Ireland, and the Isle of Man, or to their language:—*n.* the language of the Gaels.

gaff (găf), *n.* **1,** a large hook with a handle, used for getting large fish out of the water; **2,** a spar branching from the mast of a sailing vessel, to which is attached the top of a fore-and-aft sail (see illustration, page 695); **3,** *Slang,* a trial; ordeal; as, to stand the *gaff:*—*v.t.* to seize (a fish) with a gaff.

GAFF, def. 1

gaf·fer (găf/ĕr), *n.* a respectable and good old man, especially a countryman.

gag (găg), *n.* **1,** something put in the mouth to hinder speech, or to keep the mouth open; **2,** *Slang,* a practical joke; **3,** in a play, words added by an actor, or any remark, trick, or act inserted to get a laugh:—*v.t.* [gagged, gag-ging], **1,** stop up the mouth; **2,** silence by force or law:—*v.i.* to strain, as in vomiting.

¹gage (gāj), *n.* **1,** a promise; pledge; **2,** a pledge to appear and fight, as in support of a claim: indicated by the throwing down of a glove; **3,** a challenge to fight; a glove, cap, or the like, thrown down in challenge: —*v.t.* [gaged, gag-ing], to bet; wager.

²gage (gāj), *n.* the greengage, a kind of cultivated plum.

³gage (gāj), *n.* **1,** a standard of measure; **2,** an estimate or judgment; **3,** the distance between railway rails; **4,** a measuring instrument; **5,** the depth of water from the surface to the level of the keel of a floating ship:—*v.t.* [gaged, gag-ing], **1,** to measure; **2,** to judge; gauge. See **gauge.**

gai·e·ty (gā/ĕ-tĭ), *n.* [*pl.* gaieties], **1,** merriment; glee; jollity; **2,** brilliancy, as of dress. Also spelled **gay/e·ty.**

Syn. liveliness, sportiveness, fun.

Gail·lard Cut (gā/lĕrd), the deepest cut in the Panama Canal, named after Colonel David Gaillard: originally *Culebra Cut.*

gai·ly or **gay·ly** (gā/lĭ), *adv.* **1,** merrily; happily; **2,** showily; as, to dress *gai*ly.

gain (gān), *n.* **1,** advantage; profit; as, to be greedy for *gain;* **2,** increase; as, a *gain* in weight:—*v.t.* **1,** obtain, as profit or advantage; earn; **2,** win; arrive at; as, he *gained* his point; **3,** obtain through an increase; as, to *gain* ten pounds in weight:—*v.i.* **1,** improve; increase; as, *gain* in wisdom; **2,** advance; as, *gain* on the runner ahead. —*n.* **gain/er.**

gain·ful (gān/fŏŏl), *adj.* yielding profit; advantageous.—*adv.* **gain/ful·ly.**

gain·say (gān/sā′; gān/sā′), *v.t.* [gainsaid (gān/sĕd′; gān/sĕd′), gainsay-ing], to contradict; deny.

Gains·bor·ough (gānz/bŭ-rŭ; gānz/bûr-ō), Thomas (1727–1788), an English painter.

āte, ȧorta, râre, căt, ȧsk, fär, ȧllow, sofȧ; ēve, ĕvent, ĕll, writĕr, novĕl; bīte, pĭn; nō, ōbey, ôr, dŏg, tŏp, cŏllide; ūnit, ūnite, bûrn, cŭt, focŭs; nŏŏn, fŏŏt; mound; coin;

gait (gāt), *n.* a manner of walking or running; as, the old man's shuffling *gait*.

gai·ter (gā′tẽr), *n.* 1, a covering of cloth or leather for the lower leg or ankle, fitting over the top of the boot; 2, in the U.S., a shoe with elastic strips at the sides; also, a kind of overshoe with a cloth top.

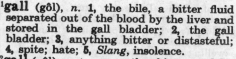

GAITERS
1, man's gaiter; 2, child's gaiter.

gal. abbreviation for *gallon, gallons.*

ga·la (gā′lá; gä′lá), *n.* a festival; celebration:—*adj.* festive; as, *gala* attire:—**gala day**, a day of pleasure; a holiday.

ga·lac·tic (gá·lăk′tĭk), *adj.* relating to a galaxy or galaxies.

Gal·a·had (găl′á·hăd), *n.* in late Arthurian legend, a knight of the Round Table, who was successful in his quest of the Holy Grail.

Ga·lá·pa·gos Is·lands (gä·lä′pä·gōs), a group of islands in the Pacific Ocean, near the equator. They are part of the Republic of Ecuador (map 2).

Ga·la·ti·a (gá·lā′shá), an ancient Roman province of central Asia Minor.

Ga·la·tians (gá·lā′shănz), *n.* 1, inhabitants of ancient Galatia; 2, a book of the New Testament, containing St. Paul's epistle, or letter, to the Galatians.

Gal·ax·y (găl′ăk·sĭ), *n.* the Milky Way; a luminous band encircling the sky. It is composed of myriads of stars including our sun:—**galaxy**, [*pl.* galaxies], 1, any vast group of stars similar to our Galaxy; 2, a gathering of splendid persons or things; as, a *galaxy* of beautiful women.

gale (gāl), *n.* 1, a strong wind, less violent than a hurricane; 2, an outburst.

ga·le·na (gá·lē′ná), *n.* a bluish-gray mineral, an important lead ore.

Ga·li·ci·a (gá·lĭsh′ĭ·á), 1, formerly, an Austrian crownland, now a part of southern Poland and U.S.S.R; 2, an old kingdom and province of northwestern Spain.

Gal·i·le·an (găl′ĭ·lē′ăn), *adj.* relating to Galilee:—*n.* a native of Galilee:—**the Galilean**, Jesus of Nazareth in Galilee.

Gal·i·lee (găl′ĭ·lē), a Roman province of northern Palestine, important in New Testament history:—**Sea of Galilee**, a lake, east of Galilee, through which the Jordan River flows: also called *Sea of Tiberias.*

Gal·i·le·o (găl′ĭ·lē′ō; *Italian,* gä′lē·lā′ō), the first name of *Galileo Galilei* (1564–1642), an Italian physicist, mathematician, and astronomer, who advanced proof that the earth travels around the sun.

¹gall (gôl), *n.* 1, the bile, a bitter fluid separated out of the blood by the liver and stored in the gall bladder; 2, the gall bladder; 3, anything bitter or distasteful; 4, spite; hate; 5, *Slang,* insolence.

²gall (gôl), *n.* a sore on the skin caused by chafing:—*v.t.* 1, to break or injure by rubbing; as, to *gall* the skin; 2, to vex; fret; harass; weary.—*adj.* **gall′ing.**

³gall (gôl), *n.* a swelling or growth on the bark or leaves of numerous plants, especially oaks, caused by, and growing around, the larvae of certain insects, especially the gallfly; a gallnut.

gal·lant (găl′ănt), *adj.* 1, brave; high-spirited; chivalrous; as, a *gallant* knight; 2, of noble or stately appearance; 3, (gă·lănt′; găl′ănt), showing elaborate courtesy and respect to women:—*n.* (găl′ănt; gă·lănt′), 1, a man of fashion; 2, a beau; a man elaborately polite to women.—*adv.* **gal′lant·ly.**—*n.* **gal′lant·ness.**

Syn., *adj.* bold, courageous, heroic.

gal·lant·ry (găl′ăn·trĭ), *n.* [*pl.* gallantries], 1, bravery; heroic courage; 2, elaborate politeness; an act of gallant conduct.

gall blad·der, a pear-shaped sac which receives and stores bile.

gal·le·on (găl′ē·ŭn), *n.* a large sailing vessel with a high stern and three or four decks, usually armed, used especially by the Spaniards from the 15th to the 17th century.

SPANISH GALLEON
(16th century)

gal·ler·y (găl′ẽr·ĭ), *n.* [*pl.* galleries], 1, a long, narrow hall, often with windows on one side only; 2, a platform projecting from the side and end walls of a theater, church, assembly room, etc., containing seats; a balcony; 3, the occupants of such seats; 4, a building or room for exhibiting works of art or the like; 5, an underground passage for communication, as in a mine or an underground fort.—*adj.* **gal′ler·ied.**

gal·ley (găl′ĭ), *n.* [*pl.* galleys], 1, a low, flat, one-decked, sea-going vessel, propelled by sails and oars, used in ancient and medieval times; 2, a large, open rowboat; 3, the cooking quarters of a ship; 4, in printing, an oblong tray to hold set-up type; also, a printer's

VENETIAN GALLEY
(14th century)

go; join; yet; sing; chin; show; thin, *th*en; hw, *wh*y; zh, azure; ü, Ger. für or Fr. lune; ö, Ger. schön or Fr. feu; n, Fr. enfant, nom; kh, Ger. ach or ich. See pages ix–x.

proof, often called *galley proof*, made from such type on a long sheet of paper.

gall-fly (gôl′flī′), *n.* [*pl.* gallflies], an insect that deposits its eggs on plants, causing a swelling of the plant tissue, called a *gall*.

Gal-li-a (găl′ĭ-ȧ), the Latin name of *Gaul*.

Gal-lic (găl′ĭk), *adj.* pertaining to ancient Gaul, or modern France.

Gal-lip-o-li (gȧ-lĭp′ō-lē), **1**, a peninsula between the Dardanelles and the Aegean Sea; **2**, a seaport of Turkey in Europe, at the entrance to the Sea of Marmara: its Turkish name is *Gelibolu*. (Map **12**).

gall-nut (gôl′nŭt′), *n.* a swelling on many plants, especially oaks. caused by developing insect larvae; a gall. See ³**gall**.

gal-lon (găl′ŭn), *n.* a unit of liquid measure; the wine gallon, or standard gallon in the U.S., being equal to four quarts or 231 cubic inches. the imperial gallon in Great Britain, to 277.420 cubic inches.

gal-lop (găl′ŭp), *n.* **1**, the fastest gait of a horse, in which he takes all four feet off the ground in the same stride; **2**, a ride at this gait:—*v.i.* **1**, to run with leaps, like a horse; **2**, to ride a horse at a gallop; **3**, to hasten; as, to *gallop* through one's work:—*v.t.* to cause to move at a gallop; as, to *gallop* a horse.

gal-lows (găl′ōz; găl′ŭs), *n.* [*pl.* gallowses], a structure consisting of two uprights with a crossbar on the top, used for hanging criminals.

gall-stone (gôl′stōn′), *n.* a lump of solid matter formed in the gall bladder or liver.

gal-op (găl′ŭp), *n.* **1**, a kind of lively dance; **2**, the music for it.

ga-lore (gȧ-lôr′), *adj.* very many; abundant: used after the noun it modifies; as, pretty girls *galore:—adv.* in great plenty.

ga-losh (gȧ-lŏsh′), *n.* any protective overshoe; especially, a high rubber overshoe: also called *arctic*.

ga-lumph (gȧ-lŭmf′), *v.i.* to "gallop in triumph"; to come bounding in glee: a made-up word from *gallop* and *triumph*, first used by Lewis Carroll in "Through the Looking Glass."

gal-van-ic (găl-văn′ĭk), *adj.* **1**, pertaining to an electric current, especially one produced from a battery; **2**, stimulating; electrifying.

gal-va-nism (găl′vȧ-nĭzm), *n.* the science which treats of electric currents, especially those arising from chemical action.

gal-va-nize (găl′vȧ-nīz), *v.t.* [galvanized, galvaniz-ing], **1**, to coat with metal, as iron with zinc, by means of electricity; **2**, to excite or shock, as if by electricity; as, to *galvanize* a person into action:—**galva-**

nized iron, iron, often in thin sheets, coated by an electric process with zinc to keep it from rusting.

gal-va-nom-e-ter (găl′vȧ-nŏm′ē-tẽr), *n.* an instrument for measuring the intensity and direction of an electric current.

Gal-ves-ton (găl′vĕs-tŭn), a seaport of southeastern Texas, on the Gulf of Mexico (map **8**)

Ga-ma (gä′mȧ), Vasco da (1469?–1524), a Portuguese navigator, discoverer of a sea route from Portugal to India.

Gam-bi-a Riv-er (găm′bĭ-ȧ), a river of French West Africa, which flows into the Atlantic Ocean.

gam-ble (găm′bl), *v.i.* [gam-bled, gam-bling], **1**, to play for money or a prize; **2**, to risk money on a possible happening; **3**, to run any great risk for the sake of uncertain gain:—*v.t.* to squander by playing for stakes; as, he *gambled* away his savings:—*n.* **1**, any game or act involving the risking of stakes; **2**, an act accompanied by uncertainty or by any special risk; as, mountain climbing is quite a *gamble*.

Syn., v. wager, hazard, venture, stake.

gam-bler (găm′blẽr), *n.* one who plays games of chance, especially habitually.

gam-bling (găm′blĭng), *n.* the practice of wagering or playing for stakes.

gam-bol (găm′bŭl), *n.* a dancing or skipping about for joy or sport; frolic:—*v.i.* [gamboled, gambol-ing], to skip and dance about in play.

¹**game** (gām), *n.* **1**, sport or amusement; fun; frolic; also, jest; as, to make *game* of a poor man; **2**, a contest carried on according to rules, success depending upon superiority in strength, skill, luck, etc.; as, the *game* of baseball, football, etc.; **3**, a single unit or division of play; as, four *games* in the first set at tennis; **4**, a scheme, plan, or undertaking, sometimes not praiseworthy; as, I've spoiled your little *game;* the *game* is up; **5**, wild animals, birds, or fish pursued by a hunter or fisherman; also, their flesh used for food:—*v.i.* [gamed, gam-ing], to play for a stake or prize:—*adj.* **1**, pertaining to animals or birds hunted or taken for sport; **2**, *Colloquial,* ready; spirited; plucky; as, he was a *game* lad.—*adv.* **game′ly**.

Syn., n. joke, play, amusement.

²**game** (gām), *adj. Colloquial,* lame or crooked; as, a *game* leg.

game-cock (gām′kŏk′), *n.* a cock bred and trained for fighting.

game-keep-er (gām′kēp′ẽr), *n.* one in charge of wild animals or birds that are to be protected or preserved for hunting.

game-some (gām′sŭm), *adj.* merry; gay.

game-ster (gām'stẽr), *n.* one who habitually bets or plays for stakes; a gambler.

gam-in (găm'ĭn), *n.* a neglected street child; an outcast boy or girl.

gam-ing (gām'ĭng), *n.* gambling.

gam-ma (găm'ȧ), *n.* the third letter of the Greek alphabet, representing G.

gam-mer (găm'ẽr), *n.* an old woman.

¹**gam-mon** (găm'ŭn), *n.* a cured ham or strip of bacon; the lower end of a side of bacon.

²**gam-mon** (găm'ŭn), *n. Colloquial,* humbug:—*v.t. Colloquial,* to deceive.

gam-ut (găm'ŭt), *n.* 1, the great scale or whole series of recognized musical notes; 2, the major scale; 3, hence, the entire range of anything; as, to run the *gamut* from joy to despair.

gam-y (gām'ĭ), *adj.* [gam-i-er, gam-i-est], 1, abounding in game; 2, plucky; ready; spirited; 3, having the flavor of game.

gan-der (găn'dẽr), *n.* 1, a male goose; 2, a simpleton.

Gan-dhi(gän'dē), Mohandas Karamchand (1869–1948), a Hindu social and religious reformer and Indian nationalist leader.

gang (găng), *n.* 1, a number of persons banded together for a particular purpose; as, a *gang* of thieves; 2, a group of workmen under one foreman; 3, an outfit or set of tools or machines arranged for use together; as, a *gang* of snowplows.

Gan-ges (găn'jēz), a great river in northern India, flowing into the Bay of Bengal (map 15).

gan-gli-on (găng'glĭ-ŭn), *n.* [*pl.* ganglia (găng'glĭ-ȧ) or ganglions (găng'glĭ-ŭnz)], a knot of nerve cells forming a nerve center.

gang-plank (găng'plăngk'), *n.* a movable platform or bridge by which to enter or leave a ship; gangway.

gan-grene (găng'grēn), *n.* the decay of some part of a living animal body:—*v.t.* [gangrened, gangren-ing], to cause to decay, as tissue.—*adj.* **gan-gre-nous** (găng'grē-nŭs).

gang-ster (găng'stẽr), *n.* a member of a lawless gang; a criminal.

gang-way (găng'wā'), *n.* 1, a movable platform or bridge between a wharf and a ship; 2, a passageway; aisle.

GANNET (¹⁄₂₄)

gan-net (găn'ĕt), *n.* a large, fish-eating bird of the North Atlantic which breeds in colonies on cliffs and rocky islands.

¹**gant-let** (gônt'lĕt; gȧnt'lĕt), *n.* 1, a former military punishment in which an offender, stripped to the waist, ran between two files of men who struck him with clubs or other weapons as he passed; 2, a similar torture practiced by Indians upon captives; 3, figuratively, a series of tests or trials; as, he ran the *gantlet* of public opinion.

²**gant-let** (gănt'lĕt; gȧnt'lĕt), *n.* a glove; a gauntlet. See **gauntlet.**

Gan-y-mede (găn'ĭ-mēd), *n.* in Greek mythology, a beautiful shepherd lad who was carried to Olympus by an eagle of Zeus, to be cupbearer to the gods.

gaol (jāl), *n.* a place of confinement; a jail: a British spelling.—*n.* **gaol'er.**

gap (găp), *n.* 1, an opening; passage; 2, a pass in a mountain ridge; 3, an unfilled interval; as, a *gap* in the conversation.

gape (gāp; găp; gȧp), *v.i.* [gaped, gap-ing], 1, to open the mouth wide, as from drowsiness, wonder, etc.; yawn; 2, to stare with open mouth, as in amazement:—*n.* 1, the act of opening the mouth and staring; 2, a yawn; 3, an opening; gap; 4, the opening between the jaws of birds or of fishes:—**the gapes,** 1, a disease of poultry; 2, a fit of yawning.

G.A.R. abbreviation for the *Grand Army of the Republic:* an organization of the Union veterans of the War between the States.

ga-rage (gȧ-räzh'; găr'äzh; găr'ĭj), *n.* a building in which automobiles are sheltered or repaired.

garb (gärb), *n.* dress; clothing, especially of a distinctive kind; as, the *garb* of a priest:—*v.t.* to clothe.

gar-bage (gär'bĭj), *n.* waste matter from a kitchen, market, store, etc.

gar-ble (gär'bl), *v.t.* [gar-bled, gar-bling], to misrepresent (facts, statements, writings, etc.) by selecting only certain parts; mutilate; as, to *garble* a quotation.

gar-den (gär'dn), *n.* a piece of ground set aside for growing flowers, fruit, vegetables, etc.; also, a place set aside for the display of plant and animal life to the public; as, the zoological *gardens:*—*v.i.* to labor in or cultivate a garden.

GARDENIA
def. 2

gar-den-er (gär'dn-ẽr; gärd'nẽr), *n.* one who gardens; also, one hired to care for a garden or an estate.

gar-de-ni-a (gär-dē'nĭ-ȧ), *n.* 1, any of a

certain group of shrubs and trees cultivated for their fragrant yellow or white flowers; **2**, the flower of any of these.

Gar-field (gär′fēld), James Abram (1831–1881), the 20th president of the U.S., assassinated in his first year of office.

Gar-gan-tu-a (gär-găn′tū-à), the gluttonous giant hero of "Gargantua," a satirical romance by Rabelais.—*adj.* **Gar-gan′-tu-an**.

gar-gle (gär′gl), *n.* a medicinal or antiseptic liquid for washing the throat or mouth:—*v.t.* [gar-gled, gar-gling], to wash or disinfect (the throat) with a medicinal liquid kept moving in it by slowly expelling the breath: —*v.i.* to use a gargle.

gar-goyle (gär′goil), *n.* a projecting stone waterspout, often in the form of a grotesquely shaped man or animal.

GARGOYLE

Ga-ri-bal-di (gä′rē-bäl′dē; gär′ĭ-băl′dĭ), Giuseppe (1807–1882), a famous Italian patriot and general: called *the Liberator*.

gar-ish (gâr′ĭsh), *adj.* gaudy; dazzling; showy; as, *garish* jewelry.—*adv.* **gar′ish-ly**.

gar-land (gär′lănd), *n.* a wreath, as of flowers, branches, or leaves, worn on the head:—*v.t.* to deck or adorn with a wreath.

gar-lic (gär′lĭk), *n.* a plant of the lily family, with a strong, biting taste and an unpleasant odor; also, the bulb of this plant, used in cooking.

gar-ment (gär′měnt), *n.* any article of clothing, as a dress, hat, or the like.

gar-ner (gär′nẽr), *n.* a storehouse for grain; a granary:— *v.t.* to gather for safekeeping; store, as in a granary; gather up; as, to *garner* grain.

gar-net (gär′nět), *n.* **1**, a semiprecious stone, used as a gem, usually deep red; **2**, a deep-red color.

GARLIC
Bulb with part of stem and leaves.

gar-nish (gär′nĭsh), *n.* **1**, an ornament or decoration; **2**, something laid about food in a dish as a decoration:—*v.t.* **1**, to adorn; **2**, to decorate (food).

gar-ni-ture (gär′nĭ-tūr), *n.* a decoration; trimming, especially of food.

Ga-ronne (gä′rôn′), a river in southwestern France flowing into the Bay of Biscay (map **12**).

gar-ret (găr′ět), *n.* the uppermost part of a house, beneath the roof; an attic.

gar-ri-son (găr′ĭ-sŭn), *n.* **1**, a body of troops stationed in a fort; **2**, the place

where such soldiers are stationed:—*v.t.* **1**, to furnish (a place) with . troops; as, to *garrison* a town; **2**, to defend by means of a fort or forts manned by soldiers; as, they built a fort to *garrison* the pass.

gar-ru-lous (găr′ū-lŭs; găr′ŏŏ-lŭs), *adj.* very talkative, especially about unimportant things.—*adv.* **gar′ru-lous-ly**.

Syn. talkative, glib, fluent, voluble.

gar-ter (gär′tẽr), *n.* a band or strap by which a stocking is held up:—**the Garter**, the badge of the Order of the Garter, the highest order of British knighthood; also, membership in the order or the order itself:—*v.t.* to bind or fasten with a garter.

garter snake, a small, harmless snake with yellow stripes along the back, common in North America.

Gar-y (gâr′ĭ), a city of Indiana, on Lake Michigan, an important center of the steel industry (map **7**).

gas (găs), *n.* **1**, any airlike fluid, without shape or volume, tending to expand indefinitely; **2**, any combustible gaseous mixture used to give light and heat; **3**, any similar fluid used as an anesthetic; especially, a mixture of nitrous oxide and oxygen: often called *laughing gas;* **4**, any fumes or vapor which make breathing difficult or impossible; as, *gases* used in warfare; **5**, *Colloquial*, gasoline:—*v.t.* [gassed, gassing], to poison by a gas.

Gas-co-ny (găs′kō-nĭ), [French **Gas-cogne** (gäs′kôny′′)], an ancient duchy (cap. Auch), in southwestern France.

gas en-gine, an engine in which the piston is driven by power produced by the explosion of a mixture of gas and air ignited within the engine cylinder; an internal-combustion engine. (See illustration on next page.)

gas-e-ous (găs′ē-ŭs), *adj.* having the nature or form of gas; as, carbon dioxide may exist in a solid or a *gaseous* state.

gash (găsh), *n.* a deep or gaping cut or wound:—*v.t.* to cut deeply; as, he *gashed* his hand with a sharp knife.

gas-ket (găs′kět), *n.* **1**, a rope or flat, plaited cord by which furled sails are tied fast to a yard or boom; **2**, braided hemp or a tallowed rope used as packing for a piston or sliding joint; hence, a similar packing made of rubber, leather, or other suitable material.

gas man-tle, a hollow, conical structure which, when placed over a gas flame and heated, gives off light.

gas mask, a covering for the face worn to prevent the inhaling of a poisonous gas.

gas-o-line or **gas-o-lene** (găs′ō-lēn; găs′-ō-lēn′), *n.* an inflammable liquid commonly obtained by distilling petroleum and used especially for fuel and cleansing.

gasp (gàsp), *n.* a quick, painful effort to catch the breath; as, his breath came in *gasps:*—*v.i.* to catch the breath with the mouth open; as, he was *gasping* for air:—*v.t.* to emit with quick, painful breaths; as, he *gasped* forth his words in terror.

gas-sy (găs´ĭ), *adj.* [gas-si-er, gas-si-est], filled with gas; like gas; inflated; gaseous.

gas-tric (găs´trĭk), *adj.* pertaining to the stomach; as, *gastric* fluid; *gastric* fever:—**gastric juice,** a thin, digestive liquid, secreted by glands in the lining of the stomach.

gat (găt), *Archaic* and *Dialectal* past tense of *get.*

gate (gāt), *n.* **1,** an opening in a wall, fence, or the like, to allow entrance or passage; **2,** a barrier, frame, or door which opens or closes such an entrance; **3,** a valve or door to stop or permit a flow, as of water, in a pipe, canal, or the like; **4,** the number of people paying to see an athletic contest; also, the amount of money taken in at the entrance gate.

gate-way (gāt´wā´), *n.* **1,** an opening in a wall or fence for entrance and exit; **2,** the frame or structure around a gate.

gath-er (găth´ẽr), *v.t.* **1,** to collect; bring together; as, to *gather* information; **2,** to pick and collect; as, to *gather* flowers; **3,** to summon; as, to *gather* one's strength; **4,** to amass gradually; as, to *gather* a fortune; **5,** to pucker; draw together; as, to *gather* a skirt to a blouse; **6,** to conclude; infer; as, they *gathered* that she was leaving:—*v.i.* **1,** to collect; come together; as, people *gathered* on all sides; **2,** to generate pus, as an abscess; **3,** to increase; as, the storm *gathers:*—*n.* one of the folds in cloth, drawn together by a thread.

gath-er-ing (găth´ẽr-ĭng), *n.* **1,** the act of bringing together; **2,** a meeting; as, a large *gathering* in the hall; **3,** any sore filled with pus.

Gat-ling gun (găt´lĭng), a machine gun consisting of clustered barrels, which are discharged in rapid succession.

Ga-tun Dam (gä-tōon´), the largest dam in the Panama Canal, on the Atlantic side of Panama, across the opening of Gatun Lake.

gaud (gôd), *n.* a piece of showy, worthless finery; a flashy ornament; bauble.

gaud-y (gôd´ĭ), *adj.* [gaud-i-er, gaud-i-est], showy; vulgarly gay or bright; as, *gaudy* imitation jewelry.—*adv.* **gaud´i-ly.**—*n.* **gaud´i-ness.**

Syn. flashy, tawdry, glittering, garish.

gauge (gāj), *n.* **1,** any of various standards of measurement; **2,** a means of estimating or judging; a test; **3,** the distance between railway rails, standard gauge being 4 feet 8 ½ inches; **4,** any measuring or recording instrument, as one for measuring rainfall, wind velocity, steam pressure, diameter of a wire, etc.; **5,** a carpenter's tool for marking a line parallel with the edge of a board:—*v.t.* [gauged, gaug-ing], **1,** to measure exactly; **2,** to ascertain the contents or capacity of; **3,** to make standard or uniform; **4,** to estimate; as, the trainer *gauged* the strength of the athlete; to *gauge* a distance. Also, **gage.**

GAUGE, def. 4

Gaul (gôl), **1,** an ancient territory which included what is now northern Italy, France, Belgium, and parts of the Netherlands, Germany, and Switzerland; **2,** an inhabitant of Gaul; **3,** a Frenchman.

gaunt (gônt; gänt), *adj.* **1,** haggard and lean, as from hunger or suffering; **2,** barren and grim; desolate; as, a *gaunt* hillside.—*adv.* **gaunt´ly.** —*n.* **gaunt´ness.**

Syn. skinny, spare, lank, lean, meager.

gaunt-let (gônt´lĕt; gänt´lĕt) or **gant-let** (gänt´lĕt; gànt´lĕt), *n.* **1,** in the Middle Ages, a mailed glove to protect the hand and wrist from wounds; **2,** a heavy glove

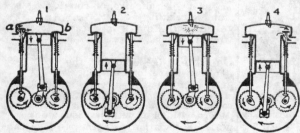

Diagram showing how a typical gas engine operates. 1, intake valve (a) open, exhaust valve (b) closed, piston ready to start down, drawing mixture of gas and air into cylinder; 2, both valves closed, piston ready to start up, compressing the mixture of gas and air; 3, spark (from spark plug), occurring at time of greatest compression, explodes the gas mixture, forcing piston down; 4, exhaust valve (b) open, piston rising, driving exhaust gas from the cylinder: on next down stroke of piston a fresh charge will be drawn in.

go; join; yet; sing; chin; show; thin, *t*hen; hw, *why*; zh, azure; ü, Ger. *für* or Fr. *lune*; ö, Ger. *schön* or Fr. *feu*; ṅ, Fr. *enfant*, nom; kh, Ger. *ach* or *ich.* See pages ix–x.

with a long cuff; **3**, that part of such a glove which covers the wrist:—**throw down the gauntlet**, to give a challenge.

gauze (gôz), *n.* a thin, light, transparent fabric of silk, cotton, or similar material.—*adj.* **gauz′y.**

gave (gāv), past tense of *give.*

gav·el (găv′ĕl), *n.* a small mallet used by a chairman or auctioneer to signal for order or attention.

Ga·wain (gä′wân; gä′wĭn), *n.* in Arthurian legend, a pure and famous knight of the Round Table, and nephew of King Arthur.

GAUNTLET (G) def. 3

gawk (gôk), *n.* a simpleton; an awkward person:—*v.i.* to stare stupidly.

gawk·y (gô′kĭ), *adj.* [gawk-i-er, gawk-i-est], awkward; clumsy.—*adv.* **gawk′i-ly.**—*n.* **gawk′i-ness.**

gay (gā), *adj.* **1**, lively; merry; full of glee; cheerful; sportive; **2**, showy; bright-colored; as, a *gay* red; **3**, addicted to pleasure; as, he leads a *gay* life.

Syn. sprightly, blithe, jovial, cheery.

gay·e·ty (gā′ĕ-tĭ), *n.* [*pl.* gayeties], joyousness. See gaiety.

gay·ly (gā′lĭ), *adv.* merrily. See gaily.

gaz. abbreviation for *gazette, gazetteer.*

gaze (gāz), *v.i.* [gazed, gaz-ing], to look earnestly or steadily; as, he *gazed* straight ahead:—*n.* a fixed, earnest look.

Syn., v. stare, gawk, glare, gape.

ga·zelle (gȧ-zĕl′), *n.* a small, swift antelope of Africa and Asia, with large black eyes.

ga·zette (gȧ-zĕt′), *n.* **1**, a newspaper; **2**, an official government journal especially one printing lists of promotions, appointments, etc.:—*v.t.* [gazetted, gȧzet-ting], to publish in a gazette.

GAZELLES (¹⁄₃₀)

gaz·et·teer (găz′ĕ-tēr′), *n.* **1**, a dictionary of geographical names; **2**, a writer or publisher of news.

G. B. abbreviation for *Great Britain.*

Gdańsk (gdänsk), a Polish seaport. See Danzig.

gear (gĭr), *n.* **1**, equipment; as, hunting and fishing *gear;* **2**, a harness for draft

animals; **3**, a unit of machinery which performs a certain function, such as transmitting power or changing timing; as, first, second, third, or reverse gears on an automobile change the speed and power of the motor; **4**, a condition in which the parts of a machine are adjusted to each other in order to act; as, a car cannot go unless it is in *gear:*—**gear wheel**, a wheel with teeth, which fit into the cogs of another wheel: also written *gearwheel:*—*v.t.* **1**, to put into gear; **2**, to provide with a gear or gears:—*v.i.* to be in, or come into, gear.

GEAR WHEEL (G) AND PINION (P)

gear·ing (gĭr′ĭng), *n.* the parts of a machine by which motion is transmitted from one section to another.

geck·o (gĕk′ō), *n.* a small, harmless house lizard, useful in destroying insects.

GECKO (⅛)

gee (jē), *interj.* a command to oxen and other animals to turn toward the right.

geese (gēs), plural of *goose.*

Gei·ger count·er (gī′gẽr), an instrument used to detect and measure radioactivity.

gei·sha (gā′shȧ), *n.* [*pl.* geisha or geishas (gā′shȧz)], in Japan, a professional singing and dancing girl.

gel·a·tin (jĕl′ȧ-tĭn) or **gel·a·tine** (jĕl′ȧ-tĭn; jĕl′ȧ-tēn), *n.* a transparent, tasteless substance extracted from the bones, hoofs, and other parts of animals by prolonged boiling; animal jelly.

ge·lat·i·nous (jĕ-lăt′ĭ-nŭs), *adj.* jellylike; of, like, or containing gelatin.

geld·ing (gĕl′dĭng), *n.* a castrated animal, especially a castrated horse.

Ge·li·bo·lu (gĕ-lē′bō-lŏŏ), the Turkish name for *Gallipoli.*

GEISHA

gem (jĕm), *n.* **1**, a precious stone; **2**, any rare object; as, a *gem* of a picture; **3**, a kind of muffin:—*v.t.* [gemmed, gem-ming], to adorn with, or as with, precious stones.

gen. abbreviation for *gender:*—**Gen.** abbreviation for *General.*

gen·darme (zhän-därm′; zhän′därm; zhän′dȧrm′), *n.* [*pl.* gendarmes (zhän-därmz′; zhän′därmz; zhän′dȧrm′)], a policeman armed and drilled as a soldier, especially in France.

gen·der (jĕn′dẽr), *n.* in English grammar, any one of the three divisions (masculine, feminine, neuter) into which nouns and pronouns are put, according to whether the objects named are regarded as male, female, or without sex.

gen·e·al·o·gist (jĕn′ĕ·ăl′ō·jĭst; jē′nē·ăl′ō·jĭst), *n.* one skilled in tracing pedigrees or descent of persons or families.

gen·e·al·o·gy (jĕn′ē·ăl′ō·jĭ; jē′nē·ăl′ō·jĭ), *n.* [*pl.* genealogies], 1, the science of investigating the descent of a person or family from an ancestor; 2, an account of such descent; a pedigree.—*adj.* gen′e·a·log′i·cal.—*adv.* gen′e·a·log′i·cal·ly.

gen·er·a (jĕn′ẽr·ȧ), plural of *genus*.

gen·er·al (jĕn′ẽr·ăl), *n.* a military officer ranking higher than a colonel and usually placed in command of an army or one of the chief divisions of an army:—*adj.* 1, pertaining to or affecting one and all; universal; as, food is the *general* need of man; a *general* epidemic; 2, indefinite; not specific or detailed; as, a *general* outline; 3, prevailing; usual; as, a *general* custom; 4, whole; not local or divided; as, a *general* vote; the *general* public; 5, not specializing in any one thing; as, a *general* store; 6, indicating superiority of rank; as, postmaster *general*.

Syn., adj. universal, common.

gen·er·al·i·ty (jĕn′ẽr·ăl′ĭ·tĭ), *n.* [*pl.* generalities], 1, the greatest part; majority; as, the *generality* of mankind; 2, a general statement, or one that is true as a rule but may have exceptions.

gen·er·al·i·za·tion (jĕn′ẽr·ăl·ĭ·zā′shŭn; -ĭ-zā′shŭn), *n.* the act of forming a general notion from particular instances.

gen·er·al·ize (jĕn′ẽr·ăl·īz), *v.t.* [generalized, generaliz-ing], to derive general principles from:—*v.i.* to draw general conclusions or notions from particular instances.

gen·er·al·ly (jĕn′ẽr·ăl·ĭ), *adv.* 1, commonly; as a rule; as, we *generally* go to the shore; 2, in a broad sense; as, *generally* speaking, children go to school; 3, extensively, but not universally; as, this condition exists *generally*.

gen·er·al·ship (jĕn′ẽr·ăl·shĭp′), *n.* 1, the office or period of office of a general; 2, military skill in leadership; as, his *generalship* saved his army; 3, leadership.

gen·er·ate (jĕn′ẽr·āt), *v.t.* [generat-ed, generat-ing], 1, to bring into existence, as plants, animals, etc.; 2, to produce, as steam in a boiler.

Syn. form, make, beget.

gen·er·a·tion (jĕn′ẽr·ā′shŭn), *n.* 1, the act or process of producing by natural or artificial means; 2, a single step in a line of succession; as, a mother and son represent two *generations*; 3, people born in the same period; as, the people of our *generation*; 4. the average period of time between generations, considered as 33 years.

gen·er·a·tive (jĕn′ẽr·ā·tĭv), *adj.* having the power to generate or produce.

gen·er·a·tor (jĕn′ẽr·ā′tẽr), *n.* one who or that which causes or produces; especially, an apparatus by which steam, electricity, or gas is produced.

gen·er·ic (jē·nĕr′ĭk), *adj.* 1, general; not specific; 2, pertaining to a genus, class, or kind.—*adv.* ge·ner′i·cal·ly.

gen·er·os·i·ty (jĕn′ẽr·ŏs′ĭ·tĭ), *n.* [*pl.* generosities], the quality of being liberal; greatness of heart; as, he showed *generosity* in his dealings with his enemies.

gen·er·ous (jĕn′ẽr·ŭs), *adj.* 1, characterized by liberality; 2, unselfish; honorable; 3, rich; abundant; noble; as, a *generous* harvest.—*adv.* gen′er·ous·ly.

Syn. liberal, beneficent, magnanimous.

gen·e·sis (jĕn′ē·sĭs), *n.* [*pl.* geneses (jĕn′ē·sēz)], the origin; beginning.

Gen·e·sis (jĕn′ē·sĭs), *n.* the first book of the Old Testament, containing the story of the creation of the world.

ge·net·ic (jē·nĕt′ĭk), *adj.* of or pertaining to origin:—**genetics,** *n.* the science of the origin and development of individuals, especially of their inherited characteristics.

Ge·ne·va (jē·nē′vȧ), a city in southwestern Switzerland, headquarters of the League of Nations:—**Lake of Geneva,** a large lake on the border between Switzerland and France. (Map 12.)

Gen·ghis Khan (jĕn′gĭz khän′), (1162?-1227), a great Mongol conqueror.

gen·ial (jĕn′yăl; jē′nĭ·ăl), *adj.* 1, favorable to comfort and growth; as, a *genial* climate; 2, kindly; sympathetic; cordial; as, a *genial* disposition.—*adv.* gen′ial·ly.

Syn. hearty, companionable, friendly.

ge·ni·al·i·ty (jē′nĭ·ăl′ĭ·tĭ; jĕn·yăl′ĭ·tĭ), *n.* the quality of being kindly; cheerfulness.

ge·nie (jē′nĭ), *n.* [*pl.* genii (jē′nĭ·ī)], a spirit; a jinni. See **jinni.**

ge·ni·i (jē′nĭ·ī), plural of *genius, genie*.

gen·i·tal (jĕn′ĭ·tăl), *adj.* pertaining to the generation of animals:—**genitals,** *n.pl.* the organs of reproduction.

gen·i·tive (jĕn′ĭ·tĭv), *adj.* naming a case, as in Latin grammar, used to express such ideas as source, origin, or possession, somewhat like the possessive case in English:—*n.* the genitive case; also, a word in that case.

gen·ius (jēn′yŭs; jē′nĭ·ŭs), *n.* [*pl.* geniuses], 1, [*pl.* genii (jē′nĭ-ī)], **a**, in Roman religion, a guardian spirit; hence, the controlling spirit of a place or person; **b**, in Mohammedan and Arabian lore, a nature spirit; a jinni; 2, remarkable ability or natural fitness for a special pursuit; as, a *genius* for music; 3, exceptional creative, intellectual, or artistic power; also, the one possessing it; 4, a person who has a powerful influence over another.

Gen-o-a (jĕn′ō-à), a seaport in northwestern Italy, home of Columbus (map 12). Its Italian name is **Ge′no-va** (jä′nō-vä).

gen-o-cide (jĕn′ō-sīd), *n.* the deliberate destruction of national, racial, or religious groups; mass murder.

gent. abbreviation for *gentleman.*

gen-teel (jĕn-tēl′), *adj.* polite; well-bred: now used only humorously or sarcastically.—*adv.* **gen-teel′ly.**

    Syn. refined, polished, courteous, civil.

gen-tian (jĕn′shǎn), *n.* any of certain plants, prized for their deep-blue flowers; especially, the tall European gentian and the U.S. fringed gentian.

Gen-tile (jĕn′tīl), *n.* one who is not a Jew:—*adj.* of or pertaining to Gentile people.

gen-til-i-ty (jĕn-tĭl′ĭ-tĭ), *n.* [*pl.* gentilities], gentle birth; refinement; good manners; as, he has no claim to *gentility.*

gen-tle (jĕn′tl), *adj.* [gen-tler, gen-tlest], 1, mild; not severe in manner; kind; 2, light; not rough; as, a *gentle* touch; 3, friendly; docile; as, a *gentle* dog; 4, gradual; as, a *gentle* slope; 5, wellborn:—*v.t.* [gen-tled, gen-tling], to train; make docile; as, to *gentle* a pony.

    Syn., adj. placid, bland, tame.

gen-tle-folk (jĕn′tl-fōk′), *n.* persons of good family and breeding.

gen-tle-man (jĕn′tl-mǎn), *n.* [*pl.* gentlemen (-mĕn)], 1, a well-bred and honorable man; 2, a man; as, show the *gentleman* in; 3, **gentlemen,** a term of polite address to a group of men or in the salutation of a letter.

gen-tle-man-ly (jĕn′tl-mǎn-lĭ), *adj.* like or befitting a gentleman; well-bred.

gen-tle-wom-an (jĕn′tl-wŏŏm′ǎn), *n.* a woman of good birth or breeding; a lady.

gen-tly (jĕn′tlĭ), *adv.* in a gentle way; quietly; kindly; as, to speak *gently.*

gen-try (jĕn′trĭ), *n.* 1, people of education and breeding; 2, in England, those ranking

GENTIAN
Fringed gentian.

next below the nobility; 3, people of a particular class: usually contemptuous.

gen-u-ine (jĕn′ū-ĭn), *adj.* 1, real; not imitation; as, a *genuine* pearl; 2, sincere; as, *genuine* affection.—*adv.* **gen′u-ine-ly.**

    Syn. true, honest.

ge-nus (jē′nŭs), *n.* [*pl.* genera (jĕn′ēr-à)], a group of plants or animals which have certain fundamental likenesses, yet differ in minor characteristics; as, the lion, tiger, and lynx are different species of the same *genus.*

ge-og-ra-pher (jē-ŏg′rà-fēr), *n.* one who knows or writes of the earth and its life.

ge-o-graph-ic (jē′ō-grăf′ĭk) or **ge-o-graph-i-cal** (jē′ō-grăf′ĭ-kǎl), *adj.* pertaining to geography:—**geographical mile,** a nautical mile, 6,080.2 feet (in British usage 6,080 feet).—*adv.* **ge′o-graph′i-cal-ly.**

ge-og-ra-phy (jē-ŏg′rà-fĭ), *n.* [*pl.* geographies], 1, the science that deals with the surface of the earth, its division into continents, its climates, plants, animals, inhabitants, and their distribution, industries, etc.; 2, the natural features of a certain area; as, the *geography* of France.

ge-o-log-ic (jē′ō-lŏj′ĭk) or **ge-o-log-i-cal** (jē′ō-lŏj′ĭ-kǎl) *adj.* pertaining to geology, or the science that studies the structure of the earth.—*adv.* **ge′o-log′i-cal-ly.**

ge-ol-o-gy (jē-ŏl′ō-jĭ), *n.* [*pl.* geologies], the science of the structure of the earth and the history of its physical changes, especially as recorded in rocks.—*n.* **ge-ol′o-gist.**

ge-o-met-ric (jē′ō-mĕt′rĭk) or **ge-o-met-ri-cal** (jē′ō-mĕt′rĭ-kǎl), *adj.* 1, pertaining to geometry; 2, having straight lines, circles, angles, etc., in a regular design.

ge-om-e-tri-cian (jē-ŏm′ē-trĭsh′ǎn; jē′ō-mē-trĭsh′ǎn), *n.* one who is skilled in that branch of mathematics called geometry.

ge-om-e-try (jē-ŏm′ē-trĭ), *n.* [*pl.* geometries], that branch of mathematics which treats of the properties and measurements of lines, angles, surfaces, and solids.

ge-o-phys-ics (jē′ō-fĭz′ĭks), *n.,* the study of the physical geography of the earth and the forces which act upon it:—*adj.* **ge-o-phys-i-cal** (jē′ō-fĭz′ĭ-kǎl).

[1]**George** (jôrj), Saint, patron saint of England, martyred 303? A.D., slayer of a legendary dragon.

[2]**George** (jôrj), the name of six kings of England, notably: 1, George III (1738–1820), king during the American Revolution; 2, George V (1865–1936); 3, George VI (1895–1952).

Geor-gette crepe or **Geor-gette** (jôr-jĕt′), a dull-finished, sheer silk fabric.

Geor-gia (jôr′jà; jôr′jĭ-à), 1, a southeastern State (cap. Atlanta), in the U.S., on

āte, āorta, râre, căt, ȧsk, fär, ăllow, sofȧ; ēve, ĕvent, ĕll, writēr, novĕl; bīte, pĭn; nō, ōbey, ôr, dŏg, tŏp, cŏllide; ūnit, ūnite, bûrn, cŭt, focŭs; nōōn, fŏŏt; mound; coin;

the Atlantic coast (map 8); **2**, a small republic (cap. Tiflis) of the U.S.S.R., south of the Caucasus Mountains, east of the Black Sea (map 12).

Ger. abbreviation for *German, Germany*.

ge-ra-ni-um (jĕ-rā′nĭ-ŭm), *n.* **1**, a plant, the *wild geranium*, with blue or rose-colored flowers; **2**, a cultivated plant with red, white, or pink flowers.

ger-fal-con (jûr′fôl′kŭn; jûr′fô/kŭn), *n.* an arctic falcon. See **gyrfalcon**.

germ (jûrm), *n.* **1**, that from which anything springs; origin; as, the *germ* of life, war, a rumor, etc.; **2**, the undeveloped beginning of an animal or plant; a sprout; seed; **3**, a microbe, especially one that may cause disease.

WILD GERANIUM
def. 1

Ger-man (jûr′măn), *adj.* pertaining to Germany, or its people or language:—*n.* **1**, a native or inhabitant of Germany; **2**, the language of Germany.—*adj.* **Ger-man′ic**.

german, a kind of lively dance; cotillion; **german silver**, a silver-white alloy of zinc, nickel, and copper.

Ger-man East Af-ri-ca, formerly, a German possession in Africa, divided between England and Belgium in 1919. The British part is now called *Tanganyika Territory*, the Belgian part was joined to Belgian Congo (map 14).

Ger-ma-ny (jûr′má-nĭ), a country in central Europe (former cap. Berlin), now divided into a West German republic (cap. Bonn), and an East German zone controlled by the U.S.S.R. (map 12).

ger-mi-cide (jûr′mĭ-sīd), *n.* a substance used to destroy germs, as carbolic acid.

ger-mi-nate (jûr′mĭ-nāt), *v.i.* [germinated, germinat-ing], to sprout or bud; begin to develop:—*v.t.* to cause to develop; as, to *germinate* seeds.

ger-mi-na-tion (jûr′mĭ-nā′shŭn), *n.* the beginning of growth in a seed, bud, or germ; the process of sprouting.

ger-und (jĕr′ŭnd), *n.* a verb form ending in *ing* and used as a noun; as, in the sentence, "Seeing is believing," both "seeing" and "believing" are *gerunds*.

ges-tic-u-late (jĕs-tĭk′ū-lāt), *v.i.* [gesticulat-ed, gesticulat-ing], to make expressive motions, especially while speaking or instead of speaking; as, an orator *gesticulates* to emphasize a point.

ges-tic-u-la-tion (jĕs-tĭk′ū-lā′shŭn), *n.* **1**, the act of making expressive motions; **2**, a gesture.

ges-ture (jĕs′tūr), *n.* **1**, a movement of the face, body, or limbs, to express an idea or emotion; **2**, something said or done as a courtesy or for effect; as, her visit was a kindly *gesture*:—*v.i.* [gestured, gestur-ing], to make expressive motions.

Syn., *n.* attitude, action, posture.

get (gĕt), *v.t.* [*p.t.* got (gŏt), *p.p.* got or got-ten (gŏt′n), *p.pr.* get-ting], **1**, to acquire; win; realize; as, to *get* a new hat; *get* first prize; *get* three wishes; **2**, to obtain by calculating; as, to *get* 40 by adding 20 and 20; **3**, to understand; as, to *get* an idea; **4**, to contract; catch; as, to *get* the measles; **5**, to receive as one's lot; as, to *get* the worst of it; to *get* ten years' imprisonment; **6**, to learn; as, to *get* a lesson; **7**, to obtain by effort or some process; as, to *get* coal from a mine; *get* power from a waterfall; also, to prepare; as, to *get* dinner; **8**, to succeed in bringing about; bring into some state; as, to *get* the grass cut; *get* him talking; **9**, *Colloquial*, to overcome; also, to catch or kill; as, he *got* his man:—*v.i.* **1**, to arrive; as, to *get* home by five; **2**, to bring oneself into a certain state; as, to *get* ready; *get* well; **3**, to become; as, to *get* hungry or tired.

get across, to make clear, or be understood; **get along**, **1**, to go; **2**, to succeed; as, to *get along* in the world; **3**, to manage; as, to *get along* without food; **4**, be friendly; as, they *get along*; **get-away**, *Slang*, an escape, as from prison; **get back**, **1**, to return; **2**, *Colloquial*, be revenged; as, I'll *get back* at you; **get out**, **1**, to betake oneself off; **2**, to become known, as a secret; **3**, to publish, as a book; **get round**, **1**, to evade, as a question or the law; **2**, to influence in one's favor; as, to *get round* the judge; **get up**, **1**, to arise from bed; **2**, to organize, as a picnic:—**get-up**, **1**, *Colloquial*, style of dress; **2**, appearance; style, as of a book.

Syn., *v.* gain, acquire, earn, attain, win.

Geth-sem-a-ne (gĕth-sĕm′á-nē), *n.* **1**, in the Bible, the garden in which Christ was betrayed and arrested (Matthew 26:36); **2**, hence, any crisis involving mental or spiritual suffering.

Get-tys-burg (gĕt′ĭz-bûrg), a borough in southern Pennsylvania, scene of a famous battle of the War between the States (map 6).

GEYSER

gew-gaw (gū′gô), *n.* a showy trifle.

gey-ser (gī′zĕr; gī′sĕr), *n.* a hot spring which frequently throws forth jets of hot water, steam, and mud.

go; join; yet; sing; chin; show; thin, *th*en; hw, *wh*y; zh, azure; ü, Ger. *für* or Fr. *lune*; ö, Ger. sch*ö*n or Fr. *feu*; n̈, Fr. e*n*fant, no*m*; kh, Ger. a*ch* or i*ch*. See pages ix–x.

Gha-na (gä′nȧ), an independent nation in western Africa, formerly British Gold Coast and Togo (map **14**).

ghast-ly (gȧst′lĭ), *adj.* **1**, deathlike; pale; **2**, horrible; as, a *ghastly* crime.
Syn. pallid, wan, hideous, shocking.

Ghent (gĕnt), a large manufacturing city in northern Belgium (map **12**).

gher-kin (gûr′kĭn), *n.* a small cucumber used for pickling.

ghet-to (gĕt′ō), *n.* [*pl.* ghettos], formerly, the only part of a city where Jews might live; now, the Jewish quarter.

ghost (gōst), *n.* **1**, the spirit of a dead person, thought of as living in an unseen world, or as returning to earth in bodily form to haunt the living; **2**, a shadowy resemblance; as, the *ghost* of a smile.
to give up the ghost, to die; **Holy Ghost**, the third being of the Trinity.
Syn. specter, phantom.

ghost-ly (gōst′lĭ), *adj.* [ghost-li-er, ghost-li-est], pertaining to or like a ghost.

ghoul (gōōl), *n.* **1**, in Oriental folklore, an evil spirit which robs graves and feeds on the dead; **2**, one whose nature and actions are repulsive to normal people.—*adj.* **ghoul′ish.**—*adv.* **ghoul′ish-ly.**

G.H.Q. abbreviation for *General Headquarters.*

gi-ant (jī′ănt), *n.* **1**, in mythology and folklore, a person of human form but of supernatural size and power; **2**, an unusually large person, animal, or plant; **3**, a person of unusual physical or mental strength or courage:—*adj.* huge; unusually powerful; monstrous.—*n.fem.* **gi′ant-ess.**

gib-ber (jĭb′ĕr; gĭb′ĕr), *v.i.* and *v.t.* **1**, to chatter rapidly and meaninglessly; as, monkeys *gibber;* **2**, to talk foolishly.

gib-ber-ish (jĭb′ĕr-ĭsh; gĭb′ĕr-ĭsh), *n.* **1**, rapid, disconnected talk; **2**, nonsense; as, his story is *gibberish.*

gib-bet (jĭb′ĕt), *n.* a kind of gallows; an upright post with an arm projecting from the top from which the bodies of executed criminals used to be hung and left as a warning:—*v.t.* **1**, to execute by hanging; **2**, to hang (the body of an executed person) on a gibbet as a warning; **3**, hence, to expose to public ridicule or scorn.

GIBBON (¼)

gib-bon (gĭb′ŭn), *n.* a small long-armed ape of southeastern Asia.

Gib-bon (gĭb′ŭn), Edward (1737–1794), an English historian, the author of "The Decline and Fall of the Roman Empire."

gibe (jīb), *n.* a taunt or scoff; sneering or sarcastic expression:—*v.t.* [gibed, gib-ing], to sneer at; taunt; as, they *gibed* him for his mistakes:—*v.i.* to sneer; scoff; as, they *gibed* at his singing. Also spelled **jibe.**
Syn., v. flout, mock, deride, jeer.

gib-lets (jĭb′lĕts), *n.pl.* the heart, liver, and gizzard of poultry.

Gi-bral-tar (jĭ-brôl′tẽr), a rock 1,396 feet high, the southernmost point of Spain, and a British fort commanding the entrance to the Mediterranean:—**Strait of Gibraltar**, a strait connecting the Atlantic Ocean and the Mediterranean (map **12**).

gid-di-ness (gĭd′ĭ-nĕs), *n.* **1**, dizziness; a whirling, confused sensation; **2**, frivolity.

gid-dy (gĭd′ĭ), *adj.* [gid-di-er, gid-di-est], **1**, lightheaded; dizzy; **2**, causing dizziness or staggering; as, a *giddy* height; **3**, frivolous; fickle; as, a *giddy* young girl.—*adv.* **gid′di-ly.**
Syn. unsteady, flighty, thoughtless.

gift (gĭft), *n.* **1**, something given; a present; **2**, the power to give or bestow; as, the position is in his *gift;* **3**, natural talent or ability; as, a *gift* for oratory.

gift-ed (gĭf′tĕd), *adj.* talented; endowed with unusual natural ability.

¹gig (gĭg), *n.* **1**, a light, two-wheeled, open carriage drawn by one horse; **2**, a ship's light boat, for the captain's use.

²gig (gĭg), *n.* a fish spear with hooks or prongs.

gi-gan-tic (jī-găn′tĭk), *adj.* huge; immense; of extraordinary size.
Syn. enormous, prodigious, vast.

gig-gle (gĭg′l), *n.* a nervous, silly laugh:—*v.i.* [gig-gled, gig-gling], to laugh in a nervous, tittering manner.—*adj.* **gig′gly.**

Gi-la mon-ster (hē′lȧ), a large, roughskinned, poisonous, black-and-orange lizard of Arizona, New Mexico, and Mexico, growing to 18 inches or more.

GILA MONSTER (1⁄16)

Gil-bert (gĭl′bẽrt), **1**, Sir Humphrey (1539?–1583), an English navigator and explorer; **2**, Sir William (1836–1911), an English poet, author of the words for Sir Arthur Sullivan's operas.

¹gild (gĭld), *v.t.* [gild-ed or gilt (gĭlt), gild-ing], **1**, to coat or cover with a thin layer of gold, or something resembling gold; **2**, to make (something) seem more attractive than it really is; gloss over; as, to *gild* a lie.—*n.* **gild′ing.**

²**gild** (gĭld), *n.* a group of people united for mutual aid; a guild. **See guild.**

Gil·e·ad (gĭl'ē-ăd), a city, a region, and a mountain in Palestine, east of the Jordan.

¹**gill** (gĭl), *n.* an organ for breathing air under water, as in fish and amphibians.

²**gill** (jĭl), *n.* a unit of liquid measure equal to one fourth of a pint.

gil·ly·flow·er (jĭl'ĭ-flou'ẽr), *n.* a popular name for the wallflower and stock.

gilt (gĭlt), past tense and past participle of *gild:*—*adj.* covered with, or of the color of, gold; as, *gilt* chairs:—*n.* a thin layer of gold or something resembling it put on a surface; as, a picture frame covered with *gilt.*

gim·crack (jĭm'krăk'), *n.* a cheap, showy article; toy; especially, a useless ornament:—*adj.* showy but useless.

gim·let (gĭm'lĕt), *n.* a small tool for boring holes.

¹**gin** (jĭn), *n.* an alcoholic liquor made from grain mash and flavored with juniper berries, etc.

²**gin** (jĭn), *n.* **1,** a trap or snare; **2,** a machine for clearing cotton fibers of seeds; a cotton gin:—*v.t.* [ginned, gin-ning], to clear (cotton) of seeds with a cotton gin.

GIMLET

gin·ger (jĭn'jẽr), *n.* **1,** a tropical plant cultivated for its spicy, sharp-tasting root; **2,** the dried, usually scraped, roots of such a plant used as a sweetmeat when candied; **3,** the powder obtained by grinding such dried roots, used as a spice or medicine; **4,** *Colloquial,* courage; vim; spirit:— **ginger ale,** a nonalcoholic drink flavored with ginger.

gin·ger·bread (jĭn'jẽr-brĕd'), *n.* **1,** a dark-colored cake sweetened with molasses and flavored with ginger, sometimes cut into fanciful shapes

GINGER, def. 1

and gilded or frosted; **2,** hence, cheap, flimsy ornamentation, especially on a house:—*adj.* gaudy; over-ornamented; as, *gingerbread* decorations.

gin·ger·ly (jĭn'jẽr-lĭ), *adv.* with extreme care; timidly:—*adj.* cautious; careful.

gin·ger·snap (jĭn'jẽr-snăp'), *n.* a thin, crisp molasses cooky flavored with ginger.

ging·ham (gĭng'ăm), *n.* a cotton dress cloth, usually in stripes, plaids, or checks, woven of dyed yarn.

gink·go (gĭngk'gō; jĭngk'gō), *n.* [*pl.* ginkgoes], a cone-bearing tree with fanshaped leaves, native to Japan and China.

gin·seng (jĭn'sĕng), *n.* **1,** a plant bearing greenish flowers in the spring and scarlet berries in the fall; **2,** the root of this plant, used by the Chinese as a medicine.

gip·sy (jĭp'sĭ), *n.* [*pl.* gipsies], one of a wandering race of dark-skinned people; a gypsy. **See gypsy.**

gi·raffe (jĭ-ràf'), *n.* a cud-chewing animal of Africa, remarkable for its long legs and neck. It has a spotted skin, and feeds on the leaves and twigs of trees.

gird (gûrd), *v.t.* [girt (gûrt) or gird-ed, gird-ing], **1,** to encircle or bind with a cord, belt, or the like; **2,** to encircle; **3,** to make ready; as, to *gird* oneself for combat.

GIRAFFE (₁⁄₃₀)

gird·er (gûr'dẽr), *n.* a main beam of wood, iron, or steel, used to support the weight of a structure; as, the steel *girders* of a bridge.

gir·dle (gûr'dl), *n.* something which surrounds, encircles, or confines, as a sash or belt:—*v.t.* [gir-dled, gir-dling], **1,** to bind or surround with, or as with, a belt; **2,** to enclose; **3,** to cut the bark of (a tree or branch) clear around.

girl (gûrl), *n.* **1,** a female child; a young unmarried woman; **2,** a female servant; **3,** *Colloquial,* a sweetheart.—*n.* **girl'hood.**

girl·ish (gûrl'ĭsh), *adj.* like, or befitting, a girl; as, a *girlish* dress.—*adv.* **girl'ish-ly.**—*n.* **girl'ish-ness.**

girl scout, a member of an American organization of girls, the "Girl Scouts" (originally "Girl Guides"), founded in 1912.

girt (gûrt), a past tense and past participle of *gird.*

girth (gûrth), *n.* **1,** a band around an animal to hold a saddle, blanket, etc., in place (see *harness,* illustration); **2,** the measure around anything; as, a man's *girth.*

gist (jĭst), *n.* the main point of a matter; as, the *gist* of a story or speech.

give (gĭv), *v.t.* [*p.t.* gave (gāv), *p.p.* giv-en (gĭv'ĕn), *p.pr.* giv-ing], **1,** to hand over as a present; as, I *gave* him a hat; **2,** to pay in exchange for something received; as, to *give* a dollar for a doll; he *gave* money for candy; **3,** to bestow freely; devote; as, he *gave* his life for his country; **4,** to administer, as medicine or gas; **5,** to deliver, as a message; as, *give* her my love; **6,** to read, recite, or utter; as, to *give* a speech; **7,** to furnish; as, fire *gives* heat; **8,** to furnish as entertainment; as, to *give* a dance; **9,** to put forth; as, *give* a jump or a shout; **10,** to impart; be the source of; as, to *give* some one a cold; the play *gave* pleasure; **11,** to allot; assign; as, to *give* a child a name; **12,** to grant; as, to *give* permission; **13,** to entrust; as, I *give* it into your charge; **14,** to pledge; as, to *give* one's word; **15,** to present for action or consideration; as, to *give* a reason; **16,** to perform; present; as, to *give* a play:—*v.i.* **1,** to present gifts; to contribute; bestow charity; as, he *gave* freely to the hospital; **2,** to yield, as to force, pressure, motion, etc.; as, the marshy ground *gave* under my feet; **3,** to afford a view or passage; as, the window *gives* on a court:—*n.* a yielding to pressure; elasticity; as, the *give* of new rubber.

give away, 1, to hand over, as a possession; **2,** to betray or expose to ridicule, as a secret or a person; **give ear,** to listen; **give in,** to yield, as in a fight or an argument; **give it to him,** *Colloquial,* punish him; **give one his due,** to admit his fine points; **give rise to,** to cause; **give up, 1,** to surrender, as a town; **2,** to hand over to the law, as a criminal; **3,** to stop trying; stop hoping; **give way, 1,** to retreat, as an army; **2,** to be supplanted by; as, sorrow *gives way* to hope; **3,** to collapse, as a bridge under a load.

giv-en (gĭv′ĕn), *adj.* **1,** inclined; disposed; as, *given* to lying; **2,** stated; as, to meet at a *given* time:—**given name,** the Christian name given to a child by his parents or guardian.

Gi-za, El (ĕl-gē′zȧ) or **Gi-zeh, El** (elgē′zĕ), a town on the Nile, famous for the pyramids and the Egyptian Sphinx (map **14).**

giz-zard (gĭz′ẽrd), *n.* the second stomach of birds, with thick, muscular walls for crushing and grinding food, often by means of pebbles previously swallowed.

Gk. abbreviation for *Greek.*

gla-cé (glȧ′sā′), *adj.* **1,** having a smooth glossy surface; **2,** coated with icing; sugarcoated, as nuts, fruit, cake, etc.

gla-cial (glā′shăl), *adj.* **1,** pertaining to ice or its action; icy; **2,** pertaining to the ice age.

gla-cier (glā′shẽr; glăs′ĭ-ẽr), *n.* a mass or river of ice, formed in high cold regions, which moves slowly down a mountain or through a valley until it melts, or else, on seacoasts, breaks off into icebergs.

glad (glăd), *adj.* [glad-der, glad-dest], **1,** joyous; cheerful; **2,** pleased; as, I am *glad* that you came; **3,** causing joy; as, *glad* news; **4,** bright; beautiful; as, a *glad* scene; a *glad* sky.—*adv.* **glad′ly.**

Syn. joyful, delighted.

glad-den (glăd′n), *v.t.* and *v.i.* to make or become happy.

Syn. cheer, comfort, please.

glade (glād), *n.* an open space in a forest.

glad-i-a-tor (glăd′ĭ-ā′tẽr), *n.* in ancient Rome, a man trained or hired to fight for the amusement of the public.

glad-i-o-lus (glăd′ĭ-ō′lŭs; glȧ-dī′ō-lŭs), *n.* [*pl.* gladioli (glăd′ĭ-ō′lī; glȧ-dī′ō-lī) or gladioluses], a plant of the iris family, with swordshaped leaves and spikes of colored, showy flowers.

glad-some (glăd′sŭm), *adj.* joyous; gay.

Glad-stone (glăd′stŭn), William Ewart (1809–1898), a British statesman, orator, and financier, prime minister four times under Queen Victoria.

glam-our or **glam-or** (glăm′ẽr), *n.* **1,** magical charm; enchantment; as, the *glamour* of the moonlight; **2,** false or alluring charm of a person, place, or thing.

GLADIOLUS

The *-our* spelling is preferred for the noun, and the *-or* spelling for the words derived from it.—*adj.* **glam′or-ous.**—*adv.* **glam′or-ous-ly.**

glance (glȧns), *n.* **1,** a swift, sidewise look; **2,** a hasty look; as, a *glance* into a room; a *glance* at a paper:—*v.i.* [glanced, glancing], **1,** to view with a quick movement of the eye; **2,** to strike at a slant and fly off; as, the stone *glanced* off his armor.

gland (glănd), *n.* an organ which secretes a special substance or substances to be used in, or discharged from, the body; as, the salivary *glands;* sweat *glands.*

glan-ders (glăn′dẽrz), *n.* a contagious disease in horses, mules, or the like, marked by fever, swelling of the glands of the lower jaw, and a discharge of mucus from the nose.

glan-du-lar (glăn′dū-lẽr), *adj.* pertaining to glands; containing glands; as, a *glandular* disease; *glandular* tissue.

glare (glâr), *n.* **1,** a brilliant light; dazzling brightness; as, the *glare* of the sun; **2,** a fierce, piercing look:—*v.i.* [glared, glaring], **1,** to shine with a dazzling light; as, the light *glared* through the windows; **2,** to look with fierce, piercing eyes; as, she *glared* at me when I spoke:—*v.t.* to express with a fierce look; as, he *glared* his hate.

glar-ing (glâr′ĭng), *adj.* **1,** dazzlingly

āte, âorta, râre, căt, ȧsk, fär, ăllow, sofȧ; ēve, êvent, ĕll, writẽr, novĕl; bīte, pĭn; nō, ōbey, ôr, dŏg, tŏp, cŏllide; ūnit, ūnite, bûrn, cŭt, focŭs; nōōn, fŏŏt; mound; coin;

bright; as, a *glaring* light; **2,** fierce; angry; as, a *glaring* eye; **3,** evident; extremely conspicuous; as, a *glaring* error.

Glas-gow (glàs′gō; glàs′kō), an important British seaport on the Clyde River, in southwestern Scotland (map **13**).

glass (glàs), *n.* **1,** a hard, brittle substance, usually transparent or translucent, made from sand mixed with soda, potash, and other chemicals, and shaped at high heat by pressing or blowing; **2,** an article made of this substance, as a mirror, a table tumbler, telescope, etc.; **3,** the amount of anything contained in a drinking tumbler; as, a *glass* of milk; **4, glasses,** spectacles; eyeglasses:—*v.t.* to put into a jar of this substance, for preservation; as, to *glass* fruits or vegetables:—*adj.* made of this substance; as, *glass* flowers.—*n.* **glass′ful.**—*n.* **glass′mak ing.**—*n.* **glass′ware.**

glass-y (glàs′ĭ), *adj.* [glass-i-er, glass-i-est], **1,** smooth, transparent, etc.; **2,** staring without expression: said of the eye or look. —*adv.* **glass′i-ly.**—*n.* **glass′i-ness.**

glaze (glāz), *v.t.* [glazed, glaz-ing], **1,** to furnish or fit (a window, case, frame, or the like) with glass; **2,** to cover or overlay with a thin coating of glass, or a substance resembling glass; hence, to make smooth and glossy; as, to *glaze* pottery or paper; **3,** in cooking, to coat with crystallized sugar; as, *glazed* fruit; **4,** to make (the eye) staring or glassy; as, death *glazed* his eyes:—*v.i.* to become staring or glassy:—*n.* **1,** a substance used for glazing; **2,** a glossy or glazed surface; as, a *glaze* of ice.

gla-zier (glā′zhẽr; glā′zĭ-ẽr), *n.* one whose trade is to set glass in windows.

glaz-ing (glā′zĭng), *n.* **1,** the act or art of fitting windows, cases, or the like, with glass, or of applying a glossy coating to pottery, porcelain, etc.; **2,** a coating of glass, or of a glossy, glasslike substance; **3,** the glass of windows.

gleam (glēm), *n.* **1,** a brief flash of light; a beam; **2,** something resembling a flash of light; as, a *gleam* of hope:—*v.i.* to send out rays of light; as, the candles *gleamed*.
    Syn., n. glimmer, glitter.

glean (glēn), *v.t.* **1,** to gather (grain, or other produce) which the reapers have left; **2,** to collect bit by bit; as, facts *gleaned* from many books:—*v.i.* to gather grain left by reapers.—*n.* **glean′er.**

glebe (glēb), *n.* **1,** *Poetic,* ground or soil; **2,** land belonging to a parish church or assigned to a minister as part of his salary.

glee (glē), *n.* **1,** gaiety; mirth; entertainment; **2,** a song, without musical accompaniment, for three or more voices, singing different parts in harmony:—**glee club,** a

club organized to sing songs in harmony.
    Syn. merriment, joviality, joy.

glee-ful (glē′fŏol), *adj.* merry; gay; as, *gleeful* children.—*adv.* **glee′ful-ly.**

glen (glĕn), *n.* a narrow secluded valley.

glib (glĭb), *adj.* [glib-ber, glib-best], speaking or spoken with readiness and ease, but often with little sincerity or thought; as, a *glib* talker; a *glib* statement.—*adv.* **glib′ly.** —*n.* **glib′ness.**

glide (glīd), *v.i.* [glid-ed, glid-ing], to flow, or move along smoothly or noiselessly; as, the boat *glided* through the water:—*n.* the act of so moving; also, a smooth, sliding step or motion, as in dancing.
    Syn., v. slip, slide.

glid-er (glī′dẽr), *n.* **1,** one who or that which moves along smoothly; **2,** a motorless airplane which is towed aloft and then flies by utilizing gravity and air currents, or is towed singly or in a train by a transport plane (see *aviation,* illustration).

glim-mer (glĭm′ẽr), *n.* **1,** a faint, unsteady light; **2,** a glimpse or hint; as, a *glimmer* of hope:—*v.i.* to flicker; shine faintly and waveringly; as, lights *glimmer* afar.
    Syn., n. gleam, glitter, glow.

glimpse (glĭmps), *n.* **1,** a hurried view; as, they caught a *glimpse* of her as she passed; **2,** a hint; a notion; as, a *glimpse* of what is to come:—*v.t.* [glimpsed, glimps-ing], to catch a hurried view of; as, they *glimpsed* the garden as they hurried by.

glint (glĭnt), *n.* a faint gleam; a flash:— *v.i.* to sparkle or flash; reflect light; as, the armor *glinted* in the sunlight.

glis-ten (glĭs′n), *v.i.* to sparkle; shine; gleam; as, her eyes *glistened* with tears:— *n.* glitter; sparkle.

glis-ter (glĭs′tẽr), *v.i.* to glitter; shine.

glit-ter (glĭt′ẽr), *v.i.* **1,** to sparkle or flash, as diamonds; **2,** to be showy, as jewels:— *n.* brilliancy; sparkle; as, the *glitter* of gold.
    Syn., v. glimmer, shine, glisten.

gloam-ing (glō′mĭng), *n.* twilight; dusk.

gloat (glōt), *v.i.* to feast the eyes or mind in triumph, greed, or spite; as, a thief *gloats* on stolen jewels; to *gloat* over an enemy's failure.

glob-al (glō′bl), *adj.* world-wide; including all parts of the earth or globe; as, *global* strategy.

GLOBE, def. 2

globe (glōb), *n.* **1,** an object which is round like a ball; a ball; a sphere; **2,** a sphere showing the map of the earth (*terrestrial globe*); a similar sphere showing the arrangement of the heavenly bodies (*celestial globe*):—**the globe**, the earth.

glob-u-lar (glŏb/ū-lẽr), *adj*. **1**, shaped like a globe; round; **2**, made up of tiny, globe-shaped particles.

glob-ule (glŏb/ūl), *n*. a tiny globe-shaped particle; as, a *globule* of fat.

gloom (glōom), *n*. **1**, partial darkness; **2**, unhappiness; low spirits; sadness:—*v.i.* **1**, to be or become cloudy or partially dark; **2**, to frown or look sullen; be sad or unhappy.
Syn., *n*. cheerlessness, dejection.

gloom-y (glōom/ĭ), *adj*. [gloom-i-er, gloom-i-est], **1**, dark; dim; as, a *gloomy* cave; **2**, dismal; sad; cheerless; as, a *gloomy* expression.—*adv.* **gloom/i-ly**.
Syn. cloudy, ill-lighted, downcast, glum.

Glor-i-a (glôr/ĭ-á), *n*. **1**, in church worship, a song of praise; especially, the *Gloria in Excelsis*, Glory be to God on High, and the *Gloria Patri*, Glory be to the Father; **2**, a musical setting of either of these:—**gloria**, in art, a halo about the head of a saint or deity.

glor-i-fy (glôr/ĭ-fī), *v.t.* [glorified, glorifying], **1**, to confer honor and splendor upon; as, to *glorify* a hero; **2**, to worship; adore; as, to *glorify* God; **3**, to give beauty and charm to; as, kindliness *glorifies* a homely face.—*n*. **glor/i-fi-ca/tion**.
Syn. praise, elevate, exalt.

glor-i-ous (glôr/ĭ-ŭs), *adj*. **1**, praiseworthy; noble; as, a *glorious* victory; **2**, of splendid beauty; magnificent; as, a *glorious* scene; **3**, *Colloquial*, delightful; as, *glorious* fun.— *adv.* **glor/i-ous-ly**.

glor-y (glôr/ĭ), *n*. [*pl.* glories], **1**, distinction, fame, or honor, given to someone or something by others; **2**, splendor; radiant beauty; as, the *glory* of the sunset; **3**, a reason for pride; as, the Colosseum was the *glory* of ancient Rome; **4**, highest state of magnificence or prosperity; as, Greece in her *glory*; **5**, praise given in worship; as, *glory* be to God; **6**, in art, a halo:—*v.i.* [gloried, glory-ing], to rejoice or exult; as, to *glory* in one's power.
Syn., *n*. brilliance, grandeur.

¹gloss (glôs), *n*. **1**, a smooth, glistening luster; as, the *gloss* of satin; **2**, an insincere or false appearance:—*v.t.* **1**, to make smooth and lustrous; **2**, to give a fair appearance to; cover up or lessen by excuses; as, to *gloss* over a mistake.

²gloss (glôs), *n*. a word or words inserted between the lines or written in the margin of a text, either as translation or to explain some word or passage.

glos-sa-ry (glŏs/á-rĭ), *n*. [*pl.* glossaries], **1**, a collection of notes explaining obso-lete, technical, or other unusual words in a book or text, or as used by some author; **2**, a dictionary of a dialect.

gloss-y (glôs/ĭ), *adj*. [gloss-i-er, gloss-i-est], shiny and smooth; as, a *glossy* table top.— *n*. **gloss/i-ness**.

glot-tis (glŏt/ĭs), *n*. the small opening at the upper part of the windpipe between the vocal cords in the larynx.

Glouces-ter (glŏs/tẽr), **1**, a seaport in northeastern Massachusetts, famous for its fisheries (map **6**); **2**, an important commercial city on the Severn River, in southwestern England (map **13**).

glove (glŭv), *n*. **1**, a covering for the hand, of leather, wool, silk, or the like, with a separate division for each finger; **2**, a padded covering to protect the hand in certain sports, as boxing, baseball, etc.

glov-er (glŭv/ẽr), *n*. a maker or seller of gloves.

glow (glō), *v.i.* **1**, to give off heat and light without flame; as, embers *glow* after a fire dies down; **2**, to be red; show brilliant color; as, the sun *glows* in the west; **3**, to be warm or flushed, as from exercise; **4**, to burn with the fervor of emotion or excitement:—*n*. **1**, intense or shining heat; **2**, redness or brightness of color; **3**, passion; ardor; **4**, warmth of body.

glow-er (glou/ẽr), *v.i.* to stare threateningly or angrily; scowl; as, the angry man *glowered* at the boy.

glow-worm (glō/wûrm/), *n*. any of various insects and their larvae which glow or flicker in the dark.

gloze (glōz), *v.t.* [glozed, gloz-ing], to smooth over or explain; as, to *gloze* a sin.

glu-cose (glōō/kōs), *n*. **1**, a form of sugar in honey and most fruits; **2**, in the U.S., a sirup made from cornstarch, and used to sweeten food: also called *corn sirup*.

glue (glōō), *n*. **1**, a substance, made by boiling fish or the skins, hoofs, etc., of animals, and used, when heated or boiled with water, for sticking things together; **2**, any substance that is like glue:—*v.t.* [glued, glu-ing], to join with glue.

glum (glŭm), *adj*. [glum-mer, glum-mest], gloomy; moody; sullen; as, a *glum* expression.—*adv.* **glum/ly**.
Syn. dismal, morose, dispirited.

glut (glŭt), *n*. too large a supply; as, a *glut* of wheat on the market:—*v.t.* [glutted, glut-ting], **1**, to more than satisfy; as, he *glutted* his appetite with rich food; **2**, to oversupply; as, to *glut* the market.
Syn., *v.* gorge, stuff, satisfy, surfeit.

glu-ten (glōō/tĕn), *n*. a nutritious and sticky substance, found in the flour of certain grains, especially wheat.

āte, âorta, râre, căt, ăsk, fär, ăllow, sofá; ēve, ĕvent, ĕll, writẽr, novĕl; bīte, pĭn; nō, ōbey, ôr, dŏg, tŏp, cŏllide; ūnit, ūnite, bûrn, cŭt, focŭs; nōōn, fŏŏt, mound; coin;

glu·ti·nous (glōō′tĭ-nŭs), *adj.* sticky; like glue.

glut·ton (glŭt′n), *n.* **1,** one who eats too much; a greedy person; **2,** a small, flesh-eating and fur-bearing animal of the northern regions; the wolverine.

glut·ton·ous (glŭt′n-ŭs), *adj.* given to overeating; greedy.—*adv.* **glut′ton·ous·ly.**

glut·ton·y (glŭt′n-ĭ), *n.* [*pl.* gluttonies], the act or habit of eating to excess.

glyc·er·in (glĭs′ĕr-ĭn) or **glyc·er·ine** (glĭs′ĕr-ĭn; glĭs′ĕr-ēn), *n.* a sweetish, colorless, sticky liquid obtained from oils, fat, etc., used in medicines, explosives, etc.

gnarl (närl), *n.* a knot in wood or on the trunk of a tree.—*adj.* **gnarl′y.**

gnarled (närld), *adj.* full of knots; distorted; twisted; as, an old, *gnarled* oak.

gnash (năsh), *v.t.* and *v.i.* to strike or grind the teeth together, as in anger or in pain.

gnat (năt), *n.* a small, two-winged insect, which stings or bites.

gnaw′ (nô), *v.t.* [*p.t.* gnawed (nôd), *p.p.* gnawed or gnawn (nôn), *p.pr.* gnaw-ing], **1,** to bite off, or eat away, little by little; to corrode; **2,** hence, to torment; as, *gnawed* by remorse:—*v.i.* **1,** to bite repeatedly; as, to *gnaw* at a crust; **2,** to torment.

gneiss (nīs), *n.* a rock composed of layers of quartz, mica, and feldspar, like granite in composition, but not in structure.

gnome (nōm), *n.* a dwarf, supposed to live in the earth to guard the earth's treasures.

gnu (nōō; nū), *n.* a South African antelope with a mane, a flowing tail, and curved horns.

GNU (1/70)

go (gō), *v.i.* [*p.t.* went (wĕnt), *p.p.* gone (gôn), *p.pr.* go-ing], **1,** to pass from place to place; travel; proceed; as, to *go* from New York to Boston; *go* ahead; gossip *goes* through a town; a telegram *goes* by wire; **2,** to move away; depart; start; as, the train *goes* at five; the train has *gone;* **3,** to follow or be guided; as, to *go* by rule; she *goes* with the fashion; **4,** to be (in a certain condition); as, to *go* dirty; *go* in daily dread; *go* prepared; **5,** to be in working order; as, a clock or an engine *goes;* **6,** to make a particular motion; as, *go* like this; **7,** to make a particular sound; as, guns *go* bang; the cat *goes* "meow"; **8,** to have a certain wording or tune; as, the song *goes* like this; **9,** to result; as, the election *went* Republican; **10,** to adopt certain views or a course of action; as, Russia *went* Communist; to *go* to war; **11,** to lead; as, the road *goes* to town; **12,** to pass by; elapse; as, an hour *goes* quickly; **13,** to be known; as, she *goes* by the name of Sue; **14,** to be sold; as, a house *goes* at auction; the ring *went* for a dollar; **15,** to be missing; as, my ring is *gone;* **16,** to disappear; be abolished or lost; as, crime must *go;* his health is *gone;* **17,** to be spent; as, my money *went* for food; **18,** to die; as, all men *go* at last; **19,** to fail; give way; collapse; as, his mind *went;* the scaffolding *went;* **20,** to attend; as, he *goes* to Yale; **21,** to become; as, to *go* crazy; *go* blind; **22,** to fit; belong; harmonize; as, this shoe *goes* on this foot; that book *goes* in that shelf; brown *goes* well with green; **23,** to be contained; as, three *goes* into nine:—**going to,** about to; intending to; as, I was just *going* to leave:—*v.t. Colloquial,* **1,** to bet; wager; as, I'll *go* you one better; **2,** to endure; tolerate; as, I can't *go* her chatter:—*n. Colloquial,* **1,** energy; enthusiasm; as, there is *go* in him yet; **2,** an agreement; as, it's a *go;* **3,** success; as, the business is a *go.*

go far, to attain fame; **go off,** to explode; **go on, 1,** to continue; as, *go on* with the story; **2,** to walk upon the stage; as, he *goes on* in the second act; **go out,** to be moved by love; as, my heart *goes out* to him; **go round,** to be enough; as, will the food *go round?* **go to sea,** to be a sailor; **go up,** to fail; as, the bank *went up.*

goad (gōd), *n.* **1,** a sharp, pointed stick to urge on cattle; **2,** anything which urges one to action:—*v.t.* to drive with a goad; as, to *goad* cattle; hence, to urge to action by irritating means; to drive; as, his taunts *goaded* me to try.

goal (gōl), *n.* **1,** a point marking the end of a race or journey; **2,** an aim; purpose; as, a *goal* in life; **3,** the place into, over, or through which the players in football, soccer, etc., must put the ball in order to score; also, the score thus made.

goat (gōt), *n.* **1,** a small, very active, cud-chewing animal, with horns and a beard, much valued for its milk, flesh, and hair; **2,** *Colloquial,* one who gets or takes the blame for another's deed; a scapegoat; one who is a butt for ridicule or jokes.—*n.* and *adj.* **goat′skin′.**

GOAT (1/15)

goat·ee (gō′tē′), *n* a pointed beard on the chin or lower lip of a man.

goat·herd (gōt′hûrd′), *n.* one who tends goats.

¹gob·ble (gŏb′l), *v.t.* [gob-bled, gob-bling], **1**, to swallow hastily or greedily; as, he *gobbled* his food; **2**, *Slang*, to seize greedily; as, to *gobble* the front seats.

²gob·ble (gŏb′l), *n.* the cry of a male turkey: —*v.i.* [gob-bled, gob-bling], to utter this cry.

gob·bler (gŏb′lĕr), *n.* a male turkey.

go·be·tween (gō′-bē-twēn′), *n.* one who goes from one person to another to make peace, do business, or settle difficulties.

Go·bi, The (gō′bē), a large desert in north central China (map **15**). Its Chinese name is *Shamo*.

gob·let (gŏb′lĕt), *n.* a drinking glass with a stem and a base, but without a handle.

gob·lin (gŏb′lĭn), *n.* an evil, mischievous, ugly spirit; gnome.

go·cart (gō′kärt′), *n.* **1**, a baby carriage with small front wheels, and a back that can be raised or lowered; **2**, a light cart.

GOBLET

god (gŏd), *n.* **1**, a being thought of as having greater than human powers and traits; especially, one to whom worship is due; **2**, anything believed to have divine powers, as an image, animal, phase of nature, or the like; **3**, a thing or person that is an object of supreme interest or devotion; as, money is his *god;* his teacher is his *god:*—**God**, the Supreme Being; the Lord: also called *Creator; the Almighty; Jehovah.*—*n.* **god′hood.**

god·child (gŏd′chīld′), *n.* a child for whose religious training a godparent or godparents promise to assume responsibility at the baptism of the child; a goddaughter or godson.

god·daugh·ter (gŏd′dô′tĕr), *n.* a girl who is a godchild.

god·dess (gŏd′ĕs), *n.* **1**, a female god; **2**, a woman of great charm or beauty.

god·fa·ther (gŏd′fä′thĕr), *n.* a man who promises, at the baptism of a child, to be responsible for its religious training.

god·head (gŏd′hĕd), *n.* the divine nature: —**Godhead**, the Supreme Deity.

god·less (gŏd′lĕs), *adj.* having no god; not believing in God; hence, wicked.

god·like (gŏd′līk′), *adj.* like, or suitable for, a god.

god·ly (gŏd′lĭ), *adj.* pious; obedient to the commands of God; as, the minister is a *godly* man.—*n.* **god′li·ness.**
 Syn. righteous, holy, religious.

god·moth·er (gŏd′mŭth′ĕr), *n.* a woman who promises, at the baptism of a child, to be responsible for its religious training.

god·par·ent (gŏd′pâr′ĕnt), *n.* a man or woman who promises, at a child's baptism, to be responsible for its religious training.

god·send (gŏd′sĕnd′), *n.* unexpected aid or good fortune which comes as if sent by God.

god·ship (gŏd′shĭp), *n.* deity; divinity.

god·son (gŏd′sŭn′), *n.* a male godchild.

God·speed (gŏd′spēd′), *n.* success: a wish for good luck, as to one going on a journey.

god·wit (gŏd′wĭt), *n.* a long-billed, long-legged bird related to the snipes.

Goe·thals (gō′thălz), George Washington (1858–1928), an American army officer and civil engineer, who built the Panama Canal.

GODWIT (₁⁄₁₂)

Goe·the (gö′tĕ), Johann Wolfgang von (1749–1832), a German poet and philosopher, author of "Faust."

gog·gle (gŏg′l), *v.i.* [gog-gled, gog-gling], to roll the eyes; stare:—*adj.* staring; prominent; rolling; as, *goggle* eyes:—*n.* **1**, a strained or affected rolling of the eyes; **2**, **goggles**, eyeglasses worn to protect the eyes from dust, sun, etc.

go·ing (gō′ĭng), *n.* **1**, departure; as, her *going* was unexpected; **2**, the state of the ground or roads, as for traveling, racing, etc.; as, the *going* is good:—*adj.* working; successful; as, a *going* concern.

goi·ter or **goi·tre** (goi′tĕr), *n.* a swelling of the thyroid gland of the neck.

gold (gōld), *n.* **1**, a precious metal, widely used for coinage and jewelry, which is heavy and easily bent, and, when pure, of a bright yellow color; **2**, money; wealth; **3**, the color of gold; **4**, precious or pure quality; as, she is *gold* all through.

Gold Coast Col·o·ny, a former British colony (cap. Accra) in western Africa, now part of Ghana (map **14**).

gold·en (gōl′dĕn), *adj.* **1**, made of, or like, gold; **2**, shining; bright like gold; **3**, excellent; as, a *golden* opportunity.
 golden age, 1, according to ancient poets, the first age of the world, a period of perfect human happiness and innocence; **2**, the period of greatest glory in the civilization, history, or literature of any country; **golden rule,** the rule given by Jesus which urges us to treat others as we wish them to treat us (Matthew 7:12).

Golden Fleece, in Greek mythology, a fleece of gold hidden in a sacred grove and guarded by a dragon, until it was won by Jason with the help of Medea.

āte, âorta, râre, căt, ȧsk, fär, ȧllow, sofȧ; ēve, ēvent, ĕll, writẽr, novĕl; bīte, pĭn; nō, ōbey, ôr, dŏg, tŏp, cŏllide; ūnit, ŭnite, bûrn, cŭt, focŭs; nōon, fŏŏt; mound; coin;

Golden Gate, the strait which forms the entrance to San Francisco Bay.

Golden Horn, an inlet of the Bosporus, forming the harbor of Istanbul.

gold·en·rod (gōl′dĕn-rŏd′), *n.* a summer- or fall-blooming plant with wandlike stems and spike-shaped clusters of small, yellow flowers.

GOLDENROD

gold·en wed·ding, the fiftieth anniversary of a marriage.

gold–filled (gōld′=fīld′), *adj.* having a heavy layer of gold over a layer of another metal.

gold-finch (gōld′fĭnch′), *n.* **1**, a brightly colored European songbird; **2**, an American songbird with a yellow body, and black crown, wings, and tail.

gold-fish (gōld′fĭsh′), *n.* a small, yellow or orange-colored fresh-water fish native to China. It is related to the carp and is often kept in ponds, bowls, or aquariums.

GOLDFINCH ($\frac{1}{4}$)
def. 2

gold leaf, sheets of gold beaten very thin, used in gilding.

Gold·smith (gōld′smĭth), Oliver (1728–1774), a British dramatist, novelist, and poet.

gold·smith (gōld′smĭth′), *n.* one who makes gold utensils and ornaments, or who deals in gold plate.

golf (gŏlf), *n.* a game played with a small, hard ball and long-handled clubs, on a

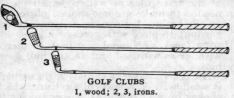

GOLF CLUBS
1, wood; 2, 3, irons.

course, or tract of land, called *links*, the object being to drive the ball into a series of holes with the fewest possible strokes:—*v.i.* to play the game of golf.

Gol·go·tha (gŏl′gŏ-thȧ), *n.* in the Bible, the place where Jesus was crucified (Matthew 27:33).

Go·li·ath (gō-lī′ăth), in the Bible, the Philistine champion, a giant killed by David with a stone from a sling (I Samuel 17:4):—**goliath**, *adj.* huge; gigantic; as, a *goliath* hammer; *goliath* frog.

Go·mor·rah (gō-mŏr′ȧ), a city of ancient Palestine, destroyed by fire because of its wickedness (Genesis 19).

gon·do·la (gŏn′dō-lȧ), *n.* **1**, a long, narrow, flat-bottomed boat, with high, pointed ends, moved, usually, by one oar, and used on the

VENETIAN GONDOLA

canals of Venice; **2**, in the U.S., an open freight car with a flat bottom and low sides; **3**, a long car slung under a dirigible balloon.

gon·do·lier (gŏn′dō-lǐr′), *n.* a man who rows a gondola.

gone (gôn), past participle of **go**:—*adj.* **1**, faint or weak; as, a *gone* feeling; **2**, departed; dead; **3**, ruined; lost.

gong (gông), *n.* a bowl-shaped, metal bell which resounds when struck; as, a dinner *gong*; a fire *gong*.

good (gŏod), *adj.* [*comp.* bet·ter, *superl.* best], **1**, adapted to the end in view; suited to its purpose; as, fish are *good* to eat; a *good* saddle horse; **2**, efficient; as, a *good* doctor; a *good* driver; **3**, satisfactory in quality; as, *good* silk; **4**, giving pleasure; as, a *good* time; **5**, not less than; complete; as, a *good* mile; **6**, real; genuine; as, *good* money; **7**, considerable; as, a *good* distance; a *good* number; **8**, well-behaved; as, a *good* child; a *good* dog; **9**, morally excellent; virtuous; as, a *good* man; **10**, kind; benevolent; as, God is *good*; **11**, right; proper; as, a *good* rule to live by; **12**, favorable; advantageous; as, *good* news; **13**, of high or respectable birth; as, to come of a *good* family; **14**, able to endure or perform; as, a coat *good* for two years; **15**, valid; sound; as, a *good* excuse; **16**, thorough; as, a *good* scolding; **17**, financially sound; trustworthy; as, *good* for a debt:—*n.* **1**, whatever is excellent, right, desirable, or sound: opposite of *evil*; as, let *good* prevail; **2**, profit; advantage; welfare; as, I tell you for your own *good*; **3**, use; as, what *good* is it?—*interj.* an exclamation of approval.

as good as, practically; as, *as good as* new; **for good and all**, forever; **a good thing**, a bargain; **have a good mind**, to be inclined; as, I *have a good mind* to go; **make good**, **1**, to succeed; **2**, to compensate; make up for; as, to *make good* a loss or a theft; **3**, to keep a promise; **to the good**, advantageous or extra; as, a pound *to the good*; **goods**, **1**, movable possessions, as household furniture; **2**, textile fabric; **3**,

---

go; join; yet; sing; chin; show; thin, *th*en; hw, *wh*y; zh, azure; ü, Ger. f*ür* or Fr. l*u*ne; ö, Ger. sch*ö*n or Fr. f*eu*; ṅ, Fr. e*n*fant, no*m*; kh, Ger. a*ch* or i*ch*. See pages ix–x.

merchandise; **goods and chattels,** personal property other than land, as clothing, furniture, money, livestock, etc..

good–by or **good–bye** (gŏŏd′–bī′), *n.* a farewell; as, a fond *good-by:—interj.* farewell! a contraction of "God be with ye."

good–for–noth-ing (gŏŏd′–fŏr–nŭth′–ĭng), *adj.* useless; worthless:—*n.* an idle, useless person.

Good Fri-day, the Friday before Easter Sunday; the anniversary of the Crucifixion.

Good Hope, Cape of, a promontory at the south western point of Africa (map **14**).

good hu-mor, a cheery mood; a kindly temper.—*adj.* **good′–hu′mored.**

good–look-ing (gŏŏd′–lŏŏk′ĭng), *adj.* handsome.

good-ly (gŏŏd′lĭ), *adj.* [good-li-er, good-li-est], **1,** handsome; **2,** of pleasing quality or character; **3,** of considerable size; as, a *goodly* sum.—*n.* **good′li-ness.**

good-man (gŏŏd′măn), *n.* [*pl.* goodmen (-měn)], *Archaic:* **1,** the head of a household; husband; **2,** a title of courtesy used for those not ranking as gentlemen: equivalent to *Master.*

good na-ture, kindness of disposition; amiability.—*adj.* **good′–na′tured.**

good-ness (gŏŏd′něs), *n.* the state or quality of being good; virtue; kindness; excellence:—*interj.* an exclamation of surprise.

good tem-per, a disposition or spirit not easily provoked or irritated; cheerfulness; good nature.—*adj.* **good′–tem′pered.**

good-wife (gŏŏd′wīf′), *n.* [*pl.* goodwives (gŏŏd′wīvz′)], *Archaic:* **1,** the mistress of a house or an establishment; **2,** a title of courtesy used for those not ranking as ladies: equivalent to *Mistress.*

good will, 1, kindly feeling; benevolence; **2,** good intention; well-wishing; as, you have my *good will;* **3,** the value to a business of its established trade. Also, **good′–will′.**

good-y (gŏŏd′ĭ), *n.* [*pl.* goodies], *Colloquial,* **1,** anything especially good to eat, as candy or a cake; **2,** one who is good in a weak, sentimental way: often, *goody-goody.*

goose (gŏŏs), *n.* [*pl.* geese (gēs)], **1,** a web-footed, flat-billed water bird, larger

GOOSE (¹⁄₁₀), def. 1

than a duck but smaller and more awkward than a swan; **2,** a female goose: in contrast to *gander;* **3,** the flesh of the goose, used as food; **4,** a silly person; a simpleton.—*adj.* **goos′y.**

goose-ber-ry (gŏŏz′běr′ĭ; gŏŏs′běr′ĭ), *n.* [*pl.* gooseberries], **1,** a sour, hairy berry, used in pies and jams; **2,** the bush that bears this berry.

goose flesh, a temporary roughness of the skin, resembling that of the skin of a plucked goose, caused by cold or fear: also called *goose skin.*

goose step, a straight-legged, stiff-kneed step, originally used by German soldiers on parade.

GOOSEBERRIES

G.O.P. abbreviation for *Grand Old Party,* the present Republican Party in the U.S.

go-pher (gō′fēr), *n.* **1,** a ground squirrel of the prairies of North America; **2,** a rat-like, burrowing animal with large cheek pouches; **3,** a burrowing land tortoise of the southern U.S.

GOPHER (¼), def. 2

Gor-di-an knot (gôr′dĭ-ăn), in Greek mythology, a very complicated knot tied by King Gordius in a leather strap, about which it was said that whoever could untie it should rule all Asia. Alexander the Great cut it with one stroke of his sword and fulfilled the prophecy:—**to cut the Gordian knot,** to solve a difficult problem by forceful means.

[1]**gore** (gôr), *n.* blood; especially, thick or clotted blood.

[2]**gore** (gôr), *n.* **1,** a three-cornered or triangular piece of cloth sewed into a dress, sail, etc., to vary its width; **2,** one of the triangular or wedge-shaped pieces needed to make a dome-shaped object, as an umbrella, balloon, etc.:—*v.t.* [gored, gor-ing], to piece with gores or a gore.

[3]**gore** (gôr), *v.t.* [gored, gor-ing], to pierce with, or as with, a horn; as, the bull *gored* him.

gorge (gôrj), *n.* **1,** the throat; **2,** that which is swallowed; **3,** a mass of anything which chokes up a channel; as, a *gorge* of ice in a river; **4,** a narrow passage, as between mountains; a ravine:—*v.t.* [gorged, gorging], **1,** to swallow greedily; to stuff; **2,** to stop up:—*v.i.* to eat greedily.

gor-geous (gôr′jŭs), *adj.* rich in color; magnificent; showy.—*adv.* **gor′geous-ly.** *Syn.* superb, grand.

Gor-gon (gôr′gŭn), *n.* in Greek mythology, one of three snake-haired sisters who were so terrible that anyone gazing on them was turned to stone:—**gorgon**, an ugly or terrible woman.

go-ril-la (gŏ-rĭl′á), *n.* an African manlike ape, the largest ape known.

gor-mand-ize (gôr′mănd-īz), *v.i.* [gormandized, gormandiz-ing], to eat greedily; devour ravenously.

gorse (gôrs), *n.* a low, evergreen shrub with yellow flowers, common throughout Europe; furze.

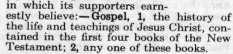
GORSE

gor-y (gôr′ĭ), *adj.* [gor-i-er, gor-i-est], bloody; bloodstained.

gos-hawk (gŏs′hôk′), *n.* any of several powerful, short-winged hawks.

Go-shen (gō′shĕn), *n.* **1,** in the Bible, the part of Egypt assigned to the Hebrews (Genesis 45:10); **2,** hence, any land of plenty.

gos-ling (gŏz′lĭng), *n.* a young goose.

gos-pel (gŏs′pĕl), *n.* **1,** good news or tidings; especially, the teachings of Jesus and the apostles; **2,** anything believed as absolutely true; as, I take his word for *gospel;* **3,** any principle which guides actions and in which its supporters earnestly believe:—**Gospel, 1,** the history of the life and teachings of Jesus Christ, contained in the first four books of the New Testament; **2,** any one of these books.

GOSHAWK
(⅛)

gos-sa-mer (gŏs′á-mer), *n.* **1,** a light film of spider's web or cobweb; **2,** any very thin, filmy fabric:—*adj.* thin; delicate; gauzy; as, a *gossamer* scarf.

gos-sip (gŏs′ĭp), *n.* **1,** familiar or idle talk; talebearing; **2,** one who makes a habit of talking about other people and their affairs:—*v.i.* to chat; tell idle tales about others; tattle.—*adj.* **gos′sip-y.**

Syn., v. babble, chat, repeat, tell.

got (gŏt), past tense and a past participle of *get.*

Gö-te-borg (yö′tĕ-bŏry′), a seaport city of southwestern Sweden (map **12**).

Gö-te-borg and Bo-hus (bō̄′hüs), a district (cap. Göteborg) in southwestern Sweden.

Goth (gŏth), *n.* **1,** one of an ancient Teutonic tribe which invaded the Roman Empire in the third and fourth centuries A.D. and settled in southwestern Europe; **2,** a crude, uncivilized person.

Goth-am (gŏth′ăm; gō′thăm), a humorous name given to New York City.

Goth-ic (gŏth′-ĭk), *adj.* **1,** characteristic of a style of architecture with pointed arches and steep roofs; **2,** relating to the Goths or their language: —*n.* **1,** a style of architecture; **2,** the language of the Goths.

GOTHIC ARCHITECTURE
Façade of cathedral at Reims, France.

got-ten (gŏt′n), a past participle of *get.*

gouge (gouj), *n.* **1,** a curved, hollow chisel for scooping out grooves or holes; **2,** a groove or hole, made with, or as with, a gouge:—*v.t.* [gouged, goug-ing], to scoop out with, or as with, a gouge. —*n.* **goug′er.**

GOUGE, def. 1

gou-lash (gōo′-läsh; gōo′läsh), *n.* a highly seasoned stew of pieces of beef or veal, and vegetables.

Gou-nod (gōo′nō′), Charles François (1818-1893), a French composer, best known for his opera, "Faust."

gourd (gôrd; gōord), *n.* **1,** any of a number of fleshy, manyseeded fruits with hard shells, related to the melon, pumpkin, etc.; also, the vine bearing this fruit; **2,** the dried shell of such fruits, used for cups, dippers, etc.; **3,** a bottle, cup, or the like, made from a gourd shell.

GOURDS, def. 1

gourde (gōord), *n.* a silver coin, the monetary unit of Haiti. (See Table, page 943.)

gour-mand (gōor′mănd), *n.* **1,** a greedy eater; glutton; **2,** a person who is very fond of eating, and is a judge of good food and drink.

gout (gout), *n.* **1,** a disease marked by painful inflammation of the joints, especially of the big toe; **2,** a splash or drop, as of rain or blood.—*adj.* **gout′y.**

Gov. abbreviation for *Governor.*

gov·ern (gŭv'ẽrn), *v.t.* **1,** to control, manage, or direct; as, to *govern* a nation or household; **2,** to decide; determine; influence; as, the financial report *governed* their decision; **3,** to require to be in a particular grammatical mood, case, etc.; as, a transitive verb *governs* a noun in the objective case:—*v.i.* to rule.

gov·ern·ess (gŭv'ẽr-nĕs), *n.* a woman employed to take care of, and often to teach, children in their own home.

gov·ern·ment (gŭv'ẽrn-mĕnt), *n.* **1,** control or management; as, the *government* of a nation; school *government;* **2,** the system of governing; method of ruling; as, a democratic *government;* **3,** a person or persons who govern; **4,** a territory or country governed.—*adj.* gov'ern·men'tal.

gov·er·nor (gŭv'ẽr-nẽr), *n.* **1,** one who governs; as, the Board of *Governors* of a hospital; especially, the head of a State in the U.S., or of a British colony; **2,** a device attached to an engine, or the like, to regulate its speed.

govt. abbreviation for *government.*

gown (goun), *n.* **1,** a woman's dress; especially, an elaborate dress; as, an evening *gown;* **2,** a long, loose robe worn by judges, priests, etc.; **3,** any loose robe or dress; as, a night*gown:*—*v.t.* to clothe with a gown.

Go·ya (gō'yä), Francisco (1746–1828), a Spanish painter and etcher, most famous for his portraits.

gr. abbreviation for *grain:*—**Gr.** abbreviation for *Greece, Greek, Grecian.*

grab (grăb), *v.t.* and *v.i.* [grabbed, grabbing], to seize suddenly; snatch; as, the thief *grabbed* the purse:—*n.* a sudden snatch at something; as, to make a *grab* at a life preserver.

grace (grās), *n.* **1,** attractiveness; charm; especially, beauty and ease of motion or manner; as, the *grace* of a dancer; **2,** favor; good will; as, in the teacher's good *graces;* **3,** hence, kindness; mercy; **4,** favor shown by granting a delay; as, three days' *grace* to pay a note already due; **5,** any charming quality, natural or affected; as, to be full of pleasant *graces;* **6,** a sense of right and wrong; as, he had the *grace* to apologize; **7,** a prayer of thanks before or after a meal; **8,** God's mercy or His divine favor:—*v.t.* **1,** [graced, grac-ing], to adorn; decorate; **2,** to honor; favor; as, the queen's presence *graced* the banquet.

Grace, the title of an archbishop, a duke, or a duchess: preceded by *your, his* or *her;* **the Graces,** in Greek ·mythology, three beautiful sister goddesses, givers of charm, beauty, and joy.

grace·ful (grās'fŏŏl), *adj.* displaying beauty in form or action; as, a *graceful* pose; a *graceful* speech.—*adv.* **grace'ful·ly.**

grace·less (grās'lĕs), *adj.* **1,** unlovely; awkward; **2,** bad; wicked; as, a *graceless* prisoner.—*adv.* **grace'less·ly.**

gra·cious (grā'shŭs), *adj.* **1,** kindly; courteous; also, merciful; as, the *gracious* king pardoned him; **2,** attractive and kind in manner and character.—*adv.* **gra'cious·ly.**

grack·le (grăk'l), *n.* **1,** any of several European birds related to the starlings; **2,** in the U.S. a blackbird; especially, the purple grackle.

PURPLE GRACKLE(¼), def. 2

gra·da·tion (grā·dā'shŭn), *n.* **1,** a gradual change from one thing to another; as, *gradation* in color from blue to purple; **2,** the act of arranging into a series in order of size, rank, color, etc.; the series so formed; a step in such a series; **3, gradations,** steps; stages; degrees.

grade (grād), *n.* **1,** a step or degree in rank, quality, order, etc.; **2,** position in a scale; as, a general holds the highest *grade* in the army; **3,** a class of persons or things of the same degree, rank, etc.; as, meat of a good *grade;* **4,** a division of the school course, consisting of a year of work; as, the elementary school has eight *grades;* also, the pupils in such a division; **5,** the mark or rating given to a pupil for school work; **6,** the rate at which a road, railroad, etc., slopes or inclines; also, the slope of a road, railroad, etc.; as, the train goes slowly on a downward *grade:*—*v.t.* [grad-ed, grad-ing], **1,** to sort out according to size, quality, rank, or value; as, to *grade* milk or fruits; to arrange into classes; as, to *grade* children according to age; **2,** to level, or to ease the slope of, as a road; **3,** to assign a mark to; as, to *grade* test papers.

grad·u·al (grăd'ū-ăl), *adj.* proceeding, or moving slowly, by degrees; not sudden; as, a *gradual* slope.—*adv.* **grad'u·al·ly.**

Syn. progressive, moderate, continuous, deliberate.

grad·u·ate (grăd'ū-āt), *v.t.* [graduat-ed, graduat-ing], **1,** to confer a degree or diploma upon; as, a university *graduates* students; **2,** to mark in grades or degrees; as, to *graduate* a measuring glass:—*v.i.* **1.** to receive a diploma or degree; as, he *graduated* from high school; **2,** to change gradually from one degree to another; as, the brightness of the light *graduates* in that sign:—*adj.* (grăd'ū-āt), **1,** having received a degree; as, a *graduate* student; **2,** designed for one who has received a degree; as, a *graduate* course:—*n.* (grăd′ū-āt), one who has received a diploma or degree; as, a *graduate* in medicine.

grad·u·a·tion (grăd′ū-ā′shŭn), *n.* **1,** the ceremony at which diplomas or degrees are given or received; school or college commencement exercises; **2,** division into degrees, as of a thermometer; **3,** the marks, or any one of the marks, on an instrument, vessel, or the like, which indicate degrees of quantity, heat, etc.

graft (grȧft), *v.t.* **1,** to insert (a shoot) from one plant into another plant, on which it continues to grow; **2,** to transplant (living tissue) from one part of the body to another; as, to *graft* skin; **3,** *Colloquial,* to get by unfair or dishonest means; as, to *graft* money or votes:—*n.* **1,** the act of grafting; also, a shoot or piece of tissue used in grafting; **2,** in the U.S., the getting of money or positions by dishonest means.—*n.* **graft′er.**

GRAFTING, def. 1

1-3, different methods of grafting; 4, graft bound in place.

gra·ham flour (grā′ăm), **1,** flour made by grinding the entire wheat kernel, without removing the bran or husk of the grain; **2,** sometimes, whole-wheat flour.

grail (grāl), *n.* cup; dish:—**Holy Grail,** in medieval legend, the cup used by Jesus at the Last Supper. It vanished because of the impurity of its keepers, and was sought by many knights, especially those of King Arthur's court, but was revealed only to a pure and perfect knight.

grain (grān), *n.* **1,** the seedlike fruit of any cereal grass, such as oats, rice, wheat, etc.; also, the plant itself; **2,** any very small, hard particle; as, a *grain* of sand or sugar; **3,** any tiny bit; as, a *grain* of salt for seasoning; a *grain* of hope; **4,** a very small unit of weight, obtained from the weight of a grain of wheat; **5,** the arrangement of fibers or the texture of wood, stone, or the like; **6,** the nature or instincts of a person; as, dishonesty goes against my *grain*:—*v.t.* to paint in imitation of the grain of wood.

gram or **gramme** (grăm), *n.* a unit or measure of weight and mass in the metric system, equal to 15.432 grains.

-gram (-grăm), a suffix meaning something written; as, tele*gram*, crypto*gram*.

gra·mer·cy (grȧ-mûr′sĭ), *interj. Archaic,* thank you.

gram·mar (grăm′ẽr), *n.* **1,** the science which deals with the forms of words and their relation to each other; **2,** the use of words according to this science; **3,** a book on this science:—**grammar school, 1,** in the U.S., the grades between the primary grades and those of the high school; **2,** in England, a school where Latin, Greek, and other subjects are taught so as to prepare a student for college.

gram·mar·i·an (grȧ-mâr′ĭ-ăn), *n.* one who knows, writes on, or teaches the science of the form and use of words.

gram·mat·i·cal (grȧ-măt′ĭ-kăl), *adj.* pertaining to grammar; according to the rules of grammar; as, "they is" is not *grammatical.*—*adv.* **gram·mat′i·cal·ly.**

Gram·o·phone (grăm′ō-fōn), *n.* a trade name for a kind of instrument for recording and reproducing sound:—**gramophone,** a machine bearing this name.

gram·pus (grăm′pŭs), *n.* a bluntheaded sea mammal related to the whales and dolphins, sometimes reaching fifteen feet in length, found

GRAMPUS (₁′₃₀), def. 1

in northern oceans. A person who puffs and blows is sometimes called a grampus.

Gra·na·da (grȧ-nä′dȧ), a city in southern Spain, once a Moorish stronghold, famous for its fortress palace, the Alhambra (map **12**).

gran·a·ry (grăn′ȧ-rĭ), *n.* [*pl.* granaries], a storehouse for grain.

grand (grănd), *adj.* **1,** main; principal; as, the *grand* entrance to a theater; **2,** magnificent; splendid; as, a *grand* ball; **3,** showing high social standing and wealth; as, a *grand* lady; **4** dignified; noble; as the *grand* manner; **5,** imposing; stately; as, a *grand* mountain; **6,** higher in rank than others of the same class; as, a *grand* duke; **7,** great in size, value, or consequence; as, a *grand* prize; *grand* climax; **8,** including everything; as, a *grand* total; **9,** *Colloquial,* very good; as, a *grand* time. *Syn.,* sublime, stately, dignified, noble, exalted, superb.

gran·dam (grăn′dăm; grăn′dăm) or **gran·dame** (grăn′dām; grăn′dăm), *n.* an old woman, especially a grandmother.

grand·aunt (grănd′ȧnt′;-änt′), *n.* an aunt of one's father or mother.

Grand Banks, a shoal in the north Atlantic Ocean, off the south and east coasts of Newfoundland, famous as a fishing ground (map **3**).

Grand Can-yon, the deep gorge cut by the Colorado River in northwestern Arizona (map **9**).

grand-child (grănd'chĭld'), *n.* [*pl.* grandchildren (grănd'chĭl'drĕn)], the child of one's son or daughter.

grand-daugh-ter (grănd'dô'tẽr), *n.* a daughter of one's son or daughter.

grand duke, 1, in certain countries of Europe, as Luxemburg, a sovereign duke, who is next below a king in rank; **2,** formerly, in Russia, a son of a czar.—**grand duch'ess.**

gran-dee (grăn-dē'), *n.* a man of high rank, especially a Spanish or Portuguese nobleman.

gran-deur (grăn'dũr), *n.* **1,** great power, rank, or fame; **2,** sublime beauty; as, the *grandeur* of the Alps; **3,** social splendor.

grand-fa-ther (grănd'fä'thẽr), *n.* the father of one's father or mother; also, any forefather.—*adj.* **grand'fa'ther-ly.**

gran-dil-o-quent (grăn-dĭl'ō-kwĕnt), *adj.* characterized by high-sounding language; bombastic.—*n.* **gran-dil'o-quence.**

gran-di-ose (grăn'dĭ-ōs), *adj.* **1,** impressive; imposing; magnificent; **2,** trying to seem great or grand.—*adv.* **gran'di-ose-ly.**

grand ju-ry, a group of jurors chosen to examine into accusations against people, and decide whether or not to send them for trial to a regular court.

grand-ma (grănd'mä'; grăn'mä'; grăm'-mä'), *n.* a grandmother. Also, **grand'-mam-ma'.**

grand-moth-er (grănd'mŭth'ẽr), *n.* the mother of one's father or mother.

grand-neph-ew (grănd'nĕf'ũ; -nĕv'ũ), *n.* the son of one's niece or nephew.

grand-niece (grănd'nēs'), *n.* the daughter of one's niece or nephew.

grand op-er-a, an elaborate dramatic composition, in which the whole dialogue is set to music.

grand-pa (grănd'pä'; grăn'pä'; grăm'pä'), *n.* a grandfather. Also, **grand'pa-pa'.**

grand-par-ent (grănd'pâr'ĕnt), *n.* either parent of one's father or mother.

Grand Rap-ids, a large city in west central Michigan (map **7**).

grand-sire (grănd'sīr'), *n. Archaic:* **1,** a grandfather or forefather; **2,** an aged man.

grand-son (grănd'sŭn'), *n.* a son of one's son or daughter.

grand-stand (grănd'stănd'), *n.* the principal seating place for spectators at a racecourse, athletic field, etc.

grand-un-cle (grănd'ŭng'kl), *n.* an uncle of one's father or mother.

grange (grānj), *n.* **1,** a farm, especially with all its buildings; **2,** in the U.S., one of the lodges of a secret national association of farmers:—**Grange,** a national association of farmers called the Patrons of Husbandry.

gran-ite (grăn'ĭt), *n.* a hard, durable rock, pink, whitish, or gray in color, used for buildings, monuments, etc.

gran-ny or **grăn-nie** (grăn'ĭ), *n.* [*pl.* grannies], a grandmother; an old woman.

Grant (grănt), Ulysses Simpson (1822–1885), a Federal general in the War between the States, and the 18th president of the U.S.

grant (grănt), *v.t.* **1,** to give or confer, especially in response to a prayer or request; as, to *grant* permission; *grant* pardon; **2,** to agree to; admit as true; as, to *grant* a point in an argument:—*n.* **1,** the act of granting; also, the thing granted; as, to receive land as a *grant* from a government; **2,** in law, a transfer of property.

Syn., v. bestow, impart, cede, allow.

gran-u-lar (grăn'ũ-lẽr), *adj.* composed of, or like, grains or granules.

gran-u-late (grăn'ũ-lāt), *v.t.* [granulat-ed, granulat-ing], **1,** to form into small grains; as, to *granulate* metal; **2,** to roughen the surface of:—*v.i.* to form into small grains; as, sirup *granulates*:—**granulated sugar,** sugar which has been whitened and made into small, separate grains.

gran-ule (grăn'ũl), *n.* a small grain.

grape (grāp), *n.* **1,** an edible, juicy berry, growing in clusters on a vine and used for making wine and raisins; **2,** the grapevine.

grape-fruit (grāp'frōōt'), *n.* a large, round, yellow fruit, related to the orange.

grape-shot (grāp'shŏt'), *n.* a cluster of small iron balls, held together in layers between plates, to be used as a charge for a cannon. The balls scatter when fired.

grape-vine (grāp'vīn'), *n.* a vine which bears grapes.

graph (grăf), *n.* a diagram showing by means of dots and lines the relationship between any two quantities or things; as, a *graph* of the temperature hour by hour.

graph (-grăf), a suffix meaning something that writes or is written; as, a tele*graph*; auto*graph*.

graph-ic (grăf'ĭk) or **graph-i-cal** (grăf'ĭ-kăl), *adj.* **1,** pertaining to the art of writing, drawing, engraving, etc.; **2,** illustrated by graphs, diagrams, or the like; **3,** vividly written or told:—**graphic arts,** drawing, painting, writing, and other arts which represent objects on a flat surface.

Syn. forcible, striking, lifelike, vivid.

āte, āorta, râre, căt, ȧsk, fär, ăllow, sofȧ; ēve, ēvent, ĕll, writẽr, novĕl; bīte, pĭn; nō, ōbey, ôr, dŏg, tŏp, cŏllide; ūnit, ūnite, bûrn, cŭt, focŭs; nōōn, fŏŏt; mound; coin;

graph-ite (grăf′īt), *n.* a kind of soft black carbon used in lead pencils.

Graph-o-phone (grăf′ō-fōn), *n.* a trade name for an instrument for recording and reproducing sounds.

-graph-y (-grăf′ĭ), a suffix meaning writing; as, tele*graphy;* also, a branch of learning or a treatise; as, geo*graphy.*

grap-nel (grăp′nĕl), *n.* 1, a small anchor with four or five hooks; 2, an instrument with iron hooks for clutching something.

GRAPNEL, def. 1

grap-ple (grăp′l), *v.t.* [grap-pled, grap-pling], to lay fast hold of:—*v.i.* to struggle in, or as in, a fight; as, to *grapple* in wrestling; to *grapple* with a problem:—*n.* 1, a close fight; a close hold, as in wrestling; 2, a mechanical device for seizing anything; a grapnel: often called a *grappling iron.*

grasp (grȧsp), *v.t.* 1, to seize; catch at; hold by clasping; as, *grasp* the rope; 2, to take hold of mentally; understand; as, to *grasp* the situation:—*v.i.* to try to seize; as, to *grasp* at power:—*n.* 1, the grip of the hand; 2, power of seizing; 3, mental hold; comprehension; control; possession.
Syn., v. clutch, clasp, grip, grab.

grasp-ing (grȧs′pĭng), *adj.* greedy.

grass (grȧs), *n.* 1, green herbage, on which grazing animals feed; especially, plants having jointed stems and narrow leaves; 2, land for grazing; any grass-covered ground: —*v.t.* 1, to cover with grass; 2, to furnish with pasture.

grass-hop-per (grȧs′hŏp′ẽr), *n.* any one of numerous slender, leaping, plant-eating insects, sometimes winged, which do great damage to crops. (See illustration under *insect.*)

grass-y (grȧs′ĭ), *adj.* [grass-i-er, grass-i-est], covered with, or like, grass.

¹grate (grāt), *v.t.* [grat-ed, grat-ing], 1, to reduce to small particles by rubbing on a rough surface; as, to *grate* cheese; 2, to rub so as to produce a rasping sound; as, to *grate* metal on stone:—*v.i.* 1, to produce a harsh noise by rubbing; 2, to cause annoyance; as, her voice *grates* on me.

²grate (grāt), *n.* 1, an iron frame of parallel or crossed bars; as, a *grate* on a prison window; 2, a framework of iron bars to hold burning fuel:—*v.t.* [grat-ed, grat-ing], to furnish with iron bars; as, to *grate* a window.

GRATE, def. 2

grate-ful (grāt′fŏŏl), *adj.* 1, thankful; ap-

preciative; 2, pleasant; soothing.—*adv.* **grate′ful-ly.**—*n.* **grate′ful-ness.**

grat-er (grāt′ẽr), *n.* an instrument, especially a kitchen utensil, with a rough surface on which to rub vegetables, cheese, etc., to reduce them to small pieces.

grat-i-fi-ca-tion (grăt′ĭ-fĭ-kā′shŭn), *n.* 1, satisfaction; 2, that which pleases; 3, reward or recompense.
Syn. enjoyment, delight.

grat-i-fy (grăt′ĭ-fĭ), *v.t.* [gratified, gratifying], to please; indulge; humor; as, to *gratify* a taste for music.

¹grat-ing (grāt′ĭng), *adj.* harsh; irritating.

²grat-ing (grāt′ĭng), *n.* a framework of crossed or parallel bars, used to cover an opening without shutting out light and air.

gra-tis (grā′tĭs; grăt′ĭs) *adv.* and *adj.* without charge; free.

grat-i-tude (grăt′ĭ-tūd), *n.* thankfulness.

gra-tu-i-tous (grȧ-tū′ĭ-tŭs), *adj.* 1, freely given; as, *gratuitous* information; 2, without cause; as, a *gratuitous* insult.

gra-tu-i-ty (grȧ-tū′ĭ-tĭ), *n.* [*pl.* gratuities], a gift of money, especially in return for services; a tip.—*Syn.* bounty, boon.

¹grave (grāv), *v.t.* [*p.t.* graved, *p.p.* grav-en (grāv′ĕn) or graved, *p.pr.* grav-ing], 1, to shape by cutting with a chisel; also, to cut, as letters, on a hard surface; 2, to impress deeply, as on the mind:—*n.* 1, a hole dug in the earth as a place of burial; any place of burial; 2, death; destruction.

²grave (grāv), *adj.* [grav-er, grav-est], 1, needing serious thought; as, a *grave* problem; 2, solemn; serious; as, a *grave* face; 3, not gay; dull; sombre; 4, low in pitch, as in music:—**grave accent,** a sign [`] over certain vowels to indicate their sound, as in French *à la carte.*—*adv.* **grave′ly.**
Syn. earnest, staid.

grav-el (grăv′ĕl), *n.* material consisting of pieces of rock and pebbles, coarser than sand:—*v.t.* [graveled, gravel-ing], to cover with gravel; as, to *gravel* a road.

grav-en (grāv′ĕn), *adj.* sculptured; carved: —**graven image,** an idol.

grav-er (grāv′ẽr), *n.* 1, a cutting tool used by engravers; 2, an engraver.

grave-stone (grāv′stōn′), *n.* a stone, usually inscribed, placed to mark a grave; a tombstone.

grave-yard (grāv′yärd′), *n.* a cemetery.

grav-i-tate (grăv′ĭ-tāt), *v.i.* [gravitat-ed, gravitat-ing], 1, to be acted upon or attracted by a force which draws all bodies in the universe toward each other; 2, to be drawn toward any center of attraction.

grav-i-ta-tion (grăv′ĭ-tā′shŭn), *n.* 1, the

force which draws all bodies in the universe toward one another; **2,** the force which draws all objects on the earth toward its center; **3,** a natural movement toward a center of attraction or influence.

grav·i·ty (grăv′ĭ-tĭ), *n.* [*pl.* gravities], **1,** seriousness; solemnity; as, the *gravity* of those attending a funeral; dignity, as of a judge; **2,** importance; serious significance; as, the *gravity* of war; **3,** the force which draws all objects on the earth toward its center; also, gravitation of any kind.

gra·vy (grā′vĭ), *n.* [*pl.* gravies], the fatty juice which comes out of meat in cooking; also, this juice made into a food dressing.

gray or **grey** (grā), *n.* any color that is formed by mixing black with white:—*adj.* **1,** of the color gray; hence, dull; as, a *gray* day; **2,** dismal; cheerless; **3,** having gray hair; old:—**gray matter, 1,** gray nerve tissue in the brain and spinal cord; **2,** *Colloquial*, brains; intelligence:—*v.t.* and *v.i.* to make or become gray.

gray-beard or **grey-beard** (grā′bērd′), *n.* an old man; hence, a wise, experienced man;—sometimes contemptuous.

gray-ish or **grey-ish** (grā′ĭsh), *adj.* somewhat gray.

gray·ling (grā′lĭng), *n.* **1,** a silver-gray fresh-water fish; **2,** a common gray or brown butterfly.

Graz (gräts), a city in southeastern Austria, nearly south of Vienna (map **12**).

GRAYLING (⅛), def. 1

¹**graze** (grāz), *v.t.* [grazed, graz·ing], **1,** to feed growing grass to; to pasture; as, to *graze* cattle; **2,** to eat grass from:—*v.i.* to eat grass.—*n.* **graz′er.**

²**graze** (grāz), *v.t.* and *v.i.* [grazed, graz·ing], to touch, rub, or scrape lightly; to scratch, or become scratched, by rubbing:—*n.* a slight rub.

gra·zier (grā′zhẽr; grā′zĭ-ẽr), *n.* one who grazes cattle for market.

Gr. Br., Gr. Brit., Gt. Br., Gt. Brit. abbreviations for *Great Britain.*

grease (grēs), *n.* **1,** melted animal fat; **2,** any thick oily substance:—*v.t.* (grēs; grēz), [greased, greas·ing], **1,** to smear with fat; **2,** to oil; to lubricate; as, to *grease* a car.

greas·er (grēs′ẽr), *n.* one who or that which lubricates the operating parts of machinery and vehicles.

greas·y (grēs′ĭ; grēz′ĭ), *adj.* [greas-i-er, greas-i-est], **1,** covered with or containing an excess of grease; as, *greasy* hands; *greasy* food; **2,** oily; hence, slippery.—*adv.* **greas′i·ly.**—*n.* **greas′i·ness.**

great (grāt), *adj.* **1,** large in size; big; vast: opposite of *small* or *little*; as, *great* plains stretch to the west; **2,** large in number; as, a *great* herd of cattle; **3,** prolonged; as, a *great* while; a *great* wait; **4,** extreme; as, *great* ignorance; *great* danger; **5,** plentiful; elaborate; as, a *great* feast; in *great* detail; **6,** of remarkable genius, skill, or character; noble; distinguished; as, a *great* artist; **7,** important; as, *great* things depend on his decision; **8,** considerable in size or intensity; as, a *great* storm; *great* pain; **9,** more than usual; as, take *great* precautions; **10,** more remote in relationship by one generation; as, a *great*-grandfather, a *great*-grandson; **11,** *Colloquial*, having unusual skill or knowledge; as, he's *great* at swimming; **12,** *Colloquial*, favorite; as, a *great* joke of his; **13,** *Colloquial*, intimate; as, *great* friends; **14,** *Slang*, excellent; as, that's *great!*—**Great War,** the war of 1914–18, which involved nearly all the important nations of the world: also called *World War I.*—*adv.* **great′ly.**—*n.* **great′ness.** *Syn., adj.* big, huge, majestic, grand.

great–aunt (grāt′-ánt′; -änt′), *n.* the aunt of one's father or mother; grandaunt.

Great Bear, a group of stars in the northern heavens containing the smaller group known as the *Dipper.*

Great Brit·ain, the island containing England, Scotland, and Wales (map **13**).

great-coat (grāt′kōt′), *n.* an overcoat.

great Dane, one of a breed of very large, powerful, short-haired dogs.

Great·er An·til·les, Cuba, Hispaniola, Jamaica, and Puerto Rico. See **Antilles.**

great–grand·child (grāt′-gränd′chĭld′), *n.* [*pl.* great-grandchildren (-chĭl′drĕn)], a child of one's grandson or granddaughter.

great–grand·fa·ther (grāt′-gränd′fä′thẽr), *n.* the father of one's grandfather or grandmother.

great–grand·moth·er (grāt′-gränd′mŭth′ẽr), *n.* the mother of one's grandfather or grandmother.

great–heart·ed (grāt′-här′tĕd), *adj.* **1,** high-spirited; brave; **2,** generous; noble.

Great Lakes, five lakes, Superior, Michigan, Huron, Ontario, and Erie, between Canada and northeastern U.S. (map **5**).

Great Salt Lake, a large salt lake in Utah (map **9**).

greaves (grēvz), *n.pl.* metal armor to protect the legs from ankle to knee.

grebe (grēb), *n.* a diving

GREBE (¹⁄₁₄).

bird with a short body, partly webbed feet, and almost no tail, related to the loon.

Gre·cian (grē′shăn), *adj.* relating to Greece or the Greeks:— *n.* 1, a Greek; 2, a Greek scholar.

Greece (grēs), a monarchy (cap. Athens) of southeastern Europe (map 12). In ancient times it was a group of independent states, and was called *Hellas.*

greed (grēd), *n.* intense and selfish hunger or desire; as, *greed* for wealth.
Syn. avidity, covetousness.

greed·y (grēd′ĭ), *adj.* [greed-i-er, greed-i-est], 1, very eager for food or drink; 2, selfishly desirous, especially for wealth.— *adv.* **greed′i-ly.** — *n.* **greed′i-ness.**

Greek (grēk), *adj.* pertaining to Greece, the Greeks, or their language:— **Greek cross,** a cross resembling a plus sign (see illustration under *cross*):— *n.* 1, a native of Greece; 2, the language of the Greeks.

Greek Church, that section of the Catholic Church dominant in eastern Europe, Asia, and Egypt, which rejects the supremacy of the Pope; the Greek Orthodox Church.

green (grēn), *n.* 1, the color of growing grass or plants; a color between blue and yellow; 2, a grass plot or common; 3, in golf, the closely cut turf around a hole; 4, **greens,** *pl.*: a, green leaves or branches cut for decorations; as, Christmas *greens;* b, spinach or similar vegetables, used for food:— *adj.* 1, having the color of, or covered with, growing grass or plants; 2, fresh; full of life; 3, having a sickly color; 4, unripe; as, *green* fruit; 5, not salted; as, *green* hams; 6, not dried; as, *green* wood; 7, untrained; inexperienced.

green-back (grēn′băk′), *n.* a piece of U.S. paper money, so called because its back is printed in green ink.

green-gage· (grēn′gāj′), *n.* a greenish-yellow plum of fine flavor.

green-horn (grēn′hôrn′), *n.* an inexperienced person; a simpleton.

green-house (grēn′hous′), *n.* a house made of glass, for growing flowers and plants.

green-ing (grēn′ĭng), *n.* any of several apples which have green skins when ripe.

green-ish (grēn′ĭsh), *adj.* somewhat green.

Green-land (grēn′lănd), a large island in the Atlantic Ocean, northeast of Canada, belonging to Denmark (map 3).

Green Moun-tains, a mountain range, part of the Appalachians, in western Vermont (map 6).

green-sward (grēn′swôrd′), *n.* smooth turf which is well covered with grass.

Green-wich (grĭn′ĭj), a borough of London, England, seat of the Royal Observatory from which longitude is reckoned.

green-wood (grēn′wŏŏd′), *n.* a forest in full leaf.

greet (grēt), *v.t.* 1, to address courteously; welcome; 2, to receive or meet, as with a demonstration; as, to *greet* the mayor with a parade; 3, to appear before; as, a view of the sea *greets* us.

greet-ing (grēt′ĭng), *n.* an expression of good will, written or spoken; a welcome.

gre-gar-i-ous (grē-gâr′ĭ-ŭs), *adj.* living in herds or flocks, as sheep.— *adv.* **gre-gar′i-ous-ly.** — *n.* **gre-gar′i-ous-ness.**

Gre-gor-i-an (grē-gôr′ĭ-ăn), *adj.* pertaining to Popes Gregory I and Gregory XIII

Gregorian calendar, the system of reckoning time introduced by Pope Gregory XIII in 1582, now in general use; **Gregorian chant,** church music used in Roman Catholic ritual, based on chants compiled by Pope Gregory I about 590 A.D.

Gre-na-da (grē-nā′dȧ), a British island in the West Indies lying north of the island of Trinidad (map 10).

gre-nade (grē-nād′), *n.* 1, a bomb containing poison gas, explosives, or the like; 2, a flask containing chemicals which scatter when the container is thrown and broken: used for putting out fires.

gren-a-dier (grĕn′ȧ-dēr′), *n.* a foot soldier who throws grenades; also, a member of the British infantry regiment called *Grenadier Guards.*

GRENADES, def. 1
1, 17th century; 2, 20th century.

Gren-fell (grĕn′fĕl), Sir Wilfred Thomason (1865–1941), a British medical missionary, noted for his work in Labrador.

Gret-na Green (grĕt′nȧ grēn′), a village in Scotland, just across the border from England, to which, because of easy Scots marriage laws, English runaway couples formerly went to be married.

grew (grōō), past tense of *grow.*

grey (grā), *adj.* and *n.* gray. See gray.

grey-beard (grā′bērd′), *n.* an old man; a graybeard. See graybeard.

grey-hound (grā′hound′), *n.* a graceful, slender dog with long legs, keen sight, and great speed, used for hunting and racing.

grid (grĭd), *n.* 1, a grate of parallel bars; a gridiron; 2, in electricity, a lead plate conducting current in a storage battery; in a vacuum tube, a plate of parallel wires which control the current (see illustration under *radio*).

grid·dle (grĭd'l), *n.* an iron, aluminum, or soapstone plate used to cook griddlecakes.

grid·dle·cake (grĭd'l-kāk'), *n.* a thin cake, usually made of wheat or buckwheat flour batter, and cooked on both sides on a griddle.

GRIDDLE

grid·i·ron (grĭd'ī'ẽrn), *n.* **1,** an iron utensil with parallel bars, used for broiling meat or fish; **2,** anything resembling a gridiron, or marked with parallel lines, as a football field.

GRIDIRON, def. 1

grief (grēf), *n.* **1,** deep sorrow as a result of trouble, a death, or the like; also, the cause of sorrow; **2,** failure; disaster; as, his plans came to *grief*.

Syn. tribulation, suffering, woe, sorrow, affliction, sadness, melancholy.

griev·ance (grēv'ăns), *n.* a real or fancied wrong or hardship; also, a cause of complaint; as, taxation without representation was the *grievance* of the Colonies.

Syn. injury, wrong.

grieve (grēv), *v.t.* [grieved, griev-ing], to cause grief to; afflict mentally; as, his death *grieved* his friends:—*v.i.* to be in sorrow; as, to *grieve* for a friend.

Syn. mourn, sorrow.

griev·ous (grēv'ŭs), *adj.* **1,** causing physical or mental suffering; severe; as, *grievous* wounds; *grievous* wrongs; **2,** showing grief; as, a *grievous* expression.—*adv.* **griev'ous·ly.**—*n.* **griev'ous·ness.**

grif·fin (grĭf'ĭn) or **grif·fon** (grĭf'ŏn), *n.* a fabled monster with the wings, head, and beak of an eagle, and the body, legs, and tail of a lion.

grill (grĭl), *n.* **1,** a gridiron for broiling food; **2,** a dish of meat or fish cooked on a gridiron; **3,** a grillroom:—*v.t.* **1,** to broil (meat, fish, etc.) on a gridiron; **2,** hence, to torment, especially with merciless questioning; as, police *grill* a criminal.

GRIFFIN

grille (grĭl), *n.* a grating of iron, bronze, or other metal forming a protecting barrier, as before a bank teller's window.

grill-room (grĭl'rōōm'), *n.* a restaurant, or dining room which specializes in chops and broiled meat.

grim (grĭm), *adj.* [grim-mer, grim-mest], **1,** stern; forbidding; threatening; as, a *grim* expression; **2,** fierce; cruel; merciless; as, a *grim* nature; **3,** ghastly; horrible; as, a *grim* story; a *grim* sight.—*adv.* **grim'ly.**—*n.* **grim'ness.**

Syn. relentless, terrible, fierce.

gri·mace (gri-mās'), *n.* a twisting of the face to show disgust or disapproval, or to provoke laughter; also, an unconscious twisting of the face in pain:—*v.i.* [grimaced, grimac-ing], to make faces.

grime (grīm), *n.* dirt rubbed or ground into the skin or other surface:—*v.t.* [grimed, grim-ing], to soil; make dirty.

Grimm (grĭm), Jakob (1785–1863), and Wilhelm (1786–1859), his brother, German scholars, who collected folklore and fairy tales.

grim·y (grīm'ĭ), *adj.* [grim-i-er, grim-i-est], much soiled; very dirty; as, *grimy* hands.—*n.* **grim'i·ness.**

grin (grĭn), *v.i.* [grinned, grin-ning], to show the teeth in smiling or as the result of pain:—*v.t.* to express by smiling; as, he *grinned* his delight:—*n.* a broad smile, or a forced smile:—**grin and bear it,** to endure pain or trouble bravely.

grind (grīnd), *v.t.* [ground (ground), grinding], **1,** to make into powder or small bits by crushing; as, to *grind* wheat; also, to make by a crushing process; as, to *grind* flour; **2,** to sharpen by wearing down to a fine edge; as, to *grind* a knife; **3,** to rub together; grate; as, to *grind* the teeth; **4,** to oppress; harass; as, to *grind* a people down; **5,** to operate by turning a crank; as, to *grind* an organ:—*v.i.* to study hard:—*n. Colloquial*, hard or tedious work; also, a student who studies hard.

grind·er (grīn'dẽr), *n.* **1,** that which sharpens or makes into powder, as a millstone; **2,** a molar tooth.

grind·stone (grīnd'stōn'), *n.* a flat, round stone which turns on an axle, used to sharpen tools.

GRINDSTONE

grip (grĭp), *n.* **1,** a tight grasp; a firm hold; as, take a *grip* on the rope; **2,** holding power; as, a dog with a strong *grip*; **3,** a handle; **4,** a particular way of clasping hands, as among members of a secret society; **5,** a mechanical device for holding something; **6,** mental or physical mastery; as, a good *grip* on the situation; **7,** *Colloquial*, a valise; **8,** grippe:—*v.t.* [gripped, grip-ping], to grasp firmly; seize:—*v.i.* to take a fast hold.

gripe (grīp), *v.t.* [griped, grip-ing], **1,** to seize; grip; **2,** to cause pain in the bowels of; **3,** to distress; oppress; as, remorse

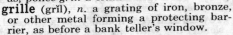

āte, āorta, râre, căt, ȧsk, fär, ȧllow, sofȧ; ēve, ĕvent, ĕll, writẽr, novĕl; bīte, pĭn; nō, ōbey, ôr, dŏg, tŏp, cŏllide; ūnit, ūnite, bûrn, cŭt, focŭs; nōōn, fŏŏt; mound; coin;

gripes the mind:—*v.i. Slang,* to find fault: —*n.* **1,** a firm hold or grip; also, control; **2,** distress; oppression; as, the *gripe* of sorrow; **3,** gripes, pains in the intestines.

grippe (grĭp), *n.* a severe cold accompanied by fever and bodily aches; influenza.

grip-ping (grĭp′pĭng), *adj.* intense; holding one's interest; as, a *gripping* book.

gris-ly (grĭz′lĭ), *adj.* [gris-li-er, gris-li-est], horrible; ghastly; gruesome; grim.

grist (grĭst), *n.* grain to be ground; also, grain that has been ground.

gris-tle (grĭs′l), *n.* a transparent, tough, elastic substance found in animal tissue; cartilage.—*adj.* **gris′tly.**

grist-mill (grĭst′mĭl′), *n.* a mill for grinding grain.

grit (grĭt), *n.* **1,** tiny, hard particles, as of sand; **2,** strength of character; courage; endurance:—*v.i.* [grit-ted, grit-ting], to make a grating sound:—*v.t.* to grind; grate; as, to *grit* the teeth.

grits (grĭts), *n.pl.* a coarsely ground breakfast food made from grain, especially oats, wheat, or corn; as, hominy *grits.*

grit-ty (grĭt′ĭ), *adj.* [grit-ti-er, grit-ti-est], **1,** like sand; also, containing sand or grit; **2,** plucky; brave.

griz-zled (grĭz′ld), *adj.* streaked with gray; gray-haired; as, a *grizzled* veteran.

griz-zly (grĭz′lĭ), *n.* [*pl.* grizzlies], a big, fierce bear of the western mountains of North America: also called *grizzly bear:*—*adj.* [griz-zli-er, griz-zli-est], somewhat gray; grizzled.

groan (grōn), *n.* a low, deep sound of pain or sorrow; a moan:—*v.i.* **1,** to utter a deep sound of pain or sorrow; **2,** to creak, as a rusty hinge; **3,** to be overburdened or oppressed:—*v.t.* to express by groans; as, the audience *groaned* its disappointment.

groat (grōt; grôt), *n.* **1,** an old English silver coin, having a value of four pence, or eight cents; **2,** any trifling sum.

gro-cer-y (grō′sĕr-ĭ), *n.* [*pl.* groceries], **1,** in the U.S., a food store; **2, groceries,** food supplies, such as tea, sugar, coffee, spices, and the like.—*n.* **gro′cer.**

grog (grŏg), *n.* an unsweetened mixture of rum or whisky with water; hence, any intoxicating liquor.

grog-gy (grŏg′ĭ), *adj.* [grog-gi-er, grog-gi-est], **1,** tipsy; drunk; **2,** dazed; staggering; as, *groggy* with sleep.—*n.* **grog′gi-ness.**

GROINS(*a, a*), def. 2

groin (groin), *n.* **1,** the curved hollow where the thigh joins the body; **2,** the curved ridge made by the intersection of two arches:—*v.t.* to build or form with such ridges; as, to *groin* a roof.

groom (grōōm), *n.* **1,** a man or boy who has charge of horses; **2,** a bridegroom; **3,** one of several officers of a royal household:—*v.t.* **1,** to feed, curry, and brush (a horse); **2,** to make neat or tidy.

grooms-man (grōōmz′măn), *n.* [*pl.* groomsmen (-měn)], one who attends a bridegroom; a best man.

groove (grōōv), *n.* **1,** a channel or furrow, especially one cut by a tool or worn by flowing water; a rut; **2,** an unchanging way of living or working; routine; habit:— *v.t.* [grooved, groov-ing], to make a groove in; as, to *groove* a panel.

grope (grōp), *v.i.* [groped, grop-ing], to feel one's way with the hands, as in the dark:—*v.t.* to search out, as in the dark; as, to *grope* one's way through a forest.

gros-beak (grōs′bēk′), *n.* any one of a number of songbirds, related to the finches, as the rose-breasted grosbeak or the cardinal grosbeak.

gros-grain (grō′grān′), *adj.* having cords or ridges running crosswise; as, *grosgrain* hatbands:—*n.* corded silk or ribbon.

GROSBEAK
Rose-breasted grosbeak (⅛)

gross (grōs), *adj.* **1,** thick; heavy; **2,** indelicate; coarse; vulgar; as, *gross* remarks; **3,** flagrant; glaring; as, *gross* errors; **4,** heavy; fat; **5,** very great; shameful; as, *gross* injustice; **6,** whole; total; as, *gross* income: distinguished from *net:*—*n.* **1,** twelve dozen; **2,** the entire amount —*adv.* **gross′ly.**—*n.* **gross′ness.**

Syn., **adj.** outrageous, unseemly.

grot (grŏt), *n. Poetic,* a grotto or cavern.

gro-tesque (grō-tĕsk′), *adj.* distorted; odd; fantastic; as, a *grotesque* mask; *grotesque* antics:—*n.* a painting or carving which combines human and animal forms in a fantastic way.

Syn., **adj.** bizarre, absurd, fanciful.

grot-to (grŏt′ō), *n.* [*pl.* grottoes or grottos], **1,** a picturesque cavern in the earth; **2,** an artificial cave, used as a retreat.

grouch (grouch), *n. Slang,* **1,** a fit of ill temper; **2,** one who indulges in fits of ill temper:—*v.i. Slang,* to sulk; complain.— *adj.* **grouch′y.**—*n.* **grouch′i-ness.**

¹**ground** (ground), past tense and past participle of *grind.*

²**ground** (ground), *n.* **1,** the surface of the earth; the soil; **2,** a topic; subject; as, to be familiar with the *ground* covered in a talk; **3,** land put to special use; as, a *playground;* **4,** distance or extent on a sur-

---

face; as, to gain *ground* in football; **5,** cause; reason; as, a *ground* for argument; **6,** in painting, a neutral background or undecorated part; **7,** the bottom of a body of water:—**grounds, 1,** lawns and gardens about a house; **2,** dregs; sediment; as, coffee or tea *grounds:*—*v.t.* **1,** to establish; as, to *ground* a government on proper principles; **2,** to bring to rest by touching the earth or bottom; as, to *ground* a boat; **3,** to teach the first principles to; as, to *ground* a class in Latin; **4,** in electricity, to connect with the earth, as a wire conductor; **5,** in aeronautics, to land an airplane, or to order a pilot to descend or remain landed; as, the storm *grounded* all planes:—*v.i.* to run upon land; as, the vessel *grounded:*—*adj.* on or near the ground; as, the *ground* floor.

ground hog, the woodchuck, a burrowing animal of the rat family.

ground-less (ground′lĕs), *adj.* without foundation or cause; as, *groundless* fear.

GROUND HOG (¹⁄₁₃)

ground swell, a heavy rolling of the sea, caused by a disturbance, such as a distant storm or an earthquake.

ground-work (ground′wûrk′), *n.* basis; foundation; fundamentals.

group (grōōp), *n.* a number of people or objects considered as a whole; also, a cluster; as, a *group* of houses:—*v.t.* to combine into a unit:—*v.i.* to gather in a unit.

grouse (grous), *n.* [*pl.* grouse], any of several game birds having, usually, a mottled reddish-brown plumage, as the partridge, or ruffed grouse, and the prairie chicken.

grove (grōv), *n.* a small wood; also, a group of cultivated fruit trees.

RUFFED GROUSE (¹⁄₁₀)

grov-el (grŏv′l; grŭv′l), *v.i.* [groveled, grovel-ing], **1,** to crawl in fear; as, to *grovel* before a king; **2,** to humble oneself basely.

grow (grō), *v.t.* [*p.t.* grew (grōō), *p.p.* grown (grōn), *p.pr.* grow-ing], to produce by cultivation, as vegetables:—*v.i.* **1,** to become bigger by natural development; as, puppies *grow* rapidly; **2,** to arise or spring up naturally; as, moss *grows* in damp places; **3,** to increase; as, to *grow* in understanding;

4, to become gradually; as, to *grow* stronger; **5,** to become attached, or become one; as, the broken bone *grew* together.

growl (groul), *n.* **1,** a deep, throaty, and threatening sound, as made by a dog; **2,** an angry, muttered complaint:—*v.i.* **1,** to snarl like a dog; **2,** to find fault in a surly tone; grumble:—*v.t.* to say in an angry muttering tone; as, he *growled* his answer.

grown (grōn), past participle of *grow:*—*adj.* mature; fully developed.

grown-up (grōn′ŭp′), *n.* an adult.—*adj.* grown′-up′.

growth (grōth), *n.* **1,** the progressive increase of animal or vegetable bodies; as, the *growth* of a plant; **2,** increase; as, *growth* in skill; **3,** that which is produced; result; as, a season's *growth* of corn; **4,** a tumor, cancer, or the like.

grub (grŭb), *v.t.* [grubbed, grub-bing], to dig up; root out of the ground, as stumps:—*v.i.* **1,** to dig in the earth; **2,** to drudge or toil; do menial labor:—*n.* **1,** the wormlike larva of some insects; **2,** *Slang,* food.

grudge (grŭj), *n.* secret ill will; as, to hold a *grudge:*—*v.t.* [grudged, grudg-ing], to envy; as, he *grudges* me my good luck; also, to begrudge; as, he *grudges* every cent he spends.—*adv.* grudg′ing-ly.

  Syn., n. spite, hatred, resentment.

gru-el (grōō′ĕl), *n.* a thin porridge made by boiling meal or flour in water or milk.

gru-el-ing (grōō′ĕl-ĭng), *adj.* exhausting; requiring great effort; as, a *grueling* race.

grue-some (grōō′sŭm), *adj.* [gruesom-er, gruesom-est], horrible; ghastly; frightful; as, a *gruesome* sight.—*adv.* grue′some-ly. —*n.* grue′some-ness.

  Syn. ghastly, hideous, repulsive.

gruff (grŭf), *adj.* rough; surly; harsh; as, a *gruff* reply; hoarse; as, a *gruff* voice.—*adv.* gruff′ly.—*n.* gruff′ness.

  Syn. blunt, rude, bearish.

grum-ble (grŭm′bl), *v.i.* [grum-bled, grum-bling], to murmur discontentedly; growl; find fault:—*v.t.* to mutter; as, he *grumbled* a reply:—*n.* a surly speech or reply; growl.—*n.* grum′bler.

grump-y (grŭmp′ĭ), *adj.* [grump-i-er, grump-i-est], surly; dissatisfied; as, a *grumpy* old man.—*adv.* grump′i-ly.—*n.* grump′i-ness.

Grun-dy, Mrs. (grŭn′dĭ), an imaginary character symbolizing conventional manners and propriety.

grunt (grŭnt), *n.* **1,** the gruff sound made by a hog; also, any similar sound; **2,** a fish that makes such a noise when caught:—*v.t.* to utter with a gruff sound; as, to *grunt* assent:—*v.i.* to make a grunting noise.

Gua-de-loupe (gwä′dĕ-lōōp′), a French

colony (cap. Basse-Terre), in the West Indies (map 10).

Guam (gwäm), a Pacific island, east of Manila (map 16). It is a U.S. naval station.

gua·no (gwä′nō), *n.* [*pl.* guanos], the solidified excrement of sea fowls, valued as a fertilizer.

gua·ra·ni (gwä′rä-nē′), *n.* the monetary unit of Paraguay. (See table, page 943.)

guar·an·tee (găr′ăn-tē′), *n.* **1,** anything that makes something else sure or certain; as, a *guarantee* of quality; **2,** a statement that something is as represented; as, a *guarantee* goes with this fountain pen; **3,** in law: **a,** a promise made by one person that another will fulfil an agreement to a third; **b,** one who becomes surety for the performance of another's promises; **c,** property pledged as security for the performance of promises:—*v.t.* [guaranteed, guaranteeing], **1,** to make sure; as, to *guarantee* success; **2,** in law, to be legally responsible for.

guar·an·tor (găr′ăn-tôr; găr′ăn-tôr′), *n.* one who acts as surety for another.

guar·an·ty (găr′ăn-tĭ), *n.* [*pl.* guaranties], **1,** a promise to answer for the payment of another's debt or obligation; guarantee; **2,** property pledged for the performance of an agreement:—*v.t.* [guarantied, guarantying], **1,** to warrant; **2,** to be responsible for.

guard (gärd), *v.t.* **1,** to protect; preserve by caution; defend; **2,** to watch over; as, to *guard* a prisoner:—*v.i.* to watch; be cautious; as, to *guard* against disease:—*n.* **1,** defense against injury or attack; **2,** a state or duty of watchfulness or attention; as, be on *guard*; **3,** a position of defense, as in fencing; **4,** a device for protection; as, a mud*guard*; **5,** a man or body of men employed for control, as in a prison; **6,** in football, either of two players in the line, one on each side of the center.
Syn., v. shelter, restrain, shield.

guard·ed (gär′dĕd), *adj.* **1,** defended; protected; as, a heavily *guarded* fort; **2,** careful; cautious; as, a *guarded* answer.—*adv.* **guard′ed·ly.**—*n.* **guard′ed·ness.**

guard·house (gärd′hous′), *n.* **1,** a military jail; **2,** a house occupied by police or soldiers acting as guards.

guard·i·an (gär′dĭ-ăn), *n.* **1,** one who legally has the care of a person or his property; a warden; as, a *guardian* of a child; **2,** one who or that which protects anything.

guard·room (gärd′rōōm′), *n.* **1,** the room occupied by a military guard on duty; **2,** a place of imprisonment for soldiers.

guards·man (gärdz′măn), *n.* [*pl.* guardsmen (-mĕn)], **1,** a man employed for defense or watching; **2,** an officer or soldier of any military body termed *Guards.*

Guar·ne·ri (gwär-nā′rē) or **Guar·ne·ri·us** (gwär-nā′rĭ-ŭs), an Italian family of celebrated violinmakers.

Gua·te·ma·la (gwä′tä-mä′lä), a republic in northwestern Central America; also, a city, its capital (map 10).

gua·va (gwä′vȧ), *n.* a tree of tropical America, yielding a pear-shaped fruit from which a jelly is made; also, the fruit.

gu·ber·na·tor·i·al (gū′bĕr-nȧ-tôr′ĭ-ăl), *adj.* pertaining to a governor or to his office; as, a *gubernatorial* election.

¹**gudg·eon** (gŭj′ŭn), *n.* **1,** a small, European, fresh-water carp, easily caught and used as bait; **2,** hence, a person easily cheated.

GUDGEON (½), def. 1

²**gudg·eon** (gŭj′ŭn), *n.* **1,** an iron pin or shaft on which a wheel revolves; **2,** a socket or ring receiving a pin that turns, as the eye of a hinge.

Guelph or **Guelf** (gwĕlf), *n.* in medieval Italy, a member of a faction that opposed the authority of the German emperors in Italy.

guer·don (gûr′dŭn), *n.* a reward, especially for courage or high deeds.

¹**Guern·sey** (gûrn′zĭ), one of the Channel Islands, northwest of France, noted for a fine breed of dairy cattle (map 13).

²**Guern·sey** (gûrn′zĭ), *adj.* designating a breed of dairy cattle from Guernsey, one of the Channel Islands:—*n.* one of this breed:—**guernsey,** a knitted woolen shirt.

guer·ril·la or **gue·ril·la** (gĕ-rĭl′ȧ), *n.* one who carries on irregular warfare; especially, one of an independent band engaged in harassing an enemy in wartime.

guess (gĕs), *n.* a hasty conclusion; an opinion formed without knowledge:—*v.t.* **1,** to form an opinion of without certain knowledge; **2,** to surmise; estimate; as, to *guess* the height of someone; **3,** to solve correctly by surmising; as, to *guess* a riddle; **4,** to think; suppose:—*v.i.* to form a chance judgment.

guess·work (gĕs′wûrk′), *n.* a result obtained by guessing; conjecture.

guest (gĕst), *n.* **1,** one who is entertained at the house or table of another; a visitor; **2,** a patron of a hotel or a restaurant.

guf·faw (gŭ-fô′), *n.* a coarse or loud burst of laughter:—*v.i.* to laugh noisily.

Gui·a·na (gē-ä′nȧ), a region on the northern coast of South America, between the Orinoco and Amazon rivers, which contains **British Guiana** (cap. Georgetown), **Dutch Guiana** or **Surinam** (cap. Paramaribo), **French Guiana** (cap. Cayenne) (map 11).

---

go; join; yet; sing; chin; show; thin, *th*en; hw, *wh*y; zh, azure; ü, Ger. *für* or Fr. l*u*ne; ö, Ger. schön or Fr. f*eu*; ṅ, Fr. e*n*fant, nom; kh, Ger. a*ch* or i*ch*.   See pages ix–x.

guid-ance (gīd'dăns), *n.* direction; leadership; influence.

guide (gīd), *n.* **1,** one who or that which directs; **2,** a person hired to conduct travelers; **3,** that by which one finds his way; a guidebook; guidepost:—*v.t.* [guid-ed, guiding], **1,** to lead; pilot; **2,** to direct; instruct.

guide-book (gīd'boŏk'), *n.* a book of information for travelers.

guid-ed mis-sile, a rocket- or jet-powered projectile flown to its target by any of various methods of remote control.

guide-post (gīd'pōst'), *n.* a post or marker to direct travelers.

guild or **gild** (gĭld), *n.* **1,** an association for mutual protection and aid of people in a common trade; **2,** a society for a useful or charitable purpose.

guil-der (gĭl'dẽr), *n.* a silver coin, the monetary unit of the Netherlands; a gulden.

guild-hall (gĭld'hôl'), *n.* the meeting place of a guild; a townhall.

guile (gīl), *n.* deceit; cunning; trickery; as, he's full of *guile.—adv.* **guile'ful-ly.**

guile-less (gīl'lĕs), *adj.* innocent; frank; as, a *guileless* child.—*adv.* **guile'less-ly.**

guil-lo-tine (gĭl'ō-tēn), *n.* a machine for cutting off a person's head by means of a knife which descends between two posts:—*v.t.* (gĭl'ō-tēn'), [guillotined, guillotin-ing], to behead with the guillotine.

guilt (gĭlt), *n.* **1,** the fact of having done a wrong, especially an act punishable by law; **2,** wrongdoing; sin; as, he led a life of *guilt* and shame.

guilt-less (gĭlt'lĕs), *adj.* innocent.

guilt-y (gĭl'tĭ), *adj.* [guilt-i-er, guilt-i-est], **1,** responsible for a crime; having committed a wrong; as, he was judged *guilty* by the jury; **2,** showing guilt; not innocent; as, a *guilty* look.—*adv.* **guilt'i-ly.**

Guin-ea (gĭn'ĭ), a coastal region of West Africa on the Gulf of Guinea, including **French Guinea** (cap. Conakry), **Portuguese Guinea** (cap. Bissau), and **Spanish Guinea** (cap. Santa Isabel), comprising Rio Muni and certain islands near the equator:— **Gulf of Guinea,** a great gulf on the west coast of Africa, near the equator. (Map 14.)

guin-ea (gĭn'ĭ), *n.* a gold coin, formerly current in England, worth 21 shillings; now, the amount of 21 shillings.

GUINEA FOWL (¹⁄₁₄)

guinea fowl, a noisy domesticated fowl, originally a native of Guinea. Its plumage is bluish gray dotted with white spots: also called *guinea* and *guinea hen.*

guinea pig, 1, a small, short-eared, short-tailed rodent, usually white, black, or tan, originally from South America, often used in scientific tests or experiments; **2,** hence, a person or thing used as the subject of a test or experiment.

GUINEA PIG (⅛)

Guin-e-vere (gwĭn'ĕ-vẽr), *n.* in Arthurian legend, the wife of King Arthur, in love with Sir Lancelot.

guise (gīz), *n.* **1,** manner or external appearance; likeness; as, the *guise* of a beggar; **2,** hence, cloak or pretense; as, to cheat under the *guise* of friendship.

gui-tar (gĭ-tär'), *n.* a long-necked musical instrument with a hollow, wooden body and six strings, played with the fingers.

gulch (gŭlch), *n.* in the western U.S., a narrow, deep valley or ravine; gorge.

gul-den (goŏl'dĕn), *n.* a silver coin of the Netherlands, also called *florin* and *guilder.*

gulf (gŭlf), *n.* **1,** an arm of the sea extending into the land, larger than a bay; **2,** a deep hollow in the earth; an abyss; **3,** a wide separation; as, the *gulf* between a king and a beggar.

GUITAR

Gulf Stream a warm ocean current that flows from the Gulf of Mexico first northward along the coast of the U.S. and then northeastward toward the British Isles.

¹**gull** (gŭl), *n.* a large, graceful, web-footed sea bird, usually white with gray or black markings, known all over the world, valuable as a harbor scavenger.

GULL (¹⁄₁₆)

²**gull** (gŭl), *v.t.* to cheat; deceive; outwit; as, *gulled* by flattery:—*n.* a person easily deceived, as by a tale; a dupe.

gul-let (gŭl'ĕt), *n.* the tube by which food travels from the mouth to the stomach; the throat. (See illustration at *epiglottis.*)

gul-li-ble (gŭl'ĭ-bl), *adj.* easily fooled.

gul-ly (gŭl'ĭ), *n.* [*pl.* gullies], a channel worn by water; a narrow ravine:—*v.t.* [gullied, gully-ing], to wear channels in.

gulp (gŭlp), *v.t.* **1,** to swallow hastily or greedily; **2,** to check; keep back; as, to *gulp* down angry words or tears:—*n.* a big swallow; a mouthful; a choke.

¹gum (gŭm), *n.* the flesh around the teeth of human beings and animals.

²gum (gŭm), *n.* **1,** a sticky substance that comes out of certain trees and shrubs and hardens on the surface; as, *gum* arabic; spruce *gum;* **2,** any natural gum prepared for some industrial use, as in drugs or chewing gum; **3,** a gum tree; **4, gums,** overshoes:— *v.t.* [gummed, gum-ming],to smear or fasten with mucilage:—*v.i.* to become stiff or sticky; to exude gum, as does a tree.—*adj.* **gum′my.**—*n.* **gum′mi-ness.**

gum ar-a-bic (är′a̍-bĭk), a gum obtained from certain species of acacia and used in the manufacture of mucilage, ink, candies, and the like.

gum-bo (gŭm′bō), *n.* [*pl.* gumbos], **1,** the okra plant or its edible pods; **2,** a soup containing okra; **3,** a soil which becomes sticky when wet.

gum-boil (gŭm′boil′), *n.* a small abscess on the gums.

gum-drop (gŭm′drŏp′), *n.* a candy made of flavored gelatin, cast in molds, and covered with sugar crystals.

gump-tion (gŭmp′shŭn), *n. Colloquial,* energy; initiative; spirit; as, he hasn't *gumption* enough to speak up for himself.

gum tree, in the U.S., a gum-yielding tree, as the sweet gum or the sour gum.

gun (gŭn), *n.* **1,** a weapon for discharging a missile through a tube by the force of an explosive, as a cannon, rifle, pistol, or revolver; **2,** any similar implement; **3,** a discharge of cannon given as an honor:— *v.i.* [gunned, gun-ning], to shoot or hunt with a gun.

gun-boat (gŭn′bōt′), *n.* a small warship.

gun-cot-ton (gŭn′kŏt′n), *n.* a highly explosive substance formed by soaking cotton in mixed nitric and sulphuric acid.

gun-fire (gŭn′fīr′), *n.* discharge of small weapons or artillery; as, intense *gunfire.*

gun-lock (gŭn′lŏk′), *n.* the mechanism of a gun which controls the hammer and fires the charge.

gun-man (gŭn′măn), *n.* [*pl.* gunmen (-měn)], an armed robber or murderer.

gun met-al, 1, a variety of bronze, formerly used in making cannon, etc., but now supplanted by steel; **2,** the color of this bronze, dark gray with a blue or purple tinge.

gun-nel (gŭn′ĕl), *n.* gunwale. See **gunwale.**

gun-ner (gŭn′ĕr), *n.* **1,** one who works a gun; **2,** one who hunts with a gun; **3,** in the navy, a warrant officer in charge of the ship's ordnance or military supplies.

gun-ner-y (gŭn′ĕr-ĭ), *n.* the science of artillery; the knowledge and use of cannon.

gun-ning (gŭn′ĭng), *n.* the hunting of game, especially small game, with a gun.

gun-ny (gŭn′ĭ), *n.* [*pl.* gunnies], a coarse sackcloth of jute or hemp; also, a bag or sack made of this material.

gun-pow-der (gŭn′pou′dĕr), *n.* an explosive powder made of sulphur, saltpeter, and charcoal, used in blasting and in guns.

gun-shot (gŭn′shŏt′), *n.* **1,** a shot fired from a gun; **2,** the range of a gun; as, within *gunshot.*

gun-smith (gŭn′smĭth′), *n.* one who makes or repairs small firearms.

gun-stock (gŭn′stŏk′), *n.* the wooden part of a firearm, to which the barrel and mechanism are fastened.

gun-wale or **gun-nel** (gŭn′ĕl), *n.* the upper edge of the side of a boat.

gur-gle (gûr′gl), *n.* a broken, bubbling sound, as of a liquid when poured from a bottle:—*v.i.* [gur-gled, gur-gling], to make a low, bubbling sound; as, a baby *gurgles;* a stream *gurgles* over stones.

gush (gŭsh), *n.* **1,** a sudden and free flow of liquid from an enclosed space, as of blood from a wound; **2,** a violent outbreak, as of anger; **3,** *Colloquial,* silly, sentimental talk or display of affection:—*v.i.* **1,** to flow out suddenly with force; flow abundantly; as, oil *gushed* from the well; **2,** *Colloquial,* to display affection and enthusiasm in a silly, showy manner.—*adj.* **gush′ing.**—*adv.* **gush′ing-ly.**

gush-er (gŭsh′ĕr), *n.* **1,** one who gushes; especially, one who makes a show of sentiment; **2,** an oil or gas well with large natural flow.

gus-set (gŭs′ĕt), *n.* **1,** a small three-cornered piece of cloth inserted in a garment to strengthen or enlarge a part; **2,** a metal bracket for strengthening an angle.

GUSSET, def. 2
A, column; B, girder; G, gusset.

gust (gŭst), *n.* **1,** a sudden rush of wind; **2,** a violent outburst, as of laughter.

gus-ta-tor-y (gŭs′ta̍-tôr′ĭ), *adj.* relating to the sense of taste; as, *gustatory* joys.

gus-to (gŭs′tō), *n.* zest; relish; enjoyment; as, to eat or drink with great *gusto.*

Syn. taste, liking, fondness.

gust-y (gŭs′tĭ), *adj.* [gust-i-er, gust-i-est], **1,** marked by bursts of wind; as, *gusty* weather; **2,** with sudden bursts; as, *gusty* laughter.—*adv.* **gust′i-ly.**

gut (gŭt), *n.* **1,** the intestinal canal; **2,**

---

go; join; yet; sing; chin; show; thin, *th*en; hw, *wh*y; zh, azure; ü, Ger. für or Fr. lune; ö, Ger. schön or Fr. feu; n̦, Fr. enfant, nom; kh, Ger. ach or ich. See pages ix–x.

catgut, as used for violin strings; **3**, a narrow channel; also, a gully:—*v.t.* [gut-ted, gut-ting], **1**, to extract the entrails from; **2**, to plunder, or empty; destroy the inside of; as, fire *gutted* the building.

Gu-ten-berg (gōō′těn-běrkh), Johannes (1397?–1468), an early German printer, the inventor of printing from movable type.

gut-ta—per-cha (gŭt′ȧ-pûr′chȧ), *n.* a grayish or yellowish substance similar to rubber, made of the juice of a tree of the Malay Archipelago; also, the tree itself.

gut-ter (gŭt′ẽr), *n.* **1**, a trough under the eaves of a building to carry off rain water (see *frame house*, illustration); **2**, a slope at the roadside to carry off surface water; **3**, any shallow trench:—*v.t.* to cut into, or make furrows in:—*v.i.* to become channeled, as the rim of a burning candle.

gut-tur-al (gŭt′ẽr-ăl), *adj.* **1**, having to do with the throat; **2**, formed in the throat; harsh; as, a *guttural* sound:—*n.* a sound formed or modified in the throat, as *g* in *go* or *goose.*—*adv.* gut′tur-al-ly.

¹**guy** (gī), *n.* a rope, chain, wire, or the like, used to secure or keep something steady; as, the *guy* of a tent pole:—*v.t.* to fasten or steady with a guy.

²**guy** (gī), *n.* **1**, a person of queer looks or dress; **2**, *Slang*, in the U.S., a fellow:—*v.t. Colloquial*, to ridicule; as, his friends *guyed* him good-naturedly.

guz-zle (gŭz′l), *v.i.* and *v.t.* [guz-zled, guzzling], to eat or drink greedily; to drink too much.—*n.* guz′zler.

gym (jĭm), *n. Colloquial*, a gymnasium.

gym-na-si-um (jĭm-nā′zĭ-ŭm), *n.* [*pl.* gymnasiums (jĭm-nā′zĭ-ŭmz) or gymnasia (jĭm-nā′zĭ-ȧ)], **1**, a room or building for athletic practice; **2**, **Gymnasium** (in Germany, gĭm-nä′zĭ-ōŏm), in Europe, a high school, preparing for the university.

gym-nast (jĭm′năst), *n.* one who is expert in physical exercises; especially, one skilled in the use of gymnasium apparatus.

gym-nas-tics (jĭm-năs′tĭks), *n.pl.* physical exercises for developing the body.

gyp (jĭp), *n. Slang*, in the U.S., a swindler; thief:—*v.t. Slang* [gypped, gyp-ping], to cheat; as, he *gypped* me out of ten cents.

gyp-sum (jĭp′sŭm), *n.* the mineral, calcium sulphate, used especially in making plaster of Paris and fertilizer.

gyp-sy (jĭp′sĭ), *n.* [*pl.* gypsies], **1**, one of an ancient wandering, dark-skinned, dark-eyed race of Eastern, probably Hindu, origin; **2**, the language of the gypsies: also called *Romany;* **3**, a person who looks or acts like a gypsy:—**gypsy moth**, a European moth, the caterpillars of which are very destructive to fruit and other trees. Also spelled **gip′sy.**

gy-rate (jī′rāt; jī-rāt′), *v.i.* [gyrat-ed, gyrat-ing], to move in a circle or spiral; go round and round; as, a cyclone *gyrates.* —*n.* gy-ra′tion.—*adj.* gy′ra-tor′y.

gyr-fal-con (jûr′fôl′kŭn; jûr′fô-kŭn), *n.* a powerful falcon found in northern or arctic regions. Also spelled **ger′fal-con.**

gy-ro-scope (jī′rŏ-skōp), *n.* an apparatus consisting of a wheel mounted in a ring so as to move freely in one or more directions. It is used

GYROSCOPE

to illustrate the laws of rotation, and to stabilize airplanes, ships, etc.—*adj.* gy′ro-scop′ic (jī′rŏ-skŏp′ĭk).

gyve (jīv), *n.* a chain for the legs; a shackle: —*v.t.* [gyved, gyv-ing], to chain; shackle.

H

H, h (āch), *n.* [*pl.* H's, h's], the eighth letter of the alphabet, following G.
h. abbreviation for *hour.*

ha (hä), *interj.* an exclamation expressing wonder, suspicion, doubt, mirth, joy, etc.

Haa-kon VII (hô′kŏn), (1872–1957), king of Norway, succeeded by his son, Olav V.

Haar-lem (här′lěm), a city in the northwestern part of the Netherlands.

Ha-bak-kuk (hȧ-băk′ŭk), a Hebrew prophet; also, a book of the Old Testament.

Ha-ban-a (hȧ-văn′ȧ; hä-bä′nä), a city, capital of Cuba (map 10). See **Ha-van′a.**

hab-er-dash-er (hăb′ẽr-dăsh′ẽr), *n.* a dealer in men's furnishings, such as socks, shirts, collars, neckties, etc.

hab-er-dash-er-y (hăb′ẽr-dăsh′ẽr-ĭ), *n.* [*pl.* haberdasheries], men's furnishings; also, a shop where they are sold.

hab-er-geon (hăb′ẽr-jŭn), *n.* a piece of armor for the neck and shoulders; a hauberk. (See illustration next page.)

ha-bil-i-ments (hȧ-bĭl′ĭ-měnts), *n.pl.* clothing; attire; raiment; garb.

hab-it (hăb′ĭt), *n.* **1**, an action so often repeated as to become a fixed characteristic; as, it is his *habit* to rise at six; the *habit* of neatness; **2,** usual physical or mental condition; as, a cheerful *habit* of mind; **3,** a woman's riding costume; **4,** the distinctive dress worn by members of a religious order; as, a nun's *habit:—v.t.* to dress; clothe.

Syn., *n.* custom, routine, practice.

hab·it·a·ble (hăb′ĭt-à-bl), *adj.* fit to be lived in; as, repairs have made the house *habitable.*

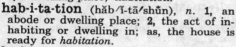

HABERGEON

A, A, A, habergeon of chain mail; B, detail showing construction of chain armor; C, leather jacket worn over habergeon; D, helmet.

hab·i·tat (hăb′ĭ-tăt), *n.* **1,** the natural abode of an animal or plant; **2,** a dwelling place; habitation.

hab·i·ta·tion (hăb′ĭ-tā′shŭn), *n.* **1,** an abode or dwelling place; **2,** the act of inhabiting or dwelling in; as, the house is ready for *habitation.*

ha·bit·u·al (hà-bĭt′ũ-ăl), *adj.* **1,** formed or acquired by custom; usual; as, *habitual* promptness; **2,** given over to a regular practice, or habit; as, a *habitual* coffee drinker.—*adv.* **ha·bit′u·al·ly.**

ha·bit·u·ate (hà-bĭt′ũ-āt), *v.t.* [habituat-ed, habituat-ing], to accustom; as, by the end of winter, he is *habituated* to cold.

ha·bit·u·é (hà-bĭt′ũ-ā′), *n.* a frequent visitor, as at a club, the theater, etc.

Habs·burg (hăps′bûrg; häps′bōŏrkh), *n.* the name of the former royal family of Austria. See **Hapsburg.**

ha·cien·da (ä-syĕn′dä; hä′sĭ-ĕn′dä), *n.* in Spanish America, a large estate or plantation, on which the owner lives.

¹hack (hăk), *v.t.* to cut unevenly or irregularly:—*v.i.* **1,** to make rough cuts; **2,** to give short dry coughs:—*n.* **1,** a cutting or notching tool, as a mattock; **2,** a cut or gash; **3,** a short, dry cough.

²hack (hăk), *n.* **1,** a horse that may be hired for work; also, a saddle or carriage horse; **2,** a carriage which may be hired; **3,** one who hires out his services for pay, especially in literary work; a drudge.

hack·le (hăk′l), *n.* the neck plumage of a domestic fowl. (See *fowl,* illustration.)

hack·ney (hăk′nĭ), *n.* [*pl.* hackneys], **1,** a horse used chiefly for riding or driving; **2,** a coach or hack kept for hire:—*adj.* let out for hire; as, a *hackney* coach.

hack·neyed (hăk′nĭd), *adj.* commonplace; trite; as, a *hackneyed* phrase.

hack saw, a close-toothed saw with a narrow blade, used for cutting metal. (See illustration at ¹*saw.*) Also, **hack′saw′.**

had (hăd), past tense and past participle of *have.*

had better, should; would be well advised to; as, you *had better* study if you want good marks; **had rather,** should or would prefer to; as, I *had rather* go with you.

had-dock (hăd′ŭk), *n.* a North Atlantic food fish of the cod family.

Ha·des (hā′dēz), *n.* **1,** in mythology, the underworld; the abode of the dead; **2,** the god of the underworld, often called *Pluto;* **3,** *Colloquial,* hell.

Ha·dri·an (hā′drĭ-ăn), (76–138), a Roman emperor;—**Hadrian's Wall,** a wall built by Hadrian in 122 to protect southern Britain from the Picts and Scots.

hae·mo·glo·bin (hē′mō-glō′bĭn; hĕm′ō-glō′bĭn), *n.* the coloring matter of red blood corpuscles. See **hemoglobin.**

haft (hăft), *n.* a handle, as of a cutting tool, dagger, or knife.

hag (hăg), *n.* **1,** a witch; **2,** an ugly old woman.

Ha·gar (hā′gẽr; hā′gär), in the Bible, the handmaid of Abraham's wife, Sarah, and the mother of his son, Ishmael.

Hag·ga·i (hăg′à-ī), in the Bible, a Hebrew prophet; also, a book of the Old Testament.

hag·gard (hăg′ẽrd), *adj.* worn and anxious in appearance; as, *haggard* from worry.

hag·gle (hăg′l), *v.i.* [hag-gled, hag-gling], to argue or wrangle; as, the woman *haggled* over the price of the butter.

Hague, The (hāg), a city near the North Sea, one of the capitals of the Netherlands: now called **'s Gravenhage** (map **12**).

Hai·dar·a·bad (hī′dẽr-ä-bäd′), a state and city in India. See **Hyderabad.**

Haig (hāg), Sir Douglas (1861–1928), commander in chief of the British forces in France from 1915 to 1919.

¹hail (hāl), *n.* **1,** small, icy particles that fall from the sky, sometimes in winter, sometimes during a thunderstorm; **2,** anything falling abundantly and with great force; as, a *hail* of shrapnel:—*v.i.* to come down in the form of hail:—*v.t.* to shower; pour down; as, they *hailed* blows upon me.

²hail (hāl), *n.* a salutation; greeting:—*v.t.* to greet; salute; accost; as, he *hailed* me as I was entering the store.

Hai·le Se·las·sie (hī′lĕ sĕ-làs′yĕ), (1893–), the ruler of Ethiopia, 1928–

hail·stone (hāl′stōn′), *n.* a single particle of hail or frozen rain.

hair (hâr), *n.* **1,** the mass of threadlike growths, forming the coat or fur of an ani-

go; join; yet; sing; chin; show; thin, *th*en; hw, *why*; zh, azure; ü, Ger. für or Fr. *lune*; ö, Ger. schön or Fr. *feu*; ṅ, Fr. e*nfant*, nom; kh, Ger. a*ch* or i*ch*. See pages ix–x.

mal, or the natural growth on a person's head; also, any one of these threadlike growths; 2, a hairlike fiber growing on the stems and leaves of plants; 3, a very small distance, degree, or quantity; as, the bullet missed him by a *hair.*—*adj.* **hair′y.** —*n.* **hair′i-ness.**—*adj.* **hair′less.**

hair-breadth (hâr′brĕdth′) or **hairs-breadth** (hârz′brĕdth′), *n.* width no greater than that of a hair; a very small distance:—*adj.* very narrow; as, a *hairbreadth* escape.

hair-cloth (hâr′klôth′), *n.* goods of horse-hair or camel's hair, often with cotton or linen warp: used mostly to cover furniture.

hair-do (hâr′dōō′), *n.* 1, any manner of arranging (a woman's) hair; coiffure; 2, hair so arranged.

hair-pin (hâr′pĭn′), *n.* a two-pronged pin, as of wire or celluloid, for holding the hair in place. (See illustration at *pin.*)

hair-split-ting (hâr′splĭt′ĭng), *adj.* show-ing or making unimportant distinctions.

hair-spring (hâr′sprĭng′), *n.* the delicate hairlike spring which regulates the balance wheel in a watch.

hair trig-ger, a secondary trigger, so ad-justed that very slight pressure on the main trigger discharges the weapon.

Hai-ti (hā′tĭ), an island in the West In-dies: see **Hispaniola:**—**Republic of Haiti** (cap. Port-au-Prince), a republic occupy-ing the western part of the island of Hispaniola (map 10).

hake (hāk), *n.* a fish of the cod family, valua-ble as food.

HAKE (1/12)

hal-berd (hăl′bĕrd) or **hal-bert** (hăl′bĕrt), *n.* a medieval weapon combining spear and battle-ax.

hal-cy-on (hăl′sĭ-ŭn), *n.* a fabled bird, identified with the kingfisher, supposed to nest at sea and bring calm weather: — *adj.* peaceful; happy; calm; as, summer's *halcyon* days.

¹**hale** (hāl), *adj.* sound in body; robust; as, a *hale* old man.

²**hale** (hāl), *v.t.* [haled, hal-ing], to drag by violence; as, they *haled* him into court.

Hale (hāl), 1, Edward Everett (1822–1909), an American clergyman and author; 2, Na-than (1755–1776), an Ameri-can patriot, hanged as a spy.

Ha-le-a-ka-la (hä′lä-ä′kä-lä′), a very large extinct crater, in the Hawaiian Islands.

HALBERD
Medieval soldier with halberd.

half (hȧf), *n.* [*pl.* halves (hȧvz)], one of two equal parts:—*adj.* forming a half; as, a *half* pound:—*adv.* 1, to the extent of a half; 2, partially; as, *half* asleep.

half–breed (hȧf′-brēd′), *n.* one whose par-ents are of different races.

half broth-er, a brother related through one parent only.

half–caste (hȧf′-kȧst′), *n.* a half-breed; one whose parents are of different races:— *adj.* of mixed blood.

half crown, an English silver coin, worth 2½ shillings.

half-heart-ed (hȧf′här′tĕd), *adj.* unin-terested; not enthusiastic; as, a *half-hearted* response to a suggestion.—*adv.* **half′heart′ed-ly.**—*n.* **half′heart′ed-ness.**

half hitch, a kind of knot, used for tem-porary fastening. (See illustration at *knot.*)

half–mast (hȧf′-mȧst′), *n.* a point near the middle of a mast or staff. A flag flies at half-mast in token of mourning or as a signal of distress.

half-pen-ny (hā′pĕn-ĭ; hăp′nĭ), *n.* [*pl.* halfpence (hā′pĕns) or halfpennies (hā′-pĕn-ĭz; hăp′nĭz)], an English bronze coin, worth half an English penny.

half sis-ter, a sister related through one parent only.

half–tone or **half-tone** (hȧf′tōn′), *n.* 1, a picture made by an engraving process which reproduces shades of light and dark; 2, in music, a half step; on a keyboard, the interval between any key and the one immediately above it, as between A and B flat, or between B and C.

half–way (hȧf′wā′), *adj.* 1, situated mid-way between two points; as, a *halfway* house; 2, midway between two states or conditions; as, twilight, the *halfway* state between night and day; 3, partial; not extreme; as, *halfway* measures:—*adv.* 1, midway; at half the distance; as, they met *halfway* between the two towns; 2, partially; as, he *halfway* consented.

half–wit-ted (hȧf′-wĭt′ĕd), *adj.* mentally lacking; feeble-minded.—*n.* **half′-wit′.**

hal-i-but (hăl′ĭ-bŭt; hŏl′ĭ-bŭt), *n.* the largest of the flatfish, prized as food.

Hal-i-fax (hăl′ĭ-făks), a city, the capital of Nova Scotia, Canada (map 4).

hal-i-to-sis (hăl′ĭ-tō′sĭs), *n.* foul or un-pleasant breath.

hall (hôl), *n.* 1, the main living room of a castle; 2, a large building or room for entertainments; as, a dance *hall;* 3, a pub-lic building; as, City *Hall;* 4, a university building used for residence, instruction, or the like; 5, a passageway in a house or other building; also, the passage or room

āte, âorta, râre, căt, ȧsk, fär, ăllow, sofȧ; ēve, êvent, ĕll, writẽr, novĕl; bīte, pĭn; nō, ōbey, ôr, dŏg, tŏp, cŏllide; ūnit, ūnite, bûrn, cŭt, focŭs; nōōn, fŏŏt; mound; coin;

through which one enters a building; **6,** in England, the residence of a landed proprietor; a manor house.

hal·le·lu·jah or **hal·le·lu·iah** (hăl′ē-lōō′yȧ), *n.* an exclamation or song of praise to God:—*interj.* praise ye Jehovah! praise be to God! Also spelled **al′le·lu′ia; al′le·lu′iah; al′le·lu′ja.**

Hal·ley (hăl′ĭ), Edmund (1656–1742), an English astronomer who, in 1682, discovered the comet later named after him.

hall-mark (hôl′märk′), *n.* a mark stamped on gold and silver articles to testify to their purity; hence, any mark of genuineness:—*v.t.* to stamp with a hallmark.

hal·lo or **hal·loa** (hă-lō′), *interj.* what ho! stop! hollo! See **hollo.**

hal·loo (hă-lōō′), *n.* [*pl.* halloos] and *interj.* a shout to attract attention or to call dogs:—*v.i.* and *v.t.* to cry out (to).

hal·low (hăl′ō), *v.t.* **1,** to make sacred; mark or set apart as holy; as, this ground has been *hallowed* by the brave men who died here; **2,** to honor as holy; reverence; as, *hallowed* be the name of the Lord.

Hal·low·een (hăl′ō-ēn′), *n.* the evening of October 31; eve of All Saints' Day.

hal·lu·ci·na·tion (hă-lū′sĭ-nā′shŭn), *n.* the seeming to see something which is not actually present or visible; a delusion.

hall·way (hôl′wā′), *n.* an entrance hall or other passage in a building.

ha·lo (hā′lō), *n.* [*pl.* halos or haloes], **1,** a circle of light around a shining body, such as the sun or moon; **2,** in pictures, a bright ring drawn or painted around the head of a holy person or saint; **3,** the splendor or glory with which one endows a person or an object highly prized:—*v.t.* to surround with a halo.

Hal·sey (hôl′sĭ), William Frederick (1882–), an American admiral in World War II.

¹halt (hôlt), *adj.* crippled or lame:—*v.i.* **1,** to limp; **2,** hence, to proceed hesitatingly; as, his lecture began smoothly, but later *halted* painfully.

²halt (hôlt), *n.* a stop or pause on a march or journey:—*v.i.* to come to a stop:—*v.t.* to bring to a stop.

HALTER, def. 1

hal·ter (hôl′tēr), *n.* **1,** a rope or strap for leading or fastening a horse or other animal; **2,** a rope for hanging criminals; as, his life will be ended by the *halter.*

halt·ing (hôl′tĭng), *adj.* **1,** lame; limping; **2,** hesitating; faltering; as, *halting* speech.

halve (hȧv), *v.t.* [halved, halv-ing], **1,** to divide into two equal parts, as an apple; to share equally; **2,** to lessen by half; as, the teacher *halved* the assignment.

halves (hȧvz), plural of *half;* as, he cut the apple into *halves.*

hal·yard (hăl′yẽrd), *n.* on a ship, a rope or tackle for hoisting and lowering a sail, yard, or flag.

ham (hăm), *n.* the thigh of an animal prepared for food; especially, the thigh of a hog, salted ánd sometimes dried in smoke; also, the meat so prepared.

ham (hăm), *n.* [Cockney abbr. of *amateur* to *am*], a licensed amateur radio operator.

Ham (hăm), in the Bible, the second son of Noah.

Ha·man (hā′măn), in the Old Testament, an enemy of the Jews, hanged on the gallows he built for his rival, Mordecai.

Ham·burg (hăm′bûrg; häm′bŏŏrkh), a city in the northern part of Germany, a commercial center and seaport (map 12).

Ham·burg steak (hăm′bûrg), finely ground beef; also, this meat when cooked.

hame (hām), *n.* one of the two curved bars on the collar of a horse's harness to which the traces are fastened.

Ham·il·ton (hăm′ĭl·tŭn), Alexander (1757–1804), an American soldier and statesman, Secretary of the Treasury under Washington, who was killed in a duel with Aaron Burr.

ham·let (hăm′lĕt), *n.* a small village.

Ham·let (hăm′lĕt), *n.* a tragedy by Shakespeare; also, the hero of the play.

ham·mer (hăm′ēr), *n.* **1,** an instrument with a handle and an iron head, used for driving nails, beating metals, etc.; **2,** anything resembling this tool; as, the *hammer* of a gunlock (see *revolver,* illustration):—*v.t.* **1,** to pound or beat with a hammer or a similar instrument; **2,** to

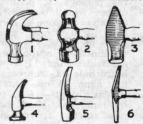

HAMMERS

1, nail hammer with claw; 2, machinist's hammer; 3, blacksmith's hammer; 4, cobbler's hammer; 5, bricklayer's hammer; 6, tack hammer.

drive into place by pounding; as, to *hammer* a nail; **3,** to produce by hard work; as, to *hammer* out a plan:—*v.i.* **1,** to strike heavy blows; **2,** to make a noise like the blow of a hammer; **3,** to work hard.

ham·mer·head (hăm′ẽr-hĕd′), *n.* a shark having a head shaped like a hammer.

ham·mock (hăm′ŭk), *n.* a swinging bed or couch, usually of network or canvas, suspended by cords at the ends.

¹**ham·per** (hăm′pẽr), *n.* a large basket, usually of wickerwork and with a cover, used for carrying or holding clothes, food, etc.

²**ham·per** (hăm′pẽr), *v.t.* to obstruct; hinder; as, the snow *hampered* the traffic.

Hamp·shire (hămp′-shĭr), a county in southern England.

ham·string (hăm′-strĭng′), *n.* in man, either of two groups of tendons at the back of the knee; in animals, the large tendon above and behind the hock:—*v.t.* [hamstrung (hăm′strŭng′), hamstring-ing], to lame or cripple by cutting the hamstring.

HAMPER

Han·cock (hăn′kŏk), John (1737–1793), an American Revolutionary patriot.

hand (hănd), *n.* **1,** that portion of the human arm extending downward from the wrist, made up of the palm, four fingers, and a thumb, and fitted for grasping objects; also, a like part on an ape, an opossum, or certain other animals that grasp; **2,** an index or pointer on a dial; as, the *hands* of a clock; **3,** a measure of four inches: used chiefly in measuring the height of horses; **4,** deftness or skill; as, try your *hand* at this game; **5,** direction to the left or right; as, on the right *hand* of the passage; **6,** penmanship; **7,** an employee who labors with his hands; **8,** a player in a game of cards; also, the cards held by a player; a single round in a game at cards; **9,** possession; control; as, the matter is in your *hands;* **10,** assistance; as, lend a *hand;* **11,** a pledge, especially of betrothal; **12,** source; as, knowledge at first *hand;* **13,** one who is skilled at a particular thing:—*v.t.* **1,** to pass or transfer by hand; as, *hand* me the book; **2,** to pass (down) from time past; as, these dishes were *handed* down to me from my grandmother; **3,** to lead or assist with the hand; as, he *handed* her into the car:—*adj.* pertaining to the hand; used or carried by the hand.—*adj.* **hand′ed.**

    hand to hand, at close quarters; as, they fought *hand to hand;* a *hand-to-hand* fight; **on the other hand,** on the contrary.

hand-bag (hănd′băg′), *n.* **1,** a satchel; **2,** a small bag to hold a purse, powder, etc.

hand-ball (hănd′bôl′), *n.* a game played in a walled court, or against a single wall, in which the players bat the ball against a wall with their hands.

hand-bar-row (hănd′băr′ō), *n.* a barrow, without a wheel, carried by four handles.

hand-bill (hănd′bĭl′), *n.* a printed advertisement distributed by hand.

hand-book (hănd′bŏŏk′), *n.* a small guidebook; a manual.

hand-breadth (hănd′brĕdth′), *n.* a measure of length equal to the width of the hand.

hand-cuff (hănd′kŭf′), *n.* one of a pair of metal braceletlike devices, locked around a prisoner's wrist to prevent his escape:—*v.t.* to restrain with handcuffs.

HANDCUFFS

Han-del (hăn′dl), George Frederick (1685–1759), a German composer, especially famous for his sacred music.

hand-ful (hănd′fŏŏl′), *n.* [*pl.* handfuls], the amount a hand can hold; hence, a small quantity or number.

hand-i-cap (hăn′dĭ-kăp′), *n.* **1,** a disadvantage imposed on a superior contestant, or an advantage granted to an inferior contestant, in order to equalize chances of winning; also, a race, contest, or game in which such a condition exists; **2,** a hindrance:—*v.t.* [handicapped, handicap-ping], **1,** to be a disadvantage to; **2,** to impose a handicap upon.

hand-i-craft (hăn′dĭ-krăft), *n.* a trade or craft requiring a skilled hand; manual skill.—*n.* **hand′i-crafts′man.**

hand-i-ly (hăn′dĭ-lĭ), *adv.* in a handy or deft manner; skilfully.

hand-i-ness (hăn′dĭ-nĕs), *n.* deftness or skill with the hands.

hand-i-work (hăn′dĭ-wûrk′), *n.* **1,** work done by hand; **2,** anything done by personal effort.

hand-ker-chief (hăng′kẽr-chĭf), *n.* a square piece of cloth for wiping the face, nose, etc.; also, one worn around the neck.

han-dle (hăn′dl), *n.* that part of a tool, vessel, etc., grasped by the hand:—*v.t.* [han-dled, han-dling], **1,** to hold, touch, or move with the hand; **2,** to manage; control; as, he *handled* the airplane with skill; **3,** to deal with or treat in a given way; as, he *handles* complaints tactfully; **4,** to buy and sell; deal in; as, a broker *handles* stocks and bonds.

hand-made (hănd′mād′), *adj.* made by hand.

hand-maid (hănd′mād′), *n.* a female servant or personal attendant.

hand or·gan, a portable musical instrument operated by a hand crank.

hand-saw (hănd′sô′), *n.* a carpenter's saw for use with one hand.

HANDSAW

hand·some (hăn′sŭm), *adj.* [handsom-er, handsom-est] **1**, pleasing to look upon; good-looking; **2**, ample; generous; as, a very *handsome* gift.—*adv.* **hand′some·ly.** *Syn.* impressive, comely, beautiful.

hand-spike (hănd′spīk′), *n.* a bar used as a lever for lifting heavy weights.

hand-spring (hănd′sprĭng′), *n.* a feat in which one places one or both hands on the ground and turns the body in the air so as to land on the feet.

HAND-SPRING

hand-writ·ing (hănd′rī′tĭng), *n.* **1**, a person's style of penmanship; **2**, writing done by hand.

hand·y (hăn′dĭ), *adj.* [hand-i-er, hand-i-est], **1**, skilful with the hands; **2**, convenient; as, a *handy* footstool near the chair.

hang (hăng), *v.t.* [*p.t.* and *p.p.* hung (hŭng) or, in def. 3, hanged (hăngd), *p.pr.* hang-ing], **1**, to attach to something above; suspend; as, to *hang* curtains; **2**, to fasten (something) so that it can swing to and fro; as, to *hang* a door; **3**, to suspend by the neck until dead; as, the murderer was *hanged;* **4**, to cause to droop; as, he *hung* his head; **5**, to decorate; as, she *hung* the wall with pictures:—*v.i.* **1**, to dangle; be suspended; **2**, to hover threateningly; as, ill fortune *hangs* over him; **3**, to rest; depend; as, my decision *hangs* on your answer; **4**, to die by hanging; **5**, to hold for support; as, *hang* on to me:—*n.* **1**, the manner in which a thing hangs; as, the *hang* of a coat; **2**, *Colloquial*: **a**, the manner of doing or using; knack; **b**, general idea; as, the *hang* of a story.

hang-ar (hăng′ẽr; hăng′gär), *n.* a shed for housing airplanes and other aircraft.

Hang-chow (hăng′chou′), a seaport city on the east coast of China (map 15).

hang-dog (hăng′dôg′), *adj.* ashamed; cowering; as, a *hangdog* expression.

hang-er (hăng′ẽr), *n.* **1**, one who hangs; as, a paper *hanger;* **2**, that by which something is hung; as, a dress *hanger;* **3**, a short, curved sword, hung from the belt.

hang-er—on (hăng′ẽr‚ŏn′), *n.* [*pl.* hangers-on], an unwelcome follower.

hang-ing (hăng′ĭng), *n.* **1**, the act of suspending; **2**, execution by suspending a person by the neck until dead; **3**, **hangings**, drapery for walls, windows, etc.

hang-man (hăng′măn), *n.* [*pl.* hangmen (-mĕn)], a public officer whose duty it is to execute convicted criminals.

hang-nail (hăng′nāl′), *n.* a small piece of loose skin around a fingernail.

hank (hăngk), *n.* a coil or skein, as of woolen or cotton yarn.

han-ker (hăng′kẽr), *v.i.* to yearn or crave; as, to *hanker* after pleasure.

Han-kow (hăn′kou′; hăng′kou′), an inland commercial city of China on the Yangtze River (map 15).

Han-ni-bal (hăn′ĭ-băl), (247–183 B.C.), a great Carthaginian general who invaded Italy in an effort to overthrow Rome.

Ha-noï (hä′noi′), chief city of Northern Vietnam (map 15). Capital of former Federation of Indo-China.

Han-o-ver (hăn′ō-vẽr) or **Han-no-ver** (hä-nō′fẽr), a city in Germany (map 12); also, a former province.

HANSOM

han-som (hăn′sŭm), *n.* a two-wheeled, covered cab, with an outside seat for the driver at the back: also called *hansom cab.*

hap (hăp), *v.i.* [happed, hap-ping], to happen; befall:—*n.* chance; lot; fortune.

hap-haz-ard (hăp′hăz′ẽrd), *adj.* accidental:—*adv.* by chance:—*n.* (hăp′hăz′ẽrd), an accident.

hap-less (hăp′lĕs), *adj.* unlucky.

hap-ly (hăp′lĭ), *adv.* perhaps; perchance.

hap-pen (hăp′ĕn), *v.i.* **1**, to occur; as, how did it *happen?* **2**, to chance; as, I *happened* to be there; **3**, to come by chance; as, we *happened* on a house in the woods.

hap-pen-ing (hăp′ĕn-ĭng), *n.* an occurrence.

hap-pi-ly (hăp′ĭ-lĭ), *adv.* **1**, luckily; **2**, in a contented manner or state; **3**, aptly; as, his thought was *happily* expressed.

hap-pi-ness (hăp′ĭ-nĕs), *n.* **1**, the state of being glad or contented; **2**, good fortune. *Syn.* joyfulness, bliss, delight.

hap-py (hăp′ĭ), *adj.* [hap-pi-er, hap-pi-est], **1**, enjoying or expressing pleasure; as, a *happy* girl with a *happy* smile; **2**, fortunate; lucky; as, a *happy* turn of events; **3**, apt; suitable; as, a *happy* remark. *Syn.* cheerful, merry, gay, contented.

hap-py—go—luck-y (hăp′ĭ-gō‚lŭk′ĭ), *adj.* **1**, gay; lighthearted; **2**, trusting to luck.

---

go; join; yet; sing; chin; show; thin, *th*en; hw, *wh*y; zh, azure; ü, Ger. *fü*r or Fr. l*u*ne; ö, Ger. sch*ö*n or Fr. f*eu*; n̊, Fr. *en*fant, *nom*; kh, Ger. a*ch* or i*ch*. See pages ix–x.

Haps·burg (hăps'bûrg; häps'bŏŏrkh), *n.* the name of a German family, founded in the twelfth century, to which many rulers of Austria, Spain, and the Holy Roman Empire belonged. Sometimes spelled **Habs'burg**.

ha·ra·ki·ri (hä'rä-kē'rĭ). *n.* a method of suicide by ripping out the bowels, practiced in Japan.

ha·rangue (hȧ-răng'), *n.* a public speech; usually a loud, ranting address:—*v.i.* and *v.t.* [harangued, harangu·ing], to address in a loud, ranting speech.

har·ass (hăr'ȧs; hȧ-răs'), *v.t.* 1, to annoy or vex; as, she was *harassed* by daily complaints; 2, to plunder; lay waste; pillage. —*n.* **har'ass·ment.**
  Syn. fret, bother, pester, besiege.

har·bin·ger (här'bĭn-jẽr), *n.* a herald; forerunner; as, the cock, *harbinger* of day.

har·bor (här'bẽr), *n.* 1, a partly sheltered portion of a sea, lake, etc., which serves as a port or haven for ships; 2, any place of refuge or safety:—*v.t.* 1, to give lodging to; shelter; 2, to cherish; indulge; as, to *harbor* resentment:—*v.i.* to find or take shelter. In British usage, **har'bour.**

hard (härd), *adj.* 1, solid; firm; not easily pierced or broken; as, *hard* bone; 2, difficult; as, a *hard* task; 3, difficult to bear; as, *hard* times; 4, hardy; strong; as, *hard* as steel; 5, done with exertion or energy; as, *hard* labor; 6, industrious; as, a *hard* worker; 7, harsh; unsympathetic; as, a *hard* master; 8, severe in action or effect; as, a *hard* winter; 9, containing a high per cent of alcohol; as, *hard* cider; 10, violent; as, a *hard* rain; 11, pronounced with the sound of *g* in "go" or *c* in "come," not soft like the *g* in "gin" or *c* in "cent":—*adv.* 1, vigorously; as, work *hard;* 2, firmly; securely; as, bound *hard* and fast; 3, with a struggle; as, love dies *hard;* 4, close, near; as, *hard* by; 5, severely; as, the loss bore *hard* on me.
  hard coal, anthracite coal; **hard water,** water that does not form lather with soap.
  Syn., adj. difficult, rigorous, relentless.

hard·en (här'dn), *v.t.* 1, to make firm, solid, or unyielding; as, to *harden* steel; *harden* one's will; 2, to toughen; make hardy; as, to *harden* the body:—*v.i.* to become firm, solid, harsh, unyielding, hardy, etc.

hard·head·ed (härd'hĕd'ĕd), *adj.* 1, having shrewd judgment; practical; 2, obstinate; stubborn.

hard·heart·ed (härd'här'tĕd), *adj.* unfeeling; cruel.—*n.* **hard'heart'ed·ness.**

har·di·hood (här'dĭ-hŏŏd), *n.* robustness; hence, boldness; audacity; impudence.

har·di·ly (här'dĭ-lĭ), *adv.* boldly.

Har·ding (här'dĭng), Warren Gamaliel (1865–1923), the 29th president of the U.S.

hard·ly (härd'lĭ), *adv.* 1, with difficulty; 2, scarcely; as, he has *hardly* recovered; 3, severely; as, to deal *hardly* with someone.

hard·ness (härd'nĕs), *n.* the quality or state of being solid, unyielding, etc.; as, *hardness* of rock; *hardness* of heart.

hard·pan (härd'păn'), *n.* 1, a bed or layer of earth which is difficult to dig; 2, a solid foundation; a firm basis.

hard·ship (härd'shĭp), *n.* that which is hard to bear, as heavy toil, privation, etc. *Syn.* suffering, misfortune, adversity.

hard·tack (härd'tăk') *n.* a large, unsalted biscuit, used in the army and navy.

hard·ware (härd'wâr'), *n.* articles manufactured from metal, as cutlery, kitchen utensils, tools, etc.

hard·wood (härd'wŏŏd'), *n.* a heavy, close-grained wood, such as oak, maple, or mahogany opposite of *softwood:—adj.* made of hardwood; as, *hardwood* floors.

har·dy (här'dĭ), *adj.* [har·di·er, har·di·est], 1, robust; capable of bearing hardship; 2, bold; resolute; 3, able to survive winter weather: used of plants.—*n.* **har'di·ness.**

Har·dy (här'dĭ), Thomas (1840–1928), an English novelist and poet.

hare (hâr), *n.* a timid, swift-footed animal, somewhat like a rabbit, with a divided upper lip, long ears, and a short fluffy tail.

HARE (¼₇)

hare·bell (hâr'bĕl'), *n.* a slender plant with blue, bell-shaped flowers; also, the flower: also called *bluebell.*

hare·brained (hâr'brānd'), *adj.* heedless; rash; as, a *harebrained* fool.

hare·lip (hâr'lĭp'), *n.* a deformity, existing from birth, in which the upper lip is divided, like that of a hare.

ha·rem (hā'rĕm; hâr'ĕm), *n.* 1, the part of a Mohammedan house where the women live; 2, a Mohammedan's wives and female relatives living in this part of the house.

hark (härk), *v.i.* to listen: often used as an exclamation; as, *Hark!* the hounds!

hark·en (här'kĕn), *v.i.* to listen; hearken. See **hearken.**

Har·lem (här'lĕm), a district in the northern part of New York City, constituting its chief Negro quarter.

Har·le·quin (här'lē-kwĭn; här'lē-kĭn), *n.* a comic character in pantomime, with

---

āte, āorta, râre, căt, ȧsk, fär, ăllow, sofȧ; ēve, ĕvent, ĕll, writẽr, novĕl; bīte, pĭn; nō, ŏbey, ôr, dŏg, tŏp, cŏllide; ūnit, ūnite, bûrn, cŭt, focŭs; nŏŏn, fŏŏt; mound; coin;

shaven head and masked face, who wears a parti-colored costume:—**harlequin**, a buffoon; clown.

har·lot (här′lŏt), *n.* a woman who engages in sexual intercourse for pay; a prostitute.

harm (härm), *n.* **1**, injury; damage; **2**, moral evil or wrongdoing:—*v.t.* to hurt or damage.

harm·ful (härm′fool), *adj.* hurtful; injurious; as, *harmful* drugs.—*adv.* **harm′ful·ly.**

harm·less (härm′lĕs), *adj.* having no power to damage or hurt; as, a *harmless* snake; also, producing no ill effect; as, a *harmless* drug.—*adv.* **harm′less·ly.**

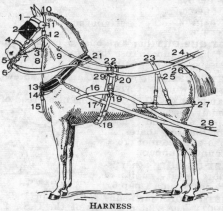

HARLEQUIN

har·mon·ic (här·mŏn′ĭk), *adj.* **1**, relating to the science dealing with musical sounds; **2**, agreeing in sound; concordant:—*n.* **1**, a tone, higher than the main tone, and heard along with it; an overtone; **2**, **harmonics**, *n.pl.* used as *sing.* the science dealing with musical sounds.

har·mon·i·ca (här·mŏn′ĭ·k*a*), *n.* a small musical wind instrument, provided with metal reeds, which is played by the mouth; a mouth organ.

HARMONICA

har·mo·ni·ous (här·mō′nĭ·ŭs), *adj.* **1**, combining so as to form a pleasing and agreeable whole; as, *harmonious* voices; **2**, agreeing in action and feeling; peaceable; friendly; as, *harmonious* neighbors.—*adv.* **har·mo′ni·ous·ly.**—*n.* **har·mo′ni·ous·ness.**

Syn. congruous, peaceable, sweet, musical.

har·mo·nize (här′mō·nīz), *v.t.* [harmonized, harmoniz-ing], **1**, to arrange in musical harmony; **2**, to bring into agreement; as, to *harmonize* colors; **3**, to cause to agree; reconcile; as, to *harmonize* conflicting opinions:—*v.i.* **1**, to play or sing in harmony; **2**, to go suitably or pleasingly together; as, these colors *harmonize*.

har·mo·ny (här′mō·nĭ), *n.* [*pl.* harmonies], **1**, the combination of parts so as to form an agreeable or connected whole; as, the *harmony* of motion in dancing; **2**, agreement in feeling, opinions, or the like; as, *harmony* in the senate; **3**, the arrangement of similar passages, as in the Bible, so as to show their points of agreement or disagreement; as, a *harmony* of the four Gospels; **4**, in music, the combination of musical tones so as to form chords, or the science treating of this; also, the composition of a piece of music with reference to its chords.

Syn. conformity, concord, melody.

har·ness (här′nĕs), *n.* the fittings used to attach a horse or other animal to a

wagon, plow, or the like:—**in harness**, working at the daily routine:—*v.t.* **1**, to put a harness upon; **2**, to make (something) produce power, by installing the necessary machinery; as, to *harness* a waterfall.

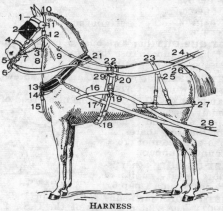

HARNESS

1-12, parts of the bridle (1, brow band; 2, blinder; 3, cheek piece; 4, noseband; 5, bit; 6, curb; 7, curb strap; 8, throatlatch; 9, checkrein; 10, crownpiece; 11, cockade; 12, guide ring (for checkrein); 13, collar; 14, collar pad; 15, martingale; 16, shaft; 17, trace; 18, girth, or belly-band; 19, shaft ring; 20, saddle; 21, ring for rein; 22, hook for checkrein; 23, hip strap; 24, reins; 25, fork; 26, crupper; 27, breeching; 28, trace buckle; 29, terret.

Har·old II (hăr′ŭld), (1022?–1066), last of the Saxon kings of England, killed in the battle of Hastings, in which he was defeated by William the Conqueror.

harp (härp), *n.* a stringed musical instrument of triangular shape, played with the fingers (see *musical instrument*, illustration):—*v.i.* **1**, to play on a harp; **2**, to dwell unduly on some particular subject.—*n.* **harp′er.**—*n.* **harp′ist.**

Har·pers Fer·ry (här′pĕrz), a town in West Virginia on the Potomac River, the scene of John Brown's raid in 1859.

har·poon (här·poon′), *n.* a long spear with a rope attached, used to strike and kill whales or large fish:—**harpoon gun**, a gun used for throwing a harpoon:—*v.t.* to strike or kill with a harpoon; as, the sailor *harpooned* the whale.—*n.* **har·poon′er.**

HARPOON GUN

harp·si·chord (härp′sĭ-kôrd), *n.* an instrument with wire strings and a keyboard, similar to the grand piano in form and arrangement, in general use before the piano.

go; join; yet; sing; chin; show; thin, *th*en; hw, *wh*y; zh, azure; ü, Ger. für or Fr. l*u*ne; ö, Ger. schön or Fr. f*eu*; ṅ, Fr. e*n*fant, no*m*; kh, Ger. a*ch* or i*ch*. See pages ix–x.

Har·py (här′pĭ), *n.* [*pl.* Harpies], in mythology, a monster with face and upper body parts like a woman's, and wings, tail, and claws of a bird: — harpy, a fierce, grasping person.

HARQUEBUS

har·que·bus (här′kwē-bŭs), *n.* an old form of hand gun in use before the musket. Also spelled **ar′que·bus.**

har·ri·dan (hăr′ĭ-dăn), *n.* an ugly, shrewish old woman; a vixen; hag.

har·ri·er (hăr′ĭ-ēr), *n.* **1,** one of a breed of small dogs, similar to the foxhound, used for hunting hares; **2,** one of a team of cross-country runners.

HARRIER (⅛)

Har·ris·burg (hăr′ĭs-bûrg), a city, capital of Pennsylvania (map 6).

Har·ri·son (hăr′ĭ-sŭn), **1,** Benjamin (1833–1901), the 23d president of the U.S.; **2,** William Henry (1773–1841), an American general, the ninth president of the U.S.

har·row (hăr′ō), *n.* a farming implement with sharp iron or wooden teeth, or sharp steel disks, for breaking up clods or covering sown seeds with earth: —*v.t.* **1,** to drive a harrow over; as, to *harrow* plowed land; **2,** to distress deeply; as, his feelings were *harrowed* by his friend's misery.

HARROW

har·ry (hăr′ĭ), *v.t.* [harried, harry-ing], **1,** to plunder; lay waste; as, the invaders *harried* the country; **2,** to annoy or vex.

harsh (härsh), *adj.* **1,** wounding the feelings; cruel; severe; as, the *harsh* father; a *harsh* command; **2,** rough or irritating to the hearing, taste, or touch; as, a *harsh* voice; a *harsh* piece of cloth; also, disagreeable; rigorous; as, a *harsh* climate. —*adv.* **harsh′ly.** —*n.* **harsh′ness.**
   Syn. strict, rigorous, gruff.

hart (härt), *n.* a male of the red deer over five years of age; a stag.

Hart·ford (härt′fērd), the capital of Connecticut, in northeastern U.S. (map 6).

harts·horn (härts′hôrn′), *n.* a solution of ammonia, formerly prepared from the horns of stags: used as smelling salts.

har·um—scar·um (hâr′ŭm-skâr′ŭm), *adj. Colloquial,* wild; thoughtless; rash; also, untidy:—*n.* a reckless, giddy person.

Har·vard (här′vērd), a university situated at Cambridge, Massachusetts.

har·vest (här′vĕst), *n.* **1,** a crop, as of grain or fruit, ready for gathering or already gathered; **2,** the gathering in of such a crop; **3,** the season, usually late summer or early fall, for gathering in a crop; **4,** result; reward; as, his good marks are the *harvest* of hard work:—*v.t.* to gather in (a crop); as, to *harvest* wheat.

har·vest·er (här′vĕs-tēr), *n.* **1,** one who gathers in a crop; a reaper; **2,** a harvesting or reaping machine.

Har·vey (här′vĭ), William (1578–1657), an English physician, the discoverer of the circulation of the blood.

has (hăz), third person singular, present indicative, of *have.*

hash (hăsh), *v.t.* **1,** to chop into small pieces, as meat; **2,** to botch; bungle:—*n.* **1,** a mixture of meat and vegetables, chopped into small pieces and cooked; also, the dish so prepared; **2,** a mixture or jumble; **3,** a botch.

hash·ish (hăsh′ēsh; hăsh′ĭsh), *n.* a preparation of Indian hemp, smoked or chewed for its intoxicating or narcotic effect.

hasp (hăsp), *n.* a hinged metal clasp for a door or a box, which folds over a staple and is fastened with a pin or padlock.

has·sock (hăs′ŭk), *n.* **1,** a heavy, stuffed cushion, used to kneel or sit upon; a footstool; **2,** a tuft of coarse grass.

HASPS
1, 2, two forms of hasp, 2 with padlock.

hast (hăst), *Archaic,* second person singular, present indicative of *have.*

haste (hāst), *n.* **1,** quickness of movement; hurry; speed; **2,** undue, rash, or excessive speed:—*v.t. and v.i.* [hast-ed, hast-ing], to hurry.

has·ten (hās′n), *v.t.* to cause (a person) to hurry; to urge (work) forward:—*v.i.* to move with speed; hurry; as, *hasten* home.
   Syn. accelerate, expedite, speed.

Has·tings (hās′tĭngz), *n.* the place and name of a battle fought in 1066 in which William the Conqueror, the Norman leader, defeated the English under Harold, and became king of England.

hast·y (hās′tĭ), *adj.* [hast-i-er, hast-i-est], **1,** speedy; hurried; as, a *hasty* departure; **2,** careless; superficial; as, *hasty* work; **3,** quick-tempered; impetuous. —*adv.* **hast′i-ly.** —*n.* **hast′i-ness.**
   Syn. quick, fast, rapid.

hast·y pud·ding, a mush made by stirring corn meal, oatmeal, or flour, into boiling milk or water.

hat (hăt), *n.* a covering for the head, usually with a crown and brim.

¹hatch (hăch), *n.* **1,** an opening in a deck, roof, floor, etc., often with a removable cover or trap door; a hatchway; **2,** a cover for a hatch.

²hatch (hăch), *v.t.* **1,** to produce young from; as, to *hatch* eggs; **2,** to produce (young) from eggs; as, to *hatch* chickens; **3,** to plot or plan; as, to *hatch* a rebellion: —*v.i.* **1,** to yield young; as, the eggs *hatched* in three weeks; **2,** to come forth from the egg, as a young chick:—*n.* the brood of young produced at one time.

hatch-er-y (hăch′ĕr-ĭ), *n.* [*pl.* hatcheries], a place where eggs, especially those of fish or poultry, are hatched.

h a t c h - e t (hăch′ĕt), *n.* a small ax with a hammer head and short handle:—**bury the hatchet,** to put an end to hostilities or to a quarrel; agree not to quarrel.

HATCHETS

hatch-ment (hăch′mĕnt), *n.* a panel bearing the coat of arms of a dead person, temporarily displayed, as on a tomb.

hatch-way (hăch′wā′), *n.* an opening, as in the deck of a vessel, for passage below; a hatch.

hate (hāt), *v.t.* [hat-ed, hat-ing], **1,** to dislike thoroughly; detest; **2,** to be averse to; dislike; as, I *hate* sewing:—*n.* extreme abhorrence or dislike; hatred.—*n.* **hat′er.**

hate-ful (hāt′fŏŏl), *adj.* deserving or causing hatred; abominable; as, murder is a *hateful* thing; also, displaying hatred; as, a *hateful* glance.—*adv.* **hate′ful-ly.**—*n.* **hate′ful-ness.**

Syn. odious, detestable, loathsome.

hath (hăth), *Archaic* or *Poetic,* third person singular, present indicative, of *have.*

Hath-a-way (hăth′à-wā), Ann (1556–1623), the maiden name of Shakespeare's wife.

ha-tred (hā′trĕd), *n.* intense dislike; enmity.

hat-ter (hăt′ĕr), *n.* a manufacturer of, or a dealer in, hats.

Hat-ter-as, Cape (hăt′ĕr-ás), a point of land on an island off the coast of North Carolina, around which navigation is dangerous (map 8).

hau-berk (hô′bûrk), *n.* a coat of chain mail worn in the Middle Ages.

haugh-ty (hô′tĭ), *adj.* [haugh-ti-er, haughti-est], proud; disdainful; as, a *haughty*

empress; a *haughty* gesture.—*adv.* **haugh′ti-ly.**—*n.* **haugh′ti-ness.**

haul (hôl), *v.t.* **1,** to pull or draw forcibly; to drag; **2,** to move or transport by pulling; as, to *haul* a load:—*v.i.* **1,** to change the course of a ship; as, the sailors *hauled* into the wind; **2,** to change direction; as, the wind *hauls* to the west:— *n.* **1,** a strong pull; **2,** a single pulling in of a net; also, the quantity of fish caught at one time; **3,** booty; loot; as, the thief made a good *haul;* **4,** the distance over which anything is drawn; as, a *haul* of 30 miles.—*n.* **haul′age.**—*n.* **haul′er.**

haunch (hônch; hänch), *n.* **1,** the hip and buttocks of a man or other animal; the hind part; **2,** of meats, the leg and loin taken together; especially, a joint of venison or mutton.

haunt (hônt; hänt), *n.* **1,** a place of frequent meeting or resort; as, the *haunt* of outlaws; **2,** (hánt; hänt), *Colloquial,* a ghost: —*v.t.* **1,** to visit frequently or habitually; **2,** to trouble persistently; as, a ghost *haunts* a house; dreams *haunt* me.

hau-teur (hō-tûr′), *n.* pride of bearing or spirit; arrogance.

Ha-van-a (hà-văn′à) or **Ha-ban-a** (hà-vän′á; ä-bä′nä), a city, capital of Cuba, on the northern shore of the island (map 10).

have (hăv), *v.t.* [*present sing.* I have, you have, he has (hăz), *pl.* have, *p.t.* and *p.p.* had (hăd), *p.pr.* hav-ing], **1,** to hold; possess; own; as, to *have* money; **2,** to be compelled; as, I *have* to sell it; **3,** to hold or harbor in one's mind; as, to *have* a grudge; **4,** in a general way, to engage in, experience, suffer, enjoy, or the like; as, to *have* a good time or an argument; to *have* a headache; **5,** to bear (a child); **6,** to cause to do or to be done; as, *have* Tom go; *have* this bill paid; **7,** to allow; permit; as, I will not *have* disobedience; **8,** to obtain; get; as, he *has* his way; **9,** to state as a fact; as, the papers *have* it that war is declared; **10,** to beat; get the better of; as, he *had* me in that argument; **11,** to show; use; as, to *have* mercy; **12,** as a helping verb, used to form the present perfect, past perfect, and future perfect tenses of verbs, indicating action occurring before the present, past, or future; as, I *have* gone; I *had* gone; I *shall have* gone.

ha-ven (hā′vĕn), *n.* **1,** a sheltered anchorage for ships; **2,** any harbor or shelter.

hav-er-sack (hăv′ĕr-săk), *n.* a strong canvas bag for carrying provisions, used especially by soldiers on the march.

hav-oc (hăv′ŭk), *n.* devastation; ruin.

Havre, Le (lĕ ȧvr′; hä′vĕr), a French seaport, on the English Channel (map 12).

HAUBERK (H,H) (13th century)

---

go; **join**; yet; **sing**; **chin**; **show**; **thin**, *th*en; **hw**, *wh*y; **zh**, a*z*ure; **ü**, Ger. f*ü*r or Fr. l*u*ne; **ö**, Ger. sch*ö*n or Fr. f*eu*; **n̈**, Fr. *en*fant, *nom*; **kh**, Ger. a*ch* or i*ch*. See pages ix–x.

¹**haw** (hô), *n.* the berrylike fruit of a hawthorn; also, a hawthorn tree.

²**haw** (hô), *n.* a hesitation or faltering in speech:—*v.i.* to speak with interruption and hesitation; as, to hem and *haw.*

³**haw** (hô), *interj.* a word meaning *left,* used in driving teams without reins: opposite of *gee:*—*v.t.* and *v.i.* to turn toward the left.

Ha·wai·i (hä-wī′ē), 1, the largest island of the Hawaiian group, near the center of the Pacific Ocean; 2, a State (cap. Honolulu) of the U.S., comprised of several islands (map 16): also called *Hawaiian Islands,* formerly *Sandwich Islands.*

Ha·wai·ian (hä-wī′yăn), *n.* a native of Hawaii; also, the language of Hawaii:—*adj.* pertaining to Hawaii or to its language or people.

¹**hawk** (hôk), *n.* any of several strong, swift-flying birds of prey, as falcons, buzzards, kites, etc.:—*v.i.* to hunt wild birds or game with the help of hawks.—*adj.* and *n.* **hawk′ing.**

²**hawk** (hôk), *v.t.* to peddle; cry out (wares) for sale as one goes from place to place.

³**hawk** (hôk), *v.i.* to clear the throat forcibly and noisily.

HAWK
Pigeon hawk (⅛)

¹**hawk·er** (hôk′ẽr), *n.* one who trains, or hunts with, hawks.

²**hawk·er** (hôk′ẽr), *n.* one who cries and sells goods in the streets; a peddler.

hawse hole (hôz; hôs), one of the holes for cables in the bow of a ship.

haw·ser (hô′zẽr; hô′sẽr), *n.* a rope or cable used to tow or moor a vessel.

haw·thorn (hô′thôrn), *n.* any of several thorny trees or shrubs, with white or pink fragrant flowers; also, the flower.

Haw·thorne (hô′thôrn), Nathaniel (1804–1864), an American prose writer.

hay (hā), *n.* various grasses, clover, etc., cut and dried for fodder:—*v.i.* to make hay.

hay·cock (hā′kŏk′), *n.* a small cone-shaped pile of hay in a field.

Hay·dn (hī′dn; hā′dn), Joseph (1732–1809), an Austrian composer, famous for his symphonies.

Hayes (hāz), Rutherford Birchard (1822–1893), the 19th president of the U.S.

hay fe·ver, a disease affecting the nose, eyes, and throat, caused by the pollen of certain plants.

hay·mow (hā′mou′), *n.* 1, a mass of hay laid up in a barn; 2, the part of a barn in which the hay is stored.

hay·rick (hā′rĭk′), *n.* a large pile of hay stacked in the open air; a haystack.

hay·stack (hā′stăk′), *n.* a stack or pile of hay in the open air; a hayrick.

haz·ard (hăz′ẽrd), *n.* 1, an old gambling game at dice; 2, chance; risk; danger; 3, in golf, an obstacle, such as rough ground, a stream, or a sand pit:—*v.t.* 1, to subject to risk, or take the risk of; as, to *hazard* one's fortune; to *hazard* a loss; 2, to offer; venture; as, to *hazard* a guess.

haz·ard·ous (hăz′ẽr-dŭs), *adj.* risky; perilous; dangerous; as, a *hazardous* climb.

¹**haze** (hāz), *n.* 1, a slight fog, mist, or smoke in the atmosphere; 2, mental vagueness or confusion.

²**haze** (hāz), *v.t.* [hazed, haz-ing], to play practical jokes upon, as in school or college initiations; bully.—*n.* **haz′er.**

ha·zel (hā′zl), *n.* 1, any of various shrubs or small trees bearing a small, rounded, edible nut; 2, the nut borne by this tree; a filbert; 3, a light, reddish-brown color:—*adj.* light reddish brown.—*n.* **ha′zel-nut′.**

ha·zy (hā′zĭ), *adj.* [ha-zi-er, ha-zi-est], 1, misty; not clear; as, a *hazy* landscape; 2, vague; uncertain; as, a *hazy* idea.—*adv.* **ha′zi-ly.**—*n.* **ha′zi-ness.**

H.C. abbreviation for *House of Commons.*

hdkf. abbreviation for *handkerchief.*

hdqrs. abbreviation for *headquarters.*

he (hē), *masc. pron.* of the third person [*nominative,* he, *possessive,* his (hĭz), *objective,* him (hĭm)], 1, one particular man or boy; as, where is Charles? *he'*s absent; 2, anyone; as, *he* who runs may read:—*n.* [*pl.* hes (hēz)], a man or boy.

head (hĕd), *n.* 1, the uppermost part of the body in man, or, in most animals, the foremost part, containing the mouth, eyes, nose, ears, and brain; 2, the top or upper end of anything, as of a flagpole, cane, stairs, page, etc.; also, the side of a coin showing a head; 3, anything resembling a head; especially, the top part of a plant, or a round compact bloom; as, a *head* of lettuce; a clover *head;* 4, imagination; intelligence; as, a story out of one's *head;* he talks over my *head;* a good *head* for figures; 5, mental calm or control; as, to keep one's *head;* 6, the front or foremost part of anything, as of a parade or an army; also, the bow of a ship; 7, the position of command or leadership; as, to be at the *head* of a firm; also, a leader or chief; 8, a separate topic; a class or subject; as, optics comes under the *head* of science; 9, a head's length; as, the horse won by a *head;* 10, a person; as, to charge so much a *head;* also, [*pl.* head], a single one; an individual; as, 50 *head* of sheep; **11,** crisis; as, the situation came to a *head;* **12,** source; beginning; as, the *head* of a river; **13,** force; pressure; as, a *head* of steam; **14,** a cape or promontory, as of land:—*adj.* **1,** principal; chief; as, a *head* clerk; **2,** coming toward one; as, a *head* wind; **3,** placed at the front or top:—*v.t.* **1,** to lead; direct; as, to *head* an expedition; **2,** to take the first place in; as, Tom *heads* his class; **3,** to get in front of; as, to *head* off a horse; prevent; as, to *head* off a quarrel:—*v.i.* **1,** to move in a given direction; as, to *head* south; **2,** to form a head, as a plant or flower; hence, to come to a climax. —*adj.* **head′less.**—*n.* **head′ship.**

head-ache (hĕd′āk′), *n.* a continuous pain in the head.

head-dress (hĕd′drĕs′), *n.* **1,** a covering, often ornamental, for the head; **2,** a manner of wearing the hair.

head-er (hĕd′ẽr), *n.* **1,** a person or machine that puts on or removes the heads of nails, barrels, etc.; **2,** a farm machine which cuts off and loads heads of grain; **3,** *Colloquial,* a plunge headfirst.

head-first (hĕd′fûrst′), *adv.* **1,** headlong; **2,** in rash, thoughtless haste.—*adv.* **head′-fore′most.**

head-gear (hĕd′gēr′), *n.* anything worn on the head.

head-ing (hĕd′ĭng), *n.* **1,** a title; caption; **2,** a division in the subject matter of a lecture, written article, or the like.

head-land (hĕd′lănd), *n.* a cape or promontory.

head-light (hĕd′līt′), *n.* a bright light on the front of a locomotive, automobile, etc.

head-line (hĕd′līn′), *n.* a heading, often in large type, at the top of a newspaper column or at the beginning of an article.

head-long (hĕd′lông), *adv.* **1,** headforemost; **2,** rashly:—*adj.* **1,** rash; violent; thoughtless; as, a *headlong* decision; **2,** plunging headfirst.

head-man (hĕd′măn), *n.* [*pl.* headmen (-mĕn)], a leader; the chief man of a tribe.

head-mas-ter (hĕd′mȧs′tẽr), *n.* the principal teacher or the principal of a school.

head-on (hĕd′-ŏn′), *adj.* with fronts facing: used especially of collisions.

head-piece (hĕd′pēs′), *n.* **1,** a covering for the protection of the head, as a helmet; also, a cap or hat; **2,** a design at the beginning of a chapter.

head-quar-ters (hĕd′kwôr′tẽrz), *n.* [*pl.* headquarters], **1,** the residence or office of a commanding officer from which orders are issued; **2,** any center of activity or authority.

heads-man (hĕdz′măn), *n.* [*pl.* headsmen (-mĕn)], a public executioner.

head-stone (hĕd′stōn′), *n.* **1,** a stone at the head of a grave; **2,** the principal or corner stone in a building.

head-strong (hĕd′strông), *adj.* ungovernable; self-willed.
Syn. determined, stubborn, obstinate.

head-wa-ters (hĕd′wô′tẽrz), *n.pl.* the source and upper waters of a stream.

head-way (hĕd′wā′), *n.* **1,** forward motion, as of a ship; progress; **2,** a clear space permitting passage under an arch, bridge, etc.

head-y (hĕd′ĭ), *adj.* [head-i-er, head-i-est], **1,** rash; ungovernable; **2,** intoxicating, as liquor; **3,** *Colloquial,* clever; intelligent.

heal (hēl), *v.t.* to restore to health; cure: —*v.i.* to become well or sound.—*n.* **heal′er.**

health (hĕlth), *n.* **1,** freedom from pain or disease; vigor of body or mind; **2,** a toast to a person's health and happiness.

health-ful (hĕlth′fŏŏl), *adj.* promoting bodily welfare; giving health; as, *healthful* exercise; a *healthful* climate.—*adv.* **health′-ful-ly.**—*n.* **health′ful-ness.**
Syn. sanitary, hygienic, wholesome.

health-y (hĕl′thĭ), *adj.* [health-i-er, health-i-est], **1,** in a sound or wholesome condition; as, a *healthy* child; **2,** showing health; as, a *healthy* look.—*adv.* **health′i-ly.** —*n.* **health′i-ness.**

heap (hēp), *n.* **1,** a number of things piled up together; **2,** a large quantity:—*v.t.* **1,** to make a pile of; **2,** to bestow generously; as, to *heap* gifts upon; **3,** to fill to overflowing; as, to *heap* a plate with food.
Syn., v. accumulate, amass.

hear (hēr), *v.t.* [heard (hûrd), hear-ing], **1,** to perceive by the ear; **2,** to attend or listen to; give heed to; **3,** to become informed of; as, to *hear* news; **4,** to grant (a favor or a prayer):—*v.i.* **1,** to have the sense of hearing; **2,** to be told; as, I *heard* of his death; **3,** to listen.—*n.* **hear′er.**
Syn. apprehend, learn.

hear-ing (hēr′ĭng), *n.* **1,** the sense by which sound is perceived; **2,** the distance over which a sound may be heard; as, to be within *hearing;* **3,** a chance to be heard; attention; as, to get a *hearing.*

heark-en or **hark-en** (här′kĕn), *v.i.* to listen; pay attention.

hear-say (hēr′sā′), *n.* rumor; gossip.

hearse (hûrs), *n.* a vehicle for carrying dead bodies to the grave.

heart (härt), *n.* **1,** a hollow, muscular organ which pumps the blood through the body (see illustration next page); **2,** hence, an essential part; as, the *heart* of a book; also, the central or inmost part; as, the *heart* of a tree; **3**, tenderness; sympathy; as, one's *heart* goes out to a child; also, courage; as, I haven't the *heart* to tell her; **4**, a conventional figure representing a heart; **5**, one of a suit, called *hearts*, of playing cards, marked with a red figure like a heart; **6**, memory; as, to learn by *heart*; **7**, liking; approval; as, after one's own *heart*; **8**, **hearts**, a card game.

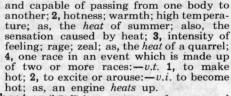

HUMAN HEART

Partly laid open to show: 1, right auricle; 2, left auricle; 3, right ventricle; 4, left ventricle; 5, aorta; 6, pulmonary artery.

heart-ache (härt′āk′), *n.* sorrow; grief.

heart-bro-ken (härt′brō′kĕn), *adj.* in despair; overwhelmed by grief.

heart-burn (härt′bûrn′), *n.* **1**, a burning sensation in the stomach, or just below the heart, caused by indigestion; **2**, jealousy; discontent.

heart-en (här′tn), *v.t.* to give courage to; to cheer or inspire.

heart-felt (härt′fĕlt′), *adj.* earnest; sincere; with true emotion.

hearth (härth), *n.* **1**, the floor or base of a fireplace, usually of brick or stone; **2**, the family circle; home.

hearth-stone (härth′stōn′), *n.* **1**, a flat stone forming a hearth; **2**, the fireside.

heart-less (härt′lĕs), *adj.* **1**, without feeling or affection; **2**, cruel; merciless.—*adv.* **heart′less-ly.**—*n.* **heart′less-ness.**

heart—rend-ing (härt′—rĕn′dĭng), *adj.* causing extreme anguish or grief; very distressing; as, *heart-rending* news.

hearts-ease or **heart's—ease** (härts′ēz′), *n.* a popular and poetic name for a number of plants, especially the violet and pansy.

heart-sick (härt′sĭk′), *adj.* distressed in mind; depressed; unhappy.

heart-strings (härt′strĭngz′), *n.pl.* **1**, in ancient anatomy, the tendons which were believed to support the heart; **2**, hence, the deepest emotions.

heart-wood (härt′wŏod′), *n.* the hard inner wood of a tree trunk.

heart-y (här′tĭ), *adj.* [heart-i-er, heart-i-est], **1**, sincere; cordial; as, a *hearty* welcome; **2**, vigorous; strong; as, a *hearty* handclasp; **3**, abundant and nourishing; as, a *hearty* meal.—*adv.* **heart′i-ly.**—*n.* **heart′i-ness.**

Syn. earnest, ardent.

heat (hēt), *n.* **1**, a form of energy due to the motion of invisible particles of matter

and capable of passing from one body to another; **2**, hotness; warmth; high temperature; as, the *heat* of summer; also, the sensation caused by heat; **3**, intensity of feeling; rage; zeal; as, the *heat* of a quarrel; **4**, one race in an event which is made up of two or more races:—*v.t.* **1**, to make hot; **2**, to excite or arouse:—*v.i.* to become hot; as, an engine *heats* up.

heat-er (hēt′ẽr), *n.* a stove or furnace used to heat a building, room, etc.

heath (hēth), *n.* **1**, a tract of waste or level land, covered with heather or other coarse vegetation, especially in Great Britain; **2**, an evergreen shrub; heather.

hea-then (hē′thĕn), *n.* [*pl.* heathens or, collectively, heathen], a person who is not of the Jewish, Christian, or Mohammedan faith; a pagan; idolater:—*adj.* pertaining to the heathen; pagan; as, a *heathen* land. —*adj.* **hea′then-ish.**

heath-er (hĕth′ẽr), *n.* a small evergreen shrub with lavender flowers, that blooms profusely in late summer: also called *heath.*—*adj.* **heath′er-y.**

HEATHER

heave (hēv), *v.t.* [*p.t.* and *p.p.* heaved (hēvd) or hove (hōv), *p.pr.* heav-ing], **1**, to hoist or lift up with effort; **2**, to utter (a sob or sigh); **3**, to throw; hurl:—*v.i.* **1**, to be lifted up; swell up; **2**, to rise and fall alternately; as, the sea *heaves;* **3**, to struggle; strain; **4**, to haul; move; as, the ship *hove* in sight:—*n.* **1**, an effort to move or pull something; a lift; **2**, the act of throwing; **3**, a swell or rising; as, a *heave* of the breast.

heav-en (hĕv′ĕn), *n.* **1**, the abode of God and the blessed; **2**, a state or condition of bliss; supreme happiness; **3**, **the heavens**, the firmament; sky.

heav-en-ly (hĕv′ĕn-lĭ), *adj.* **1**, pertaining to the sky; as, a *heavenly* body; **2**, pertaining to the abode of God; divine; as, *heavenly* joy; **3**, beyond compare; as, *heavenly* beauty.—*n.* **heav′en-li-ness.**

Syn. sacred, blessed, celestial.

heav-en-ward (hĕv′ĕn-wẽrd), *adj.* and *adv.* toward heaven. Also, *adv.* **heav′en-wards.**

heaves (hēvz), *n.pl.* used as *sing.* a disease of horses characterized by difficulty in breathing and a peculiar wheezing cough.

heav-y (hĕv′ĭ), *adj.* [heav-i-er, heav-i-est], **1**, weighty; ponderous; as, a *heavy* load; **2**, large in extent, quality, or effect; as, a *heavy* rain; **3**, oppressive; grievous; as, a *heavy* punishment; also, rough or hard to travel over; as, a *heavy* road; **4**, grave;

serious; as, *heavy* reading; **5,** dejected; sad; as, a *heavy* heart; **6,** dull; stupid; as, a *heavy* mind; **7,** powerful; loud; as, a *heavy* voice; **8,** thick; coarse; as, *heavy* linen; **9,** loaded; as, a tree *heavy* with apples; **10,** dense, as storm clouds.—*adv.* **heav′i-ly.**—*n.* **heav′i-ness.**

heav-y-weight (hĕv′ĭ-wāt′), *n.* a person of more than normal weight; especially, a boxer or wrestler over 175 pounds.

He-be (hē′bē), *n.* in Greek mythology, the goddess of youth, daughter of Zeus and Hera.

He-bra-ic (hē-brā′ĭk), *adj.* pertaining to the Hebrews or their language.

He-brew (hē′brōō), *n.* **1,** a member of one of the Semitic tribes; a Jew; **2,** the ancient language of the Hebrews:—*adj.* pertaining to the Hebrews; Jewish.

He-brews (hē′brōōz), *n.* the Epistle to the Hebrews, a book of the New Testament.

Heb-ri-des (hĕb′rĭ-dēz), a group of 500 islands off the west coat of Scotland (map **13**). Also called *Western Islands.*

He-bron (hē′brŏn), a town in Palestine.

Hec-a-te (hĕk′*a*-tē; hĕk′āt), *n.* in Greek mythology, a goddess with power over the moon, earth, and the underworld. She was associated also with magic and witchcraft.

hec-a-tomb (hĕk′*a*-tŏm; hĕk′*a*-tōōm), *n.* **1,** in ancient times, a sacrifice of 100 oxen; **2,** any great sacrifice or slaughter.

heck-le (hĕk′l), *v.t.* [heck-led, heck-ling], to question persistently, so as to annoy or confuse; as, to *heckle* a speaker.

hec-tic (hĕk′tĭk), *adj.* **1,** feverish; flushed and hot; **2,** *Colloquial,* exciting; wild: as, a *hectic* life.

Hec-tor (hĕk′tẽr), *n.* in Homer's "Iliad," the greatest of the Trojan warriors, killed by Achilles with Athena's help.

hec-tor (hĕk′tẽr), *v.t.* and *v.i.* to bully; threaten; bluster.

Hec-u-ba (hĕk′ū-b*a*), *n.* in Greek legend, the wife of Priam, king of Troy.

hedge (hĕj), *n.* **1,** a fence of bushes, shrubs, or low trees; **2,** a barrier:—*v.t.* [hedged, hedg-ing], **1,** to enclose with a border of bushes or shrubs; **2,** to obstruct; hem in; surround; as, an army *hedges* in the enemy:—*v.i.* **1,** to bet on both sides in order to protect oneself against heavy loss; **2,** to speak evasively; avoid frank speech, especially in answer to questions.

hedge-hog (hĕj′hŏg′), *n.* **1,** a spiny, insect-eating animal, with the power of rolling itself into a ball for defense; **2,** the North American porcupine.

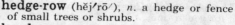

HEDGEHOG (⅓₀) def. 1

hedge-row (hĕj′rō′), *n.* a hedge or fence of small trees or shrubs.

heed (hēd), *v.t.* to notice; pay attention to; regard:—*n.* careful attention; as, give *heed.*

heed-ful (hēd′fŏŏl), *adj.* watchful; considerate; thoughtful.—*adv.* **heed′ful-ly.**—*n.* **heed′ful-ness.**

heed-less (hēd′lĕs), *adj.* careless; inattentive; neglectful.—*adv.* **heed′less-ly.**—*n.* **heed′less-ness.**
     Syn. inconsiderate, unobserving.

¹**heel** (hēl), *v.i.* to lean to one side; to list: said of a ship:—*v.t.* to cause (a ship) to list.

²**heel** (hēl), *n.* **1,** the back part of the foot; **2,** the corresponding part of a boot, shoe, or stocking (see illustration at *shoe*); **3,** anything resembling a heel in position or shape; as, the *heel* of a scythe or a golf club:—*v t.* to furnish with a heel; as, to *heel* boots.—*n.* **heel′ing.**

heft (hĕft), *n. Colloquial,* **1,** heaviness; weight; **2,** the greater part or bulk; the gist of a thing:—*v.t.* **1,** to lift; **2,** *Colloquial,* to try the weight of, by lifting.

Hei-del-berg (hī′dĕl-bûrg; hī′dĕl-bĕrkh), a city in southern Germany, famous for its university and its old castle.

heif-er (hĕf′ẽr), *n.* a young cow that has not yet calved.

height (hīt), *n.* **1,** distance from the base to the top; of man, stature; as, he is six feet in *height;* **2,** altitude; the distance anything rises above the earth or above sea level; **3,** a mountain or hill; **4,** the highest point; top; summit; hence, the utmost degree; as, the *height* of madness.

height-en (hīt′n), *v.t.* **1,** to raise; make higher; **2,** to intensify, as a color; increase; aggravate; as, to *heighten* anger:—*v.i.* to rise in height; increase.

Hei-ne (hī′nĕ), Heinrich (1797-1856), a German lyric poet.

hei-nous (hā′nŭs), *adj.* hateful; extremely wicked; as, a *heinous* crime.—*adv.* **hei′nous-ly.**—*n.* **hei′nous-ness.**

heir (âr), *n.* **1,** one who receives or has the right to receive an estate, title, etc., on the death of the owner; **2,** one who inherits anything, as property or mental qualities; as, he fell *heir* to his father's temper.
     heir apparent, one whose right to inherit cannot be annulled if he outlives the person from whom the inheritance will pass; **heir presumptive,** one who will succeed as heir if his right is not canceled by the birth of one nearer in succession.

heir-ess (âr′ĕs), *n.* a woman or girl who inherits, or is heir to, title or property.

heir-loom (âr′lōōm′), *n.* a piece of personal property handed down in a family for generations.

He·jaz (hĕ-jäz′; hĕ-zhäz′), a province (cap. Mecca) in the kingdom of Saudi Arabia.

Hel·en (hĕl′ĕn), *n.* in Greek story, the wife of Menelaus, king of Sparta, who was famed for her beauty. Her abduction by Paris, son of Priam, king of Troy, was the cause of the Trojan War, the story of which is told in Homer's "Iliad."

Hel·e·na (hĕl′ē-nȧ), a city, the capital of Montana, in the west central part of the State (map **9**).

Hel·go·land (hĕl′gō-länt′), [English **Hel·i·go·land** (hĕl′ĭ-gō-lănd′)], a German island in the North Sea.

Hel·i·con (hĕl′ĭ-kŏn; hĕl′ĭ-kŭn), a famous mountain in Boeotia, Greece, where Apollo and the Muses were thought to live.

hel·i·cop·ter (hĕl′ĭ-kŏp′tĕr), *n.* a flying machine lifted and held up by power-driven propellers revolving horizontally.

he·li·o·graph (hē′lĭ-ō-gráf′), *n.* an apparatus consisting of a mirror to catch the sun's rays and flash them to a distance: used for signaling:—*v.t.* and *v.i.* to signal by means of this instrument.

He·li·os (hē′lĭ-ŏs), *n.* in Greek mythology, the sun god, who drove daily across the sky from east to west: later called *Apollo*.

he·li·o·trope (hē′lĭ-ō-trōp), *n.* **1**, a cultivated plant bearing purplish, sweet-scented flowers; **2**, a purplish color.

he·li·um (hē′lĭ-ŭm), *n.* a rare gas, very light and not inflammable, used for inflating balloons.

hell (hĕl), *n.* **1**, the place of punishment for the wicked after death; **2**, any place or condition of extreme misery or evil; **3**, the dwelling place of the dead. —*adj.* **hell′ish.**—*n.* **hell′ish·ness.**

HELIOTROPE

Hel·las (hĕl′ȧs), Greece: so called by the ancient Greeks.

hel·le·bore (hĕl′ē-bôr), *n.* any one of several plants of the buttercup family, with deeply-cut leaves and large white, yellowish, or greenish flowers; also, the dried rootstocks of any of these plants, used in medicine and as an insecticide.

Hel·lene (hĕl′ēn), *n.* **1**, a Greek of ancient times; **2**, a native of modern Greece.

Hel·len·ic (hĕ-lĕn′ĭk; hĕ-lē′nĭk), *adj.* pertaining to the ancient Greeks, or to Greek art and literature.

Hel·len·ism (hĕl′ĕn-ĭzm), *n.* **1**, admiration or imitation of the art and literature of ancient Greece; **2**, the modern Greek national spirit.

Hel·les·pont (hĕl′ĕs-pŏnt), the ancient name of the Dardanelles (map **1**).

hell·gram·mite (hĕl′grȧ-mīt), *n.* the larva of a certain kind of insect resembling a dragonfly. It lives in the water, and is often used as fish bait.

hel·lo (hĕ-lō′), *interj.* an exclamation of informal greeting, surprise, etc.:—*n.* a salutation; greeting.

helm (hĕlm), *n.* **1**, the steering apparatus of a ship, especially the tiller or the wheel; **2**, hence, any post of command or control; as, at the *helm* of the nation.

hel·met (hĕl′mĕt), *n.* a covering, as of metal or leather, worn to protect the head.

helms·man (hĕlmz′mȧn), *n.* [*pl.* helmsmen (-mĕn)], the person who steers a ship or boat; pilot.

Hel·ot (hĕl′ŏt; hē′lŏt), *n.* one of a low class of people in ancient Sparta, between the serfs and the free men:—**helot,** a serf; slave.

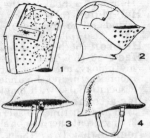

HELMETS

1, 2, European helmets of the 12th (1) and 15th (2) centuries; 3, trench helmet; 4, American helmet, World War II.

help (hĕlp), *v.t.* **1**, to give assistance to; support; **2**, to avoid; prevent; as, I cannot *help* his going; **3**, to distribute food to; serve; **4**, to remedy; as, nothing *helps* my headache:—*v.i.* to lend aid; be useful: —*n.* **1**, aid; support; **2**, remedy; relief; **3**, that which forwards or promotes; **4**, a hired servant or servants.—*n.* **help′er.**

Syn., v. aid, assist, succor.

help·ful (hĕlp′fǒǒl), *adj.* giving aid; beneficial; useful.—*n.* **help′ful·ness.**

help·ing (hĕl′pĭng), *n.* a portion of food served at table.

help·less (hĕlp′lĕs), *adj.* unable to take care of oneself; feeble; dependent.—*adv.* **help′less·ly.**—*n.* **help′less·ness.**

help·mate (hĕlp′māt′) or **help·meet** (hĕlp′mēt′), *n.* an assistant; partner; companion; especially, a wife or husband.

Hel·sin·ki (hĕl′sĕn-kĕ), [Swedish **Hel·sing·fors** (hĕl′sĭng-fôrs′)], the capital of Finland, on the Gulf of Finland (map **12**).

hel·ter—skel·ter (hĕl′tĕr=skĕl′tĕr), *adj.*

and *adv.* in hurried confusion; pell-mell:— *n.* disorder; hasty confusion.

helve (hĕlv), *n.* the handle of a tool or weapon, as of an ax or hatchet.

Hel·ve·ti·a (hĕl-vē′shĭ-à; hĕl-vē′shà), a name for Switzerland.

¹**hem** (hĕm), *n.* the edge of material turned under and sewed down to prevent fraying: —*v.t.* [hemmed, hem-ming], **1,** to fold under and sew down the edge of (a cloth or garment); **2,** to shut in; surround; as, the enemy *hemmed* us in.

²**hem** (hĕm), *interj.* expressing doubt, or used to attract attention:—*n.* the sound *hem:*—*v.i.* [hemmed, hem-ming], **1,** to utter the sound *hem;* **2,** to stammer or hesitate in speaking; as, the speaker *hemmed* and hawed.

hem·i- (hĕm′ĭ-), a prefix meaning half; as, *hemi*sphere.

hem·i·sphere (hĕm′ĭ-sfēr), *n.* a half sphere; especially, a half of the earth. The equator divides the earth into the Northern and the Southern Hemispheres. A meridian divides the earth into the Eastern Hemisphere, including Europe, Asia, Africa, and Australia, and the Western Hemisphere, including North America and South America.

hem·lock (hĕm′lŏk), *n.* **1,** any of several evergreen trees of the pine family (see illustration, page 865); also, the lumber from such a tree; **2,** any of several poisonous plants of the parsley family.

he·mo·glo·bin (hē′mō-glō′bĭn; hĕm′ō-glō′bĭn), *n.* the coloring matter of red corpuscles. Also spelled **hae·mo·glo·bin.**

hem·or·rhage (hĕm′ō-rĭj), *n.* bleeding from the lungs, arteries, veins, etc.; especially, a great or continuous flow of blood.

hemp (hĕmp), *n.* an herb of Asia, the fiber of which is used for ropes and various kinds of coarse linen. The leaves and flowers are the source of the drug hashish.

hemp·en (hĕmp′ĕn), *adj.* like, or made of, hemp.

hem·stitch (hĕm′-stĭch′), *n.* an ornamental stitch used in hemming, in which crosswise threads are pulled out and the lengthwise threads fastened into small bundles; also, needlework so finished:—*v.t.* to finish with hemstitch.

HEMP

hen (hĕn), *n.* the female of the domestic fowl; also, the female of other birds. (See illustration next column.)

hence (hĕns), *adv.* **1,** from this place, source, or time; as, a week *hence;* **2,** for this reason:—*interj.* begone!

hence·forth (hĕns′fôrth′; hĕns′fôrth′) or **hence·for·ward** (hĕns′fôr′wĕrd), *adv.* from this time on.

hench·man (hĕnch′măn), *n.* [*pl.* henchmen (-mĕn)], a trusted follower; a political supporter.

hen·na (hĕn′à), *n.* **1,** a reddish-brown dye and cosmetic made from leaves of a small Asiatic tree; **2,** a reddish-brown color.

hen·ner·y (hĕn′ĕr-ĭ), *n.* [*pl.* henneries], **1,** a chicken farm; **2,** a hen house or yard.

hen·pecked (hĕn′pĕkt′), *adj.* nagged, as a husband by his wife.—*v.t.* **hen′peck′.**

¹**Hen·ry** (hĕn′rĭ), **1,** Patrick (1736–1799), an American patriot; **2, O. Henry** (1862–1910), the pen name of *Sydney Porter*, an American short-story writer.

²**Hen·ry** (hĕn′rĭ), **1, VIII** (1491–1547), a king of England in whose reign the Church of England was established; **2, IV** (1553–1610), king of Navarre, the first Bourbon king of France.

he·pat·i·ca (hē-păt′ĭ kà), *n.* any of several spring-blooming plants of the buttercup family with hairy stems, heart-shaped leaves, and pink, lavender, or white flowers.

HEPATICA

hep·ta·gon (hĕp′tà-gŏn; hĕp′tà-gŭn), *n.* in geometry, a plane figure having seven sides and seven angles.

her (hûr), *adj.* a possessive form of *she,* belonging to her; as, *her* book:—*pron.* the objective form of *she;* as, I see *her.*

He·ra (hē′rà) or **He·re** (hē′rē), *n.* in Greek mythology, the wife of Zeus, the goddess of marriage and maternity: in Roman mythology, *Juno.*

HEPTAGON

Her·a·kles or **Her·a·cles** (hĕr′à-klēz), *n.* a hero of mythology, famous for his great strength. See Hercules.

her·ald (hĕr′ăld), *n.* **1,** an official who made s′ ate proclamations, carried important messages, and assisted at public ceremonies; **2,** a messenger; forerunner:—*v.t.* to introduce; proclaim.

HEN (₁⅕)

go; join; yet; sing; chin; show; thin, *then;* hw, *why;* zh, *a*zure; ü, Ger. für or Fr. l*u*ne; ö, Ger. schön or Fr. f*eu;* n̈. Fr. *e*nfant, nom; kh, Ger. a*ch* or i*ch.* See pages ix–x.

he·ral·dic (hĕ-răl′dĭk), *adj.* pertaining to coats of arms and to heraldry.

her·ald·ry (hĕr′ăld-rĭ), *n.* [*pl.* heraldries], **1,** the science that treats of coats of arms and of genealogies; **2,** pomp and splendor.

herb (ûrb; hûrb), *n.* a plant with a soft, juicy stem, which, after flowering, either dies completely, or withers to the ground; especially, one used for medicine, food, flavor, or the like.

her·ba·ceous (hûr-bā′shŭs), *adj.* of the nature of an herb; also, planted with herbs.

herb·age (ûr′bĭj; hûr′bĭj), *n.* grass or herbs; pasturage.

Her·bert (hûr′bĕrt), Victor (1859–1924), an American composer and conductor.

her·biv·o·rous (hûr-bĭv′ŏ-rŭs), *adj.* feeding on plants, as do horses and dairy cattle.

Her·cu·la·ne·um (hûr′kŭ-lā′nė-ŭm), an ancient Italian city on the Bay of Naples, destroyed, with Pompeii, in the eruption of Vesuvius A.D. 79 (map **1**).

Her·cu·le·an (hûr-kū′lė-ăn; hûr′kŭ-lē′ăn), *adj.* pertaining to Hercules:—**herculean, 1,** of great strength and size; as, a *herculean* fighter; **2,** very difficult; as, a *herculean* task.

Her·cu·les (hûr′kŭ-lēz), *n.* in mythology, a famous hero, son of Zeus, noted for his great strength. Also, **Her′a·kles** or **Her′a·cles** (hĕr′ȧ-klēz).

¹**herd** (hûrd), *n.* **1,** a group of animals, especially cattle, feeding or traveling together; **2,** a large crowd of people; **3,** the common people as a mass; mob:—*v.i.* **1,** to flock together, as beasts; **2,** to associate:—*v.t.* to form (cattle) into a herd.

Syn., *n.* pack, flock, shoal, swarm, band.

²**herd** (hûrd), *n.* a herdsman: now used in compounds; as, cow*herd;* shep*herd:*—*v.t.* to tend (cattle):—*v.i.* to act as herdsman.

herds·man (hûrdz′măn), *n.* [*pl.* herdsmen (-mĕn)], one who owns or tends cattle.

here (hĭr), *adv.* **1,** in this place; as, I live *here;* in answer to a roll call, present; **2,** in this direction; hither; as, look *here;* **3,** at this point or moment; as, *here* he paused; **4,** in this world; as, *here* below.

here·a·bout or **here·a·bouts** (hĭr′ȧ-bout′, hĭr′ȧ-bouts′), *adv.* in this locality.

here·aft·er (hĭr-af′tĕr), *adv.* after this; henceforth; also, in the life to come:—*n.* the future; also, the life to come.

here·by (hĭr-bī′), *adv.* by means of this.

he·red·i·tar·y (hė-rĕd′ĭ-tĕr′ĭ), *adj.* **1,** descending from a person to his heir; as, a *hereditary* estate; **2,** holding rank or position by inheritance; as, a *hereditary* ruler; **3,** passed on from parent to child; as, *hereditary* diseases or customs.

he·red·i·ty (hė-rĕd′ĭ-tĭ), *n.* [*pl.* heredities], **1,** the passing on from parent to child of physical or mental traits; **2,** hereditary traits.

here·in (hĭr-ĭn′), *adv.* in this.

here·of (hĭr-ŏv′), *adv.* of this; about this; as, we will speak further *hereof.*

here·on (hĭr-ŏn′), *adv.* on this; hereupon.

her·e·sy (hĕr′ė-sĭ), *n.* [*pl.* heresies], an opinion or doctrine contrary to those commonly accepted on such subjects as religion, politics, or art.

her·e·tic (hĕr′ė-tĭk), *n.* one who holds an opinion contrary to accepted views.

he·ret·i·cal (hė-rĕt′ĭ-kȧl), *adj.* contrary to opinions generally accepted; of the nature of heresy.—*adv.* **he·ret′i·cal·ly.**

here·to·fore (hĭr′tŏŏ-fôr′), *adv.* previously; formerly; until now.

here·un·to (hĭr′ŭn-tŏŏ′), *adv.* to this; up to the present.

here·up·on (hĭr′ŏ-pŏn′), *adv.* on this; hereon; at this point.

here·with (hĭr-wĭth′; hĭr-wĭth′), *adv.* with this; at this point.

her·it·a·ble (hĕr′ĭt-ȧ-bl), *adj.* **1,** capable of being handed down or inherited; as, *heritable* lands; **2,** able to inherit.

her·it·age (hĕr′ĭ-tĭj), *n.* that which is handed down to an heir; inheritance; also, the lot or condition into which one is born.

Her·mes (hûr′mēz), *n.* in Greek mythology, a son of Zeus, messenger of the gods, and guardian of commerce, travelers, etc.: called by the Romans *Mercury.*

her·met·ic (hûr-mĕt′ĭk) or **her·met·i·cal** (-mĕt′ĭ-kȧl), *adj.* made perfectly closed and airtight, as by soldering, so that neither air nor fluid can enter or escape; as, a *hermetic* seal.—*adv.* **her·met′i·cal·ly.**

her·mit (hûr′mĭt), *n.* one who withdraws from society and lives alone; a recluse.

her·mit·age (hûr′mĭ-tĭj), *n.* the home of a recluse or hermit.

her·ni·a (hûr′nĭ-ȧ), *n.* [*pl.* hernias (hûr′-nĭ-ȧz)], the pushing of part of the intestine through a break in the inner wall of the abdomen; a rupture.

he·ro (hĭr′ō), *n.* [*pl.* heroes], **1,** a man famed for courage or deeds of prowess; **2,** the chief character in a play, novel, etc.

Her·od (hĕr′ŭd), **1,** (73?–4 B.C.), called *the Great,* king of the Jews; **2, Antipas,** ruler of Galilee (4 B.C.–A.D. 39). He had John the Baptist beheaded, and presided at the trial of Jesus.

He·rod·o·tus (hė-rŏd′ō-tŭs), (484?–425 B.C.), an ancient Greek historian.

āte, āorta, râre, căt, ȧsk, fär, ăllow, sofȧ; ēve, ēvent, ĕll, writĕr, novĕl; bīte, pĭn; nō, ōbey, ôr, dŏg, tŏp, cŏllide; ūnit, ūnite, bûrn, cŭt, focŭs; nŏŏn, fŏŏt; mound; coin;

he-ro-ic (hē-rō′ĭk) or **he-ro-i-cal** (hē-rō′-ĭ-kăl), *adj.* **1,** having the qualities of a hero; courageous; as, a *heroic* warrior; **2,** worthy of a hero; bold; brave; as, *heroic* deeds; **3,** having to do with heroes and their deeds; as, *heroic* poetry; the *heroic* age described in Homer's "Iliad."—*adv.* **he-ro′i-cal-ly.**

Her-o-in (hĕr′ō-ĭn), *n.* a trade-mark name for a drug derived from morphine:—**heroin,** the narcotic drug bearing this name.

her-o-ine (hĕr′ō-ĭn), *n.* **1,** a woman of outstanding courage; **2,** the chief female character in a play, novel, or the like.

her-o-ism (hĕr′ō-ĭzm), *n.* heroic conduct; high and noble courage.

her-on (hĕr′ŭn), *n.* a wading bird with long legs, neck, and bill, living in marshes, and feeding on fish, frogs, and insects.

HERON (₃¹₅)

Herr (hĕr), *n.* [*pl.* Herren (hĕr′ĕn)], a German title of courtesy, equivalent to *Sir* or *Mr.*

her-ring (hĕr′ĭng), *n.* [*pl.* herring or herrings], a food fish found in North Atlantic waters.

HERRING (¹⁄₈)

her-ring-bone (hĕr′ĭng-bōn′), *adj.* composed of rows of short parallel lines slanting in opposite directions from a central rib, like the spine of a herring.

hers (hûrz), a possessive form of *she*, used alone: **1,** as *adj.*, in the predicate, belonging to her; as, whose is that hat? it is *hers;* **2,** as *pron.*, a person or thing that belongs to her; as, which hat have you? I have *hers.*

HERRINGBONE PATTERN

Her-schel (hûr′shĕl), Sir William (1738-1822), an English astronomer, who discovered the planet Uranus in 1781.

her-self (hûr-sĕlf′), *pron.* **1,** a reflexive form of *her;* as, she cut *herself;* **2,** an emphatic form of *she;* as, she did it *herself;* **3,** her normal or true self; as, she is now *herself* again.

hes-i-tan-cy (hĕz′ĭ-tăn-sĭ), *n.* [*pl.* hesitancies], indecision; hesitation.

hes-i-tant (hĕz′ĭ-tănt), *adj.* undecided; wavering; hesitating.—*adv.* **hes′i-tant-ly.**

hes-i-tate (hĕz′ĭ-tāt), *v.i.* [hesitat-ed, hesitat-ing], **1,** to be uncertain, undecided, or in doubt; as, he *hesitates* about going; also, to be unwilling; as, I *hesitate* to take the risk; **2,** to pause for a moment. *Syn.* falter, waver, delay, demur.

hes-i-ta-tion (hĕz′ĭ-tā′shŭn), *n.* **1,** uncertainty; doubt; indecision; **2,** a faltering in speech; stammering.

Hes-per-i-des (hĕs-pĕr′ĭ-dēz), *n.pl.* in mythology, the nymphs who, helped by a dragon, guarded the golden apples of Hera.

Hes-per-us (hĕs′pĕr-ŭs), *n.* the evening star: in poetry, also called *Hesper.*

Hesse (hĕs), a region in the southwestern part of Germany.

Hes-sian (hĕsh′ăn), *n.* **1,** a native of Hesse, Germany; **2,** one of the soldiers hired by George III of England to fight against the American colonists in the American Revolution:—*adj.* relating to Hesse or its people.

het-er-o- (hĕt′ĕr-ō-), a prefix meaning other or different; as, *hetero*dox.

het-er-o-dox (hĕt′ĕr-ō-dŏks), *adj.* contrary to, or holding views contrary to, accepted doctrine or belief; heretical: opposite of *orthodox.*

het-er-o-dox-y (hĕt′ĕr-ō-dŏk′sĭ), *n.* [*pl.* heterodoxies], **1,** the act or quality of differing from established doctrine; **2,** an unorthodox doctrine or opinion.

het-er-o-ge-ne-ous (hĕt′ĕr-ō-jē′nē-ŭs), *adj.* dissimilar; consisting of parts of different kinds: opposite of *homogeneous;* as, the *heterogeneous* population of the U.S.

hew (hū), *v.t.* [*p.t.* hewed, *p.p.* hewed or hewn (hūn), *p.pr.* hew-ing], **1,** to cut or chop, as with an ax; as, to *hew* wood; **2,** to cut down (trees); **3,** to cut into shape; as, to *hew* out a beam:—*v.i.* to strike blows, as with an ax.—*n.* **hew′er.**

hex (hĕks), *n.* in certain parts of the U.S., one who is supposed to practice sorcery:—*v.i.* and *v.t.* to practice sorcery (upon).

hex-a-gon (hĕk′sȧ-gŏn; hĕk′sȧ-gŭn), *n.* a plane figure with six angles and six sides.—*adj.* **hex-ag′o-nal** (hĕks-ăg′ō-năl).—*adv.* **hex-ag′o-nal-ly.**

HEXAGON

hex-am-e-ter (hĕks-ăm′ē-tēr), *n.* a line consisting of six metrical feet, as: "Now had the / season re/turned when the / nights grow / colder and / longer."

hey (hā), *interj.* an exclamation to express surprise, attract attention, etc.

hey-day (hā′dā′), *n.* the time of greatest strength, vigor, bloom, or the like; as, the *heyday* of youth.

Hez-e-ki-ah (hĕz′ē-kī′ȧ), in the Old Testament, a king of Judah.

H.H. abbreviation for *His*, or *Her, Highness* or *His Holiness* (the Pope).

---

go; join; yet; sing; chin; show; thin, *th*en; hw, *wh*y; zh, azure; ü, Ger. *für* or Fr. *lune*; ö, Ger. *schön* or Fr. *feu*; ṅ, Fr. *enfant*, nom; kh, Ger. *ach* or *ich*. See pages ix–x.

hhd. abbreviation for *hogshead.*

H.I. abbreviation for *Hawaiian Islands.*

hi-a-tus (hī-ā′tŭs), *n.* [*pl.* hiatuses or hiatus], a gap, blank space, or break, especially in a manuscript from which some word, phrase, or line is missing.

Hi-a-wa-tha (hī′a-wô′thà; hī′a-wŏth′à; hē′a-wô′thà; hē′a-wŏth′à), *n.* the legendary Indian hero of Longfellow's poem "Hiawatha": so named for an early Mohawk chief who federated the neighboring Indians into the Five Nations.

hi-ber-nate (hī′bĕr-nāt), *v.i.* [hibernat-ed, hibernat-ing], to pass the winter in a state like sleep, as does the bear; to winter; also, to be inactive.

hic-cup (hĭk′ŭp), *n.* a short, convulsive gasp:—*v.i.* [hiccuped, hiccup-ing], to have hiccups. Also spelled **hic′cough** (hĭk′ŭp).

hick-o-ry (hĭk′ō-rĭ), *n.* [*pl.* hickories], an American nut-bearing tree of the walnut family; also, the tough wood of this tree. (See illustration on page 864.)

hid (hĭd), past tense and one form of the past participle of ²*hide.*

hi-dal-go (hĭ-dăl′gō), *n.* [*pl.* hidalgos], a Spanish nobleman of lower rank.

hid-den (hĭd′n), a past participle of ²*hide:* —*adj.* concealed; out of sight; secret.

¹hide (hīd), *n.* 1, the skin, raw or dressed, of an animal; 2, the human skin:—*v.t.* [hid-ed, hid-ing], *Colloquial,* to whip with a lash.

²hide (hīd), *v.t.* [*p.t.* hid (hĭd), *p.p.* hidden (hĭd′n) or hid, *p.pr.* hid-ing], to conceal; keep secret or unknown; as, to *hide* a letter or a piece of news; also, to turn away; as, to *hide* one's face:—*v.i.* to conceal oneself or to be concealed.

    Syn. veil, cover, secrete, disguise.

hide-bound (hīd′bound′), *adj.* 1, with a hide that clings tightly; 2, hence, obstinately set in opinion; narrow-minded.

hid-e-ous (hĭd′ē-ŭs), *adj.* frightful to look upon; horrible to think of.—*adv.* **hid′e-ous-ly.**—*n.* **hid′e-ous-ness.**

    Syn. grim, ghastly, revolting.

hid-ing (hīd′ĭng), *n.* a beating; thrashing.

hie (hī), *v.i.* [hied, hy-ing or hie-ing], to make haste.

hi-er-arch-y (hī′ĕr-är′kĭ), *n.* [*pl.* hierarchies], 1, a form of government, as in a church, by various ranks and grades of officials; 2, a body of church officials, as archbishops, bishops, etc.; priesthood.

hi-er-o-glyph-ic (hī′ĕr-ō-glĭf′ĭk), *n.* 1, a picture used as one of the characters in the writing of the ancient Egyptians, Mexicans, etc.; 2, **hieroglyphics,** the

picture writing of the ancient Egyptians; hence, any writing hard to read:—*adj.* 1, pertaining to hieroglyphics; 2, symbolic; 3, illegible.

HIEROGLYPHICS

hig-gle-dy–pig-gle-dy (hĭg′l-dĭ=pĭg′l-dĭ), *adj.* jumbled together; topsy-turvy:—*adv.* in a confused manner:—*n.* confusion.

high (hī), *adj.* 1, far above the ground or sea level; as, a *high* plateau; also, tall; as, a *high* tree; a tower 30 feet *high;* 2, noble; lofty in character; as, *high* aims; 3, chief; important; as, *high* government officials; 4, elated; lively; as, *high* spirits; 5, intense or extreme; as, *high* speed; *high* favor; a *high* color; 6, strong, violent, or tempestuous; as, *high* winds; angry; as, *high* words; 7, at the full; as, a *high* tide; 8, expensive; as, food is *high;* not low; as, prices are *high;* 9, shrill or sharp; as, a *high* tone:—*adv.* 1, to a great altitude or degree; 2, extravagantly; as, to live *high;* 3, arrogantly; as, to talk *high;* 4, in a shrill or loud pitch.

high-born (hī′bôrn′), *adj.* of noble descent.

high-brow (hī′=brou′), *n.* an intellectual; especially, one who puts on an attitude of intellectual superiority.

high-flown (hī′=flōn′), *adj.* extravagant or bombastic: used of speech or writing.

high-hand-ed (hī′hăn′dĕd), *adj.* arbitrary; overbearing.

high-land (hī′lănd), *n.* high or mountainous land:—**the Highlands,** the mountainous region of Scotland.

High-land-er (hī′lăn-dĕr), *n.* a native of the Scotch Highlands:—**highlander,** a mountaineer.

high-ly (hī′lĭ), *adv.* in a high degree; as, *highly* colored; favorably; as, to speak *highly* of someone; also, at a high price or rate; as, *highly* paid.

high-mind-ed (hī′=mīn′dĕd), *adj.* honorable; having a lofty or noble character.

high-ness (hī′nĕs), *n.* the state or condition of being high; height:—**Highness,** a title of honor applied to persons of royal rank; as, His Royal *Highness.*

high-road (hī′rōd′), *n.* a chief or much-traveled road.

high school, a school including grades from the ninth to the twelfth.

high-spir-it-ed (hī′=spĭr′ĭ-tĕd), *adj.* bold; courageous; mettlesome.

high-strung (hī′=strŭng′), *adj.* sensitive; nervous; highly excitable.

HIGH-
LANDER

hight (hīt), *adj. Poetic*, called; named.

high-way (hī′wā′), *n.* **1**, a main road; highroad; **2**, any public road.

Syn. thoroughfare, road, street, avenue.

hi-jack-er (hī′jăk′ẽr), *n. U.S. Slang*, a bandit; especially, a bandit who robs those engaged in bootlegging.

hike (hīk), *Colloquial: v.i.* [hiked, hik-ing], to tramp or walk:—*n.* a long walk or march.

hi-lar-i-ous (hǐ-lâr′ǐ-ŭs; hī-lâr′ǐ-ŭs), *adj.* boisterous.—*adv.* **hi-lar′i-ous-ly.**

hi-lar-i-ty (hǐ-lăr′ǐ-tǐ; hī-lăr′ǐ-tǐ), *n.* [*pl.* hilarities], noisy merriment; jollity.

hill (hǐl), *n.* **1**, a natural elevation lower than a mountain; **2**, a small mound or heap; as, an ant *hill*:—*v.t.* to form into a mound; surround with a mound of earth; as, to *hill* potatoes.

hill-ock (hǐl′ŭk), *n.* a small hill.

hill-side (hǐl′sīd′), *n.* the side of a hill.

hill-y (hǐl′ǐ), *adj.* [hill-i-er, hill-i-est], abounding in hills; rugged; not level.—*n.* **hill′i-ness.**

hilt (hǐlt), *n.* a handle of a sword or dagger.

him (hǐm), *pron.* the objective case of *he*; as, they found *him.*

Hi-ma-la-yas, The (hǐ-mä′lȧ-yȧz; hǐm′ȧ-lā′yȧz), a mountain range between India and Tibet, the highest range in the world, containing Everest, 29,028 feet high **(map 15).**

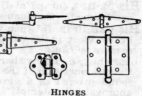

HILT (H)
Of a dagger.

him-self (hǐm-sĕlf′), *pron.* **1**, a reflexive form of *him*; as, he hurt *himself*; **2**, an emphatic form of *he*; as, he *himself* went; **3**, his normal or true self; as, he came to *himself.*

[1]**hind** (hīnd), *n.* the female of the red deer, especially one over three years old.

[2]**hind** (hīnd), *n. Archaic*, a farm servant.

[3]**hind** (hīnd), *adj.* [*comp.* hind-er, *superl.* hind-most or hind-er-most], at the rear; as, the *hind* wheels of a wagon.

[1]**hind-er** (hīn′dẽr), *adj.* [*comp.* of [3]*hind*], rear; back.

[2]**hin-der** (hǐn′dẽr), *v.t.* to keep back; slow up; as, the snow *hindered* our progress.

Syn. block, retard, prevent.

hind-most (hīnd′mōst) or **hind-er-most** (hīn′dẽr-mōst), *adj.* [*superl.* of [3]*hind*], farthest back.

hind-quar-ter (hīnd′kwôr′tẽr), *n.* the back part of half a carcass, as of beef.

hin-drance (hǐn′drȧns), *n.* the act of hindering; also, an obstruction.

Syn. impediment, encumbrance, obstacle.

Hin-du (hǐn′dōo; hǐn′dōo′), *n.* **1**, any believer in Hinduism:—*adj.* pertaining to the Hindus or to Hinduism; **2**, a native of Hindustan, or India, who belongs to the Aryan, or white, race and believes in Hinduism. Also spelled **Hin′doo.**

Hin-du-ism or **Hin-doo-ism** (hǐn′dōo-ĭzm), *n.* the religious and social system of Hindustan.

Hin-du Kush (hǐn′dōo kōosh′), a northern Afghanistan mountain range (map 15).

Hin-du-stan (hǐn′dōo-stän′), **1**, the Persian name of *India*; **2**, the predominantly Hindu areas of the peninsula of India, as opposed to Pakistan, which includes the mainly Moslem areas.

hinge (hǐnj), *n.* a jointed device or mechanism by means of which a movable part, as a door or lid, is made to turn or swing:—*v.t.* [hinged, hing-ing], to furnish or attach with a hinge:—*v.i.* to turn or depend, as on a hinge; as, my answer *hinges* on the decision you make.

HINGES

hint (hǐnt), *v.t.* to suggest slightly; refer to indirectly:—*v.i.* to make an indirect suggestion:—*n.* an indirect or veiled suggestion.

Syn., v. imply, intimate, insinuate.

hin-ter-land (hǐn′tẽr-lǎnd′), *n.* the region lying back of the lands bordering a river or the sea; an inland region; also, a region remote from towns or cities.

hip (hǐp), *n.* the widening fleshy part of the body on either side below the waist, formed by the sides of the pelvis and the upper part of the thigh; the haunch.

Hip-poc-ra-tes (hǐ-pŏk′rȧ-tēz), (460–359? B.C.), an ancient Greek physician, called the *Father of Medicine.*

Hip-po-crene (hǐp′ō-krēn), in mythology, the fount of the Muses.

hip-po-drome (hǐp′ō-drōm), *n.* **1**, an ancient Greek or Roman race course for horses and chariots; **2**, a modern arena with seats for spectators; a circus.

hip-po-pot-a-mus (hǐp′ō-pŏt′ȧ-mŭs), *n.* [*pl.* hippopotamuses or hippopotami (hǐp′ō-pŏt′ȧ-mī)], a huge land and water animal, common near rivers in Africa, with big head and mouth, thick hide, and short legs.

HIPPOPOTAMUS (1/85)

hire (hīr), *v.t.* [hired, hir-ing], **1,** to engage the service of, for a price; employ (a servant) for wages; **2,** to secure the temporary use of, for a price; to rent; as, to *hire* a horse for a day; **3,** to grant the temporary use of, for a price; as, to *hire* out a horse:—*n.* **1,** the act of hiring; **2,** the wages paid for personal service; **3,** the price paid for the use of anything.
 Syn. v. procure, secure, employ.

hire-ling (hīr′lĭng), *n.* one who serves for wages, especially one whose interest is centered in the wages rather than in the work:—*adj.* mercenary; working for pay.

his (hĭz), the possessive form of *he,* used: **1,** as *adj.,* belonging to him; as, this is *his* hat; this hat is *his;* **2,** as *pron.,* a person or thing that belongs to him; as, I have my hat, and he has *his.*

His·pa·ni·a (hĭs-pā′nĭ-a̤), the ancient Roman name for the Spanish peninsula.

His·pan·io·la (hĭs′păn-yō′la̤), an island in the West Indies (map **10**). Its former name was *Haiti.*

hiss (hĭs), *n.* **1,** the sharp sound made in the pronunciation of the letter *s;* also, this sound uttered as an exclamation of disapproval or contempt; **2,** a similar sound; as, the *hiss* of water on a hot stove; the *hiss* of a snake:—*v.i.* to make a hiss; as, they *hissed* during his speech:—*v.t.* **1,** to express contempt for by hissing; as, the audience *hissed* the actors; **2** to utter with a hiss; as, to *hiss* one's words.—*n.* **hiss′ing.**

hist (hĭst), *interj.* hush! hark! as, *hist!* what was that sound?

his·tor·i·an (hĭs-tôr′ĭ-ăn), *n.* a person who writes or studies history.

his·tor·ic (hĭs-tŏr′ĭk), *adj.* belonging to, connected with, or famous in history; as, a *historic* spot.

his·tor·i·cal (hĭs-tŏr′ĭ-kăl), *adj.* **1,** of or pertaining to history; as, *historical* studies; **2,** based on history; as, a *historical* play; **3,** true to history; not legendary; as, a *historical* event.—*adv.* **his·tor′i·cal·ly.**

his·to·ry (hĭs′tô-rĭ), *n.* [*pl.* histories], **1,** a written narrative of past facts and events affecting one or more peoples, countries, institutions, sciences, or the like, usually with comments and explanations; **2,** the branch of learning that studies, records, and explains past facts and events; **3,** past facts or events referring to a particular person, nation, or the like; as, this house has a strange *history.*
 Syn. record, annals, chronicle.

his·tri·on·ic (hĭs′trĭ-ŏn′ĭk), *adj.* pertaining to actors or acting.

hit (hĭt), *v.t.* [hit, hit-ting], **1,** to strike or give a blow to; as, to *hit* an opponent; **2,**

to bring hard against something; as, to *hit* one's head on a post; **3,** to deliver; as, to *hit* a hard blow; **4,** to touch or reach; as, to *hit* the ceiling; **5,** to wound the feelings of; as, he was hard *hit* by failure:—*v.i.* **1,** to strike or deliver a blow; as, *hit* hard! **2,** to clash or collide; as, the two cars *hit* head on; **3,** to come or light (upon); as, to *hit* upon the answer; **4,** *Colloquial,* of gasoline engines, to fire or explode; as, the motor *hits* on all six cylinders:—*n.* **1,** a stroke or blow; **2,** a success; as, the song was a *hit;* **3,** in baseball, a ball so hit as to enable the batter to reach first base successfully.—*n.* **hit′ter.**

hitch (hĭch), *v.t.* **1,** to fasten or tie; as, the pony was *hitched* to the post; **2,** to pull up with a jerk; as, *hitch* up your skirt:—*v.i.* **1,** to become fastened or entangled; **2,** to move jerkily; hobble:—*n.* **1,** a sudden pull or jerk; as, a *hitch* of the reins; **2,** a sudden stop; an obstacle; as, there was no *hitch* in the arrangements; **3,** a kind of noose or knot, used especially on shipboard for temporary fastening.

hith·er (hĭ*th*′ẽr), *adv.* to or toward this place; here:—*adj.* nearer to the speaker.

hith·er·to (hĭ*th*′ẽr-tōō′), *adv.* to this time; till now.

hith·er·ward (hĭ*th*′ẽr-wẽrd) or **hith·er·wards** (hĭ*th*′ẽr-wẽrdz), *adv.* to this place; in this direction.

Hit·ler (hĭt′lẽr), Adolf (1889–1945), leader of the German National Socialist party, and chancellor of Germany, 1933–1945.

Hit·tite (hĭt′īt), *n.* a member of an ancient people whose empire once extended over AsiaMinor; also, the language of this people.

hive (hīv), *n.* **1,** a box or house for bees; **2,** a swarm of bees in a hive; **3,** a very busy place; also, a swarming multitude:—*v.i.* [hived, hiv-ing], to enter a hive, as bees; also, to live together in swarms; as, people *hive* in a city:—*v.t.* **1,** to put (bees) into a hive; **2,** to store, as honey.

HIVE, def. 1

hives (hīvz), *n.pl.* a disease marked by the appearance of a rash accompanied by intense itching.

H.L. abbreviation for *House of Lords.*

H.M.S. abbreviation for *His,* or *Her, Majesty's Ship* or *Service.*

ho (hō), *interj.* **1,** attracting attention; **2,** expressing delight, surprise, etc. or, when repeated, mockery.

hoar (hôr), *adj.* **1,** white; as, *hoar*frost; **2,** gray with age; as, *hoar* locks.

hoard (hôrd), *n.* a secret store or treasure;

a collection of things kept in reserve:—*v.i.* to lay up money or goods:—*v.t.* to lay up or store secretly; as, to *hoard* gold.—*n.* **hoard′er.**—*n.* **hoard′ing.**

hoar-frost (hôr′frôst′), *n.* white frost; tiny ice particles from night moisture.

hoar-hound (hôr′hound′), *n.* **1,** a bitter herb; **2,** a flavoring extract or candy made from this plant. See **hore-hound.**

hoarse (hôrs), *adj.* [hoars-er, hoars-est], **1,** harsh or rough in sound; as, a *hoarse* voice; **2,** having a rough voice or making a rough rasping sound; as, a *hoarse* foghorn.—*adv.* **hoarse′ly.**—*n.* **hoarse′ness.**

hoar-y (hôr′ĭ), *adj.* [hoar-i-er, hoar-i-est], **1,** white or gray with age; as, *hoary* hair; **2,** old; venerable.

hoax (hōks), *n.* a mischievous trick or practical joke; also, a fraud:—*v.t.* to trick. *Syn., v.* deceive, cheat.

¹hob (hŏb), *n.* **1,** in a fireplace, a raised ledge along the back or sides, on which things are kept warm; **2,** the peg used as a target in such games as quoits.

²hob (hŏb), *n.* an elf:—**to play hob** or **to raise hob,** *Colloquial,* to work mischief.

Ho-bart (hō′bērt), a city, the capital of the island of Tasmania, south of Australia (map **16**).

hob-ble (hŏb′l), *v.i.* [hob-bled, hob-bling], to walk with a limp or go unevenly:—*v.t.* **1,** to make lame; **2,** to hamper, as a horse, by tying its legs:—*n.* **1,** a limping walk; **2,** a rope or fetter for hobbling horses.

hob-ble-de-hoy (hŏb′′l-dĕ-hoi′), *n.* **1,** a lad between boyhood and manhood; **2,** an inexperienced youth; an ungainly, gawky fellow.

hob-by (hŏb′ĭ), *n.* [*pl.* hobbies], a favorite interest aside from one's business.

hob-by-horse (hŏb′ĭ-hôrs′), *n.* **1,** a stick with a horse's head, on which children pretend to ride; **2,** a wooden rocking horse; **3,** a wooden horse on a merry-go-round.

hob-gob-lin (hŏb′gŏb′lĭn), *n.* **1,** a mischievous elf; **2,** an evil sprite of frightful appearance; a bogey.

hob-nail (hŏb′nāl′), *n.* a short, thick, large-headed nail for protecting the soles of heavy boots, and to prevent slipping.

hob-nob (hŏb′nŏb′), *v.i.* [hobnobbed, hob-nob-bing], to drink or talk together; be on intimate terms; as, the old cronies *hob-nobbed* all winter.

ho-bo (hō′bō), *n.* [*pl.* hobos or hoboes], an idle, shiftless vagrant; a tramp.

¹hock (hŏk), *n.* the joint in the hind leg of some animals, corresponding to the ankle in man:—*v.t.* to lame by cutting the tendons of the hock; hamstring.

²hock (hŏk), *n.* a white Rhine wine.

³hock (hŏk), *v.t. U.S. Slang,* to pawn; pledge as security for a loan.

hock-ey (hŏk′ĭ), *n.* an outdoor field game played by two teams of players with sticks curved at one end, and a ball which they try to drive through the opponents' goal: —**ice hockey,** a kind of hockey played by skaters on ice with a rubber disk, or puck, instead of a ball.

HOCKEY STICKS
1, ice-hockey stick; 2, field-hockey stick.

ho-cus-po-cus (hō′kŭs-pō′kŭs), *n.* **1,** a meaningless formula used in conjuring; **2,** a juggler's trick; sleight of hand; deception; hence, nonsense intended to cover up deception.

hod (hŏd), *n.* **1,** a wooden trough for carrying mortar or bricks; **2,** a coal scuttle.

HOD, def. 1

hodge-podge (hŏj′pŏj′), *n.* a stew of meat and vegetables; hence, any mixture or jumble.

hoe (hō), *n.* a flat-bladed, long-handled garden tool for loosening soil, removing weeds, etc.:—*v.t.* [hoed (hōd), hoe-ing], **1,** to till or loosen with a hoe; **2,** to clear of weeds; as, he *hoed* his garden every week:—*v.i.* to work with a hoe.

HOD, def. 2

Hoe (hō), Richard March (1812–1886), an American printer, inventor of a rotary printing press.

hoe-cake (hō′kāk′), *n.* a kind of thin cornmeal bread or cake.

hog (hŏg), *n.* **1,** a full-grown domestic swine; also, any of various similar animals, as the wart hog; **2,** *Colloquial,* a grasping or greedy person; also, a coarse, dirty person:—*v.t.* [hogged, hog-ging], *Slang,* to take more than a fair share of.

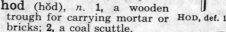

HOES
1, rake and hoe combined; 2, weeding hoe; 3-6 various types of garden hoe.

Ho-garth (hō′gärth), William (1697–1764), an English artist who in his pictures held up to ridicule the customs and fashions of his times.

hog-gish (hŏg′ĭsh), *adj.* **1,** greedy, especially in eating; selfish; **2,** filthy.—*adv.* **hog′gish-ly.**—*n.* **hog′gish-ness.**

hogs-head (hŏgz′hĕd), *n.* **1,** a liquid measure equal to 63 gallons; **2,** a large cask holding from 63 to 140 gallons.

Ho-hen-zol-lern (hō′ĕn-tsŏl′ĕrn), a family of Prussian kings of the 18th and 19th centuries, and German emperors 1871-1918.

hoist (hoist), *v.t.* to raise aloft; as, to *hoist* a flag; to raise by means of a pulley or other tackle:—*n.* **1**, an apparatus for hoisting; a tackle; an elevator; **2**, *Colloquial*, a push; a lift.

Hok·kai·do (hŏk′kī′dō), one of the islands of Japan (map **15**): formerly called *Yezo*.

¹**hold** (hōld), *n.* the interior of a ship below deck.

²**hold** (hōld), *v.t.* [*p.t.* held (hĕld), *p.p.* held or, *Archaic*, hold·en (hōl′dn), *p.pr.* hold·ing], **1**, to have in one's hand or grasp; as, to *hold* a book; also, to keep in place; support; as, a shelf *holds* books; **2**, to keep possession of; defend; as, the defenders *held* the fortress; **3**, to contain; as, this bottle *holds* a quart; **4**, to restrain or check; as, *hold* your tongue; to delay or detain; as, to *hold* a train; **5**, to believe or accept; as, to *hold* an opinion; to think; consider; as, the court *held* that the defendant was guilty; **6**, to keep in a particular state; as, to *hold* one's head erect; to *hold* someone in esteem; **7**, to maintain or carry on; as, to *hold* an argument; **8**, to conduct; as, the club *held* a meeting; also, to preside at; as, the judge *holds* court; **9**, to keep or observe (a festival); **10**, to occupy; have title to; as, to *hold* political office:—*v.i.* **1**, to keep a grasp on something; as, the anchor *holds;* **2**, to remain faithful; as, to *hold* to a purpose; **3**, to remain unbroken or unchanged; as, our ranks *held;* my offer still *holds* good; **4**, to keep going; as, to *hold* to one's course:—*n.* **1**, the act of holding; grasp; **2**, something that may be grasped for support; **3**, influence or control; as, the supernatural has a strong *hold* on him; **4**, in music, a character placed over [⌢] or under [⌣] a note or rest to show that it is to be prolonged; a pause.

   hold forth, to talk or preach; **hold one's peace**, to be still; **hold out**, to endure; last; **hold over**, to postpone; **hold up, 1**, to interrupt; **2**, to rob; **hold with**, to agree with; approve of.

hold-back (hōld′băk′), *n.* **1**, a check or hindrance; **2**, a strap used in holding back, or in backing, a carriage (see illustration under *harness*).

hold-er (hōl′dẽr), *n.* **1**, one who holds something; **2**, that which holds or can be used for holding; a handle; also, a device which holds something in position.

hold-ing (hōl′dĭng), *n.* **1**, property of any kind, as bonds, stocks, etc.; **2**, a farm or other estate rented from another.

hold—up (hōld′-up′), *n.* **1**, stoppage or delay; **2**, *Colloquial*, an armed robbery.

hole (hōl), *n.* **1**, an opening in or through something; as, a *hole* in the roof; **2**, a cavity in something solid; as, a *hole* in a tooth; **3**, an abrupt hollow in the ground, as a pit or a cave; also, a deep place in a stream; as, a swimming *hole;* **4**, the burrow of an animal; hence, a den, or hiding place; **5**, *Colloquial*, a difficulty; **6**, in golf: **a**, a cup, or hollow, in the putting green into which the ball is to be played; **b**, the part of a course from a tee to such a cup:—*v.t.* [holed, hol·ing], **1**, to drive or put into a hole; **2**, to make holes in; as, to *hole* a board for pegs:—*v.i.* **1**, to go into a hole; **2**, to make a hole; as, to *hole* through a wall; **3**, in golf, to put a ball in the hole.

hol·i·day (hŏl′ĭ-dā), *n.* **1**, a day of gaiety and joy, as in celebration of some event; **2**, a day of freedom from labor:—*adj.* festive; gay; as, in *holiday* dress.

ho·li·ness (hō′lĭ-nĕs), *n.* the state or quality of being free from sin; saintliness:—**His Holiness**, a title of the Pope.
   Syn. righteousness.

hol·land (hŏl′ănd), *n.* a linen or cotton cloth used for window shades, covers, etc.

HOLLY

Hol·land (hŏl′ănd), a kingdom in north-western Europe. See **Netherlands**.—*n.* **Hol′land·er.**

hol·lo (hŏl′ō; hŏ-lō′), *interj.* What ho! Stop! Also, **hal·io′; hal·loa′.**

hol·low (hŏl′ō), *n.* **1**, a cavity; as, the *hollow* of a tree; **2**, space between hills; a valley:—*v.t.* to scoop out; as, he *hollowed* out the sand:—*adj.* **1**, having an empty space within; as, a *hollow* shell; **2**, sunken; haggard; as, a *hollow* face; **3**, unreal; insincere; as, *hollow* words of sympathy; **4**, deep or dull; as, a *hollow* roar:—*adv.* *Colloquial*, completely; as, they beat us all *hollow.*—*adv.* **hol′low-ly.** —*n.* **hol′low-ness.**

hol·ly (hŏl′ĭ), *n.* [*pl.* hollies], a shrub or tree, the glossy leaves and red berries of which are much used as decorations at Christmas time. (See illustration above.)

hol·ly-hock (hŏl′ĭ-hŏk), *n.* a tall plant, much cultivated in gardens, that has large flowers of various colors.

HOLLYHOCK

Hol·ly·wood (hŏl′ĭ-wŏŏd), a part of the city of Los Angeles, California, famous as a center of the motion-picture industry.

holm (hōm), *n.* 1, an evergreen oak with tough, hard wood and glossy leaves, found in southern Europe: also called *holm oak;* 2, the wood of this tree.

Holmes (hōmz), 1, Oliver Wendell (1809–1894), an American physician and author; 2, Oliver Wendell (1841–1935), his son, an American jurist.

hol·o·caust (hŏl′ō-kôst), *n.* 1, a sacrifice wholly consumed by fire; 2, complete or total destruction by, or as by, fire.

Hol·stein–Frie·sian (hōl′stīn-frē′zhǎn), *n.* one of a breed of large black-and-white dairy cattle.

hol·ster (hōl′stẽr), *n.* a leather pistol case, carried at the belt or fixed to a saddle.

ho·ly (hō′lĭ), *adj.* [ho-li-er, ho-li-est], 1, dedicated to the service of God; as, *holy* ground; 2, perfect; divine; as, the *Holy* Spirit; 3, devoted to God; given over to piety; as, the *holy* saints: —*n.* [*pl.* holies], a sacred thing.

HOLSTER

Ho·ly Cit·y, Jerusalem or, sometimes, Rome; any city which is the center of religious worship and traditions; **Holy Communion,** the sacrament of the Lord's Supper; **Holy Ghost,** the third person of the Trinity; **Holy Grail,** the cup used by Jesus at the Last Supper; **holy of holies,** the innermost shrine of the Jewish tabernacle which held the sacred relics; **Holy Land,** Palestine; **Holy See,** the seat of the papacy; the authority of the Pope; **Holy Spirit,** the Holy Ghost; **Holy Week,** the week before Easter; **Holy Writ,** the Bible.

ho·ly·day (hō′lĭ-dā′), *n.* a day set aside as a religious feast day. Also written **ho′ly day.**

Ho·ly Ro·man Em·pire, a group or alliance of certain independent states in Europe, under an elected emperor, which originated with Charlemagne in 800, and continued with changes until ended by Napoleon in 1806.

ho·ly·stone (hō′lĭ-stōn′), *n.* a soft sandstone used for scouring a ship's decks:— *v.t.* [holystoned, holyston-ing], to scrub with holystone.

hom·age (hŏm′ĭj; ŏm′ĭj), *n.* 1, reverence; respect; 2, in feudal times, the ceremony in which a vassal promised loyalty and service to his lord in return for protection. *Syn.* allegiance, loyalty.

home (hōm), *n.* 1, one's fixed residence or dwelling place; hence, the unit of society formed by a family living together; 2, one's native land; 3, an institution or asylum for the care or relief of some class of persons; as, an orphans' *home;* 4, in various games, a goal:—*adv.* 1, to or at home; 2, to the heart or core; as, the blow struck *home:*—*v.i.* [homed, hom-ing], to return home, as pigeons; also, to have a home; dwell.—*adj.* **home′less.**

home base, in baseball, the base where the batter stands to bat: also called *home plate.*

home·like (hōm′līk′), *adj.* like home; comfortable; cheerful; cozy.

home·ly (hōm′lĭ), *adj.* [home-li-er, home-li-est], 1, homelike; plain; simple; as, *homely* fare; 2, plain-featured; 3, unpolished; unpretending; as, *homely* manners.

home·made (hōm′mād′), *adj.* made in the home; as, *homemade* bread.

ho·me·o·path (hō′mē-ō-pǎth; hŏm′ē-ō-pǎth), *n.* a homeopathic physician: opposite of *allopath.*—*n.* **ho′me·op′a·thist.**

ho·me·o·path·ic (hō′mē-ō-pǎth′ĭk; hŏm′-ē-ō-pǎth′ĭk), *adj.* naming or employing a method of treating disease in which medicines are given which produce in healthy persons effects similar to those of the complaint under treatment.

ho·me·op·a·thy (hō′mē-ŏp′ȧ-thĭ; hŏm′ē-ŏp′ȧ-thĭ), *n.* the method of treating disease employed by homeopathic physicians.

home plate, in baseball, the base at which the batter stands to bat: also called *home base.*

Ho·mer (hō′mẽr), (ninth century B.C.), a Greek epic poet, the traditional author of the "Iliad" and the "Odyssey."

ho·mer (hō′mẽr), *n.* in baseball, a home run.

Ho·mer·ic (hō-mẽr′ĭk), *adj.* pertaining to the Greek epic poet Homer.

home run, in baseball, a hit which allows the batter to encircle all the bases and score a run. Also called *homer.*

home·sick (hōm′sĭk′), *adj.* pining or yearning for home.—*n.* **home′sick′ness.**

home·spun (hōm′spŭn′), *n.* 1, cloth made of yarn spun at home; 2, a loosely woven, coarse, woolen fabric:—*adj.* 1, made at home; 2, plain and homely.

home·stead (hōm′stĕd), *n.* a family home with the adjoining lands and buildings.

home·ward (hōm′wẽrd), *adj.* and *adv.* toward home or one's native land; as, *homeward* bound.—*adv.* **home′wards.**

hom·i·cide (hŏm′ĭ-sīd), *n.* 1, the killing of a human being by another; 2, one who kills another.—*adj.* **hom′i·cid′al.**

hom·i·ly (hŏm′ĭ-lĭ), *n.* [*pl.* homilies], 1, a religious discourse; a sermon; 2, a tiresome moral talk delivered in private.

hom·ing pi·geon (hō′mĭng), a pigeon

trained to find its way home and carry messages from great distances.

hom·i·ny (hŏm′ĭ-nĭ), *n.* hulled Indian corn, coarsely ground or broken, used as a cereal and as a vegetable.

ho·mo·ge·ne·ous (hō′mō-jē′nē-ŭs; hŏm′-ō-jē′nē-ŭs), *adj.* uniform; of the same kind or nature; made up of like parts: opposite of *heterogeneous;* as, a *homogeneous* group.

ho·mo·gen·ize (hō′mō-jĕn-īz; hō·mŏj′ĕn-īz), *v.t.* [homogenized, homogeniz·ing], to break up the fat globules of (milk), as by forcing through very fine nozzles, to make a finer emulsion and increase digestibility.

hom·o·graph (hŏm′ō-gräf; hō′mō-gräf), *n.* one of two or more words spelled alike but different in meaning; as, *bear,* the animal, and *bear,* to carry, are *homographs.*

hom·o·nym (hŏm′ō-nĭm; hō′mō-nĭm), *n.* any of two or more words of the same sound, but different in meaning and often in spelling; as, *pair, pare,* and *pear* are *homonyms.*

hom·o·phone (hŏm′ō-fōn; hō′mō-fōn), *n.* 1, a letter or character representing the same sound as another, as *g* in *gem* and *j* in *jam;* 2, a homonym.

Hon. abbreviation for *Honorable.*

Hon·du·ras (hŏn-dōō′räs), a republic (cap. Tegucigalpa), in the northern part of Central America (map 10).

hone (hōn), *n.* a fine-grained stone for sharpening edged tools, as razors:—*v.t.* [honed, hon·ing], to sharpen on such a stone.

hon·est (ŏn′ĕst), *adj.* 1, upright; just; as, an *honest* man; truthful; sincere; as, an *honest* opinion; 2, genuine; without fraud; as, *honest* weight; 3, frank; expressing sincerity; as, an *honest* countenance.—*adv.* **hon′est·ly.**

hon·es·ty (ŏn′ĕs-tĭ), *n.* freedom from deceit; truthfulness; uprightness.
  Syn. integrity, probity, sincerity.

hon·ey (hŭn′ĭ), *n.* 1, a sweet, sticky substance, produced by bees from the nectar which they collect from flowers; 2, sweetness; 3, darling; sweet one.

hon·ey·bee (hŭn′ĭ-bē), *n.* a bee which gathers nectar from flowers to make honey. Man keeps honeybees in hives for the sake of their wax and honey.

hon·ey·comb (hŭn′ĭ-kōm), *n.* 1, a wax structure of six-sided cells made by bees to hold their honey and their eggs; 2, any similar structure:—*v.t.* and *v.i.* to fill, or become filled, with holes, passages, or cells; as, miners had *honeycombed* the ground beneath the town.

HONEYCOMB

hon·ey·dew (hŭn′ĭ-dū′), *n.* a sweet sticky substance found on the stems and leaves of certain trees and plants in hot weather, thought either to be given out by the plant itself or by certain small insects which feed on the plant.

hon·ey·dew mel·on, a smooth-skinned white melon with sweet, light-green flesh. (See illustration under *melon.*)

hon·eyed (hŭn′ĭd), *adj.* 1, covered or filled with honey; 2, sweet; coaxing; as, *honeyed* words.

hon·ey lo·cust, a large, thorny American tree bearing long, flat pods.

hon·ey·moon (hŭn′ĭ-mōōn′), *n.* a holiday spent together by a newly married couple; a wedding trip:—*v.i.* to spend a honeymoon.

hon·ey·suck·le (hŭn′ĭ-sŭk′l), *n.* a climbing plant with fragrant white, red, or yellow tube-shaped flowers.

Hong Kong (hŏng′kŏng′), a British colony (cap. Victoria) in southeastern China, on the Pacific coast (map 15).

honk (hŏngk), *n.* 1, the call of a wild goose; 2, any sound resembling this; as, the *honk* of an automobile horn:—*v.i.* to make such a sound:—*v.t.* to sound or blow (a horn).

HONEYSUCKLE

Ho·no·lu·lu (hō′nō-lōō′lōō; hŏn′ō-lōō′-lōō), a city, capital of the State of Hawaii, on the island Oahu (map 16).

hon·or (ŏn′ẽr), *n.* 1, respectful regard; high esteem; as, to show *honor* to one's parents; an outward mark of high esteem; as, military *honors;* 2, glory; fame; as, Hector fought for the *honor* of Troy; 3, distinction; as, the *honor* of being president; also, a cause of glory; a credit; as, he is an *honor* to the town; 4, uprightness; integrity; as, a man of *honor;* 5, **honors,** distinguished standing in school or college; as, he was graduated with *honors:*—**Honor,** a title of respect; as, his *Honor,* the mayor:—*v.t.* 1, to treat with respect or deference; revere; as, "*Honor* thy father and thy mother"; 2, to bestow marks of esteem upon; as, he was *honored* with the title of captain; 3, to accept and pay when due; as, the bank will *honor* my check.
  Syn. respect, reverence, renown.

hon·or·a·ble (ŏn′ẽr·à-bl), *adj.* 1, noble; illustrious; as, *honorable* deeds; 2, upright; honest; as, an *honorable* man; an *honorable* purpose; 3, in accord with honor; as, an *honorable* discharge; 4, accompanied with

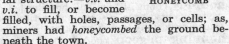

honor or marks of respect; as, *honorable* burial:—**Honorable,** a title of distinction of certain officials.—*adv.* **hon′or-a-bly.** *Syn.* creditable, just.

hon-o-rar-i-um (ŏn′ō-râr′ĭ-ŭm), *n.* [*pl.* honoraria (ŏn′ō-râr′ĭ-à) or honorariums], an honorary fee paid to a professional man as a courtesy, in recognition of a service on which custom forbids a price to be set.

hon-or-ar-y (ŏn′ẽr-ẽr′ĭ), *adj.* **1,** given as a sign of high esteem; as, an *honorary* degree; **2,** possessing a title or position by courtesy, without giving service or receiving pay; as, an *honorary* vice-president.

hon-our (ŏn′ẽr), a British spelling of *honor*. Similarly, **honourable, honourably.**

Hon-shu (hŏn′shōō), the largest island of the empire of Japan, on which the capital, Tokyo, is located (map **15**).

hood (hŏŏd), *n.* **1,** a soft wrapper or covering for the head, sometimes attached to a cloak; **2,** something resembling such a head covering in shape or use, as a folding cover for a carriage, automobile engine, etc.; **3,** an ornamental fold hanging down the back of a gown worn by a graduate of a college or university, denoting, by its color, the wearer's degree:—*v.t.* to cover, or furnish with, or as with, a hood.—*adj.* **hood′ed.**

HOOD (a), def. 3

-hood (-hŏŏd), a suffix meaning: **1,** state, quality, or character; as, child*hood*, likeli*hood*, mother*hood*; **2,** a group; as, brother*hood*, priest*hood*; **3,** an instance or example; as, false*hood*.

hood-lum (hŏŏd′lŭm), *n. Colloquial,* a rowdy; street tough; ruffian.

hoo-doo (hōō′dōō), *n. Colloquial,* a person or thing that causes ill luck:—*v.t. Colloquial,* to bring ill luck upon.

hood-wink (hŏŏd′wĭngk), *v.t.* **1,** to deceive; mislead; **2,** to blindfold.

hoof (hŏŏf), *n.* [*pl.* hoofs (hŏŏfs) or, rarely, hooves (hŏŏvz)], the horny substance covering the toes of some animals, as horses; also, the whole foot.—*adj.* **hoofed.**

hook (hŏŏk), *n.* **1,** a curved piece of metal, bone, or the like, to hold or catch something; as, a crochet *hook;* a fish*hook;* **2,** a curved instrument, as a sickle, for lopping or cutting; **3,** a sharp bend or curve, as in a river:—**by hook or by crook,** by fair means or foul:—*v.t.* to catch with, or as with, a hook; as, to *hook* a fish; hence, to steal; also, to fasten with a hook or hooks; as, *hook* the gate:—*v.i.* **1,** to bend or curve sharply; as, this road

hooks to the left; **2,** to be fastened by a hook; as, this skirt *hooks* on the side.

hook-ah or **hook-a** (hŏŏk′à), *n.* a pipe with a long tube for drawing tobacco smoke through water to cool the smoke.

hooked (hŏŏkt; hŏŏk′ĕd), *adj.* **1,** curved like a hook; as, a *hooked* nose; **2,** made with a hook; as, a *hooked* rug; **3,** furnished with hooks; as, a *hooked* dress; **4,** *Slang,* trapped.

hook-up (hŏŏk′ŭp′), *n.* the connecting with wires, as of apparatus for radio reception or transmission:—**nationwide hookup,** a network of radio stations connected so that they can all transmit the same program.

hook-worm (hŏŏk′wûrm′), *n.* a worm, most common in warm climates, that sometimes enters the intestines of man and certain animals, as through infected drinking water or food, and causes a disease marked by progressive weakness and emaciation.

HOOPS (H, H, H) def. 1

hoop (hōōp), *n.* **1,** a circular metal or wooden band to hold together the narrow, curving strips forming the sides of a cask, tub, or the like; **2,** a large circle of metal or wood rolled along the ground by children; **3,** **hoops,** a circular framework of wire, whalebone, or the like, formerly used to expand a woman's skirt; a hoop skirt; **4,** in croquet, a metal arch or wicket:—*v.t.* to bind with a hoop; encircle.

hoop skirt, a skirt expanded by means of a circular framework of wire, whalebone, or the like.

HOOP SKIRT OF 1860

hoot (hōōt), *n.* **1,** the cry of an owl; as, a long *hoot* sounded through the woods; **2,** a sound like this cry; **3,** a shout of contempt:—*v.t.* to jeer with contemptuous shouts; as, to *hoot* an actor:—*v.i.* **1,** to utter a sharp cry, as an owl; **2,** to utter shouts of derision or contempt; as, the audience *hooted* and jeered at the speaker.

Hoo-ver (hōō′vẽr), Herbert Clark (1874–), the 31st president of the U.S.

HOP
Leaves and fruit.

¹hop (hŏp), *n.* **1,** a vine with small greenish,

cone-shaped flowers; **2, hops,** the dried, ripened cones of this plant, used to give a bitter flavor to beer, ale, etc.:—*v.t.* [hopped, hop-ping], to flavor with hops:—*v.i.* to pick hops.

²**hop** (hŏp), *v.t.* [hopped, hop-ping], to jump over; as, to *hop* a fence:—*v.i.* **1,** to move by short jumps, using one leg only; **2,** to jump with both or all feet at once, as do frogs:—*n.* **1,** a short, brisk jump, especially on one leg; **2,** *Colloquial,* an informal dance.

hope (hōp), *n.* **1,** desire accompanied by expectation; anticipation; confidence; as, an invalid's *hope* of speedy recovery; **2,** the thing desired; as, success in business was his constant *hope;* **3,** a cause or source of hope; as, he was the *hope* of his parents: —*v.t.* [hoped, hop-ing], to desire; expect; as, he *hopes* his efforts will be successful: —*v.i.* to cherish a desire; as, we *hope* for better times.

Syn., n. promise, reliance.

hope-ful (hōp′fŏol), *adj.* **1,** full of confident expectation; as, he is *hopeful* that he will be able to go; **2,** promising success; as, *hopeful* news.—*adv.* **hope′ful-ly.** —*n.* **hope′ful-ness.**

Syn. assured, confident, optimistic.

hope-less (hōp′lĕs), *adj.* **1,** without expectation of good; despairing; as, *hopeless* grief; **2,** without promise of good; as, a *hopeless* situation.—*adv.* **hope′less-ly.**—*n.* **hope′less-ness.**

Syn. despondent, forlorn, cheerless.

hop-per (hŏp′ẽr), *n.* **1,** one who or that which hops; **2,** any of various leaping insects; as, the grass*hopper;* **3,** a wooden funnel through which grain passes into a mill, or any device like this.

hop-scotch (hŏp′skŏch′), *n.* a child's game, in which the players hop or skip from one space to another of a design on the ground.

Hor-ace (hŏr′ĭs), Quintus Flaccus (65–8 B.C.), a Latin poet.

Ho-ra-tius Co-cles (hō-rā′shŭs kō′klēz; hō-rā′shĭ-ŭs),*n.* in Roman legend, a famous hero who, with two comrades, guarded the bridge over the Tiber and thus saved Rome.

horde (hôrd), *n.* **1,** a wandering tribe or clan; as, a gypsy *horde;* **2,** a vast multitude, as of insects.

hore-hound (hôr′hound′), *n.* **1,** a bitter herb, with small white flowers and hairy leaves; **2,** a flavoring extract made from this plant; also, candy flavored with this extract and used for coughs and colds. Also, **hoar′hound′.**

HOP-
SCOTCH

ho-ri-zon (hō-rī′zn), *n.* **1,** the line where the sky and earth, or the sky and sea, appear to meet; **2,** the range or limit of one's mental experience or interest.

hor-i-zon-tal (hŏr′ĭ-zŏn′tăl), *adj.* parallel to, or in the direction of, the line where earth meets sky; level: opposite of *vertical.*—*adv.* **hor′i-zon′tal-ly.**

horn (hôrn), *n.* **1,** a hard, usually pointed, outgrowth on the head of certain animals, especially cattle, goats, deer, etc.; **2,** the material of which animals' horns are composed, or a similar material; **3,** anything made of or resembling the horns of an animal, as one of the ends of the moon when in crescent form; **4,** a musical wind instrument:—**horn of plenty, 1,** in mythology, a magic horn which became filled with whatever its possessor wished; **2,** hence, a horn used as a symbol of abundance; a cornucopia.

Horn, Cape, a point of land at the southern tip of South America on Horn Island in the Tierra del Fuego Archipelago (map 11).

horned toad (hôrnd tōd), a small, harmless, insect-eating lizard with scales and hornlike growths on the skin.

hor-net (hôr′nĕt), *n.* a large wasp which inflicts a severe sting.

horn-pipe (hôrn′pīp′), *n.* **1,** a lively dance, especially popular with sailors; **2,** music for this dance; **3,** a musical wind instrument, once much used in Wales.

HORNET (⅓)

horn-y (hôr′nĭ), *adj.* [horn-i-er, horn-i-est], **1,** hard like horn; **2,** made of horn; **3,** having horns.

hor-o-scope (hŏr′ō-skōp), *n.* **1,** the position of the stars at any moment, as at a person's birth; **2,** a diagram, representing the twelve divisions of the heavens, used by astrologers in foretelling future events, as of a person's life.

hor-ri-ble (hŏr′ĭ-bl), *adj.* **1,** terrible; dreadful; as, a *horrible* train wreck; **2,** *Colloquial,* severe; extreme; as, a *horrible* headache. —*adv.* **hor′ri-bly.**

Syn. awful, terrific, frightful.

hor-rid (hŏr′ĭd), *adj.* terrible; hideous; as, a *horrid* monster.

hor-ri-fy (hŏr′ĭ-fī), *v.t.* [horrified, horrifying], to fill or strike with great fear or dread.

hor-ror (hŏr′ẽr), *n.* **1,** excessive fear; extreme dread; as, they were filled with *horror* at the thought of war; **2,** great disgust or aversion; as, she has a *horror* of dirt; **3,** that which causes dread.

Syn. fright, alarm, panic.

āte, āorta, râre, căt, àsk, fär, ăllow, sofá; ēve, êvent, ĕll, writẽr, novĕl; bīte, pĭn; nō, ōbey, ôr, dŏg, tŏp, cŏllide; ūnit, únite, bûrn, cŭt, focŭs; nōon, fŏot; mound; coin;

horse (hôrs), *n.* **1,** a large, solid-hoofed, four-footed animal, used for drawing burdens or riding; **2,** mounted soldiers; cavalry; **3,** a framework for the support of anything; as, a clothes*horse;* **4,** in gymnastics, a padded and raised wooden block

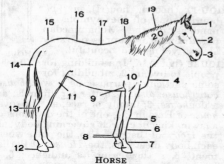

HORSE

The parts of a horse; 1, forelock; 2, face; 3, muzzle; 4, chest; 5, knee; 6, shank; 7, pastern; 8, fetlock; 9, elbow; 10, shoulder; 11, stifle; 12, hoof; 13, hock; 14, tail; 15, croup; 16, loins; 17, back; 18, withers; 19, crest; 20, mane.

used for vaulting:—**dark horse, 1,** in horse racing, a horse whose chances of success have been overlooked; especially, an unexpected winner; **2,** in politics, an unforeseen competitor:—*v.t.* [horsed, hors-ing], to mount on, or furnish with, a horse.

horse-back (hôrs/băk/), *n.* the back of a horse:—*adv.* on horseback.

horse chest-nut, a tree with large clusters of white or pink blossoms and brown, nutlike seeds growing in burs; also, the seed of this tree.

horse-fly (hôrs/-flī/), *n.* [*pl.* horse-flies], a large, two-winged fly that stings animals.

horse-hair (hôrs/-hâr/), *n.* **1,** the hair of the mane or tail of a horse; **2,** cloth made from this hair; haircloth.

HORSE CHESTNUT
Leaf, bur, and nut.

horse-hide (hôrs/hīd/), *n.* the skin of a horse, or the leather made from it.

horse-man (hôrs/măn/), *n.* [*pl.* horsemen (-měn)], **1,** a rider on horseback; **2,** a person who is clever at managing horses.—*n.fem.* **horse/wom/an.**—*n.* **horse/man-ship.**

horse pis-tol, a large pistol formerly carried by riders on horseback.

horse-play (hôrs/plā/), *n.* rough fun.

horse-pow-er (hôrs/pou/ẽr), *n.* a unit of power; the amount of power required to raise 33,000 pounds one foot in one minute.

horse—rad-ish (hôrs/-răd/ĭsh), *n.* **1,** a plant of the mustard family, the root of which is ground and used as a relish with meats, fish, etc.; **2,** the relish made from this root.

horse-shoe (hôrs/shoo/), *n.* **1,** a U-shaped metal shoe to protect the hoof of a horse; **2,** anything shaped like a horseshoe.

horseshoe crab, a crablike animal with a shell shaped like a horseshoe.

horse-sho-er (hôrs/shoo/ẽr), *n.* one whose business it is to shoe horses, or to make horseshoes.

HORSE-
SHOE
def. 1

horse-whip (hôrs/hwĭp/), *n.* a leather whip for managing horses:—*v.t.* [horsewhipped, horsewhip-ping], to flog.

hors-y (hôr/sĭ), *adj.* [hors-i-er, hors-i-est], pertaining to, or characteristic of, horses, horsemen, or horse racing.

hor-ti-cul-ture (hôr/tĭ-kŭl/tûr), *n.* the art or science of growing vegetables, fruits, and flowers.—*adj.* **hor/ti-cul/tur-al.**—*n.* **hor/ti-cul/tur-ist.**

ho-san-na (hō-zăn/ȧ), *n.* and *interj.* an exclamation of praise to God.

hose (hōz), *n.* [*pl.* hose], **1,** a covering for the leg; a stocking; **2,** a tight-fitting covering for the legs and waist, formerly worn by men; **3,** [*pl.* sometimes hoses], flexible tubing for carrying liquids; as, a *hose* for sprinkling the lawn:—*v.t.* [hosed, hos-ing], to water or drench with a hose.

Ho-se-a (hō-zē/ȧ; hō-zā/ȧ), in the Bible, a Hebrew prophet; also, a book of the Old Testament containing his prophecies.

ho-sier-y (hō/zhẽr-ĭ), *n.* stockings.

hos-pice (hŏs/pĭs), *n.* a place of shelter for travelers, especially one kept by a religious order.

hos-pi-ta-ble (hŏs/pĭ-tȧ-bl), *adj.* disposed to welcome guests with generosity and kindness; as, a *hospitable* hostess.—*adv.* **hos/pi-ta-bly.**

hos-pi-tal (hŏs/pĭ-tăl), *n.* a place for treatment and care of the sick and injured.

hos-pi-tal-i-ty (hŏs/pĭ-tăl/ĭ-tĭ), *n.* [*pl.* hospitalities], the entertaining of guests with kindness and liberality.

[1]**host** (hōst), *n.* a large army; a great number; a throng.

[2]**host** (hōst), *n.* **1,** one who entertains others; also, one who provides food and lodging for pay, as the landlord of an inn;

2, an animal or a plant organism that gives nourishment to a parasite.

Host (hōst), *n.* the consecrated bread or wafer of the Mass.

hos-tage (hŏs′tĭj), *n.* 1, a person who remains in the hands of another as a guarantee that certain conditions will be fulfilled; as, prisoners of war are sometimes held as *hostages;* 2, any pledge or guarantee.

hos-tel (hŏs′tĕl), *n.* an inn or hotel.

hos-tel-ry (hŏs′tĕl-rĭ), *n.* [*pl.* hostelries], *Archaic,* an inn or lodging house.

host-ess (hōs′tĕs), *n.* 1, a woman who receives and entertains guests; 2, the mistress of an inn; also, an attendant in a restaurant who welcomes guests, conducts them to a table, etc.

hos-tile (hŏs′tĭl; hŏs′tīl), *adj.* 1, belonging to an enemy; as, a *hostile* fleet; 2, unfriendly; as, *hostile* criticism.

hos-til-i-ty (hŏs-tĭl′ĭ-tĭ), *n.* [*pl.* hostilities], 1, unfriendliness; enmity; 2, **hostilities,** acts of warfare.
Syn. bitterness, animosity.

hos-tler (hŏs′lĕr; ŏs′lĕr), *n.* one who takes care of horses; a groom. Also spelled **ost′ler.**

hot (hŏt), *adj.* [hot-ter, hot-test], 1, of high temperature: opposite of *cold;* as, a *hot* stove; *hot* soup; 2, fiery; passionate; as, a *hot* temper; 3, having a sharp or biting taste, as spices; 4, fresh; strong; as, a *hot* scent.—*adv.* **hot′ly.**—*n.* **hot′ness.**

hot-bed (hŏt′bĕd′), *n.* 1, a bed of earth covered with glass and artificially warmed to force the growth of plants; 2, hence, any place or condition that promotes growth or activity; as, a *hotbed* of treason.

ho-tel (hō-tĕl′), *n.* an establishment where food and lodging are provided for pay.

hot-head (hŏt′hĕd′), *n.* a rash, fiery-tempered person.—*adj.* **hot′head′ed.**

hot-house (hŏt′hous′), *n.* a glass-roofed house, heated for growing or forcing flowers or vegetables.

Hot-ten-tot (hŏt′n-tŏt), *n.* one of a savage South African race; also, the language of this people.

hound (hound), *n.* any of several breeds of hunting dog, with large, drooping ears and very keen scent:—*v.t.* 1, to chase with hounds; 2, to pursue; nag; as, his debtors *hounded* him.

hour (our), *n.* 1, the 24th part of a day; 60 minutes; 2, the time of day; as, clocks tell the *hours;* 3, a particular or stated time; as, school *hours;* 4, a unit of distance reckoned by the time taken to travel it; as, three *hours* distant.—*adj.* and *adv.* **hour′ly.**

hour-glass (our′glȧs′), *n.* a device consisting of two glass bulbs, one above the other, connected by a narrow neck, used for measuring time. It takes an hour for the sand, mercury, or water with which the uppermost bulb is filled to pass through the narrow neck to the lower bulb.

hou-ri (hōō′rĭ; hou′rĭ), *n.* [*pl.* houris], one of the nymphs or maidens of the Mohammedan paradise who are supposed to stay always young and beautiful.

HOUR-
GLASS

house (hous), *n.* 1, a building for people to live in; 2, a building for some particular purpose; as, a work*house;* court*house;* also, a shelter for animals; as, a dog*house;* 3, family or race; as, the royal *house* of England; 4, one of the divisions of a lawmaking or church-governing body; as, the *House* of Bishops; also, the place where each body meets; as, the *Houses* of Parliament; 5, a theater or its audience; 6, a business firm or place of business:—*v.t.* (houz), [housed, hous-ing], 1, to shelter or lodge; 2, to store (goods); 3, to secure; put into a safe place; as, to *house* a yacht:—*v.i.* to take shelter.

House of Commons, the lower house of the British Parliament, consisting of elected representatives of the counties, boroughs, universities, etc.; **House of Lords,** the upper house of the British Parliament, consisting of archbishops, bishops, and lords; **House of Representatives,** the lower and larger branch of the United States Congress, consisting of a number of representatives from each state, the number being decided by the population of the state: often called *the House.*

house-boat (hous′bōt′), *n.* a boat fitted up and used as a residence.

house-break-er (hous′brāk′ĕr), *n.* one who breaks open and enters the dwelling of another for some unlawful purpose.—*n.* **house′break′ing.**

house-fly (hous′flī′), *n.* [*pl.* houseflies], the common domestic fly.

house-hold (hous′hōld; hous′ōld), *n.* a group of persons living together; a family:—*adj.* pertaining to a family or home; domestic; as, *household* duties.

house-hold-er (hous′hōl′dĕr), *n.* the head of a family or household.

house-keep-ing (hous′kēp′ĭng), *n.* the management of domestic affairs:—*adj.* pertaining to the management of a household; domestic.—*n.* **house′keep′er.**

house-maid (hous′mād′), *n.* a girl hired to do housework; a female servant.

house-warm-ing (hous′wôr′mĭng), *n.* a party celebrating a family's moving into a new home.

āte, ȧorta, râre, căt, ȧsk, fär, ăllow, sofȧ; ēve, ĕvent, ĕll, writẽr, novĕl; bīte, pĭn; nō, ōbey, ôr, dŏg, tŏp, cŏllide; ūnit, ūnite, bûrn, cŭt, focŭs; nōōn, fŏŏt; mound; coin;

house-wife (hous'wīf'), *n.* **1,** [*pl.* house-wives (-wīvz')], the mistress of a home; one who manages domestic affairs; **2,** (hŭz'ĭf; *pl.* hŭz'ĭvz), a small case for sewing materials.

house-work (hous'wûrk'), *n.* the work of housekeeping, as cooking, cleaning, etc.

¹**hous-ing** (hou'zĭng), *n.* **1,** the act of giving shelter; **2,** that which gives shelter; **3,** hence, provision of homes for people; as, *housing* is a problem of a large city.

²**hous-ing** (hou'zĭng), *n.* **1,** a cover; especially, a cloth under a saddle; **2,** **housings,** the decorative trappings on a horse.

Hous-ton (hūs'tŭn), a city in the eastern part of Texas (map 8).

hove (hōv), one form of the past tense and past participle of *heave*.

hov-el (hŏv'ĕl; hŭv'ĕl), *n.* a wretched little cottage; a hut.

hov-er (hŭv'ēr; hŏv'ēr), *v.i.* **1,** to flutter over or about; as, pigeons *hovered* over the square; **2,** to wait near at hand; move to and fro near a place; as, the fleet *hovers* in the bay; **3,** to waver; hesitate.

how (hou), *adv.* **1,** in what manner or way; as, *how* did you do it? **2,** to what degree or extent; as, *how* far did you go? **3,** at what price; as, *how* much did you pay for it? **4,** in what condition; as, *how* are you? **5,** with what reason or meaning; as, *how* is it that you are late?

how-be-it (hou-bē'ĭt), *conj. Archaic,* nevertheless; be this as it may.

how-dah (hou'dȧ), *n.* a seat, usually canopied and often deco-rated, for riding on an ele-phant.

how-ev-er (hou-ĕv'ēr), *adv.* in whatever manner or de-gree; as, every contribution, *however* small, is a help to the cause:—*conj.* nevertheless; as, I cannot, *however*, agree.

HOWDAH

how-itz-er (hou'ĭt-sēr), *n.* a short, light cannon that throws shells higher than an ordinary cannon does.

howl (houl), *n.* **1,** the long, wailing cry of a dog or a wolf; **2,** a cry of pain or dis-tress; **3,** a loud shout of ridicule; as, *howls* and jeers from the audience:—*v.i.* **1,** to utter a loud, wailing cry, like a dog or wolf; **2,** to utter a prolonged cry of pain or distress; lament; **3,** to roar like the wind: —*v.t.* to utter in a wailing tone.

how-so-ev-er (hou'sō-ĕv'ēr), *adv.* in what-ever manner or degree; however.

hoy-den (hoi'dn), *n.* a rude, boisterous girl; a tomboy.

h.p. abbreviation for *horsepower*.

hr. or **h.** [*pl.* hrs.], abbreviation for *hour*.

H.R. abbreviation for *Home Rule, House of Representatives.*

H.R.H. abbreviation for *His* or *Her Royal Highness.*

Hsin-king (shĭn'jĭng'), the Japanese name for a city in northeastern China, the former capital of Manchukuo (Manchuria). See **Changchun.**

H.T. abbreviation for *Hawaiian Territory.*

hub (hŭb), *n.* **1,** the central part of a wheel; **2,** anything that resembles the center of a wheel in position or importance.

hub-bub (hŭb'ŭb), *n.* uproar; tumult; as, the class was in a *hubbub* when the teacher re-turned.

huck-a-back (hŭk'ȧ-băk), *n.* a coarse, rough linen or cotton cloth, used for toweling: also called *huck.*

HUB (H) OF A WHEEL

huck-le-ber-ry (hŭk'-l-bĕr'ĭ), *n.* [*pl.* huckle-berries], the blue-black, berrylike, edible fruit of a low-growing shrub; also, the shrub.

huck-ster (hŭk'stēr), *n.* **1,** a peddler or hawker; especially, one who deals in fruit and vegetables; **2,** a mean, tricky fellow.

hud-dle (hŭd'l), *v.t.* and *v.i.* [hud-dled, hud-dling], to crowd or press together in disorder:—*n.* **1,** confusion; crowd; **2,** in foot-ball, the gathering together of the players of a team for the giving of signals, etc.

Hud-son (hŭd'sn), Henry (1576?–1611), an English navigator and explorer.

Hud-son Bay, a large bay in northeastern Canada (map 4).

Hud-son Riv-er, a river in New York, rising in the Adirondack Mountains and flowing into New York Bay (map 6).

hue (hū), *n.* color; tint; as, wild flowers of every *hue.*

    Syn. shade, dye.

hue and cry, a general outcry of alarm.

huff (hŭf), *n.* a fit of ill humor; sudden offense taken:—*v.t.* and *v.i.* to bully or offend; to take offense.

huff-y (hŭf'ĭ), *adj.* [huff-i-er, huff-i-est], easily offended.

hug (hŭg), *n.* a close embrace:—*v.t.* [hugged, hug-ging], **1,** to embrace closely; **2,** to hold fast to; cling to; as, to *hug* a belief; **3,** to keep close to; as, to *hug* the shore.

huge (hūj), *adj.* [hug-er, hug-est], **1,** of great bulk; vast; very large; as, a *huge* mountain; **2**, great; as, the party was a *huge* success.—*adv.* **huge'ly.**

Syn. colossal, enormous, immense.

Hu·go (hū'gō; ü'gō'), Victor Marie (1802–1885), a French poet, novelist, dramatist.

Hu·gue·not (hū'gē-nŏt), *n.* one of the French Protestants who lived in the 16th or 17th century.

hulk (hŭlk), *n.* **1**, the body of a wrecked or unseaworthy ship; **2**, an old, clumsy vessel; also, any clumsy object or person.

hulk·ing (hŭl'kĭng), *adj.* clumsy; bulky; as, a *hulking* fellow.

¹hull (hŭl), *n.* the outer covering of certain fruits, vegetables, and grains:—*v.t.* to shell (peas), husk (corn), etc.

²hull (hŭl), *n.* the body or frame of a ship or airship.

hul·la·ba·loo (hŭl'à-bà-lōō'; hŭl'à-bà-lōō'), *n.* clamor; uproar.

hum (hŭm), *v.i.* [hummed, hum-ming], **1**, to make a sound without opening the lips, suggesting the sound of a prolonged *m;* **2**, to make a buzzing noise, as a bee in flight; to drone; **3**, to sing with lips closed; **4**, *Colloquial*, to be in energetic motion or action; as, to make things *hum:*—*v.t.* to sing with the lips closed; as, to *hum* a song:—*n.* **1**, the noise made by bees and other insects in flying; a low sound like the letter *m;* **2**, a distant sound as of machinery in motion, airplanes in flight, and the like.

hu·man (hū'mǎn), *adj.* pertaining to, or characteristic of, man or mankind; as, *human* progress; *human* kindness:—*n.* a human being.

hu·mane (hū-mān'), *adj.* having or exhibiting the feelings proper to man; benevolent; kind; as, *humane* laws.—*adv.* **hu-mane'ly.**—*n.* **hu-mane'ness.**

hu·man·ism (hū'mǎn-ĭzm), *n.* **1**, the state of being human; **2**, liberal education; especially, study of Greek and Latin classics.—*n.* **hu'man-ist.**—*adj.* **hu'man-is'tic.**

hu·man·i·tar·i·an (hū-mǎn'ĭ-târ'ĭ-ǎn), *n.* a charitably inclined person; one who is devoted to the welfare of human beings:—*adj.* charitable; devoted to the welfare of people.—*n.* **hu-man'i-tar'i-an-ism.**

hu·man·i·ty (hū-mǎn'ĭ-tĭ), *n.* [*pl.* humanities], **1**, mankind; **2**, the nature which distinguishes man from other creatures; **3**, charity toward others; kindness; **4**, **humanities**, classical learning and literature, especially the Latin and Greek classics.

hu·man·ize (hū'mǎn-īz), *v.t.* [humanized, humaniz-ing], **1**, to make like mankind; **2**, to make humane; refine or civilize.

hu·man·kind (hū'mǎn-kīnd'), *n.* mankind collectively; human beings.

hu·man·ly (hū'mǎn-lĭ), *adv.* **1**, in a human or kind manner; as, to speak *humanly;* **2**, within human power or knowledge; as, we will do whatever is *humanly* possible.

Hum·ber Riv·er (hŭm'bêr), a river in England flowing into the North Sea (map **13**).

hum·ble (hŭm'bl), *adj.* [hum-bler, hum-blest], **1**, not proud; as, a *humble* attitude; **2**, obscure; unassuming; as, they lived in a *humble* cottage:—*v.t.* [hum-bled, hum-bling], to subdue; humiliate; as, the loss of his job *humbled* him.—*n.* **hum'ble-ness.**

hum·bug (hŭm'bŭg'), *n.* **1**, a fraud or sham; **2**, an impostor or deceiver:—*v.t.* [humbugged, humbug-ging], to swindle.

hum·drum (hŭm'drŭm'), *adj.* dull; monotonous; as, a *humdrum* life:—*n.* **1**, monotony; **2**, a stupid person; a bore.

hu·mer·us (hū'mêr-ŭs), *n.* [*pl.* humeri (hū'mêr-ī)], **1**, in man, the bone of the upper arm, from the shoulder to the elbow; **2**, the corresponding bone in the fore limb of other animals.

hu·mid (hū'mĭd), *adj.* damp; moist; as, a *humid* climate.

hu·mid·i·fy (hū-mĭd'ĭ-fī), *v.t.* [humidified, humidify-ing], to add moisture to; make (air) humid.—*n.* **hu-mid'i-fi'er.**

hu·mid·i·ty (hū-mĭd'ĭ-tĭ), *n.* dampness; moisture; as, the *humidity* of the air.

hu·mil·i·ate (hū-mĭl'ĭ-āt), *v.t.* [humiliat-ed, humiliat-ing], to humble; put to shame; as, his behavior *humiliated* me.

hu·mil·i·a·tion (hū-mĭl'ĭ-ā'shŭn), *n.* the act of putting to shame or the state of being put to shame; mortification.

hu·mil·i·ty (hū-mĭl'ĭ-tĭ), *n.* [*pl.* humilities], meekness; modesty.

hum·ming·bird (hŭm'ĭng-bûrd'), *n.* a small American bird noted for its bright colors. Its wings, during flight, move so rapidly as to make a humming noise.

HUMMINGBIRD

hum·mock (hŭm'ŭk), *n.* **1**, a small hill or rounded mound; **2**, a hump or ridge on an ice field.

hu·mor (hū'mêr; ū'mêr), *n.* **1**, a state of mind; mood; as, he is in a bad *humor;* **2**, the capacity to see or appreciate things that are funny; as, a sense of *humor;* **3**, the quality of being funny or amusing; as, the *humor* of a story:—*v.t.* to yield to the mood of; to indulge.

hu·mor·ist (hū'mêr-ĭst), *n.* an amusing or

humorous person; one whose writing or conversation is filled with humor.

hu·mor·ous (hū′mẽr-ŭs; ū′mẽr-ŭs), *adj.* full of mirth and fun; comical; witty; as, *humorous* situations.—*adv.* **hu′mor·ous·ly.** *Syn.* amusing, facetious, funny.

hu·mour (hū′mẽr; ū′mẽr), a British spelling of *humor.* Similarly, **humourist, humourous, humourously.**

hump (hŭmp), *n.* 1, a bulging lump, as that on the back of a camel; 2, an artificial hill from the top of which cars, uncoupled from a locomotive, may be rolled by gravity to their respective tracks:—*v.t.* 1, to make into such a shape; bend or curve, as the back; 2, to switch (cars) by means of a hump.

hump·back (hŭmp′băk′), *n.* 1, one with a deformed or crooked back; 2, a crooked back.—*adj.* **hump′backed′.**

humph (hm; hŭ; hŭmf), *interj.* an exclamation of doubt, surprise, disgust, etc.:—*v.i.* to utter such an exclamation.

hu·mus (hū′mŭs), *n.* a black or brown substance in soils formed by the decay of vegetable or animal matter.

Hun (hŭn), *n.* 1, one of a warlike, wandering people of Asia, who, in the fifth century, overran Europe; 2, a barbarous person.

hunch (hŭnch), *n.* 1, a hump; a rounded lump; 2, *Colloquial,* a strong feeling that something will happen, or happen in a certain way:—*v.t.* to round (the back).

hunch·back (hŭnch′băk′), *n.* 1, a person with a crooked back; 2, a crooked back.—*adj.* **hunch′backed′.**

hun·dred (hŭn′drĕd), *adj.* composed of ten times ten:—*n.* 1, the number consisting of ten times ten; 2, a sign representing this number, as 100 or c.—*adj.* and *n.* **hun′dredth.**

hun·dred·fold (hŭn′drĕd-fōld′), *adj., adv.,* and *n.* a hundred times as much or as great.

hun·dred·weight (hŭn′drĕd-wāt′), *n.* in the U.S., 100 pounds avoirdupois; in England, 112 pounds avoirdupois.

hung (hŭng), one form of the past tense and past participle of *hang.*

Hun·gar·i·an (hŭng-gâr′ĭ-ăn), *adj.* pertaining to Hungary, its language, or its people:—*n.* 1, a native of Hungary; a Magyar; 2, the language of Hungary; Magyar.

Hun·ga·ry (hŭng′gȧ-rĭ), a republic (cap. Budapest) in central Europe (map 12).

hun·ger (hŭng′gẽr), *n.* 1, a craving or need for food; 2, any strong desire; as, a *hunger* for excitement:—*v.i.* 1, to feel a desire or longing for food; 2, to long eagerly for something; as, the boy *hungered* for an education.

hun·gry (hŭng′grĭ), *adj.* [hun-gri-er, hun-gri-est], 1, having a keen appetite; feeling hunger; 2, showing hunger; as, "a lean and *hungry* look"; 3, eagerly desirous; as, *hungry* for affection.—*adv.* **hun′gri·ly.**

hunk (hŭngk), *n. Colloquial,* a lump or large piece; as, a *hunk* of meat.

hunt (hŭnt), *v.t.* 1, to pursue, or try to catch or kill (game or wild animals); 2, to search through for something; as, to *hunt* the library for a book; 3, to follow closely; hound; as, they *hunted* the fugitive over the countryside; 4, to search after; as, to *hunt* gold:—*v.i.* 1, to follow the chase; 2, to seek; as, to *hunt* for gold:—*n.* 1, the pursuing of game or wild animals; 2, an association of huntsmen; 3, a search.—*n.* **hunt′ing.** *Syn., v.* scour, track.

hunt·er (hŭnt′ẽr), *n.* 1, one who pursues game; a huntsman; 2, a horse or hound trained for use in hunting; 3, one who searches or looks for something.

Hunt·ing·ton (hŭn′tĭng-tŭn), a city in southwestern West Virginia, on the Ohio River (map 8).

hunts·man (hŭnts′măn), *n.* [*pl.* huntsmen (-mĕn)], 1, one who pursues game; 2, one who manages a hunt or chase.

hur·dle (hûr′dl), *n.* 1, a frame or framework of interwoven twigs, branches, or the like, used in making fences; 2, a fence or barrier to be leaped in steeplechasing or racing; 3, **hurdles,** a race in which such hurdles must be leaped; 4, any barrier or obstacle; 5, in England, a rude frame

HURDLE, def. 2

on which criminals were formerly dragged to execution:—*v.t.* [hur-dled, hur-dling], 1, to leap over an obstacle while running; 2, to surmount or overcome; as, to *hurdle* a difficulty.—*n.* **hur′dler.**

hur·dy–gur·dy (hûr′dĭ-gûr′dĭ), *n.* [*pl.* hurdy-gurdies], a mechanical musical instrument that is pulled through the streets on wheels, and played by turning a crank.

hurl (hûrl), *v.t.* 1, to throw with violence; fling forcibly; as, he *hurled* the javelin; 2, to cast down; overthrow; as, they *hurled* the despot from power; 3, to utter with vehemence; as, to *hurl* threats:—*v.i. Slang,* in baseball, to pitch:—*n.* a cast; a violent throw.—*n.* **hurl′er.**

hurl·y–burl·y (hûr′lĭ-bûr′lĭ), *n.* [*pl.* hurly-burlies], tumult; commotion.

Hu-ron (hū′rŏn), *n.* a member of an Iroquoian tribe of Indians, formerly living near Lakes Huron and Ontario.

Huron, Lake, one of the five Great Lakes of North America (map .5).

hur-rah (hŏŏ-rô′; hŭ-rô′; hŏŏ-rä′; hŭ-rä′), *interj.* expressing joy, triumph, applause, etc.:—*n.* a triumphant shout; a cheer:—*v.i.* to utter such a shout; to cheer.

hur-ray (hŏŏ-rā′; hŭ-rā′), *interj.* hurrah!

hur-ri-cane (hûr′ĭ-kān; hûr′ĭ-kǎn), *n.* a violent windstorm accompanied by rain, thunder, and lightning, especially common in tropical regions.

hur-ried (hûr′ĭd), *adj.* showing haste; hasty; as, a *hurried* meal.—*adv.* **hur′-ried-ly.**

hur-ry (hûr′ĭ), *v.t.* [hurried, hurry-ing], to impel to greater speed; hasten:—*v.i.* to act or move with haste; as, the woman *hurried* through the station:—*n.* haste; urgency.

    Syn., v. rush, quicken, expedite.

hurt (hûrt), *v.t.* [hurt, hurt-ing], 1, to injure or inflict pain upon; wound; as, the blow *hurt* his arm; 2, to grieve; offend; as, your indifference *hurts* me; 3, to injure; impair or damage; as, don't *hurt* the book:—*n.* 1, a wound or other injury causing physical pain; also, pain caused by such an injury; 2, an injury or loss causing mental pain; as, a *hurt* to one's pride; 3, harm or damage of any kind.

hurt-ful (hûrt′fŏŏl), *adj.* injurious; harmful.

hur-tle (hûr′tl), *v.t.* [hur-tled, hur-tling], to throw violently; fling:—*v.i.* 1, to clash; 2, to clatter; resound; 3, to dash or rush violently and noisily.

hus-band (hŭz′bǎnd), *n.* a married man:—*v.t.* to manage, direct, or use with economy; as, to *husband* one's income.

hus-band-man (hŭz′bǎnd-mǎn), *n.* [*pl.* husbandmen (-mĕn)], a tiller of the soil; farmer.

hus-band-ry (hŭz′bǎnd-rĭ), *n.* 1, agriculture; farming; 2, economical management.

    Syn. cultivation, tillage.

hush (hŭsh), *interj.* be still! silence!—*v.t.* 1, to make silent; to calm; 2, to conceal; as, to *hush* scandal:—*v.i.* to become or keep quiet:—*n.* silence; as, in the *hush* of the night.

husk (hŭsk), *n.* 1, the dry outer covering of certain fruits or seeds, as that of an ear of corn; 2, any rough, worthless outside covering:—*v.t.* to remove the husk from.—*n.* **husk′er.**

HUSK surrounding ear of co.n; *a,* silk.

husk-ing bee (hŭs′kĭng bē), a gathering of friends and neighbors to assist a farmer in husking his corn before storing it for the winter.

¹**husk-y** (hŭs′kĭ), *adj.* [husk-i-er, husk-i-est], 1, consisting of, or like, husks; 2, dry and hoarse; as, a *husky* voice.—*adv.* **husk′-i-ly.**—*n.* **husk′i-ness.**

²**hus-ky** (hŭs′kĭ), *Colloquial* in the U.S., *adj.* [hus-ki-er, hus-ki-est], well-developed; powerful:—*n.* [*pl.* huskies], a stalwart, well-developed man.

Hus-ky (hŭs′kĭ), *n.* [*pl.* Huskies], 1, an Eskimo; 2, an Eskimo dog.

hus-sar (hŏŏ-zär′), *n.* in European armies, a soldier belonging to the light cavalry.

hus-sy (hŭz′ĭ), *n.* [*pl.* hussies], 1, a worthless woman; 2, a saucy, pert girl.

hus-tle (hŭs′l), *v.t.* [hus-tled, hus-tling], 1, to push or crowd roughly; jostle; 2, *Colloquial,* to cause to be done quickly; as, to *hustle* work:—*v.i.* 1, to jostle; crowd; 2, *Colloquial,* to exhibit energy and alacrity; hurry; as, John can *hustle* if he has to:—*n.* 1, a pushing or jostling; as, *hustle* and bustle; 2, *Colloquial,* activity; vigor.—*n.* **hus′tler.**

hut (hŭt), *n.* a small, roughly-built shelter; a hovel or shanty.

hutch (hŭch), *n.* 1, a bin, box, or chest in which things may be stored; as, a grain *hutch;* 2, a coop or pen for animals; as, a rabbit *hutch.*

HUTS

huz-za (hŭ-zä′; hŏŏ-zä′), *interj.* expressing joy, triumph, or applause; hurrah!—*n.* a shout of joy or praise; a cheer:—*v.i.* to utter such a shout.

Hwang Hai (hwäng′ hī′), an inlet of the Pacific Ocean on the northeast coast of China (map 15). It is also called *Yellow Sea.*

Hwang Ho (hwäng′ hō′), a river in east central China, flowing into the Yellow Sea (map 15). It is also called *Yellow River.*

hy-a-cinth (hī′a-sĭnth), *n.* a plant of the lily family with spikes of bell-shaped, and very fragrant, white, pink, yellow, blue, or purple flowers.

hy-brid (hī′brĭd), *n.* 1, an animal or plant produced from the crossing of two distinct varieties or species; as, some roses are *hybrids;* 2, anything formed of parts of unlike origin; especially, a compound word, as *cablegram,* the elements of

HYACINTH

āte, âorta, râre, căt, ȧsk, fär, ăllow, sofȧ; ēve, ĕvent, ĕll, wrītẽr, novĕl; bīte, pĭn; nō, ōbey, ôr, dŏg, tŏp, cŏllide; ūnit, ūnite, bûrn, cŭt, focŭs; nŏŏn, fŏŏt; mound; coin;

which are derived from different languages:—*adj.* **1**, produced from two kinds or classes; as, the mule is a *hybrid* animal; **2**, composed of mixed elements; as, a *hybrid* word.—*v.t.* **hy′brid-ize.**

Hy-der-a-bad or **Hai-dar-a-bad** (hī′dĕr-ä-bäd′), **1**, a city and state in India; **2**, a city on the Indus River in Pakistan. (Map 15.)

Hy-dra (hī′drȧ), *n.* in mythology, a sea serpent with many heads, each of which, when cut off, was replaced by two more: slain by Hercules:—**hydra** [*pl.* hydras (hī′drȧz)], any evil difficult to root out or destroy.

HYDRANGEA

hy-dran-ge-a (hī-drăn′jē-ȧ), *n.* a shrub with large, round clusters of showy white, blue, or pink flowers.

hy-drant (hī′drănt), *n.* a pipe with a valve and spout through which water may be drawn from a water main.

hy-drau-lic (hī-drô′lĭk), *adj.* **1**, pertaining to liquids in motion; **2**, operated by water power; as, a *hydraulic* elevator; **3**, accomplished by water power; as, *hydraulic* mining; **4**, hardening under water; as, *hydraulic* cement:—**hydrau-lics,** *n.pl.* used as *sing.* the science that deals with liquids in motion, their use in machinery, etc.—*adv.* **hy-drau′li-cal-ly.**

HYDRANT

hy-dro- (hī′drŏ-), a prefix meaning water; as, *hydro*phobia, *hydro*plane.

hy-dro-car-bon (hī′drŏ-kär′bŏn), *n.* a compound of carbon and hydrogen.

hy-dro-chlor-ic (hī′drŏ-klôr′ĭk; hī′drŏ-klōr′ĭk), *adj.* composed of hydrogen and chlorine:—**hydrochloric acid,** a colorless, suffocating gas, soluble in water; also, a solution of this gas in water.

hy-dro-e-lec-tric (hī′drŏ-ē-lĕk′trĭk), *adj.* pertaining to electric energy generated by water power or steam.—*n.* **hy′dro-e-lec′-tric′i-ty.**

hy-dro-gen (hī′drŏ-jĕn), *n.* a colorless, tasteless, odorless, inflammable gas. It combines with oxygen to form water, and is the lightest known element.

hy-drom-e-ter (hī-drŏm′ē-tẽr), *n.* an instrument for determining the specific gravities, or relative weights, of liquids, consisting of a closed glass or metal tube, weighted so that it floats upright.

hy-dro-pho-bi-a (hī′drŏ-fō′bĭ-ȧ), *n.* a disease, rabies, usually transmitted by the bite of an infected animal, marked by dryness of the throat and inability to swallow.

hy-dro-plane (hī′drŏ-plān), *n.* **1**, a motorboat with a sloping bottom, the bow of which rises partly out of water when driven at high speed; **2**, an airplane so constructed that it can take off from, or alight on, a body of water; a seaplane.

hy-dro-pon-ics (hī′drŏ-pŏn′ĭks), *n.* the soilless growth of plants by means of chemical solutions.

hy-drox-ide or **hy-drox-id** (hī-drŏk′sīd; hī-drŏk′sĭd), *n.* a compound of an element with hydrogen and oxygen.

hy-e-na (hī-ē′nȧ), *n.* a night-prowling, flesh-eating animal, somewhat resembling a large dog, native to Africa and Asia.

HYENA (⅛)

hy-giene (hī′jēn; hī′-jĭ-ēn), *n.* the science which treats of the preservation of health.—*n.* **hy′gi-en-ist.**

hy-gi-en-ic (hī′jĭ-ĕn′ĭk), *adj.* **1**, pertaining to health or the science of health; **2**, not injurious to health; as, *hygienic* surroundings.

hy-grom-e-ter (hī-grŏm′ē-tẽr), *n.* an instrument for measuring the moisture in the atmosphere.

hy-la (hī′lȧ), *n.* a tree frog or tree toad.

Hy-men (hī′mĕn), *n.* the Greek god of marriage.

hy-me-ne-al (hī′mē-nē′ăl), *adj.* pertaining to marriage; as, *hymeneal* festivities.

hymn (hĭm), *n.* **1**, a sacred song expressing praise or adoration of God; **2**, any song of praise, thanksgiving, or the like.

hym-nal (hĭm′năl; hĭm′nl), *n.* a collection of sacred songs; a book of hymns.

hy-per- (hī′pẽr-), a prefix meaning abnormally great; excessive; as, *hyper*critical.

hy-per-bo-le (hī-pûr′bŏ-lē), *n.* obvious exaggeration, in writing or in speech, to produce an effect; as, "an endless day."—*adj.* **hy′per-bol′ic.**

hy-per-crit-i-cal (hī′pẽr-krĭt′ĭ-kăl), *adj.* too critical.

hy-per-son-ic (hī′pẽr-sŏn′ĭk), *adj.* of speed, five times the speed of sound in air, or greater.

hy-phen (hī′fĕn), *n.* a punctuation mark [-] used to join compound words, as in *self-denial*, or to divide a word into syllables, as in *hy-phen-ate:*—*v.t.* to join (words) with, or separate (syllables) by, such a mark; hyphenate.

hy-phen-ate (hī′fĕn-āt), *v.t.* [hyphenat-ed, hyphenat-ing], to insert a hyphen between (two words) or between the syllables of (a word); to hyphen.

hyp-not-ic (hĭp-nŏt′ĭk), *adj.* pertaining to, or producing, artificial sleep:—*n.* **1,** a person who can easily be hypnotized or put into a trancelike sleep; **2,** a medicine that produces sleep.—*adv.* **hyp-not′i-cal-ly.**

hyp-no-tism (hĭp′nō-tĭzm), *n.* the act or method of producing a state resembling sleep, in which the mind readily responds to suggestions, especially from the person who caused the state.—*n.* **hyp′no-tist.**

hyp-no-tize (hĭp′nō-tīz), *v.t.* [hypnotized, hypnotiz-ing], to cause to fall into an artificial trance.—*n.* **hyp′no-tiz′er.**

hy-po (hī′pō), *n.* coarse white crystals used in photography as a fixing agent; hyposulphite.

hy-po-chon-dri-a (hī′pō-kŏn′drĭ-à; hĭp′-ō-kŏn′drĭ-à), *n.* **1,** a mental disorder marked by extreme melancholy and morbid worry about one's health; **2,** low spirits; dejection.

hy-po-chon-dri-ac (hī′pō-kŏn′drĭ-ăk; hĭp′ō-kŏn′drĭ-ăk), *n.* a person who is affected with extreme melancholy or who imagines he is ill when he is not:—*adj.* pertaining to, or affected with, melancholy.

hy-poc-ri-sy (hĭ-pŏk′rĭ-sĭ), *n.* [*pl.* hypocrisies], a pretending to be what one is not; the putting on of an appearance of virtue which one does not possess.
Syn. pretense, deception, affectation.

hyp-o-crite (hĭp′ō-krĭt), *n.* one who puts on an appearance of virtue which he does not possess.—*adj.* **hyp′o-crit′i-cal.**—*adv.* **hyp′o-crit′i-cal-ly.**
Syn. dissembler, impostor, cheat.

hy-po-der-mic (hī′pō-dûr′mĭk; hĭp′ō-dûr′mĭk), *adj.* pertaining to the tissues under the skin:—**hypodermic needle,** a hollow needle attached to a small syringe for injecting liquids under the skin:—*n.* a hypodermic injection.

hy-po-sul-phite (hī′pō-sŭl′fīt), *n.* a salt, in coarse white crystals, used as a fixing agent in photography.

HYPODERMIC SYRINGE

hy-pot-e-nuse (hī-pŏt′ē-nūs; hĭ-pŏt′ē-nūs), *n.* in geometry, the side of a right-angled triangle which is opposite the right angle.

hy-poth-e-sis (hī-pŏth′ē-sĭs; hĭ-pŏth′ē-sĭs), *n.* [*pl.* hypotheses (hī-pŏth′ē-sēz; hĭ-pŏth′ē-sēz)], something which may or may not prove to be true but is assumed to be true for the sake of argument.

HYPOT-ENUSE (H)

hy-po-thet-i-cal (hī′pō-thĕt′ĭ-kǎl; hĭp′ō-thĕt′ĭ-kǎl), *adj.* assumed to be true for the purpose of reasoning. Also, **hy′po-thet′ic.**

hys-sop (hĭs′ŭp), *n.* **1,** a fragrant medicinal herb of the mint family, growing about two feet high and bearing blue flowers; also, the flowers; **2,** a plant used in ancient Jewish rites.

hys-te-ri-a (hĭs-tē′rĭ-à), *n.* a persistent nervous condition, especially of women, marked chiefly by uncontrolled emotional excitement and outbursts of senseless weeping and laughter.

hys-ter-i-cal (hĭs-tĕr′ĭ-kǎl) or **hys-ter-ic** (hĭs-tĕr′ĭk), *adj.* **1,** pertaining to, or affected by, hysteria; **2,** violently emotional; uncontrolled; as, *hysterical* laughter.—*adv.* **hys-ter′i-cal-ly.**

hys-ter-ics (hĭs-tĕr′ĭks), *n.pl.* used as *sing.* a fit of nervous and uncontrollable laughing and crying; any hysterical outburst.

I

¹I, i (ī), *n.* [*pl.* I's, i's], **1,** the ninth letter of the alphabet, following H; **2,** as a Roman numeral, 1.

²I (ī), *pron.* of the first person, [*nominative* I, *possessive* my, mine, *objective* me], the pronoun by which the speaker or writer denotes himself.

I. abbreviation for *Island:*—**i.** abbreviation for *intransitive, island.*

Ia. abbreviation for *Iowa.*

i-am-bic (ī-ăm′bĭk), *n.* **1,** a metrical foot, widely used in English poetry, consisting of one short or unaccented syllable, followed by one long, accented syllable; as,

"Ring out | the old, | ring in | the new" |; **2,** a line or stanza composed in such meter: —*adj.* designating, pertaining to, or composed of, such metrical feet.

ib. or **ibid.** abbreviation for Latin *ibidem*, meaning *in the same place.*

I-be-ri-a (ī-bē′rĭ-à), a peninsula in southwestern Europe, comprising Spain and Portugal.—*adj.* and *n.* **I-be′ri-an.**

i-bex (ī′bĕks), *n.* [*pl.* ibexes (ī′bĕk-sĕz) or ibices (ĭb′ĭ-sēz; ī′bĭ-sēz)], a wild goat, especially of the Alps and Apennines, with large, backward-curving horns.

i-bis (ī′bĭs), *n.* [*pl.* ibis or ibises], a large,

wading bird of the heron family, with a long, slender, curving beak, found in warm climates:— **sacred ibis,** an ibis found along the Nile, regarded as sacred by the ancient Egyptians.

IBIS (⅛)

-i·ble (-ĭb′l), *suffix,* another form of *-able.* See **-able.**

Ib·sen (ĭb′sĕn; ĭp′sĕn), Henrik (1828–1906), a Norwegian poet and dramatist.

-ic (-ĭk), a suffix meaning: **1,** like in nature or kind; of or belonging to; as, angel*ic,* Celt*ic,* trag*ic;* **2,** having to do with; as, publ*ic,* poet*ic,* domest*ic;* **3,** a person or thing connected with; as, mechan*ic,* crit*ic,* arithmet*ic.* The adjectives may often also end in *-ical;* as, angel*ical.*

-i·cal (-ĭk′ăl), *suffix,* another form of *-ic.* See **-ic.**

I.C.C. abbreviation for *Interstate Commerce Commission.*

ice (īs), *n.* **1,** frozen water; **2,** any substance resembling ice; as, menthol *ice;* **3,** a frozen dessert, made with fruit juices instead of cream; as, raspberry *ice;* **4,** cake frosting; icing:—*v.t.* [iced, ic-ing], **1,** to freeze; **2,** to supply with ice; **3,** to cool by ice, as beverages or fruit; **4,** to cover, as cake, with frosting:—**break the ice,** to break through formality and reserve:—*adj.* **1,** of ice; as, *ice* cubes; **2,** having to do with ice; as, *ice* hockey; an *ice*boat.

ICEBERG

AA, water line; AB, part of iceberg above water; AC, part of iceberg below water, about nine times the size of AB.

ice age, the glacial epoch, or time when ice covered large areas of the world.

ice·berg (īs′bûrg′), *n.* a large mass of ice broken off from a glacier, and floating in the sea, often rising to a great height above the water.

ice·boat (īs′bōt), *n.* **1,** a heavily-built steamboat with a very strong

ICEBOAT, def. 2

bow, used to break a channel in frozen rivers, lakes, or harbors: also called *icebreaker;* **2,** a boat or frame mounted on runners and propelled by sails over ice.

ice cream, flavored cream or custard, sweetened and frozen.

Ice·land (īs′lănd), an island in the North Atlantic, west of Norway; since 1944, an independent republic (cap. Reykjavik) (map 12).—*n.* **Ice′land**/**er.**

Ice·lan·dic (īs-lăn′dĭk), *adj.* pertaining to Iceland, or to the Icelanders or their language; as, an *Icelandic* saga:—*n.* the language of the Icelanders.

ich·neu·mon (ĭk-nū′mŏn), *n.* an Old World mongoose, a small, brave, active, weasel-like animal which feeds on mice, rats, snakes, and other small animals: held sacred by the ancient Egyptians for its supposed destruction of crocodile eggs.

ICHNEUMON (⅛)

ich·neu·mon fly, any of a large group of insects which lay their eggs upon the larvae of other insects.

i·ci·cle (ī′sĭk-l), *n.* a hanging piece of ice, tapering downward to a point, formed by the freezing of dripping water.

ic·ing (īs′ĭng), *n.* a coating or frosting for cakes, made of sugar, flavoring, etc.

i·con (ī′kŏn), *n.* [*pl.* icons (ī′kŏnz) or icones (ī′kō-nēz)], **1,** an image; statue; **2,** in the Eastern Church, a sacred image or picture, as of the Virgin Mary or a saint.

ICON

i·con·o·clast (ī-kŏn′ō-klăst); *n.* **1,** one who destroys images or icons, or who is opposed to their use in religion; **2,** one who attacks popular beliefs or traditions.

-ics (-ĭks), a suffix used to form nouns meaning: **1,** a science; as, mechan*ics,* mathemat*ics;* **2,** an occupation or condition; as, polit*ics,* hyster*ics.*

ic·y (īs′ĭ), *adj.* [ic-i-er, ic-i-est], **1,** pertaining to, like, or covered with, ice; as, *icy* pavements; cold; frosty; as, an *icy* gale; **2,** chilling in manner; indifferent; as, an *icy* welcome.—*adv.* **ic′i·ly.**

Id. or **Ida.** abbreviation for *Idaho.*

I·da (ī′dà), **1,** a mountain range, in northwestern Asia Minor, near the site of ancient Troy; **2,** a mountain in Crete, connected with the worship of Zeus. (Map 1.)

I·da·ho (ī′dà-hō), a northwestern State (cap. Boise) in the U.S. (map 9).

i·de·a (ī-dē′à), *n.* **1,** a mental picture of

---

go; join; yet; sing; chin; show; thin, *then;* hw, *why;* zh, azure; ü, Ger. für or Fr. lune; ö, Ger. schön or Fr. feu; n̈, Fr. enfant, nom; kh, Ger. ach or ich. See pages ix–x.

a thing; as, his *idea* of an elephant; **2,** an ideal; also, a plan; as, John has the *idea* of becoming an actor; **3,** the purpose or meaning of anything; as, the *idea* is to get votes; **4,** a supposition; fancy; as, I have an *idea* she will come.

Syn. thought, imagination, fancy.

i·de·al (ī-dē'ăl), *adj.* **1,** existing in imagination or fancy only; not real or practical; **2,** equal to one's highest wish; perfect; as, *ideal* weather:—*n.* any perfect person or thing, or one regarded as worthy of imitation.—*adv.* **i·de'al·ly.**

i·de·al·ism (ī-dē'ăl-ĭzm), *n.* **1,** the tendency to see things as they should be instead of as they are; **2,** the effort to live according to a standard of perfection; **3,** in art and literature, the effort to depict beauty and perfection rather than fact: opposite of *realism.*—*n.* **i·de'al·ist.**

i·de·al·ize (ī-dē'ăl-īz), *v.t.* [idealized, idealiz-ing], to look upon as perfect, regardless of fact; as, she *idealizes* her son.—*n.* **i·de'al·i·za'tion.**

i·den·ti·cal (ī-děn'tĭ-kăl), *adj.* **1,** the very same; as, the *identical* spot; **2,** exactly alike; as, no two faces are *identical.*—*adv.* **i·den'ti·cal·ly.**

i·den·ti·fy (ī-děn'tĭ-fī), *v.t.* [identified, identify-ing], **1,** to make, consider, or treat as the same; as, we *identify* sportsmanship with good character; **2,** to prove to be the same or prove as one's own; as, I *identified* my umbrella; **3,** to recognize or classify, as a plant or a person.—*n.* **i·den'ti·fi·ca'tion.**

i·den·ti·ty (ī-děn'tĭ-tĭ), *n.* [*pl.* identities], **1,** sameness or likeness; as, the *identity* of this pen with the one I lost; **2,** the fact of being as represented; as, to establish one's *identity.*

ides (īdz), *n.pl.* in the ancient Roman calendar, the 15th of March, May, July, and October; the 13th of the other months.

id·i·o·cy (ĭd'ĭ-ō-sĭ), *n.* [*pl.* idiocies], extreme lack of mind or intelligence; imbecility.

id·i·om (ĭd'ĭ-ŭm), *n.* **1,** the language of a people; also, the dialect of a group or section; as, the New England *idiom;* **2,** the peculiar form or character of a language; **3,** an expression which, as a whole, has a meaning different from the meanings of the individual words joined together, as "to be hard put to it" means "to have difficulty"; **4,** a method of expression peculiar to an individual; as, Shakespeare's *idiom.*

id·i·o·mat·ic (ĭd'ĭ-ō-măt'ĭk) or **id·i·o·mat·i·cal** (ĭd'ĭ-ō-măt'ĭ-kăl), *adj.* **1,** peculiar to a language; colloquial, especially when differing from strict grammatical construction; as, "He makes the eight o'clock train every morning" is an *idiomatic* phrase; **2,** given to, or marked by, the use of idiom; as, *idiomatic* writing.—*adv.* **id'i·o·mat'i·cal·ly.**

id·i·o·syn·cra·sy (ĭd'ĭ-ō-sĭng'krȧ-sĭ), *n.* [*pl.* idiosyncrasies], a peculiarity of thinking, acting, feeling, dressing, etc., characteristic of an individual; as, it was an *idiosyncrasy* of Mark Twain's to wear a white dress suit.

id·i·ot (ĭd'ĭ-ŭt), *n.* **1,** a person lacking in mind from birth; **2,** a fool; a dunce.

id·i·ot·ic (ĭd'ĭ-ŏt'ĭk), *adj.* **1,** pertaining to, or like, an idiot; **2,** senseless; foolish.—*adv.* **id'i·ot'i·cal·ly.**

i·dle (ī'dl), *adj.* [i·dler, i·dlest], **1,** unused; as, the house stands *idle;* **2,** useless; futile; of no importance; as, an *idle* tale; **3,** not working; lazy; as, *idle* servants:—*v.i.* [i·dled, i·dling], **1,** to waste or lose time; do nothing; **2,** to run slowly in neutral gear, as an automobile engine:—*v.t.* to waste (time); as, to *idle* time away gossiping.—*n.* **i'dle·ness.**

Syn., adj. indolent, unemployed.

i·dler (ī'dlẽr), *n.* one who wastes time in doing nothing; a lazy person.

i·dly (ī'dlĭ), *adv.* in an unoccupied or aimless manner; lazily; as, to wander *idly.*

i·dol (ī'dŭl), *n.* **1,** an image of a god used as an object of worship; **2,** a person or thing greatly loved or adored.

i·dol·a·ter (ī-dŏl'ȧ-tẽr), *n.* **1,** an idol-worshiper; one who honors images, talismans, etc.; **2,** one who loves a person or thing to excess; an ardent devotee; great admirer.—*n.fem.* **i·dol'a·tress.**

i·dol·a·trous (ī-dŏl'ȧ-trŭs), *adj.* **1,** pertaining to, or practicing, the worship of images; as, an *idolatrous* race; **2,** marked by excessive reverence or affection.

i·dol·a·try (ī-dŏl'ȧ-trĭ), *n.* [*pl.* idolatries], **1,** the worship of idols; **2,** extreme admiration for any person or thing.

i·dol·ize (ī'dŭl-īz), *v.t.* [idolized, idolizing], **1,** to worship (an image regarded as a god, or as divine); to make an idol of; **2,** to love or admire to excess; as, small boys *idolize* great football stars.

i·dyl or **i·dyll** (ī'dĭl), *n.* **1,** a short poem describing a scene or event in country life; a similar prose description; **2,** an episode suitable for such a piece.

i·dyl·lic (ī-dĭl'ĭk; ĭ-dĭl'ĭk), *adj.* **1,** pertaining to, or of the nature of, the idyl; **2,** charming and simple.

I·dylls of the King, a series of poems by Alfred Tennyson, presenting the legends of King Arthur and the Round Table.

āte, âorta, râre, căt, ȧsk, fär, ăllow, sofȧ; ēve, ĕvent, ĕll, writẽr, novĕl; bīte, pĭn; nō, ōbey, ôr, dŏg, tŏp, cŏllide; ūnit, ūnite, bûrn, cŭt, focŭs; noōn, foŏt; mound; coin;

i.e. abbreviation for Latin *id est*, meaning *that is.*

if (ĭf), *conj.* **1,** on the condition that; as, *if* I let you have the book, you must read it; supposing that; as, *if* I go to New York, what is the best train to take? **2,** whether; as, he asked *if* he might go; **3,** although; as, even *if* the answer is correct, the work is not neatly done; **4,** whenever; as, *if* I have a question, I will come to you:—*n.* a supposition or condition.

ig·loo or **ig·lu** (ĭg′lōo), *n.* an Eskimo hut, dome-shaped, usually made of blocks of snow or ice.

IGLOO
1, entrance; 2, window of ice; 3, cake of snow to reflect light through window to interior.

ig·ne·ous (ĭg′nē-ŭs), *adj.* **1,** pertaining to, or like, fire; **2,** in geology, formed under intense heat; formed by volcanic action; as, *igneous* rocks.

ig·nite (ĭg-nīt′), *v.t.* [ignit-ed, ignit-ing], to set on fire; as, to *ignite* coal:—*v.i.* to catch fire; as, the paper *ignited* from sparks.

ig·ni·tion (ĭg-nĭsh′ŭn), *n.* **1,** the act of setting on fire; kindling; **2,** the state of being ignited; **3,** the means of producing fire; **4,** the device for, or the process of, igniting the fuel mixture in gasoline engines.

ig·no·ble (ĭg-nō′bl), *adj.* **1,** of low birth; as, an *ignoble* family; **2,** of mean character or quality; degraded; vile; as, an *ignoble* act.—*adv.* **ig·no′bly.**

ig·no·min·i·ous (ĭg′nō-mĭn′ĭ-ŭs), *adj.* disgraceful; humiliating; shameful; as, an *ignominious* punishment.
    Syn. scandalous, infamous, degrading, despicable.

ig·no·min·y (ĭg′nō-mĭn-ĭ), *n.* [*pl.* ignominies], public disgrace or dishonor.
    Syn. shame, infamy, reproach.

ig·no·ra·mus (ĭg′nō-rā′mŭs), *n.* an ignorant person.

ig·no·rance (ĭg′nō-răns), *n.* lack of knowledge.

ig·no·rant (ĭg′nō-rănt), *adj.* **1,** lacking knowledge; uninformed; **2,** unaware; as, he was *ignorant* of the fact; **3,** betraying, or caused by, lack of knowledge; as, an *ignorant* reply.—*adv.* **ig′no·rant·ly.**

ig·nore (ĭg-nôr′), *v.t.* [ignored, ignor-ing], to disregard intentionally; as, to *ignore* a request; to overlook; as, to *ignore* rudeness.

i·gua·na (ĭ-gwä′nà), *n.* a tropical American lizard of green and black color which grows to a length of five or six feet. It lives either on the ground or in trees.

il- (ĭl-), *prefix,* a form of ¹*in-* or ²*in-*, used before *l.*

-ile (-īl), a suffix meaning of, like, or pertaining to; as, sen*ile:* sometimes written -*il;* as, civ*il.*

IGUANA (2/5)

Il·i·ad (ĭl′ĭ-ăd), *n.* a Greek epic poem describing the Trojan War, supposedly written by Homer.

Il·i·um (ĭl′ĭ-ŭm) or **Il·i·on** (ĭl′ĭ-ŏn), an ancient name of Troy, a city in northwestern Asia Minor (map 1). Its siege is the theme of Homer's "Iliad."

ilk (ĭlk), *n.* family; breed; kind; as, thieves and others of that *ilk.*

I'll (īl), contraction for *I will* and *I shall.*

ill (ĭl), *adj.* [*comp.* worse, *superl.* worst], **1,** sick; not well; as, the child is *ill;* **2,** disagreeable; hostile; as, *ill* humor; *ill* will; **3,** harmful; as, an *ill* turn:—*n.* **1,** evil: the opposite of *good;* **2,** something unfavorable or injurious; as, to work *ill* to one's neighbor; **3,** misfortune:—*adv.* **1,** badly; as, to fare *ill;* **2,** unkindly; as, to treat someone *ill.*

Ill. abbreviation for *Illinois.*

ill., illus., or **illust.** abbreviation for *illustrated, illustration.*

ill–bred (ĭl′-brĕd′), *adj.* badly brought up; impolite; rude.

il·le·gal (ĭl-lē′găl), *adj.* against the law; unlawful; as, it is *illegal* to drive a car without a license.—*n.* il′le·gal′i·ty (ĭl′lē-găl′ĭ-tĭ).—*adv.* il·le′gal·ly.

il·leg·i·ble (ĭl-lĕj′ĭ-bl), *adj.* not readable; difficult to read; as, an *illegible* manuscript; an *illegible* date on a coin.—*adv.* il·leg′i·bly.—*n.* il·leg′i·bil′i·ty.

il·le·git·i·mate (ĭl′lē-jĭt′ĭ-mĭt), *adj.* **1,** born out of wedlock; **2,** unlawful; illegal; as, an *illegitimate* business.

ill–fa·vored (ĭl′-fā′vĕrd), *adj.* ugly; rough-looking.

ill–hu·mored (ĭl′-hū′mĕrd), *adj.* cross; disagreeable; in a bad humor.

il·lib·er·al (ĭl-lĭb′ĕr-ăl), *adj.* **1,** narrow-minded; **2,** stingy; close; ungenerous.—*n.* il·lib′er·al′i·ty.

il·lic·it (ĭl-lĭs′ĭt; ĭ-lĭs′ĭt), *adj.* not allowed; illegal; as, *illicit* trade in drugs.

il·lim·it·a·ble (ĭl-lĭm′ĭt-à-bl), *adj.* immeasurable; vast; as, *illimitable* space.

Il·li·nois (ĭl′ĭ-noi′; ĭl′ĭ-noiz′), a north central State (cap. Springfield) of the U.S. (map 7).

---

gō; join; yet; sing; chin; show; thin, *th*en; hw, *why;* zh, a*z*ure; ü, Ger. f*ü*r or Fr. l*u*ne; ö, Ger. sch*ö*n or Fr. f*eu;* ṅ, Fr. e*n*fant, no*m;* kh, Ger. a*ch* or i*ch.* See pages ix–x.

il·lit·er·a·cy (ĭl-lĭt′ẽr-à-sĭ), *n.* [*pl.* illiteracies], want of learning; especially, inability to read and write.

il·lit·er·ate (ĭl-lĭt′ẽr-ĭt), *adj.* 1, unlearned; ignorant of letters or books; especially, unable to read or write; 2, showing lack of learning; as, an *illiterate* letter:—*n.* one unable to read or write.

   Syn., adj. uneducated, untaught.

ill—man·nered (ĭl′—măn′ẽrd), *adj.* impolite.

ill—na·tured (ĭl′—nā′tûrd), *adj.* bad-tempered; churlish; cross.

ill·ness (ĭl′nĕs), *n.* the state of being sick; also, a disease or malady.

il·log·i·cal (ĭl-lŏj′ĭ-kăl), *adj.* not sound in reasoning.

ill—tem·pered (ĭl′—tĕm′pẽrd), *adj.* cross; cranky.

ill—treat (ĭl′—trēt′), *v.t.* to treat badly or cruelly; abuse.

il·lu·mi·nate (ĭ-lū′mĭ-nāt), *v.t.* [illuminated, illuminat-ing], 1, to give light to; as, one large lamp *illuminated* the room; 2, to decorate with lights, as in token of rejoicing; 3, to make clear, as a difficult point; 4, to ornament (an initial letter or the borders of a page) with designs in colors, as in ancient manuscripts.—*n.* il·lu′mi·na′tion.

il·lu·mine (ĭ-lū′mĭn), *v.t.* [illumined, illu-min-ing], to light up; brighten; as, the moon *illumines* the night; a smile *illumined* her face.

ill—us·age (ĭl′—ūs′ĭj), *n.* wrong treatment; abuse; misuse.

ill—use (ĭl′—ūz′), *v.t.* [ill-used, ill-us-ing], to mistreat; abuse.

il·lu·sion (ĭ-lū′zhŭn), *n.* 1, an unreal or misleading appearance; as, that cloud gives the *illusion* of a castle; 2, a false idea; a delusion.

ILLUSION
The two horizontal lines appear further apart at the center than at the ends of the drawing.

il·lu·so·ry (ĭ-lū′sō-rĭ) *adj.* deceiving; misleading.—*adj.* **il·lu′sive.**

il·lus·trate (ĭl′ŭs-trāt; ĭ-lŭs′trāt), *v.t.* [illustrat-ed, illustrat-ing], 1, to make clear; as, to *illustrate* the definition of a word by a phrase in which the word is used; 2, to make plain by means of pictures or diagrams; also, to ornament with pictures.—*adj.* **il′lus-trat′ed.**

il·lus·tra·tion (ĭl′ŭs-trā′shŭn), *n.* 1, the process of making plain, or explaining, by the use of examples; 2, the art of ornamenting with pictures; 3, that which makes clear, as a comparison or an example; 4, that which decorates a text, as a picture.

il·lus·tra·tive (ĭ-lŭs′trà-tĭv; ĭl′ŭs-trā′tĭv), *adj.* tending to explain or make clear; serving as an example.

il·lus·tra·tor (ĭl′ŭs-trā′tẽr), *n.* one who makes pictures for books, magazines, etc.; especially, one who does this for a living.

il·lus·tri·ous (ĭ-lŭs′trĭ-ŭs), *adj.* famous; distinguished.—*adv.* **il·lus′tri·ous·ly.**

   Syn. celebrated, eminent.

ill will, unfriendliness.

Il·lyr·i·a (ĭ-lĭr′ĭ-à), a region in the ancient world, east of the Adriatic and north of Greece, covering what is now Yugoslavia.

Il·lyr·i·cum (ĭ-lĭr′ĭ-kŭm), a division of the Roman Empire, including what is now Yugoslavia and Albania, later extended to include also Greece and Crete (map 1).

I'm (īm), contraction for *I am.*

im- (ĭm-), *prefix,* a form of ¹*in-* or ²*in-.*

im·age (ĭm′ĭj), *n.* 1, a statue, bust, or similar representation of a person or thing; as, an *image* of the Virgin Mary; 2, a close likeness; as, he is the *image* of his brother; 3, a mental picture; an idea; 4, a reflection in a mirror or something seen through a camera lens, magnifying glass, or the like:—*v.t.* [imaged, imag-ing], 1, to form a likeness or picture of (something); portray; 2, to represent to oneself; imagine; 3, to picture vividly in words.

IMAGE OF BUDDHA

   Syn., n. effigy, icon, copy.

im·age·ry (ĭm′ĭj-rĭ; ĭm′ĭj-ẽr-ĭ), *n.* [*pl.* imageries], mental pictures, especially as conveyed in words; also, language which causes the mind to form pictures.

im·ag·i·na·ble (ĭ-măj′ĭ-nà-bl), *adj.* capable of being pictured by the mind; conceivable.

im·ag·i·nar·y (ĭ-măj′ĭ-nẽr′ĭ), *adj.* existing only in the mind; unreal.

   Syn. ideal, fanciful, illusory.

im·ag·i·na·tion (ĭ-măj′ĭ-nā′shŭn), *n.* 1, the picture-forming power of the mind; the ability to form mental pictures of things not actually present; 2, a product of this power; a mental picture or idea; a fancy.

im·ag·i·na·tive (ĭ-măj′ĭ-nā′tĭv; ĭ-măj′ĭ-nà-tĭv), *adj.* 1, having imagination or creative ability; as, an *imaginative* writer; 2, showing imagination; as, an *imaginative* poem.

im·ag·ine (ĭ-măj′ĭn), *v.t.* and *v.i.* [imagined, imagin-ing], 1, to form an idea or mental picture of (something); **2,** to suppose; fancy.

Syn. deem, picture, conceive.

im·be·cile (ĭm′bē-sĭl; ĭm′bē-sēl; ĭm′bē-sĭl), *adj.* **1,** feeble-minded; idiotic; **2,** marked by stupidity; inane; as, an *imbecile* remark:—*n.* one of weak mind.

im·be·cil·i·ty (ĭm′bē-sĭl′ĭ-tĭ), *n.* [*pl.* imbecilities], **1,** weakness of mind; **2,** hence, folly or absurdity.

im·bed (ĭm-bĕd′), *v.t.* [imbed-ded, imbedding], to enclose in surrounding matter; embed. See **embed.**

im·bibe (ĭm-bīb′), *v.t.* [imbibed, imbibing], **1,** to drink; **2,** to receive or absorb into the mind; as, to *imbibe* knowledge.

im·bro·glio (ĭm-brōl′yō), *n.* [*pl.* imbroglios], a perplexing or confused situation; a misunderstanding.

im·bue (ĭm-bū′), *v.t.* [imbued, imbu-ing], **1,** to cause to absorb; tinge deeply; dye; as, the setting sun *imbues* the lake with rose; **2,** to impress deeply; inspire; as, a soldier *imbued* with patriotism.

im·i·tate (ĭm′ĭ-tāt), *v.t.* [imitat-ed, imitating], **1,** to make a likeness of; **2,** to follow as a model or pattern; mimic; **3,** to look like; resemble; as, paper doilies are made to *imitate* lace ones.

Syn. follow, impersonate, mock, ape.

im·i·ta·tion (ĭm′ĭ-tā′shŭn), *n.* **1,** the act of copying or following a model; as, *imitation* is the sincerest form of flattery; **2,** a copy:—*adj.* made to resemble something superior; as, *imitation* lace.

im·i·ta·tive (ĭm′ĭ-tā′tĭv; ĭm′ĭ-tȧ-tĭv), *adj.* **1,** given to copying, or aping, what others do, say, or think; **2,** following a model; as, painting is an *imitative* art.

im·i·ta·tor (ĭm′ĭ-tā′tẽr), *n.* one who copies or mimics.

im·mac·u·late (ĭ-măk′ū-lĭt), *adj.* **1,** absolutely clean; as, *immaculate* hands; **2,** without fault; stainless; pure. *—adv.* **im·mac′u·late·ly.**

Im·man·u·el (ĭ-măn′ū-ĕl), *n.* a name of Jesus meaning "God with us" (Isaiah 7:14).

im·ma·te·ri·al (ĭm′mȧ-tē′rĭ-ăl), *adj.* **1,** not consisting of matter; without physical form; as, ghosts are *immaterial;* **2,** unimportant; as, *immaterial* details.

im·ma·ture (ĭm′ȧ-tūr′), *adj.* **1,** not ripe; not fully grown or developed; **2,** not finished or perfected; crude. *—adv.* **im′ma·ture′ly.** *—n.* **im′ma·tu′ri·ty.**

im·meas·ur·a·ble (ĭ-mĕzh′ẽr-ȧ-bl; ĭm-mĕzh′ẽr-ȧ-bl), *adj.* incapable of being measured; as, the *immeasurable* heavens; *immeasurable* joy.

im·me·di·ate (ĭ-mē′dĭ-ĭt), *adj.* **1,** closely related; as, one's *immediate* family; **2,** next; as, the *immediate* succession to the throne; **3,** direct; as, *immediate* cause; **4,** present; as, the *immediate* question; **5,** instant; urgent; as, *immediate* needs; **6,** *Colloquial,* near at hand; as, the *immediate* neighborhood; **7,** happening or coming at once; as, an *immediate* answer.

im·me·di·ate·ly (ĭ-mē′dĭ-ĭt-lĭ), *adv.* **1,** at once; **2,** closely; directly.

im·me·mor·i·al (ĭm′mē-môr′ĭ-ăl), *adj.* extending beyond the reach of memory or written record; as, life has existed on this earth from time *immemorial.*

im·mense (ĭ-mĕns′), *adj.* vast; enormous. *—adv.* **im·mense′ly.**

Syn. huge, colossal.

im·men·si·ty (ĭ-mĕn′sĭ-tĭ), *n.* [*pl.* immensities], hugeness; vastness.

im·merse (ĭ-mûrs′), *v.t.* [immersed, immers-ing], **1,** to plunge into some liquid; dip; as, to *immerse* clothes in water; **2,** to baptize by plunging (a person) entirely under water; **3,** to absorb the attention of; as, he was *immersed* in a book. *—adj.* **im·mersed′.**

im·mer·sion (ĭ-mûr′shŭn), *n.* **1,** the act of plunging, or the state of being plunged, into a fluid; **2,** baptism by submerging the whole of a person's body in water; **3,** concentration, as in a task.

im·mi·grant (ĭm′ĭ-grănt; ĭm′ĭ-grănt), *n.* a foreigner who enters a country to settle there permanently.

im·mi·grate (ĭm′ĭ-grāt), *v.i.* [immigrat-ed, immigrat-ing], to enter a foreign country intending to settle there permanently. *—n.* **im′mi·gra′tion.**

im·mi·nence (ĭm′ĭ-nĕns), *n.* the condition of being about to happen: said especially of disasters; as, the *imminence* of death.

im·mi·nent (ĭm′ĭ-nĕnt), *adj.* threatening; about to occur: said especially of misfortune or danger; as, *imminent* death.

im·mo·bile (ĭm-mō′bĭl; ĭm-mō′bēl), *adj.* immovable; motionless; as, *immobile* features. *—n.* **im′mo-bil′i·ty.**

im·mod·er·ate (ĭm-mŏd′ẽr-ĭt), *adj.* extreme; excessive; as, the *immoderate* use of slang. *—adv.* **im·mod′er·ate·ly.**

im·mod·est (ĭm-mŏd′ĕst; ĭ-mŏd′ĕst), *adj.* **1,** not decent or proper; as, *immodest* behavior; **2,** forward; brazen; as, *immodest* boasting.

Syn. shameless, indecent.

im·mod·es·ty (ĭm-mŏd′ĕs-tĭ; ĭ-mŏd′ĕs-tĭ), *n.* want of modesty; boldness.

im·mo·late (ĭm′ō-lāt), *v.t.* [immolat-ed,

---

go; join; yet; sing; chin; show; thin, *th***en; hw,** *wh***y; zh, a**z**ure; ü, Ger. für or Fr. lune; ö, Ger. schön or Fr. feu; ṅ, Fr. enfant, nom; kh, Ger. ach or ich. See pages ix–x.**

immolat-ing], to offer, as a victim, in sacrifice; hence, to make a sacrifice of (anything).—*n.* im′mo-la′tion.

im·mor·al (ĭm-mŏr′ăl; ĭ-mŏr′ăl), *adj.* 1, contrary to what is considered right; as, *immoral* conduct; 2, wicked; evil; unscrupulous; as, an *immoral* age.—*adv.* **immor′al-ly.**
  Syn. bad, corrupt, depraved, sinful.

im·mo·ral·i·ty (ĭm′mŏ-răl′ĭ-tĭ), *n.* [*pl.* immoralities], wickedness; vice.

im·mor·tal (ĭ-môr′tăl), *adj.* never dying; living or lasting forever; as, the Greeks considered their gods *immortal;* an *immortal* poem:—*n.* 1, one who never dies; 2, one whose fame is undying:—**the immortals,** in mythology, the gods.—*adv.* im·mor′tal-ly.
  Syn., adj. everlasting, eternal, endless.

im·mor·tal·i·ty (ĭm′ôr-tăl′ĭ-tĭ), *n.* 1, life that never ends; 2, everlasting fame.

im·mor·tal·ize (ĭ-môr′tăl-īz), *v.t.* [immortalized, immortaliz-ing], 1, to give unending life to; 2, to confer unending fame upon.

im·mov·a·ble (ĭm-mōōv′a-bl), *adj.* 1, incapable of being moved; firmly fixed; as, *immovable* rocks; 2, firm; unchanging.

im·mune (ĭ-mūn′), *adj.* 1, safe; free; as, *immune* from punishment; 2, protected from a particular disease; as, vaccination makes one *immune* to smallpox.

im·mu·ni·ty (ĭ-mū′nĭ-tĭ), *n.* [*pl.* immunities], 1, freedom from duties, burdens, obligations, or the like; as, *immunity* from taxation; 2, ability to resist disease.

im·mu·nize (ĭm′ū-nīz; ĭ-mūn′īz), *v.t.* [immunized, immuniz-ing], to protect from disease, as by inoculation; make immune.

im·mure (ĭ-mūr′), *v.t.* [immured, immuring], to confine within walls; shut up in, or as in, prison.

im·mu·ta·ble (ĭ-mū′ta-bl), *adj.* unchangeable; unalterable.

imp (ĭmp), *n.* 1, a little demon; offspring of the devil; 2, an annoying child.

imp. abbreviation for *imperative, imperfect.*

im·pact (ĭm′păkt), *n.* a collision; a forcible coming together of two objects; as, the *impact* of billiard balls.

im·pair (ĭm-pâr′), *v.t.* to make worse; lessen the quantity, excellence, value, or strength of; weaken; harm; as, reading in a dim light *impairs* the eyesight.—*n.* im·pair′ment.
  Syn. injure, mar, diminish, decrease.

im·pale (ĭm-pāl′), *v.t.* [impaled, impaling], 1, to pierce through with anything sharp; 2, to kill by thrusting through and fixing with a sharp stake.

im·pal·pa·ble (ĭm-păl′pa-bl), *adj.* 1, not touchable; as, *impalpable* shadows; 2, not easily grasped by the mind; as, *impalpable* distinctions.—*n.* im·pal′pa-bil′i-ty.

im·pan·el (ĭm-păn′ĕl), *v.t.* [impaneled, impanel-ing], 1, to enter on a list for jury duty; 2, to select (a jury) from such a list.

im·part (ĭm-pärt′), *v.t.* 1, to bestow a share or portion of; give; as, flowers *impart* beauty to a room; 2, to tell; disclose; as, to *impart* a secret.

im·par·tial (ĭm-pär′shăl), *adj.* not favoring one more than another; fair; just; as, a judge must be absolutely *impartial* in his decisions.—*adv.* im·par′tial-ly.

im·par·ti·al·i·ty (ĭm′pär-shĭ-ăl′ĭ-tĭ; ĭm′-pär-shăl′ĭ-tĭ), *n.* freedom from prejudice; unwillingness to show favoritism; fairness.

im·pass·a·ble (ĭm-pàs′a-bl), *adj.* not capable of being traversed or traveled; as, an *impassable* swamp; an *impassable* road.—*n.* im·pass′a-bil′i-ty.

im·pas·sioned (ĭm-păsh′ŭnd), *adj.* showing strong emotion; as, an *impassioned* orator; an *impassioned* appeal for aid.

im·pas·sive (ĭm-păs′ĭv), *adj.* feeling no emotion; showing no feeling; unmoved; calm; as, the Chinese have *impassive* faces.

im·pa·tience (ĭm-pā′shĕns), *n.* 1, rebelliousness against delay, restraint, or the like; restless eagerness; as, she was all *impatience* to be gone; 2, inability to tolerate or endure; intolerance; as, *impatience* of lying; 3, irritability; lack of control.

im·pa·tient (ĭm-pā′shĕnt), *adj.* 1, rebellious against delay, restraint, or the like; 2, restlessly eager; anxious; as, she is *impatient* to see the city; 3, intolerant; as, our teacher is *impatient* of carelessness; 4, showing irritability; as, an *impatient* gesture.

im·peach (ĭm-pēch′), *v.t.* 1, to charge (a person in public office), before a court, with misconduct in office; as, to *impeach* a judge; 2, to question or challenge (a person's honor, motives, or the like).—*adj.* im·peach′a-ble.

im·peach·ment (ĭm-pēch′mĕnt), *n.* 1, the calling to trial of a person for misconduct in public office; 2, an accusation that a person's motives are dishonest, his testimony false, or the like.

im·pec·ca·ble (ĭm-pĕk′a-bl), *adj.* faultless; free from sin; blameless.

im·pe·cu·ni·ous (ĭm′pē-kū′nĭ-ŭs), *adj.* lacking money; poor.

im·pede (ĭm-pēd′), *v.t.* [imped-ed, impeding], to obstruct or hinder; retard; as, snow and ice *impeded* our progress.

āte, āorta, râre, căt, àsk, fär, ăllow, sofà; ēve, ĕvent, ĕll, wrīter, novĕl; bīte, pĭn; nō, ōbey, ôr, dŏg, tŏp, cŏllide; ūnit, ūnite, bûrn, cŭt, focŭs; nōon, fŏot; mound; coin;

im·ped·i·ment (ĭm-pĕd′ĭ-mĕnt), *n.* **1,** that which hinders or obstructs; an obstacle; **2,** a defect in speech, as a stammer.

im·ped·i·men·ta (ĭm-pĕd′ĭ-mĕn′tȧ), *n.pl.* things which hinder progress; baggage; especially, the supply trains of an army.

im·pel (ĭm-pĕl′), *v.t.* [impelled, impel-ling], to drive forward; force; compel; as, fear and remorse *impelled* him to confess.
  Syn. actuate, induce, incite, instigate.

im·pend (ĭm-pĕnd′), *v.i.* **1,** to overhang; as, the sword *impending* over Damocles's head; **2,** to be at hand; threaten; as, death *impends.*

im·pen·e·tra·ble (ĭm-pĕn′ĕ-trȧ-bl), *adj.* **1,** not capable of being entered; allowing no entrance or passage; as, *impenetrable* forests; an *impenetrable* wall; **2,** not capable of being understood; as, an *impenetrable* plot; **3,** closed to reason, sympathy, etc.; as, a mind *impenetrable* to ideas.

im·pen·i·tent (ĭm-pĕn′ĭ-tĕnt), *adj.* not sorry for one's sin or wrongdoing; unrepentant:—*n.* one who is unrepentant.

im·per·a·tive (ĭm-pĕr′ȧ-tĭv), *adj.* **1,** in grammar, expressing command or exhortation; as, the *imperative* mood; **2,** commanding; peremptory; authoritative; as, an *imperative* gesture of dismissal; **3,** necessary; urgent; as, it is *imperative* to leave at once:—*n.* in grammar, the mood expressing command; also, the form of a verb used in this mood.

im·per·cep·ti·ble (ĭm′pĕr-sĕp′tĭ-bl), *adj.* **1,** so small, slow, or gradual, as hardly to be seen or felt; as, the *imperceptible* growth of a plant from day to day; **2,** too slight to be grasped by the mind; subtle; as, *imperceptible* shades of meaning.

im·per·fect (ĭm-pûr′fĕkt), *adj.* faulty; incomplete:—**imperfect tense,** tense of a verb which indicates action in the past going on but not completed; as, he *was walking:*—*n.* the imperfect tense.—*adv.* im-per′fect-ly.

im·per·fec·tion (ĭm′pĕr-fĕk′shŭn), *n.* **1,** incompleteness; faultiness; **2,** a defect.

im·pe·ri·al (ĭm-pē′rĭ-ăl), *adj.* **1,** pertaining to an empire or an emperor; as, *imperial* policies; *imperial* majesty; **2,** splendid; magnificent:—*n.* a small pointed beard.—*adv.* im-pe′ri-al-ly.

im·pe·ri·al·ism (ĭm-pē′rĭ-ăl-ĭzm), *n.* **1,** the power or government of an emperor; **2,** the policy of any nation which aims at acquisition of new territory or closer union of territory already possessed.—*adj.* im-pe′ri-al-is′tic.—*n.* im-pe′ri-al-ist.

im·per·il (ĭm-pĕr′ĭl), *v.t.* [imperiled, imperil-ing], to put in danger; endanger; as, to *imperil* one's life to save a child.

im·pe·ri·ous (ĭm-pē′rĭ-ŭs), *adj.* **1,** commanding; overbearing; **2,** urgent; as *imperious* questioning.—*adv.* im-pe′ri-ous-ly.
  Syn. domineering, dictatorial, lordly.

im·per·ish·a·ble (ĭm-pĕr′ĭsh-ȧ-bl), *adj.* indestructible; not subject to decay; enduring; as, *imperishable* fame.

im·per·son·al (ĭm-pûr′sŭn-ăl), *adj.* **1,** not relating to any particular person or thing; as, an *impersonal* discussion; **2,** not existing as a person; as, fate and luck are *impersonal* forces:—**impersonal verb,** a verb which usually has *it* for a subject, used only in the third person singular, as it *snows,* it *seems,* it *thundered,* it *follows.*—*adv.* im-per′son-al-ly.

im·per·son·ate (ĭm-pûr′sŭn-āt), *v.t.* [impersonat-ed, impersonat-ing], **1,** to play the part of, especially on the stage; **2,** to typify; represent; as, Uncle Sam *impersonates* America.—*n.* im-per′son-a′tion.—*n.* im-per′son-a′tor.

im·per·ti·nence (ĭm-pûr′tĭ-nĕns), *n.* rudeness; also, an insolent speech; a rude act.

im·per·ti·nent (ĭm-pûr′tĭ-nĕnt), *adj.* insolent; rude.—*adv.* im-per′ti-nent-ly.
  Syn. impudent, disrespectful, pert.

im·per·turb·a·ble (ĭm′pĕr-tûr′bȧ-bl), *adj.* unexcitable; also, calm; unshaken.

im·per·vi·ous (ĭm-pûr′vĭ-ŭs), *adj.* not permitting entrance or passage; as, slickers are *impervious* to rain.

im·pe·ti·go (ĭm′pē-tī′gō), *n.* a skin disease characterized by pus spots which later become crusted.—*adj.* im′pe-tig′i-nous.

im·pet·u·os·i·ty (ĭm-pĕt′ū-ŏs′ĭ-tĭ), *n.* [*pl.* impetuosities], **1,** sudden, violent energy or force; **2,** rashness; impulsiveness; as, the *impetuosity* of youth.

im·pet·u·ous (ĭm-pĕt′ū-ŭs), *adj.* **1,** rushing with force and violence; as, an *impetuous* wind; **2,** acting with sudden energy; passionate; impulsive; as, an *impetuous* child.—*adv.* im-pet′u-ous-ly.
  Syn. violent, excitable, vehement.

im·pe·tus (ĭm′pē-tŭs), *n.* **1,** the force or momentum by which a moving body tends to overcome resistance and go on moving; **2,** a moving force; stimulus; incentive; as, the desire for fame is an *impetus* to action.

im·pi·e·ty (ĭm-pī′ĕ-tĭ), *n.* [*pl.* impieties], **1,** lack of religious reverence; **2,** an act of irreverence or wickedness.

im·pinge (ĭm-pĭnj′), *v.i.* [impinged, imping-ing], **1,** to strike or dash; come into sudden contact; as, rays of light *impinge* on the retina; **2,** to encroach.

im·pi·ous (ĭm′pĭ-ŭs), *adj.* wanting in religious reverence; profane; as, *impious* remarks.—*adv.* im′pi-ous-ly.

go; join; yet; sing; chin; show; thin, *then;* **hw,** *why;* **zh,** azure; **ū,** Ger. *für* or Fr. *lune;* **ö,** Ger. *schön* or Fr. *feu;* **n,** Fr. *enfant,* nom; **kh,** Ger. a*ch* or i*ch.* See pages ix–x.

imp·ish (ĭmp'ĭsh), *adj.* like a petty demon or imp; mischievous.

im·pla·ca·ble (ĭm-plā'kȧ-bl; ĭm-plăk'ȧ-bl), *adj.* not able to be pacified or appeased; relentless; as, *implacable* hatred.
   Syn. merciless, pitiless.

im·plant (ĭm-plănt'), *v.t.* to plant or set in deeply; hence, to instil, as a belief.

im·ple·ment (ĭm'plē-měnt), *n.* an instrument, tool, or utensil; as, a surgical *implement;* a garden *implement:*—*v.t.* **1,** to fulfill or to accomplish: **2,** to make possible or to put into effect; as, to *implement* a plan.

im·pli·cate (ĭm'plĭ-kāt), *v.t.* [implicat-ed, implicat-ing], to involve deeply; as, the accusation *implicated* a dozen men.—*n.* **im'pli·ca'tion.**

im·plic·it (ĭm-plĭs'ĭt), *adj.* **1,** understood, though not expressed; implied; as, an *implicit* threat; **2,** trusting in the word or authority of another without question; complete; as, *implicit* faith; *implicit* obedience.—*adv.* **im·plic'it·ly.**
   Syn. implied, tacit, virtual.

im·plore (ĭm-plôr'), *v.t.* [implored, implor-ing], to entreat earnestly and humbly; as, to *implore* God for mercy; pray for; beg; as, to *implore* aid.—*adv.* **im·plor'ing·ly.**
   Syn. beseech, supplicate, plead.

im·ply (ĭm-plī'), *v.t.* [implied, imply-ing], **1,** to mean something not directly expressed; suggest; as, silence *implies* consent; **2,** to involve as a result; as, wealth *implies* responsibility.
   Syn. denote, signify, intimate, infer.

im·po·lite (ĭm'pō-līt'), *adj.* discourteous; rude.—*adv.* **im'po·lite'ly.**

im·pol·i·tic (ĭm-pŏl'ĭ-tĭk), *adj.* unwise; indiscreet; injudicious.

¹im·port (ĭm-pôrt'; ĭm'pôrt), *v.t.* to bring in from a foreign country, especially for commercial purposes:—*n.* (ĭm'pôrt), an article brought from a foreign country; especially, merchandise intended for sale: usually *imports.*—*n.* **im·port'er.**

²im·port (ĭm-pôrt'), *v.t.* to signify or express:—*v.i.* to have consequence; be of moment:—*n.* (ĭm'pôrt), **1,** meaning; as, the *import* of a sentence; **2,** importance; as, a decision of great *import.*
   Syn., n. sense, purport, weight.

im·por·tance (ĭm-pôr'tăns), *n.* the quality of being momentous, urgent, or weighty.
   Syn. value, gravity, moment.

im·por·tant (ĭm-pôr'tănt), *adj.* **1,** of much consequence; significant; momentous; as, an *important* election; **2,** having an air of importance; pompous.—*adv.* **im·por'tant·ly.**

im·por·ta·tion (ĭm'pôr-tā'shŭn), *n.* the act or practice of bringing merchandise into a country from abroad; also, the merchandise so imported.

im·por·tu·nate (ĭm-pôr'tū-nĭt), *adj.* persistent in asking; pressing; urgent; as, an *importunate* beggar; *importunate* demand.

im·por·tune (ĭm'pôr-tūn'; ĭm-pôr'tūn), *v.t.* [importuned, importun-ing], to ask repeatedly; beg persistently.—*n.* **im'por·tu'ni·ty.**
   Syn. beseech, entreat, implore.

im·pose (ĭm-pōz'), *v.t.* [imposed, imposing], **1,** to lay (a burden, punishment, or the like) upon persons or property; as, to *impose* taxes; **2,** to force (oneself); obtrude; as, to *impose* one's company on others:—*v.i.* to take advantage; presume; as, do not *impose* upon his kindness.

im·pos·ing (ĭm-pōz'ĭng), *adj.* stately; impressive.
   Syn. striking, majestic, august, noble.

im·po·si·tion (ĭm'pō-zĭsh'ŭn), *n.* **1,** the act of imposing a burden; **2,** the tax, punishment, or the like, imposed; also, an excessive burden imposed; **3,** a trick; fraud.

im·pos·si·bil·i·ty (ĭm-pŏs'ĭ-bĭl'ĭ-tĭ), *n.* [*pl.* impossibilities], anything which cannot exist or be done.

im·pos·si·ble (ĭm-pŏs'ĭ-bl), *adj.* **1,** not capable of occurring or existing; **2,** not convenient or easy; as, it is *impossible* to call a meeting for tomorrow; **3,** *Colloquial,* utterly objectionable; intolerable.

im·post (ĭm'pōst), *n.* a tax or duty, especially one levied by the government on goods brought into a country.

im·pos·tor (ĭm-pŏs'tēr), *n.* one who attempts to deceive others by adopting a false name or character; a swindler.

im·pos·ture (ĭm-pŏs'tūr), *n.* deception; fraud.

im·po·tence (ĭm'pō-tĕns), *n.* **1,** the state of being weak in body or mind; feebleness; **2,** utter inability to accomplish a purpose.
   Syn. weakness, incapacity, infirmity.

im·po·tent (ĭm'pō-tĕnt), *adj.* lacking physical, mental, or moral power; weak.
   Syn. feeble, helpless, infirm.

im·pound (ĭm-pound'), *v.t.* **1,** to shut up in a pound; as, to *impound* stray cattle; **2,** to collect (water) in a reservoir, as for irrigation; **3,** to take by law; confiscate.

im·pov·er·ish (ĭm-pŏv'ēr-ĭsh), *v.t.* **1,** to make poor; as, his gambling *impoverished* him; **2,** to use up the strength or fertility of; as, to *impoverish* land.

im·prac·ti·ca·ble (ĭm-prăk'tĭ-kȧ-bl), *adj.* that cannot be worked or used; as, an *impracticable* plan; an *impracticable* device.

im·prac·ti·cal (ĭm-prăk′tĭ-kăl), *adj.* not inclined to pay attention to what is useful or profitable; not practical.

im·pre·ca·tion (ĭm′prē-kā′shŭn), *n.* the calling down of evil upon someone; a curse.

im·preg·na·ble (ĭm-prĕg′nȧ-bl), *adj.* **1,** not to be captured by force; unconquerable; as, an *impregnable* fort; **2,** not to be overcome by temptation; as, a man of *impregnable* honesty.

im·preg·nate (ĭm-prĕg′nāt), *v.t.* [impregnat-ed, impregnat-ing], **1,** to make pregnant; fertilize; **2,** to cause to be filled or saturated with; as, to *impregnate* wood with creosote.—*n.* **im′preg-na′tion.**

im·pre·sa·ri·o (ĭm′prä-sä′rĭ-ō), *n.* [*pl.* impresarios], one who manages or conducts an opera or concert company.

¹im·press (ĭm-prĕs′), *v.t.* **1,** to mark by applying pressure; stamp; as, the king *impressed* the wax with the royal seal; **2,** to affect or influence deeply; as, the speech *impressed* me; **3,** to imprint or fix deeply on the mind; as, *impress* the fear of the law upon him:—*n.* (ĭm′prĕs), **1,** a mark produced by pressure, as by a stamp; **2,** a distinguishing mark.

²im·press (ĭm-prĕs′), *v.t.* **1,** to compel to enter a public service, as the army or navy; as, to *impress* sailors; **2,** to seize for public use, as goods.—*n.* **im·press′ment.**

im·pres·sion (ĭm-prĕsh′ŭn), *n.* **1,** the act of marking or stamping; also, the mark made; as, the *impression* of a seal on wax; **2,** the effect produced on the mind or emotions by something outside them; as, his first ascent in an airplane made a profound *impression* upon him; **3,** a vague notion, remembrance, or belief; as, my *impression* is that I have seen you before.

im·pres·sion·a·ble (ĭm-prĕsh′ŭn-ȧ-bl), *adj.* capable of being affected by surroundings; easily influenced; as, an *impressionable* disposition.

Syn. susceptible, sensitive.

im·pres·sive (ĭm-prĕs′ĭv), *adj.* able to influence the mind or feelings; as, an *impressive* ceremony.—*adv.* **im·pres′sive·ly.**

Syn. stirring, exciting, moving.

im·print (ĭm-prĭnt′), *v.t.* **1,** to mark by pressure; impress; **2,** to stamp or print, as letters, postmarks, etc., on paper; **3,** to impress (an idea) deeply on the mind:—*n.* (ĭm′prĭnt), **1,** an impression or mark left by something; as, the *imprint* of a foot; **2,** the printer's or publisher's name, and the place and date of publication, printed on the title page or at the end of a book.

im·pris·on (ĭm-prĭz′n), *v.t.* to put in jail or prison.—*n.* **im·pris′on·ment.**

im·prob·a·ble (ĭm-prŏb′ȧ-bl), *adj.* unlikely to happen, exist, or be true; as, an *improbable* result; an *improbable* story.—*adv.* **im·prob′a·bly.**—*n.* **im·prob′a·bil′i·ty.**

im·promp·tu (ĭm-prŏmp′tū), *adv.* and *adj.* without preparation; offhand; as, to speak *impromptu;* an *impromptu* picnic:—*n.* something, as a musical composition, that is made, done, or performed without preparation.

im·prop·er (ĭm-prŏp′ẽr), *adj.* **1,** not suited to the purpose; **2,** not according to good manners; indecent; as, *improper* conduct; **3,** incorrect; as, *improper* usage of words.—*adv.* **im·prop′er·ly.**

im·prop·er frac·tion, a fraction with a numerator which is larger than the denominator, as ⁴/₃.

im·pro·pri·e·ty (ĭm prŏ-prī′ĕ-tĭ), *n.* [*pl.* improprieties], **1,** the fact or quality of being improper; **2,** something, as in language or conduct, that is incorrect or indecent.

im·prove (ĭm-prōōv′), *v.t.* [improved, improv-ing], **1,** to make better; as, to *improve* the mind; **2,** to use to advantage; as, to *improve* an opportunity:—*v.i.* to grow better, as in health:—**improve upon,** make better.—*adj.* **im·prov′a·ble.**

Syn. amend, reform, rectify.

im·prove·ment (ĭm-prōōv′mĕnt), *n.* **1,** advancement of anything to a better condition; also, the result of this advancement; **2,** **improvements,** that by which the value of anything, especially real estate, is increased.

im·prov·i·dent (ĭm-prŏv′ĭ-dĕnt), *adj.* lacking in thrift or foresight; not providing for the future.—*adv.* **im·prov′i·dent·ly.**—*n.* **im·prov′i·dence.**

Syn. prodigal, wasteful, reckless.

im·pro·vise (ĭm′prŏ-vīz; ĭm′prō-vīz′), *v.t.* [improvised, improvis-ing], **1,** to compose without plan; make up on the spur of the moment, as verses or music; **2,** to contrive; as, we *improvised* a bed out of pine branches.—*n.* **im′pro·vi·sa′tion.**

im·pru·dence (ĭm-prōō′dĕns), *n.* **1,** lack of caution; rashness; **2,** any unwise act.

im·pru·dent (ĭm-prōō′dĕnt), *adj.* lacking caution; heedless and rash; as, it is *imprudent* to go sailing in a storm.—*adv.* **im·pru′dent·ly.**

im·pu·dence (ĭm′pū-dĕns), *n.* rudeness; forwardness; sauciness.

Syn. impertinence, insolence.

im·pu·dent (ĭm′pū-dĕnt), *adj.* insolent; rude; disrespectful; as, an *impudent* reply.

Syn. saucy, impertinent, pert, insulting.

im·pugn (ĭm-pūn′), *v.t.* to attack by

arguments; question; attack as false; as, to *impugn* a claim for damages.

im·pulse (ĭm′pŭls), *n.* **1,** a driving forward; the motion so produced, or the force producing it; **2,** a sudden, unthinking desire or inclination to act in a particular way; as, to give a beggar money under an *impulse* of pity; **3,** tendency to act without thinking; as, many people are guided by *impulse* rather than reason.

Syn. incentive, incitement, motive.

im·pul·sion (ĭm-pŭl′shŭn), *n.* **1,** the act of driving forward, or the state of being driven forward; also, the driving force; **2,** stimulation to action; as, the *impulsion* of duty; **3,** tendency to move forward; impetus; as, the *impulsion* given to medical science by Pasteur.

im·pul·sive (ĭm-pŭl′sĭv), *adj.* **1,** having the power of urging forward; as, an *impulsive* force; **2,** influenced by, or resulting from, some sudden feeling; as, *impulsive* acts; **3,** likely to act on sudden and momentary feeling; as, *impulsive* people.—*adv.* **im·pul′sive·ly.**—*n.* **im·pul′sive·ness.**

Syn. rash, headlong, impetuous.

im·pu·ni·ty (ĭm-pū′nĭ-tĭ), *n.* freedom from punishment, injury, or loss; as, you cannot break the law with *impunity.*

im·pure (ĭm-pūr′), *adj.* **1,** not clean; unwholesome; as, *impure* milk; **2,** mixed with foreign or inferior substance; as, *impure* gold; **3,** bad; corrupt in thought, word, or deed.—*adv.* **im·pure′ly.**

im·pu·ri·ty (ĭm-pū′rĭ-tĭ), *n.* [*pl.* impurities], **1,** the condition of being unclean or mixed with foreign substances; **2,** that which is, or tends to make, unclean; as, *impurities* in food.

im·pu·ta·tion (ĭm′pū-tā′shŭn), *n.* **1,** the act of laying a charge against someone; **2,** anything charged, especially discredit.

Syn. censure, charge, accusation.

im·pute (ĭm-pūt′), *v.t.* [imput-ed, imputing], to set to the account of; attribute or ascribe; as, to *impute* a theft to poverty.

in (ĭn), *prep.* **1,** within the bounds or limits of; as, lost *in* the woods; hurt *in* the hand; **2,** being surrounded by (circumstances, interests, etc.); as, *in* business; *in* trouble; **3,** within (a state, condition, occupation, or the like); as, *in* chains; *in* pain; **4,** within (a period of time); during; as, *in* winter; **5,** after; as, return *in* two days; **6,** at the time of; as, *in* the beginning; **7,** in the person or case of; as, you have a friend *in* me; **8,** in the range of; as, *in* mathematics; in the capacity of; as, it isn't *in* him to do that; **9,** made of; as, a statue *in* bronze; **10,** dressed in; as, a woman *in* black; **11,** expressed in; as, a letter *in* French; **12,** as

a means of; as, *in* explanation:—*adv.* **1,** toward the inside; as, he went *in;* **2,** inside a place; at home; as, my mother is *in:*—*adj.* **1,** incoming; as, the *in* line of traffic; **2,** in power; as, the *in* party; **3,** *Colloquial,* the richer by; as, he was *in* five dollars; **4,** *Slang,* in a certain relation; as, he's *in* bad with the officials:— **ins,** *n.pl.* those in office or power:— **ins and outs,** all the details; as, to know the *ins and outs* of a business.

in. abbreviation for *inch* or *inches.*

¹in- (ĭn-), a prefix meaning in, into, toward, within; as, *inside, inject, incline, inland:* changed to *il-, ir-,* and *im-* according to the sound that immediately follows; as, *illusion, irrigate, impart.*

²in- (ĭn-), a prefix meaning not; as, *inaudible;* lack of; as, *inability:* changed to *il-, ir-,* and *im-* according to the sound that immediately follows; as, *illogical, irregular, impractical.*

in·a·bil·i·ty (ĭn′à-bĭl′ĭ-tĭ), *n.* the condition of being unable; lack of power.

Syn. disability, incapacity.

in·ac·ces·si·ble (ĭn′ăk-sĕs′ĭ-bl), *adj.* not easy to get to or into; not obtainable or approachable; as, *inaccessible* heights.—*n.* **in′ac·ces′si·bil′i·ty.**

in·ac·cu·ra·cy (ĭn-ăk′ū-rà-sĭ), *n.* [*pl.* inaccuracies], **1,** lack of accuracy or exactness; **2,** an error; mistake; as, a page full of *inaccuracies.*

in·ac·cu·rate (ĭn-ăk′ū-rĭt), *adj.* incorrect; not exact; as, *inaccurate* figures made by *inaccurate* people.—*adv.* **in·ac′cu·rate·ly.**

in·ac·tion (ĭn-ăk′shŭn), *n.* lack of motion; idleness.

in·ac·tive (ĭn-ăk′tĭv), *adj.* unable to move or act; not active; sluggish; idle; as, an *inactive* volcano.—*n.* **in′ac·tiv′i·ty.**

in·ad·e·quate (ĭn-ăd′ē-kwĭt), *adj.* not equal to some demand; not sufficient; as, *inadequate* resources.—*adv.* **in·ad′e·quate·ly.**—*n.* **in·ad′e·qua·cy** (ĭn-ăd′ē-kwà-sĭ).

in·ad·mis·si·ble (ĭn′ăd-mĭs′ĭ-bl), *adj.* not to be granted as true; not to be allowed; as, *inadmissible* testimony.

in·ad·vert·ence (ĭn′ăd-vûr′tĕns), *n.* **1,** lack of attention; as, the mistake was due to *inadvertence;* **2,** an oversight caused by carelessness.

in·ad·vert·ent (ĭn′ăd-vûr′tĕnt), *adj.* due to heedlessness; unintentional; thoughtless; as, an *inadvertent* slight.

in·ad·vis·a·ble (ĭn′ăd-vīz′à-bl), *adj.* not to be recommended; unwise.

in·al·ien·a·ble (ĭn-āl′yĕn-à-bl; ĭn-ā′lĭ-ĕn-à-bl), *adj.* incapable of being taken away or transferred; as, liberty and freedom of speech are *inalienable* rights of man.—*adv.* **in·al′ien·a·bly.**

in·ane (ĭn-ān'), *adj.* empty; silly; as, *inane* remarks.—*adv.* **in·ane'ly.**

in·an·i·mate (ĭn-ăn'ĭ-mĭt), *adj.* **1,** without animal life; as, *inanimate* rocks; **2,** deprived of life; as, an *inanimate* human body; **3,** dull; spiritless; as, *inanimate* conversation.—*adv.* **in·an'i·mate·ly.**
Syn. apathetic, inert, dead, lifeless.

in·a·ni·tion (ĭn/ȧ-nĭsh'ŭn), *n.* emptiness; exhaustion from hunger.

in·an·i·ty (ĭn-ăn'ĭ-tĭ), *n.* [*pl.* inanities], **1,** senselessness; silliness; **2, inanities,** vanities; as, the *inanities* of fashion.

in·ap·pli·ca·ble (ĭn-ăp'lĭ-kȧ-bl), *adj.* not suitable for a definite purpose; not to be used or applied; as, that answer is *inapplicable* to this problem.

in·ap·pre·ci·a·ble (ĭn/ă-prē'shĭ-ȧ-bl), *adj.* too small to be perceived; as, an *inappreciable* difference in tone.

in·ap·pro·pri·ate (ĭn/ă-prō'prĭ-ĭt), *adj.* not suitable, fit, or proper; as, *inappropriate* dress or speech.—*adv.* **in/ap·pro'pri·ate·ly.**—*n.* **in/ap·pro'pri·ate·ness.**

in·apt (ĭn-ăpt'), *adj.* not suitable; as, an *inapt* remark; not skilful; as, an *inapt* workman.

in·ap·ti·tude (ĭn-ăp'tĭ-tūd), *n.* lack of special fitness or skill; unfitness; as, *inaptitude* for music.

in·ar·tic·u·late (ĭn/är-tĭk'ŭ-lȧt), *adj.* **1,** not expressed in words; as, *inarticulate* rage; **2,** incapable of speech; dumb; as, *inarticulate* animals; surprise made him *inarticulate*; **3,** not jointed; as, a jellyfish has an *inarticulate* body.

in·ar·tis·tic (ĭn/är-tĭs'tĭk), *adj.* **1,** not in accord with the principles of art; as, *inartistic* designs; **2,** lacking in appreciation of art; as, an *inartistic* nature; **3,** not graceful; not skilful; as, *inartistic* movements.—*adv.* **in/ar·tis'ti·cal·ly.**

in·as·much (ĭn/ăz-mŭch'), *adv.* in so far; because; as, *inasmuch* as you wish to, you may go. Also written in **as much.**

in·at·ten·tion (ĭn/ă-tĕn'shŭn), *n.* failure to fix one's mind on a matter; heedlessness; as, he failed because of *inattention.*

in·at·ten·tive (ĭn/ă-tĕn'tĭv), *adj.* paying no heed; negligent; as, an *inattentive* pupil cannot succeed.—*adv.* **in/at·ten'tive·ly.**—*n.* **in/at·ten'tive·ness.**

in·au·di·ble (ĭn-ô'dĭ-bl), *adj.* incapable of being heard; as, an *inaudible* remark.—*adv.* **in·au'di·bly.**

in·au·gu·ral (ĭn-ô'gu̇-răl), *adj.* pertaining to the dedication of a public building, the formal installation of a person in an office, etc.:—*n.* a speech made on such an occasion.

in·au·gu·rate (ĭn-ô'gu̇-rāt), *v.t.* [inaugurat-ed, inaugurat-ing], **1,** to admit or swear into office with special ceremony; as, to *inaugurate* a president; **2,** to make a formal beginning of; as, to *inaugurate* a custom; **3,** to celebrate the first public use of; as, to *inaugurate* a courthouse.—*n.* **in·au/gu·ra'tion.**

in·aus·pi·cious (ĭn/ôs-pĭsh'u̇s), *adj.* unlucky; unfavorable; as, an *inauspicious* beginning.—*adv.* **in/aus·pi'cious·ly.**

in·born (ĭn'bôrn'), *adj.* given by nature; innate; as, an *inborn* talent for music.
Syn. inbred, natural, inherent.

in·bred (ĭn'brĕd'), *adj.* **1,** innate; natural; as, *inbred* kindness; **2,** (ĭn'brĕd'), descended from closely related ancestors; as, many royal families are *inbred.*

in·breed (ĭn-brēd'), *v.t.* [inbred (ĭn-brĕd'), inbreed-ing], to mate (closely related animals).—*n.* **in'breed/ing.**

inc. abbreviation for *incorporated.*

In·ca (ĭng'kȧ), *n.* **1,** the title of the emperor of Peru before the Spanish conquest; **2,** one of the royal race of Peru.

in·cal·cu·la·ble (ĭn-kăl'kū-lȧ-bl), *adj.* **1,** beyond estimate; hence, very great; as, he did *incalculable* harm; **2,** not dependable; as, a person of *incalculable* moods.

in·can·des·cence (ĭn/kăn-dĕs'ĕns), *n.* a glowing with light from intense heat.

in·can·des·cent (ĭn/kăn-dĕs'ĕnt), *adj.* glowing with white heat; hence, brilliant; shining:—**incandescent lamp,** a kind of lamp in which a filament gives off light as a result of intense heat.

in·can·ta·tion (ĭn/kăn-tā'shŭn), *n.* **1,** the use of charms or spells, sung or spoken, as a part of a magic ritual; **2,** the words used.

in·ca·pa·ble (ĭn-kā'pȧ-bl), *adj.* **1,** not having power or ability; as, *incapable* of walking; **2,** not open to; as, *incapable* of improvement.—*n.* **in/ca·pa·bil'i·ty.**
Syn. incompetent, inadequate, unable.

in·ca·pac·i·tate (ĭn/kȧ-păs'ĭ-tāt), *v.t.* [incapacitat-ed, incapacitat-ing], to make powerless or unfit; disable; as, old age *incapacitates* one for hard labor.

in·ca·pac·i·ty (ĭn/kȧ-păs'ĭ-tĭ), *n.* [*pl.* incapacities], lack of physical or mental power; disability; as, *incapacity* for work.
Syn. inability, incompetency.

in·car·cer·ate (ĭn-kär'sĕr-āt), *v.t.* [incarcer-at-ed, incarcerat-ing], to shut up in a prison; imprison; confine.

in·car·nate (ĭn-kär'nāt), *v.t.* [incarnat-ed,

INCANDES-
CENT LAMP

incarnat-ing], **1,** to clothe with flesh; embody in flesh; as, medieval belief *incarnated* the devil in many animal forms; **2,** to give a real, or material, form to (an idea):—*adj.* (ĭn-kär′năt), embodied in human form; personified.

in-car-na-tion (ĭn′kär-nā′shŭn), *n.* **1,** the taking on of material form; embodiment in human flesh; **2,** especially, in the Christian religion, the taking upon himself of human flesh by the Son of God in the person of Jesus; **3,** a person thought of as representing a principle, ideal, etc.; as, he is the *incarnation* of honesty.

in-case (ĭn-kās′), *v.t.* [incased, incas-ing], to enclose in a box or solid covering; surround with anything; as, the medieval knights *incased* themselves in armor. Also spelled **en-case′.**

in-cau-tious (ĭn-kô′shŭs), *adj.* heedless; rash; as, *incautious* people take incautious steps.—*adv.* **in-cau′tious-ly.**

in-cen-di-a-rism (ĭn-sĕn′dĭ-à-rĭzm), *n.* the act of maliciously setting fire to property.

in-cen-di-ar-y (ĭn-sĕn′dĭ-ĕr′ĭ), *adj.* **1,** pertaining to the malicious setting on fire of property; **2,** tending to stir up passion, strife, or violence; as, an *incendiary* article: —*n.* [*pl.* incendiaries], **1,** one who maliciously sets fire to property; **2,** one who excites quarrels.

¹**in-cense** (ĭn-sĕns′), *v.t.* [incensed, incensing], to make angry; enrage; as, the lie *incensed* her.

Syn. vex, exasperate, madden.

²**in-cense** (ĭn′sĕns), *n.* **1,** any material which gives off perfume when burned; **2,** the smoke or odor of such material when burned, especially in religious rites; **3,** any pleasant odor or perfume; as, the *incense* of flowers.

in-cen-tive (ĭn-sĕn′tĭv), *adj.* arousing to action; encouraging:—*n.* that which arouses to action; motive; as, hope of gain is an *incentive* to work.

Syn., *n.* stimulus, spur, impulse.

in-cep-tion (ĭn-sĕp′shŭn), *n.* beginning; first stage; as, the movement was successful from its *inception.*

in-ces-sant (ĭn-sĕs′ănt), *adj.* unceasing; constant; repeated; as, the *incessant* dropping of water.—*adv.* **in-ces′sant-ly.**

Syn. ceaseless, continual, uninterrupted.

in-cest (ĭn′sĕst), *n.* sexual relationship between persons so closely related that their marriage is forbidden by law.—*adj.* **in-ces′tu-ous.**

inch (ĭnch), *n.* **1,** a unit of length equal to one twelfth of a foot; **2,** a small distance or degree; as, he came within an *inch* of being

struck by the automobile:—*v.i.* to move slowly; as, to *inch* along.

in-ci-dent (ĭn′sĭ-dĕnt), *adj.* apt to happen; naturally belonging; as, the dangers *incident* to a career as an aviator:—*n.* an episode; an event of small importance in relation to a larger event or experience.

in-ci-den-tal (ĭn′sĭ-dĕn′tăl), *adj.* occurring in connection with something else more important; as, a play with *incidental* music; *incidental* worries:—**incidentals,** *n.pl.* relatively unimportant items, especially minor expenses.—*adv.* **in′ci-den′tal-ly.**

in-cin-er-ate (ĭn-sĭn′ĕr-āt), *v.t.* [incinerated, incinerat-ing], to burn to ashes; consume by fire; as, to *incinerate* garbage.—*n.* **in-cin′er-a′tion.**

in-cin-er-a-tor (ĭn-sĭn′ĕr-ā′tẽr), *n.* a furnace for burning waste matter or cremating dead bodies.

in-cip-i-ent (ĭn-sĭp′ĭ-ĕnt), *adj.* beginning to be or appear; as, *incipient* tuberculosis.

in-cise (ĭn-sīz′), *v.t.* [incised, incis-ing], to engrave; cut with a sharp instrument.

in-ci-sion (ĭn-sĭzh′ŭn), *n.* **1,** the act of cutting into something; **2,** a cut made with a sharp instrument; as, a surgical *incision.*

in-ci-sive (ĭn-sī′sĭv), *adj.* sharp; cutting; also, mentally sharp; biting; as, *incisive* remarks.—*adv.* **in-ci′sive-ly.**

in-ci-sor (ĭn-sī′zẽr), *n.* a cutting tooth; in man, one of the four front teeth in either jaw. (See illustration under *dentition.*)

in-cite (ĭn-sīt′), *v.t.* [incit-ed, incit-ing], to rouse; stir up; as, hunger *incited* the mob to riot.—*n.* **in-cite′ment.**

Syn. arouse, animate, stimulate, urge.

in-ci-vil-i-ty (ĭn′sĭ-vĭl′ĭ-tĭ), *n.* [*pl.* incivilities], **1,** lack of courtesy; impoliteness; **2,** any rude act.

Syn. rudeness, discourtesy, disrespect.

in-clem-ent (ĭn-klĕm′ĕnt), *adj.* severe; not mild; hence, stormy; as, *inclement* skies.—*n.* **in-clem′en-cy.**

in-cli-na-tion (ĭn′klĭ-nā′shŭn), *n.* **1,** the act of bending or leaning towards something; especially, a bending of the head or body in reverence, recognition, etc.; a bow; **2,** a turning aside from a given direction or position; a slanting position; slope; as, the *inclination* of the Tower of Pisa; also, the amount of slant; **3,** a tendency of the mind; a liking; preference; as, an *inclination* for music.

Syn. bias, affection, attachment, liking.

in-cline (ĭn-klīn′), *v.t.* [inclined, inclining], **1,** to cause to lean; slant; as, to *incline* a board; **2,** to bow; as, to *incline* the head in prayer; **3,** to give a tendency to; turn; dispose; as, this statement *inclines*

āte, āorta, râre, căt, ȧsk, fär, ăllow, sofà; ēve, ĕvent, ĕll, writẽr, novĕl; bīte, pĭn; nō, ōbey, ôr, dŏg, tŏp, cŏllide; ūnit, ūnite, bûrn, cŭt, focŭs; nōōn, fŏŏt; mound; coin;

me to believe:—*v.i.* **1**, to turn from a given direction; slant; lean; **2**, to bow; **3**, to have a tendency or preference:—*n.* (ĭn′klĭn; ĭn-klĭn′), a slant; a sloping surface; as, we traveled up a steep *incline.*

Syn., v. slope, tend, bend.

in-cli-nom-e-ter (ĭn′klĭ-nŏm′ĕ-tēr), *n.* an instrument for measuring the inclination or slope of anything, as of an airplane while in flight.

in-close (ĭn-klōz′), *v.t.* [inclosed, inclosing], to shut in; enclose. See **enclose.**—*n.* **in-clo′sure.**

in-clude (ĭn-klōōd′), *v.t.* [includ-ed, includ-ing], to enclose within limits; contain as part of the whole; as, biology *includes* both botany and zoology.

in-clu-sion (ĭn-klōō′zhŭn), *n.* **1**, the act of enclosing or including; also, the fact or condition of being contained or included; as, the *inclusion* of unimportant details in a story; **2**, that which is enclosed or included; especially, a foreign substance, usually tiny, enclosed in a mineral mass.

in-clu-sive (ĭn-klōō′sĭv), *adj.* **1**, containing a great deal; as, an *inclusive* survey; **2**, taking in the two extremes or limits mentioned; as, study lessons one to five *inclusive.*—*adv.* **in-clu′sive-ly.**

incog. abbreviation for *incognito.*

in-cog-ni-to (ĭn-kŏg′nĭ-tō), *adv.* in disguise; under an assumed name; as, rulers often travel *incognito:*—*adj.* unknown or disguised; as, he is a prince *incognito.*

in-co-her-ence (ĭn′kō-hēr′ĕns), *n.* **1**, looseness; failure to stick together; as, the *incoherence* of sand; **2**, want of connection in thought or language; as, the essay is marked by *incoherence* of thought.

in-co-her-ent (ĭn′kō-hēr′ĕnt), *adj.* **1**, consisting of parts that do not cling together; **2**, without logical connection; rambling; as, an *incoherent* sentence.

in-com-bus-ti-ble (ĭn′kŏm-bŭs′tĭ-bl), *adj.* incapable of being consumed by fire.

in-come (ĭn′kŭm), *n.* the receipts, usually money, derived from labor, business, property, or capital; wages or salary.

in-com-ing (ĭn′kŭm′ĭng), *adj.* coming in; as, the *incoming* tide; beginning; coming into office; as, the *incoming* mayor:—*n.* the act of coming in; arrival.

in-com-men-su-rate (ĭn′kō-mĕn′shōō-rĭt), *adj.* **1**, having no common measure; incomparable; as, money and success are *incommensurate;* **2**, unequal; inadequate; as, his strength is *incommensurate* to his duties.

in-com-mode (ĭn′kŏ-mōd′), *v.t.* [incommod-ed, incommod-ing], to trouble.

Syn. annoy, plague, molest, vex.

in-com-mu-ni-ca-ble (ĭn′kŏ-mū′nĭ-ka-bl), *adj.* incapable of being shared, imparted, or told; as, *incommunicable* joys.

in-com-pa-ra-ble (ĭn-kŏm′pȧ-rȧ-bl), *adj.* not to be compared; unequaled; as, *incomparable* beauty.—*adv.* **in-com′pa-ra-bly.**

in-com-pat-i-ble (ĭn′kŏm-păt′ĭ-bl), *adj.* incapable of existing together in harmony; inconsistent; as, desires *incompatible* with one's income.—*adv.* **in′com-pat′i-bly.**—*n.* **in′com-pat/i-bil/i-ty.**

in-com-pe-tence (ĭn-kŏm′pĕ-tĕns), *n.* lack of fitness or ability; as, the *incompetence* of a worker.

Syn. incapacity, inability, unfitness.

in-com-pe-tent (ĭn-kŏm′pĕ-tĕnt), *adj.* **1**, unfit; without ability; as, an *incompetent* servant; **2**, not legally qualified.—*adv.* **in-com′pe-tent-ly.**

Syn. incapable, insufficient.

in-com-plete (ĭn′kŏm-plēt′), *adj.* not fully finished or developed; as, an *incomplete* design; not having all its parts; imperfect; as, an *incomplete* set.—*adv.* **in′com-plete′ly.**—*n.* **in′com-plete′ness.**

in-com-pre-hen-si-ble (ĭn′kŏm-prē-hĕn′-sĭ-bl), *adj.* not to be understood or grasped by the mind; as, *incomprehensible* points of view.—*adv.* **in′com-pre-hen′si-bly.**

Syn. inconceivable, unintelligible.

in-com-press-i-ble (ĭn′kŏm-prĕs′ĭ-bl), *adj.* incapable of being compressed or squeezed into a smaller space.—*n.* **in′com-press′i-bil′i-ty.**

in-con-ceiv-a-ble (ĭn′kŏn-sēv′à-bl), *adj.* incapable of being grasped by the mind or imagined; unbelievable; as, *inconceivable* cruelty.—*n.* **in′con-ceiv′a-bil′i-ty.**

in-con-clu-sive (ĭn′kŏn-klōō′sĭv), *adj.* proving nothing; unconvincing; as, *inconclusive* arguments.—*adv.* **in′con-clu′sive-ly.**

in-con-gru-i-ty (ĭn′kŏng-grōō′ĭ-tĭ), *n.* [*pl.* incongruities], unfitness; unsuitableness of one thing to another.

in-con-gru-ous (ĭn-kŏng′grŏŏ-ŭs), *adj.* unsuitable; inappropriate; as, his solemn voice was *incongruous* with the gaiety of the poem he was reciting.

Syn. conflicting, discordant, illogical.

in-con-se-quent (ĭn-kŏn′sĕ-kwĕnt), *adj.* **1**, not logically resulting from what has gone before; as, an *inconsequent* conclusion; **2**, having nothing to do with the subject at hand; as, an *inconsequent* reply; **3**, acting or thinking disconnectedly; as, an *inconsequent* mind.—*n.* **in-con′se-quence.**

in-con-se-quen-tial (ĭn-kŏn′sĕ-kwĕn′-shăl), *adj.* unrelated to the subject under discussion; hence, unimportant; as, *inconsequential* evidence.

---

in·con·sid·er·a·ble (ĭn′kŏn-sĭd′ẽr-à-bl), *adj.* not deserving consideration; trivial or unimportant; as, an *inconsiderable* difference.—*adv.* **in′con-sid′er-a-bly.**

in·con·sid·er·ate (ĭn′kŏn-sĭd′ẽr-ĭt), *adj.* not heeding the wishes, thoughts, or feelings of others; thoughtless; as, an *inconsiderate* son; an *inconsiderate* remark.—*adv.* **in′con-sid′er-ate-ly.**
  Syn. negligent, rash, heedless, careless.

in·con·sist·en·cy (ĭn′kŏn-sĭs′těn-sĭ), *n.* [*pl.* inconsistencies], **1,** lack of agreement; as, the *inconsistency* of two stories; **2,** a contradiction; as, testimony full of *inconsistencies.*

in·con·sist·ent (ĭn′kŏn-sĭs′těnt), *adj.* **1,** not in keeping (with); as, stealing is *inconsistent* with honesty; **2,** self-contradictory; not logical; as, a person *inconsistent* in argument.—*adv.* **in′con-sist′ent-ly.**
  Syn. incongruous, conflicting.

in·con·sol·a·ble (ĭn′kŏn-sōl′à-bl), *adj.* not to be comforted; as, *inconsolable* over his friend's death.—*adv.* **in′con-sol′a-bly.**

in·con·spic·u·ous (ĭn′kŏn-spĭk′ū-ŭs), *adj.* not noticeable; not prominent or striking; as, *inconspicuous* colors.—*adv.* **in′con-spic′u-ous-ly.**

in·con·stant (ĭn-kŏn′stănt), *adj.* subject to change; fickle; as, *inconstant* lovers.—*n.* **in-con′stan-cy.**

in·con·test·a·ble (ĭn′kŏn-těs′tà-bl), *adj.* not admitting of question; indisputable; as, *incontestable* rights.
  Syn. certain, unquestionable.

in·con·ti·nent (ĭn-kŏn′tĭ-něnt), *adj.* unrestrained; lacking control, especially of the passions and appetites.—*adv.* **in-con′-ti-nent-ly.**—*n.* **in-con′ti-nence.**

in·con·tro·vert·i·ble (ĭn′kŏn-trō-vûr′tĭ-bl), *adj.* not to be disproved; true; indisputable; as, *incontrovertible* facts.
  Syn. incontestable, certain, positive.

in·con·ven·ience (ĭn′kŏn-vēn′yěns), *n.* **1,** discomfort; trouble; as, an interruption in electrical service causes a great deal of *inconvenience;* **2,** that which causes trouble; a hindrance; annoyance; as, the late arrival of the train was an *inconvenience* to me:—*v.t.* to put to trouble; annoy; as, we might *inconvenience* our hosts if we stayed overnight.

in·con·ven·ient (ĭn′kŏn-vēn′yěnt), *adj.* causing trouble; annoying; uncomfortable; as, the stagecoach would be an *inconvenient* way to travel today; trailing skirts are *inconvenient.*—*adv.* **in′con-ven′ient-ly.**
  Syn. unsuitable, cumbersome.

in·con·vert·i·ble (ĭn′kŏn-vûr′tĭ-bl), *adj.* not changeable into, or exchangeable for, something else.—*n.* **in′con-vert′i-bil′i-ty.**

in·cor·po·rate (ĭn-kôr′pō-rāt), *v.t.* [incorporated, incorporat-ing], **1,** to combine into one body; unite; especially, to establish as a corporation, or group of people entitled by law to conduct a business as if they were one person; as, to *incorporate* a town or a club; **2,** to embody; include; put in; as, to *incorporate* an idea into a story; **3,** to blend; mix, as one substance with another:—*v.i.* to unite with something else to form a single body:—*adj.* (ĭn-kôr′pō-rāt), **1,** closely united; united in one body; **2,** formed into, or united with others in, a body of persons authorized by law to conduct a business as one individual.

in·cor·po·ra·tion (ĭn-kôr′pō-rā′shŭn), *n.* **1,** the formation of a combination or union; especially, the formation of a corporation, or group of persons entitled by law to conduct a business as if they were one person; the union (usually called *corporation*) so formed; **2,** the act of including; as, the *incorporation* of ideas into a story; the act of combining; as, the *incorporation* of copper with silver.

in·cor·po·re·al (ĭn′kôr-pôr′ē-ăl), *adj.* not made of matter; without bodily existence; as, a ghost is *incorporeal.*

in·cor·rect (ĭn′kŏ-rĕkt′), *adj.* **1,** not according to model or rule; faulty; as, an *incorrect* copy; **2,** not according to fact; inaccurate; as, *incorrect* information; **3,** not in accordance with what is right or proper; improper; as, *incorrect* behaviour; *incorrect* dress.—*adv.* **in′cor-rect′ly.**

in·cor·ri·gi·ble (ĭn-kŏr′ĭ-jĭ-bl), *adj.* not capable of being corrected or set right; too accustomed to a bad habit to be reformed; as, an *incorrigible* drinker or gambler.—*adv.* **in-cor′ri-gi-bly.**—*n.* **in-cor′ri-gi-bil′i-ty.**

in·cor·rupt·i·ble (ĭn′kŏ-rŭp′tĭ-bl), *adj.* **1,** incapable of destruction or decay; everlasting; **2,** incapable of being morally corrupted; especially, incapable of being bribed.—*adv.* **in′cor-rupt′i-bly.**—*n.* **in′cor-rupt′i-bil′i-ty.**

in·crease (ĭn-krēs′), *v.t.* and *v.i.* [increased, increas-ing], to make or become greater; enlarge; as, the number of students *increases* year by year:—*n.* (ĭn′krēs), **1,** growth in size, number, intensity, etc.; as, an *increase* in business; an *increase* in popularity; **2,** that which is added to the original number, stock, capital, etc.; as, an *increase* of ten students.—*adj.* **in-creas′-ing.**—*adv.* **in-creas′ing-ly.**
  Syn., v. enlarge, extend.

in·cred·i·ble (ĭn-krĕd′ĭ-bl), *adj.* hard to believe; unimaginable; as, *incredible* tales; *incredible* wealth.—*adv.* **in-cred′i-bly.**—*n.* **in-cred′i-bil′i-ty.**

āte, āorta, râre, căt, ȧsk, fär, ăllow, sofȧ; ēve, ěvent, ěll, writẽr, nověl; bīte, pĭn; nō, ōbey, ôr, dŏg, tŏp, cōllide; ūnit, ūnite, bûrn, cŭt, focŭs; nōon, fŏŏt; mound; coin;

in·cre·du·li·ty (ĭn/krē-dū/lĭ-tĭ), *n.* unbelief; skepticism.
  Syn. doubt, disbelief.

in·cred·u·lous (ĭn-krĕd/ū-lŭs), *adj.* 1, indicating lack of belief; as, an *incredulous* smile; 2, unbelieving; doubting; skeptical; as, even after the evidence was set before her, she was still *incredulous.*—*adv.* **in·cred/u·lous·ly.**

in·cre·ment (ĭn/krē-mĕnt; ĭng/krē-mĕnt), *n.* 1, increase; enlargement; 2, that which is added; especially, one of a series of small or regular additions; as, an *increment* of five dollars a year for seven years.

in·crim·i·nate (ĭn-krĭm/ĭ-nāt), *v.t.* [incriminat-ed, incriminat-ing], to charge with, or involve in, a crime; as, his words *incriminated* him.—*n.* **in·crim/i·na/tion.**

in·crust (ĭn-krŭst/), *v.t.* 1, to cover with, or as with, a crust; to coat; as, barnacles *incrust* the hulls of ships; 2, to overlay with a decorative covering, as with mosaics. Also spelled **en·crust/.**—*n.* **in/crus·ta/tion.**

in·cu·bate (ĭn/kū-bāt; ĭng/kū-bāt), *v.t.* [incubat-ed, incubat-ing], 1, to sit upon (eggs) in order to hatch them; brood; 2, to keep (eggs) under proper conditions, especially of warmth, for hatching them:—*v.i.* 1, to sit on eggs; brood; 2, to develop or hatch.—*n.* **in/cu·ba/tion.**

in·cu·ba·tor (ĭn/kū-bā/tēr; ĭng/kū-bā/tēr), *n.* 1, an apparatus for hatching eggs by artificial warmth; 2, an apparatus to help the growth of exceptionally small newborn or prematurely born babies.

in·cu·bus (ĭn/kū-bŭs; ĭng/kū-bŭs), *n.* [*pl.* incubuses or incubi (ĭn/kū-bī; ĭng/kū-bī)], 1, a nightmare; 2, any depressing weight or burden; as, the *incubus* of poverty.

in·cul·cate (ĭn-kŭl/kāt; ĭn/kŭl-kāt), *v.t.* [inculcat-ed, inculcat-ing], to impress upon the mind urgently; as, the mother tried to *inculcate* honesty on her children.—*n.* **in/cul·ca/tion.**

in·cum·bent (ĭn-kŭm/bĕnt), *adj.* 1, lying or leaning with its weight on something else; 2, pressing upon as a duty; as, it is *incumbent* upon every good citizen to vote:—*n.* the holder of an office, especially a church office.—*n.* **in·cum/ben·cy.**

in·cum·ber (ĭn-kŭm/bēr), *v.t.* to hinder or burden; encumber. See **encumber.**—*n.* **in·cum/brance.**

in·cur (ĭn-kûr/), *v.t.* [incurred, incur-ring], to meet with, fall into, or bring down upon oneself; as, to *incur* hatred, punishment, or the like.

in·cur·a·ble (ĭn-kūr/à-bl), *adj.* incapable of being healed; beyond the skill of medicine; as, an *incurable* disease:—*n.* a person diseased or crippled beyond remedy.—*adv.* **in·cur/a·bly.**—*n.* **in·cur/a·bil/i·ty.**

in·cur·sion (ĭn-kûr/zhŭn), *n.* an inroad; raid; invasion; as, an *incursion* into enemy territory.—*adj.* **in·cur/sive.**

in·curve (ĭn-kûrv/), *v.t.* and *v.i.* [incurved, incurv-ing], to bend inward.

Ind. abbreviation for *Indiana.*

in·debt·ed (ĭn-dĕt/ĕd), *adj.* 1, owing money; 2, under obligation; owing gratitude; as, I am *indebted* to you for your kindness.—*n.* **in·debt/ed·ness.**

in·de·cen·cy (ĭn-dē/sĕn·sĭ), *n.* [*pl.* indecencies], 1, want of delicacy, refinement, or good manners; 2, a word, act, picture, etc., offensive to modesty and good taste.

in·de·cent (ĭn-dē/sĕnt), *adj.* 1, unfit to be heard or seen; as, *indecent* language or pictures; 2, unbecoming; in bad taste; as, he spoke and left in *indecent* haste.—*adv.* **in·de/cent·ly.**

in·de·ci·sion (ĭn/dē-sĭzh/ŭn), *n.* inability to make up one's mind; hesitation.

in·de·ci·sive (ĭn/dē-sī/sĭv), *adj.* 1, not settling a matter; as, *indecisive* evidence; 2, not positive; uncertain; irresolute; as, an *indecisive* manner of speech.—*adv.* **in·de·ci/sive·ly.**

in·de·clin·a·ble (ĭn/dē-klīn/à-bl), *adj.* in grammar, describing a word that is not declined, or that keeps the same form in all cases.

in·dec·o·rous (ĭn-dĕk/ō-rŭs; ĭn/dē-kôr/ŭs), *adj.* in bad taste; improper; as, *indecorous* speech.—*adv.* **in·dec/o·rous·ly.**—*n.* **in·dec/o·rous·ness.**

in·deed (ĭn-dēd/), *adv.* in fact; in truth; as, I was *indeed* surprised.

in·de·fat·i·ga·ble (ĭn/dē-făt/ĭ-ga-bl), *adj.* incapable of being wearied; untiring; as, *indefatigable* workers.—*adv.* **in/de·fat/i·ga·bly.**—*n.* **in/de·fat/i·ga·bil/i·ty.**

in·de·fea·si·ble (ĭn/dē-fē/zĭ-bl), *adj.* incapable of being done away with, as a title, right, or claim.—*adv.* **in/de·fea/si·bly.**—*n.* **in/de·fea/si·bil/i·ty.**

in·de·fen·si·ble (ĭn/dē-fĕn/sĭ-bl), *adj.* without defense; especially, not capable of being held, maintained, or justified; as, an *indefensible* argument.—*n.* **in/de·fen/si·bil/i·ty.**

in·de·fin·a·ble (ĭn/dē-fīn/à-bl), *adj.* incapable of being described exactly or explained clearly; as, *indefinable* charm.

in·def·i·nite (ĭn-dĕf/ĭ-nĭt), *adj.* 1, not exact; vague; uncertain; as, his answers were *indefinite;* 2, having no fixed limit, amount, or number:—**indefinite article,** either of the words *a* or *an.*—*adv.* **in·def/i·nite·ly.**
  Syn. unsettled, unlimited, loose, lax.

in·del·i·ble (ĭn-dĕl′ĭ-bl), *adj.* incapable of being erased; as, *indelible* ink; also, incapable of being forgotten; as, an *indelible* impression.—*adv.* **in·del′i·bly.**

in·del·i·cate (ĭn-dĕl′ĭ-kĭt), *adj.* lacking in refinement; coarse.—*adv.* **in·del′i·cate·ly.** —*n.* **in·del′i·ca·cy.**

in·dem·ni·fi·ca·tion (ĭn-dĕm′nĭ-fĭ-kā′shŭn), *n.* compensation or repayment for loss, damage, injury, or expense.
Syn. reimbursement, amends, redress.

in·dem·ni·fy (ĭn-dĕm′nĭ-fī), *v.t.* [indemnified, indemnify-ing], to repay or compensate a person for loss, expense, or damage.

in·dem·ni·ty (ĭn-dĕm′nĭ-tĭ), *n.* [*pl.* indemnities], 1, insurance against loss, damage, or punishment; 2, repayment for loss or injury.

in·dent (ĭn-dĕnt′), *v.t.* 1, to give a zigzag outline to; notch; as, many small bays *indent* the coast; 2, in writing or printing, to begin (a line) with a blank space; 3, to make a depression in; dent; stamp; as, to *indent* the sand with footsteps.

in·den·ta·tion (ĭn′dĕn-tā′shŭn), *n.* 1, a small hollow or depression; a dent, as from a blow; 2, in writing or printing, a space at the beginning of a line; 3, a notch or cut.

in·den·tion (ĭn-dĕn′shŭn), *n.* 1, in writing or printing, a space at the beginning of a line; 2, a dent; an indenting.

in·den·ture (ĭn-dĕn′tŭr), *n.* 1, a dent; depression; indentation; 2, a written agreement or contract, especially one binding a servant or an apprentice to a master:— *v.t.* [indentured, indentur-ing], to bind by a written agreement, as an apprentice.

in·de·pend·ence (ĭn′dē-pĕn′dĕns), *n.* 1, freedom from support, control, or government by others; 2, an income or a sum of money sufficient for one's needs.
Syn. exemption, liberty, freedom.

Independence Day, July 4, a holiday in the U.S., celebrating the adoption of the Declaration of Independence in 1776.

in·de·pend·ent (ĭn′dē-pĕn′dĕnt), *adj.* 1, not relying on, supported by, or governed by, others; as, the American colonies declared themselves *independent* of England; 2, having enough money to live on; as, his family is *independent;* 3, not easily influenced; not biased; as, an *independent* thinker; 4, disinclined, through pride, to accept help:—*n.* one who in politics, art, literature, etc., acts or thinks for himself. —*adv.* **in′de-pend′ent·ly.**

in·de·scrib·a·ble (ĭn′dē-skrī′bȧ-bl), *adj.* 1, not sufficiently clear or definite to be described; indefinite; vague; as, an *indescribable* pain; 2, too great, beautiful, terrible, etc., to be described; beyond description; as, jewels of *indescribable* beauty.—*adv.* **in′de-scrib′a-bly.**

in·de·struct·i·ble (ĭn′dē-strŭk′tĭ-bl), *adj.* not capable of being broken up, ruined, or destroyed; durable; lasting.—*adv.* **in′de-struct′i·bly.**—*n.* **in′de-struct′i-bil′i-ty.**

in·de·ter·mi·nate (ĭn′dē-tûr′mĭ-nȧt), *adj.* not settled or fixed; indefinite; vague; as, an *indeterminate* sentence for a crime. —*adv.* **in′de-ter′mi-nate·ly.**

in·dex (ĭn′dĕks), *n.* [*pl.* indexes (ĭn′dĕk-sĕz) or indices (ĭn′dĭ-sēz)], 1, that which points out or indicates; a sign; as, busy factories are an *index* of prosperity; 2, the finger next to the thumb; 3, a pointer, as the hand on a dial; 4, a table of the contents of a book, arranged alphabetically and telling on what page each subject is treated; 5, in printing, a mark [☞] used to call attention:—*v.t.* 1, to provide (a book) with an alphabetical table of references; 2, to indicate.

Index, the *Index Librorum Prohibitorum,* a list of books regarded by the Roman Catholic Church as dangerous to the faith or morals of its members, who are forbidden to read them.

In·di·a (ĭn′dĭ-ȧ), the central peninsula of southern Asia (map 15). Most of the peninsula is now divided between the Republic of India (cap. New Delhi) and Pakistan (cap. Karachi), independent nations, members of the British Commonwealth of Nations. The Republic of India is predominantly Hindu; Pakistan predominantly Moslem. The peninsula also includes Portuguese colonies.

India ink, a black pigment used for fine drawing and painting; **India paper,** a thin paper, originally made in the Far East, used for writing and printing.

In·di·a·man (ĭn′dĭ-ȧ-măn), *n.* [*pl.* Indiamen (-mĕn)], a large merchant ship used in the India trade.

In·di·an (ĭn′dĭ-ăn), *adj.* 1, pertaining to India, the East Indies, or the British Indian Empire; 2, pertaining to the original inhabitants of America or their descendants, the American Indians; 2, made of maize, or Indian corn; as, *Indian* meal; 3, of a material, pattern, etc., made in India or by the American Indians; as, *Indian* baskets:—*n.* 1, a native of India; 2, one of the original inhabitants of America; also, the language of any of these people.

Indian club, a bottle-shaped club, swung by the hands in gymnastic exercises; **Indian corn,** an American cereal plant growing in tall stalks which

INDIAN CLUBS

bear large ears of grain; maize; **Indian file**, single file; **Indian summer**, a period of mild, pleasant, balmy weather, occurring in North America in the late fall, usually in November.

In·di·an·a (ĭn′dĭ-ăn′a̲), a north central State (cap. Indianapolis) of the U.S. (map 7).

In·di·an·ap·o·lis (ĭn′dĭ-ăn-ăp′ō-lĭs), a city, the capital of Indiana (map 7).

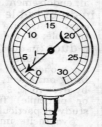

INDIAN CORN

In·di·an O·cean, one of the five great oceans of the world, lying south of Asia and east of Africa (map 15).

In·di·an Ter·ri·tor·y, a former territory of the U.S., southeast of Oklahoma, admitted to the Union in 1907 as part of the State of Oklahoma.

In·di·a rub·ber, a gummy, elastic substance; also, a piece of this, or an article made from it; rubber. See rubber.—*n.* and *adj.* **in′di·a-rub′ber.**—*adj.* **In′di·a–rub′ber.**

in·di·cate (ĭn′dĭ-kāt), *v.t.* [indicat-ed, indicat-ing], **1**, to point out; show; mark; as, signposts *indicate* the road; **2**, to suggest; also, to state briefly.
  Syn. betoken, signify, denote, disclose, intimate, hint.

in·di·ca·tion (ĭn′dĭ-kā′shŭn), *n.* **1**, the act of showing or pointing out; **2**, that which points out; a sign; symptom; evidence; as, the expression on the face is sometimes an *indication* of character.

in·dic·a·tive (ĭn-dĭk′a̲-tĭv), *adj.* **1**, pointing out; suggesting; as, cold hands are *indicative* of poor circulation; **2**, in grammar, designating, or having to do with, that mood of the verb used to state a fact or ask a direct question:—*n.* the indicative mood.—*adv.* **in·dic′a·tive·ly.**

in·di·ca·tor (ĭn′dĭ-kā′tẽr), *n.* one who or that which points out, especially a device for registering or showing something, as a rate of speed, the pressure of steam, etc.

in·di·ces (ĭn′dĭ-sēz), one form of the plural of *index.*

in·dict (ĭn-dīt′), *v.t.* to accuse; charge with a crime after finding evidence enough to warrant a trial; as, he was *indicted* for theft.—*n.* **in·dict′er; in·dict′or.**

in·dict·a·ble (ĭn-dīt′a̲-bl), *adj.* **1**, liable

INDICATOR
On dial of steam gauge

to be indicted, or charged with a crime; **2**, giving cause for indictment.

in·dict·ment (ĭn-dīt′mĕnt), *n.* **1**, a written accusation against one or more persons, laid before a grand jury, by whom in turn it is presented to the court; **2**, the act of presenting this document; **3**, the legal document containing the accusation: also called *bill of indictment.*

In·dies (ĭn′dĭz), formerly, the East Indies or the West Indies; now, usually, the East Indies.

in·dif·fer·ence (ĭn-dĭf′ẽr-ĕns), *n.* **1**, the state of not being concerned about something; absence of feeling for or against; unconcern; **2**, unimportance; insignificance; as, to win or lose was a matter of *indifference* to him.
  Syn. apathy, listlessness, coldness.

in·dif·fer·ent (ĭn-dĭf′ẽr-ĕnt), *adj.* **1**, not caring or concerned about something; feeling no interest; as, a poor ruler is *indifferent* to the wishes of his people; **2**, neither good nor bad; mediocre; as, *indifferent* work; **3**, having no preference; taking neither side, as in an argument; as, he maintained an *indifferent* attitude.

in·di·gence (ĭn′dĭ-jĕns), *n.* poverty; need.
  Syn. penury, lack, privation.

in·dig·e·nous (ĭn-dĭj′ē-nŭs), *adj.* born or produced in a particular place or country; native; as, tobacco is *indigenous* to America.—*adv.* **in·dig′e·nous·ly.**
  Syn. inborn, inherent, innate, natural.

in·di·gent (ĭn′dĭ-jĕnt), *adj.* very poor; needy; as, an *indigent* widow.

in·di·gest·i·ble (ĭn′dĭ-jĕs′tĭ-bl; ĭn′dī-jĕs′tĭ-bl), *adj.* hard or impossible to digest.—*adv.* **in′di·gest′i·bly.**

in·di·ges·tion (ĭn′dĭ-jĕs′chŭn), *n.* difficulty in digesting food; the discomfort caused by such difficulty; dyspepsia.

in·dig·nant (ĭn-dĭg′nănt), *adj.* feeling anger and scorn because of unfair treatment.—*adv.* **in·dig′nant·ly.**

in·dig·na·tion (ĭn′dĭg-nā′shŭn), *n.* anger aroused by injustice, meanness, or something low or evil; anger mixed with scorn.
  Syn. wrath, ire, resentment, fury, rage.

in·dig·ni·ty (ĭn-dĭg′nĭ-tĭ), *n.* [*pl.* indignities], an act or saying which injures the dignity of someone else; an insult; a slight.
  Syn. affront, discourtesy, rudeness.

in·di·go (ĭn′dĭ-gō), *n.* [*pl.* indigos or indigoes], **1**, a manufactured blue dye, formerly obtained from the indigo plant; **2**, a deep-violet blue: also called *indigo blue.*

indigo bird, a finch of the eastern U.S., socalled from the brilliant, indigo-blue color of the male bird: also called *indigo bunting.*

go; join; yet; sing; chin; show; thin, *th*en; hw, *why*; zh, azure; ü, Ger. für or Fr. lune; ö, Ger. schön or Fr. feu; n̈, Fr. enfant, nom; kh, Ger. ach or ich. See pages ix–x.

in·di·rect (ĭn′dĭ-rĕkt′; ĭn′dĭ-rĕkt′), *adj.*
1, not straight; not in a direct line; as, an *indirect* road; **2**, roundabout; as, *indirect* taxation; **3**, not straightforward; as, an *indirect* reply.—*adv.* **in′di-rect′ly.**—*n.* **in′di-rect′ness.**

in·dis·creet (ĭn′dĭs-krēt′), *adj.* not cautious or careful; unwise; imprudent; as, an *indiscreet* remark.—*adv.* **in′dis·creet′ly.**

in·dis·cre·tion (ĭn′dĭs-krĕsh′ŭn), *n.* **1**, rashness; lack of caution; **2**, an indiscreet or imprudent act.

in·dis·crim·i·nate (ĭn′dĭs-krĭm′ĭ-nĭt), *adj.* not distinguishing differences between one person or thing and another or others; not choosing or chosen carefully; as, an *indiscriminate* reader; *indiscriminate* reading.—*adv.* **in′dis·crim′i·nate·ly.**

in·dis·pen·sa·ble (ĭn′dĭs-pĕn′sà-bl), *adj.* not to be done without; absolutely necessary; as, food is *indispensable* to life.
Syn. essential, requisite.

in·dis·pose (ĭn′dĭs-pōz′), *v.t.* [indisposed, indispos-ing], **1**, to make unsuited or unfit; disqualify; **2**, to make ill; **3**, to make averse or unwilling; disincline.

in·dis·posed (ĭn′dĭs-pōzd′), *adj.* **1**, ill; unwell; **2**, unwilling; averse.

in·dis·po·si·tion (ĭn′dĭs-pŏ-zĭsh′ŭn), *n.* **1**, an illness, especially one that is not serious; **2**, aversion; unwillingness.
Syn. sickness, ailment, disease.

in·dis·pu·ta·ble (ĭn-dĭs′pū-tà-bl; ĭn′dĭs-pūt′à-bl), *adj.* absolutely true; beyond question.—*adv.* **in·dis′pu·ta·bly.**

in·dis·so·lu·ble (ĭn-dĭs′ō-lū-bl; ĭn′dĭ-sŏl′ū-bl), *adj.* not capable of being broken up; indestructible; as, an *indissoluble* substance; an *indissoluble* friendship.

in·dis·tinct (ĭn′dĭs-tĭngkt′), *adj.* not distinct or clear; as, an *indistinct* sound.—*adv.* **in′dis·tinct′ly.**

in·dis·tin·guish·a·ble (ĭn′dĭs-tĭng′gwĭsh-à-bl), *adj.* not capable of being made out or perceived.—*adv.* **in′dis·tin′guish·a·bly.**

in·dite (ĭn-dīt′), *v.t.* [indit-ed, indit-ing], to compose; express in words; write.

in·di·vid·u·al (ĭn′dĭ-vĭd′ū-ăl), *adj.* **1**, of or belonging to a single person or thing; as, *individual* lockers; **2**, one's own; as, an *individual* style of speaking:—*n.* a single or separate person, animal, or thing.—*adv.* **in′di·vid′u·al·ly.**

in·di·vid·u·al·ism (ĭn′dĭ-vĭd′ū-ăl-ĭzm), *n.* **1**, the conduct of a person who considers his own interests first; hence, great self-interest; selfishness; **2**, in religion and politics, a theory which favors individual development and full liberty of belief and action.

in·di·vid·u·al·ist (ĭn′dĭ-vĭd′ū-ăl-ĭst), *n.* **1**, one who thinks or acts for himself; **2**, one who believes in individualism.—*adj.* **in′di·vid′u·al·is′tic.**

in·di·vid·u·al·i·ty (ĭn′dĭ-vĭd′ū-ăl′ĭ-tĭ), *n.* [*pl.* individualities], **1**, the quality or state of existing separately, or apart from other persons or things; separate existence; **2**, the sum of all the characteristics that mark one person or thing as different and separate from another; personality; **3**, an individual person or thing.

in·di·vid·u·al·ize (ĭn′dĭ-vĭd′ū-ăl-īz), *v.t.* [individualized, individualiz-ing], **1**, to give a distinct, or individual, character to (something); as, to *individualize* instruction; **2**, to treat separately or individually.

in·di·vis·i·ble (ĭn′dĭ-vĭz′ĭ-bl), *adj.* not capable of being divided into parts.

In·do·chi·na (ĭn′dō-chī′nà), **1**, a peninsula of southeastern Asia; **2**, the associated states of Laos, Cambodia, and Vietnam (map **15**). Also **In′do-Chi′na.**

In·do–Eu·ro·pe·an (ĭn′dō-ū′rō-pē′ăn), *adj.* designating the largest family of languages in the world, including most of the languages of Europe and northern India.

in·do·lence (ĭn′dō-lĕns), *n.* love of ease; laziness; dislike for work.

in·do·lent (ĭn′dō-lĕnt), *adj.* fond of ease; avoiding labor; lazy.—*adv.* **in′do·lent·ly.**

in·dom·i·ta·ble (ĭn-dŏm′ĭ-tà-bl), *adj.* unconquerable; stubborn; unyielding; as, an *indomitable* will.—*adv.* **in·dom′i·ta·bly.**

In·do·ne·sia (ĭn′dō-nē′zhà), a republic (formerly Netherlands Indies) in southeastern Asia.

in·door (ĭn′dôr′), *adj.* pertaining to the inside of a building; living, belonging, or done, within doors; as, *indoor* sports.

in·doors (ĭn′dôrz′; ĭn′dôrz′), *adv.* in or into the house; as, play *indoors*; go *indoors.*

in·dorse (ĭn-dôrs′), *v.t.* [indorsed, indorsing], approve; endorse. See **endorse.**

in·dorse·ment (ĭn-dôrs′mĕnt), *n.* approval; endorsement. See **endorsement.**

in·du·bi·ta·ble (ĭn-dū′bĭ-tà-bl), *adj.* too clear or certain to be doubted; unquestionable; as, *indubitable* facts.

in·duce (ĭn-dūs′), *v.t.* [induced, induc-ing], **1**, to persuade; influence; prevail upon; as, money will *induce* him to go; **2**, to bring on; effect; cause; as, illness *induced* by overwork; **3**, to arrive at (a conclusion or principle) from the observation or study of particular cases.
Syn. incite, impel, urge, move, persuade.

in·duce·ment (ĭn-dūs′mĕnt), *n.* something that persuades to action, or influences conduct; motive; incentive.

in·duct (ĭn-dŭkt′), *v.t.* to introduce; put into office; install; as, to *induct* the new governor into office.

in·duc·tion (ĭn-dŭk′shŭn), *n.* 1, the introduction of a person into office; 2, in electricity, the act or process by which a conductor becomes electrified when near, but not touching, a body that is charged; 3, the process of reasoning by which a general conclusion is reached from a study of particular facts.—*adj.* **in·duc′tive.**

in·due (ĭn-dū′), *v.t.* [indued, indu-ing], 1, to put on, as clothes; 2, to furnish; equip; endue; as, man is *indued* with a sense of justice.

in·dulge (ĭn-dŭlj′), *v.t.* [indulged, indulg-ing], 1, to give way to; humor; as, the nurse *indulged* the sick child; 2, to yield to; as, to *indulge* a love of sweets:—*v.i.* to gratify one's desires, usually without restraint; as, to *indulge* in candy.

in·dul·gence (ĭn-dŭl′jĕns), *n.* 1, the pleasing or humoring of another; 2, the yielding to, or gratifying of, one's own desires; as, smoking was his only *indulgence;* 3, in the Roman Catholic Church, remission of temporal punishment still due for sin after repentance and absolution.

in·dul·gent (ĭn-dŭl′jĕnt), *adj.* yielding to the humor or wishes of another; as, an *indulgent* parent; also, too forbearing; too lenient.—*adv.* **in·dul′gent·ly.**

In·dus (ĭn′dŭs), the great river of Pakistan, flowing into the Arabian Sea (map 15).

in·dus·tri·al (ĭn-dŭs′trĭ-ăl), *adj.* of or pertaining to industry; as, *industrial* troubles; an *industrial* school.

in·dus·tri·ous (ĭn-dŭs′trĭ-ŭs), *adj.* diligent; hard-working; as, an *industrious* wife.—*adv.* **in·dus′tri·ous·ly.**

Syn. active, busy, engaged, occupied.

in·dus·try (ĭn′dŭs-trĭ), *n.* [*pl.* industries], 1, steady application to a task; diligence; 2, all forms of business and manufacture; 3, in a more limited sense, the occupations that produce goods, as distinguished from finance and commerce; 4, a particular branch of work or trade; as, the cotton *industry.*

in·e·bri·ate (ĭn-ē′brĭ-āt), *v.t.* [inebriat-ed, inebriat-ing], to make drunk; intoxicate:—*n.* (ĭn-ē′brĭ-āt), a drunkard:—*adj.* (ĭn-ē′brĭ-āt), drunken; intoxicated.—*n.* **in·e′bri·a′tion.**

in·ed·i·ble (ĭn-ĕd′ĭ-bl), *adj.* not fit to be eaten.—*n.* **in·ed′i·bil′i·ty.**

in·ef·fa·ble (ĭn-ĕf′ȧ-bl), *adj.* incapable of being expressed in words; beyond description; as, *ineffable* joy.—*adv.* **in·ef′fa·bly.**

in·ef·fec·tive (ĭn′ĕ-fĕk′tĭv), *adj.* not pro-ducing, or unable to produce, the desired result; ineffectual; as, his urgent plea was *ineffective.*—*adv.* **in′ef·fec′tive·ly.**—*n.* **in′ef·fec′tive·ness.**

in·ef·fec·tu·al (ĭn′ĕ-fĕk′tū-ăl), *adj.* without result; weak; unsuccessful; as, all his efforts were *ineffectual.*—*adv.* **in′ef·fec′tu·al·ly.**

Syn. vain, useless, ineffective.

in·ef·fi·cient (ĭn′ĕ-fĭsh′ĕnt), *adj.* 1, not producing, or not capable of producing, the desired effect; as, *inefficient* labor; 2, incapable; lacking in skill or in willingness to work well; as, an *inefficient* workman.—*adv.* **in′ef·fi′cient·ly.**—*n.* **in′ef·fi′cien·cy.**

in·e·las·tic (ĭn′ē-lăs′tĭk), *adj.* 1, not capable, when stretched or compressed, of regaining its original form; 2, unyielding; not adaptable.

in·el·e·gant (ĭn-ĕl′ē-gănt), *adj.* lacking in elegance, refinement, or good taste.—*adv.* **in·el′e·gant·ly.**—*n.* **in·el′e·gance.**

in·el·i·gi·ble (ĭn-ĕl′ĭ-jĭ-bl), *adj.* 1, unfit; unsuitable; as, a lame man is *ineligible* for the army; 2, not qualified legally for an office or position; as, his youth makes him *ineligible* for Congress.—*adv.* **in·el′i·gi·bly.**—*n.* **in·el′i·gi·bil′i·ty.**

in·ept (ĭn-ĕpt′), *adj.* 1, not fit or suitable; 2, clumsy; inefficient; as, he was an *inept* oarsman; 3, out of place; absurd; as, an *inept* remark.

in·ept·i·tude (ĭn-ĕp′tĭ-tūd), *n.* unfitness; unsuitability; also, a foolish action or remark; as, a speech full of *ineptitudes.*

in·e·qual·i·ty (ĭn′ē-kwŏl′ĭ-tĭ; ĭn′ē-kwôl′ĭ-tĭ), *n.* [*pl.* inequalities], 1, the quality of being unequal; difference of rank, station, size, number, etc.; 2, unevenness, as in surface; changeableness in the condition of a person or thing; as, *inequalities* of temper, the weather, etc.

in·eq·ui·ta·ble (ĭn-ĕk′wĭ-tȧ-bl), *adj.* not fair; unjust.—*adv.* **in·eq′ui·ta·bly.**

in·eq·ui·ty (ĭn-ĕk′wĭ-tĭ), *n.* [*pl.* inequities], lack of fairness; injustice.

in·ert (ĭn-ûrt′), *adj.* 1, without power to move; lifeless; as, an *inert* mass of rock; 2, slow; sluggish; 3, having no active chemical powers; as, an *inert* drug.—*adv.* **in·ert′ly.**—*n.* **in·ert′ness.**

Syn. passive, dead, dull, inactive.

in·er·tia (ĭn-ûr′shȧ; ĭn-ûr′shĭ-ȧ), *n.* 1, the tendency not to move, change, or exert oneself; 2, in physics, that property of matter which causes a body at rest to stay motionless, or a body in motion to continue moving in the same direction and at the same speed, unless acted upon by some outside force.

in·es·ti·ma·ble (ĭn-ĕs′tĭ-mȧ-bl), *adj.* beyond measure or price; as, the work of our public schools is of *inestimable* value.—*adv.* **in·es′ti·ma·bly.**

in·ev·i·ta·ble (ĭn-ĕv′ĭ-tȧ-bl), *adj.* not to be escaped or shunned; unavoidable; as, *inevitable* death.—*adv.* **in·ev′i·ta·bly.**—*n.* **in·ev′i·ta·bil′i·ty.**

in·ex·act (ĭn′ĕg-zăkt′), *adj.* not exact or accurate; incorrect.—*adv.* **in′ex-act′ly.**—*n.* **in′ex-act′ness.**

in·ex·cus·a·ble (ĭn′ĕks-kūz′ȧ-bl), *adj.* not to be excused or justified; as, *inexcusable* rudeness.—*adv.* **in′ex-cus′a·bly.**

in·ex·haust·i·ble (ĭn′ĕg-zôs′tĭ-bl), *adj.* 1, incapable of being used up; unfailing; as, *inexhaustible* resources; 2, of tireless power, vigor, or strength; unwearied.—*adv.* **in′ex-haust′i·bly.**

in·ex·o·ra·ble (ĭn-ĕk′sō-rȧ-bl), *adj.* not to be moved by prayers; unyielding; unrelenting; as, an *inexorable* enemy.

in·ex·pe·di·ent (ĭn′ĕks-pē′dĭ-ĕnt), *adj.* not advisable; not suitable or wise; as, it would be *inexpedient* to increase taxes now. —*n.* **in′ex-pe′di-en-cy.**

in·ex·pen·sive (ĭn′ĕks-pĕn′sĭv), *adj.* cheap; costing little.—*adv.* **in′ex-pen′sive-ly.**

in·ex·pe·ri·ence (ĭn′ĕks-pē′rĭ-ĕns), *n.* want of experience; lack of firsthand knowledge.

in·ex·pe·ri·enced (ĭn′ĕks-pē′rĭ-ĕnst), *adj.* lacking the personal knowledge and skill that comes from living a practical, active life; lacking firsthand knowledge of any special kind of work; lacking practice.

in·ex·pert (ĭn′ĕks-pûrt′), *adj.* unskilled; lacking the knowledge gained from practice.—*adv.* **in′ex-pert′ly.**

in·ex·pi·a·ble (ĭn-ĕks′pĭ-ȧ-bl), *adj.* not capable of being atoned for; as, an *inexpiable* crime.

in·ex·pli·ca·ble (ĭn-ĕks′plĭ-kȧ-bl), *adj.* not capable of being explained or understood; as, an *inexplicable* mystery.—*adv.* **in·ex′pli·ca·bly.**—*n.* **in·ex′pli·ca·bil′i·ty.**

in·ex·press·i·ble (ĭn′ĕks-prĕs′ĭ-bl), *adj.* not capable of being put into words; unutterable.—*adv.* **in′ex-press′i·bly.**

in·ex·tin·guish·a·ble (ĭn′ĕks-tĭng′gwĭsh-ȧ-bl), *adj.* that cannot be put out, as a fire; unquenchable.

in·ex·tri·ca·ble (ĭn-ĕks′trĭ-kȧ-bl), *adj.* incapable of being untied or disentangled; hopelessly confused; incapable of being solved; as, an *inextricable* difficulty.—*adv.* **in·ex′tri·ca·bly.**

inf. abbreviation for *infinitive.*

in·fal·li·ble (ĭn-făl′ĭ-bl), *adj.* 1, incapable of failing; unerring; not capable of making a mistake; as, God is *infallible;* 2, absolutely trustworthy; unfailing; as, an *infallible* remedy; an *infallible* friend.—*adv.* **in·fal′li·bly.**—*n.* **in·fal′li·bil′i·ty.**

in·fa·mous (ĭn′fȧ-mŭs), *adj.* 1, having a bad reputation; notorious; as, an *infamous* traitor; 2, villainous; as, an *infamous* plot to kill the king.—*adv.* **in′fa·mous·ly.**

Syn. shameful, scandalous, contemptible, odious.

in·fa·my (ĭn′fȧ-mĭ), *n.* [*pl.* infamies], 1, public disgrace; dishonor; 2, baseness; vileness; also, a disgraceful act.

Syn. wickedness, shame.

in·fan·cy (ĭn′făn-sĭ), *n.* 1, babyhood and early childhood; 2, the first stage of anything; as, the *infancy* of a nation.

in·fant (ĭn′fănt), *n.* 1, a baby; a young child; 2, in law, a person who has not attained the age of 21:—*adj.* pertaining to, or intended for, babies or young children; as, *infant* diet; an *infant* school; also, pertaining to the earliest stages of anything; very young; undeveloped; as, an *infant* industry.

in·fan·ti·cide (ĭn-făn′tĭ-sīd), *n.* 1, the murder of a newly born child; 2, one who kills a newly born child.

in·fan·tile (ĭn′făn-tīl; ĭn′făn-tĭl), *adj.* pertaining to babies or to the period of babyhood; as, *infantile* diseases; also, childish; as, *infantile* diversions.

in·fan·try (ĭn′făn-trĭ), *n.* soldiers who are armed, equipped, and trained for service on foot; foot soldiers.—*n.* **in′fan·try·man.**

in·fat·u·at·ed (ĭn-făt′ū-āt′ĕd), *adj.* showing foolish fondness; so inspired with an extravagant passion for something as to be wanting in sound judgment about it.

in·fat·u·a·tion (ĭn-făt′ū-ā′shŭn), *n.* 1, the state of being infatuated; 2, an extravagant, unreasoning passion.

in·fect (ĭn-fĕkt′), *v.t.* 1, to affect (a person or persons) with disease by spreading germs; as, nurses are now inoculated against typhoid fever, so that they cannot be *infected* with the disease; 2, to taint or poison (a wound, instrument, drinking water, etc.) with germs; 3, to affect or influence with a mood, feeling, or idea; as, Jane's giggles *infected* her playmates.

in·fec·tion (ĭn-fĕk′shŭn), *n.* 1, the communication of disease germs; 2, a disease communicated by germs in any manner.

in·fec·tious (ĭn-fĕk′shŭs), *adj.* 1, capable of spreading by means of germs; as, mumps and typhoid fever are *infectious* diseases; 2, readily communicated or spread; as, *infectious* gaiety.—*adv.* **in·fec′tious·ly.**

Syn. communicable, contagious.

āte, âorta, râre, căt, ȧsk, fär, ăllow, sofȧ; ēve, ĕvent, ĕll, writẽr, novĕl; bīte, pĭn; nō, ōbey, ôr, dŏg, tŏp, cŏllide; ūnit, ūnite, bûrn, cŭt, focŭs; no͞on, fŏŏt; mound; coin;

in·fe·lic·i·tous (ĭn′fē-lĭs′ĭ-tŭs), *adj.* unfortunate; unhappy; also, inapt; as, an *infelicitous* answer.

in·fer (ĭn-fûr′), *v.t.* [inferred, infer-ring], **1,** to arrive at (a conclusion) by reasoning; as, they *inferred* from the students' improved health that gymnasium work was a benefit; **2,** to give an indication of; imply; suggest; as, your haste *infers* eagerness.

in·fer·ence (ĭn′fẽr-ĕns), *n.* **1,** the act of arriving at a conclusion by reasoning; **2,** a conclusion so reached.

in·fe·ri·or (ĭn-fîr′ĭ-ẽr), *adj.* **1,** lower in place, rank, or value; secondary; as, an *inferior* court; an *inferior* officer; **2,** second-rate; poor; as, *inferior* workmanship:—*n.* one who ranks below another.

in·fe·ri·or·i·ty (ĭn-fîr′ĭ-ŏr′ĭ-tĭ), *n.* a lower state or quality:—**inferiority complex,** an exaggerated feeling that one is not equal to others in ability or station.

in·fer·nal (ĭn-fûr′năl), *adj.* **1,** belonging to, or resembling, hell; hellish; **2,** fiendish; outrageous.—*adv.* **in·fer′nal·ly.**

in·fer·no (ĭn-fûr′nō), *n.* [*pl.* infernos], **1,** the lower regions; hell; **2,** a place or a scene so horrible as to resemble hell.

in·fest (ĭn-fĕst′), *v.t.* to overrun; swarm in or over; trouble or annoy constantly or in numbers; as, moths *infested* the woolen material; pirates *infested* the coast.
Syn. molest, plague, harass.

in·fi·del (ĭn′fĭ-dĕl), *n.* one who does not believe in a certain religion; an unbeliever, as, among Mohammedans, one who is not a Mohammedan, and among Christians, one who is not a Christian:—*adj.* **1,** unbelieving; heathen; **2,** pertaining to, or like, infidels; as, *infidel* contempt for the faith.
Syn., n. unbeliever, skeptic.

in·fi·del·i·ty (ĭn′fĭ-dĕl′ĭ-tĭ; ĭn′fĭ-dĕl′ĭ-tĭ), *n.* [*pl.* infidelities], **1,** disbelief in religion, especially in the Christian religion; **2,** the breaking of a trust; unfaithfulness.

in·field (ĭn′fēld′), *n.* in baseball: **1,** the space enclosed within the base lines; the diamond as distinguished from the *outfield;* **2,** the infield players as a whole.

in·fil·trate (ĭn-fĭl′trāt), *v.t.* and *v.i.* [infiltrat-ed, infiltrat-ing], **1,** to pass slowly through very small openings; filter; percolate; **2,** to enter enemy territory, individually or in small groups, for purposes of sabotage or attack from the rear.—*n.* **in′-fil·tra′tion.**

in·fi·nite (ĭn′fĭ-nĭt), *adj.* **1,** without limit in quantity; as, *infinite* wisdom; **2,** unlimited; endless in extent; as, space is *infinite:—n.* that which has no limit:—**the Infinite,** God; the Supreme Being.—*adj.* **in′fi·nite·ly.**
Syn., adj. endless, eternal.

in·fin·i·tes·i·mal (ĭn′fĭn-ĭ-tĕs′ĭ-măl), *adj.* too small to be measured; microscopic.—*adv.* **in′fin·i·tes′i·mal·ly.**

in·fin·i·tive (ĭn-fĭn′ĭ-tĭv), *n.* in grammar, a part of the verb which expresses the general meaning of the verb without any inflection for person or number, usually having the same form as the stem of the present tense: often, though not always, used with *to;* as, he longs *to go;* this is a good road on which *to travel;* help me *finish* the job:—*adj.* pertaining to, or formed with, the infinitive; as, an *infinitive* phrase.

in·fin·i·tude (ĭn-fĭn′ĭ-tūd), *n.* the quality of being beyond measure or number; boundlessness; as, the *infinitude* of stars; the *infinitude* of space.

in·fin·i·ty (ĭn-fĭn′ĭ-tĭ), *n.* [*pl.* infinities], **1,** the state of being infinite or beyond measure in time, space, number, etc.; boundlessness; **2,** space or time considered as boundless; **3,** an infinite quantity or number.

in·firm (ĭn-fûrm′), *adj.* **1,** not well or sound physically; weak; **2,** weak of mind, will, or character; irresolute; wavering; as, a man *infirm* of purpose.—*adv.* **in·firm′ly.**
Syn. unsound, decrepit, precarious.

in·fir·ma·ry (ĭn-fûr′mȧ-rĭ), *n.* [*pl.* infirmaries], a room or building in which the sick or injured are cared for, especially in a school or institution.

in·fir·mi·ty (ĭn-fûr′mĭ-tĭ), *n.* [*pl.* infirmities], **1,** the state of being weak or sick; **2,** weakness of mind or character; frailty; as, his friends have to bear his *infirmities.*

in·flame (ĭn-flām′), *v.t.* [inflamed, inflaming], **1,** to set on fire; **2,** to excite; arouse; as, the speaker *inflamed* the crowd's anger; **3,** to put into a state of redness, swelling, and pain; as, weeping *inflames* the eyes.
Syn. anger, enrage, incense, exasperate.

in·flam·ma·ble (ĭn-flăm′ȧ-bl), *adj.* **1,** easily set on fire; as, kerosene is *inflammable;* **2,** easily excited; as, an *inflammable* temper.

in·flam·ma·tion (ĭn′flȧ-mā′shŭn), *n.* **1,** the act of inflaming; **2,** an unnatural condition of any part of the body, marked by redness, heat, swelling, and pain.

in·flam·ma·tor·y (ĭn-flăm′ȧ-tôr′ĭ), *adj.* **1,** tending to excite anger or rebellion; **2,** causing, or showing, inflammation.

in·flate (ĭn-flāt′), *v.t.* [inflat-ed, inflat-ing], **1,** to swell out with air or gas, as a balloon or a tire; **2,** to puff up; to elate; as, *inflated* with pride; **3,** to raise beyond reason, as prices:—**inflate the currency,** to increase the amount of paper money in circulation, without any addition to the gold or silver reserve, thus causing a rise in prices.

in-fla-tion (ĭn-flā′shŭn), *n.* **1,** the act of inflating, or state of being inflated; **2,** abnormal and sudden increase in the quantity of paper money in circulation or the amount of credit in use, without addition to the precious metal held in reserve.

in-flect (ĭn-flĕkt′), *v.t.* **1,** to change the pitch or tone of (the voice); **2,** to vary the form of (a word) so as to show grammatical changes in person, number, case, etc., as *he, his, him, they, their, them.*

in-flec-tion or **in-flex-ion** (ĭn-flĕk′shŭn), *n.* **1,** the rise and fall in the voice; **2,** the changes in the form of words, showing case, number, gender, tense, etc.—*adj.* **in-flec′tion-al; in-flex′ion-al.**

in-flex-i-ble (ĭn-flĕk′sĭ-bl), *adj.* **1,** not able to be bent; rigid; as, an *inflexible* rod of iron; **2,** not to be moved by entreaty; unyielding; as, he has an *inflexible* will.— *adv.* **in-flex′i-bly.**—*n.* **in-flex′i-bil′i-ty.**
Syn. unbending, rigorous, resolute.

in-flict (ĭn-flĭkt′), *v.t.* **1,** to cause by, or as if by, striking; as, to *inflict* a wound; **2,** to impose (a punishment or penalty) on someone.—*n.* **in-flic′tion.**

in-flo-res-cence (ĭn′flō-rĕs′ĕns), *n.* **1,** a blooming or flowering; **2,** the arrangement of flowers on a stem; also, a blossom, flower, or cluster of flowers.

in-flow (ĭn′flō′), *n.* a flowing in; also, that which flows in.

in-flu-ence (ĭn′flŏŏ-ĕns), *n.* **1,** a power tending to produce results by indirect or invisible means; the power of personality; moral power; as, the *influence* of a good example; **2,** power arising from wealth or station; as, political *influence;* **3,** one who, or that which, exerts a power:—*v.t.* [influenced, influenc-ing], **1,** to have power over, physically or mentally; **2,** to affect; as, weather *influences* crops.

in-flu-en-tial (ĭn′flŏŏ-ĕn′shăl), *adj.* having or exerting power; as, an *influential* citizen.—*adv.* **in′flu-en′tial-ly.**

in-flu-en-za (ĭn′flŏŏ-ĕn′za), *n.* a severe infectious disease, frequently occurring in epidemic form, characterized by inflammation of the air passages, severe muscular pains, and headache: popularly called *flu.*

in-flux (ĭn′flŭks), *n.* an inflow; a pouring in; as, an *influx* of money into a bank.

in-fold (ĭn-fōld′), *v.t.* to wrap; envelop; embrace. Also spelled **en-fold′.**

in-form (ĭn-fôrm′), *v.t.* to supply with knowledge; notify; tell:—*v.i.* to give information, especially in accusation; as, the neighbors *informed* against him.—*adj.* **in-form′a-tive.**
Syn. advise, enlighten.

in-for-mal (ĭn-fôr′măl), *adj.* not according to custom or rule; without ceremony; as, an *informal* dance; an *informal* talk. —*adv.* **in-for′mal-ly.**

in-for-mal-i-ty (ĭn′fôr-măl′ĭ-tĭ), *n.* [*pl.* informalities], want of regular, customary, or legal form or ceremony; also, an informal act; as, to walk into a neighbor's house by the back door is an *informality.*

in-form-ant (ĭn-fôr′mănt), *n.* one who gives news or information.

in-for-ma-tion (ĭn′fôr-mā′shŭn), *n.* knowledge given or acquired; especially, knowledge of facts; also, news.
Syn. tidings, intelligence.

in-form-er (ĭn-fôr′mēr), *n.* one who gives information or news; a talebearer; especially, one who informs the authorities as to some breaking of the law.

in-frac-tion (ĭn-frăk′shŭn), *n.* the act of breaking; especially, the act of breaking a law or rule.

in-fre-quent (ĭn-frē′kwĕnt), *adj.* seldom occurring; as, *infrequent* visits; *infrequent* rains.—*adv.* **in-fre′quent-ly.**—*n.* **in-fre′-quence; in-fre′quen-cy.**

in-fringe (ĭn-frĭnj′), *v.t.* [infringed, infringing], to disregard or break, as a law:—*v.i.* to trespass; as, to *infringe* upon another person's liberty.
Syn. invade, transgress.

in-fringe-ment (ĭn-frĭnj′mĕnt), *n.* **1,** the act of breaking or disregarding a law; **2,** trespass on a right, as by the unlawful use of a trade name or trade-mark; as, an *infringement* of a patent.

in-fu-ri-ate (ĭn-fū′rĭ-āt), *v.t.* [infuriat-ed, infuriat-ing], to enrage; madden; as, anything of a red color is said to *infuriate* a bull.—*n.* **in-fu′ri-a′tion.**

in-fuse (ĭn-fūz′), *v.t.* [infused, infus-ing], **1,** to introduce, as by pouring; **2,** to instil; inspire; as, to *infuse* a spirit of good will into a class; **3,** to steep in liquid; as, to *infuse* tea in boiling water.

in-fu-sion (ĭn-fū′zhŭn), *n.* **1,** a pouring in; something poured in or mingled; as, the *infusion* of new blood into old stock by breeding; **2,** the teaching, as of ideas, high principles, etc.; **3,** the process of steeping a substance in water to extract something from it; also, the liquid so obtained.

-ing (-ĭng), a suffix used to form: **1,** the present participle of verbs; as, walk*ing* down the street; a walk*ing* delegate; **2,** nouns from verb stems, naming an act; as, runn*ing* is much harder than walk*ing;* **3,** nouns meaning something that does a specified act; as, cover*ing;* **4,** nouns meaning something used for a special purpose; as, ceil*ing;* dwell*ing.*

in·gen·ious (ĭn-jēn′yŭs), *adj.* **1,** creative; gifted; clever; as, an *ingenious* mind; **2,** skilfully made or contrived; as, an *ingenious* device.—*adv.* **in·gen′ious·ly.**—*n.* **in·gen′ious·ness.**
Syn. adroit, deft.

in·ge·nu·i·ty (ĭn′jĕ-nū′ĭ-tĭ), *n.* [*pl.* ingenuities], **1,** cleverness in inventing; ingeniousness; **2,** cleverness of design or construction; as, *ingenuity* of plot.
Syn. inventiveness, originality.

in·gen·u·ous (ĭn-jĕn′ū-ŭs), *adj.* frank; innocent; sincere; as, an *ingenuous* child. —*adv.* **in·gen′u·ous·ly.**
Syn. unreserved, simple.

in·gle·nook (ĭng′gl-nōōk′), *n.* a chimney corner. Also written **in′gle nook.**

in·glor·i·ous (ĭn-glôr′ĭ-ŭs), *adj.* **1,** without fame; humble; **2,** disgraceful; shameful; as, an *inglorious* defeat.—*adv.* **inglor′i·ous·ly.**

in·got (ĭng′gŏt), *n.* a mass of cast metal, such as gold, silver, or steel.

in·graft (ĭn-grȧft′), *v.t.* to graft. See **engraft.**

in·grain (ĭn′grān′), *n.* woolen yarn dyed with a lasting color before weaving; also, a carpet made of such yarn.

in·grained (ĭn′grānd′), *adj.* thoroughly worked into the fabric, as color into yarn which is dyed before weaving; hence, permanent; deeply rooted; as, an *ingrained* prejudice.

in·grate (ĭn′grāt; ĭn-grāt′), *n.* one who is ungrateful; a thankless person.

in·gra·ti·ate (ĭn-grā′shĭ-āt), *v.t.* [ingratiat-ed, ingratiat-ing], to bring (oneself) into the good will or favor of another; as, a courtier *ingratiates* himself with a king; to *ingratiate* oneself into society.

in·grat·i·tude (ĭn-grăt′ĭ-tūd), *n.* lack of thankfulness; ungratefulness.

in·gre·di·ent (ĭn-grē′dĭ-ĕnt), *n.* a part of a compound or mixture; as, sugar is the principal *ingredient* of candy.

in·gress (ĭn′grĕs), *n.* entrance; access.

in·hab·it (ĭn-hăb′ĭt), *v.t.* to dwell in; live in; occupy; as, man *inhabits* the earth; tigers *inhabit* the jungle.—*adj.* **in·hab′-it·a·ble.**—*n.* **in·hab′i·ta′tion.**

in·hab·it·ant (ĭn-hăb′ĭ-tănt), *n.* a person, or sometimes an animal, that occupies or lives permanently in a place.

in·hale (ĭn-hāl′), *v.t.* [inhaled, inhal-ing], to draw into the lungs; to breathe in, as air, ether, or the like.—*n.* **in′ha·la′tion** (ĭn′hȧ-lā′shŭn).

in·har·mo·ni·ous (ĭn′här-mō′nĭ-ŭs), *adj.* **1,** unmusical; as, *inharmonious* sounds; **2,**

conflicting; clashing; as, *inharmonious* colors.—*adv.* **in·har·mo′ni·ous·ly.**

in·her·ent (ĭn-hēr′ĕnt), *adj.* existing in something as a permanent or essential part; inborn; as, love of beauty is *inherent* in poets.—*adv.* **in·her′ent·ly.**
Syn. innate,, inbred.

in·her·it (ĭn-hĕr′ĭt), *v.t.* **1,** to come into possession of (property, as land or money) by right of succession or by will; as, he *inherited* his father's house; **2,** to derive (mental or physical qualities) from one's ancestors; receive by birth; as, to *inherit* intelligence or a strong constitution; **3,** to be heir to.—*n.* **in·her′i·tor.**

in·her·it·ance (ĭn-hĕr′ĭ-tăns), *n.* **1,** the act of inheriting, or coming into, property; **2,** property inherited; also, a trait or quality handed down from parent to offspring.

in·hib·it (ĭn-hĭb′ĭt), *v.t.* to restrain; hold in check; as, to *inhibit* a selfish impulse. —*n.* **in′hi·bi′tion** (ĭn′hĭ-bĭsh′ŭn).
Syn. forbid, hinder, prohibit.

in·hos·pi·ta·ble (ĭn-hŏs′pĭ-tȧ-bl), *adj.* **1,** not disposed to welcome strangers or guests; as, an *inhospitable* household; **2,** barren; cheerless; as, an *inhospitable* shore. —*adv.* **in·hos′pi·ta·bly.**

in·hos·pi·tal·i·ty (ĭn-hŏs′pĭ-tăl′ĭ-tĭ), *n.* lack of friendliness toward guests; disinclination to provide shelter or food.

in·hu·man (ĭn-hū′măn), *adj.* cruel; brutal; unfeeling.—*adv.* **in·hu′man·ly.**
Syn. ruthless, merciless, fierce.

in·hu·man·i·ty (ĭn′hū-măn′ĭ-tĭ), *n.* [*pl.* inhumanities], **1,** unkindness; cruelty; as, the *inhumanity* of certain punishments; **2,** a cruel or inhuman act.

in·im·i·cal (ĭn-ĭm′ĭ-kăl), *adj.* **1,** hostile; unfriendly; **2,** harmful; as, some drugs are *inimical* to health.—*adv.* **in·im′i·cal·ly.**

in·im·i·ta·ble (ĭn-ĭm′ĭ-tȧ-bl), *adj.* matchless; impossible to imitate; as, an *inimitable* style.—*adv.* **in·im′i·ta·bly.**

in·iq·ui·tous (ĭ-nĭk′wĭ-tŭs), *adj.* wicked; grossly unjust.—*adv.* **in·iq′ui·tous·ly.**
Syn. unrighteous, unjust, criminal, atrocious.

in·iq·ui·ty (ĭ-nĭk′wĭ-tĭ), *n.* [*pl.* iniquities], **1,** wickedness; unrighteousness; **2,** a wicked act or crime; a sin.

in·i·tial (ĭ-nĭsh′ăl), *adj.* **1,** placed at the beginning; first; as, the *initial* letter of a word; **2,** marking, or pertaining to, the beginning; as, the *initial* chapter in a book; the *initial* step in an undertaking:— *n.* **1,** a letter at the beginning of a word, paragraph, etc.; **2, initials,** the first letter of each part of a person's name; as, *A. S.* are the *initials* of Adam Smith:—*v.t.* to mark with one's initial or initials.—*adv.* **in·i′tial·ly.**

in·i·ti·ate (ĭ-nĭsh′ĭ-āt), *v.t.* [initiat-ed, ini-tiat-ing], **1**, to instruct in the first principles of anything; as, to *initiate* a student into the study of French; **2**, to begin; as, to *initiate* a new fashion; **3**, to introduce into a club, secret society, tribe, etc., by special rites and ceremonies:—*n.* (ĭ-nĭsh′ĭ-āt), one who has been, or is about to be, initiated.

in·i·ti·a·tion (ĭ-nĭsh′ĭ-ā′shŭn), *n.* **1**, the introduction of a person into a club, secret society, etc.; also, the process of becoming acquainted with a new type of business, branch of literature, etc.; **2**, the rites, ceremonies, etc., with which one is made a member of a special organization.

in·i·ti·a·tive (ĭ-nĭsh′ĭ-ȧ-tĭv; ĭ-nĭsh′ȧ-tĭv), *n.* **1**, an introductory or first step; as, to take the *initiative* in a deal; **2**, a natural ability to take the lead; also, an ability to foresee what needs doing and doing it; as, people with *initiative* advance rapidly; **3**, the right, also the method, by which citizens may introduce new laws.

in·ject (ĭn-jĕkt′), *v.t.* **1**, to drive or force into; introduce, as a liquid; **2**, to throw in; interject; as, to *inject* humor into a story.

in·jec·tion (ĭn-jĕk′shŭn), *n.* **1**, a forcing in; **2**, that which is forced in; **3**, in medicine, the act of forcing a liquid into some part of the body; also, the liquid so forced in; a hypodermic.

in·ju·di·cious (ĭn′jōō-dĭsh′ŭs), *adj.* unwise; lacking in judgment; as, an *injudicious* governess; not carefully thought out; as, *injudicious* advice; an *injudicious* remark.—*adv.* **in′ju·di′cious·ly**.

in·junc·tion (ĭn-jŭngk′shŭn), *n.* **1**, a command; an order; **2**, a legal paper to command or forbid certain proceedings; as, to issue an *injunction* against a strike.

in·jure (ĭn′jẽr), *v.t.* [injured, injur-ing], to harm; damage, physically or morally.
Syn. wrong, spoil, mar, sully.

in·ju·ri·ous (ĭn-jōōr′ĭ-ŭs), *adj.* **1**, hurtful, physically or morally; harmful; as, overeating is *injurious* to health; trashy books are *injurious* to the mind; **2**, malicious; damaging; as, rumors *injurious* to his reputation.—*adv.* **in·ju′ri·ous·ly**.
Syn. harmful, detrimental.

in·ju·ry (ĭn′jẽr-ĭ), *n.* [*pl.* injuries], any hurt or harm; damage to one's person, property, rights, etc.

in·jus·tice (ĭn-jŭs′tĭs), *n.* the quality of being unfair; lack of justice; also, an injury; a wrong.
Syn. grievance, iniquity.

ink (ĭngk), *n.* a colored fluid used for writing or drawing with a pen; also, a sticky paste used for printing:—*v.t.* to mark or smear with ink.

ink·horn (ĭngk′hôrn′), *n.* formerly, a small container made of horn, wood, or other material, which was used to hold ink.

INKHORN
Inkhorn (A) at one end of a writing table.

ink·ling (ĭngk′lĭng), *n.* a faint idea or suspicion; as, an *inkling* of the truth.

ink·stand (ĭngk′stănd′), *n.* a small container for ink, pens, etc.; sometimes, a container for ink only; an inkwell.

ink·well (ĭngk′wĕl′), *n.* a cup for ink, fitted into a desk or an inkstand.

ink·y (ĭngk′ĭ), *adj.* [ink-i-er, ink-i-est], like ink; spotted with ink; black; as, an *inky* blotter; *inky* darkness.

in·laid (ĭn-lād′; ĭn′lād′), *adj.* **1**, set into a surface for ornament; as, ivory *inlaid* in ebony; **2**, ornamented with inlay.

in·land (ĭn′lănd), *adj.* **1**, pertaining to, or situated in, the interior of a country; away from the sea; as, an *inland* town; **2**, carried on within a country; as, *inland* commerce:—*adv.* (ĭn′lănd′; ĭn′lănd), toward the interior:—*n.* (ĭn′lănd; ĭn′lănd′), the interior of a country.

in·lay (ĭn-lā′), *v.t.* [in-laid (ĭn-lād′), inlaying], to ornament (a surface) by setting in pieces of ivory, wood, metal, etc.; also, to set (pieces of ivory, wood, etc.) into a surface:—*n.* (ĭn′lā′), materials for inlaying; also, a pattern or design formed by inlaying.

INLAY

in·let (ĭn′lĕt), *n.* a small bay or creek along a coast; an arm of the sea.

in·mate (ĭn′māt), *n.* a member of a family or other group of persons living under one roof; now, usually, a person confined in an institution; as, an *inmate* of a prison, a poorhouse, or the like.

in·most (ĭn′mōst), *adj.* most inward; deepest; as, the *inmost* wish of my heart is to be a great pianist.

inn (ĭn), *n.* a house for the lodging and entertainment of travelers; tavern.

in·nate (ĭn′nāt; ĭ-nāt′), *adj.* inborn; natural; as, *innate* courtesy; *innate* intelligence.—*adv.* **in′nate·ly**.
Syn. inbred, inherent, original.

in·ner (ĭn′ẽr), *adj.* **1**, internal; interior; inside; as, an *inner* lining; **2**, pertaining to the mind or soul; as, the *inner* nature of man:—**inner man**, humorously, the stomach.

āte, āorta, râre, căt, ȧsk, fär, ȧllow, sofȧ; ēve, ēvent, ĕll, writẽr, novĕl; bīte, pĭn; nō, ōbey, ôr, dŏg, tŏp, cŏllide; ūnit, ūnite, bûrn, cŭt, focŭs; nōon, fŏŏt; mound; coin;

in·ner·most (ĭn′ẽr-mōst), *adj.* farthest in from the outside; inmost.

in·ning (ĭn′ĭng), *n.* **1,** in baseball, cricket, etc., one of the divisions of the game during which one side is at bat or each side in turn is at bat once; **2, innings,** the period when a person or party is in power.

inn·keep·er (ĭn′kēp′ẽr), *n.* the owner or keeper of an inn.

in·no·cence (ĭn′ō-sĕns), *n.* **1,** freedom from sin or evil; purity; **2,** freedom from guilt, blame, or wrongdoing; as, to prove one's *innocence;* **3,** simplicity of heart; as, the *innocence* of a child.

in·no·cent (ĭn′ō-sĕnt), *adj.* **1,** free from guilt or wrongdoing; blameless; **2,** pure in heart and life; **3,** foolishly ignorant; **4,** without evil effect or meaning; as, an *innocent* joke; **5,** lacking; as, *innocent* of humor or brains:—*n.* **1,** one who is free from, or unacquainted with, sin; **2,** a simpleton. —*adv.* **in′no·cent·ly.**

Syn., adj. guiltless, sinless, stainless.

in·noc·u·ous (ĭ-nŏk′ū-ŭs), *adj.* harmless; as, an *innocuous* snake, drug, joke, etc.— *adv.* **in·noc′u·ous·ly.**

in·no·vate (ĭn′ō-vāt), *v.i.* [innovat-ed, in-novat-ing], to introduce new things; make changes in established ways or things.

in·no·va·tion (ĭn′ō-vā′shŭn), *n.* **1,** the introduction of something new; **2,** a new custom, device, style, or the like.

in·nu·en·do (ĭn′ū-ĕn′dō), *n.* [*pl.* innuendoes], an insinuation or veiled hint against someone or something; an indirect reference, usually suggesting something damaging.

in·nu·mer·a·ble (ĭ-nū′mẽr-*a*-bl; ĭn-nū′-mẽr-*a*-bl), *adj.* without number; countless; as, *innumerable* stars.—*adv.* **in·nu′mer·a·bly.**

in·oc·u·late (ĭn-ŏk′ū-lāt), *v.t.* [inoculat-ed, inoculat-ing], **1,** to produce a mild case of disease in (a person or animal) by the insertion of germs into body tissues in order to prevent future attacks; as, to *inoculate* a child against typhoid; **2,** to fill or infect the mind of (a person, community, etc.) with a feeling, opinion, or habit.

in·oc·u·la·tion (ĭn-ŏk′ū-lā′shŭn), *n.* **1,** the insertion of virus, or the poison of a disease, into body tissues, for the purpose of producing a mild form of the disease in order to ward off future attacks; **2,** an infection or spreading, as of feelings or ideas.

in·of·fen·sive (ĭn′ŏ-fĕn′sĭv), *adj.* **1,** harmless; **2,** not disagreeable or disgusting.— *adv.* **in′of·fen′sive·ly.**

in·op·er·a·tive (ĭn-ŏp′ẽr-ā′tĭv; ĭn-ŏp′ẽr-*a*-tĭv), *adj.* not active or effective; as, that law has been *inoperative* for a year.

in·op·por·tune (ĭn-ŏp′ŏr-tūn′), *adj.* happening at the wrong time; unsuitable; as, an *inopportune* remark; the *inopportune* moment.—*adv.* **in·op′por·tune′ly.**

in·or·di·nate (ĭn-ôr′dĭ-nĭt), *adj.* too much; excessive; as, it took him an *inordinate* amount of time; *inordinate* vanity.—*adv.* **in·or′di·nate·ly.**—*n.* **in·or′di·nate·ness.**

Syn. intemperate, immoderate.

in·or·gan·ic (ĭn′ôr-găn′ĭk), *adj.* without a living body; not belonging to the animal or vegetable kingdom; not part of, nor produced by, a plant or animal. Rocks and metals are inorganic substances; wood, bone, and blood are organic substances.

in·quest (ĭn′kwĕst), *n.* an official inquiry, with the aid of a jury, especially into the cause of a sudden death.

in·quire (ĭn-kwīr′), *v.t.* [inquired, inquiring], to seek after by questions; as, to *inquire* the way to the station:—*v.i.* **1,** to ask; seek information; as, *inquire* at the office; **2,** to make examination or search; as, to *inquire* into a murder; to *inquire* about something; **3,** to ask concerning the whereabouts or welfare of someone; as, to *inquire* for or after a person.—*n.* **inquir′er.**

Syn. question, examine.

in·quir·ing (ĭn-kwīr′ĭng), *adj.* given to asking questions; eager for knowledge.— *adv.* **in·quir′ing·ly.**

in·quir·y (ĭn-kwīr′ĭ; ĭn′kwĭ-rĭ), *n.* [*pl.* inquiries], **1,** the act of seeking information, knowledge, etc.; research; **2,** an investigation; **3,** a question.

Syn. examination, scrutiny, query.

in·qui·si·tion (ĭn′kwĭ-zĭsh′ŭn), *n.* inquiry; examination; especially, an official inquiry before a jury; also, the findings of the jury:—**Inquisition,** in the Roman Catholic Church, a court which was especially active in the 15th and 16th centuries in seeking out and punishing heretics, but is now chiefly concerned with heretical literature.

in·quis·i·tive (ĭn-kwĭz′ĭ-tĭv), *adj.* given to asking questions; curious; as, a gossip is *inquisitive* about her neighbors.—*adv.* **in·quis′i·tive·ly.**—*n.* **in·quis′i·tive·ness.**

in·quis·i·tor (ĭn-kwĭz′ĭ-tẽr), *n.* **1,** one who makes examinations or investigates; especially, one appointed by law to investigate; **2,** in the Roman Catholic Church, an officer of the Inquisition.

in·road (ĭn′rōd′), *n.* **1,** an invasion, especially if sudden; entry by force; as, an *inroad* into enemy territory; **2,** an advance which destroys or decreases the thing

---

go; join; yet; sing; chin; show; thin, *th***en; hw,** *wh***y; zh,** *a*zure; **ü,** Ger. f*ü*r or Fr. l*u*ne; **ö,** Ger. sch*ö*n or Fr. f*eu*; **ṅ,** Fr. e*n*fant, no*m*; **kh,** Ger. a*ch* or i*ch*. See pages ix–x.

attacked; as, the sea makes *inroads* on the land; overwork makes *inroads* on endurance.

in-rush (ĭn′rŭsh′), *n.* a pouring in; a sudden invasion; as, an *inrush* of waters.

in-sane (ĭn-sān′), *adj.* **1,** mentally disordered or ill; mad; crazy; **2,** very unreasonable or foolish; as, an *insane* desire to dance in church; **3,** intended for the mentally disordered; as, an *insane* asylum. —*adv.* **in-sane′ly.**

in-san-i-tar-y (ĭn-săn′ĭ-tĕr′ĭ), *adj.* injurious to health; as, *insanitary* plumbing.

in-san-i-ty (ĭn-săn′ĭ-tĭ), *n.* **1,** disorder of mind or intellect; mental illness; madness; **2,** extravagant folly; as, it was *insanity* to swim across the lake.

  Syn. frenzy, delirium, mania.

in-sa-ti-a-ble (ĭn-sā′shĭ-à-bl; ĭn-sā′shà-bl), *adj.* immoderate; not to be satisfied; greedy; as, an *insatiable* appetite.—*adv.* **in-sa′ti-a-bly.**—*n.* **in-sa′ti-a-bil′i-ty.**

in-sa-ti-ate (ĭn-sā′shĭ-āt), *adj.* never satisfied.—*adv.* **in-sa′ti-ate-ly.**

in-scribe (ĭn-skrīb′), *v.t.* [inscribed, inscrib-ing], **1,** to write or engrave (letters or words) on parchment, brass, etc.; as, to *inscribe* a date on a ring; **2,** to mark or engrave letters on (stone, metal, etc.); as, to *inscribe* a tablet; **3,** to stamp deeply, as on the memory; **4,** to address formally; dedicate; as, to *inscribe* a poem to a friend; **5,** to enter or enroll on a list.— *n.* **in-scrib′er.**

in-scrip-tion (ĭn-skrĭp′shŭn), *n.* **1,** the act of writing or engraving, especially in permanent form; also, anything so written, as on a monument or coin; **2,** a brief dedication, as of a book, to a person.

in-scru-ta-ble (ĭn-skrōō′tà-bl), *adj.* unreadable; not to be understood; as, his face was *inscrutable; inscrutable* Providence.—*adv.* **in-scru′ta-bly.**—*n.* **in-scru′-ta-bil′i-ty.**

in-sect (ĭn′sĕkt), *n.* any of numerous small, boneless animals, including bugs, bees, flies, etc., with three pairs of jointed legs, body divided into three sections (head, thorax, and abdomen), and, usually, wings.

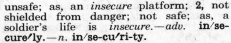

INSECT

Parts of a grasshopper: A, antennae; H, head; T, thorax; AB, abdomen; W, wings; 1,2,3, front, middle, and hind legs.

in-sec-ti-cide (ĭn-sĕk′-tĭ-sīd), *n.* a poisonous substance, either a powder or liquid, for driving away or killing destructive insects, bugs, flies, etc.

in-se-cure (ĭn′sĕ-kūr′), *adj.* **1,** not firm; unsafe; as, an *insecure* platform; **2,** not shielded from danger; not safe; as, a soldier's life is *insecure.*—*adv.* **in′se-cure′ly.**—*n.* **in′se-cu′ri-ty.**

in-sen-sate (ĭn-sĕn′sāt), *adj.* **1,** unfeeling; brutal; as, *insensate* fury; **2,** without sense; as, an *insensate* fool; **3,** without sensation; lifeless; as, *insensate* rocks.

in-sen-si-bil-i-ty (ĭn-sĕn′sĭ-bĭl′ĭ-tĭ), *n.* **1,** lack of emotion; indifference; **2,** unconsciousness; as, he lay in a state of *insensibility.*

in-sen-si-ble (ĭn-sĕn′sĭ-bl), *adj.* **1,** lacking the power to feel; indifferent; as, *insensible* to beauty or to cold; **2,** too slow, gradual, or small to be perceived; as, the *insensible* motion of a clock's hands; **3,** unconscious; as, she fell *insensible* to the ground.—*adv.* **in-sen′si-bly.**

  Syn. numb, unfeeling, dull.

in-sep-a-ra-ble (ĭn-sĕp′à-rà-bl), *adj.* incapable of being divided or parted; as, they were *inseparable* friends.—*adv.* **in-sep′a-ra-bly.**—*n.* **in-sep′a-ra-bil′i-ty.**

in-sert (ĭn-sûrt′), *v.t.* to place in something or among things; introduce; as, to *insert* a coin in a slot:—*n.* (ĭn′sûrt), that which is put in; inset; as, a colored *insert* in a book.

in-ser-tion (ĭn-sûr′shŭn), *n.* **1,** a putting in; **2,** that which is put in, as a passage in a book; **3,** a band of lace or embroidery used as trimming.

in-set (ĭn′sĕt), *n.* **1,** an extra page or pages inserted in a newspaper, magazine, etc.; **2,** a smaller drawing, map, etc., inserted within the border of a larger one: —*v.t.* (ĭn-sĕt′), [inset, inset-ting], to put in; insert.

in-shore (ĭn′shôr′), *adv.* near or toward the shore; as, to head *inshore:*—*adj.* (ĭn′-shôr′; ĭn′shôr′), near, or moving toward, the shore; as, an *inshore* current.

in-side (ĭn′sīd′), *adj.* **1,** lying or being within; as, the *inside* pages of a newspaper; **2,** *Colloquial,* private; as, *inside* information:—*adv.* within; as, to go *inside:* —*n.* **1,** that which is within; interior; as, the *inside* of a house; **2,** contents; as, to know the *inside* of a book; **3, insides,** *Colloquial,* the internal organs of the body:— *prep.* (ĭn′sīd′), within; as, *inside* the box.

in-sid-er (ĭn′sīd′ĕr), *n.* a person so situated that he is able to obtain reliable or special information not available to the public.

in-sid-i-ous (ĭn-sĭd′ĭ-ŭs), *adj.* treacherous; working harm secretly; as, *insidious* gossip.—*adv.* **in-sid′i-ous-ly.**

in-sight (ĭn′sīt′), *n.* understanding; comprehension of the inner nature of things; as, *insight* into character.

in-sig-ni-a (ĭn-sĭg′nĭ-à), *n.pl.* badges of honor or office; emblems of authority, rank, etc.; as, army *insignia*.

in-sig-nif-i-cance (ĭn′sĭg-nĭf′ĭ-kăns), *n.* unimportance; triviality; as, to rise from *insignificance* to fame.

INSIGNIA
1, U. S. Air Force Medical Corps; 2, U. S. Navy Medical Corps.

in-sig-nif-i-cant (ĭn′sĭg-nĭf′ĭ-kănt), *adj.* 1, without importance or force; as, his power is *insignificant*; 2, trifling; mean; small; as, an *insignificant* sum.—*adv.* **in′sig-nif′i-cant-ly**.
Syn. petty, trivial, unimportant.

in-sin-cere (ĭn′sĭn-sĭr′), *adj.* false; not to be trusted; as, *insincere* praise.—*adv.* **in′sin-cere′ly**.

in-sin-u-ate (ĭn-sĭn′ū-āt), *v.t.* [insinuat-ed, insinuat-ing], 1, to penetrate; push (oneself) by slow or artful means, as a courtier into a king's favor; 2, to hint or suggest indirectly; as, they *insinuated* that he lied.

in-sin-u-a-tion (ĭn-sĭn′ū-ā′shŭn), *n.* an indirect or sly hint; as, he slandered them more by *insinuations* than by direct statements.

in-sip-id (ĭn-sĭp′ĭd), *adj.* 1, without flavor; tasteless; as, *insipid* food; 2, uninteresting; dull; as, *insipid* reading.—*adv.* **in-sip′id-ly**.—*n.* **in′si-pid′i-ty** (ĭn′sĭ-pĭd′ĭ-tĭ).
Syn. flat, stale, lifeless.

in-sist (ĭn-sĭst′), *v.i.* 1, to urge, wish, or command; as, the teacher *insists* on obedience; 2, to maintain; make a stand; as, he *insists* that he is right.

in-sist-ent (ĭn-sĭs′tĕnt), *adj.* urgent; compelling attention; persistent; as, the *insistent* ringing of a bell.—*adv.* **in-sist′ent-ly**.—*n.* **in-sist′ence**.

in-snare (ĭn-snâr′), *v.t.* [insnared, insnaring], to catch in, or as in, a trap; ensnare. See **ensnare**.

in-sole (ĭn′sōl′), *n.* 1, the part of the sole inside a boot or shoe; 2, a removable sole of leather or felt put inside a shoe.

in-so-lence (ĭn′sō-lĕns), *n.* insulting or haughty language or manner; impertinence; impudence.

in-so-lent (ĭn′sō-lĕnt), *adj.* haughty or insulting; rude.—*adv.* **in′so-lent-ly**.

in-sol-u-ble (ĭn-sŏl′ū-bl), *adj.* 1, not capable of being dissolved, or hard to dissolve in some liquid; as, fats are *insoluble* in water; 2, not to be explained or solved; as, an *insoluble* mystery.—*n.* **in-sol′u-bil′i-ty**.

in-sol-vent (ĭn-sŏl′vĕnt), *adj.* unable to pay all debts; bankrupt:—*n.* a person who cannot pay his debts.—*n.* **in-sol′ven-cy**.

in-som-ni-a (ĭn-sŏm′nĭ-à), *n.* sleeplessness.

in-so-much (ĭn′sō-mŭch′), *adv.* to such a degree or extent (that).

in-spect (ĭn-spĕkt′), *v.t.* 1, to examine closely and critically, in order to find possible faults or errors, to determine quality, etc.; 2, to review and survey officially, as troops.—*n.* **in-spec′tor**.

in-spec-tion (ĭn-spĕk′shŭn), *n.* careful or critical examination.

in-spi-ra-tion (ĭn′spĭ-rā′shŭn), *n.* 1, the act of drawing air into the lungs; 2, the awakening of thought and the stirring of emotion which causes creation in art, literature, music, etc.; the effect upon the creative imagination of beauty, power, etc.; 3, the supernatural influence of the Holy Spirit, suggesting a message or a plan of action.—*adj.* **in′spi-ra′tion-al**.

in-spire (ĭn-spīr′), *v.t.* [inspired, inspiring], 1, to draw (air) into the lungs; 2, to fill with thought or feeling; as, beauty *inspires* an artist; 3, to control or guide by supernatural influence; as, God *inspired* the ancient prophets; 4, to arouse, as an idea, impulse, emotion, etc., in someone; as, his politics *inspired* his point of view.—*adj.* **in-spired′**.
Syn. animate, instil, enliven, impart, stimulate, encourage.

in-spir-it (ĭn-spĭr′ĭt), *v.t.* to give life or vitality to; cheer.—*adv.* **in-spir′it-ing-ly**.

inst. abbreviation for *instant*, meaning *of the present month*.

in-sta-bil-i-ty (ĭn′stà-bĭl′ĭ-tĭ), *n.* [*pl.* instabilities], 1, lack of steadiness; 2, lack of emotional or moral balance.
Syn. changeableness, unsteadiness.

in-stall (ĭn-stôl′), *v.t.* 1, to establish with the usual ceremonies in an office or position; 2, to put into condition or position for use; as, to *install* an electric refrigerator.

in-stal-la-tion (ĭn′stô-lā′shŭn), *n.* 1, the act of establishing in an office or position; 2, the setting up in position for service, as machinery; 3, the apparatus so set up.

in-stal-ment or **in-stall-ment** (ĭn-stôl′mĕnt), *n.* 1, the act of establishing in a position or office; 2, a portion of a sum of money that is to be paid in parts at stated times; 3, one of a number of parts of anything produced one part at a time; as, an *instalment* of a serial story.

in-stance (ĭn′stăns), *v.t.* [instanced, instanc-ing], to refer to, or offer as an example:—*n.* 1, something offered as an illustration or example; as, here is an *instance* of what I mean; 2, a suggestion; request; as, at the *instance* of the teacher, they sang.
Syn., n. specimen, sample, case.

in-stant (ĭn'stănt), *adj*. **1,** urgent; insistent; as, *instant* haste; *instant* hunger; **2,** immediate; as, *instant* death; **3,** of the present month: usually written *inst.*; as, yours of the fourth *inst.*:—*n*. a particular moment of time; as, do it this *instant;* also, a very small portion of time; as, it will take only an *instant.*

in-stan-ta-ne-ous (ĭn'stăn-tā'nē-ŭs), *adj*. done at once; happening in one moment; as, an *instantaneous* reply.

in-stan-ter (ĭn-stăn'tẽr), *adv*. immediately; without delay; as, I will go *instanter.*

in-stant-ly (ĭn'stănt-lĭ), *adv*. at once.
Syn. directly, immediately.

in-stead (ĭn-stĕd'), *adv*. **1,** in the place of; as, I will go *instead* of you; **2,** in its place; rather; as, she chose this *instead.*

in-step (ĭn'stĕp), *n*. the arched part of the upper side of the human foot between the toes and the ankle.

in-sti-gate (ĭn'stĭ-gāt), *v.t.* [instigat-ed, instigat-ing], to prompt or urge on: usually in a bad sense; as, to *instigate* a strike.—*n*. **in'sti-ga'tion.**—*n*. **in'sti-ga'tor.**
Syn. impel, incite, stimulate, encourage.

in-still or **in-stil** (ĭn-stĭl'), *v.t.* [instilled, instil-ling], **1,** to pour in by drops; **2,** to introduce gradually; infuse; as, to *instill* a sense of honor into a child.
Syn. implant, inculcate.

in-stinct (ĭn-stĭngkt'), *adj*. charged or full of; as, creatures *instinct* with life:—*n*. (ĭn'stĭngkt), **1,** a natural or inborn impulse, especially in animals, to do the necessary thing without taking conscious thought; as, it is the *instinct* of all animals to fear fire;.**2,** a natural tendency or innate ability; as, an *instinct* for music.

in-stinc-tive (ĭn-stĭngk'tĭv), *adj*. acting or prompted by natural impulse; as, self-defense is *instinctive* in all creatures.—*adv*. **in-stinc'tive-ly.**

in-sti-tute (ĭn'stĭ-tūt), *v.t.* [institut-ed, institut-ing], **1,** to establish; found; originate; **2,** to set in operation; start; as, to *institute* a new custom:—*n*. **1,** an established law or principle; **2,** an institution or place of education; as, an *institute* of music.

in-sti-tu-tion (ĭn'stĭ-tū'shŭn), *n*. **1,** the act of establishing; as, the *institution* of new rules; **2,** any established law, practice, or social custom; as, church, home, and school are fundamental *institutions;* **3,** an organized society for promoting a particular object; **4,** the building for carrying on the work of such a society; as, an *institution* for the blind.—*adj*. **in'sti-tu'-tion-al.**

in-struct (ĭn-strŭkt'), *v.t.* **1,** to teach; educate; as, to *instruct* a class in history; **2,** to furnish with orders or directions; as, to *instruct* a person to be early.
Syn. direct, train, admonish.

in-struc-tion (ĭn-strŭk'shŭn), *n*. **1,** the act of teaching; **2,** knowledge imparted; **3,** **instructions,** orders or directions.
Syn. direction, education, training.

in-struc-tive (ĭn-strŭk'tĭv), *adj*. informing; giving knowledge.—*adv*. **in-struc'-tive-ly.**

in-struc-tor (ĭn-strŭk'tẽr), *n*. **1,** one who gives knowledge; a teacher; **2,** in American colleges, a teacher ranking below a professor.—*n.fem.* **in-struc'tress.**

in-stru-ment (ĭn'strŏo-mĕnt), *n*. **1,** a person or thing used to accomplish something; a means; **2,** a tool; as, surgical *instruments;* **3,** a mechanical device for producing musical sounds; as, a horn is a wind *instrument;* **4,** in law, a formal writing; a document.

in-stru-men-tal (ĭn'strŏo-mĕn'tăl), *adj*. **1,** helping to bring about; as, he was *instrumental* in settling the quarrel; **2,** performed on, or composed for, a musical instrument or instruments.—*n*. **in'stru-men-tal'i-ty.**

in-sub-or-di-nate (ĭn'sŭ-bôr'dĭ-nĭt), *adj*. rebelling against authority; disobedient; mutinous.—*adv*. **in'sub-or'di-nate-ly.**

in-sub-or-di-na-tion (ĭn'sŭ-bôr'dĭ-nā'shŭn), *n*. rebellion against authority.

in-sub-stan-tial (ĭn'sŭb-stăn'shăl), *adj*. not solid; frail; unreal.—*adv*. **in'sub-stan'-tial-ly.**

in-suf-fer-a-ble (ĭn-sŭf'ẽr-a-bl), *adj*. not to be borne; as, *insufferable* conduct.—*adv*. **in-suf'fer-a-bly.**

in-suf-fi-cient (ĭn'sŭ-fĭsh'ĕnt), *adj*. not enough, as of quality, amount, power, etc.; as, *insufficient* light for reading.—*adv*. **in'-suf-fi'cient-ly.**—*n*. **in'suf-fi'cien-cy.**

in-su-lar (ĭn'sŭ-lẽr), *adj*. **1,** relating to an island or to the inhabitants of an island, their customs, etc.; **2,** hence, narrowminded; prejudiced.—*n*. **in'su-lar'i-ty.**

in-su-late (ĭn'sŭ-lāt; ĭn'sū-lāt), *v.t.* [insulat-ed, insulat-ing], to separate; set apart; especially, to separate by, or enclose in, a material that will not conduct electricity, heat, etc.; as, to *insulate* an electric wire or an oven.

INSULATION
(I) of an electric wire. W, wire; R,R, rubber; F, braided fabric.

in-su-la-tion (ĭn'sŭ-lā'shŭn; ĭn'sū-lā'shŭn), *n*. the act of separating by, or enclosing in, materials that will not conduct heat, electricity, or sound.

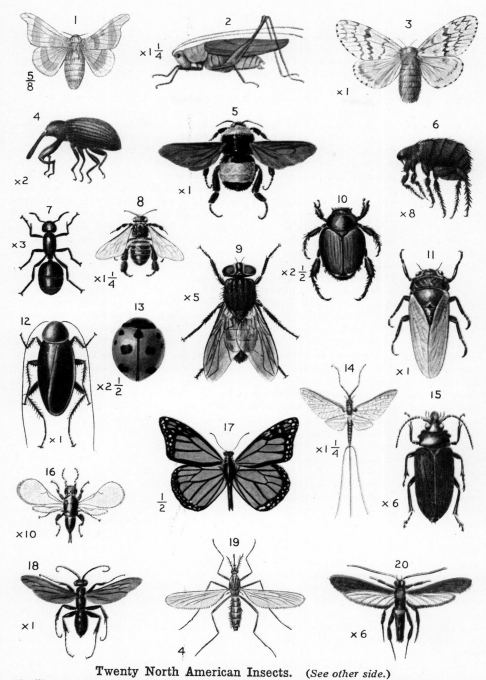

Twenty North American Insects. (*See other side.*)

1, silkworm moth; 2, grasshopper; 3, gypsy moth; 4, boll weevil; 5, bumblebee; 6, flea;
7, ant; 8, honeybee; 9, housefly; 10, Japanese beetle; 11, cicada; 12, cockroach; 13, lady;
bird; 14, May fly; 15, a boring beetle; 16, fig insect; 17, milkweed butterfly; 18, a wasp;
19, mosquito; 20, peach moth.

INSECTS

If all the insects of the earth were piled on one end of a huge seesaw and all the other animals including man were crowded on the other end, the end holding the insects would sink down and the end holding the animals would rise. It is amazing how so many million kinds of insects manage to survive. A few simple rules faithfully followed seem to explain. The rules are: "Eat, but be not eaten," "Work and fight," "Lay eggs and care for the young." Every activity of insects can be accounted for by these three rules.

The general structure of a true insect follows a common pattern. Insects have six legs. Their bodies are divided into three parts: a head containing the eyes and one pair of antennae; a thorax of three sections, each section with a pair of legs, and the last two sections each with a pair of wings; and an abdomen. But in detail insects vary. Some have strong jaws for cutting and chewing wood. Others have tubelike mouths for sucking nectar from flowers. Many have mouths like lances for piercing skin. Legs and feet also vary. Bees have hairy legs and bodies for collecting pollen. Ants have slim legs and sharp claws for running and climbing. Houseflies have suction pads on their feet, and so are able to walk on ceilings. Certain beetles are equipped for digging. Besides, the bodies of many insects are covered with a hard yet pliable substance that forms a defensive armor.

With whatever tools nature has given them, insects labor unceasingly. Some work in wood. Wood-boring insects have destroyed whole forests, and white ants can destroy a house. Many are diggers. Certain beetles will bury a dead bird or other small creature by digging the earth from under it, in order to provide food for their larvae. Hornets and certain wasps are expert paper makers. Bees make wax, honey, and beebread. In Africa, ants build 20-foot-high mounds, hard as cement, air-conditioned, drained, and divided into compartments.

Every trick imaginable is employed to secure food, especially for the young. A wasp will paralyze a worm by a sting and store the helpless victim in its nest of eggs so the young wasps will have fresh food to eat when they hatch out. Other wasps fill their nests with little live spiders. Certain ants cultivate tiny gardens; others keep aphids as men keep cows, protecting and caring for them so that the sweet liquid that aphids produce will be plentiful. The milker ants gorge themselves with the sweet fluid and carry it to the hungry workers.

But perhaps the greatest reason for the survival of insects is their ability to reproduce themselves in great numbers. You may kill a hundred beetles today and in a short time hundreds more take their place. It is a good thing that insects eat other insects, and that birds and many animals devour them, or man could not survive.

Some of the insects pictured on the previous page are useful to man and others are quite the opposite. The most useful are the honeybee, the silkworm, and the ladybird. The bee makes wax and honey, and also carries pollen from flower to flower. Without this assistance, the seed of many plants could not mature. The silkworm has been domesticated and produces millions of dollars' worth of silk each year. The ladybird helps us fight pests by eating other insects.

Butterflies and moths are so beautiful that we forget the damage that many of them do in the larva, or caterpillar, stage. You can always tell a butterfly from a moth by the position of its wings. A butterfly never folds its wings over its body.

Mosquitoes, flies, and fleas are pests and disease carriers. The destructive horde includes the boll weevil, the larva of which eats the inside of cotton bolls; the Japanese beetle, that literally devours gardens and the foliage of trees; the gypsy moth, which has destroyed so many trees; and the peach moth, which eats the tender twigs and fruit of peach trees. Three of these insects are aliens. The Japanese beetle came into New Jersey by pure chance and is now spreading to other sections of the country in spite of unceasing efforts to destroy it. From Australia, by way of Japan, came the peach moth. The gypsy moth is a native of the Old World, and came into Massachusetts, more than sixty years ago, as a stowaway.

in·su·la·tor (ĭn′sŭ-lā′tẽr; ĭn′sṳ-lā′tẽr), *n.* a material or body that does not carry electricity, heat, or sound; a nonconductor.

in·su·lin (ĭn′sṳ-lĭn), *n.* a preparation from the pancreas of oxen, and especially sheep, used in diabetes, to enable the body to utilize sugar.

INSULATORS

in·sult (ĭn′sŭlt), *n.* 1, an affront or indignity; 2, a gross abuse in word or action:—*v.t.* (ĭn-sŭlt′), to treat with intentional rudeness or abuse.

Syn., *v.* affront, outrage, mock.

in·su·per·a·ble (ĭn-sū′pẽr-à-bl), *adj.* not to be surmounted or overcome; as, *insuperable* difficulties.—*adv.* **in·su′per·a·bly.**

in·sup·port·a·ble (ĭn′sṳ-pôr′tà-bl), *adj.* unbearable; as, *insupportable* grief.—*adv.* **in′sup·port′a·bly.**

in·sur·ance (ĭn-shŏŏr′ăns), *n.* 1, a system of protection against financial loss resulting from fire, accident, death, or the like; 2, a contract whereby one party, usually a company, guarantees to repay the other party for such loss, in return for the yearly payment of a smaller sum, called a *premium*; 3, the premium; 4, the amount of payment thus guaranteed.

in·sure (ĭn-shŏŏr′), *v.t.* [insured, insur-ing], 1, to protect (a person), by a special contract, against financial loss resulting from fire, accident, theft, etc., in return for regular payments of a premium; as, to *insure* a farmer against the burning of his barn; 2, to make such a contract about (property); as, the farmer *insures* his barn; 3, to make such a contract about (one's life), providing for payment of a fixed sum to a specified person in case of one's death, or to oneself at a specified age if one lives to that age; as, he *insured* his life for $5,000.

in·sur·gent (ĭn-sûr′jĕnt), *adj.* rising against authority:—*n.* a rebel.—*n.* **in·sur′gence.**

Syn., *adj.* rebellious, mutinous.

in·sur·mount·a·ble (ĭn′sûr-moun′tà-bl), *adj.* not to be overcome; as, an *insurmountable* evil.—*adv.* **in′sur·mount′a·bly.**

in·sur·rec·tion (ĭn′sṳ-rĕk′shŭn), *n.* active or open rebellion against authority, especially against a government.—*adj.* **in′sur·rec′tion·ar′y.**

Syn. mutiny, uprising, sedition.

in·tact (ĭn-tăkt′), *adj.* entire; uninjured; untouched; as, the house was *intact* after the earthquake.

in·tagl·io (ĭn-tăl′yō; *Italian,* ēn-tä′lyȯ), *n.* [*pl.* intaglios (ĭn-tăl′yōz) or intagli (ēn-tä′lyĕ)], 1, an engraving or carving cut into or below the surface of any hard material, especially of a gem; 2, the gem or stone so ornamented: opposite of *cameo.*

in·take (ĭn′tāk′), *n.* 1, a thing taken in, as money in a store; also, a taking in, as of breath; 2, the place where a fluid enters a pipe, channel, etc.

INTAGLIO

Intaglio design from an ancient Greek gem.

in·tan·gi·ble (ĭn-tăn′jĭ-bl), *adj.* not touchable; as, ghosts are *intangible;* hence, vague; not easily expressed or defined; as, an *intangible* idea.—*adv.* **in·tan′gi·bly.**—*n.* **in·tan′gi·bil′i·ty.**

in·te·ger (ĭn′tē-jẽr), *n.* a whole number, as 1, 2, 3, etc.

in·te·gral (ĭn′tē-grăl), *adj.* 1, making a whole; complete; 2, necessary as a part; as, sincerity is an *integral* part of friendship:—*n.* a whole made up of parts.

in·te·grate (ĭn′tē-grāt), *v.t.* [integrat-ed, integrat-ing], 1, to bring together (the parts) to make a whole; 2, to give the sum total of.—*n.* **in′te·gra′tion.**

in·teg·ri·ty (ĭn-tĕg′rĭ-tĭ), *n.* 1, uprightness; virtue; honesty; as, the *integrity* of a person; 2, soundness; as, the *integrity* of an argument; 3, unbroken condition; completeness; as, the *integrity* of an army.

Syn. justice, honor, probity.

in·teg·u·ment (ĭn-tĕg′ṳ-mĕnt), *n.* a covering, as a skin or husk.

in·tel·lect (ĭn′tĕ-lĕkt), *n.* 1, the powers of the mind that know and reason: distinguished from *feeling* and *will;* the mind; 2, mental power; ability to reason; 3, a person of high intelligence.

in·tel·lec·tu·al (ĭn′tĕ-lĕk′tū-ăl), *adj.* 1, pertaining to the intellect or mind; as, *intellectual* interests; 2, possessing a high degree of intellect or understanding; as, an *intellectual* person; 3, demanding keen thinking; as, *intellectual* subjects:—*n.* a person of superior mind; as, Emerson was an *intellectual.*—*adv.* **in′tel·lec′tu·al·ly.**

Syn., *adj.* intelligent, mental.

in·tel·lec·tu·al·i·ty (ĭn′tĕ-lĕk′tū-ăl′ĭ-tĭ), *n.* [*pl.* intellectualities], mental power or ability.

in·tel·li·gence (ĭn-tĕl′ĭ-jĕns), *n.* 1, ability to learn and to use what one has learned to the best advantage; understanding; 2, information or news, particularly secret information, as that secured for the government in war time:— **intelligence department**, a government bureau for collecting information, especially military and naval information.

Syn. information, news, tidings.

in-tel-li-gent (ĭn-tĕl′ĭ-jĕnt), *adj.* 1, able to learn and to use what one has learned; possessing understanding; 2, showing understanding; as, an *intelligent* answer. —*adv.* **in-tel′li-gent-ly.**

Syn. bright, knowing, sensible.

in-tel-li-gent-si-a (ĭn-tĕl′ĭ-jĕnt′sĭ-à), *n.* the educated or intellectual classes: often used scornfully.

in-tel-li-gi-ble (ĭn-tĕl′ĭ-jĭ-bl), *adj.* capable of being understood; clear; as, an *intelligible* explanation.—*n.* **in-tel′li-gi-bil′-i-ty.**—*adv.* **in-tel′li-gi-bly.**

Syn. obvious, plain, distinct.

in-tem-per-ance (ĭn-tĕm′pēr-ăns), *n.* want of moderation or self-control; excess, especially in the use of alcoholic liquors.

in-tem-per-ate (ĭn-tĕm′pēr-ĭt), *adj.* 1, severe; not mild; as, an *intemperate* climate; 2, lacking in moderation or self-control; violent; as, *intemperate* conduct; 3, given to excess, especially in the use of alcoholic liquors.—*adv.* **in-tem′per-ate-ly.**

Syn. immoderate, inordinate.

in-tend (ĭn-tĕnd′), *v.t.* 1, to plan; mean; as, we *intend* to stay; 2, to design or destine (a person or thing) for some purpose; as, his son is *intended* for the legal profession.

in-tend-ed (ĭn-tĕn′dĕd), *adj.* 1, planned; purposed; as, the *intended* meaning of a remark; 2, *Colloquial*, betrothed; as, his *intended* wife:—*n. Colloquial*, the person to whom one is engaged to be married.

in-tense (ĭn-tĕns′), *adj.* 1, extreme; excessive; as, *intense* cold; 2, violent; eager; earnest; as, *intense* love.—*adv.* **in-tense′ly.** —*n.* **in-tense′ness.**

Syn. vehement, fervid.

in-ten-si-fy (ĭn-tĕn′sĭ-fī), *v.t.* [intensified, intensify-ing], to make greater in degree; as, to *intensify* pain.—*n.* **in-ten′si-fi-ca′-tion.**

Syn. aggravate, enhance, increase.

in-ten-si-ty (ĭn-tĕn′sĭ-tĭ), *n.* [*pl.* intensities], 1, the state or quality of being extreme; violence; as, the *intensity* of anger or joy; 2, strength or degree; as, *intensity* of light.

in-ten-sive (ĭn-tĕn′sĭv), *adj.* 1, concentrated; thorough; as, an *intensive* study of literature; *intensive* thought; 2, in grammar, giving emphasis or force; as, in the sentence, "He did it himself," the word "himself" is *intensive.*—*adv.* **in-ten′sive-ly.**

in-tent (ĭn-tĕnt′), *adj.* concentrated; closely occupied; as, he was *intent* on his work:—*n.* purpose; aim; as, study with *intent* to learn.—*adv.* **in-tent′ly.**

Syn., n. intention, purport.

in-ten-tion (ĭn-tĕn′shŭn), *n.* that which is intended or planned; purpose; aim; as, to act with good *intention.*

Syn. object, intent, plan.

in-ten-tion-al (ĭn-tĕn′shŭn-ăl), *adj.* done on purpose; as, an *intentional* wrong.—*adv.* **in-ten′tion-al-ly.**

in-ter- (ĭn′tēr-), a prefix meaning: 1, among; between; as, *inter*cede, *inter*lude; 2, together; one with the other; as, *inter*lock, *inter*weave.

in-ter (ĭn-tûr′), *v.t.* [interred, inter-ring], to bury.

in-ter-act (ĭn′tēr-ăkt′), *v.i.* to influence or act on each other; have mutual effect.

in-ter-ac-tion (ĭn′tēr-ăk′shŭn), *n.* the effect or action of one person or thing on another.

in-ter-breed (ĭn′tēr-brēd′), *v.t.* [interbred (-brĕd′), interbreed-ing], to breed by crossing different kinds or stocks:—*v.i.* to breed with each other: said of animals, plants, etc., of different races or species.

in-ter-cede (ĭn′tēr-sēd′), *v.i.* [interced-ed, interced-ing], to act as peacemaker; mediate; also, to plead for another; as, I *interceded* for him with his father.

in-ter-cept (ĭn′tēr-sĕpt′), *v.t.* 1, to seize or catch on the way; stop; as, the spy *intercepted* the message; 2, to obstruct; cut off, as a view; 3, to interfere with the course of; stop; as, to *intercept* a forward pass.—*n.* **in′ter-cep′tion.**

in-ter-ces-sion (ĭn′tēr-sĕsh′ŭn), *n.* 1, an attempt to restore friendship between persons who are unfriendly; 2, the act of pleading for someone else; a prayer.—*n.* **in′ter-ces′sor.**

in-ter-change (ĭn′tēr-chānj′), *v.t.* [interchanged, interchang-ing], 1, to exchange the position of, by putting one thing or person in the place of another; 2, to vary; alternate; as, to *interchange* study with play:—*n.* (ĭn′tēr-chānj′), 1, the exchange of two things, one for the other; as, an *interchange* of calling cards; 2, alternate succession, as of the seasons.

in-ter-change-a-ble (ĭn′tēr-chān′jà-bl), *adj.* 1, capable of being put in place of each other; 2, capable of being exchanged; alternating.—*adv.* **in′ter-change′a-bly.**

in-ter-col-le-gi-ate (ĭn′tēr-kǒ-lē′jĭ-ĭt), *adj.* 1, carried on, as games, between colleges; 2, existing, as leagues, among colleges or universities.

āte, âorta, râre, căt, àsk, fär, ăllow, sofà; ēve, êvent, ĕll, writêr, novĕl; bīte, pĭn; nō, ōbey, ôr, dôg, tŏp, cǒllide; ūnit, ûnite, bûrn, cŭt, focŭs; nōon, fŏot; mound; coin;

in·ter·com·mu·ni·cate (ĭn′tēr-kŏ-mū′-nĭ-kāt), *v.i.* [intercommunicat-ed, inter-communicat-ing], to have free passage from one to the other, as rooms:—*v.t.* to transmit or communicate to and from each other.—*n.* in′ter-com-mu/ni-ca/tion.

in·ter·cos·tal (ĭn′tēr-kŏs′tăl), *adj.* between the ribs.

in·ter·course (ĭn′tēr-kôrs), *n.* connection, correspondence, or communication between individuals, nations, etc.

in·ter·de·pend·ence (ĭn′tēr-dē-pĕn′-dĕns), *n.* the state of being dependent upon each other; as, the *interdependence* of nations.—*adj.* in′ter-de-pend′ent.

in·ter·dict (ĭn′tēr-dĭkt′), *v.t.* 1, to prohibit or forbid; 2, to cut off from the spiritual services of a church:—*n.* (ĭn′tēr-dĭkt), a formal prohibition, especially of church privileges.—*n.* in′ter-dic′tion.

Syn., *v.* inhibit, debar.

in·ter·est (ĭn′tēr-ĕst; ĭn′trĭst), *n.* 1, a feeling of concern or curiosity about something; also, that which arouses it; as, suspense gives *interest* to a story; 2, that which is of advantage; benefit; as, he acts for the public *interest*; 3, a share or part ownership; as, he has an *interest* in the business; 4, a sum paid by the borrower for the use of borrowed money; as, 2% *interest* on a loan; 5, personal influence over the actions of others; as, he used his *interest* with the president; 6, **interests**, the persons occupied in some field of business or industry, taken all together; as, the coal *interests:*—*v.t.* 1, to engage the attention of; arouse to curiosity, sympathy, or the like; as, the play *interested* him; 2, to cause to take an interest or a share in; as, he *interested* the man in insurance.

in·ter·est·ed (ĭn′tēr-ĕs-tĕd; ĭn′trĭs-tĕd), *adj.* 1, having the feelings or attention attracted and held; 2, concerned, especially for personal advantage; 3, having a share in.

in·ter·est·ing (ĭn′tēr-ĕs-tĭng; ĭn′trĭs-tĭng), *adj.* attracting and holding attention, curiosity, or emotion.

in·ter·fere (ĭn′tēr-fēr′), *v.i.* [interfered, interfer-ing], 1, to meddle; 2, to clash; be opposed; as, their views *interfered;* 3, in football, to block an opposing player.

in·ter·fer·ence (ĭn′tēr-fēr′ĕns), *n.* 1, meddling; 2, in football, the act of blocking an opposing player; also, the players who do this.

in·ter·fuse (ĭn′tēr-fūz′), *v.t.* [interfused, interfus-ing], 1, to cause to flow together or blend; 2, to spread through.

in·ter·im (ĭn′tēr-ĭm), *n.* the time or period between happenings; the meantime.

in·te·ri·or (ĭn-tē′rĭ-ēr), *adj.* 1, inner; internal; 2, far from the coast or frontier:—*n.* 1, the inside, as of a building; 2, the inland part of a country; 3, the home affairs of a nation; as, the Department of the *Interior*.

interj. abbreviation for *interjection.*

in·ter·ject (ĭn′tēr-jĕkt′), *v.t.* to put or throw in; insert; as, to *interject* a question.

in·ter·jec·tion (ĭn′tēr-jĕk′shŭn), *n.* 1, the act of throwing in or interjecting; also, that which is thrown in; an exclamation; 2, in grammar, a word used as an exclamation, having no grammatical connection with the rest of the sentence; as, "Ah!" and "Oh!" are *interjections*.

in·ter·lace (ĭn′tēr-lās′), *v.t.* and *v.i.* [interlaced, interlac-ing], to join by weaving or lacing together; to intermingle.

in·ter·lard (ĭn′tēr-lärd′), *v.t.* to mix; vary by mingling with something different; as, to *interlard* a speech with jests.

¹**in·ter·line** (ĭn′tēr-līn′), *v.t.* [interlined, interlin-ing], to write between the lines of (writing or printing).

²**in·ter·line** (ĭn′tēr-līn′), *v.t.* [interlined, interlin-ing], to fit (a garment) with an extra lining beneath the usual one.

in·ter·lock (ĭn′tēr-lŏk′), *v.t.* and *v.i.* to lock or clasp together.

in·ter·loc·u·tor (ĭn′tēr-lŏk′ū-tēr), *n.* 1, one who takes part in a conversation; a questioner; interpreter; a talker; 2, in a minstrel show, a minstrel who puts questions to other minstrels.

in·ter·lop·er (ĭn′tēr-lōp′ēr), *n.* an outsider who interferes; an intruder.

in·ter·lude (ĭn′tēr-lūd), *n.* 1, a short entertainment given between the acts of a play; 2, a short passage of music played between the stanzas of a hymn, parts of a church service, acts of an opera, etc.; 3, any event or period of time coming between; as, an *interlude* of play in a day of work.

in·ter·mar·riage (ĭn′tēr-măr′ĭj; ĭn′tēr-măr′ij), *n.* wedlock between different families, tribes, races, or the like.—*v.i.* in′ter-mar′ry.

in·ter·med·dle (ĭn′tēr-mĕd′l), *v.i.* [inter-med-dled, intermed-dling], to interfere in other people's affairs.—*n.* in′ter-med′dler.

in·ter·me·di·ar·y (ĭn′tēr-mē′dĭ-ĕr′ĭ), *adj.* 1, situated or coming between; 2, acting as a harmonizing agent; as, an *intermediary* messenger:—*n.* [*pl.* intermediaries], a go-between; as, Jim was an *intermediary* between Mary and John.

in·ter·me·di·ate (ĭn′tēr-mē′dĭ-ĭt), *adj.* existing or lying in the middle; coming between:—*n.* **1,** that which lies between; **2,** a go-between.—*adv.* **in/ter-me/di-ate-ly.**

in-ter-ment (ĭn-tûr/mĕnt), *n.* burial.

in-ter-mi-na-ble (ĭn-tûr/mĭ-n*a*-bl), *adj.* endless; exceptionally long; as, an *interminable* speech.—*adv.* **in-ter/mi-na-bly.**

in-ter-min-gle (ĭn/tĕr-mĭng/gl), *v.t.* and *v.i.* [intermin-gled, intermin-gling], to mix.

in-ter-mis-sion (ĭn/tĕr-mĭsh/ŭn), *n.* **1,** a short or temporary break; an interruption; a pause; **2,** an interval of time between two parts, as acts of a play.

in-ter-mit-tent (ĭn/tĕr-mĭt/ĕnt), *adj.* ceasing for short periods and starting again; coming and going; as, *intermittent* rain.—*adv.* **in/ter-mit/tent-ly.**

in-ter-mix (ĭn/tĕr-mĭks/), *v.t.* and *v.i.* to combine or become combined.—*n.* **in/-ter-mix/ture.**

in-ter-mon-tane (ĭn/tĕr-mŏn/tān), *adj.* situated between mountains.

in-tern (ĭn-tûrn/), *v.t.* to confine within bounds; as, in war time a nation *interns* citizens and ships of the enemy country: —*n.* (ĭn/tûrn), (also spelled *interne*), a young doctor or surgeon who is getting final training for his own practice by serving in a hospital.

in-ter-nal (ĭn-tûr/nǎl), *adj.* **1,** belonging to the inside; inner: opposite of *external;* as, the *internal* parts of an engine; **2,** inherent; coming from within the thing itself; as, *internal* evidence; **3,** having to do with affairs within a country; domestic; as, *internal* products.

in-ter-nal com-bus-tion, the process by which power is produced within an engine cylinder by the explosion of a mixture of air and a fuel, such as vaporized gasoline.—*adj.* **in-ter/nal—com-bus/tion.**

in-ter-na-tion-al (ĭn/tĕr-nǎsh/ŭn-ǎl), *adj.* relating to, or carried on between, two or more nations or their people; as, *international* trade.—*adv.* **in/ter-na/tion-al-ly.**

in-ter-ne-cine (ĭn/tĕr-nē/sĭn; ĭn/tĕr-nē/sīn), *adj.* **1,** deadly; killing; as, *internecine* strife; **2,** destructive of one another.

in-ter-play (ĭn/tĕr-plā/), *n.* the action of two things on each other; as, the *interplay* of the parts of a machine.

in-ter-po-late (ĭn-tûr/pō-lāt), *v.t.* [interpolat-ed, interpolat-ing], **1,** to insert (new or unauthorized matter) into a book or writing; **2,** to insert between other things or parts.—*n.* **in-ter/po-la/tion.**

in-ter-pose (ĭn/tĕr-pōz/), *v.t.* [interposed, interpos-ing], **1,** to place or set between; **2,** to thrust in; put forth, in order to interfere; **3,** to introduce (a remark) into a conversation:—*v.i.* **1,** to come between

parties in a quarrel; mediate; **2,** to interrupt; **3,** to be between.
Syn. arbitrate, interfere, meddle.

in-ter-po-si-tion (ĭn/tĕr-pō-zĭsh/ŭn), *n.* **1,** the act of coming between, interrupting, etc.; **2,** that which is thrust in.

in-ter-pret (ĭn-tûr/prĕt), *v.t.* **1,** to explain the meaning of; as, to *interpret* a foreign word or a difficult passage; **2,** to bring out the meaning of, as a poem, a work of art, etc.; as, to *interpret* the role of Hamlet; **3,** to take one's own meaning from (words, actions, etc.); as, to *interpret* a friend's motives.
Syn. construe, unfold, decipher.

in-ter-pre-ta-tion (ĭn-tûr/prĕ-tā/shŭn), *n·* **1,** the act of explaining the meaning of something; **2,** explanation; translation; **3,** the expression by an artist or actor of his conception of a subject, as of a landscape or a character.

in-ter-pre-ta-tive (ĭn-tûr/prĕ-tā/tĭv), *adj.* explanatory; serving to interpret.

in-ter-pret-er (ĭn-tûr/prĕ-tĕr), *n.* **1,** one who explains or makes clear; **2,** one who translates orally the words of a person speaking in a different language.

in-ter-reg-num (ĭn/tĕr-rĕg/nŭm), *n.* **1,** the time between the end of one king's reign and the beginning of the next king's reign; **2,** a break in a continuous series of events.

in-ter-re-lat-ed (ĭn/tĕr-rĕ-lāt/ĕd), *adj.* having a connection between each other; mutually connected.—*n.* **in/ter-re-la/tion.**

in-ter-ro-gate (ĭn-tĕr/ō-gāt), *v.t.* [interrogat-ed, interrogat-ing], to question; examine by asking questions; as, to *interrogate* a witness.—*n.* **in-ter/ro-ga/tor.**
Syn. inquire, ask, examine.

in-ter-ro-ga-tion (ĭn-tĕr/ō-gā/shŭn), *n.* **1,** the act of asking questions; **2,** a question; inquiry:—**interrogation point** or **mark,** a mark [?] indicating a direct question; a question mark.

in-ter-rog-a-tive (ĭn/tĕ-rŏg/*a*-tĭv), *adj.* indicating, or containing a question; as, an *interrogative* glance; an *interrogative* sentence:—*n.* in grammar, a word which asks a question, as *why, where, who,* etc.—*adv.* **in/ter-rog/a-tive-ly.**

in-ter-rog-a-tor-y (ĭn/tĕ-rŏg/*a*-tôr/ĭ), *adj.* questioning; as, an *interrogatory* remark.

in-ter-rupt (ĭn/tĕ-rŭpt/), *v.t.* **1,** to stop or hinder by breaking in upon; as, to *interrupt* a speech; to *interrupt* a speaker; **2,** to obstruct; as, a wall *interrupts* a view; **3,** to break the continuity of; as, only the clock's tick *interrupts* the silence.

in-ter-rup-tion (ĭn/tĕ-rŭp/shŭn), *n.* **1,** the state of being broken in upon, or the act of breaking in upon something, as a conversation; **2,** a hindrance; something which blocks progress or breaks in upon speech, action, etc.; **3,** a sudden ceasing.

in·ter·sect (ĭn'tĕr-sĕkt'), *v.t.* to cut across; as, one line *intersects* another:— *v.i.* to cross each other.

in·ter·sec·tion (ĭn'tĕr-sĕk'shŭn), *n.* **1,** the act of cutting across; **2,** the place of crossing; as, a street or railroad *intersection.*

INTERSECTION
The two lines intersect at the point A.

in·ter·sperse (ĭn'tĕr-spûrs'), *v.t.* [interspersed, interspers-ing], **1,** to insert here and there; as, to *intersperse* comments in the reading of a play; **2,** to scatter about; place here and there among other things; as, to *intersperse* shrubbery with flowers.

in·ter·state (ĭn'tĕr-stāt'), *adj.* between states; as, *interstate* railways.

in·ter·stice (ĭn-tûr'stĭs), *n.* [*pl.* interstices], a narrow crevice; a chink.—*adj.* in'ter·sti'tial (ĭn'tĕr-stĭsh'ăl).

in·ter·twine (ĭn'tĕr-twīn'), *v.t.* and *v.i.* [intertwined, intertwin-ing], to twist; wind or coil together.

in·ter·ur·ban (ĭn'tĕr-ûr'băn), *adj.* between cities or towns; as, an *interurban* railroad.

in·ter·val (ĭn'tĕr-văl), *n.* **1,** the time or space between events, periods, or the like; as, the *interval* between two illnesses; **2,** a space between objects; as, an *interval* of ten feet between tents; **3,** in music, the difference in pitch between two tones.

in·ter·vene (ĭn'tĕr-vēn'), *v.i.* [intervened, interven-ing], **1,** to come between (things or events); as, a minute *intervened* between his remarks; **2,** to step in; interfere, as a force to influence action; as, friends *intervened* when the two men quarreled; **3,** to be between; as, a fence *intervened* between the yards.

in·ter·ven·tion (ĭn'tĕr-vĕn'shŭn), *n.* the act of coming between; interference; as, his *intervention* ended the quarrel.

in·ter·view (ĭn'tĕr-vū), *v.t.* to question, especially in order to obtain information for the press:—*n.* **1,** a personal conference or meeting; **2,** in journalism, the act of talking with, or being questioned by, a reporter; also, the published account of such a conversation.—*n.* in'ter·view'er.

in·ter·weave (ĭn'tĕr-wēv'), *v.i.* and *v.t.* [*p.t.* interwove (-wōv'), *p.p.* interwo-ven (-wō'věn) or interwove, *p.pr.* interweaving], **1,** to twist together; **2,** to intermingle; as, to *interweave* prose and verse.

in·tes·tate (ĭn-tĕs'tāt), *adj.* not having made a will; as, to die *intestate.*

in·tes·ti·nal (ĭn-tĕs'tĭ-năl), *adj.* pertaining to the intestines; as, *intestinal* grippe. —*adv.* in·tes'ti·nal·ly.

in·tes·tine (ĭn-tĕs'tĭn), *n.* a tube extending from the stomach to the rectum, which helps to digest and absorb food and to eliminate waste matter: composed of the *large* and the *small intestine;* the bowels.

INTESTINES
S.I., small intestine; L.I., large intestine; A, appendix; R, rectum.

in·ti·ma·cy (ĭn'tĭ-mȧ-sĭ), *n.* [*pl.* intimacies], close friendship.

in·ti·mate (ĭn'tĭ-mĭt), *adj.* **1,** close in friendship; familiar; as, *intimate* friends; **2,** resulting from close study; as, an *intimate* knowledge of art; **3,** having to do with the inner nature of anything; innermost; as, a person's *intimate* feelings:—*n.* a close friend:—*v.t.* (ĭn'tĭ-māt), [intimat-ed, intimat-ing], to suggest; hint; make known indirectly; as, he *intimated* his disapproval of the plan.—*adv.* in'ti·mate·ly.

Syn., v. insinuate, imply.

in·ti·ma·tion (ĭn'tĭ-mā'shŭn), *n.* **1,** an indirect hint; **2,** an announcement.

in·tim·i·date (ĭn-tĭm'ĭ-dāt), *v.t.* [intimi-dat-ed, intimidat-ing], to frighten; over-awe, especially by threats.—*n.* in·tim'i·da'tion.

Syn. dishearten, alarm, scare.

in·to (ĭn'tōō; ĭn'tŏŏ), *prep.* **1,** to the inside of (a place, matter, occupation, state, etc.); as, come *into* the room; look *into* the affair; go *into* business; get *into* trouble; **2,** to the condition of; as, the rain later turned *into* snow.

in·tol·er·a·ble (ĭn-tŏl'ĕr-ȧ-bl), *adj.* un-bearable; not to be endured; as, *intolerable* heat; an *intolerable* insult.—*adv.* in·tol'er·a·bly.

Syn. insupportable, insufferable.

in·tol·er·ance (ĭn-tŏl'ĕr-ăns), *n.* **1,** un-willingness to permit others to follow their own opinions and beliefs, especially in matters of religion; **2,** inability to bear or endure; as, *intolerance* of extreme cold.

in·tol·er·ant (ĭn-tŏl'ĕr-ănt), *adj.* **1,** scorn-ing difference of opinion, belief, or be-havior in others, especially in religion and morals; **2,** unable to bear or endure; as, *intolerant* of pain.—*adv.* in·tol'er·ant·ly.

in·to·na·tion (ĭn'tŏ-nā'shŭn), *n.* **1,** the rise and fall of the speaking voice; **2,** chanting or intoning, as of a psalm.

---

go; join; yet; sing; chin; show; thin, *th*en; hw, *why*; zh, azure; ü, Ger. für or Fr. lune; ö, Ger. schön or Fr. feu; ṅ, Fr. enfant, nom; kh, Ger. ach or ich. See pages ix–x.

in-tone (ĭn-tōn′), *v.t.* and *v.i.* [intoned, in-ton-ing], to recite in a singing tone; chant; as, to *intone* a church service.

in-tox-i-cant (ĭn-tŏk′sĭ-kǎnt), *n.* **1,** that which makes a person drunk, as alcohol; **2,** anything that excites or elates.

in-tox-i-cate (ĭn-tŏk′sĭ-kāt), *v.t.* [intox-icat-ed, intoxicat-ing], **1,** to make drunk, as by alcoholic liquors; **2,** to excite exceed-ingly; to elate; as, happiness *intoxicated* him.—*n.* **in-tox′i-ca′tion.**

in-tra- (ĭn′trȧ-), a prefix meaning within; inside; as, *intra*mural.

in-trac-ta-ble (ĭn-trăk′tȧ-bl), *adj.* un-manageable; not easily controlled; as, an *intractable* horse; an *intractable* temper.
Syn. disobedient, perverse, unruly.

in-tra-mu-ral (ĭn′trȧ-mū′rǎl), *adj.* en-tirely within the walls or limits of a city, university, etc.; as, an *intramural* railway; *intramural* sports.

in-tran-si-tive (ĭn-trăn′sĭ-tĭv), *adj.* in grammar, not taking a direct object be-cause none is needed to complete the action or the meaning: said of verbs; as, he *sits;* he *laughed.*—*adv.* **in-tran′si-tive-ly.**

in-trench (ĭn-trĕnch′), *v.t.* **1,** to make hollows or furrows in; **2,** to surround with a ditch:—*v.i.* to intrude. See **entrench.**

in-trench-ment (ĭn-trĕnch′mĕnt), *n.* **1,** the act of enclosing within trenches; **2,** in warfare, a defensive work. See **entrench-ment.**

in-trep-id (ĭn-trĕp′ĭd), *adj.* bold; fearless; brave.—*adv.* **in-trep′id-ly.**—*n.* **in′tre-pid′-i-ty** (ĭn′trē-pĭd′ĭ-tĭ).
Syn. dauntless, courageous, heroic, gal-lant, daring.

in-tri-ca-cy (ĭn′trĭ-kȧ-sĭ), *n.* [*pl.* intri-cacies], **1,** the condition of being en-tangled or complicated; **2,** that which is entangled or involved.

in-tri-cate (ĭn′trĭ-kĭt), *adj.* entangled; complicated; involved; as, an *intricate* plot; an *intricate* carving.
Syn. difficult, complex, obscure.

in-trigue (ĭn-trēg′), *v.i.* [intrigued, in-tri-guing], **1,** to carry on a secret plot; **2,** to engage in a secret love affair:—*v.t.* **1,** to arouse curiosity in; hence, interest keenly; as, your plan *intrigues* me; **2,** to puzzle; perplex:—*n.* (ĭn-trēg′; ĭn′trēg), **1,** a plot; **2,** a secret love affair.
Syn., n. scheme, conspiracy, ruse.

in-trin-sic (ĭn-trĭn′sĭk), *adj.* relating to the inner nature; true; as, a man's *in-trinsic* worth.—*adv.* **in-trin′si-cal-ly.**
Syn. genuine, native, natural, real.

in-tro- (ĭn′trō-), a prefix meaning into; as, *intro*duce, *intro*spection.

intro. abbreviation for *introduction.*

in-tro-duce (ĭn′trō-dūs′), *v.t.* [introduced, introduc-ing], **1,** to bring in; usher in; as, he *introduced* me into the room; **2,** to bring into use or notice; as, to *introduce* a new fad; Newton *introduced* the theory of gravity; **3,** to make known, as one person to another; **4,** to put into; insert; as, to *introduce* lime into the soil; **5,** to make known or bring to notice; as, to *introduce* the poetry of Keats to a class; **6,** to present in a formal manner; as, to *introduce* a bill into Congress; **7,** to open; begin; as, a phrase may *introduce* a sentence.

in-tro-duc-tion (ĭn′trō-dŭk′shŭn), *n.* **1,** the act of introducing or being introduced; presentation, as of one person to another, a speaker to an audience, etc.; also, the making known of a new thing, idea, cus-tom, or the like; **2,** a preface, as of a book; the opening movement of a musical com-position.—*adj.* **in′tro-duc′to-ry.**

in-tro-spec-tion (ĭn′trō-spĕk′shŭn), *n.* the act or process of examining one's own thoughts or feelings.

in-tro-spec-tive (ĭn′trō-spĕk′tĭv), *adj.* in-clined to examine one's own thoughts and feelings; subjective.

in-trude (ĭn-trōōd′), *v.i.* [intrud-ed, in-trud-ing], to enter without invitation or welcome:—*v.t.* to thrust or force in; as, to *intrude* remarks into a conversation.—*n.* **in-trud′er.**

in-tru-sion (ĭn-trōō′zhŭn), *n.* the act of entering without invitation; trespassing.

in-tru-sive (ĭn-trōō′sĭv), *adj.* inclined to enter without invitation; forward.

in-trust (ĭn-trŭst′), *v.t.* to give into an-other's keeping; entrust. See **entrust.**

in-tu-i-tion (ĭn′tū-ĭsh′ŭn), *n.* knowledge that comes to one instinctively or without conscious thought or study; sudden in-sight; as, his *intuition* warned of danger.

in-tu-i-tive (ĭn-tū′ĭ-tĭv), *adj.* **1,** knowing or capable of being known by the mind without reasoning; **2,** possessing, or acting by, instinctive knowledge or feeling.—*adv.* **in-tu′i-tive-ly.**

in-un-date (ĭn′ŭn-dāt), *v.t.* [inundat-ed, inundat-ing], **1,** to fill to overflowing; flood; **2,** hence, to spread over.

in-un-da-tion (ĭn′ŭn-dā′shŭn), *n.* an overflow.

in-ure (ĭn-ūr′), *v.t.* [inured, inur-ing], to accustom; toughen; as, to *inure* oneself to cold baths:—*v.i.* to come into use; take effect; as, the fund *inured* to his benefit.

in-vade (ĭn-vād′), *v.t.* [invad-ed, invad-ing], **1,** to enter in a hostile manner; as, the Romans *invaded* Gaul; worry *invades*

āte, ȧorta, râre, căt, ȧsk, fär, ăllow, sofȧ; ēve, êvent, ĕll, writêr, novĕl; bīte, pĭn; nō, ōbey, ôr, dŏg, tŏp, cŏllide; ūnit, ŭnite, bûrn, cŭt, focŭs; nōōn, fŏŏt; mound; coin;

the mind; **2,** to infringe upon; to violate; as, to *invade* the rights of a people.

¹in-val-id (ĭn-văl′ĭd), *adj.* of no force, authority, or value; as, an *invalid* reason. —*n.* **in′va-lid′i-ty** (ĭn′và-lĭd′ĭ-tĭ).

²in-va-lid (ĭn′và-lĭd), *n.* one who is weak or sick; also, a disabled soldier or sailor:— *adj.* **1,** sick; enfeebled by ill health; **2,** for a sick person; as, an *invalid* chair:—*v.t.* **1,** to make sick or weak; **2,** to send away as sick; as, soldiers are *invalided* home.

in-val-i-date (ĭn-văl′ĭ-dāt), *v.t.* [invalidat-ed, invalidat-ing], to make null and void; as, the last will *invalidates* all others. —*n.* **in-val′i-da′tion.**
> *Syn.* cancel, overthrow, nullify, annul.

in-val-u-a-ble (ĭn-văl′ū-á-bl), *adj.* priceless; exceedingly valuable; as, his work was *invaluable* to his firm.

in-var-i-a-ble (ĭn-vâr′ĭ-á-bl), *adj.* constant; unchanging.—*adv.* **in-var′i-a-bly.**

in-va-sion (ĭn-vā′zhŭn), *n.* **1,** the act of entering in a hostile manner; **2,** an attack of anything injurious, as a disease.

in-vec-tive (ĭn-vĕk′tĭv), *n.* a violent, bitter attack in words; abusive language.
> *Syn.* reproach, vituperation.

in-veigh (ĭn-vā′), *v.i.* to speak violently and bitterly; utter blame or reproach; as, a Congressman *inveighed* against the proposed bill.—*n.* **in-veigh′er.**

in-vei-gle (ĭn-vē′gl; ĭn-vā′gl), *v.t.* [invei-gled, invei-gling], to persuade by deception or flattery; lure.—*n.* **in-vei′gle-ment.**—*n.* **in-vei′gler.**
> *Syn.* allure, decoy, entice.

in-vent (ĭn-vĕnt′), *v.t.* **1,** to create as a result of original study; originate; produce for the first time; as, to *invent* a machine; **2,** to make up; as, to *invent* a strange story.
> *Syn.* frame, discover, contrive.

in-ven-tion (ĭn-vĕn′shŭn), *n.* **1,** the act of inventing; as, the *invention* of the steam engine; also, something invented, as the radio, phonograph, or the like; **2,** a lie; as, the story is pure *invention.*

in-ven-tive (ĭn-vĕn′tĭv), *adj.* able to invent; clever and original.—*n.* **in-ven′tive-ness.**

in-ven-tor (ĭn-vĕn′tẽr), *n.* one who works out and creates something new; as, Edison was a great *inventor.*

in-ven-tor-y (ĭn′vĕn-tôr′ĭ), *n.* [*pl.* inventories], a catalog or detailed list of goods, furniture, books, etc.:—*v.t.* [inventoried, inventory-ing], to make an inventory of; to include in a list; catalog.

in-verse (ĭn-vûrs′; ĭn′vûrs), *adj.* opposite in tendency, direction, or effect; turned upside down; as, subtraction is the *inverse*

operation of addition:—*n.* the direct opposite.—*adv.* **in-verse′ly.**

in-ver-sion (ĭn-vûr′shŭn; ĭn-vûr′zhŭn), *n.* a reversal of position, order, or relation.

in-vert (ĭn-vûrt′), *v.t.* **1,** to turn upside down, inside out, or in an opposite direction; **2,** to reverse, as in meaning or order; as, to *invert* AB by making it BA.—*adj.* **in-vert′i-ble.**—*adj.* **in-vert′ed.**

in-ver-te-brate (ĭn-vûr′tĕ-brāt), *n.* an animal without backbone or spinal column: —*adj.* having no backbone; hence, weak-willed.

in-vest (ĭn-vĕst′), *v.t.* **1,** to lay out (money) for income or profit; as, he *invested* money in stocks; **2,** to clothe with an office, dignity, or the like; as, to *invest* a judge with the authority of his position:—*v.i.* to put money out for profit.

in-ves-ti-gate (ĭn-vĕs′tĭ-gāt), *v.t.* and *v.i.* [investigat-ed, investigat-ing], to examine systematically; to make careful inquiry (about); as, to *investigate* the cause of a disaster.—*n.* **in-ves′ti-ga′tor.**

in-ves-ti-ga-tion (ĭn-vĕs′tĭ-gā′shŭn), *n.* careful examination, inquiry, or search.
> *Syn.* inspection, scrutiny.

in-ves-ti-ture (ĭn-vĕs′tĭ-tūr), *n.* the ceremony of installing a person in office.

in-vest-ment (ĭn-vĕst′mĕnt), *n.* **1,** the act of investing money; also, the money invested, or that in which money is invested; as, an *investment* in stocks; real estate is sometimes a good *investment;* **2,** the act of clothing with something, as robes of office.

in-ves-tor (ĭn-vĕs′tẽr), *n.* one who puts out money for profit.

in-vet-er-ate (ĭn-vĕt′ẽr-ĭt), *adj.* **1,** of long standing; deep-rooted; as, *inveterate* hatred; **2,** habitual; as, an *inveterate* liar.
> *Syn.* confirmed, chronic.

in-vid-i-ous (ĭn-vĭd′ĭ-ŭs), *adj.* likely to provoke ill will or envy; unfairly partial.
> *Syn.* hateful, odious.

in-vig-o-rate (ĭn-vĭg′ō-rāt), *v.t.* [invig-orat-ed, invigorat-ing], to give vitality to; strengthen; as, sea air *invigorates* the weak.
> *Syn.* brace, refresh, stimulate.

in-vin-ci-ble (ĭn-vĭn′sĭ-bl), *adj.* not to be overcome or subdued; unconquerable; as, an *invincible* will.—*adv.* **in-vin′ci-bly.**—*n.* **in-vin′ci-bil′i-ty.**

in-vi-o-la-ble (ĭn-vī′ō-là-bl), *adj.* **1,** sacred; not to be violated; as, *inviolable* territory; **2,** not to be broken; as, an *inviolable* promise; *inviolable* laws.

in-vi-o-late (ĭn-vī′ō-lāt), *adj.* uninjured; unbroken; as, he kept his oath *inviolate.*

---

go; join; yet; sing; chin; show; thin, *th***en; hw,** *why;* **zh, a**zure; **ü,** Ger. f**ü**r or Fr. l**u**ne; **ö,** Ger. sch**ö**n or Fr. f**eu**; **ṅ,** Fr. enfa**n**t, no**m**; **kh,** Ger. a**ch** or i**ch.** See pages ix–x.

in·vis·i·ble (ĭn-vĭz′ĭ-bl), *adj.* not capable of being seen; out of sight; as, clouds make the stars *invisible.*—*adv.* **in-vis′i-bly.**—*n.* **in-vis′i-bil′i-ty.**

in·vi·ta·tion (ĭn′vĭ-tā′shŭn), *n.* a request to a person to come to some place or to do something; also, the written or spoken form of such a request.

in·vite (ĭn-vīt′), *v.t.* [invit-ed, invit-ing], **1,** to ask (a person) to come somewhere or to do something; as, *invite* him for a walk; **2,** to request; as, to *invite* an opinion; **3,** to tempt; as, the music *invites* us to dance.
Syn. bid, allure.

in·vit·ing (ĭn-vīt′ĭng), *adj.* tempting; alluring; as, an *inviting* meal.

in·vo·ca·tion (ĭn′vō-kā′shŭn), *n.* **1,** a prayer; a supplication, especially to a divine being; **2,** the act of conjuring up devils, or the magic words for doing so.

in·voice (ĭn′vois), *n.* **1,** a written list of goods sent to a purchaser, with their prices, quantity, and charges; **2,** the goods listed:—*v.t.* [invoiced, invoic-ing], to make an invoice of; to include in an invoice.

in·voke (ĭn-vōk′), *v.t.* [invoked, invok-ing], **1,** to address in prayer or supplication; as, to *invoke* the Lord; **2,** to ask for earnestly; as, to *invoke* a blessing; **3,** to conjure up; as, to *invoke* evil spirits.

in·vol·un·tar·y (ĭn-vŏl′ŭn-tĕr′ĭ), *adj.* **1,** not under the control of the will; as, the beating of the heart is an *involuntary* activity; **2,** against one's will; compulsory; **3,** unintentional; as, an *involuntary* sigh.—*adv.* **in-vol′un-tar/i-ly.**

in·volve (ĭn-vŏlv′), *v.t.* [involved, involv-ing], **1,** to entangle; complicate; as, he *involved* his friend in debt; **2,** to make difficult; complicate; as, these new facts certainly *involve* the mystery; **3,** to include as a necessity; require; as, a career *involves* hard work; **4,** to engage completely; as, study *involves* all my time.

in·vul·ner·a·ble (ĭn-vŭl′nĕr-à-bl), *adj.* **1,** incapable of being injured; **2,** incapable of being answered or refuted; as, an *invulnerable* argument.—*n.* **in-vul′ner-a-bil′i-ty.**

in·ward (ĭn′wĕrd), *adj.* **1,** situated within; internal; as, *inward* organs; **2,** of the inner self; as, *inward* happiness; **3,** toward the inside or center; as, an *inward* curve.

in·ward (ĭn′wĕrd) or **in·wards** (ĭn′wĕrdz), *adv.* **1,** toward the inside or center; as, to bend *inward;* **2,** into or toward the mind; as, turn the thoughts *inward.*

in·ward·ly (ĭn′wĕrd-lĭ), *adv.* internally; especially, in the mind or feelings; secretly; as, to grieve *inwardly.*

in·ward·ness (ĭn′wĕrd-nĕs), *n.* **1,** the inner meaning or real nature of a thing; **2,** spirituality; spiritual quality; as, the *inwardness* of the teachings of Christ.

in·wrap (ĭn-răp′), *v.t.* [inwrapped, inwrap-ping], to enclose in a wrapping; enwrap. See **enwrap.**

in·wrought (ĭn-rôt′; ĭn′rôt′), *adj.* **1,** worked into a fabric; as, an *inwrought* design; **2,** having a pattern worked in; as, robes *inwrought* with gold.

i·o·dide (ī′ō-dīd; ī′ō-dĭd) or **i·o·did** (ī′ō-dĭd), *n.* a compound containing iodine.

i·o·dine (ī′ō-dīn; ī′ō-dĭn; ī′ō-dēn) or **i·o·din** (ī′ō-dĭn), *n.* a black-gray crystalline element found in mineral springs, seaweed, etc. A solution of these crystals in alcohol is much used as an antiseptic.

i·o·do·form (ī-ō′dō-fôrm; ī-ŏd′ō-fôrm), *n.* a yellow crystalline powder, a compound of iodine, with a penetrating odor: used in surgical dressing and as an antiseptic.

i·on (ī′ŏn), *n.* one of the particles bearing electrical charges which transmit electric current through the air or other gases.

-i·on (-ĭ′ŏn; -ŭn), a suffix meaning: **1,** the act or process of; as, erect*ion;* **2,** the condition or state of; as, deject*ion;* **3,** that which performs the action of; as, restrict*ion;* **4,** the result of; as, object*ion.* In many words *-ion* can have more than one of these meanings, as in protect*ion.* In combination with various stem endings, it takes on a variety of forms, as *-sion, -tion, -ation, -ition.*

I·o·ni·a (ī-ō′nĭ-à), a colony of ancient Greece in western Asia Minor, on the coast of the Aegean Sea (map **1**).

I·o·ni·an Is·lands (ī-ō′nĭ-ăn), a group of islands in the Ionian Sea, off the western coast of Greece (map **12**).

I·on·ic (ī-ŏn′ĭk), *adj.* **1,** having to do with Ionia; **2,** pertaining to an order of Greek architecture having scroll-like decorations on the capitals of pillars.

IONIC
Ionic capital (1) and base (2).

i·o·ta (ī-ō′tà), *n.* **1,** the letter of the Greek alphabet which corresponds to *i;* **2,** a small or insignificant amount or degree; as, I don't care an *iota* about it.

I.O.U. abbreviation for *I owe you:*—**IOU,** a written acknowledgement of a debt.

-i·ous (-ĭ′ŭs; -ŭs), a suffix meaning: characterized by or full of: added to the stems of nouns ending in *-ion* to form the adjective; as, ambit*ious,* relig*ious,* infect*ious.*

I·o·wa (ī'ō-wà), a north central State (cap. Des Moines) of the U.S. (map 7).

ip·e·cac (ĭp'ē-kăk), *n.* 1, a tropical South American creeping plant; also, its root; 2, an extract or tincture of this root, used in medicine to cause vomiting.

i.q. abbreviation for Latin *idem quod*, meaning *the same as*.

Ir. abbreviation for *Ireland, Irish*.

ir- (ĭr-), *prefix*, a form of *in-* used before *r*.

I·ran (ē-rän'; ī-răn'), a kingdom (cap. Tehran) in southwestern Asia (map 15). It was formerly called *Persia*.

I·raq or **I·rak** (ē-räk'), a kingdom (cap. Baghdad) in the northeastern part of the Arabian peninsula (map 15): formerly called *Mesopotamia*.

i·ras·ci·ble (ī-răs'ĭ-bl; ĭ-răs'ĭ-bl), *adj.* easily excited to anger; hotheaded.—*n.* **i·ras'ci·bil'i·ty.**

Syn. irritable, peevish, quarrelsome.

i·rate (ī'rāt; ī-rāt'), *adj.* angry; enraged.

ire (īr), *n.* anger; wrath.—*adj.* **ire'ful.**

Ire. abbreviation for *Ireland*.

Ire·land (īr'lănd), one of the British Isles, divided politically into *Northern Ireland* and the Republic of Ireland (map 13).

ir·i·des·cent (ĭr'ĭ-dĕs'ĕnt), *adj.* having changing, shimmering, rainbowlike colors, as an opal.—*n.* **ir'i·des'cence.**

i·rid·i·um (ī-rĭd'ĭ-ŭm), *n.* a rare element somewhat like platinum, used to make pen points, watch and compass bearings, etc.

i·ris (ī'rĭs), *n.* [*pl.* irises], 1, the rainbow; also, a rainbowlike shimmer; 2, the colored portion of the eye around the pupil; 3, a plant with large, showy flowers and sword-shaped leaves: often called *flag*.

I·rish (ī'rĭsh), *adj.* pertaining to Ireland, its inhabitants, or its language:—*n.* the native Celtic language of the Irish; Gaelic:— **the Irish,** the people of Ireland.

Irish Free State, the former name for *Eire*, (1922–1937), now the Republic of Ireland (cap. Dublin), occupying the southern part of Ireland (map 13).

I·rish·man (ī'rĭsh-măn), *n.* [*pl.* Irishmen (-mĕn)], a man of Irish birth or race.

I·rish po·ta·to, the white potato.

Irish Sea, a body of water between Great Britain and Ireland (map 13).

irk (ûrk), *v.t.* to weary; annoy; bore; as, dull details of the business *irk* him.

irk·some (ûrk'sŭm), *adj.* tedious; wearisome; dull; as, an *irksome* lesson.

Syn. tiresome, annoying, fatiguing.

IRIS

i·ron (ī'ĕrn), *n.* 1, a silver-white metal which can be melted and worked into tools and implements: the most common of all the metals, used over almost all the world in three commercial forms, *wrought iron, cast iron,* and *steel;* 2, any tool or weapon made of iron, especially a flatiron, pistol, branding iron, or harpoon; 3, firmness; rigidity; strength; as, a man of *iron;* 4, in golf, any of several clubs with an iron head; 5, **irons,** chains or fetters:—*adj.* 1, pertaining to, or made of, iron; as, an *iron* bar; 2, resembling iron in hardness, strength, etc.; as, an *iron* will: —*v.t.* 1, to smooth with an iron; as, to *iron* clothes; 2, to fetter.

i·ron·clad (ī'ĕrn-klăd'), *n.* a warship cased with iron or steel plates:—*adj.* 1, protected with iron plates; 2, *Colloquial,* not to be evaded; strict; as, *ironclad* rules.

i·ron·i·cal (ī-rŏn'ĭ-kăl) or **i·ron·ic** (ī-rŏn'-ĭk), *adj.* 1, expressing the opposite of what is meant; disguisedly sarcastic; as, an *ironical* remark; 2, describing a circumstance the reverse of what was, or might be, expected; as, an *ironical* turn of fate made him the rival of his best friend.— *adv.* **i·ron'i·cal·ly.**

i·ron·side (ī'ĕrn-sīd'), *n.* 1, a man of great strength: 2, a warship protected with steel plates.

Ironsides, a nickname given to Oliver Cromwell for bravery, and later to his cavalrymen; **Old Ironsides,** the U.S. frigate *Constitution*, built in 1797.

i·ron·ware (ī'ĕrn-wâr'), *n.* hardware; articles made of iron.

i·ron·work (ī'ĕrn-wûrk'), *n.* 1, iron articles; 2, **ironworks,** a place where iron is smelted and articles are made from it.

i·ro·ny (ī'rō-nĭ), *n.* [*pl.* ironies], 1, hidden sarcasm; the expression of the opposite of what is really meant; as, ridicule disguised as praise is *irony;* 2, any situation or event the opposite of what would normally be expected; as, the *irony* of it was that he was killed by his own invention.

Syn. satire, ridicule, raillery.

Ir·o·quois (ĭr'ō-kwoi; ĭr'ō-kwoiz), *n.* [*pl.* Iroquois], a member of a powerful confederacy of American Indians, the Five Nations, formerly inhabiting central New York.—*adj.* and *n.* **Ir'o·quoi'an.**

ir·ra·di·ate (ĭ-rā'dĭ-āt), *v.t.* [irradiat-ed, irradiat-ing], 1, to shed light upon; brighten; as, the sun *irradiates* the world; 2, to treat by exposing to ultraviolet rays; as, to *irradiate* milk.

ir·ra·tion·al (ĭr-răsh'ŭn-ăl), *adj.* 1, lacking reasoning powers, as beasts; 2, without reason; as, an *irrational* fear.

Ir·ra·wad·dy (ĭr/à-wŏd/ĭ), a large river in central Burma, flowing south into the Bay of Bengal.

ir·re·claim·a·ble (ĭr/rē-klā/mà-bl), *adj.* incapable of being recovered, reformed, restored, etc.; as, *irreclaimable* land.

ir·rec·on·cil·a·ble (ĭr-rĕk/ŏn-sĭ/là-bl; ĭr-rĕk/ŏn-sī/là-bl), *adj.* **1,** not adjustable, as a quarrel; unchangeably hostile, as two persons who have quarreled; **2,** not in agreement; as, his actions are *irreconcilable* with his promises.—*adv.* **ir·rec/on·cil/a·bly.**

ir·re·cov·er·a·ble (ĭr/rē-kŭv/ẽr-à-bl), *adj.* not capable of being remedied or regained; as, *irrecoverable* injuries or *irrecoverable* opportunities.

ir·re·deem·a·ble (ĭr/rē-dē/mà-bl), *adj.* **1,** incapable of being restored; as, an *irredeemable* loss; **2,** not exchangeable for gold or silver: said of paper money; **3,** hopeless; not to be cured or saved; as, an *irredeemable* criminal.

ir·re·duc·i·ble (ĭr/rē-dū/sĭ-bl), *adj.* **1,** incapable of being brought to a smaller number or amount; as, *irreducible* expenses; **2,** incapable of being simplified; as, 2/3 is an *irreducible* fraction.

ir·ref·u·ta·ble (ĭ-rĕf/ū-tà-bl; ĭr/rē-fū/tà-bl), *adj.* incapable of being proved false or incorrect; as, an *irrefutable* argument.—*adv.* **ir·ref/u·ta·bly.**

ir·reg·u·lar (ĭr-rĕg/ŭ-lẽr), *adj.* **1,** not straight or symmetrical; not uniform in shape, order, etc.; as, *irregular* lines and figures; **2,** not according to rule or established method; as, an *irregular* proceeding; **3,** in grammar, not following the regular rule for conjugation or inflection; as, "go" is an *irregular* verb.—*adv.* **ir·reg/u·lar·ly.**

ir·reg·u·lar·i·ty (ĭr-rĕg/ŭ-lăr/ĭ-tĭ), *n.* [*pl.* irregularities], the quality or state of not being uniform in shape, order, etc., or of being contrary to established rules and customs; also, an instance of this; as, *irregularities* in conduct.

ir·rel·e·vant (ĭr-rĕl/ē-vănt), *adj.* not bearing upon the case; unrelated to the matter discussed; as, *irrelevant* evidence or arguments.—*adv.* **ir·rel/e·vant·ly.**—*n.* **ir·rel/e·vance;** or **ir·rel/e·van·cy.**

ir·re·li·gious (ĭr/rē-lĭj/ŭs), *adj.* lacking religion or respect for religion; profane; as, *irreligious* conduct.—*adv.* **ir/re·li/gious·ly.**

ir·re·me·di·a·ble (ĭr/rē-mē/dĭ-à-bl), *adj.* not capable of being remedied or corrected; as, *irremediable* evils.—*adv.* **ir/re·me/di·a·bly.**

ir·rep·a·ra·ble (ĭ-rĕp/à-rà-bl), *adj.* not capable of being repaired, restored, or remedied; as, his losses are *irreparable.*—*adv.* **ir·rep/a·ra·bly.**

ir·re·press·i·ble (ĭr/rē-prĕs/ĭ-bl), *adj.* incapable of being checked or controlled; as, *irrepressible* laughter.

ir·re·proach·a·ble (ĭr/rē-prō/chà-bl), *adj.* blameless; faultless; as, *irreproachable* conduct.

ir·re·sist·i·ble (ĭr/rē-zĭs/tĭ-bl), *adj.* too strong or desirable to be resisted; overpowering; as, an *irresistible* temptation.—*adv.* **ir/re·sist/i·bly.**

ir·res·o·lute (ĭ-rĕz/ō-lūt), *adj.* undecided; wavering; as, a man *irresolute* in his decisions.—*n.* **ir·res/o·lu/tion.**

ir·re·spec·tive (ĭr/rē-spĕk/tĭv), *adj.* regardless; as, all men must die, *irrespective* of rank.—*adv.* **ir/re·spec/tive·ly.**

ir·re·spon·si·ble (ĭr/rē-spŏn/sĭ-bl), *adj.* **1,** not to be held accountable; as, an *irresponsible* child; **2,** not trustworthy; as, *irresponsible* servants.—*adv.* **ir/re·spon/si·bly.**—*n.* **ir/re·spon/si·bil/i·ty.**

ir·re·triev·a·ble (ĭr/rē-trē/và-bl), *adj.* not recoverable; not to be regained; as, an *irretrievable* loss.—*adv.* **ir/re·triev/a·bly.**

ir·rev·er·ence (ĭ-rĕv/ẽr-ĕns), *n.* **1,** lack of respect or awe, especially toward sacred things; **2,** a disrespectful act or speech.

ir·rev·er·ent (ĭ-rĕv/ẽr-ĕnt), *adj.* disrespectful; showing a lack of respect or veneration, especially for things held sacred.—*adv.* **ir·rev/er·ent·ly.**

ir·re·vers·i·ble (ĭr/rē-vûr/sĭ-bl), *adj.* **1,** incapable of being turned back, upside down, or around; as, the hands on this clock are *irreversible;* **2,** incapable of being repealed, recalled, or annulled; as, an *irreversible* decision of the court.

ir·rev·o·ca·ble (ĭ-rĕv/ō-kà-bl), *adj.* incapable of being recalled or undone; as, an *irrevocable* act.

ir·ri·gate (ĭr/ĭ-gāt), *v.t.* [irrigat-ed, irrigating], **1,** to supply with water, as land under cultivation, by means of ditches, channels, etc.; **2,** to wash out, as a wound, with a flow of liquid, in order to clean or disinfect it.

ir·ri·ga·tion (ĭr/ĭ-gā/shŭn), *n.* the furnishing of a water supply, by ditches, canals, etc., to land under cultivation.

ir·ri·ta·ble (ĭr/ĭ-tà-bl), *adj.* easily annoyed or angered; cranky; also, very sensitive.—*adv.* **ir/ri·ta·bly.**—*n.* **ir/ri·ta·bil/i·ty.** *Syn.* irascible, peevish, fretful.

ir·ri·tant (ĭr/ĭ-tănt), *adj.* causing sensitiveness or inflammation:—*n.* that which causes sensitiveness or inflammation; as, dust is an *irritant* to the nasal passages.

ir·ri·tate (ĭr/ĭ-tāt), *v.t.* [irritat-ed, irritat-

ing], **1,** to annoy or make angry; as, his manner *irritates* me; **2,** to make sore; inflame; as, smoke *irritates* the eyes.
Syn. vex, aggravate, exasperate.

ir·ri·ta·tion (ĭr′ĭ-tā′shŭn), *n.* **1,** annoyance; vexation; **2,** soreness; sensitiveness; as, an *irritation* of the skin.

ir·rup·tion (ĭ-rŭp′shŭn), *n.* a bursting or rushing in; sudden invasion; as, an *irruption* of the enemy.

Ir·ving (ûr′ving), Washington (1783–1859), an American author and essayist.

is (ĭz), third person singular, present indicative, of *be*.

is. or **isl.** abbreviation for *island.*

I·saac (ī′zȧk), in the Bible, a Hebrew patriarch, son of Abraham and Sarah, and father of Jacob and Esau.

Is·a·bel·la (ĭz′ȧ-bĕl′ȧ), (1451–1504), a Spanish queen, the wife of Ferdinand. She encouraged and aided Columbus.

I·sa·iah (ī-zā′yȧ; ī-zī′ȧ), in the Bible, a great Hebrew prophet; also, the Old Testament book which contains his prophecies.

Is·car·i·ot (ĭs-kăr′ĭ-ŏt), the surname of Judas, the apostle who betrayed Jesus.

I·seult (ī-sōolt′), *n.* in medieval romance: **1,** a princess of Ireland, wife of King Mark of Cornwall, beloved by Tristram; **2,** a princess of Brittany whom Tristram later married.

-ish (-ĭsh), a suffix meaning: **1,** having to do with, or related to: added to names of places; as, Rhen*ish*, Engl*ish*; **2,** like; especially, having the undesirable traits of; as, woman*ish*; **3,** somewhat: added to adjectives; as, black*ish*.

Ish·ma·el (ĭsh′mā-ĕl), *n.* **1,** in the Bible, the exiled son of Abraham and Hagar; **2,** hence, an outcast.

i·sin·glass (ī′zĭng-glȧs′), *n.* **1,** a white, semitransparent substance or gelatin prepared from the air bladders of the sturgeon, cod, etc., used as an adhesive, for stiffening silks, linens, etc.; **2,** *Colloquial,* a mineral that readily separates into thin, semitransparent sheets; mica.

I·sis (ī′sĭs), *n.* an ancient Egyptian goddess, symbolical of fruitfulness, whose worship was popular in Rome at one time.

Is·lam (ĭs′lȧm; ĭz′lȧm; ĭs-läm′), *n.* **1,** the Mohammedan religion; **2,** the whole body of Mohammedans and the countries they occupy.—*adj.* **Is·lam′ic** (ĭs-lăm′ĭk).

is·land (ī′lănd), *n.* **1,** a tract of land surrounded by water; **2,** anything that is like an island; as, floating *islands* of ice.

is·land·er (ī′lăn-dẽr), *n.* a person who was born or is living on an island.

isle (īl), *n.* a small island: usually *Poetic,* except in proper names.

Isle of Man, a British island (cap. Douglas) in the Irish Sea (map **13**).

is·let (ī′lĕt), *n.* a small island.

ism (ĭzm), *n.* a distinctive system or theory; a fad.

-ism (-ĭzm), a suffix meaning: **1,** the action, state, condition, or quality of; as, mystic*ism*, hero*ism;* **2,** a system, doctrine, policy, etc.; as, liberal*ism;* **3,** a characteristic or peculiarity; as, American*ism;* **4,** a special condition; as, alcohol*ism.*

i·so- (ī′sŏ-), a prefix meaning equal; as, *iso*therm.

i·so·late (ī′sŏ-lāt; ĭs′ŏ-lāt), *v.t.* [isolat-ed, isolat-ing], to place alone, away from others; as, the hospital *isolates* contagious cases.

i·so·la·tion (ī′sŏ-lā′shŭn; ĭs′ŏ-lā′shŭn), *n.* a setting apart, or the state of being placed apart or in solitude; loneliness.

i·sos·ce·les (ī-sŏs′ĕ-lēz), *adj.* having two equal sides; as, an *isosceles* triangle.

i·so·therm (ī′sŏ-thûrm), *n.* a line on a map, connecting places on the earth's surface which have the same temperature.

ISOSCELES TRIANGLES

Is·ra·el (ĭz′rā-ĕl; ĭz′rĭ-ĕl), an independent Jewish republic (cap. Jerusalem), formed in 1948 from three separated parts of Palestine (map **15**);—*n.* in the Bible: **1,** the Hebrew patriarch Jacob; **2,** the descendants of Jacob; the Jews.

Is·rae·li (ĭz-rā′lĭ), *n.* a citizen of modern Israel:—*adj.* relating to modern Israel or its people.

Is·ra·el·ite (ĭz′rĭ-ĕl-īt), *n.* a descendant of Israel, or Jacob; a Hebrew; Jew.

is·sue (ĭsh′ōō), *n.* **1,** the act of passing or flowing out; **2,** an outlet; **3,** that which is sent forth or produced; as, an *issue* of bank notes; **4,** an edition of a book, newspaper, etc., especially the entire number put out at one time; **5,** offspring; progeny; as, to die without *issue;* **6,** the final result; outcome; as, the *issue* of an election; **7,** a point of contention between two parties; as, political *issues:*—*v.t.* [issued, issu-ing], **1,** to send out; discharge; as, a crater *issues* smoke; **2,** to publish; send out officially; as, to *issue* a decree; **3,** to put into circulation; as, to *issue* currency:—*v.i.* **1,** to come or pass forth; as, blood *issues* from a cut; **2,** to arise, as from a source; as, a river *issues* from a lake; **3,** to come to an end; as, the struggle *issued* in peace.—*n.* **is′su·ance.**

---

go; join; yet; sing; chin; show; thin, *th*en; hw, *wh*y; zh, azure; ü, Ger. *für* or Fr. l*u*ne; ō, Ger. sch*ö*n or Fr. f*eu*; ṅ, Fr. e*n*fant, no*m*; kh, Ger. a*ch* or i*ch*. See pages ix–x.

Is·sus (ĭs′ŭs), an ancient town in Asia Minor, where Alexander defeated the Persians in 333 B.C. (map 1).

-ist (-ĭst), a suffix meaning: **1,** one who makes a practice of doing something expressed by a verb in *-ize*; as, moral*ist*; **2,** one who pursues some branch of art or science; as, art*ist*, botan*ist*; **3,** a follower of a system, religion, political creed, etc.; as, Buddh*ist*, social*ist*.

I·stan·bul (ē′stän-bool′), a city, the former capital of Turkey, on the Strait of Bosporus, the site of ancient Byzantium (map **12**): formerly called *Constantinople*.

isth·mus (ĭs′mŭs; ĭsth′mŭs), *n.* [*pl.* isthmuses], a neck of land connecting two larger bodies of land; as, the *Isthmus* of Panama.

ISTHMUS

it (ĭt), *neut. pron.* of third person [*nominative* it, *possessive* its (ĭts), *objective* it], the thing in question; as, where is my book? *It* is on the table: also used impersonally; as, *it* is raining:—*n.* in children's games, the player whom the other players oppose.

It. abbreviation for *Italian, Italy.*

I·tal·ian (ĭ-tăl′yăn), *n.* a native of Italy; also, the language of Italy:—*adj.* relating to Italy, its language, or its people.

I·tal·ian East Af·ri·ca, a former Italian colony comprising Ethiopia, Eritrea, and Italian Somaliland.

I·tal·ian So·ma·li·land, a former Italian province, now a trusteeship of Italy.

i·tal·ic (ĭ-tăl′ĭk), *adj.* naming, or printed in, a fine sloping style of type; as, *This line is printed in italic type:* —**italics,** *n.pl.* italic type, as distinguished from Roman type.

i·tal·i·cize (ĭ-tăl′ĭ-sīz), *v.t.* [italicized, italiciz-ing], to print (words) in a slender, sloping style of type called *italics.*

It·a·ly (ĭt′a̍-lĭ), a republic (cap. Rome) of southern Europe (map **12**).

itch (ĭch), *n.* **1,** a contagious skin disease causing great irritation; **2,** a sensation of irritation in the skin; **3,** a constant and craving desire; as, an *itch* to paint:—*v.i.* **1,** to have a feeling in the skin causing a desire to scratch; **2,** to have a longing; crave; as, he *itched* to run away to sea.— *adj.* **itch′y**—*n.* **itch′i·ness.**

i·tem (ī′tĕm; ĭ′tĕm), *n.* **1,** a separate article, entry, or particular; a sum entered in an account; **2,** a newspaper paragraph.

i·tem·ize (ī′tĕm-īz), *v.t.* [itemized, itemizing], to state each part separately; as, to *itemize* a bill.

it·er·ate (ĭt′ĕr-āt), *v.t.* [iterat-ed, iterating], to say or do a second time, or again and again; as, to *iterate* a threat.

it·er·a·tion (ĭt′ĕr-ā′shŭn), *n.* a repetition of something said or done.

it·er·a·tive (ĭt′ĕr-ā′tĭv; ĭt′ĕr-a̍-tĭv), *adj.* repeating or repeated; as, an *iterative* cry.

Ith·a·ca (ĭth′a̍-ka̍), an island in the Ionian Sea, west of Greece (map **1**): in legend, the kingdom of Odysseus and Penelope.

i·tin·er·ant (ī-tĭn′ĕr-ănt; ĭ-tĭn′ĕr-ănt), *adj.* wandering from place to place; as, *itinerant* musicians.

i·tin·er·ar·y (ī-tĭn′ĕr-ĕr′ĭ; ĭ-tĭn′ĕr-ĕr′ĭ), *n.* [*pl.* itineraries], **1,** a traveler's guidebook; also, a plan for a journey; **2,** a route actually taken; also, a record of a journey.

-i·tion (-ĭsh′ŭn), a suffix equivalent to *-tion* with the connecting vowel *i.* See *-tion.*

its (ĭts), *adj.* the possessive form of the personal pronoun *it:* of or belonging to *it*; as, the tree has lost *its* leaves.

it's (ĭts), a contraction of *it is.*

it·self (ĭt-sĕlf′), *pron.* the intensive or reflexive form of *it;* as, he loved the work *itself;* the cat washes *itself.*

I've (īv), a contraction of *I have.*

i·vied (ī′vĭd), *adj.* covered with ivy.

i·vo·ry (ī′vō-rĭ), *n.* [*pl.* ivories], **1,** the hard, white substance which forms the tusks of the elephant, walrus, etc.; **2,** the color of ivory; **3,** a substance resembling ivory; **4,** an article, as a carving, made of ivory:—*adj.* made of, or like, ivory.

Ivory Coast, a French colony (cap. Abidjan) on the Atlantic coast, in northwest Africa, east of Liberia (map **14**).

i·vy (ī′vĭ), *n.* [*pl.* ivies], any of several clinging vines with shiny, green, ornamental leaves, as English ivy, Boston ivy.

IVY

I.W.W. abbreviation for *Industrial Workers of the World.*

-ize (-īz), a suffix meaning: **1,** to act like or make like; as, Anglic*ize*; **2,** treat in a certain way; as, oxid*ize*; **3,** make into; as, pulver*ize*, Christian*ize*.

Iz·mir (ĭz′mĭr′), a seaport on the west coast of Turkey in Asia (map **15**). Its former name was *Smyrna.*

iz·zard (ĭz′ĕrd), *n.* an old name for the letter *z;* as, from a to *izzard.*

āte, ā̍orta, râre, căt, a̍sk, fär, ăllow, sofa̍; ēve, ĕvent, ĕll, writĕr, novĕl; bīte, pĭn; nō, ō̍bey, ôr, dŏg, tŏp, cŏllide; ūnit, u̍nite, bûrn, cŭt, focŭs; noon, foŏt; mound; coin;

J

J, j (jā), *n.* [*pl.* J's, j's] the tenth letter of the alphabet, following I.

jab (jăb), *v.t.* and *v.i.* [jabbed, jab-bing], to stab with something pointed:—*n.* a sharp thrust; as, a *jab* of a needle.

jab-ber (jăb′ẽr), *v.i.* and *v.t.* to talk rapidly and indistinctly; chatter:—*n.* chatter; unintelligible talk.

Jab-ber-wock (jăb′ẽr-wŏk), *n.* an imaginary monster, subject of a famous nonsense poem by Lewis Carroll in "Through the Looking Glass."

ja-bot (zhȧ′bō′; zhȧ′bō), *n.* a frill or ruffle on a woman's dress front at the neck or breast, or, formerly, on a man's shirt.

jack (jăk), *n.* **1**, a young man, especially of the laboring class: often written *Jack*; **2**, hence, any one of several mechanical devices which may be considered to do the work of a laborer or assistant; as, a boot*jack*, a roasting *jack* for turning meat on a spit, or a portable device for lifting a great weight; **3**, the male of any of several animals, especially the ass; **4**, in cards, any one of the four knaves; **5**, in bowling, a small bowl used as a mark; **6**, a small flag used on a ship, as a signal or a sign of nationality; **7**, a jackstone; **8**, **jacks**, the game of jackstones —*v.t.* **1**, to raise or hoist by means of a jack, lever, block, or other mechanical device; **2**, *Colloquial*, to spur on; as, to *jack* up the lazy boy.

Jack, a nickname for John; **Jack Tar**, a sailor; **Jack-of-all-trades**, one who can do many kinds of work and is master of none.

JACK, def. 2

jack-al (jăk′ôl), *n.* **1**, a doglike, flesh-eating animal of the Old World which lives on small animals and carrion; **2**, one who does base work for another: from the false idea that the jackal hunts prey for the lion.

JACKAL (¹⁄₂₀)

jack-a-napes (jăk′ȧ-nāps′), *n.* a saucy or conceited fellow; also, a pert child.

jack-ass (jăk′ăs′), *n.* **1**, the male ass; donkey; **2**, a conceited fool; blockhead.

jack boot or **jack-boot** (jăk′bōōt′), *n.* a large boot reaching above the knee.

jack-daw (jăk′dô′), *n.* a European bird of the crow family, which can be taught to make sounds imitating human speech.

jack-et (jăk′ĕt), *n.* **1**, a short coat; **2**, a covering for protection, insulation, etc.; as, a water *jacket* for cooling an engine.

JACKDAW (¹⁄₈)

jack-in-the-pul-pit (jăk′-ĭn-thē̃-pŏŏl′-pĭt), *n.* a plant that grows in damp woods and bears inconspicuous yellow flowers on a fleshy stalk covered by a leaflike hood or spathe.

jack-knife (jăk′nīf′), *n.* [*pl.* jackknives (jăk′nīvz′)], **1**, a pocketknife larger and stronger than a penknife; **2**, a dive used in fancy diving.

jack-o'-lan-tern (jăk′-ō̃-lăn′tẽrn), *n.* **1**, a pumpkin hollowed out and cut to resemble a human face, and used as a lantern at Halloween; **2**, a will-o'-the-wisp.

jack rab-bit, a hare of western North America, having very long ears and long hind legs.

JACK-IN-THE-PULPIT

¹Jack-son (jăk′sn), **1**, Andrew (1767–1845), an American general, and seventh president of the U.S.; **2**, Thomas Jonathan (1824–1863), an American Confederate general, usually called *Stonewall Jackson.*

²Jackson, a city, capital of Mississippi (map 8).

Jack-son-ville (jăk′sn-vĭl), a city in northeastern Florida (map 8).

JACK RABBIT (¹⁄₈)

jack-stones (jăk′stōnz′), *n.pl.* a set of pebbles or small metal pieces which are picked up in various ways in a children's game; also, the game so played.

jack-straws (jăk′strôz′), *n.pl.* **1**, a game in which the players try in turn to lift light pieces of wood or metal out of a pile with a hook or magnet without moving other strips; **2**, the pieces used.

Ja-cob (jā′kŭb), a Hebrew patriarch, son of Isaac and Rebecca, ancestor of the twelve tribes of Israel: also called *Israel.*

---

go; join; yet; sing; chin; show; thin, *th*en; hw, *wh*y; zh, azure; ü, Ger. f*ü*r or Fr. l*u*ne; ö, Ger. sch*ö*n or Fr. f*eu*; ṅ, Fr. e*n*fant, no*m*; kh, Ger. a*ch* or i*ch*. See pages ix–x.

Jac·o·bite (jăk′ō-bīt), *n.* in English history, a supporter of James II after his dethronement in 1688; also, a supporter of the claim of his son or of his grandson.

¹**jade** (jād), *n.* **1,** an inferior or worn-out horse; **2,** a saucy young woman; also, a disreputable woman.

²**jade** (jād), *n.* a hard, semiprecious stone, green, white, or blue, often carved.

jad·ed (jād′ĕd), *adj.* tired; dulled; as, nothing could tempt his *jaded* appetite.

Syn. exhausted, fatigued, wearied.

Jaf·fa (yä′fä; jăf′à), a seaport in western Israel. Its ancient name was *Joppa*.

jag (jăg), *n.* a sharp projecting point; a notch:—*v.t.* [jagged (jăgd), jag-ging], to cut or tear unevenly.

jag·ged (jăg′ĕd), *adj.* notched; having sharp points or a toothed edge, as a rock.

ja·guar (jăg′wär), *n.* a fierce, cat-like, flesh-eating animal of tropical America, spotted like the leopard, but heavier and more powerful.

JAGUAR (₁⁄₁₆)

jail (jāl), *n.* a prison; especially, a lockup for persons guilty of small offenses, or for persons awaiting trial:—*v.t.* to imprison. In Great Britain, **gaol** (jāl).

jail·bird (jāl′bûrd′), *n. Colloquial*, a convict; a habitual criminal.

jail·er (jāl′ẽr), *n.* one in charge of a jail or prison. In Great Britain, **gaol′er** (jāl′ẽr).

¹**jam** (jăm), *v.t.* [jammed, jam-ming], **1,** to squeeze or press in tightly; crowd; push; as, to *jam* things into a box; block; as, to *jam* traffic; **2,** to crush or bruise; as, to *jam* one's finger in a heavy door; **3,** to render (a machine or some movable part of it) unworkable by wedging:—*v.i.* **1,** to become tightly packed; as, the logs *jammed*; **2,** to become unworkable by the wedging of some part; stick; as, the engine *jammed*.

²**jam** (jăm), *n.* a thick preserve, made by boiling fruit with sugar.

Ja·mai·ca (jà-mā′kà), a British island (cap. Kingston) in the West Indies, southeast of Cuba (map 10).

jamb (jăm), *n.* one of the side pieces of a door, window, fireplace, or other opening.

James (jāmz), **1,** in the Bible: **a,** the name of two of the twelve apostles; **b,** a book of the New Testament; **2,** the name of two kings of England.

James Riv·er, a river flowing through Virginia into the Chesapeake (map 8).

James·town (jāmz′toun′), the first successful English settlement in America. It was founded in 1607.

Jan. abbreviation for *January*.

jan·gle (jăng′gl), *v.i.* and *v.t.* [jan-gled, jan-gling], **1,** to sound harshly or out of tune, as bells; **2,** to speak or utter in a loud, wrangling manner:—*n.* **1,** a discordant sound; **2,** a wrangling.

jan·i·tor (jăn′ĭ-tẽr), *n.* **1,** a doorkeeper; **2,** the caretaker of a public building.—*n.fem.* **jan′i-tress.**

Jan·u·ar·y (jăn′ū-ĕr′ĭ), *n.* the first month of the year, having 31 days: named for the Roman god, Janus.

Ja·nus (jā′nŭs), *n.* an ancient Roman god, protector of doorways and city gates and of the state during war. He had two heads facing in opposite directions.

Jap. abbreviation for *Japan, Japanese*.

ja·pan (jà-păn′), *n.* **1,** Japanese lacquer, a hard, brilliant varnish for wood or metal; **2,** articles lacquered in the Japanese manner:—*v.t.* [japanned, japan-ning], to coat with japan or similar varnish.

Ja·pan (jà-păn′), an island empire (cap. Tokyo) off the eastern coast of Asia. Its Japanese name is *Nippon*:—**Sea of Japan,** a sea lying west of Japan. (Map **15.**)

Jap·a·nese (jăp′à-nēz′; jăp′à-nēs′), *adj.* pertaining to Japan, its inhabitants, or its language:—*n.* the language of Japan:—**the Japanese,** the people of Japan.

Jap·a·nese bee·tle, a small bronze-green beetle, very destructive to vegetation.

¹**jar** (jär), *v.i.* [jarred, jar-ring], **1,** to give out a harsh sound; be discordant; **2,** to shake; vibrate, as doors and windows in an earthquake; **3,** to strike with harsh effect; as, his laugh *jars* on my nerves:—*v.t.* **1,** to make discordant; **2,** to cause to shake; as, the blast *jarred* the house:—*n.* **1,** a harsh sound; discord; **2,** a sudden shake or quivering; **3,** a conflict of opinion.

Syn., v. jolt, quiver, disturb.

²**jar** (jär), *n.* **1,** a broad-mouthed vessel of earthenware or glass; **2,** a jar and its contents; as, I bought a *jar* of jelly; also, the amount a jar holds; as, we ate a *jar* of cookies.

JARS

1, stone jar; 2, glass jar.

jar·di·niere (jär′dĭ-nēr′; zhär′dĭ-nēr′), *n.* an ornamental container for potted plants.

jar·gon (jär′gŏn; jär′gŭn), *n.* **1,** confused

talk that cannot be understood; **2,** a mixture of two or more languages; **3,** the technical or special vocabulary of a profession, trade, etc.; cant; as, chemical *jargon;* thieves' *jargon.*

jas-mine or **jas-min** (jăs′mĭn; jăz′mĭn), *n.* a shrub of the olive family with shiny leaves and fragrant red, white, or yellow flowers; also, a perfume made from the flowers: also called *jessamine.*

JASMINE

Ja-son (jā′sŭn), *n.* in Greek mythology, the hero who organized the expedition of the Argonauts and, with Medea's help, stole the Golden Fleece.

jas-per (jăs′pĕr), *n.* **1,** an opaque, cloudy stone, usually red, brown, or yellow; **2,** in the Bible, a stone used in the breastplate of the high priest.

jaun-dice (jôn′dĭs; jän′dĭs), *n.* **1,** a disease characterized by yellowness of the eyeballs, skin, etc., caused by too much bile in the system; **2,** hence, a mental condition such as jealousy, which distorts the judgment:—*v.t.* [jaundiced, jaundic-ing], **1,** to affect with jaundice; **2,** to affect with envy or prejudice.

jaunt (jônt; jänt), *n.* a short excursion or ramble:

Syn. journey, stroll, tour.

jaun-ty (jôn′tĭ; jän′tĭ), *adj.* [jaun-ti-er, jaun-ti-est], airy; gay; carefree; as, a hat at a *jaunty* angle.—*adv.* **jaun′ti-ly.**

¹**Ja-va** (jä′vȧ), an island in the Malay archipelago, northwest of Australia; site of Djakarta, capital of Indonesia. It was the center of the Dutch East Indies (map 15).

²**Ja-va** (jä′vȧ), *n.* a kind of coffee grown in Java.

Jav-a-nese (jăv′ȧ-nēz′; jăv′ȧ-nēs′), *adj.* pertaining to Java, its inhabitants, or its language:—*n.* the language of Java:—**the Javanese,** the people of Java.

jave-lin (jăv′lĭn; jăv′ĕ-lĭn), *n.* a short, light spear to be thrown by hand.

jaw (jô), *n.* **1,** either of the two bony structures which frame the mouth and in which the teeth are set: also called *jawbone;* **2,** the lower part of the face; **3,** anything that resembles an animal's jaw in form or power of gripping; as, the *jaws* of

JAVELIN
Athlete throwing the javelin.

a vise; **4,** mouth or entrance; as, the *jaws* of a chasm.

jay (jā), *n.* any of several noisy birds of the crow family, of Europe and North America, having bright-colored plumage, and sometimes a crest; especially, in the U.S., the blue jay.

JAY (¹⁄₁₀)

jay-walk-er (jā′wôk′-ĕr), *n. Colloquial,* a pedestrian who ignores regular street crossings or traffic signals.

jazz (jăz), *n.* **1,** a kind of American music of Negro, and probably African, origin, supposedly named for Jasbo Brown, a Mississippi Negro, used especially as dance music because of its emphatic and highly syncopated rhythms; **2,** a dance to this music:—*v.t. Slang,* **1,** to play (music) so as to make it resemble jazz; **2,** to make lively; as, to *jazz* up a party:—*v.i. Slang,* to act in a gay, lively manner.

jeal-ous (jĕl′ŭs), *adj.* **1,** characterized by suspicious fear or envy; as, to be *jealous* of another's wealth; **2,** unwilling to have, or afraid of having, a rival in love; as, a *jealous* suitor; **3,** demanding exclusive worship and love: said of God; **4,** anxiously careful or watchful; as, *jealous* of a good name.—*adv.* **jeal′ous-ly.**

jeal-ous-y (jĕl′ŭs-ĭ), *n.* [*pl.* jealousies], **1,** envy; as, great wealth causes *jealousy;* **2,** resentment toward, or fear of, a rival; as, a lover's *jealousy;* **3,** insistence on exclusive affection; as, the *jealousy* of God.

jean (jēn), *n.* **1,** a kind of twilled cotton cloth; **2, jeans,** a garment of this cloth, as overalls.

Jeanne d'Arc (zhän′dȧrk′), the French peasant girl, who saved France. See **Joan of Arc.**

jeep (jēp), *n.* a small army truck carrying four persons or half a ton of equipment.

jeer (jēr), *v.t.* to sneer at; ridicule; as, the crowd *jeered* the losing team:—*v.i.* to speak in a sneering or sarcastic manner:—*n.* a sneer; coarse ridicule.

Syn. scoff, gibe, taunt.

Jef-fer-son (jĕf′ĕr-sŭn), **1,** Joseph (1829–1905), an American actor, famous in the role of Rip Van Winkle; **2,** Thomas (1743–1826), an American statesman, writer of the Declaration of Independence, and third president of the U.S.

Jef-fer-son Cit-y, a city, capital of Missouri, in the middle western U.S. (map 7).

Je-ho-vah (jē-hō′vȧ), *n.* the principal name of God in the Old Testament.

Je-hu (jē′hū), in the Bible, a warrior and

---

go; join; yet; sing; chin; show; thin, *th*en; **hw,** *wh*y; **zh,** a**z**ure; **ü,** Ger. f**ü**r or Fr. l**u**ne; **ö,** Ger. sch**ö**n or Fr. f**eu**; **ṅ,** Fr. e**n**fant, no**m**; **ͺkh,** Ger. a**ch** or i**ch.** See pages **ix-x.**

king noted for his furious driving of chariots:—**jehu**, a fast driver.

je·june (jê-jōōn′), *adj.* empty; dry; without interest; as, a *jejune* tale.

Jel·li·coe (jĕl′ĭ-kō), John Rushworth, Earl (1859–1935), an English admiral, in command at the battle of Jutland, 1916.

jel·ly (jĕl′ĭ), *n.* [*pl.* jellies], **1**, the juice of fruit, meat, etc., which becomes semisolid and semitransparent after boiling and cooling; **2**, any similar substance:—*v.i.* [jellied, jelly-ing], to become jelly:—*v.t.* to cause to become jelly.

jel·ly-fish (jĕl′ĭ-fĭsh′), *n.* any of several swimming sea animals, with boneless, disk-shaped bodies, somewhat transparent, some of which have long tentacles with stinging hairs: often called *sea nettle*.

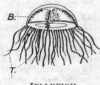

JELLYFISH
B, body; T, tentacles.

Jen·ner (jĕn′ẽr), Edward (1749–1823), an English physician, discoverer of vaccination for smallpox.

jen·net (jĕn′ĕt), *n.* a small Spanish horse.

jen·ny (jĕn′ĭ), *n.* [*pl.* jennies], **1**, a machine for spinning; **2**, a female: used before the name of an animal; as, the *jenny* wren; the *jenny* ass.

jeop·ard·ize (jĕp′ẽr-dīz), *v.t.* [jeopardized, jeopardiz-ing], to endanger; expose to risk; as, the fireman *jeopardized* his life to rescue them from the burning house.

jeop·ard·y (jĕp′ẽr-dĭ), *n.* risk; danger; as, the escape of the criminal put the safety of the community in *jeopardy*.

Syn. peril, hazard, insecurity.

Jeph·thah (jĕf′thȧ), in the Bible, a judge who, in fulfilling a vow, sacrificed his only daughter.

jer·e·mi·ad (jĕr′ê-mī′ăd), *n.* any lamentation or complaint; a sorrowful story: referring to the lamentations of Jeremiah in the Old Testament.

Jer·e·mi·ah (jĕr′ê-mī′ȧ), in the Bible, a great Hebrew prophet; also, a book of the Old Testament, containing his lamentations and prophecies.

Jer·i·cho (jĕr′ĭ-kō), an ancient city in Palestine, in the Dead Sea valley (map 1).

¹jerk (jûrk), *v.t.* **1**, to give a quick pull, twist, or push to; as, he *jerked* off his coat; to *jerk* a fish out of water; **2**, to throw with a sudden, quick movement:—*v.i.* to move with a sudden convulsive movement:—*n.* a sudden, quick pull, twist, push, or throw; as, a *jerk* of the head.

²jerk (jûrk), *v.t.* to cut into long, thin strips and dry in the sun, as beef:—*n.* beef so treated.

jer·kin (jûr′kĭn), *n.* a short, close-fitting, sleeveless coat, often made of leather, formerly worn by men.

jerk·y (jûr′kĭ), *adj.* [jerk-i-er, jerk-i-est], full of jerks; moving with sudden starts and stops; as, a *jerky* walk; not smooth; as, a *jerky* style of writing.—*adv.* **jerk′i·ly.**

JERKIN

Je·rome (jĕ-rōm′; jĕr′ŭm), Saint (340?–420), a scholar and monk who made a Latin version of the Bible known as the *Vulgate.*

¹Jer·sey (jûr′zĭ), a British island in the English Channel, northwest of France (map **13**).

²Jer·sey (jûr′zĭ), *adj.* **1**, pertaining to the island of Jersey, or to its breed of cattle; **2**, pertaining to New Jersey:—*n.* [*pl.* Jerseys], one of a breed of dairy cattle that originated in the island of Jersey:—**jersey, 1**, a close-fitting, elastic upper garment of wool or silk; **2**, a fine woolen yarn.

Jer·sey Cit·y, a manufacturing city on the Hudson River, in northern New Jersey (map **6**).

Je·ru·sa·lem (jê-rōō′sȧ-lĕm), a city, capital of Israel, northwest of the Dead Sea (maps **1, 15**). It was the ancient capital of the Hebrews, and is now a holy city for Jews, Christians, and Moslems.

jes·sa·mine (jĕs′ȧ-mĭn), *n.* a shrub bearing fragrant flowers; jasmine. See **jasmine.**

jest (jĕst), *n.* **1**, a joke; fun; as, many a true word is spoken in *jest;* **2**, the person or thing laughed at or jeered:—*v.i.* to joke; as, I was only *jesting.*

jest·er (jĕs′tẽr), *n.* **1**, one who makes jokes; **2**, in medieval times, a court fool.

Je·su (jē′sū), *Poetic,* Jesus.

Jes·u·it (jĕz′û-ĭt; jĕzh′û-ĭt), *n.* a member of the Roman Catholic Society of Jesus, founded by Loyola in 1534.—*adj.* **Jesu·it′ic; Jes′u·it/i·cal.**

Je·sus (jē′zŭs), in the Bible, the Son of Mary, founder of Christianity: also called *Jesus of Nazareth, Jesus Christ,* or *Christ.*

¹jet (jĕt), *v.t.* and *v.i.* [jet-ted, jet-ting], to shoot or spout out:—*n.* **1**, a stream of liquid or gas issuing from an opening; as, the whale spouts a *jet* of water; **2**, a spout or nozzle for the issuing of a fluid or gas; as, a gas *jet.*

²jet (jĕt), *n.* **1**, a hard, black mineral, akin to coal, which is polished and used in making ornaments and buttons; **2,** the color of jet, a deep, glossy black:—*adj.* **1,** made of, or like, jet; **2,** very black.

jet en·gine, an engine which takes in and compresses air to burn a liquid fuel, releasing the gases through a controlled opening, and thus providing thrust for propulsion.

jet plane, an airplane driven by one or more jet engines.

jet pro·pul·sion, the principle by which an object moves forward due to the push of a jet of expanding gases escaping to the rear.

jet·sam (jĕt′săm), *n.* goods thrown overboard to ease a ship in danger of sinking: especially, such goods when washed ashore.

jet·ty (jĕt′ĭ), *n.* [*pl.* jetties], **1,** a structure extending into the water, used as a pier, breakwater, or wall to direct currents; **2,** a landing pier.

Jew (joo; jū), *n.* in ancient times, a member of the tribe of Judah; now, in religion, an adherent of Judaism; in race, a Hebrew or Israelite.—*adj.* **Jew′ish.**

jew·el (joo′ĕl; jū′ĕl), *n.* **1,** a gem or precious stone; **2,** a valuable ornament or trinket set with gems; **3,** a piece of precious stone used as a bearing in the works of a watch; **4,** a person or thing of great value or dearness:—*v.t.* [jeweled, jewel-ing], to adorn or supply with jewels, as a dress or watch.

jew·el·er (joo′ĕl-ẽr; jū′ĕl-ẽr), *n.* one who makes or deals in valuable ornaments, gems, watches, etc.

jew·el·ry (joo′ĕl-rĭ; jū′ĕl-rĭ), *n.* precious stones, ornaments of gold and silver, etc.

jew·el·weed (joo′ĕl-wēd′; jū′ĕl-wēd′), *n.* a plant of the balsam family with spotted yellow or orange flowers and thin, silvery leaves. It grows in damp shady places.

JEW'S-HARP

jew's-harp or **jews'-harp** (jooz′-härp′; jūz′-härp′), *n.* a small musical instrument, with a thin, flexible metal tongue which, when placed between the teeth and struck by the finger, gives forth tones.

Jez·e·bel (jĕz′ĕ-bĕl), *n.* **1,** in the Bible, the wicked wife of Ahab, king of Israel; **2,** a bold or wicked woman.

jib (jĭb), *n.* **1,** a three-cornered sail extending from the foremast, or to the jib boom, of a vessel; **2,** the projecting arm or beam of a crane or lifting machine:— **flying jib,** a smaller, three-cornered sail set outside the

JIB (J), def. 1

jib to an extension of the jib boom called *flying jib boom* (see illustration, page 695).

jib boom or **jib-boom** (jĭb′boom′), *n.* a spar which serves to lengthen the bowsprit of a vessel, and to which a jib is attached. (See illustration, page 695.)

¹**jibe** (jīb), *v.i.* [jibed, jib-ing], **1,** to shift from one side of a vessel to the other, as a sail on its boom; **2,** to change the course of a vessel, so that the sail shifts from one side to the other; to tack:—*v.t.* to cause (a vessel, sail, or boom) to shift from one side to the other.

²**jibe** (jīb), *v.i.* [jibed, jib-ing], *Colloquial,* to agree; as, the two stories do not *jibe.*

³**jibe** (jīb), *n.* a taunt:—*v.t.* and *v.i.* [jibed, jib-ing], to mock; sneer. See gibe.

jif·fy (jĭf′ĭ), *n.* [*pl.* jiffies], *Colloquial,* an instant; a moment; as, I will do it in a *jiffy.*

jig (jĭg), *n.* **1,** a quick, lively dance; also, music for such a dance; **2,** a particular kind of fishhook:—*v.i.* [jigged, jig-ging], **1,** to dance a jig; **2,** to fish with a jig.

jilt (jĭlt), *n.* a person who discards an accepted suitor:—*v.t.* to discard or desert (a lover).

jim·my (jĭm′ĭ), *n.* [*pl.* jimmies], a short crowbar used by burglars to open doors, windows, etc.:—*v.t.* [jimmied, jimmy-ing], to force open with a jimmy.

Jim·son weed (jĭm′sn), a tall, coarse, poisonous weed of the nightshade family, with white or violet trumpet-shaped flowers and rank-smelling leaves.

JIMSON WEED

jin·gle (jĭng′gl), *n.* **1,** a sharp, tinkling sound, as of bells or of coins clinking; **2,** a pleasing or catchy succession of rimes, often with little sense:—*v.i.* [jin-gled, jin-gling], **1,** to give a tinkling sound; as, the keys *jingled* in his pocket; **2,** to sound with a pleasing or catchy succession of rimes:—*v.t.* to cause to jingle; as, to *jingle* pennies in a box.

jin·go (jĭng′gō), *n.* [*pl.* jingoes], one who favors or supports a warlike policy in foreign affairs.—*n.* **jin′go-ism.**—*adj.* **jin′go-is′tic.**

jinn (jĭn), *n.* **1,** plural of *jinni;* **2,** [*pl.* jinns], incorrectly, a jinni.

jin·ni or **jin·nee** (jĭ-nē′), *n.* [*pl.* jinn], in Mohammedan and Arabian folklore, a spirit made of fire, able to appear in both human and animal forms, and having a supernatural influence over mankind for good and evil: also called *genie* or *genius.*

jin-rik-i-sha (jĭn-rĭk′shä; jĭn-rĭk′shô), *n.* a small, two-wheeled, man-drawn Japanese carriage. Also spelled **jin-rick′sha.**

JINRIKISHA

jit-ney (jĭt′nĭ), *n.* [*pl.* jitneys], *Slang:* **1,** a five-cent piece; **2,** an automobile in which passengers are carried for a small fare.

jit-ter-bug (jĭt′tẽr-bŭg′), *n.* one who, either alone or with a partner, dances rhythmically to swing music, using improvised, acrobatic movements:—*v.i.* to dance in such a manner.

jit-ters (jĭt′ẽrz), *n.pl. Slang,* extreme nervousness.—*adj.* **jit′ter-y.**

jiu-jit-su (joo-jĭt′soo), *n.* a Japanese method of self-defense. See **jujitsu.**

jive (jīv), *n. Slang:* **1,** swing music; **2,** the special vocabulary of swing enthusiasts.

jn. abbreviation for *junction.*

Joan of Arc (jōn′ ŏv ärk′), (1412–1431), a French peasant girl who victoriously led the French against the English, was burned at the stake as a heretic, and was made a saint in 1920. She is also called *Maid of Orleans* and *Jeanne d' Arc*.

job (jŏb), *n.* **1,** a piece of work; as, a little *job* of sewing; **2,** anything one has to do; a responsibility; a duty; as, that's your *job,* not mine; **3,** any scheme for making money or securing private advantage at the expense of duty; **4,** *Colloquial,* work; a position; as, out of a *job:*—*adj.* done by the piece; as, *job* work; handled in the gross, or as a total; as, a *job* lot:—*v.i.* [jobbed, job-bing], **1,** to do an occasional piece of work for wages; **2,** to work for one's own gain in a position of trust:—*v.t.* **1,** to buy up (goods) for resale in smaller quantities; **2,** to do, or cause to be done by the lot or piece.

Job (jōb), in the Bible, the hero of a book of the Old Testament, who suffered affliction with great patience; also, the Old Testament book containing Job's story.

job-ber (jŏb′ẽr), *n.* **1,** one who buys a large amount of goods from producers and importers and sells it in smaller quantities to retail dealers; a middleman; **2,** one who works and is paid by the piece; **3,** one who transacts public business for his own private interests.

jock-ey (jŏk′ĭ), *n.* [*pl.* jockeys], **1,** a professional horseman hired to ride in a race; **2,** *Slang,* one who drives anything:—*v.t.* **1,** to ride (a horse) as a jockey; **2,** to bargain for position or advantage.

jo-cose (jŏ-kōs′), *adj.* humorous; merry; as, a *jocose* manner.—*adv.* **jo-cose′ly.**—*n.* **jo-cose′ness.**
    Syn. droll, playful, jocular, funny.

joc-u-lar (jŏk′ū-lẽr), *adj.* **1,** given to joking; as, a *jocular* person; **2,** humorous; comic; as, a *jocular* reply.—*adv.* **joc′u-lar-ly.**—*n.* **joc′u-lar′i-ty** (jŏk′ū-lăr′ĭ-tĭ).
    Syn. jocose, merry, blithe, sportive.

joc-und (jŏk′ŭnd; jō′kŭnd), *adj.* jovial; merry; as, a *jocund* laugh.

jodh-purs (jŏd′pẽrz), *n.pl.* a type of riding breeches worn over the boot.

Jo-el (jō′ĕl; jō′ĕl), in the Bible, a Hebrew prophet; also, a book of the Old Testament recording his preachings.

Joffre (zhôfr′), Joseph Jacques Césaire (1852–1931), a French marshal, noted in World War I as hero of the Marne, 1914.

jog (jŏg), *v.t.* [jogged, jog-ging], **1,** to push or shake slightly; nudge; **2,** to arouse; as, to *jog* the memory:—*v.i.* to travel along at a slow trot, as an old horse:—*n.* **1,** a slight push or shake; **2,** a slow trot; **3,** a notch; an irregularity; as, a *jog* in a road or a shore line:—**jog trot,** a slow, regular gait; hence, a dull routine; an easy-going manner.

jog-gle (jŏg′l), *v.t.* [jog-gled, jog-gling], to jerk slightly; nudge:—*v.i.* to totter:—*n.* a sudden shake; jolt.

Jo-han-nes-burg (yō-hän′ĕs-bûrg), a commercial city in southern Transvaal, Union of South Africa (map **14**).

John (jŏn), **1,** (1167?–1216), a king of England who was compelled to sign the Magna Charta in 1215; **2,** in the Bible, one of the twelve apostles; also, the Gospel written by him, or any of three Epistles attributed to him:—**John the Baptist,** a preacher of repentance who preceded Jesus (Matthew 3).

John Bull, an imaginary person typifying England; also, a typical Englishman.

john-ny-cake (jŏn′ĭ-kāk′), *n.* a flat cake of corn meal mixed with milk or water, eggs, etc., and baked.

john-ny–jump–up (jŏn′ĭ-jŭmp′-ŭp′), *n.* **1,** a wild pansy; **2,** the bird's-foot violet.

John-son (jŏn′sŭn), **1,** Andrew (1808–1875), the 17th president of the U.S.; **2,** Samuel (1709–1784), a famous English writer and dictionary maker.

Johns-town (jŏnz′toun), a city in southwestern Pennsylvania, the scene of great floods in 1889 and 1936 (map **6**).

join (join), *v.t.* **1,** to unite; connect; put or bring together; as, to *join* a hose to a faucet; *join* hands; **2,** to unite in marriage; **3,** to become a member of; as, to *join* a club; **4,** to engage in, with others; as, to *join* battle; **5,** to be next to; as, his yard *joins* ours:—*v.i.* **1,** to be in contact; **2,** to become associated or united; as, two roads *join* at this point:—*n.* a joint; a joining.
    Syn., v. consolidate, combine, add.

āte, āorta, râre, că̆t, ȧsk, fär, ăllow, sofȧ; ēve, ĕvent, ĕll, writẽr, novĕl; bīte, pĭn; nō, ōbey, ôr, dŏg, tŏp, cŏllide; ūnit, ū̆nite, bûrn, cŭt, fo̸cŭs; no͞on, fŏŏt; mound; coin;

join·er (joi′nẽr), *n.* **1**, one who or that which joins; **2**, a skilled workman who finishes the inside woodwork for houses.

joint (joint), *n.* **1**, the place where two or more things join; especially, the point where two bones of the body are joined; **2**, the part between two joinings; as, a *joint* in a grass stem; **3**, a large piece of meat cut for roasting; **4**, *Slang,* a low or disreputable resort:—*adj.* **1**, united; combined; as, *joint* efforts; **2**, used, held, or owned by two or more; as, *joint* property: —*v.t.* **1**, to connect by joints; **2**, to cut into pieces at the joints.—*adv.* **joint′ly.**

joist (joist), *n.* a piece of timber to which the boards of a floor or ceiling are fastened for support. (See illustration at *frame house.*)

joke (jōk), *n.* **1**, something said or done to cause mirth; a jest; **2**, a laughingstock; as, he was the *joke* of the town:—*v.i.* [joked, jok·ing], to jest.

jok·er (jō′kẽr), *n.* **1**, one who tells humorous stories or plays pranks; **2**, an extra card used in certain card games as the highest trump; **3**, a clause in a legislative bill, a written agreement, etc., which is inconspicuous, but which actually changes the entire meaning of the document.

Jo·li·et (jō′lĭ·ĕt; zhô′lyâ′), Louis (1645–1700), a French-Canadian explorer.

jol·li·ty (jŏl′ĭ·tĭ), *n.* [*pl.* jollities], gaiety; fun.

jol·ly (jŏl′ĭ), *adj.* [jol·li·er, jol·li·est], **1**, full of mirth; gay; as, a *jolly* time; **2**, causing or expressing mirth or gaiety; as, a *jolly* laugh:—*v.t.* [jollied, jolly-ing], *Colloquial,* to flatter; make good-humored fun of.
Syn., adj. merry, jovial, joyful, joyous.

jolt (jōlt), *v.t.* to shake by sudden jerks: —*v.i.* to have a jerky motion; as, the carriage *jolted* down the hill:—*n.* a sudden jerk; as, the train stopped with a *jolt.*

Jo·nah (jō′nà), *n.* **1**, in the Bible, one of the minor Hebrew prophets; also, the Old Testament book which tells how Jonah's presence endangered a ship, and he was thrown overboard, swallowed by a huge fish, and three days later cast ashore; **2**, hence, any person or thing that brings ill luck.

Jon·a·than (jŏn′à·thăn), in the Bible, the son of King Saul and friend of David.

JONQUIL

Jones (jōnz), John Paul (1747–1792), a noted American naval officer.

jon·quil (jŏng′kwĭl; jŏn′kwĭl), *n.* a plant of the narcissus family, with yellow or white fragrant flowers and sword-shaped leaves; also, the flower.

Jop·pa (jŏp′à), the ancient name of Jaffa, a seaport in Israel.

Jor·dan (jôr′dăn), **1**, a river in Palestine, flowing into the Dead Sea (map 1); **2**, a kingdom (cap. Amman) in western Asia: formerly called *Transjordan.*

Jo·seph (jō′zĕf), in the Bible: **1**, a Hebrew patriarch, a son of Jacob, sold into slavery in Egypt by his brothers; **2**, the husband of Mary, mother of Jesus; **3**, a rich man of Arimathea, who buried Jesus.

Josh·u·a (jŏsh′ū·à), in the Bible, the successor of Moses and leader of the Israelites into Canaan; also, a book of the Old Testament.

jos·tle (jŏs′l), *v.t.* [jos·tled, jos·tling], to push against; elbow; as, we *jostled* one another in the subway.

jot (jŏt), *v.t.* [jot·ted, jot·ting], to make a brief note of; as, to *jot* down an address: —*n.* a very small particle or quantity; as, not a *jot* of intelligence.

jounce (jouns), *v.t.* and *v.i.* [jounced, jouncing], to shake up and down; jolt:—*n.* a jolt.

jour·nal (jûr′năl), *n.* **1**, a daily record of news or events; **2**, a daily newspaper or other periodical; **3**, a diary; **4**, a book in which business transactions are entered daily; **5**, a ship's logbook; **6**, a record of the daily proceedings of a legislative body; **7**, that portion of an axle or of a rotating shaft that rests on bearings.

jour·nal·ism (jûr′năl·ĭzm), *n.* the occupation of publishing, editing, or writing for a newspaper or periodical.—*adj.* **jour′nal·is′tic.**—*n.* **jour′nal·ist.**

jour·ney (jûr′nĭ), *n.* [*pl.* journeys], **1**, a trip from one place to another; as, a *journey* from France to Spain; **2**, the amount of time consumed or space covered in travel: —*v.i.* to travel, especially by land.
Syn., n. tour, passage, expedition.

jour·ney·man (jûr′nĭ·măn), *n.* [*pl.* journeymen (-mĕn)], a mechanic who has learned a trade and works for another by the day.

joust (joust; jŭst; jōōst), *n.* a combat with lances between two mounted knights, usually as part of a tournament:—*v.i.* to engage in such a combat.

Jove (jōv), *n.* in Roman mythology, Jupiter, the chief of the gods.

jo·vi·al (jō′vĭ·ăl), *adj.* jolly; merry; gay; as, a *jovial* comrade.—*adv.* **jo′vi·al·ly.**

jowl (joul; jōl), *n.* **1**, the jaw; especially, the under jaw; **2**, the cheek.

joy (joi), *n.* **1**, a feeling of happiness; gladness; as, the holidays bring *joy;* **2**, that which causes gladness; as, "a thing of beauty is a *joy* forever": — *v.i.* to rejoice.

Syn., *n.* pleasure, delight, happiness.

joy-ful (joi′fŏol), *adj.* full of, or causing, gladness. — *adv.* **joy′ful-ly.** — *n.* **joy′ful-ness.**

Syn. joyous, jolly, jovial.

joy-less (joi′lĕs), *adj.* without gladness; sad; as, *joyless* lives. — *adv.* **joy′less-ly.**

joy-ous (joi′ŭs), *adj.* having or causing happiness; glad; as, a *joyous* occasion. — *adv.* **joy′ous-ly.** — *n.* **joy′ous-ness.**

J.P. abbreviation for *Justice of the Peace.*

Jr. abbreviation for *Junior.*

Ju. abbreviation for *June.*

ju-bi-lant (joo′bĭ-lănt), *adj.* showing great joy; exultant; as, *jubilant* over winning a game. — *adv.* **ju′bi-lant-ly.**

ju-bi-la-tion (joo′bĭ-lā′shŭn), *n.* triumphant exultation; rejoicing.

ju-bi-lee (joo′bĭ-lē), *n.* **1,** the anniversary, generally the 50th, but sometimes the 25th, of any event; **2,** any occasion of rejoicing; also, a state of rejoicing; **3,** a year of special indulgence which was formerly granted by the Pope every 25th year, but may now be granted at any time.

Ju-dah (joo′da), *n.* in the Bible: **1,** the son of Jacob and Leah; **2,** the powerful tribe descended from him, from which sprang the house of David; also, the district of southern Palestine in which the tribe lived, or the kingdom founded there.

Ju-da-ism (joo′da-ĭzm), *n.* **1,** the religious ceremonies and beliefs of the Jews; **2,** the observance of national Jewish ceremonies and customs.

Ju-das (joo′das), *n.* in the Bible: **1,** the disciple, surnamed Iscariot, who betrayed Jesus; hence, one who betrays another; **2,** another of the disciples, "not Iscariot."

Jude (jood), in the Bible, the author of one of the books of the New Testament; also, the book itself.

Ju-de-a or **Ju-dae-a** (joo-dē′a), a Roman district in southern Palestine.

judge (jŭj), *n.* **1,** the official who presides in a court of law and hears and tries cases; **2,** a person appointed to decide in a trial of skill, speed, etc., between two or more persons; **3,** one who has enough knowledge or experience to decide on the quality or value of anything; as, a *judge* of gems: — *v.t.* [judged, judg-ing], **1,** to hear and pass sentence on (a person or a matter), as in a court of law; **2,** to estimate; criticize; as, we *judged* him unfairly; **3,** to think or suppose; as, I *judged* this to be true: — *v.i.* **1,** to form an opinion after careful consideration; as, to *judge* in a debate; **2,** to hear and determine a case and pass sentence; **3,** to think; consider; hold an opinion.

Judg-es (jŭj′ĕz), *n.* a historical book of the Old Testament.

judg-ment or **judge-ment** (jŭj′mĕnt), *n.* **1,** the act of passing sentence: also, the decision of a court; **2,** the mental process by which we are able to see differences and likenesses, and by which we are able to weigh values; **3,** good sense; discernment; as, a man of *judgment;* **4,** estimate; opinion; as, in my *judgment* he is guilty; **5,** any calamity attributed to the anger of God: — **the Judgment**, the final trial of mankind by God: also called the *Last Judgment.*

ju-di-cial (joo-dĭsh′al), *adj.* **1,** pertaining to a judge, to a court of law, or to the administration of justice; as, *judicial* power; **2,** proceeding from, or inflicted by, a court of justice; as, a *judicial* decision; **3,** considering all aspects of a situation before deciding; impartial.

ju-di-ci-ar-y (joo-dĭsh′ĭ-ĕr′ĭ), *n.* [*pl.* judiciaries], the system of courts of justice in a country; also, the judges collectively: — *adj.* pertaining to judges, courts of justice, or the procedure of a court; judicial.

ju-di-cious (joo-dĭsh′ŭs), *adj.* showing good judgment; wise; as, a *judicious* choice.

Ju-dith (joo′dĭth), a Jewess who saved her people by slaying Holofernes, an Assyrian general.

JUG

jug (jŭg), *n.* **1,** a narrow-necked vessel, usually with a handle, for holding liquids; **2,** the vessel and its contents; as, a *jug* of wine; also, the amount of liquid the vessel can hold.

jug-gle (jŭg′l), *v.t.* [jug-gled, jug-gling], **1,** to perform tricks with; as, to *juggle* balls; **2,** hence, to misrepresent; as, to *juggle* facts: — *v.i.* **1,** to perform entertaining tricks; **2,** to play tricks so as to deceive.

jug-gler (jŭg′lẽr), *n.* **1,** one who entertains people by performing tricks; **2,** a trickster.

JUGGLER

Ju-go-slav (yoo′gṓ-släv′; yoo′-gṓ-släv′), *n.* a citizen of Yugoslavia. See **Yugoslav.**

Ju-go-sla-vi-a (yoo′gṓ-slä′vĭ-a), a republic in the southeastern part of Europe. See **Yugoslavia.**

jug-u-lar (jŭg′ṵ-lẽr; joo′gṵ-lẽr), *adj.* pertaining to the neck or throat: — **jugular vein**, either of two large veins on either side of the neck.

āte, ȧorta, râre, căt, ȧsk, fär, ăllow, sofȧ; ēve, ĕvent, ĕll, writẽr, novĕl; bīte, pĭn; nō, ōbey, ôr, dŏg, tŏp, cŏllide; ūnit, ŭnite, bûrn, cŭt, focŭs; noon, foot; mound; coin;

juice (joos), *n.* the liquid part of fruits, meats, etc.

juic·y (joo′sĭ), *adj.* [juic-i-er, juic-i-est], full of juice; as, *juicy* fruit.

ju·jit·su or **jiu·jit·su** (joo-jĭt′soo), *n.* the Japanese art of wrestling, which turns an opponent's own strength and weight against him.

juke box (jook), a phonograph made to play by the deposit of the required coin.

Jul. abbreviation for *July.*

ju·lep (joo′lĕp; joo′lĭp), *n.* an iced drink composed of brandy or whisky, sugar, and fresh mint.

Ju·li·an·a (joo′lĭ-ăn′à), (1909–), queen of the Netherlands.

Ju·li·et (joo′lĭ-ĕt; joo′lĭ-ĕt; joo′lĭ-ĕt′), *n.* the heroine of Shakespeare's "Romeo and Juliet," who dies with her lover.

Jul·ius Cae·sar (jool′yŭs sē′zẽr), a famous Roman. See **Caesar.**

Ju·ly (joo-lī′), *n.* the seventh month of the year, containing 31 days: named for Julius Caesar.

jum·ble (jŭm′bl), *n.* 1, a confused mass or mixture; disorder; 2, a thin round cake:— *v.t.* [jum-bled, jum-bling], to mix in a confused or disordered mass.

jump (jŭmp), *n.* 1, a spring or bound; hence, a sudden rise; as, a *jump* in temperature; 2, the space covered by a leap or bound; 3, something to be leaped or hurdled; as, the third *jump* was easy; 4, a sudden movement or start:—*v.i.* 1, to leap or spring; 2,

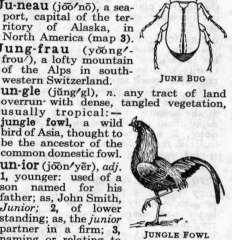

JUMP

to start suddenly; as, she *jumped* when she saw the mouse; 3, to rise suddenly; as, prices *jumped* as the supply gave out:— *v.t.* 1, to cause to leap; as, to *jump* a horse over a brook; 2, to leap on or over; 3, to jump upon or aboard; as, to *jump* a passing freight train; 4, to seize in the owner's absence; as, to *jump* a mining claim.

jump·er (jŭmp′ẽr), *n.* 1, a loose outer jacket worn by workmen; 2, a sleeveless dress, usually worn over a blouse.

Junc. abbreviation for *junction.*

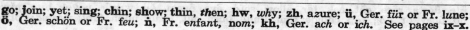

JUNCO (⅓)

jun·co (jŭng′kō), *n.* [*pl.* juncos], an American finch about the size of the English sparrow; a snowbird.

junc·tion (jŭngk′shŭn), *n.* 1, the act of joining or state of being joined; 2, a point of union; especially, a station where two or more railroad lines meet or cross.

junc·ture (jŭngk′tŭr), *n.* 1, the point at which two things join; joint; junction; 2, a union of events, especially a crisis.

June (joon), *n.* the sixth month of the year, containing 30 days:—**June bug,** a reddish-brown beetle that begins to fly about the beginning of June: also called *June beetle.*

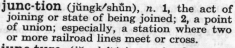

JUNE BUG

Ju·neau (joo′nō), a seaport, capital of the territory of Alaska, in North America (map 3).

Jung·frau (yoong′frou′), a lofty mountain of the Alps in southwestern Switzerland.

jun·gle (jŭng′gl), *n.* any tract of land overrun with dense, tangled vegetation, usually tropical:— **jungle fowl,** a wild bird of Asia, thought to be the ancestor of the common domestic fowl.

JUNGLE FOWL

jun·ior (joon′yẽr), *adj.* 1, younger: used of a son named for his father; as, John Smith, *Junior;* 2, of lower standing; as, the *junior* partner in a firm; 3, naming or relating to the next to the last year of a college or high-school course:—*n.* 1, a younger person; 2, one of lower standing; 3, in high schools and colleges, a student in the next to last year.

ju·ni·per (joo′nĭ-pẽr), *n.* any of several evergreen trees or shrubs of the pine family, with blue, berrylike fruits, as the common juniper and red cedar. (See illustration on page 865.)

JUNIPER
Leaves and fruit.

¹**junk** (jŭngk), *n.* a jumble of useless articles, paper, broken glass, etc.; trash:—*v.t.* to cast off as worthless or unusable; also, to destroy or make unusable.

²**junk** (jŭngk), *n.* a kind of flat-bottomed Chinese vessel with a high stern. (See illustration next page.)

jun·ket (jŭng′kĕt), *n.* 1, milk that has been curdled, sweetened, and flavored; 2, a feast; a picnic:—*v.i.* to feast or picnic.

Ju·no (joo′nō), *n.* in Roman mythology, the wife of Jupiter and goddess of marriage and childbirth: called *Hera* by the Greeks.

jun-ta (jŭn′tȧ), *n.* an assembly or council for making laws; as, the Cuban *junta*.

jun-to (jŭn′tō), *n.* [*pl.* juntos], a number of men secretly combined, especially for a political purpose.

Ju-pi-ter (jōō′pĭ-tẽr), *n.* **1**, in Roman mythology, the ruler of the gods: called *Zeus* by the Greeks; **2**, the largest planet in the solar system.

CHINESE JUNK

ju-ris-dic-tion (jōōr′ĭs-dĭk′shŭn), *n.* **1**, the right to apply legal authority; as, the *jurisdiction* of a court or state; **2**, authority of a sovereign power; **3**, the district over which any authority extends.

Syn. dominion, power, right, control.

ju-ris-pru-dence (jōōr′ĭs-prōō′dĕns), *n.* **1**, the science of law; also, a particular department of law; as, medical *jurisprudence;* **2**, a certain system of laws; as, Scottish *jurisprudence.*

ju-rist (jōōr′ĭst), *n.* one skilled in the science of law.

ju-ror (jōōr′ẽr), *n.* a member of a jury.

ju-ry (jōōr′ĭ), *n.* [*pl.* juries], **1**, a body of persons, usually twelve in number, selected and sworn to inquire into, or to try, matters of fact submitted to them in a court of law; **2**, a committee of experts selected to pass judgment on something, award prizes, etc.

ju-ry-man (jōōr′ĭ-măn), *n.* [*pl.* jurymen (-mĕn)], a member of a jury; a juror.

just (jŭst), *adj.* **1**, fair; impartial; as, the judge gave a *just* decision; **2**, based on reasonable grounds; as, a *just* accusation; **3**, exact; as, *just* weight; **4**, legally right; as, a *just* case; **5**, according to divine or human laws; upright; as, a *just* life:— *adv.* **1**, exactly; as, *just* how many? **2**, but

now; a moment ago; as, he was *just* here; **3**, only; barely; as, *just* a little; **4**, *Colloquial,* simply; quite; as, *just* beautiful.

jus-tice (jŭs′tĭs), *n.* **1**, the principle or practice of dealing uprightly with others; **2**, absolute fairness; as, the *justice* of a decision; **3**, legal administration; as, a court of *justice;* **4**, a judge:—**justice of the peace,** in the U.S., an officer having various duties, such as the administering of oaths, the judging of minor cases, and the holding of offenders charged with criminal offenses for trial by a superior court.

Syn. equity, right, impartiality.

jus-ti-fi-a-ble (jŭs′tĭ-fī′ȧ-bl), *adj.* capable of being proved right and just.

jus-ti-fi-ca-tion (jŭs′tĭ-fĭ-fĭ-kā′shŭn), *n.* **1**, the act of showing a thing to be right or just; **2**, an acceptable excuse; defense.

jus-ti-fy (jŭs′tĭ-fī), *v.t.* [justified, justifying], **1**, to show or prove to be right; warrant; as, the result *justified* the expense; **2**, to clear; free from blame:—*v.i.* to show lawful grounds for an act.

Syn. vindicate, absolve, defend.

jut (jŭt), *v.i.* [jut-ted, jut-ting], to project; stick out; as, a peninsula *juts* into the sea:—*n.* a projection.

jute (jōōt), *n.* the fiber of an East Indian plant, used for ropes, bags, etc.; also, the plant itself.

Jute (jōōt), *n.* one of a Germanic tribe which invaded and settled Britain with the Angles and Saxons in the fifth century.

Jut-land (jŭt′lănd), a peninsula, the mainland of Denmark, lying north of Germany (map **12**).

ju-ve-nile (jōō′vē-nĭl; jōō′vē-nīl), *adj.* **1**, childlike; youthful; **2**, like or for young people; as, *juvenile* literature:—*n.* **1**, a child under sixteen; **2**, a book for children; **3**, an actor in youthful roles.

jux-ta-po-si-tion (jŭks′tȧ-pō-zĭsh′ŭn), *n.* the condition of being placed close together or side by side.

K

K, k (kā), *n.* [*pl.* K's, k's], the 11th letter of the alphabet, following J.

K. abbreviation for *King.*

Ka-bul (kä′bŏŏl), a city, capital of Afghanistan, in Asia (map **15**).

Kaf-fir (kăf′ẽr) or **Ka-fir** (kä′fẽr), *n.* a member of a South African race of powerful and intelligent Negroes; also, the language of these people.

Ka-ga-wa (kä′gä-wä), Toyohiko (1888–), a Japanese social reformer and religious teacher.

kai-ser (kī′zẽr), *n.* an emperor:—**Kaiser,** the title of the former emperors of Germany and of Austria.

kale or **kail** (kāl), *n.* a plant belonging to the same family as the cabbage, with crisp, curly leaves. It is used as a vegetable.

āte, āorta, râre, căt, ȧsk, fär, ȧllow, sofȧ; ēve, ĕvent, ĕll, writẽr, novĕl; bīte, pĭn; nō, ōbey, ôr, dŏg, tŏp, cŏllide; ūnit, ūnite, bûrn, cŭt, focŭs; nōōn, fŏŏt; mound; coin;

ka·lei·do·scope (kȧ-lī′dō-skōp), *n.* **1,** an instrument containing small, loose bits of colored glass and an arrangement of mirrors, in which the bits of glass are reflected in a variety of beautiful patterns when their position is changed by rotation of the instrument; **2,** anything which shows a succession of changing aspects.—*adj.* **ka·lei′-do·scop′ic** (kȧ-lī′dō-skŏp′ĭk).

ka·lif or **kha·lif** (kā′lĭf), *n.* a Mohammedan sultan; a caliph. See **caliph.**

Ka·li·nin·grad (kȧ-lē′nĭn-grȧd′), the Russian name for Königsberg.

kal·so·mine (kăl′sō-mīn), *n.* a coating for walls and ceilings; calcimine:—*v.t.* [kalsomined, kalsomin·ing], to cover with such a coating. See **calcimine.**

Kan·dy (kän′dē), a town, the capital of Central province, Ceylon, famous for its Buddhist and Brahman temples.

kan·ga·roo (kăng′gȧ-rōō′), *n.* [*pl.* kangaroos], an animal of Australia, which has short forelegs, powerful hind legs with which it leaps, and a strong tail, used as a support in standing or leaping. The female has an external pouch in which it carries its young.

KANGAROO (₆′₀)

Kans. or **Kan.** abbreviation for *Kansas.*

Kan·sas (kăn′zȧs), a central State (cap. Topeka) of the U.S.:—**Kansas City, 1,** a city in northwestern Missouri; **2,** a city in northeastern Kansas, just across the state line from the preceding. (Map 7.)

Kant (känt; kănt), Immanuel (1724–1804), a German philosopher.

ka·o·lin (kā′ō-lĭn), *n.* a fine, pure white clay used to form the paste from which porcelain is made.

ka·pok (kā′pŏk; kăp′ŏk), *n.* the mass of silky fibers within the seed pods of a certain tropical tree, called *kapok tree:* used as stuffing for mattresses and cushions.

Ka·ra·chi (kȧ-rä′chē), a seaport city in Western Pakistan: the capital of Pakistan.

kar·a·kul or **car·a·cul** (kăr′ȧ-kŭl), *n.* **1,** a kind of Asiatic broad-tailed sheep; **2,** the curly black coat of the newborn lambs of this sheep, highly valued as a fur.

kar·at (kăr′ăt), *n.* a unit of weight for precious stones; a carat. See **carat.**

Karls·bad (kärls′bät; kärlz′băd), a health resort in northwestern Czechoslovakia. Also spelled *Carlsbad.* The Czech name is **Kar·lo·vy Va·ry** (kär′lô-vǐ vä′rǐ).

Kar·nak (kär′nȧk), a village in central Egypt on the right bank of the Nile.

Kash·mir (kăsh′mĭr′), an independent state adjacent to India, Pakistan, and Tibet.

Kat·rine, Loch (kăt′rĭn), a lake in central Scotland, scene of Scott's narrative poem "Lady of the Lake."

ka·ty·did (kā′tĭ-dĭd′), *n.* a large, green insect similar to a grasshopper, so named because of the sound it makes.

Kau·nas (kou′nȧs), a city, the former capital of Lithuania (map **12**). Its Russian name is *Kovno.*

kay·ak (kī′ăk), *n.* an Eskimo canoe, made of sealskin stretched over a light frame about sixteen feet in length, and seating one person.

KAYAK

Keats (kēts), John (1795–1821), an English poet.

kedge (kĕj), *n.* a light anchor: also called *kedge anchor:*—*v.t.* [kedged, kedg·ing], to move (a vessel, raft, etc.) by reeling in the chain of an anchor which has been grounded some distance away.

keel (kēl), *n.* **1,** the lowest timber or steel plate in the framework of a vessel, extending lengthwise along the bottom, and often projecting below the planking; **2,** anything resembling a ship's keel:—*v.t.* and *v.i.* to turn up the keel (of); turn over.

KEEL (K)

keel·son (kĕl′sn; kēl′sn) or **kel·son** (kĕl′-sn), *n.* a lengthwise beam or timber bolted to the keel of a ship, to strengthen the framework.

keen (kēn), *adj.* **1,** sharp; cutting; as, a *keen* blade; **2,** piercing; bitter; as, a *keen* wind; *keen* sarcasm; **3,** acute or sharp; as, *keen* eyesight; alert; quick; as, a *keen* mind; **4,** eager; ardent; as, a *keen* sportsman. *adv.* **keen′ly.**—*n.* **keen′ness.**
Syn. penetrating, sagacious, shrewd.

keep (kēp), *v.t.* [kept (kĕpt), keep·ing], **1,** to watch; defend; as, to *keep* goal; **2,** to take care of; as, to *keep* dogs; to provide with lodging or food; as, to *keep* boarders; **3,** to manage; as, to *keep* a shop; *keep* house; **4,** to have and retain in use, ownership, or possession; as, whatever you find you may *keep;* **5,** to observe; fulfil; as, to *keep* a holiday or a promise; **6,** to guard; as, to *keep* a secret; **7,** to detain; as, to *keep* a boy after school; **8,** to have on hand or in stock, as for sale; as, to *keep* shoes; **9,** to maintain; as, to *keep* one's health; to *keep* silence; preserve; as, to *keep* food; **10,** to maintain (a record of events, transactions, etc.); as, to *keep* books; to *keep* accounts: —*v.i.* **1,** to remain or continue; as to *keep* cheerful; to *keep* on with one's work; **2,** to continue sweet, fresh, or unspoiled; as, food will not *keep* at this time of year:— *n.* **1,** means of subsistence; maintenance; board and lodging; as, he worked for his *keep;* **2,** the stronghold of an ancient castle (see illustration under *castle*).

Syn., v. sustain, save, hold, support.

keep·er (kē′pẽr), *n.* one who keeps; especially, a person who has charge of prisoners, animals in a circus or zoo, etc.

keep·ing (kē′pĭng), *n.* **1,** maintenance; support; as, the *keeping* of bees or a dog; observance; as, the *keeping* of customs; **2,** custody; charge; as, the book was given into his *keeping;* **3,** harmony; agreement; as, a speech in *keeping* with the occasion.

keep·sake (kēp′sāk′), *n.* something kept in memory of the giver; a memento.

keg (kĕg), *n.* a small, strong barrel, with a capacity of five to ten gallons.

Kei·jo (kā′jō′), the Japanese name for Seoul, capital of Korea.

Kel·ler (kĕl′ẽr), Helen Adams (1880–), an American author, who is deaf and blind.

kelp (kĕlp), *n.* **1,** a large, brown seaweed; also, a mass or growth of seaweeds; **2,** the ashes of seaweeds, from which iodine is obtained.

KEG

kel·son (kĕl′sn), *n.* a timber in the framework of a ship; keelson. See **keelson.**

ken (kĕn), *n.* view; reach of sight or knowledge; comprehension; as, beyond one's *ken:* —*v.t.* [kenned, ken·ning], *Scottish,* to know.

Ken. or **Ky.** abbreviation for *Kentucky.*

Ken·ne·bec Riv·er (kĕn′ē-bĕk′), a river flowing through central Maine into the Atlantic Ocean (map 6).

ken·nel (kĕn′ĕl; kĕn′l), *n.* **1,** a dog house; **2, kennels,** a place where dogs are bred and raised:—*v.t.* [ken·neled, kennel·ing], to confine in a kennel; as, to *kennel* a dog:—*v.i.* to live or rest in a kennel.

Kent (kĕnt), a county in southeastern England.

KENNEL

Ken·tuck·y (kĕn-tŭk′ĭ), an east central State (cap. Frankfort) of the U.S. (map 7).

Ke·nya (kē-nyä′; kĕn′yȧ), a British crown colony and protectorate (cap. Nairobi) in central east Africa, on the Indian Ocean (map **14**).

Ke·o·kuk (kē′ō-kŭk), a city in southeastern Iowa on the Mississippi River, site of a large water-power plant.

Kep·ler (kĕp′lẽr), Johannes (1571–1630), a German mathematician and astronomer.

kept (kĕpt), past tense and past participle of *keep.*

ker·chief (kûr′chĭf), *n.* **1,** a square of cloth worn by women on the head or around the neck; **2,** a handkerchief.

kerf (kûrf), *n.* **1,** the notch or slit made by cutting or sawing; **2,** the cut end of a felled tree; **3,** something cut off; a cutting.

¹**kern** (kûrn), *n.* in printing, a part of a type face which projects beyond the body, as the tail on an ornamental capital Q.

²**kern** or **kerne** (kûrn), *n.* **1,** an Irish light-armed foot soldier; **2,** an Irish peasant.

ker·nel (kûr′nĕl; kûr′nl), *n.* **1,** a seed; a grain of wheat, corn, or other cereal; **2,** the softer, inner portion of a nut, fruit, stone, or the like, sometimes used for food; **3,** the central or important part of anything; gist; as, the *kernel* of a plan or theory.

KERNEL

1, kernel of English walnut; 2, cross section of kernel and shell.

ker·o·sene (kĕr′ō-sēn′; kĕr′ō-sēn′), *n.* a thin, colorless oil, made from petroleum, and used in lamps and stoves.

kes·trel (kĕs′trĕl), *n.* a small European falcon noted for its hovering in the air with its head always to the wind.

ketch (kĕch), *n.* a small fore-and-aft-rigged sailing vessel with two masts. (See illustration under *ship*.)

ketch·up (kĕch′ŭp), *n.* a spicy tomato sauce; catchup. See **catchup.**

ket·tle (kĕt′l), *n.* a metal vessel for heating liquids; especially, a teakettle having a handle and a spout.

ket·tle·drum (kĕt′l·drŭm′), *n.* a drum consisting of a large hollow bowl of copper or brass, with parchment stretched over the opening. (See illustration under *musical instrument*.)

KETTLES

Kew (kū), a suburb of London, England, on the Thames River, famous for its botanical gardens.

¹key (kē), *n.* **1**, a metal instrument for moving the bolt of a lock; **2**, anything resembling this instrument in use or form; as, the *key* of a clock; a fraternity *key*; **3**, that which allows or hinders entrance or control; as, Gibraltar is the *key* to the Mediterranean; **4**, that by means of which a difficulty is removed or something difficult to understand is explained; as, the *key* to a translation; a *key* to a code or cipher; **5**, in certain musical instruments, as the piano, and in typewriters and similar devices, any of a series of levers by means of which the instrument is played or operated; **6**, the general pitch or tone of the voice; as, men usually speak in a lower *key* than women; also, tone of thought or expression; as, a poem in minor *key*; **7**, an arrangement or series of musical tones bearing a fixed relation to a given note, called the keynote; as, the *key* of G major:—*v.t.* **1**, to regulate the pitch of; as, to *key* a violin; **2**, to stimulate; make tense; as, the thought of the game *keyed* him up to a state of great excitement.

²key (kē), *n.* a low, small reef or island; as, the Florida *keys.*

Key (kē), Francis Scott (1780–1843), an American lawyer, author of "The Star-spangled Banner."

key-board (kē′bôrd′), *n.* **1**, the row of keys on a piano, organ, or the like, by means of which the instrument is played; **2**, the bank of keys on a typewriter or any similar machine, by means of which the instrument is operated.

key-hole (kē′hōl′), *n.* a small opening, as in a door or lock, for inserting a key.

key-note (kē′nōt′), *n.* **1**, in music, the first note of a scale; the note on which a scale or system of tones is based; **2**, the main idea or principle; as, the *keynote* of a plan.

key-stone (kē′stōn′), *n.* **1**, the wedge-shaped stone at the topmost point of an arch, which holds the whole structure in place; **2**, something essential, on which several other connected things depend.

KEYSTONE (A)

Key West, a seaport and U.S. naval station, located on an island south of Florida, in the Gulf of Mexico (map 8).

kg. abbreviation for *kilogram.*

kha-ki (kä′kĭ), *n.* **1**, a dull, yellowish-brown or olive-drab color; **2**, a wool or cotton cloth of this color, much used for uniforms; also, a uniform of this material:—*adj.* of a dull, yellowish-brown color.

¹khan (kän; kăn), *n.* **1**, a title of princes of certain Asiatic states; **2**, in Afghanistan, Persia, and India, a title of respect.

²khan (kän; kăn), *n.* in the Orient, an inn built around a courtyard.

Kha-ni-a or **Ca-ne-a** (kä-nē′ä), a city, the capital of the island of Crete (map 12).

Khar-kov (khär′kŏf), a city, former capital of the Ukrainian Soviet Socialist Republic (map 12).

Khar-toum (khär′tōōm′), a city, capital of Sudan, and scene of a famous siege in 1885 (map 14).

khe-dive (kĕ-dēv′), *n.* formerly, the title of the Turkish governor of Egypt.

Khu-fu (kōō′fōō), another name for the Egyptian king *Cheops.* See *Cheops.*

kibe (kīb), *n.* a sore on a foot or hoof.

kib-itz-er (kĭb′ĭt-sẽr), *n. Colloquial,* one who meddles or gives advice unasked; especially, one who watches and interferes in the play at a game of cards.

kick (kĭk), *v.t.* to thrust at, or strike with the foot:—*v.i.* **1**, to strike out with the foot; **2**, to spring back, as a gun after it has been fired; **3**, *Slang,* to grumble; rebel; as, he *kicked* against staying indoors:—*n.* **1**, a blow with the foot; **2**, a backward spring, as of a gun; **3**, *Slang:* **a,** an objection or protest; **b,** thrill; excitement; as, to get a *kick* out of skiing.

kick-shaw (kĭk′shô′), *n.* **1**, a trifle; a toy; **2**, a light dish of food; a delicacy.

kid (kĭd), *n.* **1**, a young goat; also, its flesh; **2**, leather made from the skin of a kid, used especially for shoes and gloves; **3**, *Colloquial,* a child:—*adj.* made of leather called kid; as, *kid* gloves:—*v.i.* [kid-ded, kid-ding], *Slang,* to joke teasingly with someone:—*v.t. Slang,* to tease.

kid-nap (kĭd′năp), *v.t.* [kidnaped, kidnaping], to steal or carry off (a person) by force or fraud; as, to *kidnap* a child.—*n.* kid′nap′er.

kid-ney (kĭd′nĭ), *n.* [*pl.* kidneys], **1**, one of two bean-shaped glands situated in the back, near the spinal column, which separate waste matter from the blood, and pass it off in liquid form through the bladder; **2**, this organ in certain animals, used for food; **3**, sort or kind; disposition;

---

go; join; yet; sing; chin; show; thin, *th*en; hw, *wh*y; zh, *a*zure; ü, Ger. f*ü*r or Fr. l*u*ne; ö, Ger. sch*ö*n or Fr. f*eu*; ṅ, Fr. e*n*fant, no*m*; kh, Ger. a*ch* or i*ch.* See pages ix–x.

as, a man of his *kidney:*—**kidney bean,** a reddish-brown, kidney-shaped bean.

Kiel (kēl), a seaport on the Baltic Sea (map **12**):—**Kiel Canal,** a canal cut across the province of Schleswig-Holstein in northwestern Germany, connecting the Baltic and North seas.

Ki·ev (kē′yĕf), a city, capital of the Ukrainian Soviet Socialist Republic, on the Dnieper River (map **12**).

Ki·lau·e·a (kē′lou-ā′ä), the largest active crater in the world, two miles wide, on the slope of the volcano Mauna Loa, Hawaii.

Kil·i·man·ja·ro (kĭl′ĕ-män-jä′rō), the highest mountain in Africa, between Lake Victoria and the Indian Ocean (map **14**).

kill (kĭl), *v.t.* **1,** to deprive of life; as, the frost *killed* the flowers; the farmer *killed* the cow; **2,** to destroy; as, to *kill* one's hopes; **3,** to use up; as, to *kill* time; **4,** to reject; discard; as, to *kill* a legislative bill:—*v.i.* to destroy life; as, it is a crime to *kill:*—*n.* **1,** in hunting, the act of killing; **2,** the animal or animals killed.—*n.* **kill′er.**
Syn., v. execute, assassinate, murder.

Kil·lar·ney, Lakes of (kĭ-lär′nĭ), three lakes in southwestern Ireland, noted for their beauty (map **13**).

kill·deer (kĭl′dēr′), *n.* a North American bird, grayish brown and white in color, with a much repeated, penetrating cry; a plover.

kiln (kĭl; kĭln), *n.* a furnace or oven for burning, drying, or hardening something, as lime, brick, tiles, etc.

ki·lo (kē′lō; kĭl′ō), *n.* [*pl.* kilos], a shortened form of *kilogram* or *kilometer.*

kil·o· (kĭl′ō-), a prefix meaning 1,000; as, *kilo*watt, *kilo*gram.

kil·o·cy·cle (kĭl′ō-sī′kl), *n.* in electricity, especially in radio, 1,000 cycles of electric current per second. The number of *kilocycles* determines the wave length.

kil·o·gram or **kil·o·gramme** (kĭl′ō-grăm), *n.* a unit of weight equal to 1,000 grams, or 2.2046 pounds avoirdupois.

kil·o·li·ter or **kil·o·li·tre** (kĭl′ō-lē′tēr), *n.* 1,000 liters, or one cubic meter, equivalent to 264.18 gallons.

kil·o·me·ter or **kil·o·me·tre** (kĭl′ō-mē′tēr), *n.* a measure of distance equal to 1,000 meters, or 3280.8 feet.—*adj.* **kil′o·met′ric; kil′o·met/ri·cal.**

kil·o·watt (kĭl′ō-wŏt′; kĭl′ō-wôt′), *n.* a unit of electrical power equal to 1,000 watts:—**kilowatt hour,** a commercial unit of electrical energy, equal to the work done by one kilowatt acting for one hour.

kilt (kĭlt), *n.* a short plaited skirt, usually of tartan cloth, worn by men of the Scottish Highlands; also, any similar garment:—*v.t.* **1,** to form into plaits; **2,** in Scotland, to tuck up (the skirts).

kil·ter (kĭl′tēr), *n. Colloquial,* order; condition; as, the gun was out of *kilter.*

Kim·ber·ley (kĭm′bēr-lĭ), a town in the Cape province, Union of South Africa, famous for its diamond mines (map **14**).

KILT (A)

ki·mo·no (kĭ-mō′nō; kĭ-mō′na), *n.* [*pl.* kimonos], **1,** a loose outer robe, tied by a sash, worn by the Japanese; **2,** a similar garment sometimes worn as a dressing gown by women of other nations.

kin (kĭn), *n.* **1,** a person's family or relatives; kinsfolk; kindred; as, my *kin* live in England; **2,** family relationship:—*adj.* of the same ancestry; related; as, John is *kin* to me.

-kin (-kĭn), a suffix meaning small; little: used to form endearing names; as, lamb*kin,* Peter*kin.*

¹kind (kīnd), *adj.* sympathetic; inclined to be considerate of others; as, a *kind* master; also, showing such sympathy or consideration; as, a *kind* deed.

²kind (kīnd), *n.* **1,** a natural group, class, or division; as, the cat *kind;* **2,** variety; sort; as, all *kinds* of food; **3,** nature; character; style; as, prose and poetry differ in *kind.*

KIMONO

kin·der·gar·ten (kĭn′dēr-gär′tn), *n.* a school for children too young to go to regular school, in which they are taught by the use of games, toys, songs, etc.

kind-heart·ed (kīnd′här′tĕd), *adj.* sympathetic; thoughtful of others.

kin·dle (kĭn′dl), *v.t.* [kin-dled, kin-dling], **1,** to set fire to; as, the spark *kindled* the wood; **2,** to arouse or excite; stir; as, the speech *kindled* his anger; **3,** to make bright or shining; as, enthusiasm *kindled* her face:—*v.i.* **1,** to catch fire; as, the wood *kindled* rapidly; **2,** to become excited or aroused; **3,** to become bright or glowing; as, his eyes *kindled* with joy.

kin·dling (kĭn′dlĭng), *n.* material for starting a fire, such as light, dry wood.

kind·ly (kīnd′lĭ), *adj.* [kind-li-er, kind-li-est], sympathetic; gracious; kind:—*adv.* **1,** in a kind or friendly manner; **2,** naturally; as, willows take *kindly* to damp ground.—*n.* **kind′li·ness.**
Syn., adj. gentle, pleasant; friendly.

kind·ness (kīnd′nĕs), *n.* **1,** the state or

quality of being ready to do good to others; **2,** a helpful or gracious act; as, she has done us many *kindnesses.*

Syn. gentleness, clemency, tenderness.

kin-dred (kĭn′drĕd), *adj.* **1,** of like nature or character; as, football and soccer are *kindred* sports; also, congenial; as, *kindred* spirits; **2,** related by birth or marriage:— *n.* **1,** relationship by birth or marriage; kinship; **2,** one's relatives.

kine (kīn), *n. Archaic,* plural of *cow.*

ki-net-ic (kĭ-nĕt′ĭk; kī-nĕt′ĭk), *adj.* pertaining to, or resulting from, motion; as, the *kinetic* energy of falling bodies.

king (kĭng), *n.* **1,** a male sovereign or ruler; **2,** one who has power or importance that can be compared with that of a ruler or sovereign; as, a *king* of painters; a cotton *king;* **3,** the principal piece in the game of chess; **4,** in cards, a card which bears the picture of a king; **5,** in checkers, a piece which has crossed the board to the opponent's last row.

king-bird (kĭng′bûrd′), *n.* an American flycatcher.

king-bolt (kĭng′bōlt′), *n.* a vertical bolt which connects the axle of the front wheels of a vehicle to its body, and serves as a pivot in turning.

king-dom (kĭng′dŭm), *n.* **1,** a country ruled by a king or queen, or the territory comprising such a

KINGBIRD (⅙)

country; **2,** a realm or sphere in which one has control; as, the *kingdom* of the mind; his home is his *kingdom;* **3,** one of the classes into which natural objects are divided; as, the animal, mineral, and vegetable *kingdoms.*

king-fish-er (kĭng′fĭsh′ēr), *n.* any of a family of bright-colored, long-billed birds that feed on fish and insects.

king-ly (kĭng′lĭ), *adj.* [king-li-er, king-li-est], pertaining to a king; regal:—*adv.* in a manner suitable to a king.—*n.* **king′li-ness.**

KINGFISHER (1½)

Kings (kĭngz), *n.* in the Bible, two historical books of the Old Testament, recording the reigns of Jewish kings.

king-ship (kĭng′shĭp), *n.* **1,** the state, office, or dignity of a king; **2,** royal rule; monarchy; **3,** the king himself; majesty.

Kings-ley (kĭngz′lĭ), Charles (1819-1875), an English clergyman and author.

Kings-ton (kĭngz′tŭn), a seaport, capital of the Island of Jamaica (map **10**).

kink (kĭngk), *n.* **1,** a twist, curl, or loop in rope, wire, thread, hair, or the like; **2,** a notion or odd whim; a twist in one's mind or disposition:—*v.i.* to form twists or curls:—*v.t.* to make a kink in; to cause to kink.—*adj.* **kink′y.**

kins-folk (kĭnz′fōk′), *n.* relatives; kin.

kin-ship (kĭn′shĭp), *n.* relationship by birth or by marriage; also, similarity in qualities or character; as, there is close *kinship* in their ideas.

kins-man (kĭnz′măn), *n.* [*pl.* kinsmen (-mĕn)], a male relative; a man related by birth or marriage.—*n.fem.* **kins′wom′an.**

ki-osk (kē-ŏsk′), *n.* **1,** in Turkey and Persia, an open pavilion; **2,** a building of similar construction used as a newsstand, bandstand, refreshment stand, etc.

Kio-to (kyō′tō), a city of Japan. See Kyoto.

Kip-ling (kĭp′lĭng), Rudyard (1865-1936), an English author, born in India.

kip-per (kĭp′ēr), *v.t.* to cure, as salmon, by cleaning, salting, and drying or smoking:—*n.* a salmon or herring that has been cured.

kirk (kûrk; kĭrk), *n. Scottish,* a church.

kir-tle (kûr′tl), *n. Archaic:* **1,** a woman's outer petticoat or short skirt; also, a woman's dress; **2,** a man's tunic or coat.

kis-met (kĭz′mĕt; kĭs′mĕt), *n.* fate; destiny.

kiss (kĭs), *n.* **1,** a touching with the lips in a caress or greeting; **2,** a slight touch; **3,** a kind of candy:—*v.t.* **1,** to touch with the lips as a sign of affection, greeting, or the like; **2,** to touch slightly; as, a soft breeze *kissed* the flowers:—*v.i.* **1,** to touch or salute a person with the lips; **2,** to touch gently.

kit (kĭt), *n.* an outfit of tools, articles of travel, or the like; as, a plumber's *kit;* a salesman's *kit;* also, the box or bag holding such an outfit.

kitch-en (kĭch′ĕn), *n.* a room in which cooking is done:—**kitchen police,** soldiers detailed for service in preparing and serving food; also, the duty itself.

Kitch-en-er of Khar-toum (kĭch′ĕn-ēr ŏv khär′tōōm′), Horatio Herbert, Earl (1850-1916), a famous English general.

kitch-en-ette (kĭch′ĕ-nĕt′), *n.* a small, compactly arranged kitchen.

kitch-en-ware (kĭch′ĕn-wâr′), *n.* pots, pans, and other utensils used in a kitchen.

kite (kīt), *n.* **1,** a light frame of wood, covered with paper or other thin material, to be flown in the air while held by a string; **2,** a bird of the hawk family, small or medium in size, with long, narrow wings.

kith (kĭth), *n.* friends; neighbors: used in the expression *kith and kin.*

kit-ten (kĭt′n), *n.* a young cat.

Kiu-shu (kyōō′shōō), an island of Japan. See Kyushu.

klep-to-ma-ni-a (klĕp′-tō-mā′nĭ-a̍), *n.* an irresistible impulse to steal.— *n.* **klep′to-ma′ni-ac.**

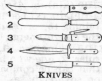

KITE (₁/₁₆)

Klon-dike (klŏn′dīk), an undefined region in Yukon Territory in northwestern Canada, famous for its gold fields (map 4).

km. abbreviation for *kilometer.*

knack (năk), *n.* cleverness in performance; ability to do something skilfully; as, she could never acquire the *knack* of tatting.

knap-sack (năp′săk′), *n.* a leather or canvas bag, worn strapped across the shoulders, for carrying toilet articles, clothes, etc.

knave (nāv), *n.* **1,** a dishonest or deceitful person; a rascal; **2,** a playing card with the figure of a soldier upon it; a jack.

knav-er-y (nāv′ẽr-ĭ), *n.* [*pl.* knaveries], dishonesty; fraud; deceit.

knav-ish (nāv′ĭsh), *adj.* dishonest; deceitful; as, a *knavish* trick.

knead (nēd), *v.t.* **1,** to mix and work into a mass, usually with the hands; as, to *knead* dough; **2,** to work over or treat with the hands or fingers; to massage.

knee (nē), *n.* **1,** in man, the joint between the thigh and the lower leg; **2,** the part of a garment covering this joint; as, the *knee* of your trousers is torn; **3,** anything resembling the human knee, especially when bent, as a sharp angle in an iron pipe.

knee-cap (nē′kăp′), *n.* a flattened, triangular, movable bone on the front part of the knee.

kneel (nēl), *v.i.* [knelt (nĕlt) or kneeled, kneel-ing], **1,** to bend the knee; as, he *knelt* to pick up his hat; **2,** to rest on bent knees; as, to *kneel* in prayer.

knee-pan (nē′păn′), *n.* the kneecap. See kneecap.

knell (nĕl), *n.* **1,** the sound of a bell, especially when tolled for a death or at a funeral; **2,** hence; a sign of the ending or extinction of something; as, "The curfew tolls the *knell* of parting day":— *v.i.* to toll dolefully.

knelt (nĕlt), one form of the past tense and past participle of *kneel.*

knew (nū), past tense of *know.*

Knick-er-bock-er (nĭk′ẽr-bŏk′ẽr), *n.* a person descended from the original Dutch settlers of New York; also, any New Yorker.

knick-er-bock-ers (nĭk′ẽr-bŏk′ẽrz), *n.pl.* short, wide breeches gathered at the knee.

knick-ers (nĭk′ẽrz), *n.pl.* knickerbockers.

knick-knack (nĭk′năk′), *n.* a trifle; toy; small ornament.

knife (nīf), *n.* [*pl.* knives (nīvz)], **1,** a cutting instrument with a sharp-edged blade or blades, set in a handle; **2,** a sharp-edged blade in a machine:— *v.t.* [knifed, knif-ing], to stab or cut with a knife.

KNIVES

1, butcher's; 2, table; 3, pocket; 4, hunting; 5, paring.

knight (nīt), *n.* **1,** in the Middle Ages, a mounted warrior who served a king or lord; especially, one of noble birth who, after serving as page and squire, and pledging himself to chivalrous conduct, was admitted by solemn ceremonies to a high military rank; **2,** in modern times in Great Britain, a man ranking next below a baronet, who has the title *Sir;* **3,** a member of any of certain orders or societies; **4,** in chess, a piece bearing the figure of a horse's head:— *v.t.* to raise (a man) to the rank of knight.

knight—er-rant (nīt′-ẽr′ănt), *n.* [*pl.* knights-errant], in the Middle Ages, a knight who went in search of adventure.

knight-hood (nīt′hŏŏd), *n.* **1,** the character, rank, or dignity of a knight; **2,** knights as a class or body.

knight-ly (nīt′lĭ), *adj.* [knight-li-er, knight-li-est], **1,** chivalrous; brave, gentle, and courteous; **2,** consisting of knights; as, a *knightly* throng.

Knight Tem-plar (tĕm′plẽr), [*pl.* Knights Templars], a member of a military order founded about 1118 to protect pilgrims on their way to the Holy Land.

knit (nĭt), *v.t.* [knit or knit-ted, knit-ting], **1,** to form (a fabric, garment, etc.) by hand or by machine, by looping or weaving a single thread or yarn on needles; as, to *knit* a sweater; **2,** to unite closely; lock together; as, he *knit* his fingers; **3,** to draw together by a tie of some kind; as, common interests *knit* them to each other; **4,** to draw (the brow) into wrinkles:— *v.i.* **1,** to weave thread or yarn in loops by the use of needles; **2,** to become closely joined or united; as, the broken bone *knit* well.

knives (nīvz), plural of *knife.*

knob (nŏb), *n.* **1,** the rounded handle of a

door, an umbrella, etc.; **2,** a round swelling, mass, or lump; **3,** a rounded hill.

knock (nŏk), *v.i.* **1,** to strike with a blow; especially, to rap on a door; **2,** to collide; bump; **3,** of machinery parts, to jar or pound noisily; **4,** *Slang,* to make unfavorable comments: — *v.t.* **1,** to strike or beat; give a blow to; **2,** to strike (something) against something else; as, to *knock* one's head against a wall; **3,** *Slang,* to criticize un-

legs bent inward so that the knees touch.

knoll (nōl), *n.* a rounded hillock; mound.

knot (nŏt), *n.* **1,** an interweaving or tying together of the parts of one or more threads, cords, ropes, etc., so that they will not slip or come apart; also, the tie so formed; **2,** something resembling a knot, as a lump or knob in a piece of wood or in a tree; **3,** a difficulty; hard problem; **4,** a

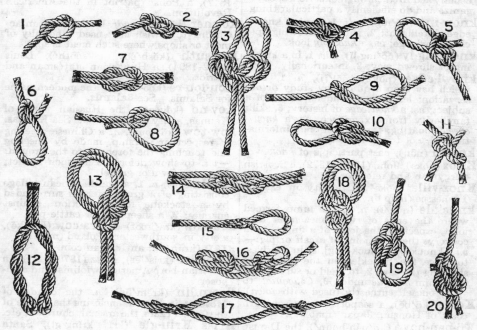

KNOTS

1, overhand knot; 2, figure-eight knot; 3, Spanish bowline knot; 4, 5, bends; 6, clinch; 7, square, or reef, knot; 8, 9, hitches; 10, running knot; 11, clove hitch; 12, cat's-paw; 13, bowline knot on a bight; 14, carrick bend; 15, eye-splice; 16, sheepshank; 17, cut splice; 18, fisherman's bend; 19, bowline knot; 20, double sheet bend.

favorably: — *n.* **1,** a sharp, quick blow; rap; **2,** a noise like that of a knock.

knock about, *Colloquial,* to wander aimlessly; **knock off, 1,** to stop; as, to *knock off* work; **2,** to deduct; as, to *knock off* a dollar from the bill.

knock-a-bout (nŏk′a̲-bout′), *n.* a small yacht carrying a mainsail and a jib (see *ship,* illustration): — *adj.* suitable for rough usage; as, *knockabout* clothes.

knock-er (nŏk′ẽr), *n.* **1,** one who knocks; **2,** a loose knob, ring, etc., attached to a door, to be used as a means of rapping.

knock–kneed (nŏk′=nēd′), *adj.* with the

group or cluster of people; **5,** a nautical mile (6,080.27 ft.), the unit used in stating the speed of a moving ship: — *v.t.* [knot-ted, knot-ting], **1,** to tie in a knot; **2,** to unite closely: — *v.i.* to form knots.

knot-hole (nŏt′hōl′), *n.* a hole in a tree or in lumber caused by the rotting or falling out of a knot.

KNOTHOLE

knot-ty (nŏt′ĭ), *adj.* [knot-ti-er, knot-ti-est], **1,** full of knots; **2,** difficult.

know (nō), *v.t.* [*p.t.* knew (nū), *p.p.* known (nōn), *p.pr.* know-ing], **1,** to perceive with the mind; understand clearly; as, he *knows*

---

go; join; yet; sing; chin; show; thin, *th*en; hw, *why*; zh, azure; ü, Ger. für or Fr. lune; ö, Ger. schön or Fr. feu; ṅ, Fr. enfant, nom; kh, Ger. ach or ich. See pages ix–x.

what he is doing; **2,** to recognize; as, he *knew* the beggar; **3,** to be familiar with; as, to *know* Spanish; **4,** to have information about; as, I *know* his reasons; **5,** to have in the memory; as, I *know* the names of all the bones; **6,** to be skilled in; as, he *knows* the art of swimming; **7,** to be certain; as, I *know* it is true:—*v.i.* to be informed; have certain knowledge.—*adj.* **know′a·ble.**

know–how (nō′-hou′), *n.* special ability, usually acquired through experience, to organize and do efficiently a particular thing.

know·ing (nō′ĭng), *adj.* **1,** having knowledge; intelligent; **2,** shrewd; showing special knowledge; as, a *knowing* look.

know·ing·ly (nō′ĭng-lĭ), *adv.* **1,** in a knowing or shrewd way; **2,** intentionally.

knowl·edge (nŏl′ĕj; nŏl′ĭj), *n.* **1,** that which has been acquired by study or observation; learning; **2,** understanding of a subject; as, a *knowledge* of history; **3,** skill; familiarity from experience; as, a *knowledge* of boating; **4,** extent of one's information; as, not to my *knowledge.*

known (nōn), past participle of *know.*

Knox (nŏks), John (1505?–1572), a Scottish clergyman and reformer.

Knox·ville (nŏks′vĭl), a city in eastern Tennessee (map **8**).

knuck·le (nŭk′l), *n.* **1,** the lump formed where the ends of two bones meet in a joint, especially the knee joint of a finger; **2,** in cookery, the knee joint of a calf or pig:—*v.i.* [knuck-led, knuck-ling], **1,** in marbles, to place the knuckles on the ground in shooting the taw; **2,** to yield or submit; as, make him *knuckle* under; **3,** *Colloquial,* to apply oneself earnestly (used with *down*).

Ko·be (kō′bĕ), a seaport on the southern coast of Honshu, Japan (map **15**).

Kö·ben·havn (kö′pĕn-houn′), the Danish name for **Copenhagen,** the capital of Denmark (map **12**).

ko·bold (kō′bŏld; kō′bōld), *n.* in German folklore, a brownie or gnome.

Ko·dak (kō′dăk), *n.* the trade-mark name for a small hand camera:—**kodak,** any camera bearing this trade name.

kohl·ra·bi (kōl′rä′bĭ), *n.* [*pl.* kohlrabies], a variety of cabbage with an enlarged, edible, turniplike stem.

Köln (köln), a city in Germany. It is also called *Cologne.* See **Cologne.**

Kö·nigs·berg (kö′nĭkhs-bĕrkh), a seaport, formerly capital of East Prussia, now in the, U.S.S.R. and called *Kaliningrad* (map **12**).

ko·peck or **ko·pek** (kō′pĕk), *n.* a Russian copper coin, one one-hundredth of a ruble.

Ko·ran (kō-rän′; kôr′ăn; kôr′ăn), *n.* the sacred book of the Mohammedans, written in Arabic, and believed by them to be the revelations of God to Mohammed.

Ko·re·a (kŏ-rē′à), a peninsula, the Republic of Korea (cap. Seoul) (map **15**).

ko·ru·na (kŏ-rōō′nä), *n.* [*pl.* koruny (kŏ-rōō′nĭ) or korun (kŏ-rōōn′)], a nickel-bronze coin, the monetary unit of Czechoslovakia. (See Table, page 943.)

Kos·ci·us·ko or **Kos·ciusz·ko** (kŏs′ĭ-ŭs′-kō; kŏsh-chōōsh′kō), Thaddeus (1746–1817), a Polish patriot in the American Revolution.

ko·sher (kō′shĕr), *adj.* lawful or clean according to Jewish law: used especially of meat or shops where such meat is sold.

Kos·suth (kŏsh′ōōt; kŏ-sōōth′), Louis (1802–1894), a Hungarian statesman and patriot.

Kou·lou·re (kōō′lōō-rē), the modern name for Salamis. See **Salamis.**

Kov·no (kôv′nō), the Russian name of Kaunas, a city in Lithuania. See **Kaunas.**

kow·tow (kō′tou′), *n.* a Chinese greeting of respect or worship, made by kneeling and touching the forehead to the ground:—*v.i.* to show deference by such an act; hence, to fawn or grovel.

kraal (kräl), *n.* **1,** a South African village consisting of a group of huts surrounded by a stockade for protection against enemies; **2,** a sheepfold, or cattle pen.

Kra·ków (krä′kŏōf) or **Cra·cow** (krä′kō), a city in southwestern Poland (map **12**).

kran (krän), *n.* an Iranian coin.

Kreis·ler (krīs′lĕr), Fritz (1875–   ), an Austrian-born American violinist and composer.

Krem·lin (krĕm′lĭn), *n.* the citadel of Moscow, in Russia, enclosing the palace of the former czars, the arsenal, churches, etc.

Kriss Krin·gle (krĭs krĭng′gl), Santa Claus; the good spirit of Christmas; Saint Nicholas.

Kris·tia·ni·a (krĭs-tyä′nē-ä), the former name of **Oslo,** the capital of Norway.

kro·na (krō′nà), *n.* [*pl.* kronor (krō′nŏr)], a silver coin, the monetary unit of Sweden. (See Table, page 943.)

kro·ne (krō′nĕ), *n.* [*pl.* kroner (krō′nĕr)], either of two silver coins, the monetary units, respectively, of Norway and Denmark. (See Table, page 943.)

Krupp (krŭp; krōōp), Alfred (1812–1887), a German manufacturer of guns.

K.T. abbreviation for *Knight Templar.*

Ku·blai Khan (kōō′blī khän′), (1216?–94), a Mongol emperor, conqueror of China.

ku·du (kōō′dōō), *n.* a large, striped antelope of Africa. (See *antelope,* illustration.)

kum·quat (kŭm′kwŏt; -kwôt), *n.* a small

citrus fruit, about the size of a large olive, used chiefly in making preserves.

Kur·di·stan (koŏr/dĭ-stän′), an undefined mountainous area of southeastern Turkey, northern Iraq, and northwestern Persia.

Ky. abbreviation for *Kentucky*.

Kyo·to or **Kio·to** (kyō/tô), a manufacturing city on the island of Honshu, the ancient capital of Japan (map **15**).

Kyu·shu or **Kiu·shu** (kyōō/shoō), the southernmost of the main group of islands of Japan (map **15**).

L

L, l (ĕl), *n.* [*pl.* L's, l's], **1,** the 12th letter of the alphabet, following K; **2,** the Roman numeral for fifty.

l. abbreviation for *left, liter* or *liters*.

L. or **£** abbreviation for *pound* or *pounds*.

la (lä), *n.* in music, the name of the sixth note of the scale.

La. abbreviation for *Louisiana*.

La·ban (lā/băn), in the Bible, the father of Leah and Rachel, the wives of Jacob.

la·bel (lā/bĕl; lā/bl), *n.* **1,** a small slip of paper, cloth, metal, etc., attached to anything, indicating its maker, contents, size, owner, destination, etc.; a tag; as, a *label* on a garment; **2,** a short phrase or catchword applied to persons or theories:—*v.t.* [labeled, label-ing], **1,** to mark with a label, as a medicine bottle; **2,** to classify; apply a descriptive word to; as, they *labeled* him a radical.

la·bi·al (lā/bĭ-ăl), *adj.* **1,** pertaining to the lips; as, a *labial* vein; **2,** formed by the lips, as the consonants *p, b,* etc.:—*n.* a sound, or a letter representing a sound, formed by the lips, as *p, b, f, v, m.*

la·bor (lā/bēr), *n.* **1,** physical or mental toil; work; **2,** a difficult task; **3,** hired workers who do physical, rather than mental, work, especially when considered as a class; as, laws benefiting *labor*:—*v.i.* **1,** to use muscular strength; toil; **2,** to be hard pressed; as, to *labor* under a difficulty; to move slowly and heavily; as, a wagon *labors* up a hill; **3,** to strive; take pains; as, he *labored* to understand the problem; **4,** to pitch and roll heavily, as a ship in a storm.

Syn., n. exertion, industry, drudgery.

lab·o·ra·to·ry (lăb/ō-rà-tôr/ĭ), *n.* [*pl.* laboratories], **1,** a place where scientific experiments and research are carried on; **2,** a place where drugs, chemicals, etc., are made, or tested for purity or strength.

La·bor Day, in most states of the U.S., a day, usually the first Monday in September, set apart as a legal holiday in honor of working people.

la·bored (lā/bērd), *adj.* produced with toil or care; not fluent; as, a *labored* speech.

la·bor·er (lā/bēr-ēr), *n.* one who toils; especially, one who does physical work requiring strength; a workman.

la·bor·i·ous (là-bôr/ĭ-ŭs), *adj.* **1,** difficult; requiring toil; as, it is a *laborious* task to cut down a tree; **2,** hard-working.

la·bor un·ion, an organization of workers which protects and advances the interests of its members.

la·bour (lā/bēr), a British spelling of *labor*. Similarly, **laboured** and **labourer**.

Lab·ra·dor (lăb/rà-dôr), part of the province of Newfoundland, on the extreme eastern coast of Canada (map **4**).

la·bur·num (là-bûr/nŭm), *n.* a poisonous tree or shrub, with hanging clusters of yellow flowers.

lab·y·rinth (lăb/ĭ-rĭnth), *n.* **1,** a maze or confusing network of passages winding into and about one another, so that it is almost impossible to find one's way through it; **2,** hence, a confusing or puzzling state of affairs:—**Labyrinth,** in Greek mythology, the intricate structure built for King Minos in Crete as a prison for the Minotaur.

lab·y·rin·thine (lăb/ĭ-rĭn/thĭn), *adj.* like a maze or network; intricate; perplexing.

lace (lās), *n.* **1,** an ornamental fabric of fine threads, as of linen, cotton, or silk, woven in a delicate open design; **2,** a cord, or string, passed through eyelets or other holes to fasten together parts of a garment, shoe, or the like:—*v.t.* [laced, lac-ing], **1,** to fasten with a lace; as, *lace* your shoes; **2,** to adorn or trim with lace; **3,** to weave or twine together; **4,** to lash; beat:—*v.i.* to be fastened with a lace; as, a blouse *laces* at the neck.

LACE

Lac·e·dae·mo·ni·an or **Lac·e·de·mo·ni·an** (lăs/ē-dē-mō/nĭ-ăn), *adj.* pertaining to the city or district of Lacedaemon or Sparta, in Greece; Spartan:—*n.* a Spartan.

lac·er·ate (lăs/ēr-āt), *v.t.* [lacerat-ed, lacerat-ing], **1,** to tear or mangle; as, the claws of the tiger *lacerated* his arm; **2,** to distress, as the feelings.—*n.* **lac/er·a/tion.**

lach·ry·mal or **lac·ri·mal** (lăk′rĭ-măl), *adj.* pertaining to, or secreting, tears; as, the *lachrymal* duct.

lac·ing (lās′ĭng), *n.* **1**, the act of fastening with a lace; **2**, a cord, string, braid, or the like, passed through eyelets to fasten something or serve as a trimming; **3**, a sound thrashing.

lack (lăk), *v.t.* to be without; not to have; as, his remarks *lack* common sense; I *lack* the money:—*v.i.* to have need; be short; as, he *lacks* in wisdom:—*n.* want; as, *lack* of fresh air.
  Syn., *n.* need, scarcity, insufficiency.

lack·a·dai·si·cal (lăk′á-dā′zĭ-kăl), *adj.* lazily indifferent; listless; as, a *lackadaisical* manner.—*adv.* **lack′a·dai′si·cal·ly.**

lack·ey (lăk′ĭ), *n.* [*pl.* lackeys], a male attendant of low rank; a footman.

lack·ing (lăk′ĭng), *adj.* wanting; needed; as, proof is *lacking*.

lack·lus·ter or **lack·lus·tre** (lăk′lŭs′tẽr), *adj.* dim; lacking brightness; as, *lackluster* eyes.

la·con·ic (lá-kŏn′ĭk), *adj.* expressing much in few words; terse; concise; also, sparing of words.—*adv.* **la·con′i·cal·ly.**
  Syn. brief, short, pithy, succinct.

lac·quer (lăk′ẽr), *n.* **1**, a transparent varnish made of shellac dissolved in alcohol, and used to protect brass, silver, etc., from tarnish and as a finish for automobiles; **2**, any of various varnishes made from resin, especially one made from the sap of certain Oriental trees, and used for polishing wood and other surfaces; **3**, Chinese or Japanese woodwork finished with a hard, polished varnish and often inlaid with gold, ivory, or the like:—*v.t.* to paint with lacquer.

lac·ri·mal (lăk′rĭ-măl), *adj.* pertaining to tears. See **lachrymal.**

la·crosse (lá-krôs′), *n.* a field game played by two teams of ten players each, in which the object is to send a small ball into the opponents' goal by means of a racket called a *crosse*.

LACROSSE

lac·te·al (lăk′tē-ăl), *adj.* pertaining to, or like, milk; milky; as, *lacteal* secretion.

lac·tic (lăk′tĭk), *adj.* pertaining to, or derived from, milk; as, *lactic* acid.

la·cu·na (lá-kū′ná), *n.* [*pl.* lacunae (lá-kū′nē) or lacunas], **1**, a space where an

omission has been made, as in a manuscript; gap; break; **2**, a small pit or hollow, as in bone or tissue.

lac·y (lās′ĭ), *adj.* [lac-i-er, lac-i-est], resembling or consisting of lace; as, a *lacy* fern; a *lacy* collar.

lad (lăd), *n.* a boy or youth; stripling.

lad·der (lăd′ẽr), *n.* **1**, a device for scaling or climbing, consisting usually of two long uprights of wood, connected by crosspieces, called *rungs*, forming steps; **2**, hence any means by which one mounts or ascends; as, the *ladder* of ambition.

lade (lād), *v.t.* [*p.t.* lad-ed, *p.p.* lad-ed or lad-en (lād′n), *p.pr.* lad-ing], **1**, to load (goods); put a cargo aboard (a ship); **2**, to lift out or in with a scoop; bail; as, to *lade* water out of a vat.

lad·en (lād′n), one form of the past participle of *lade*:—*adj.* **1**, loaded; burdened; as, *laden* with packages; **2**, oppressed or burdened in spirit; as, *laden* with sorrow.

LADDERS
1, fireman's scaling ladder; 2, extension ladder.

lad·ing (lād′ĭng), *n.* **1**, the act of loading or of bailing; **2**, freight.

la·dle (lā′dl), *n.* a deep spoon or dipper, with a long handle, for dipping out liquids:—*v.t.* [la-dled, la-dling], to dip out with a ladle.

LADLE

La·do·ga (lä′dō-gá), a lake, the largest in Europe, in the northwestern part of the U.S.S.R. (map **12**).

la·dy (lā′dĭ), *n.* [*pl.* ladies], **1**, originally, a woman of authority over a house or an estate, of the same rank as a lord; **2**, a well-bred woman; a woman of good family or of high social position; a gentlewoman.
  Our Lady, the Virgin Mary; **Lady,** in Great Britain, the title of the wife of a peer below the rank of duke, or of a knight or baronet; also, the title of the daughter of a duke, marquis, or earl; **lady in waiting,** a lady who attends a queen or princess.

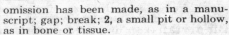

LADYBIRD
enlarged three and a half times.

la·dy·bird (lā′dĭ-bûrd′), *n.* a small, round-backed beetle, usually reddish brown with black spots: also called *ladybug*.

la-dy-like (lā′dĭ-līk′), *adj.* befitting a gentlewoman; well-bred; as, *ladylike* behavior.

la-dy-love (lā′dĭ-lŭv′), *n.* a sweetheart.

la-dy-ship (lā′dĭ-shĭp′), *n.* the position of a woman with the rank of Lady; also, a title of respect used in speaking to or of a Lady.

la-dy's—slip-per (lā′dĭz-slĭp′ẽr), *n.* any of a group of orchids with a slipper-shaped flower. Also **la′dy—slip′per.**

La-fay-ette (lä′fā-yĕt′), Marquis de (1757–1834), a French general who helped the American colonies in the War for Independence.

lag (lăg), *v.i.* [lagged, lag-ging], to move slowly; fail to keep pace; fall behind; as, to *lag* behind other runners in a race; to *lag* in one's studies:—*n.* a falling behind in movement or progress; as, a *lag* in the speed of a race or in the progress of work of any kind.

lag-gard (lăg′ẽrd), *n.* one who acts slowly; a backward person; as, he is a *laggard* in his studies:—*adj.* backward; slow.

la-goon (lȧ-gōōn′), *n.* 1, a shallow lake or channel, usually near the sea, and connected with it; 2, the shallow water inside an atoll, or ring-shaped coral island.

La-gos (lä′gōs; lā′gŏs), a seaport, capital of Nigeria, western Africa (map **14**).

La-hore (lȧ-hôr′), a city, capital of the province of Punjab, in Pakistan (map **15**).

laid (lād), past tense and past participle of ³*lay.*

lain (lān), past participle of ²*lie.*

lair (lâr), *n.* the den of a wild animal.

laird (lârd), *n.* in Scotland, the owner of a landed estate.

lais-sez faire (lâ′sā′ fâr′), [French], an expression meaning, "let well enough alone," or "let people do as they please"; in economics, a policy favoring commercial and industrial competition unhampered by government regulation.

la-i-ty (lā′ĭ-tĭ), *n.* [*pl.* laities], 1, laymen, as distinguished from the clergy; 2, those outside any particular profession.

¹**lake** (lāk), *n.* a large body of water entirely surrounded by land.

²**lake** (lāk), *n.* a deep-red color.

la-ma (lä′mȧ), *n.* a Buddhist priest of Tibet or Mongolia; also, a Buddhist monk noted for his goodness and learning.

LAMB (¹⁄₃₀)

lamb (lăm), *n.* 1, the young of sheep; 2,

the flesh of young sheep, used as food; 3, one who is gentle or innocent:—*v.i.* to bring forth lambs.

Lamb (lăm), Charles (1775–1834), an English essayist. He sometimes used *Elia* as a pen name.

lam-bent (lăm′bĕnt), *adj.* 1, playing, as light or flame, over a surface; flickering; touching lightly; 2, softly bright; as, the *lambent* light of stars.

lamb-kin (lăm′kĭn), *n.* 1, a little lamb; 2, a tenderly cherished child.

lame (lām), *adj.* [lam-er, lam-est], 1, crippled or disabled, especially in a leg or foot; also, sore; painful; as, a *lame* shoulder; 2, not sound or effective; as, a *lame* excuse:—*v.t.* [lamed, lam-ing], to cripple.—*adv.* **lame′ly** —*n.* **lame′ness.**

la-ment (lȧ-mĕnt′), *v.i.* and *v.t.* to mourn; bewail:—*n.* an expression of sorrow.—*adj.* **la-ment′ed.**

Syn., v. wail, grieve, sorrow.

lam-en-ta-ble (lăm′ĕn-tȧ-bl), *adj.* 1, regrettable; deplorable; unfortunate; as, a *lamentable* mistake; 2, mournful.

Syn. doleful, grievous, sorrowful.

lam-en-ta-tion (lăm′ĕn-tā′shŭn), *n.* an expression of grief; a lament.

Lam-en-ta-tions (lăm′ĕn-tā′shŭnz), *n.* a poetical book of the Old Testament, attributed to Jeremiah.

lam-i-na (lăm′ĭ-nȧ), *n.* [*pl.* laminae (lăm′-ĭ-nē) or laminas], 1, a thin plate, layer, flake, or scale, as of metal, rock, wood, or bone; 2, the blade, or expanded part, of a leaf.

lamp (lămp), *n.* 1, in olden days, a vessel in which oil or other inflammable liquid was burned by means of a wick to produce light; 2, in modern times, any device for producing light by gas, electricity, or the like.

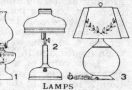

LAMPS
1, kerosene lamp; 2, gasoline lamp; 3, electric table lamp.

lamp-black (lămp′blăk′), *n.* a deep-black pigment or coloring matter, made from the soot produced by burning oil, gas, etc., and used especially in paints and printing ink.

lam-poon (lăm-pōōn′), *n.* a piece of writing holding a person up to ridicule and contempt; a satire directed at an individual:—*v.t.* to abuse or ridicule (someone) in a written article.

Lan-ca-shire (lăng′kȧ-shĭr), a county of northwestern England, on the Irish Sea. Also called **Lan′cas-ter.**

---

go; join; yet; sing; chin; show; thin, *th*en; hw, *wh*y; zh, azure; ü, Ger. für or Fr. lune; ö, Ger. schön or Fr. feu; ṅ, Fr. enfant, nom; kh, Ger. ach or ich. See pages ix–x.

Lan·cas·ter (lăng′kăs-tẽr), a seaport and municipal borough of Lancashire, England (map **13**).

Lancaster, House of, a line of English kings (1399–1471), rivals of the House of York in the Wars of the Roses, 1455–1485.

lance (láns),  *n.* **1**, a weapon consisting of a long shaft of

LANCE
Modern cavalry lance.

wood with a sharp steel head; also, a soldier equipped with a lance; **2**, any sharp-pointed instrument resembling a lance; especially, one used in spearing fish:—*v.t.*[lanced, lancing], **1**, to pierce with a lance; **2**, to cut open, as a boil, with a lancet, or surgeon's knife.

Lan·ce·lot (lán′sĕ-lŏt), *n.* the bravest and ablest of the knights of King Arthur's Round Table. He was the lover of Guinevere and the father of Galahad.

lanc·er (lán′sẽr), *n.* **1**, a person who uses a lance; **2**, a cavalry soldier armed with a lance;

LANCET

3, **lancers**, a square dance for four or more couples; also, the musical accompaniment.

lan·cet (lán′sĕt), *n.* a small, pointed, two-edged surgical knife.

Lan·chow (län′chou′; -chō′), a city in north central China on the Hwang Ho (map **15**).

land (lănd), *n.* **1**, the solid part of the surface of the globe; **2**, a division of the earth's surface marked off by natural, political, or other boundaries; a country; district; also, the people of a country; a nation; **3**, soil; ground; as, fertile *land*:—*v.t.* **1**, to set on shore; as, to *land* passengers from a ship; **2**, to capture and bring to shore; as, to *land* a fish; **3**, *Colloquial*, to win; as, to *land* a prize; **4**, to bring to a destination; as, the train *landed* him in New York on time:—*v.i.* **1**, to come or go ashore; disembark, as a passenger; **2**, to arrive at a destination; **3**, to come to the end of a course; get into a situation; as, he *landed* in jail; **4**, to alight; come to earth, as an airplane.

lan·dau (lăn′dô; lăn′dou), *n.* a four-wheeled covered carriage with a top in two sections, either of which can be raised or lowered separately; also, an automobile with a similar top.

land·ed (lăn′dĕd), *adj.* **1**, owning land; as, a *landed* proprietor; **2**, consisting of land; as, a *landed* estate.

land·hold·er (lănd′hōl′dẽr), *n.* an owner, holder, or occupier of land.

land·ing (lăn′dĭng), *n.* **1**, the act of going or putting ashore or of alighting on earth from the sky; **2**, a place or platform, as a wharf, where passengers may embark or disembark, and goods be loaded or un-

loaded; **3**, a platform, as at the end of a flight of steps.

landing craft, a type of naval vessel developed during World War II, designed to run up to the beach and let down ramps or open at the bow for discharging troops or equipment.

land·la·dy (lănd′lā′dĭ), *n.* [*pl.* landladies], **1**, a woman who rents her houses or land to others; **2**, the mistress of a boarding house or inn; also, the wife of a landlord.

land·locked (lănd′lŏkt′), *adj.* **1**, nearly surrounded by land; as, a *landlocked* bay; **2**, confined to waters shut off from the sea by some barrier; as, *landlocked* fish.

land·lord (lănd′lôrd′), *n.* **1**, one who rents his buildings or land to others; **2**, the keeper of a hotel or inn.

land·lub·ber (lănd′lŭb′ẽr), *n.* one who is awkward or inexperienced on shipboard.

land·mark (lănd′märk′), *n.* **1**, an object that marks the boundary of a tract of land; **2**, a familiar or easily seen object that serves as a guide for a traveler or a navigator; **3**, any event which marks or is associated with a stage or turning point in history; as, the discovery of fire is a *landmark* in the history of civilization.

land·scape (lănd′skāp), *n.* **1**, a stretch of land or of land and water seen as one view; **2**, a picture of a scene from nature:—*v.t.* to arrange the grounds, as around a house or in a park, to make an attractive appearance.

Land·seer (lănd′sẽr), Sir Edwin Henry (1802–1873), an English painter, noted for his pictures of animals.

Lands End or **Land's End**, a cape, Cornwall county, the westernmost point of land in England (map **13**).

land·slide (lănd′slīd′), *n.* **1**, the slipping of a mass of earth, stones, etc., down a steep slope; **2**, the material that slips down; **3**, a decisive, overwhelming victory in an election. Also, in senses **1** and **2**, **land′slip′** (lănd′slĭp′).

land·ward (lănd′wẽrd), *adj.* facing or moving toward the shore:—*adv.* toward the shore.—*adv.* **land′wards**.

lane (lān), *n.* **1**, a narrow path or byway between hedges, walls, etc.; **2**, an unpaved or little used road, or a narrow street; any narrow way or track; **3**, one of the ocean courses fixed as routes for vessels.

lan·guage (lăng′gwĭj), *n.* **1**, the power or ability to express ideas in words; human speech; **2**, the means of such expression, as sounds, words, etc., current among members of a single people; as, the German *language;* also, the means of expression, as words, phrases, etc., peculiar to special fields of knowledge; as, technical *lan-*

āte, âorta, râre, căt, ȧsk, fär, ăllow, sofȧ; ēve, ĕvent, ĕll, writẽr, novĕl; bīte, pĭn; nō, ōbey, ôr, dŏg, tŏp, cŏllide; ūnit, ūnite, bûrn, cŭt, focŭs; nōon, fŏŏt; mound; coin;

guage; **3,** any style of verbal expression; as, simple *language;* **4,** any means of expressing ideas; as, the *language* of pictures; the *language* of flowers.

Syn. tongue, dialect.

lan-guid (lăng′gwĭd), *adj.* weak, as from exhaustion; dull; listless.—*adv.* **lan′guid-ly.**—*n.* **lan′guid-ness.**

Syn. spiritless, sluggish, apathetic.

lan-guish (lăng′gwĭsh), *v.i.* **1,** to lose strength or animation; become languid; also, to pine away, as with longing; **2,** to appeal for sympathy by pretending feebleness or fatigue.

lan-guor (lăng′gĕr), *n.* **1,** lack of energy; listlessness; **2,** dreaminess; a soft, tender mood; **3,** heaviness; oppressiveness; as, the *languor* of a humid day.—*adj.* **lan′guor-ous.**—*adv.* **lan′guor-ous-ly.**

lank (lăngk), *adj.* **1,** lean; thin; as, a tall, *lank* figure; **2,** straight and limp.

Syn. gaunt, spare, bony, meager.

lank-y (lăngk′ĭ), *adj.* [lank-i-er, lank-i-est], lean; gaunt; loose-jointed.—*n.* **lank′i-ness.**

Lan-sing (lăn′sĭng), a city, the capital of Michigan, in north central U.S. (map **7**).

lan-tern (lăn′tẽrn), *n.* **1,** a transparent case enclosing a light and protecting it from wind, rain, etc.; **2,** the room at the top of a lighthouse where the light is kept.

LANTERNS
1, electric; 2, railroad; 3, farm.

lan-yard (lăn′-yẽrd), *n.* a short rope or line used on shipboard to extend or tighten stays or shrouds.

La-os (lä′ōz), a kingdom in Indochina.

¹lap (lăp), *n.* **1,** the loose part of a garment which may be doubled or folded over; the skirt of a coat or the overlapping part of a gown; **2,** that part of the clothing that rests upon the thighs and knees of a person in a sitting position; also, the part of the body thus covered; as, sit in my *lap;* **3,** a place for supporting, sheltering, or rearing; as, the *lap* of luxury; **4,** that part of an object, as a shingle, that extends over another; also, the distance or amount of such extension; as, a *lap* of two inches; **5,** the length of a course or track which has to be passed over more than once in a race:—*v.t.* [lapped, lap-ping], **1,** to lay or fold over, as cloth; also, to wrap; **2,** to place over something else so as partly to cover it; as, to *lap* one shingle over another; **3,** to enfold; surround; as, *lapped* in luxury:—*v.i.* to lie partly over something; as, the boards *lap;* also, to be folded; as, the cuff *laps* back.

²lap (lăp), *v.t.* [lapped, lap-ping], **1,** to lick up with the tongue, as liquid; **2,** to splash gently against; as, the waves *lap* the shore: —*v.i.* **1,** to take up liquid with the tongue; **2,** to make a lapping or rippling sound: —*n.* the act or sound of lapping.

la-pel (lă-pĕl′), *n.* the part of a garment which is folded back; especially, the fold at each side of a coat front, forming a continuation of the collar.

lap-i-dar-y (lăp′ĭ-dĕr′ĭ), *n.* [*pl.* lapidaries], **1,** a skilled workman who cuts and sets precious stones; **2,** a dealer in, or collector of, gems.

lap-is laz-u-li (lăp′ĭs or lā′pĭs, lăz′û-lī or lăz′û-lĭ). **1,** an opaque, semiprecious stone of a deep-blue color; **2,** a dark blue.

Lap-land (lăp′lănd), an undefined region of northern Europe, covering the northern part of the Scandinavian peninsula and Finland, and northwestern U.S.S.R. (map **12**).

Lapp (lăp), *n.* **1,** an inhabitant of Lapland: also called *Laplander;* **2,** the language of Lapland.

lap-pet (lăp′ĕt), *n.* **1,** a loose flap, as on a garment or headdress; **2,** a flap or hanging fleshy part, as an ear lobe.

lapse (lăps), *v.i* [lapsed, laps-ing], **1,** to glide or slip slowly away; as to *lapse* into unconsciousness; his attention *lapsed;* **2,** to slip or depart from a moral standard; fall into error; as, to *lapse* from good behavior; **3** to cease or to pass to another, as insurance, an estate, or the like, because of the holder's failure to fulfil certain conditions:—*n.* **1,** a gliding or passing away slowly; as, the *lapse* of time; **2,** a slight mistake; a slip, as of memory, tongue, or pen; **3,** the loss of a claim, right, etc., through failure to use or renew it; **4,** a passing into a lower rank or condition; as, a *lapse* into poverty; a *lapse* into drunkenness.—*adj.* **lapsed.**

lap-wing (lăp′wĭng′), *n.* a crested plover of the Old World with an iridescent green and violet back and white breast. It is well known for its flapping flight and shrill cry.

lar-board (lär′bôrd; lär′bẽrd), *n.* the left side of a ship as one faces the bow: now called *port:*—*adj.* naming, or pertaining to, the left, or port, side of a ship.

LAPWING (⅛)

lar-ce-ny (lär′sĕ-nĭ), *n.* [*pl.* larcenies], the unlawful taking away of another's property; theft.—*adj.* **lar′ce-nous.**

---

go; join; yet; sing; chin; show; thin, *th*en; **hw,** *why;* **zh,** azure; **ü,** Ger. *für* or Fr. *lune;*
ö, Ger. schön or Fr. *feu;* **ṅ,** Fr. e*nfant,* nom; **kh,** Ger. a*ch* or i*ch*. See pages **ix–x.**

larch (lärch), *n.* any of a group of graceful trees of the pine family, with small cones and short needlelike leaves which drop in the fall; also, the wood of these trees, which is usually durable.

lard (lärd), *n.* a white, greasy substance made from the fat of swine:—*v.t.* **1,** to smear with fat; **2,** to insert strips of bacon into (meat) before roasting.

lard·er (lär′dẽr), *n.* the place where household provisions are kept; a pantry; also, the stock or supply of food.

la·res and pe·na·tes (lā′rēz ănd pē·nā′tēz), **1,** household gods of the ancient Romans; **2,** hence, one's personal or household goods.

large (lärj), *adj.* [larg-er, larg-est], **1,** big; great in size; bulky; wide; extensive; as, a *large* estate; **2,** wide in scope; broad in understanding and sympathy; as, a *large* mind:—**at large, 1,** free; unconfined; as, the convict is *at large;* **2,** chosen to represent a whole section instead of one of its districts; as, a congressman *at large.*—*n.* **large′ness.**

Syn. huge, ample, enormous, immense.

large·ly (lärj′lǐ), *adv.* to a great extent; as, he was *largely* to blame.

lar·gess or **lar·gesse** (lär′jĕs), *n.* a generous gift; bounty; as, the king scattered *largess* as he rode; also, generous giving.

lar·go (lär′gō), *adj.* and *adv.* in music, slow; stately:—*n.* a musical composition of slow, dignified movement.

lar·i·at (lär′ǐ·ăt), *n.* **1,** a rope with a sliding noose, used for catching horses or cattle; a lasso; **2,** a rope for picketing horses.

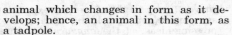

MEADOW LARK (⅒)

¹lark (lärk), *n.* **1,** any of various small European songbirds, as the skylark; **2,** any of many birds similar to larks but of different families, as the meadow lark.

²lark (lärk), *n.* a frolic; spree; an amusing adventure:—*v.i. Colloquial,* to frolic.

lark·spur (lärk′spûr), *n.* a tall plant cultivated for its showy spikes of pink, blue, or white flowers; also, the flowers.

lar·va (lär′và), *n.* [*pl.* larvae (lär′vē)], the early, often wormlike, form of insects in the stage between the egg and the pupa; also, the early form of any

LARKSPUR

animal which changes in form as it develops; hence, an animal in this form, as a tadpole.

lar·val (lär′văl), *adj.* pertaining to, or in the form of, a larva.

lar·yn·gi·tis (lär′ĭn·jī′tĭs), *n.* inflammation of the larynx, or upper end of the windpipe; a form of sore throat.

lar·ynx (lär′ĭngks), *n.* [*pl.* larynges (là·rĭn′jēz) or larynxes], an enlargement of the upper end of the windpipe, containing the vocal cords.

LARVA of Cecropia moth.

La Salle (là sȧl′), René Robert Cavelier de (1643–1687), a French explorer, founder of Louisiana.

las·civ·i·ous (lă·sĭv′ĭ·ŭs), *adj.* sensual; lewd; lustful.

¹lash (lăsh), *v.t.* **1,** to strike or beat violently with a whip; flog; also, to beat upon; as, the waves *lashed* the shore; **2,** to rebuke or scold severely; **3,** to switch backward and forward like a lash; as, the puma *lashed* his tail; **4,** to stir up or arouse; as, the orator *lashed* the crowd to fury:—*v.i.* **1,** to apply the whip; also, to rebuke severely; **2,** to rush, pour, or beat, as wind or rain:—*n.* **1,** the flexible part, or thong, of a whip; **2,** a stroke with a whip or anything used like a whip; as, a *lash* of sarcasm; **3,** one of the little hairs on the edge of the eyelid.

²lash (lăsh), *v.t.* to fasten or bind with a rope; as, they *lashed* him to the mast.

lash·ing (lăsh′ĭng), *n.* **1,** a whipping; **2,** a sharp scolding or a cutting rebuke; **3,** the act or process of binding; **4,** a cord, rope, etc., used for binding.

lass (lăs; làs), *n.* **1,** a girl or young woman; usually, a country girl; **2,** a sweetheart.

las·si·tude (lăs′ĭ·tūd), *n.* bodily or mental weariness; lack of energy.

Syn. languor, exhaustion, indifference.

las·so (lăs′ō), *n.* [*pl.* lassos or lassoes], a rope, usually of hide, with a slipknot, used for catching wild horses and cattle; a lariat:—*v.t.* to catch with a noosed rope.—*n.* **las′so·er.**

¹last (làst), *n.* a foot-shaped model in wood or metal on which shoes are made.

²last (làst), *adj.* one form of the superlative of *late:* **1,** coming after all others in time, place, order, or the like; as, the *last* man to go; **2,** next before the present; as, *last* week; **3,** authoritative; conclusive; as, his writings are regarded as the *last* word in literary criticism; **4,** least likely; least fitted; as, he is the *last* person for the position:—*adv.* **1,** after all others; **2,** on the time or occasion next preceding the present; **3,** at the end; finally:—*n.* the end:—**at last,** finally; at the end of a long period of time.

Syn., adj. latest, final.

³**last** (làst), *v.i.* **1,** to continue; as, the play *lasted* three hours; **2,** to be enough for a given time; hold out; as, this coffee will *last* a week; **3,** to wear well; endure.

last-ing (làs′tĭng), *adj.* wearing well; enduring; permanent.

Last Judg-ment, God's final trial and judgment of mankind.

last-ly (làst′lĭ), *adv.* finally; in conclusion; at the end.

Last Sup-per, Christ's meal with his disciples on the night he was betrayed.

lat. abbreviation for *latitude*:—**Lat.** abbreviation for *Latin*.

latch (lăch), *n.* a fastening device for a door or gate, made of a small bar and catch:—*v.t.* and *v.i.* to fasten with a catch.

latch-et (lăch′ĕt) *n.* a shoe-string; a strip of leather fastening a sandal.

latch-key (lăch′kē′), *n.* a key that unlocks a latch.

latch-string (lăch′strĭng′), *n.* a cord to raise a latch.

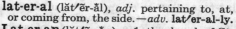

LATCH

late (lāt), *adj.* [*comp.* lat-er or lat-ter (lăt′ẽr), *superl.* lat-est or last (làst)], **1,** coming after the usual time; tardy; as, a *late* spring; **2,** far on toward the end; as, a *late* hour of the day; **3,** of recent date; as, a *late* occurrence; **4,** formerly in office; as, the *late* secretary of state; **5,** deceased; as, the *late* Mr. Smith:—*adv.* **1,** after the usual or appointed time; as, to arrive *late;* **2,** far into the day, night, etc.; as, to work early and *late:*—**of late,** recently; in the immediate past; as, I have not seen you *of late.* —*n.* late′ness.

Syn., adj. new, former, recent.

la-teen sail (lă-tēn′), a three-cornered sail attached to a yard crossed obliquely on a low mast.

late-ly (lāt′lĭ), *adv.* not long ago; recently; as, she has not been here *lately.*

la-tent (lā′tĕnt), *adj.* concealed; present, but not active; as, *latent* disease germs; *latent* discontent.—*adv.* **la′tent-ly.**

LATEEN SAILS

lat-er-al (lăt′ẽr-ăl), *adj.* pertaining to, at, or coming from, the side.—*adv.* **lat′er-al-ly.**

Lat-er-an (lăt′ẽr-ăn), *n.* **1,** the church of St. John Lateran in Rome, ranking above all other Catholic churches; **2,** the palace next to it, formerly the residence of the popes, now a museum.

la-tex (lā′tĕks), *n.* a milky juice secreted by various plants. Rubber, chicle, and gutta-percha are products made from latex.

lath (làth), *n.* [*pl.* laths (là*th*z; làths)], one of the thin, narrow strips of wood nailed to the framework of a house to support the plaster:—*v.t.* to cover with such strips.

lathe (lā*th*), *n.* a machine which holds and turns articles of wood, metal, and the like, while they are being shaped and polished.

lath-er (lă*th*′ẽr), *n.* **1,** froth made from soap and water; **2,** the foamy sweat of a horse:—*v.t.* to cover with froth or foam, as in shaving:—*v.i.* to form foam or suds. —*n.* lath′er-er.—*adj.* lath′er-y.

lath-ing (là*th*′ĭng), *n.* the thin, narrow strips of wood on which plaster is laid in building; also, the act or process of putting them in place.

Lat-in (lăt′ĭn), *adj.* **1,** pertaining to ancient Rome, its inhabitants, or its language; **2,** naming the races whose languages are derived from Latin; as, the Italians are a *Latin* race:—*n.* **1,** the language of ancient Rome; **2,** a native of ancient Rome; **3,** one whose language is derived from Latin, as a Frenchman, Italian, etc.

Lat-in A-mer-i-ca, the part of the Western Hemisphere below the southern border of the United States. So called because the official language of most of the countries is descended from Latin.

Lat-in cross, a figure like a plus sign with the lower vertical arm somewhat lengthened (see illustration under *cross*).

lat-i-tude (lăt′ĭ-tūd), *n.* **1,** the distance north or south of the equator measured in degrees; **2,** breadth; range; as, his remarks cover a wide *latitude* of subjects; **3,** degree of freedom from rules; as, he was given great *latitude* in arranging the meeting; **4,** a region or locality; as, a warm *latitude.*

La-ti-um (lā′shĭ-ŭm), an ancient division of southwestern Italy, in which Rome was situated.

lat-ter (lăt′ẽr), *adj.* one form of the comparative of *late:* **1,** the second of two things already mentioned; **2,** more recent; later; as, the *latter* half of the century.— *adv.* lat′ter-ly.

Lat-ter–day Saint, a Mormon.

---

go; join; yet; sing; chin; show; thin, *th***en; hw,** *why***; zh,** azure; **ŭ,** Ger. für or Fr. lune; **ö,** Ger. schön or Fr. feu; **ṅ,** Fr. enfant, nom; **kh,** Ger. ach or ich. See pages ix–x.

lat-tice (lăt′ĭs), *n.* crossed or interlaced openwork of metal or wood; hence, any door, window, gate, etc., made of such work:—*v.t.* [latticed, lattic-ing], **1,** to cross or interlace (strips) as in a lattice; **2,** to furnish with a lattice.—*n.* **lat′tice-work**′.

Lat-vi-a (lăt′vĭ-a), a former republic (cap. Riga) on the Baltic Sea, admitted into the Soviet Union in 1940 (map **12**).—*n.* and *adj.* **Lat′vi-an.**

LATTICE

Lat-vi-an So-vi-et So-cial-ist Re-pub-lic, Latvia.

laud (lôd), *v.t.* to praise; glorify:—*n.* a hymn extolling God; a song of praise.

laud-a-ble (lôd′a-bl), *adj.* worthy or deserving of praise; as, a *laudable* effort.

lau-da-num (lô′da-nŭm; lôd′nŭm), *n.* a solution of opium in alcohol; a poisonous narcotic drug.

laud-a-tor-y (lôd′a-tôr′ĭ), *adj.* pertaining to, or expressing, praise.

laugh (lăf), *v.i.* to express mirth, enjoyment, or derision by a series of chuckling sounds:—*v.t.* **1,** to express or utter with laughter; as, he *laughed* his pleasure; **2,** to move or affect by merriment or ridicule; as, we *laughed* her out of her pout:—*n.* the act of laughing or its sound:—**laugh up one's sleeve,** to laugh to oneself.

laugh-a-ble (lăf′a-bl), *adj.* funny; causing mirth; ridiculous.—*adv.* **laugh′a-bly.**
Syn. comical, droll, absurd, ludicrous.

laugh-ing (lăf′ĭng), *adj.* full of laughter; calling forth laughter.

laugh-ing-stock (lăf′ĭng-stŏk′), *n.* a person who makes himself ridiculous.

laugh-ter (lăf′tẽr), *n.* the act or sound of laughing.

¹launch (lônch; länch), *v.t.* **1,** to move or cause to slide into the water, as a vessel; **2,** to start off, as a business; **3,** to hurl; throw:—*v.i.* **1,** to put to sea; **2,** to plunge or start swiftly and with vigor; as, he *launched* into a torrent of abuse; **3,** to enter on a new career.

²launch (lônch; länch), *n.* **1,** the largest boat of a battleship; **2,** a large, open pleasure boat, usually motor-driven.

laun-der (lôn′dẽr; län′dẽr), *v.t.* to wash and iron (clothes).—*n.* **laun′der-er.**

laun-dress (lôn′drĕs; län′drĕs), *n.* a woman who washes and irons clothes for a living.

laun-dry (lôn′drĭ; län′drĭ), *n.* [*pl.* laundries], **1,** a commercial establishment, or a room in a home, where clothes are washed and ironed; **2,** articles sent to be washed.

laun-dry-man (lôn′drĭ-măn; län′drĭ-măn), *n.* [*pl.* laundrymen (-měn)], a man who works in or for a laundry.

lau-re-ate (lô′rĕ-ât; lô′rĕ-ĭt), *adj.* decked or crowned with laurel; hence, worthy of honor:—**poet laureate,** the official court poet of Great Britain:—*n.* a poet laureate.—*n.* **lau′re-ate-ship**′.

lau-rel (lô′rĕl; lŏr′ĕl), *n.* **1,** an evergreen shrub of southern Europe, used by the ancient Greeks and Romans as a symbol of fame and distinction: also called *bay* or *bay laurel;* **2,** any of several shrubs resembling the true laurel, especially the flowering mountain laurel; **3,** a crown or wreath of bay given as a prize or honor; **4, laurels,** fame; honor.

Lau-sanne (lō-zăn′; lō′zän′), a city on the north shore of Lake Geneva, in southwestern Switzerland.

la-va (lä′va; lăv′a), *n.* melted rock such as erupts from a volcano.

lav-a-tor-y (lăv′a-tôr′ĭ), *n.* [*pl.* lavatories], **1,** a room for washing the hands and face; **2,** a basin fixed on a stand, usually with running water, for washing.

lave (lāv), *v.i.* [laved, lav-ing], to bathe; wash oneself:—*v.t.* **1,** to wash; bathe; **2,** to flow or wash gently against; as, the calm sea *laves* the beach.

lav-en-der (lăv′ĕn-dẽr), *n.* **1,** a plant with lilac-colored flowers and narrow woolly leaves, cultivated for its perfume and used, when dried, to sweeten and scent clothes, linens, etc.; **2,** the pale-lilac color of its flowers.

la-ver (lā′vẽr), *n.* a wash basin.

lav-ish (lăv′ĭsh), *adj.* **1,** very liberal; almost too generous; **2,** excessive; as, *lavish* praise:—*v.t.* to spend or bestow liberally; squander; waste.—*adv.* **lav′ish-ly.**—*n.* **lav′ish-ness.**
Syn., *adj.* immoderate, bountiful, profuse.

LAVEN-DER

law (lô), *n.* **1,** a rule of action, established by authority or custom, for a nation or a group of people; also, a body of such rules or customs; as, maritime *law;* social *law;* **2,** an act or enactment of a legislative, or lawmaking, body; **3,** the legal profession; **4,** in sport, games, etc., the generally accepted rules of procedure; as, the *laws* of football; **5,** trial in the courts; as, take it to *law;* **6,** in science, a statement of what, under given conditions, invariably happens, or of relations between things in nature; as, the *law* of gravitation; **7,** in the Bible, the set of rules and commands given by Moses.
Syn. edict, decree, regulation, code.

law-break-er (lô′brāk′ẽr), *n.* one who breaks the law.—*n.* **law′break′ing.**

law-ful (lô′fool), *adj.* **1,** according to law; right, not wrong; as, *lawful* acts; **2,** recognized by law; rightful; as, *lawful* ownership.—*adv.* **law′ful-ly.**—*n.* **law′ful-ness.**

law-giv-er (lô′gĭv′ẽr), *n.* one who formulates or enacts a law or code of laws. Moses and Solon were lawgivers.

law-less (lô′lĕs), *adj.* **1,** without laws; **2,** not obedient to, or controlled by, authority.—*adv.* **law′less-ly.**—*n.* **law′less-ness.**

¹**lawn** (lôn), *n.* a thin, fine cotton or linen fabric used for dresses, blouses, etc.

²**lawn** (lôn), *n.* a plot of grass kept closely mowed.

lawn ten-nis, an outdoor game played on a specially marked court crossed in the middle by a net, over which a ball is driven by means of a racket: commonly called *tennis.*

Law-rence (lô′rĕns), Thomas Edward (1888–1935), called *Lawrence of Arabia,* a British soldier famed for his exploits in Arabia during the World War.

law-suit (lô′sūt′), *n.* a case in a law court to settle a claim or enforce a right.

law-yer (lô′yẽr), *n.* one who knows and practices law; an attorney.

lax (lăks), *adj.* **1,** loose; not firm, tense, or rigid; **2,** careless; inexact; not strict; as, *lax* principles.—*adv.* **lax′ly.**—*n.* **lax′ness.**

lax-a-tive (lăk′sȧ-tĭv), *adj.* loosening; causing the bowels to move:—*n.* a medicine which causes the bowels to move.

lax-i-ty (lăk′sĭ-tĭ), *n.* [*pl.* laxities], the state or quality of being loose, neglectful, or weak.

¹**lay** (lā), *n.* **1,** a short lyric or poem intended to be sung; **2,** any poem or song.

²**lay** (lā), *adj.* **1,** having to do with persons outside the clergy; as, *lay* opinion; **2,** relating to those outside any particular profession; as, the *lay* mind cannot understand all the fine points of law.

³**lay** (lā), *v.t.* [laid (lād), lay-ing], **1,** to cause to lie; place or put; as, to *lay* a card on the table; **2,** to bring or beat down; as, the blow *laid* him low; **3,** to produce and deposit (an egg); **4,** to bet; **5,** to impose, as a tax, burden, duty, or the like; **6,** to spread over a surface; as, to *lay* rugs; **7,** to keep down or quiet; suppress; make disappear; as, rain *lays* dust; to *lay* doubt; *lay* a ghost; **8,** to reduce to a certain condition; as, to *lay* waste a city; **9,** to set, in time or place; as, the scene was *laid* in ancient Rome; **10,** to place; impute; as, to *lay* blame for a crime on someone; **11,** to construct, as a floor, foundation, etc.; **12,** to present for consideration; as, to *lay* facts

before a committee:—*v.i.* **1,** to produce eggs, **2,** to bet; **3,** on shipboard, to take up a position (as specified); as, to *lay* aft:—*n.* the manner or direction in which something lies; as, the *lay* of the land.

   lay about one, to hit out to right and left; **lay hold on,** to seize; **lay out, 1,** to spend, as money; **2,** to map or plan, as a garden; **3,** to prepare (a body) for burial.

⁴**lay** (lā), past tense of ²*lie.*

lay-er (lā′ẽr), *n.* **1,** one that lays; as, a brick*layer*; **2,** one thickness; a stratum, row, coating, or the like; as, a *layer* of earth; a *layer* of paint.

lay-ette (lā-ĕt′), *n.* an outfit of clothes, bedding, etc., for a newborn child.

lay-man (lā′măn), *n.* [*pl.* laymen (-mĕn)], **1,** a person not of the clergy; **2,** a person not belonging to a particular profession.

lay-out (lā′out′), *n.* **1,** a plan or design; **2,** an outfit; as, a carpenter's *layout.*

la-zar (lā′zẽr), *n.* a beggar with a loathsome disease; a leper.

Laz-a-rus (lăz′ȧ-rŭs), in the Bible: **1,** the brother of Mary and Martha, restored to life by Jesus (John 11); **2,** in one of the parables, a beggar who lay at a rich man's door (Luke 16).

la-zy (lā′zĭ), *adj.* [la-zi-er, la-zi-est], disinclined to work; indolent; idle:—*adv.* **la′zi-ly.**—*n.* **la′zi-ness.**

lb. [*pl.* lb. or lbs.], abbreviation for *pound.*

lea (lē), *n.* a meadow; pasture land.

leach (lēch), *v.t.* **1,** to cause (a liquid) to drip, or percolate, through some material; as, to *leach* water through wood ashes to obtain lye; **2,** to wash with water to extract the soluble substances; **3,** to extract by percolation; as, to *leach* lye from ashes:—*v.i.* to be extracted or dissolved out by this process.

¹**lead** (lĕd), *n.* **1,** a soft, heavy, bluish-gray metallic element; **2,** a weight attached to a rope for sounding depths at sea; **3,** a thin strip of metal for separating lines of type in printing; **4,** a stick of graphite or black carbon in a pencil; **5, leads,** strips of lead used for framing windowpanes, stained glass, etc.:—*adj.* consisting wholly or partly of lead:—*v.t.* **1,** to cover, fit, or join with lead; **2,** in printing, to spread (lines of type) by the insertion of thin metal strips.

²**lead** (lēd), *v.t.* [led (lĕd), lead-ing], **1,** to conduct by the hand; as, to *lead* a child through a crowd; **2,** to conduct or guide by going on in advance; **3,** to guide or conduct by advice or counsel; **4,** to be first among; as, to *lead* one's class; **5,** to influence; as, hunger *led* him to steal; **6,** to direct; as, to *lead* the singing; **7,** to pass;

spend; as, to *lead* a happy life; **8**, to play (a card) as the opening play of a trick:— *v.i.* **1**, to take the first place; **2**, to act as a guide, director, or manager; **3**, to take a course; extend in a direction: **lead to**, to bring about; pave the way to; as, waste often *leads to* poverty:—*n.* **1**, guidance; example; **2**, first place or position; as, in the *lead;* also, the distance by which one competitor is in advance of another; **3**, in card games, the right to play first; also, the play thus made; **4**, something that may act as a guide; a tip or hint; **5**, the principal actor in a play; also, his part.

lead-en (lĕd′n), *adj.* **1**, made of lead; of the color or weight of lead; **2**, dull; spiritless; as, a *leaden* step.

lead-er (lēd′ẽr), *n.* **1**, one who guides, directs, or conducts; as, an orchestra *leader;* **2**, one who occupies, or is fitted to occupy, the first or chief place; as, a *leader* among men; **3**, the piece of catgut at the end of a fishing line to which the hooks are attached.—*n.* **lead′er-ship.**

   Syn. chief, commander, guide.

leaf (lēf), *n.* [*pl.* leaves (lēvz)], **1**, one of the thin, flat parts of a plant, usually green, variously shaped, and borne on a stem or growing from the roots; also, a petal; as, a rose *leaf;* **2**, foliage in general; as, a tree in *leaf;* **3**, a sheet of metal beaten thin; as, gold *leaf;* **4**, any of various thin, flat parts, especially a single page of a book, a part of a folding table top, or the like: —*v.i.* to put forth foliage:—*v.t.* to turn the pages of (a book).—*n.* **leaf′age.**

LEAF
B, blade; S, stem.

LEAVES
1, ash (white ash); 2, oak (white oak); 3, ginkgo; 4, tulip tree; 5, nasturtium; 6, lilac; 7, red maple; 8, clover (red clover); 9, dandelion.

leaf hop-per, a small, leaping insect which damages plants by sucking their juice.

leaf lard, lard which is prepared from the fat found around the kidneys of hogs.

leaf-let (lēf′lĕt), *n.* **1**, a single division of a compound leaf; **2**, a printed sheet or circular; pamphlet.

leaf-y (lēf′ĭ), *adj.* [leaf-i-er, leaf-i-est], **1**, having, or abounding in, leaves; **2**, made of, or like, leaves; as, *leafy* tracery.

¹**league** (lēg), *n.* **1**, an agreement entered into by two or more persons or nations for their common good; also, the union so formed; **2**, an organization of groups of persons with a common interest; as, a baseball *league:*—*v.t.* and *v.i.* [leagued, lea-guing], to combine for mutual interests; as, *leagued* together for protection.

   Syn., n. compact, union, coalition.

²**league** (lēg), *n.* a varying measure of distance, equal to about three miles.

League of Na-tions, an international organization established in 1920 for the preservation of peace. It was disbanded in 1946, after having been supplanted by the United Nations.

Le-ah (lē′à), in the Old Testament, the first wife of Jacob.

leak (lēk), *n.* a hole, crack, or other opening, which accidentally lets anything, especially a fluid, in or out; also, the escaping of gas or fluid; leakage:—*v.i.* **1**, to go in or out through a leak; as, air *leaks* in through a crack; **2**, to lose contents through a hole or a crack; as, a bucket *leaks;* **3**, to become gradually known; as, the news *leaked* out.

leak-age (lēk′ĭj), *n.* a leaking or escaping; also, whatever leaks in or out.

leak-y (lēk′ĭ), *adj.* [leak-i-er, leak-i-est], having a leak; as, a *leaky* pail.

leal (lēl), *adj. Poetic,* loyal.

¹**lean** (lēn), *v.i.* [leaned (lēnd), sometimes leant (lĕnt), lean-ing], **1**, to slant from an upright position; as, the *leaning* Tower of Pisa; **2**, to rest on something for support; as, to lean on a crutch; **3**, to rely; as, she *leans* on her mother in all things; **4**, to tend or be inclined; as, I *lean* toward his opinion:—*v.t.* to place in a slanting position.

²**lean** (lēn), *adj.* **1**, thin; as, a *lean* person; lacking in fat; as, *lean* meat; **2**, not productive; as, *lean* years:—*n.* meat without fat.—*n.* **lean′ness.**

   Syn., adj. meager, spare, gaunt, skinny, thin.

Le-an-der (lē-ăn′dẽr), in Greek mythology, a young man who swam the Hellespont every night to visit his sweetheart, Hero.

lean–to (lēn′=tōō′), *n.* a building that rests against another building and has a roof sloping one way only; also, a crude shelter built against a tree, rock, etc.

āte, āorta, râre, căt, ȧsk, fär, ȧllow, sofȧ; ēve, ĕvent, ĕll, writẽr, novĕl; bīte, pĭn; nō, ōbey, ôr, dŏg, tŏp, cŏllide; ūnit, ūnite, bûrn, cŭt, focŭs; nōōn, fŏŏt; mound; coin;

leap (lēp), *v.t.* [leaped (lēpt) or leapt (lĕpt), leap-ing], **1,** to pass over by a bound or jump; as, to *leap* a ditch; **2,** to cause to jump or spring; as, to *leap* a horse over a hedge:—*v.i.* **1,** to jump or spring off the ground, or from a high place; **2,** to bound or move suddenly; as, my heart *leaps* up:—*n.* **1,** the act of passing over with a bound; also, a jump; spring; **2,** the space covered in jumping.

leap-frog (lēp′frŏg), *n.* a game, in which each player in turn runs, places his hands on the bent back of another, and leaps over him.

LEAPFROG

leapt (lĕpt), one form of the past tense and past participle of *leap*.

leap year, a year of 366 days, in which February has 29 instead of 28 days.

Lear (lĭr), *n.* a legendary king of Britain, hero of Shakespeare's "King Lear," who misjudged and disinherited his devoted youngest daughter, Cordelia, in favor of her two false sisters, and died of grief over the death of Cordelia.

learn (lûrn), *v.t.* [learned (lûrnd) or learnt (lûrnt), learn-ing], **1,** to acquire knowledge of, or skill in; as, to *learn* French; **2,** to gain information of; as, I regret to *learn* the sad news; **3,** to memorize; as, to *learn* a poem:—*v.i.* to gain or receive knowledge or skill; as, she knows no algebra as yet, but *learns* quickly.—*n.* **learn′er.**

learn-ed (lûr′nĕd), *adj.* having much knowledge; scholarly; as, a *learned* professor.—*adv.* **learn′ed-ly.**

learn-ing (lûr′nĭng), *n.* **1,** the act or process of acquiring knowledge; **2,** knowledge or skill gained by study.
Syn. scholarship, lore.

lease (lēs), *n.* **1,** a written contract for the renting of land or buildings for a specified time; **2,** property so rented; also, the time for which property is so rented:—**a new lease on life,** a new chance or opportunity to live, as for a convalescent:—*v.t.* [leased, leas-ing], **1,** to grant possession of, for a specified time, by a contract or lease; as, the owner *leases* a house to a tenant; **2,** to take possession of by lease.

leash (lēsh), *n.* a thong of leather, or a long cord or chain, for holding a hawk or dog:—*v.t.* to fasten or hold with a leash.

least (lēst), *adj.* [*superl.* of *little*], smallest in degree, size, importance, etc.:—*adv.* in the lowest or smallest degree:—*n.* the smallest amount; as, to say the *least*.

leath-er (lĕth′ẽr), *n.* the skin of an animal, tanned and prepared for use; also, anything made of the skin so prepared.

leath-ern (lĕth′ẽrn), *adj.* made of leather.

leath-er-y (lĕth′ẽr-ĭ), *adj.* like leather.

¹leave (lēv), *v.t.* [left (lĕft), leav-ing], **1,** to fail to take; allow to remain behind; as, I *left* my purse at home; **2,** to have remaining at death; as, they say she *left* three children; **3,** to allow to remain or continue in the same place or condition; as, the appeal *left* him indifferent; **4,** to depart or withdraw from; as, to *leave* a job; *leave* home; **5,** to deliver; as, the postman *leaves* letters; **6,** to cease from; stop; as, *leave* your quarreling; **7,** to give by will; as, she *left* the money to charity; **8,** to refer (a matter) for decision; as, I *leave* the choice to you:—*v.i.* to go away; depart.
Syn. quit, desert.

²leave (lēv), *n.* **1,** a permission granted; **2,** departure; formal farewell.
  leave of absence, permission to be away from duty for a specified time; also, the time one is away; **take leave of,** to say good-by to.
Syn. license, liberty.

³leave (lēv), *v.i.* [leaved, leav-ing], to put forth leaves; come out in leaf.

leav-en (lĕv′ĕn), *n.* **1,** a ferment mixed with a substance to render it light, as yeast in dough; **2,** an influence which cheers or lightens; as, humor is the *leaven* of life:—*v.t.* **1,** to make light by fermentation; to cause to ferment; as, yeast *leavens* dough; **2,** to mix with some modifying element; as, he *leavens* correction with a little praise.

leaves (lēvz), plural of *leaf*.

leav-ings (lē′vĭngz), *n.pl.* what is left over; discarded remains.

Leb-a-non (lĕb′à-nŭn), **1,** an independent republic (cap. Beirut) on the Mediterranean Sea, formerly under French mandate (map 15); **2,** a mountain range in southwestern Syria, north of ancient Palestine.—*adj.* **Leb′a-nese′.**

Leb-bae-us (lĕ-bē′ŭs), in the Bible, one of the twelve apostles of Jesus: also called *Thaddeus*.

lec-ture (lĕk′tûr), *n.* **1,** a formal talk or address on any subject; **2,** a lengthy reproof; scolding:—*v.i.* [lectured, lectur-ing], to deliver a formal talk:—*v.t.* to rebuke.—*n.* **lec′tur-er.**

led (lĕd), past tense and past participle of *²lead*.

ledge (lĕj), *n.* **1,** a shelf or shelflike projection from an upright surface; as, a window *ledge*, or a *ledge* of rock; **2,** a ridge of rock, especially one under water, not far from shore.

ledg-er (lĕj′ẽr), *n.* the principal account book of a business house, in which the final summaries of debits and credits are recorded.

Lee (lē), **1,** Henry (1756–1818), often called *Light-Horse Harry*, an American general in the Revolutionary War; **2,** Robert Edward (1807–1870), his son, an American general, commander of the Confederate Army in the War between the States.

lee (lē), *n.* **1,** the direction opposite to that from which the wind blows; **2,** the side of anything which is protected from the wind; **3,** shelter; as, in the *lee* of the rock: —*adj.* **1,** pertaining to the part which is protected from the wind; as, the *lee* side of a ship; **2,** in the direction toward which the wind blows; as, a *lee* tide.

¹**leech** (lēch), *n.* **1,** any of various blood-sucking worms, usually water-dwelling, formerly much used in medicine as a means of withdrawing blood from patients; **2,** one who gets all he can out of another:—*v.t.* to bleed with leeches.

²**leech** (lēch), *n. Archaic*, a physician.

Leeds (lēdz), a manufacturing city in north central England (map **13**).

leek (lēk), *n.* an onionlike plant used as food or flavoring.

leer (lēr), *n.* a sly, sidelong look of malice or evil desire: —*v.i.* to look slyly or evilly.

lees (lēz), *n.pl.* the sediment at the bottom of a vessel containing liquor; dregs.

lee-ward (lē′wẽrd; lū′ẽrd), *adj.* pertaining to the lee; away from the wind:—*adv.* toward the lee or sheltered side:—*n.* the lee side.

LEEK

Lee-ward Is-lands (lē′wẽrd), a group of islands, most of which are part of the British West Indies, lying southeast of Puerto Rico (map **10**).

lee-way (lē′wā′), *n.* **1,** the sideward drift of a vessel caused by the wind; **2,** *Colloquial*, extra room or time for action; margin; as, he has ten minutes' *leeway* to catch the boat.

¹**left** (lĕft), past tense and past participle of ¹*leave.*

²**left** (lĕft), *adj.* **1,** naming, or relating to, that side of the human body which is toward the north when one faces east: opposite of *right;* **2,** placed or located on the left side; as, the *left* eye:—*n.* **1,** the direction or region which lies on the left side; as, look to the *left;* **2,** in politics, the liberal or radical party: so called because in some parliaments this party is often seated on the left:—*adv.* to the left.

left—hand (lĕft′-hănd′), *adj.* relating to, or situated on, the left side.

left—hand-ed (lĕft′-hăn′dĕd), *adj.* **1,** using the left hand with greater strength or skill than the right; **2,** done with, or adapted to, the left hand; **3,** awkward:— **left-handed compliment,** a compliment that carries a double meaning and is therefore of doubtful significance.

leg (lĕg), *n.* **1,** one of the limbs which support the body and by which men and animals walk; sometimes, in man, the lower limb from knee to ankle; **2,** anything resembling a leg; as, a chair *leg;* **3,** the part of a garment covering the leg; **4,** the course covered by a vessel on one tack; **5,** in mathematics, one of two sides of a triangle, the third being the base; **6,** in cards, the first game toward a rubber.

leg-a-cy (lĕg′à-sĭ), *n.* [*pl.* legacies], **1,** a gift by will; **2,** anything that has come down from one's predecessors.

le-gal (lē′găl), *adj.* **1,** pertaining to law; **2,** permitted or authorized by law; as, Sunday baseball is *legal* in some States:— **legal tender,** money or currency which by law must be accepted in payment of debts.—*adv.* **le′gal-ly.**

le-gal-i-ty (lē-găl′ĭ-tĭ), *n.* [*pl.* legalities], conformity to law; lawfulness.

le-gal-ize (lē′găl-īz), *v.t.* [legalized, legal-iz-ing], to permit by law; as, to *legalize* the sale of tobacco.

leg-ate (lĕg′ĭt), *n.* **1,** an ambassador, delegate, or envoy; **2,** in the Roman Catholic Church, a representative of the Pope.

leg-a-tee (lĕg′à-tē′), *n.* one to whom a legacy or gift is left by will.

le-ga-tion (lē-gā′shŭn), *n.* **1,** an ambassador or envoy and his associates; **2,** the official residence of a diplomatic representative in a foreign country.

le-ga-to (lā-gä′tō; lē-gä′tō), *adj.* and *adv.* in music, in a smooth, flowing manner, without breaks between notes.

leg-end (lĕj′ĕnd; lē′jĕnd), *n.* **1,** a story handed down from the past; especially, a story which centers about a historic person or event, but which cannot be proved to be true; **2,** the words of a title or inscription, as on a coin or under an illustration in a book.

leg-end-ar-y (lĕj′ĕn-dĕr′ĭ), *adj.* pertaining to, or told in, story, fable, or myth.

leg-er-de-main (lĕj′ẽr-dē-mān′), *n.* **1,** sleight of hand; the art of juggling; **2,** any deception based on trickery.

leg·ging (lĕg/ĭng), *n.* either of a pair of long gaiters worn to protect the legs from cold or wet.

Leg·horn (lĕg/hôrn; lĕg/hôrn/), a seaport in northwestern Italy (map **12**). Its Italian name is *Livorno*.

leg·horn (lĕg/hôrn; lĕg/ẽrn; lĕg/-ôrn), *n.* **1**, a braid made of fine Italian straw; **2**, a hat made of such straw:—**Leghorn**, a breed of small, domestic fowl, noted as good layers.

LEGGING

leg·i·bil·i·ty (lĕj/ĭ-bĭl/ĭ-tĭ), *n.* the quality of being easy to read; clearness.

leg·i·ble (lĕj/ĭ-bl), *adj.* capable of being read; clear; distinct.—*adv.* **leg/i·bly.**

le·gion (lē/jŭn), *n.* **1**, a division of the ancient Roman army, of 3,000 to 6,000 foot soldiers; **2**, an army; **3**, a vast number.—*adj.* and *n.* **le/gion·ar/y.**

leg·is·late (lĕj/ĭs-lāt), *v.i.* [legislat-ed, legislat-ing], to make or enact a law or laws; as, to *legislate* against gambling.—*adj.* **leg/is·la/tive.**—*n.* **leg/is·la/tor.**

leg·is·la·tion (lĕj/ĭs-lā/shŭn), *n.* **1**, the act of making a law or laws; **2**, laws made or enacted.

leg·is·la·ture (lĕj/ĭs-lā/tŭr), *n.* the law-making body of a state or nation.

le·git·i·ma·cy (lē-jĭt/ĭ-mȧ-sĭ), *n.* **1**, the state or condition of being allowed by law, or of conforming to recognized standards; **2**, of a person, the state of having been born of married parents.

le·git·i·mate (lē-jĭt/ĭ-mĭt), *adj.* **1**, lawful; rightful; as, the *legitimate* heir to a throne; **2**, born lawfully, of wedded parents; **3**, according to accepted rules; as, a *legitimate* pass in football; **4**, reasonable; just; as, illness is a *legitimate* reason for absence:—*v.t.* (lē-jĭt/ĭ-māt), [legitimat-ed, legitimat-ing], to permit or recognize by law.—*adv.* **le·git/i·mate·ly.**

leg·ume (lĕg/ūm; lē-gūm/), *n.* **1**, a type of podlike fruit, as the pea and the bean; **2**, a plant bearing such fruit; **3**, **legumes,** the seed of such fruit used as food.

le·gu·mi·nous (lē-gū/mĭ-nŭs), *adj.* composed of, or bearing, legumes; as, *leguminous* crops.

le·hu·a (lā-hōō/ä), *n.* a tree of the Pacific islands, with brilliant red flowers and hard wood.

le·i (lā/ē), *n.* in Hawaii, a wreath, usually of flowers, hung about one's neck as a token of welcome and friendship.

Leices·ter·shire (lĕs/tẽr-shĭr), a county in central England. Also called **Leices/ter.**

Lei·den (lī/dĕn), a city in the western part of the Netherlands.

Leip·zig (līp/tsĭkh), an industrial city in northwestern Saxony, Germany.

lei·sure (lē/zhẽr; lĕzh/ẽr), *n.* spare time:—*adj.* free; unoccupied by work; as, *leisure* hours.—*adj.* and *adv.* **lei/sure·ly.** *Syn.* convenience, ease.

Lem·berg (lĕm/bĕrkh), the German name for **Lwów,** a city in the U.S.S.R.

lem·ming (lĕm/ĭng), *n.* a small, mouselike animal of the arctic regions. It has a short tail and furry feet.

lem·on (lĕm/ŭn), *n.* **1**, a small tropical fruit with pale-yellow skin and very acid juice; **2**, the tree, related to the orange, which bears this fruit; **3**, a pale-yellow color:—*adj.* flavored or colored like a lemon; as, *lemon* pie; *lemon* taffeta.

lem·on·ade (lĕm/ŭn-ād/), *n.* a drink of sweetened water flavored with lemon juice.

lem·pi·ra (lĕm-pē/rȧ), *n.* the monetary unit of Honduras. (See Table, page 943.)

le·mur (lē/mẽr), *n.* any of various small sharp-nosed, tree-dwelling, woolly mammals, which are related to monkeys. They are found chiefly in Madagascar.

lend (lĕnd), *v.t.* [lent (lĕnt), lend-ing], **1**, to turn over to someone to use for a time; **2**, to give (aid); provide; as, distance *lends* enchantment; **3**, to devote; as, to *lend* oneself to a scheme:—*v.i.* to make or grant a loan.—*n.* **lend/er.**

RING-TAILED LEMUR (⅛)

lend–lease (lĕnd/-lēs/), *n.* as authorized by Congress during World War II, the disposal or transfer of such articles as aircraft, ships, munitions, and food, to a friendly nation whose safety is vital to the United States:—*adj.* pertaining to this procedure; as, a *lend-lease* program:—*v.t.* to dispose of such articles; as, to *lend-lease* food.

length (lĕngth), *n.* **1**, the measure of anything from end to end; as, the *length* of a boat; **2**, extent in space, degree, or time; as, the *length* of a journey; **3**, a specified distance, as from head to tail of a horse; **4**, a single piece, as of a series of objects that may be connected; as, a *length* of pipe; **5**, the quantity of a vowel measured by the time it takes to utter it; as, the *length* of *e* in "he":—**at length, 1**, in full detail; **2**, at last; finally.

length·en (lĕng/thĕn), *v.t.* to make long or longer; as, to *lengthen* a skirt:—*v.i.* to grow longer; as, the days *lengthen* in spring.

length·wise (lĕngth/wīz), *adj.* and *adv.*

in the direction from end to end; as, a *lengthwise* measurement; we sleep *lengthwise* in bed. Also, *adv.* **length′ways.**

length-y (lĕng′thĭ), *adj.* [length-i-er, length-i-est], long; drawn out; tedious.—*adv.* **length′i-ly.**—*n.* **length′i-ness.**

le-ni-en-cy (lē′nĭ-ĕn-sĭ; lēn′yĕn-sĭ), *n.* lack of severity; tolerance; mildness. Also, **le′ni-ence.**

le-ni-ent (lē′nĭ-ĕnt; lēn′yĕnt), *adj.* not severe; mild; merciful; as, a *lenient* judge. —*adv.* **le′ni-ent-ly.**

Len-in (lĕn′ĭn; lyĕ′nēn), Nikolay (1870–1924), the founder and first president of the Soviet government in Russia.

Len-in-grad (lĕn′in-grăd; lyĕ′nēn-grät′), a city, once the capital of Russia, known as *Saint Petersburg* until 1914, and as *Petrograd* from 1914 to 1924 (map **12**).

len-i-ty (lĕn′ĭ-tĭ), *n.* [*pl.* lenities], mercifulness of temper or action; kindliness.

lens (lĕnz), *n.* **1,** a piece of glass or other transparent substance, with one or both of its surfaces curved, used in cameras, eyeglasses, telescopes, and the like, producing a change in the direction of rays of light, as a result of which, in some lenses, the rays that pass through make an image on a screen or a camera film; **2,** a lenslike part of the eye, which focuses light on the retina.

LENS
R, parallel rays of light; L, lens; F, focus.

Lent (lĕnt), *n.* the 40 weekdays before Easter Sunday, observed in some Christian churches with fasting and penitence.

lent (lĕnt), past tense and past participle of *lend.*

Lent-en (lĕn′tĕn), *adj.* relating to, or suited to, Lent; as, *Lenten* services.

len-til (lĕn′tĭl), *n.* a pod-bearing plant, of which the small seeds are cooked as a vegetable or ground into meal, and the stalks used for fodder.

len-to (lĕn′tō), *adj.* and *adv.* in music, slow; slowly.

Le-o-nar-do da Vin-ci (lā′ō-när′dō dä vēn′chē), an Italian painter, architect, and engineer. See **Vinci.**

Le-on-i-das (lē-ŏn′ĭ-dăs), (?–480 B.C.), a king who led the Spartans against the Persians at Thermopylae.

le-o-nine (lē′ō-nīn), *adj.* like a lion; hence, powerful; majestic.

leop-ard (lĕp′ẽrd), *n.* a large carnivorous cat of southern Asia and Africa, with a black-spotted tawny coat (see illustration next column): also called *panther.*—*n.fem.* **leop′ard-ess.**

Le-o-pold III, (lē′ō-pōld), (1901–), king of the Belgians from 1934–51.

Lé-o-pold-ville (lā′ō′pōld′vēl′; lē′ō-pōld-vĭl), a city, capital of the Belgian Congo, central Africa, on the Congo River (map **14**).

lep-er (lĕp′ẽr), *n.* a person who is afflicted with leprosy.

lep-ro-sy (lĕp′rō-sĭ), *n.* [*pl.* leprosies], a loathsome, infectious skin disease marked by external ulcers and a scaling off of dead tissue: also called Hansen's disease.—*adj.* **lep′rous.**

lese maj-es-ty (lēz mǎj′ĕs-tĭ), a crime against a sovereign or government; treason.

le-sion (lē′zhŭn), *n.* a change or deterioration in any part of the body, caused by injury or disease.

less (lĕs), *adj.* [*comp.* of *little*], **1,** not so much; not so large; **2,** fewer; **3,** inferior:—*prep.* minus; as, ten *less* seven: — *adv.* in a lower degree; as, *less* famous: — *n.* a smaller quantity; as, eat *less.*

-less (-lĕs), a suffix meaning without; free from; not characterized by; as, home*less*, worth*less*, daunt*less.*

les-see (lĕs-ē′), *n.* a person who holds property under a lease; a tenant.

less-en (lĕs′n), *v.t.* to make smaller or fewer; reduce; as, to *lessen* the length of a rope; *lessen* working hours:—*v.i.* to become less. *Syn.* decrease, diminish, dwindle.

less-er (lĕs′ẽr), *adj.* [a *comp.* of *little*], smaller; inferior; less; as, the *lesser* evil.

Less-er An-til-les, a chain of small islands southeast of the Greater Antilles, in the West Indies. See **Antilles.**

Les-sing (lĕs′ĭng), Gotthold Ephraim (1729–1781), a German dramatist, critic, and philosopher.

les-son (lĕs′n), *n.* **1,** that which is assigned to a pupil to learn; **2,** the instruction given at one time; **3,** any person, thing, etc., by which one learns; as, his fate is a *lesson* to me; **4,** in Christian church services, a reading from the Bible.

lest (lĕst), *conj.* for fear that; as, in dread *lest* the thief come; so that not; as, hurry *lest* you be too late.

¹**let** (lĕt), *n.* **1,** *Archaic,* an obstacle; hindrance; **2,** in tennis, a served ball which touches the net in going over: **without let or hindrance,** without delay, difficulty, or hindrance.

LEOPARD (¹⁄₃₀)

²**let** (lĕt), *v.t.* [let, let-ting], **1,** to permit;

allow; as, *let* me try again; **2,** to rent; lease; **3,** to allow (something) to escape; as, to *let* air out of a tire:—*v.i.* to be hired or leased; as, the house *lets* for $50 a month.

let alone, 1, leave undisturbed; **2,** say nothing of; as, he can't walk one mile, *let alone* five; **let down,** fail; disappoint; as, to *let* a friend *down*; **let go of,** loosen one's hold on; set free; as, *let go of* the cat; **let off, 1,** discharge or fire, as a gun; **2,** dismiss without punishment, or with a light one; as, they *let* the thief *off* with a light sentence.

-let (-lĕt), a suffix meaning little; as, eag*let*, rivu*let*.

let-down (lĕt′doun′), *n.* a slackening; relaxing; as, a *letdown* in effort, business, etc.

le-thal (lē′thăl), *adj.* deadly; fatal; as, a *lethal* gas.

le-thar-gic (lē-thär′jĭk), *adj.* sleepy; dull; listless.

leth-ar-gy (lĕth′ẽr-jĭ), *n.* [*pl.* lethargies], **1,** unnatural drowsiness; **2,** lack of interest; listlessness.

Le-the (lē′thē), *n.* in Greek mythology, an underworld stream. Those who drank of it lost all memory of the past, so Lethe has come to symbolize forgetfulness of the past.

Le-to (lē′tō), *n.* in Greek mythology, the mother of Apollo and Artemis.

let's (lĕts), a contraction for *let us.*

let-ter (lĕt′ẽr), *n.* **1,** a mark or character used to represent a sound; an alphabetical symbol; **2,** a written or printed communication; epistle; as, a *letter* of introduction; a *letter* of thanks; **3,** the exact or word-for-word meaning; as, the *letter* of the law; **4,** letters, knowledge; learning; literature; as, men of *letters*:—*v.t.* mark with letters.

to the letter, in every detail; as, an order obeyed *to the letter*; **letter perfect, 1,** knowing something perfectly by memory, as a part in a play; **2,** of manuscript, perfect in every letter or detail.

let-ter-head (lĕt′ẽr-hĕd′), *n.* **1,** a printed form at the top of a sheet of writing paper, usually containing the name and address of the sender; **2,** a sheet of paper so printed.

let-ter-ing (lĕt′ẽr-ĭng), *n.* **1,** the process of marking with letters; **2,** the letters marked or inscribed, as on a tombstone.

let-tuce (lĕt′ŭs; lĕt′ĭs), *n.* a garden plant with tender, crisp leaves, which are used as a salad or garnish.

le-u (lĕ′ōō) or **ley** (lā), *n.* [*pl.* lei (lā)], a silver coin, the monetary unit of Rumania. (See Table, page 943.)

leu-co-cyte (lōō′kŏ-sīt), *n.* a white blood corpuscle.

leu-ke-mi-a (lōō-kē′mĭ-à), *n.* a usually fatal disease marked by rapid multiplication of the white blood cells.

lev or **lew** (lĕf), *n.* [*pl.* leva (lĕv′à)], a copper coin, the monetary unit of Bulgaria. (See Table, page 943.)

Le-vant (lē-vănt′), *n.* the Near East, or the countries about the eastern Mediterranean.

¹lev-ee (lĕv′ē; lĕ-vē′), *n.* **1,** a morning reception, especially by a person of high rank; **2,** any assemblage of guests.

²lev-ee (lĕv′ē; lĕ-vē′), *n.* **1,** a wall or embankment built along a river to keep it from flooding adjoining land; **2,** a landing place or quay.

lev-el (lĕv′ĕl; lĕv′l), *n.* **1,** an unbroken horizontal surface or line; **2,** equality of height; as, this house is on a *level* with that; **3,** a standard elevation; as, sea *level*; **4,** an instrument used to find or test a horizontal line:—*adj.* **1,** having a flat, horizontal surface; as, *level* ground; **2,** equal to something else in height or importance; **3,** steady; judicious; well-balanced; as, a *level* head:—*v.t.* [leveled, level-ing], **1,** to make smooth or flat in a horizontal plane; as, to *level* a road; **2,** to bring to the same plane, height, or condition as something else; specifically, to bring to the level of the ground; raze; **3,** to point; aim, as a gun.—*n.* **lev′el-er.**—*adv.* **lev′el-ly.**—*n.* **lev′el-ness.**

le-ver (lē′vẽr; lĕv′ẽr), *n.* **1,** a bar used to move a heavy object by prying; a crowbar; **2,** in mechanics, a rigid bar, fixed at one point, the fulcrum, around which it moves as on an axis, used to transmit or modify power.

LEVER

L, lever; F, fulcrum; W, weight.

le-ver-age (lē′vẽr-ĭj; lĕv′ẽr-ĭj), *n.* **1,** the action of a lever; **2,** the mechanical power gained by using a lever.

Le-vi (lē′vī), in the Bible, the third son of Jacob, and ancestor of the Levites.

le-vi-a-than (lē-vī′à-thăn), *n.* **1,** in the Bible, a sea animal of enormous size; **2,** anything huge, as a whale or a large ship.

Le-vite (lē′vīt), *n.* in the Bible: **1,** one of the tribe of Levi; **2,** specifically, one who assisted the priests in the rites of the tabernacle or temple.

Le-vit-i-cal (lē-vĭt′ĭ-kăl), *adj.* in the Bible, pertaining to the Levites or to their laws and customs; also, pertaining to Leviticus.

Le-vit-i-cus (lē-vĭt′ĭ-kŭs), *n.* the third book of the Old Testament, containing the laws and rituals of the priests and Levites.

lev-i-ty (lĕv′ĭ-tĭ), *n.* [*pl.* levities], lack of seriousness; unseemly frivolity.

---

go; join; yet; sing; chin; show; thin, *th*en; hw, *wh*y; zh, azure; ū, Ger. f*ü*r or Fr. l*u*ne; ö, Ger. sch*ö*n or Fr. f*eu*; ṅ, Fr. e*n*fant, no*m*; kh, Ger. a*ch* or i*ch*. See pages ix–x.

lev·y (lĕv′ĭ), *n.* [*pl.* levies], **1,** the act of collecting men or raising money under compulsion; **2,** the number or amount collected:— *v.t.* [levied, levy-ing], to raise or collect by force or order, as an army or a tax:— *v.i.* to raise money by seizing property; as, to *levy* on an estate for a debt.

lew (lĕf), *n.* the monetary unit of Bulgaria; a lev. See **lev.**

lewd (lūd), *adj.* vulgar; indecent; as, *lewd* talk.— *adv.* **lewd′ly.**— *n.* **lewd′ness.**

Lew·is (lū′ĭs), Meriwether (1774–1809), an American explorer who, with William Clark, led the first American overland expedition to the Pacific.

lex·i·cog·ra·pher (lĕk′sĭ-kŏg′ra-fẽr), one who edits or compiles a dictionary.— *n.* **lex′i-cog′ra-phy.**— *adj.* **lex′i-co-graph′ic.**

lex·i·con (lĕk′sĭ-kŏn), *n.* a dictionary, especially of an ancient language, such as Latin, Greek, Arabic, or Hebrew.

Lex·ing·ton (lĕk′sĭng-tŭn), **1,** a city of north central Kentucky (map **7**); **2,** a town in eastern Massachusetts, site of the first battle, fought in 1775, of the American Revolution.

ley (lā), *n.* the monetary unit of Rumania; leu. See **leu.**

Lha·sa (lä′sä), a city, capital of Tibet, central Asia (map **15**). It is a sacred city of the Buddhists, often called *The Forbidden City.*

L.I. abbreviation for *Long Island.*

li·a·bil·i·ty (lī′a-bĭl′ĭ-tĭ), *n.* [*pl.* liabilities], **1,** the state of being held responsible for a loss, debt, etc.; **2,** the state of being subject to something or apt to do something; tendency; as, *liability* to disease or to error; **3, liabilities,** debts; the obligations which must be paid out of assets.

li·a·ble (lī′a-bl), *adj.* **1,** answerable; responsible; as, a person is *liable* for his debts; **2,** exposed to some damage, danger, misfortune, penalty, etc.; as, a lazy student is *liable* to fail.

liai·son (lyâ′zŏṅ′; lē-ā′zŭn), *n.* a linking up; communication and co-operation, especially between separated parts of an army.

Lia·kou·ra (lyä′kōō-rà), the modern name of a mountain in Greece. See **Parnassus.**

li·ar (lī′ẽr), *n.* one who tells lies.

li·ba·tion (lī-bā′shŭn), *n.* the act of pouring out wine or other liquid in honor of a god; **2,** the liquid so poured out.

li·bel (lī′bĕl; lī′bl), *n.* a malicious written or printed statement tending to defame, or to injure the reputation of, another; also, the publishing of such a statement:— *v.t.* [libeled, libel-ing], to publish a malicious, injurious statement against; defame. — *n.* **li′bel-er.**

li·bel·ous (lī′bĕl-ŭs), *adj.* containing, or of the nature of, something that maliciously injures a person's reputation.

lib·er·al (lĭb′ẽr-ăl), *adj.* **1,** generous; **2,** abundant; plentiful; as, a *liberal* supply; **3,** free from narrowness in ideas; broadminded; **4,** in politics, in favor of social and governmental change and progress:— *n.* **1,** any freethinking person; a progressive; **2, Liberal,** a member of a liberal political party.— *adv.* **lib′er-al-ly.**

Liberal party, the progressive political party in Canada and Great Britain; **liberal arts,** such branches of learning as literature, science, history, languages, philosophy, etc.

lib·er·al·ism (lĭb′ẽr-ăl-ĭzm), *n.* liberal principles in religion, politics, etc.

lib·er·al·i·ty (lĭb′ẽr-ăl′ĭ-tĭ), *n.* [*pl.* liberalities], **1,** the quality of being generous and openhanded; **2,** mental breadth; freedom from prejudice.

lib·er·ate (lĭb′ẽr-āt), *v.t.* [liberat-ed, liberat-ing], to set free from restraint or bondage; as, to *liberate* slaves.— *n.* **lib′er-a′tor.** — *n.* **lib′er-a′tion.**

Syn. release, emancipate, discharge.

Li·be·ri·a (lī-bĭr′ĭ-à), a Negro republic (cap. Monrovia) in western Africa, southeast of Sierra Leone (map **14**).

lib·er·tine (lĭb′ẽr-tēn; lĭb′ẽr-tĭn), *n.* one who gives free rein to his evil impulses and desires:— *adj.* loose in morals.

lib·er·ty (lĭb′ẽr-tĭ), *n.* [*pl.* liberties], **1,** freedom from control or bondage; **2,** freedom to do as one pleases; **3,** an overstepping of the rules of propriety; undue freedom; as, to take *liberties* with a person; **4,** leisure; freedom from business; as, I shall be at *liberty* in an hour.

Syn. independence, immunity, license.

Lib·er·ty Is·land, a small island in New York Bay. See **Bedloe's Island.**

li·brar·i·an (lī-brâr′ĭ-ăn), *n.* one who has charge of a library.

li·brar·y (lī′brẽr-ĭ), *n.* [*pl.* libraries], **1,** a collection of books; **2,** a room or building, private or public, where such a collection is kept.

li·bret·to (lĭ-brĕt′ō), *n.* [*pl.* librettos or libretti (lĭ-brĕt′ē)], a book containing the words or text of an opera or similar musical composition; also, the text itself.— *n.* **li·bret′tist.**

Lib·y·a (lĭb′ĭ-à), **1,** a former Italian colony (cap. Tripoli) in northern Africa (map **14**), since 1951 a constitutional monarchy; **2,** an ancient Greek name for northern Africa, not including Egypt.— *n.* and *adj.* **Lib′y-an.**

Lib·y·an Des·ert (lĭb′ĭ-ăn), a desert, part

of the Sahara, in northeastern Africa, west of the Nile (map **14**).

lice (līs), plural of *louse*.

li-cense (lī'sĕns), *n.* **1,** legal authorization or permission to do something; also, the document which gives such permission; as, a fishing *license;* **2,** unrestrained liberty; abuse of freedom: — **poetic license,** the intentional deviation from fact or from recognized usage by an artist or author for the sake of effect: — *v.t.* [licensed, licensing], to authorize, or grant permission to, by law. Also spelled **li'cence.**

li-cen-tious (lī-sĕn'shŭs), *adj.* lewd; unrestrained; dissolute. — *adv.* **li-cen'tious-ly.** — *n.* **li-cen'tious-ness.**

li-chen (lī'kĕn), *n.* a flowerless, leafless plant growing flat on rocks, tree trunks, etc.

lick (lĭk), *v.t.* **1,** to pass the tongue over; as, to *lick* a lollipop; **2,** to play or pass over lightly, as do flames; **3,** *Colloquial,* to whip; also, to conquer or defeat: — *n.* **1,** the act of passing the tongue over something; **2,** a small amount; as, a *lick* of flour; **3,** a deposit of natural salt, to which animals go for salt; a salt lick.

lic-o-rice (lĭk'ō-rĭs), *n.* the dried root of a plant of the pea family, or an extract made from it, which is used in medicines and candy; also, the plant.

lic-tor (lĭk'tẽr), *n.* in Rome, one of a body of official guards who attended the chief magistrates, and carried as a badge of authority the fasces, a bundle of rods with a projecting ax.

lid (lĭd), *n.* **1,** a movable cover for an opening, as of a box; a top; **2,** the cover of the eye; eyelid.

¹lie (lī), *n.* **1,** an untrue statement; falsehood; **2,** anything that misleads or is intended to mislead: — *v.i.* [lied (līd), ly-ing], **1,** to speak a falsehood; **2,** to make false representations; as, figures never *lie.*

²lie (lī), *v.i.* [*p.t.* lay (lā), *p.p.* lain (lān), *p.pr.* ly-ing], **1,** to assume, or rest in, a reclining position; **2,** to be in a flat or horizontal position; as, the tree *lay* in the road; **3,** to be situated; as, the town *lies* yonder; also, to extend; as, there *lies* the path; **4,** to be; exist; as, the trouble *lies* in the engine; also, to remain; as, the factory *lay* idle all summer: — **lie over,** to be left for action at a future time.

lied (līd), past tense and past participle of ¹*lie.*

lief (lēf), *adv.* willingly; as, I should as *lief* go as stay.

Liége (lyāzh'; lyâzh'), a city on the Meuse River in eastern Belgium, around which occurred the first serious conflict of World War I (map **12**).

liege (lēj), *adj.* **1,** having the right to devotion and service; as, faithful to his *liege* lord; **2,** bound to give service and devotion, as to a feudal lord; **3,** hence, loyal; faithful: — *n.* **1,** one bound to give service and devotion; a vassal; **2,** a sovereign; lord and master.

li-en (lē'ĕn; lēn), *n.* a legal claim upon the property of another, entitling the claimant to hold the property until his claim is paid or settled by the owner.

lieu (lū), *n.* place; stead; as, he accepted shares of stock in *lieu* of salary.

Lieut. or **Lt.** abbreviation for *Lieutenant.*

lieu-ten-ant (lū-tĕn'ănt), *n.* **1,** one who acts for a superior: used also with names of ranks to indicate the next lower rank; as, *lieutenant* governor; *lieutenant* colonel; **2,** in the army, a commissioned officer next below a captain; **3,** in the navy, a commissioned officer ranking next below a lieutenant commander. — *n.* **lieu-ten'an-cy.**

life (līf), *n.* [*pl.* lives (līvz)], **1,** the particular quality which distinguishes an animal or a plant from rocks, earth, water, etc.; **2,** the state of being alive; existence; **3,** a living person; as, a *life* was saved by the operation; also, living beings collectively; as, human *life;* animal *life;* **4,** the period between birth and death; as, all the years of a man's *life;* **5,** a biography; as, a *life* of Tennyson; **6,** animation; vivacity; as, to be full of *life;* **7,** a manner of living; as, a *life* of hardship.

life belt, a belt of cork or other buoyant material, used as a life preserver.

life-blood (līf'blŭd'), *n.* the blood essential to life.

life-boat (līf'bōt'), *n.* a strong boat for use in rescuing persons at sea. (See illustration under *davit.*)

life buoy (boo'ĭ; boi), a float, often an airfilled ring, to keep persons from sinking.

life-guard (līf'gärd'), *n.* an expert swimmer at public bathing beaches or pools, detailed to look after the safety of bathers.

life in-sur-ance, 1, a kind of financial protection offered by an insurance company, which in consideration of specified payments called *premiums,* agrees, at the death of the insured, or at a specified time, to pay a stated sum of money to a designated person, estate, etc., called the *beneficiary;* **2,** the amount to be paid.

life-like (līf'līk'), *adj.* like a living being or a real thing; natural; realistic.

life-long (līf'lông'), *adj.* enduring throughout life; as, a *lifelong* hatred.

life pre-serv-er, 1, a jacket or belt of buoyant material, as cork, for keeping a person afloat in the water; **2,** a short stick with a loaded head, for use as a weapon; a bludgeon.

life-sav-ing (līf'sā'vǐng), *n.* the·act of saving a person, especially from drowning.

life—size (līf'=sīz'), *adj.* of the size of the object represented; as, a *life-size* statue.

life-time (līf'tīm'), *n.* the length of time that a human being lives.

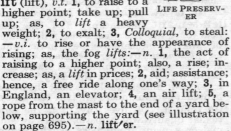

LIFE PRESERV-ER

lift (lĭft), *v.t.* **1,** to raise to a higher point; take up; pull up; as, to *lift* a heavy weight; **2,** to exalt; **3,** *Colloquial,* to steal:—*v.i.* to rise or have the appearance of rising; as, the fog *lifts:*—*n.* **1,** the act of raising to a higher point; also, a rise; increase; as, a *lift* in prices; **2,** aid; assistance; hence, a free ride along one's way; **3,** in England, an elevator; **4,** an air lift; **5,** a rope from the mast to the end of a yard below, supporting the yard (see illustration on page 695).—*n.* **lift'er.**

lig-a-ment (lĭg'å-měnt), *n.* a band of tough, fibrous tissue which connects the ends of bones or holds an organ of the body in place.

lig-a-ture (lĭg'å-tūr), *n.* a thing which unites or binds, as a bandage; especially, a thread or wire used to tie blood vessels in order to stop bleeding.

¹**light** (līt), *n.* **1,** the condition of illumination upon which sight depends; as, I need more *light;* **2,** anything which gives light, as the sun, a candle, etc.; **3,** also, the brightness or radiance given off by these; **4,** something like light that leads to mental clearness and understanding; as, to throw *light* on a problem; **5,** the state of being visible, especially in public; as, his sins were brought to *light;* **6,** brightness; shining quality; as, the *light* in her eyes; **7,** a famous or model person; as, he is a shining *light:*—*adj.* **1,** clear; bright; not dark; **2,** pale in color:—*v.t.* [light-ed or lit (lĭt), light-ing], **1,** to kindle, as a fire; also, to set on fire; **2,** to cause to shine and give forth brightness; as, *light* the lamp; **3,** to give brightness to; as, the lamp *lights* up the room; **4,** to furnish with, or guide by, a light; as, to *light* someone on his way:—*v.i.* to become bright; as, her face *lit* up when we praised her.

²**light** (līt), *adj.* **1,** not heavy; of little weight; as, a *light* package; **2,** not burdensome; easy to endure, understand, or do; as, a *light* loss; *light* reading; *light* tasks; **3,** delicate; also, graceful; nimble; as, a *light* step; **4,** cheerful; gay; as, a *light* heart; **5,** frivolous; fickle; **6,** small in amount; as, a *light* snowfall; **7,** of food,

easily digested; **8,** of wines, containing little alcohol; **9,** not heavily equipped; as, *light* infantry:—*v.i.* [light-ed or lit (lĭt), light-ing], to come down; settle; alight; as, the bird *lighted* on the lawn:—**make light of,** to treat as of little importance; disregard; as, to *make light of* one's troubles.—*adv.* **light'ly.**
  Syn., adj. flippant, inconstant.

¹**light-en** (līt'n), *v.t.* to make clear or bright; illumine:—*v.i.* **1,** to become bright; **2,** to shine with flashes of lightning.

²**light-en** (līt'n), *v.t.* **1,** to reduce in weight, as a load; **2,** to make less burdensome; as, her sympathy *lightened* my trouble.

¹**light-er** (līt'ẽr), *n.* a person or thing which causes something to give light or to burn; as, a lamp*lighter;* a cigarette *lighter.*

²**light-er** (līt'ẽr), *n.* a large open barge used in loading and unloading vessels:—*v.t.* to carry (goods or persons) in a lighter.

light—foot-ed (līt'=fŏŏt'ĕd), *adj.* nimble.

light-head-ed (līt'hĕd'ĕd), *adj.* **1,** dizzy; also, delirious, as from fever; **2,** thoughtless.

light-heart-ed (līt'här'tĕd), *adj.* free from care; gay; happy; cheerful; as, *lighthearted* laughter.—*adv.* **light'heart'ed-ly.**—*n.* **light'heart'ed-ness.**

light-house (līt'hous'), *n.* a tower or other structure with a brilliant light at the top to guide ships at night.

light—mind-ed (līt'=mīn'dĕd), *adj.* frivolous; silly.

¹**light-ness** (līt'nĕs), *n.* the state of being light or lighted; degree of illumination; as, the *lightness* of the cave surprised us.

LIGHTHOUSE

²**light-ness** (līt'nĕs), *n.* **1,** the state or quality of being light in weight; **2,** frivolity; **3,** delicacy; grace.

light-ning (līt'nĭng), *n.* a flash of light caused by electricity as it travels between clouds or from clouds to the earth.

lightning bug, a firefly.

lightning rod, a metal rod, fastened on a building and connected with the earth, to protect the building from lightning.

light-ship (līt'shĭp'), *n.* a vessel carrying a warning light and moored at sea in a dangerous place to warn other ships or to mark a channel.

light-some (līt'sŭm), *adj.* **1,** cheerful; lively; **2,** frivolous; **3,** nimble; lively; moving lightly; as, a bird on *lightsome* wing.

light-weight (līt'wāt'), *n.* a person who weighs less than the average; especially, a pugilist who weighs between 127 and 135 pounds:—*adj.* light in weight.

āte, āorta, râre, căt, ȧsk, fär, ăllow, sofȧ; ēve, ēvent, ĕll, writẽr, novĕl; bīte, pĭn; nō, ōbey, ôr, dŏg, tŏp, cŏllide; ūnit, ûnite, bûrn, cŭt, focŭs; nōōn, fŏŏt; mound; coin;

light–year (līt′yĭr′), *n.* the distance light travels in a year's time, equal to approximately 5,880,000,000,000 miles.

lig·nite (lĭg′nīt), *n.* a soft, brownish-black coal with a fibrous structure.

lik·a·ble or **like·a·ble** (lī′kȧ-bl), *adj.* attractive; so pleasant as to gain the liking and friendship of people.

¹like (līk) *adj.* [*comp.* lik-er, *superl.* lik-est, now chiefly poetical], **1,** in a mood for; as, I feel *like* reading; **2,** characteristic of; as, it was *like* him to be kind; **3,** giving indications of; as, it looks *like* rain; **4,** similar; exactly or nearly the same; as, in a *like* manner:—*prep.* in the manner of; as, act *like* a man:—*n.* the equal of a person or thing; as, I have never seen its *like*.

²like (līk), *v.t.* [liked, lik-ing], to have a taste for; enjoy; find agreeable:—*v.i.* to choose; prefer; as, we'll go, if you *like*:— **likes,** *n.pl.* the things one enjoys.

-like (-līk), a suffix meaning similar to; resembling; as, boy*like*, eel-*like*.

like·li·hood (līk′lĭ-hŏŏd), *n.* probability; as, in all *likelihood* we shall go.

like·ly (līk′lĭ), *adj.* [like-li-er, like-li-est], **1,** probable; believable; as, a *likely* tale; **2,** suitable; promising; as, a *likely* place for lunch; a *likely* fellow; **3,** expected; as, it is *likely* to snow today.

lik·en (lī′kĕn), *v.t.* to compare; as, I will *liken* him unto a wise man.

like·ness (līk′nĕs), *n.* **1,** resemblance; similarity; as, the *likeness* between the two brothers was amazing; **2,** a portrait; **3,** shape; external appearance; guise; as, an enemy in the *likeness* of a friend.

like·wise (līk′wīz′), *adv.* **1,** in a similar manner; as, watch him and do *likewise*; **2,** also; furthermore.

lik·ing (lī′kĭng), *n.* fondness; inclination; taste; as, I have a *liking* for books.

li·lac (lī′lăk), *n.* **1,** a shrub with clusters of white or pale-violet flowers; **2,** the flower of this shrub; **3,** the pale-violet color of the flowers.

Lille (lēl), a city in northeastern France, the scene of battles in World Wars I and II (map 12).

LILAC, def. 2

lilt (lĭlt), *n.* **1,** a lively song; **2,** rhythmic movement, as of verse:—*v.i.* and *v.t.* to sing with a gay, light rhythm.—*adj.* lilt′-ing.—*adv.* lilt′ing·ly.

lil·y (lĭl′ĭ), *n.* [*pl.* lilies], a plant with bell-shaped flowers and a bulblike root (see illustration in the next column):—*adj.* like a white lily; pure.

lil·y of the val·ley, a low-growing plant with stalks of fragrant, bell-shaped white flowers; also, the flowers.

Li·ma (lē′mä; lī′mȧ), a city, capital of Peru, South America (map 11).

Lima bean (lī′mȧ), a flat-podded bean; also, its seed, used as food.

limb (lĭm), *n.* **1,** a leg or arm of man or some other animal; also, a bird's wing; **2,** a main branch of a tree.

¹lim·ber (lĭm′bĕr), *n.* the detachable front part of a gun carriage.

²lim·ber (lĭm′bĕr), *adj.* **1,** flexible; **2,** supple; lithe:—*v.t.* and *v.i.* to make or become flexible or supple.—*n.* lim′ber-ness.

LILY OF THE VALLEY

lim·bo (lĭm′bō), *n.* **1,** the eternal abode of souls admitted neither to heaven nor to hell; **2,** a place of confinement or oblivion.

Lim·burg·er (lĭm′bûrg-ẽr), *n.* a soft, mild-flavored cheese with a strong odor.

¹lime (līm), *n.* a white, earth-like substance obtained by the action of heat upon limestone, marble, bones, sea shells, etc., and used in making cement, mortar, and the like:—*v.t.* [limed, lim-ing], to treat (land) with lime in order to sweeten it.

LIMBER

²lime (līm), *n.* a tree bearing a small, juicy, lemonlike fruit; also, its small, sour fruit.

³lime (līm), *n.* the linden, a much-used shade tree.

lime·light (līm′līt′), *n.* **1,** the brilliant light, formerly thrown upon the central figure or group on a stage, so called because it was produced by playing an intensely hot flame upon lime: also called *calcium light;* **2,** the bright glare of publicity.

lim·er·ick (lĭm′ẽr-ĭk), *n.* a nonsense poem of five lines, as:

"There was an old man of Tarentum
Who gnashed his false teeth till he bent 'em;
  And when asked for the cost
  Of what he had lost,
Said, 'I really don't know, for I rent 'em.'"

LILY

lime·stone (līm′stōn′), *n.* a rock used as

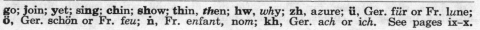

building stone, for road construction, etc. When burned it yields lime.

lime-wa-ter (līm'wô'tẽr), *n.* a solution of lime and water, used in medicine.

lim-it (līm'ĭt), *n.* **1,** a border or boundary; that which confines, ends, or checks; **2,** a point not to be passed; end; as, to reach the *limit* of one's endurance:—*v.t.* to restrict; as, his share of the profits is *limited* to 25 per cent.—*adj.* **lim'it-less.**

lim-i-ta-tion (līm'ĭ-tā'shŭn), *n.* **1,** the act of bounding or restricting; **2,** that which bounds or restrains; restriction.

lim-it-ed (līm'ĭ-tĕd), *adj.* restricted; confined:—*n.* an express train, sometimes made up of Pullman cars only.

limn (līm), *v.t.* [limned (līmd), lim-ning (līm'nĭng; līm'ĭng)], to paint or draw; portray.

lim-ou-sine (līm'ŏŏ-zēn'), *n.* a large automobile, often with a passenger compartment separated from the driver's seat.

¹limp (līmp), *n.* a lame, halting motion in walking:—*v.i.* to walk lamely.

²limp (līmp), *adj.* not stiff or firm.—*adv.* **limp'ly.**—*n.* **limp'ness.**

lim-pet (līm'pĕt), *n.* a shellfish with a flat, cone-shaped shell, found sticking tightly to rocks or piles.

lim-pid (līm'pĭd), *adj.* transparent; sparklingly clear; as, a *limpid* pool.

LIMPET SHELL

linch-pin (līnch'pĭn'), *n.* an iron pin through the end of an axle to keep the wheel from coming off.

¹Lin-coln (līng'kŭn), Abraham (1809–1865), the 16th president of the U.S., assassinated by John Wilkes Booth.

²Lin-coln (līng'kŭn), a city, capital of Nebraska (map 7).

Lind-bergh (līnd'bûrg), Charles Augustus (1902–   ), an American aviator who made the first nonstop flight from New York to Paris, in 1927.

lin-den (līn'dĕn), *n.* a large tree with heart-shaped leaves and small clusters of cream-colored flowers; the basswood: also called *lime.*

LINDEN
Leaves and fruit.

¹line (līn), *n.* **1,** a mark having length, but very little width, made with pen, pencil, or the like; **2,** a wrinkle, as in the skin; crease; **3,** a strong, slender string, cord, or the like; as, a clothes*line;* also, a wire of a telephone or telegraph system; **4,** a boundary; as, they crossed the *line* into Canada; also, a limit; **5,** a plan or method; course of action or thought; as, a *line* of reasoning; **6,** a succession of persons or objects that form a line or row; as, a long waiting *line;* a *line* of tents; **7,** a profession; branch of business; as, the restaurant *line;* **8,** a row of printed or written letters or words; **9,** family; descent; as, a *line* of kings; **10,** vehicles, cars, trains, ships, etc., making up a system of transportation; also, direction; route; as, a *line* of travel; **11,** outline; shape; as, the *line* of the face; **12, lines,** the words of a part in a play; as, the actors were not sure of their *lines:*—*v.t.* [lined, lin-ing], **1,** to draw lines upon; **2,** to form or make a line along; as, roses *line* the path; **3,** to arrange in a line, as soldiers:—*v.i.* to form a row.

²line (līn), *v.t.* [lined, lin-ing], to provide with an inside covering; as, to *line* curtains; to *line* a coat.—*n.* **lin'er.**

lin-e-age (līn'ē-ĭj), *n.* the line of one's ancestors; also, all the descendants of one ancestor.

lin-e-al (līn'ē-ăl), *adj.* **1,** pertaining to direct descent from an ancestor; as, *lineal* heirs; **2,** linear.—*adv.* **lin'e-al-ly.**

lin-e-a-ment (līn'ē-a-mĕnt), *n.* [often *lineaments*], a feature; the features; profile.

lin-e-ar (līn'ē-ẽr), *adj.* **1,** pertaining to, or composed of, lines; **2,** having, or pertaining to, length only; as, *linear* measure.

line-man (līn'măn), *n.* [*pl.* linemen (-mĕn)], *n.* **1,** a man who puts up and repairs telephone or telegraph wires; **2,** an inspector of railroad tracks; **3,** one who carries the tape, line, or chain in surveying; **4,** in football, one who plays in the front line.

lin-en (līn'ĕn), *n.* **1,** thread spun from flax; **2,** the material made of this thread; **3,** articles made of this material, as napkins, towels, collars, etc.:—*adj.* made of linen.

lin-er (līn'ẽr), *n.* **1,** a large swift ship or airplane belonging to a regular system of transport; **2,** one who or that which draws or paints lines; **3,** in baseball, a ball which, when hit, flies through the air almost parallel to the ground, and not far above it.

lines-man (līnz'măn), *n.* [*pl.* linesmen (-mĕn)], **1,** one who puts up or repairs telephone or telegraph lines; **2,** in football, an official who records the distance gained or lost in each play; **3,** in tennis, an official who decides whether the ball lands inside or outside the boundary lines of the court.

line–up (līn'ŭp'), *n.* **1.** persons arranged in a line, as for identification; **2.** the arrangement of football players just before a play; **3**, *Colloquial*, any such grouping.

lin·ger (lĭng′gẽr), *v.i.* to delay; loiter.

lin·ge·rie (lăn′zhē-rē′; popularly, län′zhē-rē), *n.* women's undergarments.

lin·go (lĭng′gō), *n.* [*pl.* lingoes], dialect; often, humorously, any queer speech; jargon; as, baseball *lingo*.

lin·guist (lĭng′gwĭst), *n.* a person who knows many languages.

lin·guis·tic (lĭng-gwĭs′tĭk), *adj.* pertaining to the study of language and languages:— **linguistics,** *n.pl.* the science of languages.

lin·i·ment (lĭn′ĭ-mĕnt), *n.* a healing or stimulating liquid rubbed on the skin.

lin·ing (lī′nĭng), *n.* an inside covering; also, material of which such a covering is made.

link (lĭngk), *n.* **1**, a single loop or division of a chain; **2**, anything that serves to connect the parts of a series; a tie; connection; as, the present is the *link* between the future and the past:—*v.t.* and *v.i.* to connect, or be connected, by a link, as facts.

links (lĭngks), *n.pl.* a golf course.

Lin·nae·us (lĭ-nē′ŭs), Carolus (1707–1778), a Swedish botanist, the first to develop the principles of biological classification.

lin·net (lĭn′ĕt), *n.* a small songbird of the finch family, common in Europe.

LINNET (⅓)

li·no·le·um (lĭ-nō′lē-ŭm), *n.* a floor covering made of a hardened mixture of ground cork and linseed oil on a backing of burlap or canvas.

Lin·o·type (lī′nō-tīp), *n.* a trade-mark name for a kind of typesetting machine which casts each line of type in one piece: —**linotype,** a machine bearing this trade name:—*v.t.* [linotyped, linotyp-ing], to set in type by means of such a machine:—*v.i.* to operate such a machine.

lin·seed (lĭn′sēd′), *n.* the seed of flax.

linseed oil, a pale-yellow oil pressed from flaxseed, used in paint, linoleum, etc.

lin·sey–wool·sey (lĭn′zĭ-wool′zĭ), *n.* a coarse cloth of wool with an admixture of linen or cotton.

lint (lĭnt), *n.* **1**, the soft down obtained by scraping linen, used for dressing wounds; **2**, ravelings from textiles.

LINTEL (L)

lin·tel (lĭn′tĕl), *n.* the horizontal piece of wood, stone, or the like over the top of a door frame or a window frame to support the structure above it.

li·on (lī′ŭn), *n.* **1**, a powerful, flesh-eating mammal of the cat family, found in Africa and southern Asia; **2**, a celebrated person who is much sought after by society.—*n. fem.* **li′on·ess.**

LION AND LIONESS (₆¹₀)

lip (lĭp), *n.* **1**, one of the two fleshy borders of the mouth; **2**, the rim of a hollow vessel; as, the *lip* of a cup:— **lip service,** something spoken but not felt.

lip·stick (lĭp′stĭk), *n.* a cosmetic preparation, usually encased in a tube, used for coloring the lips.

liq. abbreviation for *liquid, liquor.*

liq·ue·fac·tion (lĭk′wē-făk′shŭn), *n.* the changing of a solid or gas into liquid form.

liq·ue·fy (lĭk′wȧ-fī), *v.t.* [liquefied, liquefy-ing], to change into a liquid; as, to *liquefy* wax:—*v.i.* to become liquid.

li·queur (lē-kûr′; lĭ-kūr′), *n.* a strong alcoholic drink, sweetened and variously flavored; a cordial.

liq·uid (lĭk′wĭd), *adj.* **1**, not solid; freely flowing; **2**, pure and clear, or smooth and flowing in sound; as, *liquid* tones; **3**, in finance, easily and quickly salable for cash; as, *liquid* assets:—*n.* **1**, a liquid substance; **2**, either of the consonants *l* and *r*:—**liquid measure,** a system of measuring liquids, as by quarts or liters.—*n.* **li·quid′i·ty.**

liq·ui·date (lĭk′wĭ-dāt), *v.t.* [liquidat-ed, liquidat-ing], **1**, to settle the affairs of (a business, estate, etc.) by turning the assets into cash, paying the debts in whatever proportion may be possible, and dividing what is left among the owners; **2**, to pay off or settle, as a debt; **3**, to render harmless, as an enemy or rival; hence, to kill, especially by secret or violent means:—*v.i.* to wind up a business.—*n.* **liq′ui·da′tion.**

liq·uor (lĭk′ẽr), *n.* any liquid substance; especially, an alcoholic drink.

li·ra (lē′rä), *n.* [*pl.* lire (lē′rā) or liras], **1**, the monetary unit of Italy; **2**, the monetary unit of Turkey. (See Table, page 943.)

Lis·bon (lĭz′bŭn), [Portuguese **Lis·bo·a** (lēzh-bō′ä)], a city, capital of Portugal (map 12).

lisle (līl), *n.* a fine, hard-twisted cotton thread, or a fabric knitted from it, used especially for stockings, gloves, etc.

lisp (lĭsp), *v.i.* and *v.t.* to pronounce (*s* and *z*) incorrectly with the sound of *th*:—*n.* the pronunciation of *s* and *z* as *th*.

lis·some or **lis·som** (lĭs′ŭm), *adj.* nimble; swift and light in motion; lithe.

---

go; join; yet; sing; chin; show; thin, *th*en; hw, *wh*y; zh, a*z*ure; ü, Ger. für or Fr. lune; ö, Ger. schön or Fr. feu; ṅ, Fr. e*n*fant, no*m*; kh, Ger. a*ch* or i*ch*. See pages ix–x.

¹list (lĭst), *n*. **1,** a series of names, items, etc.; a catalog, roll, or register; **2,** an edge or selvage of cloth:—*v.t.* to catalog, register, or enroll.

²list (lĭst), *v.i.* to tilt toward one side, as a ship:—*n*. a leaning to one side, as of a ship.

³list (lĭst), *Archaic, v.i.* and *v.t.* to listen or hearken (to); hear.

⁴list (lĭst), *Archaic* or *Poetic, v.i.* [*p.t.* list-ed or list, *p.p.* list-ed, *p.pr.* list-ing], to please; choose; as, "the wind bloweth where it *listeth.*"

lis-ten (lĭs'n), *v.i.* **1,** to attend closely, so as to hear; hearken; **2,** to heed; obey.—*n*. **lis'ten-er.**

Lis-ter (lĭs'tẽr), Sir Joseph (1827–1912), an English surgeon, who was the first to develop and practice antiseptic surgery.

list-less (lĭst'lĕs), *adj.* lacking energy or interest; spiritless.—*adv.* **list'less-ly.**—*n*. **list'less-ness.**

lists (lĭsts), *n.pl.* in days of old, the barriers of a field where tournaments were held; hence, now, any place of contest.

Liszt (lĭst), Franz (1811–1886), a Hungarian pianist and composer.

¹lit (lĭt), one form of the past tense and past participle of ¹*light* or ²*light.*

²lit (lĭt) *n*. the monetary unit of Lithuania before its admission into the Soviet Union. Also, **li'tas** (lē'täs), [*pl.* litai (lē'tä)].

lit. abbreviation for *liter, literature.*

lit-a-ny (lĭt'á-nĭ), *n*. [*pl.* litanies], a certain form of prayer; especially, in a church service, a responsive prayer in which the clergyman repeats a series of petitions to which the congregation makes responses.

li-ter or **li-tre** (lē'tẽr), *n*. a metric unit of capacity equal to 1.0567 quarts liquid measure, or .9081 quart dry measure.

lit-er-a-cy (lĭt'ẽr-á-sĭ), *n*. the ability to read and write.

lit-er-al (lĭt'ẽr-ăl), *adj.* **1,** following the given words; exact; as, a *literal* translation; **2,** precise; not exaggerated; as, the *literal* truth; **3,** matter-of-fact.—*adv.* **lit'er-al-ly.**—*n*. **lit'er-al-ness.**

lit-er-ar-y (lĭt'ẽr-ẽr'ĭ), *adj.* relating to literature or to men of letters.

lit-er-ate (lĭt'ẽr-ĭt), *adj.* able to read and write; also, having a knowledge of literature; educated:—*n*. one who is able to read and write.

lit-er-a-ture (lĭt'ẽr-á-tůr), *n*. **1,** the written or printed productions of a country or period; especially, such poetry or prose as is notable for beauty of matter, style, etc.; **2,** the occupation of authors; **3,** the body of writings on a given subject; as, the *literature* of music; advertising *literature.*

lithe (lī*th*), *adj.* [lith-er (lī*th*'ẽr), lith-est (lī*th*'ĕst)], bending easily; supple.—*adj.* **lithe'some.**—*n*. **lithe'ness.**

lith-o-graph (lĭth'ō-gråf), *n*. a reproduction of a design drawn with greasy crayon or ink on a smooth, flat stone and etched into the stone:—*v.t.* to print from a stone.—*adj.* **lith'o-graph'ic.** —*n*. **li-thog'ra-phy** (lĭ-thŏg'rá-fĭ).—*n*. **li-thog'ra-pher** (lĭ-thŏg'rá-fẽr).

Lith-u-a-ni-a (lĭth'ū-ā'nĭ-á), a former European republic (cap. Vilna) on the Baltic Sea (map **12**). It was admitted into the Soviet Union in 1940.—*n*. and *adj.* **Lith'u-a'ni-an.**

Lith-u-a-ni-an So-vi-et So-cial-ist Re-pub-lic, Lithuania.

lit-i-gant (lĭt'ĭ-gǎnt), *n*. either party in a lawsuit:—*adj.* engaged in a lawsuit.

lit-i-ga-tion (lĭt'ĭ-gā'shŭn), *n*. the act or process of carrying on a lawsuit; also, a lawsuit.

lit-mus (lĭt'mŭs), *n*. a violet-blue dye obtained from lichens, which is turned red by an acid. It can then be turned back to blue by an alkali.

Litt.D. abbreviation for *Doctor of Letters.*

lit-ter (lĭt'ẽr), *n*. **1,** a couch with a canopy, borne on men's shoulders by means of long shafts; **2,** a cot or stretcher for carrying a sick or wounded person; **3,** straw, hay, or the like, used as

ROMAN LITTER

bedding for animals; **4,** odds and ends scattered about; **5,** young born at one time to pigs, dogs, etc; as, a *litter* of puppies:—*v.t.* **1,** to supply, as with straw, for bedding; **2,** to make (a place) untidy by scattering odds and ends about:—*v.i.* to bring forth young.

lit-tle (lĭt'l), *adj.* [*comp.* less, lesser or, *Colloquial,* lit-tler, *superl.* least or, *Colloquial,* lit-tlest], **1,** small in size or quantity; **2,** small in dignity or importance; **3,** brief in time; as, a *little* while; **4,** petty; mean; as, a *little* mind:—*adv.* in small degree; not much:—*n*. a small quantity.—*n*. **lit'tle-ness.**

Little Bear, a group of seven stars, containing the North Star, situated in the northern heavens: also called *Little Dipper.*

Little Rock, a city, capital of Arkansas, in south central U.S. (map **8**).

lit-ur-gy (lĭt'ẽr-jĭ), *n*. [*pl.* liturgies], in some Christian churches, a set form of service for public worship.

liv-a-ble (lĭv'á-bl), *adj.* **1,** fit or agreeable

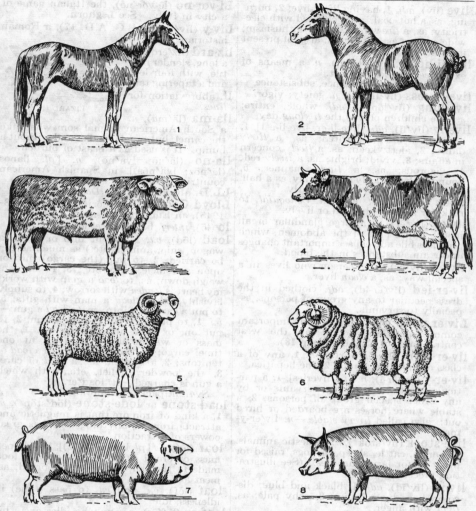

REPRESENTATIVE TYPES OF LIVESTOCK

1. DRIVING HORSE.—Tall; slender, sinewy legs; narrow but deep chest; graceful neck. **2. DRAFT HORSE.**—Stocky; heavy; strong shoulders and hips; short, muscular legs; short neck; wide chest. **3. BEEF STEER.**—Rectangular body; bones well covered; neck and legs short. **4. MILK COW.**—Pyramidal body, sloping toward rear; hip bones prominent; udder large. **5. MUTTON SHEEP.**—Plump; low-built; wide back; long, coarse fleece. **6. WOOL SHEEP.**—Thinner body; wrinkled skin; fine fleece. **7. LARD HOG.**—Chunky; fat; short legs. **8. BACON HOG.**—Rangy; firm, lean flesh; long legs.

to live in or with; **2,** endurable; as, such a life is hardly *livable.*

¹**live** (lĭv), *v.i.* [lived, liv-ing], **1,** to exist, or have life; **2,** to reside or dwell; as, to *live* in the woods; **3,** to continue to have life; as, to *live* to be old; **4,** to pass life in a particular manner; as, to *live* happily; **5,** to win a livelihood; as, to *live* by hard work; **6,** to be nourished; as, to *live* on meat:—*v.t.* to pass or spend; as, to *live* a happy life:— **live down,** to live in such a manner as to wipe out the memory of (a past mistake).

go; join; yet; sing; chin; show; thin, *th*en; **hw,** *wh*y; **zh,** azure; **ü,** Ger. *für* or Fr. *lune;* **ö,** Ger. *schön* or Fr. *feu;* **ṅ,** Fr. *enfant,* nom; **kh,** Ger. *ach* or *ich.* See pages ix-x.

²**live** (līv), *adj.* **1,** having life; alive; **2,** burning, as a hot coal; also, charged with electricity; as, a *live* wire; **3,** full of enthusiasm; wide-awake; as, a *live* club; also, of present interest; as, a *live* subject.

live-li-hood (līv′lĭ-hood), *n.* a means of existence; regular support.
  Syn. living, maintenance, subsistence.

live-li-ness (līv′lĭ-nĕs), *n.* gaiety; vigor.

live-long (lĭv′lông′), *adj.* whole; entire; as, the children played the *livelong* day.

live-ly (līv′lĭ), *adj.* [live-li-er, live-li-est], **1,** animated; brisk; spirited; as, a *lively* dance; **2,** alert; keen; as, a *lively* concern in affairs; **3,** vivid; bright; as, a *lively* red; **4,** vigorous; as, a *lively* manner; **5,** bounding back easily and quickly, as a ball.
  Syn. merry, sportive, sprightly.

liv-en (lĭv′ĕn), *v.t.* and *v.i. Colloquial,* to make or become cheerful or lively.

¹**liv-er** (lĭv′ẽr), *n.* a large glandular organ in the upper part of the abdomen, which produces bile and causes important changes in certain substances in the blood.

²**liv-er** (lĭv′ẽr), *n.* a person who lives in a special way; as, a *clean* liver.

liv-er-ied (lĭv′ẽr-ĭd), *adj.* clothed in the dress peculiar to any group of persons, especially to servants.

Liv-er-pool (lĭv′ẽr-pool), an important commercial seaport city on the west central coast of England (map **13**).

liv-er-wort (lĭv′ẽr-wûrt′), *n.* **1,** any of a class of mosslike plants; **2,** the hepatica.

liv-er-y (lĭv′ẽr-ĭ), *n.* [*pl.* liveries], **1,** a particular costume worn by servants or by any other special group of persons; **2,** a stable where horses are boarded or hired out: also called *livery stable.—n.* **liv′er-y-man.**

live-stock (līv′stŏk′), *n.* domestic animals, as horses, cattle, sheep, or hogs, raised for profit or for farm purposes. (See illustration preceding page.)

liv-id (lĭv′ĭd), *adj.* **1,** black and blue; discolored, as by a bruise; **2,** ashy pale; as, *livid* with anger.

liv-ing (lĭv′ĭng), *adj.* **1,** having life; alive; as, *living* beings; **2,** now existent; now in use; as, French is a *living* language; **3,** vigorous; active; as, a *living* hope; a *living* faith; **4,** exact; very; as, he is the *living* image of his father:—**the living,** all who are alive:—*n.* **1,** state of existence; **2,** mode of life; as, plain *living*; **3,** livelihood; as, to earn a *living*; **4,** in England, a church appointment.

Liv-ing-stone (lĭv′ĭng-stŭn), David (1813–1873), a famous Scottish missionary and explorer in Africa.

Li-vor-no (lē-vôr′nō), the Italian name of a city in Italy. See **Leghorn.**

Liv-y (lĭv′ĭ), (59 B.C.–A.D. 17), a Roman historian.

liz-ard (lĭz′ẽrd), *n.* a long, slender reptile, with four legs and a tapering tail.

LIZARD (!)

ll. abbreviation for *lines.*

lla-ma (lä′må), *n.* a South American animal somewhat like the camel, but much smaller and without a hump. It is used as a beast of burden.

lla-no (lä′nō; lyä′nō), *n.* [*pl.* llanos (lä′nōz; lyä′nōs)], in Spanish American countries, a broad, grassy plain.

LL.D. abbreviation for *Doctor of Laws.*

Lloyd George (loid′ jôrj′), David (1863–1945), an English statesman.

lo (lō), *interj.* behold! see! look!

load (lōd), *v.t.* **1,** to put into or upon (a wagon, ship, animal, etc.) as much as can be carried; **2,** to put (the cargo) into or upon a vehicle, ship, etc.; **3,** to burden; weigh down; as, to *load* a man with work; my heart is *loaded* with sorrow; **4,** to supply lavishly; as, to *load* a man with gifts; **5,** to put a cartridge into; as, to *load* a gun;—*v.i.* **1,** to put a cartridge into a gun; **2,** to put on, or take on, a cargo:—*n.* **1,** the mass or weight usually carried at one time; cargo; as, this truck carries a *load* of ten tons; **2,** a burden; as, a *load* of care; **3,** the powder, bullet, etc., with which a gun is charged.—*n.* **load′er.**
  Syn., n. pack, encumbrance.

load-stone or **lode-stone** (lōd′stōn′), *n.* **1,** a kind of iron ore that is magnetic and attracts iron; **2,** anything that has great powers of attraction.

¹**loaf** (lōf), *n.* [*pl* loaves (lōvz)], **1,** a shaped mass of bread or cake; **2,** a dish of food made in the shape of a loaf of bread; as, meat *loaf.*

²**loaf** (lōf), *v.i.* and *v.t.* to pass (time) in idleness; idle.

loaf-er (lōf′ẽr), *n.* one who idles away his time; a lazy idler.

loam (lōm), *n.* a fertile soil of clay mixed with sand and decayed vegetable matter.

loan (lōn), *n.* **1,** something that is borrowed or lent; especially, a sum of money borrowed to be returned with or without interest; **2,** the act of lending; as, the *loan* of a coat:—*v.t.* and *v.i.* to lend.

loath or **loth** (lōth), *adj.* unwilling; reluctant; as, I was *loath* to go.
  Syn. indisposed, averse, disinclined.

loathe (lōth), *v.t.* [loathed, loath-ing], to

regard with extreme dislike or disgust; detest; as, I *loathed* the sight of food when I was seasick.—*n.* **loath′ing.**

loath-some (lō*th*′sŭm), *adj.* causing disgust; detestable; as, a *loathsome* disease. *Syn.* revolting, offensive.

loaves (lōvz), plural of ¹*loaf.*

lob-by (lŏb′ĭ), *n.* [*pl.* lobbies], **1,** a hall or waiting room; **2,** persons who try to influence the votes of members of a lawmaking body:—*v.i.* [lobbied, lobby-ing], to try by personal influence to get the votes of members of a legislature for a particular measure.—*n.* **lob′by-ist.**

lobe (lōb), *n.* any rounded projection or part; as, the *lobe* of the ear.

 LOBE (L) OF EAR

lo-be-li-a (lō-bē′lĭ-a̤; lō-bēl′ya̤), *n.* a plant with red, blue, or white flowers.

lob-lol-ly (lŏb′lŏl′ĭ), *n.* [*pl.* loblollies], a pine of the southern U.S., with coarse bark and long leaves; also, its wood.

lob-ster (lŏb′stẽr), *n.* a large shellfish with five pairs of legs, the first developed into powerful pincers (see illustration below).

lo-cal (lō′kăl), *adj.* **1,** relating to a particular place or places; as, *local* customs; **2,** limited to a certain part of the body; as, a *local* sprain; **3,** of a train, making all stops; **4,** serving a limited district; as, a *local* ⬤as company:—*n.* a train which stops at all stations on a given route.

LOBELIA

lo-cal-ism (lō′kăl-ĭzm), *n.* **1,** a word, expression, or custom used in a particular region; **2,** attachment to, or interest in, one's own locality.

lo-cal-i-ty (lō-kăl′ĭ-tĭ), *n.* [*pl.* localities], a general region, place, or district; neighborhood.

lo-cal-ize (lō′kăl-īz), *v.t.* [localized, localiz-ing], to restrict to a particular place; as, the rheumatic pains were *localized* in his knees.

lo-cal-ly (lō′kăl-ĭ), *adv.* with respect to a particular place or region; as, *locally* this tree is called by another name.

LOBSTER (¹⁄₂)

Lo-car-no (lō-kär′nō), a town in southeastern Switzerland on Lake Maggiore, where a series of peace treaties was drawn up in 1925.

lo-cate (lō′kāt; lō-kāt′), *v.t.* [locat-ed, locating], **1,** to settle in a particular spot; as,

the firm *located* its office in Chicago; **2,** to mark out and determine the position of; as, to *locate* a gold mine; **3,** to find the position of; as, to *locate* the enemy:— *v.i. Colloquial,* to settle in a place.

lo-ca-tion (lō-kā′shŭn), *n.* **1,** the act of locating; **2,** position or place; as, this is a good *location* for a store; **3,** a piece of land marked out for a particular use; **4,** a site, outside a studio, on which a photoplay is filmed.

loch (lŏkh), *n. Scottish,* a lake; also, a bay or arm of the sea.

Loch-in-var (lŏkh′ĭn-vär′), the hero of a ballad in Scott's "Marmion," who boldly carries off his sweetheart as she is about to be married to another man.

¹**lock** (lŏk), *n.* **1,** a curl or tress of hair; **2,** a tuft of wool, silk, or the like.

²**lock** (lŏk), *n.* **1,** a device for fastening a door, trunk, safe, etc., so that it can be opened only by a special key or a combination of turns of a knob; **2,** an enclosure between two gates in a canal or stream, used in raising or lowering boats from one water level to another; **3,** the mechanism used to fire a gun:—*v.t.* **1,** to fasten or secure with, or as with, a lock; as, to *lock* a safe; **2,** to make secure; to confine; to shut in, out, or up; as, to *lock* up a criminal; **3,** to make fast or rigid by the linking of parts; as, to *lock* the wheels of a truck:— *v.i.* to become locked; as, the door *locks* automatically.

lock-er (lŏk′ẽr), *n.* a drawer or compartment secured by a lock; especially, a cupboard for individual use.

lock-et (lŏk′ĕt), *n.* a small, ornamental, hinged case, usually of gold or silver, made to hold a portrait or other small token, and to be worn on a necklace or chain.

LOCKERS

lock-jaw (lŏk′jô), *n.* a form of the disease tetanus, in which the jaws become firmly locked together.

lock-out (lŏk′out′), *n.* the refusal of an employer to allow his workmen to enter their place of employment, unless they accept his terms.

lock-smith (lŏk′smĭth′), *n.* a maker or repairer of locks.

LOCKET

lock-up (lŏk′ŭp′), *n.* a jail.

lo-co-mo-tion (lō′kŏ-mō′shŭn), *n.* **1,** the act of moving, or ability to move, from place to place; **2,** travel; methods of travel.

lo·co·mo·tive (lō´kō-mō´tĭv), *adj.* relating to a machine that moves about under its

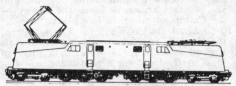

ELECTRIC LOCOMOTIVE

own power:—*n.* a steam or electric engine for drawing railway cars.

lo·co·weed (lō´kō-wēd´), *n.* a poisonous plant of the western U.S., which produces a nervous disease in the horses, cattle, and sheep which eat it.

lo·cust (lō´kŭst), *n.* 1, a grasshopper; especially, one of a certain kind, destructive to vegetation, which migrates in great swarms; 2, a cicada or seventeen-year locust; 3, a large North American tree, especially the common locust, or false acacia, having rough bark and yellow-white flowers (see illustration, page 864); also, its wood; 4, any of several other trees, as the honey locust.

LOCOWEED

lode (lōd), *n.* 1, any deposit of metallic ore containing gold, silver, etc., found in a vein or crack in a rock; 2, a vein filled with ore.

LOCUST (!)

lode·star (lōd´stär´), *n.* 1, a guiding star; especially, the polestar, or North Star; 2, hence, anything that strongly influences or attracts. Also spelled **load´star´**.

lode·stone (lōd´stōn´), *n.* a magnetic stone; loadstone. See **loadstone**.

lodge (lŏj), *v.t.* [lodged, lodg-ing], 1, to furnish with a temporary dwelling; 2, to deposit for safety; 3, to settle, or bring to rest, in some spot; as, the stone was *lodged* on a ledge; 4, to place formally before the proper authorities; as, to *lodge* a complaint:—*v.i.* 1, to be deposited or come to rest; 2, to be a lodger:—*n.* 1, a small house; cottage; 2, the den of a wild animal or group of animals; 3, a place where members of a local branch of a society meet; also, the members themselves.

lodg·er (lŏj´ẽr), *n.* one who lives in a rented room or apartment in another's house.

lodg·ing (lŏj´ĭng), *n.* 1, a place to sleep; as, *lodging* for the night; 2, **lodgings**, a room or rooms rented as living quarters.

lodg·ment or **lodge·ment** (lŏj´mĕnt), *n.* 1, the act of lodging or the state of being lodged; as, the *lodgment* of a complaint; 2, a collection of material deposited; as, a *lodgment* of mud in a hollow of rock.

Lódź (looj), [Russian **Lodz** (lôdz)], a city, capital of the province of Lódź, in western Poland (map **12**).

loft (lôft), *n.* 1, a room directly beneath a roof; an attic; 2, a floor or gallery above the main floor; as, a *loft* for hay in a barn; an organ *loft* in a church; 3, an upper floor in a warehouse or business building.

loft·i·ness (lôf´tĭ-nĕs), *n.* 1, height or elevation; 2, elevation of character, feeling, dignity, rank, style, etc.; grandeur; haughtiness.

loft·y (lôf´tĭ), *adj.* [loft-i-er, loft-i-est], 1, very high; as, a *lofty* spire; 2, dignified; proud; as, a *lofty* manner; 3, elevated in thought or language; as, *lofty* sentiments. —*adv.* **loft´i·ly**.

Syn. sublime, stately, haughty.

log (lŏg), *n.* 1, a bulky piece of felled timber, usually in its natural or unhewed state; 2, a heavy, stupid person; 3, a device consisting of a wooden float on a line and reel, used for measuring the speed of a ship through the water; 4, a book in which the record of a ship's daily progress and other items of interest are entered: also called *logbook*:—*v.t.* [logged, log-ging], 1, to fell and cut into logs, as a tree; 2, to fell and remove the timber on (a tract of woodland); 3, to enter in the logbook of a ship:—*v.i.* to cut or transport logs.

lo·gan·ber·ry (lō´găn-bĕr´ĭ), *n.* [*pl.* loganberries], 1, a plant obtained by crossing the raspberry with the blackberry; 2, the fruit of this plant.

log·a·rithm (lŏg´à-rĭthm; lŏg´à-rĭthm), *n.* 1, a figure that shows how many times a number (for ordinary uses, ten) must be multiplied by itself to produce a given number; as, the *logarithm* of 1,000 to ten is three; 2, one of a system of such numbers used to shorten arithmetical processes.

LOGANBERRY
Leaves and fruit.

log·book (lŏg´bŏŏk´), *n.* a ship's diary, or journal, recording its progress, position, daily occurrences, etc.: also called *log*.

log·ger·head (lŏg´ẽr-hĕd´), *n.* 1, a numskull; blockhead; 2, a large sea turtle:—**at loggerheads**, disagreeing; quarreling.

log·ging (lŏg´ĭng), *n.* the business of cutting down trees and getting the logs to lumber mills or to market.

log-ic (lŏj'ĭk), *n.* **1,** the science or art of reasoning; **2,** correct reasoning.

log-i-cal (lŏj'ĭ-kăl), *adj.* **1,** relating to reasoning; **2,** according to the rules of correct reasoning; as, a *logical* conclusion; reasonable; as, a *logical* explanation; **3,** skilled in reasoning; as, a *logical* thinker.

lo-gi-cian (lō-jĭsh'ăn), *n.* one skilled in the science of correct reasoning.

log-roll-ing (lŏg'rōl'ĭng), *n.* in politics, a uniting to assist in furthering the schemes of others in the expectation of receiving assistance in return.

loin (loin), *n.* **1,** that part of the body of an animal or man, on either side of the spine, between the lowest rib and the hip bone; **2,** a special cut of meat from this part of an animal (see illustration under *beef*).

Loire (lwär), a river of northern France, flowing into the Bay of Biscay (map 12).

loi-ter (loi'tẽr), *v.i.* to linger; saunter; as, don't *loiter* on your way home from school: —*v.t.* to spend idly; as, he *loitered* his time away.—*n.* **loi'ter-er.**

Lo-ki (lō'kĕ), *n.* in Norse mythology, the god of evil and mischief, who lived with the other gods and disturbed their peace.

loll (lŏl), *v.i.* **1,** to lounge at ease; as, to *loll* in a chair; **2,** to hang out loosely, as the tongue of an animal:—*v.t.* to permit (the tongue) to hang out.

lol-li-pop (lŏl'ĭ-pŏp), *n.* a lump of hard candy on a stick.

Lom-bard (lŏm'bẽrd; lŭm'bẽrd), *n.* a member of a Germanic tribe that invaded Italy in the sixth century and established the kingdom from which Lombardy gets its name; also, a native of that region.

Lom-bar-dy (lŏm'bẽr-dĭ; lŭm'bẽr-dĭ), a region (cap. Milan) of northern Italy.

Lo-mond, Loch (lō'mŭnd), a large lake in Scotland, famous in song and story.

Lon-don (lŭn'dŭn), a city (and county) of southeastern England, on the Thames River, capital of the United Kingdom and of the British Empire (map 13).

lone (lōn), *adj.* **1,** solitary; as, a *lone* star in the sky; **2,** unfrequented; as, a *lone* road.

lone-li-ness (lōn'lĭ-nĕs), *n.* **1,** the state of being solitary; solitude; **2,** low spirits due to lack of companionship.

lone-ly (lōn'lĭ), *adj.* [lone-li-er, lone-li-est], **1,** solitary; without companions; as, a *lonely* traveler; **2,** not often visited; as, a *lonely* valley; **3,** depressed because alone.

lone-some (lōn'sŭm), *adj.* [lonesom-er, lonesom-est], **1,** lonely; depressed because alone; as, to feel *lonesome;* **2,** desolate; not often visited; as, a *lonesome* place.—*adv.* **lone'some-ly.**—*n.* **lone'some-ness.**

lon. or **long.** abbreviation for *longitude.*

¹long (lông), *adj.* **1,** not short; covering great distance from end to end; as, a *long* road; **2,** extended in time; not brief; as, a *long* wait; **3,** far-reaching; as, a *long* memory; **4,** extended (to a specified measure) in space or time; as, a yard *long;* an hour *long;* **5,** of a vowel: **a,** sounded like its name: as, the *long a* in "hate," the *long e* in "eve," the *long u* in "use," etc.; **b,** taking more time to pronounce than the corresponding short sound, as the vowel in "palm" compared with the corresponding short vowel in "what":—*adv.* **1,** to a great length or extent; as, something *long* drawn out; **2,** at a distant point in time; as, *long* before the war; **3,** for a long time; as, to wait *long.*

²long (lông), *v.i.* to desire something eagerly; yearn; as, I *long* to go.

Long Beach, a commercial city and resort in southwestern California (map 9).

lon-gev-i-ty (lŏn-jĕv'ĭ-tĭ), *n.* great length of life.

Long-fel-low (lông'fĕl'ō), Henry Wadsworth (1807–1882), a famous American poet.

long-hand (lông'hănd'), *n.* ordinary handwriting, not shorthand or typewriting.

long-ing (lông'ĭng), *n.* an earnest desire; wish; as, a *longing* for wealth.—*adv.* **long'-ing-ly.**

Syn. craving, aspiration.

Long Is-land, an island southeast of New York, part of the State of New York:—**Long Island Sound,** a body of water between Connecticut and Long Island. (Map 6.)

lon-gi-tude (lŏn'jĭ-tūd), *n.* distance east or west on the earth's surface, measured in degrees, from the meridian of Greenwich, England.

lon-gi-tu-di-nal (lŏn'jĭ-tū'dĭ-năl), *adj.* **1,** relating to longitude or to length; **2,** running lengthwise; as, *longitudinal* veins on the wings of an insect.

long-play, *adj.* of phonograph records, made to be played at a speed of 33⅓ revolutions per minute. Also, **L.P.**

long-shore-man (lông'shôr'măn), *n.* [*pl.* longshoremen (-mĕn)], one who works about wharves, as in loading and unloading ships.

long-suf-fer-ing (lông'sŭf'ẽr-ĭng), *adj.* patient under injury or offense:—*n.* patience under injury.

long-wind-ed (lông'wĭn'dĕd), *adj.* tedious; long drawn out; tiresome.

look (look), *v.i.* **1,** to direct the eyes upon something; as, to *look* at a picture; **2,** to front or face; as, my windows *look* out on a garden; **3,** to appear; as, she *looks* happy; **4,** to pay attention; take care; as, *look* before you leap:—*v.t.* **1,** to show by an expression of the face; as, he *looked* his contempt; **2,** to regard or survey with the eyes; as, he *looked* the boy up and down:— *n.* **1,** the act of looking; glance; as, I took a *look* at the picture; **2,** (often *looks*), appearance; **3,** expression of face.

look for, **1,** to expect; **2,** to search for; **look forward to,** to anticipate with pleasure; **look on,** to regard; **look over,** to inspect; **look up, 1,** search for; **2,** *Colloquial,* to improve, as business conditions.

look·er-on (lŏŏk′ẽr-ŏn′), *n.* [*pl.* lookerson], a bystander; an observer.

look·ing glass, a mirror.

look·out (lŏŏk′out′), *n.* **1,** the act of watching for someone to come or something to happen; **2,** a place for watching; **3,** a person engaged in watching.

¹**loom** (lōōm), *n.* a frame or machine for weaving cloth.

²**loom** (lōōm), *v.i.* to come into view in an indistinct and enlarged form; as, the buildings *loomed* dark above the deserted street.

¹**loon** (lōōn), *n.* a fish-eating, diving bird, noted for its shrill cry.

²**loon** (lōōn), *n.* a boorish, ignorant person.

loop (lōōp), *n.* **1,** a folding or doubling of string, rope, etc., forming a ring or eye through which a cord may be run; a noose; **2,** a ring-shaped formation in a line, stream, road, etc.; **3,** a maneuver in which an airplane makes a circular turn in the air:—*v.t.* to form into, furnish with, or fasten with, loops:—*v.i.* to make a loop.

LOON (¹⁄₂₀)

loop·hole (lōōp′hōl′), *n.* **1,** a narrow opening in a wall for shooting through, as in a fort; **2,** a means of escape.

loose (lōōs), *adj.* [loos-er, loos-est], **1,** not held fast; as, a *loose* button; unbound; as, *loose* papers; **2,** free from bonds or fetters, as an escaped criminal; **3,** not tightly fitted; not snug; as, a *loose* garment; **4,** wanting in accuracy or system; as, *loose* logic; **5,** vague; unfounded; as, *loose* ideas; **6,** not close or compact in substance or texture; as, *loose* soil; **7,** lax in principles; unstable morally:—*adv.* in such a manner as not to bind:—*v.t.* [loosed, loos-ing], **1,** to set free; **2,** to relax (one's hold); **3,** to untie; unbind, as the hair; **4,** to release, as an arrow.— *adv.* **loose′ly.**—*n.* **loose′ness.**

loos·en (lōōs′n), *v.t.* **1,** to make loose; as, to *loosen* a screw; **2,** to allow to become less

rigid; as, to *loosen* discipline:—*v.i.* to become less tight, compact, or firm.

loot (lōōt), *v.t.* and *v.i.* to rob or plunder; steal:—*n.* booty thus taken.

¹**lop** (lŏp), *v.t.* [lopped, lop-ping], **1,** to cut off, as branches from a tree; **2,** to cut twigs, branches, etc., from; trim.

²**lop** (lŏp), *v.i.* [lopped, lop-ping], to hang limply:—*v.t.* to let hang limply; let flop.

lope (lōp), *n.* an easy, swinging gait, as of a horse:—*v.i.* [loped, lop-ing], to move with an easy, swinging gait.

lop·sid·ed (lŏp′sīd′ĕd), *adj.* larger or heavier on one side than on the other; hence, unevenly balanced.

lo·qua·cious (lṓ-kwā′shŭs), *adj.* talkative; garrulous.—*n.* **lo·quac′i·ty** (lṓ-kwăs′ĭ-tĭ).

lord (lôrd), *n.* **1,** a ruler or governor; master; one who has supreme power; **2,** in feudal times, a person from whom a vassal held land and to whom he owed service; **3,** in Great Britain, a nobleman; **4, Lords,** the upper house of the British Parliament: —**the Lord,** God; also, Jesus Christ:—*v.i.* to rule with absolute power.

lord·ly (lôrd′lĭ), *adj.* [lord-li-er, lord-li-est], **1,** suited to, or like, one of high rank; noble; **2,** proud; haughty.

lord·ship (lôrd′shĭp), *n.* **1,** the territory under the control of a lord; **2,** authority; control; **3,** in England, the rank of a lord: —**Lordship,** in England, a title or term of address to judges and noblemen.

Lord's Prayer, the prayer given by Jesus to his disciples (Matthew 6:9–13).

Lord's Sup·per, 1, the last supper partaken of by Jesus with his disciples, on the night before his crucifixion; **2,** the sacrament of the Holy Communion or Eucharist.

lore (lôr), *n.* knowledge; especially, the body of traditions and facts about a particular subject; as, folk*lore;* bird *lore.*

lor·gnette (lôr′nyĕt′), *n.* **1,** an eyeglass or eyeglasses fastened to a long handle; **2,** long-handled opera glasses.

lorn (lôrn), *adj.* forsaken; forlorn; lone.

Lor·raine (lṓ-rān′; lô′rân′), a region in northeastern France, bordering on the Meuse, Moselle, and Rhine rivers. Its German name is *Lothringen.*

Los An·gel·es (lŏs ăng′gĕl-ĕs; lŏs ăn′jĕl-ĕs), a city of southwestern California (map 9).

lose (lōōz), *v.t.* [lost (lôst), los-ing], **1,** to cease to have, or to be deprived of, as by death, separation, accident, negligence, etc.; as, to *lose* a son; to *lose* a finger; to *lose* money; **2,** to fail to keep or sustain; as, to *lose* one's health; to *lose* interest in one's work; **3,** to wander from; as, to *lose* one's way; **4,** to waste; let go by; as, to *lose* time; to *lose* an opportunity; **5,** to fail to keep in sight or follow mentally; as, to *lose* track of something; **6,** to fail to win; as, to *lose* a battle; **7,** to cause (a person) the loss of (a thing); as, illness *lost* him his job; **8,** to obscure; submerge; as, the stream *lost* itself in the marsh; **9,** to ruin; destroy; as, the ship was *lost* at sea:—*v.i.* **1,** to experience loss; **2,** to fail of success.

los-er (lōōz′ēr), *n.* one who fails to win, gain, or keep.

los-ing (lōōz′ĭng), *n.* **1,** the act of failing to win, gain, or keep; as, the *losing* of a game; **2, losings,** that which has been lost: —*adj.* not winning; as, a *losing* team.

loss (lôs), *n.* **1,** the state or fact of being lost or destroyed; as, the *loss* of a ship; also, that which is lost, or its value; opposite of *profit*; as, heavy *losses*; **2,** failure to keep a thing; as, *loss* of wealth; **3,** failure to win or obtain; as, the *loss* of a contract; **4,** waste; as, *loss* of gasoline; **5, losses,** the number of soldiers killed, wounded, or captured in battle.
Syn. disadvantage, damage, defeat.

lost (lôst), past tense and past participle of *lose:*—*adj.* **1,** missing; as, a *lost* child; **2,** not won; as, a *lost* race; **3,** ruined; destroyed; as, a *lost* soul; **4,** preoccupied; as, *lost* in thought; **5,** wasted; as, *lost* efforts; **6,** no longer visible; as, *lost* in the distance; **7,** insensible; as, *lost* to honor.

Lot (lŏt), in the Bible, Abraham's nephew, whose wife was turned into a pillar of salt because she looked back in her flight from Sodom (Genesis 19:26).

lot (lŏt), *n.* **1,** a method of deciding questions by drawing numbers, or by throwing blocks, dice, etc.; as, to choose by *lot*; also, the object used; **2,** what falls to a person in such a decision; share; also, fortune; one's fate; as, it is not my *lot* to become famous; **3,** a portion or parcel; especially, a plot of land; **4,** a number of objects in a group; as, the store has received a new *lot* of dresses; **5,** *Colloquial*, a great deal; as, a *lot* of money.

loth (lōth), *adj.* unwilling; loath. See **loath.**

Lo-thrin-gen (lō′trĭng-ĕn), the German name for *Lorraine*. See **Lorraine.**

lo-tion (lō′shŭn), *n.* a liquid preparation for cleansing the skin, healing a wound, etc.

lot-ter-y (lŏt′ēr-ĭ), *n.* [*pl.* lotteries], a scheme for distributing prizes by lot to persons holding tickets corresponding to numbers drawn at random.

lo-tus (lō′tŭs), *n.* **1,** a plant of the water-lily family found in Egypt, or one that is held sacred in India; **2,** in Greek legend, a fruit supposed to cause forgetfulness of care; **3,** a plant of the pea family, with red, pink, or white flowers.

loud (loud), *adj.* **1,** not low; as, *loud* music; noisy; as, *loud* streets; **2,** striking; emphatic; as, *loud* protests; **3,** *Colloquial*, showy in dress or manner; also, unpleasantly vivid; as, *loud* colors:—*adv.* not in a low manner.—*adv.* **loud′ly.**—*n.* **loud′ness.**
Syn., *adj.* clamorous, boisterous, turbulent.

LOTUS

loud—speak-er (loud′-spēk′ēr), *n.* a device on a radio for magnifying sound.

Lou-is XVI (lōō′ĭ; lōō′ĭs), (1754–1793), a king of France, guillotined during the French Revolution.

lou-is d'or (lōō ĭ dôr′), a French coin.

Lou-i-si-an-a (lōō-ē′zĭ-ăn′á), a southern State (cap. Baton Rouge) of the U.S., on the Gulf of Mexico (map 8).

Lou-is-ville (lōō′ĭ-vĭl; lōō′ĭs-vĭl), a city in northern Kentucky, on the Ohio River (map 7).

lounge (lounj), *v.i.* [lounged, loung-ing], to move, act, or recline in a lazy manner: —*n.* **1,** a couch or sofa; **2,** a comfortable and informal parlor in a hotel, club, etc.

lour (lour), *v.i.* to appear gloomy:—*n.* a scowl. See **lower.**

louse (lous), *n.* [*pl.* lice (līs)], **1,** a small, flat, wingless insect living and feeding on the bodies of animals or men; **2,** a similar insect which lives on plants.—*adj.* **lous′y** (louz′ĭ).

lout (lout), *n.* an awkward fellow; a clown.—*adj.* **lout′ish.**—*n.* **lout′-ish-ness.**

LOUSE
Enlarged four times.

Lou-vain (lōō′vân′), a city in north central Belgium.

Louvre (lōōvr′), an ancient royal palace in Paris, now used chiefly as an art museum.

lov-a-ble (lŭv′á-bl), *adj.* worthy of love; endearing.—*n.* **lov′a-ble-ness.**

love (lŭv), *n.* **1,** fond and tender attachment; as, mother *love*; also, passionate devotion; **2,** strong liking; as, *love* for music; **3,** a sweetheart:—*v.t.* [loved, lov-ing], **1,** to have a feeling of deep affection for; as, I *love* my sisters; **2,** to delight in; as, to *love* dancing:—**Love,** in Roman mythology, Cupid, the god of love: same as Greek *Eros*.

love knot, a bow or knot of ribbon, given or worn as a pledge of love.

love-li-ness (lŭv′lĭ-nĕs), *n.* beauty.

love-lorn (lŭv′lôrn′), *adj.* deserted by, or longing for, one's lover.

love-ly (lŭv′lĭ), *adj.* [love-li-er, love-li-est], 1, beautiful; charming; 2, *Colloquial*, delightful; as, *lovely* music.

lov-er (lŭv′ẽr), *n.* 1, one who has a deep affection for another of the opposite sex; 2, one who has great fondness for anything; as, a *lover* of music.

love-sick (lŭv′sĭk′), *adj.* overcome with great affection; languishing.

lov-ing (lŭv′ĭng), *adj.* affectionate; devoted; as, a *loving* friend.—*adv.* **lov′ing-ly**.

¹low (lō), *adj.* 1, not high; as, a *low* mound; 2, below the normal level; as, *low* waters; 3, deep in pitch; not loud; as, a *low* voice; 4, near the horizon; as, the sun is *low*; 5, lacking bodily or mental strength; 6, depressed; as, *low* spirits; 7, relatively small in amount, value, etc.; as, *low* prices; 8, humble; as, a *low* station in life; 9, unfavorable; as, a *low* opinion; 10, vulgar; as, *low* company; 11, slow; as, at *low* speed:—*adv.* 1, not high; as, to fly *low*; 2, at a deep pitch; 3, softly; 4, at a small price; 5, in humbleness, poverty, or disgrace.

   Syn., *adj.* soft, ignoble, abject.

²low (lō), *n.* the moo or soft call of cattle:—*v.i.* to moo.

Low Coun-tries, the Netherlands and Belgium (map **12**).

Low-ell (lō′ĕl), James Russell (1819–1891), an American poet, essayist, and diplomat.

¹low-er (lō′ẽr), *v.t.* 1, to let or bring down; let fall; as, to *lower* a curtain; 2, to reduce in price or value; as, to *lower* the rent; 3, to reduce the height of; as, to *lower* the crown of a hat; 4, to weaken; as, illness *lowers* one's resistance; 5, to humble; as, to *lower* the pride:—*v.i.* to sink; decrease; become less, as in price or value.

²low-er (lō′ẽr), *adj.* [*comp.* of ¹*low*], below in position, rank, or the like; as, a *lower* drawer; *lower* station.

³low-er (lou′ẽr) or **lour** (lour), *v.i.* 1, to appear dark, gloomy, or threatening; as, the sky *lowered*; 2, to look sullen; scowl:—*n.* a frown.—*adj.* **low′er-ing**.

Low-er Cal-i-for-ni-a, a peninsula southwest of the U.S., between the Pacific Ocean and the Gulf of California (map **10**). It is a territory of Mexico.

lower case, small letters, as abcdef or *abcdef*: opposite of *upper case* or *capitals*:—**lower-case**, *adj.* small; as, *lower-case* type.

low-er-most (lō′ẽr-mōst), *adj.* lowest: opposite of *uppermost*.

low-land (lō′lănd), *adj.* pertaining to low, flat country:—*n.* low, level country.

low-li-ness (lō′lĭ-nĕs), *n.* humbleness.

low-ly (lō′lĭ), *adj.* [low-li-er, low-li-est], humble; modest:—*adv.* modestly; humbly.

low—spir-it-ed (lō′-spĭr′ĭ-tĕd), *adj.* depressed; sad; downhearted.

loy-al (loi′ăl), *adj.* 1, faithful, especially to one's ruler or country; 2, true to friend, promise, or duty; 3, showing faithfulness.

loy-al-ist (loi′ăl-ĭst), *n.* one who supports the authority of his ruler or country, especially in time of revolt.

loy-al-ty (loi′ăl-tĭ), *n.* [*pl.* loyalties], faithfulness; constancy; devotion.

Lo-yo-la (lō-yō′lä; loi-ō′lȧ), Ignatius de (1491–1556), a Spanish priest, founder of the Society of Jesus, the members of which are known as Jesuits.

loz-enge (lŏz′ĕnj), *n.* 1, a diamond-shaped figure; 2, anything shaped in this way, as a candy or cough drop.

L.S.D. or **l.s.d.** abbreviation for *pounds, shillings, pence.*

Lt. abbreviation for *Lieutenant.*

ltd. abbreviation for *limited.*

LOZENGE

lub-ber (lŭb′ẽr), *n.* 1, an awkward fellow; 2, an untrained sailor.

Lü-beck (lü′bĕk), a port city in northern Germany (map **12**).

lu-bri-cant (lū′brĭ-kănt), *n.* a substance, as oil or grease, for oiling machine parts.

lu-bri-cate (lū′brĭ-kāt), *v.t.* [lubricat-ed, lubricat-ing], 1, to make smooth or slippery; 2, to apply oil to in order to reduce friction, as in gears.—*n.* **lu′bri-ca′tor**.

lu-bri-ca-tion (lū′brĭ-kā′shŭn), *n.* the act of oiling or the state of being oiled.

lu-cent (lū′sĕnt), *adj.* shining; bright.

Lu-cerne (lū-sûrn′; lü′sârn′), a canton in north central Switzerland; also, a city, its capital (map **12**). Its German name is **Lu-zern** (lōō-tsĕrn′).

lu-cid (lū′sĭd), *adj.* 1, clear; readily understood; as, a *lucid* explanation; 2, characterized by mental soundness or clarity; as, she has *lucid* moments; 3, clear; transparent; as, *lucid* water.

lu-cid-i-ty (lū-sĭd′ĭ-tĭ), *n.* the quality of being clear; as, *lucidity* of thought.

lu-ci-fer (lū′sĭ-fẽr), *n.* a match:—**Lucifer**, Satan.

luck (lŭk), *n.* 1, chance; fortune, whether good or bad; 2, good fortune.

luck-i-ly (lŭk′ĭ-lĭ), *adv.* fortunately.

luck-less (lŭk′lĕs), *adj.* unfortunate.

Luck-now (lŭk′nou′), a city in north central India, besieged during the famous Indian mutiny in 1857 (map **15**).

luck-y (lŭk′ĭ), *adj.* [luck-i-er, luck-i-est], 1, having good fortune; as, a *lucky* mortal;

āte, âorta, râre, căt, ȧsk, fär, ăllow, sofȧ; ēve, êvent, ĕll, writẽr, novĕl; bīte, pĭn; nō, ōbey, ôr, dŏg, tŏp, cŏllide; ūnit, ūnite, bûrn, cŭt, focŭs; nōōn, fŏŏt; mound; coin;

2, turning out well; as, a *lucky* venture; a *lucky* day.—*n.* **luck′i-ness.**

Syn. fortunate, favored, successful.

lu-cra-tive (lū′krȧ-tĭv), *adj.* profitable; money-making; as, a *lucrative* business.

lu-cre (lū′kẽr; lōō′kẽr), *n.* money; profits.

Lu-cre-ti-us (lū-krē′shĭ-ŭs; lū-krē′shŭs), (96?–55 B.C.), a Roman poet.

lu-cu-bra-tion (lū′kū-brā′shŭn), *n.* close study; also, something, as an essay, produced after long, close study.

Lu-den-dorff (lōō′dĕn-dôrf), Erich von (1865–1937), a German general in the World War.

lu-di-crous (lū′dĭ-krŭs), *adj.* ridiculous. *Syn.* laughable, droll.

luff (lŭf), *n.* **1**, the forward edge of a fore-and-aft sail; **2**, the act of sailing closer to the wind:—*v.i.* to sail nearer the wind.

¹lug (lŭg), *v.t.* [lugged, lug-ging], to pull, draw, or carry, with effort; as, there goes Mary, *lugging* a suitcase.

²lug (lŭg), *n.* an earlike projecting part; a handle; as, the *lug* of a pitcher.

lug-gage (lŭg′ĭj), *n.* baggage.

lug-ger (lŭg′ẽr), *n.* a vessel with one or more lugsails.

lug-sail (lŭg′sāl′; lŭg′sl), *n.* a four-sided sail held out by a yard, which is slung obliquely to the mast.

lu-gu-bri-ous (lū-gū′brĭ-ŭs), *adj.* mournful; sad.

LUGSAIL

Luke (lūk), in the Bible, an early Christian disciple, physician, and companion of the apostle Paul; also, the third book of the New Testament, containing Luke's account of Jesus.

luke-warm (lūk′wôrm′), *adj.* **1**, moderately warm; **2**, indifferent; not enthusiastic.

lull (lŭl), *v.t.* and *v.i.* to make or become quiet:—*n.* a lessening of noise or violence; temporary calm; as, a *lull* in a storm.

lull-a-by (lŭl′ȧ-bī′), *n.* [*pl.* lullabies], a song to lull small children to sleep.

lum-ba-go (lŭm-bā′gō), *n.* rheumatic pain in the loins and small of the back.

lum-bar (lŭm′bẽr), *adj.* relating to, or near, the loins.

¹lum-ber (lŭm′bẽr), *n.* **1**, timber that has been sawed into boards, planks, etc.; **2**, rubbish; articles of no value:—*v.i.* to cut and prepare timber for market:—*v.t.* to clutter; as, please don't *lumber* up this room.—*n.* **lum′ber-ing.**

²lum-ber (lŭm′bẽr), *v.i.* to roll heavily along; as, the truck *lumbered* up the hill.

lum-ber-man (lŭm′bẽr-măn), *n.* [*pl.* lumbermen (-mĕn)], a man engaged in cutting, or dealing in, forest timber.

lu-mi-nar-y (lū′mĭ-nẽr′ĭ), *n.* [*pl.* luminaries], **1**, a light-giving body, such as the sun or moon; **2**, a person who is a shining light, or leader, in his field.

lu-mi-nous (lū′mĭ-nŭs), *adj.* **1**, giving light; bright; as, *luminous* stars; **2**, easily understood; as, a *luminous* remark.

Syn. radiant, lustrous, shining, brilliant.

lump (lŭmp), *n.* **1**, a small, shapeless mass; as, a *lump* of clay; **2**, a swelling:—*v.t.* to unite in one body or amount; as, to *lump* expenses:—*v.i.* to form into a mass.

lump-ish (lŭmp′ĭsh), *adj.* heavy; dull.

lump-y (lŭmp′ĭ), *adj.* [lump-i-er, lump-i-est], **1**, full of lumps; as, *lumpy* bread; **2**, like a lump; lumpish.

Lu-na (lū′nȧ), *n.* in Roman mythology, the goddess of the moon.

lu-na-cy (lū′nȧ-sĭ), *n.* [*pl.* lunacies], insanity; also, extreme foolishness.

lu-nar (lū′nẽr), *adj.* relating to the moon.

lu-na-tic (lū′nȧ-tĭk), *adj.* **1**, crazy; utterly absurd; as, *lunatic* notions; **2**, relating to the insane; as, a *lunatic* asylum:—*n.* an insane person.

lunch (lŭnch), *n.* a light meal, usually eaten between breakfast and dinner; luncheon:—*v.i.* to eat a lunch.

lunch-eon (lŭn′chŭn), *n.* a light meal between breakfast and dinner; lunch; often, a lunch to which guests are invited.

lung (lŭng), *n.* either of the two organs of breathing in man and other air-breathing animals. (See illustration under *thorax*.)

lunge (lŭnj), *n.* **1**, a sudden thrust or pass with a fencing foil or a sword; **2**, a sudden leap forward:—*v.i.* [lunged, lung-ing], **1**, to make a sudden thrust; **2**, to plunge forward.

lu-pine (lū′pĭn), *n.* **1**, a garden plant of the pea family with blue, purple, yellow, or white flowers; **2**, the flower of this plant.

¹lurch (lûrch), *n.* a sudden roll to one side; as, the *lurch* of a ship; a swaying, staggering motion:—*v.i.* to stagger; as, the drunken man *lurched* down the street.

LUPINE

²lurch (lûrch), *n.* a difficult, embarrassing situation: used only in *to leave in the lurch*.

lure (lūr), *n.* **1**, anything that attracts by promising profit or pleasure; **2**, a decoy;

artificial bait; **3**, attraction; as, the *lure* of adventure:—*v.t.* [lured, lur-ing], to tempt with promise of profit or pleasure.

lu-rid (lū′rĭd), *adj.* **1**, ghastly; pale; **2**, shining with a red glow; as, a *lurid* sky; **3**, shockingly vivid; as, a *lurid* tale.

lurk (lûrk), *v.i.* **1**, to stay secretly in or about a place; as, the thief *lurked* in the shrubbery until the police had gone; **2**, to move about stealthily; **3**, to exist in secret; as, resentment *lurked* in his heart.

lus-cious (lŭsh′ŭs), *adj.* **1**, sweet and delicious; as, a *luscious* peach; **2**, pleasing to smell, hear, see, or feel.

lush (lŭsh), *adj.* **1**, juicy and luxuriant in growth; as, *lush* grass; **2**, covered with rich growth; as, *lush* meadows.

Lu-si-ta-ni-a (lū′sĭ-tā′nĭ-ȧ), a province of the Roman Empire, covering most of modern Portugal and part of western Spain.

lust (lŭst), *n.* **1**, a strong, urgent desire to possess; as, a *lust* for gold; **2**, sinful, impure desire:—*v.i.* **1**, to have a very strong desire; as, he *lusted* for power; **2**, to be filled with impure desire.—*adj.* **lust′ful**.

lus-ter or **lus-tre** (lŭs′tẽr), *n.* **1**, the quality of shining by reflected light; gloss; **2**, brightness; **3**, splendor; renown; **4**, a kind of pottery with a gleaming, metallic finish.

lust-i-ly (lŭs′tĭ-lĭ), *adv.* heartily; with vigor or energy.

lus-trous (lŭs′trŭs), *adj.* gleaming; brilliant; as, *lustrous* eyes.

lust-y (lŭs′tĭ), *adj.* [lust-i-er, lust-i-est], vigorous; healthy.

¹lute (lūt), *n.* a stringed musical instrument with a body like that of a mandolin.

²lute (lūt), *n.* a kind of cement.

LUTE, def. 1

Lu-ther (lū′thẽr; lōō′tẽr), Martin (1483–1546), the leader of the German Protestant Reformation.

Lu-ther-an (lū′thẽr-ăn), *adj.* pertaining to Martin Luther or to the church he founded:—*n.* a member of the Lutheran Church.

Lux-em-burg (lŭk′sĕm-bûrg), an independent grand duchy, southeast of Belgium; also, a city, its capital (map **12**).

Lux-or (lŭk′sôr; lōōk′sôr), a town on the Nile, in northern Egypt, the site of ancient Thebes: famous for its ruins.

lux-u-ri-ant (lŭks-ū′rĭ-ănt; lŭg-zhōōr′ĭ-ănt), *adj.* **1**, abundant and vigorous in growth; **2**, profuse or elaborate.

lux-u-ri-ate (lŭks-ū′rĭ-āt; lŭg-zhōōr′ĭ-āt), *v.i.* [luxuriat-ed, luxuriat-ing], **1**, to grow abundantly; **2**, to revel without restraint.

lux-u-ri-ous (lŭks-ū′rĭ-ŭs; lŭg-zhōōr′ĭ-ŭs),

adj. **1**, having a strong taste for costly pleasures or ease; **2**, lavishly furnished and comfortable; as, a *luxurious* hotel.

lux-u-ry (lŭk′shōō-rĭ; lŭks′ū-rĭ), *n.* [*pl.* luxuries], **1**, indulgence in costly pleasure or ease; **2**, something costly or difficult to get; **3**, anything beyond the merest necessity.

Lu-zon (lōō-zŏn′), the chief island of the Philippine Islands (map **15**).

Lwów or **Lvov** (lvōōf), a city in U.S.S.R., formerly in Poland. German name: *Lemberg*.

-ly (-lē), a suffix meaning: **1**, like; as, man*ly*; **2**, every; as, week*ly*; **3**, in the manner or degree indicated; as, bold*ly*, stupid*ly*.

ly-ce-um (lī-sē′ŭm), *n.* **1**, an association for literary study, popular lectures, debate, etc.; **2**, the building where it meets.

Ly-cur-gus (lī-kûr′gŭs), (ninth century B.C.), a Spartan lawgiver.

Lyd-i-a (lĭd′ĭ-ȧ), an ancient country in western Asia Minor, famous as the kingdom of the rich king Croesus (map **1**).

lye (lī), *n.* an alkali obtained from wood ashes, used in cleaning, making soap, etc.

¹ly-ing (lī′ĭng), present participle of ¹*lie* or ²*lie*.

²ly-ing (lī′ĭng), *n.* the act of telling lies; untruthfulness:—*adj.* untruthful.

lymph (lĭmf), *n.* a transparent, colorless fluid in animal bodies, carried in vessels called *lymphatics*.

lym-phat-ic (lĭm-făt′ĭk), *adj.* relating to, or carrying, lymph:—*n.* a tiny vessel which carries lymph.

lynch (lĭnch), *v.t.* to hang or put to death, without legal trial.

Lynn (lĭn), a manufacturing city of Massachusetts (map 6).

lynx (lĭngks), *n.* a large, fierce wildcat

LYNX. Canada Lynx (¹⁄₃₀)

with short tail, tufted ears, and valuable fur; especially, the Canada lynx.

lynx—eyed (lĭngks′-īd′), *adj.* keen-sighted.

Lyon (lyôn′) or **Ly-ons** (lī′ŭnz), a city on the Rhone, in southeastern France (map **12**).

lyre (līr), *n.* a harplike musical instrument used by the ancients to accompany singing.

lyr-ic (lĭr′ĭk), *adj.* suggesting song; like, or relating to, a song-like poem:—*n.* **1**, a short, musical poem expressing personal feelings; **2**, in music: **a**, a short, melodious song; **b**, in a musical comedy, the words of a song. Also, *adj.* **lyr′i-cal**.

LYRE

āte, āorta, râre, căt, ȧsk, fär, ăllow, sofȧ; ēve, ĕvent, ĕll, writẽr, novĕl; bīte, pĭn; nō, ōbey, ôr, dŏg, tŏp, cōllide; ūnit, ūnite, bûrn, cŭt, focŭs; nōōn, fŏŏt; mound; coin;

M

M, m (ĕm), n. [pl. M's, m's], **1,** the 13th letter of the alphabet, following L; **2,** the Roman numeral for 1,000.

m. abbreviation for *masculine, meter, mile, minute:*—**M.** [pl. MM.], abbreviation for the French *Monsieur*, equivalent of *Mr.*

M.A. abbreviation for *master of arts.*

ma (mä), n. a shortened form of *mamma*: a childish or colloquial form.

ma'am (măm; mäm), n. Colloquial, a contraction of *madam.*

mac-ad-am (măk-ăd′ăm), n. **1,** a road paved with crushed stone, closely packed and rolled; **2,** the crushed stone so used.

mac-ad-am-ize (măk-ăd′ăm-īz), v.t. [macadamized, macadamiz-ing], to build or finish (a road) with broken stone pressed and rolled to a smooth, hard surface.

mac-a-ro-ni (măk′a-rō′nĭ), n. [pl. macaronis or macaronies], **1,** a food made of a flour paste dried in long, thin tubes; **2,** in the 18th century, a dandy.

mac-a-roon (măk′a-rōōn′), n. a small cake made of white of egg, crushed almonds, and sugar.

Ma-cau-lay (ma-kô′lĭ), Thomas Babington, Lord (1800–1859), an English historian and essayist.

ma-caw (ma-kô′), n. a large, gaily colored tropical American parrot with a strong, hooked bill, a long tail, and a harsh voice.

Mac-beth (măk-bĕth′), n. the title and hero of a tragedy by Shakespeare, in which Macbeth murders the King of Scotland, takes the throne, and is also murdered.

MACAW (1/12)

Mc-Clel-lan (ma-klĕl′ăn), George B. (1826–1885), a Northern general in the War between the States.

Mac-Don-ald (măk-dŏn′ăld), James Ramsay (1866–1937), a British statesman, the first Labor premier.

Mac-Dow-ell (măk-dou′ĕl), Edward Alexander (1861–1908), an outstanding American composer and pianist.

mace (mās), n. **1,** a large and heavy club, often spiked, formerly used as a war club;

MACE, def. 1

2, a staff carried by or before an official as a symbol of power; **3,** the bearer of such a staff.

²mace (mās), n. a spice ground from the dried outer covering of the nutmeg.

Mac-e-do-ni-a (măs′ē-dō′nĭ-a), **1,** a region in the east central part of the Balkan peninsula; **2,** (often *Macedon*), an ancient province north of Greece.—n. and adj. **Mac′e-do′ni-an.**

ma-che-te (mä-chā′tā; ma-shĕt′), n. a large heavy knife used in Cuba and South America as a weapon and for cutting sugar cane.

MACHETE

Mach-i-a-vel-li (măk′ĭ-a-vĕl′ĭ), Niccolò (1469–1527), a Florentine statesman who held that any means, however treacherous or cruel, are justifiable when used to strengthen the power of the monarch.—adj. **Mach′i-a-vel′li-an.**

mach-i-na-tion (măk′ĭ-nā′shŭn), n. an evil scheme or plot; as, he escaped from the *machinations* of his enemy.

ma-chine (ma-shēn′), n. **1,** any contrivance or apparatus designed to produce or utilize power or energy; also, a mechanism which lightens human labor; as, a sewing *machine;* **2,** a vehicle, especially an automobile; **3,** one who acts without intelligence or with unfailing regularity; **4,** an organization which controls the policies of a political party.

ma-chine gun, a small, mounted gun capable of firing continuously and rapidly bullets mechanically fed it by means of a disk, belt, or clip.

MACHINE GUN

ma-chin-er-y (ma-shē′nĕr-ĭ), n. **1,** machines collectively; as, the *machinery* in a factory; also, the parts of a machine; as, the *machinery* of a clock; **2,** any means by which something is kept in action or a desired result is gained; as, the *machinery* of government or of the law.

ma-chin-ist (ma-shē′nĭst), n. one skilled in making, repairing, or attending to engines and machines.

Mach num-ber (mŏk), n. a number designating the ratio of speed of a body to the speed of sound.

Mac-ken-zie Riv-er (ma-kĕn′zĭ), a river in northwestern Canada, flowing into the Arctic Ocean (map 4).

mack·er·el (măk/ẽr-ĕl), *n.* [*pl.* mackerel], a food fish, from twelve to eighteen inches in length, found in schools in the North Atlantic: **—mackerel sky,** a sky covered with small white flecks of cloud.

MACKEREL (1/10)

Mack·i·nac, Straits of (măk/ĭ-nô), a strait between Lake Michigan and Lake Huron (map 7).

Mack·i·naw (măk/ĭ-nô), *n.* a short, heavy jacket or coat made of woolen plaid.

Mc·Kin·ley (mȧ-kĭn/lĭ), William (1843–1901), the 25th president of the U.S. He was assassinated.

McKinley, Mount, the highest peak in North America, situated in Alaska (map 3).

mack·in·tosh (măk/ĭn-tŏsh), *n.* a waterproof overcoat.

mac·ro·cosm (măk/rō-kŏzm), *n.* the whole world; universe: opposite of *microcosm.*

ma·cron (mā/krŏn; măk/rŏn), *n.* a mark [¯] over a vowel to show that it is long in quantity, as in cāme, fīne, hōpe.

mad (măd), *adj.* [mad-der, mad-dest], **1,** mentally disordered; insane; **2,** rashly foolish; as, he is *mad* to try to swim across the lake; **3,** carried away by strong feeling; excited; as, *mad* with delight; **4,** rabid; as, a *mad* dog; **5,** wild; as, a *mad* rush:—*Colloquial,* angry.—*adv.* **mad/ly.**
   Syn. crazy, violent, frantic.

Mad·a·gas·car (măd/ȧ-găs/kẽr), a large island (cap. Tananarive) under French control, east of the southern part of Africa (map 14).

mad·am (măd/ăm), *n.* [*pl.* mesdames (mā/dăm/)], a complimentary title or form of courteous address to a lady.

mad·ame (măd/ăm; mȧ/dăm/), *n.* [*pl.* mesdames (mā/dăm/)], the French title of address to a married woman.

mad·cap (măd/kăp/), *n.* a wild, thoughtless, impulsive person:—*adj.* given to wild follies; reckless.

mad·den (măd/n), *v.t.* and *v.i.* to make, or become, crazed or furious.

made (mād), past tense and past participle of *make:—adj.* contrived; artificially produced or formed; as, *made* land; *made* work.

¹**Ma·dei·ra** (mȧ-dĭr/ȧ; mä-dĕ/rȧ), a Portuguese island, west of Morocco (map 14).

²**Ma·dei·ra** (mȧ-dĭr/ȧ; mȧ-dĕ/rȧ), *n.* a sweet, amber-colored wine made on the Portuguese island of Madeira.

ma·de·moi·selle (măd/mwä/zĕl/; măd/ē-mō-zĕl/; *Colloquial,* măm/zĕl/), *n.* [*pl.* mes-demoiselles (măd/mwä/zĕl/)], Miss: a French title of address to an unmarried woman.

mad·house (măd/hous/), *n.* a house for the insane.

¹**Mad·i·son** (măd/ĭ-sŭn), a city, capital of Wisconsin (map 7).

²**Mad·i·son,** James (1751–1836), the chief author of the Constitution, and fourth president of the U.S.

mad·man (măd/măn), *n.* [*pl.* madmen (-mĕn)], a lunatic; an insane person.

mad·ness (măd/nĕs), *n.* **1,** insanity; **2,** great foolishness; as, it was *madness* to walk so far; **3,** great anger; rage.

Ma·don·na (mȧ-dŏn/ȧ), *n.* the Virgin Mary, or a picture or statue representing the Virgin Mary.

ma·dras (mȧ-drȧs/), *n.* a fabric of fine cotton, often in a fancy design, used for women's dresses, men's shirts, etc.

Ma·dras (mȧ-drȧs/), a seaport on the eastern coast of India (map 15).

Ma·drid (mȧ-drĭd/), a city, capital of Spain (map 12).

mad·ri·gal (măd/rĭ-găl), *n.* **1,** a short love poem; **2,** a musical setting for such a poem, written for three to eight or more voices, without any instrumental accompaniment.

Mael·strom (māl/strŏm), *n.* a famous whirlpool off the Norwegian coast:—**maelstrom,** any whirlpool; also, any widespread destructive force or influence; as, the *maelstrom* of war.

Mae·ter·linck (mä/tẽr-lĭngk; mä/tẽr-lĭngk; mĕt/ẽr-lĭngk), Maurice (1862–1949), a Belgian dramatist and essayist.

mag. abbreviation for *magazine.*

mag·a·zine (măg/ȧ-zēn/), *n.* **1,** (often măg/ȧ-zēn), a publication, containing articles, stories, poems, etc., and issued at regular times; **2,** a place for storing military supplies; as, a powder *magazine;* **3,** a warehouse; **4,** the cartridge chamber of a gun.

Mag·da·len (măg/dȧ-lĕn) or **Mag·da·lene** (măg/dȧ-lēn), in the Bible, Mary Magdalene:—**magdalen, magdalene,** *n.* any woman who has sinned and reformed.

Mag·de·burg (măg/dē-bûrg; măg/dē-bŏŏrkh), a commercial city on the Elbe River in Germany (map 12).

Ma·gel·lan (mȧ-jĕl/ăn), Fernando (1480?–1521), a Portuguese navigator who was the first to sail around the world.

Magellan, Strait of, a strait separating the southern end of South America from Tierra del Fuego (map 11).

ma·gen·ta (mȧ-jĕn/tȧ), *n.* a red dye made from coal tar; also, its peculiar shade of purplish red.

āte, āorta, râre, căt, ȧsk, fär, ǎllow, sofȧ; ēve, ēvent, ĕll, writẽr, novĕl; bīte, pĭn; nō, ōbey, ôr, dŏg, tŏp, cŏllide; ūnit, ūnite, bûrn, cŭt, focŭs; nōōn, fŏŏt; mound; coin;

Mag·gio·re, La·go (lä′gō mäd-jō′rä), a large lake between northern Italy and Switzerland.

mag·got (măg′ŭt), *n.* 1, the wormlike larva of an insect, especially the housefly, often found in decaying flesh, food, etc.; a grub; 2, a caprice; notion; whim.

Ma·gi (mā′jī), *n.pl.* 1, among the ancient Persians, the priestly and learned class; 2, in the Bible, the Three Wise Men from the East.

MAGGOT
1, adult fly; 2, maggot.

mag·ic (măj′ĭk), *n.* 1, the art, or pretended art, of compelling supernatural forces, as demons or spirits, to do one's bidding in the natural world: a part of all primitive religions; sorcery; witchcraft; 2, any unexplainable, bewitching power; as, the *magic* of music; 3, sleight of hand:—*adj.* pertaining to, produced by, or possessing magic; as, a *magic* touch.

Syn., n. witchery, charm.

mag·i·cal (măj′ĭ-kăl), *adj.* of, like, or produced by magic.—*adv.* **mag′i·cal·ly.**

ma·gi·cian (mȧ-jĭsh′ăn), *n.* one skilled in magic; a wizard; sorcerer.

mag·ic lan·tern, an instrument for throwing upon a screen, by means of light and lenses, enlarged images of pictures.

mag·is·te·ri·al (măj′ĭs-tē′rĭ-ăl), *adj.* relating to a magistrate or his office; judicial; authoritative; commanding.

Syn. dignified, majestic, pompous.

mag·is·trate (măj′ĭs-trāt), *n.* a government official; a local judge.

Mag·na Char·ta or **Mag·na Car·ta** (măg′nȧ kär′tȧ), 1, the Great Charter, forming the basis of English civil and personal liberty, granted by King John of England to the nobles, in 1215; 2, any constitution safeguarding personal rights.

mag·na·nim·i·ty (măg′nȧ-nĭm′ĭ-tĭ), *n.* [*pl.* magnanimities], greatness of mind or soul; freedom from pettiness; nobility.

mag·nan·i·mous (măg-năn′ĭ-mŭs), *adj.* great of mind; above pettiness; generous; noble.—*adv.* **mag·nan′i·mous·ly.**

Syn. unselfish, benevolent, munificent.

mag·nate (măg′nāt), *n.* a person of rank or importance; especially, a man of power in an industry; as, an oil *magnate*.

mag·ne·sia (măg-nē′shȧ; măg-nē′zhȧ), *n.* a white, tasteless, earthy powder, used as a medicine.

mag·ne·si·um (măg-nē′shĭ·ŭm; măg-nē′zhĭ·ŭm), *n.* a silver-white metal, light in weight. It burns with a brilliant light.

mag·net (măg′nĕt), *n.* 1, loadstone, a variety of iron ore which has the property of attracting iron; 2, a bar of iron or steel to which the power of attracting iron or steel has been artificially given; 3, a person or thing that attracts.

MAGNET

mag·net·ic (măg-nĕt′ĭk), *adj.* 1, relating to a magnet, or its power of attraction; 2, relating to the earth's magnetism; 3, having the power to attract; winning; as, a *magnetic* smile:—**magnetic needle,** a light needle of magnetized steel, which, when suspended in a compass, points in the direction of the earth's magnetism, which is approximately north and south.

mag·net·ism (măg′nĕ·tĭzm), *n.* 1, the property of a substance, naturally possessed by some substances, as loadstone, and artificially given to others, as iron or steel, of attracting certain substances according to fixed physical laws; 2, the science of magnetism; 3, personal charm.

mag·net·ize (măg′nĕ·tīz), *v.t.* [magnetized, magnetiz·ing], 1, to give magnetic properties to; make a magnet of; 2, to attract by personal charm.

mag·ne·to (măg·nē′tō), *n.* [*pl.* magnetos], a small dynamo, with permanent magnets, for generating electric current.

mag·nif·i·cent (măg-nĭf′ĭ-sĕnt), *adj.* 1, grand in appearance; splendid; as, a *magnificent* display of jewels; 2, sublime; noble; as, a *magnificent* idea.—*adv.* **mag·nif′i·cent·ly.**—*n.* **mag·nif′i·cence.**

mag·ni·fy (măg′nĭ-fī), *v.t.* [magnified, magnify·ing], 1, to cause to appear larger in size; as, a microscope *magnifies* objects seen through it; 2, to exaggerate; as, he *magnifies* the danger.

mag·nil·o·quent (măg·nĭl′ō·kwĕnt), *adj.* pompous in style of writing or speaking; boastful.

mag·ni·tude (măg′nĭ-tūd), *n.* 1, greatness of size; as, the *magnitude* of a mountain; 2, importance; as, the *magnitude* of Columbus's discovery was not recognized.

MAGNOLIA

Syn. mass, vastness, immensity.

mag·no·li·a (măg-nō′lĭ-ȧ; măg-nōl′yȧ), *n.* an ornamental tree, with shiny, dark-green leaves, large white or pink flowers, and cone-shaped fruit. It grows in Asia and North America.

mag·pie (măg′pī′), *n.* 1, a black-and-white bird of the crow family, noted for its incessant chatter; **2**, hence, one who talks continuously; a chatterer.

Mag-yar (măg′yär; mŏd′yŏr), *n.* **1**, one of the dominant race in Hungary; **2**, the language of this people:—*adj.* relating to this race or to its language.

MAGPIE (1⁄7)

ma-ha-ra-ja (mȧ-hä′rä′jȧ; mä′hä-rä′jȧ), *n.* a great king or rajah: the title of some princes in India.

Ma-hat-ma Gan-dhi (mȧ-hät′mȧ gän′-dē), a Hindu nationalist leader. See **Gandhi.**

ma-hog-a-ny (mȧ-hŏg′ȧ-nĭ), *n.* [*pl.* mahoganies], the hard, usually reddish-brown, wood of a tropical American tree, used for fine furniture; also, the tree.

Ma-hom-et (mȧ-hŏm′ĕt), an Arabian prophet. See **Mohammed.**

maid (mād), *n.* **1**, a girl or unmarried woman; **2**, a female servant.

maid-en (mād′n), *n.* a girl or unmarried woman; a maid:—*adj.* **1**, not married; as, a *maiden* lady; **2**, pure; unsoiled; **3**, earliest or first; as, a *maiden* voyage; **4**, unused; untried; as, a *maiden* sword.—*adj.* and *adv.* **maid′en-ly.**

MAIDENHAIR
Leaf of maidenhair fern.

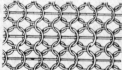

maid-en-hair (mād′n-hâr′), *n.* a delicate fern found in damp and shady woods.

maid-en-hood (mād′n-hŏŏd), *n.* the state of being a maiden.

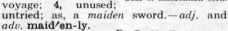

MAIL
Fragment of chain mail.

maid of hon-or, **1**, a noble lady, unmarried, who attends a queen or princess; **2**, an unmarried woman who acts as the bride's chief attendant at a wedding ceremony.

Maid of Or-leans, Saint Joan of Arc: so called because she raised the siege of Orleans. See **Joan of Arc.**

maid-serv-ant (mād′sûr′vănt), *n.* a woman servant.

¹mail (māl), *n.* **1**, body armor of steel rings, net, or scales; hence, plate or other armor; **2**, the shell-like protective coat of some animals, as the turtle.

²mail (māl), *n.* **1**, the letters, newspapers, packages, etc., delivered by post; **2**, the government system for carrying letters, packages, etc.; **3**, something that carries the mail, as an airplane or boat:—*v.t.* to post, or send by post; as, to *mail* a letter.—*adj.* **mail′a-ble.**

maim (mām), *v.t.* to deprive of the use of any necessary part of the body; cripple.

main (mān), *adj.* **1**, chief; principal; as, the *main* street; the *main* reason; **2**, sheer; as, by *main* strength:—*n.* **1**, any wide expanse; especially, the sea; as, to sail the *main*; **2**, strength: now used only in the phrase *with might and main*; **3**, a principal conduit or pipe; as, a water *main*: —in the main, for the most part. *Syn.*, *adj.* first, leading, foremost.

Main (mān; mīn), a river in northwestern Bavaria, Germany.

Maine (mān), a State (cap. Augusta) in the northeastern U.S. (map 6).

main-land (mān′lănd′; mān′lănd), *n.* a continent; a broad stretch of land, as contrasted with the islands off its coast.

main-ly (mān′lĭ), *adv.* principally; chiefly; for the most part.

main-mast (mān′mȧst′; mān′mȧst), *n.* the chief mast of a ship; in vessels of more than two masts, the second mast from the bow (see illustration on page 695).

main-sail (mān′sāl′; mān′sl), *n.* **1**, in a square-rigged vessel, the lowest and largest sail on the mainmast; **2**, in a fore-and-aft rigged vessel, the big sail on the mainmast (see illustration on page 695).

main-spring (mān′sprĭng′), *n.* **1**, the principal spring, or driving spring, in a mechanism, such as a trigger or watch; **2**, a chief motive or reason.

main-stay (mān′stā′), *n.* **1**, any of the large, strong ropes supporting the mainmast of a ship (see illustration on page 695); **2**, the chief support; as, the *mainstay* of a cause.

main-tain (mān-tān′; mĕn-tān′), *v.t.* **1**, to support or bear the expense of; as, most states *maintain* a university; **2**, to sustain; keep unimpaired; as, to *maintain* a reputation; **3**, to continue; keep up; as, to *maintain* a war; **4**, to affirm and defend by argument, as a claim; **5**, to retain possession of; hold to, as a belief. *Syn.* claim, uphold, assert.

main-te-nance (mān′tĕ-năns), *n.* **1**, the act of sustaining or defending; support; **2**, means of support; food and other necessities.

main-top (mān′tŏp′), *n.* a platform at the head of the mainmast of a ship.

āte, âorta, râre, căt, ȧsk, fär, ăllow, sofȧ; ēve, êvent, ĕll, writẽr, novĕl; bīte, pĭn; nō, ōbey, ôr, dŏg, tŏp, cŏllide; ūnit, ūnite, bûrn, cŭt, focŭs; nōōn, fŏŏt; mound; coin;

Mainz (mīnts), a fortified town on the Rhine, in Hesse, Germany (map **12**).

maize (māz), *n.* Indian corn; field corn; also, its grain.

Maj. abbreviation for *Major.*

ma-jes-tic (mȧ-jĕs′tĭk) or **ma-jes-ti-cal** (mȧ-jĕs′tĭ-kȧl), *adj.* having great dignity of person or appearance; stately.—*adv.* **ma-jes′ti-cal-ly.**
Syn. royal, splendid, magnificent.

maj-es-ty (măj′ĕs-tĭ), *n.* [*pl.* majesties], sovereign power or dignity; royal stateliness:—**Majesty,** the title of a sovereign ruler; as, His *Majesty,* the King.

ma-jor (mā′jẽr), *adj.* greater in number, extent, dignity, or quality; as, he worked the *major* part of a day:—**major scale,** in music, the most commonly used scale, consisting of eight tones arranged at intervals of a step or a half step:—*n.* **1,** .a military officer next in rank above a captain; **2,** the course of study in which a student specializes:—*v.i.* to specialize in a certain subject; as, he *majored* in history.

Ma-jor-ca (mȧ-jôr′kȧ), a Spanish island in the Mediterranean (map **12**). Its Spanish name is *Mallorca.*—*n.* and *adj.* **Ma-jor′can.**

ma-jor-do-mo (mā′jẽr-dō′mō), *n.* [*pl.* major-domos], the chief steward of a great household.

ma-jor gen-er-al, an army officer next in rank below a lieutenant general and above a brigadier general.

ma-jor-i-ty (mȧ-jŏr′ĭ-tĭ), *n.* [*pl.* majorities], **1,** the greater of two numbers looked upon as parts of a whole; also, the difference between this greater number and the smaller; as, in the class election she won by 24 to 18, a *majority* of six; **2,** the full legal age of 21 years.

make (māk), *v.t.* [made (mād), mak-ing], **1,** to build; create; fashion; as, to *make* a dress; **2,** to prepare for use; as, to *make* a garden or a bed; **3,** to get; win; as, to *make* friends; **4,** to profit or gain; clear; as, to *make* five dollars; also, to score; as, we *made* ten points in the game; **5,** to arrive at; draw near to or into sight of; as the ship *made* Boston; **6,** to cause to be or become; as, the club *made* him president; you *make* me happy; **7,** to cause; compel; as, to *make* a child behave; **8,** to perform; as, to *make* a gesture; **9,** to carry on, as war; **10,** to amount to; as, two and two *make* four; **11,** in electricity, to complete or close (a circuit):—*v.i.* **1,** to move; as, he *made* toward the goal; **2,** to prepare; as, to *make* ready for a journey; **3,** to act in a certain manner; as, to *make* merry:—*n.* **1,** character; style; build; **2,** brand; act or method

of manufacture; as, this car is of a well-known *make;* **3,** the completion of an electric circuit.
   make and break, in electricity, an automatic device for closing and opening a circuit; **make believe,** to pretend; imagine; **make fun of,** to ridicule; **make good, 1,** to fulfil, as a promise; **2,** to succeed; as, she *made good* on the stage; **make one's mark,** to become famous; **make out, 1,** to write out, as a bill; **2,** to get along; as, he *made out* well; **3,** to see; as, he could not *make out* what was on the sign; **make over,** to transfer ownership of; as, he *made over* his property to his son; **make sure,** to make oneself certain; as, *make sure* the door is locked; **make the best of,** to use most profitably; **make up, 1,** to form the parts of; as, six names *make up* each list; **2,** to invent, as a story; **3,** in printing, to arrange (type) into columns or pages for printing; **4,** to dress up; paint; as, to *make up* the face; **5,** to mend a difference or a quarrel.

make-be-lieve (māk′-bē-lēv′), *n.* pretense; pretending, as in the play of children:—*adj.* pretended; false.

mak-er (māk′ẽr), *n.* a composer, producer, or creator:—**Maker,** the Creator.

make-shift (māk′shĭft′), *n.* a thing which can be used for the time being until something better is obtained:—*adj.* temporary; as, a box may be used for a *makeshift* table.

make-up (māk′-ŭp′), *n.* **1,** the way something is put together; as, the *make-up* of a book; **2,** the arrangement of type, articles, headlines, etc., in newspapers or other printed matter; **3,** the dress, paint, powder, etc., which an actor puts on to play a part; hence, cosmetics.

mal- (măl-), a prefix meaning ill; bad; wrong; as, *mal*treat, *mal*adjusted: sometimes appearing as *male-* (măl′ē-); as, *male*diction.

Mal-a-chi (măl′ȧ-kī), in the Bible, an ancient Hebrew prophet; also, a book of the Old Testament.

mal-a-chite (măl′ȧ-kīt), *n.* a brilliant green mineral used in making ornaments.

mal-ad-just-ed (măl′ȧ-jŭs′tĕd), *adj.* poorly adjusted; out of harmony.

mal-ad-min-is-ter (măl′ăd-mĭn′ĭs-tẽr), *v.t.* to manage or conduct badly.

mal-a-droit (măl′ȧ-droit′), *adj.* unskilful; awkward; clumsy.—*adv.* **mal′a-droit′ly.**

mal-a-dy (măl′ȧ-dĭ), *n.* [*pl.* maladies], a mental or physical disease or ailment.

¹**Má-la-ga** (mä′lä-gä; măl′ȧ-gȧ), a seaport city in southern Spain (map **12**).

---

go; join; yet; sing; chin; show; thin, *th*en; **hw,** *wh*y; **zh,** a*z*ure; **ŭ,** Ger. f*ü*r or Fr. *l*une; **ö,** Ger. sch*ö*n or Fr. f*eu*; **ṅ,** Fr. e*n*fant, no*m*; **kh,** Ger. a*ch* or i*ch*. See pages ix–x.

²**Mal·a·ga** (măl′à-gà), *n.* **1,** a sweet, white, firm-fleshed grape; **2,** a kind of white wine, made in Málaga.

ma·lar·i·a (mà-lâr′ĭ-à), *n.* a disease caused by a parasite left in the blood by the bite of certain mosquitoes, and characterized by chills and fever.—*adj.* **ma·lar′i·al.**

Ma·lay (mà-lā′; mā′lā), *n.* **1,** one of the brown race of the Malay Peninsula and numerous islands off its coast; **2,** the language of these people:—*adj.* pertaining to the Malay race, country, or language. —*adj.* **Ma·lay′an.**

Ma·lay Ar·chi·pel·a·go (mà-lā′; mā′lā) or **Ma·lay·sia** (mà-lā′shà; mà-lā′zhà), a group of islands, southeast of Asia, in the Pacific and Indian oceans.

Ma·lay Pen·in·su·la, a peninsula at the southernmost tip of Asia (map **15**).

Ma·lay States, a group of native states, the Malayan Federation, in the southern part of the Malay Peninsula (map **15**).

mal·con·tent (măl′kŏn-tĕnt′), *adj.* discontented, especially with established authority:—*n.* one who is discontented with the established order of things.

male (māl), *adj.* **1,** pertaining to the sex that begets young; **2,** consisting of men or boys; masculine; as, a *male* choir:—*n.* a human being, animal, or plant of this sex.

mal·e·dic·tion (măl′ē-dĭk′shŭn), *n.* the calling down of evil upon someone; a curse.
Syn. anathema, execration, imprecation.

mal·e·fac·tor (măl′ē-făk′tēr), *n.* a wrong-doer; a criminal.— *n.* **mal′e·fac′tion.**— *n.fem.* **mal′e·fac′tress.**

ma·lev·o·lent (mà-lĕv′ô-lĕnt), *adj.* wishing evil or injury to others; spiteful.—*adv.* **ma·lev′o·lent·ly.**—*n.* **ma·lev′o·lence.**

mal·fea·sance (măl-fē′zăns), *n.* an evil deed; especially, wrongdoing by a public official.

mal·for·ma·tion (măl′fôr-mā′shŭn), *n.* faulty or abnormal structure, especially in a living body; deformity.

mal·ice (măl′ĭs), *n.* evil desire to injure others; ill will.
Syn. grudge, spite, pique.

ma·li·cious (mà-lĭsh′ŭs), *adj.* **1,** bearing ill will; filled with hatred or spite; **2,** arising from ill will; as, a *malicious* act.— *adv.* **ma·li′cious·ly.**

ma·lign (mà-līn′), *v.t.* to speak of spitefully; slander; as, to *malign* an innocent person:—*adj.* **1,** possessed of an evil disposition; malicious; **2,** tending to injure; as, *malign* influences.—*n.* **ma·lign′er.**
Syn., v. revile, vilify, abuse, asperse.

ma·lig·nant (mà-lĭg′nănt), *adj.* **1,** feeling or showing ill will; doing evil; malicious; **2,** in medical usage, tending to produce death; as, a *malignant* tumor. —*adv.* **ma·lig′nant·ly.**—*n.* **ma·lig′nan·cy.**

ma·lig·ni·ty (mà-lĭg′nĭ-tĭ), *n.* [*pl.* malignities], **1,** ill will; malice; **2,** deadly quality; malignancy.

mall (môl), *n.* **1,** a public walk shaded by trees; **2,** a mallet or maul.

mal·lard (măl′ērd), *n.* a large wild duck, especially the male, which is marked by a greenish-black head.

MALLARD DUCK (⅒)

mal·le·a·ble (măl′ē-à-bl), *adj.* capable of being hammered or rolled out without being broken; as, gold is a *malleable* metal.

mal·let (măl′ĕt), *n.* **1,** a short-handled hammer with a wooden head, used to drive a wedge or chisel; **2,** a wooden stick, hammerlike at one end, used for driving the balls in croquet or polo.

MALLET

Mal·lor·ca (mäl-yôr′kä), the Spanish name for an island in the Mediterranean Sea. See **Majorca.**

mal·low (măl′ō), *n.* a plant with showy, five-petaled flowers of pink, purple, white, or yellow color.

malm·sey (mäm′zĭ), *n.* a rich, full-flavored, sweet wine.

mal·nu·tri·tion (măl′-nū-trĭsh′ŭn), *n.* improper nourishment of the body due to lack of food, a poorly balanced diet, or poor digestion.

Mal·o·ry (măl′ô-rĭ), Sir Thomas (1430?–1470?), an English author, famous for his romance, "Morte d'Arthur," based on the King Arthur legends.

MALLOW

mal·prac·tice (măl′prăk′tĭs), *n.* any act of neglect or wrongdoing for personal gain in a position of trust, especially on the part of a physician or lawyer.

malt (môlt; mŏlt), *n.* barley or other grain which has been sprouted in water and then dried for use in brewing:—*v.t.* to make into, or work with, malt:—*adj.* made with malt; as, beer and ale are *malt* liquors.

Mal·ta (môl′tà; mŏl′tà), a British island in the Mediterranean, south of Sicily (map **12**).

Mal·tese (môl′tēz′; môl′tēs′; mŏl′tēz′;

mŏl/tēs/), *adj.* relating to the island of Malta, or to its inhabitants:— *n.* [*pl.* Maltese], a native, or the language, of Malta.

Maltese cat, a domestic cat with slate-gray fur; **Maltese cross**, a white cross on a black ground, worn by the Knights of Malta (see illustration under *cross*).

mal-treat (măl-trēt/), *v.t.* to treat with cruelty; misuse.— *n.* **mal-treat/ment.**

¹**mam-ma** (mä/mȧ; mȧ-mä/), *n.* in childish speech, mother. Also, **ma/ma.**

²**mam-ma** (măm/ȧ), *n.* [*pl.* mammae (măm/ē)], a gland which secretes milk, found in the mammals, or animals that suckle their young.

mam-mal (măm/ăl), *n.* a member of that group of animals which feed their young by means of milk glands, or mammae. Most of the common, four-footed, furry or hairy animals, as well as elephants, human beings, bats, and whales, are mammals.

mam-ma-ry (măm/ȧ-rĭ), *adj.* pertaining to the breasts, or mammae; as, the *mammary* glands.

mam-mon (măm/ŭn), *n.* wealth; worldly gain:—**Mammon**, greed, regarded as a living force; the god of greed.

mam-moth (măm/ŭth), *n.* an enormous prehistoric elephant:— *adj.* gigantic; huge; as, the pageant was a *mammoth* production.

mam-my (măm/ĭ), *n.* [*pl.* mammies], 1, mother: a childish name; 2, in the South, a Negro servant or nurse entrusted with the care of children.

SKELETON OF MAMMOTH (1/80)

man (măn), *n.* [*pl.* men (měn)], 1, a human being; also, the human race; mankind; 2, an adult male of the human race; an adult male person; 3, a male servant; valet; 4, one possessed of manly qualities in a high degree; 5, one of the pieces in chess, checkers, or similar games; also, a player in a game, whether male or female; 6, a husband; as, *man* and wife:— *v.t.* [manned, man-ning], 1, to furnish with men; as, to *man* a ship; 2, to brace or nerve (oneself); as, he *manned* himself to the unpleasant task.

Man, Isle of (măn), an island in the Irish Sea (map 13).

man-a-cle (măn/ȧ-kl), *n.* a handcuff; fetter:— *v.t.* [mana-cled, mana-cling], to place handcuffs upon; put into chains.

man-age (măn/ĭj), *v.t.* [managed, managing], 1, to carry on; conduct; as, to *man-age* a store; 2, to govern; make obedient,

as a child; 3, to bring about by clever means; contrive; as, he *managed* an escape. *Syn.* control, regulate, superintend.

man-age-a-ble (măn/ĭj-ȧ-bl), *adj.* easily managed or controlled; obedient; as, a *manageable* horse.

man-age-ment (măn/ĭj-měnt), *n.* 1, the act of directing or controlling; as, skilful *management* saves money; 2, skill in controlling or directing; 3, those in charge of a business or enterprise; as, the *management* chooses the store decorations.

man-ag-er (măn/ĭj-ẽr), *n.* 1, one who directs or conducts anything; as, the *manager* of a store; 2, a person who conducts business or household affairs with skill and economy.— *adj.* **man/a-ge/ri-al.**

man-a-tee (măn/ȧ-tē/), *n.* a large herbivorous sea mammal, about ten feet long with a broad, rounded tail; a sea cow.

Man-ches-ter (măn/chěs/tẽr), 1, a manufacturing city in southeastern New Hampshire (map 6); 2, a city and industrial center in north central England (map 13).

Man-chu (măn/chōō/; măn/chōō), *n.* 1, a member of the native Mongolian race of Manchuria, in China; 2, the language of this people:— *adj.* pertaining to Manchuria, its language or inhabitants.

Man-chu-kuo (măn/jō/kwō/; often, măn/-chōō/kwō/), the Japanese name for the state set up in Manchuria and controlled by Japan from 1932 to 1945.

Man-chu-ri-a (măn-chŏōr/ĭ-ȧ), a region in northeastern Asia belonging to China (map 15).— *n.* and *adj.* **Man-chu/ri-an.**

Man-da-lay (măn/dȧ-lā; măn/dȧ-lā/), a river port on the Irrawaddy River in central Burma (map 15).

man-da-rin (măn/dȧ-rĭn), *n.* 1, in China, a high official belonging to any one of nine grades, distinguished by a kind of button worn on the cap; 2, a kind of small orange, with easily detachable rind and sweet pulp:—**Mandarin**, the Chinese dialect of the official classes; also, the chief Chinese dialect.

man-date (măn/dāt; măn/dĭt), *n.* 1, a command; an official order; 2, a charge from the League of Nations to a member nation authorizing it to govern conquered territory; also, a territory so governed; 3, political instructions from voters to their representatives in a legislature.

man-da-tor-y (măn/dȧ-tōr/ĭ), *adj.* containing, or pertaining to, an official command; compulsory:— *n.* [*pl.* mandatories], (in legal usage, *mandatary* [pl. mandataries]), a nation or state to which the League of Nations has entrusted control and supervision of a conquered territory.

go; join; yet; sing; chin; show; thin, *th*en; hw, *wh*y; zh, azure; ü, Ger. für or Fr. lune; ö, Ger. schön or Fr. *feu*; ñ, Fr. enfant, nom; kh, Ger. ach or ich. See pages ix–x.

man-di-ble (măn′dĭ-bl), *n.* **1,** a jaw bone, usually the lower; **2,** in birds, the upper or lower part of the beak; **3,** in insects or shellfish, one of the biting jaws.

man-do-lin (măn′dō-lĭn), *n.* a musical instrument with a pear-shaped sound box and metal strings arranged in pairs.

man-drake (măn′drāk), *n.* **1,** a plant of the nightshade family with a very large, forked root and a white or purple flower; **2,** in the U.S., the May apple, a low-growing plant of the bar-berry family.

man-drill (măn′drĭl), *n.* the blue-nosed baboon of West Africa: one of the largest and most fero-cious of the baboons.

MANDO-LIN

mane (mān), *n.* the long hair on or about the neck of certain ani-mals, as the horse and the lion. (See illustra-tion under *horse.*)

ma-nes (mā′nēz), *n.pl.* among the ancient Ro-mans, the spirits of the dead; especially, an-cestral spirits worshiped as gods and guardian influences.

MANDRILL (⅒₀)

ma-neu-ver (*ma*-nōō′vẽr; *ma*-nū′vẽr), *n.* **1,** a planned and supervised movement, or change of position, of troops or ships; an evolution; in war, a strategic change of position by troops or ships; **2,** a skilful plan of action; as, a clever *maneuver:*—*v.i.* **1,** to perform certain movements: said of troops or war vessels; as, battleships *maneuvered* off the coast; **2,** to manage with art and skill; as, the driver had to *maneuver* to put the car in the garage:—*v.t.* **1,** to cause to make certain movements, as troops; **2,** to handle skilfully. Also spelled **ma-noeu′vre.**

man-ful (măn′fool), *adj.* courageous; bravely determined.—*adv.* **man′ful-ly.**
Syn. noble, brave, manly, manlike.

man-ga-nese (măng′ga-nēs; măng′ga-nēz), *n.* a hard, brittle metal of a grayish-white color tinged with red: used in making paint, glass, etc.

mange (mānj), *n.* a contagious skin dis-ease of domestic animals and sometimes man, caused by parasites.

man-ger (mān′jẽr), *n.* a feeding trough for horses or cattle.

¹**man-gle** (măng′gl), *n.* a machine for ironing cloth, especially damp linen, be-tween hot rollers:—*v.t.* [man-gled, man-gling], to iron in a mangle, as table-cloths, sheets, etc.

²**man-gle** (măng′gl), *v.t.* [man-gled, man-gling], **1,** to cut to pieces; maim; mutilate by cutting or hacking; **2,** to spoil in the making or doing.—*n.* **man′gler.**

man-go (măng′gō), *n.* [*pl.* mangoes or mangos], **1,** a tropical tree bearing a pear-shaped, juicy, yellow-red, edible fruit; **2,** the fruit.

man-grove (măng′grōv), *n.* a tropical shore tree or shrub with spreading branches that send down roots, called prop roots, which rapidly create impenetrable jungle thickets. Its bark is used in tanning.

man-gy (mān′jĭ), *adj.* [man-gi-er, man-gi-est], **1,** suffering or afflicted with the mange, a contagious skin disease; **2,** shabby; neglected.—*n.* **man′gi-ness.**

man-han-dle (măn′hăn′dl; măn-hăn′dl), *v.t.* [manhan-dled, manhan-dling], to han-dle brutally; as, to *manhandle* a prisoner.

Man-hat-tan (măn-hăt′ăn), a borough of New York City on the island of the same name at the mouth of the Hudson River.

man-hole (măn′hōl′), *n.* an opening by which workmen enter a tank or sewer.

man-hood (măn′hood), *n.* **1,** the state of being a man; **2,** men collectively; as, the *manhood* of a nation; **3,** the qualities be-longing to a man; courage; bravery.

ma-ni-a (mā′nĭ-*a*), *n.* **1,** insanity marked by excitement and violence; **2,** excessive enthusiasm; a craze; as, a *mania* for col-lecting stamps.
Syn. frenzy, madness, lunacy.

ma-ni-ac (mā′nĭ-ăk), *adj.* affected with insanity; raving; as, a *maniac* fury:—*n.* a madman.—*adj.* **ma-ni′a-cal** (*ma*-nī′*a*-kăl).

man-i-cure (măn′ĭ-kūr), *n.* **1,** the care of the hands and fingernails; **2,** one whose business is caring for people's hands and fingernails:—*v.t.* [manicured, manicur-ing], to care for (hands and fingernails).—*n.* **man′i-cur′ist.**

man-i-fest (măn′ĭ-fĕst), *adj.* clear; ap-parent to the sight or understanding; as, the truth of that statement is *manifest:*—*v.t.* **1,** to make clear; show; as, to *manifest* anger; **2,** to show the list of (a ship's cargo):—*n.* the list of a cargo to be shown to the customhouse officials.
Syn., adj. evident, open, visible, un-mistakable, obvious; *v.* reveal, display.

man-i-fes-ta-tion (măn′ĭ-fĕs-tā′shŭn), *n.* a revelation, display, or proof of the ex-istence or nature of something; as, the *manifestation* of political feeling.

man-i-fes-to (măn′ĭ-fĕs′tō), *n.* [*pl.* man-ifestoes], a public declaration, as on the part of an official or a state, concerning political measures or purposes.

---

man·i·fold (măn′ĭ-fōld), *adj.* **1,** various in kind or quality; numerous; as, *manifold* favors; **2,** comprehensive; as, *manifold* wisdom:—*v.t.* to make many copies of by means of a duplicating machine:—*n.* **1,** a copy made by a duplicating machine; **2,** a pipe with two or more outlets along its length, used for connecting one pipe with others.—*adv.* **man′i-fold′ly.**
Syn., adj. several, sundry, divers, many.

man·i·kin (măn′ĭ-kĭn), *n.* **1,** a dwarf; **2,** a model of the human body used for the study of anatomy; **3,** an artist's or dressmaker's model; a mannequin. Also spelled **man′ni-kin.**

Ma·nil·a (mȧ-nĭl′ȧ), a commercial city in the Philippine Islands (map 15):—**Manila Bay,** an inlet of the South China Sea, in the island of Luzon.

Manila hemp, a fiber made from the leaf stalks of a tree native to the Philippine Islands, used especially for making rope.

Ma·nil·a pa·per, originally, a durable paper made from Manila hemp; now, a cheap brown or buff paper made of various fibers, used especially as a wrapping paper.

ma·nip·u·late (mȧ-nĭp′ū-lāt), *v.t.* [ma-nipulat-ed, manipulat-ing], **1,** to operate or work skilfully, as tools, by means of the hands; **2,** to treat or influence artfully; control the action of, by skilful management; **3,** to falsify, as books in book-keeping.—*n.* **ma-nip′u-la′tion.**

man·i·to (măn′ĭ-tō), **man·i·tou** (măn′ĭ-tōō), or **man·i·tu** (măn′ĭ-tōō), *n.* in the religion of the Algonquian Indians, the power or spirit which rules nature.

Man·i·to·ba (măn′ĭ-tō′bȧ), a province (cap. Winnipeg) in south central Canada (map 4).

man·kind (măn′kīnd′), *n.* **1,** the human race; **2,** (măn′kīnd′), men, as distinguished from women.

man·like (măn′līk′), *adj.* like, or suitable to, a man; manly.
Syn. masculine, mannish, manful, noble.

man·li·ness (măn′lĭ-nĕs), *n.* the state or quality of possessing manly virtues.

man·ly (măn′lĭ), *adj.* [man-li-er, man-li-est], having the qualities befitting a man; courageous; noble; dignified; resolute.
Syn. masculine, vigorous.

Mann (măn), Horace (1796–1859), an American educator.

man·na (măn′ȧ), *n.* **1,** in the Old Testament, the food miraculously supplied to the Israelites during their 40 years' wandering in the wilderness; **2,** hence, anything much needed which is unexpectedly supplied.

man·ne·quin (măn′ĕ-kĭn), *n.* a person, usually a woman, employed as a model to display clothes; a manikin.

man·ner (măn′ēr), *n.* **1,** method or way of acting; as, to speak in a rapid *manner*; **2,** sort; kind; species; as, what *manner* of man is he? all *manner* of fish in the bay; **3,** personal, habitual behavior; as, his *manner* is kind; **4,** style in literature or art; as, a painting in the Chinese *manner*; **5,** habit; custom, as of a race or nation; **6, manners: a,** social behavior; as, to have good or bad *manners*; **b,** rules of social conduct; as, the *manners* of today.
Syn. way, air, look, appearance.

man·ner·ism (măn′ēr-ĭzm), *n.* an odd or peculiar action, gesture, style of speech, etc., especially if affected or habitual.

man·ner·ly (măn′ēr-lĭ), *adj.* polite:—*adv.* politely; respectfully.—*n.* **man′ner-li-ness.**

man·ni·kin (măn′ĭ-kĭn), *n.* a manikin.

man·nish (măn′ĭsh), *adj.* masculine; characteristic of a man.—*adv.* **man′nish-ly.**
Syn. noble, brave, manly, manlike.

ma·noeu·vre (mȧ-nōō′vẽr; mȧ-nū′vẽr), *n.* a military operation. See **maneuver.**

man—of—war (măn′-ŏv-wôr′), *n.* [*pl.* men-of-war (měn′-ŏv-wôr′)], a large armed vessel belonging to the navy of a country.

man·or (măn′ēr), *n.* in England, originally, a piece of land held by a nobleman, part of which he occupied, the rest being occupied and farmed by serfs; now, a landed estate held by a lord, part of which he rents to tenants.—*adj.* **ma-nor′i-al.**

man·sard roof (măn′särd), in architecture, a roof which has two slopes on all sides, the lower slope being steeper than the upper slope.

manse (măns), *n.* **1,** the residence of a Presbyterian minister, especially in Scotland; **2,** loosely, any parsonage.

man·serv·ant (măn′sûr′vănt), *n.* [*pl.* menservants (měn′-)], a male servant.

man·sion (măn′shŭn), *n.* a large residence.

man·slaugh·ter (măn′slô′tẽr), *n.* the killing of a human being by another or others, unlawfully but without intention.

man·tel (măn′tl), *n.* **1,** a structure of wood, marble, brick, etc., around and above a fireplace; **2,** the shelf above a fireplace: also called *mantelpiece.*

MANTEL
M, mantelpiece.

man·til·la (măn-tĭl′ȧ), *n.* **1,** a woman's cloak or hood; **2,** a veil worn over the head by Spanish women.

man·tis (măn′tĭs), *n.* any of several insects with long, grotesque bodies and rolling eyes, which prey on other insects and are noted for taking a position with the front legs folded as if praying: popularly called *praying mantis.*

MANTIS (⅓)

man-tle (măn′tl), *n.* **1,** a loose cloak or cape; also, any enveloping covering; as, a tree in a *mantle* of bloom; **2,** a conelike network of material that will not burn, which fits like a cap over a flame and gives light by glowing at high temperature: —*v.t.* [man-tled, man-tling], to cover with, or as with, a cloak; to disguise:—*v.i.* to become covered; as, her face *mantled* with blushes.

MANTLE def. 2

Man-tu-a (măn′tū-à), a city in northern Italy, birthplace of Vergil (map 12). Its Italian name is **Man′to-va** (män′tō-vä).

man-u-al (măn′ū-ăl), *adj.* pertaining to, or done by, the hands; as, *manual* skill; *manual* work:—*n.* **1,** a small book for easy reference; a handbook; **2,** a systematic exercise in the handling of a weapon; as, the *manual* of arms in the army:—**manual training,** a system of education which emphasizes work done with the hands, as woodworking, metalwork, leathercraft, etc.—*adv.* **man′u-al-ly.**

manuf. abbreviation for *manufactory, manufacture, manufacturer, manufacturing.*

man-u-fac-to-ry (măn′ū-făk′tō-rĭ), *n.* [*pl.* manufactories], a place where goods are manufactured.

man-u-fac-ture (măn′ū-făk′tūr), *v.t.* [manufactured, manufactur-ing], **1,** to make, as shoes, paper, etc., by hand or machinery, from raw materials; **2,** to make over into a more useful form; as, to *manufacture* yarn from wool:—*n.* **1,** the making, usually on a large scale, of articles by hand, machinery, or a combination of processes; **2,** anything made from raw material by these processes; also, such articles collectively; **3,** hence, production in general.—*n.* **man′u-fac′tur-er.**

ma-nure (må-nūr′), *n.* any fertilizing substance, especially waste from stables, used for enriching the soil:—*v.t.* [manured, manur-ing], to enrich, as a field or garden, with fertilizing substances.

man-u-script (măn′ū-skrĭpt), *adj.* written by hand:—*n.* **1,** a book or paper written by hand; especially, an author's copy of his work in handwriting or in typewriting; **2,** writing, as opposed to printing.

man-y (měn′ĭ), *adj.* [*comp.* more, *superl.* most], consisting of a great number:—*n.* a great number:—**the many,** the general public.

Ma-o-ri (mä′ō-rĭ; mou′rĭ; mä′rĭ), *n.* **1,** a member of the native brown race of New Zealand; **2,** the language of this race.

map (măp), *n.* **1,** a representation, on a flat surface, of the earth or some portion of it, showing the relative size and position of the parts or places represented; **2,** a chart of the heavens:—*v.t.* [mapped, mapping], **1,** to picture or lay down in a chart; describe clearly; **2,** to plan in detail; as, to *map* out a journey.

ma-ple (mā′pl), *n.* **1,** any of a large group of trees of the north temperate zone with deeply indented leaves and two-winged fruits, valued for their wood and for the sap of certain varieties which is used in making a kind of sugar and sirup; **2,** the wood of any of these trees, especially of the sugar maple.

Mar. or **Mch.** abbreviation for *March.*

mar (mär), *v.t.* [marred, mar-ring], **1,** to disfigure; damage; as, to *mar* a painting; **2,** to injure; ruin; as, to *mar* one's record.

mar-a-bou (măr′à-bōō), *n.* an African stork whose soft wing or tail feathers are used for dress trimming; also, the feathers.

Ma-rat (må-rà′), Jean Paul (1744-1793), a leader in the French Revolution.

Mar-a-thon (măr′à-thŏn), a village in ancient Greece, site of the defeat of the Persians in 490 B.C. (map 1).

marathon race, a long-distance foot race of 26 miles, 385 yards: so called from the run of the messenger who carried to Athens the news of the victory of Marathon.

ma-raud (må-rôd′), *v.t.* to plunder:—*v.i.* to rove in search of plunder; as, wild beasts *maraud* at night.

ma-raud-er (må-rôd′ẽr), *n.* one who roves in search of booty or plunder.

ma-raud-ing (må-rôd′ĭng), *adj.* roving in search of plunder; as, *marauding* gangs.

mar-ble (mär′bl), *n.* **1,** a hard limestone, white or of various colors, capable of taking a fine polish, used for building and sculpture; **2,** anything like such stone in hardness, smoothness, or coldness; **3,** a sculptured piece of such stone; **4,** a small clay or glass ball used as a child's plaything; **5, marbles: a,** the game played with these balls; **b,** a collection of sculpture in marble:—*adj.* **1,** made of, or like, marble; **2,** cold; hard; unfeeling:—*v.t.* [mar-bled, mar-bling], to stain or vein like marble.

mar-cel (mär-sĕl′), *n.* a deep, regular wave put in the hair by means of a special curling iron:—*v.t.* [marcelled, marcel-ing], to wave (the hair) with this iron.

¹**march** (märch), *n.* a frontier boundary; borderland.

²**march** (märch), *n.* 1, a regular, measured step or walk, especially of soldiers; 2, the distance passed over in walking with regular step from one place to another; as, a *march* of ten miles; 3, steady onward movement; as, the *march* of years; 4, a musical composition to be played as troops march: —*v.t.* 1, to cause to move at a march; 2, to cause to go by force; as, to *march* a child to bed:—*v.i.* to move with regular steps, or in military form.

Syn., *v.* tramp, tread, walk, step.

March (märch), *n.* the third month of the year, having 31 days, named for the Roman war god, Mars.

mar-chion-ess (mär´shŭn-ĕs), *n.* the wife or widow of a marquis; a woman of the rank of a marquis.

Mar-co-ni (mär-kō´nē), Guglielmo (1874-1937), an Italian scientist, inventor of the wireless telegraph.

Mar-co Po-lo (mär´kō pō´lō), (1254-1323), a Venetian traveler in Asia. See **Polo**.

Mar-di gras (mär´dē grä´), the last day before Lent, celebrated in some cities, as Rome, Paris, and New Orleans, with great merriment.

mare (mâr), *n.* the female of the horse, donkey, zebra, etc.

mare's—nest (mârz´=nĕst´), *n.* a discovery which at first seems to be wonderful but which proves to be a cheat or fake.

mar-ga-rine (mär´jȧ-rēn; mär´gȧ-rēn), *n.* oleomargarine; a butter substitute made from animal or vegetable fats.

mar-gin (mär´jĭn), *n.* 1, a border; an edge; as, the *margin* of a pool; 2, the unprinted edge of a page; 3, an amount in reserve, as of money or time; as, he allowed a *margin* of ten dollars for the trip.

Syn. rim, brink, verge, brim.

mar-gin-al (mär´jĭ-năl), *adj.* pertaining to, or placed on, the edge or border; as, a *marginal* design.

mar-gue-rite (mär´gĕ-rēt´), *n.* the common European daisy, large white flower heads with yellow centers.

Ma-rie An-toi-nette (mȧ-rē´ än´twä´nĕt´), (1755-1793), a queen of France, guillotined during the French Revolution.

mar-i-gold (măr´ĭ-gōld), *n.* 1, any of a group of strong-scented garden plants of the aster family, with showy orange, yellow, or variegated flowers; 2, any of numerous other yellow-flowered plants, as the marsh marigold; 3, the flower of any of these.

MARIGOLD

ma-ri-hua-na (mä´rĕ-hwä´nȧ), *n.*, the Indian hemp plant, used in cigarettes as a narcotic. Also **ma-ri-jua-na**.

ma-rim-ba (mȧ-rĭm´bȧ), *n.* a musical instrument consisting of graduated lengths of hardwood, each with a sounding box, played upon with mallets.

MARIMBA

ma-rine (mȧ-rēn´), *adj.* 1, pertaining to, living in, or formed by, the sea; as, *marine* plants; *marine* deposits; 2, naval; relating to commerce at sea; as, *marine* law; 3, having to do with soldiers who serve on warships; as, the *marine* corps:—*n.* 1, a soldier who serves on a warship; 2, the navy of a nation; also, the executive department dealing with naval affairs; 3, the collective shipping of a country; as, the merchant *marine*; 4, a picture of a sea scene.

Syn., *adj.* maritime, naval, nautical.

mar-i-ner (măr´ĭ-nẽr), *n.* a sailor or seaman; one of a ship's crew.

mar-i-o-nette (măr´ĭ-ō-nĕt´), *n.* a doll moved by strings or by the hand, as in a puppet show; a puppet.

mar-i-tal (măr´ĭ-tăl), *adj.* pertaining to a husband or to marriage.

mar-i-time (măr´ĭ-tīm; măr´ĭ-tĭm), *adj.* 1, pertaining to, or bordering upon, the sea; as, a *maritime* province; 2, especially, relating to sea trade or navigation.

mar-jo-ram (mär´jō-răm), *n.* any of a group of plants of the mint family, especially sweet marjoram, used as flavoring.

Mark (märk), 1, in the Bible, the Apostle, John Mark; also, the second Gospel of the New Testament written by him; 2, in Arthurian romance, a king of Cornwall, Tristram's uncle and Iseult's husband.

¹**mark** (märk), *n.* 1, the target at which one aims, as in shooting; an aim or goal; 2, a visible imprint, as a line, scratch, written word, or the like; as, an ink *mark*; 3, a sign by which anything is known; a brand, label, trade-mark, or the like; 4, a trait; distinguishing feature; as, a *mark* of intelligence; 5, high position; distinction; as, a man of *mark*; 6, a figure or letter indicating a student's grade; 7, a boundary or limit; a set standard; as, to fall below the *mark*; 8, a line, object, or the like, serving to indicate position; 9, a symbol, often a cross, made by one who cannot sign his name:—*v.t.* 1, to furnish with an identifying sign; 2, to characterize; identify or indicate, as by a sign; as, faith and courage *mark* the leader; 3, to single out or select, as by a sign; destine; as, they

go; join; yet; sing; chin; show; thin, *th*en; hw, *wh*y; zh, a*z*ure; ū, Ger. f*ü*r or Fr. l*u*ne; ŏ, Ger. sch*ö*n or Fr. f*eu*; ṅ, Fr. e*n*fant, no*m*; kh, Ger. a*ch* or i*ch*. See pages ix-x.

marked him for promotion; **4,** to notice; observe; as, I *marked* that incident; **5,** to rank or grade, as examination papers; **6,** to set apart by or as if by a boundary; as, to *mark* out a tennis court:—*v.i.* to notice; consider; observe critically.

²**mark** (märk), *n.* **1,** the gold monetary unit of the former German Empire, worth almost 24 cents; **2,** the monetary unit of the former German Republic: officially called *reichsmark.*

marked (märkt), *adj.* **1,** ranked or graded; as, *marked* papers; **2,** having a distinguishing mark or marks upon it; as, a *marked* bill; **3,** noticeable; conspicuous; clearly defined; as, *marked* ability in music.—*adv.* **mark′ed·ly** (mär′kĕd-lĭ).

mark·er (mär′kẽr), *n.* **1,** one who keeps score in a game; **2,** an instrument used for making a mark; **3,** an object used as a sign, guide, or memorial.

mar·ket (mär′kĕt), *n.* **1,** a place for the sale or purchase of goods, especially of meat, fresh vegetables, etc.; **2,** a region or country where anything can be sold; as, the U.S. is a *market* for Java coffee; **3,** the state of trade as shown by rate or price; as, a dull *market;* **4,** demand; as, there is a big *market* for radios:—*v.i.* to deal in a public place where provisions are exposed for sale; buy or sell goods or provisions:— *v.t.* to offer for sale, or to sell, in a public place.

mar·ket·a·ble (mär′kĕt-a̍-bl), *adj.* salable; in demand; as, *marketable* products.

mark·ka (märk′kä), *n.* [*pl.* markkaa (märk′kä)], a nickel-bronze coin, the monetary unit of Finland. (See Table, page 943.)

marks·man (märks′mǎn), *n.* [*pl.* marksmen (-mĕn)], one skilled in shooting.—*n.* **marks′man-ship.**

Mark Twain (märk twān), the pen name of Samuel L. Clemens. See **Twain.**

marl (märl), *n.* an earthy deposit of sand or clay, containing much lime, which is used for fertilizer and to make bricks.

mar·line (mär′lĭn), *n.* a two-stranded cord used for binding the ends of ropes.

mar·line·spike (mär′lĭn-spīk′), *n.* a pointed tool of iron used for parting the strands of a rope in splicing, or uniting two ropes by interweaving the strands.

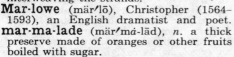

MARLINESPIKE

A, marlinespike; B, marlinespike forcing open strands of rope.

Mar·lowe (mär′lō), Christopher (1564–1593), an English dramatist and poet.

mar·ma·lade (mär′ma̍-lād), *n.* a thick preserve made of oranges or other fruits boiled with sugar.

Mar·ma·ra (mär′ma̍-rá) or **Mar·mo·ra** (mär′mō-rá), **Sea of,** an inland sea in Turkey, between the Aegean Sea and the Black Sea (map **12**).

mar·mo·set (mär′mō-zĕt), *n.* a small South or Central American monkey.

mar·mot (mär′mŭt), *n.* a small, coarse-furred, stout-bodied animal with a short bushy tail, akin to the rat and squirrel; a woodchuck.

MARMOT (²⁄₀)

Marne (märn), a river in east central France, along which were fought two of the most important battles of World War I.

¹**ma·roon** (ma̍-rōōn′), *n.* **1,** one of a class of Negroes, originally fugitive slaves, living in the wilder parts of the West Indies and Dutch Guiana; **2,** one who is left alone or abandoned on a lonely coast:—*v.t.* to abandon on a lonely coast.

²**ma·roon** (ma̍-rōōn′), *n.* a dark, brownish-red color:—*adj.* of the color of maroon.

marque (märk), *n.* formerly, seizure of an enemy's ships:—**letters of marque,** government license to a ship to plunder or capture enemy merchant ships.

mar·quee (mär-kē′), *n.* **1,** a large field tent, often used for outdoor entertainment; **2,** an awning placed as a temporary shelter, as from the street curb to the door of a church.

mar·que·try (mär′kĕ-trĭ), *n.* inlaid work, as in furniture or floors.

Mar·quette (mär′kĕt′), Jacques (1637–1675), a French missionary and explorer of the Mississippi River.

mar·quis (mär′kwĭs) or **mar·quess** (mär′kwĕs), *n.* a nobleman ranking below a duke and above an earl or count.

mar·quise (mär-kēz′), *n.* the wife or widow of a marquis; a marchioness; also, a woman of this rank.

mar·qui·sette (mär′kĭ-zĕt′; mär′kwĭ-zĕt′), *n.* a kind of sheer cotton cloth used for dresses, curtains, and the like; also, a thin silk cloth.

Mar·ra·kech (ma̍r-rä′kĕsh), a town in western Morocco, Africa (map **14**).

mar·riage (măr′ĭj), *n.* **1,** the act of legally uniting a man and woman in wedlock; the wedding ceremony; **2,** the state of being wedded; the relation existing between husband and wife.

Syn. matrimony, wedlock, wedding.

mar·riage·a·ble (măr′ĭj-a̍-bl), *adj.* fit for marriage; as, of *marriageable* age.

mar·row (măr′ō), *n.* **1,** the fatty tissue

filling the cavities and canals of bones; **2,** hence, the real meaning or significance of anything; as, the *marrow* of a speech.

¹**mar·ry** (mărʹĭ), *v.t.* [married, marry-ing], **1,** to unite as husband and wife; as, the minister *married* Tom and Mary; **2,** to take in marriage; wed; as, Tom *married* Mary; **3,** to dispose of in wedlock; as, to *marry* off a daughter:—*v.i.* to enter into the state of wedlock; take a husband or wife.

²**mar·ry** (mărʹĭ), *interj. Archaic,* indeed! a mild oath expressing surprise or assent.

Mars (märz), *n.* **1,** in Roman mythology, the god of war; **2,** the planet, noted for its red color whose orbit lies next outside the earth's in our solar system.

Mar·seil·laise (märʹsĕ-lāzʹ; márʹsâʹyâzʹ), *n.* the national song of France.

Mar·seille (márʹsâyʹ) or **Mar·seilles** (mär-sālzʹ), a French seaport city on the Mediterranean (map **12**).

marsh (märsh), *n.* a swampy tract of land.

mar·shal (märʹshăl), *n.* **1,** an official of high rank who superintends and regulates ceremonies; **2,** in some foreign armies, an officer of highest rank: also called *field marshal;* **3,** an officer who has certain police duties; sometimes, the head of a fire or police department:—*v.t.* [marshaled, marshal-ing], **1,** to arrange or dispose in order, as facts or military forces; **2,** to lead; guide.

Mar·shall (märʹshăl), John (1755–1835), a Chief Justice of the U.S. Supreme Court.

marsh mal·low, a coarse plant of the mallow family with large, five-petaled, white or rose-colored flowers, growing in salt marshes.

marsh-mal·low (märshʹmălʹō), *n.* a kind of candy, formerly made from the root of the marsh mallow, now usually made of gelatin.

marsh mar·i·gold, a plant of the butter-cup family with rounded leaves and bright-yellow flowers, growing in swamps and wet meadows.

marsh·y (märʹshĭ), *adj.* [marsh-i-er, marsh-i-est], **1,** swampy; **2,** growing in, like, or pertaining to, a swamp or fen.

mar·su·pi·al (mär-sūʹpĭ-ăl), *adj.* having a pouch: said of a class of animals that carry their young in a pouch:—*n.* one of these animals, as an opossum or kangaroo.

MARSH MARIGOLD

mart (märt), *n.* a market; a place where things are bought and sold

mar·ten (märʹtĕn), *n.* **1,** a small animal of the weasel family; **2,** the valuable fur of this animal.

Mar·tha (märʹthȧ), in the New Testament, the sister of Mary and Lazarus of Bethany.

MARTEN (¹⁄₂₀)

Mar·tha's Vine-yard (vĭnʹyĕrd), an island off the south-eastern coast of Massachusetts (map **6**).

mar·tial (märʹshăl), *adj.* **1,** of, like, or suited to, war; **2,** military; as, *martial* music.—*adv.* **marʹtial-ly.**

Syn. warlike, soldierly.

martial law, military government en-forced by the army and superseding civil government, as in time of public disorder.

Mar·ti·an (märʹshĭ-ăn; märʹshăn), *adj.* per-taining to Mars, the Roman god of war, or to the planet Mars.

mar·tin (märʹtĭn), *n.* **1,** in Europe, a bird of the swallow family which builds a mud nest on the walls of buildings; **2,** in the U.S., an insect-eating bird of the swallow family, nesting in col-onies, and having blue-black plumage and a forked tail.

MARTIN (¹⁄₆)

mar·ti·net (märʹtĭ-nĕtʹ; märʹtĭ-nĕt), *n.* one who requires and enforces strict obedience in all details; especially, a stickler for trivial details.

mar·tin·gale (märʹtĭn-gāl; märʹtĭng-gāl), or **mar·tin·gal** (märʹtĭn-găl; märʹtĭng-găl), *n.* **1.** a strap in a horse's harness, pass-ing from the girth between the forelegs for-ward and up to the reins, to keep the head down, or to the collar (see *harness,* illustra-tion); **2,** a rope or chain for holding the end of the jib boom or flying jib boom to the dol-phin striker (see illustration on page 695).

Mar·ti·nique (märʹtĭ-nēkʹ), an island (cap. Fort-de-France) in the French West Indies (map **10**).

mar·tyr (märʹtĕr), *n.* **1,** one who dies rather than forsake or betray a faith, cause, or principle; **2,** one who suffers keenly or sacrifices much, especially for a cause or principle:—*v.t.* **1,** to put to death for loyalty to some belief, especially Christianity; **2,** to persecute; torture.

mar·tyr·dom (märʹtĕr-dŭm), *n.* death or suffering for the sake of a faith or cause; as, the *martyrdom* of Joan of Arc.

mar·vel (märʹvĕl), *n.* something extraor-dinary and astonishing; a wonder:—*v.i.*

---

go; join; yet; sing; chin; show; thin, *th*en; hw, *wh*y; zh, a*z*ure; **ū,** Ger. f**ü**r or Fr. l**u**ne; **ö,** Ger. sch**ö**n or Fr. f**eu**; **ṅ,** Fr. e**n**fant, no**m**; kh, Ger. a**ch** or i**ch.** See pages ix–x.

[marveled, marvel-ing], to be struck with wonder; as, to *marvel* at a person's courage.

mar-vel-ous (mär′vĕl-ŭs), *adj.* causing wonder; scarcely to be believed; as, a *marvelous* sight.—*adv.* **mar′vel-ous-ly.**

Marx (märks), Karl (1818–1883), a German economist, and the founder of socialism.

Mar-y (mâr′ĭ), in the New Testament: **1,** the mother of Jesus; **2,** the younger sister of Martha; **3,** Mary Magdalene, a sinful woman who became a follower of Jesus.

Mar-y-land (mĕr′ĭ-lănd), a Middle Atlantic State (cap. Annapolis) in the U.S. (map 6).

Mar-y Stu-art (stū′ĕrt), (1542–1587), Queen of the Scots, beheaded by order of Queen Elizabeth of England.

mas., m., or **masc.** abbreviation for *masculine.*

mas-cot (măs′kŏt; măs′kŭt), *n.* a person or thing that is supposed to bring good luck; as, the team's *mascot* is a bulldog.

mas-cu-line (măs′kū-lĭn), *adj.* **1,** pertaining to, having the qualities of, or suitable for, a man; manly; powerful; virile; **2,** mannish: said of a woman; **3,** in gran,mar, designating the gender of words which name male persons or animals.

mash (măsh), *n.* **1,** a soft or pulpy mass; **2,** a warm mixture of bran and water for horses and other animals; **3,** bruised malt or meal soaked in hot water for making brews:—*v.t.* **1,** to mix, as malt, with hot water, in brewing; **2,** to change into a soft, pulpy state by crushing; as, to *mash* turnips.—*n.* **mash′er.**

mash-ie or **mash-y** (măsh′ĭ), *n.* [*pl.* mashies], an iron-headed golf club used for medium-length shots.

mask (måsk), *n.* **1,** a full or partial cover for the face to disguise or protect it; as, a dancer's *mask*; a baseball *mask*; also, a caricatured false face; **2,** a disguise or pretense; as, to hide sorrow under a *mask* of laughter; **3,** a likeness of a human face made of clay, wax, or a similar material; **4,** (also *masque*), a masquerade; **5,** in classical drama, a huge figure of a head worn by actors to identify the character played; **6,** (usually *masque*), an old form of drama characterized by masks, music, and pantomime:—**gas mask,** a covering for the head and face, attached to a breathing device, to protect against poisonous gases that are found in mines and are

MASKS
1, gas mask; 2, carnival mask.

used in warfare:—*v.t.* to cover with, or as with, a mask:—*v.i.* to put on a mask; be disguised.—*n.* **mask′er.**

ma-son (mā′sn), *n.* a builder in stone or brick; a bricklayer:—**Mason,** a member of the society of Freemasons.

Ma-son and Dix-on's Line (mā′sn, dĭk′snz), the southern boundary of Pennsylvania, often considered the dividing line between the North and the South.

Ma-son-ic (má-sŏn′ĭk), *adj.* of or pertaining to the society of Freemasons.

ma-son-ry (mā′sn-rĭ), *n.* [*pl.* masonries], **1,** the art or occupation of a builder in stone; **2,** a structure made of stone.

masque (måsk), *n.* **1,** a masquerade; **2,** an old form of drama, characterized by music, dancing, dialog, and spectacular pageantry, performed by bands of amateur actors in court and castle, popular in the 16th and 17th centuries. Also spelled **mask.**

mas-quer-ade (más′kĕr-ād′), *n.* **1,** a ball or festive gathering where masks are worn; **2,** an acting or living under false pretenses; as, his show of honor is a *masquerade;* **3,** a disguise:—*v.i.* [masquerad-ed, masquerad-ing], **1,** to take part in a ball where the guests are disguised; **2,** to take the part or character of another for amusement or deceit; as, to *masquerade* as the heir to a fortune.—*n.* **mas′quer-ad′er.**

Mass. abbreviation for *Massachusetts.*

mass (măs), *n.* **1,** a quantity of matter or collection of things united into one body; **2,** a large quantity or number; as, a *mass* of corrections; **3,** bulk; size; **4,** the main part:—**the masses,** the common people:—*v.t.* to collect into a lump or body; arrange in close relation; as, to *mass* shrubbery:—*v.i.* to make or gather into a lump or group.

Mass (măs), *n.* **1,** in the Roman Catholic and some Anglican Churches, the celebration of the Eucharist; **2,** the musical setting for the words of the Eucharist service.

Mas-sa-chu-setts (măs′á-chōō′sĕts), a State (cap. Boston) on the North Atlantic coast of the U.S. (map 6).

mas-sa-cre (măs′á-kĕr), *n.* the killing of many people or animals with violence and cruelty; wholesale slaughter or murder:—*v.t.* [massa-cred, (măs′á-kĕrd), massa-cring (măs′á-kĕr-ĭng; măs′á-krĭng)], to slaughter in great numbers.

mas-sage (má-säzh′), *n.* a method of treating the body, for health purposes, by rubbing and kneading with the hands:—*v.t.* [massaged, massag-ing], to rub and knead with the hands.

mas-seur (må-sûr′), *n.* one who performs the operation of massage. —*n.fem.* **masseuse′** (má-sûz′).

mas-sive (măs′ĭv), *adj.* **1,** weighty; huge; bulky; **2,** hence, imposing; impressive.— *adv.* **mas′sive-ly.**—*n.* **mas′sive-ness.**
 Syn. ponderous, unwieldy, substantial.

mass meet-ing, a general assembly of people for the discussion of some question of public interest.

mass-y (măs′ĭ), *adj.* [mass-i-er, mass-i-est], weighty; bulky.—*n.* **mass′i-ness.**

¹**mast** (måst), *n.* **1,** a long, round spar or pole of iron or timber set upright on the keel and through the decks of a vessel, to support the sails and rigging; **2,** any upright pole, as the main post of a derrick.

²**mast** (måst), *n.* nuts, especially when used as fodder for swine or other animals.

mas-ter (mås′tẽr), *n.* **1,** a man who rules or commands; a director; employer; owner; **2,** the head of a household, college, school, etc.; **3,** an expert; hence, a skilled workman; **4,** a winner in a contest; **5,** a great artist; also, a painting by a great artist; as, a gallery of old *masters;* **6,** the commander of a merchant vessel:—**Master, 1,** a person holding an advanced university degree; as, a *Master* of Arts; **2,** a title used before the names of young boys; **3,** a legal title:—*adj.* chief; skilled; as, a *master* mason:—*v.t.* to subdue or overcome; as, to *master* a task.

mas-ter-ful (mås′tẽr-fŏŏl), *adj.* **1,** commanding; powerful; as, a *masterful* speaker; **2,** domineering.—*adv.* **mas′ter-ful-ly.**

master key, a key that will open many different locks.

mas-ter-ly (mås′tẽr-lĭ), *adj.* characteristic of a chief or expert; as, he played with a *masterly* touch:—*adv.* like, or with the skill of, an expert.

mas-ter-piece (mås′tẽr-pēs′), *n.* **1,** a thing which surpasses in excellence everything else done by the maker; as, Cervantes's "Don Quixote" is his *masterpiece;* **2,** anything made with extraordinary skill.

mas-ter-y (mås′tẽr-ĭ), *n.* [*pl.* masteries], **1,** dominion; rule, as of a country; **2,** superiority or triumph, as in a contest; **3,** skill in, or full knowledge of, a subject.
 Syn. rule, sway, supremacy.

mast-head (måst′hĕd′), *n.* the top of a mast, especially the top of a lower mast, used for a lookout.

mas-tic (măs′tĭk), *n.* a yellowish gum or resin which oozes from the bark of certain trees, used in making varnishes.

mas-ti-cate (măs′tĭ-kāt), *v.t.* [masticat-ed, masticat-ing], to grind (food) with the teeth; chew.—*n.* **mas′ti-ca′tion.**

mas-tiff (mås′tĭf), *n.* one of a breed of dogs that were originally used as hunting dogs. The mastiff is extremely large and has a deep powerful chest.

mas-to-don (măs′tō-dŏn), *n.* a huge, elephantlike animal, that no longer exists on the earth.

MASTIFF (1/30)

mas-toid (măs′toid), *adj.* pertaining to a projection of the temporal bone of the skull behind the ear:—*n.* the mastoid bone.

¹**mat** (măt), *n.* **1,** a flat piece of coarse, woven fabric, made of straw, grass, rags, etc.; **2,** such a fabric placed before a door for wiping the feet; **3,** anything thickly grown or tangled, as hair, weeds, or wool; **4,** a piece of cloth, lace, asbestos, etc., placed under dishes or used as an ornament:—*v.t.* [mat-ted, mat-ting], to mass, knot, or twist together:—*v.i.* to become closely tangled.

²**mat** (măt), *adj.* dull, lusterless, but uniform: said of surfaces and colors:—*n.* **1,** a border of paper, cardboard, silk, etc., used to set off or protect a picture; **2,** a dull finish on a gilded or painted surface.

mat-a-dor (măt′à-dôr), *n.* the man chosen to kill the bull in a bullfight.

¹**match** (măch), *n.* **1,** anything which agrees with, or is exactly like, another thing; **2,** an equal; one able to cope with another; **3,** a game or contest; as, a hockey *match;* **4,** a marriage; also, a marriageable person:—*v.t.* **1,** to marry; especially, to marry advantageously; **2,** to compete with successfully; equal; as, their team *matched* ours:—*v.i.* to agree with, or be like, each other.

²**match** (măch), *n.* **1,** a slender piece of wood tipped with material that is easily set afire by friction, now almost universally used for starting fires; **2,** a wick which burns at a certain speed, used for firing cannon and guns.

match-less (măch′lĕs), *adj.* not capable of being equaled; peerless.

match-lock (măch′lŏk′), *n.* an old kind of musket set off by a match.

mate (māt), *n.* **1,** a companion or associate; as, a play*mate;* **2,** a partner in marriage; one of a pair of animals or birds for breeding; as, the lion's *mate;* **3,** one of a pair; as, the *mate* to a shoe; **4,** a ship's officer ranking below the captain:—*v.t.* and *v.i.* [mat-ed, mat-ing], **1,** to match; **2,** to marry; of animals, to pair.—*n.* and *adj.* **mat′ing.**

ma·te·ri·al (mȧ-tē′rĭ-ăl), *adj.* **1,** consisting of matter or substance; not spiritual; **2,** pertaining to bodily wants; as, the *material* needs of the poor; **3,** important; noticeable; as, a *material* loss:—*n.* the substance of which anything is made.

 Syn., adj. bodily, physical, temporal.

ma·te·ri·al·ism (mȧ-tē′rĭ-ăl-ĭzm), *n.* **1,** the doctrine that all the facts of life are the result of the nature, action, etc., of substance or matter; **2,** the tendency to give too much importance to physical well-being and matter, and too little to spiritual and intellectual life.—*n.* **ma·te′ri·al·ist.**—*adj.* **ma·te′ri·al·is′tic.**

ma·te·ri·al·ize (mȧ-tē′rĭ-ăl-īz), *v.t.* [materialized, materializ-ing], **1,** to give substance, reality, or form to; **2,** to express (an idea) through outward objects; as, to *materialize* an idea in a statue:—*v.i.* **1,** to become a fact; **2,** to assume actual form.

ma·te·ri·al·ly (mȧ-tē′rĭ-ăl-ĭ), *adv.* **1,** with respect to body or substance; **2,** actually; considerably; as, that is *materially* better.

ma·té·ri·el (mȧ-tē′rĭ-ĕl′), *n.* the physical equipment, as apparatus, supplies, etc., required for a given operation: distinguished from *personnel.*

ma·ter·nal (mȧ-tûr′năl), *adj.* pertaining to motherhood or to one's mother; as, *maternal* love.—*adv.* **ma·ter′nal·ly.**

ma·ter·ni·ty (mȧ-tûr′nĭ-tĭ), *n.* [*pl.* maternities], the state of being a mother; motherhood.

math. abbreviation for *mathematics.*

math·e·mat·i·cal (măth′ē-măt′ĭ-kăl),*adj.* **1,** pertaining to, or performed by, mathematics; **2,** exact; precise; accurate; as, they measured the distance with *mathematical* precision.—*adv.* **math′e·mat′i·cal·ly.**

math·e·ma·ti·cian (măth′ē-mȧ-tĭsh′ăn), *n.* one skilled in mathematics.

math·e·mat·ics (măth′ē-măt′ĭks), *n.pl.* used as *sing.* the science which deals with quantities, expressed in numbers or other symbols, and the relations between them.

mat·in (măt′ĭn), *adj.* pertaining to the morning:—**Matins,** *n.pl.* **1,** in the Roman Catholic Church, a service at midnight or at daybreak; **2,** in the Church of England, the morning service.—*adj.* **mat′in·al.**

mat·i·nee (măt′ĭ-nā′; măt′ĭ-nā), *n.* a play, musicale, reception, or the like, taking place in the afternoon.

mat·ri·ces (măt′rĭ-sēz), one form of the plural of *matrix.*

ma·tri·cide (mā′trĭ-sīd; măt′rĭ-sīd), *n.* **1,** the murder of a woman by her son or daughter; **2,** one who murders his mother.

ma·tric·u·late (mȧ-trĭk′ū-lāt), *v.t.* [ma-triculat-ed, matriculat-ing], to admit, especially to a college or university, by entering the name in a register; to enroll: —*v.i.* to register; as, he *matriculated* at the university.—*n.* **ma·tric′u·la′tion.**

mat·ri·mo·ni·al (măt′rĭ-mō′nĭ-ăl), *adj.* relating to marriage.

mat·ri·mo·ny (măt′rĭ-mō′nĭ), *n.* marriage.

ma·trix (mā′trĭks), *n.* [*pl.* matrices (măt′-rĭ-sēz) or matrixes], **1,** something holding, or capable of holding, embedded within it, another object to which it gives shape or form; **2,** the rock in which a fossil, mineral, or gem is embedded; **3,** a mold or form in which something is cast or shaped; as, a mold for type is a *matrix.*

ma·tron (mā′trŭn), *n.* **1,** a married woman or widow; especially, one who has borne children; **2,** a woman who superintends the housekeeping in a hospital or other institution; also, a woman whose duty it is to maintain order among women or children in a prison, dormitory, etc.

ma·tron·ly (mā′trŭn-lĭ), *adj.* like or pertaining to a matron; dignified; sedate.

mat·ted (măt′ĕd), *adj.* **1,** covered with a mat or mats; **2,** closely tangled together; as, *matted* hair.

mat·ter (măt′ẽr), *n.* **1,** substance, as opposed to mind, spirit, etc.; **2,** the substance of which physical things are made; **3,** an instance of, or occasion for, something; as, a *matter* of habit; a laughing *matter;* **4,** the content of a book or speech; as, subject *matter;* **5,** anything sent by mail; as, second-class *matter;* **6,** importance; as, no *matter;* **7,** affair; business; hence, a thing; as, this *matter* needs attention; **8,** amount; space; as, a *matter* of ten days or miles; **9,** pus; **10,** material set up in type or printed from type:—*v.i.* **1,** to be of importance; as, health *matters;* **2,** to form pus; fester.

mat·ter-of-fact (măt′ẽr-ŏv-făkt′), *adj.* literal; practical; not imaginative.

Mat·thew (măth′ū), in the Bible, one of the twelve apostles of Jesus; also, the first book of the New Testament; the Gospel of Matthew.

MATTOCK

mat·ting (măt′ĭng), *n.* a coarse fabric of straw, hemp, grass, or the like, used for covering floors.

mat·tock (măt′ŭk), *n.* a tool which has a steel head with one end flat and the other pointed like a pick, used for digging, grubbing, etc.

mat·tress (măt′rĕs), *n.* a flat case or bag made of strong material, stuffed with hair, straw, cotton, or the like, for use as a bed, or as a soft pad for a bed.

ma·ture (må-tūr′), *v.i.* [matured, maturing], **1,** to become ripe; develop fully; **2,** to fall due, as a note:—*v.t.* to bring to full growth or completion:—*adj.* [matur-er, matur-est], **1,** ripe; full-grown, as fruit; **2,** perfected; ready for use, as a plan; **3,** due, as a note.—*adv.* **ma·ture′ly.**

Syn., *adj.* developed, prime, mellow.

ma·tu·ri·ty (må-tū′rĭ-tĭ), *n.* [*pl.* maturities], **1,** ripeness; full development; **2,** the coming due of a bill or a note.

maud·lin (môd′lĭn), *adj.* **1,** easily moved to tears; weakly sentimental; as, *maudlin* sympathy; **2,** fuddled; drunkenly silly.

maul or **mall** (môl), *n.* a large, heavy hammer:—*v.t.* to beat or bruise; treat in a rough careless manner.

Mau·na Lo·a (mou′nä lō′ä), a large active volcano in the Territory of Hawaii.

MAUL

maun·der (môn′dẽr; män′dẽr), *v.i.* **1,** to talk foolishly; mumble indistinctly; as, she *maunders* on about nothing; **2,** to wander aimlessly.

mau·so·le·um (mô′sŏ-lē′ŭm), *n.* a stately, magnificent tomb.

mauve (mōv), *n.* a soft lilac or purple color.

mav·er·ick (măv′ẽr-ĭk), *n.* in the western U.S., an animal that has not been marked with the owner's brand.

ma·vis (mā′vĭs), *n.* the song thrush.

maw (mô), *n.* **1,** the stomach of an animal; **2,** in birds, the craw or crop.

mawk·ish (môk′ĭsh), *adj.* **1,** causing disgust; sickening; **2,** foolishly sentimental; as, *mawkish* love tales.– *adv.* **mawk′ish·ly.**

max. abbreviation for *maximum.*

max·il·lar·y (măk′sĭ-lẽr′ĭ), *adj.* relating to the jaw or jawbone:—*n.* [*pl.* maxillaries], either one of the jawbones, especially the upper jawbone.

max·im (măk′sĭm), *n.* a general truth or rule expressed briefly; as, "Waste not, want not" is a useful *maxim.*

Syn. adage, saying, byword, saw.

max·i·mum (măk′sĭ-mŭm), *n.* [*pl.* maxima (măk′sĭ-må) or maximums], the greatest possible number, quantity, or degree: opposite of *minimum:*—*adj.* greatest in quantity or highest in degree.

may (mā), *auxiliary v.* [*p.t.* might (mīt)], **1,** to be allowed or to be free to; as, you *may* look; **2,** to be likely, but not certain; as, it *may* rain; **3,** would that: expressing the earnest desire, or wish, of the speaker; as, *may* the report prove untrue.

May (mā), *n.* the fifth month of the year, containing 31 days.

May ap·ple, a plant with large leaves, a single, large, white flower, and a small, yellow, oval fruit; the mandrake.

may·be (mā′bē; mā′bĭ), *adv.* perhaps; possibly.

May Day, the first day of May, often celebrated by outdoor festivities, such as dancing about a garlanded pole or crowning a May queen.

May·flow·er (mā′flou′ẽr), *n.* **1,** any of several plants flowering in May or early spring, as the arbutus; **2,** the ship that brought the Pilgrims from England to America in 1620.

may·on·naise (mā′ŏ-nāz′), *n.* a thick, rich sauce or seasoned dressing made of raw egg yolks, vegetable oil, and vinegar, beaten together until thick.

may·or (mā′ẽr; mâr), *n.* the chief official of a·city or borough.

may·or·al·ty (mā′ẽr-ăl-tĭ; mâr′ăl-tĭ), *n.* [*pl.* mayoralties], the office, or term of office, of a mayor.

May·pole (mā′pōl′), *n.* a decorated pole, erected outdoors, around which May-Day revelers dance.

maze (māz), *n.* **1,** a confusing network, as of passages; a labyrinth; **2,** confusion of mind; bewilderment.

ma·zur·ka (må-zûr′kå; må-zŏŏr′kå), *n.* **1,** a lively Polish dance; **2,** music for such a dance. Also spelled **ma·zour′ka.**

ma·zy (mā′zĭ), *adj.* [ma-zi-er, ma-zi-est], hard to unravel or to trace out; winding.

M.C. abbreviation for *Member of Congress.*

Md. abbreviation for *Maryland.*

M.D. abbreviation for *Doctor of Medicine.*

M Day, abbreviation for *Mobilization Day.*

mdse. abbreviation for *merchandise.*

me (mē), *pron.* the objective case of *I.*

Me. abbreviation for *Maine.*

¹mead (mēd), *n.* an alcoholic liquor made of fermented honey and water.

²mead (mēd), *n.* Poetic, a meadow.

mead·ow (mĕd′ō), *n.* a field used for pasture; also, a field on which hay is grown.

meadow lark, a North American songbird of the oriole family, with a yellow breast marked with a black crescent.

MEADOW LARK (⅒)

mea·ger (mē′gẽr), *adj.* **1,** lacking in flesh; lean; **2,** poor; scanty; as,

a *meager* meal. Also spelled **mea/gre.**—*adv.* **mea/ger-ly.**—*n.* **mea/ger-ness.**
   Syn. lank, thin, spare.

¹**meal** (mēl), *n.* coarsely ground grain; especially, ground corn.

²**meal** (mēl), *n.* a repast; a time or occasion of taking food; also, the food eaten.

meal-y (mēl/ĭ), *adj.* [meal-i-er, meal-i-est], **1,** like meal; dry and soft; as, *mealy* soil; **2,** covered with meal; floury; **3,** pale.

¹**mean** (mēn), *v.t.* [meant (mĕnt), meaning], **1,** to intend; as, he *means* to go; he *means* mischief; **2,** to express a certain thought; signify; as, charity *means* love; **3,** to refer to; designate; as, I *mean* you; **4,** to design or intend for a purpose; as, a pitcher is *meant* for holding and pouring a liquid:—**mean well to** or **by,** to be kindly disposed toward.

²**mean** (mēn), *adj.* **1,** humble; common; as, of *mean* birth; **2,** inferior; ordinary; as, a *mean* grade of coal; **3,** poor; shabby; as, a *mean* house; **4,** lacking in generosity; stingy; as, a *mean* man; **5,** dishonorable; base; as, a *mean* motive; **6,** *Colloquial,* unkind.—*n.* **mean/ness.**
   Syn. abject, vile, degraded, pitiful.

³**mean** (mēn), *adj.* **1,** occupying the middle position between two extremes; as, a *mean* height; a *mean* course; **2,** average:—*n.* **1,** a condition, quality, course of action, or the like, which is midway between two extremes; as, gray is the *mean* between black and white; **2,** hence, moderation; **3,** **means: a,** that by which something is done or accomplished; as, a boat was the *means* of rescue; **b,** wealth; as, a man of *means.*

me-an-der (mē-ăn/dẽr), *v.i.* **1,** to follow a winding course, as a river; **2,** to wander aimlessly.

mean-ing (mēn/ĭng), *adj.* expressive; full of significance; as, a *meaning* glance:—*n.* **1,** object; intention; as, the *meaning* of her visit; **2,** that which is meant; as, the *meaning* of a word.—*adv.* **mean/ing-ly.**
   Syn., *n.* significance, import, sense.

mean-ing-less (mēn/ĭng-lĕs), *adj.* without meaning or sense; not significant.

mean-ly (mēn/lĭ), *adv.* **1,** poorly; shabbily; as, *meanly* dressed; **2,** humbly; as, *meanly* born; **3,** basely; as, *meanly* spoken.

meant (mĕnt), past tense and past participle of ¹*mean.*

mean-time (mēn/tīm/), *adv.* **1,** in the time between two occasions; **2,** at the same time:—*n.* the time between two occasions.

mean-while (mēn/hwīl/), *adv.* meantime: —*n.* the intervening time.

mea-sles (mē/zlz), *n.pl.* used as *sing.* a contagious disease, common especially among children, marked by fever and itching small red spots on the skin.

meas-ure (mĕzh/ẽr), *n.* **1,** the size, quantity, or capacity of a thing, as found by a rule or standard; **2,** a unit of measurement, as a pint, inch, etc.; also, an instrument for measuring, as a yardstick; **3,** a system of measurement; as, dry *measure;* **4,** an amount; degree; as, a small *measure* of pity; **5,** a reasonable limit; as, the normal *measure* of life is 70 years; **6,** a course of action; as, preventive *measures;* **7,** an act of legislation; **8,** rhythm, as in poetry; **9,** in music, the time of a piece; also, the group of notes between two bars on a staff:—*v.t.* [measured, measur-ing], **1,** to find out the extent, size, or volume of, by comparison with a fixed or known standard; **2,** to give out; allot; as, to *measure* out rations; **3,** mark off (size, rate, etc.); as, a speedometer *measures* the rate of speed:—*v.i.* **1,** to find dimensions, volume, or the like; **2,** to extend or be of a given length; as, the room *measures* 21 feet.—*adj.* **meas/ur-a-ble.**—*adj.* **meas/ure-less.**

meas-ured (mĕzh/ẽrd), *adj.* **1,** regulated or determined by some standard; **2,** uniform; regular; also, rhythmical; **3,** carefully considered; as, *measured* words.

meas-ure-ment (mĕzh/ẽr-mĕnt), *n.* **1,** the act of finding size, quantity, amount, etc., by a standard; **2,** the size or quantity found; **3,** a system of units of measure.

meat (mēt), *n.* **1,** animal flesh used as food; **2,** food in general; **3,** the food parts within a shell, rind, or the like; as, the *meat* of a nut.

meat-y (mēt/ĭ), *adj.* [meat-i-er, meat-i-est], like meat; full of nourishment; hence, full of material for thought; as, a *meaty* book.

Mec-ca (mĕk/á), **1,** the holy city of the Mohammedans, in Saudi Arabia (map 15); **2,** (often *mecca*), a goal at which one aims.

me-chan-ic (mē-kăn/ĭk), *n.* a skilled workman, especially one who understands the construction and use of machinery and tools:—*adj.* relating to manual labor; also, relating to machinery and tools.

me-chan-i-cal (mē-kăn/ĭ-kăl), *adj.* **1,** relating to, or made by, machinery; **2,** done without thought, as if from force of habit; as, *mechanical* movements; **3,** run by machinery; as, a *mechanical* piano.—*adv.* **me-chan/i-cal-ly.**

me-chan-ics (mē-kăn/ĭks), *n.pl.* used as *sing.* **1,** the science of machinery; **2,** the science which treats of the action of forces on bodies.

mech-a-nism (mĕk/á-nĭzm), *n.* **1,** the

āte, āorta, râre, căt, àsk, fär, ăllow, sofá; ēve, ēvent, ĕll, writẽr, novĕl; bīte, pĭn;
nō, ōbey, ôr, dŏg, tŏp, cǫllide; ūnit, ūnite, bûrn, cŭt, focŭs; nōōn, fŏŏt; mound; coin;

structure or arrangement of the working parts of a machine of any kind; **2**, a mechanical device; **3**, any system of interworking parts; as, the *mechanism* of government.

mech·a·nize (mĕk′a-nīz), *v.t.* [mechanized, mechaniz·ing], **1**, to make mechanical, as by replacing men with machines; **2**, to reduce to a routine.

med·al (mĕd′l), *n.* a coinlike piece of metal marked with a design or with words to commemorate some event, deed, etc., or to serve as a reward or decoration for merit.

MEDAL

me·dal·lion (mē-dăl′yŭn), *n.* **1**, a large medal; **2**, anything resembling a medal, as a tablet or panel with carved figures on it, a lace ornament, a design on a carpet, etc.

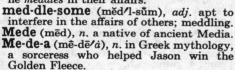

MEDALLION

med·dle (mĕd′l), *v.i.* [meddled, med·dling], to interfere with what does not concern one; as, he loses his friends, because he *meddles* in their affairs.

med·dle·some (mĕd′l-sŭm), *adj.* apt to interfere in the affairs of others; meddling.

Mede (mēd), *n.* a native of ancient Media.

Me·de·a (mē-dē′a), *n.* in Greek mythology, a sorceress who helped Jason win the Golden Fleece.

me·di·a (mē′dĭ-a), one form of the plural of *medium*.

Me·di·a (mē′dĭ-a), an ancient kingdom, now a part of northwestern Iran.

me·di·ae·val (mē′dĭ-ē′văl; mĕd′ĭ-ē′văl), *adj.* relating to the Middle Ages; medieval. See **medieval.**

me·di·al (mē′dĭ-ăl), *adj.* relating to the middle; average.

me·di·an (mē′dĭ-ăn), *adj.* in the middle: —*n.* a point or number in a series having the same number of points or numbers before as after it; as, in the series 4, 5, 8, 16, 22, the *median* is 8.

me·di·ate (mē′dĭ-āt), *v.i.* [mediat·ed, mediat·ing], to act as a peacemaker between those who are openly disagreeing: —*v.t.* to bring about by acting as an agent between enemies; as, to *mediate* a peace:— *adj.* (mē′dĭ-ĭt), not direct; acting by or through some intervening person or thing.

me·di·a·tion (mē′dĭ-ā′shŭn), *n.* **1**, the act of trying to bring about friendly relations; **2**, a plea made on behalf of another person.

me·di·a·tor (mē′dĭ-ā′tẽr), *n.* one who tries to bring about friendly relations between enemies; also, a nation acting in this capacity.

med·i·cal (mĕd′ĭ-kăl), *adj.* relating to medicine, or the treatment of disease; as, *medical* training.—*adv.* **med′i·cal·ly.**

me·dic·a·ment (mē-dĭk′a-mĕnt; mĕd′ĭ-ka-mĕnt), *n.* a medicine; anything used for healing or curing.

med·i·cat·ed (mĕd′ĭ-kāt′ĕd), *adj.* containing medicine; as, a *medicated* lotion.

Med·i·ci (mĕd′ē-chē), a famous Florentine family of statesmen, who were patrons of art and literature.

me·dic·i·nal (mē-dĭs′ĭ-năl), *adj.* having the power to cure or relieve disease.—*adv.* **me·dic′i·nal·ly.**

med·i·cine (mĕd′ĭ-sĭn; mĕd′ĭ-sn), *n.* **1**, the science which deals with the prevention, treatment, and cure of disease; **2**, any drug or remedy for the treatment and cure of disease.

medicine man, among primitive peoples, as the North American Indians, African tribes, etc., a person supposed to have magic power over evil spirits, diseases, etc.

me·di·e·val or **me·di·ae·val** (mē′dĭ-ē′văl; mĕd′ĭ-ē′văl), *adj.* relating to, or characteristic of, the Middle Ages, a period extending approximately from A.D. 500 to A.D. 1400.

Me·di·na (mā-dē′nä), a town in western Arabia, where Mohammed is buried (map 15).

me·di·o·cre (mē′dĭ-ō′kẽr; mē′dĭ-ō′kẽr), *adj.* of medium quality; commonplace; as, the actor gave a *mediocre* performance.

me·di·oc·ri·ty (mē′dĭ-ŏk′rĭ-tĭ), *n.* [*pl.* mediocrities], **1**, the quality of being ordinary or commonplace; **2**, a person of average ability.

med·i·tate (mĕd′ĭ-tāt), *v.i.* [meditat·ed, meditat·ing], to think deeply; reflect; as, to *meditate* upon revenge:—*v.t.* to consider; plan; as, to *meditate* a change.

med·i·ta·tion (mĕd′ĭ-tā′shŭn), *n.* deep, quiet thought; especially, deep pondering upon religious matters.—*adj.* **med′i·ta′-tive.**—*adv.* **med′i·ta′tive·ly.**

Med·i·ter·ra·ne·an Sea (mĕd′ĭ-tĕ-rā′nē-ăn), an inland sea between Europe and Africa (maps 12, 14).

me·di·um (mē′dĭ-ŭm), *n.* [*pl.* mediums or media (mē′dĭ-a)], **1**, that which comes between or in the middle; **2**, means; that by which or through which something is done; as, the newspaper is an advertising *medium; * **3**, the space or substance in which bodies exist or move; as, water is the *medium* in which we swim; also, a substance through which something acts or is carried; as, the air is a *medium* for sound; **4**, a person who claims to receive messages from the spirit world:—*adj.* middle; moderate; as, cloth of *medium* weight.

Syn., *n.* channel, instrument.

med·ley (měd′lĭ), *n.* [*pl.* medleys], **1,** a mixture or confused mass; **2,** in music, a composition made up of passages selected from different songs or pieces.

Syn. variety, jumble, miscellany.

me·dul·la (mē-dŭl′ä), *n.* **1,** the marrow, or substance in the center of bones; **2,** the pith, or center portion, of plants:— **medulla oblongata** (ŏb′lŏng-gā′tä), the lowest part of the brain, which joins with the spinal cord: also called *medulla.*

Me·du·sa (mē-dū′sä; mē-dū′zä), *n.* in Greek mythology, one of three sisters, called the Gorgons, who had snakes for hair, and who were so terrible to behold that one glimpse of them turned the beholder to stone.

meed (mēd), *n.* reward; that which is given in recognition of merit or worth.

meek (mēk), *adj.* **1,** mild of temper; patient; gentle; **2,** easily imposed upon; spiritless.—*adv.* **meek′ly.**—*n.* **meek′ness.**

Syn., unassuming, submissive.

meer·schaum (mēr′shŭm), *n.* **1,** a white, claylike substance; **2,** a tobacco pipe of this material.

¹**meet** (mēt), *v.t.* [met (mět), meet-ing], **1,** to come upon; come face to face with; as, he *met* her downtown; **2,** to be at the place of arrival of; as, I *met* the boat at the dock; **3,** to connect with; join; as, this path *meets* the main road; **4,** to oppose in a battle, contest, duel, or the like; **5,** to be introduced to; **6,** to experience; as, he *met* strange adventures; **7,** to be perceived by; to catch the attention of; as, to *meet* the eye; **8,** to equal; satisfy; as, will you *meet* my demands?—*v.i.* **1,** to collect in one place; assemble; **2,** to come together:—*n.* a gathering or assemblage for some definite purpose; as, a track *meet.*

²**meet** (mēt), *adj.* fitting; proper; as, it is *meet* that man should observe the law.

meet·ing (mēt′ĭng), *n.* **1,** a coming together of persons; a chance encounter; **2,** an assembly; a gathering for a special purpose, occasion, etc.; **3,** a place where two or more things come together; union; a junction, as of roads.

meet·ing·house (mēt′ĭng-hous′), *n.* a building for public worship, especially one used by Friends.

meg·a- (měg′ä-), a prefix meaning great; as, *megaphone.*

meg·a·phone (měg′ä-

MEGAPHONE

fōn), *n.* a large horn or speaking trumpet, used to increase the sound of the voice or to carry it a long distance.

mel·an·chol·y (měl′ăn-kŏl′ĭ), *n.* [*pl.* melancholies], a gloomy state of mind or mood; depression of spirits:—*adj.* dejected; downcast; sad.—*adj.* **mel′an-chol′ic.**

Syn., *adj.* dispirited, mournful.

Mel·a·ne·si·a (měl′á-nē′shĭ-á; měl′á-nē′shá; měl′á-nē′zhá), a group of islands, part of Oceania, northeast of Australia.— *n.* and *adj.* **Mel′a-ne′sian.**

Mel·bourne (měl′bērn), a seaport, capital of Victoria, in Australia (map 16).

Mel·e·a·ger (měl′ē-ā′jēr), *n.* in Greek mythology, the hero who was destined to die as soon as the brand which was burning on the hearth at his birth was consumed. His mother extinguished the brand in order to save his life, but years later threw it back into the fire to avenge Meleager's slaying of her two brothers.

me·lee (mā-lā′; mā′lā; měl′ā), *n.* a hand-to-hand fight; skirmish.

mel·lif·lu·ous (mě-lĭf′lŏo-ŭs), *adj.* smooth and sweet; honeyed; as, a *mellifluous* voice. —*adv.* **mel·lif′lu·ous·ly.**

mel·low (měl′ō), *adj.* **1,** soft, juicy, and sweet, because of ripeness; as, a *mellow* peach; **2,** of a delicate, rich flavor; well matured; as, *mellow* wine; **3,** soft; rich; as soil; **4,** pure; rich, as a color or sound; **5,** softened by age or maturity:—*v.t.* and *v.i.* to make or become ripe, gentle, or sweet; as, sorrow *mellowed* her nature.

Syn., *adj.* mature, ripe.

me·lo·di·ous (mē-lō′dĭ-ŭs), *adj.* musical; sweet; tuneful; as, a *melodious* voice.— *adv.* **me·lo′di·ous·ly.**

Syn. pleasing, harmonious.

mel·o·dra·ma (měl′ō-drä′má; měl′ō-drä′-má; měl′ō-drăm′á), *n.* **1,** a highly exciting, romantic play, with a happy ending; **2,** hence, sensational language or behavior.

mel·o·dra·mat·ic (měl′ō-drá-măt′ĭk), *adj.* **1,** relating to melodrama; **2,** highly sensational; violently emotional; as, a *melodramatic* account of her escape.—*adv.* **mel′o·dra·mat′i·cal·ly.**

mel·o·dy (měl′ō-dĭ), *n.* [*pl.* melodies], **1,** an agreeable arrangement of sounds; **2,** a song or tune; as, the *melody* was simple; **3,** the principal part in a song; the air; as, the sopranos carry the *melody.*—*adj.* **me·lod′ic** (mē-lŏd′ĭk).

mel·on (měl′ŭn), *n.* **1,** a trailing plant of the gourd family; also, its edible fruit; a muskmelon; **2,** a watermelon. (See illustration next page.)

melt (mělt), *v.i.* [*p.t.* melt-ed, *p.p.* melt-ed or, *Archaic,* mol-ten (mōl′těn), *p.pr.* melting], **1,** to be changed from a solid to a liquid state, often by heat; as, ice *melts;* **2,** to dissolve; as, sugar *melts* in the mouth; **3,** to waste away; grow gradually less; as, his anger *melts* under kindness; **4,** to disappear; vanish; as, the fog *melts* away; **5,** to become gentle or tender; as, my heart *melts;* **6,** to blend, as colors:— *v.t.* **1,** to change from a solid to a liquid state; as, heat *melts* butter; **2,** to make tender or gentle.

MELONS
1, watermelon; **2,** honeydew; **3,** cantaloupe.

Mel·ville (mĕl´vĭl), Herman (1819-1891), an American novelist and poet, most famous for "Moby Dick," a novel about whaling.

mem·ber (mĕm´bĕr), *n.* **1,** one who belongs to a group or society; as, a class *member;* **2,** a part of the body, especially a leg or arm; hence, one part of any whole.

mem·ber·ship (mĕm´bĕr-shĭp), *n.* **1,** the state of being a member; **2,** all the persons belonging to an organization.

mem·brane (mĕm´brān), *n.* a thin, soft sheet of tissue which serves as a cover, connection, or lining in an animal or vegetable body.—*adj.* **mem´bra·nous.**

me·men·to (mē-mĕn´tō), *n.* [*pl.* mementos or mementoes], that which serves as a reminder; a souvenir; token.

memo. abbreviation for *memorandum.*

mem·oir (mĕm´wär; mĕm´wôr), *n.* **1,** a memorandum; **2,** a record or account of events written from the author's personal knowledge or experience; **3,** a biography; a biographical sketch or notice.

mem·o·ra·ble (mĕm´ō-rá-bl), *adj.* worthy of being remembered; notable; as, a *memorable* battle.—*adv.* **mem´o·ra·bly.**

Syn. signal, marked, noteworthy.

mem·o·ran·dum (mĕm´ō-răn´dŭm), *n.* [*pl.* memoranda (mĕm´ō-răn´dá) or memorandums], **1,** a note to help one to remember; **2,** a brief, informal note or report.

me·mor·i·al (mē-môr´ĭ-ǎl), *adj.* in memory of a person or an event; as, a *memorial* address:—*n.* **1,** a thing serving to keep alive the memory of a place, person, etc.; as the Lincoln *Memorial;* **2,** a record or account of something; **3,** a written statement of facts addressed to a person or persons in authority, usually accompanied by a request or protest.

Memorial Day, a holiday, May 30, set aside by law in most states for honoring the U.S. soldiers and sailors who died in war: also called *Decoration Day.*

mem·o·rize (mĕm´ō-rīz), *v.t.* [memorized,

memoriz-ing], to commit to memory; to learn by heart; as, to *memorize* poetry.

mem·o·ry (mĕm´ō-rĭ), *n.* [*pl.* memories], **1,** the ability or power to remember things; **2,** a particular period or experience remembered; as, a trip to the circus is one of my earliest *memories;* **3,** the length of time within which past happenings are remembered; as, it happened within grandmother's *memory;* **4,** reputation after death; as, his *memory* is honored.

Syn. recollection, reminiscence.

Mem·phis (mĕm´fĭs), **1,** a commercial city in southwestern Tennessee (map 8); **2,** an ancient Egyptian city on the Nile (map 1).

men (mĕn), plural of *man.*

men·ace (mĕn´ĭs), *n.* a danger or evil that threatens; as, the *menace* of flood:—*v.t.* [menaced, menac-ing], to threaten; as, war *menaced* the world.—*adv.* **men´ac·ing·ly.**

me·nag·er·ie (mē-năj´ĕr-ĭ; mē-năzh´ĕr-ĭ), *n.* **1,** a place where wild animals are kept; **2,** a collection of wild animals, kept in cages, for exhibition.

mend (mĕnd), *v.t.* **1,** to repair (that which is broken or worn); as, to *mend* a torn sleeve; **2,** to make better; correct; reform; as, the prisoner *mended* his ways:—*v.i.* to grow better or stronger; improve; as, the man who had been ill *mended* rapidly:—*n.* **1,** the act of growing better; as, he is on the *mend* after his illness; **2,** a repaired part of something.

Syn., v. amend, better, rectify.

men·da·cious (mĕn-dā´shŭs), *adj.* **1,** given to lying; not truthful; **2,** false; not true, as a statement.—*adv.* **men·da´cious·ly.**—*n.* **men·dac´i·ty** (mĕn-dăs´ĭ-tĭ).

Men·del (mĕn´dĕl), Gregor (1822–1884), an Austrian monk and botanist, who formulated the law of heredity named for him.—*adj.* **Men·de´li·an** (mĕn-dē´lĭ-ǎn).

Men·de·lye·ev (mĕn´dyĕ-lyä´yĕf), Dmitri Ivanovich (1834–1907), a Russian chemist.

men·di·cant (mĕn´dĭ-kǎnt), *n.* a beggar:—*adj.* practicing begging; as, a *mendicant* rascal.

Men·e·la·us (mĕn´ĕ-lā´ŭs), *n.* in Greek mythology, a king of Sparta, who was the brother of Agamemnon and the husband of Helen.

men·ha·den (mĕn-hā´dn), *n.* a shadlike fish, about twelve to sixteen inches long, found in large numbers off the Atlantic coast, used for bait, and in making oil and fertilizer

MENHADEN (₁⁄₁₀)

go; join; yet; sing; chin; show; thin, *th*en; hw, *why;* zh, azure; ü, Ger. *für* or Fr. l*u*ne; ö, Ger. schön or Fr. *feu;* ṅ, Fr. e*n*fant, no*m;* kh, Ger. a*ch* or i*ch.* See pages ix-x.

me·ni·al (mē′nĭ-ăl; mēn′yăl), *n.* a domestic servant, especially one who does lowly or degrading work:—*adj.* relating to, or suitable for, a servant; lowly; humble; as, a *menial* task.—*adv.* **me′ni·al·ly.**

men·in·gi·tis (měn′ĭn-jī′tĭs), *n.* an inflammation of the membranes of the brain and spinal cord.

Men·non·ite (měn′ŏn-īt), *n.* a member of a Protestant sect, of which the leading features are the baptism of adults, plain living and dress, and refusal to take oaths or perform military service.

-ment (-měnt), a suffix which forms nouns meaning: **1,** the act of; as, enforce*ment;* **2,** the state of; as, content*ment;* **3,** the means or instrument; as, adorn*ment,* argu*ment;* **4,** a thing produced or result attained; as, pave*ment,* attach*ment.*

men·tal (měn′tăl), *adj.* relating to the mind; intellectual; as, *mental* exercise; done by the mind; as, to make a *mental* note of something.

men·tal·i·ty (měn-tăl′ĭ-tĭ), *n.* [*pl.* mentalities], intellectual ability, its quality or amount; mind; as, the *mentality* of the child must be developed by education.

men·tal·ly (měn′tăl-ĭ), *adv.* in the mind; as regards the mind; as, *mentally* superior.

men·thol (měn′thōl; měn′thŏl), *n.* a solid, white substance with a mintlike odor, obtained from oil of peppermint and used in medicine, toilet preparations, etc.

men·tion (měn′shŭn), *n.* a brief notice; a light or chance remark; as, he made *mention* of the fact:—*v.t.* to speak briefly of; name; refer to; as, he did not *mention* you. —*adj.* **men′tion·a·ble.**
    Syn. v. tell, impart, communicate.

men·tor (měn′tẽr; měn′tôr), *n.* a wise and faithful friend, adviser, or teacher.

men·u (měn′ū; mā′nū; mē·nü′), *n.* a bill of fare; a list of the dishes served at a meal; also, the dishes served.

mer·can·tile (mûr′kăn-tĭl; mûr′kăn-tīl), *adj.* having to do with, or engaged in, trade; relating to merchants.

mer·ca·tor's (mûr-kā′tẽrz; měr-kä′tôrz) **pro·jec·tion,** a method of representing the surface of the earth in which the meridians of longitude and parallels of latitude are drawn as straight lines, cutting each other at right angles.

mer·ce·nar·y (mûr′sē-něr′ĭ), *n.* [*pl.* mercenaries], a hired soldier:—*adj.* **1,** acting only for pay or reward; eager for money; **2,** prompted by greed; as, a *mercenary* crime.

mer·cer·ize (mûr′sẽr-īz), *v.t.* [mercerized, merceriz·ing], to treat (cotton thread or fabric) in such a way that it is strengthened,

made more capable of absorbing dyes, and given a silky luster.

mer·chan·dise (mûr′chăn-dīz), *n.* goods or articles that are bought and sold.

mer·chant (mûr′chănt), *n.* **1,** one who buys and sells goods for profit; especially, one who carries on trade on a large scale; **2,** a shopkeeper:—*adj.* relating to, or employed in, trade: as, *merchant* ships.

mer·chant·man (mûr′chănt-măn), *n.* [*pl.* merchantmen (-měn)], a trading ship.

mer·chant ma·rine, the ships of a nation which are used for trade, not for war.

mer·ci·ful (mûr′sĭ-fool), *adj.* full of mercy; tenderhearted.—*adv.* **mer′ci·ful·ly.**

mer·ci·less (mûr′sĭ-lěs), *adj.* without pity; unfeeling; cruel.—*adv.* **mer′ci·less·ly.**
    Syn. hardhearted, pitiless, unrelenting.

mer·cu·ri·al (mûr-kū′rĭ-ăl), *adj.* **1,** changeable; gay; as, *mercurial* youth; **2,** relating to, or caused by, mercury; as, *mercurial* poisoning.

mer·cu·ry (mûr′kŭ-rĭ), *n.* a heavy, liquid, silver-white metal, used in thermometers, medicines, etc.; quicksilver.

Mer·cu·ry (mûr′kū-rĭ), *n.* **1,** in Roman mythology, the messenger of the gods, inventor of the lyre, and god of commerce, wealth, etc.: identified with the Greek *Hermes;* **2,** the planet nearest to the sun.

mer·cy (mûr′sĭ), *n.* [*pl.* mercies], **1,** willingness to forgive an offender, or to treat him with kindness; pity; **2,** willingness to help suffering; **3,** an act of kindness.—**at the mercy of,** in the power of; as, the man was *at the mercy of* his captors.
    Syn. benevolence, clemency, leniency.

MERCURY

¹**mere** (mēr), *n.* a shallow lake or pool.

²**mere** (mēr), *adj.* [*superl.* mer-est], nothing but; no more than; simple; as, this error is a *mere* trifle; he is a *mere* child.

mere·ly (mēr′lĭ), *adv.* simply; purely; only; as, he is not unkind, *merely* thoughtless.

mer·e·tri·cious (měr′ē-trĭsh′ŭs), *adj.* attracting by false show; deceitfully alluring; as, *meretricious* jewelry; *meretricious* promises.

MERGANSER (¹⁄₁₅)

mer·gan·ser (měr-găn′sẽr), *n.* a kind of

fish-eating duck, often crested, with a slender, hooked, somewhat toothed bill.

merge (mûrj), *v.t.* [merged, merg-ing], to cause (something) to be absorbed into something else:—*v.i.* to be absorbed; lose separate character or identity; as, the two small banks *merged* with a larger one.
Syn. unite, blend, join, mix, mingle.

merg-er (mûr′jẽr), *n.* the legal combination of two estates, or of two or more business corporations, into one.

me-rid-i-an (mē-rĭd′ĭ-ăn), *adj.* 1, relating to the highest point reached by a heavenly body, as the sun, in its daily course; 2, relating to or characteristic of the point of greatest success or splendor (of a person, state, etc.):—*n.* 1, the highest point reached by a heavenly body; 2, the highest point, as of success, wealth, fame, etc.; 3, an imaginary circle around the earth, passing through the North and South Poles and any given place; also, a line on a map representing a meridian.

me-ringue (mē-răng′), *n.* a mixture of beaten white of egg and sugar, used as an icing on pudding or pastry, or baked into small cakes or shells.

Me-ri-no (mē-rē′nō), *n.* [*pl.* Merinos], a breed of sheep with fine wool:—**merino**, the fine cloth or yarn made from this wool.

mer-it (mĕr′ĭt), *n.* 1, due reward or punishment; usually, reward; 2, the condition of deserving, or not deserving; as, we are treated according to our *merits;* 3, excellence; worth; that which deserves praise; as, the *merit* of honesty; 4, the right or wrong of anything; as, to judge a case on its *merits:*—*v.t.* to deserve; as, to *merit* reward.

MERINO SHEEP (RAM)

mer-i-tor-i-ous (mĕr′ĭ-tôr′ĭ-ŭs), *adj.* deserving of reward or praise; as, *meritorious* conduct.—*adv.* **mer′i-tor′i-ous-ly.**

Mer-lin (mûr′lĭn), *n.* in medieval legend, a famous magician at King Arthur's court.

mer-lon (mûr′lŏn), *n.* one of the solid parts between the openings in the parapet of a castle. (See illustration under *battlement.*)

mer-maid (mûr′mād′), *n.* a sea nymph with the body of a woman and the tail of a fish.—*n.masc.* **mer′man′.**

mer-ri-ment (mĕr′ĭ-mĕnt), *n.* mirth; fun; frolic; gaiety.

mer-ry (mĕr′ĭ), *adj.* [mer-ri-er, mer-ri-est], full of mirth and fun; gay; jolly; pleasant. —*adv.* **mer′ri-ly.**
Syn. cheerful, mirthful, joyous, blithe.

mer-ry—go—round (mĕr′ĭ-gō-round′), *n.*

1, a large, revolving, circular platform fitted with wooden animals or seats, on which persons ride; a carrousel; 2, a whirl of gaiety; as, a *merry-go-round* of parties.

mer-ry-mak-ing (mĕr′ĭ-māk′ĭng), *n.* festivity:—*adj.* festive; gay.

me-sa (mā′sa̤), *n.* a tableland or plateau with steep or sloping sides.

mes-dames (mā-dȧm′), plural of *madam* or *madame.*

mes-de-moi-selles (mād′mwä-zĕl′), plural of *mademoiselle.*

mesh (mĕsh), *n.* 1, one of the openings between the threads of a net or of a wire screen; 2, hence, any network, or something that entangles; as, the *meshes* of the spider's web; 3, in machinery, the uniting, or engaging, of the teeth of two gear wheels so that power can be passed along from one to the other:—*v.t.* to catch or entangle in, or as in, a net:—*v.i.* 1, to become entangled; 2, in machinery, to unite with each other: said of gear teeth.

mes-mer-ism (mĕz′mẽr-ĭzm; mĕs′mẽr-ĭzm), *n.* the act of producing a trance or state of sleep, in which the subject's behavior is easily influenced by suggestion; hypnotism.—*n.* **mes′mer-ist.**

mes-mer-ize (mĕz′mẽr-īz; mĕs′mẽr-īz), *v.t.* [mesmerized, mesmeriz-ing], 1, to produce a hypnotic trance or sleep in; hypnotize; 2, hence, to fascinate; charm.—*n.* **mes′mer-iz′er.**

Mes-o-po-ta-mi-a (mĕs′ō-pō-tā′mĭ-a̤), a region in Asia lying between the Tigris and Euphrates Rivers.

mes-quite (mĕs-kēt′; mĕs′kēt), *n.* a small thorny tree of southwestern North America, whose sugary beanlike pods are used as food for cattle.

mess (mĕs), *n.* 1, a number of persons who take their meals together, especially soldiers or sailors; also, the meal itself; 2, enough for one meal; as, a *mess* of fish; 3, a state of dirt or confusion; a muddle; a botch:—*v.t.* 1, to provide food for; 2, *Colloquial,* to muddle; as, he *messed* the job; 3, to soil:—*v.i.* 1, to eat together, as sailors; 2, to potter; trifle.

mes-sage (mĕs′ĭj), *n.* a word, notice, etc., written, spoken, or otherwise delivered, from one person to another.

mes-sen-ger (mĕs′ĕn-jẽr), *n.* 1, one who carries a message; also, one who does errands; 2, a herald or bringer of news.

Mes-si-ah (mē-sī′a̤), *n.* 1, the expected king and deliverer of the Hebrews; the Christ; 2, in the Christian church, Jesus, called Christ, regarded as this deliverer; 3, hence, any great national savior. —*adj.* **mes′si-an′ic** (mĕs′ĭ-ăn′ĭk).

Mes·sieurs (měs′ērz; měs′yērz; mā′syö′), plural of English *Mister* and French *Monsieur.*

Mes·si·na (mě-sē′ná), a seaport in northeastern Sicily:—**Strait of Messina,** a narrow waterway between Italy and Sicily. (Map 12.)

mess·mate (měs′māt′), *n.* a companion at meals, especially on board ship; hence, a friend or companion.

Messrs. abbreviation for *Messieurs,* plural of *Mister.*

mess·y (měs′ĭ), *adj.* [mess-i-er, mess-i-est], disorderly; soiled; botched; as, a *messy* job.—*n.* **mess′i·ness.**

met (mět), past tense and past participle of *meet.*

met·al (mět′l), *n.* **1,** any of a number of solid, heavy, lustrous substances, as gold, tin, copper, etc., that conduct electricity and that can be drawn into fine threads, hammered into thin plates, and melted by heat; also, a mixture of these substances, as brass; **2,** the material, as broken stone, used for making a road or as ballast for a railroad track; **3,** spirit; temper; as, a woman of fine *metal.*

me·tal·lic (mě-tăl′ĭk), *adj.* **1,** relating to metals or a metal; **2,** having the qualities of metal; as, a *metallic* sound.

met·al·lur·gy (mět′l-ûr′jĭ; mě-tăl′ēr-jĭ), *n.* the science of separating metals from their ores, and of preparing them for use. —*adj.* **met′al·lur′gi·cal.**—*n.* **met′al·lur′gist.**

met·al·work·ing (mět′l-wûr′kĭng), *n.* the act of making something out of metal.—*n.* **met′al·work′.**—*adj.* **met′al·work′ing.**

met·a·mor·phose (mět′á-môr′fōz; mět′-á-môr′fōs), *v.t.* [metamorphosed, metamorphos-ing], to change into a different form or nature; as, the wicked fairy *metamorphosed* the princess into a bird.

met·a·mor·pho·sis (mět′á-môr′fô-sĭs; mět′á-môr-fō′sĭs), *n.* [*pl.* metamorphoses

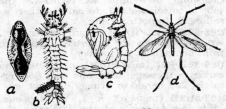

METAMORPHOSIS OF A MOSQUITO
a, egg; *b,* larva; *c,* pupa; *d,* adult.

(mět′á-môr′fô-sēz; -môr-fō′sēz)], change of form, shape, or structure; transformation;

especially, a striking change in the form and habits of an animal as it grows and develops from the egg to the adult stage; as, the *metamorphosis* of a caterpillar into a moth.—*n.* **met′a·mor′phism.**

met·a·phor (mět′á-fēr; mět′á-fôr), *n.* a figure of speech in which a name, action, or term ordinarily applied to a certain object is applied to another in order to suggest a likeness between them: distinguished from *simile* by not having *like* or *as* to introduce it. "His voice cut through the silence" is a *metaphor.*—*adj.* **met′a·phor′i·cal** (mět′á-fôr′ĭ-kăl).

met·a·phys·i·cal (mět′á-fĭz′ĭ-kăl), *adj.* **1,** having to do with the branch of philosophy that deals with the question of what is real, the existence of God, etc.; **2,** hard to understand; abstract.

met·a·phys·ics (mět′á-fĭz′ĭks), *n.pl.* used as *sing.* that branch of knowledge which tries to explain the nature, character, and causes of being and knowing.

mete (mēt), *v.t.* [met-ed, met-ing], **1,** to measure; **2,** to give out by measure; apportion; as, to *mete* out rewards.

me·te·or (mē′tē-ēr), *n.* a mass of matter coming from outer space that glows and burns as it enters and passes through the earth's atmosphere.

me·te·or·ic (mē′tē-ŏr′ĭk), *adj.* **1,** relating to, formed of, or like, a shooting star; as, a *meteoric* display; **2,** hence, swift; dazzling; rousing a passing wonder; as, a *meteoric* success.

me·te·or·ite (mē′tē-ēr-īt), *n.* a body of stone or metal which has fallen upon the earth from outer space.

me·te·or·ol·o·gy (mē′tē-ēr-ŏl′ô-jĭ), *n.* the science that studies and tells about the atmosphere and the changes of heat, cold, wind, storms, etc., that take place in it.— *adj.* **me′te·or·o·log′i·cal** (mē′tē-ŏr-ô-lŏj′-ĭ-kăl).—*n.* **me′te·or·ol′o·gist.**

-me·ter (-mē′tēr), a suffix meaning: **1,** a device for measuring; as, baro*meter;* **2,** a certain arrangement of syllables in a line of poetry; as, hexa*meter.*

¹**me·ter** or **me·tre** (mē′tēr), *n.* **1,** the arrangement of a line of poetry into measured groups of words or syllables, called feet, which gives to the line a regular beat; **2,** in music, rhythm or time.

²**me·ter** (mē′tēr), *n.* an instrument for measuring and recording the passage of liquids, gases, or electric current; as, a water *meter.*

³**me·ter** or **me·tre** (mē′tēr), *n.* the standard unit of length in the metric system; equal to 39.37 inches.

Meth. abbreviation for *Methodist.*

āte, āorta, râre, căt, ȧsk, fär, ăllow, sofȧ; ēve, ēvent, ĕll, writẽr, novĕl; bīte, pĭn; nō, ōbey, ôr, dŏg, tŏp, cŏllide; ūnit, ūnite, bûrn, cŭt, focŭs; nōon, fŏot; mound; coin;

me·thinks (mē-thǐngks′), *v.impersonal* [*p.t.* methought (mē-thôt′)], *Archaic* or *Poetic*, it appears or seems to me.

meth·od (mĕth′ŭd), *n.* 1, an established order or regular way of doing something; as, a *method* of teaching; 2, an orderly arrangement of ideas, subjects, etc. *Syn.* manner, process, rule.

me·thod·i·cal (mē-thŏd′ĭ-kǎl), *adj.* 1, arranged in order; as, a *methodical* outline; 2, devoted to order; systematic; as, a *methodical* person.—*adv.* **me·thod′i·cal·ly.**

Meth·od·ist (mĕth′ŭd-ĭst), *n.* a member of a Protestant denomination founded by John and Charles Wesley and others at Oxford, England, in 1729:—*adj.* having to do with Methodists.—*n.* **Meth′od·ism.**

me·thought (mē-thôt′), past tense of *methinks.*

Me·thu·se·lah (mē-thū′zĕ-lȧ; mē-thū′sĕ-lȧ), *n.* 1, in the Bible, a Hebrew patriarch who is recorded as having lived 969 years (Genesis 5:27); 2, hence, a very old man.

me·tic·u·lous (mē-tĭk′ū-lŭs), *adj.* too careful of trifling details.—*adv.* **me·tic′-u·lous·ly.**—*n.* **me·tic′u·lous·ness.**

me·tre (mē′tẽr), *n.* 1, the metric unit of length; 2, rhythm, as in poetry or music; meter. See ¹**meter,** ³**meter.**

met·ric (mĕt′rĭk), *adj.* having to do with some kind of measurement, especially the metric system:—**metric system,** a decimal system of weights and measures using the *meter* (39.37 inches) as the unit of length and the *gram* (equal to about a cubic centimeter of water) as the unit of weight.

met·ri·cal (mĕt′rĭ-kǎl), *adj.* 1, relating to, like, or composed in, meter or rhythm; as, a *metrical* translation; a *metrical* effect; 2, relating to measurement; metric.—*adv.* **met′ri·cal·ly.**

met·ro·nome (mĕt′rō-nōm), *n.* an instrument which beats time, used especially in practicing music.

me·trop·o·lis (mē-trŏp′ō-lĭs), *n.* the chief city or capital of a country, state, or region; also, a principal center of population and civilization.

met·ro·pol·i·tan (mĕt′rō-pŏl′ĭ-tǎn), *adj.* relating or belonging to a large city; as, *metropolitan* police:—*n.* 1, a resident of a large city; 2, an archbishop.

METRONOME

met·tle (mĕt′l), *n.* spirit; courage; as, to try one's *mettle.*—*adj.* **met′tled.**

met·tle·some (mĕt′l-sŭm), *adj.* high-spirited; fiery; as, a *mettlesome* horse.

Meuse (mōz; mūz), a river flowing through northeastern France, Belgium, and the Netherlands to the North Sea.

Meuse–Ar·gonne (mōz′-är′gôn′), a region between the Meuse River and Argonne Forest in northeastern France, the scene of some of the greatest battles in World War I.

¹**mew** (mū), *n.* a gull; especially, the common European gull.

²**mew** (mū), *n.* a cage for confining hawks:—*v.t.* to confine or enclose in, or as in, a cage or mew.

³**mew** (mū), *n.* the cry of a cat:—*v.i.* to utter a sound or cry resembling a mew.

mewl (mūl), *v.i.* to whimper like a young child:—*n.* the cry of a baby.

Mex. abbreviation for *Mexico, Mexican.*

Mex·i·can (mĕk′sĭ-kǎn), *adj.* relating to Mexico, or to its people or customs:—*n.* a native of Mexico.

Mex·i·co (mĕk′sĭ-kō), a republic in North America, south of the U.S.:—**Mexico City,** a city, its capital, in the south central part:—**Gulf of Mexico,** a large gulf, southeast of North America, touching Mexico and the U.S. (Map 10.)

mez·za·nine (mĕz′ȧ-nēn; mĕz′ȧ-nĭn), *n.* in a building, an extra floor between two others, usually the first and second, often in the form of a gallery.

mez·zo (mĕd′zō), *adj.* and *adv.* in music, middle; not extreme; moderate; as, play that piece *mezzo* piano, or moderately soft.

mf. abbreviation for Italian *mezzo forte* meaning *moderately loud.*

mfg. abbreviation for *manufacturing.*

mfr. abbreviation for *manufacturer.*

mg. abbreviation for *milligram.*

Mgr. abbreviation for *Manager, Monseigneur, Monsignor.*

M.H.R. abbreviation for *Member of the House of Representatives.*

mi (mē), *n.* in music, the name of the third note of the scale.

mi. abbreviation for *mile, miles.*

Mi·am·i (mī-ăm′ĭ), a city and resort on the southeastern coast of Florida (map 8).

mi·ca (mī′kȧ), *n.* a mineral easily separated into thin, transparent plates which are used in lanterns, stove doors, etc.: often colloquially called *isinglass.*

Mi·cah (mī′kȧ), in the Bible, a Hebrew prophet who lived about 757–700 B.C.; also, the book of the Old Testament containing his prophecies.

mice (mīs), plural of *mouse.*

Mich. abbreviation for *Michigan.*

Mi·chael (mī′kĕl; mī′kȧ-ĕl), *n.* in Jewish and Christian legend, one of the seven archangels, represented as the leader of a host of angels.

Mich·ael·mas (mĭk′ĕl-mȧs), *n.* September 29, a feast day in honor of Saint Michael.

Mi·chel·an·ge·lo (mī′kĕl-ăn′jĕ-lō), (1475–1564), a Florentine sculptor, painter, poet, and architect.

Mich·i·gan (mĭsh′ĭ-găn), a State (cap. Lansing) in the north central U.S.:— **Lake Michigan,** one of the Great Lakes, between Michigan and Wisconsin. (Map 7.)

mi·cro- (mī′krŏ-), a prefix meaning small, little, insignificant; as, *micro*cosm.

mi·crobe (mī′krōb), *n.* a living animal or plant so tiny as to be seen only under the microscope; a germ; especially, a germ that carries disease.

mi·cro·cosm (mī′krŏ-kŏzm), *n.* a little world; a world in miniature: opposite of *macrocosm.*

mi·crom·e·ter (mī-krŏm′ē-tẽr), *n.* an instrument for measuring very small distances. It is used in connection with a microscope or a telescope.

Mi·cro·ne·si·a (mī′krŏ-nē′shĭ-ȧ; mī′krŏ-nē′shȧ), a group of islands, part of Oceania, east of the Philippines.

mi·cro·or·gan·ism (mī′krŏ-ôr′găn-ĭzm), *n.* a tiny organism; a microbe.

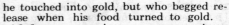
MICRO- PHONE

mi·cro·phone (mī′krŏ-fōn), *n.* an instrument which strengthens or passes along sound waves by means of electricity; as, a radio *microphone.*

mi·cro·scope (mī′krŏ-skōp), *n.* an optical instrument with a lens for making very tiny objects appear larger.

mi·cro·scop·ic (mī′krŏ-skŏp′ĭk), *adj.* **1,** seen or discovered by means of, or relating to, a microscope; **2,** having the power of a microscope; as, a *microscopic* eye; **3,** very small; invisible without a microscope; as, a *microscopic* insect or plant. Also, **mi′cro·scop′i·cal.** — *adv.* **mi′cro·scop′i·cal·ly.**

mid (mĭd), *adj.* [*superl.* mid-most], middle; as, *mid* ocean, or *mid*-ocean.

′mid (mĭd), a shortened form of *amid.*

MICROSCOPE

Mi·das (mī′dȧs), *n.* in Greek mythology, a Phrygian king to whom was granted the power to change everything he touched into gold, but who begged release when his food turned to gold.

mid·day (mĭd′dā′), *n.* the middle hours of the day; noon:—*adj.* at noon; as, the *mid-day* meal.

mid·dle (mĭd′l), *n.* a point or part halfway between two given points, ends, or sides; center; as, the *middle* of a river:— *adj.* **1,** halfway between two given points; as, the *middle* point of a line; **2,** intermediate; in-between; as, *middle* age.

mid·dle–aged (mĭd′l-ājd′), *adj.* neither young nor old: said of a person between the ages of about 40 and 60 years.

Middle Ages, the period between ancient and modern times, about A.D. 500 to about A.D. 1400.—*adj.* **Mid′dle—Age′.**

mid·dle·man (mĭd′l-măn′; mĭd′l-măn), *n.* [*pl.* middlemen (-mĕn′; -mĕn)], one who acts as a go-between; especially, one who buys goods from the producer to sell to the retail merchant.

Mid·dle·sex (mĭd′l-sĕks), a metropolitan county of England, containing northwestern London.

mid·dling (mĭd′lĭng), *adj.* of moderate rank, size, or quality; neither good nor bad; mediocre; as, a *middling* success in business:—**middlings,** *n.pl.* a mixture of coarse-ground wheat flour and fine bran.

mid·dy (mĭd′ĭ), *n.* [*pl.* middies], *Colloquial,* a midshipman, or naval cadet:— **middy blouse,** a loose sailor blouse, worn especially by children, and by women for sports.

midge (mĭj), *n.* **1,** any very small fly or gnat; **2,** a dwarf; midget.

midg·et (mĭj′ĕt), *n.* **1,** a dwarf; a little person; **2,** a small fly or gnat.

mid·i·ron (mĭd′ī′ẽrn), *n.* a golf club with an iron head on which the face is so inclined as to give the ball a moderately high path. (See *golf club,* illustration.)

mid·land (mĭd′lănd), *adj.* inland; in the central part of a country; as, a *midland* farming district:—*n.* the interior of a country:—**Midlands,** the central counties of England.

mid·most (mĭd′mōst), *adj.* in the very middle; hence, innermost.

mid·night (mĭd′nīt′), *n.* the middle of the night; twelve o'clock at night.

mid·rib (mĭd′rĭb′), *n.* in botany, the vein along the center of a leaf.

mid·riff (mĭd′rĭf), *n.* the diaphragm; the muscular partition separating the cavity of the chest from that of the abdomen.

mid·ship (mĭd′shĭp′), *adj.* relating to or at the middle of a ship.

mid·ship·man (mĭd′shĭp′măn), *n.* [*pl.* midshipmen (-mĕn)], in the U.S. Navy, one in training, usually at the Naval Academy, for an officer's commission; one who ranks next below an ensign.

midst (mĭdst), *n.* the middle; the central place; as, in the *midst* of danger:—*prep.* amidst; as, *midst* the excitement.

mid·sum·mer (mĭd′sŭm′ēr), *n.* the middle of summer; also, the period about June 21, the longest day of summer:—*adj.* (mĭd′sŭm′ēr), in or like the middle of the summer; as, *midsummer* heat.

mid·way (mĭd′wā′), *adj.* and *adv.* halfway; as, *midway* to town:—*n.* the amusement section of an exposition or fair.

mid·wife (mĭd′wīf′), *n.* [*pl.* midwives (mĭd′wivz′)], a woman who assists women in childbirth.

mid·win·ter (mĭd′wĭn′tēr), *n.* the middle of winter; also, the period about December 21, the shortest day of winter:—*adj.* (mĭd′wĭn′tēr), in or like the middle of winter.

mien (mēn), *n.* outward appearance; air; look; manner; as, a dignified *mien*.

¹**might** (mīt), past tense of *may*.

²**might** (mīt), *n.* force or power of body or mind; as, fight with all your *might*.

might·y (mīt′ĭ), *adj.* [might-i-er, might-i-est], **1**, powerful; strong; **2**, of unusual size, amount, etc.; as, a *mighty* wave:—*adv.* *Colloquial*, very or exceedingly; as, *mighty* glad.—*adv.* **might′i·ly**.

mi·gnon·ette (mĭn′yŭn·ĕt′), *n.* a fragrant garden plant with small, greenish-white flowers.

mi·graine (mī′grān; mĭ·grān′), *n.* a severe headache, usually affecting one side of the head only.

mi·grate (mī′grāt), *v.i.* [migrat-ed, migrat-ing], **1**, to move from one country or locality to another for permanent residence; **2**, to travel periodically from one climate or feeding ground to another at certain times of the year, as do many birds.—*n.* **mi·gra′tion** (mī·grā′shŭn).—*adj.* **mi′gra·tor′y** (mī′grà·tôr′ĭ).

MIGNONETTE

mi·ka·do (mĭ·kä′dō), *n.* a popular title given to the Emperor of Japan.

Mi·lan (mĭ·lăn′; mĭl′ăn), a city, capital of Lombardy, Italy (map **12**). Its Italian name is **Mi·la′no** (mē·lä′nō).

milch (mĭlch), *adj.* yielding milk; as, a *milch* cow.

mild (mīld), *adj.* **1**, gentle; kind; calm; as, a *mild* answer; **2**, moderate in quality or degree; not sharp, sour, or bitter; as, *mild* cheese; not severe; as, *mild* weather.—*adv.* **mild′ly**.—*n.* **mild′ness**.

mil·dew (mĭl′dū), *n.* **1**, any of several kinds of tiny fungi, found on plants or decaying substances; **2**, a disease of plants produced by these fungi; **3**, spots of mold caused by their growth on cloth, leather, paper, etc., usually when exposed to dampness:—*v.t.* to affect with mildew:—*v.i.* to be affected with mildew; as, leather *mildews* when it remains damp.

mile (mīl), *n.* a measure of length containing 5,280 feet:—**geographical mile**, in the U.S., 6,080.20 feet: also called *nautical mile* or *knot*.

mile·age (mīl′ĭj), *n.* **1**, an allowance for traveling expenses, at a specified rate per mile; **2**, total distance in miles, as of travel; as, the *mileage* of a trip; **3**, the use that one gets from something, expressed in miles; as, to get good *mileage* from tires.

mile·post (mīl′pōst′), *n.* a signpost stating the distance in miles to a certain point.

mile·stone (mīl′stōn′), *n.* a stone serving as a milepost; hence, any event in history, a person's life, etc., which marks a definite stage.

Mi·le·tus (mī·lē′tŭs), a ruined city of ancient Ionia, on the coast of Asia Minor (map **1**).

MILESTONE

mil·i·tant (mĭl′ĭ·tănt), *adj.* **1**, at war; also, warlike; as, a *militant* nation; **2**, combative or aggressive in promoting a cause; as, a *militant* clergyman:—*n.* one who fights; also, one who uses aggressive methods in aid of a cause.

mil·i·ta·rism (mĭl′ĭ·tà·rĭzm), *n.* **1**, a disposition to uphold a nation's power by means of a strong army and navy; **2**, a warlike policy; the policy of readiness to fight on slight grounds; **3**, rule or government by military interests.—*n.* **mil′i·ta·rist**.—*adj.* **mil′i·ta·ris′tic** (mĭl′ĭ·tà·rĭs′tĭk).

mil·i·tar·y (mĭl′ĭ·tĕr′ĭ), *adj.* **1**, relating to soldiers, arms, or war; as, *military* force; **2**, performed or supported by soldiers; as, *military* rule:—*n.* the army; troops.

mil·i·tate (mĭl′ĭ·tāt), *v.i.* [militat-ed, militat-ing], to have force or weight; tell; as, the testimony of eyewitnesses *militated* against him.

mi·li·tia (mĭ·lĭsh′à), *n.* a body of citizens enrolled and trained for the defense of a state or nation as a regular military force, but not called into active service except in an emergency.

milk (mĭlk), *n.* **1**, a white fluid produced by female mammals and used by their young as food; **2,** this fluid taken by man from certain animals, especially the cow, and used as food; **3,** the white juice of certain plants, as of the milkweed; **4,** any whitish fluid resembling milk; as, the *milk* of the coconut:—*v.t.* to draw milk from; as, to *milk* a cow.—*n.fem.* **milk′maid′.**—*n.masc.* **milk′man′.**

milk-sop (mĭlk′sŏp′), *n.* a weak, timid man.

milk-weed (mĭlk′wēd′), *n.* any of various wild plants which exude a milklike fluid when bruised.

milk-y (mĭl′kĭ), *adj.* [milk-i-er, milk-i-est], **1,** containing milk, or like milk; as, *milky* water; **2,** yielding milklike juice, as do certain plants.

MILKWEED

Milky Way, a broad band of pale light across the heavens, visible at night, consisting of countless stars not separately visible to the naked eye: also called *Galaxy.*

¹**mill** (mĭl), *n.* the thousandth part of a dollar; one tenth of a cent.

²**mill** (mĭl), *n.* **1,** a building equipped with machinery to grind grain; as, a flour *mill;* **2,** any machine for grinding solid substances, as coffee, pepper, etc., for finishing or transforming raw materials, or for extracting juice or sap; as, a cider *mill;* **3,** a manufacturing plant; as, a steel *mill;* a paper *mill;* **4,** any unpleasant or exhausting experience; as, to go through the *mill:* —*v.t.* **1,** to grind (grain), cut or saw (timber), roll or press (steel), crush (ore), etc., in a mill; **2,** to make a raised border around the edges of (a coin); **3,** to make frothy, as chocolate, by churning or whipping:—*v.i.* **1,** to move in circles; as, the cattle *milled* about the pen; **2,** to move confusedly, as a crowd.

mil-len-ni-um (mĭ-lĕn′ĭ-ŭm), *n.* [*pl.* millenniums or millennia (mĭ-lĕn′ĭ-à)], **1,** a period of 1,000 years; **2,** the time when Christ will come again and reign on earth (Revelation 20:1–4); hence, a period of great joy, prosperity, and righteousness.

mill-er (mĭl′ẽr), *n.* **1,** one who owns or works a flour mill; **2,** any moth whose wings look as if powdered with flour.

Mil-let (mē′lâ′; mĭ-lā′), Jean François (1814–1875), a French painter of scenes from peasant life.

mil-let (mĭl′ĕt), *n.* **1,** a grain-bearing grass, widely used in Europe and Asia as food for man and birds, and, in the U.S., cut for hay; **2,** the seed of this grass.

mil-li-gram or **mil-li-gramme** (mĭl′ĭ-grăm), *n.* in the metric system, one thousandth of a gram.

mil-li-me-ter or **mil-li-me-tre** (mĭl′ĭ-mē′tẽr), *n.* in the metric system, one thousandth of a meter or 0.03937 of an inch.

mil-li-ner (mĭl′ĭ-nẽr), *n.* a person, usually a woman, who deals in, makes, or trims women's hats, headdresses, etc.

mil-li-ner-y (mĭl′ĭ-nẽr′ĭ), *n.* [*pl.* millineries], **1,** such articles as milliners make or sell, as women's hats; **2,** the business of making and selling women's hats.

mil-lion (mĭl′yŭn), *n.* **1,** one thousand thousand: written 1,000,000; **2,** an indefinitely large number.—*n.* and *adj.* **mil′-lionth.**

mil-lion-aire (mĭl′yŭn-âr′), *n.* **1,** one who has a million, or more, dollars; **2,** a very rich person.

mill-race (mĭl′rās′), *n.* a channel through which water flows with a swift current to a mill wheel; also, the current driving the wheel.

mill-stone (mĭl′stōn′), *n.* **1,** one of two flat, circular stones used for grinding grain in a mill; **2,** something that crushes; a heavy burden.

mil-reis (mĭl′rās′), *n.* [*pl.* milreis], the monetary unit of Brazil, replaced by the *cruzeiro.* (See Table, page 943.)

Mil-ton (mĭl′tŭn), John (1608–1674), an English poet, author of "Paradise Lost."

Mil-wau-kee (mĭl-wô′kĭ), a port on Lake Michigan, in Wisconsin (map 7).

mime (mīm), *n.* **1,** among the Greeks and Romans, a play in which real persons and events were imitated and made fun of; **2,** an actor in such a drama; **3,** a clown.

Mim-e-o-graph (mĭm′ē-ō-grȧf′), *n.* a trade-mark name for a machine that makes copies of written or typewritten matter by means of stencils and an ink roller:— **mimeograph,** a copying machine bearing this trade name:—*v.t.* to copy by such a machine; as, to *mimeograph* a letter.

mim-ic (mĭm′ĭk), *n.* one who imitates, especially to make fun of the person or thing imitated:—*v.t.* [mimicked, mimicking], to imitate closely; especially, to ridicule (a person) by imitating his manners, characteristics, etc.:—*adj.* **1,** imitative; **2,** mock; pretending to be real; as, *mimic* warfare.

mim-ic-ry (mĭm′ĭk-rĭ), *n.* [*pl.* mimicries], **1,** the practice or art of one who imitates or mimics; **2,** the close outward likeness of various birds, animals, and insects to their surroundings, or to other more dangerous species: called *protective mimicry.*

mi·mo·sa (mĭ-mō′sȧ; mĭ-mō′zȧ), *n.* any of various plants of the pea family, including trees and shrubs, growing in warm regions.

min. abbreviation for *minute.*

min·a·ret (mĭn′ȧ-rĕt′; mĭn′ȧ-rĕt), *n.* a tall, slender tower connected with a Mohammedan mosque, or place of worship, encircled by several balconies from which the call to prayer is made by a public crier.

mince (mĭns), *v.t.* [minced, minc·ing], 1, to cut or chop into very small pieces; 2, to tell in part or by degrees; lessen the harshness of; as, to *mince* matters; 3, to utter with assumed elegance or daintiness; as, she *minces* her words:—*v.i.* 1, to talk with assumed elegance; 2, to walk primly or with assumed daintiness.

MINARETS of a mosque at Cairo, Egypt.

mince-meat (mĭns′mēt′), *n.* a mixture of raisins, suet, lemon peel, etc., and usually meat, chopped fine and used as a filling for pies.

minc·ing (mĭn′sĭng), *adj.* affected; with assumed elegance; as, *mincing* speech.—*adv.* **minc′ing·ly.**

mind (mīnd), *n.* 1, memory; recollection; as, to call to *mind;* 2, one's thoughts, opinions, etc.; as, to speak one's *mind;* 3, the part of a person that is aware, knows, thinks, feels, wills, etc.; consciousness: opposite of *matter;* 4, the understanding or intellect; as, he has a good *mind:*—*v.t.* 1, to pay attention to; as, *mind* your step; 2, to be troubled by; object to; as, to *mind* the heat; 3, to obey; as, *mind* your parents; 4, to watch; take care of; as, to *mind* the baby:—*v.i.* 1, to be troubled; feel annoyance; as, never *mind* if you can't do it; 2, to be careful; as, *mind* you put on your overcoat.

Min·da·na·o (mĭn′dä-nä′ō), a large island in the Philippine group (map 15).

mind·ed (mīnd′dĕd), *adj.* 1, disposed or inclined; intending; as, *minded* to swim; 2, having a mind of a certain kind or with a certain interest; as, pure-*minded;* mathematically-*minded.*

mind·ful (mīnd′fo͝ol), *adj.* taking thought or heed; heedful; attentive; as, *mindful* of one's duty.—*adv.* **mind′ful·ly.**

mind·less (mīnd′lĕs), *adj.* 1, forgetful; disregarding; as, *mindless* of danger; 2, without mind; stupid.

¹**mine** (mīn), *n.* 1, in mining, an excavation from which minerals, precious stones, etc., are dug; also, a deposit of ore or coal; 2, hence, an inexhaustible supply of anything, or a source of great wealth;

3, an underground passage or cavity under an enemy's fortification in which a high explosive is set off; also, a case containing high explosive, moored where it will destroy enemy ships :—*v.t.* [mined, min·ing], 1, to get by digging underground; as, to *mine* coal; 2, to dig into, as for ore or metals; 3, to destroy slowly or secretly; undermine; 4, to place explosives under (an enemy's trenches); moor submerged explosives in (a harbor, river, ocean lane, or the like):—*v.i.* 1, to carry on the work of digging for metals, coal, etc.; 2, to lay explosives, as under an enemy's trenches or in a harbor.—*n.* **min′er.**

²**mine** (mīn), a possessive form of the personal pronoun *I:* 1, as *adj.*, belonging to me· **a**, in the predicate; as, whose is that hat? it is *mine;* **b**, *Archaic* or *Poetic*, used for *my* before a vowel or *h;* as, *mine* eyes; *mine* host; 2, as *pron.*, a person or thing that belongs to me; as, which hat has he? he has *mine;* your hat is red, *mine* is blue.

min·er·al (mĭn′ēr-ȧl), *n.* 1, any substance not animal or vegetable in origin, ordinarily solid, except in the case of mercury and water; 2, ore; a substance obtained by mining:—*adj.* pertaining to, containing, or mixed with, minerals, or a mineral; as, *mineral* ore; *mineral* water.

min·er·al·o·gy (mĭn′ēr-ăl′ō-jĭ), *n.* [*pl.* mineralogies], the science of minerals.—*n.* **min er·al′o·gist.**

Mi·ner·va (mĭ-nûr′vȧ), *n.* in Roman mythology, the goddess of wisdom, handicrafts, and invention: identified with the Greek *Athena.*

min·gle (mĭng′gl), *v.t.* [min-gled, min-gling], 1, to combine by mixing; blend; 2, to associate:—*v.i.* 1, to mix or blend; 2, to enter into close relation; mix; as, to *mingle* with the crowd.

Syn. unite, join, merge.

min·i·a·ture (mĭn′ĭ-ȧ-tūr; mĭn′yȧ-tūr), *n.* 1, a very small painting, especially a portrait, usually on ivory or vellum; 2, a small model of any object:—*adj.* on a very small scale; as, a *miniature* railroad.

min·i·mize (mĭn′ĭ-mīz), *v.t.* [minimized, minimiz-ing], to reduce to the smallest degree, part, or proportion; make little of; as, to *minimize* one's illness.

min·i·mum (mĭn′ĭ-mŭm), *n.* [*pl.* minima (mĭn′ĭ-mȧ) or minimums], 1, the least quantity possible or allowable: opposite of *maximum;* 2, the lowest point reached or recorded, as of temperature:—*adj.* lowest; least possible or allowable; as, the *minimum* mark for passing.

min·ing (mīn′ĭng), *adj.* 1, relating to the excavating of metals, ores, precious stones, or the like; 2, relating to the laying of explosives:— *n.* the act of working mines for ores or minerals, or of laying explosive mines.

min·ion (mĭn′yŭn), *n.* **1,** a fawning servant or agent who obeys without question; **2,** a favorite; a pet; **3,** in printing, a small size of type (see second illustration under *type*).

min·is·ter (mĭn′ĭs-tẽr), *n.* **1,** one entrusted by the head of a government with the direction of a department; as, a *Minister* of War; **2,** a diplomatic agent sent to a foreign country to represent his own government; **3,** a clergyman or pastor of a church, especially of a Protestant church: —*v.i.* **1,** to serve or act as pastor; **2,** to give aid by doing helpful things; as, to *minister* to the poor.

min·is·te·ri·al (mĭn′ĭs-tē′rĭ-ăl), *adj.* pertaining to a minister or to the office of a minister.—*adv.* **min′is·te′ri·al·ly.**

min·is·trant (mĭn′ĭs-trănt), *adj.* serving; giving aid:—*n.* one who serves or aids.

min·is·tra·tion (mĭn′ĭs-trā′shŭn), *n.* the act of serving; aiding; as, the *ministrations* of a clergyman or priest.

min·is·try (mĭn′ĭs-trĭ), *n.* [*pl.* ministries], **1,** service; **2,** the service of one who preaches a religion; **3,** the office or duties of an officer of state; also, a department of government under the direction of a minister; as, the *Ministry* of Foreign Affairs; **4,** the clergy; **5,** the officers of state, as a group; **6,** the term of service of an officer of state or of a clergyman.

mink (mĭngk), *n.* **1,** an animal somewhat like the weasel, living part of the time in water; **2,** its valuable brown fur.

Minn. abbreviation for *Minnesota.*

Min·ne·ap·o·lis (mĭn′ē-ăp′ō-lĭs), a city in southeastern Minnesota, on the Mississippi River (map 7).

Min·ne·so·ta (mĭn′ē-sō′tȧ), a State (cap. Saint Paul) in the north central U.S. (map 7).

m i n · n o w (mĭn′ō), *n.* **1,** a tiny fresh-water fish of the carp family; **2,** loosely, any of several very small fish.

MINNOW (½)

mi·nor (mī′nẽr), *n.* **1,** a person of either sex under full legal age, which is usually 21 years; **2,** in U.S. colleges, a subject next in importance to a student's major subject:—*adj.* **1,** unimportant; as, a *minor* injury; **2,** in music, less by half a step than the major interval; hence, designating a scale, chord, or the like, in which such intervals occur.

mi·nor·i·ty (mĭ-nŏr′ĭ-tĭ; mī-nŏr′ĭ-tĭ), *n.* [*pl.* minorities], **1,** the smaller of two parts of a group; **2,** the state of being under age.

Mi·nos (mī′nŏs), *n.* in Greek mythology, a king of Crete who after death became one of the judges in Hades; in later legend, a king of Crete who built the Labyrinth and kept the Minotaur in it.

Min·o·taur (mĭn′ō-tôr), *n.* in Greek mythology, a monster, half man and half bull, which every year devoured seven youths and seven maidens, until killed by Theseus.

min·ster (mĭn′stẽr), *n.* **1,** the church of a monastery; **2,** in England, a cathedral.

min·strel (mĭn′strĕl), *n.* **1,** in the Middle Ages, a poet, singer, and musician; **2,** now, one of a group of black-face performers, who sing Negro songs, tell jokes, etc.

min·strel·sy (mĭn′strĕl-sĭ), *n.* [*pl.* minstrelsies], **1,** the art of singing and playing as practiced by minstrels of the Middle Ages; **2,** a company of minstrels; **3,** a collection of ballads or lyrics.

¹mint (mĭnt), *n.* any of a large family of spicy-leaved plants, as the peppermint.

²mint (mĭnt), *n.* **1,** a place where money is coined under government authority and supervision; **2,** an abundant supply; a vast amount; as, he has a *mint* of money; **3,** hence, any source of invention or supply: —*v.t.* **1,** to coin or stamp (money); **2,** to make into money; as, to *mint* silver.

min·u·end (mĭn′ū-ĕnd), *n.* in arithmetic, that number from which another number is to be subtracted.

min·u·et (mĭn′ū-ĕt′; mĭn′ū-ĕt), *n.* **1,** a graceful and stately dance in triple measure; **2,** the music for such a dance; also, music having a similar style and rhythm.

mi·nus (mī′nŭs), *adj.* **1,** indicating subtraction; as, the *minus* sign; **2,** indicating a negative quantity; as, a *minus* three:—*n.* the sign [—] indicating subtraction:—*prep.* less; decreased by; diminished by; as, five *minus* two.

¹min·ute (mĭn′ĭt), *n.* **1,** the 60th part of an hour or of a degree of an arc; **2,** a short time; a moment; **3,** an official note; a memorandum; **4, minutes,** the official record made of the proceedings of a meeting.

²mi·nute (mĭ-nūt′; mī-nūt′), *adj.* **1,** tiny; as, a *minute* particle; **2,** precise; detailed; as, a *minute* description.—*adv.* **mi·nute′ly.**

min·ute-man (mĭn′ĭt-măn′), *n.* [*pl.* minutemen (-mĕn′)], in the American Revolution, a citizen ready to arm at a minute's notice.

mi·nu·ti·ae (mĭ-nū′shĭ-ē; mī-nū′shĭ-ē), *n.pl.* small, precise, or trivial details.

minx (mĭngks), *n.* a bold or saucy girl.

āte, âorta, râre, căt, ȧsk, fär, ȧllow, sofȧ; ēve, êvent, ĕll, writẽr, novĕl; bīte, pĭn; nō, ōbey, ôr, dôg, tŏp, cŏllide; ūnit, ūnite, bûrn, cŭt, focŭs; nōōn, fŏŏt; mound; coin;

mir·a·cle (mĭr′ȧ-kl), *n.* an act or happening in the material or physical world which seems to depart from the laws of nature or to go beyond what is known of these laws; a wonder; a marvel.

mi·rac·u·lous (mĭ-răk′ū-lŭs), *adj.* 1, wonderful; 2, characterized by unlikeness to the known laws of nature; 3, supernatural or seemingly so.—*adv.* **mi·rac′u·lous·ly.**

mi·rage (mĭ-räzh′), *n.* the image, usually upside down and often distorted, of some object actually beyond the range of sight, reflected in the sky over deserts, oceans, and plains. Mirages are common in hot countries, especially in sandy deserts, where a traveler often imagines he sees a body of water where no water exists.

mire (mīr), *n.* deep mud; wet earth; slush; dirt:—*v.t.* [mired, mir-ing], 1, to soil; 2, to cause to be stuck in the mud; as, to *mire* the wheels of a cart:—*v.i.* to sink in mud.

mir·ror (mĭr′ẽr), *n.* 1, a looking glass; any surface that reflects images, as water or polished metal; 2, that which gives a true likeness; 3, hence, a model; a pattern:—*v.t.* to reflect; as, a lake *mirrors* a tree.

mirth (mûrth), *n.* noisy gaiety; social merriment; jollity.—*adj.* **mirth′less.**

mirth·ful (mûrth′fŏŏl), *adj.* merry; festive; jolly.—*adv.* **mirth′ful·ly.**

mis- (mĭs-), a prefix meaning bad(ly) or wrong(ly); as, *mis*direct, *mis*fit, *mis*rule.

mis·ad·ven·ture (mĭs′ăd-vĕn′tûr), *n.* bad luck; mishap; disaster.

mis·an·thrope (mĭs′ăn-thrōp; mĭz′ăn-thrōp), *n.* one who hates or distrusts mankind.—*adj.* **mis′an·throp′ic** (mĭs′ăn-thrŏp′ĭk; mĭz′ăn-thrŏp′ĭk).

mis·ap·ply (mĭs′ȧ-plī′), *v.t.* [misapplied, misapply-ing], to use or apply incorrectly or illegally, as words or funds.

mis·ap·pre·hend (mĭs′ăp-rė-hĕnd′), *v.t.* to fail to understand.—*n.* **mis′ap·pre·hen′sion.**

mis·ap·pro·pri·ate (mĭs′ȧ-prō′prĭ-āt), *v.t.* [misappropriat-ed, misappropriat-ing], to apply to a wrong use or purpose; especially, to use (another's money) as one's own.—*n.* **mis′ap·pro′pri·a′tion.**

mis·be·have (mĭs′bė-hāv′), *v.i.* [misbehaved, misbehav-ing], to act in a wrong or improper fashion.—*n.* **mis′be·hav′ior.**

misc. abbreviation for *miscellaneous.*

mis·cal·cu·late (mĭs-kăl′kū-lāt), *v.t.* [miscalculat-ed, miscalculat-ing], to make a mistake in; misjudge; as, to *miscalculate* a distance.—*n.* **mis′cal·cu·la′tion.**

mis·call (mĭs-kôl′), *v.t.* to name wrongly.

mis·car·riage (mĭs-kăr′ĭj), *n.* 1, failure; mismanagement; 2, a premature birth.

mis·car·ry (mĭs-kăr′ĭ), *v.i.* [miscarried, miscarry-ing], to go astray or go wrong.

mis·cast (mĭs-kȧst′), *v.t.* and *v.i.* to assign (an actor) to a part he is not suited to play.

mis·cel·la·ne·ous (mĭs′ĕ-lā′nė-ŭs), *adj.* 1, consisting of several kinds mixed together; 2, many-sided; consisting of various qualities.—*adv.* **mis′cel·la′ne·ous·ly.**

mis·cel·la·ny (mĭs′ĕ-lā′nĭ), *n.* [*pl.* miscellanies], 1, a collection of various things of different kinds; 2, a book containing a variety of literary compositions.

mis·chance (mĭs-chȧns′), *n.* bad luck.

mis·chief (mĭs′chĭf), *n.* 1, harm; injury; damage; misfortune; as, to do someone *mischief;* 2, discord; as, to make *mischief* between friends; 3, vexatious behavior; also, a tendency to cause annoyance; as, there was more *mischief* than evil in him.

mis·chie·vous (mĭs′chĭ-vŭs), *adj.* producing injury or damage; full of pranks; annoying.—*adv.* **mis′chie·vous·ly.**

mis·con·ceive (mĭs′kŏn-sēv′), *v.t.* and *v.i.* [misconceived, misconceiv-ing], to misunderstand; misjudge.—*n.* **mis′con·cep′tion** (mĭs′kŏn-sĕp′shŭn).

mis·con·duct (mĭs-kŏn′dŭkt), *n.* improper or wrong behavior:—*v.t.* (mĭs′kŏn-dŭkt′), to manage or handle badly; as, to *misconduct* a business.

mis·con·struc·tion (mĭs′kŏn-strŭk′shŭn), *n.* misunderstanding; the giving of a wrong meaning to something; as, the *misconstruction* of a word or an act.

mis·con·strue (mĭs′kŏn-strōō′; mĭs-kŏn′strōō), *v.t.* [misconstrued, misconstru-ing], to get the wrong meaning from; as, you *misconstrue* my words.

mis·count (mĭs-kount′), *n.* a mistake in counting:—*v.t.* and *v.i.* to count wrong.

mis·cre·ant (mĭs′krė-ănt), *n.* a villain; wrongdoer:—*adj.* villainous.

mis·deal (mĭs-dēl′), *v.t.* and *v.i.* [misdealt (mĭs-dĕlt′), misdeal-ing], to make a mistake in dealing (cards):—*n.* a mistake in dealing cards.

mis·deed (mĭs-dēd′), *n.* a wrong act; a crime.

mis·de·mean·or (mĭs′dė-mē′nẽr), *n.* a wrongdoing; especially, in law, an offense less serious than a felony. Also, **mis′de·mean′our.**

mis·di·rect (mĭs′dĭ-rĕkt′; mĭs′dī-rĕkt′), *v.t.* 1, to give false or incorrect instructions to; 2, to place a wrong address on, as a letter; 3, to apply wrongly, as one's talents.

mis·do·ing (mĭs-dōō′ĭng), *n.* wrongdoing.

mi·ser (mī′zẽr), *n.* one who accumulates money for its own sake; a greedy, stingy person.—*adj.* **mi′ser·ly.**—*n.* **mi′ser·li·ness.**

---

go; join; yet; sing; chin; show; thin, *th*en; hw, *wh*y; zh, azure; ü, Ger. für or Fr. l*u*ne; ö, Ger. schön or Fr. f*eu*; ṅ, Fr. e*n*fant, no*m*; kh, Ger. a*ch* or i*ch*. See pages ix–x.

mis·er·a·ble (mĭz′ẽr-á-bl), *adj.* **1,** very unhappy; wretched; **2,** worthless; poor in quality; as, *miserable* food; **3,** causing discomfort; as, *miserable* weather.—*adv.* **mis′er·a·bly.**
Syn. distressed, afflicted, forlorn.

mis·er·y (mĭz′ẽr-ĭ), *n.* [*pl.* miseries], extreme pain, distress, or misfortune; great unhappiness; wretchedness.

mis·fit (mĭs-fĭt′), *n.* **1,** anything which does not fit; **2,** a person in a position for which he is unfitted.

mis·for·tune (mĭs-fôr′tŭn), *n.* bad luck.

mis·give (mĭs-gĭv′), *v.t.* [*p.t.* misgave (mĭs-gāv′), *p.p.* misgiv·en (mĭs-gĭv′ĕn), *p.pr.* misgiv·ing], to cause to fail in confidence or courage; make fearful; as, my heart *misgives* me.

mis·giv·ing (mĭs-gĭv′ĭng), *n.* doubt or uncertainty; anxiety.

mis·gov·ern (mĭs-gŭv′ẽrn), *v.t.* to rule badly; mismanage, as a business, a nation, or a career.—*n.* **mis·gov′ern·ment.**

mis·guide (mĭs-gīd′), *v.t.* [misguid·ed, misguid·ing], to mislead; to influence to wrong conduct or thought.

mis·hap (mĭs-hăp′; mĭs′hăp), *n.* ill fortune; an unlucky accident.

mis·in·form (mĭs′ĭn-fôrm′), *v.t.* and *v.i.* to give incorrect or false information (to).

mis·in·ter·pret (mĭs′ĭn-tûr′prĕt), *v.t.* **1,** to misunderstand; **2,** to give a wrong explanation of.—*n.* **mis′in·ter′pre·ta′tion.**

mis·judge (mĭs-jŭj′), *v.t.* [misjudged, misjudg·ing], to form a wrong or unjust opinion of:—*v.i.* to be mistaken in opinion.

mis·lay (mĭs-lā′), *v.t.* [mislaid (mĭs-lād′), mislay·ing], to lose temporarily; put in the wrong place unintentionally.

mis·lead (mĭs-lēd′), *v.t.* [misled (mĭs-lĕd′), mislead·ing], **1,** to deceive; give a wrong idea to; **2,** to lead astray.

mis·man·age (mĭs-măn′ĭj), *v.t.* and *v.i.* [mismanaged, mismanag·ing], to manage badly.—*n.* **mis·man′age·ment.**

mis·name (mĭs-nām′), *v.t.* [misnamed, misnam·ing], to name wrongly or improperly.

mis·no·mer (mĭs-nō′mẽr), *n.* a wrong name or term.

mis·place (mĭs-plās′), *v.t.* [misplaced, misplac·ing], **1,** to put in a wrong place; **2,** to bestow, as one's affections, on an improper or undeserving object; as, he *misplaced* his trust.—*n.* **mis·place′ment.**

mis·play (mĭs-plā′), a wrong or improper play, as in baseball.

mis·print (mĭs-prĭnt′), *v.t.* to print incorrectly:—*n.* a mistake in type.

mis·pro·nounce (mĭs′prŏ-nouns′), *v.t.* and *v.i.* [mispronounced, mispronouncing], to speak with a wrong sound or accent.—*n.* **mis′pro·nun′ci·a′tion** (mĭs′prŏ-nŭn′sĭ-ā′shŭn; -shĭ-ā′shŭn).

mis·read (mĭs-rēd′), *v.t.* [misread (mĭs-rĕd′), misread·ing], **1,** to read incorrectly; as, to *misread* a letter; **2,** to misunderstand; as, to *misread* a motive.

mis·rep·re·sent (mĭs′rĕp-rē-zĕnt′), *v.t.* and *v.i.* to report incorrectly, either wilfully or through carelessness.—*n.* **mis′rep·re·sen·ta′tion.**

mis·rule (mĭs-rōōl′), *v.t.* [misruled, misrul·ing], to govern badly:—*n.* bad government.

¹miss (mĭs), *v.t.* **1,** to fail to hit; as, to *miss* the mark; **2,** to feel the need or absence of; as, he *misses* his mother; **3,** to escape by good luck; as, he just *missed* the snowstorm; **4,** to fail to meet or catch; as, to *miss* a train; **5,** to let go by; fail to grasp, attend, etc.; as, to *miss* a chance; *miss* church; **6,** to fail to hear, notice, or understand; as, he *missed* that point:—*v.i.* **1,** to fail to make a hit; **2,** to fail to secure, attain, do, etc.; as, to *miss* in spelling:—*n.* failure to hit, reach, see, obtain, etc.
Syn., v. overlook, lose.

²miss (mĭs), *n.* [*pl.* misses], a young girl:—**Miss,** a title used before the name of a girl or an unmarried woman.

Miss. abbreviation for *Mississippi.*

mis·sal (mĭs′ăl), *n.* **1,** the book containing the order of service for the Roman Catholic Mass; **2,** hence, a book of devotions or prayers.

mis·shap·en (mĭs-shāp′ĕn), *adj.* deformed; out of shape.

mis·sile (mĭs′ĭl), *n.* an object, as a spear, shot, etc., thrown or hurled as a weapon.

miss·ing (mĭs′ĭng), *adj.* lost; absent.

mis·sion (mĭsh′ŭn), *n.* **1,** the act of sending, or state of being sent, with specific powers, to do a special service; **2,** a business or duty on which one is sent; any errand; **3,** one's life work; a calling, especially to preach and spread a religion; **4,** an organization for doing religious and charitable work; also, a station or building serving as a center for such work; **5,** in military action, a task given to an individual or to a whole unit; **6,** in air warfare, a flight assignment for one airplane or a whole group of airplanes; **7, missions,** missionary work.

mis·sion·ar·y (mĭsh′ŭn-ĕr′ĭ), *n.* [*pl.* missionaries], a person who is sent to spread the knowledge of a religion and convert people to it, especially in foreign lands:—

adj. pertaining to missions or to missionaries; as, *missionary* service.

Mis·sis·sip·pi (mĭs/ĭ-sĭp/ĭ), **1,** a State (cap. Jackson) in the southern U.S. (map 8); **2,** the largest river in North America, flowing from northern Minnesota into the Gulf of Mexico (map 5).

mis·sive (mĭs/ĭv), *n.* a letter.

Mis·sou·ri (mĭ-zōōr/ĭ; mĭ-sōōr/ĭ; mĭ-zōōr/ă), **1,** a State (cap. Jefferson City) in central U.S. (map 7); **2,** a river flowing from the Rocky Mountains into the Mississippi (map 5).

mis·spell (mĭs-spĕl/), *v.t.* to spell incorrectly.

mis·spent (mĭs-spĕnt/), *adj.* spent foolishly or for the wrong purposes; wasted

mis·state (mĭs-stāt/), *v.t.* [misstat-ed, misstat-ing], to state falsely or incorrectly; misrepresent.—*n.* **mis-state/ment.**

mis·step (mĭs-stĕp/), *n.* a wrong step; hence, a wrong act.

mist (mĭst), *n.* **1,** visible water vapor in the atmosphere, at or near the earth's surface; fog; haze; **2,** anything that dims the sight or the mind:—*v.i.* to rain in very fine drops.

mis·take (mĭs-tāk/), *v.t.* [*p.t.* mistook (mĭs-tōōk/), *p.p.* mistak-en (mĭs-tāk/ĕn), *p.pr.* mistak-ing], **1,** to misunderstand; as, to *mistake* a meaning or a motive; **2,** to put wrongly in place of another person or thing; as, he *mistook* her for her sister:—*v.i.* to err in judgment or opinion; be wrong:—*n.* an error; fault; misunderstanding.—*adj.* **mis-tak/a-ble.**

mis·tak·en (mĭs-tāk/ĕn), *adj.* **1,** wrong; as, a *mistaken* idea; **2,** wrong in judgment; as, he is *mistaken;* **3,** misunderstood; as, a *mistaken* meaning.—*adv.* **mis-tak/en-ly.**

Mis·ter (mĭs/tẽr), *n.* [*pl.* Messieurs (mĕs/rz; mĕs/yẽrz)], Master: a title, usually abbreviated to *Mr.* [*pl.* Messrs.], used before a man's name or his office.

mis·tle·toe (mĭs/l-tō; mĭz/l-tō), *n.* an evergreen parasitic plant with white waxen berries, which grows and feeds on apple trees, oak trees, etc.

mis·took (mĭs-tōōk/), past tense of *mistake.*

mis·treat (mĭs-trēt/), *v.t.* to treat wrongly; abuse.

mis·tress (mĭs/trĕs), *n.* **1,** a woman at the head of a family, school, etc.; also, a woman with authority or power; as, she is *mistress* of her own business; **2,** a woman skilled in anything; as, a *mistress* of needlework; **3,** a woman courted and beloved; a sweet-

MISTLETOE

heart; **4,** a female paramour:—**Mistress,** a title formerly used before the name of a woman, married or unmarried: now *Mrs.* (mĭs/ĭz; mĭs/ĭs) for married women, and *Miss* for unmarried women.

mis·tri·al (mĭs-trī/ăl), *n.* in law, a trial made worthless by some legal error.

mis·trust (mĭs-trŭst/), *n.* lack of confidence:—*v.t.* to doubt; suspect.—*adj.* **mis-trust/ful.**

Syn., n. doubt, uncertainty, suspicion.

mist·y (mĭs/tĭ), *adj.* [mist-i-er, mist-i-est], **1,** characterized by haze or fog; **2,** dim; clouded.—*n.* **mist/i-ness.**

mis·un·der·stand (mĭs/ŭn-dẽr-stănd/), *v.t.* and *v.i.* [misunderstood (mĭs/ŭn-dẽr-stōōd/), misunderstand-ing], to take (a person, remark, etc.) in a wrong sense; mistake the meaning of (words or actions).

mis·un·der·stand·ing (mĭs/ŭn-dẽr-stăn/dĭng), *n.* **1,** disagreement; a quarrel; as, a *misunderstanding* between friends; **2,** a mistake as to meaning or motive.

mis·use (mĭs-ūs/), *n.* **1,** wrong use; **2,** abuse:—*v.t.* (mĭs-ūz/) [misused, misusing], to use wrongly; ill-treat; as, to *misuse* a horse.—*n.* **mis-us/age** (mĭs-ūs/ĭj; mĭs-ūz/ĭj).

[1]**mite** (mīt), *n.* any of various tiny animals of the spider family, which live as parasites on animals, insects, plants, and stored goods, such as cheese.

[2]**mite** (mīt), *n.* **1,** a small coin used in ancient Palestine; as, the widow's *mite* (Mark 12:42); hence, any small contribution; **2,** *Colloquial,* a very small object or quantity; a small child.

mi·ter or **mi·tre** (mī/tẽr), *n.* **1,** a kind of crown or tall cap with two peaks, worn by archbishops, bishops, and sometimes by abbots as a symbol of office at special ceremonies; **2,** a slanting joint, as at corners in moldings, edgings, etc.: also called *miter joint:*—*v.t.* **1,** to place a bishop's crown on; hence, to raise to the office of a bishop; **2,** to join on a slanting line at a corner.

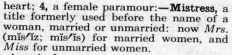

MITER, def. 1

MITER (aa), def. 2

mit·i·gate (mĭt/ĭ-gāt), *v.t.* [mitigat-ed, mitigat-ing], to make less severe or painful; soften; as, time *mitigates* grief.

Syn. relieve, diminish, alleviate.

mitt (mĭt), *n.* **1,** a kind of glove, often of lace or net, without fingers or with half fingers; **2,** a glove with a thick protective pad over the palm, used in baseball.

---

go; join; yet; sing; chin; show; thin, *th*en; hw, *why*; zh, azure; ū, Ger. für or Fr. lune; ö, Ger. schön or Fr. feu; ṅ, Fr. enfant, nom; kh, Ger. ach or ich. See pages ix-x.

mit·ten (mĭt'n), *n.* a glove for winter wear, covering the four fingers together and the thumb separately.

mix (mĭks), *v.t.* [*p.t.* and *p.p.* mixed or mixt (mĭkst), *p.pr.* mix-ing], **1,** to unite or blend into one mass or compound; **2,** to make by putting ingredients together; as, to *mix* a cake; **3,** to confuse; as, to *mix* facts:—*v.i.* **1,** to become united in a compound; as, oil will not *mix* with water; **2,** to mingle; associate; take part; as, to *mix* with the crowd; to *mix* well.

Syn. mingle, merge.

mixed (mĭkst), *adj.* **1,** composed of different kinds; as, *mixed* candy or cakes; **2,** for persons of both sexes; as, a *mixed* school; **3,** not restricted by class or condition; as, a *mixed* crowd; **4,** confused; mentally muddled; as, to be *mixed* up.

mixed num·ber, a whole number and a fraction, as 4½ or 3.1416.

mix·ture (mĭks'tŭr), *n.* **1,** the state of being blended or mingled; **2,** a compound or mass formed of two or more things.

miz·zen (mĭz'n), *n.* **1,** a fore-and-aft sail set on the mizzenmast; **2,** the lowest square sail on the mizzenmast of a full-rigged ship; **3,** a mizzenmast.

miz-zen-mast (mĭz'n-mȧst'; mĭz'n-mȧst), *n.* **1,** the mast nearest the stern in a two-masted or three-masted vessel (see illustration on page 695); **2,** the third mast from the bow in a vessel with four or more masts.

Mlle. abbreviation for *Mademoiselle.*

Mlles. abbreviation for *Mesdemoiselles.*

MM. abbreviation for *Messieurs:*—**mm.** abbreviation for *millimeter.*

Mme. abbreviation for *Madame* or *Madam.*

Mmes. abbreviation for *Mesdames.*

Mne-mos-y-ne (nē-mŏs'ĭ-nē), in Greek mythology, the goddess of memory and the mother of the Muses.

Mo. abbreviation for *Missouri:*—**mo.** abbreviation for *month:*—**M.O.** or **m.o.** abbreviation for *money order.*

Mo-ab (mō'ăb), an ancient kingdom of Syria, east of the Dead Sea.

moan (mōn), *v.i.* to utter a low sound from, or as from, pain or sorrow:—*v.t.* to utter in a low wail:—*n.* a low, drawn-out sound of sorrow or pain; hence, any similar sound; as, the *moan* of the wind.

moat (mōt), *n.* a deep ditch around a fortress or castle, usually containing water. (See illustration under *castle.*)

mob (mŏb), *n.* **1,** the common people; **2,** a rude, disorderly crowd:—*v.t.* [mobbed, mob-bing], to attack in a disorderly crowd.

Syn., n. multitude, throng, rabble.

Mo-bile (mō-bēl'), a seaport city in southwestern Alabama, on Mobile Bay:—**Mobile Bay,** an estuary of the Gulf of Mexico. (Map 8.)

mo-bile (mō'bĭl; mō'bēl), *adj.* **1,** easily moved; as, *mobile* troops; **2,** flowing freely, as some liquids; **3,** easily changing in expression; as, a *mobile* face.—*n.* **mo-bil'i-ty.**

mo-bi-lize (mō'bĭ-līz), *v.t.* [mobilized, mobiliz-ing], to call and prepare for active service; as, to *mobilize* an army or a navy. —*n.* **mo'bi-li-za'tion.**

moc-ca-sin (mŏk'ȧ-sĭn), *n.* **1,** a deerskin or other soft leather sandal worn by the North American Indians; **2,** any of several poisonous, mottled snakes of the southern U.S., especially the water moccasin; **3,** a kind of wild orchid.

MOCCASIN, def. 1

¹Mo-cha (mō'kȧ), an Arabian seaport on the Red Sea.

²Mo-cha (mō'kȧ), *n.* a fine Arabian coffee from Mocha, in Arabia.

MOCCASIN (⅙), def. 2

mock (mŏk), *v.t.* **1,** to ridicule; mimic in sport or contempt; make fun of; deride; **2,** to defy or scorn; as, to *mock* the law; **3,** to deceive; tantalize; as, the mirage in the desert *mocked* the travelers:—*n.* **1,** ridicule; **2,** a jeer or gibe; **3,** an object of ridicule:—*adj.* false; not real; as, a *mock* battle.

Syn., v. ape, imitate.

mock-er-y (mŏk'ẽr-ĭ), *n.* [*pl.* mockeries], **1,** the act of making fun of a person or thing; **2,** ridicule; **3,** a poor or disrespectful imitation; **4,** an empty sham.

mock-ing-bird (mŏk'ĭng-bûrd'), *n.* a thrush of the southern U.S., about the size of a robin, noted for imitating the calls of other birds.

mock or-ange, an ornamental shrub related to the lilac; syringa.

MOCKINGBIRD (⅛)

mode (mōd), *n.* **1,** way, method, or manner of doing something; as, a *mode* of speech; **2,** usual custom; fashion; style; as, hooped skirts are no longer the *mode;* **3,** in grammar, a certain form of a verb indicating whether or not the verb states a fact, a command, a condition, or the like; as, the indicative, imperative, or subjunctive *modes:* often called *mood.*

mod-el (mŏd'ĕl), *n.* **1,** a pattern of something to be made, copied, or imitated; a

standard copy; **2,** a small-sized, exact, and detailed representation of something to be made; as, an engine or ship *model;* a clay or wax *model* for a statue; **3,** a person who poses for a painter or sculptor; **4,** a woman who tries on costumes so that customers may see their effect; **5,** a person or thing to be imitated; as, let Lincoln be your *model:* —*v.t.* [modeled, model-ing], to form or mold; as, to *model* a head in clay:—*v.i.* **1,** to shape objects out of clay; make designs; **2,** to pose, as for an artist, or to try on costumes for customers:—*adj.* **1,** serving as a pattern; **2,** worthy of being imitated.
Syn., n. design, mold, standard.

mod-er-ate (mŏd′ẽr-āt), *v.t.* [moderat-ed, moderat-ing], **1,** to keep within bounds; make less violent, intense, or extreme; as, to *moderate* rage, heat, etc.; **2,** to preside over, as a meeting:—*v.i.* to become less violent or intense; as, the storm gradually *moderated:*—*adj.* (mŏd′ẽr-ĭt), **1,** not extreme; calm; mild; **2,** limited; mediocre; medium.—*adv.* **mod′er-ate-ly.**
Syn., adj. temperate, gentle.

mod-er-a-tion (mŏd′ẽr-ā′shŭn), *n.* **1,** the act of keeping within bounds; **2,** freedom from excess; restraint.

mod-er-a-tor (mŏd′ẽr-ā′tẽr), *n.* **1,** one who or that which regulates or restrains; as, courtesy is a *moderator* of conduct; **2,** a presiding officer, as at a meeting.

mod-ern (mŏd′ẽrn), *adj.* **1,** having to do with the present time; recent; as, *modern* inventions; **2,** relating to, or originating in, the centuries after about 1500 A.D.:—*n.* a person of recent and present times; also, one up-to-date in his views or manners.
Syn., adj. new, recent, late.

mod-ern-ism (mŏd′ẽr-nĭzm), *n.* any present-day practice, usage, taste, style, or idea:—**Modernism,** a religious movement in Catholic and Protestant churches, aiming to adapt modern scholarly and scientific knowledge to ancient creeds.—*n.* **mod′ern-ist.**—*adj.* **mod′ern-is′tic.**

mod-ern-ize (mŏd′ẽr-nīz), *v.t.* [modernized, moderniz-ing], to make like, or adapt to, present usage, taste, or speech.—*n.* **mod′ern-i-za′tion.**

mod-est (mŏd′ĕst), *adj.* **1,** not boastful or vain of one's own worth; **2,** retiring; not showy; as, the *modest* violet; **3,** not excessive or extreme; as, a *modest* ambition; **4,** pure; chaste.—*adv.* **mod′est-ly.**
Syn. virtuous, bashful, reserved.

mod-es-ty (mŏd′ĕs-tĭ), *n.* **1,** regard for what is proper in behavior or manner; **2,** reserve concerning one's own powers; lack of conceit; **3,** freedom from what is extreme; moderation; as, *modesty* in dress.
Syn. bashfulness, shyness, humility.

mod-i-fy (mŏd′ĭ-fī), *v.t.* [modified, modify-ing], **1,** to change slightly; as, to *modify* an idea; **2,** to limit; reduce; **3,** in grammar, to qualify; as, adjectives *modify* nouns.—*n.* **mod′i-fi-ca′tion.**
Syn. alter, soften, change.

mod-ish (mŏd′ĭsh), *adj.* fashionable; stylish; as, a *modish* hat.—*adv.* **mod′ish-ly.**

mod-u-late (mŏd′ū-lāt), *v.t.* [modulat-ed, modulat-ing], **1,** to vary the tone of; as, to *modulate* the voice; **2,** to tone down:—*v.i.* in music, to pass from one key to a related key.—*n.* **mod′u-la′tion.**

Mo-gul (mō-gŭl′; mō′gŭl), *n.* a person of the Mongolian race; especially, any of the Mongols who conquered India in the 16th century:—**the Great Mogul,** the ruler of their empire:—**mogul,** any imposing personage:—*adj.* relating to the Moguls or to their empire.

mo-hair (mō′hâr′), *n.* **1,** a woven material made from the hair of the Angora goat; **2,** an imitation of such a material.

Mo-ham-med (mō-hăm′ĕd), (570?–632), an Arabian prophet, founder of the Mohammedan religion. He is also called *Mahomet.*

Mo-ham-med-an (mō-hăm′ĕ-dăn), *n.* a follower of Mohammed or of the religion founded by him:—*adj.* relating to Mohammed, or to Mohammedanism.

Mo-ham-med-an-ism (mō-hăm′ĕ-dăn-ĭzm), *n.* the Moslem religion founded by Mohammed: also called *Islam.*

Mo-hawk (mō′hôk), *n.* one of a tribe of North American Indians belonging to the Five Nations, formerly occupying the Mohawk Valley, New York.

Mo-hawk Val-ley, a region in central New York State (map 6).

Mo-hi-can (mō-hē′kăn), *n.* one of a tribe of North American Indians of Algonquian stock, formerly occupying the banks of the upper Hudson, New York.

moil (moil), *n.* **1,** drudgery; labor; as, *moil* and toil; **2,** confusion.

moire (mwär; môr), *n.* a watered silk or mohair fabric.

moist (moist), *adj.* **1,** slightly wet; damp; **2,** tearful; as, *moist* eyes.
Syn. dank, humid.

mois-ten (mois′n), *v.t.* and *v.i.* to make, or become, damp or slightly wet.

mois-ture (mois′tūr), *n.* **1,** a moderate degree of dampness; **2,** water, or other liquid, in small quantity in the air as vapor, or condensed on a surface.

mo-lar (mō′lẽr), *n.* a double tooth, or grinder (see illustration under *dentition*): —*adj.* used for grinding.

mo-las-ses (mō-lăs′ĕz), *n.* [*pl.* molasses],

a dark-colored, sticky sirup, obtained as a by-product in the making of sugar.

¹mold or **mould** (mōld), *n.* fine, soft soil rich in decayed matter.

²mold or **mould** (mōld), *n.* **1,** a hollow form into which anything is poured to be shaped, as melted metals, jelly, puddings, or the like; **2,** the shape in which a thing is cast; form; **3,** kind; character; as, a man of honest *mold;* **4,** bodily shape or form:—*v.t.* **1,** to fashion in, or as in, a form; as, to *mold* a candle; to *mold* butter; **2,** to shape into a mass of the desired consistency; knead, as dough.

Syn., v. frame, shape, model, ornament.

³mold or **mould** (mōld), *n.* a fuzzy surface growth, composed of fungi, which develops chiefly on decaying animal or vegetable matter under warm, moist conditions, spreading by means of tiny spores and forming dense, feltlike mats:—*v.i.* to become covered with mold.—*adj.* **mold′y; mould′y.**

mold·er or **mould·er** (mōl′dēr), *v.i.* to crumble to dust by natural decay.

mold·ing or **mould·ing** (mōl′dĭng), *n.* **1,** anything made in or by a mold or form; **2,** an ornamental strip, usually of wood, used on a wall, picture frame, etc.

MOLDINGS

¹mole (mōl), *n.* a dark-colored spot or growth on the skin.

²mole (mōl), *n.* a tiny, burrowing, worm-eating animal with soft, blackish-brown fur, imperfectly developed eyes, and broad forefeet with which it digs underground tunnels.

³mole (mōl), *n.* a massive breakwater or stone pier, built out into the sea, sometimes to form an artificial harbor.

mol·e·cule (mŏl′ē-kūl; mō′lē-kūl), *n.* **1,** the smallest quantity of any substance which can exist separately and still retain the characteristics of the substance; a group of atoms acting as a physical unit; **2,** loosely, any tiny particle.—*adj.* **mo·lec′-u·lar** (mō-lĕk′ū-lēr).

mole·hill (mōl′hĭl′), *n.* **1,** a little mound made by the burrowing of a mole; **2,** a small, trivial hindrance or difficulty.

mo·lest (mō-lĕst′), *v.t.* to interfere with; disturb; pester.—*n.* **mo′les·ta′tion.**

Syn. plague, vex.

mol·li·fy (mŏl′ĭ-fī), *v.t.* [mollified, mollify-ing], to calm; soften; make less severe.

mol·lusk (mŏl′ŭsk), *n.* any of numerous soft-bodied, hard-shelled animals, loosely called *shellfish,* as oysters, clams, etc.

mol·ly·cod·dle (mŏl′ĭ-kŏd′l), *n.* a person, especially a man or boy, used to being petted and pampered; a sissy.

Mo·loch (mō′lŏk), *n.* **1,** in the Old Testament, a Semitic god to whom human beings were sacrificed, especially first-born children; **2,** hence, anything requiring great human sacrifice, as war or other social evils.

Mo·lo·ka·i (mō′lō-kä′ē), an island in the Hawaiian group, site of a leper colony.

molt or **moult** (mōlt), *v.i.* to cast off and renew the hair, feathers, etc.:—*v.t.* to shed, as the skin, hair, horns, etc.:—*n.* the shedding of hair, feathers, etc., or the season when such shedding takes place.

mol·ten (mōl′tĕn), a past participle of *melt.*

Mo·luc·ca Is·lands (mō-lŭk′ȧ), a group of islands in Indonesia, between Celebes and New Guinea (map 16): also called *Spice Islands.*

mo·ment (mō′mĕnt), *n.* **1,** a portion of time; an instant; **2,** the present time; as, the man of the *moment;* **3,** importance; as, news of great *moment.*

Syn. weight, significance.

mo·men·tar·y (mō′mĕn-tĕr′ĭ), *adj.* lasting only for, or done in, an instant; as, a *momentary* rage.—*adv.* **mo′men·tar′i·ly.**

Syn. passing, transient, fugitive.

mo·men·tous (mō-mĕn′tŭs), *adj.* very important; of great consequence; as, a *momentous* decision.

mo·men·tum (mō-mĕn′tŭm), *n.* **1,** in mechanics, the force of motion in a moving body as measured by the product of its weight and speed; **2,** popularly, impetus gained by motion.

Mon. abbreviation for *Monday.*

Mon·a·co (mŏn′ȧ-kō), the smallest independent state of Europe, southeast of France; also, a city, its capital (map 12).

mon·arch (mŏn′ērk), *n.* **1,** a supreme ruler or sovereign, as a king, queen, emperor, or the like; also, the hereditary ruler of a constitutional monarchy; **2,** the chief of its class or kind; as, the lion is *monarch* of all beasts.—*adj.* **mo·nar′chal** (mō-när′-kăl); **mo·nar′chi·al** (mō-när′kĭ-ăl).

mon·arch·ist (mŏn′ēr-kĭst), *n.* one who believes in, or supports, a government whose power is possessed by a king, emperor, etc.—*n.* **mon′arch·ism.**

mon·arch·y (mŏn′ēr-kĭ), *n.* [*pl.* monarchies], **1,** a state ruled by a monarch whose power is supreme: called *absolute monarchy;* **2,** a state whose constitution limits the monarch's powers: called a *limited* or *constitutional monarchy;* **3,** a kingdom; an empire.

āte, âorta, râre, căt, ȧsk, fär, ăllow, sofȧ; ēve, ĕvent, ĕll, writēr, novĕl; bīte, pĭn; nō, ōbey, ôr, dŏg, tŏp, cŏllide; ūnit, ūnite, bûrn, cŭt, focŭs; nōōn, fŏŏt; mound; coin;

mon·as·ter·y (mŏn′ăs-tĕr′ĭ), *n.* [*pl.* monasteries], a house of seclusion occupied by persons, especially monks, bound by vows to a religious life.—*adj.* **mon′as·te′ri·al.**
Syn. cloister, abbey, convent.

mo·nas·tic (mŏ-năs′tĭk) or **mo·nas·ti·cal** (mŏ-năs′tĭ-kǎl), *adj.* pertaining to religious houses called monasteries, or to monks and their manner of life; as, *monastic* discipline.—*n.* **mo·nas′ti·cism.**

Mon·day (mŭn′dĭ), *n.* the second day of the week.

mon·e·tar·y (mŏn′ē-tĕr′ĭ; mŭn′ē-tĕr′ĭ),*adj.* **1,** of or relating to money; as, a *monetary* gift; **2** pertaining to coinage or currency; as, the dollar is the *monetary* unit of the U. S.

mon·ey (mŭn′ĭ), *n.* [*pl.* moneys], **1,** coin; gold, silver, or other metal coined by a government and used as a means of exchange; **2,** bank notes, checks, drafts, etc., used as a means of exchange; **3,** wealth; **4, monies,** sums of money.
Syn. cash, currency, bullion.

mon·eyed (mŭn′ĭd), *adj.* having much money; rich.

mon·ey or·der, an order for the payment of a stated sum; especially, a form of draft sold at one post office and payable when presented by the payee at another post office.

Mon·gol (mŏng′gŏl), *adj.* pertaining to Mongolia, in Asia, to its people, or to the yellow race:—*n.* **1,** a native of Mongolia; **2,** a member of the yellow race; **3,** the Mongolian language.

Mon·go·li·a (mŏng-gō′lĭ-ȧ), a large republic in central Asia, north of China (map **15**). It was formerly a dependency of China.

Mon·go·li·an (mŏng-gō′lĭ-ăn), *adj.* **1,** relating to one of the five great races of mankind, the yellow race of Asia, including the Chinese, Japanese, Tatars, etc.; **2,** pertaining to Mongolia, its natives, or their language:—*n.* **1,** a member of the yellow race; **2,** the Mongolian language.

mon·goose (mŏng′gōōs), *n.* [*pl.* mongooses], a small, ferretlike animal of India, dingy brown in color, noted for its ability to kill poisonous snakes.

MONGOOSE (¹⁄₁₀)

mon·grel (mŭng′grĕl; mŏng′grĕl), *adj.* **1,** of a mixed breed or kind; **2,** of mixed origin: used especially of a language or a word:—*n.* an animal of mixed breed or kind.

mon·i·tor (mŏn′ĭ-tĕr), *n.* **1,** one who warns or advises; **2,** in a school, a pupil appointed to oversee the younger ones; **3,** an iron-clad warship, having low sides and one or more turrets mounted with guns; **4,** a large lizard of Africa, Asia, and Australia.

mon·i·tor·y (mŏn′ĭ-tôr′ĭ), *adj.* warning; advising.

monk (mŭngk), *n.* one of a body of men who have taken religious vows and are living in a monastery apart from the world. —*adj.* **monk′ish.**

mon·key (mŭng′kĭ), *n.* [*pl.* monkeys], in the broadest sense, any one of the highest order of animals below man; in a narrower sense, one of the smaller, long-tailed forms differing from the larger, nearly tailless forms, called *apes*:—*v.i.* to play the fool; also, to meddle:—*v.t.* to ape; imitate.

MONKEY (¹⁄₁₀)

monkey bread, the large, gourd-shaped fruit of the baobab tree, used as food by monkeys; also, the tree.

monkey gaff (găf), a spar on the mizzen-mast, for displaying signals. (See illustration on page 695.)

MONKEY WRENCH

monkey wrench, a wrench with an adjustable jaw, for turning a nut, bolt, or the like.

monks-hood (mŭngks′hŏŏd′), *n.* a plant of the buttercup family with long spikes of blue hooded flowers and extremely poisonous roots.

mon·o- (mŏn′ō-), a prefix meaning one; as, *mono*plane: appearing as *mon-* before vowels; as, *mon*arch.

mon·o·cle (mŏn′ō-kl), *n.* an eyeglass for one eye.

mo·nog·a·my (mŏ-nŏg′ȧ-mĭ), *n.* marriage with only one husband or wife at the same time.—*adj.* **mo·nog′a·mous.**—*n.* **mo·nog′a·mist.**

MONKSHOOD

mon·o·gram (mŏn′ō-grăm), *n.* a decorative character formed of two or more letters, often a person's initials, combined or interwoven.

mon·o·graph (mŏn′ō-grȧf), *n.* a scholarly paper on one particular subject.

mon·o·lith (mŏn′ō-lĭth), *n.* a pillar or column formed of a single block of stone.

mon·o·log or **mon·o·logue** (mŏn′ō-lŏg), *n.* **1,** a long speech by one person, either in conversation or in a play; **2,** a dramatic scene in which only one person speaks.

mon·o·ma·ni·a (mŏn′ō-mā′nĭ-ȧ), *n.* **1,** insanity in regard to one single subject; **2,** a

---

go; join; yet; sing; chin; show; thin, *th*en; **hw,** *wh*y; **zh,** azure; **ū,** Ger. für or Fr. l*u*ne; **ö,** Ger. schön or Fr. f*eu*; **ṅ,** Fr. e*n*fant, no*m*; **kh,** Ger. a*ch* or i*ch.* See pages ix–x.

craze; mania; as, Napoleon's *monomania* for conquest.—*n.* **mon′o-ma′ni-ac.**

mon-o-plane (mŏn′ō-plān), *n.* an airplane with but one main supporting surface, consisting of a single wing on each side of the body. (See illustration under *aviation*.)

mo-nop-o-lize (mō-nŏp′ō-līz), *v.t.* [monopolized, monopoliz-ing], 1. to gain possession of (a thing) so as to be the only producer or trader in that thing; as, to *monopolize* the sugar industry; 2, to take the whole of; gain exclusive possession of; as, to *monopolize* the attention of another. —*n.* **mo-nop′o-list.**

mo-nop-o-ly (mō-nŏp′ō-lĭ), *n.* [*pl.* monopolies], 1, the exclusive control and possession of anything, especially of some commercial product, as sugar or rubber, or of some public service, as that of providing a community with gas or electricity or water; 2, the commodity or service so controlled; 3, a company that has such control; 4, a grant, or charter, of monopoly.

mon-o-syl-lab-ic (mŏn′ō-sĭ-lăb′ĭk), *adj.* 1, having only one syllable; 2, consisting of words of one syllable; as, "Yes, do come," is a *monosyllabic* sentence.

mon-o-syl-la-ble (mŏn′ō-sĭl′a-bl), *n.* a word of one syllable. "Go," "red," and "star" are *monosyllables*.

mon-o-the-ism (mŏn′ō-thē-ĭzm), *n.* the belief in the existence of but one God.

mon-o-tone (mŏn′ō-tōn), *n.* 1, utterance of one syllable after another without change of pitch or key; 2, sameness of style or color, as in writing or painting.

mo-not-o-nous (mō-nŏt′ō-nŭs), *adj.* constantly the same; lacking variety; tiresome; as, a *monotonous* voice; a *monotonous* round of work.—*adv.* **mo-not′o-nous-ly.**

mo-not-o-ny (mō-nŏt′ō-nĭ), *n.* 1, dull sameness of tone; 2, lack of variety; tiresome sameness; as, the *monotony* of the plains.

Mon-o-type (mŏn′ō-tīp), *n.* a trade-mark name for either of two typesetting machines:—**monotype**, either typesetting machine bearing this trade name.

Mon-roe (mŭn-rō′), James (1758–1831), the fifth president of the U.S., who advanced the Monroe Doctrine.

Mon-roe Doc-trine, a policy announced by President Monroe in 1823, to the effect that the United States would view as an unfriendly act any attempt of a European nation to interfere in American affairs or to extend its holdings in the Western Hemisphere.

Mon-ro-vi-a (mŏn-rō′vĭ-á), a city, capital of Liberia, a Negro republic on the west coast of Africa (map 14).

Mon-sei-gneur (mŏn′sā-nyûr′; môń′sâ′-nyûr′), *n.* [*pl.* Messeigneurs (mĕs′á-nyûrz′; mā′sâ′nyûr′)], my lord: a French title given to princes, bishops, etc.

Mon-sieur (mē-syö′), *n.* [*pl.* Messieurs (mā′syö′)], a French title of courtesy, corresponding to English *Mister*.

Mon-si-gnor (mŏn-sē′nyôr; Italian, môn′-sē-nyôr′), *n.* [*pl.* Monsignori (môn′sē-nyō′-rē)], a title of honor conferred by the Pope.

mon-soon (mŏn-sōōn′), *n.* 1, a periodic wind in the Indian Ocean and southern Asia, which blows from the southwest from April to October, and from the northeast for the next six months; 2, the rainy season that comes with the southwest monsoon.

mon-ster (mŏn′stēr), *n.* 1, a misshapen animal or plant; as, a five-legged calf is a *monster;* 2, an imaginary animal of grotesque form, such as a dragon or the Minotaur; 3, something very huge, deformed, or hideous; 4, a person remarkable for wickedness or ugliness:—*adj.* huge.

mon-stros-i-ty (mŏn-strŏs′ĭ-tĭ), *n.* [*pl.* monstrosities], 1, the state or quality of being deformed or hideous; 2, anything unnaturally huge, hideous, or deformed; a monster.

mon-strous (mŏn′strŭs), *adj.* 1, out of the common course of nature; abnormal; 2, enormous; huge; as, a *monstrous* elephant; 3, horrible; causing disgust; as, a *monstrous* crime.—*adv.* **mon′strous-ly.** *Syn.* shocking, dreadful, immense.

Mont. abbreviation for *Montana*.

Mon-taigne (mŏn-tān′; môń′tâny′′), (1533–1592), a French essayist.

Mon-tan-a (mŏn-tăn′á; mŏn-tä′ná), a State (cap. Helena) in the northwestern U.S. (map 9).

Mon-te Car-lo (mŏn′tā kär′lō; mŏn′tē), a city of Monaco, famous as a gambling resort.

Mon-te-ne-gro (mŏn′tē-nē′grō), a former kingdom north of Albania, on the Adriatic, now a part of Yugoslavia.—*n.* and *adj.* **Mon′te-ne′grin.**

Mon-te-vid-e-o (mŏn′tē-vĭd′ē-ō; mŏn′tā-vē-thā′ō), a city, capital of Uruguay, South America (map 11).

Mont-gom-er-y (mŭnt-gŭm′ēr-ĭ; mŏnt-gŭm′ēr-ĭ), a city, capital of Alabama, in the southern U.S. (map 8).

month (mŭnth), *n.* 1, one of the twelve parts into which the year is divided, each containing about four weeks: called *calendar month;* 2, the period of 28 days from new moon to new moon: called *lunar month*.

month-ly (mŭnth′lĭ), *adj.* performed, payable, happening, or published once a month; as, a *monthly* bill, a *monthly* magazine:—*adv.* once a month; every month; as, she pays her bills *monthly*:—*n.* [*pl.* monthlies], a magazine published each month.

Mont·pel·ier (mŏnt-pēl′yẽr), a city, capital of Vermont (map 6).

Mont·re·al (mŏnt′rē-ôl′; mŭnt′rē-ôl′), the chief city of Canada, on the Saint Lawrence River (map 4).

mon·u·ment (mŏn′ū-mĕnt), *n.* 1, anything that keeps alive the memory of a person or event, as a pillar, a statue, etc.; 2, a conspicuous and lasting example; an achievement worthy to be remembered; as, a *monument* of science.

mon·u·men·tal (mŏn′ū-mĕn′tăl), *adj.* 1, connected with a monument or memorial structure; 2, like a monument; also, huge and enduring; as, "Paradise Lost" is a *monumental* poem; 3, very great; colossal.

moo (mōō), *n.* the lowing of a cow:—*v.i.* to make the sound a cow makes; to low.

¹mood (mōōd), *n.* in grammar, one of the forms that the verb can take to show the manner in which the action or state, expressed by the verb, is to be understood, whether as a fact, wish, command, etc.

²mood (mōōd), *n.* a state of mind; humor; as,. children in a merry *mood*.

mood·y (mōōd′ĭ), *adj.* [mood-i-er, mood-i-est], 1, subject to changes in the state of mind or temper; 2, often ill-humored or depressed; sullen.—*adv.* **mood′i·ly.**

moon (mōōn), *n.* 1, the heavenly body that revolves around the earth once a month; 2, any heavenly body that revolves about a planet; 3, a month; as, "the *moon* of roses"; 4, anything shaped like the moon, whether in its full or crescent phase:—*v.i.* to wander or look about listlessly.

moon·beam (mōōn′bēm′), *n.* a ray of light from the moon.

moon·light (mōōn′līt′), *n.* the light given by the moon:—*adj.* 1, lighted by the moon; 2, occurring by moonlight; as, a *moonlight* sail.

moon·lit (mōōn′lĭt′), *adj.* lighted by the moon; as, a *moonlit* scene.

moon·shine (mōōn′shīn′), *n.* 1, moonlight; 2, idle talk; high-flown ideas; nonsense; as, his ideas for reform are just so much *moonshine*; 3, *Slang*, liquor, especially whisky, smuggled or made illegally.

moon·stone (mōōn′stōn′), *n.* a semiprecious stone, lustrous and translucent.

moon·struck (mōōn′strŭk′), *adj.* bereft of one's wits, supposedly through the influence of the moon; deranged; dazed.

¹moor (mōōr), *n.* a tract of open, barren land, especially one covered with heather.

²moor (mōōr), *v.t.* to secure (a vessel) in a particular place by a cable or anchor.

Moor (mōōr), *n.* 1, a native of Morocco; 2, a Mohammedan; especially, one of the Saracens who invaded Spain, or one of their descendants:—*adj.* **Moor′ish.**

moor·age (mōōr′ĭj), *n.* a place for anchoring or fastening a vessel.

Moore (mōōr; môr), Thomas (1779–1852), an Irish poet.

moor·ings (mōōr′-ĭngz), *n.pl.* 1, the cables, anchors, etc., by which a vessel is fastened; 2, the place where a vessel is anchored or made fast.

moor·land (mōōr′-lănd′), *n.* barren land covered with heather.

MOOSE (¹⁄₅₀)

moose (mōōs), *n.* [*pl.* moose], the largest member of the deer family, related to the European elk, found in the forests of Canada and the northern U.S. It often attains a weight of 1,000 pounds or more.

moot (mōōt), *v.t.* to propose for discussion; also, to argue, debate, or discuss (a question):—*adj.* open to discussion; as, a *moot* question.

mop (mŏp), *n.* 1, a bundle of cloth, rags, or the like, fastened to the end of a long handle and used for washing floors, cleaning walls, etc.; 2, a thick head of hair like a mop:—*v.t.* [mopped, mop-ping], 1, to clean with a mop; as, to *mop* a floor; also, to remove with a mop; as, to *mop* up dust; 2, to wipe; as, to *mop* the brow.

MOP, def. 1

mope (mōp), *n.* one who is dull or out of spirits:—*v.i.* [moped, mop-ing], to be listless or low-spirited.

mo·raine (mō-rān′), *n.* a heap of earth, rocks, and gravel, gathered by a glacier and deposited at its edge.

mor·al (mŏr′ăl), *n.* 1, the lesson taught by a fable, story, or event; 2, morals, standards of conduct; also, conduct; behavior:—*adj.* 1, referring to right and wrong; ethical; as, *moral* standards; a *moral* sense; 2, virtuous; good; as, a *moral* way of living; a *moral* people; 3, able to distinguish between right and wrong; as, man is a *moral* being.

moral certainty, a probability so strong as to amount to certainty; **moral victory**, a defeat felt to be a victory because of the spiritual satisfactions, hopes, or gains.

mo·rale (mō-răl′; mō-räl′), *n.* the mental state which enables men to sustain courage, zest, hope, etc., in the face of danger or discouragement; as, defeat did not rob the team of its *morale*.

mor·al·ist (mŏr′ăl-ĭst), *n.* one who is deeply concerned with morals, as student, teacher, or author.

mo·ral·i·ty (mō-răl′ĭ-tĭ), *n.* [*pl.* moralities], **1**, morals; standards of conduct; **2**, virtuousness; upright behavior.

mor·al·ize (mŏr′ăl-īz), *v.t.* [moralized, moraliz·ing], to make moral, or improve the morals of; as, to *moralize* the heathen: —*v.i.* to talk at length about right and wrong, duty, goodness, truth, etc.

mor·al·ly (mŏr′ăl-ĭ), *adv.* **1**, according to standards of right and wrong; as, though declared innocent by law, he is *morally* guilty; **2**, virtually; practically; as, it is *morally* impossible for him to raise the money.

mo·rass (mō-răs′), *n.* a swamp; tract of soft, wet ground; bog.

mor·a·tor·i·um (mŏr′ȧ-tôr′ĭ-ŭm), *n.* a period of time over which payment of a debt may be legally delayed; also, the right, granted in an emergency, to make use of such a delay.

Mo·ra·vi·a (mō-rā′vĭ-ȧ), a former province (cap. Brno) of central Czechoslovakia.

Mo·ra·vi·an (mō-rā′vĭ-ăn), *n.* **1**, a native of Moravia; **2**, the Slavic dialect spoken in Moravia; **3**, a member of a Protestant sect which originated in 1457 in Moravia: —*adj.* **1**, pertaining to Moravia, its dialect, or its people; **2**, pertaining to the Protestant sect called Moravians or United Brethren.

mor·bid (môr′bĭd), *adj.* **1**, relating to disease; as, a *morbid* condition; **2**, sickly; hence, gloomy; unwholesome; as, a *morbid* imagination.—*adv.* **mor′bid·ly**.
  Syn. unsound, diseased, corrupt.

mor·dant (môr′dănt), *adj.* biting; keen; as, *mordant* wit:—*n.* **1**, a substance that serves to fix certain colors in dyeing; **2**, an acid that eats into a metal surface, used in etching.

Mor·de·cai (môr′dē-kī; môr′dē-kā′ī), in the Bible, the foster father of Esther who helped her save the Jews from being destroyed by Haman.

more (môr), *adj.* [*comp.* of *many* and *much*], **1**, greater in number, quality, extent, etc.; as, we know *more* people than you; you have *more* energy and *more* time than I; **2**, additional; as, one *more* word:— *adv.* **1**, to a greater degree; **2**, again; as, we shall see her once *more;* **3**, used often to form the comparative of adjectives and adverbs; as, *more* hopeful; *more* hopefully: —*n.* **1**, a greater quantity, number, etc.; **2**, something further or additional.

More (môr), Sir Thomas (1478–1535), an English statesman and philosopher, author of "Utopia."

Mo·re·a (mō-rē′ȧ), the modern name of a peninsula of Greece. See **Peloponnesus**.

more·o·ver (môr-ō′vẽr), *adv.* besides; in addition.

mor·ga·nat·ic (môr′gȧ-năt′ĭk), *adj.* relating to the marriage of a man of royal or other high rank with a woman of lower degree. Neither the wife nor children may share the man's rank or inherit his property.

morgue (môrg), *n.* a building where the bodies of unknown persons found dead are kept until they are claimed.

Mor·mon (môr′mŭn), *n.* a member of a religious sect, called officially the *Church of Jesus Christ of Latter-day Saints,* founded in 1830 by Joseph Smith.— *n.* **Mor′mon·ism.**

morn (môrn), *n. Poetic,* morning; dawn.

morn·ing (môr′nĭng), *n.* the early part of the day, not later than noon:—*adj.* pertaining to the morning; early.

morn·ing–glor·y (môr′nĭng-glôr′ĭ), *n.* [*pl.* morning-glories], a twining plant with heart-shaped leaves and red, blue, or white funnel-shaped flowers.

morning star, any of the planets Venus, Jupiter, Mars, Mercury, and Saturn, especially Venus, when it rises after midnight and can be seen in the east before sunrise.

MORNING-GLORY

Mor·o (môr′ō), *n.* [*pl.* Moros], **1**, a native Mohammedan of the southern Philippines; **2**, the language of the Moros.

Mo·roc·co (mō-rŏk′kō), a monarchy in northwestern Africa, until 1956 a protectorate of France and Spain (map 14).—*n.* and *adj.* **Mo·roc′can,**

mo·roc·co (mō-rŏk′ō), *n.* [*pl.* moroccos], a fine variety of leather made from goatskin, tanned with sumac, and used for bookbinding.

mor·on (môr′ŏn), *n.* a person whose mental ability is somewhat below normal.

mo·rose (mō-rōs′), *adj.* sullen; gloomy.

Mor·pheus (môr′fūs; môr′fē-ŭs), *n.* in Greek mythology, the god of dreams and of sleep.

mor·phine (môr′fēn; môr′fĭn), *n.* a drug made from opium and used in medicine to deaden pain or to produce sleep.

āte, āorta, râre, căt, ȧsk, fär, ăllow, sofȧ; ēve, ēvent, ĕll, writẽr, novĕl; bīte, pĭn; nō, ōbey, ôr, dŏg, tŏp, cŏllide; ūnit, ūnite, bûrn, cŭt, focŭs; nōōn, fŏŏt; mound; coin;

mor·ris (mŏr′ĭs), *n.* an old English folk dance. Also, **mor′ris dance.**

mor·row (mŏr′ō), *n.* **1,** the next day after any given day; tomorrow; **2,** *Archaic,* morning; as, good *morrow.*

Morse (môrs), Samuel Finley Breese (1791–1872), an American inventor who made the first telegraph, about 1833.

Morse code, the alphabet used in telegraphy, consisting of dots,dashes,and spaces. It was invented by Samuel F. B. Morse.

mor·sel (môr′sĕl), *n.* a small piece; a little bit; a titbit.

mor·tal (môr′tăl), *n.* a being subject to death; a human being:—*adj.* **1,** subject to death; as, *mortal* man; **2,** causing death; fatal; as, a *mortal* wound; causing spiritual death; deadly; as, *mortal* sin; **3,** involving death; as, *mortal* combat; **4,** filled with desire to kill; as, a *mortal* enemy; **5,** extreme; as, *mortal* fear; **6,** accompanying death; as, *mortal* agony; **7,** belonging to human beings; as, *mortal* fame.

mor·tal·i·ty (môr-tăl′ĭ-tĭ), *n.* [*pl.* mortalities], **1,** the condition of being subject to death; **2,** death; destruction; as, the *mortality* from war or disease; **3,** the number of deaths in a given period in a given area; death rate.

mor·tal·ly (môr′tăl-ĭ), *adv.* **1,** in such a manner as to cause death; as, *mortally* wounded; **2,** deeply; bitterly; as, *mortally* grieved.

mor·tar (môr′tẽr), *n.* **1,** a bowl-like vessel in which substances are pounded or ground with a pestle; **2,** a short cannon used for firing shells at a high angle; **3,** a building cement made of lime, sand, and water.

MORTAR AND PESTLE

mor·tar·board (môr′tẽr-bôrd), *n.* **1,** a square board with a handle on the under side, for holding mortar; **2,** an academic cap, with a flat, projecting top.

mort·gage (môr′gĭj), *n.* a legal paper given by one person, usually a borrower, to another, usually a lender, which signs over certain property of the former, as security in case the debt is not paid:—*v.t.* [mortgaged, mortgag-ing], to make over (property) as security to one to whom a debt is owed.

mort·ga·gee (môr′gĭ-jē′), *n.* a person to whom property is mortgaged as security against a loan.

mort·ga·gor (môr′gĭ-jôr′; môr′gĭ-jẽr), *n.* a person who gives a mortgage on his property as security for money he borrows.

mor·ti·fi·ca·tion (môr′tĭ-fĭ-kā′shŭn), *n.*

1, self-denial; discipline; **2,** humiliation; shame; as, the *mortification* of failing twice; also, the cause of such humiliation; **3,** gangrene; also, the death of one part of an animal body from loss of circulation.

mor·ti·fy (môr′tĭ-fī), *v.t.* [mortified, mortify-ing], **1,** to subdue by self-denial; as, to *mortify* the appetites; **2,** to embarrass; put to shame; as, his rudeness *mortified* me:—*v.i.* to be affected with gangrene, as a foot or hand.

mor·tise or **mor·tice** (môr′tĭs), *n.* a hole cut in a piece of wood, into which the shaped end, called *tenon*, of another piece of wood fits, so as to form a joint:—*v.t.* [mortised, mortis-ing], to join by a mortise and tenon.

mor·tu·ar·y (môr′tû-ẽr′ĭ), *n.* [*pl.* mortuaries], a building for the dead awaiting burial:—*adj.* connected with the burial of the dead; as, *mortuary* rites.

MORTISE (M) AND TENON (T)

Mo·sa·ic (mō-zā′ĭk), *adj.* concerning Moses or his writings; as, the *Mosaic* law.

mo·sa·ic (mō-zā′ĭk), *n.* a design made of small pieces of varicolored glass, stone, or the like, inlaid in some other material; also, a piece of work so made:—*adj.* made of or like mosaic; as, *mosaic* jewelry.

Mos·cow (mŏs′kō), [Russian **Mos-kva** (môs-kvȧ′)], a city, capital of the U.S.S.R., in east central Europe (map 12).

Mo·selle (mō-zĕl′), a river of northeastern France, flowing into the Rhine.

Mo·ses (mō′zĕs), in the Bible, the great prophet and lawgiver of the Israelites, who led them out of Egypt.

Mos·lem (mŏz′lĕm; mŏs′lĕm), *n.* a Mohammedan: also called *Mussulman:*—*adj.* relating to Mohammedans.

mosque (mŏsk), *n.* a Moslem temple.

mos·qui·to (mŭs-kē′tō), *n.* [*pl.* mosquitoes], a two-winged insect, the female of which punctures the skin of men and animals, feeding on the blood it sucks out. Some mosquitoes carry the germs of malaria and of yellow fever.

MOSQUE at Cairo, Egypt.

moss (môs), *n.* a spore-bearing, small-leaved plant, which grows like a thick mat on damp ground, trees, rocks, etc.:—**Iceland moss,** a kind of lichen.

moss-y (môs′ĭ), *adj.* [moss-i-er, moss-i-est], covered with, or like, moss; as, a *mossy* stone; a *mossy* growth.

most (mōst), *adj.* [*superl.* of *many* and *much*], greatest in number, quantity, degree, etc.; as, this house has the *most* rooms:—*n.* the greatest number, part, quantity, or value; as, give him the *most*:—*adv.* 1, in the greatest degree; as, I like plums *most*; 2, used often to form the superlative of adjectives and adverbs; as, *most* hopeful; *most* hopefully.

-most (-mōst), a suffix which forms the superlative degree; as, upper*most*, in*most*.

most-ly (mōst′lĭ), *adv.* mainly; usually.

Mo-sul (mō′sool′), a town on the Tigris River in Iraq (map 15).

mote (mōt), *n.* a tiny particle of dust.

mo-tel (mō-tĕl′), *n.* a hotel primarily for motorists.

moth (môth), *n.* [*pl.* moths (môthz; môths)], 1, any of numerous four-winged, night-flying insects, related to the butterfly, having antennae, or feelers, which are not knobbed; 2, an insect of this kind whose larva feeds on wool, fur, etc.: also called *clothes moth.*

MOTH
slightly enlarged.
1, adult clothes moth;
2, larva in its case.

moth ball, a small ball of camphor, or other substance which repels moths.

¹moth-er (mŭth′ẽr), *n.* 1, a female parent; 2, origin or source; as, oppression is the *mother* of revolt; 3, a title given to the head of a religious house for women:—*adj.* native; as, one's *mother* tongue:—*v.t.* to act as a mother to; care for.

²moth-er (mŭth′ẽr), *n.* a thick, slimy substance that forms in vinegar or wine when it is fermenting.

moth-er-hood (mŭth′ẽr-hood), *n.* 1, the state of being a mother; 2, all the mothers of a country or region.

moth-er—in—law (mŭth′ẽr-ĭn-lô′), *n.* [*pl.* mothers-in-law], the mother of one's husband or of one's wife.

moth-er-less (mŭth′ẽr-lĕs), *adj.* deprived of a mother or of a mother's care.

moth-er-ly (mŭth′ẽr-lĭ), *adj.* kind and devoted, as a mother.

moth-er—of—pearl (mŭth′ẽr-ŏv-pûrl′), *n.* the hard, rainbow-tinted lining of certain shells, used for buttons, ornaments, etc.

mo-tif (mō-tēf′), *n.* the subject or main idea of a work of art or literature; in

music, a theme which may be repeated with variations; also, a unit of design.

mo-tion (mō′shŭn), *n.* 1, the act or process of moving from one place or position to another; action, as opposed to rest; as, the ceaseless *motion* of the waves; 2, a gesture; as, a beckoning *motion*; 3, a formal proposal made in a meeting; as, a *motion* to adjourn:—*v.i.* to express one's meaning in a gesture instead of words:—*v.t.* to guide or invite by a gesture; as, he *motioned* me in.—*adj.* **mo′tion-less.**

mo-tion pic-ture, a series of pictures of persons and things in action, taken by a special camera in such a way that, when thrown on a screen rapidly, they form a continuous picture in which the action is reproduced: also called *moving picture.*

mo-ti-vate (mō′tĭ-vāt), *v.t.* [motivat-ed, motivat-ing], 1, to act as reason or impulse for; induce; as, jealousy *motivated* the murder of Desdemona; 2, to supply a motive or reason for; as, to *motivate* the action of a play.

mo-tive (mō′tĭv), *n.* 1, that which causes a person to act as he does under certain circumstances; the inner reason for any act; as, hunger might be the *motive* for stealing; 2, in art, literature, and music, the main idea or theme; motif:—*adj.* causing motion; as, *motive* power.

mot-ley (mŏt′lĭ), *adj.* 1, consisting of different colors; 2, wearing parti-colored clothing; as, a *motley* fool; 3, composed of various kinds; as, a *motley* crowd:—*n.* a garment of various colors, formerly worn by jesters.

mo-tor (mō′tẽr), *n.* 1, an engine that produces action or mechanical power; as, an electric *motor*; 2, an automobile:—*adj.* 1, having to do with motors or with motor-driven vehicles; as, a *motor* van; *motor* traffic; 2, imparting action; as, *motor* nerves:—*v.i.* to travel by automobile.

mo-tor-boat (mō′tẽr-bōt′), *n.* a boat run by a motor.

mo-tor-car (mō′tẽr-kär′), *n.* an automobile.

mo-tor-cy-cle (mō′tẽr-sī′kl), *n.* a motor-driven, two-wheeled vehicle with one or two riding seats, but sometimes with a sidecar attached.—Also *adj.* and *v.i.*

mo-tor-ist (mō′tẽr-ĭst), *n.* one who usually travels by automobile.

mo-tor-man (mō′tẽr-măn), *n.* [*pl.* motor-men (-mĕn)], one who operates a motor, especially on an electric trolley or train.

mot-tle (mŏt′l), *v.t.* [mot-tled, mot-tling], to mark with spots of various colors.

mot-to (mŏt′ō), *n.* [*pl.* mottoes], 1, a short sentence, a phrase, or a single word,

āte, āorta, râre, căt, ȧsk, fär, ȧllow, sofȧ; ēve, ĕvent, ĕll, writẽr, novĕl; bīte, pĭn; nō, ōbey, ôr, dŏg, tŏp, cŏllide; ūnit, ūnite, bûrn, cŭt, focŭs; nōon, foŏt; mound; coin;

suggesting some guiding principle; **2,** a quotation used .as a chapter heading, a slogan, or an inscription.

Syn. saying, adage, maxim.

Mouk-den (mōōk′dĕn′), a city in Manchuria. See **Mukden.** .

mould (mōld), *n.* a form of *mold* in all of its meanings. See **mold.**

mould-er (mōl′dĕr), *v.i.* to crumble. See **molder.**

moult (mōlt), *v.i.* to shed the hair, feathers, or outer skin; molt. See **molt.**

mound (mound), *n.* an artificial bank of earth or stone; also, a small hill.

¹**mount** (mount), *n.* a high hill; mountain.

²**mount** (mount), *v.t.* **1,** to climb, ascend, or get up on; as, to *mount* a platform or a horse; **2,** to set up for use; as, to *mount* cannon; also, to be equipped with; as, the fort *mounts* 30 guns; **3,** to set up or arrange for exhibition or preservation; as, to *mount* photographs or insects; **4,** to put on, or furnish with, a horse:—*v.i.* **1,** to rise or increase; as, his debts *mounted* steadily; **2,** to get up on a horse, platform, or the like:—*n.* **1,** a riding horse; **2,** that on which something, as a photograph or drawing, may be fixed or mounted.

Syn., v. arise, soar, scale, elevate.

moun-tain (moun′tĭn; moun′tĕn), *n.* **1,** a natural elevation of rock or earth rising high above the level of the surrounding country; a towering hill; **2,** anything huge.

mountain ash, a hardy tree or tall shrub bearing clusters of brilliant red berries.

moun-tain-eer (moun′tĭ-nēr′), *n.* **1,** a mountain dweller; **2,** a mountain climber.

mountain goat, a pure-white goatlike animal of the northwestern U.S.

mountain lion, the cougar or American panther.

MOUNTAIN GOAT (￼)

moun-tain-ous (moun′tĭ-nŭs), *adj.* **1,** full of mountains; as, a *mountainous* land; **2,** like a mountain; enormous.

Mount De-sert Is-land (dĕ-zûrt′; dĕz′-ĕrt), an island off the Maine coast (map **6**).

moun-te-bank (moun′tĕ-băngk), *n.* **1,** one who sells quack medicines, especially from a public platform; **2,** a person who tricks or deceives people.

mount-ing (moun′tĭng), *n.* **1,** the act of rising, climbing, etc.; **2,** a support, fixture, or setting; as, the *mounting* of a jewel; the *mounting* of a gun.

Mount Ver-non (vûr′nŭn), the home and burial place of George Washington, on the Potomac River, in Virginia.

mourn (môrn), *v.i.* and *v.t.* to grieve (for); sorrow (over); lament.—*n.* **mourn′er.**

mourn-ful (môrn′fŏŏl), *adj.* sad; sorrowful; as, a *mournful* song or mood.

mourn-ing (môr′nĭng), *n.* **1,** the act of grieving; **2,** an outward expression of sorrow, as the wearing of black clothes.

mouse (mous), *n.* [*pl.* mice (mīs)], a small rodent related to, but smaller than, the rat, with soft fur and a long tail:—*v.i.* (mouz), [moused, mous-ing], **1,** to watch for or catch mice; **2,** to prowl and pry. —*n.* **mous′er** (mouz′ẽr).

MOUSE (!)

mousse (mōōs), *n.* a frozen dessert made of whipped cream sweetened and flavored.

mous-tache (mŭs-tȧsh′; mŭs′tȧsh), *n.* the hair on a man's upper lip. See **mustache.**

mouth (mouth), *n.* [*pl.* mouths (mouthz)], **1,** the opening through which an animal takes food into the body; the space containing the teeth and tongue; **2,** this opening, as the channel of voice or speech; **3,** an opening or outlet; as, the *mouth* of a jug, tunnel, or river; **4,** a face; grimace; as, to make a *mouth*:—**mouth organ,** a small musical wind instrument, held horizontally against the lips and played by blowing or sucking air through it; a harmonica:—*v.t.* (mouth), **1,** to utter with a swelling or pompous voice; **2,** to take in the mouth; as, a dog *mouths* a bone:—*v.i.* **1,** to make faces; grimace; **2,** to declaim.

mouth-ful (mouth′fŏŏl), *n.* [*pl.* mouthfuls], **1,** as much as is usually put into the mouth at one time; **2,** a small amount.

mouth-piece (mouth′pēs′), *n.* **1,** that part of a wind instrument which is held in or against the player's mouth and through which he blows the air to produce the tone; **2,** one who speaks for others; as, he was the *mouthpiece* of the conservatives.

mov-a-ble (mōōv′ȧ-bl), *adj.* **1,** capable of being carried from one place to another; **2,** changing from one date to another; as, a *movable* holiday:—**movables,** goods or furniture that can be carried from place to place. Also, **move′a-ble.**—*adv.* **mov′a-bly; move′a-bly.**

move (mōōv), *v.t.* [moved, mov-ing], **1,** to change from one place or position to another; as, to *move* a table; **2,** to set in motion; as, the breeze *moves* the grass; **3,** to cause to act; to impel; as, no plea could *move* him to consent; **4,** to arouse the feelings of; as, to *move* an audience to tears; **5**, to put (a formal motion) before a meeting; as, I *move* we adjourn; **6**, to cause (the bowels) to act:—*v.i.* **1**, to change place or position; also, to advance; as, time *moves* on; **2**, to change one's residence; **3**, to take action; **4**, to live; to pass one's life or time; as, to *move* in society; **5**, to apply (for); as, to *move* for a new trial; **6**, to act: said of the bowels:—*n.* **1**, a changing of place or position; as, a *move* in checkers; **2**, a step in carrying out a plan; **3**, a change of residence.—*n.* **mov′er.**

move·ment (mōōv′měnt), *n.* **1**, the act of changing place; any change of position; **2**, a joint effort directed toward a desired end; as, the temperance *movement*; **3**, the delicate mechanism of a watch or clock; **4**, a main division of a long musical composition; **5**, an emptying of the bowels.

mov·ie (mōōv′ĭ), *n. Colloquial*, a motion picture, or a motion-picture theater.

mov·ing (mōōv′ĭng), *adj.* **1**, changing place or position; **2**, causing motion or action; **3**, stirring the emotions.
  Syn. impressive, exciting, touching.

mov·ing pic·ture, a series of pictures, thrown on a screen, showing persons or things in motion; a motion picture.

¹**mow** (mō), *v.t.* [*p.t.* mowed (mōd), *p.p.* mowed or mown (mōn), *p.pr.* mow-ing], **1**, to cut down with a scythe or a machine; as, to *mow* hay; **2**, to cut grass, grain, or the like, from; as, to *mow* a lawn; **3**, to kill (living beings) as if mowing down grain; as, the guns *mowed* down the enemy: —*v.i.* to cut grass, grain, or the like.

²**mow** (mou), *n.* **1**, a heap of hay, grain, or the like, stored in a barn; **2**, the compartment in a barn for hay or grain:—*v.t.* to stow in a mow.

Mo·zam·bique (mō′zăm-bēk′), a Portuguese colony (cap. Lourenço Marques) in southeastern Africa (map **14**). It is also called *Portuguese East Africa*.

Mo·zart (mō′zärt; mō′tsärt), Wolfgang Amadeus (1756–1791), an Austrian composer.

M.P. abbreviation for *Member of Parliament, Military Police*.

m.p.h. abbreviation for *miles per hour*.

Mr. (mĭs′tẽr), [*pl.* Messrs. (měs′rz)], abbreviation for *Mister*.

Mrs. (mĭs′ĭz; mĭs′ĭs), abbreviation for *Mistress*.

MS. or **ms.** [*pl.* MSS. or mss.], abbreviation for *manuscript*.

mt. abbreviation for *mountain*.

much (mŭch), *adj.* [*comp.* more, *superl.* most], great in quantity, extent, or de-

gree:—*adv.* **1**, to a great degree or extent; greatly; as, *much* obliged; **2**, nearly; as, *much* of a size:—*n.* a great quantity.

mu·ci·lage (mū′sĭ-lĭj), *n.* a fluid, gummy substance used to stick things together.

muck (mŭk), *n.* **1**, moist manure; **2**, a mixture of rich earth and decayed matter, especially when used as a fertilizer; **3**, anything filthy or dirty.—*adj.* **muck′y.**

muck·rake (mŭk′rāk′), *v.i.* [muckraked, muckrak-ing], to go about looking for and exposing the dishonesty of men in public life.

mu·cous (mū′kŭs) *adj.* pertaining to, like, or producing, mucus:—**mucous membrane**, the moist lining of the nose, throat, and other passages of the body that open to the outside.

mu·cus (mū′kŭs), *n.* the slimy substance secreted by the mucous membrane.

mud (mŭd), *n.* soft, wet earth; mire.

mud·dle (mŭd′l), *n.* a state of confusion or disorder; a mess; also, mental confusion:—*v.t.* [mud-dled, mud-dling], **1**, to confuse or stupefy; to make slightly drunk; **2**, to make a mess of; bungle; as, to *muddle* accounts:—*v.i.* to act ineffectively and at haphazard; as, to *muddle* along.

mud·dy (mŭd′ĭ), *adj.* [mud-di-er, mud-di-est], **1**, thick with mud; **2**, cloudy; not clear; as, *muddy* coffee; a *muddy* skin; **3**, confused; as, *muddy* ideas:—*v.t.* [muddied, muddy-ing], to make dirty.

mud·guard (mŭd′gärd′), *n.* a casing over a wheel, as of a bicycle, which serves as a guard against mud flying up from below.

¹**muff** (mŭf), *n.* a warm, soft cover into the ends of which the hands may be thrust for protection against cold.

²**muff** (mŭf), *n.* in games such as baseball, a clumsy miss, or failure to keep hold of a ball:—*v.t.* and *v.i.* to handle clumsily; fail to hold (a ball); bungle.

muf·fin (mŭf′ĭn), *n.* a small, usually unsweetened cake, served hot with butter.

muf·fle (mŭf′l), *v.t.* [muf-fled, muf-fling], **1**, to cover up so as to deaden the sound of; as, to *muffle* a bell; **2**, to wrap up closely and warmly.

muf·fler (mŭf′lẽr), *n.* **1**, a scarf for the throat; **2**, a device for deadening noise; as, the *muffler* of an automobile.

muf·ti (mŭf′tĭ), *n.* plain or civilian clothes, when worn by someone who ordinarily wears a uniform; as, an officer in *mufti*.

MUG

mug (mŭg), *n.* an earthen, glass, or metal cup with a handle; also, a mugful; as, bring a *mug* of ale.

āte, āorta, râre, căt, ȧsk, fär, ăllow, sofȧ; ēve, ĕvent, ĕll, writẽr, novĕl; bīte, pĭn; nō, ōbey, ôr, dŏg, tŏp, cŏllide; ūnit, ūnite, bûrn, cŭt, focŭs; nōōn, fŏŏt; mound; coin;

mug·gy (mŭg′ĭ), *adj.* [mug-gi-er, mug-gi-est], warm, damp, and close; as, a *muggy* day.

Muk·den or **Mouk·den** (mōōk′dĕn′), a walled commercial city in southeastern Manchuria (map **15**).

mu·lat·to (mŭ-lăt′ō), *n.* [*pl.* mulattoes], the child of a Negro and a white person.

mul·ber·ry (mŭl′bĕr′ĭ), *n.* [*pl.* mulberries], a tree with broad leaves and a sweet, edible, berrylike fruit. The white mulberry is grown for its leaves on which silkworms feed.

mulch (mŭlch), *n.* a layer of leaves, straw, paper, etc., used to protect the roots of trees and plants:—*v.t.* to cover or protect with mulch.

MULE (¹⁄₁₀)

mulct (mŭlkt), *v.t.* to punish with a fine; also, to take something from (a person) unjustly:—*n.* a fine.

mule (mūl), *n.* **1**, an animal bred from a donkey and a mare; **2**, *Colloquial*, a stubborn person; **3**, a kind of spinning machine.

mu·le·teer (mū′lĕ-tēr′), *n.* a driver of mules.

mul·ish (mūl′ĭsh), *adj.* stubborn; sullen.

¹**mull** (mŭl), *v.i. Colloquial*, to think deeply; ponder; as, to *mull* over a problem.

²**mull** (mŭl), *v.t.* to warm, spice, and sweeten, as ale or wine.

MULLEIN

mul·lein (mŭl′ĭn) or **mul·len** (mŭl′ĕn), *n.* a plant having coarse, fuzzy leaves and yellow flowers in tall spikes.

mul·let (mŭl′ĕt), *n.* any of a number of fresh-water and salt-water fish, some of which, as the striped mullet, the gray mullet, and the red mullet, are used as food.

mul·lion (mŭl′yŭn), *n.* an upright bar or slender column forming a division between the panes of a window, panels in a door, etc.

MULLIONS (a, a, a)

mul·ti- (mŭl′tĭ-), a prefix meaning many, much; as, *multiform*.

mul·ti·far·i·ous (mŭl′tĭ-fâr′ĭ-ŭs), *adj.* having much variety; in large numbers and not alike.

mul·ti·form (mŭl′tĭ-fôrm), *adj.* having many different forms or shapes, as clouds.

Mul·ti·graph (mŭl′tĭ-grăf), *n.* a trade-mark name for a machine that both sets type and prints:—**multigraph,** a machine bearing this trade name.

mul·ti·mil·lion·aire (mŭl′tĭ-mĭl′yŭn-âr′), *n.* the possessor of many millions.

mul·ti·ple (mŭl′tĭ-pl), *n.* a number or quantity which contains another number or quantity an exact number of times; as, 12 is a *multiple* of 6; also, the result of the multiplication of one number by another:—*adj.* **1**, having many parts; **2**, repeated many times.

mul·ti·pli·cand (mŭl′tĭ-plĭ-kănd′), *n.* a number to be multiplied by another.

mul·ti·pli·ca·tion (mŭl′tĭ-plĭ-kā′shŭn), *n.* **1**, the act or process of increasing in number; as, a *multiplication* of details; **2**, in arithmetic, the operation, shown by the sign ×, by which a number (the *multiplicand*) is taken a given number of times, (the number of times being indicated by the *multiplier*), to form a result called the *product*; as, 5 (the *multiplicand*) × 2 (the *multiplier*) = 10 (the *product*).

mul·ti·plic·i·ty (mŭl′tĭ-plĭs′ĭ-tĭ), *n.* [*pl.* multiplicities], a great number or variety; a great many; as, a *multiplicity* of duties.

mul·ti·pli·er (mŭl′tĭ-plī′ẽr), *n.* the number which tells how many times another number is to be taken or multiplied.

mul·ti·ply (mŭl′tĭ-plī), *v.t.* [multiplied, multiply-ing], **1**, to cause to increase in number or quantity; **2**, to repeat or take (a number or quantity) a given number of times; as, to *multiply* 4 by 3 means to take 4 three times, getting a result of 12:—*v.i.* to increase in number or extent; as, sorrows *multiply* as one grows old.

mul·ti·tude (mŭl′tĭ-tūd), *n.* **1**, a great number; crowd; **2**, people in general; as, the *multitude* came to hear him.
Syn. throng, host, mob, swarm.

mul·ti·tu·di·nous (mŭl′tĭ-tū′dĭ-nŭs), *adj.* consisting of a great number; very numerous.—*adv.* mul′ti·tu′di·nous·ly.

mum (mŭm), *adj.* silent:—*interj.* be silent!

mum·ble (mŭm′bl), *v.t.* and *v.i.* [mumbled, mum-bling], **1**, to mutter, or speak indistinctly; **2**, to chew (food) lightly with partly closed lips or without closing the teeth:—*n.* a muttering.

mum·mer (mŭm′ẽr), *n.* one who takes part in masked revels; an actor.

mum·mer·y (mŭm′ẽr-ĭ), *n.* [*pl.* mummeries], **1**, masquerading; **2**, ceremonies or performances regarded as silly or insincere.

mum·mi·fy (mŭm′ĭ-fī), *v.t.* [mummified, mummify-ing], to preserve (a corpse) by a drying process; embalm.

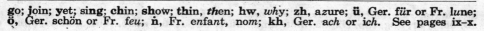

go; join; yet; sing; chin; show; thin, *th*en; hw, *wh*y; zh, azure; ü, Ger. für or Fr. lune; ö, Ger. schön or Fr. feu; ṅ, Fr. enfant, nom; kh, Ger. ach or ich. See pages ix–x.

mum-my (mŭm'ĭ), *n.* [*pl.* mummies], the body of a human being or animal embalmed in the ancient Egyptian manner.

mumps (mŭmps), *n.pl.* used as *sing.* a contagious disease marked by inflammation and swelling of the glands which secrete saliva.

munch (mŭnch), *v.t.* and *v.i.* to chew with a crunching noise, as does a horse.

mun-dane (mŭn'dān), *adj.* relating to the world; worldly; as, *mundane* desires.

Mu-nich (mū'nĭk), [German **Mün-chen** (mün'khĕn)], a city, capital of Bavaria, in southeastern Germany (map **12**).

mu-nic-i-pal (mū-nĭs'ĭ-păl), *adj.* pertaining to a city or town, or to its local self-government; as, *municipal* buildings.

mu-nic-i-pal-i-ty (mū-nĭs'ĭ-păl'ĭ-tĭ), *n.* [*pl.* municipalities], a town, city, or borough with local self-government.

mu-nif-i-cence (mū-nĭf'ĭ-sĕns), *n.* generosity; liberality.—*adj.* **mu-nif'i-cent.**

mu-ni-tion (mū-nĭsh'ŭn), *n.* ammunition and war material.

mu-ral (mū'răl), *adj.* pertaining to a wall; on a wall:—*n.* a painting on a wall.

mur-der (mûr'dẽr), *n.* the unlawful and planned killing of a human being:—*v.t.* **1,** to kill (a person) deliberately; **2,** to spoil; as, to *murder* a song.

mur-der-ous (mûr'dẽr-ŭs), *adj.* **1,** relating to murder; **2,** brutal; bloodthirsty.

murk (mûrk), *n.* darkness; gloom.

murk-y (mûr'kĭ), *adj.* [murk-i-er, murk-i-est], dark; gloomy; as, a *murky* night.

mur-mur (mûr'mẽr), *n.* **1,** a low, indistinct sound, as of voices or of a running stream; **2,** a grumbling complaint in a low, muttering tone; a grumble:—*v.i.* **1,** to make a sound like the hum of bees; speak in a low voice; **2,** to grumble:—*v.t.* to utter complainingly or in a low voice.

     Syn., v. growl, mutter.

mur-rain (mûr'ĭn), *n.* a plague, especially a fatal disease among cattle.

mus. abbreviation for *museum, music.*

mus-cle (mŭs'l), *n.* **1,** an organ of fiberlike tissue, which contracts and expands, thus producing movement in an animal body; also, the tissue of such an organ; **2,** *Colloquial,* bodily strength; physical power. —*adj.* **mus'cu-lar** (mŭs'kū-lẽr).

Muscle Shoals, a series of rapids in the Tennessee River, in Alabama, site of a huge dam built by the U.S. government.

Mus-co-vy (mŭs'kō-vĭ), an old name for *Russia.*

muse (mūz), *v.i.* [mused, mus-ing], to meditate in silence; think deeply; dream.

Muse (mūz), *n.* in Greek mythology, any one of the nine goddesses who presided over music, poetry, history, astronomy, etc.:—**muse,** the poet's inspiration.

mu-se-um (mū-zē'ŭm), *n.* a building in which objects of interest, especially of scientific, artistic, or literary interest, are kept and displayed.

mush (mŭsh), *n.* **1,** a porridge of corn meal boiled in water; hasty pudding; **2,** any soft, thick mixture like mush.—*adj.* **mush'y.**

mush-room (mŭsh'rōōm), *n.* **1,** a fast-growing fungus,' usually shaped like an umbrella, some kinds of which are poisonous and some good for food; **2,** anything like this fungus in quickness of growth:—*adj.* **1,** made from mushrooms; **2,** like mushrooms in quickness of growth.

MUSHROOMS

mu-sic (mū'zĭk), *n.* **1,** the art of making pleasing or harmonious combinations of tones; **2,** harmony; melody; **3,** a musical composition; also, the written or printed score of a musical composition; **4,** any succession of melodious sounds.

mu-si-cal (mū'zĭ-kăl), *adj.* **1,** relating to music; **2,** full of music; melodious; as, a *musical* voice; **3,** skilled in music:—**musical comedy,** a light, amusing play, with songs, choruses, etc.—*adv.* **mu'si-cal-ly.**

mu-si-cale (mū'zĭ-kàl'), *n.* a social musical entertainment, usually private.

mu-si-cal in-stru-ment, a device for making music (see illustration next page).

mu-si-cian (mū-zĭsh'ăn), *n.* one who is skilled in some field of music.

musk (mŭsk), *n.* **1,** a substance with a strong odor, obtained from the male musk deer, and used in perfumes; **2,** the odor of musk.

MUSK DEER (¹⁄₁₅)

musk deer, a small, hornless deer, found in the high parts of central Asia. From a gland of the male deer musk is obtained.

mus-kel-lunge (mŭs'kĕ-lŭnj), *n.* a large food fish found in the Great Lakes.

mus-ket (mŭs'kĕt) *n.* a riflelike gun formerly carried by foot soldiers.

mus-ket-eer (mŭs'kĕ-tēr'), *n.* a foot soldier armed with a musket. (See illustration next page.)

āte, āorta, râre, căt, àsk, fär, ăllọw, sofà; ēve, êvent, ĕll, writẽr, novĕl; bīte, pĭn; nō, ōbey, ôr, dŏg, tŏp, cŏllide; ūnit, ūnite, bûrn, cŭt, focŭs; nōon, fŏŏt; mound; coin;

mus·ket·ry (mŭs′kĕt·rĭ), *n.* **1**, the art of firing small arms; also, the fire of small arms; **2**, muskets collectively.

musk·mel·on (mŭsk′-mĕl′ŭn), *n.* the juicy, sweet, edible fruit of a trailing plant of the gourd family; also, the plant.

musk ox, a small American arctic ox, somewhat like a sheep, and having a strong odor of musk: also called *musk sheep.*

musk·rat (mŭsk′răt′), *n.* a ratlike water animal of North America, with valuable, dark-brown fur and webbed hind feet; also, the fur. (See illustration.)

FRENCH MUS-KETEER
17th century.

mus·sel (mŭs′l) *n.* any of several shellfish found in fresh and salt water, some o which are fit for food.

Mus·so·li·ni (mōōs′sŏ·lē′nĕ), Benito (1883–1945), called *Il Duce* (ēl dōō′chā), the Italian Fascist leader.

MUSSEL (⅓)

Mus·sul·man (mŭs′ŭl·măn), *n.* [*pl.* Mussulmans or Mussulmen], a Mohammedan: also called *Moslem.*

must (mŭst), *auxiliary v.* [*p.t.* must], **1**, to be obliged or compelled; as, he *must* go; **2**, to be logically necessary; as, this *must* be what he means.

mus·tache (mŭs-tăsh′; mŭs′tăsh;

MUSKRAT (1/10)

moos-tăsh′), *n.* the hair growing on a man's upper lip. Also spelled **mous-tache′.**

MUSICAL INSTRUMENTS OF A MODERN ORCHESTRA

1–4, stringed instruments played with a bow (1, violin; 2, viola; 3, violoncello; 4, contrabass); 5, harp; 6–12, wood-wind instruments (6, flute; 7, piccolo; 8, English horn; 9, bassoon; 10, oboe; 11, clarinet; 12, bass clarinet); 13–17, brass-wind instruments (13, cornet; 14, trumpet; 15, trombone; 16, French horn; 17, bass tuba); 18, saxophone; 19–22, percussion instruments (19, kettledrum; 20, bass drum; 21, cymbals; 22, snare drum).

mus·lin (mŭz′lĭn), *n.* **1**, a fine, soft cotton cloth, plain or figured, used for women's dresses, etc.; **2**, a heavier, plain cloth, used for sheets, underwear, etc.:—*adj.* made of muslin.

muss (mŭs), *n. Colloquial,* confusion; disorder:—*v.t. Colloquial,* to disarrange, as clothing; also, to soil.

mus·tang (mŭs′tăng), *n.* the small, hardy, half-wild horse of the American plains.

mus·tard (mŭs′tẽrd), *n.* **1**, a plant with yellow flowers and long, slender seed pods (see illustration on the following page); **2**, the seed of this plant, especially when

go; join; yet; sing; chin; show; thin, *th*en; hw, *why;* zh, azure; ü, Ger. für or Fr. l*u*ne; ö, Ger. schön or Fr. f*eu;* n̂, Fr. *e*nfant, nom; kh, Ger. a*ch* or i*ch.* See pages ix–x.

ground into a fine, yellow powder which is used as a seasoning.

mus-ter (mŭs′tĕr), *n.* **1**, a gathering; especially, an assembly of troops; **2**, the number of troops thus assembled:—*v.t.* **1**, to assemble, especially troops; **2**, to collect and show; as, to *muster* one's courage.

mus-ty (mŭs′tĭ), *adj.* [mus-ti-er, mus-ti-est], **1**, spoiled with damp; moldy; as, *musty* books; **2**, spoiled by age; stale.—*n.* **mus′ti-ness.**

mu-ta-ble (mū′tȧ-bl), *adj.* changeable.

mu-ta-tion (mū-tā′shŭn), *n.* change; variation.

mute (mūt), *n.* **1**, one who cannot speak or who remains silent; **2**, a contrivance to deaden or soften the sound of a musical instrument:—*adj.* **1**, silent; speechless; as, the child stood *mute;* **2**, unable to speak; dumb:—*v.t.* [mut-ed, mut-ing], to muffle the tone of.

MUSTARD

mu-ti-late (mū′tĭ-lāt), *v.t.* [mutilat-ed, mutilat-ing], to cut off or remove a necessary part of.—*n.* **mu′ti-la′tion.**
Syn. cripple, disfigure.

mu-ti-neer (mū′tĭ-nēr′), *n.* one who is guilty of rebellion against authority.

mu-ti-ny (mū′tĭ-nĭ), *n.* [*pl.* mutinies], rebellion against authority; especially rebellion of soldiers or sailors against their officers:—*v.i.* [mutinied, mutiny-ing], to rise against authority.—*adj.* **mu′ti-nous.**

mut-ter (mŭt′ĕr), *n.* a murmur:—*v.i.* **1**, to speak indistinctly in a low voice; **2**, to make a low, rumbling noise, as does thunder: —*v.t.* to utter indistinctly.

mut-ton (mŭt′n), *n.* the flesh of a sheep.

mu-tu-al (mū′tū-ăl), *adj.* interchanged; given and received; as, *mutual* admiration.

mu-zhik or **mu-zjik** (mōō-zhĭk′; mōō′zhĭk), *n.* a Russian peasant.

muz-zle (mŭz′l), *n.* **1**, the projecting jaws and nose of an animal; snout (see illustration at *horse*); **2**, a guard or cover for the mouth of an animal to prevent its biting; **3**, the mouth of a gun (see illustration at *revolver*):—*v.t.* [muz-zled, muz-zling], **1**, to enclose the mouth of, to prevent biting; **2**, to restrain from free expression of opinion; as, to *muzzle* the newspapers.

MUZZLE, def. 2

my (mī), *adj.* a possessive form of *I*: belonging or relating to me; as, it is *my* hat.

My-ce-nae (mī-sē′nē), an ancient ruined city in southeastern Greece.

myr-i-ad (mĭr′ĭ-ăd), *n.* a very large number:—*adj.* innumerable; as, *myriad* stars.

Myr-mi-don (mûr′mĭ-dŏn), *n.* in mythology, one of a band of followers of Achilles in the Trojan War:—**myrmidon,** a follower who obeys without question.

myrrh (mûr), *n.* a gummy substance obtained from a shrub of Arabia and East Africa, used in medicine, perfumes, etc.

myr-tle (mûr′tl), *n.* **1**, an evergreen shrub with glossy leaves and white or pink flowers followed by black berries; **2**, a creeping vine with dark-green leaves and blue flowers: also called *periwinkle.*

my-self (mī-sĕlf′), *pron.* [*pl.* ourselves (our-sĕlvz′)], **1**, an emphatic form of *I*; **2**, a reflexive form of *me*; as, I hurt *myself*; **3**, my natural self; as, I am not *myself* today.

MYRTLE

mys-te-ri-ous (mĭs-tē′rĭ-ŭs), *adj.* not understandable; obscure.—*adv.* **mys-te′ri-ous-ly.**

mys-ter-y (mĭs′tēr-ĭ), *n.* [*pl.* mysteries], **1**, something secret, hidden, or unexplained; as, the cause of the murder is a *mystery*; **2**, that which is beyond human understanding; as, the *mystery* of the creation of life; **3**, in the Middle Ages, a play based on incidents from the Bible.

mys-tic (mĭs′tĭk), *n.* one who believes that he can have direct spiritual communication with God:—*adj.* **1**, having a hidden meaning; mysterious; **2**, magical.

mys-ti-cal (mĭs′tĭ-kăl), *adj.* **1**, having inner, spiritual meaning, not understood by everybody; as, the *mystical* meaning of Communion; **2**, of or like mysticism.

mys-ti-cism (mĭs′tĭ-sĭzm), *n.* the belief that direct spiritual knowledge of God comes through meditation, inspiration, etc.

mys-ti-fy (mĭs′tĭ-fī), *v.t.* [mystified, mystify-ing], to bewilder; puzzle; as, his acts *mystify* me.—*n.* **mys′ti-fi-ca′tion.**

myth (mĭth), *n.* **1**, a traditional story often founded on some fact of nature, or an event in the early history of a people, and embodying some religious belief of that people; **2**, any imaginary person, thing, or event.—*adj.* **myth′i-cal.**—*adv.* **myth′i-cal-ly.**

my-thol-o-gy (mĭ-thŏl′ō-jĭ), *n.* [*pl.* mythologies], **1**, a body of myths in which are recorded a people's beliefs concerning their origin, gods, heroes, etc.; **2**, the study of these beliefs.—*n.* **my-thol′o-gist.** —*adj.* **myth′o-log′i-cal** (mĭth′ō-lŏj′ĭ-kăl).

N

N, n (ĕn), *n.* [*pl.* N's, n's], the 14th letter of the alphabet, following M.

n. abbreviation for *noun:*—**N.** abbreviation for *north.*

N.A. abbreviation for *North America.*

nab (năb), *v.t.* [nabbed, nab-bing], to catch or seize unexpectedly; grab; arrest; as, the police *nabbed* the thief.

na-bob (nā′bŏb), *n.* **1,** a native governor of a province in India under the Mogul empire; **2,** any rich or powerful man.

na-dir (nā′dẽr), *n.* **1,** that part of the heavens directly beneath the place where one stands, and opposite to the zenith; **2,** hence, the lowest point; as, the *nadir* of his hopes.

¹**nag** (năg), *n.* a small horse; hence, any horse, especially one that is worn out.

²**nag** (năg), *v.i.* [nagged, nag-ging], to scold or find fault continually, often about little things; as, she *nagged* at him to stop smoking:—*v.t.* to torment with tiresome insistence; as, the boys *nag* their mother for candy.—*adj.* **nag′ging.**

Na-ga-sa-ki (nä′gȧ-sä′kẽ), a seaport on the northwestern coast of Kyushu, the large southern island of Japan (map 15).

Na-hum (nā′hŭm), one of the Hebrew prophets; also, a book of the Old Testament.

na-iad (nā′yăd; nī′ăd), *n.* in mythology, a water nymph.

nail (nāl), *n.* **1,** the thin, horny growth at the end of a finger or a toe; **2,** a slender, short bar or rod of metal, with a head at one end, used chiefly for driving into woodwork to hold two or more pieces together:—*v.t.* **1,** to fasten with a nail; as, to *nail* a lid down; **2,** to clinch or make certain; as, I *nailed* my argument by showing the figures; **3,** to answer or disprove; as, he *nailed* the lie.

NAIL (N) def. 1

nain-sook (nān′sŏŏk; năn′-sŏŏk), *n.* a fine, soft muslin, plain or striped.

Nai-ro-bi (nī-rō′bĕ), a town, capital of Kenya Colony, British East Africa (map 14).

NAILS, def. 2
1, cut nail; 2, horseshoe nail; 3, wire finishing nail; 4, common flat-headed wire nail.

na-ive or **na-ïve** (nä-ēv′), *adj.* artless; unaffected; as, a *naïve* girl.

na-ked (nā′kĕd), *adj.* **1,** entirely undressed; nude; as, *naked* swimmers; **2,** bare; without its usual covering; as, a *naked* hillside; a *naked* sword; **3,** plain; without addition; as, the *naked* truth:—**with the naked eye,** without the aid of a telescope or similar glass.

name (nām), *n.* **1,** the term or title by which a person or thing is called or known; **2,** character; reputation; fame; as, he has made a *name* for himself in literature:—*v.t.* [named, nam-ing], **1,** to give a name to; as, they *named* the child "John"; **2,** to appoint for a special purpose; specify; as, to *name* the day; **3,** to mention or specify; as, I asked him to *name* his reasons.—*adj.* **name′less.**—*adj.* **nam′a-ble; name′a-ble.**

Syn., n. appellation, epithet, denomination.

name-ly (nām′lĭ), *adv.* that is to say; to state more particularly; as, three tools are needed, *namely,* saw, hammer, and plane.

name-sake (nām′sāk′), *n.* one who is named for another, or has the same name as another.

nan-keen or **nan-kin** (năn-kēn′), *n.* a brownish-yellow cotton cloth, formerly brought from China.

Nan-king (năn′kĭng′), a city in China, on the Yangtze River (map 15).

Nan-tuck-et (năn-tŭk′ĕt), an island off the southern coast of Massachusetts (map 6).

Na-o-mi (nā′ō-mĭ; nā-ō′mĭ; nā′ō-mĭ; nā-ō′mĭ), in the Bible, Ruth's mother-in-law.

¹**nap** (năp), *n.* a short sleep; a doze:—*v.i.* [napped, nap-ping], to take a nap, or short sleep; doze; hence, to be inattentive or off one's guard.

²**nap** (năp), *n.* short hairs or fuzz on the surface of some fabrics; the pile.

nape (nāp), *n.* in man or animals, the back of the neck.

naph-tha (năf′thȧ), *n.* a clear, inflammable liquid obtained from petroleum, coal tar, etc., somewhat like gasoline.

nap-kin (năp′kĭn), *n.* a small square piece of cloth or paper held across the lap at table for protecting the clothing or for wiping the fingers or lips.

Na-ples (nā′plz), a city on the southwestern coast of Italy (map 12). Its Italian name is **Na′po-li** (nä′pō-lē).

Na-po-le-on I (nȧ-pō′lē-ŭn), (1769-1821), emperor of the French, 1804-1815. His full name was *Napoleon Bonaparte.*—*adj.* **Na-po′le-on′ic.**

Nar-cis-sus (när-sĭs′ŭs), *n.* in mythology, a youth who fell in love with his own image.

nar-cis-sus (när-sĭs′ŭs), *n.* [*pl.* narcissuses (när-sĭs′ŭs-ĕz) or narcissi (när-sĭs′ī)], a spring-flowering plant, that grows from a bulb. The jonquil and the daffodil are kinds of narcissus.

NARCISSUS

nar·cot·ic (när-kŏt′ĭk), *n.* a drug which produces drowsiness or sleep, and which lessens pain by making the nerves dull:— *adj.* having the power to produce drowsiness, sleep, or insensibility to pain; as, opium is a *narcotic* drug.

nard (närd), *n.* a fragrant plant, the spikenard, or a fragrant ointment made from it.

nar·rate (nă-rāt′), *v.t.* [narrat-ed, narrating], to tell (a story); give an account of (events or happenings); relate; as, Sindbad *narrated* his adventures.—*n.* **nar′ra′tor.**

Syn. recount, report, describe, rehearse.

nar·ra·tion (nă-rā′shŭn), *n.* **1,** the telling of real or imaginary happenings; **2,** a story.

nar·ra·tive (năr′à-tĭv), *n.* a story or tale, or an account of real or imaginary happenings: —*adj.* having to do with storytelling; of the nature of a story; as, a *narrative* poem.

Syn., n. account, narration, relation.

nar·row (năr′ō), *adj.* **1,** not wide; of little breadth or width; as, a *narrow* lane; **2,** small; as, to move within a *narrow* range; **3,** lacking wide knowledge or breadth of view; having little imagination; as, a *narrow* mind:—*v.t.* to make smaller in width or extent; hence, to limit or restrict:—*v.i.* to become less wide.—*n.* **nar′row-ness.**— *adv.* **nar′row-ly.**

narrow escape, an escape by a small margin; **narrows,** *n. pl.,* a strait, or a narrow passage between two bodies of water.

nar·row—mind·ed (năr′ō-mīn′dĕd), *adj.* without breadth of view; intolerant; prejudiced.

nar·whal (när′hwăl), *n.* a sea mammal related to the whale, with a large, twisted tusk. The narwhal is valued in commerce for its oil and ivory.

NARWHAL (₁ₒₒ)

N.A.S. abbreviation for *National Academy of Sciences.*

na·sal (nā′zăl), *adj.* having to do with the nose; especially, pronounced through the nose; as, *m, n,* and *ng* represent *nasal* sounds: —*n.* a nasal sound, or a letter used to represent it.—*n.* **na-sal′i-ty.**—*adv.* **na′sal-ly.**

Nash·ville (năsh′vĭl), a city, capital of Tennessee (map 8)..

Nas·sau (năs′ô), a city, capital of the Bahama Islands, which lie southeast of Florida (map 10).

nas·ti·ness (năs′tĭ-nĕs), *n.* the condition of being filthy, disgusting, indecent, or nasty.

na·stur·tium (nà-stûr′shŭm), *n.* a garden plant having brilliantly colored, fragrant flowers with spurs.

NASTURTIUM

nas·ty (năs′tĭ), *adj.* [nas-ti-er, nas-ti-est], **1,** dirty; filthy; **2,** disgusting to taste or smell; as, *nasty* medicine; **3,** obscene; indecent; **4,** troublesome; as, a *nasty* cut; **5,** *Colloquial:* **a,** ill-natured; mean; **b,** unpleasant; as, a *nasty* day.

Syn. unclean, indecent, impure.

nat. abbreviation for *national.*

na·tal (nā′tăl), *adj.* pertaining to one's birth:—**natal day,** birthday.

Na·tal (nà-tăl′; nà-täl′), a province (cap. Pietermaritzburg) in the southeastern part of the Union of South Africa (map 14).

nathe·less (nāth′lĕs), *adv.* Archaic, nevertheless.

na·tion (nā′shŭn), *n.* **1,** the people of one country, as the U.S., living under one government; **2,** a race of people having the same religion and customs, but not always living in the same country or speaking the same language; as, the Jewish *nation.*

Syn. people, tribe.

na·tion·al (năsh′ŭn-ăl), *adj.* pertaining to a nation; as, *national* customs; also, pertaining to a nation as a whole; as, a *national* problem:—*n.* a member of a nation; citizen; as, a *national* of the U.S.—*adv.* **na′tion-al-ly**

na·tion·al·ism (năsh′ŭn-ăl-ĭzm), *n.* **1,** patriotic devotion or principles, often shown by glorification of one's own country with little regard for other countries; **2,** demand for, or advocacy of, national independence. —*n.* **na′tion-al-ist.**—*adj.* **na′tion-al-is′tic.**

na·tion·al·i·ty (năsh′ŭn-ăl′ĭ-tĭ), *n.* [*pl.* nationalities], one's connection with a particular nation by birth or citizenship, or one's political status because of this connection; as, he showed his French *nationality.*

na·tion·al·ize (năsh′ŭn-ăl-īz), *v.t.* [nationalized, nationaliz-ing], **1,** to put under the control of the government, as mines or railroads; **2,** to make or change into a nation; as, Garibaldi *nationalized* Italy; **3,** to admit to citizenship in a country; as, to *nationalize* an immigrant.—*n.* **na′tion-al-i-za′tion.**—*n.* **na′tion-al-iz′er.**

na·tive (nā′tĭv), *adj.* **1,** pertaining to one's birth or to the place of one's birth; as, one's *native* land or language; **2,** born or produced in, or belonging to, a country; as, *native* plants; **3,** produced by nature; not artificial; as, *native* copper; **4,** inborn; not acquired; natural; as, *native* charm:—*n.* one who is born in a given country or place.— *adv.* **na′tive-ly.**

Syn., adj. natural, indigenous.

na·tiv·i·ty (nă-tĭv′ĭ-tĭ), *n.* [*pl.* nativities], **1,** birth; **2,** the time, place, and manner of birth:—**the Nativity,** the birth of Christ.

natl. abbreviation for *national.*

LION

TIGER

LEOPARD

KANGAROO

AFRICAN ELEPHANT

BLACK BEAR

RHINOCEROS

MOOSE

GORILLA

HIPPOPOTAMUS

GIRAFFE

ZEBRA

R·BRUCE HORSFALL

All animals on this page are 1/50 natural size

Some of the Larger Wild Animals. (*See other side.*)

LARGER WILD ANIMALS

The highest class of animals suckle their young. They are called *mammals*. The animals pictured on the preceding page are all mammals. Some mammals eat only flesh. They are said to be *carnivorous*. Others live on plants. They are said to be *herbivorous*. Lions, tigers, leopards, and bears are carnivorous, though the bears like berries and honey with their meat. Mammals are further divided according to their form and habits. All cats, for example, have soft-padded feet so they can sneak up on their prey; sharp claws for catching and holding their victims; strong jaws for crunching bones and pointed teeth for tearing flesh.

Lions, tigers, and leopards are big cats. The lion is called "the king of beasts." At his loud warning cough, just before he starts on a hunt, every living creature of the jungle becomes still; then there is a wild scramble for safety. The tiger, that big cat with the tawny coat striped in black, is feared almost as much as the lion. A big tiger weighs about 500 pounds and often measures eleven feet from "nose tip to tail tip." He is a powerful fighter but avoids elephants, carabaos, and big bears. He will eat any kind of meat. Man-eaters are usually old tigers that find human beings easier to kill than wild animals. The leopard is that treacherous cat with the beautifully marked fur, prized for ladies' coats. Like all cats, except the lion, leopards are good climbers. They feed on pigs and cattle.

Contrary to belief, the bear is good-natured, but if forced to fight he proves a dangerous enemy. The black bear lives in the mountains of New York and New England. His keen senses of hearing and smell help him to survive.

Now for a glance at some of the herb eaters. The largest and strongest of all living land animals is the elephant. These giants live only in Africa and Asia, but once they roamed the world. At first the elephant had no trunk, but a tapering head with nostrils at the end of a long upper lip. The upper lip grew into a great trunk, and the eye teeth became huge tusks. Then the world had a mastodon, a creature too big to survive, although an elephant often weighs 8,000 pounds. Next in size to the elephant is the homely hippopotamus. His name means "river horse" but he is related not to the horse but to the pig. He spends most of the day in the water where he is free from insects. At night he wanders forth for food. His teeth contain ivory; his thick skin is useful; his flesh makes good food—and there is often 8,000 pounds of it. The rhinoceros is even homelier than the hippopotamus. He is about the ugliest of mammals with a head all bumps and an upright horn on his snout— one, if he comes from India, two, if from Africa. He weighs about 5,000 pounds, has short legs and clumsy feet, yet he can go crashing through the jungle at a dangerous speed. Even lions avoid him, for claws and teeth cannot pierce his armorlike skin. He has large keen ears and small dull eyes.

The tallest animal in existence is the giraffe. For ages he has been stretching his neck to reach the tender leaves of trees. His markings conceal him from other animals as he feeds. He is awkward but swifter than the fastest horse.

The most manlike animal is the gorilla. A large gorilla weighs about 300 pounds and is over five feet tall. Sugar cane and berries are his favorite foods. Gorillas live in pairs and rear their families carefully. They are seldom captured because they fight ferociously. In captivity they rarely live for any length of time.

The moose, found in Maine, Minnesota, and Canada, is the largest member of the deer family. His broad, flattened antlers are often six feet from tip to tip. They drop off in December, appear again in April, and by June are full size. With his antlers and feet a moose can kill any other beast of his domain. Only the hunter can overcome him. His food is water plants and the tender leaves of trees. The horse-like animal with the cream white suit striped all over with black is a mountain zebra. No two zebras ever have the same markings. A zebra's hide makes good leather and his flesh good food.

The kangaroo is something of a freak— a survival from the time of the mastodon. He is found only in Australia and the neighboring islands. At birth baby kangaroos are smaller than mice, and so helpless that the mother carries them in a deep fur-lined pocket. Not for several months are they permitted to leave this pocket. Animals with such pockets are called *marsupials*.

NATO (nā′tō), abbreviation for *North Atlantic Treaty Organization.*

nat-ty (năt′ĭ), *adj.* [nat-ti-er, nat-ti-est], tidy; neat; smart; trim.—*adv.* **nat′ti-ly.**—*n.* **nat′ti-ness.**

nat-u-ral (năt′ū-rǎl), *adj.* **1,** pertaining to one's nature; innate; inborn; as, *natural* gifts; **2,** occurring in the ordinary course of things; as, a *natural* result; **3,** true to life; as, a *natural* likeness; **4,** pertaining to the world and the things in it; as, *natural* science; **5,** in music, written without sharps or flats; as, the *natural* scale of C:—**natural history,** the study of plants, minerals, and natural objects in general; especially, the study of animals with relation to their life, habits, etc.:—*n.* in music, a sign [♮] placed on a line or space of the staff, to remove the effect of a preceding sharp or flat.—*n.* **nat′u-ral-ness.**

Syn., *adj.* inherent, inbred, native, indigenous.

nat-u-ral-ist (năt′ū-rǎl-ĭst), *n.* one who makes a special study of natural objects, as plants, minerals, and, especially, animals.

nat-u-ral-ize (năt′ū-rǎl-īz), *v.t.* [naturalized, naturaliz-ing], **1,** to admit (a foreigner) to citizenship; **2,** hence, to accept or adopt, as a foreign word or custom; to introduce and make grow, as a foreign plant.—*n.* **nat′u-ral-i-za′tion.**

nat-u-ral-ly (năt′ū-rǎl-ĭ), *adv.* **1,** in a natural way or manner; as, act *naturally;* **2,** by nature; as, she was *naturally* clever at music; **3,** as might be expected; as, *naturally,* I was pleased when I won the prize.

na-ture (nā′tūr), *n.* **1,** real character; the qualities that naturally belong to a person or thing; as, she is affectionate by *nature;* **2,** kind or sort; as, things of this *nature;* **3,** the outdoor world; as, the beauties of *nature;* **4,** the physical universe as a whole, including what it is and what happens in it; as, the laws of *nature.*

naught (nôt), *n.* **1,** nothing; **2,** a cipher, or zero; the character [0] used to represent an arithmetical value of nothing.

naugh-ty (nô′tĭ), *adj.* [naugh-ti-er, naugh-ti-est], bad; wayward; mischievous; disobedient.—*adv.* **naugh′ti-ly.**—*n.* **naugh′ti-ness.**

Syn. wicked, perverse, evil.

nau-se-a (nô′zhȧ; nô′zē-ȧ; nô′shȧ), *n.* **1,** sickness of the stomach, with a desire to vomit, as in seasickness; **2,** loathing; disgust.

nau-se-ate (nô′zhē-āt; nô′sē-āt), *v.t.* [nauseat-ed, nauseat-ing], to affect with nausea or with a feeling of strong disgust; sicken.

nau-seous (nô′zhŭs; nô′shŭs), *adj.* causing sickness of the stomach; disgusting.—*adv.* **nau′seous-ly.**—*n.* **nau′seous-ness.**

nau-ti-cal (nô′tĭ-kǎl), *adj.* pertaining to ships, sailors, or navigation; maritime:—**nautical mile,** 6,080.2 feet (in British usage, 6,080 feet): also called *geographical mile.*—*adv.* **nau′ti-cal-ly.**

Syn. marine, naval.

nau-ti-lus (nô′tĭ-lŭs), *n.* [*pl.* nautiluses or nautili (nô′tĭ-lī)], any of several mollusks with a spiral shell, found especially in the South Pacific and Indian oceans.

Nav-a-ho or **Nav-a-jo** (năv′ȧ-hō), *n.* [*pl.* Navahos or Navahoes; Navajos or Navajoes], a member of a tribe of North American Indians of Arizona and New Mexico.

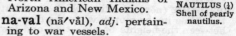

NAUTILUS (⅓). Shell of pearly nautilus.

na-val (nā′vǎl), *adj.* pertaining to war vessels.

nave (nāv), *n.* the central part of the main body of a church, from the choir to the main entrances, between the aisles (see illustration under *aisle*).

na-vel (nā′věl), *n.* the depression or mark in the center of the abdomen:—**navel orange,** a kind of orange, usually seedless, having a navel-like depression in the rind.

nav-i-ga-ble (năv′ĭ-gȧ-bl), *adj.* **1,** capable of being traveled over by a boat or an airplane; as, a *navigable* stream; **2,** capable of being steered; dirigible; as, a *navigable* balloon; an easily *navigable* boat.—*n.* **nav′i-ga-bil′i-ty.**—*n.* **nav′i-ga-ble-ness.**

nav-i-gate (năv′ĭ-gāt), *v.i.* [navigat-ed, navigat-ing], **1,** to travel by water or air; **2,** to sail or direct a ship or an airplane:—*v.t.* **1,** to travel by water in any type of ship, or by air in any airplane; **2,** to steer or manage a ship or an airplane.

nav-i-ga-tion (năv′ĭ-gā′shŭn), *n.* **1,** the act of traveling by water or air; **2,** the act or the science of managing a ship or airplane.

nav-i-ga-tor (năv′ĭ-gā′tēr), *n.* one skilled in the science of directing the course of a vessel, an airplane, or the like.

na-vy (nā′vĭ), *n.* [*pl.* navies], **1,** the warships of a nation; **2,** the sea war force of a nation, including ships, shipyards, shops, officers, men, etc.; **3,** a fleet, as of merchant ships.

nay (nā), *adv.* **1,** no; **2,** not only so, but: introducing a more definite statement; as, I suspect, *nay* I know, that he has gone:—*n.* **1,** a refusal or denial; **2,** a negative vote or reply; also, a negative voter.

Naz-a-rene (năz′ȧ-rēn′), *n.* a native of Nazareth, where Jesus spent his childhood; hence, a follower of Jesus.

Naz-a-reth (năz′ȧ-rěth), a small town in northern Palestine, the scene of the childhood of Jesus.

go; join; yet; sing; chin; show; thin, *th*en; hw, *wh*y; zh, a*z*ure; ü, Ger. f*ü*r or Fr. l*u*ne; ö, Ger. sch*ö*n or Fr. f*eu*; ṅ, Fr. e*n*fant, no*m*; kh, Ger. a*ch* or i*ch*. See pages ix–x.

Na-zi (nä′tsē), *n.* [*pl.* Nazis], a member of the National Socialist German Workers' party, founded by Adolf Hitler.

n.b. or **N.B.** abbreviation for Latin *nota bene,* meaning *note well:*—**N.B.** abbreviation for *New Brunswick.*

N.C. abbreviation for *North Carolina.*

N.C.O. abbreviation for *noncommissioned officer.*

N.D. or **N. Dak.** abbreviation for *North Dakota.*

N.E. abbreviation for *northeast, New England.*

Ne-a-pol-i-tan (nē′á-pŏl′ĭ-tăn), *adj.* pertaining to Naples, in Italy:—*n.* a native of Naples.

neap tide (nēp), the tide which occurs at that time in the month when the distance between the heights of high tide and low tide is least: opposite of *spring tide.*

near (nēr), *adj.* **1,** not far distant in time, place, or degree; close; **2,** intimate; dear; as, a *near* friend; **3,** with a narrow margin; bare; as, a *near* escape; **4,** closely akin; as, a *near* relative; **5,** direct or quick; as, to go by the *near* way; **6,** mean or stingy; **7,** on the left-hand side of a vehicle, animal, or team:—*adv.* **1,** not distant in time, place, or degree; as, Easter is *near;* **2,** almost; approximately; as, *near* dead with cold; **3,** closely; as, as *near* as I can tell:—*prep.* close to or by; as, he sat *near* the stream:—*v.i.* and *v.t.* to come close (to); approach.—*adj.* **near′ish.**—*n.* **near′ness.**

near-by or **near—by** (nēr′bī′), *adj.* not far off; close:—*adv.* (also *near by*), near; at hand.

Near East, a region comprising the Balkan States and southwestern Asia, including Turkey, Saudi Arabia, etc. (maps **12, 15**).

near-ly (nēr′lĭ), *adv.* **1,** almost; all but; as, *nearly* frozen; **2,** closely; as, *nearly* related.

near-sight-ed (nēr′sīt′ĕd), *adj.* able to see objects with distinctness only when they are quite close to the eyes.—*adv.* **near′-sight′ed-ly.**—*n.* **near′sight′ed-ness.**

neat (nēt), *adj.* **1,** tidy; trim; **2,** simple and elegant; well made; as, a *neat* costume; **3,** brief; cleverly phrased; as, a *neat* reply; **4,** skilful; deft; as, a *neat* job of carpentering.—*adv.* **neat′ly.**—*n.* **neat′ness.**

Neb. or **Nebr.** abbreviation for *Nebraska.*

Ne-bo (nē′bō), in the Bible, the mountain from which Moses saw the Promised Land.

Ne-bras-ka (nē-brăs′ká), a middle western State (cap. Lincoln) of the U.S. (map **7**).

Neb-u-chad-nez-zar (nĕb′ū-kăd-nĕz′ēr), in the Bible, a king of Babylon (604-561 B.C.), who laid waste Jerusalem and enslaved the Jews (2 Kings 24, 25).

neb-u-la (nĕb′ū-lá), *n.* [*pl.* nebulae (nĕb′-ū-lē)], a cluster of stars or a mass of luminous gas so very, very far away from our sun and its planets that it can be seen with the naked eye only as a hazy patch of light in the sky.—*adj.* **neb′u-lar.**

neb-u-lous (nĕb′ū-lŭs), *adj.* **1,** pertaining to, or like, a nebula; **2,** cloudy; indistinct; vague; as, his ideas on the matter are *nebulous.*—*n.* **neb′u-lous-ness.**

nec-es-sar-y (nĕs′ĕ-sĕr′ĭ), *adj.* **1,** existing or happening naturally; true according to natural laws; as, a *necessary* conclusion; **2,** not to be done without; essential; as, food is *necessary* to life; **3,** unavoidable; inevitable; as, the *necessary* result of an act:—**necessaries,** *n.pl.* things which cannot be done without.—*adv.* **nec′es-sar′i-ly.**

Syn., adj. needful, requisite.

ne-ces-si-tate (nē-sĕs′ĭ-tāt), *v.t.* [necessitat-ed, necessitat-ing], to make unavoidable; as, illness *necessitated* his removal.

ne-ces-si-ty (nē-sĕs′ĭ-tĭ), *n.* [*pl.* necessities], **1,** great need of aid or help; as, send for me in case of *necessity;* **2,** something greatly needed; as, sunshine is a *necessity* for health; **3,** extreme poverty; **4,** that which compels one to act in a certain way; as, he felt the *necessity* of leaving immediately; **5,** **necessities,** the things needed for a decent living.

Syn. indigence, want, need.

neck (nĕk), *n.* **1,** that part of the body connecting the head with the shoulders; **2,** the part of a garment which fits closely around the neck; the collar; **3,** a long, extended part of an object; as, the *neck* of a bottle.

neck-er-chief (nĕk′ēr-chĭf), *n.* formerly, a piece of cloth worn about the neck for protection or ornament; a scarf or muffler.

neck-lace (nĕk′lĭs), *n.* a decorative chain, as of gold, or a string of beads, jewels, or the like, worn around the neck.

neck-tie (nĕk′tī′), *n.* a narrow scarf or band worn around the neck and tied in front.

neck-wear (nĕk′wâr′), *n.* articles such as ties, collars, etc., worn around the neck.

NECKLACE

nec-ro-man-cer (nĕk′rō-măn′sēr), *n.* **1,** one who claims to be able to foretell the future by talking with spirits; **2,** a magician; conjurer.

nec-ro-man-cy (nĕk′rō-măn′sĭ), *n.* the art of foretelling the future by communication with the spirits of the dead; magic.

nec-tar (nĕk′tēr), *n.* **1,** in mythology, the wine of the gods; **2,** any delicious beverage; **3,** a sweet fluid in plants, especially in the flowers, used by bees in making honey.

āge, âorta, râre, căt, ásk, fär, ăllow, sofá; ēve, ēvent, ĕll, writēr, novĕl; bīte, pĭn; nō, ōbey, ôr, dŏg, tŏp, cŏllide; ūnit, ūnite, bûrn, cŭt, focŭs; nōon, fŏŏt; mound; coin;

nec·tar·ine (nĕk′tẽr-ēn′; nĕk′tẽr-ĭn), *n.* a kind of peach with a smooth skin.

nee (nā), *adj.* born: often placed before the maiden name of a married woman; as, Mrs. Miller, *nee* Brown.

need (nēd), *n.* **1**, lack of anything desired or useful; as, he felt the *need* of sleep; **2**, necessity; time of trouble; as, a friend in *need* is a friend indeed; **3**, urgent want; poverty:— *v.t.* to be in want of; require; have use for:— *v.i.* **1**, to be necessary; as, it *needs* to be done; **2**, to be obligated; as, I *need* not go. *Syn., n.* necessity, want.

NECTARINE

need·ful (nēd′fŏŏl), *adj.* **1**, necessary; required; **2**, needy.—*adv.* **need′ful·ly.**

nee·dle (nē′dl), *n.* **1**, a small, sharp-pointed steel instrument furnished with an eye to hold thread; **2**, a thin, straight rod used in knitting or, when hooked at the end, for crocheting; **3**, anything sharply pointed like a needle, as the leaf of a pine or fir tree; **4**, the magnetic needle, a slender piece of magnetized steel in a compass:—*v.t. Colloquial,* to tease or annoy by heckling: —**needle valve,** a valve in which a slender rod, or needle, with a cone-shaped end, fits into a funnel-shaped part, used especially for accurate control of the flow of a fluid.

NEEDLES
1, common sewing needle; 2, needle for sewing burlap, canvas, etc.; 3, crocheting needle; 4, knitting needle.

need·less (nēd′lĕs), *adj.* unnecessary; useless; not needed.— *adv.* **need′less·ly.**—*n.* **need′less·ness.**

nee·dle·wom·an (nē′dl-wŏŏm/ăn), *n.* [*pl.* needlewomen (-wĭm′ĕn)], a seamstress; a woman who sews.

nee·dle·work (nē′dl-wûrk′), *n.* hand sewing; embroidery done by hand.

NEEDLE
def. 4

needs (nēdz), *adv.* necessarily; of necessity; as, he *needs* must come.

need·y (nēd′ĭ), *adj.* [need-i-er, need-i-est], very poor; poverty-stricken.—*n.* **need′i·ness.**

ne'er (nâr), a short form of *never.*

ne'er–do–well (nâr′-dŏŏ-wĕl′), *n.* one who does nothing worth while.

ne·far·i·ous (nē-fâr′ĭ-ŭs), *adj.* very wicked; infamous.—*adv.* **ne·far′i·ous·ly.**—*n.* **ne·far′i·ous·ness.**

ne·ga·tion (nē-gā′shŭn), *n.* **1**, denial; as, he shook his head in *negation;* **2**, the opposite or absence of something real or positive; as, death is the *negation* of life.

neg·a·tive (nĕg′a-tĭv), *adj.* **1**, expressing or implying refusal or denial; as, he gave me a *negative* answer; **2**, lacking positive qualities; not forceful or influential; as, a *negative* sort of person; **3**, naming the kind of electricity made in silk by rubbing it on glass: the opposite of *positive;* **4**, in mathematics, naming a quantity to be subtracted; minus:—*n.* **1**, a refusal or denial; **2**, the side of a question which denies what the opposite side upholds; as, to support the *negative* in a debate; **3**, in mathematics, a quantity less than zero; also, its symbol; **4**, in photography, a picture made on a plate or film by exposure in a camera, in which light objects appear dark and dark objects light, and from which is printed the picture ordinarily shown as a finished photograph, called a *positive;* **5**, a word expressing denial, as the words *no, not, neither:*—*v.t.* [negatived, negativ-ing], **1**, to deny the truth of; contradict; **2**, to refuse assent to; veto; **3**, to counteract; neutralize.—*adv.* **neg′a·tive·ly.**

neg·lect (nĕg-lĕkt′), *n.* **1**, failure to do that which should be done; as, her garden showed *neglect;* **2**, habitual lack of attention; disregard; as, his friends resented his *neglect;* **3**, carelessness:—*v.t.* **1**, to fail (to act or to do something), by carelessness or design; **2**, to slight; pay little attention to; as, to *neglect* a warning; **3**, to leave uncared for; as, the boy *neglects* his dog.

neg·lect·ful (nĕg-lĕkt′fŏŏl), *adj.* **1**, careless; disregardful.—*adv.* **neg·lect′ful·ly.**

neg·li·gee (nĕg′lĭ-zhā′; nĕg′lĭ-zhā′), *n.* **1**, a loose lounging robe worn by women; **2**, easy and informal dress in general.

neg·li·gence (nĕg′lĭ-jĕns), *n.* **1**, failure to do what should be done; **2**, carelessness; **3**, disregard of appearance, manner, or style. *Syn.* heedlessness, remissness, neglect.

neg·li·gent (nĕg′lĭ-jĕnt), *adj.* **1**, careless; heedless; inattentive; **2**, neglectful.—*adv.* **neg′li·gent·ly.**

neg·li·gi·ble (nĕg′lĭ-jĭ-bl), *adj.* not worth much attention; of little account or value; as, the loss of ten cents was *negligible.*

ne·go·ti·a·ble (nē-gō′shĭ-a-bl), *adj.* capable of being converted into cash, or of being passed in the course of business from one person to another and serving the purpose of cash; as, an endorsed check is *negotiable.*—*n.* **ne·go′ti·a·bil′i·ty.**

ne·go·ti·ate (nē-gō′shĭ-āt), *v.t.* [negotiat-ed, negotiat-ing], **1**, to put through, obtain, or arrange for; as, to *negotiate* a sale, loan, treaty, peace; **2**, to sell, convert into cash, or transfer to another for a consideration; as, to *negotiate* business papers representing money value or credit, such as bonds stocks, checks, etc.; **3**, to deal with successfully; as, I knew the horse could *negotiate* the fence:—*v.i.* to treat with others in political or business affairs.—*n.* **ne-go′ti-a/tor.**

Ne-gro (nē′grō), *n.* [*pl.* Negroes], a person belonging to one of the black races of Africa:—**negro**, a black man, especially one who has some Negro blood.—*adj.* **Ne′gro; ne′gro.**

Ne-gros (nā′grōs), one of the Philippine Islands (map **15**).

Ne-he-mi-ah (nē′hē-mī′á; nē′ĕ-mī′á), in the Bible, a noted Jewish leader; also, a book of the Old Testament.

neigh (nā), *n.* the cry of a horse; a whinny:—*v.i.* to utter the cry of a horse.

neigh-bor (nā′bĕr), *n.* **1**, one who lives near another; **2**, a person or thing that is near another; **3**, a fellow being; as, love thy *neighbor* as thyself.

neigh-bor-hood (nā′bĕr-hŏŏd), *n.* **1**, the region near by; vicinity; as, it is in the *neighborhood* of the river; **2**, all the people living near one another, or within a certain range; as, the *neighborhood* welcomed us.

neigh-bor-ing (nā′bĕr-ĭng), *adj.* living or being near; adjoining.

neigh-bor-ly (nā′bĕr-lĭ), *adj.* friendly; kindly.—*n.* **neigh′bor-li-ness.**

nei-ther (nē′thẽr; nī′thẽr), *pron.* not the one nor the other; as, I want *neither* of the books:—*adj.* not either; as, *neither* book will do:—*conj.* **1**, not either; not (one or the other): often with *nor*; as, *neither* the book nor the paper; **2**, nor; nor yet; and . . . not; as, I know not, *neither* can I guess.

Nel-son (nĕl′sŭn), Horatio, Viscount (1758–1805), a British admiral.

Nem-e-sis (nĕm′ē-sĭs), *n.* in mythology, the goddess of revenge:—**nemesis**, a just punishment thought of as coming upon a person for ill deeds.

ne-o- (nē′ō-), a prefix meaning new or recent; as, *neophyte.*

ne-on (nē′ŏn), *n.* a rare gaseous element, found in the earth's atmosphere. In vacuum tubes it gives a reddish glow, and is much used in display signs.

ne-o-phyte (nē′ō-fīt), *n.* **1**, a novice; a beginner; especially, one who has just entered a convent; **2**, one recently baptized; a convert.

ne-o-plasm (nē′ō-plăzm), *n.* a new and abnormal growth in the body, as a tumor.

ne-o-prene (nē′ō-prēn), *n.* a synthetic substance used as a basis for making articles of imitation rubber.

neph-ew (nĕf′ū; nĕv′ū), *n.* the son of one's brother or sister; also, in careless use, the son of a brother-in-law or sister-in-law.

nep-o-tism (nĕp′ō-tĭzm), *n.* too great favor shown to relatives, especially by a person in power or authority, in giving them desirable positions.

Nep-tune (nĕp′tūn), *n.* in Roman mythology, the god of the sea; in astronomy, a planet of the solar system, invisible to the naked eye.

Ne-re-id (nē′rē-ĭd), *n.* a sea nymph.

nerve (nûrv), *n.* **1**, one of the cordlike fibers which connect the brain and spinal cord with all parts of the body; **2**, boldness; coolness in danger; courage; as, a high dive takes *nerve*:—*v.t.* [nerved, nerv-ing], to arouse courage or strength in; as, he *nerved* himself for the battle.

NEPTUNE
Standing beside a dolphin and holding a trident.

nerve-less (nûrv′lĕs), *adj.* **1**, without nerves; **2**, hence, lacking vigor; paralyzed; as, the pen fell from her *nerveless* grasp.—*adv.* **nerve′less-ly.**

nerv-ous (nûr′vŭs), *adj.* **1**, pertaining to, or made of, nerves; as, the *nervous* system; **2**, having weak nerves; hence, easily excited; timid; as, she is *nervous* in the dark; **3**, forceful; vigorous; as, he is full of *nervous* energy; **4**, restless or uneasy.—*adv.* **nerv′ous-ly.**—*n.* **nerv′ous-ness.**

-ness (-nĕs), a suffix added to adjectives to form nouns naming a quality or state of being; as, good*ness*, sick*ness*.

nest (nĕst), *n.* **1**, the bed or place made or chosen by a bird for the hatching of its eggs and the rearing of its young; **2**, a hatching place for insects, turtles, etc.; as, a hornet's *nest*; **3**, a cozy retreat or residence; **4**, a number of boxes, bowls, or the like, one fitting inside another:—*v.i.* to build and occupy a nest:—*v.t.* to place in a nest.

BIRD'S NEST

nest egg, **1**, an egg, usually of white porcelain, left in a nest to induce a hen to lay eggs there; **2**, a sum of money kept in reserve.

nes-tle (nĕs′l), *v.i.* [nes-tled, nes-tling], to lie close and snug; as, a child *nestles* in its mother's arms:—*v.t.* to cherish or cuddle.

WASP'S NEST

āte, âorta, râre, căt, ȧsk, fär, ȧllow, sofá; ēve, ĕvent, ĕll, writẽr, novĕl; bīte, pĭn; nō, ōbey, ôr, dŏg, tŏp, cŏllide; ūnit, únite, bûrn, cŭt, focŭs; nōon, fŏŏt; mound; coin;

nest·ling (nĕst′lĭng; nĕs′lĭng), *n.* a young bird recently hatched and not yet able to fly:—*adj.* recently hatched.

¹**net** (nĕt), *n.* **1**, a fabric made of twine knotted into meshes, used for catching birds, fish, or the like; **2**, any fine openwork fabric, very often of silk, used for bridal veils, laces, etc.; **3**, that which entraps; an entanglement; as, the criminal cannot escape the *net* of justice; a snare:—*adj.* of or like net or netting;

BUTTERFLY NET

as, a *net* dress:—*v.t.* [net-ted, net-ting], **1**, to make into a net or network; **2**, to catch in a net; hence, to entrap by clever stratagem; snare; **3**, to cover or protect with a net:—*v.i.* **1**, to make nets or network; **2**, to use nets in fishing, hunting game, etc.; as, the fishers *netted* while I watched.

²**net** (nĕt), *adj.* remaining after the deduction of all necessary expenses; as, *net* gain; also, excluding all waste, refuse, etc.: as, *net* weight:—*v.t.* [net-ted, net-ting], to earn as clear profit; as, the deal *netted* $2,000.

neth·er (nĕth′ẽr), *adj.* **1**, situated below; lying beneath; as, *nether* garments; **2**, pertaining to the regions below the heavens or the earth; as, Pluto ruled the *nether* world.

Neth·er·lands (nĕth′ẽr-lăndz), a kingdom (caps. The Hague and Amsterdam) in northwestern Europe (map 12). It is also called *Holland*.

neth·er·most (nĕth′ẽr-mōst), *adj.* lowest; farthest down; as, the *nethermost* depths of the ocean.

net·ting (nĕt′ĭng), *n.* **1**, the act or method of making nets; **2**, a fabric made of meshes; as, fish *netting*; **3**, a fabric of crossed wires, as for fences; **4**, network.

net·tle (nĕt′l), *n.* any of a group of coarse plants having prickles or stinging hairs:—*v.t.* [net-tled, net-tling], **1**, to sting, as with nettles; **2**, hence, to provoke; irritate; vex; as, his remark *nettled* me.

NETTLE

net·work (nĕt′wûrk′), *n.* **1**, an openwork fabric made by interlaced threads; **2**, any system of lines that cross like those in a net; as, a *network* of roads, vines, wires, or the like.

neu·ral (nū′răl), *adj.* pertaining to the nerves or to the nervous system.

neu·ral·gia (nū-răl′jȧ; nū-răl′jĭ-ȧ), *n.* a sharp pain along the course of a nerve.—*adj.* **neu·ral′gic.**

neu·ri·tis (nū-rī′tĭs), *n.* inflammation of a nerve or nerves.

neu·rot·ic (nū-rŏt′ĭk), *adj.* **1**, having some

nervous disease; **2**, acting on the nerves; as, a *neurotic* drug:—*n.* a person with a nervous disease.

neut. abbreviation for *neuter.*

neu·ter (nū′tẽr), *adj.* **1**, in grammar, neither masculine nor feminine; as, "book" is a *neuter* noun; **2**, in biology: **a,** having no sex, as certain plants; **b,** without fully developed sex organs; as, the worker bees are *neuter*:—*n.* a neuter word or organism.

neu·tral (nū′trăl), *adj.* **1**, not affected by a special or personal interest; indifferent; as, my feelings on the matter were altogether *neutral*; **2**, not taking sides in a quarrel, war, or the like; as, a *neutral* nation; also, belonging to a neutral nation; as, *neutral* ships; **3**, neither good nor bad; with no decided characteristics; **4**, neither acid nor alkaline; **5**, having little or no color; as, gray is a *neutral* shade:—*n.* one who does not take sides in a dispute or conflict.—*adv.* **neu′tral·ly.**

neu·tral·i·ty (nū-trăl′ĭ-tĭ), *n.* [*pl.* neutralities], **1**, the state of not taking sides in a quarrel or war; **2**, the state of being neither one thing nor the other; indifference.

neu·tral·ize (nū′trăl-īz), *v.t.* [neutralized, neutraliz-ing], **1**, to render inactive; make of no effect; counteract; as, to *neutralize* the effects of a poison; **2**, to make neutral; as, to *neutralize* small nations.—*n.* **neu′tral·i·za′tion.**

Nev. abbreviation for *Nevada.*

Ne·vad·a (nĕ-văd′ȧ; nĕ-vä′dȧ), a State (cap. Carson City) of the U.S. (map 9).

nev·er (nĕv′ẽr), *adv.* **1**, not ever; not at any time; **2**, in no degree; under no condition: used for emphasis; as, *never* fear.

nev·er·more (nĕv′ẽr-môr′), *adv.* not ever again; at no future time.

nev·er·the·less (nĕv′ẽr-thē-lĕs′), *adv.* and *conj.* notwithstanding; in spite of that; yet; however; still.

new (nū), *adj.* **1**, made for the first time; not existing before; as, a *new* dress; a *new* house; **2**, lately made, produced, invented, or discovered; as, a *new* type of engine; **3**, beginning afresh; recurring anew; as, a *new* year; a *new* start in life; **4**, freshly made or grown; as, *new* cheese; *new* peas; **5**, not yet used or worn; as, a *new* broom; a *new* suit; **6**, changed in character, health, etc.; as, I feel like a *new* man; **7**, different from that previously existing, known, or used; as, a *new* language; a *new* race of settlers:—*adv.* newly; recently; as, a field of *new*-mown hay.—*adv.* **new′ly.**—*n.* **new′ness.**

New Am·ster·dam (ăm′stẽr-dăm), the Dutch name for the city that is now called *New York.*

New-ark (nū'ẽrk), a city and industrial center in northern New Jersey (map 6).

New Bed-ford (bĕd'fẽrd), a seaport in southeastern Massachusetts (map 6).

new-born (nū'bôrn'), *adj.* 1, just born; 2, renewed; as, *newborn* energy.

New Bruns-wick (brŭnz'wĭk), a province (cap. Fredericton) in southeastern Canada (map 4).

new-com-er (nū'kŭm'ẽr), *n.* one who has lately arrived.

new-el (nū'ĕl), *n.* 1, in a winding staircase, the central upright pillar around which the steps turn; 2, the post at the foot of a stairway.

New Eng-land, the northeastern States of the U.S., comprising Maine, New Hampshire, Vermont, Massachusetts, Rhode Island, and Connecticut (map 6).

NEWEL (N) def. 2

new-fan-gled (nū'făng'gld; nū'făng'gld), *adj.* 1, new and unusual; novel: usually said in disfavor of a thing; as, *newfangled* ideas or notions; 2, easily carried away by new fashions or ideas; as, a *newfangled* teacher.

New-found-land (nū'fŭnd-lănd'; nū'fŭnd-lănd'; nū-found'lănd), an island, forming with Labrador the easternmost province (cap. St. John's) of Canada (map 4).

Newfoundland dog (nū-found'lănd), one of a breed of large and very intelligent dogs, with a coarse, dense coat.

New France, the former name of Canada.

NEWFOUNDLAND DOG (¹⁄₃₆)

New Guin-ea (gĭn'ĭ), a very large island in the East Indies (map 16): also called *Papua*.

New Hamp-shire (hămp'shĭr), a northeastern State (cap. Concord) of the U.S. (map 6).

New Ha-ven (hā'vĕn), a seaport and industrial city in southwestern Connecticut, on Long Island Sound (map 6).

New Jer-sey (jûr'zĭ), an eastern State (cap. Trenton) of the U.S. (map 6).

new-ly (nū'lĭ), *adv.* 1, recently; as, the house was *newly* completed; 2, in a new way; afresh; as, books *newly* arranged.

New Mex-i-co (mĕk'sĭ-kō), a southwestern State (cap. Santa Fe) of the U.S. (map 9).

New Neth-er-land (nĕth'ẽr-lănd), a Dutch colony along the Hudson River, in North America: so called from 1613 to 1664.

New Or-le-ans (ôr'lĕ-ănz; ôr-lēnz'), a seaport in southeastern Louisiana, on the Mississippi River (map 8).

New-port (nū'pôrt), a fashionable resort in southeastern Rhode Island (map 6).

news (nūz), *n.* recent or fresh information; as, we have no *news* of the accident; hence, recent events reported in the newspapers.
  Syn. information, intelligence, tidings.

news-boy (nūz'boi'), *n.* a boy who delivers or sells newspapers.

New South Wales, a state (cap. Sydney) in southeastern Australia (map 16).

news-pa-per (nūz'pā'pẽr), *n.* a paper printed daily or weekly, containing recent news, advertisements, pictures, etc.

news-reel (nūz'rēl'), *n.* a reel of motion pictures showing current or recent events.

newt (nūt), *n.* any of several small, harmless animals resembling lizards, found in water or damp places.

NEWT (¹⁄₃)

New Tes-ta-ment (tĕs'tá-mĕnt), one of the great divisions of the Bible, containing the accounts of the works of Jesus and his followers, and writings of some of the early Christians.

New-ton (nū'tŭn), Sir Isaac (1642–1727), an English scientist and mathematician, who discovered the law of gravitation.

New Year's Day or **New Year's**, the first day of January.

New York (yôrk), a Middle Atlantic State (cap. Albany) of the U.S.; also, a large city in southeastern New York, at the mouth of the Hudson River (map 6):—**New York State Barge Canal**, a canal in New York State, formerly called *Erie Canal.*

New York Bay, an inlet of the Atlantic at the mouth of the Hudson River.

New Zea-land (zē'lănd), a British self-governing dominion (cap. Wellington) in the Pacific, east of Australia (map 16).

next (nĕkst), *adj.* immediately following in order; nearest in time, place, degree, or rank; as, the *next* day; the *next* street; the *next* quality; *next* in order:—*adv.* immediately succeeding; in the nearest time, place, or order; as, you go *next*:—*prep.* nearest to; as, you sit *next* the end.

N.G. abbreviation for *National Guard*; also, *Slang*, abbreviation for *no good.*

N.H. abbreviation for *New Hampshire.*

Ni-ag-a-ra (nī-ăg'rá), a river between New York State and Ontario, Canada.

Niagara Falls, 1, the world-famous falls of the Niagara River; 2, a city in New York on the Niagara River (map 6).

nib (nĭb), *n.* 1, a bird's beak or bill; 2, the point of anything, especially of a pen; 3, a sharp point or prong.

nib-ble (nĭb'l), *v.t.* and *v.i.* [nib-bled, nibbling], to bite a little at a time; eat in little bites; as, the mouse *nibbled* at the cheese. —*n.* a small bite.—*n.* **nib'bler.**

nib·lick (nĭb′lĭk), *n.* in golf, a heavy, iron-headed club with a slanting face.

Nic·a·ra·gua (nĭk′à-rä′gwà), a republic (cap. Managua) in the central part of Central America (map **10**).

Nice (nēs), a city in France, on the Mediterranean, famous as a winter resort (map **12**).

nice (nīs), *adj.* [nic-er, nic-est], **1**, particular; dainty; as, *nice* in one's dress; **2**, requiring care and accuracy; exact; as, a *nice* experiment; *nice* proportions; **3**, able to find or feel small differences; as, a *nice* ear for music; **4**, requiring the best; too particular; as, he is too *nice* about his food; **5**, pleasing; agreeable; good; kind; as, she is a *nice* person to meet; **6**, well-behaved; as, they are *nice* children; **7**, *Colloquial,* pleasant; agreeable; as, to have a *nice* time.

ni·ce·ty (nī′sĕ-tĭ), *n.* [*pl.* niceties], **1**, a dainty, elegant, or delicate thing; as, the *niceties* of life; **2**, a very small difference, point, or detail; as, to learn the *niceties* of drawing; **3**, accuracy; careful attention to details; as, to describe the scene with great *nicety;* **4**, the point at which a thing is just right; as, baked to a *nicety.*

niche (nĭch), *n.* **1**, a recess or hollow in a wall, as for a statue; **2**, a condition or position especially suitable to a person or thing; as, she found a *niche* in business.

Nich·o·las, Saint (nĭk′ō-làs), (?–345?), a bishop of Asia Minor, regarded as the patron saint of children and often identified with *Santa Claus.*

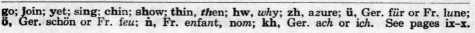

NICHE

nick (nĭk), *n.* **1**, a notch; slit; **2**, a broken place in any edge or surface; as, a *nick* in the table; **3**, the exact or critical point (of time); as, he arrived in the *nick* of time:— *v.t.* **1**, to cut notches in; **2**, to hit upon exactly; strike at the right place or proper moment.

nick·el (nĭk′l), *n.* **1**, a hard, silver-white, metallic element; **2**, in the U.S., a coin of the value of five cents, made of nickel and copper.

nick·name (nĭk′nām′), *n.* a familiar form of a given name, as "Bill" for "William," or a wholly new name given in derision, sport, or familiarity:—*v.t.* [nicknamed, nicknam-ing], to give a nickname to; call by a familiar name; as, they *nicknamed* him "Red."

Nic·o·de·mus (nĭk′ō-dē′mŭs), in the Bible, a Pharisee who consulted Jesus at night, and was told that he must be "born again."

nic·o·tine (nĭk′ō-tēn; nĭk′ō-tĭn), *n.* a pungent, colorless poison contained in tobacco.

niece (nēs), *n.* the daughter of one's brother or sister; also, the daughter of a brother-in-law or sister-in-law.

Ni·ger (nī′jẽr), a river in northwestern Africa (map **14**).

Ni·ge·ri·a (nī-jē′rĭ-à), a British colony and protectorate (cap. Lagos) in northwestern Africa, on the Gulf of Guinea (map **14**).—*n.* and *adj.* **Ni·ge′ri·an.**

nig·gard (nĭg′ẽrd), *n.* a stingy person; a miser; as, Scrooge was a *niggard:*—*adj.* miserly; stingy.

nig·gard·ly (nĭg′ẽrd-lĭ), *adj.* **1**, stingy; miserly; as, a *niggardly* person; **2**, scanty, as a meal:—*adv.* stingily; miserly; scantily; meanly.—*n.* **nig′gard-li-ness.**

nigh (nī), *adj.* **1**, near in time or place; as, the hour of his triumph is *nigh;* **2**, closely related by blood or friendship:—*adv.* **1**, near in time or place; **2**, almost; as, he was *nigh* starved:—*prep.* near to; not far from; as, the well was *nigh* the house.

night (nīt), *n.* **1**, the time from sunset to sunrise; **2**, the close of the day; **3**, the darkness of night.

night·cap (nīt′kăp′), *n.* **1**, a head covering worn in bed; **2**, *Colloquial,* a drink, especially of liquor, taken just before going to bed.

night·fall (nīt′fôl′), *n.* the coming of darkness at evening.

night·gown (nīt′goun′), *n.* a loose garment worn in bed.

night·hawk (nīt′hôk′), *n.* **1**, any of a group of American birds, not properly hawks, which fly at night; **2**, a person who stays up late at night.

Night·in·gale (nīt′ĭn-gāl; nīt′ĭng-gāl), Florence (1820–1910), an English nurse, famous for her work during the Crimean War.

night·in·gale (nīt′ĭn-gāl; nīt′ĭng-gāl), *n.* **1**, any of several small Old World thrushes noted for the melodious song of the male, heard oftenest at night; **2**, a person who sings beautifully.

night·ly (nīt′lĭ), *adj.* **1**, happening, coming, or occurring at night; as, the army made *nightly* marches; **2**, occurring every night; as, he does *nightly* exercises:— *adv.* night by night; every night; at or by night.

NIGHTINGALE (⅛)

night·mare (nīt′mâr′), *n.* **1**, a terrifying dream accompanied by a feeling of helplessness; **2**, hence, any frightful experience or haunting fear.

night·shade (nīt′shād′), *n.* any of a group of plants including the potato plant, the bittersweet, and the eggplant; especially, any of several poisonous or medicinal species, as the common nightshade.

night·shirt (nīt′-shûrt′), *n.* a man's or boy's garment to be worn in bed.

ni·hil·ism (nī′hĭ-lĭzm), *n.* 1, a socialist movement, originating in Russia, which held that existing institutions were so bad that they should be destroyed before a new order could be set up; 2, hence, in common talk, a state of violence; anarchism; terrorism. —*n.* **ni′hil·ist.**

NIGHTSHADE

nil (nĭl), *n.* 1, nothing; as, in that game his score was *nil;* 2, a thing of no account.

Nile (nīl), a river in northeastern Africa, rising in Lake Victoria and flowing into the Mediterranean (map **14**).

nim·ble (nĭm′bl), *adj.* 1, quick and active; alert; as, a *nimble* mind; 2, lively; brisk; swift; as, *nimble* feet.—*n.* **nim′ble·ness.**

nim·bly (nĭm′blĭ), *adv.* briskly; quickly; as, the boy ran *nimbly* out of the way.

Nim·rod (nĭm′rŏd), *n.* 1, in the Bible, a ruler who was described as a mighty hunter (Genesis 10:8); 2, hence, a hunter.

nine (nīn), *adj.* composed of one more than eight:—*n.* **1,** the number consisting of eight plus one; 2, a sign representing nine units, as 9 or ix.

nine·pins (nīn′pĭnz′), *n.pl.* used as *sing.* a game which consists in bowling a ball at nine wooden pins set up at one end of a bowling alley.

nine·teen (nīn′tēn′), *adj.* composed of ten more than nine:—*n.* **1,** the sum of eighteen and one; 2, a sign representing nineteen units, as 19 or xix.

nine·teenth (nīn′tēnth′), *adj.* next after the 18th: the ordinal of *nineteen:*—*n.* one of the nineteen equal parts of anything.

nine·ti·eth (nīn′tĭ-ĕth), *adj.* next after the 89th: the ordinal of *ninety:*—*n.* one of the 90 equal parts of anything.

nine·ty (nīn′tĭ), *adj.* composed of one more than 89:—*n.* [*pl.* nineties], 1, the number consisting of 89 plus one; 2, a sign representing 90 units, as 90 or xc.

Nin·e·veh (nĭn′ĕ-vĕ), an ancient city, the capital of Assyria, on the Tigris River, near modern Mosul.

nin·ny (nĭn′ĭ), *n.* [*pl.* ninnies], a foolish person; a dunce.

ninth (nīnth), *adj.* next after the eighth:

the ordinal of *nine:*—*n.* one of the nine equal parts of anything.

Ni·o·be (nī′ô-bē), *n.* in Greek mythology, the wife of Amphion, king of Thebes, whose fourteen children were slain by Apollo and Artemis, because she in her pride compared herself with Leto, their mother, who had only two children. Niobe was changed into a fountain by Zeus.

¹**nip** (nĭp), *v.t.* [nipped, nip·ping], 1, to pinch; to cut off the end of; clip; 2, to blight; blast; destroy, as by frost:—**nip in the bud,** to check suddenly; stop or destroy the growth of; as, the revolt was *nipped in the bud.*

²**nip** (nĭp), *n.* a small drink, especially of some alcoholic liquor.

nip·per (nĭp′ẽr), *n.* 1, one who or that which pinches or cuts off; 2, the large claw of a crab or lobster; 3, a horse's front tooth; 4, **nippers,** any of various tools with jaws, such as forceps, pliers, tongs, etc.

nip·ple (nĭp′l), *n.* 1, that part of a breast through which a baby or young animal draws milk; 2, the mouthpiece of a nursing bottle.

NIPPERS

Nip·pon (nĭp′pŏn′), the Japanese name of *Japan* (map **15**).

Nir·va·na (nĭr-vä′na), *n.* in the Buddhist religion, the state of perfect happiness reached by suppressing all personal desires and passions and merging into the supreme spirit.

nit (nĭt), *n.* 1, the egg of any small insect, such as a louse; 2, the young insect.

ni·ter or **ni·tre** (nī′tẽr), *n.* a white crystalline salt, potassium nitrate, used in medicine, in making gunpowder, etc. It is also called *saltpeter.*

ni·trate (nī′trāt), *n.* 1, a salt of nitric acid; 2, potassium or sodium nitrate, extensively used as a fertilizer.

ni·tric ac·id (nī′trĭk ăs′ĭd), a very powerful acid which eats into and destroys flesh, wood, metal, and other substances, and is used in etching steel and copper, in making explosives, dyestuffs, etc.

ni·tro·gen (nī′trô-jĕn), *n.* a colorless, odorless, tasteless gas, which forms four fifths of the volume of the air.

ni·trog·e·nous (nī-trŏj′ĕ-nŭs), *adj.* containing nitrogen. Nitrogenous foods, such as lean meat, white of egg, and cheese, contain some form of protein, a substance composed of nitrogen, carbon, etc.

ni·tro·glyc·er·in or **ni·tro·glyc·er·ine**

āte, âorta, râre, căt, åsk, fär, ăllow, sofá; ēve, êvent, ĕll, writẽr, novĕl; bīte, pĭn; nō, ôbey, ôr, dôg, tŏp, cŏllide; ūnit, ūnite, bûrn, cŭt, focŭs; no͞on, fŏŏt; mound; coin;

(nī′trō-glĭs′ēr-ĭn), *n.* a highly explosive, oily liquid, prepared by the action of nitric and sulphuric acids upon glycerin.

ni·trous (nī′trŭs), *adj.* resembling, obtained from, or soaked with, niter, or saltpeter.

ni·trous ox·ide (ŏk′sīd; ŏk′sĭd), a colorless gas used as an anesthetic, especially in dentistry: often called *laughing gas*.

nix (nĭks), *n.* [*pl.* nixes], in mythology, a water elf or fairy.—*n.fem.* **nix′ie.**

N.J. abbreviation for *New Jersey*.

N.M. or **N. Mex.** abbreviation for *New Mexico*.

no (nō), *n.* [*pl.* noes (nōz)], **1,** a denial; a refusal by saying "no"; as, my *no* was received in silence; **2,** a negative vote; as, my *no* lost him the election; **3, noes,** the voters in the negative:—*adv.* **1,** nay; not so; as, *No,* I cannot go: opposite of *yes;* **2,** not any; not at all; as, he is *no* better; **3,** not; as, whether or *no:*—*adj.* not any.

no. abbreviation for *number*.

No·ah (nō′ȧ), in the Bible, the Hebrew patriarch who built an ark to save his family and a pair of animals of each kind from the Flood.

nob (nŏb), *n.* a slang word for *head*.

No·bel (nō-bĕl′), Alfred Bernhard (1833–1896), a Swedish philanthropist, inventor of dynamite, and founder of the Nobel prizes for the advancement of humanity.

no·bil·i·ty (nō-bĭl′ĭ-tĭ), *n.* [*pl.* nobilities], **1,** the quality of being lofty in character, mind, or rank; **2,** the rank of persons of noble birth:—**the nobility,** the body of nobles or persons of title in a country. *Syn.* aristocracy, peerage.

no·ble (nō′bl), *adj.* [no-bler, no-blest], **1,** lofty in character or mind; as, a *noble* woman; **2,** high in rank; of ancient lineage or descent; as, of *noble* birth; **3,** stately in appearance; grand; as, *noble* architecture: —*n.* a peer or person of high rank and title. *Syn., adj.* elevated, lofty, magnificent.

no·ble-man (nō′bl-măn), *n.* [*pl.* noblemen (-mĕn)], a man of rank or title.—*n.fem.* **no′ble-wom′an.**

no·bly (nō′blĭ), *adv.* **1,** in a lofty, courageous manner; as, he served his country *nobly;* **2,** finely; splendidly; as, a statue *nobly* formed.

no·bod·y (nō′bŏd-ĭ; nō′bŭd-ĭ), *pron.* no one:—*n.* [*pl.* nobodies], a person of no importance or influence.

noc·tur·nal (nŏk-tûr′nǎl), *adj.* **1,** done or occurring at night; as, a *nocturnal* visit; **2,** active at night; as, the bat is a *nocturnal* animal.—*adv.* **noc-tur′nal-ly.**

noc·turne (nŏk′tûrn; nŏk-tûrn′), *n.* **1,** a picture of a night scene; **2,** a quiet, dreamy song without words.

nod (nŏd), *n.* **1,** a quick bending of the head, used as a sign of greeting, assent, approval, or the like; **2,** a bending of the head as a sign of supreme authority; as, the ruler's *nod:*—*v.t.* [nod-ded, nod-ding], **1,** to say by means of a nod; as, he nodded his farewells; **2,** to incline or bend with a quick movement; as, to *nod* one's head:— *v.i.* **1,** to swing or sway quickly; as, flowers *nod* in the breeze; **2,** to bend the head in token of assent or as a salute; **3,** to be drowsy; bend the head forward sleepily.— *n.* **nod′der.**

node (nōd), *n.* **1,** a knot; knob; swelling; **2,** a hard swelling on a tendon or bone; **3,** the point on the stem of a plant from which a leaf springs.

nod·ule (nŏd′ūl), *n.* a little knot, or irregular, rounded lump.—*adj.* **nod′u-lar.**

no·el (nō-ĕl′), *n.* **1,** a shout of joy, as of Christmas greeting; **2,** hence, a Christmas carol:—**Noel** (nō′ĕl), Christmas.

nog·gin (nŏg′ĭn), *n.* **1,** a small cup or mug; **2,** a liquid measure equal to one fourth of a pint.

NODES (N, N) def. 3

noise (noiz), *n.* sound, especially when confused or disagreeable:—*v.t.* [noised, nois-ing], to spread by rumor; as, the report was *noised* abroad. *Syn., n.* sound, clamor, uproar, tumult.

noise·less (noiz′lĕs), *adj.* **1,** silent; still; **2,** making little sound; as, a *noiseless* engine. —*adv.* **noise′less-ly.**—*n.* **noise′less-ness.**

nois·i·ly (noiz′ĭ-lĭ), *adv.* in a loud, disagreeable manner.

noi·some (noi′sŭm), *adj.* **1,** injurious to health; harmful; as, *noisome* gases; **2,** offensive; disgusting; as, *noisome* odors.— *adv.* **noi′some-ly.**—*n.* **noi′some-ness.** *Syn.* noxious, destructive.

nois·y (noiz′ĭ), *adj.* **1,** full of loud, confused, disagreeable sounds; as, a *noisy* city; **2,** making, or given to making, an outcry or uproar.—*n.* **nois′i-ness.**

nom. abbreviation for *nominative*.

no·mad (nō′măd), *n.* a member of a roving tribe of people, as the Arabs or gypsies, who have no fixed home but wander about in search of game, pasture, etc.: —*adj.* wandering; roving.

no·mad·ic (nō-măd′ĭk), *adj.* roving; wandering; unsettled; as, the gypsies are a *nomadic* people.

no·men·cla·ture (nō′mĕn-klā′tūr), *n.* the collection of words and terms, or the system of names, used in any art or science; as, the *nomenclature* of botany or chemistry.

nom·i·nal (nŏm'ĭ-năl), *adj.* **1,** existing in name only; not real or actual; as, though the king was the *nominal* ruler, his son governed the country; **2,** so small as to be hardly worth mentioning; as, we paid only the *nominal* sum of ten dollars for the car.

nom·i·nal·ly (nŏm'ĭ-năl-ĭ), *adv.* in name only; not really; as, the country is only *nominally* at peace.

nom·i·nate (nŏm'ĭ-nāt), *v.t.* [nominat-ed, nominat-ing], to propose or name for an office; as, to *nominate* a man for election. —*n.* **nom'i-na/tor.**

nom·i·na·tion (nŏm/ĭ-nā'shŭn), *n.* **1,** the act of naming or proposing a person for an office; **2,** choice; appointment; as, he secured the *nomination* for president.

nom·i·na·tive (nŏm'ĭ-na-tĭv), *adj.* naming the case of the subject of a verb; as, in the sentence "I am ready," "I" is in the *nominative* case:—*n.* **1,** the case of the subject of a verb; the nominative case; **2,** a word in this case.

nom·i·nee (nŏm/ĭ-nē'), *n.* one who is named or proposed for an office or duty; as, the *nominee* for president.

non- (nŏn-), a prefix used before many words with the general meaning not; as, *non*combatant; *non*resident.

nonce (nŏns), *n.* the present occasion or time; as, this will do for the *nonce*.

non·cha·lance (nŏn'sha-lăns), *n.* lack of interest; easy unconcern; jauntiness; as, he pretended *nonchalance* to cover his embarrassment.

non·cha·lant (nŏn'sha-lănt), *adj.* wanting in enthusiasm; indifferent.—*adv.* **non'-cha-lant-ly.**

non·com·bat·ant (nŏn-kŏm'ba-tănt; nŏn-kŭm'ba-tănt), *n.* **1,** a person, connected with any army or navy, whose duties do not include fighting, as a surgeon or nurse; **2,** one not in the army or navy in time of war, as a person physically unfit.

non·com·mis·sioned (nŏn/kŏ-mĭsh'-ŭnd), *adj.* not having a certificate to engage in a service:—**noncommissioned officer,** an enlisted man who has risen to the rank of sergeant or corporal.

non·com·mit·tal (nŏn/kŏ-mĭt/ăl), *adj.* not revealing one's opinion or purpose; as, his answer was wholly *noncommittal.*—*adv.* **non/com-mit/tal-ly.**

non·con·duc·tor (nŏn/kŏn-dŭk'tẽr), *n.* any substance, such as rubber, through which heat, light, electricity, or the like, will not pass readily; an insulator.

non·con·form·ist (nŏn/kŏn-fôr'mĭst), *n.*

one who does not conform to, or agree with, established beliefs, especially church beliefs.

non·con·form·i·ty (nŏn/kŏn-fôr'mĭ-tĭ), *n.* failure or refusal to make one's conduct or opinion fit the opinions regarding right and wrong held by most persons: used especially of lack of agreement with established church beliefs.

non·de·script (nŏn/dĕ-skrĭpt), *adj.* not easily described; odd; of no particular character; as, she wore a *nondescript* garment:—*n.* a nondescript thing or person.

none (nŭn), *pron.* **1,** not any; as, I will have *none* of it; **2,** not one; no one or ones: used as *sing.* or *pl.*; as, we needed a ball, but *none* was to be had; *none* of them were there:—*adv.* not at all; not in the least; as, he felt *none* the better for his trip.

non·en·ti·ty (nŏn-ĕn'tĭ-tĭ), *n.* [*pl.* nonentities], **1,** something that does not exist, or that exists only in the imagination; **2,** a person of no importance or influence; a nobody.

non·ex·ist·ent (nŏn/ĕg-zĭs'tĕnt), *adj.* having no existence; absent.—*n.* **non/ex-ist/-ence.**

non·pa·reil (nŏn/pa-rĕl'), *adj.* without equal; peerless:—*n.* **1,** a person or thing without equal; **2,** a brilliant bird of the southern U.S.; **3,** a small size of type (see illustration under *type*).

non·par·ti·san (nŏn-pär'tĭ-zăn), *adj.* not strongly in favor of, or influenced by, a cause or a party; as, a *nonpartisan* meeting.

non·plus (nŏn'plŭs), *v.t.* [nonplused or nonplussed (nŏn/plŭst), nonplus-ing or nonplus-sing], to throw into complete perplexity; bring to a standstill; as, I was *nonplused* as to how to settle the quarrel:—*n.* inability to decide or proceed.

non·res·i·dent (nŏn-rĕz/ĭ-dĕnt), *n.* **1,** one who does not live in a particular place; **2,** one who does not reside on his own estate, in his proper business location, or the like: —*adj.* **1,** not living in a particular place; as, a *nonresident* voter of the second ward; **2,** not residing where one's official duties lie. —*n.* **non·res/i-dence.**

non·sense (nŏn'sĕns), *n.* **1,** a thing without sense; language without meaning; absurdity; **2,** things of little worth; trifles; as, why spend money for such *nonsense?*— *interj.* absurd.

Syn., *n.* foolishness, folly, absurdity.

non·sen·si·cal (nŏn-sĕn/sĭ-kăl), *adj.* not making sense; foolish; absurd; as, a *nonsensical* remark.—*adv.* **non-sen/si-cal-ly.**

non·stop (nŏn/stŏp/), *adj.* and *adv.* without a stop; as, a *nonstop* flight; to fly *nonstop* from New York to Paris:—*n.* a nonstop flight or trip; as, to make a *nonstop* to Paris.

non·un·ion (nŏn-ūn'yŭn), *adj.* **1,** not belonging to a labor union; **2,** not recognizing labor unions; as, a *nonunion* factory; **3,** not agreeing with labor-union rules.

¹noo·dle (noo'dl), *n.* a stupid or silly person; a blockhead.

²noo·dle (noo'dl), *n.* a narrow strip of dried dough, resembling macaroni in appearance, and used chiefly in soups.

nook (nook), *n.* **1,** a cosy, out-of-the-way place; **2,** a corner in a room; **3,** a sheltered recess out of doors.

noon (noon), *n.* the middle of the day:— *adj.* pertaining to midday.

noon·day (noon'dā'), *n.* midday; noon:— *adj.* pertaining to midday.

noon·tide (noon'tīd'), *n.* noon.

noose (noos), *n.* **1,** a loop, made with a slipknot, as in a lasso, which binds the closer the more tightly it is drawn; **2,** any snare:—*v.t.* [noosed, noos-ing], to catch or capture in a noose.

nor (nôr), *conj.* and not: a negative connecting word used after the negatives *neither* and *not*, to continue or complete their meaning; as, he has neither money *nor* friends; not a word *nor* a sign betrayed him.

NOOSE

Nor·dic (nôr'dĭk), *adj.* belonging to, or like, the tall, blond people of northwestern Europe, especially those of Scandinavia:— *n.* a member of one of these peoples.

Nor·folk (nôr'fŭk), **1,** a seaport in southern Virginia, on the Atlantic Ocean (map 8); **2,** a county in east central England.

norm (nôrm), *n.* a rule or standard; model; pattern; type; as, to agree with the *norm*.

nor·mal (nôr'măl), *adj.* according to rule; regular; natural; serving as a standard or model:—**normal school,** a school for the training of teachers:—*n.* the usual or ordinary condition, quantity, etc.; as, the rain raised the river two feet above *normal.*— *adv.* nor'mal·ly.—*n.* nor·mal'i·ty.

Syn., adj. usual, ordinary, typical.

nor·mal·cy (nôr'măl-sĭ), *n.* the usual or ordinary condition of things; normality; especially, the state of business in time of peace and average prosperity.

Nor·man (nôr'măn), *n.* [*pl.* Normans], a native or inhabitant of Normandy:—*adj.* pertaining to Normandy or the Normans.

Nor·man·dy (nôr'măn-dĭ), an ancient duchy and province in northern France.

Norse (nôrs), *adj.* pertaining to the country, people, or language of Scandinavia,

especially ancient Norway:—*n.* **1,** the language of ancient Norway and Iceland, or of the ancient Scandinavians; **2,** [*pl.* Norse], a Norseman.

Norse·man (nôrs'măn), *n.* [*pl.* Norsemen (-měn)], a Northman; a Scandinavian of ancient times.

north (nôrth), *n.* **1,** one of the four points of the compass; the point opposite to the south, or to the left of a person facing the sunrise; **2,** a section of country lying north of another; as, the *north* of Europe:—*adj.* having to do with, situated in, or coming from, the north; as, a *north* wind:—*adv.* to the north; as, walk *north* one block.

NORTH

The weather vane is pointing toward N, standing for *north.*

North, *n.* that part of the U.S. lying generally north of the Ohio River and the southern boundary of Pennsylvania; **North Pole,** the northern end of the earth's axis; **North Star,** the star which is very nearly over the North Pole; Polaris.

North A·mer·i·ca (à-měr'ĭ-kà), a continent, the northern half of the Western Hemisphere (map 3).

North Cape, 1, the northernmost point of Europe, in Norway (map 12); **2,** the most northerly point of New Zealand (map 16).

North Car·o·li·na (kăr'ō-lī'nà), an eastern State (cap. Raleigh) of the U.S., on the Atlantic Coast (map 8).

North Da·ko·ta (dà-kō'tà), a State (cap. Bismarck) of the U.S. (map 7).

north·east (nôrth'ēst'), *n.* **1,** the point of the compass halfway between north and east; **2,** country lying in the direction of that point:—*adj.* having to do with the northeast, or in or from the northeast; as, a *northeast* wind:—*adv.* toward the northeast.—*adj.* and *adv.* north'east'ward.

north·east·er (nôrth'ēs'tēr), *n.* a violent wind or storm from the northeast.

north·east·ly (nôrth'ēs'tēr-lĭ), *adj.* and *adv.* from or toward the northeast.

north·east·ern (nôrth'ēs'tērn), *adj.* of, from, or situated in, the northeast.

north·er·ly (nôr'thēr-lĭ), *adj.* pertaining to the north, or situated in or coming from the north:—*adv.* toward the north.

north·ern (nôr'thērn), *adj.* in, from, or toward, the north; as, a *northern* course.— *adj. superl.* north'ern·most.

north·ern·er (nôr'thēr-nēr), *n.* a person living in, or coming from, the north: —**Northerner,** a person living in, or coming from, the part of the U.S. north of Mason and Dixon's line.

---

go; join; yet; sing; chin; show; thin, *th*en; hw, *wh*y; zh, azure; ü, Ger. für or Fr. lune; ö, Ger. schön or Fr. feu; n̄, Fr. enfant, nom; kh, Ger. ach or ich. See pages ix–x.

North·ern Ire·land (ĭr′lănd), a division (cap. Belfast) of the United Kingdom, in northern Ireland, comprising six counties of the former province of Ulster (map **13**).

northern lights, the aurora borealis, or streams of light seen in the sky at night, best observed in northern latitudes.

North·ern Rho·de·sia (rō-dē′zhȧ), a British colony in Africa. See **Rhodesia.**

North Is·land, the northernmost island of New Zealand (map **16**).

North·man (nôrth′măn), n. [pl. North-men (-mĕn)], a Scandinavian of ancient times; a Norseman.

North Sea, an arm of the Atlantic Ocean, east of Great Britain (map **12**).

North·um·ber·land (nôr-thŭm′bēr-lănd), a county in northern England.

North·um·bri·a (nôr-thŭm′brĭ-ȧ), an Anglo-Saxon kingdom of northern England.

north·ward (nôrth′wērd), adj. and adv. to or toward the north; leading to the north. Also, adv. **north′wards.**

north·west (nôrth′wĕst′), n. **1**, the point of the compass halfway between north and west; **2**, country lying in the direction of that point:—adj. having to do with the northwest, or in or from the northwest:—adv. toward the northwest.—adj. and adv. **north′west′ward.**

north·west·er (nôrth′wĕs′tēr), n. a strong wind or storm from the northwest.

north·west·er·ly (nôrth′wĕs′tēr-lĭ), adj. and adv. from or toward the northwest.

north·west·ern (nôrth′wĕs′tērn), adj. of, from, or situated in, the northwest.

Nor·way (nôr′wā), a kingdom (cap. Oslo), the western part of the Scandinavian peninsula, in northwestern Europe (map **12**).

Nor·we·gian (nôr-wē′jăn), n. a native of Norway; also, the language of Norway:—adj. pertaining to Norway, or its language or people.

nose (nōz), n. **1**, in man and other animals, that part of the face or head containing the nostrils and nerves of smell; **2**, the sense of smell; as, the deer has a keen nose; **3**, anything like a nose, as a spout:—v.t. [nosed, nos-ing], **1**, to smell or scent; **2**, to rub or push with the nose or front; as, horses nose each other; the boat nosed its way through the ice:—v.i. **1**, to smell or scent; **2**, to pry into another person's affairs.

TYPES OF NOSE
1, Roman; 2, Nordic (Anglo-Saxon); 3, North American Indian; 4, Negro.

nose dive, a downward plunge of an airplane; hence, any quick drop, as of prices, temperature, or the like.

nose·gay (nōz′gā′), n. a bouquet or bunch of flowers.

nos·tril (nŏs′trĭl), n. one of the two external openings in the nose.

nos·trum (nŏs′trŭm), n. **1**, a quack medicine; **2**, a pet remedy for some evil condition.

not (nŏt), adv. a word that expresses denial, prohibition, or refusal; as, he will not go.

no·ta·ble (nō′tȧ-bl), adj. **1**, worthy of attention; memorable for any reason; as, a notable event; a notable play; **2**, distinguished; as, a notable speaker was the guest of honor:—n. a person or thing of distinction.—n. **no′ta·ble·ness.**
  Syn., adj. noted, rare, signal, striking.

no·ta·bly (nō′tȧ-blĭ), adv. in a remarkable manner; strikingly; as, he was a notably clever cartoonist.

no·ta·ry (nō′tȧ-rĭ), n. [pl. notaries], an official permitted by law to witness or certify contracts or similar documents, or to record the fact that a certain person swears something is true, or the like: also called notary public [pl. notaries public].—adj. **no·tar′i·al** (nō-târ′ĭ-ăl).

no·ta·tion (nō-tā′shŭn), n. **1**, the act or practice of recording by marks or symbols; also, a note; as, he made a notation on an envelope; **2**, a system of signs or symbols used in place of language, for brevity or clearness; especially, the system of numbers, letters, and signs used in arithmetic and algebra, and the signs used in writing or printing music.

notch (nŏch), n. **1**, a small nick or V-shaped cut in the edge of something; **2**, a narrow pass through mountains:—v.t. **1**, to nick or cut into small hollows; **2**, to keep count of by nicks.

note (nōt), n. **1**, a brief memorandum to assist the memory; **2**, a brief explanation or comment; as, the notes make the book clearer; **3**, a short, informal letter; as, drop me a note about your plans; **4**, a formal letter from one government to another; **5**, characteristic quality; as, a note of gaiety in the voice; **6**, reputation; fame; distinction; as, a family of note; **7**, notice; attention; as, a matter worthy of note; **8**, a cry,

NOTES, def. 9
1, whole note; 2, half note; 3, quarter note; 4, eighth note; 5, sixteenth note.

song, or call, as of a bird; **9**, in music, a written sign or character representing the

---

āte, âorta, râre, căt, ȧsk, fär, ăllow, sofȧ; ēve, êvent, ĕll, writēr, novĕl; bīte, pĭn; nō, ōbey, ôr, dŏg, tŏp, cŏllide; ūnit, ûnite, bûrn, cŭt, focŭs; nōōn, fŏŏt; mound; coin;

pitch and relative length of a tone; also, a single tone itself, as made by a musical instrument or the voice; **10,** a legal paper acknowledging a debt, and promising payment; as, a promissory *note;* a bank *note:*—*v.t.* [not-ed, not-ing], **1,** to make a memorandum of; as, he *noted* the date in his memorandum book; **2,** to make mention of; **3,** to observe; notice; as, he *noted* her beauty; **4,** to set down in musical notation.

note·book (nōt/bŏŏk/), *n.* a book in which memoranda are made; especially, a student's book for notes, assignments, etc.

not·ed (nōt/ĕd), *adj.* well-known; celebrated; as, a *noted* musician.
 Syn. distinguished, famous.

note·wor·thy (nōt/wûr/thĭ), *adj.* worthy of notice; remarkable.—*adv.* **note/wor/-thi·ly.**—*n.* **note/wor/thi·ness.**

noth·ing (nŭth/ĭng), *pron.* not anything; as, she has *nothing* to hope for:—*n.* **1,** a thing of no value, use, or importance; **2,** a nobody:—*adv.* in no degree; not at all; as, the copy is *nothing* like the original.

noth·ing·ness (nŭth/ĭng-nĕs), *n.* **1,** nonexistence; being nothing; **2,** unimportance.

no·tice (nō/tĭs), *n.* **1,** a taking heed; attention; observation; as, to take *notice* of events; **2,** information; warning; as, he received *notice* to vacate the building; **3,** a printed announcement or sign; as, a *notice* of a death; **4,** a brief printed article or paragraph on a book, play, picture, or the like:—*v.t.* [noticed, notic-ing], **1,** to see or observe; regard; **2,** to make remarks upon; speak of; **3,** to pay polite attention to; as, she didn't even *notice* me.

no·tice·a·ble (nō/tĭs-à-bl), *adj.* **1,** capable of being observed or noticed; as, a *noticeable* lack of interest; **2,** conspicuous; likely to attract attention; **3,** worthy of attention; notable; as, his last play was a *noticeable* one.—*adv.* **no/tice·a·bly.**

no·ti·fi·ca·tion (nō/tĭ-fĭ-kā/shŭn), *n.* **1,** the act of making known; as, the *notification* occurred early in the day; **2,** notice; as, he received *notification* of his election.

no·ti·fy (nō/tĭ-fī), *v.t.* [notified, notify-ing], **1,** to give warning or information to; **2,** to make known; declare; publish.—*n.* **no/ti·fi/er.**
 Syn. acquaint, inform, advise.

no·tion (nō/shŭn), *n.* **1,** a general idea; as, I have no *notion* what he means; **2,** a theory or belief; as, that is the common *notion;* **3,** inclination; a fancy; as, to have a *notion* to do something; **4,** **notions,** in the U.S., small useful articles, such as pins, thread, etc.
 Syn. thought, whim, caprice.

no·to·ri·e·ty (nō/tō-rī/ĕ-tĭ), *n.* [*pl.* noto-

rieties], the state of being well known, especially in an undesirable or bad way.

no·tor·i·ous (nō-tôr/ĭ-ŭs), *adj.* commonly known; noted; famous: usually in a bad sense; as, a *notorious* criminal.—*adv.* **no·tor/i·ous·ly.**—*n.* **no·tor/i·ous·ness.**

Not·ting·ham (nŏt/ĭng-ăm), a manufacturing city and county in central England (map **13**).

not·with·stand·ing (nŏt/wĭth-stăn/dĭng), *prep.* in spite of; as, *notwithstanding* the rain, he went to the party:—*adv.* nevertheless; still; however; all the same; as, his mother forbade his going, but he went *notwithstanding.*

nou·gat (nōō/găt), *n.* a pasty confection containing almonds and sometimes candied fruits, usually flavored with honey.

nought (nôt), *n.* **1,** a person or thing of no importance; **2,** in arithmetic, zero [0]; a cipher; a naught.

noun (noun), *n.* in grammar, a word used to name a person or thing.

nour·ish (nûr/ĭsh), *v.t.* **1,** to feed (a plant or animal) with the material necessary to keep it alive and make it grow; **2,** to foster; encourage; as, a doctor *nourishes* hope in his patients:—*v.i.* to be nutritious; as, good food *nourishes.*
 Syn. nurture, cherish, sustain.

nour·ish·ment (nûr/ĭsh-mĕnt), *n.* that which keeps up or gives strength to the body, as food.

Nov. abbreviation for *November.*

No·va Sco·tia (nō/và skō/shà), a province (cap. Halifax) in southeastern Canada (map **4**). It was formerly called *Acadia.*

¹nov·el (nŏv/ĕl), *adj.* **1,** modern; unknown formerly; of recent origin; as, not many years ago airplanes were *novel* things; **2,** hence, new or unusual.

²nov·el (nŏv/ĕl), *n.* a story, with a plot, long enough to fill one or more volumes, presenting characters and actions as they might occur in real life.

nov·el·ist (nŏv/ĕl-ĭst), *n.* a writer of novels.

nov·el·ty (nŏv/ĕl-tĭ), *n.* [*pl.* novelties], **1,** unusualness; newness; as, the new game was fun at first, but the *novelty* soon wore off; **2,** something new; a change or innovation; as, travel by airplane is still a *novelty;* **3, novelties,** attractive manufactured articles, usually of small value, offered for sale.

No·vem·ber (nō-vĕm/bẽr), *n.* the eleventh month of the year, having 30 days.

nov·ice (nŏv/ĭs), *n.* **1,** a beginner; an inexperienced person; **2,** a monk or nun who has entered a religious house, but has not yet taken the vows.

no·vi·ti·ate or **no·vi·ci·ate** (nō-vĭsh′ĭ-āt), *n.* **1,** the state of being a beginner; **2,** the time of testing and training for admission to a religious order.

now (nou), *adv.* **1,** at the prèsent time; as, the danger is *now* over; **2,** a short time ago; quite recently; as, he left just *now;* **3,** immediately; at once; as, I am going *now;* **4,** under the present circumstances; as, *now* what can we do? **5,** used without any idea of time; as, oh, come *now,* don't do that; *now* you know better than that; *now* what do you mean?—*conj.* since; now that; as, I need not stay, *now* you are here:—*n.* the present moment.

now·a·days (nou′à-dāz′), *adv.* at the present time or age.

no·way (nō′wā′) or **no·ways** (nō′wāz′), *adv.* not at all; as, he was *noway* to blame.

no·where (nō′hwâr′), *adv.* not in, at, or to, any place.

no·wise (nō′wīz′), *adv.* not at all; noway.

nox·ious (nŏk′shŭs), *adj.* harmful; injurious; deadly; as, *noxious* gases.—*adv.* **nox′-ious·ly.**—*n.* **nox′ious·ness.**

noz·zle (nŏz′l), *n.* a projecting mouthpiece or spout, as on a hose, through which liquid can be discharged.

NOZZLE

N. T. abbreviation for *New Testament.*

nth (ĕnth), *adj.* representing an ordinal number equivalent to *n;* as, 5^n is 5 raised to the *nth* power.

Nu·bi·a (nū′bĭ-à), a region in Africa, now included in Anglo-Egyptian Sudan and Egypt (map 14).—*n.* and *adj.* **Nu′bi·an.**

nu·cle·us (nū′klē-ŭs), *n.* [*pl.* nucleuses (nū′klē-ŭs-ĕz) or nuclei (nū′klē-ī)], **1,** a kernel; a central part or thing about which other matter collects; anything that serves as the center of growth or development; as, John's few books became the *nucleus* of the town library; **2,** in biology, the central part of a seed or animal cell, necessary to growth and development.—*adj.* **nu′cle·ar.**

NUCLEUS (N) of a living cell.

nude (nūd), *adj.* bare; naked:—**in the nude,** undraped; naked.—*adv.* **nude′ly.**—*n.* **nude′ness.**—*n.* **nu′di·ty.**

nudge (nŭj), *v.t.* [nudged, nudg-ing], to touch or push gently, as with the elbow:—*n.* a gentle touch or poke, as with the elbow.

nug·get (nŭg′ĕt), *n.* a lump of native gold or other precious metal.

nui·sance (nū′sȧns), *n.* anything that offends or annoys.

null (nŭl), *adj.* of no force or value; not binding.

nul·li·fy (nŭl′ĭ-fī), *v.t.* [nullified, nullifying], **1,** to deprive of effect or legal force; as, to *nullify* a decision or a law; **2,** to make of no value; destroy.—*n.* **nul′li·fi′er.**—*n.* **nul′li·fi·ca′tion.**

Syn. invalidate, repeal, quash, cancel.

nul·li·ty (nŭl′ĭ-tĭ), *n.* [*pl.* nullities], **1,** the state of being without force; insignificance; **2,** that which is null.

numb (nŭm), *adj.* deprived of feeling or motion:—*v.t.* to deprive of sensation; benumb, as by cold.—*adv.* **numb′ly.**—*n.* **numb′ness.**

num·ber (nŭm′bĕr), *n.* **1,** a total of units, persons, or things taken together; sum; as, to find out the *number* of persons present; **2,** the figure or mark that stands for this total; as, the *number* 20; **3,** a certain numeral by which one person or thing is identified from others; as, the convict's *number* was 655; **4,** a considerable collection; as, a *number* of people were present; **5,** óne of a series; as, the October *number* of a magazine; **6,** in grammar, the characteristic of a word form whereby it refers either to one or to more than one; as, "men" is in the plural *number:*—**number one.** oneself:—**Numbers,** the fourth book of the Old Testament:—**numbers pool,** a lottery for bets on the appearance of a given number, as the last two digits of some officially published figure.—*v.t.* **1,** to count; as, to *number* the persons in the crowd; **2,** to put a number on; **3,** to amount to; as, the class *numbers* 25; **4,** to include; as, we *number* her among our friends; **5,** to limit the number of; as, her days are *numbered.*

num·ber·less (nŭm′bĕr-lĕs), *adj.* **1,** having no number; **2,** very many; countless.

nu·mer·al (nū′mĕr-ăl), *n.* a word, sign, or figure expressing a number; as, the Arabic *numerals* are 1, 2, 3, etc., the Roman *numerals* are I, II, III, etc.:—**numerals,** the figures representing the graduation year, worn by students to show excellence in some sport; as, he got his *numerals* in football.

nu·mer·ate (nū′mĕr-āt), *v.t.* [numerat-ed, numerat-ing], to count or number.—*n.* **nu′mer·a′tion.**

nu·mer·a·tor (nū′mĕr-ā′tẽr), *n.* in fractions, the number above the line. In "7/8 of a bushel," the numerator, 7, indicates that seven of the eight equal parts of a bushel are to be taken.

nu·mer·i·cal (nū-mĕr′ĭ-kăl), *adj.* having to do with, or expressed in, numbers; as, *numerical* equations.—*adv.* **nu·mer′i·cal·ly.**

āte, āorta, râre, căt, ȧsk, fär, ȧllow, sofȧ; ēve, ĕvent, ĕll, writẽr, novĕl; bīte, pĭn; nō, ōbey, ôr, dŏg, tŏp, cŏllide; ūnit, ūnite, bûrn, cŭt, focŭs; nōŏn, fŏŏt; mound; coin;

nu·mer·ous (nū/mēr-ŭs), *adj.* consisting of a great number; many.—*adv.* **nu/mer·ous·ly.**—*n.* **nu/mer·ous·ness.**

nu·mis·mat·ic (nū/mĭz-măt/ĭk; nū/mĭs-măt/ĭk), *adj.* pertaining to coins or medals: —**numismatics,** *n.pl.* used as *sing.* the science of coins and medals.

num·skull (nŭm/skŭl/), *n.* a blockhead; dunce; stupid fellow. Also, **numb/skull.**

nun (nŭn), *n.* a woman living under certain vows in a convent and devoted to a religious life. Some nuns do charitable work, nursing, teaching, etc.

nun·ci·o (nŭn/shĭ-ō), *n.* [*pl.* nuncios], a permanent ambassador or agent of the Pope, especially at a foreign court.

nun·ner·y (nŭn/ēr-ĭ), *n.* [*pl.* nunneries], a convent, or place where nuns live.

nup·tial (nŭp/shăl), *adj.* pertaining to marriage; as, the *nuptial* day:—**nuptials,** *n.pl.* a wedding; marriage.
  Syn., *n.* matrimony, wedlock.

Nu·rem·berg (nū/rĕm-bûrg), a city in northern Bavaria, Germany, noted for its quaint old buildings and the manufacture of toys (map **12**). Its German name is **Nürn/berg** (nürn/bĕrkh).

nurse (nûrs), *n.* **1,** one who cares for a young child or children; **2,** one who takes care of the sick or infirm:—*v.t.* [nursed, nurs·ing], **1,** to feed (an infant) at the breast; **2,** to take care of (a child, or young children); also, to caress or treat fondly; as, the little girl was *nursing* her doll; **3,** to care for or wait upon in sickness; **4,** to encourage; cherish; tend; make grow; as, to *nurse* an industry, a grudge, a fire, a plant, or the like:—*v.i.* **1,** to suck milk from a mother; **2,** to care for the sick or infirm.

nurs·er·y (nûr/sēr-ĭ), *n.* [*pl.* nurseries], **1,** a room where young children sleep or play; **2,** a place or garden for raising young trees and plants.

nurs·er·y·man (nûr/sēr-ĭ-măn), *n.* [*pl.* nurserymen (-mĕn)], a man who raises and sells plants.

nurs·ling (nûrs/lĭng), *n.* an infant; a child or thing needing tender care.

nur·ture (nûr/tūr), *n.* **1,** food; nourishment; **2,** feeding; promotion of growth; education; training:—*v.t.* [nurtured, nurtur·ing], **1,** to bring up; educate; **2,** to nourish; feed.

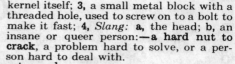
NUT, def. 1.

nut (nŭt), *n.* **1,** the dry fruit of certain trees, as the walnut, pecan, etc., consisting of a kernel, or seed, enclosed in a hard woody or leathery shell; **2,** the

NUT, def. 3
B, bolt; N, nut.

kernel itself; **3,** a small metal block with a threaded hole, used to screw on to a bolt to make it fast; **4,** *Slang:* **a,** the head; **b,** an insane or queer person:—**a hard nut to crack,** a problem hard to solve, or a person hard to deal with.

nut·crack·er (nŭt/krăk/ēr), *n.* an instrument for cracking nuts.

nut·hatch (nŭt/hăch/), *n.* any of several small birds that creep on trees and eat insects and nuts.

nut·meg (nŭt/mĕg), *n.* the hard, nutlike kernel of the seed of an East Indian tree, which is grated and used as spice.

nu·tri·ent (nū/trĭ-ĕnt), *n.* anything, as food, that nourishes and promotes growth:—*adj.* promoting growth; nourishing; as, milk is a *nutrient* fluid.

NUT-CRACKER

nu·tri·ment (nū/trĭ-mĕnt), *n.* that which provides nourishment; food.

nu·tri·tion (nū-trĭsh/ŭn), *n.* **1,** food; **2,** the process by which an animal or plant uses food to promote growth.

NUTHATCH (⅓)

nu·tri·tious (nū-trĭsh/ŭs), *adj.* promoting growth; nourishing.—*adv.* **nu·tri/tious·ly.** —*n.* **nu·tri/tious·ness.**

nu·tri·tive (nū/trĭ-tĭv), *adj.* **1,** nourishing; **2,** having to do with the process of growth in the body.

nut·shell (nŭt/shĕl/), *n.* the shell of a nut:—**in a nutshell,** briefly; in few words.

nut·ting (nŭt/ĭng), *n.* the act of gathering or searching for nuts.

nut·ty (nŭt/ĭ), *adj.* [nut-ti-er, nut-ti-est], full of, or like, nuts; as, a *nutty* flavor.

nux vom·i·ca (nŭks vŏm/ĭ-kà), an East Indian tree, whose seeds yield strychnine; also, a medicine made from the seeds.

nuz·zle (nŭz/l), *v.t.* [nuz-zled, nuz-zling], to rub or snuff with the nose; as, the puppy *nuzzled* its mother:—*v.i.* to nestle; lie close and snug; as, Bobby *nuzzled* in the hay.

N.W. abbreviation for *northwest.*

N.Y. abbreviation for *New York.*

Nya·sa·land (nyä/sä-lănd/; nī-ăs/à-lănd/), a British protectorate (cap. Zomba) in southeastern Africa (map **14**).

N.Y.C. abbreviation for *New York City.*

ny·lon (nī/lŏn), *n.* a synthetic product which may be formed into fibers, sheets, etc.: used especially as a substitute for silk.

nymph (nĭmf), *n.* in mythology, a lesser goddess of nature, living in the mountains, woods, streams, etc.

N.Z. abbreviation for *New Zealand.*

O

¹**O, o** (ō), *n.* [*pl.* O's, o's], **1,** the 15th letter of the alphabet; **2,** as a numeral, zero; **3,** anything shaped like the letter O.

²**O** (ō), *interj.* an exclamation: used in address; as, "We will praise thee, *O* God"; used also to express wonder, fear, pain, or the like; as, *O* dear!

O. abbreviation for *Ohio.*

o' (ō; ô), *prep.* a contraction of *of;* as, ten *o*'clock; also, *Colloquial,* a contraction of *on;* as, knocked *o*' the head.

oaf (ōf), *n.* **1,** formerly, a deformed child supposedly left by the fairies in place of a pretty child; a changeling; **2,** hence, an awkward or foolish person; an idiot.

O-a-hu (ō-ä′hōō), the most important island in the Hawaiian group.

oak (ōk), *n.* **1,** any of several large European and American trees bearing a one-celled fruit, the acorn, in a woody cup, and yielding a strong, tough wood used as timber; **2,** the wood of this tree; **3,** a plant that is like an oak in some respect:— *adj.* made of oak.

OAK
Leaves and acorns of: A, willow oak; B, chestnut oak; C, white oak.

oak-en (ōk′ĕn), *adj.* made of, or like, oak; as, an *oaken* bucket.

Oak-land (ōk′lănd), a city on San Francisco Bay, California (map 9).

oa-kum (ō′kŭm), *n.* loose hemp fiber obtained by untwisting old ropes, used especially for stopping leaks in boats.

OAR

oar (ôr), *n.***1,** a light pole with a broad, flat or spoon-shaped blade at one end, used for rowing or steering a boat; **2,** one who rows a boat; an oarsman:—*v.t.* to row.

oar-lock (ôr′lŏk′), *n.* a U-shaped metal device, a notch, or a pin, on the side of a boat, in which a rower rests the oar in rowing or sculling; a rowlock.

oars-man (ôrz′măn), *n.* [*pl.* oarsmen (-mĕn)], one who rows.

o-a-sis (ō-ā′sĭs; ō′á-sĭs), *n.* [*pl.* oases (ō-ā′sēz; ō′á-sēz)], a fertile place in a desert.

OATS

oat (ōt), *n.* (usually *oats*), a cereal plant or its seed, used as food, especially for horses.

oat-en (ōt′n), *adj.* **1,** made of oats or of oatmeal; **2,** made of oat straw.

oath (ōth), *n.* [*pl.* oaths (ō*th*z)], **1,** a solemn declaration that one speaks the truth, with an appeal to God as witness; **2,** a profane use of the name of God or of any sacred thing.

oat-meal (ōt′mēl′), *n.* **1,** meal made from oats; **2,** porridge or pudding made from this meal or from rolled oats.

O-ba-di-ah (ō′bá-dī′á), a Hebrew prophet in the Old Testament; also, a book of the Old Testament containing the prophecies of Obadiah.

ob-bli-ga-to (ŏb′lĭ-gä′tō), *n.* [*pl.* obbligatos or obbligati (ŏb′lĭ-gä′tē)], in music, an accompaniment, more or less independent, but indispensable to the composition, played by a single instrument.

ob-du-ra-cy (ŏb′dû-rá-sĭ; ŏb-dū′rá-sĭ), *n.* **1,** hardness of heart; **2,** stubbornness.

ob-du-rate (ŏb′dû-rât; ŏb-dū′rât), *adj.* **1,** not to be moved by appeals to the feelings; hardhearted; **2,** unrepentant; **3,** stubborn; unyielding; firm.
Syn. hard, unfeeling, obstinate.

o-be-di-ence (ō-bē′dĭ-ĕns), *n.* the act of yielding to control by others; submission to authority.—*adj.* **o-be′di-ent.**
Syn. compliance, docility.

o-bei-sance (ō-bā′săns; ō-bē′săns), *n.* a movement or bending of the body that shows obedience or respect; a bow; as, to make *obeisance* to a king.

ob-e-lisk (ŏb′ĕ-lĭsk), *n.* **1,** a four-sided, tapering stone pillar shaped at the top like a pyramid; **2,** in books, a mark of reference [†].

O-ber-am-mer-gau (ō′bĕr-äm′ĕr-gou′), a village in Bavaria, Germany, where the Passion play is given every ten years.

O-ber-on (ō′bĕr-ŏn; ŏb′ĕr-ŏn), *n.* in medieval European folklore, and in Shakespeare's "Midsummer Night's Dream," the king of the fairies and husband of Titania.

OBELISK

o-bese (ō-bēs′), *adj.* very fat.— *n.* **o-bese′ness.**

o-bes-i-ty (ō-bēs′ĭ-tĭ; ō-bĕs′ĭ-tĭ), *n.* excessive fatness.

o-bey (ō-bā′), *v.t.* **1,** to submit to the rule or authority of (a law or a person); to follow or mind; as, to *obey* the commandments; to *obey* one's parents; **2,** to respond to the guidance or control of; as, a horse *obeys* the rein:—*v.i.* to yield; do as bidden.

o-bit-u-ar-y (ō-bĭt′û-ĕr′ĭ), *n.* [*pl.* obituaries], a printed notice of the death of a person, especially one with a brief account of his life:—*adj.* pertaining to the death of a person; as, an *obituary* notice.

obj. abbreviation for *object, objective.*

¹ob-ject (ŏb-jĕkt′), *v.i.* **1,** to offer opposition; as, he *objected* to my idea; **2,** to feel or express disapproval:—*v.t.* to urge as a reason against a plan, proposal, etc.; as, he *objected* that the train left too late. —*n.* **ob-jec′tor.**

²ob-ject (ŏb′jĕkt), *n.* **1,** that which can be seen or touched; **2,** a person or thing arousing some action or feeling; as, an *object* of charity; **3,** an aim; as, my *object* in school is to learn; **4,** in grammar, a word or clause governed by a verb: called *direct object* when immediately affected by the action of the verb, and *indirect object* when less directly affected; as, in the sentence "he gave the boy money for a hat," "money" is the *direct object,* and "boy" the *indirect object,* of the verb "gave"; also, a word governed by a preposition; as, "hat" is the *object* of the preposition "for."

ob-jec-tion (ŏb-jĕk′shŭn), *n.* **1,** a feeling or expression of opposition or disapproval; **2,** a reason against anything.

ob-jec-tion-a-ble (ŏb-jĕk′shŭn-à-bl), *adj.* **1,** liable or open to opposition; **2,** arousing disapproval; undesirable; unpleasant.— *adv.* **ob-jec′tion-a-bly.**

ob-jec-tive (ŏb-jĕk′tĭv), *n.* **1,** the end or goal toward which any action is directed; an aim; **2,** that which exists outside the mind; an outward fact; reality; **3,** in grammar, the objective case; also, a word in the objective case; **4,** the lens of a microscope or telescope nearest to the object observed:—*adj.* **1,** serving as an end or goal of action or feeling; as, the *objective* point of military operations; **2,** having to do with an outward fact, or that which exists outside the mind, rather than with thoughts or feelings: opposite of *subjective;* **3,** in grammar, naming the case of the direct object of a verb or a preposition. —*adv.* **ob-jec′tive-ly.**—*n.* **ob′jec-tiv′i-ty.**

ob-jur-gate (ŏb′jĕr-gāt; ŏb-jûr′gāt), *v.t.* [objurgat-ed, objurgat-ing], to chide; scold; rebuke.—*n.* **ob′jur-ga′tion.**

ob-la-tion (ŏb-lā′shŭn), *n.* **1,** the act of making an offering or sacrifice to God or to the gods: used especially in reference to the bread and wine of the Communion; **2,** anything presented as a religious offering or sacrifice; a religious gift.

ob-li-gate (ŏb′lĭ-gāt), *v.t.* [obligat-ed, obligat-ing], to bind legally or morally, by contract or treaty, or by a sense of duty or a promise.

ob-li-ga-tion (ŏb′lĭ-gā′shŭn), *n.* **1,** the binding power of a vow, promise, contract, or sense of duty; **2,** any duty imposed by law, by social relations, or by good will; as, the *obligations* of good citizenship; **3,** the state of being bound to perform some duty or to do something burdensome; as, under *obligation* to pay a debt; **4,** a written deed or bond by which one binds himself to do a thing; a contract; a promise.

ob-lig-a-tor-y (ŏb-lĭg′à-tôr′ĭ; ŏb′lĭ-gà-tôr′ĭ), *adj.* morally or legally binding; compulsory; imposed by law, duty, etc.

o-blige (ô-blīj′), *v.t.* [obliged, oblig-ing], **1,** to compel by force, moral, legal, or physical; as, the policeman *obliged* his young prisoner to walk in front; **2,** to place under obligation; as, I was *obliged* to him for his help; **3,** to render a favor to; as, he *obliged* the audience with an encore.

o-blig-ing (ô-blīj′ĭng), *adj.* willing to do favors; courteous; kindly; as, an *obliging* neighbor.—*adv.* **o-blig′ing-ly.**

ob-lique (ŏb-lēk′), *adj.* neither horizontal nor vertical; slanting: —oblique angle, in geometry, any angle not a right angle.— *adv.* **ob-lique′ly.**—*n.* **ob-lique′ness.**

OBLIQUE
The line CD is oblique to AB.

ob-liq-ui-ty (ŏb-lĭk′wĭ-tĭ), *n.* [*pl.* obliquities], **1,** the quality possessed by lines which are neither parallel nor at right angles; **2,** divergence from a vertical or a horizontal position; **3,** a turning aside from right principles of conduct or from right ways of thinking.

ob-lit-er-ate (ŏb-lĭt′ĕr-āt), *v.t.* [obliterat-ed, obliterat-ing], to erase or blot out; destroy all traces of; as, to *obliterate* a mark; time *obliterates* sorrow.—*n.* **ob-lit′er-a′tion.** *Syn.* expunge, cancel, efface.

ob-liv-i-on (ŏb-lĭv′ĭ-ŭn), *n.* **1,** the state of being forgotten; **2,** forgetfulness of the past.

ob-liv-i-ous (ŏb-lĭv′ĭ-ŭs), *adj.* unaware; forgetful; inattentive.

ob-long (ŏb′lông), *adj.* longer than broad: said usually of a figure that is rectangular or nearly so; as, an *oblong* box:—*n.* a rectangle or figure longer than it is broad.

OBLONG

ob-lo-quy (ŏb′lō-kwĭ), *n.* [*pl.* obloquies], **1,** spoken abuse; censure; slander; **2,** the state of being in disgrace. *Syn.* shame, scandal, dishonor, infamy.

ob-nox-ious (ŏb-nŏk′shŭs), *adj.* hateful; offensive; odious.—*adv.* **ob-nox′ious-ly.**

OBOE

o-boe (ō′bō; ō′boi), *n.* a high-pitched

musical instrument of the wood-wind group with a penetrating tone.

obs. abbreviation for *obsolete*.

ob-scene (ŏb-sēn′), *adj.* offensive to modesty; impure in language or action; indecent.—*adv.* **ob-scene′ly.**

ob-scen-i-ty (ŏb-sĕn′ĭ-tĭ; ŏb-sē′nĭ-tĭ), *n.* [*pl.* obscenities], indecency; lewdness.

ob-scure (ŏb-skūr′), *adj.* **1,** not clear or distinct; as, an *obscure* view; **2,** shadowy; dim; dark; as, an *obscure* room; **3,** not easily understood; as, an *obscure* meaning; **4,** illegible; as, faint and *obscure* writing; **5,** remote; unknown; as, he lived in an *obscure* little village; **6,** humble; inconspicuous; as, he occupied an *obscure* position:—*v.t.* [obscured, obscur-ing], **1,** to darken; hide from view; **2,** to disguise; render less intelligible.—*n.* **ob-scure′ness.**

Syn., adj. indistinct, vague, hidden.

ob-scu-ri-ty (ŏb-skū′rĭ-tĭ), *n.* [*pl.* obscurities], **1,** dimness; indistinctness; **2,** lack of clearness in thought or expression; **3,** the state or fact of being unknown to fame.

ob-se-quies (ŏb′sē-kwĭz), *n.pl.* funeral rites or ceremonies.

ob-se-qui-ous (ŏb-sē′kwĭ-ŭs), *adj.* servile; fawning, usually in order to gain a selfish end.—*adv.* **ob-se′qui-ous-ly.**

ob-serv-a-ble (ŏb-zûr′vȧ-bl), *adj.* **1,** capable of being seen or noticed; noticeable; **2,** worthy of attention or note.

ob-serv-ance (ŏb-zûr′vȧns), *n.* **1,** the act of keeping, or of paying attention to, laws or customs; as, the *observance* of the Sabbath; **2,** an act, as a ceremony, performed in token of worship or respect.

ob-serv-ant (ŏb-zûr′vȧnt), *adj.* **1,** quick to notice; attentive; **2,** watchful; mindful of duties or authority.

ob-ser-va-tion (ŏb′zẽr-vā′shŭn), *n.* **1,** the act, power, or habit of seeing and noting; thorough, careful notice; **2,** that which is noticed or learned; **3,** a remark, judgment, or conclusion based on something noticed; **4,** the fact of being seen; as, he tried to avoid *observation;* **5,** the accurate examination of natural objects or events for the purpose of recording their cause, effect, etc.; as, *observation* of an eclipse.

ob-serv-a-tor-y (ŏb-zûr′vȧ-tôr′ĭ), *n.* [*pl.* observatories], **1,** a building fitted up with a telescope and other instruments for studying the heavens; **2,** a tower or other high place built to give an extensive view.

ob-serve (ŏb-zûrv′), *v.t.* [observed, observ-ing], **1,** to take notice of; **2,** to watch closely; study; **3,** to keep or celebrate; commemorate; **4,** to remark; **5,** to comply with; as, to *observe* the social conventions:—*v.i.* **1,** to take notice; **2,** to comment.

ob-serv-ing (ŏb-zûr′vĭng), *adj.* attentive; quick to notice.—*adv.* **ob-serv′ing-ly.**

ob-sess (ŏb-sĕs′), *v.t.* to rule the mind of; preoccupy; as, the idea *obsessed* him.

ob-ses-sion (ŏb-sĕsh′ŭn), *n.* **1,** the state of being ruled by one idea; **2,** a fixed idea not to be driven from one's mind.

ob-sid-i-an (ŏb-sĭd′ĭ-ȧn), *n.* a dark, glassy, volcanic rock.

ob-so-les-cent (ŏb′sō-lĕs′ĕnt), *adj.* passing out of use; as, an *obsolescent* word.—*n.* **ob′so-les′cence.**

ob-so-lete (ŏb′sō-lēt), *adj.* gone out of use; as, *obsolete* firearms; no longer practiced or accepted; as, an *obsolete* custom.

Syn. antique, ancient, antiquated.

ob-sta-cle (ŏb′stȧ-kl), *n.* that which hinders or stands in the way; an obstruction; impediment; hindrance.

ob-sti-na-cy (ŏb′stĭ-nȧ-sĭ), *n.* [*pl.* obstinacies], **1,** stubbornness; **2,** unyielding resistance to treatment; as, the *obstinacy* of a fever.

ob-sti-nate (ŏb′stĭ-nĭt), *adj.* **1,** not yielding to argument, persuasion, or entreaty; headstrong; firm in opinion or purpose; **2,** not yielding to treatment, as a disease.—*adv.* **ob′sti-nate-ly.**

Syn. headstrong, stubborn.

ob-strep-er-ous (ŏb-strĕp′ẽr-ŭs), *adj.* clamorous; noisy; turbulent; as, an *obstreperous* person.—*adv.* **ob-strep′er-ous-ly.**

ob-struct (ŏb-strŭkt′), *v.t.* **1,** to block up or close so as to prevent passage; **2,** to prevent or retard the progress of; as, to *obstruct* work; **3,** to be in the way of; cut off from sight; as, to *obstruct* the view.

Syn. bar, check, retard, hinder.

ob-struc-tion (ŏb-strŭk′shŭn), *n.* **1,** the act of blocking, or state of being blocked; **2,** anything that stops, closes, or bars the way; an obstacle.

ob-struc-tive (ŏb-strŭk′tĭv), *adj.* serving or tending to stop or to hinder progress.—*adv.* **ob-struc′tive-ly.**

ob-tain (ŏb-tān′), *v.t.* to get possession of; gain; as, to *obtain* knowledge:—*v.i.* to be established in practice or use; prevail or be in fashion; as, that custom still *obtains* here.—*adj.* **ob-tain′a-ble.**

Syn. achieve, secure, earn, attain.

ob-trude (ŏb-trōōd′), *v.t.* [obtrud-ed, obtrud-ing], to thrust forward boldly:—*v.i.* to force oneself upon others; intrude.

OBTUSE ANGLE

ob-tru-sive (ŏb-trōō′sĭv), *adj.* unduly inclined to push forward; intrusive.—*adv.* **ob-tru′sive-ly.**

ob-tuse (ŏb-tūs′), *adj.* **1,** not pointed or acute; blunt; **2,** of angles, greater than a right angle; **3,** dull or stupid; as, an *obtuse* person.—*adv.* **ob-tuse/ly.**

ob-verse (ŏb/vûrs), *n.* the front surface of anything; the side of a coin or medal having the principal design upon it: opposite of *reverse*.

ob-vi-ate (ŏb/vĭ-āt), *v.t.* [obviat-ed, obviating], to remove, or clear away, beforehand, as difficulties or objections.
Syn. forestall, preclude.

ob-vi-ous (ŏb/vĭ-ŭs), *adj.* easily understood or seen; evident; plain; as, the effect is *obvious.*—*adv.* **ob/vi-ous-ly.**
Syn. apparent, clear, manifest.

oc-ca-sion (ŏ-kā/zhŭn), *n.* **1,** a particular event or celebration; as, the king's visit was an *occasion;* **2,** occurrence; as, on the *occasion* of her last visit; **3,** something that leads to unexpected results; an incidental cause; as, his carelessness was the *occasion* of the whole trouble; **4,** need; reason; as, having *occasion* to buy food; no *occasion* for anger; **5,** a favorable chance or opportunity; as, he seized the *occasion* to speak:—*v.t.* to cause; give rise to; as, the law *occasioned* widespread revolt.
Syn. necessity, exigency, cause.

oc-ca-sion-al (ŏ-kā/zhŭn-ăl), *adj.* **1,** happening now and then, but not regularly; as, *occasional* visits; **2,** meant for, or suitable to, a special event; as, an *occasional* poem.

oc-ca-sion-al-ly (ŏ-kā/zhŭn-ăl-ĭ), *adv.* now and then; not regularly.

oc-ci-dent (ŏk/sĭ-dĕnt), *n.* the west: opposite of *orient*, or the east:—**Occident,** the countries west of Asia; western Europe and the Western Hemisphere: opposite of *Orient.*—*adj.* and *n.* **oc/ci-den/tal; Oc/ci-den/tal** (ŏk/sĭ-dĕn/tăl).

oc-cult (ŏ-kŭlt/; ŏk/ŭlt), *adj.* **1,** secret; mysterious; beyond ordinary understanding; **2,** supernatural.—*adv.* **oc-cult/ly.**

oc-cu-pan-cy (ŏk/ŭ-păn-sĭ), *n.* **1,** the act of occupying or taking possession; **2,** the period during which anything is occupied.

oc-cu-pant (ŏk/ŭ-pănt), *n.* one who dwells in, has possession of, or uses a house, property, etc.

oc-cu-pa-tion (ŏk/ŭ-pā/shŭn), *n.* **1,** the act of holding in possession, or occupying; also, the time during which a property or position is held; **2,** regular business, employment, or calling.

oc-cu-py (ŏk/ŭ-pī), *v.t.* [occupied, occupying], **1,** to take possession of; dwell in; as, to *occupy* a room; **2,** to fill or cover the time or space of; as, household duties *occupy* her day; **3,** to employ; busy; as, to *occupy* oneself with work; **4,** to hold; fill; as, to *occupy* the office of mayor.

oc-cur (ŏ-kûr/), *v.i.* [occurred, occur-ring], **1,** to happen or take place; as, the mistake must not *occur* again; **2,** to be found; exist; as, such plants *occur* in Africa; **3,** to come to mind; as, did it *occur* to you to go?

oc-cur-rence (ŏ-kûr/ĕns), *n.* a happening; event; incident.

o-cean (ō/shăn), *n.* **1,** the vast body of salt water covering three fourths of the globe; also, any one of its chief divisions; as, the Atlantic *Ocean;* **2,** a vast expanse or amount; as, an *ocean* of tears.

O-ce-an-i-a (ō/shē-ăn/ĭ-à) or **O-ce-an-i-ca** (ō/shē-ăn/ĭ-kà), a general name given to the islands in the south Pacific, including Polynesia, Micronesia, Melanesia, Australasia, and Malaysia.

o-ce-an-ic (ō/shē-ăn/ĭk), *adj.* of or relating to the ocean.

o-ce-lot (ō/sĕ-lŏt; ŏs/ĕ-lŏt), *n.* a leopardlike cat, yellowish gray with elongated fawn-colored spots edged in black, found in Central and South America.

OCELOT (⅓₀)

o-cher or **o-chre** (ō/kẽr), *n.* an earthy variety of iron ore used as coloring material in making paint, etc.; as, yellow *ocher.*

o'-clock (ŏ-klŏk/), contraction for *of the clock,* according to the clock.

Oct. abbreviation for *October.*

oc-ta-gon (ŏk/tá-gŏn; ŏk/tá-gŭn), *n.* a plane figure of eight sides and eight angles.—*adj.* **oc-tag/o-nal** (ŏk-tăg/ō-năl).

OCTAGON

oc-tave (ŏk/tāv; ŏk/tĭv), *n.* in music: **1,** an interval of eight steps, as from C in the scale to the C next above or below; **2,** the series of tones comprised in such an interval; **3,** the harmonic combination of two tones at such an interval; **4,** the eighth note in the ordinary musical scale:—*adj.* consisting of eight.

Oc-ta-vi-us (ŏk-tā/vĭ-ŭs), the first emperor of Rome. See **Augustus.**

OCTAVE
Two octaves on the keyboard of a piano.

oc-ta-vo (ŏk-tā/vō; ŏk-tä/vō), *n.* [*pl.* octavos] (-vōz), **1,** in printing, a sheet of paper folded into eight leaves or sixteen pages; **2,** a book made of such sheets:—*adj.* having eight leaves to the sheet; also, made of sheets folded in this way. It is often written 8*vo.*

Oc-to-ber (ŏk-tō/bẽr), *n.* the tenth month of the year, containing 31 days.

oc-to-pus (ŏk/tŏ-pŭs), *n.* [*pl.* octopuses

(ŏk′tŏ-pŭs-ĕz) or octopi (ŏk′tŏ-pī)], 1, a sea mollusk related to the cuttlefish, having eight arms provided with suckers with which it holds on to its prey; 2, any organization with a harmful, far-reaching hold on the public.

OCTOPUS (¹⁄₁₀)

oc·u·lar (ŏk′ū-lẽr), *adj.* 1, pertaining to the eye or to eyesight; 2, depending on, or seen by, the eye; known from actual sight; as, *ocular* evidence.

oc·u·list (ŏk′ū-lĭst), *n.* one who is skilled in the treatment of eye diseases: distinguished from *optician* and *optometrist.*

odd (ŏd), *adj.* 1, not paired or matched with another; as, an *odd* glove; 2, not exactly divisible by two; as, seven is an *odd* number; 3, left over after equal division; extra; as, you may have the *odd* one; 4, additional; as, fifty and some *odd* miles; also, plus a few more; as, thirty *odd*; 5, unusual; as, an *odd* occurrence; 6, eccentric; as, an *odd* person; 7, occasional; as, *odd* jobs; 8, not occupied; as, *odd* moments.— *adv.*—**odd′ly.**—*n.* **odd′ness.**
Syn. strange, grotesque, fantastic.

odd·i·ty (ŏd′ĭ-tĭ), *n.* [*pl.* oddities], 1, a person, thing, or quality, that is peculiar; 2, strangeness; eccentricity.

odds (ŏdz), *n.pl.* 1, inequality; 2, advantage; superiority of one as compared with another; as, the *odds* are in her favor; 3, probability; as, the *odds* are that he will succeed; 4, in betting, an advantage in the amount wagered to compensate for a smaller chance of winning; as, *odds* of ten to one.

ode (ōd), *n.* a lyric poem expressing noble sentiments in a dignified style.

O-der (ō′dẽr), a river flowing through eastern Germany into the Baltic (map **18**).

O-des·sa (ô-dĕs′a), a seaport on the Black Sea, in the Ukraine, southwestern U.S.S.R. (map **12**).

O-din (ō′dĭn), *n.* in Norse mythology, the chief god; god of wisdom, culture, and war.

o-di-ous (ō′dĭ-ŭs), *adj.* deserving of, or causing, hatred; offensive; as, his conduct was *odious.*—*adv.* **o′di-ous-ly.**
Syn. detestable, disagreeable, hateful.

o-di-um (ō′dĭ-ŭm), *n.* 1, hatred; abhorrence; 2, blame; reproach attached to a person or action; discredit.

o-dor (ō′dẽr), *n.* 1, a scent; smell, whether pleasant or offensive; 2, repute; as, to be in bad *odor.*—*adj.* **o′dor-less.**

o-dor-if-er-ous (ō′dẽr-ĭf′ẽr-ŭs), *adj.* diffusing or giving out fragrance; as, *odoriferous* spices.
Syn. fragrant, aromatic, odorous.

o-dor-ous (ō′dẽr-ŭs), *adj.* giving out an odor or scent; fragrant.

O-dys-seus (ô-dĭs′ūs; ô-dĭs′ē-ŭs), *n.* in Greek mythology, a king of Ithaca, leader in the Trojan War, and hero of Homer's "Odyssey": called by the Romans *Ulysses.*

Od-ys-sey (ŏd′ĭ-sĭ), *n.* 1, a Greek epic poem, attributed to Homer, describing the wanderings of Odysseus; 2, any long and adventurous journey.

Oed-i-pus (ĕd′ĭ-pŭs; ē′dĭ-pŭs), *n.* in Greek legend, a king of Thebes, who unwittingly killed his father and married his mother: solver of the riddle of the Sphinx.

o'er (ôr), *prep.* and *adv. Poetic,* over.

oe-soph-a-gus (ē-sŏf′a-gŭs), *n.* the gullet. See esophagus.

of (ŏv), *prep.* 1, from; as, to cure *of* a fever; born *of* a line of kings; north *of* the city; 2, forced by; as, he did it *of* necessity; 3, about; concerning; as, talk *of* success; news *of* victory; 4, in; as, quick *of* speech; 5, belonging to, related to, or connected with; as, the palace *of* the king; 6, containing; having; consisting of; as, a glass *of* milk; a man *of* brains; a line *of* trees; made from; as, a house *of* stone; 7, named; especially of political divisions; as, the state *of* Maine; 8, *Colloquial,* on; as, she died *of* a Monday; 9, *Archaic,* by; as, admired *of* men:—**of late,** recently.

off (ôf), *adv.* 1, away from a place; as, to run *off*; to stand *off* to sea; from, so as not to be on; as, take *off* your coat, gloves, hat; also, on one's way; as, he is *off* to town; 2, into the condition of; as, to drop *off* to sleep; 3, so as to stop the flow of; as, to turn *off* the gas; 4, so as to end or be rid of; as, to break *off* a friendship; to shake *off* a feeling; 5, in full; as, to pay *off* a mortgage; 6, away from work; as, he has a day *off*; 7, less; as, ten per cent *off* for cash:—*adj.* 1, on the right-hand side of a vehicle, animal, or team; 2, removed; not on; as, he stood with his hat *off*; 3, not in use; disconnected; as, the gas is *off*; the radio was *off* all day; 4, given up; canceled; as, all arrangements are *off*; 5, wrong; mistaken; as, he is *off* in his estimate; 6, out of order; not functioning properly; as, his heart is *off*; 7, unlucky; as, it is an *off* day for him; 8, not up to the usual standard; as, his playing was *off* today; 9, provided for; situated; as, he is well *off*; 10, not very probable; as, an *off* chance:—*prep.* 1, away from; as, take your hands *off* the table; removed from; as, the cover is *off* my book; 2, distant from; as, a mile *off* shore; 3, temporarily relieved of; as, he is *off* duty; **4,** less than; as ten per cent *off* the regular price:—*interj.* begone!

of·fal (ŏf′ăl), *n.* **1,** worthless scraps; refuse; **2,** waste parts of a butchered animal.

off·col·or (ôf′-kŭl′ẽr), *adj.* **1,** not of a natural or satisfactory color; as, the jewel is *off-color;* **2,** *Colloquial,* slightly improper; as, an *off-color* remark.

of·fend (ŏ-fĕnd′), *v.t.* to displease or make angry; vex or annoy:—*v.i.* **1,** to transgress; sin; as, to *offend* against the law; **2,** to do anything displeasing.

of·fend·er (ŏ-fĕn′dẽr), *n.* one who offends; one who does wrong, or breaks a law.

of·fense or **of·fence** (ŏ-fĕns′), *n.* **1,** a sin; crime; **2,** the act of offering an injury; **3,** the state of being offended; **4,** an attack or assault.—*adj.* **of·fense′less.**
Syn. affront, misdeed, transgression.

of·fen·sive (ŏ-fĕn′sĭv), *adj.* **1,** insulting; as, *offensive* actions; **2,** disagreeable; as, an *offensive* odor; **3,** used in attack; as, *offensive* weapons:—*n.* an aggressive method or attitude.—*adv.* **of·fen′sive·ly.**
Syn., adj. obnoxious, insolent, hateful.

of·fer (ôf′ẽr), *n.* **1,** a proposal; **2,** a price bid; **3,** an attempt or endeavor; as, to make an *offer* of resistance:—*v.t.* **1,** to present for acceptance or refusal; as, to *offer* money; **2,** to proffer; as, to *offer* help or advice; **3,** to propose; as, to *offer* a plan; **4,** to present in worship or sacrifice; as, to *offer* a prayer; **5,** to attempt to make or give; as, to *offer* resistance:—*v.i.* to present itself; appear; arise; as, a favorable opportunity soon *offered.*
Syn., v. extend, tender, bestow, grant.

of·fer·ing (ôf′ẽr-ĭng), *n.* **1,** the act of making a proffer or proposal; **2,** that which is offered or given; a gift.

of·fer·to·ry (ôf′ẽr-tôr′ĭ), *n.* [*pl.* offertories], **1,** that part of the church service at which the money offering is made; **2,** the offering; **3,** music played at this time.

off·hand (ôf′hănd′), *adj.* **1,** done without preparation; as, an *offhand* speech; **2,** informal; as, an *offhand* manner:—*adv.* (ôf′hănd′), without preparation.

of·fice (ôf′ĭs), *n.* **1,** a position of trust or authority; as, the *office* of President; **2,** a function; as, the *office* of the ears is to hear; **3,** a religious ceremony or rite; **4,** a duty or service; as, an *office* of kindness; **5,** a place for the transaction of business; as, a doctor's *office;* an express *office.*

of·fi·cer (ôf′ĭ-sẽr), *n.* **1,** a person empowered to perform a public duty, as a policeman; **2,** one elected to manage the affairs of an organization; **3,** in the Army or Navy, one appointed, especially by commission, to a position of rank and authority:—*v.t.* **1,** to furnish with leaders; **2,** to command.

of·fi·cial (ŏ-fĭsh′ăl), *n.* one who holds an office:—*adj.* **1,** pertaining to an office; as, *official* duties; **2,** derived from the proper authority; authorized; as, an *official* ruling.—*adv.* **of·fi′cial·ly.**

of·fi·ci·ate (ŏ-fĭsh′ĭ-āt), *v.i.* [officiat-ed, officiat-ing], **1,** to perform the duties of a divine service; **2,** to perform the duties of an office or the like.

of·fi·cious (ŏ-fĭsh′ŭs), *adj.* too bold in offering services; meddling.—*adv.* **of·fi′cious·ly.**—*n.* **of·fi′cious·ness.**
Syn. intrusive, obtrusive, meddlesome.

off·ing (ôf′ĭng), *n.* the open sea, visible from shore but beyond anchoring ground; hence, distance; future; as, a job in the *offing.*

off·ish (ôf′ĭsh), *adj.* reserved; inclined to hold aloof; rude.

off·scour·ings (ôf′skour′ĭngz), *n.pl.* refuse or cast-off filth.

off·set (ôf′sĕt′; ôf′sĕt′), *v.t.* [offset, offsetting], to make up for; compensate; balance; as, her bad manners are *offset* by her beauty:—*n.* (ôf′sĕt′), **1,** that which proceeds or develops from something else; an offshoot; **2,** one thing which makes up for another; a compensation.

off·shoot (ôf′sho͞ot′), *n.* a shoot, or branch, from a main stem; a branch, as of a family, race, etc.

off·shore (ôf′shôr′), *adj.* **1,** moving toward the sea; **2,** located out from the shore:—*adv.* (ôf′shôr′), away from, or at some distance from, the shore.

off·spring (ôf′sprĭng′), *n.* [*pl.* offspring], a child or children; a descendant or descendants of a plant or animal.

oft (ôft), *adv. Poetic,* often.

of·ten (ôf′ĕn), *adv.* frequently.

of·ten·times (ôf′ĕn-tīmz′), *adv.* often.

oft·times (ôft′tīmz′), *adv. Poetic,* often.

o·gle (ō′gl), *v.t.* [o-gled, o-gling], to eye with familiar or amorous glances:—*n.* an amorous or too familiar look.—*n.* **o′gler.**

o·gre (ō′gẽr), *n.* in fairy tales, a man-eating monster or giant; hence, a cruel, ugly person.—*n.fem.* **o′gress.**—*adj.* **o′gre·ish.**

oh (ō), *interj.* **1,** an exclamation of wonder, surprise, sorrow, shame, pain, or the like; **2,** (preferably *O*), a word used in earnest address, as in prayer.

O·hi·o (ō-hī′ō), **1,** a north central State (cap. Columbus) in the U.S.; **2,** a large river of the U.S., flowing from Pittsburgh to the Mississippi River. (Map **7.**)

---

go; join; yet; sing; chin; show; thin, *th*en; hw, *wh*y; zh, azure; ü, Ger. für or Fr. lune; ö, Ger. schön or Fr. feu; ṅ, Fr. enfant, nom; kh, Ger. ach or ich. See pages ix–x.

ohm (ōm), *n.* a unit of measure of the resistance of an electric circuit.

oil (oil), *n.* **1,** a greasy or fatty substance, of animal, vegetable, or mineral origin, and used variously as a lubricant, fuel, medicine, food, etc.; **2,** in art: **a,** a pigment mixed with oil: called *oil color* or *oil paint;* **b,** a picture painted with this material:—*v.t.* **1,** to lubricate with oil; **2,** to anoint.—*n.* **oil′er.**

oil of vitriol, the commercial name for sulphuric acid; **to burn the midnight oil,** to study late into the night.

oil-cloth (oil′klôth′), *n.* a coarse cloth coated with oil or oil paint, used for covering floors, shelves, tables, etc.

oil-skin (oil′skĭn′), *n.* **1,** a cloth treated with oil and made waterproof; **2, oilskins,** waterproof clothing made of such cloth.

oil-stone (oil′stōn′), *n.* a fine-grained stone, moistened with oil, used as a whetstone for sharpening edged tools.

oil-y (oil′ĭ), *adj.* [oil-i-er, oil-i-est], containing, or like, oil; greasy; **2,** smooth in speech or manner; smooth-tongued; as, an *oily* salesman.—*n.* **oil′i-ness.**

oint-ment (oint′mĕnt), *n.* a medicinal preparation, usually made of a fat, applied to the skin to heal or beautify.

Oise (wäz), a river in northeastern France.

Oi-sin (ŭ-shēn′), a legendary Celtic poet of the third century, son of Finn.

O.K., OK. *Colloquial,* it is so; all right.

o-ka-pi (ŏ-kä′pĭ), *n.* a small mammal of the giraffe family, with striped legs, found in the forests of central Africa.

o-kie (ō′kĭ), *n.* a wandering harvest worker in the southwestern U. S.

Okla. abbreviation for *Oklahoma.*

O-kla-ho-ma (ō′klȧ-hō′mȧ), a south central State (cap. Oklahoma City) in the U.S. (map 8).

O-kla-ho-ma Cit-y, a city, capital of Oklahoma (map 8).

o-kra (ō′krȧ; ŏk′rȧ), *n.* a West Indian plant, cultivated for the seed pods which are used as vegetables and in soups.

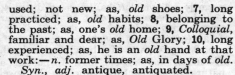
OKRA

old (ōld), *adj.* [old-er or eld-er, old-est or eld-est], **1,** having existed or lived many years; aged; as, an *old* oak; an *old* man; **2,** having an appearance of age; as, an *old* face; **3,** having reached a certain age; as, twenty-one years *old;* **4,** decayed by time; as, an *old* ruin; **5,** ancient; out of date; as, *old* customs; *old* coins; **6,** long used; not new; as, *old* shoes; **7,** long practiced; as, *old* habits; **8,** belonging to the past; as, one's *old* home; **9,** *Colloquial,* familiar and dear; as, *Old* Glory; **10,** long experienced; as, he is an *old* hand at that work:—*n.* former times; as, in days of *old.*

Syn., *adj.* antique, antiquated.

old-en (ōl′dĕn), *adj.* ancient; bygone; as, in *olden* times.

old-fash-ioned (ōld′-făsh′ŭnd), *adj.* **1,** having or adhering to old ideas or customs; as, an *old-fashioned* person; **2,** out of style; as, an *old-fashioned* coat.

Old Glor-y, the flag of the United States; a familiar term of affection.

Old Tes-ta-ment, the first of the two main divisions of the Bible.

old-time (ōld′-tīm′), *adj.* pertaining to, or characteristic of, former times.

old-world (ōld′-wûrld′), *adj.* **1,** pertaining to ancient times; **2,** (usually *Old World*), relating to the Eastern Hemisphere.

o-le-an-der (ō′lē-ăn′dẽr; ō′lē-ăn′dẽr), *n.* a poisonous, evergreen shrub with handsome, fragrant, red or white flowers.

o-le-o-mar-ga-rine (ō′lē-ō-mär′jȧ-rēn; ō′lē-ō-mär′gȧ-rēn), *n.* a fatty substance extracted from animal or vegetable fats and used in place of butter: also called *oleo.* It is also spelled o′le-o-mar′ga-rin.

ol-fac-to-ry (ŏl-făk′tō-rĭ), *adj.* pertaining to smelling; as, an *olfactory* nerve.

ol-i-garch (ŏl′ĭ-gärk), *n.* one of the rulers in a government which is controlled by a few persons.

ol-i-garch-y (ŏl′ĭ-gär′kĭ), *n.* [*pl.* oligarchies], **1,** a government in which the supreme power is in the hands of a few; **2,** a state so governed; **3,** the few who rule.

o-li-o (ō′lĭ-ō), *n.* a miscellaneous collection; a medley.

ol-ive (ŏl′ĭv), *n.* **1,** an Old World evergreen cultivated for its oily fruit; **2,** the wood of this tree; also, its fruit, brownish black when ripe; **3,** a dull yellowish-green color, as of an unripe olive:—*adj.* of a dull yellowish-green or yellowish-brown color; as, an *olive* complexion.

olive branch, a branch of the olive tree, regarded as the emblem of peace; olive oil, an oil pressed from the ripe olive, used in cookery, salad dressings, soap making, and for medicinal purposes.

OLIVE
Leaves and fruit.

Olives, Mount of, a hill on the east side of Jerusalem, at the foot of which is the Garden of Gethsemane.

O·lym·pi·a (ō-lĭm′pĭ-ȧ), **1,** a city on Puget Sound, capital of the State of Washington (map 9); **2,** a plain in ancient Elis, southwestern Greece, where the Olympic Games were held (map 1).

O·lym·pi·ad (ō-lĭm′pĭ-ăd), *n.* in ancient Greece, the period of four years between two celebrations of the Olympic games: a standard used in reckoning dates.

O·lym·pi·an (ō-lĭm′pĭ-ăn), *adj.* pertaining to Olympus; heavenly; celestial; magnificent:—*n.* in Greek mythology, any of the twelve gods who dwelt on Olympus.

O·lym·pic (ō-lĭm′pĭk), *adj.* pertaining to Olympia in Elis, Greece, or to Mount Olympus, in Thessaly:—**Olympic games, 1,** a festival of the ancient Greeks held at Olympia every four years (starting in 776 B.C.) in honor of Zeus, consisting of contests in athletics, music, and literature: also called *Olympian games;* **2,** a revival of these games, first held at Athens in 1896.

O·lym·pus (ō-lĭm′pŭs), a mountain range in Thessaly, northeastern Greece, the mythical home of the Greek gods (map 1).

O·ma·ha (ō′mȧ-hô′), a city in eastern Nebraska (map 7).

O·mar Khay·yám (ō′mȧr kī-yäm′; kī-yôm′), (?-1123), a Persian mathematician, astronomer, and poet; author of the "Rubáiyát."

o·me·ga (ō-mē′gȧ; ō′mĕ-gȧ; ō-mĕg′ȧ), *n.* **1,** the last letter of the Greek alphabet; **2,** hence, the last of anything; end.

om·e·let (ŏm′ĕ-lĕt; ŏm′lĕt), *n.* a dish consisting of eggs and milk, often with other ingredients, beaten together and browned in a pan. Also spelled **om′e·lette.**

o·men (ō′mĕn; ō′mĕn), *n.* a prophetic sign of some future event; augury.

om·i·nous (ŏm′ĭ-nŭs), *adj.* foreboding evil; threatening.—*adv.* **om′i·nous·ly.**

o·mis·sion (ō-mĭsh′ŭn), *n.* **1,** the act of omitting; state of being left out; **2,** something left out or neglected.

o·mit (ō-mĭt′), *v.t.* [omit-ted, omit-ting], to leave out; fail to include; also, to neglect; leave undone.

om·ni·bus (ŏm′nĭ-bŭs; ŏm′nĭ-bŭs), *n.* a large four-wheeled public vehicle for passenger traffic over a fixed route; bus:—*adj.* including or providing for many different objects or cases; as, an *omnibus* bill was introduced in Congress.

om·nip·o·tence (ŏm-nĭp′ō-tĕns), *n.* infinite or unlimited power:—**Omnipotence,** God, the all-powerful.

om·nip·o·tent (ŏm-nĭp′ō-tĕnt), *adj.* all-powerful:—**the Omnipotent,** God.—*adv.* **om·nip′o·tent·ly.**

om·ni·pres·ence (ŏm′nĭ-prĕz′ĕns), *n.* the state of being present everywhere at once; as, the *omnipresence* of God.

om·ni·pres·ent (ŏm′nĭ-prĕz′ĕnt), *adj.* present everywhere at the same time.

om·nis·cience (ŏm-nĭsh′ĕns; ŏm-nĭs′ĭ-ĕns), *n.* unlimited knowledge:—**Omniscience,** God, the all-knowing.

om·nis·cient (ŏm-nĭsh′ĕnt; ŏm-nĭs′ĭ-ĕnt), *adj.* knowing all; infinitely wise.

om·niv·o·rous (ŏm-nĭv′ō-rŭs), *adj.* **1,** feeding upon both vegetable and animal food; as, *omnivorous* animals; **2,** hence, all-devouring; as, an *omnivorous* reader.—*adv.* **om·niv′o·rous·ly.**

on (ŏn), *prep.* **1,** upon; supported by; as, to sit *on* a chair; **2,** in contact with the upper surface of; as, we live *on* the earth; **3,** covering; as, shoes *on* one's feet; **4,** along or by; situated by the edge of; as, Paris is *on* the Seine; **5,** in the state of; as, *on* fire; *on* sale; with a view to; as, to go *on* business; to go *on* a trip; **6,** toward; as, have pity *on* the needy; **7,** forming part of; as, *on* the committee; **8,** following; as, they are *on* his trail; **9,** in the direction of; as, the door opens *on* a lawn; from above in the direction of; as, the sun shone *on* the porch; **10,** about; concerning; as, an address *on* peace; with reference to; as, to unite *on* a plan; **11,** at the time of; as, *on* June first; **12,** against or hanging from; as, a picture *on* the wall; **13,** upon the event of; as, she saw him *on* his arrival; **14,** by means of; as, to play *on* a violin; **15,** as witness; by the strength of; as, *on* my honor; **16,** after; in addition to; as, he made error *on* error:—*adv.* **1,** forward; as, to go *on;* without interruption; longer; as, to talk *on* and *on;* at or toward something; as, to look *on;* **2,** in such a way as to cover, support, or the like; as, put *on* your coat; **3,** into action or use; as, to turn *on* the gas; **4,** in progress; as, the fight is *on.*

once (wŭns), *adv.* **1,** at one time; formerly; as, *once* upon a time; this was *once* my home; **2,** one time only; as, read it over *once;* **3,** at any time; ever; as, if *once* they lose heart, their cause will be lost:—*n.* one time:—**at once, 1,** together; as, all talk *at once;* **2,** immediately; as, do it *at once.*

on·com·ing (ŏn′kŭm′ĭng), *adj.* approaching:—*n.* approach.

one (wŭn), *adj.* **1,** a; a single; single; as, *one* person at a time; no *one* man can do that; **2,** a person named; as, I sold it to *one* Jones; a certain; as, *one* day long ago; some; we'll go there *one* day very soon; **3,** united; as, they answered with *one* voice; to be forever *one;* **4,** the same; as, don't put all your eggs in *one* basket; they were

---

go; join; yet; sing; chin; show; thin, *th***en; hw,** *wh***y; zh,** *a***zure; ü, Ger. für or Fr. lune; ō, Ger. schön or Fr. feu; ṅ, Fr. enfant, nom; kh, Ger. ach or ich. See pages ix-x.**

all going in *one* direction; **5,** only; as, the *one* thing to do:—*n.* [*pl.* ones (wŭnz)], **1,** the first number in counting by units; also, its symbol, as 1, I, or i; hence, any person or thing designated by the number; as, who has number *one*? **2,** a person or thing; as, never a *one;* pick me out some good *ones;* if this *one* is right, the other is wrong; what a *one* he is to get into trouble:—*pron.* **1,** a single person or thing; as, *one* of them was lost; may I take *one* now? they saw *one* another often; *one* by *one; one* is wise, another foolish; **2,** any person or thing; as, *one* must eat to live; *one* can hardly sleep because of the noise.

O-nei-da (ō-nī′dȧ), *n.* a member of the Oneidas, a tribe of North American Indians formerly inhabiting central New York State.

one-ness (wŭn′nĕs), *n.* singleness.

on-er-ous (ŏn′ẽr-ŭs), *adj.* burdensome; weighty; as, an *onerous* duty.
   Syn. arduous, difficult, oppressive.

one-self (wŭn-sĕlf′), *pron.* **1,** a reflexive form of *one;* **2,** an emphatic form of *one;* **3,** one's true self.

one—sid-ed (wŭn′=sīd′ĕd), *adj.* **1,** having, or appearing on, only one side; larger on one side than another; as, a *one-sided* leaf; **2,** hence, unequal; unfair; as, a *one-sided* argument.—*adv.* one′—sid′ed-ly.

one—step (wŭn′=stĕp′), *n.* a modern dance of quick movement, in two-four time.

on-ion (ŭn′yŭn), *n.* **1,** a plant of the lily family, having a strong-smelling bulb used as food; **2,** the bulb of the plant.

on-look-er (ŏn′lŏŏk′ẽr), *n.* a spectator; a casual observer.

on-ly (ōn′lĭ), *adj.* **1,** sole; single; as, the *only* man there; an *only* daughter; **2,** best; most suitable; as, he is the *only* man to choose:—*adv.* no more than; merely:—*conj.* except for the fact that; but.

On-on-da-ga (ŏn′ŏn-dô′gȧ), *n.* a member of the Onondagas, a tribe of North American Indians formerly living in New York State and Ontario.

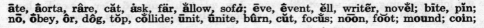
ONION

on-rush (ŏn′rŭsh′), *n.* a rushing on or forward; an assault.

on-set (ŏn′sĕt′), *n.* **1,** an assault; attack; **2,** a first step or stage; beginning.

on-slaught (ŏn′slôt′), *n.* a furious attack.

On-tar-i-o (ŏn-târ′ĭ-ō), a province (cap. Toronto) in southeastern Canada:—**Lake Ontario,** one of the five Great Lakes of North America. (Map 4.)

on-to (ŏn′tŏŏ), *prep. Colloquial,* on.

o-nus (ō′nŭs), *n.* a burden; obligation.

on-ward (ŏn′wẽrd), *adj.* advancing; as, the *onward* march of troops:—*adv.* forward; as, to move *onward.* Also, *adv.* **on′wards.**

on-yx (ŏn′ĭks; ō′nĭks), *n.* a kind of quartz in layers of various colors, such as brown, black, red, and white.

oo-mi-ak (ōō′mĭ-ăk), *n.* an Eskimo open boat; umiak. See **umiak.**

[1]**ooze** (ōōz), *n.* soft, slimy mud, especially in the bed of a river.

[2]**ooze** (ōōz), *n.* a gentle flow, as of a stream through sedges or sweat from pores:—*v.i.* [oozed, ooz-ing], **1,** to flow gently; as, the water *oozed* through a crack in the wall; **2,** to leak out gradually; as, so the news *oozed* out:—*v.t.* to give off slowly; as, the sponge *oozed* moisture.—*adj.* **oo′zy.**

o-pal (ō′păl), *n.* a stone having constantly changing and delicate colors.

o-pal-es-cent (ō′păl-ĕs′ĕnt), *adj.* having constantly changing delicate colors, like an opal.—*n.* o′pal-es′cence.

o-paque (ō-pāk′), *adj.* **1,** not allowing light to pass through; as, *opaque* window shades; **2,** having no luster; dull; not shining; as, an *opaque* surface.

ope (ōp), *Poetic: v.t.* [oped, op-ing], to open:—*adj.* open.

o-pen (ō′pĕn), *adj.* **1,** not shut; unclosed; as, an *open* door; **2,** unsealed or unstopped, as a letter or a bottle; **3,** uncovered or exposed; not enclosed; as, an *open* boat; **4,** not obstructed; as, a river *open* to navigation; **5,** clear of trees; as, *open* country; away from shore or land; as, the *open* sea; **6,** unfilled; unoccupied; as, the position is still *open;* **7,** undecided; as, an *open* question; **8,** mild; free from ice and snow; as, an *open* winter; **9,** unfolded or spread out; as, an *open* newspaper; **10,** not hidden; in plain view; as, *open* lawlessness; unreserved; as, an *open* criticism; **11,** public; free to all; as, an *open* meeting; **12,** ready to hear or to receive suggestion; as, an *open* mind; **13,** generous; as, to give with an *open* hand; **14,** frank; sincere; as, an *open* countenance:—*v.t.* **1,** to unclose or unlock, as a window or door; **2,** to spread out, as a fan; **3,** to break the seal of or untie, as an envelope or package; **4,** to remove obstructions from; as, to *open* a road; **5,** to begin; as, to *open* the discussion; **6,** to start, as a business; as, to *open* a store; **7,** to unburden; as, to *open* one's mind to a friend; **8,** to offer for settlement, use, etc.; as, to *open* undeveloped land:—*v.i.* **1,** to unclose itself; as, the door *opened;* **2,** to commence; as, the service *opened* with a hymn; **3,** to lead; as, the door *opens* into the hall; **4,** to unfold; as, the bud slowly *opened* in the sun; **5,** to become more clearly visible; as, the view *opened* before our eyes:—*n.* any wide, clear space; outdoors; as, we lived in the *open* all summer.

Syn., adj. candid, artless, ingenuous.

o·pen·hand·ed (ō′pĕn-hăn′dĕd), *adj.* generous; liberal.

o·pen·heart·ed (ō′pĕn-här′tĕd), *adj.* frank; sincere; also, generous.

o·pen·ing (ō′pĕn-ĭng; ōp′nĭng), *n.* **1,** the act of making, or the fact of becoming, open; **2,** a hole; gap; passage; as, an *opening* in a fence; **3,** a space in a woods with few trees and little undergrowth; **4,** the first steps; a beginning; as, the *opening* of a trial; **5,** an opportunity or a chance; also, a vacant position; as, John applied for the *opening* in the bank:—*adj.* first in order; as, the *opening* song in assembly.

o·pen·ly (ō′pĕn-lĭ), *adv.* without secrecy; as, he was *openly* envious of his chum.

o·pen·ness (ō′pĕn-nĕs), *n.* **1,** a being open; **2,** lack of secrecy; frankness; sincerity; as, *openness* of manner.

open shop, a shop or factory that employs both union and nonunion labor: opposite of *closed shop.*

o·pen·work (ō′pĕn-wûrk′), *n.* any work, as carving, embroidery, or the like, so made as to show open spaces in its pattern.

op·er·a (ŏp′ẽr-à), *n.* a drama set to music and produced with scenery and costumes.

opera glass, a small telescope, adapted for the use of both eyes, and used by spectators at the theater, opera, etc.: also called *opera glasses.*

OPERA GLASS

op·er·ate (ŏp′ẽr-āt), *v.i.* [operat-ed, operat-ing], **1,** to work; act; as, the engine *operates* smoothly; **2,** to produce or take a certain effect; as, many drugs *operate* harmfully on the body; **3,** to perform a surgical operation on the human body:—*v.t.* **1,** to cause to work; as, to *operate* a machine; **2,** to manage; work; as, to *operate* a coal mine.

op·er·at·ic (ŏp′ẽr-ăt′ĭk), *adj.* of, suitable for, or like, opera; as, *operatic* music.

op·er·a·tion (ŏv′ẽr-ā′shŭn), *n.* **1,** the act, method, result, etc., of operating; **2,** regular action; as, the machine is in *operation;* **3,** action; a working; as, by *operation* of the law of gravitation, objects fall to earth; **4,** a surgical treatment upon the living body to remove diseased parts, correct deformity, etc.; **5,** a series of movements of an army or fleet; as, naval *operations.*

op·er·a·tive (ŏp′ẽr-ā′tĭv; ŏp′ẽr-à-tĭv), *adj.* **1,** having the power of acting; **2,** having effect; also, in operation; as, an *operative* law;

3, concerned with work, either with the hands or with machinery; as, an *operative* art; **4,** having to do with surgical operations; as, *operative* surgery:—*n.* an artisan or workman; as, *operatives* in a factory.

op·er·a·tor (ŏp′ẽr-ā′tẽr), *n.* **1,** one who or that which works or acts; **2,** one who is employed in a telephone exchange to make connections between lines; **3,** one who runs a machine, as in a factory.

op·er·et·ta (ŏp′ẽr-ĕt′à), *n.* a short musical play, usually light and humorous.

oph·thal·mi·a (ŏf-thăl′mĭ-à), *n.* inflammation of the eye or its membranes.

o·pi·ate (ō′pĭ-āt; ō′pĭ-ĭt), *n.* **1,** a medicine containing, or made from, opium, that causes sleep; **2,** anything that soothes:—*adj.* soothing; quieting; as, an *opiate* drink.

o·pine (ō-pīn′), *v.t.* and *v.i.* [opined, opining], to think; suppose.

o·pin·ion (ō-pĭn′yŭn), *n.* **1,** belief; what one thinks about any subject; as, that is my *opinion;* **2,** estimation; as, I have a good *opinion* of him; **3,** the formal statement of an expert; as, a doctor's *opinion.*

Syn. notion, view, idea, sentiment.

o·pin·ion·at·ed (ō-pĭn′yŭn-āt′ĕd), *adj.* firm or obstinate in opinion or belief.

o·pi·um (ō′pĭ-ŭm), *n.* a powerful drug, which is used to cause sleep and dull pain. It is obtained from the juices of a certain kind of poppy.

O·por·to (ō-pôr′tō), a seaport in northwestern Portugal, on the Atlantic Coast (map **12**). Its Portuguese name is *Porto.*

o·pos·sum (ō-pŏs′ŭm), *n.* a small American animal with dark-grayish fur, which lives in trees and, if captured or in danger, pretends to be dead.

op·po·nent (ŏ-pō′nĕnt), *n.* one who works against, or takes the opposite side from, another, in a debate, race, game, or the like; a rival:—*adj.* acting against each other; as, *opponent* forces.

Syn., n. adversary, foe.

OPOSSUM (₁⅒)

op·por·tune (ŏp′ŏr-tūn′; ŏp′ŏr-tūn), *adj.* well-timed; convenient; suitable; as, this is an *opportune* time to start the campaign.—*adv.* op′por-tune′ly.

op·por·tun·ist (ŏp′ŏr-tūn′ĭst), *n.* one who takes advantage of circumstances to advance his own interest, regardless of what is right.—*n.* op′por-tun′ism.

op·por·tu·ni·ty (ŏp′ŏr-tū′nĭ-tĭ), *n.* [*pl.* opportunities], convenient time or occasion for something; a good chance; as, I have not had the *opportunity* to ask him.

op·pose (ŏ-pōz′), *v.t.* [opposed, oppos-ing], **1**, to stand in the way of; resist; to object to; as, to *oppose* a candidate's election; **2**, to set up in opposition or in contrast; as, to *oppose* one idea to another.
Syn. withstand, obstruct, prevent.

op·po·site (ŏp′ŏ-zĭt), *adj.* **1**, placed or standing in front of; facing; as, the *opposite* side of the street; the houses were *opposite* to each other; **2**, contrary; as, in the *opposite* way; **3**, antagonistic; very different; as, *opposite* opinions:—*n* one who or that which is contrary or in marked contrast; as, "slow" is the *opposite* of "fast."—*adv.* **op′po-site-ly.**

op·po·si·tion (ŏp′ŏ-zĭsh′ŭn), *n.* **1**, the act of placing one thing opposite or over against another; also, the state of being so placed; **2**, resistance; as, *opposition* to authority; **3**, one who or that which is opposite or contrary to another; especially, a political party not in power.

op·press (ŏ-prĕs′), *v.t.* **1**, to crush by hardships or severity; treat with cruelty; as, the cruel ruler *oppressed* his subjects; **2**, to weigh heavily upon; burden; as, sorrow *oppressed* him.—*n.* **op-pres′sor.**

op·pres·sion (ŏ-prĕsh′ŭn), *n.* **1**, cruel and unjust exercise of power; tyranny; as, the *oppression* suffered by a conquered nation; **2**, uneasiness or distress of mind or body; weariness; depression.

op·pres·sive (ŏ-prĕs′ĭv), *adj.* **1**, unreasonably burdensome; as, *oppressive* laws; **2**, unjustly severe; tyrannical; as, an *oppressive* ruler; **3**, overpowering; as, the *oppressive* air of a closed room.

op·pro·bri·ous (ŏ-prō′brĭ-ŭs), *adj.* **1**, expressing reproach; abusive; as, *opprobrious* language; **2**, vile; disgraceful; as, *opprobrious* conduct.—*adv.* **op-pro′bri-ous-ly.**
Syn. reproachful, insulting, offensive.

op·pro·bri·um (ŏ-prō′brĭ-ŭm), *n.* disgrace or reproach as a result of wrongdoing.

op·tic (ŏp′tĭk), *adj.* pertaining to the eye or to vision:—**optic nerve,** the nerve running from the eye to the centers of the brain which control the sense of sight.

op·ti·cal (ŏp′tĭ-kăl), *adj.* **1**, pertaining to the science of light and vision; **2**, pertaining to the eyesight; **3**, constructed to aid the vision; as, *optical* instruments.

op·ti·cian (ŏp-tĭsh′ăn), *n.* one who makes or sells eyeglasses, lenses, and other optical instruments.

op·tics (ŏp′tĭks), *n.pl.* used as *sing.* the science which treats of light, the laws of vision, and the construction of optical instruments, as microscopes, telescopes, etc.

op·ti·mism (ŏp′tĭ-mĭzm), *n.* **1**, the belief that everything in life happens for the best; **2**, the inclination to look on the best side of things: opposite of *pessimism.*

op·ti·mist (ŏp′tĭ-mĭst), *n.* one who believes that all things happen for the best; one who looks on the bright side of things: opposite of *pessimist.*

op·ti·mis·tic (ŏp′tĭ-mĭs′tĭk), *adj.* hopeful; inclined to look upon the bright side of things and to believe that everything happens for the best.
Syn. cheerful, confident, sanguine.

op·tion (ŏp′shŭn), *n.* **1**, the right or power of choosing; as, you have the *option* of taking it or leaving it; **2**, the act of choosing; choice; **3**, that which can be or is chosen; **4**, a right, usually purchased, to buy or sell something at a specified price within a specified time.
Syn. preference, alternative.

op·tion·al (ŏp′shŭn-ăl), *adj.* left to one's wish or choice; elective; as, *optional* courses of study.—*adv.* **op′tion-al-ly.**

op·tom·e·trist (ŏp-tŏm′ē-trĭst), *n.* one who examines and tests the eyes for the purpose of fitting glasses to correct any visual defect.—*n.* **op-tom′e-try.**

op·u·lence (ŏp′ū-lĕns), *n.* great riches.

op·u·lent (ŏp′ū-lĕnt), *adj.* wealthy; rich.

o·pus (ō′pŭs; ŏp′ŭs), *n.* a work; especially, a musical composition.

or (ôr), *conj.* **1**, a connecting word introducing the second of two (or the last of several) possibilities; as, this book *or* that; go *or* stay, as you please; any city, town, *or* village: often used after *either* or *whether* to complete the sense; as, we'll go either tomorrow *or* Sunday; it is all the same whether you go *or* stay; **2**, that is; in other words; as, draw a triangle, *or* a figure with three sides; **3**, otherwise; else; as, you must hurry, *or* you will be late.

-or (-ôr), a suffix meaning a person or thing that; as, navigat*or*, regulat*or*.

Or. abbreviation for *Oregon.*

or·a·cle (ôr′à-kl), *n.* **1**, among the ancients, the reply of a god, through an inspired priest, to a question or petition; **2**, the place where a god was consulted; **3**, the person through whom the god spoke; **4**, a prophet or person of great wisdom.

o·rac·u·lar (ŏ-răk′ū-lẽr), *adj.* of the nature of an oracle or prophecy; solemn; very wise; difficult to understand.

or·al (ôr′ăl), *adj.* **1**, spoken; not written; as, an *oral* quiz; **2**, of or pertaining to the mouth; as, the *oral* cavity; **3**, using the lips in instructing the deaf; as, *oral* teaching.—*adv.* **or′al-ly.**

āte, āorta, râre, căt, ȧsk, fär, ăllow, sofà; ēve, ēvent, ĕll, writẽr, novĕl; bīte, pĭn; nō, ōbey, ôr, dŏg, tŏp, cŏllide; ūnit, ūnite, bûrn. cŭt, focŭs; nōon, fŏot; mound; coin;

or-ange (ŏr'ĕnj; ŏr'ĭnj), *n*. **1,** an evergreen tree with fragrant flowers and a deep golden-colored or reddish-yellow juicy fruit; **2,** the fruit itself; **3,** the golden or reddish-yellow color of such fruit:—*adj*. **1,** pertaining to such fruit; as, an *orange* grove; **2,** of a deep golden or reddish-yellow color.

ORANGE LEAVES AND BLOSSOMS

or-ange-ade (ŏr'ĕnj-ād'; ŏr'ĭnj-ād'), *n*. a drink of orange juice, sugar, and water.

Orange Free State, a province (cap. Bloemfontein) in the eastern part of the Union of South Africa (map **14**).

Or-ange Riv-er, the principal river in southern Africa, flowing west across the continent into the Atlantic Ocean (map **14**).

o-rang-u-tan (ō-răng'ōō-tăn'; ôr'ăng-ōō'tăn) or **o-rang-ou-tang** (ō-răng'ōō-tăng'), *n*. a large, reddish-brown manlike ape of Borneo and Sumatra.

ORANGUTAN (⅟₁₆)

o-ra-tion (ō-rā'shŭn), *n*. a formal and dignified public speech, especially one delivered on a particular occasion; as, a funeral *oration*.
    Syn. address, sermon.

or-a-tor (ŏr'à-tẽr), *n*. a public speaker, especially one of skill and power.

or-a-tor-i-cal (ŏr'à-tŏr'ĭ-kăl), *adj*. relating to, or suitable to, a skilful public speaker or to eloquent and dignified public speaking; as, *oratorical* gestures.

or-a-to-ri-o (ŏr'à-tôr'ĭ-ō), *n*. [*pl*. oratorios], in music, a dramatic poem on a sacred theme, sung with orchestral accompaniment, without action, scenery, or costume.

¹**or-a-tor-y** (ŏr'à-tôr'ĭ), *n*. the art of speaking well in public; eloquence or skill in public speaking.

²**or-a-tor-y** (ŏr'à-tôr'ĭ), *n*. [*pl*. oratories], a small chapel or room, especially one for private prayer.

orb (ôrb), *n*. a globe or sphere; especially, one of the heavenly bodies, as the moon.

or-bit (ôr'bĭt), *n*. **1,** the bony cavity which contains the eye; **2,** the course followed by one heavenly body around another, as the path of the earth around the sun.

or-chard (ôr'chẽrd), *n*. a place where fruit trees are grown; also, the trees themselves.

or-ches-tra (ôr'kĕs-trȧ), *n*. **1,** a band of performers on musical instruments, especially stringed instruments; **2,** the collection of instruments on which they play; **3,** in a theater or opera house, the place occupied by the musicians; also, the front part or all of the main floor of a theater.

or-ches-tral (ôr-kĕs'trăl), *adj*. relating to, suited to, or performed by, an orchestra or its instruments; as, *orchestral* music.

or-ches-tra-tion (ôr'kĕs-trā'shŭn), *n*. the arrangement of music for an orchestra.

or-chid (ôr'kĭd), *n*. **1,** any one of a large family of plants bearing blossoms with two petals similar, and a third (the lip) usually enlarged and often queerly shaped; **2,** the blossom of any of these plants.

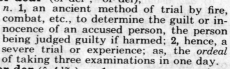

ORCHID

or-dain (ôr-dān'), *v.t*. **1,** to set apart for, or admit to, the Christian ministry or the priesthood by a special ceremony or rite; **2,** to give orders for; decree; regulate by law.

or-deal (ôr-dēl'; ôr'dēl), *n*. **1,** an ancient method of trial by fire, combat, etc., to determine the guilt or innocence of an accused person, the person being judged guilty if harmed; **2,** hence, a severe trial or experience; as, the *ordeal* of taking three examinations in one day.

or-der (ôr'dẽr), *n*. **1,** sequence; succession; as, alphabetical *order;* also, regular arrangement; as, the house is in *order;* **2,** a fixed method of acting; established custom; as, the *order* of church worship; **3,** public observance of law; as, *order* in the streets; **4,** working condition; as, the engine was out of *order;* **5,** rule; command; as, by *order* of the governor; **6,** a direction to buy, sell, or supply goods; as, an *order* for books; also, the goods bought or sold; **7,** a written direction to pay money; as, a money *order;* **8,** a rank, degree, or class in the social scale; as, the *order* of nobility; **9,** a group of persons united in a society; as, a Masonic *order;* a monastic society; as, the Franciscan *order;* **10,** the rank or degree of a priest or clergyman; as, the *order* of deacon, priest, bishop, etc.; **11,** a badge indicative of an honor or membership in a society; as, he wore all his *orders;* **12,** in botany and zoology, a group larger than the family and smaller than the class; as, the amaryllis and the iris belong to the same *order* but to different families; **13,** in architecture, the form of a column and the capital just above it; as, the Doric, Ionic, and Corinthian *orders* of Greek architecture:—*v.t.* **1,** to command; as, to *order* someone to appear before court; **2,** to regulate or manage; direct; **3,** to give an order for; as, to *order* coal.

in order that, to the end that; with the purpose in mind that; in order to, to; with the purpose of; to take orders, to enter the ministry; to order, according to directions; as, a suit made *to order*.

or·der·ly (ôr′dẽr-lǐ), *adj.* **1,** tidy; as, an *orderly* room; also, having regard for order and system; as, an *orderly* person; **2,** well conducted or managed; as, an *orderly* meeting; **3,** methodical; as, done in an *orderly* manner; **4,** peaceable; as, an *orderly* crowd:—*n.* [*pl.* orderlies], **1,** a soldier who attends an officer to carry his orders; **2,** a man who acts as attendant in a hospital.

or·di·nal (ôr′dǐ-năl), *n.* or **or·di·nal num·ber** (nŭm′bẽr), one of the numbers *first, second, third,* etc., showing order or position in a series: distinguished from *cardinal number,* as *one, two, three,* etc.

or·di·nance (ôr′dǐ-năns), *n.* an authoritative rule, law, or decree; as, a city *ordinance* against the sale of unbottled milk.

or·di·nar·i·ly (ôr′dǐ-nẽr′ǐ-lǐ; ôr′dǐ-nâr′-ǐ-lǐ), *adv.* usually; commonly.

or·di·nar·y (ôr′dǐ-nẽr′ǐ), *adj.* **1,** usual; customary; as, he followed his *ordinary* routine; **2,** commonplace; not distinguished; as, an *ordinary* dress; an *ordinary* pupil.

   Syn. regular, common, normal, average.

or·di·na·tion (ôr′dǐ-nā′shŭn), *n.* conferring of holy orders; admission to the Christian ministry.

ord·nance (ôrd′năns), *n.* **1,** the heavy guns used in warfare; **2,** military supplies.

or·dure (ôr′dūr), *n.* dung; filth.

ore (ôr), *n.* a metal-bearing mineral or rock, especially one containing sufficient metal to be commercially valuable.

Oreg. or **Ore.** abbreviation for *Oregon.*

Or·e·gon (ŏr′ē-gŏn), a northwestern State (cap. Salem) in the U.S., on the Pacific Coast (map 9).

or·gan (ôr′găn), *n.* **1,** a part of a plant or animal fitted for a special use; as, the ear is the *organ* of hearing; **2,** a medium of public communication, as a newspaper; **3,** an agency by which something is done; as, the court is an *organ* of justice; **4,** a large, musical wind instrument with one or many sets of pipes, sounded by air blown from bellows, and played by one or more keyboards.

ORGAN

or·gan·dy or **or·gan·die** (ôr′găn-dǐ), *n.* a fine, thin, stiff muslin, used for dresses, curtains, trimmings, etc.

or·gan·ic (ôr-găn′ĭk), *adj.* **1,** of, relating to, or affecting, some organ of the body; as, an *organic* disease; **2,** relating to, or derived from, something that lives or has lived; as, fossils are remains of *organic* bodies; **3,** belonging to, or inherent in, the organization or constitution of something; fundamental; as, an *organic* fault; **4,** having a systematic arrangement of parts; as, an *organic* whole.

or·gan·ism (ôr′găn-ĭzm), *n.* **1,** a living being composed of parts performing special duties, but dependent upon each other; **2,** anything like such a body in having many parts; as, the social *organism*.

or·gan·ist (ôr′găn-ĭst), *n.* a person who plays the organ.

or·gan·i·za·tion (ôr′găn-ĭ-zā′shŭn; -ĭ-zā′-shŭn), *n.* **1,** the act of grouping and arranging related parts into one whole, or the condition of being so organized; as, the *organization* of a campaign; the *organization* of a club; **2,** a body made up of parts dependent upon one another but each functioning separately; also, the way in which the separate parts of a living being are united in a whole; as, the *organization* of the human body; **3,** a body of persons united for some end or work.

or·gan·ize (ôr′găn-īz), *v.t.* [organized, organiz·ing], to cause to unite and work together in orderly fashion; as, to *organize* forces for a campaign; to arrange in good order; as, to *organize* one's facts:—*v.i.* to become organized.—*n.* or′gan·iz′er.

or·gy (ôr′jǐ), *n.* [*pl.* orgies], **1,** among the ancient Greeks and Romans, a secret celebration in honor of the gods, especially the god of wine, accompanied by wild singing, dancing, etc.; **2,** a drunken revel.

or·i·el (ôr′ĭ-ĕl), *n.* a window, either curved or with angles, projecting from the outside wall of a building and often supported by brackets.

ORIEL WINDOW

or·i·ent (ôr′ĭ-ĕnt; ôr′ĭ-ĕnt), *n.* the east: opposite of *occident* or west:—**Orient,** the countries of Asia, or the Far East, and the countries bordering the eastern Mediterranean, or the Near East: opposite of *Occident:*—*adj.* **1,** rising; dawning; **2,** bright; clear, as pearls; **3,** *Poetic,* eastern:—*v.t.* **1,** to place so as to face the east; **2,** to place (a person or oneself) in right relation to unfamiliar conditions.—*adj.* and *n.* or′i·en′tal; Or′i·en′tal (ôr′ĭ-ĕn′tăl).

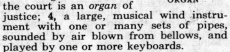

āte, âorta, râre, căt, ȧsk, fär, ăllow, sof*à*; ēve, ĕvent, ĕll, writẽr, novĕl; bīte, pĭn; nō, ōbey, ôr, dŏg, tŏp, cŏllide; ūnit, ūnite, bûrn, cŭt, focŭs; nōōn, fŏŏt; mound; coin;

or·i·en·tate (ôr′ĭ-ĕn-tāt′; ôr′ĭ-ĕn′tāt), *v.t.* [orientat-ed, orientat-ing], **1,** to place so as to face the east; **2,** to bring into a correct relation.

or·i·fice (ôr′ĭ-fĭs), *n.* a mouth or opening.

orig. abbreviation for *origin, originally.*

or·i·gin (ôr′ĭ-jĭn), *n.* **1,** a source; beginning; as, theories about the *origin* of man; **2,** hence, parentage; ancestry.
Syn. root, commencement, inception.

o·rig·i·nal (ô-rĭj′ĭ-năl), *adj.* **1,** of or relating to the beginning; first in existence or order; primary; as, the *original* edition of a book; **2,** not copied; as, an *original* painting; not translated; as, he read the story in the *original* French; **3,** new; as, an *original* idea; **4,** able to create or invent something new; as, an *original* writer:—*n.* **1,** that from which anything is copied; as, the *original* of that picture is in the museum; **2,** the literary text, or the language of such a text, from which a translation is made; **3,** an unusual person.
Syn., adj. primitive, novel, fresh.

o·rig·i·nal·i·ty (ô-rĭj′ĭ-năl′ĭ-tĭ), *n.* [*pl.* originalities], **1,** the ability to create or make something new; as, the *originality* of an inventor; **2,** the quality of being new or novel; as, the *originality* of a story.

o·rig·i·nal·ly (ô-rĭj′ĭ-năl-ĭ), *adv.* **1,** at first; as, the club *originally* had twenty members; **2,** in a new and striking manner; as, to speak or write *originally.*

o·rig·i·nate (ô-rĭj′ĭ-nāt), *v.t.* [originat-ed, originat-ing], to bring into existence; invent; create; as, to *originate* a style of dancing:—*v.i.* to begin to exist; start; as, the fire *originated* in the chemical room.—*n.* o·rig′i·na′tion.—*n.* o·rig′i·na′tor.

Or·i·no·co (ôr′ĭ-nō′kō), a large river in northern South America (map **11**).

or·i·ole (ôr′ĭ-ōl), *n.* **1,** any of various black-and-yellow songbirds of the Old World, akin to the crow, which build hanging nests; **2,** any of various American songbirds which build hanging nests, as the orange-and-black Baltimore oriole and the black-and-chestnut orchard oriole.

BALTIMORE ORIOLE
(⅛)

O·ri·on (ô-rī′ŏn), *n.* in mythology, a hunter slain by Artemis; in astronomy, a large constellation with three bright stars in a line known as the Belt, or Girdle, of Orion.

or·i·son (ôr′ĭ-zŭn), *n.* a prayer.

Ork·ney Is·lands (ôrk′nĭ), a group of islands northeast of Scotland (map **13**).

Or·lé·ans (ôr′lā′än′), or **Or·leans** (ôr′-lēnz), city in north central France, famous for its deliverance by Joan of Arc (map **12**).

or·na·ment (ôr′nȧ-mĕnt), *n.* **1,** anything that adorns; decoration; as, Christmas-tree *ornaments;* **2,** a thing or person that adds beauty, honor, or grace to the surroundings:—*v.t.* (ôr′nȧ-mĕnt), to adorn; bedeck; as, to *ornament* a hall with holly.—*adj.* or′na-men′tal.

or·na·men·ta·tion (ôr′nȧ-mĕn-tā′shŭn), *n.* **1,** the act of decorating or the state of being decorated; **2,** decorations.

or·nate (ôr-nāt′), *adj.* elaborately decorated or adorned.

or·ni·thol·o·gy (ôr′nĭ-thŏl′ō-jĭ), *n.* the scientific study of birds.—*n.* or′ni-thol′-o-gist.—*adj.* or′ni-tho-log′i-cal.

or·o·tund (ôr′ō-tŭnd; ŏr′ō-tŭnd), *adj.* **1,** having a full, clear, smooth quality; as, an *orotund* voice; **2,** imposing; pompous.

or·phan (ôr′făn), *n.* a child who has lost one or, more commonly, both parents by death:—*adj.* being without parents:—*v.t.* to deprive of a parent or parents.

or·phan·age (ôr′făn-ĭj), *n.* an institution or home for the care of orphans.

Or·pheus (ôr′fūs; ôr′fē-ŭs), *n.* in Greek mythology, a poet and musician who played with such charm that even rocks and trees wept at the sound of his lyre.

or·ris (ŏr′ĭs), *n.* a European iris or its root which, when dried and ground into a powder, is used in perfume, medicine, tooth powder, etc : also called *orrisroot.*

or·tho·dox (ôr′thō-dŏks), *adj.* **1,** holding the accepted opinion, especially in regard to religion; **2,** approved; accepted; also, conventional; as, *orthodox* behavior.

Orthodox Church, the form of the Catholic Church found in Greece, the Balkan States, and the U.S.S.R., which does not acknowledge the Pope as its head: also called the *Eastern* or *Greek Church.*

or·tho·dox·y (ôr′thō-dŏk′sĭ), *n.* [*pl.* orthodoxies], a holding to the generally accepted belief, especially in religion.

or·thog·ra·phy (ôr-thŏg′rȧ-fĭ), *n.* [*pl.* orthographies], the art of spelling words correctly; also, the method of spelling.—*adj.* or′tho-graph′ic (ôr′thō-grăf′ĭk).

or·thol·o·gy (ôr-thŏl′ō-jĭ), *n.* the art of using words correctly.—*adj.* or′tho-log′i-cal.—*n.* or′tho-lo′gi-an.

or·tho·pe·dics or **or·tho·pae·dics** (ôr′-thō-pē′dĭks), *n.pl.* used as *sing.* the prevention or treatment of deformities, especially in young children.—*adj.* or′tho-pe′dic or or′tho-pae′dic.

or·to·lan (ôr′tô-lăn), *n.* **1,** a European and African bird, much prized for its flesh; **2,** in the U.S., the bobolink.

or·y (-ôr′ĭ), a suffix meaning: **1,** concerned with; as, sens*ory*, supervis*ory;* **2,** a place for or of; as, manufact*ory*, depos*itory*.

or·yx (ôr′ĭks; ŏr′ĭks), *n.* a kind of African antelope with long, almost straight, horns. (See illustration under *antelope*.)

O·sa·ka (ō′sȧ-kȧ), a seaport on the southern coast of Honshu, Japan (map **15**).

os·cil·late (ŏs′ĭ-lāt), *v.i.* [oscillat-ed, os-cillat-ing], **1,** to swing back and forth, as the pendulum of a clock; **2,** to pass back and forth from one state to another; vary; as, to *oscillate* between two opinions.

os·cil·la·tion (ŏs′ĭ-lā′shŭn), *n.* **1,** a swinging back and forth, as of a pendulum; **2,** a wavering, as between two opinions.

os·cu·late (ŏs′kŭ-lāt), *v.t.* and *v.i.* [osculat-ed, osculat-ing], to kiss.

o·sier (ō′zhẽr), *n.* **1,** a willow, the twigs of which are used in baskets, furniture, etc.; **2,** a twig of this willow.

·os·i·ty (-ŏs′ĭ-tĭ), a suffix meaning quality or state of being; as, curi*osity*.

Os·lo (ŏs′lō), a city, capital of Norway (map **12**). Its name until 1925 was *Kristiania*.

os·prey (ŏs′prĭ), *n.* a large fish-eating hawk.

Os·sa (ŏs′ȧ), *n.* a mountain in Thessaly. In Greek mythology, the Titans, in their war with the gods, piled Pelion on Ossa in their attempt to scale Olympus, the abode of the gods.

os·si·fi·ca·tion (ŏs′-ĭ-fĭ-kā′shŭn), *n.* **1,** the act of changing into bone; **2,** the state of being changed into bone; **3,** that which has become hardened or changed into bone.

OSPREY (¹⁄₁₆)

os·si·fy (ŏs′ĭ-fī), *v.t.* and *v.i.* [ossified, ossi-fy-ing], **1,** to form or change into bone; **2,** to harden or become hardened, narrow-minded, or unprogressive.

os·ten·si·ble (ŏs-tĕn′sĭ-bl), *adj.* professed; apparent; as, an *ostensible* reason.

os·ten·si·bly (ŏs-tĕn′sĭ-blĭ), *adv.* appar-ently; seemingly; as, *ostensibly* friendly, he was in reality hostile to the cause.

os·ten·ta·tion (ŏs′tĕn-tā′shŭn), *n.* un-necessary show; ambitious or vain display.

os·ten·ta·tious (ŏs′tĕn-tā′shŭs), *adj.* fond of show; showy; also, intended for vain display; as, *ostentatious* jewelry.

os·te·o·path (ŏs′tē-ō-păth), *n.* one who practices osteopathy.—*adj.* **os′te-o-path′ic.**

os·te·op·a·thy (ŏs′tē-ŏp′á-thĭ), *n.* a sys-tem of medicine which, while recognizing the value of ordinary medical and surgical treatment, holds that disease is chiefly due to displacements of parts of the body, espe-cially of the bones of the spinal column, and in healing lays stress on working the displaced parts into place with the hands.

Ös·ter·reich (ös′tẽr-rīkh), German name for Austria.

ost·ler (ŏs′lẽr), *n.* a hostler. See **hostler.**

os·tra·cism (ŏs′trȧ-sĭzm), *n.* **1,** in ancient Greece, temporary banishment by popular vote for a period of five to ten years; **2,** exclusion from favor or privileges by general consent; as, social *ostracism*.

os·tra·cize (ŏs′trȧ-sīz), *v.t.* [ostracized, ostraciz-ing], **1,** among the ancient Greeks, to banish by popular vote; **2,** to bar from favor; as, he was *ostracized* by society.

os·trich (ŏs′trĭch), *n.* a swift-running African bird which can-not fly. It is the larg-est bird known, and is highly valued for its feathers.

O.T. abbreviation for *Old Testament*.

O·thel·lo (ô-thĕl′ō), *n.* the name of a tragedy by Shakespeare; also, the hero of the play, who, in a fit of jeal-ousy, smothered his wife, Desdemona, and later killed himself.

OSTRICH (¹⁄₅₀)

oth·er (ŭth′ẽr), *adj.* **1,** not the same; different; as, I have *other* matters to attend to; **2,** additional; more; as, I have *other* sisters; **3,** opposite; as, the *other* side of the street; **4,** alternating; second; as, every *other* line:—*adv.* other-wise; as, she could not do *other* than help him:—*pron.* and *n.* **1,** the second person or thing of two; as, one or the *other* of you must do it; some boys stayed, *others* left; they fought each *other;* **2,** a different per-son or thing; as, do good to *others;* have you any *other*? there will be many *others* here; the few *others* I have.

the other day, a day recently passed; **the other world,** the life after death.

oth·er·wise (ŭth′ẽr-wīz′), *adv.* **1,** in a different way; differently; as, you evi-dently think *otherwise;* **2,** in different conditions or respects; as, I know him professionally, but not *otherwise*:—*conj.* else; as, it was told me in confidence, *otherwise* I would tell you:—*adj.* different; as, the facts were *otherwise*.

āte, āorta, râre, căt, ȧsk, fär, ȧllow, sofȧ; ēve, ĕvent, ĕll, wrītẽr, nŏvĕl; bīte, pĭn; nō, ōbey, ôr, dŏg, tŏp, cŏllide; ūnit, ūnite, bûrn, cŭt, focŭs; nōōn, fŏŏt; mound; coin;

Ot-ta-wa (ŏt′a̤-wȧ), a city, capital of Canada, in eastern Ontario (map **4**).

ot-ter (ŏt′ĕr), *n.* **1,** a fish-eating animal which lives in and near the water and is valued for its fur; **2,** the fur of this animal.

OTTER (1/25)

Ot-to-man (ŏt′ō-măn), *adj.* Turkish:—*n.* [*pl.* Ottomans], a Turk:— **ottoman, 1,** a stuffed couch without a back; **2,** a stuffed footstool.

OTTOMAN

Ot-to-man Em-pire, the former name of the Turkish Empire. See **Turkey.**

ouch (ouch), *interj.* an exclamation of sudden pain.

¹**ought** (ôt), *v.i.* [no other form], **1,** to be or feel bound, obliged, or under obligation; as, we *ought* to finish our work; we *ought* to have paid the men; **2,** to be expected; as, this top *ought* to fit the jar; you *ought* to have been able to go; **3,** to be forced by necessity; as, we *ought* to go at once if he is to get his train; **4,** to need; as, this dress *ought* to have a collar.
   Syn. must, should.

²**ought** (ôt), *n.* **1,** anything; any part; **2,** carelessly, in arithmetic, nought or zero.

ounce (ouns), *n.* **1,** a weight of 1/16 of a pound avoirdupois; **2,** a weight of 1/12 of a pound in either troy or apothecaries' weight; **3,** a small amount; as, "an *ounce* of prevention is worth a pound of cure."

our (our), *adj.* a possessive form or the personal pronoun *we:* **1,** belonging to us; as, *our* house; **2,** of or relating to us; as, *our* children; in *our* midst.

ours (ourz), a possessive form of the personal pronoun *we,* used alone: **1,** as *adj.,* in the predicate, belonging to us; as, whose is that car? it is *ours;* **2,** as *pron.,* a person or thing that belongs to us; as, their car is black, *ours* is blue.

our-self (our-sĕlf′), *pron.* I myself: used only in formal speech or writing; as, the king said, "*ourself* will pardon him."

our-selves (our-sĕlvz′), *pron.* **1,** a reflexive form of *us;* as, we fooled *ourselves* instead; **2,** an emphatic form of *we;* as, we *ourselves* will do it.

oust (oust), *v.t.* to drive, push, or turn out; as, to *oust* a person from a position.

out (out), *adv.* **1,** outdoors; not within doors; as, stay *out* in the fresh air; not in; not at home; as, she is *out* today; not within the limits; as, he is *out* of town; at liberty; as, *out* on bail; **2,** abroad; away from home; forth; as, to go *out* to India; to send a chair *out* to be fixed; **3,** not in a state or condition; as, *out* of practice; my elbow is *out* of joint; not in power or office; as, the leaders are *out;* **4,** forth from concealment; as, the sun came *out;* he brought *out* an old bag; in or into full bloom; as, the flowers are *out;* into the open; as, the story came *out;* **5,** to or at a conclusion or end; as, the fire burned *out;* to figure *out* a problem; March went *out* like a lion; **6,** from one's possession or use to another's; as, he lends *out* money; the father parceled *out* the land to his sons; **7,** in error; as, your figures are *out;* **8,** minus; as, he is *out* five dollars; **9,** so as to clear of obstruction; as, to sweep *out* a room; **10,** on strike; as, the workers are *out;* **11,** loudly; without restraint; as, to cry *out;* **12,** in baseball: **a,** not at bat, as a team; fielding; **b,** deprived of the right to continue at bat or to continue a run around the bases for a score:—*v.i.* to come into view; to become known; as, the truth will *out.*

out—and—out (out′-ănd-out′), *adj.* complete; thorough; utter; great; as, an *out-and-out* injustice; an *out-and-out* scoundrel.

out-bid (out-bĭd′), *v.t.* [outbid, outbidding], to offer to pay more for something than (another person); as, he *outbid* all other bidders at the auction.

out-board (out′bôrd′), *adj.* located on, or attached to, the outside of a boat; as, an *outboard* motor.

out-bound (out′bound′), *adj.* outward bound; leaving a port, railway terminal, or the like; as, a ship *outbound* for Europe.

out-break (out′brāk′), *n.* **1,** a sudden bursting forth; an epidemic; as, an *outbreak* of scarlet fever; **2,** a revolt; riot.

out-build-ing (out′bĭl′dĭng), *n.* a shed or building set apart from a house.

out-burst (out′bûrst′), *n.* a breaking forth; outbreak; as, an *outburst* of anger.

out-cast (out′kȧst′), *n.* one who is driven from home, friends, or country; an exile:—*adj.* friendless; homeless; hence, also, forlorn; wretched.

out-class (out-klȧs′), *v.t.* to surpass or excel in quality, skill, etc.

out-come (out′kŭm′), *n.* the result or consequence of an act.

out-crop (out′krŏp′), *n.* something which comes to the surface, as a layer of rock through the soil:—*v.i.* (out-krŏp′), [outcropped, outcrop-ping], to come out, especially to the surface of the ground.

out-cry (out′krī′), *n.* [*pl.* outcries], a loud cry; clamor; uproar; confused noise.

go; join; yet; sing; chin; show; thin, *th*en; hw, *wh*y; zh, azure; ü, Ger. für or Fr. lune; ö, Ger. schön or Fr. feu; ṅ, Fr. enfant, nom; kh, Ger. ach or ich. See pages ix–x

out-dis-tance (out-dĭs/tăns), *v.t.* [outdistanced, outdistanc-ing], to outstrip; surpass, especially in a race.

out-do (out-dōō/), *v.t.* [*p.t.* outdid (-dĭd/), *p.p.* outdone (-dŭn/), *p.pr.* outdo-ing], to surpass; excel.

out-door (out/dôr/) or **out-doors** (-dôrz/), *adj.* 1, not inside the walls of a building; done, used, or played in the open air; 2, fond of outdoor life; as, an *outdoor* person.

out-doors (out/dôrz/), *n.* the world outside of the walls of buildings:—*adv.* (out/dôrz/), outside of a building; in the open air; as, let's go *outdoors*.

out-er (out/ẽr), *adj.* on the outside; farther out; as, *outer* garments; *outer* fortifications.

out-er-most (out/ẽr-mōst), *adj.* farthest outside; farthest from the center or inside; as, the *outermost* layer of birch bark.

out-field (out/fēld/), *n.* 1, in baseball, the part of the field outside or beyond the diamond; 2, the players who play in the outfield.—*n.* out/field/er.

out-fit (out/fĭt), *n.* all the articles required for a special purpose; equipment; as, a camping *outfit;* a baseball *outfit:*—*v.t.* (out/fĭt/), [outfit-ted, outfit-ting], to furnish with an outfit.—*n.* out/fit/ter.

out-flank (out-flăngk/), *v.t.* to go or pass around the side or wing of (an army, fleet, or the like).

out-gen-er-al (out-jĕn/ẽr-ăl), *v.t.* to excel in military skill; hence, to outwit.

out-go (out/gō/), *n.* [*pl.* outgoes], that which goes out or is paid out; outlay; as, the *outgo* was greater than the income.

out-go-ing (out/gō/ĭng), *adj.* leaving; departing; as, *outgoing* baggage; also, going out of office; as, the *outgoing* president:—*n.* 1, departure; 2, expense.

out-grow (out-grō/), *v.t.* [*p.t.* outgrew (-grōō/), *p.p.* outgrown (-grōn/), *p.pr.* outgrow-ing], 1, to excel in growing; as, weeds *outgrow* crops; 2, to grow away from; as, to *outgrow* a habit; 3, to become too big for; as, to *outgrow* clothes.

out-growth (out/grōth/), *n.* anything that grows out of anything else; a result.

out-house (out/hous/), *n.* a building belonging to, but apart from, a main house, as a barn, stable, or the like.

out-ing (out/ĭng), *n.* a short excursion or pleasure trip; especially, a party or a walk in the open air.

out-land-er (out/lăn/dẽr), *n.* one who is not a native of a country; a foreigner.

out-land-ish (out-lăn/dĭsh), *adj.* strange; unfamiliar; odd; as, *outlandish* dress.

out-last (out-làst/), *v.t.* to last longer than; outlive; as, these shoes will *outlast* the others.

out-law (out/lô/), *n.* 1, one who is deprived of the benefits and protection of the law; 2, one who flees from the law; a lawless wanderer:—*v.t.* 1, to deprive of legal benefits and protection; as, to *outlaw* a criminal; 2, to remove from legal control; to put beyond the power of the law to enforce or collect; as, to *outlaw* a debt. —*n.* out/law/ry.

out-lay (out/lā/), *n.* that which is spent, either money or effort, in an undertaking; cost; expenditure; as, an *outlay* of several thousand dollars.

out-let (out/lĕt), *n.* 1, a means of escape; as, games are an *outlet* for a child's energy; 2, a passage or way out; as, the *outlet* of a lake.

out-line (out/līn/), *n.* 1, a line showing the outer limits of an object; 2, a drawing, or manner of drawing, showing shapes or contours without light and shade; 3, a draft or sketch of a story, speech, or the like:—*v.t.* [outlined, outlin-ing], 1, to draw the outline of; 2, to state the plan of.

out-live (out-lĭv/), *v.t.* [outlived, outliv-ing], to last longer than; survive; as, the man *outlived* his wife ten years; he *outlived* his dishonor.

out-look (out/lŏŏk/), *n.* 1, a view seen from a point of vantage, as from a window; 2, the place from which such a view is obtained; lookout; 3, the present state or future prospect of things; as, a favorable *outlook;* 4, point of view; attitude; as, a happy *outlook* on life.

out-ly-ing (out/lī/ĭng), *adj.* far from the center or main body; remote; as, the *outlying* districts of the city.

out-num-ber (out-nŭm/bẽr), *v.t.* to be superior in number to; exceed in number; as, the enemy *outnumbered* us by 5,000.

out-of-date (out/≈ŏv≈dāt/), *adj.* no longer in fashion; as, *out-of-date* styles in dress.

out-of-door (out/≈ŏv≈dôr/) or **out-of-doors** (-dôrz/), *adj.* outside a building; outdoor.—*n.* and *adv.* out/—of—doors/.

out-of-the-way (out/≈ŏv≈thē≈wā/), *adj.* 1, hard to reach or find; remote; hidden; as, an *out-of-the-way* village; 2, hence, strange; unusual; as, *out-of-the-way* events.

out-post (out/pōst/), *n.* 1, a soldier or body of troops stationed at a distance from the main army to guard against a surprise attack; 2, the place so occupied.

out-pour-ing (out/pôr/ĭng), *n.* an overflow; outburst; as, an *outpouring* of enthusiasm greeted the flier's arrival.

āte, āorta, râre, căt, ȧsk, fär, ăllow, sofȧ; ēve, ēvent, ĕll, writẽr, novĕl; bīte, pĭn; nō, ōbey, ôr, dŏg, tŏp, cȯllide; ūnit, ūnite, bûrn, cŭt, focŭs; nōōn, fŏŏt; mound; coin;

out-put (out′pŏŏt′), *n.* the amount put out or produced, as from a mine, mill, or the like; the yield.

out-rage (out′rāj), *n.* gross insult or wrong; a cruel or violent act:—*v.t.* [outraged, outrag-ing], **1**, to inflict shame or wrong upon; to injure violently or grievously; **2**, to be contrary to; as, his drunkenness *outraged* all decency.
  Syn., *n.* abuse, violence, affront.

out-ra-geous (out-rā′jŭs), *adj.* atrocious; excessive; beyond all bounds of decency and right; shocking; as, his conduct was *outrageous.*—*adv.* **out-ra′geous-ly.**

out-rank (out-răngk′), *v.t.* to exceed in rank; to be superior to.

out-ride (out-rīd′), *v.t.* [*p.t.* outrode (-rōd′), *p.p.* outrid-den (-rĭd′n), *p.pr.* outrid-ing], to ride better or faster than; outstrip in riding; as, the scout *outrode* his pursuers.

out-rid-er (out′rī′dĕr), *n.* a groom who rides on horseback beside a carriage; as, the coach of the emperor was attended by six *outriders.*

out-rig-ger (out′rĭg′-ĕr), *n.* any projecting board, beam, pole, or framework attached to a ship to keep it from upsetting, to act as a means for extending sails, to support an oarlock, etc.; also, a boat thus fitted out.

OUTRIGGERS (O, O)

out-right (out′rīt′; out′rīt′), *adv.* **1**, not by instalments; all at once; as, to buy *outright;* **2**, at once; immediately; as, killed *outright;* **3**, straightforwardly:—*adj.* (out′-rīt′; out′rīt′), downright; straightforward; out-and-out; as, an *outright* denial.

out-run (out-rŭn′), *v.t.* [*p.t.* outran (-răn′), *p.p.* outrun, *p.pr.* outrun-ning], **1**, to run faster than; get ahead of by running; **2**, hence, to pass beyond; as, his ambition *outran* his ability.

out-set (out′sĕt′), *n.* a start; the beginning, as of a business or journey.

out-shine (out-shīn′), *v.t.* [*p.t.* and *p.p.* outshone (-shōn′; -shŏn′), *p.pr.* outshin-ing], **1**, to shine more brightly than; surpass in brightness; **2**, hence, to excel; as, John *outshines* the rest in arithmetic.

out-side (out′sīd′), *n.* **1**, the part of anything that is on the surface or that is seen; **2**, the farthest limit; as, I shall return in a week at the *outside:*—*adj.* **1**, of or on the surface; exterior; external; **2**, of or from one who does not belong to a group; as, *outside* help; **3**, apart from one's regular duties; as, *outside* interests:—*adv.* **1**, on or to the outer side; as, painted

green *outside;* **2**, outdoors; as, to go *outside:*—*prep.* (out′sīd′; out′sīd′), beyond the limits of; on the outer side of.

out-sid-er (out′sī′dĕr), *n.* one who does not belong to a given group, company, etc.

out-skirts (out′skûrts′), *n.pl.* edge or edges; outlying part or parts; as, she lives on the *outskirts* of the town.

out-spo-ken (out′spō′kĕn), *adj.* free or bold of speech; frank; as, he was *outspoken* in his criticism.—*adv.* **out′spo′ken-ly.**

out-spread (out-sprĕd′), *v.t.* to extend; spread out:—*v.i.* to extend; expand.

out-stand-ing (out-stăn′dĭng), *adj.* **1**, prominent, as a person; **2**, unpaid, as debts.

out-stretched (out-strĕcht′), *adj.* extended; stretched forth; as, *outstretched* hands.

out-strip (out-strĭp′), *v.t.* [outstripped, outstrip-ping], **1**, to outrun, as in a race; **2**, to excel; surpass.

out-ward (out′wĕrd), *adj.* **1**, of or on the outside; external; as, *outward* appearance; **2**, away from the shore; as, the *outward* course of a ship; **3**, visible; apparent; as, *outward* show:—*adv.* **1**, from the inside; toward the outside; as, to move *outward;* to face *outward;* **2**, away from a place; as, the ship was *outward* bound.

out-ward-ly (out′wĕrd-lĭ), *adv.* on the surface; in appearance; as, she remained *outwardly* calm.

out-wards (out′wĕrdz), *adv.* toward the outside; outward.

out-wear (out-wâr′), *v.t.* [*p.t.* outwore (-wôr′), *p.p.* outworn (-wôrn′), *p.pr.* outwear-ing], **1**, to wear out; to use up; **2**, to last longer than; as, these shoes will *outwear* those; **3**, to outlive; outgrow.

out-weigh (out-wā′), *v.t.* to surpass in weight, value, importance, etc.

out-wit (out-wĭt′), *v.t.* [outwit-ted, outwit-ting], to get the better of by superior skill or cunning; as, to *outwit* an enemy.
  Syn. foil, baffle, circumvent, thwart.

out-work (out′wûrk′), *n.* a defense or protection built beyond the main body of a fort:—*v.t.* (out-wûrk′), to work faster or better than; outdo.

out-worn (out′wôrn′), *adj.* **1**, worn out; as, *outworn* shoes; **2**, out-of-date; as, an *outworn* point of view.

o-va (ō′vȧ), plural of *ovum.*

o-val (ō′văl; ō′vl), *adj.* shaped like an egg:—*n.* anything egg-shaped; an ellipse-like curve with one end broader than the other.

OVAL.
1, ellipse; 2, oval.

o-va-ry (ō′vȧ-rĭ), *n.* [*pl.* ovaries], **1**, in a female animal, the organ in which the ova, or egg cells, are formed; **2,** the part of a plant in which the seeds are formed (see illustration under *flower*). —*adj.* **o-var'i-an** (ō-vâr'ĭ-ăn).

o-va-tion (ō-vā'shŭn), *n.* enthusiastic applause; a hearty public tribute; as, the fliers received a tremendous *ovation*.

ov-en (ŭv'ĕn), *n.* an enclosed chamber for baking, heating, or drying, especially one inside a stove or range.

ov-en-bird (ŭv'ĕn-bûrd'), *n.* a common American songbird which builds an oven-like nest on the ground.

o-ver (ō'vĕr), *prep.* **1,** above in position, authority, dignity, excellence, or the like; as, the sky is *over* our heads; a captain is *over* a lieutenant; a governor rules *over* the state; **2,** across; from one side to another; as, to jump *over* a ditch; **3,** on the surface of; upon; as, to wear a cape *over* the shoulders; to wander *over* the plains; **4,** more than; as, he spent *over* ten dollars; **5,** during; throughout; as, to stay *over* the weekend; **6,** along; as, to drive *over* a new road; **7,** on account of; as, to weep *over* defeat:—*adv.* **1,** from beginning to end; as, to talk the matter *over;* **2,** from one to another; as, to make *over* property; from one side to the other; as, to cross *over* to France; to go *over* to the enemy; **3,** in addition; remaining; as, all that is left *over;* **4,** so as to bring the under side up; as, to turn a coin *over;* so as to be upright no longer; as, to topple *over;* **5,** from end to end; throughout; as, a landscape dotted *over* with trees; **6,** again; once again; as, to do a thing *over;* **7,** down from the edge, top, or brim; as, the water is running *over;* **8,** at an end; as, all is *over;* **9,** *Colloquial,* successfully; with the effect planned; as, the play went *over* the first night.

o-ver- (ō'vĕr-), a prefix meaning: **1,** excessive or excessively; as, *over*supply, *over*confident; **2,** outer, upper, or superior position; as, *over*coat, *over*lord; **3,** motion beyond normal bounds; as, *over*flow.

o-ver-alls (ō'vĕr-ôlz'), *n.pl.* loose-fitting trousers supported by shoulder straps, worn over, or in place of, other garments.

o-ver-arch (ō'vĕr-ärch'), *v.t.* to form an arch over; as, trees *overarched* the road.

o-ver-awe (ō'vĕr-ô'), *v.t.* [overawed, overaw-ing], to hold in check through fear, respect, or the like; hold spellbound; as, the man's manner *overawed* us.

o-ver-bal-ance (ō'vĕr-băl'ăns), *v.t.* [overbalanced, overbalanc-ing], **1,** to be greater than, in weight or influence; **2,** to upset the balance of.

o-ver-bear (ō'vĕr-bâr'), *v.t.* [*p.t.* overbore (-bôr'), *p.p.* overborne (-bôrn'), *p.pr.*

overbear-ing], **1,** to bear down, as by greater physical weight or force; overthrow; **2,** to overcome; triumph over.

o-ver-bear-ing (ō'vĕr-bâr'ĭng), *adj.* haughty; domineering; as, his attitude is so *overbearing* that even his friends rebel.

o-ver-board (ō'vĕr-bôrd'), *adv.* over the side of a ship or boat, into the water.

o-ver-bur-den (ō'vĕr-bûr'dn), *v.t.* to load with too heavy a weight, as of work, anxiety, or the like.

o-ver-cap-i-tal-ize (ō'vĕr-kăp'ĭ-tăl-īz), *v.t.* [overcapitalized, overcapitaliz-ing], to issue more stock, that is, to get people to invest more money, in (a company) than the business or expected profits warrant.

o-ver-cast (ō'vĕr-kàst), *v.t.* [overcast, overcast-ing], **1,** to cover over; cloud; darken; as, the sky is *overcast;* **2,** (ō'vĕr-kàst'), to take long, loose stitches over the edges of (a seam) to prevent raveling.

o-ver-charge (ō'vĕr-chärj'), *v.t.* [overcharged, overcharg-ing], **1,** to load too heavily, as a gun; **2,** to ask too high a price from:—*n.* (ō'vĕr-chärj') **1,** too heavy a load, as of electricity; **2,** too high a price.

o-ver-cloud (ō'vĕr-kloud'), *v.t.* to cover with, or as if with, clouds; darken.

o-ver-coat (ō'vĕr-kōt'), *n.* a heavy, out-of-door coat worn in cold weather; especially, such a coat for a man or a boy.

o-ver-come (ō'vĕr-kŭm'), *v.t.* [*p.t.* overcame (-kām'), *p.p.* overcome, *p.pr.* overcom-ing], **1,** to become master of; as, to *overcome* fear; **2,** to overpower; as, terror *overcame* him.

o-ver-crowd (ō'vĕr-kroud'), *v.t.* to fill beyond normal or comfortable capacity; as, to *overcrowd* a room.—*adj.* **o'ver-crowd'ed.**

o-ver-do (ō'vĕr-dōō'), *v.t.* [*p.t.* overdid (-dĭd'), *p.p.* overdone (-dŭn'), *p.pr.* over-do-ing], **1,** to carry too far; exaggerate; **2,** to weary by overwork; **3,** to cook too long:—*v.i.* to work too hard; do too much.

o-ver-dose (ō'vĕr-dōs'), *n.* too large a dose:—*v.t.* (ō'vĕr-dōs'), [overdosed, overdos-ing], to give too large a dose to.

o-ver-draw (ō'vĕr-drô'), *v.t.* [*p.t.* overdrew (-drōō'), *p.p.* overdrawn (-drôn'), *p.pr.* overdraw-ing], **1,** to exaggerate; as, John's story of the robbery was greatly *overdrawn;* **2,** to draw against (a bank account) by writing a check for a sum greater than the amount on deposit.

o-ver-dress (ō'vĕr-drĕs'), *v.t.* and *v.i.* to dress in a manner too showy for the occasion:—*n.* (ō'vĕr-drĕs'), a garment worn over another garment and with it forming a complete dress.

āte, āorta, râre, căt, àsk, fär, ăllow, sofà; ēve, ĕvent, ĕll, writẽr, novĕl; bīte, pĭn; nō, ōbey, ôr, dŏg, tŏp, cŏllide; ūnit, ūnite, bûrn, cŭt, focŭs; nōōn, fŏŏt; mound; coin;

o·ver·due (ō′vẽr-dū′), *adj.* **1,** unpaid at the time for payment; as, an *overdue* account; **2,** not on hand at the scheduled time; as, the train is *overdue.*

o·ver·eat (ō′vẽr-ēt′), *v.i.* [*p.t.* overate (-āt′), *p.p.* overeat-en (-ēt′n), *p.pr.* overeat-ing], to eat too much; to stuff oneself with food.

o·ver·es·ti·mate (ō′vẽr-ĕs′tĭ-māt), *v.t.* [overestimat-ed, overestimat-ing], to set too high a value on; as, he *overestimates* his own ability:—*n.* (ō′vẽr-ĕs′tĭ-māt), too high a valuation, or estimate.

o·ver·flow (ō′vẽr-flō′), *n.* **1,** the spreading of water or other liquid beyond its proper limits; **2,** the excess water or liquid; also, an outlet for excess liquid; **3,** excess; superabundance; as, an *overflow* of enthusiasm:—*v.t.* and *v.i.* (ō′vẽr-flō′), to flood; overrun; spread all over.

o·ver·grow (ō′vẽr-grō′), *v.t.* [*p.t.* overgrew (-grōō′), *p.p.* overgrown (-grōn′), *p.pr.* overgrow-ing], **1,** to cover; grow over; as, the path is *overgrown* with weeds; **2,** to outgrow:—*v.i.* to grow too large or too fast.

o·ver·hand (ō′vẽr-hănd′), *adj.* **1,** down from above; as, an *overhand* blow; **2,** grasping with the hand over the object, and with the palm downward; as, an *overhand* grip; **3,** in baseball, cricket, etc., thrown or bowled

OVERHAND THROW

with the arm swung above the shoulder:—*n.* the simplest kind of knot (see illustration under *knot*):—*adv.* (ō′vẽr-hănd′), with the palm of the hand down; as, to haul in a fish line *overhand.*

o·ver·hang (ō′vẽr-hăng′), *v.t.* [overhung (-hŭng′), overhang-ing], to jut over; project above:—*v.i.* to project over and beyond something; as, the ledge *overhangs* several feet:—*n.* (ō′vẽr-hăng′), a part, as of a building or mountain, that projects.

o·ver·haul (ō′vẽr-hôl′), *v.t.* **1,** to examine thoroughly for the purpose of making repairs; **2,** to overtake; catch up with.

o·ver·head (ō′vẽr-hĕd′), *adv.* above one's head; as, stars shine *overhead:—adj.* (ō′vẽr-hĕd′), **1,** situated or operating above one's head; as, *overhead* ventilation; **2,** referring to the cost or expenses of a business which are directly chargeable not to any particular department, but to the running of the business as a whole:—*n.* (ō′vẽr-hĕd′), overhead expenses; as, rent, light, and heat are items in our *overhead.*

o·ver·hear (ō′vẽr-hēr′), *v.t.* [overheard

(-hûrd′), overhear-ing], to hear (a remark, conversation, or the like) which one is not intended to hear.

o·ver·joy (ō′vẽr-joi′), *v.t.* to make very glad; as, he was *overjoyed* at the news.

o·ver·land (ō′vẽr-lănd′), *adj.* and *adv.* across the land rather than the sea; as, an *overland* journey; to travel *overland.*

o·ver·lap (ō′vẽr-lăp′), *v.t.* [overlapped, overlap-ping], **1,** to lie so as partly to cover; as, each shingle *overlaps* the one below; also, to lay so as to cover the edge of something; **2,** to coincide partly with; as, the treasurer's duties *overlap* those of the secretary:—*v.i.* **1,** to lie so that part of one thing covers part of another; **2,** to coincide in part:—*n.* (ō′vẽr-lăp′), **1,** the extension, or amount of extension, of one thing over the edge of another; **2,** that which partly covers, or laps over, something.

OVERLAP
The shingles overlap at O,O.

o·ver·lay (ō′vẽr-lā′), *v.t.* [overlaid (-lād′), overlay-ing], to spread or cover (a surface) with something:—*n.* (ō′vẽr-lā′), that which is laid on as a covering.

o·ver·lie (ō′vẽr-lī′), *v.t.* [*p.t.* overlay (-lā′), *p.p.* overlain (-lān′), *p.pr.* overly-ing], to lie on or over.

o·ver·load (ō′vẽr-lōd′), *v.t.* to load, or burden, too heavily.—*n.* **o′ver-load′.**

o·ver·look (ō′vẽr-lōōk′), *v.t.* **1,** to look down on from above; **2,** to keep an eye on; superintend; **3,** to fail to see; miss; as, I *overlooked* part of the problem; **4,** to disregard deliberately; pass over without noticing; ignore.

o·ver·lord (ō′vẽr-lôrd′), *n.* one who is a lord over other lords.

o·ver·mas·ter (ō′vẽr-màs′tẽr), *v.t.* to overpower; subdue; defeat.—*adj.* **o′ver-mas′ter-ing.**

o·ver·match (ō′vẽr-măch′), *v.t.* to be too strong for; surpass.

o·ver·much (ō′vẽr-mŭch′), *adj.* and *adv.* too much.

o·ver·night (ō′vẽr-nīt′), *adv.* in or during the night; as, it happened *overnight:—adj.* (ō′vẽr-nīt′), **1,** lasting through a night; as, an *overnight* trip by train; **2,** used for, or remaining for, a night's stay; as, an *overnight* bag; *overnight* guests.

o·ver·pass (ō′vẽr-pàs′), *v.t.* **1,** to pass over or through; cross (mountains, a river, or the like); **2,** to exceed; surpass; as, he *overpassed* all competitors:—*n.* (ō′vẽr-pàs′), a bridge or road over a railroad track, river, etc.

o·ver·pow·er (ō′vĕr-pou′ĕr), *v.t.* **1,** to crush by superior force; **2,** to affect greatly; as, he was *overpowered* by grief and sorrow. —*adj.* **o′ver·pow′er·ing.**

o·ver·pro·duc·tion (ō′vĕr-prō-dŭk′shŭn), *n.* the raising of more crops or the manufacturing of more articles than can be sold profitably; also, the excess of crops or articles so raised or manufactured.

o·ver·rate (ō′vĕr-rāt′), *v.t.* [overrat-ed, overrat-ing], to set too high a value upon; as, to *overrate* one's ability.

o·ver·reach (ō′vĕr-rēch′), *v.t.* **1,** to defeat (oneself) by reaching too far or attempting too much; **2,** to get the better of (another) by trickery.
Syn. baffle, outwit, circumvent.

o·ver·ride (ō′vĕr-rīd′), *v.t.* [*p.t.* overrode (-rōd′), *p.p.* overrid-den (-rĭd′n), *p.pr.* overrid-ing], **1,** to trample down; **2,** to set aside tyrannically; as, to *override* a decision; **3,** to ride (a horse) to exhaustion.

o·ver·rule (ō′vĕr-rōōl′), *v.t.* [overruled, overrul-ing], **1,** to set aside; nullify; as, the judge *overruled* a previous decision; **2,** to decide against; disallow; as, the chairman *overruled* my objections.

o·ver·run (ō′vĕr-rŭn′), *v.t.* [*p.t.* overran (-răn′), *p.p.* overrun, *p.pr.* overrun-ning], **1,** to grow or spread over in great quantity or numbers; as, weeds had *overrun* the garden; the enemy *overran* the country; **2,** to run beyond; as, to *overrun* first base.

o·ver·sea (ō′vĕr-sē′) or **o·ver·seas** (ō′vĕr-sēz′), *adv.* and *adj.* across or over the sea.

o·ver·see (ō′vĕr-sē′), *v.t.* [*p.t.* oversaw (-sô′), *p.p.* overseen (-sēn′), *p.pr.* oversee-ing], to keep watch over; superintend.

o·ver·se·er (ō′vĕr-sē′ĕr), *n.* one who is in charge of workers and inspects the work that is done; a superintendent.

o·ver·shad·ow (ō′vĕr-shăd′ō), *v.t.* **1,** to darken, or obscure, with, or as with, a shadow; **2,** to cause (something) to lose importance or significance; as, his early success was *overshadowed* by his later failures.

o·ver·shoe (ō′vĕr-shōō′), *n.* a waterproof shoe, generally of rubber, worn over another shoe, for protection against wet.

o·ver·shoot (ō′vĕr-shōōt′), *v.t.* [overshot (-shŏt′), overshoot-ing], to shoot beyond or over; as, to *overshoot* the mark.

OVERSHOT WHEEL

o·ver·shot (ō′vĕr-shŏt′), *adj.* **1,** operated by water flowing over the top; as, an *overshot* wheel; **2,** with the upper jaw protruding over the lower.

o·ver·sight (ō′vĕr-sīt′), *n.* **1,** failure to see or think of something; a slip or mistake resulting from such failure; **2,** supervision; as, he has general *oversight* of the boys at recess time.
Syn. charge, direction, guidance.

o·ver·spread (ō′vĕr-sprĕd′), *v.t.* [overspread, overspread-ing], to cover the surface of; spread over; as, a mossy carpet *overspread* the ground.

o·ver·state (ō′vĕr-stāt′), *v.t.* [overstat-ed, overstat-ing], to state or express too strongly; exaggerate.—*n.* **o·ver·state′ment.**

o·ver·step (ō′vĕr-stĕp′), *v.t.* [overstepped, overstep-ping], to go beyond; exceed; as, he *overstepped* his authority.

o·ver·stock (ō′vĕr-stŏk′), *v.t.* to provide with too great a supply; fill too full:—*n.* (ō′vĕr-stŏk′), too large a supply.

o·vert (ō′vĕrt), *adj.* publicly or openly performed; not secret or hidden; as, the bombing of the city was an *overt* act of war.—*adv.* **o′vert·ly.**

o·ver·take (ō′vĕr-tāk′), *v.t.* [*p.t.* overtook (-tŏŏk′), *p.p.* overtak-en (-tāk′ĕn), *p.pr.* overtak-ing], **1,** to catch or come up with; **2,** to come upon suddenly; take by surprise; as, the storm *overtook* us.

o·ver·tax (ō′vĕr-tăks′), *v.t.* **1,** to tax too heavily; **2,** to lay too great a burden upon; as, to *overtax* one's strength.

o·ver·throw (ō′vĕr-thrō′), *v.t.* [*p.t.* overthrew (-thrōō′), *p.p.* overthrown (-thrōn′), *p.pr.* overthrow-ing], **1,** to cause to fall or to fail; as, to *overthrow* a government; **2,** to overturn; upset; as, to *overthrow* a chair:—*n.* (ō′vĕr-thrō′), ruin; defeat, as of an army.

o·ver·time (ō′vĕr-tīm′), *n.* hours of work beyond the regular hours:—*adj.* and *adv.* for or during overtime; as, *overtime* pay; to work *overtime.*

o·ver·tone (ō′vĕr-tōn′), *n.* in music, a tone, higher and fainter than the main tone, and accompanying it; a harmonic.

o·ver·top (ō′vĕr-tŏp′), *v.t.* [overtopped, overtop-ping], **1,** to rise or tower above; **2,** to surpass.

o·ver·ture (ō′vĕr-tūr), *n.* **1,** a preliminary offer or proposal; as, an *overture* of peace; **2,** music composed and played as the prelude to an opera, oratorio, or the like.

o·ver·turn (ō′vĕr-tûrn′), *v.t.* **1,** to cause to upset or turn over; as, to *overturn* a footstool; **2,** to overthrow; bring to ruin:—*v.i.* to upset:—*n.* (ō′vĕr-tûrn′), an upsetting; as, the *overturn* of a political party.

o·ver·ween·ing (ō′vĕr-wēn′ĭng), *adj.* conceited; arrogant; also, excessive; exaggerated; as, *overweening* pride.

ā̆te, â̆orta, râre, căt, ȧsk, fär, ȧllow, sofȧ; ēve, ê̆vent, ĕll, writẽr, novĕl; bīte, pĭn; nō, ō̆bey, ôr, dô̆g, tŏp, cŏllide; ūnit, ū̆nite, bûrn, cŭt, focŭs; nōōn, fŏŏt; mound; coin;

o·ver·weight (ō′vẽr-wāt′), *n.* weight greater than is usual or required:—*adj.* weighing more than is normal or necessary:—*v.t.* (ō′vẽr-wāt′), to give too great a burden to; overload.

o·ver·whelm (ō′vẽr-hwĕlm′), *v.t.* **1,** to submerge; flood; as, he was *overwhelmed* with applause; **2,** to crush utterly; as, to *overwhelm* a person by harsh criticism.—*adj.* o′ver·whelm′ing.

o·ver·work (ō′vẽr-wûrk′), *v.t.* to place too much work upon:—*v.i.* to work beyond one's strength:—*n.* (ō′vẽr-wûrk′), work beyond one's capacity; too much work.

o·ver·wrought (ō′vẽr-rôt′), *adj.* **1,** excited; unstrung; **2,** too elaborately adorned.

Ov·id (ŏv′ĭd), (43 B.C.–A.D. 17), a Roman poet, famous for his mythological tales in verse.

o·vule (ō′vūl), *n.* **1,** in plants, an undeveloped seed; **2,** in female animals, a little or undeveloped egg.

o·vum (ō′vŭm), *n.* [*pl.* ova (ō′vȧ)], the female germ cell or seed.

owe (ō), *v.t.* [owed, ow-ing], **1,** to be under obligation to pay; as, to *owe* ten dollars; **2,** to be indebted for; as, I *owe* my success to you:—*v.i.* to be in debt.

ow·ing (ō′ĭng), *adj.* due as a debt:—**owing to,** because of.

owl (oul), *n.* any one of a group of night-flying birds of prey, which have large heads and eyes, short hooked bills and sharp claws, and a peculiar call or hoot.

owl·et (oul′ĕt), *n.* a young owl; also, a small owl.

own (ōn), *adj.* **1,** belonging to the individual person or thing; as, your *own* house; the sun's *own* light; **2,** of the same parents; as, my *own* sister:—*v.t.* **1,** to be the possessor of; as, this book is mine, I *own* it; **2,** to acknowledge; as, to *own* a fault; **3,** to grant; as, I *own* the truth of your argument.

OWL (⅒)

own·er (ōn′ẽr), *n.* one who owns or possesses; a proprietor.

own·er·ship (ōn′ẽr-shĭp), *n.* right of possession; also, possession; proprietorship.

ox (ŏks), *n.* [*pl.* oxen (ŏk′sĕn)], **1,** a steer, or castrated male of the family of domestic cattle, that has been trained to do hauling and farm work; **2,** any of several animals related to domestic cattle, as the wild ox and the musk ox.

ox·a·lis (ŏk′sȧ-lĭs), *n.* any of a group of plants with small white or pink flowers, and leaves divided into three parts.

ox·eye dai·sy (ŏks′ī′ dā′zĭ), the common white daisy.

¹**Ox·ford** or **ox·ford** (ŏks′fẽrd), *n.* a low shoe, laced or tied over the instep.

²**Ox·ford** (ŏks′fẽrd), a city in south central England, famous for its university (map 13).

Oxford gray, a dark gray.

OXFORD SHOE

ox·ide (ŏk′sīd; ŏk′sĭd), *n.* a compound of oxygen with another element.

ox·i·dize (ŏk′sĭ-dīz), *v.t.* and *v.i.* [oxidized, oxidiz-ing], to combine with oxygen.—*n.* ox′i·diz′er.—*n.* ox′i·da′tion.

ox·y·gen (ŏk′sĭ-jĕn), *n.* a gas without odor, color, or taste, forming about one fifth of the total volume of the atmosphere, and essential to life. It is a part of many substances, such as water, acids, etc.

oys·ter (ois′tẽr), *n.* a shellfish, valued as food, having a rough, hinged shell.

oyster plant, a plant the root of which, when cooked, is supposed to taste like oysters: better known as *salsify.*

oz. abbreviation for *ounce, ounces.*

O·zark Moun·tains (ō′zärk), a low range of mountains between the Arkansas and Missouri rivers (map 8).

o·zone (ō′zōn; ō-zōn′), *n.* **1,** a condensed form of oxygen whose sharp, peculiar odor can often be detected in the air after a thunderstorm; **2,** pure and invigorating air.

P

P, p (pē), *n.* [*pl.* P's, p's], the 16th letter of the alphabet, following O.

p. abbreviation for *page, participle;* also, abbreviation for *piano,* meaning *softly.*

Pa. abbreviation for *Pennsylvania.*

p.a. abbreviation for *participial adjective.*

pace (pās), *n.* **1,** a step; the space covered by a step in walking; **2,** gait, or manner of moving; **3,** a certain gait of a horse; **4,**

rate of speed; as, to keep the *pace:*—*v.t.* [paced, pac-ing], **1,** to measure by steps; as, to *pace* off 50 yards; **2,** to walk over with even steps; as, the guard *paces* his round; **3,** in racing, to set the pace for:—*v.i.* **1,** to walk with long, even steps; **2,** to go at a pace, as a horse.—*n.* pac′er.

pa·cha (pȧ-shä′; pä′shȧ; päsh′ȧ), *n.* a Turkish military official or governor; pasha. See **pasha.**

go; join; yet; sing; chin; show; thin, *th*en; hw, *wh*y; zh, a*z*ure; ü, Ger. *für* or Fr. *lune;* ö, Ger. sch*ö*n or Fr. *feu;* ṅ, Fr. *enfant,* no*m;* kh, Ger. a*ch* or i*ch.* See pages ix–x.

pach·y·derm (păk′ĭ-dûrm), *n.* one of a group of thick-skinned animals, such as the elephant, rhinoceros, etc.

pa·cif·ic (pȧ-sĭf′ĭk), *adj.* 1, peacemaking; as, *pacific* words; 2, peaceful; tranquil; as, *pacific* waters.—*adv.* **pa·cif′i·cal·ly.**
Syn. calm, gentle, still, smooth.

pac·i·fi·ca·tion (păs′ĭ-fĭ-kā′shŭn; pȧ-sĭf′ĭ-kā′shŭn), *n.* 1, the act of bringing about peáce; 2, the arrangement of terms of peace, or the terms so arranged.

Pa·cif·ic O·cean (pȧ-sĭf′ĭk), the large body of water between the continents of America, Asia, and Australia (map 2).

pac·i·fist (păs′ĭ-fĭst), *n.* one who opposes war as wrong, and who works for peace between nations.—*n.* **pac′i·fism.**

pac·i·fy (păs′ĭ-fī), *v.t.* [pacified, pacify-ing], to calm; soothe; appease; as, to *pacify* an angry man.
Syn. compose, allay, tranquilize.

pack (păk), *n.* 1, a bundle tied up for carry-ing, especially on the back of a man or animal; 2, a full set of things; as, a *pack* of cards; 3, a number of animals of the same kind living or hunting together; as, a *pack* of hounds; 4, a large area of floating cakes of ice driven close together:—*v.t.* 1, to stow away, arrange compactly, or press into a bundle; as, to *pack* clothes for a trip; 2, to fill (a receptacle or space) entirely; as, to *pack* a trunk with clothes; 3, to crowd together; as, to *pack* people in a room; 4, to press into a hard mass; as, to *pack* earth; 5, to fill in (a joint or crack) to pre-vent leaking; 6, to send away; as, to *pack* him off in a hurry; 7, to arrange unfairly to suit one's own ends; as, to *pack* a jury:—*v.i.* 1, to press or crowd together into a hard mass; as, ice *packs* together; 2, to stow things for safety or for carrying; 3, to ad-mit of being stowed; as, these articles *pack* well; 4, to depart or remove in haste; as, she sent him *packing.*
Syn., n. drove, flock, herd, bevy, swarm.

pack·age (păk′ĭj), *n.* a bundle or bale of goods; a parcel; packet:—*v.t.* [pack-aged, packag-ing], to enclose in a container; to make into a bundle for the retail buyer.

pack·er (păk′ẽr), *n.* 1, one who bundles things for safety in carrying or shipping; 2, one who prepares and bundles provisions in quantities for the market.

pack·et (păk′ĕt), *n.* 1, a small bundle or parcel; package; 2, a vessel sailing between two or more ports at regular periods, carrying passengers, mail, and merchandise.

pack·ing (păk′ĭng), *n.* 1, preparing bun-dles; 2, material, as straw or paper, used to protect goods packed for carrying.

pact (păkt), *n.* an agreement or contract.

¹**pad** (păd), *v.i.* [pad-ded, pad-ding], to walk slowly and wearily; also, to walk noiselessly, as a cat does.

²**pad** (păd), *n.* 1, a soft cushion used to fill a hollow space, lessen pressure or friction, protect from blows, etc.; 2, the cushion-like part of the foot of some animals, as the dog and cat; 3, a writing or drawing tablet; 4, the floating leaf of certain water plants, as the water lily; 5, a cushioned, inked block used for inking a rubber stamp:—*v.t.* [pad-ded, pad-ding], 1, to stuff with pads; line, as a coat; 2, to expand with unnecessary material; as, to *pad* a story.

pad·ding (păd′ĭng), *n.* 1, material used to pad; stuffing; 2, material of no value used to fill up space.

¹**pad·dle** (păd′l), *n.* 1, a short oar with a broad blade at one or both ends, used to propel a canoe; 2, a short, broad-bladed instrument used for stirring, mixing, etc.; 3, one of the wide boards of a water wheel or a paddle wheel:—*v.i.* and *v.t.* [pad-dled, pad-dling], to propel (a canoe) with a paddle.

PADDLE, def. 1

²**pad·dle** (păd′l), *v.i.* [pad-dled, pad-dling], to wade; to dabble with the hands in water.

paddle wheel, a large wheel with broad paddles for propelling a steamboat.

pad·dock (păd′ŭk), *n.* 1, a small field for pasture; 2, a stable yard where horses are exercised; 3, at a racecourse, an enclosure in which horses are saddled and exercised.

pad·dy (păd′ĭ), *n.* rice in the husk, whether growing or just gathered.

Pa·de·rew·ski (pä′dĕ-rĕf′skĕ; pä′dĕ-rĕs′-kĕ), Ignace Jan (1860–1941), a famous Polish pianist, composer, and statesman.

p.adj. or **p.a.** abbreviation for *participial adjective.*

pad·lock (păd′lŏk′), *n.* a re-movable lock, which hangs by a curved bar, hinged at one end and snapped shut at the other: —*v.t.* to fasten with such a lock.

PADLOCK

pa·dre (pä′drĭ; pä′drä), *n.* 1, father: the Spanish, Portuguese, and Italian title for priest or monk; 2, in army and navy slang, a chaplain.

Pad·u·a (păd′ū-ȧ), [Italian **Pa·do·va** (pä′dō-vä)], a city in northern Italy (map 12).

pae·an (pē′ăn), *n.* a loud, joyous song of praise or triumph.

pa·gan (pā′găn), *n.* 1, a heathen; one who is not Christian, Jewish, or Moham-medan; 2, a person having no religious be-liefs:—*adj.* heathen.—*n.* **pa′gan·ism.**

¹**page** (pāj), *n.* 1, in the days of chivalry,

a boy, usually of high birth, attending on a person of distinction as the first stage in the process of his training toward knighthood; **2,** an errand boy in a legislative, or lawmaking, body; also, a uniformed serving boy, as in a hotel:—*v.t.* [paged, pag-ing], **1,** to attend as a page; **2,** to call for or summon (a person), as by page in a hotel.

²**page** (pāj), *n.* one side of a leaf, as of a book; also, what is written or printed on it:—*v.t.* [paged, pag-ing], to arrange or number in pages.

pag-eant (păj′ănt; pā′jănt), *n.* a brilliant, stately display or procession in celebration of an event or in honor of a person.

pag-eant-ry (păj′ănt-rĭ; pā′jănt-rĭ), *n.* **1,** brilliant display; pomp; show; **2,** the art of creating and staging pageants; also, such pageants collectively.

pa-go-da (pá-gō′dá), *n.* in the Far East, a sacred tower or temple of many stories, built in the form of a pyramid, and richly painted and ornamented.

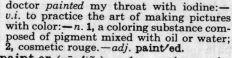

PAGODA

paid (pād), one form of the past tense and past participle of *pay.*

pail (pāl), *n.* an open vessel of wood or metal with a handle, for carrying liquids; bucket; also, the amount a pail will hold.

pail-ful (pāl′fool), *n.* [*pl.* pailfuls], the amount a pail will hold.

pain (pān), *n.* **1,** originally, penalty: now rare, except in such phrases as *on pain of death;* **2,** a suffering of body; an ache; as, a *pain* in the stomach; **3,** distress of mind; sorrow; **4, pains,** diligent effort; as, he took great *pains* with his work:—*v.t.* **1,** to cause bodily suffering to; **2,** to make uneasy; grieve; as, Mary's impoliteness *pained* her mother. — *adj.* **pained.**—*adj.* **pain′less.**

Syn., n. torture, pang, agony, misery.

pain-ful (pān′fool), *adj.* **1,** full of pain; causing pain; **2,** difficult, as a task.

pains-tak-ing (pānz′tā′kĭng), *adj.* taking great pains; careful.—*adv.* **pains′tak′ing-ly.**

paint (pānt), *v.t.* **1,** to picture in colors; as, to *paint* a portrait; **2,** to describe vividly; as, to *paint* a scene in words; **3,** to coat or cover with color; as, to *paint* a house; **4,** to coat, as with paint; as, the

PAIL

doctor *painted* my throat with iodine:—*v.i.* to practice the art of making pictures with color:—*n.* **1,** a coloring substance composed of pigment mixed with oil or water; **2,** cosmetic rouge.—*adj.* **paint′ed.**

paint-er (pān′tēr), *n.* **1.** a workman who paints houses, woodwork, etc.; **2,** one who paints pictures; an artist.

paint-ing (pān′tĭng), *n.* **1,** the act, art, or work of a painter; **2,** a picture in colors.

pair (pâr), *n.* **1,** two things of a kind, similar in form, intended to be used together, or corresponding to each other in some way; as, a *pair* of oars; a *pair* of horses; a *pair* of shoes; **2,** a single thing composed of two like parts; as, a *pair* of scissors; **3,** two members of different parties in a legislative body who agree that neither will vote on a given motion:—*v.t.* to join in couples; mate:—*v.i.* **1,** to come together in couples; as, to *pair* off in a dance; **2,** to match; form a pair.

pa-ja-mas (pá-jä′máz; pá-jăm′áz), *n.* a sleeping suit consisting, usually, of a loose coat and trousers. Also spelled **py-ja′mas.**

Pak-is-tan (păk′ĭs-tăn), an independent member (cap. Karachi) of the British Commonwealth of Nations, composed of parts of former India (map 15).

pal (păl), *n. Slang,* a chum; partner.

pal-ace (păl′ĭs; păl′ás), *n.* **1,** the official residence of a king or other ruler; **2,** a magnificent house.

pal-a-din (păl′á-dĭn), *n.* a knight; especially, one of the knights of Charlemagne.

pal-an-quin (păl′ăn-kēn′), *n.* in India and China, a covered carriage, usually for one passenger, carried on men's shoulders.

pal-at-a-ble (păl′ĭt-á-bl), *adj.* pleasing to the taste; appetizing.—*adv.* **pal′at-a-bly.**

pal-ate (păl′ĭt; păl′át), *n.* **1,** the roof of the mouth, consisting of the *hard palate,* or the bony front part of the roof of the mouth, and the *soft palate,* or the fleshy back part of the roof of the mouth (see *epiglottis,* illustration); **2,** the sense of taste; as, a delicate *palate.*

PALANQUIN

pa-la-tial (pá-lā′shăl), *adj.* pertaining to, or resembling, a palace; magnificent.

pal-a-tine (păl′á-tīn; păl′á-tĭn), *adj.* given royal privileges within one's own domains; as, a count *palatine:—n.* a count, earl, etc., given such privileges.

---

pa·lav·er (pȧ-lăv′ẽr; pȧ-lä′vẽr), *n.* **1,** in Africa, a parley, or conference, with natives; **2,** idle talk; chatter:—*v.i.* to talk idly.

¹pale (pāl), *adj.* [pal-er, pal-est], **1,** wanting in color; as, a face *pale* from illness; **2,** dim; not bright; as, *pale* blue:—*v.i.* [paled, pal-ing], to turn white, or lose color:—*v.t.* to make dim or pale.

   Syn., adj. pallid, bloodless, ghastly.

²pale (pāl), *n.* **1,** a pointed stake or fence picket; **2,** a place enclosed by such a fence; hence, a district with clearly marked bounds; **3,** limits or bounds:—*v.t.* [paled, pal-ing], to enclose or fence with pales.

pale-face (pāl′fās′), *n.* a white person: a name for the white man, said to have been used by the North American Indians.

pale-ness (pāl′nĕs), *n.* lack of color.

Pa·ler·mo (pȧ-lûr′mō; pä-lâr′mō), a seaport city in Sicily (map 12).

Pal·es·tine (păl′ĕs-tīn), Arab territory and Israel (historic cap. Jerusalem) in western Asia (map 1): also called the *Holy Land*, or in the Bible, *Canaan.*

pal·ette (păl′ĕt), *n.* **1,** a thin oval or oblong board with a hole at one end for the thumb, used by artists for mixing and holding colors; **2,** the set of colors used in painting a picture.

PALETTE

pal·frey (pôl′frĭ), *n.* [*pl.* palfreys], a saddle horse, especially a small one for a lady.

pal·ing (pā′lĭng), *n.* **1,** a fence made of narrow, upright boards, called pales, usually pointed at the top; **2,** a pale; also, wood for making pales.

pal·i·sade (păl′ĭ-sād′), *n.* **1,** a fence or fortification made of strong, pointed stakes, or pales, set close together and driven into the ground (see *castle,* illustration); **2, palisades,** a long line of cliffs, usually along a river:—*v.t.* [palisad-ed, palisad-ing], to enclose or fortify with stakes.

PALING, def. 1

Pal·i·sades (păl′ĭ-sādz′), a line of high cliffs on the west bank of the Hudson River, in New Jersey and New York.

¹pall (pôl), *n.* **1,** a heavy, velvet covering for a coffin, hearse, or tomb; also, the coffin itself; **2,** any heavy, dark covering; as, a *pall* of smoke.

²pall (pôl), *v.i.* to become distasteful or wearisome; lose power to interest; as, too much joking *palls* on him.

Pal·la·di·um (pă-lā′dĭ-ŭm), *n.* [*pl.* Palladia (pă-lā′dĭ-ȧ)], in Greek mythology, the statue of Pallas Athena at Troy, said to be necessary to the safety of the city.

Pal·las (păl′ȧs), *n.* in Greek mythology, Pallas Athena, the goddess of wisdom.

pall·bear·er (pôl′bâr′ẽr), *n.* one who helps to carry the coffin at a funeral.

pal·let (păl′ĕt), *n.* a small, rough bed.

pal·li·ate (păl′ĭ-āt), *v.t.* [palliat-ed, palliat-ing], **1,** to excuse or cause to appear less wrong; as, to *palliate* a fault; **2,** to ease without curing; as, to *palliate* a disease.

   Syn. soften, mitigate, extenuate.

pal·li·a·tive (păl′ĭ-ā′tĭv; păl′ĭ-ȧ-tĭv), *adj.* **1,** tending to excuse; **2,** serving to relieve pain or illness without curing:—*n.* that which serves to excuse guilt or to lessen disease or pain.

pal·lid (păl′ĭd), *adj.* pale; lacking in color; as, a *pallid* face.—*n.* **pal′lid-ness.**

   Syn. ghastly, bloodless, ashen, wan.

pal·lor (păl′ẽr), *n.* lack of color, as in the face; paleness.

¹palm (päm), *n.* **1,** the inner surface of the human hand, between the fingers and the wrist; **2,** a measure of length varying from three to four inches:—*v.t.* **1,** to conceal in, or about, the hand, as in a sleight-of-hand trick; **2,** hence, to pass by fraud; as, to *palm* off worthless stock on investors.

²palm (päm), *n.* **1,** a tropical tree with a crown of large fan-shaped leaves generally radiating from the summit of a slender trunk from which no large branches grow; **2,** a leaf of the tree, formerly used as an emblem of victory; hence, victory; honor.

COCONUT PALM

palm·er (päm′ẽr), *n.* a pilgrim to the Holy Land who brought back a palm branch as a token or sign of his pilgrimage.

pal·met·to (păl-mĕt′ō), *n.* [*pl.* palmettos or palmettoes], **1,** any of various palm trees growing in the West Indies and the southern part of the U.S.; **2,** palmetto leaves used in weaving.

palm·is·try (päm′ĭs-trĭ), *n.* the art of reading character or foretelling the future from the lines and marks in the palm of a person's hand.—*n.* **palm′ist.**

Palm Sun·day, the Sunday before Easter: so called in commemoration of Christ's entry into Jerusalem, when branches of palm were strewn before him.

palm·y (päm′ĭ), *adj.* [palm-i-er, palm-i-est], 1, abounding in palm trees; 2, flourishing; prosperous; as, *palmy* days.

Pal·my·ra (păl-mī′rȧ), an ancient city in Syria, famous for its architectural remains.

pal·o·mi·no (păl-ō-mē′nō), *n.* a creamy or golden colored saddle horse with white tail and mane, bred chiefly in southwestern U.S.

pal·pa·ble (păl′pȧ-bl), *adj.* 1, capable of being touched or felt; 2, easily seen; plain; as, a *palpable* error.—*adv.* **pal′pa·bly.**
Syn. manifest, obvious, evident.

pal·pi·tate (păl′pĭ-tāt), *v.i.* [palpitat-ed, palpitat-ing], to beat or throb rapidly; flutter.—*n.* **pal′pi·ta′tion.**

pal·sy (pôl′zĭ), *n.* [*pl.* palsies], paralysis; loss of sensation, or of power to move or control motion, in any part of the body:—*v.t.* [palsied, palsy-ing], to paralyze.—*adj.* **pal′sied.**

pal·ter (pôl′tẽr), *v.i.* 1, to act deceitfully; 2, to haggle; bargain.

pal·try (pôl′trĭ), *adj.* [pal-tri-er, pal-triest], worthless; contemptible; small; as, a *paltry* gift.—*n.* **pal′tri·ness.**
Syn. petty, insignificant, trifling.

pam·pas (păm′pȧz; päm′päs), *n.pl.* in South America, vast treeless plains, especially those in Argentina.

pam·per (păm′pẽr), *v.t.* to humor; gratify; indulge (a person) in every wish.

pam·phlet (păm′flĕt), *n.* a small unbound book, usually with a paper cover.

pam·phlet·eer (păm′flĕ-tĩr′), *n.* a writer of pamphlets or essays.

pan (păn), *n.* 1, a broad, shallow metal or earthenware dish for cooking and other household uses; 2, any similar vessel, as either of the dishes for holding things weighed on scales, or the shallow receptacle for washing out gold from dirt or gravel; 3, in old-fashioned guns, the hollow part of the lock that held gunpowder for firing the gun; 4, a bed or layer of solid soil or gravel: usually called *hardpan:*

PANS
—*v.t.* [panned, pan-ning], 1, in mining, to wash (gravel or dirt) in a pan to separate out the gold; 2, to cook in a pan; as, to *pan* oysters; 3, *Slang,* to ridicule without mercy:—**pan out,** 1, to yield gold, as a mine; 2, *Colloquial,* to turn out successfully.

Pan (păn), *n.* in Greek mythology, the god of flocks and herds and of the woods, represented as having a goat's legs, ears, and horns, and as playing musical pipes.

PAN

pan- (păn-), a prefix meaning all; as, *pan*acea; *pan*theon: sometimes *panto-* (păn′tō-); as, *panto*mimes.

pan·a·ce·a (păn′ȧ-sē′ȧ), *n.* a remedy for all ills; a cure-all.

¹**Pan·a·ma** (păn′ȧ-mä′; păn′ȧ-mä′), *n.* a hat of fine quality made from young leaves of a palmlike tree.

²**Pan·a·ma** (păn′ȧ-mä′), a republic (cap. Panama) in Central America:—**Isthmus of Panama,** an isthmus linking North and South America; **Panama Canal,** a canal connecting the Atlantic and Pacific Oceans. (Map 10.)

Pan–A·mer·i·can (păn′=ȧ-mẽr′ĭ-kăn), *adj.* pertaining to both North and South America, or to all Americans.—*n.* **Pan′–A·mer′i·can·ism.**

pan·cake (păn′kāk′), *n.* a thin cake made of batter fried in a pan or griddle.

pan·cre·as (păn′krē-ȧs; păng′krē-ȧs), *n.* a large, fleshy gland near the stomach, producing a fluid, called *pancreatic juice,* that helps digestion. The pancreas of animals, when cooked for food, is called *sweetbread.*—*adj.* **pan′cre·at′ic.**

pan·de·mo·ni·um (păn′dē-mō′nĭ-ŭm), *n.* 1, a place of lawless disorder; 2, wild uproar; utter confusion.

pan·der (păn′dẽr), *v.i.* to cater to the unworthy desires or prejudices of others: —*n.* one who so caters.

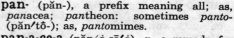
WINDOW PANES (P, P, P, etc.)

Pan·dor·a (păn-dôr′ȧ), *n.* in Greek mythology, the first mortal woman. Out of curiosity she opened a box from which escaped all evils to infest the world.

pane (pān), *n.* a square or oblong piece of glass in a window or door.

pan·e·gyr·ic (păn′ē-jĭr′ĭk), *n.* praise formally written or spoken in honor of a person or event; any high praise.

pan·el (păn′ĕl), *n.* 1, a division or section of a wall, ceiling, or door raised above, or sunk below, the surrounding parts; 2, a thin board on which a picture is painted; also, the picture itself; 3, a list of persons summoned to serve as jurors; also, an entire jury; 4, an ornamental strip placed lengthwise on a dress or skirt: —*v.t.* [paneled, panel-ing], to form, fit, or decorate with panels.—*n.* **pan′el·ing.**

PANELS (P P) IN A DOOR

pang (păng), *n.* 1, a violent, sudden pain; as, *pangs* of hunger; 2, a sudden, bitter emotion; as, *pangs* of remorse.

pan·go·lin (păng-gō′lĭn), *n.* a scaly ant-eater, found in Asia, the Malay Archipelago, and Africa.

pan·ic (păn′-ĭk), *n.* **1,** sudden, extreme fright, often groundless, or

PANGOLIN (¹⁄₁₀)

inspired by a trifling cause; **2,** general alarm and distrust in financial circles; as, the closing of several banks caused a *panic.—adj.* **pan′ick·y.**

  Syn. fear, terror, horror, dread, anxiety.

pan·i·cle (păn′ĭ-kl), *n.* a kind of branched flower cluster.

pan·ic–strick·en (păn′ĭk-strĭk′ĕn), *adj.* filled with overwhelming fear.

pan·nier (păn′yĕr; păn′ĭ-ĕr), *n.* **1,** a bread basket; **2,** one of two wicker baskets suspended across the back of an animal for carrying market produce; also, a single basket for carrying on a person's back; **3,** a framework of whalebone or steel wire, formerly used to enlarge a woman's skirts at the hips.

PANICLE

pan·o·plied (păn′ŏ-plĭd), *adj.* wearing a complete suit of armor; splendidly arrayed or covered.

pan·o·ply (păn′ŏ-plĭ), *n.* [*pl.* panoplies], **1,** a complete suit of armor; **2,** any complete covering; also, a splendid array.

PANNIERS

pan·o·ra·ma (păn′ŏ-rä′mȧ; păn′ŏ-răm′ȧ), *n.* **1,** a picture giving a view in every direction, seen from a central standpoint; **2,** a picture seen part at a time as it is unrolled or unfolded and made to pass before the spectator; **3,** a complete view of a region; **4,** a scene that moves constantly before one, as from the window of a moving train; **5,** a general view of a subject.

pan·sy (păn′zĭ), *n.* [*pl.* pansies], a common garden plant of the violet family, with blossoms of rich color and velvety texture; also, a flower of this plant; heartsease.

pant (pănt), *v.i.* **1,** to breathe rapidly; gasp; as, the walk uphill made

PANSY

him *pant;* **2,** to desire earnestly:—*v.t.* to utter with a gasp:—*n.* a short, rapid breath; also, the puff of an engine.

pan·ta·lets or **pan·ta·lettes** (păn′tȧ-lĕts′), *n.pl.* long frilled drawers, extending below the knees, formerly worn by women and girls.

pan·ta·loon (păn′tȧ-lōōn′), *n.* **1,** a clown or foolish character in pantomime; **2, pantaloons,** trousers.

pan·the·ism (păn′thē-ĭzm), *n.* the doctrine that God and nature are one.— *adj.* **pan′the·is′tic.**

PANTALETS (P)

pan·the·on (păn-thē′ŏn; păn′thē-ŏn; păn′thē-ŭn), *n.* **1,** a temple dedicated to all the gods; **2,** a building where rest the famous dead of a nation:—**Pantheon,** a circular temple in ancient Rome.

pan·ther (păn′thĕr), *n.* **1,** a large American wildcat: also called *cougar;* **2,** the leopard; **3,** less frequently, the jaguar.

pan·to·mime (păn′tŏ-mīm), *n.* **1,** a series of actions, chiefly gestures and facial expressions, that express meaning without words; **2,** a play without any talking.

pan·try (păn′trĭ), *n.* [*pl.* pantries], a room or closet for storing food, dishes, etc.

pants (pănts), *n.pl. Colloquial,* trousers; also, drawers.

pan·ty (păn′tĭ), *n.* [*pl.* panties], **1,** one leg of a pair of trousers or drawers; **2, panties,** trousers; also, drawers.

pap (păp), *n.* soft food for infants, usually bread softened in milk or water.

pa·pa (pä′pȧ; pȧ-pä′), *n.* a child's word for *father.*

pa·pa·cy (pā′pȧ-sĭ), *n.* [*pl.* papacies], the office, dignity, or jurisdiction of the Pope.

pa·pal (pā′păl), *adj.* pertaining to the Pope, or to the Roman Catholic Church:— **papal cross,** a cross with three crossbars (see illustration under *cross*).

pa·paw (pȧ-pô′; pô′pô) or **paw·paw** (pô′pô), *n.* **1,** a tree of central and southern U.S.; also, its sweet, yellowish, pulpy fruit; **2,** the papaya; also, its fruit.

pa·pa·ya (pä-pä′yä), *n.* a tropical American tree; also, its large, yellow fruit.

pa·per (pā′pĕr), *n.* **1,** a material made of finely divided fibers from rags, wood pulp, etc., commonly in the form of a thin, smooth, flexible sheet, used for writing, printing, and various other purposes; **2,** a piece or sheet of this material; **3,** a packet wrapped in this material; as, a *paper* of needles; **4,** a newspaper or journal; **5,** an

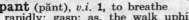

āte, âorta, râre, căt, ȧsk, fär, ȧllow, sofȧ; ēve, ĕvent, ĕll, wrītẽr, novĕl; bīte, pĭn; nō, ŏbey, ôr, dŏg, tŏp, cŏllide; ūnit, ūnite, bûrn, cŭt, focŭs; nōōn, fŏŏt; mound; coin;

essay or special article; as, a *paper* read before a club; **6**, a legal document; **7**, bank notes or bills of exchange: called *commercial paper:—adj.* **1**, having to do with paper; as, a *paper* cutter; **2**, made of paper; as, *paper* dolls; **3**, having no reality; existing only on paper; as, *paper* profits:— **paper money**, notes issued by a government, a bank, etc., and used as currency: —*v.t.* to cover or line with paper.

pa·per·y (pā′pĕr-ĭ), *adj.* having the thinness and texture of paper; as, *papery* silks of China.

pa·pier—mâ·ché (pā′pĕr=mȧ-shā′), *n.* a hard, strong material made of paper pulp mixed with glue, rosin, or the like, and molded into various shapes.

pa·pil·la (pȧ-pĭl′ȧ), *n.* [*pl.* papillae (pȧ-pĭl′ē)], a very minute projection, such as those found on the tongue.—*adj.* **pap′il·lar′y** (păp′ĭ-lĕr′ĭ; pȧ-pĭl′ȧ-rĭ).

pa·pist (pā′pĭst), *n.* a Roman Catholic: often used scornfully.—*adj.* **pa′pist.**

pa·poose (pȧ-pōōs′), *n.* a baby of North American Indian parents.

pap·ri·ka (păp′rĭ-kȧ; pȧ-prē′kȧ), *n.* a mildly pungent, red spice used in cooking, and made from the dried ripe fruit of certain peppers.

Pap·u·a (păp′ū-ȧ; pä′pōō-ä), a territory (cap. Port Moresby) in the southeastern part of the island of New Guinea (map 16). The name is sometimes applied to the whole island.

pa·py·rus (pȧ-pī′rŭs), *n.* [*pl.* papyri (pȧ-pī′rī)], **1**, a kind of Egyptian reed from which the ancients made paper; **2**, the paper made from the pith of this plant; **3**, a manuscript or writing on papyrus.

par (pär), *n.* **1**, full or normal value; as, the stock is below *par;* **2**, equality; equal footing; as, the man is not on a *par* with his associates; **3**, normal conditions; as, to feel below *par;* **4**, in golf, the standard number of strokes for a given course or hole.

Pa·rá (pä-rä′), a seaport in northeastern Brazil, South America (map 11): also called *Belém.*

PAPYRUS
(⅟₇₅)

par·a·ble (păr′ȧ-bl), *n.* a made-up story, usually about something that might naturally occur, from which a moral may be drawn.

pa·rab·o·la (pȧ-răb′ō-lȧ), *n.* a symmetrical curve, such as might be described by a ball thrown up into the air and landing some distance from the thrower.

par·a·chute (păr′ȧ-shōōt), *n.* a folding apparatus, umbrella-shaped when open, used in descending from a balloon or airplane high in the air.

pa·rade (pȧ-rād′), *n.* **1**, show; pompous display; as, a *parade* of wealth; **2**, a military display, or review of troops; **3**, a place of assembly for exercising and inspecting troops; **4**, any march or procession; as, a circus *parade;* **5**, a promenade or public place for walking:—*v.t.* [parad-ed, parading], **1**, to assemble and form (troops or the like) in military order, as for review; **2**, to march over or through; as, to *parade* the city; **3**, to make a display of:—*v.i.* **1**, to walk about so as to exhibit or show oneself; **2**, to take part in a formal march.

par·a·digm (păr′ȧ-dĭm), *n.* an example or model; especially, in grammar, a list, in proper order, of the various forms in the declension or conjugation of a word.

Par·a·dise (păr′ȧ-dīs), *n.* the garden of Eden:—**paradise**, **1**, the place in which the souls of the righteous abide after death; heaven; **2**, a place or state of bliss.

par·a·dox (păr′ȧ-dŏks), *n.* **1**, something which seems absurd or unbelievable, yet may be true; **2**, a statement that appears contradictory.

par·a·dox·i·cal (păr′ȧ-dŏk′sĭ-kȧl), *adj.* seemingly contradictory, but possibly true.

par·af·fin (păr′ă-fĭn) or **par·af·fine** (păr′-ă-fĭn; păr′ă-fēn), *n.* a tasteless, odorless, white or colorless, waxy substance obtained from wood, coal, etc., and used to make candles, to seal jars, etc.

par·a·gon (păr′ȧ-gŏn; păr′ȧ-gŭn), *n.* a model of excellence or perfection.

par·a·graph (păr′ȧ-grȧf), *n.* **1**, a small section of a piece of writing, dealing with one topic; a short passage; **2**, a reference mark [¶] indicating the beginning of a paragraph; **3**, an item in a newspaper, magazine, etc.:—*v.t.* **1**, to arrange in paragraphs; **2**, to write a brief passage about.

Par·a·guay (păr′ȧ-gwā; păr′ȧ-gwī; pä′rä-gwī′), a republic (cap. Asunción) in South America, between Argentina and Brazil (map 11).

par·a·keet (păr′ȧ-kēt), *n.* any of several small, slender-bodied parrots, usually with a long, pointed tail. Also, **par′ra·keet.**

par·al·lax (păr′ă-lăks), *n.* in astronomy, the apparent amount of change in the position of a heavenly body as seen by an observer from two different positions.

par·al·lel (păr′ă-lĕl), *adj.* **1,** equally distant from each other at all points; as, *parallel* lines; **2,** having the same course; as, *parallel* roads; **3,** similar; corresponding; as, *parallel* circumstances:—*n.* **1,** a line or plane equally distant at all points from another line or plane; **2,** one of the imaginary lines drawn on the surface of the earth, or one of the lines drawn on a map or globe, parallel to the equator, which mark degrees of latitude; **3,** a person or thing closely resembling another; **4,** a presentation of resemblance; as, to draw a *parallel* between two careers:—*v.t.* [paralleled, parallel-ing], **1,** to compare; **2,** to be parallel with; **3,** to correspond to.

PARALLEL LINES

par·al·lel·ism (păr′ă-lĕl-ĭzm), *n.* close likeness; similarity; agreement.

par·al·lel·o·gram (păr′ă-lĕl′ō-grăm), *n.* a four-sided plane figure whose opposite sides are equal and parallel.

PARALLELO-GRAMS

pa·ral·y·sis (pǎ-răl′ĭ-sĭs), *n.* [*pl.* paralyses (pǎ-răl′ĭ-sēz)], **1,** loss of feeling or of power to move in one or more parts of the body; palsy; **2,** a state of complete inactivity from lack of power to move.

par·a·lyt·ic (păr′ǎ-lĭt′ĭk), *adj.* like, or affected by, paralysis:—*n.* one who is affected by paralysis.

par·a·lyze (păr′ǎ-līz), *v.t.* [paralyzed, par-alyz-ing], **1,** to affect with paralysis; **2,** to unnerve; render useless or ineffective.

par·a·mount (păr′ǎ-mount), *adj.* above all others; supreme; as, of *paramount* importance.
Syn., dominant, superior, foremost.

par·a·mour (păr′ǎ-mōōr), *n.* one who unlawfully takes the place of husband or wife.

par·a·pet (păr′ǎ-pĕt), *n.* **1,** a low wall at the edge of a roof, platform, balcony, bridge, etc.; **2,** in fortification, a wall to protect troops from enemy fire (see *bastion*, illustration).

PARAPETS OF A BRIDGE (P. P)

par·a·pher·na·li·a (păr′ǎ-fĕr-nā′lĭ-ǎ; păr′ǎ-fĕr-nāl′yǎ), *n.pl.* **1,** small personal belongings; **2,** articles of equipment.

par·a·phrase (păr′ǎ-frāz), *n.* a free translation or explanation of a text, line of poetry, etc., which gives the meaning in other words:—*v.t.* [paraphrased, paraphras-ing], to express the meaning of (a text) in one's own words.

par·a·ple·gic (păr′ǎ-plē′jĭk), *n.* one whose lower limbs are paralyzed.

par·a·site (păr′ǎ-sīt), *n.* **1,** one who lives at another's expense, usually by flattery; a toady; **2,** an animal or plant which lives on or within another, called the host, at the latter's expense.—*adj.* **par′a-sit′ic** (păr′ǎ-sĭt′ĭk); **par′a-sit′i-cal.**

par·a·sol (păr′ǎ-sôl), *n.* a small, light umbrella used as a sunshade.

par·a·troops (păr′ǎ-trōōps), *n.pl.* soldiers landing by parachute; parachute troops.

par·boil (pär′boil′), *v.t.* to cook partially by boiling.

par·cel (pär′sĕl), *n.* **1,** a bundle or package; **2,** a separate part; as, a *parcel* of land:—*v.t.* [parceled, parcel-ing], **1,** to divide into parts; distribute; as, to *parcel* out candy; **2,** to do up in a package.

parcel post, a government system of carrying packages by mail at postal rates.

parch (pärch), *v.t.* **1,** to roast slightly; dry by heating; as, to *parch* corn; **2,** to dry up:—*v.i.* to become dry and hot.

parch·ment (pärch′mĕnt), *n.* **1,** the skin of a sheep, goat, etc., dressed and prepared for writing purposes; **2,** a deed or document on such a skin:—**parchment paper,** paper made to imitate parchment.

pard (pärd), *n.* a leopard or panther.

par·don (pär′dn), *v.t.* **1,** to free from punishment; forgive; as, to *pardon* a criminal; **2,** to overlook; excuse:—*n.* **1,** forgiveness; **2,** polite indulgence; as, I beg your *pardon;* **3,** an official act setting one free from penalty.—*adj.* **par′don-a-ble.**—*adv.* **par′don-a-bly.**—*n.* **par′don-er.**

pare (pâr), *v.t.* [pared, par-ing], **1,** to cut or shave off the outside or ends of; peel; as, to *pare* an apple; **2,** to lessen; reduce; as, to *pare* expenses.—*n.* **par′ing.**

par·ent (pâr′ĕnt), *n.* **1,** a father or mother; hence, the source of any living thing, as a plant; **2,** cause; origin.

par·ent·age (pâr′ĕn-tĭj), *n.* **1,** fatherhood or motherhood; **2,** birth or descent; as, of noble *parentage.*—*n.* **par′ent-hood.**

pa·ren·tal (pǎ-rĕn′tǎl), *adj.* like, or having to do with, parents; as, *parental* care.

pa·ren·the·sis (pǎ-rĕn′thē-sĭs), *n.* [*pl.* parentheses (pǎ-rĕn′thē-sēz)], **1,** an explanatory word, phrase, or clause put in a sentence which is grammatically complete without it: indicated by the marks ( ); **2,** either or both of the marks ( ).

par·en·thet·ic (păr′ĕn-thĕt′ĭk) or **par·en·thet·i·cal** (păr′ĕn-thĕt′ĭ-kǎl), *adj.* **1,** enclosed in parentheses; **2,** explanatory; as, a *parenthetic* remark.

pa·ri·ah (pǎ-rī′ǎ), *n.* **1,** a member of one of the low castes of southern India; **2,** an outcast; one despised by society.

¹Par·is (păr′ĭs), a city, capital of France, on the Seine River (map 12).

²Par·is (păr′ĭs), *n.* in Greek mythology, a son of Priam, king of Troy, whose stealing of Helen, wife of Menelaus, king of Sparta, brought on the Trojan War.

par·ish (păr′ĭsh), *n.* **1,** originally, a church district under the particular charge of one priest, clergyman, or minister; **2,** in England, a civil district, or part of a county, looking after its own education, charities, etc.; **3,** a congregation; also, the locality covered by its activities; **4,** in Louisiana, a state division, the same as a county in other states:—*adj.* pertaining to, or maintained by, a church, congregation, or district; as, a *parish* school.

pa·rish·ion·er (pȧ-rĭsh′ŭn-ẽr), *n.* **1,** one who belongs to a certain parish; **2,** a member of a congregation.

par·i·ty (păr′ĭ-tĭ), *n.* the state or condition of being equal or equivalent; equality.

park (pärk), *n.* **1,** a tract of ground set apart as a public place for recreation; **2,** a large extent of woods and fields attached to a country house; **3,** a train of artillery; an artillery encampment:—*v.t.* **1,** to enclose, as in a park; **2,** to collect and station in order; as, to *park* artillery; **3,** to place and leave for a time:—*v.i.* to place and leave a vehicle temporarily.

Park·man (pärk′măn), Francis (1823–1893), an American historian.

par·lance (pär′lăns), *n.* language; way of speaking; as, in legal *parlance.*

par·ley (pär′lĭ), *n.* [*pl.* parleys], a conference, especially one with an enemy:—*v.i.* to hold a conference, especially with an enemy, with a view to peace.

par·lia·ment (pär′lĭ-mĕnt), *n.* a general council; a meeting of the people or their representatives to consider matters of common interest:—**Parliament, 1,** the supreme lawmaking body of Great Britain, consisting of the House of Lords and the House of Commons; **2,** a similar assembly in certain other countries.

par·lia·men·ta·ry (pär′lĭ-mĕn′tȧ-rĭ), *adj.* **1,** according to the rules and customs of public assemblies; as, *parliamentary* order; **2,** decreed or enacted by a parliament.

par·lor (pär′lẽr), *n.* **1,** a room for conversation and the reception of visitors, in a private dwelling, inn, or club; **2,** in England, a family sitting room; **3,** in the U.S., a shop furnished with some pretensions to elegance; as, a beauty *parlor:*—**parlor car,** a railroad car with individual chairs and sofas, providing more comfortable travel than the usual coach. In British usage, **par′lour.**

par·lous (pär′lŭs), *adj.* **1,** *Archaic,* perilous; **2,** dangerously clever; shrewd; **3,** hence, *Colloquial,* surprising; shocking.

Par·nas·sus (pär-năs′ŭs), a mountain in central Greece, northwest of Athens, once sacred to Apollo and the Muses (map 1). Its modern name is *Liakoura.*

pa·ro·chi·al (pȧ-rō′kĭ-ăl), *adj.* **1,** of or pertaining to a parish, or church district; as, a *parochial* school; **2,** narrow; local.—*n.* **pa·ro′chi·al·ism.**

par·o·dy (păr′ō-dĭ), *n.* [*pl.* parodies], **1,** a humorous imitation of a serious writing; **2,** a burlesque of a musical composition; **3,** hence, a burlesque imitation of anything:—*v.t.* [parodied, parody·ing], to write a humorous imitation of.—*n.* **par′o·dist.**

Syn., n. caricature, travesty.

pa·role (pȧ-rōl′), *n.* **1,** word of honor; especially, a promise given by a prisoner of war that in return for partial freedom or privileges he will not try to escape, will not take up arms within a given time, etc.; **2,** the freeing of a prisoner before his time is up on certain conditions; also, the duration of the conditions:—*v.t.* [paroled, parol·ing], to release (a prisoner) on his word of honor to observe certain conditions.

par·ox·ysm (păr′ŏk-sĭzm), *n.* **1,** a spasm, or fit of acute pain, recurring at intervals; **2,** a sudden and violent outburst of emotion; a fit of any kind; as, a *paroxysm* of rage.—*adj.* **par′ox·ys′mal.**

par·quet (pär-kā′; pär-kĕt′), *n.* **1,** flooring made of fine, patterned, wooden inlay; **2,** the front part of the main floor of a theater: also called *orchestra:*—**parquet circle,** the part of the lower floor of a theater under the balcony.

par·quet·ry (pär′kĕt-rĭ), *n.* fine wooden inlay or mosaic work for floors.

par·ra·keet (păr′ȧ-kēt), *n.* a kind of small parrot; parakeet. See **parakeet.**

par·ri·cide (păr′ĭ-sīd), *n.* **1,** the murder of a close relative, especially a parent; **2,** one who murders a parent or other close relative.—*adj.* **par′ri·cid′al.**

par·rot (păr′ŭt), *n.* a tropical bird with a hooked bill and brilliant feathers, which can be taught to repeat words.

PARROT (¼)

par·ry (păr′ĭ), *v.t.* [parried, parry·ing], **1,**

to ward off, as a blow; **2,** to evade; as, to *parry* a question:—*v.i.* to ward off or turn something aside; as, to *parry* with the sword: —*n.* [*pl.* parries], a warding off, as of a blow.

parse (pärs), *v.t.* [parsed, pars-ing], **1,** in grammar, to analyze or describe (a sentence) by stating the parts of speech and their relation to each other; **2,** to name the part of speech of (a word) and its position in a sentence.

Par-si (pär′sē; pär-sē′), *n.* a member of the Zoroastrian religion, descended from Persian refugees who settled in India in the eighth century. Also spelled **Par′see.**

Par-si-fal (pär′sĭ-fäl), *n.* in medieval romance, Percivale, the sinless knight who found the Holy Grail. He is the hero of Wagner's opera "Parsifal."

par-si-mo-ni-ous (pär′sĭ-mō′nĭ-ŭs), *adj.* close; stingy; miserly.

  Syn. niggardly, grasping, avaricious.

par-si-mo-ny (pär′sĭ-mō′nĭ), *n.* stinginess; extreme and unnecessary economy.

pars-ley (pärs′lĭ), *n.* a garden plant, the leaves of which are used as a garnish and for flavoring.

pars-nip (pärs′nĭp), *n.* a plant with an edible carrotlike root.

par-son (pär′sn), *n.* **1,** a clergyman in charge of a parish; **2,** *Colloquial,* any minister or preacher.

par-son-age (pär′sn-ĭj), *n.* the residence of a minister in charge of a parish; especially, a house owned by a church or parish and set aside for the use of the minister.

part (pärt), *n.* **1,** something less than the whole; as, *part* of a pear; a piece, section, or division; an individual portion; **2,** a share in action, duty, or responsibility; as, to do one's *part;* **3,** an essential member or organ; as, *part* of the body; automobile *parts;* **4,** a side in a quarrel; as, they took his *part;* **5,** a character assigned to an actor in a play; also, the words spoken by that character; as, he took the *part* of Hamlet; **6,** a division of the hair of the head by a straight line; **7,** in music, one of the melodies in a harmony; as, a bass *part;* **8,** one of a given number of equal quantities into which a number, quantity, or object may be divided; as, three is the third *part* of nine; **9, parts, a,** a region or section; as, to live in these *parts;* visit foreign *parts;* **b,** ability or talent; as, a man of *parts:*—*v. t.* **1,** to divide into two or more pieces or sections; **2,** to disunite; force to go apart; **3,** to separate; as, to *part* the fighters:—*v.i.* **1,** to divide

PARSNIP

into two or more parts; break; as, the rope *parted;* **2,** to separate; as, to *part* from a friend.—*adj.* **part′ed.**

  take in good part, to take good-naturedly; **part with,** to give up.

  Syn., n. portion, division, piece.

part. or **p.** abbreviation for *participle.*

par-take (pär-tāk′), *v.i.* [*p.t.* partook (pär-tŏŏk′), *p.p.* partak-en (pär-tāk′ĕn), *p.pr.* partak-ing], **1,** to have or receive a share in common with others; as, men *partake* of the ability to talk; **2,** to take a portion; as, to *partake* of food.—*n.* **par-tak′er.**

par-terre (pär-târ′), *n.* **1,** a series of flower beds arranged ornamentally; **2,** in the U.S., that part of the floor of a theater under the galleries.

Par-the-non (pär′thē-nŏn; pär′thē-nŭn), *n.* the temple of Athena built by the ancient Greeks on the Acropolis at Athens.

Par-thi-a (pär′thĭ-ȧ), an ancient country, south of the Caucasus, in Persia.—*adj.* and *n.* **Par′thi-an.**

Par-thi-an shot (pär′thĭ-ăn), a parting shot: referring to the ancient Parthian custom of turning to flee and discharging missiles at the last moment.

par-tial (pär′shăl), *adj.* **1,** inclined to favor one side or party; **2,** having a liking for; as, she is *partial* to candy; **3,** not entire; incomplete.—*adv.* **par′tial-ly.**—*n.* **par′ti-al′i-ty** (pär′shĭ-ăl′ĭ-tĭ; pär-shăl′ĭ-tĭ).

par-tic-i-pant (pär-tĭs′ĭ-pănt), *n.* one who takes part; a sharer; as, a *participant* in a game:—*adj.* sharing; taking part.

par-tic-i-pate (pär-tĭs′ĭ-pāt), *v.i.* [participat-ed, participat-ing], to share with others; to take part; as, everyone *participated* in the fun.—*n.* **par-tic′i-pa′tor.**—*n.* **par-tic′i-pa′tion.**

par-ti-ci-ple (pär′tĭ-sĭ-pl), *n.* a part of a verb used as both verb and adjective; as, in "running, the man caught the train," the *participle* "running" shows action as a verb, and describes the noun "man" as an adjective.

par-ti-cle (pär′tĭ-kl), *n.* **1,** a very small piece; a bit; **2,** the smallest possible amount of anything; as, not a *particle* of courage; **3,** in grammar, a short, subordinate part of speech, as a conjunction, article, preposition, or interjection.

par-ti—col-ored or **par-ty—col-ored** (pär′tĭ-kŭl′ẽrd), *adj.* having various colors; as, a *parti-colored* flower.

par-tic-u-lar (pẽr-tĭk′ū-lẽr; pär-tĭk′ū-lẽr), *adj.* **1,** distinct from others; as, a *particular* kind of paint; **2,** special; as, of *particular* importance; **3,** exact; nice; as, *particular* in dress; **4,** detailed; precise; as, a *particular* report:—*n.* a detail; as, the *particulars* of the story.

Syn., adj. accurate, singular, unusual.

par·tic·u·lar·i·ty (pĕr-tĭk′û-lăr′ĭ-tĭ; pär-tĭk′û-lăr′ĭ-tĭ), *n.* [*pl.* particularities], **1,** strict attention to detail; carefulness; **2,** a peculiarity.

par·tic·u·lar·ize (pĕr-tĭk′û-lẽr-īz; pär-tĭk′û-lẽr-īz), *v.t.* [particularized, particulariz-ing], **1,** to give the details of; **2,** to make special mention of.

par·tic·u·lar·ly (pĕr-tĭk′û-lẽr-lĭ; pär-tĭk′-û-lẽr-lĭ), *adv.* **1,** in detail; in a particular manner; **2,** especially; as, he *particularly* wanted to go.

part·ing (pär′tĭng), *adj.* **1,** taking leave; hence, dying; as, a *parting* soul; **2,** given when taking leave; as, a *parting* gift:—*n.* **1,** division; **2,** the place of division; as, a *parting* of the ways; **3,** a taking leave; as, the *parting* of friends.

par·ti·san or **par·ti·zan** (pär′tĭ-zăn), *n.* a devoted, sometimes prejudiced, follower, especially of a political cause or faction:—*adj.* pertaining to, or strongly in favor of, a person, cause, or faction, especially a political party or faction.

par·ti·san·ship or **par·ti·zan·ship** (pär′tĭ-zăn-shĭp′), *n.* loyalty; especially, unreasonable loyalty to a person or cause.

par·ti·tion (pär-tĭsh′ŭn), *n.* **1,** the act of dividing or state of being divided; **2,** a sep-aration; a dividing wall, as in a building; **3,** a section or division:—*v.t.* **1,** to divide into shares or parts; **2,** to divide by walls.

PARTITIONS (P, P) in a box

part·ly (pärt′lĭ), *adv.* in part; not wholly; to some extent.

part·ner (pärt′nẽr), *n.* **1,** one who is as-sociated with another or others for mutual benefit or united action; as, a business *part-ner;* **2,** one who shares something with another; as, *partners* in misery; **3,** in games, one who plays with another on a side against opponents; **4,** one who dances with another; **5,** a husband or wife.

Syn. colleague, confederate, associate.

part·ner·ship (pärt′nẽr-shĭp), *n.* **1,** joint interest or ownership; **2,** the union of two or more persons in the same business or profession.

part of speech, in grammar, any of the several classes into which words are grouped according to their use in a sentence, as nouns, verbs, adjectives, adverbs, etc.

par·took (pär-tŏŏk′), past tense of *partake.*

par·tridge (pär′trĭj), *n.* [*pl.* partridge or partridges], **1,** any of various Old World game birds allied to the quails and pheas-ants; **2,** in the U.S., any of a number of similar game birds, as the bobwhite, quail, and ruffed grouse.

par·tridge·ber·ry (pär′trĭj-bĕr′ĭ), *n.* [*pl.* partridgeberries], an American trailing evergreen plant, bear-ing a bright red berry; also, the berry.

par·ty (pär′tĭ), *n.* [*pl.* parties], **1,** a number of persons united for a particular purpose; group; faction; as, a political *party;* **2,** one who has an interest in an affair, as one of the two sides in a lawsuit; **3,** a social gathering; as, a dinner *party.*

PARTRIDGE
Ruffed grouse (1/10)

party line, a boundary line between two adjoining properties; **party wall,** a wall built on a party line.

par·ty – col·ored (pär′tĭ-kŭl′ẽrd), *adj.* having various colors. See parti—colored.

par·ve·nu (pär′vê-nū), *n.* one who has recently risen, because of his wealth, to a position to which he is not accustomed; an upstart.

Pas·a·de·na (păs′a-dē′na), a city, north-east of Los Angeles, in California (map 9).

pa·sha (pa-shä′; pä′shä; păsh′a), *n.* in Turkey, formerly, a high military official or governor of a province; also, after a name, an honorary title. Also, **pa·cha′.**

pasque·flow·er (păsk′flou′ẽr), *n.* a plant bearing large, purplish flowers about East-er time.

pass (pàs), *v.i.* [*p.t.* passed, *p.p.* passed or past (pàst), *p.pr.* pass-ing], **1,** to go from one place or condition to another; move along; as, the parade *passes* down the street; **2,** to move from one to another; circulate freely, as money; **3,** to elapse or go by; as, the night *passed;* **4,** to make or force one's way; as, to *pass* through a crowd; **5,** to go unnoticed; as, his action *passed* without rebuke; **6,** to be approved, as a bill or law; **7,** to go through a test with success; **8,** to decide on the quality of something; as, to *pass* on someone's work; **9,** in cards, to let one's turn go by without playing or bidding; **10,** to be known or accepted; as, to *pass* for a lawyer; **11,** to end; as, old customs *pass* and new ones take their place; **12,** to happen; occur; as, see what *passed:*—*v.t.* **1,** to go by, through, beyond, etc.; as, to *pass* the house; **2,** to cause or allow to go; hand; as, to *pass* the butter; also, to give to someone; cause to circulate; as, to *pass* bad money; **3,** to spend time; as, to *pass* the day; **4,** to exceed; as, it *passes* belief; **5,** to give as a judgment; as, to *pass* sentence; **6,** to utter or pronounce; as, to *pass* an opinion; **7,** to give legal status to (a bill or law); **8,** to go through (a test) successfully:—*n.* **1,** a narrow passage, as in the mountains; **2,** a permit allowing free admission or passage; as, a railway *pass;* **3,** critical condition; as, matters have come to a sad *pass;* **4,** in fencing, a thrust.—*n.* **pass′er.**

pass away, to die; **pass off, 1,** to foist; palm off; as, to *pass off* a lame horse on an ignorant buyer; **2,** to turn attention away from; as, to *pass off* a mistake; **pass over,** to ignore; excuse; as, to *pass over* an insult; **pass through,** to experience; **come to pass,** to happen.

pass. abbreviation for *passive.*

pass-a-ble (pȧs′a̍-bl), *adj.* **1,** capable of being traveled; as, a *passable* road; **2,** not open to great objection; fairly good; as, a book in a *passable* condition; **3,** capable of being circulated, as money.

pas-sage (pȧs′ij), *n.* **1,** course or progress; as, the *passage* of time; **2,** a journey; especially, a voyage; **3,** a way by which one passes; a hall or corridor; **4,** the right to go; as, a free *passage;* **5,** legal enactment; as, the *passage* of a law; **6,** a single portion of a book, speech, etc.; **7,** a conflict; as, a *passage* at arms.

pas-sage-way (pȧs′ij-wā′), *n.* a hall or corridor connecting rooms or buildings; a passage.

pas-sé (pȧ-sā′; pȧs′ā), *adj.* past; out of date; faded.

pas-sen-ger (pȧs′ĕn-jẽr), *n.* one who travels, usually at a stated fare, by a public conveyance, as a boat, train, bus, etc.

pass-er—by (pȧs′ẽr-bī′), *n.* [*pl.* passers-by], one who goes past.

pass-ing (pȧs′ĭng), *adj.* **1,** going by, beyond, or through; as, a *passing* car; **2,** departing; fleeting; as, the *passing* hour; **3,** casual; hasty; as, a *passing* comment; **4,** noting successful completion of an examination or test; as, a *passing* mark:—*adv.* very; as, *passing* strange:—*n.* the act of passing; as, the *passing* of a law; the *passing* of time; death; as, the *passing* of a hero.

pas-sion (pȧsh′ŭn), *n.* **1,** any intense feeling or emotion, as joy, fear, love, etc.; **2,** an outburst of rage; **3,** love; intense desire; enthusiasm; as, a *passion* for music; **4,** the object of love, interest, etc.; as, poetry's my *passion;* **5, passions,** the emotions.

Passion, the sufferings of Christ on the Cross or from the Last Supper to his death; **Passion Week,** formerly, the week before Easter; now, usually, the week before Palm Sunday.

pas-sion-ate (pȧsh′ŭn-ĭt), *adj.* **1,** capable of intense feeling; swayed by emotion; ardent; as, a *passionate* advocate of liberty; **2,** intense; strongly felt; as, a *passionate* love of music.—*adv.* **pas′sion-ate-ly.**

pas-sion-flow-er (pȧsh′ŭn-flou′ẽr), *n.* a plant so named because its flower suggests the crown of thorns placed on Christ's head, the ten true apostles, etc.

pas-sion-less (pȧsh′ŭn-lĕs), *adj.* displaying no anger, intense love, ardor, etc.; tranquil; unmoved.

PASSIONFLOWER

Pas-sion play, a play showing scenes of the suffering and death of Christ, as the one given every ten years at Oberammergau, Bavaria.

pas-sive (pȧs′ĭv), *adj.* **1,** suffering without resisting; submitting; **2,** not acting but acted upon; **3,** in grammar, indicating that form of the transitive verb which carries the idea that the subject is acted upon: opposite of *active;* as, in the sentence, "the boy was thrown from the horse," the subject "boy" receives the action expressed in the *passive* form "was thrown."—*adv.* **pas′sive-ly.**—*n.* **pas-siv′i-ty** (pȧ-sĭv′ĭ-tĭ).

pass-key (pȧs′kē′), *n.* **1,** a key for opening all of a set of locks whose regular keys are not alike; **2,** a private key.

Pass-o-ver (pȧs′ō′vẽr), *n.* a Jewish feast which commemorates the sparing of the Hebrews captive in Egypt, when the Lord slew all the first-born of the Egyptians, but *passed over* the houses of the Israelites which were marked, as had been ordered, with the blood of a lamb (Exodus 12).

pass-port (pȧs′pôrt), *n.* **1,** an official paper from one's own government giving one permission to travel in a foreign country; **2,** anything that opens the way to success.

pass-word (pȧs′wûrd′), *n.* a secret word known only to those on guard and to those permitted to pass the guard; a watchword.

past (pȧst), *adj.* **1,** having formerly been; gone by; as, the *past* generation; **2,** just gone by; last; as, the *past* hour; **3,** thoroughly experienced; as, a *past* master:—*n.* **1,** time gone by; as, memories of the *past;* **2,** previous life or history; as, we know nothing of his *past;* **3,** in grammar, the past tense:—*adv.* by; beyond; as, he just walked *past:*—*prep.* beyond in time, age, or condition; as, he is *past* 21; she is *past* cure:—**past tense,** in grammar, a tense of the verb indicating time gone by; as, he *went;*

āte, āorta, râre, căt, ȧsk, fär, ȧllow, sofa̍; ēve, êvent, ĕll, writẽr, novĕl; bīte, pĭn; nō, ōbey, ôr, dŏg, tŏp, cŏllide; ūnit, ūnite, bûrn, cŭt, focŭs; nōōn, fŏŏt; mound; coin;

past perfect, a tense of the verb indicating action that took place before a time in the past; as, when we arrived, he *had gone.*

paste (pāst), *n.* **1,** a sticky mixture, often of flour and water, used for making things stick together; **2,** dough prepared for pie-crust, etc.; **3,** a preparation, as of fish, nuts, or other foods, finely ground to a creamy consistency; as, anchovy or almond *paste;* also, a jellylike confection; as, Turkish *paste;* **4,** a hard, glassy mixture used for making artificial gems:—*v.t.* [past-ed, past-ing], to cover or fasten with a sticky mixture.

paste-board (pāst′bôrd′), *n.* stiff material made by pressing paper pulp or pasting together sheets of paper.

pas-tel (păs-tĕl′; păs′tĕl), *n.* **1,** a kind of crayon made by mixing ground paints with gum dissolved in water; also, the mixture from which the crayon is made; **2,** a picture drawn with such crayon:—*adj.* light and soft in color; as, a *pastel* green.

pas-tern (păs′tĕrn), *n.* that part of the foot of certain animals between the fetlock and the hoof.

Pas-teur (päs′tûr′), Louis (1822–1895), a French scientist famous for his study of bacteria and the discovery of inoculation for hydrophobia.

PASTERN (P)

pas-teur-ize (păs′tẽr-īz; păs′tū-rīz), *v.t.* [pasteurized, pasteuriz-ing], to heat (a liquid, as milk) to a temperature high enough to destroy harmful germs without destroying the nourishing value of the liquid.—*n.* pas′teur-i-za′tion.

pas-time (păs′tīm′), *n.* diversion; sport; amusement; any activity that fills time agreeably.

pas-tor (păs′tẽr), *n.* a minister in charge of a church and congregation.

pas-to-ral (păs′tō-răl), *adj.* **1,** pertaining to the duties of a minister; as, *pastoral* calls; **2,** pertaining to shepherds or the shepherd's life; as, *pastoral* poetry:—*n.* a poem, play, or the like, depicting country life.

pas-tor-ate (păs′tẽr-ĭt), *n.* **1,** the office or parish of a clergyman; **2,** the time during which a minister holds an office.

past par-ti-ci-ple (pär′tĭ-sĭ-pl), in grammar, a participle denoting past time, action, or condition, usually ending in -d, -ed, -t, -n, or -en. *Told, painted, burnt, worn, broken* are past participles.

pas-try (pās′trĭ), *n.* [*pl.* pastries], desserts, as pies, tarts, etc., made with a rich crust enclosing, usually, fruit or meat.

pas-tur-age (pås′tûr-ĭj), *n.* land used for grazing cattle or other animals.

pas-ture (pås′tûr), *n.* land or grass on which cattle feed:—*v.t.* [pastured, pasturing], to supply with grass or pasture:—*v.i.* to graze.

¹past-y (pās′tĭ), *adj.* [past-i-er, past-i-est], covered with paste; also, like paste, as in color; as, a *pasty* complexion.

²past-y (păs′tĭ; pās′tĭ), *n.* [*pl.* pasties], a pie, usually of highly seasoned meat covered with a crust.

¹pat (păt), *n.* **1,** a light, quick blow with the hand or fingers; **2,** a small, shaped lump, as of butter; **3,** a light sound or tap:—*v.t.* [pat-ted, pat-ting], to strike gently with a flat surface, especially with the hand or fingers; stroke gently.

²pat (păt), *adj.* [pat-ter, pat-test], **1,** suitable; as, a *pat* answer; **2,** resolute; as, to stand *pat*:—*adv.* aptly; readily.

Pat-a-go-ni-a (păt′å-gō′nĭ-å), a region in southern South America, now largely in Argentina.—*adj.* and *n.* **Pat′a-go′ni-an.**

patch (păch), *n.* **1,** a piece of material, as cloth or metal, put on to cover a hole or to strengthen a worn place; **2,** a small piece; a small plot of ground; as, a garden *patch;* **3,** a spot or blotch of color; as, the cat had a *patch* of white on its side:—*v.t.* **1,** to cover or strengthen by putting on a patch; **2,** to mend clumsily; **3,** to piece together with pieces of material; as, to *patch* a quilt; **4,** to settle; mend; as, to *patch* up a quarrel.

patch-work (păch′wûrk′), *n.* **1,** a fabric made of pieces of cloth sewed together, especially pieces of various colors; **2,** hence, a jumble; work carelessly done.

pate (pāt), *n.* the head; crown of the head.

pa-tel-la (på-tĕl′å), *n.* [*pl.* patellae (på-tĕl′ē)], the kneecap; the flat, movable bone forming the front of the knee joint.

pat-ent (păt′ĕnt; pā′tĕnt), *adj.* **1,** open for anyone to view or to read: said especially of an official paper which confers a privilege; as, letters *patent;* **2,** protected by a patent; as, *patent* medicines; **3,** (usually pā′tĕnt), evident; plain; as, his honesty was *patent*:—*n.* **1,** a privilege granted by the government that gives to an inventor the sole right of making, using, or selling his invention for a definite number of years; **2,** the thing so protected; as, he owned several *patents*:—*v.t.* to grant or secure the sole right to.—*adj.* **pat′ent-a-ble.**—*adv.* **pa′tent-ly** (pā′tĕnt-lĭ).

patent leather, a leather with a hard, smooth, glossy surface, usually black: **patent medicine,** a medicine, usually sold in a package, ready for use, the name and formula of which are protected by patent.

pat·ent·ee (păt⁄ĕn-tē⁄; pā⁄tĕn-tē⁄), *n.* a person who holds a patent.

pa·ter·nal (pȧ-tûr⁄năl), *adj.* 1, pertaining to a father; as, *paternal* advice; 2, inherited from a father; as, *paternal* lands; 3, related through the father; as, a *paternal* uncle.—*adv.* **pa·ter⁄nal·ly.**

pa·ter·nal·ism (pȧ-tûr⁄năl-ĭzm), *n.* government in which those in authority seek to maintain a control over the people like that of a father over his children.

pa·ter·ni·ty (pȧ-tûr⁄nĭ-tĭ), *n.* 1, fatherhood; 2, male parentage; as, the *paternity* of the child.

pa·ter·nos·ter (pā⁄tĕr-nŏs⁄tĕr; păt⁄ĕr-nŏs⁄tĕr), *n.* 1, the Lord's Prayer, especially when said in Latin; 2, every 11th bead in a rosary, indicating where the Lord's Prayer is to be said.

Pat·er·son (păt⁄ĕr-sŭn), a manufacturing city in northeastern New Jersey (map 6).

path (påth), *n.* [*pl.* paths (påthz)], 1, a road; footpath; 2, a track; 3, a course of conduct or action.—*adj.* **path⁄less.**

pa·thet·ic (pȧ-thĕt⁄ĭk), *adj.* arousing sympathy and pity; pitiful; as, a *pathetic* cripple.—*adv.* **pa·thet⁄i·cal·ly**

path·o·log·i·cal (păth⁄ō-lŏj⁄ĭ-kăl) or **path·o·log·ic** (păth⁄ō-lŏj⁄ĭk), *adj.* 1, pertaining to the science of disease; 2, due to disease; also, diseased; as, a *pathologic* condition.—*adv.* **path⁄o·log⁄i·cal·ly.**

pa·thol·o·gy (pȧ-thŏl⁄ō-jĭ), *n.* [*pl.* pathologies], the science that treats of diseases.—*n.* **pa·thol⁄o·gist.**

pa·thos (pā⁄thŏs), *n.* that quality which excites sympathy and pity.

path·way (påth⁄wā⁄), *n.* 1, a narrow footpath; 2, any course or road.

pa·tience (pā⁄shĕns), *n.* 1, suffering without complaint; meekness; 2, endurance and perseverance; 3, forbearance; 4, the power to wait calmly; 5, a game of cards. *Syn.* composure, resignation, calmness.

pa·tient (pā⁄shĕnt), *adj.* 1, enduring pain, hardship, etc., without complaint; 2, tolerant; tender; forgiving; 3, untiring in labor; persevering; as, a *patient* worker; 4, waiting with calmness:—*n.* one under the care of a doctor.—*adv.* **pa⁄tient·ly.**

pa·ti·o (pä⁄tĭ-ō; pä⁄tyō), *n.* [*pl.* patios], an open courtyard within a house or other building. (See illustration next column.)

pa·tois (păt⁄wä; pȧ⁄twä⁄), *n.* 1, a dialect used in a certain locality, especially among peasants or illiterate people, very different from the literary language of the country; provincial speech; 2, jargon.

pa·tri·arch (pā⁄trĭ-ärk), *n.* 1, the founder or head of a family or tribe; especially, one of the early ancestors of the Jews; 2, an aged and venerable man; 3, in the Greek Church, a bishop of the highest rank.—*adj.* **pa⁄tri·ar⁄chal** (pā⁄trĭ-är⁄kăl).

pa·tri·cian (pȧ-trĭsh⁄ăn), *n.* 1, a member of the ancient Roman aristocracy: contrasted with *plebeian*; 2, a person of noble birth:—*adj.* 1, pertaining to the ancient Roman aristocracy; 2, noble; aristocratic.

Pat·rick (păt⁄rĭk), Saint (389?–461?), apostle to, and patron saint of, Ireland.

pat·ri·mo·ny (păt⁄rĭ-mō⁄nĭ), *n.* [*pl.* patrimonies], 1, property inherited from a father or other ancestor; 2, property settled upon a religious institution for its support.—*adj.* **pat⁄ri·mo⁄ni·al.**

pa·tri·ot (pā⁄trĭ-ŭt; păt⁄rĭ-ŭt), *n.* one who loves and supports his government or native country:—**Patriots' Day,** the anniversary (April 19) of the battle of Lexington, observed as a legal holiday in Massachusetts and Maine.

pa·tri·ot·ic (pā⁄trĭ-ŏt⁄ĭk; păt⁄rĭ-ŏt⁄ĭk), *adj.* showing love of one's own country.

pa·tri·ot·ism (pā⁄trĭ-ŭt-ĭzm; păt⁄rĭ-ŭt-ĭzm), *n.* love of one's country.

Pa·tro·clus (pȧ-trō⁄klŭs), *n.* a Greek hero of the Trojan War, who, while wearing the armor of his friend Achilles, was mistaken for him by Hector and slain.

pa·trol (pȧ-trōl⁄), *n.* 1, a guard; policeman; 2, the act of going the rounds of a district in order to protect it; 3, a body of soldiers on guard or reconnoitering duty; 4, a division of eight scouts in a troop of boy scouts:—*v.t.* [patrolled, patrol-ling], 1, to go or walk round in order to protect; as, a policeman *patrols* his beat; 2, to act as a guard to (a camp, sea-coast, or the like)

pa·trol·man (pȧ-trōl⁄măn), *n.* [*pl.* patrolmen (-mĕn)], a policeman or watchman whose duty it is to patrol a certain beat.

pa·tron (pā⁄trŭn), *n.* 1, a guardian or protector; 2,

PATIO

an upholder or supporter; as, a *patron* of music or painting; 3, in business, a regular customer; 4, a man who lends his support to a social or charitable event:—*adj.* aiding, or acting as guardian; as, *patron saints.—n.fem.* **pa/tron-ess** (pā/trŭn-ĕs; păt/rŭn-ĕs).

pa·tron·age (pā/trŭn-ĭj; păt/rŭn-ĭj), *n.* 1, special favor or encouragement; guardianship or protection; 2, the act of buying goods regularly at one store, of stopping regularly at one hotel, etc.; 3, politically, the power to control nominations, or to give jobs, favors, etc.

pa·tron·ize (pā/trŭn-īz; păt/rŭn-īz), *v.t.* [patronized, patroniz-ing], 1, to act as guardian or benefactor toward; support or protect; favor; 2, to treat with condescension; 3, *Colloquial,* to deal with regularly as a customer; as, to *patronize* a store.—*n.* **pa/tron-iz/er.**—*adj.* **pa/tron-iz/ing.**

pa·troon (pȧ-tro͞on/), *n.* one who received a large tract of land under the old Dutch governments of New York or New Jersey.

¹**pat·ter** (păt/ẽr), *v.i.* 1, to mumble or mutter something over and over rapidly, especially a prayer; 2, to talk glibly:—*v.t.* to mumble indistinctly:—*n.* 1, rapid, cheap, fluent talk; 2, thieves' jargon.

²**pat·ter** (păt/ẽr), *n.* a quick succession of light sounds:—*v.i.* 1, to run with quick, short steps; 2, to strike with a quick succession of light taps.

pat·tern (păt/ẽrn), *n.* 1, a model, sample, or specimen; 2, anything cut out or formed into a shape to be copied; as, a *pattern* for a dress; 3, an example to follow, especially a good example; 4, a design or figure; as, the *pattern* in a carpet:—*v.t.* 1, to make in imitation of; copy; as, to *pattern* a dress after a model; 2, to decorate, as with a design:—*v.i.* to follow a pattern or example.

pat·ty (păt/ĭ), *n.* [*pl.* patties], a small, cup-shaped shell of pastry, holding meat, oysters, or the like.

Paul (pôl), a Jew of Tarsus who became an apostle of Christ and whose epistles to the Gentiles are contained in the New Testament: originally known as *Saul.*

paunch (pônch; pänch), *n.* the abdomen; the belly and its contents.

pau·per (pô/pẽr), *n.* a very poor person, especially one who is supported by the public or by charity.—*n.* **pau/per-ism.**

pau·per·ize (pô/pẽr-īz) *v.t.* [pauperized, pauperiz-ing], to reduce to extreme poverty; to make a pauper of (a person).

pause (pôz), *n.* 1, a temporary stop or rest; interruption; as, a *pause* in the day's work; 2, an intermission or break in speaking or reading; 3, a break in writing indicated by a punctuation mark; 4, a mark in music over or under a note or rest to show that it is to be prolonged: also called

hold:—v.i. [paused, paus-ing], to make a short stop; wait; as, to *pause* for breath.

pave (pāv), *v.t.* [paved, pav-ing], 1, to cover with stones, bricks, etc.; as, to *pave* a street; 2, to make smooth or easy.

pave·ment (pāv/mĕnt), *n.* 1, a roadway or floor covered or laid with stone, brick, tile, etc.; 2, a sidewalk; 3, any material, as of stones, concrete, or the like, used in covering a road, pathway, or floor.

pa·vil·ion (pȧ-vĭl/yŭn), *n.* 1, a light, ornamental building, as in a garden; 2, a large tent with a peaked roof; 3, a temporary open building for shelter, entertainment, etc.

PAVILION, def. 2

pav·ing (pā/vĭng), *n.* 1, the surfacing of a road or sidewalk; 2, material for covering roads, walks, etc.; also, the surface itself; as, brick *paving.*

paw (pô), *n.* 1, the foot of an animal that has claws, as the cat, dog, tiger, etc.; 2, *Colloquial,* a hand:—*v.t.* 1, to scrape or beat with the feet; as, the horse *pawed* the ground; 2, *Colloquial,* to handle roughly; 3, to strike wildly with the hands; as, to *paw* the air:—*v.i.* 1, to scrape or touch something with the forefoot; 2, *Colloquial,* to handle a thing awkwardly; grope clumsily.

pawl (pôl), *n.* a short bar or catch on a machine, made to fall into notches in another part, as a wheel, in order to prevent it from turning backward.

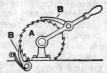

RATCHET WHEEL (A) AND PAWLS (E, B)

¹**pawn** (pôn), *n.* 1, something given or deposited as a pledge for the payment of a debt or return of a loan; 2, the state of being so pledged; as, my watch is in *pawn:—v.t.* to give as security for a loan; as, to *pawn* a ring.

²**pawn** (pôn), *n.* 1, in chess, a piece of lowest value; 2, a person deliberately used or sacrificed by another.

pawn·bro·ker (pôn/brō/kẽr), *n.* a person whose business it is to lend money on goods left with him.

pawn·shop (pôn/shŏp/), *n.* a shop run by a pawnbroker.

paw·paw (pô/pô/), *n.* a kind of tree; the papaw. See **papaw**

Paw·tuck·et (pô-tŭk/ĕt), a manufacturing city in Rhode Island (map 6).

pay (pā), *v.t.* [paid (pād), pay-ing], 1, to give money to, in return for work done or goods received;

as, to *pay* workmen; **2,** to discharge, as a debt, by giving over the money required; **3,** to be profitable to; as, it will *pay* you to do what I say; **4,** to give without any sense of obligation; as, to *pay* a compliment; **5,** to allow to run out; to pass out through the hands; as, we *payed* out all the slack in the rope:—*v.i.* **1,** to make recompense; discharge a debt; as, he always *pays* promptly; **2,** to make suitable return for effort; be worth while; as, the business *pays* well; it *pays* to be honest:—*n.* money given for work done; wages; salary.

Syn., n. allowance, compensation, fee.

pay-a-ble (pā′a̶-bl), *adj.* due, as a bill.

pay-ee (pā′ē′), *n.* one to whom money is, is to be, or has been, paid.

pay-mas-ter (pā′mȧs′tẽr), *n.* an official, as in a firm, who gives out money for wages; especially, an officer in the army or navy whose duty it is to pay the officers and men.

pay-ment (pā′mĕnt), *n.* **1,** the act of giving money for wages, a debt, etc.; **2,** that which is given to discharge a debt, duty, etc.; **3,** penalty; punishment.

payt. abbreviation for *payment*.

Paz, La (lä päs′), a city, one of the capitals of Bolivia (map 11).

p.c. abbreviation for *per cent, post card*.

pd. abbreviation for *paid*.

pea (pē), *n.* [*pl.* peas or pease (pēz)], **1,** a pod-bearing plant of the same family as the bean, widely grown as a vegetable; **2,** its round, green seed, which is used for food; **3,** a related plant; as, the sweet *pea*.

peace (pēs), *n.* **1,** a state of rest or calm; especially, freedom from war or disorder; **2,** friendly relations between persons; **3,** a treaty or agreement to end a war.

PEA
Portion of plant, showing leaves, tendrils, p o d s, and seeds.

peace-a-ble (pēs′a̶-bl), *adj.* **1,** not quarrelsome; **2,** calm; quiet.—*n.* **peace′a-ble-ness.**—*adv.* **peace′a-bly.**

peace-ful (pēs′fŏŏl), *adj.* **1,** free from war or commotion; **2,** mild; calm; undisturbed; quiet; as, a *peaceful* evening.—*adv.* **peace′ful-ly.**—*n.* **peace′-ful-ness.**

Syn. tranquil, peaceable, placid, serene.

peace-mak-er (pēs′māk′ẽr), *n.* one who restores friendly feeling between foes.

peach (pēch), *n.* **1,** a sweet, juicy fruit, with white or yellow flesh, a downy, pink-tinted skin, and a large, rough stone con-

taining one large seed; **2,** the tree bearing this fruit; **3,** a soft yellowish-pink color.

pea-cock (pē′kŏk′), *n.* the male bird of the peafowl, noted for its long, handsome tail feathers, marked with iridescent, eyelike spots.—*n. fem.* **pea′hen′** (pē′hĕn′).

PEACH
Section of fruit, showing stone.

pea-fowl (pē′foul′), *n.* a peacock or a peahen.

peak (pēk), *n.* **1,** the sharp-pointed top of a mountain or hill; **2,** a mountain standing alone; **3,** a pointed end of anything; as, the *peak* of a roof; **4,** the most intense or highest point; as, the *peak* of happiness; **5,** the visor of a cap; **6,** the narrow part of a vessel's bow or stern.

¹**peaked** (pēkt), *adj.* pointed; as, a *peaked* roof; also, projecting; as, a *peaked* cap.

²**peak-ed** (pēk′-ĕd), *adj. Colloquial,* sharp-featured; thin; wan; sickly; as, a *peaked* face.

PEACOCKS (.¹₂)

peal (pēl), *n.* **1,** a loud sound or succession of sounds, as of thunder, bells, etc.; **2,** a set of bells, or a musical phrase rung on them:—*v.i.* to give forth loud sounds, as a bell or organ:—*v.t.* to cause to sound loudly; as, to *peal* a bell.

pea-nut (pē′nŭt′), *n.* a yellow-flowered plant of the pea family, whose pods ripen under the ground; also, its nutlike fruit.

pear (pâr), *n.* **1,** a sweet, juicy, oblong-shaped fruit related to the apple; **2,** the tree which bears this fruit.

pearl (pûrl), *n.* **1,** a small, smooth, lustrous gem formed as a growth inside the shells of oysters or other shellfish; **2,** something resembling a pearl in shape, size, color, or value; **3,** a pale, grayish-white color; **4,** in printing, a small size of type (see *type,* illustration):—**mother-of—pearl,** the tinted lining of the shell of various shellfish.

PEAR
Section of fruit, showing seeds.

pearl-y (pûr′lĭ), *adj.* [pearl-i-er, pearl-i-est], **1,** like pearl or mother-of-pearl; **2,** made of, or adorned with, pearls or mother-of-pearl.

Pea-ry (pē′rĭ), Robert Edwin (1856-1920), an American arctic explorer, credited with discovering the North Pole.

peas-ant (pĕz′ȧnt), *n.* in Europe, one who

tills the soil; a farmer or farm laborer:— *adj.* rustic; as, *peasant* manners.

peas-ant-ry (pĕz′ănt-rĭ), *n.* those who till the soil; peasants; farmers.

pease (pēz), one form of the plural of *pea.*

peat (pēt), *n.* a substance formed of partly decayed vegetable matter in swamps and marshy places, and much used, as in Ireland, for fuel.—*adj.* **peat′y.**

peb-ble (pĕb′l), *n.* a small stone; a stone worn smooth by water.—*adj.* **peb′bly.**

pe-can (pē-kăn′; pē-kän′), *n.* **1,** a kind of hickory tree of southern U.S.; **2,** its oblong, smooth, thin-shelled nut.

pec-ca-dil-lo (pĕk′a-dĭl′ō), *n.* [*pl.* peccadilloes or peccadillos], a trifling fault or slight offense.

pec-ca-ry (pĕk′a-rĭ), *n.* [*pl.* peccaries], a night-roving, hoglike wild animal found in America from Texas to Paraguay.

PECCARY (¹⁄₁₆)

¹**peck** (pĕk), *n.* **1,** in dry measure, one quarter of a bushel; eight quarts; also, a vessel for measuring out a peck; **2,** a lot; a great deal; as, a *peck* of trouble.

²**peck** (pĕk), *v.t.* **1,** to strike with the beak; as the bird *pecked* my hand; **2,** to strike with a pointed instrument, as a pick; **3,** to pick up with the beak; as, the hen *pecks* corn; **4,** *Colloquial,* to eat sparingly; as, she *pecks* her food:—*v.i.* **1,** to make strokes with the beak or a sharp instrument; **2,** to pick up food with the beak:—*n.* **1,** a quick, sharp stroke, as with the beak; **2,** a mark made by a blow with a pointed instrument.

pec-to-ral (pĕk′tō-răl), *adj.* of or placed on the chest; as, a *pectoral* muscle.

pec-u-la-tion (pĕk′ū-lā′shŭn), *n.* theft of money entrusted to one's care; embezzlement.

pe-cul-iar (pē-kūl′yĕr), *adj.* **1,** one's own; individual; belonging to a particular person or place; as, a tree *peculiar* to New England; **2,** strange; queer; as, her actions are *peculiar.*—*adv.* **pe-cul′iar-ly.**
Syn. particular, singular, odd, unusual.

pe-cu-li-ar-i-ty (pē-kū′lĭ-ăr′ĭ-tĭ), *n.* [*pl.* peculiarities], **1,** something which marks a person or thing as being different from others; **2,** strangeness; oddness.

pe-cu-ni-ar-y (pē-kū′nĭ-ĕr′ĭ), *adj.* of or concerned with money; financial; as, *pecuniary* losses.

ped-a-gog or **ped-a-gogue** (pĕd′a-gŏg), *n.* a schoolteacher; often, a dull schoolmaster.

ped-a-gog-i-cal (pĕd′a-gŏj′ĭ-kăl; pĕd′a-gō′jĭ-kăl), *adj.* having to do with teaching.

ped-a-go-gy (pĕd′a-gō′jĭ; pĕd′a-gŏj′ĭ), *n.* [*pl.* pedagogies], the science, art, or practice of teaching.

ped-al (pĕd′ăl), *adj.* concerning or operated by a foot:—*n.* the treadle, or foot-operated lever, of a machine, organ, piano, or harp:—*v.t.* and *v.i.* [pedaled, pedal-ing], to move or operate by working a pedal or pedals.

ped-ant (pĕd′ănt), *n.* one who makes a show of his learning.

pe-dan-tic (pē-dăn′tĭk), *adj.* showy, or ostentatious, in the use of knowledge; as, a *pedantic* writer.—*adv.* **pe-dan′ti-cal-ly.**

ped-ant-ry (pĕd′ănt-rĭ), *n.* [*pl.* pedantries], conceited and needless display of learning; the habit of overvaluing and emphasizing trifling details of learning.

ped-dle (pĕd′l), *v.i.* [ped-dled, ped-dling], to travel about selling small wares:—*v.t.* **1,** to sell from house to house; hawk; **2,** hence, to deal out little by little.

ped-dler or **ped-lar** (pĕd′lēr), *n.* one who goes from house to house selling things.

PEDESTAL

ped-es-tal (pĕd′ĕs-tăl), *n.* **1,** the base of a column; also, the support of a statue, lamp, or the like; **2,** any base or foundation; **3,** a position of high regard or admiration; as, he put his friend on a *pedestal.*

pe-des-tri-an (pē-dĕs′trĭ-ăn), *n.* one who travels on foot, a walker:—*adj.* **1,** walking; on foot; **2,** hence, slow-moving; dull; uninspired; as, *pedestrian* argument or writing.

PEDIMENT (P)

ped-i-cel (pĕd′ĭ-sĕl), *n.* a slender flower stem branching from a peduncle.

ped-i-gree (pĕd′ĭ-grē), *n.* **1,** a record or list of ancestors; **2,** lineage; ancestry; as, a man of noble *pedigree.*

ped-i-ment (pĕd′ĭ-mĕnt), *n.* **1,** in Greek architecture, the triangular space forming the gable of a roof; **2,** hence, a similar triangular decoration over a door, window, or the like.

PEDUNCLE (A) AND PEDICEL (B)

ped-lar (pĕd′lēr), *n.* one who sells things from house to house. See **peddler.**

pe-dun-cle (pē-dŭng′kl), *n.* the main stem of a flower or cluster of flowers.

---

go; join; yet; sing; chin; show; thin, *th***en; hw,** *wh***y; zh,** *a***zure; ü, Ger. für or Fr. lune; ō, Ger. schön or Fr. feu; n, Fr. enfant, nom; kh, Ger. ach or ich.** See pages ix–x.

peek (pēk), *v.i.* to look slyly through half-closed eyes; to look through a crevice or crack; peep:—*n.* a peep; a sly glance.

peel (pēl), *v.t.* **1,** to strip off an outer covering from; as, to *peel* an orange; **2,** to strip off; as, to *peel* bark from a tree:—*v.i.* to come off; as, bark or skin *peels:*—*n.* skin or rind.

¹**peep** (pēp), *v.i.* **1,** to chirp; cry, as young birds; **2,** to speak in a weak, high voice:—*n.* **1,** a chirp; squeak; **2,** a baby chick.

²**peep** (pēp), *v.i.* **1,** to look through a crack or from a hiding place; look slyly; **2,** to begin to appear; as, the moon *peeped* from behind a cloud:—*n.* **1,** a quick, sly look; **2,** a glimpse; as, a *peep* at the first chapter made me read further; **3,** first appearance, as of the sun.

peep-er (pē′pẽr), *n.* **1,** one that peeps or chirps; especially, a young frog; **2,** a person who spies; as, Tom, the *peeper.*

¹**peer** (pēr), *n.* **1,** a person of the same or equal rank; an equal; as, a jury of his *peers;* **2,** a member of the British nobility; a nobleman.

²**peer** (pēr), *v.i.* **1,** to look closely or out of curiosity; as, they all *peered* at me; **2,** to peep out; come into sight; as, the sun *peered* from behind the cloud.

peer-age (pēr′ij), *n.* **1,** the rank or dignity of a nobleman; **2,** the whole body of noblemen; **3,** a record or list of peers, with their histories, titles, etc.

peer-ess (pēr′ĕs), *n.* the wife of a noble, or a lady of noble rank in her own right.

peer-less (pēr′lĕs), *adj.* without equal; matchless; as, a *peerless* voice.

pee-vish (pē′vĭsh), *adj.* childishly fretful; hard to please; as, a *peevish* disposition.—*adv.* **pee′vish-ly.**—*n.* **pee′vish-ness.**
    Syn. irritable, petulant, testy, cross.

peg (pĕg), *n.* **1,** a pointed wooden or metal pin used as a fastening; as, a shoe *peg;* a tent *peg;* **2,** a piece of wood serving as a nail; as, to hang one's coat on a *peg;* **3,** a step or degree; as, he took her down a *peg:* —*v.t.* [pegged, peg-ging], **1,** to fasten with pegs; as, to *peg* furniture; **2,** to mark by driving in small stakes of wood; as, to *peg* out a mining claim:—*v.i.* to work steadily; as, to *peg* away at one's lessons.

Peg-a-sus (pĕg′à-sŭs), *n.* in Greek mythology, a winged horse caught, tamed, and presented to the Muses by Minerva, and hence regarded as a symbol of poetic fancy or imagination.

Pei-ping (pā′pĭng′), a city in eastern China, capital of China (map **15**). It was formerly called **Pe-king** (pē′kĭng′) or **Pe-kin** (pē′kĭn′).

Pe-king-ese (pē′kĭng-ēz′; pē′kĭng-ēs′) or **Pe-kin-ese** (pē′kĭn-ēz′; pē′kĭn-ēs′), *n.* a small, pug-nosed, long-haired dog, originally from China.

pe-koe (pē′kō; pĕk′ō), *n.* a choice black tea from Ceylon and India.

pelf (pĕlf), *n.* **1,** stolen property; **2,** money; wealth; riches.

PEKINGESE (¹⁄₁₅)

pel-i-can (pĕl′ĭ-kăn), *n.* a large, web-footed water bird, which has a large pouch attached to the lower jaw of its huge bill.

Pe-li-on (pē′lĭ-ŏn), a mountain in Thessaly. In Greek mythology, the Titans piled Pelion on Ossa in their attempt to scale Olympus, the abode of the gods, in their war against them.

pe-lisse (pĕ-lēs′), *n.* a woman's long cloak, originally fur-lined or made entirely of fur.

pel-let (pĕl′ĕt), *n.* **1,** a little ball, as of food or medicine; **2,** a missile; bullet.

PELICANS (¹⁄₁₀)

pell—mell or **pell-mell** (pĕl′=mĕl′), *adv.* **1,** in a disorderly manner; **2,** headlong; in a great hurry; as, they rushed out *pell-mell.*

pel-lu-cid (pĕ-lū′sĭd), *adj.* **1,** transparent; clear; as, a *pellucid* stream; **2,** easily understood; as, *pellucid* language.

Pel-o-pon-ne-sus (pĕl′ō-pŏ-nē′sŭs), a peninsula (cap. Corinth), the southwest division of Greece (map **1**). Its modern name is *Peloponnesos* or *Morea.*

¹**pelt** (pĕlt), *n.* a raw hide; the untanned skin of an animal.

²**pelt** (pĕlt), *v.t.* **1,** to strike with a number of missiles; as, to *pelt* a person with snowballs; **2,** to hurl; as, to *pelt* pebbles at the windows:—*v.i.* **1,** to strike repeated blows with something thrown; **2,** to beat down heavily, as rain or hail:—*n.* **1,** a blow from something thrown; **2,** a rapid speed:—**full pelt,** (at) full speed; as, to ride *full pelt.*

pel-vic (pĕl′vĭk), *adj.* relating to the pelvis.

pel-vis (pĕl′vĭs), *n.* [*pl.* pelves (pĕl′vēz)], in man's anatomy, the basin-shaped structure of bones which supports the spinal column and to which the lower limbs are attached; in animals, a similar structure where the backbone and hip bones meet.

Pem-ba (pĕm′bà), an island off Tanganyika Territory in eastern Africa (map **14**).

pem·mi·can (pĕm′ĭ-kăn), *n*. an American Indian food made of lean meat, fat, and sometimes fruit: often dried, pounded, and pressed into cakes.

¹pen (pĕn), *n*. a small enclosure, especially one for confining animals; a coop:—*v.t.* [penned (pĕnd) or pent (pĕnt), pen-ning], to shut up in, or as if in, a pen or enclosure.

²pen (pĕn), *n*. an instrument for writing with ink, originally a quill; now, ordinarily, a split point of metal to be fitted into a holder; also, the holder and the point together:—*v.t.* [penned, pen-ning], to write; compose and put upon paper, as a letter.

pe·nal (pē′năl), *adj*. **1**, having to do with punishment or with punished persons; as, *penal* laws; *penal* labor; a *penal* colony; **2**, meriting punishment; as, a *penal* offence.

pe·nal·ize (pē′năl-īz), *v.t.* [penalized, penaliz-ing], to inflict a penalty upon; as, the referee *penalized* our football team.

pen·al·ty (pĕn′ăl-tĭ), *n*. [*pl*. penalties], **1**, legal punishment for breaking the law; as, the *penalty* for murder is death; **2**, a fine; forfeit; **3**, a punishment or handicap imposed for the breaking of a rule.

pen·ance (pĕn′ăns), *n*. **1**, an act of devotion, often prescribed, to show sorrow or repentance for a sin; **2**, hardship or suffering as a result of a mistake or wrongdoing.

pence (pĕns), in Great Britain, the plural of *penny*, used in giving a price in pennies.

pen·chant (pän′shän′; pĕn′chănt), *n*. a strong leaning or taste; as, she has a *penchant* for music.

pen·cil (pĕn′sĭl), *n*. a stick of black lead, colored chalk, etc., generally incased in wood, and used for writing, drawing, etc.:—*v.t.* [penciled, pencil-ing], to write or sketch with a pencil.—*adj.* **pen′ciled**.

pend·ant (pĕn′dănt), *n*. something hanging; especially, a hanging ornament.

pend·ent (pĕn′dĕnt), *adj*. **1**, hanging; as, *pendent* decorations; **2**, jutting over; overhanging; as, *pendent* rocks.

pend·ing (pĕn′dĭng), *adj*. not yet finished or decided; as, a *pending* trial:—*prep*. **1**, during; as, *pending* the negotiations for peace, an armistice was declared; **2**, until; awaiting; as, *pending* his arrival, we did nothing.

pen·du·lous (pĕn′dū-lŭs), *adj*. hanging so as to swing; swaying; as, *pendulous* cobwebs.

pen·du·lum (pĕn′dū-lŭm), *n*. a body suspended from a fixed point so that it is free to swing to and fro; as, the *pendulum* of a clock.

Pe·nel·o·pe (pĕ-nĕl′ō-pē), *n*. in Greek mythology, the wife of Odysseus (Ulysses) of Ithaca, who was noted for her faithfulness to her husband during his wanderings after the Trojan War.

pen·e·tra·ble (pĕn′ă-trȧ-bl), *adj*. capable of being entered or pierced.—*n*. **pen′e·tra·bil′-i·ty**.

pen·e·trate (pĕn′ă-trāt), *v.t.* [penetrat-ed, penetrat-ing], **1**, to enter into; pierce; **2**, to soak through; spread itself through; as, the dampness *penetrated* his clothes; **3**, to understand; as, to *penetrate* a secret:—*v.i.* **1**, to pierce something; **2**, to affect the feelings or mind deeply.

PENDULUM (P)

pen·e·trat·ing (pĕn′ă-trā′tĭng), *adj*. **1**, piercing; sharp; **2**, discerning; knowing; as, *penetrating* remarks.

pen·e·tra·tion (pĕn′ă-trā′shŭn), *n*. **1**, the act of entering or piercing; **2**, mental acuteness or keenness; sagacity.

pen·gö (pĕn′gö′), *n*. [*pl*. pengö or pengös], a silver coin, the former monetary unit of Hungary. See **forint**.

pen·guin (pĕn′gwĭn; pĕng′gwĭn), *n*. a large antarctic sea bird which cannot fly but uses its winglike appendages as paddles in swimming.

pen·i·cil·lin (pĕn′ĭ-sĭl′ĭn), *n*. an antibiotic produced by a mold, and used in the treatment of bacterial infections such as pneumonia.

pen·in·su·la (pĕn·ĭn′sū-là), *n*. a piece of land almost surrounded by water.—*adj.* **pen·in′su·lar**.

PENGUIN (⅟₄₀)

pen·i·tence (pĕn′ĭ-tĕns), *n*. sorrow for sin or wrongdoing; repentance.—*adj.* **pen′i·ten′tial**.

pen·i·tent (pĕn′ĭ-tĕnt), *adj*. sorry; repentant:—*n*. a person who is repentant, or sorry for sin; also, a person doing penance.

pen·i·ten·tia·ry (pĕn′ĭ-tĕn′shȧ-rĭ), *adj*. **1**, pertaining to penance; **2**, pertaining to prisons or reformatories; **3**, making a person liable to imprisonment; as, a *penitentiary* offense:—*n*. [*pl*. penitentiaries], a prison in which convicts are confined.

pen·knife (pĕn′nīf′), *n*. [*pl*. penknives (pĕn′nīvz′)], a small pocketknife.

pen·man (pĕn′măn), *n*. [*pl*. penmen (-mĕn)], a person who uses a pen; a writer.

pen·man·ship (pĕn′măn-shĭp), *n.* art or style of handwriting; as, good *penmanship*.

Penn (pĕn), William (1644-1718), an English Quaker, founder of the State of Pennsylvania.

Penn. or **Penna.** abbreviation for *Pennsylvania*.

pen name, a fictitious name used by an author instead of his own name.

pen·nant (pĕn′ănt), *n.* 1, a long, narrow naval flag or streamer; 2, a small, triangular flag; 3, a flag given to a champion team in a sport; 4, hence, championship.

pen·ni·less (pĕn′ĭ-lĕs), *adj.* without a penny; very poor; destitute.

PENNANT, def. 2

pen·non (pĕn′ŭn), *n.* 1, a flag or streamer, swallow-tailed or triangular, borne on a lance; 2, any flag or banner.

Penn·syl·va·ni·a (pĕn′sĭl-vā′nĭ-à), a State (cap. Harrisburg) in the Middle Atlantic section of the U.S. (map **6**).

pen·ny (pĕn′ĭ), *n.* [*pl.* pennies, meaning a number of coins, or pence (pĕns), meaning, generally, an amount valued in pennies], 1, in England, a coin, formerly copper, now bronze, equal to one twelfth of a shilling, or about two cents of U.S. money; 2, in the U.S., one cent.

pen·ny·roy·al (pĕn′ĭ-roi′ăl), *n.* a fragrant herb of the mint family.

pen·ny·weight (pĕn′ĭ-wāt′), *n.* a troy weight equal to 24 grains, or 1/20 of an ounce.

pen·ny–wise (pĕn′ĭ-wīz′), *adj.* saving small sums; niggardly:—**penny–wise and pound–foolish**, practicing small economies and wasteful of larger amounts.

pen·ny·worth (pĕn′ĭ-wûrth′), *n.* as much as a penny will buy.

pe·nol·o·gy (pē-nŏl′ō-jĭ), *n.* the study of prisons and of punishments for crime.

pen·sion (pĕn′shŭn), *n.* 1, a certain sum paid regularly by a government, employer, or corporation to a person retired after a long period of service; 2, an allowance paid by governments to provide for certain needy classes; as, old-age *pensions*; 3, (in French, päṅ′syôṅ′; in German, päṅ-syôṅ′), in Europe, a boarding house or boarding school:—*v.t.* to grant a regular allowance of money to.

pen·sion·er (pĕn′shŭn-ẽr), *n.* a person who receives a pension.

pen·sive (pĕn′sĭv), *adj.* 1, engaged in, or given to, serious thought; musing; as, a *pensive* mood; a *pensive* nature; 2, expressing serious thought; as, a *pensive* poem.—*adv.* **pen′sive·ly.**—*n.* **pen′sive·ness.**

Syn. meditative, reflective, dreamy.

pent (pĕnt), *adj.* shut or penned up; confined: often with *up*; as, *pent*-up rage.

pen·ta·gon (pĕn′tà-gŏn; pĕn′tà-gŭn), *n.* in geometry, a figure with five sides and five angles.—*adj.* **pen·tag′o·nal** (pĕn-tăg′ō-năl).

pen·tam·e·ter (pĕn-tăm′ē-tẽr), *n.* a verse, or line of poetry, having five metrical feet. The PENTAGON line "A horse! /a horse! / My king- /dom for/a horse! " is iambic pentameter.

Pen·ta·teuch (pĕn′tà-tūk), *n.* the first five books of the Old Testament.

Pen·te·cost (pĕn′tē-kŏst), *n.* 1, a Jewish festival celebrated on the 50th day after the second day of the Passover; 2, the Christian feast of Whitsunday, celebrating the descent of the Holy Ghost upon the disciples (Acts 2:1-4).—*adj.* **Pen′te·cos′tal.**

pent·house (pĕnt′hous′), *n.* 1, a shed or a slanting roof attached to a main wall or building; 2, a house or apartment on a roof.

pe·nult (pē′nŭlt; pē-nŭlt′), *n.* the last syllable but one.—*adj.* **pe·nul′ti·mate.**

pe·num·bra (pē-nŭm′brà), *n.* [*pl.* penumbrae (pē-nŭm′brē) or penumbras], 1, in an eclipse, the region of partial shadow around the space in complete shadow; 2, hence, any partial shadow, or partly shadowed area.

pe·nu·ri·ous (pē-nū′rĭ-ŭs), *adj.* miserly; stingy.—*n.* **pe·nu′ri·ous·ness.**

pen·u·ry (pĕn′ū-rĭ), *n.* want of the necessities of life; extreme poverty.

Syn. need, privation, destitution.

pe·on (pē′ŏn), *n.* in Spanish America and in the southern U.S., a laborer, especially one forced to work to pay a debt.—*n.* **pe′on·age.**

pe·o·ny (pē′ō-nĭ), *n.* [*pl.* peonies], a garden plant that springs up in a cluster of red shoots; also, one of its large, usually double, red, pink, or white flowers.

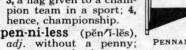

peo·ple (pē′pl), *n.* 1, a body of persons united into a community, race, tribe, nation, etc.; inhabitants; as, the American *people;* 2, men, women, and children; as, only ten *people* were present; PEONY 3, the persons of a particular place or group; as, country *people;* 4, the lower classes; the masses; as, the *people* revolted against the nobles; 5, relatives; as, my own *people:—v.t.* [peo-pled, peo-pling], to fill with inhabitants; as, to *people* a country.

Pe-or-i-a (pê-ôr′ĭ-à), a manufacturing city in central Illinois (map 7).

pep-per (pĕp′ẽr), *n.* 1, a hot seasoning made of the ground berries of an East Indian plant; also, the plant which bears these berries; 2, a plant whose red berries make a similar hot seasoning; 3, a garden plant, whose hollow red or green fruit is used as a vegetable:—*v.t.* 1, to season with pepper; 2, to sprinkle thickly; also, to shower objects upon.

PEPPER, def. 3

pep-per-corn (pĕp′ẽr-kôrn′), *n.* 1, the small dried berry of the pepper plant; 2, a trifling return or consideration.

pep-per-mint (pĕp′ẽr-mĭnt), *n.* 1, a strong-smelling plant of the mint family; 2, an oil prepared from it; 3, a candy flavored with this oil.

PEPPERMINT

pep-per-y (pĕp′ẽr-ĭ), *adj.* 1, containing pepper; 2, hot-tempered; fiery; spirited.

pep-sin (pĕp′sĭn), *n.* 1, a ferment formed in the gastric juice of animals as a natural aid to digestion; 2, a preparation from this substance used in medicine.

pep-tone (pĕp′tōn), *n.* any one of a number of substances into which proteids are converted by the gastric and pancreatic juices.

per (pûr; pĕr), *prep.* 1, through; by means of; by; as, *per* bearer; 2, in or for each; as, 1,000 feet *per* second; two dollars *per* man. **per annum** (ăn′ŭm), by the year; yearly; **per diem** (dī′ĕm), by the day; daily; **per se** (sē), by or in itself.

per- (pûr-), a prefix meaning: 1, through; throughout; as, *per*vade, *per*meate; 2, very thoroughly; as, *per*turb, *per*vert.

per-ad-ven-ture (pûr′ăd-vĕn′tũr), *adv.* Archaic, perhaps; as, *per*adventure, he will come:—*n.* doubt; question.

PERAMBULATOR

per-am-bu-late (pẽr-ăm′bū-lāt), *v.i.* [perambulat-ed, perambulat-ing], to walk about.

per-am-bu-la-tor (pẽr-ăm′bū-lā′tẽr), *n.* a baby carriage.

per-cale (pẽr-kāl′), *n.* a closely woven cotton fabric with a linen finish and, often, a printed pattern.

per cap-i-ta (pĕr kăp′ĭ-tà), by heads; hence, for each person; as, the state levied a *per capita* tax.

per-ceive (pĕr-sēv′), *v.t.* [perceived, perceiv-ing], 1, to become aware of through the senses; see, hear, feel, taste, or smell; 2, to understand; comprehend.
Syn. discern, distinguish, discriminate.

per cent (pẽr sĕnt), one unit of a whole made up of one hundred units; as, six *per cent* of a dollar is six cents.—Also, **per-cent′.**: **per cen′tum.**—*n.* and *adj.* **per-cent′.**

per-cent-age (pẽr-sĕn′tĭj), *n.* a certain part or number in each hundred; loosely, any part or proportion of a whole.

per-cep-ti-ble (pẽr-sĕp′tĭ-bl), *adj.* capable of being known through the senses.—*adv.* **per-cep′ti-bly.**—*n.* **per-cep′ti-bil′i-ty.**

per-cep-tion (pẽr-sĕp′shŭn), *n.* 1, ability to become aware of something through the senses; 2, a mental impression; understanding.

¹**perch** (pûrch), *n.* 1, a spiny-finned freshwater fish of which the yellow perch is the commonest variety; 2, any of various spiny-finned, salt-water fishes, as the sea perch or cunner, and the white perch.

²**perch** (pûrch), *n.* 1, a rod or pole on which birds sit or roost; 2, any high seat; 3, as a measure: of length, 5½ yards; a rod; of surface, 30¼ square yards; a square rod; of capacity, 24¾ cubic feet:—*v.i.* to sit on a high seat; roost.

per-chance (pẽr-chȧns′), *adv.* Archaic, perhaps; maybe.

Per-ci-vale (pûr′sĭ-văl), *n.* in medieval romance, a knight of the Round Table, pure enough to succeed in the search for the Holy Grail.

per-co-late (pûr′kō-lāt), *v.i.* [percolat-ed, percolat-ing], to pass, as a liquid, through very small spaces; to filter; as, water *per*colates through sand:—*v.t.* 1, to cause to pass through very small spaces; to filter; 2, to pass boiling water through, in order to extract a flavor; as, to *per*colate coffee.

PERCOLATOR
Water, *a,* forced up, through the tube *b* by the application of heat from below, strikes against glass lid *d,* whence it drips back through ground coffee in filter cup *c.*

per-co-la-tor (pûr′kō-lā′tẽr), *n.* anything that filters; especially, a coffeepot in which boiling water filters through ground coffee.

per ct. or **p.c.** abbreviation for *per cent.*

per-cus-sion (pĕr-kŭsh′ŭn), *n.* **1,** a violent crashing together of two bodies; **2,** the striking of sound waves against the eardrum:—**percussion instrument,** a musical instrument played by striking, as with a drumstick (see illustration under *musical instruments*).

per-di-tion (pĕr-dĭsh′ŭn), *n.* **1,** ruin; especially, loss of all happiness after death; **2,** hell; the place of lasting torment.

per-e-gri-na-tion (pĕr′ē-grĭ-nā′shŭn), *n.* a traveling about or wandering from place to place; travel.

per-emp-to-ry (pĕr-ĕmp′tō-rĭ; pĕr′ĕmp-tôr′ĭ), *adj.* positive; final; allowing no discussion; as, a *peremptory* command.— *adv.* **per-emp′to-ri-ly.**

per-en-ni-al (pĕr-ĕn′ĭ-ăl), *adj.* **1,** lasting throughout the year; as, *perennial* summer; **2,** living more than one year; living on from year to year; as, *perennial* flowers; **3,** enduring; as, *perennial* youth:—*n.* a plant that lives more than one year.

per-fect (pûr′fĕkt), *adj.* **1,** complete; finished; whole; **2,** without defect or blemish; as, a *perfect* apple; a *perfect* diamond; **3,** alike in detail; exact; as, a *perfect* likeness; **4,** of the highest type of excellence; as, a *perfect* answer; **5,** very skilled or accomplished; as, a *perfect* defense; **6,** *Colloquial,* utter; entire; as, a *perfect* stranger: —**perfect tense,** in grammar, any of three tenses of the verb, called more specifically *present perfect, past perfect,* and *future perfect,* which indicate action that has taken place before the time of the present, the past, or the future; as, I *have seen,* I *had seen,* I *shall have seen;* especially, the present perfect:—*n.* in grammar, the present perfect tense:—*v.t.* (pĕr-fĕkt′; pûr′fĕkt), **1,** to complete or finish; as, to *perfect* an invention; **2,** to bring to final excellence; as, to *perfect* one's speaking ability.

per-fec-tion (pĕr-fĕk′shŭn), *n.* **1,** completion; as, the *perfection* of the plan was left to the captain; **2,** completeness; as, to bring a plan to *perfection;* **3,** that which is faultless; also, highest excellence or skill; as, the *perfection* of the boy's playing amazed the musician.

per-fect-ly (pûr′fĕkt-lĭ), *adv.* in a faultless manner; exactly; completely.

per-fid-i-ous (pĕr-fĭd′ĭ-ŭs), *adj.* treacherous; faithless; disloyal; as, a *perfidious* friend.—*adv.* **per-fid′i-ous-ly.**
Syn. deceitful, traitorous.

per-fi-dy (pûr′fĭ-dĭ), *n.* [*pl.* perfidies], treachery; faithlessness; disloyalty.

per-fo-rate (pûr′fō-rāt), *v.t.* [perforat-ed, perforat-ing], to pierce; make a hole or a

series of holes in; as, to *perforate* checks for purposes of cancellation.—*n.* **per′fo-ra′tor.**—*adj.* **per′fo-rat′ed.**

per-fo-ra-tion (pûr′fō-rā′shŭn), *n.* **1,** the act of piercing through, or boring through; **2,** a hole, bored or punched, especially through paper; as, the *perforations* in the stamps are made by machinery.

P

PERFORATIONS (P)

per-force (pĕr-fôrs′), *adv.* necessarily.

per-form (pĕr-fôrm′), *v.t.* **1,** to do; carry out; execute; as, to *perform* a task; **2,** to discharge; fulfil; as, to *perform* a duty; **3,** to represent; render; portray; as to *perform* a part in a play:—*v.i.* **1,** to act a part; as, to *perform* on the stage; **2,** to exhibit skill in public; as, to *perform* on the piano.—*n.* **per-form′er.**
Syn. accomplish, transact, effect.

per-form-ance (pĕr-fôr′măns), *n.* **1,** the carrying out of something; completion; as, the *performance* of a duty; **2,** a thing done; deed; feat; **3,** a public exhibition, especially on the stage.

per-fume (pĕr-fūm′), *v.t.* [perfumed, perfum-ing], to fill with a pleasant odor; scent: —*n.* (pûr′fūm; pĕr-fūm′), **1,** a pleasing scent; a fragrance; **2,** a fluid especially prepared to give out a pleasing odor.—*n.* **per-fum′er.**

per-fum-er-y (pĕr-fūm′ĕr-ĭ), *n.* [*pl.* perfumeries], **1,** a perfume or perfumes in general; **2,** the place where perfumes are made or sold.

per-func-to-ry (pĕr-fŭngk′tō-rĭ), *adj.* done merely to discharge a duty; half-hearted; indifferent; as, he did the work in a *perfunctory* manner.—*adv.* **per-func′to-ri-ly.**

Per-ga-mum (pûr′gá-mŭm), an important ancient city in northwestern Asia Minor (map 1).

per-go-la (pûr′gō-lá), *n.* a latticework over a walk or veranda, used as a trellis for climbing plants; an arbor.

per-haps (pĕr-hăps′), *adv.* possibly; maybe; it may be.

per-i- (pĕr′ĭ-), a prefix meaning around; about; surrounding; as, *perimeter, periscope.*

per-i-anth (pĕr′ĭ-ănth), *n.* the sepals and petals of a flower considered together.

per-i-car-di-um (pĕr′ĭ-kär′dĭ-ŭm), *n.* [*pl.* pericardia (pĕr′ĭ-kär′dĭ-á)], the membrane that surrounds the heart.—*adj.* **per′i-car′di-ac.**

Per-i-cles (pĕr′ĭ-klēz), (495?–429 B.C.), a famous Athenian statesman, who made Athens the foremost city in Greece.

āte, āorta, râre, căt, ȧsk, fär, ăllow, sofá; ēve, ĕvent, ĕll, writĕr, novĕl; bīte, pĭn; nō, ōbey, ôr, dŏg, tŏp, cŏllide; ūnit, ūnite, bûrn, cŭt, focŭs; nōōn, fŏŏt; mound; coin;

per-il (pĕr′ĭl), *n.* exposure to injury; danger; risk; hazard:—*v.t.* [periled, peril-ing], to expose to danger or risk.

per-il-ous (pĕr′ĭ-lŭs), *adj.* dangerous; involving risk; as, a *perilous* balloon ascent.—*adv.* **per′il-ous-ly.**—*n.* **per′il-ous-ness.**

per-im-e-ter (pĕ-rĭm′ē-tẽr), *n.* the outer boundary of a body or figure, as the circumference of a circle; also, the total length of this boundary.

pe-ri-od (pē′rĭ-ŭd), *n.* **1,** a definite portion of time, the beginning and end of which are fixed; **2,** any space of time; as, a *period* of rainy weather; also, a number of years looked on as an era; as, the World War *period;* **3,** a full pause at the end of a complete sentence; **4,** a dot [.] used as a mark of punctuation at the end of a complete declarative sentence or after an abbreviation.

pe-ri-od-ic (pē′rĭ-ŏd′ĭk), *adj.* **1,** pertaining to a definite period of time; **2,** occurring at intervals; as, *periodic* fever; **3,** designating a kind of sentence so constructed that the thought is not complete until the end.

pe-ri-od-i-cal (pē′rĭ-ŏd′ĭ-kăl), *adj.* **1,** pertaining to a definite period of time; **2,** occurring at intervals; **3,** published at regular intervals:—*n.* a periodical magazine.—*adv.* **pe′ri-od′i-cal-ly.**

per-i-os-te-um (pĕr′ĭ-ŏs′tē-ŭm), *n.* [*pl.* periostea (pĕr′ĭ-ŏs′tē-à)], the tough, fibrous membrane which covers the bones except at the joints.—*adj.* **per′i-os′te-al.**

per-i-pa-tet-ic (pĕr′ĭ-pá-tĕt′ĭk), *adj.* walking about; hence, done or performed while walking about.

pe-riph-er-y (pĕ-rĭf′ẽr-ĭ), *n.* [*pl.* peripheries], **1,** in geometry, the perimeter, or boundary line, of a circle or other plane figure; **2,** the outside surface of a rounded solid, as a sphere; **3,** the outer bounds or limits of anything.—*adj.* **pe-riph′er-al.**

per-i-phras-tic (pĕr′ĭ-frăs′tĭk), *adj.* roundabout; wordy; characterized by, or expressed in, more words than are necessary; as, a *periphrastic* sentence.

per-i-scope (pĕr′ĭ-skōp), *n.* an upright tube with lenses and mirrors so arranged that a person below a certain level, as below ground or sea level, can view objects on or above that level.

per-ish (pĕr′ĭsh), *v.i.* **1,** to lose life; decay or die; **2,** to be destroyed or come to nothing; as, empires *perish.*

per-ish-a-ble (pĕr′ĭsh-á-bl), *adj.* liable to decay; easily spoiled; as, *perishable* food.

per-i-stal-tic (pĕr′ĭ-stăl′tĭk), *adj.* naming or having reference to a wavelike muscular contraction in the alimentary canal which pushes the contents onward.

per-i-to-ne-um (pĕr′ĭ-tō-nē′ŭm), *n.* [*pl.*

peritonea (pĕr′ĭ-tō-nē′á)], the thin membrane which lines the abdomen and covers the organs in it.—*adj.* **per′i-to-ne′al.**

per-i-to-ni-tis (pĕr′ĭ-tō-nī′tĭs), *n.* acute inflammation of the peritoneum, or lining membrane of the abdomen.

per-i-wig (pĕr′ĭ-wĭg), *n.* a headdress of false hair; a wig, or peruke.

¹per-i-win-kle (pĕr′ĭ-wĭng′-kl) *n.* a creeping evergreen plant, especially the common myrtle, which has shiny leaves, and blue or white flowers.

²per-i-win-kle (pĕr′ĭ-wĭng′-kl), *n.* any of various snails or their shells.

PERIWINKLE
Natural size.

per-jure (pûr′jẽr), *v.t.* [perjured, perjur-ing], to make (oneself) guilty of swearing falsely, or breaking a vow; as, to *perjure* oneself.—*n.* **per′jur-er.**

per-ju-ry (pûr′jẽr-ĭ), *n.* [*pl.* perjuries], **1,** the wilful breaking of an oath or solemn promise; **2,** wilful giving, under oath, of false testimony, usually in a court of law.

perk (pûrk), *v.t.* **1,** to lift quickly; as, the little bird *perked* up its head; **2,** to make (oneself) trim or neat:—*v.i.* **1,** to hold up the head saucily; **2,** to become brisk or jaunty.

perk-y (pûr′kĭ), *adj.* [perk-i-er, perk-i-est], pert; lively; jaunty.

per-ma-nence (pûr′má-nĕns) *n.* enduring or lasting quality. Also, **per′ma-nen-cy.**

per-ma-nent (pûr′má-nĕnt), *adj.* lasting; durable; continuing in the same state; as, *permanent* improvements to real estate.—*adv.* **per′ma-nent-ly.**

Syn. enduring, stable, fixed.

per-man-ga-nate (pẽr-măng′á-nāt), *n.* a dark-purple crystalline salt, used as an antiseptic and in tanning.

per-me-a-ble (pûr′mē-á-bl), *adj.* having tiny holes through which fluids or gases may pass; porous.—*n.* **per′me-a-bil′i-ty.**

per-me-ate (pûr′mē-āt), *v.t.* [permeat-ed, permeat-ing], **1,** to pass through the pores or crevices of; as, water *permeates* sand; **2,** to spread itself through; pervade; as, gas *permeates* a room.—*n.* **per′me-a′tion.**

per-mis-si-ble (pĕr-mĭs′ĭ-bl), *adj.* tolerable; allowable; as, *permissible* conduct.

per-mis-sion (pẽr-mĭsh′ŭn), *n.* **1,** the act of allowing; **2,** consent; leave; as, he asked *permission* to go early.

Syn. license, sufferance, allowance.

per-mis-sive (pẽr-mĭs′ĭv), *adj.* giving consent; as, a *permissive* measure.

per-mit (pẽr-mĭt′), *v.t.* [permit-ted, permit-ting], **1,** to allow by not trying to prevent; tolerate; as, swimming is *permitted* in

the creek; **2,** to give consent to; as, to
permit a marriage:—*v.i.* to give consent:
allow; as, if the weather *permits,* I shall go:
—*n.* (pûr/mĭt), a written license to do
something, as to drive an automobile.

Syn., v. suffer, endure.

Per·nam·bu·co (pĕr/năm-bōō/kŏō; pûr/-
năm-bū/kō), a city of Brazil. See **Recife.**

per·ni·cious (pĕr-nĭsh/ŭs), *adj.* highly injurious; destructive; as, a *pernicious* habit.
—*adv.* **per·ni/cious·ly.**—*n.* **per·ni/cious-
ness.**

Syn. harmful, baneful, deadly, ruinous.

per·o·ra·tion (pĕr/ō-rā/shŭn), *n.* the summing up or conclusion of a speech or oration.—*v.i.* **per/o·rate.**

per·ox·ide (pĕr-ŏk/sīd), *n.* a compound
which contains a large proportion of oxygen; as, hydrogen *peroxide.* Also spelled
per·ox/id.

per·pen·dic·u·lar (pûr/pĕn-dĭk/ū-lẽr),
adj. **1,** at right angles to a given line or
surface; **2,** perfectly upright;
also, steep; as, a *perpendicular*
hill:—*n.* **1,** a line or plane at
right angles with another; **2,**
a vertical line or direction.
—*adv.* **per/pen·dic/u·lar·ly.**

PERPENDICU-
LAR

AB is perpendic-
ular to CD.

per·pe·trate (pûr/pē-trāt),
v.t. [perpetrat-ed, perpetrat-
ing], to do; perform: usually
in a bad sense; as, to *perpetrate* a crime.—
n. **per/pe·tra/tion.**—*n.* **per/pe·tra/tor.**

per·pet·u·al (pĕr-pĕt/ū-ăl), *adj.* never ceasing; continuous; endless; everlasting.—*adv.*
per·pet/u·al·ly.

Syn. incessant, eternal, enduring.

per·pet·u·ate (pĕr-pĕt/ū-āt), *v.t.* [perpet-
uat-ed, perpetuat-ing], to make everlasting; to continue indefinitely.—*n.* **per·pet/-
u·a/tion.**—*n.* **per·pet/u·a/tor.**

per·pe·tu·i·ty (pûr/pē-tū/ĭ-tĭ), *n.* [*pl.* per-
petuities], **1,** the state of being everlasting;
endless existence; **2,** something that lasts
forever.

per·plex (pĕr-plĕks/), *v.t.* to fill with uncertainty or doubt; to puzzle; distract.—
adj. **per·plexed/.**

Syn. confuse, bewilder, mystify.

per·plex·i·ty (pĕr-plĕk/sĭ-tĭ), *n.* [*pl.* per-
plexities], **1,** the state of being puzzled;
embarrassment; **2,** that which puzzles or
confuses.

Syn. confusion, bewilderment, doubt.

per·qui·site (pûr/kwĭ-zĭt), *n.* a gain or
profit in addition to regular wages or
salary; a tip.

Per·ry (pĕr/ĭ), Oliver Hazard (1785–1819),
an American naval officer and commodore
in command at the Battle of Lake Erie.

per·se·cute (pûr/sē-kūt), *v.t.* [persecut-ed,

persecut-ing], **1,** to keep on inflicting injury
upon; to oppress, especially for religious
reasons; **2,** to harass or treat cruelly; annoy; vex.—*n.* **per/se·cu/tor.**

per·se·cu·tion (pûr/sē-kū/shŭn), *n.* **1,** the
continued infliction of unjust pain or punishment; as, religious *persecution;* **2,** the
state of being unjustly treated; repeated
injury of any kind.

Per·seph·o·ne (pĕr-sĕf/ō-nē), *n.* in Greek
mythology, the queen of the lower world:
by the Romans called *Proserpina.*

Per·seus (pûr/sūs; pûr/sē-ŭs), *n.* in Greek
mythology, the hero who slew the Gorgon
Medusa, and saved Andromeda from the
sea monster.

per·se·ver·ance (pûr/sē-vēr/ăns), *n.* refusal to give up; continued effort, especially under a handicap; persistence.

per·se·vere (pûr/sē-vēr/), *v.i.* [persevered,
persever-ing], to persist steadfastly in a
purpose or undertaking.—*adj.* **per/se·ver/-
ing.**—*adv.* **per/se·ver/ing·ly.**

Per·shing (pûr/shĭng), John Joseph
(1860–1948), an American general, commander of American forces in France from
1917 to 1918.

Per·sia (pûr/zhȧ; pûr/shȧ), the former name
for *Iran,* a country in southwestern Asia.
See **Iran.**

Per·sian (pûr/zhăn; pûr/shăn), *adj.* of or
pertaining to Persia, its people, or its
language:—*n.* **1,** a native of Persia; **2,** the
language of Persia.

Persian Gulf, an arm of the Arabian Sea,
between Iran and Arabia (map **15**).

per·si·flage (pûr/sĭ-fläzh; pĕr/sĭ-fläzh/), *n.*
light or flippant talk; banter.

per·sim·mon (pĕr-sĭm/ŭn), *n.* **1,** a pulpy,
orange-red fruit that is
good to eat only when
thoroughly ripened by
frost; **2,** the tree
bearing this fruit.

per·sist (pĕr-sĭst/; pĕr-
zĭst/), *v.i.* **1,** to continue steadily or obsti-
nately in saying or
doing something; **2,** to
continue to last or
endure; as, his cold
persists.

Syn. remain, insist.

per·sist·ence (pĕr-
sĭs/tĕns; pĕr-zĭs/tĕns), *n.* **1,** continuous
effort, especially in spite of obstacles or
opposition; **2,** lasting quality; as, the
persistence of an illness. Also, **per·sist/-
en·cy.**

per·sist·ent (pĕr-sĭs/tĕnt; pĕr-zĭs/tĕnt),

PERSIMMON
Leaves and fruit.

adj. **1,** persisting; persevering; as, a *persistent* worker; **2,** continuing; lasting; as, a *persistent* rain.—*adv.* **per-sist'ent-ly.**

per-son (pûr'sn), *n.* **1,** a human being as distinguished from a thing or an animal; an individual; **2,** the body of a human being; bodily appearance; **3,** in grammar, one of the three classes of personal pronouns, the *first person* referring to the person speaking, the *second person* to the person spoken to, the *third person* to the person or thing spoken of; also, any of the corresponding distinctions in verbs.

per-son-a-ble (pûr'sŭn-a-bl), *adj.* attractive in form and figure.

per-son-age (pûr'sŭn-ĭj), *n.* **1,** a person; especially, a man or woman of distinction; **2,** a character in a play, novel, etc.

per-son-al (pûr'sŭn-ăl), *adj.* **1,** relating to, or peculiar to, a person and his private affairs; **2,** pertaining to the outward appearance or looks; as, *personal* beauty; **3,** given, performed, etc., in person, or by oneself; as, a *personal* greeting; **4,** relating to a certain person; as, *personal* remarks; **5,** movable; as, *personal* property; **6,** in grammar, expressing person; as, *personal* endings in verbs; "I," "you," "he," "she," "it," etc., are *personal* pronouns.

per-son-al-i-ty (pûr'sŭ-năl'ĭ-tĭ), *n.* [*pl.* personalities], **1,** the quality or fact of being a person and not a thing; **2,** that which makes one human being different from another; individuality; **3,** outstanding qualities of character; also, a person who has such qualities; **4,** an offensive remark made about a person.

per-son-al-ly (pûr'sŭn-ăl-ĭ), *adv.* **1,** in person; as, to attend to business *personally;* **2,** as a person; as, *personally,* he is charming; **3,** as far as I am concerned; as, *personally,* I'd rather stay home.

per-son-ate (pûr'sŭn-āt), *v.t.* [personat-ed, personat-ing], to take the part of (a character in a drama); pretend to be (someone).—*n.* **per'son-a'tor.**

per-son-i-fi-ca-tion (pĕr-sŏn'ĭ-fĭ-kā'-shŭn), *n.* **1,** a figure of speech by which things, qualities, or abstract ideas have a personal nature given to them; as, "the cruel waves" is a *personification* of "waves"; "Giant Despair" is a *personification* of the quality "despair"; Peter Pan is a *personification* of the abstract idea of "childhood"; **2,** a striking example of some quality; as, she is the *personification* of neatness.

per-son-i-fy (pĕr-sŏn'ĭ-fī), *v.t.* [personi-fied, personify-ing], **1,** to regard or represent (a thing, quality, or idea) as a person; **2,** to be a striking example of; as, Caesar *personifies* power.

per-son-nel (pûr'sŏ-nĕl'), *n.* all the people employed in any business, public service, factory, office, etc.

per-spec-tive (pĕr-spĕk'tĭv), *n.* **1,** the art of drawing an object on a flat surface in such a way as to give the impression of looking at the object itself; **2,** a view that includes things in the distance as well as things near by; hence, the ability to see things in their right relation to each other; as, a true *perspective* of historical events; **3,** the right relationship of things to each other; as, to look at the causes of the World War in *perspective.*

per-spi-ca-cious (pûr'spĭ-kā'shŭs), *adj.* mentally acute or keen; mentally quick-sighted.—*adv.* **per'spi-ca'cious-ly.**
    Syn. astute, shrewd, sagacious.

per-spi-cac-i-ty (pûr'spĭ-kăs'ĭ-tĭ), *n.* keenness or quickness of understanding; discernment; mental clear-sightedness.

per-spi-cu-i-ty (pûr'spĭ-kū'ĭ-tĭ), *n.* clearness of thought or expression.

per-spic-u-ous (pĕr-spĭk'ū-ŭs), *adj.* clear to the understanding; plainly expressed; easily understood.—*adv.* **per-spic'u-ous-ly.**

per-spi-ra-tion (pûr'spĭ-rā'shŭn), *n.* the act of secreting sweat; also, the sweat secreted.

per-spire (pĕr-spīr'), *v.t.* and *v.i.* [perspired, perspir-ing], to sweat.

per-suade (pĕr-swād'), *v.t.* [persuad-ed, persuad-ing], to win over to a point of view; to convince by argument, advice, entreaty, etc.; as, he *persuaded* his mother to let him go.

per-sua-sion (pĕr-swā'zhŭn), *n.* **1,** the act of persuading, the power to persuade, or the state of being persuaded by argument or entreaty; **2,** a conviction; belief, generally religious; as, of the Baptist *persuasion.*

per-sua-sive (pĕr-swā'sĭv), *adj.* having power to convince or influence; as, a *persuasive* argument.—*adv.* **per-sua'sive-ly.**

pert (pûrt), *adj.* saucy; bold; as, a *pert* answer.—*adv.* **pert'ly.**

per-tain (pĕr-tān'), *v.i.* to belong; also, to relate or refer to something; as, the telegram *pertains* to business.

Perth (pûrth), a city, capital of Western Australia (map **16**).

per-ti-na-cious (pûr'tĭ-nā'shŭs), *adj.* unyielding; obstinate; holding stubbornly to an opinion, plan, etc.; as, a *pertinacious* salesman.—*adv.* **per'ti-na'cious-ly.**
    Syn. inflexible, persistent, determined.

per-ti-nac-i-ty (pûr'tĭ-năs'ĭ-tĭ), *n.* firm adherence to a purpose or opinion; unyielding perseverance; stubbornness.

per-ti-nent (pûr'tĭ-nĕnt), *adj.* fitting or appropriate; to the point; as, a *pertinent*

go; join; yet; sing; chin; show; thin, *th***en; hw,** *wh***y; zh, azure; ü, Ger. für or Fr. lune; ö, Ger. schön or Fr. feu; ṅ, Fr. enfant, nom; kh, Ger. ach or ich. See pages ix–x.**

remark.—*adv.* **per'ti·nent·ly.**—*n.* **per'ti·nence; per'ti·nen·cy.**

Syn. timely, suitable, applicable, relevant, related.

per·turb (pẽr-tûrb'), *v.t.* to agitate; disturb greatly, especially in mind.

Syn. ruffle, fluster, confuse.

per·tur·ba·tion (pûr'tẽr-bā'shŭn), *n.* **1,** disquiet of mind; **2,** disturbance.

Pe·ru (pê-rōō'), a republic (cap. Lima) on the west coast of South America (map 11).

Pe·ru·gia (pā-rōō'jä), a city in Umbria, central Italy (map 12).

pe·ruke (pê-rōōk'), *n.* a wig, sometimes resembling a natural head of hair.

pe·rus·al (pê-rōō'zăl), *n.* the act of reading carefully.

pe·ruse (pê-rōōz'), *v.t.* [perused, perusing], to read; especially, to read with care and attention.

Pe·ru·vi·an (pê-rōō'vĭ-ăn), *adj.* pertaining to Peru:—*n.* **1,** a native of Peru; **2,** the language of Peru:—**Peruvian bark,** cinchona, the bark of any of several South American trees, from which the drug quinine is obtained.

per·vade (pẽr-vād'), *v.t.* [pervad-ed, pervad-ing], to pass or spread through every part of; as, a perfume *pervades* the air.—*n.* **per·va'sion** (pẽr-vā'zhŭn).

per·va·sive (pẽr-vā'sĭv), *adj.* tending to pass through or fill every part of; as, a *pervasive* odor.—*adv.* **per·va'sive·ly.**—*n.* **per·va'sive·ness.**

per·verse (pẽr-vûrs'), *adj.* **1,** wilfully wrong; set against doing right; **2,** obstinate or stubborn, usually in a wrong action; **3,** hence, petulant; ill-tempered; as, a *perverse* child.—*adv.* **per·verse'ly.**—*n.* **per·verse'ness.**

Syn. contrary, headstrong, wilful.

per·ver·sion (pẽr-vûr'zhŭn; pẽr-vûr'shŭn), *n.* **1,** a turning from the true or proper use, purpose, or meaning; **2,** a wrong form of something, as of the spelling of a word.

per·ver·si·ty (pẽr-vûr'sĭ-tĭ), *n.* [*pl.* perversities], **1,** wilful refusal to do right; **2,** stubbornness; contrariness.

per·vert (pẽr-vûrt'), *v.t.* **1,** to turn from the true end or proper purpose; misuse; **2,** to give a wrong meaning to purposely; as, to *pervert* what someone has said:—*n.* (pûr'vûrt), one who has turned from right to wrong.—*adj.* **per·vert'ed.**

pe·se·ta (pê-sā'tä), *n.* the monetary unit of Spain. (See table, page 943.)

pe·so (pā'sō), *n.* [*pl.* pesos], **1,** the old Spanish dollar, or piece of eight; **2,** in the Philippines, a silver coin, the monetary unit; **3,** the monetary unit, equivalent usually to 100 centavos, in various Latin-American countries: Argentina, Chile, Colombia, Cuba, Dominican Republic, Mexico, and Uruguay. (See Table, page 943.)

pes·si·mism (pĕs'ĭ-mĭzm), *n.* **1,** the belief that there is more evil in the world than good; **2,** a habit of looking on the dark side of life: opposite of *optimism.*

pes·si·mist (pĕs'ĭ-mĭst), *n.* one who considers life as evil, or who looks on the worst side of things: opposite of *optimist.*

pes·si·mis·tic (pĕs'ĭ-mĭs'tĭk), *adj.* pertaining to, or marked by, the belief that the world is bad rather than good; gloomy. —*adv.* **pes'si·mis'ti·cal·ly.**

pest (pĕst), *n.* **1,** a widespread, fatal, contagious disease, as smallpox; a plague or pestilence; **2,** anything or anyone very mischievous or annoying.

pest-house (pĕst'hous'), *n.* a hospital for people having infectious or contagious diseases.

pes·tif·er·ous (pĕs-tĭf'ẽr-ŭs), *adj.* **1,** carrying disease; **2,** *Colloquial,* mischievous.—*adv.* **pes·tif'er·ous·ly.**

pes·ti·lence (pĕs'tĭ-lĕns), *n.* a widespread, infectious, fatal disease.

pes·ti·lent (pĕs'tĭ-lĕnt), *adj.* **1,** poisonous; deadly; **2,** bad for health, morals, or society; **3,** making mischief; vexatious.—*adv.* **pes'ti·lent·ly.**

MORTAR AND PESTLE

pes·ti·len·tial (pĕs'tĭ-lĕn'shăl), *adj.* **1,** pertaining to a pestilence; **2,** wicked.

pes·tle (pĕs'l; pĕs'tl), *n.* a tool for pounding substances to a powder, used chiefly by druggists:—*v.t.* and *v.i.* [pes-tled, pes-tling], to pound with a pestle.

PETALS (P)

¹pet (pĕt), *n.* **1,** a tame animal, kept, treated kindly, and played with; **2,** a person treated with special affection; a favorite:—*adj.* favorite; accustomed to fondling and indulgence:—*v.t.* [pet-ted, pet-ting], to fondle and indulge.

²pet (pĕt), *n.* a sudden fit of peevishness or ill humor.

pet·al (pĕt'ăl), *n.* one of the parts, usually bright-colored, of the flower of a plant.—*adj.* **pet'aled.**

pet cock, a small faucet for testing or draining, as on a pipe. Also written **pet'cock'** (pĕt'kŏk').

PET COCK

Pe·ter (pē'tẽr), in the Bible, one of the twelve apostles: also called *Simon* and *Simon Peter;* also, either of two books of the New Testament, containing epistles, or letters, written by Peter.

āte, āorta, râre, căt, ȧsk, fär, ȧllow, sofȧ; ēve, ēvent, ĕll, writẽr, novĕl; bīte, pĭn; nō, ōbey, ôr, dŏg, tŏp, cŏllide; ūnit, ūnite, bûrn, cŭt, focŭs; nōōn, fŏŏt; mound; coin;

Peter Pan, hero and title of a play by Sir James Barrie.

Pe-ters-burg, Saint (pē'tẽrz-bûrg), the name of the city which was formerly the capital of Russia: changed to *Petrograd* in 1914. See **Leningrad**.

pet-i-ole (pĕt'ĭ-ōl), *n.* **1**, the slender stem or stalk of a leaf; **2**, in zoology, a slender part that joins two larger parts of an insect body, as in ants, wasps, etc. —*adj.* **pet'i-o-lar.**—*adj.* **pet'-i-o-late.**

pe-tite (pĕ-tēt'), *adj.* little; small; trim of figure, as a woman or girl.

pe-ti-tion (pĕ-tĭsh'ŭn), *n.* **1**, an earnest request or prayer; **2**, a formal request from an inferior to a superior; **3**, a document containing a request supported by many signatures; as, a *petition* to the President:—*v.t.* **1**, to present a formal request to; **2**, to solicit or ask for earnestly; entreat; as, to *petition* aid for someone.—*n.* **pe-ti'tion-er.**

PETIOLE (P) OF MAPLE LEAF

Pe-trarch (pē'trärk), Francesco (1304–1374), an Italian poet, famous for his sonnets.

pet-rel (pĕt'rĕl), *n.* a strong-winged sea bird which flies far from the land.

pet-ri-fy (pĕt'rĭ-fī), *v.t.* [petrified, petrify-ing], **1**, to change into stone; **2**, to make motionless with amazement or fear; as, the approach of danger *petrified* him:—*v.i.* to become stone or of a stony hardness.—*n.* **pet'ri-fac'tion** (pĕt'rĭ-făk'shŭn).

PETREL (⅛)

Pet-ro-grad (pĕt'rō-grăd), a former name of Leningrad, a city in Soviet Russia. See **Leningrad**.

pet-rol (pĕt'rŏl; pĕt'rŭl), *n.* in Europe, gasoline.

pe-tro-le-um (pĕ-trō'lē-ŭm), *n.* a dark, yellowish-brown liquid that is obtained from the earth by means of wells, and is the source of gasoline, kerosene, etc.

pet-ti-coat (pĕt'ĭ-kōt), *n.* a loose underskirt worn by women and girls.

pet-ti-fog-ger (pĕt'ĭ-fŏg'ẽr), *n.* a lawyer who practices in small or mean cases, often using dishonest methods.

pet-tish (pĕt'ĭsh), *adj.* cross; petulant.

pet-ty (pĕt'ĭ), *adj.* [pet-ti-er, pet-ti-est], **1**, trifling; unimportant; as, a *petty* quarrel; **2**, small-minded; occupied with trivial

things; as, *petty* people:—**petty officer**, a naval officer of rank similar to that of a sergeant or corporal in the army.—*n.* **pet'ti-ness.**

Syn. trivial, insignificant, small.

pet-u-lance (pĕt'ū-lăns) or **pet-u-lan-cy** (pĕt'ū-lăn-sĭ), *n.* crossness; fretfulness.

pet-u-lant (pĕt'ū-lănt), *adj.* fretful; cross; impatient; pettish; as, a *petulant* answer. —*adv.* **pet'u-lant-ly.**

pe-tu-ni-a (pĕ-tū'nĭ-a), *n.* a common garden plant with funnel-shaped flowers, usually white, pink, or purple.

pew (pū), *n.* one of the long, fixed benches in a church.

pe-wee (pē'wē), *n.* **1**, a small American flycatcher, so named from its note: also called *wood pewee*; **2**, the phoebe.

pe-wit (pē'wĭt; pū'ĭt), *n.* **1**, the lapwing; **2**, the black-headed, or laughing, gull; **3**, the phoebe, or pewee.

PETUNIA

pew-ter (pū'tẽr), *n.* **1**, a lustrous metal, silvery gray in color, made of tin and lead, or of tin and some other metal, as copper; **2**, dishes or utensils made of this metal:— *adj.* made of pewter; as, a *pewter* tray.

pf. or **pfd.** abbreviation for *preferred*.

pfen-nig (pfĕn'ĭg), *n.* a small copper coin of Germany worth about one quarter of a cent.

Pha-ë-thon (fā'ĕ-thŏn), *n.* in Greek myths, the son of Helios, the sun god. He nearly burned up the world in trying to drive his father's chariot.

pha-e-ton (fā'ĕ-tn), *n.* **1**, a light, open, four-wheeled carriage; **2**, an open automobile with a top that folds back; a touring car.

pha-lanx (fā'lăngks; făl'ăngks), *n.* **1**, among the ancient Greeks, a company of heavy-armed soldiers drawn up in a close rank; **2**, hence, any compact body of persons united for some purpose; **3**, [*pl.* phalanges (fā-lăn'jēz)], a bone of the fingers or toes.

PHAETON

phan-tasm (făn'tăzm), *n.* **1**, an imaginary vision, as of a ghost or specter; **2**, a supposed appearance of an absent person.— *adj.* **phan-tas'mal.**

phan-ta-sy (făn'ta-sĭ; făn'ta-zĭ), *n.* [*pl.* phantasies], imagination; fancy; fantasy. See **fantasy**.

phan·tom (făn′tŭm), *n.* an apparition; spirit; ghost:—*adj.* having no substance but said to have been seen; as, a *phantom* ship.

Phar·aoh (fâr′ō; fā′rō), *n.* 1, in ancient Egypt, a king: a descriptive term or title; as, Ramses II was the *Pharaoh* of the pyramids; 2, in the Bible, the name given to many of the kings of Egypt.

Phar·i·sa·ic (făr′ĭ-sā′ĭk) or **Phar·i·sa·i·cal** (făr′ĭ-sā′ĭ-kăl), *adj.* pertaining to, or like, the Pharisees, a sect of the ancient Jews:—**pharisaic** or **pharisaical**, pretending to be religious; self-righteous; hypocritical.

Phar·i·see (făr′ĭ-sē), *n.* one of a religious sect among the ancient Jews which paid strict regard to outward observance of the law:—**pharisee**, one who observes the form rather than the spirit of religion.

phar·ma·cist (fär′må-sĭst), *n.* one skilled in the preparation of medicines; a druggist.

phar·ma·cy (fär′må-sĭ), *n.* [*pl.* pharmacies], 1, the art of preparing medicines; 2, a drugstore.

phar·ynx (făr′ĭngks), *n.* [*pl.* pharynges (fă-rĭn′jēz) or pharynxes (făr′ĭngk-sĕz)], the part of the alimentary canal between the cavity of the mouth and the esophagus.—*adj.* **pha·ryn′ge·al** (fă-rĭn′jē-ăl; făr′ĭn-jē′ăl).

phase (fāz), *n.* 1, in astronomy, a particular appearance presented by the moon or a planet, as full moon, new moon, etc.; 2, one stage or period in the development of a thing; 3, one side of a subject; as, a *phase* of history.

pheas·ant (fĕz′ănt), *n.* 1, a large, Old World game bird with brilliant feathers; 2, any of various birds that look like the pheasant, as the ruffed grouse.

phe·nol (fē′nol; fē′nŏl; fē-nōl′), *n.* a powerful poison obtained from coal tar and known popularly as *carbolic acid*.

CHINESE PHEASANT (⅒)

phe·nom·e·nal (fē-nŏm′ē-năl), *adj.* 1, pertaining to, or of the nature of, a phenomenon; 2, hence, extraordinary; unusual; as, a *phenomenal* memory.—*adv.* **phe·nom′e·nal·ly.**

phe·nom·e·non (fē-nŏm′ē-nŏn; fē-nŏm′ē-nŭn), *n.* [*pl.* phenomena (fē-nŏm′ē-nà)], 1, any natural fact or event that can be seen; 2, [*pl.* phenomenons], something uncommon, as snow in summer.

phi·al (fī′ăl), *n.* a small glass bottle.

Phid·i·as (fĭd′ĭ-ăs), (500?–432? B.C.), a famous Greek sculptor.

Phil. abbreviation for *Philip, Philippine*.

Phila. abbreviation for *Philadelphia*.

Phil·a·del·phi·a (fĭl′à-dĕl′fĭ-à), a large city in eastern Pennsylvania (map 6).

phil·an·throp·ic (fĭl′ăn-thrŏp′ĭk) or **phil·an·throp·i·cal** (-thrŏp′ĭ-kăl), *adj.* loving mankind; benevolent.—*adv.* **phil′an·throp′i·cal·ly.**

phi·lan·thro·pist (fĭ-lăn′thrō-pĭst), *n.* one who loves and seeks to benefit mankind, especially one who uses his wealth for this.

phi·lan·thro·py (fĭ-lăn′thrō-pĭ), *n.* [*pl.* philanthropies], 1, love of mankind; desire to do good to men; benevolence; 2, a benevolent act or institution.

Syn. charity, beneficence.

phi·lat·e·ly (fĭ-lăt′ē-lĭ), *n.* the collecting and study of postage stamps.—*n.* **phi·lat′e·list.**

Phi·le·mon (fĭ-lē′mŏn), *n.* a book in the New Testament that contains the Epistle, or letter, of Paul to Philemon.

Phil·ip (fĭl′ĭp), in the Bible: 1, one of the twelve apostles; 2, a deacon and preacher of the early Christian church.

Phi·lip·pi (fĭ-lĭp′ĭ), a city in northeastern Macedonia, Greece, now in ruins.

Phi·lip·pi·ans (fĭ-lĭp′ĭ-ănz), *n.* a book in the New Testament that contains the Epistle, or letter, of Paul to the church at Philippi, in Macedonia.

Phil·ip·pine (fĭl′ĭ-pēn; fĭl′ĭ-pĭn), *adj.* of or pertaining to the Philippine Islands or their inhabitants:—*n.* a native of the Philippine Islands.

Phil·ip·pine Is·lands, a group of islands (cap. Quezon City), northeast of Borneo and east of Indochina; became an independent republic July 4, 1946 (map 15): also called *Philippines*.

Phi·lis·tine (fĭ-lĭs′tĭn; fĭl′ĭs-tĭn; fĭl′ĭs-tēn), *n.* 1, in the Bible, an inhabitant of the southwestern coast of Palestine; 2, an uncultured person or one of narrow views; one who cares more for wealth than for literature, music, painting, etc.:—*adj.* 1, pertaining to, or like, the Philistines; 2, narrow-minded; uncultured.

phi·lol·o·gy (fĭ-lŏl′ō-jĭ), *n.* the scientific study of the origin, development, relationships, etc., of language.—*n.* **phi·lol′o·gist.**—*adj.* **phil′o·log′i·cal** (fĭl′ō-lŏj′ĭ-kăl).

phi·los·o·pher (fĭ-lŏs′ō-fẽr), *n.* 1, a student of philosophy; 2, one who keeps câlm and courageous in misfortune.

āte, āorta, râre, căt, åsk, fär, ållow, sofà; ēve, ēvent, ĕll, wrĭtẽr, nŏvĕl; bīte, pĭn; nō, ōbey, ôr, dôg, tŏp, cōllide; ūnit, ūnite, bûrn, cŭt, focŭs; nōon, fŏot; mound; coin;

phil·o·soph·i·cal (fĭl/ō-sŏf/ĭ-kăl) or **phil-o-soph-ic** (fĭl/ō-sŏf/ĭk), *adj.* **1**, pertaining to philosophy; **2**, wise; calm.—*adv.* **phil/o-soph/i-cal-ly.**

phi·los·o·phize (fĭ-lŏs/ō-fīz), *v.i.* [philosophized, philosophiz-ing], to reason about, or seek to explain, the causes or nature of things.—*n.* **phi·los/o·phiz/er.**

phi·los·o·phy (fĭ-lŏs/ō-fĭ), *n.* [*pl.* philosophies], **1**, the study of the principles that cause, control, or explain facts and events; **2**, the calmness of temper characteristic of a philosopher; resignation; **3**, a particular system of beliefs or views, as regarding God, existence, etc.

phil·ter or **phil·tre** (fĭl/tẽr), *n.* a charm or drink supposed to have the power to excite love.

phlegm (flĕm), *n.* **1**, thick, stringy mucus discharged from the throat, especially when one has a cold; **2**, calmness of disposition.

phleg·mat·ic (flĕg-măt/ĭk) or **phleg-mat·i·cal** (flĕg-măt/ĭ-kăl), *adj.* sluggish; not easily excited; cool; as, a *phlegmatic* person.—*adv.* **phleg-mat/i-cal-ly.**

phlox (flŏks), *n.* a plant that bears showy clusters of white, reddish, or purplish flowers.

pho·bi·a (fō/bĭ-ȧ), *n.* a morbid fear or dread: often used as a suffix; as, photo*phobia*, fear of light.

phoe·be (fē/bē), *n.* any of several small American fly-catching birds, especially a species with dark-brown upper parts and white or yellowish-white under parts, and a plaintive note: also called *pewee*.

PHLOX

Phoe·be (fē/bē), *n.* **1**, in Greek mythology, Artemis, twin sister of Phoebus Apollo and goddess of the moon and of the chase: called by the Romans *Diana*; **2**, *Poetic*, the moon.

Phoe·bus (fē/bŭs), *n.* **1**, in Greek mythology, Apollo: called *Phoebus Apollo* when regarded as the sun god; **2**, *Poetic*, the sun.

PHOEBE (⅓)

Phoe·ni·ci·a (fē-nĭsh/ĭ-ȧ), an ancient country in Asia Minor, on the northeastern shore of the Mediterranean (map 1).

Phoe·ni·cian (fē-nĭsh/ăn), *adj.* pertaining to ancient Phoenicia in Syria, or to its people or their language:—*n.* **1**, an inhabitant of Phoenicia or its colonies; **2**, the language of the people of Phoenicia.

phoe·nix (fē/nĭks), *n.* an imaginary bird, said to live 500 years in the desert of Arabia, and, after being consumed by fire, to rise again, fresh and beautiful, from its own ashes.

Phoe·nix (fē/nĭks), a city, capital of Arizona (map 9).

phone (fōn), *n. Colloquial*, a telephone:—*v.t.* and *v.i.* [phoned, phon-ing], *Colloquial*, to telephone.

pho·net·ic (fō-nĕt/ĭk), *adj.* **1**, pertaining to speech sounds; **2**, showing sounds as spoken; as, the *phonetic* spelling of "photo" is "foto."—*adv.* **pho·net/i-cal-ly.**

pho·net·ics (fō-nĕt/ĭks), *n.pl.* used as *sing.* the science of the sounds of speech, and of the symbols that represent these sounds.

phon·ic (fŏn/ĭk; fō/nĭk), *adj.* pertaining to sound, especially as in speech; acoustic.

pho·no·graph (fō/nō-grȧf), *n.* an instrument to record and reproduce accurately speech, music, or other sounds.—*adj.* **pho/no-graph/ic.**

phos·phate (fŏs/fāt), *n.* mineral substance obtained from bones, rocks, etc., and much used in fertilizers.

Phos·phor (fŏs/fõr), *n.* the morning star, especially the planet Venus; Lucifer.

PHONOGRAPH

A, disk record on revolving platform; B, reproducing mechanism; C, needle; D, sound box; E, winding crank.

phos·pho·res·cence (fŏs/fō-rĕs/ĕns), *n.* the giving of light without heat by certain bodies, as phosphorus and decaying wood and some animals.—*adj.* **phos/pho-res/cent.**

phos·pho·rus (fŏs/fō-rŭs), *n.* a yellowish, waxy, poisonous substance that has an unpleasant odor and easily bursts into flame.—*adj.* **phos/pho-rous** (fŏs/fō-rŭs; fŏs-fôr/-ŭs).

pho·to (fō/tō), *n. Colloquial*, a photograph.

pho·to·gen·ic (fō/tō-jĕn/ĭk), *adj.* having form and color such as to make an effective photograph.

pho·to·graph (fō/tō-grȧf), *n.* a picture produced by exposing to the light a plate or film which has been made sensitive to light:—*v.t.* to take a picture of (a person, scene, etc.) upon such a plate or film.

pho·tog·ra·pher (fō-tŏg/rȧ-fẽr), *n.* a person who takes photographs.

pho·to·graph·ic (fō/tō-grăf/ĭk), *adj.* per-

go; join; yet; sing; chin; show; thin, *th*en; hw, *wh*y; zh, azure; ū, Ger. für or Fr. lune; ö, Ger. schön or Fr. feu; ṅ, Fr. enfant, nom; kh, Ger. ach or ich. See pages ix–x.

taining to, like, or made by photography.
—*adv.* **pho′to-graph′i-cal-ly.**

pho-tog-ra-phy (fŏ-tŏg′rȧ-fĭ), *n.* the art or process of making pictures by the action of light on a material, as paper, glass, or celluloid, that has been coated with a film of chemicals to make it sensitive to light.

pho-tom-e-ter (fŏ-tŏm′ē-tẽr), *n.* an instrument that measures intensity of light.

pho-to-play (fō′tō-plā′), *n.* a motion-picture play.

phrase (frāz), *n.* **1**, in grammar, a group of related words not containing a subject and a predicate; as, "to the city" is a *phrase*: **2**, any brief, pithy expression containing a single idea; **3**, a characteristic style or manner of talking; as, speaking in the simple *phrase* of the day:—*v.t.* [phrased, phrasing], to put into words, especially into suitable words; as, he *phrased* his apology very carefully.

phra-se-ol-o-gy (frā′zē-ŏl′ō-jĭ), *n.* [*pl.* phraseologies], selection and arrangement of words; manner of expression; as, legal *phraseology* contains many repetitions.

phre-nol-o-gy (frē-nŏl′ō-jĭ), *n.* a system of reading character and mental abilities by studying the formation of the skull.

Phryg-i-a (frĭj′ĭ-ȧ), an ancient region (cap. Gordium), west of Galatia, in Asia Minor (map 1).—*n.* and *adj.* **Phryg′i-an.**

phy-lac-ter-y (fĭ-lăk′tẽr-ĭ), *n.* [*pl.* phylacteries], a small square leather box containing thin strips of parchment upon which certain texts from the Hebrew law are written, worn by Jews, one on the forehead and one on the left wrist, during morning prayers except on the Sabbath or holy days.

phy-lum (fī′lŭm), *n.* [*pl.* phyla (fī′lȧ)], in biology, one of the large primary divisions of the animal or plant kingdom.

phys-ic (fĭz′ĭk), *n.* **1,** *Archaic,* the science of medicine, or the art of healing; **2**, medicine in general; **3**, specifically, a medicine for cleansing the bowels; a cathartic:—*v.t.* [physicked, physick-ing], to treat with medicine, especially a cathartic.

phys-i-cal (fĭz′ĭ-kăl), *adj.* **1**, relating to natural science, or to the natural features and changes in the universe; as, *physical* geography; **2**, pertaining to the world around us, or to the material rather than to the mental or spiritual; as, the *physical* world; **3**, pertaining to the science of physics; as, *physical* changes in matter; **4**, pertaining to the body; as, *physical* weakness. —*adv.* **phys′i-cal-ly.**

phy-si-cian (fĭ-zĭsh′ăn), *n.* one skilled in the art of healing and legally qualified to treat disease; a doctor of medicine.

phys-i-cist (fĭz′ĭ-sĭst), *n.* a student or specialist in physics.

phys-ics (fĭz′ĭks), *n.pl.* used as *sing.* the science which deals with matter and its ability to perform work, including the study of mechanics, heat, light, sound, electricity, etc.

phys-i-og-no-my (fĭz′ĭ-ŏg′nō-mĭ; fĭz′ĭ-ŏn′ō-mĭ), *n.* [*pl.* physiognomies], **1**, the face; especially, the peculiar form or expression of the face; **2**, outward appearance, as of a landscape.

phys-i-og-ra-phy (fĭz′ĭ-ŏg′rȧ-fĭ), *n.* physical geography; the study of the earth and its winds, oceans, climate, etc.

phys-i-o-log-i-cal (fĭz′ĭ-ō-lŏj′ĭ-kăl), *adj.* relating to the functions or life processes of plants, animals, and human beings.

phys-i-ol-o-gy (fĭz′ĭ-ŏl′ō-jĭ), *n.* [*pl.* physiologies], that branch of biology which deals with the functions of the organs, tissues, cells, etc., in living plants, animals, and human beings.—*n.* **phys′i-ol′o-gist.**

phy-sique (fĭ-zēk′), *n.* the structure and appearance of the body; as, the football player has a powerful *physique.*

pi (pī), *n.* in mathematics, the ratio of the circumference of any circle to its diameter: usually written π. Pi is equal to 3 1/7, or 3.1416.

P.I. abbreviation for *Philippine Islands.*

pi-a-nis-si-mo (pē′ȧ-nĭs′ĭ-mō; pyä-nēs′-sē-mō), *adj.* and *adv.* in music, very soft.

pi-an-ist (pĭ-ăn′ĭst; pē′ȧ-nĭst), *n.* a person who plays the piano.

¹pi-a-no (pĭ-ä′nō), *adj.* and *adv.* in music, soft; softly.

²pi-an-o (pĭ-ăn′ō; pĭ-ä′nō), *n.* [*pl.* pianos], a large, modern musical instrument, enclosed in a case, and played from a keyboard. The keyboard, when struck, operates hammers which strike steel wires giving forth musical tones. Pianos are called *grand, upright,* etc., according to the shape of the case.

GRAND PIANO

pi-as-ter (pĭ-ăs′tẽr), *n.* any of various coins, usually silver, as a small Turkish coin worth 1/100 of a lira. Also spelled **pi-as′tre.**

pi-az-za (pĭ-ăz′ȧ), *n.* **1**, in Italy, a large, open square surrounded by buildings or columns; **2**, in the U.S., a porch, usually roofed.

pi-broch (pē′brŏkh), *n.* a wild, warlike musical selection for the Scottish bagpipes.

pi·ca (pī′kà), *n.* in printing, a large size of type; twelve-point type:—**small pica,** eleven-point type. (See second illustration under *type.*)

Pic·ar·dy (pĭk′ẽr-dĭ), an old French province on the English Channel.

pic·a·yune (pĭk′à-yōon′), *n.* **1,** a small silver coin equal to 6¼ cents, formerly used in the U.S.; **2,** a trifle; little bit.

pic·ca·lil·li (pĭk′à-lĭl′ĭ), *n.* a pickle, or relish, made of green tomatoes, onions, celery, and some spices.

pic·co·lo (pĭk′ō-lō), *n.* [*pl.* piccolos], a small, flute-shaped instrument with shrill tones an octave higher than the tones of the ordinary flute.

PICCOLO

pick (pĭk), *n.* **1,** a heavy tool for breaking earth or rock; a pickax; **2,** a pointed instrument used for piercing or pecking; as, an ice *pick;* **3,** the amount of a crop gathered at one time; a picking; **4,** choice; as, take your *pick;* **5,** the best of anything; as, the *pick* of the lot:—*v.t.* **1,** to strike or break open with a sharp instrument, or with the beak; pierce or peck; as, to *pick* a hole; **2,** to open by a sharp instrument; as, to *pick* a lock or safe; **3,** to lift or raise; as, to *pick* up something fallen; **4,** to pluck or gather; as, to *pick* berries; **5,** to choose or select; as, to *pick* the best one; **6,** hence, to bring about by choice or intention; as, to *pick* a quarrel; **7,** to rob; as, to *pick* a pocket; **8,** to separate with the fingers; as, to *pick* rags; **9,** to clean or clear of something; as, to *pick* a chicken; **10,** to pluck the strings of (a musical instrument); as, to *pick* a banjo.—*v.i.* **1,** to eat slowly and daintily; **2,** to pilfer; as, to *pick* and steal; **3,** *Colloquial,* to find fault; nag. —*n.* pick′ing.—*adj.* picked.

ICE PICK

pick·a·back (pĭk′à-băk′), *adv.* on the back or shoulders like a pack.

pick·ax or **pick·axe** (pĭk′ăks′), *n.* a hand tool for digging, with a wooden handle and a curved or straight iron head pointed at one end or at both ends.

PICKAX

pick·er (pĭk′ẽr), *n.* a person, machine, tool, etc., that picks.

pick·er·el (pĭk′ẽr-ĕl), *n.* a kind of fresh-water fish of the pike family, used for food; sometimes, the pike.

pick·et (pĭk′ĕt), *n.* **1,** an upright pointed stake, used in making fences, for tethering a horse, etc.; **2,** in warfare, a military guard stationed at a given place to prevent surprise by an enemy; **3,** one or more persons appointed by a labor union to watch at a factory, shop, etc., during a strike, to persuade, or otherwise influence, nonunion men not to work there; **4,** hence, any person or persons appointed by an organization to watch at a given place for any purpose:—*v.t.* **1,** to fence with pointed stakes; as, to *picket* a farm; **2,** to fasten to a stake; as, to *picket* a horse; **3,** to watch or guard; as, to *picket* a certain position; **4,** to place on guard; as, to *picket* men for duty:—*v.i.* to serve as a picket.

Pick·ett (pĭk′ĕt), George Edward (1825–1875), Confederate general, who led a famous charge at the Battle of Gettysburg.

pick·le (pĭk′l), *n.* **1,** brine, or a mixture of salt and water, used for preserving meat, fish, etc.; also, vinegar, with or without spices, for preserving vegetables, fruit, meat, etc.; **2,** something preserved in pickle; especially, a pickled cucumber; **3,** an embarrassment; difficulty:—*v.t.* [pickled, pick-ling], to preserve in brine or vinegar.

pick·pock·et (pĭk′pŏk′ĕt), *n.* a thief who steals purses or the contents of pockets.

pic·nic (pĭk′nĭk), *n.* a short trip by a pleasure party carrying its own food for an outdoor meal:—*v.i.* [picnicked, pic-nick-ing], to go on, or hold, an outdoor pleasure party.—*n.* pic′nick·er.

pi·cot (pē′kō), *n.* one of the small projecting loops, forming the edge of certain laces, ribbons, etc.; also, a kind of edging made by cutting through the center of a line of machine hemstitching:—*v.t.* [picoted (pē′kōd), picot-ing], to finish or edge with picots, as ribbon.

Pict (pĭkt), *n.* one of an ancient people of the Scottish Highlands.

pic·to·ri·al (pĭk-tôr′ĭ-ăl), *adj.* **1,** pertaining to, shown by, or containing, pictures; as, a *pictorial* magazine; **2,** suggesting a picture or clear mental image; as, *pictorial* description.—*adv.* pic-tor′i-al-ly.

pic·ture (pĭk′tūr), *n.* **1,** a painting, drawing, or photograph, of a person, object, scene, etc.; **2,** a likeness or image; as, she is the *picture* of her mother; representation; as, he was the *picture* of despair; **3,** a vivid portrayal in words; as, the speaker drew a *picture* of future prosperity; **4,** a mental image; as, my mind carries a *picture* of the beautiful scene; **5,** pictures, *Colloquial;* motion pictures:—*v.t.* [pictured, picturing], **1,** to represent in a painting, drawing, etc.; as, the artist *pictured* a country scene; **2,** to describe vividly in words; **3,** to form a mental image of; imagine; as, I *pictured* myself in his place.

pic·tur·esque (pĭk′tūr-ĕsk′), *adj.* **1,** giving a vivid impression, as a picture does;

as, a *picturesque* description of one's travels; **2**, suitable to be drawn or painted as an interesting or striking picture; as, *picturesque* mountain scenery.—*adv.* **pic′tur·esque′ly.**—*n.* **pic′tur·esque′ness.**

¹**pie** (pī), *n.* a prepared dish consisting of meat, fruit, or the like, baked between two layers of pastry or on one lower crust.

²**pie** (pī), *n.* the magpie, a black-and-white member of the crow family.

pie·bald (pī′bôld′), *adj.* having patches of different colors, especially black and white; as, a *piebald* horse.

piece (pēs), *n.* **1**, a part of anything; a fragment; as, a *piece* of bread; a plot or division; unit; as, a *piece* of land; **2**, a fixed quantity or size in which goods or various articles are made up for sale; as, muslin comes at twelve yards to the *piece;* **3**, a separate instance, example, or performance; as, a bad *piece* of business; **4**, a single object of a group; as, each *piece* in the set; **5**, a single, distinct, literary or artistic composition; as, a *piece* of music; **6**, the amount of work done as a distinct job; as, the work is paid for by the *piece;* **7**, a coin; as, a five-cent *piece;* **8**, a gun; as, a field *piece;* fowling *piece;* **9**, one of the counters or men with which chess, checkers, or similar games are played:—*v.t.* [pieced, piec-ing], **1**, to enlarge or mend by adding material; as, to *piece* a skirt; **2**, to make by joining sections together; as, to *piece* a quilt.

Syn., *n.* portion, section, fraction.

piece·meal (pēs′mēl′), *adv.* in portions or parts; by degrees; gradually; bit by bit; as, the work was done *piecemeal.*

piece of eight, an old Spanish and Spanish-American coin, equivalent to the dollar, and worth eight reals.

piece·work (pēs′wûrk′), *n.* work paid for by the piece: distinguished from *timework,* or work paid for by the hour, day, etc.—*n.* **piece′work′er.**

pied (pīd), *adj.* having two or more colors in blotches; piebald; as, a *pied* coat; also, wearing a many-colored coat; as, "The *Pied* Piper of Hamelin."

Pied·mont (pēd′mŏnt), a region (cap. Turin) in northwestern Italy.

pie·plant (pī′plănt′), *n.* in the U.S., the garden rhubarb, used for pies and sauce.

pier (pĭr), *n.* **1**, a support for an arch, bridge, or the like; **2**, a projecting part of a wall, such as a buttress; **3**, a wharf or dock built out over the water, for a landing place or walk.

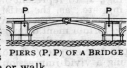
PIERS (P, P) OF A BRIDGE

Pierce (pĭrs), Franklin (1804–1869), the 14th president of the U.S.

pierce (pĭrs), *v.t.* [pierced, pierc-ing], **1**, to puncture or run through; stab; as, the knife *pierced* her hand; **2**, to make a hole in; as, she *pierced* her ears for earrings; **3**, to affect deeply; as, to *pierce* the heart with sorrow; **4**, to force a way through; as, they *pierced* the enemy lines; **5**, to see through or solve, as a mystery:—*v.i.* to enter; penetrate; as, the sun *pierced* through the clouds.

pier glass, a large high mirror, especially one used on a wall space or on a door.

Pierre (pĭr), a city, capital of South Dakota (map **7**).

pi·e·ty (pī′ĕ·tĭ), *n.* [*pl.* pieties], **1**, devotion to religion; **2**, reverence for God; **3**, honor and duty to parents.

pig (pĭg), *n.* **1**, a cloven-hoofed animal raised for its meat; a hog, especially a young one; **2**, *Colloquial,* a greedy or selfish person; **3**, an oblong mass of metal, especially of iron or lead, formed by being run into molds when melted:—*v.i.* [pigged, pig-ging], **1**, to give birth to pigs; **2**, to live like pigs.

PIG (¹⁄₆₀)

pi·geon (pĭj′ŭn), *n.* a bird, often domesticated, with stocky body, short legs, long wings, and handsome plumage; a dove.

pi·geon·hole (pĭj′ŭn·hōl′), *n.* **1**, a hole in which pigeons nest; **2**, a small, open, box-like space in a desk, case, or the like, for documents or letters:—*v.t.* [pigeonholed, pigeonhol-ing], **1**, to place (letters, documents, etc.) in such a boxlike space; to file; **2**, to lay aside and forget; shelve; as, the committee *pigeonholed* the proposal.

PIGEON

pi·geon–toed (pĭj′ŭn·tōd′), *adj.* with the toes turned in.

pig·gish (pĭg′ĭsh), *adj.* like a pig; stubborn, greedy, or dirty.—*adv.* **pig′gish·ly.**—*n.* **pig′gish·ness.**

pig·head·ed (pĭg′hĕd′ĕd), *adj.* obstinate or stubborn.

pig i·ron, crude iron as it comes from the blast furnace, usually cast into rough molds, or pigs: also called *pig.*

PIGEONHOLES def. 2

pig-ment (pĭg′mĕnt), n. 1, any substance used to give coloring; specifically, dry coloring matter which, when mixed with the proper fluid, forms paint; 2, the coloring matter in persons, animals, or plants.—adj. **pig′men-tar′y.**—n. **pig′men-ta′tion.**

pig-my (pĭg′mĭ). n. [pl. pigmies], a dwarf:—adj. very small. See **pygmy.**

pig-skin (pĭg′skĭn′), n. 1, the hide of a pig or the leather made from it; 2, Colloquial: **a,** a football; **b,** a saddle.

pig-sty (pĭg′stī′), n. [pl. pigsties], 1, a pen for pigs; 2, any very dirty place.

pig-tail (pĭg′tāl′), n. 1, hair twisted into a braid, usually hanging down from the back of the head; 2, a long twist of tobacco.

¹pike (pīk), n. a weapon formerly carried by foot soldiers, consisting of a long wooden shaft with a spearhead at one end.

PIKE (¹⁄₂₆)

²pike (pīk), n. a large, greedy fresh-water fish with a pointed head, found especially in the Great Lakes in North America.

³pike (pīk), n. 1, a road on which a charge is made for driving; a turnpike; 2, any main road.

pike-staff (pīk′stȧf′), n. a pole or shaft with a spike at the end, used especially by mountaineers to keep from slipping.

pi-las-ter (pĭ-lăs′tẽr), n. a rectangular column projecting slightly from a wall. (See illustration below.)

Pi-late (pī′lȧt), the Roman governor of Judea, under whom Christ was crucified.

¹pile (pīl), n. 1, a mass or heap; as, a pile of sand; 2, a heap of wood for burning a body; a pyre; 3, Colloquial, a great quantity; a lot; 4, Slang, a fortune:—v.t. [piled, pil-ing], 1, to place or throw in a heap; arrange; as, to pile bricks; 2, to accumulate; amass; as, he piled up a fortune; 3, to fill; load; as, to pile a car full of people:—v.i. 1, to form a mass or heap; accumulate; as, the snow piled up around the door; 2, to press forward in a mass; crowd.

SOLDIER, ABOUT 1600, WITH PIKE

²pile (pīl), n. 1, a timber driven into the ground, as for a wharf, foundation for a building, or the like; also, metal or concrete columns similarly used; 2, a

PILASTER

pointed stake or post:—**pile driver,** a machine for driving piles into the ground:—v.t. [piled, pil-ing], to drive piles into.

³pile (pīl), n. 1, nap of cloth; especially, the furry or velvety surface of velvet, plush, carpet, etc.; 2, short, soft hair; down.

piles (pīlz), n.pl. swellings in the veins about the anus, causing discomfort or soreness.

pil-fer (pĭl′fẽr), v.t. and v.i. to steal in small amounts.—n. **pil′fer-er.**

pil-grim (pĭl′grĭm), n. 1, one who travels from a distance to visit some sacred place; 2, a traveler:—**Pilgrims,** the Puritan settlers of the first colony in Massachusetts in 1620: also called Pilgrim Fathers.

pil-grim-age (pĭl′grĭ-mĭj), n. a long journey, especially to some sacred place.

pill (pĭl), n. 1, medicine prepared in the form of a small ball; 2, something disagreeable that must be accepted; as, defeat was a bitter pill.

pil-lage (pĭl′ĭj), n. 1, the act of plundering, or robbing openly, especially in war; 2, booty; spoil:—v.t. and v.i. [pillaged, pillaging], to plunder, or rob openly; despoil; sack.—n. **pil′lag-er.**

pil-lar (pĭl′ẽr), n. 1, a column to support a structure or to serve as a monument; 2, any support or mainstay; as, a pillar of society.—adj. **pil′lared.**

pil-lion (pĭl′yŭn), n. a pad put on the back of a horse behind a saddle as a seat for a second person.

pil-lo-ry (pĭl′ō-rĭ), n. [pl. pillories], an old instrument used to punish offenders publicly, consisting of a wooden frame supported by an upright post, and having holes through which the head and hands of a person were passed and secured:—v.t. [pilloried, pillory-ing], 1, to punish by putting into a pillory; 2, to expose to public disgrace.

PILLORY

pil-low (pĭl′ō), n. a case filled with feathers, down, or other soft material, to support the head of a person lying down:—v.t. to place on a pillow.

pil-low-case (pĭl′ō-kās′), n. a removable covering for a pillow.

pi-lot (pī′lŭt), n. 1, one who steers a ship; one licensed to conduct a ship in or out of a port or in waters where sailing is difficult or dangerous; 2, one who flies any kind of aircraft; 3, a guide of any sort; as, the President is the pilot of our national affairs; 4, the cowcatcher of a locomotive:—**pilot biscuit,** hardtack:—v.t. 1, to direct the course of (a vessel, airship, etc.); 2, to guide or escort through difficulties.

go; join; yet; sing; chin; show; thin, then; hw, why; zh, azure; ū, Ger. für or Fr. lune; ö, Ger. schön or Fr. feu; ṅ, Fr. enfant, nom; kh, Ger. ach or ich. See pages ix-x.

pi·lot·age (pī′lŭt-ĭj), *n.* **1,** the act or business of guiding, especially of guiding ships in or out of a port or through dangerous water; **2,** the fee paid for such service.

Pil·sen (pĭl′zĕn), a manufacturing city in Czechoslovakia (map **12**). Its Czechish name is *Plzen.*

pi·men·to (pĭ-mĕn′tō), *n.* [*pl.* pimentos], **1,** allspice, an unripe fruit, dried and used as a flavoring; also, the tree bearing it; **2,** a variety of sweet pepper; pimiento.

pi·mien·to (pē-myĕn′tō), *n.* [*pl.* pimientos], a variety of sweet pepper, used as a vegetable, stuffing for olives, etc.: often called *pimento.*

pim·per·nel (pĭm′pẽr-nĕl), *n.* a plant of the primrose family growing in cornfields and waste ground, with white, purple, or scarlet flowers which close in cloudy or rainy weather; also, the flower.

pim·ple (pĭm′pl), *n.* a small, inflamed swelling of the skin, often containing pus. —*adj.* **pim′pled.**—*adj.* **pim′ply.**

pin (pĭn), *n.* **1,** a short piece of wire with a sharp point at one end and a round head at the other, used for fastening things together; **2,** a piece of wood, metal, etc., having a similar use or appearance; as, a clothes*pin,* a hair*pin,* a hat*pin,* etc.; **3,** an ornament, badge, or jewel fitted with a pin and a clasp; as, a fraternity *pin;* **4,** a bolt or peg; **5,** a wooden roller; as, a rolling *pin;* **6,** a wooden peg, shaped like a bottle, which is a target in bowling:—*v.t.* [pinned, pinning], **1,** to fasten with, or as with, a pin; as, to *pin* a pattern on cloth; **2,** to hold fast in one position; as, the steering wheel *pinned* him in the wrecked car; **3,** to·hold or keep (a person) to an obligation, course of action, etc.; as, to *pin* him down to his promise.

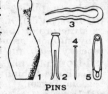

PINS

1, tenpin; 2, clothespin; 3, hairpin; 4, dressmaker's pin; 5, safety pin.

pin·a·fore (pĭn′à-fôr′), *n.* a loose sleeveless apron or covering to protect the clothing of·a child or young girl.

pin·cers (pĭn′sẽrz), *n.pl.* sometimes used as *sing.* **1,** an instrument with two handles and two jaws working on a pivot, used for gripping things; nippers; **2,** the claws of lobsters, crabs, etc. Also, **pinch′ers.**

PINCERS

pinch (pĭnch), *v.t.* **1,** to squeeze or nip between the thumb and a finger, or between two hard edges; as, to *pinch* a finger in a door; **2,** to press on so as to hurt; as, the shoe *pinches* my toe; **3,** to oppress or distress; as, to be *pinched* by poverty; **4,** to make thin or worn; as, to be *pinched* with hunger; **5,** *Slang:* **a,** to arrest; **b,** to steal:— *v.i.* **1,** to press hard; as, my shoe *pinches;* **2,** to be mean or miserly:—*n.* **1,** a squeeze or nip, as with the fingers and thumb; **2,** painful pressure; as, the *pinch* of poverty; **3,** a sudden difficulty or necessity; emergency; as, anything will do in a *pinch;* **4,** as much as can be held between the thumb and a finger; as, a *pinch* of salt.

pinch·ers (pĭn′chẽrz), *n.pl.* sometimes used as *sing.* nippers; pliers. See **pincers.**

¹pine (pīn), *n.* **1,** a kind of cone-bearing tree having clusters of evergreen needle-like leaves (see illustration, page 865); **2,** the timber of the tree; **3,** a pineapple.

²pine (pīn), *v.i.* [pined, pining], **1,** to grow thin and weak from distress, anxiety, or the like; **2,** to long intensely; as, to *pine* for friends.

Syn. languish, droop, wither, flag.

pine·ap·ple (pī′năp′l), *n.* **1,** a tropical plant with spiny leaves, bearing a large fruit somewhat resembling a pine cone; **2,** the edible, juicy fruit of this plant.

pin·feath·er (pĭn′fĕth′ẽr), *n.* a small feather just beginning to grow.

pin·hole (pĭn′hōl′), *n.* a very small hole made by, or as by, a pin.

¹pin·ion (pĭn′yŭn), *n.* a wheel, the cogs of which come into gear with those of a larger toothed wheel or of a rack, so that motion is imparted from one to the other; also, in a pair of gears, the smaller gear.

PINEAPPLE

²pin·ion (pĭn′yŭn), *n.* **1,** the last group of bones of a bird's wing; **2,** a wing; **3,** a feather:— *v.t.* **1,** to bind the wings of, or to clip the pinion of; as, to *pinion* a bird; **2,** to bind or confine; as, to *pinion* a person's arms to his sides.

PINION AND GEAR

¹pink (pĭngk), *v.t.* **1,** to cut the edges of (cloth, leather, paper, etc.) in points or scallops; **2,** to prick or pierce, as with a sword.

²pink (pĭngk), *n.* **1,** a very pale red; **2,** a garden plant with sharp-pointed leaves, and red, pink, or white flowers, which are either fringed or ruffled and have a sweet, spicy fragrance;. also, the flower; **3,** the highest degree; the peak; as, in the *pink* of perfection:—*adj.* of a very pale-red color.—*adj.* **pink′ish.**

pink-eye (pĭngk′ī′), *n.* a contagious inflammation of the eye, marked by redness of the eyeball.

pin mon-ey, money allowed to a wife by her husband for her private expenses.

pin-nace (pĭn′ĭs; pĭn′ās), *n.* **1,** a small, light, schooner-rigged vessel with oars; **2,** a man-of-war's eight-oared boat.

pin-na-cle (pĭn′ȧ-kl), *n.* **1,** a small tower or turret above the rest of a building; **2,** a high point like a spire; as, a *pinnacle* of rock; **3,** the highest point; as, few men reach the *pinnacle* of fame.

pin-nate (pĭn′āt), *adj.* having parts arranged, as in a feather, along two sides of an axis; as, in botany, a *pinnate* leaf has leaflets arranged on each side of a common stem.

PINNACLE (P)

pi-noch-le or **pi-noc-le** (pē′nŭk′l), *n.* a game of cards the object of which is the making of certain card combinations.

pi-non (pē′nyōn; pĭn′yŭn), *n.* a kind of western American pine with seeds which may be eaten; also, the seed.

pint (pīnt), *n.* a measure of capacity equal to half a quart.

pin-to (pĭn′tō; pēn′tō), *adj.* mottled; pied: —*n.* a piebald horse or pony.

PINNATE LEAVES

pi-o-neer (pī′ō-nēr′), *n.* one who goes before to prepare the way for others, especially an original settler in a frontier country:—*v.i.* to prepare a way; explore: —*v.t.* to open up (new country) or take the lead in (new causes).

pi-ous (pī′ŭs), *adj.* **1,** showing reverence for God; religious; devout; as, *pious* nuns; **2,** done under pretense of religion; as, *pious* deception.—*adv.* **pi′ous-ly.**

¹**pip** (pĭp), *n.* a small seed, as of an apple or an orange.

²**pip** (pĭp), *n.* **1,** a disease of poultry; **2,** *Slang,* humorously, any illness.

pipe (pīp), *n.* **1,** any long, hollow tube; as, a water *pipe;* **2,** a tube of clay, wood, etc., with a bowl at one end for smoking tobacco, opium, etc.; **3,** a high-pitched voice; as, the *pipe* of a child; **4,** the note or call of a bird or insect; **5,** a musical wind instrument consisting of a hollow tube, as

a flute; **6,** one of the graduated tubes in which the notes of some organs, called *pipe organs,* are produced; **7, pipes,** the bagpipe:—*v.t.* [piped, pip-ing], **1,** to play on a musical pipe; as, to *pipe* a tune; **2,** to utter in a high key; as, to *pipe* a song; **3,** to furnish with pipes; as, to *pipe* a house for water; **4,** to carry through a pipe or tube; as, to *pipe* water into a city:—*v.i.* **1,** to play on a pipe; **2,** to speak shrilly.

pip-er (pīp′ẽr), *n.* one who plays on a pipe; especially, one who plays on a bagpipe.

pip-ing (pīp′ĭng), *n.* **1,** the music of a pipe; also, a shrill sound; as, the *piping* of birds; **2,** a system of tubes for drainage, gas, etc.; **3,** a narrow fold of material used in trimming dresses.

pip-it (pĭp′ĭt), *n.* a small bird, similar to the lark, which sings as it flies.

pip-kin (pĭp′kĭn), *n.* **1,** a small earthen jar or pot; **2,** a small wooden tub.

pip-pin (pĭp′ĭn), *n.* any one of several varieties of apple.

PIPIT (⅛)

pi-quant (pē′kȧnt), *adj.* **1,** agreeably sharp to the taste; as, a *piquant* sauce; **2,** arousing interest or curiosity; having a lively charm; as, *piquant* remarks; a *piquant* face.
Syn. tart, pungent, spicy.

pique (pēk), *n.* slight anger or resentment, especially as a result of wounded pride; as, she left the party in a fit of *pique:*—*v.t.* [piqued (pēkt), pi-quing (pē′kĭng)], **1,** to wound the pride of; irritate; displease; **2,** to pride or value (oneself); as, she *piqued* herself on her ability; **3,** to stir or arouse; as, to *pique* the curiosity.
Syn., n. displeasure, irritation, vexation.

pi-qué (pē-kā′), *n.* a ribbed silk or cotton cloth.

pi-ra-cy (pī′rȧ-sĭ), *n.* [*pl.* piracies], **1,** robbery upon the high seas; **2,** the using, without permission, of another's literary work, invention, or the like, for profit.

pi-rate (pī′rĭt), *n.* **1,** a robber on the high seas; **2,** hence, anyone using lawless methods in gaining something; especially, one who uses another's literary work for profit without permission, or claims it as his own product; **3,** a ship engaged in robbery on the high seas:—*v.t.* [pirat-ed, pirat-ing], **1,** to rob at sea; **2,** to take and publish without permission or payment.—*adj.* **pi-rat′ic; pi-rat′i-cal.**

pir-ou-ette (pĭr′ōō-ĕt′), *n.* a whirling or turning about on the toes:—*v.i.* [pirouet-ted, pirouet-ting], to turn on the toes rapidly in one spot.

---

go; join; yet; sing; chin; show; thin, *th*en; hw, *wh*y; zh, azure; ü, Ger. für or Fr. lune; ö, Ger. schön or Fr. feu; n̈, Fr. enfant, nom; kh, Ger. ach or ich. See pages ix–x.

Pi-sa (pē′zà; pē′sä), a city in Tuscany, Italy, famous for its leaning tower (map 12).

pis-ca-tor-y (pĭs′kà-tôr′ĭ), *adj.* **1,** pertaining to fishes or fishing; **2,** living by fishing; as, the inhabitants of Labrador are *piscatory* people. Also, **pis′ca-tor′i-al.**

pis-ta-chi-o (pĭs-tä′shĭ-ō; pĭs-tä′shĭ-ō), *n.* [*pl.* pistachios], **1,** a small tree of Asia and southern Europe, or its nut, the kernel of which is used for flavoring; **2,** the flavor of the nut; **3,** the greenish color of the kernel.

pis-til (pĭs′tĭl; pĭs′tl), *n.* in botany, the seed-bearing organ in the center of a flower.

pis-til-late (pĭs′tĭ-lāt), *adj.* in botany, having pistils; specifically, having pistils but no stamens.

pis-tol (pĭs′tl), *n.* a small, short gun intended for use with one hand. Pistols are now usually of two types, the revolver and the automatic.

pis-ton (pĭs′tŭn), *n.* a closely fitting disk or cylinder designed to slide to and fro within a larger tube or cylinder.

PISTIL
Section of a flower showing pistil (P) and stamens (S, S).

¹**pit** (pĭt), *n.* **1,** a hole or cavity in the earth; **2,** the shaft of a mine, or the mine itself; **3,** a deep gulf; abyss; **4,** a hole used for trapping wild animals; **5,** a small scar, such as that left by smallpox; **6,** a depression in some part of the body; as, the arm-*pits;* **7,** in England, the cheaper downstairs seats in a theater; **8,** an enclosed place set aside for dogfighting, cockfighting, etc.; **9,** that part of the floor of an exchange where a special business is carried on; as, a grain *pit:*— **the pit,** hell or Hades:—*v.t.* [pit-ted, pit-ting], **1,** to mark with small pits; as, smallpox had *pitted* his face; **2,** to match or set to fight against another; as, to *pit* one's strength against a foe; **3,** to place in a pit.

PISTOL

²**pit** (pĭt), *n.* the kernel or stone of certain fruits, as the peach, cherry, date, etc.:—*v.t.* [pit-ted, pit-ting], to remove the pits of.

pit-a-pat (pĭt′à-păt′), *adv.* with quick beating; flutteringly; as, her heart went *pitapat:*—*n.* a succession of light, quick sounds.

¹**pitch** (pĭch), *n.* **1,** a thick, sticky, black substance, soft when heated, left over after distillation of coal tar or turpentine: much used in roofing and filling seams in ships: commonly called *tar;* **2,** the sticky resin of certain trees:—*v.t.* to cover or smear with pitch or tar.

²**pitch** (pĭch), *v.t.* **1,** to fix in or on the ground; set up; as, to *pitch* a tent; **2,** to throw or fling; as, to *pitch* hay; to *pitch* quoits; **3,** in music, to determine the key of; start, as a tune, by sounding the keynote:—*v.i.* **1,** to fall headlong; as, to *pitch* forward; **2,** to fix the choice; decide; as, they finally *pitched* on the right candidate; **3,** to rise alternately forward and aft, as a ship in heavy seas; to toss; **4,** in baseball, to throw the ball to the batter; act as pitcher:—*n.* **1,** a plunging forward or down; as, a headlong *pitch* from a ladder; **2,** the act or manner of throwing or tossing; as, a good *pitch* in baseball; **3,** a tossing motion, as of a ship in a storm; **4,** degree or rate; as, the highest *pitch* of excitement; **5,** the tone of a voice; **6,** slope; as, the *pitch* of a roof; **7,** the distance between two successive threads of a screw, or between the centers of two successive gear teeth; **8,** in music, the highness or lowness of a tone:— **pitched battle,** a battle for which preparations and arrangements have been made.

pitch-blende (pĭch′blĕnd′), *n.* a lustrous black, or brownish-black mineral, a source of radium and uranium.

¹**pitch-er** (pĭch′ẽr), *n.* **1,** one who throws or hurls; **2,** in baseball, the player who throws the ball to the batter.

²**pitch-er** (pĭch′ẽr), *n.* a container, usually with an open spout and a handle, used to hold or pour liquids.

pitcher plant, a plant with leaves formed into pitcher-shaped receptacles in which small insects, as flies, are caught and digested.

pitch-fork (pĭch′fôrk′), *n.* a fork with a long handle for tossing hay, straw, etc.:—*v.t.* to toss with, or as with, a pitchfork.

PITCHER

pitch-y (pĭch′ĭ), *adj.* [pitch-i-er, pitch-i-est], **1,** like, or smeared with, pitch or tar; **2,** dark; black; gloomy.

pit-e-ous (pĭt′ē-ŭs), *adj.* exciting sorrow or sympathy; mournful.—*adv.* **pit′e-ous-ly.**
Syn. miserable, pitiful, pitiable.

pit-fall (pĭt′-fôl′), *n.* **1,** a hole lightly covered, so that animals may fall into it; a trap; **2,** any hidden source of danger or temptation.

PITCHFORK

pith (pĭth), *n.* **1,** the soft, spongy substance in the center of the stem of some plants; **2,** any similar soft tissue, as the marrow in a bone; **3,** energy or force; vigor; **4,** gist; substance; as, the *pith* of his speech.—*adj.* **pith′less.**

pith·y (pĭth'ĭ), *adj.* [pith-i-er, pith-i-est], **1,** like or full of the soft, spongy substance called pith; **2,** forcible; full of meaning; as, Benjamin Franklin is noted for his *pithy* sayings.—*adv.* **pith'i·ly.**

pit·i·a·ble (pĭt'ĭ-á-bl), *adj.* **1,** deserving sympathy; as, he was in a *pitiable* condition; **2,** poor; mean; as, *pitiable* makeshifts.—*adv.* **pit'i·a·bly.**
Syn. sorrowful, sad, pitiful, piteous.

pit·i·ful (pĭt'ĭ-fŏŏl), *adj.* **1,** miserable; sad; as, a *pitiful* sight; **2,** small; meager; as, a *pitiful* amount; **3,** contemptible; as, a *pitiful* ambition.—*adv.* **pit'i·ful·ly.**
Syn. piteous, pitiable.

pit·i·less (pĭt'ĭ-lĕs), *adj.* without sympathy or mercy.—*adv.* **pit'i·less·ly.**
Syn. cruel, harsh, relentless.

Pitt (pĭt), William, Earl of Chatham (1708–1778), called *the Great Commoner,* an English statesman.

pit·tance (pĭt'ǎns), *n.* a small allowance, especially of money; any small quantity.

Pitts·burgh (pĭts'bûrg), a manufacturing city in southwestern Pennsylvania, a center of the iron and steel industry (map 6).

pi·tu·i·tar·y (pĭ-tū'ĭ-tĕr'ĭ), *adj.* pertaining to, or secreting, mucus:—**pituitary body,** a small, rounded gland in the brain.

pit·y (pĭt'ĭ), *n.* [*pl.* pities], **1,** a feeling of sorrow for the suffering of others; mercy; **2,** a reason for regret or grief; as, it is a *pity* he was not promoted with his classmates:—*v.t.* [pitied, pity-ing], to sympathize with; feel sorry for.
Syn., n. compassion, sympathy, condolence.

piv·ot (pĭv'ŭt), *n.* **1,** a fixed pin or short shaft on which some object, as a ball or wheel, turns; **2,** that on which something important depends:—*v.t.* to place on, or supply with, a pivot:—*v.i.* to turn on a pivot.

pix·y or **pix·ie** (pĭk'sĭ), *n.* [*pl.* pixies], in old folk tales, a fairy; an elf.

pk. abbreviation for *peck.*

pkg. abbreviation for *package.*

pl. abbreviation for *plural.*

PIVOT (P) OF A GYROSCOPE

plac·ard (plăk'ärd), *n.* a printed bill or notice posted in a public place, as an advertisement; a poster:—*v.t.* (plá-kärd'; plăk'ärd), **1,** to advertise by a bill posted publicly; **2,** to post a bill or notice on.

pla·cate (plā'kāt; plăk'āt; plá-kāt'), *v.t.* [placat-ed, placat-ing], to calm the anger of (a person); pacify; make friendly.

place (plās), *n.* **1,** originally, an open space, as a public square, in a town or city; sometimes, a part of a street; also, a city or town; **2,** a particular location; **3,** rank; social position; especially, high rank; **4,** a position; job; **5,** in a race, a position among the winning competitors; **6,** in arithmetic, the position occupied by a figure in relation to the other figures of a series; **7,** a building devoted to a special purpose; as, a *place* of worship; **8,** the location of a given body; as, it is out of *place;* **9,** duty; as, it is your *place* to do it; **10,** position in order; as, in the first *place;* **11,** a particular spot in a surface; as, a sore *place* on my arm:—*v.t.* [placed, placing], **1,** to put in a particular spot or position; **2,** to put in office or authority; **3,** to identify by connecting with some place, circumstance, etc.; as, we *placed* him as a former neighbor; **4,** to put; as, I *place* trust in him.

plac·er (plăs'ẽr), *n.* in mining, a place where loose surface soil or gravel contains gold or other valuable minerals.

plac·id (plăs'ĭd), *adj.* calm; peaceful.—*adv.* **plac'id·ly.**—*n.* **plac'id·ness.**
Syn. gentle, serene, tranquil.

pla·cid·i·ty (plá-sĭd'ĭ-tĭ), *n.* calmness.

plack·et (plăk'ĕt), *n.* a finished opening or slit in the upper part of a skirt or petticoat, to make it easy to put on.

pla·gi·a·rism (plā'jĭ-á-rĭzm; plā'já-rĭzm), *n.* the act of stealing and using, as one's own, another's ideas or words; literary theft.—*n.* **pla'gi·a·rist.**

pla·gi·a·rize (plā'jĭ-á-rīz; plā'já-rīz), *v.t.* and *v.i.* [plagiarized, plagiariz-ing], to steal and use (another's ideas, words, etc.) as one's own.

plague (plāg), *n.* **1,** a deadly, epidemic disease; **2,** anything very troublesome or causing misery; **3,** *Colloquial,* a nuisance:—*v.t.* [plagued, pla-guing], **1,** to afflict with disease, evil, or disaster; **2,** to trouble or annoy greatly.—*adj.* **pla'guy.**
Syn., v. harass, torment, vex, disturb.

plaid (plăd), *n.* **1,** a barred or checkered woolen cloth; **2,** a garment made of a large rectangle of such material, worn by the Highlanders of Scotland; **3,** any material with such a pattern; also, the pattern:—*adj.* having a barred or checkered pattern; as, a *plaid* dress.

PLAID (P)

plain (plān), *adj.* **1,** level; flat; even; **2,** clear; evident; as, in *plain* sight; **3,** easily understood; as, your meaning is *plain;* **4,** unlearned; unpolished; simple in manners; as, a *plain,* blunt man; **5,** frank; sincere; as, a *plain* speech; **6,** not luxurious; as, *plain* living; **7,** without ornament; as, *plain* furniture; **8,** all of one color; as, a dress of *plain* material; **9,** without beauty; homely; as, a *plain* face:—*adv.* clearly:—*n.* **1,** a wide stretch of level land; a flat expanse; **2, plains,** great tracts of level country without trees.—*adv.* **plain'ly.**—*n.* **plain'ness.**

Syn., adj. obvious, apparent, open.

plain—spo-ken (plān'-spō'kĕn), *adj.* candid; frank in speech.

plaint (plānt), *n.* **1,** *Poetic,* a mournful song; lamentation; **2,** a complaint.

plain-tiff (plān'tĭf), *n.* one who brings suit in a court of law.

plain-tive (plān'tĭv), *adj.* expressing sorrow; mournful; sad; as, a *plaintive* song.—*adv.* **plain'tive-ly.**—*n.* **plain'tive-ness.**

plait (plēt; plāt), *n.* **1,** a flattened fold made by doubling cloth over upon itself; a pleat, as in a skirt; **2,** (plăt), a braid, as of hair:—*v.t.* **1,** to double over in folds; pleat; **2,** to braid or interweave; plat.

plan (plăn), *n.* **1,** a drawing, diagram, or map, showing the outline or design of anything; as, an architect's *plan* of a building; **2,** the arrangement of parts according to a fixed design; **3,** a way of doing something; **4,** a scheme or project:—*v.t.* [planned, planning], **1,** to make a sketch or design of; outline; **2,** to arrange beforehand:—*v.i.* to make a plan; as, to *plan* for a big crowd.

PLAN FOR ONE FLOOR OF A HOUSE

Syn., n. design, purpose, intention.

¹**plane** (plān), *n.* a carpenter's tool for smoothing wood:—*v.t.* [planed, plan-ing], to make smooth with such a tool, as a board:—*v.i.* to work with a plane.

²**plane** (plān), *adj.* flat; level; even; as, a *plane* surface:—*n.* **1,** a flat or even surface; **2,** a grade or level; as, a high *plane* of living; **3,** one of the flat supporting surfaces of the wings of an airplane; **4,** an airplane.

PLANES

³**plane** (plān), *n.* any of several large trees

with broad, spreading leaves and light-brown, flaky bark, including the American sycamore, or buttonwood: also called *plane tree.*

plan-er (plān'ĕr), *n.* a machine for smoothing the surface of wood or metal.

plan-et (plăn'ĕt), *n.* in astronomy, any heavenly body revolving round the sun and shining by reflected light.

plan-e-tar-i-um (plăn'ĕ-târ'ĭ-ŭm), *n.* [*pl.* planetaria (plăn'ĕ-târ'ĭ-a)], a circular hall containing an apparatus for projecting against a domed ceiling images of the planets, stars, etc., as they appear and move in the heavens.

plan-e-tar-y (plăn'ĕ-tĕr'ĭ), *adj.* **1,** pertaining to a planet or to the planets; **2,** like a planet.

plank (plăngk), *n.* **1,** a long, broad piece of sawed timber thicker than a board; **2,** an item in the platform of a political party:—*v.t.* **1,** to cover with thick boards; **2,** *Colloquial,* to lay down, as on a plank; hence, to pay; as, to *plank* down money; **3,** to cook on a board; as, to *plank* shad.

plant (plănt), *n.* **1,** a member of the vegetable kingdom, usually with roots in the soil from which it draws part of its food in the form of minerals and water, and with stems, branches, leaves, and flowers above the ground, as a bush, herb, or tree; **2,** a sprout or young shoot ready for transplanting; **3,** the tools, machinery, fixtures, and sometimes buildings, of any trade or business; as, a manufacturing *plant;* **4,** the equipment of an institution, as a college or hospital:—*v.t.* **1,** to put into the ground for growth; as, to *plant* seed; **2,** to provide or prepare with seeds, roots, etc.; as, to *plant* a garden; **3,** to fix firmly; place; **4,** to establish, as a colony; **5,** to implant or introduce, as an idea.

Plan-tag-e-net (plăn-tăj'ĕ-nĕt), *n.* the family name of kings of England who occupied the throne from 1154 to 1485.

¹**plan-tain** (plăn'tĭn), *n.* a tropical, broad-leaved tree with an edible fruit resembling the banana; also, its fruit.

²**plan-tain** (plăn'tĭn), *n.* a common garden or roadside weed with a rosette of broad leaves, and a stalk bearing many tiny greenish flowers.

PLANTAIN, def. 2

plan-ta-tion (plăn-tā'shŭn), *n.* **1,** a place where anything is sowed, set out, or

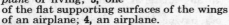

cultivated; as, a *plantation* of trees; **2,** in southern countries and in America, a large estate where cotton, sugar cane, etc., are cultivated; **3,** a new settlement or colony.

plant-er (plăn′tĕr), *n.* **1,** the owner or cultivator of a plantation; **2,** a person who sows or plants; **3,** a planting machine.

plant louse, a small, parasitic insect that sucks the juices of plants.

plaque (plăk; pläk), *n.* **1,** a flat, thin piece of metal or earthenware, upon which a picture or design is enameled or carved.

plas-ma (plăz′mȧ), *n.* **1,** the liquid part of blood, lymph, and, less commonly, of milk; **2,** blood from which the red cells have been removed. It is then treated, often dried, and preserved for use in transfusions.

plas-ter (plås′tĕr), *n.* **1,** a mixture of lime, sand, and water, which hardens on drying, used for coating walls and partitions of buildings; **2,** a substance with medicinal qualities, spread upon cloth and applied to the body as a remedy; as, a mustard *plaster*: —*v.t.* **1,** to cover with plaster; as, to *plaster* the walls; **2,** to treat with a plaster.

plas-ter-board (plås′tĕr-bôrd′), *n.* a thin board composed of plaster and paper in alternate layers.

plas-ter cast, a dressing of gauze saturated with plaster of Paris molded to a bodily part to limit movement; a plaster reproduction cast in a mold of a statue or the like.

plas-ter of Par-is, a white powdery substance which, when mixed with water, forms a quick-setting paste: used for finishing walls, making moldings, statuettes, etc.

plas-tic (plăs′tĭk), *adj.* **1,** capable of being formed or molded; as, clay is *plastic;* hence, quick to receive impressions; as, a *plastic* mind; **2,** giving form to matter; as, *plastic* art; **3,** of, pertaining to, or characteristic of, molding or modeling; **4,** made of synthetic material:—**plastic surgery,** surgery for the restoration of deformed and mutilated parts of the body:—*n.* **1,** anything which can be molded; **2,** any of a group of synthetic materials which are liquid or soft when hot and become solid when cooled. They are synthesized chemically from many plant and animal materials, and are used as substitutes for natural materials as wood, metal, glass, leather, and the like; **3,** an article made from such material.—*n.* **plas-tic′i-ty** (plăs-tĭs′ĭ-tĭ).—*n.* **plas-ti-ci′zer.**

¹plat (plăt), *v.t.* [plat-ted, plat-ting], to braid; plait:—*n.* a braid.

²plat (plăt), *n.* **1,** a small plot of ground; **2,** a plan, map, etc.:—*v.t.* [plat-ted, plat-ting], to map.

Pla-ta Riv-er (plä′tä), a river of Argentina and Uruguay, South America (map 11).

plate (plāt), *n.* **1,** a thin, flat piece of metal or glass, rigid, and of uniform thickness; as, armor *plate;* **2,** a shallow, usually circular, dish from which food is eaten; **3,** as much food as such a plate will hold; a plateful; also, food served to one person at a meal; **4,** a piece of metal on which something is engraved; as, a door *plate;* **5,** a print made from an engraved metal surface; also, the surface; **6,** in photography, a thin sheet of glass treated with chemicals to make it sensitive to light, on which a picture is taken; **7,** household articles of gold or silver; **8,** a thin piece of rubber, metal, etc., fitted to the mouth, and holding artificial teeth; also, a device for straightening irregular teeth; **9,** in baseball, the home base; **10,** a cut of beef from the lower part of the side; **11,** in architecture, a horizontal timber upon which the lower ends of the rafters are set; **12,** the mold of a page or section of type:—*v.t.* [plat-ed, plat-ing], **1,** to coat with metal; **2,** to cover with sheets of metal.

pla-teau (plă-tō′), *n.* [*pl.* plateaus], an elevated tract of flat land; tableland.

plate glass, a fine glass, rolled in plates, ground smooth, and polished.

plat-form (plăt′fôrm′), *n.* **1,** a structure raised above the level of the ground, as along the tracks in a railroad station, or above the level of the main floor, as a stage for public speakers; **2,** a level, raised area for mounting guns or launching rockets; **3,** a statement of principles and policies, as of a political party.

plat-ing (plā′tĭng), *n.* **1,** the art of overlaying with a thin coating of metal; **2,** a coating of metal or of thin metal sheets.

plat-i-num (plăt′ĭ-nŭm), *n.* a heavy, silver-white, precious metal much used for chemical utensils and for jewelry.

plat-i-tude (plăt′ĭ-tūd), *n.* **1,** commonplaceness or dulness in speaking or writing; **2,** a trite, commonplace remark, especially if uttered as new or original; as, "It never rains but it pours," is a *platitude.*

Pla-to (plā′tō), (427?–347 B.C.), a Greek philosopher.

Pla-ton-ic (plȧ-tŏn′ĭk), *adj.* pertaining to, or characteristic of, Plato or his philosophy:—**Platonic love** or **friendship,** an affection between the sexes based solely on mental and spiritual attraction.

PLATTER

pla-toon (plȧ-tōōn′), *n.* a body of soldiers, usually consisting of two to four squads.

plat-ter (plăt′ĕr), *n.* a large, flat dish for serving meat, poultry, etc.

---

go; join; yet; sing; chin; show; thin, *th*en; hw, *wh*y; zh, azure; ū, Ger. für or Fr. lune; ö, Ger. schön or Fr. *feu*; ṅ, Fr. enfant, nom; kh, Ger. ach or ich. See pages ix–x.

plat-y-pus (plăt′ĭ-pŭs), *n.* a small, burrowing water animal of Australia, which lays eggs, but suckles its young; the duckbill.

plau-dit (plô′dĭt), *n.* approval; enthusiastic applause, usually expressed by clapping or by shouting.

plau-si-ble (plô′zĭ-bl), *adj.* **1,** seeming to be true; having the appearance of truth; as, a *plausible* excuse; **2,** fair-spoken; persuasive; as, a *plausible* speaker.—*n.* **plau-si-bil′i-ty.**—*adv.* **plau′si-bly.**
Syn. apparent, specious, ostensible.

play (plā), *v.i.* **1,** to move lightly or capriciously; flicker, as a shadow; flutter, as leaves in the wind; **2,** to sport or frolic; exercise actively; **3,** to take part in a game; also, to gamble; **4,** to perform on a musical instrument; **5,** to act on the stage; **6,** to behave thoughtlessly; dally; trifle:—*v.t.* **1,** to take part in (a game or contest); as, to *play* checkers; also, to compete with, in a game; as, our team *played* the high-school team; **2,** to put into action in a game or contest, as by laying a card on the table; **3,** to imitate in sport; as, to *play* school; **4,** to perform; as, to *play* a comedy; *play* a waltz on the piano; also, to perform music on; as, to *play* the violin; **5,** to act in the character of; as, to *play* Othello; *play* the fool; **6,** to work; set in action; as, to *play* a trick; **7,** to operate continuously or repeatedly; as, to *play* a hose on the grass:—*n.* **1,** brisk, lively, sometimes irregular, motion; as, the *play* of light and shade; **2,** freedom or room to act; as, to give one's arm full *play* in throwing a ball; **3,** action or use; as, all their resources were brought into *play*; **4,** exercise, especially in a contest of strength or skill; as, the *play* of a duelist's sword; **5,** an athletic or other contest; a game or sport; **6,** recreation; frolic; **7,** gambling; as, to lose money at *play;* **8,** any single action in a game; also, one's turn to move a piece, lay down a card, etc., in a game; as, it is your *play;* **9,** fun; jest; as, she did it in *play;* **10,** conduct; manner of dealing; as, fair *play;* **11,** a drama intended for stage performance; also, the performance of a drama:—**a play on words,** a pun; the use of words in a double meaning.
Syn., n. pastime, diversion, game, sport.

play-er (plā′ẽr), *n.* **1,** one who takes part in a game; **2,** a musical performer; **3,** an actor; **4,** a gambler.

play-er pi-an-o, a piano operated by a mechanical playing device.

play-fel-low (plā′fĕl′ō), *n.* a playmate.

play-ful (plā′fŏŏl), *adj.* full of play; lively; as, a *playful* kitten.—*adv.* **play′-ful-ly.**—*n.* **play′ful-ness.**

play-ground (plā′ground′), *n.* a plot of ground set aside for children's play.

play-house (plā′hous′), *n.* **1,** a theater; **2,** a house for children's play.

play-ing card, one of the cards of a pack used for playing games; especially, one of a pack of 52 cards divided into four suits: diamonds, hearts, spades, and clubs.

play-mate (plā′māt′), *n.* one who takes part in games with another; a playfellow.

play-thing (plā′thĭng′), *n.* a toy.

play-wright (plā′rīt′), *n.* a writer of plays; dramatist.

pla-za (plä′zȧ; plăz′ȧ), *n.* an open square or market place surrounded by buildings.

plea (plē), *n.* **1,** an excuse or apology; **2,** an entreaty; **3,** the defendant's answer to the charges in a lawsuit.

plead (plēd), *v.i.* [*p.t.* and *p.p.* plead-ed or, *Colloquial,* plead (plĕd), *p.pr.* plead-ing], **1,** to argue or reason in support of a cause against another; **2,** to argue before a court of law; as, to *plead* for an acquittal; **3,** to beg earnestly; pray; as, to *plead* for mercy:—*v.t.* **1,** to defend by arguments; as, to *plead* a case; **2,** to answer, as to a charge; as, to *plead* not guilty; **3,** to offer as an excuse; as, to *plead* poverty.—*n.* **plead′er.**
Syn. urge, beseech, entreat.

plead-ings (plēd′ĭngz), *n.pl.* the written record of the statements made by the two parties in a lawsuit.

pleas-ant (plĕz′ănt), *adj.* **1,** pleasing; delightful; agreeable; as, a *pleasant* smell; **2,** characterized by charming manners or behavior; cheerful; as, a *pleasant* fellow.—*adv.* **pleas′ant-ly.**—*n.* **pleas′ant-ness.**
Syn. comfortable, merry, amiable.

pleas-ant-ry (plĕz′ănt-rĭ), *n.* [*pl.* pleasantries], **1,** merriment; lively talk; gaiety; **2,** a laughable speech; a joke.
Syn. raillery, banter, playfulness.

please (plēz), *v.t.* [pleased, pleas-ing], **1,** to gratify; give enjoyment to; **2,** to be the will of; suit; as, *please* God, we may return safely:—*v.i.* **1,** to give satisfaction or enjoyment; as, we strive to *please;* **2,** to like or choose; as, to do as you *please.*
Syn. delight, charm, gladden.

pleas-ing (plēz′ĭng), *adj.* giving enjoyment; agreeable.—*adv.* **pleas′ing-ly.**

pleas-ur-a-ble (plĕzh′ẽr-ȧ-bl), *adj.* delightful; gratifying; as, a *pleasurable* occasion.—*adv.* **pleas′ur-a-bly.**

pleas-ure (plĕzh′ẽr), *n.* **1,** a feeling of delight or satisfaction; enjoyment; **2,** a source of delight; a joy; **3,** choice; wish; as, I await your *pleasure.*
Syn. satisfaction, comfort, happiness.

āte, āorta, râre, căt, ásk, fär, ȧllow, sofȧ; ēve, ĕvent, ĕll, wrītẽr, novĕl; bīte, pĭn; nō, ōbey, ôr, dŏg, tŏp, cŏllide; ūnit, ūnite, bûrn, cŭt, focŭs; no͞on, fŏŏt; mound; coin;

pleat (plēt), *n.* a fold, as of cloth doubled over upon itself:—*v.t.* to fold in pleats. Also spelled **plait**.

ple-be-ian (plē-bē′yăn; plē-bē′ăn), *adj.* **1,** originally, pertaining to the plebs, or common people, of ancient Rome; **2,** hence, vulgar or common; as, *plebeian* tastes:—*n.* **1,** one of the common people of ancient Rome: opposite of *patrician;* **2,** any person of common breeding.

pleb-i-scite (plĕb′ĭ-sīt; plĕb′ĭ-sĭt; plē′bĭ-sīt), *n.* a direct vote of all the people, as to determine a form of government.

pledge (plĕj), *n.* **1,** anything given or considered as a security or guarantee; a pawn; **2,** the state of being given as security; as, goods held in *pledge;* **3,** a drinking of a health as an expression of good will; also, a person so pledged; **4,** an agreement or promise to do or not to do something; **5,** a token or sign of good will; as, a *pledge* of friendship:—*v.t.* [pledged, pledg-ing], **1,** to give as security or guarantee; as, to *pledge* one's honor; to put in pawn; as, he *pledged* his watch; **2,** to bind by a promise; as, to *pledge* oneself to secrecy; **3,** to drink to the health of.

Ple-iad (plē′yăd; plī′ăd), *n.* any one of the Pleiades.

Ple-ia-des (plē′yȧ-dēz; plē′ȧ-dēz; plī′ȧ-dēz), *n.pl.* **1,** in Greek mythology, the seven daughters of Atlas, changed into stars; **2,** a cluster of seven small stars.

ple-na-ry (plē′nȧ-rĭ; plĕn′ȧ-rĭ), *adj.* full; complete; as, *plenary* authority.

plen-i-po-ten-ti-ar-y (plĕn′ĭ-pō-tĕn′shĭ-ĕr′ĭ; plĕn′ĭ-pō-tĕn′shȧ-rĭ), *adj.* having full power; unlimited:—*n.* [*pl.* plenipotentiaries], an ambassador or government agent to a foreign court, given full powers.

plen-i-tude (plĕn′ĭ-tūd), *n.* fulness; abundance; as, a *plenitude* of power.

plen-te-ous (plĕn′tē-ŭs), *adj.* abundant; amply sufficient; plentiful.—*adv.* **plen′-te-ous-ly.**—*n.* **plen′te-ous-ness.**

plen-ti-ful (plĕn′tĭ-fŏŏl), *adj.* **1,** yielding abundance; as, a *plentiful* harvest; **2,** existing in great quantity.—*adv.* **plen′ti-ful-ly.**—*n.* **plen′ti-ful-ness.**

Syn. abundant, ample, bountiful, rich.

plen-ty (plĕn′tĭ), *n.* [*pl.* plenties], abundance; a full supply; more than enough.

pleth-o-ra (plĕth′ō-rȧ), *n.* **1,** overabundance; excess; **2,** specifically, an excess of blood.—*adj.* **ple-thor′ic** (plē-thŏr′ĭk).

pleu-ri-sy (plŏŏr′ĭ-sĭ), *n.* [*pl.* pleurisies], inflammation of the membrane lining the chest and covering the lungs.

plex-us (plĕk′sŭs), *n.* [*pl.* plexuses or plexus], a network, as of veins, nerves, etc.:—**solar plexus**, a network of nerve fibers behind the stomach radiating to the abdominal organs.

pli-a-ble (plī′ȧ-bl), *adj.* **1,** easily bent; flexible; **2,** easily influenced; docile.—*adv.* **pli′a-bly.**—*n.* **pli′a-bil′i-ty.**

pli-ant (plī′ănt), *adj.* **1,** easily bent; pliable; as, a *pliant* twig; **2,** easily influenced.—*adv.* **pli′ant-ly.**—*n.* **pli′an-cy.**

pli-ers (plī′ẽrz), *n.pl.* used as *sing.* small pincers for bending wire, handling small objects, etc.

PLIERS

¹**plight** (plīt), *n.* a state or condition, usually unfavorable or dangerous; predicament; as, a sorry *plight.*

²**plight** (plīt), *n.* a pledge or solemn promise:—*v.t.* **1,** to pledge, as one's faith; **2,** to betroth.

plinth (plĭnth), *n.* the lowest, rectangular part of the base of a column or pedestal.

plod (plŏd), *v.i.* [plod-ded, plod-ding], **1,** to walk slowly and heavily; trudge; **2,** to drudge or toil steadily and with perseverance:—*v.t.* to walk over heavily and slowly.—*n.* **plod′der.**

plot (plŏt), *n.* **1,** a small area of ground; **2,** a plan of a piece of land, an estate, or the like; a diagram; chart; map; **3,** a scheme or plan; especially, a secret conspiracy; **4,** the plan of a play, novel, etc.:—*v.t.* [plot-ted, plot-ting], **1,** to lay plans for; scheme; as, to *plot* a crime; **2,** to make a plan or map of; **3,** to locate or show on a map or chart:—*v.i.* to scheme; as, to *plot* against an enemy.—*n.* **plot′ter.**

Syn., v. conspire, plan, contrive.

plough (plou), *n.* a farm implement; the plow. See **plow**.

plov-er (plŭv′ẽr; plō′vẽr), *n.* a shore bird with a short bill, long, pointed wings, and short tail.

plow or **plough** (plou), *n.* **1,** a farming implement for cutting and turning up the soil in preparation for planting; **2,** any implement that works in a similar way by cutting, shoving, furrowing, etc.; as, a snowplow:—*v.t.* to turn up with such an implement; till; as, to *plow* a field:—*v.i.* **1,** to break or turn up soil

PLOVER (⅛)

PLOW. P, Plowshare.

with, or as with, a plow; **2,** to move onward by cutting or pushing a way; as, the ship *plowed* on; we *plowed* through the mud.

plow-boy or **plough-boy** (plou′boi′), *n.* **1,** a boy who guides the plow, or leads the team in plowing; **2,** a country boy.

plow-man (plou′măn), *n.* [*pl.* plowmen (-měn)], one who operates a plow; hence, a farmer. Also, **plough′man.**

plow-share or **plough-share** (plou′-shâr′), *n.* the strong, pointed blade of the plow, which cuts the soil.

pluck (plŭk), *v.t.* **1,** to pull off, out, or up; as, to *pluck* weeds; **2,** to pick or gather; harvest; as, to *pluck* grapes; **3,** to pull or twitch; as, to *pluck* the strings of a banjo; **4,** to strip completely of feathers; as, to *pluck* a goose:—**pluck up,** to summon; as, *pluck up* your courage:—*v.i.* to give a sudden pull; tug:—*n.* **1,** spirit; courage; as, a man of *pluck;* **2,** a pull; snatch; tug.
Syn., n. gameness, bravery, valor.

pluck-y (plŭk′ĭ), *adj.* [pluck-i-er, pluck-i-est], brave; courageous.—*adv.* **pluck′i-ly.**

plug (plŭg), *n.* **1,** a piece of wood, rubber, metal, or the like, used to fill or stop a hole; **2,** a device to make an electrical connection; **3,** a cake of pressed tobacco; **4,** a point in a water system where a hose may be attached; a fire hydrant:—*v.t.* [plugged, plug-ging], to stop or make tight with a piece of wood, cork, etc.; as, to *plug* a leak:—*v.i. Colloquial,* to work hard; plod:—**plug in,** to make an electrical connection by inserting a plug in a socket.

PLUGS, def. 2

plum (plŭm), *n.* **1,** a tree somewhat like the peach and cherry; also, its red, green, purple, or yellow, smooth-skinned fruit; **2,** something like this fruit in sweetness or shape; as, a sugar*plum;* **3,** a raisin when used in cooking; **4,** a dark-purple color; **5,** a choice or best part; a desirable job or appointment.

plum-age (plōō′mĭj), *n.* **1,** a bird's feathers; **2,** bright and ornamental costume.

PLUM
Section of fruit, showing stone.

plumb (plŭm), *n.* **1,** a small weight, fastened to a cord, used by builders to test the accuracy of vertical work: also called *plumb bob;* **2,** a similar weight used to find the depth of water; a plummet; **3,** the perpendicular or vertical:—*adj.* vertical; upright:—*adv.* **1,** vertically; **2,** *Slang,* completely; entirely; as, *plumb* crazy:—*v.t.* **1,** to test with a plumb line;

2, to straighten; make vertical; as, to *plumb* up a wall; **3,** to sound (the depth of water) by a plummet; hence, to get to the bottom of; solve.

plumb-er (plŭm′ẽr), *n.* a workman who supplies, repairs, or installs bathroom fixtures, water and gas pipes, etc.

plumb-ing (plŭm′ĭng), *n.* **1,** the occupation of putting in or repairing the piping and other fittings for the water or gas supply or sewage disposal of a building; **2,** the pipes and fittings so installed.

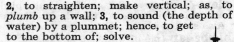

PLUMB
def. 1

plumb line, 1, a cord attached to a plumb; **2,** an exact vertical line.

plume (plōōm), *n.* **1,** a long and beautiful feather or tuft of feathers; **2,** a feather worn as an ornament:—*v.t.* [plumed, pluming], **1,** to clean and adjust; as, a bird *plumes* its feathers; **2,** to adorn with feathers or with fine clothes; **3,** to feel proud of (oneself); as, to *plume* oneself on one's skill.

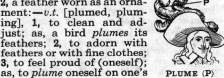

PLUME (P)

plum-met (plŭm′ĕt), *n.* a weight attached to a plumb line.

¹plump (plŭmp), *adj.* well-filled or rounded out; as, a *plump* figure:—*v.i.* to grow round or full:—*v.t.* to cause to fill out or become round.

²plump (plŭmp), *v.i.* to fall or sink down heavily and abruptly; as, to *plump* into a chair:—*v.t.* to cause to fall heavily:—*adj.* blunt; direct; as, a *plump* contradiction:—*adv.* heavily; as, he fell *plump* into the water:—*n. Colloquial,* a sudden fall.

plum pud-ding, a rich boiled pudding made of flour, suet, raisins, currants, and spices.

plu-mule (plōō′mūl), *n.* a small or downy feather; a first feather.

plum-y (plōō′mĭ), *adj.* plumelike; feathery; covered with plumes.

plun-der (plŭn′dẽr), *n.* the act of robbing or taking by force; also, that which is taken; booty:—*v.t.* to rob by open force, especially in war.—*n.* **plun′der-er.**

plunge (plŭnj), *v.t.* [plunged, plung-ing], **1,** to thrust suddenly into a liquid, or into any substance that can be penetrated; **2,** hence, to place suddenly in an unexpected condition; as, to *plunge* a friend into difficulty:—*v.i.* **1,** to dive, fall, or rush, as into water; **2,** to enter suddenly; as, to *plunge* into danger:—*n.* a sudden dive or leap; a headlong rush.

plung-er (plŭn′jẽr), *n.* **1,** one who speculates or gambles extravagantly or rashly;

2, a device, such as the piston of a pump or the dasher of a churn.

plup. abbreviation for *pluperfect.*

plu-per-fect tense (plōo′pûr′fĕkt; plōo′pûr′fĕkt), a tense of a verb which shows an event or action that has been completed before another action, also in the past. In "he *had gone* before I arrived," "had gone" is in the pluperfect tense.

plur. or **pl.** abbreviation for *plural.*

plu-ral (ploŏr′ăl), *adj.* **1,** consisting of more than one; **2,** in grammar, relating to the form of a word that names more than one; as, "girls" is a *plural* noun:—*n.* in grammar, that form of a word that names more than one; as, *churches* is the plural of *church,* *men* of *man,* *oxen* of *ox,* *daughters-in-law* of *daughter-in-law,* *axes* of *axis.*

plu-ral-i-ty (ploŏ-răl′ĭ-tĭ), *n.* [*pl.* pluralities], **1,** the state of consisting of more than one; **2,** the larger number; the majority; **3,** in U.S. politics, the excess of votes cast for one candidate for an office over those for any other candidate.

plus (plŭs), *adj.* **1,** extra; as, *plus* value; **2,** and more; as, 100 *plus;* **3,** indicating addition; as, the *plus* sign; **4,** indicating a positive quantity; as, a *plus* three:—*n.* **1,** an extra quantity; an addition; **2,** the plus sign [+]:—*prep.* with the addition of; and; as, 4 *plus* 2 makes 6.

plush (plŭsh), *n.* thick, soft cloth with a pile or nap longer than that of velvet.

Plu-tarch (plōo′tärk), (46?–120?), a Greek biographer and historian.

Plu-to (plōo′tō), *n.* **1,** in Greek mythology, the god of the underworld; **2,** in astronomy, a remote planet discovered in 1930.

plu-toc-ra-cy (plōo-tŏk′rà-sĭ), *n.* [*pl.* plutocracies], **1,** rule or government by the rich; **2,** the wealthy class.

plu-to-crat (plōo′tō-krăt), *n.* one who has power or influence because of wealth.

plu-to-ni-um (plōo-tō′nĭ-ŭm), *n.* a radioactive element produced from uranium and used in atomic bombs.

¹ply (plī), *v.t.* [plied, ply-ing], **1,** to work at steadily; as, to *ply* a trade; **2,** to use diligently or earnestly; as, to *ply* an oar; **3,** to urge; offer something persistently to; as, to *ply* one with food:—*v.i.* to run regularly on a fixed course between two ports or places, as does a boat.

²ply (plī), *n.* [*pl.* plies], **1,** a thickness or layer, as in a carpet; **2,** a turn or twist, as in yarn or thread.

Plym-outh (plĭm′ŭth), **1,** a town in southeastern Massachusetts, where the Pilgrims landed in 1620 (map **6**); **2,** a city and naval station in southwestern England (map **13**).

ply-wood (plī′wŏŏd′), *n.* two or more thin layers of wood glued together.

Pl-zen (pŭl′zĕny′), the Czechish name for a town in Bohemia. See **Pilsen.**

p.m. or **P.M.** abbreviation for Latin *post meridiem,* meaning *after noon:*—**P.M.** abbreviation for *Postmaster.*

pneu-mat-ic (nū-măt′ĭk), *adj.* **1,** pertaining to air; **2,** inflated with air; as, a *pneumatic* tire; **3,** made to work by air pressure or vacuum; as, a *pneumatic* drill.

pneu-mo-ni-a (nū-mō′nĭ-à), *n.* inflammation of the tissues of the lungs.

Po (pō), a river in northeastern Italy (map **12**).

P.O. abbreviation for *Postal Order, Post Office.*

¹poach (pōch), *v.t.* to cook (eggs) by breaking (them) into boiling water.

²poach (pōch), *v.t.* and *v.i.* to hunt or fish, without permission, on another's property. —*n.* **poach′er.**

Po-ca-hon-tas (pō′kà-hŏn′tàs), (1595?–1617), the daughter of Powhatan, an Indian chief.

pock (pŏk), *n.* **1,** a slight swelling on the skin filled with pus, as in smallpox; **2,** the scar it leaves; a pockmark.

pock-et (pŏk′ĕt), *n.* **1,** a small pouch or bag attached to a garment, for carrying small articles; **2,** a small netted bag in a pool table for catching the balls; **3,** in a mine, a cavity or place where a deposit of ore is found; as, a gold *pocket;* **4,** in airplane travel, a region marked by a sudden variation in the density of the air, which causes the plane to drop suddenly:—*v.t.* **1,** to put into a pocket; **2,** to take unlawfully, as profits:—*adj.* small-sized; as, a *pocket* Bible.

pock - et - book (pŏk′ĕt-bŏŏk′), *n.* a small case or folder for carrying money, papers, etc., in the pocket.

pock - et - knife (pŏk′ĕt-nīf′), *n.* [*pl.* pocketknives (-nīvz′)], a small knife with blades that close into the handle.

pock-mark (pŏk′märk′), *n.* a scar or small hole, as one left by smallpox.

pod (pŏd), *n.* a seed vessel, especially of the pea or bean.

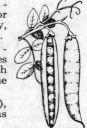

PEA PODS

Poe (pō), Edgar Allan (1809–1849), an American poet and short-story writer.

po-em (pō′ĕm), *n.* a composition in verse; a piece of poetry.

po-e-sy (pō′ĕ-sĭ; pō′ĕ-zĭ), *n.* [*pl.* poesies], the art of writing poetry; also, poetry.

po·et (pō'ĕt), *n.* one who writes verses; especially, one who writes such verse or poetry as is characterized by beauty of thought and language.—*n. fem.* **po'et·ess.**

po·et·ic (pō-ĕt'ĭk) or **po·et·i·cal** (pō-ĕt'-ĭ-kȧl), *adj.* **1,** connected with, or characteristic of, poetry or poets; as, *poetic* language; **2,** written in verse; as, Milton's *poetical* works.—*adv.* **po·et'i·cal·ly.**

po·et·ry (pō'ĕt-rĭ), *n.* **1,** the art of expressing beautiful or elevated thought or feeling in verse; **2,** a poem or poems.

poign·ant (poin'yȧnt; poin'ȧnt), *adj.* **1,** acute; as, *poignant* thirst; **2,** piercing; keenly felt; as, *poignant* regrets; **3,** keen; as, *poignant* wit.—*n.* **poign'an·cy.**

poin·set·ti·a (poin-sĕt'ĭ-ȧ; poin-sĕt'ȧ), *n.* a plant on which tiny greenish flowers are surrounded by large, showy, bright-red petal-like leaves.

point (point), *n.* **1,** the sharp or tapering end of a thing; as, the *point* of a pin; a pencil *point;* a *point* of land; **2,** a particular or separate part; detail; as, the *points* of an argument; a trait; as, *points* of character; also, the most important feature of a speech, story, action, or the like; as, you missed the *point;* **3,** purpose; as, she gained her *point;* **4,** a particular spot or position; as, a certain *point* on a road; also, a definite degree or stage; as, the boiling *point;* a turning *point;* **5,** the unit of scoring in many games; **6,** a dot printed or written; period; decimal point; **7,** one of the 32 equal divisions of the compass or one of the points marking them; **8,** a physical feature in an animal, especially one by which excellence is judged: —*adj.* made with the needle; as, *point* lace:—*v.t.* **1,** to sharpen; as, to *point* a pencil; **2,** to give liveliness or force to; show the purpose of; as, to *point* a moral; **3,** to show the direction of; as, to *point* the way; **4,** to direct or aim; as, to *point* a gun; **5,** to separate with a decimal point; as, to *point* off figures; **6,** to fill the joints of (masonry) with mortar and smooth with a trowel; **7,** to show the presence of (game) by standing in a certain position, as some hunting dogs do; **8,** to indicate; direct attention to; as, to *point* out errors:—*v.i.* **1,** to call attention by extending the finger; **2,** to face; tend (to or toward); be directed; **3,** to indicate the presence of game by standing in a certain position, as do some dogs.

POINSETTIA

point—blank (point'=blăngk'), *adj.* aimed straight at the mark; hence, direct; blunt; as, a *point-blank* question:—*adv.* (point'=blăngk'), directly.

point·ed (poin'tĕd), *adj.* **1,** sharpened; having a sharp end, as a needle; **2,** direct; telling; as, *pointed* repartee; also, having a personal application; as, a *pointed* allusion.

point·er (poin'tẽr), *n.* **1,** a thing that points, or shows position; **2,** a breed of large hunting dog with short hair and long ears, trained to point, that is, to stop and show the place where game is hidden; **3,** *Colloquial,* a timely hint; suggestion; tip.

point·less (point'lĕs), *adj.* **1,** without a point; blunt; as, a *pointless* pencil; **2,** meaningless; as, a *pointless* anecdote.
Syn. flat, insipid, inane, irrelevant.

poise (poiz), *n.* **1,** equilibrium; balance; **2,** the manner of carrying the head and body; **3,** mental balance; self-possession:—*v.t.* and *v.i.* [poised, pois-ing], to balance.

poi·son (poi'zn), *n.* **1,** a substance which causes injury or death to a living body by chemical action when taken in or absorbed; **2,** an influence that damages the character:—*v.t.* **1,** to injure or kill by some deadly substance; **2,** to put a deadly substance into or upon; as, to *poison* food; **3,** to corrupt.

poi·son i·vy, a common vine with compound leaves formed of three leaflets, the mere touch of which brings out, on many persons, a painful, itching rash.

POISON IVY

poi·son·ous (poi'-zn-ŭs), *adj.* **1,** likely to injure or kill because of some deadly quality or substance; as, a *poisonous* snake; a *poisonous* plant; **2,** morally harmful.

¹**poke** (pōk), *n.* the pokeweed, a tall American plant with white flowers and purple berries. See **pokeweed.**

²**poke** (pōk), *v.t.* [poked, pok-ing], **1,** to thrust or push against, especially with a pointed object; prod; as, to *poke* the fire; **2,** to thrust (in or out); as, to *poke* one's head out of the door:—*v.i.* **1,** to thrust or push; as, to *poke* at the fire; **2,** to move lazily; dawdle:—*n.* **1,** a thrust or push; **2,** a projecting brim on the front of a woman's bonnet; **3,** a

POKE BONNET

bonnet with a projecting rim: also called *poke bonnet.*

¹pok·er (pō′kĕr), *n.* a rod of metal used for stirring fires.

²pok·er (pō′kĕr), *n.* a card game in which two or more

POKER

players bet on the value of their hands, the winner taking the pool.

poke·weed (pōk′wēd′) or **poke** (pōk), *n.* a common American plant with white flowers, purple berries, and poisonous root.

pok·y or **poke·y** (pō′kĭ), *adj.* [pok-i-er, pok-i-est], **1,** slow; dull; **2,** small; shabby.

Po·land (pō′lănd), a republic (cap. Warsaw) in north-central Europe (map **12**).

po·lar (pō′lẽr), *adj.* **1,** pertaining to, or situated near, either pole of the earth; **2,** pertaining to either pole of a magnet.

polar bear, the large, white bear of the arctic regions.

Po·lar Re·gions, the territory around the North Pole and the South Pole.

¹pole (pōl), *n.* **1,** either of the two ends of the axis of a sphere; especially, either of the two ends of the earth's axis, called the *North Pole* and the *South Pole;* **2,** either of the two terminals or ends of a magnet, electric battery, or the like.

²pole (pōl), *n.* **1,** a long piece of wood or metal; as, a fishing *pole;* also, an upright timber, such as a mast; as, a telegraph *pole;* **2,** a rod, or linear measure equal to 16½ feet, or 5¹₂ yards:—*v.t.* [poled, poling], to push with a pole; as, to *pole* a boat.

Pole (pōl), *n.* a person who was born in Poland or who is a citizen of Poland.

pole·cat (pōl′kăt′), *n.* **1,** a small, flesh-eating European animal of the weasel family, which throws out a strong, offensive odor, and is valued for its dark-brown fur; **2,** in the U.S., a skunk.

POLECAT (¹⁄₁₅), def. 1

po·lem·ic (pō-lĕm′ĭk), *adj.* having to do with controversy; as, *polemic* writings:—*n.* an argument or controversy; a paper written to uphold one side of a controversy.—*adj.* po·lem′i·cal.

pole·star (pōl′stär′), *n.* **1,** the North Star, or Polaris, a guide to navigators and explorers; **2,** hence, a guiding light; guide.

pole vault, in sports, a leap over a high bar with the aid of a pole.

po·lice (pō-lēs′), *n.* **1,** that part of a government which enforces the laws, investigates crimes, makes arrests, and keeps order; **2,** the men in this department:—*v.t.* [policed, polic-ing], **1,** to watch,

protect, and keep in order by means of policemen; **2,** in the U.S. Army, to clean up (quarters or a camp):—*adj.* connected with the police; as, *police* protection.

po·lice·man (pō-lēs′măn), *n.* [*pl.* policemen (-mĕn)], a member of a police force.

¹pol·i·cy (pŏl′ĭ-sĭ), *n.* [*pl.* policies], **1,** wise management of public affairs; **2,** a course of conduct; especially, the conduct of a government, business corporation, or the like; as, an immigration *policy.*

²pol·i·cy (pŏl′ĭ-sĭ), *n.* [*pl.* policies], a document containing a contract of insurance between an insurance company and the person or persons insured.

pol·i·o·my·e·li·tis (pŏl′ĭ-ō-mī′ĕ-lī′tĭs), *n.* an inflammation and wasting of the gray matter of the spinal cord: **acute anterior poliomyelitis,** an infectious form which especially attacks children, causing a paralysis, sometimes permanent, of various muscles of the arms and legs: also called *infantile paralysis,* or *polio.*

Pol·ish (pō′lĭsh), *adj.* pertaining to Poland, its language, or its people:—*n.* the language of the Poles.

pol·ish (pŏl′ĭsh), *v.t.* **1,** to make smooth or glossy by rubbing; as, to *polish* brass; **2,** to make polite or cultured:—*v.i.* to become smooth or glossy:—*n.* **1,** the act of polishing; **2,** a smooth, glossy surface; **3,** a mixture for making a surface smooth and glossy; as, shoe *polish;* **4,** elegance of manners.—*n.* pol′ish·er.

Syn., v. shine, rub, burnish, furbish.

po·lite (pō-līt′), *adj.* [polit-er, polit-est], **1,** well-bred; refined; as, *polite* society; **2,** courteous; as, a *polite* child.—*adv.* po·lite′ly.—*n.* po·lite′ness.

Syn. courteous, genteel, civil.

pol·i·tic (pŏl′ĭ-tĭk), *adj.* **1,** prudent; shrewd; as, a *politic* adviser; **2,** useful; advisable; as, a *politic* decision:—**body politic,** a political body; the state.

Syn. discreet, diplomatic, cautious.

po·lit·i·cal (pō-lĭt′ĭ-kăl), *adj.* associated with the science of government or the management of public affairs.

political economy, the science which studies the production, distribution, and use of wealth; economics; **political science,** the science which studies the organization and management of government.

pol·i·ti·cian (pŏl′ĭ-tĭsh′ăn), *n.* a person who occupies himself with politics, especially one who works for a political party.

pol·i·tics (pŏl′ĭ-tĭks), *n.pl.* used as *sing.* **1,** the science or art of government; political science; **2,** one's political opinions; the party to which one belongs.

pol·i·ty (pŏl′ĭ-tĭ), *n.* [*pl.* polities], **1,** the

organization of the government of a state, church, etc.; **2,** any community living under an organized system of government.

Polk (pōk), James Knox (1795–1849), the 11th president of the U.S.

pol·ka (pōl′kȧ), *n.* **1,** a lively dance of Bohemian origin, performed by two persons; **2,** music suitable for such a dance.

poll (pōl), *n.* **1,** the head, especially the part of it on which hair grows; **2,** a count of persons, or the resulting number; hence, a list of persons, as of those entitled to vote at an election; **3,** an election; **4,** the number of votes recorded at an election; **5,** (usually *polls*), the place where votes are cast; **6,** a tax on each person: also called *poll tax:*—*v.t.* **1,** to lop, clip, or shear; as, to *poll* trees or sheep; also, to cut the horns of (cattle); **2,** to enroll, as for voting; **3,** to examine or record the votes of; as, to *poll* a jury; **4,** to receive votes from; as, he *polled* a large majority; **5,** to cast or drop in a ballot box; as, to *poll* one's vote.

pol·len (pŏl′ĕn), *n.* the fine powder produced by the anthers of a flower, which, when carried to the pistil, usually of another flower, fertilizes the seeds.

pol·li·nate (pŏl′ĭ-nāt), *v.t.* [pollinat-ed, pollinat-ing], to carry and drop pollen upon the pistil of (a flower) for fertilization, as bees do.—*n.* **pol′li·na′tion.**

pol·li·wog (pŏl′ĭ-wŏg), *n.* a tadpole.

poll tax, a tax on each person, or head: also called *poll.*

pol·lute (pŏ-lūt′), *v.t.* [pollut-ed, polluting], **1,** to make unclean; as, to *pollute* water with filth; **2,** to destroy the purity of; corrupt.

pol·lu·tion (pŏ-lū′shŭn), *n.* **1,** the act of making unclean; **2,** uncleanness; impurity.

Pol·lux (pŏl′ŭks), *n.* in Greek mythology, the twin brother of Castor.

Po·lo (pō′lō), Marco (1254–1323), a Venetian who traveled to the Far East, and on his return wrote of his adventures.

po·lo (pō′lō), *n.* a game similar to field hockey, in which the players are mounted on ponies and equipped with long-handled mallets:—**water polo,** a ball game played in the water by swimmers.

POLO

po·lo·naise (pō′lō-nāz′; pŏl′ō-nāz′), *n.* **1,** a garment worn in the 18th century, consisting of a bodice and skirt open from the waist down and looped back to show an elaborate petticoat; **2,** a stately Polish dance; also, the music for it.

pol·troon (pŏl-trōōn′), *n.* a coward.

pol·y- (pŏl′ĭ-), a prefix meaning many; as, *poly*gamy, *poly*gon.

po·lyg·a·my (pō-lĭg′ȧ-mĭ), *n.* the practice or state of having more than one wife or more than one husband at the same time. —*adj.* **po·lyg′a·mous.**

pol·y·glot (pŏl′ĭ-glŏt), *adj.* containing, or knowing, many languages:—*n.* **1,** a book, often the Bible, with the same text in several languages; **2,** one who can use or understand several languages.

pol·y·gon (pŏl′ĭ-gŏn; pŏl′ĭ-gŭn), *n.* a plane figure with five or more sides and angles.—*adj.* **po·lyg′-o·nal**(pō-lĭg′ō-nȧl).

POLYGONS

Pol·y·ne·si·a (pŏl′ĭ-nē′shĭ-ȧ; pŏl′ĭ-nē′shȧ), a group of islands, part of Oceanica, in the Pacific Ocean.—*adj.* and *n.* **Pol′y·ne′sian.**

pol·yp (pŏl′ĭp), *n.* a small salt-water animal, as the coral, with a tubelike body, one end of which forms a mouth surrounded by tentacles, the other end being attached to shells, rocks, etc. (See illustration under *coral.*)

pol·y·syl·la·ble (pŏl′ĭ-sĭl′ȧ-bl), *n.* a word of three or more syllables.—*adj.* **pol′y·syl·lab′ic.**

pol·y·tech·nic (pŏl′ĭ-tĕk′nĭk), *adj.* pertaining to many arts and sciences, especially in their practical application.

pol·y·the·ism (pŏl′ĭ-thē-ĭzm), *n.* belief in the existence of more than one god.

po·made (pō-mād′; pō-mäd′), *n.* a perfumed ointment for the hair. Also, **po·ma′tum** (pō-mā′tŭm; pō-mä′tŭm).

pome·gran·ate (pŏm′grăn′ĭt; pŭm′grăn′ĭt; pŏm-grăn′ĭt; pŭm-grăn′ĭt), *n.* **1,** a tropical Asiatic tree yielding a fruit with a thick rind and a very seedy, crimson pulp, which has a pleasant, acid taste; **2,** the fruit of this tree.

POMEGRANATE

pom·mel (pŭm′ĕl), *n.* **1,** the knob on a sword hilt; **2,** the ridge on the front of a saddle:—*v.t.* [pommeled, pommel-ing], to beat, especially with the fists. Also spelled **pum′mel.**

pomp (pŏmp), *n.* display; magnificence. *Syn.* ceremony, ostentation, pageantry.

pom·pa·dour (pŏm′pȧ-dôr; pŏm′pȧ-dōōr), *n.* a style of wearing the hair

āte, āorta, râre, căt, ȧsk, fär, ăllow, sofȧ; ēve, ēvent, ĕll, writẽr, novĕl; bīte, pĭn; nō, ōbey, ôr, dŏg, tŏp, cŏllide; ūnit, ūnite, bûrn, cŭt, focŭs; nōōn, fŏŏt; mound; coin;

brushed back from the forehead without a part, and often over a roll.

Pom-pe-ii (pŏm-pā′yē; pŏm-pē′ī), an ancient city near Naples in Italy, buried by the eruption of Vesuvius in A.D. 79 (map 1).—*adj.* and *n.* **Pom-pe′ian.**

Pom-pey (pŏm′pĭ), (106–48 B.C.), sometimes called *the Great*, a Roman general.

pom-pon (pŏm′pŏn), *n.* **1**, an ornamental ball, or puff, of feathers, ribbon, silk, or the like, especially for women's wear.

pom-pous (pŏm′pŭs), *adj.* self-important; pretentious; as, a *pompous* orator.
Syn. showy, ostentatious.

Pon-ce de Le-ón (pŏn′thä dā lā-ōn′; pŏns dē lē′ŭn), Juan (1460?–1521), a Spanish explorer who discovered Florida, while seeking the Fountain of Youth.

pon-cho (pŏn′chō), *n.* [*pl.* ponchos], **1**, in Spanish America, a loose cloak consisting of a blanket with a hole in the middle for the head; **2**, a cloak made on the same plan, used chiefly as a raincoat.

pond (pŏnd), *n.* a small body of still water: —**pond lily,** a water lily.

pon-der (pŏn′dĕr), *v.t.* to consider carefully; think about:—*v.i.* to reflect.
Syn. study, meditate, muse, deliberate.

pon-der-ous (pŏn′dĕr-ŭs), *adj.* **1**, very heavy; **2**, labored; dull; as, a *ponderous* style of writing.

pone (pōn), *n.* bread made of corn meal, with or without milk or eggs: also called *corn pone.*

pon-gee (pŏn-jē′; pŭn-jē′), *n.* a soft, thin, unbleached silk from China; also, any similar dyed silk fabric.

pon-iard (pŏn′yĕrd), *n.* a dagger.
PONIARD

pon-tiff (pŏn′tĭf), *n.* a bishop; especially, the Pope.

pon-tif-i-cal (pŏn-tĭf′ĭ-kăl), *adj.* pertaining to a bishop, especially the Pope:— **pontificals,** *n.pl.* the official robes worn by a bishop.

pon-tif-i-cate (pŏn-tĭf′ĭ-kāt), *n.* the dignity, office, or term of office, of a bishop, especially the Pope.

Pon-tius Pi-late (pŏn′shŭs pī′lăt; pŏn′tĭ-ŭs), in the Bible, the Roman governor of Judea under whose authority Christ was crucified.

pon-toon (pŏn-tōōn′), *n.* **1**, a small, low, flat-bottomed boat; **2**, a flatboat, a raft, a hollow metal cylinder, or the like, used to support a floating bridge, called a *pontoon bridge* (see illustration under *bridge*); **3**, a boatlike attachment on the bottom of an airplane, to enable it to land on water (see illustration under *aviation*).

Pon-tus (pŏn′tŭs), an ancient country in Asia Minor, south of the eastern part of the Black Sea (map 1).

po-ny (pō′nĭ), *n.* [*pl.* ponies], **1**, a horse of any one of certain small breeds; as, a Shetland *pony;* **2**, in the U.S., a literal translation into English of some foreign text, used by students in preparing lessons; a trot.

poo-dle (pōō′dl), *n.* one of a breed of intelligent, black or white, curly-haired dogs.

pooh (pōō; pŏŏ), *interj.* an exclamation of scorn or contempt; pshaw! nonsense!

pooh–pooh (pōō′-pōō′), *v.t.* to laugh at; speak of with contempt.

¹**pool** (pōōl), *n.* **1**, a small body of still water; a pond; **2**, also, a small body of any standing liquid.

²**pool** (pōōl), *n.* **1**, a game played on a special table, with balls which are shot with a cue into the pockets at the edge of the table; **2**, in betting games, the total amount of the players' bets; the money at stake; **3**, a combination of persons, rival business corporations, or the like, united for some special purpose, intended to result in profit to all involved; also, the resources combined in furtherance of this end:—*v.t.* to put into a common fund for a joint undertaking, or in order to share the profits.

poop (pōōp), *n.* the raised deck in the stern of a vessel; also, the stern itself.

poor (pŏŏr), *adj.* **1**, having little or no means; lacking riches; **2**, lacking in good qualities such as strength, beauty, or dignity; **3**, inferior in skill or execution; as, a *poor* piece of work; **4**, wretched; feeble; also, spiritless; **5**, of no great value; as, in my *poor* opinion; **6**, not fertile; as, *poor* soil; scanty; as, a *poor* harvest.—*adv.* **poor′ly.**

POOP DECK

poor-house (pŏŏr′hous′), *n.* a place where paupers live at public expense; an almshouse.

pop (pŏp), *n.* **1**, a short, sharp, quick sound; **2**, a shot from a small firearm; **3**, a bubbling nonintoxicating drink; as, soda *pop:*—*v.t.* [popped, pop-ping], **1**, to cause to burst open by heat; as, to *pop* corn; **2**, to fire (a gun); **3**, to push or thrust suddenly; as, she *popped* her head through the door:—*v.i.* **1**, to make a short, sharp, quick sound; **2**, to move quickly; dart; as, to *pop* in or out; **3**, come suddenly into view; to burst open with a sound:—*adv.* suddenly.

pop-corn (pŏp′kôrn′), *n.* **1**, a kind of Indian corn with small, hard grains which, when exposed to heat, burst open with a sharp noise, or pop, and become white and puffy; **2,** the white, puffed kernels.

Pope (pōp), *n.* the bishop of Rome and head of the Roman Catholic Church:— **pope,** a church dignitary with great power.

pop-gun (pŏp′gŭn′), *n.* a toy gun that goes off with a pop.

pop-in-jay (pŏp′ĭn-jā), *n.* **1,** formerly, a parrot; **2,** now, a vain, conceited fellow who chatters like a parrot.

pop-ish (pōp′ĭsh), *adj.* pertaining to the Roman Catholic Church: a scornful term.

pop-lar (pŏp′lẽr), *n.* a fast-growing, slender tree with shiny, heart-shaped leaves, rough bark, and soft wood; also, the wood.

pop-lin (pŏp′lĭn), *n.* a finely ribbed fabric, usually of silk or silk and worsted. It is used for dresses, curtains, etc.

Po-po-ca-te-petl (pō-pō′kä-tā′pĕtl), a volcano in Mexico, southeast of Mexico City (map **10**).

pop-o-ver (pŏp′ō′vẽr), *n.* a hot bread made of a batter of eggs, milk, and flour, thoroughly beaten. When baked it becomes a hollow shell.

pop-py (pŏp′ĭ), *n.* [*pl.* poppies], any of a number of plants with showy red, yellow, or white flowers; also, the flower of a poppy plant.

pop-u-lace (pŏp′ū-lĭs; pŏp′ū-lås), *n.* the common people; the masses.

pop-u-lar (pŏp′ū-lẽr), *adj.* **1,** having to do with the common people; as, *popular* taste; a *popular* form of government; **2,** suitable for the majority; as, *popular* music; **3,** held in favor by many people; as, a *popular* writer; **4,** within the means of the average purchaser; as, *popular* prices.—*adv.* **pop′u-lar-ly.**

POPPY
Flower, leaves, and fruit.

pop-u-lar-i-ty (pŏp′ū-lăr′ĭ-tĭ), *n.* the state of being liked and admired by many people.

pop-u-lar-ize (pŏp′ū-lẽr-īz), *v.t.* [popularized, populariz-ing], to make pleasing or familiar to, or adapt to the use of, the majority.

pop-u-late (pŏp′ū-lāt), *v.t.* [populat-ed, populat-ing], **1,** to furnish with inhabitants; as, to *populate* a country; **2,** to inhabit.

pop-u-la-tion (pŏp′ū-lā′shŭn), *n.* **1,** the total number of people of a country, state, town, or the like; **2,** the people themselves; also, any one group of the people; as, the adult *population;* **3,** the process of furnishing with inhabitants.

pop-u-lous (pŏp′ū-lŭs), *adj.* containing many inhabitants.—*n.* **pop′u-lous-ness.**

por-ce-lain (pôr′sĕ-lĭn; pôrs′lĭn), *n.* **1,** a fine, white, glazed earthenware, which is unusually hard, and so thin that light can be seen through it; **2,** dishes or ornaments of such ware:—*adj.* made of porcelain.

porch (pôrch), *n.* **1,** a covered approach to a doorway, usually extending from the main wall of the building, with a roof of its own; **2,** a veranda; piazza.

por-cu-pine (pôr′kū-pīn), *n.* an animal akin to the rat and beaver, with spines or sharp quills in its hairy coat which protect it from its enemies.

PORCUPINE (₂₅)

¹**pore** (pôr), *n.* a tiny hole or opening, especially one of many in the skin through which perspiration is discharged.

²**pore** (pôr), *v.i.* [pored, por-ing], to study with close attention; ponder; as, to *pore* over lessons.

por-gy (pôr′gĭ), *n.* [*pl.* porgies], a saltwater food fish found in the Mediterranean Sea and the Atlantic Ocean.

pork (pôrk), *n.* the flesh of pigs or hogs, used for food.

pork-er (pôr′kẽr), *n.* a pig or hog fattened for food.

por-ous (pôr′ŭs), *adj.* full of tiny holes through which a fluid may pass or be absorbed.—*n.* **po-ros′i-ty** (pō-rŏs′ĭ-tĭ).

por-phy-ry (pôr′fĭ-rĭ), *n.* [*pl.* porphyries], a rock, found in Egypt, consisting of a dark crimson base in which crystals of feldspar and quartz are embedded. It is a hard rock, and takes a high polish.

por-poise (pôr′pŭs), *n.* **1,** a sea animal, five to eight feet long, related to the whales, and, like the whale, a mammal; **2,** a dolphin.

PORPOISE (₆₆)

por-ridge (pŏr′ĭj), *n.* a food made by boiling a cereal or a vegetable slowly in water or milk until it thickens; as, oatmeal *porridge.*

por-rin-ger (pŏr′ĭn-jẽr), *n.* a small dish or bowl, from which broth, porridge, or the like, may be eaten.

¹**port** (pôrt), *n.* **1,** a place where vessels arrive and depart; harbor; as, the *port* of New York; **2,** a harbor town.

²**port** (pôrt), *n.* **1,** a round opening or window in the side of a ship, through which air and light may enter, or out of which cannon may be discharged; a loophole in a wall, fort, or the like: also called *porthole;* **2,** an outlet, as for steam or water.

³**port** (pôrt), *n.* the way one carries oneself.

⁴**port** (pôrt), *n.* the left side of a ship as one faces the bow: formerly called *larboard:* opposite of *starboard:—adj.* on the left side of a ship; as, a *port* cabin:—*v.t.* to turn to the port, or left, side of a ship; as, to *port* the helm.

⁵**port** (pôrt), *n.* a strong, sweet wine, usually dark red in color.

port-a-ble (pôr′tȧ-bl), *adj.* capable of being easily carried; as, a *portable* typewriter.

por-tage (pôr′tĭj), *n.* **1,** the carrying of boats, goods, etc., overland from one navigable lake or river to another; also, the overland route taken; **2,** any cargo to be carried, or the cost of such carriage.

por-tal (pôr′tăl), *n.* a gateway; entrance.

Port Ar-thur, a fortified port in Manchuria, leased by China to Russia in 1898, held by Japan 1905–1945, now controlled by China (map **15**).

port-cul-lis (pôrt-kŭl′ĭs), *n.* a strong grating hung over the gateway of a fortress or castle, capable of being let down to close the gate and aid in defense.

porte—co-chere (pôrt′-kŏ-shâr′), *n.* **1,** a large gateway through which a carriage may drive into a courtyard; **2,** an extension of a porch roof over a drive to permit carriages to stop under cover.

PORTCULLIS

por-tend (pôr-tĕnd′), *v.t.* to give advance warning of (something that is to happen); as, clouds *portend* a storm.

por-tent (pôr′tĕnt; pôr′tĕnt), *n.* an omen or sign, especially of calamity to come.

por-ten-tous (pôr-tĕn′tŭs), *adj.* **1,** foreshadowing evil; threatening; as, a *portentous* dream; **2,** remarkable; extraordinary.

Por-ter (pôr′tĕr), **1,** David Dixon (1813–1891), an American admiral; **2,** William Sydney (1862–1910), an American short-story writer, better known by his pen name, *O. Henry.*

¹**por-ter** (pôr′tĕr), *n.* a doorkeeper.

²**por-ter** (pôr′tĕr), *n.* **1,** one who carries baggage, as at railway stations and hotels; **2,** an attendant in a sleeping car or parlor car; **3,** a dark-brown, bitter beer.

por-ter-house steak (pôr′tĕr-hous′), a choice cut of beef, consisting chiefly of tenderloin. (See illustration under *beef.*)

port-fo-li-o (pôrt-fō′lĭ-ō; pôrt-fōl′yō), *n.* [*pl.* portfolios], **1,** a case for carrying loose papers, drawings, etc.; a brief case; **2,** the office of a minister of the government; as, the *portfolio* of war.

port-hole (pôrt′hōl′), *n.* **1,** a round opening, or window, in the side of a ship; **2,** an opening in the wall of a fort, blockhouse, or the like, through which to shoot.

Por-ti-a (pôr′shȧ; pôr′shĭ-ȧ), *n.* **1,** the heroine of Shakespeare's play, "The Merchant of Venice"; **2,** in Shakespeare's "Julius Caesar," the wife of Brutus.

por-ti-co (pôr′tĭ-kō), *n.* [*pl.* porticoes or porticos], a colonnade or walk covered by a roof supported on columns; especially, a porch with columns at the front of a building.

por-tiere (pôr′tyâr′; pôr′tĭ-âr′), *n.* a curtain or drapery hanging at a doorway.

por-tion (pôr′shŭn), *n.* **1,** a piece or part of anything; as, a *portion* of pie; **2,** hence, a share, or a part given; a part of an estate left to an heir; also, a dowry:—*v.t.* **1,** to divide into shares; **2,** to give a share to.

Syn., n. allotment, lot, parcel.

PORTICO

Port-land (pôrt′lănd), **1,** a city in Maine, on the Atlantic coast (map **6**); **2,** a large city in northwestern Oregon (map **9**).

port-ly (pôrt′lĭ), *adj.* [port-li-er, port-li-est], **1,** corpulent; stout; as, a *portly* chef; **2,** stately and dignified; as, a man of *portly* mien.—*n.* port′li-ness.

port-man-teau (pôrt-măn′tō), *n.* a traveling bag; suitcase.

Por-to (pōr′tŏō), the Portuguese name for a city in Portugal (map **12**). See **Oporto.**

Port of Spain (pôrt′ ŏv spān′), a town, capital of the island of Trinidad, British West Indies (map **11**).

Por-to Ri-co (pôr′tō rē′kō), the former name of an island in the West Indies. See **Puerto Rico.**

por-trait (pôr′trāt; pôr′trĭt), *n.* a picture of a person; a likeness.

por-trai-ture (pôr′trȧ-tūr), *n.* **1,** the art

or practice of making likenesses of people; **2**, a portrait, or likeness.

por·tray (pôr-trā'), *v.t.* **1**, to make a likeness of; **2**, to describe; **3**, to play the part of; as, to *portray* Hamlet.

por·tray·al· (pôr-trā'ăl), *n.* **1**, the making of a picture of anything by drawing or painting it, or by describing it in words; also, the playing of a part on the stage; **2**, a picture; description; representation.

Port Sa·id (sä-ēd'), a seaport city in Egypt, at the northern end of the Suez Canal (map 14).

Ports·mouth (pôrts'mŭth), a seaport city in Hampshire, southern England, the chief naval base of England (map 13).

Por·tu·gal (pôr'tŭ-găl), a republic (cap. Lisbon) on the western coast of the Spanish peninsula, including the Azores and Madeira (map 12).

Por·tu·guese (pôr'tŭ-gēz; pôr'tŭ-gēs), *adj.* relating to Portugal, its people, or its language:—*n.* **1**, the language of Portugal; **2**, [*pl.* Portuguese], a native of Portugal.

Por·tu·guese East Af·ri·ca, a Portuguese colony in Africa. See **Mozambique**.

Por·tu·guese West Af·ri·ca, a Portuguese colony in Africa. See **Angola**.

por·tu·la·ca (pôr'tŭ-lā'kȧ; pôr'tŭ-lăk'ȧ), *n.* a garden plant with leaves like fleshy needles, and flowers of various colors.

¹**pose** (pōz), *v.i.* [posed, pos-ing], **1**, to assume and keep an attitude; as, the model *posed* for an hour; **2**, to pretend to be what one is not; as, he *posed* as an expert:—*v.t.* **1**, to place in a suitable attitude; as, to *pose* a person for a portrait; **2**, to put or set forth; as, he *posed* a question:—*n.* **1**, attitude or position; **2**, a mental attitude assumed for the sake of effect.

²**pose** (pōz), *v.t.* [posed, pos-ing], to perplex.

Po·sei·don (pŏ-sī'dŏn), *n.* in Greek mythology, the god of the sea: called *Neptune* by the Romans.

Po·sen (pō'zĕn), a city in western Poland, now called Poznan. See **Poznan**.

po·sey (pō'zĭ), [*pl.* poseys], **1**, a flower or a bouquet; **2**, a verse. See **posy**.

po·si·tion (pŏ-zĭsh'ŭn), *n.* **1**, the place where a thing is set or placed; situation; as, the *position* of a house; **2**, the manner in which anything is placed or arranged; as, an awkward sleeping *position*; **3**, social standing or rank; **4**, employment; job; **5**, mental attitude toward any subject; as, a conservative *position*; **6**, correct or proper place; as, take your *positions*.

pos·i·tive (pŏz'ĭ-tĭv), *adj.* **1**, clearly stated; as, a *positive* assertion; uttered with authority; as, *positive* instructions; **2**, leaving no doubt; as, proof *positive*; **3**, of real, practical value; as, self-reliance is a *positive* virtue; **4**, confident; sure; as, people were once *positive* that the sun moved round the earth; **5**, in grammar, naming the simplest form of an adjective or adverb; as, "easy" is a *positive* form, "easier" is comparative; **6**, in arithmetic, a quantity larger than zero; a plus quantity; **7**, naming the kind of electricity formed on a glass rod when it is rubbed with silk: opposed to the electricity on the silk, which is called *negative*; **8**, in photography, matching the original in the distribution of light and shade: opposite of *negative*; **9**, *Colloquial*, utter; absolute; as, a *positive* beauty:—*n.* **1**, in grammar, the simplest degree of comparison; also, an adjective or adverb in that degree; **2**, a photographic plate, film, or slide, reproducing the light and shade of the original: opposite of *negative*, in which the light and shade of the original are reversed.—*adv.* **pos'i-tive-ly**.

pos·se (pŏs'ē), *n.* a number of men summoned by a sheriff to assist in carrying out the law.

pos·sess (pŏ-zĕs'), *v.t.* **1**, to own; have; as, to *possess* great wealth; to *possess* great patience; **2**, to control; as, to *possess* one's soul in patience; **3**, to occupy; seize; as, to *possess* a city during war:—**possessed**, *adj.* as if in the power of evil spirits; crazy.

pos·ses·sion (pŏ-zĕsh'ŭn), *n.* **1**, control; occupancy; as, *possession* of a town by an enemy; **2**, the thing owned; as, a small *possession*; **3**, **possessions**, property.

pos·ses·sive (pŏ-zĕs'ĭv), *adj.* **1**, showing ownership, or a desire to own; as, a *possessive* manner; **2**, in grammar, naming the case used to express ownership, origin, or a similar relation, as "Mary's" in the expression "Mary's book":—*n.* the possessive case; also, a word in that case.

pos·ses·sor (pŏ-zĕs'ẽr), *n.* one who owns or holds something.

pos·si·bil·i·ty (pŏs'ĭ-bĭl'ĭ-tĭ), *n.* [*pl.* possibilities], **1** anything that may happen; as, snow is a *possibility* today; **2**, the chance that a thing may happen; as, the *possibility* of failure.

pos·si·ble (pŏs'ĭ-bl), *adj.* **1**, capable of existing or coming into being; capable of happening; as, the *possible* result of an act; **2**, available; worth considering; as, a *possible* candidate.—*adv.* **pos'si-bly**.

pos·sum (pŏs'ŭm), *n. Colloquial*, in the U.S., an opossum.

¹**post** (pōst), *n.* an upright piece of timber, metal, or the like, used especially as a support for something:—*v.t.* **1**, to fasten, as a notice, to a wall; **2**, to make known by

means of notices fastened to a wall; **3,** to place (a person's name) on such a notice; **4,** to put notices upon (a place) forbidding entrance or warning against use; as, to *post* a hunting preserve or an unsafe bridge.

²post (pōst), *n.* **1,** formerly, one of a number of riders, placed at fixed stations along a road, each of whom in turn carried the mail forward to the next station; a postman; also, formerly, one of the stations where relays of horses were kept for such riders; **2,** a system of carrying and delivering letters; the mail:—*v.i.* to travel with speed:—*v.t.* **1,** to send by mail; especially, to drop, as a letter, into a letter box; **2,** in bookkeeping, to transfer (an entry or item) from journal to ledger; **3,** *Colloquial,* to inform fully:—*adv.* speedily.

³post (pōst), *n.* **1,** a place where a person or thing is stationed; **2,** a position of trust; **3,** a trading settlement; **4,** a military station; also, the soldiers occupying it:—*v.t.* to station.

post- (pōst-), a prefix meaning behind; after; as, *post*graduate, *post*pone.

post-age (pōs'tĭj), *n.* the cost of sending letters by mail:—**postage stamp,** a government stamp to be pasted on mail as a sign that postage has been paid.

post-al (pōs'tăl), *adj.* of or pertaining to the post office or mail service; as, *postal* rates:—**postal card, 1,** a card for mailing, with a postage stamp officially printed on it; **2,** a post card.

post card, a private card for mailing, to which a stamp must be attached. Also written **post'card'.**

post chaise (pōst shāz), a carriage with fast horses, in which mail and passengers were formerly carried along regular routes more quickly than by coach.

post-er (pōs'tĕr), *n.* a placard or bill put up in a public place, as on a wall, to advertise or announce something.

pos-te-ri-or (pŏs-tē'rĭ-ēr), *adj.* **1,** later; **2,** rear; hinder:—*n.* often in *pl.,* the rump; buttocks.—*n.* **pos-te'ri-or'i-ty** (pŏs-tē'rĭ-ŏr'ĭ-tĭ).

pos-ter-i-ty (pŏs-tĕr'ĭ-tĭ) *n.* **1,** a person's descendants, considered as a group; **2,** future generations.

pos-tern (pōs'tĕrn; pŏs'tĕrn), *n.* **1,** formerly, a back door or gate; private entrance; **2,** in a fort, an underground passage, closed by a door, leading inward from the trench:—*adj.* behind; private; rear.

post-grad-u-ate (pōst-grăd'ŭ-āt), *adj.* relating to, or engaging in, studies after graduation from a school or college:—*n.* a person pursuing such studies.

post-haste (pōst'hāst'), *adv.* quickly.

post-hu-mous (pŏs'tū-mŭs), *adj.* **1,** born after the death of the father; as, a *posthumous* child; **2,** published after the death of an author; as, a *posthumous* book; **3,** arising or occurring after one's death; as, *posthumous* fame.—*adv.* **post'hu-mous-ly.**

pos-til-ion or **pos-til-lion** (pōs-tĭl'yŭn; pŏs-tĭl'yŭn), *n.* a person who rides the lefthand horse of a carriage team, to guide it.

post-man (pōst'măn), *n.* [*pl.* postmen (-mĕn)], a letter carrier.

post-mark (pōst'märk'), *n.* a mark stamped upon mail to show the place and date of mailing:—*v.t.* to stamp thus.

post-mas-ter (pōst'mȧs'tĕr), *n.* **1,** the superintendent of a post office; **2,** formerly, one who furnished horses for traveling:—**postmaster general,** [*pl.* postmasters general], the chief officer of the post-office department.

post me-ri-di-em (pōst mē-rĭd'ĭ-ĕm), a Latin phrase meaning *after noon.*

post-mis-tress (pōst'mĭs'trĕs), *n.* a woman superintendent of a post office.

post-mor-tem (pōst'-môr'tĕm), *adj.* happening after death; as, the *post-mortem* examination of a body:—*n.* an examination of a body made after death, as to find the cause of death; an autopsy.

post of-fice 1, the department of a government which handles the mail; **2,** any local office of this department.

post-paid (pōst'pād'), *adj.* having the postage paid in advance.

post-pone (pōst-pōn'), *v.t.* [postponed, postpon-ing], to put off to another time.—*n.* **post-pone'ment.**
  Syn. procrastinate, delay, defer.

post-script (pōst'skrĭpt), *n.* a written addition to a book, article, or the like; especially, a paragraph added to a letter after the writer's signature.

pos-tu-late (pŏs'tū-lāt), *v.t.* [postulat-ed, postulat-ing], to assume without proof; as, to tell someone to do a thing *postulates* that it can be done:—*n.* (pŏs'tū-lāt), **1,** a statement which may be taken for granted; **2,** something assumed in order to account for something else.

pos-ture (pŏs'tūr). *n.* the way one holds parts of the body in relation to the whole body; carriage:—*v.t.* [postured, postur-ing], to place in a particular attitude:—*v.i.* to take a certain position, especially an artificial or affected pose.

post-war (pōst'wâr'), *adj.* after any war, as contrasted with *prewar.*

po-sy (pō'zĭ), *n.* [*pl.* posies], **1,** a flower or a bunch of flowers; **2,** a motto or verse sent with a bouquet or inscribed in a ring. Also spelled **po'sey.**

---

go; join; yet; sing; chin; show; thin, *th*en; **hw,** *wh*y; **zh,** azure; **ü,** Ger. f*ü*r or Fr. l*u*ne; **ö,** Ger. sch*ö*n or Fr. f*eu*; **n,** Fr. e*n*fant, no*m*; **kh,** Ger. a*ch* or i*ch.* See pages ix–x.

pot (pŏt), *n.* **1,** a metal or earthenware vessel used for cooking; **2,** the quantity such a vessel will hold; **3,** such a vessel with its contents; **4,** a vessel of earthenware for holding growing plants; **5,** *Slang:* **a,** a sum of money made up as a bet by contributions from a group, to go to one of them; **b,** a large sum of money:—*v.t.* [pot-ted, pot-ting], **1,** to preserve in a pot, as meat; **2,** to transplant into a pot; **3,** to shoot (a bird or animal) for food.

POTS
1, bean pot; 2, coffeepot.

pot-ash (pŏt′ăsh′), *n.* a salt of potassium; especially, impure potassium carbonate, a white salt obtained from wood ashes, and used in making soap and glass.

po-tas-si-um (pō-tăs′ĭ-ŭm), *n.* a soft, very light, bluish-white metal, found only in union with other substances. It is used in making fertilizers, glass, etc.

po-ta-tion (pō-tā′shŭn), *n.* **1,** the act of drinking; **2,** a drink.

po-ta-to (pō-tā′tō), *n.* [*pl.* potatoes], **1,** a plant related to the tomato, grown for its starchy, edible tubers: also called *white potato* and *Irish potato;* **2,** one of these tubers used as food; **3,** the sweet potato:—**potato bug,** a beetle with yellow and black stripes, which destroys the leaves of the potato and related plants.

POTATO BUG (?)

po-ten-cy (pō′těn-sĭ), *n.* [*pl.* potencies], power, physical or mental; authority. Also, **po′tence.**

po-tent (pō′těnt), *adj.* **1,** powerful; mighty; as, a *potent* drug; **2,** having great authority or influence.—*adv.* **po′tent-ly.**

po-ten-tate (pō′těn-tāt), *n.* a ruler who has great power; a monarch.

po-ten-tial (pō-těn′shăl), *adj.* **1,** capable of existing, but not yet in existence; possible, but not actual; as, Alaska has great *potential* wealth; **2,** in grammar, expressing power or possibility, as the word "can" in the sentence "I can come":—*n.* the amount of electrical force in an electrical conductor, usually measured in volts. —*adv.* **po-ten′tial-ly.**

po-ten-ti-al-i-ty (pō-těn′shĭ-ăl′ĭ-tĭ), *n.* [*pl.* potentialities], **1,** possibility of development; as, the *potentialities* of a new business; **2,** power; ability.

poth-er (pŏth′ẽr), *n.* fuss; bustle:—*v.i.* to make a stir:—*v.t.* to worry; bother.

pot-herb (pŏt′ûrb′; pŏt′hûrb′), *n.* **1,** any plant used as greens, as spinach; **2,** any herb, as parsley, sage, thyme, etc., used to flavor or season soups and stews.

pot-hook (pŏt′hŏŏk′), *n.* **1,** an S-shaped iron hook for hanging a pot over an open fire; **2** a curved, hooked iron rod for lifting hot pots and stove lids; **3,** a hooked stroke used in teaching penmanship.

po-tion (pō′shŭn), *n.* a drink, especially of liquid medicine.

pot-luck (pŏt′lŭk′), *n.* whatever may happen to be ready for a meal.

Po-to-mac (pô-tō′măk), a river flowing from West Virginia, between Virginia and Maryland, to Chesapeake Bay (map 8).

POT-HOOK

pot-pie (pŏt′pī′), *n.* **1,** a meat pie; **2,** a meat stew with dumplings.

pot-pour-ri (pō′pŏŏ′rē′; pŏt′pŏŏr′ĭ), *n.* **1,** a mixture of dried flower petals, spices, and the like, kept in an ornamental jar, and occasionally opened to scent a room; **2,** such a jar; **3,** a musical or literary medley.

pot shot, 1, an easy shot at an animal or bird to kill it for food, and not for sport; **2,** a shot fired at an animal or person within easy range.

pot-tage (pŏt′ĭj), *n.* a stew or thick soup of meat and vegetables, or of both.

¹**pot-ter** (pŏt′ẽr), *n.* a maker of vessels of earthenware, stoneware, and the like.

²**pot-ter** (pŏt′ẽr) or **put-ter** (pŭt′ẽr), *v.i.* to work lazily, or with little purpose; as, to *potter* around at gardening.

potter's field, a plot of ground set aside for the burial of criminals, of unidentified persons, and of persons who have neither friends nor money.

pot-ter-y (pŏt′ẽr-ĭ), *n.* [*pl.* potteries], **1,** pots, dishes, vases, and the like, molded from moistened clay and hardened in ovens or kilns; **2,** a place where such ware is manufactured; **3,** the art of making it.

pouch (pouch), *n.* **1,** a bag or sack of any sort; as, a tobacco *pouch;* **2,** in certain animals, any baglike part, as that in which the kangaroo carries its young:—*v.t.* **1,** to put (something) into a small bag; as, to *pouch* money; **2,** to give a pouchlike form to (part of a dress or the like):—*v.i.* to form a pouchlike cavity.

poul-tice (pōl′tĭs), *n.* a moist mixture of bread, herbs, or the like, usually heated, spread on a cloth, and applied to a sore or inflamed spot:—*v.t.* [poulticed, poultic-ing], to apply such a mixture to (a sore place).

poul-try (pōl′trĭ), *n.* domestic fowls, as chickens, turkeys, and the like.

pounce (pouns), *n.* a sudden swooping

āte, āorta, râre, căt, àsk, fär, ǎllow, sofà; ēve, ēvent, ĕll, wrïtẽr, novĕl; bīte, pĭn; nō, ōbey, ôr, dŏg, tŏp, cŏllide; ūnit, ūnite, bûrn, cŭt, focŭs; nōōn, fŏŏt; mound; coin;

attack:—*v.i.* [pounced, pounc-ing], to spring suddenly or unexpectedly; as, the terrier *pounced* on the rat.

¹**pound** (pound), *n.* **1**, a measure of avoirdupois weight, equal to sixteen ounces; also, a measure of troy weight, equal to twelve ounces; **2**, the standard of money in Great Britain, called the *pound sterling* (see Table, page 943).

²**pound** (pound), *n.* **1**, a place for confining or keeping stray animals; as, a dog *pound;* **2**, a shelter for livestock; **3**, an enclosure for trapping wild animals; **4**, an area or space where fish are caught or kept:—*v.t.* to confine, as in a pound.

³**pound** (pound), *v.t.* **1**, to beat; strike forcibly; **2**, to reduce to powder; **3**, to make solid by blows; tamp, as loose earth; **4**, to walk with heavy steps:—*v.i.* to deal blows; beat heavily or steadily, as waves against the seashore:—*n.* **1**, a blow; **2**, the sound of a blow.

pour (pôr), *v.t.* **1**, to cause to flow in a stream; **2**, to send forth freely; utter freely:—*v.i.* to flow down freely:—*n.* a heavy rain.

pout (pout), *v.i.* to push out the lips, as in sullenness, contempt, or displeasure; look sulky:—*v.t.* to push (the lips) out; pucker:—*n.* **1**, a sullen puckering of the lips; **2**, **pouts**, a fit of sullenness.

pout-er (pou′tĕr), *n.* a kind of pigeon which puffs out its crop.

pov-er-ty (pŏv′ĕr-tĭ), *n.* **1**, the state of being poor; necessity; want; **2**, any lack of excellence in quality; scarcity; as, a *poverty* of good books.
Syn. destitution, need, indigence.

POUTER PIGEON (¼)

pov-er-ty–strick-en (pŏv′ĕr-tĭ=strĭk′ĕn), *adj.* extremely poor; destitute.

pow-der (pou′dĕr), *n.* **1**, any dry substance in fine particles; a fine dust; **2**, an explosive in powder form; as, blasting *powder;* **3**, a fine, dustlike cosmetic for use on the skin; **4**, a medicine in powder form; also, a dose of this; as, a sleeping *powder:*—*v.t.* **1**, to reduce to powder; pulverize; **2**, to dust with powder; to decorate, as with powder; as, a box *powdered* with gilt stars; **3**, to sprinkle for flavoring; as, to *powder* cake with sugar:—*v.i.* **1**, to use powder; as, she *powders* lightly; **2**, to be reduced to powder; as, sugar *powders* easily.

pow-der horn, a container for gunpowder; especially, one made of the horn of an ox. (See illustration next column.)

pow-der-y (pou′dĕr-ĭ), *adj.* **1**, like powder; in the form of powder; **2**, covered or sprinkled with powder.

pow-er (pou′ĕr), *n.* **1**, ability to act or to do something; as, the *power* to fly; the *power* to think; **2**, strength; vigor; as, the *power* of a blow; **3**, rule; influence; as, to have *power* over a group; also, official right to rule; authority; as, the *power* to levy taxes; **4**, a person or thing of great influence; as, he is a *power* in the city; **5**, an influential nation; as, Spain was once a great *power;* **6**, any form of force or energy to do work; as, mechanical or electrical *power;* **7**, the magnifying capacity of a lens; **8**, the result of multiplying a number by itself a given number of times; as, 27 is the third *power* of three, that is $3 \times 3 \times 3 = 27$.
Syn. energy, force.

pow-er-boat (pou′ĕr-bōt′), *n.* a boat propelled by a motor or engine; a motorboat.

pow-er-ful (pou′ĕr-fŏŏl), *adj.* having great power, influence, or strength; as, a *powerful* man, engine, telescope, odor, etc.—*adv.* **pow′er-ful-ly**.
Syn. vigorous, effectual, influential.

pow-er-less (pou′ĕr-lĕs), *adj.* **1**, weak; **2**, unable to bring about an effect; as, *powerless* to help her.—*n.* **pow′er-less-ness**.
Syn. feeble, ineffectual, impotent.

pow-er of at-tor-ney, a legal writing by which a person authorizes another to do business for him.

Pow-ha-tan (pou′há-tăn′), (1550?–1618), an Indian chief of Virginia, father of Pocahontas.

pow-wow (pou′wou′), *n.* **1**, a public feast or dance, especially one intended to secure religious or magical aid in a hunt, war, or the like, as among the North American Indians; **2**, the working of magic, as in the cure of disease; **3**, a worker of magic; medicine man; **4**, *Colloquial*, in the U.S., a meeting; especially, a noisy meeting, often a political one:—*v.i.* (pou′wou′; pou′wou′), to hold such a meeting.

pox (pŏks), *n.* a disease marked by an eruption, or breaking out, on the skin.

Poz-nań (pôz′näny′), a city in western Poland (map 12): formerly called *Posen.*

p.p. abbreviation for *past participle:*—**pp.** abbreviation for *pages:*—**pp** abbreviation for Italian *pianissimo,* a musical term meaning *very softly.*

p.pr. or **ppr.** abbreviation for *present participle.*

pr. abbreviation for *pair.* POWDER HORN

POWDER HORN

prac-ti-ca-ble (prăk′tĭ-ká-bl), *adj.* capable of being done, practiced, or used; as, fire prevention is *practicable;* a *practicable* idea.—*adv.* **prac′ti-ca-bly.**—*n.* **prac′ti-ca-bil′i-ty.**

Syn. usable, feasible.

prac-ti-cal (prăk′tĭ-kăl), *adj.* **1,** relating to, or obtained through, experience or use; as, *practical* wisdom; **2,** capable of being put to use; useful; as, a *practical* suggestion; **3,** inclined to useful action rather than thought; as, a *practical* disposition; **4,** skilled, but without complete training; as, a *practical* nurse.—*n.* **prac′ti-cal′i-ty.**

practical joke, a trick played upon a person to make him appear ridiculous.

prac-ti-cal-ly (prăk′tĭ-kăl-ĭ), *adv.* **1,** really; as, his painting is *practically* worthless; **2,** through actual experience or practice; as, he is *practically* familiar with all types of radio; **3,** virtually; in fact, though not in name; as, he is *practically* the president.

¹**prac-tice** (prăk′tĭs), *v.t.* [practiced, practic-ing], **1,** to do in reality; as, *practice* what you preach; **2,** to do frequently or as a rule; as, to *practice* plain eating; **3,** to work at, as a profession; as, to *practice* law; **4,** to perform in order to learn; as, to *practice* baseball:—*v.i.* **1,** to do something as a habit; **2,** to follow a profession; **3,** to do something often in order to learn. Also spelled **prac′tise.**—*n.* **prac′tic-er.**

²**prac-tice** (prăk′tĭs), *n.* **1,** custom; habit; **2,** the putting of knowledge to actual use; as, the *practice* of good manners; **3,** the exercise of any profession; as, the *practice* of medicine; **4,** regular exercise as a means to learning; as, *practice* in writing.

Syn. usage, manner, routine.

prac-ticed or **prac-tised** (prăk′tĭst), *adj.* skilled; expert; as, he is a *practiced* hand at the game of lawn tennis.

prac-ti-tion-er (prăk-tĭsh′ŭn-ẽr), *n.* a person who is engaged in any profession, especially medicine or law.

prae-tor or **pre-tor** (prē′tŏr), *n.* a Roman magistrate, ranking next below a consul, and acting as judge, general, and administrator.

prae-tor-i-an (prē-tôr′ĭ-ăn), *adj.* **1,** relating to a praetor; **2,** relating to the bodyguard of a Roman emperor:—*n.* **1,** a man with the rank of praetor; **2,** a soldier of a Roman emperor's bodyguard. Also spelled **pre-tor′i-an.**

prag-mat-ic (prăg-măt′ĭk) or **prag-mat-i-cal** (prăg-măt′ĭ-kăl), *adj.* **1,** practical; **2,** relating to everyday matters; commonplace.—*adv.* **prag-mat′i-cal-ly.**

Prague (präg; prāg), a large city, the capital of Czechoslovakia (map 12). Its Czechish name is **Pra′ha** (prä′hä).

prai-rie (prâr′ĭ), *n.* a large, treeless tract of level or rolling grassland, especially in the central U.S.

prai-rie chick-en, a large grouse of the prairies of the Mississippi River Valley.

prairie dog, a small animal resembling a woodchuck: so called because it barks. It lives in large, underground colonies in the western U.S.

PRAIRIE DOG (½)

prai-rie schoon-er, *Colloquial,* in the U.S., a large, canvas-covered wagon, formerly used by emigrants to the West.

prairie wolf, a small wolf of western North America; a coyote.

praise (prāz), *n.* **1,** approval; applause; **2,** glorification of God:—*v.t.* [praised, prais-ing], **1,** to speak well of; approve; **2,** to glorify (God).

PRAIRIE SCHOONER

Syn., v. commend, extol, laud, flatter, applaud, eulogize.

praise-wor-thy (prāz′wûr′thĭ), *adj.* deserving approval.—*n.* **praise′wor′thi-ness.**

prance (prăns), *v.i.* [pranced, pranc-ing], **1,** to move by springing or bounding from the hind legs, as a high-spirited horse; **2,** to ride a prancing horse; **3,** to swagger; strut; **4,** *Colloquial,* to dance; caper:—*v.t.* to cause (an animal) to prance:—*n.* a prancing or swaggering.—*n.* **pranc′er.**

¹**prank** (prăngk), *n.* a mischievous trick.

²**prank** (prăngk), *v.t.* and *v.i.* to dress showily; prink.

prate (prāt), *v.i.* [prat-ed, prat-ing], to talk idly:—*v.t.* to prattle; talk idly.

prat-tle (prăt′l), *v.t.* and *v.i.* [prat-tled, prat-tling], to babble like a child; chatter:—*n.* childish talk.—*n.* **prat′tler.**

prawn (prôn), *n.* an edible shellfish like a shrimp, but larger, and found in either fresh or salt water.

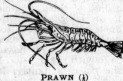

Prax-it-e-les (prăks-ĭt′ĕ-lēz), (about 340 B.C.), a famous Greek sculptor.

PRAWN (⅛)

pray (prā), *v.i.* **1,** to make request or confession, or offer praise, especially to God; **2,** to make a petition to a human being or authority:—*v.t.* **1,** to make request of; as, to *pray* the court for relief; **2,** to make request for; as, we *pray* Thy forgiveness; **3,** to bring about by praying.

Syn. entreat, implore, plead, petition.

prayer (prâr), *n.* earnest entreaty, especially that offered to God with thanks and praise.

prayer book, a book of prayers for use in public and private worship; **Prayer Book,** a book containing the prayers and forms of divine service used in the Episcopal Church.

prayer-ful (prâr′fŏŏl), *adj.* given to devout appeal to God.—*adv.* **prayer′ful-ly.**

pre- (prē-), a prefix meaning before; as, *prepay, precede, predict.*

preach (prēch), *v.i.* and *v.t.* **1,** to talk or teach publicly on a religious subject, especially from a text of Scripture; as, to *preach* eloquently; to *preach* Christ; **2,** to advise on moral, religious, or social subjects; as, his teacher *preached* to him.

preach-er (prēch′ěr), *n.* **1,** a clergyman; **2,** a person who strongly urges something.

preach-ment (prēch′měnt), *n.* a sermon or moral lecture, especially if tedious.

pre-am-ble (prē′ăm′bl; prē-ăm′bl), *n.* **1,** an introduction to a speech or writing; **2,** an introduction to a statute or law, giving the reason for passing the law; as, the *preamble* to the Constitution.

pre-car-i-ous (prē-kâr′ĭ-ŭs), *adj.* depending on circumstances; uncertain; hence, dangerous; risky.—*adv.* **pre-car′i-ous-ly.**

Syn. uncertain, insecure.

pre-cau-tion (prē-kô′shŭn), *n.* care taken beforehand to prevent harm, loss, etc.

pre-cau-tion-ar-y (prē-kô′shŭn-ěr′ĭ), *adj.* marked by care taken beforehand; intended to prevent harm or loss.

pre-cede (prē-sēd′), *v.t.* and *v.i.* [preced-ed, preced-ing], to go before in time, place, rank, or importance.

pre-ced-ence (prē-sē′děns), *n.* **1,** the act of going before another or others in time, order, rank, importance, etc.; **2,** superiority in rank; specifically, the right of going before others in ceremonies and social formalities. Also, **pre-ced′en-cy.**

prec-e-dent (prĕs′ē-děnt), *n.* something said or done in the past, that serves as a model for the future:—*adj.* (prē-sēd′ěnt), going before.

pre-ced-ing (prē-sē′dĭng), *adj.* happening or coming just before something else.

Syn. previous, prior, antecedent.

pre-cept (prē′sěpt), *n.* a rule of conduct or action to be used as a guide.

pre-cep-tor (prē-sěp′těr), *n.* a teacher.—*n.fem.* **pre-cep′tress.**

pre-cinct (prē′sĭngkt), *n.* **1,** a boundary; also, the region within it; **2,** a small district marked off, as for voting or police purposes; **3, precincts,** the surrounding regions.

pre-cious (prěsh′ŭs), *adj.* **1,** of great price or value; as, *precious* metals; **2,** very dear; as, my *precious* child; highly esteemed; as, a *precious* privilege; **3,** *Colloquial,* thorough; extreme; as, a *precious* nuisance.

prec-i-pice (prĕs′ĭ-pĭs), *n.* the steep, nearly vertical face of a cliff or rock.

pre-cip-i-tant (prē-sĭp′ĭ-tănt), *adj.* too hasty; rash; as, *precipitant* flight:—*n.* in chemistry, anything that, added to a liquid in which certain substances have been dissolved, causes one or more of the dissolved substances to separate from the liquid as a solid and settle to the bottom.

pre-cip-i-tate (prē-sĭp′ĭ-tāt), *v.t.* [precipitat-ed, precipitat-ing], **1,** to throw headlong; **2,** to hurry on rashly; bring to a crisis; as, his act *precipitated* the disaster; **3,** to cause to change from vapor to liquid or solid, and fall, as rain or snow; **4,** in chemistry, to cause to separate in solid form from a solution, as salt crystals from brine:—*n.* (prē-sĭp′ĭ-tāt; prē-sĭp′ĭ-tĭt), any solid substance which separates from a solution:—*adj.* (prē-sĭp′ĭ-tāt), **1,** rash; hasty; as, a *precipitate* departure; **2,** falling or rushing headlong, as a waterfall.—*adv.* **pre-cip′i-tate-ly** (prē-sĭp′ĭ-tāt-lĭ).

pre-cip-i-ta-tion (prē-sĭp′ĭ-tā′shŭn), *n.* **1,** a headlong fall or descent; **2,** rashness; **3,** in chemistry, the process of causing the solid part of a solution to separate from the liquid and sink; **4,** moisture condensed from the atmosphere and falling as rain, snow, or the like.

pre-cip-i-tous (prē-sĭp′ĭ-tŭs), *adj.* very steep, as a cliff.

Syn. sheer, steep, abrupt.

pre-cise (prē-sīs′), *adj.* **1,** exact; careful; as, a *precise* speaker; *precise* measurements; **2,** keeping closely to rule; prim; strict.—*adv.* **pre-cise′ly.**

Syn. particular, correct.

pre-ci-sion (prē-sĭzh′ŭn), *n.* exactness; definiteness; accuracy; as, *precision* of movement; *precision* of thought.

pre-clude (prē-klōōd′), *v.t.* [preclud-ed, preclud-ing], to shut out; prevent.

pre-co-cious (prē-kō′shŭs), *adj.* showing unusual mental development for his or her age; as, a *precocious* child.

pre-coc-i-ty (prē-kŏs′ĭ-tĭ), *n.* unusually early development, especially of mind.

pre-con-ceive (prē′kŏn-sēv′), *v.t.* [preconceived, preconceiv-ing], to form (an idea) before having actual knowledge.

pre·con·cep·tion (prē′kŏn-sĕp′shŭn), *n.* an idea formed before actual knowledge has been obtained.

pre·con·cert (prē′kŏn-sûrt′), *v.t.* to agree upon or arrange beforehand; as, to *preconcert* a plan.—*adj.* **pre′con·cert′ed.**

pre·cur·sor (prē-kûr′sẽr), *n.* a person or thing that goes before, to show that someone or some event is about to follow; a forerunner.

pred·a·to·ry (prĕd′à-tôr′ĭ), *adj.* living by plunder, or by preying on others; as, a *predatory* tribe or beast.

pred·e·ces·sor (prĕd′ē-sĕs′ẽr; prĕd′ē-sĕs′-ẽr; prē′dē-sĕs′ẽr), *n.* a person who has gone before another, as in the same office, position, etc.: opposite of *successor.*

pre·des·ti·nate (prē-dĕs′tĭ-nāt), *v.t.* [predestinat-ed, predestinat-ing], to decree or determine beforehand, or from the very beginning.—*n.* **pre·des′ti·nar′i·an.**

pre·des·ti·na·tion (prē-dĕs′tĭ-nā′shŭn), *n.* **1,** the act of determining beforehand; **2,** fate; destiny; **3,** the belief that whatever happens was decreed by God from the very beginning.

pre·des·tine (prē-dĕs′tĭn), *v.t.* [predestined, predestin-ing], to decree or determine beforehand; predestinate:—**predestined,** *adj.* fated; as, *predestined* to succeed.

pre·de·ter·mine (prē′dē-tûr′mĭn), *v.t.* and *v.i.* [predetermined, predetermin-ing], to decide or resolve beforehand; predestine.—*n.* **pre′de·ter′mi·na′tion.**

pre·dic·a·ment (prē-dĭk′à-mĕnt), *n.* an unpleasant or dangerous situation.
Syn. quandary, plight, dilemma.

pred·i·cate (prĕd′ĭ-kāt), *v.t.* [predicat-ed, predicat-ing], to declare (something) to be true or characteristic of something else; as, to *predicate* wetness of water:—*n.* (prĕd′ĭ-kĭt), in grammar, the part of a sentence which makes a statement about the subject; as, in the sentence, "Tom caught the ball," the expression "caught the ball" is the *predicate:*—*adj.* (prĕd′ĭ-kĭt), belonging in the predicate; as, in the sentence, "This is my hat," the word "hat" is a *predicate* noun.

pre·dict (prē-dĭkt′), *v.t.* and *v.i.* to tell or make known beforehand; foretell.—*n.* **pre-dic′tor.**—*adj.* **pre·dic′tive.**

pre·dic·tion (prē-dĭk′shŭn), *n.* the foretelling of a future event; a prophecy.

pre·di·gest (prē′dĭ-jĕst′; prē′dī-jĕst′), *v.t.* to treat (food) artificially so that it is partly digested before being eaten.

pre·di·lec·tion (prē′dĭ-lĕk′shŭn; prĕd′ĭ-lĕk′shŭn), *n.* a preference; partiality; as, he has a *predilection* for rich food.

pre·dis·pose (prē′dĭs-pōz′), *v.t.* [predis-posed, predispos-ing], **1,** to incline beforehand; as, good humor in strangers *predisposes* us to like them; **2,** to make liable or subject, as to a disease; as, to be *predisposed* to tuberculosis.

pre·dis·po·si·tion (prē′dĭs-pô-zĭsh′ŭn), *n.* a previous inclination or tendency; bias.

pre·dom·i·nance (prē-dŏm′ĭ-nǎns), *n.* superiority in strength or influence.

pre·dom·i·nant (prē-dŏm′ĭ-nǎnt), *adj.* superior in numbers, strength, influence, or the like.—*adv.* **pre·dom′i·nant·ly.**
Syn. ruling, dominant, prevailing.

pre·dom·i·nate (prē-dŏm′ĭ-nāt), *v.i.* [predominat-ed, predominat-ing], to be superior in power or influence; prevail.

pre·em·i·nence (prē-ĕm′ĭ-nĕns), *n.* superiority to all others in merit or rank.

pre·em·i·nent (prē-ĕm′ĭ-nĕnt), *adj.* highly superior to others; distinguished from others who are eminent.

pre·empt (prē-ĕmpt′), *v.t.* **1,** to take possession of, before others can; as, to *preempt* a parking space; **2,** to establish the first claim to (public land):—*v.i.* to establish a right to purchase public land by filing a claim to it and settling upon it.—*adj.* **pre·emp′tive.**—*n.* **pre·emp′tion.**

preen (prēn), *v.t.* **1,** to cleanse and smooth (the feathers) with the beak; **2,** to dress or groom (oneself) with care.

pre·ex·ist (prē′ĕg-zĭst′), *v.i.* to exist before the present life.—*n.* **pre′·ex·ist′ence.**—*adj.* **pre′·ex·ist′ent.**

pref. abbreviation for *preface, prefix.*

pre·fab·ri·cate (prē′făb′rĭ-kāt), *v.t.* to manufacture all standardized parts at a factory, before their shipment for assembly into one unit; as, to *prefabricate* a house.—*n.* **pre′fab·ri·ca′tion.**

pref·ace (prĕf′ĭs), *n.* an introduction, as to a book, preceding the body of the work:—*v.t.* [prefaced, prefac-ing], **1,** to introduce (a book, speech, or the like) by some act or statement; **2,** to serve as an introduction to; as, the program was *prefaced* by a talk.—*adj.* **pref′a·tor·y.**

pre·fect (prē′fĕkt), *n.* **1,** in the Roman Empire, a civil or military officer of high rank, as the governor of a province; **2,** in modern France, the governor of a department or district.—*n.* **pre′fec·ture.**

pre·fer (prē-fûr′), *v.t.* [preferred, prefer-ring], **1,** to like (something) more than something else; as, to *prefer* candy to cake; **2,** to offer for consideration; as, to *prefer* a claim.
Syn. choose, elect, favor.

pref·er·a·ble (prĕf′ẽr-à-bl), *adj.* more desirable; as, death is *preferable* to slavery.

āte, åorta, râre, căt, åsk, fär, ållow, sofà; ēve, ĕvent, ĕll, writẽr, novĕl; bīte, pĭn; nō, ōbey, ôr, dŏg, tŏp, cŏllide; ūnit, ūnite, bûrn, cŭt, focŭs; nōon, fŏŏt; mound; coin;

pref·er·a·bly (prĕf′ẽr-ȧ-blĭ), *adv.* rather than something else; by choice; as, come soon, *preferably* in the morning.

pref·er·ence (prĕf′ẽr-ĕns), *n.* 1, choice of one thing rather than another; 2, that which is favored or chosen.

pref·er·en·tial (prĕf′ẽr-ĕn′shăl), *adj.* showing a preference or favor for one person or thing as against others.

pre·fer·ment (prĕ-fûr′mĕnt), *n.* promotion to higher rank or office; as, political *preferment*; also, a high post of honor or profit, especially in the church.

pre·fig·ure (prē-fĭg′ūr), *v.t.* [prefigured, prefigur-ing], to represent beforehand; show beforehand by a figure or symbol.— *n.* **pre-fig′u-ra′tion.**

pre·fix (prē′fĭks), *n.* a syllable, or syllables, placed at the beginning of a word to modify its meaning, as *sub-* in the word "subway," and *super-* in the word "superfine":—*v.t.* (prē-fĭks′), to place before, or at the beginning of, anything; as, he *prefixed* "Doctor" to his name.

preg·nan·cy (prĕg′năn-sĭ), *n.* 1, the condition of being about to have young; 2, significance; suggestiveness; weightiness; as, *pregnancy* of thought.

preg·nant (prĕg′nănt), *adj.* 1, about to have young; carrying unborn young; 2, fruitful; fertile; 3, full of meaning; important; as, a *pregnant* thought.

pre·hen·sile (prē-hĕn′sĭl), *adj.* capable of grasping; as, a monkey has a *prehensile* tail.

pre·his·tor·ic (prē′hĭs-tŏr′ĭk) or **pre·his·tor·i·cal** (prē′hĭs-tŏr′ĭ-kăl), *adj.* relating to the time before there were written records.

pre·judge (prē-jŭj′), *v.t.* [prejudged, prejudg-ing], to judge in advance or without waiting to learn all of the facts in the case. —*n.* **pre-judg′ment; pre-judge′ment.**

prej·u·dice (prĕj′ŏo-dĭs), *n.* 1, an opinion, often unfavorable, formed without a fair examination of the facts; bias; 2, injury or harm resulting from hasty or unfair judgment:—*v.t.* [prejudiced, prejudic-ing], to cause to form an opinion, usually unfavorable, before examination of the facts; as, your story *prejudiced* me against him.
Syn., *n.* unfairness, partiality.

prej·u·di·cial (prĕj′ŏo-dĭsh′ăl), *adj.* injurious; damaging; as, his bad record was *prejudicial* to him.—*adv.* **prej′u-di′cial-ly.**

prel·a·cy (prĕl′ȧ-sĭ), *n.* [*pl.* prelacies], 1, the position of a clergyman of high rank, as a bishop; 2, the bishops of a church, taken together; 3, church government by the higher orders of clergy.

prel·ate (prĕl′ĭt), *n.* a clergyman of high rank, as a bishop or archbishop.

pre·lim·i·nar·y (prē-lĭm′ĭ-nĕr′ĭ), *adj.* introductory; preparatory:—*n.* [*pl.* preliminaries], an introductory act or step.

prel·ude (prĕl′ūd; prē′lūd), *n.* 1, a preface; something preceding and preparing for something of greater importance; as, a lie may be the *prelude* to a quarrel; 2, a piece of music played at the opening of church services, or as an introduction to a musical composition:—*v.t.* and *v.i.* [prelud-ed, prelud-ing], to precede; preface; introduce.

pre·ma·ture (prē′mȧ-tūr′; prē′mȧ-tūr), *adj.* coming before the usual or proper time; untimely; as, a *premature* winter.— *adv.* **pre′ma-ture′ly.**

pre·med·i·tate (prē-mĕd′ĭ-tāt), *v.t.* and *v.i.* [premeditat-ed, premeditat-ing], to think over carefully or plan beforehand.

pre·med·i·ta·tion (prē′mĕd-ĭ-tā′shŭn), *n.* forethought; the act of planning or arranging beforehand.—*adj.* **pre-med′i-ta′tive.**

pre·mi·er (prē′mĭ-ẽr; prĕm′yẽr), *adj.* 1, foremost; chief; 2, earliest in time:—*n.* (prē′mĭ-ẽr; prē-mēr′; prĕm′yẽr), the chief officer of a state; a prime minister.

¹prem·ise (prĕm′ĭs), *n.* 1, a statement accepted as true, from which a conclusion is to be drawn; especially, in logic, one of the first two statements of a form of argument called a syllogism; as, major *premise*, men must eat to live; minor *premise*, John is a man; conclusion, John must eat to live; 2, **premises: a,** facts previously stated, as in a legal document; **b,** the property, such as lands, houses, etc., which is the subject of a legal document; **c,** hence, a house or building with its grounds.

²pre·mise (prē-mīz′), *v.t.* [premised, premis-ing], to preface or introduce with explanations or the like; as, to *premise* a speech about transcontinental air travel with a short history of aviation.

pre·mi·um (prē′mĭ-ŭm), *n.* 1, a reward or prize for excelling, as in a competition; 2, a sum agreed upon as the price to be paid for a contract of insurance; 3, an amount exceeding the par value of something; as, the stock sold at a *premium;* 4, that which is given in return for a loan of money, over and above the interest; as, he paid a *premium* of $5 for a loan of $100.

pre·mo·ni·tion (prē′mō-nĭsh′ŭn), *n.* 1, a warning in advance; as, a *premonition* of a flood; 2, a foreboding; a feeling that something is about to happen.—*adj.* **pre-mon′i-tor′y** (prē-mŏn′ĭ-tôr′ĭ).

pre·oc·cu·pa·tion (prē-ŏk′ū-pā′shŭn), *n.* the state of being lost in thought or wrapped up in one's own affairs.

---

go; join; yet; sing; chin; show; thin, *th*en; hw, *wh*y; zh, a*z*ure; ü, Ger. f*ür* or Fr. l*u*ne; ö, Ger. sch*ö*n or Fr. f*eu*; ṅ, Fr. e*n*fant, no*m*; kh, Ger. a*ch* or i*ch*. See pages ix–x.

pre·oc·cu·pied (prē-ŏk′ū-pīd), *adj.* **1,** lost in thought; absorbed; **2,** already occupied or in use.

pre·oc·cu·py (prē-ŏk′ū-pī), *v.t.* [preoccupied, preoccupy-ing], to fill the mind of; hold the attention of.

pre·or·dain (prē′ôr-dān′), *v.t.* to decree or determine beforehand.

prep. abbreviation for *preposition.*

pre·paid (prē-pād′), past tense and past participle of *prepay.*

prep·a·ra·tion (prĕp′a·rā′shŭn), *n.* **1,** the act of making fit or ready for use; as, the *preparation* of dinner took an hour; **2,** a state of readiness; **3,** that which makes fit or ready; as, *preparations* for war; **4,** a substance, as a medicine or a salve, made up or compounded for a special use.

pre·par·a·tor·y (prē-păr′a·tôr′ĭ), *adj.* serving to make ready or fit for something further; as, *preparatory* measures.

pre·pare (prē-pâr′), *v.t.* [prepared, preparing], **1,** to fit for some purpose or make ready for use; as, to *prepare* a house for occupancy; to *prepare* food; **2,** to make (a person) mentally ready or fit for something; as, we *prepared* him for bad news; **3,** to provide or fit out; as, to *prepare* an expedition:—*v.i.* to make things or oneself ready; as, to *prepare* for cold weather; to *prepare* for bad news.

pre·par·ed·ness (prē-pâr′ĕd-nĕs; prē-pârd′nĕs), *n.* the state of being ready; especially, readiness for military activity.

pre·pay (prē-pā′), *v.t.* [prepaid, prepaying], to pay, or pay for, in advance.—*n.* **pre·pay′ment.**

pre·pon·der·ance (prē-pŏn′dēr-ăns), *n.* superiority in power, influence, number, or amount; as, there was a *preponderance* of women in the audience.

pre·pon·der·ant (prē-pŏn′dēr-ănt), *adj.* greater in weight, power, influence, number, etc.—*adv.* **pre·pon′der·ant·ly.**

pre·pon·der·ate (prē-pŏn′dēr-āt), *v.i.* [preponderat-ed, preponderat-ing], to exceed others in power, number, etc.; as, dark-haired people *preponderate* in Spain.

prep·o·si·tion (prĕp′ō-zĭsh′ŭn), *n.* in grammar, a part of speech, as *to, from, by,* and the like, used with a noun or pronoun in the objective case, to show the relation between the noun or pronoun and some other word or words in the sentence; as, in "a bag for the mail," the word "for" is a *preposition* showing a relation between "bag" and "mail."—*adj.* **prep′o·si′tion·al.**

pre·pos·sess (prē′pŏ·zĕs′), *v.t.* **1,** to occupy beforehand; **2,** to influence beforehand, especially to a favorable opinion.

pre·pos·sess·ing (prē′pŏ·zĕs′ĭng), *adj.* tending to win favor, love, affection, confidence, or the like; attractive.

pre·pos·ses·sion (prē′pŏ·zĕsh′ŭn), *n.* an opinion, usually favorable, formed in advance of actual knowledge.

pre·pos·ter·ous (prē-pŏs′tēr-ŭs), *adj.* contrary to common sense; foolish; absurd.

pre·req·ui·site (prē-rĕk′wĭ-zĭt), *n.* that which is required before something else can follow; as, reading is a *prerequisite* of all other studies:—*adj.* required before something else can follow.

pre·rog·a·tive (prē-rŏg′a·tĭv), *n.* a right or privilege belonging to a person, class, or body of persons, by virtue of rank or position; as, the *prerogatives* of a President, of a citizen, etc.

pres. abbreviation for *present:*—**Pres.** abbreviation for *President.*

¹**pres·age** (prĕs′ĭj), *n.* **1,** a sign or omen foretelling what is going to happen; **2,** a feeling of what is going to happen; a foreboding.

²**pre·sage** (prē-sāj′), *v.t.* [presaged, presaging], **1,** to give a warning or sign of; **2,** to foretell.

pres·by·ter (prĕz′bĭ-tēr; prĕs′bĭ-tēr), *n.* **1,** in the early Christian church, a priest or elder; **2,** in the Episcopal Church, a minister, ranking between bishop and deacon; **3,** in the Presbyterian Church, a minister or elder.

Pres·by·te·ri·an (prĕz′bĭ-tē′rĭ-ăn; prĕs′bĭ-tē′rĭ-ăn), *adj.* naming, or pertaining to, a church or churches governed by ministers and elders:—*n.* a member of a Presbyterian church.

pres·by·ter·y (prĕz′bĭ-tēr′ĭ; prĕs′bĭ-tēr′ĭ), *n.* [*pl.* presbyteries], **1,** in the early Christian church, a body of elders; **2,** in the Presbyterian Church, a court composed of all the ministers and one elder from each congregation in a district; also, the district; **3,** the front part of the church, reserved for the clergy; **4,** a priest's residence.

pre·sci·ence (prē′shĭ-ĕns; prĕsh′ĭ-ĕns), *n.* the knowing of events before they take place; foreknowledge.

pre·sci·ent (prē′shĭ-ĕnt; prĕsh′ĭ-ĕnt), *adj.* foreseeing; knowing the future.

pre·scribe (prē-skrīb′), *v.t.* [prescribed, prescrib-ing], **1,** to advise the use of (a medicine or treatment); **2,** to set down as a rule of action:—*v.i.* **1,** to write or give medical directions; **2,** to give laws, rules, or directions.

pre·scrip·tion (prē-skrĭp′shŭn), *n.* a written direction for the preparation and use of a medicine; also, the medicine.

āte, âorta, râre, căt, àsk, fär, ăllow, sofà; ēve, ēvent, ĕll, writēr, novĕl; bīte, pĭn; nō, ōbey, ôr, dŏg, tŏp, cŏllide; ūnit, ūnite, bûrn, cŭt, focŭs; nōōn, fŏŏt; mound; coin;

pres·ence (prĕz'ĕns), *n.* **1,** the state of being in a certain place; **2,** nearness; immediate neighborhood; as, in the *presence* of danger; **3,** one's appearance or bearing; as, a girl of pleasing *presence:*—**presence of mind,** quickness of thought or action in an emergency.

¹pres·ent (prĕz'ĕnt), *adj.* **1,** being at hand or in sight at a given place; as, all people here *present;* **2,** existing now; as, my *present* situation:—*n.* **1,** the time now here; as, I do not know at *present;* **2,** the present tense:—**present tense,** a tense of the verb which indicates an action now going on; as, he *runs;* **present perfect,** in grammar, a tense of the verb indicating: **1,** action begun in the past and continuing to the present; as, I *have waited* an hour; **2,** an action the results of which are still going on; as, he *has stolen* my dog; **3,** an action just completed; as, I *have done* the deed.

²pres·ent (prē·zĕnt'), *v.t.* **1,** to introduce (one person) to another; as, let me *present* Mrs. Brown to you; **2,** to bring (oneself) into the presence of someone; as, he *presented* himself before the judge; **3,** to bring to the view or attention of the public; as, to *present* a play; **4,** to submit; hand in; as, to *present* a bill; **5,** to give as a gift; as, we *presented* a book to him; also, to give a gift to; as, we *presented* him with a book; **6,** to display; offer to view; as, he *presented* a sad appearance.

³pres·ent (prĕz'ĕnt), *n.* a gift.

pres·ent·a·ble (prē·zĕn'ta·bl), *adj.* **1,** suitable to be offered, given, or introduced; **2,** suitable in appearance; fit to be seen.

pres·en·ta·tion (prĕz'ĕn·tā'shŭn; prē'zĕn·tā'shŭn), *n.* **1,** a formal introduction; as, *presentation* at court; **2,** the act of offering to view; as, the *presentation* of a play; also, a show; a play; **3,** the act of bestowing (a gift); as, the *presentation* of a medal.

pres·en·ti·ment (prē·zĕn'tĭ·mĕnt), *n.* a feeling that some particular thing is going to happen; a foreboding.

pres·ent·ly (prĕz'ĕnt·lĭ), *adv.* soon; before long; as, I shall be there *presently.*

pres·ent·ment (prē·zĕnt'mĕnt), *n.* the act of presenting to view; also, that which is presented, as a play, picture, etc.

pres·er·va·tion (prĕz'ĕr·vā'shŭn), *n.* the act of keeping, or the state of being kept, from injury or decay.

pre·serv·a·tive (prē·zûr'va·tĭv), *n.* a substance which tends to prevent decay or injury:—*adj.* acting as a preservative.

pre·serve (prē·zûrv'), *v.t.* [preserved, preserv-ing], **1,** to keep from injury; save; **2,** to keep (fruit or vegetables) from spoiling by canning, pickling, cooking with sugar, or the like; **3,** to keep up; maintain; as, to *preserve* peace:—*n.* **1,** (usually *preserves*), fruit or vegetables preserved with sugar; **2,** a place set apart for keeping game, fish, or the like, for sport.

Syn., v. keep, guard, shield.

pre·serv·er (prē·zûr'vẽr), *n.* a person or thing that saves, protects, or defends.

pre·side (prē·zīd'), *v.i.* [presid-ed, pre-sid-ing], **1,** to direct or control; as, to *preside* over a home; **2,** to act as chairman of a meeting; as, Mr. Jones *presided.*

pres·i·den·cy (prĕz'ĭ·dĕn·sĭ), *n.* [*pl.* presidencies], the office, or term of office, of a president.

pres·i·dent (prĕz'ĭ·dĕnt), *n.* **1,** the 'chief officer of a company, college, club, etc.; **2,** (often *President*), the highest executive officer of a modern republic.

pres·i·den·tial (prĕz'ĭ·dĕn'shăl), *adj.* pertaining to a president, or to his office.

press (prĕs), *v.t.* **1,** to bear down upon; **2,** to compress; squeeze; as, to *press* fruit to extract juice; also, to squeeze out; as, to *press* juice from a fruit; **3,** to thrust or push; as, to *press* a crowd back; **4,** to embrace; hug; as, she *pressed* the baby to her; **5,** to urge; entreat; as, we *pressed* him to stay; **6,** to hasten or urge; as, heavy anxiety *pressed* him on; **7,** to thrust upon others; impose; as, she *pressed* gifts upon them; **8,** to smooth or shape by pressure; as, to *press* clothes; **9,** to place in an urgent situation; as, to be *pressed* for time:—*v.i.* **1,** to bear down

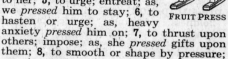

FRUIT PRESS

PRINTING PRESS

heavily; **2,** to hasten; strive eagerly; as, we *pressed* to the gate; **3,** to urge or impel to action; as, time *presses:*—*n.* **1,** the act of pushing forward; **2,** a dense crowd; **3,** a machine which presses or stamps anything; as, a printing *press;* **4,** newspaper and magazine literature, or those who write or publish it; as, the power of the *press;* a statement issued by the *press;* **5,** urgent demand; as, the *press* of business; **6,** an upright cupboard, as for clothes.

Press·burg (prĕs'bŏŏrkh), the German name for Bratislava, a city in southwestern Czechoslovakia. See **Bratislava.**

press·ing (prĕs'ĭng), *adj.* persistent; urgent; as, a *pressing* engagement.

press·man (prĕs'măn), *n.* [*pl.* pressmen (-mĕn)], one who manages or operates a press, especially a printing press.

pres·sure (prĕsh′ẽr), *n.* **1,** a bearing down upon; as, the *pressure* of a roller on a lawn; **2,** weight on the mind; distress; as, the *pressure* of worry; **3,** burden; oppression; as, the *pressure* of high expenses; **4,** weight of influence or authority; as, parental *pressure* changed his mind; **5,** urgent demand on one's time or energies; as, the *pressure* of work; **6,** in physics, force exerted on a body so as to tend to change its shape or lessen its volume:—**pressure cooker,** a closed vessel in which foods may be cooked under steam pressure.

pres·ti·dig·i·ta·tor (prĕs′tĭ-dĭj′ĭ-tā′tẽr), *n.* a sleight of hand performer; a juggler.

pres·tige (prĕs-tēzh′; prĕs′tĭj), *n.* reputation or influence resulting from past achievement or associations.

pres·to (prĕs′tō), *adv.* **1,** quickly; suddenly: used as an exclamation by a magician; **2,** in music, rapidly.

pre·sum·a·ble (prē-zū′má-bl), *adj.* probable; to be expected; as, the *presumable* results of an act.—*adv.* **pre·sum′a·bly.**

pre·sume (prē-zūm′), *v.t.* [presumed, presum-ing], **1,** to take for granted; suppose; **2,** to venture; dare (to do something); as, to *presume* to offer advice:—*v.i.* to take liberties; act with unwarranted boldness.

pre·sump·tion (prē-zŭmp′shŭn), *n.* **1,** boldness; arrogance; **2,** acceptance and belief of something not fully proved; as, the argument is based on *presumption;* **3,** that which is taken for granted.

pre·sump·tive (prē-zŭmp′tĭv), *adj.* **1,** affording reasonable grounds for belief; as, *presumptive* evidence; **2,** based on presumption or likelihood; as, the heir *presumptive.*—*adv.* **pre·sump′tive·ly.**

pre·sump·tu·ous (prē-zŭmp′tū-ŭs), *adj.* bold or overconfident.

pre·sup·pose (prē′sŭ-pōz′), *v.t.* [presupposed, presuppos-ing], to take for granted in advance.

pre·sup·po·si·tion (prē′sŭp-ō-zĭsh′ŭn), *n.* **1,** the forming of a belief in advance of actual knowledge; **2,** a belief previously formed.

pre·tend (prē-tĕnd′), *v.t.* **1,** to make believe; as, he *pretends* to be a prince; **2,** to make a false show of; as, to *pretend* friendship:—*v.i.* **1,** to put forward a claim, true or false; as, to *pretend* to a title; **2,** to play at make-believe. *Syn.* feign, sham, counterfeit.

pre·tend·er (prē-tĕn′dẽr), *n.* one who lays claim, especially a false claim, to anything; as, the *pretender* to a throne.

pre·tense (prē-tĕns′; prē′tĕns), *n.* **1,** make-believe; a putting on of a false appearance in order to hide what is real; deception; as, she made a *pretense* of friendship; **2,** a false show; display; as, a man without *pretense;* **3,** a claim; as, she had no *pretense* to beauty. Also spelled **pre-tence′.**

pre·ten·sion (prē-tĕn′shŭn), *n.* **1,** a claim made, whether true or false; **2,** outward show; display.

pre·ten·tious (prē-tĕn′shŭs), *adj.* **1,** making claims to importance, worth, etc.; as, a *pretentious* book; **2,** made or done for show or display; as, a *pretentious* house.—*adv.* **pre·ten′tious·ly.**—*n.* **pre·ten′tious·ness.**

pret·er·it or **pret·er·ite** (prĕt′ẽr-ĭt), *adj.* in grammar, past; expressing a past action or state; as, the *preterit* tense of a verb:—*n.* the past tense or a verb in that tense; as, in the sentence "he ran," the verb "ran" is in the *preterit.*

pre·ter·nat·u·ral (prē′tẽr-năt′ū-răl), *adj.* unlike ordinary occurrences; extraordinary.—*adv.* **pre′ter·nat′u·ral·ly.**

pre·text (prē′tĕkst), *n.* a pretense or excuse; a false motive put forward to conceal the real one.

pre·tor (prē′tŏr), *n.* a Roman magistrate; praetor. See **praetor.**

Pre·tor·i·a (prē-tôr′ĭ-á), a city, the capital of the Transvaal and the Union of South Africa (map 14).

pret·ty (prĭt′ĭ), *adj.* [pret-ti-er, pret-ti-est], **1,** pleasing to look at; attractive; **2,** nice; fine; as, a *pretty* wit: often used slightingly; as, a *pretty* mess:—*adv.* fairly; moderately; as, *pretty* well.—*adv.* **pret′ti·ly.**—*n.* **pret′ti·ness.** *Syn.,* *adj.* fair, comely, beautiful.

pret·zel (prĕt′sĕl), *n.* a hard biscuit, made in a twisted form and glazed and salted on the outside.

pre·vail (prē-vāl′), *v.i.* **1,** to be victorious; triumph; as, right will *prevail;* **2,** to be or become widespread; be in general use; as, the English language *prevails* in America; **3,** to persuade; as, she finally *prevailed* on him to go.—*adj.* **pre·vail′ing.**

prev·a·lence (prĕv′á-lĕns), *n.* widespread occurrence; common practice; as, the *prevalence* of crime in certain districts.—*adj.* **prev′a·lent.**—*adv.* **prev′a·lent·ly.**

pre·var·i·cate (prē-văr′ĭ-kāt), *v.i.* [prevaricat-ed, prevaricat-ing], to stray from the truth; lie.—*n.* **pre·var′i·ca′tor.** *Syn.* evade, equivocate.

pre·var·i·ca·tion (prē-văr′ĭ-kā′shŭn), *n.* a turning aside from the truth; a lie.

pre·vent (prē-vĕnt′), *v.t.* to stop or keep from happening, doing, etc.; hinder.—*adj.* **pre·vent′a·ble; pre·vent′i·ble.** *Syn.* obstruct.

pre·ven·tion (prē-vĕn′shŭn), *n.* **1,** the

āte, āorta, râre, căt, ȧsk, fär, ăllow, sofȧ; ēve, ēvent, ĕll, writēr, novĕl; bīte, pĭn; nō, ōbey, ôr, dŏg, tŏp, cŏllide; ūnit, ūnite, bûrn, cŭt, focŭs; nōon, fŏot; mound; coin;

act of hindering or obstructing; **2,** any hindrance or obstruction.

pre-ven-tive (prĕ-vĕn′tĭv), *adj.* serving to hinder:—*n.* that which hinders; especially, something that wards off disease.

pre-view (prē′vū′), *n.* a private showing of a painting, motion picture, or the like, before it is shown publicly.

pre-vi-ous (prē′vĭ-ŭs), *adj.* earlier; preceding; as, he spoke of you in a *previous* letter.—*adv.* **pre′vi-ous-ly.**
Syn. former, foregone.

pre-war (prē-wôr′; prē′wôr′), *adj.* before any war, as contrasted with *postwar.*

prey (prā), *n.* **1,** any animal hunted or killed by another animal for food; **2,** hence, a person who is a victim of another person or of anything which is hostile or evil:—**bird,** or **beast, of prey,** a bird or beast that devours other animals:—*v.i.* **1,** to plunder for the sake of booty; **2,** to seize and devour an animal as food; **3,** to exert a destructive influence; as, his guilt *preyed* upon his mind.

Pri-am (prī′ăm), *n.* in Greek legend, the last king of Troy, slain in the sack of Troy.

price (prīs), *n.* **1,** worth; value; as, pearls of great *price;* **2,** something, usually money, given or asked in exchange for a thing; cost; **3,** reward; as, to set a *price* on a criminal's head; **4,** the cost at which something is obtained; as, the *price* of victory was the loss of a thousand lives:—*v.t.* [priced, pric-ing], **1,** to set a price on; **2,** *Colloquial,* to inquire the price of; as, to *price* goods in various stores.
Syn. *n.* expense, outlay, cost.

price-less (prīs′lĕs), *adj.* too valuable to be bought at any price; invaluable.

prick (prĭk), *n.* **1,** a dot or mark made by a pointed instrument; also, the instrument; **2,** a sharp, stinging pain; hence, remorse:—*v.t.* **1,** to pierce with something pointed; **2,** to mark out by puncturing; **3,** to pain or sting, as with remorse; **4,** to erect or raise; as, a dog *pricks* up its ears; **5,** to spur; urge; as, to *prick* a horse on:—*v.i.* to feel a sharp, stinging pain.

prick-er (prĭk′ẽr), *n.* a sharp, pointed instrument; a prickle.

prick-le (prĭk′l), *n.* **1,** a sharp point; especially, a small, slender projection growing from the surface of a plant; **2,** a slight stinging sensation:—*v.t.* [prick-led, prick-ling], **1,** to give a stinging sensation to (the skin); **2,** to cover with small dots:—*v.i.* to tingle.

prick-ly (prĭk′lĭ), *adj.* [prick-li-er, prick-li-est], **1,** full of thorns or sharp points; as, a *prickly* blackberry bush; **2,** stinging; tingling; as, a *prickly* sensation:—**prickly**

pear, a cactus bearing a pear-shaped fruit covered with small thorns; also, its edible fruit.—*n.* **prick′li-ness.**

pride (prīd), *n.* **1,** a high opinion of one's own qualities; conceit; **2,** haughtiness; disdain; **3,** dignity; self-respect:—*v.t.* [prid-ed, prid-ing], to be proud of; as, he *prides* himself on his speech.

PRICKLY PEAR

priest (prēst), *n.* one with authority to perform religious rites and services.

priest-ess (prēs′tĕs), *n.* a woman priest, especially in pagan times.

priest-hood (prēst′hŏŏd), *n.* **1,** the whole body of priests; **2,** the office or duties of a priest.

priest-ly (prēst′lĭ), *adj.* [priest-li-er, priest-li-est], pertaining to a priest.

prig (prĭg), *n.* a conceited person who is overparticular about speech, conduct, etc.

prig-gish (prĭg′ĭsh), *adj.* tending to be too particular about speech, manners, etc.—*adv.* **prig′gish-ly.**—*n.* **prig′gish-ness.**

prim (prĭm), *adj.* [prim-mer, prim-mest], extremely neat or precise.—*adv.* **prim′ly.**

pri-ma-cy (prī′mȧ-sĭ), *n.* [*pl.* primacies], **1,** the state of being first in rank, importance, time, etc.; **2,** the office or dignity of an archbishop; **3,** in the Roman Catholic Church, the supreme power of the Pope.

pri-ma don-na (prē′mȧ dŏn′ȧ), [*pl.* prima donnas], the principal female singer in an opera or concert.

pri-mal (prī′mȧl), *adj.* **1,** first; original; **2,** primary; chief.

pri-ma-ri-ly (prī′mẽr-ĭ-lĭ; prī-mâr′ĭ-lĭ), *adv.* **1,** at first; originally; **2,** principally; pre-eminently.

pri-ma-ry (prī′mẽr-ĭ; prī′mȧ-rĭ), *adj.* **1,** first in time; original; as, the *primary* meaning of a word; **2,** naming the first three grades of elementary school; **3,** basic; fundamental; as, the *primary* colors; **4,** chief; principal; as, a *primary* purpose; **5,** pertaining to the large flight feathers of a bird's wing:—*n.* [*pl.* primaries], **1,** that which is first in rank, place, or importance; **2,** in the U.S., a district meeting of the voters of a party to name candidates for a coming election; **3,** (also *primary election*), a preliminary election in which parties nominate their respective candidates; **4,** one of the large flight feathers in a bird's wing (see *bird,* illustration); **5,** one of the primary colors.

pri-mate (prī′mĭt), *n.* **1,** an honorary title given to the archbishop, or, sometimes, to the bishop, who holds first place in a district or districts; **2,** (prī'māt), a member of the highest order (*Primates*) of mammals, which includes man, monkeys, apes, etc.

¹prime (prīm), *adj.* **1,** first in time; original; **2,** chief; principal; as, a matter of *prime* importance; **3,** first in excellence or value; as, a *prime* grade of beef:—*n.* **1,** the early stage or beginning, as of a day, year, etc.; **2,** the spring of life; youth; also, the period of the greatest health, beauty, etc.; as, a man in the *prime* of life; **3,** the best one of a group or the best part of anything.

prime minister, in some countries, the chief officer of the government; **prime ·number,** a number which can be divided equally only by itself and 1, as 5 and 13.

²prime (prīm), *v.t.* [primed, prim·ing], **1,** to prepare (a gun) for firing; also, to prepare (a pump) to lift water, by pouring water into it; **2,** to cover with the first coat of paint or plaster; **3,** to instruct (a person) beforehand as to what must be said; as, the lawyer *primed* the witness. —*n.* prim'er (prī'mĕr).—*n.* prim'ing.

¹prim·er (prĭm'ẽr), *n.* **1,** a small book from which children receive their first lessons in reading; **2,** a textbook containing the first principles of any subject.

²prim·er (prĭm'ẽr), *n.* in printing, either of two sizes of book type:—**great primer,** eighteen-point type:—**long primer,** ten-point type. (See illustration under *type*.)

pri·me·val (prī-mē'văl), *adj.* pertaining to the earliest age or time; primitive; original.—*adv.* pri·me'val·ly.

prim·i·tive (prĭm'ĭ-tĭv), *adj.* **1,** belonging to the earliest ages; first; as, *primitive* man lived by hunting and fishing; **2,** characterized by the style of early times; hence, simple or crude; as, the savages used *primitive* weapons.

pri·mo·gen·i·ture (prī'-mō-jĕn'ĭ-tūr), *n.* **1,** the state of being the first-born of the children in a family; **2,** in law, the exclusive right of the first-born to inherit all his parents' property.

pri·mor·di·al (prī-môr'dĭ-ăl), *adj.* existing from the beginning; first in order; original.—*adv.* pri·mor'di·al·ly.

prim·rose (prĭm'rōz'), *n.* a plant bearing flowers which are usually pale yellow and which blossom in the early spring; also, the flower:—*adj.* pale yellow.

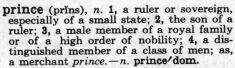

PRIMROSE

prince (prĭns), *n.* **1,** a ruler or sovereign, especially of a small state; **2,** the son of a ruler; **3,** a male member of a royal family or of a high order of nobility; **4,** a distinguished member of a class of men; as, a merchant *prince*.—*n.* prince'dom.

Prince Ed·ward Is·land, an island province in the Gulf of St. Lawrence (map 4).

prince·ly (prĭns'lĭ), *adj.* [prince-li-er, prince-li-est], **1,** pertaining to a prince; **2,** like, or worthy of, a prince.

prin·cess (prĭn'sĕs), *n.* **1,** the daughter or granddaughter of a sovereign; **2,** the wife of a prince; **3,** a female member of a royal family.

prin·ci·pal (prĭn'sĭ-păl), *adj.* highest in rank, value, or importance; main; foremost; chief; as, the *principal* reason for his failure was his lack of confidence: —*n.* **1,** a leader; the chief person in authority; **2,** the head of a school; **3,** a sum of money drawing interest; **4,** a person or group of persons for whom an agent acts. —*adv.* prin'ci·pal·ly.

prin·ci·pal·i·ty (prĭn'sĭ-păl'ĭ-tĭ), *n.* [*pl.* principalities], the territory of a prince or the country from which he obtains his title.

prin·ci·ple (prĭn'sĭ-pl), *n.* **1,** a truth or law on which other truths, laws, etc., are based; as, *principles* of government; **2,** a settled rule of action; as, *principles* of conduct; **3,** honesty; uprightness; as, a man of *principle;* **4,** a natural law; especially, one which is utilized in the construction and operation of a machine; as, an automobile engine works on the *principle* of the expanding power of gases.

Syn. motive, impulse, maxim.

prink (prĭngk), *v.t.* and *v.i.* to dress up in a showy fashion.

print (prĭnt), *n.* **1,** a mark or character made by pressure; as, a foot*print;* **2,** a stamp or die for making an impression; also, that which has received the impression; **3,** letters produced from type; as, the child's book was in large *print;* **4,** the state of being in published form; as, the story has just got into *print;* **5,** anything produced by type or from an engraved plate, as a newspaper, engraving, etc.; **6,** cloth decorated with a printed design:—*v.t.* **1,** to make an impression on; as, their feet *print* the sand; **2,** to fix or stamp in or on something; as, to *print* footsteps in the sand; **3,** to reproduce from type, engraved plates, etc., as books, pictures, newspapers, etc.; **4,** to make in letters, like those of type; as, a child *prints* a letter; **5,** in photography, to produce (a picture) from a negative:—*v.i.* to make letters like those used in type; as, the child *prints* well.

āte, âorta, râre, căt, ȧsk, fär, ăllow, sofȧ; ēve, ĕvent, ĕll, writẽr, novĕl; bīte, pĭn; nō, ōbey, ôr, dŏg, tŏp, cŏllide; ūnit, ūnite, bûrn, cŭt, focŭs; no͞on, fo͝ot; mound; coin;

print·er (prĭn′tẽr), *n.* one whose trade is the setting of type or the making of impressions from type.

print·ing (prĭnt′ĭng), *n.* the setting of reading matter in type, or the making of printed books, magazines, etc.

printing press, a machine for printing on paper, wood, etc., impressions from the inked surface of type, plates, or the like.

pri·or (prī′ẽr), *adj.* going before in time, order, or importance; previous:—*n.* the head of a monastery; also, in an abbey, the religious officer next below an abbot. —*n. fem.* **pri′or·ess.**

pri·or·i·ty (prī-ŏr′ĭ-tĭ), *n.* the state of being first in rank, time, or place.

pri·o·ry (prī′ō-rĭ), *n.* [*pl.* priories], a house of a religious order ruled by a prior or prioress.

prism (prĭzm), *n.* 1, a solid object with ends that are parallel and exactly the same in size and shape, and sides  PRISMS that are parallelograms; 2, such a solid, usually three-sided, made of glass or a similar substance, which breaks up a ray of sunlight into the colors of the rainbow.

pris·mat·ic (prĭz-măt′ĭk), *adj.* 1, like, or pertaining to, a prism; 2, formed by a prism:—**prismatic colors,** the seven colors of the rainbow.

pris·on (prĭz′n), *n.* a place of confinement or detention for criminals; a jail.

pris·on·er (prĭz′n-ẽr; prĭz′nẽr), *n.* anyone held against his will, as a person under arrest, in jail, or captured in war.

pris·tine (prĭs′tēn; prĭs′tĭn; prĭs′tīn), *adj.* belonging to the far past; ancient; primitive; as, *pristine* simplicity.

prith·ee (prĭth′ē), *interj. Archaic,* please.

pri·va·cy (prī′vȧ-sĭ), *n.* [*pl.* privacies], 1, the state of being away from public view; seclusion; retirement; 2, secrecy; as, to plot a scheme in *privacy.*

pri·vate (prī′vĭt), *adj.* 1, concerning or belonging to oneself alone; personal; not public; as, one's *private* affairs; 2, away from public view or knowledge; secret; as, he obtained *private* information; 3, not holding a public position; as, a *private* citizen:—*n.* a common soldier.

pri·va·teer (prī′vȧ-tēr′), *n.* 1, an armed ship, privately owned, but permitted by the government to attack the enemy's ships; 2, the commander or one of the crew of such a ship:—*v.i.* to sail in, or as, a privateer.

pri·vate·ly (prī′vĭt-lĭ), *adv.* secretly; not in public.

pri·va·tion (prī-vā′shŭn), *n.* need; hardship; want of the usual comforts of life.

priv·et (prĭv′ĕt) *n.* a shrub with dark-green leaves and small white flowers, much used for hedges.

priv·i·lege (prĭv′ĭ-lĭj), *n.* a special favor or right granted to a person or body of persons:—*v.t.* [privileged, privileg-ing], to give some particular right to; as, employees are *privileged* to buy at a discount.

Syn., n. exemption, immunity, benefit.

priv·y (prĭv′ĭ), *adj.* 1, for private, not public, use; personal; as, the *privy* purse; 2, secretly informed; as, to be *privy* to a plot:—*n.* [*pl.* privies], an out-of-door toilet. —*adv.* **priv′i·ly.**

prize (prīz), *n.* 1, a reward offered or won in a contest; 2, anything of value; 3, that which is taken from an enemy in war; especially, a captured vessel:—*adj.* 1, given a prize; as, a *prize* painting; 2, worthy to be given a prize; as, a *prize* pupil; 3, given as a prize; as, he won the *prize* box of candy:—*v.t.* [prized, priz-ing], to value or esteem highly; as, to *prize* a gift.

pro (prō), *adv.* on the affirmative side; as, they argued *pro* and con.

pro- (prō-), a prefix meaning: 1, in front of; as, *pro*tection; 2, forward; to the front; as, *pro*ceed; 3, in behalf of; favoring; as, *pro*war; 4, instead of; as, *pro*noun; 5, according to; as, *pro*portion.

prob·a·bil·i·ty (prŏb′ȧ-bĭl′ĭ-tĭ), *n.* [*pl.* probabilities], 1, the quality or state of being likely; 2, something likely to happen; 3, chance; as, the *probabilities* at present are against war.

prob·a·ble (prŏb′ȧ-bl), *adj.* 1, likely; expected; as, it is *probable* that we shall all go; 2, giving grounds for belief; having the appearance of truth; as, a *probable* explanation.—*adv.* **prob′a·bly.**

pro·bate (prō′bāt), *n.* official legal proof; especially, proof that a will is genuine:—*v.t.* [probat-ed, probat-ing], to prove the genuineness of (a will).

pro·ba·tion (prō-bā′shŭn), *n.* 1, a trial or test of a person's character, ability, etc.; also, the period of trial; 2, a system of permitting young offenders against the law to go free, though under police supervision.

pro·ba·tion·er (prō-bā′shŭn-ẽr), *n.* one who is undergoing a test or trial, as a nurse in the first period of her training.

probe (prōb), *n.* 1, a slender surgical instrument for examining a wound, cavity, etc.; 2, a searching inquiry:—*v.t.* [probed, prob-ing], 1, to examine with a probe, or slender instrument; **2,** to inquire into closely.

prob·i·ty (prŏb'ĭ-tĭ; prō'bĭ-tĭ), *n.* uprightness; honesty.

Syn. rectitude, integrity, soundness.

prob·lem (prŏb'lĕm; prŏb'lĕm), *n.* **1,** a question hard to understand; a matter hard to solve or settle; **2,** in mathematics, something that is to be worked out or solved.

prob·lem·at·i·cal (prŏb'lĕm-ăt'ĭ-kăl), *adj.* questionable; doubtful; difficult to decide or solve. Also, **prob'lem·at'ic.**

pro·bos·cis (prō-bŏs'ĭs), *n.* [*pl.* proboscises or proboscides (prō-bŏs'ĭ-dēz)], **1,** the trunk of an elephant; **2,** the long flexible snout of certain other animals, as the tapir; **3,** the elongated mouth parts of certain insects.

pro·ce·dure (prō-sē'dŭr), *n.* **1,** a course of action; a proceeding; as, his *procedure* in the hearing was fair; **2,** a system of proceeding; manner of conducting a business transaction, a lawsuit, etc.; **3,** the established manner of conducting a meeting.

pro·ceed (prō-sēd'), *v.i.* **1,** to go on or forward; advance; continue acting, speaking, etc.; as, to *proceed* on a journey; *proceed* with your speech; **2,** to issue; result; as, the tides *proceed* from the attraction of the sun and moon; **3,** to carry on a series of actions in a systematic manner.

pro·ceed·ing (prō-sē'dĭng), *n.* **1,** a transaction, as in business; **2,** a course of conduct; **3, proceedings,** the record of the business accomplished at a meeting of a society, board of directors, or the like.

pro·ceeds (prō'sēdz), *n.pl.* results from a transaction; especially, the amount of money realized from a sale.

proc·ess (prŏs'ĕs; prō'sĕs), *n.* **1,** progress; course; as, the house is in *process* of construction; **2,** a continuous action or series of actions which lead to the accomplishment of a result; as, getting an education is a long *process;* **3,** in industry, especially manufacturing, a method of operation or treatment which brings about a certain result; as, the Bessemer *process* of making steel; **4,** an official written summons to appear in court; **5,** an outgrowth or projecting part, especially on a bone:—*v.t.* to subject to a special treatment or process; as, to *process* leather.

pro·ces·sion (prō-sĕsh'ŭn), *n.* **1,** the act of going on or forward; **2,** a formal parade; as, a religious *procession.*

pro·ces·sion·al (prō-sĕsh'ŭn-ăl), *adj.* pertaining to a procession:—*n.* **1,** a hymn sung at the beginning of a church service; **2,** organ music suitable for a procession.

pro·claim (prō-klām'), *v.t.* to make known publicly; declare; publish abroad.

Syn. announce, publish, broadcast.

proc·la·ma·tion (prŏk'lȧ-mā'shŭn), *n.* **1,** the act of announcing publicly; **2,** that which is announced; a formal announcement.

pro·con·sul (prō-kŏn'sŭl), *n.* a Roman official who performed the duties of a consul, or chief magistrate, outside of Rome, especially as governor of a province.

pro·cras·ti·nate (prō-krăs'tĭ-nāt), *v.i.* [procrastinat-ed, procrastinat-ing], to delay; put off action from day to day.—*n.* **pro·cras'ti·na'tion.**

Syn. retard, postpone, defer.

proc·tor (prŏk'tẽr), *n.* an officer who maintains order in a school or university.

pro·cur·a·ble (prō-kūr'ȧ-bl), *adj.* capable of being obtained.

proc·u·ra·tor (prŏk'ū-rā'tẽr), *n.* **1,** one who acts for another in legal matters; an agent; **2,** in Roman times, an officer who collected taxes and attended to various other duties in a province of the empire.

pro·cure (prō-kūr'), *v.t.* [procured, procur-ing], **1,** to get; obtain; **2,** to cause or bring about; as, she *procured* his arrest.

Syn. acquire, gain, earn, attain, win.

prod (prŏd), *n.* **1,** a pointed implement for pricking, as a goad or pointed stick; **2,** a prick; hence, a poke or dig:—*v.t.* [prodded, prod-ding], **1,** to punch or poke with a pointed instrument; **2,** hence, to goad or urge.

prod·i·gal (prŏd'ĭ-găl), *adj.* reckless with money; lavish; wasteful:—*n.* a spendthrift.—*adv.* **prod'i·gal·ly.**

prod·i·gal·i·ty (prŏd'ĭ-găl'ĭ-tĭ), *n.* [*pl.* prodigalities], reckless extravagance.

pro·di·gious (prō-dĭj'ŭs), *adj.* **1,** unusually great in size, quantity, or the like; vast; enormous; **2,** marvelous; amazing.

Syn. extraordinary, astonishing.

prod·i·gy (prŏd'ĭ-jĭ), *n.* [*pl.* prodigies], **1,** anything both unusual and unnatural; as, comets were once thought of as *prodigies;* **2,** anything causing wonder; a marvel; as, a *prodigy* of learning; **3,** a person, especially a child, unusually gifted or precocious.

¹pro·duce (prō-dūs'), *v.t.* [produced, produc-ing], **1,** to exhibit or bring to view; as, he *produced* the papers from the safe; **2,** to yield or bring forth; as, trees *produce* fruit; **3,** to manufacture; **4,** to lead to; as, wealth *produces* comfort; **5,** to present upon the stage, as a play.

²prod·uce (prŏd'ūs), *n.* that which is brought forth or yielded; especially, the products of farm and garden.

āte, âorta, râre, căt, ȧsk, fär, ăllow, sofȧ; ēve, êvent, ĕll, wrĭtẽr, novĕl; bīte, pĭn; nō, ōbey, ôr, dŏg, tŏp, cŏllide; ūnit, ūnite, bûrn, cŭt, focŭs; nōōn, fŏŏt; mound; coin;

pro-duc-er (prō-dū'sẽr), *n.* 1, one who manufactures goods or raises crops; 2, one who presents plays.

prod-uct (prŏd'ŭkt; prŏd'ŭkt), *n.* 1, that which is yielded by nature, or made by labor, thought, manufacture, etc.; as, farm or factory *products;* poetry is a *product* of the imagination; 2, in arithmetic, the result obtained by multiplying two or more numbers together; as, the *product* of 1, 3, and 5, is 15.

pro-duc-tion (prō-dŭk'shŭn), *n.* 1, that which is yielded by nature or made by labor, thought, etc.; 2, a performance on the stage; 3, the act of producing.

pro-duc-tive (prō-dŭk'tĭv), *adj.* 1, having the power to create something; creative; 2, creating in abundance; fertile; as, *productive* soil; 3, causing to exist; as, experience is *productive* of wisdom; 4, making or yielding something of value; as, *productive* labor.—*n.* pro'duc-tiv'i-ty.

pro-em (prō'ĕm), *n.* a preface; foreword.

prof. abbreviation for *professor.*

prof-a-na-tion (prŏf'a-nā'shŭn), *n.* the treatment of sacred things in an irreverent way; also, the abuse of anything that should be held in reverence or respect.

pro-fane (prō-fān'), *adj.* 1, not sacred or holy; hence, having to do with this world only; as, *profane* history; 2, showing disrespect or irreverence toward God or sacred things; as, *profane* language:—*v.t.* [profaned, profan-ing], 1, to treat (something sacred) with irreverence, contempt, or abuse; 2, to put to an improper or ignoble use.—*adv.* pro-fane'ly.

pro-fan-i-ty (prō-făn'ĭ-tĭ), *n.* [*pl.* profanities], irreverent conduct or speech.

pro-fess (prō-fĕs'), *v.t.* 1, to make a public statement of (one's belief, intentions, etc.); as, to *profess* allegiance to the flag; 2, to pretend; claim; as, to *profess* friendship; he *professed* to have expert knowledge.

pro-fes-sion (prō-fĕsh'ŭn), *n.* 1, the act of declaring; declaration; as, a *profession* of friendship; 2, a calling or vocation, especially one that requires special education; as, the *professions* of medicine and law; 3, all the persons engaged in any one calling of this kind.

pro-fes-sion-al (prō-fĕsh'ŭn-ăl), *adj.* 1, pertaining to or associated with a profession; as, *professional* duties; 2, pertaining to sport engaged in for profit or pay, or to the act or practice of engaging in a sport for pay; as, a *professional* boxer; *professional* golf:—*n.* one who engages in a sport or other pleasurable pursuit for gain: opposite of *amateur.*—*adv.* pro-fes'sion-al-ly.—*n.* pro-fes'sion-al-ism.

pro-fes-sor (prō-fĕs'ẽr), *n.* 1, a teacher of the highest rank in a college or university; 2, loosely, a teacher; 3, one who makes an open declaration of his opinions, especially concerning religion.—*adj.* pro'-fes-sor'i-al (prō'fĕ-sôr'ĭ-ăl; prŏf'ĕ-sôr'ĭ-ăl).

pro-fes-sor-ship (prō-fĕs'ẽr-shĭp), *n.* the office or position of a teacher of highest rank in a college or university.

prof-fer (prŏf'ẽr), *v.t.* to offer for acceptance; as, to *proffer* help:—*n.* an offer.

pro-fi-cien-cy (prō-fĭsh'ĕn-sĭ), *n.* knowledge, skill, or expertness.

pro-fi-cient (prō-fĭsh'ĕnt), *adj.* thoroughly skilled; expert; as, *proficient* in drawing:—*n.* an expert.—*adv.* pro-fi'cient-ly.

pro-file (prō'fīl; prō'fēl), *n.* 1, outline or contour; as, the *profile* of a mountain; 2, a side view of a human face, or a drawing, photograph, or the like, made from it.

PROFILE
def. 2

prof-it (prŏf'ĭt), *n.* 1, gain in money; the amount by which income exceeds expenses in a given time: opposite of *loss;* 2, profits, the gain, as from the operation of a business, after all expenses, charges, etc., have been met; 3, benefit or advantage:—*v.i.* and *v.t.* to benefit; as, to *profit* from a transaction; the transaction *profited* him.—*adj.* prof'it-less.

prof-it-a-ble (prŏf'ĭt-a-bl), *adj.* yielding gain or benefit; useful; paying; as, a *profitable* business.—*adv.* prof'it-a-bly.

prof-it-eer (prŏf'ĭ-tēr'), *n.* one who makes undue or unjust profits, as during a period of scarcity:—*v.i.* to make, or try to make, undue profits.—*n.* prof'it-eer'ing.

prof-li-gate (prŏf'lĭ-gāt), *adj.* 1, given up to vice; dissolute; 2, recklessly extravagant:—*n.* a vicious or immoral person.—*n.* prof'li-ga-cy (prŏf'lĭ-ga-sĭ).

Syn., adj. abandoned, depraved, corrupt.

pro-found (prō-found'), *adj.* 1, deep, as to space; as, the *profound* depths of ocean; 2, deep, as to mental state; thorough; as, *profound* thought; *profound* learning; 3, deep, as to feeling; intense; as, *profound* sorrow; 4, of a bow, low, as indicating humility; 5, coming from the depths; as, a *profound* sigh.—*adv.* pro-found'ly.—*n.* pro-found'ness.

Syn. fathomless, penetrating, solemn.

pro-fun-di-ty (prō-fŭn'dĭ-tĭ), *n.* [*pl.* profundities], 1, deepness; depth; 2, depth of thought, knowledge, feeling, or the like; 3, that which is deep in any sense.

pro-fuse (prō-fūs'), *adj.* 1, pouring forth freely; giving or given with great generosity; as, *profuse* kindness; 2, produced or

go; join; yet; sing; chin; show; thin, *th*en; hw, *wh*y; zh, a*z*ure; ü, Ger. für or Fr. lune; ö, Ger. schön or Fr. feu; ṅ, Fr. enfant, nom; kh, Ger. ach or ich. See pages ix–x.

shown in great abundance; as, *profuse* foliage.—*adv.* **pro-fuse′ly.**—*n.* **pro-fuse′ness.**
Syn. prodigal, copious, bountiful, liberal, lavish.

pro-fu-sion (prō-fū′zhŭn), *n.* **1,** abundance; as, a *profusion* of flowers; **2,** lavishness; as, the *profusion* of nature.

pro-gen-i-tor (prō-jĕn′ĭ-tẽr), *n.* an ancestor; forefather.

prog-e-ny (prŏj′ĕ-nĭ), *n.* offspring; children; descendants or a descendant.

prog-nos-ti-cate (prŏg-nŏs′tĭ-kāt), *v.t.* [prognosticat-ed, prognosticat-ing], to foretell (an event); predict.—*n.* **prog-nos′ti-ca⁄tor.**

prog-nos-ti-ca-tion (prŏg-nŏs′tĭ-kā′shŭn), *n.* **1,** the act of foretelling what is to come to pass; **2,** a forecast or prediction.

pro-gram or **pro-gramme** (prō′grăm), *n.* **1,** a brief outline giving in order the features that make up a public entertainment, ceremony, etc.; as, a concert *program*; **2,** the features that make up such an entertainment; **3,** a clearly defined plan of action in any undertaking.

¹**prog-ress** (prŏg′rĕs; prō′grĕs), *n.* **1,** a moving forward; as, the *progress* of a boat; hence, advancement or improvement; as, the patient made slow *progress* to recovery; **2,** growth or development; as, the *progress* of a campaign.

²**pro-gress** (prō-grĕs′), *v.i.* **1,** to move forward; as, time *progresses;* **2,** to grow; improve; develop; as, science *progresses.*

pro-gres-sion (prō-grĕsh′ŭn), *n.* the act or method of advancing.
  arithmetical progression, a series of numbers in which each number differs from the one that follows it by the same amount; as, 3, 6, 9, 12, 15, are in *arithmetical progression;* **geometric progression,** a series of numbers in which each number is multiplied by the same figure to produce the one that follows; as, 3, 9, 27, 81, are in *geometric progression.*

pro-gres-sive (prō-grĕs′ĭv), *adj.* **1,** moving forward step by step; as, *progressive* improvement; **2,** ready to accept new ideas or to introduce changes for the sake of improvement; as, a *progressive* schoolteacher; **3,** in grammar, designating a form (of a verb) that expresses an action as going on; as, I *am thinking;* in December he *was working.*—*n.* one who believes in, and works for, changes and reforms, especially in political matters.—*adv.* **pro-gres′sive-ly.** —*n.* **pro-gres′sive-ness.**

pro-hib-it (prō-hĭb′ĭt), *v.t.* **1,** to forbid by law; as, to *prohibit* the sale of liquor; **2,** to hinder; prevent.

pro-hi-bi-tion (prō′ĭ-bĭsh′ŭn; prō′hĭ-bĭsh′ŭn), *n.* **1,** the act of forbidding; especially, the forbidding by law of the manufacture and sale of intoxicating drinks; **2,** a law or injunction forbidding something.—*n.* **pro′hi-bi′tion-ist.**

pro-hib-i-tive (prō-hĭb′ĭ-tĭv), *adj.* tending to forbid, prevent, or hinder; as, *prohibitive* prices keep us from buying.—*adj.* **pro-hib′i-tor-y.**

¹**pro-ject** (prō-jĕkt′), *v.t.* **1,** to throw or shoot forward; **2,** to cause (a beam of light, a shadow, or the like) to fall on a surface; as, to *project* a picture on a screen; **3,** to plan (something to be done, a course of action, etc.):—*v.i.* to jut out; extend forward; as, a bay window *projects.*

²**proj-ect** (prŏj′ĕkt), *n.* **1,** a design; scheme; plan; **2,** in school, a problem or lesson intended to make pupils rely on their own effort and natural ability.

pro-jec-tile (prō-jĕk′tĭl), *n.* something thrown or shot forward; especially, a ball, shell, torpedo, or the like, intended to be shot from a cannon.

pro-jec-tion (prō-jĕk′shŭn), *n.* **1,** the act or state of extending or jutting out; **2,** something that juts out.

pro-jec-tor (prō-jĕk′tẽr), *n.* **1,** one who makes schemes or plans; **2,** an optical instrument for throwing a picture upon a screen by means of a system of lenses.

pro-le-tar-i-an (prō′lē-târ′ĭ-ăn), *n.* a person of the wage-earning class:—*adj.* pertaining to the wage-earning class of society.

pro-le-tar-i-at (prō′lē-târ′ĭ-ăt), *n.* the wage-earning class of society.

pro-lif-ic (prō-lĭf′ĭk), *adj.* **1,** producing young or fruit abundantly; fertile; as, a *prolific* vine; **2,** producing ideas or results abundantly; as, a *prolific* writer.

pro-lix (prō-lĭks′; prō′lĭks), *adj.* long drawn out; tedious; wordy; as, a *prolix* speech.
Syn. long, prolonged, tiresome, prosaic.

pro-lix-i-ty (prō-lĭk′sĭ-tĭ), *n.* [*pl.* prolixities], tediousness; wordiness.

pro-log or **pro-logue** (prō′lŏg), *n.* **1,** an introduction or preface to a poem, drama, or the like; especially, verses spoken or sung by an actor before the performance of a play or an opera; **2,** the actor by whom these verses are delivered.

pro-long (prō-lông′), *v.t.* to lengthen in time or space; draw out; extend; as, to *prolong* a conversation; to *prolong* a line.

pro-lon-ga-tion (prō′lông-gā′shŭn), *n.* **1,** a lengthening in time or space; **2,** the part added by lengthening.

prom-e-nade (prŏm′ĕ-näd′; prŏm′ĕ-nād′),

n. 1, a walk for pleasure or exercise; 2, a place for walking; 3, a ball or dance:—*v.i.* [promenad-ed, promenad-ing], to walk for pleasure.

Pro-me-theus (prŏ-mē′thūs; prŏ-mē′thē-ŭs), *n.* in Greek mythology, a Titan who stole fire from heaven for men, and who, as a punishment, passed many years chained to Mount Caucasus.—*adj.* **Pro-me′the-an.**

prom-i-nence (prŏm′ĭ-nĕns), *n.* 1, the state or quality of jutting out or projecting; 2, the quality of being distinguished or noticeable.

prom-i-nent (prŏm′ĭ-nĕnt), *adj.* 1, standing or jutting out; projecting; 2, conspicuous; noticeable; as, a *prominent* shop-window; 3, distinguished; as, a *prominent* diplomat.

Syn. eminent, marked, important.

pro-mis-cu-ous (prŏ-mĭs′kū-ŭs), *adj.* 1, confused; mixed; made up of many different elements jumbled together; as, a *promiscuous* assembly; 2, not limited to any particular person or class; not discriminating; as, *promiscuous* hospitality. —*n.* **prom′is-cu′i-ty** (prŏm′ĭs-kū′ĭ-tĭ; prō′mĭs-kū′ĭ-tĭ).

Syn. indiscriminate, haphazard.

prom-ise (prŏm′ĭs), *n.* 1, a pledge that one will or will not do something; 2, a cause or ground for hope or expectation; as, a *promise* of fair weather:—*v.i.* [promised, promis-ing], 1, to pledge or engage to do or not to do something; 2, to give reason for hope or expectation; as, the garden *promises* well:—*v.t.* 1, to pledge or engage (to do or not to do); as, he *promised* to go; 2, to agree to give to, or get for, someone; as, he *promised* her a position; 3, to give reason to expect (something); as, the day *promised* rain.—*n.* **prom′is-er.**

Promised Land, in the Bible, the land promised to the Israelites by God; Canaan; hence, any place of promised happiness.

prom-is-ing (prŏm′ĭs-ĭng), *adj.* likely to be successful; as, a *promising* youth; *promising* plans.—*adv.* **prom′is-ing-ly.**

prom-is-sor-y (prŏm′ĭ-sôr′ĭ), *adj.* containing an agreement to do or not to do something:—**promissory note,** a written agreement to pay a certain sum of money on demand or at a fixed date.

prom-on-tor-y (prŏm′ŭn-tôr′ĭ), *n.* [*pl.* promontories], a high point of land extending into a body of water; a headland.

pro-mote (prŏ-mōt′), *v.t.* [promot-ed, promot-ing], 1, to raise to a higher rank or class; as, the teacher *promoted* Mary to the sixth grade; 2, to set on foot or organize (a business venture); 3, to help the growth or development of; as, to *promote* interest in outdoor sports.

pro-mot-er (prŏ-mō′tĕr), *n.* one who encourages or forwards an undertaking; especially, one whose business it is to start new companies, encourage sales, etc.

pro-mo-tion (prŏ-mō′shŭn), *n.* 1, advancement to a better position or higher class or rank, in school, business, etc.; 2, the furthering of any cause or purpose; as, the *promotion* of learning.

prompt (prŏmpt), *adj.* 1, ready and quick to act; as, *prompt* to forgive; 2, done or given without delay; as, *prompt* service; 3, on time; not tardy; as, you must learn to be *prompt*:—*v.t.* 1, to rouse to action; incite; 2, to suggest; inspire; as, generosity *prompted* the gift; 3, to remind or help (a speaker at a loss for words).—*n.* **prompt′er.**

Syn., adj. alert, ready, punctual.

promp-ti-tude (prŏmp′tĭ-tūd), *n.* quickness of decision and action; readiness.

pro-mul-gate (prŏ-mŭl′gāt; prŏm′ŭl-gāt), *v.t.* [promulgat-ed, promulgat-ing], to make known formally and officially; proclaim; as, to *promulgate* a law.—*n.* **pro′mul-ga′-tion** (prō′mŭl-gā′shŭn; prŏm′ŭl-gā′shŭn).

pron. abbreviation for *pronoun.*

prone (prōn), *adj.* 1, naturally disposed or inclined; as, she is *prone* to forget; 2, lying face downward.

prong (prŏng), *n.* one of the pointed ends of a fork; also, any sharp point or sharp-pointed instrument.

prong-horn (prŏng′hôrn′), *n.* a cud-chewing animal resembling an antelope, found on the western plains of North America.

PRONGHORN (1⁄30)

pro-nom-i-nal (prŏ-nŏm′ĭ-năl), *adj.* pertaining to, or like, a pronoun, or word standing for a noun:—**pronominal adjective,** a word which may modify a noun, or which may be used alone as a pronoun, as "this" and "that" in the sentence *this* dog barked at *that.*

pro-noun (prō′noun), *n.* a word which refers to, or is used in the place of, a noun or name, as, "this," "which," "he," "who," etc.

pro-nounce (prŏ-nouns′), *v.t.* [pronounced, pronounc-ing], 1, to utter the sounds of; as, to *pronounce* a name; 2, to declare; as, they *pronounced* him a failure; 3, to speak or utter with formal solemnity; as, to *pronounce* a benediction:—*v.i.* 1, to utter words, especially with care and precision; enunciate; 2, to speak with confidence or authority.—*adj.* **pro-nounce′a-ble.**

---

go; join; yet; sing; chin; show; thin, *th*en; hw, *why*; zh, azure; ü, Ger. für or Fr. lune; ö, Ger. schön or Fr. feu; n̄, Fr. enfant, nom; kh, Ger. ach or ich. See pages ix–x.

pro-nounced (prō-nounst′), *adj.* strongly marked; decided; as, a *pronounced* change in the weather.

pro-nounce-ment (prō-nouns′mĕnt), *n.* a formal or public announcement.

pro-nun-ci-a-tion (prō-nŭn′sĭ-ā′shŭn; prō-nŭn′shĭ-ā′shŭn), *n.* the act or manner of uttering the sounds which form words.

proof (prōof), *n.* **1,** the means by which something is shown to be true or correct; **2,** convincing evidence; as, *proof* of guilt; **3,** a test or trial; as, "the *proof* of the pudding is in the eating"; **4,** in photography, a trial print from a negative; **5,** in printing, an impression taken from type for correction:—*adj.* **1,** used in proving or testing; **2,** of a standard strength or purity; as, *proof* whisky; **3,** capable of resisting; as, *proof* against infection.
Syn., n. evidence, experiment.

-proof (-prōof), a suffix meaning: **1,** not penetrable by; as, water*proof,* bullet*proof;* **2,** not admitting; as, dust*proof,* light*proof;* **3,** not subject to the action of; able to resist; as, rust*proof,* moth*proof;* **4,** incapable of being; as, shatter*proof.*

proof-read (prōof′rēd′), *v.t.* [proofread (prōof′rĕd′), proofread-ing], to read and correct (printer's proof).—*n.* **proof′read′er.**

prop (prŏp), *v.t.* [propped, prop-ping], **1,** to support by placing something under or against; as, to *prop* up a book; **2,** to sustain; support; as, to *prop* up a friend's courage: —*n.* a support or stay.

prop-a-gan-da (prŏp′a-găn′da), *n.* **1,** any organization or scheme for spreading special opinions or beliefs; **2,** the opinions or beliefs thus spread.—*n.* **prop′a-gan′dist.**

prop-a-gate (prŏp′a-gāt), *v.t.* [propagated, propagat-ing], **1,** to cause to increase or multiply by natural reproduction; as, to *propagate* plants; **2,** to spread from person to person; as, to *propagate* news.— *n.* **prop′a-ga′tor.**—*n.* **prop′a-ga′tion.**
Syn. circulate, increase, scatter.

pro-pel (prō-pĕl′), *v.t.* [propelled, propelling], to push or urge forward; drive onward; as, to *propel* ships by steam.

pro-pel-ler (prō-pĕl′ẽr), *n.* one who or that which drives forward; especially, a device, usually a revolving shaft with blades, for causing an airplane or a ship to move forward.

PROPELLERS
1, three-bladed propeller for a boat; 2, 3, two-bladed and four-bladed propellers for aircraft.

pro-pen-si-ty (prō-pĕn′sĭ-tĭ), *n.* [*pl.* propensities], natural inclination or tendency; as, a *propensity* to exaggerate.

prop-er (prŏp′ẽr), *adj.* **1,** suitable; fitting; appropriate; as, *proper* clothes for wet weather; **2,** belonging naturally to some person or thing; characteristic; as, trees *proper* to a region; **3,** according to accepted usage; correct; conventional; respectable; as, *proper* table manners; **4,** in a narrow or restricted sense; as, the spider is not an insect *proper.*
   proper fraction, a fraction of which the numerator is less than the denominator; **proper noun,** a noun which names one individual as distinct from other individuals of the same class, as "Troy," "James." —*adv.* **prop′er-ly.**

prop-er-ty (prŏp′ẽr-tĭ), *n.* [*pl.* properties], **1,** any quality or attribute that belongs to a thing, or one that especially marks it; as, sourness is a *property* of vinegar; **2,** ownership; as, the duties and rights of *property;* **3,** the thing owned; possessions, namely real estate, movable goods, etc.; **4, properties,** all the stage furnishings and articles required by actors in performing a play, except stage scenery and the costumes of the actors.

proph-e-cy (prŏf′ē-sĭ), *n.* [*pl.* prophecies], a foretelling or prediction of future events, especially one made under divine influence.

proph-e-sy (prŏf′ē-sī), *v.t.* [prophesied, prophesy-ing], to foretell, especially under divine influence.

proph-et (prŏf′ĕt), *n.* **1,** in the Bible, one inspired by God to teach His will to men and to announce future events; **2,** one who foretells the future:—**the Prophet,** Mohammed.—*n.fem.* **proph′et-ess.**

proph-et-ic (prō-fĕt′ĭk), *adj.* **1,** pertaining to the foretelling of future events, or to one who foretells; as, the *prophetic* gift; **2,** containing a prophecy; as, a *prophetic* vision.

pro-phy-lac-tic (prō′fĭ-lăk′tĭk; prŏf′ĭ-lăk′tĭk), *adj.* tending to ward off, or protect against, disease; as, a *prophylactic* treatment:—*n.* anything that prevents, or helps to prevent, disease.

pro-pin-qui-ty (prō-pĭng′kwĭ-tĭ), *n.* nearness in time, place, or blood relationship; proximity.

pro-pi-ti-ate (prō-pĭsh′ĭ-āt), *v.t.* [propitiat-ed, propitiat-ing], to win over (one who is offended or angry); conciliate.—*n.* **pro-pi′ti-a′tion.**—*adj.* **pro-pi′ti-a-tor′y.**

pro-pi-tious (prō-pĭsh′ŭs), *adj.* **1,** favorably inclined; gracious; **2,** favorable; suitable; as, *propitious* weather.
Syn. auspicious, fortunate.

pro-por-tion (prō-pôr′shŭn), *n.* **1,** the relation between the size, amount, or degree of one thing and the size, amount, or degree of another; ratio; as, the *proportion* of weekdays to Sundays is six to one; **2,** proper or just share; as, what is my *proportion* of the profits? **3,** in mathematics, a statement of equality between two ratios; as, 4 : 8 = 6 : 12 is a *proportion;* **4, proportions,** dimensions; size; as, the *proportions* of a rug:—*v.t.* to cause (one thing) to be in suitable relation to another; as, to *proportion* one's expenses to one's income; also, to give suitable dimensions to; as, this room is beautifully *proportioned.*

pro-por-tion-al (prō-pôr′shŭn-ăl), *adj.* corresponding in amount or degree; in proportion; as, *proportional* representation: —*n.* in mathematics, one of the terms of a proportion.—*adv.* **pro-por′tion-al-ly.**

pro-por-tion-ate (prō-pôr′shŭn-ĭt), *adj.* in reasonable relation or proportion; commensurate; as, success *proportionate* to effort; profits *proportionate* to investment.

pro-pos-al (prō-pō′zăl), *n.* **1,** the act of offering something for acceptance; **2,** a plan; proposition; as, a business *proposal;* **3,** an offer of marriage.

pro-pose (prō-pōz′), *v.t.* [proposed, proposing], **1,** to put forward for consideration; suggest; as, he *proposed* that I should go; I *proposed* a later date; **2,** to suggest the name of, for an office; nominate:—*v.i.* **1,** to make an offer of marriage; **2,** to form a plan; make known a plan; hence, to intend; purpose; as, I *propose* to stay at home.—*n.* **pro-pos′er.**

prop-o-si-tion (prŏp′ō-zĭsh′ŭn), *n.* **1,** that which is offered for consideration; a proposal; **2,** the formal statement of a topic to be discussed; **3,** in mathematics, the statement of a theorem or problem for solution.

pro-pound (prō-pound′), *v.t.* to offer for discussion or debate; to set forth, as a question, problem, or the like.

pro-pri-e-tar-y (prō-prī′ĕ-tĕr′ĭ), *n.* [*pl.* proprietaries], **1,** an owner or group of owners; **2,** an individual or group to whom a colony was granted in America by the king of England:—*adj.* **1,** associated with an individual owner, or proprietary; as, *proprietary* government; **2,** made and marketed by owners who have the exclusive right to make and sell; as, *proprietary* foods.

pro-pri-e-tor (prō-prī′ĕ-tĕr), *n.* one who has a legal title to property; an owner; as, the *proprietor* of a farm.—*n.fem.* **pro-pri′e-tress.**—*n.* **pro-pri′e-tor-ship′.**

pro-pri-e-ty (prō-prī′ĕ-tĭ), *n.* [*pl.* proprieties], **1,** fitness or suitability; espe-

cially, correctness of manners or conduct; **2, proprieties,** the manners expected in polite society.

pro-pul-sion (prō-pŭl′shŭn), *n.* **1,** the act or process of driving forward; **2,** a force or power that drives or urges forward.

pro ra-ta (prō rā′tȧ; rä′tȧ), in proportion; proportionate(ly).

pro-rogue (prō-rōg′), *v.t.* [prorogued, pro-ro-guing], to discontinue (a session of parliament) for an indefinite time by royal command.

pro-sa-ic (prō-zā′ĭk), *adj.* commonplace; unimaginative; as, a *prosaic* person; dull; as, a *prosaic* speech.

pro-scribe (prō-skrīb′), *v.t.* [proscribed, proscrib-ing], **1,** to put (a person) outside the protection of the law; outlaw; banish; **2,** to condemn; prohibit; as, free speech is still *proscribed* in some quarters of the world.—*n.* **pro-scrib′er.**

pro-scrip-tion (prō-skrĭp′shŭn), *n.* the act of outlawing; also, the condition of being outlawed.

prose (prōz), *n.* ordinary spoken or written language without the meter or rhythm of poetry: distinguished from *verse:*—*v.i.* [prosed, pros-ing], to write or speak tediously and at length:—*adj.* pertaining to composition that is not verse.

pros-e-cute (prŏs′ĕ-kūt), *v.t.* [prosecut-ed, prosecut-ing], **1,** to follow up or pursue (an undertaking) in order to complete it; as, to *prosecute* an investigation; **2,** to bring legal proceedings against (someone):—*v.i.* **1,** to conduct the case against a person accused of crime; **2,** to carry on a lawsuit.

pros-e-cu-tion (prŏs′ĕ-kū′shŭn), *n.* **1,** the following up of an undertaking in order to complete it; **2,** the starting and carrying on of a lawsuit; **3,** the party starting the suit or proceeding against the accused.

pros-e-cu-tor (prŏs′ĕ-kū′tĕr), *n.* **1,** one who carries on a lawsuit against another; **2,** an attorney who brings suit on behalf of a city, state, or the like, especially in criminal cases.

pros-e-lyte (prŏs′ĕ-līt), *n.* a convert; a person won over from one religion, belief, or party, to another:—*v.t.* [proselyt-ed, proselyt-ing], to try to win over to a different opinion, belief, party, etc.:—*v.i.* to try to obtain followers.

Pro-ser-pi-na (prō-sûr′pĭ-nȧ), *n.* in Roman mythology, the daughter of Jupiter and Ceres, who was carried off by Pluto to be queen of the lower world. The Greeks called her *Persephone.*

pros-o-dy (prŏs′ō-dĭ), *n.* the science that deals with the study or writing of verse,

---

go; join; yet; sing; chin; show; thin, *th*en; **hw,** *wh*y; **zh,** azure; **ü,** Ger. f*ü*r or Fr. l*u*ne; **ö,** Ger. sch*ö*n or Fr. f*eu;* **n̈,** Fr. *en*fant, nom; **kh,** Ger. a*ch* or i*ch.* See pages **ix-x.**

especially with the arrangement of words or syllables in metrical feet and verses.

pros-pect (prŏs′pĕkt), *n.* **1,** a scene spread out before the sight; view; outlook; as, a *prospect* of green, rolling prairie; **2,** a looking forward or, especially, that which one looks forward to, or expects; expectation; as, a *prospect* of fair weather; **3,** a possible customer or client:—*v.t.* and *v.i.* to search or explore, especially for gold, oil, etc.

pro-spec-tive (prŏ-spĕk′tĭv), *adj.* **1,** concerned with the future; **2,** expected; hoped for; as, *prospective* profits.—*adv.* pro-spec′tive-ly.

pros-pec-tor (prŏs′pĕk-tẽr; prŏ-spĕk′tẽr), *n.* one who explores a region, searching for oil, gold, silver, or similar products of the earth.

pro-spec-tus (prŏ-spĕk′tŭs), *n.* [*pl.* prospectuses], **1,** an outline of a proposed undertaking; **2,** a brief description, as of a book to be published; **3,** a catalog, as of a school, hotel, etc.

pros-per (prŏs′pẽr), *v.i.* to thrive; make progress; flourish.

pros-per-i-ty (prŏs-pĕr′ĭ-tĭ), *n.* the state of flourishing or thriving; success.

Pros-per-o (prŏs′pẽr-ō), *n.* in Shakespeare's "Tempest," the rightful Duke of Milan, exiled to a remote island, who by magic raises a tempest which shipwrecks his usurping brother, Antonio.

pros-per-ous (prŏs′pẽr-ŭs), *adj.* flourishing; successful; as, a *prosperous* business; a *prosperous* businessman.

pros-ti-tute (prŏs′tĭ-tūt), *v.t.* [prostitut-ed, prostitut-ing], to put to low and unworthy purpose for the sake of money; as, to *prostitute* talent:—*n.* a woman who engages in sexual intercourse for pay; a harlot.

pros-trate (prŏs′trāt), *adj.* **1,** lying face down on the ground; bending to the ground in token of defeat, humility, or worship; as, the vanquished foe, *prostrate* before the victor; **2,** flung down to the ground; as, the *prostrate* pillars of a ruined temple; **3,** overcome, as with emotion; also, drained of vitality; lifeless; as, a *prostrate* industry:—*v.t.* [prostrat-ed, prostrat-ing], **1,** to humble (oneself) by lying face down on the ground; as, to *prostrate* oneself before God; **2,** to exhaust; as, she is *prostrated* with fatigue.

pros-tra-tion (prŏs-trā′shŭn), *n.* **1,** the act of throwing oneself down, or the condition of lying face down; **2,** self-abasement; humility; **3,** a state of exhaustion.

pros-y (prōz′ĭ), *adj.* [pros-i-er, pros-i-est], commonplace; tedious; dull; as, a *prosy* lecturer.

Prot. abbreviation for *Protestant.*

pro-te-an (prō′tē-ăn; prŏ-tē′ăn), *adj.* readily taking on different shapes or forms; like Proteus, the sea god, who changed himself at will into any form.

pro-tect (prŏ-tĕkt′), *v.t.* to shield from harm; guard; shelter; as, a lightning rod *protects* a building against fire from lightning. *Syn.* preserve, defend.

pro-tec-tion (prŏ-tĕk′shŭn), *n.* **1,** the act of keeping in safety; **2,** the state of being kept in safety; **3,** that which keeps safe; defense; security; as, an overcoat is a *protection* against a cold wind; **4,** the placing of duties on imported goods for the encouragement of home industry, a policy opposed to that of free trade.

pro-tec-tive (prŏ-tĕk′tĭv), *adj.* **1,** serving to keep safe; as, the *protective* coloring of animals; **2,** encouraging home industry; as, *protective* duties on goods from abroad.

pro-tec-tor (prŏ-tĕk′tẽr), *n.* **1,** a defender; guardian; **2,** anything that serves to shield or protect; as, a chest *protector.*

pro-tec-tor-ate (prŏ-tĕk′tẽr-ĭt), *n.* **1,** government by a person appointed to rule in place of a king; **2,** the relation of a great nation to a weak one which it defends and partly controls; also, the period during which this control is maintained; **3,** the nation so defended and controlled.

pro-té-gé (prō′tĕ-zhā; prŏ′tā-zhā′), *n.* one who is under the guardianship or care of another.—*n.fem.* **pro′té-gée.**

pro-te-in (prō′tē-ĭn; prō′tēn), *n.* a substance containing nitrogen, found as a vital element in all living organisms, animal and vegetable. Protein is an essential part of any diet, and is contained in such foods as meat, milk, butter, cheese, eggs, nuts, peas, and beans.

pro tem. abbreviation for Latin *pro tempore*, meaning *for the time being.*

pro-test (prŏ-tĕst′), *v.i.* to make a formal declaration of disapproval or dissent:—*v.t.* **1,** to affirm or assert; as, the defendant *protested* that he was telling the absolute truth; **2,** to object to; dissent from; as, to appeal to a higher court is to *protest* the judgment of the lower; **3,** to make a formal statement of refusal to honor or pay; as, to *protest* a check:—*n.* (prō′tĕst), **1,** a formal declaration of opinion against something; **2,** a formal notification that a note, check, or the like, will not be honored or paid.

prot-es-tant (prŏt′ĕs-tănt), *adj.* making a protest; declaring an opposing opinion:—*n.* one who declares an opinion opposing those which are generally accepted.

āte, āorta, râre, căt, ȧsk, fär, ȧllow, sofȧ; ēve, êvent, ĕll, writẽr, novĕl; bīte, pĭn; nō, ōbey, ôr, dŏg, tŏp, cŏllide; ūnit, ūnite, bûrn, cŭt, focŭs; nōōn, fŏŏt; mound; coin;

Prot·es·tant (prŏt/ĕs-tănt), *adj.* naming, or pertaining to, any of the branches of the Christian church which separated from the Roman Catholic Church in the 16th century:—*n.* a member of a Protestant church.—*n.* **Prot/es-tant-ism.**

Prot·es·tant E·pis·co·pal Church, in the United States, the church which corresponds to the Church of England.

prot·es·ta·tion (prŏt/ĕs-tā/shŭn), *n.* 1, a solemn declaration; as, *protestations* of friendship; 2, a formal objection or protest; as, a *protestation* against war.

Pro·teus (prō/tūs; prō/tē-ŭs), *n.* in mythology, a god of the sea with prophetic powers, who could change himself into any form at will.

pro·to·col (prō/tō-kŏl), *n.* 1, an original copy or record; especially, the first draft of a treaty or agreement, often signed, used as a basis for a final treaty; 2, a formal or official statement of points agreed upon; 3, the code of etiquette in diplomatic affairs and state ceremonies.

pro·ton (prō/tŏn), *n.* the active part of the nucleus of an atom. It carries a positive charge of one elementary unit of electricity, the electrical opposite of the *electron*.

pro·to·plasm (prō/tō-plăzm), *n.* the essential living substance of both animal and plant cells. It is usually a colorless, jellylike substance, in which tiny grains of solid matter are suspended.

pro·to·type (prō/tō-tīp), *n.* the first or original example of anything.

pro·tract (prō-trăkt/), *v.t.* 1, to draw out; prolong, as a meeting; 2, to draw to scale.—*n.* pro-trac/tion.—*adj.* pro-tract/ed.

pro·trac·tor (prō-trăk/tẽr), *n.* an instrument for measuring or drawing angles.

pro·trude (prō-trōōd/), *v.t.* and *v.i.* [protrud-ed, protrud-ing], to stick out; project; as, to *protrude* the tongue; pencils *protrude* from his pocket.

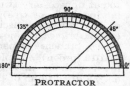

PROTRACTOR

pro·tru·sion (prō-trōō/zhŭn), *n.* 1, the act of thrusting out, or the state of being thrust out; 2, that which is thrust out or projects; as, the brow is a *protrusion* over the eyes.

pro·tu·ber·ance (prō-tū/bẽr-ăns), *n.* 1, a swelling or bulging; 2, something that protrudes; a bulge.—*adj.* pro-tu/ber-ant.

proud (proud), *adj.* 1, having or exhibiting too great self-esteem; overbearing; haughty; as, a *proud* lady with her *proud* airs; 2, having worthy self-respect; as, too

proud to beg; 3, having a feeling of glad satisfaction; gratified; as, *proud* of his boy's success; 4, noble, magnificent; as, a *proud* old castle.—*adv.* proud/ly.

prove (prōōv), *v.t.* [*p.t.* proved (prōōvd), *p.p.* proved or, *Archaic,* prov-en (prōōv/ĕn), *p.pr.* prov-ing], 1, to test by an experiment; as, to *prove* the purity of copper; 2, to demonstrate by reasoning or evidence; as, to *prove* a theorem in geometry; 3, to cause to be accepted as genuine; as, to *prove* a will:—*v.i.* to turn out to be; be found to be; as, the new coat *proved* warm.

prov·en (prōō/vĕn), *Archaic,* a past participle of *prove:—adj.* found to be genuine.

Pro·ven·çal (prō/vän-säl/; prō/vän/sȧl/), *adj.* pertaining to Provence, France, or its people:—*n.* 1, a native of Provence; 2, the medieval language of Provence.

Pro·vence (prō/väṅs/), an ancient province (cap. Aix) in southeastern France.

prov·en·der (prŏv/ĕn-dẽr), *n.* dry feed for livestock, as hay, oats, or corn.

prov·erb (prŏv/ûrb), *n.* 1, a short, homely saying, expressing a truth in few words; an adage, as "a stitch in time saves nine"; 2, a byword.

Prov·erbs (prŏv/ûrbz), *n.* a book of the Old Testament containing the practical wisdom of the wise men of Israel.

pro·ver·bi·al (prō-vûr/bĭ-ăl), *adj.* 1, contained in, or resembling, proverbs; as, *proverbial* wisdom; 2, widely spoken of or known; as, her kindness is *proverbial.*—*adv.* pro-ver/bi-al-ly.

pro·vide (prō-vīd/), *v.t.* [provid-ed, pro-vid-ing], 1, to supply or furnish (a thing) for use; as, to *provide* food and lodging; also, to outfit or equip (a person); as, to *provide* a child with books; 2, to set forth as a condition; stipulate; as, her will *provided* that a new hospital be built:—*v.i.* to make preparations in advance; as, to *provide* for the future; to *provide* against cold weather.

pro·vid·ed (prō-vī/dĕd), *conj.* on condition that; if; as, I'll go, *provided* you go.

Prov·i·dence (prŏv/ĭ-dĕns), a city, capital of Rhode Island (map 6).

prov·i·dence (prŏv/ĭ-dĕns), *n.* 1, prudence; foresight; also, prudent management; thrift; 2, an instance of divine care; as, her recovery was God's special *providence:—***Providence,** God; as, to trust in *Providence.*

prov·i·dent (prŏv/ĭ-dĕnt), *adj.* 1, mindful of the future; prudent; 2, economical; thrifty.—*adv.* prov/i-dent-ly.

prov·i·den·tial (prŏv/ĭ-dĕn/shăl), *adj.* 1, of or by divine foresight; as, a *providential* recovery from illness; 2, fortunate.—*adv.* prov/i-den/tial-ly.

---

go; join; yet; sing; chin; show; thin, *th***en; hw,** *wh***y; zh,** a**zure; ü,** Ger. f*ü*r or Fr. l*u*ne; **ö,** Ger. sch*ö*n or Fr. f*eu*; **ṅ,** Fr. e*n*fant, no*m*; **kh,** Ger. a*ch* or i*ch*. See pages ix–x.

prov·ince (prŏv′ĭns), *n.* **1,** a division of an empire or country; as, Alberta is a *province* of Canada; **2,** a country governed by a distant authority; **3,** limits or range; a proper sphere of action; as, this task is outside your *province;* **4, provinces,** regions remote from a capital or a very large city; as, the theatrical company left London for the *provinces.*

pro·vin·cial (prŏ-vĭn′shăl), *adj.* **1,** of or belonging to a division of an empire or country; as, *provincial* government; **2,** countrified; crude; **3,** restricted to the ideas and customs of one special region; hence, narrow; limited:—*n.* an inhabitant of a province; hence, an uncultivated person.

pro·vin·cial·ism (prŏ-vĭn′shăl-ĭzm), *n.* **1,** a word, expression, mannerism, or way of thinking peculiar to an outlying district or to a particular locality; **2,** devotion to the ideas and customs of one special region; narrow-mindedness.

pro·vi·sion (prŏ-vĭzh′ŭn), *n.* **1,** preparation; care beforehand; as, *provision* must be made for a long journey; **2,** (often *provisions*), a supply or stock of food; as, *provisions* for the winter; **3,** a condition; proviso; stipulation; as, a *provision* in a contract:—*v.t.* to supply with food, especially on a large scale.

pro·vi·sion·al (prŏ-vĭzh′ŭn-ăl), *adj.* serving for present use; temporary; as, a *provisional* government; also, conditional; as, a *provisional* contract.—*adv.* **pro·vi′sion·al·ly.**

pro·vi·so (prŏ-vī′zō), *n.* [*pl.* provisos or provisoes], a conditional clause or stipulation, as in a deed or will.

prov·o·ca·tion (prŏv′ŏ-kā′shŭn), *n.* **1,** that which excites to anger or resentment; as, he fairly rages on the slightest *provocation;* **2,** the act of provoking; as, the *provocation* of a quarrel.

pro·voc·a·tive (prŏ-vŏk′à-tĭv), *adj.* tending to rouse or call forth an action, thought, or emotion; as, a remark *provocative* of anger or laughter.

pro·voke (prŏ-vōk′), *v.t.* [provoked, pro-vok-ing], **1,** to excite; stir up; as, to *provoke* criticism; **2,** to cause; as, to *provoke* a laugh; **3,** to irritate; rouse; incite; as, to *provoke* another to anger.—*adj.* **pro-vok′ing.**

prov·ost (prŏv′ŭst), *n.* **1,** a person appointed to be the head of a cathedral church, college, or the like; **2,** the chief magistrate of a city in Scotland.

prow (prou), *n.* the forward end or part, as the nose of an airplane or bow of a ship.

prow·ess (prou′ĕs), *n.* **1,** daring; bravery; valor; **2,** very great skill or ability; as, he was noted for his *prowess* as a wrestler.

prowl (proul), *v.i.* to move about stealthily; as, wolves *prowl* for food:—*v.t.* to roam over, as woods or fields, in search of prey:—*n.* a roving for prey or plunder; as, beasts on the *prowl.*—*n.* **prowl′er.**

prox·im·i·ty (prŏks-ĭm′ĭ-tĭ), *n.* nearness; closeness; as, *proximity* to danger.

prox·i·mo (prŏk′sĭ-mō), *adv.* in or of the coming month; as, the 12th *proximo.*

prox·y (prŏk′sĭ), *n.* [*pl.* proxies], **1,** authority to act for another; hence, the document giving the authority; as, to vote by *proxy;* **2,** a person who is given authority to act for another, especially in a given situation.
Syn. agent, representative, delegate.

prude (prōōd), *n.* a person who is extremely or affectedly proper in dress, speech, or behavior.

pru·dence (prōō′dĕns), *n.* wisdom or discretion in practical matters; good judgment, especially in one's own affairs.
Syn. care, judgment, discretion, wisdom.

pru·dent (prōō′dĕnt), *adj.* **1,** mindful of the future; using judgment and foresight; cautious; as, a *prudent* housewife; **2,** showing forethought; as, a *prudent* act.
Syn. frugal, farseeing, forehanded, wary.

pru·den·tial (prōō-dĕn′shăl), *adj.* **1,** proceeding from, or marked by, careful thought or wisdom; **2,** using sound judgment.—*adv.* **pru-den′tial-ly.**

prud·er·y (prōō′dĕr-ĭ), *n.* [*pl.* pruderies], extreme propriety or modesty in conduct, either genuine or assumed; primness.

prud·ish (prōō′dĭsh), *adj.* unusually precise and prim; also, too precise and prim.—*adv.* **prud′ish-ly.**—*n.* **prud′ish-ness.**

¹prune (prōōn), *v.t.* [pruned, prun-ing], **1,** to cut unnecessary twigs or branches from (a vine, bush, or tree); trim; **2,** to cut out or clear away the useless parts of; as, the author *pruned* his novel:—*v.i.* to remove useless branches or parts.—*n.* **prun′er.**

²prune (prōōn), *n.* a plum capable of being dried without undergoing fermentation; also, a dried plum of this kind.

Prus·sia (prŭsh′à), a former state (cap. Berlin) in Germany.

Prus·sian (prŭsh′ăn), *adj.* pertaining to Prussia or to its people:—*n.* a native of Prussia.

prus·sic ac·id (prŭs′ĭk), a highly poisonous liquid, much used for destroying harmful insects.

¹pry (prī), *v.i.* [pried, pry-ing], to look or peer closely and inquisitively; inquire into anything and everything; as, some people *pry* into other people's affairs.—*adj.* **pry′ing.**

²pry (prī), *v.t.* [pried, pry-ing], **1,** to raise

āte, āorta, râre, căt, ȧsk, fär, ăllow, sofȧ; ēve, ēvent, ĕll, writĕr, novĕl; bīte, pĭn; nō, ōbey, ôr, dŏg, tŏp, cŏllide; ūnit, ūnite, bûrn, cŭt, focŭs; nōōn, fŏŏt; mound; coin;

or open with a lever; **2,** to budge or move with difficulty; as, you can't *pry* Sally away from the piano:—*n.* a lever.

P.S. abbreviation for *postscript.*

psalm (säm), *n.* a sacred song or poem.

psalm-ist (säm′ĭst), *n.* a composer of psalms or sacred hymns:—**the Psalmist**, David.

psal-mo-dy (săl′mŏ-dĭ; säm′ŏ-dĭ), *n.* [*pl.* psalmodies], **1,** the act or art of singing psalms; **2,** the arrangement of psalms for singing; also, psalms so arranged.

Psalms (sämz), *n.* a book of the Old Testament containing sacred songs.

Psal-ter (sôl′tẽr), *n.* the Old Testament Book of Psalms; also, a book or part of a book containing the Book of Psalms.

psal-ter-y (sôl′tẽr-ĭ), *n.* [*pl.* psalteries], a zitherlike, stringed musical instrument, used by the ancient Hebrews.

pseu-do (sū′dō), *adj.* false; pretended; not real; as, a *pseudo* prophet.

pseu-do-nym (sū′dŏ-nĭm), *n.* a false name used by a writer who does not wish his real name known; as, Mark Twain was the *pseudonym* of Samuel L. Clemens.

pshaw (shô), *interj.* an expression showing contempt, scorn, or impatience.

Psy-che (sī′kē), *n.* in Greek mythology, a beautiful maiden who was the personification of the human soul. She was the beloved of Cupid.

psy-chi-a-try (sī-kī′ȧ-trĭ; sī′kĭ-ăt′rĭ), *n.* the scientific study and treatment of mental disorders.—*adj.* **psy-chi′a-trist.**—*adj.* **psy′chi-at′ric** (sī′kĭ-ăt′rĭk).

psy-chic (sī′kĭk), *n.* a person sensitive to forces which cannot be explained by any known laws; a medium:—*adj.* **1,** concerning the soul or mind; spiritual; **2,** lying outside the realm of known physical processes; as, *psychic* forces; **3,** sensitive to forces of this kind; as, a *psychic* person. Also, *adj.* **psy′chi-cal.**

psy-chol-o-gy (sī-kŏl′ŏ-jĭ), *n.* [*pl.* psychologies], the science that studies the mind, particularly the human mind, and its activities.—*adj.* **psy′cho-log′i-cal** (sī′kŏ-lŏj′ĭ-kăl).—*n.* **psy-chol′o-gist.**

psy-cho-path-ic (sī′kŏ-păth′ĭk), *adj.* mentally disordered; as, a *psychopathic* patient; also, reserved for the mentally afflicted; as, the *psychopathic* ward in a hospital.

pt. abbreviation for *pint, point, port.*

ptar-mi-gan (tär′mĭ-găn), *n.* a northern grouse whose gray or black plumage turns white in winter. (See illustration next column.)

PT boat, a small, very fast boat, armed with antiaircraft guns and torpedoes: originally called *MPT boat,* for *motor patrol torpedo boat.*

Ptol-e-my (tŏl′ē-mĭ), **1,** the name given to Greek rulers of Egypt from 323 to 30 B.C.; **2, Claudius Ptolemy** (second century A.D.), a famous Greek-Egyptian astronomer, geographer, and mathematician.

pto-maine or **pto-main** (tō′mān; tō-mān′), *n.* a substance, usually poisonous, found in decaying organic matter.

pu-ber-ty (pū′bẽr-tĭ), *n.* the age, about fourteen years for boys and twelve for girls, which is recognized as the time at which a boy or girl outgrows childhood and begins to be a man or woman.

pub-lic (pŭb′lĭk), *adj.* **1,** pertaining to the people as a whole; as, the *public* welfare; **2,** common to all; open to general use; as, a *public* park; a *public* library or school; **3,** generally known; not secret; as, the facts were made *public;* **4,** serving the people; as, a *public* utility:—*n.* **1,** the people in general or as a whole; **2,** a special section or group of the people; as, the voting *public.*—*adv.* **pub′lic-ly.**

pub-li-can (pŭb′lĭ-kăn), *n.* **1,** in Great Britain, one who keeps an inn or public house; **2,** in ancient Rome or in the Bible, a collector of taxes and public revenues.

pub-li-ca-tion (pŭb′lĭ-kā′shŭn), *n.* **1,** the act or business of printing and placing on sale; as, the *publication* of books; **2,** a book, magazine, etc.; **3,** a making known to the public; as, this fact is not for *publication.*

public house, an inn or tavern; especially, in Great Britain, a place where alcoholic liquors are sold and drunk.

pub-li-cist (pŭb′lĭ-sĭst), *n.* **1,** one familiar with the laws that govern the relations between nations; **2,** a writer on topics of political and economic interest.

pub-lic-i-ty (pŭb-lĭs′ĭ-tĭ), *n.* **1,** the state of being open to common knowledge; notoriety; public notice; as, unfavorable *publicity;* a *publicity* seeker; **2,** news that advertises; as, theatrical *publicity.*

pub-lic—spir-it-ed (pŭb′lĭk-spĭr′ĭ-tĕd), *adj.* devoted to the public welfare.

pub-lish (pŭb′lĭsh), *v.t.* **1,** to make generally known; as, to *publish* one's intentions; also, to proclaim, as an edict; **2,** to print and offer for sale, as a book, magazine, etc.

Syn. declare, promulgate.

PTARMIGAN (¹⁄₁₀)

pub-lish-er (pŭb′lĭsh-ẽr), *n.* a person or a

firm whose business is the printing and distributing of books, magazines, etc.

¹puck (pŭk), *n.* in English folklore, a mischievous fairy or goblin:—**Puck,** the elf Robin Goodfellow.

²puck (pŭk), *n.* in hockey, a hard rubber disk pushed or driven along the ice with a stick.

puck-er (pŭk′ẽr), *v.t.* to draw up into small folds; wrinkle; as, in perplexity he *puckered* up his brow:—*v.i.* to become drawn up into folds; as, the cloth *puckered* badly after being wet:—*n.* a small fold or wrinkle.

pud-ding (pŏŏd′ĭng), *n.* **1,** a kind of soft food, often a dessert, made of flour, milk, eggs, etc.; **2,** a kind of sausage; as, blood *pudding.*

pud-dle (pŭd′l), *n.* **1,** a small pool of dirty water; **2,** a mixture of clay and water used as a watertight covering or filling:—*v.t.* [pud-dled, pud-dling], **1,** to make muddy; **2,** to work water into (clay) so as to make a mixture through which water cannot pass; **3,** to stir (molten pig iron) so as to produce wrought iron.—*n.* pud′-dler.—*n.* pud′dling.

pudg-y (pŭj′ĭ), *adj.* [pudg-i-er, pudg-i-est], short and fat; as, a *pudgy* hand.—*n.* pudg′i-ness.

pueb-lo (pwĕb′lō), *n.* [*pl.* pueblos], **1,** a building made of sun-dried brick by the Indians of New Mexico, Arizona, etc., often several stories high, housing the entire village or tribe; **2,** in the U.S. and Spanish America, an Indian or Spanish village:—**Pueblo,** a member of one of the tribes of Indians who live in pueblos.

pu-er-ile (pū′ẽr-ĭl; pū′ẽr-īl), *adj.* childish; foolish; trivial; as, a *puerile* argument.—*n.* pu′er-il′i-ty (pū′ẽr-ĭl′ĭ-tĭ).

Puer-to Ri-co (pwâr′tō rē′kō), an island (cap San Juan), a self-governing commonwealth of the U. S. in the West Indies (map **10**). Formerly its name was *Porto Rico.*

puff (pŭf), *n.* **1,** a short, quick blast, as of wind, steam, gas, breath, or the like; also, the accompanying sound or vapor; as, one may both hear and see the *puffs* of a locomotive; **2,** a soft pad; as, a powder *puff;* **3,** a light pastry shell filled with whipped cream, custard, etc.; as, a cream *puff;* **4,** in dressmaking, a piece of material gathered on two sides so as to stand out in the center; **5,** exaggerated praise; as, the critic gave the new play quite a *puff;* **6,** a loose mass or roll of hair:—*v.i.* **1,** to send out air, smoke, breath, etc., in puffs; **2,** to breathe quickly and hard, as a runner; **3,** to swell with air; **4,** to swell with importance:—*v.t.* **1,** to emit or blow out, with

whiffs or little blasts; **2,** to cause to swell, as with wind, or, figuratively, with importance; as, to *puff* out the cheeks; **3,** to praise in too high terms; as, to *puff* a book; **4,** to arrange in puffs, as the hair, dress material, etc.

puff-ball (pŭf′bôl′), *n.* a ball-shaped fungus, somewhat similar to a mushroom, which, when dried and broken open, sends out a dustlike puff of spores.

puf-fin (pŭf′ĭn), *n.* a northern sea bird, related to the auk, with a short neck and large bill.

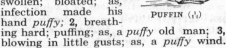

puff-y (pŭf′ĭ), *adj.* [puff-i-er, puff-i-est], **1,** swollen; bloated; as, infection made his hand *puffy;* **2,** breathing hard; puffing; as, a *puffy* old man; **3,** blowing in little gusts; as, a *puffy* wind. —*n.* puff′i-ness.

PUFFIN (¹⁄₁₂)

pug (pŭg), *n.* a small, stocky dog with a short, broad nose, wrinkled face, and tightly curled tail: also called *pug dog.*

Pu-get Sound (pū′jĕt), a long arm of the Pacific Ocean, extending into the northwest part of the State of Washington (map 9).

PUG (¹⁄₁₆)

pu-gil-ism (pū′jĭ-lĭzm), *n.* the art or sport of fighting with the fists; professional boxing; prize fighting.

pu-gil-ist (pū′jĭ-lĭst), *n.* a prize fighter; a boxer.—*adj.* pu′gil-is′tic.

pug-na-cious (pŭg-nā′shŭs), *adj.* quick to fight; quarrelsome.—*adv.* pug-na′cious-ly.

pug-nac-i-ty (pŭg-năs′ĭ-tĭ), *n.* inclination to fight; quarrelsomeness.

pug nose, a turned-up nose, broadened at the tip.—*adj.* pug′-nosed′.

pu-is-sance (pū′ĭ-săns; pū-ĭs′ăns; pwĭs′-ăns), *n. Poetic,* power; strength; vigor.

pu-is-sant (pū′ĭ-sănt; pū-ĭs′ănt; pwĭs′-ănt), *adj.* powerful; strong; mighty; as, a *puissant* monarch.—*adv.* pu′is-sant-ly.

pule (pūl), *v.i.* [puled, pul-ing], to cry weakly; whine; whimper, as a sickly child.

Pu-lit-zer (pū′lĭt-sẽr), Joseph (1847–1911), an American journalist, founder of the Pulitzer prize awards.

pull (pŏŏl), *v.t.* **1,** to draw out or toward one by exerting force; as, to *pull* a nail; *pull* a tooth; **2,** to draw in any direction; drag; haul; **3,** to pluck up by the roots; as, to *pull* weeds; **4,** to rend or tear; as, to *pull* a dress to pieces; **5,** to work by stretching; as, to *pull* candy:—*v.i.* to draw forcibly; tug:—*n.* **1,** the act of pulling; a tug; as, he gave my sleeve a *pull;* **2,** a hard climb; as, a long *pull* up the mountain; **3,** a handle or cord by which something is pulled; **4,** *Slang,* influence; unfair advantage.

pul-let (pŏŏl′ĕt), *n.* a young hen.

pul-ley (pŏŏl′ĭ), *n.* [*pl.* pulleys], a tackle which consists of a wood or metal frame for a wheel with a grooved rim, into which fits a rope. A pulley is used for hauling, lifting, and pulling, or for changing the direction of a pull: **pulley block,** a pulley with its frame.

PULLEY

Pull-man car (pŏŏl′măn), a railway car with sleeping berths and staterooms; also, a car with individual chairs. Also, **Pull′man.**

pul-mo-nar-y (pŭl′mō-nĕr′ĭ), *adj.* pertaining to the lungs; as, *pulmonary* cells.

Pul-mo-tor (pŭl′mō′tĕr), *n.* a trade-mark name for a machine which produces artificial breathing by forcing air into the lungs:—**pulmotor,** a machine bearing this trade name

pulp (pŭlp), *n.* **1,** the soft fleshy part of fruit, plant stems, etc.; **2,** the inner fleshy part of a tooth; **3,** any soft, wet mass; as, wood *pulp;* paper *pulp;* **4, pulps,** magazines printed on cheap paper, dealing principally with mystery, adventure, or sex.

pul-pit (pŏŏl′pĭt), *n.* **1,** a raised platform or desk in a church, from which the sermon is delivered; **2,** the preaching profession; as, the voice of the *pulpit.*

pulp-y (pŭl′pĭ), *adj.* [pulp-i-er, pulp-i-est], consisting of, or like, a soft, moist mass of matter; soft; fleshy.

PULPIT

pul-sate (pŭl′sāt; pŭl-sāt′), *v.i.* [pulsat-ed, pulsat-ing], **1,** to throb; beat, as the heart; **2,** to quiver; vibrate with life or feeling; as, a *pulsating* voice.

pul-sa-tion (pŭl-sā′shŭn), *n.* **1,** a single throb or beat, as of the heart; **2,** the regular throbbing or beating of the heart.

¹**pulse** (pŭls), *n.* **1,** the throbbing or beating in an artery, as the blood is pumped through; **2,** a stroke or beat occurring at regular intervals:—*v.i.* [pulsed, puls-ing], to beat or throb, as an artery.

²**pulse** (pŭls), *n.* the seeds of such plants as peas, beans, and lentils, which are cooked and used as food; also, the plants themselves.

pul-ver-ize (pŭl′vĕr-īz), *v.t.* [pulverized, pulveriz-ing], to crush, grind, or beat into powder or dust; as, to *pulverize* sugar:—*v.i.* to become dust; as, even rocks *pulverize* in the course of centuries.

pu-ma (pū′má), *n.* a large, tawny, American wildcat; the mountain lion, or cougar.

PUMA (1/15)

pum-ice (pŭm′ĭs), *n.* a hard, light, porous, volcanic rock, used for cleaning or polishing: also called *pumice stone.*

pum-mel (pŭm′ĕl), *n.* a pommel:—*v.t.* to beat with the fists; pommel. See **pommel.**

¹**pump** (pŭmp), *n.* a machine for raising or moving liquids or for compressing gases by means of pressure or suction:—*v.t.* **1,** to raise or draw, as water, by means of a pump; **2,** to remove water or gases from; as, to *pump* a boat dry; **3,** to draw out by artful questions; as, to *pump* a secret, or a friend; **4,** to force, as does a pump; as, the heart *pumps* blood to all parts of the body:—*v.i.* **1,** to work a pump; as, to *pump* faster; **2,** to work like a pump; as, your heart *pumps* too fast.—*n.* **pump′er.**

PUMP
V, V. valves.

²**pump** (pŭmp), *n.* a low lightweight shoe, especially one without a lace, strap, or other fastening.

pump-kin (pŭmp′kĭn; *Colloquial,* pŭng′kĭn), *n.* a vine or plant that bears large yellow or orange fruit, like squashes; also, the fruit, used especially for pies and as feed for animals.

PUMP

pun (pŭn), *n.* a form of jesting expression in which one word is used with two meanings, or two different words pronounced nearly alike are used close together, as in "*stand* by what you say or you will *stand* the penalty" and "he went and *told* the sexton and the sexton *tolled* the bell":—*v.i.* [punned, pun-ning], to make or utter a pun; as, he is always *punning.*

PUMPKIN

¹**punch** (pŭnch), *n.* **1,** a tool for making dents or holes; **2,** a machine tool for stamping and forming sheet-metal articles; **3,** a blow or thrust, especially with the closed fist:—*v.t.* **1,** to strike with the

fist; **2,** to drive along; as, to *punch* cattle; **3,** to press the key or keys of (a machine); as, to *punch* a typewriter; **4,** to make (a hole) in; **5,** to cut or mark with a tool:—*v.i.* **1,** to hit with the fist; as, to *punch* hard; **2,** to make a hole; as, this tool *punches* cleanly.

PUNCH

²**punch** (pŭnch), *n.* a drink made of rum, whisky, or other liquor, with water, lemon juice, sugar, etc.; also, a drink made from fruit juices, sweetened and flavored.

Punch (pŭnch), *n.* the hunchbacked, hook-nosed husband of Judy:— **Punch—and—Judy show,** an amusing puppet show in which the quarrelsome Punch gets into difficulties with his wife.

pun-cheon (pŭn′chŭn), *n.* a large liquor cask of varying capacity, especially one which holds 84 gallons of wine.

punc-til-i-o (pŭngk-tĭl′ĭ-ō;ʹ pŭngk-tĭl′yō), *n.* [*pl.* punctilios], a minute point of etiquette in conduct, manners, or dress; also, formal correctness; formality.

punc-til-i-ous (pŭngk-tĭl′ĭ-ŭs), *adj.* very nice or precise in conduct; paying careful attention to details of dress, speech, or the like; as, *punctilious* in table manners.— *adv.* **punc-til′i-ous-ly.**—*n.* **punc-til′i-ous-ness.**

Syn. scrupulous, correct, particular.

punc-tu-al (pŭngk′tū-ăl), *adj.* prompt; arriving or appearing at the proper time.— *adv.* **punc′tu-al-ly.**

punc-tu-al-i-ty (pŭngk′tū-ăl′ĭ-tĭ), *n.* arrival on time; promptness in keeping an appointment or engagement.

punc-tu-ate (pŭngk′tū-āt), *v.t.* [punctuat-ed, punctuat-ing], **1,** to mark or set off the parts of, with a period, comma, semicolon, etc.; as, to *punctuate* a paragraph; **2,** to emphasize; as, he *punctuated* his remarks with gestures; **3,** to interrupt at intervals, or now and then; as, cheers *punctuated* the speaker's words.

punc-tu-a-tion (pŭngk′tū-ā′shŭn), *n.* in writing or printing, the marking, or setting off, of words, phrases, sentences, etc., by the use of certain special marks:— **punctuation marks,** the comma [,], semicolon [;], colon [:], period [.], interrogation mark [?], exclamation mark [!], dash [—], parentheses [( )], brackets [ ], double quotation marks [". . ."], and single quotation marks ['. . .'].

punc-ture (pŭngk′tŭr), *n.* a hole or wound made by something pointed; as, a *puncture* in a tube; also, deflation, as of a balloon:—*v.t.* [punctured, punctur-ing],

1, to make a hole in, or pierce, as with a pointed instrument; prick; **2,** to deflate; destroy; as, a sharp reproof may *puncture* pride.

pun-gen-cy (pŭn′jĕn-sĭ), *n.* sharpness; tartness; biting quality; as, the *pungency* of an odor.

pun-gent (pŭn′jĕnt), *adj.* **1,** stinging; pricking; biting; as, a *pungent* acid; **2,** piercing; keen; as, *pungent* wit; **3,** sarcastic; caustic; as, *pungent* satire.—*adv.* **pun′gent-ly.**

Syn. acrid, sharp, stimulating, bitter.

pun-ish (pŭn′ĭsh), *v.t.* **1,** to cause (a person) to pay the penalty for a crime or fault; as, to *punish* a child; **2,** to inflict penalty for (something); as, to *punish* disobedience.

Syn. discipline, chastise.

pun-ish-a-ble (pŭn′ĭsh-à-bl), *adj.* deserving of, or liable to, a penalty or punishment; as, a crime *punishable* by death.

pun-ish-ment (pŭn′ĭsh-mĕnt), *n.* **1,** the penalty inflicted for a crime or fault; as, the *punishment* of imprisonment; **2,** the act of punishing or state of being punished; as, *punishment* may fail to produce results; Mary resents *punishment.*

pu-ni-tive (pū′nĭ-tĭv), *adj.* having to do with, or inflicting, punishment; as, *punitive* laws; a *punitive* expedition.

Pun-jab (pŭn-jäb′), a province divided between Pakistan and India.

punk (pŭngk), *n.* **1,** partly decayed wood; tinder; **2,** a substance, made of decayed vegetable matter, which is used to light fireworks.

pun-ster (pŭn′stĕr), *n.* a person who habitually makes puns.

¹**punt** (pŭnt), *n.* a long flat-bottomed boat, square at the ends, propelled by a pole thrust against the bottom of shallow water:—*v.t.* **1,** to propel (a boat), by pushing with a pole; **2,** to transport in a punt.—*n.* **punt′er.**

²**punt** (pŭnt), *n.* in football, the kicking of the ball, when dropped from the hand, before it touches the ground; also, the kick so made:—*v.t.* and *v.i.* to kick (a football so dropped) before it touches the ground.

pu-ny (pū′nĭ), *adj.* [pu-ni-er, pu-ni-est], **1,** undersized; weak; as, a *puny* baby; **2,** hence, feeble; halfhearted; as, a *puny* effort.

pup (pŭp), *n.* **1,** a young dog; a puppy; **2,** the young of several other mammals, as of the seal:—**pup tent,** *Slang,* a small shelter tent, with sloping sides, used by soldiers and campers.

pu-pa (pū′pà), *n.* [*pl.* pupae (pū′pē) or pupas], the stage in the life of an insect

---

āte, āorta, râre, căt, ȧsk, fär, ȧllow, sofȧ; ēve, ēvent, ĕll, writĕr, novĕl; bīte, pĭn; nō, ōbey, ôr, dŏg, tŏp, cŏllide; ūnit, ūnite, bûrn, cŭt, focŭs; noon, foŏt; mound; coin;

when it is in a cocoon or case. The pupa is the stage between the caterpillar and the butterfly.—*adj.* **pu′pal.**

¹**pu-pil** (pū′pĭl; pū′pĭl), *n.* a young person under the care and instruction of a teacher. —*n.* **pu′pil-age.**

²**pu-pil** (pū′pĭl; pū′pĭl), *n.* the dark center in the iris of the eye, through which rays of light pass to the retina.

pup-pet (pŭp′ĕt), *n.* **1,** a small doll or figure, especially one moved by wires from behind a screen in a mock drama, called a *puppet show;* a marionette; **2,** one who, though properly his own master, is under the control of another; as, the king was the *puppet* of his ministers.

PUPPET

pup-py (pŭp′ĭ), *n.* [*pl.* puppies], **1,** a young dog; **2,** a conceited, silly young man.—*adj.* **pup′py-ish.**

pur (pûr), *v.* [purred, pur-ring], and **pur,** *n.* purr. See **purr.**

pur-blind (pûr′blīnd′), *adj.* almost without sight; partly blind.—*adv.* **pur′blind′ly.** —*n.* **pur′blind′ness.**

pur-chase (pûr′chĭs), *v.t.* [purchased, purchas-ing], to get by paying money; buy:— *n.* **1,** the act or process of buying; as, the *purchase* and sale of goods or land; **2,** the thing bought; as, he examined his *purchase;* **3,** a firm hold or grasp to help one to move something or to keep oneself from slipping; as, to take a *purchase* on a rock with a crowbar.—*n.* **pur′chas-er.**—*adj.* **pur′chas-a-ble.**

pure (pūr), *adj.* [pur-er, pur-est], **1,** free from any foreign matter that might lower its quality; clear; clean; **2,** free from sin; chaste; innocent; **3,** sheer; mere; nothing but; as, *pure* foolishness.—*n.* **pure′ness.**

Syn. undefiled, stainless, genuine.

pure-ly (pūr′lĭ), *adv.* entirely; merely; as, I have a *purely* unselfish interest in it.

pu-rée (pū-rā′; pū′rā), *n.* a thick soup made of meat and vegetables boiled and forced through a sieve.

pur-ga-tive (pûr′gȧ-tĭv), *adj.* having the power of cleansing:—*n.* a medicine for the purpose of cleansing the system of waste and impurities; a cathartic or physic.

pur-ga-tor-y (pûr′gȧ-tôr′ĭ), *n.* **1,** in the Roman Catholic belief, the state and place after death in which souls are purified before they can enter into heaven; **2,** hence, any place or state of temporary suffering or misery.—*adj.* **pur′ga-tor′i-al.**

purge (pûrj), *v.t.* [purged, purg-ing], **1,** to cleanse or free from impurities; **2,** to clear of guilt; free from sin; as, to *purge* one's

mind of evil thoughts; **3,** to cleanse (the bowels) by the action of a cathartic medicine:—*n.* **1,** the act or process of cleansing or freeing from impurities; **2,** a purgative.

pu-ri-fi-ca-tion (pū′rĭ-fĭ-kā′shŭn), *n.* **1,** a cleansing from guilt or sin; **2,** a making free of impurities; as, air and sunshine aid in the *purification* of water in reservoirs.

pu-ri-fy (pū′rĭ-fī), *v.t.* [purified, purifying], **1,** to make clean; also, to free from impurities; **2,** to make ceremonially clean, as by baptism.—*n.* **pu′ri-fi′er.**

pur-ist (pūr′ĭst), *n.* one who is exceedingly careful and precise in his choice of words.—*adj.* **pu-ris′tic.**

pu-ri-tan (pū′rĭ-tăn), *n.* one who is very strict in his religious life or in his attitude toward worldly pleasures; often, one who is bigoted and narrow-minded: —**Puritan,** in England and her American colonies in the 17th century, a person who tried to reform the Church of England and insisted upon simpler forms of worship.

PURITAN COSTUME

pu-ri-tan-i-cal (pū′rĭ-tăn′ĭ-kăl), *adj.* strict and precise in religious duties and moral conduct; also, enforcing strict morality; as, *puritanical* laws.—*adv.* **pu′ri-tan′i-cal-ly.**—*n.* **pu′ri-tan′i-cal-ness.**

pu-ri-ty (pū′rĭ-tĭ), *n.* **1,** freedom from impurities; as, *purity* of spring water; **2,** virtue; innocence; freedom from evil; as, *purity* of thought; **3,** accuracy; refined elegance; as, *purity* of style.

¹**purl** (pûrl), *n.* in knitting, a stitch that is the opposite or reverse of the regular stitch:—*v.t.* and *v.i.* to knit with the purl stitch.

²**purl** (pûrl), *v.i.* to bubble or flow with a gentle murmur; to swirl gently in flowing; as, the brook *purled* on its way:—*n.* the sound or motion of purling water.

pur-lieu (pûr′lū), *n.* **1,** a neighboring or outlying district; **2, purlieus,** outskirts; as, the *purlieus* of a city.

pur-loin (pûr-loin′), *v.t.* to steal; pilfer; filch.—*n.* **pur-loin′er.**

pur-ple (pûr′pl), *n.* **1,** a color resulting from a mixture of red and blue; formerly, a deep crimson; **2,** a robe of this color formerly worn by royalty; **3,** hence, royal power or dignity; also, great wealth or high rank; as, born to the *purple:*—*adj.* of the color of blended blue and red.

pur-plish (pûr′plĭsh), *adj.* like purple; somewhat purple.

pur-port (pûr′pôrt), *n.* meaning; sense; substance; as, the *purport* of his reply was that he would do what we wished:—*v.t.* (pûr-pôrt′; pûr′pôrt), to profess; as, the book *purported* to be a real account of the author's experiences in the jungle.

pur-pose (pûr′pŭs), *n.* **1,** settled intention; design; aim; as, his *purpose* in consenting was merely to help his friends; **2,** end; result; as, he saved his money, but to little *purpose*, because his children spent it foolishly:—*v.t.* [purposed, purpos-ing], to intend; resolve; as, I *purpose* to go on with my studies.

   Syn., *n.* intent, object, plan.

pur-pose-ly (pûr′pŭs-lĭ), *adv.* intentionally; deliberately; on purpose; as, he hit me *purposely*.

purr or **pur** (pûr), *n.* a low murmuring sound, such as that made by a cat when it is comfortable or contented:—*v.i.* [purred, purr-ing], to utter such a sound.

purse (pûrs), *n.* **1,** a small bag or pouch for money; **2,** a sum of money collected for a purpose; as, they made up a *purse* for the widow; also, a sum of money offered as a prize; **3,** money; treasury; as, the public *purse*:—*v.t.* [pursed, purs-ing], to pucker or wrinkle; as, to *purse* the lips.

purs-er (pûr′sẽr), *n.* on shipboard, the officer who has charge of the accounts.

purs-lane (pûrs′lān; pûrs′lĭn), *n.* a low-growing, fleshy-leafed plant, used as a salad or a potherb.

pur-su-ance (pẽr-sū′ăns), *n.* the act of pursuing or carrying out; as, in *pursuance* of her original plan, she left by airplane.

pur-su-ant (pẽr-sū′ănt), *adj.* pursuing; following out:—**pursu-ant to,** in accordance with; in accord with; as, *pursuant to* a plan previously decided upon, the army re-crossed the river.

PURSLANE

pur-sue (pẽr-sū′), *v.t.* [pursued, pursu-ing], **1,** to follow with the aim of over-taking; chase; as, to *pursue* a thief; **2,** to seek; engage in; as, to *pursue* pleasure; **3,** to go on with; continue; as, to *pursue* an inquiry; **4,** to follow; engage in (studies, a profession, etc.).—*n.* **pur-su′er.**

   Syn. hunt, succeed.

pur-suit (pẽr-sūt′), *n.* **1,** the act of following or seeking; chase; as, the *pursuit* of

game; **2,** occupation; employment; as, scientific or mercantile *pursuits.*

pur-sui-vant (pûr′swĭ-vănt), *n.* **1,** an attendant or follower; **2,** a state messenger.

pu-ru-lent (pū′rŏō-lĕnt; pūr′ū-lĕnt), *adj.* discharging, or containing, pus.

pur-vey (pûr-vā′), *v.t.* to provide; supply, as provisions for an army:—*v.i.* to make a business of supplying provisions or food to others.

pur-vey-ance (pûr-vā′ăns), *n.* **1,** the act of providing; **2,** provisions supplied; **3,** the former right of the English sovereign to commandeer provisions or services at a fixed price.

pur-vey-or (pûr-vā′ẽr), *n.* a person who makes a business of supplying or furnishing provisions to others.

pur-view (pûr′vū), *n.* **1,** extent or scope of a law, statute, writing, etc.; **2,** range of vision, concern, activity, etc.

pus (pŭs), *n.* the white or yellowish-white substance produced by inflammation in sores, abscesses, etc.; matter.—*adj.* **pus′sy.**

push (pŏŏsh), *v.t.* **1,** to press against with force, for the purpose of moving; **2,** to urge forward or extend by effort; as, to *push* one's interests; **3,** to dun urgently; press; urge; as, to *push* a debtor:—*v.i.* **1,** to make a steady forward effort; as, the army *pushed* on; **2,** to press hard in order to move:—*n.* **1,** a thrust; force applied; a shove; **2,** *Colloquial,* enterprise; energy; as, I admire his *push.*

   Syn., v. shove, thrust, force.

push-er (pŏŏsh′ẽr), *n.* a person who or that which pushes:—**pusher airplane,** an airplane with the propeller placed back of the main supporting surfaces.

pu-sil-lan-i-mous (pū′sĭ-lăn′ĭ-mŭs), *adj.* cowardly; mean-spirited; fainthearted; as, he was too *pusillanimous* to defend the reputation of his friend.—*adv.* **pu′sil-lan′i-mous-ly.**—*n.* **pu′sil-la-nim′i-ty** (pū′sĭ-lȧ-nĭm′ĭ-tĭ).

   Syn. weak, timid.

puss (pŏŏs), *n.* a cat; pussy.

puss-y (pŏŏs′ĭ), *n.* [*pl.* pussies], a cat.

puss-y-foot (pŏŏs′ĭ-fŏŏt′), *v.i.Colloquial,* **1,** to walk as quietly and carefully as a cat; **2,** to fail to take a decided stand; to hedge.

puss-y wil-low, a dwarf willow which in the spring bears silky, furry buds along its branches.

put (pŏŏt), *v.t.* [put, put-ting], **1,** to move so as to place (something) in some position; place; set; as, *put* on your hat; **2,** hence, to cause

PUSSY
WILLOW

to be in a certain condition; as, to *put* things in order; *put* one's parents to shame; 3, to state; propose; as, to *put* a question; 4, to assign; set a value on (a thing); as, *put* a price on the desk; 5, to express; as, to *put* a thought into words; 6, to apply; set; as, he *put* himself to the task; 7, to throw or hurl with an upward and forward motion of the arm; as, to *put* a shot; 8, to force or urge; as, to *put* a horse through its paces:—*v.i.* to go; proceed; as, to *put* out to sea.

put about, to alter the course of (a ship); **put by**, to save, as money; **put in**, to head toward shore; **put off**, 1, to postpone (an action); 2, to turn (a person) aside from a purpose; **put on**, to assume, as airs; **put out**, 1, to vex; 2, to inconvenience; 3, to send forth, as buds or shoots; 4, to extinguish (fire); 5, to publish; **put over**, *Slang*, to accomplish or bring about; **put through**, to carry out successfully; **put up**, 1, to offer for sale, especially at auction; 2, to raise (a price); 3, to can or preserve (fruit); 4, to offer or advance (funds), as on a bet; 5, to lodge; 6, to nominate, as for membership; 7, to lay aside (work); 8, to build; **put up to**, to incite (a person) to (mischief or daring); **put up with**, to tolerate; bear.

pu·tre·fac·tion (pū/trē-făk/shŭn), *n.* 1, the act or process of decaying; 2, decomposition; rottenness.

pu·tre·fy (pū/trē-fī), *v.t.* [putrefied, putrefy-ing], to rot; corrupt:—*v.i.* to decay or become rotten.

pu·trid (pū/trĭd), *adj.* 1, corrupt; rotten; 2, foul; as, a *putrid* odor.—*n.* **pu/trid-ness.** —*n.* **pu-trid/i-ty.**

putt (pŭt), *n.* in golf, a short stroke to play the ball into a hole:—*v.t.* and *v.i.* to drive (a golf ball) into a hole.

put·tee (pŭt/ĭ), *n.* 1, a gaiter made of cloth wrapped spirally from ankle to knee, worn by soldiers or sportsmen; 2, a stiff leather legging.

[1]**putt·er** (pŭt/ẽr), *n.* in golf, a short club, usually with a brass or iron head, used for playing the ball into a hole; also, one who putts with such a club. (See illustration under *golf club*.)

PUTTEES
1, spirally wrapped put-tee; 2, a leather puttee.

[2]**put·ter** (pŭt/ẽr), *v.i.* to busy oneself with trifles; potter.

putt·ing green (pŭt/ĭng), in golf, the plot of smooth turf around a hole into which the ball is played.

put·ty (pŭt/ĭ), *n.* a cement of whiting and linseed oil used for filling cracks, holding panes in window sashes, etc.:—*v.t.* [puttied, putty-ing], to fill, as a crack or a hole, with such cement.

puz·zle (pŭz/l), *n.* 1, something that perplexes, confuses, or bewilders; 2, a toy or problem made to tax one's skill or ingenuity; 3, a problem; riddle:—*v.i.* [puz-zled, puz-zling], to be perplexed; as, to *puzzle* over a mystery:—*v.t.* 1, to perplex; entangle; 2, to solve by clever thinking; as, to *puzzle* out a riddle.—*n.* **puz/zler.**

Syn., v. bewilder, confuse, mystify.

pyg·my (pĭg/mĭ), *n.* [*pl.* pygmies], a very small person or thing; dwarf:— **Pygmy**, one of a race of dwarf people native to central Africa:—*adj.* dwarflike; very small; as, *pygmy* plants. Also spelled **pig/my; Pig/my.**

py·ja·mas (pĭ-jä/măz; pà-jä/màz), *n.* a sleeping or lounging suit. See **pajamas.**

py·lon (pī/lŏn), *n.* 1, in Egyptian architecture, a gateway in the form of a pyramid without an apex, or of two such pyramids; 2, a tower used as a marker in an airplane course, or as a support for a span of wire.

py·or·rhe·a (pī/ŏ-rē/à), *n.* 1, a discharge of pus; 2, popularly, a disease of the gums, in which pus forms at the sockets of the teeth, and the teeth become loose.

pyr·a·mid (pĭr/à-mĭd), *n.* 1, in geometry, a solid body standing on a triangular, square, or polygonal base, with triangular sides which meet in a point at the apex or top; 2, anything having the shape of a pyramid:—

PYRAMIDS
1, triangular; 2, square; 3, pentagonal.

The Pyramids, a group of Egyptian monuments built by the early kings to serve as their tombs:— *v.t.* and *v.i.* to build in the form of a pyramid; to pile up.—*adj.* **py-ram/i-dal** (pĭ-răm/ĭ-dăl).

EGYPTIAN PYRAMIDS

pyre (pīr), *n.* a pile of wood for burning a corpse; a funeral pile.

Pyr·e·nees (pĭr/ē-nēz), a mountain range between France and Spain (map 12).

py·rite (pī/rīt), *n.* a yellow mineral with a bright luster, formed of iron and sulphur; iron pyrites.

py·ri·tes (pī-rī/tēz; pĭ-rī/tēz; pī/rīts), *n.* a compound of sulphur with iron, copper, or the like, as pyrite.

py·ro·tech·nic (pī/rŏ-těk/nĭk; pīr/ŏ-těk/nĭk), *adj.* pertaining to fireworks or the

go, join; yet; sing; chin; show; thin, *then*; hw, *why*; zh, azure; ü, Ger. für or Fr. *lune*; ö, Ger. schön or Fr. *feu*; ṅ, Fr. *enfant*, nom; kh, Ger. *ach* or *ich*. See pages ix–x.

art of making them:—**pyrotechnics,** *n.pl.* **1,** fireworks or the art of making them; **2,** hence, any brilliant display, as of wit.

Pyr-rhic vic-to-ry (pĭr′ĭk), a victory gained at too great cost: so called from the victory of Pyrrhus over the Romans at Asculum, 279 B.C., in which a great many men were killed.

Pyr-rhus (pĭr′ŭs), **1,** in mythology, a Greek hero of the Trojan War, the son of Achilles; **2,** a king of Epirus in Greece (318?–272 B.C.).

Py-thag-o-ras (pĭ-thăg′ō-răs), (582–507? B.C.), a Greek philosopher and mathematician.—*n.* and *adj.* **Py-thag′o-re′an.**

Pyth-i-as (pĭth′ĭ-ăs), *n.* in Greek legend, a youth famed for his faithful friendship with Damon.

py-thon (pī′thŏn; pī′thŭn), *n.* a large, non-poisonous Old World serpent which crushes its prey.

Q

Q, q (kū), *n.* [*pl.* Q's, q's], the 17th letter of the alphabet, following P.

Q.M. abbreviation for *Quartermaster.*

qt. [*pl.* qt.], abbreviation for *quart.*

¹**quack** (kwăk), *n.* the cry of a duck, or a harsh sound like it:—*v.i.* to utter a quack.

²**quack** (kwăk), *n.* **1,** an ignorant person who claims to have skill in medicine; **2,** hence, one who pretends to have knowledge which he does not really possess:—*adj.* making false claims; not genuine.— *n.* **quack′er-y.**

quad-ran-gle (kwŏd′răng′-gl; kwôd′-; kwŏd-răng′-gl; kwôd′-), *n.* **1,** in geometry, a plane figure with four angles and four sides; **2,** a four-sided court, surrounded by buildings, especially on a college campus.

QUADRANGLE, def. 2

quad-ran-gu-lar (kwŏd-răng′-gṳ-lẽr; kwôd-), *adj.* having four angles.

quad-rant (kwŏd′rănt; kwôd′-), *n.* **1,** one fourth of the circumference of a circle, or an arc of 90 degrees; **2,** the area bounded by such an arc and the lines from its ends to the center of the circle; **3,** an instrument used in surveying, astronomy, etc., to measure altitude.

QUADRANT def. 1

quad-ren-ni-al (kwŏd-rĕn′ĭ-ăl; kwôd-), *adj.* **1,** lasting four years; **2,** happening once in four years; as, a *quadrennial* election.

quad-ri-lat-er-al (kwŏd′rĭ-lăt′ẽr-ăl;

1, square; 2, rhomboid; 3, trapezoid.
QUADRILATERALS

kwôd′-), *n.* a plane figure bounded by four straight lines:—*adj.* having four sides.

qua-drille (kwŏ-drĭl′), *n.* an old-fashioned square dance for four couples; also, the musical accompaniment.

quad-ru-ped (kwŏd′rŏŏ-pĕd; kwôd′-), *n.* a four-footed animal:—*adj.* having four feet.

quad-ru-ple (kwŏd′rŏŏ-pl; kwôd′-; kwŏd-rōō′pl; kwôd-), *adj.* fourfold; composed of, or including, four parts:—*n.* (kwŏd′rŏŏ-pl; kwôd′-), a sum or quantity four times as great as another:—*v.t.* (kwŏd-rōō′pl; kwôd-; kwŏd′rŏŏ-pl; kwôd′-), [quadrupled, quadru-pling], to multiply by four:— *v.i.* to increase fourfold.

quad-ru-plet (kwŏd′rŏŏ-plĕt; kwôd′-), *n.* **1,** a combination of four of one kind; **2,** one of four children born at one birth.

quaff (kwȧf), *v.t.* to drink in deep draughts: —*v.i.* to drink deeply.

quag-mire (kwăg′mīr′; kwŏg′mīr′; kwôg′-), *n.* soft ground which yields under the feet; a bog; marsh.

¹**quail** (kwāl), *n.* [*pl.* quail or quails], any of several small game birds, as the European quail and the bobwhite: often called *partridge.*

²**quail** (kwāl), *v.i.* to shrink from pain or danger; lose heart; cower.

quaint (kwānt), *adj.* pleasingly odd in appearance or manner; especially, attractive because of an old-fashioned daintiness or prettiness.—*n.* **quaint′ness.**

EUROPEAN QUAIL

quake (kwāk), *v.i.* [quaked, quak-ing], **1,** to shake from internal shock or convulsion; as, the earth *quakes;* **2,** to tremble or shake with fear, cold, etc.; quiver:—*n.* a shaking or trembling; especially, an earthquake.

Quak-er (kwā′kẽr), *n.* a member of a religious sect, officially called *Religious Society of Friends,* founded in England about 1650.—*n.fem.* **Quak′er-ess.**

qual·i·fi·ca·tion (kwŏl′ĭ-fĭ-kā′shŭn; kwôl-/), *n.* **1,** the act of making, or the state of being, fit or qualified; **2,** that which makes a person or thing fit for a special task, position, etc.; fitness; **3,** that which limits; a restriction; as, he told the story with the *qualification* that it be kept secret for a week.

qual·i·fied (kwŏl′ĭ-fīd; kwôl-/), *adj.* **1,** fitted; adapted; as, she is well *qualified* for the task; **2,** limited; as, *qualified* praise.

qual·i·fi·er (kwŏl′ĭ-fī′ẽr; kwôl-/), *n.* **1,** that which limits or modifies; **2,** in grammar, a word, as an adjective or adverb, which limits the meaning of another word.

qual·i·fy (kwŏl′ĭ-fī; kwôl-/), *v.t.* [qualified, qualify-ing], **1,** to make fit for any office, occupation, sport, etc.; as, his work *quali- fied* him to compete for the prize; **2,** to alter slightly; change; limit; as, to *qualify* a statement; **3,** to moderate; lessen; soften; as, to *qualify* a rebuke; **4,** to give legal authorization to; as, the state has *qualified* him to practice medicine; **5,** in grammar, to limit the meaning of (a word); as, ad- verbs *qualify* verbs, adjectives, or other adverbs:—*v.i.* to be or become competent or fit for any office or employment; as, he *qualified* for the college crew.

qual·i·ta·tive (kwŏl′ĭ-tā′tĭv; kwôl-/), *adj.* pertaining to quality or kind, as opposed to quantity or amount; as, *qualitative* anal- ysis.—*adv.* **qual′i-ta′tive-ly.**

qual·i·ty (kwŏl′ĭ-tĭ; kwôl-/), *n.* [*pl.* quali- ties], **1,** that which distinguishes one person or thing from others, as color, weight, skill, etc.; **2,** the essential nature of a person or thing; a characteristic; as, elasticity is a *quality* of rubber; **3,** degree of excellence; as, a fine *quality* of wool; **4,** worth.
Syn. attribute, property.

qualm (kwäm; kwôm), *n.* **1,** a feeling of sickness or faintness that lasts only a moment; **2,** hence, a sudden fear; **3,** un- easiness of conscience.—*adj.* **qualm′ish.**

quan·da·ry (kwŏn′dȧ-rĭ; kwôn′-), *n.* [*pl.* quandaries], a state of hesitation or doubt; uncertainty.

quan·ti·ta·tive (kwŏn′tĭ-tā′tĭv; kwôn′-), *adj.* pertaining to quantity or amount, as opposed to quality or kind; as, *quantitative* analysis.—*adv.* **quan′ti-ta′tive-ly.**

quan·ti·ty (kwŏn′tĭ-tĭ; kwôn′-), *n.* [*pl.* quantities], **1,** amount; bulk; as, this bag contains one bushel in *quantity;* **2,** any un- certain, usually considerable, amount; as, to buy ice in *quantity;* **3,** the relative time occupied in uttering a sound or syllable;

4, in mathematics, anything that can be increased, divided, or measured.

quar·an·tine (kwŏr′ăn-tēn; kwôr′-), *n.* **1,** the time during which an incoming vessel may not dock, while its passengers are in- spected for contagious diseases; hence, the means taken to enforce this inspection; also, the place where the ships are held; **2,** any enforced restriction placed on a person or thing because of contagious disease:— *v.t.* (kwŏr′ăn-tēn; kwôr′-; kwŏr′ăn-tēn′; kwôr′-), [quarantined, quarantin-ing], to keep (a person or thing) away from others.

¹**quar·rel** (kwŏr′ĕl; kwôr′-), *n.* **1,** an angry dispute; a petty fight; **2,** a cause for dis- pute; as, he has no *quarrel* with us; **3,** a disagreement or falling out; a breach of friendship:—*v.i.* [quarreled, quarrel-ing], **1,** to dispute violently; fight; **2,** to dis- agree; fall out; **3,** to find fault; as, to *quarrel* with a decision.—*n.* **quar′rel-er.**

²**quar·rel** (kwŏr′ĕl; kwôr′-), *n.* a heavy arrow with a square head, for- merly used with the crossbow.

QUARREL

quar·rel·some (kwŏr′ĕl-sŭm; kwôr′-), *adj.* inclined to dispute, find fault, or fight.

¹**quar·ry** (kwŏr′ĭ; kwôr′ĭ), *n.* [*pl.* quarries], an open excavation or hole from which stone is obtained by cutting or blasting:— *v.t.* [quarried, quarry-ing], to dig or take from an excavation or hole.

²**quar·ry** (kwŏr′ĭ; kwôr′ĭ), *n.* [*pl.* quarries], an animal that is hunted, caught or killed, as in a chase; game.

quart (kwôrt), *n.* **1,** a mea- sure of capacity; two pints, or one fourth of a gallon, or, in dry measure, one eighth of a peck; **2,** a vessel containing a quart; also, its contents.

QUART
MEASURE

quar·ter (kwôr′tẽr), *n.* **1,** one of the four equal parts into which a thing may be, or is, divided; **2,** three months or a fourth of one year; **3,** one half of a semester at school or college; **4,** a fourth of a dollar, or 25 cents; also, a silver coin of this value; **5,** one of the four cardinal points of the compass; hence, any part or di- vision of the earth; as, men came from all *quarters;* **6,** a particular place or dis- trict; as, the French *quarter* in New Orleans; **7,** one of the four limbs of an ani- mal with the parts near it; as, a *quarter* of beef; **8,** a measure for grain, consisting of eight bushels; **9,** one of the four equal parts of the monthly period of the moon; also, its position after the first or third of these; **10,** life granted to a captive or enemy; mercy; as, to give no *quarter;* **11,**

---

go; join; yet; sing; chin; show; thin, *th*en; **hw,** *why;* **zh,** a**z**ure; **ü,** Ger. f**ü**r or Fr. l**u**ne; **ö,** Ger. sch**ö**n or Fr. f**eu;** **ṅ,** Fr. e**n**fant, no**m;** **kh,** Ger. a**ch** or i**ch.** See pages ix–x.

the after part of a ship's side; **12, quarters**, lodging; as, bachelor *quarters:*—*adj.* consisting of, or equal to, a fourth part of something; as, a *quarter* hour:—*v.t.* **1**, to divide into fourths, or quarters; **2**, to furnish with food and lodging; as, to *quarter* soldiers in a town.

quar·ter–deck (kwôr′tẽr-dĕk′), *n.* that part of the upper deck of a ship between the stern and mizzenmast, used as a promenade for officers.

quar·tered oak (kwôr′tẽrd ōk), oak lumber made by sawing the trunk lengthwise through the center into quarters and then sawing these in such a way as to bring out the grain of the wood.

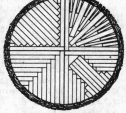

QUARTERED OAK

Section of log, showing different methods of sawing.

quar·ter·ly (kwôr′tẽr-lĭ), *n.* [*pl.* quarterlies], a publication issued once every three months:—*adj.* **1**, consisting of, or containing, a fourth part; **2**, coming, or falling due, once every three months:—*adv.* once in each quarter.

quar·ter·mas·ter (kwôr′tẽr-màs′tẽr), *n.* **1**, in the army, an officer whose duty it is to provide lodgings, food, clothing, and other supplies for soldiers; **2**, in the navy, a petty officer who attends to the steering, signals, soundings, etc., of ships.

quar·ter sec·tion, in the surveying systems of the United States and Canadian governments, 160 acres.

quar·ter·staff (kwôr′tẽr-stàf′), *n.* [*pl.* quarterstaves (-stāvz′; -stàvz′)], a stout stick from six to eight feet long, formerly used in England as a weapon.

quar·tet or **quar·tette** (kwôr-tĕt′), *n.* **1**, a musical composition for four voices or instruments; **2**, the four performers of such a composition; **3**, anything made up of four.

quar·to (kwôr′tō), *n.* [*pl.* quartos], the size of a page obtained by folding a sheet of printing paper twice so as to form four leaves; also, a book made of paper so folded:—*adj.* having four leaves in a sheet; of the size and shape of a quarto.

quartz (kwôrts), *n.* a very common, hard mineral, found in brilliant crystals or in masses. Many semiprecious stones, such as agates, amethysts, onyx, and jasper are forms of quartz.

quash (kwŏsh; kwôsh), *v.t.* **1**, to subdue or crush, as an uprising; **2**, in law, to stop, as a suit; set aside, as an indictment.

qua·si (kwā′sī; kwä′sĭ), as if; almost; seemingly; in a manner: used as an adjective or adverb, or as a prefix with a verb, adjective, adverb, or noun; as, a *quasi* truth; a *quasi*-historical statement; a *quasi*-serious remark.

quat·rain (kwŏt′rān; kwôt′rān), *n.* a four-line stanza, in which, usually, the first and third lines rime, and the second and fourth.

qua·ver (kwā′vẽr), *n.* **1**, a shaking or trembling, as of the voice; **2**, a trill in singing or playing; **3**, in music, an eighth note:—*v.i.* to quiver; vibrate:—*v.t.* to utter or sing with trills.

quay (kē), *n.* a permanent wharf, often of masonry, where ships may load or unload.

Que. abbreviation for *Quebec*.

quea·sy (kwē′zĭ), *adj.* [quea-si-er, quea-si-est], nauseated; easily upset; as, a *queasy* stomach; hence, squeamish; over-scrupulous; as, a *queasy* conscience.

Que·bec (kwē-bĕk′), a province in eastern Canada; also, a city, its capital, on the Saint Lawrence River (map 4).

queen (kwēn), *n.* **1**, a woman who rules a country in her own right; **2**, the wife of a king; **3**, a woman who is a leader in a certain sphere; as, a social *queen;* **4**, the perfect female of bees, ants, or the like, usually the only female in the group able to lay eggs; **5**, a playing card bearing a conventional drawing of a queen; **6**, in chess, the piece ranking next to the king; **7**, the best or chief of her kind; as, the *queen* of beauty.

queen consort, the wife of a reigning king; **queen dowager**, the widow of a king; **queen mother**, a king's widow who is also mother of a reigning sovereign; **queen regent**, **1**, a queen reigning during the childhood,- absence, or incapacity of the actual sovereign; **2**, a queen reigning in her own right: also called *queen regnant*.

queen·ly (kwēn′lĭ), *adj.* [queen-li-er, queen-li-est], like a queen.—*n.* **queen′li·ness**.

queen post, one of two upright timbers in the framework of a roof which are placed at equal distances from the apex, or point.

Queens·land (kwēnz′lănd; kwēnz′lănd), a state (cap. Brisbane) in northeastern Australia (map 16).

Queens·town (kwēnz′toun; kwēnz′tŭn), the former name of a city in Ireland. See **Cóbh**.

queer (kwĭr), *adj.* **1**, differing from the ordinary or normal; droll; strange; **2**, giddy; faint; as, a *queer* feeling; •**3**, *Colloquial*: **a**, mentally unsound; **b**, open to question:—*v.t.* **1**, to spoil; upset; to interfere with; as, to *queer* one's chances for a job; **2**, to place in an embarrassing situation; as, he *queered* himself at the party.—*adv.* **queer'-ly.**—*n.* **queer'ness.**

Syn. eccentric, erratic, odd, singular.

quell (kwĕl), *v.t.* to suppress or subdue; put an end to; as, to *quell* a riot.

quench (kwĕnch), *v.t.* **1,** to put out; extinguish; as, to *quench* a fire; hence, to suppress; stifle; as, to *quench* a desire for revenge; **2,** to relieve; slake; as, to *quench* thirst.—*adj.* **quench'a-ble.**

quer-u-lous (kwĕr'ū-lŭs; kwĕr'ŏŏ-lŭs), *adj.* **1,** complaining; fretful; as, a *querulous* old man; **2,** whining; as, a *querulous* voice.—*n.* **quer'u-lous-ness.**

que-ry (kwĭ'rĭ), *n.* [*pl.* queries], **1,** a question; an inquiry; **2,** a question mark [?]:—*v.t.* [queried, query-ing], **1,** to inquire into; ask; **2,** to express a doubt in regard to; as, to *query* his loyalty:—*v.i.* to ask questions.

quest (kwĕst), *n.* **1,** a search; as, an animal in *quest* of food; **2,** in medieval romance, an expedition for a particular object; as, the *quest* for the Holy Grail:—*v.i.* to make search; to seek.

ques-tion (kwĕs'chŭn), *n.* **1,** the act of asking or inquiring; **2,** that which is asked; **3,** the subject under discussion or to be decided upon; as, the *question* before the meeting; **4,** dispute, doubt, or objection; as, beyond *question*, these are the facts:—**question mark,** an interrogation point; a mark [?] of punctuation in writing or printing put at the end of a question:—*v.t.* **1,** to ask; examine by queries; **2,** to consider doubtful; **3,** to challenge; take exception to; as, I *question* that statement:—*v.i.* to make inquiries.—*n.* **ques'tion-er.**

Syn. query, distrust, uncertainty.

ques-tion-a-ble (kwĕs'chŭn-*a*-bl), *adj.* **1,** open to question or doubt; **2,** arousing suspicion; as, a *questionable* character.

ques-tion-naire (kwĕs'chŭn-âr'), *n.* a series of questions given to a number of persons whose replies often serve as a basis of a report on the subject of the questions.

quet-zal (kĕt-säl') or **que-zal** (kĕ-säl'), *n.* **1,** a Central American bird; **2,** monetary unit of Guatemala. (See page 943).

QUEUE (Q), def. 1
18th century.

queue (kū), *n.* **1,** a braid of hair hanging down the back; a pigtail; **2,** a line of people, automobiles, or the like, awaiting their turn to proceed. Also spelled *cue.*

Quezon City (kā'sôn), capital city of the Philippine Republic (map 16).

quib-ble (kwĭb'l), *n.* a skilful evasion of the point in question by advancing a trifling argument or by using words with a double meaning:—*v.i.* [quib-bled, quib-bling], to avoid the truth by a skilful but trifling objection.—*n.* **quib'bler.**

quick (kwĭk), *adj.* **1,** rapid; swift; as, *quick* in action; **2,** nimble; as, *quick* on one's feet; **3,** prompt to respond to impressions; alert; as, a *quick* mind; **4,** accurate; unhesitating; ready; as, a *quick* eye; *quick* wit; **5,** easily excited; hasty; as, a *quick* temper; **6,** sensitive; as, a *quick* ear:—*adv.* with haste; rapidly:—*n.* **1,** living beings; **2,** the living flesh; as, to cut the nails down to the *quick;* hence, the seat of the feelings; as, she was hurt to the *quick.*—*adv.* **quick'ly.**—*n.* **quick'ness.**

Syn., adj. brisk, lively, speedy, fast.

quick-en (kwĭk'ĕn), *v.i.* **1,** to come to life; become alive; **2,** to act or move more rapidly:—*v.t.* **1,** to increase the speed of; hasten; as, to *quicken* one's steps; **2,** to bring to life; **3,** to make keen; arouse; kindle; as, the walk *quickened* our appetites.—*n.* **quick'en-er.**

quick-lime (kwĭk'līm'), *n.* lime produced by burning limestone, shells, etc.: changed by the addition of water into *slaked lime,* and used in cement, mortar, etc.

quick-sand (kwĭk'sănd'), *n.* a bed of wet, loose sand that sucks into it any heavy object that comes upon it.

quick-sil-ver (kwĭk'sĭl'vĕr), *n.* mercury.

quick—wit-ted (kwĭk'-wĭt'ĕd), *adj.* clever; alert; as, a *quick-witted* reply.

quid (kwĭd), *n.* a piece of something, as of tobacco, held in the mouth and chewed.

qui-es-cent (kwī-ĕs'ĕnt), *adj.* calm; still; tranquil.—*n.* **qui-es'cence.**

qui-et (kwī'ĕt), *adj.* **1,** without sound; silent; as, a *quiet* night; **2,** not moving; still; as, *quiet* hands; **3,** tranquil; peaceful; secluded; as, a *quiet* countryside; **4,** peaceable; gentle; as, a *quiet* disposition; **5,** informal; as, a *quiet* wedding; **6,** not showy; as, *quiet* colors:—*v.t.* to make peaceful; as, to *quiet* a child:—*v.i.* to become still or calm; as, the sea has *quieted:*—*n.* **1,** freedom from motion, noise, or disturbance; **2,** gentleness or composure of manner; **3,** peace; rest.—*n.* **qui'et-ness.**

Syn., n. tranquillity, serenity, quietude.

qui-e-tude (kwī'ĕ-tūd), *n.* tranquillity.

qui-e-tus (kwī-ē'tŭs), *n.* **1,** the final settlement of an account; **2,** anything which puts an end to action; especially, death.

QUILL, def. 2

quill (kwĭl), *n.* **1,** a large, strong feather; also, the hollow shaft of a feather; **2,** a pen made from a feather; **3**, a long, sharp spine, as of a porcupine.

quilt (kwĭlt), *n.* a bedcover made by stitching together two layers of fabric, usually in an ornamental pattern, with a layer of cotton or wool between; also, any warm bedcover:—*v.t.* to stitch and interline (layers of cloth) in the manner of a quilt:—*v.i.* to do quilting.

quilt-ing (kwĭl′tĭng), *n.* **1**, the act or process of making quilted work; **2**, the material for such work; also, the finished work.

quince (kwĭns), *n.* **1**, a tree related to the apple; **2**, the hard yellowish fruit of this tree, used for preserves and jellies.

QUINCE
Leaves and fruit.

qui-nine (kwī′nīn; kwĭ-nēn′), *n.* a bitter drug obtained from bark of the cinchona tree and used especially in treating malaria.

quin-quen-ni-al (kwĭn-kwĕn′ĭ-ăl), *adj.* **1**, lasting five years; **2**, occurring once in five years.

quin-sy (kwĭn′zĭ), *n.* severe soreness of the tonsils and throat.

quin-tes-sence (kwĭn-tĕs′ĕns), *n.* **1**, the pure essence, or most refined extract, as of a drug; **2**, the perfect example of some quality; as, he is the *quintessence* of wit.

quin-tet or **quin-tette** (kwĭn-tĕt′), *n.* **1**, a musical composition for five voices or instruments; **2**, the five performers of such a piece; **3**, any set of five.

quin-tu-ple (kwĭn′tŭ-pl), *adj.* fivefold; multiplied by five, or arranged in fives.

quin-tu-plet (kwĭn′tŭ-plĕt), *n.* **1**, a combination of five of one kind; **2**, one of five children born at one birth.

quip (kwĭp), *n.* **1**, a clever or sarcastic remark; **2**, an evasion of a point by clever use of words; a quibble; **3**, something odd.

quire (kwīr), *n.* a pack of 24 or 25 uniform sheets of paper.

Quir-i-nal (kwĭr′ĭ-năl; kwĭ-rī′năl), *n.* **1**, one of the hills upon which Rome was built; **2**, the palace of the king of Italy, which stands on this hill; **3**, hence, the monarchical government in Italy.

quirk (kwûrk), *n.* **1**, a sudden twist or turn, as of a pen in writing; **2**, a quick turn of fancy; a quip; **3**, a clever evasion.

quirt (kwûrt), *n.* a short-handled riding whip with a lash of braided rawhide.

quis-ling (kwĭz′lĭng), *n.* a person who uses a position of authority in his own country to betray it to its enemies.

quit (kwĭt), *v.t.* [quit or quit-ted, quit-ting], **1**, to pay off (a debt); **2**, to stop; give up; as, to *quit* work; **3**, to go away from; as, to *quit* a neighborhood:—*v.i.* to stop doing something; as, to *quit* at noon:—*adj.* free; as, we're *quit* of that fellow.

quit-claim (kwĭt′klām′), *n.* in law, a deed by which a person gives up claim to a property.

quite (kwīt), *adv.* **1**, totally; completely; as, *quite* mistaken; **2**, *Colloquial*, to a considerable extent; rather; as, *quite* cold.

Qui-to (kē′tō), a city, the capital of Ecuador, South America (map 11).

quits (kwĭts), *adj.* even or equal (with someone), as upon the repayment of a favor or an injury; as, now we're *quits*.

quit-tance (kwĭt′ăns), *n.* **1**, release from a debt; **2**, repayment of a favor or wrong.

quit-ter (kwĭt′ēr), *n.* one who gives up; especially, a shirk or a coward.

¹quiv-er (kwĭv′ēr), *n.* a light case for carrying arrows.

²quiv-er (kwĭv′ēr), *n.* a trembling or shivering:—*v.i.* to shake, as from excitement.
Syn., *v.* shudder, tremble.

ANCIENT
QUIVER

qui vive (kē′ vēv′), a call of a French sentry, corresponding to "Who goes there?":—**on the qui vive**, keen; alert.

Quix-ote, Don (dŏn kwĭk′sŏt; dŏn kē-hō′tā), the ridiculously chivalrous hero of a satirical Spanish romance of that name by Cervantes.

quix-ot-ic (kwĭks-ŏt′ĭk), *adj.* absurdly chivalrous, romantic, or idealistic.

quiz (kwĭz), *n.* [*pl.* quizzes], **1**, an informal examination of a pupil or class; a test; **2**, a puzzling question:—*v.t.* [quizzed, quizzing], to examine informally.

quiz-zi-cal (kwĭz′ĭ-kăl), *adj.* comical; humorously serious; as, a *quizzical* look.

quoin (koin; kwoin), *n.* a cornerstone.

quoit (kwoit; koit), *n.* **1**, a flat iron ring about six inches across; **2**, quoits, a game in which players pitch such rings at a peg.

QUOIT, def. 1

quon-dam (kwŏn′dăm), *adj.* former; as, a *quondam* friend.

quor-um (kwôr′ŭm), *n.* the number of members of an assembly that the rules require to be present in order that business may legally be transacted.

quo-ta (kwō′tȧ), *n.* the part of a total that any individual or group is to contribute or receive; a share; as, each class paid its *quota* toward the school picnic.

āte, ȧorta, râre, căt, ȧsk, fär, ăllow, sofȧ; ēve, êvent, ĕll, writēr, novĕl; bīte, pĭn; nō, ōbey, ôr, dŏg, tŏp, cŏllide; ūnit, ūnite, bûrn, cŭt, focŭs; nōōn, fŏŏt; mound; coin;

quot·a·ble (kwō'tȧ-bl), *adj.* suitable for quoting from, as an author or a poem.

quo·ta·tion (kwō-tā'shŭn), *n.* 1, the repeating of another's words; 2, the words repeated; 3, a passage from a book, poem, or the like; 4, the current market price of something, or a statement of this; as, a *quotation* on wheat:—**quotation mark**, a mark of punctuation placed at the beginning ["] and end ["] of a word or passage to show that it is quoted. A quotation within a quotation is usually enclosed in single quotation marks [' ']; as, "the boy said, 'I am going home.'"

quote (kwōt), *v.t.* [quot-ed, quot-ing], 1, to repeat (another's words, either written or spoken); as, I *quoted* your poem; 2, to repeat a passage from; refer to as an authority; as, to *quote* Ruskin; 3, to give the present price of:—*v.i.* to repeat the words of another; as, he *quoted* accurately:—*n.* in printing, a quotation mark.

quoth (kwōth), *v.t. Archaic,* said; spoke; as, "I met a fool," *quoth* he.

quo·tient (kwō'shĕnt), *n.* the result obtained when one number is divided by another; as, if 10 is divided by 5, the *quotient* is 2.

R

R, r (är), *n.* [*pl.* R's, r's], the 18th letter of the alphabet, following Q:—**the three R's,** reading, 'riting, and 'rithmetic.

R. abbreviation for *river*.

R.A. abbreviation for *Rear Admiral*.

Ra·bat or **Rab·bat** (rȧ-bät'), a seaport and chief capital of Morocco in northwestern Africa (map 14).

rab·bi (rāb'ī), *n.* [*pl.* rabbis or rabbies (rāb'īz)], in the Jewish religion, a teacher and interpreter of the law and ritual.

rab·bit (rāb'ĭt), *n.* a small, short-tailed animal of the hare family. Its fur is used to make imitations of expensive furs.

rab·ble (rāb'l), *n.* a noisy crowd or mob:—**the rabble,** the common people, especially those of the lowest class. *Syn.* populace, throng, crowd, mob.

RABBIT (⅛)

Ra·be·lais (rȧ'bĕ-lā'), François (1490?-1553), a French monk, physician, traveler, and author of famous satires.

rab·id (rāb'ĭd), *adj.* 1, furious; raging; 2, extremely unreasonable; excessively zealous; as, a *rabid* reformer; 3, infected with rabies; as, a *rabid* dog.

ra·bi·es (rā'bĭ-ēz; rā'bēz), *n.* an infectious and often fatal disease of the dog and other animals, especially flesh-eating animals; hydrophobia. It may be transmitted to man by the bite of an infected animal.

rac·coon or **ra·coon** (rȧ-kōōn'), *n.* 1, a grayish-brown, tree-dwelling animal of North America, with a bushy, ringed tail: often called *coon;* 2, its fur, often made into coats.

¹race (rās), *n.* 1, a swift current of water, or the channel for such a current; as, a mill *race;* 2, course of life; career; as, my

race is run; 3, a competitive contest of speed, as in running or swimming; also, any contest or rivalry; as, a political *race:*—*v.i.* [raced, rac-ing], 1, to run swiftly; 2, to compete in speed:—*v.t.* 1, to cause to move swiftly; as, to *race* a motor; 2, to try to beat in a speed contest; as, I'll *race* you to the corner.

²race (rās), *n.* 1, the descendants of a common ancestor; a family; 2, a people or group of peoples united by a common language, religion, or culture; as, the English *race;* 3, a division of mankind, made up of tribes and nations descended from a common stock; as, the Negro *race;* 4, a class of persons with common interests and traits; as, the *race* of poets.

ra·ceme (rȧ-sēm'; rā-sēm'), *n.* a flower cluster in which the flowers on slender stems are arranged at intervals on a flower stalk, as in the lily of the valley.

RACEME of lily of the valley.

rac·er (rā'sẽr), *n.* 1, a person who engages in a speed contest; also, anything that can go at great speed, as an unusually swift horse; 2, a swift snake, especially the American black snake.

Ra·chel (rā'chĕl), in the Bible, the wife of Jacob and mother of Joseph and Benjamin.

ra·cial (rā'shăl), *adj.* pertaining to a race or division of mankind; as, *racial* customs.—*adv.* **ra·cial·ly.**

RACK (R), def. 4

¹rack (rāk), *n.* 1, a framework on or in which articles are hung, arranged, held, or displayed; as, a meat *rack;* a towel *rack;* 2, a frame of bars above a manger for holding fodder; **3,** a framework fitted to a wagon for hauling hay; **4,** a bar with teeth on one side that engage the teeth of a gear.

²rack (răk), *n.* **1,** in former times, an instrument for torturing the body by stretching and straining the limbs; **2,** intense physical or mental anguish:—*v.t.* **1,** to stretch, as on the rack; **2,** to subject to great pain or anguish; as, remorse *racked* him; **3,** to strain; exert to the utmost; as, to *rack* one's brain for a word.

Syn., *v.* torture, torment, distort.

³rack (răk), *n.* wreck; ruin: used only in the expression *rack and ruin.* See **wrack.**

¹rack·et (răk'ĕt), *n.* **1,** a clattering noise; din; noisy talk or play; **2,** a dishonest trick or scheme; especially, an organized activity of the criminal underworld, such as the extortion of money by threats of violence:—*v.i.* to make a loud and confused noise.

Syn., *n.* hubbub, uproar, commotion.

²rack·et or **rac·quet** (răk'ĕt), *n.* a network bat used in tennis and similar games.

TENNIS RACKET

rack·et·eer (răk'ě·tîr'), *n.* a person who, alone or as a gang member, extorts money by threats.

rac·y (rā'sĭ), *adj.* [rac·i·er, rac·i·est], **1,** having a marked flavor suggestive of the source from which a thing comes; **2,** colorful; vivid; as, he writes in a *racy* style.—*n.* **rac'i·ness.**

ra·dar (rā'där), *n.* a system for detecting and locating objects, as aircraft or ships, by transmitting high frequency radio waves which rebound when they strike an obstruction; also, the apparatus used in this way.

ra·di·al (rā'dĭ·ăl), *adj.* arranged like the spokes of a wheel.—*adv.* **ra'di·al·ly.**

ra·di·ance (rā'dĭ·ăns), *n.* brilliancy; luster. Also, **ra'di·an·cy** (rā'dĭ·ăn·sĭ).

ra·di·ant (rā'dĭ·ănt), *adj.* **1,** sending out rays of light or heat; as, the *radiant* sun; also, shining; brilliant; as, *radiant* beauty; **2,** beaming with joy, delight, etc.; as, a *radiant* face; **3,** coming out in rays from some source; as, the *radiant* energy of the sun.—*adv.* **ra'di·ant·ly.**

Syn. luminous, beaming, brilliant.

ra·di·ate (rā'dĭ·āt), *v.t.* [radiat-ed, radiat-ing], **1,** to send out in rays; as, a lamp *radiates* light; **2,** to spread abroad; as, to *radiate* happiness:—*v.i.* **1,** to send forth beams; shine; glow; **2,** to come out in rays, as heat from a fire; **3,** to come out from a center; as, the spokes of a wheel.

ra·di·a·tion (rā'dĭ·ā'shŭn), *n.* **1,** the act of issuing and spreading from a center; as, the *radiation* of heat from a stove; **2,** that which spreads from a center; **3,** the rays or particles given off by radioactive substances.

ra·di·a·tor (rā'dĭ·ā'tẽr), *n.* **1,** a set of pipes heated by hot water or steam, for heating a room; **2,** an appliance used to cool a motor.

rad·i·cal (răd'ĭ·kăl), *adj.* **1,** having to do with a root or origin; deep-seated; fundamental; as, a *radical* cure; **2,** advocating extreme change; as, a *radical* speech:—*n.* (often *Radical*), a person who wishes to root out old customs and institutions, rather than to reform them; especially, in politics, an extremist.

RADIATOR
def. 1

ra·di·o (rā'dĭ·ō), *n.* [*pl.* radios], **1,** the equipment for broadcasting and receiving messages, music, or the like by means of electromagnetic waves without the use of wires between sender and receiver; especially, the instrument for receiving such broadcasts; **2,** the system of such wireless communication; as, we heard the news by *radio*; **3,** any

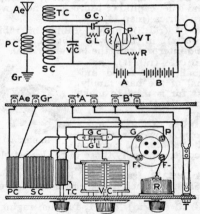

A SIMPLE VACUUM TUBE RADIO RECEIVING SET

Current is received from aerial *Ae,* and passes through coil *PC* to ground *Gr,* thus making up a circuit. Current is thereby induced in coil *SC* (turned to required wave length by condenser *VC*) and passes to filament *F* and grid *G* in vacuum tube *VT. F* is heated by a current, regulated by rheostat *R,* from battery *A,* which passes through grid *G* to plate *P.* From *P* current passes through coil *TC,* to earphones *T,* where the electrical vibrations are transformed to sound vibrations. Grid condenser *GC* and grid leak *GL* aid vacuum tube in changing current from alternating to direct.

message or program transmitted or received in this manner:—used in many one- and two-word combinations meaning: **1,** having to do with radio; as, *radio* program; or with radio waves; as, *radio* star; **2,** radioactive; as, *radio*carbon, *radio* gold; **3,** using radium or other radiation; as, *radio*therapy.

āte, āorta, râre, căt, àsk, fär, ăllow, sof*a*; ēve, ĕvent, ĕll, writẽr, novĕl; bīte, pĭn; nō, ōbey, ôr, dŏg, tŏp, cŏllide; ūnit, ūnite, bûrn, cŭt, focŭs; nōon, fŏŏt; mound; coin;

ra·di·o·ac·tive (rā′dĭ-ō-ăk′tĭv), *adj*. sending forth, as do radium and uranium, certain invisible rays or particles that go through most substances and are harmful to living tissues.—*n*. **ra′di·o·ac·tiv′i·ty**.

ra·di·o bea·con, a radio transmitting station, usually located at a landing field, which continually sends out signals that help a flyer to determine his position, especially in darkness or fog.

rad·ish (răd′ĭsh), *n*. a garden plant of the mustard family, with a pungent root; also, the root, which is eaten raw.

ra·di·um (rā′dĭ-ŭm), *n*. a rare white metal found in various minerals. Its atoms break down through various stages into lead, giving off rays which are used in treating cancer, and in other ways.

RADISH

ra·di·us (rā′dĭ-ŭs), *n*. [*pl*. radii (rā′dĭ-ī) or radiuses], **1**, a straight line from the center of a circle to its circumference, or from the center of a sphere to its surface; **2**, an area about a point, bounded by a circle with a given radius; as, within a *radius* of a mile from the post office.

ra·don (rā′dŏn), *n*. a radioactive gaseous element formed by disintegration of radium.

raf·fi·a (răf′ĭ-à), *n*. **1**, the fiber of a Madagascar palm, used in weaving hats, baskets, and the like; **2**, the palm itself.

raf·fle (răf′l), *n*. a kind of lottery in which each person pays a small sum for a chance of winning a large prize:—*v.t.* [raf-fled, raf-fling], to dispose of by means of a raffle; as, to *raffle* off a turkey:—*v.i.* to take part in a raffle; as, *to raffle* for a turkey.

RADIUS (R) def. 1

raft (răft), *n*. a floating framework of logs, etc.:—*v.t.* to convey on such a float.

raft·er (răf′tẽr), *n*. a sloping beam that helps support the roof of a house.

rag (răg), *n*. **1**, a worn or torn piece of cloth; a shred; **2**, **rags**, tattered or worn-out clothes:—*v.t.* [ragged (răgd), rag-ging], **1**, *Colloquial*, to play (music) with a catchy shifting of the beat; play in ragtime; **2**, *Slang*, to tease; also, to scold.

rag·a·muf·fin (răg′à-mŭf′ĭn), *n*. a ragged, dirty child, especially a boy.

rage (rāj), *n*. **1**, uncontrolled anger; **2**, extreme violence; fury, as of a storm; **3**, *Colloquial*, anything for the moment extremely popular or fashionable; as, colored shoes are the *rage* this spring:—*v.i.*

[raged, rag-ing], **1**, to be furious with anger; **2**, to act or speak violently; **3**, to have furious force or effect; as, the tornado *raged* through the town.

rag·ged (răg′ĕd), *adj*. **1**, having holes or tears resulting from wear; torn; as, a *ragged* coat; **2**, clothed in tatters; as, a *ragged* fellow; **3**, rough; jagged; as, a *ragged* stone.

ra·gout (rà-gōō′), *n*. a stew of meat and vegetables highly seasoned.

rag·time (răg′tīm′), *n*. in music, especially in Negro melodies, a distinct rhythm in which the accent of the melody often falls just before the regular beat of the accompaniment; syncopated music; also, the jerky, catchy rhythm of such music.

rag·weed (răg′wēd′), *n*. a coarse weed with small, yellowish-green flowers. Its pollen often causes hay fever.

raid (rād), *n*. **1**, a hostile invasion; a sudden attack; as, a cavalry *raid;* an air *raid;* **2**, a forced entrance by the police, to make arrests or seize stolen goods.—*v.t.* **raid**.

RAGWEED

¹**rail** (rāl), *n*. **1**, a bar of wood or metal placed level between two posts, as in a fence; **2**, a wooden or iron barrier to keep persons from falling; as, a hand*rail;* **3**, one of the two metal bars forming a track for trolley cars or trains; **4**, a railroad; as, to travel by *rail:*—*v.t.* to enclose with bars; as, to *rail* off part of a hall; to *rail* in an exhibit.

RAIL FENCE

²**rail** (rāl), *n*. a wading bird resembling a small crane.

³**rail** (rāl), *v.i.* to use bitter, scornful, or reproachful language; as, to *rail* at a beggar; to *rail* against fate.—*n*. and *adj*. **rail′ing**.

rail·ing (rāl′ĭng), *n*. **1**, material for rails; **2**, a fence or barrier made of rails and held up by posts.

RAIL (¹⁄₅)

rail·ler·y (rā′lẽr-ĭ; răl′ẽr-ĭ), *n*. [*pl*. railleries], good-natured ridicule or banter.

rail·road (rāl′rōd′), *n*. **1**, a permanent track formed of two parallel rails, on which trains move; **2**, a railroad system, including land, equipment, etc.:—*v.t. Colloquial*, to put through rapidly; as, to *railroad* a bill through a legislature.

rail·way (rāl′wā′), *n.* 1, a railroad; 2, any track with rails for wheels to run on.

rai·ment (rā′měnt), *n.* clothing; attire.

rain (rān), *n.* 1, water falling in drops condensed from moisture in the air; 2, the fall of such drops; as, a heavy *rain;* 3, a shower of anything; as, a *rain* of bullets:— *v.i.* to fall in drops, or like rain:—*v.t.* to pour down like rain; as, to *rain* blows on someone.—*adj.* **rain′less.**

rain·bow (rān′bō′), *n.* an arc or bow, containing the colors of the spectrum, formed in the sky opposite the sun by the reflection of the sun's rays from drops of falling rain, spray, or mist.

rain·coat (rān′kōt′), *n.* a coat or cloak made of waterproof material.

rain·drop (rān′drŏp′), *n.* a single drop of rain.

rain·fall (rān′fôl′), *n.* 1, a shower; 2, the amount of rain that falls during a definite period on any given area.

Rai·nier, Mount (rā-nēr′), a peak in the Cascade Range in the State of Washington, north of the Columbia River (map 9).

rain·y (rā′nĭ), *adj.* [rain-i-er, rain-i-est], abounding in rain; showery; wet.—*n.* **rain′i-ness.**

raise (rāz), *v.t.* [raised, rais-ing], 1, to set upright; as, to *raise* a flagpole; lift up; as, to *raise* a weight; 2, to stir up (game); to rouse from sleep; also, to restore (the dead) to life; 3, to erect; construct; as, to *raise* a building; 4, to cause to come into existence; as, to *raise* a smile; to *raise* trouble; 5, to grow; breed (crops, cattle, etc.); 6, to procure; collect; muster; as, to *raise* money, armies, etc.; 7, to bring up for consideration (a question, claim, or the like); 8, to cause to increase in degree, amount, intensity, etc.; as, to *raise* prices, the voice, one's courage; 9, to terminate; put an end to (a blockade); 10, to cause (bread) to rise; 11, to make higher in rank or power; as, to *raise* a prince to the throne; 12, to rear; bring up (children):—**raise Cain,** *Slang,* to cause a disturbance:—*n.* an increase, as in wages or salary.—*n.* **rais′er.**

rai·sin (rā′zn), *n.* a variety of sweet grape, often sold in dried form.

ra·ja or **ra·jah** (rä′jȧ), *n.* a Hindu king or prince.

¹rake (rāk), *n.* a farm or garden tool with teeth at one end of a long handle, used for loosening or smoothing soil, or for gathering loose matter, such as dead leaves, hay, or the like:—*v.t.* [raked, rak-ing], 1, to gather, smooth, or loosen with a rake; as, to *rake* the lawn; 2, to gather by

RAKE

diligent effort; as, to *rake* up evidence; to *rake* a few dollars together; 3, to search carefully; as, to *rake* the library for a special book; 4, in military language, to fire along the length of; as, to *rake* the deck of a ship:—**rake over the coals,** *Colloquial,* to scold vigorously; as, John's mother *raked* him *over the coals:—v.i.* 1, to work with a rake; 2, to make a close search.

²rake (rāk), *n.* a man of loose morals.

³rake (rāk), *n.* a slant or tilt; as, the *rake* of a hat; also, a slant from the perpendicular, as of a ship's mast or funnel:— *v.i.* and *v.t.* [raked, rak-ing], to slant, or cause to slant, as a mast.

rak·ish (rā′kĭsh), *adj.* 1, speedy-looking, as a ship with slanting masts or funnels; 2, jaunty; dashing, as a cap set at an angle.

¹Ra·leigh (rô′lĭ), Sir Walter (1552–1618), an English navigator and courtier.

²Ra·leigh (rô′lĭ), a city, capital of North Carolina, near the center of the state (map 8).

¹ral·ly (răl′ĭ), *v.t.* [rallied, rally-ing], 1, to bring together (troops in flight) and restore (them) to order; 2, to call together for any purpose; as, to *rally* voters:—*v.i.* 1, to return to order; as, the troops *rallied;* 2, to come together for action; be aroused to vigorous action; as, *rally* round the flag; 3, to recover strength; as, to *rally* from fever; 4, in tennis, to send the ball rapidly back and forth over the net:—*n.* [*pl.* rallies], 1, a restoring or recovery of order and discipline, as among defeated troops; 2, a quick sharp rise after a dip; as, a *rally* in prices; 3, a mass meeting; 4, in tennis, the repeated return of the ball in play until one player misses.

²ral·ly (răl′ĭ), *v.t.* [rallied, rally-ing], to tease good-naturedly; banter; as, to *rally* a boy on his first long trousers.

ram (răm), *n.* 1, a male sheep; 2, in war, a heavy pole for battering a wall; a battering ram:—*v.t.* [rammed, ramming], 1, to strike or butt against; 2, to pack with sharp blows; as, to *ram* earth into a hole; also, to pack hastily; cram.

RAM (¹⁄₂₀), def. 1

ram·ble (răm′bl), *v.i.* [ram-bled, rambling], 1, to wander or rove aimlessly about; to stroll for pleasure; 2, to talk or write at length and aimlessly; 3, to grow or spread at random, as vines:—*n.* a leisurely, aimless stroll.

ram·bler (răm′blẽr), *n.* 1, a person who

wanders aimlessly; **2,** a climbing rose.

ram·bling (răm′blĭng), *adj.* **1,** wandering at will; **2,** built on no single plan; growing or spreading at random; as, a *rambling* garden; **3,** loose and unorganized; as, a *rambling* tale.

Ram·e·ses (răm′ē-sēz), the name of several ancient Egyptian kings. See **Ramses.**

ram·i·fy (răm′ĭ-fī), *v.i.* [ramified, ramifying], to divide into branches or divisions, as a road.—*n.* **ram/i-fi-ca′tion.**

ram·jet (răm-jĕt), *n.* a jet engine which uses its forward motion to force air through its open front end into the combustion chamber.

ram·mer (răm′ẽr), *n.* one who or that which batters or rams.

¹ramp (rămp), *v.i.* **1,** to rear up on the hind legs in a threatening manner; **2,** to rage; storm about.

²ramp (rămp), *n.* a sloping roadway, by which persons or vehicles may go from one level to another.

ram·page (răm′pāj; răm-pāj′), *n.* a fit of excitement or rage:—*v.i.* (răm-pāj′; răm′-pāj), [rampaged, rampag-ing], to dash about in a wild rage.

ramp·ant (răm′pănt), *adj.* **1,** showing a fierce, high spirit; violent; as, the *rampant* foe; **2,** bold and unchecked; as, *rampant* crime; also, growing rankly, as weeds; **3,** reared on the hind legs, with one foreleg raised above the other, as a lion on a coat of arms.

LION RAMPANT def. 3

ram·part (răm′pärt; răm′pẽrt), *n.* **1,** an embankment or earthen wall, built around a fort for better defense; **2,** any protection against danger.

ram·rod (răm′rŏd′), *n.* a rod used for ramming down the charge of a gun which loads through the muzzle.

Ram·ses (răm′sēz), *n.* the name of several kings of ancient Egypt; especially, **Ramses II,** called *the Great* (about 1324–1258 B.C.), a great conqueror and builder. Also spelled **Ram/e-ses.**

ram·shack·le (răm′shăk′l), *adj.* loose; out of repair; rickety; as, a *ramshackle* house.

ran (răn), past tense of *run.*

ranch or **ranche** (rănch), *n.* **1,** in western U.S. and Canada, a farm for the raising of cattle, horses, or sheep in large herds; **2,** a large farm for a special crop; as, a fruit *ranch:—v.i.* to manage, or work on, a ranch.—*n.* **ranch′er.**—*n.* **ranch′man.**

ran·cid (răn′sĭd), *adj.* having the rank, tainted smell or taste of spoiled fat.—*n.* **ran′cid-ness.**

ran·cor (răng′kẽr), *n.* deep spite or malice; a bitter, cherished grudge. In British usage, **ran′cour.**—*adj.* **ran′cor-ous.**

Syn. hostility, resentment, animosity.

ran·dom (răn′dŭm), *adj.* done without aim or purpose; guided by chance:—**at random,** without definite direction or aim; as, books picked *at random.*

Syn. haphazard, casual.

rang (răng), past tense of *ring.*

range (rānj), *v.t.* [ranged, rang-ing], **1,** to set in a row or in regular order; as, to *range* cups on a shelf; also, to classify; as, to *range* books by subjects; **2,** to put (oneself) in a certain position with reference to others; as, he *ranged* himself with the rebels; **3,** to wander over; as, cattle *range* the plains:—*v.i.* **1,** to wander; roam; as, he lets his fancy *range;* **2,** to vary within certain limits; as, these apes *range* in height from five to six feet; **3,** to be found, or to occur, over a certain area; as, the magnolia *ranges* northward to Ohio:—*n.* **1,** a line or row; series; chain, as of hills or mountains; **2,** direct line; as, in *range* with my window; **3,** the limits of space or time included or covered; scope; extent; as, the whole *range* of history; **4,** the limits within which something varies; as, her voice has a *range* of two octaves; **5,** a tract of land over which cattle graze; **6,** the distance to which a gun, cannon, or the like, can shoot; as, a *range* of one mile; also, the distance of the target from the gun; **7,** a place for target practice; as, a rifle *range;* **8,** the area over which a plant or animal may be found; as, the *range* of the violet; **9,** a large cooking stove.

rang·er (rān′jẽr), *n.* **1,** in England, the keeper of a royal park; **2,** a wanderer; rover; **3,** a member of a corps of mounted men who police a large region; **4,** in America, a forest guard.

Ran·goon (răng-gōon′; răng′gōon), a city, capital of Burma, near the western coast of Indochina (map 15).

rang·y (rān′jĭ), *adj.* [ran-gi-er, ran-gi-est], **1,** having a tendency to roam; able to wander far and wide; **2,** hence, long-limbed and muscular. Also spelled **ran′gey.**

¹rank (răngk), *n.* **1,** a row or line of persons or objects; also, an orderly arrangement; especially, a line of soldiers drawn up side by side; **2,** high station or position; as, a man of *rank;* **3,** a grade of social or official position; as, the *rank* of duke; the *rank* of admiral; **4,** degree of worth or eminence; as, a poet of the first *rank;* **5, ranks: a,** the army as a whole; **b,** the body of privates, as distinguished from the officers; as, the captain was reduced to the *ranks* for disobedience:—**rank and file,** the whole body of common soldiers; hence, the common people:—*v.t.* **1**, to place in rows; draw up (soldiers) in line; **2**, to include in a certain class, order, or division; as, to *rank* students by their marks; **3**, to be of higher rank than (another); outrank; as, a major *ranks* a captain:—*v.i.* **1**, to hold a certain grade or position; as, she *ranks* high in her classes.

    Syn., *n.* order, degree.

²rank (răngk), *adj.* **1**, plentiful and coarse in growth; as, *rank* grass; **2**, producing too freely; as, *rank* soil; **3**, coarse; strong in taste or smell; as, *rank* fat; **4**, gross; inexcusable; extreme; as, *rank* carelessness. —*adv.* **rank′ly.**—*n.* **rank′ness.**

ran-kle (răng′kl), *v.i.* [ran-kled, ran-kling], **1**, to fester or cause to fester; **2**, to cause mental pain or irritation; as, the insult *rankled.*

ran-sack (răn′săk), *v.t.* **1**, to make a thorough search of; as, I *ransacked* my desk in vain; **2**, to pillage; to plunder; as, the enemy *ransacked* the town.

ran-som (răn′sŭm), *n.* **1**, the returning of a captive or seized property upon payment of a price; as, they negotiated the *ransom* of the prisoners from the pirates; **2**, the sum so paid or demanded:—*v.t.* **1**, to free from prison, slavery, or punishment, by a payment; **2**, to set free on receipt of a payment.

rant (rănt), *n.* noisy, empty speech:—*v.i.* to speak loudly and at great length; to rave on.—*n.* **rant′er.**—*adj.* **rant′ing.**

¹rap (răp), *v.i.* [rapped, rap-ping], to strike a quick, sharp blow; to knock:—*v.t.* **1**, to strike sharply; **2**, to utter sharply; as, to *rap* out a command.

²rap (răp), *n.* an old coin of little value; hence, the saying, "not worth a *rap.*"

ra-pa-cious (rȧ-pā′shŭs), *adj.* **1**, given to robbery; seizing by violence; as, *rapacious* highwaymen; **2**, greedy; grasping; as, a *rapacious* pawnbroker.—*adv.* **ra-pa′cious-ly.**—*n.* **ra-pa′cious-ness.**

ra-pac-i-ty (rȧ-păs′ĭ-tĭ), *n.* [*pl.* rapacities], excessive greed.

¹rape (rāp), *v.t.* [raped, rap-ing], to take by force:—*n.* a taking or carrying off by force.

²rape (rāp), *n.* a plant of the mustard family, used as food for sheep and hogs. From its seeds an oil is obtained.

Raph-a-el (răf′ȧ-ĕl; rä′fȧ-ĕl), **1**, (1483–1520), a famous Italian painter; **2**, in Jewish and Christian legend, one of the seven archangels.

rap-id (răp′ĭd), *adj.* very quick or swift; as, to run at a *rapid* rate; a *rapid* runner: —**rapids**, *n.pl.* a place in a river where

the water rushes swiftly because of a steep slope in the river bed.—*adv.* **rap′id-ly.**

    Syn. fast, fleet, hasty, speedy.

ra-pid-i-ty (rȧ-pĭd′ĭ-tĭ), *n.* swiftness in motion; speed.

ra-pi-er (rā′-pĭ-ẽr), *n.* a straight, slender, light, two-edged sword.

RAPIER

rap-ine (răp′ĭn), *n.* the act of plundering or of carrying off property by force; destruction.

    Syn. plunder, pillage, robbery.

rap-scal-lion (răp-skăl′yŭn), *n.* a rascal.

rapt (răpt), *adj.* **1**, carried away with delight; enraptured; **2**, absorbed; engrossed; as, he gave *rapt* attention to his book.

    Syn. entranced, charmed, absorbed.

rap-ture (răp′tŭr), *n.* the state of being transported or carried away with great joy; extreme delight or pleasure.—*adj.* **rap′tur-ous.**—*adv.* **rap′tur-ous-ly.**

    Syn. bliss, ecstasy.

¹rare (râr), *adj.* [rar-er, rar-est], **1**, thin; not dense; as, a *rare* atmosphere; **2**, scarce; not frequent; as, on one of his *rare* visits to the country; **3**, unusual; precious; as, *rare* old lace.—*n.* **rare′ness.**—*adv.* **rare′ly.**

    Syn. extraordinary, incomparable.

²rare (râr), *adj.* [rar-er, rar-est], not cooked through; underdone; as, *rare* beef.

rare-bit (râr′bĭt), *n.* a Welsh rabbit, a cheese dish.

rar-e-fy (râr′ē-fī), *v.i.* and *v.t.* [rarefied, rarefy-ing], to become, or cause to become, thin or less dense; as, air *rarefies* as one ascends.—*n.* **rar′e-fac′tion.**

rar-i-ty (răr′ĭ-tĭ; râr′ĭ-tĭ), *n.* [*pl.* rarities], **1**, uncommonness; scarcity; as, the *rarity* of great men; also, an instance of scarcity; as, a century plant in bloom is a *rarity*; **2**, thinness; as, the *rarity* of the air on the mountain top.

ras-cal (răs′kăl), *n.* a scoundrel; rogue.— *adj.* and *adv.* **ras′cal-ly.**—*n.* **ras-cal′i-ty.**

    Syn. vagabond, scamp.

¹rash (răsh), *n.* an eruption of the skin, showing red spots, as in scarlet fever.

²rash (răsh), *adj.* **1**, hasty in thought or act; reckless; as, he was *rash* to drive that car; **2**, done, made, or given through lack of caution; as, a *rash* promise.—*adv.* **rash′ly.**—*n.* **rash′ness.**

rash-er (răsh′ẽr), *n.* a thin slice of bacon or ham.

rasp (rȧsp), *v.t.* **1**, to rub or scrape with, or as with, a file or other rough instrument; **2**, to irritate; as, her voice *rasps* my nerves:—*v.i.* **1**, to scrape or grate roughly; 2, to make a harsh, grating noise: —*n.* 1, a rough file with a toothed rather than a ridged surface; 2, the act of rasping or scraping; also, a harsh, grating noise; as, the *rasp* of rusty hinges.

rasp-ber-ry (răz′bĕr′ĭ), *n.* [*pl.* raspberries], the red, black, yellow, or white seedy, edible fruit of a prickly shrub or vine; also, the shrub or vine.

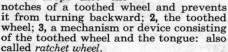

RASPBERRY
Leaves and berries.

rat (răt), *n.* a gnaw-ing animal that looks like a mouse but is larger:—*v.i.* [rat-ted, rat-ting], to hunt or catch rats.—*n.* **rat′ter.**

ra-tan (ră-tăn′), *n.* a kind of palm; rattan. See **rattan.**

ratch-et (răch′ĕt), *n.* 1, a hinged tongue, or pawl, which drops into the notches of a toothed wheel and prevents it from turning backward; 2, the toothed wheel; 3, a mechanism or device consisting of the toothed wheel and the tongue: also called *ratchet wheel.*

RAT (½)

¹**rate** (rāt), *n.* 1, the amount or number of one thing measured in units of another; as, a *rate* of 50 miles an hour; 2, a fixed charge for a certain amount of material, piece of work, length of time, etc.; as, the *rate* of wages is $15 a week; 3, a relative standard in respect to manner, style, etc.; as, to drive at a fast *rate;* to spend at an extravagant *rate;* also, class; quality; as, first-*rate* food:—**at any rate,** in any case:—*v.t.* [rat-ed, rat-ing], 1, to settle or fix the value, rank, or degree of; 2, to consider; regard; as, we *rate* him among the best authors:—*v.i.* to be estimated or ranked; as, he *rated* very high in his class.

RATCHET WHEEL (A) AND PAWLS (B, B)

²**rate** (rāt), *v.t.* and *v.i.* [rat-ed, rat-ing], to scold sharply; berate.

Syn. reprove, upbraid, chide.

rath-er (ráth′ẽr), *adv.* 1, more gladly; sooner; as, I should *rather* read than write; 2, on the contrary; instead; as, ask *rather* those who really know; 3, more accurately; as, a pale purple, or *rather,* a deep lavender; 4, somewhat; to a certain extent; as, I *rather* like it that way.

rat-i-fi-ca-tion (răt′ĭ-fĭ-kā′shŭn), *n.* a formal approval; confirmation; as, the *ratification* of the Constitution.

rat-i-fy (răt′ĭ-fī), *v.t.* [ratified, ratify-ing], to approve; endorse; make valid by sign-ing; as, the States *ratified* the amend-ment.—*n.* **rat′i-fi′er.**

Syn. accept, sanction.

rat-ing (rā′tĭng), *n.* 1, the act of classifying according to relative value; 2, rank; class; as, a high scholastic *rating.*

ra-ti-o (rā′shĭ-ō; rā′shō), *n.* [*pl.* ratios], the relation in number, degree, or quantity, existing between two things; proportion; as, our school has average students and brilliant students in the *ratio* of 10 to 1.

ra-tion (rā′shŭn; răsh′ŭn), *n.* 1, a definite quantity of food or supplies allowed daily to a soldier or sailor in the service; 2, any fixed or stated share; as, a daily *ration* of sugar:—*v.t.* to furnish (soldiers) with a fixed allowance of food, supplies, etc.; also, to distribute (food, supplies, etc.) on a limited basis.

ra-tion-al (răsh′ŭn-ăl), *adj.* 1, having the power to reason, or think connectedly; as, man is a *rational* being; 2, based on, or in accord with, reason; intelligent; not foolish; as, *rational* thought or conduct.— *adv.* **ra′tion-al-ly.**

Syn. reasonable, sensible, sound.

ra-tion-al-i-ty (răsh′ŭn-ăl′ĭ-tĭ), *n.* [*pl.* rationalities], the ability or power to reason; the possession or use of the power of reasoning.

rat-line or **rat-lin** (răt′-lĭn), *n.* 1, one of a series of small cross ropes forming a ladder in a ship's shrouds; 2, light, tarred rope used for this.

RATLINES AND SHROUDS

rat-tan or **ra-tan** (ră-tăn′), *n.* 1, a climbing palm with long, smooth, reedlike stems; 2, the stems of such a palm, used particularly in making wicker furniture; 3, a walking stick or cane of rattan.

rat-tle (răt′l), *v.i.* [rat-tled, rat-tling], 1, to produce short, sharp noises in quick succession; clatter; as, a door *rattles* in the wind; 2, to talk in a noisy, rapid manner; prattle; as, she *rattled* on for an hour; 3, to move with a clatter; as, the wagon *rattled* along the road:—*v.t.* 1, to cause to make a succession of rapid, sharp noises; as, the wind *rattles* the shutters; 2, to utter in a rapid, noisy way; as, he *rattled* off his speech; 3, *Colloquial,* to con-fuse or daze; as, this unexpected news *rattled* him:—*n.* 1, a series of short, sharp, clattering sounds following one another quickly; as, the *rattle* of hail against the windows; 2, anything for making a rattling sound, as a child's toy.

rat·tler (răt′lĕr), *n*. **1,** anything that makes a rattling noise; **2,** a rattlesnake.

rat·tle-snake (răt′l-snāk′), *n*. a poisonous snake with hard bony rings or scales on the tail which make a rattling sound.

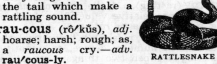

RATTLESNAKE

rau·cous (rô′kŭs), *adj*. hoarse; harsh; rough; as, a *raucous* cry.—*adv*. **rau′cous-ly.**

rav·age (răv′ĭj), *v.t.* [ravaged, ravag-ing], to lay waste; pillage; plunder; as, the enemy *ravaged* the country:—*v.i.* to work havoc:—*n*. destruction by violence; ruin; waste; as, the *ravages* of the storm.
Syn., v. overrun, devastate, destroy.

rave (rāv), *v.i.* [raved, rav-ing], **1,** to act or talk madly; **2,** to speak enthusiastically; as, he *raved* about her singing; **3,** to rage, as a high wind.—*adj*. **rav′ing.**

rav·el (răv′ĕl), *v.t.* [raveled, ravel-ing], to draw out the threads of (a woven or knitted fabric):—*v.i.* to become unwoven or unknit; as, a stocking *ravels* out:—*n*. a pulled-out thread; raveled material.

rav·el·ing (răv′ĕl-ĭng), *n*. a thread drawn from woven or knitted material; something that has raveled.

ra·ven (rā′vĕn), *n*. a large bird of the crow family, noted for its glossy-black color:—*adj*. like a raven; jet black and shining.

rav·en·ing (răv′ĕn-ĭng), *adj*. greedy; seeking eagerly for prey; as, *ravening* wolves.

RAVEN (⅛)

Ra·ven·na (ra̤-vĕn′a̤), a city in northeastern Italy, near the Adriatic Sea (maps **1, 12**).

rav·en·ous (răv′ĕn-ŭs), *adj*. mad for food; starving; as, *ravenous* beasts of prey; also, extremely sharp; as, a *ravenous* appetite.—*adv*. **rav′en-ous-ly.**

ra·vine (ra̤-vēn′), *n*. a long, deep hollow, worn by the action of a stream or torrent; a mountain gorge; gully.

rav·ish (răv′ĭsh), *v.t.* **1,** to seize and remove by force; **2,** to affect overpoweringly, as with delight, rapture, grief, etc.; as, they were *ravished* by the divine music.—*n*. **rav′ish-er.**—*n*. **rav′ish-ment.**
Syn. enrapture, enchant, delight.

rav·ish·ing (răv′ĭsh-ĭng), *adj*. very charming; entrancing; as, a *ravishing* voice.

raw (rô), *adj*. **1,** uncooked; as, a *raw* potato; **2,** without the covering of the skin; as, a *raw* spot on the hand; **3,** in its natural form or state; unprepared; as, *raw*

silk; **4,** crude; inexperienced; unpracticed; as, *raw* judgment; *raw* troops; **5,** cold and damp; as, *raw* weather.—*n*. **raw′ness.**

raw-boned (rô′bōnd′), *adj*. with but little flesh on the bones; gaunt; thin.

raw-hide (rô′hīd′), *n*. **1,** untanned skin or hide, as of cattle; **2,** a whip made of a roll or braid of tanned leather.

¹**ray** (rā), *n*. **1,** a single line of light appearing to stream from a bright center or source; as, a *ray* of sunlight; also, light or illumination; as, they studied by the *ray* of the lamp; **2,** a glimmer; trace; as, a *ray* of hope; **3,** one of a number of thin lines spreading from a common center like the spokes of a wheel; **4,** a beam of energy, electricity, etc.; as, an X *ray*; **5,** something that resembles a ray, as one of the yellow, petal-like flowers around the dark disk of a black-eyed Susan, one of the radiating arms of a starfish, etc.:—*v.t.* to send forth (light):—*v.i.* to shine forth; radiate.—*adj*. **ray′less.**

²**ray** (rā), *n*. a fish with a broad, flat body and a thin tail. The skate and the torpedo are rays. (See illustration below.)

RAYS (R) OF A STARFISH

ray-on (rā′ŏn), *n*. a shiny, silklike fabric made from wood fiber spun into thread.

raze (rāz), *v.t.* [razed, razing], to level to the ground; tear down, as a building.

ra-zor (rā′zẽr), *n*. a sharp-edged instrument used in shaving. (See illustration below.)

R.C. abbreviation for *Red Cross, Roman Catholic.*

R.C.Ch. abbreviation for *Roman Catholic Church.*

Rd. abbreviation for *road:* —**rd.** abbreviation for *rod.*

R.D. abbreviation for *Rural Delivery.*

RAY (⅛)

re (rā; rē), *n*. in music, the name of the second note of the scale.

re- (rē-), a prefix meaning: **1,** back; backward; as, *recall, recline;* **2,** again; anew; as, *reread, reconquer;* **3,** in return; mutually; as, *react, reciprocal.*

reach (rēch), *v.t.* **1,** to stretch out; as, the children *reached* out their hands for pennies; **2,** to touch or grasp; as, they could not *reach* the railing;

RAZORS

3, to pass or deliver to another; to hand; as, please *reach* me my coat; **4,** to arrive at or come to; attain; as, to *reach* a goal; **5,** to extend as far as; penetrate to; as, this road *reaches* the lake:—*v.i.* **1,** to extend the hand so as to touch or seize something; **2,** to endeavor to obtain something; as, to *reach* for fame; **3,** to extend in time, space, amount, etc.; as, the cost *reaches* into thousands; **4,** to cover a distance as does the eye; as, water extended as far as eye could *reach:*—*n.* **1,** the act or power of stretching out the arm in order to touch or grasp something; also, the distance one can stretch; as, he has a long *reach;* **2,** the distance within which one can touch, observe, etc.; as, he lives within *reach* of town; **3,** an unbroken stretch, as of water.

¹**re—act** (rē-ăkt′), *v.t.* to act or perform a second time; as, to *re-act* a play.

²**re-act** (rē-ăkt′), *v.i.* **1,** to rebound; act as a boomerang; as, John's cruelty to his friend *reacted* on John and made him suffer; **2,** to respond to an influence or stimulus; as, the patient *reacted* favorably to the doctor's treatment; **3,** in chemistry, to undergo change; as, some substances are inert, that is, slow to *react.*

re-ac-tion (rē-ăk′shŭn), *n.* **1,** the effect of an action on the person responsible for it; as, a deed of spite has a damaging *reaction* on the doer; **2,** a wish or tendency to return to a former, or opposite, state of things; as, a *reaction* against new ideas; **3,** an impulse in response to some influence; as, my first *reaction* was to scoff; **4,** in chemistry, the changes that take place in substances when they are combined.

re-ac-tion-ar-y (rē-ăk′shŭn-ĕr′ĭ), *n.* [*pl.* reactionaries], **1,** a person who favors a return to former conditions; **2,** one who seeks to block social or political progress: —*adj.* pertaining to, or favoring, a return to a former state of affairs; as, a *reactionary* political party.

¹**read** (rēd), *v.t.* [read (rĕd), read-ing], **1,** to look at and understand the meaning of (something written or printed); to peruse; as, to *read* a book; **2,** to utter aloud (something written or printed); as, he *reads* his sermons; **3,** to discover, by observation, the meaning of certain lines or marks on; as, to *read* palms; to *read* a thermometer; **4,** to make a study of; as, to *read* law; **5,** to interpret (dreams or riddles); also, to foretell (the future); **6,** to show; indicate; as, the meter *reads* 35 miles:— *v.i.* **1,** to peruse written or printed matter; **2,** to learn from written or printed matter; as, to *read* about politics; **3,** to utter aloud written or printed words; as, he often *reads* to us; **4,** to have a special form; as,

the passage *reads* thus:—**read between the lines,** to see more than meets the eye.

²**read** (rĕd), *adj.* informed by reading; learned; as, he is a well-*read* man.

read-a-ble (rē′dȧ-bl), *adj.* **1,** easy and pleasant to read; interesting; **2,** legible; plainly written.—*n.* **read′a-ble-ness.**—*n.* **read′a-bil′i-ty.**

read-er (rē′dẽr), *n.* **1,** one who reads; as, he is a *reader* of poetry; **2,** a textbook for the study of reading.

Read-ing (rĕd′ĭng), a city in southeastern Pennsylvania (map 6).

read-ing (rē′dĭng), *n.* **1,** the act of one who reads; perusal of written or printed matter; **2,** utterance aloud of the words of books, letters, and the like; **3,** a public recital; as, to give a *reading* from Kipling; **4,** a form of a particular passage in a book; as, various *readings* of a passage may be found in different editions of Shakespeare; **5,** written or printed matter to be perused; as, "Ivanhoe" is good *reading;* **6,** the manner of interpreting something written; as, an actor's *reading* of his lines; **7,** that which is shown by an instrument; as, the *reading* of our gas meter is taken monthly.

re-ad-just (rē′ȧ-jŭst′), *v.t.* to set in order again; set to rights once more.

read-y (rĕd′ĭ), *adj.* [read-i-er, read-i-est], **1,** in condition for immediate action; as, I am *ready* to go; prepared for instant use; as, your dress is *ready;* **2,** quick; prompt; as, *ready* payment; **3,** mentally fit or prepared; willing; as, *ready* to obey; **4,** on the point of; about to; as, that tree is *ready* to fall; **5,** awaiting use; available; as, *ready* cash.— *adv.* **read′i-ly.**—*n.* **read′i-ness.**

read-y—made (rĕd′ĭ-mād′), *adj.* **1,** not made to individual order; made in standard forms; as, *ready-made* clothing; **2,** prepared beforehand; as, a *ready-made* speech.

re-a-gent (rē-ā′jĕnt), *n.* a chemical substance known to react in certain ways under specific conditions, and therefore used in analysis and measurement of chemical compounds.

¹**re-al** (rē′ăl), *adj.* **1,** actually existing as a thing, or occurring as a fact; as, *real* events; a *real* illness; **2,** genuine; not imitation; as, *real* silk; **3,** in law, pertaining to land or buildings; as, *real* property.

    Syn. actual, certain, sure, authentic.

²**re-al** (rē′ăl; rä-äl′), *n.* [*pl.* reals (rē′ălz) or reales (rä-ä′läs)], a former Spanish coin worth about one eighth of a dollar. This is why the dollar was called a "piece of eight."

re-al es-tate, land and all related property, such as trees, fences, buildings, etc.

---

go; **join;** yet; **sing; chin; show;** thin, *then;* **hw,** *why;* zh, azure; **ü,** Ger. *für* or Fr. **lune;** **ö,** Ger. schön or Fr. *feu;* **ṅ,** Fr. e*nfant,* no*m;* **kh,** Ger. a*ch* or i*ch.* **See pages ix–x.**

re·al·ism (rē′ăl-ĭzm), *n.* **1,** in art and literature, the effort to represent people and scenes as they appear in real life: opposite of *idealism;* **2,** in philosophy, the belief that objects which can be seen or touched do actually exist.—*n.* **re′al·ist.**

re·al·is·tic (rē′ăl-ĭs′tĭk), *adj.* presenting people and scenes as they actually are; true to fact and life; as, a *realistic* novel.— *adv.* **re′al·is′ti·cal·ly.**

re·al·i·ty (rē-ăl′ĭ-tĭ), *n.* [*pl.* realities], **1,** the state or quality of being real or actual; as, we believe in the *reality* of what we see; **2,** that which exists or is actual; a fact; as, the *reality* proved less horrible than his fear.

re·al·i·za·tion (rē′ăl-ĭ-zā′shŭn; rē′ăl-ī-zā′shŭn), *n.* **1,** accomplishment; fulfilment; as, the *realization* of an ambition; **2,** full or keen appreciation; as, he had a full *realization* of his danger; **3,** the turning of property into money.

re·al·ize (rē′ăl-īz), *v.t.* [realized, realiz-ing], **1,** to bring into actual existence; hence, to accomplish; as, he *realized* his plan to go abroad; **2,** to see clearly; understand; as, he *realized* his error; **3,** to obtain as profit; as, he *realized* $50 from the sale:—*v.i.* to turn property into money; as, to *realize* on a building.

Syn. obtain, get, acquire, comprehend.

re·al·ly (rē′ăl-ĭ), *adv.* actually; as a matter of fact.

realm (rĕlm), *n.* **1,** a kingdom; an empire; **2,** hence, any region or state; as, the *realm* of dreams.

re·al·tor (rē′ăl-tēr), *n.* a dealer in real estate, affiliated with the National Association of Real Estate Boards: a trade term.

re·al·ty (rē′ăl-tĭ), *n.* [*pl.* realties], land and buildings; real estate.

¹ream (rēm), *n.* twenty quires, or about 480 sheets, of paper.

²ream (rēm), *v.t.* to enlarge or taper (a hole), especially in metal.

REAMER, def. 1

ream·er (rē′mēr), *n.* **1,** one who or that which reams; especially, a tool with sharp edges for enlarging or tapering holes; **2,** a device for squeezing fruit, consisting of a dish with a ridged, cone-shaped center.

re·an·i·mate (rē-ăn′ĭ-māt), *v.t.* [reanimat-ed, reanimat-ing], to bring back to life; give new strength to; encourage.

REAMER, def. 2

reap (rēp), *v.t.* **1,** to cut down with a scythe, sickle, or machine; gather in; as,

to *reap* grain; **2,** to cut a crop from; as, to *reap* a field; **3,** to receive as reward; as, to *reap* the benefit of hard study:—*v.i.* to cut and gather grain.—*n.* **reap′er.**

re·ap·pear (rē′ă-pĭr′), *v.i.* to come into view again.

¹rear (rĭr), *n.* **1,** the back or back part; as, the door at the *rear* of the room; **2,** that part of a fleet or an army behind the rest: —*adj.* pertaining to, or situated at, the back part; as, *rear* stairs.

²rear (rĭr), *v.t.* **1,** to raise or lift up; as, a snake *rears* its head; **2,** to construct; erect; as, to *rear* a palace; **3,** to bring up and educate; as, to *rear* children; **4,** to breed; grow; as, to *rear* horses:—*v.i.* to rise up on the hind legs, as a horse.

rear ad·mi·ral, in the U.S. Navy, an officer ranking next above a commodore.

re·ar·range (rē′ă-rānj′), *v.t.* [rearranged, rearrang-ing], to put back in order or place; to change the position of.—*n.* **re′ar·range′-ment.**

rear·ward (rĭr′wērd), *adj.* and *adv.* at or toward the rear.

re·as·cend (rē′ă-sĕnd′), *v.t.* and *v.i.* to climb or rise again.

rea·son (rē′zn), *n.* **1,** an explanation given for a belief, act, or the like; as, she gave no *reason* for leaving; **2,** the grounds for an opinion or the motive of an act; as, there were *reasons* for his belief; **3,** the power to understand or think; as, the sick man lost his *reason;* **4,** sanity; common sense; as, to bring a child to *reason:*—*v.i.* **1,** to exercise the power of thinking; to draw logical conclusions; **2,** to argue; as, you cannot *reason* with a stubborn person:— *v.t.* **1,** to persuade by argument; as, to *reason* a child out of his fears; **2,** to prove or explain by means of the intellect; as, to *reason* out a solution.—*n.* **rea′son·er.**

Syn. argument, cause, motive.

rea·son·a·ble (rē′zn-ȧ-bl), *adj.* **1,** having the power to think clearly and to reach sound conclusions; as, a *reasonable* being; **2,** governed by reason; just; as, a *reasonable* employer; **3,** moderate or fair; as, a *reasonable* charge; **4,** sound or sensible; as, a *reasonable* decision.—*adv.* **rea′son·a·bly.** —*n.* **rea′son·a·ble·ness.**

rea·son·ing (rē′zn-ĭng), *n.* **1,** the process of reaching conclusions by careful and connected thinking; **2,** a line of argument; a presentation of reasons; as, the pupils understood the teacher's *reasoning.*

re·as·sem·ble (rē′ă-sĕm′bl), *v.t.* [reassem-bled, reassem-bling], to put together again; as, to *reassemble* a motor.

re·as·sert (rē′ă-sûrt′), *v.t.* to declare or state again; as, to *reassert* an old claim.

āte, āorta, râre, căt, àsk, fär, ăllow, sofȧ; ēve, ĕvent, ĕll, writĕr, novĕl; bīte, pĭn; nō, ōbey, ôr, dŏg, tŏp, cōllide; ūnit, ūnite, bûrn, cŭt, focŭs; nōōn, fŏŏt; mound; coin;

re·as·sume (rē/ă-sūm/), v.t. [reassumed, reassum-ing], to take again; resume.

re·as·sure (rē/ă-shŏŏr/), v.t. [reassured, reassur-ing], to give back courage to; give new confidence to.—n. **re/as·sur/ance.**

re·a·wak·en (rē/å-wā/kĕn), v.t. and v.i. to rouse or wake again.

re·bate (rē/bāt; rē-bāt/), n. money paid back; discount; as, John got a *rebate* of two dollars on the books he bought.

Re·bek·ah or **Re·bec·ca** (rē-bĕk/å), in the Bible, the wife of Isaac and mother of Esau and Jacob.

re·bel (rē-bĕl/), v.i. [rebelled, rebel-ling], 1, to take up arms against the law or government; 2, to resist any authority:—n. (rĕb/ĕl), 1, one who takes up arms against his government or resists its laws; 2, one who resists any authority:—adj. opposing or resisting authority.

re·bel·lion (rē-bĕl/yŭn), n. 1, the act of taking up arms, or the state of being in revolt, against the government or its laws; 2, defiance of any authority.
    Syn. insurrection, mutiny, revolution.

re·bel·lious (rē-bĕl/yŭs), adj. 1, opposing or resisting law or government; 2, resisting control; unmanageable; as, a *rebellious* child.—adv. **re·bel/lious·ly.**—n. **re·bel/lious-ness.**

re·bind (rē-bīnd/), v.t. [rebound, rebind-ing], to bind or cover again, as a book.

re·birth (rē-bûrth/; rē/bûrth/), n. 1, a second birth; 2, a revival of life or spirit; as, the *rebirth* of learning.

re·born (rē-bôrn/), adj. born again or anew; taking on new life.

re·bound (rē-bound/), v.i. to spring or fly back from that which has been struck; as, the ball *rebounded* from the wall:—n. (rē-bound/; rē/bound/), the act of springing back or rebounding.

re·buff (rē-bŭf/), n. a sudden check; repulse; defeat:—v.t. to refuse or repel sharply; snub (someone).

re·build (rē-bĭld/), v.t. [rebuilt (rē-bĭlt/), rebuild-ing], to construct again or anew.

re·buke (rē-būk/), n. a sharp reproof; scolding:—v.t. [rebuked, rebuk-ing], to censure sharply; as, to *rebuke* a child.
    Syn., v. admonish, reprimand, scold.

re·bus (rē/bŭs), n. a puzzle in which words, phrases, or sentences are represented by signs and pictures of objects; as, "2 Y's" is a *rebus* for "too wise."

re·but (rē-bŭt/), v.t. [rebut-ted, rebut-ting], to oppose or refute with argument, or proof, as in a debate.—n. **re·but/tal.**

rec. abbreviation for *receipt.*

re·cal·ci·trant (rē-kăl/sĭ-trănt), adj. obstinately refusing to submit; unruly.—n. **re·cal/ci·trance.**

re·call (rē-kôl/), v.t. 1, to order or summon back; as, to *recall* an ambassador; 2, to remember; recollect; as, to *recall* a name; 3, to withdraw; annul; as, to *recall* a decision:—n. 1, the act of summoning or calling back; 2, the power by which an unsatisfactory public official may be put out of office by vote of the people.

re·cant (rē-kănt/), v.t. to withdraw publicly (something previously believed or said):—v.i. to renounce formally an opinion previously held.—n. **re/can·ta/-tion.**
    Syn. recall, revoke, abjure.

re·ca·pit·u·late (rē/kå-pĭt/ū-lāt), v.t. [recapitulat-ed, recapitulat-ing], to sum up the chief points of; as, after listening to the speakers, he *recapitulated* their main arguments:—v.i. to repeat briefly what has already been said at length.

re·cap·ture (rē-kăp/tūr), n. the act of seizing or taking again; as, the *recapture* of a town:—v.t. [recaptured, recaptur-ing], to seize or take again; also, to recollect.

re·cast (rē-kást/), v.t. [recast, recast-ing], 1, to plan or lay out anew; as, I must *recast* the first chapter; 2, to mold or cast again; as, to *recast* a medal.

recd. abbreviation for *received.*

re·cede (rē-sēd/), v.i. [reced-ed, reced-ing], 1, to fall back; retire; as, the tide *recedes;* 2, to withdraw, as from a claim or proposal; 3, to slope or incline backward; as, his forehead *recedes.*

re·ceipt (rē-sēt/), n. 1, the act of getting, or state of having received, something given, sent, etc.; as, the *receipt* of a letter; in *receipt* of news; 2, a written acknowledgment of anything, usually money or goods, had from another; as, he signed a *receipt* for the package; 3, especially in cookery, a direction for making something by mixing certain ingredients; a recipe; 4, (usually *receipts*), that which is taken in, as distinguished from what is paid out:—v.t. to sign (a paper) in acknowledgment of payment or of something received; as, to *receipt* a bill.

re·ceiv·a·ble (rē-sē/và-bl), adj. due; payable; as, accounts *receivable.*

re·ceive (rē-sēv/), v.t. [received, receiving], 1, to get (a gift, message, payment, or the like) from another; as, I *received* your letter; 2, to be informed of; as, to *receive* news; 3, to admit to one's company; greet; entertain; as, to *receive* guests; 4, to serve as a holder for; as, a box to *receive* books; 5, to get; experience;

as, to *receive* a shock; to *receive* a sword thrust:—*v.i.* 1, to entertain; welcome guests; as, she *receives* on Wednesdays; 2, to change or convert electric waves into sounds that one can hear, as does a radio.

re·ceiv·er (rĕ-sē′vĕr), *n.* 1, one who or that which takes or holds; 2, a receptacle; as, a trash *receiver;* 3, the part of a telephone which receives the electric waves and turns them into sound; 4, a person appointed by a court to hold and manage the property of a bankrupt person or firm.

TELEPHONE RE-CEIVER (R) AND TRANSMITTER (T)

re·ceiv·er·ship (rĕ-sē′vĕr-shĭp), *n.* 1, the condition of having one's affairs taken charge of by a receiver appointed by the court; 2, the position or office of a receiver.

re·cent (rē′sĕnt), *adj.* 1, pertaining to time not long past; as, a *recent* occurrence; 2, new; modern; fresh; as, a *recent* book.—*adv.* re′cent·ly.—*n.* re′cent·ness.

Syn. late, new.

re·cep·ta·cle (rĕ-sĕp′tă-kl), *n.* 1, anything, such as a cup, barrel, or vault, used to hold other things; 2, in a plant, the part of the stalk to which the parts of the flower are attached.

RECEPTACLE Diagram of a flower showing: P, pistil; St, stamen; Pe, petal; S, sepal; R, receptacle.

re·cep·tion (rĕ-sĕp′shŭn), *n.* 1, the act of receiving, or the state of being received; as, the *reception* of news; 2, the act or manner of welcoming; as, a cool *reception;* 3, a formal entertainment; as, a *reception* was held in honor of the Mayor.

re·cep·tive (rĕ-sĕp′tĭv), *adj.* having the ability to take in or contain; quick to take in ideas or impressions; as, a *receptive* mind.—*adv.* re·cep′tive·ly.—*n.* re·cep′tive-ness.—*n.* re′cep·tiv′i·ty.

re·cess (rĕ-sĕs′; rē′sĕs), *n.* 1, a receding part or space that breaks the line of a wall; an alcove or niche; 2, a natural hollow or indentation in a coast line, a mountain range, or the like; 3, a brief time during which work ceases; an intermission; as, the school *recess:*—*v.t.* (rĕ-sĕs′), to put back; set into a recess:—*v.i. Colloquial,* to take a recess or intermission.

re·ces·sion (rĕ-sĕsh′ŭn), *n.* the act of going back or retiring; withdrawal.

re·ces·sion·al (rĕ-sĕsh′ŭn-ăl), *n.* 1, a hymn sung, or music played, at the close of a church service as the clergy and choir leave the chancel; 2, music played when a service, performance, etc., is over and the audience is leaving:—*adj.* pertaining to withdrawal or retirement.

re·ces·sive (rĕ-sĕs′ĭv), *adj.* receding; tending to recede, or go back.

Re·ci·fe (rä-sē′fĕ), a city on the eastern coast of Brazil (map 11). It is also called *Pernambuco.*

rec·i·pe (rĕs′ĭ-pē), *n.* 1, a set of directions for mixing or preparing anything, as in cookery; as, a good *recipe* for cake; 2, general directions for accomplishing a result; as, there is no *recipe* for success.

re·cip·i·ent (rĕ-sĭp′ĭ-ĕnt), *n.* one who receives; as, a *recipient* of high honors:—*adj.* receiving or ready to receive.

re·cip·ro·cal (rĕ-sĭp′rŏ-kăl), *adj.* 1, mutual; done, given, or offered by each to the other; as, *reciprocal* benefits; 2, corresponding; equivalent; as, to ask for *reciprocal* privileges; 3, in grammar, showing mutual action or relation: used of certain pronouns; as, in the sentence, "John and Jim spoke to each other," "each" and "other" are *reciprocal* pronouns, showing that John spoke to Jim and Jim spoke to John:—*n.* 1, that which is given or done by each to the other; an equivalent; 2, in mathematics, the quotient obtained by dividing the number 1 by another number; as, the *reciprocal* of 3 is ⅓.—*adv.* re·cip′ro·cal·ly.

re·cip·ro·cate (rĕ-sĭp′rŏ-kāt), *v.t.* [reciprocat-ed, reciprocat-ing], 1, to give and take in exchange; as, they *reciprocate* each other's affection; 2, to give something in return for; as, to *reciprocate* a favor; 3, in mechanics, to cause to move to and fro:—*v.i.* 1, in mechanics, to move to and fro; 2, to interchange; make an exchange with one another; 3, to pay back; make a return; as, she *reciprocated* with a gift.—*n.* re·cip′ro·ca′tion.

rec·i·proc·i·ty (rĕs′ĭ-prŏs′ĭ-tĭ), *n.* [*pl.* reciprocities], 1, a condition in which there is mutual action, giving and taking, etc., between two parties; co-operation; as, *reciprocity* between teacher and pupil; 2, a relationship or policy under which each of two nations grants the other special advantages in trade.

re·cit·al (rĕ-sī′tăl), *n.* 1, a telling of the details of an event; narration; as, a *recital* of one's adventures; also, the thing told; a story; 2, an entertainment, usually consisting of one type of music, instrumental or vocal; as, a piano *recital.*

rec·i·ta·tion (rĕs′ĭ-tā′shŭn), *n.* 1, a public delivery of prose or poetry from memory; 2, the selection of prose or poetry so delivered; as, the pupils liked John's *recitation* in assembly; **3,** the reciting by pupils in a classroom of a lesson prepared in advance; as, a *recitation* in history.

rec·i·ta·tive (rĕs/ĭ-tȧ-tēv′), *n.* a kind of singing that resembles speaking, used in certain parts of operas and oratorios; also, the music for such a passage:—*adj.* not conforming to strict musical rhythm; sung with the accents of speech.

re·cite (rē-sīt′), *v.t.* [recit-ed, recit-ing], **1,** to repeat aloud from memory; declaim; as, to *recite* a poem; **2,** to tell in detail; relate; as, to *recite* the story of a trip; **3,** to repeat (a lesson) to a teacher:—*v.i.* to repeat something from memory.

reck (rĕk), *v.t.* and *v.i. Archaic,* to care for; heed; as, he *recks* not of danger.

reck·less (rĕk/lĕs), *adj.* heedless of consequences or danger; rash; careless; as, a *reckless* driver; *reckless* spending.—*adv.* **reck/less·ly.**—*n.* **reck/less·ness.**
Syn. foolhardy, daring, regardless.

reck·on (rĕk/ŭn), *v.t.* **1,** to count or number; compute; as, to *reckon* the cost; **2,** to look upon as being; consider; as, we *reckon* him a friend; **3,** *Colloquial,* to think; suppose; as, I *reckon* it will rain:—*v.i.* **1,** to depend or rely; as, he *reckoned* on our votes; **2,** to make calculations:—**reckon with,** to settle accounts with.

reck·on·ing (rĕk/ŭn-ĭng), *n.* **1,** the act of one who counts or computes; as, by my *reckoning* the amount is too high; also, the result of such counting or calculation; **2,** an accounting for one's actions or conduct; as, the day of *reckoning* will come; **3,** a bill at a hotel, tavern, or the like; **4,** the calculation of the position of a ship, or the position so determined.

re·claim (rē-klām′), *v.t.* **1,** to demand or obtain the return of; as, to *reclaim* a book; **2,** to reform; as, to *reclaim* a drunkard; **3,** to bring under cultivation; as, to *reclaim* swampy land.—*adj.* **re·claim/a·ble.**

rec·la·ma·tion (rĕk/lȧ-mā/shŭn), *n.* the act of recovering or restoring; especially, the making of wasteland productive, as through irrigation in the western U.S.

re·cline (rē-klīn′), *v.i.* [reclined, reclining], to lie down for rest or repose:—*v.t.* to cause to lean or lie back; as, he *reclined* his tired body on the cot.

re·cluse (rē-kloōs′; rĕk/lūs), *n.* one who lives alone; a hermit.

rec·og·ni·tion (rĕk/ŏg-nĭsh/ŭn), *n.* **1,** an identifying of something previously known; as, my *recognition* of your handwriting; **2,** formal approval or commendation; as, *recognition* of a brave deed; **3,** special notice; acknowledgment; as, his singing won him *recognition* by the critics; **4,** a

formal acknowledgment of the independence of a country; as, America's *recognition* of Cuba.

re·cog·ni·zance (rē-kŏg/nĭ-zȧns; rē-kŏn/ĭ-zȧns), *n.* a legal agreement to do, or keep from doing, some particular act; also, the sum of money to be paid, or forfeited, if the agreement is not kept.

rec·og·nize (rĕk/ŏg-nīz), *v.t.* [recognized, recogniz-ing], **1,** to know the identity of; recall as having known before; as, to *recognize* a voice; **2,** to admit acquaintance with; salute; as, she *recognized* her old friend with a smile; **3,** to take formal notice of; acknowledge; as, America *recognized* Cuba; **4,** to appreciate; as, to *recognize* true worth; **5,** to concede as true; admit; as, I *recognize* that you are right; **6,** in a meeting, to acknowledge (someone) as the person entitled to be heard at the time.—*adj.* **rec/og·niz/a·ble.**

re·coil (rē-koil′), *v.i.* **1,** to start back or shrink, as in horror, fear, etc.; as, they *recoiled* at the sight of the mangled body; **2,** to spring back; kick, as a gun; **3,** to retreat or fall back; as, the enemy *recoiled;* **4,** to come back to the starting point; as, evil *recoils* on the doer:—*n.* **1,** a shrinking back; **2,** a rebound; **3,** the springing back or kick of a gun or spring; also, the distance it moves.

rec·ol·lect (rĕk/ŏ-lĕkt′), *v.t.* to call back to the mind; remember.

rec·ol·lec·tion (rĕk/ŏ-lĕk/shŭn), *n.* **1,** the act of remembering; also, the power of remembering; as, age impairs the *recollection;* **2,** a person's memory or the time over which it extends; as, the coldest winter in my *recollection;* **3,** something remembered; as, boyhood *recollections.*

re·com·bine (rē/kŏm-bīn′), *v.t.* [recombined, recombin-ing], to put together again; combine anew.

re·com·mence (rē/kŏ-mĕns′), *v.t.* and *v.i.* [recommenced, recommenc-ing], to start or begin again.

rec·om·mend (rĕk/ŏ-mĕnd′), *v.t.* **1,** to give in charge or trust, as to God; **2,** to offer to the favor, attention, or use of another; speak in favor of; as, to *recommend* a servant; **3,** to advise; suggest; as, I *recommend* a change of diet; **4,** to make attractive or deserving; as, her gentleness *recommends* her.

rec·om·men·da·tion (rĕk/ŏ-mĕn-dā/shŭn), *n.* **1,** the act of offering to favorable notice; **2,** something that procures or deserves favorable attention; as, a neat appearance is a good *recommendation;* **3,** something recommended or advised; as, the committee's *recommendation* is to wait.

---

go; join; yet; sing; chin; show; thin, *th*en; hw, *why;* zh, azure; ü, Ger. *für* or Fr. *lune;* ö, Ger. schön or Fr. *feu;* ṅ, Fr. e*n*fant, no*m;* kh, Ger. a*ch* or i*ch.* See pages ix–x.

re·com·mit (rē′kŏ-mĭt′), *v.t.* [recommit-ted, recommit-ting], **1,** to send or order back; as, he was *recommitted* to prison; **2,** to send (a bill or measure) back to a com-mittee.

rec·om·pense (rĕk′ŏm-pĕns), *v.t.* [recom-pensed, recompens-ing], **1,** to give an equivalent to (a person); reward; repay; as, she *recompensed* him for his devotion; **2,** to make amends for; atone for; as, to *recompense* a loss:—*n.* something given by way of reward or amends.

rec·on·cile (rĕk′ŏn-sīl), *v.t.* [reconciled, reconcil-ing], **1,** to restore peace between; as, to *reconcile* brothers who have quar-reled; **2,** to adjust; settle; as, to *reconcile* differences; **3,** to make content or sub-missive; as, to *reconcile* a person to his fate; **4,** to make consistent; as, it is hard to *reconcile* her words with her actions.—*n.* **rec′on·cil′er.**—*n.* **rec′on·cile′ment.**—*adj.* **rec′on·cil′a·ble.**

rec·on·cil·i·a·tion (rĕk′ŏn-sĭl′ĭ-ā′shŭn), *n.* **1,** a renewing of friendship after dis-agreement; **2,** a settlement or adjustment of differences; compromise.

rec·on·dite (rĕk′ŭn-dīt; rē-kŏn′dīt), *adj.* very difficult for the ordinary mind to understand; abstruse.—*adv.* **rec′on-dite-ly.**—*n.* **rec′on-dite-ness.**

Syn. hidden, secret, mysterious.

re·con·nais·sance (rē-kŏn′ĭ-sǎns), *n.* a survey or examination of a territory, as for military or scientific purposes.

rec·on·noi·ter (rĕk′ŏ-noi′tẽr; rē′kŏ-noi′-tẽr), *v.t.* and *v.i.* to explore and investi-gate, especially for military or scientific purposes. Also spelled **rec′on-noi′tre.**

re·con·quer (rē-kŏng′kẽr), *v.t.* to over-come or subdue again.

re·con·sid·er (rē′kŏn-sĭd′ẽr), *v.t.* **1,** to think over or ponder again; as, to *recon-sider* a proposal; **2,** in a legislative body, to bring up (a bill or motion) for renewed deliberation.—*n.* **re′con-sid′er-a′tion.**

re·con·sti·tute (rē-kŏn′stĭ-tūt), *v.t.* [re-constitut-ed, reconstitut-ing], to set up, or form, again.

re·con·struct (rē′kŏn-strŭkt′), *v.t.* to rebuild; remodel; as, to *reconstruct* a ship.

re·con·struc·tion (rē′kŏn-strŭk′shŭn), *n.* a rebuilding or remodeling; as, the *re-construction* of an old church:—**the Re-construction,** the reorganization of the South as states of the Union after the War between the States.

¹re·cord (rē-kôrd′), *v.t.* **1,** to write out or set down in some permanent form; as, to *record* events; to *record* a voice by means of a phonograph; **2,** to register; as, to *record* a deed; **3,** to mark or indicate; as, the clock *records* time.

²rec·ord (rĕk′ẽrd; rĕk′ôrd), *n.* **1,** the act of writing down or recording facts or events for the purpose of history or evi-dence; also, what is written or recorded; as, a family *record;* **2,** an official report, written or printed, of public acts; as, a legislative *record;* a court *record;* **3,** the body of facts, known and preserved, giving the history of a person or thing; as, the prisoner's *record;* **4,** the cylinder, disk, or paper roll for re-producing sounds in phonographs, me-chanical pianos, or the like; **5,** in sports, the best performance so far officially recognized; as, the track team broke two *records:*—*adj.* best, greatest, or most remarkable of its kind up to a given time; as, *record* heat.

PHONOGRAPH RECORD

Syn., n. chronicle, annals, history.

re·cord·er (rē-kôr′dẽr), *n.* **1,** a person whose business it is to keep an official record; as, a *recorder* of wills; **2,** in some cities, a judge or a magistrate; **3,** any of various devices that register mechanically.

¹re·count (rē-kount′), *v.t.* to tell or re-peat in full the particulars of; recite.

Syn. relate, describe, narrate, rehearse.

²re·count (rē-kount′), *v.t.* to count or enumerate again:—*n.* (rē-kount′; rē′-kount′), a counting again.

re·coup (rē-kōōp′), *v.t.* **1,** to make good; recover; as, to *recoup* a loss; **2,** to repay; reimburse; as, to *recoup* oneself for a loss.

re·course (rē-kôrs′; rē′kôrs), *n.* **1,** an appeal for aid or protection; **2,** the person to whom one appeals, or the thing to which one turns.

¹re·cov·er (rē-kŭv′ẽr), *v.t.* **1,** to get back or regain; as, to *recover* one's health; to *recover* lost property; **2,** to obtain by judgment in a court of law; as, to *recover* damages; **3,** to make up for; make good the loss or waste of; as, to *recover* lost time; **4,** to find again; as, to *recover* a scent:—*v.i.* **1,** to regain health, strength, or any former state; **2,** to win a law-suit.—*adj.* **re·cov′er·a·ble.**

²re·cov·er (rē-kŭv′ẽr), *v.t.* to put a new covering on; as, to *re-cover* a chair.

re·cov·er·y (rē-kŭv′ẽr-ĭ), *n.* [*pl.* recov-eries], **1,** the act of regaining something; as, the *recovery* of a lost book; **2,** a return to health, prosperity, or any former, de-sirable, state or condition.

rec·re·ant (rĕk′rē-ănt), *n.* **1,** a faithless person; a traitor; **2,** a coward:—*adj.* **1,** cowardly; **2,** unfaithful to one's duty or to a cause; false; as, a *recreant* knight.

re·cre·ate (rē′-krē-āt′), *v.t.* [re-creat-ed, re-creat-ing], to make or create anew.

rec·re·a·tion (rĕk/rē-ā/shŭn), *n.* refreshment of mind or body after toil; play.
Syn. sport, pastime, amusement.

re·crim·i·na·tion (rē-krĭm/ĭ-nā/shŭn), *n.* the act of answering an accusation, or charge, with another; a counteraccusation.

re·cross (rē-krôs/), *v.t.* to cross again.

re·cruit (rē-krōōt/), *n.* **1,** a man newly enlisted in an army or a navy; **2,** one who has just joined any cause:—*v.t.* **1,** to gather together; to add to, or supply with, fresh members; as, to *recruit* an army, a party, an association; also, to enlist (soldiers, sailors, etc.); **2,** to build up; restore; as, to *recruit* one's strength:—*v.i.* **1,** to obtain fresh supplies of men or members; **2,** to recover health and strength.

rec·tan·gle (rĕk/tăng/gl), *n.* a four-sided figure with four right angles.

rec·tan·gu·lar (rĕk-tăng/gu̇-lẽr), *adj.* shaped like a rectangle.

RECTANGLES

rec·ti·fy (rĕk/tĭ-fī), *v.t.* [rectified, rectifying], **1,** to correct; as, to *rectify* an error; to remedy; as, to *rectify* abuses; **2,** to refine or purify (liquids) by distillation; **3,** in electricity, to change (an electric current) from alternating to direct.—*n.* **rec/ti-fi/er.**—*n.* **rec/ti-fi-ca/tion.**

rec·ti·tude (rĕk/tĭ-tūd), *n.* rightness of intention and action; honesty; uprightness.
Syn. justice, integrity, goodness.

rec·tor (rĕk/tẽr), *n.* **1,** in the Protestant Episcopal Church, a clergyman in charge of a parish; **2,** in the Roman Catholic Church, the head of a religious house for men; also, the head of a parish; **3,** the head of a university, college, or school.

rec·to·ry (rĕk/tō-rĭ), *n.* [*pl.* rectories], **1,** the house of a rector; **2,** in England, a rector's benefice, including the church, the rector's residence, lands, etc.

rec·tum (rĕk/tŭm), *n.* the lower end of the large intestine.

re·cum·bent (rē-kŭm/bĕnt), *adj.* lying down; reclining; as, a *recumbent* figure.

re·cu·per·ate (rē-kū/pẽr-āt), *v.t.* [recuperat-ed, recuperat-ing], to regain (one's health):—*v.i.* to recover from illness, losses, etc.; as, it took her months to *recuperate.*—*n.* **re-cu/per-a/tion.**—*adj.* **re-cu/per-a/tive.**

re·cur (rē-kûr/), *v.i.* [recurred, recur-ring], **1,** to go back, as in memory or in speech; as, he *recurred* to his former opinion; **2,** to come back or return; as, a thought *recurs* to the mind; **3,** to come again, or at intervals, as malaria.

re·cur·rence (rē-kûr/ĕns), *n.* a return; repetition; as, the *recurrence* of a fever.

re·cur·rent (rē-kûr/ĕnt), *adj.* **1,** coming back at intervals; as, a *recurrent* fever; **2,** turning back in a reverse direction; as, a *recurrent* nerve.

red (rĕd), *n.* **1,** the color of blood; that part of the visible spectrum having the longest wave length; **2,** any coloring matter that produces this color; **3,** (often *Red*), a communist or revolutionary socialist; also, loosely, any radical:—*adj.* [red-der, reddest], **1,** of the color of blood; **2,** pertaining to or favoring revolution.—**to be in the red,** to show a net loss: said of an account; hence, of a person, to be in debt, rather than making money.

red·bird (rĕd/bûrd/), *n.* any of various birds of a red color, as the cardinal.

red·breast (rĕd/brĕst/), *n.* the robin.

red·coat (rĕd/kōt/), *n.* **1,** one who wears a red coat; **2,** formerly, a soldier of the British army.

red cross, a red Greek cross on a white ground, adopted by the Geneva Convention, in 1864, as the sign of neutrality in war:—**Red Cross,** a society for helping the sick and wounded during war, and giving aid and relief in times of calamity.

red deer, the common European stag.

red·den (rĕd/n), *v.t.* to make red:—*v.i.* to become red; blush; flush.

red·dish (rĕd/ish), *adj.* somewhat red; tinged with red.

re·deem (rē-dēm/), *v.t.* **1,** to buy back; **2,** to rescue or free from bondage or claim by paying a ransom or price; **3,** to ransom or free from sin and its consequences; **4,** to make good; perform; as, to *redeem* a promise; **5,** to make up for; as, to *redeem* a fault; **6,** to pay off (a promissory note); also, to pay off (bank notes) in coin; **7,** to recover (mortgaged property) by paying a price.—*adj.* **re-deem/a-ble.**
Syn. rescue, deliver, save.

re·deem·er (rē-dē/mẽr), *n.* one who saves or redeems:—**the Redeemer,** Jesus Christ.

re·demp·tion (rē-dĕmp/shŭn), *n.* **1,** the act of redeeming or buying back; as, the *redemption* of a mortgage; **2,** the salvation of mankind by Jesus Christ.

red·hand·ed (rĕd/-hăn/dĕd), *adj.* having bloodstained hands; hence, in the very act of committing a crime; as, the thief was caught *red-handed.*

red·hot (rĕd/-hŏt/), *adj.* **1,** heated to redness; **2,** fiery; excited; extreme.

re·dis·cov·er (rē/dĭs-kŭv/ẽr), *v.t.* to find again; come upon once more.

red·let·ter (rĕd/-lĕt/ẽr), *adj.* memorable; lucky; as, a *red-letter* day.

red-ness (rĕd'nĕs), *n.* the state or quality of being red.

red-o-lent (rĕd'ō-lĕnt), *adj.* **1,** giving off a pleasing odor; fragrant; as, the air was *redolent* of roses; **2,** suggestive; as, a scene *redolent* of romance.—*n.* **red'o-lence.**
Syn. odorous, scented, aromatic.

re-dou-ble (rē-dŭb'l; rĕ-dŭb'l), *v.t.* [re-dou-bled, redou-bling], **1,** to make twice as great; increase; **2,** in bridge, to double an opponent by whom one has been doubled:—*v.i.* to become twice as great.

re-doubt (rē-dout'), *n.* a small enclosed fortification, often temporary.

re-doubt-a-ble (rē-dout'a-bl), *adj.* inspiring fear or dread; formidable; valiant; as, a *redoubtable* foe.

re-dound (rē-dound'), *v.i.* to add or contribute; as, his acts *redound* to his glory.

red pep-per, cayenne pepper. See **cayenne.**

re-dress (rē-drĕs'), *v.t.* **1,** to right (a wrong); **2,** to correct or do away with (abuses):—*n.* (rē-drĕs'; rē'drĕs), **1,** the act of setting right; as, *redress* of grievances; **2,** compensation for a wrong or loss; as, to seek *redress* in the courts.

Red Riv-er, a river rising in northwestern Texas and flowing into the Mississippi River (map 5).

Red Sea, a branch of the Indian Ocean, between Arabia and Egypt (map 15).

red-skin (rĕd'skĭn'), *n.* a North American Indian.

red-start (rĕd'stärt'), *n.* **1,** a small European bird of the thrush family; **2,** a North American warbler.

red tape, excessive attention to details, rules, or forms in the conduct of business: so called from the custom of tying official papers with red tape.—*adj.* **red'-tape'.**

re-duce (rē-dūs'), *v.t.* [reduced, reducing], **1,** to make less in value, size, or the like; lessen; lower; as, to *reduce* a debt; **2,** to bring from a higher to a lower rank or position; degrade; as, to *reduce* an officer to the ranks; **3,** to subdue; conquer; as, to *reduce* a hostile tribe; **4,** to bring into order; as, to *reduce* spelling to rules; **5,** to bring to a specified condition; as, she *reduced* her family to despair; **6,** to change into some other physical state; as, to *reduce* sugar to sirup; **7,** in arithmetic, to change from one form to another without changing the value, as gallons to pints; **8,** in chemistry, to remove nonmetallic elements from; as, to *reduce* iron ore; **9,** in surgery, to restore (a displaced part) to its right position; also, to set; as, to *reduce* a fracture.—*adj.* **re-duc'i-ble.**

re-duc-tion (rē-dŭk'shŭn), *n.* **1,** the act of cutting down or reducing; also, the state of being reduced; **2,** the amount by which something is reduced; as, a *reduction* of ten pounds in weight; **3,** a duplicate on a smaller scale; as, the *reduction* of a map.

re-dun-dan-cy (rē-dŭn'dăn-sĭ), *n.* [*pl.* redundancies], an excessive amount; a quantity greater than is needful or useful; especially, the use of more words than are necessary to convey one's meaning.—Also, **re-dun'dance.**

re-dun-dant (rē-dŭn'dănt), *adj.* exceeding what is needed; superfluous in writing or speaking; too full or too wordy.

re-du-pli-cate (rē-dū'plĭ-kāt), *v.t.* [redu-plicat-ed, reduplicat-ing], to make double; multiply.—*n.* **re-du'pli-ca'tion.**

red-wing (rĕd'wĭng'), *n.* **1,** in America, the red-winged blackbird; **2,** in Europe, a thrush with red wing feathers.

red-wood (rĕd'wo͝od'), *n.* **1,** a very large California evergreen tree; **2,** the big tree. Both trees are sequoias.

re-ech-o (rē-ĕk'ō), *v.t.* to echo, or repeat the sound of, again:—*v.i.* to resound:—*n.* [*pl.* re-echoes], a repeated echo; a second echo.

reed (rēd), *n.* **1,** any of certain tall, coarse grasses that grow in wet places; also, one of their jointed hollow stems; **2,** a musical pipe made of the hollow stem of a plant; **3,** a thin, elastic tongue attached to the mouthpiece of certain musical instruments, as the clarinet; **4,** *Poetic,* an arrow.—*adj.* **reed'y.**—*n.* **reed'i-ness.**

reed-bird (rēd'bûrd'), *n.* the bobolink.

¹reef (rēf), *n.* that part of a sail which can be drawn in and secured by small ropes in shortening sail:—**reef knot,** a common knot, used for fastening two ends of rope or cord together: also called *square knot* (see illustration under *knot*):—*v.t.* to reduce (a sail) by drawing in or folding up part of it.

²reef (rēf), *n.* a sand bar or a shelf of rock at or just below the surface of the water.

reef-er (rē'fēr), *n.* **1,** one who reefs, or takes in, sail; hence, a midshipman; **2,** a short, tight-fitting, usually double-breasted jacket.

reek (rēk), *n.* vapor or steam; also, a disagreeable odor:—*v.i.* to send out vapor or unpleasant fumes.—*adj.* **reek'y.**

FISHING REEL AND LINE

¹reel (rēl), *n.* **1,** any of various devices with a revolving frame for winding yarn, wire, rope, or the like; **2,** a spool or bobbin for holding thread; **3,** in motion pictures, a strip of film, usually either 1,000 or 2,000 feet long, held by one spool:—*v.t.* **1,** to wind on a frame or bobbin; **2,** to draw in by winding a line on a reel; as, to *reel* in a trout; **3,** to tell rapidly and easily; as, to *reel* off a long story.

²**reel** (rēl), *v.i.* **1,** to stagger or sway from side to side in walking; **2,** to turn round and round; feel dizzy; as, his head *reeled;* **3,** to give way; waver; as, the whole line *reeled:*—*n.* the act of staggering or swaying.

³**reel** (rēl), *n.* **1,** a lively country or folk dance; **2,** the music for such a dance.

re—e-lect (rē/-ē-lĕkt/), *v.t.* to elect (a person) to another term.

re—e-lec-tion (rē/-ē-lĕk/shŭn), *n.* the election of a person to an office which he has held before.

re—en-ter (rē-ĕn/tẽr), *v.t.* and *v.i.* to enter (a place) again.

re—en-try (rē-ĕn/trĭ), *n.* [*pl.* re-entries], a second or new entry or appearance.

re—es-tab-lish (rē/-ĕs-tăb/lĭsh), *v.t.* to fix firmly again; restore; establish anew.—*n.* re/-es-tab/lish-ment.

re—ex-am-ine (rē/-ĕg-zăm/ĭn), *v.t.* [re-examined, re-examin-ing], to scrutinize again; examine again, as a book or a student.

re-fec-tion (rĕ-fĕk/shŭn), *n.* a light repast or lunch; refreshment.

re-fec-to-ry (rĕ-fĕk/tō-rĭ), *n.* [*pl.* refectories], a dining hall, especially in a monastery, convent, or school.

re-fer (rĕ-fûr/), *v.t.* [referred, refer-ring], **1,** to submit to another person or authority for information or decision; as, they *referred* the question to experts; **2,** to direct or send somewhere for information, help, or the like; as, to *refer* students to the encyclopedia; **3,** to explain as due to a certain cause; as, I *refer* his actions to ignorance:—*v.i.* **1,** to make mention of something; allude; as, he *referred* frequently to progress; **2,** to turn to something; apply; as, he *referred* frequently to his notes; **3,** to point or call attention; as, that sign *refers* to a footnote; **4,** to direct one person to another for information or recommendation; as, he had permission to *refer* to Mr. Jones.—*adj.* **ref/er-a-ble** (rĕf/ẽr-a-bl); **re-fer/ri-ble** (rĕ-fûr/ĭ-bl).
Syn. attribute, ascribe.

ref-er-ee (rĕf/ẽr-ē/), *n.* one to whom a matter in dispute is handed over for decision and settlement; an umpire:—*v.t.* and *v.i.* to umpire.

ref-er-ence (rĕf/ẽr-ĕns), *n.* **1,** the act of submitting a matter for settlement, or of applying for information; **2,** a source of information which may be consulted; as, a dictionary is a book of *reference;* **3,**

a passing allusion; as, he made no *reference* to politics; **4,** a passage or note in a book, article, etc., directing attention to some other book or passage; also, the book or passage to which attention is directed; **5,** a person to whom inquiries may be addressed regarding another person; **6,** a written statement about a person's character or ability; **7,** regard; respect; as, with *reference* to your request.

ref-er-en-dum (rĕf/ẽr-ĕn/dŭm), *n.* [*pl.* referendums (rĕf/ẽr-ĕn/dŭmz) or referenda (rĕf/ẽr-ĕn/dä)], **1,** the submitting of a legislative act to the vote of the people for approval or rejection; **2,** the right of the people to vote upon a legislative act; **3,** a direct popular vote on a proposed measure.

re-fill (rē/fĭl), *n.* a new or additional filling for a container; as, a *refill* of lead for a pencil:—*v.t.* (rē-fĭl/), to fill again.

re-fine (rĕ-fīn/), *v.t.* [refined, refin-ing], **1,** to make pure; clear from dross or worthless matter; as, to *refine* sugar; **2,** to free from imperfections; improve; as, he has *refined* his manners in the last year.

re-fined (rĕ-fīnd/), *adj.* **1,** freed from impurities; as, *refined* ore; **2,** well-bred; polished; as, *refined* speech.

re-fine-ment (rĕ-fīn/mĕnt), *n.* **1,** a freeing from impurities; **2,** freedom from what is coarse or lacking in good taste; culture.

re-fin-er-y (rĕ-fīn/ẽr-ĭ), *n.* [*pl.* refineries], a place where anything is refined or made pure; as, a sugar *refinery.*

re-fit (rē-fĭt/), *v.t.* [refit-ted, refit-ting], to equip or make ready for use again:—*v.i.* to be repaired or obtain fresh supplies; as, the ship had to *refit* in a week.

re-flect (rĕ-flĕkt/), *v.t.* **1,** to throw or give back (rays of light, heat, or sound); **2,** to give back or show an image of, as does a mirror; **3,** to give back as a result; as, his act *reflects* honor upon him:—*v.i.* **1,** to consider carefully; think; **2,** to cast reproach, blame, etc.; as, his faulty grammar *reflects* upon his early schooling.
Syn. ponder, muse, meditate.

re-flec-tion (rĕ-flĕk/shŭn), *n.* **1,** the act of throwing back; as, the *reflection* of light; **2,** that which is reflected, as an image; also, an effect or influence; as, the *reflection* of early associations on the character; **3,** careful consideration or thinking; as, this question requires prolonged *reflection;* **4,** criticism; reproach; as, a *reflection* on one's honesty; **5,** a remark, thought, or opinion; as, that was a profound *reflection;* **6,** in anatomy and zoology, the bending, turning, or folding of a part back on itself.
Syn. deliberation, meditation, musing.

---

go; join; yet; sing; chin; show; thin, *th*en; **hw,** *wh*y; **zh,** azure; **ü,** Ger. für or Fr. l*u*ne; **ö,** Ger. schön or Fr. f*eu*; **ṅ,** Fr. e*n*fant, no*m*; **kh,** Ger. a*ch* or i*ch*. See pages ix–x.

re-flec-tive (rĕ-flĕk′tĭv), *adj.* **1,** reflecting or throwing back images; as, the *reflecitve* surface of a pond; **2,** thoughtful; as, a *reflective* turn of mind.

re-flec-tor (rĕ-flĕk′tẽr), *n.* anything that reflects; especially, a polished, often hollowed, surface for reflecting heat or light; also, a device for reflecting sound.

REFLECTORS
1, for a candle (18th century); **2,** for an incandescent lamp.

re-flex (rē′flĕks), *adj.* **1,** thrown back; recoiling; as, *reflex* consequences; **2,** in physiology, showing automatic response to some outside stimulus; as, *reflex* action:—*n.* **1,** an image or reflection; as, public opinion is often a *reflex* of the newspapers; **2,** in physiology, an involuntary movement of some part of the body in response to a stimulus.

re-flex-ive (rĕ-flĕk′sĭv), *adj.* in grammar, indicating an action which the subject performs upon himself; as, "cut" in the sentence "he cut himself" is a *reflexive* verb:—**reflexive pronoun,** a pronoun which, though used as the object of a verb, is invariably identical with the subject, as "himself" in the sentence "he hurt himself accidentally."—*adv.* **re-flex′ive-ly.**

re-flux (rē′flŭks), *n.* a flowing back; ebb, as of the tide:—*adj.* flowing back.

re-for-est (rē-fŏr′ĕst), *v.t.* to plant anew with trees:—*v.i.* to set out trees again.—*n.* **re′for-est-a′tion.**

¹**re—form** (rē=fôrm′), *v.t.* and *v.i.* to shape or form again or anew.

²**re-form** (rē-fôrm′), *v.t.* to improve or make better by changing the form, removing the faults, or correcting or ending abuses; as, to *reform* the calendar, a thief, the courts:—*v.i.* to abandon evil ways:— *n.* a change for the better; a removal of some evil or abuse; as, *reforms* in the school system; also, improvement in character:— *adj.* pertaining to reform; as, a *reform* movement.

Syn., *v.* reclaim, rectify, mend.

ref-or-ma-tion (rĕf′ŏr-mā′shŭn), *n.* the act of changing for the better; improvement, especially in social, political, or religious affairs:—**Reformation,** the great religious movement begun by Martin Luther in the 16th century which resulted in the establishment of Protestantism.

re-form-a-to-ry (rĕ-fôr′mȧ-tôr′ĭ), *n.* [*pl.* reformatories], an institution or school for correcting the habits and conduct, especially of young offenders:—*adj.* tending to correct; as, *reformatory* schools.

re-form-er (rē-fôr′mẽr), *n.* one who sponsors or advocates reform in religion, politics, or the like.

re-fract (rĕ-frăkt′), *v.t.* to bend from a straight line; as, a prism *refracts* light rays. —*adj.* **re-frac′tive.**—*n.* **re-frac′tor.**

re-frac-tion (rĕ-frăk′shŭn), *n.* the bending or turning of rays of light, heat, or sound, as they pass obliquely from one medium into another.

re-frac-to-ry (rĕ-frăk′tō-rĭ), *adj.* **1,** disobedient; stubborn; unmanageable; as, a *refractory* boy; **2,** not yielding to treatment; as, a *refractory* disease; **3,** resisting heat; hard to work or fuse; as, *refractory* ore.

REFRACTION
J, jar partly filled with water. A ray of light starting at D, and passing into the air at B, is refracted to the direction BA, so that an object at D will appear to be at C.

¹**re-frain** (rĕ-frān′), *n.* a phrase or verse repeated at intervals in a poem or song.

²**re-frain** (rĕ-frān′), *v.i.* to hold oneself back; restrain oneself; as, to *refrain* from comment.

Syn. abstain, withhold, cease.

re-fresh (rĕ-frĕsh′), *v.t.* **1,** to make fresh again; revive; as, to *refresh* flowers; **2,** to restore after fatigue; as, rest *refreshes* the body; **3,** to quicken; as, to *refresh* the mind.

Syn. invigorate, recreate, strengthen.

re-fresh-ment (rĕ-frĕsh′mĕnt), *n.* **1,** the act of reviving, or state of being revived; restoration of strength, liveliness, etc.; **2,** that which restores or revives, especially food, drink, or rest; **3, refreshments,** food and drink served to guests.

re-frig-er-ate (rĕ-frĭj′ẽr-āt), *v.t.* and *v.i.* [refrigerat-ed, refrigerat-ing], to cool or become cool.—*n.* **re-frig′er-a′tion.**

re-frig-er-a-tor (rĕ-frĭj′ẽr-ā′tẽr), *n.* a receptacle or a room where food and other perishable things are kept cool by ice, cold air, or other means.

ref-uge (rĕf′ūj), *n.* **1,** a place of safety from trouble or danger; a shelter or secure retreat; as, to seek *refuge* from the storm; **2,** one who or that which protects or defends from danger or misfortune; as, he is my *refuge.*

Syn. protection, harbor, cover.

ref-u-gee (rĕf′ū-jē′), *n.* one who flees for safety, especially from political or religious persecution, to a foreign land.

re-ful-gent (rĕ-fŭl′jĕnt), *adj.* casting a brilliant light; splendid.—*adv.* **re-ful′gent-ly.**—*n.* **re-ful′gence.**

Syn. flashing, bright, radiant.

re-fund (rĕ-fŭnd′), *v.t.* and *v.i.* to give

back or pay back (money); as, the game was canceled and the money for the tickets *refunded:—n.* (rē-fŭnd′; rē′fŭnd), money paid back.

re-fus-al (rē-fū′zăl), *n.* 1, the act of rejecting or denying; 2, the right to refuse or take something before others are given an opportunity to take it; as, to have the *refusal* of an office.

¹**re-fuse** (rē-fūz′), *v.t.* [refused, refus-ing], 1, to decline to take; be unwilling to accept; 2, to decline to do or grant; deny; as, to *refuse* aid:—*v.i.* to decline to take an offer; decline to do something.
   Syn. reject, renounce, repel.

²**ref-use** (rĕf′ūs), *n.* waste material; trash; rubbish:—*adj.* worthless.
   Syn., n. dregs, sediment, scum, leavings.

re-fute (rē-fūt′), *v.t.* [refut-ed, refut-ing], to prove to be false or wrong; to overthrow by argument or proof.—*adj.* **ref′u-ta-ble** (rĕf′ū-tá-bl; rē-fūt′á-bl).—*n.* **ref′u-ta′tion.**

re-gain (rē-gān′), *v.t.* 1, to get back; recover; as, to *regain* a fortune; 2, to reach again; as, to *regain* shelter.

re-gal (rē′găl), *adj.* royal; fit for a king; hence, resplendent; magnificent.

re-gale (rē-gāl′), *v.t.* [regaled, regal-ing], to entertain; feast; as, to *regale* guests with choice food.

re-ga-li-a (rē-gā′lĭ-á; rē-gāl′yá), *n.pl.* 1, the signs or emblems of royalty, such as the crown and scepter; 2, personal decorations, as of a fraternal order.

re-gard (rē-gärd′), *v.t.* 1, to observe closely; look upon attentively; as, she *regarded* him with a frown; 2, to consider; as, I *regard* her as an enemy; 3, to heed; respect; as, *regard* my words; she does not *regard* her mother's wishes; 4, to relate to; concern; as, the matter *regards* your happiness; 5, to esteem; admire; as, I *regard* him highly: —*n.* 1, a look or gaze; close attention or notice; 2, care; consideration; as, *regard* for others; 3, respect; affection; as, I hold him in high *regard;* 4, **regards,** good wishes; as, my best *regards* to your mother:— **in regard to** or **with regard to,** concerning; about; as, *with regard to* your request, I have some interesting news.
   Syn., n. esteem, heed, observance.

re-gard-ful (rē-gärd′fŏŏl), *adj.* 1, taking notice; heedful; 2, respectful.

re-gard-ing (rē-gär′dĭng), *prep.* about; in respect to.

re-gard-less (rē-gärd′lĕs), *adj.* careless; negligent; heedless; as, *regardless* of danger.

re-gat-ta (rē-găt′á), *n.* a boat race or a series of boat races.

re-gen-cy (rē′jĕn-sĭ), *n.* [*pl.* regencies], 1, the office of a temporary ruler; 2, a person or body of persons governing for another; 3, the office, powers, or government of such a person or body; 4, the period during which someone rules for another.

re-gen-er-ate (rē-jĕn′ĕr-āt), *v.t.* [regenerat-ed, regenerat-ing], 1, to renew spiritually; 2, to make a change for the better in; reform; as, the economic system needs to be *regenerated;* 3, to produce anew; as, the body *regenerates* tissue; also, to fill with new life or power:—*adj.* (rē-jĕn′ĕr-ĭt), 1, having new life; 2, spiritually reborn; as, a *regenerate* soul.—*adj.* **re-gen′er-a′tive.**— *n.* **re-gen′er-a′tion.**

re-gent (rē′jĕnt), *n.* 1, a person appointed to govern while the rightful ruler is unable to do so, or until he is able to take the throne; 2, in certain universities, a member of the governing board:—*adj.* ruling in place of another; as, prince *regent.*

reg-i-cide (rĕj′ĭ-sīd), *n.* the murder or the murderer of a king.

re-gime (rā-zhēm′), *n.* 1, a system of government, social or political; 2, a systematized method of living; as, he follows a daily *regime.*

reg-i-men (rĕj′ĭ-mĕn), *n.* 1, orderly government; control; 2, a system of diet, exercise, sleep, and daily routine, prescribed for some special purpose.

reg-i-ment (rĕj′ĭ-mĕnt), *n.* an organized body of soldiers under the command of a colonel.

reg-i-men-tal (rĕj′ĭ-mĕn′tăl), *adj.* pertaining to a regiment; as, *regimental* quarters:—**regimentals,** *n.pl.* the uniform worn by the soldiers of a regiment.

re-gion (rē′jŭn), *n.* 1, an indefinitely large section of land; a district; as, the Rocky Mountain *region;* 2, one of the divisions or portions into which the earth, the sea, or the air may be thought of as divided; as, the inner *regions* of the earth; the upper *regions* of the atmosphere; 3, a division or part of the body; as, the *region* of the liver.—*adj.* **re′gion-al.**

reg-is-ter (rĕj′is-tẽr), *n.* 1, an official written record; as, a *register* of births and deaths; also, a book for keeping such a record; 2, a person who keeps a record; as, a *register* of deeds; 3, a device that records; as, a cash *register;* 4, a device for regulating the entrance of heated air to a room; 5, the compass or range of a voice or an instrument:—*v.t.* 1, to enter in a list or formal record; enroll; as, to *register* securities; to *register* students; 2, to mark or read; as, the thermostat *registers* 60 degrees; 3, to indicate by facial expression; as, to *register* surprise:—*v.i.* to write one's name in a list or record; as, to *register* at a hotel.

---

go; join; yet; sing; chin; show; thin, *th***en; hw,** *wh***y; zh,** a**zure; ŭ,** Ger. f*ür* or Fr. l*u*ne; **ö,** Ger. sch*ö*n or Fr. f*eu;* **ṅ,** Fr. e*n*fant, no*m*; kh, Ger. a*ch* or i*ch.* See pages ix–x.

reg·is·trar (rĕj′ĭs-trär; rĕj′ĭs-trär′), *n.* an official who keeps records; as, a *registrar* in a college or university.

reg·is·tra·tion (rĕj′ĭs-trā′shŭn), *n.* **1**, the act of entering names, facts, etc., in a register; also, an item entered in a register; **2**, total enrollment.

reg·is·try (rĕj′ĭs-trĭ), *n.* [*pl.* registries], **1**, the act of entering on a record; **2**, a written account or record, as of births, deaths, or the like; **3**, the place where such a record is kept.

re·gress (rē′grĕs), *n.* **1**, a passage back; way of return; as, a place which offers no *regress*; **2**, the power or privilege of returning; as, the right of free egress and *regress*: —*v.i.* (rē-grĕs′), to go back; return.—*n.* **re·gres′sion.**—*adj.* **re·gres′sive.**

re·gret (rē-grĕt′), *v.t.* [regret-ted, regret-ting], **1**, to look back upon, or recall, with remorse or distress; as, to *regret* one's mistakes; **2**, to feel sorry about or grieve over; as, he *regretted* leaving:—*n.* **1**, sorrow for the loss or want of something; as, *regret* for vanished wealth; **2**, distress of mind over some past event with the wish that it had been otherwise; as, *regret* for harsh words; **3**, sadness; disappointment; as, I hear with *regret* that you will not come; **4**, **regrets**, a polite expression of refusal in answer to an invitation.

re·gret·ful (rē-grĕt′fŏŏl), *adj.* remembering with distress; expressing regret.—*adv.* **re·gret′ful·ly.**—*n.* **re·gret′ful·ness.**

re·gret·ta·ble (rē-grĕt′á-bl), *adj.* arousing regret; deplorable; as, a *regrettable* accident.—*adv.* **re·gret′ta·bly.**

reg·u·lar (rĕg′ū-lẽr), *adj.* **1**, according to some established rule, order, or custom; occurring on a fixed date; as, a *regular* holiday; without a break; as, in *regular* succession; fully qualified; as, a *regular* student; orthodox; as, a *regular* Republican; orderly or methodical; as, *regular* habits; unvarying, steady, or uniform; as, a *regular* pulse; **2**, following a certain design; symmetrical; as, *regular* features; **3**, belonging to a religious order; bound by religious rule; as, *regular* clergy; **4**, permanent; as, the *regular* army; **5**, in grammar, following the usual rules of declension, comparison, or conjugation; **6**, *Colloquial*, thorough; as, she is a *regular* bookworm:—*n.* **1**, a soldier belonging to a standing army; **2**, a member of the clergy who belongs to a religious order.—*adv.* **reg′u·lar·ly.**

Syn., *adj.* normal, typical, customary.

reg·u·lar·i·ty (rĕg′ū-lăr′ĭ-tĭ), *n.* [*pl.* regularities], the state of being normal; orderly occurrence or arrangement.

reg·u·late (rĕg′ū-lāt), *v.t.* [regulat-ed, regulat-ing], **1**, to govern according to rule, method, or established custom; as, to *regulate* one's conduct; **2**, to put or keep in proper order; as, to *regulate* a household; **3**, to adjust to some desired or standard condition; as, to *regulate* a thermostat.—*adj.* **reg′u·la·tive.**

Syn. direct, manage, rule.

reg·u·la·tion (rĕg′ū-lā′shŭn), *n.* **1**, the act of adjusting; as, the *regulation* of temperatures; also, the state of being adjusted; **2**, a rule or law; as, hospital *regulations*:—*adj.* conforming to a regular style, method, or rule; as, a *regulation* uniform.

reg·u·la·tor (rĕg′ū-lā′tẽr), *n.* **1**, one who or that which controls or governs in accordance with rules; **2**, a device for controlling speed; as, the *regulator* of a clock; **3**, a clock of finest mechanism and accuracy used as a standard of time.

re·ha·bil·i·tate (rē′há-bĭl′ĭ-tāt), *v.t.* [rehabilitat-ed, rehabilitat-ing], **1**, to restore to a former state, rank, or privilege; reinstate; **2**, to clear the character or reputation of; re-establish in social position; **3**, to put into useful or working condition again.—*n.* **re′ha·bil′i·ta′tion.**

re·hash (rē-hăsh′), *v.t.* to use again or work into a new form:—*n.* (rē′hăsh), something made over into a new form; as, a *rehash* of an old plot.

re·hears·al (rē-hûr′sǎl), *n.* **1**, the act of practicing in private; also, a private recital or practice in advance of a public performance; as, the *rehearsal* of a play; **2**, a telling over; as, a *rehearsal* of one's summer experiences in Europe.

re·hearse (rē-hûrs′), *v.t.* [rehearsed, rehears-ing], **1**, to narrate; tell the story of; as, she *rehearsed* the most interesting events of her career; **2**, to practice in preparation for a public performance; as, to *rehearse* a play or a piano solo.

reichs·mark (rīkhs′märk′), *n.* the monetary unit of Germany, established in 1924 (see Table, page 943).

reign (rān), *n.* **1**, supreme rule; royal power; **2**, the time during which a ruler holds sway:—*v.i.* **1**, to exercise royal authority; rule; **2**, to hold sway; prevail; as, terror *reigned* in the village.

re·im·burse (rē′ĭm-bûrs′), *v.t.* [reimbursed, reimburs-ing], to repay (a person); as, to *reimburse* a man for the loss of his time.—*n.* **re′im·burse′ment.**

Syn. compensate, indemnify.

Reims (rēmz; răṅs), a city in northeastern France, famous for its cathedral (map 12). Also spelled **Rheims.**

rein (rān), *n.* **1**, either of two leather

straps fastened to rings in the ends of the bit of a horse or other animal as a means of guiding and controlling it; **2,** (often *reins*), any means of restraint or control; as, the *reins* of government:—**give rein to,** allow to be unchecked or uncontrolled; as, to *give rein to* grief:—*v.t.* **1,** to hold in, direct, or stop, by means of reins; as, to *rein* a horse; **2,** to restrain; control; as, to *rein* one's anger.

re·in·car·na·tion (rē'ĭn-kär-nā'shŭn), *n.* a new embodiment or incarnation; especially, in certain cults and religions, the rebirth of the soul in another body; also, the new body inhabited by the soul.

rein·deer (rān'dēr'), *n.* [*pl.* reindeer], a large deer with branched antlers, found in northern countries, and used as a draft animal. Its flesh and hide are used for food and clothing.

REINDEER (₁/₆₀)

re·in·force (rē'ĭn-fôrs'), *v.t.* [reinforced, reinforcing], to give new strength to; support; strengthen; as, to *reinforce* the foundations of a building.

re·in·force·ment (rē'ĭn-fôrs'mĕnt), *n.* **1,** the act of strengthening; also, the state of being strengthened; **2,** anything that strengthens or supports; any additional support; **3, reinforcements,** additional troops or ships.

re·in·state (rē'ĭn-stāt'), *v.t.* [reinstated, reinstating], to restore to a former position; as, to *reinstate* a suspended pupil.— *n.* **re·in·state'ment.**

re·is·sue (rē-ĭsh'oo), *v.t.* [reissued, reissuing], to give out again; as, to *reissue* an edict:—*v.t.* to go forth again; emerge again.

re·it·er·ate (rē-ĭt'ēr-āt), *v.t.* [reiterated, reiterating], to do or say again and again; as, to *reiterate* a denial.— *n.* **re·it'er·a'tion.** —*adj.* **re·it'er·a'tive.**

re·ject (rē-jĕkt'), *v.t.* **1,** to throw away as worthless; discard; as, to *reject* all imperfect specimens; **2,** to refuse to take; decline; as, to *reject* an offer of assistance; **3,** to refuse to grant, believe, or agree to; as, to *reject* a suggestion.— *n.* **re·jec'tion.**

re·joice (rē-jois'), *v.i.* [rejoiced, rejoicing], to feel or express joy or gladness; as, I *rejoice* in your happiness:—*v.t.* to make joyful; gladden; as, the sight of her gifts *rejoiced* Mary greatly.— *n.* **re·joic'ing.**

re·join (rē-join'), *v.t.* to join again; re-

turn to after separation:—*v.i.* (rē-join'), to make answer to a reply; retort.

re·join·der (rē-join'dēr), *n.* a reply; retort.

re·ju·ve·nate (rē-jōō'vē-nāt), *v.t.* [rejuvenated, rejuvenating], to renew the youth of; cause to feel young again.— *n.* **re·ju've·na'tion.**

re·kin·dle (rē-kĭn'dl), *v.t.* [rekindled, rekindling], to set fire to anew; as, to *rekindle* a dying blaze:—*v.i.* to take fire again.

re·lapse (rē-lăps'), *v.i.* [relapsed, relapsing], to fall back into a former bad state or habit; as, he *relapsed* into unpunctuality; also, to fall back into illness after a state of partial recovery:—*n.* a slipping back; a setback.

re·late (rē-lāt'), *v.t.* [related, relating], **1,** to tell (a story); recite; narrate; **2,** to show a connection between; as, to *relate* poverty and crime:—*v.i.* to refer or allude (to); have to do (with); as, the letter *relates* to his success.—*adj.* **re·lat'ed.**

re·la·tion (rē-lā'shŭn), *n.* **1,** the act of narrating or telling; also, the thing narrated or told; **2,** a connection between two or more things; as, the *relation* of lack of nourishment to disease; **3,** reference; regard; as, in *relation* to the matter of which you spoke; **4,** connection by birth or marriage; also, a relative; **5, relations,** dealings; affairs; as, foreign *relations;* business *relations.*— *n.* **re·la'tion·ship.**

rel·a·tive (rĕl'á·tĭv), *n.* **1,** that which refers to, or is thought of in its connection with, something else; **2,** a person connected with another by blood or marriage; **3,** in grammar, a word, such as the pronouns *who, which, that,* which refers to an antecedent:—*adj.* **1,** having or expressing connection with, or reference to, something; as, their conversation was *relative* to business; **2,** comparative; as, the *relative* speed of field hockey and ice hockey; **3,** having meaning only in connection with something else; as, "more" and "less" are *relative* terms; **4,** in grammar, referring to an antecedent; as, a *relative* pronoun.—*adv.* **rel'a·tive·ly.**— *n.* **rel'a·tiv'i·ty.**

re·lax (rē-lăks'), *v.t.* **1,** to slacken; make less tight or firm; as, to *relax* one's hold; **2,** to make less strict, harsh, or severe; as, to *relax* rules of conduct; **3,** to relieve from strain; ease; as, seeing a good comedy *relaxes* one's mind:—*v.i.* **1,** to become less tight, firm, or severe; **2,** to cease from effort; lessen tension; rest; as, to *relax* after the day's labor.

re·lax·a·tion (rē'lăk-sā'shŭn), *n.* **1,** the act of letting up or relaxing; a lessening of tension or restraint; **2,** that which

go; join; yet; sing; chin; show; thin, *th*en; hw, *wh*y; zh, a*z*ure; ü, Ger. f*ür* or Fr. l*u*ne; ö, Ger. sch*ö*n or Fr. f*eu*; ñ, Fr. e*n*fant, no*m*; kh, Ger. a*ch* or i*ch.* See pages ix–x.

eases and relaxes; amusement; pastime; as, everyone needs *relaxation* occasionally.

re-lay (rĕ-lā′; rē′lā), *n.* a new or additional supply of men, horses, or the like, held ready to replace or relieve others:—**relay race**, a race in which a number of contestants replace one another, each covering a definite part of the course:—*v.t.* (rē-lā′), to send as if by successive messengers; as, to *relay* a message across the border.

re-lease (rē-lēs′), *v.t.* [released, releas-ing], **1,** to set free; as, the man was *released* from prison; **2,** to free from obligation or penalty; as, to *release* a person from a promise; **3,** to deliver from pain, care, etc.; **4,** to permit the showing or sale of; as, to *release* a book:—*n.* **1,** the act of setting free; the state of being set free; **2,** deliverance from pain, anxiety, distress, etc.; **3,** a freeing from an obligation or a penalty; as, *release* from debt; **4,** a device for holding or freeing part of a machine; as, a *release* on an automobile clutch; **5,** a placing on the market or before the public; as, the *release* of a film.

Syn., *v.* discharge, liberate, acquit.

rel-e-gate (rĕl′ē-gāt), *v.t.* [relegat-ed, rel-egat-ing], **1,** to send away; exile; hence, to remove, usually to a worse or less desirable place or situation; as, to *relegate* furniture to the attic; **2,** to turn over (a task, duty, etc.) to someone else; as, a sheriff may *relegate* certain duties to a deputy.—*n.* rel′e-ga′tion.

re-lent (rē-lĕnt′), *v.i.* to become less harsh, severe, or cruel; to become more merciful; as, the tyrant *relented.*—*adj.* re-lent′less.—*adv.* re-lent′less-ly.—*n.* re-lent′less-ness.

rel-e-vant (rĕl′ē-vănt), *adj.* having to do with, or relating to, the case in hand; pertinent; as, a *relevant* remark.—*n.* rel′e-vance; rel′e-van-cy.

Syn. fit, proper, suitable, appropriate.

re-li-a-bil-i-ty (rē-lī′a̍-bĭl′ĭ-tĭ), *n.* the quality of meriting trust or confidence, or of being dependable.

re-li-a-ble (rē-lī′a̍-bl), *adj.* trustworthy; fit to be depended upon; as, *reliable* servants; *reliable* news.—*adv.* re-li′a-bly.

re-li-ance (rē-lī′ăns), *n.* **1,** the act of trusting or depending; also, the state of being confident; hence, confidence; trust; as, the passengers placed perfect *reliance* in the skill of the driver; **2,** that on which one depends; a foundation for trust.

re-li-ant (rē-lī′ănt), *adj.* having confidence; depending; as upon a person or thing.

rel-ic (rĕl′ĭk), *n.* **1,** that which remains; a survival; a trace or memorial, as of a custom, period, people, etc.; as, arrow-heads are *relics* of primitive peoples; **2,** anything held in religious reverence as having belonged to a martyr or saint.

rel-ict (rĕl′ĭkt), *n.* a widow.

re-lief (rē-lēf′), *n.* **1,** the release in whole or in part from pain, grief, want, etc.; hence, comfort; ease; **2,** that which aids or relieves; as, exercise is a *relief* from overstudy; **3,** release from a task or duty; as, the *relief* of a sentinel by another; **4,** charitable help given to the poor; also, help given in time of danger or difficulty; **5,** fresh supplies of men, animals, food, etc.; especially, fresh troops, coming to take the place of those tired out in action; **6,** the raising of a sculptured design from a flat surface; as, the figures carved in *relief* on an altar; hence, sharpness of outline, due to contrast; as, a tower in bold *relief* against the sky.

RELIEF, def. 6

Syn. succor, aid, assistance, redress.

re-lieve (rē-lēv′), *v.t.* [relieved, reliev-ing], **1,** to remove; reduce in severity; lessen; as, to *relieve* pain; **2,** to free from suffering, distress, or the like; to help; as, to *relieve* a famine-stricken people; **3,** to release from a post; take the place of; as, he *relieved* the guard at midnight; **4,** to set off; bring out by contrast; as, a white collar *relieves* a black dress.

Syn. ease, assuage, allay, lighten.

re-li-gion (rē-lĭj′ŭn), *n.* **1,** belief in a divine or superhuman power, especially in a personal God, to whom obedience and honor are due; **2,** the outward acts and practices of life that grow out of the worship of such a god; **3,** any system of faith and worship; as, the Christian *religion.*

re-li-gious (rē-lĭj′ŭs), *adj.* **1,** feeling and living in accordance with a belief in a divine power to whom honor and obedience are due; devout; pious; **2,** pertaining to religion; as, *religious* literature; **3,** strict; conscientious; as, he did the work with *religious* care:—*n.* one who is bound by religious vows; a monk or nun.—*adv.* re-li′gious-ly.

re-lin-quish (rē-lĭng′kwĭsh), *v.t.* to give up; leave; surrender; as, to *relinquish* a claim.—*n.* re-lin′quish-ment.

Syn. resign, forsake, forgo, abandon.

rel-ish (rĕl′ĭsh), *n.* **1,** a taste or preference; as, a *relish* for adventure; also, enjoyment; as, he ate his meal with *relish;* **2,** the quality that makes a thing pleasurable; as, novelty gave *relish* to the journey; **3,**

a sauce, catchup, or the like, that adds flavor to food and stimulates the appetite: —*v.t.* **1,** to enjoy; take pleasure in; as, to *relish* gossip; **2,** to eat with pleasure or zest; as, he *relishes* his dinner.

re·load (rē-lōd′), *v.t.* and *v.i.* to fill or load again.

re·luc·tance (rē-lŭk′tăns), *n.* unwillingness; hesitation; as, to leave a party with *reluctance.* Also, **re·luc′tan·cy.**

re·luc·tant (rē-lŭk′tănt), *adj.* **1,** unwilling; disinclined; as, *reluctant* to admit defeat; **2,** marked by unwillingness; as, a *reluctant* acceptance.—*adv.* **re·luc′tant·ly.**
Syn. averse, loath, indisposed.

re·ly (rē-lī′), *v.i.* [relied, rely-ing], to trust; have confidence; depend; as, you can *rely* on John.

re·main (rē-mān′), *v.i.* **1,** to stay behind when others go; as, only he *remained* in the room; **2,** to be left after a part has been used, taken away, lost, or destroyed; as, the walls of the house *remain;* **3,** to be left for further consideration or action; as, that *remains* to be seen; **4,** to continue in the same state; as, he *remains* a bachelor.

re·main·der (rē-mān′dĕr), *n.* **1,** the portion left after anything is taken away; the rest; as, the *remainder* of one's life; **2,** in arithmetic, the quantity left after subtraction; as, 9 − 3 leaves a *remainder* of 6; also, the part, less than the divisor, left over after division.

re·mains (rē-mānz′), *n.pl.* **1,** the part or parts left; as, the *remains* of a meal; **2,** ruins; relics, especially of antiquity; as, the extensive *remains* of ancient Rome; **3,** a dead body; corpse.

re·mand (rē-mănd′), *v.t.* to send back; especially, to commit to custody again; as, to *remand* a prisoner:—*n.* the sending back of a prisoner to custody.

re·mark (rē-märk′), *v.t.* **1,** to take note of; observe; as, we *remarked* his worried look; **2,** to utter briefly and casually; mention; as, he *remarked* that he would be in New York today:—*v.i.* to comment upon something:—*n.* **1,** observation; notice; comment; as, her dress made her an object of *remark;* **2,** a brief, casual comment or statement; as, we laughed at his *remarks.*

re·mark·a·ble (rē-mär′kȧ-bl), *adj.* worthy of observation or comment; extraordinary; as, *remarkable* wit.—*adv.* **re·mark′a·bly.**
Syn. famous, wonderful.

re·mar·ry (rē-măr′ĭ), *v.t.* and *v.i.* [remarried, remarry-ing], to marry again.

Rem·brandt van Rijn or **Ryn** (rĕm′-brănt; *Dutch* rĕm′bränt vän rīn′), (1606–1669), a famous Dutch painter and etcher.

re·me·di·a·ble (rē-mē′dĭ-ȧ-bl), *adj.* capable of being cured or corrected; as, a *remediable* fault.—*adv.* **re·me′di·a·bly.**

re·me·di·al (rē-mē′dĭ-ăl), *adj.* affording, or used as, a cure; as, *remedial* treatment.

rem·e·dy (rĕm′ė-dĭ), *n.* [*pl.* remedies], **1,** anything designed to cure or relieve illness; a helpful medicine; **2,** that which removes or corrects an evil; a relief:—*v.t.* [remedied, remedy-ing], **1,** to cure, or cause to improve, with medicine; as, to *remedy* a cough; **2,** to repair; make right; correct (an evil).
Syn., n. help, corrective, redress, cure.

re·mem·ber (rē-mĕm′bĕr), *v.t.* **1,** to retain or keep in the mind; recall; as, I don't *remember* how to play checkers; **2,** to keep in mind carefully; know by heart; as, to *remember* a poem; **3,** to carry greetings from; as, *remember* me to her; **4,** to give a present to; tip; as, *remember* the porter:—*v.i.* to possess or use the faculty of memory; as, he doesn't *remember* from one day to the next.

re·mem·brance (rē-mĕm′brăns), *n.* **1,** the act or power of recalling to, or keeping in, the mind; recollecting; **2,** the state of being held in, or recalled to, mind; memory; as, in *remembrance* of someone; **3,** the length of time over which one's memories extend; as, the most remarkable event in my *remembrance;* **4,** that which is remembered; also, a memento or keepsake; **5,** **remembrances,** greetings showing regard; as, give her my *remembrances.*

re·mind (rē-mīnd′), *v.t.* to bring to the mind of; cause to recollect; as, *remind* me to go.—*n.* **re·mind′er.**

rem·i·nis·cence (rĕm′ĭ-nĭs′ĕns), *n.* the recollection of past experiences; remembrance; also, a particular event or experience which is remembered and told.

rem·i·nis·cent (rĕm′ĭ-nĭs′ĕnt), *adj.* **1,** bringing memories of the past; as, a *reminiscent* scene; **2,** given to recalling the past; dwelling on the past; as, a *reminiscent* letter; **3,** suggestive; as, a poem *reminiscent* of Burns.

re·miss (rē-mĭs′), *adj.* careless in matters of duty, business, etc.; neglectful; lax; as, he is apt to be *remiss* in keeping his engagements.—*n.* **re·miss′ness.**
Syn. slack, slothful, negligent.

re·mis·sion (rē-mĭsh′ŭn), *n.* **1,** the act of canceling, as a fine or debt; also, forgiveness, as of sins or other offenses; **2,** temporary lessening; as, a *remission* of pain.

re·mit (rē-mĭt′), *v.t.* [remit-ted, remit-ting], **1,** to forgive or pardon; as, to *remit* sins; **2,** to send (money) in payment of debts or bills due; **3,** to refrain from demanding or insisting upon; as, to *remit* a fine; **4,** to make less severe; relax; as, to *remit* one's watchfulness:—*v.i.* **1,** to abate; lessen in force; slacken; **2,** to send money, as in payment of goods.

re·mit·tance (rė-mĭt′ăns), *n.* **1,** the sending of money, especially to someone at a distant place; **2,** the sum so sent.

rem·nant (rĕm′nănt), *n.* that which is left over; remainder; especially, a short length of fabric, the last of a piece, offered at a low price.

Syn. residue, portion, balance.

re·mod·el (rė-mŏd′l), *v.t.* [remodeled, remodel-ing], to put into new shape; make over; as, to *remodel* a dress.

re·mon·strance (rė-mŏn′străns), *n.* a strong objection to, or protest against, something; a reproof.

re·mon·strate (rė-mŏn′strāt), *v.i.* [remonstrat-ed, remonstrat-ing], to urge or put forward strong reasons against some act or course; as, to *remonstrate* against low wages.

Syn. protest, complain, expostulate.

re·morse (rė-môrs′), *n.* anguish of mind caused by a sense of guilt; bitter reproach of oneself; repentance.—*adj.* **re·morse′ful.** —*n.* **re·morse′ful-ness.**

re·morse·less (rė-môrs′lĕs), *adj.* cruel; merciless; pitiless.

re·mote (rė-mōt′), *adj.* [remot-er, remotest], **1,** far off in time; as, *remote* centuries; **2,** distant in place; as, *remote* lands; **3,** far removed; not closely related; as, his remarks were *remote* from the subject; a *remote* cousin; **4,** slight; not plainly seen; as, a *remote* likeness; a *remote* possibility. —*adv.* **re·mote′ly.**—*n.* **re·mote′ness.**

Syn. irrelevant, foreign, alien.

re·mount (rė-mount′), *v.t.* to get up on again; as, the fireman *remounted* the ladder:—*v.i.* to mount a horse again; as, the captain *remounted* quickly:—*n.* a fresh horse to replace one killed or fatigued.

re·mov·al (rė-mōō′văl), *n.* **1,** the act of taking away; as, the *removal* of the tenements pleased everyone; **2,** the state of being removed; as, this patient will not stand *removal;* **3,** dismissal, as from office.

re·move (rė-mōōv′), *v.t.* [removed, removing], **1,** to take from its place; transfer from one place to another; as, to *remove* toys from a counter; **2,** to put an end to; push out of the way; as, to *remove* a hindrance; **3,** to dismiss; displace; as, to *remove* a man from office:—*v.i.* to go from one place to another; change residence:— *n.* a step or interval; as, unemployment is but one *remove* from poverty.—*n.* **re·mov′er.**—*adj.* **re·mov′a-ble.**

re·mu·ner·ate (rė-mū′nėr-āt), *v.t.* [remunerat-ed, remunerat-ing], to pay (someone) in return for service, time spent, etc. —*adj.* **re·mu′ner-a′tive.**—*n.* **re·mu′ner-a′tion.**

Syn. recompense, reimburse, satisfy.

Re·mus (rē′mŭs), *n.* in Roman legend, the brother of Romulus. See **Romulus.**

ren·ais·sance (rĕn′ė-säns′; rė-nā′săns), *n.* a revival of interest and effort in any line of endeavor, especially in art or literature:—**Renaissance,** the period of a great revival of learning and classical art in Europe during the 15th and 16th centuries, marking the transition from medieval to modern civilization. Also spelled **re·nas′cence; Re·nas′cence.**

re·name (rē-nām′), *v.t.* [renamed, renaming], to name again.

re·nas·cence (rė-năs′ĕns), *n.* rebirth; renaissance:—**Renascence,** the Renaissance.

ren·coun·ter (rĕn-koun′tėr), *n.* **1,** a contest; **2,** an unexpected meeting.

rend (rĕnd), *v.t.* [rent (rĕnt), rend-ing], **1,** to tear apart with violence; split; as, the wind *rends* the sail; **2,** to take away by force or violence.

Syn. break, sever, sunder.

ren·der (rĕn′dėr), *v.t.* **1,** to give in return; pay back; as, to *render* blow for blow; **2,** to pay, as something owed; as, to *render* homage; **3,** to present for payment; as, to *render* an account; **4,** to utter as final; as, to *render* a decision; **5,** to yield; as, to *render* one's life; **6,** to furnish; give; as, to *render* aid; **7,** to cause to be; make; as, to *render* a house fit for habitation; **8,** to translate; as, to *render* French into English; **9,** to express or interpret; as, to *render* music; **10,** to extract and purify by melting; as, to *render* lard.

ren·dez·vous (rän′dė-vōō; rĕn′dė-vōō), *n.* [*pl.* rendezvous (rän′dė-vōōz; rĕn′dė-vōōz)], **1,** an appointed place of meeting; **2,** a meeting by appointment; as, John had a *rendezvous* with his chums at the store:— *v.i.* and *v.t.* to meet or bring together at a certain place.

ren·di·tion (rĕn-dĭsh′ŭn), *n.* **1,** the act of producing or rendering; also, something rendered; as, the *rendition* of a symphony; **2,** a version or translation.

ren·e·gade (rĕn′ė-gād), *n.* one who denies or gives up his faith; a deserter.

re·new (rė-nū′), *v.t.* **1,** to cause to become new once more; bring back the youth and strength of; revive; as, spring *renews* the earth; **2,** to take up again; resume; as, Mary *renewed* her piano lessons; **3,** to grant or obtain an extension of; as, to *renew* a loan; to continue; as, to *renew* a

---

āte, åorta, râre, căt, åsk, fär, ăllow, sofà; ēve, ĕvent, ĕll, writēr, novĕl; bīte, pĭn; nō, ōbey, ôr, dŏg, tŏp, cŏllide; ūnit, ūnite, bûrn, cŭt, focŭs; nōon, fŏot; mound; coin;

magazine subscription; **4,** to replace; as, to *renew* furniture.—*adj.* **re-new'a-ble.**—*n.* **re-new'al.**

Re-no (rē'nō), a large city in western Nevada (map **9**).

re-nounce (rē-nouns'), *v.t.* [renounced, renounc-ing], **1,** to disown; cast off; as, to *renounce* an heir; **2,** to abandon; surrender; as, to *renounce* a claim.

   Syn. discard, disclaim.

ren-o-vate (rĕn'ō-vāt), *v.t.* [renovat-ed, renovat-ing], to make as good as new; restore to a former or better condition of freshness; as, to *renovate* a house.—*n.* **ren'o-va'tor.**—*n.* **ren'o-va'tion.**

   Syn. renew, revive, regenerate, refresh.

re-nown (rē-noun'), *n.* fame; celebrity; as, a man of great *renown.*

re-nowned (rē-nound'), *adj.* famous; distinguished.

¹rent (rĕnt), past tense and past participle of *rend:*—*n.* a tear; a hole or slit made by tearing, as in cloth.

   Syn., n. breach, fissure, separation.

²rent (rĕnt), *n.* a fixed amount payable at a stated time or times for the use of property:—*v.t.* **1,** to lease; hire; hold or use without ownership, in consideration of stated, regular payments; as, to *rent* a house from the owner; **2,** to give possession of, in return for rent; lease; as, to *rent* a house to a tenant:—*v.i.* to be leased or to let; as, the house *rents* for $900 a year.

rent-al (rĕn'tăl), *n.* the amount of money paid or received as rent.

rent-er (rĕn'tẽr), *n.* a person who rents something, as a house, a typewriter, etc.

re-nun-ci-a-tion (rē-nŭn'sĭ-ā'shŭn; rē-nŭn'shĭ-ā'shŭn), *n.* the act of disowning, casting off, or giving up.

   Syn. disavowal, abandonment, repudiation.

re-o-pen (rē-ō'pĕn), *v.t.* and *v.i.* to open again; as, to *reopen* an argument; the store *reopened* yesterday.

re-or-der (rē-ôr'dẽr), *v.t.* to order another supply of; as, to *reorder* coffee.

re-or-gan-ize (rē-ôr'găn-īz), *v.t.* and *v.i.* [reorganized, reorganiz-ing], to arrange or organize anew; change to a more satisfactory form or system; as, to *reorganize* a club.—*n.* **re'or-gan-i-za'tion.**

rep (rĕp), *n.* a silk, wool, or silk-and-wool fabric with a finely corded surface.

Rep. or **Repub.** abbreviation for *Republic, Republican.*

re-paid (rē-pād'), past tense and past participle of *repay.*

¹re-pair (rē-pâr'), *v.i.* to go; resort; as, to *repair* to the country.

²re-pair (rē-pâr'), *v.t.* **1,** to put in good condition again after decay, injury, or the like; mend; renovate; as, to *repair* a roof; **2,** to remedy; set right; as, to *repair* a mistake:—*n.* **1,** the act of restoring to a sound condition, or the state of being thus restored; **2,** (usually *repairs*), the results of such restoration; as, he made the needed *repairs* on the barn; **3,** general condition in regard to soundness, need of repair, etc.; as, the house is in good *repair.*— *adj.* **re-pair'a-ble.**—*n.* **re-pair'er.**

rep-a-ra-ble (rĕp'a-ra-bl), *adj.* capable of being repaired or made good; as, *reparable* damage.

rep-a-ra-tion (rĕp'a-rā'shŭn), **1,** the act of remedying a mistake, a wrong, an injury, or the like; as, he made *reparation* for his neglect; **2,** that which is done by way of amends; **3,** **reparations,** money paid in compensation, as for war damages.

   Syn. recompense, satisfaction, redress.

rep-ar-tee (rĕp'ẽr-tē'), *n.* a quick-witted, clever reply; also, a conversation full of such replies; as, she is expert at *repartee.*

re-pass (rē-pás'), *v.t.* and *v.i.* to pass again; retrace (one's steps).

re-past (rē-pást'), *n.* a meal; food.

re-pay (rē-pā'), *v.t.* [repaid (rē-pād'), re-pay-ing], **1,** to pay back, as money; **2,** to pay back money or the like to; as, to *repay* a creditor; **3,** to make a return to; as, to *repay* one for kindness.—*n.* **re-pay'ment.**

re-peal (rē-pēl'), *v.t.* to cancel; take back; revoke; as, to *repeal* an amendment:—*n.* a canceling; an abolition; as, the *repeal* of a law.—*adj.* **re-peal'a-ble.**

   Syn., v. annul, rescind.

re-peat (rē-pēt'), *v.t.* **1,** to do or speak a second time; as, to *repeat* a command; **2,** to say over from memory; recite; as, to *repeat* the alphabet; **3,** to say after another; tell; as, to *repeat* gossip:—*v.i.* to say or do anything over again:—*n.* **1,** the act of doing or saying over again; also, something done or said again; repetition; **2,** in music, a sign [:] or [⁝] placed at the beginning and end, or only at the end, of a part to be played twice.

re-peat-ed (rē-pē'tĕd), *adj.* done or said again, or over and over; frequent; as, *repeated* hammer blows.—*adv.* **re-peat'ed-ly.**

re-peat-er (rē-pē'tẽr), *n.* **1,** one who or that which says or does a thing over; **2,** a revolver or rifle which fires several shots without being loaded again.

re-pel (rē-pĕl'), *v.t.* [repelled, repel-ling], **1,** to force back; check the advance of; as, to *repel* invaders; **2,** to reject; refuse to consider; as, to *repel* an offer; **3,** to cause disgust in; as, the idea *repels* me.

---

go; join; yet; sing; chin; show; thin, *th*en; hw, *why*; zh, azure; ū, Ger. für or Fr. lune; ö, Ger. schön or Fr. feu; ṅ, Fr. enfant, nom; ḳh, Ger. ach or ich. See pages ix–x.

re·pel·lent (rĕ-pĕl′ĕnt), *adj.* **1**, driving back; as, a *repellent* force; **2**, causing disgust; as, a *repellent* sight; **3**, tending to keep at a distance; forbidding; as, a *repellent* manner.

re·pent (rĕ-pĕnt′), *v.i.* **1**, to feel regret or sorrow on account of something done or left undone; **2**, to change one's ways because of regret for sin:—*v.t.* to feel regret or sorrow for; as, to *repent* hasty words.

re·pent·ance (rĕ-pĕn′tăns), *n.* regret and sorrow for wrongdoing, with desire to mend one's ways.

Syn. remorse, contrition.

re·pent·ant (rĕ-pĕn′tănt), *adj.* feeling or showing sorrow because of wrongdoing; penitent.—*adv.* **re·pent′ant·ly**.

re·per·cus·sion (rē′pĕr-kŭsh′ŭn), *n.* **1**, a throwing or forcing back of something; also, a rebound; **2**, a reverberation or echo, as of waves, sounds, firearms, etc.

rep·er·toire (rĕp′ĕr-twär; rĕp′ĕr-twôr′), *n.* the stock of roles, plays, operas, etc., which a performer or a company is ready to present; a repertory.

rep·er·tor·y (rĕp′ĕr-tôr′ĭ), *n.* [*pl.* repertories], **1**, a place where things are so arranged that they can readily be found; **2**, a collection, especially of information, facts, etc.; **3**, a list of dramas, operas, etc., ready for performance; a repertoire.

rep·e·ti·tion (rĕp′ē-tĭsh′ŭn), *n.* the act of doing or saying something more than once; a repeating; also, that which is repeated; as, this work is a *repetition* of what you did yesterday.—*adj.* **rep′e·ti′tious**.

re·pine (rĕ-pīn′), *v.i.* [repined, repin-ing], to fret; complain; feel discontent.

re·place (rĕ-plās′), *v.t.* [replaced, replacing], **1**, to put back in place; as, to *replace* a dish on a shelf; **2**, to fill the place of; as, a new house *replaces* the old one; **3**, to supply an equivalent in place of; as, to *replace* a broken doll.—*n.* **re·place′ment**.

re·plant (rē-plănt′), *v.t.* to plant again.

re·plen·ish (rĕ-plĕn′ĭsh), *v.t.* to fill up again; stock in abundance; as, to *replenish* food supplies.

re·plete (rĕ-plēt′), *adj.* completely filled, especially with food.

re·ple·tion (rĕ-plē′shŭn), *n.* the state of being full to excess; surfeit.

rep·li·ca (rĕp′lĭ-ká), *n.* **1**, a copy of a picture or statue; especially, a copy made by the original artist or sculptor; **2**, any exact copy or duplicate.

re·ply (rĕ-plī′), *n.* [*pl.* replies], **1**, something spoken, written, or done by way of an answer; a response; as, he sent in his *reply* to the advertisement; **2**, the act of

answering:—*v.i.* [replied, reply-ing], to say or write something in answer; as, to *reply* to a request.

Syn., *n.* rejoinder, repartee, retort.

re·port (rĕ-pôrt′), *v.t.* **1**, to give an oral or written account of; as, to *report* the results of an investigation; **2**, to make a charge or accusation against; as, to *report* an offender:—*v.i.* **1**, to make, prepare, or present, a written or oral statement; **2**, to present oneself at a given place; as, to *report* for work:—*n.* **1**, an official or authorized presentation of facts; as, a government *report;* the *report* of a case at law; a school *report;* **2**, something widely talked of; rumor; hearsay; hence, fame; reputation; as, a man of good *report;* **3**, a loud and sudden noise; the sound of an explosion; as, the *report* of a pistol.

re·port·er (rĕ-pôr′tĕr), *n.* one who reports; especially, a person who collects news for a newspaper.

¹**re·pose** (rĕ-pōz′), *v.t.* [reposed, repos-ing], to lay or place; as, to *repose* one's faith in God.

²**re·pose** (rĕ-pōz′), *v.t.* [reposed, repos-ing], to place in a position of rest; lay down to rest; as, to *repose* oneself on a bed:—*v.i.* to lie at rest; hence, to sleep:—*n.* **1**, rest; sleep; **2**, quietness of manner.

Syn., *n.* ease.

re·pos·i·tor·y (rĕ-pŏz′ĭ-tôr′ĭ), *n.* [*pl.* repositories], a place for the storing and safekeeping of goods, as a bank or warehouse.

re·pos·sess (rē′pŏ-zĕs′), *v.t.* to recover possession of.

rep·re·hend (rĕp′rē-hĕnd′), *v.t.* **1**, to blame; charge with a fault; **2**, to censure or criticize; as, to *reprehend* rudeness.

Syn. reprimand, rebuke, reproach.

rep·re·hen·si·ble (rĕp′rē-hĕn′sĭ-bl), *adj.* blamable; deserving reproof or rebuke.

rep·re·sent (rĕp′rē-zĕnt′), *v.t.* **1**, to show a likeness of; portray; as, this statue *represents* Paul Revere; **2**, to make (oneself) out to be; describe (oneself); as, she *represents* herself as belonging to the nobility; **3**, to act for or speak in place of; as, he *represents* his father in the business; **4**, to take or act the part of; as, he *represented* a clown in the play; **5**, to stand for; as, letters *represent* sounds.

rep·re·sen·ta·tion (rĕp′rē-zĕn-tā′shŭn), *n.* **1**, the act of standing for, or representing; also, the state of being represented, especially in a legislative body; as, each of the 48 States is given *representation* in Congress; **2**, a picture, statue, etc., that portrays something; an image; as, a *representation* of a saint; **3**, a statement of fact; also, an argument in behalf of some-

---

āte, âorta, râre, căt, ásk, fär, ăllow, sofá; ēve, ĕvent, ĕll, writĕr, novĕl; bīte, pĭn; nō, ōbey, ôr, dŏg, tŏp, cŏllide; ūnit, ūnite, bûrn, cŭt, focŭs; nōōn, fŏŏt; mound; coin;

one or something; **4**, a sign or symbol; as, figures are the *representations* of numbers. *Syn.* delineation, portraiture, emblem.

rep·re·sent·a·tive (rĕp′rē-zĕn′tȧ-tĭv), *n.* **1**, one who or that which stands as a type, or shows the marked features of a group; as, the boy was a splendid *representative* of the American Indian; **2**, one who has power or authority to act for another or others; **3**, a member of a legislative body, elected by the people:—**Representative**, in the U.S., a member of the lower house in Congress, or in a State legislature:—*adj.* **1**, serving to represent; portraying; **2**, acting, or having power to act, for another or others, especially in government; also, founded on representation by delegates; as, *representative* government; **3**, characteristic of; typical; as, they made a *representative* selection of the author's work.

re·press (rē-prĕs′), *v.t.* **1**, to keep under control; check; as, to *repress* a wish; **2**, to crush; subdue; as, to *repress* a rebellion.— *n.* **re·pres′sion**.—*adj.* **re·pres′sive**. *Syn.* restrain, curb, suppress.

re·prieve (rē-prēv′), *n.* **1**, a temporary delay in carrying out the sentence of a judge; **2**, a temporary relief from pain or escape from danger:—*v.t.* [reprieved, repriev·ing], **1**, to grant a delay in the execution of; as, to *reprieve* a condemned prisoner; **2**, to free for a time from pain or danger.

rep·ri·mand (rĕp′rĭ-mănd), *n.* a severe reproof or rebuke:—*v.t.* (rĕp′rĭ-mănd; rĕp′-rĭ-mănd′), to rebuke severely for a fault; especially, to reprove officially. *Syn., v.* censure, upbraid, scold.

re·print (rē-prĭnt′), *v.t.* to print again; print a new copy or edition of:—*n.* (rē′-prĭnt; rē-prĭnt′), a second or new edition or impression of any printed work.

re·pris·al (rē-prī′zăl), *n.* **1**, in war, injury or loss inflicted upon an enemy in return for an injury or loss suffered; **2**, any repayment of injury with injury.

re·proach (rē-prōch′), *n.* **1**, the act of scolding or rebuking; censure; as, a *reproach* for tardiness; **2**, the cause or object of blame, scorn, or shame; as, the tenement district is a *reproach* to the town:—*v.t.* **1**, to charge with something wrong or disgraceful; rebuke or blame; as, he *reproached* the clerk for carelessness; **2**, to bring shame or dishonor upon; disgrace.

re·proach·ful (rē-prōch′fŏŏl), *adj.* expressing rebuke or censure; as, a *reproachful* look.

rep·ro·bate (rĕp′rō-bāt), *n.* a sinful or wicked person; a scoundrel:—*v.t.* [reprobat·ed, reprobat·ing], to disapprove of strongly; condemn:—*adj.* given up to sin; wicked.

rep·ro·ba·tion (rĕp′rō-bā′shŭn), *n.* **1**, the act of strongly disapproving or censuring; strong condemnation; as, the cowardly act met with public *reprobation;* **2**, the state of being censured or condemned.

re·pro·duce (rē′prō-dūs′), *v.t.* [reproduced, reproduc·ing], **1**, to bring about or show again; repeat; as, to *reproduce* a play, a sound, or a gesture; **2**, to bear, yield, or bring forth (offspring); **3**, to copy; make an image of; as, to *reproduce* a person's features in marble.—*n.* re′pro·duc′er.

re·pro·duc·tion (rē′prō-dŭk′shŭn), *n.* **1**, the act, power, or process of producing again; revival; **2**, a copy, as of a work of art; **3**, the process of producing offspring.

re·pro·duc·tive (rē′prō-dŭk′tĭv), *adj.* pertaining to, or employed in, the process of bringing forth; as, the *reproductive* organs. —*n.* re′pro·duc′tive·ness.

re·proof (rē-prōōf′), *n.* the act of censuring; a rebuke; as, a gentle *reproof*.

re·prove (rē-prōōv′), *v.t.* [reproved, reprov·ing], to blame; rebuke; as, to *reprove* a child. *Syn.* chide, censure, scold, reprimand.

rep·tile (rĕp′tĭl), *n.* **1**, any of a class of cold-blooded, air-breathing, scaly animals, usually egg-laying, as snakes, lizards, alligators, and turtles; **2**, a mean, debased person.

Repub. abbreviation for *Republic, Republican.*

re·pub·lic (rē-pŭb′lĭk), *n.* a state or country in which the supreme power is held by the voting public, which elects its own representatives and executive officers, who are responsible directly to the people; also, the form of government of such a state or country.

re·pub·li·can (rē-pŭb′lĭ-kăn), *adj.* pertaining to, characteristic of, or believing in, government by representatives of the people:—*n.* one who favors government by representatives of the people.

Re·pub·li·can (rē-pŭb′lĭ-kăn), *adj.* naming, or relating to, the Republican party: —**Republican party**, one of the two major political parties in the U.S., established in 1854:—**Republican**, *n.* a member of the Republican party.

re·pub·lish (rē-pŭb′lĭsh), *v.t.* to put forth or issue anew, as a book.—*n.* re′pub·li·ca′tion.

re·pu·di·ate (rē-pū′dĭ-āt), *v.t.* [repudiated, repudiat·ing], **1**, to refuse to recognize; disown; as, to *repudiate* an old friend; **2**, to decline to acknowledge or pay; as, to *repudiate* a debt; **3**, to reject; refuse to honor; as, to *repudiate* authority; to *repudiate* a statement.—*n.* re·pu′di·a′tion. *Syn.* discard, renounce.

---

go; join; yet; sing; chin; show; thin, *th*en; hw, *wh*y; zh, azure; ü, Ger. für or Fr. l*u*ne; ŏ, Ger. schön or Fr. f*eu*; ṅ, Fr. enfant, nom; kh, Ger. a*ch* or i*ch*. See pages ix–x.

re·pug·nance (rē-pŭg/năns), *n.* extreme dislike; disgust.

re·pug·nant (rē-pŭg/nănt), *adj.* 1, highly distasteful or disagreeable; as, a *repugnant* task; 2, contrary; opposed; as, a course *repugnant* to one's principles.

re·pulse (rē-pŭls/), *v.t.* [repulsed, repulsing], 1, to drive back; beat off; as, to *repulse* an attack; 2, to drive away by coldness, lack of sympathy, or the like:—*n.* 1, the act of forcefully driving back; also, a defeat or setback; as, the army met with a *repulse;* 2, a decided refusal; rejection; as, his request met with another *repulse.*

re·pul·sion (rē-pŭl/shŭn), *n.* 1, the act of driving back; also, the fact of being driven back; 2, a feeling of great disgust; strong dislike.

re·pul·sive (rē-pŭl/sĭv), *adj.* disgusting; loathsome; as, a *repulsive* sight.—*adv.* re·pul/sive·ly.—*n.* re·pul/sive·ness.

rep·u·ta·ble (rĕp/ū-tȧ-bl), *adj.* having a good reputation; decent, respectable.—*adv.* rep/u·ta·bly.

rep·u·ta·tion (rĕp/ū-tā/shŭn), *n.* 1, good name or standing; honor; as, the artist has achieved world *reputation;* 2, the general opinion held of a person, whether good or bad; as, he has a *reputation* for meanness.

re·pute (rē-pūt/), *v.t.* [reput-ed, reputing], to regard or consider; as, he is *reputed* to be rich:—*n.* the estimation, good or bad, in which a person, place, or thing is held; also, fame; as, a man of *repute:*—**by repute,** by report or gossip.

re·put·ed (rē-pū/tĕd), *adj.* supposed; considered as being; as, a *reputed* scholar.

re·quest (rē-kwĕst/), *n.* 1, the act of asking for something; as, a *request* for information; 2, that which is asked for; as, to grant a *request;* 3, the condition of being in demand; as, he is in great *request* as a public speaker:—*v.t.* 1, to ask for; express a wish for; as, to *request* a favor; 2, to ask (someone) to do something; as, she *requested* him to make haste.

re·qui·em (rē/kwĭ-ĕm; rĕk/wĭ-ĕm), *n.* any hymn or solemn musical service in honor of the dead:—**Requiem,** in the Roman Catholic Church: 1, a Mass sung for the repose of the souls of the dead; 2, the music for such a Mass.

re·quire (rē-kwīr/), *v.t.* [required, requiring], 1, to demand or insist upon; as, to *require* promptness at school; 2, to have need of; call for; as, this will *require* haste.

re·quire·ment (rē-kwīr/mĕnt), *n.* 1, that which is called for or demanded; an essential condition; as, college entrance *requirements;* 2, that which is needed; as, the body's *requirement* of food and rest.

req·ui·site (rĕk/wĭ-zĭt), *n.* anything that cannot be done without; a necessity; as, honesty is a *requisite* of fine character:—*adj.* so needful that it cannot be done without; necessary; as, a *requisite* amount of food.

   Syn., adj. required, essential, needed.

req·ui·si·tion (rĕk/wĭ-zĭsh/ŭn), *n.* 1, a written demand or claim made by right or authority; as, a *requisition* for office supplies; 2, the condition of being demanded or put to use; as, his new bicycle was in constant *requisition* for family errands:—*v.t.* 1, to demand; claim by authority; as, to *requisition* supplies; 2, to make a demand upon, as for supplies; especially, to require (a country invaded in war) to deliver horses, food, or other military supplies.

re·quite (rē-kwīt/), *v.t.* [requit-ed, requiting], 1, to repay (someone) for something; compensate; as, to *requite* a person for a kindness; 2, to repay (something) with something else; as, to *requite* kindness with ingratitude.—*n.* re·quit/al.

   Syn. remunerate, recompense.

re·scind (rē-sĭnd/), *v.t.* to repeal; annul or cancel; as, to *rescind* a law.

res·cue (rĕs/kū), *n.* deliverance from danger, imprisonment, or violence; as, the police aided in the *rescue* of the kidnaped boy:—*v.t.* [rescued, rescu-ing], to set free from danger, evil, violence, or imprisonment; save; as, the firemen *rescued* the entire family.—*n.* res/cu·er.

re·search (rē-sûrch/; rē/sûrch), *n.* careful study or investigation in an effort to find new information in history, science, literature, etc., by experiment or by a thorough examination of sources; as, much time, money, and effort are being devoted to cancer *research.*

re·sem·blance (rē-zĕm/blȧns), *n.* a likeness; similarity of outward appearance or of qualities; as, the *resemblance* between sisters.

re·sem·ble (rē-zĕm/bl), *v.t.* [resem-bled, resem-bling], to be similar to in appearance or character; as, the brothers *resemble* each other.

re·sent (rē-zĕnt/), *v.t.* to be angry because of; be indignant at; as, to *resent* criticism. —*adj.* re·sent/ful.—*adv.* re·sent/ful·ly.

re·sent·ment (rē-zĕnt/mĕnt), *n.* strong anger or displeasure, often accompanied by a feeling of ill will, because of a real or fancied wrong, insult, or the like.

res·er·va·tion (rĕz/ẽr-vā/shŭn), *n.* 1, the act of holding back or hiding; 2, a limiting condition; as, they gave their consent with *reservations;* 3, accommodations arranged for in advance, as on a sleeping

---

āte, āorta, râre, căt, ȧsk, fär, ăllow, sofȧ; ēve, ēvent, ĕll, writēr, novĕl; bīte, pĭn; nō, ōbey, ôr, dŏg, tŏp, cŏllide; ūnit, ūnite, bûrn, cŭt, focŭs; nōͦn, fŏͦt; mound; coin;

car, on a steamship, in a hotel, etc.; **4,** a tract of public land set aside for some special use; as, an Indian *reservation.*

re·serve (rĕ-zûrv′), *v.t.* [reserved, reserving], **1,** to hold back for later use; as, to *reserve* the best till last; arrange for in advance; as, to *reserve* a room; **2,** to keep as one's own; keep control of; as, he *reserves* all rights in this book:—*n.* **1,** the act of setting aside, keeping back, or excepting; restriction; qualification; as, to accept a report without *reserve;* **2,** that which is kept in store for future use or for a particular purpose; extra supply; as, a large *reserve* of ammunition; **3,** a tract of land set apart for a special purpose; as, a game *reserve;* **4,** restraint in speech and manner; **5,** funds kept on hand by a bank as a basis for credits; **6, reserves,** a body of troops withheld from action and kept in readiness as reinforcements.

re·served (rĕ-zûrvd′), *adj.* **1,** keeping one's thoughts and feelings to oneself; also, undemonstrative; as, a *reserved* manner; **2,** set aside; arranged for, or capable of being arranged for, in advance; as, *reserved* seats.

res·er·voir (rĕz′ĕr-vwôr; rĕz′ĕr-vwär), *n.* **1,** a place where anything, especially water, is collected and stored for current and future use; **2,** a part of an apparatus or instrument in which a liquid is held; as, the *reservoir* of an oil lamp; **3,** a reserve; a storehouse; as, natural resources are a *reservoir* of wealth.

re·set (rē-sĕt′), *v.t.* [reset, reset·ting], to place in position again; set again; as, to *reset* type; to *reset* a jewel.

re·side (rē-zīd′), *v.i.* [resid·ed, resid·ing], **1,** to dwell for a length of time; live; as, they *reside* in the country; **2** to exist as a fixed or essential quality, characteristic, right, or the like; as, the power to issue currency *resides* in the national government.

res·i·dence (rĕz′ĭ-dĕns), *n.* **1,** the place where one lives; a settled or permanent home; **2,** the act or fact of living in a place for a period of time; also, the period during which one lives in a place; as, during his *residence* abroad.

res·i·dent (rĕz′ĭ-dĕnt), *n.* **1,** one who lives in a place; as, a *resident* of Boston; **2,** a government agent at a foreign court:—*adj.* living in a place; as, the *resident* physician of a hospital.

res·i·den·tial (rĕz′ĭ-dĕn′shǎl), *adj.* pertaining to, connected with, or suitable for, dwelling places; as, the *residential* section of a city.

re·sid·u·al (rē-zĭd′ū-ǎl), *adj.* forming a residue or remainder; as, pitch is a *residual* product of coal tar.

res·i·due (rĕz′ĭ-dū), *n.* **1,** that which remains after a part has been removed by filtration, burning, or the like; as, ash is the *residue* of coal; **2,** that part of an estate remaining after payment of all debts, charges, and particular bequests.
Syn. remnant, leavings, balance.

re·sid·u·um (rē-zĭd′ū-ŭm), *n.* [*pl.* residua (rē-zĭd′ū-ả)], that which is left after any process of subtraction, purification, evaporation, or the like.

re·sign (rē-zīn′), *v.t.* **1,** to give up; surrender; as, to *resign* an office; to *resign* hope; **2,** to submit calmly; reconcile; as, she *resigned* herself to staying at home:—*v.i.* to withdraw from a position or office.

res·ig·na·tion (rĕz′ĭg-nā′shŭn; rĕs′ĭg-nā′-shŭn), *n.* **1,** the act of giving up or yielding; a withdrawal; also, the official or written notice of such withdrawal; as, he handed in his *resignation;* **2,** patient submission; a bowing to misfortune; as, she accepted the loss with *resignation.*

re·signed (rē-zīnd′), *adj.* submissive; patiently uncomplaining.

re·sil·i·ent (rē-zĭl′ĭ-ĕnt), *adj.* **1,** springing back to a former position; elastic; as, the *resilient* bough of a young tree; **2,** having power of recovery; buoyant; as, the *resilient* spirit of a carefree child.—*n.* **re·sil′-i·ence; re·sil′i·en·cy.**

res·in (rĕz′ĭn), *n.* a hardened or dried brownish or yellowish substance obtained from certain trees, such as the pine and the fir, and used in making varnish, medicine, etc. The resin obtained from pine is often called *rosin.*—*adj.* **res′in·ous.**

re·sist (rē-zĭst′), *v.t.* **1,** to stop or repel; to succeed in standing against, warding off, etc.; as, the armor *resisted* all weapons; **2,** to strive against; oppose; as, the boys *resisted* the plan:—*v.i.* to offer opposition; refuse to obey or agree.—*adj.* **re·sist′i·ble.**

re·sist·ance (rē-zĭs′tăns), *n.* **1,** the act of opposing; as, the thief offered no *resistance* when caught; **2,** power of opposing; as, an underfed child has little *resistance* to disease; **3,** a force that acts to retard motion; as, the *resistance* of air to bodies passing through it.—*adj.* **re·sist′ant.**

re·sist·less (rē-zĭst′lĕs), *adj.* **1,** not to be withstood; as, a gypsy has a *resistless* desire to travel; **2,** having no power to oppose or withstand; powerless.—*adv.* **re·sist′less·ly.**—*n.* **re·sist′less·ness.**

res·o·lute (rĕz′ô-lūt), *adj.* having a fixed purpose; determined; firm; as, a *resolute* will.—*adv.* **res′o·lute·ly.**—*n.* **res′o·lute·ness.**
Syn. steady, steadfast, inflexible.

---

go; join; yet; sing; chin; show; thin, *th***en; hw,** *wh***y; zh,** *a***zure; ü,** Ger. f*ü***r** or Fr. l*u***ne; ö,** Ger. sch*ö***n** or Fr. f*eu***; ṅ,** Fr. e*n***fant,** nom**; kh,** Ger. a*ch* or i*ch***.** See pages ix–x.

res·o·lu·tion (rĕz′ō-lū′shŭn), *n.* **1,** fixed determination; purpose, or firmness of purpose; as, a man of *resolution;* **2,** that which is determined; as, we seldom keep our New Year's *resolutions;* **3,** a formal proposal or statement voted on in a legislative assembly or public meeting; **4,** the act of reducing a chemical compound to a simpler form or to component parts.

re·solve (rē-zŏlv′), *v.t.* [resolved, resolving], **1,** to determine by vote; decide; as, they *resolved* that no additional funds should now be paid out; **2,** to explain; clear up; as, he *resolved* all doubts by confessing everything; **3,** to reduce by breaking up; transform; as, the argument *resolves* itself into three heads:—*v.i.* **1,** to come to a determination; decide firmly; as, he *resolved* to do better; **2,** to change to some simpler form or state; **3,** to pass or adopt a resolution:—*n.* **1,** fixed purpose; determination; **2,** that which has been determined on; a resolution.

re·solved (rē-zŏlvd′), *adj.* firm in purpose; determined.

res·o·nance (rĕz′ō-nǎns), *n.* a round, full, vibrating quality of sound; as, the *resonance* of an organ.

res·o·nant (rĕz′ō-nǎnt), *adj.* **1,** echoing; resounding; continuing to sound; **2,** having the ability to return, increase, or prolong sound; as, *resonant* walls.

re·sort (rē-zôrt′), *v.i.* **1,** to go often, habitually, or in numbers; betake oneself; **2,** to apply or turn to something for help, relief, or the gaining of an end; as, to *resort* to law:—*n.* **1,** the act of turning to something; as, a *resort* to arms; **2,** a thing to which, or a person to whom, one applies for aid; a refuge; as, charity was their last *resort;* **3,** a place much visited; as, a seashore *resort.*

¹re·sound (rē-zound′), *v.i.* **1,** to sound loudly; as, his voice *resounded* far; **2,** to be full of sound; echo; as, the woods *resound* with song; **3,** *Poetic,* to be famous; as, his name *resounded* far and wide.

²re·sound (rē-sound′), *v.i.* and *v.t.* to sound, or cause to sound, again.

re·source (rē-sôrs′; rē′sôrs), *n.* **1,** knowledge of what to do in an emergency or difficulty; as, a man of *resource;* **2,** that to which one turns in a difficulty or emergency; as, flight was his only *resource;* **3,** resources, a stock or reserve upon which one can draw when necessary; wealth in money, property, raw materials, etc.; as, a country's natural *resources.*
Syn. resort, contrivance, means.

re·source·ful (rē-sôrs′fŏŏl), *adj.* **1,** abounding in resources or riches; as, a *resourceful* country; **2,** capable of meeting unusual demands or sudden needs; as, a *resourceful* housekeeper can make ends meet when funds are low.—*n.* **re·source′-ful·ness.**

re·spect (rē-spĕkt′), *n.* **1,** regard for worth; honor and esteem; as, the world's *respect* for a great man; regard; as, *respect* for property; consideration; as, *respect* for old age; **2,** **respects,** expression of good will or regard; as, to pay one's *respects;* **3,** a special point or particular; as, in certain *respects* the book is good; **4,** relation, reference, or regard; as, with *respect* to your question:—*v.t.* **1,** to honor or esteem; as, the world *respects* a good man; also, to obey; as, *respect* the law; **2,** to regard as important; heed; as, to *respect* the advice of parents; **3,** to have relation to; as, the matter *respects* our welfare; **4,** to avoid intruding upon; as, *respect* his privacy.
Syn., n. deference, notice.

re·spect·a·ble (rē-spĕk′tà-bl), *adj.* **1,** worthy of regard or esteem; as, an honest and *respectable* merchant; **2,** of moderate excellence or size; passably good; as, a *respectable* income; **3,** presentable; as, a *respectable* suit of clothes.—*adv.* **re·spect′a·bly.**—*n.* **re·spect′a·bil′i·ty.**

re·spect·ful (rē-spĕkt′fŏŏl), *adj.* showing, or marked by, proper regard, esteem, or courtesy; polite; as, *respectful* manners.—*adv.* **re·spect′ful·ly.**—*n.* **re·spect′ful·ness.**

re·spect·ing (rē-spĕk′tĭng), *prep.* with regard or relation to; concerning; as, *respecting* his conduct, the less said the better.

re·spec·tive (rē-spĕk′tĭv), *adj.* belonging to each of several persons or things; particular; as, the boys took their *respective* positions in line.

re·spec·tive·ly (rē-spĕk′tĭv-lĭ), *adv.* as relating to each; in the order named; as, the red, blue, and green ties are for James, George, and William *respectively.*

res·pi·ra·tion (rĕs′pĭ-rā′shŭn), *n.* the act or process of breathing; as, artificial means are used to produce *respiration* in persons rescued from the sea.

re·spir·a·tor·y (rē-spīr′à-tôr′ĭ; rĕs′pĭ-rà-tôr′ĭ), *adj.* having to do with breathing; as, a *respiratory* disease.

re·spire (rē-spīr′), *v.t.* and *v.i.* [respired, respiring], to breathe; inhale and exhale.

res·pite (rĕs′pĭt), *n.* **1,** a putting off; postponement, especially in the carrying out of a sentence; as, the murderer was granted a *respite;* **2,** a brief period of rest; as, a *respite* from labor:—*v.t.* [respit-ed, respit-ing], to grant a respite to.
Syn., n. pause, interval, reprieve, stay.

re·splend·ent (rē-splĕn′dĕnt), *adj.* shining brilliantly; intensely bright; as, the heavens were *resplendent* with stars.

re-spond (rĕ-spŏnd′), *v.i.* **1,** to return an answer; make a reply; as, to *respond* to a question; **2,** to act, or show some feeling, in answer or sympathy; as, to *respond* to a friend's need; **3,** to react; as, to *respond* quickly to medicine.

re-sponse (rĕ-spŏns′), *n.* **1,** the act of answering; an answer or reply; as, a *response* to an inquiry; **2,** an act or feeling called forth by something; as, a sympathetic *response* to an appeal for help.

re-spon-si-bil-i-ty (rĕ-spŏn′sĭ-bĭl′ĭ-tĭ), *n.* [*pl.* responsibilities], **1,** the state or fact of being answerable or accountable; as, I will assume no *responsibility* for debts contracted by you; **2,** that for which one is answerable or accountable; a duty or charge; as, this work is your *responsibility*; **3,** ability to meet obligations; as, a bank checks a man's *responsibility* before granting him a loan.

re-spon-si-ble (rĕ-spŏn′sĭ-bl), *adj.* **1,** involving trust, duty, or obligation; as, he is capable of holding a *responsible* position; **2,** answerable; accountable; as, a guardian is *responsible* to the law; I will not be *responsible* for his debts; **3,** able to answer for one's conduct; trustworthy; as, only a *responsible* person can hold this position.

re-spon-sive (rĕ-spŏn′sĭv), *adj.* **1,** answering; as, a *responsive* look; **2,** containing responses; as, *responsive* reading in a church service; **3,** easily moved; sympathetic; as, an audience.—*adv.* **re-spon′-sive-ly.**—*n.* **re-spon′sive-ness.**

MUSICAL RESTS

¹rest (rĕst), *n.* **1,** freedom from motion; as, a machine at *rest*; freedom from work or activity; as, a day of *rest*; freedom from disturbance of mind or spirit; peace of mind; as, a *rest* from worry; **2,** sleep; as, a good night's *rest*; **3,** a place of quiet or repose; a shelter or lodging place; as, a sailors' *rest*; **4,** that on which anything leans for support; as, a back *rest*; **5,** in music and in reading aloud, a pause or a sign indicating such a pause:—*v.i.* **1,** to stop moving or acting; pause; relax; as, to *rest* from work; **2,** to take repose: sleep; as, I *rested* well all night; **3,** hence, to lie dead; as, the unknown soldier *rests* in his tomb; **4,** to be supported; as, the house *rests* upon its foundation; to lean; as, her hand *rested* upon the arm of the chair; to be fixed; as, his eyes *rested* on the book; **5,** to rely; depend; as, the success of this campaign

a, whole; *b,* half; *c,* quarter (two forms); *d,* eighth; *e,* sixteenth; *f,* thirty-second.

rests on you; to be based or founded; as, the case *rested* on the evidence of one man; **6,** to remain for action or accomplishment; as, the matter *rests* with you:—*v.t.* **1,** to place at rest or in repose; as, *rest* yourself after a hard day's work; **2,** to lean; as, he *rested* his arm on the table; **3,** to base or ground; as, we *rest* our hopes in him.

²rest (rĕst), *n.* that which remains or is left; as, the *rest* of the book; the others; those who remain; as, the *rest* of the party: —*v.i.* to be and to continue to be; stay; as, we *rest* satisfied.

re-state (rē-stāt′), *v.t.* [restat-ed, restating], to state or express over again or in a new way.—*n.* **re-state′ment.**

res-tau-rant ′(rĕs′tō-rănt), *n.* a public place which serves meals or refreshments.

rest-ful (rĕst′fool), *adj.* **1,** giving repose; as, *restful* sleep; **2,** tranquil; peaceful; as, a *restful* hour.

res-ti-tu-tion (rĕs′tĭ-tū′shŭn), *n.* **1,** the act of giving back to the rightful owner that which has been taken away or lost; **2,** the act of making good any loss, injury, or damage.

Syn. return, restoration, compensation, amends, redress, reparation.

res-tive (rĕs′tĭv), *adj.* **1,** actively resisting control; unruly; as, a *restive* horse; **2,** rebellious; as, a people *restive* under slavery; **3,** restless; uneasy; as, the children grew *restive* in church.

Syn. fidgety, nervous.

rest-less (rĕst′lĕs), *adj.* **1,** always active or in motion; as, a *restless* child; *restless* waves; **2,** eager for change; as, a *restless* spirit; **3,** affording no repose; uneasy; as, a *restless* night.—*adv.* **rest′less-ly.**—*n.* **rest′less-ness.**

Syn. wandering, roving, unsettled.

res-to-ra-tion (rĕs′tō-rā′shŭn), *n.* **1,** the act of bringing back, or the state of being brought back, to a former condition or plan; as, *restoration* to health or to office; **2,** the process of bringing back a building, a fossil, or a work of art, to something like its original form; also, a representation of the original form; as, a *restoration* of the Roman Forum.

re-stor-a-tive (rĕ-stôr′a-tĭv), *adj.* having the power to bring back to a former condition or place; as, a *restorative* medicine: —*n.* something which has power to restore; especially, a medicine used to bring back health or to restore consciousness.

re-store (rĕ-stôr′), *v.t.* [restored, restoring], **1,** to bring back to a former or original condition; as, to *restore* health; to *restore* a painting; *restore* a person to office; **2,** to bring back to the owner; as, to *restore* a lost pet.

go; join; yet; sing; chin; show; thin, *th*en; hw, *why*; zh, a*z*ure; ü, Ger. f*ür* or Fr. l*u*ne; ö, Ger. sch*ö*n or Fr. f*eu*; ṅ, Fr. e*n*fant, no*m*; kh, Ger. a*ch* or i*ch*. See pages ix-x.

re-strain (rē-strān′), *v.t.* to check; hold back; as, I could not *restrain* my desire to laugh.

Syn. suppress, bridle, confine, curb.

re-straint (rē-strānt′), *n.* **1,** the act of holding back or hindering from action of any kind; **2,** the state of being held back or hindered; **3,** that which limits or hinders; **4,** reserve; as, to speak with *restraint.*

re-strict (rē-strĭkt′), *v.t.* to keep within bounds; to confine or limit; as, to *restrict* a patient to a certain diet.—*adj.* **re-strict′ed.**

re-stric-tion (rē-strĭk′shŭn), *n.* **1,** the act of limiting; as, the *restriction* of immigration; **2,** the condition of being limited; **3,** that which limits; as, *restrictions* on trade. —*adj.* **re-stric′tive.**

re-sult (rē-zŭlt′), *n.* **1,** consequence; outcome; as, the *result* of hard work; **2,** in arithmetic, the answer to a problem or example:—*v.i.* **1,** to follow as a consequence or effect; as, benefits will *result* from this law; **2,** to end; lead to something as an outcome; as, the quarrel *resulted* in a fight.

Syn. **n.** conclusion, effect, issue.

re-sult-ant (rē-zŭl′tănt), *n.* that which follows as a consequence:—*adj.* following as a consequence; as, the *resultant* damage to the crops.

re-sume (rē-zūm′), *v.t.* [resumed, resuming], **1,** to take up again after interruption; begin again; as, to *resume* work; **2,** to take or occupy again after leaving; as, he *resumed* his seat.

ré-su-mé (rā′zū-mā′), *n.* a synopsis or summary; as, a *résumé* of a book.

re-sump-tion (rē-zŭmp′shŭn), *n.* the act of taking up again after interruption, or of beginning again; as, *resumption* of study.

res-ur-rect (rĕz′ŭ-rĕkt′), *v.t.* **1,** to raise from the dead; **2,** to bring again to notice or use; as, to *resurrect* an old style.

res-ur-rec-tion (rĕz′ŭ-rĕk′shŭn), *n.* **1,** a rising again from the dead; **2,** a springing into new life and freshness:—**the Resurrection,** the rising of Christ from the dead.

re-sus-ci-tate (rē-sŭs′ĭ-tāt), *v.t.* [resuscitated, resuscitating], to bring back to life from apparent death; as, artificial respiration to *resuscitate* a drowning person.—*n.* **re-sus′ci-ta′tion.**

re-tail (rē′tāl), *n.* the sale of goods in small quantities: opposite of *wholesale:*—*adj.* pertaining to, or engaged in, the sale of goods in small quantities; as, *retail* price; *retail* store; *retail* merchant:—*v.t.* (rē′tāl; rē-tāl′), **1,** to sell in small quantities; **2,** to tell in detail; pass on to others; as, to *retail* gossip:—*v.i.* to sell at retail price; as, this cloth *retails* for two dollars a yard.

re-tail-er (rē′tā-lēr; rē-tā′lēr), *n.* a person who sells goods in small quantities.

re-tain (rē-tān′), *v.t.* **1,** to hold or keep in possession, practice, control, use, or the like; as, the Scotchman *retained* his accent; **2,** to engage by payment of a fee beforehand; as, to *retain* a lawyer; **3,** to keep in mind; as, he *retained* the memory of that experience for years.

re-tain-er (rē-tā′nẽr), *n.* **1,** one kept in the service of a person of high rank or position; as, a lord's *retainers;* **2,** a person or thing that keeps possession; **3,** an advance fee paid to a lawyer, adviser, etc.

re-take (rē-tāk′), *v.t.* [*p.t.* retook (rē-tŏŏk′), *p.p.* retak-en (rē-tā′kĕn), *p.pr.* retak-ing], **1,** to take or receive again; as, to *retake* a town; **2,** to photograph again:—*n.* (rē′tāk′), *Colloquial,* another taking of a photograph or of a scene or scenes of a motion picture.

re-tal-i-ate (rē-tăl′ĭ-āt), *v.i.* [retaliat-ed, retaliat-ing], to give like for like, especially evil for evil; as, to *retaliate* upon a man for an insult:—*v.t.* to repay (an injury) with something of the same kind.—*n.* **re-tal′i-a′tion.**

re-tard (rē-tärd′), *v.t.* to cause to move less quickly; to hinder; delay; as, the heavy snow *retarded* traffic.

retch (rĕch), *v.i.* to vomit or try to vomit; strain, as in vomiting.

re-tell (rē-tĕl′), *v.t.* [retold (rē-tōld′), re-tell-ing], to relate again; as, to *retell* a story.

re-ten-tion (rē-tĕn′shŭn), *n.* **1,** the act of keeping in one's power or possession; **2,** the state of being kept in possession; **3,** the act or power of keeping things in mind; memory.

re-ten-tive (rē-tĕn′tĭv), *adj.* tending, or having the power, to keep; as, a *retentive* memory.—*n.* **re-ten′tive-ness.**

ret-i-cence (rĕt′ĭ-sĕns), *n.* the act or habit of keeping silent or of not telling all one knows or thinks; restraint in speech.

ret-i-cent (rĕt′ĭ-sĕnt), *adj.* disposed to be silent; reserved in speech.

ret-i-na (rĕt′ĭ-na), *n.* the inner sensitive coating of the eyeball containing the ends of the nerves of sight. Upon the retina are focused the images of objects.

ret-i-nue (rĕt′ĭ-nū), *n.* the body of persons who attend a prince or person of distinction; a train of attendants.

re-tire (rē-tīr′), *v.i.* [retired, retir-ing], **1,** to go to a place of privacy; as, to *retire* to a monastery; **2,** to withdraw; retreat; as, to *retire* from a battle; **3,** to withdraw from business or from official or active life;

4, to go to bed:—*v.t.* **1,** to withdraw; as, to *retire* forces; **2,** to withdraw (currency) from circulation, or (securities) from the market; **3,** to cause to give up active service; as, to *retire* an employee with a pension.

re-tired (rĕ-tīrd′), *adj.* **1,** apart or withdrawn from society; secluded; as, a *retired* life; **2,** having given up business or active life; as, a *retired* physician.

re-tire-ment (rĕ-tīr′mĕnt), *n.* **1,** the act of withdrawing from business or public life; **2,** the state of being so withdrawn; as, during his *retirement;* **3,** a place removed from public notice.

re-tir-ing (rĕ-tīr′ĭng), *adj.* modest; shy.

¹re-tort (rĕ-tôrt′), *n.* a quick, witty, or angry reply; as, her insulting remark brought a quick *retort:*— *v.t.* and *v.i.* to answer sharply, wittily, or angrily.

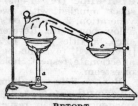

RETORT

a, gas burner; *b,* retort containing liquid; *c,* flask to receive distilled liquid.

²re-tort (rĕ-tôrt′), *n.* a vessel or container, usually of glass, with a long neck, in which substances are heated to a high temperature for purposes of distillation or decomposition.

re-touch (rĕ-tŭch′), *v.t.* to touch up; improve by going over; as, to *retouch* a painting.

re-trace (rĕ-trās′), *v.t.* [retraced, retracing], to go over again; as, to *retrace* one's steps.

re-tract (rĕ-trăkt′), *v.t.* and *v.i.* **1,** to draw back or in; as, the cat can *retract* its claws; muscles *retract;* **2,** to take back (something said or written).

Syn. disavow, recant, repudiate.

re-trac-tion (rĕ-trăk′shŭn), *n.* **1,** the act of drawing in or back; also, the act of taking back something said or written; as, the *retraction* of a false statement; **2,** the state of being withdrawn.

re-treat (rĕ-trēt′), *n.* **1,** the act of withdrawing or retiring; especially, the retiring of troops before an enemy; also, the signal for retiring; **2,** a place of safety or shelter; as, the birds' forest *retreat:*—*v.i.* to withdraw; retire.

Syn., n. refuge, shelter, solitude.

re-trench (rĕ-trĕnch′), *v.t.* **1,** to reduce; as, to *retrench* expenses; **2,** to take away; as, to *retrench* privileges:—*v.i.* to cut down expenses.—*n.* **re-trench′ment.**

Syn. decrease, diminish, curtail.

re-tri-al (rē-trī′ăl), *n.* another trial or test; a second trial.

ret-ri-bu-tion (rĕt′rĭ-bū′shŭn), *n.* reward or punishment suitable to a good or bad action; especially, loss or suffering considered as just punishment for sins.

re-trib-u-tive (rĕ-trĭb′ū-tĭv), *adj.* punishing for a wrong done; as, *retributive* justice.

re-trieve (rĕ-trēv′), *v.t.* [retrieved, retrieving], **1,** to recover; regain; as, to *retrieve* a lost book; **2,** to restore; revive; as, to *retrieve* one's good name; **3,** to repair the harm done by; as, to *retrieve* a misfortune; **4,** in hunting, to fetch (wounded or killed game):—*v.i.* to find and bring in dead or wounded game; as, the hunter trained his dog to *retrieve.*

re-triev-er (rĕ-trē′vĕr), *n.* a dog trained to find and bring in game after it has been killed or wounded by the hunter.

ret-ro-ac-tive (rĕt′rō-ăk′tĭv; rē′trō-ăk′-tĭv), *adj.* having the power to affect past acts; as, a *retroactive* law.

ret-ro-grade (rĕt′rō-grād; rē′trō-grād), *adj.* **1,** moving backward; retreating; reversed; as, the *retrograde* motion of an engine; **2,** going from a better to a worse state or character; as, a *retrograde* people: —*v.i.* [retrograd-ed, retrograd-ing], to go, or appear to go, backward; to deteriorate.

ret-ro-gres-sion (rĕt′rō-grĕsh′ŭn; rē′-trō-grĕsh′ŭn), *n.* **1,** the act of going or moving backward; **2,** a change to a worse condition.—*adj.* **ret′ro-gres′sive.**

ret-ro-spect (rĕt′rō-spĕkt; rē′trō-spĕkt), *n.* a looking back on things past; a review of the past; as, life is pleasant in *retrospect.*

ret-ro-spec-tion (rĕt′rō-spĕk′shŭn; rē′-trō-spĕk′shŭn), *n.* **1,** the act of meditating upon things past; **2,** a calling to remembrance; a reviewing of the past.

ret-ro-spec-tive (rĕt′rō-spĕk′tĭv; rē′trō-spĕk′tĭv), *adj.* **1,** looking back, or given to looking back, on things past; **2,** pertaining to the past.

re-try (rĕ-trī′), *v.t.* [retried (rĕ-trīd′), retry-ing] to try, or put on trial, again; as, to *retry* a prisoner.

re-turn (rĕ-tûrn′), *v.i.* **1,** to come or go back to a place, person, or condition; as, to *return* to one's home; **2,** to begin or appear again; as, spring *returns;* **3,** to come or go back in thought or consideration; as, to *return* to the subject; **4,** to reply; make answer:—*v.t.* **1,** to bring, send, carry, or put back; restore; as, to *return* a borrowed book; **2,** to say in reply; as, to *return* an answer; also, to repay; as, to *return* a visit; **3,** to yield; as, the fields *returned* a good crop; **4,** to give back (an official report); as, to *return* the results of an election; **5,** in various games, to strike or play (the ball) back:—*n.* **1,** a coming or going back; as, a *return* from a vacation; **2,** a restoring or giving back; as, a *return* of lost keys; **3,** that which is restored or given back; **4,** profit or yield; as, a good *return* on an investment; **5, returns,** results; as, election *returns;* also, proceeds; as, the *returns* from the sale:—*adj.* pertaining to a return; as, a *return* journey; a *return* engagement.—*adj.* **return′a-ble.**

re-un-ion (rē-ūn′yŭn), *n.* **1,** the act of coming or bringing together again; **2,** a gathering of persons who were once closely associated but who have been separated; as, a class *reunion.*

re-u-nite (rē′ū-nīt′), *v.t.* [reunit-ed, re-unit-ing], **1,** to bring together again; **2,** to reconcile:—*v.i.* to become joined again.

rev abbreviation for *revise, revised, revolution:—***Rev.** abbreviation for *Revelation, Reverend.*

Re-val (rā′väl), the German name for the capital of Estonia. See **Tallinn.**

re-vamp (rē-vămp′), *v.t.* **1,** to supply (a shoe) with a new vamp, or upper; **2,** hence, to patch; make over; as, to *revamp* a play.

re-veal (rē-vēl′), *v.t.* **1,** to make known; disclose; as, a chance word *revealed* his secret ambition; **2,** to display; unveil; expose to view; as, the curtain rose to *reveal* a forest scene.

re-veil-le (rĕv′ĕ-lē′; rĕv′ĕ-lē′), *n.* the early morning drumbeat or bugle call that rouses the soldier or sailor to duty.

rev-el (rĕv′ĕl), *v.i.* [reveled, revel-ing], **1,** to make merry; be wildly gay; **2,** to take great delight; as, to *revel* in music:—*n.* a gay or noisy festivity; merrymaking.—*n.* **rev′el-er.**

rev-e-la-tion (rĕv′ĕ-lā′shŭn), *n.* **1,** the telling or making known of something secret or private; **2,** that which is made known:—**Revelation,** the last book of the New Testament; the Apocalypse.

rev-el-ry (rĕv′ĕl-rĭ), *n.* [*pl.* revelries], uproarious merrymaking; festivity.

re-venge (rē-vĕnj′), *v.t.* [revenged, re-veng-ing], **1,** to inflict pain or injury in return for; as, to *revenge* an insult; **2,** to avenge a wrong done to; as, to *revenge* oneself:—*n.* **1,** the returning of injury for injury; **2,** the desire to return evil for evil; as, his heart was still filled with *revenge;* **3,** a chance to obtain satisfaction; as, to give a loser at cards his *revenge.*—*adj.* **re-venge′ful.**

Syn., v. retaliate, requite, vindicate.

rev-e-nue (rĕv′ĕ-nū), *n.* **1,** the sum that is yielded by an investment of any kind; income; **2,** the general income of a government from taxes, customs, and other sources.

re-ver-ber-ate (rē-vûr′bēr-āt), *v.i.* [re-verberat-ed, reverberat-ing], to resound; re-echo; as, thunder *reverberates* in the mountains:—*v.t.* to cause (sound) to echo; also, to reflect (heat or light).—*n.* **re-ver′-ber-a′tion.**

Re-vere (rē-vēr′), Paul (1735–1818), an American patriot.

re-vere (rē-vēr′), *v.t.* [revered, rever-ing], to regard with respectful and affectionate awe; to honor; venerate.

rev-er-ence (rĕv′ēr-ĕns), *n.* **1,** deep respect mingled with awe and affection; veneration; **2,** an act or sign of respect, as a low bow:—**his Reverence, your Reverence,** a title given to the clergy:—*v.t.* [reverenced, reverenc-ing], to regard with affectionate respect; hold in high respect or esteem.

Syn., n. deference, homage, honor.

rev-er-end (rĕv′ēr-ĕnd), *adj.* worthy of reverence or deep respect:—**Reverend,** a title of respect given to clergymen.

rev-er-ent (rĕv′ēr-ĕnt), *adj.* feeling or expressing respect and affection mingled with awe or fear; deeply respectful.—*adj.* **rev′er-en′tial.**—*adv.* **rev′er-ent-ly.**

rev-er-ie (rĕv′ēr-ĭ), *n.* deep musing; dreaminess; the state of being lost in thought or dreams. Also spelled **rev′er-y.**

re-verse (rē-vûrs′), *adj.* **1,** turned backward; opposite; as, the *reverse* order of subject and verb in an interrogative sentence; **2,** causing an opposite motion; as, the *reverse* gear in an automobile:—*n.* **1,** the direct contrary or opposite; as "right" is the *reverse* of "left"; **2,** an opposite, generally a backward, motion; as, a car in *reverse;* **3,** the back or less important side, as of a coin: opposite of *obverse;* **4,** a change for the worse; as, business *reverses;* also, a check or defeat; as, the enemy met with a *reverse:*—*v.t.* [reversed, revers-ing], **1,** to turn back; **2,** to cause to move in an opposite direction; **3,** to exchange; transpose; as, to *reverse* positions; **4,** to set aside or annul; as, to *reverse* a judgment:—*v.i.* to move in an opposite direction.

re-vers-i-ble (rē-vûr′sĭ-bl), *adj.* **1,** capable of being turned back; **2,** capable of being used on both sides; as, *reversible* cloth; **3,** capable of being, or liable to be, set aside or annulled; as, a *reversible* judgment.

re-ver-sion (rē-vûr′shŭn; rē-vûr′zhŭn), *n.* **1,** the right to future enjoyment or possession; as, the *reversion* of a title; **2,** in biology, a return of descendants to the physical type, mode of life, etc., of their ancestors.

re-vert (rĕ-vûrt′), *v.i.* **1,** to go back to an idea, purpose, or the like; **2,** to return to the original owner or his heirs; **3,** in biology, to return to an earlier type.

rev-er-y (rĕv′ẽr-ĭ), *n.* [*pl.* reveries], daydreaming; reverie. See **reverie**.

re-view (rĕ-vū′), *n.* **1,** a going over anything again to consider or examine it; **2,** an examination by a higher court of a decision of a lower court; **3,** a lesson studied or recited again; **4,** a general survey; as, a *review* of the news; **5,** a criticism, especially of a new publication or a work of art; **6,** a magazine or newspaper featuring criticisms of new books, timely essays, or the like; **7,** a military inspection:—*v.t.* **1,** to study or examine again; as, to *review* a legal decision; **2,** to go over in order to make corrections; revise; examine critically; also, to write a critical notice of; as, to *review* a concert; **3,** to look back on; as, to *review* one's life; **4,** to inspect (troops): —*v.i.* to write criticisms of books, works of art, or the like.—*n.* **re-view′ing.**

re-view-er (rĕ-vū′ẽr), *n.* a person whose business it is to write criticisms of books, plays, etc.

re-vile (rĕ-vīl′), *v.t.* [reviled, revil-ing], to address with abusive language; heap abuse upon; as, to *revile* an enemy.
Syn. abuse, slander, malign, vilify.

re-vise (rĕ-vīz′), *v.t.* [revised, revis-ing], **1,** to go over and examine in order to correct; also, to change and correct; as, to *revise* a manuscript; **2,** to reconsider; amend; as, to *revise* one's judgment.—*n.* **re-vis′er.**

re-vi-sion (rĕ-vĭzh′ŭn), *n.* **1,** the act of examining manuscript, statutes, etc., for the purpose of correction; **2,** that which has been examined and corrected; a new and amended edition.

re-vis-it (rĕ-vĭz′ĭt), *v.t.* to visit again; return to.

re-viv-al (rĕ-vī′văl), *n.* **1,** a bringing back, or the state of being brought back, to life, consciousness, or energy; as, the *revival* of flagging spirits; a *revival* of trade; **2,** a bringing or coming back to public attention and use; as, the *revival* of an old fashion; also, a new performance of an old play or opera; **3,** a religious awakening or reawakening of a community; also, the series of meetings held with this purpose in view.—*n.* **re-viv′al-ist.**

re-vive (rĕ-vīv′), *v.i.* [revived, reviv-ing], **1,** to come back to life; **2,** to return to consciousness, as after a faint; **3,** to return to

vigor or activity; as, learning *revived* in the 15th century:—*v.t.* **1,** to restore to life; **2,** to give new vigor to; refresh; as, efforts to *revive* interest in handicrafts; **3,** to bring back from a state of neglect; as, to *revive* folk songs; **4,** to recall (memories).— *n.* **re-viv′er.**

rev-o-ca-ble (rĕv′ô-kȧ-bl), *adj.* capable of being canceled or repealed.

rev-o-ca-tion (rĕv′ô-kā′shŭn), *n.* the act of annulling; reversal; repeal; as, the *revocation* of a license.

re-voke (rĕ-vōk′), *v.t.* [revoked, revok-ing], to cancel; repeal; annul; as, to *revoke* a law or a license:—*v.i.* in card playing, to fail to follow suit when one could and should:—*n.* in card playing, a failure to follow suit when one could and should.

re-volt (rĕ-vōlt′; rĕ-vŏlt′), *n.* an uprising against authority; rebellion:—*v.i.* **1,** to rebel; **2,** to turn from something in disgust or loathing; as, the civilized mind *revolts* against cannibalism:—*v.t.* to disgust; as, snakes *revolt* me.—*n.* **re-volt′er.**
Syn., n. mutiny, sedition, insurrection.

re-volt-ing (rĕ-vōl′tĭng; rĕ-vŏl′tĭng), *adj.* **1,** disgusting, loathsome; **2,** rebelling; as, a *revolting* province.

rev-o-lu-tion (rĕv′ô-lū′shŭn), *n.* **1,** the turning of a body, especially a heavenly body, around a central point or axis; rotation; **2,** the course or motion of such a body around another body in a fixed orbit; as, the *revolution* of the earth around the sun; also, the time it takes to complete such a revolution; **3,** any far-reaching change in habits of thought, methods of labor, manner of life, or the like; as, one century has seen a *revolution* in transportation from sail to steamships, and from horse power to railroads, automobiles, and aircraft; **4,** a sudden change in the government of a country; the overthrow of one form of government and the setting up of another, as illustrated in the French Revolution.
Syn. rebellion, sedition, insurrection.

rev-o-lu-tion-ar-y (rĕv′ô-lū′shŭn-ĕr′ĭ), *adj.* associated with a sudden and complete change in thought, method, government, or the like:—*n.* [*pl.* revolutionaries], a believer in sudden and complete change.

Revolutionary War, the American Revolution (1775–1783), as a result of which the American colonies became independent of Great Britain.

rev-o-lu-tion-ist (rĕv′ô-lū′shŭn-ĭst), *n.* one who advocates sudden and complete change, especially in government.

rev-o-lu-tion-ize (rĕv′ô-lū′shŭn-īz), *v.t.* [revolutionized, revolutioniz-ing], to cause an entire change in the government, af-

---

go; join; yet; sing; chin; show; thin, *then;* hw, *why;* zh, azure; ü, Ger. für or Fr. *lune;* ö, Ger. schön or Fr. *feu;* ṅ, Fr. e*n*fant, no*m;* kh, Ger. a*ch* or i*ch.* See pages ix–x.

fairs, or character of; as, electricity *revolutionized* all kinds of industry.

re·volve (rē-vŏlv′), *v.i.* [revolved, revolving], **1**, to turn around on an axis; rotate; as, the earth *revolves* once in 24 hours; wheels *revolve;* **2**, to move in a curved path around a center, as the moon around the earth; **3**, to occur regularly; come round again and again; as, the seasons *revolve:—v.t.* **1**, to turn over and over in the mind, as an idea or plan; **2**, to cause to turn.—*adj.* **re·volv′ing.**

re·volv·er (rē-vŏl′vĕr), *n.* something that turns round or revolves; specifically, a pistol with several bullet chambers in a cylinder that

REVOLVER
1, muzzle; 2, sight; 3, barrel; 4, extractor; 5, cylinder; 6, firing pin; 7, hammer; 8, cylinder release; 9, trigger; 10, trigger guard; 11, grip.

revolves, bringing a fresh cartridge into position, so that the pistol may be fired several times without reloading.

re·vul·sion (rē-vŭl′shŭn), *n.* a sudden and violent change, especially of feeling; a sharp recoil; as, a *revulsion* of feeling from a popular favorite.

Rev. Ver. abbreviation for *Revised Version.*

re·ward (rē-wôrd′), *n.* **1**, something given in return; as, this prize is a *reward* for diligence; **2**, money offered for service or for the return of something lost:—*v.t.* to make a return to (somebody) or for (something); as, to *reward* a soldier; to *reward* his courage.

Syn., n. pay, remuneration, compensation.

re·word (rē-wûrd′), *v.t.* to state in different words; change the wording of.

re·write (rē-rīt′), *v.t.* and *v.i.* [*p.t.* rewrote (rē-rōt′), *p.p.* rewrit·ten (rē-rĭt′n), *p.pr.* rewrit·ing], to write in different words; write (something) again.

Rey·kja·vik (rā′kyȧ-vēk′), a seaport, capital of Iceland, on the southwestern coast of the island (map 12).

Reyn·ard (rĕn′ẽrd; rā′närd), *n.* in poetry and legend, a fox.

Reyn·olds (rĕn′ŭlz; rĕn′ŭldz), Sir Joshua (1723–1792), a famous English portrait painter.

R.F.D. abbreviation for *Rural Free Delivery*, an earlier term for *Rural Delivery.*

rhap·so·dy (răp′sō-dĭ), *n.* [*pl.* rhapsodies], **1**, a piece of literature, highly emotional in tone; **2**, an utterance of extravagant feeling; as, on Christmas morning there were *rhapsodies* of delight; **3**, in music, an instrumental composition, emotional in tone and irregular in form.

Rheims (rēmz; răns), a city in France, famous for its cathedral. See **Reims.**

Rhen·ish (rĕn′ĭsh), *adj.* pertaining to the river Rhine or the country around it:—*n.* wine from the Rhine vineyards.

rhe·o·stat (rē′ō-stăt), *n.* an instrument for controlling the flow of electric current by varying the resistance in the circuit.

rhet·o·ric (rĕt′ō-rĭk), *n.* **1**, the art of correct and forceful language, written or spoken; **2**, the use of words to make a fine show.

rhe·tor·i·cal (rē-tŏr′ĭ-kăl), *adj.* **1**, pertaining to the art of fine writing or speaking; **2**, showy in language:—**rhetorical question**, a question asked, not to be answered, but only for emphasis or effect.

rhet·o·ri·cian (rĕt′ō-rĭsh′ăn), *n.* **1**, a master or teacher of the art of literary composition; **2**, a showy writer or speaker.

rheum (rōōm), *n.* a watery discharge from the mucous membrane of the eyes or nose; hence, catarrh; a cold.

rheu·mat·ic (rōō-măt′ĭk), *adj.* pertaining to, affected with, or caused by, rheumatism:—*n.* a sufferer from rheumatism.

rheu·ma·tism (rōō′mȧ-tĭzm), *n.* a disease causing stiffness and pain in the muscles and joints.

Rhine (rīn), [German **Rhein** (rīn)], a river in western Europe, rising in the Alps and flowing into the North Sea (map 12):—**Rhine Province** or **Rhenish Prussia**, a former province (cap. Coblenz) in the western part of Prussia, Germany.

rhine·stone (rīn′stōn′), *n.* a colorless paste gem made in imitation of a diamond.

rhi·noc·er·os (rī-nŏs′ẽr-ŏs), *n.* a massive thick-skinned, three-toed, herb-eating

RHINOCEROS (⅓₀)

animal of tropical Asia and Africa, having either one or two hornlike projections on the snout.

rhi·zome (rī′zōm), *n.* a stem growing horizontally underground.

Rhode Is·land (rōd), a northeastern State (cap. Providence) in the U.S. (map 6).

Rhodes (rōdz), an island in the Aegean Sea (map 1).

Rhodes (rōdz), Cecil John (1853-1902), an English administrator in South Africa, who provided for Oxford University scholarships which bear his name.

āte, āorta, râre, căt, ȧsk, fär, ăllow, sofȧ; ēve, ĕvent, ĕll, writẽr, novĕl; bīte, pĭn; nō, ōbey, ôr, dŏg, tŏp, cŏllide; ūnit, ūnite, bûrn, cŭt, focŭs; nōōn, fŏŏt; mound; coin;

Rho-de-si-a (rō-dē′zhĭ-à; rō-dē′zĭ-à), a region in South Africa, comprising the British colonies of *Northern Rhodesia* (cap. Lusaka) and *Southern Rhodesia* (cap. Salisbury) (map 14).

RHODODENDRON

rho-do-den-dron (rō′dŏ-dĕn′drŏn), *n,* a shrub with shiny, usually evergreen, leaves and large clusters of variously colored flowers.

rhom-boid (rŏm′-boid), *n.* a four-sided plane figure with equal opposite sides and two acute and two obtuse angles.

Rhone (rōn), a river in western Europe, rising in the Alps and flowing south through France into the Mediterranean (map 12).

RHOMBOID

rhu-barb (rōō′bärb), *n.* **1,** a plant with large green leaves and long, fleshy, reddish stems or stalks; **2,** the stalks of this plant used as food; **3,** a medicine made from the roots of a certain kind of rhubarb.

RHUBARB

rhyme (rīm), *n.* **1,** the identity in sound of the final syllable or syllables of two or more words; **2,** words with identical final sounds; **3,** verse or poetry which employs like sounds at the ends of lines:— *v.i.* [rhymed, rhym-ing], **1,** to end in similar sounds; **2,** to compose verses:— *v.t.* to make lines of verse end in like sounds. See **rime.**

rhyme-ster (rīm′stĕr), *n.* one who fancies himself a poet. See **rimester.**

rhythm (rĭth′ăm; rĭthm), *n.* **1,** in prose and poetry, the harmonious rise and fall of the sounds of language, produced by patterns, more or less regularly repeated, of stressed and unstressed syllables; **2,** in music, the ebb and flow of sound in measured intervals of time set off by beats; **3,** in any action, the regular repetition of movement or sound; as, the *rhythm* of the pulse.

rhyth-mi-cal (rĭth′mĭ-kál) or **rhyth-mic** (rĭth′mĭk), *adj.* characterized by regularly repeated movement or accent; as, the *rhythmic* flow of the tide; *rhythmical* sounds. —*adv.* **rhyth′mi-cal-ly.**—*n.* **rhyth′mics.**

R.I. abbreviation for *Rhode Island.*

ri-al (rē-ăl′), *n.* a coin, the monetary unit of Iran. (See Table, page 943.)

rib (rĭb), *n.* **1,** in man and other animals, one of the set of long, flat, curved bones joined in pairs to the spine, which encircle and protect the cavity of the chest; **2,** anything like a rib, as a ridge in fabrics or knitted work, a rod in an umbrella frame, one of the curved pieces of timber that shape and strengthen the side of a ship, etc.; **3,** the main vein of a leaf:—*v.t.* [ribbed, rib-bing], to enclose, strengthen, or mark with, or as with, ribs; as, to *rib* a ship; to *rib* an umbrella.—*adj.* **ribbed.**

rib-ald (rĭb′ăld), *adj.* **1,** given to low jesting; **2,** coarse; low; as, a *ribald* song.

rib-ald-ry (rĭb′ăld-rĭ), *n.* [*pl.* ribaldries], low jesting; vulgar jokes.

rib-bon (rĭb′ŭn), *n.* **1,** a woven strip of fabric, such as silk or velvet, used for trimming, tying back the hair, etc.; **2,** a fabric strip used for a special purpose; as, a typewriter *ribbon;* **3,** a strip or shred; as, a curtain torn to *ribbons;* **4,** a war decoration; a prescribed portion of the ribbon worn in place of the medal on service uniforms.

rice (rīs), *n.* **1,** a grass, valuable for its seed, grown in wet soil in a warm climate; **2,** the seed or grain itself, the chief article of food in China, India, and Japan.

rice-bird (rīs′bûrd′), *n.* the bobolink: so called in the southern U.S. because in the autumn it feeds on rice.

RICE

rich (rĭch), *adj.* **1,** having much money or many possessions; wealthy; **2,** expensive; valuable; as, *rich* clothing; **3,** great in amount; abundant; as, *rich* crops; **4,** fertile; as, *rich* soil; productive; as, a *rich* mine; **5,** heavily spiced or seasoned; made with large quantities of butter, eggs, sugar, etc.; as, a *rich* pudding; **6,** having depth and vividness; as, a *rich* color; **7,** mellow and full in sound; as, a *rich* voice; **8,** highly humorous or entertaining; as, a *rich* situation:—**the rich,** those who have wealth.—*n.* **rich′ness.**—*adv.* **rich′ly.**

Syn. opulent, affluent, fruitful.

Rich-ard (rĭch′ĕrd), the name of three kings of England, notably: **Richard I** (1157-1199), called *the Lionhearted,* who ruled from 1189 to 1199.

Ri-che-lieu (rē′shĕ-lyö′; rĭsh′ĕ-lōō), Duc de (1585-1642), a famous French cardinal and prime minister.

rich-es (rĭch′ĕz), *n.pl.* wealth; plenty.

Rich-mond (rĭch'mŭnd), a city, capital of Virginia, on the James River (map 8).

rick (rĭk), *n.* a stack, or rounded pile, as of hay or straw, in the open air:—*v.t.* to pile or heap into a stack.

rick-ets (rĭk'ĕts), *n.* a disease of children caused by insufficient or improper nourishment, and marked by softness and curving of the bones.

rick-et-y (rĭk'ĕ-tĭ), *adj.* **1,** affected with rickets; **2,** shaky; as, a *rickety* table.

rick-sha (rĭk'shä; rĭk'shô), *n. Colloquial,* a two-wheeled carriage. Also spelled **rick-shaw.** See **jinrikisha.**

ric-o-chet (rĭk'ō-shā'; rĭk'ō-shĕt'), *n.* the rebounding or skipping of anything along the ground or along the surface of water:—*v.i.* [ricocheted (rĭk'ō-shād') or ricochetted (rĭk'ō-shĕt'ĕd), ricochet-ing (rĭk'ō-shā'ĭng) or ricochet-ting (rĭk'ō-shĕt'ĭng)], to rebound by touching the ground or the surface of the water and glancing off, as a bullet or a flat stone; to skip; skim:—*v.t.* to cause to rebound or skip.

rid (rĭd), *v.t.* [rid or rid-ded, rid-ding], to free, as of a burden; clear; as, to *rid* oneself of an unpleasant task; *rid* a room of flies:—**be rid of** or **get rid of,** to be, or become, free from; as, to *get rid of* weeds.

rid-dance (rĭd'ăns), *n.* the act of freeing, or the state of being freed, from something unpleasant; as, so he's gone at last; that's a good *riddance.*

rid-den (rĭd'n), past participle of *ride.*

¹**rid-dle** (rĭd'l), *n.* **1,** a question or problem so worded that one is puzzled to find the answer; **2,** a person or thing that is difficult to understand; a mystery:—*v.t.* [rid-dled, rid-dling], to explain; solve; as, *riddle* me this:—*v.i.* to speak with doubtful meaning.
Syn., n. conundrum, paradox, puzzle.

²**rid-dle** (rĭd'l), *n.* a coarse sieve, as for sifting ashes or gravel, or for sorting potatoes by size:—*v.t.* [rid-dled, rid-dling], **1,** to sift through a coarse sieve; **2,** to pierce with many holes; as, to *riddle* a board with shot.

ride (rīd), *v.i.* [*p.t.* rode (rōd), *p.p.* rid-den (rĭd'n), *p.pr.* rid-ing], **1,** to be carried on the back of a horse or other animal; **2,** to be borne in a vehicle, on a boat, etc.; **3,** of a vessel, to lie at anchor; **4,** to serve as a means of travel; as, this horse *rides* well:—*v.t.* **1,** to sit upon and manage; as, to *ride* a horse; **2,** to be carried on; as, to *ride* the waves; **3,** to take part in, as a race; **4,** to cause to ride; as, he *rode* the baby on his back; **5,** to oppress; as, the foreman *rode* his men:—*n.* a journey on horseback, in a vehicle, on a boat, etc.; as, a horseback *ride;* a *ride* in a train or automobile.

rid-er (rī'dēr), *n.* **1,** one who travels on a horse or other animal, or in a vehicle; **2,** a section or clause added to a legislative bill while in course of passage.

ridge (rĭj), *n.* **1,** a range of hills or mountains; **2,** the projecting backbone of an animal; **3,** the angle formed by the meeting of two sloping sides; as, the *ridge* of a roof; **4,** any raised strip or line; as, the *ridges* in plowed ground:—*v.t.* and *v.i.* [ridged, ridging], to mark, or become marked, with raised lines, or ridges.

ridge-pole (rĭj'pōl'), *n.* **1,** the horizontal timber along the ridge of a sloping roof, to which the rafters are nailed; **2,** the horizontal pole at the top of a tent.

rid-i-cule (rĭd'ĭ-kūl), *n.* words, looks, or acts intended to make fun of someone, or to make something seem absurd:—*v.t.* [ridiculed, ridicul-ing], to make fun of.
Syn., n. irony, derision, mockery.

ri-dic-u-lous (rĭ-dĭk'ū-lŭs), *adj.* deserving or exciting ridicule or laughter.
Syn. comical, funny, ludicrous, absurd.

rife (rīf), *adj.* **1,** common; widespread; as, gossip is *rife* in the town; **2,** abounding; as, the town is *rife* with gossip.

riff-raff (rĭf'răf'), *n.* **1,** trash; **2,** the rabble; lowest class; as, the *riffraff* of society.

¹**ri-fle** (rī'fl), *v.t.* [ri-fled, ri-fling], **1,** to ransack and rob; as, the safe was *rifled;* **2,** to make off with; steal.

²**ri-fle** (rī'fl), *n.* a firearm with the barrel spirally grooved inside to secure greater

RIFLE

accuracy in firing:—*v.t.* [ri-fled, ri-fling], to groove (a gun barrel) spirally.

ri-fle-man (rī'fl-măn), *n.* [*pl.* riflemen (-mĕn)], a person, especially a soldier, armed with, or skilled in the use of, a rifle.

rift (rĭft), *n.* **1,** an opening made by splitting; a cleft, as a crevice in a rock; **2,** any opening or separating; as, a *rift* in friendship; a *rift* in a fog:—*v.t.* and *v.i.* to split; burst open.

rig (rĭg), *v.t.* [rigged, rig-ging], **1,** to furnish (a ship) with spars, ropes, sails, etc.; **2,** to make; equip; as, to *rig* up a fishing pole; **3,** to dress; as, she *rigged* herself out in an old costume:—*n.* **1,** a special arrangement of sails, masts, etc., on a ship; as, a square *rig;* **2,** *Colloquial,* an odd style of dress; outfit; as, a cowboy's *rig.*

Ri-ga (rē'gȧ), a seaport city of Latvia, U.S.S.R., on the Gulf of Riga:—**Gulf of Riga,** an inlet of the Baltic Sea between Latvia and Estonia. (Map 12.)

āte, āorta, râre, căt, åsk, fär, ȧllow, sofȧ; ēve, ĕvent, ĕll, writēr, novĕl; bīte, pĭn; nō, ōbey, ôr, dŏg, tŏp, cŏllide; ūnit, ūnite, bûrn, cŭt, focŭs; nōon, fŏŏt; mound; coĭn;

rig-ging (rĭg′ĭng), *n.* **1,** the ropes, chains, etc., by which the masts and spars of a vessel are supported, and the sails trimmed or set (see illustration, page 695); **2,** any gear or tackle.

right (rīt), *adj.* **1,** straight; as, a *right* line; **2,** just; honorable; as, it is *right* to fulfil one's obligations; **3,** fit; suitable; as, the *right* man for the job; **4,** correct; not mistaken; as, his opinion is usually *right;* **5,** in good condition; well; healthy; as, to be all *right;* **6,** meant to be placed or worn so as to be seen; as, the *right* side of a rug; the *right* side of a blouse; **7,** naming the side of the body on which are the arm and hand which most people naturally use for writing, carrying, etc.: opposite of *left:—adv.* **1,** in a direct line; as, he went *right* to the place; **2,** justly; honorably; truthfully; as, to act *right;* **3,** suitably; properly; as, nothing has been done *right;* **4,** exactly; as, *right* now; **5,** in the direction of the right side; as, then you should turn *right;* **6,** very; as, *right* honorable:—*n.* **1,** that which is proper, just, honorable: opposite of *wrong;* as, to fight for the *right;* **2,** the right-hand side; **3,** something to which one has a moral or legal claim; as, to defend one's *rights;* **4,** in politics, the conservative party: opposite of *left:—v.t.* **1,** to restore to proper condition; correct; as, to *right* an injustice; **2,** to make straight or upright; as, to *right* a chair:—*v.i.* to go back to a natural, generally an upright, position.

by right or **by rights,** if right were done; as, *by rights* you should have had a better mark than I; **to rights,** *Colloquial,* in order; as, to put a house *to rights;* **right of way, 1,** the right to pass over privately owned land; **2,** the right to move first; precedence, as in traffic.

Syn., adj. lawful, honest, true, fair.

right an-gle, an angle of 90 degrees formed by two straight lines perpendicular to each other.

RIGHT ANGLES (ABC AND ABD)

right-eous (rī′chŭs), *adj.* **1,** just; upright; honorable; as, a *righteous* sovereign; **2,** justifiable; as, *righteous* indignation.—*adv.* **right′eous-ly.**—*n.* **right′eous-ness.**

right-ful (rīt′fŏŏl), *adj.* **1,** having a just claim according to law; as, the *rightful* heir; **2,** just; fair; as, a *rightful* claim; **3,** held by just claim; as, a *rightful* inheritance.—*n.* **right′ful-ness.**

right—hand (rīt′-hănd′), *adj.* **1,** pertaining to, or situated on, the right; **2,** chiefly relied upon; as, my *right-hand* man; **3,** intended for the right hand, as a glove.

right—hand-ed (rīt′-hăn′dĕd), *adj.* **1,** able to use the right hand more skilfully than

the left; **2,** done or used with the right hand; **3,** turning in the same direction as the hands of a clock seen from the front; as, a *right-handed* screw.

right-ly (rīt′lĭ), *adv.* **1,** honestly; uprightly; as, duty *rightly* performed; **2,** properly; suitably; as, he is *rightly* called our benefactor; **3,** correctly; in accordance with fact; as, you are *rightly* informed.

right tri-an-gle, a triangle with one right angle.

rig-id (rĭj′ĭd), *adj.* **1,** stiff; immovable; as, the *rigid* bone of the upper jaw; **2,** strict; severe; as, *rigid* discipline.—*adv.* **rig′-id-ly.**—*n.* **rig′id-ness.**—*n.* **ri-gid′i-ty** (rĭ-jĭd′ĭ-tĭ).

RIGHT TRIANGLE

Syn. firm, hard, stern, harsh, austere.

rig-ma-role (rĭg′mȧ-rōl), *n.* foolish, disconnected talk; nonsense.

rig-or (rĭg′ẽr), *n.* **1,** strictness; severity; as, to enforce a law with *rigor;* **2,** severity of climate; hardship; as, the *rigors* of Arctic life. In British usage, **rig′our.**

Syn. exactness, austerity, inclemency.

rig-or-ous (rĭg′ẽr-ŭs), *adj.* **1,** marked by sternness or severity; as, *rigorous* discipline; **2,** exact; strict; as, *rigorous* honesty; **3,** harsh; as, a *rigorous* climate.

Syn. austere, relentless, stern.

rile (rīl), *v.t.* [riled, ril-ing], *Colloquial:* **1,** to make muddy by stirring; **2,** to vex. See **roil.**

Ri-ley (rī′lĭ), James Whitcomb (1853–1916), an American poet.

rill (rĭl), *n.* a very small stream; rivulet.

rim (rĭm), *n.* a border, edge, or margin, especially when round or raised; as, spectacle *rims:—v.t.* [rimmed, rim-ming], **1,** to furnish with a border or edge; **2,** to serve as a border around; as, silver *rims* the cup.

Syn., n. brim, verge, brink, coast.

¹rime (rīm), *n.* hoarfrost; white frost.

²rime (rīm), *n.* **1,** the identity in sound of the final sounds or syllables of two or more words; as, the words "bewail" and "nightingale," and "willow" and "billow," form *rimes;* **2,** words with identical final sounds; as, "flame" and "name" are *rimes;* **3,** verse or poetry that consists of lines ending in like sounds:—*v.i.* [rimed, rim-ing], **1,** to end in identical sounds; as, "bone" and "stone" *rime;* also, to end in words that end in identical sounds; as, the lines "Tell me where is fancy bred" and "Or in the heart or in the head" *rime;* **2,** to compose verses:—*v.t.* to make lines of poetry end in like sounds. Also spelled **rhyme.**—*n.* **rim′er.**

rime-ster or **rhyme-ster** (rīm′stẽr), *n.* a person who writes ordinary or poor verse.

rind (rīnd), *n.* the outer skin or coat of a thing; as, the *rind* of a lemon; the *rind* of cheese; also, the bark of a tree.

¹ring (rĭng), *n.* 1, any circular band or hoop; especially, a small ornamental hoop, as of gold or platinum, often set with gems, worn as an ornament or distinctive mark; as, an engagement *ring;* a class *ring;* 2, an ornament for the ear; as, an ear*ring;* 3, anything circular in shape; as, a key *ring;* a *ring* of smoke; any circular arrangement; as, a *ring* of dancers; 4, an arena or space used for contests or displays; as, a circus with three *rings;* 5, a group of persons working together secretly, often towards some unlawful end:— *v.t.* [ringed, ring-ing], 1, to put a ring around; encircle; hem in; 2, to fit or decorate with a ring or rings; 3, to put a ring through; as, to *ring* the nose of a bull; 4, in certain games, to throw a loop over (a peg).

RINGS

²ring (rĭng), *v.i.* [*p.t.* rang (răng), *p.p.* rung (rŭng), *p.pr.* ring-ing], 1, to sound musically or resound, as a bell when struck; 2, to cause a bell to sound; as, to *ring* for breakfast; 3, to sound loudly and clearly; as, his voice *rang* out; 4, to give the impression of a quality; as, his excuse *rings* false; 5, to be filled with a buzzing sound; as, my ears *ring;* 6, to resound; echo; as, the woods *ring* with song; 7, to be known far and wide; be famous; as, his deeds *ring* through the country:— *v.t.* 1, to cause (particularly a bell or other metal object) to give forth a resonant sound; 2, to announce or proclaim by a bell; as, to *ring* the hours; 3, to summon, control, or otherwise affect by a bell signal; as, to *ring* up a friend on the telephone; *ring* up the curtain:— *n.* 1, the sound made by a blow on metal; as, the *ring* of a hammer on iron; also, any similar sound; as, the musical *ring* of glass; 2, a summons by, or as by, a bell; as, the *ring* of an alarm; 3, a characteristic quality of spoken or written words; as, his words have the *ring* of sincerity; 4, any echoing or repeated sound; as, the *ring* of applause.

ring-lead-er (rĭng′lē′dẽr), *n.* the leader of a number of persons banded together, usually for some unlawful act.

ring-let (rĭng′lĕt), *n.* 1, a small ring; 2, a curl, or lock, of hair.

ring-worm (rĭng′wûrm′), *n.* a contagious skin disease marked by circular patches.

rink (rĭngk), *n.* 1, an expanse of ice marked off for skating; 2, an artificial sheet of ice in a building, for skating, or a floor for roller skating; also, the building.

rinse (rĭns), *v.t.* [rinsed, rins-ing], 1, to put through clear water to remove all traces of soap; as, to *rinse* clothes; 2, to wash lightly; as, to *rinse* the mouth:— *n.* a light wash, especially to remove soap.

Ri-o de Ja-nei-ro (rē′ō dā zhȧ-nā′rō), a seaport, capital of Brazil, on the central Atlantic coast of South America (map 11).

Ri-o Gran-de (rē′ō grän′dā), a river, the boundary line between Texas and Mexico, flowing into the Gulf of Mexico (map 5).

Ri-o Mu-ni (rē′ō moo′nē), a Spanish territory in western Africa, part of Spanish Guinea, on the Gulf of Guinea (map 14).

ri-ot (rī′ŭt), *n.* 1, disorderly or uproarious behavior; revelry; 2, a disturbance of the public peace by a number of persons who are ready for violence; as, a bread *riot;* 3, unrestrained display or growth; as, a *riot* of color; a *riot* of weeds:— *v.i.* 1, to raise an uproar; engage in a public disturbance; 2, to eat and drink without restraint; revel.— *n.* **ri′ot-er.**

Syn., *n.* disorder, uproar, tumult.

ri-ot-ous (rī′ŭt-ŭs), *adj.* 1, connected with violent disturbance of the peace; as, *riotous* crowds; 2, unrestrained; wild; as, *riotous* living.— *adv.* **ri′ot-ous-ly.**

Syn. noisy, clamorous.

¹rip (rĭp), *v.t.* [ripped, rip-ping], 1, to tear or cut with violence; as, she *ripped* open the package; he *ripped* off the bandage from his arm; 2, to undo the seam of, by cutting or pulling out the stitches; as, please *rip* both sleeves; 3, to saw (wood) along, or with, the grain:— *v.i.* to become torn apart:— *n.* a rent made by the breaking of stitches; also, a tear.

²rip (rĭp), *n.* 1, a stretch of water roughened by the meeting of cross currents or tides; 2, a part of a current roughened by passing over shallows.

ripe (rīp), *adj.* [rip-er, rip-est], 1, grown to maturity; ready for harvest; 2, just right for use; mellow; as, *ripe* ale; 3, advanced to a high degree; mature; as, *ripe* wisdom; 4, ready; prepared; as, *ripe* for action.— *adv.* **ripe′ly.**— *n.* **ripe′ness.**

Syn. complete, perfected, seasoned.

rip-en (rī′pĕn), *v.t.* and *v.i.* to bring or come to maturity or completion.

rip-ple (rĭp′l), *n.* 1, a tiny wave on the surface of water; 2, any slight, curling wave; as, *ripples* of hair; 3, the sound made by gentle waves of water, or a sound like it; as, a *ripple* of mirth:— *v.t.* [rip-pled, rip-pling], to make small curling waves upon or in; as, the wind *ripples* the water:— *v.i.* 1, to become ruffled or waved on the surface; 2, to sound like running water; as, the laughter of children *rippled* below us.

āte, āorta, râre, căt, ȧsk, fär, ăllow, sofȧ; ēve, ēvent, ĕll, writẽr, novĕl; bīte, pĭn; nō, ōbey, ôr, dŏg, tŏp, cŏllide; ūnit, ūnite, bûrn, cŭt, focŭs; nōͦn, fŏͦt; mound; coin;

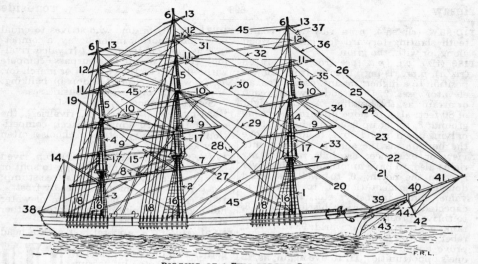

RIGGING OF A FULL-RIGGED SHIP

1, foremast; 2, mainmast; 3, mizzenmast; 4, 4, 4, topmasts; 5, 5, 5, topgallant masts; 6, 6, 6, royal and skysail masts; 7, 7, yards (fore and main); 8, crossjack yard; 9, 9, 9, lower topsail yards; 10, 10, 10, upper topsail yards; 11, 11, 11, topgallant yards; 12, 12, 12, royal yards; 13, 13, 13, skysail yards; 14, spanker gaff; 15, trysail gaff; 16, 16, 16, lower shrouds; 17, 17, 17, upper shrouds; 18, 18, 18, backstays; 19, monkey gaff; 20, forestay; 21, fore-topmast stay; 22, jib stay; 23, outer jib stay; 24, fore-topgallant stay; 25, fore-royal stay; 26, fore-skysail stay; 27, mainstay; 28, main-topmast lower stay; 29, main-topmast upper stay; 30, main-topgallant stay; 31, main-royal stay; 32, main-skysail stay; 33, lift; 34, lower-topsail lift; 35, upper-topsail lift; 36, topgallant lift; 37, royal lift; 38, spanker boom; 39, bowsprit; 40, jib boom; 41, flying jib boom; 42, dolphin striker, with stays running forward to jib boom and flying jib boom; 43, bobstays; 44, back ropes; 45, 45, 45, braces for adjusting sails to wind, named for yards to which they belong.

FULL-RIGGED SHIP UNDER SAIL

1, foresail; 2, mainsail; 3, crossjack; 4, spanker; 5, 5, 5, lower topsails; 6, 6, 6, upper topsails; 7, 7, 7, topgallant sails; 8, 8, 8, royals; 9, 9, 9, skysails; 10, fore-topmast staysail; 11, jib; 12, outer jib; 13, flying jib; 14, main-topmast lower staysail; 15, main-topmast upper staysail; 16, main-topgallant staysail; 17, main-royal staysail; 18, mizzen staysail; 19, mizzen-topmast staysail; 20, mizzen-topgallant staysail; 21, mizzen-royal staysail; 22, 22, 22, braces for adjusting sails to wind, named for yards to which they belong; 23, reef points on sails.

rip-saw (rĭp′sô′), *n.* a saw with coarse teeth slanting forward for cutting wood along, or with, the grain.

rise (rīz), *v.i.* [*p.t.* rose (rōz), *p.p.* ris-en (rĭz′n), *p.pr.* ris-ing], **1**, to go from a lower position to a higher; mount; ascend; as, an elevator *rises;* **2**, to extend upward; reach or attain; as, the building *rises* to a height of 80 feet; also, to slope upward; as, *rising* ground; **3**, to get up from kneeling, sitting, or lying down; stand up; **4**, to appear above the horizon, as the sun; **5**, to come into view or existence; as, hills *rose* on my right; also, to have an origin; as, this river *rises* in the north; **6**, to swell, as bread dough in fermentation; **7**, to increase in value, force, intensity, etc.; as, milk is expected to *rise* in price; his fears *rose;* **8**, to thrive; prosper; also, to be promoted in rank; as, to *rise* in the world; **9**, to revolt; rebel; as, to *rise* against authority; **10**, to prove equal to something; as, to *rise* to one's opportunities; **11**, to live again; as, to *rise* from the dead:—*n.* **1**, the act of going up; ascent; **2**, the distance anything ascends; as, the *rise* of a step; **3**, a small hill; **4**, appearance above the horizon; as, the *rise* of the sun; **5**, origin; source; as, the *rise* of a river; **6**, increase in value, amount, or the like; as, a steady *rise* in prices; **7**, advance in power or rank; **8**, rebellion.

ris-er (rī′zẽr), *n.* **1**, one who rises, especially with reference to the hour of rising; as, we are all late *risers;* **2**, the upright part of a step or stair.

ris-i-bil-i-ty (rĭz′ĭ-bĭl′ĭ-tĭ), *n.* [*pl.* risibilities], readiness to laugh; laughter.

RISER (R) AND TREAD (T) OF A STEP

ris-i-ble (rĭz′ĭ-bl), *adj.* **1**, able to laugh; as, man is the only *risible* animal; **2**, laughable; ridiculous; **3**, used in laughing; as, the *risible* muscles.

risk (rĭsk), *n.* possibility of loss or injury; peril:—*v.t.* **1**, to expose to danger; as, to *risk* life and limb; **2**, to hazard; as, to *risk* a battle.—*adj.* **risk′y.**

Syn., *n.* jeopardy, hazard.

ris-qué (rĭs′kā′; rēs′kā′), *adj.* somewhat improper; daring; as, a *risqué* remark.

rite (rīt), *n.* the prescribed form for conducting a solemn ceremony; also, the ceremony; as, funeral *rites.*

Syn. observance, form, formality.

rit-u-al (rĭt′ū-ăl), *adj.* pertaining to formal, solemn ceremonies; as, *ritual* observances:—*n.* **1**, a set form for conducting a solemn, especially a religious, ceremony; **2**, a book of such forms; **3**, a set of ceremonies used in any church or order.—*n.* **rit′u-al-ism.**—*adj.* **rit′u-al-is′tic.**

riv. abbreviation for *river.*

ri-val (rī′văl), *n.* one who strives to equal or surpass another in some way; a competitor; as, *rivals* in tennis:—*v.t.* [rivaled, rivaling], to try to equal or surpass; compete with; also, to be the equal of or match for; as, New York *rivals* London in banking:—*adj.* competing; as, *rival* businesses.

Syn., *n.* opponent, antagonist.

ri-val-ry (rī′văl-rĭ), *n.* [*pl.* rivalries], the act of trying to equal or excel; competition; as, the *rivalry* between schools is often very keen.

rive (rīv), *v.t.* [*p.t.* rived (rīvd), *p.p.* rived or riv-en (rĭv′ĕn), *p.pr.* riv-ing], to split or tear apart; cleave; as, to *rive* a tree stump:—*v.i.* to be split apart, as trees by frost.

riv-er (rĭv′ẽr), *n.* a large stream of water flowing in a definite channel into another stream, or into a lake or sea.

riv-et (rĭv′ĕt), *n.* a metal bolt with a head on one end, used to fasten together two or more pieces of wood, metal, etc., by passing it through holes and hammering down the plain end to form another head:—*v.t.* **1**, to secure with, or as with, such a bolt; as, to *rivet* parts of a ship; **2**, to make firm or secure; as, to *rivet* a friendship; **3**, to fix (the eyes, mind, etc.) attentively.—*n.* **riv′et-er.**

RIVETS

Ri-vie-ra (rĭ-vĭ-âr′ä; rē-vyâ′rä), an extended region in France and Italy along the northwestern Mediterranean, famous for its winter resorts.

riv-u-let (rĭv′ū-lĕt), *n.* a little stream.

Ri-yadh (rē-yäd′), a city, one of the two capitals of Saudi Arabia (map **15**).

ri-yal (rē-yäl′), *n.* the monetary unit of Saudi Arabia. (See table, page 943.)

rm. abbreviation for *ream.*

¹roach (rōch), *n.* a household insect pest; a cockroach.

²roach (rōch), *n.* a silvery-green European fresh-water fish related to the carp.

ROACH (⅒)

road (rōd), *n.* **1**, a public way for travel; highway; **2**, a way or means by which anything is reached; as, the *road* to happiness; **3**, a place near the shore where ships may ride at anchor; a roadstead.

Syn. thoroughfare, street, avenue.

road-bed (rōd′bĕd′), *n.* **1**, in railroads, the foundation for the ties and rails; **2**, in road construction, the foundation of rock, gravel, etc., beneath the top surface.

road-side (rōd′sīd′), *n.* a strip of land along a road or highway:—*adj.* situated by the side of a road; as, a *roadside* stand.

āte, âorta, râre, cặt, ặsk, fär, ặllow, sofặ; ēve, ēvent, ĕll, writẽr, novĕl; bīte, pĭn; nō, ōbey, ôr, dŏg, tŏp, cŏllide; ūnit, ūnite, bûrn, cŭt, focŭs; nōon, fŏot; mound; coin;

road-stead (rōd′stĕd), *n.* an anchorage for ships offshore, less sheltered than a harbor.

road-ster (rōd′stẽr), *n.* **1**, an open automobile, usually for two passengers; **2**, a horse used for light driving.

road-way (rōd′wā′), *n.* a road, especially the part that is used by vehicles.

ROADSTER, def. 1

roam (rōm), *v.i.* to wander about aimlessly; ramble:—*v.t.* to wander over; as, to *roam* the countryside.

roan (rōn), *adj.* reddish brown, black, or chestnut, thickly sprinkled with gray or white; as, a *roan* horse:—*n.* **1**, a roan color; **2**, a horse of roan color.

Ro-a-noke (rō′a-nōk′), a city in southwestern Virginia (map **8**).

roar (rôr), *n.* **1**, the deep, full cry of a large animal; as, the *roar* of a tiger; **2**, any loud, confused noise; as, the *roar* of traffic; **3**, loudly expressed mirth; as, a *roar* of laughter:—*v.i.* **1**, to cry with a loud, full, deep sound; as, a bull *roars;* **2**, to cry loudly, as in pain, distress, or anger; **3**, to laugh loudly; **4**, to make a loud, confused noise, as wind, waves, passing vehicles, etc.:—*v.t.* to utter boisterously; cry aloud; as, he *roared* his defiance.

roast (rōst), *v.t.* **1**, to cook before a fire or in a closed oven; **2**, to dry and parch under the action of heat; as, to *roast* peanuts:—*v.i.* to be cooked by heat, as before a fire or in an oven:—*n.* a piece of meat cooked, or suitable to be cooked, before a fire or in an oven; as, a *roast* of veal:—*adj.* roasted.

roast-er (rōs′tẽr), *n.* **1**, a pan for roasting; also, a kind of oven; **2**, something suitable for roasting; especially, a large-sized young chicken.

rob (rŏb), *v.t.* [robbed, rob-bing], **1**, to take something forcibly away from; as, to *rob* a man; to steal from; as, to *rob* a bank; **2**, to deprive (a person) of something unjustly; as, to *rob* people of their rights:—*v.i.* to commit a theft.

rob-ber (rŏb′ẽr), *n.* one who takes what is not his; a thief.

rob-ber-y (rŏb′ẽr-ĭ), *n.* [*pl.* robberies], the unlawful and forcible taking away of the money or goods of others.

  Syn. piracy, theft, plunder, larceny.

robe (rōb), *n.* **1**, a long, loose outer garment, especially one indicating rank or honor; **2**, **robes**, state or ceremonial costume; as, *robes* of office; **3**, a wrap or covering:—*v.t.* and *v.i.* [robed, rob-ing], to dress in, or put on, a robe.

Ro-bes-pierre (rō′bĕs-pyär′; rō′bĕs-pēr;

rōbz′pēr), Maximilien de (1758–1794), a famous French revolutionist.

rob-in (rŏb′ĭn), *n.* **1**, a small European bird of the thrush family; the robin redbreast; **2**, an American thrush somewhat like the English robin, but larger.

Rob-in Good-fel-low (gōōd′fĕl′ō), in English folklore, a mischievous and good-natured elf: also called *Puck*.

Robin Hood, in English legend, a gallant outlaw.

Rob-in-son Cru-soe (rŏb′ĭn-sŭn krōō′sō), the title of Defoe's most famous story; also, the hero of the book.

ro-bot (rō′bŏt; rŏb′ŏt), *n.* a machine made to look and act somewhat like a human being; hence, a person who acts mechanically.

ro-bust (rô-bŭst′), *adj.* strong; vigorous; sturdy; as, *robust* health.

roc (rŏk), *n.* in Arabian and Persian legend, a bird of prey of gigantic size.

Roch-es-ter (rŏch′ĕs-tẽr), a city in western New York, on Lake Ontario (map **6**).

¹**rock** (rŏk), *n.* **1**, a large mass of stone or of stony matter; **2**, mineral matter; a bed or mass of one mineral; **3**, that which resembles such a mass in firmness; a firm support; **4**, anything that may bring a person or thing to ruin; as, the business was wrecked on the *rock* of extravagance.

²**rock** (rŏk), *v.t.* **1**, to move to and fro, or backward and forward; as, to *rock* a cradle; also, to move or swing (a baby) in a cradle; **2**, to lull to sleep; **3**, to cause to shake; as, the explosion *rocked* the building:—*v.i.* **1**, to move backward and forward; as, to *rock* in a rocking chair; **2**, to sway:—*n.* a rocking movement.

rock crys-tal, a transparent, usually colorless, variety of quartz.

rock-er (rŏk′ẽr), *n.* **1**, one who or that which rocks; **2**, one of the curved pieces upon which a rocking chair or cradle sways back and forth; **3**, a rocking chair.

rock-et (rŏk′ĕt), *n.* **1**, a firework which shoots high into the air and bursts into a shower of sparks; used in displays and in signaling; **2**, in warfare, a highly explosive missile, usually released from an airplane, a ship, or a land-based launching platform:—*v.i.* to mount high and fast.

ROCKERS (R, R) OF A ROCKING CHAIR

Rock-ford (rŏk′fẽrd), a city in northern Illinois, near Lake Michigan (map **7**).

rock-ing chair, a chair with legs set on curved pieces, or rockers; a rocker.

rock salt, common salt which exists in nature in solid mineral form.

rock·y (rŏk′ĭ), *adj.* [rock-i-er, rock-i-est], **1,** full of rocks or stones; as, a *rocky* road; **2,** like a rock; hard.

Rock·y Moun·tains or **Rock·ies,** the longest mountain range in North America, extending from Mexico to the arctic regions (map 3).

ro·co·co (rō-kō′kō; rō′kŏ-kō′), *n.* **1,** a showy style of decoration, popular in the 17th and 18th centuries, consisting of leaves, shells, scrolls, etc.; **2,** a piece of work in this style:—*adj.* **1,** pertaining to this style; **2,** over-decorated; hence, in bad taste.

rod (rŏd), *n.* **1,** a straight, slender stick of wood or metal; **2,** a fishing pole; **3,** a switch or whip; hence, correction or discipline; as, to spare the *rod;* **4,** *U.S. Slang,* a revolver; **5,** a measure of length containing 5 ½ yards or 16 ½ feet.

rode (rōd), past tense of *ride.*

ro·dent (rō′dĕnt), *n.* any one of various gnawing animals, such as rats, mice, squirrels, and beavers:—*adj.* gnawing.

ro·de·o (rō′dē-ō; rō-dā′ō), *n.* **1,** a roundup or driving together of cattle to be branded; **2,** an exhibition of cowboys' skill in cattle roping, horsemanship, etc.

Ro·din (rô′dăn′), Auguste (1840–1917), a French sculptor.

¹roe (rō), *n.* **1,** a small deer of Europe and Asia; **2,** sometimes, a doe of the red deer.

²roe (rō), *n.* the eggs of a fish.

roe·buck (rō′bŭk′), *n.* the male of the roe deer; also, any roe deer.

Roent·gen (rönt′gĕn; rĕnt′gĕn), Wilhelm Konrad (1845–1923), a German physicist, discoverer of the X ray. Also spelled **Rönt′gen.**

Roentgen ray or **Röntgen ray,** a form of radiating energy; X ray. See **X ray.**

ROEBUCK (⅕)

rogue (rōg), *n.* **1,** a dishonest person; cheat; **2,** a mischievous person; as, a playful little *rogue.*

ro·guer·y (rō′gĕr-ĭ), *n.* [*pl.* rogueries], **1,** dishonest practices; cheating; **2,** playful mischief; as, the *roguery* of children.

ro·guish (rō′gĭsh), *adj.* **1,** dishonest; cheating; **2,** playfully mischievous; as, a *roguish* trick.—*adv.* **ro′guish·ly.**—*n.* **ro′guish·ness.**

roil (roil), *v.t.* **1,** to make muddy by stirring; as, to *roil* a stream; **2,** to vex or irritate; disturb; as, to *roil* the temper.

roist·er (rois′tĕr), *v.i.* to swagger; boast; also, to revel noisily.—*n.* **roist′er·er.**

Ro·land (rō′lănd), the most celebrated of the knights of Charlemagne.

role or **rôle** (rōl), *n.* **1,** a part or character taken by an actor in a play; **2,** any assumed part; as, she played the *role* of mother to the orphaned child.

roll (rōl), *v.t.* **1,** to cause to move onward by turning over and over; as, to *roll* a ball; **2,** to move or push along on casters or wheels; as, to *roll* a wheel chair; **3,** to wrap upon itself or on some other object; as, *roll* a rug; **4,** to wrap up; as, to *roll* oneself in a blanket; **5,** to cause to sway sidewise, as a ship; **6,** to utter or express with a deep, vibrating sound; as, the organ *rolls* forth its music; **7,** to level with a heavy revolving cylinder; as, to *roll* a lawn; **8,** to pronounce with a prolonged trilling sound; as, to *roll* one's r's:—*v.i.* **1,** to move onward by turning over and over; as, a ball *rolls;* **2,** to run on wheels; as, the wagon *rolls* along; **3,** to rock, as does a ship; **4,** to sweep along, as do waves; **5,** to give forth a long, deep, rumbling sound; as, the thunder *rolls;* **6,** to form, when being wound, the shape of a ball or cylinder; as, the cloth *rolls* easily; **7,** to rise and fall in gentle slopes, as land; **8,** to flatten under some kind of roller; as, dough *rolls* easily; **9,** *Colloquial,* to pile up; as, debts *roll* up quickly:—*n.* **1,** the act of turning over and over, or of tossing from side to side; **2,** the state of being rolled; **3,** that which revolves; roller; as, a towel *roll;* **4,** anything wrapped upon itself in the form, or nearly the form, of a cylinder; as, a *roll* of oilcloth; **5,** a list of persons, generally official in character; as, a class *roll;* **6,** a kind of biscuit or bread, rolled or rounded; **7,** a continued, deep sound, as of a beaten drum, thunder, or the like; **8,** a swell or unevenness on a surface, as of a rough sea.

Rol·land (rô′län′), Romain (1866–1944), a French writer and critic.

roll call, 1, the act or time of calling a list of names to find out who are present; as, I arrived at school for *roll call;* **2,** a signal for roll call, as a bell.

roll·er (rōl′ĕr), *n.* **1,** anything that turns round and round, or over and over; **2,** a heavy cylinder used for grinding, smoothing, etc.; as, a hand *roller;* **3,** a small wheel on which something moves along, as on a roller skate; **4,** a long, huge wave; **5,** one of the cylinders on a clothes wringer; **6,** a

ROLLER, def. 2

rod on which to roll up a curtain; **7,** a kind of pigeon which turns somersaults in the air; **8,** a canary with a trilling song.

roller skate, a skate with (usually four) wheels, for skating on a smooth surface other than ice:— **roller–skate** (rōl′-ẽr⹀skāt′), *v.i.* [roller-skat-ed, roller-skat-ing], to skate on roller skates.

ROLLER SKATE

rol·lick (rŏl′ĭk), *v.i.* to frolic or sport in a joyous, carefree manner.

rol·lick·ing (rŏl′ĭk-ĭng), *adj.* very jovial or gay; as, *rollicking* fun.

roll·ing (rōl′ĭng), *adj.* **1,** moving along by turning over and over; as, a *rolling* ball; **2,** moving on, or as on, wheels; as, a *rolling* chair; **3,** rising and falling in gentle slopes; as, *rolling* country; **4,** rumbling; as, *rolling* thunder:—**rolling stock,** the wheeled equipment, as engines, cars, etc., of a railway:—*n.* **1,** the act of a person or thing that rolls; also, a person who works with a rolling tool; **2,** a deep, full sound, as of thunder.

rolling mill, a mill in which iron or steel is rolled into bars, plates, wires, etc.

rolling pin, a long, smooth cylinder, made of wood or glass, for rolling out dough.

ROLLING PIN

Rom. abbreviation for *Roman, Romans.*

Ro·man (rō′măn), *n.* a native or citizen of ancient or modern Rome; also, a member of the Roman Catholic Church:—**roman,** the upright type ordinarily used in printing:—*adj.* **1,** relating to Rome or its people; **2,** relating to the Roman Catholic Church:—**roman,** naming the ordinary type used in printing: distinguished from *italic.*

Roman candle, a kind of firework, in the form of a candle, which sends forth showers of sparks and, at intervals, balls of fire; **Roman nose,** a nose with a high or prominent bridge; **Roman numerals,** the figures i, ii, iii, or I, II, III, etc., distinguished from Arabic numerals, as 1, 2, 3, etc.

Ro·man Cath·o·lic, pertaining to the church of which the Pope in Rome is the head; also, a member of this church.

ro·mance (rō-măns′; rō′măns), *n.* **1,** a long prose or poetical tale of adventure, chivalry, etc., as Malory's "Morte d'Arthur"; **2,** a novel or prose narrative full or imagination and adventure, as "Ivanhoe"; **3,** a series of acts or happenings that are strange and fanciful; **4,** a disposition to delight in what is fanciful; **5,** a falsehood:

—*v.i.* [romanced, romanc-ing], **1,** to invent fanciful stories; **2,** to indulge in dreamy imaginings.—*n.* **ro-manc′er.**

Ro·mance lan·guag·es, any of the languages descended from the Latin spoken by the Romans, such as French, Spanish, Italian, etc.

Ro·man Em·pire, the ancient Empire of Rome, founded by Augustus in 27 B.C. and divided, after the death of the emperor Theodosius the Great in A.D. 395, into the *Western Roman Empire* and the *Eastern Roman Empire.*

Ro·man·esque (rō′-măn-ĕsk′), *n.* a style of architecture developed from the Roman and distinguished by its rounded arches:—*adj.* naming, or relating to, this style of architecture.

ROMANESQUE ARCHITECTURE

Ro·man·ism (rō′măn-ĭzm), *n.* the Roman Catholic religion.

Ro·man·ist (rō′măn-ĭst), *n.* **1,** a member of the Roman Catholic church; **2,** one who makes a study of the law and institutions of ancient Rome.

Ro·mans (rō′mănz), *n.* a book of the New Testament, containing the Epistle of Paul to the Christians at Rome.

ro·man·tic (rō-măn′tĭk), *adj.* **1,** pertaining to, or like, what is imaginary, sentimental, or idealistic; hence, fanciful; impractical; as, *romantic* ideas; **2,** pertaining to, or suggesting, what is strange or heroic; as, *romantic* literature; **3,** of a disposition to ignore what is real and delight in what is fanciful; as, a *romantic* girl; **4,** strangely wild and picturesque; as, *romantic* scenery; **5,** pertaining to a style of literature, art, or music, which places more value on imagination and fancy than on things as they are.

Syn. fictitious, dreamy, poetic.

ro·man·ti·cism (rō-măn′tĭ-sĭzm), *n.* **1,** the quality of being imaginative, sentimental, or extravagantly idealistic; **2,** in literature, the movement in Europe in the late 18th and early 19th centuries which emphasized imagination and natural beauty rather than conventionality and formal beauty.

Rom·a·ny (rŏm′à-nĭ), *n.* [*pl.* Romanies], a gypsy; also, the language of the gypsies.

Rome (rōm), **1,** a city, the capital of Italy (maps **1, 12**); **2,** the Roman Empire.

go; join; yet; sing; chin; show; thin, *th*en; **hw,** *wh*y; **zh,** azure; **ū,** Ger. **für** or Fr. **l***u***ne; ö,** Ger. **sch***ö***n** or Fr. **f***eu***; ṅ,** Fr. **e***n***fant, no***m***; kh,** Ger. **a***ch* or *ich.* See pages ix–x.

Ro·me·o (rō'mē-ō), *n.* the hero of Shakespeare's play, "Romeo and Juliet."

romp (rŏmp), *n.* **1,** one who plays boisterously; a tomboy; **2,** rough, noisy play:—*v.i.* to play in a rough, boisterous manner.

romp·ers (rŏmp'ẽrz), *n.pl.* an outer garment consisting of a waist with bloomers attached, worn by small children at play.

Rom·u·lus (rŏm'ū-lŭs), *n.* in Roman mythology, a son of Mars, thrown into the Tiber River with his twin brother Remus. Both were rescued and reared by a she-wolf. Romulus later became the founder of Rome.

Rönt·gen (rŏnt'gĕn; rĕnt'gĕn), Wilhelm Konrad, a German scientist. See **Roentgen.**

Rönt·gen ray, a form of radiating energy; X ray. More often spelled **Roent'gen ray.** See **X ray.**

rood (rōōd), *n.* **1,** a cross with the figure of Christ upon it; a crucifix, especially over an altar; **2,** a measure equal to one fourth of an acre, or 40 square rods.

roof (rōōf), *n.* **1,** the top covering of a building; **2,** any similar top covering, as of a car or a cave:—*v.t.* to cover with a roof. —*n.* **roof'er.**

roof·ing (rōō'fĭng), *n.* **1,** the act of putting a covering on a building; **2,** materials for constructing a roof; also, the roof.

roof·less (rōōf'lĕs), *adj.* **1,** having no top covering; **2,** without a shelter or home.

¹rook (rŏok), *n.* **1,** a European bird with glossy black plumage, similar to the crow; **2,** a cheat, especially at dice or cards:—*v.t.* and *v.i.* to cheat; defraud.

²rook (rŏok), *n.* a piece used in chess: also called *castle.*

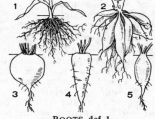

ROOK (½), def. 1

rook·er·y (rŏok'ẽr-ĭ), *n.* [*pl.* rookeries], **1,** a place where rooks gather and build their nests; **2,** a colony of these birds; **3,** a place where other birds or animals, as gulls or seals, gather and breed; **4,** a wretched tenement or group of tenements in a slum area.

room (rōōm), *n.* **1,** a space separated by partitions from the rest of the structure in which it is located; a chamber; as, a living *room;* **2,** space; as, there is *room* in this closet for their coats; **3,** opportunity; as, *room* for development:—*v.i.* to occupy a room or rooms:—*v.t.* to accommodate with a room or lodgings.—*n.* **room'ful.**

room·er (rōō'mẽr), *n.* a lodger; one who rents a room, especially temporarily.

room·mate (rōōm'māt'), *n.* one of two or more persons who share the same room,

especially in school or college.

room·y (rōō'mĭ), *adj.* [room-i-er, room-i-est], having plenty of room; spacious; as, a *roomy* garage.—*n.* **room'i·ness.**

Roo·se·velt (rō'zĕ-vĕlt), **1,** Franklin Delano (1882–1945), the 32d president of the U.S.; **2,** Theodore (1858–1919), the 26th president of the U.S.

roost (rōōst), *n.* **1,** the pole, perch, etc., upon which a bird rests at night; **2,** a number of fowls resting together; **3,** a temporary resting place:—*v.i.* to sit or sleep upon a perch or pole.

roost·er (rōōs'tẽr), *n.* the domestic cock; a male fowl.

ROOSTER (¹⁄₂₀)

¹root (rōōt), *n.* **1,** that part of a plant, usually growing downward into the soil, which holds the plant in place, and absorbs and stores food; **2,** in popular usage, any underground part of a plant; especially, a large part suitable for food, as a beet, turnip, etc.; **3,** anything like a root in position, use, etc.; as, the *root* of a tooth; **4,** a cause or source; as, laziness is the *root* of his poverty; **5,** in arithmetic, a number which, used as a factor a given number of times, produces a given number; as, since $2 \times 2 \times 2 = 8$, 2 is the third *root* of 8; **6,** the basic part of a word, considered apart from prefixes, suffixes, etc.; as, "roll" is the *root* of "roller" and "enroll":—*v.t.* **1,** to plant and fix in the earth; **2,** to implant deeply; as, his dislike was *rooted* in fear; **3,** to tear or dig up by the roots; to destroy; as, to *root* out vice:—*v.i.* **1,** to take root; as, the bulbs began to *root* in February; **2,** to become firmly or permanently established.

²root (rōōt), *v.t.* **1,** to dig with the snout, as swine; **2,** to get by searching or hunting; as, to *root* out a secret:—*v.i.* **1,** to turn up the earth with the snout; **2,** to rummage.

³root (rōōt), *v.i.* Slang, to encourage by cheering; as, they *rooted* for our team.—*n.* **root'er.**

ROOTS, def. 1

1, grass; **2,** dahlia; **3,** beet; **4,** carrot; **5,** radish. **3, 4,** and **5** are taproots.

root-let (rōōt′lĕt), *n.* a little root.

rope (rōp), *n.* **1,** a thick, stout cord made of several strands of hemp, cotton, etc., twined together; **2,** a collection of things braided or twined together in a line or string; as, a *rope* of pearls; **3,** a stringy thread formed in a liquid:—*v.t.* [roped, rop-ing], **1,** to fasten, bind, or tie with a rope; **2,** to mark or enclose by means of a rope; as, to *rope* off a field; **3,** to lasso; as, to *rope* a steer:—*v.i.* to form stringy threads, as sirup does.—*adj.* **rop′y.**—*n.* **rop′i-ness.**

ro-sa-ry (rō′za-rĭ), *n.* [*pl.* rosaries], **1,** a string of beads for counting a series of prayers to be said one after the other in a certain order; also, the series of prayers thus recited; **2,** a rose bed or rose garden; a place where roses grow.

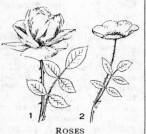

¹rose (rōz), *n.* **1,** a thorny shrub, erect or climbing, bearing showy, fragrant flowers; also, the flower; **2,** the most typical color of a rose; deep pink; **3,** a certain shape in which diamonds are cut.

ROSES
1, cultivated rose; 2, wild rose.

²rose (rōz), past tense of *rise.*

ro-se-ate (rō′zē-āt), *adj.* rose-colored.

rose-bud (rōz′bŭd′), *n.* the bud of a rose.

rose-bush (rōz′bŏŏsh′), *n.* a shrub which bears roses.

rose-mar-y (rōz′mâr′ĭ), *n.* [*pl.* rosemaries], a fragrant evergreen shrub. The leaves are used as a seasoning and in making perfume.

ROSEMARY

ro-sette (rō-zĕt′), *n.* an ornament, as a knot or bunch of ribbon, made into the shape of a rose.

rose wa-ter, toilet water scented with roses.

rose-wood (rōz′wŏŏd′), *n.* a valuable, hard, dark-red wood, yielded by various tropical trees and used for fine furniture; also, a tree from which such wood is obtained.

ROSETTE

ros-in (rŏz′ĭn), *n.* the resin, or solid substance, that remains after distilling crude turpentine:—*v.t.* to rub with rosin; as, to *rosin* the bow of a violin.

Ross (rôs) Betsy, (1752–1836), an American woman, who, at the request of George Washington, made the first American flag.

ros-ter (rŏs′tẽr), *n.* **1,** an enrollment or list of names; **2,** a schedule or program; as, the *roster* of the day's events.

ros-trum (rŏs′trŭm), *n.* [*pl.* rostra (rŏs′-trȧ) or rostrums], a pulpit, platform, or stage for public speaking.

ros-y (rōz′ĭ), *adj.* [ros-i-er, ros-i-est], **1,** like a rose; red; blooming; blushing; **2,** favorable; hopeful; as, *rosy* prospects.—*adv.* **ros′i-ly.**—*n.* **ros′i-ness.**

rot (rŏt), *v.i.* [rot-ted, rot-ting], to decay; as, the fruit was *rotting* in the orchard:—*n.* **1,** the process of decay; **2,** the state of being decayed; **3,** decayed matter; **4,** a disease of certain animals, especially sheep; as, foot *rot;* also, a disease or decay of plant tissues; as, dry *rot.*

ro-ta-ry (rō′tȧ-rĭ), *adj.* **1,** turning or rotating; **2,** having parts that turn around; as, a *rotary* engine.

ro-tate (rō′tāt; rō-tāt′), *v.t.* [rotat-ed, ro-tat-ing], **1,** to cause to turn on, or as on, an axis; as, to *rotate* a wheel; **2,** to alternate or change about; as, to *rotate* crops:—*v.i.* **1,** to turn around on its own center or axis; revolve; **2,** to take turns at anything; as, the members of the club *rotated* in office.—*n.* **ro-ta′tion.**

ro-ta-tor-y (rō′tȧ-tôr′ĭ), *adj.* **1,** relating to movement on, or as on, an axis; as, *rotatory* speed; **2,** following one another in regular sequence; as, *rotatory* assemblies.

R.O.T.C. abbreviation for *Reserve Officers′ Training Corps,* or *Camp.*

rote (rōt), *n.* the repeating of words over and over to learn them, without paying much attention to their meaning; as, to learn rules by *rote.*

ro-to-gra-vure (rō′tṓ-grȧ-vūr′; rō′tṓ-grā′-vūr), *n.* **1,** a process for the rapid printing of illustrations from plates etched on cylinders; **2,** an illustration so printed.

ro-tor (rō′tŏr), *n.* in machinery, a part which revolves around, or in, a stationary part; as, the *rotor* of a helicopter.

rot-ten (rŏt′n), *adj.* **1,** decayed; as, *rotten* food; **2,** likely to break; not firm; as, a *rotten* plank; **3,** corrupt; dishonest.—*adv.* **rot′ten-ly.**—*n.* **rot′ten-ness.**

Rot-ter-dam (rŏt′ẽr-dăm′), a seaport in the southwestern part of the Netherlands, connected with the North Sea by a ship canal (map **12**).

ro-tund (rō-tŭnd′), *adj.* **1,** round from plumpness; rounded out; as, a *rotund* figure; **2,** full and ample; as, a *rotund* style of writing.—*n.* **ro-tun′di-ty.**

ro·tun·da (rô-tŭn′dá), *n.* **1,** a circular building, especially one with a dome; **2,** a large, round room; as, the *rotunda* of a museum.

rou·ble (rōō′bl), *n.* a coin of the U.S.S.R.; the ruble. See **ruble.**

Rou·en (rōō-än′), a city, the ancient capital of Normandy, in northern France, famous for its cathedral (map 12).

rouge (rōōzh), *n.* a red powder or paste used for coloring the cheeks and lips:— *v.t.* and *v.i.* [rouged, roug-ing], to color with rouge; redden.

rough (rŭf), *adj.* **1,** having an uneven surface; not smooth; as, a *rough* road; *rough* cloth; **2,** not polished; unfinished; as, *rough* diamonds; *rough* sketches; **3,** harsh; severe; violent; as, *rough* treatment; *rough* sports; also, stormy; as, *rough* weather; **4,** not refined; rude in character; as, *rough* people: —*n.* **1,** a low, coarse fellow; a rowdy; **2,** a crude or unfinished condition; as, diamonds in the *rough;* **3,** in golf, the long grass bordering a fairway: — *v.t.* **1,** to make rough; ruffle; as, the bird *roughed* its feathers; **2,** to shape or sketch roughly; as, to *rough* in an outline:—**rough it,** to do without conveniences, as on a camping trip.—*adv.* **rough′ly.**—*n.* **rough′ness.**
Syn., adj. jagged, abrupt, rustic.

rough·age (rŭf′ĭj), *n.* **1,** coarse stuff; rubbish; **2,** coarse, bulky food, as bran or leafy vegetables.

rough·en (rŭf′n), *v.t.* to destroy the smoothness of; as, the wind *roughens* one's skin:—*v.i.* to become uneven or coarse on the surface.

rough·hew (rŭf′hū′), *v.t.* [*p.t.* rough-hewed (-hūd′), *p.p.* roughhewed or rough-hewn (-hūn′), *p.pr.* roughhew-ing], to cut (timber) without smoothing.

rough·rid·er (rŭf′rī′dẽr; rŭf′rī/dẽr), *n.* one who breaks horses for riding or who is a skilled rider of untrained horses.

rough·shod (rŭf′shŏd′), *adj.* shod, as a horse, with shoes having calks, or projecting pieces of metal, to prevent slipping:— **to ride roughshod over,** to have one's own way regardless of the welfare and feelings of others.

rou·lette (rōō-lĕt′), *n.* **1,** a game of chance played with a rotating wheel; **2,** an instrument with a toothed wheel used for making dotted lines or perforations, as on a sheet of postage stamps.

Rou·ma·ni·a (rōō-mā′nĭ-á), a republic in Europe. See **Rumania.**

round (round), *adj.* **1,** like, or nearly like, a circle or sphere in shape; as, a *round* plate; an apple is *round;* **2,** having a curved surface; as, a *round* cheek; **3,** semi-circular, as opposed to pointed; as, a *round* arch; also, moving in a circle; as, a *round* dance; **4,** full or whole; as, a *round* dozen; **5,** going from, and returning to, the same place; as, a *round* trip; **6,** full in sound; not jarring; as, the *round* tones of a voice; **7,** outspoken; frank; as, a *round* scolding; **8,** brisk; as, a good *round* pace:—**in round numbers,** expressed approximately, as in even tens, dozens, etc.:—*n.* **1,** a circle or sphere; also, a curved part; **2,** a fixed course or route; a beat; routine; as, the day's *round* of duties; **3,** a series of events or acts; as, a *round* of gaiety; **4,** one of a series of regular periods, especially in a game or contest; as, the *rounds* in a fight; **5,** a rung of a ladder; **6,** a cut of beef between the rump and the leg (see illustration under *beef*); **7,** a simultaneous volley of shots, each soldier firing once; also, the ammunition needed for such a volley, or enough for a single shot; **8,** a song sung by several persons or groups starting one after the other at intervals:—*v.t.* **1,** to give a curved or rounded form to; **2,** to travel or pass around; as, they *rounded* the cape; **3,** to bring to complete perfection or finish; as, to *round* out a plan; **4,** to drive in, or gather together; as, to *round* up cattle:— *v.i.* **1,** to become curved, spherical, or circular in form; **2,** to grow full, complete, or perfect; develop:—*adv.* **1,** in the neighborhood; near by; as, they waited *round* for orders; **2,** in a circle or group; as, to gather *round;* **3,** in a circular motion; as, the earth goes *round;* **4,** from one side or party to another; as, he came *round* to our belief; **5,** in a complete circuit from person to person, or point to point; as, food to go *round;* **6,** by outside measure; as, a hole two inches *round;* **7,** so as to face in the opposite direction; as, to turn *round:*—*prep.* **1,** about; on every side of; as, a wall *round* a town; **2,** taking a curved or bent course to the other side of; as, walk *round* the corner.—*n.* **round′ness.**

round·a·bout (round′á-bout′), *adj.* indirect; not straightforward; as, *rounda-bout* methods:—*n.* **1,** a merry-go-round; **2,** a short jacket, as for boys or sailors.

roun·de·lay (roun′dĕ-lā), *n.* **1,** a song with a simple melody often repeated; **2,** a round dance.

round·house (round′hous′), *n.* **1,** the cabin on the after part of a ship's quarter-deck; **2,** a circular building for storing and repairing locomotives.

round·ish (roun′dĭsh), *adj.* tending to be round.

round–shoul·dered (round′-shŏl′dẽrd), *adj.* not erect; having stooped shoulders.

Round Ta·ble, in Arthurian legend: **1,** the table at which sat King Arthur and his knights; **2,** the knights of King Arthur's court.

round-up (round′ŭp′), *n.* **1,** the herding together and corralling of cattle; **2,** the men and horses that herd them; **3,** any similar drive or roundup; as, a *roundup* of voters.

rouse (rouz), *v.t.* [roused, rous-ing], **1,** to awaken; also, to stir to thought or action; **2,** to bring into existence; as, to *rouse* indignation:—*v.i.* **1,** to awake from sleep; **2,** to show signs of activity; as, the crowd *roused* at the sound of a shot.

Rous·seau (rōō′sō′), Jean Jacques (1712–1778), a French writer and philosopher.

roust·a·bout (roust′à-bout′), *n.* **1,** a wharf laborer; a deck hand on a river steamboat; **2,** a man who tramps around the country, doing odd jobs for a living.

¹**rout** (rout), *n.* **1,** a total defeat and flight, as of an army; **2,** disorder resulting from such defeat; **3,** a noisy crowd; mob:—*v.t.* to defeat and put to flight.

   Syn., v. overpower, conquer, repulse.

²**rout** (rout), *v.t.* **1,** to root up, as with the snout; **2,** to dig out, as with a gouging tool; **3,** *Colloquial,* to drag by force; as, to *rout* someone out of bed.

route (rōōt; rout), *n.* a way or road traveled; course; journey:—*v.t.* [rout-ed, rout-ing], to send or ship forward, as freight or express, by a certain road or railway.

rou·tine (rōō-tēn′), *n.* a customary course of action in business, pleasure, or duty.

   Syn. system, habit, custom, practice.

rove (rōv), *v.t.* and *v.i.* [roved, rov-ing], to wander aimlessly (over); ramble; as, buffaloes *roved* over the land.

rov·er (rōv′ẽr), *n.* **1,** a pirate; **2,** a wanderer.

¹**row** (rō), *n.* **1,** a series of persons or things in a line; **2,** a line of houses side by side on a street; also, the street.

²**row** (rō), *v.i.* **1,** to move a boat by means of oars; as, John has learned to *row;* **2,** to be moved by means of oars; as, the boat *rows* easily:—*v.t.* **1,** to propel by means of oars; **2,** to carry in a boat; as, he *rowed* her across:—*n.* the act of moving a boat by oars; also, a ride taken in a rowboat.

³**row** (rou), *n. Colloquial,* a noisy quarrel; brawl; fight:—*v.i. Colloquial,* to quarrel.

row-boat (rō′bōt′), *n.* a boat propelled by means of oars.

ROWBOAT

row·dy (rou′dĭ), *n.* [*pl.* rowdies], a rough fellow; ruffian:—*adj.* [row-di-er, row-di-est], disorderly; noisy and rude.

row·el (rou′ĕl), *n.* the small, sharp-pointed wheel of a spur:—*v.t.* [roweled, rowel-ing], to prick (a horse) with the wheel of a spur.

row·er (rō′ẽr), *n.* one who rows a boat.

ROWEL

row-lock (rō′lŏk; rŭl′ŭk), *n.* a notch, a pair of wooden pins, or a piece of metal with a U-shaped top, in which the oar rests in a rowboat: also called *oarlock.*

roy·al (roi′ăl), *adj.* **1,** pertaining to, or belonging to, a king; kingly; as, the *royal* household; **2,** pertaining to, or connected with, a kingdom; as, the *royal* navy; **3,** suited to or like a king; regal; as, *royal* dignity:—*n.* a small sail above the topgallant sail and under the skysail (see illustration on page 695).

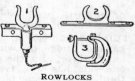

ROWLOCKS
1, swivel; 2, fixed; 3, racing.

roy·al·ism (roi′ăl-ĭzm), *n.* the belief in, and support of, government by a king; also, this form of government.—*n.* **roy′-al·ist.**

roy·al·ly (roi′ăl-ĭ), *adv.* in a grand manner.

roy·al·ty (roi′ăl-tĭ), *n.* [*pl.* royalties], **1,** the station, dignity, etc., of a king; **2,** the king himself; also, any person of sovereign rank; as, *royalty* was present at the theater; **3,** kingly nature or quality; **4,** a tax paid to the crown; **5,** a share of the profits paid to the owner for the use of a property; **6,** a percentage paid to an inventor or author for the use of a patent or copyright; as, *royalties* from the sale of a book.

R.R. abbreviation for *Railroad.*

R.S.F.S.R. or **RSFSR** abbreviation for *Russian Soviet Federated Socialist Republic.*

R.S.V.P. abbreviation for a French phrase meaning *answer if you please; please reply.*

rub (rŭb), *v.t.* [rubbed, rub-bing], **1,** to cause (a surface) to undergo friction and pressure; as, to *rub* one's face with a towel; **2,** to touch with a scraping or brushing movement; as, the wheel *rubbed* my dress; **3,** to cause to move over something with pressure; as, to *rub* the eraser over the paper; **4,** to cleanse or scour by rubbing; as, she *rubbed* the silver with a cloth; **5,** to erase; as, to *rub* out a mark; **6,** to cause to penetrate; spread; as, to *rub* wax on a floor:—*v.i.* **1,** to move along a surface with pressure; scrape; as, two things *rub* together; **2,** to get along with difficulty; as, to *rub* along somehow:—*n.* **1,** the use of friction and pressure upon a surface; a rubbing; as, give the table a good *rub;* 2, that which makes progress difficult; a hindrance; as, what's the *rub?*

¹rub·ber (rŭbّẽr), *n.* 1, one who polishes, erases, massages, or rubs in any way; 2, anything used for erasing, polishing, or the like; as, a *rubber* on a pencil; 3, the prepared, solidified sap from various tropical trees, used for waterproofing, insulating, etc.; caoutchouc: also called *India rubber;* 4, an article made of this, as an overshoe or an elastic band:—*adj.* made of, like, or pertaining to, rubber.

²rub·ber (rŭbّẽr), *n.* specifically, in the game of bridge, the winning of two games out of three; also, the games played until one side has won two; sometimes, the third, decisive game played after each side has won one; hence, generally, any game that breaks a tie.

rub·bish (rŭbّĭsh), *n.* anything valueless; trash.

rub·ble (rŭb'l), *n.* 1, rough, broken stones or bricks; 2, masonry built of them.

Ru·bens (rōōّbĕnz), Peter Paul (1577–1640), a Flemish painter.

Ru·bi·con (rōō'bĭ-kŏn), a small river in northern Italy, flowing into the Adriatic Sea. It formed the northern boundary of ancient Italy. By leading his army over the Rubicon into Italy, against the orders of the Senate, Caesar started a civil war which made him supreme in the Roman Republic:—**to cross the Rubicon,** to take a decided step or a decisive action.

ru·bi·cund (rōō'bĭ-kŭnd), *adj.* inclined to redness; flushed.

ru·ble or **rou·ble** (rōō'bl), *n.* a silver coin, the monetary unit of the U.S.S.R. (See Table, page 943.)

ru·bric (rōō'brĭk), *n.* 1, in a prayer book, the directions for a religious service, formerly printed in red; 2, the title or heading of a law, chapter, etc.

ru·by (rōō'bĭ), *n.* [*pl.* rubies], 1, a precious stone, varying in color from carmine to crimson; 2, the color of the stone.

rud·der (rŭdّẽr), *n.* 1, a broad, flat piece of wood or metal, hinged vertically to the stern of a vessel and used for steering; 2, a similar part in an airplane.—*adj.* **rud'der-less.**

rud·dy (rŭd'ĭ), *adj.* [ruddi-er, rud-di-est], 1, red or reddish; as, a warm, *ruddy* glow; 2, having the color of good health; as, a *ruddy* complexion.

RUDDER
A, rudder; B, tiller.

rude (rōōd), *adj.* [rud-er, rud-est], 1, primitive; uncivilized; as, a *rude* people; 2, impolite; disrespectful; as, *rude* behavior; 3, crude; unskilful; as, a *rude* carving; 4, rough; severe; as, a *rude* awakening.

Syn. uncouth, discourteous, vigorous.

ru·di·ment (rōō'dĭ-mĕnt), *n.* 1, one of the first principles of an art, science, etc.; as, the *rudiments* of algebra; 2, in biology, a part or organ partially developed; as, the *rudiments* of antlers.

ru·di·men·ta·ry (rōō'dĭ-mĕn'tȧ-rĭ), *adj.* 1, elementary; as, *rudimentary* instruction; 2, undeveloped; as, *rudimentary* wings.

¹rue (rōō), *n.* an Old World yellow-flowered plant with strong odor and bitter taste.

²rue (rōō), *v.t.* [rued, ru-ing], to be sorry for; wish undone; as, he shall *rue* his wicked deeds:—*n.* remorse; regret.

rue·ful (rōō'fōōl), *adj.* 1, showing sorrow or pity; sad; as, a *rueful* smile; 2, arousing sorrow; pitiable; as, a *rueful* sight.

ruff (rŭf), *n.* 1, a large pleated or fluted collar, worn in the 16th and 17th centuries; 2, anything like such a collar, as a prominent growth of feathers round the neck of a bird.

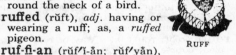

RUFF

ruffed (rŭft), *adj.* having or wearing a ruff; as, a *ruffed* pigeon.

ruf·fi·an (rŭf'ĭ-ăn; rŭf'yăn), *n.* a brutal, lawless fellow; one given to cruel deeds:—*adj.* brutal; cruel.

ruf·fle (rŭf'l), *n.* a pleated or gathered strip of material used as a trimming:—*v.t.* [ruf-fled, ruf-fling], 1, to draw into folds or pleats; 2, to furnish or adorn with pleated or gathered strips; 3, to cause to stand up or out; as, a bird *ruffles* its feathers; 4, to disturb slightly or make ripples upon; as, the wind *ruffled* the pond; 5, to disarrange; disorder (the hair); 6, to annoy or vex:—*v.i.* 1, to form small folds; 2, to become vexed or annoyed.

rug (rŭg), *n.* 1, a heavy floor covering, usually made in one piece and often of a size to cover only part of the floor; 2, a skin or a piece of heavy cloth used as a robe or blanket.

¹Rug·by (rŭg'bĭ), a small city in Warwickshire, central England, famous for its boys' school (map 13).

²Rug·by (rŭg'bĭ), *n.* a game of football developed at Rugby school, in England.

rug·ged (rŭg'ĕd), *adj.* 1, having an uneven surface; rough; as, *rugged* country; also, steep and rocky; as, a *rugged* cliff; 2, crude; plain; as, a *rugged* peasant; 3, hard; austere; harsh; as, a *rugged* character; 4, healthy; strong.—*n.* **rug'ged-ness.**

āte, âorta, râre, căt, àsk, fär, ăllow, sofȧ; ēve, êvent, ĕll, writêr, novĕl; bīte, pĭn; nō, ōbey, ôr, dŏg, tŏp, cŏllide; ūnit, ūnite, bûrn, cŭt, focŭs; nōōn, fŏŏt; mound; coin;

Ruhr (rōōr), a river in western Prussia, flowing into the Rhine. The valley is a center of iron and coal production.

ru·in (rōō'ĭn), *n.* **1,** overthrow; destruction; downfall; as, political *ruin;* also, a cause of destruction; **2, ruins,** the remains of a building destroyed or fallen into decay; as, the *ruins* of an old castle; **3,** the state of decay or desolation:—*v.t.* to pull down, overthrow, or destroy; as, the scandal *ruined* his career.

    Syn., v. deface, demolish.

ru·in·a·tion (rōō'ĭ·nā'shŭn), *n.* destruction; downfall.

ru·in·ous (rōō'ĭ·nŭs), *adj.* **1,** bringing or causing ruin; destructive; as, a *ruinous* war; **2,** dilapidated; as, a barn in a *ruinous* state.—*adv.* **ru'in·ous·ly.**

rule (rōōl), *n.* **1,** a standard or principle of conduct; as, the golden *rule;* school *rules;* an established usage or law, as in arithmetic or grammar; **2,** government; authority; as, a country under foreign *rule;* **3,** usual course of action; as, he works late as a *rule;* **4,** that which may be generally expected; as, scholarship is the *rule* in a university; **5,** a straight-edged strip of wood or metal, marked off in inches, used in drawing lines or measuring:—*v.t.* [ruled, rul-ing], **1,** to govern; as, to *rule* a country; **2,** to guide, influence, or control; as, he was *ruled* by hatred; **3,** to establish by a decision, as does a court; **4,** to mark with lines by the use of a ruler:—*v.i.* **1,** in law, to decide a point; **2,** to exercise superior authority; as, he *ruled* over the country for ten years.

    Syn., v. manage, direct.

rul·er (rōō'lẽr), *n.* **1,** one who governs; as, a wise *ruler;* **2,** a strip of wood, metal, etc., used in drawing lines or in measuring.

rul·ing (rōō'lĭng), *adj.* chief; predominant:—*n.* **1,** a decision laid down by a judge or court; **2,** the act of making lines; also, ruled lines.

¹rum (rŭm), *n.* **1,** a strong, alcoholic liquor made from molasses or the juice of the sugar cane; **2,** any intoxicating drink.

²rum (rŭm), *adj.* [rum-mer, rum-mest], *Slang,* odd; queer.

Ru·ma·ni·a or **Rou·ma·ni·a** (rōō·mā'nĭ·ả), a republic (cap. Bucharest) in southeastern Europe, on the Black Sea (map 12).—*adj.* and *n.* **Ru·ma'ni·an.**

RUMBLE (R), def. 3

rum·ble (rŭm'bl), *n.* **1,** a low, heavy, rolling sound; as, the *rumble* of city traffic; **2,**

a seat for servants at the back of a carriage; **3,** in an automobile, a folding outside seat at the back: also called *rumble seat:*—*v.i.* and *v.t.* [rum-bled, rum-bling], to make, or cause to make, rumbling sounds.

ru·mi·nant (rōō'mĭ·nănt), *n.* any of certain hoofed animals that chew the cud, as oxen, sheep, goats, deer, camels:—*adj.* **1,** chewing the cud; **2,** meditative.

ru·mi·nate (rōō'mĭ·nāt), *v.i.* [ruminat-ed, ruminat-ing], **1,** to chew the cud; **2,** to meditate or muse; reflect; as, to *ruminate* on the future.—*adj.* **ru'mi·na·tive.**

ru·mi·na·tion (rōō'mĭ·nā'shŭn), *n.* **1,** the act or process of chewing the cud; **2,** thoughtful meditation; as, he gave much time to *rumination* on past events.

rum·mage (rŭm'ĭj), *n.* a thorough search made by turning things over in a disorderly way:—*v.t.* [rummaged, rummaging], to search thoroughly by turning over the contents of; ransack:—*v.i.* to make a thorough but disorderly search; as, to *rummage* in a closet.

rummage sale, a sale of unclaimed or secondhand goods, odds and ends, etc.

rum·my (rŭm'ĭ), *n.* **1,** a kind of card game; **2,** [*pl.* rummies], *Slang,* a drunkard:—*adj.* [rum-mi-er, rum-mi-est], *Slang,* queer; odd.

ru·mor (rōō'mẽr), *n.* **1,** talk; hearsay; **2,** a current story that has not been verified; as, a *rumor* of strikes:—*v.t.* to spread by report. In British usage, **ru'mour.**

rump (rŭmp), *n.* the hind part of an animal; the buttocks; also, a cut of beef from this part. (See illustration under *beef.*)

rum·ple (rŭm'pl), *n.* a wrinkle or crease:—*v.t.* and *v.i.* [rum-pled, rum-pling], to wrinkle; muss; as, to *rumple* cloth.

rum·pus (rŭm'pŭs), *n. Colloquial,* a disturbance; row; brawl.

run (rŭn), *v.i.* [*p.t.* ran (răn), *p.p.* run, *p.pr.* run-ning], **1,** to go on the feet at a speed faster than a walk; depart suddenly; **2,** to hurry; rush; as, he *ran* through his work too fast; **3,** to travel; proceed; as, the express *runs* 60 miles an hour; **4,** to make regular trips; as, a bus *runs* between New York and Boston; **5,** to move in a stream; flow, as a river; **6,** to act; be in action; operate; as, the engine will not *run;* **7,** to extend; be placed; as, a path *runs* round the house; **8,** to become unfastened; ravel; as, a thread *runs* in a stocking; **9,** to engage in a contest; be a competitor; as, to *run* for office; **10,** to climb; creep; trail; as, the vine *runs* along the wall; **11,** to be written or related; as, so the story *runs;* **12,** to spread or dissolve; as, dye *runs;* **13,** to discharge a fluid; ooze;

---

as, the nose *runs;* a sore *runs:—v.t.* **1,** *Colloquial,* to cause to move or operate; as, to *run* an engine; to *run* a theater; **2,** to thrust; stick; as, to *run* a pin into one's finger; **3,** to drive or dash forcibly; as, to *run* one's head against a wall; **4,** to do by running; as, to *run* errands; **5,** to go through (some danger) successfully; as, to *run* a blockade; **6,** to expose oneself to; as, to *run* a risk; **7,** to permit to mount up, as debts; **8,** to sew with small, even stitches; as, to *run* a seam:—*n.* **1,** the act or power of going at a pace swifter than a walk; **2,** a trip or journey; progress; as, the boat made its usual *run;* **3,** the act of flowing or that which flows; as, a *run* of maple sap; **4,** a course or succession; repetition; as, a *run* of ill luck; **5,** the average kind; as, the *run* of workers; **6,** a place passed over frequently by animals; also, an enclosed place for animals; **7,** a herd of animals or school of fish moving together; **8,** a period of operation; as, the play had a year's *run;* **9,** sudden and pressing demand; as, a *run* on a bank; **10,** in baseball, cricket, etc., the unit of scoring, made by running once over a specified course; **11,** a brook; **12,** *Colloquial,* free use or enjoyment; as, the *run* of a friend's house.

run down, 1, to cease going, as a clock; **2,** to knock down, as with an automobile; **3,** to pursue and catch; as, to *run down* a thief; **4,** to speak against; **5,** to weaken, or be weak, as in health; **run out of,** to reach the end of a supply of; use up; **run through, 1,** to use quickly and wastefully, as a fortune; **2,** to inspect rapidly, as a book; **3,** to stab or pierce, as with a sword.

run·a·bout (rŭn′a·bout′), *n.* **1,** a light, open automobile or carriage; **2,** a light motorboat; **3,** one who gads about.

run·a·gate (rŭn′a·gāt), *n.* **1,** a fugitive; **2,** a wanderer; vagabond.

run·a·way (rŭn′a·wā′), *n.* **1,** one who escapes; a fugitive; **2,** the act of escaping; also, a horse of which the driver has lost control:—*adj.* **1,** out of control; as, a *runaway* engine; **2,** brought about by eloping; as, a *runaway* wedding.

rune (rōōn), *n.* **1,** a letter of the earliest Teutonic alphabet, dating from the second century, used by the Scandinavians and Anglo-Saxons; **2,** a magic mark or a mysterious saying or verse.

¹**rung** (rŭng), past participle of *ring.*

²**rung** (rŭng), *n.* a crosspiece or round of a ladder or a chair.

run·let (rŭn′lĕt) or **run·nel** (rŭn′ĕl), *n.* a rill or brook.

run·ner (rŭn′ẽr), *n.* **1,** one who runs, as a racer, a messenger, or the like; **2,** one of

the long, narrow pieces on which a sleigh, skate, or sled moves; **3,** a long strip of linen or carpet; **4,** a vertical rip in a stocking; **5,** a slender, trailing branch that takes root at the end or at the joints; also, a plant that spreads in this way.

run·ning (rŭn′ĭng), *n.* **1,** the act of moving swiftly; **2,** the power or ability to run, as of machinery; **3,** management; as, the *running* of an office:—*adj.* **1,** moving swiftly; **2,**

RUNNERS OF STRAWBERRY PLANT

a, original plant; *b,* runner; *c,* new plant.

being in operation or action; **3,** successive; continuous; as, two days *running;* **4,** discharging pus; as, a *running* ear.

running board, a narrow step along the side of a vehicle; **running gear,** the wheels, axles, etc., of a vehicle, as distinct from the body; **running knot,** a slipknot; a knot tied to slip along the string, rope, or cord in which it is tied (see illustration at *knot*); **running noose,** a slipknot; **in the running,** with a good chance to win; **out of the running,** with no chance to win.

Run·ny·mede (rŭn′ĭ-mēd), a meadow on the Thames in Surrey, England, where King John signed the Magna Charta, June 15, 1215.

runt (rŭnt), *n.* **1,** any undersized animal; especially, the smallest and weakest of a litter; **2,** a person of stunted growth.

run·way (rŭn′wā′), *n.* **1,** a beaten way or path along which animals pass; **2,** a track, as for the take-off of airplanes; **3,** a fenced place; as, a *runway* for dogs.

ru·pee (rōō-pē′), *n.* the monetary unit of the Union of India and of Pakistan.

ru·pi·ah (rōō-pē′a), *n.* the monetary unit of Indonesia. (See table, page 943.)

rup·ture (rŭp′tũr), *n.* **1,** a bursting or breaking apart; **2,** the state of being broken or violently burst apart; **3,** a breach or an interruption of friendly relations; **4,** a hernia:—*v.t.* [ruptured, ruptur-ing], **1,** to burst violently apart; **2,** to cause a hernia to; **3,** to bring about a breach of (friendship):—*v.i.* to suffer a breach or break.

ru·ral (rōōr′ăl), *adj.* pertaining to, or like, the country or country life:—**rural delivery,** mail delivery in country districts, formerly called *rural free delivery.*

Rus. or **Russ.** abbreviation for *Russia, Russian.*

ruse (rōōz), *n.* a trick; fraud or deceit.

¹**rush** (rŭsh), *n.* any of certain plants growing in wet ground, having long hollow stems which are used for caning chairs.

R

R

RUNGS (R, R) OF A LADDER

²**rush** (rŭsh), *v.i.* **1,** to move with great speed; press forward with violent haste; **2,** to act with extraordinary haste or eagerness; as, to *rush* through one's work:— *v.t.* **1,** to cause to move or act with great speed; hurry; as, to *rush* an order; **2,** to make an attack on and occupy; as, to *rush* a fortification:— *n.* **1,** a driving forward with eagerness and haste; **2,** a sudden migration; as, a gold *rush;* **3,** *Colloquial,* extraordinary activity; as, the Christmas *rush:*— *adj.* requiring haste; as, a *rush* job.

rusk (rŭsk), *n.* a kind of sweetened bread baked until it is crisp and dry; also, a kind of sweetened raised biscuit.

Rus-kin (rŭs´kĭn), John (1819–1900), an English essayist and art critic.

rus-set (rŭs´ĕt), *n.* **1,** a reddish-brown color; **2,** cloth, especially homespun, of such color; **3,** a kind of winter apple:— *adj.* reddish brown in color.

Rus-sia (rŭsh´à), a former empire (cap. Saint Petersburg) in Eastern Europe and northern and western Asia, whose territory corresponded closely to that of the present Union of Soviet Socialist Republics, or U.S.S.R.:— **Soviet Russia** or **Russian Soviet Federated Socialist Republic** (R.S.F.S.R.), the largest republic (cap. Moscow) in the U.S.S.R. (map 12). See **Union of Soviet Socialist Republics.**

Rus-sian (rŭsh´ăn), *n.* a native or inhabitant of Russia; also, the language of Russia:— *adj.* pertaining to Russia, its language, or its people.

rust (rŭst), *n.* **1,** the reddish matter formed on iron and steel and some other metals through exposure to air; red oxide of iron; **2,** anything like rust, as mildew on wheat, corn, etc.:— *v.i.* **1,** to form rust; **2,** to grow worthless because of idleness:— *v.t.* to cause to rust.

rus-tic (rŭs´tĭk), *n.* a person reared in the country, especially one who is unpolished:— *adj.* **1,** relating to the country; **2,** simple; artless; **3,** awkward; crude.

   Syn., adj. rude, plain, uncouth, coarse.

rus-tic-i-ty (rŭs-tĭs´ĭ-tĭ), *n.* [*pl.* rusticities], the quality of being rustic; homely or countrylike manners; awkwardness.

rus-tle (rŭs´l), *n.* a soft, crackling sound, such as that made by leaves:— *v.i.* [rustled, rus-tling], to make a soft, crackling sound, as taffeta when moved:— *v.t.* **1,** to cause to make such a sound; **2,** to steal (cattle).— *n.* **rus´tler.**

rust-y (rŭs´tĭ), *adj.* [rust-i-er, rust-i-est], **1,** covered with rust; **2,** harmed by inactivity or idleness, as an engine; hence, out of practice; behind the times.— *adv.* **rust´i-ly.** — *n.* **rust´i-ness.**

rut (rŭt), *n.* **1,** a hollow track or groove made by a wheel; **2,** a fixed habit:— *v.t.* [rut-ted, rut-ting], to cut into hollows; make wheel tracks in.— *adj.* **rut´ty.**

ru-ta-ba-ga (rōō´tà-bā´gà), *n.* a large, yellow turnip, used as food.

Ruth (rōōth), *n.* in the Bible, a book of the Old Testament; also, its heroine.

Ru-the-ni-a (rōō-thē´nĭ-à), a region in southwestern U.S.S.R., formerly in Czechoslovakia.

ruth-less (rōōth´lĕs), *adj.* cruel; without mercy; savage; as, a *ruthless* fighter.— *adv.* **ruth´less-ly.**

Rut-land (rŭt´lănd), a city in western Vermont, noted for its marble quarries (map 6).

R.V. abbreviation for *Revised Version* (of the Bible).

Ry. abbreviation for *Railway.*

rye (rī), *n.* a hardy cereal plant closely related to wheat; also, its seed, used in making bread and whisky.

RYE

S

S, s (ĕs), *n.* [*pl.* S's, s's], **1,** the 19th letter of the alphabet; **2,** anything having the shape of an S.

S. abbreviation for *Saint, South.*

s. abbreviation for *second* or *seconds, shilling* or *shillings.*

S.A. abbreviation for *Salvation Army, South America, South Africa.*

Saar Ba-sin (zär), a small territory of southwestern Germany, famous for its coal and iron mines, governed from 1919 to 1935 by the League of Nations, now governed internationally.

Sab-bath (săb´àth), *n.* **1,** the seventh day of the week, observed by the Jews and certain others as a day of rest, commencing at sunset on Friday and ending at sunset on Saturday; **2,** the Christian Sunday, or first day of the week, observed as a day of rest and worship.

sab-bat-i-cal (să-băt´ĭ-kăl) or **sab-bat-ic** (să-băt´ĭk), *adj.* pertaining to, or like, the Sabbath; as, *sabbatical* peace:— **sabbatical year,** every seventh year; especially, a year or half year granted to a teacher or professor for study or rest after six consecutive years of service.

go; join; yet; sing; chin; show; thin, *th*en; hw, *wh*y; zh, *a*zure; ü, Ger. für or Fr. l*u*ne; ö, Ger. schön or Fr. f*eu*; ṅ, Fr. e*n*fant, no*m*; kh, Ger. a*ch* or i*ch*. See pages ix-x.

sa·ber or **sa·bre** (sā′bēr), *n.* a cavalry sword with a curved blade:—*v.t.* to cut down with a saber.

Sa·bine (sā′bīn), *n.* one of an ancient tribe in Italy conquered by the Romans.—*adj.* **Sa′bine.**

sa·ble (sā′bl), *n.* **1,** a small flesh-eating animal valued for its handsome, dark fur; **2,** the fur of this animal:—*adj.* **1,** made of the fur of the sable; as, a *sable* coat: **2,** very dark; black; as, *sable* night.

sa·bot (sȧ′bō′; săb′ō), *n.* **1,** a wooden shoe worn by peasants; **2,** a shoe with a leather top and a wooden sole.

sab·o·tage (săb′ō-täzh′; săb′ō-tĭj), *n.* **1,** the wilful damaging or destroying of machinery or materials by workmen during labor troubles; **2,** similar interference with government activities in time of war or emergency.

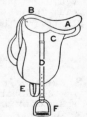
SABER

sac (săk), *n.* a baglike part of a plant or an animal, often containing a fluid.

sac·cha·rin (săk′ȧ-rĭn) or **sac·cha·rine** (săk′ȧ-rĭn; săk′ȧ-rēn), *n.* a white crystalline product of coal tar, very much sweeter than cane sugar. It is used as a substitute for sugar by diabetics.

SABOTS
1, wood; 2, leather.

sac·cha·rine (săk′ȧ-rĭn; săk′ȧ-rīn), *adj.* containing sugar; also, very sweet.

sac·er·do·tal (săs′ēr-dō′tăl), *adj.* pertaining to priests; as, *sacerdotal* privileges.

sa·chem (sā′chĕm), *n.* a North American Indian chief of highest rank.

sa·chet (să-shā′), *n.* a small bag or cushion filled with a perfume in the form of powder; also, the powder itself.

¹sack (săk), *n.* **1,** a bag; especially, a large coarse bag open at one end, for holding grain, potatoes, etc.; **2,** a sackful; as, a *sack* of sugar; **3,** (often *sacque*), a loose jacket worn by women and children; **4,** *Slang,* dismissal; as, to get the *sack:*—*v.t.* to put into a bag.—*n.* **sack′ful.**

²sack (săk), *n.* the plundering by soldiers of a town taken in war; as, the *sack* of Rome by the Vandals:—*v.t.* **1,** to plunder or pillage; ravage; **2,** to rob; ransack.

³sack (săk), *n.* any of several dry, white wines, originally imported from Spain.

sack·cloth (săk′klôth′), *n.* **1,** a coarse material of which sacks are made; **2,** a coarse, rough cloth worn in ancient times as a token of mourning or repentance.

sack coat, a man's short, loose coat.

sack·ing (săk′ĭng), *n.* coarse materials used for making sacks or bags.

sacque (săk), *n.* a loose jacket worn by women and children; a sack.

sac·ra·ment (săk′rȧ-mĕnt), *n.* **1,** a religious act or ceremony regarded as an outward, visible sign of inward, spiritual grace, as baptism and the Eucharist, or Lord's Supper; **2,** (also *Sacrament*), the consecrated elements of the Eucharist.—*adj.* **sac′ra·men′tal.**

Sac·ra·men·to (săk′rȧ-mĕn′tō), a city, capital of California (map 9).

sa·cred (sā′krĕd), *adj.* **1,** set apart for religious uses; consecrated; holy; as, a *sacred* edifice; **2,** pertaining to religion; as, *sacred* literature; **3,** to be treated with reverence; not to be violated; as, a *sacred* trust.
Syn. hallowed, divine, inviolable.

sac·ri·fice (săk′rĭ-fīs; săk′rĭ-fīz), *n.* **1,** the act of presenting an offering to God or to a god; **2,** that which is offered; anything offered or consecrated to God; **3,** the giving up of something in order to gain something else; as, the *sacrifice* of leisure time for money; also, self-sacrifice; **4,** a price below cost; as, the house sold at a *sacrifice:*—*v.t.* (săk′rĭ-fīz; săk′rĭ-fīs), [sacrificed, sacrific-ing], **1,** to offer to God or to a god; **2,** to give up for the sake of some other person or object; as, to *sacrifice* health for riches; **3,** to sell at a loss:—*v.i.* to offer up a sacrifice.—*adj.* **sac′ri·fi′cial** (săk′rĭ-fĭsh′ăl).

sac·ri·le·gious (săk′rĭ-lē′jŭs; săk′rĭ-lĭj′ŭs), *adj.* treating sacred things irreverently; profane.—*n.* **sac′ri·lege.**

sac·ris·ty (săk′rĭs-tĭ), *n.* [*pl.* sacristies], the room in a church where the sacred vessels, the minister's robes, etc., are kept; a vestry.

sac·ro·sanct (săk′rō-săngkt), *adj.* very sacred; most holy.

sad (săd), *adj.* [sad-der, sad-dest], **1,** full of grief; mournful; doleful; **2,** causing mournfulness; as, a *sad* event.—*adv.* **sad′ly.**—*n.* **sad′ness.**
Syn. downcast, melancholy, depressed.

sad·den (săd′n), *v.t.* and *v.i.* to make or become mournful or sorrowful.

sad·dle (săd′l), *n.* **1,** a padded leather seat for a rider on horseback; also, the seat of a bicycle; **2,** the part of a horse's harness which rests on the horse's back; **3,** anything shaped like a saddle, as a cut of meat consisting of the

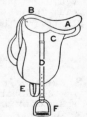
SADDLE
A, seat; B, pommel; C, flap; D, stirrup strap; E, girth; F, stirrup.

two loins; **4,** a ridge between two hills or summits:—*v.t.* [sad-dled, sad-dling], **1,** to equip with a seat for a rider; **2,** to burden or embarrass; as, to be *saddled* with debt.

sad-dle-bag (săd'l-băg'), *n.* one of a pair of bags or pouches attached to a saddle, for carrying small articles.

sad-dle-bow (săd'l-bō'), *n.* the pommel, or front part, of a saddle.

sad-dler (săd'lẽr), *n.* one whose business it is to make and repair saddles and harness.

¹**safe** (sāf), *adj.* [saf-er, saf-est], **1,** free from danger or harm; as, *safe* and sound; **2,** out of danger; secure; as, the soldier was *safe* from pursuit; **3,** incapable of doing injury or harm; securely kept, as a prisoner; **4,** reliable; trustworthy; involving no risk of loss; as, a *safe* investment.—*adv.* **safe′ly.** —*n.* **safe′ness.**

²**safe** (sāf), *n.* a steel chest, usually fireproof or burglar-proof, specially designed for safeguarding money and other valuables.

safe—con-duct (sāf′-kŏn′dŭkt), *n.* safe passage through an enemy's country in time of war; also, the passport or pass guaranteeing safe passage.

safe-guard (sāf′gärd′), *n.* a person or thing that guards or protects; a means of security; defense; as, traffic lights are a *safeguard* for both pedestrians and motorists: —*v.t.* to protect or defend.

SAFE

safe-keep-ing (sāf′kēp′ĭng), *n.* care; protection.

safe-ty (sāf′tĭ), *n.* freedom from danger, injury, or damage; security:—*adj.* protecting against accident or injury; as, *safety* devices.

safety valve, a valve which permits steam to escape from a boiler when the pressure reaches a certain danger point.

saf-fron (săf′rŭn), *n.* **1,** a purple-flowered, fall-booming species of crocus; **2,** the yellow color obtained from the dried stigmas of this plant, used as a dye and in medicine; **3,** a deep-yellow color:—*adj.* deep yellow.

S.Afr. abbreviation for *South Africa.*

sag (săg), *v.i.* [sagged, sag-ging], **1,** to sink or droop in the middle, from weight or pressure; as, the wire *sags;* **2,** to lean to one side; become lopsided; as, the door *sags;* **3,** to lose firmness; weaken; as, his spirits *sagged:*—*n.* the fact or the extent of sinking or drooping under weight or pressure; as, the *sag* of a door.

sa-ga (sä′gȧ; sā′gȧ), *n.* **1,** in medieval Scandinavian literature, a realistic prose story of heroic deeds, historical, legendary, or mythical, centering about one or more heroes or about one family; **2,** hence, any narrative, prose, or verse, celebrating heroic deeds.

sa-ga-cious (sȧ-gā′shŭs), *adj.* having good judgment; shrewd; as, a *sagacious* ruler.

sa-gac-i-ty (sȧ-găs′ĭ-tĭ), *n.* keen and sound judgment; shrewdness.

sag-a-more (săg′ȧ-môr), *n.* among certain North American Indian tribes, a chief.

¹**sage** (sāj), *adj.* [sag-er, sag-est], wise; shrewd:—*n.* an extremely wise man.

²**sage** (sāj), *n.* **1,** a plant of the mint family, whose spicy, dull-green leaves are used for flavoring meats, soups, etc.; **2,** the American sagebrush.

sage-brush (sāj′brŭsh′), *n.* a low shrub of the plains of the western U.S.

Sag-i-naw (săg′ĭ-nô), a city on the Saginaw River, in east central Michigan (map **7**).

sa-go (sā′gō), *n.* [*pl.* sagos], **1,** a powdered starch used in puddings, soups, etc., obtained from the pith of certain East Indian palms; **2,** a palm tree from which sago is made: also called *sago palm.*

SAGEBRUSH

Sa-ha-ra (sȧ-hä′rȧ; sȧ-hâr′ȧ), a desert region in northern Africa (map **14**).

Sa-hib (sä′ĭb), *n.* lord; master; sir: a word always used by the natives of India when addressing or referring to a European gentleman or a titled Indian.

said (sĕd), past tense and past participle of *say:*—*adj.* already referred to; mentioned before; as, the *said* John Jones.

sail (sāl), *n.* **1,** a sheet of canvas or cloth which is rigged to the masts and spars of a vessel and extended to catch the wind; **2,** all the sails of a ship; as, under full *sail;* **3,** (*pl.* sail), any ship; as, a squadron of 50 *sail;* **4,** an excursion in a sailboat; as, we went for a *sail;* **5,** anything resembling a sail, as the arms of a windmill:—*v.i.* **1,** to be driven or propelled by the force of the wind upon spread canvas; **2,** hence, to go by water; as, we *sailed* to Liverpool; **3,** to begin a voyage; as, the ship *sailed* at noon; **4,** to glide smoothly;

SAGO
A, fruit.

as, the eagle *sailed* through the air:—*v.t.*
1, to pass over in a ship; as, to *sail* the
seas; **2,** to navigate or steer (a ship).

sail-boat (sāl′bōt′), *n.* a boat provided
with a sail or sails.

sail-fish (sāl′fĭsh′), *n.* a large game fish with
a large sail-like dorsal fin. As in the sword-
fish, its upper
jaw lengthens out
into a swordlike
projection.

sail-or (sāl′ẽr), *n.*

SAILFISH (⅓₀)

1, a member of
the crew of a ves-
sel; a seaman; **2,** a straw hat with a flat
brim and crown:—**good sailor,** a person
who does not get seasick.

saint (sānt), *n.* **1,** a person
of exceptionally upright or
holy life; **2,** one of the
blessed in heaven; **3,** in the
Roman Catholic Church, an
exceptionally godly person,
who, after death, is de-
clared holy by the church:
—*v.t.* to canonize; declare
officially to be a saint.

SAILOR, def. 2

Saint Au-gus-tine (ô′gŭs-tēn′), a seaport and health resort in northeastern
Florida (map **8**). Founded by the Spaniards in 1565, it is the oldest town in the U.S.

¹**Saint Ber-nard** (bẽr-närd′; săn′-
bâr′når′), either of two mountain passes
in the Alps; especially, the Great Saint
Bernard Pass, noted for its hospice founded by Saint Bernard, from which the Saint
Bernard dogs are sent to rescue travelers.

²**Saint Ber-nard** (bẽr-närd′), a large,
powerful dog, formerly bred chiefly at a
hospice at Great Saint Bernard Pass in the
Swiss Alps. These dogs are famous for
rescuing lost travelers.

Saint Croix (kroi), one of the Virgin
Islands. See **Virgin Islands.**

saint-ed (sān′tĕd), *adj.* **1,** pious; also,
sacred; holy; **2,** canonized.

Saint–É-tienne (săn′-tā′tyĕn′), a city in
southeastern France (map **12**).

Saint Got-thard (gŏt′ẽrd; gŏth′ẽrd; sân′-
gô′tår′), **1,** a mountain range of the Alps
in south central Switzerland; **2,** a pass
over this range; also, the nine-mile tunnel
under the pass.

Saint He-le-na (hĕ-lē′nå), a British island
in the South Atlantic, west of Angola,
Africa, on which Napoleon was exiled
from 1815 until his death in 1821 (map **14**).

Saint John (jŏn), one of the Virgin Islands. See **Virgin Islands.**

Saint John's (jŏnz), a seaport city, capital of Newfoundland (map **4**).

Saint Jo-seph (jō′zĕf), a city in northwestern Missouri, on the Missouri River
(map **7**).

Saint Law-rence (lô′rĕns), a river flowing from Lake Ontario into the Gulf of
Saint Lawrence:—**Gulf of Saint Lawrence,** an inlet of the Atlantic Ocean,
between Canada and Newfoundland.
(Map **3**.)

Saint Lou-is (lōō′ĭs; lōō′ĭ), the chief
city of Missouri, on the Mississippi
River (map **7**).

saint-ly (sānt′lĭ), *adj.* [saint-li-er, saint-
li-est], godly; pious; befitting a saint.—*n.*
saint′li-ness.

Saint Nich-o-las (nĭk′ô-lås), **1,** a bishop
of Asia Minor in the fourth century; **2,**
the legendary bringer of Christmas gifts;
Santa Claus.

Saint Paul (pôl), a city, capital of Minnesota, on the Mississippi River (map **7**).

Saint Pe-ters-burg (pē′tẽrz-bûrg), the
capital of the former Russian Empire.
See **Leningrad.**

Saint Thom-as (tŏm′ås), one of the
Virgin Islands (cap. Charlotte Amalie). See
Virgin Islands.

Saint Val-en-tine's Day (văl′ĕn-tīnz),
February 14, the day on which anonymous love letters or tokens are sent.

Saint Vi-tus's dance (vī′tŭs-ĕz), a nervous disease characterized by involuntary
twitchings of the muscles.

saith (sĕth), *Archaic* or *Poetic,* a form of
says.

sake (sāk), *n.* **1,** purpose; cause; as, for
the *sake* of argument; **2,** one's own welfare
or the welfare of others; as, for my own
sake; for my country's *sake.*

sa-laam or **sa-lam** (så-läm′), *n.* **1,** an
Oriental greeting, meaning "Peace"; **2,** a
low formal bow:—*v.i.* to make a low formal
bow:—*v.t.* to greet with such a bow.

sal-a-ble (sāl′å-bl), *adj.* capable of being
sold; easily sold; as, a *salable* commodity.
Also spelled **sale′a-ble.**—*n.* **sal′a-ble-ness.**
—*n.* **sal′a-bil′i-ty.**

sa-la-cious (så-lā′shŭs), *adj.* lewd; indecent.—*adv.* **sa-la′cious-ly.**—*n.* **sa-la′-
cious-ness.**

sal-ad (săl′åd), *n.* a cold dish, as of lettuce
with vegetables, fruit, meat, fish, or the
like, mixed with, or covered by, dressing.

Sal-a-din (săl′å-dĭn), (1137–1193), a sultan of Egypt and Syria, the Mohammedan
leader against whom the Crusaders under
Richard I of England took the field.

sal-a-man-der (săl′å-măn′dẽr), *n.* **1,** a
small, lizardlike but scaleless, animal living

in water or damp places: formerly fabled to live unharmed in fire; **2,** hence, one who can bear intense heat.

Sal·a·mis (săl′á-mĭs), a small island off the coast of Greece, where the Greeks defeated the Persians under Xerxes in 480 B.C. (map **1**). Its modern name is *Kouloure*.

SALAMANDER (!)

sal·a·ried (săl′á-rĭd), *adj.* receiving a stated amount in pay; on a salary; as, a *salaried* accountant.

sal·a·ry (săl′á-rĭ), *n.* [*pl.* salaries], a regular, periodic payment for services; as, teachers receive a monthly *salary*.
Syn. wage, hire, pay, compensation, stipend.

sale (sāl), *n.* **1,** the act of selling; the exchange of a commodity or goods for an agreed price; as, to arrange for the *sale* of a house; **2,** a disposal of goods at a reduced price, by auction or in some other special way; as, the store is holding its annual *sale*; **3,** a chance to dispose of goods; a demand for goods; as, there is a great *sale* for toys at Christmas.

sale·a·ble (sāl′á-bl), *adj.* capable of being sold; salable. See **salable.**

Sa·lem (sā′lĕm), **1,** an old seaport city of Massachusetts (map **6**); **2,** a city, capital of Oregon (map **9**).

sal·e·ra·tus (săl′ĕ-rā′tŭs), *n.* sodium bicarbonate; baking soda.

sales·man (sālz′măn), *n.* [*pl.* salesmen (-mĕn)], a man whose business it is to sell goods.—*n.fem.* **sales′wom′an.**

sales·man·ship (sālz′măn-shĭp), *n.* skill or success in selling.

sa·li·ent (sā′lĭ-ĕnt), *adj.* outstanding; noticeable; as, the *salient* feature of a face; the *salient* point of an argument.

sa·line (sā′līn), *adj.* **1,** consisting of, or containing, salt; as, a *saline* solution; **2,** salty; as, a *saline* taste:—*n.* **1,** a salt spring, lake, etc.; **2,** any salty substance.

Salis·bur·y (sôlz′bĕr′ĭ; sôlz′bĕr-ĭ), a cathedral town of southern England (map **13**).

sa·li·va (sá-lī′vá), *n.* the watery fluid secreted by the salivary glands and discharged into the mouth; spit.

sal·i·var·y (săl′ĭ-vĕr′ĭ), *adj.* pertaining to saliva or to the glands secreting it.

sal·low (săl′ō), *adj.* of a pale, sickly yellow color; as, the *sallow* complexion of a confined invalid.—*n.* **sal′low-ness.**

sal·ly (săl′ĭ), *n.* [*pl.* sallies], **1,** a sudden rushing forth of troops from a fortified place to attack the enemy; **2,** a sudden outburst of wit or fancy; as, his *sally* made the crowd laugh:—*v.i.* [sallied, sally-ing], **1,** to rush out, as troops from a besieged town; **2,** to set out, as on a pleasure trip.

salm·on (săm′ŭn), *n.* [*pl.* salmon], **1,** a silver-scaled, salt-water or fresh-water fish, prized as a game and food fish; **2,** the orange-pink color of cooked salmon flesh:—*adj.* of an orange-pink color.

SALMON (¹⁄₂₀)

sa·lon (sá-lôn′), *n.* [*pl.* salons (sá-lôn′; sá-lônz′)], **1,** a large reception room; **2,** a group of distinguished persons who meet from time to time for discussions or social intercourse; **3,** an art gallery; also, the paintings or sculpture exhibited there.

Sa·lo·ni·ka (sä′lō-nē′ká), a seaport in northern Greece (map **12**). Its Greek name is *Thessalonikē*.

sa·loon (sá-lōon′), *n.* **1,** a large room or apartment in a hotel or on a steamship, often elaborately decorated and used for exhibitions, receptions, etc.; as, a dining *saloon*; **2,** in the U.S., a tavern or barroom where liquors are sold.

sal·si·fy (săl′sĭ-fĭ), *n.* a plant grown for its oyster-flavored root, which is used as a vegetable: also called *oyster plant*.

sal so·da (săl′ sō′dá), sodium carbonate; washing soda. Also written **sal′so′da.**

salt (sôlt), *n.* **1,** a white, crystalline substance found in sea water, mineral springs, etc., and used universally for seasoning foods and preserving meats; **2,** anything which, like salt, gives flavor or character; savor; **3,** in chemistry, a compound, generally crystalline, formed by the union of an acid with a base; **4, salts,** in medicine, a substance resembling salt, used as a cathartic; **5,** *Colloquial,* a sailor:—*adj.* **1,** flavored or seasoned with salt; **2,** preserved with salt; **3,** growing in salt water; as, *salt* weed:—*v.t.* **1,** to preserve with salt; as, to *salt* meat; **2,** to sprinkle or season with salt; **3,** to furnish with salt; as, to *salt* cattle.—*adj.* **salt′y.**—*n.* **salt′i-ness.**

salt·cel·lar (sôlt′sĕl′ẽr), *n.* a dish or shaker used on the table to hold salt.

Sal·til·lo (säl-tēl′yō), a city in northeastern Mexico (map **10**).

Salt Lake Cit·y, a city, capital of Utah, in western U.S. (map **9**).

salt lick, a place where natural salt is found on the surface of the earth, and where animals satisfy their craving for salt.

salt·pe·ter (sôlt′pē′tẽr), *n.* a white, crystalline compound used in making gunpowder and matches, and in preserving foods.

sa-lu-bri-ous (sȧ-lū′brĭ-ŭs), *adj.* healthful; promoting health; as, a *salubrious* climate.—*adv.* **sa-lu′bri-ous-ly.**

sal-u-ta-tion (săl′ū-tā′shŭn), *n.* the act or manner of addressing or greeting another; also, the words or the gestures used.

sa-lute (sȧ-lūt′), *n.* **1**, a greeting; **2**, a gesture, bow, or the like, expressing welcome, respect, etc.; **3**, in the army and navy, a gesture or position prescribed for respectful recognition of a superior officer, consisting of raising the fingers to the cap; also, the discharge of cannon, the lowering and raising again of a flag, etc., as a mark of honor:—*v.t.* [salut-ed, salut-ing], **1**, to address with words or gestures of greeting; **2**, in the army and navy, to honor or receive with an official salute or with a formal demonstration, as a discharge of guns, the lowering of a flag, etc.; as, the private *saluted* the captain; the fleet *saluted* the President with a discharge of 21 guns:—*v.i.* to make a gesture of respect.

SALUTES
1, British; 2, American.

Sal-va-dor (săl′vȧ-dôr), a commercial seaport in eastern Brazil, formerly called Bahia (map **11**).

Sal-va-dor, El (ĕl săl′vȧ-dôr; ĕl säl′vä-thôr′), a republic (cap. San Salvador) in the northwestern part of Central America (map **10**).

sal-vage (săl′vĭj), *n.* **1**, the act of saving a ship or goods from the sea, from a wreck, from a fire, etc.; **2**, the ship or the goods so saved; **3**, payment given to those who help to save property under such circumstances:—*v.t.* [salvaged, salvag-ing], to save (a ship or goods) from destruction.

sal-va-tion (săl-vā′shŭn), *n.* **1**, the act of saving; rescue; **2**, the setting free of the soul from sin and from eternal punishment; **3**, that which saves or rescues; as, a raft was their *salvation* from the sea.

Sal-va-tion Ar-my, a religious body, organized for the purpose of relieving poverty and giving spiritual comfort.

salve (săv), *n.* **1**, an ointment or greasy mixture, used for the relief and healing of wounds and sores on the skin; **2**, anything that calms, soothes, or pacifies; as, the *salve* of kindness heals many hurts:—*v.t.* [salved, salv-ing], to soothe; as, the compliment *salved* his wounded pride.

sal-ver (săl′vĕr), *n.* a tray on which anything is served or presented.

sal-vi-a (săl′vĭ-ȧ), *n.* a plant of the mint family grown for its showy, scarlet flowers.

sal-vo (săl′vō), *n.* [*pl.* salvos or salvoes], **1**, the simultaneous firing of a number of guns; **2**, the loud cheers of a crowd.

S.Am. or **S.Amer.** abbreviation for *South America, South American.*

Sa-mar-i-a (sȧ-mâr′ĭ-ȧ), a district in Palestine; also, a city, its capital.

Sa-mar-i-tan (sȧ-măr′ĭ-tăn), *n.* a native or inhabitant of Samaria, the central district of ancient Palestine:—**Good Samaritan**, **1**, in the Bible, a character in one of the parables of the New Testament, rescuer of a Jew who had been beaten and robbed, and had been left helpless by a priest and a Levite; **2**, hence, a person willing to aid those in distress.

SALVIA

same (sām), *adj.* **1**, being one; identical; as, he goes to the *same* school as his sister; **2**, similar in kind or quality; as, suits of the *same* cloth; **3**, equal; as, the *same* distance; **4**, just mentioned; as, these *same* words:—*pron.* the identical person or thing; as, give me more of the *same.*

same-ness (sām′nĕs), *n.* **1**, the condition of being exactly alike; similarity; as, the *sameness* of the writing proves that one person wrote both notes; **2**, monotony; as, the *sameness* of the work wearied him.

Sa-mo-a (sä-mō′ȧ), a group of islands in the Pacific, northeast of Australia (map **16**).

Sa-mo-an (sȧ-mō′ăn), *adj.* pertaining to the Samoa Islands, or to their inhabitants:—*n.* **1**, a native of Samoa; **2**, the language of the people of Samoa.

sam-o-var (săm′ō-vär; săm′ō-vär′), *n.* a metal vessel of Russian origin, with a heating tube through the center, used to heat water for making tea.

SAMOVAR

samp (sămp), *n.* hulled, crushed Indian corn; coarse hominy.

SAMPAN

sam-pan (săm′păn), *n.* a flat-bottomed boat, used along the coasts and on the rivers of China and Japan.

sam-ple (săm′pl), *n.* a specimen; model; pattern; also, a part of something, by which the whole is judged; as, she showed us a *sample* of the silk:—*v.t.* [sam-pled, sam-pling], to test by trying a small piece; as, to *sample* candy.

sam-pler (săm′plĕr), *n.* **1,** one who makes a business of testing goods by means of samples; **2,** a piece of ornamental needlework made as an exhibition of skill.

Sam-son (săm′sn) or **Samp-son** (sămp′-sŭn; săm′sn), *n.* **1,** in the Bible, a judge of Israel, noted for his great strength; **2,** hence, any person of unusual strength.

Sam-u-el (săm′û-ĕl), in the Bible, a Hebrew prophet, the last of the judges; also, either of two books in the Old Testament which give his history.

San An-to-ni-o (săn ăn-tō′nĭ-ō), a large city in Texas, once its capital (map **8**).

san-a-tor-i-um (săn′a̍-tôr′ĭ-ŭm), *n.* [*pl.* sanatoria (săn′a̍-tôr′ĭ-a̍) or sanatoriums], **1,** a health resort; **2,** an institution for the care of invalids; a sanitarium.

sanc-ti-fy (săngk′tĭ-fī), *v.t.* [sanctified, sanctify-ing], **1,** to make holy; set apart for some sacred use; as, "God blessed the seventh day and *sanctified* it"; **2,** to purify (human beings) from sin.

sanc-ti-mo-ni-ous (săngk′tĭ-mō′nĭ-ŭs), *adj.* having the appearance of, or making a show of, piety or holiness; hypocritical.

sanc-tion (săngk′shŭn), *n.* formal approval or consent by those in authority:—**sanctions**, a legal term given to measures imposed for securing obedience to law:—*v.t.* to approve; authorize; as, their parents *sanctioned* the marriage.

Syn., v. encourage, support, ratify.

sanc-ti-ty (săngk′tĭ-tĭ), *n.* [*pl.* sanctities], **1,** holiness; purity; **2,** sacredness; solemnity; as, the *sanctity* of a cathedral; **3, sanctities**, sacred objects, duties, etc.

sanc-tu-ar-y (săngk′tū-ĕr′ĭ), *n.* [*pl.* sanctuaries], **1,** a consecrated place; a church or temple; **2,** the part of a Christian church nearest the altar; **3,** a place of shelter and protection; as, a *sanctuary* for wild fowl; **4,** hence, security; shelter; as, to seek *sanctuary* from the world.

sanc-tum (săngk′tŭm), *n.* **1,** a sacred place; **2,** a private room or study.

sand (sănd), *n.* **1,** dry soil composed of fine particles of crushed or worn rock, found chiefly along the shores of large bodies of water or in deserts; **2, sands,** moments; time: from the custom of measuring time by sand in an hourglass; as, the *sands* of life run fast:—*v.t.* to sprinkle, mix, or rub with sand; as, to *sand* floors.

san-dal (săn′dăl), *n.* **1,** a kind of low shoe, worn by the ancient Greeks and Romans, consisting of a sole without uppers fastened by straps over the instep and around the ankle; **2,** in modern times, a similar shoe

for children; also, an openwork street shoe or evening slipper; **3,** a low overshoe.

san-dal-wood (săn′dăl-wōŏd′), *n.* **1,** a tree that grows in the Malay Archipelago and India; **2,** the close-grained and fragrant wood of this tree, used for fine carving, and valued for the perfume which it yields.

ROMAN SANDAL

sand-bag (sănd′băg′), *n.* a bag filled with sand, used as ballast, as a material for the parapets of trenches, or as a weapon to give a heavy, stunning blow, etc.:—*v.t.* [sandbagged, sandbag-ging], to slug or stun with a sandbag.

sand dol-lar, a flat, circular sea urchin. (See illustration at *sea urchin*.)

A MODERN SANDAL

sand-glass (sănd′glȧs′), *n.* a reversible instrument designed to measure intervals of time by the running of sand. See **hourglass.**

San Di-e-go (săn dē-ā′gō), a seaport and naval base in southern California, near the Mexican border (map **9**).

sand-man (sănd′măn′), *n.* a nursery character, supposed to bring sleep to children.

sand-pa-per (sănd′pā′pĕr), *n.* a heavy paper with a coating of sand on one side, used for smoothing and polishing:—*v.t.* to smooth or polish with sandpaper.

sand-pip-er (sănd′-pīp′ĕr), *n.* a small wading bird which feeds along sandy or muddy shores.

SANDPIPER (!)

sand-stone (sănd′stōn′), *n.* a rock composed chiefly of quartz sand hardened into a solid mass by a natural cement.

sand-wich (sănd′wĭch), *n.* two or more slices of fresh or toasted bread with meat, cheese, or other filling between them:—*v.t.* to place (a person or thing) between two others.

Sandwich Is-lands, the former name of the *Hawaiian Islands.* See **Hawaii.**

sand-y (săn′dĭ), *adj.* [sand-i-er, sand-i-est], **1,** entirely or chiefly composed of sand; as, *sandy* soil; **2,** of a yellowish-red color; as, *sandy* hair.—*n.* **sand′i-ness.**

sane (sān), *adj.* [san-er, san-est], **1,** mentally sound or healthy; **2,** coming from a sound mind; sensible; as, a *sane* suggestion.

San Fran·cis·co (săn frăn-sĭs'kō), an important port and city in California: —**San Francisco Bay,** a bay on the coast of California. (Map 9.)

sang (săng), past tense of *sing*.

san·gui·nar·y (săng'gwĭ-nĕr'ĭ), *adj*. 1, attended with much bloodshed; as, a *sanguinary* attack; 2, bloodthirsty; cruel; as, a *sanguinary* pirate.
Syn. inhuman, savage.

san·guine (săng'gwĭn), *adj*. 1, of the color of blood; ruddy; as, a *sanguine* complexion; 2, hopeful; confident; as, *sanguine* of victory.
Syn. optimistic, buoyant, cheerful.

san·i·tar·i·um (săn'ĭ-târ'ĭ-ŭm), *n*. [*pl.* sanitariums or sanitaria (săn'ĭ-târ'ĭ-à)], a place for the care of invalids or the treatment of certain diseases; also, a sanatorium; health resort.

san·i·tar·y (săn'ĭ-tĕr'ĭ), *adj*. 1, relating to health; as, *sanitary* laws; 2, preserving health; hygienic; as, *sanitary* conditions.

san·i·ta·tion (săn'ĭ-tā'shŭn), *n*. the science and practice of bringing about conditions that protect health; hygiene.

san·i·ty (săn'ĭ-tĭ), *n*. soundness of mind; mental balance.

San Juan (săn' hwän'; sän' hwän'), 1, a seaport city, capital of Puerto Rico (map 10); 2, a hill near Santiago, Cuba, captured by U.S. troops during the Spanish American War, in 1898.

sank (săngk), past tense of *sink*.

sans (sănz; *French* säṅ), *prep*. without: chiefly in old or poetic usage.

San Sal·va·dor (săn săl'và-dôr; sän'säl'-vä-thôr'), 1, a city, capital of El Salvador (map 10); 2, the island in the Bahamas where Columbus is thought to have landed before touching the mainland (map 10): also called *Watling Island*.

San·skrit (săn'skrĭt), *n*. the ancient written language of the Hindus of India, the oldest of a great group of Indo-European languages to which most of the languages of modern Europe, including English, belong: —*adj*. relating to, or written in, this language.

San·ta Claus or **San·ta Klaus** (săn'tà klôz), in the nursery lore of many countries, the jolly white-bearded old man who brings gifts to children on Christmas Eve; Saint Nicholas.

San·ta Fe (săn'tà fā'), a city, capital of New Mexico, founded about 1605 (map 9).

San·ti·a·go (săn'tē-ä'gō), a city, capital of Chile, South America (map 11).

San·ti·a·go de Cu·ba (săn'tē-ä'gō dā kōō'bä), a seaport in southeastern Cuba, near which the most important engage-

ments of the Spanish American War took place (map 10).

San·to Do·min·go (sän'tō dō-mǐng'gō), the former name for Ciudad Trujillo. See **Ciudad Trujillo.**

São Pau·lo (souṅ'pou'lŏŏ), a state in southeastern Brazil; also, a city, its capital (map 11).

São Sal·va·dor (souṅ' säl'và-thôr'), a city in eastern Brazil. See **Salvador.**

¹sap (săp), *n*. the watery juice of a tree or plant. From the sap of certain trees come products useful to man, as rubber, sugar, etc.—*adj*. **sap'less.**

²sap (săp), *v.t.* [sapped, sap-ping], 1, to wear away by digging beneath; undermine; as, the flood waters *sapped* the foundations of the house; 2, to weaken; wear away; as, continual defeats *sapped* his courage.

sa·pi·ence (sā'pĭ-ĕns), *n*. wisdom.

sa·pi·ent (sā'pĭ-ĕnt), *adj*. wise; full of knowledge.—*adv*. **sa'pi·ent·ly.**

sap·ling (săp'lĭng), *n*. 1, a flexible young tree; 2, hence, a youth.

sap·phire (săf'īr), *n*. 1, a precious stone, hard and transparent, and of a deep-blue color; 2, the deep-blue color of this gem.

sap·py (săp'ĭ), *adj*. [sap-pi-er, sap-pi-est], 1, full of sap or juice, as a plant; 2, *Colloquial,* foolish; silly.

sap·suck·er (săp'sŭk'ẽr), *n*. a small American woodpecker which feeds partly on the sap of trees.

sap·wood (săp'wŏŏd'), *n*. the soft living wood between the bark and the hard inner wood of most trees.

SAPSUCKER (⅛)

Sar·a·cen (săr'à-sĕn), *n*. 1, in ancient times, an Arab; 2, during the Crusades, the name given by the Christians to any Moslem; hence, a Moslem.

Sar·ah or **Sar·a** (sâr'à), in the Bible, the wife of Abraham and mother of Isaac.

Sa·ra·je·vo (sä'rà-yĕ'vō), a city, formerly the capital of Bosnia, in central Yugoslavia (map 12). The assassination here of Archduke Francis Ferdinand of Austria on June 28, 1914, set off World War I.

sar·casm (sär'kăzm), *n*. a bitter, cutting remark; also, ironical language expressing scorn or contempt.

sar·cas·tic (sär-kăs'tĭk), *adj*. bitterly scornful; cutting; as, a *sarcastic* letter; a *sarcastic* teacher.—*adv*. **sar·cas'ti·cal·ly.**

sar·coph·a·gus (sär-kŏf'à-gŭs), *n*. [*pl.* sarcophagi (sär-kŏf'à-jī) or sarcophaguses], a stone coffin or tomb.

āte, âorta, râre, căt, ȧsk, fär, ăllow, sofà; ēve, êvent, ĕll, wrȳtẽr, novĕl; bīte, pĭn; nō, ōbey, ôr, dŏg, tŏp, cŏllide; ūnit, ûnite, bûrn, cŭt, focŭs; nŏŏn, fŏŏt; mound; coin;

sar·dine (sär-dēn′; sär′dēn), *n.* a small fish of the herring family, preserved in oil for use as food.

Sar·din·i·a (sär-dĭn′ĭ-*ȧ*), an island in the Mediterranean, west of Italy (map 12).

SARDINE (⅓)

sar·don·ic (sär-dŏn′ĭk), *adj.* bitter; mocking; derisive.—*adv.* **sar·don′i·cal·ly.**

sar·do·nyx (sär′dō-nĭks), *n.* a variety of onyx, usually reddish brown and white.

Sar·gas·so Sea (sär-găs′ō), a large area in the North Atlantic Ocean (map 3): so named because of a floating seaweed, called *sargasso,* which is found there.

Sark (särk), one of the Channel Islands. See **Channel Islands.**

sar·sa·pa·ril·la (sär′sȧ-pȧ-rĭl′ȧ), *n.* 1, a tropical American plant, the root of which is used as medicine or for flavoring; 2, a cooling drink of soda water flavored with extract of sarsaparilla.

sar·tor·i·al (sär-tôr′ĭ-ăl), *adj.* having to do with a tailor or tailoring, or with men's clothes; as, *sartorial* elegance.

¹**sash** (săsh), *n.* [*pl.* sashes], an ornamental band, ribbon, etc., worn around the waist or over the shoulder.

²**sash** (săsh), *n.* [*pl.* sashes or sash], a window frame, or a part of a door, made to hold panes of glass.

SASH

A, top rail; B, bottom rail; C, C, stiles; D, sash bars.

Sas·katch·e·wan (săs-kăch′ĕ-wŏn), a province (cap. Regina) of western Canada (map 4).

sas·sa·fras (săs′ȧ-frăs), *n.* 1, a tree of the laurel family, whose root, wood, and flowers have a spicy smell and a pungent taste; 2, the root bark of this tree, used in medicine and for flavoring.

sat (săt), past tense and past participle of *sit.*

Sat. abbreviation for *Saturday.*

Sa·tan (sā′tăn), *n.* the Devil.

sa·tan·ic (sȧ-tăn′ĭk), *adj.* pertaining to, or like, Satan; devilish; wicked.

SASSAFRAS
Leaves and fruit.

satch·el (săch′ĕl), *n.* a small bag, usually of fabric or of leather, in which to carry small personal belongings, papers, etc.

sate (sāt), *v.t.* [sat-ed, sat-ing], 1, to satisfy fully (an appetite or desire); 2, to disgust or weary with an excess of something; as, he was *sated* with flattery.

Syn. glut, surfeit, satiate, cloy.

sa·teen (să-tēn′), *n.* a cotton fabric with a glossy, satinlike finish.

sat·el·lite (săt′ĕ-līt), *n.* 1, a heavenly body revolving round a larger one; as, the moon is a *satellite* of the earth; 2, a persistent attendant or follower of a great person; as, Boswell was Johnson's *satellite.*

sa·ti·a·ble (sā′shĭ-ȧ-bl), *adj.* capable of being satisfied; as, *satiable* desires.

sa·ti·ate (sā′shĭ-āt), *v.t.* [satiat-ed, satiating], to gratify to excess; as, to *satiate* one's appetite for sweets.

sa·ti·e·ty (sȧ-tī′ĕ-tĭ), *n.* the condition of being filled or satisfied beyond desire; as, no food can tempt one filled to *satiety.*

sat·in (săt′ĭn), *n.* a closely woven, glossy silk:—*adj.* made of, or like, this silk.—*adj.* **sat′in·y.**

sat·in·wood (săt′ĭn-wŏŏd′), *n.* 1, an East Indian tree; 2, the yellowish-brown wood of this tree, which has a satiny sheen.

sat·ire (săt′īr), *n.* 1, a poem, essay, story, etc., exposing and ridiculing evil or folly; 2, biting sarcasm or ridicule.—*adj.* **sa·tir′ic** (sȧ-tĭr′ĭk); **sa·tir′i·cal.**

sat·i·rist (săt′ĭ-rĭst), *n.* 1, one who writes satire; 2, one who uses biting sarcasm or ridicule.

sat·i·rize (săt′ĭ-rīz), *v.t.* [satirized, satirizing], to attack by ridiculing; hold up to ridicule; as, to *satirize* a hypocrite.

sat·is·fac·tion (săt′ĭs-făk′shŭn), *n.* 1, the act of supplying a need or desire; also, the act of paying off, compensating, contenting, or the like; 2, the condition of having one's wishes filled, or of being gratified, paid off, contented, etc.; contentment; 3, that which satisfies or gratifies; as, your visit will be a great *satisfaction.*

Syn. enjoyment, comfort, gratification.

sat·is·fac·to·ry (săt′ĭs-făk′tō-rĭ), *adj.* sufficient; adequate; producing satisfaction; as, her progress at school was *satisfactory.*—*adv.* **sat′is·fac′to·ri·ly.**

sat·is·fy (săt′ĭs-fī), *v.t.* [satisfied, satisfying], 1, to content; fill the wishes of; as, they were *satisfied* with the new house; also, to gratify to the full; as, to *satisfy* one's hunger; 2, to free from doubt; convince; as, the explanation *satisfied* the child; 3, to pay off; as, to *satisfy* a creditor: —*v.i.* to give gratification; as, riches do not always *satisfy.*

sa·trap (sā′trăp; săt′răp), *n.* 1, the governor of a province in ancient Persia; 2, hence, any petty ruler acting under a despotic superior.—*n.* **sa′trap·y.**

---

go; join; yet; sing; chin; show; thin, *th*en; hw, *wh*y; zh, a*z*ure; ü, Ger. für or Fr. l*u*ne; ö, Ger. schön or Fr. f*eu*; ṅ, Fr. *en*fant, nom; kh, Ger. a*ch* or i*ch*. See pages ix–x.

sat·u·rate (săt′ū-rāt), *v.t.* [saturat-ed, saturat-ing], to cause to become soaked; to fill to the limit of the capacity for absorbing; as, to *saturate* the ground with water.—*n.* **sat′u·ra′tion.**

Sat·ur·day (săt′ĕr-dĭ; săt′ĕr-dā), *n.* the seventh day of the week.

Sat·urn (săt′ĕrn), *n.* **1,** the second largest planet, notable for the three rings that surround it; **2,** in Roman mythology, a god of agriculture.

Sat·ur·na·li·a (săt′ĕr-nā′lĭ-ȧ), *n.pl.* an ancient Roman festival in honor of the god Saturn, celebrated in December with merrymaking:—**saturnalia,** *pl.* often used as *sing.* a period of riotous merrymaking.

sat·ur·nine (săt′ĕr-nīn), *adj.* gloomy; dismal; as, a *saturnine* disposition.

sat·yr (săt′ĕr; sā′tĕr), *n.* in mythology, a forest god, represented with long, pointed ears, short horns, and the tail of a horse or goat, who indulged in riotous merriment and wantonness.

sauce (sôs), *n.* **1,** a dressing or seasoning for food; also, any highly seasoned mixture of ingredients, used as a relish; as, chili *sauce;* **2,** stewed fruit; as, apple-*sauce;* **3,** *Colloquial,* insolence; pertness:—*v.t.* [sauced, sauc-ing], **1,** to put seasoning into; add flavor to; **2,** *Colloquial,* to treat with pertness or sauciness.

sauce·pan (sôs′păn′), *n.* a small metal pan, with a handle, used in cooking.

SAUCEPAN

sau·cer (sô′sĕr), *n.* a shallow dish, especially one to hold a cup.

sau·cy (sô′sĭ), *adj.* [sau-ci-er, sau-ci-est], pert; impudent; also, roguish; as, a *saucy* smile.—*adv.* **sau′ci·ly.**—*n.* **sau′ci·ness.**
Syn. impertinent, rude, insolent.

Sa·u·di A·ra·bi·a (sä-ōō′dē), a kingdom (caps. Riyadh and Mecca) occupying most of the peninsula of Arabia (map **15**).

sauer·kraut (sour′krout′), *n.* finely sliced cabbage, fermented in a brine made of its own juice.

Saul (sôl), in the Bible: **1,** the first king of Israel; **2,** the apostle Paul.

saun·ter (sôn′tĕr; sän′tĕr), *v.i.* to wander idly; stroll; as, to *saunter* along the beach:—*n.* **1,** a leisurely manner of walking; **2,** an idle walk or ramble.

sau·sage (sô′sĭj), *n.* meat, usually pork, ground fine and highly seasoned. It is often stuffed into a thin, tubelike casing.

sau·té (sō-tā′), *adj.* fried quickly and lightly in a pan containing very little grease; as, *sauté* mushrooms.

sav·age (săv′ĭj), *adj.* **1,** relating to the forest or wilderness; wild; as, *savage* country; **2,** cruel; fierce; as, *savage* beasts; **3,** uncivilized; barbaric; as, *savage* tribes:—*n.* **1,** an uncivilized person; a barbarian; **2,** a fierce, brutal person.—*adv.* **sav′age·ly.**—*n.* **sav′age·ness.**

sav·age·ry (săv′ĭj-rĭ), *n.* [*pl.* savageries], **1,** the condition of being wild or uncivilized; **2,** brutal roughness or cruelty.

sa·van·na or **sa·van·nah** (sȧ-văn′ȧ), *n.* an open plain or meadow without trees.

Sa·van·nah (sȧ-văn′ȧ), **1,** a river on the boundary between Georgia and South Carolina; **2,** a city and port on the Savannah River, in eastern Georgia. (Map **8.**)

sa·vant (să-vän′; săv′ănt), *n.* [*pl.* savants (să-vänz′; săv′ănts)], a learned man; a scholar.

¹save (sāv), *v.t.* [saved, sav-ing], **1,** to bring out of danger; deliver; rescue; as, the soldier *saved* his comrade's life; also, to preserve from damage, decay, etc.; as, rubbers *save* shoes; **2,** to spare; avoid; as, to *save* trouble; prevent the waste of; as, to *save* time; **3,** to refrain from spending; hoard; as, to *save* money; **4,** to free from the power and result of sin; as, to *save* souls:—*v.i.* **1,** to refrain from spending or wasting money or supplies; **2,** to lay by money a little at a time.—*n.* **sav′er.**

²save (sāv), *prep.* except; not including; as, he attended every game *save* one.

sav·ing (sāv′ĭng), *adj.* **1,** preserving from sin or destruction; as, *saving* faith; **2,** redeeming; compensating; as, a *saving* sense of humor; **3,** economical; not wasteful; as, a very *saving* individual:—*n.* **1,** economy; as, he early learned the habit of *saving;* **2,** rescue; as, the *saving* of a life; **3,** **savings,** money saved:—*prep.* except.
Syn., adj. thrifty, sparing, provident.

savings bank, a bank devoted particularly to depositors who wish to leave money there at interest.

sav·ior or **sav·iour** (sāv′yĕr), *n.* one who rescues or saves:—**Saviour,** Jesus Christ, the Redeemer.

Sav·o·na·ro·la (săv′ō-nȧ-rō′lȧ), (1452–1498), an Italian monk and religious and political reformer, influential in Florence.

sa·vor (sā′vĕr), *n.* flavor; taste; as, a spicy *savor:*—*v.t.* **1,** to flavor; as, to *savor* a soup; **2,** to taste or smell with delight:—*v.i.* to partake of a quality or characteristic; as, this book *savors* of personal prejudice.—*adj.* **sa′vor·less.**

¹sa·vor·y (sā′vĕr-ĭ), *adj.* with appetizing taste or smell; as, a *savory* stew.

²sa·vor·y (sā′vĕr-ĭ), *n.* a fragrant herb of the mint family, used in cooking.

āte, āorta, râre, căt, ȧsk, fär, ăllow, sofȧ; ēve, ĕvent, ĕll, wrīter, novĕl; bīte, pĭn; nō, ōbey, ôr, dŏg, tŏp, cŏllide; ūnit, ūnite, bûrn, cŭt, focŭs; nōōn, fŏŏt; mound; coin:

[1]saw (sô), *n.* a cutting tool with a thin, toothed blade, worked mechanically or by hand; also, a cutting machine having one or more such blades:—*v.t.* [*p.t.* sawed (sôd), *p.p.* sawed or sawn (sôn), *p.pr.* saw-ing], 1, to cut with a saw; as, to *saw* wood; 2, to form or fashion with such a

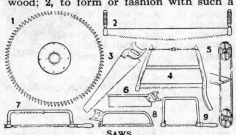

SAWS

1, circular saw; 2, two-handed, or crosscut, saw; 3, handsaw; 4, bucksaw; 5, band saw; 6, backsaw; 7, hack saw; 8, butcher's saw; 9, coping saw.

tool; as, he *sawed* the board so that it fitted into place; 3, to make motions as if sawing; as, the excited speaker *sawed* the air:—*v.i.* 1, to be cut with a saw; as, the wood *saws* easily; 2, to use a saw; also, to make motions as if using a saw; 3, to perform the function of a saw.

[2]saw (sô), *n.* a proverb; an adage; as, "Well begun is half done" is an old *saw*.

[3]saw (sô), past tense of [1]*see*.

saw-buck (sô′bŭk′), *n.* a sawhorse.

saw-dust (sô′dŭst′), *n.* the fine particles or chips that fly when wood is sawed.

saw-horse (sô′hôrs′), *n.* a rack or frame to hold sticks of wood while they are being sawed by hand; a saw-buck.

saw-mill (sô′mĭl′), *n.* a mill where logs are sawed into lumber by machines; also, a sawing machine.

SAWHORSE

sawn (sôn), one of the past participles of [1]*saw*.

saw-yer (sô′yẽr), *n.* a person whose occupation is the sawing of logs or timber.

sax-horn (săks′hôrn′), *n.* any of a family of brass wind instruments, as the tuba.

sax-i-frage (săk′sĭ-frĭj), *n.* a low-growing plant with white, red, or yellow flowers.

Sax-on (săk′sŭn), *n.* 1, a member of a Germanic tribe which, in the fifth and sixth centuries, with the Angles and the Jutes, conquered and settled England; also, a member of the nation which grew up after this

SAXHORN

conquest; an Anglo-Saxon; 2, an inhabitant of modern Saxony in Germany; 3, the language of the ancient Saxons; also, the language of the people of modern Saxony, a dialect of German:—*adj.* having to do with the ancient Saxons, or with modern Saxony.

Sax-o-ny (săk′sô-nĭ), 1, a state (cap. Dresden) in east central Germany; 2, a former province (cap. Magdeburg) in Prussia, Germany.

sax-o-phone (săk′sô-fōn), *n.* a musical instrument consisting of a metal tube with keys and a reed mouthpiece.

SAXOPHONE

say (sā), *v.t.* [said (sĕd), say-ing], 1, to utter in words; tell; 2, to declare; state as a decision; assert; as, I *say* he shall go; 3, to estimate; assume; as, *say* he has ten houses, how long will he keep them? 4, to recite; repeat; as, to *say* a poem:—*n.* 1, something that one has said or intends to say; as, to have one's *say*; 2, one's turn or right to express an opinion; as, it's your *say* next; also, the right to decide; as, the teacher has the whole *say*.

say-ing (sā′ĭng), *n.* that which is often said; a proverb or maxim.

    Syn. saw, byword, truism.

Sc. abbreviation for *Scotch, Scottish, Scots.*

S.C. abbreviation for *South Carolina.*

scab (skăb), *n.* 1, a crust formed over a wound or sore; 2, a disease of animals, especially sheep, characterized by spots that resemble scabs; also, a similar disease of plants; 3, a worker who accepts lower wages than those set by the trade-union; also, a worker who takes a striker's job.

scab-bard (skăb′ẽrd), *n.* the case in which the blade of a sword, bayonet, or the like is sheathed.

scaf-fold (skăf′ōld; skăf′ŭld), *n.* 1, a temporary timber structure serving as a support for workmen while building, painting, or the like; 2, an elevated platform on which the execution of criminals takes place by hanging, beheading, etc.

scaf-fold-ing (skăf′ōl-dĭng; skăf′ŭl-dĭng), *n.* 1, a scaffold or series of scaffolds; 2, the materials used in erecting scaffolds.

scal-a-wag or **scal-la-wag** (skăl′á-wăg), *n.* 1, originally, a stunted, inferior animal; 2, hence, a worthless person; scamp; rascal

scald (skôld), *v.t.* 1, to burn or injure, as

does hot liquid; also, to burn with steam; **2,** hence, to pain as if by burning; as, hot tears *scalded* her face; **3,** to bring near to the boiling point; as, to *scald* milk; **4,** to rinse or dip in boiling water; as, to *scald* dishes; to *scald* tomatoes:—*n.* a burn or injury from hot liquid or steam.

¹scale (skāl), *n.* **1,** one of the pans or dishes of a balance; **2,** (usually *scales*), the balance itself; **3,** any instrument or machine for weighing:—*v.t.* [scaled, scal-ing], to weigh by means of scales.

SCALES, def. 2

²scale (skāl), *n.* **1,** one of the thin, bony or horny plates forming the outer covering of many fishes, lizards, snakes, etc.; **2,** any thin plate resembling a scale; **3,** one of the small flaky pieces of dead skin which fall off in certain diseases:— *v.t.* [scaled, scal-ing], to strip (a fish) of scales:—*v.i.* **1,** to form or drop scales; separate and come off in thin layers; **2,** to become rough and hard; become crusted.

COUNTER SCALES

³scale (skāl), *n.* **1,** a measure consisting of a series of marks, laid down at definite, regular distances along a line; as, the *scale* on a tape measure; **2,** a basis for a system of numbering; as, the decimal *scale;* **3,** a series of numbers, similar objects, or the like, which progress from a low to a high point or degree; as, the *scale* of marks in the arithmetic test ranged from 47 to 98; **4,** the relation between the actual size of an object and the size of the object as it appears in a drawing, painting, etc.; as, a drawing of a house on the *scale* of five feet to one inch; **5,** any standard for judging or estimating; **6,** in music, a series of tones in a regular order, whether ascending or descending; also, a succession of tones beginning on a certain keynote; as, the *scale* of F:—*v.t.* [scaled, scal-ing], **1,** to climb up; as, to *scale* a wall; **2,** to reduce in accordance with a settled ratio or scale; as, to *scale* down expenses; **3,** to make (a drawing, etc.) in accordance with a definite scale.

scal-la-wag (skăl′a-wăg), *n.* a rascal; scalawag. See **scalawag.**

scal-lion (skăl′yŭn), *n.* an onionlike plant; a leek.

scal-lop (skŏl′ŭp; skăl′ŭp) or **scol-lop** (skŏl′ŭp), *n.* **1,** a salt-water shellfish with two fan-shaped, usually ribbed, shells that are hinged together; **2,** the muscle by which the shell is closed, valued for food; **3,** one of a series of curves that form an ornamental edge, as on lace, linens, etc.: —*v.t.* **1,** to cut the edge or border of, in a series of curves; **2,** to mix with crumbs, butter, etc., and bake; as, to *scallop* tomatoes.

SCALLOP SHELL
(½)

scalp (skălp), *n.* the skin on the top of the head, normally covered with hair:—*v.t.* to torture or kill by cutting off the skin and hair of the head; as, the Indians *scalped* the prisoners.

scal-pel (skăl′pĕl), *n.* a surgeon's keen-edged, sharp-pointed knife.

SCALLOPS, def. 3
Collar with scalloped edge.

scal-y (skā′lĭ), *adj.* [scal-i-er, scal-i-est], like, or provided with, scales.—*n.* **scal′i-ness.**

¹scamp (skămp), *n.* a rascal; a good-for-nothing fellow.

²scamp (skămp), *v.t.* to perform (work) carelessly, hastily, and with poor material.

SCALPEL

scam-per (skăm′pĕr), *v.i.* to run or skip; as, the frightened rabbit *scampered* to cover:—*n.* a hasty flight.

scan (skăn), *v.t.* [scanned, scan-ning], **1,** to look at the details of; scrutinize; as, Columbus *scanned* the horizon for land; **2,** to read or mark (a line of poetry) to show the number and kind of metrical feet used; **3,** in transmitting or receiving television, to create or reproduce an image as a series of light and dark dots or lines.—*n.* **scan′ner.**

scan-dal (skăn′dăl), *n.* **1,** a cause of reproach; also, shame; disgrace; as, the tenement district was a *scandal* to the city; **2,** careless or malicious gossip injurious to another's reputation; backbiting.—*adj.* **scan′dal-ous.**

scan-dal-ize (skăn′dăl-īz), *v.t.* [scandalized, scandaliz-ing], to offend or shock by an opinion, action, etc.

scan-dal-mon-ger (skăn′dăl-mŭng′gĕr), *n.* a person who listens to and repeats gossip.

Scan-di-na-vi-a (skăn′dĭ-nā′vĭ-à), **1,** Norway, Sweden, Denmark, and Iceland; **2,** in a restricted sense, the peninsula of Norway and Sweden (map **12**).

Scan-di-na-vi-an (skăn′dĭ-nā′vĭ-ăn), *n.* a native of Scandinavia; also, the languages, or any one of the languages, of Scandinavia:—*adj.* pertaining to Scandinavia, its languages, or its people.

scant (skănt), *adj.* **1,** having only a small

amount; short; as, *scant* of material; **2,** barely enough; as, a *scant* supply of food; also, a little less than; as, it weighs a *scant* pound:—*v.t.* to stint; limit the supply of.

scant·ling (skănt′lĭng), *n.* a piece of lumber of small size, especially one used as an upright in a partition of a building.

scant·y (skăn′tĭ), *adj.* [scant-i-er, scant-i-est], barely sufficient; scarcely enough; as, *scanty* supplies.

   Syn. bare, sparse, insufficient.

scape·goat (skāp′gōt′), *n.* **1,** in an ancient Jewish custom, a goat selected by lot, on whose head the high priest laid the sins of the people, after which it was driven into the wilderness; **2,** hence, one who bears the blame for others.

scape·grace (skāp′grās′), *n.* an irresponsible, unprincipled person.

scar (skär), *n.* **1,** the mark left after a wound or burn heals; **2,** any mark like a scar; as, knife *scars* on the table; **3,** a lasting effect caused by grief, trouble, or the like:—*v.t.* [scarred, scar-ring], to mark with, or as with, a scar:—*v.i.* to form a scar.

scar·ab (skăr′ăb), *n.* **1,** a kind of beetle; especially, a beetle held sacred by the ancient Egyptians as a symbol of immortality; **2,** a gem or seal cut in the form of this beetle.

SCARAB, def. 1 (⅓)

scarce (skârs), *adj.* [scarc-er, scarc-est], **1,** not common; rarely seen; as, real emeralds are *scarce*; **2,** not plentiful; not equal to the demand; as, peaches are *scarce* this year.—*n.* **scarce′ness.**

scarce·ly (skârs′lĭ), *adv.* **1,** surely not; hardly; as, you can *scarcely* run as fast as that; **2,** almost not; barely; as, I *scarcely* saw him before he left.

scar·ci·ty (skâr′sĭ-tĭ), *n.* **1,** lack; insufficiency; dearth; **2,** rareness.

scare (skâr), *v.t.* [scared, scar-ing], to strike with sudden terror; frighten:—*n.* a sudden fright or panic.—*adj.* **scar′y.**

scare·crow (skâr′krō′), *n.* **1,** a figure, usually a crude representation of a man, dressed in ragged clothes, set up to frighten birds and animals away from crops; **2,** anything which frightens without real cause; **3,** a person dressed in rags.

scarf (skärf), *n.* [*pl.* scarves (skärvz) or scarfs], **1,** a neckerchief or necktie; **2,** a strip of lace, silk, wool, etc., worn loosely, for ornament or warmth, about the neck, head, or shoulders; **3,** a cover, often long and narrow, used on a bureau, piano, sideboard, etc.

scar·i·fy (skăr′ĭ-fī), *v.t.* [scarified, scarifying], to scratch; cut, as the skin.

scar·let (skär′lĕt), *n.* a bright-red color tinged with orange:—*adj.* of a scarlet color.

scar·let fe·ver (fē′vĕr), a highly contagious disease, characterized by a severe sore throat, high fever, and scarlet rash.

scath·ing (skāth′ĭng), *adj.* severe; bitter; as, *scathing* remarks.—*adv.* **scath′ing·ly.**

scat·ter (skăt′ĕr), *v.t.* **1,** to throw here and there; strew; as, to *scatter* clothes about a room; *scatter* seed; **2,** to drive apart; disperse; as, the soldiers *scattered* the mob:—*v.i.* to separate and go in different directions; as, the class *scattered* when the bell rang.

scaup duck (skôp dŭk), any of various northern salt-water ducks; especially, a duck the male of which has a glossy black head and neck and a white belly.

SCAUP DUCK (¹⁄₁₀)

scav·en·ger (skăv′ĕn-jĕr), *n.* **1,** a man employed to keep the streets clean by carrying off all filth, refuse, etc.; **2,** any animal, bird, or fish, that eats refuse.

sce·na·ri·o (sē-nä′rĭ-ō; sē-nâr′ĭ-ō), *n.* [*pl.* scenarios], the complete, detailed story of the plot of a photoplay, including the cast of characters and acting directions.

scene (sēn), *n.* **1,** one of the parts into which an act of a play is divided; **2,** the painted background, hangings, etc., used on the stage to picture the place where the action is going on; **3,** the time, place, or circumstances in which the action of a play, story, etc., takes place; as, the *scene* of the play is a farm; **4,** a particular episode or happening of a story, play, etc.; as, the storm *scene* in "David Copperfield"; **5,** a display of feeling or emotion; as, John made quite a *scene* when told to go home; **6,** a landscape; view.

scen·er·y (sēn′ĕr-ĭ), *n.* **1,** painted hangings, screens, etc., used on a stage; the background; **2,** a landscape; as, mountain *scenery*.

sce·nic (sē′nĭk; sĕn′ĭk), *adj.* **1,** pertaining to the stage; **2,** pertaining to a landscape; also, offering beautiful views of nature.

scent (sĕnt), *n.* **1,** odor; fragrance; **2,** the sense of smell; as, hounds have a keen *scent*; **3,** an odor left lingering about a place by a person or animal; as, the dogs caught the wolf by following his *scent*; **4,** hence, the trail or track, as of a criminal; **5,** a perfume:—*v.t.* **1,** to smell; **2,** hence, to get a hint of; as, to *scent* trouble; **3,** to perfume; as, handkerchiefs *scented* with lavender.—*adj.* **scent′less.**

scep·ter or **scep·tre** (sĕp′tẽr), *n.* a ruler's staff; an emblem of authority or power.

scep·tic (skĕp′tĭk), *n.* one who doubts; a skeptic.—*adj.* **scep′ti·cal.** See **skeptic.**

scep·ti·cism (skĕp′tĭ-sĭzm), *n.* an unbelieving, doubting state of mind; skepticism. See **skepticism.**

sched·ule (skĕd′ūl), *n.* **1,** a written or printed paper containing a list or inventory; as, a *schedule* of household goods; **2,** a list of things to be done in a certain order of time; as, according to the *schedule,* the job will take a month; also, a timetable:—*v.t.* [scheduled, schedul-ing], **1,** to make a list or schedule of; as, to *schedule* one's possessions; **2,** to include in a list or schedule; as, I'll *schedule* your speech among those for Tuesday.

Scheldt (skhĕlt) or **Schel·de** (skhĕl′dē), a river flowing through northern Belgium into the North Sea.

scheme (skēm), *n.* **1,** a carefully arranged and systematic plan; a system; as, a *scheme* for old-age pensions; **2,** an underhand plan; plot; as, a *scheme* to rob a house; **3,** an arrangement or system in which everything is related or in harmony; as, the color *scheme* of a costume:—*v.t.* [schemed, schem-ing], to design or plan; plot:—*v.i.* to form a plot or plan.—*n.* **schem′er.**—*adj.* **schem′ing.**

Sche·nec·ta·dy (skĕ-nĕk′tạ-dĭ), a city in eastern New York State, on the Mohawk River (map 6).

scher·zo (skĕr′tsō), *n.* [*pl.* scherzos], in music, a lively movement.

Schil·ler (shĭl′ẽr), Johann Christoph Friedrich von (1759–1805), a German poet and dramatist.

schil·ling (shĭl′ĭng), *n.* the Austrian monetary unit. (See Table, page 943.)

schism (sĭzm), *n.* **1,** a split or division; especially, a split in the Christian church; **2,** the offense of causing such a split or division; **3,** a group that has separated from the main body of the church.—*adj.* **schis·mat′ic.**

Schles·wig–Hol·stein (shläs′vĭkh᠊hōl′shtīn), a province (cap. Kiel) in northwestern Germany.

schol·ar (skŏl′ẽr), *n.* **1,** one who attends a school or learns from a teacher; **2,** one who has acquired thorough and expert knowledge in one or more fields of learning.

schol·ar·ship (skŏl′ẽr-shĭp), *n.* **1,** the knowledge and attainments of a learned man; learning; erudition; **2,** money given to a student to enable him to follow or continue a course of study.

scho·las·tic (skŏ-lăs′tĭk), *adj.* relating to schools, education, academic life, etc.

¹school (skōōl), *n.* **1,** a place where instruction is given; a schoolhouse; as, the new *school* was opened yesterday; **2,** a regular meeting or session at which instruction is given and received; as, there will be no *school* tomorrow afternoon; **3,** the whole body of pupils in any educational institution; as, the *school* is happy over the victory; **4,** the followers or imitators of a teacher or leader; as, the Platonic *school* of philosophy; **5,** a division of a university devoted to one branch of learning; as, a *school* of dentistry:—*v.t.* to train or instruct in, or as in, a school.

²school (skōōl), *n.* a great number of fish feeding or swimming together; a shoal:—*v.i.* to swim together in great numbers.

school·book (skōōl′bŏŏk′), *n.* a book used in schools; a textbook.

school·boy (skōōl′boi′), *n.* a boy who attends school.

school·fel·low (skōōl′fĕl′ō), *n.* a companion at school; a schoolmate.

school·girl (skōōl′gûrl′), *n.* a girl who attends school.

school·house (skōōl′hous′), *n.* a building where school is held.

school·ing (skōō′lĭng), *n.* instruction in school; education.

school·mas·ter (skōōl′mȧs′tẽr), *n.* a man who teaches in, or is the head of, a school.—*n.fem.* **school′mis′tress.**

school·mate (skōōl′māt′), *n.* a companion or associate at school; schoolfellow.

school·room (skōōl′rōōm′), *n.* a room in which pupils are taught.

school·teach·er (skōōl′tē′chẽr), *n.* one who teaches in a school.

schoon·er (skōō′nẽr), *n.* **1,** a vessel with two or more masts, rigged fore-and-aft (see *ship,* illustration); **2,** in the U.S., a covered wagon, formerly used by pioneers on the western prairies; a prairie schooner.

Schu·bert (shōō′bẽrt), Franz (1797–1828), an Austrian composer.

schuss (shŏŏs), *n.* in skiing, a straight downhill run on a very steep course.

sci·ence (sī′ĕns), *n.* **1,** knowledge, or the pursuit of knowledge, of things as they are, and of why they act as they do; also, the classification and systematic arrangement of such knowledge, and the formulation, where possible, of general laws, or

SCEPTER

truths, deduced from it; **2,** a special branch of such knowledge; as, the *science* of botany; the *science* of economics.

sci·ence fic·tion, stories about possible future scientific developments, especially those about travel through space or time.

sci·en·tif·ic (sī/ĕn-tĭf/ĭk), *adj.* **1,** relating to, or used in, a science; as, *scientific* instruments; **2,** in accordance with the methods of science; following or using the laws of science; as, *scientific* mining.—*adv.* **sci/en·tif/i·cal·ly.**

sci·en·tist (sī/ĕn-tĭst), *n.* a person who is learned in science; also, one whose profession is scientific research:— **Scientist,** a Christian Scientist.

Scil·la (shēl/lä), a headland in Italy. See **Scylla.**

scim·i·tar or **scim·i·ter** (sĭm/ĭ-tẽr), *n.* an Oriental sword with a curved blade.

scin·til·la (sĭn-tĭl/ä), *n.* a spark; particle; as, there is not a *scintilla* of evidence to prove his guilt.

scin·til·late (sĭn/tĭ-lāt), *v.i.* [scintillat-ed, scintillat-ing], **1,** to give forth sparks or flashes of fire or light; to sparkle; twinkle; **2,** hence, to flash; glow; as, his speech *scintillated* with humor.—*n.* **scin/til·la/tion.**

SCIM-ITAR

sci·on (sī/ŭn), *n.* **1,** the sprout or shoot of a plant, cut off and used for planting or grafting; **2,** a descendant; heir, especially of a noble family.

Scip·i·o (sĭp/ĭ-ō), the name of two famous Roman generals: **1,** *the Elder* (237–183? B.C.), who defeated Hannibal; **2,** *the Younger* (185?–129 B.C.), who destroyed Carthage.

scis·sors (sĭz/ẽrz), *n.pl.* an instrument, smaller than shears, with two sharp blades which open and close on a pivot, and cut when they meet.

scoff (skôf), *n.* an expression of scorn or contempt; also, an object of scorn or contempt; a laughingstock:—*v.i.* to show scorn or contempt by mocking language; to jeer; as, do not *scoff* at the mistakes of others.—*adv.* **scoff/ing·ly.**
Syn., v. mock, sneer.

SCISSORS

scoff·er (skôf/ẽr), *n.* one who is inclined to mock and jeer.

scold (skōld), *v.i.* to chide sharply or rudely:—*v.t.* to find fault with; rebuke severely; as, the teacher *scolded* him for being late:—*n.* one who habitually finds fault; especially, a rude, quarrelsome woman.
Syn., v. reprove, reprimand, upbraid.

scold·ing (skōl/dĭng), *n.* the act of one who scolds; also, angry reproaches.

scol·lop (skŏl/ŭp), *n.* a shellfish:—*v.t.* to mix with crumbs and butter and bake; scallop. See **scallop.**

sconce (skŏns), *n.* an ornamental bracket, fastened to a wall, holding one or more candlesticks.

scone (skōn), *n.* **1,** a Scotch batter cake of barley, oatmeal, or wheat, baked on a griddle; **2,** a rich baking-powder biscuit with currants.

scoop (skōōp), *n.* **1,** a large long-handled ladle for skimming or dipping out liquids; **2,** a shovel for snow, coal, etc.; also, a small utensil, shaped like a shovel, for dipping out flour, sugar, etc.; **3,** the act of dipping out or making a hollow; **4,** any gesture or motion like that made with a scoop; as, with a *scoop* of his hand, he splashed water into my face; **5,** the hollow left from scooping; **6,** the quantity dipped out in one scoop; as, two *scoops* will be enough; **7,** the scooplike bucket of a dredging machine, water wheel, etc.:—*v.t.* **1,** to take out or up with a scoop; **2,** to make hollow.

SCONCE

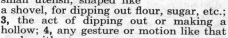
SCOOP, def. 2

scoot (skōōt), *v.i. Colloquial,* to walk or run hastily; dart; as, when he saw me, he *scooted* around the corner.

scoot·er (skōō/tẽr), *n.* **1,** a flat-bottomed sailboat with runners, for sailing through water or over ice; **2,** a child's toy vehicle consisting of a narrow board, hung low on two tandem wheels, and a long handle for steering.

scope (skōp), *n.* **1,** extent of understanding; range of mental activity; as, a book beyond the *scope* of high-school pupils; **2,** the field covered; range of subjects embraced; as, a book limited in *scope;* **3,** room or outlet for action; as, he craved ample *scope* for his abilities.

SCOOTER, def. 2

scorch (skôrch), *v.t.* **1,** to burn the surface of; as, to *scorch* linen; **2,** to parch; wither; as, a hot sun *scorches* grass.

score (skôr), *n.* **1,** a line, groove, or mark that has been drawn, cut, or scratched on a surface; **2,** a debt; bill; also, a grudge; as, to pay off old *scores;* **3,** reason; ground;

as, he was freed on the *score* of insufficient evidence; **4,** the number of points, runs, etc., made in a game or contest; as, the *score* was five to one; **5,** [*pl.* score], twenty; as, three *score* and ten; **6,** in music, a copy of a composition showing all the parts for all the instruments or voices; **7, scores,** a great many; as, *scores* of people were there:— *v.t.* [scored, scor-ing], **1,** to notch or mark with lines, scratches, etc., as wood or paper; **2,** to make a record of; **3,** to win (a run, a point, etc.); hence, to achieve (a hit, success, etc.); **4,** to grade (test papers); also, to remove by marking out; as, to *score* out a paragraph; **5,** to blame; find fault with:— *v.i.* **1,** to keep the tally in a game; **2,** to win points in a game.

scorn (skôrn), *n.* **1,** extreme contempt; haughty disdain and indignation; **2,** an object of contempt; as, the *scorn* of the neighborhood:— *v.t.* **1,** to hold in extreme disdain; reject with contempt; as, to *scorn* underhand methods; **2,** *Archaic,* to taunt; scoff at; as, to *scorn* a liar.

    Syn., v. abhor, detest, mock, deride.

scorn-ful (skôrn′fŏŏl), *adj.* full of, or expressing, contempt; disdainful; as, *scornful* pride.— *adv.* **scorn′ful-ly.**

scor-pi-on (skôr′pĭ-ŭn), *n.* an animal of the same class as the spider, two to eight inches in length. Each of the front legs is equipped with a pair of pincers, and the tip of the tail has a poisonous sting.

Scot (skŏt), *n.* a native or inhabitant of Scotland.

Scot. abbreviation for *Scotch, Scottish, Scotland.*

Scotch (skŏch), *adj.* pertaining to Scotland, its inhabitants, or its language:— *n.* English as spoken by the Scotch:—**the Scotch,** the people of Scotland.

scotch (skŏch), *v.t.* **1,** to scratch; cut; notch; **2,** to wound without killing; disable; as, to *scotch* a snake.

Scotch-man (skŏch′-măn), *n.* [*pl.* Scotchmen (-měn)], a native of Scotland; a Scot.

sco-ter (skō′tẽr), *n.* a northern sea duck.

scot—free (skŏt′-frē′), *adj.* safe; unpunished; as, the prisoner went *scot-free.*

Sco-tia (skō′shȧ), *Poetic,* Scotland.

Scot-land (skŏt′lănd), a country (cap. Edinburgh), the northern division of Great Britain (map **13**).

SCORPION (½)
S, sting.

SCOTER (⅛)

Scots (skŏts), *adj.* pertaining to the Scottish people; Scottish; as, the *Scots* parliament:— *n.* English as spoken by the Scotch.

Scots-man (skŏts′măn), *n.* [*pl.* Scotsmen (-měn)], a Scotchman; a Scot.

Scott (skŏt), Sir Walter (1771–1832), a Scotch poet and novelist, author of the Waverley novels.

Scot-tish (skŏt′ĭsh), *adj.* pertaining to Scotland, its inhabitants, its language or literature.

scoun-drel (skoun′drĕl), *n.* a low, worthless rascal.

¹scour (skour), *v.t.* **1,** to rub hard with some rough material, in order to make clean and shiny; as, we *scoured* the pots and pans; **2,** to wash or clear of dirt, grease, etc., by rubbing with soap and water, flushing, etc.; as, to *scour* a rug; to *scour* a pipe:— *n.* the act of scouring; as, she gave the floor a good *scour.*— *n.* **scour′er.**

²scour (skour), *v.t.* to go through thoroughly, as on a search; as, the police *scoured* the city for the criminal.

scourge (skûrj), *n.* **1,** a whip used to inflict pain or punishment; **2,** a means of inflicting punishment; hence, harsh punishment; **3,** one who or that which afflicts or destroys; as, the *scourge* of pestilence:— *v.t.* [scourged, scourg-ing], **1,** to whip severely; **2,** to grieve or torment greatly; harass; as, the plague *scourged* the land.

¹scout (skout), *n.* **1,** a person sent out to obtain and bring back information; especially, a soldier sent out to obtain information about the enemy; **2,** the act of gathering such information; **3,** a member of the Boy Scouts or the Girl Scouts:— *v.i.* **1,** to act as a scout; to go about for purposes of securing information; especially, to ascertain the movements, position, strength, etc., of an enemy; **2,** to perform the duties of a boy scout or a girl scout.

²scout (skout), *v.i.* to mock; scoff; jibe:— *v.t.* to reject with disdain; as, she *scouted* all objections to her plan.

scow (skou), *n.* a large flat-bottomed boat with square ends, used especially to carry garbage and other refuse to be dumped.

scowl (skoul), *v.i.* to wrinkle the brows in displeasure, anger, or the like:— *n.* an angry wrinkling of the brow.

scrab-ble (skrăb′l), *v.i.* [scrab-bled, scrab-bling], **1,** to move along on the hands and knees; as, to *scrabble* up a hill; **2,** to scrape, scratch, or paw with the hands, as if to find or collect something; as, she *scrabbled* in the box for her thimble; **3,** hence, to drudge for a living:— *v.t.* to gather hurriedly; scrape together; as, he *scrabbled* up his belongings:—*n.* a scramble; a hasty gathering up or together.

scrag (skrăg), *n.* **1,** a thin, scrawny person or animal; **2,** the back of a sheep's neck:—*v.t.* [scragged, scrag-ging], *Colloquial,* to wring the neck of.

scrag-gly (skrăg′lĭ), *adj.* [scrag-gli-er, scrag-gli-est], unkempt; as, a *scraggly* beard; also, jagged; craggy.

scrag-gy (skrăg′ĭ), *adj.* [scrag-gi-er, scrag-gi-est], **1,** lean, thin, and scrawny; **2,** rough, with uneven points; broken; jagged.

scram-ble (skrăm′bl), *v.i.* [scram-bled, scram-bling], **1,** to clamber or move along on the hands and feet; as, to *scramble* over sand dunes; **2,** to struggle eagerly or roughly for something; as, the children *scrambled* for the candy:—*v.t.* **1,** to toss together at random; **2,** to prepare (eggs) by cooking the mixed yolks and whites:—*n.* a rude, disorderly struggle or climb.

Scran-ton (skrăn′tŭn), a city in northeastern Pennsylvania (map 6).

¹scrap (skrăp), *n.* **1,** a small piece, cut or broken off; **2,** worn out, discarded, or broken machinery, or used and discarded metal of any kind; junk metal; **3, scraps,** odds and ends; especially, small pieces of food left over from a meal:—*adj.* in the form of scrap; as, *scrap* metal:—*v.t.* [scrapped, scrap-ping], to break up; discard, as broken machinery.

²scrap (skrăp), *Slang: n.* a fight; quarrel:—*v.i.* [scrapped, scrap-ping], to fight.

scrap-book (skrăp′book′), *n.* a blank book in which to paste clippings from books, magazines, etc.

scrape (skrāp), *v.t.* [scraped, scrap-ing], **1,** to drag harshly or gratingly; as, to *scrape* a chair along the floor; **2,** to remove by rubbing with something sharp or rough; as, to *scrape* paint from a door; also, to remove paint, paper, etc., from; as, to *scrape* furniture; *scrape* walls; **3,** to gather or accumulate in small amounts, with effort; as, to *scrape* together a small sum:—*v.i.* to manage by being extremely economical; as, to pinch and *scrape:—n.* **1,** the act, noise, or effect of harsh rubbing or grating; **2,** a difficult or awkward situation; as, if he had obeyed his mother, he would not be in this *scrape.—n.* **scrap′er.**

scrap-ple (skrăp′l), *n.* a food made by boiling together seasoned, chopped meat, usually pork, and corn meal or flour. It is served in fried slices.

scratch (skrăch), *v.t.* **1,** to mark or tear the surface of, with something rough or pointed; as, to *scratch* a table with a pin; **2,** to cancel or erase; as, *scratch* this item out; **3,** to scrape or rub lightly with the fingernails, etc.; as, he *scratched* his cheek; **4,** to strike on an uneven surface; as, to *scratch* matches:—*v.i.* **1,** to make a grating noise; as, the chalk *scratches;* **2,** to cause irritation or pain by rubbing; as, the collar *scratches:—n.* **1,** a mark or tear made by something pointed or rough; **2,** a slight wound or cut, as that made by a pin; **3,** a grating sound, as of chalk on a slate; **4,** the starting line in a race; also, the beginning; as, we will start this work from *scratch.—n.* **scratch′er.**—*adj.* **scratch′y.**

scrawl (skrôl), *v.t.* and *v.i.* to write or draw hastily, or in badly formed characters:—*n.* careless handwriting; a scribble.

scraw-ny (skrô′nĭ), *adj.* [scraw-ni-er, scraw-ni-est], lean; skinny.

scream (skrēm), *n.* a sharp, shrill cry, as of fear or pain:—*v.i.* to utter such a cry:—*v.t.* to utter in a loud, piercing voice; as, to *scream* a warning.

screech (skrēch), *n.* a harsh, shrill cry, as of fright or pain:—*v.i.* to utter a harsh, shrill cry:—*v.t.* to cry out in a shrill harsh voice.

screech owl, an owl that utters a shrill, screeching cry instead of hooting.

screen (skrēn), *n.* **1,** a light, covered framework, partition, or curtain, that protects or conceals; as, the nurse put a *screen* around his bed; **2,** anything in the nature of a protective curtain; as, a smoke *screen;* the villain was concealed behind a *screen* of shrubbery; **3,** a frame covered with wire or cotton fabric to exclude insects; as, a window *screen;* **4,** a coarse sieve for separating coal, gravel, etc., into different sizes; **5,** a surface on which images are projected by a motion-picture machine or a magic lantern; **6,** hence, motion pic-tures:—*v.t.* **1,** to shut off from danger, observation, etc.; shelter or conceal; protect; **2,**

SCREEN def. 1

SCREEN, def. 4

to sift through a coarse sieve; **3,** to project (a picture) upon a screen with a motion-picture machine or magic lantern; **4,** to select (personnel) by standard tests.

screw (skroō), *n.* **1,** a slender, nail-like, round bar of metal, with a spiral groove, or thread, for holding together pieces of wood, metal, or the like; **2,** anything resembling such a device; **3,** a contrivance to propel steamships, motorboats, etc.: also called *screw propeller;* **4,** a turn of a screw; as, give it another screw:—*v.t.* **1,** to tighten or fasten with, or as with, a screw; **2,** to twist or distort; as, to *screw* up one's face; **3,** to force (something) from someone as if by the use of screws; as, to *screw* information out of a prisoner:—

SCREWS, def. 1

v.i. to turn with a motion like a screw.

screw driv-er (drīv′ẽr), a tool with a blunt blade, the tip of which fits into a slot in the head of a screw, and is used for turning the screw. Also written **screw′driv′er.**

SCREW DRIVER

scrib-ble (skrĭb′l), *v.t.* [scrib-bled, scrib-bling], **1,** to write hastily and carelessly; **2,** to cover (paper, books, etc.) with careless or meaningless scrawls:—*v.i.* to scrawl; as, a small child *scribbles:*—*n.* hasty, careless writing.

scrib-bler (skrĭb′lẽr), *n.* one who writes carelessly and hastily; especially, an author who writes poor books.

scribe (skrīb), *n.* **1,** a skilled penman; especially, in former times, one who copied manuscripts, or acted as an official or public secretary; **2,** among the Jews, in ancient times, a teacher and lawgiver; **3,** humorously, an author.

scrim (skrĭm), *n.* a thin, loosely woven but strong, fabric of cotton or linen, used especially in making curtains.

scrim-mage (skrĭm′ĭj), *n.* **1,** a general quarrel or fight; a tussle; **2,** in football, any play following the snapping back of the ball when both teams are lined up.

scrimp (skrĭmp), *v.t.* **1,** to make too small; as, to *scrimp* a dress; **2,** to be sparing of; as, to *scrimp* material; also, to be niggardly to; stint:—*v.i.* to be sparing or stingy.

scrimp-y (skrĭmp′ĭ), *adj.* [scrimp-i-er, scrimp-i-est], *Colloquial,* scanty; also, stingy; miserly.

¹scrip (skrĭp), *n. Archaic,* a small pouch or wallet, formerly used by beggars or pilgrims.

²scrip (skrĭp), *n.* **1,** a certificate of ownership; **2,** paper money of a denomination less than a dollar used during and after the War between the States; **3,** substitute money issued as wages by a corporation, municipality, etc., in an emergency when legal currency is scarce.

script (skrĭpt), *n.* **1,** ordinary handwriting; written characters; also, style of writing; **2,** type that is an imitation of writing; **3,**

in motion pictures, a written summary of the action, the cast of characters, etc.

Scrip-ture (skrĭp′tŭr), *n.* the Bible; the books of both the Old and the New Testaments, or of either one: often called *The Holy Scriptures:*—**scripture,** any sacred writing; as, the Buddhist *scriptures.*—*adj.* **scrip′tur-al.**

scrive-ner (skrĭv′nẽr; skrĭv′ẽn-ẽr), *n.* formerly, a clerk; especially, one who copied documents, drew up contracts, wrote letters, etc.; a scribe; hence, a writer.

scrof-u-la (skrŏf′ū-là), *n.* a disease marked by swelling of glands, particularly those of the neck, and inflammation of bones and joints. It occurs most often in children.

SCROLL, def. 1

scroll (skrōl), *n.* **1,** a manuscript of paper or parchment in the form of a roll; **2,** a spiral, ornamental design in carving or printing; **3,** an ornamental flourish to a signature.

scroll saw, a very narrow saw for cutting thin wood in intricate, ornamental patterns.

Scrooge (skro͞oj), *n.* in Dickens's story "A Christmas Carol," the old miser whose heart was softened by a vision he saw on Christmas Eve.

SCROLLS, def. 2

¹scrub (skrŭb), *v.t.* [scrubbed, scrub-bing], **1,** to wash by hard rubbing; as, to *scrub* clothes; **2,** to rub hard with a wet cloth or brush; as, to *scrub* floors, woodwork, hands, etc.:—*v.i.* to do cleaning and scouring; as, she *scrubs* for a living:—*n.* the act or process of cleaning by hard rubbing.

²scrub (skrŭb), *n.* **1,** a shrub, tree, bush, or the like, stunted or inferior in growth; also, a growth or thicket of such stunted trees; as, pine *scrub;* **2,** anything, as a person, plant, or animal, that is inferior in size, quality, or breed; also, a member of a second or inferior team; as, the varsity played the *scrubs:*—*adj.* **1,** mean or small; also, below normal size; stunted; **2,** consisting of, or pertaining to, players who are not members of a regular team; as, a *scrub* game.

scrub-by (skrŭb′ĭ), *adj.* [scrub-bi-er, scrub-bi-est], **1,** mean and small; stunted in growth; **2,** covered with brushwood.

scruff (skrŭf), *n.* the back of the neck; the loose skin at the back of the neck.

scru-ple (skro͞o′pl), *n.* **1,** an apothecaries'

āte, āorta, râre, căt, ȧsk, fär, ăllow, sofȧ; ēve, ĕvent, ĕll, writẽr, novĕl; bīte, pĭn; nō, ōbey, ôr, dŏg, tŏp, cȯllide; ūnit, ūnite, bûrn, cŭt, focŭs; no͞on, fo͝ot; mound; coin;

weight of twenty grains or one third of a dram; **2,** a very small quantity; **3,** a feeling of doubt, uneasiness, or uncertainty arising from one's conscience; as, he had *scruples* about disregarding his mother's advice:—*v.i.* [scru-pled, scru-pling], to hesitate on grounds of conscience; as, he *scrupled* to leave his work so long.

scru·pu·lous (skrōō′pŭ-lŭs), *adj.* **1,** conscientious; attentive to details; as, a *scrupulous* student; **2,** unswerving; strict; as, *scrupulous* honesty.

scru·ti·nize (skrōō′tĭ-nīz), *v.t.* and *v.i.* [scrutinized, scrutiniz-ing], to inspect closely; examine carefully.

scru·ti·ny (skrōō′tĭ-nĭ), *n.* [*pl.* scrutinies], close inspection or examination; as, a careful *scrutiny* detected no flaws.
    Syn. inquiry, investigation.

scud (skŭd), *v.i.* [scud-ded, scud-ding], to run or move swiftly; of a ship, to run before a gale of wind with little or no sail spread:—*n.* **1,** the act of scudding; **2,** foam or spray driven by the wind.

scuff (skŭf), *v.t.* **1,** to wear a rough place on the surface of; as, to *scuff* new shoes; **2,** to shuffle or drag (the feet):—*v.i.* **1,** to become rough on the surface; as, soft leather *scuffs* easily; **2,** to drag the feet in a slovenly manner:—*n.* a rough or worn spot.

scuf·fle (skŭf′l), *v.i.* [scuf-fled, scuf-fling], **1,** to fight or struggle in a confused, disorderly manner; **2,** to drag the feet in a slovenly fashion; scuff:—*n.* a close grappling; a confused or disorderly struggle or fight.

scull (skŭl), *n.* **1,** one of a pair of short, light oars; **2,** an oar used at the stern of a boat and worked from side to side to propel the boat forward; **3,** a boat, usually for racing, propelled by short sculls:—*v.i.* and *v.t.* to propel or move (a boat) with a scull.—*n.* **scull′er.**

SCULL, def. 2

scul·ler·y (skŭl′ẽr-ĭ), *n.* [*pl.* sculleries], a room where cooking utensils are washed and kept; also, a back kitchen for rough work, such as cleaning pots and pans.

scul·lion (skŭl′yŭn), *n.* a servant who cleans cooking utensils and does other menial service in the kitchen.

sculp·tor (skŭlp′tẽr), *n.* one who practices the art of carving, cutting, or modeling figures or designs in wood, stone, or any other material.—*n.fem.* **sculp′tress.**

sculp·ture (skŭlp′tŭr), *n.* **1,** the art of

fashioning figures or other objects in stone, metal, wood, or clay; **2,** a piece of such work:—*v.t.* [sculptured, sculptur-ing], to carve, chisel, model, cast, in stone, wood, clay, or metal.
—*adj.* **sculp′tur-al.**

scum (skŭm), *n.* **1,** a layer of impurities which forms on the surface of a liquid; **2,** anything worthless or vile; hence, low, worthless people.

scup·per (skŭp′ẽr), *n.* a hole, tube, or gutter in the side of a ship to carry off water from the deck.

scurf (skûrf), *n.* **1,** white, flaky scales on the skin, especially on the scalp; dandruff; **2,** anything like flakes or scales sticking to a surface.

SCULPTURE
def. 2

scur·ril·ous (skûr′ĭ-lŭs), *adj.* **1,** using abusive, indecent language; **2,** containing abuse; as, *scurrilous* language.—*adv.* **scur′ril-ous-ly.**—*n.* **scur′ril-ous-ness.**—*n.* **scurril′i-ty** (skŭ-rĭl′ĭ-tĭ).

scur·ry (skûr′ĭ), *v.i.* [scurried, scurry-ing], to hasten or move rapidly along:—*n.* [*pl.* scurries], a scampering; hurrying.

scur·vy (skûr′vĭ), *n.* a disease caused by lack of fresh vegetable food, and marked by great weakness, thinness of the body, bleeding gums, etc.:—*adj.* [scur-vi-er, scur-vi-est], contemptible; mean; as, a *scurvy* trick.

scutch·eon (skŭch′ŭn), *n.* a surface bearing a coat of arms; an escutcheon. See **escutcheon.**

¹scut·tle (skŭt′l), *v.i.* [scut-tled, scut-tling], to hasten or hurry away:—*n.* a hurried flight.

²scut·tle (skŭt′l), *n.* a small opening with a lid, as in the roof of a house, or in the deck, bottom, or side of a ship; also, the lid covering such an opening:—*v.t.* [scuttled, scut-tling], to sink (a ship) by cutting holes in the bottom or sides.

³scut·tle (skŭt′l), *n.* a deep metal vessel or hod for holding a small quantity of coal.

Scyl·la (sĭl′à), *n.* **1,** in mythology, a hideous female sea monster, surrounded by barking dogs, feared by sailors; **2,** her supposed abode, a dangerous headland in southwestern Italy on the Strait of Messina, opposite which is Charybdis, a whirlpool on the coast of Sicily (map 1):
—**between Scylla and Charybdis,** between two dangers, either of which is difficult to avoid without running into the other.

³SCUTTLE

scythe (sīth), *n.* a cutting instrument for mowing grain, grass, or the like, by hand.

Scyth·i·a (sĭth′ĭ·a̤), the name given in ancient times to the entire region north and northeast of the Black Sea, included in what is now the U.S.S.R.

S.D. or **S.Dak.** abbreviation for *South Dakota.*

S.E. abbreviation for *southeast.*

sea (sē), *n.* **1,** a body of salt water, smaller than an ocean; as, the Caribbean *Sea;* **2,** an inland body of water; as, the *Sea* of Galilee; **3,** the ocean as a whole; **4,** a billow or large wave; the swell of the ocean or other body of water in a storm; as, the high *sea* kept on after the storm; **5,** a large quantity; anything like the sea in vastness; as, a *sea* of troubles; a *sea* of faces:—**at sea, 1,** on the ocean; out of sight of land; **2,** puzzled; uncertain.

sea a·nem·o·ne (a̤-nĕm′ṓ-nē), a polyp or low form of sea animal, often large, beautifully colored, and growing singly.

sea-board (sē′bôrd′), *n.* the land bordering the sea or ocean; the seacoast:—*adj.* near or on the seacoast.

sea-coast (sē′kōst′), *n.* the coast of the sea or ocean; seashore.

sea cow, any of several large, fishlike sea mammals, as the manatee.

sea dog, 1, any of various seals; especially, the common seal of northern seas; **2,** the dogfish; **3,** an old sailor.

sea-far-er (sē′fâr′ẽr), *n.* a person who travels by sea or follows the life of a sailor.

sea-far-ing (sē′fâr′ĭng), *adj.* following the life of a sailor.

sea-girt (sē′gûrt′), *adj.* surrounded by the sea; as, *seagirt* islands.

sea-go-ing (sē′gō′ĭng), *adj.* **1,** seafaring; **2,** suitable or fitted for use on the open sea; as, a *seagoing* yacht.

sea gull, any bird of the gull family that remains near the sea.

sea horse, 1, in mythology, a fabulous creature, half horse and half fish; **2,** a small fish with a head resembling that of a horse.

SEA HORSE (½) def. 2

¹seal (sēl), *n.* **1,** any of various flesh-eating sea animals, found chiefly in polar regions, and hunted for their hide and oil, and, in some species, for their valuable fur; **2,** the dressed fur of this animal; sealskin; **3,** a leather made from the skin of the seal:—*v.i.* to hunt seals.

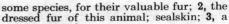

SEAL (¹⁄₂₀), def. 1

²seal (sēl), *n.* **1,** a stamp or die engraved with a device, image, or the like, used for making an impression in wax or some similar substance; **2,** wax or a similar substance fixed upon a letter or document and stamped with an emblem or design as proof of genuineness; **3,** anything that closes another thing securely in order to prevent its being opened or tampered with; hence, anything that secures; a pledge; as, a *seal* of silence on his lips; **4,** a decorative stamp used in sealing a letter or package; as, a Christmas *seal:*—*v.t.* **1,** to fasten with a device so that it cannot be tampered with; as, to *seal* a letter; **2,** to set or affix a seal to; as, to *seal* a deed; **3,** to ratify or confirm; as, the bargain was *sealed;* **4,** to keep secure or secret; as, to *seal* documents for later examination; **5,** to settle (a person's fate) once and for all; **6,** to enclose; confine; as, a fly *sealed* in amber; **7,** to close tightly, as a pipe, a jar of fruit, etc.; also, to fill up the cracks of.

seal brown, a rich, dark-brown color like that of the fur of the seal after it is dyed.

sea lev-el, the level of the sea halfway between high and low tide: used as the standard in measuring the height of land; as, 300 feet above *sea level.*

seal-ing wax, a kind of wax that softens when heated and hardens quickly on cooling, used for sealing letters, packages, etc.

sea li-on, any of several large seals of the Pacific Ocean.

seal-skin (sēl′skĭn′), *n.* the skin of a fur seal or a garment made of it.

seam (sēm), *n.* **1,** the line formed by sewing together two edges of material; **2,** a visible line of junction or union, as between two boards; **3,** a scar; also, a wrinkle; **4,** a layer or bed of mineral or rock; as, a *seam* of copper ore:—*v.t.* **1,** to join or sew together, as the parts of a garment; **2,** to scar; line; as, the wind had *seamed* his face with wrinkles.—*adj.* **seam′less.**

SEA LION (¹⁄₃₀)

sea-man (sē′măn), *n.* [*pl.* seamen (-mĕn)], a sailor; mariner.—*n.* **sea′man-ship.**

sea mew (mū), a sea gull; especially, one of the common European sea gulls.

seam-stress (sēm′strĕs; sĕm′strĕs), *n.* a woman who does sewing; a needlewoman.

seam-y (sēm′ĭ), *adj.* [seam-i-er, seam-i-est], **1,** showing or having seams, especially roughly finished seams; **2,** hence, rough; harsh and unpleasant; as, the *seamy* side of life.

sé-ance (sā′äns′; sā′äns), *n.* **1,** a meeting or session; **2,** a meeting of spiritualists to receive spirit messages.

sea-plane (sē′plān′), *n.* an airplane so constructed that it can alight or travel upon the surface of water. (See illustration under *aviation*.)

sea-port (sē′pôrt′), *n.* a town, harbor, or port that can be reached by seagoing vessels.

sear (sēr), *v.t.* **1,** to cause to dry up or wither; scorch; as, the summer sun *sears* the fields; **2,** to burn to dryness and hardness on the surface; cauterize; as, to *sear* a wound; **3,** to render callous or unfeeling, as the conscience:—*adj.* (also *sere*), withered; dried, as vegetation.

search (sûrch), *v.t.* **1,** to seek; as, to *search* out the truth; **2,** to look for something by examining carefully the contents of (a place or object), the clothing of (a person), etc.; as, to *search* a room; to *search* a prisoner for weapons; **3,** to probe; try or test; as, to *search* one's heart:—*n.* **1,** the act of seeking or looking for something; **2,** a careful investigation; examination.

search-ing (sûr′chĭng), *adj.* penetrating; thorough; keen; as, a *searching* analysis; a *searching* glance.—*adv.* **search′ing-ly.**

search-light (sûrch′līt′), *n.* a powerful electric light that can throw a beam of light in any direction; also, the beam of light.

search war-rant, a written order giving a police officer authority to search a house.

sea-shore (sē′shôr′), *n.* the land bordering the sea; seacoast.

sea-sick (sē′sĭk′), *adj.* suffering from nausea caused by the pitching and rolling of a boat.—*n.* **sea′sick′ness.**

SEARCHLIGHT

sea-side (sē′sīd′), *n.* the shore along the sea; the seashore.

sea-son (sē′zn), *n.* **1,** one of the four periods into which the year is divided, as spring, summer, autumn, and winter; **2,** any particular time; as, the holiday *season;* **3,** a suitable, convenient, or legal time; as, the shooting *season:*—**in season and out of season,** at all times:—*v.t.* **1,** to bring to the best state for use; as, to *season* timber; **2,** to make palatable, as with salt or spices; also, to make more agreeable or delightful; as, he *seasoned* his lecture with humor:—*v.i.* to become fit for use; as, timber *seasons* well in the open air.

sea-son-a-ble (sē′zn-á-bl), *adj.* **1,** occurring or coming in good or proper time; as, *seasonable* advice; **2,** in keeping with the time of year; as, *seasonable* weather.

sea-son-al (sē′zn-ăl), *adj.* relating to or influenced by certain periods of the year; as, *seasonal* rates; *seasonal* diseases; *seasonal* trades; *seasonal* labor.—*adv.* **sea′son-al-ly.**

sea-son-ing (sē′zn-ĭng), *n.* that which is added to give relish to food, as salt, pepper, spices, etc.

seat (sēt), *n.* **1,** an object on which one sits; a bench, chair, or stool; **2,** that part of a chair, stool, or bench, on which one sits; **3,** that part of the body on which one sits; also, the part of a garment covering it; as, the *seat* of one's trousers; **4,** the place where anything flourishes; location; site; as, the brain is the *seat* of the intellect; a university is a *seat* of learning; **5,** a capital town or city; as, a county *seat;* **6,** the right to sit; specifically, membership; as, a *seat* on the stock exchange; **7,** room or space for a spectator; as, *seats* for a football game:—*v.t.* **1,** to place on a chair or bench; cause to sit down; **2,** to furnish with places to sit; as, this hall *seats* 800 persons; **3,** to repair the bottom of; as, to *seat* a chair.

Se-at-tle (sē-ăt′l), a city on Puget Sound, in the State of Washington (map **9**).

sea ur-chin (ûr′chĭn), a small sea animal with a thin shell covered with movable spines.

sea wall, a wall or embankment to break the force of the waves and prevent damage by the sea.

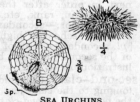

SEA URCHINS

A, sea urchin with long spines; B, sand dollar with most of spines (Sp.) removed to show skeleton.

sea-ward (sē′wĕrd), *adj.* going toward, or situated in the direction of, the sea:—*adv.* toward the sea.—*adv.* **sea′wards.**

sea-weed (sē′wēd′), *n.* any plant growing in the sea, as kelp.

sea-wor-thy (sē′wûr′thĭ), *adj.* fit for a voyage on the open sea; as, a *seaworthy* boat.—*n.* **sea′wor′thi-ness.**

se·ba·ceous (sē-bā′shŭs), *adj.* **1,** pertaining to, or resembling, fat; **2,** containing or secreting fat; as, *sebaceous* glands.

sec. abbreviation for *second* or *seconds, section, secretary.*

se·cede (sē-sēd′), *v.i.* [seced-ed, seced-ing], to withdraw formally from fellowship, union, or association; especially, to withdraw from a political or religious body.

se·ces·sion (sē-sĕsh′ŭn), *n.* a deliberate and formal withdrawal from a group, union, or organization.—*n.* **se·ces′sion-ist.**

se·clude (sē-klood′), *v.t.* [seclud-ed, seclud-ing], to withdraw or keep apart from others; to place in solitude.

se·clu·sion (sē-kloo′zhŭn), *n.* withdrawal from others; privacy.—*adj.* **se·clu′sive.**

sec·ond (sĕk′ŭnd), *adj.* **1,** immediately following the first; next to the first in order of place or time; **2,** next to the first in value, excellence, merit, dignity, or importance; as, a *second* choice; **3,** being of the same kind as another that has gone before; another; as, a *second* Lincoln; additional; as, a *second* helping; **4,** in music, rendering a part next to the highest in pitch and importance; as, a *second* violin: —*n.* **1,** one who or that which is next to the first in place, rank, excellence, or power; **2,** one who attends another, as in a duel or boxing match; **3,** a unit of time; the 60th part of a minute; **4,** hence, *Colloquial,* a short space of time; as, wait just a *second;* **5,** an article of merchandise of a grade inferior to the best; as, these *seconds* are very cheap:—*v.t.* **1,** to act as an assistant or supporter of; assist; **2,** in parliamentary practice, to support (a motion, resolution, or nomination) proposed by another.

sec·ond·ar·y (sĕk′ŭn-dĕr′ĭ), *adj.* following next in order after the first; of second place, origin, rank, etc.; hence, subordinate; inferior:—**secondary school,** a high school or school of high-school rank:—*n.* [*pl.* secondaries], any of the quill feathers of the second joint of a bird's wing (see illustration under *bird*).

sec·ond–class (sĕk′ŭnd-klàs′), *adj.* belonging to the class just below the first or the best; as, a *second-class* passage.

sec·ond-hand (sĕk′ŭnd-hănd′), *adj.* **1,** not new; as, *secondhand* furniture; **2,** dealing in goods that are not new; as, a *secondhand* shop; **3,** heard or learned indirectly; as, *secondhand* news.

sec·ond-ly (sĕk′ŭnd-lĭ), *adv.* in the next place; in the second place.

sec·ond–rate (sĕk′ŭnd-rāt′), *adj.* not first-class; second in rank or quality; as, a *second-rate* hotel.

se·cre·cy (sē′krĕ-sĭ), *n.* [*pl.* secrecies], **1,** the state or quality of being secret or hidden; concealment; as, done in *secrecy;* **2,** the habit of keeping information to oneself.

se·cret (sē′krĕt), *adj.* **1,** concealed; private; as, *secret* information; **2,** withdrawn from public view or knowledge; as, a *secret* treaty; also, operating· in secrecy; as, a *secret* society; **3,** permitting concealment; secluded; as, a *secret* chamber; **4,** mysterious; unknown; as, the *secret* operations of nature:—**secret service,** government detective service:—*n.* **1,** that which is purposely concealed or left untold; **2,** something not widely known; as, the *secrets* of science; **3,** a hidden reason or cause; as, unselfishness is the *secret* of his happiness; **4,** secrecy; as, prepared in *secret.*—*adv.* **se′cret·ly.**

Syn., adj. clandestine, sly, underhand.

sec·re·tar·y (sĕk′rĕ-tĕr′ĭ), *n.* [*pl.* secretaries], **1,** one who does writing for another; especially, one who attends to records, letters, etc., for an individual or an organization; **2,** an official of a company or society in charge of records and correspondence; **3,** a state executive who superintends the business of a government department; as, the *Secretary* of State; **4,** a writing desk.—*adj.* **sec′re·tar′i·al** (sĕk′rĕ-târ′-ĭ-ăl).

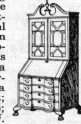

SECRETARY
def. 4

secretary bird, a large bird of prey, native to Africa, so called because of a crest of long feathers suggesting pens stuck behind the ear. It eats snakes and insects, and is often tamed and used in ridding places of reptiles.

SECRETARY BIRD (¹⁄₃₀)

se·crete (sē-krēt′), *v.t.* [secret-ed, secret-ing], **1,** to hide or conceal; **2,** to separate from the blood and make into a new substance; produce; as, the liver *secretes* bile.

Syn. mask, cloak, disguise.

se·cre·tion (sē-krē′shŭn), *n.* **1,** the producing of a new substance out of materials separated from the blood; as, the *secretion* of saliva; **2,** any substance so produced; as, bile is a *secretion* of the liver.

se·cre·tive (sē-krē′tĭv), *adj.* inclined to keep things to oneself; not frank or open; reticent.—*adv.* **se·cre′tive·ly.**—*n.* **se·cre′-tive·ness.**

āte, āorta, râre, căt, ȧsk, fär, ăllow, sofȧ; ēve, ĕvent, ĕll, writēr, novĕl; bīte, pĭn; nō, ōbey, ôr, dŏg, tŏp, cŏllide; ūnit, ūnite, bûrn, cŭt, focŭs; noōn, fŏŏt; mound; coin;

sect (sĕkt), *n.* a number of persons who, following a teacher or leader, hold certain opinions in common, especially certain religious opinions.

sec-tar-i-an (sĕk-târ′ĭ-ăn), *adj.* pertaining to a denomination or sect; as, a *sectarian* school; hence, narrow-minded; bigoted:— *n.* a member of a denomination or sect.

sec-tion (sĕk′shŭn), *n.* **1,** the act of cutting; separation by cutting; **2,** a part or portion cut off; **3,** a representation of an object cut in two crosswise or lengthwise; as, the cross *section* of a tomato; **4,** a division or subdivision of a chapter, often marked with the character [§]; **5,** a distinct part of a country,

SECTION, def. 3
Cross section of a tomato.

people, community, or class; as, the business *section* of the city; **6,** in a sleeping car, a compartment including an upper and a lower berth:— *v.t.* to divide or cut into sections.

sec-tion-al (sĕk′shŭn-ăl), *adj.* **1,** relating to a section or district; local; as, *sectional* strife; **2,** consisting of parts; as, a *sectional* bookcase.

sec-tion-al-ism (sĕk′shŭn-ăl-ĭzm), *n.* sectional or local prejudice, feeling, or the like; devotion to local interests rather than to the welfare of the country at large.

sec-tor (sĕk′tẽr), *n.* **1,** in geometry, a figure bounded by two radii of a circle and the part of the circumference cut off by them; **2,** one of the parts into which an area of military defense is divided, each assigned to a separate commander.

SECTOR (S) of a circle.

sec-u-lar (sĕk′ū-lẽr), *adj.* **1,** relating to things of the world or to things not sacred; worldly; as, *secular* art; of the state as opposed to the church; as, *secular* courts; **2,** not bound by monastic vows or living in monastic communities; as, a parish priest belongs to the *secular* clergy.

Syn. earthly, terrestrial, temporal.

sec-u-lar-ize (sĕk′ū-lẽr-īz), *v.t.* [secularized, seculariz-ing], **1,** to transfer from sacred to secular or common use, as church property; to transfer from church to state control; as, to *secularize* education; **2,** to make worldly or unspiritual; as, to *secularize* the Sabbath; **3,** to release temporarily from sacred or monastic vows; as, to *secularize* a priest.

se-cure (sē-kūr′), *adj.* **1,** free from fear, care, or worry; **2,** safe; free from danger; as, *secure* against attack; in safekeeping; as, the prisoners are *secure;* affording safety;

as, a *secure* retreat; firm or steady; as, a *secure* foundation; **3,** confident; as, *secure* of welcome; certain; assured; as, the victory is *secure:—v.t.* [secured, secur-ing], **1,** to make safe; protect; **2,** to guarantee repayment of; as, he gave a mortgage to *secure* the loan; also, to protect oneself against the loss of; as, he took a mortgage to *secure* the loan; **3,** to make fast; latch or lock; as, to *secure* a door; also, to place in custody; as, to *secure* a prisoner; **4,** to gain possession of; as, to *secure* wealth.— *adv.* **se-cure′ly.**

se-cu-ri-ty (sē-kū′rĭ-tĭ), *n.* [*pl.* securities], **1,** the state or quality of being safe or protected; certainty; **2,** a means of safety or protection; as, insurance offers security; **3,** something given as a guarantee of performance or payment; as, he offered stock as *security* for the loan; **4,** one who becomes responsible for another; a surety; **5, securities,** bonds or stock that may be bought and sold.

secy. or **sec.** abbreviation for *secretary.*

se-dan (sē-dăn′), *n.* **1,** a portable covered chair or vehicle accommodating one passenger, usually slung between two poles and carried by two men: also called *sedan chair;* **2,** a closed automobile for four or more persons (see illustration under *automobile*).

SEDAN CHAIR

Se-dan (sē-dän′), a town in northeastern France, on the Meuse River, scene of battles during the World War.

se-date (sē-dāt′), *adj.* calm; composed; serious; as, a *sedate* young lady.—*adv.* **se-date′ly.**—*n.* **se-date′ness.**

sed-a-tive (sĕd′à-tĭv), *adj.* tending to calm or soothe; quieting:— *n.* something that has a calming, soothing effect.

sed-en-tar-y (sĕd′ĕn-tẽr′ĭ), *adj.* **1,** accustomed to sitting most of the day; **2,** requiring much sitting; as, *sedentary* work.

sedge (sĕj), *n.* any of many grasslike herbs or plants growing in marshes.

sed-i-ment (sĕd′ĭ-mĕnt), *n.* **1,** the solid substance which settles at the bottom of a liquid; dregs; **2,** sand, gravel, mud, or the like, deposited, as by water.

sed-i-men-ta-ry (sĕd′ĭ-mĕn′tà-rĭ), *adj.* **1,** pertaining to dregs or sediment; **2,** in geology, formed of material deposited by water or, sometimes, by wind; as, *sedimentary* rocks; *sedimentary* sands.

se·di·tion (sĕ-dĭsh′ŭn), *n.* agitation against a government, just short of insurrection or treason; the stirring up of discontent, rebellion, or resistance against lawful authority.

Syn. rebellion, revolt, mutiny.

se·di·tious (sĕ-dĭsh′ŭs), *adj.* 1, pertaining to rebellion against lawful authority; as, *seditious* writings; 2, engaged in rebellion or in stirring up rebellion; as, a *seditious* person.—*adv.* **se·di′tious·ly.**

Syn. rebellious, turbulent, mutinous.

se·duce (sĕ-dūs′), *v.t.* [seduced, seduc-ing], to lead away from the paths of right, duty, or virtue, by flattery, promises, or the like; lead astray; tempt to do wrong.—*n.* **se·duc′er.**

se·duc·tion (sĕ-dŭk′shŭn), *n.* 1, the act of tempting and leading astray; 2, something that may lead astray; a temptation; as, the *seductions* of pleasure.

se·duc·tive (sĕ-dŭk′tĭv), *adj.* tending to lead astray; alluring; enticing.

sed·u·lous (sĕd′ū-lŭs), *adj.* steadily industrious; hard-working; diligent; tireless.—*adv.* **sed′u·lous·ly.**

¹**see** (sē), *v.t.* [*p.t.* saw (sô), *p.p.* seen (sēn), *p.pr.* see-ing], 1, to perceive with the eyes; behold; 2, to discern mentally; understand; as, to *see* a meaning; 3, to accompany or escort; as, he *saw* the visitor to the door; 4, to find out or learn by observation or experience; as, he wished to *see* what the result would be; 5, to have personal experience of; as, he *saw* service in the war; 6, to make sure; as, *see* that you address him properly; 7, to visit, call on, or talk with; as, we went to *see* her; 8, to admit to one's presence; receive; as, she refused to *see* us:—*v.i.* 1, to possess or use the power of sight; 2, to understand or discern; 3, to consider; reflect; as, will you do it? I will *see*; 4, to take care; attend; as, *see* to the dinner; 5, to look: used only in the imperative; as, *See!* here he comes!

²**see** (sē), *n.* the official local seat of a bishop; the diocese of a bishop; the office or authority of a bishop:—**Holy See,** the seat of the papacy; the papal court or authority.

seed (sēd), *n.* [*pl.* seed or seeds], 1, that part of a flowering plant that holds the germ of life, capable of developing into another plant; 2, any small, seedlike fruit; as, dandelion or grass *seed;* 3, a source or origin; as, *seeds* of discord; 4, offspring; descendants; as, the *seed* of Jacob:—**to go to seed,** 1, to develop seed; 2, *Colloquial,* to become shabby; to lose vitality or vigor:—*v.i.* 1, to sow seed; 2, to mature or produce seed; also, to shed seed:—*v.t.* 1, to sow with seed, as a lawn; 2, to remove the seeds from.—*n.* **seed′er.**—*adj.* **seed′less.**

seed-case (sēd′kās′), *n.* a dry, hollow fruit containing seeds, as the pod of a pea.

seed-ling (sēd′lĭng), *n.* 1, a plant grown from a seed; 2, a young plant or tree.

seeds-man (sēdz′măn), *n.* [*pl.* seedsmen (-mĕn)], one who sows or sells seed.

seed-y (sēd′ĭ), *adj.* [seed-i-er, seed-i-est], 1, full of seed; having run to seed; 2, *Colloquial,* shabby; threadbare.

see-ing (sē′ĭng), *n.* the act or power of sight; vision:—*conj.* in view of the fact; since; as, *seeing* you are going, I shall go too.

seek (sēk), *v.t.* [sought (sôt), seek-ing], 1, to go in search of; 2, to aim at; as, to *seek* wealth; 3, to ask or appeal for; as, to *seek* aid; 4, to resort to; as, he *sought* the theater for recreation; 5, to attempt or try; as, he *sought* to undo the harm he had done:—*v.i.* to make search; inquire; make efforts to find someone or something.—*n.* **seek′er.**

seem (sēm), *v.i.* 1, to appear; look; have the semblance of; as, the sky *seems* clear; 2, to appear to exist; as, there *seems* little difference of opinion; 3, to appear to one's own mind or imagination; as, I *seemed* to be floating in space.

seem-ing (sēm′ĭng), *adj.* apparent; often, having appearance without reality; as, *seeming* truth:—*n.* appearance; show; especially, false show.—*adv.* **seem′ing·ly.**

seem-ly (sēm′lĭ), *adj.* [seem-li-er, seem-li-est], fit or becoming; decent; proper; as, *seemly* behavior.—*n.* **seem′li·ness.**

seen (sēn), past participle of *see.*

seep (sēp), *v.i.* to leak out slowly; ooze.

seep-age (sēp′ĭj), *n.* 1, a slow leaking through; 2, the liquid that leaks through.

se-er (sē′ẽr), *n.* 1, one who sees; 2, (sēr) one who claims to foresee the future; a prophet.

seer-suck-er (sēr′sŭk′ẽr), *n.* a cotton or linen dress fabric, woven in alternating smooth and crinkly stripes.

SEESAW

see-saw (sē′sô′), *n.* 1, a game in which children, sitting or standing on opposite ends of a balanced plank, move alternately up and down; also, the plank; 2, any movement to and fro or up and down:—*v.i.* to move up and down or to and fro.

seethe (sēth), *v.i.* [*p.t.* seethed, *p.p.* seethed or, rarely, sod-den (sŏd′n), *p.pr.* seeth-ing], **1,** to boil; as, a *seething* pot; to move in violent agitation; as, a *seething* whirlpool; **2,** to be violently agitated; as, the crowd *seethed* with excitement.

seg-ment (sĕg′mĕnt), *n.* **1,** any of the parts into which an object naturally separates or divides; a section; as, a *segment* of an orange; **2,** in geometry, a part cut off from a figure by one or more lines; especially, the part of a circle included between an arc and its chord.

SEGMENT (S) of a circle.

seg-re-gate (sĕg′rē-gāt), *v.t.* [segregat-ed, segregat-ing], to separate from others; set apart; as, to *segregate* a person who has scarlet fever.—*n.* **seg′re-ga′tion.**

sei-gneur (sēn-yûr′), *n.* in feudal times, a lord. Also, **seign′ior** (sēn′yẽr).

seine (sān; sēn), *n.* a large fishing net equipped with sinkers and floats:—*v.t.* [seined, sein-ing], to catch (fish) with such a net:—*v.i.* to fish with a seine.

Seine (sān), a river of northern France, flowing northwest through Paris to the English Channel (map **12**).

seis-mic (sīz′mĭk; sīs′mĭk), *adj.* relating to an earthquake; as, *seismic* tremors.

seis-mo-graph (sīz′mõ-gráf; sīs′mõ-gráf), *n.* an instrument for recording the time, duration, direction, and intensity of an earthquake.—*adj.* **seis′mo-graph′ic.**

seis-mol-o-gy (sīz-mŏl′õ-jĭ; sīs-mŏl′õ-jĭ), *n.* the scientific study of earthquakes, especially of their causes and effects.—*n.* **seis-mol′o-gist.**—*adj.* **seis′mo-log′i-cal.**

seize (sēz), *v.t.* [seized, seiz-ing], **1,** to take possession of forcibly or suddenly; as, soldiers *seized* the fort; **2,** to grasp; snatch; take hold of; as, *seize* him by the arm; **3,** to take into legal custody on a warrant; as, the officers *seized* the kidnapers; **4,** to grasp mentally; understand.

seiz-ing (sēz′ĭng), *n.* **1,** the act of taking hold or grasping; **2,** on boats, the fastening or lashing together of things with rope; also, the rope used.

sei-zure (sē′zhẽr), *n.* **1,** the act of taking forcible possession; **2,** a sudden attack, as of a disease; a fit.

sel-dom (sĕl′dŭm), *adv.* rarely; not often.

se-lect (sē-lĕkt′), *adj.* **1,** carefully chosen or picked out; **2,** hence, of great excellence; choicest or best; as, a volume of *select* poems; **3,** exclusive; made up of chosen persons; as, a *select* club:—*v.t.* to pick out from among a number; choose.—*n.* **se-lec′tor.**—*adj.* **se-lec′tive.**
Syn., v. pick, cull, elect.

se-lec-tion (sē-lĕk′shŭn), *n.* **1,** the act of choosing; choice; as, the *selection* of one from so many is difficult; **2,** the thing or things chosen; as, the Scott novel is my *selection;* **3,** a part of a book, a piece of music, or the like; as, he read a *selection* from Shakespeare.

se-lect-man (sē-lĕkt′măn), *n.* [*pl.* selectmen (-mĕn)], one of a board of officials chosen annually in most New England towns to carry on the public business of the town.

self (sĕlf), *n.* [*pl.* selves (sĕlvz)], **1,** the entire person or character of an individual; that which makes one person quite different from others; personality; **2,** a phase or side of a person's character which may show itself under certain conditions or at specific times; as, her nobler *self;* **3,** personal or private interest; as, *self* was always present in his thoughts:—*adj.* same or very: now used only in the compound *selfsame;* as, I bought some of the *self*same material.

self- (sĕlf-), a prefix (used freely to form compounds, generally hyphenated) meaning: **1,** action by oneself or itself; as, *self*-acting, *self*-starter; **2,** action directed upon or toward oneself or itself; as, *self*-government, *self*-control.

self—act-ing (sĕlf′-ăk′tĭng), *adj.* having the power to act or move of itself; automatic.—*n.* **self′—ac′tion.**

self—as-ser-tion (sĕlf′-ă-sûr′shŭn), *n.* **1,** insistence on one's own opinions, rights, or claims; **2,** a putting oneself forward in an overbearing manner.

self—as-ser-tive (sĕlf′-ă-sûr′tĭv), *adj.* inclined to put oneself forward or to insist on one's own rights or opinions.

self—com-mand (sĕlf′-kō-mănd′), *n.* control of one's actions and emotions; selfcontrol; self-possession.

self—com-pla-cent (sĕlf′-kŏm-plā′sĕnt), *adj.* pleased with oneself and with one's opinions and conduct; self-satisfied.

self—con-ceit (sĕlf′-kŏn-sēt′), *n.* too great confidence in one's own abilities.

self—con-fi-dence (sĕlf′-kŏn′fĭ-dĕns), *n.* belief in one's own ability; sometimes, too great belief in oneself; conceit.—*adj.* **self′—con′fi-dent.**

self—con-scious (sĕlf′-kŏn′shŭs), *adj.* too keenly aware of one's own actions, manner, feelings, etc.; embarrassed in the presence of others; ill at ease.

self—con-tained (sĕlf′-kŏn-tānd′), *adj.* **1,** sufficient or complete in itself; **2,** in full control of one's words and actions; **3,** cautious in expressing oneself; reserved; not inclined to talk.

go; join; yet; sing; chin; show; thin, *th*en; hw, *wh*y; zh, azure; **ü**, Ger. f*ü*r or Fr. l*u*ne; **ö**, Ger. schön or Fr. f*eu*; **n̄**, Fr. e*n*fant, no*m*; **kh**, Ger. a*ch* or i*ch*. See pages ix–x.

self–con·trol (sĕlf´-kŏn-trōl´), *n.* control of one's desires, acts, and emotions.

self–de·fense or **self–de·fence** (sĕlf´-dĕ-fĕns´), *n.* the act of protecting one's person, property, or name against attack.

self–de·ni·al (sĕlf´-dĕ-nī´ăl), *n.* refusal to consider one's own wishes or needs; self-sacrifice.—*adj.* **self´–de·ny´ing.**

self–de·ter·mi·na·tion (sĕlf´-dĕ-tûr´mĭ-nā´shŭn), *n.* **1,** the making of one's own decisions without help from others; **2,** the choice, made by the people of a territory, of the form of government which that territory shall have.

self–es·teem (sĕlf´-ĕs-tēm´), *n.* **1,** proper respect for oneself; self-respect; **2,** too high an opinion of oneself; conceit.

self–ev·i·dent (sĕlf´-ĕv´ĭ-dĕnt), *adj.* entirely clear, without need of explanation; obviously true, without need of proof.

self–ex·pres·sion (sĕlf´-ĕks-prĕsh´ŭn), *n.* expression of one's own feelings, ideas, etc.

self–gov·ern·ment (sĕlf´-gŭv´ĕrn-mĕnt), *n.* **1,** government of a nation by the united action of its people, as in a republic; **2,** a similar form of government in a state, town, school, etc.; **3,** of persons, self-control.—*adj.* **self´–gov´ern·ing.**

self–im·por·tant (sĕlf´-ĭm-pôr´tănt), *adj.* having an exaggerated idea of one's own importance; pompous.—*n.* **self´–im·por´tance.**

self–in·ter·est (sĕlf´-ĭn´tĕr-ĕst; -ĭn´trĭst), *n.* concern for one's own welfare, regardless of the rights of others; selfishness.

self·ish (sĕl´fĭsh), *adj.* **1,** putting one's own wishes and advantages before the wishes and advantages of others; **2,** prompted or marked by undue regard for oneself; as, a *selfish* act.—*adv.* **self´ish·ly.**—*n.* **self´ish·ness.**

self–made (sĕlf´-mād´), *adj.* having risen by one's own efforts from poverty and obscurity to wealth and power.

self–pos·sessed (sĕlf´-pŏ-zĕst´), *adj.* having, or seeming to have, composure and calmness; poised.—*n.* **self´–pos·ses´sion.**

self–pres·er·va·tion (sĕlf´-prĕz´ĕr-vā´shŭn), *n.* the keeping of oneself from harm or danger; especially, the instinct to protect oneself when danger threatens.

self–re·li·ance (sĕlf´-rĕ-lī´ăns), *n.* confidence in, and dependence on, one's own ability, efforts, or judgment.—*adj.* **self´–re·li´ant.**

self–re·spect (sĕlf´-rĕ-spĕkt´), *n.* proper regard or respect for oneself; self-esteem. —*adj.* **self´–re·spect´ing.**

self–re·straint (sĕlf´-rĕ-strānt´), *n.* self-control; self-command.

self–right·eous (sĕlf´-rī´chŭs), *adj.* convinced of one's own uprightness.

self–sac·ri·fice (sĕlf´-săk´rĭ-fīs; -săk´rĭ-fīz), *n.* the sacrifice of one's personal interests or of one's life, whether from affection for another person, or devotion to a duty or cause.—*adj.* **self´–sac´ri·fic´ing.**

self–same (sĕlf´-sām´), *adj.* the very same; identical.

self–sat·is·fied (sĕlf´-săt´ĭs-fīd), *adj.* entirely pleased with oneself; complacent.—*n.* **self´–sat´is·fac´tion.**

self–seek·ing (sĕlf´-sēk´ĭng), *n.* the act or practice of looking out for one's own interests:—*adj.* selfish.

self–start·er (sĕlf´-stär´tĕr), *n.* an automatic device for starting an engine.

self–styled (sĕlf´-stīld´), *adj.* given a name or designation by oneself alone; as, a *self-styled* cook.

self–suf·fi·cient (sĕlf´-sŭ-fĭsh´ĕnt), *adj.* **1,** needing no help from others; **2,** having undue confidence in oneself; self-confident. —*n.* **self´–suf·fi´cien·cy.**

self–sup·port·ing (sĕlf´-sŭ-pôr´tĭng), *adj.* **1,** earning one's own living; **2,** paying for itself without outside help; as, a *self-supporting* institution.

self–willed (sĕlf´-wĭld´), *adj.* bent on having one's own way; stubborn; wilful.

sell (sĕl), *v.t.* [sold (sōld), sell-ing], **1,** to give in return for a price, especially for money; as, this store *sells* shoes; also, to act as a salesman of; as, he *sells* insurance; **2,** to betray for a reward; as, to *sell* one's country:—*v.i.* **1,** to dispose of goods for a price; **2,** to find a market; as, eggs *sell* at a lower price in summer than in winter.

sell·er (sĕl´ĕr), *n.* **1,** one who sells; **2,** an article sold; as, this novel is a best *seller*.

sel·vage or **sel·vedge** (sĕl´vĭj), *n.* the edge of cloth so woven as to prevent raveling.

selves (sĕlvz), plural of *self*.

se·man·tics (sĕ-măn´tĭks), *n.pl.* used as *sing.,* the science of the meaning and sense development of words.—*adj.* **se·man´tic.**

sem·a·phore (sĕm´á-fôr), *n.* **1,** an apparatus for signaling, by day or night, by means of mechanical arms, lanterns, flags, etc. (see illustration next page); **2,** in the army, a system of signaling in which the operator uses a flag in each hand, the letters of the alphabet being represented by various positions of the arms in relation to the body and to each other.

sem·blance (sĕm´blăns), *n.* **1,** image; representation; as, a crucifix is the *semblance* of Christ crucified; **2,** outward appearance; hence, pretense; as, a *semblance* of truth.

se·mes·ter (sĕ-mĕs´tĕr), *n.* **1,** a half year;

āte, āorta, râre, căt, åsk, fär, ăllow, sofá; ēve, ēvent, ĕll, writēr, novĕl; bīte, pĭn; nō, ōbey, ôr, dŏg, tŏp, cŏllide; ūnit, ūnite, bûrn, cŭt, focŭs; nōōn, fŏŏt; mound; coin;

2, specifically, one of the two terms of a college or university year.

sem·i- (sĕm′ĭ-), a prefix, attached freely, and usually without hyphen, meaning half or about half; as, *semi*circumference, *semi*-civilized.

sem·i-an·nu·al (sĕm′ĭ-ăn′û-ăl), *adj.* occurring, published, due, etc., each half year, or twice a year; as, *semiannual* interest payments.—*adv.* **sem′i-an′nu-al-ly.**

sem·i-cir·cle (sĕm′ĭ-sûr′kl), *n.* half of a circle.

sem·i-cir·cu·lar (sĕm′ĭ-sûr′kû-lẽr), *adj.* shaped like half of a circle.

sem·i-cir-cum·fer·ence (sĕm′ĭ-sẽr-kŭm′-fẽr-ĕns), *n.* an arc of 180°; half of a circumference.

sem·i-civ·i-lized (sĕm′ĭ-sĭv′ĭ-līzd), *adj.* only partly reclaimed from savagery; partly civilized.

sem·i-co·lon (sĕm′ĭ-kō′lŏn), *n.* a mark of punctuation [;], indicating a separation in the parts of a sentence greater than that marked by a comma.

sem·i-month·ly (sĕm′ĭ-mŭnth′lĭ), *adj.* occurring or done every half month, or twice a month:—*n.* [*pl.* semimonthlies], anything published or produced twice a month:—*adv.* at intervals of half a month.

sem·i-nar·y (sĕm′ĭ-nẽr′ĭ), *n.* [*pl.* seminaries], **1,** a private school or academy, usually one which prepares pupils for college; **2,** a school or college which prepares students for the priesthood or the ministry.

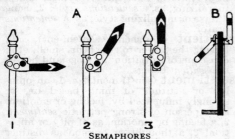

SEMAPHORES

A, railway semaphore, signaling: 1, stop; 2, approach; 3, proceed. B, marine semaphore signaling the letter *k*.

sem·i-pre·cious (sĕm′ĭ-prĕsh′ŭs), *adj.* not among the most valuable: used of gems, such as the opal and amethyst, to distinguish them from *precious* gems, such as the diamond and ruby.

Sem-ite (sĕm′īt; sē′mīt), *n.* a member of a Caucasian race to which the ancient Phoenicians, Babylonians, etc., belonged. It is now represented chiefly by the Arabs and the Jews.

Se·mit·ic (sē-mĭt′ĭk), *adj.* referring to the Semites or to their languages.

sem·i-week·ly (sĕm′ĭ-wēk′lĭ), *adj.* occurring, published, or produced twice a week: —*n.* [*pl.* semiweeklies], anything published or produced twice a week.

Sen. or **sen.** abbreviation for *senate, senator, senior.*

sen·ate (sĕn′ĭt; sĕn′át), *n.* **1,** in ancient Rome, the supreme legislative and administrative body; **2,** in modern times, an assembly or council of citizens with governmental powers; a legislative body:—**Senate,** the upper and smaller branch of the legislature, in such countries as the U.S., France, and Australia.

sen·a·tor (sĕn′á-tẽr), *n.* a member of the senate, or upper house of a legislature.

sen·a·tor·i·al (sĕn′á-tôr′ĭ-ăl), *adj.* **1,** referring to, or befitting, a senator or a senate; as, *senatorial* dignity; **2,** entitled to elect a senator; as, a *senatorial* district.

send (sĕnd), *v.t.* [sent (sĕnt), send-ing], **1,** to cause to go, often to some special destination; as, to *send* a messenger; to *send* a child to school; **2,** to cause to be carried; as, to *send* a letter, greetings, or news; **3,** to cause to come or happen; bestow; as, fate *sent* much happiness to him; **4,** to throw or drive, as a ball:—*v.i.* to send word of some kind; as, he *sent* for me; I *sent* to warn him.—*n.* **send′er.**

[1]Sen·e·ca (sĕn′ê-ká), Lucius Annaeus (4? B.C.–A.D. 65), a Roman Stoic philosopher and author.

[2]Sen·e·ca (sĕn′ê-ká), *n.* a member of the Senecas, a tribe of North American Indians, the most numerous and warlike of the Five Nations.

Sen·e·gal (sĕn′ê-gôl′), a French colony on the west coast of Africa, north of the Gambia River (map **14**).—*n.* and *adj.* **Sen′e-gal-ese′.**

sen·es·chal (sĕn′ĕ-shăl), *n.* in the Middle Ages, an important official in the castle of a great noble.

se·nile (sē′nīl; sē′nĭl), *adj.* characteristic of, or belonging to, old age; as, *senile* quavers; *senile* insanity.—*n.* **se-nil′i-ty** (sē-nĭl′ĭ-tĭ).

sen·ior (sēn′yẽr), *adj.* **1,** superior in dignity, rank, or office; older in standing; as, the *senior* member of the firm; **2,** older in years: generally used after a person's name, often in abbreviated form, *Sr.*, to distinguish the older of two persons having the same name; as, John Moore, *Sr.*; **3,** connected with the last year of a high-school or college course:—*n.* **1,** one who is older than others, or superior in dignity, rank, or office; **2,** a student in the final year of his high-school or college course.—*n.* **sen-ior/-i-ty** (sēn-yŏr/ĭ-tĭ).

sen-na (sĕn/*à*), *n.* the dried leaves of the cassia plant, used as a laxative medicine; also, the cassia plant.

Sen-nach-er-ib (sĕ-năk/ĕr-ĭb), (?–681 B.C.), a king of ancient Assyria.

se-ñor (sā-nyôr/), *n.* [*pl.* señores (sā-nyō/-rās)], a Spanish title of courtesy, meaning *Mr.* or *Sir;* a gentleman.

se-ño-ra (sā-nyō/rä), *n.* a Spanish title of courtesy, meaning *Mrs.* or *Madam;* a lady.

se-ño-ri-ta (sā/nyō-rē/tä), *n.* a Spanish title of courtesy, meaning *Miss;* a young lady.

sen-sa-tion (sĕn-sā/shŭn), *n.* 1, a bodily feeling, usually produced by an external object or condition; as, a *sensation* of warmth; also, a mental feeling or emotion; as, a *sensation* of fear; 2, a state of general excitement or interest; as, the new pianist produced a great *sensation;* also, the cause of the excitement.

sen-sa-tion-al (sĕn-sā/shŭn-ăl), *adj.* 1, pertaining to bodily sensation; 2, extraordinary; as, a *sensational* escape; 3, melodramatic; as, a *sensational* novel.

sense (sĕns), *n.* 1, any one of the special faculties of the body by which impressions are received from the outside world; as, the *senses* of sight, smell, hearing, taste, touch, etc.; 2, bodily feeling; sensation; as, a *sense* of pleasure or pain, heat or cold; 3, understanding; judgment; as, he is a man of *sense;* a *sense* of the fitness of things; 4, lively appreciation; as, a *sense* of humor: —*v.t.* [sensed, sens-ing], 1, to perceive; be aware of; as, to *sense* hostility; 2, *Colloquial,* to understand; as, I *sense* your meaning.

sense-less (sĕns/lĕs), *adj.* 1, without feeling; unconscious, as a person in a faint; 2, stupid; meaningless; as, a *senseless* argument.—*n.* **sense/less-ness.**

sense or-gan, one of the organs of the body, through which sensations are received. The eyes, ears, nose, tongue, and skin are sense organs.

sen-si-bil-i-ty (sĕn/sĭ-bĭl/ĭ-tĭ), *n.* [*pl.* sensibilities], 1, the capacity to feel; as, the *sensibility* of the skin; 2, sensitiveness; capacity for emotion, in contrast to intellect; especially, acute feelings of delight, sorrow, appreciation, etc., in response to impressions; as, the *sensibility* of an artist or poet.

sen-si-ble (sĕn/sĭ-bl), *adj.* 1, capable of affecting the senses; noticeable; as, a *sensible* rise in temperature; 2, capable of being grasped by the mind; as, a *sensible* difference; 3, conscious; aware; as, I am *sensible* of your kindness to me; 4, having good common sense; reasonable.

sen-si-tive (sĕn/sĭ-tĭv), *adj.* 1, quick to receive impressions from external objects or conditions; as, a *sensitive* skin; 2, responding to or recording slight shades or changes of sound, light, etc.; as, a *sensitive* photographic film; 3, easily moved; impressionable; also, easily offended; touchy.—*n.* **sen/si-tive-ness.**

sen-so-ry (sĕn/sō-rĭ), *adj.* 1, pertaining to the senses or to sensation; as, *sensory* impressions; 2, conveying messages from the organs of sense, as the eyes, ears, etc., to the brain; as, *sensory* nerves.

sen-su-al (sĕn/shŏŏ-ăl; sĕn/sū-ăl), *adj.* 1, associated with the pleasures of the body; not mental or spiritual; as, a *sensual* life; 2, indulging in the pleasures of the body.

sen-su-ous (sĕn/shŏŏ-ŭs; sĕn/sū-ŭs), *adj.* 1, appealing to the senses; as, *sensuous* music; 2, sensitive to the beauty of color, tone, texture, etc.—*adv.* **sen/su-ous-ly.**

sent (sĕnt), past tense and past participle of *send.*

sen-tence (sĕn/tĕns), *n.* 1, in grammar, a series of words containing a subject and a predicate, and expressing a complete thought; 2, in law, judgment pronounced by a court; also, a penalty imposed:—*v.t.* [sentenced, sentenc-ing], to pronounce judgment or impose a penalty upon; as, the judge *sentenced* the thief to two months' imprisonment.

sen-ten-tious (sĕn-tĕn/shŭs), *adj.* 1, full of proverbs or terse, pithy sayings; hence, moralizing; as, a *sententious* style; 2, using a terse or moralizing style; as, a *sententious* orator.

sen-tient (sĕn/shĕnt; sĕn/shĭ-ĕnt), *adj.* having the power to see, hear, smell, etc.; conscious of sensation; as, dogs and horses are *sentient* beings.

sen-ti-ment (sĕn/tĭ-mĕnt), *n.* 1, an opinion or attitude of mind based on, or strongly influenced by, feeling or emotion; as, a person of strong patriotic *sentiment;* 2, a feeling or emotion, as of pity or affection; 3, a thought or opinion as distinct from the words in which it is expressed; as, I like the *sentiment* but do not like the language.

sen-ti-men-tal (sĕn/tĭ-mĕn/tăl), *adj.* 1, easily moved to pity, sympathy, etc.; also, given to indulging one's emotions freely, or too freely; as, a *sentimental* girl; 2, appealing to the emotions; as, *sentimental* poetry.—*adv.* **sen/ti-men/tal-ly.**—*n.* **sen/-ti-men-tal/i-ty.**

sen-ti-nel (sĕn/tĭ-nĕl), *n.* a person who watches or guards; especially, a soldier on guard at a camp or fort; a sentry.

āte, āorta, rāre, căt, àsk, fär, ăllow, sof*à*; ēve, ĕvent, ĕll, writĕr, novĕl; bīte, pĭn; nō, ōbey, ôr, dŏg, tŏp, cŏllide; ūnit, ūnite, bûrn, cŭt, focŭs; nōōn, fŏŏt; mound; coin;

sen·try (sĕn′trĭ), *n.* [*pl.* sentries], a person stationed as a sentinel or guard.

Se·oul (sē-ōol′; sē′ōol), the capital of Korea. Formerly Japanese Keijo. (Map 15.)

se·pal (sē′păl; sĕp′ăl), *n.* one of the leaflike sections of the calyx, outside the colored petals of a flower.

sep·a·ra·ble (sĕp′a·ra·bl), *adj.* capable of being divided, disunited, or distinguished one from another.

sep·a·rate (sĕp′a·rāt), *v.t.* [separat-ed, separat-ing], 1, to part or divide; disunite; set apart; as, please *separate* the pens

SEPALS (S, S)

from the pencils; 2, to come in between; keep apart; as, a hedge *separates* the two gardens:—*v.i.* to part; withdraw from each other or from one another; scatter; as, rain began to fall, and the crowd *separated* in a hurry:—*adj.* (sĕp′a·rĭt), 1, divided; no longer united; as, they have turned the second floor into two *separate* apartments; 2, distinct; single; as, each *separate* item on a bill.—*adv.* **sep′a·rate·ly.**—*n.* **sep′a·ra′tion.**

Syn., *v.,* sever, detach, estrange, split.

sep·a·ra·tor (sĕp′a·rā′tẽr), *n.* a person or thing that separates; especially, a mechanical device that removes dust from grain, or one that separates cream from milk.

SEPARATOR

A, supply bowl from which milk flows into a revolving bowl inside of the case B; B, outlet for cream; C, outlet for skimmed milk; E, crank handle.

se·pi·a (sē′pĭ-a), *n.* 1, a dark-brown pigment made from an inky fluid ejected by the European cuttlefish; 2, this cuttlefish; also, the inky fluid; 3, a dark-brown color.

se·poy (sē′poi), *n.* an Indian native employed as a soldier by a European government, especially by Great Britain.

sep·sis (sĕp′sĭs), *n.* blood poisoning.

Sept. abbreviation for *September.*

Sep·tem·ber (sĕp-tĕm′bẽr), *n.* the ninth month of the year, containing 30 days.

sep·tic (sĕp′tĭk), *adj.* 1, produced by, or associated with, germs such SEPOY as those that cause blood poisoning; as, *septic* fever; 2, not sterile; infected; as, a *septic* wound.

Sep·tu·a·gint (sĕp′tū-a-jĭnt), *n.* a Greek version of the Old Testament, still used in the Eastern Church.

sep·ul·cher (sĕp′ŭl-kẽr), *n.* a grave or tomb; a place of burial:—*v.t.* to bury; entomb. Also spelled **sep′ul·chre.**

se·pul·chral (sē-pŭl′kral), *adj.* 1, pertaining to a tomb or to the burial of the dead; 2, gloomy or funereal; as, a *sepulchral* mansion; 3, deep and solemn; as, a *sepulchral* voice.

sep·ul·ture (sĕp′ŭl-tūr), *n.* burial.

se·quel (sē′kwĕl), *n.* 1, a succeeding part; continuation; as, the *sequel* to a book; 2, result; as, the *sequel* of his fiery ·speech was a riot.

se·quence (sē′kwĕns), *n.* 1, the act of following; the coming of one thing after another; as, the *sequence* of cause and effect; 2, the order in which things occur or are arranged; as, the *sequence* of words in a sentence; 3, a series; as, a *sequence* of plays in a game; 4, an event that follows another.

se·ques·ter (sē-kwĕs′tẽr), *v.t.* in law: 1, to take possession of (property) until some claim against the owner is paid or satisfied; 2, to confiscate.

se·ques·tered (sē-kwĕs′tẽrd), *adj.* secluded; retired; quiet.

se·quin (sē′kwĭn; sĕk′ĭn), *n.* 1, one of the tiny metal disks used as ornamentation for dresses; 2, a gold coin, formerly in use in Italy and Turkey.

se·quoi·a (sē-kwoi′a), *n.* either of two evergreen trees of California, called *big tree* and *redwood* respectively, which grow to immense size. (See illustration, page 865.)

se·ragl·io (sē-răl′yō; sē-räl′yō), *n.* [*pl.* seragli (sē-răl′yē; sē-räl′yē) or seraglios], the women's apartments of a Mohammedan palace; a harem.

ser·aph (sĕr′ăf), *n.* [*pl.* seraphim (sĕr′a-fĭm) or seraphs], an angel of the highest order of angels.

se·raph·ic (sē-răf′ĭk), *adj.* pertaining to, befitting, or like, a seraph; angelic.

ser·a·phim (sĕr′a-fĭm), a form of the plural of *seraph.*

Serb (sûrb), *n.* 1, an inhabitant of Serbia; especially, a member of the dominant Slavic race in Serbia; 2, the Serbian language.

Serb–Cro·at–Slo·vene State (sûrb′-krō′ăt-slō-vēn′), the name given, between 1918 and 1929, to the area now called Yugoslavia. See **Yugoslavia.**

Ser·bi·a (sûr′bĭ-a), formerly, a Balkan kingdom (cap. Belgrade); now, the southeastern part of Yugoslavia.

go; join; yet; sing; chin; show; thin, *then;* hw, *why;* zh, a*z*ure; ü, Ger. f*ür* or Fr. l*u*ne; ö, Ger. sch*ö*n or Fr. f*eu;* ṅ, Fr. *en*fant, *nom;* kh, Ger. a*ch* or i*ch.* See pages ix–x.

Ser·bi·an (sûr′bĭ-ăn), *adj.* pertaining to Serbia, its language, or its natives, who are now citizens of Yugoslavia:—*n.* **1,** a native or an inhabitant of Serbia; **2,** the language of the Serbians.

sere (sēr), *adj. Poetic,* dry; withered; as, a *sere* leaf.

ser·e·nade (sĕr′ĕ-nād′), *n.* **1,** music sung or played at night, often by a lover under his lady's window; **2,** a piece of music suitable to such an occasion:—*v.t.* and *v.i.* [serenad-ed, serenad-ing], to sing or play a serenade in honor of (a person).

se·rene (sĕ-rēn′), *adj.* **1,** clear and calm; as, a *serene* summer day; **2,** placid; composed.—*adv.* **se·rene′ly.**—*n.* **se·ren′i·ty** (sĕ-rĕn′ĭ-tĭ).

Syn. quiet, tranquil, peaceful.

serf (sûrf), *n.* **1,** originally, a slave; **2,** in the Middle Ages, a tiller of the soil who belonged to the land he tilled, and stayed with the land whenever it was sold.—*n.* **serf′dom.**

serge (sûrj), *n.* a woolen material, woven with fine diagonal ridges, used for dresses, suits, and coats.

ser·geant (sär′jĕnt), *n.* **1,** a sergeant at arms; **2,** a police officer of minor rank; **3,** a noncommissioned officer of the army or the marines, ranking next above a corporal:—**sergeant major** [*pl.* sergeants major], the chief sergeant and highest noncommissioned officer of a regiment.

sergeant at arms [*pl.* sergeants at arms], an officer of a judicial, legislative, or deliberative body, who is responsible for keeping order at meetings.

se·ri·al (sē′rĭ-ăl), *adj.* consisting of parts or units which follow one another; especially, published in successive parts or numbers; as, a *serial* story:—*n.* a story, photoplay, or the like, appearing in successive instalments.—*adv.* **se′ri·al·ly.**

se·ries (sē′rēz; sē′rĭz), *n.* [*pl.* series], a number of similar things or events following one another in regular order or succession; as, a short *series* of lectures.

se·ri·ous (sē′rĭ-ŭs), *adj.* **1,** responsible; earnest; as, a *serious* student; **2,** not trifling; not comic; as, a *serious* play; **3,** demanding thought and attention; as, *serious* reading; **4,** disastrous; as, *serious* consequences.—*adv.* **se′ri·ous·ly.**—*n.* **se′ri·ous·ness.**

Syn. solemn, sober.

ser·mon (sûr′mŭn), *n.* **1,** a formal talk or lecture on a moral or religious subject, often based on Scripture and usually delivered by a priest or a minister; **2,** any serious talk or address.

Syn. discourse, exhortation, oration.

ser·pent (sûr′pĕnt), *n.* **1,** a snake; a reptile, especially a large one; **2,** a sly, deceitful person.

ser·pen·tine (sûr′pĕn-tēn; sûr′pĕn-tīn), *adj.* **1,** snakelike; winding in coils or curves; as, the *serpentine* course of a stream; **2,** sly and crafty; as, *serpentine* wisdom:—*n.* (sûr′pĕn-tēn), a kind of dull-green, sometimes mottled, rock which takes a high polish.

ser·ried (sĕr′ĭd), *adj.* close; crowded; as, *serried* ranks.

se·rum (sē′rŭm), *n.* **1,** the yellowish, clear, watery fluid which remains after blood has coagulated; **2,** such a fluid, taken from the blood of an animal which has been inoculated with a given disease, and used to fight the disease in human beings.

ser·vant (sûr′vănt), *n.* a person who works for wages; especially, one who performs domestic duties in return for board, lodging, and wages:—**public servant,** a government employee.

serve (sûrv), *v.t.* [served, serv-ing], **1,** to attend or wait upon; work for; **2,** to obey and honor; as, to *serve* God; **3,** to put on the table and distribute, as food; also, to wait upon (persons) at table or in a shop; **4,** to be of use to; as, the car *served* him very well all summer; the coat *served* her for a pillow; **5,** to defend; take the part of; as, to *serve* one's country; also, to promote; make a contribution to; as, to *serve* science; **6,** to treat; deal with; act toward; as, he *served* me shamefully; **7,** to supply (customers) at regular or stated times; as, the milkman *serves* us with milk every morning; **8,** to deliver, as a legal writ or summons; **9,** to undergo; as, to *serve* a prison sentence; **10,** in games, such as tennis, to put (the ball) into play:—*v.i.* **1,** to be employed by another; be a servant, slave, or employee; **2,** to discharge the duties of an office or employment; as, to *serve* in the army or navy; to *serve* on a committee; **3,** to be sufficient; act as substitute; answer the purpose; as, rain will not *serve* as an excuse for absence; **4,** in games, such as tennis, to put the ball into play by sending it to an opponent as the first stroke:—*n.* in games, as tennis, the act of serving the ball; also, the ball as served or the turn for serving; as, whose *serve* is it?—*n.* **serv′er.**

serv·ice (sûr′vĭs), *n.* **1,** the state or position of a servant; as, she was in *service* for ten years before her marriage; **2,** duty or function performed or required; as, have you need of our *services?* also, the manner of performing work; as, poor hotel *service;* **3,** a set of implements for special use; as, a silver tea *service;* **4,**

public worship; as, the evening *service;* also, any formal religious ceremony; as, the funeral *service;* **5,** professional or official functions or duties; as, a lawyer's *services;* military *service;* **6,** employment; also, a special division of public employment; as, civil *service;* **7,** benefit; advantage; as, an education is often of great *service;* **8,** in games, such as tennis, that stroke of the ball which puts it into play: —*v.t.* [serviced, servic-ing], to put into, or maintain in, condition; put back into good shape; as, to *service* a radio set.

serv-ice-a-ble (sûr′vĭs-*a*-bl), *adj.* **1,** useful; helpful; as, colonies may in many ways be *serviceable* to the parent country; **2,** having good wearing qualities; durable; as, *serviceable* material.

ser-vi-ette (sûr′vĭ-ĕt′), *n.* a table napkin.

ser-vile (sûr′vĭl; sûr′vīl), *adj.* **1,** pertaining to a slave; as, of *servile* origin; **2,** characteristic of a slave; as, *servile* fear; **3,** cringing; slavishly humble; as, a *servile* flatterer.—*n.* **ser-vil′i-ty.**

ser-vi-tor (sûr′vĭ-tẽr), *n.* a servant.

ser-vi-tude (sûr′vĭ-tūd), *n.* **1,** slavery; bondage; **2,** service or labor enforced as a punishment; as, penal *servitude.*

ses-a-me (sĕs′*a*-mê), *n.* an East Indian plant bearing seeds from which an oil is obtained; also, the seeds:—**Open sesame,** in the Arabian Nights' tale of Ali Baba and the Forty Thieves, a magic formula used to open the door of the robbers' cave; hence, (often *open sesame*), mysterious or magical means for gaining admission to what is usually inaccessible.

ses-sion (sĕsh′ŭn), *n.* **1,** a meeting of a school, court, legislative body, or the like; **2,** a series of such meetings; **3,** the time occupied by a single meeting or by a series of meetings; as, a two-hour *session;* a two-month *session.*

set (sĕt), *v.t.* [set, set-ting], **1,** to place or fix in a certain position; as, they *set* the basket on the floor; **2,** to put (a hen) upon a nest of eggs, or (eggs) under a hen; **3,** to put in order; make ready for use; as, to *set* a table; *set* a trap; **4,** to regulate (a clock); **5,** to cause to become stiff, as jelly; to make permanent or fast, as colors; **6,** to prepare (a broken bone) to knit; **7,** to fix (a price); **8,** to adapt, as words to music; **9,** to put into a special condition; as, to *set* a house on fire; **10,** to arrange (type) in words; **11,** to fix or determine; as, to *set* one's mind on, to, or against something:—*v.i.* **1,** to sink below the horizon, as the sun; **2,** to become firm, as jelly, or rigid, as cement; **3,** to apply oneself; as, to *set* to work; **4,** to flow or tend; as, the current *sets* to the north; **5,**

to start; as, to *set* out on a journey; **6,** to fit; as, this coat *sets* well; **7,** to sit; hatch eggs; as, a *setting* hen:—*adj.* **1,** fixed or established; as, a *set* wage; **2,** immovable; obstinate; as, *set* in his ways; **3,** regular; formal; as, a *set* speech:—*n.* **1,** a number of things of the same kind, to be used in conjunction; as, a *set* of golf clubs; a *set* of surgical instruments; also, apparatus; as, a radio receiving *set;* **2,** a congenial group of persons; clique; as, the younger *set;* **3,** a series of games which counts as a unit, as in tennis; **4,** a setting, either on a stage or in a photoplay; **5,** posture; as, the *set* of the head; **6,** fit; as, the *set* of a coat.

set-back (sĕt′băk′), *n.* a check to progress or advancement; a reverse.

Seth (sĕth), in the Bible, the third son of Adam.

set-tee (sĕ-tē′), *n.* a long seat or short sofa with arms and a back.

SETTEE

set-ter (sĕt′ẽr), *n.* **1,** one who or that which sets; as, a type*setter;* **2,** a long-haired hunting dog trained to stand rigid and point on scenting game.

set-ting (sĕt′ĭng), *n.* **1,** that in which something is fastened, as the mounting of a jewel; **2,** the scenery and stage properties for a play or a scene in a play; the background of a story; **3,** music composed for a written text; **4,** the eggs placed under a hen for hatching.

ENGLISH SETTER (½)

¹**set-tle** (sĕt′l), *v.t.* [set-tled, set-tling], **1,** to place in a fixed state or position; as, *settle* yourself in this hammock; also, to establish in business or in a home; as, they were finally *settled* in the new house; **2,** to make calm; free from unrest; as, you must *settle* your nerves; **3,** to agree on; as, to *settle* a price; adjust, as a quarrel; pay, as a bill; **4,** to free of dregs by causing them to sink; as, to *settle* coffee; **5,** to make firm or solid; as, to *settle* a roadway; **6,** to colonize; as, the Quakers *settled* Pennsylvania; **7,** to dispose of; as, to *settle* an estate; bestow legally; as, to *settle* an annuity on someone; put into shape, as one's affairs:—*v.i.* **1,** to become fixed; assume a lasting form; **2,** to come to rest, as a bird; establish a residence, as a colonist; **3,** to become established in business or in a way of life; as, to *settle* down; **4,** to sink to the bottom of a liquid, as dregs; be cleared of dregs, as coffee; **5,** to become firm or solid, as a roadbed;

find a permanent level, as the foundations of a building; **6,** to determine; as, to *settle* on a course of conduct; **7,** to pay a bill.

²**set·tle** (sĕt′l), *n.* a long, wooden bench with arms, a straight, high back, and, often, an enclosed boxlike base.

SETTLE

set·tle·ment (sĕt′l-mĕnt), *n.* **1,** the act of settling or establishing; also, the state of being fixed or established, as in a business or profession; **2,** the payment of an account; adjustment of a dispute; **3,** a legal gift; as, a marriage *settlement;* **4,** the process of colonizing; also a colony, especially one in a state of development; **5,** a small town or village; **6,** in a poor and crowded section of a large city, an institution providing instruction, entertainment, etc., for the people of the neighborhood.

set·tler (sĕt′lẽr), *n.* a colonist.

set–to (sĕt′=tōō′), *n.* [*pl.* set-tos (sĕt′=tōōz′)], *Colloquial,* a bout, usually brief, of fist fighting, argument, or the like.

sev·en (sĕv′ĕn), *adj.* composed of one more than six:—*n.* **1,** the sum of one and six; **2,** a sign representing seven units, as 7 or vii.

sev·en·fold (sĕv′ĕn-fōld′), *adj.* **1,** multiplied seven times; seven times as great; **2,** consisting of seven parts:—*adv.* (sĕv′-ĕn-fōld′), seven times as much or as many.

sev·en·teen (sĕv′ĕn-tēn′), *adj.* composed of ten more than seven:—*n.* **1,** the sum of sixteen and one; **2,** a sign representing seventeen units, as 17 or xvii.

sev·en·teenth (sĕv′ĕn-tēnth′), *adj.* next after the 16th: the ordinal of *seventeen:—n.* one of the seventeen equal parts of anything.

sev·enth (sĕv′ĕnth), *adj.* next after the sixth: the ordinal of *seven:—n.* one of the seven equal parts of anything.

sev·en·ti·eth (sĕv′ĕn-tĭ-ĕth), *adj.* next after the 69th: the ordinal of *seventy:—n.* one of the 70 equal parts of anything.

sev·en·ty (sĕv′ĕn-tĭ), *adj.* composed of one more than 69:—*n.* [*pl.* seventies], **1,** the number consisting of 69 plus one; **2,** a sign representing 70 units, as 70 or lxx.

sev·er (sĕv′ẽr), *v.t.* **1,** to divide or separate with violence; cut; as, they *severed* the cords that bound him; **2,** to put apart (two or more persons or things); divide:—*v.i.* to part; be torn apart.

Syn. detach, disjoin, break, rend.

sev·er·al (sĕv′ẽr-ăl), *adj.* **1,** distinct; separate; as, they went their *several* ways;

2, more than two but not many; some; as, *several* members of the club arrived late.

sev·er·ance (sĕv′ẽr-ăns), *n.* **1,** the act of cutting or separating; **2,** the state of being cut off or divided; separation.

se·vere (sẽ-vēr′), *adj.* [sever-er, sever-est], **1,** strict; stern; as, *severe* methods of discipline; **2,** austere; grave in manner; **3,** extremely plain; as, a gown of a *severe* style; **4,** extreme; sharp; violent; as, *severe* anguish; **5,** hard to bear or undergo; trying; as, a *severe* test.—*adv.* **se·vere′ly.**

se·ver·i·ty (sẽ-vĕr′ĭ-tĭ), *n.* [*pl.* severities], **1,** the quality of being stern or strict; **2,** seriousness; gravity; **3,** plainness; lack of ornament, as in dress; **4,** violence; harshness, as of the weather.

Sev·ern (sĕv′ẽrn), a river of England and Wales, flowing into the Bristol Channel (map **13**).

Sev·ille (sĕv′ĭl; sẽ-vĭl′), [Spanish **Se-vil-la** (sã-vēl′yä)], a city in southwestern Spain (map **12**).

sew (sō), *v.i.* [*p.t.* sewed (sōd), *p.p.* sewed or sewn (sōn), *p.pr.* sew-ing], **1,** to work with needle and thread; **2,** to do dressmaking for a living:—*v.t.* **1,** to put together, as a dress, etc. by means of stitches; **2,** to join or fasten to something with stitches, as a ruffle on a skirt; **3,** to close or mend by sewing, as, to *sew* up a tear.

sew·age (sū′ĭj), *n.* foul liquids or waste matter carried off by sewers.

sew·er (sū′ẽr), *n.* an underground pipe to carry off water, waste, etc.; public drain.

sew·er·age (sū′ẽr-ĭj), *n.* **1,** drainage by sewers; **2,** the system of sewers used in the drainage of a town or city; **3,** refuse matter carried off by a sewer; sewage.

sew·ing (sō′ĭng), *n.* **1,** the occupation of one who sews; **2,** needlework.

sewn (sōn), a past participle of *sew.*

sex (sĕks), *n.* **1,** the physical characteristics that make a human being, animal, or plant, distinctively male or female; **2,** one of the two divisions of animals or plants, called male and female.

sex·tant (sĕks′tănt), *n.* an instrument used by mariners especially for observing the altitude of the sun in order to determine latitude and longitude at sea.

SEXTANT

sex·tet or **sex·tette** (sĕks-tĕt′), *n.* **1,** a musical composition for six performers; also, the six performers rendering such a composition; **2,** any group of six.

sex·ton (sĕks′tŭn), *n.* an underofficial or janitor of a church, whose duty is to take care of the church building and property, attend to burials, etc.

sex·u·al (sĕk′shŏŏ-ăl; sĕks′ū-ăl), *adj.* pertaining to sex or the sexes.

's Gra·ven·ha·ge (skhrä′vĕn-hä′gē), one of the capitals of the Netherlands. Also called *The Hague.*

Sgt. abbreviation for *sergeant.*

shab·by (shăb′ĭ), *adj.* [shab-bi-er, shab-bi-est], **1,** threadbare or worn; as, *shabby* clothes; **2,** poorly dressed; seedy; **3,** petty or unworthy; mean; as, that was a *shabby* trick.—*adv.* **shab′bi·ly.**—*n.* **shab′bi·ness.**

shack (shăk), *n. Colloquial,* a hut; hovel.

shack·le (shăk′l), *n.* **1,** (usually *shackles*), anything that confines the arms or legs so as to prevent free action, as a strap or chain; a fetter; handcuff; **2,** hence, anything which restrains or prevents free action; **3,** any of various fastenings, as a link for coupling cars:—*v.t.* [shack-led, shack-ling], **1,** to chain; manacle; fetter; **2,** to embarrass or hinder; **3,** to join or fasten with a shackle.

shad (shăd), *n.* [*pl.* shad], a large food fish of the herring family, found along the Atlantic coast of the United States.

shad·bush (shăd′bŏŏsh′), *n.* a white-flowering, tall shrub or small tree, bearing purple, edible, berrylike fruit.

shade (shād), *n.* **1,** partial darkness caused by cutting off rays of light; **2,** a spot not exposed to the sun; a shady place; hence, a secluded retreat; **3,** something which cuts off or softens the rays of light; especially, a screen or curtain fitting close to a window-pane and adjustable so as to regulate the amount of light admitted; **4,** a special degree or variety of a color; as, this *shade* of blue is difficult to match; often, a dark color; as, tints and *shades;* **5,** a slight degree or amount; a trace; as, there was a *shade* of doubt in his voice; **6,** a shadow; a ghost or phantom; an unreal thing; **7, shades,** the shadows that gather as light fails; darkness; dimness; as, the *shades* of night:—*v.t.* [shad-ed, shad-ing], **1,** to screen from light or heat; **2,** to darken or make dim; **3,** to mark or paint with varying degrees of light or color:—*v.i.* to merge or change by slight degrees; as, the sunset *shaded* from a flame color to pale yellow.

Syn., n. tint, hue, color, tinge.

SHADE (S) for electric lamp.

WINDOW SHADE

shad·ow (shăd′ō), *n.* **1,** comparative darkness, or shade, caused by cutting off the direct rays coming from the sun or other source of light; **2,** a dark figure or image projected by a body or person cutting off the direct light from a given source; as, his figure cast a *shadow* on the wall; **3,** that which follows inseparably; a constant companion; as, Jane is Mary's *shadow;* **4,** a reflection, as in water; hence, an imaginary likeness; **5,** the darker portion of a picture; **6,** protection; as, under the *shadow* of the Almighty; **7,** a weakened counterpart; a mere semblance; as, after her illness, she was only a *shadow* of her former self; **8,** a ghost; phantom; wraith; **9,** an unsubstantial or unreal thing; **10,** slightest trace; as, without a *shadow* of excuse:—*v.t.* **1,** to darken; cloud; **2,** to indicate indirectly or in outline; **3,** to keep under observation; as, the detective *shadowed* his man.—*adj.* **shad′ow·y.**

shad·y (shād′ĭ), *adj.* [shad-i-er, shad-i-est], **1,** giving shade or shelter; as, a *shady* tree; **2,** sheltered from the glare of light or heat; as, a *shady* path; **3,** *Colloquial,* questionable; of doubtful honesty; as, *shady* business deals.—*n.* **shad′i·ness.**

shaft (shăft), *n.* **1,** the long stem or handle of an arrow or similar missile; also, an arrow; spear; dart; **2,** any long, slender part resembling the stem of an arrow, as the stalk of a plant or the handle of a golf club; **3,** the long, narrow, vertical or slanted entrance to a mine; **4,** the pole of a wagon or carriage (see illustration under *harness*); **5,** in an engine or a machine, a bar to hold or to help move wheels or other rotating parts; **6,** an open well-like space through which air and light reach the windows of a building, as a tenement or factory; also, the vertical well in which an elevator runs; **7,** the body of a column between the base and the top.

shag (shăg), *n.* **1,** coarse or rough hair, wool, etc.; **2,** a kind of cloth with a long coarse nap; also, the nap.

shag·bark (shăg′bärk′), *n.* a nut-bearing tree with ragged bark; a hickory.

shag·gy (shăg′ĭ), *adj.* [shag-gi-er, shag-gi-est], **1,** rough-haired; as, a *shaggy* dog; **2,** unkempt; tangled.—*n.* **shag′gi·ness.**

shah (shä), *n.* the title of the ruler of Iran, and of other Eastern countries.

shake (shāk), *v.t.* [*p.t.* shook (shŏŏk), *p.p.* shak-en (shāk′ĕn), *p.pr.* shak-ing], **1,** to move with a quick back and forth motion; as, a terrier *shakes* a rat; **2,** to cause to tremble; as, chills *shook* his body; **3,** to cause (a person) to waver or doubt; also, to weaken; impair; as, to *shake* a person's faith; **4,** to throw off or dispel; as, to *shake* off sleepiness; **5,** to loosen; unfasten; as, to *shake* out a sail:—*v.i.* to tremble; quake:—*n.* the act of moving or causing to move with a quick short motion.

Syn., v. quiver, shiver, shudder.

shak-er (shāk'ẽr), *n.* **1,** one who shakes; **2,** that from which something is shaken; as, a salt *shaker:*—**Shaker,** one of a religious sect living in community settlements in the U.S.

Shake - speare (shāk'spēr), William (1564–1616), an Elizabethan poet and dramatist, considered England's greatest dramatist.

FLOUR SHAKER

Shake-spear-e-an (shāk-spēr'-ē-ăn), *adj.* relating to Shakespeare or his works.

shak-o (shăk'ō), *n.* [*pl.* shakos], a kind of high military cap, usually cylindrical, with an upright plume.

shak-y (shāk'ĭ), *adj.* [shak-i-er, shak-i-est], **1,** ready to fall to pieces; unsound; as, a *shaky* table; **2,** feeble; tottering.

shale (shāl), *n.* a rock of clayey origin, easily split into sheets, and somewhat resembling slate.

shall (shăl), *auxiliary v.* [*p.t.* should (shŏŏd)], used in the first person to express simple futurity, and in the second and third persons to express command, determination, promise, etc.; as, I *shall* be in town tomorrow; "Curfew *shall* not ring tonight."

SHAKO

shal-lop (shăl'ŭp), *n.* a small, light, open boat with sails or oars, or both.

shal-low (shăl'ō), *adj.* **1,** not deep; as, a *shallow* stream; **2,** having no mental depth; superficial; as, a *shallow* mind:—*n.* a place where the water is not deep; a shoal.

shalt (shălt), second person singular, present indicative, of *shall.*

sham (shăm), *n.* **1,** one who or that which deceives; a trick, fraud, or pretense; **2,** an ornamental cover for a pillow or bolster:—*adj.* **1,** feigned; false; as, the fleet engaged in a *sham* attack; **2,** unreal; pretentious; as, *sham* finery:—*v.t.* [shammed, sham-ming], to make a pretense of, in order to deceive; feign; as, to *sham* death.

sham-ble (shăm'bl), *v.i.* [sham-bled, sham-bling], to walk awkwardly and uncertainly, as if with weak knees; shuffle:—*n.* a shuffling gait.—*adj.* **sham'bling.**

sham-bles (shăm'blz), *n.pl.* sometimes used as *sing.* **1,** a slaughterhouse; **2,** any scene of bloody slaughter.

shame (shām), *n.* **1,** a painful feeling caused by the knowledge that one has been guilty of something wrong, immodest, or dishonorable; also, that which causes a feeling of shame; **2,** disgrace; dishonor; **3,** a restraining sense of modesty or decency:—*v.t.* [shamed, sham-ing], **1,** to cause to blush with shame or guilt; **2,** to disgrace; as, to *shame* one's family; **3,** to make (a person) do a thing through a sense of decency; as, his friends *shamed* John into apologizing.

Syn., n. humiliation, distress, chagrin.

shame-faced (shām'fāst'), *adj.* bashful; also, showing embarrassment or shame.

shame-ful (shām'fŏŏl), *adj.* causing disgrace; disgraceful; as, *shameful* conduct.

shame-less (shām'lĕs), *adj.* without shame; without decency; brazen.

Sha-mo (shä'mō'), the Chinese name for a desert in central Asia. See **Gobi, The.**

sham-poo (shăm-pŏŏ'), *v.t.* to cleanse and rub (the head and hair) with soap and water, or other cleansing preparation:—*n.* **1,** the act of washing the hair; **2,** a preparation used in washing the hair.

sham-rock (shăm'rŏk), *n.* a kind of three-leaved plant of the clover family. It is the national emblem of Ireland.

Shang-hai (shăng'hī'), a seaport city in eastern China (map 15).

shang-hai (shăng-hī'; shăng'-hī), *v.t.* [shanghaied, shang-hai-ing], to drug and kidnap for service as a sailor.

SHAMROCK

shank (shăngk), *n.* **1,** the leg; especially, in man, the leg from the knee to the ankle; the shin; also, a corresponding part in animals (see *fowl, horse,* illustrations); **2,** in dressed beef, a cut from the upper part of the foreleg; **3,** the portion of a tool, implement, etc., between the cutting or working part and the handle, as the stem of a key, bit, or drill, or the central part of an anchor; **4,** in a shoe, the part of the sole under the instep.

Shan-non (shăn'ŭn), a river in Ireland, flowing into the Atlantic Ocean (map 13).

shan't (shȧnt), *Colloquial,* contraction of *shall not.*

Shan-tung (shän'tŏŏng'), a province (cap. Tsinan) and peninsula of eastern China, bordering on the Yellow Sea.

shan-ty (shăn'tĭ), *n.* [*pl.* shanties], a rude shack or cabin.

shape (shāp), *n.* **1,** the form or figure of a person or thing; outline; as, the *shape* of a boat; **2,** that which has form or figure, whether real or imaginary; a person or thing indistinctly seen; hence, a ghost; **3,** a pattern for guiding a cutter; a mold;

āte, âorta, râre, căt, ȧsk, fär, ăllow, sofȧ; ēve, êvent, ĕll, writẽr, novĕl; bīte, pĭn; nō, ōbey, ôr, dŏg, tŏp, cŏllide; ūnit, ûnite, bûrn, cŭt, focŭs; nŏŏn, fŏŏt; mound; coin;

4, concrete or definite form; as, to whip an idea into *shape;* 5, *Colloquial,* condition or state of being; as, his affairs were in bad *shape:— v.t.* [shaped, shap-ing], 1, to make into a certain form; fashion; as, eyebrows *shaped* in a long curve; 2, to adapt to a particular end; regulate; adjust; as, to *shape* plans:— *v.i.* to take form; develop; give signs of future form or fate.

shape-less (shāp′lĕs), *adj.* formless; irregular; lacking beauty of proportion.

shape-ly (shāp′lĭ), *adj.* [shape-li-er, shape-li-est], well-formed.— *n.* **shape′li-ness.**

shard (shärd), *n.* a fragment of brittle material, as of earthenware.

¹**share** (shâr), *n.* 1, a certain portion or part that falls to an individual; as, he has had more than his *share* of trouble; 2, an equitable part given or belonging to one of a number of persons claiming or owning something jointly; as, he received his *share* of the estate; 3, one's proportional contribution of any kind to a joint undertaking; as, he gave his *share* of time and money to the club; 4, one of the equal portions into which a company's capital stock is divided, each represented by a certificate entitling the holder to a proportionate part of the earnings:— *v.t.* [shared, shar-ing], 1, to give away a part of; divide and distribute; as, to *share* one's wealth; 2, to possess in common; partake of, or experience, with others:— *v.i.* to take part; as, to *share* in the fun:— **share crop-per,** a tenant farmer who pays his rent with a portion of the crop which he raises.

²**share** (shâr), *n.* the part of a plow which cuts the earth; the blade; plowshare.

share-hold-er (shâr′hōl′dẽr), *n.* one who owns one or more shares of stock in a corporation; a stockholder.

shark (shärk), *n.* 1, a large, carnivorous, sharp-toothed fish, found mostly in warm

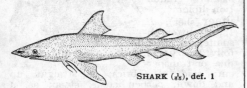

SHARK (₆₀₀), def. 1

seas; 2, a swindler or cheat; 3, *Slang,* a person unusually talented in some special line; as, a *shark* at mathematics.

Shar-on (shăr′ŭn), in the Bible, a fertile plain in western Palestine.

sharp (shärp), *adj.* 1, having a very thin, fine edge; as, a *sharp* knife; 2, ending in a fine point; as, a *sharp* needle; 3, well-defined; distinct; as, *sharp* features; 4, angular; abrupt; as, a *sharp* bend in the road; 5, quick; keen; alert; as, a *sharp* eye; also, clever; shrewd; intelligent; 6, close in dealing; hence, dishonest; unscrupulous; as, a *sharp* dealer; 7, severe; intense; as, a *sharp* pain; 8, piercing; shrill; penetrating; as, a *sharp* voice; 9, acid; sour; tart; as, a *sharp* taste; 10, frosty; cutting; as, *sharp* cold; 11, quick; hasty; as, a *sharp* temper; 12, sarcastic; bitter; as, a *sharp* tongue; 13, fierce; violent; as, a *sharp* contest; 14, in music: **a,** above the true pitch; as, a *sharp* note; **b,** raised by a half step; as, C *sharp:— adv.* 1, in music, above the true pitch; 2, *Colloquial,* promptly; precisely; as, six o'clock *sharp;* 3, in a sharp manner; alertly; as, look *sharp:— n.* in music, a tone or note raised a half step in pitch; also, the sign [#] showing that a note is to be so raised:— *v.t.* and *v.i.* in music, to make (a note) higher in pitch by a half step; also, to sing or play above the correct pitch.

sharp-en (shär′pĕn), *v.t.* to make keen or keener; give point or keenness to; as, to *sharpen* a tool:— *v.i.* to become sharp.— *n.* **sharp′en-er.**

sharp-er (shär′pẽr), *n.* one who drives a close bargain; hence, a cheat; swindler.

sharp-shoot-er (shärp′shōōt′ẽr), *n.* an expert marksman, especially with a rifle.

shat-ter (shăt′ẽr), *v.t.* 1, to break violently into many pieces; smash; as, to *shatter* a vase; 2, to derange or disorder; as, the accident *shattered* his nerves; 3, to defeat; ruin; as, hopes that are *shattered:— v.i.* to fly into pieces; break.

shat-ter-proof (shăt′ẽr-prōōf′), *adj.* not able to be splintered; as, *shatterproof* glass.

shave (shāv), *v.t.* [*p.t.* shaved (shāvd), *p.p.* shaved or shav-en (shāv′ĕn), *p.pr.* shav-ing], 1, to cut off or remove with a razor or similar sharp-edged instrument; free (the face, chin, etc.) of hair; 2, to cut in very thin slices; as, to *shave* citron; 3, to come very close to; graze:— *v.i.* to use the razor to remove hair:— *n.* 1, the act or operation of removing hair with a razor; 2, any of various woodworking instruments for paring or smoothing the surface of wood; 3, *Colloquial,* a very small time or distance; also, a narrow escape; as, a close *shave.— n.* and *adj.* **shav′ing.**

shav-er (shāv′ẽr), *n. Colloquial,* a little boy.

shawl (shôl), *n.* a scarf made of a square or oblong piece of cloth, used chiefly by women as a loose outer covering for the shoulders.

shay (shā), *n. Colloquial,* a chaise; a light carriage; as, the one-horse *shay.*

---

go; join; yet; sing; chin; show; thin, *th*en; hw, *wh*y; zh, azure; ū, Ger. für or Fr. l*u*ne; ö, Ger. schön or Fr. f*eu*; ṅ, Fr. *en*fant, nom; kh, Ger. a*ch* or i*ch*. See pages ix–x.

she (shē), *fem.pron.* of the third person personal pronoun [*nominative* she, *possessive* her (hûr) or hers (hûrz), *objective* her], **1,** one particular woman or girl, previously mentioned; as, where is Ann? *she* is here; **2,** any female animal, or thing personified as female:—*n.* a woman; any female.

sheaf (shēf), *n.* [*pl.* sheaves (shēvz)], **1,** a quantity of cut grain, laid lengthwise and bound together; **2,** any bundle of things tied together, as arrows, papers, etc.

shear (shēr), *v.t.* [*p.t.* sheared (shērd), *p.p.* sheared or shorn (shôrn), *p.pr.* shearing], **1,** to cut off or clip (hair, wool, etc.), especially with large scissors or shears; **2,** to cut or clip wool or hair from; as, to *shear* sheep:—*n.* **1,** a machine for cutting or clipping metal; **2,** **shears: a,** any of various large cutting instruments, working much like scissors, by the crossing of cutting blades or edges; **b,** large scissors.—*n.* **shear′er.**

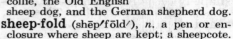

SHEARS

sheath (shēth), *n.* [*pl.* sheaths (shēthz)], **1,** a close-fitting cover or case for a sword or knife; a scabbard; **2,** any covering enclosing a part or organ, as the wing case of an insect.

sheathe (shēth), *v.t.* [sheathed, sheathing], **1,** to put into, furnish, or cover with, a case; as, to *sheathe* a sword; **2,** to incase or protect with a covering; as, to *sheathe* a roof with tin.

sheath-ing (shēth′ĭng), *n.* that which covers, or protects; especially, the protective boarding on the outside of a frame house. (See illustration at *frame house.*)

¹sheave (shēv), *n.* a grooved wheel on which a rope is worked; the wheel of a pulley.

²sheave (shēv), *v.t.* [sheaved, sheav-ing], to gather and bind into bundles, as grain.

sheaves (shēvz), plural of *sheaf.*

She-ba (shē′bȧ), an ancient kingdom in southwestern Arabia.

¹shed (shĕd), *v.t.* [shed, shed-ding], **1,** to pour out; drop; spill; as, to *shed* tears; **2,** to cause to flow; as, to *shed* blood; **3,** to pour forth; spread about; as, the sun *sheds* light; **4,** to cause to flow off; as, oilskins *shed* water; **5,** to cast away; let fall; as, birds *shed* their feathers:—*v.i.* to cast off or let fall hair, feathers, etc.

²shed (shĕd), *n.* a small building, often with the front or sides open, used for sheltering animals, or for storing supplies, farm implements, etc.

sheen (shēn), *n.* luster; radiance.

sheep (shēp), *n.* [*pl.* sheep], **1,** a timid, cud-chewing animal, related to the goat, valued for its wool, skin, and flesh; **2,** a timid, defenseless person; **3,** leather made of sheepskin and used in bookbinding.

SHEEP (₃⁄₁₀)

sheep-cote (shēp′kōt′; shēp′kŏt′), *n.* a pen for sheep; a sheepfold.

sheep dog, a dog used to herd sheep. Well-known varieties are the collie, the Old English sheep dog, and the German shepherd dog.

sheep-fold (shēp′fōld′), *n.* a pen or enclosure where sheep are kept; a sheepcote.

sheep-ish (shēp′ĭsh), *adj.* awkwardly bashful; somewhat silly; as, a *sheepish* look.

sheep-shank (shēp′shăngk′), *n.* a knot for temporarily shortening a rope. (See illustration under *knot.*)

sheeps-head (shēps′hĕd′), *n.* a common and valuable food fish of the Atlantic coast of the U.S.: so called from the resemblance of its incisor teeth to those of a sheep.

1, Old English Sheep Dog (₃⁄₁₀)
2, German Shepherd Dog (₃⁄₁₀)

sheep-skin (shēp′skĭn′), *n.* **1,** the dressed skin of a sheep, preserved with the wool on, and used for garments; **2,** leather or parchment made from the skin of sheep; **3,** a document written on parchment; hence, *Colloquial*, a graduation diploma.

¹sheer (shēr), *adj.* **1,** pure; utter; absolute; as, *sheer* folly; **2,** very thin, fine, or transparent: said of fabrics; **3,** straight up and down; perpendicular; steep; as, a *sheer* precipice:—*adv.* **1,** steeply; straight up and down; **2,** quite; completely.

SHEEPSHEAD (₁⁄₂)

²sheer (shēr), *v.i.* to turn from the course; swerve; as, the ship *sheered* to the north.

sheet (shēt), *n.* **1,** a large, broad, thin piece of any substance, as of cloth, glass, or metal; **2,** a broad piece of linen or cotton, used as bedding; **3,** a single piece of paper; **4,** a newspaper; **5,** a broad expanse or surface; as, a *sheet* of ice; **6,** a rope attached to the lower corner of a sail to hold and regulate it.

sheet·ing (shēt′ĭng), *n.* material for making sheets.

Shef·field (shĕf′ēld), a manufacturing city in north central England, famous for its steel blades and silver plate (map **13**).

Sheffield plate, plate made by rolling and soldering a thin coating of silver on copper or some other material.

sheik (shēk; shāk), *n.* the head of an Arab family, tribe, or clan. Also, **sheikh.**

shek·el (shĕk′ĕl), *n* an ancient Hebrew unit of weight and money; a coin.

shel·drake (shĕl′- drāk′), *n.* a fish-eat- ing wild duck of the Old World, which re- sembles the goose.

SHELDRAKE (¹⁄₈)

shelf (shĕlf), *n.* [*pl.* shelves (shĕl v z)], **1,** a flat board, usu- ally long and narrow, fastened to a wall or set into a bookcase or cupboard; **2,** something resembling a shelf in appearance or position, as a sandbank or a reef; **3,** a flat projecting ledge of rock.

shell (shĕl), *n.* **1,** a hard outside case or covering, as on a fruit, egg, nut, or seed, or on certain animals, as a crab or oyster; also, a husk, as on corn; **2,** the covering of a tortoise or a manufactured material re- sembling it, used in making combs, spec- tacle frames, etc.; **3,** a framework or skeleton, as of a building; **4,** a very light, long, narrow racing boat; **5,** a metal or paper case holding ammunition for a rifle, pistol, or the like; **6,** [*pl.* shell], a metal projectile filled with explosive, for use in a cannon or mortar:—*v.t.* **1,** to take from the shell, pod, etc., as peas from the pod; **2,** to separate from the cob, as corn; **3,** to bombard; as, to *shell* an enemy fort.

shel·lac (shĕ·lăk′; shĕl′ăk), *n.* a sticky, resinous substance used in making sealing wax, varnish, etc.; also, a solution of dry shellac, especially in alcohol, used as a varnish:—*v.t.* [shellacked, shellack-ing], to coat or treat with this substance.

Shel·ley (shĕl′ĭ), Percy Bysshe (bĭsh), (1792–1822), a great English lyric poet.

shell-fish (shĕl′fĭsh′), *n.* a water animal having a shell, as a clam, lobster, etc.

shell shock, a mental disorder among soldiers, believed to be caused by exposure to prolonged bombardment and the gen- eral wear and tear of modern warfare.

shel·ter (shĕl′tĕr), *n.* **1,** anything that protects, covers, or shields; a refuge, es- pecially from the weather; a house or cabin; **2,** the state of being protected, covered, or shielded; safety:—*v.t.* to pro- tect; defend:—*v.i.* to take refuge; as, dur- ing the storm we *sheltered* in the cave.

¹shelve (shĕlv), *v.t.* [shelved, shelv-ing], **1,** to place on a shelf; **2,** to dismiss from service; as, to *shelve* an officer; **3,** to postpone indefinitely; as, to *shelve* a peti- tion; **4,** to furnish with shelves, as a closet.

²shelve (shĕlv), *v.i.* [shelved, shelv-ing], to slope; as, the bottom *shelves* from the shore.

She·ol (shē′ōl), *n.* among the Hebrews, the home of the dead; also, the grave.

shep·herd (shĕp′ērd), *n.* **1,** one who tends sheep; **2,** one who guides the religious life of others; a pastor; minister:—*v.t.* to tend or guard, as sheep; also, to protect; lead. —*n. fem.* **shep′herd-ess.**

sher·bet (shûr′bĕt), *n.* **1,** a cooling drink of sweetened fruit juices; **2,** a water ice, usually with a fruit flavor.

Sher·i·dan (shĕr′ĭ-dăn), **1,** Philip Henry (1831–1888), an American general, famous in the War between the States; **2,** Richard Brinsley (1751–1816), a British dramatist, author of "The School for Scandal."

sher·iff (shĕr′ĭf), *n.* the chief law-enforcing officer of a county.

Sher·man (shûr′măn), William Tecumseh (1820–1891), a famous general in the War between the States.

sher·ry (shĕr′ĭ), *n.* [*pl.* sherries], a white wine made in Jerez, Spain; also, a similar, stronger, darker wine.

Sher·wood For·est (shûr′wŏŏd), a forest in central England, famous as the home of the outlaw Robin Hood.

Shet·land Is·lands (shĕt′lănd), a group of islands in the Atlantic Ocean, northeast of Scotland (map **13**).

shew (shō), in British use, a form of *show*.

shib·bo·leth (shĭb′ō-lĕth), *n.* the pet phrase or catchword of a party or sect; a political slogan.

shield (shēld), *n.* **1,** a broad piece of metal or wood, or a frame covered with

SHIELDS
1, Greek; 2, Roman; 3, medieval French.

leather or a similar material, carried on the arm to protect the body in fighting; **2,** hence, any person or thing that serves to ward off attack or injury:—*v.t.* to protect with, or as with, a shield; defend.

shift (shĭft), *v.t.* **1,** to transfer; as, to *shift* the blame; **2,** to exchange; substitute; as, to *shift* places in a boat:—*v.i.* **1,** to change position; as, sand dunes *shift*; also, to veer; as, the wind *shifted* to the north; **2,** to make one's way; as, to *shift* for oneself:—*n.* **1,** a turning from one thing to another; change; substitution; as, a *shift* of public enthusiasm toward a new leader; **2,** an expedient; as, to make one's way by *shifts*; hence, a trick; **3,** the system of working groups in relays; any one of these groups; as, an early *shift*; also, the working time of each group; as, an eight-hour *shift*; **4,** in football, a change in position of the line just before the ball is snapped.

shift-less (shĭft′lĕs), *adj.* lazy; thriftless; taking no thought for the future.

shift-y (shĭf′tĭ), *adj.* [shift-i-er, shift-i-est], **1,** able to turn circumstances to advantage; **2,** hence, not to be trusted.

shil-ling (shĭl′ĭng), *n.* a British silver coin, equivalent to twelve pence.

shil-ly—shal-ly (shĭl′ĭ=shăl′ĭ), *v.i.* [shilly-shallied, shilly-shally-ing], to hesitate; be irresolute:—*n.* trifling; weak indecision.

Shi-loh (shī′lō), a town in ancient Palestine.

shim-mer (shĭm′ẽr), *v.i.* to shine waveringly; gleam and glitter, as moonlight on the water:—*n.* **1,** a tremulous gleam; flicker; **2,** gloss; sheen, as of satin.

shin (shĭn), *n.* the front part of the leg between the ankle and knee; shank:—*v.i.* [shinned, shin-ning], to climb a tree, pole, or the like, by gripping it alternately with the arms and legs.

shine (shīn), *v.i.* [shone (shōn; shŏn; shin-ing], **1,** to emit or give forth rays of light, as the sun or moon; also, to reflect light; gleam; sparkle; as, the lake *shone* in the sunlight; **2,** to be brilliant; excel in some particular line; as, he *shines* in English:—*v.t.* [*p.t.* and *p.p.* shined (shīnd)], *Colloquial,* to cause to glisten; polish; as, to *shine* an automobile:—*n.* **1,** luster; sheen; **2,** bright weather; sunshine; as, rain and *shine*; **3,** *Colloquial,* a polish; as, my shoes need a *shine*.—*adj.* **shin′ing.**

shin-er (shīn′ẽr), *n.* one of many varieties of small silvery fishes.

¹**shin-gle** (shĭng′gl), *n.* **1,** one of the thin, oblong pieces of wood, slate, or the like, used in overlapping rows for roofing and siding (see *frame house,* illustration); **2,** *Colloquial,* a signboard, as on a doctor's office:—*v.t.* [shin-gled, shin-gling], **1,** to

cover, as a roof, with shingles; **2,** to cut (the hair) progressively shorter toward the nape of the neck, so as to reveal the outline of the back of the head.

²**shin-gle** (shĭng′gl), *n.* rounded seashore pebbles, coarser than ordinary gravel.

shin-gles (shĭng′glz), *n.pl.* used as *sing.* an inflammatory skin disease, of nervous origin, characterized by groups of small blisters and severe pain or intense itching.

shin-ny (shĭn′ĭ), *n.* [*pl.* shinnies], a kind of hockey played by boys; also, one of the sticks used in playing this game.

shin-y (shīn′ĭ), *adj.* [shin-i-er, shin-i-est], bright; glossy; shining.

ship (shĭp), *n.* **1,** any large seagoing vessel; **2,** a large sailing vessel with three, four, or five square-rigged masts; **3,** an airship or airplane:—*v.t.* [shipped, ship-ping], **1,** to load on a vessel; as, to *ship* cargo; **2,** to carry or transport by water; **3,** to send through any regular channel of transportation, as by rail; **4,** to fix in its proper place or position on a ship, as a mast or a rudder; **5,** to hire for service on a ship; as, to *ship* sailors:—**ship a sea,** to have a wave break over the decks:—*v.i.* **1,** to engage oneself for service on a vessel, as a sailor; **2,** to embark on a ship; as, to *ship* for Spain.

-ship (-shĭp), a suffix meaning: **1,** state or quality; as, hard*ship,* kin*ship;* **2,** office, dignity, or profession; as, king*ship,* judge*ship;* **3,** art or skill; as, penman*ship,* horseman*ship.*

ship bis-cuit (bĭs′kĭt), hardtack; a kind of coarse, hard biscuit made for use on shipboard.

ship-board (shĭp′bôrd′), *n.* the side or deck of a ship; hence, a ship: used chiefly in the phrase *on shipboard.*

ship-mas-ter (shĭp′màs′tẽr), *n.* the captain or master of a merchant ship, or of any ship other than a war vessel.

ship-mate (shĭp′māt′), *n.* a fellow sailor.

ship-ment (shĭp′mĕnt), *n.* **1,** the act of having goods transported; **2,** the goods transported.

ship of the line formerly, a ship of war of sufficient size to have a place in the front line of battle.

ship-per (shĭp′ẽr), *n.* one who sends goods by any transportation agency.

ship-ping (shĭp′ĭng), *n.* **1,** the act or business of one who ships goods; **2,** all the ships in a port or harbor; all the ships belonging to a country; tonnage.

ship-shape (shĭp′shāp′), *adj.* neat; in good order:—*adv.* neatly; in an orderly way.

āte, āorta, râre, căt, àsk, fär, ăllow, sofà; ēve, êvent, ĕll, writẽr, novĕl; bīte, pĭn; nō, ōbey, ôr, dŏg, tŏp, cŏllide; ūnit, ūnite, bûrn, cŭt, focŭs; nōōn, fŏŏt; mound; coin;

TYPES OF SAILING BOATS AND SHIPS

1, dinghy; 2, catboat; 3, knockabout; 4, Chesapeake Bay boat; 5, sloop; 6, yawl; 7, ketch; 8, 9, schooners; 10, brig 11, bark; 12, brigantine; 13, barkentine. (See also full-page illustration of *Rigging and Sails*, page 695.)

ship-worm (shǐp′wûrm′), *n.* a wormlike mollusk that bores into ship timbers, wharf piles, etc.

ship-wreck (shǐp′rĕk′), *n.* **1,** the destruction of a ship by disaster at sea, or by grounding, hitting a rock, etc.; **2,** a wrecked ship; **3,** utter ruin; as, the *shipwreck* of a life:—*v.t.* **1,** to destroy by, or cause to suffer, shipwreck; **2,** to ruin.

ship-yard (shǐp′yärd′), *n.* a place where ships are built or repaired.

shire (shīr; as an ending, -shĭr; -shēr), *n.* in England, a district or county.

shirk (shûrk), *v.t.* and *v.i.* **1,** to neglect (work, etc.) purposely; **2,** to shun or evade (responsibility):—*n.* one who purposely neglects or evades work or obligation.

shirr (shûr), *n.* in sewing, a puckering made in a fabric by means of parallel gathers:—*v.t.* **1,** to draw up (cloth), by gathering it in parallel lines; **2,** to bake (eggs) in a buttered dish with cream.

shirt (shûrt), *n.* **1,** a man's sleeved blouse, usually worn under a coat or vest; **2,** a close-fitting undergarment for the upper part of the body.

shirt-ing (shûrt′ĭng), *n.* material suitable for making outer shirts and blouses.

shirt-waist (shûrt′wāst′), *n.* a woman's sleeved blouse, made long enough to be tucked under a skirt.

¹shiv-er (shǐv′ẽr), *v.i.* to tremble, as from cold or fright; to quiver; shake:—*n.* a trembling from cold, fear, or the like.—*adj.* **shiv′er-y.**

²shiv-er (shǐv′ẽr), *v.i.* and *v.t.* to break, or cause to break, into small pieces; shatter:—*n.* a small fragment splintered off by a fall or blow; a sliver.

¹shoal (shōl), *n.* a large number; as, a *shoal* of fish.

²shoal (shōl), *adj.* of little depth; shallow; as, *shoal* water:—*n.* **1,** a shallow place in any body of water; a shallow; **2,** a sandbank or bar which shows only at low tide; **3,** hence, a hidden or unexpected danger: —*v.i.* to grow shallow.

shoat (shōt), *n.* a young hog; shote.

¹shock (shŏk), *n.* **1,** a forcible blow; impact; violent jar; as, the *shock* of a collision; **2,** an unexpected and violent jarring of the feelings; as, a *shock* of grief; **3,** the effect of the passage of an electric current through the body; as, he got a *shock* when he touched the live wire; **4,** a condition of extreme physical exhaustion caused by the pain of severe wounds or blows, loss of blood, or the like:—*v.t.* to strike with surprise, horror, disgust, or the like; as, the crime *shocked* the country.

²shock (shŏk), *n.* a stack of sheaves of grain set upright together in a field:—*v.t.* to collect and stack (sheaves of grain).

³shock (shŏk), *n.* a bushy mass, as of hair.

shock-ing (shŏk′ĭng), *adj.* **1,** emotionally disturbing; as, a *shocking* accident; **2,** offensive; as, a *shocking* remark.

shod (shŏd), past tense and past participle of *shoe.*

shod-dy (shŏd′ĭ), *n.* [*pl.* shoddies], **1,** fibers obtained by picking apart waste cotton or woolen fabrics; also, yarn spun from these fibers, or an inferior cloth made from this yarn; **2,** rubbish; waste; **3,** hence, an inferior thing made to have an appearance of superiority:—*adj.* [shod-di-er, shod-di-est], **1,** made of such inferior material; as, *shoddy* clothing; **2,** not genuine; sham; as, *shoddy* aristocracy.

shoe (shoo), *n.* **1,** an outer covering for the human foot, made of leather, suède, satin, or the like; **2,** a U-shaped metal bar nailed on the hoof of a horse, donkey, etc., **3,** something resembling a shoe in form or use, as the strip of steel fastened on the runners of a sleigh, or the outer covering of an automobile tire:—*v.t.* [shod (shŏd), shoe-ing], **1,** to furnish with a shoe or shoes; as, the blacksmith *shod* the horse; **2,** to protect, strengthen, or ornament, by adding a tip, rim, etc., of harder material; as, to *shoe* a wooden pole with an iron point.

SHOE
1, toe; 2, vamp; 3, sole; 4, shank; 5, heel; 6, top.

shoe-horn (shoo′hôrn′), *n.* a curved, smooth piece of metal or other material, used as an aid in putting on a shoe.

shoe-mak-er (shoo′māk′ẽr), *n.* a person whose business it is to make or mend shoes.—*n.* **shoe′mak′ing.**

shone (shōn; shŏn), one form of the past tense and past participle of *shine.*

shoo (shoo), *v.t.* and *v.i.* to scare away animals, especially fowl; drive by a cry of "shoo"; as, to *shoo* chickens into a coop: —*interj.* an exclamation used to drive away animals.

shook (shŏok), past tense of *shake.*

shoot (shoot), *v.t.* [shot (shŏt), shoot-ing], **1,** to let fly, send out, or discharge with sudden force; as, to *shoot* an arrow; **2,** to strike, kill, or wound with a missile discharged from a gun; **3,** to fire or discharge (a missile, weapon); **4,** to streak with different colors; as, the setting sun *shot* the sky with crimson; **5,** to move (a bolt) into or out of a fastening; **6,** to push forward; stick out; as, the snake *shot* out its tongue; **7,** to throw; as, to *shoot* dice; **8,** to flip or propel by a sharp, quick movement of the thumb or fingers; as, to *shoot* marbles; **9,** to pass or rush rapidly through or over; as, to *shoot* the rapids in a canoe; **10,** in motion pictures, to photograph (a scene):—*v.i.* **1,** to protrude or project; jut; as, the peninsula *shoots* out into the sea; **2,** to rush or flash along swiftly; as, the meteor *shot* through the sky; **3,** to bud; sprout; **4,** to dart with a stabbing sensation; as, a sharp pain *shot* up her arm; **5,** to discharge a missile from a gun; cause a gun, bow, etc., to let fly a missile; **6,** to grow rapidly; grow taller; **7,** to stream forth; spurt:—*n.* **1,** a young branch or growth; **2,** a shooting match; a hunt.

shoot-ing star, a luminous body that enters and passes through the earth's atmosphere; a meteor.

shop (shŏp), *n.* **1,** a room or building where goods are sold at retail; a store; **2,** a place where mechanics carry on their trade; as, an automobile repair *shop;* **3,** (usually *shops*), a factory; **4,** one's own business as a subject of conversation; as, to talk *shop:*—*v.i.* [shopped, shop-ping], to visit stores to look over or purchase goods.—*n.* and *adj.* **shop′ping.**

shop-keep-er (shŏp′kēp′ĕr), *n.* a tradesman who sells goods at retail in a store.

shop-lift-er (shŏp′lĭf′tĕr), *n.* a person who steals goods from a shop while pretending to buy or inspect.—*n.* **shop′lift′ing.**

shop-worn (shŏp′wôrn′), *adj.* soiled or worn from having been kept a long time in stock or on display in a shop.

¹**shore** (shōr), *n.* the land bordering on a body of water, as on the sea, a lake, or a river.

SHORES, supporting a ship.

Syn. beach, strand, coast.

²**shore** (shōr), *n.* a prop set slantwise against or beneath a ship, wall, or the like, as a temporary support:—*v.t.* [shored, shor-ing], to support or steady with props.

shorn (shôrn), one of the forms of the past participle of *shear.*

short (shôrt), *adj.* **1,** brief in time; as, a *short* vacation; **2,** not long; of little length; as, a *short* piece of string; a *short* walk; **3,** below the average height; not tall; as, a *short* man; **4,** scant; deficient; as, a *short* supply of food; also, insufficiently provided with; as, to be *short* of cash; **5,** curt; abrupt; uncivil; as, a *short* answer; **6,** rich; flaky, as pastry; **7,** of vowels: **a,**

taking less time to pronounce than the corresponding long sound, as the vowels in "fed" and "foot" compared with those in "fare" and "food"; **b,** sounded like *a* in "hat," *e* in "met," *i* in "sit," *o* in "hot," *oo* in "look," *u* in "but":—**short ton,** a weight of 2,000 pounds: called *ton:*—**shorts,** *n.pl.* short, loose trousers:—*adv.* **1,** abruptly; suddenly; **2,** less than the desired or regular distance; as, to fall *short* of the mark.

Syn., adj. brief, concise, terse.

short-age (shôr′tĭj), *n.* the amount by which anything is short; a deficit; as, his accounts last year showed a *shortage.*

short-cake (shôrt′kāk′), *n.* a cake resembling biscuit in texture, or a sweetened sponge cake, split and served with fruit between the layers; as, strawberry *shortcake.*

short cir-cuit, a circuit made through a conductor of low resistance.

short-com-ing (shôrt′kŭm′ĭng; shôrt′-kŭm′ĭng), *n.* a failing; fault.

short-en (shôr′tn), *v.t.* **1,** to make short or shorter in time, extent, or measure; lessen; as, the new road will *shorten* our trip to town; **2,** to make crisp or short, as pastry, by using butter, lard, or the like:—*v.i.* to grow or become shorter or briefer.

short-en-ing (shôr′tn-ĭng), *n.* that which makes pastry crisp, as lard, butter, etc.

short-hand (shôrt′hănd′), *n.* a system of rapid writing in which characters, symbols, or abbreviations are used for letters, words, phrases, etc.; stenography.

SHORTHAND SYMBOLS

short-hand-ed (shôrt′hăn′dĕd), *adj.* lacking the regular number of servants or workmen.

short-horn (shôrt′hôrn′), *n.* one of a large, heavy breed of beef cattle with short horns.

short—lived (shôrt′=līvd′), *adj.* living or lasting a short time; as, a butterfly is *short-lived;* his power was *short-lived.*

short-ly (shôrt′lĭ), *adv.* **1,** soon; **2,** in a few words; concisely; **3,** curtly; abruptly.

short-sight-ed (shôrt′sīt′ĕd), *adj.* **1,** seeing clearly at short distances only; unable to see far; **2,** due to, or marked by, lack of foresight; imprudent; as, a *shortsighted* business venture.

short-stop (shôrt′stŏp′), *n.* in baseball, a player stationed between second base and third base.

short—wind-ed (shôrt′=wĭn′dĕd), *adj.* affected with shortness of breath; likely to be so affected under the strain of exertion.

¹**shot** (shŏt), past tense and past participle

of *shoot:—adj.* variegated in color; as, rose silk *shot* with silver.

²**shot** (shŏt), *n.* **1,** the discharge of a fire-arm; **2,** a bullet, shell, cannon ball, etc.; also, anything let fly or discharged with force; **3,** [*pl.* shot], a small pellet or a number of such pellets combined in one charge, to be fired from a shotgun; **4,** the distance which is or can be covered by a missile; hence, range; as, the soldiers were within gun*shot;* **5,** in certain games, a stroke, throw, or the like; **6,** hence, an attempt; a try; **7,** a marksman; as, he is a good *shot;* **8,** in sports, a heavy ball-shaped weight to be thrown in competition for distance; **9,** in motion pictures, the film record of a scene; also, the process of photographing a single scene; **10,** *Colloquial,* an innocula-tion, especially by hypodermic injection, against disease.

shote (shōt), *n.* a young hog; shoat.

shot-gun (shŏt′gŭn′), *n.* a gun with a smooth bore, for firing at short range.

should (shŏŏd), *auxiliary v.* past tense of *shall,* used: **1,** in quoting a thought or ex-pression in which *shall* was originally used; as, "I *shall* stay until six" becomes "I said that I *should* stay until six"; "he *shall* not leave" becomes "I said that he *should* not leave"; **2,** to express doubt, uncertainty, condition, etc.; as, if it *should* rain, don't try to go; I *should* like to see the play, if it were a good one; **3,** to express obligation that ought to be or ought to have been fulfilled; as, he *should* telephone this after-noon; he *should* have telephoned yesterday.

shoul-der (shōl′dĕr), *n.* **1,** either of the two projecting parts of the human body between the neck and the place where the arm joins the trunk; **2,** in animals, the fore-quarter; also, a cut of meat consisting of the upper joint of the foreleg and adjacent parts of the animal; **3,** the part of a gar-ment that covers the shoulder; **4,** anything resembling a shoulder; as, the *shoulder* of a vase; **5,** the graded edge of a road:—*v.t.* **1,** to take upon the shoulder; as, to *shoulder* a pack; **2,** hence, to assume the responsi-bility of; as, to *shoulder* an obligation; **3,** to push with the shoulders; hence, to make (one's way) by pushing with the shoulders; as, he *shouldered* his way through the mob.

shoulder blade, the flat triangular bone of the shoulder.

shoulder board, the insignia worn on the shoulder of naval officers to show rank.

shoulder strap, 1, one of a pair of straps of fabric, ribbon, lace, etc., worn over the shoulders to support an article of clothing; **2,** a narrow strap worn on the shoulder by army officers to bear the insignia of rank.

shouldst (shŏŏdst), the second person singular of *should.*

shout (shout), *n.* a loud and sudden cry, as of joy, command, encouragement, or the like:—*v.i.* to make an outcry; as, he *shouted* with joy:—*v.t.* to utter with a loud voice; as, he *shouted* out his orders.

shove (shŭv), *n.* a forcible push:—*v.t.* [shoved, shov-ing], **1,** to push (something) along; as, to *shove* a book across the table; **2,** to jostle; crowd; as, she *shoved* me against the door:—*v.i.* to crowd against others:—**shove off,** to push off from shore in a boat.

shov-el (shŭv′l), *n.* **1,** a tool consisting of a broad, flat scoop with a handle, for lifting and throwing coal, grain, etc., or for digging; **2,** anything which re-sembles a shovel in shape or use; **3,** the amount that a shovel holds; as, a *shovel* of ashes:—*v.t.*° [shoveled, shovel-ing], **1,** to take up and throw with such a tool; **2,** to gather up with, or as with, a shovel; as, to *shovel* one's food; **3,** to dig, clear, or clean out with this tool; as, to *shovel* a path through snow.

SHOVELS

shov-el-er (shŭv′l-ẽr), *n.* **1,** one who uses a shovel; **2,** a river duck with a long and very broad bill.

show (shō), *v.t.* [*p.t.* showed (shōd), *p.p.* shown (shōn) or showed, *p.pr.* show-ing], **1,** to present to view; exhibit; as, *show* your stamps to me; to *show* anger; **2,** to make known; disclose; as, a fortuneteller claims to *show* the future; **3,** to make clear or ex-plain (something); as, let me *show* just what I mean; hence, to teach; as, *show* me how to skate; **4,** to prove; demonstrate; as, I shall *show* that he is wrong; **5,** to indi-cate; point out; as, this *shows* who did it; **6,** to direct; as, to *show* a person to his seat; **7,** bestow or manifest; as, to *show* mercy: —*v.i.* to be visible or noticeable; as, pity *showed* in his face; the stain still *shows:*— *n.* **1,** the act of exhibiting or displaying; **2,** an exhibition or display; as, a dog *show;* **3,** an imposing or proud display; as, a *show* of wealth; **4,** a deceitful appearance or pre-tense; as, a *show* of enthusiasm; **5,** *Collo-quial,* a theatrical performance.

show up, *Colloquial:* **1,** to expose; as, to *show up* a fraud; **2,** to put in an appear-ance; **show off,** *Colloquial,* to make a dis-play in order to impress others with one's own importance.

show-case (shō′kās′), *n.* a glass case for displaying and protecting wares in stores, articles or exhibits in museums, etc.

show-down (shō′doun′), *n.* **1,** in the game of poker, a laying of cards, face up, on the table; **2,** hence, a full disclosure of facts or plans; as, to force a *showdown.*

show-er (shou′ẽr), *n.* **1,** a brief fall of rain, sleet, or hail; **2,** something resembling a shower; a brief outburst; as, a *shower* of stones; a *shower* of abuse; **3,** a party at which gifts are given to a future bride; **4,** a shower bath:—*v.t.* **1,** to cause a liquid to fall upon; as, he *showered* me with water; **2,** to bestow liberally upon a person; as, honors were *showered* on the hero:—*v.i.* **1,** to rain for a short time; **2,** to fall in a shower.—*adj.* **show′er-y.**

show-ing (shō′ĭng), *n.* a display or exhibition; as, a *showing* of fall clothes; also, the impression made by a person's appearance or actions, or by a presentation of facts; as, a poor financial *showing.*

show-man (shō′măn), *n.* [*pl.* showmen (-měn)], one who displays; especially, the manager of a traveling exhibition.

shown (shōn), a form of the past participle of *show.*

show-y (shō′ĭ), *adj.* [show-i-er, show-i-est], attracting attention; gaudy; as, a *showy* dress; a *showy* garden.—*adv.* **show′i-ly.**—*n.* **show′i-ness.**

shrank (shrăngk), a form of the past tense of *shrink.*

shrap-nel (shrăp′něl), *n.* a shell, filled with bullets, and timed to explode and scatter over a desired point.

shred (shrĕd), *n.* a long, narrow strip torn or cut off; a scrap or fragment; as, to tear a handkerchief to *shreds:*—*v.t.* [*p.t.* and *p.p.* shred or shred-ded, *p.pr.* shred-ding], to tear or cut into strips; as, to *shred* cabbage.

SHRAPNEL Section of shell, showing bullets.

Shreve-port (shrēv′pôrt), a city in northwestern Louisiana, on the Red River (map 8).

shrew (shrōō), *n.* **1,** a scolding, quarrelsome woman; **2,** a mouselike animal with a long snout, which feeds chiefly on insects and worms.

shrewd (shrōōd), *adj.* sharp-witted; clever in practical affairs; keen; as, a *shrewd* buyer.

Syn. astute, sagacious, farsighted.

SHREW (⅓), def. 2

shrew-ish (shrōō′ĭsh), *adj.* scolding; sharp-tongued; as, a *shrewish* wife.

shriek (shrēk), *v.t.* and *v.i.* to cry out sharply; scream; as, "Fire!" he *shrieked;* he *shrieked* for help:—*n.* a piercing scream; a shrill outcry.

shrift (shrĭft), *n. Archaic,* confession to a priest, especially a deathbed confession:—**short shrift,** the brief time allowed for confession before dying; hence, a short delay between sentence and execution.

shrike (shrīk), *n.* any of various birds which feed chiefly on insects, but which sometimes kill smaller birds, mice, etc.

SHRIKE (⅓)

shrill (shrĭl), *adj.* sharp and piercing in tone; as, a *shrill* cry:—*v.i.* and *v.t.* to speak in a piercing, sharp tone.—*adv.* **shril′ly.**

shrimp (shrĭmp), *n.* **1,** a small shellfish used for food; **2,** a puny person; one of little account.

shrine (shrīn), *n.* **1,** a case or box in which sacred relics are kept; **2,** the tomb of a saint; **3,** any consecrated place or object, as a chapel or the statue of a saint; also, a place considered sacred because of its history; as, Keats's tomb is a *shrine* for lovers of poetry:—*v.t.* [shrined, shrin-ing], to cherish as sacred; put in a sacred place; enshrine.

SHRIMP (⅓), def. 1

shrink (shrĭngk), *v.i.* [*p.t.* shrank (shrăngk) or shrunk (shrŭngk), *p.p.* shrunk or, especially as *adj.,* shrunk-en (shrŭngk′ĕn), *p.pr.* shrink-ing], **1,** to contract; become smaller or shorter; as, the blanket *shrank* when it was washed; **2,** to draw back; recoil; as, to *shrink* from punishment or an unpleasant sight:—*v.t.* to cause to contract or grow smaller; as, to *shrink* flannel by washing.

shrink-age (shrĭngk′ĭj), *n.* a contraction or shrinking; also, the amount lost by shrinking; as, try washing a sample of the goods to find out the *shrinkage.*

shrive (shrīv), *v.t.* [*p.t.* shrived (shrīvd) or shrove (shrōv), *p.p.* shriv-en (shrĭv′ĕn) or shrived, *p.pr.* shriv-ing], *Archaic,* to hear the confession of and give absolution to; as, to *shrive* a dying man.

shriv-el (shrĭv′l), *v.t.* and *v.i.* [shriveled, shrivel-ing], to wrinkle, wither, or dry up; as, the heat *shriveled* the leaves of the plant; some plants *shrivel* quickly.

Syn. wither, blight, fade.

Shrop-shire (shrŏp′shĭr), a county in west central England.

shroud (shroud), *n.* **1,** a dress or covering for the dead; **2,** anything that envelops and conceals; as, a *shroud* of mystery; **3,**

shrouds, a set of ropes, usually two to five, connected by rope rungs, or ratlines, which support and steady the masts of a vessel:— *v.t.* **1,** to clothe (a corpse) in a shroud; **2,** to hide or conceal with a covering; veil; as, the hills were *shrouded* in gray mist.

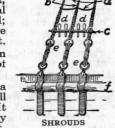

SHROUDS

a, ratlines; *b,* shrouds; *c,* rail for belaying pins, *d, d; e, e,* deadeyes; *f,* wale.

shrove (shrōv), a form of the past tense of *shrive.*

shrub (shrŭb), *n.* a woody plant not so tall as a tree; a bush. It usually has many separate stems starting near the ground.— *adj.* **shrub'by.**

shrub-ber-y (shrŭb'ĕr-ĭ), *n.* [*pl.* shrubberies], **1,** a group or collection of shrubs; **2,** ground planted with shrubs.

shrug (shrŭg), *v.t.* and *v.i.* [shrugged, shrug-ging], to draw up or hunch (the shoulders) in doubt, surprise, contempt, or the like:— *n.* a drawing up or hunching of the shoulders; as, his answer was a *shrug.*

shrunk (shrŭngk), one of the forms of the past tense and past participle of *shrink.*

shrunk-en (shrŭngk'ĕn), a form of the past participle of *shrink:—adj.* shriveled; contracted; dried up.

shuck (shŭk), *n.* a husk or pod; the outer covering of a nut; a shell:— *v.t.* to shell, as peanuts; husk, as corn.

shud-der (shŭd'ĕr), *v.i.* to tremble or shake, as with fear or cold; to quake; shiver:— *n.* a sudden trembling, as from fear, horror, aversion, cold, or excitement.

shuf-fle (shŭf'l), *v.t.* [shuf-fled, shuf-fling], **1,** to shift from place to place or from person to person; as, we *shuffled* the money from hand to hand; **2,** to rearrange or mix up the order of (cards in a pack); **3,** to jumble together in a disorderly heap; as, to *shuffle* papers into a desk; **4,** to drag or trail (the feet) in walking or dancing; **5,** to slip off carelessly; as, to *shuffle* off a burden:— *v.i.* **1,** to shift things from one position to another; **2,** to rearrange the cards in a pack; **3,** to drag the feet in a slow, lagging manner; scuffle; as, he *shuffled* along in his big slippers; also, to dance with a sliding or scraping motion of the feet; **4,** to do something in a careless, clumsy manner; as, to *shuffle* through one's work:— *n.* **1,** the act of shifting, rearranging, or the like; especially, the rearranging of cards in a pack; **2,** a lazy, dragging gait or movement; also, a dance characterized by a scraping or sliding motion of the feet.

shun (shŭn), *v.t.* [shunned, shun-ning], to avoid; keep clear of; as, to *shun* evil.

shunt (shŭnt), *v.t.* to turn off or switch to one side; as, to *shunt* a train to a side-track:— *v.i.* to turn aside or off; switch:— *n.* a turning off, as of a car, to a side rail; a switch.

shut (shŭt) *v.t.* [shut, shut-ting], **1,** to close, so as to prevent entrance or exit; as, to *shut* a gate; **2,** to bar or deny entrance to; as, the country *shut* its ports to trade; **3,** to prevent the entrance of; as, to *shut* out certain imports; **4,** to confine; imprison; as, to *shut* a child in his room; **5,** to keep from functioning by turning a screw, dial, or the like; as, to *shut* off the radio; **6,** to bring together the folding parts of; as, to *shut* an umbrella or a book:— *v.i.* **1,** to become closed; as, the door *shut* with a bang; **2,** to cease working; as, the factory *shut* down for six weeks.

shut-ter (shŭt'ĕr), *n.* **1,** a movable metal or wood cover or screen for a window; **2,** in photography, a device for regulating the exposure of a sensitive plate to light.

shut-tle (shŭt'l), *n.* **1,** in weaving, an instrument used to carry the thread of the weft, or woof, back and forth through the warp; **2,** in a sewing machine, the sliding holder which encloses the bobbin and carries the lower thread to meet the upper thread in order to form a single stitch; **3,** any similar device, as one used in tatting; **4,** a train making short trips back and forth between two points: also called *shuttle train:—v.t.* and *v.i.* [shut-tled, shut-tling], to move backwards and forwards like a shuttle.

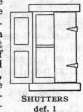

SHUTTERS
def. 1

shut-tle-cock (shŭt'l-kŏk'), *n.* **1,** a rounded cork stuck with feathers and driven with a battledore or light racket; **2,** the game played with this ball and bat: usually called *battledore and shuttlecock.*

¹**shy** (shī), *adj.* [shi-er or shy-er, shi-est or shy-est], **1,** easily scared away; timid, as a fawn; **2,** reserved; bashful; as, a *shy* girl; **3,** *Slang,* short; lacking; as, this pack is one card *shy:—v.i.* [shied, shy-ing], to start suddenly aside, as from fear; as, a horse that *shies.—adv.* **shy'ly.—***n.* **shy'ness.**

Syn., adj. diffident, modest.

SHUTTLE-COCK

²**shy** (shī), *v.t.* [shied, shy-ing], to throw with a jerk; fling; as, the boy *shied* a large stone at the kitten:— *n.* [*pl.* shies], **1,** a fling; throw; **2,** *Colloquial,* a try; a trial.

Shy-lock (shī′lŏk), *n.* **1,** a hardhearted moneylender in Shakespeare's "Merchant of Venice"; **2,** hence, a merciless creditor.

si (sē), *n.* in music, the seventh note of the scale: now often called *ti.*

S.I. abbreviation for *Staten Island.*

Si-am (sī-ăm′; sī′ăm), a kingdom (cap. Bangkok) of southeastern Asia (map **15**): now called *Thailand.*

Si-be-ri-a (sī-bē′rĭ-à), the northern part of the U.S.S.R. between the Ural Mountains and the Pacific Ocean; also, a geographical division of the U.S.S.R. comprising part of this territory. (Map **15.**)

Si-be-ri-an (sī-bē′rĭ-ăn), *adj.* pertaining to Siberia or its people:—*n.* one of the inhabitants of Siberia.

sib-yl (sĭb′ĭl; sĭb′l), *n.* a woman who claims to foretell the future; a prophetess.

sic (sĭk), [Latin], *adv.* so; thus: used after a debatable word in a quotation to emphasize that it is quoted accurately.

Sic-i-ly (sĭs′ĭ-lĭ) or **Si-cil-ia** (sē-chēl′yä), an island (cap. Palermo) belonging to Italy, in the Mediterranean (map **12**).— *adj.* and *n.* **Si-cil′i-an.**

sick (sĭk), *adj.* **1,** in ill-health; indisposed; **2,** affected with nausea; inclined to vomit; **3,** tired (of); as, *sick* of flattery; **4,** longing (for); as, *sick* for recognition; **5,** used by, or set apart for the use of, a person who is ill; as, a *sick*bed; a *sick* benefit:—**the sick,** those who are ill.

sick-en (sĭk′ĕn), *v.i.* **1,** to become ill; as, to *sicken* and die; **2,** to become tired (of); as, to *sicken* of vain effort:—*v.t.* **1,** to make ill; as, the tainted meat *sickened* me; **2,** to disgust; as, she is *sickened* by vulgarity.

sick-en-ing (sĭk′ĕn-ĭng), *adj.* making sick; nauseating; as, a *sickening* odor.

sick-ish (sĭk′ĭsh) *adj.* **1,** somewhat ill; slightly nauseated; **2,** apt to nauseate one; as, *sickish* sweets.—*adv.* **sick′ish-ly.**

sick-le (sĭk′l), *n.* a hand tool consisting of a curved steel blade fitted into a short handle, used to cut grass, trim lawns, etc.

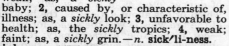

SICKLE

sick-ly (sĭk′lĭ), *adj.* [sick-li-er, sick-li-est], **1,** habitually ailing; weak; as, a *sickly* baby; **2,** caused by, or characteristic of, illness; as, a *sickly* look; **3,** unfavorable to health; as, the *sickly* tropics; **4,** weak; faint; as, a *sickly* grin.—*n.* **sick′li-ness.**

sick-ness (sĭk′nĕs), *n.* **1,** illness; ill-health; **2,** a particular disease; as, sleeping *sickness*; **3,** nausea; vomiting or inclination to vomit.

side (sīd), *n.* **1,** one of the edges or lines that bound a surface; especially, in a rectangle, one of the longer lines as distinguished from the ends; **2,** one of the surfaces of a solid object; as, one of the six *sides* of a box; also, either of the surfaces of an object that has no appreciable thickness; as, the shiny *side* of a piece of silk; **3,** the particular surfaces or a structure which are not the top, bottom, front, or back; as, the *sides* of a house; **4,** a position to the right or to the left of the center; as, he kicked the ball to the right *side* of the field; **5,** either lengthwise half of a person or an animal; as, a *side* of beef; **6,** a party or group upholding one view or aspect of a cause; **7,** line of descent through the father or mother; as, a cousin on my mother's *side*:—*adj.* **1,** pertaining to a side or sides; **2,** directed from or toward one side; as, a *side* step; **3,** placed or situated on one side; as, a *side* door; **4,** minor; incidental; as, a *side* issue:—*v.i.* [sid-ed, sid-ing], to take the part of one against another; as, he invariably *sided* with them.

side-board (sīd′bôrd′), *n.* a piece of dining-room furniture with drawers and compartments for holding flat silverware, dishes, linens, and other articles used on the table.

sid-ed (sīd′ĕd), *adj.* with sides or surfaces: now used in compounds; as, four-*sided.*

side-long (sīd′lông′), *adv.* sideways:— *adj.* directed to one side; as, a *sidelong* glance.

si-de-re-al (sī-dē′rē-ăl), *adj.* **1,** pertaining to the stars; **2,** measured by the apparent motion of the fixed stars; as, *sidereal* time.

side-sad-dle (sīd′săd′l), *n.* a woman's saddle with one stirrup for the left foot and a horn over which to hook the right knee, both feet thus being on one side of the horse.

side-track (sīd′trăk′), *v.t.* **1,** to transfer (a car or train) from the main track to a siding; **2,** *Colloquial,* to put off for consideration at some future time; set aside; as, to *sidetrack* a legislative bill:—*v.i.* to run a train upon a siding:—*n.* a siding.

side-walk (sīd′wôk′), *n.* a path or pavement beside a road or street for foot travel.

side-ways (sīd′wāz′), *adv.* **1,** toward the side; as, to glance *sideways*; **2,** from the side; as, to see a thing *sideways*; **3,** with the side foremost; as, to turn *sideways*:—*adj.* directed or turned to one side; as, a *sideways* look.

side-wise (sīd′wīz′), *adv.* and *adj.* sideways.

sid-ing (sīd′ĭng), *n.* a short railroad track by the side of the main track, to which cars may be switched; a sidetrack.

---

go; join; yet; sing; chin; show; thin, *th*en; hw, *wh*y; zh, a*z*ure; ü, Ger. f*ü*r or Fr. l*u*ne; ö, Ger. sch*ö*n or Fr. f*eu*; ṅ, Fr. e*n*fant, no*m*; kh, Ger. a*ch* or i*ch*. See pages ix–x.

si-dle (sī'dl), *v.i.* [si-dled, si-dling], to move sideways; edge along, as if from shyness or fear; as, the timid girl *sidled* up to us.

Sid-ney (sĭd'nĭ), Sir Philip (1554–1586), an English soldier, statesman, and poet.

siege (sēj), *n.* **1,** the surrounding of a fortified place by an army or fleet to compel its surrender; **2,** a prolonged or persistent attempt to gain possession of something; as, he laid *siege* to her heart.

si-er-ra (sĭ-ĕr'à), *n.* a mountain chain or range rising in irregular peaks.

Si-er-ra Le-o-ne (sĭ-ĕr'à lē-ō'nē), a British colony (cap. Freetown) in western Africa (map 14).

Si-er-ra Ne-vad-a (sĭ-ĕr'à nĕ-văd'à; nĕ-vä'dà), a mountain range extending north and south through California (map 9).

si-es-ta (sĭ-ĕs'tà), *n.* a midday or afternoon rest or nap.

sieve (sĭv), *n.* a utensil with meshes usually of wire, for separating the finer from the coarser parts of a substance; as, a flour *sieve*.

SIEVE

sift (sĭft), *v.t.* **1,** to separate, as the finer part from the coarser, with a sieve; **2,** to put through a sieve; also, to sprinkle with a sieve; as, the cook *sifted* flour over the meat; **3,** to examine critically; as, the jury *sifted* the facts in he case.—*n.* **sift'er.**

sigh (sī), *n.* **1,** a deep, audible breath expressing fatigue, sorrow, etc.; as, to heave a *sigh*; **2,** a similar sound; as, the *sigh* of the wind:—*v.i.* **1,** to breathe a sigh; as, to *sigh* with regret; **2,** to long; grieve; as, the old lady *sighs* for the past; **3,** to make a sound like sighing; as, trees murmur and *sigh*:—*v.t.* .to express by sighs; as, she *sighed* her relief.

sight (sīt), *n.* **1,** the power of seeing; vision; as, eyeglasses help to correct defects in *sight*; **2,** the act of seeing; as, she was thrilled by her first *sight* of mountains; **3,** that which is seen; a view or spectacle; as, the sunset was a *sight* to remember; also, something ludicrous or grotesque; a fright; as, my hair is a *sight* on a windy day; **4,** the limit or range within which a person can see, or an object can be seen; as, in *sight*; out of *sight*; **5,** manner of looking at or considering something; opinion; as, in his *sight*, she did well; **6,** inspection; as, this report is intended for the *sight* of the committee only; **7,** any of several devices, as on a gun, optical instrument, etc., to help in guiding the eye or aim; **8,** careful aim or observation taken by means of such a device; as, take *sight* before firing:—**at sight, on sight,** as soon as seen; upon presentation to sight:—*v.t.* **1,** to see with the eye;

as, to *sight* land in the distance; **2,** to look at through, or as through, a sight; as, to *sight* an object through the telescope; **3,** to direct by means of an aiming device; as, to *sight* a gun:—*v.i.* **1,** to aim a gun by means of a sight; **2,** to look carefully in a certain direction.

sight-less (sīt'lĕs), *adj.* having no power to see; blind.—*n.* **sight'less-ness.**

sight-ly (sīt'lĭ), *adj.* [sight-li-er, sight-li-est], **1,** pleasing to the eye; comely; **2,** affording a fine view; as, a *sightly* location.—*n.* **sight'li-ness.**

sight—see-ing (sīt'-sē'ĭng), *adj.* engaged in or used for visiting objects or places of interest; as, *sight-seeing* busses:—*n.* the act of visiting objects or places of interest.—*n.* **sight'-se'er.**

sign (sīn), *n.* **1,** a symbol, emblem, or character typifying or representing an idea; as, the *sign* of the cross; **2,** that by which anything is made known; a mark; token; proof; as, his gift was a *sign* of his love; also, indication; evidence; as, there was no *sign* of anyone stirring in the house at that hour; **3,** an omen; as, the breaking of a mirror is said to be a *sign* of bad luck; **4,** a gesture or motion used instead of words to express some thought, command, or wish; as, the teacher gave the *sign* to rise; **5,** a lettered board or plate displaying the name of a business, giving information, etc.; as, a shoemaker's *sign*; a *sign* to keep off the grass; **6,** one of the twelve equal divisions of the zodiac or its symbol; **7,** in arithmetic, a symbol for adding, subtracting, multiplying, or dividing, as $+$, $-$, $\times$, or $\div$:—*v.t.* **1,** to write one's name at the end of; as, to *sign* a letter; **2,** to transfer (a right to property) by putting one's signature to a document; as, the old man *signed* away all his property; **3,** to hire by getting the signature of; as, to *sign* a person for a particular job:—*v.i.* **1,** to write one's signature; as, I am ready to *sign*; **2,** to signal; motion; as, he *signed* for them to approach.—*n.* **sign'er.**

sign off, in radio, to announce the close of a broadcast, mentioning the name of the station; **sign up,** *Colloquial,* to join by, or as by, signing a contract.

sig-nal (sĭg'năl), *n.* **1,** a sign agreed upon for sending information, giving notice of danger, etc.; as, a train *signal*; **2,** that which brings about action; as, the blowing of the fire whistle was the *signal* for panic:—*adj.* memorable; extraordinary; remarkable; as, a *signal* success:—*v.t.* [signaled, signal-ing], to communicate with, by means of flags, lights, etc.; make signs to; as, the scoutmaster *signaled* the boys to return to camp:—*v.i.* to make signs.

āte, âorta, râre, căt, ȧsk, fär, ăllow, sofà; ēve, êvent, ĕll, writẽr, novĕl; bīte, pĭn; nō, ōbey, ôr, dŏg, tŏp, cŏllide; ūnit, ûnite, bûrn, cŭt, focŭs; nōōn, fŏŏt; mound; coin;

sig·nal·ize (sĭg′năl-īz), *v.t.* [signalized, signaliz-ing], to make noteworthy; to mark; as, his reign was *signalized* by great social reform.

sig·nal·ly (sĭg′năl-ĭ), *adv.* in an extraordinary or striking manner.

sig·na·ture (sĭg′nȧ-tûr), *n.* 1, the name of a person in his own handwriting; an autograph; 2, in music, the signs at the beginning of a staff indicating key and time.

sig·net (sĭg′nĕt), *n.* 1, a seal; especially, in England, one of the private seals of the monarch; 2, an imprint made by, or as by, a seal.

sig·nif·i·cance (sĭg-nĭf′ĭ-kȧns), *n.* 1, meaning; as, the full *significance* of his remark escaped me; 2, importance; as, he must realize this is a matter of some *significance;* 3, expressiveness; as, he gave the boy a look of deep *significance.*

sig·nif·i·cant (sĭg-nĭf′ĭ-kȧnt), *adj.* 1, full of meaning; expressive; also, suggestive; having some concealed or special meaning; as, a *significant* silence; 2, important; conspicuous; as, *significant* progress.—*adv.* **sig·nif′i·cant·ly.**

sig·ni·fy (sĭg′nĭ-fī), *v.t.* [signified, signifying], 1, to show by a sign, mark, or token; make known; declare; as, to *signify* one's consent; 2, to denote; mean; as, that gesture *signifies* refusal:—*v.i.* to be of importance; to matter or count.—*n.* **sig′ni·fi·ca′tion** (sĭg′nĭ-fĭ-kā′shŭn).

si·gnor (sē′nyôr), *n.* 1, a title of address or respect among the Italians, used before a man's name, corresponding to *master, mister* (*Mr.*); 2, a form of address used without the name; Sir; 3, an Italian nobleman or gentleman.

si·gno·ra (sē-nyō′rä), *n.* [*pl.* signore (sē-nyō′rā)], 1, a title of respectful address to an Italian lady, corresponding to *Mrs.* or *Madam;* 2, an Italian lady.

si·gno·re (sē-nyō′rā), *n.* [*pl.* signori (sē-nyō′rē)], a title of address or respect among the Italians, corresponding to *Sir;* used without the person's name.

si·gno·ri·na (sē′nyō-rē′nä), *n.* [*pl.* signorine (sē′nyō-rē′nä)], 1, among the Italians, a title of address to a young lady, corresponding to *Miss;* 2, a young Italian lady.

sign·post (sīn′pōst′), *n.* 1, a guidepost; 2, a pole which bears signs.

Si·kang (shē′käng′), a province of south-central China (cap. Yaan).

Sikh (sēk), *n.* one of a Hindu religious sect famous as soldiers.

si·lage (sī′lĭj), *n.* corn, clover, and other cattle food, usually cut fine and stored, while green, in a silo to ferment.

si·lence (sī′lĕns), *n.* 1, the state of being still or mute; as, he listened in *silence;* 2, entire absence of sound or noise; general stillness; as, there was *silence* in the courtroom; 3, absence of mention; as, to pass over a subject in *silence:*—*v.t.* [silenced, silenc-ing], 1, to cause to be still; as, to *silence* the dogs; 2, to quiet; put to rest; as, to *silence* opposition; 3, to force (guns) to cease firing.

si·lenc·er (sī′lĕn-sẽr), *n.* a person or thing that muffles or dulls sound or noises; especially, a device which may be attached to the muzzle of a firearm to reduce the sound when the gun is fired.

si·lent (sī′lĕnt), *adj.* 1, saying nothing; mute; also, not given to frequent or copious words; as, a *silent* man; 2, quiet; still; free from noise; as, a *silent* place; 3, not expressed; not spoken; as, a *silent* command; 4, having a share, not publicly acknowledged, in a business; as, a *silent* partner; 5, written, but not pronounced: said of a letter; as, the "b" in "doubt" is *silent.*—*adv.* **si·lent·ly.**

Syn. dumb, speechless.

Si·le·nus (sī-lē′nŭs), *n.* in Greek mythology, a woodland god, companion of Bacchus. He is usually represented as a fat, drunken old man with pointed ears.

Si·le·si·a (sĭ-lē′shĭ-ȧ; sĭ-lē′shȧ), a central European district divided between Czechoslovakia and Poland.

sil·hou·ette (sĭl′ŏŏ-ĕt′), *n.* 1, an outline drawing, especially a profile portrait, filled in with solid color, usually black; 2, the figure cast by a shadow, as on a wall or screen:—*v.t.* [silhouetted, silhouet-ting], to cause to appear in outline or silhouette; as, his form was *silhouetted* against the wall.

SILHOUETTE

sil·i·ca (sĭl′ĭ-kȧ), *n.* a hard, white or colorless substance, one of the commonest of minerals, occurring as quartz, rock crystal, flint, sea sand, etc. It is used in the manufacture of glass.

sil·i·cate (sĭl′ĭ-kāt), *n.* any of a great number of natural salts, found in nature as topaz, mica, etc.

sil·i·con (sĭl′ĭ-kŏn), *n.* a nonmetallic element or substance found abundantly in rocks and sand.

silk (sĭlk), *n.* 1, a fine, soft, lustrous fabric made from threads spun by silkworm larvae to form their cocoons; 2, the thread as produced by the larvae; 3, any similar thread, as that spun by certain spiders; **4,** anything like silk, as the down of the milk-weed pod:—*adj.* made of silk.—*adj.* **silk'-en.**—*adj.* **silk'y.**—*n.* **silk'i-ness.**

silk-worm (sĭlk'wûrm'), *n.* the larva of a certain kind of moth. The silkworm makes

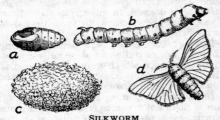

SILKWORM

a, pupa; *b,* larva (caterpillar); *c,* silk cocoon enclosing pupa; *d,* adult female moth.

a strong silk fiber in spinning its cocoon.

sill (sĭl), *n.* **1,** a horizontal piece forming the foundation, or part of the foundation, of a structure (see illustration under *frame house*); **2,** a threshold; as, a door*sill*; **3,** the bottom or lowest piece in a window frame.

sil-ly (sĭl'ĭ), *adj.* [sil-li-er, sil-li-est], **1,** weak-minded; **2,** stupid; absurd; as, a *silly* answer.—*n.* **sil'li-ness.**

si-lo (sī'lō), *n.* [*pl.* silos], a pit or tower, airtight and watertight, for storing and preserving green fodder.

silt (sĭlt), *n.* mud or fine earth carried in, or deposited by, water; also, a deposit of such mud or fine earth:—*v.t.* to choke or block up by such a deposit:—*v.i.* to become blocked by such a deposit.

Si-lu-ri-an (sĭ-lū'rĭ-ăn; sī-lū'rĭ-ăn), *adj.* pertaining to an early period in the earth's development, marked by the appearance of the first air-breathing land animals.

sil-van (sĭl'văn), *adj.* pertaining to woods or trees; sylvan. See **sylvan.**

sil-ver (sĭl'vẽr), *n.* **1,** a soft, shining, white metal, used for table implements, dishes, jewelry, etc.; **2,** anything made of this metal, as silverware or money; **3,** anything that has the luster or color of silver; as, cloth of *silver:*—*adj.* **1,** made of silver; as, a *silver* cup; **2,** having a soft, silvery luster; as, *silver* dew; **3,** soft and clear, as the tones of a silver bell; hence, eloquent; as, a *silver* tongue; **4,** relating to silver; as, *silver* legislation; a *silver* mill:—*v.t.* **1,** to cover or coat with silver, or with something resembling it; **2,** to give a silverlike polish to; make the color of silver:—*v.i.* to turn silvery white or gray; as, her hair *silvered* at a very early age.—*adj.* **sil'ver-y.**

sil-ver-smith (sĭl'vẽr-smith'), *n.* one who makes articles of silver.

sil-ver-ware (sĭl'vẽr-wâr'), *n.* silver plate; knives, forks, spoons, dishes, vases, etc., made of silver.

sim-i-an (sĭm'ĭ-ăn), *adj.* pertaining to, or like, an ape:—*n.* an ape.

sim-i-lar (sĭm'ĭ-lẽr), *adj.* **1,** having a general likeness; like, but not exactly the same; as, pink and rose are *similar* colors; **2,** in geometry, shaped alike, but not of the same size, position, etc.; as, *similar* triangles.—*adv.* **sim'i-lar-ly.**

Syn. corresponding, alike.

sim-i-lar-i-ty (sĭm'ĭ-lăr'ĭ-tĭ), *n.* [*pl.* similarities], **1,** resemblance or likeness; **2,** a point or respect in which things are alike.

sim-i-le (sĭm'ĭ-lē), *n.* a figure of speech in which two different things having some likeness are compared by the use of *like* or *as;* as, the ice is *like* glass; the night is black *as* ink.

si-mil-i-tude (sĭ-mĭl'ĭ-tūd), *n.* similarity; likeness; as, modern painting no longer aims at exact *similitude.*

sim-mer (sĭm'ẽr), *v.t.* **1,** to boil gently; **2,** to cook in liquid at or just below the boiling point:—*v.i.* **1,** to cook at or just below the boiling point; as, let the stew *simmer;* **2,** to make a gentle, low, murmuring sound, as a liquid about to boil; **3,** to be in a state of suppressed emotion; to be on the verge of breaking out; as, the savage tribes were *simmering* with revolt:—*n.* **1,** a heated state at or near the boiling point; as, to cook meat at a *simmer;* **2,** a state of suppressed emotion or excitement.

Si-mon (sī'mŭn), in the Bible: **1,** an apostle: usually called *Simon Peter* or *Peter;* **2,** a disciple of Jesus: usually called *Simon Zelotes* (zē-lō'tēz); **3,** a sorcerer who offered to buy the power of giving the Holy Ghost: also called *Simon Magus* (mā'gŭs).

sim-o-ny (sĭm'ô-nĭ; sī'mô-nĭ), *n.* the act of buying or selling church offices or positions of honor.

si-moom (sĭ-mōōm') or **si-moon** (sĭ-mōōn'), *n.* a hot, suffocating, dust-laden wind which blows from the deserts of Arabia or from the Sahara.

sim-per (sĭm'pẽr), *v.i.* to smile in an affected, silly, or self-conscious manner; smirk:—*n.* an affected smile; a smirk.

sim-ple (sĭm'pl), *adj.* [sim-pler, sim-plest], **1,** not mixed or compounded; as, a *simple* fraction; not divided into parts; as, a *simple* leaf; **2,** not involved or elaborate; easy to solve or understand; as, *simple* words; a *simple* problem; **3,** plain; as, *simple* food; unadorned; as, *simple* clothes; **4,** mere; unqualified; as, a *simple* fact; **5,** sincere; straightforward; as, a *simple*, unaffected manner; **6**, humble; of low rank or degree; as, *simple* folk; **7**, weak in intellect; foolish.—*n.* **sim'ple-ness.**

sim-ple-ton (sĭm'pl-tŭn), *n.* one who is foolish or weak-minded.

sim-plic-i-ty (sĭm-plĭs'ĭ-tĭ), *n.* [*pl.* simplicities], **1**, the state or quality of being clear, plain, or unaffected; as, *simplicity* of language; *simplicity* of dress; **2**, lack of cunning; sincerity; **3**, lack of common sense, or of average ability to judge.

sim-pli-fy (sĭm'plĭ-fī), *v.t.* [simplified, simplify-ing], to make easier; make plainer to the understanding.—*n.* **sim'pli-fi-ca'tion.**

sim-ply (sĭm'plĭ), *adv.* **1**, plainly; clearly; as, to write *simply;* **2**, without elaborate show; as, to dress *simply;* **3**, only; merely; as, it is *simply* a question of money; **4**, absolutely; as, you *simply* must go.

Sims (sĭmz), William S. (1858–1936), an American admiral in the World War.

sim-u-late (sĭm'ū-lāt), *v.t.* [simulat-ed, simulat-ing], to make a pretense of; as, to *simulate* goodness; also, to imitate; take the appearance of; as, some moths *simulate* leaves.—*n.* **sim'u-la'tion.**
Syn. dissimulate, dissemble, feign.

si-mul-ta-ne-ous (sī'mŭl-tā'nē-ŭs; sĭm'-ŭl-tā'nē-ŭs), *adj.* happening, done, or existing at the same time; as, *simultaneous* explosions.—*adv.* **si'mul-ta'ne-ous-ly.**

sin (sĭn), *n.* **1**, the breaking or violation of God's laws; also, any instance of such violation, as dishonesty; **2**, any serious offense:—*v.i.* [sinned, sin-ning], **1**, to transgress, offend, or neglect the law of God in any way; **2**, to commit evil deeds.

Si-nai (sī'nī; sī'nā-ī), **1**, a peninsula of Arabia, extending into the north end of the Red Sea; **2**, a mountain in the southern part of this peninsula where Moses received the Ten Commandments. (Map **14**.)

since (sĭns), *adv.* **1**, from a certain past time until now; as, he left six years ago and has not been seen *since;* **2**, at some time after a certain past event and before now; as, he was then treasurer, but has *since* been elected president; **3**, before this; ago; as, not long *since:*—*prep.* from the time of; during the time after; ever after; as, *since* his departure, I have never seen him:—*conj.* **1**, from and after a time when; as, I have not seen him *since* that happened; **2**, seeing that; because; as, *since* that is the case, I shall go.

sin-cere (sĭn-sēr'), *adj.* [sincer-er, sincer-est], honest; frank; as, a *sincere* man; genuine; as, a *sincere* friend; also, honestly felt or intended; as, *sincere* wishes for your success.—*adv.* **sin-cere'ly.**
Syn. candid, hearty, straightforward.

sin-cer-i-ty (sĭn-sĕr'ĭ-tĭ), *n.* the state or quality of being true or genuine; honesty; as, to speak in all *sincerity.*

Sind-bad the Sail-or (sĭnd'băd; sĭn'-băd), in the "Arabian Nights," a wealthy merchant of Bagdad, who tells of his extraordinary voyages.

si-ne-cure (sī'nē-kūr; sĭn'ē-kūr), *n.* a salaried office or position to which little work or responsibility is attached.

sin-ew (sĭn'ū), *n.* **1**, a tendon or tough piece of tissue joining muscle to bone; **2**, strength; power; energy; **3**, anything supplying strength; the mainstay of anything; as, money, the *sinews* of war.—*adj.* **sin'-ew-y.**—*adj.* **sin'ew-less.**

sin-ful (sĭn'fŏŏl), *adj.* full of wickedness; tainted with sin; as, *sinful* men commit *sinful* deeds.—*n.* **sin'ful-ness.**

sing (sĭng), *v.i.* [*p.t.* sang (săng), *p.p.* sung (sŭng), *p.pr.* sing-ing], **1**, to make musical sounds with the voice; **2**, to make a shrill or humming noise; as, a flying arrow *sings;* **3**, to make pleasant, melodious sounds; as, the brook *sings* merrily; **4**, to celebrate some event in verse; as, Vergil *sang* of the deeds of Aeneas; **5**, to ring with a constant humming or buzzing sound; as, my ears are *singing:*—*v.t.* **1**, to utter with musical tones of the voice; as, to *sing* a song; to chant; as, to *sing* Mass; **2**, to celebrate in poetry; **3**, to lull by singing; as, to *sing* a child to sleep.

sing. abbreviation for *singular.*

Sin-ga-pore (sĭng'gȧ-pôr'), a British island south of the Malay Peninsula; also a city, its capital (map **15**).

singe (sĭnj), *v.t.* [singed, singe-ing], **1**, to burn slightly or on the surface; scorch; **2**, to pass over a flame to remove the feathers or down; as, to *singe* a plucked chicken before cooking it:—*n.* a slight burn.
Syn., v. sear, char, scorch.

sin-gle (sĭng'gl), *adj.* **1**, consisting of one only; as, a *single* page; **2**, not married; as, they employ *single* girls only; **3**, performed by one person; having only one on each side; as, *single* combat; **4**, for the use of one person only; as, a *single* room; **5**, straightforward; sincere; as, a man of *single* purpose; **6**, in botany, having only one row of petals; as, a *single* tulip:—*v.t.* [sin-gled, sin-gling], to select (one person or thing) from others; as, they *singled* him out for honorable mention:—*v.i.* to make a base hit:—*n.* **1**, in baseball, a base hit; **2**, in golf, a game between two players; in tennis, (usually *singles*), a game with only one person on each side.

single file, a line of persons one behind the other.

sin·gle—foot (sĭng′gl̵-foŏt′), *n.* a horse's gait in which each foot strikes the ground singly at regular intervals, in the order: right hind, right fore, left hind, left fore.

sin·gle-hand-ed (sĭng′gl-hăn′dĕd), *adj.* done without aid or assistance.

sin·gle-heart-ed (sĭng′gl-här′tĕd), *adj.* straightforward; free from deceitfulness.

sin·gle—mind-ed (sĭng′gl-mīn′dĕd), *adj.* having but one purpose; also, sincere.

sin·gle-ness (sĭng′gl-nĕs), *n.* **1**, the state of being separate or alone; the state of being unmarried; **2**, freedom from selfish ends; sincerity; as, *singleness* of purpose.

sin·gle-tree (sĭng′gl-trē′), *n.* the swinging bar on a cart, carriage, etc., to which the traces of the harness are fastened.

sin·gly (sĭng′glĭ), *adv.* **1**, individually; one by one; as, we took up each matter *singly;* **2**, without others; alone; singlehanded.

sing-song (sĭng′sông′), *n.* **1**, song or verse having an unvaried, monotonous rhythm; **2**, a monotonous tone:—*adj.* monotonous in tone or rhythm; as, a *singsong* voice.

sin·gu·lar (sĭng′gṳ-lẽr), *adj.* **1**, in grammar, relating to the form of a word naming one person or thing; as, the word "girl" is a *singular* noun; **2**, extraordinary; exceptional; as, *singular* strength; **3**, peculiar; strange; as, *singular* habits:—*n.* in grammar, that form of a word naming one person or thing; as, "man" is the *singular* of "men."—*adv.* **sin′gu·lar·ly**.

Syn., *adj.* uncommon, queer, eccentric.

sin·gu·lar·i·ty (sĭng′gṳ-lăr′ĭ-tĭ), *n.* **1**, uncommonness; strangeness; as, the *singularity* of his foreign clothes; **2**, a quality or thing that is uncommon, odd, or peculiar.

sin·is·ter (sĭn′ĭs-tẽr), *adj.* **1**, ill-omened; threatening; evil; as, a *sinister* look; **2**, base; dishonest; as, *sinister* intentions; **3**, left: applied in heraldry to the side of a shield on the left side of the person bearing it.

sink (sĭngk), *v.i.* [*p.t.* sank (săngk) or sunk (sŭngk), *p.p.* sunk, *p.pr.* sink-ing], **1**, to become wholly or partly submerged, as in water; **2**, to descend gradually; as, the sun *sinks;* to slope downward; as, land *sinks* to the sea; **3**, to decline gradually, as in strength; also, to degenerate, as in morals; **4**, to become hollow: often said of the cheeks; **5**, to enter deeply; as, a thought *sinks* into the mind:—*v.t.* **1**, to cause to go to the bottom; as, to *sink* a boat in a river; **2**, to make by digging downward; as, to *sink* a well; also, to place in an excavation thus made; as, to *sink* a pipe; **3**, to invest or spend unprofitably; as, to *sink* money in worthless stocks:—*n.* **1**, a kind of basin, as in a kitchen, with a drain to carry off dirty or excessive water; **2**, any slight hollow of land, especially one that has little or no water outlet; **3**, a place of vice and corruption.

sink-er (sĭngk′ẽr), *n.* that which drops down or causes to drop down, as a small weight attached to a fishing line.

sin-less (sĭn′lĕs), *adj.* without guilt; blameless; as, a *sinless* life.

sin-ner (sĭn′ẽr), *n.* one who breaks the law of God or man; an offender.

Sinn Fein (shĭn fān) an Irish movement and party, organized about 1905, to revive Irish national culture, as industries, language, literature, etc., and to promote political independence.

sin-u-ous (sĭn′ṳ-ŭs), *adj.* curving in and out; winding; as, the path took a *sinuous* course up the hill:—*adv.* **sin′u-ous-ly**.—*n.* **sin′u-os′i-ty** (sĭn′ṳ-ŏs′ĭ-tĭ).

si-nus (sī′nŭs), *n.* a natural cavity or hollow in bone, especially an air cavity in a bone of the skull.

Si-on (sī′ŭn), *n.* a certain hill in Jerusalem; figuratively, heaven; Zion. See **Zion**.

-sion (-shŭn), a suffix meaning: **1**, the act or process of; as, intru*sion;* **2**, the condition or state of; as, delu*sion;* **3**, that which performs the action of; as, provi*sion;* **4**, the result of; as, allu*sion.* In many words *-sion* can have more than one of these meanings; as, in admis*sion.*

Sioux (soō), *n.* [*pl.* Sioux (soō; soōz)], one of an important and warlike tribe of North American Indians.

Sioux Cit-y (soō), a city in Iowa, on the Missouri River (map **7**).

sip (sĭp), *v.t.* [sipped, sip-ping], to drink by taking a small portion at a time; as, she *sips* her chocolate:—*v.i.* to drink a liquid, in sips:—*n.* a small taste or mouthful.

si-phon (sī′fŏn; sī′fŭn), *n.* **1**, a pipe or tube bent like an inverted U, with one leg longer than the other, used for drawing off liquids from a higher to a lower level; **2**, a bottle for plain soda water, fitted with a siphon, through which the water is forced by pressure of the gas in the bottle:—*v.t.* to draw off by such a tube.

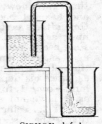

SIPHON, def. 1

Sir (sûr), *n.* the title of respect used before the Christian name of a baronet or knight; as, *Sir* James Barrie:—**sir**, a term of respect in addressing a man without using his name; as, Are you there? Yes, *sir.*

sire (sīr), *n.* **1,** (*Sire*), a title of respect used in addressing a sovereign or king; **2,** a father; the head of a family; **3,** among animals, the male parent:—*v.t.* [sired, sir-ing], to be or become the father of: used especially of animals.

si·ren (sī/rĕn), *n.* **1,** (often *Siren*), in Greek mythology, one of the sea nymphs who captivated sailors by their sweet singing; **2,** an alluring or captivating woman; **3,** a device for producing a shrill sound; as, a *siren* on an ambulance:—*adj.* **1** pertaining to, or like, a siren; **2,** bewitching.

SIREN, def. 3
As used on fire engines, automobiles, etc.

Sir·i·us (sĭr/ĭ-ŭs), *n.* the Dog Star, the most brilliant star in the sky.

sir·loin (sûr/loin/), *n.* a choice cut of beef, taken from the upper part of the loin. (See illustration under *beef*.)

si·roc·co (sĭ-rŏk/ō), *n.* [*pl.* siroccos], **1,** a hot, dusty wind blowing north from the Sahara; **2,** any hot wind.

sir·rah (sĭr/ȧ), *n. Archaic,* fellow; sir: a term used in contempt, arrogant command, displeasure, or the like.

sir·up or **syr·up** (sĭr/ŭp), *n.* **1,** a thick, sticky liquid made from the juice of fruits, herbs, or the like, boiled with sugar; **2,** any similar liquid; as, maple *sirup;* cough *sirup.*—*adj.* sir/up-y; syr/up-y.

si·sal (sī/săl; sē/săl; sĕ-säl/), *n.* the fiber obtained from a West Indian plant, used in making rope; also, the plant itself.

sis·ter (sĭs/tẽr), *n.* **1,** a woman or girl who has the same father and mother as another person; also, a woman or girl who is a very good friend; as, she's been a *sister* to me; **2,** a woman of the same religious society, order, or community as others; a nun.—*adj.* sis/ter-ly.

sis·ter·hood (sĭs/tẽr-hood), *n.* **1,** the relationship between sisters; **2,** a number of women united by a common interest, as a religious society.

sis·ter–in–law (sĭs/tẽr=ĭn-lô/), *n.* [*pl.* sisters-in-law], **1,** a husband's or wife's sister; **2,** a brother's wife.

Sis·y·phus (sĭs/ĭ-fŭs), *n.* in Greek mythology, a greedy king of Corinth who was condemned in Hades to roll uphill a huge stone, which kept falling back again.

sit (sĭt), *v.i.* [sat (săt), sit-ting], **1,** to rest with the weight of the body on the lower part of the trunk; occupy a seat; as, to *sit* on a bench; to *sit* on the porch; **2,** to perch;

as, the birds *sit* in the tree; **3,** to have place or position; be situated; as, the box *sits* on the floor; **4,** to fit; suit; as, the dress *sits* well; **5,** to press or weigh, as sorrow on the mind; **6,** to occupy a seat officially; be a member of a council or assembly; as, to *sit* in Parliament; **7,** to meet or hold a session, as a court; **8,** to cover eggs to be hatched, as does a fowl; **9,** to pose; as, to *sit* for a portrait:—*v.t.* **1,** to have, or keep, a seat upon; as, to *sit* a horse; **2,** to seat (oneself).—*n.* sit/ter.

site (sīt), *n.* **1,** position or place; as, the *site* of a battle; **2,** a plot of land suitable for a building.

sit·ting (sĭt/ĭng), *adj.* **1,** resting on the haunches; seated; as, a *sitting* figure; **2,** pertaining to, or used for sitting; as, a *sitting* room:—*n.* **1,** the position or act of one who sits; **2,** a session or meeting; **3,** the time during which one sits; as, a long *sitting;* **4,** a set of eggs for hatching.

sit·u·at·ed (sĭt/ū-āt/ĕd), *adj.* having a position; located; placed.

sit·u·a·tion (sĭt/ū-ā/shŭn), *n.* **1,** position; location; as, the *situation* of a hospital; **2,** a combination of circumstances; as, a ludicrous *situation;* **3,** a position of employment; as, a *situation* as nurse.
  Syn. condition, plight, predicament.

six (sĭks), *adj.* composed of one more than five:—*n.* **1,** the number consisting of five plus one; **2,** a sign representing six units, as 6 or vi.

six·fold (sĭks/fōld/), *adj.* **1,** multiplied six times; six times as great; **2,** consisting of six parts:—*adv.* (sĭks/fōld/), six times as much or as many.

six·pence (sĭks/pĕns), *n.* a small British silver coin, of the value of six English pence, or about twelve cents.

six·teen (sĭks/tēn/), *adj.* composed of ten more than six:—*n.* **1,** the sum of fifteen plus one; **2,** a sign representing sixteen units, as 16 or xvi.

six·teenth (sĭks/tēnth/), *adj.* next after the 15th: the ordinal of *sixteen:—n.* one of the sixteen equal parts of anything.

sixth (sĭksth), *adj.* next after the fifth: the ordinal of *six:—n.* one of the six equal parts of anything.

six·ti·eth (sĭks/tĭ-ĕth), *adj.* next after the 59th: the ordinal of *sixty:—n.* one of the 60 equal parts of anything.

six·ty (sĭks/tĭ), *adj.* composed of one more than 59:—*n.* [*pl.* sixties], **1,** the number consisting of 59 plus one; **2,** a sign representing 60 units, as 60 or lx.

siz·a·ble or **size·a·ble** (sīz/ȧ-bl), *adj.* of considerable bulk; quite large.—*adv.* siz/a-bly; size/a-bly.

go; join; yet; sing; chin; show; thin, *then;* hw, *why;* zh, azure; ü, Ger. für or Fr. lune; ö, Ger. schön or Fr. feu; n̄, Fr. enfant, nom; kh, Ger. ach or ich. See pages ix-x.

¹**size** (sīz), *n.* any of various thin, sticky washes, used by painters, papermakers, etc., for glazing the surface of various materials:—*v.t.* [sized, siz-ing], to prepare, stiffen, or cover with thin glue.—*n.* **siz′ing.**

²**size** (sīz), *n.* **1,** dimensions; bigness; as, to measure the *size* of a room; **2,** a measure showing how large something is; as, a *size* four shoe:—*v.t.* [sized, siz-ing], **1,** to arrange in order of bulk, height, volume, or extent; **2,** *Colloquial,* to form a conclusion about; as, to *size* up a situation.

siz-zle (sĭz′l), *v.i.* [siz-zled, siz-zling], to make a hissing sound, as in frying:—*n.* a hissing sound.

¹**skate** (skāt), *n.* a broad, flat-bodied fish with a very narrow tail.

SKATE (⅟₁₀)

²**skate** (skāt), *n.* **1,** a frame, with a metal runner attached, shaped to fit a shoe, or fastened permanently to a shoe, and used for gliding over ice; **2,** a device consisting of small wheels attached to a frame which clamps to the sole of the shoe, or is fastened permanently to the shoe; a roller skate:—*v.i.* [skat-ed, skat-ing], to move or glide along on skates.—*n.* **skat′er.**

skein (skān), *n.* a quantity of thread or yarn, coiled together.

SKATES
1, ordinary clamp skate and key; 2, tubular hockey skate attached to shoe; 3, roller skate.

skel-e-tal (skĕl′ē-tăl), *adj.* pertaining to a skeleton or bony framework; as, *skeletal* muscles.

skel-e-ton (skĕl′ē-tŭn), *n.* **1,** the bony framework of man and other animals; **2,** a supporting framework, as of a building.

skeleton key, a key with part of the bit filed away so that it will open a number of locks.

skep-tic or **scep-tic** (skĕp′tĭk), *n.* **1,** a person of doubting mind; **2,** one who doubts the truth of any fact or theory, and questions the possibility of human knowledge of anything; **3,** one who doubts the truth of a religious belief, as Christianity.—*adj.* **skep′ti-cal; scep′ti-cal.**
    Syn., doubter, infidel, unbeliever.

skep-ti-cism or **scep-ti-cism** (skĕp′tĭ-sĭzm), *n.* **1,** an unbelieving, doubting state of mind; **2,** doubt or denial of the doctrines of Christianity.

sketch (skĕch), *n.* **1,** a simple, quickly made drawing; as, a crayon *sketch;* **2,** an outline; a rough draft or preliminary study; as, a *sketch* for a story; **3,** a short, simple piece of literature or music; also, a short, simple, dramatic performance:—*v.t.* to make an outline or sketch of; as, to *sketch* plans; to *sketch* a flower:—*v.i.* to make a sketch.—*n.* **sketch′er.**

sketch-book (skĕch′bŏŏk′), *n.* **1,** a book of or for drawings; **2,** a book of notes or outlines, as of stories to be written.

sketch-y (skĕch′ĭ), *adj.* [sketch-i-er, sketch-i-est], of the nature of a sketch; given in outline only; incomplete; as, a *sketchy* description.—*adv.* **sketch′i-ly**

skew (skū), *adj.* twisted or turned to one side:—*n.* a deviation from a straight line; a twist, turn, or slant.

skew-er (skū′ẽr), *n.* a pin of wood or metal for holding meat in shape while cooking:—*v.t.* to fasten with, or as with, a skewer.

SKEWER

ski (skē), *n.* [*pl.* skis (skēz) or ski], one of a pair of long, narrow pieces of wood, to be fastened one on each foot for sliding or traveling over snow:—*v.i.* [s k i e d (skēd), ski-ing], to slide or travel on skis.—*n.* **ski′-er.**

skid (skĭd), *n.* **1,** a device used on the wheel of a vehicle to check its motion; **2,** one of a pair or set of logs, rails, etc., used to form a track down which heavy objects roll or slide; **3,** a piece of timber on which a boat rests during the process of building or repair; **4,** a runner attached under an airplane to aid in landing (see illustration under *airplane*); **5,** the act of sliding or slipping sideways; as, a *skid* on the ice:—*v.t.* [skid-ded, skid-ding], **1,** to cause to move on skids; **2,** to protect or check with a drag or skid:—*v.i.* to slip sideways on the road: said of an automobile.

SKIS
a, top view; *b*, side view; *c, c*, ski poles.

skiff (skĭf), *n.* a small, light boat that can be rowed.

skil-ful or **skill-ful** (skĭl′fŏŏl), *adj.* **1,** having expert training; clever; as, a *skilful* worker; **2,** showing expertness; as, *skilful* work.—*adv.* **skil′ful-ly; skill′ful-ly.**
    Syn. adroit, apt, deft.

skill (skĭl), *n.* knowledge of any art or science, with ability to use it; dexterity; as, *skill* in surgery.

skilled (skĭld), *adj.* **1,** expert; as, *skilled* in painting; **2,** having or requiring special training; as, *skilled* labor.

Syn. trained, skilful, competent.

skil-let (skĭl′ĕt), *n.* **1,** a shallow, metal vessel with a handle, used for frying; a frying pan; **2,** a long-handled saucepan.

SKILLET, def. 1

skim (skĭm), *v.t.* [skimmed, skim-ming], **1,** to remove floating substances from the top of; as, to *skim* milk; **2,** to take from the surface of a liquid, with a ladle or spoon; as, to *skim* cream from milk; **3,** to touch the surface of, lightly; as, the boat *skims* the water; **4,** to read hurriedly:—*v.i.* **1,** to pass lightly over a surface; also, to glide, as through the air; **2,** to read without thoroughness; as, to *skim* through a book:—**skim milk**, milk from which the cream has been taken.

skim-mer (skĭm′ĕr), *n.* **1,** one who or that which skims; especially, a shallow, perforated spoon or ladle for removing scum or floating substances from a liquid; **2,** a long-winged marine bird.

skimp (skĭmp), *Colloquial: v.t.* **1,** to do badly or carelessly; to slight; **2,** to be sparing with; as, to *skimp* material in making a dress:—*v.i.* to save; be miserly.—*adj.* **skimp′y.**

SKIMMER

skin (skĭn), *n.* **1,** in man and other animals, the outer covering of the body; **2,** the pelt of an animal after it is removed from the body; as, a fur coat made of valuable *skins;* **3,** rind; as, an orange *skin;* **4,** a vessel made of an animal's skin, used to hold liquids; **5,** anything like a skin, as the outside covering of an airship:—*v.t.* [skinned, skin-ning], **1,** to strip the skin from; as, to *skin* a rabbit; **2,** *Slang,* to get the better of; cheat:—*v.i.* to become covered over with skin, as a wound.

skin diving, a sport in which a swimmer submerges under water, for spear fishing or exploring, without a diving suit, but using a mask and often artificial fins.

skin-flint (skĭn′flĭnt′), *n.* a stingy person.

skin-ny (skĭn′ĭ), *adj.* [skin-ni-er, skin-ni-est], **1,** like skin in appearance or texture; **2,** lean; without much flesh.

skip (skĭp), *v.t.* [skipped, skip-ping], **1,** to jump lightly over; as, to *skip* rope; **2,** to pass over or omit; as, he *skipped* three pages in reading; she was bright enough to *skip* a grade in school:—*v.i.* **1,** to leap or bound lightly; move with light trips and hops; **2,** to pass along rapidly; hurry along, omitting portions, as in reading:—*n.* **1,** a light leap or bound, **2,** an omission; a passing over.

¹**skip-per** (skĭp′ĕr), *n.* **1,** one who or that which moves with a light leaping or tripping step; **2,** a maggot found in cheese; **3,** a butterfly with a small but stout body, and swift jerky flight.

²**skip-per** (skĭp′ĕr), *n.* the master of a small trading or fishing vessel; the master or captain of any ship.

skir-mish (skûr′mĭsh), *n.* **1,** a brisk fight between small parties of soldiers during a war; **2,** any slight struggle or encounter:—*v.i.* to engage in a skirmish.—*n.* **skir′mish-er.**

Syn., n. attack, battle, conflict, action.

skirt (skûrt), *n.* **1,** the lower and loose part of a coat, dress, or other garment; **2,** an outer garment for women and girls, covering the body below the waist; **3,** an edge or border; **4, skirts,** the outskirts or suburbs; **5,** on a saddle, one of the side flaps:—*v.t.* to border; run or pass along the edge of; as, we *skirted* the town.

skit (skĭt), *n.* a short literary composition or play, usually humorous or satirical.

skit-tish (skĭt′ĭsh), *adj.* **1,** easily frightened; quick to shy; as, a *skittish* horse; **2,** playful; lively; also, capricious; fickle.

skit-tles (skĭt′lz), *n.pl.* used as *sing.* a game resembling ninepins.

skulk (skŭlk), *v.i.* to hide or get out of the way in a sneaking or underhand manner:—*n.* an idle, good-for-nothing fellow.—*n.* **skulk′er.**

skull (skŭl), *n.* **1,** in man and other animals, the skeleton or framework of the head; **2,** the head, as the seat of intelligence.

skull-cap (skŭl′kăp′), *n.* a soft, brimless, tight-fitting cap.

SKUNK (⅒)

skunk (skŭngk), *n.* **1,** a small American mammal, usually black with white markings, which gives forth a liquid of very offensive odor when frightened or attacked; **2,** the skin of this animal, valued as fur; **3,** *Colloquial,* a contemptible person.

sky (skī), *n.* [*pl.* skies], **1,** the heavens or upper atmosphere; the region of the clouds and winds; **2,** heaven.

sky blue, the color of a clear sky; azure.

¹**sky-lark** (skī′lärk′), *n.* a small Old World lark, noted for its song.

²**sky-lark**(skī′lärk′), *v.i.* to frolic; play.

sky-light (skī′līt′), *n.* a window in a roof or in the ceiling of a room.

sky-line (skī′līn′), *n.* **1,** the line where land and sky, or water and sky, seem to meet; the horizon; **2,** the outline of mountains, trees, buildings, or the like, against the sky.

SKYLARK (⅛)

sky-rock-et (skī′rŏk′ĕt), *n.* a kind of firework that mounts high in the air and explodes there.

sky-sail (skī′sāl′; skī′sl), *n.* the sail at the top of a mast, above the royal. (See illustration on page 695.)

sky-scrap-er (skī′skrā′pĕr), *n.* a building many stories high.

sky-ward (skī′wẽrd), *adj.* and *adv.* toward the sky.—*adv.* **sky′wards.**

slab (slăb), *n.* a thick piece of anything, as of marble, wood, or stone; also, a thick slice, as of bread or cheese.

slack (slăk), *adj.* **1,** slow; lacking in vigor or energy; as, a *slack* pace; **2,** sluggish, as a backwater; **3,** relaxed; not tight; as, a *slack* wire; **4,** lazy; careless; as, a *slack* housekeeper; **5,** inactive; slow; as, business is *slack*:—*n.* **1,** that part of a wire, rope, etc., which is not stretched taut; **2,** a dull period, as in business; **3, slacks,** wide, loosely fitting trousers:—*v.t.* **1,** to loosen or slacken (a rope); **2,** to slake (lime):—*v.i.* to be or become sluggish or slack.—*adv.* **slack′ly.**—*n.* **slack′ness.**

slack-en (slăk′ĕn), *v.i.* **1,** to become less firm, tense, or rigid; **2,** to let up; become slower; as, the coal business *slackens* in warm weather:—*v.t.* **1,** to make slower; relax; as, to *slacken* speed or efforts; **2,** to loosen; as, do not *slacken* the rope.

slack-er (slăk′ẽr), *n.* a person who shirks his work or his duty.

slag (slăg), *n.* **1,** the dross or dregs of melted metal; **2,** lava from a volcano.

slain (slān), past participle of *slay.*

slake (slāk), *v.t.* [slaked, slak-ing], **1,** to quench; render less active; appease; as, to *slake* one's thirst; **2,** to combine chemically with water; as, to *slake* lime:—*v.i.* to be chemically mixed with water.

slam (slăm), *v.t.* [slammed, slam-ming], **1,** to shut violently and noisily; **2,** to put, or throw, with force and loud noise; as, to *slam* down a book:—*v.i.* to bang; as, the door *slams*:—*n.* **1,** a blow; a bang; **2,** the act of shutting noisily.

grand slam, in some card games, the taking of all the tricks; **small slam** or **little slam,** the taking of all the tricks but one.

slan-der (slăn′dẽr), *n.* the utterance of false reports about a person in order to defame or injure him; also, the reports themselves:—*v.t.* to injure the reputation of (a person) by spreading false reports.—*n.* **slan′der-er.**—*adj.* **slan′der-ous.**

Syn., n. aspersion, scandal.

slang (slăng), *n.* **1,** those words or phrases which, though regarded as not permissible in formal or written language, are used in popular speech for the sake of picturesqueness or novelty; **2,** the language or jargon of a particular group or profession; as, thieves' *slang.*—*adj.* **slang′y.**

slant (slănt), *n.* **1,** an inclined plane; a slope; as, the *slant* of a roof; **2,** *Colloquial,* a point of view; attitude; as, he has a modern *slant* on the problem:—*v.t.* to give a sloping direction to; as, *slant* your ruler a little more:—*v.i.* to slope; as, tilt the easel so that it *slants* a bit:—*adj.* sloping.—*adj.* **slant′ing.**—*adv.* **slant′ing-ly.**

slant-wise (slănt′wīz′), *adv.* slantingly.

slap (slăp), *n.* **1,** a blow with the open hand; **2,** an insult; a repulse:—*v.t.* [slapped, slap-ping], **1,** to strike with the open hand; **2,** *Colloquial,* to lay down with, or as with, a bang.

slap-jack (slăp′jăk′), *n.* **1,** a pancake; **2,** a game that children play with cards.

slash (slăsh), *v.t.* **1,** to cut by striking violently and aimlessly; **2,** to cut slits in (a garment) to expose the material beneath; **3,** to lash with a whip; **4,** to criticize harshly; as, the critics *slashed* the novel unmercifully:—*v.i.* to strike out violently and at random:—*n.* **1,** a long cut or gash; **2,** the stroke of a whip; **3,** a slit, as in a sleeve, showing other material beneath.—*n.* **slash′er.**

slat (slăt), *n.* a thin, narrow strip of wood or metal.

slate (slāt), *n.* **1,** a kind of fine-grained rock that splits into thin layers; **2,** the dark bluish-gray color of this rock; **3,** a thin plate of this rock prepared for use, as for roof covering, blackboards, writing tablets, or the like; **4,** a list of proposed candidates for nomination or election:—*v.t.* [slat-ed, slat-ing], **1,** to cover with slate; **2,** to register or suggest (a person) for an office, a role, or an appointment.—*n.* **slat′er.**—*adj.* **slat′y.**

slat-tern (slăt′ẽrn), *n.* a slovenly woman. —*adj.* and *adv.* **slat′tern-ly.**

āte, āorta, râre, căt, ȧsk, fär, ăllow, sofȧ; ēve, ēvent, ĕll, writēr, novĕl; bīte, pĭn; nō, ōbey, ôr, dŏg, tŏp, cŏllide; ūnit, ūnite, bûrn, cŭt, focŭs; no͞on, fŏŏt; mound; coin;

slaugh-ter (slô′tẽr), *n.* **1,** the act of killing; great and wanton destruction of life; **2,** the killing of animals for food:—*v.t.* **1,** to kill with violence; **2,** to butcher (animals) for the market.—*n.* **slaugh′ter-er.**
Syn., n. butchery, bloodshed, massacre.

slaugh-ter-house (slô′tẽr-hous′), *n.* a place where animals are butchered for the market.

Slav (släv; slăv), *n.* a member of one of the great divisions of the Aryan race, widely spread over southeastern and eastern Europe, and including Russians, Poles, Czechs, and natives of the Balkan states.

slave (slāv), *n.* **1,** a person owned by another; a bondsman; **2,** one who works like a slave; a drudge; **3,** a person in the power of a habit or vice; as, a *slave* to drink:—*adj.* pertaining to slaves; as, *slave* labor:—*v.i.* [slaved, slav-ing], to work like a drudge; toil.

slave-hold-er (slāv′hōl′dẽr), *n.* one who owns or keeps slaves.

¹slav-er (slăv′ẽr), *v.i.* to let saliva run from the mouth; drool:—*v.t.* to cover or dribble with saliva:—*n.* saliva running from the mouth.

²slav-er (slāv′ẽr), *n.* a vessel or person engaged in the slave trade

slav-er-y (slāv′ẽr-ĭ), *n.* [*pl.* slaveries], **1,** the condition of being a slave; **2,** the practice of owning slaves; **3,** a condition resembling slavery; complete submission to the will of another or to some influence or vice; **4,** drudgery.
Syn. thraldom, captivity, vassalage.

Slav-ic (släv′ĭk; slăv′ĭk), *adj.* pertaining to the Slavs or the peoples of eastern or southeastern Europe:—*n.* the language of any of the Slavs.

slav-ish (slāv′ĭsh), *adj.* **1,** characteristic of slaves; servile; mean; base; **2,** without originality or independence; as, *slavish* opinions.—*n.* **slav′ish-ness.**

slaw (slô), *n.* sliced cabbage mixed with a dressing, served as a relish or salad.

slay (slā), *v.t.* [*p.t.* slew (slōō), *p.p.* slain (slān), *p.pr.* slay-ing], to kill or put to death by violence.
—*n.* **slay′er.**

slea-zy (slā′zĭ; slē′-zĭ), *adj.* [slea-zi-er, slea-zi-est], lacking firmness; thin; as, *sleazy* silk.

sled (slĕd), *n.* a vehicle on runners, used for coasting, or for carrying loads, on snow or ice:—*v.i.* and *v.t.* [sled-ded, sled-ding], to travel or carry by sled.—*n.* **sled′ding.**

SLED
With flexible runners.

¹sledge (slĕj), *n.* a vehicle on runners for carrying heavy loads over snow or ice:—*v.i.* and *v.t.* [sledged, sledg-ing], to travel or carry on a sledge.

²sledge (slĕj), *n.* a large, heavy hammer, used by blacksmiths: also called *sledge hammer.*

SLEDGE

sleek (slēk), *adj.* **1,** smooth; glossy; as, the *sleek* coat of a seal; **2,** smooth or flattering in speech; as, a *sleek* betrayer:—*v.t.* to make smooth or shiny, especially by rubbing or brushing.—*n.* **sleek′ness.**

sleep (slēp), *n.* **1,** the condition of not being conscious or awake; slumber; **2,** any condition like sleep; as, death is called eternal *sleep*:—*v.i.* [slept (slĕpt), sleep-ing], **1,** to be asleep; slumber; **2,** to be motionless; remain inactive:—*v.t.* **1,** to rest in (sleep); as, he *slept* a sound sleep; **2,** to spend, waste, or rid oneself of, by sleeping; as, he *slept* away half the morning; he *slept* off his headache; **3,** *Colloquial,* to provide with a place to sleep; as, we *slept* three guests overnight.—*adj.* **sleep′less.**

sleep-er (slēp′ẽr), *n.* **1,** one who sleeps; hence, one who likes to sleep; a lazy person; **2,** a horizontal beam, on or near the ground level, that serves as support for some structure above, as railroad ties for rails; **3,** a sleeping car.

sleep-walk-ing (slēp′wôk′ĭng), *n.* the act or habit of walking in one's sleep.—*n.* **sleep′walk′er.**

sleep-y (slēp′ĭ), *adj.* [sleep-i-er, sleep-i-est], **1,** inclined to, or ready for, slumber; **2,** producing drowsiness; as, *sleepy* weather; **3,** drowsy; inactive; as, a *sleepy* town.—*adv.* **sleep′i-ly.**—*n.* **sleep′i-ness.**

sleet (slēt), *n.* driving rain that is partly frozen or that freezes as it falls:—*v.i.* to shower frozen rain.

sleet-y (slēt′ĭ), *adj.* [sleet-i-er, sleet-i-est], of or like half-frozen rain.

sleeve (slēv), *n.* **1,** the part of a garment that covers the arm; **2,** something, as a part of a machine, that covers or protects another part.—*adj.* **sleeve′less.**

sleigh (slā), *n.* a vehicle, equipped with runners, for use on snow or ice:—*v.i.* to travel by sleigh.

SLEIGH

sleigh-ing (slā′ĭng), *n.* **1,** the act of riding in a sleigh; **2,** the condition of snow which permits such travel.

sleight (slīt), *n.* a trick done so expertly and quickly as to deceive the eye: now used chiefly in the phrase *sleight of hand,* meaning the tricks or skill of a juggler or magician.

slen-der (slĕn′dẽr), *adj.* 1, narrow in proportion to length or height; slim; 2, scanty; slight; scarcely sufficient; as, *slender* meals; *slender* opportunities.

slept (slĕpt), past tense and past participle of *sleep.*

sleuth (slōōth), *n.* 1, a bloodhound; 2, a detective. Also, **sleuth′hound′.**

¹slew (slōō), past tense of *slay.*

²slew (slōō), *v.t.* and *v.i.* to turn around; slue. See **slue.**

slice (slīs), *n.* a thin, broad piece cut from something; as, a *slice* of bread:—*v.t.* [sliced, slic-ing], 1, to cut into thin pieces or layers; as, *slice* the entire cake; also, to cut into; as, *slice* open the melon; 2, to cut (a layer) from something; as, to *slice* off a piece of meat.—*n.* **slic′er.**

slick (slĭk), *adj.* 1, smooth; sleek; as, *slick* hair; slippery, as wet roads; 2, too smooth in speech and manners; 3, *Slang:* **a,** tricky; sly; **b,** first-rate; as, a *slick* time:—*v.t.* to make smooth or glossy, as hair.

slick-er (slĭk′ẽr), *n.* a loose waterproof coat.

SLICKER

slid (slĭd), past tense and one of the forms of the past participle of *slide.*

slide (slīd), *v.i.* [*p.t.* slid (slĭd), *p.p.* slid or slid-den (slĭd′n), *p.pr.* slid-ing], 1, to move smoothly over a surface, as over ice; glide; 2, to move quietly or secretly; slip; as, he *slid* into a seat; 3, to move or pass gradually or without being noticed; as, time *slides* by:—**to let slide,** to let (something) take care of itself; as, I'll *let* my lessons *slide* until tomorrow:—*v.t.* 1, to push along; cause to slip into place; as, they *slid* the canoe into the water; 2, to put quietly; slip; as, he *slid* his left hand into his pocket:—*n.* 1, the act of sliding; 2, a surface of snow or ice for sliding; 3, any smooth slope or incline; 4, a mass of earth, rock, or snow that slides down a mountain; 5, a thin glass plate upon which is a picture to be projected on a screen; also, a plate of glass upon which is mounted a specimen for examination under a microscope; 6, that part of a device upon which anything slides; also, the part that slides.

slid-ing (slīd′ĭng), *adj.* 1, moving in, or as in a groove; as, a *sliding* door; 2, varying with changing conditions; as, a *sliding* scale of wages.

slight (slīt), *adj.* 1, slender; frail; not strong; as, a *slight* figure; 2, small in amount or degree; as, a *slight* trace of gas; 3, not important; trivial; as, a *slight* difference in color:—*v.t.* 1, to treat with indifference; as, she *slighted* her guests; 2, to neglect or perform carelessly; as, she was so engrossed in her music that she *slighted* her studies:—*n.* an act of discourtesy; a snub.—*n.* **slight′ness.**

Syn., v. scorn, disregard, snub.

slight-ing (slī′tĭng), *adj.* showing indifference or discourtesy.

slight-ly (slī′tlĭ), *adv.* 1, to a small or trifling extent; as, *slightly* annoyed; 2, slenderly; as, *slightly* built.

slim (slĭm), *adj.* [slim-mer, slim-mest], 1, slender; as, a *slim* figure; 2, scant; slight; insufficient; as, a *slim* excuse.

slime (slīm), *n.* 1, soft, sticky mud; any sticky, dirty substance; 2, a sticky external secretion of certain animals, such as fishes and snails, and of certain plants.—*adj.* **slim′y.**

sling (slĭng), *n.* 1, an implement for hurling a missile, as a stone; 2, the act of hurling or flinging; a throw; 3, any of various devices for hoisting or lowering heavy articles, or for suspending a gun, pack, or the like, from the shoulder; 4, a supporting bandage, as for a wounded arm:—*v.t.* [slung (slŭng), sling-ing], 1, to hurl with, or as with, a sling; 2, to hang (a hammock) so that it will swing; 3, to place or suspend in a device for hoisting or lowering.

SLING

sling-shot (slĭng′shŏt′), *n.* a forked stick with a rubber band attached, for shooting small stones.

slink (slĭngk), *v.i.* [slunk (slŭngk), slinking], to go furtively; sneak or steal along.

slip (slĭp), *v.i.* [slipped, slip-ping], 1, to glide or slide smoothly; as, the drawers *slip* in and out easily; 2, to miss one's foothold; lose one's balance; 3, to move or pass without being seen; as, she *slipped* into the room; 4, to move suddenly out of place; as, the knife *slipped;* 5, to escape; as, the address has *slipped* from my mind:—*v.t.* 1, to put on or off with ease; as, to *slip* on a ring; *slip* off a coat; 2, to cause to slide; as, to *slip* a rod into place; 3, to lose or allow to escape; as, to *slip* a stitch; to cause to slide off; as, the horse *slips* his bridle; 4, to escape from; as, his name has *slipped* my mind; 5, to cut a small shoot from, in order to grow a new plant; as, to *slip* a rosebush:—*n.* 1, the act of sliding or missing one's foothold; also, an escaping or eluding; as, to give someone the *slip;* **2,** a fault; an error; as, a *slip* in grammar; **3,** a cutting from a plant; **4,** a space between wharves for vessels; a dock; **5,** something that may be put on or off with ease, as a kind of undergarment, a pillowcase, etc.; **6,** a long narrow piece of something; a strip; **7,** a slim person; as, a mere *slip* of a girl.

slip-knot (slĭp'nŏt'), *n.* a knot which slips along the cord around which it is formed.

SLIPKNOT

slip-per (slĭp'ẽr), *n.* a low, comfortable shoe, usually intended for indoor wear.—*adj.* **slip'pered.**

slip-per-y (slĭp'ẽr-ĭ), *adj.* [slipper-i-er, slip-per-i-est], **1,** having a surface so smooth or slimy as to yield no firm hold or footing; as, a *slippery* pavement; **2,** of persons, shifty; not trust-worthy.—*n.* **slip'per-i-ness.**

slip-shod (slĭp'shŏd'), *adj.* **1,** wearing shoes down at the heel; **2,** hence, slovenly; careless.

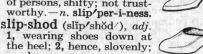
SLIPPERS

slit (slĭt), *v.t.* [slit (slĭt), slit-ting], **1,** to cut or tear lengthwise or into long strips; as, to *slit* cloth for band-ages; **2,** to cut or make a lengthwise open-ing in; as, to *slit* a skirt for a placket:— *n.* **1,** a long cut or tear; **2,** a narrow open-ing.—*n.* **slit'ter.**

slith-er (slĭth'ẽr), *v.i.* to slip or slide; as, to *slither* over icy streets.—*adj.* **slith'er-y.**

sliv-er (slĭv'ẽr), *n.* a long, thin, sharp-point-ed piece, as of wood; a splinter:—*v.t.* and *v.i.* to break off or split into long, thin pieces.

slob-ber (slŏb'ẽr), *v.i.* **1,** to let saliva dribble from the mouth; drool; **2,** to show or express feeling gushingly:—*v.t.* to wet by letting liquid run from the mouth; as, to *slobber* a dress; to spill so as to soil something; as, to *slobber* milk over a dress.

sloe (slō), *n.* the bitter, plumlike fruit of a shrub of the rose family; also, the shrub, which bears small white flowers before it leafs.

slo-gan (slō'găn), *n.* **1,** a war cry or rally-ing cry; **2,** a word or phrase used as a motto by a party or group, or as a catch-word to advertise a product.

sloop (slōōp), *n.* a one-masted vessel with a fore-and-aft rig, a mainsail, and a single jib. (See illustration under *ship*.)

slop (slŏp), *n.* **1,** water or other liquid carelessly spilled; **2,** poor or weak liquid food: used contemptuously; **3,** (often *slops*): **a,** refuse or dirty water from kitch-en or bedrooms; **b,** refuse or garbage used as food for swine:—*v.t.* [slopped,

slop-ping], **1,** to soil by letting liquid fall upon; as, to *slop* the floor; **2,** to spill; as, to *slop* water on the floor:—*v.i.* to be spilled; also, to overflow.

slope (slōp), *n.* **1,** a slanting line; also, a tilted surface; **2,** the degree of such a slant or tilt; as, a steep *slope;* **3,** any stretch of descending ground; specifically, the land that descends toward the ocean; as, the Pacific *slope:*—*v.i.* and *v.t.* [sloped, slop-ing], to incline; slant; as, the ground *slopes;* to *slope* a roof.

slop-py (slŏp'ĭ), *adj.* [slop-pi-er, slop-pi-est], **1,** wet or muddy; as, *sloppy* weather; **2,** soiled with liquid; **3,** *Colloquial,* slov-enly; careless; as, *sloppy* work.—*adv.* **slop'pi-ly.**—*n.* **slop'pi-ness.**

slot (slŏt), *n.* **1,** a narrow groove or de-pression in which something fits or moves snugly; **2,** a narrow opening through which something can be slipped; as, a mail *slot* in a door; a *slot* for a coin:—**slot machine,** a machine that operates on the insertion of a coin in a slot, for selling candy, gum, etc.:—*v.t.* [slot-ted, slot-ting], to cut a slot or slots in.

sloth (slōth; slôth), *n.* **1,** laziness; indolence; **2,** a tree-dwelling ani-mal of South and Cen-tral America which clings upside down to the branches: so called from its slow move-ments.

SLOTH (⅒), def. 2

sloth-ful (slōth'fool; slôth'fool), *adj.* lazy; slow; idle; sluggish; indolent.—*adv.* **sloth'-ful-ly.**

slouch (slouch), *n.* **1,** a stooping or droop, as of the head or shoulders; **2,** an incom-petent, lazy fellow:—**slouch hat,** a soft hat with a flexible brim:—*v.i.* to stand or move in a loose, ungainly manner.

slouch-y (slouch'ĭ), *adj.* [slouch-i-er, slouch-i-est], slovenly; drooping.

¹**slough** (slou; in def. 2, slōō), *n.* **1,** a miry place; a mudhole; **2,** (slōō), a swamp; also, an inlet from a river: also spelled *slue;* **3,** a state of depression or gloom into which one sinks and from which it is difficult to free oneself; as, the *slough* of despair.

²**slough** (slŭf), *n.* **1,** the castoff skin of a snake or other animal; **2,** anything that has been or can be cast off, as dead tissue, a bad habit, or the like:—*v.i.* **1,** to come off or be shed, as the skin of a snake; **2,** to shed or cast the skin:—*v.t.* to cast off, as the skin; hence, to discard.

Slo-vak (slō'văk; slō-văk'), *n.* **1,** one of a Slavic people, or their language, of Central Europe which with the Czechs of Bohemia and Moravia form the Republic of Czechoslovakia.—*n.* and *adj.* **Slo-vak′i-an** (slō-văk′ĭ-ăn; slō-vä′kĭ-ăn).

Slo-va-ki-a (slō-vä′kĭ-*a*), a province (cap. Bratislava) of eastern Czechoslovakia.

slov-en (slŭv′ĕn), *n.* a person who is untidy, careless, or slipshod.

slov-en-ly (slŭv′ĕn-lĭ), *adj.* [sloven-li-er, sloven-li-est], untidy in appearance; careless; not neat.—*n.* **slov′en-li-ness.**

slow (slō), *adj.* **1,** not rapid in motion; as, a *slow* march; **2,** not prompt; as, *slow* in arriving; **3,** taking a long time; as, a *slow* journey; **4,** not rash or hasty; as, *slow* to anger; **5,** behind the correct time; as, the clock is *slow;* **6,** mentally dull; as, a *slow* pupil; **7,** tending to hinder rapid motion; as, a *slow* track; **8,** *Colloquial,* dull; not lively; as, a *slow* party:—*adv.* in a manner not rapid:—*v.i.* to move with less and less speed; as, the train *slowed* down:—*v.t.* **1,** to cause to move with less speed; as, to *slow* down a car; **2,** to delay; as, heavy rains *slowed* up the haying.—*adv.* **slow′ly.**
  Syn., adj. sluggish, tardy.

slow match, a fuse that burns slowly, used for firing a blast, mine, etc.

sludge (slŭj), *n.* **1,** slush; mire; sticky mud; **2,** floating ice.

¹slue (slōō), *v.t.* [slued, slu-ing], to cause to turn around a fixed point or pivot:—*v.i.* to slide around, as on a slippery surface; to turn about. Also spelled **slew.**

²slue (slōō), *n.* a swamp; slough. See **¹slough.**

¹slug (slŭg), *n.* **1,** an animal like a snail, except that it has no shell or only a very thin one; **2,** a sluglike larva or caterpillar; **3,** *Archaic,* a sluggard.

SLUG (1)

²slug (slŭg), *n.* a small, unshaped piece of metal; specifically, a kind of small, rough bullet.

³slug (slŭg), *v.t.* [slugged, slug-ging], to strike hard, especially with the fist, as in boxing:—*n.* a hard blow, as with the fist or a club.—*n.* **slug′ger.**

slug-gard (slŭg′ẽrd), *n.* a person who is naturally lazy and idle:—*adj.* lazy.

slug-gish (slŭg′ish), *adj.* **1,** habitually lazy and idle; dull; slothful; **2,** inactive; slow; as, a *sluggish* river.
  Syn. indolent, languid, tardy.

sluice (slōōs), *n.* **1,** an artificial channel for conducting water, having a gate, called *sluice gate,* to regulate the flow; **2,** a floodgate for controlling the flow of water; **3,** a channel through which anything flows; **4,** an inclined trough for washing gold ore, carrying down logs, etc.:—*v.t.* [sluiced, sluic-ing], **1,** to wash with water from, or as from, a sluice; as, to *sluice* gold; **2,** to draw off (water) by a channel or floodgate; **3,** to transport (logs) by such means.

slum (slŭm), *n.* **1,** a dirty, densely populated street or district of a town or city; **2, slums,** a neighborhood composed of such streets:—*v.i.* [slummed, slum-ming], to visit such neighborhoods for the purpose of study or charity, or out of curiosity.

slum-ber (slŭm′bẽr), *v.i.* **1,** to sleep peacefully; **2,** to be in a state of rest or inactivity; as, his suspicions *slumbered:*—*n.* sleep.

slum-ber-ous (slŭm′bẽr-ŭs) or **slumbrous** (slŭm′brŭs), *adj.* **1,** sleepy; drowsy; heavy with sleep; **2,** bringing sleep; as, *slumberous* music; **3,** placid; peaceful; as, a *slumberous* landscape.

slump (slŭmp), *v.i.* **1,** to fall or sink suddenly, as into a marsh; **2,** to sink down heavily; as, he *slumped* in his chair; **3,** to fall or decline suddenly, as prices, stocks, business, etc.:—*n.* **1,** the act of sinking down; **2,** a sudden drop or decline; as, a *slump* in business.

slung (slŭng), past tense and past participle of *sling.*

slunk (slŭngk), past tense and past participle of *slink.*

slur (slûr), *v.t.* [slurred, slur-ring], **1,** to pass over hurriedly or briefly; as, to *slur* over an incident; **2,** to pronounce hastily or indistinctly (a sound or syllable); **3,** in music, to sing or sound (two or more successive tones of different pitch) without a break; also, to mark (notes that are to be so sounded) with the sign [⌢ or ⌣]:—*n.* **1,** a stain or blot; **2,** a slight reproach, or a remark conveying such reproach; **3,** in music, a mark [⌢ or ⌣] connecting notes that are to be sung or played without a break; also, the notes to be so treated.

slush (slŭsh), *n.* **1,** partly melted snow; **2,** silly, sentimental talk or writing:—*v.t.* **1,** to wet or splash with slush; **2,** *Colloquial,* to wash by dashing water upon.—*adj.* **slush′y.**

slut (slŭt), *n.* a dirty, untidy woman.—*adj.* **slut′tish.**

sly (slī), *adj.* [sli-er or sly-er, sli-est or sly-est], **1,** furtive; working or acting secretly; underhand; deceitful; as, a *sly* schemer; a *sly* scheme; **2,** playfully mischievous; roguish:—**on the sly,** in secret.—*adv.* **sly′ly.**—*n.* **sly′ness.**
  Syn. artful, subtle, wily, crafty.

¹smack (smăk), *n.* a slight taste or flavor; tinge:—*v.i.* to convey a suggestion; as, this *smacks* of treason.

āte, âorta, râre, căt, àsk, fär, ållow, sofà; ēve, ĕvent, ĕll, writẽr, novĕl; bīte, pĭn; nō, ōbey, ôr, dŏg, tŏp, cŏllide; ūnit, únite, bûrn, cŭt, focŭs; no͞on, fŏŏt; mound; coin;

²**smack** (smăk), *n.* **1,** a quick, sharp noise made with the lips; **2,** a loud, hearty kiss; **3,** a quick, resounding blow or slap:—*v.t.* **1,** to make a loud noise with (the lips); **2,** to strike or slap.

³**smack** (smăk), *n.* a small sailing vessel used in fishing; a fishing sloop.

smack-ing (smăk′ĭng), *adj.* **1,** making a sharp noise; **2,** lively; brisk; as, the wind blew up a *smacking* breeze.

small (smôl), *adj.* **1,** little in size, amount, number, degree, or the like; as, a *small* boy; a *small* school; a *small* dose; **2,** not important; insignificant; as, his opinion is of *small* value; **3,** doing business in a limited way; as, a *small* farmer; **4,** petty; not generous; narrow; as, a *small* mind.—*adj.* **small′ish.**—*n.* **small′ness.**

the small hours, the early hours after midnight; **small talk,** light conversation or gossip; **small change,** coins of small denomination.

small-pox (smôl′pŏks′), *n.* a contagious disease marked by fever and a characteristic skin eruption.

smart (smärt), *v.i.* **1,** to feel a sharp stinging pain; as, my hand *smarts;* **2,** to cause a stinging sensation; as, iodine *smarts;* **3,** to suffer; have one's feelings wounded:—*n.* **1,** a quick, lively pain; **2,** a pang of grief:—*adj.* **1,** causing a sharp, stinging sensation; also, severe; as, a *smart* thrashing; **2,** brisk; fresh; as, a *smart* breeze; **3,** clever; shrewd; as, a *smart* businessman; also, quick to learn; as, a *smart* child; **4,** amusingly witty; as, a *smart* saying; **5,** up-to-date; fashionable; as, a *smart* gown; the *smart* set.—*adv.* **smart′ly.**—*n.* **smart′ness.**

smart-en (smär′tn), *v.t.* to make smart or spruce; as, to *smarten* up a gown.

smash (smăsh), *v.t.* to break (something) into pieces by dropping it, hitting it, or striking it against something else; as, to *smash* a vase, window, car:—*v.i.* **1,** to break into many pieces; as, fine glass *smashes* easily; **2,** to rush or be thrown violently against something; as, the car *smashed* into the fence; **3,** to go to pieces, as a business that fails:—*n.* **1,** an act or the sound of breaking to pieces; a crash; **2,** a violent collision; **3,** complete destruction or ruin.

smat-ter (smăt′ẽr), *n.* a slight knowledge of anything.

smat-ter-ing (smăt′ẽr-ĭng), *n.* slight, superficial knowledge.

smear (smēr), *v.t.* **1,** to spread with anything greasy, oily, or sticky; daub; **2,** to spread (oil, paint, or the like) over something:—*n.* a blot or stain; a streak.

smell (smĕl), *v.t.* [*p.t.* and *p.p.* smelled (smĕld) or smelt (smĕlt), *p.pr.* smell-ing],

1, to perceive by means of the nose; obtain the scent of; as, to *smell* smoke; **2,** to inhale the odor of; as, to *smell* a flower; **3,** to suspect; detect; as, to *smell* trouble:—*v.i.* to have an odor; as, this room *smells* of lilacs:—*n.* **1,** that quality of things which is perceived by the nose; an odor; **2,** the sense by which odors are perceived; **3,** the act of smelling.—*adj.* **smell′y.**

Syn., n. fragrance, scent, perfume.

smell-ing salts, an aromatic, often scented, preparation used to relieve faintness or headache.

¹**smelt** (smĕlt), *n.* a small, silvery food fish found in northern waters.

²**smelt** (smĕlt), *v.t.* to fuse or melt (ore) in order to refine the metal; also, to obtain (metal) by this process.

SMELT (⅟₁)

smelt-er (smĕl′tẽr), *n.* **1,** a person who smelts or refines ore; **2,** a place where ores or metals are smelted and refined.

smile (smīl), *n.* an expression on the face, particularly around the mouth, indicating amusement, pleasure, or affection; also, a facial expression conveying irony or contempt:—*v.i.* [smiled, smil-ing], **1,** to show a smile; look pleasant; as, the photographer told her to *smile;* **2,** to show pleasure or amusement, contempt or disdain, by smiling; **3,** to look with favor or approval; as, Fortune *smiled* upon his efforts; **4,** to present a gay or cheerful aspect; as, a *smiling* landscape:—*v.t.* to express by smiling; as, to *smile* assent.

smirch (smûrch), *v.t.* **1,** to smear; soil; stain; **2,** to bring disgrace upon:—*n.* a smear or stain.

smirk (smûrk), *v.i.* to smile affectedly or conceitedly:—*n.* an affected smile.

smite (smīt), *v.t.* [*p.t.* smote (smōt), *p.p.* smit-ten (smĭt′n), *p.pr.* smit-ing], **1,** to hit; strike with the hand, or with a weapon or implement; **2,** to strike with disaster; afflict; as, Jehovah *smote* Egypt with plagues; **3,** to cause to strike; as, he *smote* his staff upon the ground; **4,** to affect with the suddenness of a blow; as, a cry *smote* the silence; **5,** to affect with any strong feeling, as love, grief, fear, or the like; **6,** to cause to feel regret or sorrow; as, his conscience *smote* him.

smith (smĭth), *n.* one who works or shapes metal with hammer and anvil.

Smith, John (1580–1631), one of the founders of Jamestown, the first permanent English settlement in America.

smith-y (smĭth′ĭ; smĭth′ĭ), *n.* [*pl.* smithies], a forge; a blacksmith's shop.

smit-ten (smĭt'n), past participle of *smite:—adj.* **1,** afflicted; as, *smitten* with illness; *smitten* with sorrow; **2,** *Colloquial,* enamored; as, he was *smitten* with her beauty.

smock (smŏk), *n.* a long, loose blouse or garment worn to protect the clothing:—*v.t.* to trim (a blouse or dress) with gathers fastened into a pattern by fancy stitches.—*n.* **smock'ing.**

smoke (smōk), *n.* **1,** the visible gas that escapes from a burning substance; **2,** a column, cloud, or mass of smoke; **3,** the act of inhaling the fumes of burning tobacco, opium, etc.; **4,** anything that resembles smoke, as fumes or vapor:—*v.t.* [smoked, smok-ing], **1,** to preserve (fish or meat) by exposure to smoke; **2,** to inhale and puff out the fumes of; as, to *smoke* tobacco; **3,** to force out by smoke; as, to *smoke* out snakes:—*v.i.* **1,** to give out fumes, as a chimney; **2,** to inhale and puff out the fumes of tobacco, opium, etc.; **3,** to give off anything like smoke.

SMOCK

smok-er (smōk'ẽr), *n.* **1,** a person who smokes tobacco; **2,** a railway car, or a compartment in a car, in which passengers may smoke; **3,** a social gathering for men at which smoking is permitted.

smoke-less (smōk'lĕs), *adj.* burning with little or no smoke; as, *smokeless* powder.

smoke-stack (smōk'stăk'), *n.* a tall chimney, as on a factory or steamship.

smok-y (smōk'ĭ), *adj.* [smok-i-er, smok-i-est], **1,** giving out, or filled with, smoke; as, a *smoky* stove; a *smoky* town; **2,** like smoke in flavor or appearance; as, a *smoky* taste; a *smoky* gray.—*n.* **smok'i-ness.**

smol-der or **smoul-der** (smōl'dẽr), *v.i.* **1,** to burn slowly, giving forth smoke without flame; **2,** to burn beneath the surface; as, hate *smoldered* in his heart.

smooth (smōōth), *adj.* **1,** not rough; even in surface or texture, as a road; **2,** perfectly blended; free from lumps; as, *smooth* gravy; **3,** gently flowing, as a river; hence, serene; calm; pleasant; **4,** easy and polished; as, a *smooth* style in speaking or writing; **5,** flattering; fluent; as, *smooth* words; a *smooth* talker; **6,** without beard; as, a *smooth* face; **7,** steady in motion; not jerky or jarring; as, the *smooth* running of a car; **8,** of liquors, aged; free from sharpness; pleasant:—*adv.* in a smooth manner:—*v.t.* **1,** to remove roughness from; **2,** to make even, steady, or calm; **3,** to soothe; as, to *smooth* a person's feelings; **4,** to make easy; as, to *smooth* a person's way; also, to remove; as, to *smooth* away difficulties.—*n.* **smooth'ness.**—*adv.* **smooth'ly.**

smooth-bore (smōōth'bôr'), *adj.* having a smooth, ungrooved bore, as a gun.

smooth—faced (smōōth'=fāst'), *adj.* without beard or mustache.

smote (smōt), past tense of *smite.*

smoth-er (smŭth'ẽr), *v.t.* **1,** to kill by depriving of air; stifle; also, to deaden by suffocating, as a fire; **2,** to suppress or conceal; cover up; as, to *smother* one's anger; **3,** in cookery, to cover, as with onions, and cook in a covered dish:—*v.i.* **1,** to be deprived of air; **2,** to be restrained:—*n.* a dense smoke or thick dust.

smoul-der (smōl'dẽr), *v.i.* to burn without flame; smolder. See **smolder.**

smudge (smŭj), *n.* **1,** a smear or stain; **2,** a smouldering fire that produces a dense smoke for protecting fruit trees from frost or for keeping off insects:—*v.t.* [smudged, smudg-ing], **1,** to smear or stain; **2,** to keep away by a smudge.

smug (smŭg), *adj.* [smug-ger, smug-gest], **1,** precise; rather too prim; **2,** self-satisfied; pleased with oneself.—*adv.* **smug'ly.**—*n.* **smug'ness.**

smug-gle (smŭg'l), *v.t.* and *v.i.* [smuggled, smug-gling], to bring or send (goods) into or out of a country secretly, without paying duties.—*n.* **smug'gler** (smŭg'lẽr).

smut (smŭt), *n.* **1,** a spot or stain made by soot or dirt; also, that which causes the spot; **2,** a disease affecting corn, wheat, or the like; **3,** foul or indecent language:—*v.t.* [smut-ted, smut-ting], to soil or blacken with, or as with, soot:—*v.i.* **1,** to become blackened by soot; also, to be affected by mildew or smut, as grain.

smutch (smŭch), *v.t.* to soil with smoke, soot, or coal:—*n.* a dirty spot.

smut-ty (smŭt'ĭ), *adj.* [smut-ti-er, smut-ti-est], **1,** soiled or stained with dirt or soot; **2,** indecent; **3,** of grain, diseased.

Smyr-na (smûr'nà), the former name for Izmir, a seaport in Turkey. See **Izmir.**

snack (snăk), *n.* a slight, hurried meal.

snaf-fle (snăf'l), *n.* a horse's bit jointed in the middle and without a curb:—*v.t.* [snaf-fled, snaf-fling], to put such a bit in the mouth of (a horse); also, to control by means of such a bit.

snag (snăg), *n.* **1,** the stump of a branch projecting from the trunk of a tree; **2,** some part of a tree sticking up from the bottom of a river or lake and dangerous to boats; **3,** a broken or decayed tooth; **4,** any unexpected obstacle or difficulty:—*v.t.* [snagged, snag-ging], **1,** to catch or damage on a snag; **2,** to clear of obstructions or snags.

SNAFFLE

snail (snāl), *n.* **1,** a small land or water animal with a spiral shell into which it withdraws for protection; **2,** a person slow-moving as a snail.

SNAIL (½)

snake (snāk), *n.* **1,** a long, legless, slim-bodied reptile which preys on insects and small animals; **2,** a treacherous person:—*v.t.* [snaked, snaking], *Colloquial*, to drag, especially at full length; jerk; as, to *snake* a log out of a swamp: —*v.i.* to crawl along like a snake.— *adj.* **snak′y.**

SNAKE

snap (snăp), *v.i.* [snapped, snap-ping], **1,** to break suddenly; as, the glass *snapped* in my hand; **2,** to snatch at something suddenly, especially with the teeth; as, a dog *snaps* at a bone; **3,** to produce a sharp, sudden sound; as twigs *snap* underfoot; **4,** to speak crossly or angrily; **5,** to sparkle; as, her eyes *snapped:*—*v.t.* **1,** to break off short; crack; **2,** to seize suddenly; as, the fish *snapped* up the bait; **3,** to cause to make a sudden, sharp sound; **4,** to close with a sharp sound; as, to *snap* down a lid; **5,** in football, to put (the ball) in play by passing it back from the line of scrimmage; **6,** to take a quick photograph of:—*n.* **1,** the act of seizing suddenly; **2,** the sudden breaking of something stiff or tightly stretched; as, the *snap* of a wire; **3,** a sudden, sharp sound; **4,** a spring lock or catch; **5,** a kind of thin, crisp cooky; a gingersnap; **6,** a sudden, short period of severe weather; **7,** *Colloquial*, energy or vim:—*adj.* **1,** done in haste or without much thought; as, a *snap* decision; **2,** closing with a click, or with a special closing device; as, a *snap* bracelet; **3,** *Colloquial*, easy; requiring little effort.

snap-drag-on (snăp′drăg′-ŭn), *n.* a plant with showy white, yellow, or reddish flowers.

snap-per (snăp′ẽr), *n.* **1,** a fighting, edible fish inhabiting warm seas; **2,** a fresh-water turtle, highly valued as food.

snap-pish (snăp′ĭsh), *adj.* **1,** likely to snap or bite; as, a *snappish* dog; **2,** sharp in speech; easily irritated.—*n.* **snap′pish-ness.**

SNAPDRAGON

snap-py (snăp′ĭ), *adj.* [snap-pi-er, snap-pi-est], **1,** sharp and irritable in speech; **2,** *Colloquial:* **a,** lively; brisk, as conversation; **b,** stylish; smart, as clothes.

snap-shot (snăp′shŏt′), *n.* a photograph taken quickly or instantaneously.

snare (snâr), *n.* **1,** a running noose or a loop of cord or wire, for catching an animal or a bird; **2,** hence, anything that entangles or entraps:—*v.t.* [snared, snar-ing], to catch with, or as with, a snare.—*n.* **snar′er.**

snare drum, a small drum with catgut strings, or snares, stretched across the lower head to produce a rattling sound, when the upper head is beaten. (See *musical instrument,* illustration.)

¹**snarl** (snärl), *v.i.* **1,** to make a growling noise, as an angry dog; **2,** to speak in harsh, surly tones:—*v.t.* to utter in a growl or in a harsh, surly tone:—*n.* **1,** the act of growling; **2,** a surly tone.

²**snarl** (snärl), *n.* a tangle or knot, as of yarn or hair; hence, a state of confusion; a complicated situation:—*v.t.* and *v.i.* to make or become tangled.

snatch (snăch), *v.t.* to seize suddenly or rudely:—*v.i.* to try to seize something suddenly; as, the child *snatched* at a flower:— *n.* **1,** a hasty catch; **2,** a small fragment; as, *snatches* of verse; **3,** a brief period; as, to work in *snatches.*—*n.* **snatch′er.**

sneak (snēk), *v.i.* **1,** to creep or move about secretly or slyly; slink; **2,** to act in a cowardly or mean way:—*n.* **1,** a mean, cowardly fellow; **2,** a petty thief; **3,** **sneak-ers,** canvas shoes with rubber soles.—*adj.* **sneak′y.**

sneak-ing (snēk′ĭng), *adj.* **1,** cowardly; mean; **2,** secret; not acknowledged; as, a *sneaking* respect for a person.

sneer (snēr), *v.i.* **1,** to show contempt by an expression of the face, as by curling the lips; **2,** to speak contemptuously or with ridicule:—*n.* **1,** contempt or scorn shown in speech; **2,** a contemptuous smile.

 Syn., *v.* taunt, scoff, jeer, gibe.

sneeze (snēz), *n.* a sudden brief spasm of the breathing organs, causing a violent and audible rush of air out through the mouth and nostrils:—*v.i.* [sneezed, sneezing], to be seized with such a spasm.

snick-er (snĭk′ẽr) or **snig-ger** (snĭg′ẽr), *n.* a half-suppressed laugh; a giggle:—*v.i.* to laugh slyly; giggle.

sniff (snĭf), *v.i.* **1,** to draw in the breath audibly through the nose; to clear the nose; **2,** to express contempt; as, he *sniffed* at the suggestion:—*v.t.* **1,** to smell quickly and audibly; **2,** to smell out; as, to *sniff* danger:—*n.* **1,** the act of smelling; **2,** an audible, often scornful, inhaling through the nose.

snif-fle (snĭf′l), *v.i.* [snif-fled, snif-fling], to draw air through the nose audibly and repeatedly; to snuffle.

---

go; join; yet; sing; chin; show; thin, *th***en; hw,** *wh***y; zh,** *a***zure; ü, Ger. für or Fr. lune; ö, Ger. schön or Fr.** *feu***; ṅ, Fr. e***n***fant, no***m***; kh, Ger. a***ch* **or** *ich***. See pages ix–x.**

snip (snĭp), *v.t.* [snipped, snip-ping], to cut or clip, with scissors or shears, in short, quick strokes:—*n.* **1,** a single cut with scissors; a clip; **2,** a small piece; bit.

snipe (snīp), *n.* [*pl.* snipe], a long-billed shore bird akin to the woodcock:—*v.i.* [sniped, snip-ing], **1,** to hunt such birds; **2,** in war, to shoot at enemy soldiers, one by one, from ambush:—*v.t.* to shoot or shoot at (soldiers) in this way.

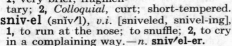

SNIPE (⅛)

snip-py (snĭp′ĭ), *adj.* [snip-pi-er, snip-pi-est], **1,** very brief; fragmentary; **2,** *Colloquial,* curt; short-tempered.

sniv-el (snĭv′l), *v.i.* [sniveled, snivel-ing], **1,** to run at the nose; to snuffle; **2,** to cry in a complaining way.—*n.* **sniv′el-er.**

snob (snŏb), *n.* one who apes and is slavishly humble to persons of wealth or position and ignores those he considers socially inferior.—*adj.* **snob′bish.**—*n.* **snob′ber-y.**

snood (snōōd), *n.* a band or ribbon formerly worn around the head by young women to hold back the hair.

snoop (snōōp), *v.i.* to peer or pry in a sneaking way:—*n.* one who thus pries.

snooze (snōōz), *Colloquial: v.i.* [snoozed, snooz-ing], to take a nap; doze:—*n.* a nap.

snore (snôr), *v.i.* [snored, snor-ing], to breathe with a hoarse sound through the nose, or nose and mouth, in sleep:—*n.* a noisy breathing in sleep.—*n.* **snor′er.**

snort (snôrt), *v.i.* **1,** to force the air out through the nose with a loud sound; **2,** to express feeling by such a sound; as, to *snort* with anger:—*n.* a loud, abrupt sound so made; as, a *snort* of rage.

snout (snout), *n.* **1,** the projecting nose, and often jaws, of a beast, especially of a hog; the muzzle; **2,** anything like a snout.

snow (snō), *n.* frozen water vapor in the form of white, feathery flakes, or crystals, falling through the air; also, masses of such flakes lying on the ground:—*v.i.* to fall in frozen crystals:—*v.t.* **1,** to pour out thickly like falling snow, as confetti; **2,** to obstruct or shut in with masses of snow.

snow-ball (snō′bôl′), *n.* **1,** a mass of snow pressed together in the form of a ball; **2,** a shrub or tree of the honeysuckle family, bearing ball-like clusters of white flowers:—*v.i.* to throw snowballs:—*v.t.* to storm or attack with snowballs.

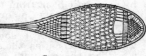

SNOWBIRD (¼)

snow-bird (snō′bûrd′), *n.* **1,** the junco, an American finch blue-gray and white in color; **2,** the snow bunting.

snow—blind (snō′-blīnd′), *adj.* temporarily blind from the glare of the sun on snow.—**snow blind′ness.**

snow-bound (snō′bound′), *adj.* shut in by a heavy snowstorm.

snow bun-ting (bŭn′tĭng), a black-and-white finch nesting in the arctic regions. Its winter plumage is white, overcast with brown.

snow-drift (snō′drĭft′), *n.* a mass of snow heaped up by the wind.

snow-drop (snō′drŏp′), *n.* **1,** a plant with white flowers, which blooms in very early spring; **2,** its flower; also, its bulb.

snow-fall (snō′fôl′), *n.* the quantity of snow which falls in the course of a single storm, or in a single place.

snow-flake (snō′flāk′), *n.* a white feathery crystal or small mass of snow.

SNOWDROPS

snow-plow or **snow-plough** (snō′plou′), *n.* a machine used to clear roads, tracks, etc., of heavy snow.

snow-shoe (snō′shōō′), *n.* a network of rawhide stretched upon a racket-shaped wooden frame, fastened by thongs to the foot and worn for traveling over deep snow.

SNOWSHOE

snow-y (snō′ĭ), *adj.* [snow-i-er, snow-i-est], **1,** covered with, or full of, snow; **2,** white like fresh snow; as, *snowy* linen.

snub (snŭb), *v.t.* [snubbed, snub-bing], **1,** to check, answer, or interrupt with rude or scornful words; **2,** to treat with scorn; slight intentionally; **3,** to check the motion of; as, to *snub* a boat by means of a rope wound round a post:—*n.* **1,** an intentional slight; **2,** a check:—*adj.* short and slightly turned up; as, a *snub* nose.

¹snuff (snŭf), *v.t.* **1,** to draw in through the nose; **2,** to smell; sniff at:—*n.* **1,** the act of snuffing; **2,** powdered tobacco to be inhaled through the nose.—*n.* **snuff′er.**

²snuff (snŭf), *n.* the burned part of a wick:—*v.t.* **1,** to cut or pinch the charred part from; as, to *snuff* a candle; **2,** to put out (a candle); hence, to put a sudden end to; as, the accident *snuffed* out his life.

snuff-ers (snŭf′ẽrz), *n.pl.* a device resembling small tongs, for snuffing a candle.

snuf-fle (snŭf′l), *v.i.* [snuf-fled, snuffling], to speak or breathe noisily through the nose, especially when it is stopped up:

āte, âorta, râre, căt, ȧsk, fär, ăllow, sofȧ; ēve, ēvent, ĕll, writẽr, novĕl; bīte, pĭn; nō, ōbey, ôr, dŏg, tŏp, cŏllide; ūnit, ŭnite, bûrn, cŭt, focŭs; nōon, fŏŏt; mound; coin;

—*n.* **1**, a noisy breathing through the nose; **2**, **snuffles**, a cold in the head.

snug (snŭg), *adj.* [snug-ger, snug-gest], **1**, sheltered and warm; as, a *snug* house; **2**, fitting closely; as, a *snug* jacket; **3**, sufficient; as, a *snug* fortune.—*adv.* **snug′ly.**

snug-gle (snŭg′l), *v.i.* [snug-gled, snug-gling], to nestle close for warmth and comfort:—*v.t.* to hold close and comfortably.

¹**so** (sō), *adv.* **1**, in like manner or degree; as, I can run fast, *so* can she; today is not *so* hot as yesterday; **2**, to such a degree; as, this fabric is *so* old that it tears; **3**, as stated, indicated, or implied; as, I told you she would come and *so* she did; hold your needle *so*; **4**, well: expressing surprise; as, *so* here you are:—*pron.* **1**, a person or thing already indicated; as, he is a poor student and will always remain *so*; **2**, approximately that which has been indicated; a little more or less; as, it costs a dollar or *so*:—*conj.* therefore; consequently.

²**so** (sō) or **sol** (sōl; sŏl), *n.* in music, the fifth note of the scale.

soak (sōk), *v.t.* **1**, to wet thoroughly; as, the rain *soaked* him; **2**, to wet so as to soften; as, to *soak* dried apricots before cooking; **3**, to absorb; as, blotting paper *soaks* up ink:—*v.i.* **1**, to become thoroughly wet; **2**, to enter by pores or small openings; as, water *soaks* into a sponge; also, to penetrate the mind, as words or ideas:—*n.* the act or process of wetting thoroughly.

soap (sōp), *n.* a substance for cleansing, made by combining fats or oils with an alkali:—*v.t.* to cover or wash with soap.

soap op-er-a, *Colloquial*, a radio serial dealing with domestic problems in a highly dramatic manner.

soap-stone (sōp′stōn′), *n.* a kind of soft, grayish stone with a smooth surface, supposed to feel like soap; talc; also, the same substance when powdered.

soap-y (sōp′ĭ), *adj.* [soap-i-er, soap-i-est], covered with, like, or containing soap.

soar (sôr), *v.i.* **1**, to fly high, as a bird; mount upward with wings; **2**, to rise far above what is usual; as, prices *soared*.

sob (sŏb), *v.i.* [sobbed, sob-bing], to catch the breath convulsively; also, to weep with a convulsive heaving of the breast:—*v.t.* to utter while catching the breath; as, to *sob* out a confession:—*n.* **1**, a convulsive sigh; **2**, any similar sound.

so-ber (sō′bẽr), *adj.* **1**, temperate by habit, especially in the use of intoxicating liquors; **2**, not intoxicated; **3**, calm; steady; as, *sober* judgment; **4**, solemn; grave; as, a *sober* face; **5**, plain; subdued; as, *sober* colors:—*v.t.* and *v.i.* to make or become sober.—*adv.* **so′ber-ly.**

so-bri-e-ty (sō-brī′ĕ-tĭ), *n.* **1**, moderation; temperance, especially in the use of liquor; **2**, calmness; seriousness; gravity.

so-bri-quet (sō′brĭ-kā) or **sou-bri-quet** (sōō′brē′kā̇), *n.* a nickname; a fanciful or assumed name.

so—called (sō′=kôld′), *adj.* usually thus named or termed, but often inaccurately.

soc-cer (sŏk′ẽr), *n.* a form of football in which the ball is advanced by the feet, legs, body, or head, the use of the hands and arms being prohibited.

so-cia-ble (sō′shȧ-bl), *adj.* **1**, friendly; companionable; **2**, giving opportunity for friendly companionship; as, a *sociable* neighborhood; **3**, marked by friendliness; not formal:—*n.* an informal, friendly party.—*adv.* **so′cia-bly.**—*n.* **so′cia-bil′i-ty.**

so-cial (sō′shăl), *adj.* **1**, pertaining to human beings living in association with one another; **2**, relating to human life in general; as, *social* welfare; **3**, pertaining to the life of people of wealth and fashion; as, the *social* whirl; **4**, pertaining to insects, living in organized communities, as ants or bees:—*n.* an informal gathering.—*adv.* **so′cial-ly.**

so-cial-ism (sō′shăl-ĭzm), *n.* the economic, social, and political doctrine which holds that, for the greatest good of the people, the resources of a country and its industries should be placed permanently under public or government ownership and operation.—*n.* and *adj.* **so′cial-ist.**—*adj.* **so′cial-is′tic.**

so-cial-ize (sō′shăl-īz), *v.t.* [socialized, socializ-ing], **1**, to make social; fit (a person) for society; **2**, to conduct (an enterprise, business, etc.) according to the principles of socialism; as, to *socialize* a factory; **3**, to put under the control of a group rather than of an individual; as, to *socialize* a class recitation.

So-cial Se-cur-it-y Act an act of Congress, providing Federal old-age insurance, Federal help in regulating state unemployment compensation, and Federal grants to help states with the public care of the needy.

so-ci-e-ty (sō-sī′ĕ-tĭ), *n.* [*pl.* societies], **1**, people in general, considered as living in relationship with one another; **2**, people of culture and of good standing in any community: sometimes applied only to people of wealth and fashion; **3**, an organized body of persons united by a common interest or purpose; as, a debating *society*; **4**, association; companionship; as, her *society* was pleasant for us.

so-ci-ol-o-gy (sō′sĭ-ŏl′ō-jĭ; sō′shĭ-ŏl′ō-jĭ), *n.* the science of human relationships, dealing with the problems of the family, church, and society as a whole.—*adj.* **so/ci-o-log/i-cal.**—*n.* **so/ci-ol/o-gist.**

sock (sŏk), *n.* a short stocking not reaching the knee.

sock-et (sŏk/ĕt), *n.* a hollow into which something is fitted; as, the *socket* of the eye; the *socket* of an electric-light bulb.

Soc-ra-tes (sŏk/rȧ-tēz), (469–399 B.C.), a famous Greek philosopher.

SOCKETS
1, for incandescent lamp; 2, for curtain pole.

sod (sŏd), *n.* **1,** the top layer of the soil, containing the roots of grass; turf; **2,** a piece of turf, usually cut square; **3,** the surface of the ground:—*v.t.* [sod-ded, sod-ding], to cover with turf or pieces of turf.

so-da (sō/dȧ), *n.* **1,** the name given to either of two compounds of sodium: **a,** a white powdery substance, sodium bicarbonate, or baking soda; **b,** a white crystalline substance, sodium carbonate, or washing soda; **2,** soda water; also, a soft drink made from soda water.

so-da foun-tain, a counter equipped for serving soda water, ice cream, beverages, sandwiches, etc.

so-dal-i-ty (sō-dăl/ĭ-tĭ), *n.* [*pl.* sodalities], a religious or charitable association of members of the Roman Catholic Church.

so-da wa-ter, water charged with carbon dioxide, usually flavored with a fruit sirup.

sod-den (sŏd/n), *adj.* **1,** soaked; heavy with moisture; as, *sodden* shoes; **2,** badly cooked or baked; as, *sodden* piecrust; **3,** spiritless; dull; as, a *sodden* crowd.

so-di-um (sō/dĭ-ŭm), *n.* a silvery-white, alkaline metallic element always occurring in nature in combination, as in common salt, rock salt, borax, or the like.

sodium bicarbonate, a compound of sodium and carbon, used in cookery, medicine, etc.; baking soda; **sodium carbonate,** a compound of sodium and carbon, used extensively in the manufacture of glass, soap, paper, for softening water, as a bleach, etc.: also called *wash-ing soda.*

Sod-om (sŏd/ŭm), a city of ancient Palestine, noted for its wickedness.

SOFA

so-fa (sō/fȧ), *n.* a long, upholstered seat with a back and arms.

So-fi-a (sō/fē-yȧ; sō-fē/ȧ), a city, capital of Bulgaria (map 12).

soft (sôft), *adj.* **1,** easily yielding to pressure; lacking in hardness; as, *soft* clay; **2,** easily molded or shaped; as, *soft* wax; **3,** smooth and yielding to the touch; as, *soft* fur; **4,** not glaring; as, a *soft* light; **5,** not loud; as, *soft* music; **6,** kind; courteous; mild or gentle; as, a *soft* answer; **7,** easily touched or moved; as, a *soft* heart; **8,** mild; as, *soft* winds; **9,** weak; unmanly; **10,** pronounced with the sound of "c" in "cell" or "g" in "gem"; not hard, like the "c" in "case" or "g" in "gate"; **11,** *Colloquial:* **a,** not in good physical condition; flabby; as, *soft* muscles; **b,** containing no alcohol; as, *soft* drinks: —*adv.* quietly.—*adv.* **soft/ly.**—*n.* **soft/ness.**

soft coal, bituminous coal; **soft water,** water that easily forms a lather with soap.

Syn., *adj.* mellow, mature, ripe.

sof-ten (sô/fn; sô/fĕn), *v.t.* and *v.i.* to make or become less hard, loud, glaring, severe, or rude.

soft-wood (sôft/wŏŏd/), *n.* any light, easily worked wood, especially that of cone-bearing trees, such as the spruce or pine: opposite of *hardwood.* Also written **soft wood.**

sog-gy (sŏg/ĭ), *adj.* [sog-gi-er, sog-gi-est], soaked; as, *soggy* clothes; also, wet and heavy; as, *soggy* cake.—*n.* **sog/gi-ness.**

¹**soil** (soil), *n.* **1,** the loose top layer of the earth's surface, as distinguished from solid rock; ground; earth; **2,** land; the country; as, to go back to the *soil.*

²**soil** (soil), *v.t.* **1,** to make dirty; stain; as, to *soil* the hands; **2,** to mar or sully, as a reputation:—*v.i.* to become stained or dirty:—*n.* **1,** dirt; stain; **2,** manure.

soi-rée (swä-rā/), *n.* an evening party, as a reception or ball.

so-journ (sō-jûrn/; sō/jûrn), *v.i.* to dwell for a time:—*n.* (sō/jûrn; sō-jûrn/), a short stay.—*n.* **so-journ/er.**

Sol (sŏl), *n.* the sun; the name of the Roman god of the sun.

¹**sol** (sōl; sŏl), *n.* in music, the fifth note of the scale; so.

²**sol** (sōl), *n.* [*pl.* sols (sōlz) or soles (sō/läs)], a silver coin, the monetary unit of Peru. (See table, page 943.)

sol-ace (sŏl/ĭs), *n.* comfort in sorrow; consolation; as, to find *solace* in music:—*v.t.* [solaced, solac-ing], to comfort in sorrow; console.

so-lar (sō/lẽr), *adj.* pertaining to, measured by, or proceeding from, the sun; as, *solar* rays; *solar* time:—**solar system,** the sun together with the planets and the other bodies that circle round it; hence, any star with the planets and other bodies revolving around it.

so-lar-i-um (sō-lâr′ĭ-ŭm), *n.* [*pl.* solaria (sō-lâr′ĭ-*à*)], a porch or room enclosed with glass and exposed to the sun.

so-lar plex-us (plĕk′sŭs), **1,** the great network of nerves lying back of the stomach; **2,** *Colloquial,* the pit of the stomach.

sold (sōld), past tense and past participle of *sell.*

sol-der (sŏd′ẽr), *n.* a metal or metallic alloy used, when melted, to join metal surfaces, or to mend breaks in metal:— *v.t.* to join or patch with such an alloy.

sol-dier (sōl′jẽr), *n.* **1,** a man engaged in military service; **2,** a private as distinguished from a commissioned officer; **3,** a man of military experience:—**soldier of fortune,** an adventurer; especially, a military adventurer:—*v.i.* **1,** to serve in the army; **2,** to pretend to be working; shirk.

sol-dier-ly (sōl′jẽr-lĭ), *adj.* pertaining to a soldier or soldiers; military.

sol-dier-y (sōl′jẽr-ĭ), *n.* military forces; troops.

¹sole (sōl), *n.* a kind of flatfish used for food.

SOLE (1⁄10)

²sole (sōl), *n.* **1,** the under side of the foot; **2,** the bottom of a shoe or slipper:— *v.t.* [soled, sol-ing], to furnish with a sole.

³sole (sōl), *adj.* alone; only; single; as, the *sole* survivor.—*adv.* **sole′ly.**

sol-e-cism (sŏl′ē-sĭzm), *n.* **1,** a mistake in the use of words or in the structure of a sentence; an error in grammar; **2,** a rude or absurd breach of manners.

sol-emn (sŏl′ĕm), *adj.* **1,** attended with sacred rites or ceremonies; as, a *solemn* religious service; **2,** inspiring awe or fear; as, a *solemn* occasion; **3,** sober; serious; as, a *solemn*-expression; **4,** grave; deliberate; as, a *solemn* oath.—*adv.* **sol′emn-ly.** —*n.* **sol′emn-ness.**

so-lem-ni-ty (sō-lĕm′nĭ-tĭ), *n.* [*pl.* solemnities], **1,** a sacred rite or ceremony; **2,** a formal and grave celebration; **3,** impressiveness; seriousness; gravity.

sol-em-nize (sŏl′ĕm-nīz), *v.t.* [solemnized, solemniz-ing], **1,** to perform (rites) in a ceremonious or legally formal manner; **2,** to celebrate; as, to *solemnize* a festival. *Syn.* honor, observe, dignify.

so-lic-it (sō-lĭs′ĭt), *v.t.* to ask for urgently; implore; entreat; seek; as, to *solicit* a favor; to *solicit* trade:—*v.i.* to seek orders, support, votes, etc.—*n.* **so-lic′i-ta′tion.**

so-lic-i-tor (sō-lĭs′ĭ-tẽr), *n.* **1,** one who seeks trade, votes, etc.; **2,** an attorney or lawyer; **3,** the civil law officer of a city, town, department, or government.

so-lic-it-ous (sō-lĭs′ĭ-tŭs), *adj.* anxious; concerned; also, eager; as, *solicitous* to repay a debt.

so-lic-i-tude (sō-lĭs′ĭ-tūd), *n.* anxiety; worry; as, *solicitude* for another's health. *Syn.* uneasiness, concern, care.

sol-id (sŏl′ĭd), *adj.* **1,** keeping its shape despite pressure; not in the form of a liquid or a gas; **2,** not hollow; as, a *solid* rubber ball; **3,** firm; dependable; as, a *solid* foundation; also, substantial; as, a man of *solid* means; **4,** all of a piece; the same throughout; as, *solid* silver or gold; **5,** unbroken; as, a *solid* line of defense; **6,** *Colloquial,* whole; uninterrupted; as, a *solid* hour:— *n.* **1,** a body whose shape cannot be changed by pressure; a substance not liquid nor gaseous; **2,** in geometry, a body having length, breadth, and thickness; as, a prism is a *solid.*—*n.* **sol′id-ness.** *Syn., adj.* rigid, stable.

sol-i-dar-i-ty (sŏl′ĭ-dăr′ĭ-tĭ), *n.* the condition of being united in opinion, interests, and effort; as, the *solidarity* of a nation.

so-lid-i-fy (sō-lĭd′ĭ-fī), *v.t. and v.i.* [solidified, solidify-ing], to make or become hard or firm.

so-lid-i-ty (sō-lĭd′ĭ-tĭ), *n.* [*pl.* solidities], **1,** the quality of being solid; hardness; firmness; **2,** moral, mental, or financial soundness.

so-lil-o-quize (sō-lĭl′ō-kwīz), *v.i.* [soliloquized, soliloquiz-ing], to talk to oneself; converse with oneself.

so-lil-o-quy (sō-lĭl′ō-kwĭ), *n.* [*pl.* soliloquies], a talk to oneself; especially, a monologue in a play.

sol-i-taire (sŏl′ĭ-târ′), *n.* **1,** a game of cards played by one person; **2,** a gem, especially a diamond, mounted alone.

sol-i-tar-y (sŏl′ĭ-tẽr′ĭ), *adj.* **1,** living by oneself; without companions; as, a *solitary* hermit; **2,** done, passed, or suffered alone; as, *solitary* confinement; **3,** rarely visited; remote; secluded; as, a *solitary* house; a *solitary* inn; **4,** only; single; as, a *solitary* example. *Syn.* deserted, desolate, alone.

sol-i-tude (sŏl′ĭ-tūd), *n.* **1,** the state of being by oneself; loneliness; seclusion; **2,** a remote and lonely place.

so-lo (sō′lō), *n.* [*pl.* solos (sō′lōz) or soli (sō′lē)], **1,** a musical composition, or a part of one, played or sung by a single person; **2,** any performance, as an airplane flight, by one person:—*adj.* done by one person; as, a *solo* flight; also, performing alone; as, a *solo* violinist.—*n.* **so′lo-ist.**

Sol·o·mon (sŏl′ō-mŭn), the son of David and Bathsheba, king of Israel in the tenth century B.C., and famous for his wisdom: **Solomon Islands**, a group of islands in the Pacific Ocean, east of New Guinea (map 16).

Sol·o·mon's—seal (sŏl′ō-mŭnz-sēl′), _n._ a plant of the lily family, with small, drooping, yellowish-green flowers.

So·lon (sō′lŏn; sō′lŭn), (639?–559 B.C.), an Athenian lawgiver. He was regarded as very wise, and we now speak of a wise man as a Solon.

sol·stice (sŏl′stĭs), _n._ either of the two points in the sun's path at which the sun is farthest north or south of the equator. **summer solstice**, June 21 or 22, the longest day in the northern year; **winter solstice**, December 21 or 22, the shortest day in the northern year.

sol·u·ble (sŏl′ū-bl), _adj._ **1**, capable of being dissolved in a fluid, as sugar in water; **2**, capable of being solved or explained.—_n._ **sol′u·bil′i·ty.**

so·lu·tion (sō-lū′shŭn), _n._ **1**, the process of solving, or arriving at the answer to, a problem; an answer; **2**, the process by which a gas, liquid, or solid is dissolved in and mixed with a liquid; also, the liquid which results from such a process; as, an ammonia _solution._

solve (sŏlv), _v.t._ [solved, solv-ing], **1**, to explain; find out; especially, to find the answer to (a problem); **2**, to make clear; as, to _solve_ a mystery.

sol·ven·cy (sŏl′vĕn-sĭ), _n._ the condition of being able to pay all one's debts.

sol·vent (sŏl′vĕnt), _adj._ **1**, capable of dissolving another substance; as, turpentine has a _solvent_ action; **2**, able to pay one's debts:—_n._ any liquid, as water, alcohol, etc., capable of dissolving other substances.

So·ma·li (sō-mä′lē) or **So·mal** (sō-mäl′), _n._ a member of a Mohammedan tribe inhabiting Somaliland.

So·ma·li·land (sō-mä′lē-lănd′), a peninsula of Africa between the Indian Ocean and the Gulf of Aden:—**British Somaliland**, a protectorate (cap. Hargeisa) on the Gulf of Aden; **French Somaliland**, a protectorate (cap. Djibouti) northwest of British Somaliland; **Italian Somaliland**, a former Italian colony (cap. Mogadiscio) on the Indian Ocean now under Italian trusteeship. (Map 14.)

som·ber or **som·bre** (sŏm′bĕr), _adj._ **1**, dull; dark; **2**, dismal; gloomy.

som·bre·ro (sŏm-brĕ′rō), _n._ [_pl._ sombreros], a kind of broad-brimmed hat worn especially in Latin America and southwestern U.S. (See illustration next column.)

some (sŭm), _adj._ **1**, a certain; particular, but not named; as, _some_ boy did it; _some_ other time; there were _some_ men here today; **2**, of an indefinite number, amount, extent, etc.; as, have _some_ potatoes; I have _some_ money:—_pron._ **1**, particular persons not named; as, _some_ came early; **2**, an indefinite number or amount; as, I'll have _some_ of these pencils; _some_ of the cake:—_adv._ **1**, about; nearly; as, _some_ ten men came; **2**, _Colloquial_, somewhat; as, _some_ colder.

-some (-sŭm), a suffix meaning: **1**, naturally disposed to; as, meddle_some_, frolic_some;_ **2**, of such a kind as to; as, tire_some_, weari_some;_ **3**, producing or engaged in; as, bother_some_, venture_some;_ **4**, rather or somewhat; as, blithe_some_, light_some_.

some·bod·y (sŭm′bŏd′ĭ; sŭm′bŭd-ĭ), _pron._ a person unknown or not named:—_n._ [_pl._ somebodies], a person of importance.

some·how (sŭm′hou), _adv._ in one way or another; by some means.

some·one (sŭm′wŭn′), _pron._ a person unknown or not named; somebody.

som·er·sault (sŭm′ĕr-sôlt), _n._ a spring or leap in which one turns heels over head.

som·er·set (sŭm′ĕr-sĕt), _n._ a somersault.

Som·er·ville (sŭm′ĕr-vĭl), a city, a suburb of Boston, in Massachusetts (map 6).

some·thing (sŭm′thĭng), _pron._ **1**, a thing not definitely known, named, decided, or stated; **2**, a thing of unnamed amount or degree; as, one should give _something_ to charity; **3**, a person or thing of importance.

some·time (sŭm′tīm′), _adv._ **1**, at a time not exactly known or not definitely stated; as, _sometime_ in June; **2**, at a time in the future, not yet decided upon:—_adj._ former.

some·times (sŭm′tīmz′), _adv._ once in a while; now and then.

some·what (sŭm′hwŏt′; -hwŏt′), _pron._ **1**, an indefinite amount; **2**, a person or thing to some extent like another; as, he was _somewhat_ of a shirker:—_adv._ to an indefinite degree or extent; rather; as, _somewhat_ tired.

some·where (sŭm′hwâr′), _adv._ **1**, in one place or another; **2**, in, at, or to, a place not named or not known.

som·nam·bu·list (sŏm-năm′bū-lĭst), _n._ a person who walks in his sleep.—_n._ **som·nam′bu·lism.**

som·no·lent (sŏm′nō-lĕnt), _adj._ **1**, sleepy; drowsy; **2**, causing sleepiness.

SOMBRERO

son (sŭn), _n._ **1**, a male child; a boy or man in relation to his parent or parents; **2**, any male descendant; **3**, a native of a particular country; **4,** a person thought of as the product of an age, civilization, or the like; as, a true *son* of the Middle Ages:—**the Son,** Jesus Christ: also called *Son of God.*

so-nar (sō'när), *n.* a device for detecting underwater objects by means of reflected high frequency vibrations.

so-na-ta (sŏ-nä'tä), *n.* a musical composition in three or four movements, usually for the piano.

song (sông), *n.* **1,** a series of rhythmic and tuneful musical sounds uttered vocally, as by a bird; **2,** music produced by the human voice; **3,** poetry; especially, a lyric or ballad which can be set to music; **4,** a musical composition to be sung; **5,** *Colloquial,* a mere trifle; as, he sold it for a *song.*

song-bird (sông'bûrd'), *n.* a singing bird.

Song of Sol-o-mon, in the Bible, one of the poetical books of the Old Testament: also called *Song of Songs.*

song-ster (sông'stẽr), *n.* **1,** a person who sings; also, a singing bird; **2,** one who writes songs or lyric poetry.—*n.fem.* **song'stress.**

son-ic (sŏn'ĭk), *adj.* **1,** of or pertaining to sound; **2,** pertaining to the speed of sound in air (about 738 miles per hour).

son-ic bar-ri-er, the point at which speed in flight becomes greater than that of sound, long thought to be unsurpassable.

son—in—law (sŭn'=ĭn=lô'), *n.* [*pl.* sons-in-law], the husband of one's daughter.

son-net (sŏn'ĕt), *n.* a poem, usually of fourteen lines, arranged in any one of several rime schemes.

so-nor-ous (sŏ-nôr'ŭs), *adj.* **1,** resonant; giving a full or loud sound; as, *sonorous* bells; **2,** having a full, rich sound.

soon (sōōn), *adv.* **1,** in a short time; in the near future; as, it will *soon* be dark; **2,** shortly; quickly; as, he came *soon* afterwards:—**as soon as not,** gladly; willingly.

soot (sŏŏt; sōōt), *n.* the very fine black powder which colors smoke, formed when anything is burned, and which is deposited in chimneys, stovepipes, etc.

sooth (sōōth), *n. Archaic,* truth.

soothe (sōōth), *v.t.* [soothed, sooth-ing], **1,** to make quiet or calm; comfort or console; **2,** to make less severe, as pain.
Syn. assuage, mitigate, pacify.

sooth-say-er (sōōth'sā'ẽr), *n.* one who claims to have the power of foretelling the future; a fortuneteller.—*n.* **sooth'say'ing.**

soot-y (sŏŏt'ĭ; sōō'tĭ), *adj.* [soot-i-er, soot-i-est], **1,** pertaining to, or covered with, soot; **2,** dusky; black.—*n.* **soot'i-ness.**

sop (sŏp), *n.* **1,** anything soaked, dipped or softened in a liquid, as bread in broth; **2,** something given to pacify; as, a *sop* to

injured feelings:—*v.t.* [sopped, sop-ping]' **1,** dip or soak, as crullers in coffee; **2,** mop up, as gravy with bread.—*adj.* **sop'py.**

soph-ist (sŏf'ĭst), *n.* one whose reasoning is clever but unsound.

so-phis-ti-cat-ed (sŏ-fĭs'tĭ-kāt'ĕd), *adj.* wise in the ways of the world.—*n.* **so-phis'ti-ca'tion.**

soph-ist-ry (sŏf'ĭs-trĭ), *n.* [*pl.* sophist-ries], clever but unsound reasoning; also, an argument containing such reasoning.

Soph-o-cles (sŏf'ŏ-klēz), (496?–406 B.C.), a Greek writer of tragedies.

soph-o-more (sŏf'ŏ-môr), *n.* in universities, colleges, and U.S. high schools, a student in the second year of a four-year course.

so-pra-no (sŏ-prä'nō; sŏ-prăn'ō), *n.* [*pl.* sopranos], **1,** the highest singing voice; **2,** a singer with such a voice; **3,** a musical part for such a voice.—*adj.* **so-pra'no.**

sor-cer-er (sôr'sẽr-ẽr), *n.* a magician; con-jurer.—*n.fem.* **sor'cer-ess.**

sor-cer-y (sôr'sẽr-ĭ), *n.* [*pl.* sorceries], witchcraft; magic; enchantment.

sor-did (sôr'dĭd), *adj.* **1,** filthy; squalid; as, *sordid* slums; **2,** vile; base; degraded; as, a *sordid* soul.—*adv.* **sor'did-ly.**

sore (sôr), *adj.* [sor-er, sor-est], **1,** tender or painful to the touch; inflamed; **2,** afflicted; grieved; as, her heart was *sore;* **3,** *Colloquial,* vexed; annoyed; resentful:—*adv.* grievously; severely; deeply:—*n.* **1,** a painful or diseased spot on the body; an ulcer; **2,** a cause of trouble or distress.

sor-ghum (sôr'gŭm), *n.* a canelike grass yielding a sweet juice from which sirup is made; also, the molasses or sirup prepared from the juice.

so-ror-i-ty (sŏ-rŏr'ĭ-tĭ), *n.* [*pl.* sororities], a club or society of girls or women in a school or college.

¹**sor-rel** (sŏr'ĕl), *n.* any of several flowering herbs with sour juice.

²**sor-rel** (sŏr'ĕl), *adj.* reddish brown:—*n.* **1,** a reddish-brown color; **2,** a reddish-brown horse.

sor-row (sŏr'ō), *n.* **1,** mental pain caused by loss, regret, disappointment, or the like; grief; **2,** that which causes grief; trouble:—*v.i.* to feel sorrow; grieve.—*n.* **sor'row-er.**
Syn., n. remorse, affliction, tribulation.

SORREL

sor-row-ful (sŏr'ō-fŏŏl), *adj.* unhappy; sad; as, a *sorrowful* mood; also, expressing sorrow; as, a *sorrowful* smile.—*adv.* **sor'-row-ful-ly.**—*n.* **sor'row-ful-ness.**
Syn. mournful, disconsolate.

---

go; join; yet; sing; chin; show; thin, *th*en; **hw,** *wh*y; **zh,** a*z*ure; **ü,** Ger. f*ü*r or Fr. l*u*ne; **ö,** Ger. sch*ö*n or Fr. f*eu*; **ṅ,** Fr. e*n*fant, no*m*; **kh,** Ger. a*ch* or i*ch.* See pages ix–x.

sor-ry (sŏr′ĭ), *adj.* [sor-ri-er, sor-ri-est], **1,** feeling regret for one's own loss, disappointment, wrongdoing, etc.; **2,** feeling pity or regret for another; **3,** wretched; shabby; as, a *sorry* fellow; also, dismal; miserable; as, a *sorry* plight.

sort (sôrt), *n.* **1,** a kind or species; as, there are many *sorts* of roses; **2,** quality; character; as, material of this *sort* wears longest:—**out of sorts,** ill; out of humor:—*v.t.* to place in different classes, according to kind; as, to *sort* beads by color.

sor-tie (sôr′tē), *n.* **1,** a sudden sally of troops from a defensive position; **2,** in air warfare, a single round trip of one airplane on a military mission.

SOS (ĕs′ō′ĕs′), the international signal call of distress.

so-so (sō′sō′), *Colloquial, adj.* neither very good nor very bad; passable; tolerable:—*adv.* passably. Also, **so′-so′; so so.**

sot (sŏt), *n.* a confirmed drunkard.

sot-tish (sŏt′ĭsh), *adj.* **1,** given to excessive drinking; **2,** like a drunkard.

sou (sōō), *n.* **1,** the name of a former French coin; **2,** the bronze, prewar five-centime piece, the 20th part of a franc.

sou-bri-quet (sōō′brē′kâ′), *n.* a nickname; sobriquet. See **sobriquet.**

souf-flé (sōō′flā′; sōō′flā), *n.* a delicate dish of eggs, milk, and a principal ingredient, such as cheese or fish, made light and fluffy by mixing in the beaten whites of eggs just before baking.

sough (sŭf; sou), *n.* a hollow murmuring or sighing sound, such as is made by the wind blowing gently through trees:—*v.i.* to murmur or sigh, as the wind.

sought (sôt), past tense and past participle of *seek.*

soul (sōl), *n.* **1,** that part of man which is supposed to be the center of his mental and spiritual life, and which by many is believed to survive death; **2,** the part that gives vigor and character; as, the *soul* of art; **3,** a person who leads and inspires; as, the *soul* of the company; **4,** a person; as, not a *soul* was there; **5,** personification; as, the *soul* of honor.

soul-ful (sōl′fŏŏl), *adj.* appealing to the deeper emotions; as, *soulful* music.

soul-less (sōl′lĕs), *adj.* **1,** without a soul; lacking nobility; as, a *soulless* wretch; **2,** spiritless; dull; as, *soulless* verse.—*n.* **soul′less-ness.**

¹**sound** (sound), *adj.* **1,** whole; not hurt; in good condition; as, safe and *sound;* **2,** deep; as, *sound* slumber; **3,** healthy; not decayed; as, a *sound* tooth; **4,** founded on what is believed to be true and right; free from error; as, *sound* doctrine; carefully

thought out; as, a *sound* plan; **5,** conservative; dependable; as, a *sound* businessman; solvent; as, a *sound* business; **6,** legal; valid; as, a *sound* title; **7,** firm; safe; as, a *sound* floor; **8,** thorough; as, a *sound* thrashing:—*adv.* deeply; thoroughly; as, *sound* asleep.—*n.* **sound′ness.**

²**sound** (sound), *n.* **1,** that which is heard; the sensation perceived through the ear; as, the *sound* of a drum; a loud *sound;* **2,** meaning attached to what is heard; as, I don't like the *sound* of what you say; **3,** the distance to which a sound is audible; as, within *sound* of the bell:—*v.t.* **1,** cause to make a sound; as, to *sound* a bell; **2,** cause (a sound) to be heard; utter, play, etc.; as, to *sound* a high note; **3,** examine or test by causing to give forth sound; as, to *sound* the walls of a house; **4,** order or announce by sound; as, to *sound* an alarm:—*v.i.* **1,** make a noise or sound; **2,** be played upon, as an instrument; make music; **3,** give a certain impression when heard; as, her voice *sounds* sad.

³**sound** (sound), *v.t.* **1,** to measure the depth of (water, etc.), as by lowering a weighted line from the surface; to fathom; **2,** to examine indirectly; try to find out the opinions or attitude of: often with *out;* as, to *sound* out the members:—*v.i.* **1,** to measure the depth of water; **2,** to dive deeply, as do whales.—*n.* **sound′er.**

⁴**sound** (sound), *n.* **1,** a long stretch of water, wider than a strait, connecting two large bodies of water, or lying between the mainland and an island; as, Long Island *Sound;* **2,** the air bladder of a fish.

sound-ing (soun′dĭng), *n.* **1,** the act of measuring the depth of water, especially by letting down a weighted line from the surface, or, more recently, by the use of sonar; **2,** the result or measurement thus obtained; **3, soundings,** a place where the water is shallow enough to permit depth measurements to be taken by a hand line.

sound-less (sound′lĕs), *adj.* silent.

sound-ly (sound′lĭ), *adv.* **1,** thoroughly; as, *soundly* thrashed; **2,** deeply; as, he sleeps *soundly;* **3,** well and wisely; as, *soundly* reasoned.

sound track, the part of a motion picture film on which sound is recorded.

soup (sōōp), *n.* liquid food, or broth, made by simmering meat or vegetables, or both together, in a large quantity of liquid.

sour (sour), *adj.* **1,** having a sharp, biting taste, as vinegar or green fruit; **2,** acid, especially as a result of fermentation; as, *sour* cream; **3,** disagreeable; cross; as, a *sour* disposition:—*v.t.* **1,** cause to become acid or fermented; **2** cause to become cross and disagreeable:—*v.i.* become acid or fermented.

āte, āorta, râre, căt, ȧsk, fär, ăllow, sofȧ; ēve, ĕvent, ĕll, writẽr, novĕl; bīte, pĭn; nō, ōbey, ôr, dŏg, tŏp, cŏllide; ūnit, ūnite, bûrn, cŭt, focŭs; nōōn, fŏŏt; mound; coin;

source (sôrs), *n.* **1,** a spring or fountain; the beginning of a stream; **2,** that from which anything rises or originates; as, books are a *source* of information.

Sou-sa (sōō′sȧ), John Philip (1854–1932), called the *March King*, an American bandmaster and composer.

souse (sous), *v.t.* [soused, sous-ing], **1,** to steep or soak in brine or vinegar; to pickle; **2,** to dip or plunge into any liquid; as, to *souse* linen in soapsuds; **3,** to pour or dash; as, to *souse* water on a fire:—*n.* **1,** something soaked or preserved in pickle, as pigs' feet or fish; **2,** the pickling fluid; **3,** the process of pickling.

south (south), *n.* **1,** one of the four points of the compass; the point opposite to the north, or to the right of a person facing the sunrise; **2,** the section of a country lying to the south; as, the *south* of France:—*adj.* having to do with, or coming from, the south; as, a *south* wind:—*adv.* to the south; as, turn *south*.
    South, that part of the U.S. lying generally south of the Ohio River and the southern boundary of Pennsylvania; **South Pole,** the southern end of the earth's axis.

South Af-ri-ca, Un-ion of, a British self-governing dominion (caps. Pretoria and Capetown), composed of the provinces of Cape of Good Hope, Natal, Orange Free State, and Transvaal (map 14).

South A-mer-i-ca, the southern continent of the Western Hemisphere (map 11).

South-amp-ton (south-ămp′tŭn), a seaport in the south of England (map 13).

South Aus-tral-ia (ôs-trāl′yȧ; ôs-trā′lĭ-ȧ), a state (cap. Adelaide) of the Commonwealth of Australia (map 16).

South Bend, a city in Indiana (map 7).

South Car-o-li-na (kăr′ō-lī′nȧ), a southern State (cap. Columbia) of the U.S. (map 8).

South Chi-na Sea, a sea south of China, between Indo-China and the Philippine Islands (map 15).

South Da-ko-ta (dȧ-kō′tȧ), a north central State (cap. Pierre) in the U.S. (map 7).

south-east (south′ēst′), *n.* **1,** the point of the compass halfway between south and east; **2,** a region lying in the direction of that point:—*adj.* having to do with the southeast, or in or from the southeast; as, a *southeast* wind:—*adv.* toward the southeast.—*adj., adv.,* and *n.* **south′east′ward.**

south-east-er (south′ēs′tẽr), *n.* a storm or gale coming from the southeast.

south-east-er-ly (south′ēs′tẽr-lĭ), *adj.* and *adv.* from or toward the southeast.

south-east-ern (south′ēs′tẽrn), *adj.* of, from, or situated in, the southeast.

south-er-ly (sŭth′ẽr-lĭ), *adj.* pertaining to, situated in, or coming from, the south:—*adv.* toward the south.

south-ern (sŭth′ẽrn), *adj.* in, from, or toward, the south:—**Southern,** pertaining to the South, or the southern United States.—*adj.* **south′ern-most.**

south-ern-er (sŭth′ẽr-nẽr), *n.* a person living in, or coming from, the south:—**Southerner,** a person living in, or coming from, the part of the United States south of the Ohio River and Pennsylvania.

South-ern Rho-de-si-a (rō-dē′zhĭ-ȧ), a British South African colony. See **Rhodesia.**

South Is-land, the larger of the two chief islands of New Zealand (map 16).

South Sea Is-lands, the islands in the South Pacific Ocean.

south-ward (south′wẽrd), *adj.* and *adv.* to or toward the south; leading to the south. Also, *adv.* **south′wards** (south′wẽrdz).

south-west (south′wĕst′), *n.* **1,** the point of the compass halfway between south and west; **2,** a region lying in the direction of that point:—*adj.* having to do with the southwest, or in or from the southwest; as, a *southwest* wind:—*adv.* toward the southwest.—*adj., adv.,* and *n.* **south′west′ward.**

South—West Af-ri-ca, a territory, formerly German (cap. Windhoek) in southwest Africa, now managed by the Union of South Africa (map 14).

south-west-er (south′wĕs′tẽr), *n.* a strong wind or storm from the southwest.

south-west-er-ly (south′wĕs′tẽr-lĭ), *adj.* and *adv.* from or toward the southwest.

south-west-ern (south′wĕs′tẽrn), *adj.* of, from, or situated in, the southwest.

sou-ve-nir (sōō′vĕ-nēr′; sōō′vĕ-nēr), *n.* a thing by which to remember a person or an event; a memento or keepsake.

sou'-west-er (sou′wĕs′- tẽr), *n.* **1,** a southwester; **2,** a painted canvas or oilskin hat with a brim that is wide at the back, worn in stormy weather by sailors and fishermen.

SOU'WESTER
def. 2

sov-er-eign (sŏv′ẽr-ĭn; sŏv′rĭn; sŭv′ẽr-ĭn; sŭv′rĭn), *adj.* **1,** chief; supreme; as, *sovereign* power; **2,** possessing absolute and independent power; as, a *sovereign* state; **3,** principal; greatest; also, best and most effective; as, a *sovereign* remedy:—*n.* **1,** a ruler, as a king, emperor, or queen; **2,** a British gold coin equal to twenty shillings.

---

go; join; yet; sing; chin; show; thin, *th*en; hw, *wh*y; zh, a*z*ure; ü, Ger. f*ür* or Fr. l*u*ne; ö, Ger. schön or Fr. f*eu*; ṅ, Fr. e*n*fant, no*m*; kh, Ger. a*ch* or i*ch*. See pages ix–x.

sov·er·eign·ty(sŏv/ĕr-ĭn-tĭ;sŏv/rĭn-tĭ;sŭv/-ĕr-ĭn-tĭ; sŭv/rĭn-tĭ), *n.* [*pl.* sovereignties], supreme power or dominion, whether vested in a monarch, or in the people.

so·vi·et (sō/vĭ-ĕt/; sō/vĭ-ĕt), *n.* **1,** a council; **2,** (usually *Soviet*), one of the local councils or governing bodies of the Union of Soviet Socialist Republics, which are elected by the people, and which send delegates to the higher congresses.—*n.* **so/vi-et/ism.**

So·vi·et Rus·sia, the Russian Soviet Federated Socialist Republic, the largest republic in the U.S.S.R. See **Russia.**

¹sow (sou), *n.* a female hog.

²sow (sō), *v.t.* [*p.t.* sowed (sōd), *p.p.* sown (sōn) or sowed, *p.pr.* sow-ing], **1,** to strew, as seed, upon the earth; **2,** to strew seed in, on, or over; as, to *sow* a lawn; **3,** to cause to grow or spread; as, to *sow* discord:—*v.i.* to strew seed for growing.

soy (soi), *n.* **1,** an oriental sauce made from fermented soybeans:—also called **soya; 2,** the soybean plant.

soy·bean (soi/bēn), *n.* **1,** an Asiatic plant of the legume family, valuable as a rotation crop. It is used for food and fodder, and in the making of many plastics and oil products; **2,** the seed or bean of this plant.

Sp. abbreviation for *Spain, Spaniard, Spanish.*

spa (spä), *n.* **1,** a mineral spring; **2,** a resort or locality where there are mineral springs.

space (spās), *n.* **1,** the boundless expanse in which our universe moves, and all known things exist; **2,** all that lies beyond the earth's atmosphere; **3,** a definite, or limited, distance or area; room; as, the *space* between the desk and the wall; **4,** length of time; as, in the *space* of a few months; **5,** in music, one of the open places between the lines of the staff; **6,** in typewritten or printed matter, one of the open spaces separating letters or words:—*v.t.* [spaced, spac-ing], to arrange, as letters or words, by separating them with spaces.—*adj.* **spa/tial** or **spa/cial.**

space·ship (spās/shĭp), *n.* a fictional craft, usually rocket-powered, for travel in outer space.

SPADE def. 1

spa·cious (spā/shŭs), *adj.* **1,** capacious; roomy; as, a *spacious* house; **2,** extensive; as, a *spacious* domain.

   Syn. large, vast, expansive.

spade (spād), *n.* **1,** a digging tool, consisting of a broad, flat blade of iron with a long handle; **2,** one of a suit, called *spades*, of playing cards, marked with a black figure like a pointed spade:—*v.t.* [spad-ed, spad-ing], to dig or work (ground) with a spade; as, to *spade* a garden.

spa·dix (spā/dĭks), *n.* [*pl.* spadices (spā-dī/sēz)], a spikelike flower head on a fleshy axis, often enclosed in a spathe, or leaflike envelope, as in the jack-in-the-pulpit. (See cut-out in illustration at *spathe.*)

spa·ghet·ti (spȧ-gĕt/ĭ), *n.* a flour product like macaroni, except that each piece is solid, and smaller in circumference.

Spain (spān), a country (cap. Madrid) in southwestern Europe (map **12**). It is officially a monarchy.

spake (spāk), an old form of the past tense of *speak.*

span (spǎn), *n.* **1,** the distance from the end of the thumb to the tip of the little finger when the thumb and fingers are extended wide open; also, regarded as a measure of length, nine inches; **2,** a short space of time; **3,** any extent having two definite bounds; as, the *span* of a river; **4,** the distance between the supports of an arch, a beam, etc.; also, the section of an arch, beam, etc., between two supports; **5,** a pair of horses, harnessed as a team:—*v.t.* [spanned, spanning], **1,** to measure by the extended thumb and fingers; **2,** to extend across; as, a plank *spanned* the gully.

span·gle (spǎng/gl), *n.* **1,** one of the tiny, shining, metallic disks used to ornament dresses; **2,** any small, glittering ornament:—*v.t.* [span-gled, span-gling], to adorn with bits of shining material.

Span·iard (spǎn/yẽrd), *n.* a native or citizen of Spain.

span·iel (spǎn/yĕl), *n.* any of various small or medium-sized dogs with drooping ears and long, silky hair.

COCKER SPANIEL (⅛)

Span·ish (spǎn/ĭsh), *adj.* pertaining to Spain, its language, or its people:—*n.* the people of Spain; also, their language.

Span·ish A·mer·i·ca, those countries of America in which Spanish is the national language, including Mexico, Cuba, Puerto Rico, the Dominican Republic, all of Central America except British Honduras, and all of South America except Brazil and the Guianas (maps **10, 11**).

Span·ish Guin·ea (gĭn/ĭ), a colony in western Africa. See **Guinea.**

Spanish Main, the mainland of South America bordering the Caribbean Sea; also, in careless use, the Caribbean Sea itself.

spank (spǎngk), *v.t.* to strike; punish by striking the buttocks with the open hand, a slipper, or the like:—*n.* a slap.

spank·er (spǎngk/ẽr), *n.* a fore-and-aft sail attached to the mast nearest the stern of a square-rigged vessel.

āte, âorta, râre, căt, ȧsk, fär, ȧllow, sofȧ; ēve, ĕvent, ĕll, writẽr, novĕl; bīte, pĭn; nō, ōbey, ôr, dŏg, tŏp, cŏllide; ūnit, ūnite, bûrn, cŭt, focŭs; nōōn, fŏŏt; mound; coin;

spank-ing (spăngk′ĭng), *adj.* **1** moving with a quick, lively step, as horses; **2**, fresh; brisk; as, a *spanking* breeze.

¹**spar** (spär), *n.* a crystalline mineral, which can be broken up into smooth layers, and has a shiny luster.

²**spar** (spär), *n.* a mast, yard, boom, etc., on a vessel:—*v.t.* [sparred, spar-ring], to fit with spars.

³**spar** (spär), *v.i.* [sparred, spar-ring], **1**, to fight with the fists; to box; especially, to box skilfully or scientifically; **2**, to engage in a contest of words; wrangle.

spare (spâr), *v.t.* [spared, spar-ing], **1**, to use in a frugal or saving manner; use rarely; as, *spare* the rod; **2**, to do without conveniently; as, can you *spare* this book? **3**, to refrain from; omit; as, I shall *spare* no expense; **4**, to save (a person) from something; as, this will *spare* me trouble; **5**, to avoid injuring; treat carefully; as, to *spare* a person's feelings:—*adj.* [spar-er, spar-est], **1**, thin; lean; **2**, held in reserve; as, a *spare* tire; also, extra; as, *spare* cash: —*n.* **1**, a spare part; especially, a spare tire; **2**, in bowling, the knocking over of all the pins in two attempts; also, the score for this.

Syn., *adj.* gaunt, lank, meager.

spare-rib (spâr′rĭb′), *n.* a cut of pork, consisting of the ends of a set of ribs with what little meat is attached to them.

spar-ing (spâr′ĭng), *adj.* **1**, frugal; as, a *sparing* housewife; **2**, limited; as, a *sparing* use of salt.—*adv.* **spar′ing-ly.**—*n.* **spar′ing-ness.**

¹**spark** (spärk), *n.* **1**, a tiny, burning particle thrown off by a body that is on fire; **2**, any bright, small flash; **3**, hence, any sudden flash; as, a *spark* of genius; **4**, a small sign or particle; as, not a *spark* of life remained; **5**, the flash of light produced by a discharge of electricity between two conductors; **6**, the discharge of electricity in a spark plug; also, the mechanism controlling this discharge:—*v.i.* **1**, to send out sparks; **2**, to produce an electric spark.

²**spark** (spärk), *n.* a gay, dashing, young fellow; a beau; gallant:—*v.i.* and *v.t. Colloquial*, to play the gallant; court.

spar-kle (spär′kl), *v.i.* [spar-kled, spar-kling], **1**, to give off light in small flashes; glisten; gleam; **2**, to flash; scintillate, as wit; **3**, to bubble, as wine:—*n.* a gleam or glitter, as of gems; also, a flash, as of wit.—*n.* **spar′kler.**

spark plug, a device used in many engines, such as the engine of an automobile, for igniting a mixture of air and gasoline vapor by means of an electric spark.

SPARK PLUG

spar-row (spăr′ō), *n.* a common bird of the finch family, small, not brightly colored, found in most parts of the world.

sparrow hawk, a small North American falcon which feeds on small insects, especially grasshoppers, and sometimes on small birds.

SPARROW (⅓)

sparse (spärs), *adj.* [spars-er, spars-est], thinly scattered; scant and thinly distributed; as, *sparse* vegetation.—*adv.* **sparse′ly.**—*n.* **sparse′ness.**

Spar-ta (spär′tȧ), an ancient city of southern Greece (map 1).

Spar-tan (spär′tăn), *adj.* **1**, pertaining to Sparta in ancient Greece, whose people were noted for their bravery and obedience to stern military discipline; **2**, hence, unwavering in courage and endurance:—*n.* **1**, formerly, a citizen of Sparta; **2**, a person who faces hardships without flinching.

spasm (spăzm), *n.* **1**, a sudden, violent, involuntary contraction, or shortening, of the muscles; **2**, a sudden, violent, but brief, movement, emotion, or the like.

spas-mod-ic (spăz-mŏd′ĭk), *adj.* **1**, accompanied by spasms; convulsive; as, a *spasmodic* cough; **2**, violent but short-lived; in fits and starts; as, *spasmodic* efforts.

Syn. fitful, jerky, intermittent, convulsive, unstable, impulsive.

spas-tic (spăs′tĭk), *adj.* pertaining to a spasm, especially a long-continued spasm.

¹**spat** (spăt), *n.* the eggs or spawn of shellfish, especially oysters; also, young oysters:—*v.i.* [spat-ted, spat-ting], to spawn: said of oysters.

²**spat** (spăt), *Colloquial*, *n.* **1**, a slight blow with the open hand; a slap; **2**, a spatter, as of rain; **3**, a petty quarrel:—*v.i.* [spat-ted, spat-ting], to engage in a petty quarrel:—*v.t.* to slap.

SPATS, def. 3

³**spat** (spăt), *n.* a kind of short cloth gaiter, fastened under the instep.

⁴**spat** (spăt), one form of the past tense and of the past participle of *spit*.

spathe (spāth), *n.* a leaflike envelope enclosing a spadix, and growing from the same stem, as in the jack-in-the-pulpit.

SPATHE

---

go; join; yet; sing; chin; show; thin, *th*en; hw, *wh*y; zh, azure; ü, Ger. für or Fr. lune; ö, Ger. schön or Fr. feu; ṅ, Fr. enfant, nom; kh, Ger. ach or ich. See pages ix–x.

spa-tial (spā′shăl), *adj.* pertaining to distance or area. Also, **spa′cial.**—*adv.* **spa′-tial-ly.**

spat-ter (spăt′ẽr), *v.t.* **1,** to splash a liquid upon; soil by splashing; as, to *spatter* the tablecloth with grease; **2,** to scatter in drops or by splashing; as, to *spatter* milk over the floor; **3,** to cover, as with splashes; as, a field *spattered* with flowers:—*v.i.* to splash in drops:—*n.* **1,** a splashing or sprinkling; **2,** a spot so made; **3,** a pattering, as of rain.

SPATULAS

spat-u-la (spăt′ū-lȧ), *n.* an instrument with a flat, flexible, dull-edged blade, used for mixing or spreading paints, etc.

spav-in (spăv′ĭn), *n.* a disease of horses, causing lameness by a deposit of bony matter in the hock.—*adj.* **spav′ined.**

spawn (spôn), *n.* **1,** the eggs of fish, oysters, and other water animals which lay great numbers of small eggs; **2,** offspring:—*v.t.* and *v.i.* **1,** to lay or produce (eggs or spawn); **2,** to produce (offspring) in great numbers.

S.P.C.A. abbreviation for *Society for the Prevention of Cruelty to Animals.*

S.P.C.C. abbreviation for *Society for the Prevention of Cruelty to Children.*

speak (spēk), *v.i.* [*p.t.* spoke (spōk) or, *Archaic,* spake (spāk), *p.p.* spo-ken (spō′-kěn), *p.pr.* speak-ing], **1,** to utter words; talk; **2,** to tell; mention; as, do not *speak* of this; **3,** to make an address or speech; **4,** to sound, as a gun; **5,** to convey ideas, though not in words; as, our actions *speak* for us:—*v.t.* **1,** to utter, as a word; pronounce; **2,** to express in words; as, to *speak* the truth; **3,** to use, or be able to use, in conversation; as, he *speaks* four languages; **4,** to address or hail, as a ship.

speak-er (spē′kẽr), *n.* **1,** a person who speaks, especially in public; **2,** the presiding officer of a meeting or assembly.

speak-ing (spē′kĭng), *adj.* **1,** having the power of speech; **2,** eloquent; expressive; as, a *speaking* countenance; **3,** vivid; lifelike; as, a *speaking* likeness.

spear (spēr), *n.* **1,** a weapon with a long shaft and sharp, pointed head; to be thrust or thrown; a lance; **2,** an instrument with barbed prongs for catching fish; **3,** a slender blade or shoot; as, a *spear* of grass:—*v.t.* to pierce or kill with a spear.—*n.* **spear′man.**

SPEAR, def: 1
Hunting spear, 16th century.

spear-mint (spēr′mĭnt′), *n.* a common mint resembling peppermint, used as flavoring.

spe-cial (spěsh′ăl), *adj.* **1,** characterizing a single person or thing, or a single class; as, the *special* qualities of a leader; **2,** designed for a particular purpose; as, a *special* course of study; **3,** particular; unusual; as, a *special* favor; a *special* point of interest; **4,** esteemed beyond others; intimate; as, a *special* companion.—*adv.* **spe′cial-ly.**

spe-cial-ist (spěsh′ăl-ĭst), *n.* a person who limits himself to one particular field of work or study; as, an eye *specialist.*

spe-cial-ize (spěsh′ăl-īz), *v.i.* [specialized, specializ-ing], to pursue a particular line of action or course of study; as, to *specialize* in science:—*v.t.* to modify or adapt for a particular purpose or use.

spe-cial-ty (spěsh′ăl-tĭ), *n.* [*pl.* specialties], **1,** a line of study or work to which a person especially devotes himself; as, his *specialty* is music; **2,** an article dealt in particularly or exclusively; as, the *specialty* of the store was fruit; **3,** a mark or feature particularly characteristic of a person or thing.

spe-cie (spē′shĭ), *n.* gold or silver coin, as distinguished from paper money.

spe-cies (spē′shĭz; spē′shēz), *n.* [*pl.* species], **1,** a kind; variety; **2,** a group of animals or plants differing from one another in unimportant respects, and having certain common characteristics which clearly distinguish the group from other groups.

spe-cif-ic (spē-sĭf′ĭk), *adj.* **1,** pertaining to a species; as, a *specific* name; **2,** definite or particular; precise; as, *specific* information; **3,** having some particular curing or healing quality; as, a *specific* medicine:—*n.* anything that is suited to a particular use or purpose; especially, a remedy for a certain disease.

spe-cif-i-cal-ly (spē-sĭf′ĭ-kăl-ĭ), *adv.* **1,** with respect to one particular point; **2,** definitely; in particular.

spec-i-fi-ca-tion (spěs′ĭ-fĭ-kā′shŭn), *n.* **1,** the act of stating or specifying in detail; **2, specifications,** the items of a detailed statement of requirements for carrying out some work or project; also, the statement; as, the *specifications* for a building.

spe-cif-ic grav-i-ty (spē-sĭf′ĭk grăv′-ĭ-tĭ), the weight of a substance expressed in relation to the weight of water or air. The specific gravity of iron is about 8; that is, iron is 8 times as heavy as water.

spec-i-fy (spěs′ĭ-fī), *v.t.* [specified; specifying], to mention or name particularly; state fully and clearly.

āte, âorta, rāre, căt, ȧsk, fär, ȧllow, sofȧ; ēve, ĕvent, ĕll, writẽr, nŏvĕl; bīte, pĭn; nō, ōbey, ôr, dŏg, tŏp, cŏllide; ūnit, ūnite, bûrn, cŭt, focŭs; nōōn, fŏŏt; mound; coin;

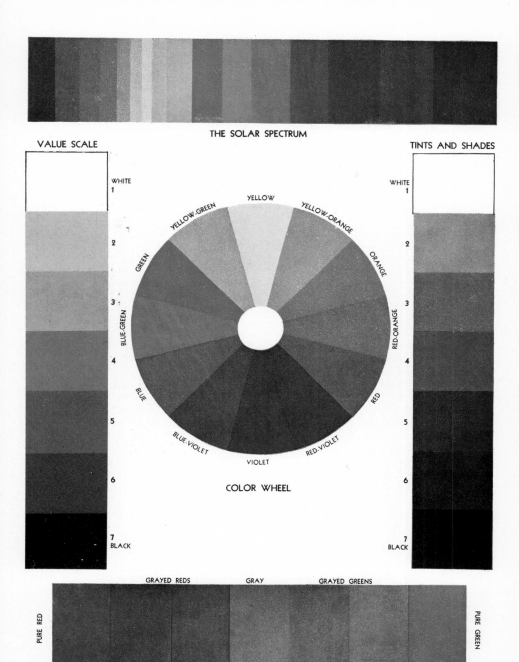

THE SOLAR SPECTRUM

VALUE SCALE

TINTS AND SHADES

WHITE
1

WHITE
1

2

2

3

3

4

4

5

5

6

6

7
BLACK

7
BLACK

YELLOW
YELLOW-GREEN
YELLOW-ORANGE
GREEN
ORANGE
BLUE-GREEN
RED-ORANGE
BLUE
RED
BLUE-VIOLET
RED-VIOLET
VIOLET

COLOR WHEEL

GRAYED REDS
GRAY
GRAYED GREENS

PURE RED
PURE GREEN

GRAYED COLOR

Solar Spectrum and Color Charts. (*See other side.*)

COLOR AND ITS QUALITIES

We usually think of daylight as being without color, or nearly so, but long ago it was found that seemingly white or colorless light is made up of all the colors of the rainbow, so blended, or mixed, that no color predominates.

The simplest way to prove that this is true, is to hold a glass prism in a beam of light and study the band of color that falls upon a screen or on a wall beyond. This band of color is called a *spectrum*. It contains all the colors of the rainbow, separated out of the beam of light by passing through the prism.

At the top of the previous page, you will see a band of these spectrum colors. It progresses gradually, like the colors of the rainbow, from violet to indigo, to blue, to green, to yellow, to orange, until finally at the opposite end, it stops with red.

If you were to bend this band of colors into a circle, and join the two ends by a rectangle of red-violet, you would obtain a continuous arrangement of colors very similar to that of the color wheel shown at the center of the page, except that in the color wheel a smaller number of colors is shown, and the steps between them are more regular.

In the color wheel, the three colors that we call primaries, namely yellow, blue, and red, have been placed at equal intervals, that is, yellow is the same distance from blue that blue is from red, and red from yellow. In between the primary colors, also at equal intervals, are placed the secondary colors, orange between yellow and red, violet between red and blue, and green between blue and yellow. Finally, between each primary and the nearest secondary, and between that and the next primary, and so on around the wheel, are placed the intermediate colors yellow-orange, red-orange, red-violet, blue-violet, blue-green, and yellow-green.

Every spot of color that you may see, whether it is in a painting, or a dress, or a flower, or the sky, has three qualities, or attributes, by which it may be distinguished from other spots of color. The first of these, well illustrated in the color wheel, is *hue*. Hue is the quality by which we distinguish a color as red, or blue, or green, and so on, and by which all of these colors differ from neutral gray.

The second quality of color is *value*, or *brilliance*. It is lightness or darkness, irrespective of hue. Two spots of color may be of exactly the same hue, say red, but one may approach white in lightness, as in the case of pink, while the other may approach black in darkness, as in the case of maroon.

A spot of color may have value, or brilliance, but no hue at all, in which case we call it white, or black, or neutral gray; but every spot of color which has a hue, also has a value, or degree of lightness and darkness. A light hue, as pink, is often called a *tint*, a dark hue, as maroon, is often called a *shade*.

The eye can distinguish many degrees of lightness and darkness. In the value scale on the previous page, white is placed at the top, black at the bottom. In between are placed five degrees of neutral gray, which gradually become darker and darker as you pass from white to black. In this scale there is no hue of any kind.

On the opposite side of the page, you will find a scale which shows both hue and value. Both scales start with white and end with black, and in between white and black both scales have the same number of intermediate values, but in the righthand scale these values are tints and shades of a single hue, namely red. A similar scale could be made for any hue in the color wheel.

Besides hue and value, there is a third quality, or attribute, of color which has been called *purity*, or *intensity*, or *saturation*. This quality is illustrated in the chart at the bottom of the preceding page. Two spots of color may be of the same hue and the same value, but one may be strong or vivid, the other lacking in life or distinctness of hue, in which case we are apt to say that the color is *grayed*. Grayed color can be produced by mixing with it more or less of its complementary color. Thus if we take our purest red and gradually add green to it, we can produce a succession of reds that are less and less pure or intense until finally we have nothing left but neutral gray. Similarly, we can start with green and by adding red, produce less and less intense greens until, again, we arrive at neutral gray.

spec-i-men (spĕs′ĭ-mĕn), *n.* **1,** a part which represents, or shows the quality of, the whole; as, a *specimen* of ore; **2,** one of a group from which the characteristics of the entire group may be studied; as, an insect *specimen*.

Syn. example, instance, sample.

spe-cious (spē′shŭs), *adj.* at first sight appearing to be honest, just, or fair, but not really so; as, a *specious* argument.

speck (spĕk), *n.* **1,** a spot or flaw; blemish; as, a *speck* of decay in fruit; **2,** a very small thing; particle; as, a *speck* of dust:—*v.t.* to spot, or stain with small spots; speckle.

speck-le (spĕk′l), *n.* a small spot in or on something:—*v.t.* [speck-led, speck-ling], to mark with speckles.

spec-ta-cle (spĕk′tȧ-kl), *n.* **1,** something displayed to view, especially something unusual or worthy of notice; a public exhibition; pageant; **2, spectacles,** a pair of lenses for assisting or correcting vision, set in a frame, with a bridge to fit over the nose and bows to pass over the ears.

SPECTACLES

spec-tac-u-lar (spĕk-tăk′ū-lẽr), *adj.* of the nature of a public show, or spectacle; making, or like, a great display; designed to excite wonder; imposing.

spec-ta-tor (spĕk-tā′tẽr; spĕk′tā-tẽr), *n.* one who looks on, as at a theater or parade; an observer.

spec-ter or **spec-tre** (spĕk′tẽr), *n.* a ghost.

spec-tral (spĕk′trăl), *adj.* **1,** pertaining to, or like, a ghost; ghostly; as, a *spectral* light; **2,** pertaining to a spectrum; as, *spectral* analysis.—*adv.* **spec′tral-ly.**

spec-tro-scope (spĕk′trō-skōp), *n.* an instrument for breaking up light into the rays of which it is composed, and for examining the image, or spectrum, so produced.

spec-trum (spĕk′trŭm), *n.* [*pl.* spectra (spĕk′trȧ) or spectrums], the image formed when light is broken up into its constituent parts and these are arranged according to their different wave lengths, as in the rainbow or when light passes through a prism.

spec-u-late (spĕk′ū-lāt), *v.i.* [speculat-ed, speculat-ing], **1,** to meditate; consider a subject from every side before forming an opinion; **2,** to buy or sell, with the idea of profiting by a rise or fall in prices.

spec-u-la-tion (spĕk′ū-lā′shŭn), *n.* **1,** meditation or theorizing on a subject; also, the result of this; a conjecture; guess; as, science requires that *speculations* be supported by proof; **2,** the buying or selling of shares of stock, goods, etc., with the idea of profiting by a rise or fall in prices.

spec-u-la-tive (spĕk′ū-lā′tĭv), *adj.* **1,** given to theorizing; also, thoughtful; reflective; as, a *speculative* turn of mind; **2,** pertaining to financial or commercial transactions, in which the high risk of loss is offset by the hope of large profits; as, a *speculative* venture.—*adv.* **spec′u-la′tive-ly.**

spec-u-la-tor (spĕk′ū-lā′tẽr), *n.* **1,** a person who engages in financial or commercial ventures in which the high risk of loss is offset by the hope of large profit; **2,** a person who meditates or theorizes.

sped (spĕd), past tense and past participle of *speed*.

speech (spēch), *n.* **1,** the power of uttering sounds or words that are understandable; **2,** the expression of thought in words; the act of speaking; **3,** manner of speaking; as, his *speech* is indistinct; **4,** that which is spoken; words; remarks; **5,** a language or dialect; as, Italian is a musical *speech;* **6,** a formal talk, delivered in public.—*adj.* **speech′less.**

Syn. oration, harangue, sermon.

speed (spēd), *n.* **1,** swiftness of motion; **2,** rate of motion; **3,** *Archaic,* good fortune; success; as, he wished her all *speed:*—*v.t.* [sped (spĕd) or speed-ed, speed-ing], **1,** to bid farewell to; as, to *speed* the parting guest; **2,** to favor; to aid; as, may God *speed* you; **3,** to cause to move faster; as, to *speed* an engine; he *sped* the job to completion:—*v.i.* **1,** to move quickly; as, the car *sped* toward him; **2,** [speed-ed, speed-ing], to move at too great speed.—*n.* **speed′er.**

speed-om-e-ter (spēd-ŏm′ē-tẽr), *n.* an instrument for indicating speed. The speedometer on an automobile shows the rate of motion in miles per hour at which the car goes, and the total number of miles gone.

speed-way (spēd′wā′), *n.* a course or track made for fast driving or racing.

speed-well (spēd′wĕl), *n.* an herb which bears small blue, white, pink, or purple flowers.

speed-y (spē′dĭ), *adj.* [speed-i-er, speed-i-est], swift; prompt.—*adv.* **speed′i-ly.**

Syn. fast, rapid.

¹spell (spĕl), *n.* **1,** a spoken word, or words, supposed to act as a charm; **2,** hence, fascination.

²spell (spĕl), *v.i.* [spelled (spĕld) or spelt (spĕlt), spell-ing], to form words with letters:—*v.t.* **1,** to give, in order, the proper letters of (a word); **2,** to make out or decipher with difficulty; as, to *spell* out an inscription; **3,** to make up or form; as, the letters d, o, g, *spell* "dog"; **4,** to indicate or mean; as, war *spells* hardship.

³spell (spĕl), *n.* **1,** a turn at work to relieve another; as, a *spell* at the oars; **2,**

any short period of time; as, a hot *spell;*
3, *Colloquial,* a short attack of illness; as,
a dizzy *spell:—v.t.* [spelled, spell-ing], to
take the place of, or do a turn of work for;
as, let me *spell* you at the oars.

spell-bind (spĕl′bīnd′), *v.t.* [spellbound
(-bound′), spellbind-ing], to hold as by a
spell; fascinate.—*n.* **spell′bind′er.**

spell-bound (spĕl′bound′), *adj.* fasci-
nated; enchanted.

spell-er (spĕl′ẽr), *n.* **1,** one who spells, especially one who spells in a particular
way; as, a good *speller;* a poor *speller;* **2,**
a book with exercises for teaching pupils
how to spell; a spelling book.

spell-ing (spĕl′ĭng), *n.* **1,** the act of forming words with letters; **2,** the way in which
any particular word is spelled.

¹**spelt** (spĕlt), one form of the past tense
and past participle of ²*spell.*

²**spelt** (spĕlt), *n.* a kind of wheat cultivated in ancient times, and still raised to
some extent in Germany and Switzerland.

spend (spĕnd), *v.t.* [spent (spĕnt), spend-
ing], **1,** to pay out, as money; expend or
use up, as strength or energy; **2,** to squan-
der; exhaust; **3,** to pass (time); as, I *spent*
an hour shopping.

spend-thrift (spĕnd′thrĭft′), *adj.* wasteful; extravagant:—*n.* a person who spends
money foolishly or wastefully.

spent (spĕnt), past tense and past participle of *spend:—adj.* exhausted; worn out;
without energy or force.

sperm (spûrm), *n.* the fertilizing fluid
of male animals; also, one of the many
living germ cells which it contains.

sper-ma-ce-ti (spûr′må-sē′tĭ; spûr′må-
sĕt′ĭ), *n.* a white, waxy substance obtained from a large cavity in the head of
the sperm whale. It is used in making
ointments and candles.

sperm oil, a yellowish oil obtained from
the sperm whale, especially from a large
cavity in the head.

sperm whale, a large whale found in
w a r m
seas, val-
ued for
the sperm
oil and
for a wax-
like sub-

SPERM WHALE (₁₀₀)

stance, spermaceti, both obtained from a
large cavity in the head.

spew (spū), *v.t.* and *v.i.* **1,** to vomit; **2,** to
cast forth; eject.

sp. gr. abbreviation for *specific gravity.*

sphere (sfēr), *n.* **1,** a round, solid body,
with a continuous surface every point of

which is equally distant from the point
within called its center; **2,** a globe or
globelike body; a ball; also, a planet; **3,**
extent or range of knowl-
edge, influence, action, etc.;
as, to seek a wider *sphere* for
one's abilities.

spher-i-cal (sfĕr′ĭ-kăl), *adj.*
round, like a sphere or
globe.

SPHERE

sphe-roid (sfē′roid), *n.* a
body that is nearly a sphere in shape; as,
the earth is a *spheroid* flattened at the
poles.—*adj.* **sphe-roi′dal.**

sphinx (sfĭngks), *n.* [*pl.* sphinxes (sfĭngk′-
sĕz)], **1,** in
Greek mythol-
ogy, a mon-
ster with the
b o d y o f a
winged lion
and a wom-
an's head and
breasts; **2,**
Sphinx, the
s p h i n x a t
Thebes, who
slew passers-
by when they
c o u l d n o t
s o l v e t h e
riddle she set
them; **3,** in
Egyptian art,
a creature rep-
resented with a lion's body and a hawk's,
ram's, or man's head; **4,** a mysterious
person, whose life or character is not
easily guessed.

SPHINXES
1, Greek sphinx; 2, Egyptian sphinx.

spice (spīs), *n.* **1,** an aromatic vegetable
substance, sometimes ground or powdered,
used for seasoning, as cinnamon, nutmeg,
or pepper; **2,** that which gives flavor or
zest; relish; as, a *spice* of humor:—*v.t.*
[spiced, spic-ing], to season or flavor with
spice or spices.—*adj.* **spic′y.**

Spice Is-lands, a group of islands in the
East Indies. See **Molucca Islands.**

spick—and—span (spĭk′⸗ănd⸗spăn′), *adj.*
fresh and new; absolutely clean and neat;
as, *spick-and-span* white gloves; a *spick-
and-span* cupboard.

spi-der (spī′dẽr), *n.* **1,** a
small, insectlike animal,
wingless, with four pairs
of legs, capable of spinning
silken threads of which it
makes cocoons for eggs,
and, in some instances,
webs for catching prey; **2,**
anything thought to resemble or recall a
spider; **3,** a cast-iron frying pan.

SPIDER

āte, âorta, râre, căt, ăsk, fär, ăllow, sofå; ēve, êvent, ĕll, wrītẽr, novĕl; bīte, pĭn;
nō, ōbey, ôr, dŏg, tŏp, cŏllide; ūnit, ûnite, bûrn, cŭt, focŭs; nōōn, fŏŏt; mound; coin;

spig-ot (spĭg′ŭt), *n.* **1**, a plug or peg used to stop a cask; **2**, a faucet.

¹**spike** (spīk), *n.* **1**, a sharp point; **2**, any slender pointed object, as a kind of large nail; **3**, one of the metal pieces fastened to the soles of certain shoes used in sports, to prevent slipping:—*v.t.* [spiked, spik-ing], **1**, to fasten or equip with large nails or sharp points; **2**, to run through with a sharp point; **3**, to make (a gun, cannon, etc.) useless by driving a spike into an opening; **4**, hence, to make ineffective; as, to *spike* gossip.

²SPIKE def. 2

²**spike** (spīk), *n.* **1**, an ear of grain; **2**, a long, often tapering, flower cluster, in which the flowers grow along the sides of the stalk, as in the hyacinth.

spike-let (spīk′lĕt), *n.* in botany, a small spike, as the flower cluster of some grasses.

spike-nard (spīk′nẽrd; spīk′närd), *n.* **1**, a precious ointment in Bible times; also, the plant from which it is supposed to have come; **2**, a tall, fragrant plant with greenish flower clusters.

spik-y (spī′kĭ), *adj.* [spik-i-er, spik-i-est], **1**, fitted with spikes; as, a *spiky* iron fence; **2**, sharp and pointed; as, a *spiky* thorn.

spile (spīl), *n.* **1**, a large timber driven into the ground as part of a foundation; a pile; **2**, a wooden plug; **3**, a spout driven into a sugar maple to drain off the sap.

¹**spill** (spĭl), *n.* a thin strip of wood or small roll of paper for lighting a fire.

²**spill** (spĭl), *v.t.* [spilled (spĭld) or spilt (spĭlt), spill-ing], **1**, to permit to run over, or fall out of, a vessel or other container; as, don't *spill* the water; **2**, to cause to be scattered, wasted, lost, or the like; as, to *spill* blood:—*v.i.* to flow over, fall out, be scattered, or the like:—*n.* **1**, an overflowing or downpour, as of liquid or rain; **2**, a fall or tumble; as, a bad *spill* from a horse; **3**, the overflow of a dam.

spill-way (spĭl′wā′), *n.* a passage for water overflow, as from a dam or reservoir.

spin (spĭn), *v.t.* [*p.t.* spun (spŭn) or, *Archaic,* span (spăn), *p.p.* spun, *p.pr.* spin-ning], **1**, to draw out and twist (fiber) into threads; as, to *spin* cotton; **2**, to form (a web or cocoon) by drawing out threads of fluid from a gland: said of spiders, silkworms, etc.; **3**, to draw out to some length; as, to *spin* a long story; **4**, to cause to whirl rapidly, as a top:—*v.i.* **1**, to engage in drawing out and twisting fiber into threads, or in making a thread as a spider does; **2**, to whirl; **3**, *Colloquial,* to move swiftly; as, to *spin* along on a bicycle:—*n.* **1**, the act of spinning; especially, a rapid whirling; as,

the *spin* of a wheel; **2**, *Colloquial,* a short drive, as in an automobile.—*n.* **spin′ner.**—*n.* **spin′ning.**

spin-ach (spĭn′ĭj; spĭn′ĭch), *n.* a common garden vegetable, the leaves of which are cooked and eaten.

spi-nal (spī′năl), *adj.* pertaining to the backbone, or spinal column; as, the *spinal* fluid; a *spinal* puncture.

spi-nal col-umn (kŏl′ŭm), the backbone, a series of small, similar bones joined by cartilage, extending from the base of the skull to the pelvis.

spinal cord, a cord of nervous tissue running lengthwise through the spinal column.

spin-dle (spĭn′dl), *n.* **1**, in spinning, a long, thin rod, or a tapering stick, used for twisting and winding the thread; **2**, a slender rod or pin on which something turns.

spin-dle—leg-ged (spĭn′dl-lĕg′ĕd; -lĕgd′), *adj.* having long, slender legs; as, a *spindle-legged* table.

spin-dle-shanks (spĭn′dl-shăngks′), *n.pl.* **1**, long, thin legs; **2**, *pl.* used as *sing.* a tall person with long, thin legs.—*adj.* **spin′dle—shanked′.**

spin-dling (spĭn′dlĭng), *adj.* tall and slim; especially, too thin in proportion to height; as, a *spindling* child or plant.

spin-drift (spĭn′drĭft′), *n.* foam or spray blown up from the surface of the sea.

spine (spīn), *n.* **1**, the backbone, or spinal column; **2**, something like the backbone in position or function; hence, that which supports or strengthens; endurance or courage; **3**, a stiff, thorn-shaped or pointed growth on a plant, as the hawthorn or barberry, or on an animal, as the hedgehog.—*adj.* **spine′less.**—*adj.* **spi′nous;** **spi′nose.**

spin-et (spĭn′ĕt; spĭ-nĕt′), *n.* a musical instrument like the harpsichord, but smaller; an early form of piano.

spin-na-ker (spĭn′à-kẽr), *n.* a large sail, triangular in shape, used chiefly by a racing vessel running before the wind.

spin-ner-et (spĭn′ẽr-ĕt), *n.* in spiders, silkworms, etc., the organ that spins silk.

spin-ning wheel, a household machine consisting of a spindle turned by a large wheel, used formerly for spinning fibers of cotton, linen, wool, etc., into thread or yarn. (See illustration next page.)

spin-ster (spĭn′stẽr), *n.* a woman who has not married.—*n.* **spin′ster-hood.**

spin-y (spī′nĭ), *adj.* [spin-i-er, spin-i-est],

SPINDLE
A, distaff; B, spindle.

full of, or covered with, thorny prongs or points; prickly, as the hawthorn.

spi-ra-cle (spī′rȧ-kl; spĭr′ȧ-kl), *n.* **1,** any of the small breathing holes in insects and some fishes; **2,** a hole for breathing in the head of a whale, porpoise, etc.

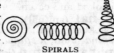

SPIRALS

spi-ral (spī′rȧl), *adj.* **1,** winding around a fixed point or center in increasingly larger circles, like a watch spring; **2,** winding about a cylindrical surface, like the thread of a screw, or the stripes on a barber pole:—*n.* a spiral curve; a curve like that of a watch spring or the thread of a screw:—*v.i.* and *v.t.* [spiraled, spiral-ing], to follow, or cause to follow, a spiral course; as, the smoke slowly *spiraled* upward; the airplane *spiraled* downward.—*adv.* **spi′ral-ly.**

¹spire (spīr), *n.* **1,** a spiral or single turn of a spiral; **2,** the upper part of a spiral shell.

²spire (spīr), *n.* **1,** a slender leaf or blade, as of grass; **2,** a form that tapers to a point; especially, the slender, tapering top of a tower or steeple; also, a steeple.

spi-re-a (spī-rē′ȧ), *n.* a shrub of the rose family, cultivated or wild, bearing small white or pink flowers.

²SPIRE def. 2

spir-it (spĭr′ĭt), *n.* **1,** the soul; the immortal, nonphysical part of man; **2,** a supernatural being, as a sprite or fairy; a ghost; also, a being without a body; as, departed *spirits;* **3,** a person considered with reference to qualities of mind or character; as, the poet is a noble *spirit;* **4, spirits,** state of mind; mood; as, to be in low *spirits;* **5,** courage; energy and vim; as, the troops advanced with *spirit;* **6,** enthusiasm for an object; as, school *spirit;* **7,** intent; real meaning; as, I expect you to keep the *spirit* as well as the words of your promise; also, the chief characteristic or influence; as, the scientific *spirit* of the

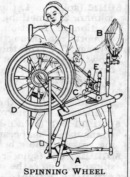

SPINNING WHEEL

A, treadle by which the wheel (D) is turned; B, distaff from which fibers are drawn, twisted, and fed to revolving spindle (E) connected with wheel (D) by belt, or double cord (C).

20th century; **8,** (usually *spirits*): **a,** any strong distilled alcoholic liquor, as brandy, whisky, etc.; **b,** an alcoholic solution of certain drugs which evaporate easily; as, *spirits* of ammonia:—**Spirit,** the third person of the Trinity: also called *Holy Spirit, Holy Ghost:*—*v.t.* to carry off (a person) suddenly and secretly.

spir-it-ed (spĭr′ĭ-tĕd), *adj.* full of vigor or life; animated; lively; as, a *spirited* horse.

spir-it-less (spĭr′ĭt-lĕs), *adj.* listless; lacking courage or animation; as, a *spiritless* address.—*adv.* **spir′it-less-ly.**

spir-it-u-al (spĭr′ĭt-ū-ăl), *adj.* **1,** pertaining to the mind or spirit, as distinguished from matter; **2,** pertaining to the soul or higher nature of man; pure; holy; **3,** pertaining to sacred or religious things; as, *spiritual* guidance:—*n.* a hymn or sacred song, especially one originating among the negroes of the southern U.S.—*adv.* **spir′it-u-al-ly.**—*n.* **spir′it-u-al′i-ty.**

spir-it-u-al-ism (spĭr′ĭt-ū-ăl-ĭzm), *n.* the belief that the spirits of the dead communicate with the living, especially through a medium.—*n.* **spir′it-u-al-ist.**

spir-it-u-ous (spĭr′ĭt-ū-ŭs), *adj.* containing alcohol; distilled; intoxicating.

spirt (spûrt), *v.i.* and *v.t.* to pour forth suddenly:—*n.* a gushing. See **spurt.**

¹spit (spĭt), *n.* **1,** a long pointed rod or bar, used to hold meat for roasting over an open fire; **2,** a point of land extending into the sea:—*v.t.* [spit-ted, spit-ting], to pierce with a spit; impale.

²spit (spĭt), *v.t.* [spat (spăt) or, sometimes, spit, spit-ting], **1,** to eject (saliva or blood) from the mouth; **2,** to eject or expel; as, the cannon *spat* fire:—*v.i.* **1,** to eject saliva from the mouth; **2,** to make a hissing noise: said especially of cats:—*n.* **1,** saliva; **2,** the act of ejecting saliva; **3,** exact likeness; as, she is the *spit* and image of her mother.

spite (spīt), *n.* ill will or hatred toward another; malice:—**in spite of,** in defiance of; notwithstanding:—*v.t.* [spit-ed, spit-ing], to show malice toward; try to injure or baffle; annoy.

Syn., n. enmity, resentment, animosity.

spite-ful (spīt′fŏŏl), *adj.* full of ill will; malicious; having a desire to injure or annoy.—*adv.* **spite′ful-ly.**—*n.* **spite′ful-ness.**

spit-fire (spĭt′fīr′), *n.* a hot-tempered person.

spit-tle (spĭt′l), *n.* saliva; spit.

spit-toon (spĭ-tōōn′), *n.* a vessel into which one may spit; a cuspidor.

spitz dog (spĭts), a small dog with a sharp

muzzle, long, silky white hair, and bushy tail: also called *spitz*.

splash (splăsh), *v.t.* **1**, to spatter or toss about; as, to *splash* water; **2**, to spatter or soil with water, mud, or the like:—*v.i.* **1**, to dash or spatter a liquid about in drops; as, don't *splash*; **2**, to move or proceed with a splashing noise; as, to *splash* into, or through, a puddle; **3**, to fall or fly about in drops; as, the paint *splashed* over the floor:—*n.* **1**, a spot or daub; as, I have a *splash* of mud on my dress; **2**, an irregular spot of color; a blotch; as, the dog has a *splash* of black on his head; **3**, a noise as from sudden, violent contact with water; as, he plunged into the pool with a *splash*.

splat-ter (splăt′ẽr), *v.t.* and *v.i.* to spatter; splash.

splay (splā), *v.t.* to slope or slant (the side of a door or window frame):—*n.* an opening with beveled or sloped surfaces, for a window; an embrasure:—*adj.* spread out; broad and flat; as, *splay* feet.

spleen (splēn), *n.* **1**, one of the ductless glands near the stomach, supposed by the ancients to be the seat of anger, melancholy, etc.; **2**, hence, ill temper, melancholy, or spite.

splen-did (splĕn′dĭd), *adj.* magnificent; gorgeous; inspiring; as, a *splendid* spectacle.—*adv.* **splen′did-ly.**

splen-dor (splĕn′dẽr), *n.* **1**, dazzling brightness; as, the *splendor* of diamonds; **2**, magnificence; pomp; as, the *splendor* of a king's court. In British usage, **splen′dour.**
Syn. luster, grandeur, brilliance.

sple-net-ic (splē-nĕt′ĭk), *adj.* peevish; melancholy; ill-tempered.
Syn. morose, sullen, gloomy.

splice (splīs), *v.t.* [spliced, splic-ing], **1**, to unite without knots, as two ropes, by interweaving the ends of the strands (see illustration under *knot*); **2**, to connect (pieces of wood or metal) by overlapping and making fast the ends:—*n.* the union, or place of union, of ropes, timbers, etc., by splicing.

SPLICES

splint (splĭnt), *n.* **1**, one of a number of thin strips of wood interwoven to form chair seats, baskets, etc.; **2**, a device or appliance for holding in place a broken or fractured bone until it knits.

splin-ter (splĭn′tẽr), *n.* a thin sliver of wood, metal, etc., split or torn off lengthwise; a fragment:—*v.t.* and *v.i.* to split into long, thin pieces.—*adj.* **splin′ter-y.**

split (splĭt), *v.t.* [split, split-ting], **1**, to di-

vide or cut lengthwise; as, to *split* wood; **2**, to rend or tear apart; as, the frost *splits* rocks; **3**, to divide or break up into parts; as, to *split* a large class into several sections:—**split hairs**, to make too fine distinctions:—*v.i.* **1**, to burst; break apart; as, my sleeve *split*; **2**, to divide lengthwise, or with the grain; as, wood *splits* easily; **3**, to separate into groups; as, a political party *splits*:—*n.* **1**, a rent or crack; **2**, a division or separation, as in an organization.

split-ting (splĭt′ĭng), *adj.* of a headache, very severe; of the head, afflicted with a violent headache.

splotch (splŏch), *n.* a stain; daub; blotch:—*v.t.* to mark with stains or blotches.—*adj.* **splotch′y.**

splurge (splûrj), *Colloquial:* *n.* a showy or vulgar display, as of wealth:—*v.i.* [splurged, splurg-ing], to make a vulgar display; as, the newly rich are apt to *splurge*.

splut-ter (splŭt′ẽr), *v.i.* **1**, to speak hastily and confusedly; as, to *splutter* with excitement; **2**, to make a hissing noise; sputter; as, the candles *spluttered* in their holders:—*v.t.* *Colloquial*, to utter in a quick, incoherent manner:—*n.* a confused noise; stir.

spoil (spoil), *v.t.* [spoiled (spoild) or spoilt (spoilt), spoil-ing], **1**, to damage or impair the good qualities of; mar; as, the rain *spoiled* the crops; **2**, to indulge (a child) with harmful effects on its character; pamper:—*v.i.* to decay; as, food sometimes *spoils* in warm weather:—*n.* **1**, pillage; plunder; booty; as, they shared the *spoil*; **2**, **spoils**, public offices and the gain derived from them, appropriated as plunder by the successful party in an election.—*n.* **spoil′er.**
Syn., v. injure, destroy, corrupt.

Spo-kane (spō-kăn′), a large commercial city in the State of Washington (map **9**).

¹spoke (spōk), past tense of *speak*.

²spoke (spōk), *n.* **1**, one of the bars of a wheel connecting the hub with the rim; **2**, a round or rung of a ladder.

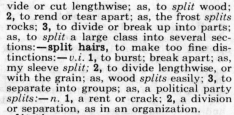

SPOKES
of a wheel.

spo-ken (spō′kĕn), past participle of *speak*.

spoke-shave (spōk′shāv′), *n.* a carpenter's tool with a handle on either end of a short blade, used in planing the curved surfaces of woodwork.

spokes-man (spōks′măn), *n.* [*pl.* spokesmen (-měn)], a person who speaks for others; an agent or representative.

spo·li·a·tion (spō/lǐ-ā/shŭn), *n.* the plundering of neutral ships in time of war.

sponge (spŭnj), *n.* **1,** the porous elastic mass of horny fibers forming the skeleton of certain salt-water animals and capable of absorbing a large amount of water; also, any one of these animals; **2,** the act of bathing or cleaning with a sponge; **3,** any light and porous substance, as raised dough:— *v.t.* [sponged, spong-ing], **1,** to cleanse, wipe out, or dampen with a sponge; as, to *sponge* cloth; **2,** to take up or absorb, as with a sponge; **3,** *Colloquial,* to obtain by imposing upon someone; as, to *sponge* a dinner:— *v.i.* **1,** *Colloquial,* to live as a parasite upon others, or to get something without paying for it, by imposing upon someone; **2,** to gather sponges.—*n.* **spong'er.**

spon·gy (spŭn/jǐ), *adj.* [spon-gi-er, spon-gi-est], full of small holes and easily compressed; absorbent.

spon·sor (spŏn/sẽr), *n.* **1,** one who endorses or lends support to a person, movement, or the like; as, the *sponsor* of a radio program; **2,** a godfather or godmother:— *v.t.* to endorse or support; as, to *sponsor* a bill in Congress.

SPOOL

spon·ta·ne·ous (spŏn-tā/nē-ŭs), *adj.* **1,** acting or springing from natural impulse; as, *spontaneous* applause; **2,** produced by internal forces rather than by an external cause; as, *spontaneous* combustion. —*n.* **spon'ta-ne'i-ty** (spŏn/tȧ-nē/ǐ-tǐ)

SPOONS

spook (spook), *n.* a ghost or spirit; an apparition.—*adj.* **spook'y.**

spool (spool), *n.* a hollow cylinder or reel of wood or metal, with a rim at each end, for winding thread, wire, etc.:— *v.t.* to wind on a spool.

spoon (spoon), *n.* **1,** a utensil with a shallow bowl at the end of a handle, used in preparing, serving, or eating food; **2,** something resembling a spoon, as an oar with a curved blade:— *v.t.* to take up with, or as with, a spoon.—*n.* **spoon'ful.**

SPOONBILL (₁⁄₁₆)

spoon·bill (spoon/bǐl/), *n.* a wading bird

with long legs and a bill which is extremely broad and flattened at the tip.

spoon·drift (spoon/drǐft/), *n.* spray blown from sea waves; spindrift.

spoor (spoor), *n.* the track, trail, or scent of any wild animal.

spo·rad·ic (spō-răd/ǐk), *adj.* occurring here and there in a scattered manner; occasional; as, *sporadic* cases of smallpox.— *adv.* **spo·rad/i·cal·ly.**

spore (spōr), *n.* a very small cell, occurring in flowerless plants, such as ferns, and in certain plantlike animals. It is capable of developing into a new plant or a new animal.

spor·ran (spŏr/ăn), *n.* the large purse or pouch, covered with hair or fur, worn in front of the kilt in the full-dress costume of a Scottish Highlander.

SPORRAN (S)

sport (spôrt), *n.* **1,** pastime; amusement; **2,** jest or pleasantry; as, he said it in *sport;* **3,** mockery or derision; as, they made *sport* of him; **4,** outdoor play or recreation, as hunting or shooting; also, an athletic game, as baseball or hockey; **5,** a person willing to take a chance; a good loser: often called *good sport:*— *v.i.* **1,** to play or frolic; **2,** to make merry or jest; trifle:— *v.t. Colloquial,* to show off, or wear in public; as, to *sport* a diamond ring:— *adj.* (also **sports**), relating to, or suitable for, outdoor games or recreation; also, adapted to informal outdoor wear; as, *sports* clothes.—*adj.* **sport'ing.**

spor·tive (spôr/tǐv), *adj.* frolicsome; playful.—*adv.* **spor'tive·ly.**—*n.* **spor'tive·ness.**

sports·man (spôrts/măn), *n.* [*pl.* sportsmen (-měn)], **1,** one who engages in sports, especially hunting, racing, or fishing; **2,** one who is fair and honorable in sports.—*adj.* **sports'man·like/.**—*n.* **sports'man·ship.**— *n. fem.* **sports'wom/an.**

spot (spŏt), *n.* **1,** a blot or mark; a discolored place or stain; as, a *spot* of ink; **2,** a blemish; as, a *spot* on his reputation; **3,** locality; place; as, the exact *spot* where he fell; **4,** a small part of a surface, differing from the background in color; as, *spots* on a playing card:— *v.t.* [spot-ted, spot-ting], **1,** to mark with spots; discolor; stain; **2,** to disgrace or blemish; **3,** *Colloquial,* to mark or note; recognize; as, we *spotted* the guilty man: —*v.i.* to become marked or stained; as, velvet always *spots* with water.

spot·less (spŏt/lĕs), *adj.* immaculately clean; unblemished.—*adv.* **spot'less·ly.**

spot·light (spŏt/līt/), *n.* **1,** a brilliant beam of light directed so as to single out

āte, ãorta, râre, căt, ȧsk, fär, ăllow, sofȧ; ēve, ĕvent, ĕll, writẽr, novĕl; bīte, pǐn; nō, ōbey, ôr, dǒg, tŏp, cŏllide; ūnit, ŭnite, bûrn, cŭt, focŭs; nōon, fŏŏt; mound; coin;

a particular object or person, as an actor on a stage; also, the lamp or apparatus which throws this light; **2,** hence, prominence; public notice; as, his fight against gangsters brought him into the *spotlight.*

spot-ted (spŏt′ĕd), *adj.* marked with spots or stains; as, a dress *spotted* with ink.

spot-ty (spŏt′ĭ), *adj.* [spot-ti-er, spot-ti-est], **1,** full of, or marked with, spots; **2,** irregular; now good, now poor; as, *spotty* trade.

spouse (spouz), *n.* either one of a married couple.

spout (spout), *v.t.* **1,** to throw out (liquid) forcibly in a jet or stream, as does a pipe; **2,** to utter pompously; as, to *spout* poetry:—*v.i.* **1,** to come forth with violence in a jet or stream, as blood from a wound; **2,** to force out fluid in a jet or stream, as does a whale; **3,** to speak in a pompous manner:—*n.* **1,** the projecting tube, nozzle, or the like, through which a liquid pours; as, the *spout* of a teapot; also, a trough or pipe for carrying off rain from a roof; **2,** a stream or jet of liquid.

sprain (sprān), *n.* a severe twisting or straining of the muscles or ligaments around a joint:—*v.t.* to injure by wrenching or twisting severely; as, to *sprain* a wrist.

sprang (sprăng), one form of the past tense of *spring.*

sprat (sprăt), *n.* a small herringlike fish.

sprawl (sprôl), *v.i.* **1,** to lie or sit in a careless, ungraceful position; **2,** to move or crawl along awkwardly, as does a very young puppy; **3,** to spread in an irregular, straggling manner, as a plant, or a person's handwriting:—*v.t.* to spread or cause to spread awkwardly or ungracefully:—*n.* an awkward spreading position or movement.

¹**spray** (sprā), *n.* a small branch of a tree or plant, bearing leaves or flowers; sprig.

²**spray** (sprā), *n.* **1,** water driven in small drops or particles by the wind, the dashing of waves, etc.; **2,** medicine or other liquid applied, in the form of vapor, by an atomizer or spray machine; **3,** an instrument for throwing fine drops of liquid or vapor; an atomizer:—*v.t.* **1,** to apply fine drops of liquid to; as, to *spray* trees; **2,** to scatter (a liquid) in fine drops.

spread (sprĕd), *v.t.* [spread (sprĕd), spreading], **1,** to cause to cover a surface; as, to *spread* butter on bread; also, to cover (a surface) with something; as, to *spread* bread with jam; **2,** to unfold; stretch forth; expand; as, the peacock *spreads* his tail; **3,** to publish or make widely

known; as, to *spread* the good news; **4,** to place food upon; as, to *spread* the table; **5,** to communicate or carry from person to person; as, flies *spread* disease:—*v.i.* **1,** to be extended over a surface; as, smoke *spread* over the city; **2,** to be dispersed or scattered; as, rumors *spread;* **3,** to be forced apart, as rails:—*n.* **1,** extension; growth; as, the *spread* of civilization; **2,** the limit or area of expansion; as, the *spread* of an eagle's wings; **3,** a covering for a bed, table, etc.; **4,** *Colloquial,* a table set with provisions; a feast; **5,** any substance, as butter or jam, used to spread on bread.

spread-er (sprĕd′ĕr), *n.* anything that spreads, as, on a ship, a bar serving to hold two stays or guys apart.

spree (sprē), *n.* **1,** a merry frolic; **2,** a drunken debauch.

sprig (sprĭg), *n.* **1,** a small branch; a twig or shoot; **2,** an ornamental figure or design in the form of a spray.

spright-ly (sprīt′lĭ), *adj.* [spright-li-er, spright-li-est], vivacious; gay.—*n.* **spright′-li-ness.**

    Syn. lively, brisk, cheerful.

spring (sprĭng), *v.i.* [*p.t.* sprang (sprăng) or sprung (sprŭng), *p.p.* sprung, *p.pr.* spring-ing], **1,** to leap; bound; **2,** to rise suddenly; dart out, as an animal from a covert; **3,** to start up or forth; appear; as, a breeze has *sprung* up; **4,** to result; have a beginning; as, superstitions *spring* from fear; **5,** to recoil; rebound; as, an elastic *springs* back; **6,** to become warped or bent, as a board:—*v.t.* **1,** to reveal or produce with unexpected suddenness; as, to *spring* a surprise; **2,** to release the catch of (a trap); also, to explode or discharge (a mine); **3,** to weaken by a crack or strain; as, I have *sprung* my tennis racket; also, to develop (an opening) at the seams; as, the roof *sprung* a leak:—*n.* **1,** the act of springing; a leap; also, the length of the leap; **2,** a contrivance, usually of metal, that yields to pressure and returns to its original form when the force is removed; as, automobile *springs;* **3,** the quality of being elastic; as, the *spring* of a rubber band; also, the shooting back from a tense position; recoil; **4,** cause; origin; as, the *springs* of conduct; **5,**

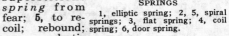

SPRINGS

1, elliptic spring; 2, 5, spiral springs; 3, flat spring; 4, coil spring; 6, door spring.

a natural fountain or supply of water rising to the surface of the earth; **6,** the season of the year between winter and summer; usually, in the Northern Hemisphere, from March 21 to June 21:—*adj.* pertaining to the spring.

spring-board (spring'bôrd/), *n.* a springy, elastic board used to give added spring to acrobats and athletes in jumping and to swimmers in diving.

spring-bok (spring'bŏk/), *n.* the South African gazelle, noted for its graceful form and agility.

SPRINGBOK (⅟₅₀)

Spring-field (spring'fēld), **1,** a city, capital of Illinois (map 7); **2,** a city in southern Massachusetts (map 6).

spring tide, the tide, occurring near the time of new moon and of full moon, when the variation between high tide and low tide is greatest: opposite of *neap tide.*

spring-tide (spring'tīd/), *n.* the spring season: also called *springtime.*

spring-y (spring'ĭ), *adj.* [spring-i-er, spring-i-est], elastic; full of spring; as, a *springy* gait; a *springy* board.

sprin-kle (spring'kl), *v.t.* [sprin-kled, sprin-kling], **1,** to scatter in small drops or particles; as, to *sprinkle* salt on food; **2,** to spray with small drops or particles; as, to *sprinkle* the lawn:—*v.i.* to rain lightly:—*n.* **1,** a light shower of rain; **2,** a small quantity; as, a *sprinkle* of salt.

sprint (sprint), *n.* **1,** a short run at full speed; **2,** a race over a short distance:—*v.i.* to run a rather short distance at full speed; dash.—*n.* **sprint'er.**

SPRITSAIL
Boat rigged with spritsail. *a*, sprit; *b*, sail.

sprit (sprit), *n.* a small spar running diagonally from the bottom of the mast to the top outside corner of a sail, which it elevates and extends.

sprite (sprit), *n.* an elf, goblin, or fairy.

s p r i t - s a i l (sprit'-sāl/; sprit'sl), *n.* a fore-and-aft sail extended by a sprit.

sprock-et (sprŏk'ĕt), *n.* **1,** a toothlike projection as on the outer rim of a wheel, shaped so as to engage with

SPROCKET
WHEEL AND
CHAIN

the links of a driving chain; **2,** a wheel having such teeth on its rim.

sprout (sprout), *v.i.* **1,** to begin to grow; **2,** to put forth shoots, as the seed of a plant:—*v.t.* to cause to put forth shoots; as, plants may be *sprouted* indoors:—*n.* a new shoot; bud.

¹spruce (sprōōs), *adj.* [spruc-er, spruc-est], smart; trim; neat:—*v.i.* and *v.t.* [spruced, spruc-ing], *Colloquial,* to dress smartly; arrange in a neat and tidy manner.

²spruce (sprōōs), *n.* an evergreen tree bearing cones and needle-shaped leaves; also, its wood. (See illustration on page 865.)

sprung (sprŭng), one form of the past tense of *spring;* also, the past participle.

spry (sprī), *adj.* [spri-er or spry-er, spriest or spry-est], nimble; active; agile.

spud (spŭd), *n.* **1,** a sharp, narrow spade, especially for digging up large-rooted weeds; **2,** *Colloquial,* a potato.

spume (spūm), *n.* froth; foam; scum.

spun (spŭn), one form of the past tense of *spin;* also, the past participle.

spunk (spŭngk), *n. Colloquial,* courage; spirit; pluck.—*adj.* **spunk'y.**

spur (spûr), *n.* **1,** a pointed instrument worn on the heel of a horseman's boot, used to urge on a horse; **2,** anything that urges to action; an incentive; as, to offer a prize as a *spur* to good work; **3,** anything resembling a spur, as the hollow, projecting part of the flower in the larkspur and the columbine; **4,** a mountain ridge running out to the side from a range of mountains; **5,** the stiff, sharp spine on a rooster's leg; **6,** a short railway line connected with a main line at only one end; a short railway branch line over which regular service is not maintained:—*v.t.* [spurred, spur-ring], **1,** to prick with a spur; as, to *spur* a horse; **2,** to excite or drive on to action:—*v.i.* to travel with haste; press onward.

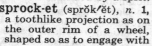

SPUR

spu-ri-ous (spū'rĭ-ŭs), *adj.* not genuine; false; not authentic; as, *spurious* coins. *Syn.* artificial, fraudulent, sham.

spurn (spûrn), *v.t.* **1,** to push away, as with the foot; **2,** to reject with contempt; scorn to accept; as, to *spurn* a suitor.

spurred (spûrd), *adj.* wearing or having a spur or spurs.

spurt (spûrt), *v.i.* to gush forth suddenly in a stream or jet; as, water *spurted* from the leak in the pipe:—*v.t.* to throw or force out in a stream or jet; squirt:—*n.* **1,** a sudden gushing forth of liquid; **2,** any brief and sudden outbreak, as of pas-

āte, āorta, râre, căt, ȧsk, fär, ȧllow, sofȧ; ēve, ĕvent, ĕll, writēr, novĕl; bīte, pĭn; nō, ōbey, ôr, dŏg, tŏp, cŏllide; ūnit, ūnite, bûrn, cŭt, focŭs; nōōn, fŏŏt; mound; coin;

sion or anger; **3,** a sudden and extraordinary burst of strength or energy for a brief period, as in a race; also, a sharp and sudden increase in business. Also, **spirt.**

sput-ter (spŭt′ĕr), *v.i.* **1,** to throw out small particles, as sparks from burning wood; **2,** to spit small, scattered drops of saliva, as in rapid or excited speech; **3,** to speak rapidly and indistinctly:—*v.t.* to utter in an excited or confused way:—*n.* **1,** the act of sputtering; also, the sound; **2,** excited and indistinct talk; **3,** fuss; bustle. —*n.* **sput′ter-er.**

spu-tum (spū′tŭm), *n.* saliva; spit.

spy (spī), *n.* [*pl.* spies], **1,** a person who enters the enemy's territory secretly in time of war, to gain information; **2,** one who keeps watch on others; a secret agent: —*v.t.* [spied, spy-ing], **1,** to catch sight of, especially at a distance; as, she *spied* a friend in the crowd; **2,** to watch closely or explore secretly; as, to *spy* out the land:— *v.i.* **1,** to make a careful examination; **2,** to act as a spy.

spy-glass (spī′glås′), *n.* a small telescope for viewing distant objects.

sq. abbreviation for *square.*

squab (skwŏb; skwôb), *n.* a young pigeon.

squab-ble (skwŏb′l; skwôb′l), *n.* a noisy quarrel; dispute:—*v.i.* [squab-bled, squabbling], to wrangle; dispute noisily.

squad (skwŏd; skwôd), *n.* **1,** a small party of soldiers assembled for drill, etc.; **2,** any small group of persons engaged in a common effort; as, a *squad* of police.

squad-ron (skwŏd′rŭn; skwôd′rŭn), *n.* **1,** any group of men in regular formation; **2,** in the U.S. Army, a division of a cavalry regiment containing from two to four troops; **3,** in the Navy, a group of war vessels employed on some particular service; **4,** a unit of an airplane fleet.

squal-id (skwŏl′ĭd; skwôl′ĭd), *adj.* extremely dirty and neglected; wretched; as, a *squalid* tenement.

¹squall (skwôl), *n.* **1,** a sudden and violent gust of wind, often accompanied by rain, sleet, or snow; **2,** *Colloquial,* trouble or danger of any sort.—*adj.* **squall′y.**

²squall (skwôl), *v.i.* and *v.t.* to weep, scream, or utter violently, as a child in pain:—*n.* a loud, harsh scream.

squal-or (skwŏl′ĕr; skwôl′ĕr), *n.* a condition of filth and misery; sordid poverty.

squan-der (skwŏn′dĕr; skwôn′dĕr), *v.t.* to spend lavishly or wastefully.

square (skwâr), *n.* **1,** a plane figure with four right angles and four equal sides; **2,** anything shaped like a square; as, silk *squares* for patchwork; **3,** a city block consisting of a four-sided space on each side

of which is a street; **4,** the distance from one cross street to the next; as, the nearest store is three *squares* from our house; **5,** an open space or area, often used as a small park; **6,** an instrument, consisting usually of two straight edges at right angles to each other, used for measuring or laying out right angles; **7,** in mathematics, the product obtained by multiplying a number by itself; as, 4 is the *square* of 2:—

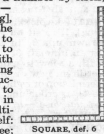

SQUARE def. 1

v.t. [squared, squar-ing], **1,** to give (an object) the shape of a square; **2,** to cause (a line or side) to make a right angle with another; also, to bring into a position producing such an angle; **3,** to balance (accounts); **4,** in mathematics, to multiply (a number) by itself: —*v.i.* to accord or agree; coincide; fit; as, his story does not *square* with mine:—*adj.* **1,** having the same shape as a square; **2,** forming a right angle; rectangular; as, a *square* outline; **3,** straight and angular, rather than curved, in outline; as, a *square* jaw; **4,** true; honest; just; as, a man who is *square* in his dealings; **5,** balanced; settled, as accounts; **6,** *Colloquial,* satisfying; substantial; as, a *square* meal:—*adv.* directly; as, he hit the nail *square* on the head.—*adv.* **square′ly.**—*n.* **square′ness.**

SQUARE, def. 6

square inch, foot, etc., in surface measure, a unit area which is equal to that of a square surface an inch, a foot, etc., on each side; **square dance,** an old-fashioned dance consisting of a series of set figures, or steps, for an even number of couples; **square knot,** a reef knot (see illustration under *knot*).

square-rigged (skwâr′-rĭgd′), *adj.* having rectangular sails stretched along yards which are slung horizontally to the mast. A brig is a square-rigged craft.

¹squash (skwŏsh; skwôsh), *n.* a green, yellow, or white gourdlike fruit, used as a vegetable; also, the vine bearing the fruit.

SQUASHES

²squash (skwŏsh; skwôsh), *v.t.* **1,** to beat or mash into pulp; to crush; **2,** to put down or suppress; as, to *squash* a rumor:—*v.i.* **1,** to fall in a soft mass; be crushed to a pulp, as from a fall; **2,** *Colloquial,* to make a noise like that of a sodden mass falling: —*n.* **1,** a crushed object or mass; **2,** the sudden fall of something soft and heavy; also, the noise made when such a thing falls; **3,** a game similar to tennis, played in a walled court with rackets and a ball.

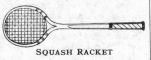

SQUASH RACKET

squash-y (skwŏsh′ĭ; skwôsh′ĭ), *adj.* [squash-i-er, squash-i-est], **1,** easily crushed; mushy; **2,** soft and wet; miry; as, *squashy* slush.—*n.* **squash′i-ness.**

squat (skwŏt; skwôt), *v.i.* [squat-ted, squatting], **1,** to sit on the heels, or with knees drawn up; **2,** to crouch on the ground, as an animal; **3,** to settle on public land with a view to gaining title to it; also, to settle on new or unoccupied land without permission or right:—*adj.* [squat-ter, squattest], **1,** crouching; **2,** short and thick; as, a *squat* vase:—*n.* a squatting position.—*n.* **squat′ter.**—*adj.* **squat′ty.**

squaw (skwô), *n.* an American Indian woman.

squawk (skwôk), *n.* a loud, harsh cry, as of a duck or hen:—*v.i.* to utter a loud, harsh cry.

squeak (skwēk), *n.* a short, shrill, sharp sound; as, the *squeak* of a mouse:—*v.i.* **1,** to utter a short, shrill, sharp cry; **2,** to make a grating, disagreeable noise, as a rusty hinge.—*adj.* **squeak′y.**

squeal (skwēl), *n.* a shrill, prolonged cry, as of a pig:—*v.i.* **1,** to utter a shrill, prolonged cry; **2,** *Colloquial,* to betray a plot or a companion in a crime or fault.—*n.* **squeal′er.**

squeam-ish (skwēm′ĭsh), *adj.* **1,** easily nauseated; **2,** prudish; easily shocked; **3,** fastidious; too fussy about trifles.
Syn. scrupulous, finical.

squeeze (skwēz), *v.t.* [squeezed, squeezing], **1,** to exert pressure on; compress; as, clothes *squeezed* into a bag; **2,** to draw forth by pressure; extract; as, to *squeeze* water from a wet garment; also, to cause to yield juice; as, to *squeeze* a lemon; **3,** to thrust forcibly; crowd into too small a space; as, to *squeeze* people into a hall:—*v.i.* to press; force one's way; push; as, to *squeeze* through a crowd:—*n.* **1,** pressure; a crowding together; **2,** the act of squeezing.—*n.* **squeez′er.**

squelch (skwĕlch), *v.t.* to crush; silence by a rebuke; as, to *squelch* a quarrelsome child:—*v.i.* to make a squashing sound, such as is made by walking through slush.

squib (skwĭb), *n.* **1,** a firecracker which burns with a hissing sound or explodes with a crack; **2,** a short, witty or sarcastic speech or writing.

squid (skwĭd), *n.* a kind of ten-armed cuttlefish with a tapering body.

squint (skwĭnt), *n.* **1,** the condition of being cross-eyed; **2,** a sidelong, stealthy glance:—*v.i.* **1,** to look sideways; **2,** to have the eyes half closed, as in bright sunlight; **3,** to be cross-eyed:—*v.t.* to half close (the eyes):—*adj.* **1,** looking sideways; **2,** cross-eyed.

SQUID (¹⁄₁₀)

squire (skwīr), *n.* **1,** formerly, the shield-bearer of a knight; **2,** in the U.S., a justice of the peace; **3,** in England, the chief landholder of a district; **4,** a lady's escort:—*v.t.* [squired, squir-ing], to accompany (a lady) as a squire or escort.

squirm (skwûrm), *v.i.* to twist about like an eel or a snake; wriggle; writhe.

squir-rel (skwûr′ĕl), *n.* a small, bushy-tailed, gray, black, or reddish-brown animal that lives mostly in trees and feeds largely on grains and nuts; also, its fur.

squirt (skwûrt), *v.i.* to gush forth in a stream or jet from a small opening; to spurt:—*v.t.* to force out in a quick jet; as, a squid *squirts* an inky liquid:—*n.* **1,** a small stream or jet squirted forth; **2** an instrument for squirting water or other liquid.

SQUIRREL (⅛)

Sr. abbreviation for *Senior.*

S.S. abbreviation for *Steamship, Sunday School.*

St. abbreviation for *Saint, Strait, Street.*

stab (stăb), *v.t.* [stabbed, stab-bing], **1,** to pierce with a pointed weapon; **2,** to wound the feelings of; as, conscience *stabbed* him with remorse:—*v.i.* **1,** to pierce something with a pointed weapon; **2,** to wound a person's feelings:—*n.* **1,** a thrust with a sharp-pointed weapon; **2,** a wound so made.

sta-bil-i-ty (stá-bĭl′ĭ-tĭ), *n.* **1,** firmness; the ability to withstand change or onslaught: as, the *stability* of a government; **2,** firmness of character or purpose.

sta-bi-lize (stā′bĭ-līz; stăb′ĭ-līz), *v.t.* [stabilized, stabiliz-ing], **1,** to make firm, steady, regular, or dependable; as, to *stabilize* one's life, or one's income; **2,** to secure or maintain the balance of (a boat or aircraft) by a special device.—*n.* **sta′bi-li-za′tion.**—*n.* **sta′bi-liz′er.**

¹**sta-ble** (stā′bl), *adj.* **1,** firm; securely established; hence, having permanence; con-

tinuing without change; as, *stable* institutions; **2,** steadfast; unwavering; as, a man of *stable* purpose.

Syn. inflexible, steady, solid.

²**sta-ble** (stā′bl), *n.* a building, usually divided into stalls, in which horses, or sometimes cattle, are housed:—*v.t.* [sta-bled, sta-bling], to put into, or keep in, such a building:—*v.i.* to be so lodged.

stac-ca-to (stȧ-kä′tō), *adj.* **1,** in music, played in an abrupt, disconnected fashion; as, *staccato* notes; **2,** marked by quick, sharp accents; as, *staccato* cries:—*adv.* in a staccato manner.

stack (stăk), *n.* **1,** a large quantity of hay, wood, etc., piled up in orderly fashion; **2,** a somewhat orderly mass or heap; as, a *stack* of letters; **3,** a chimney; often, a vent for smoke, as on a factory; **4,** rifles, bean poles, or the like, arranged to form a pyramid; **5,** a rack or set of shelves for books:—*v.t.* to heap or pile up.

sta-di-um (stā′dĭ-ŭm), [*pl.* stadia (stā′-dĭ-ȧ); stadiums], *n.* a large structure consisting of seats arranged in tiers around a field which is used for outdoor athletic contests.

staff (stȧf), *n.* [*pl.* staves (stāvz; stȧvz) or staffs], **1,** a pole, rod, or stick used as a support in walking or climbing, as a means of defense, or as an emblem or evidence of authority; **2,** a long, slender pole serving as a support; as, a flag*staff;* **3,** [*pl.* staffs], a body of persons engaged in a single task; as, a teaching *staff;* an office *staff;* also, in the army, a body of assistant advisory officers; **4,** [*pl.* staffs], in music, the set of five horizontal lines and four intervening spaces on which the notes are written: also called *stave.*

stag (stăg), *n.* the full-grown male of the red deer and certain other large deer.

stage (stāj), *n.* **1,** a raised platform, as in a theater or concert hall; **2,** the theater; the theatrical profession; as, she is reluctant to leave the *stage;*

STAG (⅟₆₀)

3, a place or field of action; as, the political *stage;* the scene of any celebrated event or career; as, London was the *stage* of her debut; **4,** a part, or lap, as of a journey; **5,** degree of progress in any business, process, or the like; a point or period of development; as, an advanced *stage* of civilization; **6,** a stagecoach:—*v.t.* [staged, stag-ing], to put (a play) on the stage:—*v.i.* to be adapted to the stage; as, but few poetic plays *stage* well.

stage-coach (stāj′kōch′), *n.* in former times, a four-wheeled coach, having seats within and usually on top, running on schedule and carrying passengers and mail.

stag-ger (stăg′ẽr), *v.i.* to totter or reel; walk unsteadily; as, a drunkard *staggers:* —*v.t.* **1,** to cause to totter or reel; **2,** to shock; as, the truth *staggered* him; **3,** to make less sure or certain; as, the setback *staggered* his self-confidence; **4,** to arrange in shifts; as, working hours were *staggered* so that some workers came at 8, some at 8:30, some at 9; also, to arrange alternately on opposite sides of the center, as the hub ends of the spokes of a wheel: —*n.* **1,** a reeling or tottering; **2, staggers,** *n.pl.* used as *sing.* a nerve disease of horses, sheep, and cattle, marked by staggering and falling: often called *blind staggers.*

stag-ing (stā′jĭng), *n.* **1,** a temporary structure of boards; **2,** the art or business of putting on a play.

stag-nant (stăg′nȧnt), *adj.* **1,** not flowing; stale or foul from standing; as, *stagnant* water; **2,** not brisk; sluggish; as, the mind grows *stagnant* with disuse.

stag-nate (stăg′nāt), *v.i.* [stagnat-ed, stagnat-ing], **1,** to cease to flow or run; be motionless; **2,** to be or become inactive or dull.—*n.* **stag-na′tion.**

stag-y (stā′jĭ), *adj.* [stag-i-er, stag-i-est], theatrical; artificial; as, a *stagy* voice or manner.—*n.* **stag′i-ness.**

staid (stād), *adj.* quiet; sedate; steady.

stain (stān), *n.* **1,** a discolored spot or blot; **2,** a dye; as, walnut *stain;* **3,** the taint of guilt or crime; as, a reputation without *stain:*—*v.t.* **1,** to blot or spot; as, to *stain* a tie; **2,** to tinge with coloring matter; as, to *stain* walls; **3,** to tarnish or dim:—*v.i.* to take or give a dye or stain.—*adj.* **stain′less.**

stair (stâr), *n.* **1,** any one of a set of steps or treads connecting different levels; **2,** (usually *stairs*), a flight of steps.

stair-case (stâr′kās′), *n.* a flight of steps; a stairway.

stair-way (stâr′wā′), *n.* a flight of steps; a staircase.

stake (stāk), *n.* **1,** a strong stick sharpened at one end for fixing in the ground as a marker or support; **2,** the post to which a person condemned to be burned is bound; hence, death by burning; **3,** (often *stakes*), money wagered or risked on an event; as, to play for high *stakes:*—**at stake,** risked or hazarded:—*v.t.* [staked, stak-ing], **1,** to fasten, support, or provide with stakes; as, to *stake* tomatoes; **2,** to mark the limits of; as, to *stake* a claim;

3, to wager; risk; pledge; as, he *staked* all he had on the success of his invention.

sta·lac·tite (stȧ-lăk′tīt; stăl′ăk-tīt), *n.* an iciclelike formation of carbonate of lime, hanging from the roof of a cave.

sta·lag·mite (stȧ-lăg′mīt; stăl′ăg-mīt), *n.* a tapering cone of carbonate of lime deposited on the floor of a cave by water dripping from the roof.

stale (stāl), *adj.* [stal-er, stalest], **1,** not fresh or new; tasteless; dried out: used especially of food; **2,** worn out by constant repetition or use; as, a *stale* plot; **3,** out of condition,

STALACTITES (A) AND STALAGMITES (B)

as an athlete who is not in training or who has trained too hard or too long:—*v.t.* [staled, stal-ing], to make stale; destroy the novelty of:—*v.i.* to lose newness or freshness; wear out.

stale·mate (stāl′māt′), *n.* **1,** in chess, a draw; **2,** hence, a standstill or deadlock:—*v.t.* [stalemat-ed, stalemat-ing], to bring to a standstill.

Sta·lin (stä′lēn), Joseph (1879–1953), a Russian political leader and premier of the U.S.S.R.

Sta·lin·grad (stä-lēn-gräd′), a city of the U.S.S.R. on the Volga River (map **12**).

¹stalk (stôk), *n.* **1,** the stem of a plant, or of a leaf, flower, or fruit; **2,** any stemlike support, as of a goblet.

²stalk (stôk), *v.t.* to approach (game) cautiously and under cover:—*v.i.* to walk in a haughty manner:—*n.* **1,** the act of creeping up on game; **2,** a proud, haughty step.

stalk·ing–horse (stôk′ĭng-hôrs′), *n.* **1,** a horse, or figure of a horse, behind which a hunter hides in stalking game; **2,** hence, a pretense; a blind.

stall (stôl), *n.* **1,** a stable; cattle shed; also, an enclosed space in a stable for one animal; **2,** a table on which goods are exposed for sale; as, a flower *stall;* **3,** a seat in the choir of a church; also, a church pew:—*v.t.* **1,** to place or keep in a stall; **2,** to cause to stick fast or stop; as, the snowdrifts *stalled* the train; unskilled driving *stalled* the engine:—*v.i.* **1,** to stick fast, as in mud; **2,** to come to a forced standstill; cease running.

stal·lion (stăl′yŭn), *n.* an uncastrated male horse.

stal·wart (stôl′wẽrt; stŏl′wẽrt), *adj.* **1,** sturdy; strong and muscular; as, a man of *stalwart* build; **2,** brave; daring; as, a *stalwart* fighter:—*n.* a firm, loyal partisan.

sta·men (stā′mĕn), *n.* the pollen-bearing part of a flower. (See *flower,* illustration.)

stam·i·na (stăm′ĭ-nȧ), *n.* bodily strength; power of endurance; vigor; as, it requires great *stamina* to run a marathon race.

stam·mer (stăm′ẽr), *v.i.* to hesitate or falter in speaking; stutter:—*v.t.* to utter with difficulty or hesitation; as, he *stammered* out an excuse:—*n.* **1,** hesitating or faltering speech; **2,** any difficulty in pronouncing; a stutter.—*n.* **stam′mer-er.**

stamp (stămp), *v.t.* **1,** to mark with a design by means of a die, pattern, etc.; as, to stamp a coin; **2,** to put a postage or other official stamp upon; as, to *stamp* a letter; **3,** to label; brand; as, our acts *stamp* our characters; **4,** to set (the foot) down heavily; **5,** to crush or grind (ore) into powder; **6,** to shape or cut out, as by pressure of a die or stamp:—**stamp out,** to destroy; end; as, to *stamp out* crime:—*v.i.* to bring down the foot forcibly or with pressure:—*n.* **1,** a mark or design impressed upon a surface; as, the *stamp* on a coin; **2,** a die; **3,** a small piece of paper, sold by the government and stuck to a letter, document, etc., to show payment of a fee or tax; as, a revenue *stamp;* **4,** a characteristic mark or imprint; as, his actions bear the *stamp* of refinement; **5,** a heavy downward blow with the foot.

stam·pede (stăm-pēd′), *n.* **1,** a sudden, wild running away, as of a herd of animals; **2,** any sudden, impulsive movement on the part of a crowd; a general rush; as, a *stampede* for the exits:—*v.t.* [stamped-ed, stamped-ing], to put to sudden flight; as, to *stampede* cattle:—*v.i.* **1,** to start off in a general panic; **2,** to act together from a sudden impulse.

stance (stăns), *n.* **1,** posture; **2,** in golf, the position of a player's feet when he prepares to make a stroke.

stanch (stänch; stȧnch), *v.t.* **1,** to stop the flow of; as, to *stanch* blood; **2,** to stop a flowing from; as, to *stanch* a wound:—*adj.* **1,** seaworthy, as a ship; **2,** loyal; firm; strong; as, a *stanch* friend. Also spelled **staunch.**

stan·chion (stăn′shŭn), *n.* an upright support, post, or pillar.

stand (stănd), *v.i.* [stood (stŏod), stand-ing], **1,** to be stationary on the feet in an erect position; **2,** to be in a certain condition, attitude, or position; as, I *stand* ready to pay; he *stands* acquitted; **3,** to be a substitute; as, a pronoun *stands* for a noun; **4,** to remain firm or in force; as, the agreement *stands;* **5,** to maintain a certain attitude toward a question or a principle; as, he *stands* for free trade:—

STAND

āte, ȧorta, râre, căt, ȧsk, fär, ȧllow, sofȧ; ēve. ĕvent, ĕll, writẽr, novĕl; bīte, pĭn; nō, ōbey, ôr, dŏg, tŏp, cŏllide; ūnit, ūnite, bûrn, cut, focŭs; nōōn, fŏŏt; mound; coin;

v.t. **1,** to set on the feet, or on end, in an upright position; put in place; as, *stand* the broom in the corner; **2,** to put up with; endure; as, to *stand* pain:—*n.* **1,** a stop or halt to maintain a position or to offer resistance; as, they made a *stand* at the river; **2,** position; place of standing; as, he took his *stand* behind the counter; **3,** an outdoor platform for spectators, usually with seats in tiers; **4,** a booth or station used for business; as, a cigar *stand;* **5,** a piece of furniture on which things may be placed or kept; a small table; **6,** a standing growth; as, a good *stand* of wheat.

stand by, 1, to support; uphold; as, to *stand by* one's friends; **2,** to live up to; as, to *stand by* one's word; **3,** in radio, to remain in readiness either to send or to receive messages; **stand out, 1,** to be conspicuous or excellent; as, your work *stands out* from the rest; **2,** to resist; hold out; as, he *stood out* as long as he could.

stand-ard (stăn′dĕrd), *n.* **1,** a figure, flag, or the like, used as an emblem; as, to rally around the *standard;* **2,** an established measure of weight, length, quality, or the like; **3,** any state or degree that is accepted as the desirable one; as, a high *standard* of living; **4,** an upright support; as, a lamp on a tall *standard:*—*adj.* **1,** serving as an accepted basis for comparison, reference, etc.; as, *standard* time; **2,** of a certain or recognized level of excellence; as, *standard* English.

Syn., n. test, ideal, criterion.

stand-ard-ize (stăn′dĕr-dīz), *v.t.* [standardized, standardiz-ing], to bring to a certain level or standard; to make uniform; as, to *standardize* the equipment of automobiles, the sizes of iron pipe, etc.

stand-ing (stăn′dĭng), *n.* **1,** duration; as, a habit of long *standing;* **2,** reputation; rank; as, he is in good *standing:*—*adj.* **1,** stagnant; not flowing; as, *standing* water; **2,** lasting; open indefinitely; as, a *standing* invitation.

Stan-dish (stăn′dĭsh), Miles (1584?–1656) a Puritan leader in Plymouth Colony.

stand-pipe (stănd′pīp′), *n.* a high tower or reservoir, into which water is pumped to secure pressure in a water system.

stand-point (stănd′point′), *n.* a position, principle, or standard from which things are considered or judged; as, from the *standpoint* of justice, the man should be given a fair trial.

stand-still (stănd′stĭl′), *n.* a ceasing of action; a halt or stop; rest; as, the car came to a *standstill.*

stank (stăngk), one form of the past tense of *stink.*

Stan-ley (stăn′lĭ), Sir Henry Morton (1841–1904), a British explorer of Africa.

stan-za (stăn′zȧ), *n.* a group of lines or verses, varying in number, forming a unit or section of a poem or song.

¹**sta-ple** (stā′pl), *n.* **1,** the chief thing produced in a district; as, cotton is the *staple* of the South; **2,** the principal part, or an important element, of something; chief item; as, bread is a *staple* of food; **3,** raw material for manufacture; **4,** the fiber of cotton, flax, or wool; as, wool of long, fine *staple:*—*adj.* **1,** important because produced regularly and in large amounts; as, *staple* goods; **2,** in commerce, fixed; as, a *staple* demand:—*v.t.* [sta-pled, sta-pling], to sort according to the quality of its fiber; as, to *staple* wool.

²**sta-ple** (stā′pl), *n.* a small, U-shaped piece of metal which may be driven into wood, and into which is fitted a hook or other locking device, as on a door or gate; also, a small piece of light wire bent to hold papers together.

STAPLE

star (stär) *n.* **1,** any heavenly body seen as a point of light; **2,** a figure whose points make it look like a star, as an asterisk; **3,** in astrology, a planet supposed to influence a person's life; **4,** a brilliant, outstanding person, especially on the

STARS, def. 2

stage or in athletics:—*v.t.* [starred, starring], **1,** to deck or adorn with stars; **2,** to cast (a person) as the principal actor in a play:—*v.i.* **1,** to be illustrious or prominent; **2,** to appear as the principal actor in a play.—*adj.* **star′less.**—*adj.* **star′like′.**—*adj.* **starred.**

star-board (stär′bôrd; stär′bĕrd), *n.* the right side of the ship as one faces the bow: opposite of *port:*—*adj.* on the right side of a ship; as, a *starboard* cabin:—*v.t.* to turn to the starboard side of a ship; as, to *starboard* the helm.

starch (stärch), *n.* **1,** a white, odorless, tasteless substance obtained commercially from grain and potatoes, but found in nearly all plants; **2,** a commercial preparation of this substance used in laundering to stiffen fabrics or clothes; **3,** hence, stiffness of conduct or manner:—*v.t.* to stiffen with starch.—*adj.* **starch′y.**

stare (stâr), *v.i.* [stared, star-ing], **1,** to look with eyes wide open; gaze fixedly in one direction; **2,** to glare, as, lights or bright colors:—*v.t.* to be visible to; confront; as, disaster *stared* them in the face; also, to embarrass or dismay by staring; as, she *stared* him into silence:—*n.* a fixed steady look with wide-open eyes.

---

go; join; yet; sing; chin; show; thin, *th*en; hw, *wh*y; zh, azure; ü, Ger. f*ü*r or Fr. l*u*ne; ö, Ger. sch*ö*n or Fr. f*eu*; ṅ, Fr. *en*fant, n*om*; kh, Ger. a*ch* or i*ch*. See pages ix–x.

star-fish (stär′fĭsh′), *n.* a sea animal with a body shaped like a star. It usually has five arms or rays.

star-gaz-er (stär′gāz′ẽr), *n.* a person who gazes at the stars, especially an astrologer; a dreamer.

stark (stärk), *adj.* 1, stiff; rigid; as, *stark* with cold; 2, utter; complete; as, *stark* nonsense:—*adv.* wholly; as, *stark* naked.—*adv.* **stark′ly.**

star-light (stär′līt′), *n.* light from the stars:—*adj.* lighted by the stars.

STARFISH (⅛)

star-ling (stär′lĭng), *n.* a bird, varying in plumage from brown with light speckles in winter to greenish black in summer, brought to America from Europe and now something of a pest. The starling is a sociable bird, flying in flocks and building near human habitations.

star-lit (stär′lĭt′), *adj.* made light by the stars; as, *starlit* waters.

star-ry (stär′ĭ), *adj.* [star-ri-er, star-ri-est], 1, spangled or lighted with stars; as, a *starry* night; 2, shining like stars; as, *starry* eyes. —*n.* **star′ri-ness.**

STARLING (¼)

Stars and Stripes, the flag of the U.S.

star—span-gled (stär′-spăng′gld), *adj.* thickly set or dotted with stars.

Star—Span-gled Ban-ner, The, the national anthem of the U.S., the words of which were written by Francis Scott Key during the War of 1812.

start (stärt), *v.i.* 1, to spring suddenly; leap; bound; 2, to make a sudden involuntary movement, as of surprise, pain, or shock; 3, to begin; set out; as, to *start* on a journey; to *start* in business; 4, to become loosened, as a nail or screw:—*v.t.* 1, to originate action in; set going; as, to *start* a clock; 2, to rouse suddenly, as game; 3, to originate; begin; as, to *start* a quarrel; 4, to loosen (a nail); 5, to cause or help (a person) to begin; as, to *start* a man in business:—*n.* 1, a sudden leap or bound; an involuntary movement, caused by surprise, fear, or joy; as, the prisoner gave a *start* when he heard the sentence; 2, a brief effort; as, to work by fits and *starts;* 3, a beginning; as, a *start* in business; 4, a lead or advantage; as, he had a good *start.*

Syn., v. jerk, twitch, flinch, wince.

star-tle (stär′tl), *v.t.* [star-tled, star-tling], to cause to start or move suddenly; scare; shock; as, the noise *startled* her.

star-tling (stär′tlĭng), *adj.* causing sudden alarm or surprise; as, a *startling* announcement.

star-va-tion (stär-vā′shŭn), *n.* 1, suffering or death from lack of food; 2, the act of depriving others of food; as, deliberate *starvation* of prisoners was charged against the enemy.

starve (stärv), *v.i.* [starved, starv-ing], to suffer or die from extreme hunger:—*v.t.* to cause to suffer or die from hunger.

starve-ling (stärv′lĭng), *n.* one who is weak from lack of food; also, a thin, weak animal or plant:—*adj.* hungry; weak; lean.

state (stāt), *n.* 1, the condition in which a person or thing is; as, a *state* of health; a confused *state* of affairs; 2, great style or formal dignity; as, to receive an ambassador in *state;* 3, a body of people united under one government; a commonwealth; 4, the territory or the civil powers of such a commonwealth; 5, (often *State*), one of several political units forming a federation; as, the *State* of Texas:—*adj.* 1, pertaining to a state; as, a *state* tax; 2, formal; ceremonious; as, *state* occasions:—*v.t.* [stat-ed, stat-ing], to set forth clearly and formally; tell; declare; as, to *state* the facts.

state-craft (stāt′kraft′), *n.* the art of managing the political affairs of a commonwealth or state; statesmanship.

stat-ed (stā′tĕd), *adj.* fixed; regular; as, a *stated* meeting; at *stated* times.

State-house (stāt′hous′), *n.* a building in which a State legislature meets. Also written **State house.**

state-ly (stāt′lĭ), *adj.* [state-li-er, state-li-est], having a grand or imposing appearance or manner; noble; majestic; as, a *stately* princess.—*n.* **state′li-ness.**

state-ment (stāt′mĕnt), *n.* 1, the act of presenting or expressing formally in words; also, that which is so expressed; 2, a report or summary of financial condition; as, a bank *statement.*

state-room (stāt′room′), *n.* a private room or compartment on a passenger vessel or in a railroad car.

states-man (stāts′măn), *n.* [pl. statesmen (-měn)], one skilled in public affairs and the art of government.—*adj.* **states′-man-like′.**—*n.* **states′man-ship.**

stat-ic (stăt′ĭk), *n.* in radio, a sharp, jarring noise made by electrical disturbances, such as thunderstorms, in the air:—*adj.* 1, pertaining to bodies at rest, or to forces in balance; 2, standing still; inactive; 3, in radio, caused by static.

āte, āorta, râre, căt, ȧsk, fär, ăllow, sofȧ; ēve, ēvent, ĕll, writẽr, novĕl; bīte, pĭn; nō, ōbey, ôr, dôg, tŏp, cŏllide; ūnit, ūnite, bûrn, cŭt, focŭs; no͞on, foŏt: mound; coin;

sta·tion (stā′shŭn), *n.* **1,** a place where a person or thing usually remains; position; as, the guard took his *station* before the door; **2,** the place to which a person or force is appointed for duty; as, a fire *station;* **3,** a regular stopping place on a railroad; also, the buildings there; **4,** rank; standing; as, a man of high *station:* —*v.t.* to set or place in a certain position; assign; as, to *station* troops on the border.

sta·tion·ar·y (stā′shŭn-ĕr′ĭ), *adj.* **1,** not to be moved; fixed; as, a *stationary* tub; **2,** without change in condition, numbers, etc.; stable; as, a *stationary* population.

sta·tion·er (stā′shŭn-ĕr), *n.* one who deals in writing materials.

sta·tion·er·y (stā′shŭn-ĕr′ĭ), *n.* paper and other writing materials.

stat·is·ti·cian (stăt′ĭs-tĭsh′ăn), *n.* a person whose business it is to collect and interpret numerical data, or statistics.

sta·tis·tics (stȧ-tĭs′tĭks), *n.pl.* **1,** numerical facts or data relating to a community, a special industry, or the like, collected and arranged for study; **2,** *pl.* used as *sing.* the science of collecting and interpreting such data.—*adj.* **sta·tis′ti·cal.**

stat·u·ar·y (stăt′ū-ĕr′ĭ), *n.* **1,** the art of sculpture; **2,** a collection of statues.

stat·ue (stăt′ū), *n.* the figure of a person or an animal, sculptured, as in marble, or cast, as in bronze.

stat·u·esque (stăt′ū-ĕsk′), *adj.* like a statue; having the beauty or formal dignity of a statue.

stat·u·ette (stăt′ū-ĕt′), *n.* a little statue or modeled figure.

stat·ure (stăt′ūr), *n.* the height of a person or an animal; as, a man of average *stature.*

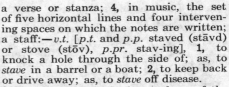

STATUE OF APOLLO

sta·tus (stā′tŭs), *n.* [*pl.* statuses], **1,** the position, state, or condition of a person; standing; as, the *status* of an alien; **2,** the position or condition of affairs; as, what is the present *status* of the negotiations?

stat·ute (stăt′ūt), *n.* an ordinance or law passed by a lawmaking body.

stat·u·tor·y (stăt′ū-tôr′ĭ), *adj.* defined or enacted by statute or law; as, a *statutory* crime or penalty.

staunch (stônch; stänch), *v.t.* to stop the flow of, or a flow from:—*adj.* firm; stanch. See **stanch.**

stave (stāv), *n.* **1,** a staff or heavy stick; **2,** one of the curved, narrow strips of wood forming the sides of a cask or barrel; **3,**

a verse or stanza; **4,** in music, the set of five horizontal lines and four intervening spaces on which the notes are written; a staff:—*v.t.* [*p.t.* and *p.p.* staved (stāvd) or stove (stōv), *p.pr.* stav-ing], **1,** to knock a hole through the side of; as, to *stave* in a barrel or a boat; **2,** to keep back or drive away; as, to *stave* off disease.

staves (stāvz; stȧvz), **1,** one form of the plural of *staff;* **2,** (stāvz), plural of *stave.*

STAVES (S, S, S)

stay (stā), *v.t.* **1,** to put off; postpone; as, to *stay* a trial; **2,** to satisfy for a time; as, to *stay* the stomach:—*v.i.* **1,** to remain; wait; as, you must *stay* until I return; **2,** to dwell temporarily; as, to *stay* at a hotel; *stay* south for the winter:—*n.* **1,** a postponement; as, the *stay* of a trial; **2,** a prop or support; especially, a rope or wire used to steady or support a mast or spar on a vessel; **3,** one that supports; as, he is the *stay* of the family; **4,** a stop or halt; sojourn; **5, stays,** a corset.

stay-sail (stā′sāl′; stā′sl), *n.* any sail attached to a stay. (See *rigging,* illustration, page 695.)

stead (stĕd), *n.* **1,** the place which another had or might have; as, to go to war in another's *stead;* **2,** use; service; advantage; as, it will stand you in good *stead.*

stead·fast or **sted·fast** (stĕd′făst), *adj.* **1,** fixed firmly; immovable; as, the troops stood *steadfast;* **2,** steady; constant; as, *steadfast* faith.—*adv.* **stead′fast·ly.**

stead·y (stĕd′ĭ), *adj.* [stead-i-er, stead-i-est], **1,** firmly fixed or supported; as, a *steady* foundation; **2,** constant in feeling or purpose; resolute; unwavering; as, a *steady* faith; **3,** regular; uniform; even; as, a *steady* tread; **4,** sober; industrious; as, a *steady* young man:—*v.t.* and *v.i.* [steadied, steady-ing], to make or become steady.— *adv.* **stead′i·ly.**—*n.* **stead′i·ness.**

steak (stāk), *n.* a slice of beef or other meat, cut for broiling or frying.

steal (stēl), *v.t.* [*p.t.* stole (stōl), *p.p.* sto-len (stō′lĕn), *p.pr.* steal-ing], **1,** to take by theft; take without leave or right; **2,** to take or get by craft or surprise; as, to *steal* a kiss; **3,** to gain gradually; as, the child *stole* its way into the man's heart:— *v.i.* **1,** to take what belongs to another; **2,** to move or act stealthily or secretly; as, to *steal* about on tiptoes:—*n.* an act of theft; also, that which is stolen.

stealth (stĕlth), *n.* secret means used to accomplish an object; secret action.

stealth·y (stĕl′thĭ), *adj.* [stealth-i-er,

stealth-i-est], acting slyly; done secretly; furtive; as, a *stealthy* approach.—*adv.* **stealth′i-ly.**—*n.* **stealth′i-ness.**

steam (stēm), *n.* **1,** the visible vapor which rises from boiling water; **2,** this vapor used as a source of power; as, the engine was driven by *steam:*—*v.i.* **1,** to throw off visible vapor; as, a teakettle *steams;* **2,** to rise or pass off in visible vapor; as, moisture *steams* from the earth; **3,** to move under the power of steam; as, the vessel *steamed* away:—*v.t.* to expose to, or treat by, steam.

steam-boat (stēm′bōt′), *n.* a boat driven by steam.

steam en-gine, a locomotive or a stationary engine operated by the power of steam.

paratus which records weight on a horizontal bar.

¹**steep** (stēp), *adj.* **1,** having a sharp pitch or slope; nearly vertical; as, a *steep* cliff; **2,** *Colloquial,* very high; as, *steep* prices: —*n.* a cliff or precipice.—*adv.* **steep′ly.**
  Syn., *adj.* abrupt, precipitous.

²**steep** (stēp), *v.t.* **1,** to soak, usually in a liquid just below the boiling point; as, to *steep* tea; **2,** to soak or dye; hence, to saturate; fill thoroughly; as, the sun *steeped* the valley in sunshine:—*v.i.* to be soaked or steeped in a liquid.

stee-ple (stē′pl), *n.* a high tapering tower above the roof of a church.

stee-ple-chase (stē′pl-chās′), *n.* **1,** a cross-country race on horseback; **2,** any

STEAM LOCOMOTIVE

steam-er (stēm′ẽr), *n.* **1,** a steamship; **2,** an apparatus in which articles are subjected to steam.

steam fit-ter, one who installs or repairs steam pipes and steam fittings.

steam roll-er, 1, a heavy machine, operated by steam, used to press down and level roads; **2,** *Colloquial,* any great power, as in politics, used to crush opposition.

steam-ship (stēm′shĭp′), *n.* a vessel driven by steam power.

steam shov-el, an excavating machine operated by steam.

sted-fast (stĕd′fȧst), *adj.* firm; constant; steadfast. See **steadfast.**

steed (stēd), *n.* a horse, especially a spirited war or parade horse.

steel (stēl), *n.* **1,** an alloy of iron and carbon, treated to make a hard, tough metal; **2,** any instrument or weapon of steel; **3,** a piece of steel for striking fire from flint:— *adj.* made of steel; as, a *steel* blade:—*v.t.* to make hard or strong; as, to *steel* one's courage.—*adj.* **steel′y.**

STEELYARD

steel-yard (stēl′yärd′), *n.* a weighing ap-

race over a course made difficult with artificial obstacles.—*n.* **stee′ple-chas′ing.**

stee-ple jack, a workman who climbs high structures, such as smokestacks, to make repairs.

¹**steer** (stēr), *n.* a bull, or male of the family of domestic cattle, that has been castrated, especially one that is to be slaughtered for market.

²**steer** (stēr), *v.t.* to direct or guide (a ship, automobile, etc.) by means of a rudder, wheel, or other gear:—*v.i.* **1,** to direct a ship, vehicle, etc., in its course; **2,** to direct one's course in a given direction; as, *steer* toward shore; **3,** to obey the helm; be steered.

STEEPLE

steer-age (stēr′ĭj), *n.* that part of a ship set aside for passengers paying the lowest rates.

steer-ing wheel, the wheel by which an automobile, motorboat, or the like, is steered or controlled.

steers-man (stērz′măn), *n.* [*pl.* steersmen (-mĕn)], one who steers; a helmsman.

stein (stīn), *n.* a mug, generally of earthenware, used especially for beer.

---

stel-lar (stĕl′ẽr), *adj.* of or like the stars or a star.

¹**stem** (stĕm), *n.* **1,** the main stalk of a plant; also, any slender stalk that bears a leaf, flower, or fruit; **2,** any shaft, support, or handle, resembling the stalk of a plant; as, the *stem* of a wineglass; **3,** the curved wooden or metal piece to which the two sides of a ship are joined in the front; as, from *stem* to stern; **4,** the part of a word to which various endings may be attached:—*v.t.* [stemmed, stem-ming], to pluck the stem or stems from; as, to *stem* cherries.

STEM
(S)
def. 2

²**stem** (stĕm), *v.t.* [stemmed, stem-ming], **1,** to stop or check; dam up; as, to *stem* a flow of water; **2,** to make headway against; as, to *stem* the tide.

stench (stĕnch), *n.* a strong, disagreeable odor; very bad smell; stink.

sten-cil (stĕn′sĭl), *n.* **1,** a thin sheet of metal, paper, or the like, cut with an open pattern, so that, when it is placed on a surface and color is brushed over it, the design appears on the surface beneath; **2,** a design or decoration so made:—*v.t.* [stenciled, stencil-ing], to mark or decorate in this manner.

STENCIL

ste-nog-ra-pher (stĕ-nŏg′rá-fẽr), *n.* a person whose business it is to take and transcribe shorthand notes.—*adj.* **sten′o-graph′ic** (stĕn′ō-grăf′ĭk).

ste-nog-ra-phy (stĕ-nŏg′rá-fĭ), *n.* a rapid, abbreviated method of writing; shorthand; also, the process of taking dictation in shorthand notes and transcribing them.

sten-tor-i-an (stĕn-tôr′ĭ-ăn), *adj.* extremely loud or powerful; as, a *stentorian* voice.

step (stĕp), *v.i.* [stepped, step-ping], **1,** to move the feet alternately, as in walking forward, backward, or sidewise; **2,** to walk, especially a short distance; as, to *step* across the street; **3,** to take possession without effort; as, to *step* into a fortune; **4,** to place the foot (on); as, to *step* on a tack:—*v.t.* **1,** to set or place (the foot); **2,** to measure by steps; as, to *step* off a yard; **3,** to place the heel, or foot, of (a mast) in the socket:—*n.* **1,** the complete movement made in raising and setting down the foot, as in walking or dancing; a pace; **2,** the distance gained in one such movement; hence, any short distance; **3,** a degree of progress; as, a *step* nearer fame; **4,** a tread in a stairway; **5,** one of a series of actions or measures; as, the first *step* in an undertaking; **6,** in music,

the interval between two successive degrees on a scale or staff.—*n.* **step′per.**

step- (stĕp-), a prefix, showing a relationship not by blood, but by remarriage; as, *step*father, *step*child.

step-broth-er (stĕp′brŭth′ẽr), *n.* the son, by a previous marriage, of one's stepfather or stepmother.

step-child (stĕp′chīld′), *n.* [*pl.* stepchildren (-chĭl′drĕn)], the child, by a previous marriage, of one's husband or wife.

step-daugh-ter (stĕp′dô′tẽr), *n.* the daughter, by a previous marriage, of one's husband or wife.

step-fa-ther (stĕp′fä′thẽr), *n.* the husband of one's mother by a later marriage.

step-lad-der (stĕp′lăd′ẽr), *n.* a short, portable set of steps, supported at the back by a hinged prop.

step-moth-er (stĕp′mŭth′ẽr), *n.* the wife of one's father by a later marriage.

steppe (stĕp), *n.* a vast level plain without forests, as in Siberia.

step-sis-ter (stĕp′sĭs′tẽr), *n.* the daughter, by a previous marriage, of one's stepfather or stepmother.

STEPLADDER

step-son (stĕp′sŭn′), *n.* the son, by a previous marriage, of one's husband or wife.

ster-e-op-ti-con (stĕr′ē-ŏp′tĭ-kŏn; stē′rē-ŏp′tĭ-kŏn), *n.* a kind of magic lantern for magnifying and projecting pictures, usually photographs, on a screen.

ster-e-o-scope (stĕr′ē-ō-skōp′; stē′rē-ō-skōp′), *n.* an optical instrument with two lenses, through which a person looks at two photographs of the same scene taken from slightly different angles, and sees a single picture in which the objects stand out in sharp relief.

STEREOSCOPE

ster-e-o-type (stĕr′ē-ō-tīp′; stē′rē-ō-tīp′), *n.* a plate made by pouring metal into a mold made from the original type.

ster-e-o-typed (stĕr′ē-ō-tīpt′; stē′rē-ō-tīpt′), *adj.* **1,** printed from a stereotype; **2,** hence, always the same; monotonous; as, a *stereotyped* remark.

ster-ile (stĕr′ĭl), *adj.* **1,** not fertile or fruitful; barren; not producing fruit, seed, crops, or young; **2,** free from living germs or microbes; as, a *sterile* bandage.—*n.* **ste-ril′i-ty.**

ster-i-lize (stĕr′ĭ-līz), *v.t.* [sterilized, steriliz-ing], **1,** to make fruitless or barren;

go; join; yet; sing; chin; show; thin, *th*en; hw, *wh*y; zh, azure; ü, Ger. für or Fr. lune; ö, Ger. schön or Fr. feu; ṅ, Fr. enfant, nom; kh, Ger. ach or ich. See pages ix–x.

deprive of the power of reproduction; as, to *sterilize* an animal; **2,** to free from germs; as, to *sterilize* a needle.—*n.* **ster′i-li-za′tion.**

ster-ling (stûr′lĭng), *n.* English money; as, *sterling* rose when the U.S. went off the gold standard:—*adj.* **1,** of standard weight or purity; as, *sterling* silver; **2,** pure; genuine; of acknowledged worth; as, a *sterling* character.

¹stern (stûrn), *adj.* **1,** severe; rigorous; strict; as, *stern* discipline; **2,** forbidding; repelling; as, a *stern* look.—*adv.* **stern′ly.**

²stern (stûrn), *n.* the aft or rear part of a vessel.

ster-num (stûr′nŭm), *n.* the breastbone.

steth-o-scope (stĕth′ō-skōp), *n.* an instrument used by doctors to examine the heart or lungs by listening through it to the sounds which they make.

ste-ve-dore (stē′vĕ-dôr′), *n.* one who loads or unloads the cargoes of ships.

Ste-ven-son (stē′vĕn-sŭn), Robert Louis (1850–1894), a Scottish writer of prose and verse, author of "Treasure Island."

stew (stū), *v.t.* and *v.i.* to boil slowly; simmer:—*n.* **1,** a dish of food, usually of meat and vegetables, prepared by simmering; **2,** *Colloquial,* nervous anxiety; worry.

stew-ard (stū′ẽrd), *n.* **1,** one who manages the household affairs of a family or institution; also, the manager of a large estate or farm; **2,** a person employed at a hotel, club, or on board ship, as a waiter or an attendant in staterooms; **3,** one who controls financial affairs; as, the *steward* of a church.—*n.fem.* **stew′ard-ess.**

¹stick (stĭk), *n.* **1,** a piece of wood, generally long and slender; a small branch from a tree or shrub; **2,** something long and slender, as a long piece of candy, a cane, the baton of a musical director, etc.; **3,** *Colloquial,* a stiff or dull person.

²stick (stĭk), *v.t.* [stuck (stŭk), stick-ing], **1,** to puncture with a pointed instrument; prick, pierce; as, he *stuck* his hand with a pin; to cause (a pin or a needle) to go through fabric; **2,** to attach or hold in place by means of a point; as, to *stick* a pickle on a fork; also, to fasten in place by causing to adhere; as, to *stick* a stamp on an envelope; **3,** to push or thrust (something); as, he *stuck* the letter under the door:—*v.i.* **1,** to penetrate by means of a pointed end; as, the pin *stuck* in his arm; **2,** to adhere closely; as, dough *sticks* to the hands; **3,** to stay in one place; as, to *stick* at home; **4,** to hold fast; as, he *sticks* to his ideals; **5,** to persist; persevere; as,

to *stick* to a job; **6,** to protrude; as, his handkerchief *stuck* out of his pocket; **7,** to be checked; lose the power of motion; as, to *stick* in a rut; hence, to become blocked or jammed; as, an engine *sticks;* **8,** to be checked by fear; hesitate; as, to *stick* at nothing.

stick-le (stĭk′l), *v.i.* [stick-led, stick-ling], to argue or hold out stubbornly, usually for little reason; as, do not *stickle* at trifles.

stick-ler (stĭk′lẽr), *n.* one who stubbornly insists, especially about small matters; as, a *stickler* for details.

stick-y (stĭk′ĭ), *adj.* [stick-i-er, stick-i-est], **1,** tending to stick or adhere, like glue; **2,** *Colloquial,* hot and humid; as, *sticky* weather.—*n.* **stick′i-ness.**

stiff (stĭf), *adj.* **1,** not easily bent; rigid; firm; as, *stiff* cardboard; also, moved or bent with difficulty or with pain; as, a *stiff* knee; **2,** not easily operated; not working smoothly; as, a *stiff* engine; **3,** strong; fresh; as, a *stiff* breeze; **4,** unnatural; formal; as, a *stiff* manner; **5,** firm; thick; not fluid; as, *stiff* gelatin; **6,** difficult; as, a *stiff* test; **7,** *Colloquial,* high; dear; as, a *stiff* charge.—*adv.* **stiff′ly.**

stiff-en (stĭf′ĕn), *v.t.* and *v.i.* to make or become rigid, stiff, or less flexible.

stiff—necked (stĭf′-nĕkt′), *adj.* stubborn; obstinate; as, *stiff-necked* pride.

¹sti-fle (stī′fl), *v.t.* [sti-fled, sti-fling], **1,** to suffocate; smother; **2,** to put out (a fire); also, to stop or muffle (sounds); **3,** to suppress; choke back; as, to *stifle* a yawn. —*adj.* **sti′fling.**

²sti-fle (stī′fl), *n.* the joint above the hock in the hind leg of the horse and dog. (See illustrations under *horse, dog.*)

stig-ma (stĭg′mȧ), *n.* **1,** [*pl.* stigmas], a mark of disgrace or dishonor; as, the *stigma* attached to a prison term; **2,** [*pl.* stigmata (stĭg′mȧ-tȧ)], a distinguishing mark; especially, the sign of some particular disorder; as, the *stigmata* of hysteria; **3,** **stigmata,** marks resembling the wounds on the body of Christ, said to have appeared on the bodies of certain saints; **4,** [*pl.* stigmas], the upper part of a flower pistil on which the pollen falls (see illustration under *flower*).

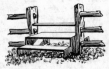

STILE, def. 1

stig-ma-tize (stĭg′mȧ-tīz), *v.t.* [stigmatized, stigmatiz-ing], to hold up to disgrace; as, to *stigmatize* a man as a traitor.

stile (stīl), *n.* **1,** a set of steps leading over a fence or wall; also, a turnstile; **2,** in framing or paneling, a vertical sidepiece (see illustration under *sash*).

sti-let-to (stĭ-lĕt′ō), *n.* [*pl.* stilettos or stilettoes], **1,** a small, slender dagger; **2,** a tool for making holes in needle-work.

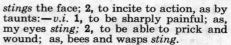
STILETTO

¹still (stĭl), *adj.* **1,** motionless; also, peaceful and calm; tranquil; as, a *still* pond; **2,** quiet; silent; as, a *still* evening:—*n. Poetic,* stillness; profound silence:—*adv.* **1,** up to this time; up to any particular time; as, he is *still* sleeping; he was *still* sleeping when I saw him; **2,** nevertheless; in spite of something; as, though he failed, his friends loved him *still;* **3,** even; as, louder *still:*—*conj.* however; yet; as, he was in pain, *still* he uttered no sound:—*v.t.* to check motion, disturbance, or sound in; calm; put at rest; as, to *still* a baby; *still* one's fears.

Syn., v. lull, allay, subdue, pacify.

²still (stĭl), *n.* an apparatus for distilling liquids, as water or alcoholic liquors.

still-born (stĭl′bôrn′), *adj.* dead at the time of birth.

still-y (stĭl′ĭ), *adj.* [still-i-er, still-i-est], calm; quiet; as, "oft in the *stilly* night."

stilt (stĭlt), *n.* one of a pair of wooden poles, each with an elevated footrest. They are used to hold one high above the ground in walking.

stilt-ed (stĭl′tĕd), *adj.* stiff; formal; as, a *stilted* speech.

stim-u-lant (stĭm′ū-lănt), *n.* **1,** that which excites or spurs on; **2,** that which quickens some bodily function for a short time; as, coffee is a heart *stimulant.*

stim-u-late (stĭm′ū-lāt), *v.t.* [stimulat-ed, stimulat-ing], **1,** to rouse to activity; animate; as, danger *stimulated* us to action; **2,** to produce greater activity in; as, coffee *stimulates* the heart.—*n.* stim′u-la′tion.

STILTS

stim-u-lus (stĭm′ū-lŭs), *n.* [*pl.* stimuli (stĭm′ū-lī)], **1,** something that rouses to action; **2,** something that excites an organ or tissue to a specific activity.

sting (stĭng), *n.* **1,** the sharp, often poisonous, organ with which certain animals, as the scorpion and bee, are armed; **2,** the thrust of such an organ; also, the wound made by it; **3,** keen, smarting, mental or physical pain:—*v.t.* [stung (stŭng), sting-ing], **1,** to prick or wound with a sharp point; cause a sharp, smarting pain to; as, cold

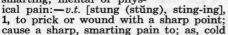
STING (S) OF SCORPION

stings the face; **2,** to incite to action, as by taunts:—*v.i.* **1,** to be sharply painful; as, my eyes *sting;* **2,** to be able to prick and wound; as, bees and wasps *sting.*

sting ray, a kind of tropical fish which has a broad, flat body, and a tail with bony spines that can inflict severe wounds. Also written **sting′ray′.**

stin-gy (stĭn′jĭ), *adj.* [stin-gi-er, stin-gi-est], **1,** meanly saving of money; miserly; **2,** scanty; meager; as, a *stingy* portion.—*n.* **stin′gi-ness.**

stink (stĭngk), *n.* an offensive odor; disgusting smell:—*v.i.* [*p.t.* stank (stăngk), or stunk (stŭngk), *p.p.* stunk, *p.pr.* stinking], to throw off a strong, offensive odor.

stink-bug (stĭngk′bŭg′), *n.* any of various small bugs which give forth an unpleasant odor.

stint (stĭnt), *v.t.* to keep within narrow limits; skimp; as, to *stint* food; to limit to a scant allowance; as, to *stint* a child:—*v.i.* to be sparing or frugal:—*n.* **1,** a limit or bound; as, generosity without *stint;* **2,** a task assigned; as, his weekly *stint* was to cut the grass.—*adj.* **stint′ed.**

sti-pend (stī′pĕnd), *n.* fixed pay or salary for services; remuneration.

stip-u-late (stĭp′ū-lāt), *v.t.* [stipulat-ed, stipulat-ing], to arrange or settle definitely; specify, as part of an agreement; as, he *stipulated* that he be paid in advance.—*n.* **stip′u-la′tion.**

stip-ule (stĭp′ūl), *n.* one of two small leaflike attachments at the base of some leaves, as in the rose.

stir (stûr), *v.t.* [stirred, stirring], **1,** to change the position of; move; as, he *stirred* neither hand nor foot; **2,** to set in motion; as, the wind *stirred* the leaves; **3,** to shake or mix up the parts of, by moving, beating, poking, etc., with some utensil; as, *stir* the cake with a spoon; *stir* the fire with a poker; **4,** to move or rouse;

STIPULE (S)

as, to *stir* men to pity:—*v.i.* **1,** to move or be moved; budge; as, he would not *stir* from his chair; **2,** to be in motion; as, the leaves *stirred* in the trees; **3,** to be roused; as, pity *stirred* in his heart:—*n.* **1,** the act of stirring or mixing; as, give the soup a *stir;* **2,** hustle; excitement; as, his announcement created quite a *stir.*

stir-rup (stĭr′ŭp; stûr′ŭp), *n.* one of a pair of loop-shaped supports for the feet of a horseback rider, attached to the saddle by a strap. (See illustration under *saddle.*)

---

go; join; yet; sing; chin; show; thin, *th*en; hw, *wh*y; zh, a*z*ure; ü, Ger. f*ü*r or Fr. l*u*ne; ö, Ger. sch*ö*n or Fr. f*eu;* ṅ, Fr. *en*fant, no*m;* kh, Ger. a*ch* or i*ch.* See pages ix–x.

stitch (stĭch), *n.* **1,** in sewing, a single passing of a threaded needle in and out of the material; also, the section of thread left in the fabric; **2,** in knitting, crocheting, and such work, a single complete movement of the needle or hook; also, the link or loop so formed; **3,** a particular type of stitch or arrangement of stitches, as the buttonhole stitch in needlework; **4,** a sudden, sharp pain; as, a *stitch* in the side: —*v.t.* to join by stitches; hence, to sew; also, to ornament by stitches:—*v.i.* to sew.—*n.* **stitch′er.**

sti·ver (stī′vẽr), *n.* **1,** a Dutch coin of little value; **2,** anything of little value:— **not a stiver,** not a bit; nothing.

stoat (stōt), *n.* the European ermine or weasel, especially in its summer coat of reddish brown; also, any ermine or weasel.

stock (stŏk), *n.* **1,** a wooden stump or block; **2,** hence, a dull or senseless person; also, the object or butt of some action or notice; as, a laughing*stock;* **3,** the main stem or trunk of a plant or tree; also, a growing plant in which a graft is placed; as, a quince *stock;* **4,** the race

STOCK, def. 11

or line of a family; ancestry; as, he comes of old *stock;* **5,** the part of an implement or machine that serves as the body or main support for other parts, as the part of a gun to which the barrel, lock, etc., are attached, the crosspiece of an anchor, etc. (see illustrations under *anchor, die*); **6,** the capital of a corporation in the form of shares; **7,** the supply of goods which a merchant keeps on hand;

STOCKS, def. 14

as, to replenish *stock;* **8,** hence, a supply of anything; as, a *stock* of information; **9,** domestic animals kept on a farm; livestock; **10,** raw material ready for manufacture; as, paper *stock;* also, the juices of meats or vegetables from which soups, gravies, etc., are made; **11,** a close-fitting wide band or cloth for the neck; **12,** a company of actors presenting one play after another; **13,** a commonly cultivated plant with single or double sweet-scented flowers growing along the stalk: also called *gillyflower;* **14, stocks,** an old instrument of punishment for minor offenses, consisting of a wooden frame with holes in which to confine the hands, feet, and, sometimes, the head of offenders:— *v.t.* to lay in a stock or supply of.

stock-ade (stŏk-ād′), *n.* **1,** a fence of upright posts or logs set close together in the earth, used as a defensive barrier or to form an enclosure for cattle; **2,** the space so enclosed:— *v.t.* [stockad-ed, stockad-ing], to surround with, or defend by, such a fence.

STOCKADE

stock-bro-ker (stŏk′brō′kẽr), *n.* one who buys and sells shares of stock for others.

stock com-pa-ny, 1, a corporation, the capital of which is divided into shares of stock; **2,** a company of actors presenting a series of plays.

stock ex-change, 1, an association of stockbrokers; **2,** a place where shares of stock are bought and sold.

stock-hold-er (stŏk′hōl′dẽr), *n.* one who owns a share or shares of stock:

Stock-holm (stŏk′hōlm; stŏk′hōm), a city, capital of Sweden (map **12**).

stock-ing (stŏk′ĭng), *n.* a woven or knit covering for the foot and leg.

stock mar-ket, 1, a place where shares of stock are bought and sold; a stock exchange; **2,** the trend in the prices of stocks; as, the *stock market* is up today.

stock-still (stŏk′stĭl′), *adj.* still as a post; motionless.

stock-y (stŏk′ĭ), *adj.* [stock-i-er, stock-i-est], short and stoutly built; thickset.

stock-yard (stŏk′yärd′), *n.* a large pen for cattle, swine, and sheep, usually for those which are to be slaughtered.

stodg-y (stŏj′ĭ), *adj.* [stodg-i-er, stodg-i-est], **1,** solid; heavy; as, *stodgy* food; **2,** dull; uninteresting; as, a *stodgy* book.

sto-gie or **sto-gy** (stō′gĭ), *n.* [*pl.* stogies], a long, coarse, slender cigar.

sto-gy (stō′gĭ), *n.* [*pl.* stogies], **1,** a coarse boot or shoe; brogue; **2,** a stogie.

Sto-ic (stō′ĭk), *n.* one of the followers of the Greek philosopher Zeno, who taught that virtue is the highest good, that man should be governed by reason, control all emotion, and be alike indifferent to joy and pleasure, grief and pain:—**stoic,** a person who suffers without complaint.

sto-ic (stō′ĭk) or **sto-i-cal** (stō′ĭ-kăl), *adj.* self-controlled; able to suffer without complaining.—*adv.* **sto′i-cal-ly.**

Sto-i-cism (stō′ĭ-sĭzm), *n.* the philosophy of the Stoics:—**stoicism,** endurance of suffering without protest or complaint.

stoke (stōk), *v.t.* and *v.i.* [stoked, stok-ing], to tend (a fire or furnace).

āte, āorta, râre, căt, ȧsk, fär, ăllow, sofȧ; ēve, êvent, ĕll, writẽr, novĕl; bīte, pĭn; nō, ōbey, ôr, dŏg, tŏp, cŏllide; ūnit, ūnite, bûrn, cŭt, focŭs; nōōn, fŏŏt; mound; coin:

stoke-hold (stōk′hōld′), *n.* **1,** in a steamship, the space in front of the boilers, from which the fires are fed: also called *stokehole;* **2,** the room containing the ship's boilers.

stoke-hole (stōk′hōl′), *n.* **1,** in a steamship, the space in front of the boilers: also called *stokehold;* **2,** the mouth of a furnace.

stok-er (stōk′ẽr), *n.* **1,** one who feeds fuel to a furnace, especially on a steamship or locomotive; a fireman; **2,** a mechanical feeder for a furnace.

¹**stole** (stōl), *n.* **1,** a long, narrow scarf worn by bishops and priests during services; **2,** a woman's long, narrow scarf, often of fur.

²**stole** (stōl), past tense of *steal.*

sto-len (stō′lĕn), past participle of *steal.*

stol-id (stŏl′ĭd), *adj.* not easily aroused or excited.—*adv.* **stol′id-ly.**—*n.* **sto-lid′i-ty.**

stom-ach (stŭm′ăk), *n.* **1,** a part of the digestive tract; in man, the sac at the end of the gullet to which food goes when it is swallowed; **2,** desire; inclination; as, he had no *stomach* for revenge:—*v.t.* to put up with; tolerate.

stom-ach-er (stŭm′ăk-ẽr), *n.* formerly, the part of a woman's dress covering the stomach, and usually forming the lower part of the bodice.

stone (stōn), *n.* **1,** a small piece of rock; **2,** the hard, nonmetallic mineral matter of which rock consists; **3,** a piece of rock cut and shaped for a special use; as, a hearth*stone;* **4,** a gem; as, a perfect ruby is a rare *stone;* **5,** in Great Britain, a measure of weight equal to fourteen pounds; **6,** something resembling a small stone in hardness and shape; as, a hail*stone:*—*v.t.* [stoned, ston-ing], **1,** to pelt with pieces of rock; kill by hurling pieces of rock; **2,** to remove the stones, or pits, from; as, to *stone* dates:—*adj.* made of stoneware or earthenware.—**stone—blind,** entirely blind.—*adj.* **ston′y.**

stone-ware (stōn′wâr′), *n.* a kind of hard, coarse, glazed pottery or earthenware.

stone-work (stōn′wûrk′), *n.* **1,** any piece of work built of stone; **2,** the process of working in stone.

stood (stŏŏd), past tense and past participle of *stand.*

stool (stōōl), *n.* **1,** a seat without a back, having three or four legs; **2,** a rest for the feet; also, a rest for the knees in kneeling.

STOOL

stool pi-geon, 1, a pigeon trained to help trap other pigeons; **2,** a person employed, usually by the police, to trap a criminal.

¹**stoop** (stōōp), *v.i.* **1,** to bend the body down and, usually, forward; also, to carry the head and shoulders habitually bowed forward; **2,** to condescend; as, the king *stooped* to dine with the peasant; **3,** to submit; yield:—*n.* a bending down and forward, especially of the head and shoulders.

²**stoop** (stōōp), *n.* a small porch or veranda at the entrance to a house.

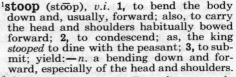
STOOP, def. 2

stop (stŏp), *v.t.* [stopped, stop-ping], **1,** to fill up (a hole or an opening); also, to close (a container); as, to *stop* a keg; **2,** to obstruct or make impassable; as, to *stop* a road; **3,** to check the progress or motion of; cause to come to a state of rest; as, to *stop* a car; cause to cease; as, to *stop* an annoyance; **4,** to desist from; as, *stop* all that noise:—*v.i.* **1,** to cease; desist; halt; **2,** *Colloquial,* to tarry; lodge; as, to *stop* at an inn:—*n.* **1,** a pause or delay; **2,** a halt; also, a halting place; **3,** a punctuation mark; **4,** any of several devices, as a block, peg, plug, or pin, to regulate or check motion, or to keep a movable part in place; as, a window *stop;* **6,** in music, any means or device for regulating pitch; also, in an organ, a set of pipes producing tones of the same quality.

stop-gap (stŏp′găp′), *n.* **1,** that which closes an opening; **2,** hence, a makeshift; temporary substitute.

stop-o-ver (stŏp′ō′vẽr), *n.* a stop or halt, as between trains, or overnight, in the course of a journey.

stop-page (stŏp′ĭj), *n.* the arresting of motion or action; also, the state of arrested motion; obstruction.

stop-per (stŏp′ẽr), *n.* a plug, as of glass, wood, or cork, that closes a bottle, cask, or jug.

stop-ple (stŏp′l), *n.* a stopper:—*v.t.* [stoppled, stop-pling], to close with a cork, stopper, or the like.

stop watch, a watch, which can be stopped or started instantly, used in timing races and other athletic contests.

stor-age (stôr′ĭj), *n.* the placing of goods in a warehouse for safekeeping; also, the space thus occupied or the price charged for the service.

stor-age bat-ter-y, a battery which gives out, as desired, the electricity stored in its cells.

store (stôr), *n.* **1,** a great quantity or number; **2,** (often *stores*), an accumulation or supply kept in reserve or ready for use;

3, a shop where goods are kept for sale:— **in store,** in reserve:—*v.t.* [stored, stor-ing], **1,** to furnish or stock; equip; as, he *stored* his mind with stories; **2,** to collect; hoard; **3,** to put in a warehouse for safekeeping. —*n.* **store/house/.**—*n.* **store/room/.**

store-keep-er (stôr/kēp/ẽr), *n.* one who manages a shop or retail store.

stor-ey (stôr/ĭ), *n.* [*pl.* storeys], a floor; a story. See ¹**story.**

¹**stor-ied** (stôr/ĭd), *adj.* having floors or stories; as, a three-*storied* building.

²**stor-ied** (stôr/ĭd), *adj.* celebrated in story, history, or legend.

stork (stôrk), *n.* a kind of wading bird with long legs and a long bill.

storm (stôrm), *n.* **1,** a violent disturbance of the atmosphere, often with a heavy fall of rain, snow, or hail; also, a thunderstorm; **2,** an outburst of passion or excitement; as, a *storm* of rage; **3,** a sudden, violent attack on a fortified place:—

STORK (₂⁄₄)

v.t. to attack suddenly with violence; as, to *storm* a fort:—*v.i.* **1,** to blow violently, or to rain, hail, snow, etc.; **2,** to rage.

storm-y (stôr/mĭ), *adj.* [storm-i-er, storm-i-est], **1,** marked by tempest or furious winds; as, *stormy* weather; **2,** passionate; turbulent; as, a *stormy* life.—*adv.* **storm/-i-ly.**—*n.* **storm/i-ness.**

¹**stor-y** (stôr/ĭ), *n.* [*pl.* stories], a floor of a building, usually divided into rooms. Also spelled **stor/ey.**

²**stor-y** (stôr/ĭ), *n.* [*pl.* stories], **1,** real or imagined events narrated in prose or verse; a tale, either written or spoken; **2,** a report or statement; rumor; **3,** *Colloquial,* a lie.

stoup (stoop), *n.* **1,** a drinking vessel; a cup or flagon; as, a *stoup* of wine; **2,** a basin for holy water in the entrance of a church.

stout (stout), *adj.* **1,** brave; resolute; as, a *stout* heart; **2,** tough; strong; as, the *stout* oak; **3,** bulky; thickset; as, a *stout* figure:—*n.* strong, dark porter, ale, or beer.—*adv.* **stout/ly.**—*n.* **stout/ness.**
Syn., *adj.* portly, corpulent, stocky.

¹**stove** (stōv), *n.* an apparatus of iron, steel, or the like, for producing heat with which to cook, warm a room, etc.

²**stove** (stōv), one of the forms of the past tense and past participle of *stave.*

stow (stō), *v.t.* **1,** to fill by close packing;

as, to *stow* a trunk with articles; **2,** to store (a cargo) compactly; **3,** to hide away; conceal.

stow-a-way (stō/à-wā/), *n.* one who hides on a ship, train, etc., to travel free.

Stowe (stō), Harriet Beecher (1812–1896), an American novelist, author of "Uncle Tom's Cabin."

strad-dle (străd/l), *v.t.* [strad-dled, strad-dling], **1,** to stand or sit astride of; as, to *straddle* a fence; **2,** *Colloquial,* to support, or seem to support, both sides of; as, to *straddle* an issue:—*v.i.* **1,** to sit, stand, or walk with the legs wide apart; **2,** *Colloquial,* to support, or seem to support, both sides of a question:—*n.* the act of strad-dling; also, the space between the legs of one who straddles.

Strad-i-va-ri-us (străd/ĭ-vā/rĭ-ŭs), *n.* a stringed instrument, especially a violin, made by Antonio Stradivari (strä/dē-vä/rē), (1644–1737), of Cremona, Italy.

strag-gle (străg/l), *v.i.* [strag-gled, strag-gling], **1,** to wander away from the main group; stray; ramble; as, on the hike, certain boys *straggled* behind the rest; **2,** to spread about; occur here and there; grow unevenly; as, weeds *straggle* along a roadside.—*n.* **strag/gler.**—*adj.* **strag/gly.**

straight (strāt), *adj.* **1,** not crooked or curved; extending directly without change in direction; as, a *straight* line; **2,** honest; upright; as, *straight* living; **3,** logical; clear; as, *straight* thinking; **4,** accurate; in order, as accounts; **5,** orderly; tidy:—*adv.* directly; without swerving; as, the arrow flew *straight.*—*n.* **straight/ness.**

straight-en (strāt/n), *v.t.* **1,** to make free of turns or curves; as, to *straighten* a road; **2,** to arrange in a desired position or con-dition; as, to *straighten* a necktie; to *straighten* a room; **3,** to make clear; as, to *straighten* out a mystery:—*v.i.* to become straight.

straight-for-ward (strāt/fôr/wẽrd), *adj.* proceeding in a direct course or manner; hence, honest.—*n.* **straight/for/ward-ness.**

straight-way (strāt/wā/), *adv.* at once.

¹**strain** (strān), *n.* **1,** stock; race; line of descent; hence, family ancestry; breed; **2,** inborn disposition; tendency; **3,** manner; tone; as, to speak in lofty *strain;* **4,** a vein or streak; as, a *strain* of humor; **5,** a tune or melody.

²**strain** (strān), *v.t.* **1,** to put to its utmost strength; exert as much as possible; as, to *strain* every muscle; stretch even beyond proper limits; as, to *strain* the law; **2,** to weaken or injure by excessive use; as, to *strain* one's voice; **3,** to put through a sieve; as, to *strain* soup; also, to re-

move by filtering:—*v.i.* **1**, to make violent efforts; strive; **2**, to pass through a sieve or filter; be strained; **3**, to become injured by excessive use or exertion:—*n.* **1**, extreme stretching; tension; **2**, a violent effort; **3**, injury due to violent effort or to overwork.

strained (strānd), *adj.* **1**, put through a sieve; as, *strained* orange juice; **2**, showing effects of great effort; as, the athlete's face had a *strained* expression; **3**, injured; as, a *strained* muscle; **4**, unnatural; as, a *strained* laugh.

strain-er (strā′nēr), *n.* a device having meshes or pores through which a liquid is passed to separate it from solid or foreign matter; as, a coffee *strainer*.

STRAINER

strait (strāt), *n.* **1**, a narrow passage of water connecting two larger bodies of water; as, the *Strait* of Magellan; **2**, **straits**, perplexity; difficulties; as, financial *straits*:—*adj.* narrow; confining; strict; as, the *strait* and narrow path; a *strait* jacket.

strait-ened (strā′tnd), *adj.* contracted; narrowed:—**straitened circumstances**, poverty.

strait jack-et, a strong, tight coat, so made as to prevent the use of the arms. It is used to restrain criminals and the violently insane.

strait—laced (strāt′⸗lāst′), *adj.* very strict in manners or morals.

Straits Set-tle-ments, a former British crown colony (cap. Singapore), including the southern part of the Malay Peninsula, and several small islands (map **15**).

¹**strand** (strănd), *n.* the shore, as of an ocean:—*v.t.* **1**, to drive ashore; run aground; as, the storm *stranded* the ship on a reef; **2**, to leave in a state of embarrassment or difficulty; as, he was *stranded* in Paris:—*v.i.* to run aground.

²**strand** (strănd), *n.* one of a number of flexible strings, as of wire or hemp, twisted together into a rope; also, any similar string, as of pearls, beads, or hair.

strange (strānj), *adj.* [strang-er, strang-est], **1**, belonging to some other person or place; as, to sleep in a *strange* bed; **2**, not familiar; as, a *strange* voice; **3**, odd; remarkable; unusual; as, *strange* ideas; **4**, reserved; shy; timid; as, to feel *strange* in company; **5**, inexperienced; as, he is *strange* to the new work.—*adv.* **strange′ly**. —*n.* **strange′ness**.

Syn. peculiar, singular, queer.

stran-ger (strān′jēr), *n.* **1**, a person from another place; as, "a *stranger* in a strange land"; **2**, a newcomer; visitor; as, *strangers* are welcome in this church; **3**, a person not known to one; as, he was a *stranger* to me.

stran-gle (străng′gl), *v.t.* [stran-gled, stran-gling], **1**, to choke; kill by squeezing the throat; **2**, to suppress; as, to *strangle* an impulse:—*v.i.* to be choked or suffocated.—*n.* **stran′gler**.

strap (străp), *n.* **1**, a narrow strip of leather or like material, used to fasten objects together or hold them in place; as, a book *strap*; **2**, a razor strop:—*v.t.* [strapped, strap-ping], **1**, to fasten or bind with a strap; **2**, to flog with a strap; **3**, to sharpen (a razor) on a strop.

strap-ping (străp′ĭng), *adj.* *Colloquial*, tall; robust; as, a *strapping* fellow.

Stras-bourg (străs′bŏŏr′; străs′bûrg), [German **Strass-burg** (shträs′bŏŏrkh)], a famous cathedral city in France (map **12**).

stra-ta (strā′tà; străt′à), one form of the plural of *stratum*.

strat-a-gem (străt′à-jĕm), *n.* **1**, a trick for deceiving an enemy, especially in war; **2**, any trick for gaining some advantage.

stra-te-gic (strà-tē′jĭk), *adj.* skilfully adapted to the end in view; advantageous; as, a *strategic* position on a hill.

strat-e-gy (străt′ê-jĭ), *n.* **1**, the art or science of war; the art of maneuvering troops or ships on a large scale; **2**, skill in managing any affair; **3**, the use of a ruse or a trick; artifice.—*n.* **strat′e-gist**.

Strat-ford up-on A-von (străt′fērd ŭ-pŏn′ ā′vŭn), a small borough in central England, where Shakespeare was born and where he was buried (map **13**).

strat-i-fy (străt′ĭ-fī), *v.t.* and *v.i.* [stratified, stratify-ing], to form in strata, or layers.—*n.* **strat′i-fi-ca′tion**.

stra-to (strā′tō), *adj.* pertaining to the stratosphere; as, *strato* pilots.

stra-to-sphere (strā′tō-sfīr; străt′ō-sfīr), *n.* the portion of the earth's atmosphere seven miles or more above the earth.

stra-tum (strā′tŭm; străt′ŭm), *n.* [*pl.* strata (strā′tà; străt′à) or stratums] **1**, one of a series of layers of rock or earth; as, a *stratum* of rock between *strata* of clay; **2**, a class in society; as, he belongs to the upper *stratum*.

Strauss (shtrous), **1**, Johann (1825–1899), an Austrian composer; **2**, Richard (1864–1949), a German composer and conductor.

straw *n.* (strô), **1**, the stalk of grain; **2**, such stalks when cut and threshed, used for fodder, packing, etc.; **3**, anything practically worthless; as, he is not worth a *straw*; **4**, a hollow stalk, or something resembling one; as, she drank her soda through a *straw*; *adj.*—**1**, made of straw;

as, a *straw* hat; stuffed with straw; as, a *straw* mattress; **2,** of the color of straw.

straw-ber-ry (strô′bĕr′ĭ), *n.* [*pl.* strawberries], a tart, fleshy, edible berry, red when fully ripe; also the low-growing plant of which it is the fruit.

straw vote, a sample and unofficial vote showing the trend of public opinion.

stray (strā), *v.i.* to wander from one's path; hence, to wander from the path of duty; err:—*adj.* **1,** wandering; lost; as, a *stray* dog; **2,** occasional; incidental; as, a *stray* remark:—*n.* a lost person or domestic animal; as, the cow is a *stray.*

Syn., v. digress, deviate.

STRAWBERRY
Leaves and fruit.

streak (strēk), *n.* **1,** a line differing in color from its background; a stripe; **2,** a trait of character; as, a *streak* of meanness; **3,** a layer; as, the *streaks* of lean in bacon:—*v.t.* to mark with streaks.—*adj.* **streak′y.**—*n.* **streak′i-ness.**

stream (strēm), *n.* **1,** flowing water; a creek, small river, etc.; **2,** anything flowing forth like a stream; as, a *stream* of people; a *stream* of light; **3,** hence, a continued flow; drift; course; as, the *stream* of civilization:—*v.i.* **1,** to flow or move continuously; run in a current; **2,** to pour or drip; as, an umbrella *streams* with rain; **3,** to float; as, banners *stream* in the air.

stream-er (strē′mẽr), *n.* **1,** a long, narrow pennant or ribbon; **2,** a shaft of light, as in the northern lights; **3,** a newspaper headline which stretches across the page.

stream-let (strēm′lĕt), *n.* a little stream.

stream-line (strēm′līn′), *adj.* shaped in long smooth curves so as to offer the least resistance to air or water; as, *streamline* design:—*v.t.* to make or re-model in such a form; hence, to modernize or reorganize for efficiency.

STREAMLINER

stream-lin-er (strēm′lī-nẽr), *n.* a streamlined passenger train.

street (strēt), *n.* a public way in a city or town, usually lined with buildings.

Syn. thoroughfare, avenue, road.

street-car (strēt′kär′), *n.* a car, usually an electric passenger car, run on tracks laid on the surface of a street.

strength (strĕngth; strĕngkth), *n.* **1,** the quality of being strong; muscular force; also, the ability to do or endure; **2,** firmness; toughness; as, the *strength* of a rope; **3,** power; vigor; intensity; as, *strength* of will; **4,** force in numbers; as, the *strength* of an army.

strength-en (strĕng′thĕn; strĕngk′thĕn), *v.t.* and *v.i.* to make or become stronger.

stren-u-ous (strĕn′ū-ŭs), *adj.* **1,** urgent; zealous; as, a *strenuous* reformer; **2,** full of effort or exertion; as, a *strenuous* life.

strep-to-my-cin (strĕp′tō-mī′sĭn), *n.* an antibiotic extracted from a bacterium found in the soil, used in the treatment of tuberculosis, certain kinds of meningitis, etc.

stress (strĕs), *n.* **1,** impelling force; pressure; as, the *stress* of work; **2,** importance; emphasis; as, to lay *stress* on a particular fact; **3,** in physics, a force, especially one causing change of shape or volume:—*v.t.* **1,** to emphasize; **2,** to accent; as, *stress* the first word; **3,** in physics, to subject to mechanical pressure.

stretch (strĕch), *v.t.* **1,** to draw out in length or width; hence, to draw taut; as, to *stretch* a rubber band; **2,** to extend; as, to *stretch* out an arm; to extend between two points; as to *stretch* a tennis net; **3,** to strain; exert to the utmost; as, *stretch* every effort to get there; **4,** to exaggerate; as, to *stretch* the truth; **5,** to make the most of; as, *stretch* the pennies:—*v.i.* **1,** to spread; reach; as, the rope *stretched* across the street; **2,** to admit of being extended; as, elastic *stretches*; **3,** to extend or spread the body or limbs:—*n.* **1,** the act of straining or extending; **2,** reach; scope; extent; **3,** a continuous line, space, or time; as, a *stretch* of good road.

stretch-er (strĕch′ẽr), *n.* **1,** a device which stretches something or draws it out to the desired shape; as, a curtain *stretcher*; **2,** a frame, usually covered with canvas, for carrying the disabled.

strew (strōō), *v.t.* [*p.t.* strewed (strōōd), *p.p.* strewed or strewn (strōōn), *p.pr.* strew-ing], **1,** to scatter; let fall loosely; as, to *strew* flowers on a path; **2,** to cover by scattering small objects; as, to *strew* a walk with pebbles.

strick-en (strĭk′ĕn), *adj.* afflicted; affected by illness, age, misfortune, etc.

strict (strĭkt), *adj.* **1,** exacting; severe; as, *strict* laws; **2,** rigid; unswerving; as, *strict* honesty; **3,** accurate; precise; as, the *strict* sense of a word.—*adv.* **strict′ly.**

Syn. harsh, austere, stern.

stric-ture (strĭk′tŭr), *n.* **1,** the abnormal narrowing of a passage of the body; **2,** severe criticism or blame.

stride (strīd), *n.* a long step; also, the space covered by a long step:—*v.i.* [*p.t.* strode (strōd), *p.p.* strid-den (strĭd′n), *p.pr.* strid-ing], to walk with long steps:—*v.t.* to straddle; hence, to ride (a horse).

āte, âorta, râre, căt, ȧsk, fär, ăllow, sofȧ; ēve, ĕvent, ĕll, writẽr, novĕl; bīte, pĭn; nō, ōbey, ôr, dŏg, tŏp, cŏllide; ūnit, ŭnite, bûrn, cŭt, focŭs; nōōn, fŏŏt; mound; coin;

stri-dent (strī'dĕnt), *adj.* harsh; grating; as, *strident* tones.—*adv.* **stri'dent-ly.**

strife (strīf), *n.* conflict; hostilities; rivalry.

strike (strīk), *v.t.* [*p.t.* struck (strŭk), *p.p.* struck or, in senses 5 and 8 in the passive, also strick-en (strĭk'ĕn), *p.pr.* striking], **1,** to hit; dash against; **2,** to deal (a blow); also, to deal a blow to; as, John *struck* him in the face; **3,** to collide, or cause to collide, with; as, my foot *struck* the table; **4,** to come to the mind of; occur to; as, an idea *struck* her; **5,** to afflict or affect; as, to be *struck* with horror; to be *stricken* with illness; **6,** to come upon, as gold; **7,** to conclude, as a bargain; **8,** to cancel; as, the remarks were then *struck* (or *stricken*) from the record; **9,** to cause (a match) to ignite; **10,** to produce by printing; as, to *strike* off a new issue of stamps; **11,** to cause to sound; as, to *strike* a bell; also, to announce by sound; as, the clock *strikes* twelve; **12,** to lower (a flag or sail) as a sign of submission:—*v.i.* **1,** to deal a quick blow or thrust; make an attack; fight; **2,** to hit; collide; become stranded, as a ship; **3,** to proceed; as, they *struck* into the woods; **4,** to sound, as a bell or a clock; **5,** to cease from work in order to secure or prevent a change in working conditions or pay:—*n.* **1,** the act of hitting; **2,** a stopping of work by a number of employees in order to secure or prevent a change in working conditions, rate of pay, etc.; **3,** a fortunate discovery of ore or oil; hence, any sudden success; **4,** in baseball, an unsuccessful attempt by the batter to hit the ball, or a ball so pitched that the batter should have struck at it; **5,** in bowling, the upsetting, by a player, of all the pins with the first ball bowled; also, the score so made; **6,** in air warfare, an attack by one airplane, or a combined attack by a formation of airplanes; also, a series of attacks, extending over several days.

strike-break-er (strīk'brā'kĕr), *n.* a workman hired to take the place of one out on strike.

strik-er (strī'kĕr), *n.* **1,** a person or thing that hits; **2,** a workman who with others quits work in protest against existing or proposed conditions.

strik-ing (strī'kĭng), *adj.* very noticeable; surprising.—*adv.* **strik'ing-ly.**

string (strĭng), *n.* **1,** a thin cord; thick thread; twine; also, something used for tying; as, apron *strings;* **2,** a set of things, as beads, arranged on a cord; also, a series of things in, or as in, a line; as, a *string* of jokes; a *string* of cars; **3,** a vegetable fiber, as of string beans; **4,** a tightly stretched cord for musical instruments; **5, strings,** stringed musical instruments:

—*v.t.* [strung (strŭng), string-ing], **1,** to furnish (a bow, violin, etc.) with a string or strings; **2,** to thread on a cord, as beads; **3,** to form into a line or series; **4,** to fasten or hang with a cord; as, to *string* pictures on a wall; **5,** to take the strings from (beans):—*v.i.* **1,** to form strings; become stringy, as glue; **2,** to move along in a single file.

string bean, a kind of bean, grown for its edible pods; also, one of the pods.

stringed (strĭngd), *adj.* fitted with strings, as the violin, cello, mandolin, etc.

strin-gen-cy (strĭn'jĕn-sĭ), *n.* **1,** severity or strictness, as of laws; **2,** scarcity or tightness, as of money.

strin-gent (strĭn'jĕnt), *adj.* strict; severe; as, *stringent* rules.—*adv.* **strin'gent-ly.**

STRING BEANS

string-er (strĭng'ĕr), *n.* **1,** in building, a long heavy timber used to connect uprights, support floors, or the like; **2,** in railroading, a long piece of timber or metal which carries the track, especially over bridges.

string-y (strĭng'ĭ), *adj.* [string-i-er, string-i-est], **1,** long and thin; as, a *stringy* youth; **2,** full of fibers or strings; as, *stringy* meat; **3,** capable of being drawn out into strings, as glue.

strip (strĭp), *v.t.* [stripped, strip-ping], **1,** to make naked; deprive of a covering; hence, to rob; bare; as, to *strip* a man of his riches; to *strip* a tree of apples; **2,** to pull off (a covering); as, to *strip* bark from a tree; **3,** to milk (a cow) dry:—*v.i.* to undress:—*n.* a long, narrow piece of anything.

stripe (strīp), *n.* **1,** a line, band, or streak; **2,** a strip of different color or material attached to anything; as, a *stripe* on a uniform; **3,** a discolored bruise on the skin made by the blow of a whip; also, a blow by a whip; **4,** distinctive sort or kind; as, they are persons of the same *stripe:*—*v.t.* [striped, strip-ing], to mark with lines or bands.

striped (strīpt; strī'pĕd), *adj.* marked with stripes or bands of color.

strip-ling (strĭp'lĭng), *n.* a youth; lad.

strive (strīv), *v.i.* [*p.t.* strove (strōv), *p.p.* striv-en (strĭv'ĕn), *p.pr.* striv-ing], **1,** to make an effort; try hard; as, to *strive* for success; **2,** to struggle; battle; as, the swimmer *strove* against the current.

strode (strōd), past tense of *stride*.

stroke (strōk), *n*. **1,** the act of dealing a blow or the blow dealt; as, the *stroke* of a hammer; **2,** a sudden action or effect suggesting the violence of a blow; as, a *stroke* of apoplexy; **3,** a single effort, or the result produced; as, a *stroke* of business; **4,** a gentle touch; as, a *stroke* of the hand; **5,** a single movement with an instrument; as, a pencil *stroke;* the result or mark made by such a movement; **6,** the sound of a bell or clock; also, the time marked; as, at the *stroke* of three; **7,** one of a series of repeated movements in air or water; as, the *stroke* of a swimmer; **8,** in rowing, the oarsman nearest the stern who sets the time:—*v.t.* [stroked, strok-ing], **1,** to rub gently with the hand; **2,** to set the pace for (rowers); as, he *stroked* the crew for two years.

Syn., *n.* knock, lash, shock, cuff.

stroll (strōl), *n.* a quiet walk or ramble:—*v.i.* to wander on foot from place to place; to ramble.—*n.* **stroll′er.**

strong (strông), *adj.* **1,** physically powerful; muscular; robust; as, a *strong* horse; a *strong* physique; **2,** upright; firm; as, a *strong* character; **3,** powerful in wealth, numbers, or other resources; as, a *strong* party; also, of a specified numerical force; as, 9,000 *strong;* **4,** violent, as a high wind; **5,** ardent or warm, as the affections; **6,** vigorous or forceful, as an argument; **7,** stable or settled, as a government; **8,** intense, as a bright light; concentrated; as, *strong* tea or coffee; also, containing alcohol; as, *strong* drink; **9,** firm in opinion; ardent; as, a *strong* partisan; **10,** deeply rooted; positive; as, *strong* beliefs; **11,** solid; not easily broken; as, a *strong* plank:—**strong verb,** in English grammar, a verb which forms its past tense and past participle by a vowel change, as *sing, sang, sung; speak, spoke, spoken.*—*adv.* **strong′ly.**

strong-hold (strông′hōld′), *n.* a fort or fortress; a place of refuge.

strop (strŏp), *n.* a strip of leather, as for sharpening a razor:—*v.t.* [stropped, strop-ping], to sharpen (a razor) on a strop.

STROP

strove (strōv), past tense of *strive*.

struck (strŭk), past tense and one form of the past participle of *strike*.

struc-ture (strŭk′tûr), *n.* **1,** that which is built, as a bridge or a house; **2,** the manner in which something is built; as, the *structure* of ships has been improved; **3,** the form or arrangement of parts or ele-

ments; as, the *structure* of a flower.—*adj.* **struc′tur-al.**—*adv.* **struc′tur-al-ly.**

strug-gle (strŭg′l), *v.i.* [strug-gled, struggling], **1,** to put forth violent effort, as in trying to escape from a grasp; **2,** to labor; strive; as, he *struggled* to get a start:—*n.* **1,** a violent effort; **2,** a contest; strife.

strum (strŭm), *v.t.* and *v.i.* [strummed, strum-ming], to play badly and noisily on (a stringed instrument):—*n.* the act of so playing, or the sound of strumming.

strum-pet (strŭm′pĕt), *n.* an immoral woman; a harlot.

strung (strŭng), past tense and past participle of *string*.

¹strut (strŭt), *v.i.* [strut-ted, strut-ting], to walk with a proud step or false dignity:—*n.* a proud and haughty step.

²strut (strŭt), *n.* a brace or bar to support or receive weight or pressure in the direction of its length.

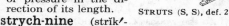

STRUTS (S, S), def. 2

strych-nine (strĭk′nĭn; strĭk′nēn; strĭk′nīn), *n.* a powerful poison obtained from certain plants and used in small doses to stimulate the nerves and the heart. Also spelled **strych′nin.**

Stu-art (stū′ẽrt), *n.* the name of a royal family of Scotland and England, to which belonged, notably, Mary Stuart of Scotland and Charles I of England.

stub (stŭb), *n.* **1,** the stump of a tree; **2,** the short, blunt, remaining part of anything, as of a cigar; **3,** the part of a leaf left in a checkbook after a check is torn out, used for a memorandum; **4,** a pen with a short, blunt point:—*v.t.* [stubbed, stub-bing], to strike (one's toe) against some fixed object.

STUB (S), def. 3.

stub-ble (stŭb′l), *n.* **1,** the stumps of grain left in the ground after cutting; **2,** a short growth of beard.

stub-born (stŭb′ẽrn), *adj.* **1,** fixed in opinion or purpose; determined; obstinate; as, a *stubborn* child; **2,** obstinately followed or held to; as, a *stubborn* attempt; **3,** hard to treat; as, a *stubborn* cold.—*adv.* **stub′-born-ly.**—*n.* **stub′born-ness.**

Syn. headstrong, perverse.

stuc-co (stŭk′ō), *n.* [*pl.* stuccoes or stuccos], a kind of plaster used on inside walls or on the outside of houses:—*v.t.* [stuccoed (stŭk′ōd), stucco-ing (stŭk′ō-ing)], to cover with stucco.

stuck (stŭk), past tense and past participle of *stick*.

¹**stud** (stŭd), *n.* **1,** an upright timber in walls to which the laths are nailed; **2,** an ornamental boss or knob projecting from a surface; as, a belt with brass *studs;* **3,** a device like a button used as a fastener; as, shirt *studs:—v.t.* [stud-ded, stud-ding], **1,** to furnish with upright props; **2,** to adorn or set with studs; **3,** to be set thickly in; as, stars *stud* the sky.

²**stud** (stŭd), *n.* **1,** a collection of horses, especially one kept for breeding; also, the place where they are kept; **2,** a stallion.

stud-ding (stŭd′ĭng), *n.* collectively, the upright beams in walls to which laths are nailed. (See illustration under *frame house.*)

stu-dent (stū′dĕnt), *n.* **1,** a person who attends school; **2,** a person devoted to books or learning; **3,** a close observer; as, a *student* of life.

stud-ied (stŭd′ĭd), *adj.* carefully considered; deliberate; as, a *studied* compliment.

stu-di-o (stū′dĭ-ō), *n.* [*pl.* studios], **1,** the workroom of an artist; **2,** a place where motion pictures are filmed; **3,** a room equipped for the broadcasting of radio programs.

stu-di-ous (stū′dĭ-ŭs), *adj.* **1,** given to study; fond of books; as, a *studious* youth; **2,** thoughtful; earnest; as, *studious* attention.—*n.* **stu′di-ous-ness.**

stud-y (stŭd′ĭ), *n.* [*pl.* studies], **1,** the application of the mind to books, science, etc., for the gaining of knowledge; **2,** a special branch of learning; as, mathematics is a difficult *study;* **3,** careful examination of a particular question; as, a *study* of foreign trade; also, the result of such examination; as, this book is a *study* of the tariff; **4,** reverie; deep thought; as, to be in a brown *study;* **5,** in painting, a preliminary sketch for a picture; **6,** in music, a piece for a special kind of practice; **7,** earnest effort; aim; as, his constant *study* is how to please; **8,** a room set apart for reading or writing:—*v.i.* [studied, study-ing], to devote oneself to the gaining of knowledge; as, he is *studying* at college:—*v.t.* **1,** to learn the details of; as, to *study* Latin; **2,** to investigate or examine closely; think over carefully; as, to *study* labor disputes.

stuff (stŭf), *n.* **1,** the material of which anything is composed or may be made; **2,** the essential part of anything; as, he is of the *stuff* of heroes; **3,** woven fabrics or cloth; **4,** belongings; portable property; **5,** refuse or waste matter; hence, nonsense; as, *stuff* and nonsense:—*v.t.* **1,** to crowd, cram, or pack; as, to *stuff* clothes into a bag; also, to fill by cramming; as, to *stuff* a bag with clothes; **2,** to fill with specially prepared material; as, to *stuff* a chicken; **3,** to fill the skin of (a dead animal) so as to make it look lifelike; **4,** to put dishonest votes into (a ballot box).

stuff-ing (stŭf′ĭng), *n.* material used in filling something; especially, a mixture of bread crumbs, seasoning, etc., for stuffing meat and fowl.

stuff-y (stŭf′ĭ), *adj.* [stuff-i-er, stuff-i-est], **1,** close or badly ventilated; as, a *stuffy* room; **2,** choked or stopped up, as with a cold in the head.—*n.* **stuff′i-ness.**

stul-ti-fy (stŭl′tĭ-fī), *v.t.* [stultified, stulti-fy-ing], to cause (a person or thing) to seem foolish; also, to make (oneself) appear ridiculous.

stum-ble (stŭm′bl), *v.i.* [stum-bled, stum-bling], **1,** to trip or fall in walking; **2,** to walk in an unsteady manner; **3,** to fall into error:—**stumble on** or **upon,** to come upon by chance; as, to *stumble on* a valuable secret:—*n.* **1,** a tripping, as in walking; **2,** an error or blunder.—*adv.* **stum′bling-ly.**

stum-bling block, an obstacle; a hindrance.

stump (stŭmp), *n.* **1,** that part of a tree which remains in the ground after the trunk is cut down; **2,** the part, as of an arm, tail, etc., remaining after the main part has been removed; **3,** a platform for political speaking: from the early custom of speaking from tree stumps:—*v.i.* to walk heavily:—*v.t. Colloquial:* **1,** to canvass (a district) making political speeches; **2,** to block or hinder; as, he was *stumped* and could go no further.

stun (stŭn), *v.t.* [stunned, stun-ning], **1,** to make senseless by a blow; **2,** to confuse, daze, or overpower.—*n.* **stun′ner.**

stung (stŭng), past tense and past participle of *sting.*

stunk (stŭngk), one form of the past tense of *stink;* also, the past participle.

stun-ning (stŭn′ĭng), *adj. Slang,* striking; very handsome; as, *stunning* clothes.

¹**stunt** (stŭnt), *v.t.* to check the growth or development of; dwarf.

²**stunt** (stŭnt), *n. Colloquial,* a striking feat or performance, as of bodily strength or skill.

stu-pe-fac-tion (stū′pē-făk′shŭn), *n.* **1,** a numbed or dazed condition of mind or body; **2,** a state of utter amazement.

stu-pe-fy (stū′pē-fī), *v.t.* [stupefied, stupefy-ing], to dull the senses of.

stu-pen-dous (stū-pĕn′dŭs), *adj.* overpowering the senses by great size, speed, etc.; amazing; remarkable.

---

go; join; yet; sing; chin; show; thin, *th*en; hw, *wh*y; zh, azure; ü, Ger. für or Fr. lune; ö, Ger. schön or Fr. feu; ṅ, Fr. enfant, nom; kh, Ger. ach or ich. See pages ix–x.

stu·pid (stū′pĭd), *adj.* dull; unintelligent; as, a *stupid* scholar; also, foolish; as, a *stupid* error.—*adv.* **stu′pid·ly.**

stu·pid·i·ty (stū-pĭd′ĭ-tĭ), *n.* [*pl.* stupidities], great dulness of mind; slowness; foolishness.

stu·por (stū′pĕr), *n.* a condition of more or less complete unconsciousness; lethargy.

stur·dy (stûr′dĭ), *adj.* [stur-di-er, stur-di-est], **1,** hardy; robust; stout; as, a *sturdy* oak; **2,** firm and unyielding; as, a man of *sturdy* principles.

stur·geon (stûr′jŭn), *n.* a large food fish, having rows of bony plates along the body.

STURGEON (¹⁄₁₀)

stut·ter (stŭt′ĕr), *v.i.* in speaking, to hesitate over or repeat the initial sounds of words; to stammer:—*v.t.* to utter with difficulty:—*n.* a stammer.

Stutt·gart (shtŏŏt′gärt), a city, capital of the state of Württemberg, Germany (map 12).

¹**sty** (stī), *n.* [*pl.* sties], **1,** a pen for swine; **2,** a filthy or vile place.

²**sty** (stī), *n.* [*pl.* sties], an inflamed swelling of the eyelid.

Styg·i·an (stĭj′ĭ-ăn), *adj.* pertaining to the river Styx, or to Hades, the region it encircles; hence, dark; gloomy; dismal.

¹**style** (stīl), *n.* **1,** a pointed instrument used by the ancients for writing upon wax tablets; hence, any of various similar instruments, as an engraver's tool; **2,** a characteristic manner of writing or speaking; as, a polished *style;* also, literary excellence; as, the speech lacked *style;* **3,** mode of expression or execution in any art; as, the Colonial *style* in architecture; **4,** manner of conduct or action; as, a graceful *style* of dancing; also, fine or dashing appearance; as, she has *style;* **5,** fashion; as, a coat of the latest *style:*—*v.t.* [styled, styl-ing], to term, name, or call; as, Washington is *styled* the Father of his Country.

Syn., n. diction, phraseology, mode.

²**style** (stīl), *n.* the stemlike part of the pistil of a flower. (See illustration under *flower.*)

styl·ish (stīl′ĭsh), *adj.* very fashionable; modern.—*adv.* **styl′ish·ly.**—*n.* **styl′ish·ness.**

styl·ist (stīl′ĭst), *n.* a person, especially a writer, who concerns himself with form or style

sty·lus (stī′lŭs), *n.* a style; a sharp-pointed instrument.

sty·mie (stī′mĭ), *n.* in golf, a situation

on the green in which the ball nearer the hole lies directly in the line of play of the other ball.

styp·tic (stĭp′tĭk), *adj.* used to stop bleeding; as, a *styptic* pencil:—*n.* a substance that stops bleeding, as alum.

Styx (stĭks), *n.* in Greek mythology, the river which encircled Hades, the abode of the dead. Across it the souls of the dead had to be ferried by Charon.

sua·sion (swā′zhŭn), *n.* persuasion.

suave (swäv; swāv), *adj.* polite; agreeably smooth; bland.—*adv.* **suave′ly.**

suav·i·ty (swăv′ĭ-tĭ; swä′vĭ-tĭ), *n.* [*pl.* suavities], agreeableness; pleasantness; smooth politeness.

sub- (sŭb-), a prefix meaning: **1,** under or beneath the surface; as, *sub*marine, *sub*merge; **2,** near or next to; as, *sub*urb; **3,** inferior in rank; as, *sub*lieutenant; **4,** lower of two; lowered; as, *sub*way; **5,** not up to a standard; as, *sub*normal; **6,** at the end; as, *sub*scribe; **7,** a part of something larger; as, *sub*committee; into still smaller parts; as, *sub*divide.

sub·al·tern (sŭb-ôl′tẽrn), *n.* a military officer who ranks below a captain; also, a person in a subordinate position:—*adj.* ranking below a captain; subordinate.

sub·con·scious (sŭb-kŏn′shŭs), *adj.* pertaining to the activities that go on in a person's mind without his being aware of them.—*adv.* **sub-con′scious·ly.**

sub·di·vide (sŭb′dĭ-vīd′), *v.t.* [subdivided, subdivid-ing], to separate the parts of into other parts:—*v.i.* to divide or separate again.

sub·di·vi·sion (sŭb′dĭ-vĭzh′ŭn), *n.* **1,** the separation of a part or parts into smaller parts; **2,** a part of a larger part.

sub·due (sŭb-dū′), *v.t.* [subdued, subduing], **1,** to conquer; vanquish; as, to *subdue* an enemy; **2,** to bring under control; master, as an impulse; **3,** to tone down or soften; as, a *subdued* light.

sub·floor (sŭb′flôr′), *n.* a layer of rough boards laid directly upon the floor joists, upon which the flooring is laid.

sub·ject (sŭb′jĕkt), *adj.* **1,** under the power or control of another; as, a *subject* nation; **2,** exposed; liable; as, he is *subject* to malaria; **3,** dependent on; as, a plan *subject* to your approval:—*n.* **1,** a person under the control of another; especially, one who owes allegiance to a government or a sovereign; **2,** a person, animal, or thing made to undergo an operation or treatment; as, the *subject* of an experiment; **3,** the matter, theme, or topic, about which something is said or written; **4,** in a sentence, the word or group of words of

---

āte, āorta, râre, căt, ȧsk, fär, ăllow, sofȧ; ēve, ȇvent, ĕll, writẽr, novĕl; bīte, pĭn; nō, ōbey, ôr, dŏg, tŏp, cŏllide; ūnit, ūnite, bûrn, cŭt, focŭs; nōon, fŏŏt; mound; coin;

which something is said or asked; as, in "our vacation begins tomorrow" the *subject* is "our vacation":—*v.t.* (sŭb-jĕkt′), **1,** to bring under control; **2,** to make liable; expose; as, to be *subjected* to insult; **3,** to cause to undergo; as, to *subject* iron to heat.

sub-jec-tion (sŭb-jĕk′shŭn), *n.* **1,** the act of bringing others under one's own rule; **2,** the state of being under the control of another.

sub-jec-tive (sŭb-jĕk′tĭv; sŭb-jĕk′tĭv), *adj.* **1,** existing in the mind; belonging to the thoughts and feelings of a person rather than to outward objects: opposite of *objective*; as, a *subjective* view of life; **2,** in literature and art, dealing with thoughts and feelings rather than with action and things in the world outside; also, reflecting the thoughts and feelings of the author or artist; personal; **3,** relating to the thinker, rather than the object of thought.—*adv.* **sub-jec′tive-ly.**

sub-ject mat-ter, the subject under consideration, as in a book or speech.

sub-ju-gate (sŭb′jōō-gāt), *v.t.* [subjugated, subjugat-ing], to conquer; subdue, as savage tribes.—*n.* **sub′ju-ga′tion.**
　Syn. overcome, defeat, enslave.

sub-junc-tive (sŭb-jŭngk′tĭv), *adj.* in grammar, pertaining to that mood of a verb which expresses state or action, not as a fact, but as something possible, desired, feared, or doubtful:—*n.* the subjunctive mood.

sub-lease (sŭb′lēs′), *n.* a lease given by a tenant, who thus becomes the landlord of a third person:—*v.t.* (sŭb-lēs′), [subleased, subleas-ing], to lease (property already rented from another).

sub-let (sŭb-lĕt′), *v.t.* [sublet, sublet-ting], to let or lease (property already leased from another); sublease.

sub-li-mate (sŭb′lĭ-māt), *v.t.* [sublimated, sublimat-ing], to divert (natural impulses or energy) through education or effort into more useful channels.

sub-lime (sŭb-līm′), *adj.* [sublim-er, sublim-est], **1,** inspiring a feeling of awe, reverence, greatness, power, or grandeur; **2,** exalted; noble:—*n.* that which is lofty, awe-inspiring, or grand:—*v.t.* [sublimed, sublim-ing], to exalt or dignify.—*adv.* **sub-lime′ly.**—*n.* **sub-lim′i-ty** (sŭb-lĭm′ĭ-tĭ).

sub-ma-rine (sŭb′mȧ-rēn′), *adj.* living, situated, or used, beneath the surface of the sea; as, *submarine* plant life:—*n.* (sŭb′mȧ-rēn′), a vessel, usually a war vessel, which can be operated under water.

sub-merge (sŭb-mûrj′), *v.t.* [submerged, submerg-ing], **1,** to put or sink under water; as, to *submerge* a boat; **2,** to cover

with water; flood; overwhelm:—*v.i.* to sink under water or out of sight.

sub-mer-sion (sŭb-mûr′shŭn; sŭb-mûr′-zhŭn), *n.* the act of sinking under water or the condition of being sunk under water.

sub-mis-sion (sŭb-mĭsh′ŭn), *n.* **1,** the act of referring to the judgment, or yielding to the power or authority, of another; **2,** humility or meekness.—*adj.* **sub-mis′sive.**

sub-mit (sŭb-mĭt′), *v.t.* [submit-ted, submit-ting], **1,** to yield (oneself) to the will of another; **2,** to present for, or refer to, the judgment of another; as, to *submit* an offer:—*v.i.* to yield or surrender.

sub-nor-mal (sŭb-nôr′mȧl), *adj.* below the normal or usual.

sub-or-di-nate (sŭ-bôr′dĭ-nĭt), *adj.* **1,** lower in rank, value, power, or importance; as, a *subordinate* rank; **2,** subject to another; as, a *subordinate* official; **3,** in grammar, designating the dependent clause in a complex sentence, or any conjunction which introduces it:—*n.* one who is below another in rank, power, or the like:—*v.t.* (sŭ-bôr′dĭ-nāt),[subordinat-ed, subordinating], **1,** to place in a lower order or rank; **2,** to make subject or obedient.—*n.* **sub-or′di-na′tion.**

sub-orn (sŭb-ôrn′; sŭb-ôrn′), *v.t.* in law, to induce (someone) to give false testimony.

sub-poe-na (sŭb-pē′nȧ; sŭ-pē′nȧ), *n.* a written order commanding a person to appear in court:—*v.t.* [subpoenaed (sŭb-pē′nȧd; sŭ-pē′nȧd), subpoena-ing (sŭb-pē′nȧ-ĭng; sŭ-pē′nȧ-ĭng)], to serve or summon with such a written order. Also spelled **sub-pe′na.**

sub-scribe (sŭb-skrīb′), *v.t.* [subscribed, subscrib-ing], **1,** to write or put (one's name) to a paper or document; **2,** to sign one's name at the end of (a document); **3,** to give or promise (a sum of money) to a cause; as, he *subscribed* $40 to the milk fund:—*v.i.* **1,** to sign one's name to a letter or other document; **2,** to give assent; agree; as, to *subscribe* to a protest; **3,** to promise to give a certain sum; as, to *subscribe* to a charity; also, to agree to take or buy something.—*n.* **sub-scrib′er.**

sub-scrip-tion (sŭb-skrĭp′shŭn), *n.* **1,** the act of signing one's name by way of agreement; **2,** a formal agreement to give or contribute a sum of money; also, the sum of money promised; **3,** an order for a certain number of issues of a periodical.

sub-se-quent (sŭb′sē-kwĕnt; sŭb′sē-kwĕnt), *adj.* following; coming after; as, *subsequent* events.—*adv.* **sub′se-quent-ly.**

sub-serve (sŭb-sûrv′), *v.t.* [subserved, subserv-ing], to serve; advance; as, to *subserve* the interests of another.

sub·ser·vi·ence (sŭb-sûr′vĭ-ĕns), *n.* degrading subjection of oneself to the will of another; servility. Also, **sub-ser′vi-en-cy.**

sub·ser·vi·ent (sŭb-sûr′vĭ-ĕnt), *adj.* servile; cringing.—*adv.* **sub-ser′vi-ent-ly.**

sub·side (sŭb-sīd′), *v.i.* [subsid-ed, subsid-ing], **1,** to sink or fall to the bottom; settle, as sediment; **2,** to sink to a lower level; fall; as, the swollen river will *subside;* **3,** to become quiet or less violent, as anger, fever, a storm, or the like.

sub·sid·i·ar·y (sŭb-sĭd′ĭ-ĕr′ĭ), *adj.* **1,** assisting; secondary or subordinate; **2,** in business, owned or controlled by another organization; as, *subsidiary* companies:—*n.* [*pl.* subsidiaries], **1,** an assistant or a subordinate; **2,** in business, a corporation owned or controlled by another corporation.

sub·si·dize (sŭb′sĭ-dīz), *v.t.* [subsidized, subsidiz-ing], to aid or furnish with financial help.

sub·si·dy (sŭb′sĭ-dĭ), *n.* [*pl.* subsidies], **1,** a gift of money granted someone as an aid; **2,** money granted in time of war by one friendly government to another; **3,** a government grant of money to encourage or support a private enterprise that serves the public.

sub·sist (sŭb-sĭst′), *v.i.* **1,** to continue to be; exist; **2,** to be supported; live; as, to *subsist* on fish.

sub·sist·ence (sŭb-sĭs′tĕns), *n.* livelihood; the means of supporting life.

sub·soil (sŭb′soil′), *n.* the layer of earth lying just beneath the surface soil.

sub·stance (sŭb′stăns), *n.* **1,** the real or essential part of anything; **2,** the stuff, matter, or material of which something is made; **3,** the gist or real point of a speech or an article; **4,** wealth; property; as, a man of *substance.*

sub·stan·tial (sŭb-stăn′shăl), *adj.* **1,** having real existence; actual; not imaginary; **2,** made of good substance; solid; strong; as, a car *substantial* enough to stand ordinary wear and tear; **3,** of real worth; considerable; as, a *substantial* gift; also, nourishing; ample; as, *substantial* food; **4,** prosperous; responsible; as, *substantial* businessmen; **5,** real or true for the most part; virtual; as, the two stories were in *substantial* accord.—*adv.* **sub-stan′tial-ly.**

sub·stan·ti·ate (sŭb-stăn′shĭ-āt), *v.t.* [substantiat-ed, substantiat-ing], to establish the truth of (a claim, rumor, theory, etc.) by proof or evidence; prove or verify.—*n.* **sub-stan′ti-a′tion.**

Syn. confirm, ratify, sustain.

sub·stan·tive (sŭb′stăn-tĭv), *adj.* **1,** real; permanent; substantial; **2,** in grammar:

a, expressing existence; as, "to be" is a *substantive* verb; **b,** of the nature of a noun or used as a noun; as, a *substantive* clause:—*n.* a noun or a group of words used as a noun.—*adv.* **sub′stan-tive-ly.**

sub·sti·tute (sŭb′stĭ-tūt), *n.* a person or thing that takes the place of another:—*v.t.* [substitut-ed, substitut-ing], to put in the place of another person or thing:—*v.i.* to take the place of another; as, to *substitute* for a teacher.

sub·sti·tu·tion (sŭb′stĭ-tū′shŭn), *n.* the putting of a person or thing in the place of another.

sub·stra·tum (sŭb-strā′tŭm), *n.* [*pl.* substrata (sŭb-strā′tȧ)], **1,** an under layer, as of soil or rock; **2,** hence, that which forms the groundwork or support of some other structure; a foundation.

sub·ter·fuge (sŭb′tĕr-fūj), *n.* a scheme, excuse, or trick by which one seeks to escape from a difficulty.

sub·ter·ra·ne·an (sŭb′tĕ-rā′nē-ăn), *adj.* **1,** below the surface of the earth; underground; as, a *subterranean* cave; **2,** hidden; secret; as, *subterranean* maneuvers.

sub·tle (sŭt′l), *adj.* [sub-tler, sub-tlest], **1,** delicate; elusive; as, a *subtle* odor; **2,** clever; discerning; keen; as, a *subtle* mind; **3,** artful; crafty; cunning; as, a *subtle* scheme; **4,** intricate; hard to follow; as, *subtle* reasoning.—*adv.* **sub′tly** (sŭt′lĭ).

Syn. wily, sly, penetrating, shrewd.

sub·tle·ty (sŭt′l-tĭ), *n.* [*pl.* subtleties], **1,** keenness of mind; **2,** cunning; artfulness; **3,** elusiveness; delicacy.

sub·tract (sŭb-trăkt′), *v.t.* to take away (a part) from the whole.—*n.* **sub-trac′tion.**

sub·tra·hend (sŭb′trȧ-hĕnd′), *n.* a number to be subtracted from another.

sub·trop·i·cal (sŭb-trŏp′ĭ-kăl), *adj.* pertaining to the regions bordering the tropical zone.—*n.pl.* **sub-trop′ics.**

sub·urb (sŭb′ûrb), *n.* a residential district on the outskirts of a city.

sub·ur·ban (sŭb-ûr′băn; sŭb-ûr′băn), *adj.* situated in, living in, or characteristic of, a suburb.

sub·ver·sion (sŭb-vûr′shŭn; sŭb-vûr′-zhŭn), *n.* the act of overturning or the condition of being overturned; ruin; overthrow.—*adj.* **sub-ver′sive.**

sub·vert (sŭb-vûrt′), *v.t.* **1,** to turn upside down; overthrow (a government); **2,** to ruin or corrupt, as a person's principles.

sub·way (sŭb′wā′), *n.* **1,** an underground passage for water or gas pipes, wires, etc.; **2,** an underground electric railway.

suc- (sŭk-), *prefix,* a form of *sub-* used before *c;* as, *succeed, succor.*

āte, āorta, râre, căt, ȧsk, fär, ăllow, sofȧ; ēve, ēvent, ĕll, wrīter, novĕl; bīte, pĭn; nō, ōbey, ôr, dŏg, tŏp, cŏllide; ūnit, ūnite, bûrn, cŭt, focŭs; noon, foŏt; mound; coin;

suc-ceed (sŭk-sēd′), *v.t.* **1,** to take the place of; be the successor of (a ruler); **2,** to follow; as, Friday *succeeds* Thursday:— *v.i.* **1,** to become heir (to); as, he *succeeded* to the family estate; **2,** to be successful; meet with success; as, his plans *succeed*; he *succeeded* in finding the lost book.

suc-cess (sŭk-sĕs′), *n.* **1,** the favorable end or result of an undertaking; the gaining of wealth, fame, or the like; **2,** a person or thing that turns out well; as, his book was a great *success.—adj.* **suc-cess′ful.—adv.** **suc-cess′ful-ly.**

suc-ces-sion (sŭk-sĕsh′ŭn), *n.* **1,** a following of one person or thing after another; as, things happened in quick *succession;* also, a series; as, a *succession* of misfortunes; **2,** the act or right of succeeding to the place, office, property, title, or throne of another.

suc-ces-sive (sŭk-sĕs′ĭv), *adj.* following in regular order or in a series without omission; consecutive.

suc-ces-sor (sŭk-sĕs′ẽr), *n.* one who follows, or takes the place of, another: opposite of *predecessor.*

suc-cinct (sŭk-sĭngkt′), *adj.* clearly expressed in a few words; concise; terse.

suc-cor (sŭk′ẽr), *v.t.* to help or relieve (someone) in difficulty or distress:—*n.* **1,** relief; aid; help; **2,** one who or that which brings help.

Syn., v. aid, comfort, assist, sustain.

suc-co-tash (sŭk′ō-tăsh), *n.* corn and beans stewed together.

suc-cu-lent (sŭk′ū-lĕnt), *adj.* full of juice, as fruit.—*n.* **suc′cu-lence; suc′cu-len-cy.**

suc-cumb (sŭ-kŭm′), *v.i.* **1,** to yield or submit; **2,** hence, to die.

such (sŭch), *adj.* **1,** of that kind; of the like kind; as, pens, pencils, and *such* things; **2,** the same; as, this flour is *such* as I have always used; **3,** a certain or particular; as, on *such* a date; **4,** so great, so good, so bad, or the like; as, he is *such* a fool; he did *such* work that he took honors:—*pron.* a certain person or thing; also, these or those; as, *such* of you as are going may start.

suck (sŭk), *v.t.* **1,** to draw (a liquid) into the mouth by action of the lips and tongue; as, to *suck* juice from an orange; **2,** to draw a liquid from (something) with the mouth; as, to *suck* an orange; **3,** to drink in or absorb; as, a blotter *sucks* up moisture; **4,** to draw in or engulf, as does quicksand:— *v.i.* to draw milk from the breast or udder: —*n.* the act of drawing in a liquid.

suck-er (sŭk′ẽr), *n.* **1,** a person or thing that sucks; a young animal; a suckling; **2,** a shoot of a plant from the roots or the lower part of the stem; **3,** a fresh-water fish

with thick, soft lips; **4,** in some animals, a disk-shaped organ by which they adhere to other animals; **5,** *Colloquial,* a lollipop.

SUCKER (⅛), def. 3

suck-le (sŭk′l), *v.t.* [suck-led, suck-ling], to nurse at the breast:—*v.i.* to suck; take the breast.

suck-ling (sŭk′lĭng), *n.* a baby or young animal that nurses at the breast.

su-cre (sōō′krā), *n.* the monetary unit of Ecuador. (See table, page 943.)

Su-cre (sōō′krā), a city, one of the capitals of Bolivia.

suc-tion (sŭk′shŭn), *n.* **1,** the act or condition of sucking; **2,** the drawing of liquid, dust, or the like, into a container as air is withdrawn from it; as, liquid is drawn into a syringe by *suction;* **3,** the sticking together of two bodies when the air between them is removed.

Su-dan (sōō-dăn′; sōō-dän′), **1,** a large region in Africa south of the Sahara Desert, extending from the Red Sea to Guinea. **2,** an independent country (cap. Khartoum), formerly *Anglo-Egyptian Sudan.*

Anglo-Egyptian Sudan, a territory south of Egypt, formerly governed by Egypt and Great Britain. **French Sudan,** a French colony (cap. Bamako) in French West Africa. (Map 14.)—*adj.* and *n.* **Su′da-nese′** (sōō′dá-nēz′;—nēs′).

sud-den (sŭd′n), *adj.* **1,** happening unexpectedly; as, a *sudden* turn for the worse; **2,** quickly done; hasty; as, a *sudden* change. —*adv.* **sud′den-ly.—***n.* **sud′den-ness.**

suds (sŭdz), *n.pl.* soapy water; also, the froth or bubbles floating on it.

sue (sū), *v.t.* [sued (sūd), su-ing (sū′ĭng)], to start an action in law against (a person); prosecute; as, to *sue* a man for libel:—*v.i.* **1,** to entreat, beg, or petition; as, to *sue* for pardon; **2,** to pay court; as, to *sue* for a lady's hand; **3,** to begin a lawsuit.

suède (swād), *n.* soft, unglazed kid with a slight nap, used for gloves, shoes, etc.

su-et (sū′ĕt), *n.* the hard fat around the kidneys and loins of mutton and beef. It is used in cooking and for making tallow.

Su-ez, Isth-mus of (sōō-ĕz′; sōō′ĕz), a strip of land joining Asia and Africa, between the Red Sea and the Mediterranean: —**Suez Canal,** a canal across the Isthmus of Suez, 100 miles long, from Port Said to the city of Suez (map 14).

suf- (sŭf-), *prefix,* a form of *sub-* used before *f;* as, *suffuse.*

suf-fer (sŭf′ẽr), *v.t.* **1,** to feel or endure; as, to *suffer* pain; bear up under; as, to *suffer*

a wrong; **2**, to experience; as, all things *suffer* change; **3**, to permit; allow:—*v.i.* **1**, to feel pain, distress, or loss; **2**, to sustain loss or damage; as, illness made his work *suffer.*—*adj.* **suf′fer-a-ble.**—*n.* **suf′fer-er.**
   Syn. support, stand, tolerate.

suf-fer-ance (sŭf′ẽr-ăns), *n.* **1**, implied consent or permission; as, he remained in the house on *sufferance* only; **2**, the ability to endure; endurance; as, cruelty beyond *sufferance.*

suf-fer-ing (sŭf′ẽr-ĭng), *n.* **1**, the bearing of physical or mental pain; **2**, the pain borne; the loss or injury endured.

suf-fice (sŭ-fīs′; sŭ-fīz′), *v.i.* [sufficed, suffic-ing], to be enough or sufficient:— *v.t.* to be sufficient for; satisfy; as, the small amount *sufficed* him.
   Syn. content, do, serve.

suf-fi-cien-cy (sŭ-fĭsh′ĕn-sĭ), *n.* [*pl.* sufficiencies], enough of anything; a supply equal to the need; as, only one town had a *sufficiency* of food during the flood.

suf-fi-cient (sŭ-fĭsh′ĕnt), *adj.* equal to the need; enough; as, *sufficient* coal for the winter.—*adv.* **suf-fi′cient-ly.**

suf-fix (sŭf′ĭks), *n.* a syllable or syllables, added at the end of a word or word stem, to form a new word related in meaning, as *-ant* in "dependant" or *-ion* in "erection":—*v.t.* (sŭ-fĭks′), to add (a syllable) to the end of a word in order to form a new word.

suf-fo-cate (sŭf′ō-kāt), *v.t.* [suffocat-ed, suffocat-ing], to kill by stopping the breath of; smother; stifle:—*v.i.* to be choked or stifled.—*n.* **suf′fo-ca′tion.**

Suf-folk (sŭf′ŭk), formerly, a county of eastern England: now divided into the counties of *East Suffolk* and *West Suffolk.*

suf-fra-gan (sŭf′rȧ-găn), *n.* an assistant bishop:—*adj.* assistant; subordinate.

suf-frage (sŭf′rĭj), *n.* **1**, a vote upon a measure or candidate; **2**, the right to vote; also, the act of voting.

suf-fra-gette (sŭf′rȧ-jĕt′), *n.* a woman who believes in, and works for, the right of women to vote.

suf-fra-gist (sŭf′rȧ-jĭst), *n.* one who believes in, and works for, the right of women to vote.

suf-fuse (sŭ-fūz′), *v.t.* [suffused, suffus-ing], to spread over; as, a blush *suffused* her cheeks.—*n.* **suf-fu′sion.**

sug- (sŭg-), *prefix,* a form of *sub-* used before *g;* as, **suggest.**

sug-ar (shoog′ẽr), *n.* **1**, a sweet substance obtained usually from the sugar cane or sugar beet, but also from many other plants, such as the maple; **2**, any sweet substance like sugar obtained from corn,

milk, etc.:—*v.t.* **1**, to mix or sprinkle with sugar; as, to *sugar* berries; **2**, to make less disagreeable:—*v.i.* to turn into sugar; as, sirup *sugars* if boiled too long.

   sugar beet, a variety of the common garden beet, with large white roots from which sugar is obtained; **sugar cane,** a tall, jointed, maizelike grass from the sap of which sugar is obtained; **sugar loaf, 1,** a cone-shaped loaf or mass of hard, refined sugar; **2,** something shaped like a cone of sugar, as a conical hill; **sugar maple,** the hard maple of the eastern U.S., from the sap of which maple sugar is made; **sugar of milk,** a sweet white powder used in infants' food.

SUGAR CANE

sug-ar-plum (shoog′ẽr-plŭm′), *n.* a bonbon; sweetmeat.

sug-ar-y (shoog′ẽr-ĭ), *adj.* like, made of, or containing, sugar; sweet.

sug-gest (sŭg-jĕst′), *v.t.* **1**, to propose, as a plan or method; **2**, to cause (an idea) to come to a person's mind through some natural connection or relationship; as, crocuses *suggest* spring.

sug-ges-tion (sŭg-jĕs′chŭn), *n.* **1**, the act of proposing something; also, the thing proposed; as, we accepted his *suggestion* for a ride; **2**, the process by which an idea causes another idea to come to mind through some natural connection; also, the idea thus brought to mind.

sug-ges-tive (sŭg-jĕs′tĭv), *adj.* **1**, tending to bring thoughts, ideas, etc., to the mind; **2**, tending to bring to mind something improper or indecent.

su-i-cid-al (sū′ĭ-sī′dȧl), *adj.* **1**, pertaining to the taking of one's own life; **2**, fatal to one's own interests; as, *suicidal* plans.

su-i-cide (sū′ĭ-sīd), *n.* **1**, the act of intentionally taking one's own life; **2**, a person who kills himself intentionally.

suit (sūt), *n.* **1**, the act of seeking favor, especially in wooing or courtship; **2**, an action or process at law; **3**, a set or number of things used together; as, a *suit* of clothes; **4**, any of the four sets in a deck of cards:—*v.t.* **1**, to fit; adapt; as, *suit* your words to the occasion; **2**, to be proper or suitable to; become; befit; as, your behavior does not *suit* your position; **3**, to please; satisfy; as, I hope this will *suit* you.

suit-a-ble (sūt′ȧ-bl), *adj.* fitting; becoming; appropriate.—*adv.* **suit′a-bly.**—*n.* **suit′a-ble-ness.**—*n.* **suit′a-bil′i-ty.**

āte, āorta, râre, căt, ȧsk, fär, ȧllow, sofȧ; ēve, ĕvent, ĕll, wrītẽr, novĕl; bīte, pĭn; nō, ōbey, ôr, dŏg, tŏp, cŏllide; ūnit, ūnite, bûrn, cŭt, focŭs; noon, foot; mound; coin;

suit-case (sōōt'kās'), *n.* a flat traveling bag for carrying clothes, toilet articles, etc.

suite (swēt), *n.* **1,** a corps of attendants; as, a king and his *suite;* **2,** a series or set, as of rooms, furniture, etc.

suit-or (sōō'tẽr), *n.* one who sues or entreats; especially, a man who courts or woos a woman.

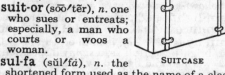

SUITCASE

sul-fa (sŭl'fà), *n.* the shortened form used as the name of a class of drugs useful in treating bacterial diseases, as **sulfanilamide, sulfadiazine.**

sul-fate (sŭl'fāt), *n.* a salt of sulfuric acid.

sul-fur (sŭl'fẽr), *n.* **1,** a yellow, nonmetallic element found in many places and in various forms, which burns with a blue flame and a suffocating odor, and is used in manufacturing gunpowder and matches, as a disinfectant, in medicine, etc.; **2,** a small yellow butterfly, usually spotted or streaked with black. Also, **sul'phur.**—*adj.* **sul'fu-rous** (sŭl'fŭ-rŭs; sŭl-fū'rŭs).

sul-fu-ric (sŭl-fū'rĭk), *adj.* pertaining to, or obtained from, sulfur.

sul-fu-ric ac-id, a heavy, oily, colorless, highly acid and corrosive fluid.

sulk (sŭlk), *v.i.* to be sullen or ill-humored: —**sulks,** *n.pl.* a sullen mood.

sulk-y (sŭl'kĭ), *adj.* [sulk-i-er, sulk-i-est], moody; sullen:—*n.* [*pl.* sulkies], a light, two-wheeled vehicle for one person.

sul-len (sŭl'ĕn), *adj.* **1,** gloomy; unsociable; as, a *sullen* disposition; **2,** dismal; lowering; as, *sullen* weather.—*adv.* **sul'len-ly.**

Syn. surly, morose, sulky, grim.

Sul-li-van (sŭl'ĭ-văn), Sir Arthur Seymour (1842-1900), an English composer, associated with Sir William Gilbert, who wrote the words for his operas.

sul-ly (sŭl'ĭ), *v.t.* [sullied, sully-ing], to tarnish or soil; dirty or stain.

sul-phur (sŭl'fẽr), *n.* **1,** a yellow nonmetallic element; **2,** a butterfly. See **sulfur.**

sul-tan (sŭl'tăn; sŏŏl-tän'), *n.* a Mohammedan ruler:—**Sultan,** formerly, the emperor of Turkey.

sul-tan-a (sŭl-tăn'à; sŭl-tä'nà), *n.* the wife, daughter, mother, or sister, of a sultan.

sul-tan-ate (sŭl'tăn-āt), *n.* the rule, rank, or territory of a Mohammedan ruler.

sul-try (sŭl'trĭ), *adj.* [sul-tri-er, sul-tri-est], very hot, close, moist, and oppressive; as, a *sultry* day.

sum- (sŭm-), *prefix,* a form of *sub-* used before *m;* as, *sum*mon.

sum (sŭm), *n.* **1,** the total of two or more numbers, quantities, or the like; the whole; **2,** the amount resulting from addition; as, 5 is the *sum* of 3 + 2; **3,** a problem in arithmetic; **4,** a quantity, as of money; **5,** summary; substance; as, the *sum* of the evidence:—*v.t.* [summed, summing], **1,** to add into one amount; **2,** to condense into few words:—*v.i.* to make a summary; as, and now, let me *sum* up.

su-mac or **su-mach** (shōō'măk; sōō'măk), *n.* **1,** a shrub or small tree with divided green leaves turning to a vivid red in the fall, and clusters of flowers followed by red or white berries; **2,** the dried leaves and roots of the sumac, used in tanning and dyeing.

SUMAC
Leaves and fruit.

Su-ma-tra (sōō-mä'trà), an island of the Indonesian Republic, south of the Malay Peninsula (map **15**).

sum-ma-rize (sŭm'à-rīz), *v.t.* [summarized, summariz-ing], to sum up.

sum-ma-ry (sŭm'à-rĭ), *n.* [*pl.* summaries], a brief account containing the sum or substance of a fuller account; an abridgment: —*adj.* **1,** giving the general idea; brief; concise; **2,** performed instantly and without formalities; as, *summary* punishment.

sum-mer (sŭm'ẽr), *n.* the hottest season of the year; the season of the year when the sun shines most directly; in the northern hemisphere, the period from the summer solstice, about June 21st, to the autumnal equinox, about September 22d:—*adj.* of or characteristic of summer:—*v.i.* to pass the summer; as, to *summer* at the shore:—*v.t.* to care for during the summer; as, to *summer* horses in a pasture.

sum-mit (sŭm'ĭt) *n.* the top or highest point; as, the *summit* of a hill.

sum-mon (sŭm'ŭn), *v.t.* **1,** to require the presence of; order to appear in court; **2,** to send for; call; as, to *summon* a doctor; **3,** to arouse; gather up; as, to *summon* one's strength.

sum-mons (sŭm'ŭnz), *n.* [*pl.* summonses (sŭm'ŭn-zĕz)], **1,** an order to appear in court on a certain day; **2,** a document containing such a notice; **3,** a call to duty.

sump-ter (sŭmp'tẽr), *n.* an animal, as a horse or mule, for carrying burdens.

sump-tu-ous (sŭmp'tū-ŭs), *adj.* costly; lavish; as, a *sumptuous* feast.

---

go; join; yet; sing; chin; show; thin, *th*en; hw, *wh*y; zh, azure; ū, Ger. für or Fr. lune; ö, Ger. schön or Fr. feu; ṅ, Fr. enfant, nom; kh, Ger. ach or ich. See pages ix-x.

sun (sŭn), *n.* **1,** the heavenly body round which the earth and other planets of our solar system revolve, and which gives us light and heat; **2,** a heavenly body which, like our sun, is the center of a system of planets; **3,** sunshine:—*v.t.* [sunned, sunning], to expose to the sun's rays for warming, drying, sterilizing, or bleaching purposes.

Sun. abbreviation for *Sunday.*

sun-beam (sŭn′bēm′), *n.* a ray of sunlight.

sun-bon-net (sŭn′bŏn′ĕt), *n.* a woman's or child's bonnet, with a brim projecting about the face, and a cape at the back, for protection from the sun.

sun-burn (sŭn′bûrn′), *n.* an inflammation of the skin caused by exposure to the sun:—*v.t.* and *v.i.* to burn by exposure to the sun. SUNBONNET

sun-dae (sŭn′dĭ), *n.* a serving of ice cream topped with a sirup, fruit, or nuts.

Sun-day (sŭn′dĭ), *n.* the first day of the week; the Christian Sabbath, or the Lord's Day.

sun-der (sŭn′dẽr), *v.t.* to divide or sever; separate; as, friends long *sundered.*

SUNDIAL

sun-dew (sŭn′-dū′), *n.* a bog plant with leaves that secrete a dewlike sticky fluid, by which it captures insects.

sun-di-al (sŭn′dī′ăl), *n.* a device that shows the time of day by a shadow which a pointer casts upon a dial.

sun-down (sŭn′-doun′), *n.* sunset.

sun-dry (sŭn′drĭ), *adj.* various; several:—**sundries**, *n.pl.* various trifles too small or too numerous to be specified.

SUNFISH (¼), def. 2

sun-fish (sŭn′fĭsh′), *n.* **1,** a very large, round, short-tailed fish, found in all warm seas, basking in the sun near the surface; **2,** a small American fresh-water fish.

sun-flow-er (sŭn′flou′ẽr), *n.* a tall plant with large leaves and round, flattened, showy yellow flower heads. (See illustration next column.)

sung (sŭng), an archaic form of the past tense of *sing;* also, the past participle.

sunk (sŭngk), one form of the past tense of *sink;* also, the past participle.

sunk-en (sŭngk′ĕn), *adj.* **1,** on a lower level; as, *sunken* gardens; below the surface of a body of water; especially, lying at the bottom; as, *sunken* treasure; **2,** fallen in; hollow; as, *sunken* eyes.

sun-light (sŭn′lĭt′), *n.* the light of the sun.

sun-lit (sŭn′lĭt′), *adj.* lighted by the sun.

sun-ny (sŭn′ĭ), *adj.* [sun-ni-er, sun-ni-est], **1,** bright; cheerful; as, a *sunny* disposition; **2,** warmed and lighted by the sun.

sun-rise (sŭn′rīz′), *n.* **1,** the coming up of the sun from below the horizon; **2,** the time of the sun's rising; **3,** the brightening of the sky at that time; **4,** the east.

sun-set (sŭn′sĕt′), *n.* **1,** the daily disappearance of the sun below the horizon; **2,** the time at which the sun disappears; **3,** the colors of the sunset sky; **4,** the west.

sun-shine (sŭn′shīn′), *n.* **1,** the light or rays of the sun; also, the place where they fall; **2,** brightness; cheer.

sun-spot (sŭn′spŏt′), *n.* one of the dark, irregular patches or spots visible at periodic intervals on the sun's disk.

sun-stroke (sŭn′strōk′), *n.* a sudden illness, often fatal, due to exposure to the sun or to other intense heat.

sun-tan (sŭn′tăn′), *n.* a browning of the skin brought about by exposure to the sun.

sup (sŭp), *v.t.* [supped, sup-ping], to take into the mouth a little at a time; sip:—*v.i.* **1,** to take supper; **2,** to sip:—*n.* a small mouthful of liquid; a sip.

sup- (sŭp-), *prefix,* a form of *sub-* used before *p;* as, *sup*press.

su-per (sōo′pẽr), *n.* the removable upper story of a beehive where honey is stored (see illustration under *beehive*):—*adj.* especially good or fine; superfine.

su-per- (sōo′pẽr-), a prefix meaning: **1,** above; over; as, *super*position, *super*intendent; **2,** going beyond; more than; as, *super*natural; *super*human; **3,** in excess; as, *super*abundance; *super*fluous.

su-per-a-bun-dant (sōo′pẽr-à-bŭn′dănt), *adj.* much more than is sufficient; excessive.—*n.* su′per-a-bun′dance.

su-per-an-nu-at-ed (sōo′pẽr-ăn′ū-ā′tĕd), *adj.* rendered unfit for work because of old age; also, pensioned because of old age or infirmity.

SUNFLOWER

su-perb (sū-pûrb′), *adj.* **1,** grand; proud; stately; as, a *superb* residence; **2,** rich;

āte, āorta, râre, căt, àsk, fär, ăllow, sofà; ēve, ĕvent, ĕll, writẽr, novĕl; bīte, pĭn; nō, ōbey, ôr, dŏg, tŏp, cŏllide; ūnit, ūnite, bûrn, cŭt, focŭs; nōon, fŏot; mound; coin;

elegant; as, *superb* attire; **3,** exceedingly good; of finest quality; as, *superb* acting.

su·per·car·go (soo′pẽr-kär′gō), *n*. [*pl*. supercargoes or supercargos], an agent on a merchant ship who has charge of its cargo and business affairs during the voyage.

su·per·cil·i·ous (soo′pẽr-sĭl′ĭ-ŭs) *adj*. contemptuously haughty; proud; overbearing.

su·per·fi·cial (soo′pẽr-fĭsh′ăl), *adj*. **1,** lying on the surface only; not deep; as, *superficial* wounds; **2,** not thorough; as, a *superficial* investigation.

su·per·fine (soo′pẽr-fīn′), *adj*. **1,** of the very choicest quality, or finest grind; **2,** very subtle; too nice; as, a *superfine* distinction.

su·per·flu·ous (soo′pẽr-pûr′floo-ŭs), *adj*. beyond what is necessary or desirable; excessive; as, *superfluous* remarks.— *n*. **su′per·flu′i·ty.**

su·per·high·way (soo′pẽr-hī′wā′), *n*. a modern public road, especially designed and constructed for safe high-speed travel.

su·per·hu·man (soo′pẽr-hū′măn), *adj*. **1,** beyond what is human; seeming to exceed human powers; as, *superhuman* strength; **2,** supernatural; divine; as, *superhuman* beings.

su·per·im·pose (soo′pẽr-ĭm-pōz′), *v.t*. [superimposed, superimpos-ing], to lay (something) on something else.

su·per·in·tend (soo′pẽr-ĭn-tĕnd′), *v.t*. to have, or exercise, the charge or oversight of; supervise and direct.— *n*. **su′per-in-tend′en·cy; su′per-in-tend′ence.**

su·per·in·tend·ent (soo′pẽr-ĭn-tĕn′dĕnt), *n*. one who directs or controls; a manager.

su·per·ri·or (soo′pĭr′ĭ-ẽr), *adj*. **1,** higher in place, position, rank, dignity, or office; as, a *superior* officer; **2,** of higher or better quality; preferable; as, this cloth is far *superior;* **3,** not stooping (to); not yielding (to); as, *superior* to petty jealousies; **4,** pretending to greater rank or dignity than that of others; arrogant; as, a *superior* attitude:— *n*. **1,** one who is better, greater, or higher in rank; **2,** the head of a religious house; as, a Mother *Superior.* — *n*. **su·pe′ri·or′i·ty.**

Syn., adj. principal, foremost.

Superior, Lake, the largest of the Great Lakes of North America (map **5**).

superl. abbreviation for *superlative.*

su·per·la·tive (soo′pûr′lȧ-tĭv), *adj*. **1,** best, highest, or greatest in degree; as, a man of *superlative* wisdom; **2,** in grammar, naming that form of an adjective or adverb, as *greatest* or *best,* that expresses the highest degree of the quality indicated by the simple word in the positive degree:— *n*. the superlative degree; also, a superlative form; as, "best" is the *superlative* of "good."

su·per·man (soo′pẽr-măn′), *n*. [*pl*. supermen(-mĕn′), a man of unusual strength and ability, or with more than human powers.

su·per·mar·ket (soo′pẽr-mär′kĕt), *n*. a large food store with most articles so arranged that customers can wait on themselves. Also, **super market.**

su·per·nat·u·ral (soo′pẽr-năt′û-răl), *adj*. outside, or exceeding, the laws of nature; miraculous:— *n*. that which is outside the usual course of nature.

su·per·nu·mer·ar·y (soo′pẽr-nū′mẽr-ẽr′ĭ), *n*. [*pl*. supernumeraries], **1,** a person or thing beyond the stated number, or beyond what is necessary or usual; **2,** an actor employed merely to appear in a performance, often as one of a group or crowd, with no speaking part:— *adj*. more than the desired or usual number.

su·per·scrip·tion (soo′pẽr-skrĭp′shŭn), *n*. words written or engraved on the outside or top of something; especially, the address on a letter or envelope.

su·per·sede (soo′pẽr-sēd′), *v.t*. [superseded, supersed-ing], to take the place of; supplant; as, automobiles *superseded* carriages.

su·per·son·ic (soo′pẽr-sŏn′ĭk), *adj*. of sound, having a frequency higher than can be heard by the human ear; of speed, faster than the speed of sound in air (about 738 miles per hour).

su·per·sti·tion (soo′pẽr-stĭsh′ŭn), *n*. **1,** belief in, fear of, or reverence for, the unknown or mysterious; **2,** beliefs or practices, often of a religious character, based on fear of the unknown; also, any popular belief in the power of omens, charms, etc.

su·per·sti·tious (soo′pẽr-stĭsh′ŭs), *adj*. pertaining to, believing in, or influenced by fear of or reverence for, the unknown.

su·per·struc·ture (soo′pẽr-strŭk′tûr), *n*. **1,** any structure built on something else; **2,** that part of a building which is above the basement or foundation.

su·per·vene (soo′pẽr-vēn′), *v.i*. [supervened, superven-ing], to come as something additional; follow closely upon something else; as, fire *supervened* upon flood.

su·per·vise (soo′pẽr-vīz′), *v.t*. [supervised, supervis-ing], to oversee; superintend.— *n*. **su′per-vi′sor.**— *adj*. **su′per-vi′so·ry.**— *n*. **su′per-vi′sion** (soo′pẽr-vĭzh′ŭn).

su·pine (soo-pīn′), *adj*. **1,** lying on the back; **2,** careless; indifferent; listless.

sup·per (sŭp′ẽr), *n*. the evening meal; the last meal of the day.— *adj*. **sup′per-less.**

sup·plant (sŭ-plănt′), *v.t*. **1,** to take the place of; as, electric lighting has *supplanted* gas lighting; **2,** to take the place of (another), sometimes by underhand means.

sup·ple (sŭp′l), *adj*. [sup-pler, sup-plest], **1,** easily bent; flexible; **2,** submissive.

Syn. limber, pliant, elastic.

sup·ple·ment (sŭp′lē-mĕnt), *n*. that which completes an unfinished thing or adds something to a completed thing; especially, a part at the end of a book or an article adding information or making corrections:— *v.t.* (sŭp′lē-měnt), to make additions to; complete.— *adj.* **sup′ple-men′-tal.**

sup-ple-men-ta-ry (sŭp′lē-měn′tȧ-rĭ), *adj.* **1,** additional; added to supply some lack; as *supplementary* evidence; **2,** of angles or arcs, making a total of 180 degrees when added.

sup-pli-ant (sŭp′lĭ-ănt), *n.* one who implores or entreats:— *adj.* **1,** asking earnestly and humbly; **2,** expressive of entreaty; as, bend the *suppliant* knee.

sup-pli-cant (sŭp′lĭ-kănt), *n.* one who entreats or asks earnestly and humbly:— *adj.* asking humbly; beseeching.

sup-pli-cate (sŭp′lĭ-kāt), *v.t.* [supplicat-ed, supplicat-ing], **1,** to ask for humbly and earnestly; as, to *supplicate* Heaven's blessing; **2,** to address or appeal to in prayer:— *v.i.* to pray or beseech humbly and earnestly.— *n.* **sup′pli-ca′tion.**

sup-ply (sŭ-plī′), *v.t.* [supplied, supplying], **1,** to furnish; provide; as, to *supply* men with food; to *supply* food for men; **2,** to make up for; fill; as, to *supply* a lack:— *n.* [*pl.* supplies], **1,** the act of furnishing what is needed; that which is needed; an amount required; as, a winter's *supply* of coal; **3,** the total amount available.

sup-port (sŭ-pôrt′), *v.t.* **1,** to bear the weight of; as, the pedestal *supports* the statue; **2,** to endure; bear; as, he *supported* his agony bravely; **3,** to encourage; sustain; **4,** to verify; prove; as, the figures *support* my claim; **5,** to aid, favor, or defend, as a political party; **6,** to provide for; as, to *support* a family:— *n.* **1,** the act of maintaining or upholding; **2,** one who or that which maintains or upholds; a prop; pillar; as, he is the chief *support* of the cause; the column is a strong *support* for the roof; **3,** maintenance; livelihood; **4,** one who furnishes means of living; as, she is the *support* of the family.— *n.* **sup-port′er.**

sup-pose (sŭ-pōz′), *v.t.* [supposed, supposing], **1,** to accept as true; imagine; think; **2,** to assume as a basis of argument; as, but *suppose* you lose; **3,** to imply; require as a condition; as, creation *supposes* a creator:— *v.i.* to think; imagine.— *adj.* **sup-pos′-a-ble.**

sup-posed (sŭ-pōzd′), *adj.* accepted as true, though not necessarily so; imagined.— *adv.* **sup-pos′ed-ly** (sŭ-pōz′ĕd-lĭ).

sup-po-si-tion (sŭp′ŏ-zĭsh′ŭn), *n.* the belief that a theory or hypothesis may prove to be true; also, the theory; as, our government was built on the *supposition* that all men are created equal.

sup-press (sŭ-prĕs′), *v.t.* **1,** to subdue;

crush; as, to *suppress* a revolt; **2,** to keep in; restrain; as, to *suppress* a cough; **3,** to conceal; also, to stop the publication of; as, to *suppress* news.

sup-pu-rate (sŭp′ū-rāt), *v.i.* [suppurat-ed, suppurat-ing], to form pus; fester.

su-pra-re-nal (sū′prȧ-rē′nȧl), *adj.* in anatomy, naming two small glands near the kidneys: also called *adrenal glands:*— *n.* a suprarenal gland.

su-prem-a-cy (sū-prĕm′ȧ-sĭ; sŏŏ-prĕm′ȧ-sĭ), *n.* the highest authority or power.

su-preme (sū-prēm′; sŏŏ-prēm′), *adj.* **1,** highest in power or authority; as, a *supreme* court; **2,** highest in degree; greatest possible; as, *supreme* indifference; **3,** crucial; most important; as, the climax is the *supreme* moment in the play.

Supreme Being, God.

Supreme Court, 1, the highest court in the United States, consisting of a chief justice and eight associate justices; **2,** any court resembling this, as in many of the States and in other countries.

Supt. abbreviation for *superintendent.*

su-rah (sŏŏ′rȧ; sū′rȧ), *n.* a soft, twilled silk material: also called *surah silk.*

sur-charge (sûr′chärj′; sûr-chärj′), *n.* **1,** an excessive or added charge, load, or burden; a charge beyond what is just and right; **2,** an additional word, mark, etc., officially printed on the face of a postage stamp to change its value or use:— *v.t.* (sûr-chärj′), [surcharged, surcharg-ing], **1,** to overcharge; put an extra charge upon; **2,** to overload; overburden; **3,** to print additional words on (a postage stamp).

sur-cin-gle (sûr′sĭng′gl), *n.* a belt passed round the body of a horse or other animal to hold a saddle or blanket in place.

sur-coat (sûr′kōt′), *n.* an outer coat; especially, the long, loose cloak, often brilliantly adorned, worn by a knight over his armor.

sure (shŏŏr), *adj.* [sur-er, sur-est], **1,** knowing and believing; confident; as, I am *sure* you will succeed; **2,** destined; certain; as, you are *sure* to succeed; **3,** dependable; reliable; as, the only *sure* way; **4,** firmly fixed; as, a *sure* foundation:— *adv.* surely; as, *sure* as fate.— *n.* **sure′ness.**

sure—foot-ed (shŏŏr′-fŏŏt′-ĕd), *adj.* not in the least likely to stumble.

sure-ly (shŏŏr′lĭ), *adv.* **1,** with certainty; as, slowly but *surely;* **2,** undoubtedly; as, he will *surely* come.

sure-ty (shŏŏr′tĭ; shŏŏr′ē-tĭ), *n.* [*pl.* sure-

SURCOAT
Knight, 13th century, wearing surcoat over armor.

ties], **1,** certainty; **2,** that which makes for security; especially, a guarantee against loss or damage; **3,** one who makes himself responsible for certain acts of another, as for the payment of a debt.

surf (sûrf), *n.* the waves of the sea as they break in foam upon the shore.

sur-face (sûr′fĭs), *n.* **1,** the outside part of a solid body, or the upper face of a body of liquid; as, a rough *surface;* the *surface* of a lake; **2,** external or outward appearance: —*adj.* **1,** pertaining to the top or surface; **2,** insincere; as, *surface* politeness:—*v.t.* [surfaced, surfac-ing], to give an outside covering or polish to:—*v.i.* to come to the surface from below, as a submarine.

sur-feit (sûr′fĭt), *n.* **1,** indulgence to excess, especially in eating or drinking; **2,** fulness or sickness caused by such excess: —*v.t.* to feed to excess; cloy; glut; satiate.

surge (sûrj), *n.* **1,** a large wave, swell, or billow; **2,** a great rolling motion; rush; as, the *surge* of a mob:—*v.i.* [surged, surging], to rise high and roll; swell.

sur-geon (sûr′jŭn), *n.* a doctor trained to perform operations.

sur-ger-y (sûr′jēr-ĭ), *n.* [*pl.* surgeries], the science and practice of treating injuries, deformities, or diseases by operations, especially by the use of the knife.

sur-gi-cal (sûr′jĭ-kăl), *adj.* pertaining to surgeons or to surgery, the science and practice of performing operations.

Su-ri-nam (soo′rĭ-näm′), a Dutch colony in South America. See **Guiana.**

sur-ly (sûr′lĭ), *adj.* [sur-li-er, sur-li-est], ill-humored; uncivil; rudely abrupt.
   Syn. rude, gruff, sullen, gloomy.

sur-mise (sûr-mīz′; sûr′mīz), *n.* a thought or conjecture based upon little evidence; a guess:—*v.t.* and *v.i.* (sûr-mīz′), [surmised, surmis-ing], to guess, or make a guess on insufficient evidence.

sur-mount (sûr-mount′), *v.t.* **1,** to overcome; conquer; as, to *surmount* difficulties; **2,** to be situated at the top of; as, a castle *surmounts* the hill.

sur-name (sûr′nām′), *n.* originally, a name, often descriptive, added to the Christian name, as in "Charles the Bold"; now, the last or family name, shared by all the members of one family:—*v.t.* (sûr′nām′; sûr-nām′), [surnamed, surnam-ing], to give a surname, or additional name, to; as, Alexander was *surnamed* the Great.

sur-pass (sēr-pás′), *v.t.* **1,** to exceed; go beyond the limits of; as, wonders that *surpass* belief; **2,** to excel; be superior to.

sur-plice (sûr′plĭs), *n.* an outer white linen garment with wide sleeves, worn in some churches by the clergy and the choir.

sur-plus (sûr′plŭs; sûr′plŭs), *n.* that which remains over and above what is used or required; excess: opposite of *deficit:*—*adj.* exceeding what is used or needed.

sur-prise (sēr-prīz′), *n.* **1,** the act of coming upon or attacking unexpectedly; as, the enemy was taken by *surprise;* **2,** the feeling aroused by what is sudden and strange; wonder; astonishment; **3,** a sudden or unexpected event or fact; as, his dismissal came as a *surprise:*—*v.t.* [surprised, surpris-ing], **1,** to take unawares; come upon or attack without warning; as, they *surprised* the conspirators; **2,** to strike with wonder, as does something unexpected; **3,** to hurry (a person) into doing something unintended; as, to *surprise* a thief into confessing.

sur-ren-der (sŭ-rĕn′dēr), *v.t.* **1,** to yield (oneself) under pressure to the power of another; **2,** to resign possession of; give up; as, to *surrender* arms; *surrender* one's claim to property; **3,** to yield (oneself) to an influence or emotion:—*v.i.* to yield; give up the struggle:—*n.* the act of yielding to an outside influence; also, the giving up of a claim or privilege.

sur-rep-ti-tious (sûr′ĕp-tĭsh′ŭs), *adj.* stealthy; secret; clandestine.

sur-rey (sûr′ĭ), *n.* [*pl.* surreys], a light, four-wheeled ′carriage with two seats.

SURREY

sur-ro-gate (sûr′ō-gāt), *n.* **1,** a person appointed to act for another; **2,** in certain states, a court officer who deals with the probating, or proving, of wills, and the administration of estates.

sur-round (sŭ-round′), *v.t.* **1,** to enclose on all sides; as, the city is *surrounded* by suburbs; **2,** to encircle or cause to be encircled; as, to *surround* oneself with luxuries.

sur-round-ings (sŭ-roun′dĭngz), *n.pl.* neighborhood; environment.

sur-tax (sûr′tăks′), *n.* an additional tax over and above a normal tax.

sur-veil-lance (sûr-vāl′ăns; sûr-vāl′yăns), *n.* a close watch; supervision.

sur-vey (sēr-vā′), *v.t.* **1,** to look at, as from a height; take a broad, general view of; as, to *survey* a landscape; *survey* a series of events; **2,** to examine closely, with respect to condition, value, etc.; as, to *survey* a factory; **3,** to measure and determine the boundaries or other features of (a portion of land):—*n.* (sûr′vā; sēr-vā′), **1,** the act of looking over or examining carefully; **2,** an investigation, often of official nature; as, a

---

go; join; yet; sing; chin; show; thin, *th***en; hw,** *wh***y; zh,** a**zure; ŭ,** Ger. f**ür** or Fr. l**une;**
ō, Ger. sch**ön** or Fr. f**eu;** **ṅ,** Fr. e**nfant,** no**m; kh,** Ger. a**ch** or i**ch.** See pages **ix–x.**

survey of unemployment; **3,** a summary or outline; **4,** the process of determining the exact measurements, outline, position, etc., of any part of the earth's surface; also, an accurate plan and description, based on these measurements.—*n.* **sur-vey′or.**

sur-vey-ing (sĕr-vā′ing), *n.* the science, act, or business, of measuring, determining, and recording the boundaries, position, etc., of any part of the earth's surface.

sur-viv-al (sĕr-vīv′ăl), *n.* **1,** the fact of living or continuing after the others of the same kind have disappeared; as, the *survival* of an old custom; **2,** something that has outlived others of the same kind.

sur-vive (sĕr-vīv′), *v.t.* [survived, surviving], to live longer than (others); to outlive; also, to live beyond or through (an event, state, or the like); as, to *survive* a tornado:—*v.i.* to remain alive or in existence.—*n.* **sur-vi′vor.**

sus-cep-ti-ble (sŭ-sĕp′tĭ-bl), *adj.* **1,** capable of; admitting; as, a statement *susceptible* of proof; **2,** capable of being changed, influenced, or easily affected; as, a person *susceptible* to flattery; **3,** sensitive; impressionable; as, *susceptible* youth. —*n.* **sus-cep′ti-bil′i-ty.**

sus-pect (sŭs-pĕkt′), *v.t.* **1,** to conjecture; surmise; as, I *suspect* that illness kept her home; **2,** to believe in the possible guilt of, without having proof; **3,** to consider as questionable; doubt; as, to *suspect* the accuracy of a report:—*n.* (sŭs′pĕkt; sŭs-pĕkt′), a person believed, but not proved, to be guilty of crime.

sus-pend (sŭs-pĕnd′), *v.t.* **1,** to cause to hang down; as, to *suspend* a rope from a roof; **2,** to hold, as if hanging; as, particles of dust are *suspended* in the air; **3,** to delay; hold undecided; as, to *suspend* judgment; **4,** to set aside or waive temporarily; disregard for a time; as, to *suspend* a rule; **5,** to debar, or keep out, for a time, from some privilege, office, or the like; as, to *suspend* a pupil from school.

sus-pend-ers (sŭs-pĕn′dĕrz), *n.pl.* two straps or bands worn over the shoulders to hold up the trousers.

sus-pense (sŭs-pĕns′), *n.* a state of uncertainty, doubt, or anxiety.

sus-pen-sion (sŭs-pĕn′shŭn), *n.* **1,** the act of hanging, or state of being hung, from a support; also, the act of floating unattached, as of dust in the air; **2,** the act of holding back or delaying; as, *suspension* of judgment; **3,** the act of removing for a time, or the state of being removed, from a position, office, privilege, etc.; **4,** a temporary interruption; as, *suspension* of payments, hostilities, or a law:—**suspension bridge,** a bridge, the roadway of which is

hung, unsupported from below, from cables stretched across the interval bridged (see illustration under *bridge*).

sus-pi-cion (sŭs-pĭsh′ŭn), *n.* **1,** the feeling or imagining that something is wrong; mistrust; doubt; **2,** a notion or inkling; as, a *suspicion* of trouble; **3,** a very small amount; hint; as, a *suspicion* of humor. *Syn.* misgiving, distrust.

sus-pi-cious (sŭs-pĭsh′ŭs), *adj.* **1,** inclined to imagine without proof; distrustful; as, a *suspicious* parent; **2,** open to, or exciting, unbelief; as, a *suspicious* alibi; **3,** showing, or suggesting, doubt or suspicion; as, a *suspicious* glance.

Sus-que-han-na (sŭs′kwĕ-hăn′ȧ), a river in New York, Pennsylvania, and Maryland, flowing into Chesapeake Bay (map 6).

Sus-sex (sŭs′ĕks), a former county of southeastern England, now divided into *East Sussex* and *West Sussex.*

sus-tain (sŭs-tān′), *v.t.* **1,** to support, as weight or pressure; **2,** to maintain or keep up, as an argument; **3,** to keep going; as, food *sustains* life; **4,** to suffer; undergo, as a loss; **5,** to bear up under; receive, as a blow; **6,** to keep up the spirit of; as, his faith *sustained* him; **7,** to confirm; bear out; as, to *sustain* an accusation with proof; **8,** to uphold, as a decision.

sus-te-nance (sŭs′tĕ-năns), *n.* **1,** the act of supporting; also, support or maintenance; as, he is responsible for the *sustenance* of his brother's family; **2,** that which supports life; food.

sut-ler (sŭt′lĕr), *n.* a person who follows an army to sell food, liquor, etc.

su-ture (sū′tūr), *n.* **1,** the drawing together of the edges of a wound by stitches; also, the thread used, as silk or catgut; **2,** the lines or seams where bones, as those of the skull, are united.

su-ze-rain (sū′zĕ-rān; sōō′zĕ-rān), *n.* **1,** formerly, a feudal lord with authority over vassals who owed him loyalty and service in return for the use of land; **2,** a state holding sovereign power over a semi-independent state.

su-ze-rain-ty (sū′zĕ-rān-tĭ; sōō′zĕ-rān-tĭ), *n.* the position or power of a suzerain.

svelte (svĕlt), *adj.* slender; supple; lithe.

Sverd-lovsk (svĕrd-lôfsk′), the present name of Ekaterinburg, the Russian city where Czar Nicholas II of Russia was assassinated (map 15).

S.W. abbreviation for *southwest.*

swab (swŏb; swôb), *n.* **1,** a mop for cleaning decks, floors, etc.; **2,** a bit of sponge or cotton, usually fastened to the end of a thin stick, used to clean, or apply medicine to, the mouth, throat, etc.:—*v.t.* [swabbed,

---

āte, āorta, râre, căt, ȧsk, fär, ȧllow, sofȧ; ēve, ĕvent, ĕll, writẽr, novĕl; bīte, pĭn; nō, ōbey, ôr, dŏg, tŏp, cŏllide; ūnit, ūnite, bûrn, cŭt, focŭs; nōōn, fŏŏt; mound; coin;

swab-bing], to clean, or apply medicine to, with a swab. Also spelled **swob.**—*n.* **swab′ber.**

swad-dle (swŏd′l; swôd′l), *v.t.* [swad-dled, swad-dling], to wrap or swathe (a new-born infant) with cloths or bandages.

swag (swăg), *n. Slang,* booty; plunder.

swag-ger (swăg′ẽr), *v.i.* to strut about; also, to boast noisily; bluster:—*n.* an affected, insolent walk or strut; also, noisy boastfulness.

swain (swān), *n.* 1, a country lad; 2, a young suitor.

SWALLOW (¹⁄₁)

¹**swal-low** (swŏl′ō; swôl′ō), *n.* any one of several small migratory birds, with long, forked tail and pointed wings, noted for graceful, swift flight.

²**swal-low** (swŏl′ō; swôl′ō), *v.t.* 1, to transfer, as food, from the mouth to the stomach through the gullet; 2, to absorb; as, expenses *swallow* up income; engulf; as, night *swallowed* the earth; 3, to endure quietly, as an insult; 4, to accept readily as true without asking for proof; as, to *swallow* an improbable story:—*v.i.* to perform the act of taking down food or liquid; as, to *swallow* quickly:—*n.* the act of swallowing; also, the amount swallowed at one time.

swal-low—tailed (swŏl′ō-tāld′; swô′lō-tāld′), *adj.* 1, with a tail forked like a swallow's tail; 2, with two long, tapering skirts; as, a *swallow-tailed* coat.

swam (swăm), past tense of *swim.*

swamp (swŏmp; swômp), *n.* wet, marshy land:—*v.t.* 1, to cause to sink in a swamp or bog; 2, to sink by filling with water; as, to *swamp* a boat; 3, to overwhelm; submerge; as, the business was *swamped* by old debts.—*adj.* **swamp′ish.** —*adj.* **swamp′y.**

SWAN (¹⁄₂₀)

swan (swŏn; swŏn), *n.* a large, graceful aquatic bird with a long neck:—**swan song,** 1, the beautiful song which the swan was supposed to sing just before its death; 2, hence, a last utterance or writing.

swan dive, a graceful kind of fancy dive.

SWAN DIVE

swank (swăngk), *n. Colloquial,* swagger; pretentiousness.—*adj.* **swank′y.**

swan's—down (swŏnz′=doun′; swŏnz′= doun′), *n.* 1, the soft feathers of the swan, often used as trimming; 2, (usually *swans-down*), a soft, thick cloth resembling down.

Swan-sea (swŏn′sē; swŏn′zē), a city in Wales on the Bristol Channel (map 13).

swap (swŏp; swôp), *Colloquial: v.t.* and *v.i.* [swapped, swap-ping], to exchange or trade; as, to *swap* horses:—*n.* an exchange.

sward (swôrd), *n.* a stretch of land covered thickly with short grass; turf.

sware (swâr), *Archaic,* past tense of *swear.*

swarm (swôrm), *n.* 1, a large number of moving birds, animals, insects, or the like; as, a *swarm* of locusts; 2, a large number of honeybees, accompanied by a queen, leaving one hive to establish a new home in another; also, a colony of bees settled in a hive permanently; 3, a great number; a crowd; as, *swarms* of people:—*v.i.* 1, to move about in great numbers; as, people *swarmed* into the theater; 2, to be crowded; as, the town *swarmed* with soldiers; 3, of bees, to leave a hive in a swarm to form a new colony:—*v.t.* to throng; as, people *swarmed* the streets.

swarth-y (swôr′thĭ; swôr′thĭ), *adj.* [swarth-i-er, swarth-i-est], of a dusky color; dark-skinned.—*n.* **swarth′i-ness.**

swash (swŏsh; swôsh), *v.i.* to dash or wash with a splashing sound, as water against a boat:—*v.t.* to splash (water) about:—*n.* the dashing of water, as against rocks.

swash-buck-ler (swŏsh′bŭk′lẽr; swôsh′-bŭk′lẽr), *n.* a blustering bully; a swaggerer.

swas-ti-ka or **swas-ti-ca** (swŏs′tĭ-ka; swôs′tĭ-ka; swăs′tĭ-ka), *n.* a crosslike symbol, dating from ancient times, shaped like four capital L's joined together; adopted by the Nazis as the national emblem of Germany.

SWASTIKA

swat (swŏt; swôt), *v.t.* [swat-ted, swat-ting], to strike violently:—*n.* a smart rap.

swath (swŏth; swôth), *n.* 1, a line or row of grass or grain, as cut down by a mower; 2, the reach of a mowing machine or scythe; 3, the space cleared in one course.

swathe (swāth), *v.t.* [swathed, swath-ing], 1, to bind with a band or bandage; 2, to wrap; enclose; as, to *swathe* oneself in furs: —*n.* a bandage.

sway (swā), *v.i.* 1, to move or swing from side to side, or backward and forward, as treetops in a breeze; 2, to lean to one side; waver; as, the tightrope dancer *swayed* and fell:—*v.t.* 1, to cause to bend or to move backward and forward, or from side to side; 2, to cause to lean to one side; bias; as, to *sway* opinion; 3, to influence by power; direct; rule; as, to *sway* the lives of a people:—*n.* **1,** the act of swaying; **2,** a controlling force or influence; as, under the *sway* of anger; **3,** rule or control; as, the *sway* of the press over public opinion.

sway–backed (swā′-băkt′), *adj.* having an abnormally sagging back; as, a *sway-backed* horse. Also, **sway′—back′.**

Swa-zi-land (swä′zē-lănd′), a small district, under British control, in the Union of South Africa (map 14).

swear (swâr), *v.i.* [*p.t.* swore (swôr) or, *Archaic,* sware (swâr), *p.p.* sworn (swôrn), *p.pr.* swear-ing], **1,** to make a solemn declaration, with an appeal to God as witness, to the truth of what is affirmed; **2,** to make a solemn vow or promise; **3,** to give evidence on oath; **4,** to use prŏfane language:— *v.t.* **1,** to declare solemnly, with an appeal to God or to some sacred object; **2,** to vow or promise solemnly; **3,** to cạuse (a person) to take an oath; as, to *swear* a witness.—*n.* **swear′er.**—*n.* **swear′ing.**

sweat (swĕt), *n.* **1,** the moisture which is given off through the pores of the skin; perspiration; **2,** moisture given off by any substance; **3,** the act of perspiring; also, the condition of one who is perspiring:—*v.i.* [*p.t.* and *p.p.* sweat or sweat-ed, *p.pr.* sweat-ing], **1,** to perspire; **2,** to form moisture in drops on the outside; as, a glass of water *sweats;* **3,** *Colloquial,* to labor hard; drudge:—*v.t.* **1,** to cause to perspire freely; as, to *sweat* a horse; **2,** to wet with perspiration; **3,** to employ at long hours of hard work for very low wages.—*adj.* **sweat′y.**

sweat-er (swĕt′ēr), *n.* **1,** a person who overworks and underpays those who work for him; **2,** a knitted or crocheted jacket.

sweat-shop (swĕt′shŏp′), *n.* a factory which employs persons for long hours of hard work at low wages.

Swede (swēd), *n.* a native of Sweden.

Swe-den (swē′dn), a kingdom (cap. Stockholm) occupying the eastern part of the Scandinavian Peninsula (map 12).

Swed-ish (swē′dĭsh), *adj.* pertaining to Sweden, its inhabitants, or its language:— *n.* the language of Sweden.

sweep (swēp), *v.t.* [swept (swĕpt), sweep-ing], **1,** to brush or clean with a broom, brush, etc.; as, to *sweep* a rug; **2,** to remove or clean away; as, to *sweep* up bits of paper; **3,** to drive, flow over, or carry along or off, with force; as, waves *swept* the deck; **4,** to pass lightly over or across; as, to *sweep* the strings of a guitar; **5,** to scan or gaze at; move over or traverse swiftly; as, to *sweep* the seas:—*v.i.* **1,** to clean or clear away dirt with a brush, broom, etc.; **2,** to pass with speed or force; as, the cavalry *swept* down the field; **3,** to move with stateliness or dignity; **4,** to extend in

a continuous line or curve; as, the lawn *sweeps* down to the river:—*n.* **1,** the act of sweeping, clearing out, or getting rid of; **2,** a sweeping motion; as, a *sweep* of the arm; **3,** the range of such a motion; **4,** a bend or curve, as of a drive; **5,** one who makes a business of cleaning chimneys; **6,** a long pole, attached to a post, for drawing a bucket from a well; **7,** a long oar for moving or steering a boat.—*n.* **sweep′er.**

sweep-ing (swē′pĭng), *adj.* of great scope or range; broad; as, a *sweeping* assertion: —**sweepings,** *n.pl.* a collection of dirt and particles swept up; rubbish.

sweep-stakes (swēp′stāks′), *n.* **1,** a horse race in which the purse is made up by the owners of the horses, the winner taking all; **2,** the whole amount put up on such a race; **3,** a form of gambling, as on a horse race, in which individuals buy tickets, the stakes being distributed among a limited number of the ticket holders determined by lot.

sweet (swēt), *adj.* **1,** tasting like sugar; **2,** not stale or sour; as, *sweet* milk; **3,** not salt; as, *sweet* butter; **4,** fragrant; **5,** pleasing in sound; soft; as, the *sweet* tones of a violin; **6,** charming or attractive in manner or appearance; **7,** gentle; mild; as, a *sweet* disposition:—*n.* **1,** one dearly loved; a darling; **2,** a tart, pudding, etc.; dessert; **3, sweets,** confectionery or candy.

sweet a-lys-sum (ạ-lĭs′ŭm), a low-growing garden plant with white flowers.

sweet-bread (swēt′brĕd′), *n.* the pancreas of a calf or lamb, cooked for food.

sweet-bri-er or **sweet-bri-ar** (swēt′brī′-ẽr), *n.* a thorny shrub bearing fragrant, single, pink flowers: also called *eglantine.*

sweet corn, a sweet kind of Indian corn, usually eaten when the ears are young.

sweet-en (swēt′n), *v.t.* to make sweet; as, to *sweeten* tea:—*v.i.* to become sweet.

sweet-en-ing (swēt′n-ĭng; swĕt′nĭng), *n.* a substance which sweetens.

sweet-heart (swēt′härt′), *n.* one who is beloved; a lover.

sweet-ish (swē′tĭsh), *adj.* rather sweet.

sweet mar-jo-ram (mär′-jō-răm), a fragrant mint used as a flavoring in cooking: also called *marjoram.*

SWEET PEA

sweet-meat (swēt′mēt′), *n.* a piece of crystallized fruit, ginger, or the like; a candy.

sweet-ness (swēt′nĕs), *n.* the quality or condition of being sweet.

sweet pea, a plant with slender, climbing

stems and fragrant, winged flowers of various colors; also, the flower.

sweet po-ta-to, the sweet, starchy root of a tropical American vine, used as a vegetable; also, the vine.

sweet Wil-liam, a plant of the pink family with small flowers of various colors in dense flat clusters.

SWEET WIL-LIAM

swell (swĕl), *v.i.* [*p.t.* swelled (swĕld), *p.p.* swelled or swol-len (swŏl′ĕn), *p.pr.* swell-ing], **1**, to increase in size, volume, force, importance, value, etc.; as, her sprained ankle began to *swell*; it is hoped that profits will *swell* this year; the music *swelled* to a climax; **2**, to be inflated or bulge, as sails; **3**, to be puffed up; as, to *swell* with pride; **4**, to rise above the surrounding surface; as, the ground *swells*:—*v.t.* **1**, to cause to rise or increase; fill; puff up; **2**, to inflate with pride; **3**, in music, to play or sing (notes) with gradual increase and decrease of volume:—*n.* **1**, the act of swelling; an increase in volume, force, value, etc.; **2**, in music, gradual increase and decrease of sound; **3**, a long, continuous wave; **4**, *Colloquial*, a very fashionable person.

swell-ing (swĕl′ĭng), *n.* **1**, increase or expansion; **2**, a swollen part; a lump.

swel-ter (swĕl′tĕr), *v.i.* to suffer from the heat; perspire freely.

swept (swĕpt), past tense and past participle of *sweep*.

swerve (swûrv), *v.i.* and *v.t.* [swerved, swerv-ing], to turn, or cause to turn, aside from a course:—*n.* a sudden turning aside.

Swift (swĭft), Jonathan (1667–1745), an English satirical writer, author of "Gulliver's Travels."

swift (swĭft), *adj.* rapid; quick; alert:—*n.* a bird, related to the hummingbird, but resembling the swallow.

SWIFT (⅓)

swig (swĭg), *Colloquial*: *v.t.* [swigged, swig-ging], to drink in deep drafts; gulp:—*n.* a deep drink, as of liquor.

swill (swĭl), *v.t.* and *v.i.* to drink or gulp greedily in large quantities:—*n.* **1**, drink taken in large quantities; **2**, food for animals, especially for swine; **3**, garbage.

swim (swĭm), *v.i.* [*p.t.* swam (swăm), *p.p.* swum (swŭm), *p.pr.* swim-ming], **1**, to propel or push oneself forward in the water, with the arms and legs, as does man, with fins and tail, as do fish, etc.; **2**, to float on a liquid; **3**, to be carried along smoothly by a current; **4**, to overflow; as, eyes *swimming* with tears; **5**, to be dizzy; as, my head *swims*; also, to reel or seem to reel; as, the room *swam* before her eyes:—*v.t.* **1**, to cause to swim or float; as, to *swim* cattle across a stream; **2**, to traverse by swimming; as, to *swim* a lake:—*n.* swimming, especially as a sport:—**in the swim**, in the main current of affairs.—*n.* **swim′mer**.

swim-ming-ly (swĭm′ĭng-lĭ), *adv.* easily and smoothly; successfully.

swin-dle (swĭn′dl), *v.t.* and *v.i.* [swin-dled, swin-dling], to get money or something else from (someone) on false pretenses; cheat:—*n.* the act of cheating; also, a fraudulent scheme.—*n.* **swin′dler**.

 Syn., *v.* steal, trick, delude.

swine (swīn), *n.* [*pl.* swine], **1**, any animal of the hog family; **2**, a person with greedy or coarse habits.

swine-herd (swīn′hûrd′), *n.* a tender of hogs or swine.

swing (swĭng), *v.i.* [swung (swŭng), swing-ing], **1**, to move to and fro regularly, as the pendulum of a clock; **2**, to turn on, or as on, a hinge, or axis; as, the gate *swings* open; **3**, to move with a loose, free, swaying gait; **4**, to turn or wheel round; veer, as the wind:—*v.t.* **1**, to cause to move to and fro; as, to *swing* a child in a hammock; **2**, to move or wave to and fro; brandish, as a cane; **3**, to cause to turn or wheel about; **4**, to put up so as to hang freely; as, to *swing* a hammock; hang on hinges; as, to *swing* a gate; **5**, to manage successfully; as, to *swing* a business deal:—*n.* **1**, the act of swinging; also, the distance through which an object swings; **2**, a loose, free gait; **3**, an apparatus for swinging, as a rope holding a seat; **4**, strongly marked rhythm, as of poetry or music; **5**, swing music:—*adj.* designating a kind of jazz music played with improvised and complicated rhythms and variations of the music as originally written.

SWING

swipe (swīp), *n.* a vigorous blow, as with a club:—*v.t.* [swiped, swip-ing], **1**, to hit with force; **2**, *Slang*, to steal.

swirl (swûrl), *v.i.* to move with a circular or whirling motion:—*v.t.* to cause to eddy or whirl:—*n.* a whirl, eddy, or twist.

swish (swĭsh), *n.* a rustling sound, or the movement that makes it:—*v.t.* to brandish, as a cane; cause to make a rustling sound:—*v.i.* to move with a rustling sound.

Swiss (swĭs), *adj.* pertaining to Switzerland or its people:—*n.* [*pl.* Swiss], a native or citizen of Switzerland.

switch (swĭch), *n.* **1,** a thin, flexible twig or rod; **2,** a blow with such a switch or whip; **3,** a movable section of rail for shifting cars from one track to another; **4,** a device for making, breaking, or shifting electric circuits; **5,** a tress of false hair, used by women in dressing the hair:—*v.t.* **1,** to whip or lash with a switch; **2,** to swing or jerk; as, the horse *switched* its tail; **3,** to shift (cars) to another track; **4,** to shift to another circuit, or on or off a circuit; as, to *switch* off the electric light:—*v.i.* **1,** to shift to another track; **2,** hence, to change course suddenly.

switch-back (swĭch′băk′), *n.* a railway up a steep incline. The tracks are laid not in a straight line, but in a series of zigzag curves to offset the steepness of the grade.

switch-board (swĭch′bôrd′), *n.* an apparatus fitted with plugs that control electric currents; as, a telephone *switchboard.*

Switz-er-land (swĭt′zẽr-lănd), a republic (cap. Bern) in central Europe (map 12).

swiv-el (swĭv′l), *n.* **1,** anything that turns on a headed bolt or pin; as, the *swivel* of a watch chain; **2,** a link in two parts connected by a bolt or pin, so that each part can turn independently:—*v.t.* and *v.i.* [swiveled, swivel-ing], to turn on a swivel.

SWIVEL

swob (swŏb; swôb), *n.* **1,** a mop; **2,** a piece of cotton used in applying medicine:—*v.t.* [swobbed, swob-bing], to clean, or apply medicine to, with a swob; swab. See **swab.**

swol-len (swōl′ĕn), one form of the past participle of *swell.*

swoon (swōōn), *v.i.* to faint:—*n.* a fainting fit.

swoop (swōōp), *v.i.* to sweep (down) swiftly and suddenly; pounce; as, the eagle *swoops* down upon its prey:—*n.* a sudden downward plunge, as of a bird of prey.

sword (sôrd), *n.* **1,** a weapon consisting of a long pointed blade, with one or with two sharp edges, set in a handle or hilt, and kept, when not in actual use, in a sheath or scabbard; **2,** the symbol of military power, of justice, or of vengeance; **3,** conflict or war; as, to resort to the *sword.*

SWORD

sword-fish
(sôrd′fĭsh′), *n.* a large, edible sea fish, whose upper jaw lengthens out into a swordlike projection.

SWORDFISH (ₒ¹₀₀)

sword-play (sôrd′plā′), *n.* the act or art of wielding a sword; also, fencing.

swords-man (sôrdz′măn), *n.* [*pl.* swordsmen (-mĕn)], **1,** a person who uses the sword; hence, a soldier; **2,** one skilled in the use of the foil; a fencer.

swore (swôr), past tense of *swear.*

sworn (swôrn), past participle of *swear.*

swum (swŭm), past participle of *swim.*

swung (swŭng), past tense and past participle of *swing.*

syc-a-more (sĭk′à-môr), *n.* **1,** the American buttonwood; **2,** a fig tree of Syria and Egypt; **3,** in Europe and Asia, a kind of maple.

syc-o-phant (sĭk′ō-fănt), *n.* a toady.

Syd-ney (sĭd′nĭ), a seaport city, capital of New South Wales, Australia (map 16).

syl-lab-ic (sĭ-lăb′ĭk), *adj.* pertaining to a syllable or syllables; as, a *syllabic* hyphen.

syl-lab-i-cate (sĭ-lăb′ĭ-kāt), *v.t.* [syllabicat-ed, syllabicat-ing], to divide into syllables; syllabify.—*n.* **syl-lab′i-ca′tion.**

syl-lab-i-fy (sĭ-lăb′ĭ-fī), *v.t.* [syllabified, syllabify-ing], to divide into syllables.—*n.* **syl-lab′i-fi-ca′tion.**

syl-la-ble (sĭl′à-bl), *n.* **1,** a unit of pronunciation consisting of a vowel sound, or a vowel sound grouped with one or more consonant sounds, pronounced by a single impulse of the voice, and forming either a complete word or one of the units which, together, make a word; as, "dog" is the first *syllable* of "dog-mat-ic"; **2,** the written or printed letters corresponding, though not always exactly, to a syllable as pronounced.

syl-la-bus (sĭl′à-bŭs), *n.* [*pl.* syllabuses (sĭl′à-bŭs-ĕz)], a brief summary of a book, subject, course of study, etc.

syl-lo-gism (sĭl′ō-jĭzm), *n.* a logical form of reasoning, consisting of a major premise, a minor premise, and a conclusion. This is a *syllogism:* all dogs can bark (major premise); Pal is a dog (minor premise); therefore, Pal can bark (conclusion).

sylph (sĭlf), *n.* **1,** an imaginary being living in the air; **2,** a slender, graceful young woman.—*adj.* **sylph′like′.**

syl-van or **sil-van** (sĭl′văn), *adj.* **1,** pertaining to woods, forests, or trees; rustic; as, a *sylvan* deity; **2,** abounding in woods; wooded; as, a *sylvan* scene.

sym-bol (sĭm′bŭl), *n.* **1,** something that stands for or represents something else; an emblem; as, the hearth is the *symbol* of home; **2,** a mark, character, combination of letters, etc.; as, the letters of the alphabet are *symbols;* the sign ÷ is the *symbol* of division; H₂O is the chemical *symbol*

āte, āorta, râre, căt, àsk, fär, ăllow, sofà; ēve, ēvent, ĕll, writẽr, novĕl; bīte, pĭn; nō, ōbey, ôr, dŏg, tŏp, cŏllide; ūnit, ūnite, bûrn, cŭt, focŭs; nōōn, fŏŏt; mound; coin;

for water.—*adj.* **sym-bol'ic** (sĭm-bŏl'ĭk); **sym-bol'i-cal.**—*adv.* **sym-bol'i-cal-ly.**
   Syn. token, figure, sign.

sym-bol-ism (sĭm'bŭl-ĭzm), *n.* the practice or art of using symbols; in literature and the fine arts, the tendency to give imaginative meanings to well-known objects, or to represent emotions by means of symbols.

sym-bol-ize (sĭm'bŭl-īz), *v.t.* [symbolized, symboliz-ing], to stand for, or represent; as, the lily *symbolizes* purity; also, to represent by means of a symbol.

sym-met-ri-cal (sĭ-mĕt'rĭ-kăl), *adj.* regular or even; having a harmonious relation between parts; well-balanced; as, a *symmetrical* design.—*adv.* **sym-met'ri-cal-ly.**

sym-me-try (sĭm'ĕ-trĭ), *n.* [*pl.* symmetries], **1,** the balanced structure of an object, the halves of which are alike; as, the *symmetry* of a sphere; **2,** beauty of proportion.

sym-pa-thet-ic (sĭm'på-thĕt'ĭk), *adj.* **1,** congenial; understanding or sharing the feelings of another; as, a *sympathetic* friend; **2,** compassionate; **3,** harmonious; **4,** *Colloquial,* inclined to favor; as, the teacher was *sympathetic* to the pupils' request.—*adv.* **sym'pa-thet'i-cal-ly.**

sym-pa-thize (sĭm'på-thīz), *v.i.* [sympathized, sympathiz-ing], **1,** to understand and share the sentiments, emotions, etc., of another; **2,** to feel or express compassion; **3,** to be interested or favorably inclined; as, to *sympathize* with reform movements.—*n.* **sym'pa-thiz'er.**

sym-pa-thy (sĭm'på-thĭ), *n.* [*pl.* sympathies], **1,** the sharing of another's emotions; as, I feel *sympathy* with your indignation; **2,** compassion for another's trouble; **3,** harmony or agreement of affections or tastes; congeniality; **4,** friendly understanding and interest.

sym-pho-ny (sĭm'fō-nĭ), *n.* [*pl.* symphonies], **1,** harmony of sound; an agreeable blending of any kind; as, a *symphony* in blue and gray; **3,** an elaborate musical composition, consisting of three or four movements, for a full orchestra:—**symphony orchestra,** a large concert orchestra which plays symphonies and other similar musical compositions.

sym-po-si-um (sĭm-pō'zĭ-ŭm), *n.* [*pl.* symposia (sĭm-pō'zĭ-å) or symposiums], **1,** a conference or meeting for discussion of a particular subject; also, loosely, a general discussion; **2,** a number of short articles or talks by different persons, presenting various opinions on a given topic.

symp-tom (sĭmp'tŭm), *n.* **1,** any change or special condition in the body or its functions, as an evidence of disease; **2,** a sign

of the existence of something; as, strikes are *symptoms* of social unrest.

symp-to-mat-ic (sĭmp'tŏ-măt'ĭk), *adj.* serving as a sign or indication of; as, fever is *symptomatic* of illness.

syn- (sĭn-), a prefix meaning: **1,** along with; together; as, *synthesis, synchronize;* **2,** associated with; like; as, *synonym.*

syn-a-gogue (sĭn'å-gŏg), *n.* **1,** an assembly or gathering of Jews for worship; **2,** the building used for such worship.

syn-chro-nize (sĭng'krō-nīz), *v.i.* [synchronized, synchroniz-ing], **1,** to happen at the same time; coincide; **2,** to agree in speed, rate of vibration, etc., as two clocks when they keep together:—*v.t.* **1,** to cause to agree in time, speed, etc., as clocks; **2,** in motion pictures, to add sound effects or dialog, timing them to accompany the action.—*adj.* **syn'chro-nous.**

syn-co-pate (sĭng'kō-pāt), *v.t.* [syncopat-ed, syncopat-ing], **1,** to shorten (a word) by omitting a letter or letters from the middle, as in "e'er" for "ever"; **2,** in music, to begin (a note) on an unaccented beat and hold it into the next accented beat, thus shifting the rhythmic accent, as in jazz.—*n.* **syn'co-pa'tion.**

syn-di-cate (sĭn'dĭ-kåt), *n.* a group or company of persons formed to carry out a particular enterprise, especially one requiring much capital; as, a motion-picture *syndicate:*—*v.t.* (sĭn'dĭ-kāt), [syndicat-ed, syndicat-ing], **1,** to form into a syndicate; **2,** to manage, control, or sell through a syndicate; as, to *syndicate* a bond issue.

syne (sīn), *adv. Scottish,* since:—**auld lang syne,** days of long ago.

Synge (sĭng), John Millington (1871–1909), an Irish dramatist and poet.

syn-od (sĭn'ŭd), *n.* **1,** a church council or meeting; also, an ecclesiastical court; **2,** any assembly or council.

syn-o-nym (sĭn'ō-nĭm), *n.* a word having the same or nearly the same meaning as another; as, "keen" is a *synonym* of "sharp": opposite of *antonym.*

syn-on-y-mous (sĭ-nŏn'ĭ-mŭs), *adj.* alike or equivalent in meaning: used of words.

syn-op-sis (sĭ-nŏp'sĭs), *n.* [*pl.* synopses (sĭ-nŏp'sēz)], a condensed statement or summary, as of a book or play.

syn-tax (sĭn'tăks), *n.* that part of grammar which treats of the relationship of the words in a sentence to one another; sentence structure.—*adj.* **syn-tac'ti-cal** (sĭn-tăk'tĭ-kăl); **syn-tac'tic.**

syn-the-sis (sĭn'thĕ-sĭs), *n.* [*pl.* syntheses (sĭn'thĕ-sēz)], the combining of separate elements, substances, or parts to make a new form or whole.

---

go; join; yet; sing; chin; show; thin, *th*en; hw, *wh*y; zh, a*z*ure; **ü,** Ger. f*ü*r or Fr. l*u*ne; **ö,** Ger. sch*ö*n or Fr. f*eu*; **ṅ,** Fr. e*n*fant, no*m*; kh, Ger. a*ch* or i*ch.* See pages ix–x.

syn-thet-ic (sĭn-thĕt′ĭk), *adj.* **1,** pertaining to the putting together of elements in a new form; as, a *synthetic* manufacturing process; **2,** produced by artificial means; as, *synthetic* rubber.—*adv.* **syn-thet′i-cal-ly.**—*n.pl.* **syn-thet′ics.**

syph-i-lis (sĭf′ĭ-lĭs), *n.* a contagious venereal disease.

Syr-i-a (sĭr′ĭ-á), a country south of Turkey in Asia Minor (cap. Damascus), since 1941 an independent republic (map 15).—*adj.* and *n.* **Syr′-i-an.**

sy-rin-ga (sĭ-rĭng′gá), *n.* a kind of ornamental garden shrub with white or cream-colored flowers: also called *mock orange.*

SYRINGA

syr-inge (sĭr′ĭnj), *n.* an appliance for injecting a liquid into the body:—*v.t.* [syringed, syring-ing], to inject a fluid into, or cleanse, by the use of a syringe.

syr-up (sĭr′ŭp), *n.* a thick, very sweet, sticky liquid; sirup. See **sirup.**

sys-tem (sĭs′tĕm), *n.* **1,** a group or combination of parts or units functioning together as a whole according to some common law or purpose; as, the solar *system;* **2,** an orderly collection of rules and principles; as, a *system* of laws; **3,** an orderly grouping of facts and objects; as, a filing *system;* **4,** regular routine; hence, efficiency; as, this office needs *system;* **5,** the human body considered as a unit.—*adj.* **sys-tem′ic.**

sys-tem-at-ic (sĭs′tĕm-ăt′ĭk) or **sys-tem-at-i-cal** (-ăt′ĭ-kăl), *adj.* **1,** characterized by system; methodical; orderly; as, *systematic* reading; **2,** carried on with regularity and persistence; as, *systematic* practice.—*adv.* **sys′tem-at′i-cal-ly.**

sys-tem-a-tize (sĭs′tĕm-á-tīz), *v.t.* [systematized, systematiz-ing], to reduce to a system or plan; as, to *systematize* one's reading.

Sze-ged (sĕ′gĕd), [German **Sze-ge-din** (sĕ′gĕ-dĭn)], a city in southern Hungary (map 12).

T

T, t (tē), *n.* [*pl.* T's, t's], **1,** the 20th letter of the alphabet, following S; **2,** anything with the shape of a T:—*adj.* shaped like a T; as, a *T* bone.

T. abbreviation for *Territory, Tuesday.*

tab (tăb), *n.* **1,** a small flap or tag attached to the edge of something; as, shoulder *tabs;* **2,** *Colloquial,* account; check; as, to keep close *tab* on the students' work.

tab-ard (tăb′ẽrd), *n.* a loose garment worn by knights over armor; also, a coat worn by a herald and decorated with the arms of his sovereign.

Ta-bas-co (tá-băs′kō), *n.* a trade-mark name for a sauce made from red peppers:—**tabasco,** a peppery sauce bearing this trade name.

tab-by (tăb′ĭ), *n.* [*pl.* tabbies], a domestic cat, especially a female, yellowish gray and marked with black.

tab-er-nac-le (tăb′ẽr-năk′l), *n.* **1,** a place of worship, especially one erected temporarily; also, a large and imposing church; **2,** a Jewish temple; **3,** in some churches, an ornamental box resting on the altar and containing the sacred Host; **4,** a temporary dwelling; a tent:—**Tabernacle,** the movable structure used by the Israelites as a place of worship in the wilderness.

ta-ble (tā′bl), *n.* a piece of furniture consisting of a flat smooth top supported by legs; **2,** the persons sitting around a table; as, a *table* of bridge; **3,** food; fare in general; as, a hotel noted for its good *table;* **4,** an arrangement of words, facts, figures, etc., in systematic order for reference; as, statistical *tables;* **5,** a thin slab of wood, stone, metal, etc., with a flat surface, especially one on which an inscription may be written or carved:—*v.t.* [ta-bled, ta-bling], **1,** to lay aside so as to postpone consideration of; as, to *table* a report; **2,** to lay (cards, money, etc.) on a table; **3,** to put in list form; tabulate.

TABLE

tab-leau (tăb′lō; tá′blō′), *n.* [*pl.* tableaux (tăb′lōz; tá′blō′) or tableaus (tăb′lōz)], a representation, as of a scene from history, in which silent and motionless living models pose.

table d'hote (tábl′ dōt′; tä′bl), [*pl.* tables d'hôte (tábl′; tä′blz)], a complete meal of several courses served at a fixed price: opposite of *à la carte.*

ta-ble-land (tā′bl-lănd′), *n.* a plateau, or elevated level stretch of land.

ta-ble-spoon (tā′bl-spoon′), *n.* a large spoon used in preparing and serving meals,

---

āte, âorta, râre, căt, àsk, fär, ăllow, sofá; ēve, êvent, ĕll, writẽr, novĕl; bīte, pĭn; nō, ōbey, ôr, dŏg, tŏp, cŏllide; ūnit, ûnite, bûrn, cŭt, focŭs; nōon, fŏŏt; mound; coin;

and holding three times as much as a teaspoon.—*n.* **ta'ble-spoon'ful.**

tab-let (tăb'lĕt), *n.* **1,** a small flat piece of some hard material, as wood or ivory, for writing upon; **2,** blank sheets of paper fastened together at one end and used for writing; a writing pad; **3,** a flat panel, often of stone, brass, or bronze, fastened in a wall and bearing an inscription; **4,** medicine in the form of a small flat disk; **5,** a small, flat cake of soap, candy, etc.

tab-loid (tăb'loid), *n.* a daily newspaper, small in size, and usually containing many photographs:—*adj.* condensed; brief; as, *tabloid* news.

ta-boo or **ta-bu** (tă-boo'), *n.* a system or practice, among primitive races, in which certain things are held sacred, and contact with them forbidden; hence, a ban or prohibition:—*v.t.* to place under a ban; forbid; prohibit:—*adj.* **1,** set apart; made untouchable or sacred; **2,** prohibited by social custom; as, bad manners are *taboo.*

ta-bor (tā'bẽr), *n.* a small drum, shaped like a tambourine.

Ta-briz (tă-brēz'), a city in northwestern Iran, noted for its rugs (map **15**).

tab-u-lar (tăb'ŭ-lẽr), *adj.* **1,** arranged in the form of a table; set in columns; as, the report was in *tabular* form; **2,** reckoned from sets of figures; **3,** having a broad, flat top; as, a *tabular* mountain.

tab-u-late (tăb'ŭ-lāt), *v.t.* [tabulat-ed, tabulat-ing], to set up, or arrange in, a systematic outline, usually in columns; as, to *tabulate* data.—*n.* **tab'u-la'tion.**

ta-chom-e-ter (tă-kŏm'ê-tẽr), *n.* an instrument for measuring engine speed in airplanes, motorboats, etc., by indicating the number of revolutions per minute.

tac-it (tăs'ĭt), *adj.* silent, not spoken; implied, but not stated outright; as, a *tacit* agreement.—*adv.* **tac'it-ly.**

tac-i-turn (tăs'ĭ-tûrn), *adj.* silent or reserved; disinclined to talk.—*adv.* **tac'i-turn-ly.**—*n.* **tac'i-tur'ni-ty.**

tack (tăk), *n.* **1,** a small, sharp-pointed nail with a flat head; as, upholstery *tacks;* **2,** a rope for lashing down the lower forward corner of certain sails; also, the corner of the sail so held down; **3,** the direction of a ship as determined by the position of her sails; **4,** a change in a ship's direction to take advantage of side winds; **5,** hence, any course or policy of action:—*v.t.* **1,** to fasten with tacks; as, to *tack* down matting; **2,** to stitch lightly together; attach; as, to *tack* a bow on a dress; **3,** to change

TACKS, def. 1
1, ordinary tack; 2, matting tack; 3, thumb tack.

the course of (a vessel) by using the helm and shifting the sails:—*v.i.* to change the course of a vessel by shifting the position of its sails.

tack-le (tăk'l), *n.* **1,** an instrument consisting of pulleys and ropes, used for raising or lowering weights; especially, on a vessel, the pulleys and ropes for managing sails and spars, taking on cargo, etc.; **2,** equipment; gear; as, fishing *tackle;* **3,** in football, the act of seizing and stopping an opponent who is running with the ball; also, a player in the line next to either end player, or the position next to either end position:—*v.t.* [tack-led, tack-ling], **1,** to grapple with (a person); try to solve (a problem); **2,** to fasten with ropes and pulleys; **3,** to seize and stop by a tackle, as in football.

TACKLES
1, single; 2, double.

Ta-co-ma (tă-kō'mă), a city in the State of Washington, on Puget Sound (map **9**).

tact (tăkt), *n.* natural ability to deal wisely with others; skill in saying and doing the appropriate thing.—*adj.* **tact'ful.**—*n.* **tact'ful-ness.**

tac-ti-cal (tăk'tĭ-kăl), *adj.* **1,** pertaining to military or naval science; as, *tactical* maneuvers; **2,** marked by clever tactics; as, the team developed a *tactical* defense.

tac-ti-cian (tăk-tĭsh'ăn), *n.* one who is skilled in tactics or maneuvers.

tac-tics (tăk'tĭks), *n.pl.* **1,** the science or practice of handling military or naval forces in the presence of an enemy; **2,** any skilful maneuvering to gain an end.

tact-less (tăkt'lĕs), *adj.* lacking, or not showing, readiness to say and do the most suitable thing; lacking tact, or diplomacy.—*adv.* **tact'less-ly.**—*n.* **tact'less-ness.**

Ta-djik (tă-zhĭk') or **Ta-jik-i-stan** (tă-zhĭk'ĭ-stän'), a republic of the U.S.S.R. Its official name is *Tadjik Soviet Socialist Republic.*

Ta-djik So-vi-et So-cial-ist Re-pub-lic, a republic (cap. Stalinabad) of the U.S.S.R., in south central Asia between Afghanistan and Sinkiang (map **15**).

t a d - p o l e (tăd'pōl'), *n.* a frog or toad in an immature stage, with gills and a tail.

TADPOLE
1, egg of frog; 2–5, tadpole in different stages of development.

tael (tāl), *n.* **1,** a Chinese unit of money; **2,** a Chinese weight of from one to two and a half ounces.

taf-fe-ta (tăf′ē-tȧ), *n.* a shiny, fine, rustling silk or rayon, slightly stiffened.

taff-rail (tăf′rāl), *n.* the rail around the stern of a ship.

taf-fy (tăf′ĭ), *n.* **1,** candy made of brown sugar, or molasses, and butter; **2,** *Colloquial,* flattery.

Taft (tăft), William Howard (1857–1930), the 27th president of the U.S., later Chief Justice of the U.S. Supreme Court.

tag (tăg), *n.* **1,** an attached identifying card or label; as, a price *tag;* **2,** a children's game in which one chases the others in order to touch, or "tag," them; **3,** a reinforcement at the end of a shoestring, as to stiffen it; **4,** a loose end:—*v.t.* [tagged, tag-ging], **1,** to fix a tag to; **2,** in the game of tag, to catch by touching; **3,** *Colloquial,* to follow closely and persistently:—*v.i. Colloquial,* to follow another closely.

Ta-hi-ti (tä-hē′tē; tä′ē-tĭ; tä′hē-tē), a French island (cap. Papeete), one of the Society Islands, in the South Pacific Ocean (map 16).—*adj.* and *n.* **Ta-hi′ti-an.**

Ta-hoe (tä′hō; tā′hō), the largest lake in the Sierra Nevada, between California and Nevada (map 9).

tail (tāl), *n.* **1,** the hindmost part of an animal, extending beyond the rest of the body; **2,** hence, something resembling a tail in position, shape, etc.; as, a comet's *tail;* **3,** the end part of anything; as, the *tail* of a parade; **4,** the side of a coin opposite the side bearing the impression of a head; **5,** a plane or planes at the rear of an airplane to give it balance:—*v.t.* to furnish with a tail:—*v.i.* to follow close behind; tag.

tail-less (tāl′lĕs), *adj.* without a tail.

tai-lor (tā′lẽr), *n.* one whose business it is to make and repair outer garments for men and women:—*v.i.* to follow the trade of a tailor.—*n.fem.* **tai′lor-ess.**

tai-lor-ing (tā′lẽr-ĭng), *n.* the occupation or business of a tailor.

tail skid, a runner at the rear of early airplanes to keep the tail off the ground.

tail spin, a circling, downward motion of an airplane, in which the tail describes larger arcs than the nose.

taint (tānt), *n.* a spot, trace, or tinge of decay, corruption, or pollution:—*v.t.* **1,** to spoil by mixing with something unpleasant or poisonous; infect; **2,** to defile; corrupt:— *v.i.* to become spoiled, as meat.

Tai-wan (tī′wän′), an island (cap. Taihoku) southwest of Japan, and north of the Philippines (map 15). It is now called *Formosa.*

Ta-jik-i-stan (tä-zhĭk′ĭ-stän′), a republic of the U.S.S.R. Its official name is *Tadjik Soviet Socialist Republic.*

Taj Ma-hal (täj mȧ-häl′), a white marble building, renowned for its beauty, erected at Agra, India, by the emperor Shah Jehan in memory of his favorite wife.

take (tāk), *v.t.* [*p.t.* took (tŏŏk), *p.p.* tak-en (tāk′ĕn), *p.pr.* tak-ing], **1,** to lay hold of, as with the hands; grasp; as, to *take* a man by the throat; also, to seize or capture; as, the troops *took* the city; **2,** to assume possession of; as, he *took* the store on a year's lease; also, to buy regularly; subscribe to; as, I *take* this magazine every month; **3,** to eat, drink, or inhale; as, to *take* breakfast; to *take* gas; **4,** to carry; as, *take* your purse; also, to conduct or escort; as, to *take* a guest home; **5,** to remove; subtract; as, to *take* three from five; also, to steal; as, to *take* another's idea; **6,** to experience; feel; as, to *take* pride in one's work; **7,** to perform, do, make, etc.; as, to *take* exercise; to *take* a picture; **8,** to require; as, it *takes* two to make a bargain; **9,** to pick out; choose; as, *take* the largest plum; **10,** to be infected with; catch; as, to *take* cold; **11,** to attract the attention of; please; as, the hat *took* her fancy:— *v.i.* **1,** to have the intended effect; act; be successful; as, the vaccination *took;* **2,** to proceed; go; as, they *took* to the boats; **3,** to prove attractive; as, the song *took:*— *n.* the amount or quantity received or taken: said especially of fish.—*n.* **tak′er.**

take after, to be similar to; resemble; **take down, 1,** to lower (a flag); **2,** to write down (a speech) while it is being delivered; **3,** to humble; **take in, 1,** to receive (work); **2,** to grasp with the mind; **3,** to reduce (a garment) to a smaller size; **4,** to deceive; **take off, 1,** to remove; **2,** to leave a place; as, the plane *took off* easily; **3,** to give a parody of; imitate; **take on, 1,** to add (weight); **2,** to put on; as, he *took on* the appearance of virtue; **3,** to attempt; **4,** to hire; **take place,** to occur; **take to, 1,** to begin; fall into the habit of; **2,** to form a liking for; **take up, 1,** to lift; **2,** to absorb; **3,** to start the study of (a subject); **4,** to pay off (a loan).

take-off (tāk′-ôf′), *n.* **1,** a parody; as, a *take-off* of an actress; **2,** a place from which one makes a start in running or jumping, an airplane flight, or the like; also, the act of taking off.

tak-ing (tā′kĭng), *adj.* **1,** attractive; pleasing; as, *taking* manners; **2,** contagious, as a disease:—*n.* **1,** the act of gaining possession; **2, takings,** the amount taken or received; receipts.

talc (tălk), *n.* a soft mineral, greasy to

the touch, used in rubber manufacture, toilet powders, etc.: also called *soapstone*.

tal·cum (tăl′kŭm), *n.* talc:—**talcum powder,** a toilet powder of finely pulverized talc.

tale (tāl), *n.* 1, that which is told; a story; fable; 2, a false report or piece of gossip; 3, a count; a summing or sum; as, the *tale* of bricks made in a day.

tal·ent (tăl′ĕnt), *n.* 1, an ancient weight and coin; 2, mental ability; skill; cleverness; 3, a special gift for a particular business, art, or profession; as, the school boasts a variety of *talent;* 4, skilled persons.—*adj.* **tal′ent·ed.**

ta·ler or **tha·ler** (tä′lẽr), *n.* [*pl.* taler, thaler], a former German silver coin, worth three marks.

tal·is·man (tăl′ĭs·măn; tăl′ĭz·măn), *n.* [*pl.* talismans], a figure engraved on a stone or ring, supposed to possess magical powers; a charm; an amulet.

talk (tôk), *v.i.* 1, to utter words; express and try to communicate thoughts through speech; 2, to speak familiarly; converse; 3, to confer; discuss; as, to *talk* with one's doctor; 4, to chatter; gossip; 5, to communicate ideas without speech; as, to *talk* by gestures:—*v.t.* 1, to speak of; discuss; as, to *talk* business; 2, to speak a language freely; as, to *talk* French; 3, to influence or affect by speech; as, they *talked* him over to their side:—*n.* 1, speech; conversation; as, an evening of friendly *talk;* 2, a subject of discussion; as, the *talk* of the town; 3, rumor; as, there is *talk* of a strike; 4, meaningless speech; as, idle *talk;* 5, a conference; as, the settlers held a *talk* with the Indians; 6, an informal address; as, a short *talk* on art.—*adj.* **talk′ing.**

talk·a·tive (tôk′á·tĭv), *adj.* given to much talking; garrulous.

    Syn. communicative, voluble, fluent.

talk·ing pic·ture, a motion picture in which the words and other sounds belonging to the scene pictured are reproduced mechanically, timed with the action: often shortened to *talkie.*

tall (tôl), *adj.* 1, of more than average height; as, a *tall* boy; 2, of a certain specified height; as, a man six feet *tall.*

Tal·la·has·see (tăl′á·hăs′ē), a city, capital of Florida (map 8).

Tal·linn (tàl′lĭn), a city, capital of Estonia (map 12). Also called *Reval.*

tal·low (tăl′ō), *n.* the fat of animals, as beef or mutton suet, melted and used for making candles, soap, etc.:—*adj.* made of tallow.—*adj.* **tal′low·y.**

tal·ly (tăl′ĭ), *n.* [*pl.* tallies], 1, originally, a stick on which scores were recorded by notches; 2, anything on which a score or

account is kept; also, the score; 3, a duplicate; counterpart:—*v.t.* [tallied, tally·ing], to keep score of; count; reckon:—*v.i.* to match; balance; as, the two accounts *tally.*

tal·ly·ho (tăl′ĭ·hō′), *interj.* the huntsman's cry to urge on his hounds:—*n.* (tăl′ĭ·hō′), [*pl.* tallyhos], 1, a coach drawn by four horses; 2, the cry "tallyho."

Tal·mud (tăl′mŭd), *n.* the collection of Jewish civil and canonical laws together with the extensive commentaries on them.

tal·on (tăl′ŭn), *n.* the claw of a bird of prey; as, the *talon* of a hawk or eagle.

TALON

tam·a·ble (tām′á·bl), *adj.* capable of being made gentle.

ta·ma·le (tá·mä′lē), *n.* a Mexican dish of chopped meat and corn meal, seasoned with red pepper, wrapped in corn husks, dipped in oil, boiled or steamed, and served hot.

tam·a·rack (tăm′á·răk), *n.* an American larch tree.

tam·a·rind (tăm′á·rĭnd), *n.* a tall tropical tree having yellow flowers striped with red; also, its podlike fruit, the acid pulp of which is used to make cooling drinks.

tam·bou·rine (tăm′bŏŏ·rēn′), *n.* a small hand drum, with pairs of little metallic disks in the hoop or rim. The performer in playing shakes it or strikes it with the knuckles.

TAMBOURINE

tame (tām), *adj.* [tam-er, tam-est], 1, changed from a wild state; made useful to man; 2, harmless; gentle; also, without fear; as, these squirrels are very *tame;* 3, tedious; dull; as, the debate was *tame:—v.t.* [tamed, tam·ing], 1, to make (an animal) useful to man; as, to *tame* an elephant; also, to make less wild or timid; as, to *tame* a bird; 2, to crush the spirit or courage of; subdue.—*adv.* **tame′ly.**—*n.* **tame′ness.**

Tam·ma·ny (tăm′á·nĭ), *n.* a political organization of New York City Democrats.

tam-o′-shan·ter (tăm′-ŏ·shăn′tẽr), *n.* a Scotch cap with a tight band, and a loose, round top: often called *tam.*

tamp (tămp), *v.t.* 1, in blasting, to fill in (a hole containing the charge) with clay, earth, or similar material; 2, to drive in or down by repeated light strokes; as, the gardener has *tamped* down the sod.—*n.* **tamp′er.**

TAM-O′-SHANTER

Tam·pa (tăm′pá), a commercial city on the western coast of Florida (map 8).

tam-per (tăm′pēr), v.i. to meddle so as to injure or alter anything; as, to *tamper* with a lock.

tan (tăn), n. 1, oak bark, or other bark containing tannic acid, used in treating hides; 2, a yellowish-brown color, like that of such bark; 3, a brown color given to the skin by exposure to the sun:—v.t. [tanned, tan-ning], 1, to convert (rawhide) into leather by treating with tannic acid or with mineral salts; 2, to make brown by exposure to the sun; 3, *Colloquial*, to thrash; beat:—v.i. 1, to be made into leather; 2, to become brown in the sun:—adj. yellowish brown.

tan-a-ger (tăn′a-jer), n. any of a family of American songbirds closely related to the finches, and usually of brilliant plumage, as the scarlet tanager.

Ta-na-na-rive (tà′nà′nà′rēv′), a city, capital of Madagascar (map 14).

tan-bark (tăn′bärk′), n. oak or other bark containing tannic acid, used in treating hides, and, when the acid is exhausted, for making a soft surface, as on race tracks.

tan-dem (tăn′dĕm), adv. one behind another:—adj. arranged one behind the other, as horses, or seats on a bicycle:—n. 1, a pair of horses harnessed one before

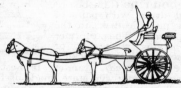

TANDEM, def. 2

the other; 2, a carriage with horses tandem, or a bicycle with seats tandem.

tang (tăng), n. 1, a strong sharp taste or flavor; 2, the part of a knife or similar tool that fits into the handle.

Tan-gan-yi-ka, Lake (tăn′găn-yē′kà), a lake in east central Africa:—**Tanganyika Territory**, a British trusteeship in East Africa (cap. Dar-es-Salaam) (map 14).

tan-gent (tăn′jĕnt), adj. 1, touching; 2, in geometry, touching a line or surface at one point only, but not passing through it:—n. a tangent line or surface:—**fly off at a tangent** or **go off at a tangent**, to change hastily from a usual course of action.

tan-ge-rine (tăn′jĕ-rēn; tăn′jĕ-rēn′), n. a small, deep-colored, sweet orange.

tan-gi-ble (tăn′jĭ-bl), adj. 1, touchable; capable of being felt by the touch; 2, definite; real; as, *tangible* proof.

Tan-gier (tăn-jēr′), an international area

and city in northern Morocco, Africa, on the Strait of Gibraltar (map 14).

tan-gle (tăng′gl), v.t. [tan-gled, tan-gling], to knot so as to make difficult to unravel; entangle:—v.i. to be or become entangled:—n. 1, a snarl; a confused mass; as, a *tangle* of string; 2, hence, a confused state. —adj. **tan′gled**.

tan-go (tăng′gō), n. [pl. tangos], a dance, originally from South America, in two-four time and with a great variety of steps.

tank (tăngk), n. 1, a large cistern, basin, or circular container for holding water or other fluid; as, an oil *tank;* a gasoline *tank;* 2, a kind of armored motorcar, built like a caterpillar tractor and equipped with guns: used in modern warfare for advancing over rough ground:—v.t. to put or store in a tank.

TANK, def. 1

tank-ard (tăngk′ērd), n. a large drinking vessel with one handle, and a hinged cover.

tank-er (tăngk′ēr), n. a ship especially built with tanks for carrying oil, molasses, etc., in bulk.

tan-ner (tăn′ēr), n. one whose business is the tanning of hides into leather.

tan-ner-y (tăn′ēr-ĭ), n. [pl. tanneries], a place where hides are tanned into leather.

TANKARD

tan-nic (tăn′ĭk), adj. pertaining to, or obtained from, any bark, as oak or hemlock, which produces tan:—**tannic acid**, a strong acid obtained from tea, sumac, etc., and used in tanning, dyeing, and medicine: also called *tannin*.

tan-nin (tăn′ĭn), n. a strong vegetable acid used in tanning and in making ink.

tan-ning (tăn′ĭng), n. the process of making hides into leather.

tan-sy (tăn′zĭ), n. [pl. tansies], an herb with small heads of yellow flowers, and bitter, aromatic leaves.

tan-ta-lize (tăn′ta-līz), v.t. [tantalized, tantaliz-ing], to tease by exciting hopes or fears which will not be realized.

Tan-ta-lus (tăn′ta-lŭs), n. in mythology, a son of Zeus who, in punishment for his crimes, had to stand up to his chin in water which receded when he stooped to drink.

tan-ta-mount (tăn′ta-mount′), adj. equivalent to in effect or importance; as, a wish *tantamount* to a command.

tan-trum (tăn′trŭm), n. *Colloquial*, a sudden outburst of temper or passion.

āte, āorta, râre, căt, àsk, fär, ăllow, sofà; ēve, ĕvent, ĕll, writēr, novĕl; bīte, pĭn; nō, ōbey, ôr, dŏg, tŏp, cŏllide; ūnit, ūnite, bûrn, cŭt, focŭs; nōōn, fŏŏt; mound; coin;

¹**tap** (tăp), *n.* **1,** a pipe or cock through which liquor is drawn from a cask; also, a faucet or spigot for drawing water; **2,** a place where liquor is drawn and sold; a taproom; **3,** liquor drawn from a cask; **4,** a tool for cutting screw threads on an inner surface, as of a nut; **5,** in electricity, a device for making connection with a wire:—*v.t.* [tapped, tap-ping], **1,** to furnish with a cock or spigot; pierce (the side of a cask or the bark of a tree), in order to draw out liquid; **2,** to draw or let out (liquid); **3,** to make connections so as to draw from or extract from; as, to *tap* secret sources of information; **4,** to make connection with (a wire) so as to draw off current.

²**tap** (tăp), *v.t.* [tapped, tap-ping], **1,** to strike or touch lightly; as, he *tapped* me on the shoulder; **2,** to cause to strike or touch lightly; as, he *tapped* his foot impatiently;—*v.i.* to strike light blows:—*n.* a light blow or touch; pat; rap.

ta-pa (tä′pä), *n.* the bark of an Asiatic tree resembling the mulberry, used in Pacific islands for making cloth.

tape (tāp), *n.* **1,** a narrow woven band of linen or cotton, used for tying packages, in sewing, etc.; **2,** the narrow strip of paper on which a telegraph or stock ticker prints; **3,** the rope or line stretched across the track to mark the finish of a race; **4,** a narrow strip of cloth, paper, or steel, marked for measuring length:—*v.t.* [taped, tap-ing], **1,** to supply, secure, or cover with tape; as, he *taped* the handle of his tennis racket; **2,** to measure off with a tape.

tape-line (tāp′līn′), *n.* a strip of fabric, metal, etc., marked for measuring.

ta-per (tā′pĕr), *n.* **1,** a long, slender candle; **2,** a gradual lessening of thickness toward a point; as, the *taper* of a cone:—*v.i.* and *v.t.* **1,** to narrow to a point; **2,** to decrease gradually; as, a boxer *tapers* off his training as the date for the fight draws near.

tap-es-try (tăp′ĕs-trĭ), *n.* [*pl.* tapestries], an ornamental fabric in which a picture or design is woven, used as a wall hanging.

tape-worm (tāp′wûrm′), *n.* a long, flat, many-jointed worm which infests the intestines of man and other animals.

TAPIR (¹⁄₁₆)

tap-i-o-ca (tăp′ĭ-ō′kà), *n.* a starchy, granular substance prepared from the roots of a South American plant called the cassava, used for puddings and as a thickening.

ta-pir (tā′pĕr), *n.* a heavy, brownish-black,

short-legged animal with a flexible snout, found in South and Central America.

tap-room (tăp′rŏŏm′), *n.* a place where liquors are kept ready to be drawn and sold.

tap-root (tăp′rŏŏt′), *n.* the main root of a plant, growing straight downward and sending off few or many small branches, as in the carrot, radish, dandelion, etc.

taps (tăps), *n.pl.* in the U.S. army and navy, the last signal of the day, on drum or bugle, ordering lights out. Taps are also sounded over the grave of a soldier or sailor.

tap-ster (tăp′stĕr), *n.* one whose business it is to draw liquor.

¹**tar** (tär), *n.* a thick, black, oily substance obtained from wood, coal, peat, etc.:—*v.t.* [tarred, tar-ring], to cover with, or as with, tar; as, the sailors *tarred* the ropes.

TAP-ROOT

²**tar** (tär), *n. Colloquial,* a sailor; seaman.

tar-an-tel-la (tăr-ăn-tĕl′à), *n.* **1,** a lively Italian dance, once supposed to cure the bite of the tarantula; **2,** the music for this dance.

ta-ran-tu-la (tà-răn′tū-là), *n.* a large, hairy, poisonous spider, found in many warm countries.

tar-dy (tär′dĭ), *adj.* [tar-di-er, tar-di-est], **1,** moving or progressing slowly; as, *tardy* growth; **2,** not prompt; late.—*adv.* **tar′di-ly.** —*n.* **tar′di-ness.**

Syn. sluggish, slow.

TARANTULA

¹**tare** (târ), *n.* an allowance of weight made to a purchaser by subtracting the weight of the container:—*v.t.* [tared, tar-ing], to weigh (a container) in order to find the allowance of weight to be deducted.

²**tare** (târ), *n.* in the Bible, a weed.

tar-get (tär′gĕt), *n.* **1,** formerly, a small shield or buckler; **2,** a mark set up for archery, rifle, or artillery practice; **3,** one who or that which is made the object of attack, criticism, ridicule, etc.; as, he is the *target* of all their scorn.

tar-iff (tăr′ĭf), *n.* **1,** a schedule of duties or taxes placed by a government on goods entering, or leaving, the country; **2,** a tax or duty levied according to such a schedule; **3,** any schedule of rates, charges, etc.

ARCHER'S TARGET

go; join; yet; sing; chin; show; thin, *th***en; hw,** *wh***y; zh,** a**zure; ŭ,** Ger. f**ü**r or Fr. l**u**ne; **ō,** Ger. sch**ö**n or Fr. f**eu**; **ṅ,** Fr. e**n**fant, no**m**; **kh,** Ger. a**ch** or i**ch.** See pages ix–x.

tar-la-tan (tär′la-tăn), *n.* a thin, stiff, open-meshed muslin used for caps, etc.

tarn (tärn), *n.* a small mountain lake.

tar-nish (tär′nĭsh), *v.t.* to dull the brightness of; discolor or stain:—*v.i.* to lose brightness; as, silver *tarnishes* easily:—*n.* dulness; loss of polish; stain.

ta-ro (tä′rō), *n.* [*pl.* taros], a tropical plant grown especially in Pacific islands, where its root is used for food; also, the root of this plant.

tar-pau-lin (tär-pô′lĭn), *n.* 1, heavy waterproof canvas used for covering a ship's hatches, boats, etc.; 2, a hat or coat of waterproof canvas.

tar-pon (tär′pŏn), *n.* a large game fish found in West Indian waters and along the coasts of Georgia and Florida.

TARPON (₁/₁₅)

¹**tar-ry** (tär′ĭ), *adj.* [tar-ri-er, tar-ri-est], of, like, or covered with, tar; hence, dirty.

²**tar-ry** (tăr′ĭ), *v.i.* [tarried, tarry-ing], 1, to live in a place for a time; stay; as, he *tarried* there for a week; 2, to be late; delay; linger.

Tar-sus (tär′sŭs), a city in Asiatic Turkey, birthplace of the Apostle Paul (map 1).

tar-sus (tär′sŭs), *n.* [*pl.* tarsi (tär′sī)], 1, the ankle, or instep; also, the group of bones that form the ankle; 2, in birds, the shank or part of the leg between the knee and foot (see illustration under *bird*).

¹**tart** (tärt), *adj.* sharp to the taste; as, a *tart* jelly; hence, severe; cutting; as, a *tart* reply.—*adv.* **tart′ly.**—*n.* **tart′ness.**
   Syn. piquant, biting, stinging.

²**tart** (tärt), *n.* a small pastry shell without a top crust, filled with fruit or jam.

tar-tan (tär′tăn), *n.* a woolen cloth, woven with a plaid pattern, worn particularly in the Scottish Highlands:—*adj.* made from, or in the pattern of, tartan.

Tar-tar (tär′tẽr), *n.* a member of one of the nomadic Mongol races of central Asia; a Tatar: see **Tatar:**— **tartar,** a person of irritable temper.

TARTAN

tar-tar (tär′tẽr), *n.* 1, a whitish-yellow substance often found on teeth; 2, an acid substance, present in grape juice, which is deposited on the inside of wine casks during fermentation; also, a purified form, called *cream of tartar*, used in baking powder.

tar-tar-ic (tär-tär′ĭk; tär-tär′ĭk), *adj.* pertaining to, or derived from, tartar:—**tartaric acid,** an acid found in the juice of grapes, oranges, etc.

Tar-ta-rus (tär′ta-rŭs), *n.* in mythology, an abyss below Hades; also, Hades.

Tar-ta-ry (tär′ta-rĭ), the name of a region in central Asia. See **Tatary.**

task (tàsk), *n.* a piece of work given out to be done; as, daily *tasks:*—**take to task,** to censure:—*v.t.* to burden with work.
   Syn., n. undertaking, toil, drudgery.

task-mas-ter (tàsk′màs′tẽr), *n.* one who gives out, or assigns, work to be done.

Tas-ma-ni-a (tăz-mā′nĭ-a), an island (cap. Hobart) south of Australia (map 16). It is a state in the Commonwealth of Australia.

tas-sel (tăs′l), *n.* 1, a hanging ornament made of a tuft of threads or cords of silk, wool, etc.; 2, the hanging flower or head of certain plants; as, corn *tassels:*—*v.i.* [tasseled, tasseling], to put forth hanging flowery heads:—*v.t.* to trim with, or make into, tassels.

taste (tāst), *v.t.* [tast-ed, tast-ing], 1, to perceive or know by the tongue and palate; as, I *taste* vanilla in the cocoa; 2, to test the flavor of, by eating or drinking a little; as, to *taste* tea; 3, to experience; as, to *taste* the joys of living:—*v.i.* 1, to try food by the tongue or palate; 2, to have a certain flavor; as, candy *tastes* sweet:—*n.* 1, the flavor of a substance as perceived by the tongue and palate; as, a spicy *taste;* 2, a little bit or piece; especially, a small portion tasted; as, take a *taste;* 3, the sense by which the flavor of substances is perceived; 4, liking or inclination; as, a *taste* for reading; 5, ability to see what is beautiful; as, she has good *taste* in clothes.

TASSEL def. 1

taste-ful (tāst′fŏŏl), *adj.* marked by good taste.—*adv.* **taste′ful-ly.**—*n.* **taste′ful-ness.**

taste-less (tāst′lĕs), *adj.* 1, without flavor; flat; 2, marked by lack of good taste; unattractive; as, a *tasteless* hat.

tast-y (tās′tĭ), *adj.* [tast-i-er, tast-i-est], having a fine flavor; as, a *tasty* sauce.

tat (tăt), *v.t.* and *v.i.* [tat-ted, tat-ting], to make (trimming or lace) by looping and knotting thread wound on a shuttle.

Ta-tar (tä′tẽr), *n.* a member of one of the nomadic Mongol races of central Asia. Also spelled **Tar′tar.**—*adj.* **Ta′tar.**—*adj.* **Ta-tar′i-an** (tä-târ′ĭ-ăn).

Ta-ta-ry (tä′ta-rĭ) or **Tar-ta-ry** (tär′ta-rĭ), the name given to a large indefinite region in central Asia, extending from the Sea of Japan to the Caspian Sea.

tat-ter (tăt′ẽr), *n.* **1,** a loose-hanging rag; **2,** tatters, ragged clothing.—*adj.* **tat′tered.**

tat-ter-de-mal-ion (tăt′ẽr-dĕ-māl′yŭn; -măl′yŭn), *n.* a ragged fellow; ragamuffin.

tat-ting (tăt′ĭng), *n.* a kind of narrow lace, or edging, made with a small hand shuttle; also, the art of making such lace.

tat-tle (tăt′l), *v.i.* [tat-tled, tat-tling], to chatter; to tell tales:—*v.t.* to tell (tales or secrets):—*n.* trifling or idle talk; gossip. —*n.* **tat′tler.**—*n.* **tat′tling.**

¹**tat-too** (tă-tōō′), *n.* a drum or bugle signal to call soldiers to their quarters; also, a continuous beating or strumming; as, he beat a *tattoo* on the desk.

²**tat-too** (tă-tōō′), *n.* [*pl.* tattoos], a design made by puncturing the skin and rubbing indelible stain or dye into the punctures:—*v.t.* [tattooed (tă-tōōd′), tattoo-ing], to mark with tattoos.—*n.* **tat-too′ing.**—*n.* **tat-too′er.**

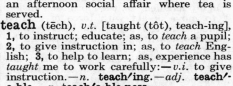

TATTOO

taught (tôt), past tense and past participle of *teach.*

taunt (tônt; tänt), *n.* a bitter or mocking gibe:—*v.t.* to ridicule with bitter, sarcastic, or insulting language; as, they *taunted* John on his failure to pass the examination.

Syn., v. deride, mock, jeer, sneer, gibe.

taupe (tōp), *n.* a dark-gray color with a slight tinge of dull yellow.

taut (tôt), *adj.* **1,** tight, as a stretched rope; **2,** in good condition; shipshape.

tau-tog (tô-tŏg′), *n.* a medium-sized food fish found off the Atlantic coast of North America: also called *blackfish.*

tau-tol-o-gy (tô-tŏl′ŏ-jĭ), *n.* [*pl.* tautologies], a useless repetition of the same idea in different words; also, an example of such a repetition. "A panacea for all ills" is an example of tautology because "panacea" itself means "a cure for all ills."—*adj.* **tau′to-log′i-cal** (tô′tô-lŏj′ĭ-kăl).—*adv.* **tau′to-log′i-cal-ly.**

tav-ern (tăv′ẽrn), *n.* **1,** an inn; a hotel, especially one in a rural section; **2,** an establishment whose business is the selling of liquor to be drunk on the premises.

taw (tô), *n.* **1,** a mark or line from which players shoot in playing marbles; **2,** the game of marbles; **3,** a marble, especially one with which a player shoots.

taw-dry (tô′drĭ), *adj.* [taw-dri-er, taw-dri-est], showy but cheap; gaudy; as, *tawdry* jewelry.—*n.* **taw′dri-ness.**

taw-ny (tô′nĭ), *adj.* [taw-ni-er, taw-ni-est], tan-colored; of a yellowish-brown color; as, the puma has a *tawny* coat.—*n.* **taw′ni-ness.**

tax (tăks), *n.* **1,** a charge or duty on income or property, imposed by a government; as, public schools are supported by the *taxes* paid by the people; **2,** a heavy or oppressive burden; as, a *tax* on one's patience:—*v.t.* **1,** to impose a rate or duty upon, especially for the support of a government; as, to *tax* all incomes above a certain amount; **2,** to burden; oppress; as, to *tax* the mind with too much detail; **3,** to accuse; as, to *tax* a person with bribery. —*adj.* **tax′a-ble.**

Syn., n. toll, assessment.

tax-a-tion (tăks-ā′shŭn), *n.* **1,** the act or system of raising money for public use by imposing a charge or duty upon persons or property; **2,** the sum, or tax, imposed.

tax-i (tăk′sĭ), *n.* [*pl.* taxis], a taxicab:—*v.i.* [taxied, taxi-ing or taxy-ing], **1,** of an airplane, to run along on water or land, as when preparing to rise or after landing; **2,** to ride in a taxicab.

tax-i-cab (tăk′sĭ-kăb′), *n.* a motor-driven cab provided with a meter that measures the distance traveled and records the fare.

tax-i-der-my (tăk′sĭ-dûr′mĭ), *n.* the art of preparing, stuffing, and mounting the skins of animals to give them a lifelike appearance.—*n.* **tax′i-der′mist.**

tax-pay-er (tăks′pā′ẽr), *n.* a person who pays a tax; especially, one who pays a tax on real estate.

Tay-lor (tā′lẽr), Zachary (1784–1850), the 12th president of the U.S.

t.b. *Slang,* abbreviation for *tuberculosis.*

Tchai-kov-sky (chī-kôf′skĕ), Peter Ilyitch (1840–1893), a Russian composer.

tea (tē), *n.* **1,** a shrub of eastern Asia, cultivated for its leaves; **2,** the dried leaves of the tea plant; **3,** the drink obtained by pouring boiling water on these leaves; **4,** any of various mild beverages resembling tea; as, beef *tea;* **5,** a light afternoon meal at which tea is served; **6,** hence, an evening meal, when dinner is eaten in the middle of the day; **7,** an afternoon social affair where tea is served.

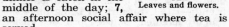

TEA
Leaves and flowers.

teach (tēch), *v.t.* [taught (tôt), teach-ing], **1,** to instruct; educate; as, to *teach* a pupil; **2,** to give instruction in; as, to *teach* English; **3,** to help to learn; as, experience has *taught* me to work carefully:—*v.i.* to give instruction.—*n.* **teach′ing.**—*adj.* **teach′a-ble.**—*n.* **teach′a-ble-ness.**

---

go; join; yet; sing; chin; show; thin, *th***en; hw,** *wh***y; zh,** *a***zure; ü,** Ger. *fü***r** or Fr. *lu***ne; ö,** Ger. *schö***n** or Fr. *feu;* **ṅ,** Fr. *e***nfant,** *no***m; kh,** Ger. *a***ch** or *i***ch.** See pages ix–x.

teach-er (tē′chĕr), *n.* a person whose profession is instructing.

tea-cup (tē′kŭp′), *n.* **1,** a cup, usually smaller than a coffee cup, in which tea is served; also, any cup of this size; **2,** the amount such a cup holds; a teacupful.

teak (tēk), *n.* **1,** a tall East Indian tree the leaves of which yield a red dye; **2,** the hard, durable timber of this tree, much used in the making of ships and furniture.

tea-ket-tle (tē′kĕt′l), *n.* a covered kettle with a spout and handle, in which water is heated.

teal (tēl), *n.* a swift, small, fresh-water wild duck.

team (tēm), *n.* **1,** two or more horses, oxen, or other animals, harnessed together to one plow, cart, or carriage; **2,** a number of persons working or playing together; as, a basketball *team:*—*v.t.* **1,** to join together in a team; as, to *team* horses; **2,** to transport with a team; as, to *team* lumber:—*v.i.* **1,** to make one's living by driving a team; **2,** to work with a group or team; as, he *teamed* up with the other boys.

TEAL (⅟₁₃)

team-mate (tēm′māt′), *n.* a member of the same team.

team-ster (tēm′stĕr), *n.* **1,** the driver of a team of horses or other animals; **2,** one whose business is hauling, with draft animals or by truck.

team-work (tēm′wûrk′), *n.* work done by several persons acting as a unit, as distinguished from work done by one person alone; as, superior *teamwork* won for our side.

tea-pot (tē′pŏt′), *n.* a vessel with a spout, handle, and cover, for making and serving tea.

TEAPOT

¹**tear** (târ), *v.t.* [*p.t.* tore (tôr), *p.p.* torn (tôrn), *p.pr.* tear-ing], **1,** to pull apart; rend; as, I *tore* my dress when I fell; **2,** to cut deeply; gash; as, to *tear* the flesh; **3,** to produce or cause by the action of rending; as, to *tear* a hole in paper; **4,** to remove by force; as, he *tore* the plant up by the roots; **5,** to cause great pain to; as, it *tore* his heart to leave his friend:—*v.i.* **1,** to part on being pulled or roughly handled; as, the cloth *tears* easily; **2,** to move or act with force or excited haste; as, to *tear* across the street:—*n.* **1,** the act of tearing; also, damage caused by tearing; **2,** a rent: a hole made by pulling apart; as, there is a large *tear* in my coat.

²**tear** (tĭr), *n.* a small drop of salty, watery liquid secreted by a gland of the eye.—*n.* **tear′drop′.**—*adj.* **tear′less.**

tear-ful (tĭr′fŏŏl), *adj.* shedding tears; weeping.—*adv.* **tear′ful-ly.**

tease (tēz), *v.t.* [teased, teas-ing], **1,** to comb or unravel (wool or flax); separate the fibers of; **2,** to roughen the surface of; as, to *tease* cloth; **3,** to annoy by petty requests or by good-natured ridicule:—*n. Colloquial,* one who teases.—*n.* **teas′er.**—*n.* and *adj.* **teas′ing.**—*adv.* **teas′ing-ly.**

tea-sel (tē′zl), *n.* **1,** an herb bearing stiff, hooked spines and white or purplish flowers in dense, long heads; **2,** the dried flower head, used to raise the nap on woolen cloth; **3,** any mechanical device substituted for the flower heads of this plant in raising the nap on woolen cloth.

TEASEL, def. 1

tea-spoon (tē′spōon′), *n.* a small spoon, the ordinary size for table use, which holds about one third as much as a tablespoon.—*n.* **tea′spoon-ful.**

teat (tēt), *n.* the nipple on the breast or udder through which milk passes.

tech-ni-cal (tĕk′nĭ-kăl), *adj.* **1,** having to do with the industrial or mechanical arts and sciences; as, a *technical* school; **2,** having to do with a specific occupation or science; as, "raceme" is a *technical* botanical word; **3,** having to do with technique; as, she has mastered the *technical* details of poetry.—*adv.* **tech′ni-cal-ly.**

tech-ni-cal-i-ty (tĕk′nĭ-kăl′ĭ-tĭ), *n.* [*pl.* technicalities], **1,** the quality characterizing a specific field; as, the *technicality* of scientific language; **2,** a small point, often of a quibbling nature; as, he was acquitted on a *technicality.*

tech-ni-cian (tĕk-nĭsh′ăn), *n.* **1,** one trained to perform and record details of experiments in a laboratory; as a laboratory *technician*; medical *technician;* **2,** a person skilled in an art, as music. Also, **tech′ni-cist.**

tech-nique (tĕk-nēk′), *n.* the method of handling details in any fine art or in doing anything that requires special skill.

tech-nol-o-gy (tĕk-nŏl′ō-jĭ), *n.* **1,** the science of industrial arts and manufactures; as, to study engineering, a student should go to a school of *technology*; **2,** the application of science to the various arts.

ted (tĕd), *v.t.* [ted-ded, ted-ding], to turn or spread for drying; as, to *ted* hay.

Te De-um (tē dē′ŭm), an ancient Christian hymn of praise or thanksgiving, beginning with the words "Te Deum laudamus" (We praise thee, O God), sung as part of the service in some churches; also, a musical setting of this hymn.

te·di·ous (tē′dĭ-ŭs; tēd′yŭs; tē′jŭs), *adj.* wearisome; tiresome; as, *tedious* work.—*adv.* **te′di·ous·ly**.—*n.* **te′di·ous·ness**.

te·di·um (tē′dĭ-ŭm), *n.* tediousness; tiresomeness; monotony; as, the *tedium* of long hours of work.

tee (tē), *n.* 1, in golf, the place at the beginning of each hole from which the ball is first driven; also, a small cone of sand, wood, or the like, on which the ball may be placed; 2, the mark aimed at in certain games, as in quoits:—*v.t.* [teed, tee-ing], in golf, to place (the ball) on a tee:—*v.i.* in golf, to start play; as, to *tee off*.

teem (tēm), *v.i.* to be very productive; be full; be stocked or crowded to overflowing; as, the city *teemed* with tourists.

teens (tēnz), *n.pl.* the years of one's age marked by numbers ending in -*teen*, from thirteen to nineteen; as, a girl in her *teens*.

tee·pee (tē′pē), *n.* a wigwam; tepee. See **tepee.**

tee·ter (tē′tēr), *v.t.* and *v.i.* to seesaw; sway from side to side:—*n.* a seesaw; a swaying motion.

teeth (tēth), plural of *tooth.*

teethe (tēth), *v.i.* [teethed, teeth-ing], to cut teeth; also, to grow or develop teeth.

tee·to·tal (tē-tō′tl), *adj.* 1, *Colloquial,* entire; total; 2, pertaining to total abstinence from intoxicating liquor; as, a *teetotal* pledge.—*n.* **tee·to′tal·er.**

tee·to·tum (tē-tō′tŭm), *n.* a kind of toy for children, like a top, spun with the fingers.

teg·u·ment (tĕg′ū·mĕnt), *n.* a natural external covering, as the human skin, the shell of a turtle, etc.

TEETOTUM

Te·hran or **Te·heran** (tē-hrän′; tē-ē-rän′), a city, the capital and chief city of Iran (map 15).

tel. abbreviation for *telephone, telegram, telegraph.*

Tel A·viv (tĕl′ ȧ-vēv′), a city, the main seaport of Israel.

tel·e·cast (tel′ē·kast′), *n.* a television program; the reproduction on a screen of distant objects, actions, or events.

tel·e·gram (tĕl′ē·grăm), *n.* a message sent by telegraph.

tel·e·graph (tĕl′ē·gràf), *n.* an equipment or system for sending and receiving signals, or messages, at a distance by means of electricity:—*v.t.* to send by means of such an instrument; as, to *telegraph* news; also, to send a message to, by such means;

as, to *telegraph* a friend:—*v.i.* to send a message by telegraph.—*adj.* **tel′e·graph′ic.**—*n.* **te·leg′ra·pher** (tē-lĕg′rȧ-fēr; tĕl′ē-grȧf′ēr).

te·leg·ra·phy (tē-lĕg′rȧ-fĭ), *n.* the science or process of sending messages by telegraph.

te·lep·a·thy (tē-lĕp′ȧ-thĭ), *n.* the passage of thought from one person to another without the use of words or signs.—*adj.* **tel′e·path′ic** (tĕl′ē-păth′ĭk).

tel·e·phone (tĕl′ē·fōn), *n.* an instrument for transmitting speech over a distance by means of electricity:—*v.t.* [telephoned, telephon-ing], to send (a message) by telephone; also, to communicate with, by telephone; as, to *telephone* a friend:—*v.i.* to send a message by telephone.

TELEPHONES

1, ordinary telephone; 2, French telephone with transmitter and receiver on handle.

te·leph·o·ny (tē-lĕf′ō-nĭ; tĕl′ē-fō′nĭ), *n.* the science, art, or process of sending sounds to a distance by telephone.

tel·e·scope (tĕl′ē·skōp), *n.* an optical instrument used for viewing objects at a distance, especially the moon, stars, etc.:—*v.t.* [telescoped, telescop-ing], to drive or force together, as colliding railway cars, so that one part slides into another, like sections of a collapsible telescope:—*v.i.* to be forced together in this manner.

tel·e·scop·ic (tĕl′ē-skŏp′ĭk), *adj.* 1, pertaining to, or made by, the telescope; 2, visible only by means of the telescope; as, *telescopic* stars; 3, farseeing; as, *telescopic* vision; 4, capable of being extended or shortened by means of parts sliding one into another; as, a *telescopic* spyglass.

tel·e·vise (tĕl′ē-vīz′), *v.t.* to broadcast by television.

tel·e·vi·sion (tĕl′ē-vĭzh′ŭn), *n.* the process of sending and receiving, by means of radio waves, images of events as they are happening; as, by the use of *television*, we can see, as well as hear, people singing over the radio. *Syn.*, video.

tell (tĕl), *v.t.* [told (tōld), tell-ing], 1, to count; mention one by one; as, to *tell* the beads of a rosary; 2, to relate in words; narrate; as, to *tell* a story; also, to say; utter; as, to *tell* a falsehood; 3, to disclose; confess; as, to *tell* a secret; 4, to decide; as, I cannot *tell* what is best to do; also, to recognize; as, to *tell* the difference; 5, to order; as, he *told* her to buy meat:—*v.i.* 1, to give an account; as, he *told* of days gone by; **2,** *Colloquial,* to play the informer; as, John *told* on Billy; **3,** to have a marked effect; as, hardship *tells* on him.

Tell, Wil·liam, a legendary Swiss peasant who, because he refused to salute the hat of Gessler, the Austrian governor, was ordered to shoot an apple from the head of his son.   This he did with bow and arrow.

tell·er (tĕl'ẽr), *n.* **1,** one who tells, discloses, narrates, etc.; as, a story writer is sometimes called a *teller* of tales; **2,** a bank clerk who receives and pays out money over the counter; **3,** one who counts the votes in a legislative body, meeting, etc.

tell·ing (tĕl'ĭng), *adj.* striking; impressive; as, his words had a *telling* effect.

tell·tale (tĕl'tāl'), *n.* a talebearer; an informer; one who betrays secrets or makes known private affairs:—*adj.* betraying; giving information of what is meant to be secret; as, a *telltale* blush.

te·mer·i·ty (tĕ-mĕr'ĭ-tĭ), *n.* boldness; rashness; as, the clerk had the *temerity* to criticize the firm before the manager's son.

tem·per (tĕm'pẽr), *v.t.* **1,** to mix to the proper degree of softness; as, to *temper* clay; also, to soften; as, to *temper* a rebuke with a smile; **2,** to bring to the proper degree of hardness or toughness; as, to *temper* steel; **3,** to reduce; moderate; as, sympathy *tempers* grief:—*n.* **1,** the degree of hardness, softness, toughness, etc., of a substance, as of steel, clay or mortar; consistency; **2,** disposition or mood; as, he is in a bad *temper* today; **3,** anger; as, to show *temper;* **4,** control of one's anger; as, to lose one's *temper.*—*adj.* **tem'pered.**

tem·per·a·ment (tĕm'pẽr-á-mĕnt), *n.* disposition; the characteristic mental and emotional make-up of a person; as, an artistic *temperament.*

tem·per·a·men·tal (tĕm'pẽr-á-mĕn'tăl), *adj.* **1,** arising from, or pertaining to, a person's mental or emotional make-up; as, he has a *temperamental* aptitude for the life of a monk; **2,** sensitive; liable to sudden changes of mood; as, a *temperamental* actress.

tem·per·ance (tĕm'pẽr-ăns), *n.* **1,** moderation; avoidance of extremes, especially in eating and drinking; **2,** moderation in, or abstinence from, the use of alcoholic liquors.

tem·per·ate (tĕm'pẽr-ĭt), *adj.* **1,** inclined not to eat or drink to excess; moderate; also, seldom or never using alcoholic liquors; **2,** calm; restrained; as, a *temperate* disposition; **3,** free from extremes of heat or cold; as, a *temperate* climate.—*adv.* **tem'per·ate·ly.**—*n.* **tem'per·ate·ness.**

tem·per·a·ture (tĕm'pẽr-á-tūr), *n.* the degree or amount of heat or cold as meas-

ured by a thermometer; also, the degree of heat of the human body or an excess of this heat above the normal; as, a child, when ill, often has a high *temperature.*

tem·pest (tĕm'pĕst), *n.* **1,** a violent windstorm, usually accompanied by rain, hail, etc.; **2,** any violent tumult or agitation; as, a *tempest* of fury.

tem·pes·tu·ous (tĕm-pĕs'tū-ŭs), *adj.* stormy; agitated; as, *tempestuous* seas.

Tem·plar (tĕm'plẽr), *n.* a member of a military and religious order, founded early in the 12th century in Jerusalem, to protect pilgrims and the Holy Sepulcher.

TEMPLAR

¹**tem·ple** (tĕm'pl), *n.* **1,** a building dedicated to the worship of a deity; as, a *temple* of Jupiter; **2,** a building for Christian public worship; especially, a Protestant church in France:—**the Temple,** any one of three successive edifices built in Jerusalem for the worship of Jehovah.

²**tem·ple** (tĕm'pl), *n.* the flat part of the head at each side, between the eye and the upper part of the ear.

tem·po (tĕm'pō), *n.* [*pl.* tempos or tempi (tĕm'pē)], in music, the rate of speed at which a composition should be, or is, given.

¹**tem·po·ral** (tĕm'pŏ-răl), *adj.* **1,** limited in time; not eternal or everlasting; also, worldly or earthly; **2,** pertaining to civil matters, or to affairs of political life; secular; not of the church; as, *temporal* powers.

²**tem·po·ral** (tĕm'pŏ-răl), *adj.* pertaining to or situated near the temples, or sides of the forehead; as, the *temporal* bone.

tem·po·rar·y (tĕm'pŏ-rẽr'ĭ), *adj.* continuing for a limited time only; not permanent; as, *temporary* relief.—*adv.* **tem'po·rar'i·ly.**

tem·po·rize (tĕm'pŏ-rīz), *v.i.* [temporized, temporiz·ing], **1,** to yield temporarily to current opinion or circumstances; **2,** to adopt a policy of delay.

tempt (tĕmpt), *v.t.* **1,** to persuade, or try to persuade, to evil ways; to entice; as, he was *tempted* to cheat; **2,** to attract; invite; as, some foods *tempt* me much more than others.—*adj.* **tempt'ing.**

temp·ta·tion (tĕmp-tā'shŭn), *n.* **1,** the act of leading, or the state of being led, into evil; an effort to lure, especially to evil; as, the *temptation* of Christ by Satan; **2,** an enticement; that which allures; as, the chance to fly was a great *temptation.*

tempt·er (tĕmp'tẽr), *n.* one who seeks to lead others into evil:—**the Tempter,** Satan; the Devil.—*n.fem.* **tempt'ress.**

 āte, âorta, râre, căt, ȧsk, fär, ăllow, sofȧ; ēve, ĕvent, ĕll, writẽr, novĕl; bīte, pĭn; nō, ōbey, ôr, dŏg, tŏp, cŏllide; ūnit, ŭnite, bûrn, cŭt, focŭs; nōon, fŏŏt; mound; coin;

ten (tĕn), *adj.* composed of one more than nine, or twice five:—*n.* **1,** the number consisting of five and five; **2,** a sign representing ten units, as 10 or x.

ten-a-ble (tĕn′à-bl), *adj.* capable of being held, defended, etc.; as, a *tenable* viewpoint.

te-na-cious (tē-nā′shŭs), *adj.* **1,** holding fast or firmly; as, the *tenacious* grip of a bulldog; a miser is *tenacious* of his gold; also, stubborn in holding fast to one's purpose; **2,** sticky, as glue; **3,** tough, as steel; **4,** capable of holding or retaining; as, a *tenacious* mind.—*adv.* **te-na′cious-ly.**

te-nac-i-ty (tē-năs′ĭ-tĭ), *n.* **1,** firmness in holding to one's purpose; also, the power, as of the memory, to retain; **2,** that quality of a body which keeps it from being pulled apart; as, the *tenacity* of wire; also, the quality of sticking to other objects; adhesiveness.

ten-an-cy (tĕn′ăn-sĭ), *n.* [*pl.* tenancies], the temporary use of land or houses on the payment of rent to the owner; also, the length of such use or occupancy.

ten-ant (tĕn′ănt), *n.* **1,** one who has use or possession of property for a certain length of time on the payment of rent; **2,** an occupant or dweller; as, Eskimos are the only *tenants* of this icy waste:—*v.t.* to hold as a tenant; occupy.—*adj.* **ten′-ant-less.**

ten-ant-ry (tĕn′ănt-rĭ), *n.* [*pl.* tenantries], the entire group of tenants occupying land and houses on one estate.

Ten Com-mand-ments, the commands or precepts of God, given to Moses on Mount Sinai.

¹tend (tĕnd), *v.i.* **1,** to move or go in a certain direction; as, the point to which an argument *tends;* also, to exhibit a natural tendency toward something; as, her talents *tend* toward music; **2,** to be likely to have a certain result; as, ill health *tends* to make some people irritable.

²tend (tĕnd), *v.t.* to attend to; watch over; protect; as, the shepherd *tends* his sheep; to have charge of; as, to *tend* a machine.

tend-en-cy (tĕn′dĕn-sĭ), *n.* [*pl.* tendencies], **1,** direction; trend or movement in some direction; as, there was a *tendency* toward anarchy in the state; **2,** natural bent or inclination; as, he had a *tendency* to get angry easily.

¹tend-er (tĕn′dẽr), *n.* **1,** one who attends or takes care of; as, a bar*tender;* **2,** a small car containing coal and water, attached behind a locomotive; **3,** a small vessel attending and supplying a larger one, with fuel, provisions, etc.; **4,** a small boat used to land passengers from a ship.

²ten-der (tĕn′dẽr), *v.t.* **1,** to offer for

acceptance; as, to *tender* one's resignation; **2,** to offer (money) in payment of a debt:—*n.* an offer, bid, or proposal for acceptance; also, the thing offered:—**legal tender,** currency that a lender must, by law, accept when it is offered in repayment of money due him.

³ten-der (tĕn′dẽr), *adj.* **1,** easily broken, chewed, or cut; **2,** not hardy or tough; as, the *tender* shoots of a plant; also, easily hurt or injured; as, a *tender* skin; **3,** easily touched by pain, grief, love, or kindness; as, a *tender* heart; also, gentle; kind; loving; as, *tender* words; **4,** immature; youthful; as, a *tender* age.—*adv.* **ten′der-ly.**

ten-der-foot (tĕn′dẽr-fŏŏt′), *n.* [*pl.* tenderfeet (-fēt′)], **1,** one who has had no experience of rough living or hardships; especially, a greenhorn or newcomer to pioneer life in the western U.S.; **2,** the beginning rank, or class, of the Boy Scouts and the Girl Scouts; also, a member of this class.

ten-der-heart-ed (tĕn′dẽr-här′tĕd), *adj.* readily touched by the pain or grief of others; sympathetic.

ten-der-loin (tĕn′dẽr-loin′), *n.* the tenderest part of the loin of beef or pork.

ten-der-ness (tĕn′dẽr-nĕs), *n.* the state or quality of being easily cut, injured, touched, etc.; as, *tenderness* of meat; *tenderness* of the skin; *tenderness* of heart.

ten-don (tĕn′dŭn), *n.* a tough cord or band of fibrous tissue attaching a muscle to a bone, to another muscle, or to an organ of the body.

ten-dril (tĕn′drĭl), *n.* **1,** a slender, twining plant structure, which attaches itself to a support, thus enabling the plant to climb or to hold itself up; **2,** anything resembling this, as a curl or ringlet.

ten-e-ment (tĕn′ĕ-mĕnt), *n.* **1,** in law, any kind of permanent property rented by one person from another; **2,** a dwelling house; **3,** an apartment, or set of rooms, usually of inferior grade:—**tene-ment house,** a large building containing many sets of rooms, each set occupied by a family: used commonly of buildings occupied by families of small means.

TENDRIL (T)

ten-et (tĕn′ĕt), *n.* a creed, principle, or belief.

ten-fold (tĕn′fōld′), *adj.* ten times as much or as many.—*adv.* **ten′fold′.**

Tenn. abbreviation for *Tennessee.*

Ten-nes-see (tĕn′ĕ-sē′), **1,** a south central State (cap. Nashville) of the U.S. (map

8); **2,** a river rising in Tennessee and flowing into the Ohio (map 8).

ten-nis (tĕn′ĭs), *n.* a game in which a ball is batted back and forth, with rackets, over a net stretched at a height of 3 feet across a specially marked surface called a court.

Ten-ny-son (tĕn′ĭ-sŭn), Alfred, Lord (1809–1892), an English poet, author of "Idylls of the King."

ten-on (tĕn′ŭn), *n.* a projection at the end of a piece of wood cut to fit into a hole in another piece of wood:— *v.t.* **1,** to cut a tenon at the end of (a timber); **2,** to join (two timbers) with a mortise and tenon.

MORTISE (M) AND TENON (T)

ten-or (tĕn′ẽr), *n.* **1,** settled tendency, direction, or course; as, the even *tenor* of the life of a nun; **2,** general character; nature; purport; as, the *tenor* of a conversation; **3,** the highest of adult male voices; also, a part written for this voice; **4,** one who sings such a part; also, an instrument, as the viola, which plays it.

ten-pins (tĕn′pĭnz′), *n.* a bowling game played with ten pins set up at one end of a bowling alley.

TENPINS
Two alleys with pins set up and balls being returned to bowlers.

¹**tense** (tĕns), *adj.* [tens-er, tens-est], stretched taut; rigid; as, *tense* muscles; also, showing or feeling mental strain; highstrung.—*adv.* **tense′ly.**

²**tense** (tĕns), *n.* in grammar, the form a verb takes to indicate the time of an action or state of being.

ten-sile (tĕn′sĭl), *adj.* **1,** pertaining to tension or the act of stretching; as, the *tensile* strength of wire; **2,** capable of being stretched or strained; as, *tensile* wire.

ten-sion (tĕn′shŭn), *n.* **1,** the act of stretching or straining; **2,** the state of being stretched or strained; **3,** mental strain; intensity of feeling; **4,** strained relations; as, *tension* between relatives.

tent (tĕnt), *n.* a portable shelter, usually of canvas, stretched over poles and fastened down by ropes attached to pegs driven into the ground (see illustration next column):—*v.i.* to camp out in a tent.

ten-ta-cle (tĕn′tȧ-kl), *n.* **1,** a thin, flexible feeler, or organ, attached to the mouth parts or to the head of certain insects, fishes, etc., and used to aid feeling, moving, etc. (see illustration next column); **2,** a feeler on the leaf of a plant.

ten-ta-tive (tĕn′tȧ-tĭv), *adj.* made or done as an experiment; not complete or final; as, a *tentative* schedule; a *tentative* offer.—*adv.* **ten′ta-tive-ly.**

ten-ter-hook (tĕn′tẽr-hŏŏk′), *n.* one of the sharp, hooked nails set on a tenter, or frame for stretching cloth:—**on tenterhooks,** in suspense or anxiety.

tenth (tĕnth), *adj.* next after the ninth; the ordinal of *ten*:—*n.* one of the ten equal parts of anything.

ten-u-ous (tĕn′ū-ŭs), *adj.* **1,** slender; fragile; as, *tenuous* cobwebs; **2,** rare; not dense or heavy; as, *tenuous* air; **3,** of little importance; weak; as, a *tenuous* argument.—*adv.* **ten′u-ous-ly.**—*n.* **ten′u-ous-ness.**

ten-ure (tĕn′ūr), *n.* **1,** the right, or manner, of holding real estate or employment; as, some teachers have permanent *tenure;* **2,** time during which anything is held.

TEPEE

te-pee (tē′pē; tĕp′ē), *n.* the cone-shaped tent, or wigwam, of the North American Indians. Also spelled **tee′pee.**

TENTS
1, soldier's pup tent; 2, army squad tent; 3, wall tent with fly; 4, outing tent with front flap raised as an awning.

tep-id (tĕp′ĭd), *adj.* moderately warm; lukewarm; as, a *tepid* bath.

ter-cen-te-nar-y (tûr-sĕn′tē-nĕr′ĭ), *n.* [pl. tercentenaries], the 300th anniversary of an event.

term (tûrm), *n.* **1,** a fixed period of time; the time during which a thing lasts; as, a *term* of office; the school's fall *term;* a prison *term;* **2,** a word or expression, especially one belonging to a particular art, business, etc.; as, chemical *terms;* **3,** in mathematics, one of the parts of a proportion or ratio; **4, terms: a,** conditions or arrangements; as, *terms* of a sale; **b,** rela-

TENTACLES (T) of jellyfish.

tionships; footing; as, to be on good *terms* with a person:—*v.t.* to name or call; as, the police *termed* his mysterious death murder.

ter-ma-gant (tûr′mȧ-gănt), *n.* a noisy, violent, quarrelsome woman:—*adj.* noisy and quarrelsome.

ter-mi-nal (tûr′mĭ-năl), *adj.* **1,** forming the end; growing at the end of a shoot or branch; as, a *terminal* bud; **2,** having to do with the end of a railroad, bus, or air line; as, a *terminal* station:—*n.* **1,** a limit or boundary; an end; **2,** the end of a railroad line, including the station, switches, etc.; **3,** one end of an electrical circuit.

ter-mi-nate (tûr′mĭ-nāt), *v.t.* [terminated, terminat-ing], **1,** to limit or bound; **2,** to bring to an end; finish; as, the two countries *terminated* friendly relations:—*v.i.* **1,** to be limited or bounded; **2,** to come to an end; as, the contract *terminates* in June.

   Syn. end, cease, conclude.

ter-mi-na-tion (tûr′mĭ-nā′shŭn), *n.* **1,** the act of bringing to an end; **2,** end; conclusion.

ter-mi-nol-o-gy (tûr′mĭ-nŏl′ō-jĭ), *n.* [*pl.* terminologies], the special or technical expressions used in a science, art, or business; as, legal *terminology*.

ter-mi-nus (tûr′mĭ-nŭs), *n.* [*pl.* termini (tûr′mĭ-nī) or terminuses], **1,** a limit or goal; **2,** an end of a railway, bus, or air line; also, the town and station at that place.

ter-mite (tûr′mīt), *n.* the white ant, which lives in large colonies, and is extremely destructive to books, timbers, etc.

tern (tûrn), *n.* a sea bird resembling the gull, but generally smaller, slenderer, and swifter in flight. It has long, deeply forked wings, and a slim, straight bill.

TERN (⅟₁₁)

terr. abbreviation for *territory*.

ter-race (tĕr′ĭs; tĕr′ȧs), *n.* **1,** a raised level space or platform of earth with sloping sides; as, a garden *terrace*; **2,** a row of houses set along the top of a bank or slope; also, a short street lined with such a row of houses:—*v.t.* [terraced, terrac-ing], to form into, or supply with, a terrace or terraces; as, to *terrace* a lawn.

ter-ra cot-ta (tĕr′ȧ kŏt′ȧ), pottery of baked clay or earth; also, its reddish-brown or yellowish-brown color.

ter-ra fir-ma (tĕr′ȧ fûr′mȧ), firm or solid earth, as distinguished from water.

ter-ra-pin (tĕr′ȧ-pĭn), *n.* a North Amer-

ican turtle living in fresh and brackish water; also, its flesh used as food.

ter-res-tri-al (tĕ-rĕs′trĭ-ăl), *adj.* **1,** consisting of earth or land; as, the *terrestrial* globe; consisting of land as distinguished from water; as, *terrestrial* portions of the earth; **2,** belonging to the earth, not to the heavens; as, a *terrestrial* being; **3,** existing on land, not in the water, trees, or air; as, *terrestrial* animals.

TERRAPIN (⅟₁₁)

ter-ret (tĕr′ĕt), *n.* one of the rings on a harness pad, through which the driving reins pass. (See illustration at *harness*.)

ter-ri-ble (tĕr′ĭ-bl), *adj.* **1,** exciting or causing fear or dread; dreadful; as, a *terrible* disaster; **2,** *Colloquial,* extreme; excessive; as, a *terrible* hurry.—*adv.* **ter′ri-bly.**

   Syn. shocking, grim, horrible.

ter-ri-er (tĕr′ĭ-ĕr), *n.* an active, intelligent dog, usually of small size, and noted for its alertness and gameness, especially in killing rats and mice, and in digging out game that has burrowed in the ground.

ter-rif-ic (tĕ-rĭf′ĭk), *adj.* **1,** such as to cause fear or terror; alarming; dreadful; as, a *terrific* explosion; **2,** *Colloquial,* excessive; extreme; as, a *terrific* amount of work.

TERRIER (AIREDALE) (⅟₂₄)

ter-ri-fy (tĕr′ĭ-fī), *v.t.* [terrified, terrifying], to fill with great alarm or terror; frighten greatly; as, the storm *terrified* her.

ter-ri-tor-i-al (tĕr′ĭ-tôr′ĭ-ăl), *adj.* **1,** pertaining to a given region of land, especially to a division of a national domain; as, *territorial* disputes; **2,** limited to a particular district; as, *territorial* laws; **3,** pertaining to forces organized for the defense of a particular district:—**Territorial,** pertaining to the Territories of the U.S.:—*n.* a soldier enrolled in the territorial defense, or home reserves.

ter-ri-tor-y (tĕr′ĭ-tôr′ĭ), *n.* [*pl.* territories], **1,** a large tract of land; region; as, Canada covers a large *territory*; also, an assigned district; as, the salesman's *territory* covers the entire state; **2,** the entire extent of land and water under the control of one ruler or government; as, British *territory*:—**Territory,** in the U.S., a region or portion of the country not yet admitted into the Union as a State.

ter-ror (tĕr′ẽr), *n.* **1,** very great fear; alarm; **2,** one who or that which causes such fear; as, the tyrant was a *terror* to his subjects.

Syn. consternation, horror, panic.

ter-ror-ism (tĕr′ẽr-ĭzm), *n.* **1,** the act of filling, or the state of being filled, with great alarm or terror; **2,** a system of government, or opposition to government, by methods which arouse fear.

ter-ror-ist (tĕr′ẽr-ĭst), *n.* one who governs by violent methods which arouse fear.

ter-ror-ize (tĕr′ẽr-īz), *v.t.* [terrorized, terroriz-ing], **1,** to fill with great alarm or fear; reduce to a state of terror; **2,** to govern by methods which arouse fear.

terse (tûrs), *adj.* [ters-er, ters-est], concise or brief; exactly to the point; as, a *terse* literary style.—*adv.* **terse′ly.**—*n.* **terse′ness.**

Syn. pointed, succinct, curt.

ter-tian (tûr′shăn), *adj.* occurring every other day:—*n.* fever returning every other day.

ter-ti-ar-y (tûr′shĭ-ẽr′ĭ; tûr′shȧ-rĭ), *adj.* third in order of time or rank.

test (tĕst), *n.* **1,** trial; proof; as, his character was put to a *test;* examination; as, a *test* in typewriting; **2,** a criterion, or standard, by which a person or thing may be gauged; as, self-control is the *test* of a man's power; **3,** in chemistry, an experiment for discovering the presence of any particular substance in a compound:—*v.t.* **1,** to put to test; try; as, to *test* a man's ability; **2,** in chemistry, to try to find a particular substance in; as, to *test* alcohol for poison.

Syn., n. ordeal, criterion.

tes-ta-ment (tĕs′tȧ-mĕnt), *n.* a written document in which a person provides for the disposal of his property after his death: usually in the phrase *last will and testament:*—**Testament, 1,** either of the two main parts of the Bible; **2,** a book containing only the New Testament.

tes-ta-men-ta-ry (tĕs′tȧ-mĕn′tȧ-rĭ), *adj.* **1,** pertaining to a will, or to the administration or settlement of a will; as, letters *testamentary;* **2,** given or bequeathed by will; **3,** done according to, provided or appointed by, a will or testament; as, a *testamentary* guardian.

tes-tate (tĕs′tāt), *adj.* having made and left a will; as, he died *testate.*

tes-ta-tor (tĕs-tā′tẽr), *n.* a man who leaves a valid will at his death.—*n.fem.* **tes-ta′trix.**

tes-ti-fy (tĕs′tĭ-fī), *v.i.* [testified, testifying], **1,** to bear witness; to declare under oath before a court of law; as, the witness

testified in the prisoner's behalf; **2,** to serve as evidence; as, his works *testify* to his industry:—*v.t.* to declare solemnly on oath; bear witness to.—*n.* **tes′ti-fi′er.**

tes-ti-mo-ni-al (tĕs′tĭ-mō′nĭ-ăl), *n.* **1,** a writing or certificate regarding the character, ability, etc., of a person, or the value of a thing; **2,** a token of respect, gratitude, or the like, presented to a person.

tes-ti-mo-ny (tĕs′tĭ-mō′nĭ), *n.* [*pl.* testimonies], **1,** evidence; proof; as, fossil-bearing rocks give *testimony* of life in former ages; **2,** in law, a spoken or written declaration furnished by a witness under oath; **3, testimonies,** the Scriptures.

tes-ty (tĕs′tĭ), *adj.* [tes-ti-er, tes-ti-est], touchy; irritable.—*adv.* **tes′ti-ly.**—*n.* **tes′-ti-ness.**

Syn. fretful, impatient.

te-ta-nus (tĕt′ȧ-nŭs), *n.* an acute and usually fatal disease causing muscular spasms: called *lockjaw* when confined to the muscles of the lower jaw.

tête-à-tête (tāt′-ȧ-tāt′; tâ′-tȧ-tât′), *n.* confidential, friendly talk between two persons:—*adj.* face to face; confidential.

teth-er (tĕth′ẽr), *n.* **1,** a rope or chain to fasten an animal; **2,** hence, power; endurance; as, she was at the end of her *tether:*—*v.t.* to tie with a rope or chain.

Teu-ton (tū′tŏn), *n.* **1,** a member of an ancient German tribe of unknown origin; **2,** a member of a race of people including the Germans, Dutch, Danes, Swedes, Norwegians, and English; **3,** a German.

Teu-ton-ic (tū-tŏn′ĭk), *adj.* pertaining to a group of peoples including the ancient Goths, Scandinavians, Anglo-Saxons, Germans, etc., inhabiting central and northern Europe, or their descendants.

Tex. abbreviation for *Texan, Texas.*

Tex-as (tĕk′sȧs), the largest State (cap. Austin) of the U.S., bordering on Mexico and the Gulf of Mexico (map 8).

Tex-as tow-er, a tower, anchored in the sea, off the coast, which houses a radar station; so called because of its resemblance to an oil derrick.

text (tĕkst), *n.* **1,** the main body of any piece of written or printed matter as distinguished from the illustrations, notes, etc.; **2,** a verse of Scripture forming the subject of a sermon; **3,** the subject of a discussion, speech, etc.; theme.

text-book (tĕkst′book′), *n.* a standard book of instruction in a branch of study.

tex-tile (tĕks′tĭl; tĕks′tīl), *adj.* **1,** pertaining to weaving; as, a *textile* mill; **2,** woven; suitable for weaving:—*n.* woven goods.

tex-tu-al (tĕks′tū-ăl), *adj.* **1,** based on a

text, especially of the Scriptures; **2,** pertaining to, or contained in, the printed or written words of a book or manuscript.

tex-ture (těks′tūr), *n.* **1,** the structure or arrangement of threads making up a fabric; as, damask has a smooth *texture;* **2,** composition; as the compact *texture* of clay.

T.H. abbreviation for *Territory of Hawaii.*

-th (-th) or **-eth** (-ĕth), a suffix used: **1,** in ordinal numbers; as, seven*th,* thirtie*th;* **2,** *Archaic,* in the third singular present indicative of verbs; as, "He com*eth* in the name of the Lord."

Thack-er-ay (thăk′ĕr-ĭ), William Makepeace (1811–1863), an English novelist, author of "Vanity Fair."

Thad-dae-us (thă-dē′ŭs), in the Bible, one of the twelve apostles of Christ: also called *Lebbaeus.*

Thai-land (tī′lănd), a kingdom (cap. Bangkok) in southeastern Asia (map **15**): formerly called *Siam.*

tha-ler (tä′lĕr), *n.* [*pl.* thaler], a German silver coin; a taler. See **taler.**

thal-lus (thăl′ŭs), *n.* [*pl.* thalli (thăl′ī)], a simple plant body, not divided into stem, leaves, and root, as in seaweeds and lichens.

Thames (tĕmz), the principal river of southern England, on which is located the city of London (map **13**).

than (thăn), *conj.* **1,** in comparison with; as, you are taller *than* James; also, in comparison with one's desire; as, I'd rather stay *than* go; **2,** besides; but; as, none other *than* my parents can help me.

thane (thān), *n.* among the Anglo-Saxons, a member of a class between an ordinary freeman and a noble, usually attached to the service of a lord.

thank (thăngk), *v.t.* to express gratitude to:—**thanks,** *n.pl.* expression of gratitude.

thank-ful (thăngk′fo͝ol), *adj.* feeling or expressing gratitude; grateful. — *adv.* **thank′ful-ly.**—*n.* **thank′ful-ness.**

thank-less (thăngk′lĕs), *adj.* **1,** ungrateful; not feeling or expressing gratitude; as, a *thankless* child; **2,** not gaining gratitude; unprofitable; as, a *thankless* task.— *adv.* **thank′less-ly.**—*n.* **thank′less-ness.**

thanks-giv-ing (thăngks-gĭv′ĭng; thăngks′gĭv′ĭng), *n.* the act of expressing gratitude; especially, a form of prayer expressing thanks to God.

Thanksgiving Day, in the U.S., usually the last Thursday in November, a day set apart as a legal holiday for gratitude and praise to God: also called *Thanksgiving.*

that (thăt), *adj.* [*pl.* those (thōz)], **1,** indicating someone or something at a distance in time or space; the farther; yon; as, please take *that* chair upstairs; who are

those people? **2,** pointing out a single, particular, or known thing or person; as, ask *those* people best able to pay; **3,** the other; the second; the latter; as, on this side and *that* side:—*demonstrative pron.* **1,** a person or thing at a distance; not this; as, *that* is not fair; these must stay, *those* may go; **2,** a person or thing already indicated or to be indicated; as, so *that* is what he said; *that* is the man you mean; **3,** the other, second, or farther person or thing; as, this wood is softer than *that:*—*relative pron.* **1,** who or whom; which; as, the man *that* you saw; **2,** in, on, or at which; when; as, all those years *that* he was gone; also, for which; as, the reason *that* he came:— *conj.* **1,** used to introduce a clause which is the object or the subject of a verb; as, he said *that* he would come; *that* he lied is bad; **2,** with a purpose; as, work *that* you may succeed; **3,** with the result; as, I am so sleepy *that* I can hardly see; **4,** I wish; as, oh, *that* you were here!

thatch (thăch), *n.* a roof or covering made of straw, reeds, or the like; also, the material used:—*v.t.* to cover with, or as with, a roof of straw, reeds, or the like.

THATCH
House with thatched roof.

thaw (thô), *v.i.* **1,** to melt or become liquid, as ice or snow; **2,** to grow warm enough to melt ice and snow; **3,** to become milder or more genial; to unbend; as, his manner *thawed* perceptibly:—*v.t.* to cause to melt or dissolve:—*n.* the melting of ice or snow as a result of warm weather; also, a state of weather when ice and snow melt.

¹**the** (*the* when unaccented before a consonant, as in *the* cat; *the* or th*ĭ* when unaccented before a vowel, as in *the* ear; *the* when emphatic or alone), *adj.* or *definite article* **1,** pointing out a specific or known person or thing; as, *the* boy in the back row; *the* book I gave you; **2,** a; any; every; as, *the* cow is a useful animal; **3,** that which is, or those who are; as, *the* beautiful; *the* great; **4,** being best, greatest, or most important; as, *the* event of the year: —*prep.* a; to each; as, 20 lines the page.

²**the** (*the*; *the*), *adv.* usually in such phrases as *the* sooner, *the* better, with the meanings: by however much . . . . by so much.

the-a-ter or **the-a-tre** (thē′ȧ-tĕr), *n.* **1,** a building where plays, motion pictures, or other dramatic performances are given; **2,** dramatic art; the drama; **3,** a place where important action takes place; as, Gettysburg was once the *theater* of battle.

---

go; join; yet; sing; chin; show; thin, *th*en; hw, *wh*y; zh, azure; ū, Ger. für or Fr. lune; ö, Ger. schön or Fr. feu; ṅ, Fr. enfant, nom; kh, Ger. ach or ich. See pages ix–x.

the-at-ric (thē-ăt′rĭk), *adj.* artificial; showy; as, she indulged in *theatric* clothes.

the-at-ri-cal (thē-ăt′rĭ-kăl), *adj.* 1, pertaining to the theater, a dramatic performance, or actors; as, *theatrical* costumes; 2, suitable for, or characteristic of, the stage; conspicuous; as, a *theatrical* entrance:—**theatricals**, *n.pl.* dramatic performances, especially by amateurs.—*adv.* **the-at′ri-cal-ly.**

Thebes (thēbz), 1, an ancient capital of Egypt on the Nile River, south of Cairo; 2, an ancient city of Greece, northwest of Athens (map 1).

thee (thē), *pron.* objective case of *thou:* used mainly in prayer, poetry, or in poetic prose.

theft (thĕft), *n.* 1, the act of stealing; robbery; 2, the property stolen; as, the *theft* amounted to ten dollars.

their (thâr), *adj.* a possessive form of the personal pronoun *they:* 1, belonging to them; of them; as, *their* house; 2, coming from them; as, *their* kindness.

theirs (thârz), a possessive form of *they,* used alone: 1, as *adj.* in the predicate, belonging to them; as, whose is that car? it is *theirs;* 2, as *pron.,* a person or thing that belongs to them; as, our car is blue, *theirs* is black.

the-ism (thē′ĭzm), *n.* the belief in the existence of a god or gods; especially, the belief in a personal God as the creator and supreme ruler of the universe.

them (thĕm), *pron.* objective case of *they.*

theme (thēm), *n.* 1, the subject or topic of a speech, essay, etc.; 2, a short essay or composition on a given subject; 3, in music, a series of notes forming the subject of a composition or movement.

them-selves (thĕm-sĕlvz′), *pron.* the plural form of *himself, herself,* and *itself;* the emphatic form of *they* or reflexive form of *them;* as, they *themselves* are going; they caused *themselves* much trouble.

then (thĕn), *conj.* in that case; therefore; in consequence; as, *then* you need not go; if you are able, *then* do it:—*adv.* 1, next; immediately after; as, wash it, *then* dry it; 2, at that time; as, *then* Rome fell; 3, later; at another time; as, come *then:*—*adj.* existing at the time mentioned; as, the *then* poet laureate:—*n.* a time mentioned; as, by *then* he was ready.

thence (thĕns), *adv.* 1, from that place; as, he departed *thence;* 2, from or after that time; as, a week *thence;* 3, from that cause, fact, or source.

thence-forth (thĕns′fôrth′; thĕns′fôrth′), *adv.* from then on; thereafter.

thence-for-ward (thĕns′fôr′wĕrd), *adv.* forward; from that time or place.

the-oc-ra-cy (thē-ŏk′rà-sĭ), *n.* [*pl.* theocracies], government by God directly or by his representatives; hence, government by an organized church.

The-o-do-si-us (thē′ō-dō′shĭ-ŭs), called *the Great* (346?–395), a Roman emperor.

the-o-lo-gi-an (thē′ō-lō′jĭ-ăn), *n.* a person skilled in theology, or the theory of religion; a professor of theology.

the-ol-o-gy (thē-ŏl′ō-jĭ), *n.* [*pl.* theologies], the study of the nature, powers, and laws of God, especially as they affect man; divinity; the science of religion.—*adj.* **the′o-log′i-cal** (thē′ō-lŏj′ĭ-kăl).

the-o-rem (thē′ō-rĕm), *n.* 1, that which can be shown to be true and has been established as a principle or law; 2, in geometry, a proposition to be proved.

the-o-ret-i-cal (thē′ō-rĕt′ĭ-kăl) or **the-o-ret-ic** (thē′ō-rĕt′ĭk), *adj.* 1, pertaining to, or depending on, abstract principles or theories; 2, based on ideas rather than on fact or experience; not practical; as, *theoretical* knowledge.—*adv.* **the′o-ret′i-cal-ly.**

the-o-rist (thē′ō-rĭst), *n.* one who draws conclusions from abstract principles or theories rather than from facts; a dreamer.

the-o-rize (thē′ō-rīz), *v.i.* [theorized, theoriz-ing], to form beliefs intended to explain facts; to speculate; as, to *theorize* about the origin of the universe.

the-o-ry (thē′ō-rĭ), *n.* [*pl.* theories], 1, a statement of the fundamental principles of an art or science rather than the method of practicing it; as, the *theory* of music; 2, an opinion, based on observed facts, offered by a person to explain how something has been brought about; as, the *theory* of evolution; also, a view or opinion, not necessarily based on facts; a guess; conjecture; as, his *theory* of the crime.

Syn. scheme, conjecture.

ther-a-peu-tic (thĕr′à-pū′tĭk), *adj.* pertaining to healing; curative; as, *therapeutic* baths:—**therapeutics**, *n.pl.* used as *sing.* the science of treating diseases; therapy.

ther-a-py (thĕr′à-pĭ), *n.* the treatment of disease; therapeutics.

there (thâr), *adv.* 1, in or at that place; not here; as, put the book *there;* 2, to or toward that place; as, I will go *there* today; 3, in that matter, respect, etc.; as, you're wrong *there,* I think; 4, used preceding a verb or in questions to introduce a sentence; as, is *there* time? *there* is time:—*interj.* 1, expressing defiance, triumph, etc.; as, I won't go, so *there!* 2, expressing sympathy; as, *there, there,* don't fret.

āte, âorta, râre, căt, ȧsk, fär, ăllow, sofȧ; ēve, ĕvent, ĕll, writĕr, novĕl; bīte, pĭn; nō, ōbey, ôr, dŏg, tŏp, cōllide; ūnit, ūnite, bûrn, cŭt, focŭs; nōōn, fŏŏt; mound; coin;

there-a-bouts (*thâr′ȧ-bouts′*) or **there-a-bout** (*thâr′ȧ-bout′*), *adv.* near that place, time, number, etc.; nearly.

there-aft-er (*thâr-ȧf′tẽr*), *adv.* after that; thereupon.

there-at (*thâr-ăt′*), *adv.* **1**, at that place; there; **2**, on that account; therefore.

there-by (*thâr-bī′*), *adv.* **1**, by that means; **2**, near by; **3**, in that connection; as, *thereby* hangs a tale.

there-for (*thâr-fôr′*), *adv.* for that or this; as, we give thanks *therefor*

there-fore (*thâr′fôr*), *adv.* for that reason; on that account.

there-from (*thâr-frŏm′*), *adv.* from this or that place, time, cause, etc.

there-in (*thâr-ĭn′*), *adv.* **1**, in or into this or that place, time, etc.; **2**, in this or that respect; as, *therein* you are right.

there-of (*thâr-ŏv′*; *thâr-ŏf′*), *adv.* **1**, of that or this; **2**, from this or that cause.

there-on (*thâr-ŏn′*), *adv.* **1**, on that or this place or thing; **2**, thereafter; consequently.

there-to (*thâr-tōō′*), *adv.* **1**, to that or this place or thing; **2**, moreover; also.

there-un-to (*thâr′ŭn-tōō′*; *thâr′ŭn′tōō*), *adv.* **1**, thereto; to that or this place or thing; **2**, in addition; moreover.

there-up-on (*thâr′ŭ-pŏn′*), *adv.* **1**, thereon; upon that; **2**, therefore; by reason of that; **3**, immediately; thereafter.

there-with (*thâr-wĭth′*; *thâr-wĭth′*), *adv.* **1**, with that or this; **2**, at the same time.

there-with-al (*thâr′wĭth-ôl′*), *adv. Archaic:* **1**, at the same time; **2**, in addition.

ther-mal (*thûr′măl*), *adj.* **1**, pertaining to heat; as, *thermal* units; **2**, hot; as, *thermal* baths:—*n.* a current of air blowing upward:—**thermal soaring**, sailing in a glider on rising currents of air.

ther-mom-e-ter (*thẽr-mŏm′ē-tẽr*), *n.* an instrument for measuring temperature and temperature changes, especially one consisting of a sealed glass tube partly filled with mercury or colored alcohol, the degree of the expansion or contraction of which, corresponding to heat changes, is indicated on a graduated scale. **Fahrenheit thermometer,** one with a scale marking the freezing point of water at 32 degrees and the boiling point at 212 degrees; **centigrade thermometer,** one with a scale marking the freezing point at 0 and the boiling point at 100 degrees.

THERMOM-ETER

Ther-mop-y-lae (*thẽr-mŏp′ĭ-lē*), a narrow defile between Thessaly and Greece where Leonidas died resisting the Persians in 480 B.C. (map **1**).

Ther-mos bot-tle (*thûr′mŏs*), a trademark name for a bottle provided with a vacuum to keep its contents at the same temperature:—**thermos bottle,** a container bearing this trade name.

ther-mo-stat (*thûr′mō-stăt*), *n.* an automatic apparatus for controlling temperature, by regulating dampers, the flow of fuel oil, etc.

the-sau-rus (*thē̇-sô′rŭs*), *n.* [*pl.* thesauri (*thē̇-sô′rī*)], **1**, a place where treasure is kept; **2**, a storehouse of words; a lexicon.

these (*thēz*), plural of *this:* opposite of *those.*

The-seus (*thē′sūs*; *thē′sē̇-ŭs*), *n.* in Greek mythology, a hero famed for many exploits. He slew the Minotaur and conquered the Amazons.

the-sis (*thē′sĭs*), *n.* [*pl.* theses (*thē′sēz*)], **1**, something laid down or stated; especially, a statement by a person who undertakes to support it by argument; **2**, a long essay, based on original research, offered by a candidate for an advanced degree at a college or university.

Thes-pi-an (*thĕs′pĭ-ăn*), *adj.* referring to the theater or to dramatic art:—*n.* an actor or actress.

Thes-sa-lo-ni-ans (*thĕs′ȧ-lō′nĭ-ănz*), *n.* in the Bible, either of two books of the New Testament, consisting of letters written by the apostle Paul to the people of the ancient city of Thessalonica, the present name of which is Salonika.

Thes-sa-lo-ni-kē (*thĕs′ȧ-lō-nē′kē*), a city in northeastern Greece. See **Salonika.**

Thes-sa-ly (*thĕs′ȧ-lĭ*), the northeastern section of Greece (map **1**).

The-tis (*thē′tĭs*), *n.* in Greek mythology, the mother of Achilles.

thews (*thūz*), *n.pl.* muscles; sinews; hence, muscular power or strength.

they (*thā*), *personal pron.* **1**, nominative plural of *he, she,* or *it;* **2**, people in general; men; as, so *they* say.

thick (*thĭk*), *adj.* **1**, large in diameter; coarse; as, a *thick* stem; **2**, of specified, or relatively great, depth between two opposite surfaces; as, a board two inches *thick;* a *thick* book; **3**, of compact or dense texture, consistency, or the like; as, *thick* glue; **4**, close together; abundant; as, *thick* foliage; also, densely set or overgrown; as, a garden *thick* with weeds; **5**, stupid; dense; **6**, not clear; muddy; foggy; as, the air was *thick* with smoke; **7**, throaty; hoarse; as, a *thick* voice; **8**, *Col-*

loquial, extremely friendly or intimate; as, she's too *thick* with Mary:—*adv.* close together; following closely or quickly; as, the blows came *thick* and fast:—*n.* **1**, the thickest part of anything; as, the *thick* of the thumb; **2**, the most intense moment; the place where action is liveliest; as, the *thick* of the combat:—**through thick and thin**, through fortune and misfortune; under all conditions.—*n.* **thick′ness**.

thick-en (thĭk′ĕn), *v.t.* to make (a liquid) less thin; as, to *thicken* gravy:—*v.i.* **1**, to become denser; as, the clouds *thicken;* **2**, to become complicated; as, the plot *thickens*.

thick-et (thĭk′ĕt), *n.* a dense growth of tangled shrubs, trees, etc.

thick-ly (thĭk′lĭ), *adv.* **1**, densely; closely; as, *thickly* strewn; **2**, in a muffled or hoarse voice.

thick-set (thĭk′sĕt′), *adj.* **1**, closely planted; **2**, having a short, stout body; as, a *thickset* fighter.

thief (thēf), *n.* [*pl.* thieves (thēvz)], a person who steals or robs.

thieve (thēv), *v.t.* and *v.i.* [thieved, thieving], to steal; rob.

thiev-er-y (thē′vẽr-ĭ), *n.* [*pl.* thieveries], the act or habit of stealing.

thiev-ish (thē′vĭsh), *adj.* given to stealing; also, like a thief; sneaking; sly.—*adv.* **thiev′ish-ly**.—*n.* **thiev′ish-ness**.

thigh (thī), *n.* **1**, in man, the muscular part of the leg between the knee and the trunk; **2**, the corresponding part in other animals.

thim-ble (thĭm′bl), *n.* a cap of metal, celluloid, etc., worn to protect the tip of the finger in sewing.

thin (thĭn), *adj.* [thin-ner, thin-nest], **1**, small in diameter; fine; slim; slender; **2**, having the two opposite surfaces close together; of little thickness; as, a *thin* board; **3**, transparent; sheer; as, *thin* muslin; **4**, hence, easily seen through; slight; shallow; as, a *thin* excuse; **5**, lacking density; rarefied; as, *thin* air; **6**, high-pitched; shrill; faint; as, a *thin* voice; **7**, lacking roundness or plumpness of figure; gaunt; **8**, scanty; lacking substance or vigor; as, *thin* blood; **9**, lacking abundance; scanty; as, *thin* vegetation:—*v.t.* [thinned, thin-ning], **1**, to make thin or less dense; **2**, to reduce in numbers:—*v.i.* to become less dense or numerous:—*n.* a kind of small, dry biscuit.—*n.* **thin′ness**.

Syn., *adj.* lean, meager, spare, lank.

THIMBLE

thine (thīn), *Archaic* or *Poetic*, a possessive form of *thou:* **1**, as *adj.*, belonging or relating to thee: **a**, in the predicate; as, whose is the glory? it is *thine;* **b**, used in place of *thy* before a vowel sound; as,

thine own self; guard *thine* honor; **2**, as *pron.*, a person or thing belonging to thee; as, joy to thee and *thine*.

thing (thĭng), *n.* **1**, any object which may be perceived through the senses, as a stone, a book, etc.; also, anything which may be made an object of thought, or which exists in the imagination only, as courage or valor, a fairy, etc.; **2**, a particular act, course, or affair; as, this *thing* must not occur again; **3**, a person or animal: usually a term of pity, sympathy, affection, or contempt; as, poor *thing!* **4**, **things: a**, wraps; personal possessions, as property or baggage; **b**, circumstances; as, *things* are bad.

think (thĭngk), *v.i.* [thought (thôt), thinking], **1**, to develop ideas; to form a conception, opinion, or judgment; **2**, to consider; to meditate; muse; **3**, to have in mind, or call to mind, a thought, idea, or image of something; as, to *think* of a picture; **4**, to have an opinion or judgment; as, he *thinks* well of you; **5**, to purpose, plan, or intend; as, I had not *thought* of going until tomorrow:—*v.t.* **1**, to occupy the mind with; imagine; as, *think* no evil; **2**, to review or examine mentally; as, to *think* out a problem; **3**, to hold as an opinion; as, you may *think* what you please.—*n.* **think′er**.

third (thûrd), *adj.* next after the second: the ordinal of *three:*—*n.* one of the three equal parts of anything.

third-ly (thûrd′lĭ), *adv.* in the third place.

third—rate (thûrd′=rāt′), *adj.* **1**, third in rank or quality; **2**, very poor; quite inferior.

thirst (thûrst), *n.* **1**, a desire for drink; also, the sensation relieved only by drinking, usually a feeling of dryness and heat in the mouth, throat, and stomach; **2**, a great craving; a yearning; as, a *thirst* for fame:—*v.i.* **1**, to desire drink; **2**, to be eager; as, to *thirst* for revenge.

thirst-y (thûrs′tĭ), *adj.* [thirst-i-er, thirst-i-est], **1**, feeling desire for drink; **2**, without moisture; parched.—*adv.* **thirst′i-ly**.—*n.* **thirst′i-ness**.

thir-teen (thûr′tēn′), *adj.* composed of one more than twelve:—*n.* **1**, the sum of twelve plus one; **2**, a sign representing thirteen units, as 13 or xiii.

thir-teenth (thûr′tēnth′), *adj.* next after the 12th: the ordinal of *thirteen:*—*n.* one of the thirteen equal parts of anything.

thir-ti-eth (thûr′tĭ-ĕth), *adj.* next after the 29th: the ordinal of *thirty:*—*n.* one of the 30 equal parts of anything.

thir-ty (thûr′tĭ), *adj.* composed of one more than 29:—*n.* **1**, the sum of 29 plus one; **2**, a sign representing 30 units, as 30 or xxx.

this (thĭs), *adj.* [*pl.* these (thēz)], **1**, indicating something or someone near in

āte, āorta, râre, căt, ȧsk, fär, ăllow, sofȧ; ēve, ĕvent, ĕll, writẽr, novĕl; bīte, pĭn; nō, ōbey, ôr, dŏg, tŏp, cŏllide; ūnit, ūnite, bûrn, cŭt, focŭs; nōōn, fŏŏt; mound; coin;

time or space; as, will you mail *this* letter for me? *these* guests came; 2, pointing out a single, particular, or known thing or person; as, *this* whole matter is a joke; *these* students best able to work; 3, the first; the nearer; the former; as, *this* side and that:—*demonstrative pron.* 1, a person or thing near at hand; not that; as, *this* is my house; 2, a person or thing just indicated; as, I have heard *this* before; *this* is my friend; 3, the first or nearer person or thing; as, *this* is a better cake than that.

this-tle (thĭs′l), *n.* a plant of the aster family with rough, thorny stems, finely divided, prickly leaves, and yellow, purple, or white flowers.

this-tle-down (thĭs′l-doun′), *n.* the downy fluff from ripe thistle flowers.

thith-er (thĭth′ẽr), *adv.* Archaic, to that place; in that direction.

thole (thōl), *n.* a pin in the side of a boat that keeps the oar in place: also called *tholepin.*

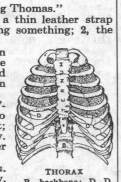

THISTLE

Thom-as (tŏm′ás), in the Bible, the apostle who would not believe in Jesus's resurrection until he had proof, and is therefore sometimes called "doubting Thomas."

THOLES

thong (thŏng), *n.* 1, a thin leather strap or string for fastening something; 2, the lash of a whip.

Thor (thôr), *n.* in Norse mythology, the god of thunder and strength, for whom Thursday is named.

tho-rac-ic (thō-răs′ĭk), *adj.* pertaining to the thorax, or chest; as, the *thoracic* cavity. (See illustration under *diaphragm.*)

thor-ax (thôr′ăks), *n.* 1, in the human body, the chest, containing the heart, lungs, etc.; 2, in insects, the middle of the three main sections of the body.

THORAX
B, backbone; D, D, diaphragm; H, heart; L, L, lungs.

Tho-reau (thō′rō; thō-rō′), Henry David (1817–1862), an American author, philosopher, and naturalist.

thorn (thôrn), *n.* 1, in plants, a stiff, sharp-pointed, slender projection, as on the locust; in animals, a similar sharp projection, usually called *spine;* 2, any tree or shrub bearing thorns; 3, hence, anything that annoys; a source of worry.—*adj.* **thorn′y.**—*adj.***thorn′less.**—*n.***thorn′i-ness.**

thor-ough (thûr′ō), *adj.* 1, finished; complete; not superficial; as, a *thorough* cleaning; 2, accurate; careful; as, a *thorough* worker.—*n.* **thor′ough-ness.**
Syn. trustworthy, reliable.

thor-ough-bred (thûr′ō-brĕd′), *adj.* 1, of pure and unmixed breed; as, a *thoroughbred* dog; 2, showing the characteristics of good birth and breeding; 3, high-spirited: —*n.* 1, an animal of pure breed; 2, a person of fine breeding.

thor-ough-fare (thûr′ō-fâr′), *n.* a street, road, or passage open at both ends.

thor-ough-go-ing (thûr′ō-gō′ĭng), *adj.* leaving nothing undone; complete; thorough; as, a *thoroughgoing* analysis.

those (thōz), plural of *that:* opposite of *these.*

thou (thou), *pron.* [nominative thou, possessive thy (thī) or thine (thīn), objective thee (thē); *pl.* nominative ye (yē) or you (yōō), possessive your (yōōr) or yours (yōōrz), objective you], *Archaic* or *Poetic,* the personal pronoun of the second person.

though (thō), *conj.* 1, notwithstanding the fact that; as, I shall go, *though* it is late; 2, even if; as, *though* he go, I'll stay: —**as though**, as if; as, he ate *as though* he were hungry:—*adv.* nevertheless; however.

¹thought (thôt), *n.* 1, mental activity; meditation; reflection; 2, that which the mind conceives, considers, remembers, or imagines; an idea; opinion; notion; 3, the power of imagining and reasoning; intellect; as, man is endowed with *thought;* 4, concern; care; worry; as, take *thought* for the morrow; 5, a way of thinking, or a group of ideas or beliefs, characteristic of a period, nation, class, society, or the like; as, modern *thought;* 6, a little bit; a trifle; as, she was a *thought* reckless.
Syn. contemplation, deliberation.

²thought (thôt), past tense and past participle of *think.*

thought-ful (thôt′fool), *adj.* 1, thinking; full of thought; 2, considerate of other people; kind.—*adv.* **thought′ful-ly.**

thought-less (thôt′lĕs), *adj.* 1, not thinking; careless; 2, without consideration for others.—*adv.* **thought′less-ly.**

thou-sand (thou′zănd), *adj.* 1, composed of ten times 100; indefinitely great in number:—*n.* 1, the number consisting of ten hundreds; 2, a sign representing this number, as 1,000 or M; 3, a large number.

go; join; yet; sing; chin; show; thin, *th*en; hw, *why;* zh, azure; ü, Ger. für or Fr. lune; ö, Ger. schön or Fr. feu; ň, Fr. enfant, nom; kh, Ger. ach or ich. See pages ix-x.

Thou·sand Is·lands, a group of about 1,700 islands in the Saint Lawrence River, between New York State and Ontario, Canada.

thou·sandth (thou′zăndth), *adj.* next after the 999th: the ordinal of *thousand:—n.* one of the 1,000 equal parts of anything.

Thrace (thrās), the name for an ancient division of the eastern part of the Balkan peninsula, north of Macedonia (map 1).— *adj.* **Thra′cian.**

thral·dom or **thrall·dom** (thrôl′dŭm), *n.* serfdom or slavery; bondage.

thrall (thrôl), *n.* 1, a slave or serf; 2, slavery or bondage; as, held in *thrall.*

thrash (thrăsh), *v.t.* 1, (preferably *thresh*), to beat out (grain) from the hull or husk; 2, to discuss thoroughly, or over and over; as, to *thrash* out the solution to a problem; 3, to beat or flog:—*v.i.* 1, (preferably *thresh*), to beat out grain; 2, to toss or move wildly; as, the patient with a high fever *thrashed* about in bed.

thrash·er (thrăsh′ẽr), *n.* 1, a person who thrashes; 2, a North American thrushlike bird; 3, a large shark: also called *thrasher shark,* preferably *thresher shark.*

thrash·ing (thrăsh′-ĭng), *n.* a flogging.

thread (thrĕd), *n.* 1, a thin, twisted strand of flax, cotton, silk, or other fibrous substance; 2, a filament; anything threadlike; as, a *thread* of glass or metal; a fiber; 3, something running through and connecting the parts of anything; as, the *thread* of a story; 4, the spiral ridge of a screw or nut:—*v.t.* 1, to provide with, or as with, a thread; as, to *thread* a screw; 2, to put a thread through the eye of (a needle); 3, to string (beads); 4, to pass or pierce through; as, to *thread* a narrow street; also, to make (one's way) with difficulty. —*adj.* **thread′y.**—*adj.* **thread′like′.**

BROWN THRASHER (⅟₄)

THREADS (T) of a screw.

thread-bare (thrĕd′bâr′), *adj.* 1, worn down to the threads; shabby; as, *threadbare* upholstery; 2, hackneyed or worn-out; as, a *threadbare* plot.

threat (thrĕt), *n.* 1, the declaration of an intention to hurt or punish; as, he never carried out his *threats;* 2, a warning of coming evil or danger.

threat·en (thrĕt′n), *v.i.* to give notice of coming evil or danger:—*v.t.* 1, to warn of punishment or injury; as, the law *threatens* criminals with punishment; 2, to portend; give evidence of (a coming event or coming calamity); as, the clouds *threaten* a storm.—*adj.* **threat′en·ing.**—*adv.* **threat′-en·ing·ly.**

three (thrē), *adj.* composed of one more than two:—*n.* 1, the number consisting of two plus one; 2, a sign representing three units, as 3 or iii.

three—base hit, in baseball, a hit which allows the batter to reach third base.

three-fold (thrē′fōld′), *adj.* triple; in three layers, forms, etc.; consisting of three:— *adv.* (thre′fōld′), in a threefold manner; triply.

three-score (thrē′skôr′), *n.* three times twenty; sixty.

thresh (thrĕsh), *v.t.* 1, to beat out (grain) from the husk or (husks) from grain; 2, (usually *thrash*), to discuss thoroughly; 3, (usually *thrash*), to beat or flog:—*v.i.* 1, to beat out grain; 2, (usually *thrash*), to toss or move wildly.

thresh·er (thrĕsh′ẽr), *n.* 1, a person or a machine that threshes; 2, a large shark with a long tail: also called *thresher shark.*

thresh·old (thrĕsh′ōld; thrĕsh′hōld), *n.* 1, the stone, plank, or piece of timber under a door; a doorsill; 2, an entrance; the place or time of entrance; as, on the *threshold* of manhood.

threw (thrōō), past tense of *throw.*

thrice (thrīs), *adv.* 1, three times; 2, in a threefold manner or degree.

thrift (thrĭft), *n.* careful management; frugality; economy.

thrift·i·ly (thrĭf′tĭ-lĭ), *adv.* economically; in a thrifty manner.

thrift·less (thrĭft′lĕs), *adj.* extravagant; wasteful.—*n.* **thrift′less·ness.**

thrift·y (thrĭf′tĭ), *adj.* [thrift-i-er, thrift-i-est], 1, saving; not extravagant; 2, prosperous; thriving; also, growing well; flourishing; as, a *thrifty* plant.—*n.* **thrift′i·ness.** *Syn.* sparing, provident, prudent, chary.

thrill (thrĭl), *v.t.* to fill with intense emotion; stir deeply; as, the great actress *thrilled* her audience:—*v.i.* 1, to experience a sharp tingling sensation or a wave of emotion; as, they *thrilled* with delight; 2, to quiver; as, his voice *thrilled* with anger:—*n.* 1, a tingling, vibrating sensation; 2, a quiver of emotion.

thrive (thrīv), *v.i.* [*p.t.* throve (thrōv) or thrived, *p.p.* thrived or thriv-en (thrĭv′ĕn), *p.pr.* thriv-ing], 1, to prosper by industry, economy, and good management; 2, to increase or prosper in any way; succeed; 3, to grow sturdily; increase or flourish.

throat (thrōt), *n.* 1, the front part of the neck between the collarbone and the chin;

also, the passage through it; **2,** hence, a narrow entrance or passage; as, the *throat* of a cannon.

throat-latch (thrōt/lăch/), *n.* the part of a horse's bridle which passes under the throat. (See illustration under *harness*.)

throat-y (thrōt/ĭ), *adj.* [throat-i-er, throat-i-est], guttural; harsh; as, *throaty* sounds.

throb (thrŏb), *v.i.* [throbbed, throb-bing], **1,** to beat, as the pulse; sometimes, to beat with more than usual force; palpitate; **2,** hence, to thrill, as with joy:—*n.* **1,** a strong pulsation or beat; **2,** a thrill; as, a *throb* of joy.

throe (thrō), *n.* agony; violent pain; extreme anguish.

throne (thrōn), *n.* **1,** the chair of state of a king, bishop, or other high dignitary; **2,** sovereign or kingly power; also, one who holds sovereign power:—*v.t.* [throned, thron-ing], to place in a position of kingly power; raise to the throne.

throng (thrông), *n.* a multitude or great number; a crowd:—*v.t.* to crowd into; fill; as, soldiers *thronged* the streets:—*v.i.* to come in multitudes or great numbers.
Syn., *n.* mob, rabble, populace.

thros-tle (thrŏs/'l), *n.* a thrush.

throt-tle (thrŏt/'l), *v.t.* [throt-tled, throt-tling], **1,** to strangle or choke by pressure on the windpipe; **2,** to shut off fuel from; as, to *throttle* an engine:—*n.* a valve to control the supply of fuel to an engine.

through (thrōō), *prep.* **1,** from beginning to end; as, *through* life; *through* a tunnel; *through* thick and thin; **2,** into at one place and out of at another; as, to bore *through* a plank; **3,** in the midst of; as, to walk *through* the woods; **4,** by means of; as, *through* the influence of a friend; **5,** on account of; by reason of; as, he departed *through* fear of being discovered:—*adv.* **1,** from end to end, or from side to side; as, to drive a nail *through*; **2,** from the beginning to the end; as, he played the music *through*; **3,** to the end or to a conclusion; as, we will put the job *through*:—*adj.* **1,** extending from one place or point to another; as, a *through* passage; a *through* bolt; **2,** transporting passengers or freight from one place to another without stop or change of cars; as, a *through* train.

through-out (thrōō-out/), *adv.* everywhere; in every part; as, the jewelry is gold *throughout*:—*prep.* during; in every part of; as, *throughout* the year.

throve (thrōv), one form of the past tense of *thrive*.

throw (thrō), *v.t.* [*p.t.* threw (thrōō), *p.p.* thrown (thrōn), *p.pr.* throw-ing], **1,** to fling or hurl with the arm; pitch; toss; as,

to *throw* a stone; **2,** to give forth or cast; as, the lamp *threw* a faint light; she *threw* him a quick glance; **3,** to upset; to make (someone) fall in any way; as, his horse *threw* him; the wrestler *threw* his opponent; **4,** to put or place in a particular position, state, or the like; as, the fire *threw* the people into confusion:—*n.* **1,** the act of twirling, casting, or flinging; **2,** a cast of dice.
a stone's throw, the distance one can throw a stone; hence, a short distance; **throw cold water on,** to discourage by indifference or disapproval; **throw over,** *Colloquial*, to desert in favor of another; **throw up, 1,** to resign; **2,** to recall tauntingly; **3,** *Colloquial*, to vomit.

thrown (thrōn), past participle of *throw*.

thrum (thrŭm), *v.t.* [thrummed, thrumming], **1,** to play idly or listlessly on (a stringed musical instrument); to strum; **2,** to drum on or tap; as, he *thrummed* the table with his fingers:—*v.i.* **1,** to play idly on a stringed instrument; strum; **2,** to drum or tap on a table, board, or the like:—*n.* a monotonous tapping or drumming.

thrush (thrŭsh), *n.* any of a large family of songbirds, most often of plain color, but sometimes with spotted throat and breast.

thrust (thrŭst), *v.t.* [thrust, thrust-ing], **1,** to push or shove forcibly; as, he *thrust* me into the car; **2,** to pierce; as, their swords *thrust* him through:—*v.i.* to attack, with a pointed weapon; as, to *thrust* with a dagger:—*n.* **1,** a violent or sudden push; **2,** a stab; as, the *thrust* of a sword.
Syn., *v.* force, press.

WOOD THRUSH (¼)

thud (thŭd), *n.* a dull sound:—*v.i.* [thudded, thud-ding], to make a dull sound; to strike so as to make a dull sound; as, the apples *thudded* on the ground.

thug (thŭg), *n.* an assassin; a ruffian.

thumb (thŭm), *n.* **1,** the thickest finger of the human hand, consisting of two joints only; **2,** the part of a glove which covers the thumb:—*v.t.* **1,** to turn rapidly with the thumb, as leaves of a book; **2,** to rub or soil with the thumb or by handling; as, his new book is already *thumbed*; **3,** to ask for or obtain (a ride) by signaling with the thumb

THUMBSCREW

thumb-screw (thŭm/skrōō/), *n.* **1,** a screw with a flattened head, made so that it can be turned by the forefinger and thumb; **2,** an old instrument of torture for squeezing the thumb.

---

go; join; yet; sing; chin; show; thin, *th*en; hw, *why*; zh, azure; ü, Ger. *für* or Fr. *lune*; ö, Ger. schön or Fr. *feu*; ṅ, Fr. *enfant*, nom; kh, Ger. *ach* or *ich*. See pages ix–x.

thump (thŭmp), *n.* **1,** a hard, heavy blow; as, he hit him a *thump* on the back; **2,** a heavy fall, or the sound of it; as, the man fell with a *thump:—v.t.* to pound; strike or beat with dull, heavy blows; as, he *thumped* the door:—*v.i.* to pound or throb, as the heart.

thun·der (thŭn′dẽr), *n.* **1,** the noise which is heard immediately after a flash of lightning; **2,** any similar loud noise; as, the *thunder* of the guns:—*v.i.* **1,** to send forth peals of thunder; **2,** to send forth a sound like thunder; as, the sea *thundered* against the rocks.—*adj.* **thun′der·ous.**

thun·der·bolt (thŭn′dẽr-bōlt′), *n.* **1,** a flash of lightning accompanied by a clap of thunder; **2,** something swift, sudden, and terrible, like lightning and thunder; as, the news of the bank's failure was a *thunderbolt.*

thun·der·clap (thŭn′dẽr-klăp′), *n.* the quick, sharp, crashing noise heard immediately after a flash of lightning.

thun·der·cloud (thŭn′dẽr-kloud′), *n.* a dark, heavy cloud charged with electricity, which produces a thunderstorm.

thun·der·show·er (thŭn′dẽr-shou′ẽr), *n.* a brief fall of rain, accompanied by thunder and lightning.

thun·der·storm (thŭn′dẽr-stôrm′), *n.* a downpour of rain, accompanied by thunder and lightning.

thun·der·struck (thŭn′dẽr-strŭk′), *adj.* astonished; struck dumb, as by terror.

Thurs., Thur., or **Th.** abbreviation for *Thursday.*

Thurs·day (thûrz′dĭ), *n.* the fifth day of the week.

thus (thŭs), *adv.* **1,** in this or that manner; as, write it *thus;* **2,** to this degree or extent; as, *thus* far; **3,** so; therefore; as, *thus* we see that plants need light.

thwack (thwăk), *v.t.* to strike with something flat and heavy; thump:—*n.* a heavy blow with something flat; a thump.

thwart (thwôrt), *adj.* situated or placed across something:— *n.* a rower's seat in a boat, extending from side to side:— *v.t.* to oppose; baffle; outwit; as, to *thwart* an enemy.

    Syn., v. frustrate, hinder.

thy (thī), *Archaic* or *Poetic,* a possessive form of the personal pronoun *thou:* belonging or relating to thee; as, honor *thy* father and *thy* mother.

THYME

thyme (tīm), *n.* an herb with small aromatic leaves, used for seasoning.

thy·mus (thī′mŭs), *n.* **1,** in infants, a gland located at the base of the throat, which gradually wastes away until it disappears; **2,** a similar gland in animals: called *sweetbread* in the lamb and calf.

thy·roid (thī′roid), *n.* a large gland located in the neck. It has an important effect upon growth and development. An enlargement of the thyroid is known as *goiter.*

thy·self (thī-sĕlf′), *pron.* an emphatic or reflexive form of *thee* and *thou;* as, thou *thyself* must be the judge; know *thyself.*

ti (tē), *n.* in music, the seventh note of the scale: formerly called *si.*

ti·ar·a (tī-âr′à; tē-ä′rà), *n.* **1,** the triple crown worn by the Pope; **2,** a coronet for the head; as, a *tiara* of diamonds.

TIARA, def. 2

Ti·ber (tī′bẽr), a river in central Italy, on which is located the city of Rome (map 1).

Ti·be·ri·as, Sea of (tī-bē′-rĭ-ăs), a sea in Palestine. See **Galilee.**

Ti·bet (tĭ-bĕt′; tĭb′ĕt), a country (cap. Lhasa), a dependency of China, in the southern portion of Central Asia (map 15). —*adj.* **Ti·bet′an.**

tib·i·a (tĭb′ĭ-à), *n.* [*pl.* tibiae (tĭb′ĭ-ē) or tibias], the inner and larger of the two bones of the leg, extending from knee to ankle; the shin bone.—*adj.* **tib′i·al.**

tic (tĭk), *n.* a twitching of the muscles, especially of the face.

¹tick (tĭk), *v.i.* to make a slight, quick, regularly repeated sound; as, a watch *ticks:—v.t.* **1,** to mark or check off with dots or other small marks; as, he *ticked* each item as he came to it; **2,** to mark off (time) by repeated ticking sounds, as does a clock:—*n.* **1,** a light, repeated ticking sound; **2,** time shown by the sound made by a clock; an instant; as, I'll do it in a *tick;* **3,** a tiny mark, as a dot, check, or the like, used in checking off, or in marking something for attention.

²TICK, def. 2
Sheep tick,
enlarged.

²tick (tĭk), *n.* **1,** a tiny, blood-sucking spider which attaches itself to the skin of man and other animals; **2,** an insect which attaches itself to the skin of animals and sucks their blood; as, the bat *tick;* sheep *tick.*

²TICK, def. 1
Cattle tick,
enlarged.

³tick (tĭk), *n.* the strong cloth case or cover which contains the feathers or other filling of a mattress, pillow, etc.

tick·er (tĭk′ẽr), *n.* **1,** one who checks or marks off; or that which makes a light, clicking sound; **2,** a telegraphic instrument which automatically prints, on a strip of paper, stock quotations and other market or general news.

tick-et (tĭk′ĕt), *n.* **1,** a certificate or card which entitles the holder to certain stated privileges, such as admission to an entertainment, transportation by rail or boat, etc.; **2,** a small card stating price, size, etc., of goods; a label or tag; **3,** a list of candidates to be voted for; as, the Democratic *ticket:—v.t.* to mark by a label.

tick-ing (tĭk′ĭng), *n.* a strong, closely woven cloth, used to make cases or covers for mattresses, pillows, etc.

tick-le (tĭk′l), *v.t.* [tick-led, tick-ling], **1,** to touch lightly so as to produce a peculiar nervous tingle; **2,** to please or amuse; as, your speech *tickled* me:—*v.i.* to feel a tingling sensation; as, my ear *tickles:—n.* a peculiar thrill or tingle, or the touch causing this sensation.

tick-ler coil (tĭk′lẽr), in radio, a coil used to intensify the sound. (See illustration under *radio.*)

tick-lish (tĭk′lĭsh), *adj.* **1,** easily tickled; **2,** delicate to handle or cope with; as, a *ticklish* problem; **3,** risky; unstable; unsteady; as, *ticklish* footing; **4,** of persons, oversensitive; touchy; easily disturbed; as, she is *ticklish* on that point.—*n.* **tick′lish-ness.**—*adv.* **tick′lish-ly.**

Ti-con-der-o-ga (tī-kŏn′dẽr-ō′gà), an historic fort on Lake Champlain (map 6).

tid-al (tīd′ăl), *adj.* pertaining to, or affected by, the tide; as, a *tidal* river; *tidal* flats.

tid-bit (tĭd′bĭt′), *n.* a choice bit; titbit. See **titbit.**

tide (tīd), *n.* **1,** time; season; used especially in combination; as, Easter*tide;* spring*tide;* **2,** the regular rise and fall twice every day of the oceans and the bodies of water connected with them, due to the unequal attraction of the sun and the moon on the waters; **3,** anything which increases and decreases, like the tide; as, the economic *tide:—v.t.* [tid-ed, tid-ing], **1,** to carry along with the current or tide; **2,** to help (a person) along; assist in time of need; as, this money will *tide* him along until he gets a job.

tide-wa-ter (tīd′wô′tẽr), *n.* **1,** water affected by the rise and fall of the tide; **2,** land bordered by such water.

ti-dings (tī′dĭngz), *n.pl.* news; information; a message; as, glad *tidings.*

ti-dy (tī′dĭ), *adj.* [ti-di-er, ti-di-est], **1,** trim; neat; orderly; **2,** *Colloquial,* considerable; as, a *tidy* sum of money:—*v.t.* and *v.i.* [tidied, tidy-ing], to make neat; put things in proper order:—*n.* an ornamental,

removable cover for protecting the back or arms of a chair.—*n.* **ti′di-ness.**
Syn., adj. cleanly, prim, dapper.

tie (tī), *v.t.* [tied, ty-ing], **1,** to attach by a cord or rope drawn together and knotted; as, to *tie* a tag to a box; to *tie* flowers in a bunch; **2,** to bind together the parts of, by a cord that is drawn up and knotted; as, to *tie* a shoe; **3,** to make a knot or bow in; as, to *tie* a scarf; also, to form (a knot, bow, etc.) by looping and securing the ends of a cord or rope; **4,** to restrict or limit; as, his business *ties* him down; **5,** to equal in score; make the same score as; as, we *tied* the other team in football; **6,** in music, to unite (two notes) by a curved line:—*v.i.* **1,** to form a bow or knot; as, the sash *ties* in the back; **2,** to make the same score:— *n.* **1,** something, as a band, rope, or ribbon, used to bind, draw, or fasten together; **2,** a plank or rod to which the rails of a railroad track are attached; **3,** something tied, as a ribbon, and used as a fastening or ornament; especially, a necktie; **4,** a relationship or connection; as, business *ties;* **5,** a common interest which unites; as, a strong family *tie;* **6,** equality of numbers, as of votes; equal scores in a contest, race, etc.; **7,** in music, a curved line

TIE, def. 7

[⌢] connecting two notes of the same pitch, to indicate that only the first note is to be sung or played but that this note is to be held the length of the two notes.

Tien-tsin (tyĕn′tsēn′), a treaty port in northern China (map 15).

tier (tēr), *n.* a row or rank; especially, one of a set of such rows arranged one above the other; as, a *tier* of seats in a theater.

tierce (tērs), *n.* a cask, between a barrel and a hogshead in size.

Tier-ra del Fue-go (tyĕr′rä dĕl fwä′gō), a group of islands at the southern extremity of South America, separated from the mainland by the Strait of Magellan (map 11).

tiff (tĭf), *n.* **1,** a fit of anger; huff; **2,** a slight quarrel; disagreement.

Tif-lis (tĭf′lĭs; tĭf-lēs′), a city, capital of the Georgian Soviet Socialist Republic in the southern U.S.S.R. (map 12).

ti-ger (tī′gẽr), *n.* a large, fierce Asiatic beast of prey of the cat family, having yellow fur with black cross stripes.—*n.fem.* **ti′gress.**

ti-ger bee-tle, a beetle which eats flesh, lives in dry or sandy places, and flies very rapidly. (See illustration at *antenna.*)

ti-ger lil-y, a lily which bears orange-colored flowers spotted with black.

tight (tīt), *adj.* **1,** not loose; fastened

firmly; as, a *tight* knot; compact; as, a *tight* weave; 2, closely built, so that water or other liquid cannot pass through; as, a *tight* barrel; 3, fitting close to a part of the body, usually too close for comfort; as, a *tight* glove; 4, taut or stretched; as, a *tight*rope; 5, not easily obtained; not plentiful; as, during a depression, money is *tight*; 6, *Colloquial*, stingy:—*adv.* tightly; firmly; as, he closed the window *tight*:— **tights**, *n.pl.* close-fitting garments for the lower part of the body, worn by actors, acrobats, etc.—*adv.* **tight/ly.**—*n.* **tight/ness.**

   Syn., *adj.* fast, secure, firm.

tight-en (tīt/n), *v.t.* and *v.i.* to make or become tight; as, to *tighten* a screw.

tight-rope (tīt/rōp/), *n.* a taut or stretched rope or cable on which acrobats balance themselves while performing.

TIGHTROPE
Acrobat walking tightrope with aid of a balancing pole.

Ti-gris (tī/grĭs), a river in Asiatic Turkey and Iraq, emptying into the Euphrates River (map 15).

til-de (tĭl/dĕ; tĭl/dĭ), *n.* 1, a mark [~] used, as in *señor, cañon,* etc., to indicate that the *n* should be pronounced like the *ni* in onion; 2, in this book, a mark used over *e* to indicate an intermediate or characterless pronunciation, as in writĕr, thĕ boy.

tile (tīl), *n.* 1, a thin slab of baked clay, stone, etc., used for roofing, floors, wall decoration, etc.; 2, a pipe made of baked clay and used as a drain:—*v.t.* [tiled, til-ing], to cover with tiles.

ROOF OF TILES

¹**till** (tĭl), *n.* a money drawer.

²**till** (tĭl), *prep.* to the time of; as far as; as, wait *till* one o'clock:—*conj.* 1, until; to the time when; as, wait *till* I return; 2, before; unless; as, he won't come *till* you call him.

³**till** (tĭl), *v.t.* to prepare for seed, as by plowing; cultivate; as, to *till* the soil.—*n.* **till/er.**—*adj.* **till/a-ble.**

till-age (tĭl/ĭj), *n.* 1, the act or art of tilling land; 2, land under cultivation.

till-er (tĭl/ĕr), *n.* a steering lever for turning the rudder of a vessel.

TILLER
a, rudder; *b,* tiller.

tilt (tĭlt), *v.i.* 1, to lean or tip; keel over; 2, to fight or make a charge on horseback,

armed with a lance:—*v.t.* to raise at one end; tip; as, to *tilt* a stone:—*n.* 1, the act of tipping; the state of being tipped; as, the *tilt* of her head; 2, that which slopes; an incline; 3, a military combat between opponents on horseback armed with lances or spears with which each one tries to unhorse the other.

tilth (tĭlth), *n.* 1, the act or science of cultivating land; 2, cultivated land.

tim-ber (tĭm/bĕr), *n.* 1, wood suitable for carpentry, shipbuilding, etc.; 2, a large thick piece of wood prepared for use; 3, wooded land from which timber may be obtained:—*v.t.* to furnish or construct with timber.

tim-bered (tĭm/bĕrd), *adj.* 1, built with timber, or with a timber framework; 2, covered with trees; wooded; as, *timbered* land.

tim-ber hitch, a kind of knot used to fasten a rope end to a spar. (See illustration under *knot.*)

tim-bre (tĭm/bĕr; *French* tȧnbr/), *n.* the quality, or tone character, by which one voice or instrument is recognized as differing from another.

tim-brel (tĭm/brĕl), *n.* a small drum or tambourine.

time (tīm), *n.* 1, the moment when something happens or occurs; as, his father was away at the *time* of the fire; 2, the period during which something is going on; as, the play continued for two hours' *time;* 3, the regular or appointed hour when something is supposed to begin, take place, or end; as, it is *time* for lunch; 4, the proper moment for something to happen; opportunity; as, this is the *time* for you to buy a new bicycle; 5, a definite or precise moment as shown by a clock; as, the *time* for his departure is five o'clock; 6, a period with more or less definite limits; an age; as, in the *time* of Julius Caesar; ancient *times;* 7, a period marked by definite physical characteristics; as, summer*time;* day*time;* 8, a period characterized by special qualities, experiences, or conditions; as, to have a good *time;* hard *times;* 9, the period required or consumed in performing an action; as, the winner's *time* was 11.5 seconds; 10, one of a series of repeated actions; as, do this exercise five *times;* 11, the lapse or passing of all the days, months, and years, taken as a whole; as, *time* will make him forget; 12, a system of reckoning or measuring the passage of hours, days, etc.; as, solar *time;* standard *time;* 13, the rate at which something is done; as, to run in double-quick *time;* 14, in music, the arrangement of the rhythmic beats of a composition into equal measures included be-

āte, âorta, râre, căt, ȧsk, fär, ăllow, sofȧ; ēve, ĕvent, ĕll, writĕr, novĕl; bīte, pĭn; nō, ōbey, ôr, dŏg, tŏp, cŏllide; ūnit, ūnite, bûrn, cŭt, focŭs; nōon, fŏŏt; mound; coin;

tween successive bars; as, two-four *time;* also, the tempo at which a passage or composition should be, or is, played; **15,** a period long enough for something to be done; as, I have no *time* to finish this work; **16, times,** an indication that one number is to be multiplied by another: often used in place of the multiplication sign (×); as, five *times* two is ten:—*v.t.* [timed, tim-ing], **1,** to adapt to the occasion; arrange the time of; as, I will *time* my visit to suit your convenience; **2,** to regulate; as, to *time* the speed of a machine; **3,** to find out or record the speed of; as, to *time* a runner.

time–hon-ored (tīm′-ŏn′ērd), *adj.* respected because of age or long usage.

time-keep-er (tīm′kēp′ēr), *n.* one who or that which keeps, records, regulates, or indicates time.

time-ly (tīm′lĭ), *adj.* [time-li-er, time-li-est], suitable to the moment or occasion; well-timed; as, *timely* help.—*n.* **time′li-ness.**

time-piece (tīm′pēs′), *n.* any instrument that records the time; a clock or watch.

time-ta-ble (tīm′tā′bl), *n.* a systematically arranged list of the dates and hours for events; especially, a list of trains, boats, etc., with their times of arrival and departure from various stations.

tim-id (tĭm′ĭd), *adj.* shy; wanting in courage.—*adv.* **tim′id-ly.**
   Syn. afraid, diffident, timorous.

ti-mid-i-ty (tĭ-mĭd′ĭ-tĭ), *n.* want of courage; shyness.

tim-ing (tīm′ĭng), *n.* regulation or adjustment of the time or of the rate of speed at which anything is done or produced; as, the *timing* of a blow; the *timing* of a spark in a gas engine.

tim-or-ous (tĭm′ēr-ŭs), *adj.* **1,** fearful of danger; lacking in courage; timid; as, a *timorous* cur; **2,** expressing fear or alarm; as, a *timorous* look.
   Syn. shy, afraid, diffident.

tim-o-thy (tĭm′ŏ-thĭ), *n.* a valuable grass with long, closely packed flower spikes, used for hay: also called *timothy grass.*

Tim-o-thy (tĭm′ŏ-thĭ), in the Bible, a companion and follower of Saint Paul, to whom Paul wrote two epistles, or letters, known as *First* and *Second Timothy;* also, either of these Epistles.

tin (tĭn), *n.* **1,** a silvery-white, soft metal from which many useful articles are made, such as boxes, cans, and pans; **2,** thin plates of iron or steel covered with this metal; **3,** ware made of tin plate:—*v.t.* [tinned, tin-ning], **1,** to cover with tin, or with tinned iron; **2,** in Great Britain, to preserve in tins, as food.

tinc-ture (tĭngk′tŭr), *n.* **1,** a medicinal

substance in an alcoholic solution; as, *tincture* of iodine; **2,** a small amount; touch; as, a *tincture* of hope:—*v.t.* [tinctured, tinctur-ing], to color; tinge; imbue.

tin-der (tĭn′dēr), *n.* any material which catches fire easily, especially when used to kindle a fire from a spark.

tin-der-box (tĭn′dēr-bŏks′), *n.* a metal box designed to hold the tinder and, usually, the flint and steel, formerly used in kindling a fire.

TINDERBOX

a, flint; *b,* steel; *c,* tinder; *d,* tinderbox; *e,* lid; *f,* candlestick and candle; *g,* extinguisher.

tine (tīn), *n.* a tooth or spike; prong.

tin foil, tin, or tin and lead, rolled into very thin sheets, and used as a wrapping for candy, tobacco, etc.

tinge (tĭnj), *v.t.* [tinged, tinge-ing or ting-ing], **1,** to stain slightly with color; dye faintly; **2,** to give a certain characteristic flavor or quality to; as, envy *tinged* all his remarks:—*n.* **1,** a slight degree of some color; tint; **2,** a touch; trace; as, there was a *tinge* of sarcasm in his remarks.

TINES (T) of a fork

tin-gle (tĭng′gl), *v.i.* [tin-gled, tin-gling], to feel or have a stinging sensation or pricking pain; as, his fingers *tingled* with the cold:—*n.* a stinging sensation or pain, as from cold or a slap.

tink-er (tĭngk′ēr), *n.* **1,** a mender of metal pots, kettles, etc.; **2,** a person able to do almost any kind of small repairing:—*v.t.* to mend, especially in a bungling way; to patch:—*v.i.* **1,** to try in a bungling way to mend metalware; **2,** to work at anything in a bungling or careless manner.

tin-kle (tĭng′kl), *n.* a small, quick, sharp, ringing sound; as, the *tinkle* of a bell:—*v.i.* and *v.t.* [tin-kled, tin-kling], to make or cause to make such a sound.

tin-ny (tĭn′ĭ), *adj.* [tin-ni-er, tin-ni-est], **1,** pertaining to, or containing, tin; **2,** having a flat taste, as of tin; **3,** having a thin, metallic sound; as, a *tinny* piano.

tin plate, thin sheet iron or steel coated with tin.

tin-sel (tĭn′sĕl), *n.* **1,** a fabric originally of silk, or silk and wool, covered or woven with gold and silver threads; **2,** strips of glittering, metallic material, used as an inexpensive trimming, as for Christmas trees; **3**, something showy but of little value; hence, false show; pretense:—*v.t.* [tinseled, tinsel-ing], to decorate with, or as with, tinsel.

tin-smith (tĭn′smĭth′), *n.* one who makes or deals in tinware.

tint (tĭnt), *n.* **1**, a slight coloring; a pale tinge; as, just a *tint* of gold in the hair; **2**, a delicate or pale color or a pale tinge of a color; as, her dress and shoes were different *tints* of blue:—*v.t.* to give a slight coloring to.

Syn., *n.* dye, stain, shade.

tin-tin-nab-u-la-tion (tĭn′tĭ-năb′ū-lā′-shŭn), *n.* a tinkling, as of bells.

tin-ware (tĭn′wâr′), *n.* articles, especially household articles, made of tin plate.

ti-ny (tī′nĭ), *adj.* [ti-ni-er, ti-ni-est], very small; wee.

-tion (-shŭn), a suffix meaning: **1**, the act or process of; as, assump*tion;* **2**, the condition or state of; as, atten*tion;* **3**, that which performs the action of; as, decep*tion;* **4**, the result of; as, prescrip*tion*. In many words *-tion* can have more than one of these meanings, as in descrip*tion*.

¹**tip** (tĭp), *n.* **1**, the point or end of anything; as, the *tip* of a finger; **2**, a small piece or part attached to the end of a thing; as, the *tip* of a cane:—*v.t.* [tipped, tip-ping], **1**, to form or put a point on; **2**, to cover the end of.

²**tip** (tĭp), *v.t.* [tipped, tip-ping], **1**, to slant or tilt; raise at one end or side; as, to *tip* a chair; **2**, to overturn; cause to lose balance; as, to *tip* a vase over; **3**, to raise (one's hat) in greeting:—*v.i.* to lean, slant, or fall over; as, the boat *tipped* dangerously.

³**tip** (tĭp), *v.t.* [tipped, tip-ping], **1**, to strike or hit lightly; to give a slight blow to; as, his bat just *tipped* the ball; **2**, *Colloquial,* to give a private hint to; as, *tip* me off on this race; **3**, to give a small present to for service; as, to *tip* a waiter:—*v.i.* to give a fee or present, as to a servant:—*n.* **1**, a light blow or tap; **2**, a present, as to a servant; **3**, a friendly hint; secret or advance information.

tip-pet (tĭp′ĕt), *n.* a neck scarf or small shoulder cape made of fur, wool, or other warm material.

tip-ple (tĭp′l), *v.i.* [tip-pled, tip-pling], to drink liquor habitually but in small amounts; also, to sip liquor:—*v.t.* to drink (liquor), especially in small amounts:—*n.* liquor; drink.—*n.* **tip′pler.**

tip-sy (tĭp′sĭ), *adj.* [tip-si-er, tip-si-est], almost drunk; unsteady or foolish from the effect of liquor.

tip-toe (tĭp′tō′), *n.* the end or point of a toe or the toes:—**on tiptoe,** on the tips of the toes; hence, alert; expectant:—*v.i.* [tiptoed, tiptoe-ing], to walk or stand on the balls of the toes; walk softly; as, the nurse *tiptoed* down the hall.

tip-top (tĭp′tŏp′), *n.* the highest point or degree; the best of anything:—*adj.* **1**, at the highest point or degree; **2**, *Colloquial,* fine; without equal.

ti-rade (tī′rād; tĭ-rād′), *n.* a violent, abusive speech.

Ti-ra-na (tē-rä′nä), a city, the capital and chief city of Albania (map **12**).

¹**tire** (tīr), *n.* a band or hoop of steel or rubber, which is placed on the rim of a wheel of an automobile, wagon, carriage, etc.: —*v.t.* [tired, tir-ing], to furnish (a wheel) with a tire.

²**tire** (tīr), *v.t.* [tired, tir-ing], to exhaust or wear out the strength, interest, or patience of; as, hard work *tired* him:—*v.i.* to become physically weary; as, he *tires* easily.

tired (tīrd), *adj.* weary; exhausted; fatigued; as, a *tired* mother.

tire-less (tīr′lĕs), *adj.* unwearying; not to be wearied; as, *tireless* hands.—*adv.* **tire′-less-ly.**

tire-some (tīr′sŭm), *adj.* wearisome; tedious; as, a *tiresome* journey; also, annoying; boring; as, *tiresome* talk.—*adv.* **tire′some-ly.**—*n.* **tire′some-ness.**

Syn. fatiguing, irksome, troublesome.

Tir-ol (tĭr′ŏl; tē-rōl′), an Alpine province (cap. Innsbruck) of western Austria. Also spelled **Tyr′ol.**

Tir-pitz (tĭr′pĭts), Alfred von (1849–1930), a German statesman and admiral in the World War.

'tis (tĭz), a contraction of *it is.*

tis-sue (tĭsh′ū; tĭsh′ōō), *n.* **1**, a woven fabric or cloth, especially thin, transparent silk material; fine cloth or gauze; **2**, the cells and connecting parts that form the structure and substance of any part of an animal or plant; as, bone *tissue;* **3**, a web or network; as, a *tissue* of lies:—**tissue paper,** very thin, gauzelike paper used to wrap up delicate articles, protect engravings, etc.

tit (tĭt), *n.* any one of several small birds, especially the titmouse.

Ti-tan (tī′tăn), *n.* in Greek mythology, one of the giant gods, including Prometheus and Atlas, who at one time ruled the world

TIRE
Section of pneumatic automobile tire. A, rubber shoe with raised tread; B, fabric; C, inner tube; D, valve stem; E, valve cap.

āte, âorta, râre, căt, åsk, fär, ăllow, sofá; ēve, ĕvent, ĕll, writēr, novĕl; bīte, pĭn; nō, ōbey, ôr, dŏg, tŏp, cŏllide; ūnit, ūnite, bûrn, cŭt, focŭs; nōon, fŏŏt; mound; coin;

but were overthrown by the Olympian gods:—**titan**, a person of giant strength.

Ti-ta-ni-a (tǐ-tā′nǐ-à; tǐ-tā′nǐ-à), *n.* the wife of Oberon and queen of the fairies in Shakespeare's "A Midsummer Night's Dream."

ti-tan-ic (tī-tăn′ĭk), *adj.* huge; of enormous strength or size.

tit-bit (tĭt′bĭt′), *n.* **1,** a small bit or choice morsel of food; **2,** hence, a choice bit, as of gossip. Also spelled **tid′bit′** (tĭd′bĭt′).

tit for tat, blow for blow; a fair return.

tithe (tīth), *n.* **1,** the tenth part of anything; especially, the tenth part of one's income or possessions given to the support of the church; **2,** loosely, any small part:— *v.t.* [tithed, tith-ing], **1,** to grant or pay a tenth of, especially to the support of the church; **2,** to impose tithes upon.

Ti-tian (tĭsh′ăn), (1477–1576), a famous Venetian painter.

Ti-ti-ca-ca (tē′tē-kä′kä), a lake on the boundary between Bolivia and Peru (map 11).

tit-il-late (tĭt′ǐ-lāt), *v.t.* [titillat-ed, titillat-ing], to tickle; also, to rouse pleased excitement in.—*n.* **tit′il-la′tion.**

tit-lark (tĭt′lärk′), *n.* a small songbird, resembling the lark; a pipit.

ti-tle (tī′tl), *n.* **1,** the name of a book, poem, play, etc.; **2,** a designation of dignity, rank, or distinction, generally used in front of a person's name; **3,** a claim or right; as, a *title* to respect; **4,** the legal right to property, especially real estate; as, a *title* to land; also, the paper giving such right:—*v.t.* [ti-tled, ti-tling], to entitle; give a name to:— **titled,** having a title, especially of nobility.

title page, the page at the beginning of a book, giving its name, author, publisher, etc.

ti-tlist (tī′tlĭst), *n.* the holder of the championship; as, the *titlist* in a tennis tournament.

tit-mouse (tĭt′mous′), *n.* [*pl.* titmice (tĭt′mīs′)], any one of a number of small songbirds, including the chickadee, the tufted titmouse, etc.

TITMOUSE (⅓)

Ti-to (tē′tō), Marshal (1891–   ), (real name *Josip Broz*) premier of Yugoslavia.

tit-ter (tĭt′ẽr), *v.i.* to laugh or giggle in a suppressed fashion:—*n.* a suppressed giggle.

tit-tle (tĭt′l), *n.* **1,** a very small part or particle; **2,** a mark over a letter to distinguish it in form or pronunciation, as the dot over the j.

tit-tle—tat-tle (tĭt′l=tăt′l), *n.* trifling talk; senseless chatter; gossip:—*v.i.* [tittle-tattled, tittle-tat-tling], to gossip.

tit-u-lar (tĭt′ū-lẽr), *adj.* **1,** pertaining to a title; **2,** existing in name or title only; having the honors but not the duties of an office or rank; as, a king is often only the *titular* head of a nation.

Ti-tus (tī′tŭs), **1,** in the Bible, a disciple of Paul; also, a book of the New Testament containing the epistle written by Paul to Titus; **2,** (40-81), a Roman emperor who conquered Jerusalem.

TNT or **T.N.T.** abbreviation for *trinitrotoluene, trinitrotoluol.*

to (tōō; when not emphatic, tŏō), *prep.* **1,** in the direction of; toward; as, on my way *to* work; the earth turns from west *to* east; **2,** as far as; so as to arrive at or be in; as, he came *to* my office today; **3,** opposite; as, face *to* face; compared with; as, the score was six *to* four; **4,** into the possession of; as, give the book *to* John; **5,** in agreement or harmony with; as, words set *to* music; true *to* life; **6,** fitting; for; as, a key *to* the car; ten pounds *to* a bag; a room *to* himself; **7,** within the scope of; as, *to* my knowledge he has not come; **8,** till or until; as, I shall stay *to* midnight; before; as, ten minutes *to* five:—used to introduce an infinitive: **a,** in a noun construction; as, she began *to* sing; *to* err is human; **b,** expressing purpose; as, we work *to* succeed; **c,** completing the meaning of a preceding adjective or noun; as, fit *to* wear:—*adv.* **1,** in or into a position or contact; as, the wind blew the door *to;* **2,** to the normal position or condition; as, she came *to* slowly:—**to and fro,** back and forth.

toad (tōd), *n.* a tailless, leaping, froglike animal, which breeds in water, but lives on land and eats worms, flies, etc.

toad-stool (tōd′stōōl′), *n.* any umbrella-shaped fungus which grows on decaying matter; especially, a poisonous mushroom.

TOAD (⅓)

toad-y (tō′dĭ), *n.* [*pl.* toadies], one who caters to the rich or powerful for the sake of gain or favor:—*v.t.* and *v.i.* [toadied, toady-ing], to flatter in order to gain reward.

¹**toast** (tōst), *n.* sliced bread browned by heat:—*v.t.* **1,** to brown or heat at a fire; as, to *toast* bread; **2,** to heat or warm thoroughly; as, *toast* your hands at the fire. —*n.* **toast′er.**

²**toast** (tōst), *n.* **1,** the act of drinking or proposing a drink in honor of some person or thing; as, they called for a *toast* to the winner; **2,** the person or thing toasted; as, she was the *toast* of the evening:—*v.t.* to drink or propose a toast to.

toast-mas-ter (tōst′mȧs′tẽr), *n.* a person who presides at a dinner, proposing the toasts and introducing the speakers.

to-bac-co (tō-băk′ō), *n.* [*pl.* tobaccos], **1,** a large-leaved plant with pink or white trumpet-shaped flowers; **2,** the dried leaves of this plant treated in various ways and used for smoking and chewing, or as snuff.

to-bog-gan (tō-bŏg′ăn), *n.* a kind of long, flat sled without runners, curving up at the front and often carrying four or more persons: used in winter sports: —*v.i.* to ride or coast on such a sled.

toc-sin (tŏk′sĭn), *n.* **1,** a bell for sounding an alarm; also, the sounding of the alarm; **2,** any alarm signal.

TOBACCO
Leaves and flowers.

to-day or **to—day** (tŏŏ-dā′), *adv.* **1,** on the present day; as, you must go *today;* **2,** in these times; as, *today* many people travel by airplane:—*n.* **1,** the present day; as, *today* is Tuesday; **2,** this present time or age; as, the fashions of *today* change fast.

tod-dle (tŏd′l), *v.i.* [tod-dled, tod-dling], to walk with short, uncertain steps.—*n.* **tod′dler.**

TOBOGGAN

tod-dy (tŏd′ĭ), *n.* [*pl.* toddies], **1,** a drink made of the sap of certain palm trees of East India; **2,** a sweetened mixture of liquor and hot water.

toe (tō), *n.* **1,** one of the five separate divisions or digits of the foot; **2,** the front of the foot, or of a stocking or other foot covering; as, he tore the *toe* of his sock; **3,** anything resembling a toe:—*v.t.* [toed, toe-ing], to touch, reach, or strike with the toe; as, to *toe* the mark in a race.

to-ga (tō′gȧ), *n.* [*pl.* togas], the loose outer garment worn in public by the citizens of ancient Rome.

to-geth-er (tŏŏ-gĕth′ẽr), *adv.* **1,** in company or association; as, to live *together;* **2,** without interruption; at a stretch; as, we talked for hours *together;* **3,** at the same time; simultaneously; as, the firecrackers exploded *together.*

tog-ger-y (tŏg′ẽr-ĭ), *n.* [*pl.* toggeries], *Colloquial,* clothes; dress.

togs (tŏgz), *n.pl.* clothes, especially for a particular use; as, tennis *togs.*

¹toil (toil), *v.i.* **1,** to work hard or long; labor; **2,** to move with difficulty; plod; trudge:—*n.* work or effort that exhausts the body or mind.—*n.* **toil′er.**

²toil (toil), *n.* **1,** *Archaic,* a trap, as of net or cord, for ensnaring game; **2, toils,** figuratively, a snare; as, in the *toils* of crime.

toi-let (toi′lĕt), *n.* **1,** the act or process of washing and dressing, arranging the hair, etc.; **2,** style of dress; also, a particular costume; **3,** in the U.S., a lavatory, especially one with a water closet; also, a water closet.

toi-let wa-ter, a fragrant liquid, milder than a perfume, used in the bath, or after bathing.

toil-some (toil′sŭm), *adj.* laborious; tiresome; wearisome.

to-ken (tō′kĕn), *n.* **1,** a mark, sign, symbol, representation, or indication; as, the four-leaf clover is a *token* of good luck; **2,** a memento; keepsake; as, the old locket was a *token* from her sister; **3,** a piece of metal used as money, the face value of which exceeds its real value; hence, any piece of currency, as a bill or note; **4,** a coinlike piece of metal issued at a fixed price and used in payment of a streetcar or railroad fare.

To-kyo or **To-kio** (tō′kyō), a city, the capital of Japan, situated on the southeast coast of the island of Honshu (map **15**).

told (tōld), past tense and past participle of *tell.*

To-le-do (tō-lē′dō), **1,** a manufacturing city in Ohio (map **7**); **2,** a city in central Spain (map **12**).

tol-er-a-ble (tŏl′ẽr-ȧ-bl), *adj.* **1,** capable of being suffered or endured; **2,** passable; fairly good.—*adv.* **tol′er-a-bly.**

tol-er-ance (tŏl′ẽr-ăns), *n.* willingness to bear with others whose views and opinions differ from one's own.

tol-er-ant (tŏl′ẽr-ănt), *adj.* willing or inclined to put up with views or opinions which are different from one's own.—*adv.* **tol′er-ant-ly.**

tol-er-ate (tŏl′ẽr-āt), *v.t.* [tolerat-ed, tolerat-ing], **1,** to permit to exist or continue without interference; endure; as, he could not *tolerate* their dishonesty any longer; **2,** in medicine, to be able to take (a drug or treatment) without evil effects.

tol-er-a-tion (tŏl′ẽr-ā′shŭn), *n.* the act of permitting to exist or continue without interference; especially, the recognition of the rights of the private individual to his own opinions and practices; as, religious *toleration.*

¹toll (tōl), *n.* **1,** a tax paid for some special privilege, as for using a bridge, highway, or canal; **2,** in telephoning, the charge made for a call.

Syn. custom, impost, assessment, duty.

²toll (tōl), *v.t.* **1,** to cause to sound with

slow strokes spaced at regular intervals; as, the sexton *tolls* the bell; **2,** to sound or strike; as, "the curfew *tolls* the knell of parting day":—*v.i.* to give forth a slow, regular, ringing sound, as a bell in announcing a death.

toll-gate (tōl′gāt′), *n.* a gate, as on a bridge or road, where toll is paid.

Tol-stoy (tŏl′stoi), Leo Nikolaevich, Count (1828–1910), a Russian novelist and social reformer.

tom-a-hawk (tŏm′à-hôk), *n.* a kind of hatchet or ax used by the North American

TOMAHAWK

Indians as a weapon in war and as a tool:—*v.t.* to strike, cut, or kill with a tomahawk.

to-ma-to (tō-mā′tō; tō-mä′tō), *n.* [*pl.* tomatoes], a garden plant with yellow flowers, and a red or yellow fruit which is used for food; also, the fruit.

tomb (tōōm), *n.* a grave or vault for the dead:—*v.t.* to put into a grave or vault.

TOMATO

tom-boy (tŏm′hoi), *n.* a girl who acts like a lively, noisy boy.

tomb-stone (tōōm′stōn′), *n.* a stone marking a grave.

tom-cat (tŏm′kăt′), *n.* a male cat.

tome (tōm), *n.* a book, especially a large, heavy book.

tom-fool-er-y (tŏm′fool′ĕr-ĭ), *n.* [*pl.* tom-fooleries], nonsense; silliness.

to-mor-row or **to-mor-row** (tōō-mŏr′ō), *n.* the day after the present day:—*adv.* on, or for, the morrow.

tom-tom (tŏm′-tŏm′), *n.* a primitive drum, often beaten with the hands: used in the East Indies and among most barbaric peoples.

ton (tŭn), *n.* any of various relatively large measures of weight; specifically, the weight of 2,240 pounds used in Great Britain, commonly called a *long ton*; the weight of 2,000 pounds, used in the U.S., Canada, etc., often called a *short ton*; or the weight of 2,204.6 pounds, called a *metric ton*.

TOM-TOM

ton-al (tōn′ăl), *adj.* pertaining to the character or quality of sound.

tone (tōn), *n.* **1,** a sound or the quality of

a sound; as, the loud *tones* of music; **2,** the voice, as expressive of feeling; as, she spoke in an imploring *tone*; **3,** one of the larger intervals in a musical scale, as that from C to D: preferably called *step*; **4,** normal or healthy condition; as, good muscular *tone*; **5,** the quality and harmony of the colors of a painting; **6,** a hue, tint, or shade of color; as, a gray *tone*; **7,** the general character or spirit; as, I did not like the *tone* of the letter:—*v.t.* [toned, ton-ing], **1,** to bring to a required shade or color; as, to *tone* a photographic print, a painting, etc.; **2,** to give a particular sound, character, etc., to:—*v.i.* to harmonize in color; as, the wallpaper *tones* with the curtains.

tong (tŏng), *n.* a Chinese secret society.

Ton-ga Is-lands (tŏng′gà), a group of about 180 islands east of Fiji in the south Pacific Ocean (map 16). They are also called *Friendly Islands*.

tongs (tŏngz), *n.pl.* a device with two arms joined by a hinge, used for grasping, lifting, etc.; as, sugar *tongs*; fire *tongs*.

tongue (tŭng), *n.* **1,** the muscular organ in the mouth, used in tasting, and also, in man, for speech; **2,** a language; as, his native *tongue*; **3,** manner of speaking; as, a sharp *tongue*; **4,** anything resembling a tongue in shape, position, or use, as the clapper or hammer of a bell, the point of a flame, the vibrating reed in the mouthpiece of some musical instruments, etc.:—*adj.* **tongue′less.**

ICE TONGS

Syn. speech, dialect.

tongue—tied (tŭng′-tīd′), *adj.* **1,** unable to speak clearly because of a defect of the tongue; **2,** hence, unable to speak normally because of fear, shyness, etc.

ton-ic (tŏn′ĭk), *adj.* **1,** tending to strengthen; bracing; as, the *tonic* effect of a high altitude; **2,** pertaining to sounds; **3,** in music, pertaining to the keynote:—*n.* **1,** a strengthening medicine; **2,** in music, the keynote of a scale or composition.

to-night or **to-night** (tōō-nīt′), *n.* the present night or the night of today:—*adv.* on, or during, the present or coming night.

ton-nage (tŭn′ĭj), *n.* **1,** the weight of goods carried in a ship; **2,** the carrying capacity of a vessel, stated in tons; **3,** the duty or toll on vessels, based on the burden carried; **4,** the entire shipping of any port or country, stated in tons.

ton-neau (tŭn-ō′; tô′nō′), *n.* [*pl.* tonneaus (tŭn-ōz′) or tonneaux (tŭn-ōz′; tô′nō′)], in certain automobiles, an enclosed part of the body containing the back seats and separated by a partition from the driver's seat.

go; join; yet; sing; chin; show; thin, *th*en; hw, *wh*y; zh, azure; ü, Ger. für or Fr. lune; ö, Ger. schön or Fr. feu; n̈, Fr. enfant, nom; kh, Ger. ach or ich. See pages ix–x.

ton·sil (tŏn′sĭl), *n.* a mass of tissue, on either side of the base of the tongue.—*n.* **ton′sil·li′tis** or **ton′sil·i′tis.**

ton·sure (tŏn′sher), *n.* **1,** the act of cutting the hair, or of shaving the crown, of the head, especially of persons entering the priesthood; **2,** the part of a monk's head left bare by such shaving:—*v.t.* [tonsured, tonsur-ing] to shave the crown of the head of; as, to *tonsure* a monk.

too (tōō), *adv.* **1,** also; likewise; as, he is going, *too;* **2,** more than enough; as, *too* long; **3,** so much more than enough as to be painful, intolerable, etc.; as, that is *too* annoying; **4,** *Colloquial,* exceedingly; very; as, I am *too* happy to see you.

took (tŏŏk), past tense of *take.*

tool (tōōl), *n.* **1,** an instrument used in doing work, especially one used with the hand, as a chisel, hammer, saw, etc.; **2,** a person used as the agent of another; as, Tom was William's *tool* in the scheme; **3,** anything used as a tool, as books, money, etc.:—*v.t.* **1,** to shape with a tool; **2,** to mark (leather) with a design pressed on it with a heated tool; **3,** to prepare machinery for specialty manufacture; as, to *tool* a factory for airplane production.

Syn., n. utensil, implement.

toot (tōōt), *v.t.* to cause (a horn, whistle, etc.) to sound:—*v.i.* to give forth short, quick sounds:—*n.* a short blast on a horn.

tooth (tōōth), *n.* [*pl.* teeth (tēth)], **1,** one of the hard, bony structures set in the jaws and used for biting and chewing, and sometimes for attacking and defending; **2,** any projection resembling a tooth, as on a gear wheel, a comb, a rake, or a saw:—*v.t.* **1,** to indent or form into jagged points; as, to *tooth* a saw; **2,** to supply with projections or teeth: **—by the skin of one's teeth,** narrowly; barely; **fight tooth and nail,** to fight with every bit of strength; **in the teeth of,** directly against; as, *in the teeth of* great odds, he won; **show one's teeth,** to bare the teeth, as a dog; hence, to threaten.

TOOTH
a, enamel covering crown; *b,* pulp; *c,* dentine; *d, d,* cement covering roots.

tooth-ache (tōōth′āk′), *n.* a pain in a tooth or in the teeth.

tooth-brush (tōōth′brŭsh′), *n.* [*pl.* toothbrushes], a brush for cleaning the teeth.

tooth-less (tōōth′lĕs), *adj.* without teeth.

tooth-pick (tōōth′pĭk′), *n.* a pointed piece of wood, a quill, or the like, used to clear the spaces between the teeth.

tooth-some (tōōth′sŭm), *adj.* pleasant to the taste; as, a *toothsome* bit of food.

¹**top** (tŏp), *n.* **1,** the highest part; summit; as, the *top* of a hill; **2,** the upper surface, side, or part, as of a table, a carriage, a shoe, or a page; **3,** head; upper end; as, the *top* of a street; **4,** the most important person, place, or rank; as, the *top* of his profession; **5,** the crown of the head; **6,** the part of a plant above the ground: used of plants with edible roots; **7,** the very highest step or degree; as, he has reached the *top* of his ambition; **8,** a small platform at the upper end of the lower mast of a ship:—*v.t.* [topped, topping], **1,** to put a cover on; cap; as, to *top* a box; to *top* a bottle; **2,** to be at the head of; as, she *tops* the list of graduates; **3,** to surmount; reach or go over the top of; as, to *top* a hill; **4,** to surpass; as, he *topped* his own record; **5,** to cut off the upper part of (a plant):—*v.i.* **1,** to rise to a height; tower; **2,** to excel; surpass:—*adj.* **1,** pertaining to the highest part; highest; as, the *top* shelf; **2,** highest in degree; greatest; as, at *top* speed.

²**top** (tŏp), *n.* a child's cone-shaped toy with a point on which it can be made to spin rapidly by means of a spring or string.

TOPS

to·paz (tō′păz), *n.* a mineral often used as a gem, varying in color from yellow to blue or green.

top-coat (tŏp′kōt′), *n.* a light, outer coat.

To·pe·ka (tô-pē′kȧ), a city, capital of Kansas (map **7**).

top·er (tōp′ẽr), *n.* one who drinks to excess; a drunkard.

top-gal-lant (tŏp′găl′ȧnt; tô-găl′ȧnt), *adj.* situated next above the topmast, or second section of the mast of a vessel; as, a *topgallant* sail:—*n.* such a mast or sail (see illustration on page 695).

top-ic (tŏp′ĭk), *n.* the subject of conversation, argument, literary composition, etc.: **—topic sentence,** a sentence which gives the principal or main thought of a paragraph, composition, or the like, generally near the beginning: also called *topical sentence.*

top-i-cal (tŏp′ĭ-kȧl), *adj.* **1,** of local or current interest; as, articles on *topical* subjects; **2,** pertaining to the topic or subject of a conversation, composition, etc.; as, a *topical* remark.—*adv.* **top′i-cal-ly.**

top-knot (tŏp′nŏt′), *n.* a tuft of hair on the head; a crest of feathers on a bird's head.

top-mast (tŏp′mȧst′; tŏp′mȧst), *n.* the second mast above the deck of a ship, erected on top of the mainmast, foremast, etc. (See illustration on page 695.)

top-most (tŏp′mōst), *adj.* highest; at the very top or summit.

āte, āorta, râre, căt, ȧsk, fär, ăllow, sofȧ; ēve, ēvent, ĕll, writẽr, novĕl; bīte, pĭn; nō, ōbey, ôr, dŏg, tŏp, cŏllide; ūnit, ūnite, bûrn, cŭt, focŭs; nōōn, fŏŏt; mound; coin;

to·pog·ra·phy (tŏ-pŏg′rȧ-fĭ), *n.* [*pl.* topographies], **1,** the surface features of the earth or of a particular region, including such physical characteristics as mountains, rivers, cities, communication routes, etc.; also, a detailed description or representation on a map of these features; **2,** the science which treats of such features; also, the science or art of making a map or other drawing on which the physical characteristics of a region are shown.

top·ple (tŏp′l), *v.t.* [top-pled, top-pling], to overturn:—*v.i.* to fall top foremost; as, the flagstaff *toppled* in the wind.

top·sail (tŏp′sāl′; tŏp′sl), *n.* **1,** the second sail from the deck of a square-rigged vessel (see illustration on page 695); **2,** a sail which is set above, or sometimes on, the gaff of a fore-and-aft-rigged vessel:—**topsail schooner,** a two-masted schooner with square-rigged topsails on the foremast (see illustration under *ship*).

top·sy–tur·vy (tŏp′sĭ-tûr′vĭ), *adv.* and *adj.* **1,** upside down; **2,** in confusion:—*n.* a state of upset or confusion.

toque (tōk), *n.* a woman's close-fitting hat with no projecting brim.

torch (tôrch), *n.* **1,** a light, made by burning wood, flax, or the like, carried at the end of a pole or handle; **2,** any of various devices which give out a flare or hot flame; as, a plumber's *torch.*

torch-light (tôrch′līt′), *n.* the light given by torches.

tore (tôr), past tense of *tear.*

tor·e·a·dor (tŏr′ĕ-ȧ-dôr′; tŏr′ĕ-ȧ-dôr′), *n.* a bullfighter, especially one who fights on horseback.

To·ri·no (tō-rē′nō), the Italian name for a city in northern Italy. See **Turin.**

tor·ment (tôr′mĕnt), *n.* **1,** extreme mental or physical suffering; **2,** that which causes pain or anguish:—*v.t.* (tôr-mĕnt′), **1,** to put to extreme pain of mind or body; torture; as, he was *tormented* with doubt and fear; **2,** to tease; annoy; as, he *tormented* his mother with questions.— *n.* **tor-men′tor;** **tor-ment′er.**

TOREADOR

torn (tôrn), past participle of *tear.*

tor·na·do (tôr-nā′dō), *n.* [*pl.* tornadoes], a violent storm of whirling, destructive wind, produced from a funnel-shaped cloud that travels rapidly along a narrow path.

To·ron·to (tō-rŏn′tō), a city, capital of Ontario, Canada (map **4**).

tor·pe·do (tôr-pē′dō), *n.* [*pl.* torpedoes], **1,** a cigar-shaped, self-moving, underwater projectile, containing explosives which may be set off by contact with a vessel, by a timing apparatus, or by radio: usually

TORPEDO, def. 1

launched from a submarine or torpedo boat; **2,** any shell or case filled with explosives, as an undersea mine; **3,** a kind of cartridge that is placed on a railroad track and, when exploded by a locomotive wheel, warns the engineer of danger; **4,** a kind of firework which explodes when thrown against a hard surface; **5,** a fish which gives an electric shock:—*v.t.* to destroy or blow up with a torpedo; as, to *torpedo* a ship.

torpedo boat, a small, fast, war vessel equipped with tubes for firing torpedoes.

tor·pid (tôr′pĭd), *adj.* **1,** inactive; sluggish; as, a *torpid* liver; **2,** dormant; as, a snake is *torpid* in winter; **3,** dull; stupid; as, a *torpid* intellect.

tor·por (tôr′pēr), *n.* **1,** loss of feeling or of the power of motion; **2,** dulness; listlessness.

tor·rent (tŏr′ĕnt), *n.* **1,** a violent, raging stream; **2,** hence, any similar violent flow; as, a *torrent* of words; *torrents* of rain. —*adj.* **tor-ren′tial** (tŏ-rĕn′shăl).

tor·rid (tŏr′ĭd), *adj.* dried by the sun's heat; extremely hot; as, a *torrid* desert.

tor·so (tôr′sō), *n.* [*pl.* torsos], the trunk of a human body; also, the body of a statue, especially one without head or limbs.

tor·toise (tôr′tŭs; tôr′tĭs), *n.* a turtle, especially one that lives on land.

tor·toise bee·tle, a small beetle shaped like a tortoise.

tor·toise shell, the horny outer surface of the shell of certain

TORTOISE (⅛)

turtles, used in making combs, fans, etc.:— *adj.* **tortoise–shell,** made of tortoise shell, or having the mottled brown and yellow color of a tortoise shell.

tor·tu·ous (tôr′tŭ-ŭs), *adj.* **1,** crooked; winding; as, a *tortuous* channel; **2,** not straightforward; as, *tortuous* business policies.—*adv.* **tor′tu-ous-ly.**—*n.* **tor′tu-ous-ness.**

tor·ture (tôr′tūr), *n.* **1,** agony of mind or body; extreme pain; **2,** the inflicting of extreme pain or torment; as, they used *torture* to make the man confess:—*v.t.* [tortured, tortur-ing], to inflict extreme agony upon, as a punishment or as a means of persuasion.

Tor·y (tôr′ĭ), *n.* [*pl.* Tories], **1,** in English politics, one who opposed changes in the established order in church and state: distinguished from *Whig;* **2,** in America, at the time of the Revolutionary War, one who favored continued allegiance to Great Britain.

toss (tôs), *v.t.* **1,** throw upward; pitch; as, to *toss* a ball; **2,** to lift or throw up quickly; as, to *toss* the head; **3,** to put into violent motion; cause to rise and fall; as, the waves *tossed* the vessel:—*v.i.* **1,** to throw oneself from side to side; be restless; as, to *toss* in pain; **2,** to be made to rise and fall; as, the ship *tossed* on the sea:—*n.* **1,** a throwing upward; pitch; **2,** a fling, as of the head.

tot (tŏt), *n.* a small child.

to·tal (tō′tăl), *adj.* **1,** whole; not divided; as, the *total* amount; **2,** complete; utter; as, *total* silence:—*n.* the whole sum or amount:—*v.t.* [totaled, total-ing], **1,** to find the sum of; add; as, to *total* figures; **2,** to amount to; as, the costs *total* $500. *Syn., n.* aggregate, entirety, mass.

to·tal·i·tar·i·an (tō-tăl′ĭ-târ′ĭ-ăn), *adj.* pertaining to a system of government which exercises supreme control over all phases of existence and admits of no opposition by the people.—*n.* **to·tal′i·tar′i·an·ism.**

to·tal·i·ty (tō-tăl′ĭ-tĭ), *n.* **1,** wholeness; completeness; **2,** the time during which an eclipse is complete.

to·tal·ly (tō′tăl-ĭ), *adv.* completely; entirely; as, *totally* blind.

to·tem (tō′tĕm), *n.* **1,** an animal or object thought of by a savage people as being closely related to their tribe or clan; **2,** a carved or painted representation of this animal or plant, as a pole or post.

tot·ter (tŏt′ẽr), *v.i.* **1,** to be unsteady on one's feet; stagger; **2,** to shake as if about to collapse; lose strength and firmness; as, the building *tottered.*

TOTEM POLE

tou·can (tōō-kän′; tōō′kăn), *n.* a noisy, fruit-eating bird with a very large beak and bright plumage, found in Central and South America.

touch (tŭch), *v.t.* **1,** to come into contact with; extend the hand so as to come into contact with; as, don't *touch* the wet paint; **2,** to bring into contact with; as, he *touched* his hand to his hat; **3,** to be in contact with; join; as, the two estates *touch* each other; **4,** to strike lightly; play on; as, he *touched* the keys of the piano; **5,** to add a light stroke to; also, to improve; as, he *touched* up the drawing; **6,** to mark slightly with some aspect of color; as, the sky was *touched* with rose and gold at sunset; **7,** to take a portion of; taste; as, he has not *touched* food for three days; **8,** to affect; injure or hurt; as, the books were not *touched* by the fire; this decision does not *touch* you; **9,** to affect mentally; derange; as, he has been *touched* by sorrow; **10,** to affect the senses or feelings of; as, her sorrow *touches* us deeply; **11,** to refer to; as, to *touch* a subject in conversation; **12,** to reach; as, to *touch* one's goal; **13,** to equal; compare with; as, your books can't *touch* mine; **14,** *Slang,* to borrow from; as, he *touched* me for a dollar:—*v.i.* **1,** to be in contact; as, the two benches *touch;* **2,** to speak of a subject briefly; as, to *touch* on art; **3,** to call at a port: said of ships:—*n.* **1,** the act or state of coming into, or being in, contact; **2,** a slight tap; as, she attracted my attention by a *touch* on the arm; **3,** the sense of feeling; **4,** a distinctive manner of execution; as, the *touch* of a master in painting; **5,** the manner of action of the fingers or hand; as, she plays the piano with a light *touch;* **6.** a single delicate stroke on a painting, drawing, or the like; also, the result produced by such a stroke; **7,** communication; as, she kept in *touch* with her family while she was away; **8,** a very slight amount; as, a *touch* of pepper; a light attack; as, a *touch* of influenza.— *adj.* **touch′a·ble.**—*n.* **touch′er.**

touch-down (tŭch′doun′), *n.* in football, the carrying of the ball across the opponents' goal line; also, the score made by so doing.

touch·ing (tŭch′ĭng), *adj.* arousing sympathy; pathetic; as, a *touching* tale of a dog's devotion.

touch-stone (tŭch′stōn′), *n.* **1,** a kind of black stone by means of which gold and silver are tested, the color of the streak left on the stone when it is rubbed with the metal indicating the purity of the metal; **2,** a standard or test by which the value of something is determined; as, time is the *touchstone* of literary merit.

touch·y (tŭch′ĭ), *adj.* [touch-i-er, touch-i-est], irritable; peevish; easily offended.

tough (tŭf), *adj.* **1,** standing great strain without breaking; not easily broken or split; as, *tough* wood; hard to cut or chew; as, *tough* meat; **2,** able to endure hardship or strain; as, a *tough* body; **3,** hard to change; stubborn; as, a *tough* will; **4,** difficult; as, a *tough* problem; **5,** rough and bad; as, a *tough* district:—*n.* a rough fellow; a rowdy.—*n.* **tough′ness.**

TOUCAN (¹⁄₁₂)

tough·en (tŭf′ĕn), *v.t.* and *v.i.* **1,** to make or become hard to break or divide; **2,** to make or become strong, stubborn, etc.

tou·pee (tŏo-pē′), *n.* a small wig or patch of false hair, used to cover a bald spot.

tour (tŏor), *n.* a journey; an excursion or a trip; as, to make a *tour* of America:—*v.i.* to make a journey:—*v.t.* to make a trip through; as, to *tour* the country.

tour·ing car, a large open automobile for five or more passengers. (See illustration under *automobile.*)

tour·ist (tŏor′ĭst), *n.* one who makes a journey, usually for sight-seeing; a traveler for pleasure.

tour·ma·line (tŏor′mȧ-lĭn; tŏor′mȧ-lēn), *n.* a mineral that is usually black, but sometimes red, blue, green, or, rarely, colorless. It is often used as a gem.

tour·na·ment (tŏor′nȧ-mĕnt; tûr′nȧ-mĕnt), *n.* **1,** in the Middle Ages, a contest with blunt lances or swords, by knights on horseback; also, a complete series of such contests occurring at one meeting; **2,** in modern times, any meeting for a trial of skill; especially, a series of meetings to determine a championship, as in tennis.

tour·ney (tŏor′nĭ; tûr′nĭ), *n.* [*pl.* tourneys], a tournament or trial of skill:—*v.i.* to take part in a tournament.

tour·ni·quet (tŏor′nĭ-kĕt), *n.* a device for compressing a blood vessel to control the flow of blood, consisting of a bandage twisted tight by a stick, an elastic rubber bandage, a pad that can be pressed tight by a screw, etc.

TOURNIQUET

tou·sle (tou′zl), *v.t.* [tou-sled, tou-sling], *Colloquial,* **1,** to pull about roughly; tussle with; **2,** to put into disorder; dishevel (hair):—*n.* a tumbled or disordered mass, especially of hair.

¹tow (tō), *v.t.* to pull or drag by a rope or line; as, to *tow* a boat; *tow* an automobile:—*n.* **1,** the act of pulling or the condition of being pulled; as, a boat in *tow;* **2,** anything pulled along by, or as by, a rope; **3,** a rope or line used in pulling.

²tow (tō), *n.* the short, coarse part of flax or hemp, made ready for spinning.

¹to·ward (tō′ĕrd; tôrd; tŏo-wôrd′) or **to·wards** (tō′ĕrdz; tôrdz; tŏo-wôrdz′), *prep.* **1,** in the direction of; as, go *toward* the city; **2,** with respect to; regarding; as, his attitude *toward* free trade; **3,** near to; close upon; as, *toward* evening; **4,** with a view to; for; contributing to; as, take this money *toward* your charity drive.

²to·ward (tō′ĕrd; tôrd), *adj.* **1,** *Archaic,* ready to learn; promising; **2,** going on; being done; as, what's *toward?*

tow·boat (tō′bōt′), *n.* a boat, especially a small, powerful steam vessel, used for pulling other vessels; a tug.

tow·el (tou′ĕl), *n.* a cloth for drying anything wet; also, a piece of absorbent paper so used.

tow·el·ing (tou′ĕl-ĭng), *n.* material from which towels are made.

tow·er (tou′ĕr), *n.* **1,** a high structure, rising above its surroundings, and either standing alone or attached to a building; as, a church *tower;* **2,** a citadel or fortress; **3,** anything resembling a tower in actual height or in being above other things or people in strength, endurance, or the like:—*v.i.* to rise to a height; overtop other objects or persons; as, the giant *towered* above everyone.

TOWER

tow·er·ing (tou′ĕr-ĭng), *adj.* **1,** very high; lofty; as, a *towering* tree; **2,** intense; violent; as, a *towering* fury.

town (toun), *n.* **1,** any collection of houses, buildings, etc., making a distinct place with a name, larger than a village but not organized as a city; **2,** the citizens or voters of such a place; as, the *town* opposed the new taxes; **3,** the business or shopping center; as, I'm going to *town;* **4,** the city as opposed to the country.

town hall, a public building with offices for officials and a hall for public meetings.

towns·folk (tounz′fōk′), *n.* the people of a town or community.

town·ship (toun′shĭp), *n.* **1,** a district or unit of local government; **2,** a land unit six miles square divided into 36 sections, of one square mile each; **3,** a division of a Canadian province.

towns·man (tounz′măn), *n.* [*pl.* townsmen (-mĕn)], an inhabitant or citizen of a town; also, a fellow citizen.

towns·peo·ple (tounz′pē′pl), *n.* the people living in a town; townsfolk; the people living in a town distinguished from those living in the country.

tow·path (tō′pȧth′), *n.* a path beside a canal or other stream, along which men or animals walk when towing boats.

tox·e·mi·a or **tox·ae·mi·a** (tŏks-ē′mĭ-ȧ), *n.* a poisoned condition of the blood.

tox·ic (tŏk′sĭk), *adj.* pertaining to, or produced by, poison; as, *toxic* symptoms.

---

go; join; yet; sing; chin; show; thin, *th*en; hw, *wh*y; zh, a*z*ure; ü, Ger. f*ü*r or Fr. l*u*ne; ö, Ger. sch*ö*n or Fr. f*eu*; ṅ, Fr. e*n*fant, no*m*; kh, Ger. a*ch* or i*ch*. See pages ix–x.

tox-in (tŏk′sĭn), *n.* a poison produced by action within animal or vegetable tissue.

toy (toi), *n.* 1, a child's plaything; 2, something of no real value; a trinket; 3, a thing very small of its kind; as, her dog won the prize among the *toys:—v.i.* to play with something; handle or treat something idly; as, she *toyed* with her purse; to *toy* with the idea of going abroad:—*adj.* like, or made as, a plaything; as, a *toy* soldier.

¹**trace** (trās), *n.* either of the side straps, chains, etc., connecting the collar or breastplate of a harness with the vehicle. (See illustration under *harness.*)

²**trace** (trās), *v.t.* [traced, trac-ing], 1, to draw or sketch by means of lines; 2, to copy by following the lines of, as with a pencil on transparent paper placed over the original; 3, to form (characters in writing) laboriously or with extreme care; 4, to follow up; study out; as, to *trace* a family record; 5, to follow, as by tracking; as, to *trace* a fox; 6, to decorate with ornamental lines:—*v.i.* to make one's way; follow a trail:—*n.* 1, a mark, indication, or sign left by something that has passed by or disappeared; as, there were *traces* of carriage wheels in the snow; 2, a small quantity or portion of something; as, a *trace* of poison was found in the food.—*adj.* **trace′a-ble.**

trac-er (trā′sẽr), *n.* a small firework which, burning slowly, shows the path of a projectile to which it is attached.

trac-er-y (trā′sẽr-ĭ), *n.* [*pl.* traceries], graceful, ornamental work made by lines which branch out and interlace to form a design, as in carved stone.

TRACERY

tra-che-a (trā′kē-á; trá-kē′á), *n.* [*pl.* tracheae (trā′kē-ē; trá-kē′ē)], the windpipe; the air tube leading to the lungs. (See illustration under *bronchi.*)

trac-ing (trā′sĭng), *n.* 1, the act of one who follows up or copies; 2, that which is traced or copied, as a copy of a pattern or design made by marking on thin paper over the original.

track (trăk), *n.* 1, a mark or impression left by the foot, a wheel, or the like; a trace; 2, a beaten path; road; as, a *track* has been worn through the woods; also, the path which something takes; as, the *track* of a storm; 3, the state of maintaining contact with current events, people, etc.; as, he kept *track* of all the graduates of the school; 4, a course laid out for a special purpose, as for horse racing, foot races, etc.; also, the sports which take place on such a track; 5, a set of metal rails supported by ties, upon which cars or trains run:—*v.t.* 1, to seek or follow by means of traces or marks; to trail; as, to *track* a deer; 2, to make footprints upon or with; as, to *track* a floor with dirt; to *track* dirt across a floor.—*n.* **track′er.**

¹**tract** (trăkt), *n.* a pamphlet, usually on some moral or religious subject.

²**tract** (trăkt), *n.* 1, a region or area of land; as, a sandy *tract;* 2, *Poetic*, a period of time; 3, in the body, an entire system of related organs, performing a specific function; as, the digestive *tract.*

trac-ta-ble (trăk′tá-bl), *adj.* 1, docile; easily led or managed; as, a *tractable* child; 2, easily handled or worked, as gold.

trac-tion (trăk′shŭn), *n.* 1, the act of drawing or pulling anything over a surface; 2, the power used in pulling; as, electric *traction;* 3, the force, or friction, which tends to keep a moving body on the surface on which it moves.

trac-tor (trăk′tẽr), *n.* anything that draws or hauls; especially, a heavy motor vehicle for pulling trailers, plows, etc. (See also illustration under *trailer.*)

FARM TRACTOR

trade (trād), *n.* 1, an occupation; business; 2, a particular means of livelihood, usually manual or mechanical, which a person learns and engages in; as, he is a mason by *trade;* 3, buying and selling for money; commerce; 4, all the persons engaged in a particular business; as, he deals with the clothing *trade;* 5, the total amount of business transacted at one place; 6, a deal; bargain; also, an exchange; as, a horse *trade;* 7, **trades**, the trade winds:—*adj.* relating to business or a particular line of business; as, a *trade* journal:—*v.i.* [trad-ed, trad-ing], 1, to buy and sell goods; as, to *trade* in furs; 2, to take unfair advantage; as, to *trade* on a person's sympathy:—*v.t.* to exchange.—*n.* **trad′er.**

Syn., n. pursuit, calling, craft.

trade–mark or **trade-mark** (trād′märk′), *n.* a word, mark, or design, used by a merchant or manufacturer to distinguish his goods from the goods made or sold by others.

trade name, 1, the name given by a merchant or manufacturer to an article to distinguish it from other articles of the same class; a trade-mark; a name; 2, the name by which an article is known in the industry that uses it; 3, the business name of a firm.

trades-man (trādz′măn), *n.* [*pl.* tradesmen (-mĕn)], a shopkeeper.

trade–un·ion (trād/=ūn/yŭn; trād/=ūn/-yŭn) or **trades–un·ion** (trādz/=; trādz/=), *n.* an association of workers in any particular industry, organized to better wages, hours, and working conditions.

trade wind, a wind in or near the Torrid Zone which blows steadily toward the equator from an easterly direction.

tra·di·tion (trȧ-dĭsh/ŭn), *n.* **1,** the handing down of information, opinions, doctrines, practices, etc., by word of mouth, from generation to generation; **2,** that which is so handed down; as, family *traditions;* **3,** an old custom so well established as to be almost as effective as a law.

tra·di·tion·al (trȧ-dĭsh/ŭn-ăl), *adj.* **1,** relating to customs, stories, beliefs, etc., handed down from generation to generation; **2,** customary; usual; as, it is *traditional* to have fancy eggs at Easter.

tra·duce (trȧ-dūs/), *v.t.* [traduced, traducing], to defame or slander.—*n.* **tra·duc/er.**

Traf·al·gar, Cape (trăf/ăl-gär/; trȧ-făl/gẽr) a cape near the Strait of Gibraltar, off which Lord Nelson's naval victory over the French took place in 1805.

traf·fic (trăf/ĭk), *n.* **1,** interchange of goods; business or trade; as, the liquor *traffic;* **2,** the transportation business done by a railway, steamship line, etc., carrying persons or goods; **3,** the passing of vehicles, persons, or animals, in a street; as, city *traffic:*—*v.i.* [trafficked, traffick-ing], **1,** to barter; buy or sell goods; as, to *traffic* in hides; **2,** to do business in a mean or dishonest way.—*n.* **traf/fick-er.**

tra·ge·di·an (trȧ-jē/dĭ-ăn), *n.* **1,** a writer of tragedies; **2,** an actor who plays tragic parts.

tra·ge·di·enne (trȧ-jē/dĭ-ĕn/), *n.* [*pl.* tragediennes (trȧ-jē/dĭ-ĕnz/)], an actress who plays tragic parts.

trag·e·dy (trăj/ĕ-dĭ), *n.* [*pl.* tragedies], **1,** a play which ends unhappily, arousing pity or terror by the misfortunes that befall the principal characters; **2,** a story, poem, etc., of similar character; **3,** a melancholy occurrence; a fatal event; calamity.

trag·ic (trăj/ĭk) or **trag·i·cal** (trăj/ĭ-kăl), *adj.* **1,** relating to tragedy; as, a *tragic* play; **2,** terrible; sad; as, a *tragic* accident.—*adv.* **trag/i-cal-ly.**

trag·i·com·e·dy (trăj/ĭ-kŏm/ĕ-dĭ), *n.* [*pl.* tragicomedies], a play containing both tragic and comic scenes.

trail (trāl), *v.t.* **1,** to draw or drag along behind; as, to *trail* oars in the water; **2,** to hunt or follow by tracking; as, the hunters *trailed* the bear:—*v.i.* **1,** to fall or hang down so as to sweep along the ground; as, her dress *trailed;* **2,** to grow to some length; as, the morning-glory *trails* along the wall; **3,** to follow; also, to move in a long and straggling line; as, they *trailed* home one by one; **4,** to lag behind; be last; as, to *trail* in a race:—*n.* **1,** a track left by a person, an animal, or a moving object; as, the hurricane left a *trail* of ruin; **2,** a footpath or track through a wilderness; **3,** the scent followed in hunting; as, the dogs lost the *trail* when they came to the river; hence, a trace or clue; **4,** anything drawn out in the wake of something; as, a *trail* of dust followed the car.

trail·er (trāl/ẽr), *n.* **1,** a person or animal that follows behind; **2,** a vehicle, car, sledge, or the

TRAILER (T)

like, pulled along by a motorcar, wagon, or trolley; **3,** a creeping or trailing plant.

train (trān), *n.* **1,** a connected line of railroad cars; **2,** that part of a dress or robe that trails on the ground; **3,** a retinue or body of servants; **4,** a line of men, animals, vehicles, etc., moving in procession; **5,** any series of connected things; as, a *train* of ideas; **6,** a line of gunpowder laid to fire a charge:—*v.t.* **1,** to instruct by practice; to drill; discipline; educate; **2,** to aim or point, as a gun; as, to *train* ratillery on a town; **3,** to teach to perform certain motions, tricks, etc.; as, to *train* seals; *train* horses; **4,** to direct the growth of; as, to *train* a plant:—*v.i.* to prepare oneself for a contest of strength or skill; drill.—*n.* **train/er.**

train·ing (trān/ĭng), *n.* **1,** the act of instructing, drilling, etc.; as, a school for the *training* of nurses; **2,** the condition or process of becoming drilled, instructed, or educated; as, to be in *training* for a cross-country race.

train oil, oil obtained from the blubber of whales and other sea animals.

trait (trāt), *n.* a feature or characteristic; as, a *trait* of character.

trai·tor (trā/tẽr), *n.* a person guilty of treason; one who betrays his country, cause, or friends.—*n.fem.* **trai/tress.**—*adj.* **trai/tor-ous.**

tra·jec·to·ry (trȧ-jĕk/tō-rĭ), *n.* [*pl.* trajectories], the curve made by a body moving through space, as the path of a bullet discharged from a gun.

tram (trăm), *n.* **1,** a kind of coal wagon used in mines; **2,** in England, a streetcar.

tram·car (trăm/kär/), *n.* **1,** in England, a streetcar that runs on tracks; **2,** a four-wheeled car on tracks in a mine.

---

go; join; yet; sing; chin; show; thin, *th*en; hw, *wh*y; zh, *a*zure; ü, Ger. für or Fr. l*u*ne; ö, Ger. schön or Fr. f*eu;* ṅ, Fr. e*n*fant, nom; kh, Ger. a*ch* or i*ch.* See pages ix–x.

tram-mel (trăm′ĕl), *n.* 1, a net used for catching birds, fish, or the like; 2, a kind of harness for controlling the gait of a horse; 3, anything that hinders progress, action, or freedom; 4, an S-shaped hook from which pots are hung in a fireplace:— *v.t.* [trammeled, trammel-ing], to hamper. *Syn., n.* fetter, bond, chain, impediment.

tramp (trămp), *v.t.* 1, to step upon forcibly and repeatedly; as, to *tramp* the grass down; 2, to travel over on foot; as, to *tramp* the hills:—*v.i.* 1, to wander on foot; 2, to walk with a heavy step:— *n.* 1, a foot traveler; especially, a roving, shiftless person; 2, a walk or hike; 3, the sound of heavy footsteps; 4, a freight steamer that picks up a cargo wherever it can.

tram-ple (trăm′pl), *v.t.* [tram-pled, trampling], to tread down under the feet; as, don't *trample* the grass:—*v.i.* to tread heavily; hence, to inflict hurt or grief by unkind treatment; as, to *trample* on a person's feelings.

tram-way (trăm′wā′), *n.* 1, in England, a street railway; 2, a road or track for heavy hauling, as in a mine.

trance (tràns), *n.* 1, a condition of the body in which the mind and senses cannot be aroused; a daze; stupor; 2, a deep sleep due to illness or hypnotism.

tran-quil (trăng′kwĭl; trăn′kwĭl), *adj.* [tranquil-er, tranquil-est], calm; quiet; serene; as, a *tranquil* mind; a *tranquil* scene.—*adv.* **tran′quil-ly.**

tran-quil-ize (trăng′kwĭl-īz), *v.t.* [tranquilized, tranquiliz-ing], to make peaceful. *Syn.* soothe, allay, appease, pacify.

tran-quil-li-ty (trăn-kwĭl′ĭ-tĭ; trăng-kwĭl′ĭ-tĭ), *n.* calm; quiet. Also spelled **tran-quil′i-ty.**

trans- (trănz-; trăns-), a prefix meaning: 1, across; beyond; as, *trans*port, *trans*atlantic; 2, through; as, *trans*fix; 3, altogether; as, *trans*form, *trans*figure.

trans-act (trăns-ăkt′; trăn-zăkt′), *v.t.* to conduct or manage, as business; also, to close; complete; as, to *transact* a deal.

trans-ac-tion (trăns-ăk′shŭn; trăn-zăk′-shŭn), *n.* 1, the management of any business or affair; 2, that which is done or performed; a business deal; 3, **transactions,** the minutes, or records, of the proceedings of a society. *Syn.* negotiation, occurrence.

trans-at-lan-tic (trăns-ăt-lăn′tĭk), *adj.* 1, beyond the Atlantic; 2, crossing the Atlantic; as, a *transatlantic* flight.

Trans-cau-ca-sian Fed-er-a-tion (trăns′kô-kā′shăn; -kā′zhăn; -kăsh′ăn; -kăzh′ăn), a former republic of the U.S.S.R. Its official name was *Transcaucasian Soviet Socialist Republic.*

Transcaucasian Soviet Socialist Republic, a federated republic from 1921 to 1936 (cap. Tiflis) in the U.S.S.R., lying between the Caspian and Black seas (map 12).

tran-scend (trăn-sĕnd′), *v.t.* 1, to rise above or go beyond; exceed; as, miracles *transcend* human knowledge; 2, to surpass; excel; as, his ability *transcends* mine.

tran-scend-ent (trăn-sĕn′dĕnt), *adj.* of surpassing excellence; superior or supreme; as, the *transcendent* beauty of a sunset.

tran-scen-den-tal (trăn′sĕn-dĕn′tăl), *adj.* 1, superior; supreme; 2, beyond human experience or knowledge.

trans-con-ti-nen-tal (trăns′kŏn-tĭ-nĕn′-tăl), *adj.* extending across a continent; as, a *transcontinental* road.

tran-scribe (trăn-skrīb′), *v.t.* [transcribed, transcrib-ing], 1, to copy in writing; as, the medieval monks *transcribed* many manuscripts; 2, to translate (shorthand notes) into longhand.

tran-script (trăn′skrĭpt), *n.* 1, a written or typewritten copy; 2, any copy; an imitation.

tran-scrip-tion (trăn-skrĭp′shŭn), *n.* 1, the act of copying; 2, a written copy; 3, a rearrangement of a musical composition to fit an instrument or voice other than that for which it was written.

tran-sept (trăn′sĕpt), *n.* that part of a cross-shaped church which crosses at right angles the main body of the building.

trans-fer (trăns-fûr′), *v.t.* [transferred, transfer-ring], 1, to convey or carry from one person or place to another; as, to *transfer* baggage; 2, in law, to give or make over the possession or ownership of; as, to *transfer* a piece of land; 3, to copy from one surface to another; as, to *transfer* designs by a stencil:—*v.i.* to change from one streetcar, train, bus, or the like, to another at a junction point:—*n.* (trăns′fûr), 1, the making over of a right, title, property, or the like, from one person to another; 2, a removal from one place to another; 3, a ticket permitting a person to change from one streetcar, bus, or the like, to another.—*adj.* **trans-fer′a-ble** (trăns-fûr′á-bl; trăns′fẽr-á-bl). *Syn., v.* move, shift, transport.

trans-fer-ence (trăns-fûr′ĕns; trăns′fẽr-ĕns), *n.* 1, the act of carrying, or state of being carried, from one place to another; 2, a making over of property to another.

trans-fig-u-ra-tion (trăns-fĭg′ū-rā′shŭn), *n.* a change in appearance:—**the Transfiguration,** the wonderful change in the appearance of Jesus Christ on the mount (Matthew 17:2); also, the church festival on August 6, celebrating this event.

āte, âorta, râre, căt, àsk, fär, ăllow, sofá; ēve, ēvent, ĕll, wrītẽr, novĕl; bīte, pĭn; nō, ôbey, ôr, dôg, tŏp, cŏllide; ūnit, ūnite, bûrn, cŭt, focŭs; nōon, fŏŏt; mound; coin;

trans-fig-ure (trăns-fĭg′ŭr), *v.t.* [transfigured, transfigur-ing], **1,** to change the form or appearance of; **2,** to make glow or shine; illumine; as, hope *transfigured* his face.

trans-fix (trăns-fĭks′), *v.t.* **1,** to pierce with a pointed weapon; **2,** hence to render motionless; as, he stood *transfixed* by fear.

trans-form (trăns-fôrm′), *v.t.* **1,** to change the shape or appearance of; to change into something else; **2,** to change the nature of; convert; as, to *transform* a child by kindness; **3,** to change (an electric current) from higher to lower, or from lower to higher, voltage; **4,** to change (one form of energy) into another.

trans-for-ma-tion (trăns′fôr-mā′shŭn), *n.* **1,** a changing, or the state of being changed, in shape, appearance, nature, or the like; **2,** a kind of wig worn by women.

trans-form-er (trăns-fôr′mĕr), *n.* **1,** one who or that which transforms; **2,** a device for tranforming an electric current.

trans-fuse (trăns-fūz′), *v.t.* [transfused, transfus-ing], to transfer from one vessel to another by pouring; also, to transfer (blood) from the blood vessels of one person to those of another.

trans-fu-sion (trăns-fū′zhŭn), *n.* a transference, as of blood from the blood vessels of one person to those of another.

trans-gress (trăns-grĕs′), *v.i.* to break a law, rule, or the like; sin:—*v.t.* **1,** to break, sin against, or violate; as, to *transgress* a law; **2,** to go beyond (any limit or bounds); as, to *transgress* the bounds of good manners.—*n.* **trans-gres′sor.**

trans-gres-sion (trăns-grĕsh′ŭn), *n.* the breaking of a law, rule, social convention, or the like; sin.

tran-sient (trăn′shĕnt), *adj.* **1,** fleeting; brief; passing; as, *transient* hopes; **2,** coming and going; temporary; as, *transient* lodgers:—*n.* a temporary lodger.—*adv.* **tran′sient-ly.**

trans-it (trăn′sĭt; trăn′zĭt), *n.* **1,** a passing through or over; passage; as, rapid *transit;* **2,** the act of carrying over or through; conveyance; as, goods lost in *transit;* **3,** in surveying, an instrument for measuring angles.

tran-si-tion (trăn-zĭsh′ŭn; trăn-sĭzh′ŭn; trăn-sĭsh′ŭn), *n.* the passage from one place, period, state, subject, or the like, to another; in music, an abrupt change from one key to another.

tran-si-tion-al (trăn-zĭsh′ŭn-ăl; trăn-sĭzh′ŭn-ăl; trăn-sĭsh′ŭn-ăl), *adj.* pertaining to transition, or change; as, the tadpole is a *transitional* form between egg and frog.—*adv.* **tran-si′tion-al-ly.**

tran-si-tive (trăn′sĭ-tĭv), *adj.* in grammar, requiring or taking a direct object to complete the meaning; as, "wrote" and "mailed" in the sentence "I wrote a card and mailed it" are *transitive* verbs.

tran-si-tor-y (trăn′sĭ-tôr′ĭ), *adj.* brief; lasting but a short time; quickly passing; as, this *transitory* life.

Syn. transient, ephemeral.

trans-late (trăns-lāt′), *v.t.* [translat-ed, translat-ing], **1,** to change from one language into another; as, to *translate* a story from French into English; **2,** to remove to another place or position; specifically, to remove to heaven without death; as, Elijah did not die; he was *translated.*—*n.* **trans-la′tor.**

trans-la-tion (trăns-lā′shŭn), *n.* **1,** the act of changing from one language into another; also, the translated form of a book, article, or the like; **2,** the removal of a person from one state or condition to another; specifically, the removal of a person to heaven without death.

trans-lu-cent (trăns-lū′sĕnt), *adj.* permitting light to go through, but not transparent; as, frosted glass is *translucent.*

Syn. lucid, lucent.

trans-mi-gra-tion (trăns′mī-grā′shŭn; trăns′mĭ-grā′shŭn), *n.* **1,** the going from one place to another; **2,** the passing of the soul at death from one body to another.

trans-mis-sion (trăns-mĭsh′ŭn), *n.* **1,** the act of passing, or the state of being passed, through or over; as, the *transmission* of news or disease; **2,** that part of an automobile which transfers power from the engine to the driving shaft.

trans-mit (trăns-mĭt′), *v.t.* [transmit-ted, transmit-ting], **1,** to cause or allow to pass over or through something; as, to *transmit* news by wire; **2,** to conduct; as, iron *transmits* heat; **3,** to transfer from one person to another; pass on, as a title.

trans-mit-ter (trăns-mĭt′ĕr), *n.* a person by whom, or a thing through which, something is sent; especially, a device for transmitting, as the mouthpiece of a telephone, the sending instrument of a telegraph, or a radio transmitting set.

TELEPHONE RECEIVER (R) AND TRANSMITTER (T)

trans-mute (trăns-mūt′), *v.t.* [transmut-ed, transmut-ing], to change from one form, nature, substance, or class, into another; as, the medieval alchemists attempted to *transmute* metals like zinc or lead into gold.—*n.* **trans′mu-ta′tion.**—*n.* **trans-mut′er.**

tran·som (trăn′sŭm), n. **1**, a crossbar, as in a window or over a door; **2**, a window over a door or other window, usually hinged to the crossbar. (See illustrations below.)

trans·par·en·cy (trăns-pâr′ĕn-sĭ), n. [pl. transparencies], **1**, the quality of being seen through clearly; **2**, that which is seen through; especially, a picture or inscription on glass, thin cloth, or the like, made visible by a light behind it; **3**, simplicity of mind or character.

trans·par·ent (trăns-pâr′ĕnt), adj. **1**, so clear or thin that one can see through it; as, transparent glass; transparent gauze; **2**, easy to understand; easily detected; as, a transparent lie.

TRANSOMS (T,T) in a window. def. 1

tran·spire (trăn-spīr′), v.i. [transpired, transpir-ing], **1**, to pass off as vapor; **2**, to send out vapor or moisture, as through the skin; **3**, to become known or public; as, the true story of the attack has not transpired; **4**, to happen; occur; as, what transpired at camp?—v.t. to throw off (a vapor); exhale or breathe out.—n. tran·spi·ra′tion (trăn′spĭ-rā′shŭn).

trans·plant (trăns-plănt′), v.t. to remove and establish in another place, as trees or people.

TRANSOM, def. 2

trans·port (trăns-pôrt′), v.t. **1**, to carry from one place to another; as, to transport supplies or soldiers; **2**, to carry away emotionally; as, he was transported with delight; **3**, to banish or deport (a convicted criminal) from a country:—n. (trăns′pôrt), **1**, the act of conveying or of being conveyed; as, the transport of grain; **2**, a means of conveyance; especially, a vessel for transporting troops, stores, etc.; **3**, a strong burst of emotion; as, a transport of rage.

trans·por·ta·tion (trăns′pôr-tā′shŭn), n. **1**, the act of carrying, or state of being carried, from one place to another; **2**, a means of conveyance; also, the charge for conveyance; **3**, the act of banishing, or sending away, a convicted criminal.

trans·pose (trăns-pōz′), v.t. [transposed, transpos-ing], **1**, to change the place or order of; as, to transpose letters in a word; **2**, in music, to change the key of; **3**, in algebra, to change (a term) from one side of an equation to the other.—n. trans′po·si′tion.—n. trans·pos′er.

trans·ship (trăns-shĭp′), v.t. [transshipped, transship-ping], to transfer from one ship, car, or the like, to another for further shipment.—n. trans·ship′ment.

tran·sub·stan·ti·a·tion (trăn′sŭb-stăn′-shĭ-ā′shŭn), n. **1**, a changing into another substance; **2**, the doctrine held by the Roman Catholic and Orthodox Churches that the bread and wine of the Eucharist are changed in substance into the body and blood of Christ, only the appearance of bread and wine remaining.

Trans·vaal (trăns-väl′), a state (cap. Pretoria) in the Union of South Africa (map 14).

trans·verse (trăns-vûrs′; trăns′vûrs), adj. lying across, or crosswise; as, transverse lines:—n. anything that lies crosswise.—adv. trans·verse′ly.

¹trap (trăp), n. a kind of fine-grained rock used in road building. Also called traprock.

²trap (trăp), n. **1**, a device, such as a snare or pitfall, for catching animals; **2**, an ambush; a means of tricking people; also, a hazard on a golf course; **3**, a device, as an S-shaped or a U-shaped bend, for sealing a drainpipe with water against the return of sewer gas; **4**, any of various straining or separating devices; **5**, a device for throwing into the air clay disks, balls, or the like, to be shot at; **6**, a trap door; **7**, a light, two-wheeled carriage:—v.t. [trapped, trapping], **1**, to catch in, or as in, a snare or spring; as, to trap rabbits; **2**, to ambush (an enemy); to capture by trickery:—v.i. to set traps for game.

trap door, a door which lifts up, as in a floor.

tra·peze (trȧ-pēz′), n. a swinging horizontal bar suspended by ropes.

tra·pe·zi·um (trȧ-pē′zĭ-ŭm), n. a plane figure with four sides, no two of which are parallel.

TRAPEZE

trap·e·zoid (trăp′ė-zoid), n. a plane figure with four sides, only two of which are parallel.

trap·per (trăp′ẽr), n. one who snares or traps animals, especially fur-bearing animals, for their skins.

TRAPEZOID   TRAPEZIUM

trap·pings (trăp′ĭngz), n.pl. **1**, ornamental coverings or harness for a horse; **2**, hence, ornamental dress; decorations.

trash (trăsh), n. anything that is worthless or useless; refuse; rubbish.

trav·ail (trăv′āl; trăv′l), n. **1**, the suffering endured in childbirth; **2,** physical or mental agony or severe pain; as, a mind in *travail:—v.i.* to suffer in childbirth.

trav-el (trăv′ĕl), *v.i.* [traveled, travel-ing], **1,** to journey from place to place for pleasure, recreation, or adventure; **2,** to journey from place to place in the course of business; as, he *travels* for a paint firm; **3,** to move onward or proceed; as, a train *travels* faster than a horse:—*v.t.* to journey over or through; as, to *travel* a hard road; he has *traveled* the South from end to end:—*n.* **1,** a journey or journeying; as, to seek health in *travel;* a record of one's *travels;* **2,** the number of persons, vehicles, etc., on the road; traffic; as, heavy *travel.*

Syn., n. transit, trip, voyage.

trav-eled (trăv′ĕld), *adj.* **1,** experienced in traveling; as, a *traveled* man; **2,** used by many travelers; as, a *traveled* route.

trav-el-er (trăv′ĕl-ēr), *n.* **1,** one who or that which journeys; **2,** a traveling salesman.

trav-e-log or **trav-e-logue** (trăv′ĕ-lŏg), *n.* a lecture on travel or travels usually illustrated.

trav-erse (trăv′ẽrs), *v.t.* [traversed, travers-ing], **1,** to cross in traveling; travel or pass over; as, to *traverse* a city; also, to move forward and backward over; cross and recross; as, the beams of a searchlight *traverse* the sky; **2,** to extend across; as, canals *traverse* the country:—*n.* something placed or lying across something else; a crosspiece:—*adj.* lying across.

trav-es-ty (trăv′ĕs-tĭ), *n.* [*pl.* travesties], **1,** a burlesque or parody; any deliberate imitation with intent to ridicule; **2,** any likeness that is fantastic or ridiculous:—*v.t.* [travestied, travesty-ing], **1,** to burlesque or parody; **2,** to be a ridiculous likeness or imitation of.

trawl (trôl), *n.* **1,** a large, bag-shaped net used in sea fishing; **2,** a very long fishing line to which are attached many short lines with hooks:—*v.t.* and *v.i.* to fish with such a net or line.—*n.* **trawl′ing.**

trawl-er (trôl′ēr), *n.* **1,** one who fishes with a trawl; **2,** a vessel used in trawling.

tray (trā), *n.* a flat, shallow receptacle of wood, metal, or the like, with a raised rim.

treach-er-ous (trĕch′ẽr-ŭs), *adj.* **1,** betraying a trust or pledge; **2,** not to be trusted in spite of appearances; as, a *treacherous* friend; not safe; as, a *treacherous* floor.—*adv.* **treach′-er-ous-ly.**

TRAY

Syn. traitorous, disloyal, false, untrue.

treach-er-y (trĕch′ẽr-ĭ), *n.* [*pl.* treacheries], a betrayal of faith or confidence; disloyal or treasonable conduct.

trea-cle (trē′kl), *n.* the sirup obtained in refining crude sugar; molasses.

tread (trĕd), *v.i.* [*p.t.* trod (trŏd), *p.p.* trod-den (trŏd′n) or trod, *p.pr.* tread-ing], **1,** to step or walk; as, *tread* carefully on the carpet; **2,** to press something beneath the foot; trample; as, don't *tread* on my toes:—*v.t.* **1,** to walk on; **2,** to press or crush under the feet; as, peasants *tread* grapes; **3,** to dance; as, to *tread* a minuet:—*n.* **1,** a walking or stepping; also, the manner or style of walking; as, a firm *tread;* **2,** in a flight of stairs, the horizontal surface of a step; **3,** the part of a wheel or tire that touches the road or rail; also, the mark or rut left by a wheel or tire on a road.

TREAD, def. 2
R, riser; T, tread.

trea-dle (trĕd′l), *n.* a flat piece attached to a crank and worked by the foot for running a lathe, sewing machine, or the like:—*v.i.* [trea-dled, trea-dling], to operate a treadle.

tread-mill (trĕd′mĭl), *n.* **1,** a mill worked by persons or animals walking on a wheel or endless belt; **2,** any tiresome routine.

treas. abbreviation for *treasurer, treasury.*

trea-son (trē′zn), *n.* **1,** the betrayal of one's country; an attempt to overthrow the government of one's country; in a monarchy, an attempt to injure the sovereign; **2,** treachery; betrayal of faith.—*adj.* **trea′son-ous.**

trea-son-a-ble (trē′zn-ȧ-bl), *adj.* pertaining to treason, or disloyalty to one's country; as, a *treasonable* speech.—*adv.* **trea′son-a-bly.**—*n.* **trea′son-a-ble-ness.**

Syn. treacherous, disloyal, traitorous, false, untrue.

treas-ure (trĕzh′ēr), *n.* **1,** a hoard, as of money or jewels; abundance or wealth; **2,** anything highly valued; a person dear to one:—*v.t.* [treasured, treasur-ing], **1,** to lay up or store for future use; hoard; also, to retain in the mind; as, to *treasure* up memories; **2,** to value highly; as, to *treasure* an heirloom.

treas-ur-er (trĕzh′ēr-ēr), *n.* one who has charge of receiving and paying out money.

treas-ure-trove (trĕzh′ēr-trōv′), *n.* money, jewels, or the like, found in the earth or in any secret hiding place, and claimed by no owner.

treas-ur-y (trĕzh′ēr-ĭ), *n.* [*pl.* treasuries], **1,** a place where wealth is stored; especially, a place where public funds, or the funds of an organization, are kept and paid out; also, the funds; **2,** (also *Treasury*): **a,** that department of a government which has charge of the public funds; **b,** the officials of such a department:—**treasury note,** a piece of paper money issued by the U.S.

treat (trēt), *v.t.* **1,** to handle, deal with, or manage; as, the speaker *treated* his subject cleverly; **2,** to behave or act toward; as, to *treat* others kindly; **3,** to regard or consider; as, to *treat* a matter lightly; **4,** to cause (something) to undergo a process for a special purpose; as, to *treat* corn with lye to make hominy; **5,** to entertain; as, he *treated* his guests to music; also, to pay the cost of entertainment for (someone); **6,** to deal with, for some desired result; as, a doctor *treats* his patients; to *treat* a cold:—*v.i.* **1,** to discuss or deal with; as, the book *treats* of Russia; **2,** to negotiate; as, they were ready to *treat* with the outlaws:—*n.* **1,** the act of paying for entertainment, food, etc., for a friend; also, the entertainment or food so given; **2,** something which gives great pleasure; as, the circus is a *treat.*

trea-tise (trē′tĭs), *n.* a long, written discussion or essay on a particular subject; as, a *treatise* on birds.

treat-ment (trēt′mĕnt), *n.* **1,** manner of dealing with a person, problem, etc.; as, a firm's generous *treatment* of employees; **2,** medical or surgical care of a person.

trea-ty (trē′tĭ), *n.* [*pl.* treaties], an agreement or contract between nations, as for settling differences or arranging commercial relations.

treaty port, a seaport or other city kept open by treaty to foreign trade.

tre-ble (trĕb′l), *adj.* **1,** threefold or triple; **2,** in music, relating to the highest vocal or instrumental part; of high pitch:—*n.* **1,** in music, the highest part; **2,** a soprano singer or instrument; also, a high-pitched voice or sound:—*v.t.* and *v.i.* [tre-bled, trebling], to make or become three times as great.

tre-bly (trĕb′lĭ), *adv.* three times as much; in three ways; as, *trebly* tormented.

tree (trē), *n.* **1,** a large woody plant with a high main trunk, branches, and leaves (see illustration on pages 864, 865); **2,** sometimes, a bush trained to grow like a tree; **3,** a piece of timber used as part of a structure; as, an axle*tree:*—**family tree,** an outline or diagram, sometimes shaped like a tree, showing family descent and relationships:—*v.t.* [treed, tree-ing], to drive up a tree; as, to *tree* an opossum.

tree fern, a large tropical fern with a single, straight, woody stem or trunk.

tree toad, a toad that lives in trees, but breeds in water: often called *tree frog.* (See illustration under *amphibian.*)

tre-foil (trē′foil), *n.* **1,** any three-leaved plant, such as the clover; **2,** an ornamental design like a three-lobed leaf.

TREFOIL def. 2

trek (trĕk), *v.i.* [trekked, trekking], **1,** to pull a vehicle or load: said generally of oxen; **2,** to travel by wagon, especially in search of a new settlement:—*n.* a journey, especially by wagon.—*n.* **trek′ker.**

trel-lis (trĕl′ĭs), *n.* a frame of wood or metal network to support climbing vines; a latticework:—*v.t.* to provide with a lattice for vines; train (vines) on a lattice.

trem-ble (trĕm′bl), *v.i.* [trem-bled, trembling], **1,** to shake or shiver, as with fear or cold; shudder; **2,** to quaver, as a sound:—*n.* an involuntary shaking; a shiver; shudder.—*n.* **trem′bler.**

Syn., v. vibrate, waver, flutter, quiver.

trem-bling (trĕm′blĭng), *adj.* shaking, as with fear or cold:—*n.* a shaking or quivering.—*adv.* **trem′bling-ly.**

tre-men-dous (trē-mĕn′dŭs), *adj.* **1,** exciting fear or terror because of unusual size or violence; terrible; as, a *tremendous* crash; **2,** *Colloquial,* astonishing; extraordinary; as, a *tremendous* feat.

trem-o-lo (trĕm′ō-lō), *n.* [*pl.* tremolos], a trembling or quivering of a tone in singing or instrumental music.

trem-or (trĕm′ẽr; trē′mẽr), *n.* **1,** a trembling, quivering, or shaking; as, an earthquake *tremor;* **2,** a thrill or quiver of excitement.

trem-u-lous (trĕm′ū-lŭs), *adj.* **1,** trembling; quivering; shaking; **2,** showing fear or timidity; as, a *tremulous* voice; **3,** marked by unsteadiness; as, *tremulous* writing.—*adv.* **trem′u-lous-ly.**

trench (trĕnch), *n.* **1,** a long, narrow ditch in the earth; an open ditch for draining; **2,** a deep ditch dug in a zone of battle and held as a defensive position or as a base from which to attack:—*v.t.* **1,** to cut a ditch in; to drain by ditches; **2,** to dig trenches for (an army):—*v.i.* to encroach, as upon someone's property.

trench-ant (trĕn′chănt), *adj.* **1,** sharp; keen; as, a *trenchant* sword; also, cutting or biting; as, *trenchant* satire; **2,** forceful and clear; as, a *trenchant* explanation.

trench-er (trĕn′chẽr), *n.* a large wooden plate or platter on which, in the old days, food was carved or served.

trend (trĕnd), *n.* the general direction taken by something; as, the northeasterly *trend* of the Gulf Stream; general tendency or drift; as, the *trend* of public opinion:— *v.i.* **1**, to take a particular direction or course; **2**, to have a general tendency; as, prices are *trending* upward.

Tren-ton (trĕn′tŭn), a city, capital of New Jersey, situated on the Delaware River (map 6).

trep-i-da-tion (trĕp′ĭ-dā′shŭn), *n.* **1**, a trembling or vibration; **2**, a state of nervous alarm; fear mingled with uncertainty.

tres-pass (trĕs′pȧs), *v.i.* **1**, to commit any offense; sin; as, to *trespass* against the Lord; **2**, to enter unlawfully upon the property of another; **3**, to make an inroad upon a person's time, presence, attention, etc.:— *n.* **1**, a violation of a moral law; a sin; **2**, an unlawful encroachment on the property of another.— *n.* **tres′pass-er**.

Syn., *n.* offense, intrusion.

tress (trĕs), *n.* a long curl or lock of hair, especially of woman's hair.

-tress (-trĕs), a suffix forming the feminine of words ending in *-tor* and *-ter;* as, proprie*tress*, hun*tress*.

tres-tle (trĕs′l), *n.* **1**, a movable frame, made of a horizontal beam and spreading legs, for supporting a platform, table top, or the like; **2**, a rigid framework of timbers or steel for supporting a road or bridge across a ravine or gully.

tres-tle-work (trĕs′l-wûrk′), *n.* a series of trestles built to support an elevated road or a bridge.

tri- (trī-), a prefix meaning three or threefold; as, *tri*angle, *tri*color.

tri-ad (trī′ăd), *n.* a set or group of three; three similar things; as, a *triad* of virtues.

tri-al (trī′ăl), *n.* **1**, the act of testing or putting to a test; as, the *trial* of the new airplane proved it unsatisfactory; **2**, the state of being tested; a chance to make good; as, give this coffee a

TRIANGLES, def. 1

week's *trial;* **3**, hardship; as, a time of *trial* and suffering; **4**, a person or thing that puts faith, mercy, or patience to the test; as, he was a great *trial* to his family; **5**, the hearing and deciding of a case in law court.

Syn. test, experiment.

TRIANGLE, def. 3, and rod for sounding.

tri-an-gle (trī′ăng′gl), *n.* **1**, a plane figure with three sides and three angles; **2**, anything shaped like a triangle; **3**, a musical instrument used in orchestras and bands, consisting of a steel rod bent in the form of a triangle open at one corner, sounded with a light metal rod.

tri-an-gu-lar (trī-ăng′gū-lẽr), *adj.* **1**, having three angles; three-sided; three-cornered; **2**, concerned with, or comprising, three persons, parts, elements, or the like; as, a *triangular* treaty.

tribe (trīb), *n.* **1**, a group of uncivilized people, usually consisting of several clans, under one chief; as, a Tatar *tribe;* loosely, any similar group; as, a gypsy *tribe;* **2**, among the ancient Israelites, one of the twelve divisions of the nation; as, the *tribe* of Judah; **3**, a group of people akin to one another because of a common occupation or trait; as, the *tribe* of moneylenders; **4**, a class or division of plants or animals.— *adj.* **trib′al**.

trib-u-la-tion (trĭb′ū-lā′shŭn), *n.* severe affliction or distress; deep sorrow; also, a cause of affliction or distress.

Syn. suffering, trouble, grief.

tri-bu-nal (trī-bū′năl; trī-bū′năl), *n.* **1**, the seat occupied by a judge or magistrate; **2**, a court of justice; any judicial assembly; **3**, any final authority; as, the *tribunal* of conscience.

¹trib-une (trĭb′ūn), *n.* **1**, a Roman magistrate elected by the people to protect their liberties; **2**, hence, one who champions the rights of the people.

²trib-une (trĭb′ūn), *n.* in ancient Rome, a raised stand for public speakers.

trib-u-tar-y (trĭb′ū-tĕr′ĭ), *adj.* **1**, paying tribute or taxes; hence, subordinate or subject; as, *tributary* states; **2**, flowing into another; as, a *tributary* river:— *n.* [*pl.* tributaries], **1**, a state or government which pays taxes to, or is under the control of, a superior government; **2**, a river flowing into a larger river or into a lake.

trib-ute (trĭb′ūt), *n.* **1**, an annual or stated sum of money paid by one state or ruler to another to acknowledge submission, obtain protection, or to fulfil the terms of a treaty; **2**, an acknowledgment of worth, service rendered, or the like; praise; as, *tribute* paid to a national hero.

¹trice (trīs), *v.t.* [triced, tric-ing], to pull and tie with a small rope; as, to *trice* up a sail.

²trice (trīs), *n.* a very short space of time; as, I'll be there in a *trice*.

trick (trĭk), *n.* **1**, a clever, crafty, or deceitful device or action, used in order to gain an advantage; a stratagem; artifice; **2**, a foolish or stupid act; as, why did he do such a *trick?* **3**, an exhibition of skill and dexterity; as, a card *trick;* **4**, a mischievous, sometimes annoying, prank; **5**, a peculiarity of manner; habit; as, a *trick* of

---

go; join; yet; sing; chin; show; thin, *th*en; hw, *wh*y; zh, azure; ü, Ger. für or Fr. lune; ö, Ger. schön or Fr. feu; ṅ, Fr. enfant, nom; kh, Ger. ach or ich. See pages ix–x.

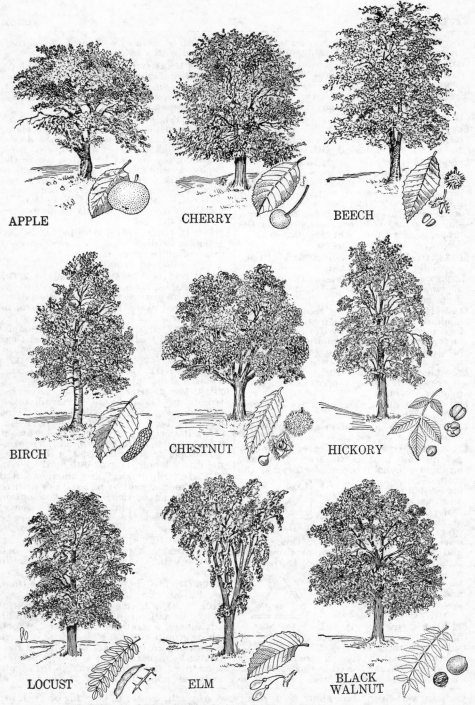

APPLE

CHERRY

BEECH

BIRCH

CHESTNUT

HICKORY

LOCUST

ELM

BLACK
WALNUT

TYPICAL NORTH AMERICAN TREES, WITH THEIR LEAVES AND FRUITS

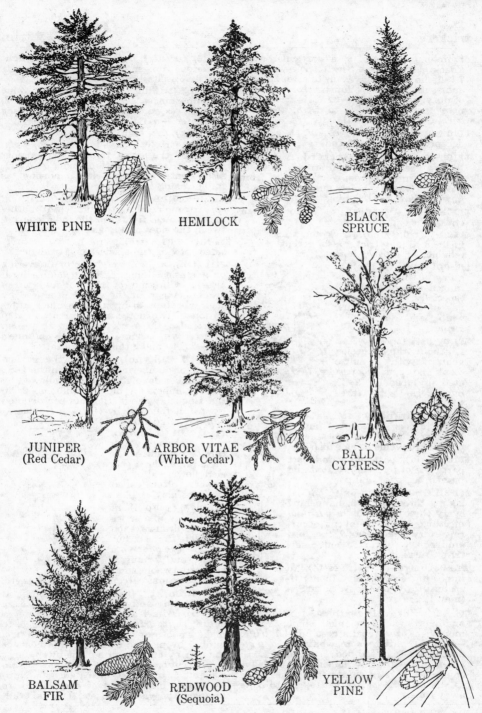

WHITE PINE

HEMLOCK

BLACK SPRUCE

JUNIPER
(Red Cedar)

ARBOR VITAE
(White Cedar)

BALD
CYPRESS

BALSAM
FIR

REDWOOD
(Sequoia)

YELLOW
PINE

TYPICAL NORTH AMERICAN TREES, WITH THEIR LEAVES AND FRUITS

twitching the ears; **6,** a particular skill; knack; as, there is a *trick* to pole vaulting; **7,** all the cards played in one round of a game; as, they took four *tricks*; **8,** a turn of duty, as on a ship:—*v.t.* **1,** to cheat; impose upon; deceive; **2,** to dress; deck; as, *tricked* out in new clothes.

trick-er-y (trĭk/ẽr-ĭ), *n.* [*pl.* trickeries], deception; cheating; fraud.

trick-le (trĭk/l), *v.i.* [trick-led, trick-ling], to flow gently in a small stream; also, to drip; fall in drops; as, water *trickled* from the faucet:—*n.* a small amount of liquid flowing gently or dripping.

trick-ster (trĭk/stẽr), *n.* a cunning or crafty cheat or deceiver.

trick-y (trĭk/ĭ), *adj.* [trick-i-er, trick-i-est], inclined to play tricks; also, deceptive; unreliable; as, a *tricky* horse.

tri-col-or (trī/kŭl/ẽr), *n.* a flag of three colors arranged in equal stripes; especially, the national flag of France, of blue, white, and red vertical stripes.

tri-cy-cle (trī/sĭk-l), *n.* **1,** a light, three-wheeled vehicle, with a single seat, and usually operated by pedals; **2,** a motorcycle with three wheels.

TRICYCLE

tri-dent (trī/dĕnt), *n.* **1,** a weapon with three prongs, especially that carried by Neptune, the god of the sea; **2,** a three-pronged implement, as a fish gig.

tried (trīd), past tense and past participle of *try*:—*adj.* tested and proved; as, *tried* abilities.

tri-en-ni-al (trī-ĕn/ĭ-ăl), *adj.* **1,** lasting three years; **2,** happening every three years; as, a *triennial* meeting:—*n.* **1,** an event occurring every three years; **2,** the third anniversary of an event.—*adv.* **tri-en/ni-al-ly.**

Tri-este (trē-ĕst/; trē-ĕs/tĕ) an important seaport city in northeastern Italy, on the Adriatic Sea (map 12).

TRIDENT

tri-fle (trī/fl), *n.* **1,** anything of little value or importance; **2,** a small amount, as of money; as, the repairs cost only a *trifle*: —**a trifle,** rather; somewhat; as, *a trifle* disturbed:—*v.i.* [tri-fled, tri-fling], **1,** to act or talk without seriousness; **2,** to dally; toy; play; as, she *trifled* with her necklace as she talked:—*v.t.* to waste; as, to *trifle* away time.

tri-fler (trī/flẽr), *n.* **1,** one who makes light of serious things; **2,** one who talks or acts idly and uselessly; a time-waster.

tri-fling (trī/flĭng), *adj.* **1,** of small value or importance; as, a *trifling* matter; **2,** thoughtless or shallow; as, a *trifling* character:—*n.* dallying; time-wasting.

trig (trĭg), *adj.* trim; neat; shipshape.

trig-ger (trĭg/ẽr), *n.* a lever which, when pulled by the finger, releases the hammer of a gun (see illustration under *revolver*); also, a catch serving a similar purpose, as for springing a trap.

trig-o-nom-e-try (trĭg/ō-nŏm/ē-trĭ), *n.* [*pl.* trigonometries], the branch of mathematics which treats of the relations between the sides and angles of triangles.

tri-lat-er-al (trī-lăt/ẽr-ăl), *adj.* three-sided; having three sides, as a triangle.

trill (trĭl), *n.* **1,** a trembling or quavering on a musical tone; as, the *trill* of a bird; also, a vibration of the tongue, as in pronouncing *r*, or the sound produced by such vibration; **2,** in music, a quick alternation of two notes a step or a half step apart; also, the mark indicating this:—*v.t.* to utter with a vibration; as, to *trill* one's r's:—*v.i.* to make the voice vibrate.

tril-lion (trĭl/yŭn), *n.* **1,** in the French system of numbering, followed in the U.S., the number denoted by a unit followed by twelve ciphers; a million millions; **2,** in the English system, the number denoted by a unit followed by eighteen ciphers.— *adj.* and *n.* **tril/lionth.**

tril-li-um (trĭl/ĭ-ŭm), *n.* a plant with three leaves surrounding a large, three-petaled flower; also, the flower: often called *wake-robin*.

tril-o-gy (trĭl/ō-jĭ), *n.* [*pl.* trilogies], a series of three dramas, each complete in itself, but with a common theme, and forming a connected whole; similarly, three musical compositions, novels, etc.

TRILLIUM

trim (trĭm), *v.t.* [trimmed, trim-ming], **1,** to make tidy and neat; set in order; as, a bird *trims* its feathers; **2,** to decorate or adorn; as, to *trim* a dress with lace; **3,** to make smooth or ready for use; as, to *trim* lumber by planing it; **4,** to make neat, as the hair by cutting, or a plant by clipping; also, to cut or clip (unnecessary parts) from a plant; **5,** to adjust or balance (a ship) by proper distribution of cargo; also, to arrange (the yards and sails) to take ad-

---

āte, åorta, râre, căt, åsk, fär, ăllow, sofá; ēve, ēvent, ĕll, writẽr, novĕl; bīte, pĭn; nō, ōbey, ôr, dôg, tŏp, cŏllide; ūnit, ūnite, bûrn, cŭt, focŭs; no͞on, fŏŏt; mound; coin;

vantage of the wind; **6,** *Colloquial,* to defeat; as, we were *trimmed* by 40 points: —*v.i.* to maintain a middle course; try to please both sides or parties at the same time:—*n.* **1,** order; adjustment; suitable condition; **2,** dress; style; appearance; **3,** the inside woodwork of a building around the windows, doors, etc.; **4,** of a vessel, fitness for sailing; also, its position in the water:—*adj.* [trim-mer, trim-mest], neat; tidy; as, a *trim* cabin.—*adv.* **trim′ly.** —*n.* **trim′mer.**—*n.* **trim′ness.**

trim·ming (trĭm′ĭng), *n.* **1,** the act or process of arranging, decorating, etc.; **2,** adornment; decoration, especially for clothes; **3, trimmings: a,** parts removed by cutting off the edges; as, the *trimmings* of meat; **b,** *Colloquial,* the garnishings of a dish; as, roast duck with *trimmings.*

Trin·i·dad (trĭn′ĭ-dăd′), a British island (cap. Port of Spain) in the West Indies, off the northeast coast of Venezuela (map 10).

tri·ni·tro·tol·u·ene (trī-nī′trō-tŏl′ū-ēn), *n.* a substance in the form of brownish crystals, used as an explosive: often called *TNT.* Also, **tri·ni·tro·tol′u·ol** (trī-nī′trō-tŏl′ū-ōl; -tŏl′ū-ŏl).

Trin·i·ty (trĭn′ĭ-tĭ), *n.* **1,** the union of the Father, the Son, and the Holy Ghost in one Godhead; **2,** Trinity Sunday:—**trinity,** [*pl.* trinities], any union of three in one; a trio.

trin·ket (trĭng′kĕt), *n.* **1,** a small ornament or jewel; **2,** a trifle; toy.

tri·o (trē′ō; trī′ō), *n.* [*pl.* trios], **1,** a set of three; **2,** in music, a composition for three performers; also, a group of three musicians, either vocal or instrumental.

trip (trĭp), *v.i.* [tripped, trip-ping], **1,** to run or step lightly or nimbly; take short, quick steps; skip; **2,** to stumble; hence, to make a mistake; err:—*v.t.* **1,** to perform with light, agile steps, as a dance; **2,** to cause to stumble or trip; as, the rug *tripped* me; **3,** to catch in a mistake or deception; as, I *tripped* you up that time; **4,** to release or set free by opening a catch, trigger, or the like:—*n.* **1,** a quick, short step; **2,** a misstep or mistake; **3,** a journey or excursion.

tri·par·tite (trī-pär′tīt; trĭp′ĕr-tīt), *adj.* **1,** in three parts, as a clover leaf; also, having three similar parts or copies; **2,** made or existing among three persons or groups of persons; as, a *tripartite* agreement.

tripe (trīp), *n.* a part of the stomach of the ox or cow, used for food.

trip ham·mer, a heavy power hammer, which falls by gravity. Also written **trip′- ham′mer.**—*adj.* **trip′ham′mer.**

tri·ple (trĭp′l), *adj.* **1,** being in threes; threefold; as, a *triple* window; **2,** three times as much or as many; three times the size, strength, value, etc.; also, done three times; as, a *triple* knock:—**triple measure,** in music, a measure of three beats, with the accent on the first beat:—*n.* **1,** a group or combination of three; **2,** in baseball, a three-base hit:—*v.t.* [tri-pled, tri-pling], to increase threefold; multiply by three; as, he *tripled* his efforts:—*v.i.* **1,** to increase to three times as much; **2,** in baseball, to make a three-base hit.

trip·let (trĭp′lĕt), *n.* **1,** a set of three of a kind or three united; **2,** one of three children born at one birth.

trip·li·cate (trĭp′lĭ-kāt), *adj.* threefold; made in sets of three; as, a *triplicate* record:—*n.* something which matches two others exactly alike; the third of a set of three; also, any one of the three; as, a *triplicate* of a letter:—*v.t.* (trĭp′lĭ-kāt), [triplicat-ed, triplicat-ing], to reproduce in a set of three, all alike; produce by threes.

tri·pod (trī′pŏd), *n.* **1,** a three-legged support, as for a surveying instrument; **2,** any article, such as a stool or vase, with three feet or legs.

Trip·o·li·ta·ni·a (trĭp′ō-lĭ-tā′nĭ-à), a district (cap. Tripoli) of Libya in northern Africa (map 14).

TRIPOD

trip·ping (trĭp′ĭng), *adj.* with light or graceful motion; as, a *tripping* gait.

tri·reme (trī′rēm), *n.* in ancient times, a warship with three banks of oars.

Tris·tram (trĭs′trăm), *n.* in medieval romance, a knight, nephew of King Mark of Cornwall, who unwittingly drank a love potion with Iseult of Ireland while bringing her to Cornwall to become Mark's wife.

TRIREME

trite (trīt), *adj.* worn out; used far too much; commonplace; as, a *trite* reply.
   Syn. old, banal, hackneyed, ordinary.

Tri·ton (trī′tŏn), *n.* a Greek demigod of the sea, part man and part fish, who used a shell trumpet to raise or calm the sea.

tri·umph (trī′ŭmf), *n.* **1,** exultation over success; **2,** in ancient Rome, a grand parade and celebration in honor of a victorious general; **3,** a marked success or conquest; as, the new singer scored a *triumph:—v.i.* **1,** to rejoice in success; **2,** to be successful or victorious.—*adj.* **tri·um/phal** (trī-ŭm/făl).

tri·um·phant (trī-ŭm/fănt), *adj.* victorious; rejoicing in victory or success.

tri·um·vir (trī-ŭm/vẽr), *n.* [*pl.* triumvirs or triumviri (trī-ŭm/vĭ-rī)], in ancient Rome, one of three magistrates who together governed the republic.

tri·um·vi·rate (trī-ŭm/vĭ-rât), *n.* **1,** government by three men having equal authority; also, the office or authority of the three; **2,** hence, a group of three; as, a *triumvirate* of friends.

triv·et (trĭv/ĕt), *n.* **1,** a three-legged stand for holding a kettle near or over an open fire; **2,** a short-legged metal plate on which to set hot dishes.

triv·i·al (trĭv/ĭ-ăl), *adj.* trifling; insignificant; of little worth or importance.

triv·i·al·i·ty (trĭv/ĭ-ăl/ĭ-tĭ), *n.* [*pl.* trivialities], insignificance; pettiness; also, an insignificant or petty matter.

-trix (-trĭks), a suffix forming the feminine of words ending in *-tor;* as, avia*trix.*

tro·chee (trō/kē), *n.* in poetry, a foot of two syllables, the first long or accented and the second short or unaccented, as "Tell me / not in / mournful / numbers." —*adj.* **tro·cha/ic** (trō-kā/ĭk).

trod (trŏd), past tense and one form of the past participle of *tread.*

trod·den (trŏd/n), one form of the past participle of *tread.*

Tro·i·lus (trō/ĭ-lŭs), *n.* in medieval romances based on Homer's "Iliad," the lover of Cressida.

Tro·jan (trō/jăn), *adj.* pertaining to the ancient city of Troy in Asia Minor, or its people:—*n.* **1,** an inhabitant of Troy; **2,** an industrious and fearless person; as, he worked like a *Trojan.*

¹troll (trōl), *v.t.* **1,** to sing the parts of (a song) in succession, as in a round like "Scotland's Burning"; also, to carol lustily; **2,** to fish for, or in, by dragging a line from a boat; as, to *troll* pike; to *troll* a stream:— *v.i.* **1,** to share in a round or part song; also, to sing a song lustily; **2,** to fish, as for pike, with a hook and line drawn along through the water from a moving boat:—*n.* **1,** a round, or part song; **2,** the rod, line, etc., used in trolling.

TROLLEY, def. 2

²troll (trōl), *n.* in Scandinavian folk tales, a giant or, later, a dwarf, supposed to live in caves.

trol·ley (trŏl/ĭ), *n.* [*pl.* trolleys], **1,** a kind of truck running on an overhead track and carrying a load suspended from it; **2,** on an electric car, a grooved metal wheel at the end of a pole forming a contact with a live electric wire to convey current to the car; **3,** an electric car; a streetcar. Also spelled **trol/ly** [*pl.* trollies].

trom·bone (trŏm/bōn; trŏm-bōn/), *n.* a long brass wind instrument with a U-shaped sliding tube by which variations in tone are produced.

TROMBONE

troop (trōōp), *n.* **1,** a number of persons, or sometimes of animals, gathered together; a company; **2,** in the Boy Scouts and the Girl Scouts, a unit consisting of from two to four patrols; **3,** a unit of cavalry, under the command of a captain; **4, troops,** armed forces; soldiers:—*v.i.* to move in crowds; flock together.

troop·er (trōōp/ẽr), *n.* **1,** a member of a troop of mounted police or soldiers; **2,** a cavalry horse.

troop·ship (trōōp/shĭp/), *n.* a vessel carrying soldiers, a military transport.

trope (trōp), *n.* a word or expression figuratively used for effect. "The little tree shivered and whispered in the wind" is a trope.

tro·phy (trō/fĭ), *n.* [*pl.* trophies], **1,** anything captured in battle and kept in memory of a military victory, as arms, flags, cannon, etc.; **2,** any memento of deeds, achievements, etc.; as, an explorer's *trophies;* also, a prize in a contest; as, a tennis *trophy.*

trop·ic (trŏp/ĭk), *n.* **1,** either of the two imaginary circles on the earth's surface, parallel to the equator, at a distance of 23° 30′ north and south of it, called *Tropic of Cancer* and *Tropic of Capricorn* respectively, marking the limits of the Torrid Zone; **2, tropics,** the region of the earth lying between these two circles; the Torrid Zone.

trop·i·cal (trŏp/ĭ-kăl) or **trop·ic** (trŏp/ĭk), *adj.* pertaining to, living in, or produced in, the tropics; as, *tropical* flowers.

trop·ic bird, a white and salmon-colored bird with webbed feet and elongated tail, somewhat larger than a pigeon, which is found in tropical waters.

trot (trŏt), *n.* **1,** a jogging pace, as of a horse, faster than a walk, in which the right forefoot and left hind foot are lifted together, and then the left forefoot and right hind foot; **2,** any jogging gait:—*v.i.* [trot-ted, trot-ting], **1,** to move at a trot; **2,** to run in a jogging gait:—*v.t.* to cause (a horse) to trot.

āte, āorta, râre, căt, ȧsk, fär, ȧllow, sofȧ; ēve, ēvent, ĕll, writẽr, novĕl; bīte, pĭn; nō, ōbey, ôr, dŏg, tŏp, cŏllide; ūnit, ūnite, bûrn, cŭt, focŭs; nōōn, fŏŏt; mound; coin;

troth (trôth; trōth), *n.* **1,** faith or fidelity; as, to plight one's *troth;* **2,** truth to one's word; as, by my *troth;* **3,** *Archaic,* betrothal.

trot-ter (trŏt′ẽr), *n.* a trotting horse.

trou-ba-dour (trōō′bà-dōōr; trōō′bà-dôr), *n.* one of a class of poets and singers of love songs, who flourished in France and Italy during the 11th, 12th, and 13th centuries.

trou-ble (trŭb′l), *v.t.* [trou-bled, trou-bling], **1,** to distress, perturb, or worry; as, he was *troubled* by her silence; **2,** to cause inconvenience to; as, may I *trouble* you for a glass of water? **3,** to stir up or agitate, as water:—*v.i.* to take pains; put oneself out; as, don't *trouble* to apologize: —*n.* **1,** mental excitement, distress, or worry; **2,** the cause of such disturbance; as, a wayward child is a great *trouble* to his parents; **3,** inconvenience; effort; as, she goes to much *trouble* to entertain her friends; **4,** illness; an ailment; as, heart *trouble.*—*adj.* **trou′ble-some.**

Syn., n. misfortune, calamity, disaster.

trou-blous (trŭb′lŭs), *adj.* disturbed; full of, or bringing, distress and trouble; as, *troublous* times.

trough (trôf), *n.* **1,** a long, shallow, uncovered container of wood, metal, or concrete, for watering or feeding livestock; **2,** any similar container, for kneading dough, washing ore, etc.; **3,** a long, narrow, uncovered gutter or drain for carrying off water; as, a pump *trough;* an eaves *trough;* **4,** any long, natural hollow; as, the *trough* between ocean waves, or between hills.

trounce (trouns), *v.t.* [trounced, trouncing], to beat soundly; flog; also, to overcome or get the better of (an opponent).

troupe (trōōp), *n.* a company, as of actors or acrobats.

trou-sers (trou′zẽrz), *n.pl.* an outer garment covering the body from the waist to the knees, or ankles, and so divided as to cover each leg separately.

trous-seau (trōō′sō′; trōō′sō), *n.* [*pl.* trousseaux (trōō′sō′) or trousseaus (trōō′- sōz′; trōō′sōz)], a bride's outfit.

trout (trout), *n.* [*pl.* trout], **1,** a medium-sized, fresh-water food fish of the salmon family, as the brook trout; **2,** any of various similar fishes.

trow (trō), *v.t. Archaic,* to think; believe.

trow-el (trou′ĕl), *n.* **1,** a flat-bladed hand tool, used by bricklayers, masons, and plasterers, for spreading mortar, plaster, or the like; **2,** a scoop-shaped tool used by gardeners for moving small plants.

TROWELS
Gardener's (above) and bricklayer's.

Troy (troi), an ancient city in northwestern Asia Minor, south of the Hellespont, famous as the scene of Homer's "Iliad" (map 1).

troy weight, a system of weights with twelve ounces to the pound, used for gold, silver, etc.

tru-ant (trōō′ănt), *n.* **1,** a pupil who stays away from school without permission; **2,** a shirker or loafer:—*adj.* playing the truant; idle; wandering; as, a *truant* lad; *truant* fancies.—*n.* **tru′an-cy.**

truce (trōōs), *n.* **1,** a temporary peace or interruption of war by mutual agreement; an armistice; **2,** a lull in a period of stress and strain.

¹**truck** (trŭk), *v.t. and v.i.* to give in exchange; barter:—*n.* **1,** commodities for sale; articles of commerce; **2,** the system of paying wages in commodities instead of in money; **3,** fresh vegetables cultivated for sale; **4,** *Colloquial:* **a,** useless articles or rubbish; as, the old house is full of *truck;* **b,** dealings; as, have no *truck* with a cheat.—*n.* **truck′er.**—*n.* **truck′man.**

²**truck** (trŭk), *n.* **1,** originally, a strong, small wheel; **2,** now, a wheeled vehicle for carrying heavy or bulky loads, especially a large motor vehicle for this purpose; **3,** a strong frame or platform on wheels used for hauling baggage in railroad stations; **4,** a set of wheels, or a frame mounted on wheels, to support one end of a locomotive, railroad car, or the like:—*v.t.* to carry by truck:—*v.i.* **1,** to carry goods by truck; **2,** to drive a truck for a livelihood.

TRUCK
Two-wheeled warehouse truck.

¹**truck-ing** (trŭk′ĭng), *n.* the business of growing vegetables for market.

²**truck-ing** (trŭk′ĭng), *n.* the business of carting goods by truck.

truck-le (trŭk′l), *n.* a trundle bed: also called *truckle bed:*—*v.i.* [truck-led, truckling], to yield without opposition to the will of another; be subservient.

truc-u-lent (trŭk′ū-lĕnt; trōō′kŭ-lĕnt), *adj.* **1,** fierce; savage; ready to attack; **2,** harsh; scathing; as, *truculent* satire.—*n.* **truc′u-lence; truc′u-len-cy.**

trudge (trŭj), *v.i.* [trudged, trudg-ing], to travel on foot, usually with effort or labor:—*n.* a long or fatiguing walk; as, a long *trudge* to the station.

true (trōō), *adj.* [tru-er, tru-est], **1,** in accord with fact or reality; as, hers was the only *true* account of the robbery; **2,** faithful and loyal; reliable; as, a *true* friend; **3,** genuine; not pretended; as, *true* love; **4,** rightful; legitimate; as, the *true* heir; **5,** corresponding to a standard; as, a *true* color; **6,** correct; exact; as, a *true* square:—*adv.* **1,** truthfully; **2,** accurately; as, the hunter aimed *true*:—*n.* the condition of being accurate; as, the wall is out of *true*:—*v.t.* [trued, ru-ing or trueing], to make accurate; as, to *true* a door frame.

truf-fle (trŭf'l; trōō'fl; trōōf'l), *n.* an edible potato-shaped fungus that grows underground, usually at the roots of oak or birch trees; also, its edible fruit.

tru-ism (trōō'izm), *n.* an obvious and well-known truth or fact; also, a hackneyed, tiresome statement of fact.

   Syn. adage, maxim, proverb, axiom.

Tru-jil-lo (trōō-hēl'yō), a city, the capital of the Dominican Republic. See **Ciudad Trujillo.**

tru-ly (trōō'lĭ), *adv.* **1,** in agreement with truth or fact; precisely; as, *truly* told; **2,** sincerely; honestly; as, *truly* grateful; **3,** in fact; indeed; as, *truly,* I am sorry.

Tru-man (trōō'măn), Harry S. (1884–), the 33d president of the U.S.

¹**trump** (trŭmp), *n. Poetic,* a trumpet or trumpet call.

²**trump** (trŭmp), *n.* in cards, the suit which temporarily outranks the other suits; also, any card of this suit:—*v.t.* **1,** to play a trump on when trump has not been led; as, to *trump* a trick; **2,** to think up or invent; as, to *trump* up an excuse:—*v.i.* to play trump when trump has not been led: —*adj.* relating to the suit named as trump.

trump-er-y (trŭmp'ẽr-ĭ), *n.* [*pl.* trumperies], worthless finery; rubbish:—*adj.* showy but worthless; trashy.

trum-pet (trŭm'pĕt), *n.* **1,** a metal wind instrument formed of a single curved tube with a bell-shaped mouth, regulating keys, valves, etc. (see *musical instruments,* illustration); **2,** something shaped like this instrument; as, a speaking *trumpet;* an ear *trumpet;* **3,** a sound like that of a trumpet; as, the elephant's *trumpet* in the jungle:—*v.t.* to noise abroad:—*v.i.* to utter a sound like that of a trumpet.—*n.* **trum'pet-er.**

trun-cate (trŭng'-kāt), *v.t.* [truncat-ed, truncat-ing], to cut the top or end from; cut down:—*adj.* having a flat top as if cut off evenly; having a broad end as if cut off squarely.

TRUNCATED CONE AND TRUNCATED PYRAMID

trun-cheon (trŭn'chŭn), *n.* **1,** *Archaic,* a stout club or cudgel; **2,** a staff of authority; especially, a policeman's club.

trun-dle (trŭn'dl), *v.t.* [trun-dled, trun-dling], to roll, as a hoop; to cause to move on wheels; as, to *trundle* a gocart:—*v.i.* to roll along; move on, or as on, small wheels:—*n.* **1,** a small wheel; caster; **2,** a kind of low-wheeled truck; **3,** a kind of low bed on casters: also called *trundle bed.*

trundle bed, a low bed that runs on casters, so that, when not in use, it may be rolled under a high bed; a truckle bed.

trunk (trŭngk), *n.* **1,** the upright stem or body of a tree; **2,** in man and other animals, the body exclusive of the head and limbs; **3,** the chief part, or stem, of anything that branches; as, the *trunk* of a nerve; **4,** the elongated nose, or proboscis, of an elephant; **5,** a large box or chest to hold clothes and other personal belongings for a journey; **6, trunks,** short breeches reaching about halfway to the knee, worn by athletes, acrobats, etc.; in the 16th and 17th centuries, very full and wide dress breeches of about the same length: known also as *trunk hose:*—*adj.* pertaining to a main line; as, a *trunk* line on a railroad.

TRUNK

truss (trŭs), *n.* **1,** a brace or framework of timbers or bars supporting a roof or bridge; **2,** a bandage or support for a rupture; **3,** a weighed measure, or a bundle, of hay or straw:—*v.t.* **1,** to bind or fasten with skewers and string; as, to *truss* a turkey; **2,** to support with a brace, framework, or the like.

trust (trŭst), *n.* **1,** confidence; faith; belief in someone's goodness; also, the source of faith and belief; as, God is our *trust;* **2,** expectation or hope; as, she put no *trust* in the future; **3,** credit granted to a buyer or borrower, because of belief in his honesty; as, to sell goods on *trust;* **4,** something involving duties and responsibilities; as, he regarded his wealth as a public *trust;* **5,** property, or an interest in property, held and managed by one party (the trustee) for the benefit of another; as, the will created *trusts* for the children; also, the state of property so held, as, the estate was held in *trust* for him; **6,** a combination of business or commercial interests into a corporation so large that it has a virtual monopoly in its field, and is able to fix prices, etc.:—*v.t.* **1,** to place confidence in; rely upon; as, to *trust* one's own judgment; **2,** to believe; as, I *trust* his word; **3,** to entrust to someone's care; **4,** to sell to on credit; **5,** to hope with confidence; as, we *trust* that you will come

---

āte, ȧorta, râre, căt, ȧsk, fär, ăllow, sofȧ; ēve, ĕvent, ĕll, writẽr, novĕl; bīte, pĭn; nō, ōbey, ôr, dŏg, tŏp, cŏllide; ūnit, ūnite, bûrn, cŭt, focŭs; nōon, fŏŏt; mound; coin;

again:—*v.i.* to have confidence; as, *trust* in the Lord:—*adj.* held in charge for someone else; as, a *trust* fund.

trus-tee (trŭs-tē′), *n.* a person or firm to whom property, or the management of property, is entrusted.

trust-ful (trŭst′fŏŏl), *adj.* ready to believe in others; confiding.—*adv.* **trust′-ful-ly.**—*n.* **trust′ful-ness.**

trust fund, money, securities, or other property held in trust.

trust-ing (trŭs′tĭng), *adj.* inclined to believe in others; unsuspicious.

trust-wor-thy (trŭst′wûr′thĭ), *adj.* reliable; meriting trust.

trust-y (trŭs′tĭ), *adj.* [trust-i-er, trust-i-est], faithful; as, a *trusty* messenger; reliable; as, a *trusty* sword:—*n.* a person to be trusted; especially, a convict found worthy of special privileges in prison.

truth (trōōth), *n.* **1,** the quality of being according to fact; agreement with facts; as, his testimony has the ring of *truth;* also, correctness; accuracy; **2,** sincerity of speech and action; as, there is no *truth* in him; **3,** a generally accepted or proved fact; as, the *truths* of science.

truth-ful (trōōth′fŏŏl), *adj.* **1,** according to the facts; true; as, a *truthful* statement; **2,** naturally given to telling the truth; as, a *truthful* nature.—*adv.* **truth′ful-ly.**—*n.* **truth′ful-ness.**

try (trī), *v.t.* [tried, try-ing], **1,** to put to a trial or experiment; test; as, to *try* a new dish in cooking; **2,** to become acquainted with, by actual use; as, to *try* a new brand of tea; **3,** to subject to trouble, affliction, or annoyance; as, she *tries* her parents sorely; **4,** to test the strength or endurance of; as, she *tries* my patience; **5,** to strain; weary; as, bright light *tries* the eyes; **6,** to decide by argument or contest; as, to *try* an issue by war; **7,** to attempt; endeavor; to use; as, I have *tried* argument in vain; **8,** to melt or render; as, to *try* out fat; **9,** in law: **a,** to examine (the case of an accused person) before a court, as does a lawyer; **b,** to act as judge at the trial of (a person or case):—*v.i.* to make an effort; as, do *try* to come:—*n.* [*pl.* tries], an attempt; as, to succeed after several *tries.*

try-ing (trī′ĭng), *adj.* annoying; hard to bear; distressing.

try-sail (trī′sāl′; trī′sl), *n.* a fore-and-aft sail, suspended from a gaff set on the foremast or mainmast of a sailing vessel. It is used chiefly in rough weather. (See illustration on page 695.)

try square, a tool used by carpenters and joiners for laying off and testing right angles. (See illustration next column.)

tryst (trĭst; trīst), *n.* **1,** an agreement to meet at a certain place and time; as, a lovers' *tryst;* **2,** a meeting; **3,** the place of meeting: also called *trysting place.*

Tsang-po (tsäng′pō′), a river rising in Tibet. See **Brahmaputra.**

tsar (tsär), *n.* the title of the former emperors of Russia. See **czar.**

tsa-ri-na (tsä-rē′nà), *n.* the title of the former empresses of Russia. See **czarina.**

tset-se (tsĕt′sē), *n.* **1,** a small African fly which by its bite causes germs to enter the blood of domestic animals, producing a severe disease; **2,** another fly of this kind which in the same way produces in man a disease called sleeping sickness. It is also called *tsetse fly.*

TSETSE FLY
Enlarged.

T square, a ruler with a cross-bar at one end, used in mechanical drawing.

Tu. abbreviation for *Tuesday:*—

T.U. abbreviation for *Trade Union.*

T SQUARE

tub (tŭb), *n.* **1,** an open circular vessel of wood or metal, used for washing and other household purposes; **2,** a large, deep, stationary receptacle in a laundry, kitchen, or bathroom, used for washing, bathing, etc.; **3,** a small wooden cask for lard, butter, or the like; **4,** the amount contained in a tub; as, a *tub* of water; **5,** *Colloquial:* **a,** a bath; as, a hot *tub;* **b,** a slow or clumsy boat:—*v.t.* and, *Colloquial, v.i.* [tubbed, tubbing], to bathe in a tub.

tu-ba (tū′bà), *n.* a large brass wind instrument, very low in pitch, used in bands and orchestras.

TUB

tube (tūb), *n.* **1,** a hollow cylinder, much longer than it is wide, of glass, rubber, metal, etc., for holding or conveying liquids or gases; as, a test *tube;* also, any living structure of similar shape; as, the bronchial *tubes;* **2,** a small cylinder of flexible metal, fitted with a screw cap, for holding lotions, cold cream, etc.; **3,** an underground tunnel; a subway; hence, an underground railway; **4,** a bulb or tube containing a more or less perfect vacuum; as, the vacuum *tube,* one form of which is used to produce X rays and another, in radio to detect and amplify sound waves.

TRY SQUARE

tu·ber (tū′bẽr), *n.* a thick, roundish part of an underground stem, bearing small buds or eyes. The potato is a tuber.

tu·ber·cle (tū′bẽr-kl), *n.* **1,** a natural healthy, knoblike growth, as on a bone or on the root of a plant; **2,** a small diseased lump on the skin or in the soft tissues of the body, characteristic of tuberculosis.

tu·ber·cu·lar (tū-bûr′kū-lẽr), *adj.* **1,** having to do with the small growths called *tubercles;* **2,** in careless usage, affected with tuberculosis; tuberculous.

tu·ber·cu·lo·sis (tū-bûr′kū-lō′sĭs), *n.* a wasting, infectious disease characterized by the growth of tubercles in any part of the body; especially, this disease affecting the lungs: commonly called *consumption.*— *adj.* **tu·ber′cu·lous.**

tube-rose (tūb′rōz′; tū′bẽr-ōs), *n.* a Mexican plant, growing from a bulb, cultivated for its spike of fragrant white flowers.

tu·ber·ous (tū′bẽr-ŭs), *adj.* **1,** covered with knoblike swellings; **2,** consisting of, like, or producing, tubers.

tub·ing (tūb′ĭng), *n.* **1,** a piece of tube; **2,** cylindrical material for tubes; also, a set or series of tubes.

TUBEROSE

tu·bu·lar (tū′bū-lẽr), *adj.* pertaining to, shaped like, or consisting of, one or more hollow cylinders, or tubes.

tuck (tŭk), *v.t.* **1,** to roll or fold; as, to *tuck* up one's sleeves; also, to turn under the loose ends of; as, to *tuck* up one's hair; **2,** to cover snugly; as, to *tuck* a child into bed; **3,** to stow away neatly or into a small space; as, to *tuck* bills into a purse; **4,** to make and sew folds in; as, to *tuck* a skirt:— *n.* a stitched fold.

tuck·er (tŭk′ẽr), *n.* **1,** a machine or a special device on a sewing machine for stitching cloth into folds; also, the operator of a tucking machine; **2,** a piece of lace, linen, or other fine material, folded across the front, or forming the top part, of a woman's dress:— *v.t. Colloquial,* to tire; as, the long march *tuckered* him out.

Tuc·son (tōō-sŏn′), a city in Arizona, noted as a health resort (map **9**).

Tu·dor (tū′dẽr), *n.* the family name of the English sovereigns who ruled from 1485 to 1603:— *adj.* pertaining to this royal house, or to the period of its rule, especially to the drama and architecture of the period.

Tues., Tu., or **T.** abbreviation for *Tuesday.*

Tues-day (tūz′dĭ), *n.* the third day of the week.

tuft (tŭft), *n.* **1,** a small, compact bunch of feathers, threads, or other fibers, growing together or held together at the base; as, a *tuft* of grass; *tufts* in a mattress; **2,** a cluster or clump; as, a *tuft* of asters:— *v.t.* to provide with a tuft or tufts; specifically, to reinforce (mattresses, quilts, upholstery, etc.) with thread drawn through tightly at regular intervals, tied, and finished with cotton tufts or buttons.— *adj.* **tuft′ed.**

tug (tŭg), *v.t.* [tugged, tug-ging], **1,** to pull or haul with an effort; **2,** to tow with a tugboat:— *v.i.* to pull; as, the child *tugs* at his mother's skirt:— *n.* **1,** a strain or pull with great effort; also, a struggle; **2,** a rope or chain used for pulling; especially, a trace of a harness; **3,** a small powerful boat for towing vessels:—**tug of war,** a contest in which two groups of persons pull on a rope against each other.

tug-boat (tŭg′bōt′), *n.* a small steam or power vessel, used to tow, or push, heavy boats, as passenger ships. Also, **tug.**

Tui·ler·ies (twē′lẽr-ĭz; twē′lẽ-rē′), *n.* a royal palace in Paris, burned by the revolutionists in 1871.

tu·i·tion (tū-ĭsh′ŭn), *n.* **1,** instruction; teaching; **2,** the fee charged for instruction.

tu·lip (tū′lĭp), *n.* a plant of the lily family, bearing brilliantly colored, cup-shaped flowers; also, its bulb or its flower.

tulip tree, an American tree of the magnolia family, bearing greenish-yellow flowers resembling a double tulip.

Tul·sa (tŭl′sȧ), a large city in Oklahoma, one of the centers of the oil industry.

tum·ble (tŭm′bl), *v.i.* [tumbled, tum-bling], **1,** to fall suddenly and hard; **2,** to roll in play; **3,** to perform acrobatic feats, such as somersaults; **4,** to move in a careless, blundering fashion; as, he *tumbled* into the chair:— *v.t.* **1,** to fling down; **2,** to cause to roll over and over; **3,** to rumple; as, to *tumble* a heap of clothes:— *n.* **1,** a fall; **2,** a state of confusion; also, a disordered heap.

TULIP

tum·ble·bug (tŭm′bl-bŭg′), *n.* a kind of beetle that rolls up balls of dung and uses them as places in which to lay its eggs.

TUMBLERS, def. 1

tum·bler (tŭm′blẽr), *n.* **1,** a person who performs feats of leaping, somersaulting, or the like; an acrobat; **2,** a stemless drinking glass with straight sides; also, the amount it holds; as, a *tumbler* of milk; **3**, that part of a lock which must be put into a certain position, generally by a key, before the lock will open; **4**, a kind of pigeon which turns somersaults in the air: also called *tumbler pigeon*.

tum·brel (tŭm'brĕl) or **tum·bril** (tŭm'brĭl), *n.* a rude cart; especially, a cart used in the French Revolution to take condemned prisoners to the guillotine.

TUMBLER def. 2

tu·mid (tū'mĭd), *adj.* **1**, bulging; swollen, as parts of the body in disease; **2**, full of high-sounding words.—*n.* **tu·mid'i·ty**.

tu·mor (tū'mẽr), *n.* an abnormal swelling or growth of tissue within or upon the body.—*adj.* **tu'mor·ous**.

tu·mult (tū'mŭlt), *n.* **1**, such noise and confusion as proceeds from a crowd of excited people; **2**, violent agitation, as of the mind.

Syn. uproar, turbulence, clamor.

tu·mul·tu·ous (tū-mŭl'tū-ŭs), *adj.* **1**, marked by, or full of, noisy confusion; **2**, agitated, as the feelings; **3**, stormy; rough, as the sea.—*adv.* **tu·mul'tu·ous·ly**.

Syn. turbulent, riotous, boisterous.

tun (tŭn), *n.* **1**, a large cask; **2**, formerly, a measure of wine equal to 252 gallons.

tu·na (tōō'nȧ), *n.* [*pl.* tuna or tunas], a large game and food fish found in warm seas; the tunny: also called *tuna fish*.

tun·dra (tōōn'drȧ; tŭn'drȧ), *n.* a stretch of the flat or rolling marshy land found in northern arctic regions. Mosses and lichens, but no trees, grow on tundras.

tune (tūn), *n.* **1**, a series of musical tones having rhythm and melody and forming a complete theme; an air or melody; **2**, a musical setting, as for a hymn or ballad; also, any easy, simple musical composition; as, I love an old *tune*; **3**, the state of giving forth tones of the proper pitch; **4**, proper adjustment in respect to musical sounds; as, the piano and the violin are in *tune*; **5**, state of harmonious adjustment; fitting mood; as, to be in *tune* with one's surroundings:—*v.t.* [tuned, tun-ing], **1**, to cause to give forth the proper sounds; adjust (a voice or an instrument) to the correct musical pitch; **2**, to put into harmony with something; as, he was *tuned* with the gaiety of the party; **3**, to put into proper working condition; as, to *tune* a motor; **4**, to adjust (a radio receiver) to a certain wave length or frequency:—*v.i.* to be in harmony:—**tune in**, **tune out**, in radio, to adjust a receiving set so as to bring in, or shut out, a given sound.—*adj.* **tune'less**.

tune·ful (tūn'fŏŏl), *adj.* full of music or melody; harmonious; as, a *tuneful* voice.

tun·er (tūn'ẽr), *n.* **1**, one who adjusts musical instruments to their proper pitch; as, a piano *tuner;* **2**, a device for tuning.

tung·sten (tŭng'stĕn), *n.* a metal which in its impure form is hard, brittle, and gray. It is used as an alloy of steel and for the filaments of electric lamps.

tu·nic (tū'nĭk), *n.* **1**, a kind of shirt worn as an undergarment by both men and women in ancient Greece and Rome; **2**, nowadays, a woman's loose outer garment or overblouse reaching down to, or below, the hips; **3**, the close-fitting short coat of a soldier's or policeman's uniform.

tun·ing fork, a fork-shaped piece of steel which, when struck, gives out a fixed tone. It is used in determining pitch and in tuning musical instruments.

Tu·nis (tū'nĭs), a city, capital of Tunisia, in Africa (map 14).

Tu·nis·i·a (tū-nĭsh'ĭ-ȧ; tū·nĭsh'ȧ), a country (cap. Tunis) in northern Africa, on the Mediterranean, formerly a French protectorate (map 14).

tun·nel (tŭn'ĕl), *n.* an underground passage cut through a hill or under a river; as, a railroad *tunnel;* also, an underground passage dug by a burrowing animal:—*v.i.* and *v.t.* [tunneled, tunnel-ing], to make or dig a tunnel (through); as, to *tunnel* through a hill; *tunnel* a hill.

tun·ny (tŭn'ĭ), *n.* [*pl.* tunnies], a food and game fish found in all warm seas; the tuna fish. Largest of the mackerel family, it sometimes attains a length of ten feet and a weight of 1,000 pounds.

TUNNY (¹⁄₇₅)

tu·pe·lo (tōō'pē-lō), *n.* [*pl.* tupelos], a North American tree with blue-black berries and hard, close-grained wood; also, the wood of this tree.

tur·ban (tûr'bȧn), *n.* **1**, in the Orient, a man's headdress, consisting of a cap around which a scarf is wrapped, worn especially by Mohammedans; **2**, any similar headdress, as the bandanna worn by Negro mammies; **3**, a small close-fitting, brimless hat for women; a toque.

TURBAN

tur·bid (tûr'bĭd), *adj.* **1**, having the sediment stirred up; hence, muddy; thick; as, *turbid* waters; **2**, unsettled; confused; as, a *turbid* state of mind; *turbid* thoughts.

go; join; yet; sing; chin; show; thin, *th*en; hw, *w*hy; zh, azure; ü, Ger. *f*ür or Fr. *l*une; ȫ, Ger. schön or Fr. *f*eu; ṅ, Fr. *e*nfant, *no*m; kh, Ger. a*ch* or i*ch*. See pages ix–x.

tur·bine (tûr′bĭn; tûr′bīn), *n.* a form of motor in which the power is derived from water, steam, or air, driven against curved vanes or cups on the rim of a wheel.

tur·bot (tûr′bŭt), *n.* a large European fish of the flounder family, greatly valued as food; also, any similar flounder, or flatfish, as the halibut.

tur·bu·lent (tûr′bū-lĕnt), *adj.* **1,** violent; not easily controlled; as, *turbulent* emotions; **2,** agitated; wild, as a stormy sea; **3,** riotous; creating disturbance; as, a *turbulent* crowd.—*n.* **tur′bu·lence.**

tu·reen (tū-rēn′; tŏŏ-rēn′), *n.* a deep covered dish for serving soup at table.

turf (tûrf), *n.* **1,** the top layer of ground, containing plant débris, matted grass roots, etc.; sod; also, a piece of sod; **2,** peat:—**the turf, 1,** a track for horse racing; **2,** horse racing:— *v.t.* to cover with grassy sod.

TUREEN

tur·gid (tûr′jĭd), *adj.* **1,** swollen; puffed out; **2,** bombastic; pompous.

Tu·rin (tū′rĭn; tū-rĭn′), a large city of northwestern Italy (map 12). Its Italian name is *Torino.*

Turk (tûrk), *n.* **1,** a native of Turkey; **2,** any member of the race from which the Ottomans are descended; **3,** a Mohammedan, especially one dwelling in Turkey.

Tur·ke·stan(tûr′kĕ-stăn′;tŏŏr′kĕ-stän′)or **Tur·ki·stan** (tûr′kĭ-stăn′; tŏŏr′kĕ-stän′), a region of central Asia (map 15).

Tur·key (tûr′kĭ), a republic (cap. Ankara) in southeastern Europe and Asia Minor (maps 12, 15). It was formerly known as the *Turkish* or *Ottoman Empire.*

tur·key (tûr′kĭ), *n.* [*pl.* turkeys], a large wild or domestic American fowl; also, its flesh used as food.

tur·key buz·zard, a large carrion-eating vulture of South and Central America and the southern U.S.: also called *turkey vulture.*

TURKEY COCK (¼)

Turk·ish (tûr′kĭsh), *adj.* pertaining to Turkey or the Turks:—*n.* the language of the Turks.

Turk·men·i·stan (tûrk′mĕn-ĭ-stăn′; tŏŏrk′mĕn-ē-stän′), or **Tur·ko·man** (tûr′kō-măn), a republic of the U.S.S.R. Its official name is *Turkmen Soviet Socialist Republic.*

Turkmen Soviet Socialist Republic, a republic (cap. Ashkhabad) of the U.S.S.R. on the Caspian Sea, north of Iran (map 15).

tur·mer·ic (tûr′mĕr-ĭk), *n.* an East Indian plant; also, its root, which is reduced to a powder and used in chemistry and as a seasoning:

tur·moil (tûr′moil), *n.* confusion and disturbance; upheaval; agitation.

turn (tûrn), *v.t.* **1,** to cause to revolve or go round; as, to *turn* a wheel; hence, to revolve in the mind or ponder; as, to *turn* over a new idea; **2,** to do or perform by means of a revolving motion; as, to *turn* a handspring; **3,** to shape by revolving against a sharp edge, as in a lathe; **4,** to change the direction, attitude, or position of; as, to *turn* an automobile; **5,** to unsettle or upset (the stomach); **6,** to change (something) into something else; as, to *turn* failure into success; **7,** to cause to go; send; as, to *turn* a beggar away; to *turn* an employee off; **8,** to move to the other side of; go around; as, to *turn* a corner; **9,** to invert; reverse; as, to *turn* a blouse; **10,** to spoil; sour; as, the hot weather *turned* the cream:—*v.i.* **1,** to have a circular motion; revolve; rotate; as, the earth *turns* on its axis; **2,** to depend; hinge; as, my action *turns* on yours; **3,** to change one's direction or position; as, he *turned* away; also, to change one's attitude; as, he *turned* against his friend; **4,** to seem to whirl or spin; reel; as, my head is *turning;* **5,** to change in condition; as, the cider *turned* to vinegar:—*n.* **1,** the act of revolving; a single revolution or twisting; as, the *turn* of a wheel; **2,** a change of direction; also, a bend or curve; as, a *turn* in the road; **3,** a short walk for exercise; **4,** a deed or act; as, you did me a good *turn;* **5,** the time for some act which one does in rotation with others; as, it's your *turn* now; **6,** a change in condition; as, his fortune took a *turn* for the better; **7,** tendency; bent; particular cast of mind; as, he is of a mechanical *turn;* **8,** a short piece or act on the stage; **9,** *Colloquial,* a startling surprise or shock; as, the news gave me a *turn.*

turn in, *Colloquial,* to go to bed; **turn on** or **off,** to cause to flow, shine, operate, etc., or to stop the flowing, shining, operating, etc., as by turning a key or knob; as, to *turn on* the water, the electric light, the radio; **turn out, 1,** to result or prove to be; as, it *turned out* to be a sunny day; the cake *turned out* well; **2,** *Colloquial,* to come out, as for the theater, a meeting, or the like; **turn the tables,** to make the winner the loser, and vice versa; **turn to, 1,** to set to work; **2,** to refer to or consult; as, *turn to* the dictionary; **turn turtle,** to turn upside down, as an automobile; **turn up**, to occur or happen; as, who knows what will *turn up*; **to a turn**, to just the right degree.

turn-coat (tûrn′kōt′), *n.* a person who forsakes his principles; one who goes over to the opposite camp; a deserter; renegade.

turn-er (tûr′nẽr), *n.* **1,** one who or that which turns; as, a pancake *turner*; **2,** a person who shapes articles with a lathe.

tur-nip (tûr′nĭp), *n.* **1,** the fleshy, rounded, edible root, white or yellow, of a certain plant, the leaves of which may also, when tender, be cooked and eaten; **2,** the plant.

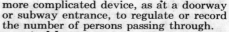
TURNIP

turn-key (tûrn′kē′), *n.* [*pl.* turnkeys], a person who has charge of the keys of a prison or penitentiary.

turn-out (tûrn′out′), *n. Colloquial,* a public gathering of persons; attendance at a meeting; a crowd.

turn-o-ver (tûrn′ō′vẽr), *n.* **1,** the act or result of upsetting, reversing position, or the like; an upset; **2,** a pie or tart made by folding one half of the crust over the other half, with filling between; **3,** in commercial usage, the series of steps by which a business operation is brought to completion, ready for repetition, as when goods are sold and a fresh stock purchased, or when money is invested in a business and later returned by it; also, the total amount involved in any such operation, and the speed with which it is put through; **4,** any similar cycle, or length of cycle, referring to the taking on and the discharge of employees, hospital patients, hotel guests, etc.:—**labor turnover,** the number of employees who leave and are replaced in a definite period of time:—*adj.* made with a part folded over.

turn-pike (tûrn′pīk′), *n.* **1,** a gate or bar to stop wagons, carriages, etc., until toll is paid; a tollgate; **2,** a road which now has or once had tollgates; **3,** loosely, a main highway: also called *turnpike road* or *pike.*

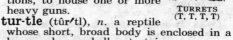
TURNSTILE

turn-spit (tûrn′spĭt′), *n.* a person who turns the slender, pointed rod, or spit, used for holding meat which is being roasted over an open fire.

turn-stile (tûrn′stīl′), *n.* **1,** formerly, a gate at the entrance of a road, bridge, or the like, made of four arms pivoted on the top of a post and turning to let persons through, one by one; **2,** now, a similar but more complicated device, as at a doorway or subway entrance, to regulate or record the number of persons passing through.

turn-ta-ble (tûrn′tā′bl), *n.* a circular platform that may be revolved, as for switching a locomotive on to another track or for turning it around.

tur-pen-tine (tûr′pĕn-tīn), *n.* **1,** the sap obtained from certain trees, such as the pine and fir; **2,** commonly, a light-colored fluid distilled from this sap, used in paints and varnishes, and also in medicine.

tur-pi-tude (tûr′pĭ-tūd), *n.* shameful wickedness.

tur-quoise (tûr′koiz; tûr′kwoiz), *n.* **1,** an opaque, light-blue or greenish-blue stone, much used as a gem; **2,** the greenish-blue color of this stone.

tur-ret (tûr′ĕt), *n.* **1,** a small tower, usually at the corner of a building, sometimes merely decorative; **2,** a low towerlike, rotating structure or platform, mounted on battleships or in fortifications, to house one or more heavy guns.

TURRETS (T, T, T, T)

tur-tle (tûr′tl), *n.* a reptile whose short, broad body is enclosed in a bony or horny shell; a tortoise.

tur-tle-dove (tûr′tl-dŭv′), *n.* any of several Old World doves, especially a European dove, noted for its gentleness and its soft cooing.

tush (tŭsh), *interj.* an expression of contempt, reproof, or restraint.

GREEN TURTLE (¼)

tusk (tŭsk), *n.* **1,** one of the two outside pointed teeth which project from the mouth, when closed, of certain animals, such as the elephant and walrus; **2,** any abnormally large, projecting tooth.

tus-sah (tŭs′à), *n.* an Oriental silkworm that produces a strong, coarse, brownish silk; also, the silk.

tus-sle (tŭs′l), *n.* a scuffle, as in sport:—*v.i.* [tus-sled, tus-sling], to scuffle or struggle.

tus-sock (tŭs′ŭk), *n.* a tuft of grass; a hummock of grass or twigs.

tut (tŭt), *interj.* hush! be quiet! an expression of rebuke, impatience, or the like.

tu-te-lage (tū′tē-lĭj), *n.* **1,** the acting as guardian; guardianship; **2,** the state of being under a tutor or guardian.

tu-te-lar-y (tū′tē-lĕr′ĭ) or **tu-te-lar** (tū′tē-lẽr), *adj.* **1,** acting as guardian; as, a *tutelary* deity; **2,** relating to a guardian.

---

go; join; yet; sing; chin; show; thin, *th*en; hw, *why*; zh, a*z*ure; ü, Ger. f*ü*r or Fr. l*u*ne; ö, Ger. sch*ö*n or Fr. f*eu*; ṅ, Fr. *en*fant, no*m*; kh, Ger. a*ch* or i*ch.* See pages ix–x.

tu-tor (tū′tĕr), *n.* **1,** a person whose profession it is to teach; especially, a private teacher; **2,** in some American colleges, a teacher ranking below an instructor:—*v.t.* to instruct or teach privately:—*v.i.* **1,** to do the work of a tutor; **2,** *Colloquial,* to be taught privately; as, he had to *tutor* in Latin.—*adj.* **tu-tor′i-al** (tū-tôr′ĭ-ăl).

Tux-e-do (tŭk-sē′dō), *n.* [*pl.* Tuxedos or Tuxedoes], a man's dinner jacket or evening dress for semiformal occasions. Also written **tux-e′do.**

TV, abbreviation for *television.*

twad-dle (twŏd′l; twôd′l), *n.* silly talk:—*v.i.* [twad-dled, twad-dling], to talk in a silly or foolish manner.—*n.* **twad′dler.**

Twain, Mark (twān), (1835–1910), the pen name of *Samuel Langhorne Clemens,* American humorist and writer, author of "Tom Sawyer" and "Huckleberry Finn."

twain (twān), *Poetic* or *Archaic: adj.* two:—*n.* a pair; two.

twang (twăng), *n.* **1,** a sharp, quick, vibrating sound; **2,** a sharp nasal tone in speech; as, a Yankee *twang:*—*v.t.* to cause to sound with a twang:—*v.i.* to sound or speak with a twang.

'twas (twŏz), a contraction of *it was.*

tweak (twēk), *v.t.* to pinch or twist with a jerk:—*n.* a sudden, sharp pinch.

tweed (twēd), *n.* a twilled fabric, usually woolen, showing two or more colors generally mixed in the yarn.

tweet (twēt), *n.* a low, chirping bird note.

TWEEZERS

tweez-ers (twē′zĕrz), *n.pl.* a small instrument for taking hold of, or pulling out, something tiny, as a hair.

twelfth (twĕlfth), *adj.* next after the 11th: the ordinal of *twelve:*—*n.* one of the twelve equal parts of anything.

Twelfth—night (twĕlfth′=nīt′), *n.* the twelfth night after Christmas; Epiphany evening: sometimes used of Epiphany Eve.

twelve (twĕlv), *adj.* composed of one more than eleven:—*n.* **1,** the number consisting of eleven plus one; a dozen; **2,** a sign representing twelve units, as 12 or xii:—**the Twelve,** the twelve disciples of Jesus.

twelve-month (twĕlv′mŭnth′), *n.* a period of twelve calendar months; a year.

twen-ti-eth (twĕn′tĭ-ĕth), *adj.* next after the 19th: the ordinal of *twenty:*—*n.* one of the twenty equal parts of anything.

twen-ty (twĕn′tĭ), *adj.* composed of one more than nineteen:—*n.* [*pl.* twenties], **1,** the number consisting of nineteen plus one; a score; **2,** a sign representing twenty units, as 20 or xx.

twice (twīs), *adv.* **1,** two times; as, I told him *twice;* **2,** doubly; as, *twice* as old.

twid-dle (twĭd′l), *v.t.* [twid-dled, twid-dling], to twirl; as, to *twiddle* one's thumbs.

twig (twĭg), *n.* a small branch or shoot.

twi-light (twī′līt′), *n.* **1,** the faint light that prevails after sunset; **2,** partial light; dimness:—*adj.* **1,** pertaining to the time between sunset and darkness; **2,** dim; obscure.

twill (twĭl), *n.* **1,** a weave of cloth that shows diagonal lines or ribs on the surface; **2,** a fabric woven with such ribs, as serge:—*v.t.* to weave (cloth) so as to show diagonal lines or ribs.

'twill (twĭl), a contraction of *it will.*

twin (twĭn), *adj.* **1,** made of two separate, but equal, parts; double; as, *twin* towers; **2,** very like each other; **3,** born at the same birth; as, *twin* brothers:—*n.* **1,** one of two born at one birth; **2,** a person or thing very like another.

twine (twīn), *n.* **1,** a kind of strong thread or string; **2,** a twist or tangle:—*v.t.* [twined, twin-ing], **1,** to make by twisting; as, to *twine* a garland; **2,** to encircle; as, to *twine* a pole with ribbons:—*v.i.* to wind; as, the vine *twines* over the porch.

twinge (twĭnj), *n.* a sudden, darting pain.

twin-kle (twĭng′kl), *v.i.* [twin-kled, twin-kling], **1,** to shine with a gleam that grows alternately dimmer and brighter; flicker; as, a star *twinkles;* hence, to sparkle, as the eyes; **2,** to flash in and out rapidly, as the feet in dancing:—*v.t.* to open and shut (the eyelids) rapidly; wink:—*n.* **1,** a flicker or quiver; **2,** a sparkle or gleam; **3,** the time occupied by a wink; a moment; twinkling.

twin-kling (twĭng′klĭng), *n.* **1,** the time occupied by a wink or a brief flash; a moment; an instant; **2,** a flash or flicker, as of a star.

twirl (twûrl), *v.t.* **1,** to turn (something) around rapidly; whirl; as, to *twirl* a cane; **2,** *Slang,* in baseball, to pitch:—*v.i.* **1,** to rotate rapidly; **2,** *Slang,* to pitch:—*n.* a quick, circular motion; a twist.

twist (twĭst), *v.t.* **1,** to wind (strands) together; also, to form (a rope or twine) by this means; **2,** to twine or wind; as, to *twist* a scarf around one's neck; **3,** to wrench or turn; as, to *twist* one's wrist:—*v.i.* **1,** to become joined by winding; also, to form knots; as, this silk *twists* badly; **2,** to become wrenched or turned; as, my ankle *twisted;* **3,** to take a winding course; as, the stream *twists* round the bend:—*n.* **1,** the act or manner of winding or twining; **2,** something made by winding strands together, as certain kinds of silk or cotton thread; **3,** a wrench, as of a muscle; **4,** a special tendency of mind; as, a poetical *twist.*

twist-er (twĭs'tẽr), *n.* a tornado.

twit (twĭt), *v.t.* [twit-ted, twit-ting], to upbraid or tease, often good-naturedly, by reminding a person of a mistake or fault.

twitch (twĭch), *v.i.* **1.** to pull at something with a sudden jerk; **2,** to move jerkily; as, her fingers *twitched:—n.* **1,** a sudden jerk or pull; **2,** a short, jerky contraction of a muscle.

twit-ter (twĭt'ẽr), *v.i.* **1,** to chirp; make a series of small, sharp sounds, as does a bird; **2,** to feel a slight nervous excitement: *—v.t.* to utter in short, broken sounds:— *n.* **1,** a series of short, broken sounds; **2,** a nervous trembling.

'twixt (twĭkst), a contraction of *betwixt.*

two (to͞o), *adj.* composed of one more than one:—*n.* [*pl.* twos], **1,** the sum of one and one; **2,** a sign representing two units, as 2 or ii.

two—base hit, in baseball, a hit which allows the batter to reach second base.

two-fold (to͞o'fōld'), *adj.* made of two parts; double; as, a *twofold* errand:—*adv.* (to͞o'-fōld'), doubly.

two-pence (tŭp'ĕns; if used as two words, to͞o pĕns), *n.* **1,** the sum of two English pennies; **2,** a coin worth that amount of money.

two-pen-ny (tŭp'ĕn-ĭ), *adj.* **1,** worth twopence; **2,** cheap or commonplace.

two—ply (to͞o'-plī'), *adj.* **1,** made of two strands or thicknesses; **2,** woven double.

two—step (to͞o'-stĕp'), *n.* **1,** a kind of dance in march or two-four time; **2,** the music for such a dance.

'twould (two͝od), a contraction of *it would.*

-ty (-tē), a suffix meaning quality or state; as, loyal*ty:* sometimes, *-ity;* as, civili*ty.*

Ty-ler (tī'lẽr), John (1790–1862), the tenth president of the U.S.

tym-pa-num (tĭm'pȧ-nŭm), *n.* [*pl.* tympanums or tympana (tĭm'pȧ-nȧ)], **1,** the eardrum, or middle ear; **2,** the thin membrane dividing the outer from the middle ear: also called *tympanic membrane.—adj.* **tym-pan'ic** (tĭm-păn'ĭk).

Tyn-dale (tĭn'dȧl), William (?–1536), an English reformer and martyr, and a translator of the Bible.

TYPE

type (tīp), *n.* **1,** a person or thing possessing the characteristic qualities of a group; an example; as, many of Dickens's characters are *types* of middle-class English

life; **2,** a particular class or kind; as, a high *type* of person; a juicy *type* of apple; **3,** a group of persons or things having common characteristics; as, men of an athletic *type;* also, in biology, a group or division of animals, plants, etc., having a common structure or form; as, an animal of the cat *type;* **4,** in printing: **a,** a metal or wooden block bearing on one end a raised letter, figure, or other character, an impression of which may be transferred, after inking, to paper; **b,** a series or group of such blocks; **c,** the impression from them:—*v.t.* [typed, typ-ing], to write on a typewriter.

NOTE.—The size of type was formerly given by name, and in England the name system is still often followed. In America, the point system is used, with approximately 72 points to the inch, meaning that in 72-point the type is one inch high. Types may be cut in any size; below are given the commonly used point sizes from 24 point to 5 point, with the name of the nearest equivalent size in the name system:

24	point	two-line pica	abcde
18	point	great primer	abcdefgh
14	point	English	abcdefghij
12	point	pica	abcdefghijkl
11	point	small pica	abcdefghijklm
10	point	long primer	abcdefghijklmn
9	point	bourgeois	abcdefghijklmno
8	point	brevier	abcdefghijklmnop
7	point	minion	abcdefghijklmnopq
6	point	nonpareil	abcdefghijklmnopqrst
5½	point	agate	abcdefghijklmnopqrstu
5	point	pearl	abcdefghijklmnopqrstuv

type-set-ter (tīp'sĕt'ẽr), *n.* a person or machine that arranges type in words for printing.—*n.* **type'set'ting.**

type-write (tīp'rīt'), *v.t.* and *v.i.* [*p.t.* typewrote (-rōt'), *p.p.* typewrit-ten (-rĭt'n), *p.pr.* typewrit-ing], to write on a typewriter; type.

type-writ-er (tīp'rīt'ẽr), *n.* **1,** a machine, with a keyboard operated by the fingers, which produces writing similar to printing; **2,** one who writes on a typewriter.

type-writ-ing (tīp'rīt'ĭng), *n.* **1,** the art or practice of using a typewriter; **2,** manuscript made on a typewriter.

ty-phoid (tī'foid), *n.* an infectious, often fatal, disease, traceable to germ-infected

go; join; yet; sing; chin; show; thin, *th***en; hw,** *wh***y; zh,** a**zure; ü,** Ger. f**ü**r or Fr. l**u**ne; **ō,** Ger. sch**ö**n or Fr. f**eu; ṅ,** Fr. e**n**fant, no**m; kh,** Ger. a**ch** or i**ch.** See pages ix–x.

food or drinking water: also called *typhoid fever.*

ty·phoon (tī-fōōn′), *n.* a violent tornado, usually occurring in the China Seas.

ty·phus (tī′fŭs), *n.* a serious contagious fever, spread by the bites of infected lice, marked by an eruption of red spots, weakness, and delirium.—*adj.* **ty′phous.**

typ·i·cal (tĭp′ĭ-kăl), *adj.* **1,** characteristic; like others of its class; as, Penrod is *typical* of all small boys; a *typical* country store; **2,** symbolic; representing a whole class.— *adv.* **typ′i·cal·ly.**

typ·i·fy (tĭp′ĭ-fī), *v.t.* [typified, typify-ing], **1,** to bear or show the striking characteristics of (a class or group); represent; as, the cat *typifies* a family of animals; **2,** to symbolize; as, the lamb *typifies* meekness.

typ·ist (tī′pĭst), *n.* one whose business it is to operate a typewriting machine.

ty·pog·ra·phy (tī-pŏg′rà-fī; tĭ-pŏg′rà-fī), *n.* [*pl.* typographies], the art of printing from type; also, the appearance or arrangement of printed matter.—*n.* **ty·pog′-ra·pher.**—*adj.* **ty′po-graph′ic** (tī′pŏ-grăf′-ĭk; tĭp′ŏ-grăf′ĭk); **ty′po-graph′i·cal.**

ty·ran·ni·cal (tĭ-răn′ĭ-kăl; tī-răn′ĭ-kăl), *adj.* unjustly severe; despotic; as, a *tyrannical* master; *tyrannical* laws.

tyr·an·nize (tĭr′à-nīz), *v.i.* [tyrannized, tyranniz-ing], to act like a despot; rule severely and cruelly; as, the father *tyrannized* over his daughter.

tyr·an·nous (tĭr′à-nŭs), *adj.* unjustly severe and cruel; tyrannical.

tyr·an·ny (tĭr′à-nĭ), *n.* [*pl.* tyrannies], **1,** the government or conduct of a cruel and unjust ruler; **2,** undue severity.

ty·rant (tī′rănt), *n.* **1,** an absolute monarch; a despot; **2,** a ruler or master who uses his power to oppress those under him.

Tyre (tīr), an ancient city and port, capital of Phoenicia (map 1).

Tyr·i·an (tĭr′ĭ-ăn), *adj.* pertaining to ancient Tyre in Phoenicia:—**Tyrian purple,** a famous purple or crimson dye, obtained by the ancient Greeks and Romans from certain mollusks, or shellfish.—*n.* **Tyr′i·an.**

ty·ro (tī′rō), *n.* [*pl.* tyros], a beginner.

Tyr·ol (tĭr′ŏl; tĕ-rōl′), a province of western Austria. See Tirol.

U

U, u (ū), [*pl.* U's, u's], *n.* **1,** the 21st letter of the alphabet, following T; **2,** anything with the shape of a U.

u·biq·ui·tous (ū-bĭk′wĭ-tŭs), *adj.* being, or seeming to be, everywhere at the same time.—*n.* **u·biq′ui·ty.**

U—boat (ū′-bōt′), *n.* in World War I, a German or Austrian submarine.

ud·der (ŭd′ẽr), *n.* in certain animals, a baglike milk gland with teats.

U·gan·da (ū-găn′dà; ōō-gän′dä), a British protectorate (cap. Entebbe) in central Africa, east of the Belgian Congo (map 14).

ug·ly (ŭg′lĭ), *adj.* [ug-li-er, ug-li-est], **1,** displeasing to the eye; hideous; **2,** morally repulsive; evil; as, *ugly* deeds; **3,** *Colloquial:* **a,** suggesting trouble; as, an *ugly* rumor; **b,** quarrelsome; as, an *ugly* disposition.—*n.* **ug′li·ness.**

u·kase (ū-kās′; ū′kās), *n.* **1,** in Russia under the czars, an imperial decree taking effect as law; **2,** hence, any official ruling or mandate.

U·kraine (ū′krān; ū-krān′), a republic in the U.S.S.R. Its official name is *Ukrainian Soviet Socialist Republic.*

Ukrainian Soviet Socialist Republic, a republic (cap. Kiev) in the U.S.S.R., north of the Black Sea (map 12).

u·ku·le·le (ū′kŭ-lā′lĕ), *n.* a four-stringed guitar-shaped Hawaiian instrument of Portuguese origin.

ul·cer (ŭl′sẽr), *n.* **1,** an open sore which secretes pus; **2,** hence, a corrupt influence; a public evil.—*adj.* **ul′cer-ous.**

ul·cer·ate (ŭl′sẽr-āt), *v.t.* [ulcerated, ulcerat-ing], to affect with a pus-discharging sore, or ulcer:— *v.i.* to form an ulcer.—*n.* **ul′cer-a′tion.**

Ul·ster (ŭl′stẽr), **1,** a former province of northern Ireland; **2,** Northern Ireland, now part of the United Kingdom.

ul·ster (ŭl′stẽr), *n.* a long, loose overcoat.

UKULELE

ult. abbreviation for Latin *ultimo,* meaning *in the month preceding the current month.*

ul·te·ri·or (ŭl-tĭr′ĭ-ẽr), *adj.* **1,** lying beyond; more distant; **2,** beyond what is expressed or admitted; as, an *ulterior* purpose.

ul·ti·mate (ŭl′tĭ-mĭt), *adj.* **1,** last; final; as, the *ultimate* decision; **2,** fundamental; basic; as, *ultimate* facts of nature.—*adv.* **ul′ti·mate·ly.**

ul·ti·ma·tum (ŭl′tĭ-mā′tŭm), *n.* [*pl.*

ultimatums or ultimata (ŭl´tĭ-mā´tȧ)], a final condition; one's last word on a matter; especially, the final terms stated by one nation to another, the rejection of which may be expected to lead to war.

ul·ti·mo (ŭl´tĭ-mō), *adv.* in the month preceding the current month.

ul·tra (ŭl´trȧ), *adj.* extreme; going to extremes; as, an *ultra* conservative.

ul·tra- (ŭl´trȧ-), a prefix meaning: **1,** beyond; as, *ultra*violet; **2,** excessively; beyond the usual; as, *ultra*modern.

ul·tra·ma·rine (ŭl´trȧ-mȧ-rēn´), *n.* **1,** a blue coloring matter made from the gem lapis lazuli; **2,** hence, a bright, deep blue.

ul·tra·mod·ern (ŭl´trȧ-mŏd´ẽrn), *adj.* extremely modern, fashionable, or radical.

ul·tra·vi·o·let (ŭl´trȧ-vī´ō-lĕt), *adj.* having a wave length shorter than that of the violet ray. Ultraviolet rays are invisible to the human eye, but affect some photographic plates, and are useful in the treatment of certain diseases.

U·lys·ses (ū-lĭs´ēz), *n.* the hero of Homer's "Odyssey" and the wisest and craftiest of the Greek chiefs in the Trojan War. The Greeks called him *Odysseus.*

um·bel (ŭm´bĕl), *n.* a flower cluster in which all the flower stalks, of nearly equal length, grow from a common center, and spread to form a flat or rounded head.

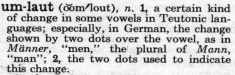

UMBEL

um·ber (ŭm´bẽr), *n.* **1,** a brown earth used as coloring matter; **2,** a rich, dark-brown color:—*adj.* umber-colored.

um·brage (ŭm´brĭj), *n.* **1,** formerly, shade or obscurity; **2,** hence, a sense of injury, as if from being put in the shade; offense.

um·brel·la (ŭm-brĕl´ȧ), *n.* a device for protection against rain, sun, etc., consisting of a folding frame, covered with silk, cotton, or the like, on a stick which ends in a handle.

Um·bri·a (ŭm´brĭ-ȧ), a department in central Italy.

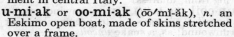

UMIAK

u·mi·ak or **oo·mi·ak** (ōō´mĭ-ăk), *n.* an Eskimo open boat, made of skins stretched over a frame.

um·laut (ōōm´lout), *n.* **1,** a certain kind of change in some vowels in Teutonic languages; especially, in German, the change shown by two dots over the vowel, as in *Männer,* "men," the plural of *Mann,* "man"; **2,** the two dots used to indicate this change.

um·pire (ŭm´pīr), *n.* a person chosen to decide a controversy; especially, one who oversees a game, to enforce the rules and decide disputed points:—*v.t.* and *v.i.* [umpired, umpir·ing], to supervise or decide as an umpire.

¹un- (ŭn-), a prefix meaning: **1,** not; the opposite of; as, *un*fair, *un*fairness, *un*fairly, *un*seen; **2,** lack of; as, *un*employment, *un*rest, *un*concern.

²un- (ŭn-), a prefix meaning action undoing or reversing the action implied in the original word; as, *un*twist, *un*lock.

NOTE.—The prefix ¹*un-*, and to a less extent ²*un-*, can be attached to a very large number of words, forming compounds of which the meaning is usually self-evident. Only the more important or especially difficult compounds are listed.

U.N. abbreviation for *United Nations.*

un·a·bashed (ŭn´ȧ-băsht´), *adj.* unembarrassed; not cast down.

un·a·ble (ŭn-ā´bl), *adj.* incapable; not able; lacking power or ability.

un·a·bridged (ŭn´ȧ-brĭjd´), *adj.* not shortened; as, an *unabridged* edition of a book.

un·ac·count·a·ble (ŭn´ȧ-koun´tȧ-bl), *adj.* **1,** not capable of explanation; as, an *unaccountable* delay; **2,** not responsible; irresponsible.—*adv.* **un´ac·count´a·bly.**

un·ac·cus·tomed (ŭn´ȧ-kŭs´tŭmd), *adj.* **1,** not usual or customary; as, *unaccustomed* speed; **2,** not familiar with or used to; as, she is *unaccustomed* to the work.

un·ad·vised (ŭn´ăd-vīzd´), *adj.* **1,** not discreet or prudent; rash; as, an *unadvised* person; an *unadvised* act; **2,** without having received advice.—*adv.* **un´ad·vis´ed·ly** (ŭn´ăd-vīz´ĕd-lĭ).

un·af·fect·ed (ŭn´ȧ-fĕk´tĕd), *adj.* **1,** without pretense; natural in manner; **2,** not influenced.—*adv.* **un´af·fect´ed·ly.**

u·na·nim·i·ty (ū´nȧ-nĭm´ĭ-tĭ), *n.* united opinion; absolute agreement.

u·nan·i·mous (ū-năn´ĭ-mŭs), *adj.* **1,** united in a single opinion; agreeing; as, we were *unanimous* in our decision; **2,** showing that all agree; as, a *unanimous* vote.

un·armed (ŭn-ärmd´), *adj.* without weapons; defenseless.

un·as·sum·ing (ŭn´ȧ-sūm´ĭng), *adj.* modest; unaffected.

un·a·vail·ing (ŭn´ȧ-vāl´ĭng), *adj.* without

effect; useless; as, *unavailing* efforts to rescue a person from drowning.

un-a-void-a-ble (ŭn/ȧ-void/ȧ-bl), *adj.* not to be escaped; inevitable; as, an *unavoidable* accident.—*adv.* **un/a-void/a-bly.**

un-a-ware (ŭn/ȧ-wâr/), *adj.* not knowing; ignorant of; as, he was *unaware* of my presence.

un-a-wares (ŭn/ȧ-wârz/), *adv.* 1, without previous planning; 2, by surprise; as, they caught the enemy *unawares*.

un-bal-anced (ŭn-băl/ănst), *adj.* 1, of unequal weight; out of equilibrium; as, *unbalanced* scales; 2, hence, mentally disordered; slightly insane.

un-bar (ŭn-bär/), *v.t.* [unbarred, unbarring], to remove a bar from (a gate or door); unlock.

un-be-com-ing (ŭn/bē-kŭm/ĭng), *adj.* 1, not suitable or fit; improper; as, conduct *unbecoming* a lady; 2, not suited to one's appearance; as, an *unbecoming* hat.

un-be-lief (ŭn/bē-lēf/), *n.* lack of positive faith or belief; especially, refusal to accept the teachings of religion.
Syn. incredulity, disbelief, doubt.

un-be-liev-er (ŭn/bē-lēv/ẽr), *n.* 1, one who lacks faith; a doubter; 2, one who refuses to accept the teachings of religion.—*adj.* **un/be-liev/ing.**

un-bend (ŭn-bĕnd/), *v.t.* [unbent (ŭn-bĕnt/), unbend-ing], 1, to make straight; loosen; as, to *unbend* a bow; 2, to free from strain; relax; as, to *unbend* the mind; 3, to unfasten (a sail) from a spar:—*v.i.* 1, to become straight; 2, to become less severe or stiff; become gracious.

un-bend-ing (ŭn-bĕn/dĭng), *adj.* 1, stiff; rigid; 2, unyielding; obstinate.

un-bi-ased or **un-bi-assed** (ŭn-bī/ăst), *adj.* impartial; without prejudice.

un-bind (ŭn-bīnd/), *v.t.* [unbound (ŭn-bound/), unbind-ing], 1, to make loose; untie; as, to *unbind* a bandage; 2, to release; free (a person) from bonds.

un-bolt (ŭn-bōlt/), *v.t.* to draw back a bolt from; unfasten; as, to *unbolt* a gate.—*adj.* **un-bolt/ed.**

un-bolt-ed (ŭn-bōl/tĕd), *adj.* coarse; not sifted; as, *unbolted* flour.

un-born (ŭn-bôrn/), *adj.* not yet born; hence, yet to come; future.

un-bos-om (ŭn-bŏoz/ŭm), *v.t.* to unburden (oneself) of a secret:—*v.i.* to free one's mind by telling one's thoughts.

un-bound (ŭn-bound/), past tense and past participle of *unbind*:—*adj.* not bound; as, *unbound* pamphlets.

un-bound-ed (ŭn-boun/dĕd), *adj.* 1, without limits; as, *unbounded* space; 2, extreme; as, *unbounded* admiration.

un-bri-dled (ŭn-brī/dld), *adj.* 1, not fastened with a bridle; 2, not restrained; as, an *unbridled* tongue.

un-buck-le (ŭn-bŭk/l), *v.t.* [unbuck-led, unbuck-ling], to undo the buckle or buckles of; as, to *unbuckle* a belt.

un-bur-den (ŭn-bûr/dn), *v.t.* 1, to relieve of a burden; as, to *unburden* oneself of a secret; 2, to throw off (a burden).

un-but-ton (ŭn-bŭt/n), *v.t.* to unfasten the button or buttons of.

un-called-for (ŭn-kôld/-fôr/), *adj.* not needed; out of place; as, an *uncalled-for* comment.

un-can-ny (ŭn-kăn/ĭ), *adj.* not to be explained by reason; unearthly.

un-cer-tain (ŭn-sûr/tĭn), *adj.* 1, not sure; doubtful; as, the result is *uncertain*; 2, indefinite as to quantity or quality; as, an *uncertain* number; an *uncertain* flavor; 3, not positive; not decided; as, we are *uncertain* about going; 4, not steady; as, the platform gave but *uncertain* support; 5, changing; fluctuating; as, the *uncertain* tide.
Syn. variable, fitful, precarious.

un-cer-tain-ty (ŭn-sûr/tĭn-tĭ), *n.* [*pl.* uncertainties], the state or quality of being doubtful; also, something about which there is considerable doubt.

un-chain (ŭn-chān/), *v.t.* to unfasten the chains of; let loose; as, to *unchain* a dog.

un-char-i-ta-ble (ŭn-chăr/ĭ-tȧ-bl), *adj.* 1, not generous toward the needy; 2, unkind; harsh in judging others.

un-chris-tian (ŭn-krĭs/chăn), *adj.* 1, heathen; 2, unbecoming to, or unlike, a Christian; as, *unchristian* conduct.

un-civ-il (ŭn-sĭv/ĭl), *adj.* rude; discourteous.

un-civ-i-lized (ŭn-sĭv/ĭ-līzd), *adj.* savage; barbarous.

un-clasp (ŭn-klȧsp/), *v.t.* to release the clasp of; as, to *unclasp* a necklace; to unfasten; as, to *unclasp* one's fingers.

un-cle (ŭng/kl), *n.* 1, the brother of one's father or mother; 2, the husband of one's aunt; 3, *Colloquial*, an old man.

un-clean (ŭn-klēn/), *adj.* 1, soiled; filthy; 2, impure; obscene.

Uncle Sam, *Colloquial*, the United States government: from the abbreviation *U.S.*

un-clothe (ŭn-klōth/), *v.t.* [unclothed, uncloth-ing], to remove the clothes or covering from; undress.

un-coil (ŭn-koil/), *v.t.* to unwind; as, to *uncoil* a spring:—*v.i.* to become loose or unwound; as, a snake *uncoils*.

āte, āorta, râre, căt, ȧsk, fär, ăllow, sofȧ; ēve, ēvent, ĕll, writẽr, novĕl; bīte, pĭn; nō, ōbey, ôr, dŏg, tŏp, cŏllide; ūnit, ūnite, bûrn, cŭt, focŭs; nōon, fŏŏt; mound; coin;

un·com·fort·a·ble (ŭn-kŭm′fẽrt-*a*-bl), *adj.* 1, not at ease physically or mentally; 2, causing discomfort; as, an *uncomfortable* chair.—*adv.* **un·com′fort·a·bly.**

un·com·mon (ŭn-kŏm′ŭn), *adj.* out of the ordinary; rare; strange.

un·com·pro·mis·ing (ŭn-kŏm′prŏ-mīz′-ĭng), *adj.* not willing to make concessions; unyielding; as, an *uncompromising* man.

un·con·cern (ŭn′kŏn-sûrn′), *n.* lack of interest or anxiety.

un·con·cerned (ŭn′kŏn-sûrnd′), *adj.* 1, not anxious; 2, uninterested.

un·con·di·tion·al (ŭn′kŏn-dĭsh′ŭn-ăl), *adj.* without any limitations; absolute; as, an *unconditional* promise.—*adv.* **un′con·di′tion·al·ly.**

un·con·scion·a·ble (ŭn-kŏn′shŭn-*a*-bl), *adj.* 1, unreasonable; as, *unconscionable* anger; 2, not influenced by the conscience.

un·con·scious (ŭn-kŏn′shŭs), *adj.* 1, without consciousness; without apparent life; 2, without realization or understanding; as, a person *unconscious* of ridicule; 3, not deliberate; accidental; as, an *unconscious* omission.—*n.* **un·con′-scious·ness.**

un·con·sti·tu·tion·al (ŭn′kŏn-stĭ-tū′-shŭn-ăl), *adj.* not in accord with the constitution or political principles of a country.—*n.* **un′con·sti·tu′tion·al′i·ty.**

un·cork (ŭn-kôrk′), *v.t.* to open by pulling out the cork of; as, to *uncork* a jug.

un·cou·ple (ŭn-kŭp′l), *v.t.* [uncou-pled, uncou-pling], to set free; to unleash; also, to unloose from a coupling; detach; as, to *uncouple* a locomotive.

un·couth (ŭn-kōōth′), *adj.* 1, awkward; ungainly; 2, crude; boorish.

un·cov·er (ŭn-kŭv′ẽr), *v.t.* 1, to remove a top or cover from; 2, to take the hat or cap from; 3, to make known; bring to light, as a plot:—*v.i.* to take off the hat or cap; as, to *uncover* for the flag.

unc·tion (ŭngk′shŭn), *n.* 1, the act of anointing as a sign of consecration; 2, an ointment; hence, anything soothing; 3, excessive courtesy; a smooth, oily manner.

unc·tu·ous (ŭngk′tū-ŭs), *adj.* 1, oily; smooth; 2, bland; insincerely suave; as, an *unctuous* speech.—*n.* **unc′tu·ous·ness.**

un·cul·ti·vat·ed (ŭn-kŭl′tĭ-vāt′ĕd), *adj.* 1, untilled; as, *uncultivated* land; also, undeveloped; as, an *uncultivated* talent; 2, uncivilized; unrefined.

un·curl (ŭn-kûrl′), *v.t.* to cause to straighten out; as, to *uncurl* feathers:—*v.i.* to become straight.

un·daunt·ed (ŭn-dôn′tĕd; ŭn-dän′tĕd), *adj.* not dismayed; bold.

un·de·ceive (ŭn′dĕ-sēv′), *v.t.* [undeceived, undeceiv-ing], to free from error or mistake; enlighten.

un·de·cid·ed (ŭn′dĕ-sīd′ĕd), *adj.* 1, doubtful; unsettled; as, an *undecided* issue; 2, wavering; as, *undecided* what to do.

un·de·filed (ŭn′dĕ-fīld′), *adj.* not corrupted; pure.

un·de·fined (ŭn′dĕ-fīnd′), *adj.* 1, without definite limits; indefinite; as, *undefined* boundaries; 2, unexplained; as, an *undefined* word.

un·de·ni·a·ble (ŭn′dĕ-nī′*a*-bl), *adj.* 1, not to be contradicted; unquestionable; as, he possesses *undeniable* skill; 2, decidedly good; as, a person of *undeniable* character. —*adv.* **un′de·ni′a·bly.**

un·der (ŭn′dẽr), *prep.* 1, below or beneath; as, *under* a ladder; *under* the skin; *under* the sea; also, lower than, in position, authority, excellence, or value; as, a captain is *under* a major; cotton sells *under* silk; 2, less than, in height, weight, age, or number; as, *under* six feet; *under* ten years; *under* five dollars; 3, subject to the action or effect of; as, *under* treatment; *under* a strain; *under* orders; 4, because of; as, *under* the circumstances; 5, in conformity with; as, *under* a rule of the firm; classified beneath; as, *under* this topic; 6, during the rule of; as, England *under* the Tudors:—*adj.* 1, lower in position; as, the *under* surface; 2, lower in rank; as, an *under* waiter:—*adv.* in or to a lower place or subordinate position.

un·der- (ŭn′dẽr-), a prefix meaning: 1, below; as, *underground*; 2, below standard or need; as, *undervalue*, *underfed*; 3, subordinate; as *undergraduate*, *understudy*.

un·der·bid (ŭn′dẽr-bĭd′), *v.t.* [underbid, underbid-ding], to outdo (a person), as in competitive bidding, by offering to sell or do something at a lower price.

un·der·brush (ŭn′dẽr-brŭsh′), *n.* bushes, shrubs, and small trees growing thickly in a forest; undergrowth.

un·der·clothes (ŭn′dẽr-klōthz′), *n.pl.* garments worn beneath other clothes; underwear: also called *underclothing*.

un·der·cur·rent (ŭn′dẽr-kûr′ĕnt), *n.* 1, a current, as of air or water, below another current or below the surface; 2, hence, a concealed tendency of thought or feeling; as, an *undercurrent* of opposition.

un·der·done (ŭn′dẽr-dŭn′; ŭn′dẽr-dŭn′), *adj.* cooked too little; not thoroughly done.

un·der·fed (ŭn′dẽr-fĕd′), *adj.* given insufficient food; undernourished.

un·der·foot (ŭn′dẽr-fŏŏt′), *adv.* beneath the feet; as, it is slushy *underfoot*.

---

go; join; yet; sing; chin; show; thin, *th*en; hw, *wh*y; zh, a*z*ure; ü, Ger. f*ür* or Fr. l*u*ne; ö, Ger. sch*ö*n or Fr. f*eu*; ṅ, Fr. e*n*fant, no*m*; kh, Ger. a*ch* or i*ch*. See pages ix–x.

un·der·gar·ment (ŭn′dĕr-gär′mĕnt), *n.* a garment worn under the outer clothing.

un·der·go (ŭn′dĕr-gō′), *v.t.* [*p.t.* underwent (-wĕnt′), *p.p.* undergone (-gôn′), *p.pr.* undergo-ing], to be subjected to; experience; as, to *undergo* an operation.

un·der·grad·u·ate (ŭn′dĕr-grăd′ū-āt), *n.* a college or university student who has not yet taken his first, or bachelor's, degree.

un·der·ground (ŭn′dĕr-ground′), *adj.* **1,** below the surface of the earth; as, an *underground* railway; **2,** acting in secret; as, an *underground* system of spying:—*adv.* (ŭn′dĕr-ground′), beneath the earth's surface:—*n.* (ŭn′dĕr-ground′), something below the surface of the earth; as, in London, the subway is called the *underground.*

un·der·grown (ŭn′dĕr-grōn′), *adj.* below normal size; not fully grown.

un·der·growth (ŭn′dĕr-grōth′), *n.* low shrubs and bushes in a forest; underbrush.

un·der·hand (ŭn′dĕr-hănd′), *adj.* **1,** acting secretly or deceitfully; also, characterized by deceit; as, *underhand* methods; **2,** of a ball, thrown with an upward swing of the arm, with the palm of the hand turned up:—

UNDERHAND THROW

adv. (ŭn′dĕr-hănd′), **1,** secretly; **2,** unfairly.

un·der·hand·ed (ŭn′dĕr-hăn′dĕd), *adj.* dishonest; not aboveboard; underhand.—*adv.* **un·der·hand·ed·ly.**

un·der·lie (ŭn′dĕr-lī′), *v.t.* [*p.t.* underlay (-lā′), *p.p.* underlain (-lān′), *p.pr.* underly-ing], **1,** to lie or be beneath; **2,** hence, to be at the bottom of; serve as the basis of; as, what motives *underlie* his acts?

un·der·line (ŭn′dĕr-līn′), *v.t.* [underlined, underlin-ing], *v.t.* to draw a line beneath; underscore; as, to *underline* a word.

un·der·ling (ŭn′dĕr-lĭng), *n.* a person occupying a low position; a subordinate.

un·der·ly·ing (ŭn′dĕr-lī′ĭng), *adj.* essential; basic; as, the *underlying* cause.

un·der·mine (ŭn′dĕr-mīn′), *v.t.* [undermined, undermin-ing], **1,** to dig beneath; form a tunnel under; **2,** hence, to weaken; work against secretly; as, to *undermine* one's health; *undermine* one's influence.

un·der·most (ŭn′dĕr-mōst), *adj.* lowest in place, position, or rank.

un·der·neath (ŭn′dĕr-nēth′; ŭn′dĕr-nēth′), *adv.* and *prep.* beneath; below.

un·der·rate (ŭn′dĕr-rāt′), *v.t.* [underrat-ed, underrat-ing], to place too low a value or estimate upon; as, to *underrate* a person's abilities.

un·der·score (ŭn′dĕr-skôr′), *v.t.* [underscored, underscor-ing], to draw a line under; underline.

un·der·sea (ŭn′dĕr-sē′), *adj.* beneath the surface of the sea; submarine; as, *undersea* plants.—*adv.* **un·der·sea′; un·der·seas′.**

un·der·sell (ŭn′dĕr-sĕl′), *v.t.* [undersold (-sōld′), undersell-ing], to sell at a lower price than (another).

un·der·shirt (ŭn′dĕr-shûrt′), *n.* a garment for the upper half of the body, worn under other clothing, next to the skin.

un·der·shot (ŭn′dĕr-shŏt′), *adj.* **1,** driven by water passing underneath, as a water wheel; **2,** having a prominent or protruding lower jaw.

UNDERSHOT WHEEL

un·der·sign (ŭn′dĕr-sīn′), *v.t.* [undersigned, undersign-ing], to write one's name below, or at the end of; as, to *undersign* a petition:—**the undersigned,** the person or persons signing a document.

un·der·skirt (ŭn′dĕr-skûrt′), *n.* a skirt worn under an outer garment; a petticoat.

un·der·stand (ŭn′dĕr-stănd′), *v.t.* [understood (-stŏŏd′), understand-ing], **1,** to comprehend or grasp; as, she doesn't *understand* what you mean; **2,** to know thoroughly; as, to *understand* one's business; **3,** to see clearly; realize; as, you do not *understand* what the consequences will be; **4,** to accept as a fact without positive knowledge; believe; as, I *understand* he will come; **5,** in grammar, to supply mentally (a word which is not expressed); as, in the phrase, "red roses and white," "roses" may be *understood* after "white":—*v.i.* to comprehend; as, say no more; I *understand.*

un·der·stand·ing (ŭn′dĕr-stăn′dĭng), *adj.* intelligent; also, sympathetic:—*n.* **1,** knowledge; as, an *understanding* of algebra; **2,** ability to understand; intelligence; as, John is superior to him in *understanding;* **3,** the agreement of two minds; as, the perfect *understanding* between them.

Syn., n. reason, discernment, judgment.

un·der·state (ŭn′dĕr-stāt′), *v.t.* [understat-ed, understat-ing], to tell less than the truth about; state (facts) too weakly.

un·der·stood (ŭn′dĕr-stŏŏd′), past tense and past participle of *understand.*

un·der·stud·y (ŭn′dĕr-stŭd′ĭ), *v.t.* and *v.i.* [understudied, understudy-ing], to learn (another actor's part) in order to take his place if necessary.—*n.* **un·der·stud·y.**

un·der·take (ŭn′dĕr-tāk′), *v.t.* [*p.t.* undertook (-tŏŏk′), *p.p.* undertak-en (-tāk′-

ĕn), *p.pr.* undertak-ing], **1,** to take upon oneself; attempt; as, to *undertake* a task; **2,** to contract to do; promise; as, he *undertook* to finish the work by June.

un-der-tak-er (ŭn′dẽr-tāk′ẽr), *n.* one who makes a business of preparing the dead for burial, and of conducting funerals.

un-der-tak-ing (ŭn′dẽr-tāk′ĭng), *n.* **1,** the taking upon oneself of a task or responsibility; **2,** task or enterprise; **3,** (ŭn′-dẽr-tāk′ĭng), the business of preparing the dead for burial, and of managing funerals.

un-der-tone (ŭn′dẽr-tōn′), *n.* **1,** a low or subdued pitch of voice or sound; **2,** a subdued shade of any color.

un-der-took (ŭn′dẽr-tŏŏk′), past tense of *undertake.*

un-der-tow (ŭn′dẽr-tō′), *n.* a current below the surface of water, moving in a direction opposite to the current of the surface; especially, at the seashore, the outgoing current below the incoming breakers.

un-der-val-ue (ŭn′dẽr-văl′ū), *v.t.* [undervalued, undervalu-ing], to rate or value below actual worth.

un-der-waist (ŭn′dẽr-wāst′), *n.* an undergarment for the upper part of the body.

un-der-wear (ŭn′dẽr-wâr′), *n.* garments worn under the ordinary outer clothing.

un-der-weight (ŭn′dẽr-wāt′), *adj.* weighing less than is considered normal.

un-der-went (ŭn′dẽr-wĕnt′), past tense of *undergo.*

un-der-world (ŭn′dẽr-wûrld′), *n.* **1,** Hades, or the abode of the dead; **2,** the degraded and criminal classes.

un-der-write (ŭn′dẽr-rīt′), *v.t.* [*p.t.* underwrote (-rōt′), *p.p.* underwrit-ten (-rĭt′n), *p.pr.* underwrit-ing], **1,** to write something underneath or below; **2,** to assume (an insurance risk), guaranteeing payment in event of loss; **3,** to subscribe to (a project requiring capital); especially, to agree to buy, on a given date at a specified price, (an issue of bonds or stocks) to be sold to the public:—*v.i.* to carry on an insurance business.—*n.* **un′der-writ′er.**

un-did (ŭn-dĭd′), past tense of *undo.*

un-dis-guised (ŭn′dĭs-gīzd′), *adj.* frank; open; not disguised.

un-dis-tin-guished (ŭn′dĭs-tĭng′gwĭsht), *adj.* not unusual; commonplace.

un-do (ŭn-dōō′), *v.t.* [*p.t.* undid (-dĭd′), *p.p.* undone (-dŭn′), *p.pr.* undo-ing], **1,** to do away with the result of; as, going out in the rain will *undo* the effect of the medicine; **2,** to destroy; ruin; as, evil company will *undo* him; **3,** to loosen; unfasten; as, to *undo* a knot.—*n.* **un-do′er.**

un-do-ing (ŭn-dōō′ĭng), *n.* **1,** a setting aside, or reversal, of something that has been done; **2,** ruin; downfall; as, gambling was his *undoing.*

un-done (ŭn-dŭn′), past participle of *undo:*—*adj.* **1,** made null and void; **2,** ruined; **3,** unfinished.

un-doubt-ed (ŭn-dout′ĕd), *adj.* certain; not to be doubted; as, an *undoubted* fact.

un-draw (ŭn-drô′), *v.t.* [*p.t.* undrew (-drōō′), *p.p.* undrawn (-drôn′), *p.pr.* undraw-ing], to draw back, as curtains.

un-dress (ŭn-drĕs′), *v.i.* to take off one's clothes; strip:—*v.t.* to take off the clothes or covering of; strip:—*n.* (ŭn′drĕs; ŭn-drĕs′), everyday clothes:—*adj.* (ŭn′drĕs′), informal; as, an *undress* uniform.

un-due (ŭn-dū′; ŭn′dū′), *adj.* **1,** wrong or illegal; as, an *undue* course of action; **2,** more than is proper or suitable; excessive; as, *undue* attention to trifles.

un-du-late (ŭn′dŭ-lāt), *v.i.* and *v.t.* [undulat-ed, undulat-ing], to move, or cause to move, with a wavy motion; as, a field of grain *undulates* in the wind.—*n.* **un′du-la′tion.**

un-du-ly (ŭn-dū′lĭ), *adv.* **1,** improperly; **2,** excessively.

un-dy-ing (ŭn-dī′ĭng), *adj.* lasting; seeming to last forever; eternal.

un-earth (ŭn-ûrth′), *v.t.* **1,** to take from the earth; dig from underground; uncover; **2,** hence, to bring to light; discover; as, to *unearth* a crime.

un-earth-ly (ŭn-ûrth′lĭ), *adj.* **1,** not according to, or like, nature; supernatural; **2,** weird; uncanny; as, an *unearthly* light.

un-eas-y (ŭn-ēz′ĭ), *adj.* [uneas-i-er, uneas-i-est], **1,** not at ease in mind or body; disturbed; anxious; as, John's failure in school made him *uneasy;* **2,** awkward in manner; constrained.—*n.* **un-eas′i-ness.**

un-em-ployed (ŭn′ĕm-ploid′), *adj.* **1,** not being used; as, *unemployed* funds; **2,** out of work:—**the unemployed,** all the people out of work.—*n.* **un′em-ploy′ment.**

un-e-qual (ŭn-ē′kwăl), *adj.* **1,** not of the same strength, amount, size, etc.; as, *unequal* triangles; **2,** not well balanced or matched; as, *unequal* teams; **3,** not sufficiently large, strong, or able; as, *unequal* to the job; **4,** irregular.—*adv.* **un-e′qual-ly.**

un-e-quiv-o-cal (ŭn′ē-kwĭv′ō-kăl), *adj.* unmistakably clear or plain; definite; as, an *unequivocal* refusal.

un-err-ing (ŭn-ûr′ĭng; ŭn-ĕr′ĭng), *adj.* making no mistakes; accurate.

un-e-ven (ŭn-ē′vĕn), *adj.* **1,** not level; not smooth or flat; as, an *uneven* board; **2,** not uniform; as, *uneven* pressure; **3,** not even;

odd; as, seven is an *uneven* number.—*n.*
un-e′ven-ness.

un-ex-am-pled (ŭn′ĕg-zăm′pld), *adj.* so
unusual that there is nothing like it; new;
as, a man of *unexampled* villainy.

un-ex-celled (ŭn′ĕk-sĕld′), *adj.* best of its
kind; unsurpassed.

un-ex-cep-tion-a-ble (ŭn′ĕk-sĕp′shŭn-*a*-
bl), *adj.* not open to blame or criticism;
beyond reproach.

un-ex-pect-ed (ŭn′ĕks-pĕk′tĕd), *adj.* not
looked for.—*n.* **un′ex-pect′ed-ness.**

un-fail-ing (ŭn-fāl′ĭng), *adj.* **1,** not likely
to fail; as, an *unfailing* water supply; **2,** reliable; as, an *unfailing* friend.

un-fair (ŭn-fâr′), *adj.* not fair; not impartial.—*adv.* **un-fair′ly.**—*n.* **un-fair′ness.**

un-faith-ful (ŭn-fāth′fŏŏl), *adj.* **1,** false;
untrue; **2,** not exact; not reliable.—*adv.*
un-faith′ful-ly.—*n.* **un-faith′ful-ness.**

un-fa-mil-iar (ŭn′f*a*-mĭl′yẽr), *adj.* **1,**
strange; unknown; **2,** without knowledge;
not acquainted; as, *unfamiliar* with law.

un-fas-ten (ŭn-fàs′n), *v.t.* to untie; loosen:
—*v.i.* to become untied.

un-fath-om-a-ble (ŭn-făth′ŭm-*a*-bl), *adj.*
so deep that it cannot be measured; hence,
so strange that it cannot be understood.

un-fa-vor-a-ble (ŭn-fā′vẽr-*a*-bl), *adj.* disapproving; adverse; as, an *unfavorable*
opinion.—*adv.* **un-fa′vor-a-bly.**

un-feel-ing (ŭn-fēl′ĭng), *adj.* **1,** cruel;
brutal; **2,** without feeling or sensation.

un-feigned (ŭn-fānd′), *adj.* real; sincere;
without pretense; as, *unfeigned* liking.

un-fin-ished (ŭn-fĭn′ĭsht), *adj.* **1,** not complete; imperfect; **2,** not perfected; lacking
artistic finish.

un-fit (ŭn-fĭt′), *v.t.* [unfit-ted, unfit-ting],
to make unsuitable or unable:—*adj.* not
suitable; not qualified.—*n.* **un-fit′ness.**

un-fledged (ŭn-flĕjd′), *adj.* **1,** without
feathers, as a very young bird; **2,** hence,
undeveloped; immature.

un-fold (ŭn-fōld′), *v.t.* **1,** to spread open,
as a pocket map; **2,** to reveal by degrees:—
v.i. to open, as a flower.

un-for-tu-nate (ŭn-fôr′tū-nĭt), *adj.* **1,** not
lucky; not prosperous; **2,** badly chosen; regrettable; as, an *unfortunate* speech:—*n.*
an unlucky or unsuccessful person.

un-found-ed (ŭn-foun′dĕd), *adj.* **1,** without basis; not established; **2,** hence, without basis of fact; as, an *unfounded* rumor.

un-friend-ly (ŭn-frĕnd′lĭ), *adj.* not
friendly; hostile; not favorable.

un-furl (ŭn-fûrl′), *v.t.* to loose from its
fastenings and spread out, as a flag or sail:
—*v.i.* to be spread out or unfolded.

un-gain-ly (ŭn-gān′lĭ), *adj.* clumsy; uncouth; as, a tall, *ungainly* figure.

un-god-ly (ŭn-gŏd′lĭ), *adj.* wicked; sinful;
unholy.—*n.* **un-god′li-ness.**

un-gov-ern-a-ble (ŭn-gŭv′ẽr-n*a*-bl), *adj.*
uncontrollable; unruly; rebellious; as, an
ungovernable temper.

un-gra-cious (ŭn-grā′shŭs), *adj.* rude;
discourteous.

un-grate-ful (ŭn-grāt′fŏŏl), *adj.* not
thankful; not appreciative.—*adv.* **un-
grate′ful-ly.**—*n.* **un-grate′ful-ness.**

un-ground-ed (ŭn-groun′dĕd), *adj.* **1,**
without reason; baseless; as, *ungrounded*
fear; **2,** without instruction; untaught.

un-guent (ŭng′gwĕnt), *n.* any ointment
used as a salve for burns, sores, etc.

un-hal-lowed (ŭn-hăl′ōd), *adj.* **1,** not set
apart as sacred; **2,** wicked; godless.

un-hand (ŭn-hănd′), *v.t.* to let go of; release from one's grasp.

un-hand-y (ŭn-hăn′dĭ), *adj.* [unhand-i-er,
unhand-i-est], clumsy; awkward; inconvenient.

un-hap-py (ŭn-hăp′ĭ), *adj.* [unhap-pi-er,
unhap-pi-est], **1,** sorrowful; wretched; **2,**
unfortunate; unsuccessful; as, an *unhappy*
venture; **3,** unsuitable; as, an *unhappy*
choice.—*adv.* **un-hap′pi-ly.**—*n.* **un-hap′-
pi-ness.**

un-health-y (ŭn-hĕl′thĭ), *adj.* [unhealth-
i-er, unhealth-i-est], **1,** not well; sickly; **2,**
harmful to health.

un-heard (ŭn-hûrd′), *adj.* **1,** not heard; as,
an *unheard* cry; **2,** not given a hearing:—
unheard—of, not heard of before; strange.

un-hinge (ŭn-hĭnj′), *v.t.* [unhinged, un-
hing-ing], **1,** to remove from hinges; **2,**
to unsettle; as, trouble *unhinged* his mind.

un-ho-ly (ŭn-hō′lĭ), *adj.* [unho-li-er, un-
ho-li-est], not sacred; godless; wicked.—
adv. **un-ho′li-ly.**—*n.* **un-ho′li-ness.**

un-horse (ŭn-hôrs′), *v.t.* [unhorsed, un-
hors-ing], to throw or drag from the back
of a horse; unseat.

u-ni- (ū′nĭ-), a prefix meaning
one; single; as, *unicorn, uni-
formity, unify.*

u-ni-corn (ū′nĭ-kôrn), *n.* a
fabulous animal resembling a
horse, with one straight horn
projecting from its forehead. **UNICORN**

u-ni-fi-ca-tion (ū′nĭ-fĭ-kā′shŭn), *n.* **1,** the
act of uniting, or the state of being united,
into a whole; **2,** the act of making, or the
state of being made, alike or uniform.

u-ni-form (ū′nĭ-fôrm), *adj.* **1,** not changing in form, degree, or character; unvarying; as, a *uniform* climate; **2,** like one

---

āte, âorta, râre, căt, ȧsk, fär, ăllow, sof*a*; **ēve, ĕvent, ĕll, writ***ẽr***, nov***ĕl***; bīte, pĭn;
nō, ōbey, ôr, dŏg, tŏp, cŏllide; ūnit, ūnite, bûrn, cŭt, foc***ŭs***; nōōn, fŏŏt; mound; coin;**

another; as, the two cities have *uniform* traffic laws:—*n.* an official or regulation dress belonging to a particular class or profession:—*v.t.* to furnish with uniforms. —*adv.* **u′ni·form′ly.**

u·ni·form·i·ty (ū′nĭ-fôr′mĭ-tĭ), *n.* continued and unvarying sameness; also, the state of being of the same form as others.

u·ni·fy (ū′nĭ-fī), *v.t.* [unified, unify-ing], 1, to form into one; unite; 2, to make alike in form.

un·im·peach·a·ble (ŭn′ĭm-pē′chȧ-bl), *adj.* unquestionable; not to be doubted as regards honesty.

un·in·tel·li·gi·ble (ŭn′ĭn-tĕl′ĭ-jĭ-bl), *adj.* incapable of being understood.

un·ion (ūn′yŭn), *n.* 1, the act of joining two or more things into one whole; the state of being so joined; 2, that which is made one by the joining of parts; 3, a confederation; league; 4, an association of workers formed for mutual benefit and protection: often called *labor* or *trade-union;* 5, a coupling for connecting pipes or rods; 6, agreement; harmony; as, we work together in perfect *union:*—**the Union,** the United States of America.—*n.* **un′ion·ism.**—*v.t.* **un′ion·ize.**

un·ion·ist (ūn′yŭn-ĭst), *n.* 1, a believer in union; 2, an advocate or member of a labor union:—**Unionist,** one who supported the national government in the War between the States.

union jack, a jack, or small flag, emblematic of union:—**Union Jack,** the British flag; also, a U.S. naval flag with 48 white stars on a blue ground.

UNION JACK OF GREAT BRITAIN

Un·ion of South Af·ri·ca, a union of states in South Africa. See **South Africa, Union of.**

Un·ion of So·vi·et So·cial·ist Re·pub·lics, a state (cap. Moscow) of federated socialist republics in Europe and Asia (maps **12, 15**); Russia. Its abbreviation is *U.S.S.R.*

UNION JACK OF THE UNITED STATES

u·nique (ū-nēk′), *adj.* 1, unlike anything else; without an equal; 2, extremely unusual; striking; as, a *unique* design.

u·ni·son (ū′nĭ-sŭn; ū′nĭ-zŭn), *n.* 1, harmony; agreement; concord; 2, a selection or passage of music in which all performers sing or play the same part together; also, this manner of performing music; as, the third line of the song is sung in *unison.*

u·nit (ū′nĭt), *n.* 1, one person or thing of a number constituting a group; as, each citizen is a *unit* in the national body; also,

a single group in an association made up of groups; as, a patrol is one of the *units* of a scout troop; 2, in mathematics, the smallest whole number; one; 3, a fixed amount, quantity, distance, etc., taken as a standard of measurement; as, the pound is a *unit* of weight.—*adj.* **u′ni·tar′y.**

U·ni·tar·i·an (ū′nĭ-târ′ĭ-ȧn), *n.* a member of a Christian church which was founded upon the belief that God is only one person:—*adj.* pertaining to Unitarians or their beliefs.—*n.* **U′ni·tar′i·an·ism.**

u·nite (ū-nīt′), *v.t.* [unit-ed, unit-ing], 1, to join together; combine so as to make one; as, to *unite* states into a nation; 2, to bring into close association; ally, as to be *united* in fellowship:—*v.i.* 1, to be joined together; 2, to act together; as, let us *unite* to make this a success.—*adj.* **u·nit′ed.**—*adv.* **u·nit′ed·ly.** *Syn.* merge, connect, mingle, blend.

U·nit·ed King·dom, an island kingdom of northwest Europe, composed of Great Britain (England, Scotland, and Wales) and Northern Ireland (map **13**).

U·nit·ed Na·tions, an international organization for cooperation in the preservation of peace, formed after World War II on a charter drawn up in San Francisco in 1945. It has three main bodies: a Security Council, General Assembly, and Secretariat, along with many specialized agencies. Its permanent headquarters are in New York City.

FLAG OF THE UNITED NATIONS

U·nit·ed States of A·mer·i·ca, The, a federal republic (cap. Washington, D.C.) consisting of 50 states and the District of Columbia, together with island possessions and the Commonwealth of Puerto Rico (map **5**).

u·ni·ty (ū′nĭ-tĭ), *n.* [*pl.* unities], 1, the state of being one; union of parts; 2, harmony; agreement; as, to act in *unity;* 3, the number one.

univ. abbreviation for *university.*

u·ni·ver·sal (ū′nĭ-vûr′sǎl), *adj.* 1, pertaining to the entire universe; as, the *universal* law of gravitation; also, embracing or including the whole; prevailing everywhere; as, *universal* peace; 2, entire; whole:—**universal joint,** a coupling or joint that permits the turning of two connected parts in any direction.

UNIVERSAL JOINT

u·ni·ver·sal·i·ty (ū′nĭ-vûr-sǎl′ĭ-tĭ), *n.* the state or quality of existing everywhere or being universal; limitless extent.

---

go; join; yet; sing; chin; show; thin, *th*en; hw, *wh*y; zh, a*z*ure; **ü,** Ger. f*ü*r or Fr. l*u*ne; **ö,** Ger. sch*ö*n or Fr. f*eu;* **ṅ,** Fr. e*n*fant, no*m;* kh, Ger. a*ch* or i*ch.* See pages ix–x.

u·ni·verse (ū/nĭ-vûrs), *n.* the whole system of existing material things; all creation; loosely, the world.

u·ni·ver·si·ty (ū/nĭ-vûr/sĭ-tĭ), *n.* [*pl.* universities], an institution for instruction and study in the higher branches of learning, as in the arts, medicine, law, etc.

un·just (ŭn-jŭst/), *adj.* unfair; not just.— *adv.* **un·just/ly.**—*n.* **un·just/ness.**

un·kempt (ŭn-kĕmpt/), *adj.* 1, not combed; disheveled; 2, slovenly.

un·kind (ŭn-kīnd/), *adj.* not kind or sympathetic; harsh; as, *unkind* words.—*adv.* **un·kind/ly.**—*n.* **un·kind/ness.**

un·lace (ŭn-lās/), *v.t.* [unlaced, unlac-ing], to undo the lacing of; as, to *unlace* a shoe.

un·law·ful (ŭn-lô/fŏol), *adj.* contrary to law; illegal.—*adv.* **un·law/ful·ly.**

un·learn·ed (ŭn-lûr/nĕd), *adj.* 1, ignorant; without schooling; 2, betraying lack of knowledge; 3, (ŭn-lûrnd/), not acquired by experience or study; as, truths *unlearned.*

un·leav·ened (ŭn-lĕv/ĕnd), *adj.* not raised; made without yeast or other leavening.

un·less (ŭn-lĕs/), *conj.* if not; except when; as, we can't pass the examination *unless* we study.

un·let·tered (ŭn-lĕt/ĕrd), *adj.* untaught; also, unable to read or write.
    Syn. ignorant, untutored.

un·like (ŭn-līk/), *adj.* having no resemblance; different.—*n.* **un·like/ness.**

un·like·ly (ŭn-līk/lĭ), *adj.* [unlike-li-er, unlike-li-est], 1, not probable; not likely to happen; 2, not giving promise of success; as, an *unlikely* plan.

un·lim·it·ed (ŭn-lĭm/ĭ-tĕd), *adj.* without boundaries; as, an *unlimited* area; also, without restriction; as, *unlimited* power.

un·load (ŭn-lōd/), *v.t.* 1, to remove freight or a cargo from; as, to *unload* a wagon; 2, to remove from a car, wagon, ship, etc.; as, to *unload* freight; 3, to free or relieve from care or trouble:—*v.i.* to discharge freight.

un·lock (ŭn-lŏk/), *v.t.* 1, to unfasten; to release the catch on (a door, trunk, etc., that has been fastened with a lock); 2, to make clear; reveal; as, to *unlock* a mystery.

un·loose (ŭn-lōōs/), *v.t.* [unloosed, unloos-ing], to unfasten; set at liberty.

un·luck·y (ŭn-lŭk/ĭ), *adj.* [unluck-i-er, unluck-i-est], 1, not lucky or fortunate; as, an *unlucky* speculator; 2, accompanied by, or tending to bring, bad luck; as, an *unlucky* day.—*adv.* **un·luck/i·ly.**

un·man (ŭn-măn/), *v.t.* [unmanned, unman-ning], to rob of courage and strength.

un·man·ly (ŭn-măn/lĭ), *adj.* [unman-li-er, unman-li-est], not manly; lacking courage.

un·man·ner·ly (ŭn-măn/ĕr-lĭ), *adj.* rude; without courtesy; impolite.

un·mask (ŭn-måsk/), *v.t.* to remove a disguise from; show the true nature of:—*v.i.* to lay aside a mask; also, to reveal one's true nature.

un·mean·ing (ŭn-mēn/ĭng), *adj.* senseless; without significance.

un·meet (ŭn-mēt/), *adj.* not proper or fitting.

un·mer·ci·ful (ŭn-mûr/sĭ-fŏol), *adj.* without kindness or pity; cruel.—*adv.* **un·mer/-ci·ful·ly.**—*n.* **un·mer/ci·ful·ness.**

un·mis·tak·a·ble (ŭn/mĭs-tāk/à-bl), *adj.* incapable of being mistaken or misunderstood; clear.—*adv.* **un/mis·tak/a·bly.**

un·mor·al (ŭn-mŏr/ăl), *adj.* not concerned with right and wrong.

un·nat·u·ral (ŭn-năt/ū-răl), *adj.* 1, not like or representing nature; artificial; 2, cruel; inhuman.

un·nec·es·sar·y (ŭn-nĕs/ĕ-sĕr/ĭ), *adj.* not needed.—*adv.* **un·nec/es·sar/i·ly.**

un·nerve (ŭn-nûrv/), *v.t.* [unnerved, unnerv-ing], to deprive of control, strength, or courage; as, the accident *unnerved* him.

un·num·bered (ŭn-nŭm/bĕrd), *adj.* 1, not counted; 2, countless; numerous.

un·pack (ŭn-păk/), *v.t.* 1, to take out; as, to *unpack* books from a box; 2, to remove the contents of; as, to *unpack* a box.

un·par·al·leled (ŭn-păr/ă-lĕld), *adj.* unrivaled; without an equal; having no parallel.

un·par·lia·men·ta·ry (ŭn/pär-lĭ-mĕn/tà-rĭ), *adj.* not conforming to the rules of parliamentary procedure.

un·pin (ŭn-pĭn/), *v.t.* [unpinned, unpin-ning], to unfasten by taking out pins.

un·pleas·ant (ŭn-plĕz/ănt), *adj.* disagreeable; distasteful.—*n.* **un·pleas/ant·ness.**

un·pop·u·lar (ŭn-pŏp/ū-lĕr), *adj.* not generally liked or approved.

un·prec·e·dent·ed (ŭn-prĕs/ē-dĕn/tĕd), *adj.* without precedent; unusual; novel.

un·prej·u·diced (ŭn-prĕj/ŏŏ-dĭst), *adj.* impartial; fair; without bias.

un·pre·med·i·tat·ed (ŭn/prē-mĕd/ĭ-tāt/-ĕd), *adj.* not planned beforehand.

un·pre·pared (ŭn/prē-pârd/), *adj.* not ready; not equipped; done without preparation.

un·pre·ten·tious (ŭn/prē-tĕn/shŭs), *adj.* not showy; without affectation or display.

un·prin·ci·pled (ŭn-prĭn/sĭ-pld), *adj.* lacking moral standards; unscrupulous.

āte, âorta, râre, căt, àsk, fär, ăllow, sofà; ēve, ĕvent, ĕll, writĕr, novĕl; bīte, pĭn; nō, ŏbey, ôr, dŏg, tŏp, cŏllide; ūnit, ūnite, bûrn, cŭt, focŭs; nōōn, fŏŏt; mound; coin;

un-qual-i-fied (ŭn-kwŏl′ĭ-fīd; ŭn-kwôl′ĭ-fīd), *adj.* **1,** lacking the proper qualifications; unfit; **2,** absolute; utter; as, *unqualified* disapproval.

un-ques-tion-a-ble (ŭn-kwĕs′chŭn-á-bl), *adj.* not to be doubted or questioned; indisputable.—*adv.* **un-ques′tion-a-bly.**

un-qui-et (ŭn-kwī′ĕt), *adj.* noisy; disturbed; not at peace.

un-rav-el (ŭn-răv′ĕl), *v.t.* [unraveled, unravel-ing], **1,** to untangle; pull out, as knitting; **2,** to solve, as a mystery:—*v.i.* to become untangled or solved.

un-rea-son-a-ble (ŭn-rē′zn-á-bl), *adj.* **1,** not influenced or controlled by reason; **2,** demanding too much; exorbitant; as, *unreasonable* prices.—*adv.* **un-rea′son-a-bly.**

un-re-served (ŭn′rē-zûrvd′), *adj.* **1,** not held in reserve; **2,** frank; outspoken.

un-rest (ŭn-rĕst′), *n.* uneasiness; anxiety; a state of disturbance.

un-ri-valed (ŭn-rī′văld), *adj.* unequaled; without a rival; peerless.

un-roll (ŭn-rōl′), *v.t.* **1,** to open out (something which is rolled); **2,** to display:—*v.i.* to unfold; develop.

un-ruf-fled (ŭn-rŭf′ld), *adj.* **1,** smooth; not rough; **2,** calm; tranquil.

un-rul-y (ŭn-rōōl′ĭ), *adj.* paying no attention to rules or commands; hard to manage; ungovernable.—*n.* **un-rul′i-ness.**

un-sad-dle (ŭn-săd′l), *v.t.* [unsad-dled, unsad-dling], **1,** to remove a saddle from; **2,** to unhorse.

un-sa-vor-y (ŭn-sā′vĕr-ĭ), *adj.* **1,** lacking taste or seasoning; **2,** disagreeable to taste or smell; **3,** morally bad. In British usage, **un-sa′vour-y.**

un-say (ŭn-sā′), *v.t.* [unsaid (ŭn-sĕd′), unsay-ing], to take back (something that has been said).

un-screw (ŭn-skrōō′), *v.t.* **1,** to take the screws from; **2,** to take out or loosen by turning; as, to *unscrew* a nut.

un-scru-pu-lous (ŭn-skrōō′pŭ-lŭs), *adj.* unprincipled; indifferent to right and wrong.—*n.* **un-scru′pu-lous-ness.**

un-seal (ŭn-sēl′), *v.t.* to open by breaking or removing the seal.

un-search-a-ble (ŭn-sûr′chá-bl), *adj.* incapable of being traced or searched out; hidden; mysterious.

un-sea-son-a-ble (ŭn-sē′zn-á-bl), *adj.* **1,** coming at an ill-chosen time; untimely; as, an *unseasonable* request; **2,** out of season.

un-seat (ŭn-sēt′), *v.t.* **1,** to remove from a seat; also, to unhorse; **2,** to depose; deprive of the right to sit as representative; as, to *unseat* a senator or congressman.

un-seem-ly (ŭn-sēm′lĭ), *adj.* improper; not fitting:—*adv.* in an unsuitable manner.

un-seen (ŭn-sēn′), *adj.* **1,** not seen; beyond the range of vision; **2,** invisible.

un-self-ish (ŭn-sĕl′fĭsh), *adj.* not selfish; generous; thoughtful of others.

un-set-tle (ŭn-sĕt′l), *v.t.* [unset-tled, unset-tling], to change from a firm position or state; disturb; make uncertain.

un-set-tled (ŭn-sĕt′ld), *adj.* **1,** not determined; undecided; as, an *unsettled* question; **2,** not settled; uncertain, as weather; **3,** unpaid; as, an *unsettled* bill; **4,** uninhabited by settlers; **5,** disturbed; disordered; as, *unsettled* times.

un-shak-a-ble (ŭn-shāk′á-bl), *adj.* firm; determined; as, an *unshakable* belief.

un-sheathe (ŭn-shē*th*′), *v.t.* [unsheathed, unsheath-ing], to take from its scabbard, as a dagger or sword.

un-sight-ly (ŭn-sīt′lĭ), *adj.* not pleasant to see; ugly.

un-skil-ful or **un-skill-ful** (ŭn-skĭl′fŏŏl), *adj.* not expert or skilful; awkward.—*adv.* **un-skil′ful-ly.**—*n.* **un-skil′ful-ness.**

un-skilled (ŭn-skĭld′), *adj.* not expert; untrained; not having learned a trade.

un-so-phis-ti-cat-ed (ŭn′sŏ-fĭs′tĭ-kāt′ĕd), *adj.* not experienced in the ways of the world; simple; guileless.

un-sound (ŭn-sound′), *adj.* not sound; not healthy; weak.—*n.* **un-sound′ness.**

un-speak-a-ble (ŭn-spēk′á-bl), *adj.* **1,** not to be expressed or described in words; as, *unspeakable* happiness; **2,** too bad to be mentioned; as, an *unspeakable* crime.—*adv.* **un-speak′a-bly.**

un-spot-ted (ŭn-spŏt′ĕd), *adj.* without stain; flawless; guiltless.

un-sta-ble (ŭn-stā′bl), *adj.* not firm or stable; easily unbalanced.

un-stead-y (ŭn-stĕd′ĭ), *adj.* not steady; shaky; as, *unsteady* nerves; also, unreliable.

un-strung (ŭn-strŭng′), *adj.* **1,** having the strings loosened or missing, as a harp, banjo, violin, etc.; **2,** nervously upset; unnerved.

un-sub-stan-tial (ŭn′sŭb-stăn′shăl), *adj.* **1,** not strong; not firmly put together; **2,** fanciful; imaginary; not real.

un-suit-ed (ŭn-sūt′ĕd), *adj.* not suited; not appropriate.

un-sung (ŭn-sŭng′), *adj.* not praised in story or song; not sung.

un-tan-gle (ŭn-tăng′gl), *v.t.* [untan-gled, untan-gling], to take out knots or snarls from; as, to *untangle* yarn.

un-think-a-ble (ŭn-thĭngk′á-bl), *adj.* incapable of being thought of or imagined.

un-think-ing (ŭn-thĭngk′ĭng), *adj.* not using or showing thought; careless; inconsiderate.—*adv.* **un-think′ing-ly.**

un-ti-dy (ŭn-tī′dĭ), *adj.* [unti-di-er, unti-di-est], not neat; slatternly; slovenly.— *adv.* **un-ti′di-ly.**—*n.* **un-ti′di-ness.**

un-tie (ŭn-tī′), *v.t.* [untied, unty-ing], to unfasten by loosening (a knot); to unfasten (an object) by loosening the knot that holds it; as, to *untie* a necktie; to *untie* a shoe; hence, to loose or set free; as, to *untie* a dog:—*v.i.* to become unfastened.

un-til (ŭn-tĭl′), *prep.* to or up to; as, he played *until* noon:—*conj.* to the degree, time, or place that; as, he talked *until* he became hoarse; he studied *until* the sun was high.

un-time-ly (ŭn-tīm′lĭ), *adj.* not at the right moment or on the right occasion; happening too soon:—*adv.* inopportunely; too soon.

un-tir-ing (ŭn-tīr′ĭng), *adj.* never wearying or tiring.

un-to (ŭn′tōō; ŭn′tŏŏ), *prep. Archaic or Poetic,* to; as, "Suffer little children to come *unto* me."

un-told (ŭn-tōld′), *adj.* 1, not expressed or revealed; 2, not numbered; hence, very great; as, *untold* riches.

un-to-ward (ŭn-tō′ẽrd; ŭn-tôrd′), *adj.* 1, wayward; perverse; stubborn; 2, uncouth; awkward; 3, unfortunate; inconvenient; as, an *untoward* meeting.

un-true (ŭn-trōō′), *adj.* 1, false; contrary to the truth; 2, not faithful to one's duty; disloyal; 3, varying from a standard; not straight, as lines, angles, etc.

un-truth (ŭn-trōōth′), *n.* 1, lack of adherence to fact; incorrectness; 2, a falsehood, or lie.
Syn. falsity, mendacity.

un-tu-tored (ŭn-tū′tẽrd), *adj.* not taught; having little learning.

un-used (ŭn-ūzd′), *adj.* 1, not put to use; 2, not accustomed; as, *unused* to luxury.

un-u-su-al (ŭn-ū′zhōō-ăl), *adj.* uncommon; strange; remarkable.—*adv.* **un-u′su-al-ly.**

un-ut-ter-a-ble (ŭn-ŭt′ẽr-a-bl), *adj.* unspeakable; not to be expressed in words; as, *unutterable* grief.—*adv.* **un-ut′ter-a-bly.**

un-veil (ŭn-vāl′), *v.t.* to reveal by taking off a veil or covering; uncover, as a monument:—*v.i.* to take off one's veil.

un-war-rant-a-ble (ŭn-wŏr′ăn-ta-bl; ŭn-wôr′ăn-ta-bl), *adj.* not to be justified.

un-war-y (ŭn-wâr′ĭ), *adj.* not cautious; careless; heedless.—*adv.* **un-war′i-ly.**

un-wield-y (ŭn-wēl′dĭ), *adj.* difficult to move or manage because of size, shape, or weight; bulky; clumsy.—*n.* **un-wield′i-ness.**

un-will-ing (ŭn-wĭl′ĭng), *adj.* reluctant; not willing; disinclined.—*adv.* **un-will′ing-ly.**—*n.* **un-will′ing-ness.**

un-wind (ŭn-wīnd′), *v.t.* and *v.i.* [unwound (ŭn-wound′), unwind-ing], to loosen or become loose by uncoiling.

un-wise (ŭn-wīz′), *adj.* lacking good judgment; indiscreet.—*adv.* **un-wise′ly.**

un-wit-ting (ŭn-wĭt′ĭng), *adj.* unaware; unconscious; not deliberate; as, he was the *unwitting* cause of all our trouble.—*adv.* **un-wit′ting-ly.**

un-wont-ed (ŭn-wŭn′tĕd), *adj.* unusual; uncommon; as, *unwonted* kindness.

un-world-ly (ŭn-wûrld′lĭ), *adj.* free from sordid or worldly motives; spiritually minded.

un-wor-thy (ŭn-wûr′thĭ), *adj.* [unwor-thi-er, unwor-thi-est], 1, lacking merit; hence, discreditable; as, an *unworthy* suggestion; 2, not deserving; as, he is *unworthy* of our confidence; 3, not suitable or becoming; as, such conduct is *unworthy* of you.—*adv.* **un-wor′thi-ly.**—*n.* **un-wor′-thi-ness.**

un-writ-ten (ŭn-rĭt′n), *adj.* 1, not expressed or recorded in writing; as, *unwritten* legends; 2, blank; without writing; as, an *unwritten* page.

up (ŭp), *adv.* 1, from a lower to a higher position or degree: opposite of *down;* as, to go *up* in an elevator; come *up* from a mine; 2, into notice or consideration; as, to bring *up* a question; 3, at or to a higher scale, price, or volume; as, the prices are going *up;* to swell *up;* 4, even with something in time, degree, space, amount, etc.; as, to catch *up* in a race; keep *up* with the news; 5, on one's feet; out of bed; 6, to a person, point, or place; as, he came *up* to us to ask directions; 7, used with many verbs to give emphasis or to indicate that the action is finished; as, to tear *up* a report; to store *up* wealth; to finish *up* a job; to nail *up* a box; to be swallowed *up* in a crowd; the stream has dried *up:*—*prep.* 1, from a lower to a higher place on or along; as, to walk *up* the hill; 2, toward the source of; as, *up* the river; also, toward the interior of (a country or region); 3, to, at, or near the top of; as, to climb *up* a rope:—*adj.* 1, leading, moving, or sloping toward a higher place; upward; as, on the *up* grade; 2, in golf, ahead of an opponent; as, two holes *up;* 3, well-informed; abreast of the times; as, *up* on politics; 4, exhausted; at an end; as, my stay is *up;* 5, above the horizon; as, the sun is *up;* 6, out of bed; as, the patient will be *up* tomorrow: **—ups and downs,** alternate states of good and bad fortune.

up-braid (ŭp-brād′), *v.t.* to chide or blame; reprove severely.

  Syn. censure, rebuke, berate.

up-bring-ing (ŭp-brĭng′ĭng), *n.* rearing; training during childhood and youth.

up-grade (ŭp′grād′), *n.* **1,** an ascent, as in a road; **2,** *Colloquial,* a rise to a better condition; as, on the *upgrade.*—Also *adj.* and *adv.*

up-heav-al (ŭp-hēv′ăl), *n.* **1,** a lifting from below; especially, an elevation of some part of the earth's crust, as in an earthquake; **2,** a violent political or social disturbance, as a revolution.

up-hill (ŭp′hĭl′), *adv.* to a higher level or point on a slope; upward; as, we climbed *uphill:*—*adj.* (ŭp′hĭl′), **1,** sloping upward; ascending; **2,** hence, tiresome; difficult; as, study is sometimes *uphill* work.

up-hold (ŭp-hōld′), *v.t.* [upheld (-hĕld′), uphold-ing], **1,** to support; hold up; keep erect; **2,** to encourage or aid; also, to defend; as, to *uphold* the right of free speech; **3,** to maintain or confirm; as, the umpire's decision was *upheld.*

up-hol-ster (ŭp-hōl′stẽr), *v.t.* to provide (furniture) with cushions, springs, and coverings.—*n.* **up-hol′ster-er.**

up-hol-ster-y (ŭp-hōl′stẽr-ĭ), *n.* [*pl.* upholsteries], **1,** the business of an upholsterer; **2,** the materials used in making cushions and coverings for furniture.

up-keep (ŭp′kēp′), *n.* the maintaining of a house, automobile, etc., in good order and repair; also, the cost of maintenance.

up-land (ŭp′lănd′; ŭp′lănd), *n.* an elevated region, especially in the interior of a country:—*adj.* pertaining to an elevated region or to hilly land.

up-lift (ŭp-lĭft′), *v.t.* **1,** to raise; elevate; **2,** to better the condition of, especially morally, socially, or intellectually:—*n.* (ŭp′-lĭft′), **1,** an elevation; **2,** hence, a tendency or move toward a higher standard.

up-on (ŭ-pŏn′), *prep.* **1,** on; resting on the top or surface of; as, *upon* the shelf; **2,** against; as, *upon* the wall; **3,** at the moment of; as, *upon* arrival; **4,** so as to meet or find; as, to come *upon* a bargain.

up-per (ŭp′ẽr), *adj.* **1,** higher in place, position, rank, or the like; as, the *upper* story of a house; the *upper* classes; **2,** farther inland; as, the *upper* Nile:—**the upper hand,** the advantage:—*n.* the part of a shoe above the sole.

upper case, capital letters, as ABCDEF: **—upper-case,** *adj.* capital, or printed in capital letters.

up-per-most (ŭp′ẽr-mōst), *adj.* highest in place, rank, or authority: opposite of *lowermost.*—Also **up′most.**

up-raise (ŭp-rāz′), *v.t.* [upraised, upraising], to lift up; raise.

up-rear (ŭp-rēr′), *v.t.* to raise; bring up.

up-right (ŭp′rīt′; ŭp-rīt′), *adj.* **1,** standing erect; in a vertical position; **2,** just; honest; honorable:—*adv.* in an erect position:—*n.* (ŭp′rīt′), something set or standing straight up, as a timber supporting a beam. —*n.* **up′right/ness.**

up-rise (ŭp-rīz′), *v.i.* [*p.t.* uprose (-rōz′), *p.p.* upris-en (-rĭz′n), *p.pr.* upris-ing], **1,** to get up; rise; **2,** to ascend or rise into view; as, the sun then *uprose.*

up-ris-ing (ŭp-rīz′ĭng; ŭp′rīz′ĭng), *n.* a rebellion against authority; revolt.

up-roar (ŭp′rôr′), *n.* tumult; confusion.

  Syn. racket, commotion, noise, clamor.

up-root (ŭp-rōōt′), *v.t.* to pull up by the roots; hence, to remove; get rid of.

up-set (ŭp-sĕt′), *v.t.* [upset, upset-ting], **1,** to knock over; overturn; as, to *upset* a chair; also, to interfere with; as, our arrangements have been *upset;* **2,** to disturb the normal mental or physical condition of; as, the news of the accident *upset* her: —*v.i.* to overturn; as, the car *upset* at the corner:—*adj.* **1,** overturned; also, interfered with; **2,** physically or mentally disturbed:—*n.* (ŭp′sĕt′), **1,** the act of overturning or disturbing; **2,** the state of being overturned; **3,** mental or physical disturbance.

up-shot (ŭp′shŏt′), *n.* final result; conclusion; outcome.

up-side (ŭp′sīd′), *n.* the upper part:—**upside down,** with the top part at the bottom; topsy-turvy.

up-stairs (ŭp′stârz′), *adv.* toward or on an upper floor:—*adj.* (ŭp′stârz′), belonging to, or on, an upper floor; as, an *upstairs* room:—*n.* (ŭp′stârz′), the part of a building above the first floor.

up-start (ŭp′stärt′), *n.* a person who has suddenly risen from obscurity to wealth, power, or honor, especially one who presumes on his success:—*v.i.* and *v.t.* (ŭp-stärt′), to start or cause to start up.

up-stream (ŭp′strēm′), *adv.* toward the source of a stream; against the current.

up-to-date (ŭp′≠tŏō-dāt′), *adj.* up to the minute in style, fads, information, etc.

up-town (ŭp′toun′), *adj.* relating to, or in, the upper part of a town or city, especially, the residential section:—*adv.* (ŭp′toun′), towards or in the upper part of a town or city; as, the car sped *uptown.*

---

go; **join;** yet; **sing; chin; show; thin,** *th*en; hw, *why;* zh, *a*zure; ü, Ger. *für* or Fr. l*u*ne; ö, Ger. sch*ö*n or Fr. f*eu;* ṅ, Fr. *en*fant, no*m;* kh, Ger. a*ch* or i*ch.* See pages ix-x.

up-turn (ŭp-tûrn'), *v.t.* to turn upward or over; as, to *upturn* sod:—*n.* (ŭp'tûrn'), a change for the better; as, there has been an *upturn* in business.

up-ward (ŭp'wẽrd), *adj.* moving toward a higher place or level; as, an *upward* march.

up-ward (ŭp'wẽrd) or **up-wards** (ŭp'-wẽrdz), *adv.* **1,** in an ascending direction; from lower to higher; **2,** toward a higher rank or position; as, to climb *upward* in a profession; **3,** toward the source; as, the explorers followed the river *upward;* **4,** indefinitely more; as, children of three years and *upward.*

Ur (ûr), an ancient district and city in Babylonia, northwest of the Persian Gulf.

U-ral (ū'răl), **1,** a mountain system in the U.S.S.R. between Asia and Europe; **2,** a river rising in the Ural Mountains and flowing into the Caspian Sea. (Map 12.)

u-ra-ni-um (ū-rā'nĭ-ŭm), *n.* a hard, heavy, white, radioactive metallic element, found chiefly in pitchblende; basic to the atomic bomb.

U-ra-nus (ū'rȧ-nŭs), *n.* a planet, appearing to the naked eye as a faint star.

ur-ban (ûr'băn), *adj.* pertaining to a city or town; as, *urban* residents.

ur-bane (ûr-bān'), *adj.* courteous; refined and polished in manner.—*adv.* **ur-bane'ly.** —*n.* **ur-ban'i-ty** (ûr-băn'ĭ-tĭ).

ur-chin (ûr'chĭn), *n.* a small boy, especially a mischievous one.

-ure (-ūr), a suffix meaning: **1,** action; as, censure, seizure; **2,** state; as, temperature, moisture; **3,** result; as, mixture, sculpture.

u-re-a (ū-rē'ȧ; ū'rē-ȧ), *n.* a substance found in urine.

urge (ûrj), *v.t.* [urged, urg-ing], **1,** to force onward; drive faster; as, he *urged* on his steed; **2,** to advocate strongly; as, to *urge* the necessity of help; **3,** to try to influence (a person) by arguments, entreaties, etc.; as, we *urged* him to accept the nomination.
Syn. push, encourage, promote.

ur-gen-cy (ûr'jĕn-sĭ), *n.* the pressure of necessity; need for instant action; as, the *urgency* of the case is unquestioned.

ur-gent (ûr'jĕnt), *adj.* **1,** calling for immediate attention; pressing; as, an *urgent* need; **2,** insistent; eager; as, an *urgent* plea.

U-ri-el (ū'rĭ-ĕl), *n.* in Christian and Jewish legend, one of the seven archangels.

u-ri-nal (ū'rĭ-năl), *n.* **1,** a receptacle for urine; **2,** a place for urinating.

u-ri-nate (ū'rĭ-nāt), *v.i.* [urinat-ed, urinating], to pass urine.—*n.* **u'ri-na'tion.**

u-rine (ū'rĭn), *n.* the fluid secreted by the kidneys, and cast off as waste.

urn (ûrn), *n.* **1,** a kind of vase, usually with a rounded body and a base or pedestal; **2,** a closed vessel with a tap and a heating device, used for making and keeping hot such beverages as tea and coffee.

Ur-sa Ma-jor (ûr'sȧ mā'jẽr), the Great Bear, the most prominent of the northern constellations, containing the seven stars that form the Big Dipper.

Ur-sa Mi-nor (ûr'sȧ mī'nẽr), the Little Bear, a constellation in the northern heavens, containing the Little Dipper. The end star of the handle is the North Star.

COFFEE URN

U-ru-guay (ū'rŏŏ-gwā; ōō'rŏŏ-gwī'), a republic (cap. Montevideo) on the southeastern coast of South America (map 11).

us (ŭs), objective case of *we.*

URN, def. 1.

U.S. abbreviation for *United States.*

U.S.A. abbreviation for *United States of America, United States Army.*

us-a-ble (ūz'ȧ-bl), *adj.* fit to be employed or used.

us-age (ūs'ĭj; ūz'ĭj), *n.* **1,** the way of using; treatment; as, the furniture shows rough *usage;* **2,** settled habit or custom; established use; as, in accordance with the best *usage.*
Syn. use, fashion, practice.

use (ūz), *v.t.* [used, us-ing], **1,** to make use of; employ; as, to *use* the best material; **2,** to practice or make habitual use of; as, to *use* economy; **3,** to treat, act, or behave toward; as, she *uses* her servants harshly; **4,** to make accustomed; as, man is *used* to ease:—*v.i.* to be accustomed; as, they *used* to work together:—*n.* (ūs), **1,** the act of employing; the application of anything to a particular purpose; as, the *use* of steel for rails; **2,** the condition of being used; as, this room is in *use;* **3,** the method of using; treatment; **4,** familiarity; custom; continued practice; **5,** practical worth; utility; as, an ornament of no *use;* also, advantage; as, there is no *use* in apologizing; **6,** reason for employing; as, we have no *use* for the goods.—*adj.* **use'ful.**—*adv.* **use'ful-ly.**—*n.* **use'ful-ness.**—*n.* **us'er.**

use-less (ūs'lĕs), *adj.* **1,** having, or being of, no practical worth; as, *useless* rubbish; **2,** without results; as, *useless* efforts.—*adv.* **use'less-ly.**—*n.* **use'less-ness.**

ush-er (ŭsh'ẽr), *n.* **1,** one who escorts or directs persons to seats in a church, theater, or the like; **2,** in England, an assistant teacher:—*v.t.* **1,** to escort or accompany; **2,** to announce; herald; as, high winds often *usher* in the month of March.

U.S.N. abbreviation for *United States Navy.*

U.S.S.R. or **USSR** abbreviation for *Union of Soviet Socialist Republics.*

u·su·al (ū′zhŏŏ-ăl), *adj.* customary; regular; as, come at the *usual* time.—*adv.* **u′su·al·ly.**—*n.* **u′su·al·ness.**

u·su·rer (ū′zhŏŏ-rẽr), *n.* a person who lends money and demands an unlawfully high rate of interest.

u·su·ri·ous (ū-zhŏŏr′ĭ-ŭs), *adj.* practicing usury; lending money at an unlawful rate of interest; also, involving usury.

u·surp (ū-zûrp′), *v.t.* to take possession of by force or unjust means; as, to *usurp* the power of a king.—*n.* **u·surp′er.**—*n.* **u′sur·pa′tion** (ū′zûr-pā′shŭn).

u·su·ry (ū′zhŏŏ-rĭ), *n.* **1,** the practice of lending money at a rate higher than the lawful rate; **2,** a very high rate of interest.

Ut. abbreviation for *Utah.*

U·tah (ū′tô; ū′tä), a State (cap. Salt Lake City) in the U.S., west of the Rocky Mountains (map 9).

u·ten·sil (ū-tĕn′sĭl; ū-tĕn′sl), *n.* an implement or vessel for use in practical work; especially, one for use in housework.

u·ter·us (ū′tẽr-ŭs), *n.* [*pl.* uteri (ū′tẽr-ī)], the womb of a female mammal; the organ in which the young are carried before birth.

U·ti·ca (ū′tĭ-k*a*), a city on the Mohawk River, in central New York (map 6).

u·til·i·tar·i·an (ū-tĭl′ĭ-târ′ĭ-ăn; ū′tĭl-ĭ-târ′ĭ-ăn), *adj.* characterized primarily by usefulness rather than by beauty of appearance.—*n.* **u·til′i·tar′i·an·ism.**

u·til·i·ty (ū-tĭl′ĭ-tĭ), *n.* [*pl.* utilities], **1,** the quality or state of being suitable for use; general usefulness; **2,** (often *public utility*),

an organization, as a gas or electric company, a railroad, etc., that sells a service to a community.

u·ti·lize (ū′tĭ-līz), *v.t.* [utilized, utiliz-ing], to make profitable; make use of; as, surgery now *utilizes* X rays.—*n.* **u′ti·li·za′tion.**

ut·most (ŭt′mōst), *adj.* **1,** greatest; of the highest degree; as, use the *utmost* care; **2,** most removed in space or time; farthest; as, the radio reaches the *utmost* points of the globe:—*n.* **1,** the extreme limit; as, he can be trusted to the *utmost;* **2,** all that is possible; as, I will do my *utmost* to aid.

U·to·pi·a (ū-tō′pĭ-*a*), *n.* **1,** an imaginary land, described in Sir Thomas More's "Utopia," where there was perfection in society and government; **2,** (often *utopia*) hence, any picture of a perfect country or condition.—*adj.* **U·to′pi·an; u·to′pi·an.**

U·trecht (ū′trĕkt), a city in the northern part of the Netherlands.

¹**ut·ter** (ŭt′ẽr), *adj.* entire; absolute; complete; as, *utter* absurdity; *utter* gloom.

²**ut·ter** (ŭt′ẽr), *v.t.* to speak; sound.

ut·ter·ance (ŭt′ẽr-ăns), *n.* **1,** expression by the voice; speech; also, style of speaking; as, indistinct *utterance;* **2,** something, usually of importance, expressed in words.

ut·ter·ly (ŭt′ẽr-lĭ), *adv.* fully; totally; altogether; as, *utterly* useless.

ut·ter·most (ŭt′ẽr-mōst), *adj.* utmost; in the farthest, greatest, or highest degree:—*n.* the farthest extent or degree; as, he worked to the *uttermost* to finish the job.

u·vu·la (ū′vū-l*a*), *n.* the small, fleshy projection hanging from the soft palate above the back part of the tongue.

Uz·bek (ŏŏz′bĕk; ŭz′bĕk), a republic in the U.S.S.R. Its official name is *Uzbek Soviet Socialist Republic.*

Uzbek Soviet Socialist Republic, a republic (cap. Tashkent) of the U.S.S.R. in south central Asia (map 15).

V

V, v (vē), *n.* [*pl.* V's, v's], **1,** the 22d letter of the alphabet, following U; **2,** anything shaped like the letter V; **3,** the Roman numeral for five.

V. abbreviation for *verb* or for Latin *vide,* meaning *see.*

Va. abbreviation for *Virginia.*

va·can·cy (vā′kăn-sĭ), *n.* [*pl.* vacancies], **1,** the state of being empty; emptiness; **2,** an office or a position open to applicants; **3,** a room or rooms offered for rent; **4,** an empty space; blank.

va·cant (vā′kănt), *adj.* **1,** empty, as an unoccupied room; **2,** lacking thought or expression; as, a *vacant* look.—*adv.* **va′cant·ly.**

    Syn. void, unfilled, blank.

va·cate (vā′kāt), *v.t.* [vacat-ed, vacat-ing], to make empty; give up the possession of; as, to *vacate* a house:—*v.i.* to give up a house, office, or the like; move out.

va·ca·tion (v*a*-kā′shŭn), *n.* a time of recreation or rest from regular duties:— *v.i.* to pass one's vacation.

---

go; join; yet; sing; chin; show; thin, *th*en; hw, *why;* **zh, a**zure; **ū,** Ger. f**ü**r or Fr. l**u**ne; **ö,** Ger. sch**ö**n or Fr. f**eu;** **ṅ,** Fr. e**n**fant, no**m;** **kh,** Ger. a**ch** or i**ch.** See pages ix–x.

vac·ci·nate (văk′sĭ-nāt), *v.t.* [vaccinat-ed, vaccinat-ing], to inoculate, or give a mild form of a disease to, in order to prevent a severe attack of the disease; especially, to make immune to smallpox.

vac·ci·na·tion (văk′sĭ-nā′shŭn), *n.* inoculation with a virus to prevent disease.

vac·cine (văk′sēn; văk′sĭn), *n.* 1, a virus, or poison, obtained from cows affected with a disease called cowpox, and injected into the human body to prevent smallpox; 2, any substance used for inoculation.

vac·il·late (văs′ĭ-lāt), *v.i.* [vacillat-ed, vacillat-ing], to be changeable or uncertain in opinion, course of action, or the like.—*n.* vac′il·la′tion.

va·cu·i·ty (vă-kū′ĭ-tĭ), *n.* [*pl.* vacuities], 1, space not filled or occupied; 2, mental inactivity or emptiness; 3, lack of intelligence in facial expression.

vac·u·ous (văk′ū-ŭs), *adj.* 1, empty; vacant; 2, blank; stupid; expressionless.

vac·u·um (văk′ū-ŭm), *n.* 1, a space entirely empty of matter; 2, a sealed space, such as the inside of an incandescent lamp bulb, emptied or nearly emptied of air by artificial means.

    vacuum bottle, a bottle having two sides or walls with a vacuum between them, used to keep liquids hot or cold; **vacuum cleaner,** a machine for cleaning rugs, curtains, and the like, by means of suction which draws dust into a bag; **vacuum tube,** a sealed tube or bulb that contains very little air and hence permits electricity to pass easily between the metal electrodes that extend into the tube, used in the production of X rays, the detection of radio waves, etc.

vag·a·bond (văg′a-bŏnd), *n.* one who roams about with no permanent abode; especially, an idle fellow without honest means of support; a vagrant or tramp:—*adj.* wandering about without a fixed dwelling place; roaming.

va·gar·y (va-gâr′ĭ), *n.* [*pl.* vagaries], a wild or extravagant notion or act; eccentricity; freak of fancy; whim; as, *vagaries* of conduct; the *vagaries* of fortune.

va·grant (vā′grănt), *adj.* wandering from place to place without purpose and without a settled home:—*n.* a tramp.

    Syn., *n.* beggar, vagabond.

vague (vāg), *adj.* [va-guer, va-guest], not clearly seen, stated, or understood; hazy; as, a *vague* answer.—*adv.* **vague′ly.**—*n.* **vague′ness.**

    Syn. indistinct, obscure, indefinite.

vain (vān), *adj.* 1, valueless; empty; idle; as, *vain* boasting; 2, without force or effect; useless; as, *vain* efforts; 3, proud

of small accomplishments or of personal appearance; conceited:—**in vain,** without success; to no purpose.—*adv.* **vain′ly.**

vain·glor·i·ous (vān′glôr′ĭ-ŭs), *adj.* boastful; full of excessive pride or vanity.

vain·glor·y (vān′glôr′ĭ), *n.* excessive vanity or pride in oneself or one's accomplishments.

val·ance (văl′ăns), *n.* a short curtain hung across the top of a window or around a bedstead.

vale (vāl), *n.* *Poetic*, a valley.

val·e·dic·tor·i·an (văl′ē-dĭk-tôr′ĭ-ăn), *n.* a member of a graduating class in a school or college, usually chosen because highest in academic standing, who makes the farewell oration at commencement.

VALANCE (V)

val·e·dic·to·ry (văl′ē-dĭk′tō-rĭ), *n.* [*pl.* valedictories], a farewell speech; especially, a farewell address at a commencement.

Va·len·ci·a (va-lĕn′shĭ-a; va-lĕn′sha), a large city in Spain, on the Mediterranean (map 12).

Va·len·ciennes (va-lä̇n′syĕn′; va-lĕn′sĭ-ĕnz′), *n.* a fine lace, originally made at Valenciennes, France.

val·en·tine (văl′ĕn-tīn), *n.* 1, a greeting card or gift sent on Saint Valentine's Day, February 14; 2, a sweetheart chosen on Saint Valentine's Day.

va·le·ri·an (va-lē′rĭ-ăn), *n.* 1, an herb with small pink or white flowers and a peculiarly pungent odor; 2, a drug obtained from the dried root of this plant.

val·et (văl′ĕt; văl′ā), *n.* a manservant who personally attends a man, taking care of his apartment, clothes, etc.:—*v.t.* to serve (someone) as a valet.

Val·hal·la (văl-hăl′a), *n.* in Norse mythology, the palace in which dwell the souls of heroes who were slain in battle.

VALERIAN

val·iant (văl′yănt), *adj.* brave; heroic; as, *valiant* warriors; *valiant* deeds.

val·id (văl′ĭd), *adj.* 1, based on fact; sound; as, a *valid* argument; 2, executed with all formalities required by law; legally binding; as, a *valid* contract.—*adv.* **val′id·ly.**—*n.* **va·lid′i·ty** (va-lĭd′ĭ-tĭ).

val·i·date (văl′ĭ-dāt), *v.t.* [validat-ed, validat-ing], to ratify; confirm; make valid.

va·lise (và-lēs′; và-lēz′), *n.* a traveling bag, usually of leather, for holding clothes and toilet articles.

Val·kyr·ie (văl-kĭr′ĭ; văl-kī′rĭ; văl′kĭ-rĭ), *n.* in Norse mythology, one of Odin's handmaidens who watched over the battlefields, chose those who were to be slain, and conducted to Valhalla the souls of the worthy heroes. Also written **val-kyr′ie.**

VALISE

val·ley (văl′ĭ), *n.* [*pl.* valleys], low land between hills or mountains.

Valley Forge, a village in Pennsylvania, about 30 miles northwest of Philadelphia, Washington's headquarters in 1777–1778.

val·or (văl′ẽr), *n.* fearlessness in facing danger; bravery. In British usage, **val′-our.**
 Syn. heroism, gallantry, courage, pluck.

val·or·ous (văl′ẽr-ŭs), *adj.* brave; fearless; courageous.—*adv.* **val′or·ous·ly.**

Val·pa·rai·so (văl′pà-rī′zō; väl′pä-rä-ē′sō), a seaport city in Chile (map 11).

valse (vàls; vôls), *n.* a waltz, especially one composed for concert performance.

val·u·a·ble (văl′ū-à-bl), *adj.* 1, costly, or worth a good price; as, a *valuable* jewel; 2, of great importance or use; as, a *valuable* hint:—**valuables,** *n.pl.* costly possessions, especially small personal things, as jewelry.

val·u·a·tion (văl′ū-ā′shŭn), *n.* 1, the act of estimating the worth of something; 2, an estimated worth or price.

val·ue (văl′ū), *n.* 1, worth; the quality which makes a thing worth possessing; as, this ring has only a sentimental *value;* 2, a fair or adequate return; as, to receive *value* for money spent; 3, worth in money; as, the *value* of the property increased; 4, estimated worth; as, he gives his ability a high *value:*—*v.t.* [valued, valu-ing], 1, to estimate the worth of; put a price on; as, to *value* an estate; 2, to esteem highly; hold dear; as, to *value* a friendship.—*n.* **val′u·er.**—*adj.* **val′ue·less.**

valve (vălv), *n.* 1, a mechanical device for opening and closing a pipe, and thus regulating or directing the movement through it of a gas, liquid, or the like (see illustration under *gas engine*); 2, a device, as in a blood vessel, consisting often of two or more folds, or flaps, that open in the direction of the flow of the blood and are closed by a reversal of the flow; 3, either of the two pieces of the shell of a clam, oyster, etc.

va·moose (và-mōos′), *v.i.* and *v.t.* [vamoosed, vamoos-ing], *Slang,* to run away; leave quickly; desert.

vamp (vămp), *n.* 1, the part of a shoe just above the sole, covering the toes and extending to the sides (see illustration under *shoe*); 2, anything patched up; especially, a literary work based on old material:—*v.t.* to patch up with new material.

vam·pire (văm′pīr), *n.* 1, according to superstition, a ghost, or a corpse restored to life, supposed to suck the blood of sleeping persons; 2, one who makes a living at the expense of others; 3, any of various South American blood-sucking bats.

¹van (văn), *n.* the front line or front part of an army or fleet; hence, a pioneering or leading position; as, in the *van* of progress.

²van (văn), *n.* a large covered truck.

va·na·di·um (và-nā′dĭ-ŭm), *n.* a metallic element, used especially as an alloy in steel.

Van Bu·ren (văn bū′rĕn), Martin (1782–1862), the eighth president of the U.S.

Van·cou·ver (văn-kōō′vẽr), 1, an island off the west coast of Canada, a part of British Columbia; 2, a large city in southwestern British Columbia. (Map 4.)

Van·dal (văn′dăl), *n.* one of a Teutonic race which ravaged Gaul, Spain, northern Africa, and Rome during the fourth and fifth centuries:—**vandal,** one who wilfully destroys or defaces anything beautiful or valuable, especially a work of art.—*n.* **van′dal·ism.**

vane (vān), *n.* 1, a movable device fastened to an elevated object to show which way the wind blows; a weathercock; 2, a flat surface that is moved around an axis by wind or water; as, the *vane* that turns the wheel of a windmill into the wind; 3, the flat spreading part of a feather (see illustration under *feather*).

VANE (V), def. 2

van·guard (văn′gärd′), *n.* the first line or advance guard of an army; the van.

va·nil·la (và-nĭl′à), *n.* 1, a tropical American climbing plant of the orchid family; 2, the pod or bean of various species of this plant, used to make a flavoring extract; 3, the flavoring so obtained.

van·ish (văn′ĭsh), *v.i.* 1, to disappear; fade from sight; as, the ship *vanished* beyond the horizon; 2, to pass out of existence; be lost; as, hopes *vanish.*

van·i·ty (văn′ĭ-tĭ), *n.* [*pl.* vanities], 1, shallow pride, as in one's appearance or attainments; conceit; 2, the quality of being worthless; futility; as, the *vanity* of

VANILLA
Leaves and beans.

go; join; yet; sing; chin; show; thin, *th*en; hw, *wh*y; zh, azure; ü, Ger. für or Fr. lune; ö, Ger. schön or Fr. feu; ṅ, Fr. enfant, nom; kh, Ger. ach or ich. See pages ix–x.

human pomp; **3,** a small case, usually of metal, containing a mirror, face powder, and rouge.

van·quish (văng′kwĭsh), *v.t.* to conquer; subdue; defeat; as, to *vanquish* an enemy. —*n.* **van′quish·er.**

van·tage (vån′tĭj), *n.* **1,** a superior position or opportunity; advantage; as, to gain a point of *vantage* in a battle; **2,** in tennis, advantage; the first point scored following deuce.

vap·id (văp′ĭd), *adj.* lacking life or spirit; flat; pointless; as, *vapid* talk.—*adv.* **vap′id·ly.**—*n.* **vap′id·ness.**
Syn. dull, insipid, stale, stupid.

va·por (vā′pẽr), *n.* **1,** the gaseous form of a liquid or solid; as, water *vapor*, or steam, is formed when water is boiled; **2,** moisture floating in the air, as fog or mist; also, a cloudlike substance floating in the air and robbing it of clearness, as smoke. —*adj.* **va′por·ish.**—*adj.* **va′por·y.**

va·por·ize (vā′pẽr·īz), *v.t.* and *v.i.* [vaporized, vaporiz-ing], to change, or be changed, into vapor.

va·por·ous (vā′pẽr·ŭs), *adj.* **1,** full of, or like, vapor, gas, etc.; **2,** unreal; without substance.

va·pour (vā′pẽr), a British spelling of *vapor.* Similarly, **vapourish, vapoury.**

var·i·a·ble (vâr′ĭ·à·bl), *adj.* changeable; inconstant; fitful; as, a *variable* wind:—*n.* that which is subject to change.—*adv.* **var′i·a·bly.**—*n.* **var′i·a·bil′i·ty.**—*n.* **var′i·a·ble·ness.**

var·i·ance (vâr′ĭ·ăns), *n.* **1,** the state of being changeable or different; change; difference; also, the degree of change; as, a *variance* of several dollars in price; **2,** a difference of opinion; discord; as, it is painful to be at *variance* with one's friends.

var·i·ant (vâr′ĭ·ănt), *adj.* differing from others in the same general class; showing variation; as, a *variant* form of a word:—*n.* something that differs from another thing in form; as, "colour" is a *variant* of "color."

var·i·a·tion (vâr′ĭ·ā′shŭn), *n.* **1,** a modification or change; diversity; as, dahlias show great *variations* in color; **2,** amount or extent of change or difference; as, there is little *variation* in the temperature; **3,** in music, the repetition of a single melody with changes and elaborations.

var·i·col·ored (vâr′ĭ·kŭl′ẽrd), *adj.* spotted, streaked, or marked with various colors; as, a *varicolored* mosaic.

var·ied (vâr′ĭd), *adj.* **1,** of different sorts; diversified; as, a *varied* collection of pictures; **2,** variegated.

var·i·e·gate (vâr′ĭ·ĕ·gāt; vâr′ĭ·gāt), *v.t.*

[variegat-ed, variegat-ing], to change the appearance of, by marking with different colors; streak; spot.

var·i·e·ga·tion (vâr′ĭ·ĕ·gā′shŭn; vâr′ĭ·gā′shŭn), *n.* variety; diversity in coloring or marking.

va·ri·e·ty (và·rī′ĕ·tĭ), *n.* [*pl.* varieties], **1,** the state of being different; diversity; change; as, we like the *variety* of city life; **2,** a collection of unlike objects; as, she received a *variety* of gifts; **3,** a plant or animal differing in some details from others of the same general class or kind; as, one *variety* of palm bears dates, another *variety* bears coconuts.

var·i·ous (vâr′ĭ·ŭs), *adj.* **1,** different; diverse; of several sorts; as, the *various* colors of autumn leaves; **2,** several; as, he met the man on *various* occasions.—*adv.* **var′i·ous·ly.**—*n.* **var′i·ous·ness.**

var·let (vär′lĕt), *n. Archaic,* a scoundrel.

var·nish (vär′nĭsh), *n.* **1,** a liquid preparation of resin used for giving gloss to the surface of wood, metal, etc.; **2,** the coating or gloss resulting from an application of varnish; **3,** superficial smoothness or polish; outside show:—*v.t.* **1,** to cover with varnish; give a gloss to; **2,** to cover up the defects of; gloss over.—*n.* **var′nish·er.**

var·y (vâr′ĭ), *v.t.* [varied, vary-ing], to alter in appearance, shape, substance, or the like; change; as, to *vary* the order of events:—*v.i.* to undergo a change; differ; as, the price *varies* from day to day.

vas·cu·lar (văs′kŭ·lẽr), *adj.* pertaining to the vessels of an animal or vegetable body which carry or convey fluids, as blood and lymph vessels in animals, and sap ducts in plants.

vase (vās; vāz), *n.* a vessel of glass, pottery, or the like, used as an ornament or for holding flowers.

Vas·e·line (văs′ĕ·lēn; văs′ĕ·lĭn), *n.* a trade-mark name for various products, the chief of which is petroleum jelly, a jelly-like substance obtained from petroleum, used as an ointment and lubricant; also, a product bearing this trade-mark name.

vas·sal (văs′ăl), *n.* **1,** in the feudal system, one who placed himself under the protection of a lord or master, and in return rendered homage and service; one who held land under feudal tenure; **2,** a servant.
Syn. serf, dependent.

vas·sal·age (văs′ăl·ĭj), *n.* **1,** the condition of a serf or vassal; **2,** servitude.

vast (våst), *adj.* very great in size, extent, amount, or the like; as, a *vast* plain; a *vast* fortune.—*n.* **vast′ness.**
Syn. enormous, huge, colossal.

āte, āorta, râre, căt, åsk, fär, ållow, sofà; ēve, ēvent, ĕll, wrītẽr, novĕl; bīte, pĭn; nō, ōbey, ôr, dŏg, tŏp, cŏllide; ūnit, ūnite, bûrn, cŭt, focŭs; nōon, fŏŏt; mound; coin;

vat (văt), *n.* a large tank, tub, or vessel, especially one for holding liquors, dyes, etc., in process of manufacture.

Vat-i-can (văt′ĭ-kăn), *n.* the papal palace in Rome:—**Vatican City,** a small independent state enclosing the Vatican.

vaude-ville (vōd′vĭl; vô′dĕ-vĭl), *n.* a kind of theatrical performance consisting of a series of songs, dances, acrobatic feats, short dramatic sketches, etc.

¹vault (vôlt), *n.* a leap or jump made with the use of the hands or with the aid of a pole:—*v.i.* and *v.t.* to leap over; jump; as, to *vault* a fence.—*n.* **vault′er.**

²vault (vôlt), *n.* **1,** an arched roof or ceiling; also, any arched covering; especially, the arch of the sky; **2,** storage space, as in a cellar; **3,** a cavern; tomb; **4,** a steel room, as in a bank, in which valuables are kept:—*v.t.* to shape like a vault; provide with an arched ceiling.

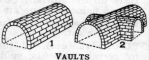

VAULTS
1, simple vault; 2, intersecting vault.

vaunt (vônt; vänt), *v.i.* to brag:—*v.t.* to boast of; display boastfully; as, to *vaunt* one's courage:—*n.* a boast; brag; vain display.—*adj.* **vaunt′ing.**

vb. abbreviation for *verb, verbal.*

veal (vēl), *n.* the meat of the calf.

veer (vēr), *v.t.* and *v.i.* to change in direction; shift; as, the ship *veered* suddenly to the south.

Ve-ga (vē′gȧ), *n.* a bluish-white star of the first magnitude.

veg-e-ta-ble (věj′ĕ-tȧ-bl), *n.* **1,** a plant, especially one cultivated for food, as potatoes, corn, beans, etc.; **2,** the edible portion of such a plant:—*adj.* **1,** pertaining to plants; **2,** derived from plants; as, *vegetable* fats.

veg-e-tar-i-an (věj′ĕ-târ′ĭ-ăn), *n.* one who avoids meat as an element of diet, and considers plants the only proper source of food for man:—*adj.* **1,** pertaining to vegetarians; **2,** consisting of vegetables; as, a *vegetarian* diet.

veg-e-tate (věj′ĕ-tāt), *v.i.* [vegetat-ed, veg-etat-ing], to grow as a plant does; hence, of persons, to lead an idle, unthinking existence.—*adj.* **veg′e-ta′tive.**

veg-e-ta-tion (věj′ĕ-tā′shŭn), *n.* **1,** the act of growing or vegetating; **2,** plant life; plants in general; as, the dense *vegetation* of the jungle.

ve-he-mence (vē′ĕ-měns), *n.* **1,** violence, as of a storm; **2,** passionate earnestness or vigor, as of an orator.

ve-he-ment (vē′ĕ-měnt), *adj.* **1,** very violent; furious; as, a *vehement* wind; **2,** passionate; earnest; as, *vehement* words.—*adv.* **ve′he-ment-ly.**
Syn. fiery, impetuous, ardent.

ve-hi-cle (vē′ĭ-kl; vē′hĭ-kl), *n.* **1,** any kind of conveyance, especially one used on land, as a car, wagon, bicycle, etc.; **2,** anything which may be used as a medium for communicating thought, feeling, knowledge, or the like, as a newspaper, radio, etc.

veil (vāl), *n.* **1,** a thin, gauzy, ornamental covering for the face; **2,** a piece of fabric hanging from the head over the shoulders, as worn by a nun; **3,** a curtain or covering which conceals something; as, a *veil* of clouds over the mountains; **4,** anything which hides; as, a *veil* of mystery:—**to take the veil,** to become a nun:—*v.t.* **1,** to cover with, or as with, a veil or curtain; **2,** to hide.

veil-ing (vāl′ĭng), *n.* thin, gauzy material, as for veils; also, a veil.

vein (vān), *n.* **1,** one of the tubelike vessels which carry the blood to or toward the heart; **2,** one of the branching ribs of a leaf or of the wing of an insect; **3,** a crack or seam in rock; also, ore or other material filling a fissure in rock; as, a *vein* of coal; **4,** a long streak of a different color, as in wood or marble; **5,** a particular strain or disposition; peculiarity of mood, speech, etc.; as, he spoke in a solemn *vein*:—*v.t.* to cover, fill, or form with veins.—*adj.* **veined** (vānd).

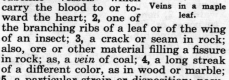

VEIN, def. 2
Veins in a maple leaf.

Ve-lás-quez (vĕ-läs′kĕth), Diego (1599–1660), a Spanish painter.

veld (vĕlt; fĕlt), *n.* in South Africa, open pasture land or thinly wooded country. Also spelled **veldt.**

vel-lum (vĕl′ŭm), *n.* **1,** a fine parchment, usually made of calfskin, intended for binding books, writing upon, etc.; **2,** a kind of paper or cotton cloth made in imitation of this.

ve-loc-i-pede (vĕ-lŏs′ĭ-pēd), *n.* **1,** a light vehicle for children, with a large wheel in front and two small wheels behind, and moved by pedals; **2,** an early form of the bicycle or tricycle.

ve-loc-i-ty (vĕ-lŏs′ĭ-tĭ), *n.* [*pl.* velocities], the rate of motion of a moving object; speed; swiftness; as, the *velocity* of a bullet.

VELOCIPEDE
def. 1

ve-lours (vĕ-lŏor′), *n.* [*pl.* velours (vĕ-lŏorz′)], any of various woven fabrics having a pile, or nap, like that of velvet.

vel-vet (vĕl′vĕt), *n.* a closely woven silk material with a short, thick pile, or nap, of fine upright threads:—*adj.* **1,** made of velvet; **2,** as soft as velvet.—*adj.* **vel′vet-y.**

vel-vet-een (vĕl′vĕ-tēn′), *n.* a cotton material resembling velvet; imitation velvet.

ve-nal (vē′năl), *adj.* **1,** willing to sacrifice honor and principle for sordid gain; open to bribes; as, a *venal* person; **2,** to be obtained by purchase or hire; as, *venal* services.—*adv.* **ve′nal-ly.**—*n.* **ve-nal′i-ty** (vē-năl′ĭ-tĭ).

vend (vĕnd), *v.t.* to sell; offer for sale.

ven-det-ta (vĕn-dĕt′a), *n.* a private feud for revenge by bloodshed, usually carried on by the relatives of a murdered man.

ven-dor or **vend-er** (vĕn′dĕr), *n.* a seller; usually, a hawker or peddler.

ve-neer (vĕ-nĭr′), *v.t.* **1,** to overlay with a thin surface of more valuable or beautiful material; as, to *veneer* a pine table with walnut; **2,** hence, to cover or conceal (something cheap or mean) with a surface polish; give a gloss to:—*n.* **1,** a thin surface of fine wood overlaying wood of a poorer quality; **2,** outside show; pretense; surface elegance; as, a *veneer* of fine manners.

VENEER, def. 1

a, layer of veneer, partly cut away to show board beneath.

ven-er-a-ble (vĕn′ĕr-a-bl), *adj.* **1,** so old and wise as to be worthy of reverence; as, a *venerable* judge; **2,** sacred by reason of associations of a religious or historic nature; as, a *venerable* cathedral.—*adv.* **ven′er-a-bly.** *Syn.* respected, revered.

ven-er-ate (vĕn′ĕr-āt), *v.t.* [venerat-ed, venerat-ing], to regard with the highest respect and honor; reverence.

ven-er-a-tion (vĕn′ĕr-ā′shŭn), *n.* **1,** deep respect and reverence; **2,** the act of venerating; worship. *Syn.* adoration, honor, respect.

ve-ne-re-al (vĕ-nĭr′ē-ăl), *adj.* pertaining to sexual intercourse; specifically, resulting from intercourse with an infected person; as, a *venereal* disease.

Ve-ne-tian (vĕ-nē′shăn), *n.* a native of Venice, in Italy:—*adj.* pertaining to Venice or its people.:—**Venetian blind,** a window blind made of horizontal slats held in position by tapes, and regulated by cords which raise and lower or tilt the slats.

Ven-e-zue-la (vĕn′ē-zwē′la), a republic (cap. Caracas) on the north coast of South America (map **11**).

venge-ance (vĕn′jăns), *n.* punishment inflicted for a wrong endured; repayment for an offense; as, he swore *vengeance* on his enemy:—**with a vengeance,** vehemently; with great fury; also, in greater amount or degree than expected.

venge-ful (vĕnj′fŏŏl), *adj.* filled with a desire for vengeance.—*adv.* **venge′ful-ly.**

ve-ni-al (vē′nĭ-ăl), *adj.* not beyond forgiveness:—**venial sin,** in the Roman Catholic Church, a fault that may be forgiven.

Ven-ice (vĕn′ĭs), a city of northeastern Italy on the Adriatic Sea (map **12**). Its Italian name is **Ve-ne′zia** (vä-nĕt′syä).

ven-i-son (vĕn′ĭ-zn; vĕn′zn), *n.* deer's flesh used for meat.

ven-om (vĕn′ŭm), *n.* **1,** the poison secreted by certain serpents, spiders, etc., which makes their bite or sting injurious and sometimes fatal; **2,** spite; malignity.

ven-om-ous (vĕn′ŭm-ŭs), *adj.* **1,** full of poison; **2,** capable of giving a poisonous bite or sting; as, a *venomous* snake; **3,** spiteful; as, a *venomous* rumor.—*adv.* **ven′om-ous-ly.**—*n.* **ven′om-ous-ness.**

vent (vĕnt), *n.* **1,** a small opening for the passage of air, smoke, etc.; **2,** an outlet; free play; utterance; as, to give *vent* to one's indignation:—*v.t.* **1,** to let out through a hole, as steam; **2,** to give an outlet to; relieve by speech or action; as, she *vented* her displeasure in words.

ven-ti-late (vĕn′tĭ-lāt), *v.t.* [ventilat-ed, ventilat-ing], **1,** to provide with a proper circulation of air, by letting in fresh and driving out stale air, as through open windows, shafts, etc.; **2,** to purify by exposure to fresh air; **3,** to bring out (a subject) for public examination and discussion.

ven-ti-la-tion (vĕn′tĭ-lā′shŭn), *n.* **1,** the act of providing with a proper circulation of air; also, a means for doing this; **2,** proper circulation of air.

ven-ti-la-tor (vĕn′tĭ-lā′tĕr), *n.* a contrivance for admitting fresh air and letting out foul or stagnant air.

ven-tral (vĕn′trăl), *adj.* pertaining to, or situated on or near, the abdomen, or belly of an animal; as, the *ventral* fins of a fish.

ven-tri-cle (vĕn′trĭ-kl), *n.* either of the two lower chambers of the heart, from which blood is forced into the arteries.

ven-tril-o-quism (vĕn-trĭl′ŏ-kwĭzm), *n.* the art of speaking in such a way that the voice appears to come from another person or place.—*n.* **ven-tril′o-quist.**

ven·ture (vĕn′tûr), *n.* **1**, a dangerous or daring undertaking; **2**, an enterprise involving risk; as, a business *venture:*—*v.t.* [ventured, ventur-ing], **1**, to risk; expose to danger; as, he *ventured* his life in the attempt; also, to stake; as, he *ventured* all his money in the enterprise; **2**, to hazard; give; as, to *venture* a guess:—*v.i.* **1**, to dare; **2**, to take a chance; run a risk.—*n.* **ven′tur-er.**

Syn., *n.* chance, peril, stake.

ven·ture·some (vĕn′tûr-sŭm), *adj.* **1**, daring; bold; as, a *venturesome* spirit; **2**, dangerous; as, a *venturesome* undertaking.

ven·tur·ous (vĕn′tûr-ŭs), *adj.* **1**, fearless; venturesome; **2**, full of risks.

Ve·nus (vē′nŭs), *n.* **1**, the Roman goddess of beauty and love: called *Aphrodite* by the Greeks; **2**, the most brilliant of the planets.

ve·ra·cious (vĕ-rā′shŭs), *adj.* **1**, habitually telling the truth; **2**, true; reliable; as, a *veracious* report.

ve·rac·i·ty (vĕ-răs′ĭ-tĭ), *n.* [*pl.* veracities], **1**, truthfulness; **2**, truth; accuracy; as, the *veracity* of a statement.

Ve·ra·cruz (vĕr′ȧ-krōōz′), a city, the chief seaport of Mexico, on the Gulf of Mexico (map 10).

ve·ran·da or **ve·ran·dah** (vĕ-răn′dȧ), *n.* a long open porch, usually roofed.

verb (vûrb), *n.* that part of speech which expresses action, state of being, or condition; a word which states something; as, in the sentence "John studied his lesson," the *verb* is "studied."

ver·bal (vûr′băl), *adj.* **1**, pertaining to words; also, consisting merely of words; as, his penitence was only *verbal;* **2**, spoken; not written; as, a *verbal* agreement; **3**, pertaining to a verb; as, a *verbal* prefix; **4**, literal; word for word, as a translation:—**verbal noun,** a noun formed by adding *-ing* to a verb; as, in "Seeing is believing," "seeing" and "believing" are *verbal* nouns.—*adv.* **ver′bal-ly.**

ver·ba·tim (vûr-bā′tĭm), *adv.* word for word; literally; as, to report a speech *verbatim:*—*adj.* literal; word for word.

ver·be·na (vĕr-bē′nȧ), *n.* a garden plant with large heads of flowers of various colors and spicy fragrance.

ver·bi·age (vûr′bĭ-ĭj), *n.* wordiness; the use of more words than necessary.

VERBENA

ver·bose (vûr-bōs′), *adj.* wordy; using too many words.—*n.* **ver-bose′ness.**

ver·bos·i·ty (vûr-bŏs′ĭ-tĭ), *n.* [*pl.* verbosities], the use of too many words; wordiness.

ver·dant (vûr′dănt), *adj.* **1**, covered with fresh green grass or foliage; fresh; green; as, a *verdant* landscape; **2**, fresh and untried in knowledge or judgment; inexperienced.

Verde, Cape (vûrd), the western extremity of Africa (map **14**).

ver·dict (vûr′dĭkt), *n.* **1**, the decision of a jury on a case in court; as, the jury's *verdict* was for acquittal; **2**, the expression of any important decision.

ver·di·gris (vûr′dĭ-grēs; vûr′dĭ-grĭs), *n.* a greenish or bluish rust which forms on copper, bronze, brass, etc.

Ver·dun (vâr′dûṅ), a town and fortress on the Meuse River, in northeastern France, scene of battles in World War I.

ver·dure (vûr′dūr), *n.* **1**, greenness or freshness, especially of grass and growing plants; **2**, green grass, growing plants, etc.

verge (vûrj), *n.* a boundary; brink; an extreme edge; as, the country was on the *verge* of revolution:—*v.i.* [verged, verg-ing], **1**, to approach closely; be on the border; as, his actions *verge* on treason; **2**, to tend; incline; as, a day *verging* toward its close.

Syn., *n.* margin, border, limit.

Ver·gil or **Vir·gil** (vûr′jĭl), (70–19 B.C.), a Roman poet, author of the "Aeneid."

ver·i·fi·ca·tion (vĕr′ĭ-fĭ-kā′shŭn), *n.* the act of proving the accuracy of a statement, figures, dates, etc.; also, the proof.

ver·i·fy (vĕr′ĭ-fī), *v.t.* [verified, verify-ing], to check the truth or correctness of; as, to *verify* the answer to an arithmetic problem.—*n.* **ver′i-fi′er.**

ver·i·ly (vĕr′ĭ-lĭ), *adv.* in truth; truly.

ver·i·ta·ble (vĕr′ĭ-tȧ-bl), *adj.* actual; genuine; true; as, the rain was a *veritable* godsend.—*adv.* **ver′i-ta-bly.**

ver·i·ty (vĕr′ĭ-tĭ), *n.* [*pl.* verities], the quality or state of being true; reality; also, that which is true; a truth; fact.

ver·meil (vûr′mĭl; vûr′ml), *n.* **1**, *Poetic,* vermilion or its brilliant red color; **2**, gilded silver, bronze, etc:—*adj.* vermilion.

ver·mi·cel·li (vûr′mĭ-sĕl′ĭ; vûr′mĭ-chĕl′ĭ), *n.* a food made of fine flour paste like that used in macaroni or spaghetti, and prepared in long slender threads.

ver·mic·u·lite (vûr-mĭk′ū-līt), *n.* a type of mica which is expanded at extremely high temperature to somewhat wormlike structure honeycombed with air cells. It is used for insulating, fireproofing, sound deadening, packaging, and gardening.

ver·mi·form (vûr′mĭ-fôrm), *adj.* shaped like a worm:—**vermiform appendix,** a small, closed tube, now without use to the body, attached to the large intestine; the seat of appendicitis.

ver·mil·ion (vẽr-mĭl′yŭn), *n.* a brilliant red pigment; a vivid red color like this pigment:—*adj.* of the color of vermilion.

ver·min (vûr′mĭn), *n.* [*pl.* vermin], usually in *pl.*, harmful and offensive insects or small animals, as flies, lice, rats, etc.

Ver·mont (vẽr-mŏnt′), a New England State (cap. Montpelier) in the U.S. (map 6).

ver·nac·u·lar (vẽr-năk′ū-lẽr), *adj.* pertaining to the spoken language or idiom of a country; colloquial rather than literary:—*n.* 1, the spoken language of a country; 2, the prevailing fashion of speech among the people in any locality, business, or profession; as, the *vernacular* of the stage.

ver·nal (vûr′năl), *adj.* 1, pertaining to, or appearing in, the spring; as, *vernal* breezes; 2, springlike; hence, youthful.

Ver·sailles (vâr′sáy′; vẽr-sālz′), a city near Paris, France, noted chiefly for its magnificent palace (map 12).

ver·sa·tile (vûr′sȧ-tĭl; vûr′sȧ-tīl), *adj.* capable of dealing with many subjects, or of doing many things equally well; as, a *versatile* writer; a *versatile* workman.

ver·sa·til·i·ty (vûr′sȧ-tĭl′ĭ-tĭ), *n.* skill in many different lines of activity.

verse (vûrs), *n.* 1, a single metrical line in poetry; 2, loosely, a group of metrical lines; a stanza; 3, a form of literary composition possessing rhythm; poetry: distinguished from *prose;* 4, any of the short divisions of a chapter in the Bible.

versed (vûrst), *adj.* thoroughly trained; skilled; learned; as, *versed* in law.

ver·si·fi·ca·tion (vûr′sĭ-fĭ-kā′shŭn), *n.* 1, the art or practice of composing verses, as of poetry; 2, the metrical framework, or structure, of poetry.

ver·si·fy (vûr′sĭ-fī), *v.i.* [versified, versifying], to make verses:—*v.t.* to put into verse. —*n.* **ver′si·fi′er.**

ver·sion (vûr′zhŭn; vûr′shŭn), *n.* 1, a translation from one language into another; as, a revised *version* of the Bible; 2, a report or description of an occurrence from an individual point of view; as, his *version* of the accident differs from mine.

vers libre (vâr′ lēbr′), [French], verse not following a fixed metrical form.

verst (vûrst), *n.* a Russian measure of distance equal to 3,500 feet, or about two thirds of a mile.

ver·sus (vûr′sŭs), *prep.* against; as, Army *versus* Navy.

ver·te·bra (vûr′tē-brȧ), *n.* [*pl.* vertebrae (vûr′tē-brē) or vertebras (vûr′tē-brȧz)], one of the single bones, or segments, which are joined together to make the backbone.

ver·te·brate (vûr′tē-brȧt), *adj.* having a backbone, or spinal column:—*n.* an animal with a spinal column.

ver·tex (vûr′tĕks), *n.* [*pl.* vertexes (vûr′-tĕk-sēz) or vertices (vûr′tĭ-sēz)], the highest point; top; apex; as, the *vertex* of a pyramid.

ver·ti·cal (vûr′tĭ-kăl), *adj.* upright; in the direction in which a tree grows: opposite of *horizontal;* as, the flagpole in our school-yard is *vertical.*—*adv.* **ver′ti·cal·ly.**

ver·ti·go (vûr′tĭ-gō), *n.* [*pl.* vertigoes], giddiness; extreme dizziness.

verve (vûrv), *n.* enthusiasm, energy, or vigor, especially in literary or artistic work.

ver·y (vĕr′ĭ), *adj.* [ver-i-er, ver-i-est], 1, absolute; complete; as, the *very* truth; 2, identical; the same; as, that is the *very* dress; 3, mere; as, the *very* thought of an accident frightens me:—*adv.* in a high degree; extremely; as, she does *very* good work; the book was *very* dull.

ves·per (vĕs′pẽr), *adj.* 1, pertaining to the evening; 2, **Vesper,** pertaining to an evening prayer service; as, *Vesper* hymns:—*n.* 1, *Poetic,* evening; 2, **Vesper,** the evening star, or Hesperus; especially, the planet Venus as the evening star.

Ves·pers (vĕs′pẽrz), *n.pl.* a prayer or song service held in the early evening or late afternoon.

Ves·puc·ci (vĕs-pōōt′chē), Amerigo, an Italian navigator. See **Amerigo Vespucci.**

ves·sel (vĕs′l), *n.* 1, a hollow container, usually for liquids, as a barrel, cup, etc.; 2, a tube or canal in the body through which a fluid passes; as, a blood *vessel;* 3, a ship; boat, especially a large one.

vest (vĕst), *n.* 1, a waistcoat; a man's sleeveless garment, worn beneath the coat; also, a similar jacket worn by women; 2, a woven or knitted undershirt; an undervest; 3, an ornamental insertion in the front of a woman's dress or jacket; vestee: —*v.t.* 1, to dress in a garment; as, they *vested* the choir in white robes; 2, to clothe or endow with authority, power, or the like; as, the church *vests* its bishops with certain powers; 3, to put into the care of another; as, the management of the company is *vested* in its officials:—*v.i.* to clothe oneself with vestments.

Ves·ta (vĕs′tȧ), *n.* the Roman virgin goddess of the hearth, in whose temple the sacred fire was kept by the vestal virgins.

ves·tal (vĕs′tăl), *adj.* pertaining to the Roman goddess Vesta, or to the virgins who served in her temple; hence, suitable to a virgin or nun:—*n.* 1, a virgin consecrated to the service of Vesta; 2, hence, a virgin; also, a nun.

āte, âorta, râre, căt, ȧsk, fär, ȧllow, sofȧ; ēve, ĕvent, ĕll, writẽr, novĕl; bīte, pĭn; nō, ōbey, ôr, dŏg, tŏp, cŏllide; ūnit, ūnite, bûrn, cŭt, focŭs; nōōn, fŏŏt; mound; coin;

vest-ed (vĕs′tĕd), *adj.* **1,** clothed, especially in priestly or other ceremonial garments; **2,** fixed; having rights established by law; as, *vested* interests.

vest-ee (vĕs′tē′), *n.* a small vest, or a piece of material forming a V-shaped front in a woman's blouse or dress.

ves-ti-bule (vĕs′tĭ-būl), *n.* a small, enclosed entry between the outer and inner doors of a house or other building; also, an enclosed entrance to a railway coach.

ves-tige (vĕs′tĭj), *n.* originally, a footprint or track; hence, a visible sign or trace of something that is gone or has disappeared; as, not a *vestige* of the house remained.

vest-ment (vĕst′mĕnt), *n.* a robe; especially, an official or ceremonial garment, or one worn by priests, ministers, choir, etc., during services.

ves-try (vĕs′trĭ), *n.* [*pl.* vestries], **1,** a room in a church where the clergy put on their vestments, or where the sacred vessels of the service are kept; **2,** in some Protestant churches, a room or building attached to a church, and used as a chapel or Sunday-school room; **3,** in the Protestant Episcopal Church, a body of men who direct the affairs of a parish.—*n.* **ves′try-man.**

ves-ture (vĕs′tūr), *n.* clothing; garments.

Ve-su-vi-us (vē-sū′vĭ-ŭs), an active volcano near Naples, Italy (map 1).

vetch (vĕch), *n.* a plant of the pea family, often used as fodder.

vet-er-an (vĕt′ẽr-ăn), *adj.* possessing experience due to age; long trained or practiced, especially as a soldier:—*n.* **1,** a person of age and experience; one grown old in service; **2,** a soldier of any age who has seen active service in war.

vet-er-i-nar-y (vĕt′ẽr-ĭ-nĕr′ĭ), *adj.* pertaining to the treatment of diseases and injuries of animals; as, a *veterinary* surgeon:—*n.* [*pl.* veterinaries], one who practices veterinary medicine or surgery.—*n.* **vet′er-i-nar′i-an.**

ve-to (vē′tō), *n.* [*pl.* vetoes], the right of a president, governor, or other executive, to prevent temporarily or permanently the enactment of a measure as law; a prohibition by someone in authority:—*v.t.* to prohibit; refuse to approve; as, the teacher *vetoed* the idea of a class party; especially, to refuse assent to (a bill) so as to prevent its becoming a law, or to cause its reconsideration.—*n.* **ve′to-er.**

vex (vĕks), *v.t.* **1,** to irritate by small annoyances; harass; make angry; **2,** to agitate; disquiet; as, angry winds *vexed* the sea.

    Syn. provoke, annoy, exasperate.

vex-a-tion (vĕks-ā′shŭn), *n.* annoyance; displeasure; irritation; as, he plainly showed his *vexation;* also, a source of annoyance; as, the sore finger was a *vexation*

    Syn. chagrin, mortification, trouble.

vex-a-tious (vĕks-ā′shŭs), *adj.* causing annoyance; irritating; provoking; as, *vexatious* delays.

v.i. abbreviation for *verb intransitive.*

vi-a (vī′à), *prep.* by the way of; as, he traveled *via* the Great Lakes.

vi-a-duct (vī′à-dŭkt), *n.* a bridge, usually built of arched masonry or of steel, for carrying a road or a railway over a valley or ravine.

VIADUCT

vi-al (vī′ăl), *n.* a small glass bottle with a stopper, as for medicines; a phial.

vi-and (vī′ănd), *n.* **1,** an article of food; **2, viands,** provisions; food.

vi-at-i-cum (vī-ăt′ĭ-kŭm), *n.* [*pl.* viatica (vī-ăt′ĭ-kà) or viaticums], in the Roman Catholic church, the Communion given to one on the verge of death.

vi-brant (vī′brănt), *adj.* **1,** vigorous; full of life and feeling; **2,** resonant; resounding; as, the *vibrant* tones of a violin.

vi-brate (vī′brāt), *v.i.* [vibrat-ed, vibrating], **1,** to move back and forth with a regular motion; **2,** to quiver, as the voice; make a tremulous sound:—*v.t.* **1,** to cause to move to and fro; **2,** to cause to quiver.

vi-bra-tion (vī-brā′shŭn), *n.* a quivering or trembling, as of the voice; also, regular motion to and fro.

vi-bra-tor (vī′brā-tẽr), *n.* that which quivers or which causes to-and-fro motion; especially, a rubber-tipped electric appliance, used in massaging.

vic-ar (vĭk′ẽr), *n.* **1,** in the Roman Catholic Church, a member of the clergy acting as representative of one of the higher clergy; **2,** in the Protestant Episcopal Church, a minister who is the head of one chapel in a large parish; also, a bishop's representative in charge of a church.

vic-ar-age (vĭk′ẽr-ĭj), *n.* the office, position, or residence of a vicar.

vi-car-i-ous (vī-kâr′ĭ-ŭs; vĭ-kâr′ĭ-ŭs), *adj.* **1,** acting for another; **2,** done or endured in place of another; as, many people enjoy *vicarious* adventures through motion pictures.—*adv.* **vi-car′i-ous-ly.**

---

go; join; yet; sing; chin; show; thin, *th*en; hw, *wh*y; zh, azure; ü, Ger. f*ü*r or Fr. l*u*ne; ö, Ger. sch*ö*n or Fr. f*eu*; ṅ, Fr. e*n*fant, no*m*; kh, Ger.·a*ch* or i*ch*. See pages ix–x.

¹vice (vīs), *n.* **1**, a debasing practice or habit, as drunkenness; **2**, wickedness; corruption; **3**, a bad trick or habit, as of a horse, dog, or the like.

²vice (vīs), *n.* a vise. See **vise.**

vice— (vīs-), a prefix, usually set off by a hyphen, meaning next in rank to, or acting in the place of, another; as, *vice*-principal.

vice—pres·i·dent (vīs′-prĕz′ĭ-dĕnt), *n.* the officer next in rank below a president, who takes the place of the president during the latter's absence or disability. Also written **vice president.**

vice·re·gal (vīs′rē′găl), *adj.* pertaining to a viceroy.

vice·roy (vīs′roi), *n.* a ruler of a colony or province, representing, and ruling with the authority of, the king; as, the *viceroy* of India.—*n.* **vice′roy′al·ty** (vīs′roi′ăl-tĭ).

vi·ce ver·sa (vī′sē vûr′sȧ), the terms being reversed; the other way around; as, that man calls black white and *vice versa* (that is, he calls white black).

vi·cin·i·ty (vĭ-sĭn′ĭ-tĭ), *n.* [*pl.* vicinities], **1**, nearness; closeness; **2**, a region about or near; neighborhood.

vi·cious (vĭsh′ŭs), *adj.* **1**, faulty; defective; as, *vicious* reasoning; **2**, corrupt; depraved; wicked; as, a *vicious* life; **3**, bad-tempered; malicious; as, *vicious* remarks. —*adv.* **vi′cious·ly.**—*n.* **vi′cious·ness.**

vi·cis·si·tude (vĭ-sĭs′ĭ-tūd), *n.* a complete, unexpected change of circumstances; as, the *vicissitudes* of war.

Vicks·burg (vĭks′bûrg), a city in Mississippi, the scene of a decisive battle in the War between the States (map 8).

vic·tim (vĭk′tĭm), *n.* **1**, a living being sacrificed in a religious ceremony; **2**, a person or animal injured or killed in some misfortune or calamity; **3**, a sufferer from mental or physical disease; **4**, a person who is cheated; a dupe.—*v.t.* **vic′tim·ize.**

vic·tor (vĭk′tẽr), *n.* a conqueror; one who wins:—*adj.* conquering.

Vic·tor Em·man·u·el III (vĭk′tẽr ĕ-măn′ū-ĕl), (1869–1947), the king of Italy from 1900 to 1946.

vic·to·ri·a (vĭk-tôr′ĭ-ȧ), *n.* a low four-wheeled carriage with a top that may be lowered, and a high seat in front for the coachman. (See illustration next column.)

¹Vic·to·ri·a (vĭk-tôr′ĭ-ȧ), **1**, a city, capital of British Columbia, Canada (map 4); **2**, a state (cap. Melbourne) of southeastern Australia (map 16):—**Victoria Falls,** falls in the Zambezi River in Rhodesia, Africa (map 14).

²Vic·to·ri·a (vĭk-tôr′ĭ-ȧ), Alexandrina (1819–1901), queen of Great Britain and Ireland, 1837–1901, and empress of India, 1876–1901.

VICTORIA

Vic·to·ri·an (vĭk-tôr′ĭ-ăn), *adj.* pertaining to the reign of Queen Victoria, or characteristic of English life and sentiment of that time; as, the *Victorian* era.

Vic·to·ri·a Nyan·za (nyän′zä), a large lake in east central Africa (map 14). It is often called *Lake Victoria.*

vic·to·ri·ous (vĭk-tôr′ĭ-ŭs), *adj.* **1**, having conquered in battle or contest; triumphant; as, a *victorious* army; **2**, marked by or ending in victory.—*adv.* **vic·tor′i·ous·ly.**—*n.* **vic·tor′i·ous·ness.**

vic·to·ry (vĭk′tō-rĭ), *n.* [*pl.* victories], **1**, the defeat of an enemy; **2**, any triumph.

Vic·tro·la (vĭk-trō′lȧ), *n.* a trade-mark name for a make of phonograph:—**victrola,** a phonograph of this make.

vict·ual (vĭt′l), *v.t.* to supply or stock with food:—**victuals,** *n.pl.* food for human beings; provisions.

vi·cu·ña (vĭ-kōōn′yȧ; vĭ-kū′nȧ), *n.* a cud-chewing animal of the high Andes, similar to the llama and alpaca, and furnishing a soft, reddish wool.

vid·e·o (vĭd′ē-ō), *adj.* pertaining to television; as, *video* channel:—*n.* television.

vid. or **v.** abbreviation for Latin *vide* (vī′dē), meaning *see.*

vie (vī), *v.i.* [vied, vy·ing], to compete, as in games, schoolwork, etc.; contend for superiority.

VICUÑA (1/30)

Vi·en·na (vē-ĕn′ȧ), the capital of Austria, on the Danube River (map 12). Its German name is *Wien.*

Vi·et·nam (vē′ĕt-näm′), a country in Indochina. (Map 15.)

view (vū), *n.* **1**, the act of seeing; inspection; as, this is worth a nearer *view;* **2**, that which is seen; scene; as, a splendid *view* of the river; **3**, a range of mental perception; as, to take a broad *view* of the matter; **4**, range of vision; as, the top of the hill is beyond our *view;* **5**, a picture of a scene, object, or person; **6**, a way of looking at anything mentally; opinion; as, he held advanced *views;* **7**, purpose or aim; as, to make your plans with a *view* to success:—*v.t.* **1,** to see; gaze at; look upon; **2,** to survey mentally; form an opinion of. —*n.* **view′er.**—*adj.* **view′less.**

in view of, in consideration of; **with a view to,** with the purpose of; **on view,** open to public inspection.

view-point (vū′point′), *n.* the position or place from which one looks at or something; especially, a way of looking at or judging things; as, a person of very narrow *viewpoint*.

vig-il (vĭj′ĭl), *n.* **1,** a keeping awake during a time usually devoted to sleep; watchfulness; **2,** (usually *vigils*), religious devotions in the evening or night; **3,** the eve of a feast day.

vig-i-lance (vĭj′ĭ-lăns), *n.* watchfulness; alertness to avoid danger.

vig-i-lant (vĭj′ĭ-lănt), *adj.* keenly watchful; alert.—*adv.* **vig′i-lant-ly.**

Syn. wakeful, wary, observant.

vig-or (vĭg′ẽr), *n.* physical or mental strength or energy; vitality.

vig-or-ous (vĭg′ẽr-ŭs), *adj.* **1,** full of strength and health; forceful; **2,** energetic; as, a *vigorous* shaking.—*adv.* **vig′or-ous-ly.**

vi-king (vī′kĭng), *n.* one of the Scandinavian or Norse sea rovers, who terrorized the coasts of Europe from the eighth to the tenth century.

VIKING BOAT

vile (vīl), *adj.* [vil-er, vil-est], **1,** mean; ignoble; **2,** morally base or impure; as, a *vile* person; **3,** foul or offensive; bad; as, *vile* odors.—*adv.* **vile′ly.**—*n.* **vile′ness.**

vil-i-fy (vĭl′ĭ-fī), *v.t.* [vilified, vilify-ing], to defame; slander; speak evil of; as, to *vilify* a man.—*n.* **vil′i-fi-ca′tion.**

Syn. debase, revile.

vil-la (vĭl′ȧ), *n.* a large suburban or country residence, usually set in extensive grounds.

vil-lage (vĭl′ĭj), *n.* a small group of houses in a country district, smaller than a town; also, the people who live in a village.—*n.* **vil′lag-er** (vĭl′ĭj-ẽr).

vil-lain (vĭl′ĭn), *n.* **1,** a wicked person; scoundrel; **2,** in a play or novel, the character who opposes the hero; **3,** (usually *villein*), a feudal serf.

vil-lain-ous (vĭl′ĭn-ŭs), *adj.* evil; base; also, *Colloquial*, very bad; abominable.—*adv.* **vil′lain-ous-ly.**

Syn. infamous, heinous, detestable.

vil-lain-y (vĭl′ĭn-ĭ), *n.* [*pl.* villainies], **1,** wickedness; **2,** an act of wickedness; a crime.

vil-lein or **vil-lain** (vĭl′ĭn), *n.* under the feudal system, a serf, or half-free tiller of the soil, bound to his lord but legally free in his relations with other people.

Vil-na (vĭl′nȧ), a city in the U.S.S.R., capital of Lithuanian S.S.R. See **Wilno.**

vim (vĭm), *n.* energy; vitality.

Vin-ci (vēn′chē) Leonardo da (1452–1519), an Italian sculptor, painter, engineer, and architect. The most famous of his paintings are "Mona Lisa" and "The Last Supper."

vin-di-cate (vĭn′dĭ-kāt), *v.t.* [vindicat-ed, vindicat-ing], to defend successfully against unjust accusation; clear from suspicion of wrong or dishonor.—*n.* **vin′di-ca′tor.**—*n.* **vin′di-ca′tion.**

vin-dic-tive (vĭn-dĭk′tĭv), *adj.* revengeful; inclined to hold a grudge.—*adv.* **vin-dic′-tive-ly.**—*n.* **vin-dic′tive-ness.**

vine (vīn), *n.* **1,** a climbing, woody-stemmed plant; especially, the grapevine; **2,** any climbing or trailing plant.

vin-e-gar (vĭn′ē-gẽr), *n.* a sour liquid obtained by the fermentation of cider, wine, etc., and used to season or preserve food.

vine-yard (vĭn′yẽrd), *n.* a place where grapevines are cultivated.

vi-nous (vī′nŭs), *adj.* of, pertaining to, or like, wine; as, *vinous* spirits.

vin-tage (vĭn′tĭj), *n.* **1,** the act of, or the season for, gathering grapes and making wine; **2,** the yearly produce of a vineyard, or of the vineyards of a country; **3,** the wine produced in a given season; as, the *vintage* of 1872.

vint-ner (vĭnt′nẽr), *n.* a wine merchant.

Vi-nyl-ite (vī′nĭl-īt), *n.* the trade-mark name for a synthetic plastic used to make unbreakable phonograph records, protective coatings, etc.

vi-ol (vī′ŭl), *n.* a medieval musical instrument, the forerunner of the violin.

¹vi-o-la (vē-ō′lȧ; vī-ō′lȧ), *n.* a stringed instrument of the violin class, between the violin and violoncello in size and range. (See illustration under *musical instrument*.)

²vi-o-la (vī′ō-lȧ), *n.* any of a group of plants of the violet family, including the common violet and the pansy.

vi-o-late (vī′ō-lāt), *v.t.* [violat-ed, violating], **1,** to treat roughly or severely; ill-use; **2,** to trespass upon; **3,** to treat irreverently; as, to *violate* a tomb; **4,** to transgress; as, to *violate* the law; also, to disregard or break, as a promise.—*n.* **vi′o-la′tor.**

Syn. abuse, desecrate.

---

go; join; yet; sing; chin; show; thin, *th*en; hw, *why*; zh, azure; ü, Ger. für or Fr. lune; ö, Ger. schön or Fr. feu; ǹ, Fr. enfant, nom; kh, Ger. ach or ich. See pages ix–x.

vi·o·la·tion (vī/ō-lā/shŭn), *n.* **1,** interruption; disturbance; as, *violation* of a person's privacy; **2,** irreverent treatment, as of sacred or venerable things; **3,** the act of breaking a promise, law, or the like.

vi·o·lence (vī/ō-lĕns), *n.* **1,** great strength; as, the *violence* of the wind; **2,** furious, vehement feeling or action; **3,** an outrage; attack; **4,** injury to something that should be respected; as, to do *violence* to a shrine.
Syn. severity, intensity, vehemence.

vi·o·lent (vī/ō-lĕnt), *adj.* **1,** marked by, or acting with, great physical force; as, a *violent* storm; **2,** marked by or due to strong feeling; intense; as, a *violent* dislike; **3,** resulting from the use of force; as, a *violent* death; **4,** extreme; as, a *violent* shock.—*adv.* **vi/o·lent·ly.**
Syn. boisterous, vehement.

vi·o·let (vī/ō-lĕt), *n.* **1,** a color made up of blue and a small amount of red; a bluish-purple color; the color of the common violet; **2,** a low-growing plant with violet, yellow, or white flowers; also, the flower: —*adj.* of a violet color.

vi·o·lin (vī/ō-lĭn/), *n.* **1,** the smallest and highest tuned of modern four-string musical instruments played with a bow (see illustration under *musical instrument*); **2,** a violin player.

vi·o·lin·ist (vī/ō-lĭn/ĭst), *n.* one who plays a violin.

vi·o·lon·cel·lo (vē/ō-lŏn-chĕl/ō; vī/ō-lŏn-sĕl/ō), *n.* [*pl.* violoncellos], a large four-string instrument of the violin class, tuned below the viola: often shortened to 'cello or *cello* (see illustration under *musical instrument*).—*n.* **vi/o·lon·cel/list.**

vi·per (vī/pĕr), *n.* **1,** a kind of Old World poisonous snake; an adder; also, less correctly, any poisonous snake; **2,** hence, a malignant or evil person.

vi·ra·go (vĭ-rā/gō; vī-rā/gō), *n.* [*pl.* viragoes or viragos], a quarrelsome woman; a scold.

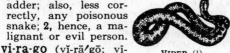
VIPER (⅛)

vir·e·o (vĭr/ē-ō), *n.* [*pl.* vireos], any of a family of small, American, insect-eating songbirds, olive-green or gray in color, as the red-eyed vireo, the yellow-throated vireo, etc.

Vir·gil (vûr/jĭl), a Roman poet. See **Vergil.**

VIREO (⅙)

vir·gin (vûr/jĭn), *n.* a maid; a chaste woman:—*adj.* **1,** chaste; maidenly; **2,** spotless; undefiled; as, *virgin* white; **3,** fresh; untouched; as, *virgin* soil.—*n.* **vir·gin/i·ty.**

vir·gin·al (vûr/jĭ-năl; vûr/jĭ-nl), *adj.* pertaining to a maid; chaste.

Vir·gin·i·a (vẽr-jĭn/ĭ-à; vẽr-jĭn/yà), a southern State (cap. Richmond) in the U.S. (map 8).—*adj.* and *n.* **Vir·gin/i·an.**

Vir·gin·i·a creep·er, a North American woody vine, with leaves divided into five or seven parts and bluish-black berries: also called *woodbine* or *American ivy.*

Vir·gin Is·lands, a group of small islands in the West Indies, some of which belong to the United States and some to Great Britain:—**Virgin Islands of the United States,** a group of islands (cap. Charlotte Amalie) east of Puerto Rico, including Saint Thomas, Saint John, and Saint Croix (map 10); these were formerly the *Danish West Indies.*

VIRGINIA CREEPER

Vir·gin Mar·y, in the Bible, the mother of Jesus of Nazareth (Matthew 1:18; Luke 2: 5–7).

vir·ile (vĭr/ĭl; vī/rĭl), *adj.* **1,** characteristic of, or befitting, a man; masculine; as, *virile* strength; **2,** forceful; masterful.—*n.* **vi·ril/i·ty** (vĭ-rĭl/ĭ-tĭ; vī-rĭl/ĭ-tĭ).

vir·tu·al (vûr/tū-ăl), *adj.* existing in effect, though not in fact; as, his words amounted to a *virtual* confession of guilt.—*adv.* **vir/tu·al·ly.**

vir·tue (vûr/tū), *n.* **1,** moral excellence; uprightness; goodness; **2,** a particular kind of goodness; as, patience is a *virtue;* **3,** excellence or merit; as, this room has the *virtue* of being cool in summer; **4,** efficacy or effectiveness; as, the *virtue* of physical exercise; **5,** chastity; purity:—**by virtue of,** because of; as, he won *by virtue of* superior strength.

vir·tu·o·so (vûr/tū-ō/sō; vĭr/tōō-ō/sō), *n.* [*pl.* virtuosos or virtuosi (vûr/tū-ō/sē; vĭr/tōō-ō/sē)], **1,** one with a special knowledge of, or taste for, objects of art, curios, or the like; a collector; **2,** one skilled in the technique of an art, especially a musical art, as in playing the violin.

vir·tu·ous (vûr/tū-ŭs), *adj.* possessing or showing moral uprightness; chaste.—*adv.* **vir/tu·ous·ly.**—*n.* **vir/tu·ous·ness.**

vir·u·lence (vĭr/ū-lĕns; vĭr/ōō-lĕns), *n.* **1,** poisonous quality; deadliness; **2,** bitter hostility.

vir·u·lent (vĭr/ū-lĕnt; vĭr/ōō-lĕnt), *adj.* **1,** poisonous; deadly; as, a *virulent* disease; **2,** hostile; bitter; as, *virulent* abuse.

vi·rus (vī/rŭs), *n.* **1,** an agent of disease, smaller than bacteria and able to grow only in the presence of living cells. Common virus diseases are influenza, measles, mumps, the common cold, etc.; **2,** venom; **3,** hence, a poison that affects the mind or soul.

vi·sa (vē′zȧ), *n.* a consul's official endorsement on a passport showing he has examined it and approved its holder for entrance into his country:—*v.t.* [visaed (vē′-zȧd), visa-ing (vē′zȧ-ĭng)], to examine (a document or passport) and mark as approved. Also spelled **vi′sé.**

vis·age (vĭz′ij), *n.* the face.

Vi·sa·yan Is·lands (vē-sä′yȧn), a group of islands in the Philippines (map 15). They are also called the *Bisayas.*

vis·cer·a (vĭs′ẽr-ȧ), *n.pl.* the organs inside the body, as the heart, liver, intestines, etc.—*adj.* **vis′cer·al** (vĭs′ẽr-ăl).

vis·cid (vĭs′ĭd), *adj.* sticky or gluelike.

vis·count (vī′kount′), *n.* a title of nobility next below earl or count and next above baron.—*n.fem.* **vis′count′ess.**

vis·cous (vĭs′kŭs), *adj.* thick and sticky; gluelike.—*n.* **vis·cos′i·ty** (vĭs-kŏs′ĭ-tĭ).

vise (vīs), *n.* a device with two jaws which may be drawn together to hold objects firmly while work is being done on them. Also spelled **vice.**

vi·sé (vē′zā; vē-zā′), *n.* an official endorsement; visa:—*v.t.* [viséed (vē′zād; vē-zād′), visé-ing], to mark approved; visa. See **visa.**

VISES

vis·i·ble (vĭz′ĭ-bl), *adj.* **1,** in sight; as, the ocean is *visible* from here; **2,** apparent; open; as, *visible* signs of grief.—*adv.* **vis′-i·bly.**—*n.* **vis′i·bil′i·ty.**

Vis·i·goth (vĭz′ĭ-gŏth), *n.* one of the West Goths, an ancient Teutonic race.

vi·sion (vĭzh′ŭn), *n.* **1,** the sense of sight; also, the act or faculty of seeing; sight; as, the accident impaired his *vision;* **2,** that which is seen in a dream or trance; as, the *visions* of a prophet; also, a phantom; **3,** a mental image; a picture created by the fancy; as, a boy's *visions* of glory; **4,** imagination; foresight; as, a leader must be a man of *vision:*—*v.t.* to see in, or as in, a vision; imagine.

vi·sion·ar·y (vĭzh′ŭn-ẽr′ĭ), *adj.* **1,** dreamy; inclined to accept fancies as realities; **2,** not practical; as, a *visionary* plan—*n.* [*pl.* visionaries], an impractical person.

vis·it (vĭz′ĭt), *v.t.* **1,** to go or come to see, as on pleasure, friendship, business, or courtesy; **2,** to come upon, either as a blessing or as an affliction; as, *visit* us with thy mercies; the city was *visited* with an epidemic:—*v.i.* to be a guest:—*n.* **1,** a brief stay as a guest; **2,** an official or professional call; **3,** the act of going to see a person, place, or thing; as, a *visit* to Rome.

vis·it·ant (vĭz′ĭ-tănt), *n.* a guest; a visitor:—*adj.* visiting.

vis·it·a·tion (vĭz′ĭ-tā′shŭn), *n.* **1,** the act of visiting, or state of being visited; **2,** reward or punishment from God; hence, any unusual event causing pleasure or pain; especially, a severe affliction.

vis·it·ing card (vĭz′ĭ-tĭng), a small card bearing a name and, sometimes, an address, to be left by a visitor or caller.

vis·i·tor (vĭz′ĭ-tẽr), *n.* one who pays a visit; a guest.

vi·sor or **vi·zor** (vī′zẽr), *n.* **1,** the movable front piece of a helmet that protects the upper part of the face, so made that it can be pushed up; **2,** the brim of a cap.

vis·ta (vĭs′tȧ), *n.* **1,** a long, narrow view, as between trees or buildings; also, the trees, buildings, etc., forming such a view; **2,** a mental view of a series of events.

VISOR (V)

Vis·tu·la (vĭs′tū-lȧ), a river of Poland, flowing from the Carpathian Mountains to the Baltic Sea (map 12).

vis·u·al (vĭzh′ū-ăl), *adj.* **1,** concerned with, or used in, seeing; **2,** capable of being seen; visible; **3,** received through the sense of sight; as, *visual* impressions.—*adv.* **vis′u·al·ly.**

vis·u·al·ize (vĭzh′ū-ăl-īz), *v.t.* and *v.i.* [visualized, visualiz-ing], to form a mental picture (of); see in fancy.

Vi·ta·glass (vī′tȧ-glȧs′), *n.* a trade-mark name for a kind of glass which, unlike ordinary glass, permits passage of ultraviolet rays:—**vitaglass,** glass bearing this trade name.

vi·tal (vī′tăl), *adj.* **1,** pertaining to, or concerned with, life; as, *vital* functions; **2,** essential to life; as, air is a *vital* necessity; **3,** affecting life; ending life; as, a *vital* wound; **4,** hence very important; as, a *vital* question:—**vitals,** *n.pl.* the parts of the body necessary to life, as the heart, lungs, etc.—*adv.* **vi′tal·ly.**

vi·tal·i·ty (vī-tăl′ĭ-tĭ), *n.* **1,** ability to sustain life; **2,** strength; energy.

vi·tal·ize (vī′tăl-īz), *v.t.* [vitalized, vitalizing], to fill or endow with life.

vi·ta·min (vī′tȧ-mĭn) or **vi·ta·mine** (vī′-tȧ-mĭn; vī′tȧ-mīn), *n.* any of a class of substances which are present in certain foods in minute quantities in their natural state and which are necessary to the health and normal growth of people and animals.

vi·ti·ate (vǐsh/ǐ-āt), *v.t.* [vitiat-ed, vitiating], **1,** to make worthless; invalidate; **2,** to impair the quality of; contaminate; as, escaping gas *vitiates* the air.

vit·re·ous (vǐt/rē-ŭs), *adj.* of or like glass; as, *vitreous* rocks:— **vitreous humor,** the jellylike substance filling the eyeball.

vit·ri·fy (vǐt/rǐ-fī), *v.t.* and *v.i.* [vitrified, vitrify-ing], to make or be made into glass or a glassy substance; glaze.

vit·ri·ol (vǐt/rǐ-ŭl), *n.* **1,** sulphuric acid: also called *oil of vitriol;* **2,** any of several of the salts of this acid, as blue vitriol, or copper sulphate; **3,** anything sharp or biting, as sarcasm.—*adj.* **vit·ri·ol·ic** (vǐt/rǐ-ŏl/ǐk).

vi·tu·per·ate (vī-tū/pẽr-āt; vǐ-tū/pẽr-āt), *v.t.* [vituperat-ed, vituperat-ing], to heap abuse upon; berate.—*n.* **vi·tu·per·a/tion.** —*adj.* **vi·tu/per·a/tive.**

vi·va·cious (vī-vā/shŭs; vǐ-vā/shŭs), *adj.* lively; gay; full of spirit.—*adv.* **vi·va/cious·ly.**—*n.* **vi·va/cious·ness.**
Syn. sportive, merry, jocose, mirthful.

vi·vac·i·ty (vī-văs/ǐ-tǐ; vǐ-văs/ǐ-tǐ), *n.* [*pl.* vivacities], liveliness; gaiety.

viv·id (vǐv/ǐd), *adj.* **1,** brilliant; intense: said of light or colors; as, a *vivid* red; **2,** active; clear; realistic; as, a *vivid* description; a *vivid* imagination.

viv·i·fy (vǐv/ǐ-fī), *v.t.* [vivified, vivify-ing], to fill with life; animate.

viv·i·sect (vǐv/ǐ-sĕkt; vǐv/ǐ-sĕkt/), *v.t.* to dissect or experiment upon (a living animal), for scientific study:— *v.i.* to operate or experiment upon a living animal.—*n.* **viv/i-sec/tion.**—*n.* **viv/i-sec/tion-ist.**

vix·en (vǐk/sn), *n.* **1,** a female fox; **2,** a quarrelsome, ill-tempered woman.

viz. abbreviation for Latin *videlicet,* meaning *namely.*

vi·zier (vǐ-zēr/; vǐz/yẽr; vǐz/ǐ-ẽr), *n.* a high official in Mohammedan countries. Also spelled **vi·zir/** (vǐ-zēr/).

vi·zor (vī/zẽr), *n.* the movable front part of a helmet; a visor. See **visor.**

Vla·di·vos·tok (vlà/dǐ-vôs-tôk/), a town in Siberia, U.S.S.R., on the Sea of Japan (map **15**).

vocab. abbreviation for *vocabulary.*

vo·cab·u·lar·y (vō-kăb/ū-lẽr/ǐ), *n.* [*pl.* vocabularies], **1,** a list or collection of words arranged alphabetically and explained or translated; **2,** the stock of words employed by a language, class, or individual.
Syn. diction, phraseology.

vo·cal (vō/kăl), *adj.* **1,** pertaining to, or uttered by, the voice; as, a *vocal* protest;

2, expressing oneself by the voice; hence, loud; vehement; as, he was *vocal* in his denial of guilt:— **vocal cords,** either of two pairs of bands of fibrous tissue, called the *false* and the *true* vocal cords, situated in the larynx, the voice being produced by the vibration of the lower pair, or true vocal cords, as the air is passed out through them.—*adv.* **vo/cal·ly.**

vo·cal·ist (vō/kăl-ĭst), *n.* a singer.

vo·ca·tion (vō-kā/shŭn), *n.* **1,** occupation; trade; profession; as, his *vocation* is the law; **2,** a calling to lead a religious life. —*adj.* **vo·ca/tion·al.**

vo·cif·er·ate (vō-sǐf/ẽr-āt), *v.i.* and *v.t.* [vociferat-ed, vociferat-ing], to cry out in a loud, determined voice; exclaim noisily.

vo·cif·er·ous (vō-sǐf/ẽr-ŭs), *adj.* making a loud outcry; clamorous; noisy.

vod·ka (vŏd/kȧ), *n.* a Russian intoxicating liquor, made from rye, potatoes, or maize.

vogue (vōg), *n.* **1,** the fashion of the moment; as, long skirts are the *vogue;* **2,** popularity; as, his books had a great vogue.

voice (vois), *n.* **1,** sound proceeding from the mouth; especially, human utterance; specifically, sound produced by the vibration of the vocal cords; **2,** the power of speech; as, he lost his *voice;* **3,** anything resembling or likened to human speech or utterance; **4,** opinion, or an expression of opinion; as, the *voice* of the majority; **5,** the right to express a choice or opinion; as, she had no *voice* in the decision; **6,** in grammar, the form of the verb showing whether the subject acts or is acted upon; as, active or passive *voice:— v.t.* [voiced, voic-ing], to give expression to; put into speech; as, he *voiced* his protest.—*adj.* **voiced.** —*adj.* **voice/less.**

void (void), *adj.* **1,** empty; vacant; **2,** lacking; wanting; as, *void* of humor; **3,** without effect; useless; especially, in law, having no force; as, a *void* contract:— *v.t.* **1,** to cause to be empty; **2,** to annul or cancel; as, to *void* a law:— *n.* a vacuum; an empty space.

voile (voil), *n.* a thin, semitransparent dress material of silk, cotton, or wool.

vol. abbreviation for *volume.*

vol·a·tile (vŏl/ȧ-tǐl; vŏl/ȧ-tl), *adj.* **1,** readily evaporating or changing into vapor; as, ether is a *volatile* liquid; **2,** hence, lively; gay; also, changeable; fickle.

vol·can·ic (vŏl-kăn/ĭk), *adj.* **1,** pertaining to, like, or produced by, a volcano; **2,** violent; powerful; explosive.

vol·ca·no (vŏl-kā/nō), *n.* [*pl.* volcanoes or volcanos], an opening in the earth's sur-

---

āte, āorta, râre, căt, ȧsk, fär, ăllow, sofȧ; ēve, ĕvent, ĕll, writẽr, novĕl; bīte, pǐn; nō, ōbey, ôr, dŏg, tŏp, cŏllide; ūnit, ūnite, bûrn, cŭt, focŭs; nōon, fŏŏt; mound; coin;

face, generally surrounded by a mass of ejected material forming a hill or mountain, from which molten rock, gases, and steam are expelled.

vole (vōl), n. any of several ratlike animals of the fields and damp meadows, including the water rat and field mouse.

Vol·ga (vŏl′gȧ), a river in the U.S.S.R., the longest in Europe (map 12). VOLE (½)

vo·li·tion (vō-lĭsh′ŭn), n. **1**, the exercise or use of the will; choice; as, he came of his own volition; **2**, the power of willing. —adj. **vo·li′tion·al**.
   Syn. desire, preference, choice.

vol·ley (vŏl′ĭ), n. [pl. volleys], **1**, the throwing of many missiles, as arrows, bullets, etc., at the same time; also, the missiles so thrown; **2**, a sudden burst of any sort; as, a volley of words:—**volley ball**, a game in which two groups of players attempt with the hands to keep a large ball moving from side to side over a net without letting the ball touch the ground:—v.t. and v.i. to discharge, or be discharged, all at the same time.

volt (vōlt), n. a unit for measuring the force needed to cause a current of electricity to flow through a conductor against resistance.

volt·age (vōl′tĭj), n. the total number of volts in a particular electrical current, measuring its electrical power.

Vol·taire (vŏl′târ′), (1694–1778), a French philosopher and dramatist.

volt·me·ter (vōlt′mē′tẽr), n. an instrument for measuring the voltage of an electric current.

vol·u·bil·i·ty (vŏl′ū-bĭl′ĭ-tĭ), n. too great readiness in speech; talkativeness.

vol·u·ble (vŏl′ū-bl), adj. smooth or ready in speech; talkative.—adv. **vol′u·bly**.

vol·ume (vŏl′ŭm), n. **1**, a number of printed sheets bound together; a book; **2**, one of the books within a series of books that form a complete work; as, the second volume of an encyclopedia; **3**, the amount of space occupied by a body, as measured by cubic units; as, the volume of water in a tank; **4**, a large quantity; **5**, fulness of tone; as, a voice lacking in volume.

vo·lu·mi·nous (vō-lū′mĭ-nŭs), adj. **1**, large; bulky; **2**, filling many volumes; as, a voluminous history.

vol·un·tar·y (vŏl′ŭn-tẽr′ĭ), adj. **1**, done or made freely; not forced by another; as, a voluntary choice; **2**, acting of one's own free will; as, a voluntary worker; **3**, intentional; deliberate; as, voluntary manslaugh-

ter; **4**, controlled by the will; as, voluntary muscles.—adv. **vol′un·tar′i·ly**.

vol·un·teer (vŏl′ŭn-tēr′), n. one who enters into any service of his own free will; especially, one who offers himself for military service of his own free will:—v.i. to offer one's services freely:—v.t. to offer freely of one's own accord; as, to volunteer information:—adj. pertaining to free services; voluntary.

vo·lup·tu·ar·y (vō-lŭp′tū-ẽr′ĭ), n. [pl. voluptuaries], a person devoted to luxury and the pleasures of the senses.

vo·lup·tu·ous (vō-lŭp′tū-ŭs), adj. **1**, giving delight to the senses; sensuous; **2**, devoted to luxurious pleasures; as, voluptuous living.—n. **vo·lup′tu·ous·ness**.

vom·it (vŏm′ĭt), v.i. to throw up the contents of the stomach; spew:—v.t. **1**, to throw up from the stomach; **2**, to discharge with violence; belch forth:—n. matter thrown up by the stomach.

voo·doo (vōō′dōō; vōō-dōō′), n. **1**, a form of sorcery practiced as a religion by certain Negroes, especially in Haiti; **2**, a person who practices such sorcery:—adj. pertaining to voodoo:—v.t. to bewitch by voodoo.—n. **voo′doo·ism**.

vo·ra·cious (vō-rā′shŭs), adj. **1**, greedy in eating; as, the wolf is a voracious animal; **2**, marked by greediness; as, a voracious appetite; **3**, extremely eager in any pursuit; as, a voracious reader.—adv. **vo·ra′cious·ly**.—n. **vo·rac′i·ty** (vō-răs′ĭ-tĭ).

vor·tex (vôr′tĕks), n. [pl. vortexes (vôr′tĕk-sĕz) or vortices (vôr′tĭ-sēz)], air or water with a rotary motion tending to suck bodies caught in it into a depression or vacuum at the center; an eddy or whirlpool.

Vosges Moun·tains (vōzh), a mountain chain in northeastern France.

vo·ta·ry (vō′tȧ-rĭ), n. [pl. votaries], a person bound by a vow or promise to some service; as, a nun is a votary of the church; also, one devoted to any pursuit; as, a votary of music.—n.fem. **vo′ta·ress**.—n. **vo′ta·rist**.

vote (vōt), n. **1**, a formal expression of the choice, judgment, or wish of a person or group of persons, as in an election; as, a president is elected by the vote of the people; **2**, the means of expressing such choice; as, an oral vote; **3**, the right to express such choice; as, women were given the vote; **4**, the entire number of such expressions; as, the vote was 55 to 30; also, such expressions of a particular class or group taken as a whole; as, the student vote; **5**, a resolution resulting from the formal expression of the choice or will of a majority; as, a vote of thanks:—v.t.

go; join; yet; sing; chin; show; thin, then; hw, why; zh, azure; ü, Ger. für or Fr. lune; ö, Ger. schön or Fr. feu; n, Fr. enfant, nom; kh, Ger. ach or ich. See pages ix–x.

[vot-ed, vot-ing], **1,** to declare or authorize by a vote; as, to *vote* a reform; **2,** to grant; as, to *vote* money; **3,** *Colloquial,* to pronounce, by general consent; as, we *voted* the meeting a failure:—*v.i.* to cast a ballot.

vot-er (vōt′ẽr), *n.* **1,** one who casts a ballot; **2,** one who has a legal right to vote.

vo-tive (vō′tĭv), *adj.* given, offered, etc., in consecration or fulfilment of a vow; as, *votive* offerings.

vouch (vouch), *v.i.* to bear witness; to give evidence or assurance; as, I can *vouch* for the truth of his statement.

vouch-er (vouch′ẽr), *n.* a paper, or the like, which bears witness to something; specifically, a receipt for payment.

vouch-safe (vouch-sāf′), *v.t.* [vouchsafed, vouchsaf-ing], to deign to grant or give; concede; as, to *vouchsafe* an opinion.

vow (vou), *n.* **1,** a solemn promise or pledge, especially one made to God or some deity; **2,** a pledge of love and faithfulness:—*v.t.* to promise or assert solemnly; swear:—*v.i.* to make a solemn promise; to declare with emphasis.

vow-el (vou′ĕl), *n.* **1,** a simple vocal sound made with the mouth and lips more or less open and the vocal cords vibrating; **2,** a letter representing such a sound, as *a, e, i, o, u*:—*adj.* pertaining to a vowel.

vox po-pu-li (vŏks pŏp′ū-lī), a Latin phrase meaning *the voice of the people;* hence, public opinion; popular choice.

voy-age (voi′ĭj), *n.* a journey by water, especially a long one:—*v.i.* [voyaged, voyag-ing], to make a journey by water:—*v.t.* to sail, or travel, over; traverse.—*n.* **voy′ag-er** (voi′ĭj-ẽr).

V.P. abbreviation for *Vice-President.*

vs. abbreviation for *versus.*

Vt. abbreviation for *Vermont.*

v.t. abbreviation for *verb transitive.*

Vul-can (vŭl′kăn), *n.* in Roman mythology, the god of fire and of metalworking.

vul-can-ize (vŭl′kăn-īz), *v.t.* [vulcanized, vulcaniz-ing], to harden (rubber, etc.) by treating, especially with sulphur, at a high temperature.—*n.* **vul′can-i-za′tion.**

Vulg. abbreviation for *Vulgate.*

vul-gar (vŭl′gẽr), *adj.* **1,** pertaining to the common people; **2,** unrefined; in bad taste. —*adv.* **vul′gar-ly.**
     Syn. coarse, base, gross, vile.

vul-gar-ism (vŭl′gẽr-ĭzm), *n.* a phrase or common expression not in use by cultivated speakers.

vul-gar-i-ty (vŭl-găr′ĭ-tĭ), *n.* [*pl.* vulgarities], lack of good taste and refinement in manners, dress, speech, etc.; also, an instance of such commonness.

vul-gar-ize (vŭl′gẽr-īz), *v.t.* [vulgarized, vulgariz-ing], to make coarse, cheap, or low.

Vul-gate (vŭl′gāt), *n.* a Latin translation of the Bible in use in the Roman Catholic Church, made originally by St. Jerome in the fourth century A.D.

vul-ner-a-ble (vŭl′nẽr-ȧ-bl), *adj.* **1,** capable of being wounded or hurt; **2,** open to injury or criticism; as, a *vulnerable* reputation. —*n.* **vul′ner-a-bil′i-ty.**

vul-ture (vŭl′tūr), *n.* a large bird of prey that feeds on carrion, and is allied to the hawks and eagles.

VULTURE (1/20)

vy-ing (vī′ĭng), present participle of *vie.*—*adv.* **vy′ing-ly.**

W

W, w (dŭb′l-ū), *n.* [*pl.* W's, w's], the 23d letter of the alphabet, following V.

w. abbreviation for *week.*

W. abbreviation for *West, Western.*

wab-ble (wŏb′l; wôb′l), *v.i.* and *v.t.* [wab-bled, wab-bling], to move unsteadily from side to side; wobble. See **wobble.**

wad (wŏd; wôd), *n.* **1,** a small mass or bundle of soft material; **2,** a soft bunch of cotton, wool, rope, etc., used to stop an opening, pad a garment, etc.; **3,** a plug to hold a charge of powder or shot in position in a muzzle-loading gun or in a cartridge (see illustration under *cartridge*):—*v.t.* [wad-ded, wad-ding], **1,** to form, as some soft material, into a compact mass or bunch; **2,** to insert a wad into; close, as an opening, with a small compact mass; **3,** to provide with a pad.

wad-dle (wŏd′l; wôd′l), *v.i.* [wad-dled, wad-dling], to sway from side to side in walking; walk with short, clumsy steps, as does a short, fat person, or an animal like a duck with short legs set wide apart:—*n.* a clumsy, rocking gait.—*n.* **wad′dler.**

wade (wād), *v.i.* [wad-ed, wad-ing], **1,** to

āte, âorta, râre, căt, ȧsk, fär, ȧllow, sofȧ; ēve, ĕvent, ĕll, writẽr, novĕl; bīte, pĭn; nō, ōbey, ôr, dŏg, tŏp, cŏllide; ūnit, ūnite, bûrn, cŭt, focŭs; nōōn, fŏŏt; mound; coin;

walk through water, mud, snow, or other substance that hinders progress; **2,** hence, to proceed with difficulty; as, to *wade* through a tiresome lesson; **3,** to go at something with great force; as, to *wade* into one's work:—*v.t.* to cross by walking through water, mud, etc.

wa-fer (wā′fẽr), *n.* **1,** a thin cake or biscuit; **2,** a thin disk of unleavened, or unraised, bread, used in the communion service in certain churches: in the Roman Catholic Church, called the *Host;* **3,** a small, colored disk of adhesive paper, paste, etc., for fastening letters, sealing documents, etc.

waf-fle (wŏf′l; wôf′l), *n.* a flat batter cake baked in a waffle iron:—**waffle iron,** a device for baking waffles, consisting of a pair of iron plates, hinged so as to close over batter poured upon one of them.

waft (wȧft), *v.i.* and *v.t.* to float along through the air or on the water; as, the current *wafted* the leaves downstream:—*n.* a gust or puff, as of wind.

¹wag (wăg), *v.t.* [wagged, wag-ging], to move, or cause to swing, from side to side; as, to *wag* a finger:—*v.i.* to move from side to side:—*n.* a wagging movement.

²wag (wăg), *n.* a practical joker; a wit.

wage (wāj), *v.t.* [waged, wag-ing], to engage in vigorously; carry on; as, to *wage* war:—*n.* that which is paid or received for services; as, a weekly *wage.*

wage earner, 1, one who works for wages; **2,** hence a member of a family whose earnings support the family.

wa-ger (wā′jẽr), *n.* something risked on an uncertainty; a bet:—*v.t.* and *v.i.* to bet.

wag-es (wāj′ĕz), *n.pl.* money paid or received for labor, reckoned by the hour, day, week, etc.
  Syn. pay, fee, salary.

wag-ger-y (wăg′ẽr-ĭ), *n.* [*pl.* waggeries], good-humored jesting; foolery.

wag-gish (wăg′ĭsh), *adj.* **1,** fond of playing good-natured jokes on others; **2,** done in good-humored jesting; mischievous.— *adv.* **wag′gish-ly.**—*n.* **wag′gish-ness.**

wag-gle (wăg′l), *v.i.* and *v.t.* [wag-gled, wag-gling], to move from side to side; wag:—*n.* a wagging.

Wag-ner (väg′nẽr), Wilhelm Richard (1813–1883), a famous German composer.

Wag-ne-ri-an (väg-nĭr′ĭ-ăn), *adj.* pertaining to Wagner, to his work, or to his characteristic style.

wag-on (wăg′ŭn), *n.* a four-wheeled vehicle, used for hauling freight or other goods, and drawn by draft animals. (See illustration next column.) Also, **wag′gon.** —*n.* **wag′on-er; wag′gon-er.**

waif (wāf), *n.* a homeless wanderer; a lost person or animal; especially, a lost child.

wail (wāl), *v.t.* to mourn or lament aloud: —*v.i.* to utter a cry of lament; make a mournful sound:—*n.* a mournful cry.

wain (wān), *n. Archaic* and *Poetic,* a wagon.

wain-scot (wān′skŭt; wān′skŏt), *n.* a wooden lining, generally paneled, of a room wall or the lower portion of it:— *v.t.* [wainscot-ed, wainscot-ing], to line or face (the walls of a room) with wood.

wain-scot-ing (wān′skŭt-ĭng; wān′skŏt-ĭng), *n.* wall lining or paneling.

waist (wāst), *n.* **1,** the narrowest part of the body, just below the ribs; **2,** a garment, or that section of a garment, which covers the body from shoulders to waist; **3,** the middle part of a vessel's deck, between the forecastle and quarter-deck.

waist-coat (wāst′kōt′; wĕs′kŭt), *n.* a short, sleeveless garment for men, formerly ornamental, worn under the coat; a vest.

wait (wāt), *v.i.* **1,** to linger or tarry; remain; **2,** to continue in a state of expecting; as, to *wait* for news:—**wait upon, 1,** to attend or serve; **2,** to call on formally; as, he *waited upon* the President:—*v.t.* **1,** to expect or tarry for; as, to *wait* permission; **2,** *Colloquial,* to delay; as, to *wait* supper: —*n.* **1,** the act of delaying or lingering; **2,** the length of time during which one lingers in expectation; delay; as, a *wait* of half an hour; **3,** ambush; hiding; as, to lie in *wait* for an enemy; **4,** one of a band of musicians who play and sing carols in the streets at Christmas time.

wait-er (wā′tẽr), *n.* **1,** a man who serves at table; **2,** a serving tray for dishes.

wait-ing (wā′tĭng), *n.* **1,** the act or state of delaying, lingering, etc.; **2,** service; attendance:—**in waiting,** in attendance; as, ladies *in waiting* to the queen:—*adj.* attendant; serving; as, *waiting* maid.

waiting room, a place or room where one waits, as for a train, airplane, etc.

WAGON

wait-ress (wā′trĕs), *n.* a female waiter.

waive (wāv), *v.t.* [waived, waiv-ing], to give up a claim to; forgo; forbear to insist upon; as, to *waive* an inheritance.

waiv-er (wā′vẽr), *n.* the voluntary giving

up of a right, especially a legal right; also, a document affirming such an act.

¹**wake** (wāk), *v.i.* [*p.t.* waked or woke (wōk), *p.p.* waked, *p.pr.* wak-ing], **1,** to cease to sleep; as, to *wake* at ten o'clock; also, to be roused from sleep; **2,** to be aroused, excited, or made aware; as, let us *wake* to the danger; to *wake* to duty; the principal *woke* to the situation; **3,** to keep a watch or vigil at night:—*v.t.* **1,** to rouse from sleep; awake; as, John *woke* his father; **2,** to make active; arouse; as, music *wakes* the soul:—*n.* a vigil; especially, a keeping awake to watch over a dead body before burial.

²**wake** (wāk), *n.* the trail left behind a moving ship; hence, a track or trail; as, in the *wake* of explorers come merchants.

wake-ful (wāk′fŏol), *adj.* **1,** free from sleepiness; unable to sleep; **2,** watchful; vigilant; as, a *wakeful* sentinel.—*n.* **wake′-ful-ness.**

Syn. vigilant, heedful.

Wake Is-land, a small island in the Pacific, belonging to the U.S. (map **16**).

wak-en (wāk′ĕn), *v.t.* **1,** to rouse from sleep or inaction; **2,** to excite; move to action:—*v.i.* to become awake.

wake-rob-in (wāk′-rŏb′ĭn), *n.* in the U.S., one of a number of plants, as the jack-in-the-pulpit and the trillium.

wale (wāl), *n.* **1,** a mark produced on flesh by flogging: also, *wheal* or *weal;* **2,** a rib or ridge on the surface, as of cloth; hence, the texture of certain cloth; **3,** a heavy plank along the side of a vessel, just below the gunwale (see illustration under *shroud*).

WAKE-ROBIN

Wales (wālz), a principality in southwestern Great Britain, west of England (map **13**).

walk (wôk), *v.i.* **1,** to go by foot; proceed by steps at a moderate pace: distinguished from *run;* **2,** to take a stroll:—*v.t.* **1,** to pass over on foot; as, to *walk* a golf course; **2,** to cause to go on foot; as, the guide *walked* us ten miles; also, to ride or drive at a slow pace; as, to *walk* a horse:—*n.* **1,** a proceeding on foot without running; also, a stroll or promenade; **2,** manner of walking; gait; **3,** a special place for walking, as a path around a lake; **4,** a distance that may be covered by walking; as, the park is a short *walk* from here; **5,** one's circle or environment; as, he was from a humble *walk* of life.—*n.* **walk′er.**

walk-ing stick (wôk′ĭng), **1,** a cane; **2,** an insect with a long, slender body resembling a small stick.

walk-out (wôk′out′), *n. Colloquial,* in the U.S., a labor strike.

wall (wôl), *n.* **1,** a solid structure, usually vertical, which forms any one of the sides of a building or the side of a room; **2,** a structure of stone, brick, etc., serving as an enclosure, a defense, etc.; **3,** the side or inside surface of any cavity, vessel, or receptacle; **4, walls,** fortifications:—*v.t.* **1,** to surround with, or as with, a structure for enclosure, security, or defense; **2,** to fill in or close up, as an opening.

wal-la-by (wŏl′á-bĭ; wôl′á-bĭ), *n.* [*pl.* wallabies], a small Australian kangaroo.

Wal-lace (wŏl′ĭs; wôl′ĭs), **1,** Lew (1827–1905), an American general and writer, author of "Ben Hur"; **2,** Sir William (1272?–1305], a Scottish hero and patriot.

wal-la-roo (wŏl′á-rōō′; wôl′á-rōō′), *n.* a kind of large Australian kangaroo.

wal-let (wŏl′ĕt; wôl′ĕt), *n.* **1,** a bag or knapsack for the articles necessary for a journey; **2,** a folding pocketbook.

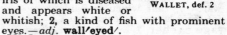

WALLET, def. 2

wall-eye (wôl′ī′), *n.* **1,** an eye, as of a horse, the iris of which is diseased and appears white or whitish; **2,** a kind of fish with prominent eyes.—*adj.* **wall′eyed′.**

wall-flow-er (wôl′flou′ẽr), *n.* **1,** a plant of the mustard family, with sweet-scented yellow, orange, or red flowers; **2,** *Colloquial,* at a dance, one who, for lack of a partner, sits idle at the side of the room.

Wal-loon (wŏ-lōōn′; wô-lōōn′), *n.* **1,** a member of a mixed race of people living in southern Belgium and parts of France, mainly Celtic and Italic; **2,** their language, a French dialect.

wal-lop (wŏl′ŭp; wôl′ŭp), *v.t.* **1,** *Colloquial,* to beat soundly; flog; **2,** *Slang,* to strike very hard; as, to *wallop* a ball:—*n. Slang,* a very hard blow.

wal-low (wŏl′ō; wôl′ō), *v.i.* **1,** to roll about in, or as in, mud, as a hog does; **2,** to live in and enjoy; as, to *wallow* in luxury:—*n.* **1,** the act of rolling or reveling in mud, vice, or the like; **2,** a muddy place in which an animal rolls about.

wall-pa-per (wôl′pā′pẽr), *n.* paper for covering the inner walls of houses.

Wall Street, a street in New York which is the chief financial center of the U.S.

wal-nut (wôl′nŭt; wôl′nŭt), *n.* **1,** any of several trees bearing edible nuts, especially the black walnut tree and the English walnut tree (see illustration on page 864);

2, the nut of such a tree; **3,** the wood of the tree, valuable in making furniture.

wal-rus (wôl′rŭs; wŏl′rŭs), *n.* a large arctic sea animal related to the seal, and valuable for its blubber, skin, and tusks.

WALRUS (1/20)

waltz (wôlts), *n.* **1,** a smooth, graceful dance in triple time; **2,** music for such a dance:—*v.i.* to dance a waltz.—*n.* **waltz′er.**

wam-pum (wŏm′pŭm; wŏm′pŭm), *n.* beads made of shells, strung into strands, or woven into belts, used by the North American Indians as money, ornaments, etc.

wan (wŏn; wŏn), *adj.* [wan-ner, wan-nest], pale; sickly; languid; as, a *wan* child; a *wan* smile.—*adv.* **wan′ly.**

wand (wŏnd; wŏnd), *n.* a slender rod.

wan-der (wŏn′dĕr; wôn′dĕr), *v.i.* **1,** to ramble; stroll about with no definite purpose or direction; **2,** to stray; as, he *wandered* from the right path; **3,** to come slowly in a long, winding course; as, the sheep *wandered* back to the fold; **4,** to be delirious:—*n.* the act of wandering.—*n.* **wan′der-er.**

wan-der-lust (vän′dĕr-lŏŏst′; wŏn′dĕr-lŭst′; wôn′dĕr-lŭst′), *n.* a strong impulse to travel.

wane (wān), *v.i.* [waned, wan-ing], **1,** to grow smaller; decrease; applied especially to the moon; **2,** to decline in power, importance, etc.:—*n.* **1,** the decrease in the visible bright part of the moon from full to new; also, the period of that decrease; **2,** decrease, as of power, importance, etc.

want (wŏnt; wŏnt), *n.* **1,** state of being without; lack; scarcity; as, there is a *want* of supplies in this district; **2,** state of being without necessaries; hence, poverty; as, a family in *want;* **3,** a thing needed or greatly desired; a necessity; as, my *wants* are few:—*v.t.* **1,** to be without; lack; as, the soldier does not *want* courage; **2,** to need; require; as, we *want* food when we are hungry; **3,** to desire; as, I *want* to take a trip to Europe:—*v.i.* to be in poverty.

Syn., n. destitution, penury.

want-ing (wôn′tĭng; wŏn′tĭng), *adj.* **1,** short of; lacking; as, one o'clock *wanting* two minutes; **2,** falling short of what is expected; as, *wanting* in courage; **3,** missing; as, one page *wanting.*

wan-ton (wŏn′tŭn; wŏn′tŭn), *adj.* **1,** sportive; playful; as, a *wanton* wind, child, etc.; **2,** unrestrained; unruly; as, *wanton* curls;

3, loose in morals; **4,** heartless; outrageous; as, a *wanton* murder:—*n.* a person of loose morals, especially a woman:—*v.i.* to sport and play.—*adv.* **wan′ton-ly.**

wap-i-ti (wŏp′ĭ-tĭ; wôp′ĭ-tĭ), *n.* [*pl.* wapitis or wapiti], a large American elk, reddish buff in color, with large, heavy antlers. It is similar to the European red deer but very much larger.

WAPITI (1/40)

war (wôr), *n.* **1,** a conflict by force of arms between nations, or parts of the same nation; also, the condition created by such a conflict; as, to be at *war;* **2,** the science or art of the profession of arms; as, skilled in *war;* **3,** any contest or contention; as, a *war* of words:—*v.i.* [warred, war-ring], **1,** to engage in an armed conflict; fight; **2,** to contend.

War between the States, a war fought in the U.S. (1861–1865) between the North (Federals) and the South (Confederates), over the questions of slavery and States' rights.

war-ble (wôr′bl), *v.i.* [war-bled, war-bling], to trill; carol, as a bird; also, to make a melodious sound, as a stream:—*v.t.* to sing with trills; also, to relate in verse:—*n.* **1,** the act of warbling; **2,** a soft, sweet flow of sounds; a carol.

war-bler (wôr′blĕr), *n.* **1,** one who carols; a singer; **2,** any of several small, singing birds, often brightly colored.

WARBLER (1/8)

ward (wôrd), *v.t.* **1,** to turn aside; avert; as, to *ward* off an attack; **2,** *Archaic,* to guard:—*n.* **1,** the act of guarding; protection; **2,** a person under guard or protection; especially, a person who, because of youth, insanity, or the like, is placed under protection of the court or of a person chosen as guardian; **3,** one of the sections into which a town or city is divided for election or other purposes; **4,** a section of a hospital or prison.—*n.* **ward′ship.**

-ward (-wĕrd) or **-wards** (-wĕrdz), a suffix meaning toward, in the direction of; as, back*ward,* up*ward,* west*ward.*

ward-en (wôr′dn), *n.* **1,** one who keeps watch; a guardian; **2,** a keeper; especially, the head keeper of a prison; **3,** in England, the chief officer of government in a college or guild; **4,** an officer in a church.

ward·er (wôr′dẽr), *n.* a guard or keeper.

ward·robe (wôrd′rōb′), *n.* **1,** a closet or cabinet for clothes; **2,** one's stock of wearing apparel.

¹ware (wâr), *n.* **1,** manufactured articles; as, glazed *ware;* silver*ware;* **2, wares,** articles for sale; as, the merchant peddled his *wares.*

²ware (wâr), *v.t.* to beware of: used in such phrases as *ware hounds:—adj. Archaic,* aware of; heedful; wary.

war·head (wôr′hĕd), *n.* the explosive, or other destructive material, carried in the nose of a projectile.

ware·house (wâr′hous′), *n.* a building for storing goods.

war·fare (wôr′fâr′), *n.* open hostilities between enemies; armed conflict.

war·i·ly (wâr′ĭ-lĭ), *adv.* cautiously.

war·i·ness (wâr′ĭ-nĕs), *n.* the state or quality of being wary or cautious.

war·like (wôr′līk′), *adj.* **1,** fit for, or fond of, military life or fighting; as, *warlike* peoples; **2,** of or for war; as, *warlike* preparations; **3,** threatening war.

warm (wôrm), *adj.* **1,** moderately heated; not cold; as, *warm* water; *warm* weather; **2,** having little cold weather; as, a *warm* climate; **3,** giving out warmth; as, a *warm* fire; also, serving to keep heat near the body; as, *warm* fur; **4,** heated with passion, anger, excitement, or the like; as, a *warm* dispute; **5,** kindly; affectionate; as, a *warm* greeting; **6,** having tones which give a feeling of warmth, as red, yellow, or orange:— *v.t.* and *v.i.* **1,** to make or become warm; as, to *warm* milk; **2,** to make or become eager, excited, etc.—*adj.* **warm′ly.**

warm–blood·ed (wôrm′-blŭd′ĕd), *adj.* **1,** having blood like that of mammals and birds, which remains, regardless of the temperature of the surroundings, at approximately the same temperature; **2,** easily aroused or excited.

warmth (wôrmth), *n.* **1,** the quality or state of having moderate heat; as, the *warmth* of the climate; **2,** earnestness; zeal; as, the *warmth* of an appeal.

warn (wôrn), *v.t.* **1,** to put on guard; make aware of possible danger; caution; as, we *warned* him not to go out in the storm; **2,** to notify; as, why didn't you *warn* us that you were coming?

warn·ing (wôr′nĭng), *n.* previous notice, especially of danger; as, the black clouds gave *warning* of an approaching storm; also, that which notifies or cautions; as, let this be a *warning* to you.

War of In·de·pend·ence, the American Revolution, 1775–1783, the war which made the American colonies independent of Great Britain.

warp (wôrp), *n.* **1,** the lengthwise thread in weaving: distinguished from *woof;* **2,** a rope attached at one end to a fixed object, used in towing a boat; **3,** a twist, as in a board:— *v.t.* **1,** to turn or twist out of shape; as, dampness *warps* wood; his mind is *warped* by misfortune; **2,** to tow (a vessel) with a warp:— *v.i.* to become twisted.

war·rant (wŏr′ănt; wôr′ănt), *n.* **1,** an official paper giving authority to receive money, to make an arrest, etc.; also, authorization so given; **2,** that which vouches for or guarantees anything; as, his presence is a *warrant* of his sincerity; **3,** justification; as, he acted without *warrant:—v.t.* **1,** to guarantee; as, this silver is *warranted* sterling; **2,** to give (a person) authority to do something; also, to authorize (a course of action); **3,** to justify; give just grounds for or to; as, this state of affairs *warrants* action; **4,** *Colloquial,* to declare as certain; as, I *warrant* this will happen.—*adj.* **war′-rant·a·ble.**

war·rant of·fi·cer, **1,** in the U.S. Navy, an officer subordinate in rank to a commissioned officer but superior to petty officers, appointed by the President; **2,** in the U.S. Army, an officer of subordinate rank appointed by the Secretary of War.

war·ren (wŏr′ĕn; wôr′ĕn), *n.* a place for breeding rabbits or other small animals; also, a place where small animals abound.

war·ri·or (wŏr′ĭ-ẽr; wôr′ĭ-ẽr; wôr′yẽr), *n.* a soldier; a man in military life.

War·saw (wôr′sô), a city, capital of Poland, on the Vistula River (map 12).

war·ship (wôr′shĭp′), *n.* a government ship equipped and used for war.

wart (wôrt), *n.* **1,** a small, usually hard, lump on the skin; **2,** a similar lump on a plant stem.—*adj.* **wart′y.**

wart hog, a wild hog of Africa, with two pairs of warty growths on the face, and large tusks.

War·wick·shire (wŏr′ĭk-shĭr; wŏr′ĭk-shẽr), a county in central England. Also called **War′wick.**

WART HOG (1/30).

war·y (wâr′ĭ), *adj.* [war-i-er, war-i-est], **1,** constantly on guard; as, a *wary* foe; **2,** marked by caution; as, *wary* speeches.
Syn. watchful, prudent, circumspect.

was (wŏz), past indicative singular, first and third persons, of the verb *be*.

wash (wŏsh; wôsh), *v.t.* 1, to cleanse with a liquid, usually water; as, to *wash* the hands; 2, to cover with water; flow against; as, the breakers *wash* the shore; 3, to take away, or remove, by the action of water; as, the flood *washed* the bridge away; 4, to overlay with a thin coat of metal, color, etc.:—*v.i.* 1, to become clean by the use of water; 2, to cleanse clothes, linen, etc., in water; as, she *washes* on Monday; 3, to stand without injury the process of being cleaned in water; as, this material will *wash* well; 4, to be removed or worn away by the action of water; as, the spot will *wash* out; the bank has *washed* away; 5, to move with a flowing, lapping sound; to splash:—*n.* 1, the act of washing; 2, a collection of articles which are to be, or have been, washed; as, there are six sheets in the *wash*; 3, the dash or sound of a body of water; 4, material deposited by water, as wreckage on a beach; 5, disturbed water behind the propellers, oars, etc., of a boat; also, disturbed air behind a moving airplane; 6, liquid with which anything is tinted or washed; as, white*wash*; eye*wash*; 7, waste liquid; especially, kitchen waste for feeding pigs.—*adj.* **wash′a-ble.**

Wash. abbreviation for *Washington*.

wash-board (wŏsh′bôrd′; wôsh′bôrd′), *n.* a board with a ridged metal or glass surface, on which clothes are rubbed in being washed.

wash-er (wŏsh′ẽr; wôsh′ẽr), *n.* 1, one who or that which washes; specifically, a machine for washing dishes, clothes, etc.; 2, a flat ring of metal, leather, etc., used to secure the tightness of a joint or screw.

wash-er-wom-an (wŏsh′ẽr-wŏom′ăn; wôsh′ẽr-), *n.* [*pl.* -women (-wĭm′ĕn)], a woman who earns a living by washing clothes.

WASH-BOARD

wash-ing (wŏsh′ĭng; wôsh′ĭng), *n.* 1, the act of cleansing; 2, articles that have been, or are to be, washed:—*adj.* pertaining to washing; as, a *washing* machine.

WASHER

¹Wash-ing-ton (wŏsh′ĭng-tŭn; wôsh′ĭngtŭn), George (1732–1799), an American Revolutionary general, the first president of the U.S.

²Wash-ing-ton (wŏsh′ĭng-tŭn; wôsh′ĭngtŭn), 1, a western State (cap. Olympia) of the U.S. (map 9); 2, a city in the District of Columbia, capital of the U.S. (map 6).

wash-out (wŏsh′out′; wôsh′out′), *n.* 1, the carrying away of earth, rocks, etc., as by heavy rain; 2, a place where earth, rocks, etc., have been so carried away.

wasp (wôsp; wŏsp), *n.* an insect with strong wings, very slender body, and powerful sting.

WASP (⅔)

wasp-ish (wôs′pĭsh; wŏs′pĭsh), *adj.* 1, resembling a wasp in form; slender of waist; 2, irritable; peevish.—*adv.* **wasp′ish-ly.**

was-sail (wŏs′l; wŏs′-ăl; wăs′l; wăs′ăl), *n.* 1, in ancient times, an expression of good will uttered on a solemn or festive occasion when drinking a health; 2, the liquor, especially a spiced ale, in which healths were drunk on such occasions; 3, a riotous celebration; drinking bout.

wast (wŏst), *Archaic* or *Poetic*, the second person singular, past tense, of the verb *be*.

waste (wāst), *v.t.* [wast-ed, wast-ing], 1, to lay in ruins; destroy; 2, to wear away gradually the strength of; as, disease *wastes* the body; 3, to spend recklessly, as, to *waste* money:—*v.i.* to lose vigor, substance, or strength gradually; as, she is *wasting* away with the disease:—*adj.* 1, useless or unused, as unproductive land; 2, desolate; dreary; 3, discarded; no longer useful; as, *waste* products; 4, used for carrying away or holding waste products; as, a *waste* pipe:—*n.* 1, the act or process of spending carelessly, of wearing gradually away, destroying, etc.; also, the state of being destroyed, used up, etc.; 2, that which is of no value; refuse; 3, something thrown aside in a manufacturing process; as, cotton *waste*; 4, that which is devastated, desolate, or unproductive; a desert.

waste-ful (wāst′fŏol), *adj.* spending or consuming extravagantly or uselessly.—*adv.* **waste′ful-ly.**—*n.* **waste′ful-ness.**

wast-rel (wās′trĕl), *n.* a wasteful person.

watch (wŏch; wôch), *n.* 1, wakefulness for the purpose of guarding or protecting; a vigil; 2, the state of being alert or on the lookout; as, always on the *watch*; close observation; as, keep a good *watch* over the child; 3, a watchman; guard; 4, the time a guard is on duty; also, any one of the periods into which the day is divided, during which a given part of a ship's crew is on duty; 5, a spring-driven pocket timepiece:—*v.i.* 1, to be or keep awake; as, to *watch* at night by the bedside of the sick; 2, to keep guard; 3, to be on the lookout; 4, to wait; as, to *watch* for an opening to speak:—*v.t.* 1, to tend; guard; as, the shepherd *watches* his flock; 2, to keep in sight; observe; as, to *watch* a game; 3, to wait for; as, *watch* your turn.—*n.* **watch′er.**

watch-dog (wŏch′dôg′; wôch′dôg′), *n.* a dog quick to detect the approach of strangers, kept to protect property.

watch-ful (wŏch′fŏŏl; wôch′fŏŏl), *adj.* vigilant; on the lookout; as, a *watchful* guard. —*adv.* **watch′ful-ly.**—*n.* **watch′ful-ness.**

watch-mak-er (wŏch′mā′kẽr; wôch′-mā′kẽr), *n.* one who makes or repairs watches.

watch-man (wŏch′măn; wôch′măn), *n.* [*pl.* watchmen (-mĕn)], a guard; as, a night *watchman.*

watch-tow-er (wŏch′tou′ẽr; wôch′tou′ẽr), *n.* 1, in medieval times, a fortified tower in which a sentinel was placed; 2, any tower or high platform used as a lookout.

watch-word (wŏch′wûrd′; wôch′wûrd′), *n.* 1, a password; 2, a rallying cry.

wa-ter (wô′tẽr), *n.* 1, the common liquid which forms lakes, rivers, etc., and which comes from the clouds as rain; also, this liquid used for cooking, washing, drinking, etc.; 2, any clear liquid like or containing water, as tears; 3, a body of water, as a sea, river, lake, etc.; as, to cross the *water* in a steamer; 4, a kind of wavy, shiny pattern, as in some silks, metals, etc.:—*v.t.* 1, to moisten, sprinkle, or provide with water; as, to *water* the lawn; 2, to treat (fabric) so as to produce a wavy, shiny pattern upon it; 3, to flow through; irrigate; as, the Columbia River *waters* a large valley; 4, to give a drink to; as, to *water* the horses; 5, to dilute with water; as, to *water* wine:—*v.i.* 1, to obtain or take in water; also, to drink water: said usually of animals; 2, to secrete or fill with liquid; as, his eyes *watered:*—*adj.* 1, used for holding or conducting water; 2, living, feeding, etc., in, on, or near water.

in deep water, undergoing difficulty; **in hot water,** in trouble; **of the first water,** of the best quality; **throw cold water on,** to discourage; **throw bread upon the waters,** to do good which will later react to one's advantage.

wa-ter-buck (wô′tẽr-bŭk′), *n.* [*pl.* waterbuck or waterbucks], a large antelope of Central Africa, found near water.

wa-ter buf-fa-lo, the East Indian buffalo, often domesticated for its milk and used as a draft animal: also called *carabao.*

water bug, 1, a small, winged cockroach; **2,** a bug that lives in the water and propels itself by means of long oarlike legs; **3,** a

WATCHTOWER

bug which cannot swim but which walks about on the surface of the water.

Wa-ter-bur-y (wô′tẽr-bĕr′ĭ), a manufacturing city in Connecticut, the center of the watch and clock industry (map 6).

water clock, an instrument which measures time by the flow of water.

wa-ter col-or, 1, a paint prepared for use by being moistened with water; **2,** a picture made with paints of this kind, as distinguished from one painted with oil colors; **3,** the art of painting with such colors.

wa-ter-course (wô′tẽr-kôrs′), *n.* **1,** a stream of water; **2,** a channel for water.

water cress (krĕs), a plant that grows in running water; also, its pungent leaves, used as a salad or garnish.

wa-ter-fall (wô′tẽr-fôl′), *n.* a steep descent or fall of water; a cataract.

water flea, an extremely small crustacean which swims with a springing movement. (See illustration under *crustacean.*)

wa-ter-fowl (wô′tẽr-foul′), *n.* [*pl.* waterfowl or waterfowls], a bird which lives on or close to a body of water, as a wild duck; also, all such birds as a class.

water front, a part of a town which lies along a body of water.

water hole, a natural watering place for cattle in a desert or other dry country.

wa-ter-ing place (wô′tẽr-ĭng), **1,** a place for getting water; **2,** a pleasure resort, noted either for mineral springs or for bathing beaches.

wa-ter jack-et, a case for holding water, or through which water may circulate for cooling purposes, as on an engine.

wa-ter lil-y, a plant which grows in the water, bearing a fragrant, beautiful flower and broad, flat, floating leaves; also, the flower itself.

water line, any of several lines or watermarks on the sides of a vessel, showing the water level at various weights of load. Also written **wa′ter-line′.**

wa-ter-logged (wô′tẽr-lŏgd′), *adj.* so soaked or filled with water as to be heavy and unmanageable.

Wa-ter-loo (wô′tẽr-lōō′; wô′tẽr-lōō′), a village in Belgium where Napoleon was defeated in 1815.

wa-ter-man (wô′tẽr-măn), *n.* [*pl.* watermen (-mĕn)], **1,** a man who runs or manages a boat for hire; **2,** a man who works or lives on a boat.

WATER LILY

wa·ter·mark (wô′tĕr-märk′), *n.* **1,** a mark that shows the height or limit of the rise of water; **2,** a faintly visible marking or design in some kinds of paper, seen when the paper is held to the light.

wa·ter·mel·on (wô′tĕr-mĕl′ŭn), *n.* a trailing plant of the cucumber family cultivated for its large, edible fruit which has a green rind and red, sweet, juicy pulp; also, the fruit. (See illustration under *melon*.)

wa·ter ou·zel (oo′zl), a wrenlike songbird: often called *dipper*.

wa·ter po·lo (pō′lō), a game played in the water by teams of swimmers with a large ball like that used in soccer.

wa·ter pow·er, power from falling or running water, used to run machinery.

wa·ter·proof (wô′tĕr-proof′), *adj.* not permitting water to come through; as, *waterproof* garments:—*n.* (wô′tĕr-proof′), any material treated so as to shed water; especially, a raincoat made of such material:—*v.t.* to make secure against water; as, to *waterproof* a fabric.

water rat, 1, a small, ratlike animal which lives in wet meadows; a vole; **2,** a muskrat.

wa·ter·shed (wô′tĕr-shĕd′), *n.* **1,** a height or ridge of land lying between areas drained by different river systems; **2,** an area drained by a single river or lake system.

water snake, a snake that lives in the water, especially in fresh water.

wa·ter·spout (wô′tĕr-spout′), *n.* **1,** a column of water drawn up by a whirlwind at sea to meet a descending funnel-shaped cloud; **2,** a spout for the discharge of water, especially of rain water.

wa·ter·tight (wô′tĕr-tīt′), *adj.* so closely made or fastened as to permit no water to leak out or to enter.

wa·ter·way (wô′tĕr-wā′), *n.* **1,** a channel for water; **2,** a body of water permitting navigation.

water wheel, a wheel turned by the direct action of flowing or falling water.

wa·ter·works (wô′tĕr-wûrks′), *n.pl.* a pumping station, a system for supplying water to a city, town, etc.

wa·ter·y (wô′tĕr-ĭ), *adj.* **1,** pertaining to, or like, water; **2,** containing or discharging water; as, *watery* eyes; **3,** soggy; soft; as, *watery* potatoes.

Wat·ling Is·land (wŏt′lĭng; wôt′lĭng), an island in the Bahamas. See **San Salvador.**

Watt (wŏt; wôt), James (1736–1819), a Scotchman, inventor of the steam engine.

watt (wŏt; wôt), *n.* a unit of electric power.

wat·tle (wŏt′l; wôt′l), *n.* **1,** a twig; a rod easily bent; also, a framework of pliant rods; **2,** material made of pliant twigs twisted together and used for walls, fences, etc.; **3, wattles,** rods used in a roof to support thatch made of straw, etc.; **4,** the folds of loose red flesh under the throat of certain birds or reptiles:—*v.t.* [wattled, wat-tling], **1,** to twist or interweave (twigs or rods) into a framework, fence, etc; **2,** to cover or fence in with rods.—*adj.* **wat′tled.**

WATTLE (W)
def. 4

wave (wāv), *n.* **1,** a swell on the surface of water; a billow; **2,** the wavelike motion by which sound, light, or the like, is carried; **3,** anything like a wave, whether natural or artificial; as, *waves* in hair; **4,** a steady increase or sweeping advance of any feeling, condition, etc.; as, a *wave* of enthusiasm; a crime *wave;* a heat *wave;* **5,** an up-and-down motion, as with the hand; also, a signal made by motions of the hand or some object:—*v.i.* [waved, wav-ing], **1,** to move up and down or back and forth; as, the flag *waved* in the breeze; **2,** to signal by such a motion; as, he *waved* to us to stop; **3,** to form into ripples; as, her hair *waves* beautifully:—*v.t.* **1,** to cause to move back and forth; as, to *wave* a banner; **2,** to signal by such a movement; as, to *wave* good-by; **3,** to form into ripples; as, to *wave* the hair.

wa·ver (wā′vĕr), *v.i.* **1,** to tremble; sway; flicker, as a flame; **2,** to hesitate, as in opinion; **3,** to begin to give way; as, the line of troops *wavered.*—*adj.* **wa′ver·ing.**

wav·y (wāv′ĭ), *adj.* [wav-i-er, wav-i-est], moving to and fro in waves or swells; as, *wavy* grass; full of waves or curves; as, *wavy* lines.—*adv.* **wav′i·ly.**—*n.* **wav′i·ness.**

WAVY LINES

¹**wax** (wăks), *v.i.* **1,** to increase in size, power, degree, etc.; grow: used of the moon in its first and second quarters; **2,** to pass gradually into a specified condition; become; as, the party *waxed* gay.

²**wax** (wăks), *n.* **1,** a sticky, yellowish substance, made by bees, from which the honeycomb is built; beeswax; **2,** any similar substance; as, ear*wax;* sealing *wax:*—*v.t.* to smear, polish, or treat the surface of, with wax; as, to *wax* floors:—*adj.* made of or like wax; as, a *wax* candle.

wax·en (wăks′sĕn), *adj.* **1,** made of, or covered with, wax; as, a *waxen* image; **2,** resembling wax; as, *waxen* paleness.

---

go; join; yet; sing; chin; show; thin, *th*en; hw, *wh*y; zh, azure; **ū,** Ger. f**ür** or Fr. l**une; ŏ,** Ger. sch**ön** or Fr. f**eu;** ñ, Fr. e**nfant,** no**m;** kh, Ger. a**ch** or i**ch.** See pages ix–x.

wax myr·tle (mûr′tl), an evergreen shrub or tree from the waxy berries of which candles are made: also called *bayberry*.

wax·wing (wăks′wǐng′), *n.* a crested, brownish bird with waxy red tips on certain wing feathers, as the cedarbird, or cedar waxwing.

wax·y (wăk′sǐ), *adj.* [wax-i-er, wax-i-est], **1,** resembling wax; **2,** made of, or coated with, wax. — *n.* **wax′i-ness.**

CEDAR WAXWING (⸓)

way (wā), *n.* **1,** a road, street, path, or passage; as, a covered *way;* hence, room for passing; as, make *way* for the procession; **2,** the route from one place to another; the direction or best route to go; as, please tell me the *way* to the post office; also, distance in general; as, it is a long *way* to China; **3,** progress; advance; headway; as, the ship gathers *way;* he made his *way* in business; **4,** manner; as, she has a winning *way;* also, methods or means; as, Franklin found a *way* to succeed; find a *way* to do it; **5,** a habitual or determined course of action or mode of life; as, she goes her *way* through life; he was set in his *ways;* have your own *way* about it; **6,** aspect; feature; respect; as, in some *ways* it proved a success; **7,** the line of the weave in cloth; **8, ways,** a structure of timbers on which a ship is built and down which it slides when being launched; **9,** *Colloquial,* neighborhood; as, out our *way;* **10,** *Colloquial,* condition; state; as, we're in a bad *way.*

by the way, incidentally; **by way of, 1,** passing through on the way; via; as, he went to Washington *by way of* Philadelphia; **2,** as a substitute for; as, he said that *by way of* an apology; **right of way, 1,** the right to pass over privately owned land; **2,** the right to move first; precedence, as in traffic; **to give way,** to give passage; hence, to yield or break down, as under pressure; **to pave the way,** to make things easy; serve as introduction; as, he *paved the way* for his request; **under way,** in motion or progress, as a ship or a project; **ways and means,** methods and means of accomplishing an end, especially of meeting expenses.

Syn. highway, avenue, thoroughfare.

way·bill (wā′bǐl′), *n.* a paper containing shipping instructions for goods carried by train or steamer.

way·far·er (wā′fâr′ẽr), *n.* a traveler, especially one who goes on foot.

way·far·ing (wā′fâr′ǐng), *adj.* traveling, especially on foot; as, a *wayfaring* man.

Way·land (wā′lănd), *n.* a smith of English legend, often called *Wayland Smith.*

way·lay (wā′lā′; wā′lā′), *v.t.* [waylaid (-lād′; -lād′), waylay-ing], to lie in wait for with intent to rob, kill, etc.; to seize or attack on the way. — *n.* **way′lay′er.**

Wayne (wān), Anthony (1745–1796), often called *Mad Anthony,* an American Revolutionary general.

-ways (-wāz), a suffix indicating position, manner, etc.; as, side*ways*, al*ways*.

way·side (wā′sīd′), *n.* the edge of a road or path:—*adj.* located or growing near the edge of the road; as, *wayside* flowers.

way sta·tion, a small station between larger ones on a railroad.

way·ward (wā′wẽrd), *adj.* **1,** disobedient; as, a *wayward* son; **2,** freakish; unaccountable. — *adv.* **way′ward-ly.** — *n.* **way′wardness.**

Syn. obstinate, headstrong, wilful.

we (wē), *pron.* the first person plural of the personal pronoun *I* [*nominative* we, *possessive* our, ours, *objective* us], **1,** the pronoun by which the writer or speaker denotes himself and the group of which he is a part; **2,** the pronoun sometimes used by sovereigns and writers instead of the singular *I* in official proclamations, unsigned articles, editorials, etc.

weak (wēk), *adj.* **1,** lacking in strength of body or in endurance; as, he is *weak* from illness; also, not capable of supporting a heavy weight; as, a *weak* platform; **2,** easily overcome; as, *weak* objections; **3,** wanting in mental or moral strength; easily influenced; as, a *weak* will; **4,** faulty; below standard; as, a *weak* point in the plan; *weak* in arithmetic; **5,** faint in sound; feeble; as, a *weak* cry; also, diluted; thin; watery; as, *weak* wine; **6,** not skilful, experienced, or the like; as, a *weak* swimmer:—**weak verb,** in grammar, a verb which forms its past tense and past participle by the addition of *-ed, -d,* or *-t;* as, *talk, talked, talked; love, loved, loved; weep, wept, wept.*

weak·en (wēk′ĕn), *v.t.* and *v.i.* to make or become less strong.

weak·fish (wēk′fǐsh′), *n.* an edible sea fish found along the Atlantic Coast: so named from its tender mouth.

weak·ling (wēk′lǐng), *n.* a person lacking strength of body or character.

weak·ly (wēk′lǐ), *adj.* [weak-li-er, weak-li-est], sickly; not strong:—*adv.* in a feeble or faint manner.

weak·ness (wēk′nĕs), *n.* **1,** lack of strength, power, or force; as, tuberculosis is marked by great *weakness;* **2,** a fault or defect; as, there is a *weakness* in your plan; **3,** a liking for; as, she has a *weakness* for candy.

¹**weal** (wēl), *n. Archaic,* happiness; prosperity; welfare; as, the public *weal.*

²**weal** (wēl), *n.* a ridge or mark made on the skin by flogging; a wale or wheal.

wealth (wĕlth), *n.* 1, riches; large amounts of money or worldly possessions; 2, abundance of anything; as, there is a *wealth* of detail in this story.

wealth-y (wĕl'thĭ), *adj.* [wealth-i-er, wealth-i-est], rich; marked by abundance.

wean (wēn), *v.t.* 1, to accustom (a child or any young animal) to substitute other food for the mother's milk; 2, to draw away the affections or interests of (a person or animal) from any object or habit; as, they *weaned* him from smoking.

weap-on (wĕp'ŭn), *n.* any instrument for fighting or for defense.

wear (wâr), *v.t.* [*p.t.* wore (wôr), *p.p.* worn (wôrn), *p.pr.* wear-ing], 1, to carry on or about the body; as, to *wear* a coat; 2, to bear or maintain about one; to show; as, to *wear* a careless manner; 3, to use up or consume, wholly or in part, especially by personal use; as, he *wears* clothes out rapidly; 4, to diminish or lessen the quality or value of, by rubbing, scraping, or the like; as, the steps were *worn* by the children's feet; hence, to weaken; weary; fatigue; as, anxiety *wore* the woman out; 5, to bring about by use, friction, or the like; as, to *wear* a hole in a rug:—*v.i.* 1, to go through, or endure, the process of being used; as, these gloves *wear* like iron; 2, to become used up; be diminished in value as a result of use; as, these shoes *wore* out too soon; 3, to pass gradually; as, the night *wore* on:—*n.* 1, the act of using or state of being used; use; as, suits for spring *wear;* 2, garments; clothing; as, they deal in children's *wear;* 3, damage caused by use; as, to show *wear;* 4, lasting quality; service; as, these stockings will give you good *wear.*

wea-ri-some (wē'rĭ-sŭm), *adj.* causing fatigue; tedious; as, *wearisome* work.

wea-ry (wē'rĭ), *adj.* [wea-ri-er, wea-ri-est], 1, fatigued; tired; as, *weary* in body and mind; 2, exhausted, as in patience, by continuance of something tiresome; 3, characteristic of, or showing, fatigue; as, a *weary* sigh; 4, causing, or accompanied by, fatigue; as, to walk many *weary* miles:—*v.t.* [wearied, weary-ing], 1, to wear out or make tired; 2, to harass or worry by something irksome:—*v.i.* to become weary.—*adv.* **wea'ri-ly.**—*n.* **wea'ri-ness.**

WEASEL (⅙)

wea-sel (wē'zl), *n.* a small, active animal of the same family as the mink and skunk,

with a pointed face and a long, thin body: destructive to poultry, mice, etc.

weath-er (wĕth'ẽr), *n.* the state of the air or atmosphere as to cold, heat, wetness, dryness, etc.; as, fair *weather:*—*v.t.* 1, to expose to the air; season by exposure to the elements; also, to wear away; as, wind and water *weather* rocks; 2, to sail to the windward of; 3, to endure or resist; withstand; as, to *weather* a gale at sea:—*v.i.* to undergo action of the air, sun, rain, etc.:—*adj.* windward; facing the wind.

weath-er-beat-en (wĕth'ẽr-bēt'n), *adj.* 1, toughened by the action of sun, rain, etc.; as, *weather-beaten* skin; 2, worn by the weather; as, *weather-beaten* shingles.

weath-er-board (wĕth'ẽr-bôrd'), *n.* a board used to form an outer protective covering for part of a building; especially, a board cut and fitted to overlap the boards above and below it, so that it will shed water easily. (See illustration under *frame house.*)

weath-er-cock (wĕth'ẽr-kŏk'), *n.* a figure, often shaped like a cock, fastened to a high spire, roof, pole, etc., and turning with the wind to show which way it is blowing; a weather vane.

weath-er-glass (wĕth'ẽr-glås'), *n.* an instrument, as a barometer, for predicting the weather, usually by indicating changes in the pressure of the atmosphere.

WEATHER-COCK

weather strip, a strip of felt or other material placed at a joint or crack, as about a window or door, to keep out wind, rain, or snow.

weather vane, a movable device fastened to a spire, roof, or pole to show which way the wind blows; a weathercock: also called *vane.*

weave (wēv), *v.t.* [*p.t.* wove (wōv) or, sometimes, weaved, *p.p.* wo-ven (wō'vĕn) or wove, *p.pr.* weav-ing], 1, to twist or interlace, as threads; 2, to form by interlacing or twisting, as cloth on a loom; 3, to spin; as, the spider *weaves* a web; 4, to compose or fabricate; as, to *weave* a story; 5, to direct (one's way) in a winding course, as through a crowd:—*v.i.* 1, to make cloth on a loom; to spin a web; 2, to become twisted together or interlaced; 3, to wind in and out:—*n.* a particular pattern in weaving; as, cloth with a plain *weave.*

weav-er (wēv'ẽr), *n.* one whose trade is making cloth on a loom.

web (wĕb), *n.* 1, a woven fabric, especially a whole piece of cloth; 2, a substance or piece of material resembling woven cloth; specifically, a cobweb; **3,** anything of complicated structure or arrangement, as an intricate plot; **4,** the skin between the toes of many water birds and some water animals:— *v.t.* [webbed, web-bing], to unite or surround with, or as with, a web; entangle.

webbed (wĕbd), *adj.* **1,** having a web; **2,** having fingers or toes joined by webs; as, the *webbed* hind feet of beavers.

web–foot-ed (wĕb′=fŏŏt′ĕd), *adj.* having toes which are joined by webs; as, swans are *web-footed*.

Web-ster (wĕb′stẽr), **1,** Daniel (1782–1852), an American statesman and orator; **2,** Noah (1758–1843), an American dictionary writer.

wed (wĕd), *v.t.* [*p.t.* wed-ded, *p.p.* wed-ded or wed, *p.pr.* wed-ding], **1,** to marry; **2,** to join in marriage:— *v.i.* to marry.

we'd (wēd), contraction for *we had* or *we would*, and often for *we should*.

Wed. abbreviation for *Wednesday*.

wed-ded (wĕd′ĕd), *adj.* **1,** married; as, a *wedded* pair; **2,** attached; devoted; as, he is *wedded* to his art.

wed-ding (wĕd′ing), *n.* **1,** a marriage; a marriage ceremony; **2,** a marriage anniversary; as, a golden *wedding*.
Syn. matrimony, wedlock, nuptials.

wedge (wĕj), *n.* **1,** a piece of wood or metal, thick at one end and thin at the other, used for splitting wood or rocks, raising heavy objects, etc.; **2,** anything of a similar shape; as, a *wedge* of land; **3,** any action used to create an opening or lead to further developments:— *v.t.* [wedged, wedg-ing], **1,** to split or force apart with a wedge; **2,** to fasten with a wedge, as a door or wheel; **3,** to force in (something) to serve as a wedge; to press or crowd in; as, to *wedge* packing into a crack.

WEDGE
def. 1

wed-lock (wĕd′lŏk), *n.* the state of being married; matrimony.
Syn. wedding, marriage, nuptials.

Wednes-day (wĕnz′dĭ), *n.* the fourth day of the week.

wee (wē), *adj.* [we-er, we-est], very little; tiny.

¹weed (wēd), *n.* a wild plant that grows in cultivated fields, and is unsightly or useless:— *v.t.* **1,** to root out or remove, as undesirable plants; **2,** to free from wild and useless plants; as, to *weed* a garden; **3,** to remove from a group (the inferior, useless, and harmful parts); as, to *weed* out the troublemakers:— *v.i.* to take out weeds or anything obnoxious.

²weed (wēd), *n.* **1,** a garment; **2,** **weeds,** mourning garments; as, widow's *weeds*.

weed-y (wēd′ĭ), *adj.* [weed-i-er, weed-i-est], **1,** pertaining to, resembling, or abounding with, weeds; **2,** *Colloquial,* unhealthily tall and thin.

week (wēk), *n.* **1,** a period of seven days; **2,** the six working days of the week; as, the museum is open during the *week*.

week-day (wēk′dā′), *n.* any day of the week except Sunday.

week end, **1,** the time from Friday night or Saturday noon to Monday morning, usually free from business; **2,** a holiday or party at this time.— *adj.* **week′–end′.**

week-ly (wēk′lĭ), *adj.* **1,** of a week; for a week; as, a *weekly* wage; **2,** happening or coming every seven days; as, a *weekly* paper:— *adv.* once a week:— *n.* [*pl.* weeklies], a paper or magazine issued once every seven days.

ween (wēn), *v.t.* and *v.i. Archaic,* to suppose; think.

weep (wēp), *v.i.* [wept (wĕpt), weep-ing], **1,** to shed tears; cry; **2,** to give forth moisture; as, the skies *weep*:— *v.t.* **1,** to shed, as tears; **2,** to shed tears for; hence, to lament or mourn.— *n.* **weep′er.** — *n.* and *adj.* **weep′ing.**

wee-vil (wē′vl; wē′vĭl), *n.* a small hard-shelled beetle having the head extended into a beak with mouth parts at the end: destructive to grain, nuts, fruits, leaves, etc.

weft (wĕft), *n.* in weaving, the threads that cross the warp, or lengthwise threads; woof; also, yarn used for the weft.

WEEVIL
Slightly
enlarged.

weigh (wā), *v.t.* **1,** to find the heaviness of, by use of a scale or balance, or by lifting; as, I *weighed* the stone in my hand; **2,** to ponder; reflect on carefully; as, to *weigh* the evidence; **3,** to distribute in definite quantities, as by the use of scales; as, to *weigh* out sugar; **4,** to press heavily upon; as, care *weighs* him down; **5,** to raise: used only in *to weigh anchor*:— *v.i.* **1,** to have a certain weight; as, these bricks *weigh* over a ton; **2,** to bear heavily; **3,** to be considered important; as, his testimony didn't *weigh* much with the jury.

weight (wāt), *n.* **1,** heaviness; the tendency of bodies to fall toward the earth; **2,** a system of units used in finding the heaviness or quantity of objects or substances; as, apothecaries' *weight*; **3,** a unit of weight, as pound, ounce, gram, ton; **4,** the amount a thing weighs; as, her *weight* is 100 pounds; **5,** degree of heaviness; as, two boys of the same *weight;* **6,** a piece of metal used as a balance in finding the heaviness of other bodies; **7,** a heavy object; as, the *weight* in a clock; **8,** something oppressive; as, care is a *weight* on the mind; **9,** power; importance; as, a man of great *weight* in the community: — *v.t.* **1,** put weight upon; load down; as, to *weight* a sack with stones; **2,** oppress with a load; as, he's *weighted* down with cares.

weight-less (wāt′lĕs), *adj.* beyond the pull of the earth's gravity; at zero gravity, as a body would be during travel in space. —*n.* **weight′less-ness.**

weight-y (wā′tĭ), *adj.* [weight-i-er, weight-i-est], **1,** heavy; as, a *weighty* body; hence, burdensome; as, *weighty* cares; **2,** important; influential; as, *weighty* considerations; **3,** serious in aspect; as, a *weighty* countenance.—*adv.* **weight′i-ly.**—*n.* **weight′i-ness.**

weir (wĭr), *n.* **1,** a dam placed in a stream to stop and raise the water, in order to lead it into a mill, or into ditches for irrigation, or the like; **2,** a fence of brush or stakes set in a stream for catching fish.

weird (wĭrd), *adj.* pertaining to the supernatural; uncanny or unearthly.—*adv.* **weird′ly.**—*n.* **weird′ness.**

wel-come (wĕl′kŭm), *adj.* **1,** received with gladness or hospitality; as, a *welcome* guest; producing gladness; as, *welcome* gifts; **2,** permitted gladly; as, you're *welcome* to stay:—*n.* a kindly greeting:—*v.t.* [welcomed, welcom-ing], to greet with kindness; receive with hospitality.

weld (wĕld), *v.t.* **1,** to join (pieces of metal) by heating to the melting point and pressing or hammering together or permitting to flow together; **2,** hence, to unite closely; as, he *welded* the tribes into a nation:— *v.i.* to become welded, or firmly joined together; as, iron *welds* easily:—*n.* **1,** the state of being welded; **2,** a welded joint.

wel-fare (wĕl′fâr), *n.* the state or condition of having good health, prosperity, etc.:—*adj.* pertaining to welfare:—**welfare work,** organized endeavor by a community to improve the social condition of its poorer classes by the distribution of money, food, medical information, and the like.

wel-kin (wĕl′kĭn), *n. Poetic,* the sky.

we'll (wēl), contraction of *we will, we shall.*

¹well (wĕl), *n.* **1,** a spring or fountain; **2,** a shaft sunk deep in the earth, for obtaining water, gas, oil, or the like; **3,** an enclosed or sunken space resembling such a shaft; **4,** a source of steady or continuous supply:—*v.i.* to flow, as from a spring; as, tears *welled* into her eyes.

²well (wĕl), *adv.* [*comp.* bet-ter, *superl.* best], **1,** in a right, just, or praiseworthy manner; as, the work was *well* done; **2,**

satisfactorily or suitably; as, to dine *well;* **3,** with reason; justifiably; as, he may *well* question the verdict; **4,** fortunately; favorably; as, the store is *well* situated; **5,** to a considerable extent or degree; as, a man *well* over 50; **6,** intimately; as, we are *well* acquainted with him; **7,** definitely; clearly; as, they knew perfectly *well* the outcome: —*adj.* **1,** in good health; **2,** in a satisfactory state; as, all is *well:*—*interj.* an exclamation of wonder, relief, resignation, or the like.

well-a-day (wĕl′ȧ-dā′) or **well-a-way** (wĕl′ȧ-wā′), *interj.* an exclamation of grief and sorrow; alas!

well—be-ing (wĕl′-bē′ĭng), *n.* general health and prosperity; welfare.

well—born (wĕl′bôrn′), *adj.* born of a good family; formerly, of noble birth.

well—bred (wĕl′-brĕd′), *adj.* refined in manners; cultivated; polite.

¹Wel-ling-ton (wĕl′ĭng-tŭn), Arthur Wellesley, Duke of (1769–1852), a British general, whose forces defeated Napoleon at Waterloo in 1815.

²Wel-ling-ton (wĕl′ĭng-tŭn), a seaport city, capital of New Zealand (map **16**).

well—known (wĕl′-nōn′), *adj.* familiar; famed; generally recognized; as, a *well-known* nursery tale; a *well-known* author.

well—nigh (wĕl′-nī′), *adv.* very nearly; almost; as, *well-nigh* exhausted.

well—spring (wĕl′sprĭng′), *n.* **1,** a flow of water issuing from the earth; a spring; **2,** a source of never-failing supply.

well—to-do (wĕl′-tȧ-dōō′), *adj.* prosperous; moderately wealthy.

Welsh (wĕlsh), *adj.* pertaining to Wales, its people, or its language:—*n.* the language of Wales.

the Welsh, the people of Wales; **Welsh rabbit,** a dish of melted cheese, cooked with milk, ale, or beer, seasoned, and served on toasted bread or crackers: often incorrectly called *Welsh rarebit.*

Welsh-man (wĕlsh′măn), *n.* [*pl.* Welshmen (-mĕn)], a native or inhabitant of Wales.

welt (wĕlt), *n.* **1,** an edge or border fastened to something, for strengthening or ornamenting it, as the narrow strip of leather around a shoe between the upper and the sole; **2,** *Colloquial,* a red, swollen mark raised on the skin by a blow:—*v.t.* **1,** to secure or ornament with a welt, or narrow strip; **2,** *Colloquial,* to flog.

wel-ter (wĕl′tĕr), *v.i.* **1,** to roll; wallow, as a pig in mire; **2,** to rise and fall with violent tossing, as a ship in a storm:—*n.* **1,** a violent tossing or rolling, as of waves; **2,** a state of confusion.

wel-ter-weight (wĕl′tĕr-wāt′), *n.* in box-

go; join; yet; sing; chin; show; thin, *th*en; hw, *why;* zh, azure; ü, Ger. für or Fr. lune; ö, Ger. schön or Fr. feu; ṅ, Fr. enfant, nom; kh, Ger. ach or ich. See pages **ix–x.**

ing and wrestling, a contestant weighing more than a lightweight and less than a middleweight.

wen (wĕn), *n.* a harmless tumor of the skin.

wench (wĕnch), *n.* **1**, a young girl or woman; **2**, a female servant.

wend (wĕnd), *v.i.* to go; journey:—*v.t.* to direct or continue; as, to *wend* one's way.

went (wĕnt), past tense of *go*.

wept (wĕpt), past tense and past participle of *weep*.

we're (wēr), a contraction of *we are*.

were (wûr; wâr), **1**, past indicative plural of *be*; as, we *were;* you *were;* they *were;* **2**, past subjunctive, singular and plural, of *be;* as, if I *were* you, I would go.

were-wolf (wēr′wŏolf′; wûr′wŏolf′), *n.* [*pl.* werewolves (-wŏolvz′)], in folklore, a person turned into a wolf, or one who could assume a wolf's shape at will.

Wer-fel (vĕr′fĕl), Franz (1890–1945), a German writer.

wert (wûrt), *Archaic* or *Poetic*, second person singular, past indicative and subjunctive, of *be*.

Wes-ley (wĕs′lĭ), **1**, Charles (1707–1788), an English Methodist preacher and hymn writer; **2**, John (1703–1791), his brother, a preacher, the founder of Methodism.

Wes-ley-an (wĕs′lĭ-ăn; wĕz′lĭ-ăn), *adj.* pertaining to John Wesley, or to the Methodist religious denomination which he founded:—*n.* **1**, a follower of John Wesley; **2**, a Methodist.

Wes-sex (wĕs′ĕks), an ancient Anglo-Saxon kingdom in southern England; also, a corresponding section of modern England.

west (wĕst), *n.* **1**, that part of the heavens where the sun is seen to set; one of the four points of the compass: opposite of *east;* **2**, the part of the earth lying toward the sunset:—**West**, **1**, the Occident; Europe and the Americas, as distinguished from Asia, or the the Orient; **2**, in the U.S., the territory lying between the Mississippi River and the Pacific Ocean:—*adj.* coming from the west; as, a *west* wind; in the direction of the west; as, a *west* door:—*adv.* toward the west; as, facing *west*.

west-er-ly (wĕs′tẽr-lĭ), *adj.* **1**, toward the west; **2**, from the west, as a wind:—*adv.* in the direction of the west:—*n.* [*pl.* westerlies], a wind blowing from the west.

west-ern (wĕs′tẽrn), *adj.* **1**, grown or produced in the west; as, *western* apples; **2**, situated in the west; as a *western* city; also, going toward, or coming from, the west; as, a *western* train:—*n.* a type of novel or motion picture showing cowboy and pioneer life in the western United

States:—**Western**, relating to any district or region called the West.

West-ern Aus-tral-ia, a state (cap. Perth) of Australia (map **16**).

West-ern Hem-i-sphere, the half of the earth, as represented on the globe, which includes the continents of North and South America (maps **3, 11**).

West-ern Is-lands, islands west of Scotland. See **Hebrides**.

West In-dies (ĭn′dĭz), a group of islands in the Atlantic Ocean, east of Central America, including the Greater and the Lesser Antilles and the Bahamas (map **10**).

West-min-ster (wĕst′mĭn′stẽr), a city and borough of London in which the Houses of Parliament are located.

West-min-ster Ab-bey (ăb′ĭ), a famous old church in Westminster, begun in 1050 and rebuilt after 1245, where English sovereigns are crowned, and noted soldiers, statesmen, and poets are buried.

West-pha-li-a (wĕst-fā′lĭ-à) a former province (cap. Münster) in Prussia, Germany.

West Point, a military reservation in New York State, site of U.S. Military Academy.

West Vir-gin-i-a (vẽr-jĭn′ĭ-à; vẽr-jĭn′yà), an east central State (cap. Charleston) in the U.S. (map **8**).

¹**west-ward** (wĕst′wẽrd), *adj.* toward the west; as, steer a *westward* course.

²**west-ward** (wĕst′wẽrd) or **west-wards** (-wẽrdz), *adv.* toward the west; as, to travel *westward*.—*adv.* **west′ward-ly**.

wet (wĕt), *v.t.* [wet or wet-ted, wet-ting], to moisten or soak with water or some other liquid:—*n.* **1**, water; moisture; also, rainy or misty weather; **2**, *Colloquial*, an opponent of prohibition:—*adj.* [wet-ter, wet-test], **1**, containing, consisting of, or soaked with, water or some other liquid; as, *wet* streets; also, of paint, varnish, ink, etc., not dry; **2**, rainy or misty; as, *wet* weather; **3**, *Colloquial*, favoring the manufacture and sale of alcoholic beverages.

wet-back (wĕt′băk′), *n.* a person who has entered the United States illegally from Mexico.

weth-er (wĕ*th*′ẽr), *n.* a castrated male sheep.

we've (wēv), a contraction of *we have*.

whack (hwăk), *n. Colloquial*, a smart, resounding blow : —*v.t. Colloquial*, to strike with a smart, resounding blow.

WHALE (⅟₄₀₀)

¹**whale** (hwāl), *n.* a huge, warm-blooded, air-breathing

sea mammal with finlike fore limbs, no external hind limbs, and a fishlike tail, valued for oil, whalebone, etc.:—*v.i.* [whaled, whaling], to hunt whales.—*n.* **whal′ing.**

²**whale** (hwāl), *v.t.* [whaled, whal-ing], *Colloquial*, **1,** to flog or beat soundly; **2,** to hit hard; as, he *whaled* the ball for a home run.

whale-boat (hwāl′bōt′), *n.* a long, narrow rowboat, sharp and slanting at both ends, first used by whale fishermen.

whale-bone (hwāl′bōn′), *n.* **1,** a stiff, springy substance in the upper jaw of certain whales; **2,** something made of whalebone.

whal-er (hwāl′ẽr), *n.* **1,** anyone engaged in the trade of whale fishing; **2,** a vessel used by whale fishermen.

wharf (hwôrf), *n.* [*pl.* wharves (hwôrvz) or wharfs], a structure of wood, steel, or stone built at the water's edge, at which ships may be moored; a pier or quay.

wharf-age (hwôr′fĭj), *n.* **1,** the use of, or accommodation at, a wharf; **2,** the fee collected for the use of a wharf or pier; **3,** the entire wharf space at a port.

what (hwŏt; hwôt), *pron.* **1,** in questions, which thing or things; as, *what* is wrong? *what* is your business? **2,** in relative clauses, that or those which; the thing or things that; as, *what* you have just said is wrong; also, anything that; everything that; all that; as, give him *what* he wants; I'll give *what* I can; **3,** in exclamations, what things; how much; as, *what* he has suffered! —*adj.* **1,** in questions, which; as, *what* trade do you follow? how much; as, *what* good will that do? **2,** in relative clauses, that or those which; which in particular; as, I want to know *what* car I should take; also, any; all; whatever; as, I'll contribute *what* flowers I have; as many as; as, take *what* pencils you please; as much as; as, take *what* ink you need; what sort of; as, I wonder *what* magazines he likes; **3,** in exclamations, how great, strange, unusual, or the like; as, *what* recklessness!—*adv.* **1,** partly; in part; as, *what* with the cold and *what* with the darkness, we could go no farther; **2,** in questions, how much; in what way; as, *what* does it profit a man? **3,** in exclamations, such; as, *what* bright colors!—*conj.* that; as, I do not know but *what* it is true:—**what though,** even though; even granting that; as, *what though* we failed today, all is not lost:—*interj.* an exclamation expressing surprise; as, *what!* the boat stolen?

what-ev-er (hwŏt-ĕv′ẽr; hwôt-), *pron.* **1,** all that; anything that; as, give *whatever* you can; **2,** no matter what; as, we must have sugar, *whatever* its cost; **3,** used inter-rogatively, as an emphatic form of *what*, expressing surprise, wonder, etc.; as, *whatever* made you do it?—*adj.* of any kind; as, he owns no property *whatever*. Also, *Poetic,* **what-e'er′** (hwŏt-âr′).

what-not (hwŏt′nŏt′; hwôt′-), *n.* a set of ornamental, open shelves for holding bric-a-brac.

what-so-ev-er (hwŏt′sō-ĕv′ẽr; hwôt′-), *pron.* and *adj.* an emphatic form of *whatever*.

wheal (hwēl), *n.* a ridge raised on the flesh, as by flogging; a wale or weal.

wheat (hwēt), *n.* **1,** a tall, slender, cultivated grass bearing long spikes of seeds, the most important of the cereal grains; **2,** the seed of this grass, used in the making of flour and cereals.

wheat-en (hwēt′n), *adj.* pertaining to, or made from, wheat; as, *wheaten* bread.

whee-dle (hwē′dl), *v.t.* [wheedled, whee-dling], **1,** to persuade by flattery; cajole; coax; as, she *wheedled* her father into consenting; **2,** to get by coaxing or flattery:—*v.i.* to coax.

WHEAT
A, without beard; B, with beard.

wheel (hwēl), *n.* **1,** a circular frame or disk designed to turn on a central axis or axle; **2,** a vehicle or machine in which a frame or disk of this kind is a characteristic or essential part, as a bicycle; **3,** something resembling a wheel, as a circular, revolving firework; **4,** a complete turning around; hence, a turn made by a line of troops or of ships moving abreast, by pivoting at one end of the line; **5, wheels,** the inner workings of anything; as, the *wheels* of state:—*v.t.* **1,** to move (something) on wheels; **2,** to cause to turn, as a line of troops:—*v.i.* **1,** to turn on, or as if on, an axis; **2,** to move on wheels, as a vehicle.—*adj.* **wheeled.**

WHEEL, def. 1 H, hub

wheel-bar-row (hwēl′băr′ō), *n.* a light vehicle with two handles and usually one wheel, used for moving small loads.

wheel-wright (hwēl′rīt′), *n.* one who makes or repairs wheels and wheeled vehicles.

wheeze (hwēz), *v.i.* [wheezed, wheez-ing], **1,**

WHEELBARROW

to breathe noisily and with difficulty; **2,** to make a whistling or gasping sound; as, the pump *wheezes:—n.* a whistling or gasping breath, as in asthma.

wheez-y (hwēz'ĭ), *adj.* [wheez-i-er, wheez-i-est], **1,** having difficulty in breathing; **2,** making a whistling or gasping sound; as, a *wheezy* old organ.

whelk (hwĕlk), *n.* a kind of large, spiral-shelled, marine snail, used for food in Europe.

whelm (hwĕlm), *v.t.* to engulf; overwhelm.

whelp (hwĕlp), *n.* **1,** the young of a dog, lion, fox, etc.; a cub; **2,** a worthless, disagreeable child or youth:—*v.t.* and *v.i.* of animals, to give birth to (young).

WHELK (‡)

when (hwĕn), *adv.* **1,** in questions, at or during what time; as, *when* are you coming? **2,** in relative clauses, at which time; as, he knew *when* he had to work:—*conj.* **1,** at or after the time; as, *when* he came, it was too late; on any occasion that; whenever; at whatever time; as, *when* I meet him, he does not speak; as soon as; as, *when* dinner is over, you may leave; **2,** whereas; while on the contrary; in spite of the fact that; as, he gave me ten dollars *when* he owed me only five:—*pron.* **1,** what time; as, since *when* have you been here? **2,** the time or occasion just spoken of; as, since *when*, his work has improved.

whence (hwĕns), *adv.* **1,** in questions, from what place, source, or origin; hence, for what reason; **2,** in relative clauses, from which; as, the place *whence* I came.

whence-so-ev-er (hwĕns'sō-ĕv'ẽr), *adv.* and *conj.* from whatever place or origin.

when-ev-er (hwĕn-ĕv'ẽr), *adv.* and *conj.* at whatever time; as often as. Also, *Poetic,* **when-e'er'** (hwĕn-âr').

when-so-ev-er (hwĕn'sō-ĕv'ẽr), *adv.* and *conj.* at whatever time; whenever.

where (hwâr), *adv.* **1,** in questions, at or in what place; as, *where* do they live? hence, in what part; in what respect; as, *where* am I wrong? to what place; whither; as, *where* are you going? from what source or place; as, *where* did you get that? **2,** in relative clauses, in, at, or to which; as, the house *where* I lived; in, at, or to whatever place; wherever; as, stay *where* you are:—*conj.* whereas; as, he did much, *where* we expected little:—*pron.* the place at, in, or to which; as, that is *where* I made my mistake.

where-a-bouts (hwâr'ȧ-bouts'), *adv.* in or near what place:—*n.* (also *whereabout*) the place where a person or thing is; as, her *whereabouts* is still unknown.

where-as (hwâr-ăz'), *conj.* **1,** considering that; it being the case that; **2,** while on the contrary; as, he thought he was late, *whereas* he was early.

where-at (hwâr-ăt'), *adv.* **1,** in relative clauses, at or upon which; **2,** whereupon; on which account.

where-by (hwâr-bī'), *adv.* **1,** in relative clauses, by which; **2,** in questions, by what means; how.

where-fore (hwâr'fôr), *adv.* **1,** in relative clauses, for which reason; **2,** in questions, why:—*n.* a cause or reason; as, the whys and *wherefores*.

where-in (hwâr-ĭn'), *adv.* **1,** in relative clauses, in which; in which time, place, respect, or the like; **2,** in questions, in what; as, *wherein* am I mistaken?

where-of (hwâr-ŏv'; hwâr-ŏf'), *adv.* **1,** in relative clauses, of which; of whom; **2,** in questions, of what.

where-on (hwâr-ŏn'), *adv.* **1,** in relative clauses, on which; **2,** in questions, on what; as, *whereon* do you rely?

where-so-ev-er (hwâr'sō-ĕv'ẽr), *adv.* and *conj.* in or to whatever place; wherever.

where-to (hwâr-tōō'), *adv.* **1,** in relative clauses, to which; **2,** in questions, to what; to what end or place.

where-un-to (hwâr'ŭn-tōō'), *adv. Archaic,* unto which; whereto.

where-up-on (hwâr'ŭ-pŏn'), *adv.* **1,** in relative clauses, upon which; as the result of which; after which; as, *whereupon* he rose to speak; **2,** in questions, upon what; upon what grounds.

wher-ev-er (hwâr-ĕv'ẽr), *adv.* at, to, or in, whatever place.

where-with (hwâr-wĭth'; hwâr-wĭth'), *adv.* **1,** in relative clauses, with which; as, he had no tools *wherewith* to work; **2,** in questions, with what:—*pron.* that with which; as, he has *wherewith* to buy a car.

where-with-al (hwâr'wĭth-ôl'), *adv.* with which:—*pron.* wherewith:—*n.* (hwâr'with-ôl'), that with which a thing can be bought or done; as, he has the *wherewithal* to buy a house.

wher-ry (hwĕr'ĭ), *n.* [*pl.* wherries], **1,** a light, shallow rowboat; **2,** in Great Britain, a light barge or fishing vessel.

whet (hwĕt), *v.t.* [whet-ted, whet-ting], **1,** to sharpen on or with a whetstone; as, to *whet* an axe; **2,** to make eager; stimulate; as, the rumor *whets* my curiosity.

wheth-er (hwĕth'ẽr), *conj.* **1,** in case that; no matter if; as, *whether* you go or *whether* you stay, I shall help you; *whether* he fails or not, it's worth trying; **2,** if; as, I wonder *whether* they will come today.

āte, āorta, râre, căt, ȧsk, fär, ȧllow, sofȧ; ēve, ēvent, ĕll, writẽr, novĕl; bīte, pĭn; nō, ōbey, ôr, dŏg, tŏp, cŏllide; ūnit, ūnite, bûrn, cŭt, focŭs; nōōn. fŏŏt; mound; coin;

whet-stone (hwĕt′stōn′). *n.* a fine-grained stone for sharpening edged tools.

whew (hwū; hū), *interj.* an exclamation expressing surprise, disgust, or dismay.

whey (hwā), *n.* the thin, watery part of milk, which may be separated from the curds, as in making cheese.

which (hwĭch), *pron.* **1,** in questions, what one or ones (of several); as, *which* is your book? **2,** in relative clauses: **a,** that; as, the books *which* we have read; *Archaic,* who or whom; as, Our Father *which* art in heaven; **b,** the one that; as, point out *which* is yours; also, any that; whichever; as, take *which* of these books you please: —*adj.* **1,** in questions, what; as, *which* house is yours? **2,** in relative clauses, what; as, after a month, during *which* time he did nothing; point out *which* hat is yours.

which-ev-er (hwĭch-ĕv′ĕr), *pron.* any one or ones that; as, take *whichever* you please: —*adj.* no matter which; any; whatever; as, *whichever* book you choose.

which-so-ev-er (hwĭch′sō-ĕv′ĕr), *pron.* and *adj.* whichever.

whiff (hwĭf), *n.* **1,** a sudden breath or gust, as of air or smoke; a puff; **2,** a faint odor; a trace: —*v.t.* and *v.i.* to puff or blow out or away in sudden breaths; waft.

whif-fle-tree (hwĭf′l-trē′; hwĭf′l-trĭ), *n.* a whippletree. See **whippletree.**

Whig (hwĭg), *n.* **1,** a member of a former political party in the U.S. with principles somewhat similar to those of the Republican party, founded in 1834 and lasting until the War between the States; **2,** a supporter of the American Revolution; **3,** in England, a member of a liberal political party which originated in the 17th century, and developed into the Liberal party: distinguished from *Tory.*

while (hwīl), *n.* **1,** a period of time; as, he stayed only a little *while;* **2,** time or pains required in doing something; as, it will be worth your *while* to go: —*conj.* **1,** as long as; during the time that; at the same time that; as, you might read *while* I am gone; **2,** less correctly, although; as, *while* I like fruit, I dislike apples: —*v.t.* [whiled, whil-ing], to cause to pass; spend; as, to *while* away the time between trains.

whiles (hwīlz), *Archaic:* *adv.* sometimes: —*conj.* while.

whi-lom (hwī′lŭm), *Archaic:* *adv.* formerly; once: —*adj.* former; onetime; as, his *whilom* friends deserted him.

whilst (hwīlst), *conj.* while.

whim (hwĭm), *n.* a fancy; caprice; notion.

whim-per (hwĭm′pĕr), *v.i.* to cry in a low, whining voice: —*n.* a fretful whining.

whim-sey (hwĭm′zĭ), *n.* [*pl.* whimseys], a fancy; whim. Also, **whim′sy** [*pl.* whimsies].

whim-si-cal (hwĭm′zĭ-kăl), *adj.* **1,** full of odd or fanciful notions; capricious; **2,** odd; quaint; as, *whimsical* fancies.—*adv.* **whim′si-cal-ly.**

whine (hwīn), *v.i.* [whined, whin-ing], **1,** to utter a plaintive, long-drawn cry; especially, to show distress by such a cry; as, the dog *whined* to be let in; **2,** to coax or complain in a plaintive or fretful tone: —*v.t.* to utter in a fretful or complaining way: —*n.* **1,** a plaintive tone or cry; **2,** a weak, fretful complaining.

whin-ny (hwĭn′ĭ), *v.i.* [whinnied, whinny-ing], to neigh: —*n.* [*pl.* whinnies], a neigh.

whip (hwĭp), *v.t.* [whipped or whipt (hwĭpt), whip-ping], **1,** to strike, as with a lash or rod; beat; **2,** to beat into froth, as cream; **3,** to move or take suddenly; snatch; jerk; as, he *whipped* off his coat; **4,** *Colloquial,* to defeat in a contest; conquer: —*v.i.* **1,** to thrash about, as a loose sail; **2,** to move quickly or nimbly; as, the fox *whipped* out of sight: —*n.* **1,** a flexible rod, often tapering to a lash, or a rod with a lash attached; **2,** anyone who uses such a rod or lash; a driver; **3,** in cookery, a preparation, usually a dessert, which is made up largely of cream or the whites of eggs, beaten stiff.—*n.* **whip′per.**

whip hand, 1, the hand holding the whip in driving; **2,** hence, mastery; control; advantage; as, to gain the *whip hand* of a foe.

whip-pet (hwĭp′ĕt), *n.* a very fleet smooth-coated dog, resembling a greyhound, but somewhat smaller, used especially for racing.

WHIPPET (¹⁄₂₄)

whip-ple-tree (hwĭp′l-trē′; hwĭp′l-trĭ), *n.* a bar pivoted crosswise at the front of a carriage or wagon, to the ends of which the traces of the harness are fastened: also called *whiffletree.*

whip-poor-will (hwĭp′-pŏŏr-wĭl′; hwĭp′pŏŏr-wĭl′), *n.* a small American bird, mottled brown, black, and buff: so called from its frequently repeated note.

whip-stock (hwĭp′-stŏk′), *n.* the handle of a whip.

WHIPPOORWILL (¹⁄₁₆)

whir (hwûr), *v.i.* [whirred, whir-ring], to move, fly, or revolve with a buzzing noise: —*n.* a buzzing noise caused by rapid motion; as, the *whir* of an airplane propeller.

---

go; join; yet; sing; chin; show; thin, *th*en; hw, *wh*y; zh, a*z*ure; ü, Ger. f*ü*r or Fr. l*u*ne; ö, Ger. sch*ö*n or Fr. f*eu*; ṅ, Fr. *en*fant, *nom*; kh, Ger. a*ch* or i*ch*. See pages ix–x.

whirl (hwûrl), *v.t.* **1,** to turn or cause to revolve rapidly; as, to *whirl* a hat on one's finger; **2,** to carry onward or away quickly, with a revolving motion:—*v.i.* **1,** to revolve with great speed; as, the earth *whirls* on its axis; **2,** to move along swiftly; as, the carriage *whirled* away; **3,** to seem to spin around; as, my brain *whirled*:—*n.* **1,** a rapid rotation or circular motion; **2,** something revolving rapidly; as, a *whirl* of dust; **3,** confused and bustling activity; as, the *whirl* of social life.

whirl-i-gig (hwûr′lĭ-gĭg′), *n.* **1,** a child's toy that spins or whirls round; **2,** a merry-go-round; **3,** anything that turns or whirls around rapidly.

whirl-pool (hwûrl′pōōl′), *n.* a swift-moving, circling eddy or current in a river or sea, with a central depression into which floating objects are drawn by suction.

whirl-wind (hwûrl′wĭnd′), *n.* a violent windstorm marked by a whirling, spiral motion of the air.

whisk (hwĭsk), *v.t.* **1,** to sweep or brush lightly and rapidly; **2,** to take or carry off with a quick, sweeping motion; as, the wind *whisked* away the scrap of paper; **3,** to beat (eggs, cream, etc.) into a froth:—*v.i.* to move rapidly and nimbly; as, the squirrel *whisked* up the tree:—*n.* **1,** the act of brushing with a quick motion; **2,** a quick, nimble movement; **3,** a small broom or brush with a short handle; **4,** a kitchen utensil for whipping eggs, cream, etc.

WHISK

whisk-er (hwĭs′kẽr), *n.* **1,** (usually *whiskers*), the hair growing on the side of a man's face, or on his upper lip or his chin; **2,** one of the long, bristly hairs growing near the mouth of a cat, rat, or other animal.—*adj.* **whisk′ered.**

whis-ky (hwĭs′kĭ), *n.* [*pl.* whiskies], a strong alcoholic liquor distilled from grains, as corn or rye. Also, **whis′key**[*pl.* whiskeys].

whis-per (hwĭs′pẽr), *v.i.* **1,** to speak in a low voice or under the breath; **2,** to rustle; as, leaves *whispered* in the breeze:—*v.t.* to say under the breath; tell privately:—*n.* **1,** a low, hushed tone of voice; **2,** a hint or suggestion; rumor; as, a *whisper* of scandal; **3,** a soft, rustling sound.

¹whist (hwĭst), *n.* a card game for four persons, from which the modern game of bridge has been developed.

²whist (hwĭst), *interj. Archaic,* hush! be silent!—*adj. Archaic,* hushed or quiet.

whis-tle (hwĭs′l), *v.i.* [whis-tled, whis-tling], **1,** to make a shrill sound by forcing the breath between the teeth or puckered lips, or by forcing air, steam, or the like, through a small opening, as in a valve; **2,** to make any similar shrill sound; as, the wind *whistles;* **3,** to go or pass swiftly with a sharp, shrill sound; as, arrows *whistled* past him:—*v.t.* **1,** to utter by whistling; as, to *whistle* a tune; **2,** to call or signal by whistling:—*n.* **1,** the shrill noise made by forcing air, steam, etc., through an opening; **2,** an instrument to produce such a sound.—*n.* **whis′tler.**

Whis-tler (hwĭs′lẽr), James Abbott Mc-Neill(1834-1903),an American-born painter and etcher. He lived in London.

whit (hwĭt), *n.* the smallest particle; as, there is not a *whit* of truth in the rumor.

white (hwīt), *adj.* [whit-er, whit-est], **1,** of the color of clean snow: opposite of *black;* **2,** hence, pure; innocent; **3,** silvery; gray, as hair; **4,** fair-skinned:—*n.* **1,** the color of clean snow; **2,** a Caucasian, or white person; **3,** white clothing; as, nurses wear *white;* **4,** the albumen of an egg.—*n.* **white′ness.**

to **show the white feather,** to betray cowardice; **white lie,** a harmless fib or falsehood, as one told to save the feelings of another.

white ant, a tropical insect, the termite, most abundant in Africa. It is destructive to books, wooden structures, and the like.

WHITEFISH (½)

white-cap (hwīt′kăp′), *n.* a wave crest whitened with foam.

white-fish (hwīt′fĭsh′), *n.* an edible, freshwater fish of the salmon family.

white flag, a flag of truce or surrender.

White House, the official residence, at Washington, of the President of the United States.

White Moun-tains, a mountain range in northern New Hampshire (map **6**).

whit-en (hwī′tn), *v.t.* to bleach or make white:—*v.i.* to become white, as linen in the sun.

THE WHITE HOUSE

White Russian Soviet Socialist Republic, a Soviet republic on the western border of the U.S.S.R. (map **12**).

White Sea, an arm of the Arctic Ocean, extending southward into northern European U.S.S.R. (map **12**).

āte, âorta, râre, căt, ȧsk, fär, ăllow, sofȧ; ēve, ĕvent, ĕll, writẽr, novĕl; bīte, pĭn; nō, ōbey, ôr, dŏg, tŏp, cŏllide; ūnit, ūnite, bûrn, cŭt, focŭs; nōōn, fŏŏt; mound; coin;

white-wash (hwīt′wŏsh′; -wôsh′), *n.* a white mixture of lime and water, for coating walls, fences, etc.:—*v.t.* **1,** to cover with whitewash; **2,** hence, to gloss over the faults or misdeeds of.—*n.* **white′wash′er.**

whith-er (hwĭ*th*′ẽr), *adv.* **1,** in questions, to what place; as, *whither* goest thou? **2,** anywhere; wherever; as, go *whither* you will; you will go *whither* you are sent.

whith-er-so-ev-er (hwĭ*th*′ẽr-sŏ-ĕv′ẽr), *adv.* to whatever place; wherever.

whit-ing (hwīt′ĭng), *n.* **1,** a sea fish, much used as food; **2,** a powdered preparation of chalk used in the manufacture of putty, in polishing silverware, etc.

Whit-man (hwĭt′măn), Walt (1819-1892), an American poet.

Whit-ney (hwĭt′nĭ), Eli (1765-1825), the American inventor of the cotton gin.

Whitney, Mount (hwĭt′nĭ), a mountain, the highest in the U.S., in central California in the Sierra Nevada range (map **9**).

Whit-sun-day (hwĭt′sŭn′dĭ; hwĭt′sŭn-dā′), *n.* the seventh Sunday after Easter.

Whit-sun-tide (hwĭt′sŭn-tīd′), *n.* the week following Whitsunday; especially, the first three days, which are called *Whitsunday, Whitmonday,* and *Whit-Tuesday.*

Whit-ti-er (hwĭt′ĭ-ẽr), John Greenleaf (1807-1892), an American poet.

Whit-ting-ton (hwĭt′ĭng-tŭn), Dick, a poor orphan boy who, as is told in a famous old legend, became Lord Mayor of London.

whit-tle (hwĭt′l), *v.t.* [whit-tled, whit-tling], **1,** to cut, shape, or carve with a knife; as, to *whittle* a toy; **2,** to reduce bit by bit by, or as if by, cutting away:—*v.i.* to shape a piece of wood slowly with a knife.

whiz or **whizz** (hwĭz), *v.i.* [whizzed, whizzing], to move rapidly with a humming or hissing sound; as, the car *whizzed* past us:—*n.* a humming or hissing noise.

who (hōō), *pron.* [nominative who, *possessive* whose (hōōz), *objective* whom (hōōm)], **1,** in questions, what person or persons; as, *who* else was there with you? *whom* did you choose? also, what sort of person or persons; as, *who* am I to be so honored? **2,** in relative clauses, that; as, Mr. Smith, *who* lives near me; the one that; the person that; as, I know *who* was there; I don't know *who* you are; he that or they that; whoever; as, "*who* steals my purse, steals trash."

whoa (hwō), *interj.* stop! hold! stand still!

who-ev-er (hōō-ĕv′ẽr), *pron.* anyone or everyone who; whatever person or persons; as, *whoever* wishes, may come along.

whole (hōl), *adj.* **1,** in good health; uninjured; **2,** not defective or broken; intact; **3,** not divided into parts; not broken, cut up, or ground; as, *whole* cloves; hence, undivided in devotion, allegiance, etc.; as, to work with one's *whole* heart and soul; **4,** complete; entire; containing all the parts or members; as, the *whole* school:—*n.* all the parts or members of something taken together; a total; as, the *whole* of a nation.—*n.* **whole′ness.**

whole-heart-ed (hōl′här′tĕd), *adj.* sincere; completely earnest; hearty; as, *wholehearted* co-operation.

whole num-ber, an integer; a number expressed without the use of a fraction, as 5, 12, 23.

whole-sale (hōl′sāl′), *n.* the sale or purchase of goods in large quantities: opposite of *retail:*—*adj.* buying or selling in large quantities; also, pertaining to such trade:—*v.t.* [wholesaled, wholesal-ing], to sell at wholesale.

whole-sal-er (hōl′sāl′ẽr), *n.* a person who sells goods to dealers rather than direct to consumers.

whole-some (hōl′sŭm), *adj.* [wholesom-er, wholesom-est], **1,** tending to promote health of body or mind; as, a *wholesome* meal; **2,** characteristic of, or suggesting, health; as, a *wholesome* appearance.

whole–wheat (hōl′=hwēt′), *adj.* made of flour milled from the whole grain of the wheat; as, *whole-wheat* bread.

whol-ly (hōl′lĭ; hōl′ĭ), *adv.* completely; entirely; altogether; as, he was *wholly* satisfied with his purchase.

whom (hōōm), *pron.* the objective case of *who.*

whom-so-ev-er (hōōm′sō-ĕv′ẽr), *pron.* the objective case of *whosoever.*

whoop (hōōp), *v.i.* **1,** to utter a loud and prolonged cry; shout; halloo; **2,** to make the gasping sound that follows a fit of coughing in whooping cough:—*v.t.* to drive, call, or urge with loud cries or shouts:—*n.* **1,** a loud shout; **2,** a gasping sound following a fit of coughing.

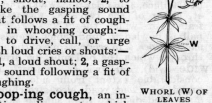

WHORL (W) OF LEAVES

whoop-ing cough, an infectious disease to which children are particularly susceptible, characterized by violent coughing.

whore (hôr), *n.* a harlot; prostitute.

whorl (hwûrl; hwôrl), *n.* **1,** the circular arrangement of leaves, petals, or the like, at one level on a stem; **2,** one of the turns of a spiral shell.—*adj.* **whorled.**

whose (hōoz), *pron.* the possessive case of *who.*

who·so (hōo′sō), *pron.* whoever.

who·so·ev·er (hōo′sō-ĕv′ẽr), *pron.* any person who; whoever.

why (hwī), *adv.* **1,** in questions, for what reason, with what motive, or for what purpose; on what account; wherefore; as, *why* did you leave? **2,** in relative clauses, on account of which; for which; as, the reason *why* he went I don't know; the reason for which; as, I do not understand *why* he is so angry:—*n.* [*pl.* whys (hwīz)], a cause or reason; motive; as, psychology explains the *why* of human conduct:—*interj.* expressing surprise; as, *why!* it's snowing!

Wich·i·ta (wĭch′ĭ-tô), a city in southern Kansas (map 7).

wick (wĭk), *n.* the cord or tape of twisted fibers in a candle or lamp, through which the melted tallow or oil is drawn to feed the flame.

WICK (W) OF CANDLE

wick·ed (wĭk′ĕd), *adj.* **1,** evil; sinful; base; immoral; as, a *wicked* sinner; **2,** mischievous; roguish; as, a *wicked* look; **3,** harmful; dangerous; as, a *wicked* blow. —*adv.* **wick′ed·ly.**—*n.* **wick′ed·ness.**
Syn. infamous, vicious, bad, naughty.

wick·er (wĭk′ẽr), *n.* **1,** a pliant twig; especially, a pliant willow rod; **2,** such twigs woven into baskets, furniture, etc.:— *adj.* made of wicker; as, a *wicker* table.

wick·er·work (wĭk′ẽr-wûrk′), *n.* articles such as tables, chairs, baskets, etc., made of wicker.

wick·et (wĭk′ĕt), *n.* **1,** a small door or gate, especially one in a larger gate or door; **2,** a windowlike opening, especially one with a grill or grate, as in a ticket office; **3,** in cricket, either of the two frames at which the ball is bowled, behind which stands the *wicketkeeper;* **4,** in croquet, one of the arches through which the ball must be driven.

WICKET, def. 3
A, wicketkeeper; B, wicket; C, batsman.

wide (wīd), *adj.* [wid·er, wid·est], **1,** of considerable extent from side to side; broad; as, a *wide* road; also, stretching for a specified distance from side to side; as, the room is nine feet *wide;* **2,** vast; spacious; as, a *wide* domain; **3,** inclusive of much; comprehensive; as, a person of *wide* experience; **4,** far from a point aimed at; as, *wide* of the mark; **5,** opened to the fullest extent; as, eyes *wide* with wonder: —*adv.* **1,** over or to a considerable distance or extent; widely; as, his fame spread

far and *wide;* **2,** of a door, gate, window, etc., fully open; **3,** far from the point aimed at.—*adv.* **wide′ly.**—*n.* **wide′ness.**

wide–a·wake (wīd′-à-wāk′), *adj.* entirely awake; alert; vigilant.

wid·en (wī′dn), *v.t.* and *v.i.* to make or become broader or larger; as, here the river *widens.*

wide-spread (wīd′sprĕd′), *adj.* **1,** opened or spread to the fullest extent; as, a *widespread* fan; **2,** widely distributed; as, English is a *widespread* language.

widg·eon (wĭj′ŭn), *n.* a wild, fresh-water duck.

wid·ow (wĭd′ō), *n.* a woman whose husband is dead. —*adj.* **wid′owed.**

wid·ow·er (wĭd′ō-ẽr), *n.* a man whose wife is dead.

wid·ow·hood (wĭd′ō-hŏod), *n.* the state or condition of being a widow.

WIDGEON (1/15)

width (wĭdth), *n.* the extent of a thing from side to side; breadth; as, this lot is 50 feet in *width.*

wield (wēld), *v.t.* **1,** to use with the hands; as, to *wield* an ax; **2,** to exercise (power, authority, etc.).—*n.* **wield′er.**

Wien (vēn), the German name for Vienna, a city in Austria. See **Vienna.**

Wies·ba·den (vēs′bä′dĕn), a city in western Germany. It is famous as a health resort.

wife (wīf), *n.* [*pl.* wives (wīvz)], a married woman.—*n.* **wife′hood.**—*adj.* **wife′ly.**

wig (wĭg), *n.* an artificial covering of hair for the head, to conceal baldness, to adorn, or to form part of official dress.

wig·gle (wĭg′l), *v.i.* and *v.t.* [wiggled, wig-gling], to squirm; wriggle.

wight (wīt), *n. Archaic,* a creature; as, poor, luckless *wight.*

Wight, Isle of (wīt), an island off the southern coast of England (map 13).

WIGS
A, plaited wig of about 1710; B, modern wig as worn by an English judge; C,D, wigs as worn about 1780.

wig·wag (wĭg′-wăg′), *v.t.* and *v.i.* [wigwagged, wigwag-ging], **1,** to move back and forth; **2,** to signal with flags or lights, moved or flashed according to a code.

wig-wam (wĭg′wŏm; wĭg′wôm), *n.* a hut made of a framework of poles, covered with bark or hides, used by the North American Indians.

wild (wīld), *adj.* **1,** living in the natural state; untamed; as, the lion is a *wild* animal; also, not cultivated; as, *wild* flowers; **2,** not civilized; savage; as, a *wild* tribe; **3,** of a region, uninhabited; like a wilderness; **4,** uncontrolled; as, *wild* anger; **5,** fantastic; unreasonable; as, a *wild* scheme; **6,** wide of the mark; **7,** *Colloquial,* eager; as, I am *wild* to go:—*adv.* without control; wildly:—**wilds,** *n.pl.* a desert or wilderness. —*adv.* **wild′ly.**— *n.* **wild′ness.**

wild boar, an undomesticated European hog, from which the domestic hog has been developed.

WILD BOAR (⅒)

wild-cat (wīld′-kăt′), *n.* a savage catlike animal, as the lynx and the Texas wildcat: also written *wild cat:—adj.* risky; unreliable; as, *wild-cat* banks.

wil-de-beest (wĭl′dĕ-bēst′; vĭl′dĕ-bāst′), *n.* [*pl.* wildebeests or, sometimes, wildebeest], in Dutch South Africa, the gnu, a short-horned antelope.

wil-der-ness (wĭl′dĕr-nĕs), *n.* a wild un-cultivated region; not inhabited by man.

wild-fire (wīld′fīr′), *n.* a composition, as of certain chemicals, that catches fire readily and is hard to put out; hence, anything that spreads swiftly; as, the story spread like *wildfire.*

wile (wīl), *n.* a subtle, crafty trick or sub-tle words, meant to lure or deceive:— *v.t.* [wiled, wil-ing], **1,** to obtain by trickery; as, she *wiled* the secret from him; **2,** to pass (time): incorrect for *while.*

wil-ful or **will-ful** (wĭl′fool), *adj.* **1,** headstrong; stubborn; as, a *wilful* child; **2,** intentional; deliberate; as, *wilful* mur-der.—*adv.* **wil′ful-ly.**—*n.* **wil′ful-ness.**

Wil-hel-mi-na (vĭl′hĕl-mē′nä), (1880–), queen of the Netherlands, 1890–1948.

wil-i-ness (wīl′ĭ-nĕs), *n.* craft; trickiness.

Wilkes—Bar-re (wĭlks′ₔbăr′ĭ), a mining and manufacturing city in northeastern Pennsylvania (map 6).

¹**will** (wĭl), *n.* **1,** the power of the mind to decide upon and carry out a course of action; **2,** control exercised over impulse; self-control; as, *will* conquers habit; **3,** a deliberate choice, desire, intention, or de-termination directed towards a special end or purpose; as, the *will* to live helps a patient to recover; **4,** strong determina-tion; hence, enthusiasm; energy; as, he went to work with a *will;* **5,** that which has been desired, or determined upon; as, thy *will* be done; he always had his *will;* **6,** the power to act as one wishes or sees fit; as, he comes and goes at *will;* **7,** dis-position or attitude towards others; as, peace on earth and good *will* toward men; **8,** a legal paper in which a person directs how his property is to be disposed of after his death; as, his last *will* and testament: —*v.t.* [willed, will-ing], **1,** to have as a wish or determination; to have in mind as a purpose; as, to *will* success is partly to win it; **2,** to influence or compel by exercising the power of the mind; as, she *willed* him to turn around; **3,** to bequeath; as, he *willed* half his estate to his cousin:— *v.i.* to decide, choose, or determine; as, if God so *wills,* we'll win this struggle yet.

²**will** (wĭl), *v.t.* [*sing.* I will, thou wilt, he will, *pl.* will; *p.t.* would (wo͝od); no other parts], *Archaic,* to wish or desire; as, what *will* you?—*v.i.* and *auxiliary* **1,** is or are go-ing to; as she *will* like this novel; they *will* be there; **2,** to wish to; want to; as, which *will* you have? come and go as you *will;* **3,** to wish; as, it shall be as you *will:* often with the subject omitted; as, *would* it were spring; **4** to be willing to; consent to; intend to; to be inclined or dis-posed to; as, he *will* not work any more; also, in polite commands, to be ordered to; as, you *will* please take this report to your father; **5,** to be determined to; as, I *will* do it whether you approve or not; he *will* go in spite of the weather; **6,** to be des-tined to; as, children *will* grow up; acci-dents *will* happen; **7,** to be accustomed to; as, she *would* sit and read for hours on end; **8,** to be able to; can; as, the bridge *will* not bear so heavy a load.

will-ful (wĭl′fool), *adj.* headstrong; de-liberate; wilful. See **wilful.**

Wil-liam I (wĭl′yăm), (1027?–1087), called *the Conqueror,* a duke of Normandy who became king of England in 1066.

Wil-liams (wĭl′yămz), Roger (1604?–1683), an English colonist who founded Rhode Island.

will-ing (wĭl′ĭng), *adj.* **1,** cheerfully ready; not lazy or slow; as, a *willing* worker; **2,** given or done freely or gladly; as, a *willing* service; **3,** favorably disposed; as, he is *willing* to buy it.—*adv.* **will′ing-ly.**—*n.* **will′ing-ness.**

will-o'-the-wisp (wĭl′ₔŏ-thē̆-wĭsp′), *n.* **1,** a light that is seen flitting above marshy ground at night; **2,** anything that misleads one or eludes one's grasp.

wil-low (wĭl′ō), *n.* a tree or shrub with slender flexible branches, usually growing near water; also, its wood, used in making baskets, furniture, etc.:—**weeping willow,** a species of willow whose drooping branches are a symbol of grief.

wil·low·y (wĭl'ō-ĭ), *adj.* **1,** like a willow in slenderness and grace; **2,** abounding in willow trees.

wil·ly-nil·ly (wĭl'ĭ-nĭl'ĭ), *adv.* by compulsion; whether one likes it or not; as, he must accept the verdict, *willy-nilly.*

Wil·ming·ton (wĭl'mĭng-tŭn), a manufacturing city and port in Delaware (map 6).

Wil·no (vēl'nō), the Polish name for Vilna, now the capital of the Lithuanian Soviet Socialist Republic (map **12**).

Wil·son (wĭl'sŭn), (Thomas) Woodrow (1856–1924), the 28th president of the United States.

¹wilt (wĭlt), *v.i.* **1,** to wither or droop, as a flower; **2,** to lose strength; become faint or weak:—*v.t.* to cause to wither.

²wilt (wĭlt), second person singular present of *²will.*

wil·y (wī'lĭ), *adj.* [wil-i-er, wil-i-est], cunning; crafty; as, the *wily* fox.
   Syn. artful, sly, subtle.

wim·ble (wĭm'bl), *n.* a boring tool, as an auger or a gimlet.

wim·ple (wĭm'pl), *n.* a covering of linen, silk, or the like, for the head, neck, and chin, worn by women generally in medieval times, and still part of the dress of some orders of nuns:—*v.t.* [wimpled, wim-pling], **1,** to clothe with such a covering; **2,** to lay in folds:—*v.i.* to lie in folds; also, to ripple, as a stream.

WIMPLE

win (wĭn), *v.i.* [won (wŭn), win-ning], to gain a victory; prevail; as, to *win* in a battle:—*v.t.* **1,** to acquire by effort or perseverance; obtain; as, to *win* promotion; earn, as a living; **2,** to gain in a contest; as, he *won* the prize; **3,** to be victorious in; as, to *win* a game; **4,** to persuade; induce; as, try to *win* him over to our side.
   Syn. acquire, achieve, attain, procure.

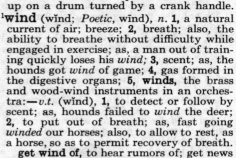

WINCH

a, a, cranks turned by hand; *b,* drum on which rope is wound; *c,* lever for disengaging pinion from gear; *d,* brake handle; *e,* pawl to prevent unwinding.

wince (wĭns), *v.i.* [winced, winc-ing], to shrink or draw back suddenly, as from a blow; flinch:—*n.* the act of flinching.

winch (wĭnch), *n.* a hoisting machine or windlass in which a rope or chain is wound up on a drum turned by a crank handle.

¹wind (wĭnd; *Poetic,* wīnd), *n.* **1,** a natural current of air; breeze; **2,** breath; also, the ability to breathe without difficulty while engaged in exercise; as, a man out of training quickly loses his *wind;* **3,** scent; as, the hounds got *wind* of game; **4,** gas formed in the digestive organs; **5, winds,** the brass and wood-wind instruments in an orchestra:—*v.t.* (wĭnd), **1,** to detect or follow by scent; as, hounds failed to *wind* the deer; **2,** to put out of breath; as, fast going *winded* our horses; also, to allow to rest, as a horse, so as to permit recovery of breath.
   get wind of, to hear rumors of; get news of; **take the wind out of someone's sails,** to surprise or disconcert someone, as by telling a story he expected to tell.

²wind (wīnd; wĭnd), *v.t.* [wound (wound), wind-ing], to blow (a horn or a blast on a horn); as, the hunter *wound* his horn.

³wind (wīnd), *v.i.* [wound (wound), winding], **1,** to turn; move with changing direction; as, the stream *winds* through the valley; **2,** to twine round and round; as, the ivy *winds* around the tree:—*v.t.* **1,** to twist or coil around on something; as, to *wind* yarn on a spool; **2,** to cover with something wrapped around; as, to *wind* a tire with tape; **3,** to tighten the springs of, by turning; as, to *wind* a watch or a music box; **4,** to make or pursue (one's way); as, he *wound* his course across hill and dale:—**wind up, 1,** in baseball, to give a preparatory swing to the arm before pitching a ball; **2,** *Colloquial,* to come to an end; as, how did the affair *wind up?* **3,** to bring to an end; settle; as, to *wind up* someone's business affairs:—*n.* a bend; coil; twist.—*n.* **wind'er.**

wind·break (wĭnd'brāk'), *n.* a shelter or protection from the wind, as a wall or a grove of trees.

wind·fall (wĭnd'fôl'), *n.* **1,** something blown down by the wind, as ripe fruit; **2,** an unexpected piece of good fortune, as a legacy.

wind·flow·er (wĭnd'flou'ēr), *n.* the anemone.

wind in·stru·ment (wĭnd), a musical instrument, as, the flute, oboe, or clarinet, sounded by a current of air blown into it. The organ is also a wind instrument.

WINDLASS

wind·jam·mer (wĭnd'jăm'ēr), *n. Colloquial,* a sailing vessel.

wind·lass (wĭnd'lăs), *n.* a machine for hoisting or hauling; a winch.

OTTER

RABBIT

SQUIRREL

WEASEL

RED FOX

RACCOON

COYOTE

SKUNK

SABLE

MUSKRAT

BEAVER   MINK

All animals on this page are 1/12 natural size

Some of the Smaller Wild Animals. (*See other side.*)

SOME OF OUR SMALLER WILD ANIMALS

The animals pictured on the preceding page are among the best known of our smaller wild animals. They belong to various families, but all of them are *mammals*, or animals that suckle their young, and all are *carnivorous*, or flesh-eating, except the rabbit, squirrel, beaver, and muskrat, and the latter likes fresh-water clams and fish. Excepting the coyote, all have valuable fur—rabbit being the cheapest and sable the costliest.

The sable, mink, weasel, otter, and skunk belong to the weasel family. Nature has equipped the skunk with a scent sac of odoriferous fluid which the little black-and-white rascal can squirt with disgusting accuracy. When he raises that plumelike tail as if to say, "Stand still or else —," even a bear will stop. Skunks are found from Northern Canada to Central America. They prefer brushy creek bottoms, but can live at sea level or on mountains. They like to live near man's abode, and make their home under a house, in a hollow log, or in an abandoned burrow. The young remain with the parents until the next spring. Skunks hunt at night for mice, frogs, weasels, birds, and poultry.

The other members of the weasel family look much alike. All have long, round bodies, short legs, and pointed heads and are famous for their silky, dusky-brown fur. Weasels and sables are notorious killers. The weasel is said to be a perfect killing machine. Certainly he is blood-thirsty, for in one night's raid he will suck the warm blood of a dozen fowl. He also eats rats and mice. Weasels are found in Northern Europe and Asia, and in the United States. A close relative is the mink, a partially webfooted, aquatic little animal that feeds largely on fishes, but will eat small animals, eggs, and chickens. The otter is an entirely aquatic animal that lives along streams or lakes and is noted for its grace and agility in the water. On land it moves by leaps. Its home is a den in the bank of a stream; its food, fish. The sable does not kill just for sport as the weasel seems to do, but for food—and hate. He is cold and cruel even to his own, except during the mating season. After the young are born, he clears out, and if he meets one of his own kind, even his mate,

he fights to kill. If a pair are imprisoned together, the male often murders his cell mate by biting a hole in her skull. He is nervous, quick, and bold, but stupid about traps, so, although he lives in the deep North Woods, trappers find him easy prey. The sable lives mostly on minks, weasels, squirrels, frogs, fish, and beetles.

The raccoon, that fellow wearing a black mask, walks on the flat of his foot, like a bear, or a man. He prowls about at night in search of frogs, crayfish, birds, eggs, nuts or—green corn. He will risk his gray-and-black coat for a feast of green corn. Raccoons are found from Southern Canada to Mexico. They are easily tamed and make amusing pets.

To the dog family belong the red fox and the coyote. The fox is noted for his cunning, the coyote for his weird night howling. The fox chooses a life mate and the cubs, usually eight or nine, are carefully tended and trained. A fox eats mice, snakes, insects, and fowl. The coyote, really a prairie wolf, has neither the ferocity nor the size of the great timber wolf, yet he can run swiftly, outwit most of his enemies and out-howl all of them. The coyote lives on rabbits, prairie dogs, and rats, and raises a family of sometimes fourteen cubs.

The rodents are represented by the beaver, muskrat, rabbit, and squirrel. The beaver and muskrat have much in common. Both live along fresh water. Both dig underground passages, with underwater entrances, to their cone-shaped houses of clay and sticks. The beaver is, in equipment and intelligence, superior to the muskrat. A beaver builds dams, fells trees, constructs houses, digs canals, and stores up food for winter. This food consists of bark and tender twigs. The rabbit is a ground dweller and lives about old fields. His home is a burrow; his food, vegetables. In some places the rabbit is destructive to crops. The gray squirrel has long legs for leaping, paws for digging, and strong teeth for cracking nuts. In the "Big Top" of our great trees he is a star performer, leaping safely from limb to limb or running along slim branches high overhead. He makes his home and raises his young in a tree. For food he eats nuts, grain, maple buds, and acorns.

wind-mill (wĭnd′mĭl′), *n.* a mill operated by a large wheel whose oblique sails or vanes are turned as they catch the wind:— **to fight windmills,** to fight a fancied wrong or an imaginary opponent: so called because Don Quixote fought windmills, imagining they were giants.

win-dow (wĭn′dō), *n.* 1, an opening in the wall of a building, the side of an automobile or railroad car, etc., to let in light and air; 2, the framework and glass which fills such an opening.

win-dow-pane (wĭn′dō-pān′), *n.* one of the pieces of glass in the frame of a window.

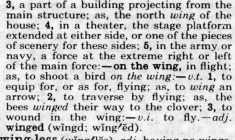

WINDMILLS
1, old Dutch windmill; 2, modern windmill for pumping water.

wind-pipe (wĭnd′pīp′), *n.* the trachea, or breathing tube, leading from the larynx to the lungs. (See illustration under *bronchi*.)

wind-row (wĭnd′rō′; wĭn′rō′), *n.* a long, low ridge of raked hay, or a row of sheaves of grain stacked in a line, and left to dry.

wind-shield (wĭnd′shēld′), *n.* a pane of glass attached to an automobile or airplane, in front of the seats, to shield the passengers from wind, rain, dust, etc.

Wind-sor Cas-tle (wĭn′zẽr), a residence of the King of England, near London.

Windsor, House of, the name of the royal house of England, adopted in 1917.

wind—swept (wĭnd′-swĕpt′), *adj.* blown clean or bare by steady winds; as, a *windswept* peak or plain.

wind-ward (wĭnd′wẽrd), *n.* the direction from which the wind is blowing:—*adj.* on the side from which the wind blows:—*adv.* toward the wind.

Wind-ward Is-lands, the islands forming the southern part of the Lesser Antilles, in the West Indies (map **10**).

wind-y (wĭn′dĭ), *adj.* [wind-i-er, wind-i-est], 1, characterized by winds; breezy; as, March is a *windy* month; also, exposed to the wind; as, the *windy* side of the house; 2, noisy, wordy, or boastful; as, a *windy* braggart.—*n.* wind′i-ness.

wine (wīn), *n.* 1, the fermented juice of grapes, used as a drink; 2, the fermented juice of other fruits or plants used similarly:—*v.t.* [wined, win-ing], to furnish or entertain with wine, as a guest.

wing (wĭng), *n.* 1, one of the broad, flat organs or parts of birds, insects, and bats, by means of which they fly; 2, one of the main supporting surfaces of an airplane;

3, a part of a building projecting from the main structure; as, the north *wing* of the house; 4, in a theater, the stage platform extended at either side, or one of the pieces of scenery for these sides; 5, in the army or navy, a force at the extreme right or left of the main force:—**on the wing,** in flight; as, to shoot a bird *on the wing*:—*v.t.* 1, to equip for, or as for, flying; as, to *wing* an arrow; 2, to traverse by flying; as, the bees *winged* their way to the clover; 3, to wound in the wing:—*v.i.* to fly.—*adj.* **winged** (wĭngd; wĭng′ĕd).

wing-less (wĭng′lĕs), *adj.* having no wings.

wink (wĭngk), *v.i.* 1, to close and open quickly one or both eyelids; blink; 2, to convey a hint or signal by a quick motion of one eyelid; 3, to keep oneself from seeing something; as, to *wink* at slight errors; 4, to twinkle; gleam at regular intervals, as the light of a lighthouse:—*v.t.* 1, to close and open quickly, as the eyelids; 2, to remove by winking; as, to *wink* the tears away:—*n.* 1, the act of winking; especially, the act of closing one eye for a moment as a signal; also, a hint or command thus given; 2, the time required for a wink; an instant; as, he came a *wink* too soon:—**forty winks,** a short nap.

win-ner (wĭn′ẽr), *n.* a person or thing that wins; a victor; hence, anything exceptionally good.

win-ning (wĭn′ĭng), *adj.* 1, successful, as in a competition; as, the *winning* horse; 2, attractive; charming; as, a *winning* personality:—*n.* 1, the act of gaining or conquering; 2, **winnings,** that which one gains; especially, money won in gambling.

Win-ni-peg (wĭn′ĭ-pĕg), 1, a city, capital of Manitoba province, Canada; 2, a large lake in Manitoba province, Canada. (Map **4**.)

win-now (wĭn′ō), *v.t.* 1, to blow chaff and refuse from (grain) by a current of air; 2, to sift; separate; as, to *winnow* truth from falsehood:—*v.i.* to separate chaff from grain by winnowing.—*n.* win′now-er.

win-some (wĭn′sŭm), *adj.* attractive; charming.—*adv.* win′some-ly.

Win-ston—Sa-lem (wĭn′stŭn-sā′lĕm), an industrial city in western North Carolina (map **8**).

win-ter (wĭn′tẽr), *n.* 1, the coldest season of the year; in any region, that one of the four seasons of the year when the sun shines least directly; in the Northern Hemisphere, the period from the winter solstice, about December 21, to the vernal equinox, about March 21; 2, any time, as of gloom or sorrow, suggesting winter; also, figuratively, a year of life:—*adj.* pertaining to winter:—*v.i.* to pass the months of the cold season; as, snakes *winter* in the ground:—*v.t.* to keep during the cold season; as, to *winter* cattle.

win-ter-green (wĭn′-tẽr-grēn′), *n.* **1**, a low-growing, woody, evergreen plant that bears white blossoms, pungent red berries, and leaves which yield an aromatic oil called *oil of wintergreen;* **2**, this oil; also, its flavor.

WINTERGREEN

win-try (wĭn′trĭ), *adj.* [win-tri-er, win-tri-est], pertaining to, or like, winter; cold; chilling; as, a *wintry* day; a *wintry* greeting.—*n.* **win′tri-ness.**

wipe (wīp), *v.t.* [wiped, wip-ing], **1**, to dry or cleanse by rubbing with something soft; as, to *wipe* dishes; to *wipe* furniture; **2**, to remove by rubbing; as, to *wipe* away tears; *wipe* off dirt:—**wipe out,** *Colloquial* to destroy utterly; as, the drought *wiped out* the crops:—*n.* the act of cleansing or rubbing.—*n.* **wip′er.**

wire (wīr), *n.* **1**, metal drawn out into a strand of comparatively small, often minute, diameter, usually flexible and of great length; **2**, such metal used, either singly or in cables, in telephone and telegraph systems; **3**, *Colloquial*, a telegram; as, to send a *wire:*—**to pull wires,** to use indirect influence in order to gain an end:—*v.t.* [wired, wir-ing], **1**, to bind, fit, or provide with wire; as, to *wire* a house for electricity; *wire* a broken chair together; **2**, *Colloquial*, to send (a message), or send a message to (a person), by telegraph; as, *wire* him to come.

wire-less (wīr′lĕs), *adj.* without the use of wires; as, *wireless* telegraphy or telephony:—*n.* a wireless telegraph or telephone system; as, to send news by *wireless;* also, a message transmitted thus:—*v.t.* (chiefly in British usage), to send (a message), or send a message to (a person), by wireless; to radio; as, they *wirelessed* the news of the discovery.

wir-y (wīr′ĭ), *adj.* [wir-i-er, wir-i-est], **1**, like wire; stiff; **2**, lean and slight, but sinewy; as, a *wiry* child.—*n.* **wir′i-ness.**

Wis. abbreviation for *Wisconsin.*

Wis-con-sin (wĭs-kŏn′sĭn), a north central State (cap. Madison) in the U.S. (map 7).

wis-dom (wĭz′dŭm), *n.* **1**, the ability to form sound judgments; common sense; **2**, learning; knowledge:—**wisdom tooth,** the third molar, or extreme back tooth, on each side in each jaw.

-wise (-wīz), a suffix indicating position, direction, manner, etc.; as, cross*wise,* clock*wise,* other*wise.*

¹wise (wīz), *adj.* [wis-er, wis-est], having knowledge and the ability to use it; having good judgment; sage:—**Three Wise Men,** the three Magi who came from the East bearing gifts for the infant Jesus.—*adv.* **wise′ly.**

²wise (wīz), *n.* way; manner; mode; as, in such *wise* it happened.

wise-a-cre (wīz′ā-kẽr), *n.* a stupid person who imagines he knows a great deal.

wish (wĭsh), *v.i.* to have a strong desire; as, I *wish* to stay; we *wish* for peace:—*v.t.* **1**, to desire; as, what do you *wish?* also, to express (a desire); as, I *wish* I had a dog; **2**, to express (a hope, etc.) for, or against, someone; as, to *wish* a person good fortune; also, to express (a greeting); as, I *wish* you good morning:—**to wish on someone,** to foist on someone; as, he *wished* an old car *on me:*—*n.* **1**, a strong or eager desire; **2**, the object or thing desired; as, popularity in school was his only *wish;* **3**, a request.—*n.* **wish′er.**

Syn., n. longing, yearning.

wish-bone (wĭsh′bōn′), *n.* in domestic fowl and other birds, the forked bone in front of the breastbone.

wish-ful (wĭsh′fŏŏl), *adj.* full of longing; desirous.

WISHBONE

wish-y-wash-y (wĭsh′ĭ-wŏsh′ĭ; -wôsh′ĭ), *adj.* weak; thin, as a diluted liquid; hence, of persons, weak; lacking in spirit and vigor.

wisp (wĭsp), *n.* **1**, a handful or small bundle, as of straw or hay; **2**, a thin fragment or bit, as of smoke, cotton, etc.

wist (wĭst), *Archaic,* past tense and past participle of ¹*wit.*

wis-ta-ri-a (wĭs-tā′rĭ-ȧ) or **wis-te-ri-a** (wĭs-tē′rĭ-ȧ), *n.* a climbing shrub of the pea family, with drooping clusters of lavender flowers.

WISTARIA

wist-ful (wĭst′fŏŏl), *adj.* pensive; longing; wishful; as, a *wistful* expression.—*adv.* **wist′-ful-ly.**—*n.* **wist′ful-ness.**

¹wit (wĭt), *v.t.* and *v.i.* [*sing.* I wot (wŏt; wôt), thou wot-test, he wot, *pl.* wite (wīt), *p.t.* and *p.p.* wist (wĭst), *p.pr.* wit-ting], *Archaic* or *Poetic,* to know:—**to wit,** namely; that is to say.

²wit (wĭt), *n.* **1**, wisdom; intelligence; as, he hasn't the *wit* to meet an emergency; **2**, **wits,** mental faculty or power; as, keep your *wits* about you; **3,** the ability quickly to perceive that which is odd or amusing in a situation or idea and to express it in an unexpected and amusing way; **4,** a person noted for this ability; also, the clever or brilliant things he says or writes: —**at one's wit's end,** at the end of one's mental resources; at a loss.

Syn. humor, shrewdness.

witch (wĭch), *n.* **1,** a woman supposed to have supernatural powers given her by the devil or by evil spirits; enchantress; **2,** an old crone; a hag; **3,** *Colloquial,* a charming young woman:—*v.t.* to bewitch; enchant.

witch-craft (wĭch'kràft'), *n.* dealings with evil spirits; sorcery; magic.

witch-er-y (wĭch'ẽr-ĭ), *n.* [*pl.* witcheries], **1,** fascination; compelling charm; **2,** witchcraft.

witch ha-zel (hā'zl), **1,** a shrub with small yellow flowers which appear after the leaves have gone; **2,** an extract from the bark of this shrub, used as a lotion.

witch-ing (wĭch'ĭng), *adj.* relating to witchcraft; weird; as, the *witching* hour.

with (wĭth; wĭth), *prep.* **1,** by the side of; as, put the glove *with* its mate; in the employ, association, or company of; as, he has been *with* the firm for years; favorable to; as, we have the wind *with* us; **2,** between oneself and another: as, we trade *with* England; **3,** in the care, keeping, or possession of; as, leave the child *with* me; **4,** characterized by; as, a man *with* a sad expression; **5,** by means of; as, slain *with* a dagger; **6,** in the state, condition, or manner of; as, he performed *with* ease; **7,** as a result of; as, to perish *with* hunger; **8,** in spite of; as, *with* all his learning, he was a fool; **9,** during; as, the river rose higher *with* every minute; at the same time as; as, he was up *with* the sun; **10,** from; as, we parted *with* our friends at noon; **11,** in opposition to; against; as, I played tennis *with* my brother.

with-al (wĭth-ôl'), *adv. Archaic,* moreover; likewise; as, a melancholy scene, impressive *withal.*

with-draw (wĭth-drô'; wĭth-drô'), *v.t.* [*p.t.* withdrew (-drōō'), *p.p.* withdrawn (-drôn'), *p.pr.* withdraw-ing], **1,** to remove; take away; as, the school *withdrew* its team from the tournament; **2,** to retract; take back; as, to *withdraw* a charge in court:—*v.i.* to leave; depart.

with-draw-al (wĭth-drô'ăl; wĭth-drô'ăl), *n.* a removal; also, a taking back; as, the *withdrawal* of a promise.

with-drew (wĭth-drōō'; wĭth-drōō'), past tense of *withdraw.*

withe (wĭth; wĭth; wĭth), *n.* a tough, flexible twig for tying or binding; a withy.

with-er (wĭth'ẽr), *v.t.* to cause to shrink, fade, droop, or decay:—*v.i.* to lose sap or juice; dry up or fade; languish.

with-ers (wĭth'ẽrz), *n.pl.* the part of a horse's back between the shoulder blades. (See illustration under *horse.*)

with-held (wĭth-hĕld'; wĭth-hĕld'), past tense and past participle of *withhold.*

with-hold (wĭth-hōld'; wĭth-hōld'), *v.t.* [withheld (wĭth-hĕld'; wĭth-hĕld'), with-hold-ing], **1,** to hold back, as from action; restrain; **2,** to keep back; refuse to give; as, to *withhold* payment.

with-in (wĭth-ĭn'), *adv.* **1,** in the inner part; inside; **2,** inwardly; **3,** in the house; indoors:—*prep.* **1,** inside of; **2,** in the limits of; as, *within* an hour; *within* hail.

with-out (wĭth-out'), *adv.* **1,** outside; **2,** outwardly; **3,** outdoors:—*prep.* **1,** outside of; **2,** beyond; as, *without* question; **3,** in the absence of; lacking in; as, *without* hope.

with-stand (wĭth-stănd'; wĭth-stănd'), *v.t.* [withstood (-stŏŏd'), withstand-ing], to oppose; resist; endure; as, to *withstand* a siege.

with-y (wĭth'ĭ; wĭth'ĭ), *n.* [*pl.* withies], a flexible willow twig used for tying or binding; a withe.

wit-less (wĭt'lĕs), *adj.* lacking sense or judgment; foolish; as, a *witless* remark.— *adv.* **wit'less-ly.**—*n.* **wit'less-ness.**

wit-ness (wĭt'nĕs), *n.* **1,** testimony; evidence; as, his friends bore *witness* to his good character; **2,** a person or thing that gives evidence; as, a receipted bill is *witness* that the bill has been paid; **3,** a person who tells in court under oath what he knows of a fact or event; **4,** one who puts his signature to a document to show that he has seen it signed; **5,** one who from actual presence knows of an occurrence: also called *eyewitness:*—*v.t.* **1,** to give evidence of, as in court; **2,** to reveal; betray; as, her startling pallor *witnessed* her sudden fear; **3,** to sign (a document) to indicate knowledge of another's signing; **4,** to see or know personally; as, to *witness* a performance of a play:—*v.i.* to testify.

wit-ti-cism (wĭt'ĭ-sĭzm), *n.* a witty remark; a clever saying.

wit-ting-ly (wĭt'ĭng-lĭ), *adv.* with knowledge; intentionally; as, I would not *wittingly* hurt your feelings.

wit-ty (wĭt'ĭ), *adj.* [wit-ti-er, wit-ti-est], **1,** having the faculty of arousing laughter by a clever and amusing way of expressing ideas; **2,** marked by wit.—*adv.* **wit'ti-ly.**— *n.* **wit'ti-ness.**

wive (wīv), *v.t.* and *v.i.* [wived, wiv-ing], *Archaic,* to marry.

wives (wīvz), plural of *wife.*

wiz-ard (wĭz′ẽrd), *n.* **1**, a magician; conjurer; **2**, *Colloquial*, a very clever person; as, a financial *wizard*.—*n.* **wiz′ard-ry**.

wiz-ened (wĭz′nd), *adj.* dried up; shriveled.

wk. [*pl.* wks.], abbreviation for *week*.

W. long. abbreviation for *west longitude*.

wob-ble (wŏb′l; wôb′l), *v.i.* [wob-bled, wob-bling], **1**, to move unsteadily from side to side; **2**, to be undecided in opinion or actions:—*v.t.* to cause to waver or totter:—*n.* a swaying motion. Also, **wab′ble**.—*adj.* **wob′bly**.

Wo-den or **Wo-dan** (wō′dn), *n.* in Germanic mythology, the chief of the gods: called by the Norse *Odin*.

woe or **wo** (wō), *n.* **1**, deep sorrow; inconsolable grief; **2**, the cause of sorrow or grief; an affliction.

woe-be-gone or **wo-be-gone** (wō′bē-gŏn′), *adj.* overwhelmed with woe; showing great grief or misery; as, a *woebegone* appearance.

woe-ful or **wo-ful** (wō′fŏŏl), *adj.* **1**, sorrowful; miserable; **2**, mean; paltry; wretched.—*adv.* **woe′ful-ly**.

woke (wōk), a past tense of ¹*wake*.

wold (wōld), *n.* an uncultivated, treeless tract of land; a down or moor.

wolf (wŏŏlf), *n.* [*pl.* wolves (wŏŏlvz)], **1**, a savage, flesh-eating animal of the dog family, usually a tawny gray in color, which hunts in packs, and preys on sheep and other animals; **2**, a fierce, greedy, or destructive person.

to keep the wolf from the door, to keep away want; **a wolf in sheep's clothing,** one who hides unfriendly intentions under a guise of friendliness.

Wolfe (wŏŏlf), James (1727–1759), an English general, famous for his victory at Quebec, in the French and Indian War.

wolf-hound (wŏŏlf′hound′), *n.* any of several breeds of tall, swift dogs, formerly used for hunting wolves.

wolf-ish (wŏŏl′fĭsh), *adj.* like a wolf; savage; hungry. — *n.* **wolf′ish-ness**.

wolfs-bane (wŏŏlfs′bān′), *n.* a European plant of the buttercup family; monkshood.

WOLVERINE (¹⁄₃₀)

wol-ver-ine or **wol-ver-ene** (wŏŏl′vẽr-ēn′), *n.* a ferocious, flesh-eating animal of Canada and the northern U.S., between two and three feet long, with a thick-set form and shaggy blackish fur.

wolves (wŏŏlvz), plural of *wolf*.

wom-an (wŏŏm′ăn), *n.* [*pl.* women (wĭm′ĕn)], **1**, an adult female of the human race; **2**, the female sex; **3**, a female servant.—*n.* **wom′an-hood**.—*adj.* **wom′an-ish**.

wom-an-kind (wŏŏm′ăn-kīnd′), *n.* the women of the human race.

wom-an-ly (wŏŏm′ăn-lĭ), *adj.* like, or befitting, a woman; feminine; as, *womanly* modesty.—*n.* **wom′an-li-ness**.

womb (wŏŏm), *n.* the organ which holds the young of mammals before birth.

WOMBAT (¹⁄₁₅)

wom-bat (wŏm′bat; wôm′băt), *n.* an Australian animal which carries its young in a pouch like the kangaroo and resembles a small bear.

wom-en (wĭm′ĕn), plural of *woman*.

¹**won** (wŭn), past tense and past participle of *win*.

²**won** (wän), *n.* a coin, the monetary unit of Korea. (See table, page 943.)

won-der (wŭn′dẽr), *n.* **1**, the state of mind produced by anything new, strange, unexpected, or surprising; astonishment; **2**, a cause of surprise; marvel; miracle:—**seven wonders of the world,** the seven most remarkable structures in ancient times: the Egyptian pyramids, the mausoleum erected by Artemisia at Halicarnassus, the temple of Artemis at Ephesus, the hanging gardens and the walls of Babylon, the Colossus at Rhodes, the statue of Zeus by Phidias at Olympia, and the Pharos, or lighthouse at Alexandria:—*v.i.* to feel surprise or amazement; be astonished; **2**, to feel doubt or curiosity; speculate:—*v.t.* to be doubtful about; have a desire to know; as, *I wonder* what I ought to do.—*n.* **won′der-ment**.

won-der-ful (wŭn′dẽr-fŏŏl), *adj.* astonishing; strange; marvelous.—*adv.* **won′der-ful-ly**.—*n.* **won′der-ful-ness**.

won-drous (wŭn′drŭs), *adj.* marvelous; remarkable.—*adv.* **won′drous-ly**.

wont (wŭnt; wōnt), *adj.* used or accustomed; as, she is *wont* to give much to charity:—*n.* habit or custom; as, he dined late, as was his *wont*.

won't (wōnt; wŭnt), *Colloquial*, a contracted form of *will not*.

wont-ed (wŭn′tĕd; wōn′tĕd), *adj.* habitual; customary; as, his *wonted* tasks.

woo (wŏŏ), *v.t.* **1**, to court or make love to; **2**, to coax; entreat; **3**, to seek; as, to *woo* success:—*v.i.* to go courting.

wood (wŏŏd), *n.* **1**, a large number of trees growing on an extensive tract of land; a grove or forest; **2**, the hard part of a tree under the bark; **3**, trees cut for firewood

āte, āorta, râre, căt, ȧsk, fär, ȧllow, sofȧ; ēve, ĕvent, ĕll, writẽr, novĕl; bīte, pĭn; nō, ōbey, ôr, dŏg, tŏp, cŏllide; ūnit, ūnite, bûrn, cŭt, focŭs; nŏŏn, fŏŏt; mound; coin;

or trimmed ready for use in building; lumber; timber; **4, woods,** used as *sing.* or *pl.*, a thick growth of trees; forest.

wood·bine (wŏŏd′bīn), *n.* any of several vines of the honeysuckle family, including the wild honeysuckle and the Virginia creeper.

wood·chuck (wŏŏd′chŭk′), *n.* a coarse-furred, grayish-brown animal of the rat family, about eighteen

WOODCHUCK (⅛)

inches long, which burrows in the ground and hibernates in winter, found in the U.S. and Canada: also called *ground hog.*

wood·cock (wŏŏd′kŏk′), *n.* a small brown game bird with a long, straight bill and a short, rounded tail.

WOODCOCK (¼)

wood·craft (wŏŏd′kráft′), *n.* knowledge of the woods and woodland life, together with skill in hunting, trapping, camping, etc.

wood·ed (wŏŏd′ĕd), *adj.* abounding in trees; as, a *wooded* slope.

wood·en (wŏŏd′n), *adj.* **1,** made or consisting of wood; as, a *wooden* bucket; **2,** stiff; awkward; as, a *wooden* pose; also, dull; spiritless; as, a *wooden* smile.

wood·land (wŏŏd′lănd′; wŏŏd′lănd), *n.* land covered with trees; a forest:—*adj.* peculiar to, or dwelling in, the woods.

wood louse, any of several small crustaceans which live on land and are found under old logs, stones, etc. (See *crustacean,* illustration.)

wood·peck·er (wŏŏd′pĕk′ẽr), *n.* a bird with feet and tail feathers adapted for climbing, and a strong beak for piercing the bark of trees for insects.

wood pe·wee, a small bird which resembles the phoebe, but lives in the woods and has a high-pitched, plaintive call.

woods·man (wŏŏdz′măn), *n.* [*pl.* woodsmen (-měn)], one who lives or works in the woods, as a hunter, trapper, or lumberman.

wood thrush, a migratory North American thrush with a bell-like note: also called *wood robin.*

wood winds, in an orchestra, the wooden wind instruments collectively, including oboe, bassoon, clarinet, English horn, flute, and piccolo. (See illustration under *musical instrument.*)

wood·work (wŏŏd′wûrk′), *n.* objects, or

parts of objects, made of wood; especially, the wooden finishings of a house, as stairways, doors, etc.—*n.* **wood′work′er.**

wood·y (wŏŏd′ĭ), *adj.* [wood-i-er, wood-i-est], **1,** covered with, or abounding in, woods; **2,** consisting of, or containing, wood; as, a *woody* shrub; **3,** like, or characteristic of, wood; as, a *woody* smell.

woo·er (wŏŏ′ẽr), *n.* a man who courts a woman; a suitor.

woof (wŏŏf), *n.* **1,** in weaving, the threads carried back and forth by the shuttle, as distinguished from *warp,* the threads fixed in the loom; **2,** the texture of a fabric.

wool (wŏŏl), *n.* **1,** the soft, curly coat of the sheep and some related animals; **2,** anything like the hair of sheep; **3,** yarn or cloth made of this hair.

wool·en (wŏŏl′ĕn), *adj.* **1,** made of sheep's hair; as, *woolen* blankets; **2,** pertaining to sheep's hair fabrics; as, a *woolen* manufacturer:—**woolens,** *n.pl.* cloth made of sheep's hair; also, garments made of such fabric. Also spelled **wool′len.**

wool-gath·er·ing (wŏŏl′găth′ẽr-ĭng), *n.* indulgence in idle dreaming.

wool·ly (wŏŏl′ĭ), *adj.* [wool-li-er, wool-li-est], consisting of, or like wool. Also, **wool′y.**

Worces·ter (wŏŏs′tẽr), a manufacturing city in eastern Massachusetts (map 6).

word (wûrd), *n.* **1,** a sound or combination of sounds used in any language as a symbol of an idea, and forming a grammatical part of speech; **2,** the printed or written letters or other characters which represent the spoken word; **3,** a brief speech; saying; remark; as, a *word* of praise; **4,** information; message; report; as, he received *word* of their arrival; **5,** a password; **6,** a command; **7,** a promise; as, to keep one's *word;* **8, words,** language used in anger; as, they had *words* yesterday:—*v.t.* to express in words; as, to *word* a message.

word·ing (wûr′dĭng), *n.* the manner in which anything is expressed in words.

word·less (wûrd′lĕs), *adj.* having nothing to say; without words.

Words·worth (wûrdz′wûrth), William (1770–1850), a great English poet.

word·y (wûr′dĭ), *adj.* [word-i-er, word-i-est], **1,** expressed in too many words; as, a *wordy* argument; **2,** using too many words; as, a *wordy* person.—*adv.* **word′i·ly.**—*n.* **word′i·ness.**

wore (wôr), past tense of *wear.*

work (wûrk), *v.i.* [worked (wûrkt) or, in certain meanings, wrought (rôt), work-ing], **1,** to put forth physical or mental effort; labor; toil; **2,** to be occupied in business; be employed; as, he *works* in the steel mill; **3,** to act, operate, or run; especially, to act effectively; as, the machine *works* well; **4,** to ferment, as liquors; **5,** to progress slowly or laboriously; as, the nail *worked* loose:—*v.t.* **1,** to operate, manage, or set in motion; as, to *work* a mine; **2,** to prepare for use; manipulate; as, to *work* the soil; **3,** to bring or move gradually or laboriously; as, he *worked* the stone into place; **4,** to perform, produce, or cause; as, he *wrought* marvelous cures; **5,** to make or fashion; also, to embroider; as, the metal was beautifully *wrought;* she *worked* the linen with fine stitches; **6,** to exact labor from; cause to labor, as horses; **7,** to solve; as, to *work,* or work out, a problem; **8,** to canvass in the interest of one's trade; as, a salesman *works* a town:—*n.* **1,** physical or mental effort directed to some end or purpose; toil; labor; **2,** occupation; employment; job; **3,** a task; undertaking; **4,** a product of mental or physical effort; as, the *works* of Shakespeare; **5,** manner or style of working; as, painstaking *work;* **6, works: a,** the moving parts of any machinery; as, the *works* of a watch; **b,** structures connected with engineering projects, as bridges, docks, dams, embankments, etc.; **c,** often used as *sing.,* a manufacturing plant or the like, with its contents, outbuildings, etc.; as, a dye *works.*—*n.* **work′er.**

Syn., n. labor, toil, drudgery.

work-a-ble (wûr′ka-bl), *adj.* **1,** practicable, as a plan; **2,** capable of being manipulated, as soil or putty.

work-day (wûrk′dā′), *n.* a day for labor, as distinguished from Sundays, holidays, etc.; also, the length of such a day.

work-house (wûrk′hous′), *n.* **1,** a house of correction in which petty offenders are confined at labor; **2,** a public institution where the able-bodied poor are supported and made to labor; a poorhouse.

work-ing (wûr′kĭng), *adj.* pertaining to or engaged in labor; as, *working* people:—*n.* functioning; method of operation; as, the *working* of an engine.

work-ing-man (wûr′kĭng-măn′), *n.* [*pl.* workingmen (-měn′)], a man who labors with his hands; a laboring man.—*n.fem.* **work′ing-wom′an.**

work-man (wûrk′măn), *n.* [*pl.* workmen (-měn)], a man who is employed in labor with his hands; especially, a skilled laborer; mechanic.—*adj.* **work′man-like′.**

work-man-ship (wûrk′măn-shĭp), *n.* **1,** the skill and methods of a workman; **2,** the finish or peculiar quality of anything made.

work-out (wûrk′out′), *n.* training or practice, usually in preparation for a contest; a trial; exercise.

world (wûrld), *n.* **1,** the earth with all living things and the traces of them, especially man and his works; **2,** any one of the planets or stars imagined as similar to the earth; as, are there other *worlds* than ours? **3,** some special branch of civilization; as, the Roman *world;* **4,** any separate system, state, or sphere of existence, conceived as a whole; as, the literary *world;* the *world* of dreams; **5,** the inhabitants of the earth and their affairs; especially, people in general as the bearers of public opinion; as, the *world* admired him; **6,** those people who are especially devoted to pleasure; also, material affairs as opposed to spiritual.

man of the world, a man who knows and is experienced in the ways of men, especially in the ways of fashionable living; **New World,** the Western Hemisphere; **Old World,** the Eastern Hemisphere.

world-ly (wûrld′lĭ), *adj.* [world-li-er, world-li-est], earthly; devoted to the pleasures and advantages of this life.

World War I, the war of 1914-19, which involved nearly all the important nations of the earth: also called *the Great War.*

World War II, the war of 1939-45, in which Germany, Italy, Japan, and their allies opposed most of the other nations.

world-wide (wûrld′-wīd′), *adj.* universal; extending to every part of the earth; as, *world-wide* renown.

worm (wûrm), *n.* **1,** any small, slender, creeping or crawling, legless animal, usually having a soft, hairless body, as an earthworm; **2,** any device resembling such an animal, as a short rotating screw, made to mesh with a worm wheel; **3,** an insignificant or contemptible person: used in scorn or disgust; **4, worms,** any illness due to worms living in the body:—**worm wheel,** a wheel fitted with teeth which gear with a short rotating screw, or worm:—*v.t.* to bring out, put in, or move along, by methods suggesting a worm's motion; as, to *worm* his secret from him; he *wormed* himself into favor.

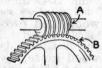

WORM, def. 2
A, worm; B, worm gear, or worm wheel.

worm-wood (wûrm′wŏŏd′), *n.* **1,** a plant of the aster family, used in the preparation of certain bitter liquors, and in medicine; **2,** hence, something distressing or bitter; as, the *wormwood* of remorse.

worm-y (wûr′mĭ), *adj.* [worm-i-er, worm-i-est], **1,** infested with worms; eaten by worms; **2,** like a worm.

worn (wôrn), past participle of *wear.*

worn—out (wôrn′-out′), *adj.* **1,** used until past repair; as, *worn-out* shoes; **2,** exhausted; **3,** hackneyed; as, a *worn-out* phrase.

wor-ri-some (wûr'ĭ-sŭm), *adj.* **1,** causing anxiety; troublesome; **2,** fretful.

wor-ry (wûr'ĭ), *v.t.* [worried, worry-ing], **1,** to shake, tear, or mangle with the teeth; as, the cat *worried* the mouse; **2,** to trouble; tease; harass; as, John *worried* his father:—*v.i.* to be anxious; fret; as, he *worried* about the safety of the children: —*n.* [*pl.* worries], anxiety; disturbance of mind.—*n.* **wor'ri-er.**

Syn., n. care, solicitude, concern.

worse (wûrs), *adj.* [*comp.* of *bad* or *ill*], **1,** more bad, ill, or evil; more extreme in degree; as, he's a *worse* liar than his brother; **2,** less well in health; sicker; as, the sick man is *worse:*—*adv.* [*comp.* of *badly* or *ill*], **1,** in a more evil or extreme manner; less well; as, John plays the piano *worse* than Peter; **2,** less; as, even *worse* suited to one business than to another:—*n.* a thing or state even more undesirable than another; as, the patient took a turn for the *worse.*

wor-ship (wûr'shĭp), *n.* **1,** the act of paying reverence, adoration, or homage, especially to God; **2,** excessive admiration; devotion; adoration; as, hero *worship:*— *v.t.* [worshiped, worship-ing], **1,** to adore or show honor to (a divinity); **2,** to admire excessively; idolize:—*v.i.* **1,** to perform religious service; **2,** feel excessive admiration.—*n.* **wor'ship-er.**

wor-ship-ful (wûr'shĭp-fŏŏl), *adj.* **1,** worthy of respect or honor; **2,** honorable: a title of respect used in formal address.

worst (wûrst), *adj.* [*superl.* of *bad* or *ill*], bad, evil, or ill in the highest degree:—*adv.* in the most bad or evil way; most extreme in degree; least well:—*n.* that which is most bad or evil; as, I'm afraid the *worst* has happened:—*v.t.* to defeat; as, our team *worsted* theirs.

wor-sted (wŏŏs'tĕd), *n.* **1,** a twisted yarn spun out of wool; also, the cloth made from such yarn; **2,** a softer woolen yarn, twisted little or not at all, used in knitting and embroidery.

worth (wûrth), *n.* **1,** excellence or desirable qualities; merit; as, a person of great *worth;* a gift of much *worth;* **2,** value as expressed in money; as, the *worth* of the chair is three dollars; **3,** personal wealth; as, his total *worth* is in the millions:— *adj.* **1,** meriting; as, *worth* attention; **2,** of the actual value of; as, *worth* the price; **3,** priced at; as, *worth* ten dollars; **4,** possessed of; as, he is *worth* a million dollars.

worth-less (wûrth'lĕs), *adj.* having no value, merit, or excellence; useless; as, a *worthless* person; a *worthless* play.

worth—while (wûrth'-hwīl'), *adj.* deserving or repaying the cost or trouble; as, a *worth-while* effort.

wor-thy (wûr'thĭ), *adj.* [wor-thi-er, wor-thi-est], **1,** having value or excellence; as, a *worthy* man; **2,** deserving; as, a *worthy* charity:—*n.* [*pl.* worthies], a person of distinction: often used humorously.— *adv.* **wor'thi-ly.**—*n.* **wor'thi-ness.**

wot (wŏt; wôt), *Archaic,* first and third person singular, present tense, of ¹*wit.*

would (wŏŏd), past tense of ²*will,* used to express: **1,** intention; as, he said he *would* go; **2,** determination; as, you *would* play, although you were told not to; **3,** expectation; as, he said you *would* return soon; **4,** wish; as, I *would* spring were here; **5,** custom or habit; as, he *would* come to see us every day.

would-n't (wŏŏd'nt), a contraction of *would not.*

¹**wound** (wŏŏnd; *Archaic,* wound), *n.* **1,** a hurt or injury caused by violence; a cut; stab; as, he had a bullet *wound* in his foot; **2,** an injury to one's feelings or good name:—*v.t.* to hurt by violence; cut; slash; also, to hurt the feelings of.

²**wound** (wound), past tense and past participle of ²*wind* and ³*wind.*

wove (wōv), past tense and one form of the past participle of *weave.*

wo-ven (wō'vĕn), a past participle of *weave.*

wrack (răk), *n.* **1,** wreck; ruin: now used only in the phrase *wrack and ruin:* also spelled *rack;* **2,** seaweed, etc., cast ashore by the sea.

wraith (rāth), *n.* the ghostly image of a person, supposed to be seen just before or just after his death; hence, a specter.

wran-gle (răng'gl), *v.i.* [wran-gled, wran-gling], to dispute noisily:—*n.* a noisy, angry dispute.—*n.* **wran'gler.**

wrap (răp), *v.t.* [wrapped, wrap-ping], **1,** to roll or fold around something; as, *wrap* the blanket around the child; **2,** to envelop; conceal by enveloping with something; as, Mary *wrapped* her doll in a towel; **3,** to do up securely; as, *wrap* the book in paper: —**wrapped up in,** intensely interested in; as, *wrapped up in* music:—*n.* **1,** an article of dress to be folded around a person; **2,** **wraps,** outer garments, such as coats.

wrap-per (răp'ẽr), *n.* **1,** a person or thing which enfolds or covers; as, a candy *wrapper;* **2,** a loose garment resembling a dressing gown, worn indoors by women.

wrap-ping (răp'ĭng), *n.* covering, as for a package, parcel, bundle, or the like.

wrath (răth), *n.* **1,** rage; deep indignation; violent anger; fury; **2,** punishment; vengeance.

wrath-ful (răth'fŏŏl), *adj.* deeply angry; furious; raging.

wreak (rēk), *v.t.* to give rein to; inflict; as, he *wreaked* his fury on the dog.

wreath (rēth), *n.* [*pl.* wreaths (rēthz)], **1**, flowers or leaves wound or twined into a circular band; a garland or chaplet; **2**, something curled or twisted into circular form.

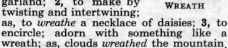

WREATH

wreathe (rēth), *v.t.* [wreathed, wreath-ing], **1**, to give a turned or twisted form to; as, to *wreathe* a garland; **2**, to make by twisting and intertwining; as, to *wreathe* a necklace of daisies; **3**, to encircle; adorn with something like a wreath; as, clouds *wreathed* the mountain.

wreck (rĕk), *n.* **1**, destruction by collision, fire, storm, etc.; especially, the destruction of a vessel afloat; shipwreck; **2**, anything that has been ruined or disabled, as a ship, automobile, house, etc.:—*v.t.* **1**, to ruin or disable by violence; as, the accident *wrecked* his health; **2**, to involve in destruction or ruin; **3**, to dismantle; as, to *wreck* a building.

wreck-age (rĕk′ĭj), *n.* the remains of a destroyed ship, train, building, etc.

wreck-er (rĕk′ẽr), *n.* **1**, one who causes destruction or ruin; **2**, a person or vessel employed to recover wrecked vessels or goods; **3**, *Colloquial*, a train or car with apparatus for clearing away wreckage; **4**, one whose work is tearing down old buildings.

wren (rĕn), *n.* a small, brown, singing bird with a short, perky, erect tail.

wrench (rĕnch), *n.* **1**, a violent turn; a sideways pull or twist; **2**, a sprain, as at a joint; **3**, a pang; a sudden distressed feeling; **4**, a tool for grasping and turning nuts, bolts, etc.:—*v.t.* **1**, to twist; wring or pull sideways with effort; wrest; as, to *wrench* the top off a box; **2**, to twist; sprain; as, she *wrenched* her ankle.

WRENCHES
1, S wrench; 2, monkey wrench; 3, pipe wrench.

wrest (rĕst), *v.t.* to turn or wrench, especially from a normal state; pull or take away by force or violence; as, he *wrested* the football from my arms.

wres-tle (rĕs′l), *v.i.* [wres-tled, wres-tling], **1**, to grapple with an opponent in an effort to force him to the ground; **2**, to struggle; strive earnestly, especially with something difficult; as, to *wrestle* with arithmetic: —*n.* a wrestling match; also, a hard struggle. —*n.* **wres′tler.**—*n.* **wres′tling.**

wretch (rĕch), *n.* **1**, an unfortunate or miserable person; **2**, a mean, contemptible person.

wretch-ed (rĕch′ĕd), *adj.* **1**, miserable; unhappy; **2**, causing misery; as, *wretched* health; **3**, mean; as, a *wretched* hovel; **4**, poor; as, *wretched* work.

wretch-ed-ness (rĕch′ĕd-nĕs), *n.* misery; unhappiness.

wrig-gle (rĭg′l), *v.i.* [wrig-gled, wrig-gling], **1**, to move by twisting and turning; squirm; as, the pupils *wriggled* in their seats; **2**, hence, to proceed by trickery or underhand means; as, to *wriggle* out of a lie:—*n.* the act of twisting or squirming; a squirming motion.—*n.* **wrig′gler.**

wright (rīt), *n.* a workman; one who makes something; as, a ship*wright*, a play*wright*.

Wright (rīt), Orville (1871–1948) and Wilbur (1867–1912), his brother, American aviators and inventors.

wring (rĭng), *v.t.* [wrung (rŭng), wring-ing], **1**, to twist and squeeze; as, to *wring* wet clothes; **2**, to force out by twisting or pressure; extort; as, to *wring* water from clothes; to *wring* a confession; **3**, to give pain to, as if by twisting; distress.

wring-er (rĭng′ẽr), *n.* **1**, a person or thing that twists, strains, etc.; **2**, a machine which squeezes water from clothes after they are washed.

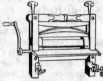

WRINGER, def. 2

[1]**wrin-kle** (rĭng′kl), *n.* a slight ridge or crease caused by folding, puckering, or rumpling:—*v.t.*[wrin-kled, wrin-kling], to form small ridges or creases in; pucker; as, the rain *wrinkled* his suit:— *v.i.* to become creased; as, my dress *wrinkles* easily.—*adj.* **wrin′kly.**

[2]**wrin-kle** (rĭng′kl), *n. Colloquial*, a valuable hint; clever device; good idea.

wrist (rĭst), *n.* the joint between the hand and forearm.

wrist-band (rĭst′bănd′; rĭst′bănd; rĭz′-bănd), *n.* the part of a sleeve, especially of a shirt sleeve, that covers the wrist.

[1]**writ** (rĭt), *n.* **1**, anything written: mainly applied to Scripture; as, Holy *Writ;* **2**, a written order of a court of justice.

[2]**writ** (rĭt), *Archaic*, past tense and past participle of *write.*

write (rīt), *v.t.* [*p.t.* wrote (rōt) or, *Archaic*, writ (rĭt), *p.p.* writ-ten (rĭt′n) or, *Archaic*, writ, *p.pr.* writ-ing], **1**, to trace, as letters, etc., on a surface with an instrument, as a, pen, pencil, etc.; **2**, to express in words or characters on paper with a pen or

āte, āorta, râre, căt, ásk, fär, ăllow, sofà; ēve, ĕvent, ĕll, writĕr, novĕl; bīte, pĭn; nō, ōbey, ôr, dŏg, tŏp, cŏllide; ūnit, ûnite, bûrn, cŭt, focŭs; nōōn, fŏŏt; mound; coin;

pencil; as, to *write* one's name; **3,** to produce as an author; compose; as, he *wrote* a book of adventure; **4,** to leave traces on; as, trouble is *written* on his face; **5,** to compose and send a letter to; as, I *wrote* my sister today:—*v.i.* **1,** to form letters, as with a pen; **2,** to compose; write books or the like; **3,** to communicate by letter.

writ-er (rīt′ẽr), *n.* **1,** one who writes; as, the *writer* of this letter is known to me; **2,** a person whose occupation in life is writing; as, Mark Twain was a versatile *writer*.

write–up (rīt′-ŭp′), *n.* a written account or record, as of an event.

writhe (rīth), *v.i.* [writhed, writh-ing], to squirm or twist, as from acute pain or distress; also, to be shamed or bitterly annoyed; as, to *writhe* at an insult.

writ-ing (rī′tĭng), *n.* **1,** the act of forming letters with a pen, pencil, etc., as on paper; **2,** that which is so set down, as an essay; **3,** the art of literary production; **4,** **writings,** things written; literary work; as, his *writings* include poetry and prose.

writ-ten (rĭt′n), past participle of *write*.

Wroc-law (vrôts′läf), a city in Poland on the Oder River. See **Breslau.**

wrong (rông), *adj.* **1,** not morally right or just; wicked; as, it is *wrong* to cheat; **2,** not according to fact; incorrect; as, he gave me the *wrong* directions; **3,** amiss; out of order; as, the clock is *wrong;* **4,** contrary to law; illegal; **5,** of a side of a piece of cloth, garment, etc., meant to be turned away from view:—*n.* that which is con-trary to moral right, fact, principles, intention, etc.; evil; injury; crime: opposite of *right;* as, you are in the *wrong:*—*adv.* **1,** in a manner not right morally; as, to go *wrong;* **2,** incorrectly; as, to guess *wrong:*—*v.t.* to treat unjustly; harm.—*adv.* **wrong′ly.**

wrong-do-er (rông′dōō ẽr; rông dōō′ẽr), *n.* one who does evil; an offender against the law.—*n.* **wrong′do′ing.**

wrong-ful (rông′fool), *adj.* evil; injurious; unjust.—*adv.* **wrong′ful-ly.**

wrong-head-ed (rông′hĕd′ĕd), *adj.* stubborn in sticking to incorrect opinions.

wrote (rōt), past tense of *write*.

wroth (rôth), *adj.* wrathful; indignant.

wrought (rôt), a past tense and past participle of *work:*—*adj.* worked; fashioned or molded from the rough; as, *wrought* silver: —**wrought iron,** iron of low carbon content, tough, and easily drawn out into wire or hammered into shape.

wrung (rŭng), past tense and past participle of *wring*.

wry (rī), *adj.* [wri-er, wri-est], twisted out of shape; as, a *wry* mouth.—*adv.* **wry′ly.**

wt. abbreviation for *weight*.

Würt-tem-berg (vür′tĕm-bĕrkh), a state (cap. Stuttgart) in southwestern Germany.

W. Va. abbreviation for *West Virginia*.

Wyo. or **Wy.** abbreviation for *Wyoming*.

Wy-o-ming (wī-ō′mĭng; wĭ′ō-mĭng), a western State (cap. Cheyenne) of the U.S. (map **9**).

X

X, x (ĕks), *n.* [*pl.* X's, x's], **1,** the 24th letter of the alphabet, following W; **2,** the Roman numeral for ten.

Xan-thip-pe (zăn-tĭp′ē), the wife of Socrates, noted for her scolding temper.

Xav-i-er (zăv′ĭ-ẽr), Saint Francis (1506–1552), a Jesuit missionary.

xe-bec (zē′bĕk), *n.* an old type of three-masted sailing ship.

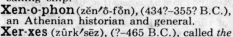

XEBEC

Xen-o-phon (zĕn′ō-fŏn), (434?–355? B.C.), an Athenian historian and general.

Xer-xes (zûrk′sēz), (?–465 B.C.), called *the Great,* a king of Persia.

Xmas. abbreviation for *Christmas*.

X ray (ĕks rā), **1,** a ray produced by an electric discharge in a vacuum tube, now known to be similar to a light ray, but of very short wave length, capable of penetrating many substances, as the human body, which ordinary light rays cannot penetrate: also called *Roentgen ray* or *Röntgen ray;* **2,** a photograph, as of an internal diseased part of the human body, of a bone fracture, etc., made with the aid of such rays.

xy-lem (zī′lĕm), *n.* the woody tissue of plants.

xy-lo-phone (zī′lō-fōn; zĭl′ō-fōn), *n.* a musical instrument

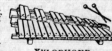

XYLOPHONE

of great antiquity, made of parallel wooden bars of graduated length which are struck with two small, flexible, wooden mallets.

Y

Y, y (wī), *n.* [*pl.* Y's, y's], the 25th letter of the alphabet, following X.

y. abbreviation for *year.*

¹-y (-ē), a suffix meaning: **1,** similar to; containing; as, silk*y*, thorn*y;* **2,** little; as, doll*y*, ladd*y*.

²-y (-ē), a suffix meaning the result of; as, dowr*y*, treat*y*.

³-y (-ē), a suffix meaning the state or quality of; as, honest*y*.

yacht (yŏt), *n.* a light vessel, propelled by sails, steam, or electricity, used for pleasure or racing:—*v.i.* to sail in a yacht.—*n.* **yacht′ing.**

yak (yăk), *n.* a wild or domesticated ox of central Asia, with a hump and with long hair hanging from its shoulders, sides, and tail.

YAK (⅒)

Yale (yāl), *n.* a university situated at New Haven, Connecticut.

Ya-lu (yä′lü′), a river between Manchuria and Korea, flowing into the Yellow Sea.

yam (yăm), *n.* **1,** a tropical vine with edible, potatolike roots; also, the root; **2,** in the southern U.S., a kind of sweet potato.

Yang-tze (yäng′tsĕ′) or **Yang-tze Kiang** (kyäng′; jyäng′), a great river in China, flowing into the East China Sea (map 15).

yank (yăngk), *v.t. Colloquial,* to jerk or pull quickly; as, to *yank* a coat from a hook:—*n. Colloquial,* a hard, sudden pull.

Yan-kee (yăng′kē), *n.* **1,** a citizen of New England; in Great Britain, a native of the U.S.; **2,** a Northerner:—*adj.* relating to, or like, Yankees.

yap (yăp; yȧp), *v.i.* [yapped, yap-ping], to bark or yelp:—*n.* a bark or yelp.

Yap (yäp), an island in the western Pacific, formerly under Japanese mandate (map 16).

¹yard (yärd), *n.* **1,** the standard unit of linear measure, equal to three feet, or 36 inches; **2,** a measuring rod of 36 inches; yardstick; **3,** a slender spar slung crosswise to a mast, used to support a sail (see illustration, page 695).—*n.* **yard′stick′.**

²yard (yärd), *n.* **1,** a small piece of enclosed ground beside or around a building; as, a front *yard;* **2,** a space, often enclosed, where a specific kind of work is carried on; as, a railroad *yard.*

yard-arm (yärd′ärm′), *n.* either end of a yard that supports a square sail.

yarn (yärn), *n.* **1,** a spun thread; especially, thread used for weaving, or heavy woolen thread used for knitting; **2,** *Colloquial,* an exaggerated story.

Yar-row (yăr′ō), a small river in southern Scotland, famous in song.

yar-row (yăr′ō), *n.* a plant having a strong smell and taste, bearing small white flowers and finely divided leaves.

YARROW

yaw (yô), *v.i.* of a ship or an airplane, to fail to hold a steady course; also, of a pilot, to steer off the straight line of a course:—*n.* a temporary change from a straight course, as of a ship or an airplane.

yawl (yôl), *n.* **1,** a two-masted, fore-and-aft rigged sailing vessel with the smaller mast aft of the rudder post; **2,** a ship's small boat.

YAWL

yawn (yôn), *n.* an unintentional opening of the jaws, as from sleepiness:—*v.i.* **1,** to open the mouth wide, as from hunger, surprise, etc.; **2,** especially, to open the mouth unintentionally as wide as possible while inhaling deeply, as the result of sleepiness or boredom; **3,** to open wide; as, the mouth of a cave *yawned* before us.

y-clept or **y-cleped** (ĭ-klĕpt′), *adj. Archaic,* named; as, a knight *y-clept* Galahad.

yd. abbreviation for *yard.*

ye (yē), *pron. Archaic* and *Poetic,* a nominative plural form of *you.*

yea (yā), *adv. Archaic,* yes; indeed; truly: —*n.* (now usually *aye*), an affirmative vote.

year (yēr), *n.* **1,** the length of time it takes the earth to make one complete revolution around the sun, or 365 days, 5 hours, 48 minutes, and 46 seconds; **2,** a period of twelve months, consisting of 365 days, or, in the case of leap year, 366 days; **3,** a period of time, usually less than a year, devoted to some particular activity; as, the college *year.*

āte, ȧorta, râre, căt, ȧsk, fär, ăllow, sofȧ; ēve, ȇvent, ĕll, wrītẽr, nŏvĕl; bīte, pĭn; nō, ōbey, ôr, dôg, tŏp, cŏllide; ūnit, ūnite, bûrn, cŭt, focŭs; nōōn, fŏŏt; mound; coin;

year-book (yēr/bŏŏk/), *n.* **1**, a book giving facts about the current year, such as its seasons, holidays, etc.; **2**, a book either published or revised annually, each issue containing new information.

year-ling (yēr/lǐng; yûr/lǐng), *n.* an animal between one and two years old:—*adj.* one year old; of a year's duration.

year-ly (yēr/lǐ; yûr/lǐ), *adj.* **1**, occurring once a year or every year; as, a *yearly* visit; **2**, by the year; as, a *yearly* rent; **3**, for a year; as, a *yearly* lease.

yearn (yûrn), *v.i.* to be filled with longing, compassion, or tenderness; as, to *yearn* for rest; *yearn* over a child.

yeast (yēst), *n.* a growth of minute cells, causing fermentation in sugar solutions and starchy substances, used in making beer, and in causing bread dough to rise.

yell (yĕl), *n.* **1**, a sharp, loud cry, as of pain, rage, or terror; a shriek; **2**, a characteristic shout, as used in warfare or by a group of persons; as, a college *yell*:—*v.t.* to cry out loudly; as, to *yell* defiance:—*v.i.* to cry out, as with pain.

yel-low (yĕl/ō), *adj.* **1**, of the color of gold, buttercups, etc.; **2**, cowardly; mean; dishonorable; as, that boy has a *yellow* streak; **3**, melodramatic; sensational; as, a *yellow* newspaper:—*n.* **1**, a bright elementary color, between orange and green; **2**, any dye or paint that gives this color; **3**, the yolk of an egg.

yel-low fe-ver, a dangerous, infectious fever of the tropics, marked by a yellow skin, vomiting, etc., and carried to man by the bite of a certain species of mosquito.

yel-low-ish (yĕl/ō-ĭsh), *adj.* colored somewhat like yellow; having a yellow tinge.

yellow jack, **1**, yellow fever; **2**, the yellow quarantine flag of all nations; **3**, a West Indian golden and silvery food fish.

yel-low jack-et, any of several American wasps, with a black abdomen marked with yellow: often called *hornet*. Wasps live in colonies; one kind builds nests of a paper-like material; others nest in the ground.

Yel-low Riv-er, a river in China. See **Hwang Ho.**

Yellow Sea, an inlet of the Pacific Ocean. See **Hwang Hai.**

YELLOW JACKET

Yel-low-stone Na-tion-al Park (yĕl/ō-stōn/), the largest U.S. national park, most of it in northwestern Wyoming, famous for its scenery (map 9).

yelp (yĕlp), *v.i.* to utter a sharp bark, as a dog when hurt:—*n.* a sharp, quick bark.

yen (yĕn), *n.* the monetary unit of Japan, (see Table, page 943); also, a gold or silver coin of this value.

yeo-man (yō/măn), *n.* [*pl.* yeomen (-mĕn)], **1**, in England, a soldier of the royal bodyguard; **2**, in England, a small landowner; **3**, in the U.S. Navy, a petty officer with clerical duties.

yeo-man-ry (yō/măn-rǐ), *n.* **1**, yeomen collectively; **2**, in England, the common people, especially the farming class.

yes (yĕs), *adv.* **1**, it is so: the affirmative answer to a question, opposite of *no;* **2**, furthermore; more than this; as, he is strong, yes, very strong.

yes-ter (yĕs/tẽr), *adj.* pertaining to a period of time just past: usually in compounds; as, *yester*year; *yester*morn.

yes-ter-day (yĕs/tẽr-dǐ; yĕs/tẽr-dā), *n.* **1**, the day before today; **2**, hence, a recent day; as, it seems only *yesterday* that we came:—*adv.* on the day before today.

yes-ter-night (yĕs/tẽr-nīt/), *n.* the night before tonight:—*adv.* on the night before tonight.

yet (yĕt), *adv.* **1**, up until now; as, he has not come *yet;* **2**, now as previously; still; as, I have your present *yet;* **3**, even; still; besides; as, more important *yet;* **4**, sooner or later; as, the day will *yet* come; **5**, even though this is so; as, *yet* I cannot understand:—*conj.* **1**, nevertheless; however; **2**, although; though.

yew (yū), *n.* **1**, a large, cone-bearing, evergreen tree of the Old World, with dark-green leaves; also, its fine-grained wood, used for making bows; **2**, a small evergreen tree of Pacific North America; **3**, a dwarf evergreen shrub of the eastern U.S.

Yez-o (yĕz/ō), the former name of an island in Japan. See **Hokkaido.**

Yid-dish (yĭd/ĭsh), *n.* a kind of German dialect, differing slightly in different countries, spoken by Jews and written or printed in Hebrew characters.

yield (yēld), *v.t.* **1**, to produce; as, the land *yields* wheat; **2**, to concede; as, I *yield* the point; **3**, to surrender; **4**, to afford; permit; as, to *yield* space; **5**, to give as return for labor, money invested, etc.:—*v.i.* **1**, to assent; comply; **2**, to give way; submit; **3**, to give a return; produce:—*n.* the return for labor expended or for capital invested.

yield-ing (yēl/dǐng), *adj.* **1**, easily bent; **2**, inclined to give way; submissive.

Y. M. C. A. abbreviation for *Young Men's Christian Association.*

yo-del (yō/dl), *v.t.* and *v.i.* [yodeled, yo-del-ing], to sing or call with sudden changes in the voice from chest tones to falsetto:—*n.* a call or song so sung. Also spelled **yo′dle.**

yoke (yōk), *n.* **1,** a wooden frame to couple together draft animals, especially oxen, for work; **2,** two animals so coupled together; as, a *yoke* of oxen; **3,** a frame of wood fitted to a person's shoulders,

YOKE, def. 1

for carrying buckets hung from each end; **4,** the upper part of a garment made to fit the neck and shoulders; also, the upper part of a skirt made to fit the hips; **5,** that which binds; a bond or tie; **6,** hence, bondage; as, the *yoke* of slavery:—*v.t.* [yoked, yok-ing], **1,** to put a yoke on; as, to *yoke* oxen; **2,** to couple or link.

YOKE (Y) OF A DRESS

yoke-fel-low (yōk′fĕl′ō), *n.* a person bound to another by some tie, especially by marriage; hence, a husband or a wife; also, an associate in work.

yo-kel (yō′kĕl), *n.* a country fellow.

Yo-ko-ha-ma (yō′kō-hä′mä), a seaport on the southeast coast of Japan (map 15).

yolk (yōk; yōlk), *n.* the yellow part of an egg, surrounded by the white.

yon (yŏn), *adj.* and *adv. Poetic,* yonder.

yon-der (yŏn′dẽr), *adj.* **1,** situated at a distance, but in sight; over there; as, *yonder* hills; **2,** more distant; as, the *yonder* side of the valley:—*adv.* at that place; there; as, situated *yonder.*

Yon-kers (yŏng′kẽrz), a city on the Hudson River, in New York (map 6).

yore (yôr), *n.* time long since past; as, days of *yore.*

York (yôrk), a city in north central England, noted for its cathedral (map 13).

York, House of, an English royal house, 1461–1485, the rival of the House of Lancaster in the Wars of the Roses.

York-shire (yôrk′shĭr; yôrk′shẽr) or **York,** a large county in northern England.

York-town (yôrk′toun), a town in Virginia, on the Chesapeake Bay, the scene of the surrender of Lord Cornwallis in 1781.

Yo-sem-i-te (yō-sĕm′ĭ-tē), a large national park in east central California (map 9).

you (yū), *pron.* the second person of the personal pronoun (*sing.* or *pl.,* but always taking a plural verb), [*nominative* you, *possessive* your, yours, *objective* you], **1,** the person or persons spoken to; as, how are *you?* **2,** one; anyone; a person; people; as, *you* pay when *you* leave.

young (yŭng), *adj.* **1,** being in the early part of life or growth; as, a father with his *young* son; **2,** vigorous; fresh; strong; as, old in body, but *young* in heart:—*n.* **1,** those who are young; as, *young* and old came to hear him; **2,** the offspring of animals; as, a wolf with its *young.*

young-ling (yŭng′lĭng), *n.* a person in early years; also, a young animal or plant.

young-ster (yŭng′stẽr), *n.* a person in early years; a child or youth; a lad.

Youngs-town (yŭngz′toun), a manufacturing city in northeastern Ohio (map 7).

your (yŏor), *adj.* a possessive form of the personal pronoun *you:* **1,** belonging to you; as, *your* coat; **2,** coming from, or relating to, you; as, *your* kindness.

yours (yŏorz), a possessive form of the personal pronoun *you,* used alone: **1,** as *adj.,* in the predicate, belonging or relating to you; as, whose is this glass? it is *yours;* **2,** as *pron.,* a person or thing that belongs to you; as, which car shall we use? let's take *yours.*

your-self (yŏor-sĕlf′), *pron.* [*pl.* yourselves (-sĕlvz′)], **1,** a reflexive form of *you;* as, you fooled *yourself;* **2,** an emphatic form of *you;* as, you *yourself* must go.

youth (yūth), *n.* [*pl.* youths (yūths; yū_th_z)], **1,** the state or quality of being young; **2,** the time of life between childhood and maturity; **3,** a young man; **4,** young people; as, the *youth* of a nation.

youth-ful (yūth′fŏol), *adj.* **1,** not old; as, a *youthful* person; **2,** pertaining or fitting to youth; as, *youthful* pleasures.

yowl (youl), *n.* a howl; a long, wailing cry, as of a cat:—*v.i.* to howl or yell.

Ypres (ēpr′; ē′prĕz), a town in Belgium, scene of many battles in World War I.

yr. abbreviation for *year.*

yu-an (yü-än′), *n.* [*pl.* yuan], the monetary unit of the Chinese Republic: also called *yuan dollar.* (See table, page 943.)

Yu-ca-tán (yōo′kä-tän′), **1,** a peninsula in southeastern Mexico, extending north into the Gulf of Mexico; **2,** a state (cap. Mérida) in southeastern Mexico. (Map 10.)

yuc-ca (yŭk′å), *n.* a plant of the lily family, having long, pointed leaves and white flowers; also, the flowers.

YUCCA

Yu-go-slav (yōo′gō-släv′; yōo′gō-släv′), *n.* a native or a citizen of Yugoslavia; also, the language of Yugoslavia:—*adj.* pertaining to Yugoslavia, its language, or its people. Also spelled **Ju·go-slav′** (yōo′gŏ-).

Yu·go-sla-vi-a (yōo′gŏ-slä′vĭ·á), a republic (cap. Belgrade) in southeastern Europe (map **12**). It was a kingdom until 1945. Also spelled **Ju′go-sla′vi·a** (yōo′-gŏ-).

Yu-kon (yōo′kŏn), **1,** a territory in northwestern Canada (map **4**); **2,** a river in Canada and Alaska, flowing into the Pacific (map **3**).

yule (yūl), *n.* Christmas or the Christmas feast:—**yule log,** a huge log brought indoors for an open fire on Christmas Eve.

yule-tide (yūl′tīd′), *n.* Christmas time.

Yün-nan (yōon′nän′; yün′nän′), a province (cap. Kun·ming) in southwestern China.

BRINGING IN THE YULE LOG

Y. W. C. A. abbreviation for *Young Women's Christian Association.*

Z

Z, z (zē), *n.* [*pl.* Z's, z's], the 26th letter of the alphabet, following Y.

Za-greb (zä′grĕb), an industrial town in northern Yugoslavia (map **12**). Its German name is *Agram.*

Zam-be-zi (zăm-bē′zĭ; zàm-bā′zē), a river in south central Africa, flowing into the Indian Ocean (map **21**).

za-ny (zā′nĭ), *n.* [*pl.* zanies], **1,** a fool or clown; buffoon; **2,** a stupid person.

Zan-zi-bar (zăn′zĭ-bär′; zăn′zĭ-bär′), a city, situated on an island of the same name off the east coast of Africa (map **21**). It is under British control.

Za-ra-thus-tra (zä′rà-thōos′trà), a Persian prophet. See **Zoroaster.**

zeal (zēl), *n.* ardor; great earnestness.

Zea-land (zē′-lănd), a large island forming a part of Denmark. On it is located Copenhagen, the capital of Denmark.

ZEBRA (⅙₀)

zeal-ot (zĕl′ŭt), *n.* an enthusiast; a person of too great zeal.

zeal-ous (zĕl′ŭs), *adj.* eager; enthusiastic.—*adv.* zeal′ous-ly.

Zeb-e-dee (zĕb′ē-dē), in the Bible, the father of the apostles James and John.

ze-bra (zē′brà), *n.* an African wild animal belonging to the horse family, especially one with dark stripes on a white or tawny body.

ZEBU (¼)

ze-bu (zē′bū), *n.* a domestic animal of India with long ears, short horns, and a large hump on the shoulders.

Zech-a-ri-ah (zĕk′à-rī′à), in the Bible, a Hebrew prophet; also, a book of the Old Testament.

zed (zĕd), *n.* the English name for Z.

ze-nith (zē′nĭth), *n.* **1,** that part of the heavens directly above the place where one stands: opposite of *nadir;* **2,** the greatest height.

Ze-no (zē′nō), (third century B.C.), a Greek philosopher, founder of the Stoic school of philosophy.

Zeph-a-ni-ah (zĕf′à-nī′à), in the Bible, a Hebrew prophet; also, a book of the Old Testament.

zeph-yr (zĕf′ẽr), *n.* the west wind.

Zep-pe-lin (zĕp′ē-lĭn), *n.* a large, metal-framed, cigar-shaped balloon driven by motors, and able to fly long distances carrying a heavy cargo.

ze-ro (zē′rō), *n.* [*pl.* zeros or zeroes], **1,** a cipher; **2,** nothing; **3,** the point on a scale from which reckoning begins; **4,** the lowest point; as, her courage sank to *zero.*

zest (zĕst), *n.* relish; keen enjoyment; eager enthusiasm; as, *zest* for a race.

Zeus (zūs; zōos), *n.* in Greek mythology, the ruler of the gods: corresponding to the Roman *Jupiter.*

zig-zag (zĭg′zăg′), *n.* **1,** one of a number of short, sharp angles or turns; **2,** something characterized by sharp turns, as a path: —*adj.* having short, sharp turns; as, a *zigzag* line:—*adv.* crookedly; with sharp turns; as, the path climbs *zigzag*:—*v.t.* and *v.i.* [zigzagged, zigzag-ging], to move or be in, or form, quick, sharp turns; as, to *zigzag* one's way; a path *zigzags* up the hill.

ZIGZAG LINES

zinc (zĭngk), *n.* a bluish-white metal, which can stand exposure to air and moisture:

used in paint making, in electric cells, and as a protective coating on iron sheets, wire, etc.

zin·ni·a (zĭn'ĭ-à), *n.* a plant bearing bright-colored, showy flowers; also, a flower of this plant.

Zi·on (zī'ŭn) or **Si·on** (sī'ŭn), *n.* **1,** a hill in Jerusalem, the royal residence of King David and his successors, the seat of the temple, and the center of Hebrew life; **2,** the chosen people; the Jewish race; **3,** the Church of God; **4,** the new Jerusalem, or heaven.

Zi·on·ism (zī'ŭn-ĭzm), *n.* a movement among modern Jews to return to Palestine to establish a nation.—*n.* **Zi'on·ist.**

ZINNIA

zip (zĭp), *n.* a sudden hissing sound, like the whiz of a bullet; hence, speed; energy.

zip·per (zĭp'ẽr), *n.* a fastening device for galoshes, purses, tobacco pouches, clothing, etc., sewed on both edges of an opening, with a locking mechanism pulled by an attached tab which causes the two edges to lock together.

zith·er (zĭth'ẽr), *n.* a musical instrument with about 36 strings over a shallow sounding box, played with a small piece of metal or ivory.

ZITHER

zlo·ty (zlô'tĭ), *n.* [*pl.* zlotys or zloty], a nickel coin, the monetary unit of Poland. (See Table, page 943.)

zo·di·ac (zō'dĭ-ăk), *n.* an imaginary belt encircling the heavens, extending eight degrees on each side of the path of the sun, containing the paths of the moon and the important planets, and divided into twelve equal parts, called signs:—**signs of the zodiac,** the twelve divisions of the zodiac, each with a specific name.

zone (zōn), *n.* **1,** any encircling belt, band, stripe, or path; as, a *zone* of color; **2,** any one of the five sections into which the earth's surface is divided by imaginary lines, north and south of the equator; as, the Torrid *Zone* (about the equator), the two Frigid *Zones* (about the poles), and the two Temperate *Zones* (lying between); **3,** in the U.S. parcel-post system, telephone system, etc., a specified area throughout which a certain rate is charged; **4,** an area or region distinct because of its use, its natural characteristics, or the like; as, a safety *zone*; a cotton *zone*:—*v.t.* [zoned, zon-ing], **1,** to divide into areas or zones; as, the city is *zoned* into five sections; **2,** to include within an area or zone:—*v.i.* to be divided into zones.

zoo (zōō), *n.* a park or other large enclosure in which living animals are kept for public exhibition; a zoological garden.

zo·o·log·i·cal (zō'ō-lŏj'ĭ-kăl), *adj.* pertaining to zoology, the science of animal life:—**zoological garden,** a park in which animals are kept for exhibition; a zoo.

zo·ol·o·gist (zō-ŏl'ō-jĭst), *n.* a person trained in the science of animal life.

zo·ol·o·gy (zō-ŏl'ō-jĭ), *n.* the branch of biology dealing with animal life.

zoom (zōōm), *v.i.* **1,** to move with a humming or buzzing sound; **2,** in aviation, to climb for a short time at a very steep angle:—*v.t.* to cause (an airplane) to zoom.

Zor·o·as·ter (zôr'ō-ăs'tẽr), (about 1000 B.C.), the founder of the ancient Persian religion. He is also called *Zarathustra.*—*n.* and *adj.* **Zor'o·as'tri·an.**

Zou·ave (zōō-äv'; zōō-äv'), *n.* **1,** in the French army, one of a body of infantry, originally Algerians, wearing a brightly colored uniform; **2,** one of a body of soldiers in the War between the States with similar uniforms.

ZOUAVE

zounds (zoundz), *interj. Archaic,* expressing anger or wonder.

Zui·der Zee (zī'dẽr zā'; zī'dẽr zē'), an inlet of the North Sea, in the Netherlands, now closed off by a dike (map 12).

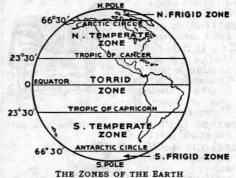

THE ZONES OF THE EARTH

Zu·lu (zōō'lōō), *n.* one of a warlike native tribe of Natal, South Africa.

Zu·lu·land (zōō'lōō-lănd'), a territory in the Union of South Africa.

Zu·rich (zōōr'ĭk) or **Zü·rich** (tsü'rĭkh), a manufacturing city in northern Switzerland (map 12).

zwie·back (tsvē'bäk'; tswē'bäk'; swī'băk'; zwī'băk'), *n.* a kind of bread baked in a loaf, sliced, and baked again.

APPENDIX

TABLES OF WEIGHTS, MEASURES, AND STANDARDS

THE METRIC SYSTEM

The metric system is a system of weights and measures that originated in France in the latter part of the 18th century. It has been adopted by law in most of the civilized countries of the world, and is almost universally used for scientific measurements.

The fundamental units of the metric system are: the *meter*, the unit of length; the *liter*, the unit of capacity; and the *gram*, the unit of mass, or weight.

The standard *meter* is the distance between two lines on a bar of platinum preserved at the International Bureau of Weights and Measures at Sèvres, near Paris, France. The meter is exactly 39.37 inches long. It was intended to be, and approximately is, the ten millionth part of a quadrant of a terrestrial meridian.

The *liter* is equivalent to the space occupied by one kilogram of pure water at the temperature of its greatest density (4° Centigrade). It is, approximately, a cubic decimeter.

The *gram* is one thousandth of the mass of a piece of platinum deposited with the International Bureau of Weights and Measures. It was intended to have the same mass as a cubic decimeter of pure water at 4° Centigrade.

The other units of the metric system are decimally related to the fundamental units; that is, each unit in each table is ten times the unit next smaller, and one tenth of the unit next larger. To express this relationship, the following prefixes are used: *milli-*, one thousandth; *centi-*, one hundredth; *deci-*, one tenth; *deka-*, ten times; *hecto-*, one hundred times; *kilo-*, one thousand times; *myria-*, ten thousand times.

MEASURES OF LENGTH AND SURFACE

Length

Metric Denominations and Values		Equivalents
1 myriameter	10,000 meters	6.2137 miles
1 kilometer	1,000 meters	0.62137 mile, or 3,280 feet 10 inches
1 hectometer	100 meters	328 feet 1 inch
1 decameter	10 meters	393.7 inches
1 meter	1 meter	39.37 inches
1 decimeter	1/10 meter	3.937 inches
1 centimeter	1/100 meter	0.3937 inch
1 millimeter	1/1,000 meter	0.0394 inch
1 micron	1/1,000,000 meter	1/1,000 millimeter
1 millimicron	1/1,000,000,000 meter	1/1,000 micron

Surface

1 square kilometer	1,000,000 square meters	0.3861 square mile
1 hectare	10,000 square meters	2.471 acres: equivalent to a square 328′ 1″ on a side
1 are	100 square meters	119.6 square yards
1 centare	1 square meter	1,550 square inches
1 square decimeter	0.01 square meter	15.50 square inches
1 square centimeter	0.0001 square meter	0.155 square inch
1 square millimeter	0.000001 square meter	0.00155 square inch

MEASURES OF CAPACITY AND VOLUME

Metric Denominations and Values	Cu. In.	Equivalents Dry Measure	Liquid Measure	Approximate Cubic Measure[1]
1 kiloliter[1]	1,000 liters	61025.0	1.308 cubic yards	264.18 gallons	1 cubic meter[1], or 1 stere[2]
1 hectoliter	100 liters	6102.50	2.8378 bushels	26.418 gallons	1/10 cubic meter
1 decaliter	10 liters	610.250	1.1351 pecks	2.6418 gallons	10 cubic decimeters
1 liter	1 liter	61.0250	0.9081 quart	1.0567 quarts	1 cubic decimeter
1 deciliter	1/10 liter	6.10250	0.18162 pint	0.8454 gill	1/10 cubic decimeter
1 centiliter	1/100 liter	0.610250	0.6102 cubic inch	0.3381 fluid ounce	10 cubic centimeters
1 milliliter	1/1,000 liter	0.0610250	0.0610 cubic inch	0.2705 fluid dram	1 cubic centimeter

[1] The cubic meter = 61,023.38 cubic inches; 1 kiloliter = 61,025 cubic inches.—[2] By definition, 1 stere = 1 cubic meter; that is, 1,000.027 liters, or 1.000027 kiloliters; 1 hectostere = 100 cubic meters.

MEASURES OF MASS (WEIGHTS)

Metric Denominations and Values		Quantity of Water	Equivalents Avoirdupois Weight	Troy Weight
1 tonne (metric ton)	1,000,000 grams	1 cubic meter (nearly)	1.102311 short tons	
1 quintal	100,000 grams	1 hectoliter	220.46 pounds	
1 myriagram	10,000 grams	10 liters	22.046 pounds	
1 kilogram or kilo	1,000 grams	1 liter	2.2046 pounds	2.6792 pounds
1 hectogram	100 grams	1 deciliter	3.5274 ounces	3.2151 ounces
1 decagram	10 grams	1 milliliter	0.3527 ounce	0.3215 ounce
1 gram	1 gram	1 cubic centimeter	0.0353 ounce	0.0322 ounce
1 decigram	1/10 gram	1/10 cubic centimeter		1.5432 grains
1 centigram	1/100 gram	10 cubic millimeters		0.1543 grain
1 milligram	1/1,000 gram	1 cubic millimeter		0.0154 grain

METRIC EQUIVALENTS OF DOMESTIC MEASURES

Length

1 inch	2.54 centimeters
1 foot	0.3048 meter
1 yard	0.9144 meter
1 rod	5.029 meters
1 mile	1,609.35 meters

Surface

1 square inch	6.452 square centimeters
1 square foot	0.0929 square meter
1 square yard	0.8361 square meter
1 square rod	25.293 square meters
1 acre	4046.87 square meters
1 acre	40.469 ares
1 square mile	259.000 hectares

Capacity

1 cubic inch	16.387 cubic centimeters
1 cubic inch	0.0164 liter, cubic decimeter
1 cubic foot	28.316 liters, 28.317 cubic decimeters
1 cubic yard	764.539 liters, 764.559 cubic decimeters
1 cord	3.625 steres
1 quart, dry measure	1.1012 liters
1 peck (U. S.)	8.8096 liters
1 bushel (U. S.)	35.24 liters

1 fluid dram	3.70 cubic centimeters
1 fluid ounce	29.57 cubic centimeters
1 fluid ounce	0.0296 liter
1 gill	0.1183 liter
1 quart, liquid measure	0.9463 liter
1 gallon (231 cubic inches)	3.785 liters

English Measures (used also in Canada)

1 British quart	1.2009 U. S. liquid quarts
1 British quart	1.0320 U. S. dry quarts
1 U. S. dry quart	0.9690 British quart
1 U. S. liquid quart	0.8327 British quart

Weights

1 grain[1]	64.80 milligrams
1 ounce, avoirdupois	28.3495 grams
1 ounce, troy	31.103 grams
1 pound, avoirdupois	0.45359 kilogram
1 pound, troy	0.3732 kilogram
1 short ton (2,000 pounds)	907.2 kilograms
1 short ton (2,000 pounds)	0.9072 metric ton
1 long ton (2,240 pounds)	1.016 metric tons

[1] The troy, avoirdupois, and apothecaries' grain are the same.

THE METRIC SYSTEM SIMPLIFIED

The following tables of the metric system of weights and measures have been simplified as much as possible by omitting such denominations as are not in practical, everyday use in the countries where the system is used.

TABLES OF THE SYSTEM

Length

The denominations in practical use are the millimeter (mm.), centimeter (cm.), meter (m.), and kilometer (km.).

10 millimeters	1 centimeter
10 centimeters	1 decimeter
10 decimeters	1 meter
1,000 meters	1 kilometer

Weight

The denominations in use are the milligram (mg.), gram (g.), kilogram (kg.), and ton (metric ton).

1,000 milligrams	1 gram
1,000 grams	1 kilogram
1,000 kilograms	1 metric ton

Capacity

The denominations in use are cubic centimeter (c.c.) and liter (l.).

1,000 cubic centimeters	1 liter
100 liters	1 hectoliter

Relation of capacity and weight to length: a cubic decimeter is, approximately, a liter, and a liter of water weighs one kilogram.

APPROXIMATE EQUIVALENTS

A meter (39.37 inches) is about a yard.
A kilogram (2.2 pounds) is about two pounds.
A liter (0.91 dry qt. and 1.06 liquid qts.) is about a quart.
A centimeter (0.39 inch) is about one half inch.
A metric ton (2204.6 pounds) is about a long ton.
A kilometer (0.62 mile, or 3280 feet) is about ⅝ mile.
A cubic centimeter is about a thimbleful.
A nickel weighs about five grams.
For postal purposes fifteen grams are considered the equivalent of one half ounce avoirdupois. At the mint a half dollar is considered to weigh 12.5 grams.

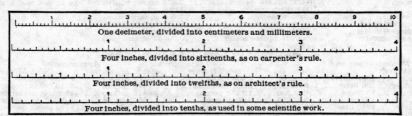

One decimeter, divided into centimeters and millimeters.

Four inches, divided into sixteenths, as on carpenter's rule.

Four inches, divided into twelfths, as on architect's rule.

Four inches, divided into tenths, as used in some scientific work.

THE DECIMETER AND THE INCH

DOMESTIC WEIGHTS AND MEASURES

Long Measure

12 inches	1 foot
3 feet	1 yard
5½ yards	1 rod or pole
40 rods	1 furlong
8 furlongs	1 statute mile (1,760 yards, or 5,280 feet)
3 miles	1 league

Mariners' Measure

6 feet	1 fathom
100 fathoms	1 cable length, or about 1/10 nautical mile
5,280 feet	1 statute mile
6,080.20 feet	1 nautical mile

Surveyors' Measure

1 link	7.92 inches
100 links, or 1 chain	22 yards
10 square chains	1 acre

Square Measure

144 square inches	1 square foot
9 square feet	1 square yard
30¼ square yards	1 square rod
40 square rods	1 rood
4 roods, 160 square rods	1 acre

[An acre contains 43,560 square feet; an area 208' 8½' square is approximately one acre.]

640 acres	1 square mile
100 square feet	1 square: used in roofing, etc.

Cubic Measure

1,728 cubic inches	1 cubic foot
27 cubic feet	1 cubic yard
24¾ cubic feet	1 perch

Wood Measure

24¾ cubic feet	1 perch
16 cubic feet	1 cord foot
8 cord feet, or 128 cubic feet	1 cord

[A pile 8 ft. long, 4 ft. wide, and 4 ft. high contains 1 cord.]

Dry Measure

2 pints	1 quart
8 quarts	1 peck
4 pecks	1 bushel
1 quart, dry measure	67.2 cubic inches
1 bushel, level	2150.42 cubic inches

Liquid Measure

4 gills	1 pint
2 pints	1 quart
4 quarts	1 gallon
31½ gallons	1 barrel
2 barrels	1 hogshead

[A standard U. S. gallon, the unit of liquid measure, is the same as the English wine gallon, and contains 231 cubic inches. A gallon of water weighs about 8⅓ pounds. A barrel contains about 4⅕ cubic feet.]

Apothecaries' Fluid Measure

60 minims	1 fluid dram
8 fluid drams	1 fluid ounce
16 fluid ounces	1 pint
8 pints	1 gallon

Apothecaries' Weight

20 grains	1 scruple
3 scruples	1 dram
8 drams	1 ounce
12 ounces	1 pound

Avoirdupois Weight

16 drams	1 ounce (437½ grains)
16 ounces	1 pound (7,000 grains)
25 pounds	1 quarter
4 quarters, or 100 pounds	1 short hundredweight
112 pounds	1 long hundredweight
20 hundredweight	1 ton
2,000 pounds (20 short hundredweight)	1 short ton
2,240 pounds (20 long hundredweight)	1 long ton

Troy Weight

24 grains	1 pennyweight
20 pennyweights	1 ounce (480 grains)
12 ounces	1 pound (5,760 grains)
3⅙ grains	1 carat

[The metric carat, 200 milligrams, is now generally used by jewelers.]

Angular Measure

60 seconds (″)	1 minute (′)
60 minutes	1 degree (°)
90 degrees	1 right angle, or quadrant
360 degrees	1 circle, or circumference
1 radian	57.296°

Time Measure

60 seconds	1 minute
60 minutes	1 hour
24 hours	1 day
7 days	1 week
28 to 31 solar days	1 month
365 solar days	1 common year
366 solar days	1 leap year

[1 tropical, or solar, year = 365 days, 5 hours, 48 minutes, 46 seconds; 1 Julian year = 365¼ days.]

FOREIGN MONETARY UNITS

The following list gives the values, in the money of the United States, of the monetary units of the countries named as of December 1959. For countries marked with an asterisk (*), no official value has been established. Because of present political and economic conditions, the exchange values fluctuate and those given here are in most cases approximate. Most metropolitan newspapers give daily or weekly quotations of foreign exchange. Where large daily newspapers are not available, this information can be obtained from local banks.

Country	Monetary Unit	Value
Argentina	Peso	$0.0127
Australia	Pound	2.2537
Austria	Schilling	.0390
Belgium	Franc	.0200
Bolivia	Boliviano	.0001
Brazil	Cruzeiro	.0550
British Colonies in Australasia and Africa	Pound sterling	2.8237
British Honduras	Dollar	.7078
Bulgaria	Lev [*pl.* leva]	.1470
Canada	Dollar	1.0387
Ceylon	Rupee	.2117
Chile	Peso	.0001
China (Nationalist)	Dollar	.0278
(Communist)	People's Dollar	*
Colombia	Peso	.1265
Costa Rica	Colon	.1790
Cuba	Peso	1.0000
Czechoslovakia	Koruna	.1400
Denmark	Krone [*pl.* kroner]	.1452
Dominican Republic	Peso	1.0000
Ecuador	Sucre	.0666
Egypt	Pound	2.8825
Finland	Markka	.0032
France	Franc	.0020
Ghana	Pound	2.8162
Great Britain	Pound sterling	2.8162
Greece	Drachma	.0335
Guatemala	Quetzal	1.0000
Haiti	Gourde	.2000
Honduras	Lempira	.5000
Hong Kong	Dollar	.1750
Hungary	Forint	.0861
Iceland	Krona	.0615
India	Rupee	.2112
Indonesia	Rupiah	.0881
Iran	Rial	$0.0135
Iraq	Dinar	2.8162
Ireland	Pound	2.8162
Israel	Pound	.5600
Italy	Lira [*pl.* lire]	.0016
Japan	Yen [*pl.* yen]	.0028
Korea	Won	.0020
Lebanon	Pound	.3190
Liberia	Dollar	1.0000
Mexico	Peso	.0801
Netherlands	Guilder (florin)	.2650
New Zealand	Pound	2.8062
Nicaragua	Córdoba	.1430
Norway	Krone [*pl.* kroner]	.1405
Pakistan	Rupee	.2115
Panama	Balboa	1.0000
Paraguay	Guarani	.0167
Peru	Sol [*pl.* soles]	.0370
Philippine Republic	Peso	.4990
Poland	Zloty	.2500
Portugal	Escudo	.0351
Rumania	Leu [*pl.* lei]	.1666
Salvador, El	Colon	.4000
Saudi Arabia	Riyal	.2675
Singapore	Dollar	.3300
South Africa, Union of	Pound sterling	2.8200
Spain	Peseta	.0240
Sweden	Krona [*pl.* kronor]	.1935
Switzerland	Franc	.2312
Thailand (Siam)	Baht	.0480
Turkey	Lira	.3575
Union of Soviet Socialist Republics	Ruble	.2500
Uruguay	Peso	.1150
Venezuela	Bolivar	.3010
West Germany	Mark	.2391
Yugoslavia	Dinar	.0033

SIGNS AND SYMBOLS

ASTRONOMY

○ the Sun; Sunday. Also, ⊙.
☽, ☾ or ☾ the Moon; Monday. Also ☽, ☾.
● new moon; ☽, ☽ first quarter.
○, ⊕ full moon; ☾, ☾ last quarter.
☿ Mercury; Wednesday.
♀ Venus; Friday;
⊕, ⊖, ♁ the Earth; ♂ Mars; Tuesday.
♃ Jupiter; Thursday; ♄ Saturn; Saturday.
♅, ♅ Uranus; ♆ Neptune; ♇ Pluto.
☄ comet; ✳, ✱ fixed star.

COMMERCE AND FINANCE

$ dollar; dollars; as, $1; $5.
¢ cent; cents; as, 1¢; 12¢.
/ shillings; as, 1/6 = 1s. 6d.
£ pound (sterling); pounds; from the initial letter of Lat. *libra*, pound; as, £1; £5.
£E Egyptian pound or pounds.
₱ peso or pesos; as, ₱25.
lb pound (in weight); pounds; as, 1 ℔; 2 ℔.
@ at; as, gingham @ $.50 per yard; also, to; as, butter, per lb. 45¢ @ 50¢.
% per cent; also, order of; care of.
% account; as, Wm. Jones % with J. Brown.
B/L bill of lading.

MATHEMATICS

+ plus, and, more; as 3+2=5.
− minus, less; as 6−3=3.
± plus or minus; as the square root of 4 is±2.
× multiplied by; as 6×2=12.
÷ divided by; as 6÷2=3.
> is greater than; as 6>5.
< is less than; as 5<6.
: is to; as 6:3 : : 8:4.
: : as; as 6:3 : : 8:4.
∠ angle; as, ∠ABC = ∠CEF.
√ the square root; as √9 =3.
°, ′, ″ degrees, minutes, seconds of arc.

MEDICINE AND PHARMACY

ā ā [Gk. *ana*], of each.
℞ [Lat. *recipe*, take], take; written on prescriptions.
S [Lat. *signa*], mark preceding directions for taking medicine; often written Sig.
℔ [Lat. *libra*], pound; ℥ ounce.
℈ dram; a weight of 60 grains or ⅛ ounce; a fluid dram, ⅛ fluid ounce (of water, about a teaspoonful, or 60 drops).
℈ scruple; ℳ or ℳ minim, drop.

MISCELLANEOUS

© copyrighted. ℗ Associated Press (news item).
& ampersand: and; as, Smith & Co.
&c and the rest; and so forth; for *etc*. [Lat. *et cetera*.]
′ feet; ″ inches; as, a room 12′ 6″ long.
× by: used in dimensions: as, a room 8′ × 16′.
♣ club; ♦ diamond; ♥ heart; ♠ spade; marks of the suits on playing cards.
♯ number; also, pound.
c/o or c/o care of.
☌ or ♂, *Zoöl.*, male; ♀, female.
○ *Zoöl.*, of undetermined sex.
† died: used in genealogies.

PUNCTUATION

, comma.
; semicolon.
: colon.
. period.
? interrogation.
! exclamation.
( ) parentheses.
[ ] brackets.
' apostrophe.
— dash.
- hyphen.
′ acute accent.
\ grave accent.
^ circumflex accent.
~ circumflex; tilde.
— long accent; macron.

˘ short; breve.
¨ diaeresis
¸ cedilla.
∧ caret.
* * * ellipsis.
. . . ellipsis.
——— ellipsis.
* asterisk.
† dagger; obelisk.
‡ double dagger.
§ section.
‖ parallel.
¶ paragraph.
☞ index.
⁎, ⁎*⁎ asterism.

UNITED STATES WEATHER BUREAU SIGNALS

KEY: ☐ white; ▨ red; ■ black; ▤ blue.

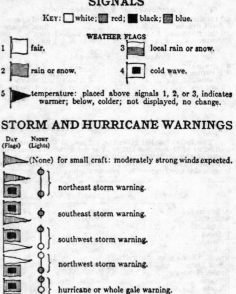

WEATHER FLAGS

1 fair.   3 local rain or snow.

2 rain or snow.   4 cold wave.

5 temperature: placed above signals 1, 2, or 3, indicates warmer; below, colder; not displayed, no change.

STORM AND HURRICANE WARNINGS

DAY (Flags)   NIGHT (Lights)

(None) for small craft: moderately strong winds expected.

northeast storm warning.

southeast storm warning.

southwest storm warning.

northwest storm warning.

hurricane or whole gale warning.

UNITED STATES WEATHER BUREAU SYMBOLS

(Used on Daily Weather Map)

○ clear.   ⊛ rain.   ▲ hail.
◑ partly cloudy. ⊗ snow.   △ sleet.
● cloudy.   ® report missing. ⏀ thunderstorm.
➤○➤ storm warning.

♂ ♀ etc. Arrows attached to other symbols indicate wind direction; arrows fly with the wind.
▤ Shaded area indicates precipitation of 0.01 inch or more during last 24 hours.

SIGNAL CODES

(945)

THE PRESIDENTS OF THE UNITED STATES

Name	State	Party	Term of Office	Name	State	Party	Term of Office
1. George Washington	Va.		1789–1797	18. Ulysses S. Grant	Ill.	Rep.	1869–1877
2. John Adams	Mass.	Fed.	1797–1801	19. Rutherford B. Hayes	O.	Rep.	1877–1881
3. Thomas Jefferson	Va.	Rep.*	1801–1809	20. James A. Garfield†	O.	Rep.	1881
4. James Madison	Va.	Rep.*	1809–1817	21. Chester A. Arthur	N. Y.	Rep.	1881–1885
5. James Monroe	Va.	Rep.*	1817–1825	22. Grover Cleveland	N. Y.	Dem.	1885–1889
6. John Quincy Adams	Mass.	Rep.*	1825–1829	23. Benjamin Harrison	Ind.	Rep.	1889–1893
7. Andrew Jackson	Tenn.	Dem.	1829–1837	24. Grover Cleveland	N. Y.	Dem.	1893–1897
8. Martin Van Buren	N. Y.	Dem.	1837–1841	25. William McKinley†	O.	Rep.	1897–1901
9. William Henry Harrison†	O.	Whig	1841	26. Theodore Roosevelt	N. Y.	Rep.	1901–1909
10. John Tyler	Va.	Dem.	1841–1845	27. William H. Taft	O.	Rep.	1909–1913
11. James Knox Polk	Tenn.	Dem.	1845–1849	28. Woodrow Wilson	N. J.	Dem.	1913–1921
12. Zachary Taylor†	La.	Whig	1849–1850	29. Warren G. Harding†	O.	Rep.	1921–1923
13. Millard Fillmore	N. Y.	Whig	1850–1853	30. Calvin Coolidge	Mass.	Rep.	1923–1929
14. Franklin Pierce	N. H.	Dem.	1853–1857	31. Herbert C. Hoover	Calif.	Rep.	1929–1933
15. James Buchanan	Pa.	Dem.	1857–1861	32. Franklin D. Roosevelt†	N. Y.	Dem.	1933–1945
16. Abraham Lincoln†	Ill.	Rep.	1861–1865	33. Harry S. Truman	Mo.	Dem.	1945–1953
17. Andrew Johnson	Tenn.	Rep.	1865–1869	34. Dwight D. Eisenhower	Kans.	Rep.	1953–

Abbreviations: *Fed.*, Federalist; *Dem.*, Democrat; *Rep.*, Republican.
*The party named Republican by Thomas Jefferson was later called Democratic or Democratic-Republican. It was succeeded by the Democratic party in 1828. The modern Republican party originated in 1854. The Whig party opposed the Democratic party from about 1834–1856. †Seven Presidents have died in office. In each case, the Vice-President succeeded to the Presidency.

THE STATES OF THE UNITED STATES

Name	Abbreviation	Capital	Entered the Union	Popular Name	State Flower
Alabama	Ala.	Montgomery	Dec. 14, 1819	Cotton State	Goldenrod
Alaska		Juneau	Jan. 3, 1959		Forget-Me-Not
Arizona	Ariz.	Phoenix	Feb. 14, 1912	Grand Canyon State	Cactus
Arkansas	Ark.	Little Rock	June 15, 1836	Wonder State	Apple Blossom
California	Calif.	Sacramento	Sept. 9, 1850	Golden State	Golden Poppy
Colorado	Colo.	Denver	Aug. 1, 1876	Centennial State	Columbine
Connecticut	Conn.	Hartford	*Jan. 9, 1788	Nutmeg State	Mountain Laurel
Delaware	Del.	Dover	*Dec. 7, 1787	Diamond State	Peach Blossom
Florida	Fla.	Tallahassee	Mar. 3, 1845	Everglade State	Orange Blossom
Georgia	Ga.	Atlanta	*Jan. 2, 1788	Cracker State	Cherokee Rose
Hawaii		Honolulu	†June 27, 1959		Red Hibiscus
Idaho	Id. or Ida.	Boise	July 3, 1890	Gem State	Syringa
Illinois	Ill.	Springfield	Dec. 3, 1818	Prairie State	Wood Violet
Indiana	Ind.	Indianapolis	Dec. 11, 1816	Hoosier State	Zinnia
Iowa	Ia.	Des Moines	Dec. 28, 1846	Hawkeye State	Wild Rose
Kansas	Kans.	Topeka	Jan. 29, 1861	Sunflower State	Sunflower
Kentucky	Ky.	Frankfort	June 1, 1792	Bluegrass State	Goldenrod
Louisiana	La.	Baton Rouge	April 8, 1812	Creole State	Magnolia
Maine	Me.	Augusta	Mar. 15, 1820	Pine-Tree State	Pine Cone and Tassel
Maryland	Md.	Annapolis	*April 28, 1788	Old Line State	Black-eyed Susan
Massachusetts	Mass.	Boston	*Feb. 6, 1788	Bay State	Mayflower (Arbutus)
Michigan	Mich.	Lansing	Jan. 26, 1837	Wolverene State	Apple Blossom
Minnesota	Minn.	St. Paul	May 11, 1858	Gopher State	Moccasin Flower
Mississippi	Miss.	Jackson	Dec. 10, 1817	Magnolia State	Magnolia
Missouri	Mo.	Jefferson City	Aug. 10, 1821	Ozark State	Hawthorn
Montana	Mont.	Helena	Nov. 8, 1889	Bonanza State / Treasure State	Bitterroot
Nebraska	Nebr.	Lincoln	Mar. 1, 1867	Cornhusker State	Goldenrod
Nevada	Nev.	Carson City	Oct. 31, 1864	Silver State / Sagebrush State	Sagebrush
New Hampshire	N. H.	Concord	*June 21, 1788	Granite State	Purple Lilac
New Jersey	N. J.	Trenton	*Dec. 18, 1787	Garden State	Violet
New Mexico	N. Mex.	Santa Fe	Jan. 6, 1912	Sunshine State / Spanish State	Yucca
New York	N. Y.	Albany	*July 26, 1788	Empire State	Rose
North Carolina	N. C.	Raleigh	*Nov. 21, 1789	Tarheel State	Dogwood
North Dakota	N. Dak.	Bismarck	Nov. 2, 1889	Sioux State	Wild Prairie Rose
Ohio	O.	Columbus	Mar. 1, 1803	Buckeye State	Scarlet Carnation
Oklahoma	Okla.	Oklahoma City	Nov. 16, 1907	Sooner State	Mistletoe
Oregon	Ore.	Salem	Feb. 14, 1859	Beaver State	Oregon Grape
Pennsylvania	Pa.	Harrisburg	*Dec. 12, 1787	Keystone State	Mountain Laurel
Rhode Island	R. I.	Providence	*May 29, 1790	Little Rhody	Violet
South Carolina	S. C.	Columbia	*May 23, 1788	Palmetto State	Yellow Jessamine
South Dakota	S. Dak.	Pierre	Nov. 2, 1889	Coyote State	Pasqueflower
Tennessee	Tenn.	Nashville	June 1, 1796	Volunteer State	Iris
Texas	Tex.	Austin	Dec. 29, 1845	Lone-Star State	Bluebonnet
Utah	Ut.	Salt Lake City	Jan. 4, 1896	Beehive State	Sego Lily
Vermont	Vt.	Montpelier	Mar. 4, 1791	Green Mountain State	Red Clover
Virginia	Va.	Richmond	*June 25, 1788	Old Dominion	Dogwood
Washington	Wash.	Olympia	Nov. 11, 1889	Evergreen State	Rhododendron
West Virginia	W. Va.	Charleston	June 20, 1863	Panhandle State	Rhododendron
Wisconsin	Wis.	Madison	May 29, 1848	Badger State	Violet
Wyoming	Wyo.	Cheyenne	July 10, 1890	Equality State	Painted Cup (or Indian Paintbrush)

*Date of ratification of the Constitution. †Date of Hawaiian vote.

AREA AND POPULATION OF THE UNITED STATES

Name	Land Area Sq. Miles	Population 1950	Name	Land Area Sq. Miles	Population 1950
Alabama	51,078	3,061,743	North Carolina	49,142	4,061,929
Alaska	586,400	128,643	North Dakota	70,054	619,636
Arizona	113,580	749,587	Ohio	41,122	7,946,627
Arkansas	52,725	1,909,511	Oklahoma	69,283	2,233,351
California	156,803	10,586,223	Oregon	96,350	1,521,341
Colorado	103,967	1,325,089	Pennsylvania	45,045	10,498,012
Connecticut	4,899	2,007,280	Rhode Island	1,058	791,896
Delaware	1,978	318,085	South Carolina	30,594	2,117,027
District of Columbia	61	802,178	South Dakota	76,536	652,740
Florida	54,262	2,771,305	Tennessee	41,961	3,291,718
Georgia	58,518	3,444,578	Texas	263,644	7,711,194
Hawaii	6,433	499,794	Utah	82,346	688,862
Idaho	82,808	588,637	Vermont	9,278	377,747
Illinois	55,947	8,712,176	Virginia	39,899	3,318,680
Indiana	35,205	3,934,224	Washington	66,977	2,378,963
Iowa	55,986	2,621,073	West Virginia	24,090	2,005,552
Kansas	82,113	1,905,299	Wisconsin	54,715	3,434,575
Kentucky	40,109	2,944,806	Wyoming	97,506	290,529
Louisiana	45,177	2,683,516			
Maine	31,040	913,774	United States	2,384,295	151,325,798
Maryland	9,887	2,343,001			
Massachusetts	7,907	4,690,514			
Michigan	57,022	6,371,766	**POSSESSIONS AND DEPENDENCIES**		
Minnesota	80,009	2,982,483			
Mississippi	47,420	2,178,914	American Samoa	76	18,937
Missouri	69,270	3,954,653	Guam	206	59,498
Montana	146,316	591,024	Midway Islands	28	437
Nebraska	76,653	1,325,510	Panama Canal Zone	553	52,822
Nevada	109,802	160,083	Puerto Rico	3,435	2,210,703
New Hampshire	9,024	533,242	Virgin Islands	133	26,665
New Jersey	7,522	4,835,329			
New Mexico	121,511	681,187	Totals	4,431	2,369,062
New York	47,929	14,830,192			

CHIEF CITIES OF THE UNITED STATES

(Including all cities having 35,000 inhabitants or more in 1950 census, and all capitals of States)

Abilene, Tex.	45,570	Binghamton, N. Y.	80,674	Clifton, N. J.	64,511	East St. Louis, Ill.	82,295
Akron, Ohio	274,605	Birmingham, Ala.	326,037	Colorado Springs, Colo.	45,472	Easton, Pa.	35,632
Alameda, Calif.	64,430	*Bismarck, N. D.	18,640	*Columbia, S. C.	86,914	Eau Claire, Wis.	36,058
*Albany, N. Y.	134,995	Bloomfield, N. J.	49,307	Columbus, Ga.	79,611	Elgin, Ill.	44,223
Albuquerque, N. M.	96,815	*Boise, Idaho	34,393	*Columbus, Ohio	375,901	Elizabeth, N. J.	112,817
Alexandria, Va.	61,787	*Boston, Mass.	801,444	Compton, Calif.	47,991	Elkhart, Ind.	35,556
Alhambra, Calif.	51,359	Bridgeport, Conn.	158,709	*Concord, N. H.	27,988	Elmira, N. Y.	49,716
Allentown, Pa.	106,756	Bristol, Conn.	35,961	Corpus Christi, Tex.	108,287	El Paso, Tex.	130,485
Altoona, Pa.	77,177	Brockton, Mass.	62,860	Council Bluffs, Iowa	45,529	Enid, Okla.	36,017
Amarillo, Tex.	74,246	Brookline, Mass.	57,589	Covington, Ky.	64,452	Erie, Pa.	130,803
Anderson, Ind.	46,820	Brownsville, Tex.	36,066	Cranston, R. I.	55,060	Essex, Md.	35,000
*Annapolis, Md.	10,047	Buffalo, N. Y.	580,132	Cumberland, Md.	37,679	Euclid, Ohio	41,396
Ann Arbor, Mich.	48,251	Burbank, Calif.	78,577			Eugene, Oreg.	35,879
Arlington, Mass.	44,353			Dallas, Tex.	434,462	Evanston, Ill.	73,641
Arlington, Va.	135,449	Cambridge, Mass.	120,740	Danville, Ill.	37,864	Evansville, Ind.	128,636
Asheville, N. C.	53,000	Camden, N. J.	124,555	Danville, Va.	35,066	Everett, Mass.	45,982
*Atlanta, Ga.	331,314	Canton, N. C.	74,906	Davenport, Iowa	74,549		
Atlantic City, N. J.	61,657	Canton, Ohio	116,912	Dayton, Ohio	243,872	Fall River, Mass.	111,963
Auburn, N. Y.	36,722	*Carson City, Nev.	3,082	Dearborn, Mich.	94,994	Fargo, N. Dak.	38,256
Augusta, Ga.	71,508	Cedar Rapids, Iowa	72,296	Decatur, Ill.	66,269	Fitchburg, Mass.	42,691
*Augusta, Me.	20,913	Champaign, Ill.	39,563	*Denver, Colo.	415,786	Flint, Mich.	163,143
Aurora, Ill.	50,576	Charleston, S. C.	70,174	*Des Moines, Iowa	177,965	Fort Lauderdale, Fla.	36,328
*Austin, Tex.	132,459	*Charleston, W. Va.	73,501	Detroit, Mich.	1,849,568	Fort Lewis, Wash.	35,000
		Charlotte, N. C.	134,042	*Dover, Del.	6,223	Fort Smith, Ark.	47,942
Baltimore, Md.	949,708	Chattanooga, Tenn.	131,041	Downey, Calif.	35,000	Fort Wayne, Ind.	133,607
*Baton Rouge, La.	125,629	Chelsea, Mass.	38,912	Dubuque, Iowa	49,671	Fort Worth, Tex.	278,778
Battle Creek, Mich.	48,666	Chester, Pa.	66,039	Duluth, Minn.	104,511	*Frankfort, Ky.	11,916
Bay City, Mich.	52,523	*Cheyenne, Wyo.	31,935	Dundalk, Md.	40,182	Fresno, Calif.	91,669
Bayonne, N. J.	77,203	Chicago, Ill.	3,620,962	Durham, N. C.	71,311		
Beaumont, Tex.	94,014	Chicopee, Mass.	49,211			Gadsden, Ala.	55,725
Bellflower, Calif.	40,000	Cicero, Ill.	67,544	East Bakersfield, Calif.	38,177	Galveston, Tex.	66,568
Berkeley, Calif.	113,805	Cincinnati, Ohio	503,998	East Chicago, Ind.	54,263	Gary, Ind.	133,911
Berwyn, Ill.	51,280	Cleveland, Ohio	914,808	East Cleveland, Ohio	40,047	Glendale, Calif.	95,702
Bethlehem, Pa.	66,340	Cleveland Heights, Ohio	59,141	East Orange, N. J.	79,340	Grand Rapids, Mich.	176,515
Biloxi, Miss.	37,425			E. Providence, R. I.	35,871	Great Falls, Mont.	39,214

* designates capitals

(947)

City	Pop.	City	Pop.	City	Pop.	City	Pop.
Green Bay, Wis.	52,735	Macon, Ga.	70,252	*Pierre, S. D.	5,715	South Gate, Calif.	51,116
Greensboro, N. C.	74,389	*Madison, Wis.	96,056	Pine Bluff, Ark.	37,162	Spartanburg, S. C.	36,795
Greenville, S. C.	58,161	Malden, Mass.	59,804	Pittsburgh, Pa.	676,806	Spokane, Wash.	161,721
Greenwich, Conn.	40,835	Manchester, N. H.	82,732	Pittsfield, Mass.	55,348	*Springfield, Ill.	81,628
		Mansfield, Ohio	43,546	Plainfield, N. J.	42,366	Springfield, Mass.	162,399
Hagerstown, Md.	36,260	Marion, Ohio	38,817	Pomona, Calif.	35,405	Springfield, Mo.	66,731
Hamilton, Ohio	57,951	Mayagüez, Puerto		Ponce, Puerto Rico	126,451	Springfield, Ohio	78,508
Hammond, Ind.	87,594	Rico	87,038	Pontiac, Mich.	73,681	Stamford, Conn.	74,293
Hamtramck, Mich.	43,355	McKeesport, Pa.	51,502	Port Arthur, Tex.	57,530	Steubenville, Ohio	35,872
*Harrisburg, Pa.	89,544	Medford, Mass.	66,113	Port Huron, Mich.	35,725	Stockton, Calif.	70,853
*Hartford, Conn.	177,397	Memphis, Tenn.	396,000	Portland, Me.	77,634	Superior, Wis.	35,325
Haverford, Pa.	39,641	Meriden, Conn.	44,088	Portland, Oreg.	373,628	Syracuse, N. Y.	220,583
Haverhill, Mass.	47,280	Meridian, Miss.	41,893	Portsmouth, Ohio	36,798		
Hazleton, Pa.	35,491	Miami, Fla.	249,276	Portsmouth, Va.	80,039	Tacoma, Wash.	143,673
*Helena, Mont.	17,581	Miami Beach, Fla.	46,282	Poughkeepsie, N. Y.	41,023	*Tallahassee, Fla.	27,237
Highland Park, Mich.	46,393	Milwaukee, Wis.	637,392	*Providence, R. I.	248,674	Tampa, Fla.	124,681
High Point, N. C.	39,973	Minneapolis, Minn.	521,718	Pueblo, Colo.	63,685	Taunton, Mass.	40,109
Hoboken, N. J.	50,676	Mobile, Ala.	129,009			Terre Haute, Ind.	64,214
Hollywood, Calif.	179,749	Moline, Ill.	37,397	Quincy, Ill.	41,450	Toledo, Ohio	303,616
Holyoke, Mass.	54,661	Monroe, La.	38,572	Quincy, Mass.	83,835	*Topeka, Kans.	78,791
*Honolulu, Hawaii	245,612	Montclair, N. J.	43,297			*Trenton, N. J.	128,009
Houston, Tex.	596,163	*Montgomery, Ala.	106,525	Racine, Wis.	71,193	Troy, N. Y.	72,311
Huntington, W. Va.	86,353	*Montpelier, Vt.	8,599	*Raleigh, N. C.	65,679	Tucson, Ariz.	45,454
		Mt. Vernon, N. Y.	71 899	Reading, Pa.	109,320	Tulsa, Okla.	182,740
Independence, Mo.	36,963	Muncie, Ind.	58,479	Revere, Mass.	36,763	Tuscaloosa, Ala.	46,396
*Indianapolis, Ind.	427,173	Muskegon, Mich.	48,429	Richmond, Calif.	99,545	Tyler, Tex.	38,968
Inglewood, Calif.	46,185	Muskogee, Okla.	37,289	Richmond, Ind.	39,539		
Irvington, N. J.	59,201			*Richmond, Va.	230.310	Union, N. J.	38,004
		*Nashville, Tenn.	174,307	Riverside, Calif.	46,764	Union City, N. J.	55,538
Jackson, Mich.	51,088	Newark, N. J.	438,776	Roanoke, Va.	91,921	University City, Mo.	39,892
*Jackson, Miss.	98,271	New Bedford, Mass.	109,185	Rochester, N. Y.	332,488	Upper Darby, Pa.	84,951
Jacksonville, Fla.	204,517	New Britain, Conn.	73,726	Rockford, Ill.	92,927	Utica, N. Y.	101,531
Jamestown, N. Y.	43,354	New Brunswick, N. J.	38,811	Rock Island, Ill.	48,710		
*Jefferson City, Mo.	25,099	New Castle, Pa.	48,834	Rome, N. Y.	41,682	Van Nuys, Calif.	90,000
Jersey City, N. J.	299,017	New Haven, Conn.	164,443	Royal Oak, Mich.	46,898	Venice, Calif.	58,871
Johnstown, Pa.	63,232	New Orleans, La.	570,445				
Joliet, Ill.	51,601	Newport, R. I.	37,564	*Sacramento, Calif.	137,572	Waco, Texas	84,706
Joplin, Mo.	38,711	Newport News, Va.	42,358	Saginaw, Mich.	92,918	Waltham, Mass.	47,187
*Juneau, Alaska	5,818	New Rochelle, N. Y.	59,725	St. Joseph, Mo.	78,588	Warren, Ohio	49,856
		Newton, Mass.	81,994	St. Louis, Mo.	856,796	Warwick, R. I.	43,028
Kalamazoo, Mich.	57,704	New York, N. Y.	7,891,957	*St. Paul, Minn.	311,349	Washington, D. C.	802,178
Kansas City, Kans.	129,553	Niagara Falls, N. Y.	90,872	St. Petersburg, Fla.	96,738	Waterbury, Conn.	104,477
Kansas City, Mo.	456,622	Norfolk, Va.	213,513	*St. Thomas (Charlotte		Waterloo, Iowa	65,198
Kearney, N. J.	39,952	Norristown, Pa.	38,126	Amalie) Virgin Is.	9,801	Watertown, Mass.	37,329
Kenosha, Wis.	54,368	North Bergen, N. J.	41,560	Salem, Mass.	41,880	Waukegan, Ill.	38,946
Knoxville, Tenn.	124,769	North Little Rock,		*Salem, Oreg.	43,140	West Allis, Wis.	42,959
Kokomo, Ind.	38,672	Ark.	44,097	*Salt Lake City, Utah	182,121	West Hartford, Conn.	44,402
		Norwalk, Conn.	49,460	San Angelo, Tex.	52,093	West New York, N. J.	37,683
La Crosse, Wis.	47,535	Norwood, Ohio	35,001	San Antonio, Tex.	408,442	West Palm Beach, Fla.	43,162
Lafayette, Ind.	35,568			San Bernardino, Calif.	63,058	Wheeling, W. Va.	58,891
Lake Charles, La.	41,272	Oakland, Calif.	384,575	San Diego, Calif.	334,387	White Plains, N. Y.	43,466
Lakewood, Ohio	68,071	Oak Park, Ill.	63,529	San Francisco, Calif.	775,357	Wichita, Kans.	168,279
Lancaster, Pa.	63,774	Ogden, Utah	57,112	San Jose, Calif.	95,280	Wichita Falls, Tex.	68,042
*Lansing, Mich.	92,129	*Oklahoma City, Okla.	243,504	*San Juan, Puerto		Wilkes-Barre, Pa.	76,826
Laredo, Texas	51,910	*Olympia, Wash.	15,819	Rico	223,949	Williamsport, Pa.	45,047
Lawrence, Mass.	80,536	Omaha, Nebr.	251,117	San Mateo, Calif.	41,782	Wilmington, Del.	110,356
Levittown, N. Y.	40,000	Orange, N. J.	38,037	San Pedro, Calif.	74,000	Wilmington, N. C.	45,043
Lewiston, Me.	40,974	Orlando, Fla.	52,367	Santa Ana, Calif.	45,533	Winston-Salem, N. C.	87,811
Lexington, Ky.	55,534	Oshkosh, Wis.	41,084	Santa Barbara, Calif.	44,913	Woodbridge, N. J.	35,758
Lima, Ohio	50,246			*Santa Fe, N. Mex.	27,998	Woonsocket, R. I.	50,211
*Lincoln, Nebr.	98,884	Parkersburg, W. Va.	40,492	Santa Monica, Calif.	71,595	Worcester, Mass.	203,486
*Little Rock, Ark.	102,213	Pasadena, Calif.	104,577	Savannah, Ga.	119,638	Wyandotte, Mich.	36,846
Long Beach, Calif.	250,767	Passaic, N. J.	57,702	Schenectady, N. Y.	91,785		
Lorain, Ohio	51,202	Paterson, N. J.	139,336	Scranton, Pa.	125,536	Yakima, Wash.	38,486
Los Angeles, Calif.	1,970,358	Pawtucket, R. I.	81,436	Seattle, Wash.	467,591	Yonkers, N. Y.	152,798
Louisville, Ky.	369,129	Pensacola, Fla.	43,479	Sheboygan, Wis.	42,365	York, Pa.	59,953
Lowell, Mass.	97,249	Peoria, Ill.	111,856	Shreveport, La.	127,206	Youngstown, Ohio	168,330
Lubbock, Tex.	71,747	Perth Amboy, N. J.	41,330	Sioux City, Iowa	83,991		
Lynchburg, Va.	47,727	Petersburg, Va.	35,054	Sioux Falls, S. D.	52,696	Zanesville, Ohio	40,517
Lynn, Mass.	99,738	Philadelphia, Pa.	2,071,605	Somerville, Mass.	102,351		
		*Phoenix, Ariz.	106,818	South Bend, Ind.	115,911		

AREA AND POPULATION OF FOREIGN COUNTRIES

Name	Area in Square Miles	Estimated Population	Name	Area in Square Miles	Estimated Population
Abyssinia (Ethiopia)	350,000	15,000,000	France	212,659	42,600,000
Afghanistan	250,000	12,000,000	Germany	143,200	69,421,000
Albania	10,629	1,122,000	Greece	50,270	7,776,000
Andorra	191	5,230	Guatemala	45,452	2,890,000
Argentina	1,079,965	18,056,000	Haiti	10,204	3,200,000
Australia	2,974,581	8,829,000	Honduras	44,275	1,513,000
Federal Capital	940	15,156	Hungary	35,875	9,460,000
New South Wales	309,432	2,985,464	Iceland	40,437	148,000
Northern Territory	523,620	10,868	India (Republic of India)	1,345,410	367,000,000
Queensland	670,500	1,106,269	Iran (Persia)	628,000	19,519,000
South Australia	380,070	646,216	Iraq	116,600	5,100,000
Tasmania	26,215	257,117	Ireland (Republic of Ireland)	27,137	2,942,000
Victoria	87,884	2,055,252	Israel	5,500	1,651,000
Western Australia	975,920	502,731	Italy	119,713	47,015,000
Austria	32,393	6,949,000	Japan	141,800	86,700,000
Belgium	11,775	8,706,000	Jordan	37,264	1,320,000
Bolivia	414,470	3,089,000	Korea	85,000	25,120,174
Brazil	3,275,510	55,772,000	Liberia	43,000	2,000,000
British Commonwealth	12,974,710	612,000,000	Liechtenstein	65	14,000
British Isles	94,279	50,592,000	Luxembourg	999	302,000
England and Wales	50,874	43,940,000	Mexico	767,168	28,053,000
Northern Ireland	5,237	1,375,000	Monaco	8	21,000
Scotland	30,405	5,114,000	Morocco	172,104	9,823,000
Isle of Man, Channel Islands, etc.	296	159,000	Netherlands	12,551	10,377,000
Bulgaria	42,825	7,390,000	New Zealand	103,722	2,047,000
Canada	3,737,606	14,781,000	Nicaragua	60,000	1,088,000
Alberta	255,285	936,501	Norway	124,556	3,327,000
British Columbia	366,255	1,165,210	Pakistan	361,007	75,342,165
Manitoba	246,512	776,541	Panama	32,380	864,000
New Brunswick	27,985	515,697	Paraguay	163,400	1,464,000
Newfoundland	42,743	361,416	Peru	482,133	9,035,000
Northwest Territory	1,309,682	16,004	Philippine Republic	115,000	21,023,000
Nova Scotia	21,068	642,584	Poland	120,000	24,976,926
Ontario	412,582	4,597,542	Portugal	34,254	8,621,000
Prince Edward Island	2,184	98,429	Rumania	91,671	16,300,000
Quebec	594,534	4,055,681	Salvador, El	13,176	2,054,000
Saskatchewan	251,700	831,728	San Marino	38	13,000
Yukon Territory	207,076	9,096	Saudi Arabia	600,000	7,000,000
Ceylon	25,332	7,941,000	South Africa, Union of	472,550	13,153,000
Chile	296,717	5,932,000	Spain	196,607	28,528,000
China	3,380,692	463,500,000	Sweden	173,157	7,125,000
Colombia	439,997	12,033,000	Switzerland	16,000	4,884,000
Costa Rica	23,000	850,000	Syria	54,300	3,500,000
Cuba	44,164	5,471,000	Thailand (Siam)	200,148	19,556,000
Czechoslovakia	38,190	14,429,000	Tunisia	296,500	24,797,000
Denmark	16,576	4,334,000	Turkey	294,416	22,461,000
Dominican Republic	19,325	2,236,000	Union of Soviet Socialist Republics	8,306,316	193,000,000
Ecuador	276,000	3,350,000	Uruguay	72,153	2,353,000
Egypt	383,000	21,425,000	Venezuela	352,143	5,440,000
Finland	134,000	4,140,000	Yugoslavia	95,558	17,004,000

ESTIMATED POPULATION OF FOREIGN CITIES

City	Population
Aachen, Germany	129,811
Aberdeen, Scotland	182,714
Addis Ababa, Ethiopia	400,000
Adelaide, Australia	382,000
Agra, India	375,000
Ahmadabad, India	788,333
Aleppo, Syria	320,167
Alexandria, Egypt	919,024
Algiers, Algeria	266,165
Amoy, China	234,000
Amritsar, India	325,747
Amsterdam, Netherlands	803,847
Ankara, Turkey	286,781
Antwerp, Belgium	263,233
Asmara, Eritrea	131,000
Asunción, Paraguay	205,000
Athens, Greece	559,250
Auckland, New Zealand	127,406
Augsburg, Germany	185,183
Avellaneda, Argentina	273,839
Baghdad, Iraq	364,049
Bahia, Brazil	395,993
Baku, U.S.S.R.	809,347
Bangalore, India	778,977
Bangkok, Thailand	620,830
Barcelona, Spain	1,280,179
Basel, Switzerland	183,543
Beirut, Lebanon	233,970
Belém, Brazil	230,181
Belfast, No. Ireland	443,670
Belgrade, Yugoslavia	367,816
Benares, India	355,777
Bergen, Norway	113,000
Berlin, Germany	3,336,975
Bern, Switzerland	146,499
Birmingham, England	1,112,340
Bloemfontein, So. Africa	80,559
Bochum, Germany	289,804
Bogotá, Colombia	524,870
Bologna, Italy	349,326
Bolton, England	167,162
Bombay, India	2,839,270
Bonn, Germany	155,394
Bordeaux, France	253,751
Bradford, England	292,394
Bratislava, Czechoslovakia	172,664
Bremen, Germany	444,549
Brisbane, Australia	402,000
Bristol, England	442,281
Brno, Czechoslovakia	273,127
Brussels, Belgium	184,838
Bucharest, Rumania	886,110
Budapest, Hungary	1,058,288
Buenos Aires, Argentina	2,981,043
Cairo, Egypt	2,090,654
Calcutta, India	2,548,677
Calgary, Canada	129,060
Canberra, Australia	15,000
Canton, China	1,495,694
Cape Town, South Africa	440,181
Caracas, Venezuela	487,903
Cardiff, Wales	243,627
Catania, Sicily	300,000
Cawnpore, India	705,383
Charlottetown, Canada	15,000
Chemnitz, Germany	250,188
Chengtu, China	749,770
Christchurch, New Zealand	123,548
Chungking, China	1,038,683
Ciudad Trujillo, Dominican Republic	181,533
Cologne, Germany	594,941
Colombo, Ceylon	362,074
Córdoba, Argentina	369,886
Coventry, England	258,211
Croydon, England	249,592
Dairen, Manchuria	1,054,465
Dakar, Fr. W. Africa	83,390
Damascus, Syria	286,310
Danzig (see Gdansk).	
Delhi, India	914,790
Derby, England	141,264
Djakarta, Indonesia	435,184

Dnepropetrovsk, U.S.S.R.	500,662	Kingston, Jamaica	109,056	Nice, France	211,165
Dortmund, Germany	507,349	Kingston upon Hull, England	299,068	Ningpo, China	249,000
Dresden, Germany	467,966	Kishnev, Rumania	112,500	Nottingham, England	306,008
Dublin, Ireland	521,322	Kobe, Japan	765,435	Nuremberg, Germany	362,459
Duisburg-Hamborn, Germany	410,783	Köbenhavn, Denmark	768,105		
Dundee, Scotland	177,333	Krakow, Poland	347,517	Odessa, U.S.S.R.	604,223
Durban, South Africa	430,256	Kuybyshev, U.S.S.R.	390,262	Omsk, U.S.S.R.	280,000
Düsseldorf, Germany	500,516	Kyoto, Japan	1,101,854	Oporto, Portugal	279,738
				Oran, Algeria	244,594
Edinburgh, Scotland	466,770	Lagos, Nigeria	230,000	Osaka, Japan	1,956,136
Edmonton, Canada	159,631	Lahore, Pakistan	849,333	Oslo, Norway	433,000
Essen, Germany	605,411	Lanchow, China	224,028	Ottawa, Canada	202,045
		La Paz, Bolivia	321,073		
Florence, Italy	390,832	La Plata, Argentina	207,031	Palermo, Italy	501,005
Foochow, China	328,000	Leeds, England	504,954	Panama, Panama	127,874
Frankfurt, Germany	532,037	Leicester, England	285,061	Paris, France	2,725,374
Fredericton, Canada	16,000	Leipzig, Germany	607,655	Peiping, China	1,940,290
Fukuoka, Japan	392,649	Leningrad, U.S.S.R.	3,191,304	Piraeus, Greece	184,980
		Leopoldville, Belgian Congo	208,662	Perth, Australia	272,528
Gdansk, Poland	191,000	Lhasa, Tibet	20,000	Pietermaritzburg, So. Africa	63,546
Gelsenkirchen, Germany	315,460	Liége, Belgium	156,208	Plymouth, England	208,985
Geneva, Switzerland	145,473	Lille, France	200,265	Poona, India	480,982
Genoa, Italy	683,023	Lima, Peru	520,000	Port-au-Prince, Haiti	142,840
Ghent, Belgium	166,096	Lisbon, Portugal	783,919	Pôrto Alegre, Brazil	381,964
Glasgow, Scotland	1,089,555	Liverpool, England	785,532	Port Said, Egypt	177,703
Gorki, U.S.S.R.	644,116	Lódz, Poland	622,495	Portsmouth, England	233,464
Göteborg, Sweden	354,381	London, England (Greater London)	8,346,137	Poznán, Poland	327,192
Graz, Austria	226,271	Lucknow, India	496,861	Prágue, Czechoslovakia	922,284
Guadalajara, Mexico	378,423	Luxemburg, Luxemburg	61,590	Pretoria, So. Africa	229,877
Guatemala, Guatemala	283,100	Lwow, U.S.S.R.	318,000		
		Lyon, France	460,748	Quebec, Canada	164,016
Hague, The, Netherlands	532,998			Quezon City, Philippine Rep.	107,977
Halifax, Canada	85,589	Madras, India	1,416,056	Quito, Ecuador	212,873
Halle, Germany	222,505	Madrid, Spain	1,618,435		
Hamburg, Germany	1,605,606	Magdeburg, Germany	236,326	Rabat, Morocco	161,416
Hamilton, Canada	208,321	Malmö, Sweden	192,670	Rangoon, Burma	500,800
Hankow, China	750,000	Managua, Nicaragua	107,444	Recife, Brazil	522,466
Hanoi, Vietnam	237,500	Manchester, England	703,175	Regina, Canada	71,319
Hanover, Germany	444,296	Manila, Phil. Rep.	983,906	Reykjavik, Iceland	38,196
Harbin, Manchuria	661,984	Mannheim, Germany	245,634	Riga, U.S.S.R.	393,211
Havana, Cuba	659,883	Marrakech, Morocco	238,237	Rio de Janeiro, Brazil	2,303,063
Havre, France	106,934	Marseille, France	636,264	Riyadh, Saudi Arabia	80,000
Helsinki, Finland	367,462	Mecca, Hejaz, Saudi Arabia	90,000	Rome, Italy	1,695,477
Hiroshima, Japan	285,712	Medina, Hejaz, Saudi Arabia	12,000	Rosario, Argentina	467,937
Hong Kong, China (see Victoria, Hong Kong)		Melbourne, Australia	1,226,000	Rostov, U.S.S.R.	510,253
Honolulu (see Cities of the U.S.)		Meshed, Iran	191,794	Rotterdam, Netherlands	646,248
Hyderabad, India	1,085,722	Messina, Italy	220,790		
		Mexico City, Mexico	2,233,709	Saigon, Vietnam	698,000
Isfahan, Iran	196,134	Milan, Italy	1,272,934	Saint-Etienne, France	177,966
Istanbul, Turkey	1,000,022	Monrovia, Liberia	10,000	Saint John's, Newfoundland	52,873
Izmir, Turkey	230,508	Montevideo, Uruguay	536,533	Salford, England	178,036
		Montreal, Canada	1,320,232	Salonika, Greece	191,847
Jerusalem, Palestine	137,500	Moscow, U.S.S.R.	4,137,018	Samarkand, U.S.S.R.	134,346
Johannesburg, South Africa	630,297	Mosul, Iraq	203,273	San José, Costa Rica	86,909
Juneau, Alaska	5,956	Mukden, Manchuria	1,551,317	San Juan, Puerto Rico	224,767
		Munich, Germany	831,937	San Salvador, El Salvador	160,380
Kabul, Afghanistan	154,134			Santiago, Chile	639,546
Kaliningrad, U.S.S.R.	372,164	Nagasaki, Japan	241,805	São Paulo, Brazil	2,041,716
Karachi, Pakistan	1,006,000	Nagoya, Japan	1,030,635	Saratov, U.S.S.R.	376,000
Kassel, Germany	162,132	Nagpur, India	449,099	Seoul, Korea	1,446,019
Kaunas, U.S.S.R.	102,750	Nanking, China	1,020,000	Seville, Spain	376,627
Kazan, U.S.S.R.	401,665	Nantes, France	200,265	Shanghai, China	5,406,644
Kharkov, U.S.S.R.	833,432	Naples, Italy	1,027,800	Sheffield, England	512,834
Kiel, Germany	254,449	Newcastle, England	291,723	Sian, China	559,127
Kiev, U.S.S.R.	846,293				

Singapore, Federation of Malaya	679,659
Sofia, Bulgaria	434,888
Soochow, China	339,517
Southampton, England	178,326
Stalingrad, U.S.S.R.	445,476
Stockholm, Sweden	744,431
Stoke on Trent, England	275,095
Strasbourg, France	177,966
Stuttgart, Germany	497,677
Sucre, Bolivia	40,128
Sunderland, England	181,515
Surabaya, Indonesia	341,675
Sverdlovsk, U.S.S.R.	425,544
Swansea, Wales	160,832
Sydney, Australia	1,500,000
Szczecin, Poland	200,217
Tabriz, Iran	279,168
Taipeh, Formosa	503,086
Tallinn, U.S.S.R.	146,388
Tananarive, Madagascar	174,153
Tangier, Morocco	84,628
Tashkent, U.S.S.R.	585,005
Tbilisi, U.S.S.R.	519,175
Tegucigalpa, Honduras	99,948
Tehran, Iran	618,976
Tientsin, China	1,785,813
Tirana, Albania	80,000
Tokyo, Japan	5,385,071
Toronto, Canada	675,754
Tottenham, England	126,921
Toulouse, France	264,411
Trieste, Italy and Yugoslavia	271,452
Tripoli, Libya	135,858
Tsinan, China	642,275
Tunis, Tunisia	364,593
Turin, Italy	720,032
Utrecht, Netherlands	185,246
Valencia, Spain	509,075
Valparaiso, Chile	209,945
Vancouver, Canada	344,833
Venice, Italy	323,216
Ventiane, Laos	10,000
Victoria, Canada	51,331
Victoria, Hong Kong	766,800
Vienna, Austria	1,760,784
Vladivostok, U.S.S.R.	206,432
Warsaw, Poland	641,877
Wellington, New Zealand	120,072
Wenchow, China	631,276
West Ham, England	170,987
Willesden, England	179,647
Winnipeg, Canada	235,710
Wroclaw, Poland	341,419
Wuhan, China	1,008,205
Wuppertal, Germany	363,224
Yerevan, U.S.S.R.	200,000
Yokohama, Japan	951,189
Zagreb, Yugoslavia	279,623
Zürich, Switzerland	390,020